Chilton's
AUTOMATIC TRANSMISSION MANUAL
1980-1984

Managing Editor John H. Weise, S.A.E. ☐ **Assistant Managing Editor** David H. Lee, A.S.E., S.A.E.

Service Editors Arthur I. Birney, Nick D'Andrea,
Robert McAnally, Michael D. Powers, S.A.E., John T. Kaufmann, Lawrence Braun
Editorial Consultants Edward K. Shea, S.A.E., Stan Stephenson

Production Manager John Cantwell
Manager Editing & Design Dean F. Morgantini
Production Coordinator Robin S. Miller
Mechanical Artists Margaret A. Stoner, Bill Gaskins

National Sales Manager Albert M. Kushnerick ☐ **Assistant** Jacquelyn T. Powers
Regional Managers Joseph Andrews, Jr., James O. Callahan, David Flaherty

OFFICERS
President Lawrence A. Fornasieri
Vice President & General Manager John P. Kushnerick

CHILTON BOOK COMPANY Chilton Way, Radnor, Pa. 19089

Manufactured in USA © 1984 Chilton Book Company
ISBN 0-8019-7390-2   ISSN 0743-8923   Library of Congress Catalog Card No. 83-45327
1234567890 3210987654

ACKNOWLEDGEMENTS

Chilton Book Company expresses appreciation to the following firms for their cooperation and technical assistance:

ATRA—Automatic Transmission Rebuilders Association, Ventura, California
    Special Thanks to: Mr. Gene Lewis—Executive Director
                Mr. John Maloney—National President
                Mr. Robert D. Cherrnay—Technical Director
                Mr. Michael Abell—Service Engineering
                Mr. C. W. Smith—Technical Staff
ASC—Automotive Service Councils, Inc.® Elmhurst, Illinois
    Special Thanks to: Mr. Del Wright—Chairman of the Board
                Mr. John F. Mullins, Jr.—Vice Chairman of the Board
                Mr. George W. Merwin, III—President
American Motors Corporation and Regie Nationale des Usines Renault, Detroit, Michigan
American Honda Motor Company, Gardena, California
American Isuzu Motors, Inc., Whittier, California
Audi, Division of Volkswagen of America Incorporated, Englewood Cliffs, New Jersey
Brandywine Transmission Service, Inc., Wilmington, Delaware
Borg Warner Transmission Service Center, Ramsey, New Jersey
    Special Thanks to: Mr. Michael LePore
Chrysler Corporation, Detroit, Michigan
Detroit Diesel Allison, Division of General Motors Corporation, Indianapolis, Indiana
Ford Motor Company, Dearborn, Michigan
Fuji Heavy Industries, Ltd., Tokyo, Japan
General Motors Corporation, Flint, Michigan
Hydra-Matic, Division of General Motors Corporation, Ypsilanti, Michigan
Jaguar, Rover, Triumph Motor Company, Inc., Leonia, New Jersey
Japanese Automatic Transmission Company, Tokyo, Japan
Lee's Auto Service, Trainer, Chester, Pennsylvania
Mazda Motors of America, Incorporated, Montvale, New Jersey
Mercedes Benz of North America, Incorporated, Montvale, New Jersey
Nissan Motor Corporation of USA, Carson, California
Ralph's Garage, Chester, Pennsylvania
Seuro Transmissions, Incorporated, Pittsburgh, Pennsylvania
Subaru of America, Incorporated, Pennsauken, New Jersey
Toyota Motor Sales USA, Incorporated, Torrence, California
Transmissions By Lucille, Pittsburgh, Pennsylvania
Volkswagen of America, Incorporated, Englewood Cliffs, New Jersey
Volvo of America Corporation, Rockleigh, New Jersey
ZF of North America, Inc., Chicago, Illinois

There are six major sections in this manual. And each is appropriately numbered for easy location:

1. **GENERAL INFORMATION**
2. **DOMESTIC CAR TRANSMISSIONS/TRANSAXLES**
3. **DOMESTIC TRUCK TRANSMISSIONS**
4. **IMPORT CAR, PICK-UP TRUCK TRANSMISSIONS/TRANSAXLES**

Further, each section is indexed and organized by the following functions:

APPLICATIONS
GENERAL DESCRIPTION
MODIFICATIONS
TROUBLE DIAGNOSIS
ON CAR SERVICES
REMOVAL AND INSTALLATION PROCEDURES
BENCH OVERHAUL
SPECIFICATIONS
SPECIAL TOOLS

Graphic symbols throughout the manual aid in the location of sections and speed the pinpointing of information.

METRIC NOTICE

Certain parts are dimensioned in the metric system. Many fasteners are metric and should not be replaced with a customary inch fastener.

It is important to note that during any maintenance procedure or repair, the metric fastener should be salvaged for reassembly. If the fastener is not reusable, then the equivalent fastener should be used.

A mismatched or incorrect fastener can result in component damage or possibly, personal injury.

SAFETY NOTICE

Proper service and repair procedures are vital to the safe, reliable operation of all motor vehicles, as well as the personal safety of those performing repairs. This manual outlines procedures for servicing and repairing vehicles using safe, effective methods. The procedures contain many NOTES, CAUTIONS and WARNINGS which should be followed along with standard safety procedures to eliminate the possibility of personal injury or improper service which could damage the vehicle or compromise its safety.

It is important to note that repair procedures and techniques, tools and parts for servicing motor vehicles, as well as the skill and experience of the individual performing the work, vary widely. It is not possible to anticipate all of the conceivable ways or conditions under which vehicles may be serviced, or to provide cautions as to all of the possible hazards that may result. Standard and accepted safety precautions and equipment should be used when handling toxic or flammable fluids, and safety goggles or other protection should be used during cutting, grinding, chiseling, prying, or any other process that can cause material removal or projectiles.

Some procedures require the use of tools specially designed for a specific purpose. Before substituting another tool or procedure, you must be completely satisfied that neither your personal safety, nor the performance of the vehicle will be endangered.

INDEX

GENERAL INFORMATION

Introduction

With this second volume of Chilton's Automatic Transmission Manual, we continue to assist the professional Automatic Transmission repair trade to perform quality repairs and adjustments for that "like new" dependability of the automatic transmission.

This concise, but comprehensive service manual places emphasis on diagnosing, troubleshooting, adjustments, testing, disassembly and assembly of the automatic transmission.

This manual will consist of the following major sections:
1. General Information section
2. Domestic Car Automatic Transmission section
3. Domestic Truck Automatic Transmission section
4. Import Cars and Light Truck Automatic Transmission section
5. Modification section—Automatic Transmissions covered in first volume
6. Correction section—Corrections to first volume.

Within the Automatic Transmission sections, the following information is included:
1. Transmission Application Chart
2. General description—to include:
   Model and type
   Capacities
   Fluid specifications
   Checking fluid level
3. Transmission modifications
4. Trouble diagnosis—to include:
   Hydraulic System Operation
   Oil Pressure Test
   Air Pressure Test
   Stall Test
   Control Pressure Specifications
   Shift Speed Specifications (when available)
5. On Car services—to include:
   Adjustments
   Removal and installation
6. Transmission/Transaxle removal and installation

7. Bench overhaul—to include:
   Transmission/Transaxle Disassembly
   Internal Component Disassembly and Assembly
   Transmission/Transaxle Assembly
8. Specifications
9. Factory recommended tools.

Metric Fasteners and Inch System

Metric bolt sizes and thread pitches are more commonly used for all fasteners on the automatic transmissions/transaxles now being manufactured. The metric bolt sizes and thread pitches are very close to the dimensions of the similar inch system fasteners and for this reason, replacement fasteners must have the same measurement and strength as those removed.

Do not attempt to interchange metric fasteners for inch system fasteners. Mismatched and incorrect fasteners can result in dam-

Chilton's Professional Automatic Transmission Manual, Volume 1

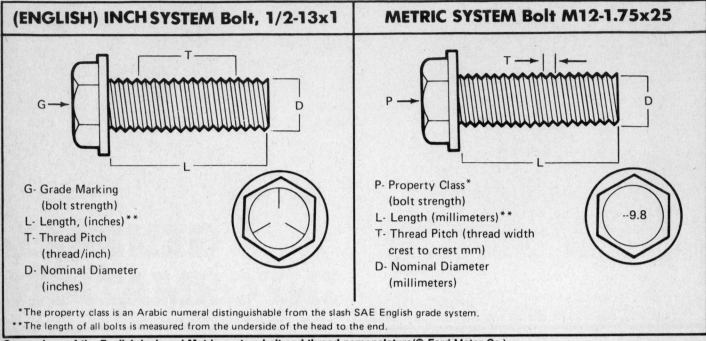

(ENGLISH) INCH SYSTEM Bolt, 1/2-13x1

G- Grade Marking
   (bolt strength)
L- Length, (inches)**
T- Thread Pitch
   (thread/inch)
D- Nominal Diameter
   (inches)

METRIC SYSTEM Bolt M12-1.75x25

P- Property Class*
   (bolt strength)
L- Length (millimeters)**
T- Thread Pitch (thread width
   crest to crest mm)
D- Nominal Diameter
   (millimeters)

*The property class is an Arabic numeral distinguishable from the slash SAE English grade system.
**The length of all bolts is measured from the underside of the head to the end.

Comparison of the English Inch and Metric system bolt and thread nomenclature(© Ford Motor Co.)

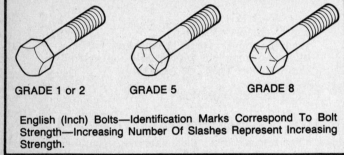

GRADE 1 or 2   GRADE 5   GRADE 8

English (Inch) Bolts—Identification Marks Correspond To Bolt Strength—Increasing Number Of Slashes Represent Increasing Strength.

Typical English Inch bolt head identification marks
(© Ford Motor Co.)

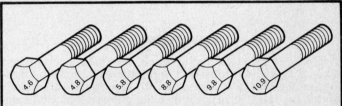

Metric Bolts—Identification Class Numbers Correspond To Bolt Strength—Increasing Numbers Represent Increasing Strength. Common Metric Fastener Bolt Strength Property Are 9.8 And 10.9 With The Class Identification Embossed On The Bolt Head.

Typical Metric bolt head identification marks
(© Ford Motor Co.)

(ENGLISH) INCH SYSTEM		METRIC SYSTEM	
Grade	Identification	Class	Identification
Hex Nut Grade 5	3 Dots	Hex Nut Property Class 9	Arabic 9
Hex Nut Grade 8	6 Dots	Hex Nut Property Class 10	Arabic 10
Increasing dots represent increasing strength.		May also have blue finish or paint daub on hex flat. Increasing numbers represent increasing strength.	

Comparison of English Inch and Metric hex nut strength identification marks(© Ford Motor Co.)

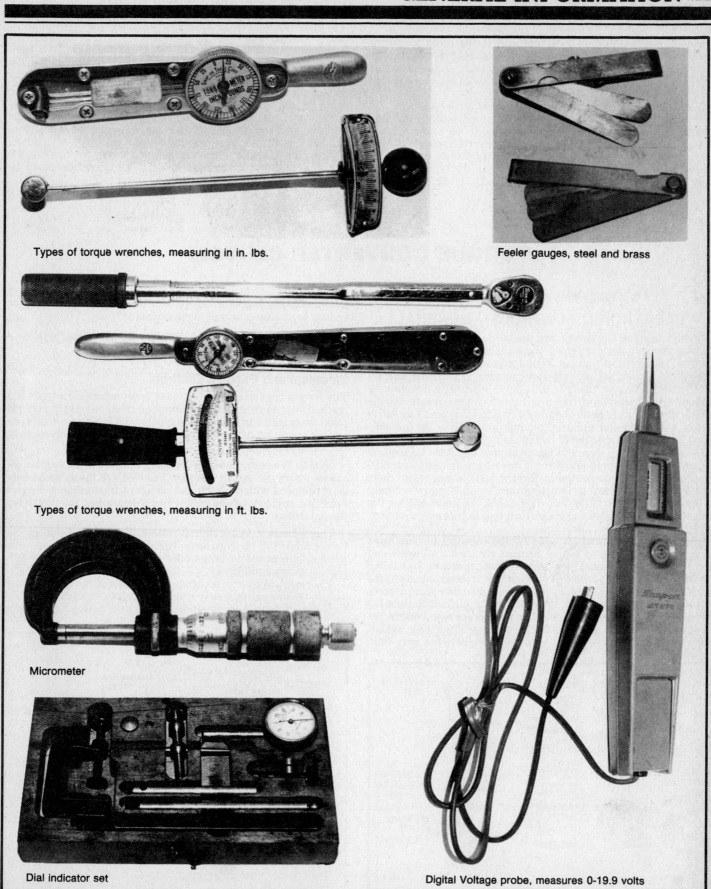

Types of torque wrenches, measuring in in. lbs.

Feeler gauges, steel and brass

Types of torque wrenches, measuring in ft. lbs.

Micrometer

Dial indicator set

Digital Voltage probe, measures 0-19.9 volts

Typical precision measuring tools

age to the transmission/transaxle unit through malfunction, breakage or possible personal injury. Care should be exercised to re-use the fasteners in their same locations as removed, when ever possible. If any doubt exists in the re-use of fasteners, install new ones.

To avoid stripped threads and to prevent metal warpage, the use of the torque wrench becomes more important, as the gear box assembly and internal components are being manufactured from light weight material. The torque conversion charts should be understood by the repairman, to properly service the requirements of the torquing procedures. When in doubt, refer to the specifications for the transmission/transaxle being serviced or overhauled.

Critical Measurements

With the increase use of transaxles and the close tolerances needed throughout the drive train, more emphasis is placed upon making the critical bearing and gear measurements correctly and being assured that correct preload and turning torque exists before the unit is re-installed in the vehicle. Should a comeback occur because of the lack of proper clearances or torque, a costly rebuild can result. Rather than rebuilding a unit by "feel", the repairman must rely upon precise measuring tools, such as the dial indicator, micrometers, torque wrenches and feeler gauges to insure that correct specifications are adhered to.

TORQUE CONVERTER CLUTCH

Principles of Operation

ELECTRONIC CONTROLS—GENERAL

Many changes in the design and operation of the transmission/transaxles have occurred since the publishing of our first Automatic Transmission Manual. New transaxles and transmissions have been developed, manufactured and are in use, with numerous internal changes made in existing models. The demand for lighter, smaller and more fuel efficient vehicles has resulted in the use of electronics to control both the engine spark and fuel delivery at a more precise time and quantity, to achieve the fuel efficient results that are required by law. Certain transmission/transaxle assemblies are a part of the electronic controls, by sending signals of vehicle speed and throttle opening to an on-board computer, which in turn computes these signals, along with others from the engine assembly, to determine if spark occurence should be changed or the delivery fo fuel should be increased or decreased. The computed signals are then sent to the respective controls and/or sensors as required.

Automatic transmissions with microcomputers to determine gear selections are now in use. Sensors are used for engine and road speeds, engine load, gear selector lever position, kick down switch and a status of the driving program to send signals to the microcomputer to determine the optimum gear selection, according to a preset program. The shifting is accomplished by solenoid valves in the hydraulic system. The electronics also control the modulated hydraulic pressure during shifting, along with regulating engine torque to provide smooth shifts between gear ratio changes. This type of system can be designed for different driving programs, such as giving the operator the choice of operating the vehicle for either economy or performace.

ELECTRICAL CONTROL FOR TORQUE CONVERTER CLUTCH

Electrical and Vacuum Controls

The torque converter clutch should apply when the engine has reached near normal operating temperature in order to handle the slight extra load and when the vehicle speed is high enough to allow the operation of the clutch to be smooth and the vehicle to be free of engine pulses.

NOTE: When the converter clutch is coupled to the engine, the engine pulses can be felt through the vehicle in the same manner as if equipped with a clutch and standard transmission. Engine condition, engine load and engine speed determines the severity of the pulsations.

The converter clutch should release when torque multiplication is needed in the converter, when coming to a stop, or when the mechanical connection would affect exhaust emissions during a coasting condition.

The electrical control components consists of the brake release switch, the low vacuum switch and the governor switch. Some vehicle models have a thermal vacuum switch, a relay valve and a

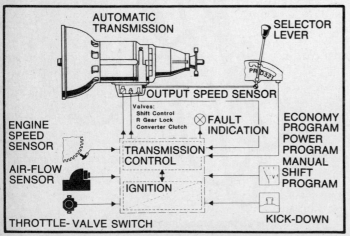

Typical schematic of Electronic gear selection with microcomputer control(© ZF of North America, Inc.)

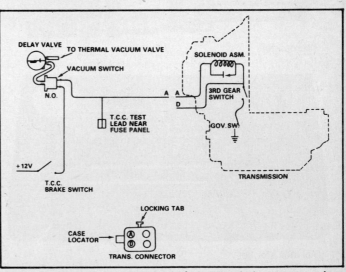

Use of electrical and vacuum controls to operate torque converter clutch(© General Motors Corp.)

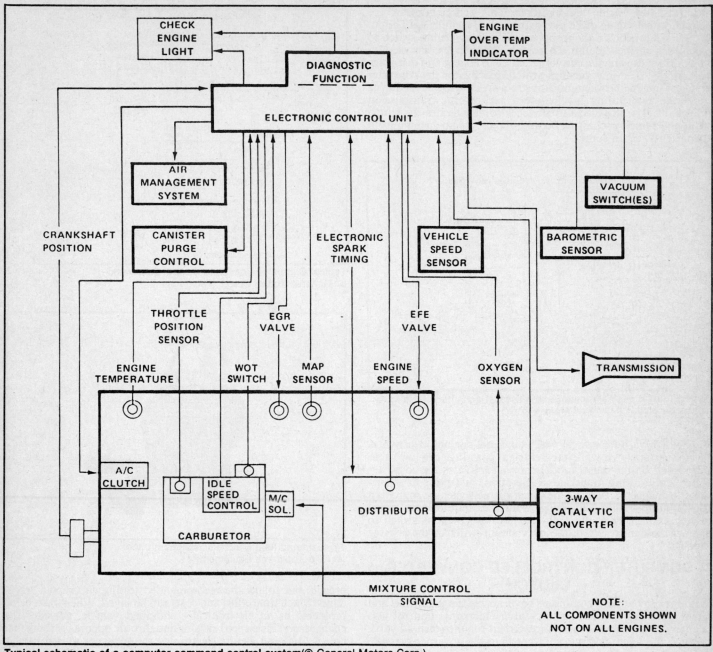

Typical schematic of a computer command control system(© General Motors Corp.)

delay valve. Diesel engines use a high vacuum switch in addition to certain above listed components. These various components control the flow of current to the apply valve solenoid. By controlling the current flow, these components activate or deactivate the solenoid, which in turn engages or disengages the transmission converter clutch, depending upon the driving conditions as mentioned previously. The components have the two basic circuits, electrical and vacuum.

ELECTRICAL CURRENT FLOW
All of the components in the electrical circuit must be closed or grounded before the solenoid can open the hydraulic circuit to engage the converter clutch. The circuit begins at the fuse panel and flows to the brake switch and as long as the brake pedal is not depressed, the current will flow to the low vacuum switch on the gasoline engines and to the high vacuum switch on the diesel engines. These two switches open or close the circuit path to the so-

lenoid, dependent upon the engine or pump vacuum. If the low vacuum switch is closed (high vacuum switch on diesel engines), the current continues to flow to the transmission case connector, into the solenoid and to the governor pressure switch. When the vehicle speed is approximately 35-50 mph, the governor switch grounds to activate the solenoid. The solenoid, in turn, opens a hydraulic circuit to the converter clutch assembly, engaging the unit.

It should be noted that external vacuum controls include the thermal vacuum valve, the relay valve, the delay valve, the low vacuum switch and a high vacuum switch (used on diesel engines). Keep in mind that all of the electrical or vacuum components may not be used on all engines, at the same time.

VACUUM FLOW
The vacuum relay valve works with the thermal vacuum valve to keep the engine vacuum from reaching the low vacuum valve

switch at low engine temperatures. This action prevents the clutch from engaging while the engine is still warming up. The delay valve slows down the response of the low vacuum switch to changes in engine vacuum. This action prevents the low vacuum switch from causing the converter clutch to engage and disengage too rapidly. The low vacuum switch deactivates the converter clutch when engine vacuum drops to a specific low level during moderate acceleration just before a part-throttle transmission downshift. The low vacuum switch also deactivates the clutch while the vehicle is coasting because it receives no vacuum from its ported vacuum source.

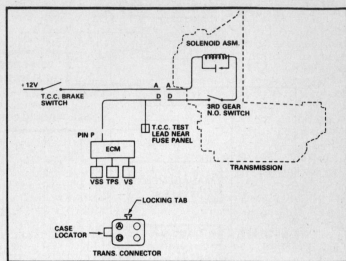

Typical Computer Command Control schematic
(© General Motors Corp.)

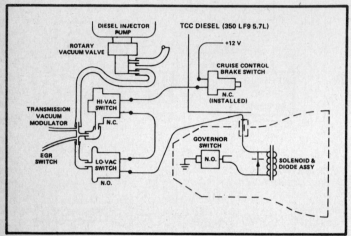

Typical diesel engine vacuum and electrical schematic for torque converter clutch(© General Motors Corp.)

The high vacuum switch, when on diesel engines, deactivates the converter clutch while the vehicle is coasting. The low vacuum switch on the diesel models only deactivates the converter clutch only during moderate acceleration, just prior to a part-throttle downshift. Because the diesel engine's vacuum source is a rotary pump, rather than taken from a carburetor port, diesel models require both the high and the low vacuum switch to achieve the same results as the low vacuum switch on the gasoline models.

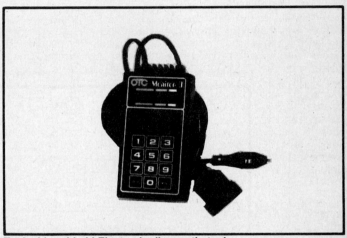

Typical hand held Electronic diagnostic tool
(© OTC Tools and Equipment)

COMPUTER CONTROLLED CONVERTER CLUTCH

With the use of micro-computers governoring the engine fuel and spark delivery, the converter clutch electronic control was changed to provide the grounding circuit for the solenoid valve through the micro-computer, rather than the governor pressure switch. Sensors are used in place of the formerly used switches and send signals back to the micro-computer to indicate if the engine is in its proper mode to accept the mechanical lock-up of the converter clutch.

Normally a coolant sensor, a throttle position sensor, an engine vacuum sensor and a vehicle speed sensor are used to signal the micro-computer when the converter clutch can be applied. Should a sensor indicate the need for the converter clutch to be deactivated, the grounding circuit to the transmission solenoid valve would be interrupted and the converter clutch would be released.

Diagnostic Precautions

We have entered into the age of electronics and with it, the need for the diagnostician to increase the skills needed for this particular field. By learning the basic components, their operation, the testing procedures and by applying a "common sense" approach to the diagnosis procedures, repairs can be made accurately and quickly. Avoid the "short-cut" and "parts replacement" ap-

proach, but follow the recommended testing and repair procedures. Much time effort and costs can be saved. When diagnosing problems of an electronically equipped vehicle, consider the changes in vehicle speed sensing and throttle opening sensing that are encountered. Before electronics, the governor sensed vehicle speed and by allowing more governor pressure to be produced, overcame throttle and main line pressures to move the shifting valves. Now, the vehicle speed is sensed from a small electric producing generator, mounted on or near the speedometer or cable and is activated by the rotation of the speedometer cable. This signal is then directed to the micro-computer for computation on when the converter clutch should be engaged or disengaged.

The governor operation still remains the same as to the shifting and producing of governor pressure, but its importance of being the vehicle speed sensor has now diminished. A throttle positioner switch has been added to the carburetor to more precisely identify the position of the throttle plates in regards to vehicle speed and load. The throttle cable or modulator are still used to control the throttle pressure within the transmission/transaxle assemblies. Added pressure switches are mounted to the various passages of the valve bodies to sense gear changes, by allowing electrical current to either pass through or be blocked by the switches. The repairman must be attentive when overhauling or replacing the valve body, to be sure the correct pressure switch is installed in the correct hydraulic passage, because the switches have either normally closed (N.C.) contacts or normally open (N.O.) contacts and would be identified on the electrical schematic as such. To interchange switches would cause malfunctions and possible costly repairs to both the transmission and to the electronic system components.

The many types of automatic transmissions that employ the electronic controlled converter clutch, do not follow the same electronic or hydraulic routings nor have the same sensors, oil pressure switches and vacuum sensing applications. Therefore, before diagnosing a fault in the converter clutch assembly, the electric, the electronic or hydraulic circuits, identify the automatic transmission as to its model designation and code.

NOTE: Refer to the proper diagnostic outline in the individual automatic transmission outline or to the General Motors Turbo Hydra-Matic Converter Clutch Diagnostic outline, at the beginning of the General Motors Automatic Transmission Sections.

HYDRAULIC CONVERTER CLUTCH OPERATION

Numerous automatic transmissions rely upon hydraulic pressures to sense, determine when and to apply the converter clutch assembly. This type of automatic transmission unit is considered to be a self-contained unit with only the shift linkage, throttle cable or modulator valve being external. Specific valves, located within the valve body or oil pump housing, are caused to be moved when a sequence of events occur within the unit. For example, to engage the converter clutch, most all automatic transmissions require the gear ratio to be in the top gear before the converter clutch control valves can be placed in operation. The governor and throttle pressures must maintain specific fluid pressures at various points within the hydraulic circuits to aid in the engagement or disengagement of the converter clutch. In addition, check valves must properly seal and move to exhaust pressured fluid at the correct time to avoid "shudders" or "chuckles" during the initial application and engagement of the converter clutch.

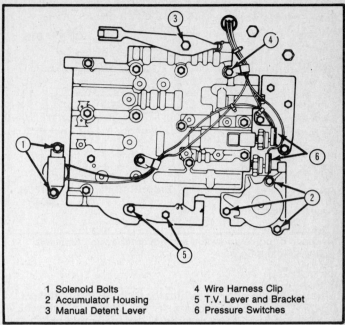

1 Solenoid Bolts	4 Wire Harness Clip
2 Accumulator Housing	5 T.V. Lever and Bracket
3 Manual Detent Lever	6 Pressure Switches

Valve body components and pressure switches
(© General Motors Corp.)

CENTRIFUGAL TORQUE CONVERTER CLUTCH OPERATION

A torque converter has been in use that mechanically locks up centrifugally without the use of electronics or hydraulic pressure. At specific input shaft speeds, brake-like shoes move outward from the rim of the turbine assembly, to engage the converter housing, locking the converter unit mechanically together for a 1:1 ratio. Slight slippage can occur at the low end of the rpm scale,

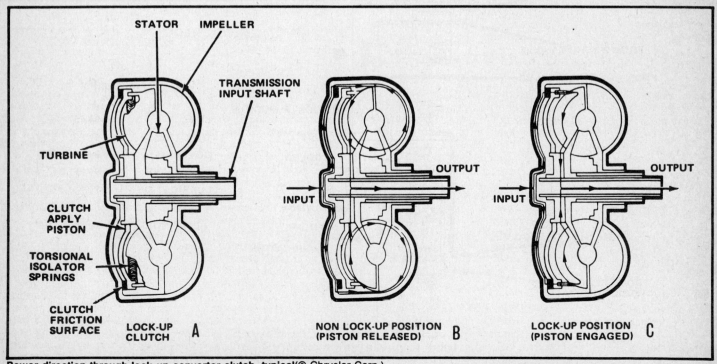

Power direction through lock-up converter clutch, typical(© Chrysler Corp.)

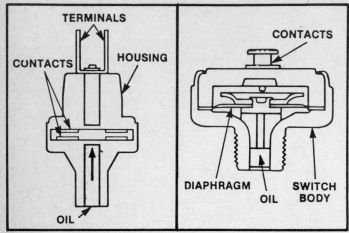

**Comparison of pressure switch and governor switch terminals
(© General Motors Corp.)**

MECHANICAL CONVERTER LOCK-UP OPERATION

An other type of converter lock-up is the Ford Motor Company's AOD Automatic Overdrive transmission, which uses a direct drive input shaft splined to the damper assembly of the torque converter cover to the direct clutch, bypassing the torque converter reduction components. A second shaft encloses the direct drive input shaft and is coupled between the converter turbine and the reverse clutch or forward clutch, depending upon their applied phase. With this type of unit, when in third gear, the input shaft torque is split, 30% hydraulic and 70% mechanical. When in the overdrive or fourth gear, the input torque is completely mechanical and the transmission is locked mechanically to the engine.

CONFIRMING LOCK-UP OF TORQUE CONVERTER

To confirm the lock-up of the torque converter has occurred, check the engine rpm with a tachometer while the vehicle is being driven. If the torque converter is locked-up, the engine rpm will decrease approximately 200-400 rpm, at the time of lock-up.

Overdrive Units

With need for greater fuel economy, the automatic transmission/transaxles were among the many vehicle components that have been modified to aid in this quest. Internal changes have been made and in some cases, additions of a fourth gear to provide the

but the greater the rpm, the tighter the lock-up. Again, it must be mentioned, that when the converter has locked-up, the vehicle may respond in the same manner as driving with a clutch and standard transmission. This is considered normal and does not indicate converter clutch or transmission problems. Keep in mind if engines are in need of tune-ups or repairs, the lock-up "shudder" or "chuckle" feeling may be greater.

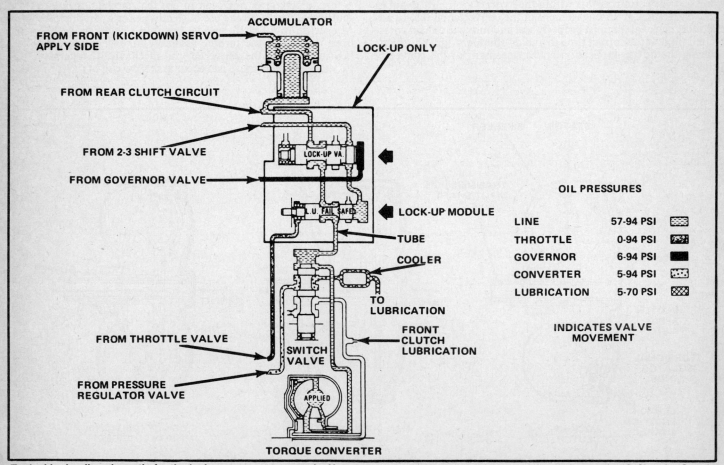

Typical hydraulic schematic for the lock-up converter controls. Note governor pressure reaction area on the lock-up valve(© Chrysler Corp.)

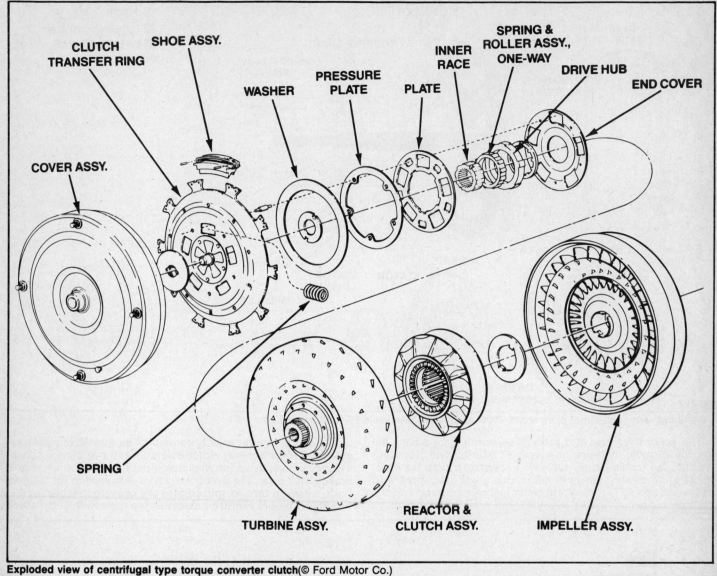

COVER ASSY.

CLUTCH TRANSFER RING

SHOE ASSY.

WASHER

PRESSURE PLATE

PLATE

INNER RACE

SPRING & ROLLER ASSY., ONE-WAY

DRIVE HUB

END COVER

SPRING

TURBINE ASSY.

REACTOR & CLUTCH ASSY.

IMPELLER ASSY.

Exploded view of centrifugal type torque converter clutch(© Ford Motor Co.)

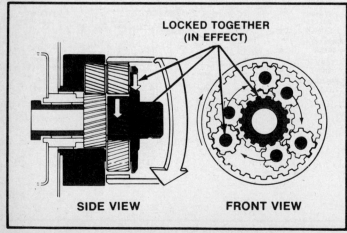

LOCKED TOGETHER (IN EFFECT)

SIDE VIEW   FRONT VIEW

Planetary gear rotation in direct drive(© Ford Motor Co.)

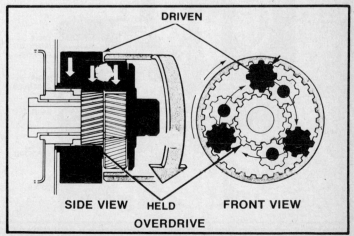

DRIVEN

SIDE VIEW   HELD   FRONT VIEW

OVERDRIVE

Planetary gear rotation in overdrive(© Ford Motor Co.)

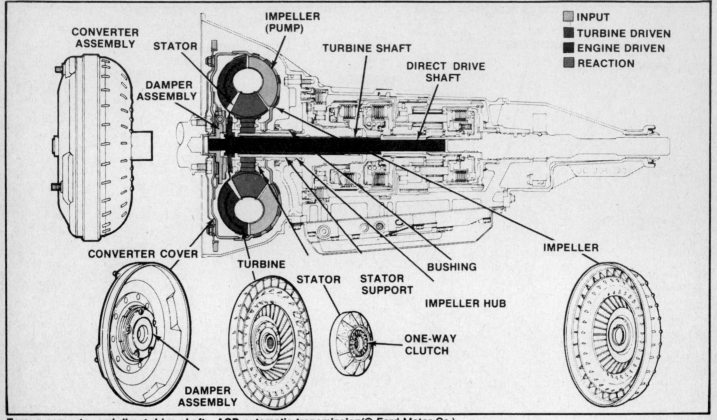

Torque converter and direct drive shaft—AOD automatic transmission(© Ford Motor Co.)

overdirect or overdrive gear ratio. The reasoning for adding the overdrive capability is that an overdrive ratio enables the output speed of the transmission/transaxle to be greater than the input speed, allowing the vehicle to maintain a given road speed with less engine speed. This results in better fuel economy and a slower running engine.

The overdrive unit usually consists of an overdrive planetary gear set, a roller one-way clutch assembly and two friction clutch assemblies, one as an internal clutch pack and the second for a brake clutch pack. The overdrive carrier is splined to the turbine shaft, which in turn, is splined into the converter turbine.

Another type of overdrive assembly is a separation of the over-

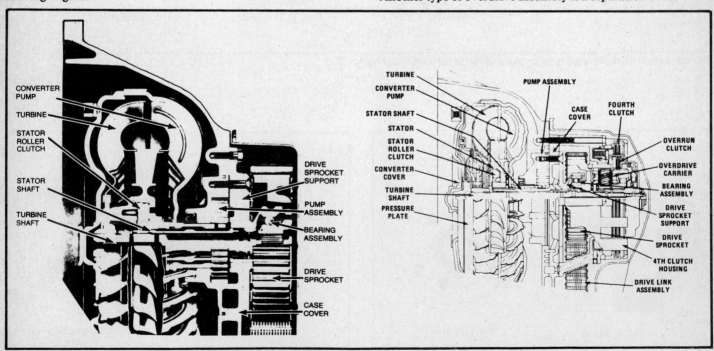

The addition of an overdrive unit and converter clutch assembly to an existing transaxle, changes its top end operation (© General Motors Corp.)

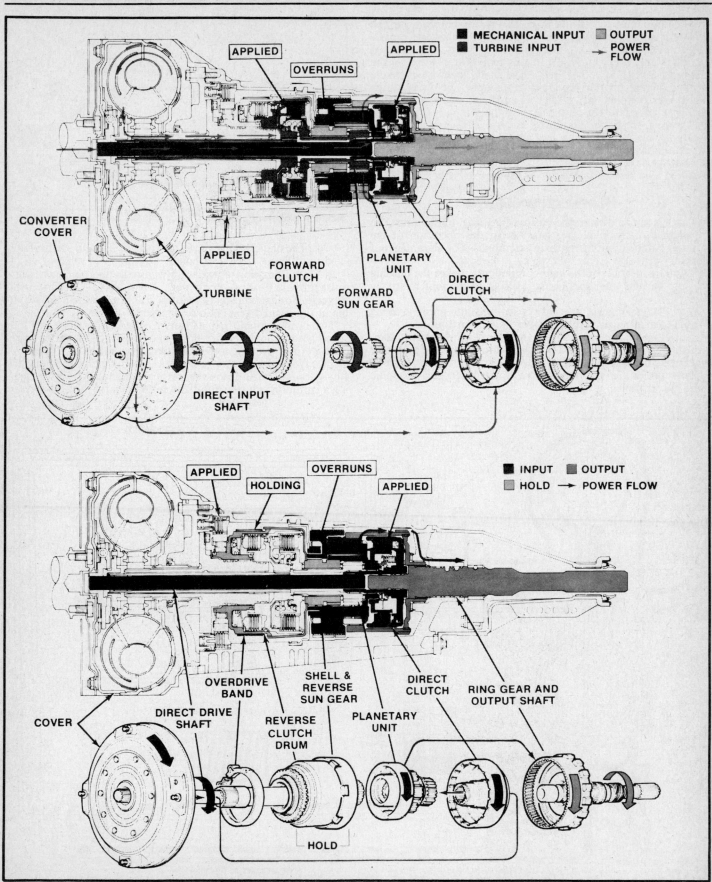

Comparison of direct drive and overdrive power flows(© Ford Motor Co.)

drive components by having them at various points along the gear train assembly and also utilizing them for other gear ranges. Instead of having a brake clutch pack, an overdrive band is used to lock the planetary sun gear. In this type of transmission, the converter cover drives the direct drive shaft clockwise at engine speed, which in turn drives the direct clutch. The direct clutch then drives the planetary carrier assembly at engine speed in a clockwise direction. The pinion gears of the planetary gear assembly "walk around" the stationary reverse sun gear, again in a clockwise rotation. The ring gear and output shaft are therefore driven at a faster speed by the rotation of the planetary pinions. Because the input is 100% mechanical drive, the converter can be classified as a lock-up converter in the overdrive position.

Planetary Gears

Our aim is not to discuss the basics of gearing, but to stress the importance of the planetary gear set in the operation of the automatic transmission/transaxle assemblies. The advantages of planetary gear sets are as follows;

a. The location of the gear components makes the holding of the various members or the locking of the unit relatively easy.

b. Planetary gears are always in constant mesh, making quick gear changes without power flow interruption.

c. Planetary gears are strong and sturdy. The gears can handle larger torque loads as it is passed through the the planetary gear set, because the torque load is distributed over several planet pinion gears, allowing more tooth contact area to handle the power flow.

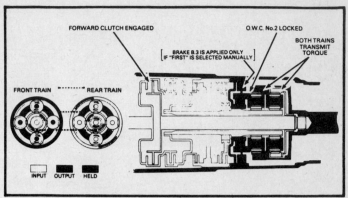

Simpson planetary gear set(© Borg Warner, Ltd.)

d. The planetary gear set is compact in size and easily adapted to different sized gear boxes.

In the automatic transmission/transaxle, the planetary gears must provide Neutral, Reduction, Direct Drive, Overdrive and Reverse. To accomplish this, certain gear or gears are held, resulting in the desired gear ratio or change of direction.

Two or more planetary gear sets are used in the three and four speed automatic units, providing the different gear ratios in reduction or to provide a separate overdrive ratio.

Two types of planetary gear sets are used, the Simpson and the Ravigneaux. The Simpson gear set is two planetary gear sets sharing a common sun gear shaft and output shaft. The Ravigneaux

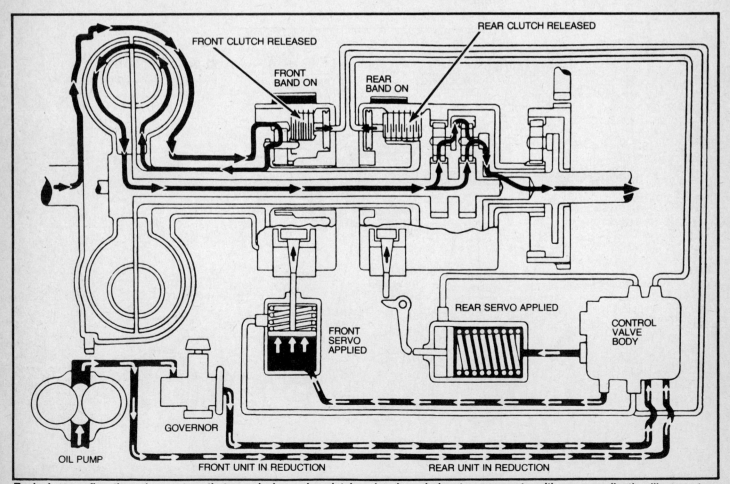

Typical power flow through an automatic transmission, using clutches, bands and planetary gear sets, with servo application illustrated

gear set utilizes a dual pinion planetary carrier, two sun gears and a ring gear. The pinion gears consists of short pinions (primary) and long pinions (secondary). Most automatic gear boxes use the Simpson type planetary gear assemblies.

HOLDING OR LOCKING-UP COMPONENTS OF THE PLANETARY GEARS

The holding or locking-up of the planetary gears is accomplished by hydraulic pressure, directed to a specific component, by the opening or closing of fluid passages in the transmission/transaxle assembly by spool type valves, either operated manually or automatically. The holding components are either clutch packs, internal or external, bands or overrunning "one-way" clutch units. Depending upon the design of the transmission/transaxle assembly, would dictate the holding of a specific part of the planetary gear unit by the holding components. It is important for the repairman to refer to the clutch and band application chart to determine the holding components in a particular gear ratio.

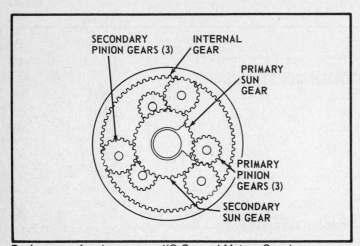

Ravigneaux planetary gear set(© General Motors Corp.)

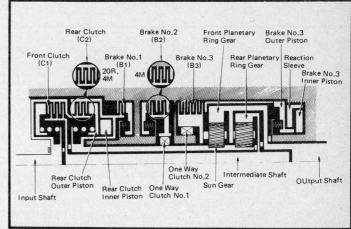

Typical component arrangement using clutch brakes instead of bands(© Toyota Motor Co.)

DIAGNOSING AUTOMATIC TRANSMISSION/TRANSAXLE MALFUNCTIONS

Diagnosing automatic transmission problems is simplified following a definite procedure and understanding the basic operation of the individual transmission that is being inspected or serviced. Do not attempt to "short-cut" the procedure or take for granted that another technician has performed the adjustments or the critical checks. It may be an easy task to locate a defective or burned-out unit, but the technician must be skilled in locating the primary reason for the unit failure and must repair the malfunction to avoid having the same failure occur again.

Each automatic transmission manufacturer has developed a diagnostic procedure for their individual transmissions. Although the operation of the units are basically the same, many differences will appear in the construction, method of unit application and the hydraulic control systems.

The same model transmissions can be installed in different makes of vehicles and are designed to operate under different load stresses, engine applications and road conditions. Each make of vehicle will have specific adjustments or use certain outside manual controls to operate the individual unit, but may not interchange with another transmission/vehicle application from the same manufacturer.

The identification of the transmission is most important so that the proper preliminary inspections and adjustments may be done and if in need of a major overhaul, the correct parts may be obtained and installed to avoid costly delays.

CUSTOMER EXPLANATION OF MALFUNCTION

The customer should be approached and questioned in a professional, but friendly and courteous manner as to the malfunction that could exist in the gearbox. By evaluating the answers, a pattern could emerge as to why this problem exists, what to do to correct it and what should be done to prevent a recurrence. Should the vehicle be towed because of apparent transmission failure, the cause should be determined before the unit is re-

Obtaining customer explanation of malfunction(© Ford Motor Co.)

moved to be certain a stalled engine, a broken or worn drive line component, broken drive plate or lack of fluid could be the cause. Again, question the owner/driver as to what happened, when and where the malfunction took place, such as engine flare-up, starting from a stop and/or on a hill. From the answers given, usually the correct diagnosis can be determined. Physical inspection of the vehicle components is the next step, to verify that either the outer components are at fault or the unit must be removed for overhaul.

SYSTEMATIC DIAGNOSIS

Transmission/transaxle manufacturers have compiled diagnostic aids for the use of technicians when diagnosing malfunctions through oil pressure tests or road test procedures. Diagnostic symptom charts, operational shift speed charts, oil pressure specifications, clutch and band application charts and oil flow schematics are some of the aids available.

Numerous manufacturers and re-manufacturers require a diag-

AUTOMATIC TRANSMISSION	CUSTOMER QUESTIONNAIRE

1. How long have you had the condition?   R. O. _____

    ☐ Since car was new
    ☐ Recently (when?) _____
    ☐ Came on gradually   ☐ Suddenly

2. Describe the condition?

	P-R-N-D-2-1 SELECTOR POSITION(S)	CHECK AS APPROPRIATE WHICH GEAR?		
		HIGH	INTERMEDIATE	LOW
☐ Slow Engagement				
☐ Rough Engagement				
☐ Slip				
☐ No Drive				
☐ No Upshift				
☐ No Downshift				
☐ Slip During Shift				
☐ Wrong Shift Speed(s)				
☐ Rough Shift				
☐ Mushy Shift				
☐ Erratic Shift				
☐ Engine "runaway or "buzzy"				
☐ No Kickdown				
☐ Starts in high gear in D				
☐ Starts in intermediate gear in D				
☐ Oil leak (where?)				

3. Which of the following cause or affect the condition?

    ☐ Transmission cold   ☐ Engine at fast (cold) idle
    ☐ After warm-up   ☐ Normal idle
    ☐ High speed   ☐ Wet road
    ☐ Cruising speed   ☐ Dry road
    ☐ Low Speed   ☐ Braking
    ☐ Accelerating   ☐ Coasting down

4. Does the engine need a tune-up?

    ☐ Yes   ☐ No   ☐ When was last tune-up? _____

5. Describe any strange noises

    ☐ Rumble   ☐ Squeak
    ☐ Knock   ☐ Grind
    ☐ Chatter   ☐ Hiss
    ☐ Snap or pop   ☐ Scrape
    ☐ Buzz   ☐ Other (describe)_____
    ☐ Whine

Ford
Ford Parts and Service Division
Training and Publications Department

SERVICE ADVISOR HELPER

Customer questionnaire, published by Ford Motor Co., for use by their Dealer body diagnostic personnel. Typical of other manufacturers (© Ford Motor Co.)

nosis check sheet be filled out by the diagnostician, pertaining to the operation, fluid level, oil pressures (idling and at various speeds), verification of adjustments and possible causes and the needed correction of the malfunctions. In certain cases, authorization must be obtained before repairs can be done, with the diagnostic check sheet accompanying the request for payment or warranty claim, along with the return of defective parts.

It is a good policy to use the diagnostic check sheet for the evaluation of all transmission/transaxles diagnosis and include the completed check sheet in the owners service file, should future reference be needed.

Many times, a rebuilt unit is exchanged for the defective unit, saving down time for the owner and vehicle. However, if the diagnostic check sheet would accompany the removed unit to the rebuilder, more attention could be directed to verifying and repairing the malfunctioning components to avoid costly comebacks of the rebuilt unit, at a later date. Most large volume rebuilders employ the use of dynamometers, as do the new unit manufacturers, to verify proper build-up of the unit and its correct operation before it is put in service.

GENERAL DIAGNOSIS

Should the diagnostician not use a pre-printed check sheet for the diagnosing of the malfunctioning unit, a sequence for diagnosis of the gear box is needed to proceed in an orderly manner. A suggested sequence is as follows:
1. Inspect and correct the fluid level.
2. Inspect and adjust the throttle or kick-down linkage.
3. Inspect and adjust the manual linkage.
4. Install one or more oil pressure gauges to the transmission as instructed in the individual transmission sections.

Use the oil pressure gauge(© General Motors Corp.)

5. Road test the vehicle (with owner if possible).

NOTE: During the road test, use all the selector ranges while noting any differences in operation or changes in oil pressures, so that the unit or hydraulic circuit can be isolated that is involved in the malfunction.

Engine Performance

When engine performance has declined due to the need of an engine tune-up or a system malfunction, the operation of the transmission is greatly affected. Rough or slipping shift and overheating of the transmission and fluid can occur, which can develop into serious internal transmission problems. Complete the adjustments or repairs to the engine before the road test is attempted or transmission adjustments made.

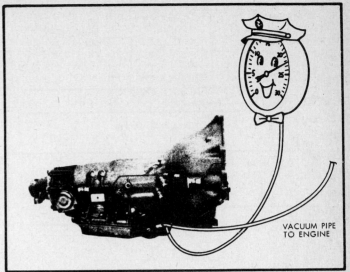

Use the vacuum gauge as required(© General Motors Corp.)

Using the hand operated vacuum pump as required (© General Motors Corp.)

Inspection of the Fluid Level

Most automatic transmissions are designed to operate with the fluid level between the ADD or ONE PINT and FULL marks on the dipstick indicator, with the fluid at normal operating temperature. The normal operating temperature is attained by operating the engine-transmission assembly for at least 8 to 15 miles of driving or its equivalent. The fluid temperature should be in the range of 150° to 200°F when normal operating temperature is attained.

NOTE: If the vehicle has been operated for long periods at high speed or in extended city traffic during hot weather, an accurate fluid level check cannot be made until the fluid cools, normally 30 minutes after the vehicle has been parked, due to fluid heat in excess of 200° F.

The transmission fluid can be checked during two ranges of temperature.
1. Transmission at normal operating temperature.
2. Transmission at room temperature.
During the checking procedure and adding of fluid to the transmission, it is most important not to overfill the reservoir to avoid foaming and loss of fluid through the breather, which can cause slippage and transmission failure.

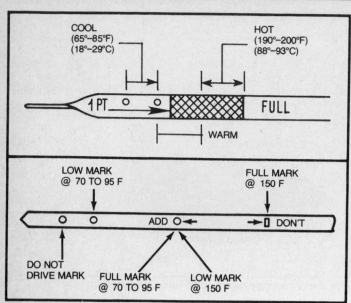

Typical fluid level indicators

TRANSMISSION AT NORMAL OPERATING TEMPERATURE

(150° to 200° F.—Dipstick hot to the touch)

1. With the vehicle on a level surface, engine idling, wheels blocked or parking brake applied, move the gear selector lever through all the ranges to fill the passages with fluid.

2. Place the selector lever in the Park position and remove the dipstick from the transmission. Wipe clean and reinsert the dipstick to its full length into the dipstick tube.

3. Remove the dipstick and observe the fluid level mark on the dipstick stem. The fluid level should be between the ADD and the FULL marks. If necessary, add fluid through the filler tube to bring the fluid level to its proper height.

4. Reinstall the dipstick and be sure it is sealed to the dipstick filler tube to avoid the entrance of dirt or water.

TRANSMISSION AT ROOM TEMPERATURE

(65° to 95° F.—Dipstick cool to touch)

——————— CAUTION ———————

The automatic transmissions are sometimes overfilled because the fluid level is checked when the transmission has not been operated and the fluid is cold and contracted. As the transmission is warmed to normal operating temperature, the fluid level can change as much as ¾ inch.

1. With the vehicle on a level surface, engine idling, wheels blocked or parking brake applied, move the selector lever through all the ranges to fill the passages with fluid.

2. Place the selector lever in the Park position and remove the dipstick from the transmission. Wipe clean and re-insert it back into the dipstick tube.

3. Remove the dipstick and observe the fluid level mark on the dipstick stem. The fluid should be directly below the FULL indicator.

NOTE: Most dipsticks will have either one mark or two marks, such as dimples or holes in the stem of the dipstick, to indicate the cold level, while others may be marked HOT or COLD levels.

4. Add enough fluid, as necessary, to the transmission, but do not overfill.

——————— CAUTION ———————

This operation is most critical, due to the expansion of the fluid under heat.

FLUID TYPE SPECIFICATIONS

The automatic transmission fluid is used for numerous functions such as a power-transmitting fluid in the torque converter, a hydraulic fluid in the hydraulic control system, a lubricating agent for the gears, bearings and bushings, a friction-controlling fluid for the bands and clutches and a heat transfer medium to carry the heat to an air or cooling fan arrangement.

Because of the varied automatic transmission designs, different frictional characteristics of the fluids are required so that one fluid cannot assure freedom from chatter or squawking from the bands and clutches. Operating temperatures have increased sharply in many new transmissions and the transmission drain intervals have been extended or eliminated completely. It is therefore most important to install the proper automatic transmission fluid into the automatic transmission designed for its use.

Types of Automatic Transmission Fluid

DEXRON® II

This fluid supersedes the Dexron® type fluid and meets a more severe set of performance requirements, such as improved high temperature oxidation resistance and low temperature fluidity. The Dexron® II is recommended for use in all General Motors, Chrysler, American Motors and certain imported vehicles automatic transmissions. This fluid can replace all Dexron® fluid with a B- number designation.

Container Identification number—D-XXXXX

DEXRON® II—SERIES D

This fluid was developed and is used in place of the regular Dexron® II fluids.

The container identification is with a "D" prefix to the qualification number on the top of the container.

TYPE F

Ford Motor Company began developing its own specifications for automatic transmission fluid in 1959 and again updated its specifications in 1967, requiring fluid with different frictional characteristics and identified as Type F fluid.

Beginning with the 1977 model year, a new Type CJ fluid was specified for use with the C-6 and newly introduced Jatco model PLA-A transmissions. This new fluid is not interchangeable with the Type F fluid.

Prior to 1967, all Ford automatic transmissions use fluids in containers marked with qualification number IP-XXXXXX, meeting Ford specification number ESW-M2C33-D.

Fluids in containers marked with qualification number 2P-XXXXXX meets Ford specification ESW-M2C33-F and is used in the Ford automatic transmissions manufactured since 1967, except the 1977 and later C-6, the Automatic Overdrive, and Jatco models PLA-A, PLA-A1, PLA-A2 transmissions.

The container identification number for the new fluid is Ford part number D7AZ-19582-A and carries a qualification number ESP-M2C138-CJ.

TYPE CJ

——————— CAUTION ———————

The CJ fluid is NOT compatible with clutch friction material of other Ford transmissions and must only be used in the 1977 and later C-6, the Automatic Overdrive and Jatco models PLA-A, PLA-A1 and PLA-A2 automatic transmissions.
Do not mix or interchange the fluids through refills or topping off as the Type F and the Type CJ fluids are not compatible.

A technical bulletin has been issued by Ford Motor Company, dated 1978, advising the compatibility of Dexron® II, series D fluid with the CJ fluid. It can be substituted or mixed, if necessary, in the 1977 and later C-6, the Automatic Overdrive and the Jatco PLA-A, PLA-A1 and PLA-A2 automatic transmissions.

With approved internal modifications, CJ or Dexron® II, series D automatic transmission fluid can be used in the past models of the C-4 transmissions. To insure the proper fluid is installed or added, a mylar label is affixed or is available to be affixed to the dipstick handle with the proper fluid designation on the label.

TYPE H

With the introduction of the C-5 automatic Transmission, Ford Motor Company developed a new type fluid, designated "H", meeting Ford's specification ESP-M2C166-H. This fluid contains a special detergent which retains in suspension, particles generated during normal transmission operation. This suspension of particles results in a dark discoloration of the fluid and does not indicate need for service. It should be noted that the use of other fluids in the C-5 automatic transmission could result in a shuddering condition.

TYPE G

The type G fluid is an improvement over the type F fluid and meets Ford Motor Company specification of M2C-33G.

Type G fluid has the capability of reducing oxidization at higher transmission operating temperatures. Should an automatic transmission be filled with type G fluid, type F fluid can be used to top off the level. However, the more type F fluid that is mixed with the type G fluid, will proportionally reduce the maximum working temperature of the type G fluid.

FLUID CONDITION

During the checking of the fluid level, the fluid condition should be inspected for color and odor. The normal color of the fluid is deep red or orange-red and should not be a burned brown or black color. If the fluid color should turn to a green/brown shade at an early stage of transmission operation and have an offensive odor, but not a burned odor, the fluid condition is considered normal and not a positive sign of required maintenance or transmission failure.

With the use of absorbent white paper, wipe the dipstick and examine the stain for black, brown or metallic specks, indicating clutch, band or bushing failure, and for gum or varnish on the dipstick or bubbles in the fluid, indicating either water or anti-freeze in the fluid.

Should there be evidence of water, anti-freeze or specks of residue in the fluid, the oil pan should be removed and the sediment inspected. If the fluid is contaminated or excessive solids are found in the removed oil pan, the transmission should be disassembled, completely cleaned and overhauled. In addition to the cleaning of the transmission, the converter and transmission cooling system should be cleaned and tested.

Fluid Overfill Problems

When the automatic transmission is overfilled with fluid, the rotation of the internal units can cause the fluid to become aerated. This aeration of the fluid causes air to be picked up by the oil pump and causes loss of control and lubrication pressures. The fluid can also be forced from the transmission assembly through the air vent, due to the aerated condition.

Fluid Underfill Problems

When the fluid is low in the transmission, slippage and loss of unit engagement can result, due to the fluid not being picked up by the pump. This condition is evident when first starting after the vehicle has been sitting and cooled to room temperature, in cold weather, making a turn or driving up a hill. This condition should be corrected promptly to avoid costly transmission repairs.

Throttle Valve and Kickdown Control Inspection

Inspect the throttle valve and kickdown controls for proper operation, prior to the road test. Refer to the individual transmission section for procedures.

THROTTLE VALVE CONTROLS

The throttle valve can be controlled by linkage, cable or engine vacuum.

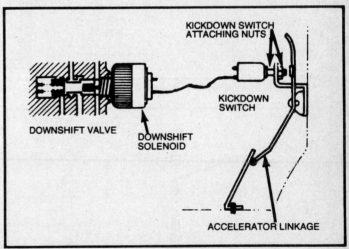

Typical kickdown switch and controls(© Ford Motor Co.)

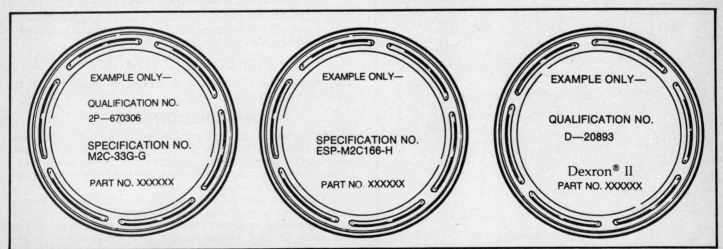

Comparison of types H, G and Dexron® II identifying codes found on container tops—typical

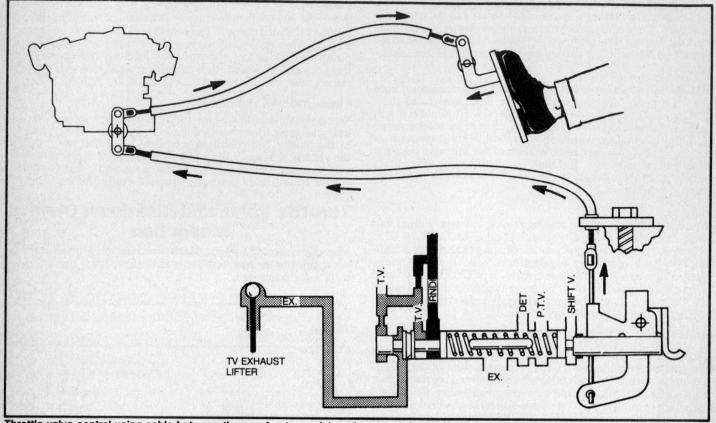

Throttle valve control using cable between the accelerator pedal, carburetor and control valve (© Borg Warner, Ltd.)

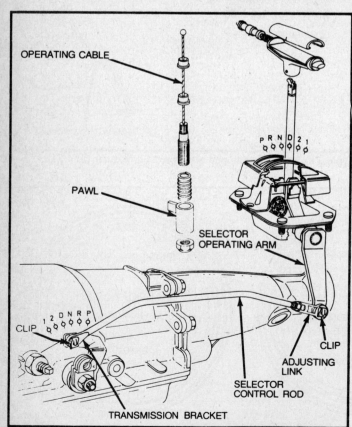

Manual Control linkage phasing—typical(© Ford Motor Co.)

LINKAGE CONTROL

Inspect the linkage for abnormal bends, looseness at the bellcrank connections and linkage travel at the wide open throttle stop. Be sure the linkage operates without binding and returns to the closed position upon release of the accelerator.

CABLE CONTROL

Inspect the cable for sharp bends or crimps, secured retainers, freedom of cable movement throughout the full throttle position and the return to the closed throttle position without binding or sticking, and connection of the throttle return spring.

ENGINE VACUUM CONTROLS

Inspect for sufficient engine vacuum, vacuum hose condition and routing, and signs of transmission fluid in the vacuum hoses indicating a leaking vacuum diaphragm (modulator).

KICKDOWN CONTROLS

The transmission kickdown is controlled by linkage, cable or electrical switches and solenoid.

LINKAGE CONTROLS

The linkage control can be a separate rod connected to and operating in relation with the carburetor throttle valves, or incorporated with the throttle linkage. Inspect for looseness, bends, binding and movement into the kickdown detent upon the movement of the throttle to the wide open stop.

NOTE: It is a advisable to inspect for the wide open throttle position at the carburetor from inside the vehicle, by depressing the accelerator pedal, rather than inspecting movement of the linkage from under the hood. Carpet matting, dirt or looseness of the accelerator can prevent the opening of the throttle to operate the kickdown linkage.

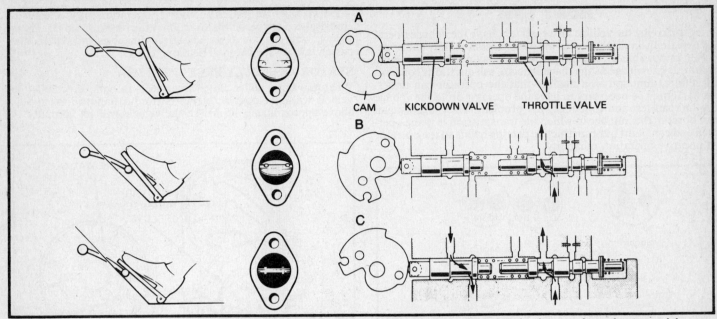

Typical throttle and kickdown valve operation through three possible operating positions of the throttle plates and accelerator pedal (© Borg Warner, Ltd.)

CAM   KICKDOWN VALVE   THROTTLE VALVE

CABLE CONTROLS

The kickdown cable control can be a separate cable or used with the throttle valve control cable. It operates the kickdown valve at the wide open throttle position. Inspect for kinks and bends on bracket retention of the cable. Inspect for freedom of movement of the cable and see that the cable drops into the kickdown detent when the accelerator pedal is fully depressed and the throttle valves are fully open.

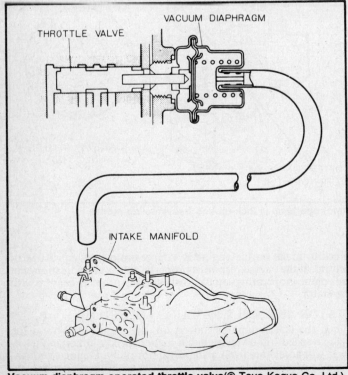

THROTTLE VALVE   VACUUM DIAPHRAGM

INTAKE MANIFOLD

Vacuum diaphragm operated throttle valve(© Toyo Kogyo Co. Ltd.)

ELECTRICAL CONTROLS

The electrical kickdown controls consist of a switch, located on the accelerator linkage and a solenoid control, either mounted externally on the transmission case or mounted internally on the control valve body, in such a position as to operate the kickdown valve upon demand of the vehicle operator. Inspect the switch for proper operation which should allow electrical current to pass through, upon closing of the switch contacts by depressing the accelerator linkage. Inspect the wire connector at the transmission case or the terminals of the externally mounted solenoid for current with the switch contacts closed. With current present at the solenoid, either externally or internally mounted, a clicking noise should be heard, indicating that the solenoid is operating.

Manual Linkage Control Inspection

The manual linkage adjustment is one of the most critical, yet the most overlooked, adjustment on the automatic transmission. The controlling quadrant, either steering column or console mounted, must be properly phased with the manual control valve detent. Should the manual valve be out of adjustment or position, hydraulic leakage can occur within the control valve assembly and can result in delay of unit engagement and/or slippage of the clutches and bands upon application. The partial opening of apply passages can also occur for clutches and bands not in applying sequence, and result in dragging of the individual units or bands during transmission operation.

Inspect the selector lever and quadrant, the linkage or cable control for looseness, excessive wear or binding. Inspect the engine/transmission assembly for excessive lift during engine torque application, due to loose or broken engine mounts, which can pull the manual valve out of position in the control valve detent.

CAUTION

The neutral start switch should be inspected for operation in Park and Neutral positions, after any adjustments are made to the manual linkage or cable.

Road Test

Prior to driving the vehicle on a road test, have the vehicle operator explain the malfunction of the transmission as fully and as accurate as possible. Because the operator may not have the same technical knowledge as the diagnostician, ask questions concerning the malfunction in a manner that the operator can understand. It may be necessary to have the operator drive the vehicle on the road test and to identify the problem. The diagnostician can observe the manner in which the transmission is being operated and can point out constructive driving habits to the operator to improve operation reliability.

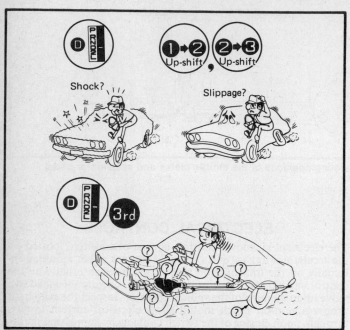

Road Test vehicle to determine malfunctions(© Toyota Motor Co.)

Many times, an actual transmission malfunction can occur without the operator's knowledge, due to slight slippages occurring and increasing in duration while the vehicle is being driven. Had the operator realized that a malfunction existed, minor adjustments possibly could have been done to avoid costly repairs.

As noted previously in this section, be aware of the engine's performance. For example, if a vacuum modulator valve is used to control the throttle pressure, an engine performing poorly cannot send the proper vacuum signals to the transmission for proper application of the throttle pressure and control pressure, in the operation of the bands and clutches. Slippages and changes in shift points can occur.

Perform the road test with the customer, whenever possible, to determine the cause of the malfunction

During the road test, the converter operation must be considered. Related converter malfunctions affecting the road test are as follows, with the converter operation, diagnosis and repairs discussed later in the General Section.

STATOR ASSEMBLY FREE WHEELS

When the stator roller clutch freewheels in both directions, the vehicle will have poor acceleration from a standstill. At speeds above approximately 45 MPH, the vehicle will act normally. A

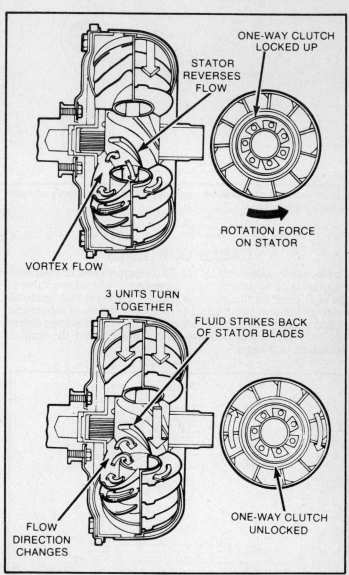

Stator operation in lock-up and freewheeling modes

check to make on the engine is to accelerate to a high RPM in neutral. If the engine responds properly, this is an indication that the engine is operating satisfactorily and the problem may be with the stator.

STATOR ASSEMBLY REMAINS LOCKED UP

When the stator remains locked up, the engine RPM and the vehicle speed will be restricted at higher speeds, although the vehicle will accelerate from a standstill normally. Engine overheating may be noticed and visual inspection of the converter may reveal a blue color, resulting from converter overheating.

Clutch and Band Application

During the road test, operate the transmission/transaxle in each gear position and observe the shifts for signs of any slippage, variation, sponginess or harshness. Note the speeds at which the up-shifts and downshifts occur. If slippage and engine flare-up occurs in any gears, clutch, band or overrunning clutch problems are indicated and depending upon the degree of wear, a major overhaul may be indicated.

The clutch and band application chart in each transmission/transaxle section provides a basis for road test analysis to determine the internal units applied or released in a specific gear ratio.

NOTE: Certain transmission/transaxles use brake clutches in place of bands and are usually indicated as B-1 and B-2 on the unit application chart. These components are diagnosed in the same manner as one would diagnose a band equipped gearbox.

EXAMPLES

Using the Borg Warner Model 66 Clutch and Band application chart as a guide, the following conditions can be determined.

1. A customer complaint is a slippage in third speed and reverse. By referring to the clutch and band application chart, the commonly applied component is the rear clutch unit, applied in both third speed and reverse. By having a starting point, place the gear selector in the reverse position and if the slippage is present and slippage is verified on the road in third speed, all indications would point to rear clutch failure.

Broken input shaft can operate intermittently at low torque applications, until worn smooth as illustrated

2. A customer complaint is a flare-up of engine speed during the 1-2 shift, D position, with a delayed application or sponginess in the second gear. By referring to the clutch and band application chart, the application of the components can be located during each shift and gear ratio level. With the front clutch unit applied in each of the gear ranges and the front band applied only in the second speed, the complaint can then be pinpointed to either the front band being out of adjustment, worn out or a servo apply problem. Because the front clutch is applied in the three forward speeds and no apparent slippage or flare-up occurs in the first or third speeds, the front clutch unit is not at fault.

Many times, malfunctions occur within a unit that are not listed on a diagnosis chart. Such malfunctions could be breakage of servo or clutch return springs, stripped serrated teeth from mated components or broken power transfer shaft, just to name a few. When a malfunction of this type occurs, it can be difficult to diagnose, but by applying the information supplied in a clutch and band application chart, the use of an oil pressure gauge, when necessary, and using a "common sense" approach, the malfunction can be determined.

SUMMARY OF ROAD TEST

This process of elimination is used to locate the unit that is malfunctioning and to confirm the proper operation of the transmission. Although the slipping unit can be defined, the actual cause of the malfunction cannot be determined by the band and clutch application charts. It is necessary to perform hydraulic and air pressure tests to determine if a hydraulic or mechanical component failure is the cause of the malfunction.

Pressure Tests
OIL PRESSURE GAUGE

The oil pressure gauge is the primary tool used by the diagnostician to determine the source of malfunctions of the automatic transmissions.

Oil pressure gauges are available with different rates, ranging from 0-100, 0-300 and 0-500 PSI that are used to measure the pressures in the various hydraulic circuits of the automatic transmissions. The high-rated pressure gauges (0-300, 0-500 PSI) are used to measure the control line pressures while the low-rated gauge (0-100 PSI) is used to measure the governor, lubrication and throttle pressures on certain automatic transmissions.

The gauges may be an individual unit with a 4- to 10-foot hose attached, or may be part of a console unit with other gauges, normally engine tachometer and vacuum. The diagnostician's preference dictates the type used.

CLUTCH AND BAND APPLICATION CHART
Borg Warner Model 66

Gear	Front Clutch	Rear Clutch	Front Band	Rear Band	One-Way Clutch
Drive 1st	Applied	—	—	—	Holding
Drive 2nd	Applied	—	Applied	—	—
Drive 3rd	Applied	Applied	—	—	—
1—Low	Applied	—	—	Applied	—
2—1st	Applied	—	—	—	Holding
2—2nd	Applied	—	Applied	—	—
Reverse	—	Applied	—	Applied	—

NOTE: Rear band is released in "N", but applied in "P" for constructional reasons only.

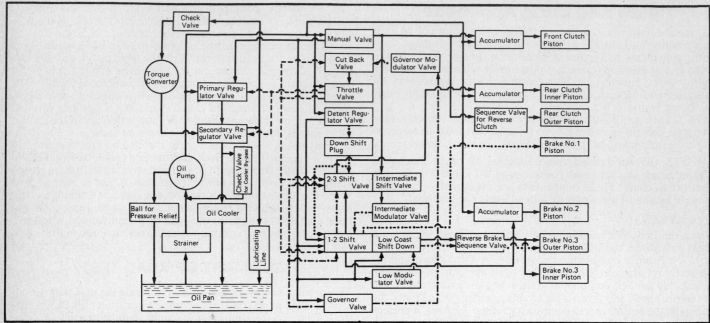

Typical hydraulic control system(© Toyota Motor Co.)

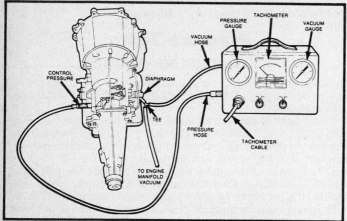

Typical installation of oil pressure and vacuum gauges on transmission(© Ford Motor Co.)

To measure the hydraulic pressures, select a gauge rated over the control pressure specifications and install the hose fitting into the control pressure line tap, located either along the side or the rear of the transmission case. Refer to the individual automatic transmission sections for the correct locations, since many transmission cases have more than one pressure tap to check pressures other than the control pressure.

The pressure gauges can be used during a road test, but care must be exercised in routing the hose from under the vehicle to avoid dragging or being entangled with objects on the roadway.

The gauge should be positioned so the dial is visible to the diagnostician near the speedometer area. If a console of gauges is used, the console is normally mounted on a door window or on the vehicle dash.

─── **CAUTION** ───

During the road test, traffic safety must be exercised. It is advisable to have a helper to assist in the reading or recording of the results during the road test.

CONTROL PRESSURE TESTING

The methods of obtaining control pressure readings when conducting a pressure test, vary from manufacturer to manufacturer when vacuum modulators are used to modulate the throttle pressures. Since engine vacuum is the controlling factor as the vehicle is being driven, the amount of vacuum must be controlled when testing. The use of a motorized vacuum pump, a hand held mechanically operated vacuum pump or an air bleed valve may be recommended by the manufacturer.

Before any vacuum tests are performed on the modulator, the engine, being the primary vacuum source, must be checked to ascertain that vacuum is available to the modulator. The hose at the modulator should be disconnected and a vacuum gauge attached to the hose. With the brakes set and the engine idling at normal operating temperature, the engine vacuum reading should be in

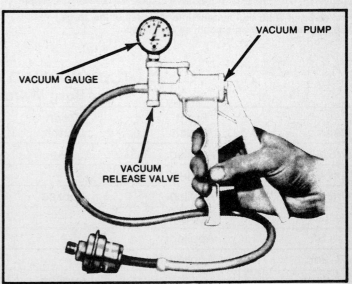

Typical vacuum pump used to test vacuum diaphrams on and off the transmission(© Ford Motor Co.)

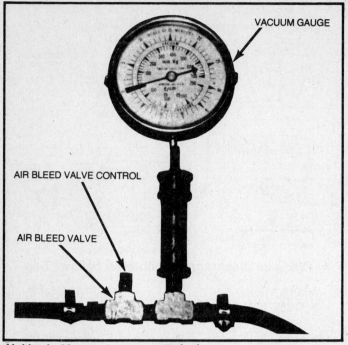

Air bleed with vacuum gauge attached

the 17 to 20 in. Hg range. Should the vacuum be low, check the vacuum reading at the engine and compare the two readings. If the vacuum reading is lower at the modulator end of the hose than at the engine, look for leaking or defective hoses or lines. If both readings are low, the engine is not producing sufficient vacuum to properly operate the modulator at road speeds or under specific road conditions, which could result in transmission malfunctions and premature internal wear. To correct this condition, the reason for the low engine vacuum would have to be determined and repaired.

CAUTION

To install a rebuilt unit under this type of vacuum condition would invite operational problems.

An air bleed valve was placed in the vacuum line from the engine to the modulator to control the amount of vacuum reacting on the diaphragm, simply by allowing more or less atmospheric air to enter the vacuum line, controlled by a screw valve. This type of testing has been replaced by the use of the hand held mechanical vacuum pump, in most cases.

Testing Control Pressure—Typical

To illustrate a typical control pressure test, the following explanation is given concerning the accompanying chart.

NOTE: Refer to the individual transmission sections for correct specifications.

TRANSMISSION MALFUNCTION RELATED TO OIL PRESSURE

③ Drive Brakes Applied 1000 RPM	③ Reverse Brakes Applied 1000 RPM	③ Super or Lo Brakes Applied 1000 RPM	Neutral Brakes Applied 1000 RPM	③ Drive 1000 RPM Brakes on Detent* Activated	Drive Idle	① Drive 30 MPH Closed Throttle	Drive—from 1000 to 3000 RPM Wheels free to move	Pressure Test Conditions
15-20" vacuum applied to modulator							0" vacuum to modulator	
60-90	85-150	85-110	55-70	90-110	60-85	55-70	Pressure drop of 10 PSI or more	Normal Results Note2
							DROP	Malfunction in Control Valve Assembly
							NO DROP	Malfunction in Governor or Governor Feed System
ALL PRESSURES HIGH WITH LESS THAN 35 PSI BETWEEN PRESSURE READINGS							—	Malfunction in Detent System
ALL PRESSURES HIGH WITH MORE THAN 35 PSI BETWEEN PRESSURE READINGS							—	Malfunction in Modulator
Low					—	Low to Normal	—	Oil Leak in Feed System to the Direct Clutch
Low		Low to Normal		Low to Normal	—	Low to Normal	—	Oil Leak in Feed System to the Forward Clutch
				Low			—	Detent System

A blank space = Normal pressure
A dash (—) in space = Pressure reading has no meaning
① Coast for 30 mph—read before reaching 20 mph

② If high line pressures are experienced see "High Line Pressures" note.

③ Cable pulled or blocked thru detent position or downshift switch closed by hand

NOTE: It is assumed the oil pressure gauge, the vacuum gauge, the vacuum pump, and the tachometer are attached to the engine/transmission assembly, while having the brakes locked and the wheels chocked. The fluid temperature should be at normal operating temperature.

1. Start the engine and allow to idle.

2. Apply 15-20 inches of vacuum to the vacuum modulator with the vacuum hand pump.

3. Place the selector lever in the Drive position and increase the engine speed to 1000 RPM. The pressure reading should be 60-90 PSI, as indicated on the chart.

4. Taking another example from the chart, place the selector lever in the Super or Low position and increase the engine speed to 1000 RPM. As indicated on the chart, the pressure should read 85-110 PSI.

5. Referring to the chart column to test pressures with the detent activated, the following must be performed. Place the selector lever in the Drive position and increase the engine speed to 1000 RPM. With the aid of a helper, if necessary, pull the detent cable through the detent, or if the transmission is equipped with an electrical downshift switch, close the switch by hand. The pressure reading should be 90-110 PSI, as indicated on the chart.

6. A pressure test conditions column is included in the chart to assist the diagnostician in determining possible causes of transmission malfunctions from the hydraulic system.

——————— CAUTION ———————

Do not use the above pressure readings when actually testing the control pressures. The above readings are only used as a guide for the chart explanation. Refer to the individual transmission section for the correct specifications and pressure readings.

HIGH CONTROL PRESSURE

If a condition of high control pressure exists, the general causes can be categorized as follows.
1. Vacuum leakage or low vacuum
2. Vacuum modulator damaged
3. Pump pressure excessive
4. Control valve assembly
5. Throttle linkage or cable misadjusted

LOW CONTROL PRESSURE

If a condition of low control pressure exists, the general causes can be categorized as follows.
1. Transmission fluid low
2. Vacuum modulator defective
3. Filter assembly blocked or air leakage
4. Oil pump defective
5. Hydraulic circuit leakage
6. Control valve body

NO CONTROL PRESSURE RISE

If a control pressure rise does not occur as the vacuum drops or the throttle valve linkage/cable is moved, the mechanical connection between the vacuum modulator or throttle valve linkage/cable and the throttle valve should be inspected. Possible broken or disconnected parts are at fault.

Vacuum Modulator

TESTING

A defective vacuum modulator can cause one or more of the following conditions.
- a. Engine burning transmission fluid
- b. Transmission overheating
- c. Harsh upshifts
- d. Delayed shifts
- e. Soft up and down shifts

Whenever a vacuum modulator is suspected of malfunctioning, a vacuum check should be made of the vacuum supply.

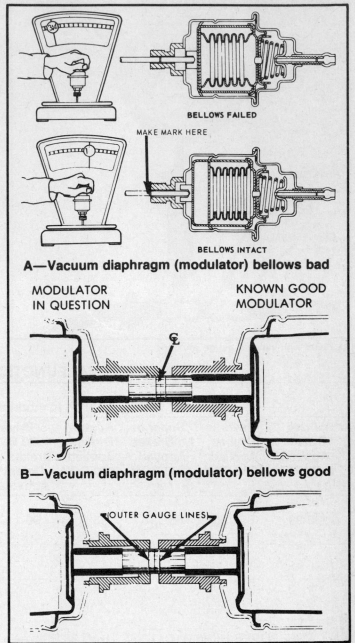

A—Vacuum diaphragm (modulator) bellows bad

MODULATOR IN QUESTION   KNOWN GOOD MODULATOR

B—Vacuum diaphragm (modulator) bellows good

Other methods used to test vacuum diaphragms

1. Disconnect the vacuum line at the transmission vacuum modulator connector pipe.

2. With the engine running, the vacuum gauge should show an acceptable level of vacuum for the altitude at which the test is being performed.

3. If the vacuum reading is low, check for broken, split or crimped hoses and for proper engine operation.

4. If the vacuum reading is acceptable, accelerate the engine quickly. The vacuum should drop off and return immediately upon release of the accelerator. If the gauge does not register a change in the vacuum reading, indications are that the vacuum lines are plugged, restricted or connected to a reservoir supply.

5. Correct the vacuum supply as required.

When the vacuum supply is found to be sufficient, the vacuum modulator must be inspected and this can be accomplished on or off the vehicle.

On Vehicle Tests

1. Remove the vacuum line and attach a vacuum pump to the modulator connector pipe.

2. Apply 18 inches of vacuum to the modulator. The vacuum should remain at 18 inches without leaking down.

3. If the vacuum reading drops sharply or will not remain at 18 inches, the diaphragm is leaking and the unit must be replaced.

4. If transmission fluid is present on the vacuum side of the diaphragm or in the vacuum hose, the diaphragm is leaking and the unit must be replaced.

NOTE: Gasoline or water vapors may settle on the vacuum side of the diaphragm. Do not diagnose as transmission fluid.

Off Vehicle Tests

1. Remove the vacuum modulator from the transmission.

2. Attach a vacuum pump to the vacuum modulator connector pipe and apply 18 inches of vacuum.

3. The vacuum should hold at 18 inches, if the diaphragm is good and will drop to zero if the diaphragm is leaking.

4. With the control rod in the transmission side of the vacuum modulator, apply vacuum to the connector pipe. The rod should move inward with light finger pressure applied to the end of the rod. When the vacuum is released, the rod will move outward by pressure from the internal spring.

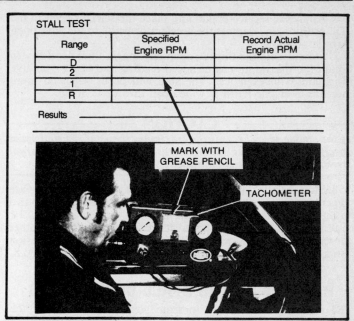

Preparation for stall test (© Ford Motor Co.)

Stall Speed Tests

The stall speed test is performed to evaluate the condition of the transmission as well as the condition of the engine.

The stall speed is the maximum speed at which the engine can drive the torque converter impeller while the turbine is held stationary. Since the stall speed is dependent upon the engine and torque converter characteristics, it can vary with the condition of the engine as well as the condition of the automatic transmission, so it is most important to have a properly performing engine before a stall speed test is attempted, thereby eliminating the engine from any malfunction that may be present.

Because engines perform differently between high and low altitudes, the stall speeds given in specification charts are for vehicles tested at sea level and cannot be considered representative of stall speed tests performed at higher altitudes. Unless specific stall speed tests specification charts are available for use at higher altitudes, representative stall speeds can be determined by testing several vehicles known to be operating properly, averaging the results and recording the necessary specifications for future reference.

EFFECT OF ALTITUDE ON ENGINE VACUUM

Elevation in Feet	Number of Engine Cylinders		
	FOUR	SIX	EIGHT
Zero to 1000	18 to 20	19 to 21	21 to 22
1000 to 2000	17 to 19	18 to 20	19 to 21
2000 to 3000	16 to 18	17 to 19	18 to 20
3000 to 4000	15 to 17	16 to 18	17 to 19
4000 to 5000	14 to 16	15 to 17	16 to 18
5000 to 6000	13 to 15	14 to 16	15 to 17

PERFORMING THE STALL SPEED TESTS

1. Attach a tachometer to the engine and an oil pressure gauge to the transmission control pressure tap. Position the tachometer and oil pressure gauge so the operator can read the dials.

2. Mark the specified maximum engine RPM on the tachometer clear cover with a grease pencil so that the operator can immediately check the stall speed to see if it is over or under specifications.

3. Start the engine and bring to normal operating temperature.

4. Check the transmission fluid level and correct as necessary.

5. Apply the parking brake and chock the wheels.

— CAUTION —

Do not allow anyone in front of the vehicle during the preparation or during the stall speed test.

SAMPLE STALL TEST DIAGNOSIS CHART

Selector Lever Range	Specified Engine RPM	Actual Engine RPM	Control Pressure PSI	Holding Members Applied
D (Drive)				
1				
2				
R (Reverse)				

NOTE: The range identifications are to be taken from the selector quadrant of the vehicle being tested. Before stall test, fill in the specified engine RPM and the holding members applied columns from the clutch and band application and specification charts of the automatic transmission being tested.

6. Apply the service brakes and place the selector lever in the "D" position and depress the accelerator pedal to the wide open throttle position.

7. Do not hold the throttle open any longer than necessary to obtain the maximum engine speed reading and never over five (5) seconds for each test. The stall will occur when no more increase in engine RPM at wide open throttle is noted.

— CAUTION —

If the engine speed exceeds the maximum limits of the stall speed specifications, release the accelerator immediately as internal transmission slippage is indicated.

8. Shift the selector lever into the Neutral position and operate the engine from 1000 to 1500 RPM for at least 30 seconds to two minutes to cool the transmission fluid.

9. If necessary, the stall speed test can be performed in other forward and reverse gear positions. Observe the transmission fluid cooling procedure between each test as outlined in step 8.

RESULTS OF THE STALL SPEED TESTS

The stall speed RPM will indicate possible problems. If the engine RPM is high, internal transmission slippage is indicated. If the engine RPM is low, engine or converter problems can exist.

The transmission will not upshift during the stall test and by knowing what internal transmission members are applied in each test range, an indication of a unit failure can be pinpointed.

It is recommended a chart be prepared to assist the diagnostician in the determination of the stall speed results in comparison to the specified engine RPM, and should include the range and holding member applied.

LOW ENGINE RPM ON STALL SPEED TEST

The low engine RPM stall speed indicates either the engine is not performing properly or the converter stator one-way clutch is not holding. By road testing the vehicle, the determination as to the defect can be made.

If the stator is not locked by the one-way clutch, the performance of the vehicle will be poor up to approximately 30-35 MPH. If the engine is in need of repairs or adjustments, the performance of the vehicle will be poor at all speeds.

HIGH ENGINE RPM ON STALL SPEED TEST

When the engine RPM is higher than specifications, internal transmission unit slippage is indicated. By following the holding member application chart, the defective unit can be pinpointed.

It must be noted that a transmission using a one-way overrunning clutch while in the "D" position, first gear, and having a band applied in the "2" position, first gear (for vehicle braking purposes while going downhill), may have the band slipping unnoticed during the stall test, because the overruning clutch will hold. To determine this, a road test must be performed to place the transmission in a range where the band is in use without the overrunning clutch.

NORMAL ENGINE RPM ON STALL SPEED TEST

When the engine RPM is within the specified ranges, the holding members of the transmission are considered to be operating properly.

A point of interest is if the converter oneway clutch (overrunning) is seized and locks the stator from turning either way, the engine RPM will be normal during the test, but the converter will be in reduction at all times and the vehicle will probably not exceed a speed of 50-60 miles per hour. If this condition is suspected, examine the fluid and the converter exterior for signs of overheating, since an extreme amount of heat is generated when the converter remains in constant reduction.

Transmission Noises

During the stall speed test and the road test, the diagnostician must be alert to any abnormal noises from the transmission area or any excessive movement of the engine/transmission assembly during torque application or transmission shifting.

— CAUTION —

Before attempting to diagnose automatic transmission noises, be sure the noises do not orginate from the engine components, such as the water pump, alternator, air conditioner compressor, power steering or the air injection pump. Isolate these components by removing the proper drive belt and operate the engine. Do not operate the engine longer than two minutes at a time to avoid overheating.

1. Whining or siren type noises—Can be considered normal if occurring during a stall speed test, due to the fluid flow through the converter.

2. Whining noise (continual with vehicle stationary)—If the noise increases and decreases with the engine speed, the following defects could be present.

   a. Oil level low

   b. Air leakage into pump (defective gasket, "O"-ring or porosity of a part)

   c. Pump gears damaged or worn

   d. Pump gears assembled backward

   e. Pump crescent interference

3. Buzzing noise—This type of noise is normally the result of a pressure regulator valve vibrating or a sealing ring broken or worn out and will usually come and go, depending upon engine/transmission speed.

4. Rattling noise (constant)—Usually occurring at low engine speed and resulting from the vanes stripped from the impeller or turbine face or internal interference of the converter parts.

5. Rattling noise (intermittent)—Reflects a broken flywheel or flex plate and usually occurs at low engine speed with the transmission in gear. Placing the transmission in "N" or "P" will change the rattling noise or stop it for a short time.

6. Gear noise (one gear range)—This type of noise will normally indicate a defective planetary gear unit. Upon shifting into another gear range, the noise will cease. If the noise carries over to the next gear range, but at a different pitch, defective thrust bearings or bushings are indicated.

7. Engine vibration or excessive movement—Can be caused by transmission filler or cooler lines vibrating due to broken or disconnected brackets. If excessive engine/transmission movement is noted, look for broken engine/transmission mounts.

— CAUTION —

When necessary to support an engine equipped with metal safety tabs on the mounts, be sure the metal tabs are not in contact with the mount bracket after the engine/transmission assembly is again supported by the mounts. A severe vibration can result.

8. Squeal at low vehicle speeds—Can result from a speedometer driven gear seal, a front pump seal or rear extension seal being dry.

The above list of noises can be used as a guide. Noises other than the ones listed can occur around or within the transmission assembly. A logical and common sense approach will normally result in the source of the noise being detected.

Air Pressure Tests

The automatic transmission have many hidden passages and hydraulic units that are controlled by internal fluid pressures, supplied through tubes, shafts and valve movements.

The air pressure test are used to confirm the findings of the fluid pressure tests and to further pinpoint the malfunctioning area. The air pressure test can also confirm the hydraulic unit operation after repairs have been made.

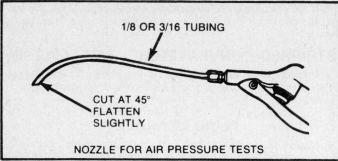

Type of air nozzle to be used in the air pressure tests
(© Ford Motor Co.)

To perform the air pressure test, the control valve body must be removed from the transmission case, exposing the case passages. By referring to the individual transmission section, identify each passage before any attempt is made to proceed with the air pressure test.

CAUTION

It is a good practice to protect the diagnostician's face and body with glasses and protective clothing and the surrounding area from the oil spray that will occur when air pressure is applied to the various passages.

NOTE: The air pressure should be controlled to approximately 25 psi and the air should be clean and dry.

When the passages have been identified and the air pressure applied to a designated passage, reaction can be seen, heard and felt in the various units. Should air pressure be applied to a clutch apply passage, the piston movement can be felt and a soft dull thud should be heard. Some movement of the unit assembly can be seen.

When air pressure is applied to a servo apply passage, the servo rod or arm will move and tighten the band around the drum. Upon release of the air pressure, spring tension should release the servo piston.

When air pressure is applied to the governor supply passage, a whistle, click or buzzing noise may be heard.

When failures have occurred within the transmission assembly and the air pressure tests are made, the following problems may exist.
1. No clutch piston movement
2. Hissing noise and excessive fluid spray
3. Excessive unit movement
4. No servo band apply or release

Torque Converter

The torque converter is a simple, but yet complex torque multiplication unit, designed and applied to specific engine/transmis-

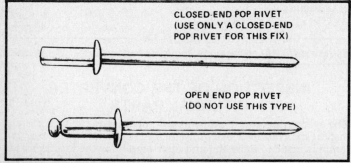

Comparison of closed end "POP" rivet and open end "POP" rivet

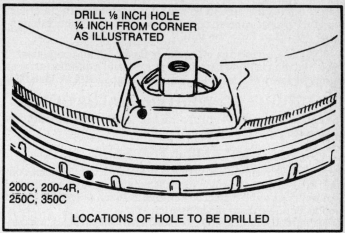

Location of hole to be drilled in the converters of models THM 325, 200C, 200-4R, 250C and 350C transmissions
(© General Motors Corp.)

sion/transaxle applications. Manufacturers apply different ratings for their application to a specific engine. An example is the use of the "K" factor method by several of the vehicle manufacturers to indicate the performance curve of a given engine size. The larger the "K" factor, the smaller the engine size, which gives more engine break-away torque at lower speeds.
Example:

$$K = \frac{RPM}{\sqrt{Torque\ (Nm)}}$$

$$K = \frac{2200}{\sqrt{100}}$$

$$K = \frac{2200}{10}$$

$$K = 220$$

NOTE: Torque of 100 N•m is usually constant for the finding of the "K" factor.

NOTE: Performance cars are rated differently.

Regardless of the type of rating used, the correct torque converter must be coupled to the specific engine/transmission/transaxle assembly to achieve the desired operational efficiency. Converter rebuilders are supplying quality rebuilt units to the trade, that in most cases, equal the performance of the new converter units. In cases where problems occur, it is generally the use of a converter assembly that does not match the desired performance curve of the engine/transmission/transaxle assembly.

DRAINING AND FLUSHING THE CONVERTER

When the converter has become filled with contaminated fluid that can be flushed out and the converter reused, the different manufacturers recommend procedures that should be followed for their respective converters. All recommend the use of a commercial flushing machine, if available. Certain converters will have drain plugs that can be removed to allow the fluid to drain. Other manufacturers recommend the drilling of drain holes and the use of a rivet plug to close the hole after the fluid has been drained and the converter flushed. With the use of lock-up converters, the drilling of a drain hole in the converter shell must be done correctly or the lock-up mechanism can be damaged. Various after-market suppliers have drill and tap guide kits available to drill a hole in the converter, tap threads in the shell and install a threaded plug or a kit with a drill, pop rivets and instructions on the location of the hole to be drilled. Certain manufacturers require that a contaminated converter be replaced without attempting to drain and flush the unit.

NOTE: Be certain the oil cooler is flushed of all contaminates before the vehicle is put back in service. Should a question arise as to the efficiency of the cooler, a replacement should be installed.

TORQUE CONVERTER EVALUATION

The following is a "rule of thumb" as to the determination regarding the replacement or usage of the converter.

CONTAMINATED FLUID

1. If the fluid in the converter is discolored but does not contain metal particles, the converter is not damaged internally and does not need to be replaced. Remove as much of the discolored fluid as possible from the converter.

2. If the fluid in the converter contains metal particles, the converter is damaged internally and must be replaced.

3. If the fluid contamination was due to burned clutch plates, overheated fluid or engine coolant leakage, the unit should be flushed. The degree of contamination would have to be decided by the repairman in regards to either the replacement or flushing of the unit.

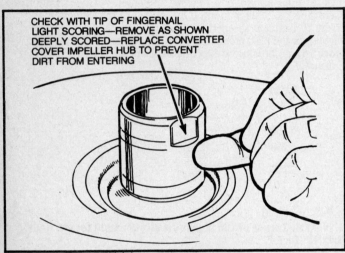

CHECK WITH TIP OF FINGERNAIL
LIGHT SCORING—REMOVE AS SHOWN
DEEPLY SCORED—REPLACE CONVERTER
COVER IMPELLER HUB TO PREVENT
DIRT FROM ENTERING

Checking converter hub for light or heavy scoring
(© Ford Motor Co.)

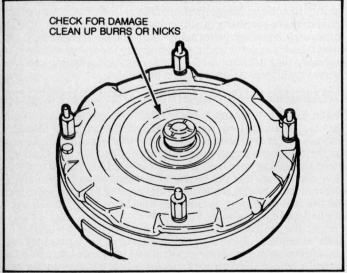

CHECK FOR DAMAGE
CLEAN UP BURRS OR NICKS

Checking converter cover for nicks or burrs (© Ford Motor Co.)

4. If the pump gears or cover show signs of damage or are broken, the converter will contain metal particles and must be replaced.

STRIPPED CONVERTER BOLT RETAINERS

1. Inspect for the cause, such as damaged bolt threads. Repair the stripped bolt retainers, using Heli-coils or its equivalent.

FLUID LEAKAGE

1. Inspect the converter hub surface for roughness, scoring or wear that could damage the seal or bushing. If the roughness can be felt with a fingernail, the front seal could be damaged. Repair the hub surface with fine crocus cloth, if possible, and replace the front seal.

2. Inspect the inside of the bell housing. If fluid is present, leakage is indicated and the converter should be leak tested. If leaks are found in the converter, the unit should be replaced.

CAUTION
Do not attempt to re-weld the converter.

CONVERTER NOISE OR SLIPPAGE

1. Check for loose or missing flywheel to converter bolts, a cracked flywheel, a broken converter pilot, or other engine parts that may be vibrating. Correct as required.

NOTE: Most converter noises occur under light throttle in the "D" position and with the brakes applied.

2. Inspect the converter for excessive end play by the use of the proper checking tools. Replace the converter if the turbine end play exceeds the specifications (usually 0.050 in.).

3. Inspect the converter for damages to the internal roller bearings, thrust races and roller clutch. The thrust roller bearing and thrust races can be checked by viewing them when looking into the converter neck or feeling through the opening to make sure they are not cracked, broken or mispositioned.

4. Inspect the stator clutch by either inserting a protected finger into the splined inner race of the roller clutch or using special tools designed for the purpose, and trying to turn the race in either direction. The inner race should turn freely in a clockwise direction, but not turn or be very difficult to turn in a counterclockwise direction. The converter must be replaced if the roller bearings, thrust races or roller clutch are damaged.

CONVERTER VIBRATION

1. Isolate the cause of the vibration by disconnecting other engine driven parts one at a time. If the converter is determined to be the cause of the vibration, check for loss of balance weights and should they be missing, replace the converter. If the weights are in place, relocate the converter 120 degrees at a time to cancel out engine and converter unbalanced conditions. Washers may be used on the converter to flywheel bolts to isolate an area of unbalance.

CAUTION
Be sure sufficient clearance is available before starting the engine.

INSPECTION OF THE CONVERTER INTERNAL PARTS

The average automatic transmission repair shop can and should inspect the converter assembly for internal wear before any attempt is made to reuse the unit after rebuilding the transmission unit. Special converter checking tools are needed and can be obtained through various tool supply channels.

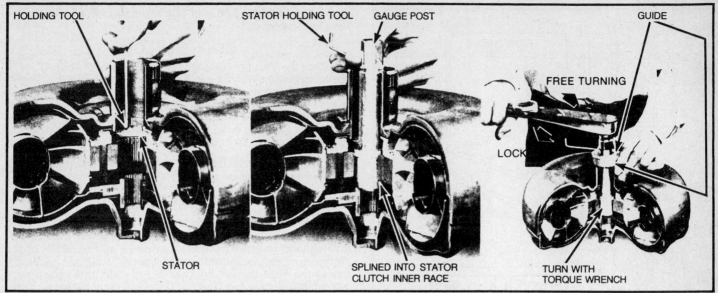

Preparing tool to inspect converter stator overrunning clutch operation(© Ford Motor Co.)

CHECKING CONVERTER END PLAY (STATOR AND TURBINE)

1. Place the converter on a flat surface with the flywheel side down and the converter hub opening up.
2. Insert the special end play checking tool into the drive hub opening until the tool bottoms.

NOTE: Certain end play checking tools have a dual purpose, to check the stator and turbine end play and to check the stator one-way clutch operation. The dual purpose tool will have an expandable sleeve (collet) on the end, along with splines to engage the internal splines of the stator one-way clutch inner race.

3. Install the cover or guide plate over the converter hub and tighten the screw nut firmly to expand the split sleeve (collet) in the turbine hub.
4. Attach a dial indicator tool on the tool screw and position the indicator tip or button on the converter hub or the cover. Zero the dial indicator.
5. Lift the screw upward as far as it will go, carrying the dial indicator with it. Read the measurement from the indicator dial. The reading represents the converter end play.
6. Refer to the individual automatic transmission sections for the permissible converter end play.
7. Remove the tools from the converter assembly. Do not leave the split sleeve (collet) in the turbine hub.

STATOR TO IMPELLER INTERFERENCE CHECK

1. Place the transmission oil pump assembly on a flat surface with the stator splines up.
2. Carefully install the converter on oil pump and engage the stator splines.
3. Hold the pump assembly and turn the converter counterclockwise.
4. The converter should turn freely with no interference. If a slight rubbing noise is heard, this is considered normal, but if a binding or loud scraping noise is heard, the converter should be replaced.

STATOR-TO-TURBINE INTERFERENCE CHECK

1. Place the converter assembly on a flat surface with the flywheel side down and the converter hub opening up.

2. Install the oil pump on the converter hub. Install the input shaft into the converter and engage the turbine hub splines.
3. While holding the oil pump and converter, rotate the input shaft back and forth.
4. The input shaft should turn freely with only a slight rubbing noise. If a binding or loud scraping noise is heard, the converter should be replaced.

STATOR ONE-WAY CLUTCH CHECK

Because the stator one-way clutch must hold the stator for torque multiplication at low speed and free-wheel at high speeds during the coupling phase, the stator assembly must be checked while the converter is out of the vehicle.

1. Have the converter on a flat surface with the flywheel side down and the hub opening up.
2. Install the stator race holding tool into the converter hub opening and insert the end into the groove in the stator to prevent the stator from turning.
3. Place the special tool post, without the screw and split sleeve (collet), into the converter hub opening. Engage the splines of the tool post with the splines of the stator race. Install the cover or guide plate to hold the tool post in place.
4. With a torque wrench, turn the tool post in a clockwise manner. The stator should turn freely.
5. Turn the tool post with the torque wrench in a counterclockwise rotation and the lock-up clutch should lock up with a 10 ft.-lb. pull.
6. If the lock-up clutch does not lock up, the one-way clutch is defective and the converter should be replaced.

Certain vehicle manufacturers do not recommend the use of special tools or the use of the pump cover stator shaft as a testing device for the stator one-way clutch unit. Their recommendations are to insert a finger into the converter hub opening and contact the splined inner race of the one-way clutch. An attempt should be made to rotate the stator inner race in a clockwise direction and the race should turn freely. By turning the inner race in a counter-clockwise rotation, it should either lock-up or turn with great difficulty.

— CAUTION —

Care should be exercised to remove any metal burrs from the converter hub before placing a finger into the opening. Personal injury could result.

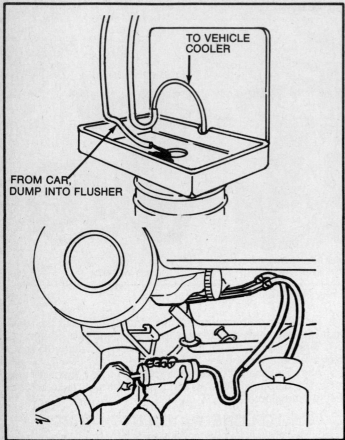

To Vehicle Cooler

FROM CAR,
DUMP INTO FLUSHER

Two methods of flushing transmission cooler and lines

CONVERTER LOCK-UP CLUTCH AND PISTON

Unless a direct malfunction occurs and/or fluid contamination exists from the converter clutch unit, it is extremely difficult to diagnose an internal wear problem. The diagnostician should exercise professional expertise when the determination is made to replace or reuse the converter unit, relating to mileage, type of operation and wear of related parts within the gearbox.

Flushing the Fluid Cooler and Lines

Much reference has been made to the importance of flushing the transmission/transaxle fluid coolers and lines during an overhaul procedure. With the increased use of converter clutch units and the necessary changes to the internal fluid routings, the passage of contaminated fluid, sludge or metal particles to the fluid cooler is more predominate. In most cases, the fluid returning from the fluid cooler is directed to the lubrication system and should the system be deprived of lubricating fluid due to blockage, premature unit failure will occur.

GENERAL FLUSHING PROCEDURES

Two methods of flushing the fluid cooling system can be used.
  a. Disconnect both fluid lines from the cooler and the transmission/transaxle and flush each line and cooler separately.
  b. Disconnect both fluid lines from the transmission/transaxle assemblies, leaving the lines attached to the cooler. Add a length of hose to the return line and place in a container. Flush both lines and the cooler at the same time.
When flushing the cooling components, use a commercial flushing fluid or its equivalent. Reverse flush the lines and cooler with the flushing fluid and pulsating air pressure. Continue the flushing process until clean flushing fluid appears. Remove the

flushing fluid by the addition of transmission fluid through the lines and cooler.

COOLER FLOW

To check the fluid flow through the cooler, place the return line to the transmission/transaxle in a clean container of approximately one quart capacity. Overfill the transmission/transaxle by one quart of fluid, start the engine with the shift in the neutral position. Run the engine for exactly twenty (20) seconds. If the cooler flow is less than one quart in the twenty (20) seconds, have the radiator fluid cooler reconditioned or replaced.

NOTE: Commercial flushing machines are available that flush the fluid cooling system and measure the rate of flow.

Special Tools

There are an unlimited amount of special tools and accessories available to the transmission rebuilder to lessen the time and effort required in performing the diagnosing and overhaul of the automatic transmission/transaxles. Specific tools are necessary during the disassembly and assembly of each unit and its subassemblies. Certain tools can be fabricated, but it becomes the responsibility of the repair shop operator to obtain commercially manufactured tools to insure quality rebuilding and to avoid costly "come backs."

The commercial labor saving tools range from puller sets, bushing and seal installer sets, compression tools and presses (both mechanically and hydraulically operated), holding fixtures, oil pump aligning tools (a necessity on most automatic transmissions) to work bench arrangements, degreaser tanks, steam cleaners, converter flushing machines, transmission jacks and lifts, to name a few. For specific information concerning the various tools, a parts and tool supplier should be consulted.

In addition to the special tools, a complete tool chest with the necessary hand tools should be available to the repairman.

BASIC MEASURING TOOLS

The use of the basic measuring tools has become more critical in the rebuilding process. The increased use of front drive transaxles, in which both the automatic transmission and the final drive gears are located, has required the rebuilder to adhere to specifications and tolerances more closely than ever before.

Bearings must be torqued or adjusted to specific preloads in order to meet the rotating torque drag specifications. The end play and backlash of the varied shafts and gears must be measured to avoid excessive tightness or looseness. Critical tensioning bolts must be torqued to their specifications to avoid warpage of components and proper mating of others.

Dial indicators must be protected and used as a delicate measuring instrument. A mutilated or un-calibrated dial indicator invites premature unit failure and destruction. Torque wrenches are available in many forms, some cheaply made and others, accurate and durable under constant use. To obtain accurate readings and properly applied torque, recalibration should be applied to the torque wrenches periodically, regardless of the type used. Micrometers are used as precise measuring tools and should be properly stored when not in use. Instructions on the recalibration of the micrometers and a test bar usually accompany the tool when it is purchased.

Other measuring tools are available to the rebuilder and each in their own way, must be protected when not in use to avoid causing mis-measuring in the fitting of a component to the unit. A good example of poorly cared-for tools is the lowly feeler gauge blades. Many times a bent and wrinkled blade is used to measure clearances that, if incorrect, can cause the failure of a rebuilt unit. Why risk the failure of a $1000.00 unit because of a $2.98 feeler gauge? Good tools and the knowledge of how to use them reflects upon the longevity of the rebuilt unit.

STANDARD TORQUE SPECIFICATIONS
AND CAPSCREW MARKINGS

Newton/Metre has been designated as the world standard for measuring torque and will gradually replace the foot-pound and kilogram-meter torque measuring standard. Torquing tools are still being manufactured with foot-pounds and kilogram-meter scales, along with the new Newton-Metre standard. To assist the repairman, foot-pounds, kilogram-meter and Newton-Metre are listed in the following charts, and should be followed as applicable.

U. S. BOLTS

SAE Grade Number	1 or 2			5			6 or 7			8		
Capscrew Head Markings Manufacturer's marks may vary. Three-line markings on heads shown below, for example, indicate SAE Grade 5. 	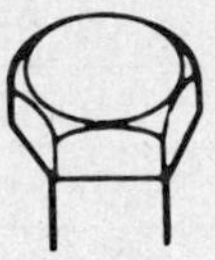											
Usage	Used Frequently			Used Frequently			Used at Times			Used at Times		
Quality of Material	Indeterminate			Minimum Commercial			Medium Commercial			Best Commercial		
Capacity Body Size (inches)—(Thread)	**Torque** Ft-Lb	kgm	Nm	**Torque** Ft-Lb	kgm	Nm	**Torque** Ft-Lb	kgm	Nm	**Torque** Ft-Lb	kgm	Nm
¼-20	5	0.6915	6.7791	8	1.1064	10.8465	10	1.3630	13.5582	12	1.6596	16.2698
-28	6	0.8298	8.1349	10	1.3830	13.5582				14	1.9362	18.9815
⁵/₁₆-18	11	1.5213	14.9140	17	2.3511	23.0489	19	2.6277	25.7605	24	3.3192	32.5396
-24	13	1.7979	17.6256	19	2.6277	25.7605				27	3.7341	36.6071
⅜-16	18	2.4894	24.4047	31	4.2873	42.0304	34	4.7022	46.0978	44	6.0852	59.6560
-24	20	2.7660	27.1164	35	4.8405	47.4536				49	6.7767	66.4351
⁷/₁₆-14	28	3.8132	37.9629	49	6.7767	66.4351	55	7.6065	74.5700	70	9.6810	94.9073
-20	30	4.1490	40.6745	55	7.6065	74.5700				18	10.7874	105.7538
½-13	39	5.3937	52.8769	75	10.3725	101.6863	85	11.7555	115.2445	105	14.5215	142.3609
-20	41	5.6703	55.5885	85	11.7555	115.2445				120	16.5860	162.6960
⁹/₁₆-12	51	7.0533	69.1467	110	15.2130	149.1380	120	16.5960	162.6960	155	21.4365	210.1490
-18	55	7.6065	74.5700	120	16.5960	162.6960				170	23.5110	230.4860
⅝-11	83	11.4789	112.5329	150	20.7450	203.3700	167	23.0961	226.4186	210	29.0430	284.7180
-18	95	13.1385	128.8027	170	23.5110	230.4860				240	33.1920	325.3920
¾-10	105	14.5215	142.3609	270	37.3410	366.0660	280	38.7240	379.6240	375	51.8625	508.4250
-16	115	15.9045	155.9170	295	40.7985	399.9610				420	58.0860	568.4360
⅞-9	160	22.1280	216.9280	395	54.6285	535.5410	440	60.8520	596.5520	605	83.6715	820.2590
-14	175	24.2025	237.2650	435	60.1605	589.7730				675	93.3525	915.1650
1-8	236	32.5005	318.6130	590	81.5970	799.9220	660	91.2780	894.8280	910	125.8530	1233.7780
-14	250	34.5750	338.9500	660	91.2780	849.8280				990	136.9170	1342.2420

SUGGESTED TORQUE FOR COATED BOLTS AND NUTS

Metric Sizes		6&6.3	8	10	12	14	16	20
Nuts and All Metal Bolts	N·m	0.4	0.8	1.4	2.2	3.0	4.2	7.0
	In. Lbs.	4.0	7.0	12	18	25	35	57
Adhesive or Nylon Coated Bolts	N·m	0.4	0.6	1.2	1.6	2.4	3.4	5.6
	In. Lbs.	4.0	5.0	10	14	20	28	46

Inch Sizes		¼	⁵/₁₆	⅜	⁷/₁₆	½	⁹/₁₆	⅝	¾
Nuts and All Metal Bolts	N·m	0.4	0.6	1.4	1.8	2.4	3.2	4.2	6.2
	In. Lbs.	4.0	5.0	12	15	20	27	35	51
Adhesive or Nylon Coated Bolts	N·m	0.4	0.6	1.0	1.4	1.8	2.6	3.4	5.2
	In. Lbs.	4.0	5.0	9.0	12	15	22	28	43

METRIC BOLTS

Description	Torque ft-lbs. (Nm)			
Thread for general purposes (size x pitch) (mm)	Head mark 4		Head mark 7	
6 x 1.0	2.2 to 2.9	(3.0 to 3.9)	3.6 to 5.8	(4.9 to 7.8)
8 x 1.25	5.8 to 8.7	(7.9 to 12)	9.4 to 14	(13 to 19)
10 x 1.25	12 to 17	(16 to 23)	20 to 29	(27 to 39)
12 x 1.25	21 to 32	(29 to 43)	35 to 53	(47 to 72)
14 x 1.5	35 to 52	(48 to 70)	57 to 85	(77 to 110)
16 x 1.5	51 to 77	(67 to 100)	90 to 120	(130 to 160)
18 x 1.5	74 to 110	(100 to 150)	130 to 170	(180 to 230)
20 x 1.5	110 to 140	(150 to 190)	190 to 240	(160 to 320)
22 x 1.5	150 to 190	(200 to 260)	250 to 320	(340 to 430)
24 x 1.5	190 to 240	(260 to 320)	310 to 410	(420 to 550)

CAUTION: Bolts threaded into aluminum require much less torque.

DECIMAL AND METRIC EQUIVALENTS

Fractions	Decimal In.	Metric mm.	Fractions	Decimal In.	Metric mm.
1/64	.015625	.397	33/64	.515625	13.097
1/32	.03125	.794	17/32	.53125	13.494
3/64	.046875	1.191	35/64	.546875	13.891
1/16	.0625	1.588	9/16	.5625	14.288
5/64	.078125	1.984	37/64	.578125	14.684
3/32	.09375	2.381	19/32	.59375	15.081
7/64	.109375	2.778	39/64	.609375	15.478
1/8	.125	3.175	5/8	.625	15.875
9/64	.140625	3.572	41/64	.640625	16.272
5/32	.15625	3.969	21/32	.65625	16.669
11/64	.171875	4.366	43/64	.671875	17.066
3/16	.1875	4.763	11/16	.6875	17.463
13/64	.203125	5.159	45/64	.703125	17.859
7/32	.21875	5.556	23/32	.71875	18.256
15/64	.234375	5.953	47/64	.734375	18.653
1/4	.250	6.35	3/4	.750	19.05
17/64	.265625	6.747	49/64	.765625	19.447
9/32	.28125	7.144	25/32	.78125	19.844
19/64	.296875	7.54	51/64	.796875	20.241
5/16	.3125	7.938	13/16	.8125	20.638
21/64	.328125	8.334	53/64	.828125	21.034
11/32	.34375	8.731	27/32	.84375	21.431
23/64	.359375	9.128	55/64	.859375	21.828
3/8	.375	9.525	7/8	.875	22.225
25/64	.390625	9.922	57/64	.890625	22.622
13/32	.40625	10.319	29/32	.90625	23.019
27/64	.421875	10.716	59/64	.921875	23.416
7/16	.4375	11.113	15/16	.9375	23.813
29/64	.453125	11.509	61/64	.953125	24.209
15/32	.46875	11.906	31/32	.96875	24.606
31/64	.484375	12.303	63/64	.984375	25.003
1/2	.500	12.7	1	1.00	25.4

Work Area

The size of the work area depends upon the space available within the service shop to perform the rebuilding operation by having the necessary benches, tools, cleaners and lifts arranged to provide the most logical and efficient approach to the removal, disassembly, assembly and installation of the automatic transmission. Regardless of the manner in which the work area is arranged, it should be well lighted, ventilated and clean.

Precautions to Observe When Handling Solvents

All solvents are toxic or irritating to the skin to some degree. The amount of toxicity or irritation normally depends upon the skin exposure to the solvent. It is a good practice to avoid skin contact with solvent by using rubber gloves and parts drainers when cleaning the transmission parts.

CAUTION

Do not, under any circumstances, wash grease from hands or arms by dipping into the solvent tank and air drying with compressed air. Blood poison can result.

Drive Line Service

Drive line vibrations can affect the operation and longevity of the automatic transmission/transaxles and should be diagnosed during the road test and inspected during the unit removal phase. The drive shafts are designed for specific applications and the disregard for the correct application can result in drive shaft failure with extremely violent and hazardous consequences. A replace-

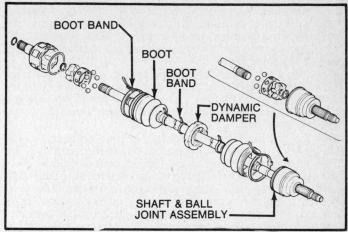

Typical front drive axle assembly using CV joint components on both ends of shaft(© Toyo Kogyo Co. Ltd.)

ment shaft assembly must always be of the same design and material specifications as the original to assure proper operation.

Natural drive line vibrations are created by the fluctuations in the speed of the drive shaft as the drive line angle is changed during a single revolution of the shaft. With the increased use of the front drive transaxles, the drive shafts and universal joints must transfer the driving power to the front wheels and at the same time, compensate for steering action on turns. Special universal joints were developed, one a constant velocity (CV) or double offset type, and a second type known as the tripod joint. The constant velocity joint uses rolling balls in curved grooves to obtain

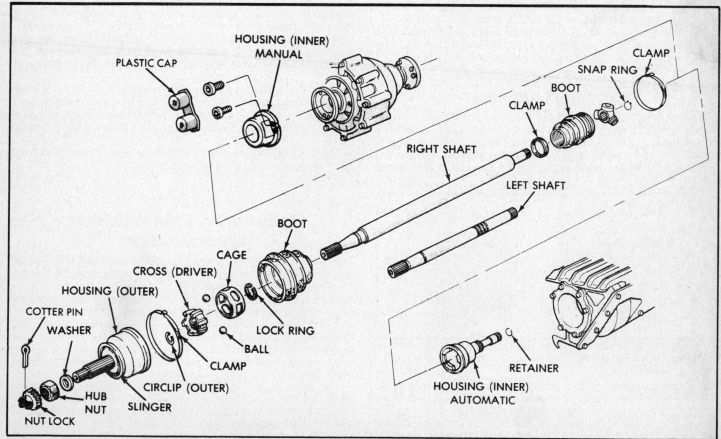

Typical front drive axle assembly using CV and Tri-pot joint components(© Chrysler Corp.)

uniform motion. As the joint rotates in the driving or steering motion, the balls, which are in driving contact between the two halves of the joint coupling, remain in a plane which bisects the angle between the two shafts, thus cancelling out the fluctuations of speed in the drive shaft.

The tripod type uses a three legged spider, with needle bearing and balls incased in a three grooved housing. With the spider attached to the driveshaft, the joint assembly is free to roll back and forth in the housing grooves as the shaft length varies in normal drive line operation.

The front driveshafts are normally of two different lengths from the transaxle to the drive wheels, due to the location of the engine/transaxle mounting in the vehicle. Care should be exercised when removing or replacing the driveshafts, as to their locations (mark if necessary), removal procedures and handling so as not to damage the boots covering the universal joints, or if equipped, with boots covering the transaxle driveshaft opening. Should the boots become torn or otherwise damaged, premature failure of the universal joint would result due to the loss of lubricant and entrance of contaminates.

ATTACHMENT OF THE DRIVESHAFT TO THE TRANSAXLE

The attachment of the driveshafts to the transaxle is accomplished in a number of ways and if not familiar with the particular shaft attachment, do not pry or hammer until the correct procedure is known.

The shafts can be attached by one of the following methods:

1. Driveshaft flange to transaxle stub shaft flange, bolted together. Mark flanges and remove bolts.
2. Circlips inside differential housing. Remove differential cover, compress circlips and push axle shafts outward.
3. Spring loaded circlip mounted in groove on axle shaft and mating with a groove in the differential gear splines. Is usually pryed or taped from differential gear with care.
4. Universal joint housing, axle shaft flange or axle shaft stub end pinned to either the differential stub shaft or differential gear flange with a roll pin. Mark the two components and drive the pin from the units.

BOOT REPLACEMENT

The most common repairs to the front driveshafts are boot replacement and boot retaining ring replacement. Many automatic transmission repair shops are requested to perform this type of repairs for their customers. EOM and after-market replacement boots are available, with special tools used to crimp and tighten

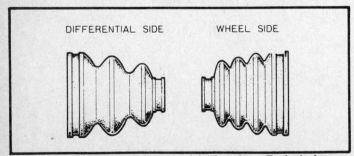

DIFFERENTIAL SIDE   WHEEL SIDE

Look for boot differences between joint locations. Typical of one manufacturer's drive axle (© Toyo Kogyo Co. Ltd.)

the retaining rings. Most boot replacement procedures require the removal of the driveshafts. A boot kit is available that provides a split boot that can be installed without driveshaft removal. The boot is then sealed with a special adhesive along its length and the procedure finished with the installation of the boot retaining rings.

DRIVE LINE DIAGNOSIS—FRONT WHEEL DRIVE

Clicking Noise In Turns

1. Worn or damaged outboard joint. (Check for cut or damaged seals).

"Clunk" When Accelerating From "Coast" To "Drive"

1. Worn or damaged inboard joint

Shudder Or Vibration During Acceleration

1. Excessive joint angle
   a. Excessive toe-in.
   b. Incorrect spring heights.
2. Worn or damaged inboard or outboard joints.
3. Sticking inboard joint assembly (Double Offset Design).
4. Sticking spider assembly (Tri-Pot Design).

Vibration At Highway Speeds

1. Out of balance front wheels or tires.
2. Out of round front tires.

Towing

Proper towing is important for the safe and reliable transfer of an inoperative vehicle from one point to another.

The basic towing instructions and procedures are general in nature and the towing procedures may not apply to the same make, model or vehicle throughout the model years without procedure changes, modification to equipment or the use of auxiliary equipment designed for a specific purpose.

It is important to minimize the risk of personal injury, to avoid damage to the towed vehicle or to render it unsafe while being towed. There are many conceivable methods of towing with possible hazardous consequences for each method. Therefore, it is the responsibility of the tow truck operator to determine the correct connection of the towing apparatus in a safe and secure manner.

Towing manuals are available from varied sources, explaining the vehicle manufacturer's recommended lifting procedures, towing speeds and towing distances. The operating instructions for the towing truck should be understood and followed by the operator.

The disabled vehicle should never be pushed or pulled on a highway because of safety reasons.

Automatic Transmission Identification

The need to identify automatic transmissions occurs when transmission units are obtained; for example, through bulk buying for overhaul and storage as replacement units. To assist the repairman in coupling the proper transmission to the vehicle/engine combination, a listing is given of automatic transmission codes and their corresponding vehicle model and engine usage. The torque converter identification is difficult, as most replacement converters are rebuilt and distributed to suppliers for resale. The transmission model and serial number should be considered when converter replacement is required.

The following listings contain the transmission models or codes for the most commonly used automatic transmissions. Should a model or code be needed for a non-listed vehicle or transmission, refer to the individual transmission section and, if available, the model or code will be noted along with the model and code location.

AMERICAN CAR MANUFACTURER'S BODY CODES

AMERICAN MOTORS CORPORATION

Year	Series	Model
1980-82	01	Concord
1980-83	30	Eagle
1980-83	40	Spirit
1980	40	AMX
1981-83	50	SX-4, Kammback
1980	60	Pacer

Chrysler Corporation

Year	Series	Model
1980-82	L	M-Horizon/TC3, Z-Omni/024
1984	L	M-Horizon/turismo, Z-Omni/Charger
1980	F	H-Volare, N-Aspen
1980-81	M	B-Caravelle, F-LeBaron, G-Diplomat
1982	M	V-Dodge 400, C-LeBaron, G-Diplomat
1984	M	G-Diplomat/Gran Fury, F-New Yorker/Fifth Avenue
1980-84	J	X-Mirida, S-Cordoba
1980-81	R	J-Gran Fury, E-Saint Regis, T-Newport/New Yorker
1982	R	B-Gran Fury, F-New Yorker
1981-84	Y	Y-Imperial
1981-84	K	D-Aries, P-Reliant
1984	CV	V-Dodge 400, C-LeBaron
1984	E	E-Chrysler E class, New Yorker, Dodge 600, 600ES

Ford Motor Company

Year	Series	Model
1980-82		LTD, Marquis, Continental
1984	L	LTD, Marquis, Continental
1980-82		Thunderbird, Cougar
1984	S	Thunderbird, Cougar
1980-82		Town Car, Mark VI
1984	Panther	LTD Crown Victoria, Grand Marquis, Town Car, Mark VI
1980-82		Fairmont, Zephyr, Mustang, Capri

Ford Motor Company

Year	Series	Model
1984	Fox	Fairmont, Zephyr, Mustang, Capri
1980		Pinto, Bobcat
1980-82		Granada, Monarch[1]
1981-82		Escort, Lynx, EXP, LN7
1984	Erika	Escort, Lynx, EXP, LN7
1984	Topaz	Tempo, Topaz

[1] 1980 only

General Motors Corporation

Year	Series	Model
1980-81	A	Century, Regal, Malibu, El Camino, Monte Carlo, Cutlass, LeMans, Grand AM, Safari
1982-84	A	Century, Celebrity, Ciera, 6000
1980-81	B	LeSabre, Estate Wagon, Impala, Caprice, Delta 88, Catalina, Bonneville
1982-84	B	LeSabre, Impala, Caprice, Delta 88
1980-84	C	Electra, Limited, Fleetwood Cp.[1] Deville, Ninety-Eight
1980-84	E	Riviera, Eldorado, Toronado
1980	H	Skyhawk, Monza, Starfire, Sunbird
1980-84	X	Skylark, Citation, Omega, Phoenix
1982-84	J	Skyhawk, Cimarron, Firenza, Cavalier, 2000
1980-82	D	Fleetwood Sedan, Limousine
1984	D	Fleetwood, Limousine
1980-84	K	Seville
1980-84	Z	Commercial Chassis
1980-84	F	Camaro, Firebird
1980-84	T	Chevette
1982-84	T	1000
1980-84	Y	Corvette
1982-84	G	Regal, Malibu, El Camino, Monte Carlo, Cutlass, Bonneville, Grand Prix

[1] 1984 Fleetwood Brougham

GENERAL MOTORS CORPORATION
Automatic Transmission/Transaxle Listing

Year	Model	Engine	Trans. code
		THM 125 (M34,MD9)	
1980-81	Skylark, Citation, Omega	151 eng.	PZ
	Phoenix	173 eng.	CT,CV
1982-84	Century, Celebrity, Citation, Ciera, Omega, Phoenix, 6000	151 eng.	PL,PW,PI,PD,PZ
		173 eng.	CE,CL,CT,CW,CC
	Century, Ciera	3.0L eng.	BL,BF
	Century, Celebrity, Ciera 6000	260 eng. (diesel)	OP
	Cavalier, Cimarron, Firenza, Skyhawk, J2000	112 eng. (1.8L)	PG,P3,C1,CU,CF,C3,HV,CA,CJ,PE, PJ
	Cavalier, Cimarron, Firenza, Skyhawk	122 eng. (2.0L)	CB,CA,CF
	Fiero	151 eng.	PF
		THM 180 (MD2,MD3)	
1980-81	Chevette	1.6L eng.	Trans. Code unavailable
		THM 180 C	
1982	Chevette, T1000	1.6L eng.	VQ
1983	Chevette, T1000	1.6L eng.	JY,TN
1984	Chevette, T1000	1.6L eng.	TP
		THM 200 (MV9, M29)	
1980	Chevette	1.6L eng.	CN
	Monza, Starfire, Sunbird	151 eng.	PB,PY
	El Camino, Grand Am, LeMans, Malibu, Monte Carlo	229 eng.	CA,CK
	Century, Grand Am, Grand Prix, LeMans, Cutlass, Regal	231 eng.	BZ
	Bonneville, Catalina, Century, Grand Am, Grand Prix, LeMans Regal	260 eng.	PG
	Delta 88	260 eng.	OW
	Caprice, Impala	267 eng.	CE
	Century, Grand AM, Grand Prix, LeMans, LeSabre, Regal	301 eng.	PW
	Firebird	301 eng.	PD
	Cutlass, El Camino, Malibu, Monte Carlo	305 eng.	CC
	Bonneville, Catalina, LeSabre,	350 eng. (Gas)	BA
	Delta 88	350 eng. (Gas)	OS
	Bonneville, Catalina, Cutlass, Delta 88, Electra, LeSabre, Olds. 98	350 eng. (Diesel)	OT
	DeVille, Fleetwood	350 eng. (Diesel)	AS
1981	Chevette	1.6L eng.	CN
	Chevette	1.8L eng. (Diesel)	CY
	Starfire	151 eng.	PB,PY
	El Camino, Grand Prix, LeMans, Malibu, Monte Carlo	229 eng.	CA

GENERAL MOTORS CORPORATION
Automatic Transmission/Transaxle Listing

Year	Model	Engine	Trans. code
1981	Century, Cutlass, El Camino. Grand Prix, LeMans, Malibu, Monte Carlo, Regal	231 eng.	BZ
	Delta 88	260 eng.	OW
	Bonneville, Catalina, Century, Grand Prix, LeMans, Regal	260 eng.	DW,PG
	Firebird	260 eng.	PF
	Camaro, El Camino, Malibu, Monte Carlo	267 eng.	CE
	Cutlass	267 eng.	WA
	Grand Prix, LeMans	301 eng.	PD,PE
	Cutlass, El Camino, Malibu, Monte Carlo	305 eng.	CC
	LeSabre	307 eng.	OG
	Bonneville, Catalina, Caprice, Century, Cutlass, Delta 88, Electra, Grand Prix, Impala, LeMans, LeSabre, Olds. 98, Regal	350 eng. (Diesel)	OT
	DeVille, Fleetwood	350 eng. (Diesel)	AS
1982-83	Chevette, T1000	1.8L eng. (Diesel)	JY,CY
	Cutlass, El Camino, Malibu, Monte Carlo, Regal	260 eng. (Diesel)	OR
1984	Chevette, T1000	1.8L eng. (Diesel)	JY
	Bonneville, Caprice, Cutlass, Delta 88, El Camino, Grand Prix, Impala, LeSabre, Monte Carlo, Parisienne, Regal	231 eng.	BH
	Cutlass	260 eng. (Diesel)	OR
	Cutlass, Delta 88, LeSabre	307 eng.	OI
	Bonneville, Caprice, Cutlass, Delta 88, El Camino, Grand Prix, Impala, LeSabre, Monte Carlo, Parisienne	350 eng. (Diesel)	OU
THM 200-4R (MW9)			
1981	DeVille, Fleetwood, LeSabre	252 eng.	BM,BY
	Caprice, Impala	305 eng.	CU
	Bonneville, Catalina, Delta 88, Electra, Olds. 98	307 eng.	OG
1982-83	Regal	231 eng.	BR
	DeVille, Electra, Fleetwood LeSabre, Olds. 98	252 eng. (V-6)	BY
	Regal	252 eng. (V-6)	BT
	DeVille, Fleetwood	252 eng. (V-8)	AA,AP
	Caprice, Impala	267 eng.	CQ
	Caprice, Impala	305 eng.	CR

GENERAL MOTORS CORPORATION
Automatic Transmission/Transaxle Listing

Year	Model	Engine	Trans. code
1982-83	Cutlass	307 eng.	OZ
	Electra, LeSabre	307 eng.	OG
	Caprice, Delta 88, Deville, Electra, Fleetwood, Impala, LeSabre, Olds. 98,	350 eng. (Diesel)	OM
	THM 250 (M31)		
1980	Caprice, Impala	229 eng.	WK
	Firebird	260 eng.	MC
	Caprice, Impala, El Camino, Malibu, Monte Carlo	267 eng.	WH,XL
	Bonneville, Catalina, Century, Grand AM, Grand Prix, LeMans, LeSabre, Regal	301 eng.	MD,TB
	Cutlass, El Camino, Malibu, Monte Carlo	305 eng.	WL
	Delta 88	307 eng.	TT
1981	Camaro, Caprice, Impala	229 eng.	TA
	Cutlass, El Camino, Grand Prix LeMans, Malibu, Monte Carlo	231 eng.	XX
	El Camino, Malibu, Monte Carlo	267 eng.	XS
	El Camino, Malibu, Monte Carlo	305 eng.	XK
	Cutlass, Delta 88, LeSabre	307 eng.	XL,XA
1982-84	Caprice, El Camino, Impala, Malibu, Monte Carlo	229 eng.	XP,XE
	Bonneville, Cutlass, El Camino, Grand Prix, Malibu, Monte Carlo Regal	231 eng.	WK
	Bonneville, El Camino, Grand Prix, Malibu, Monte Carlo, Caprice	305 eng.	XK
	Cutlass	307 eng.	XN
	Delta 88, LeSabre	307 eng.	XL
	El Camino, Monte Carlo	229 eng.	CH
	Regal	231 eng.	BQ
	LeSabre, Electra, Regal	252 eng. (V6)	BY,BT
	Fleetwood	252 eng. (V8)	AA,AP
	Cutlass, Regal	260 eng. (Diesel)	OF,OY
	Cutlass, Regal	305 eng.	HG
	Bonneville, El Camino, Grand Prix, Monte Carlo	305 eng.	CQ,CR
	Delta 88, Electra, LeSabre, Olds. 98	307 eng.	OG,OJ,OZ
	Bonneville, Cutlass, Delta 88, El Camino, Electra, Grand Prix, LeSabre, Monte Carlo, Olds. 98, Parisienne, Regal	350 eng. (Diesel)	OM

GENERAL MOTORS CORPORATION
Automatic Transmission/Transaxle Listing

Year	Model	Engine	Trans. code
		THM 325 (M32)	
1980-81	Riviera	231 eng.	BJ
	Riviera, Toronado	252 eng.	BE
	Eldorado, Seville	252 eng.	AG
	Riviera, Toronado	307 eng.	OH
	Riviera, Toronado	350 eng. (Gas)	OJ
	Eldorado, Seville	350 eng. (Gas)	AJ
	Riviera, Toronado	350 eng. (Diesel)	OK
	Eldorado, Seville	350 eng. (Diesel)	AK
	Eldorado, Seville	368 eng.	AF
		THM 325 4SP. (M57)	
1982-84	Riviera	231 eng.	BJ
	Eldorado, Seville	252 eng. (V-6)	AM
	Eldorado, Seville	252 eng. (V-8)	AB,AJ,AE
	Riviera, Toronado	252 eng.	BE
	Riviera, Toronado	307 eng.	OJ
	Eldorado, Seville	350 eng. (Diesel)	AL
	Riviera, Toronado	350 eng. (Diesel)	OK
		THM 350	
1980	Caprice, Impala	229 eng.	JA,XY
	Bonneville, Catalina, Caprice, Century, Cutlass, Delta 88, El Camino, Grand Am, Grand Prix, Impala, LeMans, Malibu, Monte Carlo	231 eng.	KJ,KT,KC,KS,KH
	Camaro, Firebird	231 eng.	KF
	Skyhawk, Starfire, Sunbird	231 eng.	KA
	DeVille, Electra, Fleetwood LeSabre	252 eng.	KD
	Cutlass	260 eng.	LC,LD
	Camaro, El Camino, Malibu, Monte Carlo	267 eng.	JJ,JN
	Bonneville, Catalina, Grand Am, Grand Prix, LeMans	301 eng.	MS
	Camaro, Firebird	301 eng.	MJ,MT
	Bonneville, Caprice, Catalina, Century, Cutlass, El Camino, Grand Am, Grand Prix, Impala, LeMans, Malibu, Monte Carlo, Regal	305 eng.	JE,JK,LJ
	Camaro, Firebird	305 eng.	JK,JD
	Corvette	305 eng.	JC
	Bonneville, Catalina, Delta 88, LeSabre	350 eng. (Gas)	KN,LA,TV
	Camaro	350 eng. (Gas)	JL

GENERAL MOTORS CORPORATION
Automatic Transmission/Transaxle Listing

Year	Model	Engine	Trans. code
		THM 350	
1980	Caprice, El Camino, Impala, Malibu, Monte Carlo	350 eng. (Diesel)	JS
1981	Bonneville, Catalina, Caprice, Century, Cutlass, Delta 88, El Camino, Grand Prix, LeMans, LeSabre, Impala, Malibu, Monte Carlo, Regal	231 eng.	KD,KT
	Camaro, Firebird	231 eng.	KY
	Electra, LeSabre	252 eng.	KK
	Cutlass, Grand Prix, LeMans	260 eng.	LC
	Firebird	301 eng.	MC
	Grand Prix, LeMans	301 eng.	MA
	Camaro	350 eng. (Gas)	JC
	Corvette	350 eng. (Gas)	JD
	Bonneville, Catalina, Caprice, Delta 88, Impala, LeSabre	350 eng. (Diesel)	LA,LD
1982	Caprice, El Camino, Impala, Malibu, Monte Carlo	229 eng.	WP
	Caprice, El Camino, Impala, Malibu, Monte Carlo	267 eng.	WC
	Bonneville, Cutlass, El Camino, Grand Prix, Malibu, Monte Carlo, Regal	350 eng. (Diesel)	WX
	Caprice, Delta 88, Electra, Impala, LeSabre, Olds. 98	350 eng. (Diesel)	WT
		THM 350C—(Lock-up Converter)	
1980	Caprice, Impala	267 eng.	TZ
	El Camino, Malibu, Monte Carlo	267 eng.	XN
	Bonneville, Catalina, LeSabre	301 eng.	WB
	Corvette	305 eng.	TW
	Caprice, Cutlass, El Camino, Impala, Malibu, Monte Carlo	305 eng.	WD
	Delta 88	307 eng.	WA
	All Models	350R eng. (Gas)	TY
	Bonneville, Catalina	350X eng. (Gas)	TV
	Bonneville, Catalina, Caprice, Delta 88, Impala, LeSabre	350 eng. (Diesel)	WC
1981	El Camino, Malibu, Monte Carlo	229 eng.	WP
	Caprice, Cutlass, El Camino, Impala, Malibu, Monte Carlo	267 eng.	WC
	Camaro, Caprice, El Camino, Impala, Malibu, Monte Carlo	305 eng.	WD
	Caprice, El Camino, Impala, Malibu, Monte Carlo	350 eng. (Gas)	WE
	Caprice, Impala	350 eng. (Diesel)	WS,WW

GENERAL MOTORS CORPORATION
Automatic Transmission/Transaxle Listing

Year	Model	Engine	Trans. code
	THM 350C—(Lock-up Converter)		
1982	Bonneville, Caprice, El Camino Cutlass, Delta 88, Impala, Electra, Grand Prix, Malibu, Monte Carlo, Regal	231 eng.	KA
	Bonneville, Electra, Grand Prix, Regal	252 eng.	KE,KK
	Cutlass, Delta 88	260 eng.	LA
	Bonneville, El Camino, Grand Prix, Malibu, Monte Carlo	350 eng. (Diesel)	LB
	Caprice, Delta 88, Electra, Impala, Regal	350 eng. (Diesel)	LD
1983	Bonneville, Caprice, Cutlass, Delta 88, Electra, Impala Grand Prix, Regal	231 eng.	KA
	Electra	252 eng.	KE,KK
	Bonneville, El Camino, Grand Prix, Malibu, Monte Carlo	305 eng.	WD,WE
	Caprice, Delta 88, Impala	350 eng. (Diesel)	LD,LJ
	Bonneville, Cutlass, El Camino, Grand Prix, Malibu, Monte Carlo	350 eng. (Diesel)	LB
	Electra, Regal	350 eng. (Diesel)	LB,LJ
1984	El Camino, Monte Carlo	305 eng.	WS
	Impala, Caprice	305 eng.	WW
	THM 400 (M40)		
1980	Electra, LeSabre	350 eng.	BB,OB
	Fleetwood, DeVille	368 eng.	AB,AD,AE
	Limo, Comm. Ch.	368 eng.	AD,AN
1981-84	Fleetwood, DeVille	368 eng.	AE
	Limo	368 eng.	AN
	Comm. Ch.	368 eng.	AD
	THM 700 (MD8)		
1982	Caprice, Impala	267 eng.	Y4,YL
	Caprice, Impala	305 eng.	Y3,YK
	Corvette	350 eng. (Gas)	YA
1983	Caprice, Impala	305 eng.	YK
1984	Camaro, Firebird	151 eng.	PQ
	Camaro, Firebird	173 eng.	YF
	Camaro, Firebird	305 eng.	YG,YP
	Caprice, Impala, Parisienne	305 eng.	YK
	Corvette	350 eng.	Y9,YW
	THM 440-T4 (ME9)		
1984	Celebrity, Century, Ciera, 6000	260 eng. (Diesel)	OB,OV

CHRYSLER CORPORATION
Transmission Listing

Year	Assy. No.	Engine Cu. In.	Type Trans.	Other Information
				AMERICAN MOTORS CORPORATION CARS
1980	3235770	2.5 Litre	A-904	Standard—Non-Lockup (4 Cyl)
	3237269	258	A-904	Standard—Lockup
	3236581	258	A-998	4-Wheel Drive—Non-Lockup
	3238455	258	A-998	Export Non-Lockup
	3238767	282	A-998	Mexico—Lockup
	3235220	258/304	A-999	Jeep CJ 4-Wheel Drive—Non-Lockup
	5359402	258/360	A-727	Jeep SR 4-Wheel Drive—Non-Lockup
1981	3238777	2.5 Litre	A-904	Wide Ratio—Non Lockup
	3238772	2.5 Litre	A-904	4x4 Wide Ratio—Non Lockup
	3238778	2.5 Litre	A-904	CJ-7 4x4 Wide Ratio—Non Lockup
	3240107	258	A-904	Standard—Lockup
	3238771	258	A-998	4x4 Eagle—Lockup
	3240296	258/282	A-998	VAM—Lockup
	3238773	258/304	A-999	CJ-7 4x4 Lockup (2.73 Axle)
	3239816	258/304	A-999	CJ-7 4x4 Lockup (3.31 Axle)
	3240219	258	A-999	CJ-7 4x4 Export—Non Lockup
	3238774	360	A-727	Sr Jeep 4x4 Lockup (2.73 Axle)
	3239817	258/360	A-727	Sr Jeep 4x4 Lockup (3.31-3.73 Axle)
	3240255	258/360	A-727	Sr Jeep 4x4 Export—Non Lockup
1982	3238772	2.5 Litre	A-904	4x4—Non-Lockup
	3238777	2.5 Litre	A-904	Non-Lockup
	—	2.5 Litre	A-904	CJ7 4x4—Non-Lockup
	5567640	2.5 Litre	A-904	AM General-Post Office Trucks
	3240229	258	A-904	Lock-up
	3241099	258	A-998	4x4 Eagle-Lockup
	3241100	6 & V8	A-998	VAM—Non-Lockup
	3240231	258	A-999	CJ7 4x4—Lockup
	3240231	258	A-999	SR Jeep 4x4—Lockup (2.73 Axle)
	—	258/304	A-999	CJ7 4x4—Lockup (3.31 Axle)
	3241098	258	A-999	CJ7 4x4 Export—Non-Lockup
	3238774	360	A-727	SR Jeep 4x4—Lockup (2.73 Axle)
	3239817	258/360	A-727	SR Jeep 4x4—Lockup (3.31/3.73 Axle)
	3240255	258/360	A-727	SR Jeep 4x4 Export—Non-Lockup
1983-84	8933000864	2.5 Litre	A-904	4x4—Non Lockup
	8933000863	2.5 Litre	A-904	Non Lockup
	8923000028	2.5 Litre	A-904	AM General—Post Office Truck
	8953000847	2.46 Litre	A-904	XJ 4x4—Lockup
	3240229	258	A-904	Lockup
	8933000916	258	A-998	4x4 Eagle—Lockup
	3241100	6 & 8	A-998	VAM—Non Lockup
	8933000913	258	A-999	CJ7-8 4x4—Lockup
				SJ 4x4—Lockup (2.73 Axle)
	8933000917	258	A-999	CJ 4x4 Export—Non Lockup
	8933000915	360	A-727	SJ 4x4—Lockup (2.73 Axle)
	8933000914	258/360	A-727	SJ 4x4—Lock (3.31/3.73 Axle)
	8933000918	258/360	A-727	SJ 4x4 Export—Non Lockup

CHRYSLER CORPORATION
Transmission Listing

Year	Assy. No.	Engine Cu. In.	Type Trans.	Other Information
			CHRYSLER CORPORATION CARS	
1980	4130951	225	A-904	Standard—Lockup
	4130953	225	A-904	Wide Ratio Gear Set—Lockup
	4202095	225	A-904	Wide Ratio Gear Set—Non-Lockup
	4130952	225	A-904	Heavy Duty—Lockup
	4202094	225	A-904	Heavy Duty—Non-Lockup
	4130955	318	A-998	Standard—Lockup
	4130956	318	A-998	Wide Ratio Gear Set—Lockup
	4130957	360	A-999	Standard—Lockup
	4202084	1.6 Litre	A-904	MMC (Colt-Arrow)—Non-Lockup
	4202085	2.0 Litre	A-904	MMC (Colt-Arrow) Non-Lockup
	4202086	2.6 Litre	A-904	MMC (Colt-Arrow) Non-Lockup
	4202064	318	A-727	Standard—Lockup
	4130976	360	A-727	Hi-Performance—Lockup
	4058376	360	A-727	Hi-Performance—Non-Lockup
	5224442	1.7 Litre	A-404	Federal & California—3.48 Axle
1981	4202662	225	A-904	Wide Ratio—Non Lockup
	4202663	225	A-904	Wide Ratio—Lockup
	4202664	225	A-904	Heavy Duty—Wide Ratio—Non Lockup
	4058383	225	A-904T	Heavy Duty—Wide Ratio—Lockup
	4058398	318	A-999	Wide Ratio—Lockup
	4202675	318	A-999	Wide Ratio—Lockup
	4202729	318	A-999	"Imperial"-Wide Ratio—Lockup
	4202572	1.6 Litre	A-904	MMC (Arrow-Colt)—Non Lockup
	4202573	2.0 Litre	A-904	MMC (Arrow-Colt)—Non Lockup
	4202574	2.6 Litre	A-904	MMC (Arrow-Colt)—Non Lockup
	4202571	318	A-727	Hi-Performance—Lockup
	4058393	360	A-727	Export—Non-Lockup
1982	4202662	225	A-904	Non-Lockup
	4202663	225	A-904	Lockup
	4202664	225	A-904	Heavy Duty—Non Lockup
	4058383	225	A-904T	Heavy Duty—Lockup Also used in truck
	4058398	318	A-999	Lockup—Also used in truck
	4202675	318	A-999	Lockup
	4202729	318	A-999	"Imperial" lockup
	4269051	1.6 Litre	A-904	MMC Non-Lockup
	4269052	2.0 Litre	A-904	MMC Non-Lockup
	4269053	2.6 Litre	A-904	MMC Non-Lockup
	4202571	318 HP	A-727	Hi-Performance Lockup
	4058393	360	A-727	Export—Non-Lockup
1983	4202662	225	A-904	Non-Lockup
	4202663	225	A-904	Lockup
	4202664	225	A-904	Heavy Duty—Non Lockup
	4058398	318	A-999	Lockup-Also used in Truck
	4202675	318	A-999	Lockup
	4202729	318	A-999	"Imperial" lockup
	4269932	1.6 Litre	A-904	MMC Non Lockup
	4269933	2.0 Litre	A-904	MMC Non Lockup
	4269934	2.6 Litre	A-904	MMC Non Lockup

CHRYSLER CORPORATION
Transmission Listing

Year	Assy. No.	Engine Cu. In.	Type Trans.	Other Information
1983	4202898	2.6 Litre	A-904	MMC 4x4 Non Lockup
	4202571	318 HP	A-727	Hi-Performance Lockup
	—	360	A-727	Export—Non Lockup
1984	4295512	2.2 Litre	Transaxle	2.78 Overall Ratio
	4295763	2.2 Litre	Transaxle	3.22 Overall Ratio
	4295513	2.2 Litre (E.F.I)	Transaxle	3.02 Overall Ratio
	4329827	2.2 Litre (Turbo)	Transaxle	3.02 Overall Ratio
	4295515	2.6 Litre	Transaxle	3.02 Overall Ratio
	4295517	2.6 Litre	Transaxle	3.22 Overall Ratio
	4295887	318	A904	Lock-up 2.24 Axle
	4329436	318	A904	Lock-up 2.26 Axle
	4058398	318	A904	Lock-up 2.94 Axle
	4329631	318	A904	Non Lock-up 2.94 Axle

DODGE TRUCK TRANSMISSIONS

Year	Assy. No.	Engine Cu. In.	Type Trans.	Other Information
1980	4058376	360	A-727	Hi-Perf. Long Extension—Non-Lockup
	4058371	225	A-727	Long Extension—Lockup
	4058355	225	A-727	4-Wheel Drive—Lockup
	4058351	318/360	A-727	Short Extension—Lockup
	4058375	318/360	A-727	Short Extension—Non-Lockup
	4058373	318/360	A-727	Long Extension—Lockup
	4058374	318/360	A-727	Long Heavy Duty Ext.—Lockup
	4058372	318/360	A-727	Long Heavy Duty Ext.—Non-Lockup
	4058356	318/360	A-727	4-Wheel Drive-Lockup
	4058358	318/360	A-727	4-Wheel Drive—Non-Lockup
	4058336	446	A-727	Medium Extension—Non-Lockup
1981	4058383	225	A-904T	Wide Ratio—Lockup
	4058398	318	A-999	Wide Ratio—Lockup
	4058384	225	A-727	Long Ext.—Lockup
	4058385	225	A-727	4x4—Lockup
	4058388	318/360	A-727	Short Ext.—Lockup
	4058389	318/360	A-727	Short Ext.—Non-Lockup
	4058392	318/360	A-727	Long Ext.—Lockup
	4058394	318/360	A-727	HD Long Ext.—Lockup
	4058395	318/360	A-727	HD Long Ext.—Non Lockup
	4058396	318/360	A-727	4x4—Lockup
	4058397	318/360	A-727	4x4—Non-Lockup
1982	4058383	225	A-904T	Lockup
	4058398	318	A-999	Lockup
	4058384	225	A-727	Long Ext.—Lockup
	4058385	225	A-727	4x4—Lockup
	4058388	318/360	A-727	Short Ext.—Lockup
	4058389	318/360	A-727	Short Ext.—Non-Lockup
	4058394	318/360	A-727	HD Long Ext.—Lockup
	4058395	318/360	A-727	HD Long Ext.—Non-Lockup
	4058396	318/360	A-727	4x4—Lockup
	4058397	318/360	A-727	4x4—Non-Lockup

CHRYSLER CORPORATION
Transmission Listing

Year	Assy. No.	Engine Cu. In.	Type Trans.	Other Information
			DODGE TRUCK TRANSMISSIONS	
1983	4058383	225	A-904T	Lockup
	4058398	318	A-999	Lockup
	4058384	225	A-727	Long Ext.—Lockup
	—	225	A-727	4x4—Lockup
	—	318/360	A-727	Short Ext.—Lockup
	4058389	318/360	A-727	Short Ext.—Non-Lockup
	—	318/360	A-727	HD Long Ext.—Lockup
	4058395	318/360	A-727	HD Long Ext.—Non Lockup
	—	318/360	A-727	4x4—Lockup
	4058397	318/360	A-727	4x4—Non Lockup
1984	4058384	225	A-727	Long Ext.—Lockup
	4295941	225	A-727	Long Ext.—Non Lockup
	4329438	318	A-727	Long Ext.
	4329468	360	A-727	Long Ext.
	4329482	318/360	A-727	Short Ext.
	4329458	318	A-727	4x4
	4329488	360	A-727	4x4
	4058383	225	A-904	Long Ext.
	4058398	318	A-999	Long Ext.—Lockup

Other Transmission Usage

Year	Assy. No.	Engine Cu. In.	Type Trans.	Other Information
			EXPORT	
1980	4193341	—	A-727	Aston-Martin—Non-Lockup
	4193390	—	A-727	Aston-Martin—Lockup
	4058377	225/Diesel	A-727	United Kingdon Export Short Ext.
			AM GENERAL TRANSMISSION	
	5565798	2.0L	A-904	Standard—Non-Lockup (4 Cyl)
			INTERNATIONAL HARVESTER CORP. TRANSMISSION	
	492448-C91	304/345	A-727	Scout 4-Wheel Drive—Non-Lockup
			MARINE AND INDUSTRIAL TRANSMISSIONS	
	4142312	225	A-727	Short Extension—Non-Lockup
	4142313	225	A-727	Medium Extension—Non-Lockup
	4142321	318/360	A-727	Medium Extension—Non-Lockup
	4142362	Diesel	A-727	Short Extension—Non-Lockup
	4142363	Diesel	A-727	Medium Extension—Non-Lockup
	4142364	Diesel	A-727	Long Extension—Non-Lockup
			EXPORT	
1981	4025739	—	A-727	Aston-Martin Lockup
	4058387	225/Diesel	A-727	UK Export—Short Ext.—Non Lockup
			MARINE & INDUSTRIAL TRANSMISSIONS	
	4142312	225	A-727	Short Ext.—Non Lockup
	4142313	225	A-727	Medium Ext.—Non Lockup
	4142321	318/360	A-727	Medium Ext.—Non Lockup
			MARINE AND INDUSTRIAL TRANSMISSIONS	
	4142362	Diesel	A-727	Short Ext.—Non Lockup
	4142363	Diesel	A-727	Medium Ext.—Non Lockup
	4142364	Diesel	A-727	Long Ext.—Non Lockup

CHRYSLER CORPORATION
Transmission Listing

Other Transmission Usage

EXPORT

1982	4058387	225/Diesel	A-727	UK Export—Short Non-Lockup
	4025739	—	A-727	Aston Martin—Lockup
	4202717	—	A-727	Roadmaster Rail—Medium Non-Lockup
	3836023	—	A-727	Land Rover 4x4—Non-Lockup
	3836024	Diesel	A-727	IVECO—Medium Ext—Non-Lockup

MARINE AND INDUSTRIAL TRANSMISSIONS

	4142312	225	A-727	Short Ext—Non-Lockup
	4142313	225	A-727	Medium Ext—Non-Lockup
	4142321	318/360	A-727	.Medium Ext—Non-Lockup
	4142362	Diesel	A-727	Short Ext—Non-Lockup
	4142363	Diesel	A-727	Medium Ext—Non-Lockup
	4142364	Diesel	A-727	Long Ext—Non-Lockup

EXPORT

1983	4058387	225/Diesel	A-727	UK Export-Short Non-Lockup
	4025739	—	A-727	Aston Martin-Lockup
	4202717	—	A-727	Roadmaster Rail—Med. Non-Lockup
	3836023	—	A-727	Land Rover 4x4—Non Lockup
	3836024	Diesel	A-727	IVECO—Med. Ext. Non-Lockup
	3836040	—	A-727	Maserati—Lockup

MARINE AND INDUSTRIAL TRANSMISSIONS

	4142312	225	A-727	Short Ext—Non Lockup
	4142313	225	A-727	Med. Ext—Non Lockup
	4142321	318/360	A-727	Med. Ext—Non Lockup
	4142362	Diesel	A-727	Short Ext—Non Lockup
	4142363	Diesel	A-727	Med. Ext—Non Lockup
	4142364	Diesel	A-727	Long Ext—Non Lockup

FORD MOTOR CO.
Automatic Transmission/Transaxle Listing

Year	Model	Engine	Trans-code
C-3 TRANS.			
1980	Pinto—Bobcat	2.3L eng.	80DT-AA,-AB
	Mustang—Capri	2.3L eng. wo/turbo	800T-CA,-CB
		2.3L eng. w/turbo	800T-CDA,-CDB
		200 eng.	80DT-EA,-EB
	Fairmont—Zephyr	2.3L eng. wo/turbo	80DT-CA,-CB,-HA,-HB
		2.3L eng. w/turbo	80DT-CDA,-CDB
		200 eng.	80DT-EA,-EB,-LA,-LB,-CEB
	Thunderbird—Cougar	200 eng.	80DT-LB
1981	Mustang—Capri	2.3L eng.	81DT-CFA,-CHA
		200 eng.	81DT-DAA,-DAB,-DEA,-DEB
	Cougar-XR7—Granada Fairmont—Zephyr	2.3L eng.	81DT-CFA,-CHA,-CKA,-CMA
		200 eng.	81DT-DAA,-DAB,-DDA,-DDB,-DEA-DEB,-DGA,-DGB
	Thunderbird	200 eng.	81DT-DDA,-DDB,-DGA,-DGB

FORD MOTOR CO.
Automatic Transmission/Transaxle Listing

Year	Model	Engine	Trans-code
1982	Mustang—Capri	2.3L eng.	82DT-AAA,-ACA
		200 eng.	82DT-BBA
	Cougar-XR7—Granada	2.3L eng.	82DT-AAA,-ABA,-ACA,-ADA,-ARA
	Fairmont—Zephyr	2.3L eng.	82DT-AAA,-ABA,-ACA,-ADA
		200 eng.	82DT-BAA,-BBA
1983	Mustang—Capri	2.3L eng.	83DT-AAB
	LTD—Marquis	2.3L eng.	83DT-AAB,-ABB,-AGB,-AHB
	Fairmont—Zephyr	2.3L eng.	83DT-AAB,-ABB
		200 eng.	83DT-BAA,-BBA
	Cougar-XR7—Thunderbird	232 eng.	PKA-BH1,2,3
		255 eng.	PKA-AH5,6,7,8
	Lincoln Continental	232 eng.	PKA-BF1,2,3,4
		302 eng.	PKA-BD1,2,3,4
	Lincoln Towncar—Mark VI	302 eng.	PKA-M8-M13,14,15,16-BC1,2,3
1983	Ford—Mercury	302 eng.	PKA-AG17-AU17-AY12-BB12
		351 eng.	PKA-C25-AS17
	Cougar-XR7—Thunderbird	232 eng.	PKA-BR-BT
		302 eng.	PKA-K
	Lincoln Continental	302 eng.	PKA-BD12
	Lincoln Towncar—Mark VI	302 eng.	PKA-M25-BC5
	Marquis—LTD	232 eng.	PKA-BR-BT
1984	Ford—Mercury	302 eng.	PKA-AG23,24-AU23,24 -AY18,19-BB18,19
		351 eng.	PKA-C31,32-AS,23
	Mustang—Capri	232 eng.	PKA-BZ,1-CD,1
		302 eng.	PKA-BW,1
	Cougar-XR7—LTD Marquis—Thunderbird	232 eng.	PKA-BT6,7-CB6,7
	Cougar-XR7—Thunderbird	302 eng.	PKA-K6,7
	Lincoln Continental	302 eng.	PKA-BD18
	Lincoln Towncar	302 eng.	PKA-M31-BC12
	Lincoln Mark VII	302 eng.	PKA-BV

ATX TRANS.

Year	Model	Engine	Trans-code
1981	Escort—Lynx	1.6L eng.	PMA-A1,2
	LN7—EXP	1.6L eng.	PMA-K,1
1982	Escort—Lynx—LN7—EXP	1.6L eng.	PMA-A3-K2
		1.6L eng.(H.O.)	PMA-R
1983	Escort—Lynx—LN7—EXP	1.6L eng.	PMA-K3,PMB-A1
		1.6L eng.w/E.F.I.	PMA-P
		1.6L eng.(H.O.)	PMA-R1
1984	Tempo—Topaz	2.3L eng.	PMA-N
	Tempo, Topaz	2.3L eng.(Canada)	PMA-AA
	Escort—Lynx—EXP	1.6L eng.w/E.F.I.	PMA-U1,2-PMB,D
		1.6L eng.(w/H.O.)	PMA-V3-PMB-C2
	Tempo—Topaz	2.3L eng.	PMA-N-N1-N2

FORD MOTOR CO.
Automatic Transmission/Transaxle Listing

Year	Model	Engine	Trans-code
		C-3 TRANS.	
1984	Mustang—Capri	140 eng.	84DT-AAA,-ACA,-AJA
	LTD—Marquis	140 eng.	83DT-AGB,-AHB 84DT-ABA,-ACA,-ADA,-AKA
	Thunderbird—Cougar XR7	140 eng.	84DT-AEA,-AFA
		C-4 TRANS.	
1980	Ford—Mercury	302 eng.	PEE-DZ3,4,5,6,7,-EA3,4,5,6,7- EM3,4-FC1,2-FE1,2,3,4,5
	Mustang—Capri	2.3L eng. 200 eng. 255 eng.	PEJ-AC1,2,3 PEB-P4,5,6,7 PEM-B1,2,3,4-E1,2,3,4-N1,2,3,4
	Granada—Monarch	250 eng. 255 eng. 302 eng.	PEL-A1,2,3-B1,2,3,-C1-D1 PEM-J1,2,3,4-K1,2,3,4-P1-R1 PEE-CW5,6,7,8,9-FP1,2,3,4- FR1,2,3,4
	Pinto—Bobcat	2.3L eng.	PEJ-Z1,2,3
	Fairmont—Zephyr	2.3L eng. 200 eng. 255 eng.	PEJ-AC1,2,3-AD1,2,3 PEB-N6,7,8,9,-P4,5,6,7-S3,4- T1,2,3,4-U1,2,3 PEM-C1,2,3,4-D1,2,3,4-E1,2,3,4-G1- H1,2,3,4-M1,2,3,4-L1,2,3,4- N1,2,3,4
	Cougar—Thunderbird	200 eng. 255 eng. 302 eng.	PEB-T3,4 PEM-D1,2,3,4-L1,2,3,4 PEE-F1,2,3,4-FN1,2,3,4
	Versailles	302 eng.	PEE-EY2,3,4,5,6-FV1,2,3,4
1981	Mustang—Capri	2.3L eng. 200 eng. 255 eng.	PEJ-AC3-AC4 PEB-P8,P9,P10-A1-B1 PEM-E5-E6-W-W1-AD-AD1-AK-AK1
	Fairmont—Zephyr	2.3L eng. 200 eng. 255 eng.	PEJ-AC3-AC4-AD3-AD4 PEB-N10-N11—P8,P9,P10,U4-U5- Z-Z1 PEM-C5-C6-D5-D6-E5-E6-AC- AC1-AD-AD1-AL-AL1-AM- AM1-AN-AN1-AN2
	Cougar-XR7	2.3L eng. 200 eng. 255 eng.	PEJ-AC3-AC4-AD3-AD4 PEB-N10-N11-P8,P9,P10-Z-Z1 PEN-A-A1-B-B1 PEM-C5-C6-D6-D5-E5-E6- AC-AC1-AD-AD1-AE-AE1- AL-AL1-AM-AM1-AN-AN1- AN2
	Granada	2.3L eng. 200 eng. 255 eng.	PEJ-AC3-AC4-AD3-AD4 PEB-N10-N11-P8-P9-P10 PEN-A-A1-B-B1 PEM-C5-C6-E5-E6-AC-AC1- AD-AD1-AL-AL1-AM-AM1- AN-AN1-AN2
	Thunderbird	200 eng.	PEB-A-Z1-D5-D6-AC-AC1-AE- AE1-AN2

FORD MOTOR CO.
Automatic Transmission/Transaxle Listing

Year	Model	Engine	Trans-code
		C-5 TRANS.	
1982	Mustang—Capri	200 eng.	PEN-G-W
		255 eng.	PEM-AM3-AP
	Cougar-XR7—Granada	200 eng.	PEB-Z2-C-G-J-K-P-S
		232 eng.	PEP-B-D-E-F-G-H-N-P
	Fairmont—Zephyr	200 eng.	PEN-C-G-P-V-W
		255 eng.	PEM-AL3
1983	Mustang—Capri	232 eng.	PEP-B1-R
	Cougar-XR7—Thunderbird	232 eng.	PEP-V-W
	Fairmont—Zephyr	200 eng.	PEN-G1-P1-AA-AB-BA-CA
	Marquis—LTD	200 eng.	PEN-S1-U-Y-Z
		232 eng.	PEP-R-W
1984	Mustang—Capri	232 eng.	PEP-AF
	Cougar-XR7—Thunderbird	232 eng.	PEP-AD-AE
	LTD—Marquis	232 eng.	PEP-AC-AE-Z
		C-6 TRANS.	
1980	Ford—Mercury	302 eng.	PDG-BH5-CU5
		351 eng.	PGD-DD-DE-DG
		FMX TRANS.	
1980	Ford—Mercury	302 eng.	PHB-BH2-BH3
		351 eng.	PHB-BK-BK1-BP-BP1-BT-BT1-BU-BU1
1981	Ford—Mercury	302 eng.	PHB-BH2,3-BN
		JATCO TRANS.	
1980	Granada—Monarch	250 eng.	PLA-A2-A3
		A.O.T. TRANS.	
1980	Ford—Mercury	302 eng.	PKA-E1,2,3,4,5,6-W1,2,3
		351 eng.	PKA-C1,2,3,4,5,6-R1,2,3,4,5,6 T1,2,3,4,5,6-Z1,2,3,4,5,6
	Cougar-XR7—Thunderbird	302 eng.	PKA-Y1,2,3,4,5,6
	Lincoln—Mark VI	302 eng.	PKA-M1m2m3m4m5m6
		351 eng.	PKA-D1,2,3,4,5,6-U1,2,3,4,5,6
1981	Ford—Mercury	255 eng.	PKA-AF-AF5-AT-AT5
		302 eng.	PKA-E6-AG-AG5-AG50-AL-AV-AU5
		351 eng.	PKA-C6-C8-C13-R8-T8-Z8-AR-AS-AS5-AV
	Cougar-XR7—Thunderbird	255 eng.	PKA-AH-AH5
		302 eng.	PKA-Y8
	Lincoln—Mark VI	302 eng.	PKA-=M8-M13
1982	Ford	255 eng.	PKA-AF5,6-AT5
		302 eng.	PKA-AG-AG5-AU5-AU6-AY,1-BB,1
		351 eng.	PKA-C13,14-AS5,6
	Mercury	255 eng.	PKA-AF,5,6,7,8,-AT,5,6,7,8
		302 eng.	PKA-AG-AG5,6,7,8-AU-AU5,6,7,8-AY1,2,3-BB1,2,3
		351 eng.	PKA-C13,14,15,16-AS-AS5,6,7,8

INDEX

CHRYSLER CORPORATION
A404 • A413 • A415 • A470

Chrysler Corporation Transaxles

MODELS A-404, A-413 and A-470

1980—Omni/024, Horizon/TC3
1981—Omni/024, Horizon/TC3, Aries, Reliant
1982—LeBaron, Aries, Reliant, 400, Rampage,
  Horizon/TC3/Turismo/Miser/E-Type
  Omni/024/Miser/Charger/E-Type
1983—LeBaron, Aries, 600, Reliant, E-Class, New Yorker,
  400, Scamp, Rampage, Horizon/Turismo, Omni/Charger
1984—Laser, Voyager, LeBaron, New Yorker/E-Class,
  Reliant, Horizon/Turismo, Daytona, Caravan, 600,
  Aries, Omni/Charger

Vehicle Line Letter Code Identification

References will be made to the vehicle models by a letter code, throughout the section. An explanation, by year, follows:

1980
Z   Omni/024
M   Horizon/TC3

1981
Z   Omni/024
M   Horizon/TC3
P   Reliant
D   Aries

1982
C   LeBaron
     LeBaron Medallion
     Town and Country
D   Aries
     Aries Custom
     Aries S.E.
M   TC3 Miser
     Horizon Miser
     TC3
     Horizon
     TC3 Turismo
     E-Type
P   Reliant
     Reliant Custom
     Reliant S.E.
V   400
     400 LS
Z   024 Miser
     Omni Miser
     024
     Rampage
     Omni
     024 Charger 2.2
     E-Type

1983
C   LeBaron
     Town and Country
D   Aries
     Aries Custom
     Aries S.E.
E   600
     600 ES
J,L Caravelle (Canada)
M   Scamp
     Horizon Custom
     Horizon
     Turismo
     Scamp 2.2
P   Reliant
     Reliant Custom
     Reliant S.E.
T   E-Class
     New Yorker
V   400
Z   Rampage Sport
     Omni Custom
     Rampage
     Omni
     Charger

1984
C   LeBaron
D   Aries
E   600
J,L Caravelle (Canada)
M   Horizon
P   Reliant
T   New Yorker and E-Class
Z   Omni
V   Daytona (Dodge)
C   Laser (Chrysler)

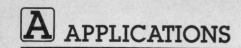

CHRYSLER CORPORATION
Transaxles Models A-404, A-413, A-415 and A-470

Year	Assy. No.	Engine	Trans Type	Over-all Ratio	Other Information
1980	5224442	1.7L	A-404	3.48	Fed. & Calif. Emissions
1981	4207088	1.7L	A-404	3.48	L-Car
	4269522	2.2L	A-413	2.78	K-Car
	4269523	2.2L	A-413	2.78	L-Car
	5224475	2.6L	A-470	2.78	K-Car
1982	4207296	2.6L	A-470	2.78	K-Car
	4207293	1.7L	A-404	3.48	L-Car
	4207294	2.2L	A-413	2.78	C,V,E,T, L & K Car
	4269544	2.2L	A-413	3.22	C,V,E,T, L & K Hi-Alt.
1983	4269686	2.6L	A-470	2.78	K-Car
	4295231	1.7L	A-404	3.50	L-Car
	4269683	2.2L	A-413	2.78	L & K Car
	4269685	2.2L	A-413	3.22	K-Car/Mex
	4269684	2.2L	A-413	3.02	L & K Car
	4269791	2.6L	A-470	3.02	K-Car
1984	4329551	1.6L	A-415	3.02	M,Z
	4295512	2.2L	A-413	2.78	M,Z,P,D
	4329552	2.2L	A-413	3.02	—
	4329553	2.2L	A-413	3.22	—
	4329827	2.2L	A-413	3.02	V,C,ET,VC
	4295763	2.2L	A-413	3.22	H,K
	4295513	2.2L	A-413	3.02	M,Z,P,D, VC,ET
	4295515	2.6L	A-470	3.02	P,D,V,C,E,T
	4295517	2.6L	A-470	3.22	H,K,P,D,C

ENGINE TO TRANSAXLE APPLICATION

Engine Liter	Transaxle Models
1.6	A-415
1.7	A-404
2.2	A-413
2.6	A-470

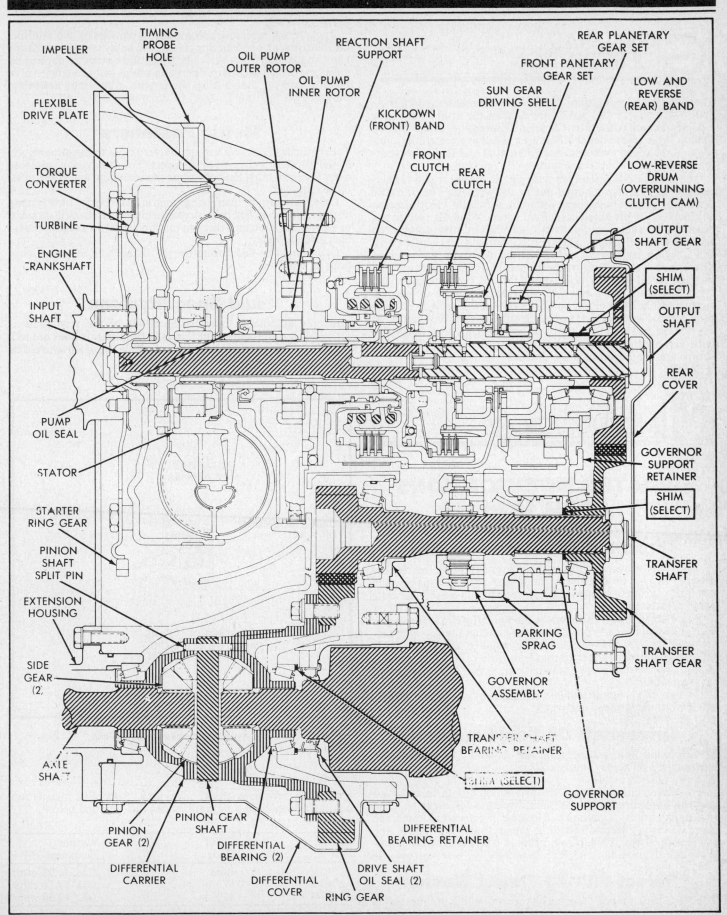

Cross section of TorqueFlite transaxle (©Chrysler Corp.)

GENERAL DESCRIPTION

The Chrysler Corporation TorqueFlite Transaxles, Models A-404, A-413, A-415 and A-470, are used on the front wheel drive vehicles, manufactured by Chrysler Corporation in the United States. These transaxles combine a torque converter, a fully automatic three speed transmission, differential and final drive gearing into a front wheel drive unit.

The transaxle is assembled with metric fasteners and numerous special tools are required during its overhaul. The transaxle operation requirements are different for each vehicle/engine combination, with different internal parts used in the specific application. It is important to refer to the parts number stamped on the transaxle oil pan flange when obtaining replacement parts. The torque converter is a sealed unit and cannot be disassembled for repairs. The cooling of the transaxle fluid is accomplished through an oil-to-water type cooler, located in the radiator side tank. The transaxle sump was separated from the differential sump until the 1983 models, when both were combined as a common sump. The later type can be identified by the elimination of the fill hole and plug from the cover, which is not interchangeable with earlier models. Both the later transaxle and differential sumps are vented through the dipstick.

The internal mechanical components consists of two multiple disc clutches, an overrunning clutch, two apply servos, two bands and two planetary gear sets. The hydraulic system is supplied by an engine driven oil pump, operating valves within a single valve body to control the shifting, along with a governor assembly, mounted on the transfer shaft of the transaxle assembly.

Metric Fasteners

The metric fastener dimensions are very close to the dimensions of the familiar inch system fasteners. For this reason, replacement fasteners must have the same measurement and strength as those removed.

Do not attempt to interchange metric fasteners for inch system fasteners. Mismatched or incorrect fasteners can result in damage to the transmission unit through malfunctions, breakage or possible personal injury.

Care should be taken to re-use the fasteners in the same locations as removed.

Fluid Specifications

Use only automatic transmission fluids of the type marked Dexron® II or its equivalent. Chrysler Corporation does not recommend the use of additives, other than the use of a dye to aid in the determination of fluid leaks.

MODIFICATIONS

UPDATED MODIFICATIONS FROM 1978

Throttle Cable Retaining Clip

A new wider transaxle throttle cable grommet retaining clip has recently entered production on the subject models. This new clip retains the grommet more securely, resulting in a more accurate cable adjustment.

When servicing a vehicle where the retaining clip is missing or a vehicle with the early production narrow clip, the new wider retaining clip, P/N 5214484, should be installed and proper cable adjustment made. Proper transaxle throttle cable adjustment is *necessary* to ensure proper automatic transaxle shift quality and performance.

If a new clip is not available, a replacement can be easily fabricated from .021″ sheet steel stock.

Driveshaft Oil Seal Leakage

Transmission fluid leakage from the driveshaft oil seal may be encountered on some Omni and Horizon models equipped with an automatic transaxle.

To correct this condition, the driveshaft should be removed and the inner driveshaft seal area inspected for nicks or burrs which may cause seal failure and leakage. If defects are found, the inner driveshaft section should be replaced. In all instances, the driveshaft oil seal, blue in color, should be replaced with an improved seal, green in color, P/N 5205591.

"Select Fit" #3 Thrust Washer

The No. 3 thrust washer located on the front of the output shaft is

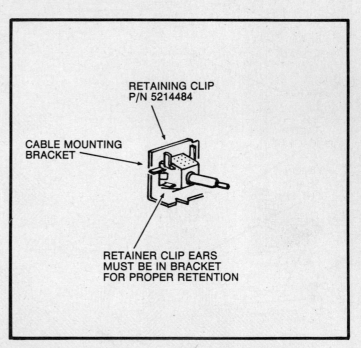

Installation of cable mounting bracket retaining clip
(©Chrysler Corp.)

serviced in three sizes (thicknesses) for a "Select Fit" installation on all Chrysler built automatic transaxles, as listed below:

Washer Part No.	Color Code	Washer Thickness
5224039	Blue	.078″ (1.98 mm)
5224040	White	.085″ (2.16 mm)
5224041	Yellow	.092″ (2.34 mm)

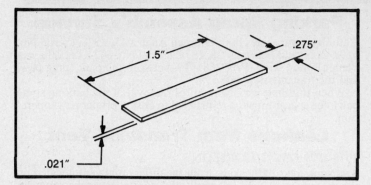

Fabrication of retaining clip (©Chrysler Corp.)

The function of No. 3 thrust washer is to set input shaft end play. The procedure for measuring input shaft end play is as follows:

Measuring Input Shaft End Play

Measure input shaft end play prior to disassembly; which will indicate whether a thrust washer change is required. If, during repair, the input and/or output shafts are replaced, it will be necessary to assemble the transaxle and measure "Input Shaft End Play"; this will allow you to select the proper No. 3 thrust washer.

1. Attach a dial indicator to the transaxle bell housing with its plunger seated against the end of the input shaft.

Move the input shaft in until it bottoms and zero the dial indicator. Pulling on the input shaft, measure the amount of input shaft end play. Input shaft end play should be .030" to .106".

2. Note the amount of end play. When assembling the transaxle, select the No. 3 thrust washer that will provide the minimum amount of specified end play.

EXAMPLES: 1. End play as measured   .037 inch
            Original Thrust Washer   .078 inch (Blue)
            Corrected End Play   In Specification

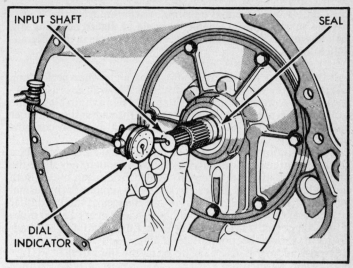

Measuring input shaft seal (©Chrysler Corp.)

2. End play as measured   .027 inch
   Original Thrust Washer   .085 inch (White)
   Replacement Thrust Washer   .078 inch (Blue)
   Corrected End Play   .034 inch

Capacity

CHECKING FLUID LEVEL

1981-82

Place the selector in "PARK" and allow the engine to idle. The fluid should be at operating temperature (180°). Check the dipstick. The fluid level is correct if it is between the "FULL" and "ADD" marks. Do not overfill.

CAPACITY CHART

Year	Transaxle	Engine (Liter)	U.S. Quarts	Liters	Imperial Quarts
1981-82	A-404	1.7	7.3	6.9	6.2
	A-413	2.2	7.5	7.1	6.3
	A-470	2.6	8.5	8.1	7.0

NOTES: 1. Differential capacity—1.2 U.S. quarts, 1.1 liter, 1.0 Imperial quart.
       2. Replacement fluid volume is approximately 3.0 U.S. quarts, 2.8 liter, 2.5 Imperial quarts.

Year	Transaxle	Engine (Liter)	U.S. Quarts	Liters	Imperial Quarts
1983-84	A-404	1.7	8.4	7.9	7.0
	A-413	2.2 Except Fleet	8.9	8.4	7.4
	A-415	1.6	8.9	8.4	7.4
	A-470	2.6 Except Fleet	8.9	8.4	7.4
	A-413	2.2 Fleet only	9.2	8.7	7.6
	A-470	2.6 Fleet only	9.2	8.7	7.6

NOTES: 1. Differential sump included with transaxle sump.
       2. Replacement fluid volume is approximately 4.0 U.S. quarts, 3.8 liters, 3.7 Imperial quarts.

NOTE: The differential oil sump is separate from the "transmission sump." Special emphasis should be placed on filling and maintaining the differential oil level to the fill hole in the differential cover.

It is necessary to treat these units separately when performing lubricant changes or oil level inspections. The transaxle assembly does not have the conventional filler tube, nor a drain plug in the pan or converter. The transaxle is filled through a die cast filler (and dipstick) hole in the case. The differential assembly contains both a fill and drain plug.

Both the automatic transaxle and differential assembly require Dexron® automatic transmission fluid. Although they share the same housing, they are internally sealed from each other. Both should have their fluid levels checked every six months in normal service. Although in normal service no changes of fluid and filter are necessary the transaxle should be serviced every 15,000 miles if used for severe service. At that time, fluid, filter and band adjustment should be done. The refill capacity is 3 quarts of Dexron® adding, if necessary, to bring the fluid to the "FULL" mark when warmed up.

1983 AND LATER

Place the vehicle on a level surface with the engine/transaxle at or near normal operating temperature (minimum operating time of six minutes) to stablize the oil level between the transaxle and the differential. Apply the parking brake and momentarily place the gear selector in each gear position, ending in the P (Park) position.

Remove the dipstick, wipe clean and check the fluid to determine if it is hot or warm. If the fluid is approximately 180°F (82°C) and cannot be held comfortably between the fingers, it would be considered at normal operating temperature. If the fluid is between 85 to 125°F (29 to 52 C) and can be held comfortably between the fingers, it is considered to be warm.

Re-insert the dipstick to its seat on the cap seal, remove the dipstick and note the oil level indication. If the fluid temperature is considered hot, the reading should be in the crosshatched area marked 'OK' (Between the two dots in the dipstick). If the fluid temperature is considered warm, the fluid level should be between the bottom of the dipstick and the lower dot.

If the fluid level indicates low, add sufficient fluid to bring the level to within the marks indicated for the appropriate fluid temperature.

The Automatic Transaxle fluid and filter should be changed, and the bands adjusted if the vehicle is used under severe usage, at 15,000 miles (24,000 km). Severe usage is defined as more than 50% operation in heavy city traffic during hot weather (above 90°F (32°C). A band adjustment and filter change should be made at the time of the transaxle fluid change, regardless of vehicle usage.

Parking Sprag Assembly Service

Automatic transaxles built between August 17, 1978, (Serial No. 6198-xxxx) and February 28, 1979, (Serial No. 6424-xxxx) have a Planet Pinion Ring, P/N 3681949, between the park sprag pawl and the transmission case.

When transaxle service requires removal of the parking sprag pawl, the spacer must be reinstalled to ensure proper pawl operation.

Leakage from Transaxle Vent

1978-1979 OMNI/HORIZON

Transmission fluid leakage from the differential vent, located on the extension, may be the result of a porous or cracked transfer bearing and oil seal retainer, a leaking oil seal or a nicked or broken "O" ring(s).

If vent leakage exists, it will be necessary to remove the transfer shaft bearing and oil seal retainer to allow complete inspection of the retainer for defects. If the retainer is found to be defective, it should be replaced with P/N 5222120. To improve sealing of the retainer, a second "O" ring has been added to the retainer on transaxles with a starting transaxle serial number of 6324-xxxx.

If either the transfer shaft or transfer shaft bearing and oil seal retainer are replaced, the procedure for setting transfer shaft end play contained in the transaxle assembly procedure must be followed.

The transfer shaft bearing cup should be reused whenever the transfer shaft bearing retainer is replaced, unless the cup is damaged during removal. The Transfer Shaft Oil Seal, P/N 5222015, and Transfer Shaft Bearing Retainer "O" Ring(s), P/N 6500169, must always be replaced.

Automatic Transaxle Gear and Bearing Noise Diagnosis and Repair

ALL 1978 THROUGH 1980 OMNI AND HORIZON EQUIPPED WITH AUTOMATIC TRANSAXLE

Abnormal gear and bearing noises must be distinguished to facilitate proper repair of the A-404 automatic transaxle for these conditions.

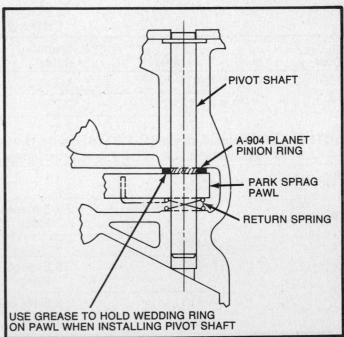

Use of planet pinion ring between park sprag pawl and case (©Chrysler Corp.)

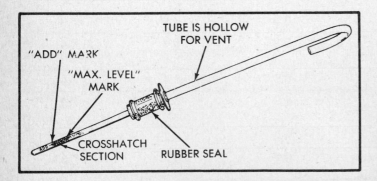

Dipstick assembly with internal vent (©Chrysler Corp.)

Before attempting any repair for a noise condition on an A-404 automatic transaxle, a thorough road test should be performed to determine whether such repairs are warranted or unnecessary.

NOTE: The automatic transaxle by its design characteristics (a multi-angle gear drive unit), being located in front of the driver, develops higher levels of gear noise than conventional rear wheel drive units.

GEAR NOISE DIAGNOSIS

Planetary Gear Noise:

Low frequency gear whine which occurs in low and second gear but not in direct drive (high gear). This is similar in sound and pitch to rear wheel drive automatic transmission planetary gear noise.

Transfer Gear Noise:

High frequency gear whine most noticeable in direct drive or on coast below 25 mph. This noise may occur at any car speed.

Final Drive Gear Noise (Differential Gear):

Low frequency gear whine most noticeable above 40 mph in direct drive (high gear) or coast (the audible frequency is usually ⅓ that of transfer gear noise).

BEARING NOISE DIAGNOSIS

Bearing noise is a low frequency, rumbling type noise which is apparent throughout the entire speed range. Bearing noise is not torque sensitive, whereas gear noise usually changes with torque and speed.

NOTE: Do not mistake front wheel bearing noise for transaxle bearing noise. Transaxle bearing noise is not sensitive to steering direction, whereas front wheel bearing noise is sensitive to changes in steering direction.

Once the source of gear or bearing noise has been determined, the gear set or bearing must be replaced properly to assure correction of the noise condition.

NOTE: When gear set replacement is required, the replacement gears should be replaced in a matched set. This will ensure proper gear tooth contact and reduction in gear noise.

When bearing replacement is required, replace both the bearing cup and cone. The replacement of both the cup and cone will ensure maximum bearing life.

SERVICE COMPONENTS FOR CORRECTION OF ABNORMAL GEAR AND BEARING NOISE

Planetary Gear Set Components

Replace all components shown for planetary gear noise

Description	Part Number
Rear Annulus Gear	5222047
Rear Annulus Bearing Cone	5224300
Rear Annulus Bearing Cup	5224299
Rear Carrier Assembly	5205740
Sun Gear Assembly	5205733
Front Carrier Assembly	5222495
Front Annulus Assembly (Service Component Parts)	
Snap Rings (2)	5205725
Gear	5212201
Support Assembly	5212203

Transfer Gear Set Components

Replace all components shown for transfer gear set noise.

Description	Part Number
Transfer and Output Gear Set	4131048
Output Shaft Gear Bearing Cone	5224300
Output Shaft Gear Bearing Cup	5224299
Transfer Shaft Gear Bearing Cone	5224301
Transfer Shaft Gear Bearing Cup	5222259

Final Drive Gear Set Components

Replace all components shown for final drive gear noise.

Description	Part Number	
	3.48 (1978/1979 FEDERAL) (1980 ALL)	**3.67** (1978/1979 CALIF)
Ring Gear and Transfer Shaft Set	4131049 (54T gear-19T shaft)	4131050 (54T gear-18T shaft)
Transfer Shaft Bearing Cone	5224301	5224301
Transfer Shaft Bearing Cup	5222259	5222259

——— CAUTION ———

Ring Gear Service Package, P/N 4131050, has an identification groove on the O.D. of the gear teeth. Extreme care must be exercised to use this ring gear with the 18-tooth transfer shaft only.

NOTE: Improperly seated bearing cups and cones are subject to low mileage failures.

When servicing the transaxle for gear or bearing noise, particular attention should be given to the following points:
   a. All bearing adjustments, except transfer shaft bearing, must be made with no other gear train component interference or in gear mesh.
   b. Used (original) bearings may lose up to 50% of the original drag torque after break-in.
   c. When replacement of either the output or transfer gear is required, both gears should be replaced in a matched set.

After servicing the transaxle and installing the unit back in the vehicle, remember the transmission and differential have separate oil sumps and fill each sump to the proper specification. Check and adjust shift linkage and throttle cable adjustments.

Driveline Vibration— Automatic Transaxle

1979 & 1980 OMNI/HORIZON MODELS

Driveline vibration sensed at speeds from 25 to 35 mph, primarily felt through the steering column, may be caused by excessive transfer shaft runout.

If abnormal driveline vibration is present, use the following procedure to verify the condition.
   a. Road test vehicle. This condition cannot be effectively diagnosed on a hoist.
   b. Verify that condition occurs between 25 to 35 mph and in both drive and coast. This condition is extremely speed sensitive and is most noticeably transferred through the steering column.
   Tire balance or C/V joint malfunction can also cause driveline vibration.

a. TIRE BALANCE—most often causes vibration above 40 mph

b. C/V JOINT—most noticeable in direct gear in drive, **not** coast, and in long smooth straight away areas.

When transfer shaft runout condition is incurred, it will be necessary to replace the following parts.

Description	Part Number	
	3.48 (1978/1979 FEDERAL) (1980 ALL)	**3.67** (1978/1979 CALIF)
Ring Gear and Transfer Shaft Set	4131049 (54T gear-19T shaft)	4131050 (54T gear-18T shaft)
Transfer Shaft Bearing Cone	5224301	5224301
Transfer Shaft Bearing Cup	5222259	5222259

--------- CAUTION ---------

Ring Gear Service Package, P/N 4131050, has an identification groove on the O.D. of the gear teeth. Extreme care must be exercised to use this ring gear with the 18-tooth transfer shaft only.

When servicing the transaxle for gear or bearing noise, particular attention should be given to the following points:

a. All bearing adjustments, except transfer shaft bearing, must be made with no other gear train components interference or in gear mesh.

b. Used (original) bearings may lose up to 50% of the original drag torque after break-in.

c. When replacement of either the output or transfer gear is required, both gears must be replaced in a matched set.

After servicing the transaxle and installing the unit back in the vehicle, remember the transmission and differential have separate oil sumps and fill each sump to the proper specification. Check and adjust shift linkage and throttle cable adjustment.

Transfer Shaft Bearing Service A-404, 413 & 470 Automatic Transaxle

OMNI, HORIZON, ARIES, RELIANT

Transfer shaft bearing and bearing cup retainer service in many instances may be difficult, due to the pressed fit of the transfer shaft bearing cup in the bearing retainer.

To improve service of the bearing and its retainer, a service package has been released. This package, PN #4205899, consists of:

1—Transfer Shaft Bearing Cone
1—Transfer Shaft Bearing Cup
1—Transfer Shaft Retainer
1—Transfer Shaft Oil Seal
2—Transfer Shaft Retainer 'O' Ring

This package will have the bearing cup pressed into the retainer. Use the package in its entirety, **Do Not Use Individual Parts.**

Simplifying the service of the transaxle should provide easier and better repair.

Automatic Transaxle Kickdown Band Adjustment & Application

1981 & 1982 OMNI/HORIZON, ARIES/RELIANT

The kickdown band adjustment for automatic transaxle assemblies released for the 1982 subject model vehicles differs from the

1981 model assemblies. The adjustment is changed from 2 turns for the 1981 assembly to 2¾ turns for the 1982 assembly.

Since 1981 and 1982 transaxle assemblies may have been interchanged on a limited number of late built 1981 and early built 1982 subject model vehicles, it is important that the transaxle part number be observed prior to adjusting the kickdown on these vehicles.

NOTE: Remember that kickdown band adjustment is accomplished by tightening the kickdown band adjustment screw to 72 inch pounds (8 N•m), then backing the screw out 2 or 2¾ turns depending on model year, then tightening the lock nut.

The list below gives the model year, transaxle part number, engine application, and kickdown band adjustment for the transaxles involved.

Model Year	Transaxle Part• No. & Model	Engine Application	Kickdown Band Adjustment
81	4269534-A-413	2.2L	2 turns
81	4269535-A-470	2.6L	2 turns
82	4207294-A-413	2.2L	2¾ turns
82	4207296-A-470	2.6L	2¾ turns
82	4269544-A-413	2.2L (Hi Alt.)	2¾ turns

Automatic Transaxle—Transfer Gear Noise Reduction

1981 OMNI, HORIZON, ARIES, RELIANT; 1982 OMNI, HORIZON, ARIES, RELIANT, LEBARON & DODGE 400

On some 1981 and 1982 vehicles equipped with automatic transaxle, light gear noise may be noticeable between 40 and 60 miles per hour (MPH).

To properly determine this condition a road test must be performed. The gear noise will be high pitch in sound.

To reduce this noise a Rubber Shift Cable Sleeve, PN 4269881, must be installed on the gear shift selector cable between the selector cable mounting on the transaxle and the firewall using the following procedure:

1. Open hood and locate gear selector cable.
2. Unravel the sleeve from the center and wrap it around the gear shift selector cable.

NOTE: For best performance the sleeve should be centered between the firewall and the mounting bracket.

Speedometer pinion gear failure

1981 OMNI, HORIZON, ARIES, RELIANT; 1982 OMNI, HORIZON, ARIES, RELIANT, LEBARON, DODGE 400

Check the routing of the speedometer cable or cables. Make certain the cable is not misrouted or improperly bound by any component that may shorten its length or restrict its travel.

NOTE: Speedometer cable travel is the movement of the cable during engine rock (movement when shifting gears or accelerating).

Inspect the cable for damage due to improper routing and replace if necessary. Proper cable routing should prevent pinion gear failures in all applications. See the attached illustrations for proper cable routing.

On vehicles equipped with the 2.6 litre engine and speed control that have experienced speedometer pinion gear failure, the following procedure should be used:

REPAIR PROCEDURE

VEHICLES EQUIPPED WITH 2.6 LITRE ENGINE & SPEED CONTROL

Speedometer pinion gear failures on these vehicles may be due to engine movement pulling on the speedometer cable. In this application the cable length may be shortened due to routing. This results in side loading of the speedometer adapter, deflecting the drive pinion gear away from the drive shaft and failing of the pinion gear.

To correct this condition and insure unrestricted cable travel, install a new 5" longer Speedometer Cable (PN 4047761).

Transaxle Oil Leak at Oil Pan Bolt

ALL 1981-1982 OMNI, HORIZON, RELIANT, ARIES; RAMPAGE, & LEBARON

Oil leak at transaxle oil pan which appears to be a result of improper application of RTV sealer at the oil pan.

The leak may be due to porosity of the case between the governor pressure port and the nearest oil pan tapped hole. The porosity may allow oil to leak from the governor circuit, into the oil pan bolt hole, and out around the bolt. Use the following procedure to correct.

Parts Required: RTV Sealer—PN 4026070
1. Remove the oil pan bolt from tapped hole.
2. Check for transmission fluid presence in the hole and on the bolt threads.
3. Thoroughly clean the bolt and the hole of transmission fluid. Use Mopar Brake and Carburetor Parts Cleaner, PN 3879889, or equivalent to clean the parts. Blow dry with compressed air.
4. Apply RTV sealer to the bolt threads, reinstall and torque bolt to 165 inch pounds (19 N•m).

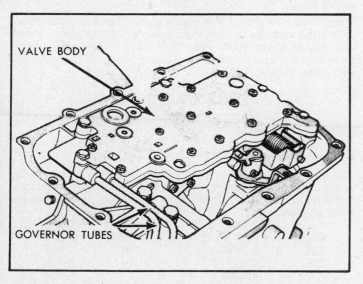

Location of possible fluid leakage at oil pan tapped bolt hole (©Chrysler Corp.)

Shift Cable Adjustment

1981 & 1982 OMNI, HORIZON, ARIES, RELIANT, LEBARON & DODGE 400 EQUIPPED WITH AUTOMATIC TRANSMISSION

Transmission cable adjustment procedures have been clarified for subject model vehicles equipped with automatic transmissions.

Note that the following adjustment methods vary depending on the type of shift (column versus console shift) and/or the model vehicle being serviced.

Adjustment Procedure

1. Place the gear shift lever in "P" (Park).

2. Loosen the cable retaining clamp on the cable mounting bracket of the automatic transmission.
3. Apply loading as follows while retightening the cable retaining clamp bolt to 90 inch pounds (10 N•m).
All models equipped with column shift—apply a 10 pound load in the forward direction on the cable housing isolator.
Aries, Reliant, LeBaron and Dodge 400 models equipped with console shift—apply a 10 pound minimum load in the forward direction on the console shift lever knob.
Omni and Horizon models equipped with console shift—apply a 10 pound load in the forward direction on the transmission lever (at the transmission).
4. Check adjustment by moving the shift lever through all positions while attempting to key start. Engine should start only in the Park and Neutral positions.

TRANSAXLE MANUFACTURING RUNNING CHANGES

1980 Changes

OVER-ALL RATIO
The optional 3.67 over-all ratio for California cars was dropped this year.

THROTTLE VALVE SPRING
The A404 throttle valve spring was replaced by the current A904/A727 throttle valve spring. This change will produce lower vehicle speed upshifts, improve fuel economy and reduce part throttle downshift sensitivity.

VALVE BODY AND TRANSFER PLATE ASSEMBLY
A new valve body and transfer plate assembly was introduced as a running change in preparation for major hydraulic changes that took place in the 1981 Model Year. The parts involved are: Valve body casting, transfer plate casting, steel plate, torque converter switch valve, throttle valve, regulator valve cover, and an additional cover on top of the valve body. These individual parts are not interchangeable with previous style parts, however, the complete valve body and transfer plate assembly can be used on all prior model transaxles.

OUTPUT SHAFT BEARINGS
The two output shaft bearings were moved six millimeters further apart in the over running clutch race. This improves the alignment between the input and output shafts, thus reducing output plug wear and rear clutch disc spline wear. The parts involved in this change are: over running clutch race, output shims, output shaft, transfer gear, and end cover. The transaxle assembly part number with these changes is 4207442 for the 1.7 liter engine application. The parts are not interchangeable with the previous style parts.

1981 Changes

In 1981 two new models were introduced into the transaxle family—one for the 2.2 liter Chrysler-built engine and one for the 2.6 liter MMC engine. The two new models each have a new case configuration, making a total of four transaxle cases.

WIDE RATIO
All models have a wide ratio planetary gear set (similar to the A-904). The gear ratios are 2.69 (low) and 1.55 (second) as compared to the previous standard ratios of 2.48 and 1.48. The wide ratio transaxle offers fuel economy improvements with little loss of performance because it is used with lower final drive ratios.

M MODIFICATIONS

The wide ratio gear set consists of a new larger front annulus gear, support, snap ring, front carrier, stepped diameter sun gear, carrier thrust washers, and drive shell thrust plate, along with rear clutch discs and plates which have larger inside diameters. These parts are unique to the wide ratio and are not interchangeable with previous model transaxles.

DIFFERENTIAL BEARING RETAINER

The differential bearing retainer was changed from aluminum to steel. This adds stability and reduces deflection of the retainer, which is required for the higher torque engines. The steel retainer requires the use of shorter bolts, and maybe used on all prior model transaxles.

LOW-REVERSE ADJUSTABLE LEVER

A two piece low-reverse lever with an adjustment screw and a new narrow strut is used in transaxles for the 2.2 and 2.6 liter engines. The adjustment on this lever is 3½ turns backed off from 41 inch pounds. This lever cannot be used in prior model transaxles.

KICKDOWN LEVER

A 3.00 to 1 ratio kickdown lever instead of the 2.76 to 1 ratio is used in transaxles for the 2.2 and 2.6 liter engines. The adjustment for the 3.00 lever is 2 turns backed off from 72 inch pounds. A new configuration 2.76 ratio lever is used with the new servo. This lever may be used on all previous models.

TRANSFER GEAR SET

A new transfer gear set having a lower ratio was introduced for use with the 2.2 and 2.6 liter engines. The gear set consists of a 57 tooth output gear and a 52 tooth transfer shaft gear.

FINAL DRIVE GEARS

A new final drive gear set with a 20-61 tooth combination was introduced for use with the 2.6 liter engine. An 18-55 tooth combination set previously used in 1978 is used with the 2.2 liter engine.

REAR CLUTCH

All 1981 transaxles have a 3 disc rear clutch assembly instead of a 2 disc assembly as in prior models. The 3 disc assembly consists of a new retainer which is longer and a new waved snap ring, belleville spring, discs and plates which have a larger inside diameter to fit the wide ratio front annulus gear (mentioned above). These parts are not interchangeable with the previous style parts.

SUN GEAR DRIVE SHELL

The drive shell configuration was slightly modified to clear the longer rear clutch retainer. This part may be used on previous models.

FRONT CLUTCH

A redesigned front clutch assembly was introduced, consisting of a new retainer, smaller outside diameter piston, outer seal (same as A-904), thicker separator plates and a thinner reaction plate. A two disc front clutch with two separator plates between the discs is used in transaxles for the 1.7 liter and Simca engines. A three disc front clutch with one separator plate between each disc is used in transaxles for the 2.2 and 2.6 liter engines. These new front clutch parts are not interchangeable with the previous style parts.

VALVE BODY

The valve body was redesigned to improve shift quality, reduce internal leakage and to provide lower line pressures. Several of the changes were made as running 1980 model year changes as previously stated. The parts involved in the 1981 changes are: valve body, steel plate, shuttle valve and plug, regulator valve, springs and the additional bypass valve. None of these parts or the complete valve body and transfer plate assembly are interchangeable with prior model parts.

KICKDOWN PISTON

The diameter of the kickdown piston was increased. The large diameter is the same as the A-904 and uses the same seal ring; the small diameter is the same as the A-998 and uses the same seal ring. The inner piston, o-ring, snap ring and rod are A-904 parts. A new kickdown guide was also required. The case piston bore is larger, therefore making none of these parts interchangeable with the previous style parts. This change was made to accommodate the lower line pressures and to improve shift quality with the larger engines.

GOVERNOR

The size of the governor valves and governor body bores were redesigned to accommodate the lower line pressures and wide ratio which require different shift points. The parts are not interchangeable with the previous style parts.

LOW-REVERSE SERVO

The low-reverse servo was modified to give more stroke to improve neutral to reverse shift quality. The servo stem length was modified, cushion spring wire diameter was reduced, and the spring retainer replaced with the A-904 MMC spring retainer. These parts, as a group, can be used on prior models.

DIFFERENTIAL COVER AND FILL PLUG

The differential cover fill plug thread boss was changed from a welded-on boss to one extruded from the sheet metal cover. A new length plug and washer assembly is used. These parts reduce plug leaks and can be used on all prior model transaxles.

GOVERNOR

The governor for the 1.7 liter engine application was modified to reduce the wide open throttle shift speeds. The secondary valve was replaced by the Simca valve which was a hole through its center and the spring load decreased. This governor can be used in all wide ratio transaxles for the 1.7 liter engine.

1982 Changes

KICKDOWN PISTON

The length of the bore for the inner piston was increased by 2.5mm. The purpose was to improve shift quality throughout the operating temperature range. With this servo, the Kickdown Band adjustments are:

Engine	Trans. Part No.	Turns	Trans Model
2.2L	4207294	2¾	A-413
2.6L	4207296	2¾	A-470
1.7L	4207293	3	A-404
2.2L	4269544 (Hi Alt.)	2¾	A-413

This piston may be used in 1981 model transaxles with the above kickdown band adjustments.

VALVE BODY AND TRANSFER PLATE

The regulator valve line pressure plug and sleeve were eliminated and the regulator valve throttle pressure plug replaced with a longer plug having a different diameter. With this system, a new regulator valve throttle plug spring is required. The transfer plate cast passages were modified in the area of the regulator valve. The 1-2 and 2-3 shift valve springs were changed to the springs used in 1980 Model Year. These individual parts are not interchangeable with previous style parts, however, the complete valve body and transfer plate assembly may be used on 1981 Model Year transaxles.

TRANSFER GEAR SET

A new transfer gear set was introduced in 1982 for high altitude and Mexican applications. The tooth combination is a 53 tooth output shaft gear and a 56 tooth transfer shaft gear.

GOVERNOR VALVE

The primary governor valve used in the high altitude and Mexican applications was made lighter by making a stepped diameter hole in it, this increases the shift speeds.

TEFLON SEAL RINGS

Teflon seal rings for the Kickdown and Accumulator pistons and the Input Shaft were incorporated. They may be used in previous model transaxles.

DIFFERENTIAL ASSEMBLY

The 18-55 tooth combination was replaced with the 20-61 tooth combination.

FRONT PUMP SEAL

A Vamac (black) front pump seal replaced the Silicone (orange) seal. This seal may be used on all prior model transaxles.

DIFFERENTIAL COVER AND PLUG

The differential cover and plug was changed from the threaded plug to a push-in rubber plug, similar to conventional rear axles. This cover and plug can be use on all prior model transaxles.

EXTENSION

The extension speedo bore was re-designed giving a machined pilot bore for the and of the speedometer pinion. This extension can be used on all prior model transaxles.

MAIN OIL PAN BOLT

A nylon sealing patched bolt was incorporated for use in the main oil pan screw hole which is next to the governor pressure circuit. This bolt reduces leakage, due to porosity, between the governor circuit and the tapped hole thus reducing external leaks.

1983 Changes
COMMON TRANSMISSION AND DIFFERENTIAL OIL SUMP

This change makes a common reservoir of oil for the differential and the transmission. The purpose of "Common Sump" is to reduce the possibility of transfer shaft bearing failures due to low differential oil level. The intent is to signal the customer via changes in transmission performance (slipping) when the oil level is too low. If the oil level is not corrected, a rear clutch failure will occur before a more serious and costly transfer shaft or differential bearing failure occurs. The possibility of leaks is reduced since the differential cover plug and extension vent are eliminated.

Following is a description of the parts that changed:

CASE—There is a machined passage between the transmission and differential cavities. This case is not interchangeable with previous models.

TRANSFER SHAFT BEARING RETAINER—One O-ring groove and the transfer shaft seal has been eliminated. The outside and inside diameter of the hub where the seal went is reduced in size to 17.8mm. This part is not interchangeable with previous model parts.

PUMP HOUSING GASKET—The gasket was modified by adding a torque converter circuit bleed hole which feeds oil to the differential cavity under all conditions, and a cut out to match the case passage hole. This gasket may be used on all previous model transaxles.

PUMP HOUSING—The casting was changed to accommodate the revised gasket and to make a space for oil to flow between the differential and transmission cavities.

EXTENSION—The machined vent hole and the vent were eliminated. This extension is not interchangeable with previous models.

DIFFERENTIAL COVER—The fill hole and fill plug were eliminated. This cover cannot be used on previous models.

DIFFERENTIAL THRUST WASHERS—The thrust washers in the differential assembly were changed from free spinning washers to tabbed washers to reduce the possibility of dirt contamination to the transmission as the washers were. Differential carriers with these washers may be used in all previous model transaxles.

VALVE BODY OIL FILTER—A new style body filter which has the filter material in a partially enclosed plastic and steel case is used. This style filter does not have to be completely immersed in oil to avoid sucking air. With common sump the filter at times may be tipped out of the oil reservoir and exposed to air within the transmission.

A gasket is used between the filter and the transfer plate.

This new filter requires a new deeper main oil pan.

This filter can be used on all prior model transaxles but must be accompanied by the pan and gasket.

DIFFERENTIAL OIL RETAINER—A new different oil retainer with a revised shape and smaller inside diameter which improves lubrication to the differential half shaft journal is used. The left side hub of the differential carrier was reduced in length by 1mm to accommodate this retainer. The oil retainer cannot be used in previous model transaxles.

OIL DIPSTICK—A new length oil dipstick is required for the common sump transaxles. The "FULL" mark is 101mm from the washer face, 1982 models had the "FULL" mark 90mm from the washer face.

COOLER LINE FITTING

The cooler line fitting was redesigned in order to reduce cooler line leakage. The new fitting has a nippled extension on it to accommodate a rubber hose and clamp instead of the inverted flare tube joint. This fitting may be used on all previous model transaxles with the proper rubber hoses.

DIFFERENTIAL GEAR SETS

The 19-54 tooth combination gear set was replaced by a higher capacity 21-60 tooth combination gear set. This gear set may be used to replace the 19-54 set on prior models.

REAR SERVO SEAL

The material of the rear servo seal was changed to Viton to improve its resistance to high temperatures. This seal may be used in all prior model transaxles.

1983 Model transaxles may be used to service all prior models, it is important that the 1983 Models have the correct dipstick.

TRANSAXLE GOVERNOR REPLACEMENT
A-404, A-413, A-415 and A-470

Model Year	Transmission P/N	Gov. Body	Primary Valve	Secondary Valve	Spring
1978	5212256 5222187	4269501	5222457 or 5224390	5222458 or 5224391	5222459-Plain
1979	5224023 5224196	4269501	5222457 or 5224390	5222458 or 5224391	5222459-Plain
1980	5224442 4207442	4269501	5222457 or 5224390	5222458 or 5224391	5222459-Plain
1981	5224442 4207442	4269501	5222457 or 5224390	5222458 or 5224391	5222459-Plain

NOTE: Governor repair package 4186092 can be used to service the above transmissions. The size of the governor valves and governor body bores were redesigned for use with wide ratio and low line pressure transmissions introduced in 1981. The new parts *shown below* are not interchangeable with previous parts.

Model Year	Transmission P/N	Gov. Body	Primary Valve	Secondary Valve	Spring
1981	4207088 4207215	4207055	4207186-Solid	4207183-Hole	4207193-Blue
1981	4269522-4269523 4269534-4269535 5224473-5224474 5224475	4207055	4207186-Solid	4207185-Solid	4207193-Blue
1982	4207293	4207055	4207186-Solid	4207183-Hole	4207193-Blue
1982	4207294 4207296	4207055	4207186-Solid	4207185-Solid	4207193-Blue
1982	4269544 4269651	4207055	4269641-2 Dia Hole	4207183-Hole	4207194-Orange

TROUBLE DIAGNOSIS

CLUTCH AND BAND APPLICATION CHART
A-404, A-413, A-415 and A-470 TorqueFlite Transaxles

Lever Position	Clutches Front	Rear	Over-running	Bands (Kickdown) Front	(Low-Rev.) Rear
P—PARK	—	—	—	—	—
R—REVERSE	X	—	—	—	X
N—NEUTRAL	—	—	—	—	—
D—DRIVE					
First	—	X	X	—	—
Second	—	X	—	X	—
Direct	X	X	—	—	—
2—SECOND					
First	—	X	X	—	—
Second	—	X	—	X	—
1—LOW (First)	—	X	—	—	X

—Not applicable

CHILTON'S THREE "C's" TRANSAXLE DIAGNOSIS CHARTS
A-404, A-413, A-415 and A-470 TorqueFlite Transaxles

Condition	Cause	Correction
Harsh engagement from Neutral to D	a) Engine idle speed too high b) Valve body malfunction c) Hydraulic pressure too high d) Worn or faulty rear clutch	a) Adjust to specification b) Clean or overhaul c) Adjust to specifications d) Overhaul rear clutch
Harsh engagement from Neutral to R	a) Low/reverse band mis-adjusted (A-413, A-470) b) Engine idle speed too high c) Low/reverse band worn out d) Low/reverse servo, band or linkage malfunction e) Hydraulic pressure too high f) Worn or faulty rear clutch	a) Adjust to specifications b) Adjust to specifications c) Overhaul d) Overhaul e) Adjust to specifications f) Overhaul rear clutch
Delayed engagement from Neutral to D	a) Hydraulic pressure too low b) Valve body malfunction c) Malfunction in low/reverse servo, band or linkage d) Low fluid level e) Manual linkage adjustment f) Oil filter clogged g) Faulty oil pump h) Bad input shaft seals i) Idle speed too low j) Bad reaction shaft support seals k) Bad front clutch l) Bad rear clutch	a) Adjust to specification b) Clean or overhaul c) Overhaul d) Add as required e) Adjust as required f) Change filter and fluid g) Overhaul pump h) Replace seal rings i) Adjust to specifications j) Replace seal rings k) Overhaul l) Overhaul
Delayed engagement from Neutral to R	a) Low/reverse band mis-adjusted (A-413, A-470) b) Hydraulic pressures too low c) Low/reverse band worn out d) Valve body malfunction or leakage e) Low/reverse servo, band or linkage malfunction f) Low fluid level g) Manual linkage adjustment h) Faulty oil pump i) Worn or broken input shaft seal rings j) Aerated fluid k) Idle speed too low l) Worn or broken reaction shaft support seal rings m) Worn or faulty front clutch n) Worn or faulty rear clutch o) Oil filter clogged	a) Adjust to specifications b) Adjust to specifications c) Overhaul d) Clean or overhaul e) Overhaul f) Add as required g) Adjust as required h) Overhaul pump i) Replace seal rings j) Check for overfilling k) Adjust to specifications l) Replace support seal rings m) Overhaul n) Overhaul o) Change filter and fluid
Runaway upshift	a) Hydraulic pressure too low b) Valve body malfunction c) Low fluid level d) Oil filter clogged e) Aerated fluid f) Manual linkage adjustment g) Bad reaction shaft support seals h) Malfunction in kickdown servo, band or linkage i) Bad front clutch	a) Adjust to specifications b) Clean or overhaul c) Add as required d) Change filter and fluid e) Check for overfilling f) Adjust as required g) Replace seal rings h) Overhaul i) Repair as needed

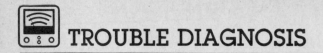

CHILTON'S THREE "C's" TRANSAXLE DIAGNOSIS CHARTS
A-404, A-413, A-415 and A-470 TorqueFlite Transaxles

Condition	Cause	Correction
No upshift	a) Hydraulic pressure too low b) Valve body malfunction c) Low fluid level d) Manual linkage adjustment e) Incorrect throttle linkage adjustment f) Bad seals on governor support g) Bad reaction shaft support seals h) Governor malfunction i) Malfunction in kickdown servo, band or linkage j) Bad front clutch	a) Adjust to specifications b) Clean or overhaul c) Add as required d) Adjust as required e) Adjust as required f) Replace seals g) Replace seal rings h) Service or replace unit i) Overhaul j) Overhaul
3-2 Kickdown runaway	a) Hydraulic pressure too low b) Valve body malfunction c) Low fluid level d) Aerated fluid e) Incorrect throttle linkage adjustment f) Kickdown band out of adjustment g) Bad reaction shaft support seals h) Malfunction in kickdown servo, band or linkage i) Bad front clutch	a) Adjust to specifications b) Clean or overhaul c) Add as required d) Check for overfilling e) Adjust as required f) Adjust to specifications g) Replace seal rings h) Overhaul i) Overhaul
No kickdown or normal downshift	a) Valve body malfunction b) Incorrect throttle linkage adjustment c) Governor malfunction d) Malfunction in kickdown servo, band or linkage	a) Clean or overhaul b) Adjust as required c) Service or replace unit d) Service or replace parts as required
Shifts erratic	a) Hydraulic pressure too low b) Valve body malfunction c) Low fluid level d) Manual linkage adjustment e) Oil filter clogged f) Faulty oil pump g) Aerated fluid h) Incorrect throttle linkage adjustment i) Bad seals on governor support j) Bad reaction shaft support seals k) Governor malfunction l) Malfunction in kickdown servo, band or linkage m) Bad front clutch	a) Adjust to specifications b) Clean or overhaul c) Add as required d) Adjust as required e) Change filter and fluid f) Overhaul oil pump g) Check for overfilling h) Adjust as required i) Replace seals j) Replace seal rings k) Service or replace unit l) Overhaul m) Overhaul
Slips in forward drive positions	a) Hydraulic pressure too low b) Valve body malfunction c) Low fluid level d) Manual linkage adjustment e) Oil filter clogged f) Faulty oil pump g) Bad input shaft seals h) Aerated fluid i) Incorrect throttle linkage adjustment	a) Adjust to specifications b) Clean or overhaul c) Add as required d) Adjust as required e) Change filter and fluid f) Overhaul pump g) Replace seal rings h) Check for overfilling i) Adjust as required

CHILTON'S THREE "C's" TRANSAXLE DIAGNOSIS CHARTS
A-404, A-413, A-470 TorqueFlite Transaxles

Condition	Cause	Correction
Slips in forward drive positions	j) Overrunning clutch not holding	j) Overhaul or replace
	k) Bad rear clutch	k) Overhaul
Slips in reverse only	a) Hydraulic pressure too low	a) Adjust as required
	b) Low/reverse band out of adjustment	b) Adjust to specifications
	c) Valve body malfunction	c) Clean or overhaul
	d) Malfunction in low/reverse servo, band or linkage	d) Service or replace parts as required
	e) Low fluid level	e) Add as required
	f) Manual linkage adjustment	f) Adjust as required
	g) Faulty oil pump	g) Overhaul pump
	h) Aerated fluid	h) Check for overfilling
	i) Bad reaction shaft support seals	i) Replace seal rings
	J) Bad front clutch	j) Overhaul
Slips in all positions	a) Hydraulic pressure too low	a) Adjust as required
	b) Valve body malfunction	b) Clean or overhaul
	c) Low fluid level	c) Add as required
	d) Oil filter clogged	d) Change fluid and filter
	e) Faulty oil pump	e) Overhaul pump
	f) Bad input shaft seals	f) Replace seal rings
	g) Aerated fluid	g) Check for overfilling
No drive in any position	a) Hydraulic pressure too low	a) Adjust to specifications
	b) Valve body malfunction	b) Clean or overhaul
	c) Low fluid level	c) Add as required
	d) Oil filter clogged	d) Change filter and fluid
	e) Faulty oil pump	e) Overhaul pump
	f) Planetary gear sets broken or seized	f) Replace affected parts
No drive in forward drive positions	a) Hydraulic pressure too low	a) Adjust to specifications
	b) Valve body malfunction	b) Clean or overhaul
	c) Low fluid level	c) Add as required
	d) Bad input shaft seals	d) Replace seal rings
	e) Overrunning clutch not holding	e) Overhaul or replace
	f) Bad rear clutch	f) Overhaul
	g) Planetary gear sets broken or seized	g) Replace affected parts
No drive in reverse	a) Hydraulic pressure too low	a) Adjust to specifications
	b) Low/reverse band out of adjustment	b) Adjust to specifications
	c) Valve body malfunction	c) Clean or overhaul
	d) Malfunction in low/reverse servo, band or linkage	d) Overhaul
	e) Manual linkage adjustment	e) Adjust as required
	f) Bad input shaft seals	f) Replace seal rings
	g) Bad front clutch	g) Overhaul
	h) Bad rear clutch	h) Overhaul
	i) Planetary gear sets broken or seized	i) Replace affected parts
Drives in neutral	a) Valve body malfunction	a) Clean or overhaul
	b) Manual linkage adjustment	b) Adjust as required
	c) Insufficient clutch plate clearance	c) Overhaul clutch pack
	d) Bad rear clutch	d) Overhaul
	e) Rear clutch dragging	e) Overhaul

CHILTON'S THREE "C's" TRANSAXLE DIAGNOSIS CHARTS
A-404, A-413, A-415 and A-470 TorqueFlite Transaxles

Condition	Cause	Correction
Drags or locks	a) Stuck lock-up valve	a) Clean or overhaul
	b) Low/reverse band out of adjustment	b) Adjust to specifications
	c) Kickdown band adjustment too tight	c) Adjust to specifications
	d) Planetary gear sets broken or seized	d) Replace affected parts
	e) Overrunning clutch broken or seized	e) Overhaul or replace
Grating, scraping or growling noise	a) Low/reverse band out of adjustment	a) Adjust to specifications
	b) Kickdown band out of adjustment	b) Adjust to specifications
	c) Output shaft bearing or bushing bad	c) Replace
	d) Planetary gear sets broken or seized	d) Replace affected parts
	e) Overrunning clutch broken or seized	e) Overhaul or replace
Buzzing noise	a) Valve body malfunction	a) Clean or overhaul
	b) Low fluid level	b) Add as required
	c) Aerated fluid	c) Check for overfilling
	d) Overrunning clutch inner race damaged	d) Overhaul or replace
Hard to fill, oil blows out filler tube	a) Oil filler clogged	a) Change filter and fluid
	b) Aerated fluid	b) Check for overfilling
	c) High fluid level	c) Bad converter check valve
	d) Breather clogged	d) Clean, change fluid
Transmission overheats	a) Engine idle speed too high	a) Adjust to specifications
	b) Hydraulic pressure too low	b) Adjust to specifications
	c) Low fluid level	c) Add as required
	d) Manual linkage adjustment	d) Adjust as required
	e) Faulty oil pump	e) Overhaul pump
	f) Kickdown band adjustment too tight	f) Adjust to specifications
	g) Faulty cooling system	g) Service vehicle's cooling system
	h) Insufficient clutch plate clearance	h) Overhaul clutch pack
Harsh upshift	a) Hydraulic pressure too low	a) Adjust to specifications
	b) Incorrect throttle linkage adjustment	b) Adjust as required
	c) Kickdown band out of adjustment	c) Adjust to specifications
	d) Hydraulic pressure too high	d) Adjust to specifications
Delayed upshift	a) Incorrect throttle linkage adjustment	a) Adjust as required
	b) Kickdown band out of adjustment	b) Adjust as required
	c) Bad seals on governor support	c) Replace seals
	d) Bad reaction shaft support seals	d) Replace seal rings

CHILTON'S THREE "C's" TRANSAXLE DIAGNOSIS CHARTS
A-404, A-413, A-415 and A-470 TorqueFlite Transaxles

Condition	Cause	Correction
Delayed upshift	e) Governor malfunction	e) Service or replace unit
	f) Malfunction in kickdown servo, band or linkage	f) Overhaul
	g) Bad front clutch	g) Overhaul

DIAGNOSIS TEST

Automatic Transaxle problems are caused by five general conditions. These are:

1. Poor engine performance (out of tune, improperly maintained).
2. Incorrect fluid levels (too low or too high).
3. Improper linkage, band or control pressure adjustments.
4. Malfunctions in the hydraulic system.
5. Actual break down of mechanical parts.

Two procedures can be followed in checking out a vehicle with transaxle problems. If the vehicle can be driven, follow this procedure:

1. Check the level of the transaxle fluid. Note the condition, color and appearance of the fluid. (Air bubbles, metal particles, burnt smell, etc.)
2. If the complaint was that the shifts were delayed, erratic or harsh, adjust the throttle and shift linkages before road testing. Check for obvious faults like broken linkage, etc.
3. If the complaint was that the acceleration is slow, or sluggish, or if an unusual amount of throttle is needed to keep up road speed, then a stall test should be performed.
4. Road test vehicle, preferably with the vehicle operator doing the driving. Observe for any malfunction, noting speed, load, any unusual noises or vibrations, gear range, etc.
5. Perform hydraulic pressure test.
6. Perform air pressure test of clutch and band operation.

If the vehicle cannot be driven, follow the procedure shown below.

1. Check the level of the transaxle fluid. Note the condition, color and appearance of the fluid. (Air bubbles, metal particles, burnt smell, etc.)
2. Check for broken or disconnected throttle linkage.
3. Check for broken cooler lines, and loose or missing pressure port plugs, thus causing massive fluid loss.
4. Raise the car, start engine, shift into gear and check:
   (a.) If drive shafts turns but not the wheels, then the problem is in the differential or axle shaft, and not in the transaxle.
   (b.) If drive shafts do not turn, and transaxle is noisy, immediately stop engine, remove the pan and check for debris lying in the pan. If debris is not found, then the transaxle must be removed. Check for broken drive plate, attaching bolts, broken converter hub shafts or oil pump.
   (c.) If drive shafts do not turn and transaxle is not noisy, perform a hydraulic pressure test to determine if the problem is caused by a hydraulic or mechanical component.

FLUID LEVEL AND CONDITION

Since the torque converter fills in both the Park and Neutral positions, place the selector in Park and allow the engine to idle. The fluid should be at operating temperature (180°). Check the dipstick. The fluid level is correct if it is between the "Full" and "Add" marks. Do not overfill, or the fluid will be churned into foam and cause the same symptoms of low fluid level and can lead to transmission overheating, and fluid being forced from the vent. Check the condition of the fluid, examining the fluid for metal bits or friction material particles. A milky appearance indicates water contamination, possibly from the cooling system. Check for a burned smell. If there is any doubt about the condition of the fluid, drain out a sample for a better check.

MANUAL LINKAGE

A quick way to check the manual linkage adjustment is to check the operation of the neutral safety switch. If the starter operates in both Park and Neutral, the manual linkage is properly adjusted. If not, either the neutral switch is bad or the linkage needs adjustment. See the section "On Car Services" for the procedure.

THROTTLE CABLE

The throttle cable adjustment is critical to the proper operation of the transmission, because it controls a valve in the valve body which determines shift speed, shift quality and part throttle downshift sensitivity. If the setting is to short, early shifts and slippage between shifts may happen. If the setting is too long, shifts may be delayed and the part throttle downshifts will be sensitive.

Diagnostic Test Sequence

The following order should be used when trouble shooting a TorqueFlite transaxle.

1. Road Test
2. Hydraulic Pressure Test
3. Stall Test
4. Air Pressure Test
5. Check diagnosis charts for probable cause of malfunction.

ROAD TEST

Before road testing, check for obvious faults, such as low fluid level, disconnected linkage, bad fluid leaks, etc.

During the road test, observe the engine performance. An out of tune engine will often cause symptoms mistaken for transmission difficulties. It is a good idea to let the vehicle operator drive so that the service technician is free to record any problems. The transaxle should be shifted to each position to check for slipping or any variation in shifting. Take note whether the shifts feel spongy or are too harsh. Record the speed at which the downshifts and upshifts occur. Listen for engine speed flare up or slippage. In most cases the clutch or band that is slipping can be determined by checking how the transaxle operates in each shift position.

For example, the rear clutch is applied in both "D" first gear and "1" first gear positions, but the overrunning clutch is applied "D" first and the low and reverse band is applied in "1" first. If the transaxle slips in "D" first gear but does not slip in "1" first gear, then the overrunning clutch must be the unit that is slipping.

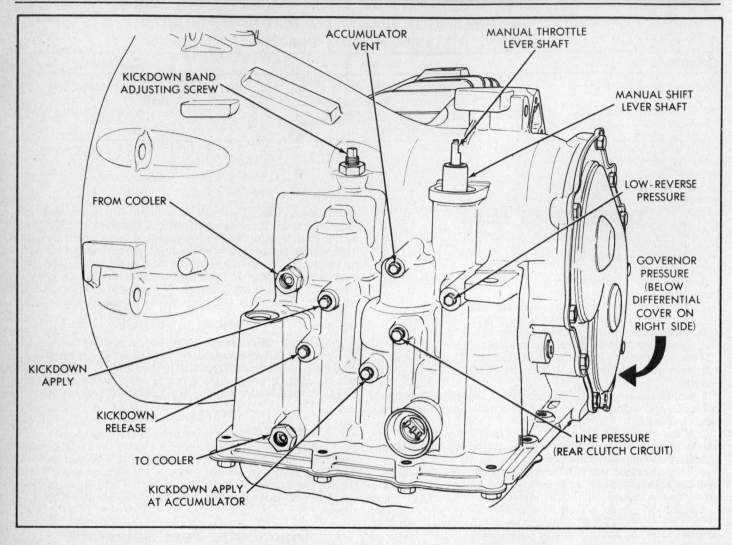

Location of pressure point taps, manual control and band adjustment screw, left side of transaxle (©Chrysler Corp.)

In the same way, if the transaxle slips in any two forward gears, then the rear clutch is the slipping unit. Using this same procedure, notice that the rear clutch and front clutch are applied in "D" third gear. So if the slippage is in the third gear, then either the front clutch or rear clutch is slipping. By shifting to another gear which does not use one of those units, the unit that is slipping can be determined. This process of elimination can be used to detect any unit which slips as well as to confirm proper operation of good units.

Although a road test analysis can usually diagnose the slipping units, the actual cause usually cannot be determined. Any of the above conditions can be caused by leaking hydraulic circuits or sticking valves. So before attempting to disassemble the transaxle, a hydraulic pressure test should be done.

CONTROL PRESSURE TEST

Before starting on a pressure test, make sure the fluid level is correct and the linkage is adjusted properly. Fluid should be at operating temperature (approx. 180°F).

Test Procedure

1. Hook up engine tachometer and route wires so that it can be read under the car.

2. Raise vehicle on hoist so that the front wheels can turn. It may be helpful to disconnect the throttle valve and shift controls so that they can be shifted from under the vehicle. Two size gauges are needed, one 150 psi and the other a 300 or 400 psi. The higher pressure gauge is required for the "reverse test."

TEST ONE (Selector in "1")

The purpose of this test is to check pump output, the pressure regulation and also to check on the condition of the rear clutch and servo hydraulic circuits.

1. Hook up gauges to the "line pressure" port and "low-reverse pressure" port (rear servo).
2. Adjust engine speed to 1000 rpm.
3. Shift into "1" position (selector lever on transaxle all the way forward).
4. Read pressures on both gauges as the throttle lever on the transaxle is moved from the full forward position to full rearward position.
5. Line pressure should read 60 to 66 psi (1981 and later—52 to 58 psi), with the throttle lever forward and it should gradually increase as the lever is moved rearward, to 97 to 103 psi (1981 and later—80 to 88 psi).
6. Rear servo pressure should read the same as the line pressure to within 3 psi.

TEST TWO (Selector in "2")

The purpose of this test is to check pump output, the pressure regulation and also to check on the condition of the rear clutch and lubrication hydraulic circuits.

1. Hook up gauge to "line pressure" port and, with a "tee" fitting, hook into the lower cooling line to read "lubrication" pressure.
2. Adjust engine speed to 1000 rpm.
3. Shift into "2" position. (This is one "detent" rearward from the full forward position).
4. Read pressures on both gauges as the throttle lever on the transaxle is moved from the full forward position to full rearward position.
5. Line pressure should read 60 to 66 psi (1981 and later—52 to 58 psi), with the throttle lever forward and it should gradually increase as the lever is moved rearward, to 97 to 103 psi (1981 and later—80 to 88 psi).
6. Lubrication pressure should read 10 to 25 psi with the lever forward and 10 to 35 psi with the lever rearward.

TEST THREE (Selector in "D")

The purpose of this test is to check pump output, the pressure regulation and also to check on the condition of the rear clutch and front clutch hydraulic circuits.

1. Attach gauges to the "line pressure" port and "kickdown *release*" port (front servo *release*).
2. Adjust engine speed to 1600 rpm.
3. Shift into "D" position. (This is two "detents" rearward from the full forward position of the selector lever.)
4. Read pressures on both gauges as the throttle lever on the transaxle is moved from the full forward position to the full rearward position.
5. Line pressure should read 60 to 66 psi (1981 and later—52 to 58 psi), with the throttle lever forward and it should gradually increase as the lever is moved rearward.
6. The "kickdown release" port is pressurized only in direct drive and should be the same as the line pressure within 3 psi, up to the downshift point.

TEST FOUR (Selector in "Reverse")

The purpose of this test is to check pump output, pressure regulation and the condition of the front clutch and rear hydraulic circuits. Also, at this time, a check can be made for leakage into the rear servo due to case porosity, cracks, valve body or case warpage which can cause reverse band burn out.

1. Attach the 300 psi gauge to the "low-reverse pressure" port (rear servo).
2. Adjust engine speed to 1600 rpm.
3. Shift into "R" position. (This is four "detents" rearward from the full forward position of the selector lever.)
4. Read pressure on the gauge. It should read 176 to 180 psi (1981 and later—160 to 180 psi), with the throttle lever forward and it should gradually increase as the lever is moved rearward to 270 to 280 psi (1981 and later—250 to 300 psi).
5. Move the selector lever on the transaxle to "D" position. The rear servo pressure should drop to zero since even a little pressure can cause the band to apply and burn up.

Analyzing the Pressure Test

1. If the pressure readings from minimum to maximum are correct, the pump and pressure regulator are working properly.
2. If there is low pressure in "D 1, 2" but correct pressure in "R," then there is leakage in the rear clutch circuit.
3. If there is low pressure in "D and R" but correct pressure in "1," then there is leakage in the front clutch circuit.
4. If there is low pressure in "R and 1" but correct pressure in "2," then there is leakage in the rear servo circuit.
5. If there is low line pressure in all positions then there could be a band pump, stuck pressure regulator valve or clogged filter.

GOVERNOR PRESSURE

The governor pressure only needs to be tested if the transaxle shifts at the wrong vehicle speeds, when the throttle cable adjustment has been verified correct.

1. Connect a gauge that will read 0 to 150 psi to the "governor pressure" port which is on the lower side of the transaxle case, below the differential cover.
2. With the engine running and in third gear, read the pressures and compare the speeds shown in the chart.

If the pressures are wrong at a given speed, the governor valves are probably sticking. The pressure should respond smoothly to any change in rpm and should drop to 0 to 3 psi when the vehicle is stopped. If there is high pressure at standstill (more than 3 psi) then the transaxle will be prevented from downshifting.

THROTTLE PRESSURE

The TorqueFlite Transaxle has no provision for testing throttle pressure with a gauge. The only time incorrect throttle pressure should be suspected is if the part throttle upshift speeds are either too slow in coming or occur too early in relation to vehicle speeds. Engine "runaway" on either upshifts or downshifts can also be an indicator of incorrect (low) throttle pressure setting. The throttle pressure really should not be adjusted until the throttle cable has been checked and adjustment has been verified to be right.

STALL TEST

The stall test involves determining the maximum engine speed obtainable at full throttle in "D" position. This test checks on the torque converter's stator clutch and the clutches' holding ability. The transaxle oil level should be checked and temperatures brought to normal operating levels.

— CAUTION —

Never allow anyone to stand in front of the car when performing a stall test. Both the parking and service brakes must be fully applied during the test.

NOTE: Do not hold the throttle open any longer than necessary and never longer than five seconds at a time. If more than one stall test is required, operate the engine at 1,000 rpm in neutral for at least 20 seconds to cool the transmission fluid between runs.

1. After checking the fluid level, blocking wheels and setting the brakes, use the tachometer (previously hooked up for the pressure test) to record the maximum engine rpm by opening the throttle completely in drive, "D."
2. If engine speed exceeds 2000-2400 rpm, release accelerator immediately. This indicates that the transaxle is slipping.
3. Shift transaxle into Neutral; operate engine for at least 20 seconds at 1,000 rpm to cool the transmission fluid before shutting off engine.

STALL SPEED TOO HIGH

If the stall speed is more than 200 rpm above specifications, clutch slippage is the likely problem. The hydraulic pressure tests and air pressure will help pinpoint the problem unit.

STALL SPEED TOO LOW

Low stall speeds with a properly tuned engine would indicate a problem in the torque converter stator clutch. This condition should be confirmed by road testing prior to converter replacement.

If the stall speed is 250 to 350 rpm below what it should be and the vehicle runs properly on the highway, but has poor acceleration through the gears, then the stator over-running clutch is slipping, and the converter must be replaced.

If both the stall speed and acceleration are normal, but an unusually large amount of throttle is needed to keep up highway speeds, then the stator clutch has seized and the converter must be replaced.

AUTOMATIC SHIFT SPEEDS AND GOVERNOR PRESSURE CHART
(Approximate Miles and Kilometers Per Hour)

1980	—Carline— Federal (M,Z)		—Carline— California (M,Z)	
Engine (liter)	1.7		1.7	
Axle ratio	3.48		3.67	
Throttle Minimum	MPH	Km/h	MPH	Km/h
1-2 Upshift	8-15	13-24	7-14	11-23
2-3 Upshift	11-21	18-34	10-19	16-31
3-1 Downshift	8-15	13-24	7-14	11-23
Throttle Wide Open				
1-2 Upshift	32-44	51-71	30-41	48-66
2-3 Upshift	52-65	84-105	48-60	77-97
Kickdown Limit				
3-2 WOT Downshift	48-61	77-98	44-57	71-92
3-2 Part Throttle Downshift	35-50	56-80	32-46	50-74
3-1 WOT Downshift	30-37	48-60	28-34	45-55
Governor Pressure①				
15 psi	21-23	34-37	19-21	31-34
40 psi	35-41	56-66	32-38	51-61
60 psi	50-56	80-90	46-52	74-84

1981	—Carline— M and Z		—Carline— M, Z, P and D	
Engine (liter)	1.7		2.2 and 2.6	
Overall Top Gear Ratio	3.48		2.78	
Throttle Minimum	MPH	Km/h	MPH	Km/h
1-2 Upshift	9-14	14-23	9-13	14-21
2-3 Upshift	15-18	24-29	14-17	23-27
3-1 Downshift	9-13	14-21	8-12	13-19
Throttle Wide Open				
1-2 Upshift	27-39	43-63	33-45	53-72
2-3 Upshift	51-62	82-100	57-69	92-111
Kickdown limit				
3-2 WOT Downshift	48-59	77-95	54-66	87-106
3-2 Part Throttle Downshift	36-47	58-76	42-53	68-85
3-1 WOT Downshift	27-35	43-56	29-37	47-60
Governor Pressure①				
15 psi	22-23	35-37	21-23	34-37
60 psi	52-59	83-95	59-66	95-106

1982	—Carline— M and Z		—Carline— M,Z,P,D,C,V		—Carline— M,Z,P,D,C,V High Altitude	
Engine (Liter)	1.7L.		2.2 and 2.6L.		2.2L.	
Overall Top Gear Ratio	3.48		2.78		3.22	
Throttle Minimum	MPH	km/h	MPH	km/h	MPH	km/h
1-2 Upshift	11-15	18-24	10-14	16-23	11-15	18-24
2-3 Upshift	16-21	26-34	15-20	24-32	16-22	26-35
3-1 Downshift	11-14	18-23	10-13	16-21	11-15	18-24
Throttle Wide Open						
1-2 Upshift	33-39	53-63	37-44	60-71	33-38	53-61
2-3 Upshift	55-64	89-103	61-71	98-114	62-73	100-117

AUTOMATIC SHIFT SPEEDS AND GOVERNOR PRESSURE CHART

(Approximate Miles and Kilometers Per Hour)

1982	—Carline— M and Z		—Carline— M,Z,P,D,C,V		—Carline— M,Z,P,D,C,V High Altitude	
Kickdown Limit						
3-2 WOT Downshift	51-60	82-97	57-66	92-106	56-66	90-106
3-2 Part Throttle Downshift	28-32	45-51	26-30	42-48	29-33	47-53
3-1 WOT Downshift	30-35	48-56	32-38	51-61	31-36	50-58
Governor Pressure①						
15 psi	23-26	37-42	22-24	35-39	24-27	39-43
50 psi	54-61	87-98	61-68	98-109	61-68	98-109

1983	—Carline— M and Z		—Carline— M,Z,P,D,C,V,L		—Carline— M,Z,P,D,C,V,L,J,E,T High Altitude	
Engine (Liter)	1.7L.		2.2 and 2.6L.		2.2 and 2.6L.	
Overall Top Gear Ratio	3.50		2.78		3.02	
Throttle Minimum	MPH	km/h	MPH	km/h	MPH	km/h
1-2 Upshift	11-15	18-24	10-14	16-23	12-15	20-25
2-3 Upshift	16-21	26-34	15-20	24-32	17-22	28-35
3-1 Downshift	11-14	18-23	10-13	16-21	11-15	20-25
Throttle Wide Open						
1-2 Upshift	33-39	53-63	37-44	60-71	35-39	57-62
2-3 Upshift	55-64	89-103	63-71	101-114	60-70	92-113
Kickdown Limit						
3-2 WOT Downshift	51-60	82-97	58-66	93-106	54-64	87-103
3-2 Part Throttle Downshift	28-32	45-51	43-54	70-87	39-49	62-79
3-1 WOT Downshift	30-35	48-56	31-39	50-62	33-36	53-58
Governor Pressure①						
15 psi	23-26	37-42	22-24	35-39	26-29	42-47
50 psi	54-61	87-98	61-68	98-109	59-66	95-106

1984	—Carline— M,Z,P,D		—Carline— H,K,P,D,C		—Carline— M,Z,P,D,C,H,K,E,T		—Carline— C,V	
Engine (Liter)	2.2L		2.6L		2.2 and 1.6L		2.2L	
Overall Top Gear Ratio	2.78		3.22		3.02 (except turbocharged)		3.02 (turbocharged)	
Throttle Minimum	MPH	km/h	MPH	km/h	MPH	km/h	MPH	km/h
1-2 Upshift	13-17	21-27	13-16	21-26	13-17	21-27	15-19	24-31
2-3 Upshift	17-21	27-34	17-21	27-34	18-22	29-35	21-25	34-40
3-2 Downshift	13-16	21-26	12-15	19-24	13-16	21-26	15-19	24-31
Throttle Wide Open								
1-2 Upshift	35-42	56-68	34-42	55-68	36-44	58-71	38-42	61-68
2-3 Upshift	61-68	98-109	59-66	95-106	63-71	101-114	70-80	113-129
Kickdown Limit								
3-2 WOT Downshift	56-64	90-103	55-62	89-100	58-66	93-106	64-74	103-119
3-2 Part Throttle Downshift	44-52	71-84	44-51	71-82	46-54	74-87	47-55	76-89
3-1 WOT Downshift	31-38	50-61	30-37	48-60	32-39	51-63	37-40	60-64
Governor Pressure								
15 psi	23-25	37-40	24-27	39-43	26-29	42-47	28-31	45-50
50 psi	59-65	95-105	57-63	92-101	61-68	98-109	69-76	111-122

NOTE: Changes in tire size will cause shift points to occur at corresponding higher or lower vehicle speeds.
Km/h. = Kilometers per hour
① Governor pressure should be from zero to 3 psi at stand still or downshift may not occur.

NOTE: A siren-like noise, or a whining is normal on some converters during the stall test due to the fluid flow. However, loud metallic noises or banging from loose parts indicate a defective converter. To make sure, operate the vehicle on a lift at light throttle in both "D" and then "N," listening under the transaxle bell housing to confirm the area from which the noise originates.

AIR PRESSURE TESTS

Even though all fluid pressures are correct and the hydraulic pressure test checks out, it is still possible to have a "no drive" condition, due to inoperative clutches or bands. By testing with air pressure instead of hydraulic pressure, the defective unit can be pinpointed.

NOTE: Compressed air should be limited to 30 psi and must be free from dirt and moisture.

1. After the car is safely supported, remove the oil pan and carefully remove the valve body.
2. Locate the front clutch "apply" passage and apply air pressure. Listen for a dull "thud" and/or place fingertips on the front clutch housing to feel piston movement, confirming that the front clutch is operating. Look for excessive oil leaking.
3. Locate the rear clutch "apply" passage and apply air pressure. As before, listen for a dull "thud" and/or place fingertips on the rear clutch housing to feel piston movement confirming that the rear clutch is operating, and again looking for excessive oil leaks.
4. Locate the kickdown servo "on" passage (front servo apply) and apply air pressure. This tests the kickdown servo and operation is indicated by the front band tightening. The spring on the servo piston should release the band.
5. Locate the low-reverse servo "apply" passage (rear servo) and apply air pressure. This tests the low and reverse servo and operation is indicated by the rear band tightening. The spring on the servo piston should release the band.

If, after the air pressure tests, correct operation of the clutches

and servos are confirmed, and the complaint was no upshift or erratic shifts, then the problem has been narrowed down to the valve body.

FLUID LEAKAGE DIAGNOSIS

Fluid leakage can be deceptive as to its origin, in and around the transaxle and converter areas, due to engine oil leakages. Factory fill fluid for the automatic transaxles is red in color and should easily be distinguished from engine oil. However, with contaminants in the automatic transaxle fluid, its color appearance can change to that of engine oil. Therefore, the leaking fluid should be examined closely and its point of origin be determined before repairs are started.

1. The following leaks may be corrected without removing the transaxle assembly:
   a. Manual lever shaft oil seal.
   b. Pressure gauge plugs.
   c. Neutral start switch.
   d. Oil pan sealer.
   e. Oil cooler fittings or lines.
   f. Extension housing to case bolts.
   g. Speedometer adapter "O" ring.
   h. Front band adjusting screw.
   i. Extension housing axle seal.
   j. Differential bearing retainer axle seal.
   k. Rear end cover sealer.
   l. Extension housing "O" ring.
   m. Differential bearing retainer sealer.
2. The following leaks require the removal of the transaxle and torque converter assemblies for repairs.
   a. Transaxle fluid leaking from the lower edge of the converter housing, caused by the front pump oil seal.
   b. Pump to case seal.
   c. Torque converter weld.
   d. Cracked or porous transaxle case.

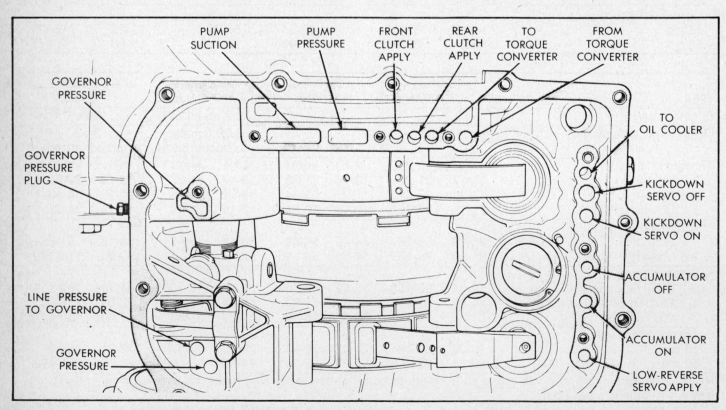

Air pressure test locations in transaxle case (©Chrysler Corp.)

OIL COOLERS AND TUBES REVERSE FLUSHING

When a transaxle failure has contaminated the fluid, the oil cooler(s) should be flushed and the torque converter replaced with an exchange unit to insure that metal particles or sludged oil are not later transferred back into the reconditioned or replaced transaxle assembly.

Procedure

1. Place a length of hose over the end of the lower oil cooler tube (from cooler) and insert the other end of the hose into a waste oil container.
2. Apply compressed air into the upper oil cooler hose in short, sharp blasts.
3. Pump approximately one quart of automatic transaxle fluid into the upper oil cooler hose (to cooler).
4. Repeat the short, sharp blasts of air into the lower cooler line. Repeat if necessary.
5. If the reverse flushing of the cooler system fails to clear all the obstructions from the system, the cooler and/or radiator assembly must be replaced.

NOTE: The fluid flow through the cooler should be, as a rule of thumb, one quart in 20 seconds, the transaxle in neutral and the engine at curb idle.

ABNORMAL NOISE DIAGNOSIS

1. Examine fluid level and condition.
2. Road test vehicle to determine if an abnormal noise exists.
3. Identify the type of noise, the driving ranges and conditions when the noise occurs.

Gear Noise

1. Check for correct location of rubber insulator sleeve on the center of the shift cable.
2. Planetary gear noise—Necessary to remove the transaxle assembly and replace the planetary gear set.
3. Transfer Shaft Gear noise—Necessary to remove the transaxle assembly and replace the output and transfer shaft gears.
4. Differential gear noise—Necessary to remove the transaxle assembly and replace the transfer shaft and ring gears and/or the differential carrier gears.

Grinding Noise

1. Remove the transaxle/converter assembly.
2. Disassemble, clean and inspect all parts. Clean the valve body, install all new seals, rings and gaskets.
3. Replace all worn or defective parts.

Knock, Scrape or Clicking Noise

1. Remove the converter dust shield and inspect for loose or cracked converter drive plate.
2. Inspect for contact of the starter drive with the starter ring gear.

Whine or Buzzing Noise

1. Determine source of noise, from either the transaxle or converter.
2. If the transaxle has the buzzing or whining noise, remove all three pans and inspect for debris indicating worn or failed parts. If no debris, check valve body.
3. If the converter has the buzzing or whining noise, replace the converter assembly.

TORQUEFLITE TRANSAXLE STALL SPEED CHART

Year	Engine Liter	Transaxle Type	Converter Diameter	Stall R.P.M.
1980-81	1.7	A-404	9½ inches (241 millimetres)	2250-2450
	2.2	A 413	9½ inches (241 millimetres)	2190-2410
	2.6	A-470	9½ inches (241 millimetres)	2400-2630
1982-83	1.6	A-415	9½ inches (241 millimetres)	2250-2450
	1.7	A-404	9½ inches (241 millimetres)	2300-2500
	2.2	A-413	9½ inches (241 millimetres)	2200-2410
	2.6	A-470	9½ inches (241 millimetres)	2400-2630
1984	1.6	A-415	9½ inches (241 millimetres)	2250-2450
	2.2	A-413	9½ inches (241 millimetres)	2200-2400
	2.2 EFI	A-413	9½ inches (241 millimetres)	2280-2480
	2.2 EFI (turbocharged)	A-413	9½ inches (241 millimetres)	3020-3220
	2.6	A-470	9½ inches (241 millimetres)	2400-2600

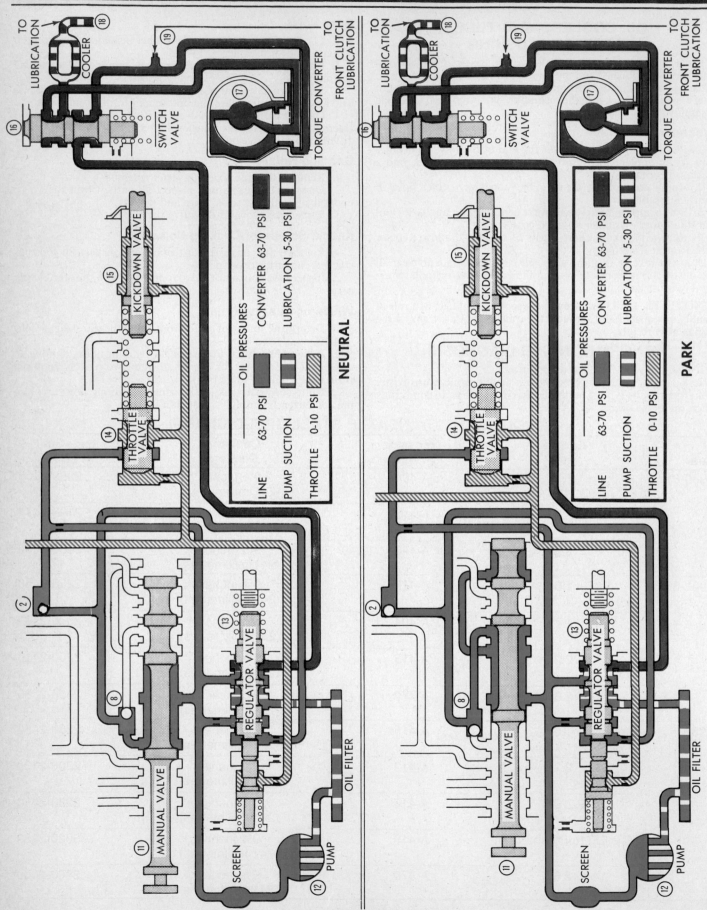

NEUTRAL

PARK

Neutral—park (1982) (©Chrysler Corp.)

NEUTRAL—PARK POSITIONS
(1982)

Units Applied—None

THE PRESSURE SUPPLY SYSTEM

The oil pump ⑫ is operating and supplying fluid to the pressure regulator valve ⑬.

THE PRESSURE REGULATING SYSTEM

The fluid pressure is being regulated by the pressure regulator valve ⑬ with fluid being directed to the throttle valve ⑭ and the kick-down valve ⑮ at a lower pressure value. The manual valve ⑪, being in the neutral position, blocks off the fluid supply to the governor ㉖. Note the change in the pressure regulator valve assembly and the changes in the main line pressure routings.

THE FLOW CONTROL VALVE SYSTEM

Main line pressured fluid is directed from the regulator valve ⑬ as converter pressure, to the switch valve ⑯. The fluid is then directed into the converter ⑰ and back to the switch valve. A metered passage ⑲ is included in the fluid passage to the converter for the purpose of front clutch lubrication. The switch valve directs the converter return fluid to the cooler and lubrication system ⑱.

THE CLUTCHES, BAND SERVOS AND ACCUMULATOR SYSTEM

Fluid is not directed to the clutches, band servos or accumulator, therefore, none are applied and the transaxle is in neutral.

THE CHECK VALVE OPERATION

Check valves are used to prevent the pressure from entering other passages in the main line circuits. The manual valve check valve ⑧ is used to control the direction of fluid in the neutral position and to control the fluid in another direction in the park position. The throttle valve check valve ② is now used in a different manner, since the passage routings have been changed. Its main purpose is to control throttle pressure when the transaxle is in reverse.

With the movement of the manual valve ⑪ to the Park position, the main line pressure is routed through a different passage in the valve body and with the use of the manual valve check valve ⑧, the pressured fluid is prevented from applying the clutches, band servos or accumulator. The transaxle remains in neutral and the parking mechanism is operated by the manual valve linkage.

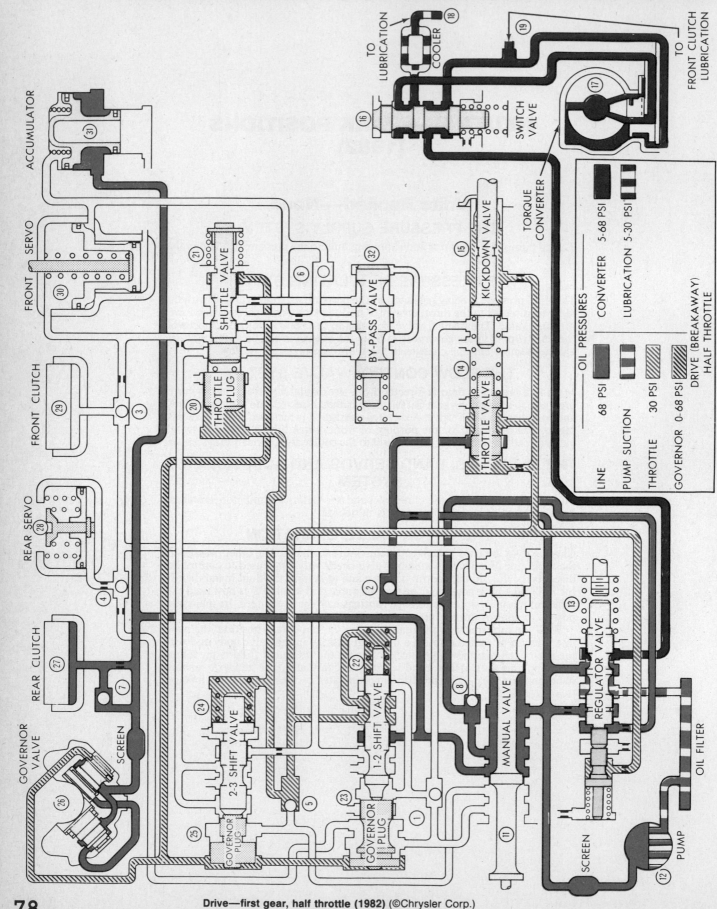

Drive—first gear, half throttle (1982) (©Chrysler Corp.)

DRIVE—FIRST GEAR
(1982)

Units Applied—Rear Clutch, Overrunning Clutch

The selector lever is in the Drive position and the transmission is in the first gear. The vehicle is moving and the throttle is in the half open position.

THE PRESSURE SUPPLY SYSTEM

The oil pump ⑫ is operating and supplying fluid to the main line passages, opened by the movement of the manual valve ⑪ and the pressure regulator valve ⑬.

THE PRESSURE REGULATING SYSTEM

The pressure regulator valve ⑬ maintains a specific level of pressure within the transaxle and operates in conjunction with throttle pressure. Note the changes in the pressure regulator valve assembly and the changes in the main line pressure routings.

THE FLOW CONTROL VALVE SYSTEM

The manual valve ⑪ directs main line pressure to the land of the 1-2 shift valve ㉒, the accumulator ㉛, the rear clutch apply ㉗, the governor assembly ㉖ and to the throttle valve ⑭, from which the governor and throttle pressures are obtained respectively. To prevent the shift from first to second until a predetermined speed is reached in conjunction with the throttle opening, the throttle pressure is routed to one end of the 1-2 shift valve ㉒, the 2-3 shift valve ㉔, the shuttle valve throttle plug ⑳ and to the kick-down valve ⑮ to oppose the governor pressure which is routed to the front of the 1-2 shift valve governor plug ㉓ and the front of the 2-3 shift valve governor plug ㉕. Governor pressure is also routed to the shuttle valve ㉑, but is blocked by a land on the valve. The pressure regulator valve ⑬, routes main line pressure to the switch valve ⑯. The switch valve routes pressure to and from the converter ⑰. The return pressure is metered and directed to the cooler and lubrication ⑱ circuit at a lesser pressure psi. A passage is provided for the front clutch lubrication ⑲. A by-pass valve ㉜ has been added to the hydraulic circuit to aid in smooth application of the kickdown band (front) during the 1-2 upshift and is not in operation during the first speed mode.

THE CLUTCHES, BAND SERVOS AND ACCUMULATOR SYSTEM

The rear clutch ㉗ is applied hydraulically while the overrunning clutch is operated mechanically. The accumulator ㉛ is applied to act as an engagement softener for the rear clutch application.

THE CHECK VALVE OPERATION

The 2-3 shift valve check valve ⑤ is blocking throttle pressure from entering the 2-3 shift valve governor plug bore ㉕. The manual valve check valve ⑧ is blocking main line pressure from entering other apply passages. The remaining check valves are either allowing fluid to pass or not in a charged passage.

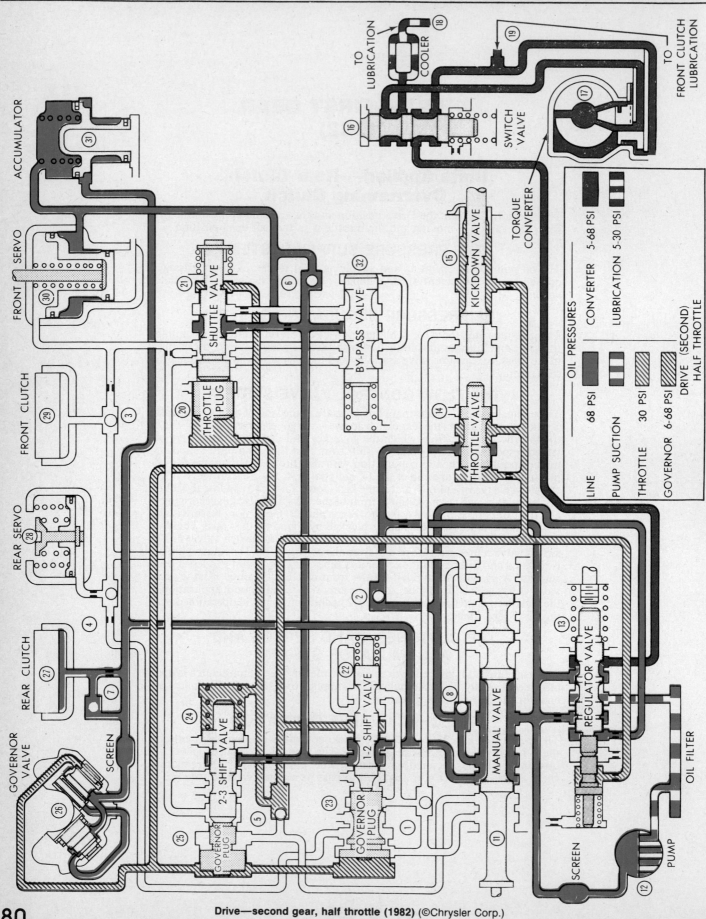

Drive—second gear, half throttle (1982) (©Chrysler Corp.)

DRIVE—SECOND GEAR
(1982)

Units Applied—Rear Clutch, Front Brake Band (Kickdown)

The selector lever is in the Drive position and governor pressure has overcome throttle pressure and caused the transmission to shift into the second speed. The vehicle is traveling at moderate speed and the throttle is in the half open position.

THE PRESSURE SUPPLY SYSTEM

The oil pump ⑫ is operating and supplying fluid to the main line passages.

THE PRESSURE REGULATING SYSTEM

The pressure regulator valve ⑬ maintains a specific level of pressure within the transmission and operates in conjunction with the throttle pressure.

Note the changes in the pressure regulator valve assembly and the changes in the main line pressure routings.

THE FLOW CONTROL VALVE SYSTEM

The manual valve ⑪ directs main line pressure to governor valve ㉖, the rear clutch apply piston ㉗, the front servo ㉚, the accumulator ㉛, the 1-2 shift valve ㉒ and through it to the 2-3 shift valve ㉔, where it is blocked by a land on the shift valve. The throttle pressure resists the increase in governor pressure until the speed of the output shaft has increased to provide higher governor pressure in the shifting system to allow the 2-3 shift valve ㉔ to be moved for the 2-3 up-shift.

As the 1-2 shift valve ㉒ is positioned in the second speed position, main line pressure is directed to the shuttle valve ㉑. The shuttle valve ㉑ is moved against the throttle plug ⑳ by main line pressure, allowing governor pressure to react on the end of the shuttle valve ㉑. The by-pass valve ㉜ stops the main line pressure on one of its lands. The fluid flow is then directed to the apply side of the front servo ㉚ and to the release side of the accumulator ㉛. With the aid of the accumulator return spring, the accumulator piston is placed in the released position. The rear clutch ㉗ remains in the applied position.

The regulator valve ⑬ routes main line pressure to the switch valve ⑯. The switch valve routes pressure to and from the converter ⑰. The return pressure is metered and directed to the cooler and lubrication ⑱ system at a lesser pressure psi. A passage is provided for the front clutch lubrication ⑲.

THE CLUTCHES, BAND SERVOS AND ACCUMULATOR SYSTEM

The rear clutch ㉗ remains applied. The front servo ㉚ is applied, which in turn applies the front band (kickdown). The accumulator ㉛ is controlling the apply pressure for the front servo.

THE CHECK VALVE OPERATION

The 2-3 shift valve check valve ⑤ is blocking throttle pressure, while the manual valve check valve ⑧ is blocking main line pressure. The remaining check valves are either allowing pressured fluid to pass or are not in charged passages.

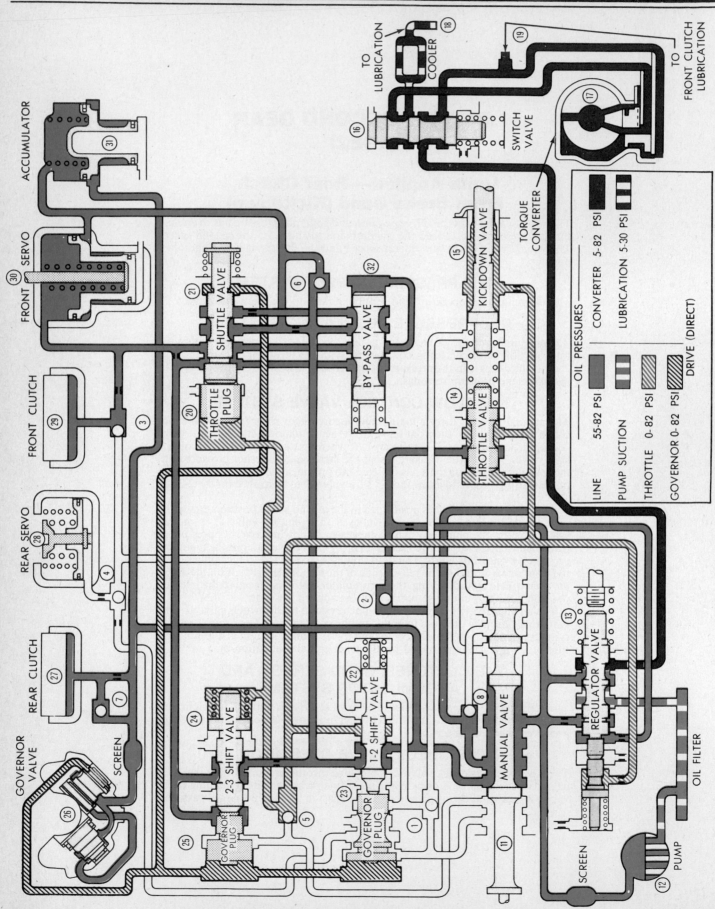

Drive—direct, third gear (1982) (©Chrysler Corp.)

DRIVE—DIRECT
(1982)

Units Applied—Rear Clutch, Front Clutch

The selector lever is in the Drive position and the 2-3 shift has occurred. The transmission is now in the Direct gear ratio (3rd Speed), with the vehicle moving at a moderate rate of speed.

THE PRESSURE SUPPLY SYSTEM

The oil pump ⑫ is operating and supplying fluid to the main line passages.

THE PRESSURE REGULATING SYSTEM

The pressure regulator valve ⑬ maintains a specific level of pressure within the transmission and operates in conjunction with the throttle pressure. Note the changes in the pressure regulator valve assembly and the changes in the main line pressure routings.

THE FLOW CONTROL VALVE SYSTEM

The manual valve directs main line pressure to the governor valve ㉖, the rear clutch apply piston ㉗, (which remains engaged), the front clutch ㉙, the release side of the front servo ㉘, the release side of the accumulator ㉛, the shuttle valve ㉑ and through both the 1-2 and the 2-3 shift valves ㉒ and ㉔. The throttle valve is being served by the main line pressure and throttle pressure is being developed.

As the 2-3 shift is made, increased governor pressure is developed and overcomes the throttle pressure. The increase in governor pressure forces the shuttle valve ㉑ to move against the throttle plug ⑳, opening the other main line pressure passages in the by-pass valve ㉜. This allows main line pressure to be directed around the by-pass valve ㉜ and to its end, forcing the valve against its return spring and opening other passages for the main line pressure to be routed.

The regulator valve ⑬ routes main line pressure to the switch valve ⑯. The switch valve routes pressure to the converter ⑰ and back again. The return pressure is metered and directed to the cooler and lubrication system ⑱ at a lesser pressure psi. A passage is provided for the front clutch lubrication ⑲.

THE CLUTCHES, BAND SERVOS AND ACCUMULATOR SYSTEM

The rear clutch ㉗ remains applied. The front servo ㉚ has been released and the front clutch ㉙ has been applied. The accumulator ㉛ is in the released position.

THE CHECK VALVE OPERATION

The 2-3 shift valve check valve ⑤ is blocking throttle pressure while the manual valve check valve ⑧ is blocking main line pressure to the rear servo circuit. The front clutch check valve ③ is in a blocking position to prevent main line pressure from applying the rear servo. The remaining check valves are either allowing pressure to pass or are not in charged passages.

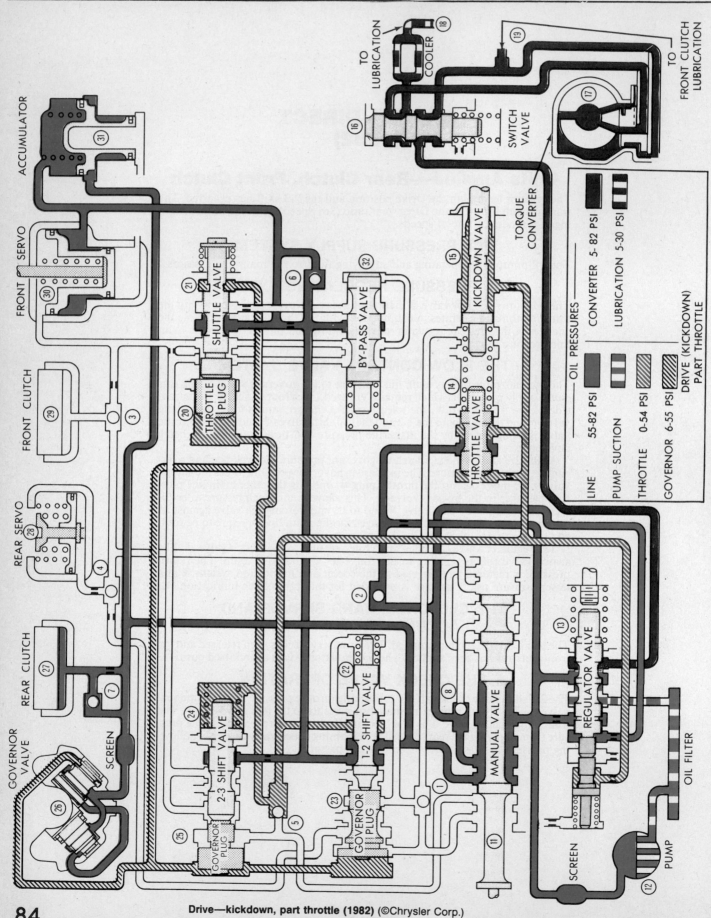

Drive—kickdown, part throttle (1982) (©Chrysler Corp.)

DRIVE—PART THROTTLE KICKDOWN (1982)

Units Applied—Rear Clutch, Front Band (Kickdown)

The selector lever is in the Drive position and the vehicle is moving at a speed of less than 30 MPH. An increase in the throttle opening has occurred to increase the vehicle speed, but not at wide open throttle (W.O.T.). The transmission automatically downshifts from 3rd to 2nd speed.

THE PRESSURE SUPPLY SYSTEM

The oil pump ⑫ is supplying fluid to the main line passages.

THE PRESSURE REGULATING SYSTEM

The pressure regulator valve ⑬ maintains a specific level of pressure within the transmission and operates in conjunction with the throttle pressure. Note the changes in the pressure regulator valve assembly and the changes in the main line pressure routings.

THE FLOW CONTROL VALVE SYSTEM

The slowing of the output shaft RPM has lowered the governor pressure to the affected valves. The movement of the throttle linkage causes the throttle valve to move and increase the throttle pressure to a higher psi than the governor pressure. This change in pressure causes the 2-3 shift valve ㉔ to move to its original position to block main line pressure to the front clutch ㉙ and to the release side of the front servo ㉚. The apply side of the front servo is charged with main line pressure which applies the front band (kickdown). The rear clutch ㉗ remains applied and the transmission has downshifted from 3rd speed to 2nd speed. The shuttle valve ㉑ is moved by the throttle pressure during the shifting operation, to block the main line pressure to the release side of the front servo.

The by-pass valve ㉜ main line pressure circuits are closed off by the shuttle valve ㉑ movement, allowing the by-pass return spring to move the valve to the off position.

The oil flow circuits are the same as in the second speed after the downshift has occurred. The converter ⑰, and the lubrication and cooler passages ⑱ are charged from the switch valve. A passage ⑲ is provided for front clutch lubrication.

THE CLUTCHES, BAND SERVOS AND ACCUMULATOR SYSTEM

The rear clutch ㉗ remains applied. The front clutch ㉙ has been released and the front servo ㉘ has been applied to apply the front band (kickdown). The accumulator has been charged to control the application of the front servo.

THE CHECK VALVE OPERATION

The manual valve check valve ⑧ is blocking main line pressure, while the 2-3 shift valve check valve ⑤ is blocking throttle pressure. The remaining check valves are either allowing passages of fluid or are in a passage that is not charged.

85

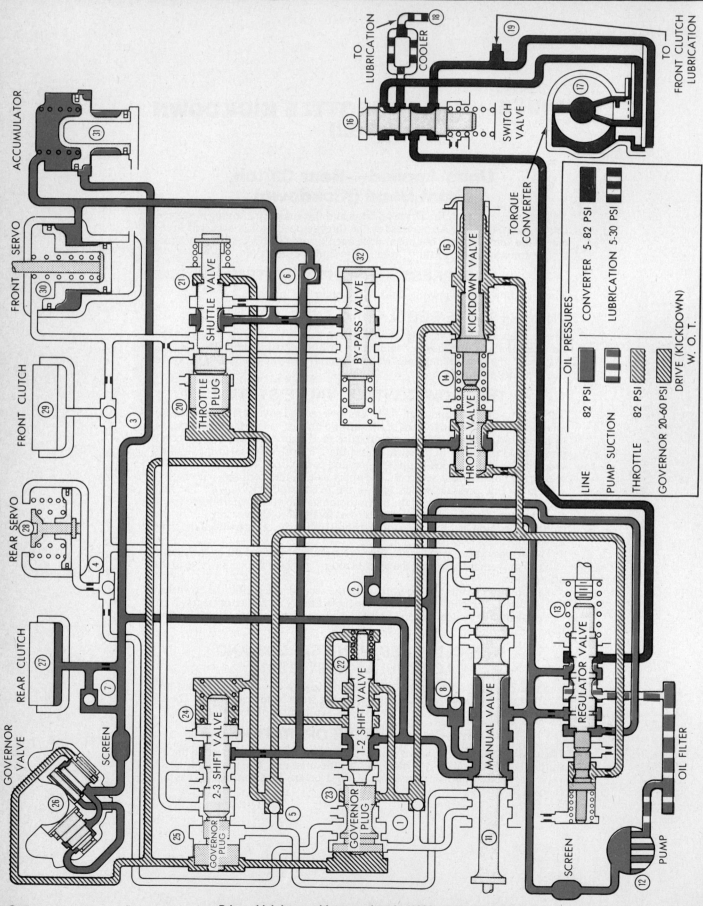

Drive—kickdown, wide open throttle (1982) (©Chrysler Corp.)

DRIVE—FULL THROTTLE KICKDOWN (1982)

Units Applied—Rear Clutch, Front Band (Kickdown)

The selector lever is in the Drive position and the vehicle is moving at a speed of 50 MPH or more.

The accelerator has been depressed to the wide open throttle position (W.O.T.) and the transmission automatically downshifts from 3rd to 2nd speed.

THE PRESSURE SUPPLY SYSTEM

The oil pump ⑫ is supplying fluid to the main line passages.

THE PRESSURE REGULATING SYSTEM

The pressure regulator valve ⑬ maintains a specific level of fluid pressure within the transmission and operates in conjunction with the throttle pressure. Note the changes in the pressure regulator valve assembly and the changes in the main line pressure routings.

THE FLOW CONTROL VALVE SYSTEM

The full opening of the accelerator moves the kickdown valve ⑮ (allowing main line pressure to enter the throttle pressure passage at the throttle valve ⑭) which quickly raises the throttle pressure for the downshift procedure. Main line pressure is directed to the 1-2 shift valve ㉒ lands to prevent its movement. The increased throttle pressure acts upon the 2-3 shift valve ㉔ and moves it to its original position in the valve body, causing the front clutch ㉙ to be released and the front band servo ㉚ to be applied.

Throttle pressure is routed to the throttle plug ⑳, and blocks the movement of the shuttle valve. The remaining fluid circuits remain the same as in the DRIVE—2nd speed gear range. The converter ⑰, the lubrication and cooler system ⑱ is being charged from the switch valve ⑯. A passage ⑲ is provided for front clutch lubrication.

The by-pass valve ㉜ is inoperative and remains in the off position.

THE CLUTCHES, BAND SERVOS AND ACCUMULATOR SYSTEM

The rear clutch ㉗ remains applied and the front clutch ㉙ is released as the front band (kickdown) is applied. The transmission is in the 2nd speed gear ratio. The accumulator is charged with fluid to assist the front band application.

THE CHECK VALVE OPERATION

Numbers ① and ⑤ check valves are positioned to block throttle pressure from acting upon the 2-3 shift valve governor plug ㉓. The number ⑧ check ball is positioned to block main line pressure from one circuit of the manual valve assembly. The remaining check valves are either allowing fluid to pass or are not in a charged passage.

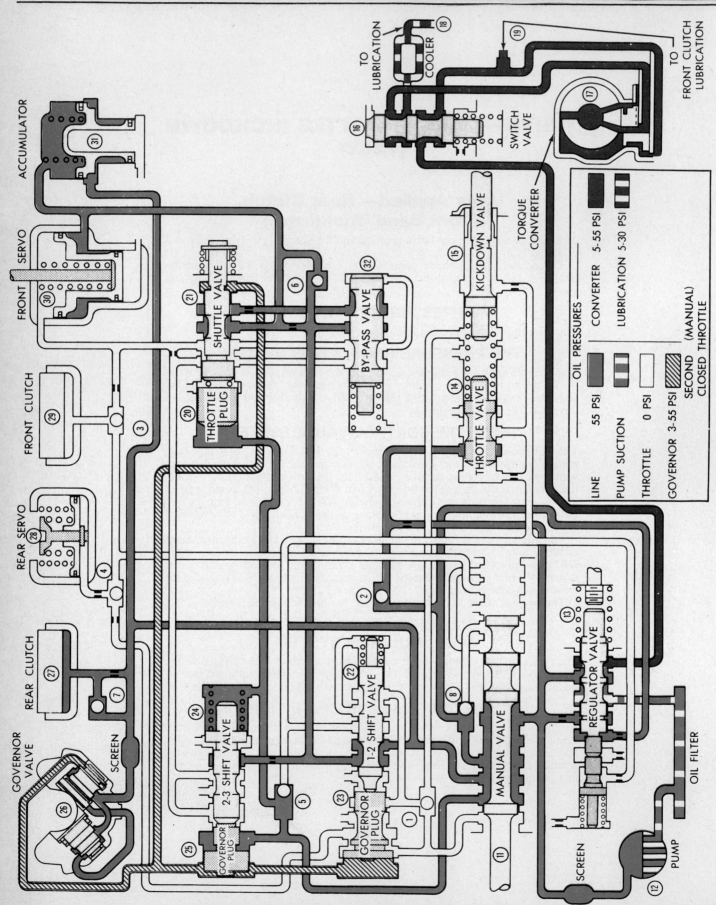

Second—manual position, closed throttle (1982) (©Chrysler Corp.)

SECOND-MANUAL—CLOSED THROTTLE
(1982)

Units Applied—Rear Clutch, Front Band
(Kickdown)

The selector lever is positioned in the Second position (manual Second). The vehicle is moving slowly with a closed throttle. Governor pressure is being developed from the governor by the rotation of the output shaft.

THE PRESSURE SUPPLY SYSTEM

The oil pump ⑫ is operating and charging the main line passages.

THE PRESSURE REGULATING SYSTEM

The pressure regulator valve ⑬ maintains a specific pressure level and operates in conjunction with the throttle pressure. Note the changes in the pressure regulator assembly and the changes in the main line pressure routings.

THE FLOW CONTROL VALVE SYSTEM

The manual valve ⑪ is positioned to allow main line pressure to be routed to the governor ㉖ assembly, where governor pressure is developed. Main line pressure is routed to the rear of the 2-3 shift valve ㉔ and to the 2-3 shift valve governor plug ㉕ to prevent the govenor pressure from shifting them. Main line pressure is also routed to the throttle plug ⑳ to prevent the shuttle valve ㉒ from passing throttle pressure through the passages. Main line pressure is also directed to the by-pass valve ㉜, but the valve remains inoperative. The transmission is locked into the 2nd speed because no throttle pressure is developed to oppose the governor pressure. The converter ⑰, the lubrication and cooler systems ⑱ are fed from the switch valve. A passage ⑲ is provided for front clutch lubrication.

THE CLUTCHES, BAND SERVOS AND
ACCUMULATOR SYSTEM

The rear clutch ㉗ and the front servo ㉚ are applied. The accumulator ㉛ is in a position to receive pressured fluid to cushion the front band application.

THE CHECK VALVE OPERATION

The check valves, number ⑤ and ⑧, are positioned to prevent main line pressure from being routed to the pressure regulator valve to prevent the throttle pressure from being built up. The remaining check valves are either allowing fluid to pass or are not in a charged passage.

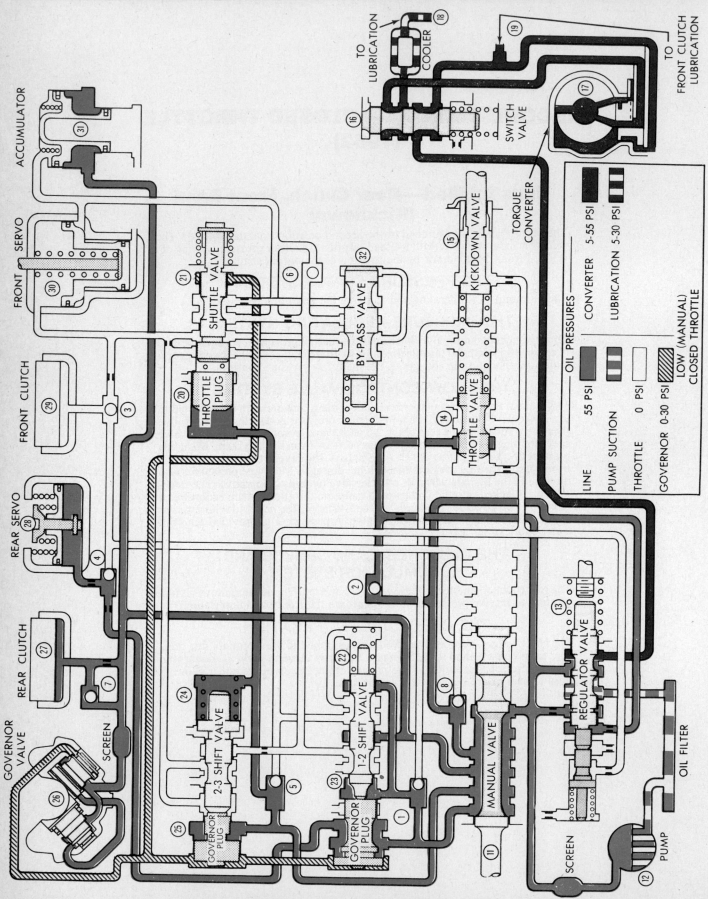

Low—manual position, closed throttle (1982) (©Chrysler Corp.)

LOW-MANUAL—CLOSED THROTTLE
(1982)

Units Applied—Rear Clutch, Rear Band (Low-Reverse)

The selector lever is in the Low position (manual Low) with the throttle closed and the vehicle moving slowly.

THE PRESSURE SUPPLY SYSTEM

The oil pump ⑫ is operating and charging the main line passages.

THE PRESSURE REGULATING SYSTEM

The pressure regulator valve ⑬ maintains a specific amount of fluid pressure and operates in conjunction with the throttle pressure. Note the pressure regulator valve assembly changes and the re-routing of the main line pressure from the regulator valve.

THE FLOW CONTROL VALVE SYSTEM

The manual valve is positioned to allow main line pressure to be routed to the rear clutch ㉗ and apply the unit. Main line pressure is routed to the 1-2 shift vale governor plug ㉓ to oppose governor pressure and prevent the shifting of the 1-2 shift valve ㉒. Main line pressure is routed through the grooves of the 1-2 shift valve governor plug ㉓ and to the rear servo ㉘ to apply the rear band (low-reverse). Main line pressure is directed to the throttle plug ⑳ and the shuttle valve ㉑ to hold them in a non-shifting position. The main line pressure is not directed to the by-pass ㉜ valve, therefore, it remains inoperative. Throttle pressure is not developed to oppose governor pressure, therefore the transmission is locked in the 1st gear range. The converter ⑰, the cooler and lubrication system ⑱ is charged from the switch valve ⑯. A passage ⑲ is provided for front clutch lubrication.

THE CLUTCHES, BAND SERVOS AND ACCUMULATOR SYSTEM

The accumulator ㉛ is applied by main line pressure. The rear clutch ㉗ and the rear servo ㉘ are applied to provide the low range.

THE CHECK VALVE OPERATION

The check valves, numbers①, ④, ⑤, and ⑧ are used to prevent main line pressure from entering passages that would allow movements of valves and create pressures not needed. The remaining check valves are in passages not charged or are ineffective.

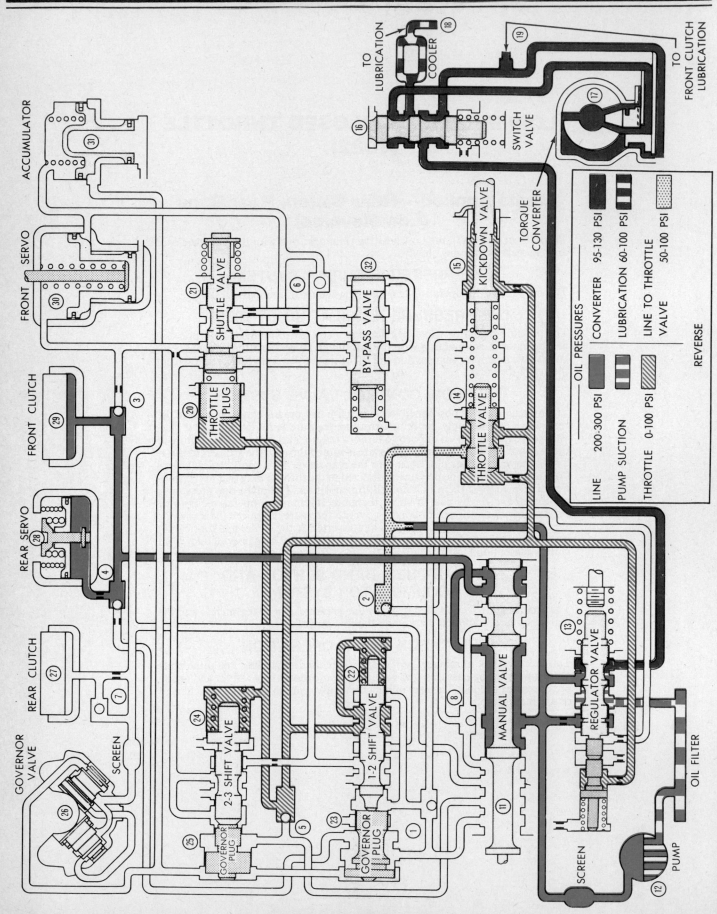

Reverse (1982) (©Chrysler Corp.)

REVERSE (1982)

Units Applied—Rear Servo (Low-Reverse Band), Front Clutch

The selector lever is in the Reverse position and the vehicle is stationary with the throttle closed.

THE PRESSURE SUPPLY SYSTEM

The oil pump ⑫ is operating and providing fluid to the main line passages.

THE PRESSURE REGULATING SYSTEM

The pressure regulator valve ⑬ supplies a specific amount of pressure within the transmission. The pressure regulator operates in conjunction with throttle pressure, when it is present. Note the changes in the pressure regulator valve assembly and the changes in the main line pressure routings.

THE FLOW CONTROL VALVE SYSTEM

The reverse gear needs higher pressures to apply the units and hold, necessary due to the increase of torque in the reverse mode. To accomplish this, the pressure regulator must increase the pressure to over double of its normal operation. To accomplish this, throttle pressure is directed to a specific land on the pressure regulator valve, to assist in holding the pressure regulator valve and increasing the resistance so that main line pressure can be increased. The main line pressure increases from approximately 65 psi to 250-300 psi by this procedure. This increased pressure is then directed to the applying units. Governor pressure is not produced so that throttle pressure is unopposed to hold the valves from shifting.

The pressure regulator supplies pressure to the switch valve ⑯ at lower pressure, and is directed to the converter ⑰, the front clutch lubrication outlet ⑲ and to the lubrication and cooler circuits ⑱.

THE CLUTCHES, BAND SERVOS AND ACCUMULATOR SYSTEM

The increased main line pressure is directed to the rear clutch ㉗ and applies the unit. Main line pressure is directed to the rear servo ㉘, which in turn applies the Low-Reverse band. All other units are unused.

THE CHECK VALVE OPERATION

The rear servo check valve ④ and the front clutch check valve ③ are used to prevent the pressure fluid from passing into other passages. The throttle valve check valve ② and the governor plug check valve ⑤ are used to prevent the throttle pressure from entering shift valve passages.

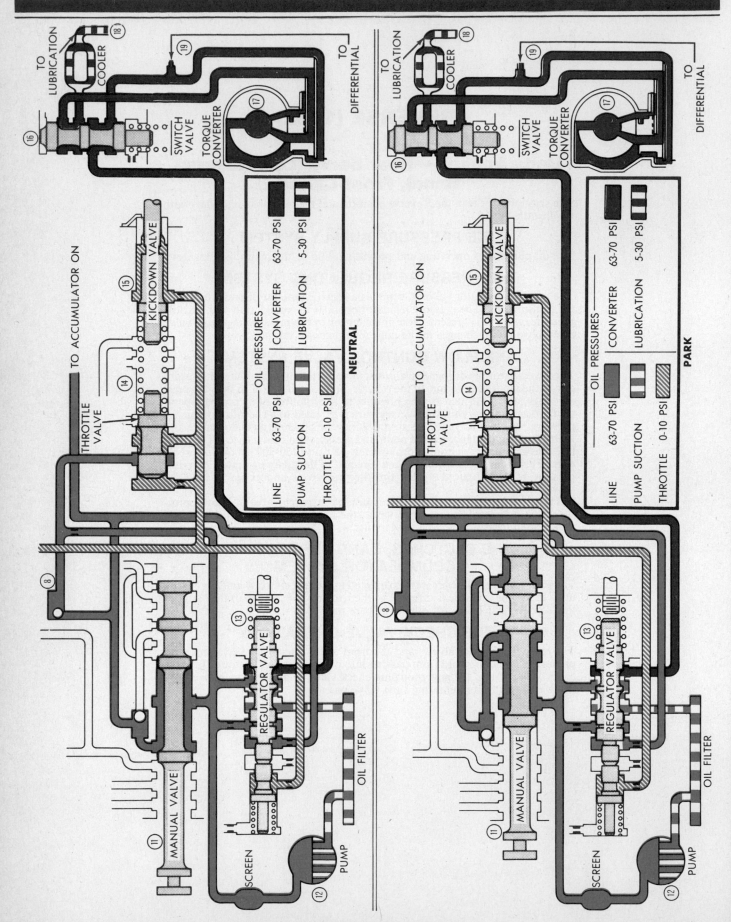

Neutral—park (1983-84) (©Chrysler Corp.)

NEUTRAL—PARK POSITIONS
(1983-84)

Units Applied—None
THE PRESSURE SUPPLY SYSTEM

The oil pump ⑫ is operating and supplying fluid to the pressure regulator valve ⑬.

THE PRESSURE REGULATING SYSTEM

The fluid pressure is being regulated by the pressure regulator valve ⑬ with fluid being directed to the throttle valve ⑭ and the kick-down valve ⑮ at a lower pressure value. The manual valve ⑪, being in the neutral position, blocks off the fluid supply to the governor ㉖. Note the change in the pressure regulator valve assembly and the changes in the main line pressure routings.

THE FLOW CONTROL VALVE SYSTEM

Main line pressured fluid is directed from the regulator valve ⑬ as converter pressure, to the switch valve ⑯. The fluid is then directed into the converter ⑰ and back to the switch valve. A metered passage ⑲ is included in the fluid passage to the converter for the purpose of differential lubrication. The switch valve directs the converter return fluid to the cooler and lubricaton system ⑱.

THE CLUTCHES, BAND SERVOS AND
ACCUMULATOR SYSTEM

Fluid is not directed to the clutches, band servos or accumulator, therefore, none are applied and the transaxle is in neutral.

THE CHECK VALVE OPERATION

Check valves are used to prevent the pressure from entering other passages in the main line circuits. The manual valve check valve ⑧ is used to control the direction of fluid in the neutral position and to control the fluid in another direction in the park position. The throttle valve check valve ② is now used in a different manner, since the passage routings have been changed. Its main purpose is to control throttle pressure when the transaxle is in reverse.

With the movement of the manual valve ⑪ to the Park position, the main line pressure is routed through a different passage in the valve body and with the use of the manual valve check valve ⑧, the pressured fluid is prevented from applying the clutches, band servos or accumulator. The transaxle remains in neutral and the parking mechanism is operated by the manual valve linkage.

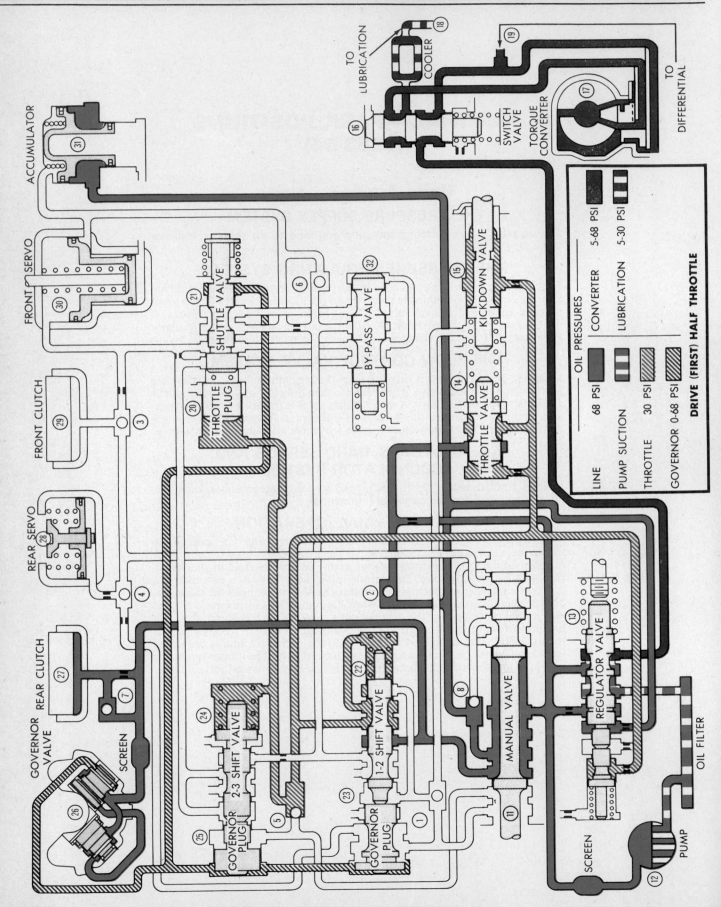

Drive—first gear, half throttle (1983-84) (©Chrysler Corp.)

DRIVE—FIRST GEAR
(1983-84)

Units Applied—Rear Clutch, Overrunning Clutch

The selector lever is in the Drive position and the transmission is in the first gear. The vehicle is moving and the throttle is in the half open position.

THE PRESSURE SUPPLY SYSTEM

The oil pump ⑫ is operating and supplying fluid to the main line passages, opened by the movement of the manual valve ⑪ and the pressure regulator valve ⑬.

THE PRESSURE REGULATING SYSTEM

The pressure regulator valve ⑬ maintains a specific level of pressure within the transaxle and operates in conjunction with throttle pressure. Note the changes in the pressure regulator valve assembly and the changes in the main line pressure routings.

THE FLOW CONTROL VALVE SYSTEM

The manual valve ⑪ directs main line pressure to the land of the 1-2 shift valve ㉒, the accumulator ㉛, the rear clutch apply ㉗, the governor assembly ㉖ and to the throttle valve ⑭, from which the governor and throttle pressures are obtained respectively. To prevent the shift from first to second until a predetermined speed is reached in conjunction with the throttle opening, the throttle pressure is routed to one end of the 1-2 shift valve ㉒, the 2-3 shift valve ㉔, the shuttle valve throttle plug ⑳ and to the kick down valve ⑮ to oppose the governor pressure which is routed to the front of the 1-2 shift valve governor plug ㉓ and the front of the 2-3 shift valve governor plug ㉕. Governor pressure is also routed to the shuttle valve ㉑, but is blocked by a land on the valve. The pressure regulator valve ⑬, routes main line pressure to the switch valve ⑯. The switch valve routes pressure to and from the converter ⑰. The return pressure is metered and directed to the cooler and lubrication ⑱ circuit at a lesser pressure psi. A passage is provided for the differential lubrication ⑲. A by-pass valve ㉝ has been added to the hydraulic circuit to aid in smooth application of the kickdown band (front) during the 1-2 upshift and is not in operation during the first speed mode.

THE CLUTCHES, BAND SERVOS AND ACCUMULATOR SYSTEM

The rear clutch ㉗ is applied hydraulically while the overrunning clutch is operated mechanically. The accumulator ㉛ is applied to act as an engagement softener for the rear clutch application.

THE CHECK VALVE OPERATION

The 2-3 shift valve check valve ⑤ is blocking throttle pressure from entering the 2-3 shift valve governor plug bore ㉕. The manual valve check valve ⑧ is blocking main line pressure from entering other apply passages. The remaining check valves are either allowing fluid to pass or not in a charged passage.

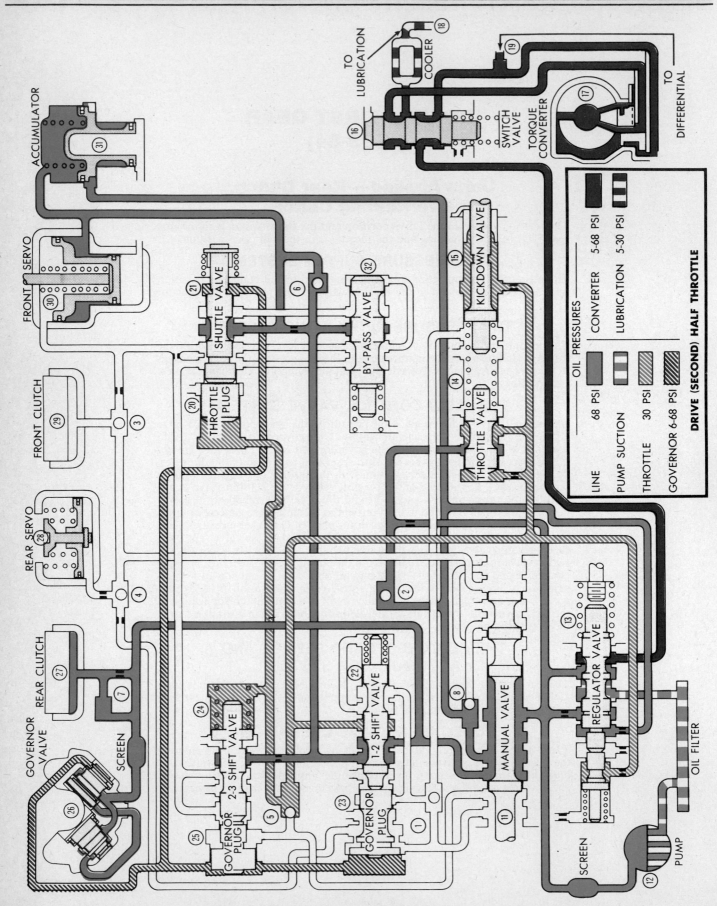

Drive—second gear, half throttle (1983-84) (©Chrysler Corp.)

DRIVE—SECOND GEAR
(1983-84)

Units Applied—Rear Clutch, Front Brake Band (Kickdown)

The selector lever is in the Drive position and governor pressure has overcome throttle pressure and caused the transmission to shift into the second speed. The vehicle is traveling at moderate speed and the throttle is in the first half open position.

THE PRESSURE SUPPLY SYSTEM

The oil pump ⑫ is operating and supplying fluid to the main line passages.

THE PRESSURE REGULATING SYSTEM

The pressure regulator valve ⑬ maintains a specific level of pressure within the transmission and operates in conjunction with the throttle pressure.

Note the changes in the pressure regulator valve assembly and the changes in the main line pressure routings.

THE FLOW CONTROL VALVE SYSTEM

The manual valve ⑪ directs main line pressure to governor valve ㉖, the rear clutch apply piston ㉗, the front servo ㉚, the accumulator ㉛, the 1-2 shift valve ㉒ and through it to the 2-3 shift valve ㉔, where it is blocked by a land on the shift valve. The throttle pressure resists the increase in governor pressure until the speed of the output shaft has increased to provide higher governor pressure in the shifting system to allow the 2-3 shift valve ㉔ to be moved for the 2-3 up-shift.

As the 1-2 shift valve ㉒ is positioned in the second speed position, main line pressure is directed to the shuttle valve ㉑. The shuttle valve ㉑ is moved against the throttle plug ⑳ by main line pressure, allowing governor pressure to react on the end of the shuttle valve ㉑. The by-pass valve ㉜ stops the main line pressure on one of its lands. The fluid flow is then directed to the apply side of the front servo ㉚ and to the release side of the accumulator ㉛. With the aid of the accumulator return spring, the accumulator piston is placed in the released position. The rear clutch ㉗ remains in the applied position.

The regulator valve ⑬ routes main line pressure to the switch valve ⑯. The switch valve routes pressure to and from the converter ⑰. The return pressure is metered and directed to the cooler and lubrication ⑱ system at a lesser pressure psi. A passage is provided for the differential lubrication ⑲.

THE CLUTCHES, BAND SERVOS AND ACCUMULATOR SYSTEM

The rear clutch ㉗ remains applied. The front servo ㉚ is applied, which in turn applies the front band (kickdown). The accumulator ㉛ is controlling the apply pressure for the front servo.

THE CHECK VALVE OPERATION

The 2-3 shift valve check valve ⑤ is blocking throttle pressure, while the manual valve check valve ⑧ is blocking main line pressure. The remaining check valves are either allowing pressured fluid to pass or are not in charged passages.

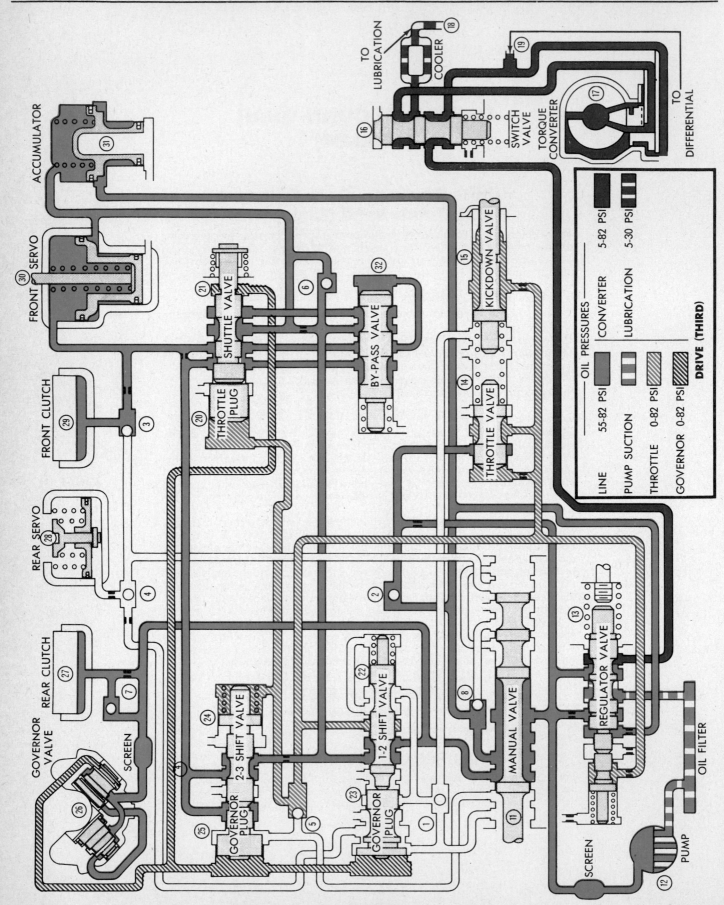

Drive—direct, third gear (1983-84) (©Chrysler Corp.)

DRIVE—DIRECT
(1983-84)

Units Applied—Rear Clutch, Front Clutch

The selector lever is in the Drive position and the 2-3 shift has occurred. The transmission is now in the Direct gear ratio (3rd Speed), with the vehicle moving at a moderate rate of speed.

THE PRESSURE SUPPLY SYSTEM

The oil pump ⑫ is operating and supplying fluid to the main line passages.

THE PRESSURE REGULATING SYSTEM

The pressure regulator valve ⑬ maintains a specific level of pressure within the transmission and operates in conjunction with the throttle pressure. Note the changes in the pressure regulator valve assembly and the changes in the main line pressure routings.

THE FLOW CONTROL VALVE SYSTEM

The manual valve directs main line pressure to the governor valve ㉖, the rear clutch apply piston ㉗, (which remains engaged), the front clutch ㉙, the release side of the front servo ㉘, the release side of the accumulator ㉛, the shuttle valve ㉑ and through both the 1-2 and the 2-3 shift valves ㉒ and ㉔. The throttle valve is being served by the main line pressure and throttle pressure is being developed.

As the 2-3 shift is made, increased governor pressure is developed and overcomes the throttle pressure. The increase in governor pressure forces the shuttle valve ㉑ to move against the throttle plug ⑳, opening the other main line pressure passages in the by-pass valve ㉜. This allows main line pressure to be directed around the by-pass valve ㉜ and to its end, forcing the valve against its return spring and opening other passages for the main line pressure to be routed.

The regulator valve ⑬ routes main line pressure to the switch valve ⑯. The switch valve routes pressure to the converter ⑰ and back again. The return pressure is metered and directed to the cooler and lubrication system ⑱ at a lesser pressure psi. A passage is provided for the differential lubrication ⑲.

THE CLUTCHES BAND SERVOS AND ACCUMULATOR SYSTEM

The rear clutch ㉗ remains applied. The front servo ㉚ has been released and the front clutch ㉙ has been applied. The accumulator ㉛ is in the released position.

THE CHECK VALVE OPERATION

The 2-3 shift valve check valve ⑤ is blocking throttle pressure while the manual valve check valve ⑧ is blocking main line pressure to the rear servo circuit. The front clutch check valve ③ is in a blocking position to prevent main line pressure from applying the rear servo. The remaining check valves are either allowing pressure to pass or are not in charged passages.

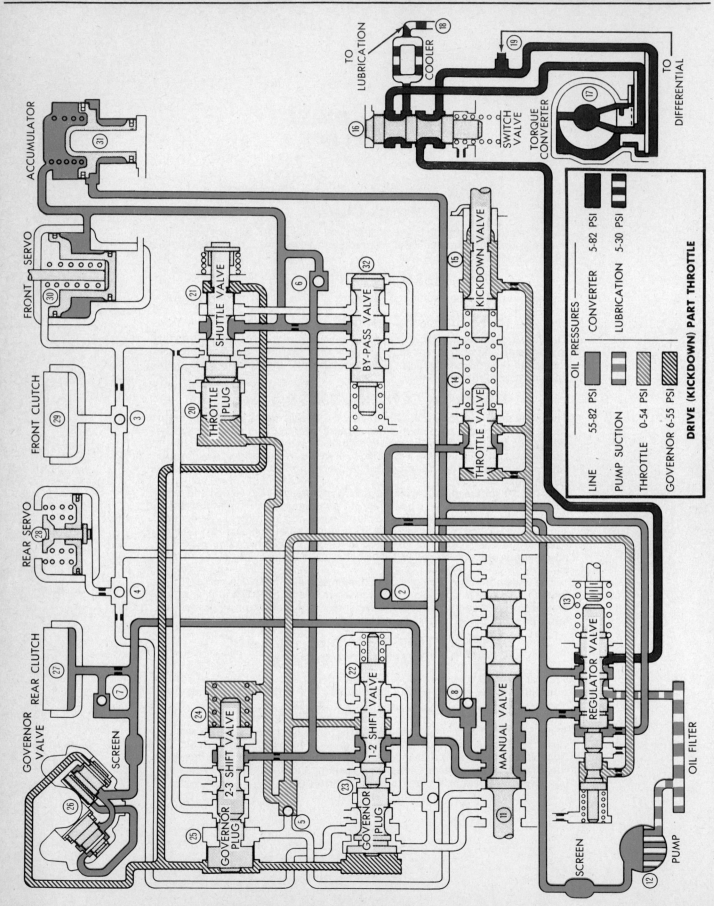

Drive—kickdown, part throttle (1983-84) (©Chrysler Corp.)

DRIVE—PART THROTTLE KICKDOWN (1983-84)

Units Applied—Rear Clutch, Front Band (Kickdown)

The selector lever is in the Drive position and the vehicle is moving at a speed of less than 30 MPH. An increase in the throttle opening has occurred to increase the vehicle speed, but not at wide open throttle (W.O.T.). The transmission automatically downshifts from 3rd to 2nd speed.

THE PRESSURE SUPPLY SYSTEM

The oil pump ⑫ is supplying fluid to the main line passages.

THE PRESSURE REGULATING SYSTEM

The pressure regulator valve ⑬ maintains a specific level of pressure within the transmission and operates in conjunction with the throttle pressure. Note the changes in the pressure regulator valve assembly and the changes in the main line pressure routings.

THE FLOW CONTROL VALVE SYSTEM

The slowing of the output shaft RPM has lowered the governor pressure to the affected valves. The movement of the throttle linkage causes the throttle valve to move and increase the throttle pressure to a higher psi than the governor pressure. This change in pressure causes the 2-3 shift valve ㉔ to move to its original position to block main line pressure to the front clutch ㉙ and to the release side of the front servo ㉚. The apply side of the front servo is charged with main line pressure which applies the front band (kickdown). The rear clutch ㉗ remains applied and the transmission has downshifted from 3rd speed to 2nd speed. The shuttle valve ㉑ is moved by the throttle pressure during the shifting operation, to block the main line pressure to the release side of the front servo ㉚.

The by-pass valve ㉜ main line pressure circuits are closed off by the shuttle valve ㉑ movement, allowing the by-pass return spring to move the valve to the off position.

The oil flow circuits are the same as in the second speed after the downshift has occurred. The converter ⑰, and the lubrication and cooler passages ⑱ are charged from the switch valve. A passage is provided for differential lubrication ⑲.

THE CLUTCHES, BAND SERVOS AND ACCUMULATOR SYSTEM

The rear clutch ㉗ remains applied. The front clutch ㉙ has been released and the front servo ㉘ has been applied to apply the front band (kickdown). The accumulator has been charged to control the application of the front servo.

THE CHECK VALVE OPERATION

The manual valve check valve ⑧ is blocking main line pressure, while the 2-3 shift valve check valve ⑤ is blocking throttle pressure. The remaining check valves are either allowing passage of fluid or are in a passage that is not charged.

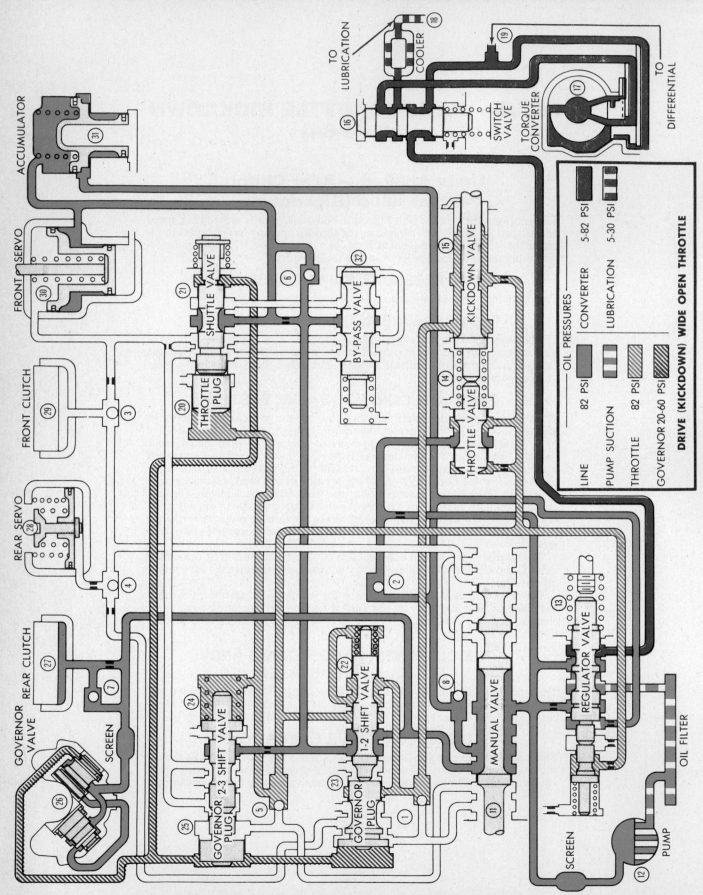

Drive—kickdown, wide open throttle (1983-84) (©Chrysler Corp.)

DRIVE—FULL THROTTLE KICKDOWN (1983-84)

Units Applied—Rear Clutch, Front Band (Kickdown)

The selector lever is in the Drive position and the vehicle is moving at a speed of 50 MPH or more.

The accelerator has been depressed to the wide open throttle position (W.O.T.) and the transmission automatically downshifts from 3rd to 2nd speed.

THE PRESSURE SUPPLY SYSTEM

The oil pump ⑫ is supplying fluid to the main line passages.

THE PRESSURE REGULATING SYSTEM

The pressure regulator valve ⑬ maintains a specific level of fluid pressure within the transmission and operates in conjunction with the throttle pressure. Note the changes in the pressure regulator valve assembly and the changes in the main line pressure routings.

THE FLOW CONTROL VALVE SYSTEM

The full opening of the accelerator moves the kickdown valve ⑮ (allowing main line pressure to enter the throttle pressure passage at the throttle valve ⑭) which quickly raises the throttle pressure for the downshift procedure. Main line pressure is directed to the 1-2 shift valve ㉒ lands to prevent its movement. The increased throttle pressure acts upon the 2-3 shift valve ㉔ and moves it to its original position in the valve body, causing the front clutch ㉙ to be released and the front band servo ㉚ to be applied.

Throttle pressure is routed to the throttle plug ⑳, and blocks the movement of the shuttle valve. The remaining fluid circuits remain the same as in the DRIVE—2nd speed gear range. The converter ⑰, the lubrication and cooler system ⑱ is being charged from the switch valve ⑯. A passage ⑲ is provided for differential lubrication.

The by-pass valve ㉜ is inoperative and remains in the off position.

THE CLUTCHES, BAND SERVOS AND ACCUMULATOR SYSTEM

The rear clutch ㉗ remains applied and the front clutch ㉙ is released as the front band (kickdown) is applied. The transmission is in the 2nd speed gear ratio. The accumulator is charged with fluid to assist the front band application.

THE CHECK VALVE OPERATION

Numbers ① and ⑤ check valves are positioned to block throttle pressure from acting upon the 2-3 shift valve governor plug ㉓. The number ⑧ check ball is positioned to block main line pressure from one circuit of the manual valve assembly. The remaining check valves are either allowing fluid to pass or are not in a charged passage.

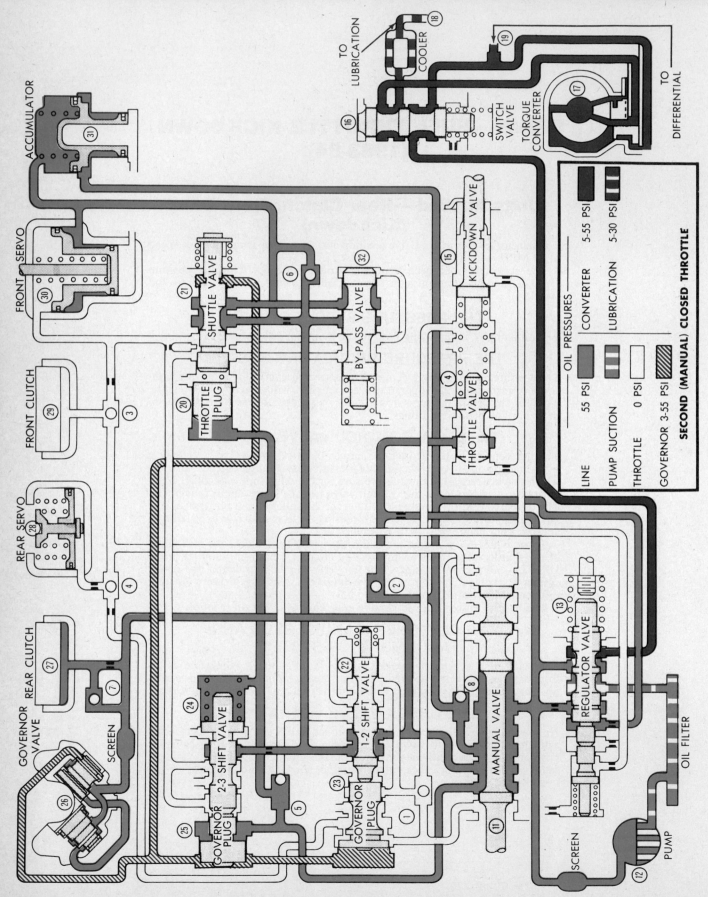

Second—manual position, closed throttle (1983-84) (©Chrysler Corp.)

SECOND-MANUAL—CLOSED THROTTLE
(1983-84)

Units Applied—Rear Clutch, Front Band (Kickdown)

The selector lever is positioned in the Second position (manual Second). The vehicle is moving slowly with a closed throttle. Governor pressure is being developed from the governor by the rotation of the output shaft.

THE PRESSURE SUPPLY SYSTEM

The oil pump ⑫ is operating and charging the main line passages.

THE PRESSURE REGULATING SYSTEM

The pressure regulator valve ⑬ maintains a specific pressure level and operates in conjunction with the throttle pressure. Note the changes in the pressure regulator assembly and the changes in the main line pressure routings.

THE FLOW CONTROL VALVE SYSTEM

The manual valve ⑪ is positioned to allow main line pressure to be routed to the governor ㉖ assembly, where governor pressure is developed. Main line pressure is routed to the rear of the 2-3 shift valve ㉔ and to the 2-3 shift valve governor plug ㉕ to prevent the governor pressure from shifting them. Main line pressure is also routed to the throttle plug ⑳ to prevent the shuttle valve ㉑ from passing throttle pressure through the passages. Main line pressure is also directed to the by-pass valve ㉜, but the valve remains inoperative. The transmission is locked into the 2nd speed because no throttle pressure is developed to oppose the governor pressure. The converter ⑰, the lubrication and cooler systems ⑱ are fed from the switch valve. A passage ⑲ is provided for differential lubrication.

THE CLUTCHES, BAND SERVOS AND ACCUMULATOR SYSTEM

The rear clutch ㉗ and the front servo ㉚ are applied. The accumulator ㉛ is in a position to receive pressured fluid to cushion the front band application.

THE CHECK VALVE OPERATION

The check valves, number ⑤ and ⑧, are positioned to prevent main line pressure from being routed to the pressure regulator valve to prevent the throttle pressure from being built up. The remaining check valves are either allowing fluid to pass or are not in a charged passage.

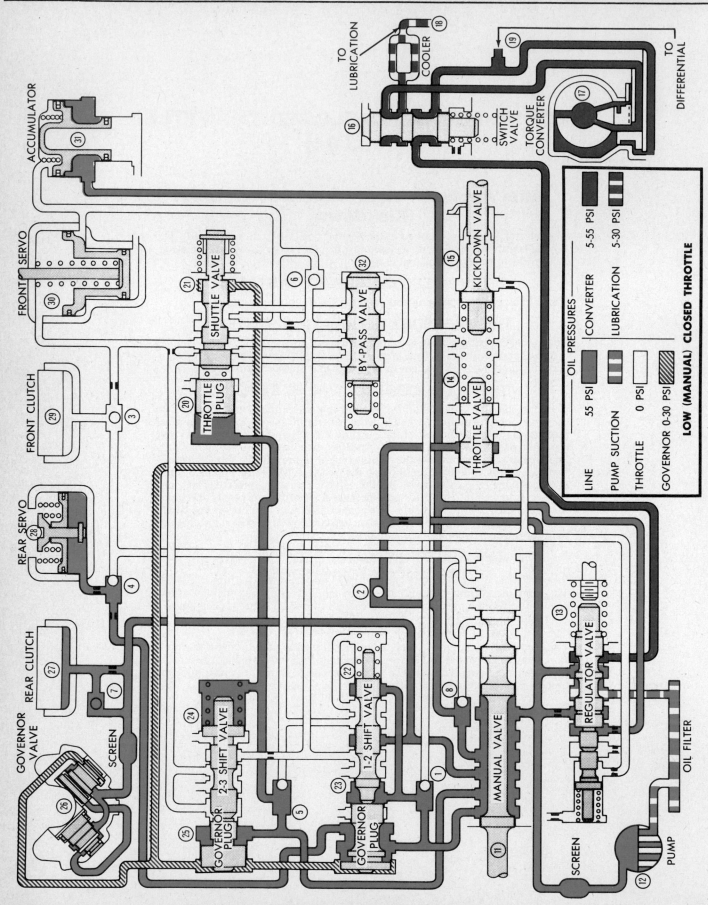

Low—manual position, closed throttle (1983-84) (©Chrysler Corp.)

LOW-MANUAL—CLOSED THROTTLE
(1983-84)

Units Applied—Rear Clutch, Rear Band (Low-Reverse)

The selector lever is in the Low position (manual Low) with the throttle closed and the vehicle moving slowly.

THE PRESSURE SUPPLY SYSTEM

The oil pump ⑫ is operating and charging the main line passages.

THE PRESSURE REGULATING SYSTEM

The pressure regulator valve ⑬ maintains a specific amount of fluid pressure and operates in conjunction with the throttle pressure. Note the pressure regulator valve assembly changes and the re-routing of the main line pressure from the regulator valve.

THE FLOW CONTROL VALVE SYSTEM

The manual valve is positioned to allow main line pressure to be routed to the rear clutch ㉗ and apply the unit. Main line pressure is routed to the 1-2 shift valve governor plug ㉓ to oppose governor pressure and prevent the shifting of the 1-2 shift valve ㉒. Main line pressure is routed through the grooves of the 1-2 shift valve governor plug ㉓ and to the rear servo ㉘ to apply the rear band (low-reverse). Main line pressure is directed to the throttle plug ⑳ and the shuttle valve ㉑ to hold them in a non-shifting position. The main line pressure is not directed to the by-pass ㉜ valve, therefore, it remains inoperative. Throttle pressure is not developed to oppose governor pressure, therefore the transmission is locked in the 1st gear range. The converter ⑰, the cooler and lubrication system ⑱ is charged from the switch valve ⑯. A passage ⑲ is provided for differential lubrication.

THE CLUTCHES, BAND SERVOS AND ACCUMULATOR SYSTEM

The accumulator ㉛ is applied by main line pressure. The rear clutch ㉗ and the rear servo ㉘ are applied to provide the low range.

THE CHECK VALVE OPERATION

The check valves, numbers ①, ④, ⑤, and ⑧ are used to prevent main line pressure from entering passages that would allow movements of valves and create pressures not needed. The remaining check valves are in passages not charged or are ineffective.

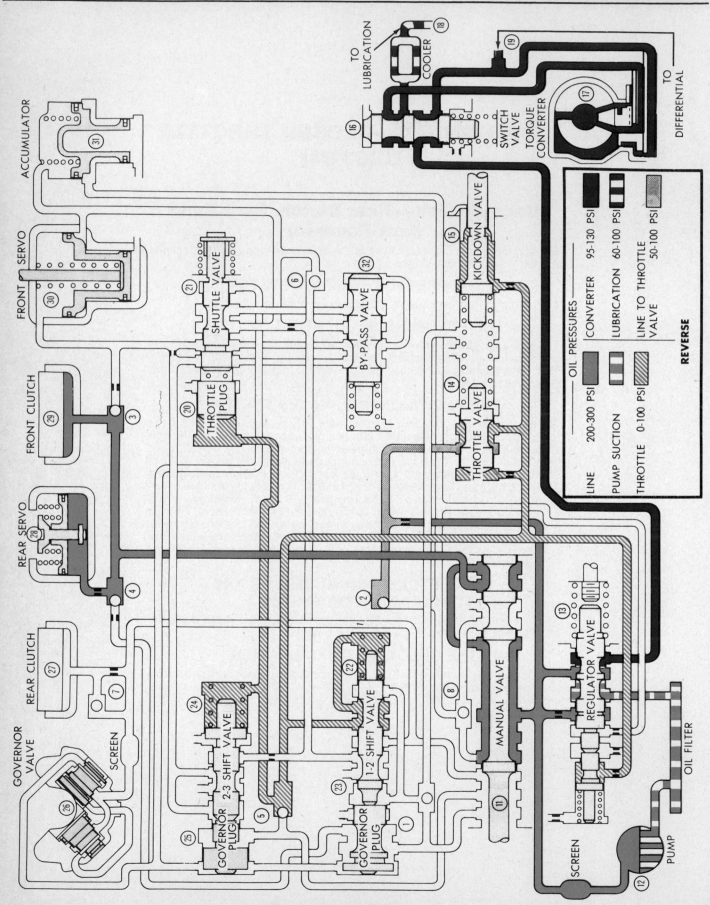

Reverse (1983-84) (©Chrysler Corp.)

REVERSE (1983-84)

Units Applied—Rear Servo (Low-Reverse Band), Front Clutch

The selector lever is in the Reverse position and the vehicle is stationary with the throttle closed.

THE PRESSURE SUPPLY SYSTEM

The oil pump ⑫ is operating and providing fluid to the main line passages.

THE PRESSURE REGULATING SYSTEM

The pressure regulator valve ⑬ supplies a specific amount of pressure within the transmission. The pressure regulator operates in conjunction with throttle pressure, when it is present. Note the changes in the pressure regulator valve assembly and the changes in the main line pressure routings.

THE FLOW CONTROL VALVE SYSTEM

The reverse gear needs higher pressures to apply the units and hold, necessary due to the increase of torque in the reverse mode. To accomplish this, the pressure regulator must increase the pressure to over double of its normal operation. To accomplish this, throttle pressure is directed to a specific land on the pressure regulator valve, to assist in holding the pressure regulator valve and increasing the resistance so that main line pressure can be increased. The main line pressure increases from approximately 65 psi to 250-300 psi by this procedure. This increased pressure is then directed to the applying units. Governor pressure is not produced so that throttle pressure is unopposed to hold the valves from shifting.

The pressure regulator supplies pressure to the switch valve ⑯ at lower pressure, and is directed to the converter ⑰, the differential lubrication outlet ⑲ and to the lubrication and cooler circuits ⑱.

THE CLUTCHES, BAND SERVOS AND ACCUMULATOR SYSTEM

The increased main line pressure is directed to the rear clutch ㉗ and applies the unit. Main line pressure is directed to the rear servo ㉘, which in turn applies the Low-Reverse band. All other units are unused.

THE CHECK VALVE OPERATION

The rear servo check valve ④ and the front clutch check valve ③ are used to prevent the pressured fluid from passing into other passages. The throttle valve check valve ② and the governor plug check valve ③ are used to prevent the throttle pressure from entering shift valve passages.

ADJUSTMENTS
Gearshift Linkage

If it should be necessary to take the linkage apart, the plastic grommets that are used as retainers should be replaced with new ones. Use a prying tool (large screwdriver) to force rod from grommet, then cut away old grommet. Use pliers to snap new grommet into the lever and to snap the rod into the grommet.

1980 MODELS

1. Make sure that the adjustable swivel block is free to slide on the shift cable. Disassemble and clean or repair, to assure free action, as necessary.

2. With all linkage assembled and free and the adjustable swivel lock bolt loose, place the gearshift lever in Park, then move the shift lever on the transaxle all the way to the rear detent position.

3. Tighten the swivel lock bolt to 90 in. lbs. (10N•m).

4. To check operation, key start must work only when the gear shift lever is in Park or Neutral.

1981 AND LATER MODELS

1. Place the gear shift lever in the "P" (Park) position.

2. Loosen the cable retaining clamp on the cable mounting bracket of the automatic transaxle.

3. Apply the loading as follows while tightening the cable retaining clamp bolt to 90 in. lbs. (10N•m).

   a. All models equipped with column shift—Apply a 10 pound load in the forward direction on the cable housing isolator.

   b. All models except Omni and Horizon equipped with console shift—Apply a 10 pound load minimum, in the forward direction on the console shift lever knob.

   c. Omni and Horizon Models equipped with console shift—Apply a 10 pound load in the forward direction on the transaxle lever, at the transaxle.

4. Check the adjustment by moving the shift lever through all positions while attempting to start the engine with the key. The engine should only start with the transaxle shift lever in the Park or Neutral positions.

Throttle Linkage

Bring engine to operating temperature and be sure the carburetor is off fast idle. Check idle speed with tachometer. Disconnect choke if necessary to keep carburetor off fast idle.

1. Loosen the adjustment bracket lock screw. The bracket must be free to slide on its slot. If necessary, disassemble and clean or repair. Lube with a good quality light grease.

2. a. 1980-82—Hold the transaxle throttle lever firmly rearward against its internal stop, and then tighten the adjusting lock screw to 105 in. lbs. (12N•m). This automatically removes cable backlash.

   b. 1983 and Later—Slide the bracket to the left (towards the engine) to the limit of its travel. Release the bracket and move the throttle lever fully to the right against its internal stop and tighten the adjusting bracket lock screw to 105 in. lbs. (12N•m).

3. Connect choke if it was disconnected. Test for freedom of movement by pushing the lever forward and slowly release it to confirm that it will return fully rearward.

Band Adjustment
KICKDOWN (FRONT) BAND

The kickdown band (front band) has its adjusting screw located on the top front (left side) of the transaxle case. Adjustment is as follows:

1. Loosen the lock nut and back off about five turns.

2. Tighten the adjusting screw to 72 in. lbs. (8N•m):

3. Back off the adjusting screw 3 turns from 72 in. lbs. on the A-404 and A-415 models. Back off the adjusting screw 2¾ turns from 72 in. lbs. on the 1982 and later A-413 and A-470 transaxles. 1981 A-413 and A-470 models require the adjusting screw to be backed off 2 turns.

4. Hold the adjusting screw in this position and tighten the locknut to 35 ft. lbs. (47 N•m).

LOW-REVERSE BAND

A-404

The Low-reverse band (rear) is not adjustable. If excessive band wear is suspected, the following procedure should be used to verify wear.

1. Remove the transaxle oil pan and pressurize the low-reverse servo with 30 psi of air pressure.

2. With the low-reverse servo pressurized, measure the gap between the band ends. If the gap is less than 0.080 inch (2.0 mm) the band has worn excessively and should be replaced.

A-413 and A-470

The low-reverse band is adjustable. However, before adjustments are done, the procedure outlined to check the low-reverse band for the A-404 transaxle should be done to verify that the proper end gap exists on these transaxle models. To adjust the band, follow the outlined procedure.

1. Loosen and back off the lock nut approximately 5 turns.

2. With an inch pound torque wrench, tighten the adjusting screw to 41 inch pound (5N•m) torque.

3. Back off the adjusting screw 3½ turns from the 41 in. lbs. (5N•m) torque.

4. While holding the adjusting screw, tighten the lock nut to 10 ft. lbs. (14N•m) torque.

SERVICES

Fluid Change and/or Oil Pan Removal

1. Raise the vehicle and support safely. Loosen, but do not remove the oil pan bolts. Gently pull one corner of the oil pan downward so the fluid will drain into a container with a large opening.

— CAUTION —

If the fluid is hot, do not allow it to touch the person. Burns can result.

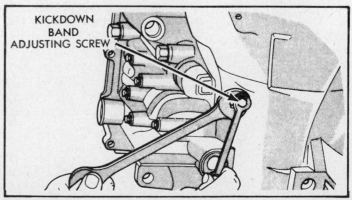

Adjusting kickdown band (©Chrysler Corp.)

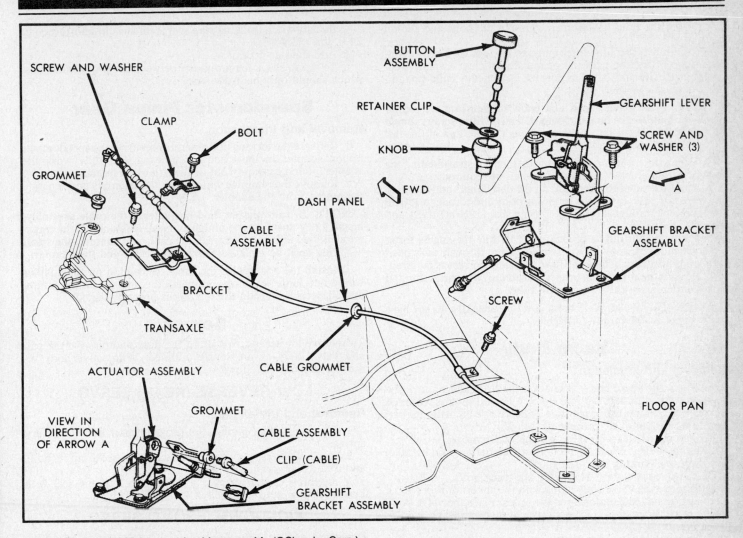

Console model shift linkage and cable assembly (©Chrysler Corp.)

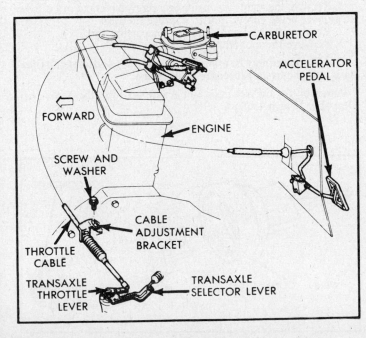

Throttle linkage assembly (©Chrysler Corp.)

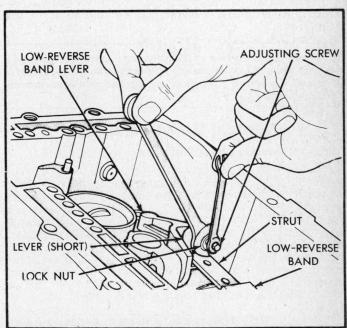

Adjusting low-reverse band, A-413 and A-470 models (©Chrysler Corp.)

2. When the fluid has drained, remove the bolts and the oil pan.

3. Carefully inspect the filter and pan bottom for a heavy concentration of friction material or metal particles. A small accumulation can be considered as normal, but a heavy build-up indicates damaged or worn parts.

NOTE: Filter replacement and band adjustments are recommended whenever the fluid is changed. The oil filter screws should be torqued to 35 in. lbs., (7N•m) through 1980, and 40 in. lbs. (5N•m), 1981 and later.

4. Check the oil pan carefully for distortion, straightening the flanges with a block of wood and mallet, as required.

5. Apply a bead of RTV sealant on the pan flanges and install to the transaxle case. Install the retaining bolts and torque to 150 in. lbs. (16N•m) through 1980, and 165 in. lbs. (19N•m), 1981 and later.

6. Fill with four quarts of Dexron R II. Idle the engine for at least six minutes, moving the selector lever through each position, ending in Park. Check the fluid level and correct as required.

7. Be sure the dipstick is properly seated to prevent water and dirt from entering the transaxle fill tube.

NOTE: The A-404, A-413 and A-470 transaxles do not have drain plugs on the torque converters.

Valve Body

Removal and Intallation

To remove the valve body, first drain the fluid and remove the pan as outlined under "Oil Pan R&R." The oil filter is removed next which requires the proper size Torx® drive bit. After the pan and filter are removed, proceed as follows:

1. Unscrew the neutral safety switch and remove.

2. Remove the "E" clip that connects the parking rod to its lever. Remove parking rod.

3. Remove the seven valve body attaching bolts.

4. Remove the valve body along with the governor tubes being very careful not to bend or force the tubes. Place the valve body where it will be protected from damage if other transaxle work is to be done.

5. To install the valve body assembly, reverse the removal procedure. Torque the valve body attaching bolts to 40 in. lbs. (5N•m).

——————————— CAUTION ———————————

Do not clamp any portion of the valve body or transfer plate in a vise. Distortion can occur causing sticking valves. Do not use force on any valve or spring. Identify all springs and valves for reassembly identification.

Neutral Safety Switch

Testing, Removal and Installation

The neutral safety switch used on this transaxle includes provision for the backup lamp switch function. The neutral start circuit is through the center pin on the three terminal switch. It provides a ground for the starter solenoid circuit through the center pin when in Park or Neutral. The two outside terminals of the neutral switch are for the circuit feeding the backup lamps. To test and/or replace the switch, follow this procedure:

1. Remove the wiring connector and with a test light or voltmeter, check for continuity between the center pin of the switch and the transaxle case. There should be continuity only in Park or Neutral. If switch tests "bad" check gearshift cable for proper adjustment.

2. If switch needs replacement, unscrew from transaxle case. Expect fluid to run out; keep container close.

3. Move selector lever to Park and Neutral to see if the lever in the transaxle is centered in the switch opening.

4. Install switch (making sure seal is on switch) and torque to 24 ft. lbs. (33N•m).

5. Add fluid as necessary.

6. To retest, check for continuity between the two outside pins, which should only be in Reverse.

Speedometer Pinion Gear

Removal and Installation

1. Remove the locking bolt assembly securing the speedometer pinion adapter in the extension housing. Carefully work the adapter/pinion assembly out of the extension housing.

2. Remove the retaining spring from the assembly and separate the pinion from the adapter.

NOTE: If transmission fluid has entered the cable assembly, install a new speedometer pinion and seal assembly. If the transmission fluid is leaking between the cable and adapter, the small "O" ring must be replaced between the cable and the adapter.

3. Install the adapter on the cable, the pinion on the adapter with a new large "O" ring and install the retainer on the pinion and adapter. Be certain the retainer is properly seated.

Servos

To remove the servos, first drain the fluid and remove the pan and valve body as previously outlined. With valve body removed, proceed as follows:

LOW-REVERSE (REAR) SERVO

Removal and Installation

1. Remove the snap ring, the servo retainer and the return spring.

2. The low-reverse servo assembly can be pulled from its bore, and if necessary, have the lip seal renewed.

3. Assembly is the reverse, being sure to lube the seal with Dexron® II or petroleum jelly.

KICKDOWN (FRONT) SERVO

Removal and Installation

1. Remove the snap ring, using two screwdrivers to pry it from its groove, being careful not to damage the case.

2. Remove the rod guide, spring and piston rod.

3. Remove the kickdown piston.

NOTE: There may be minor variations due to different applications, but the basic procedure is the same.

Assembly is the reverse, being sure to lube the seals with Dexron® II or petroleum jelly.

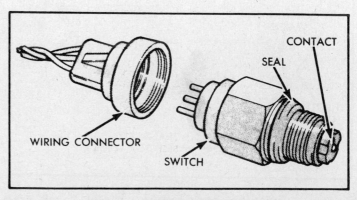

Neutral start and back-up lamp switch (©Chrysler Corp.)

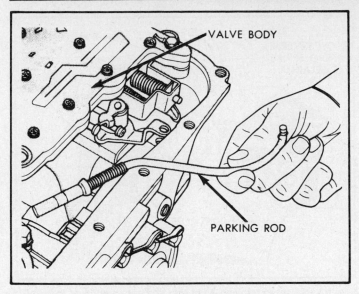

Removing park rod from valve body (©Chrysler Corp.)

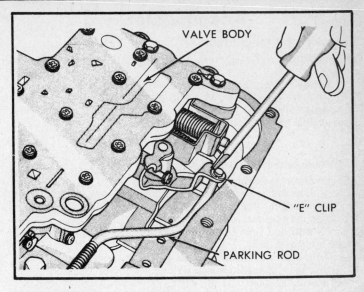

Removing parkrod "E" clip retainer (©Chrysler Corp.)

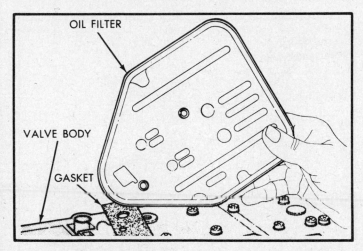

Oil filter removal (©Chrysler Corp.)

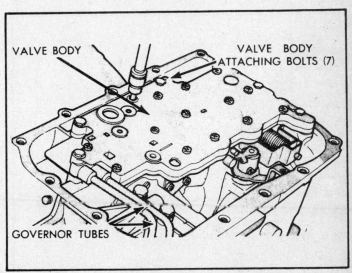

Valve body attaching bolts and governor tube location (©Chrysler Corp.)

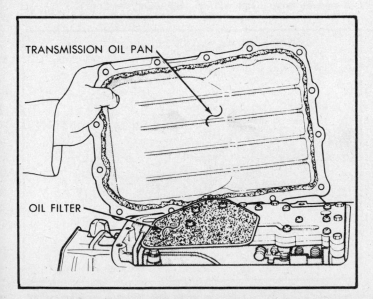

Transaxle oil pan removal and filter location (©Chrysler Corp.)

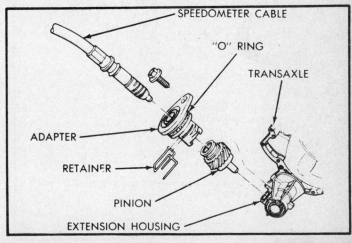

Exploded view of speedometer drive assembly (©Chrysler Corp.)

Accumulator

Removal and Installation

The accumulator is easily removed in much the same manner as the servos.

1. Remove the snap ring and accumulator plug.
2. Remove the spring and accumulator piston.
3. Assembly is the reverse, being sure to lube the seals with Dexron® II or petroleum jelly.

Governor

Removal and Installation

The governor assembly is a special offset design. No shaft runs through it and so it can be removed for service without removing the transaxle gear cover, transfer gear or governor support. The governor may be serviced by the following procedure:

1. As outlined previously, remove the transaxle oil pan and valve body assembly.
2. Unbolt the governor from the governor support and remove for cleaning or reconditioning. When cleaning or assembling the governor, make sure that the valves move freely in their bores.
3. When installing the governor, torque the bolts to 60 in. lbs. (7N•m).

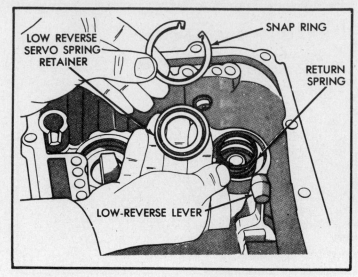

Low-reverse servo retainer, snap ring and spring removal or installation (©Chrysler Corp.)

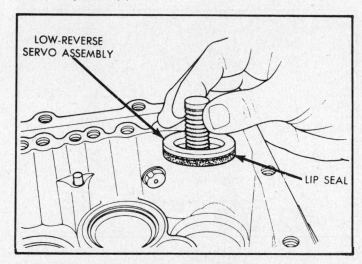

Low-reverse servo piston with lip seal (©Chrysler Corp.)

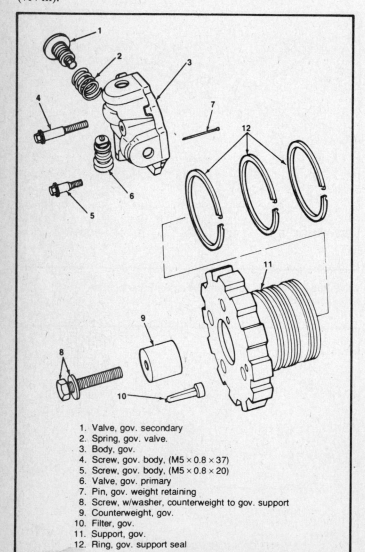

1. Valve, gov. secondary
2. Spring, gov. valve.
3. Body, gov.
4. Screw, gov. body, (M5 × 0.8 × 37)
5. Screw, gov. body, (M5 × 0.8 × 20)
6. Valve, gov. primary
7. Pin, gov. weight retaining
8. Screw, w/washer, counterweight to gov. support
9. Counterweight, gov.
10. Filter, gov.
11. Support, gov.
12. Ring, gov. support seal

Exploded view of governor assembly (©Chrysler Corp.)

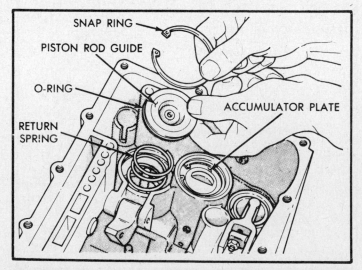

Kickdown servo rod guide and snap ring removal or installation (©Chrysler Corp.)

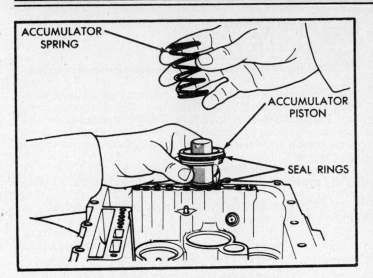

Accumulator piston assembly removal or installation
(©Chrysler Corp.)

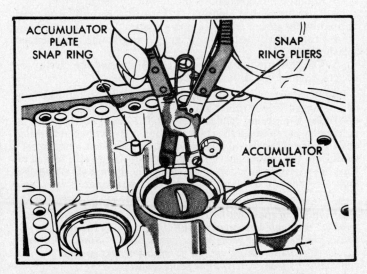

Removal or installation of accumulator plate (©Chrysler Corp.)

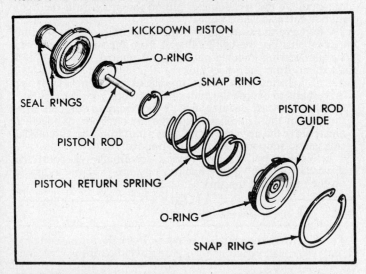

Exploded view of controlled load kickdown servo assembly
(©Chrysler Corp.)

Typical engine support fixture (©Chrysler Corp.)

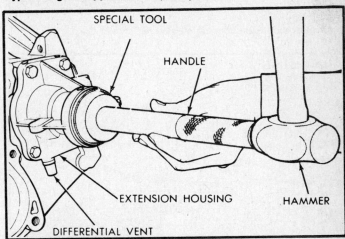

Installation of extension housing oil seal using special driver tool
(©Chrysler Corp.)

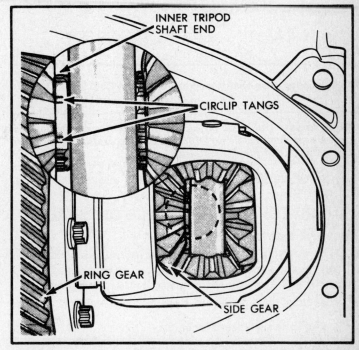

Circlip location within the differential carrier assembly
(©Chrysler Corp.)

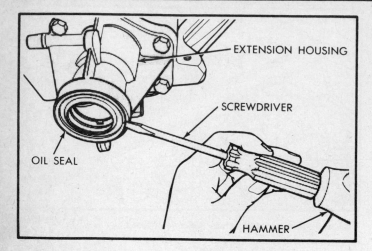

Removal of extension housing oil seal (©Chrysler Corp.)

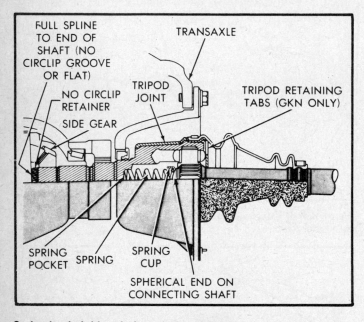

Spring loaded drive shaft assembly (©Chrysler Corp.)

While the removal of the transaxle does not require the removal of the engine, it should be noted that care must be used to prevent damage to the converter drive plate. The drive plate will not support any weight, so the transaxle and converter must be removed as an assembly. Do not let any of the weight of the transaxle or converter rest.

1. Disconnect the negative battery cable.

2. Disconnect the throttle and shift linkage from the transaxle levers.

3. With the vehicle on the floor and foot brakes applied, loosen the hub and wheel nuts.

4. Remove the upper and lower cooler lines at the transaxle.

5. Position an engine support fixture to the engine and tighten to equalize the engine weight from the mounts.

NOTE: This step can be done later in the procedure, at the discretion of the repairman.

6. Remove the upper bolts of the bell housing.

7. Raise the vehicle, remove the wheel/tire assemblies and the hub nut with washer from the drive shaft.

8. From under the left front fender, remove the inner fender splash panel.

9. Vehicles equipped with driveshafts having the circlip retainers, remove the differential cover.

NOTE: Driveshafts were changed from a circlip retainer to a spring loaded Tripod (inner joint) during the 1982 model year. To determine if a spring loaded joint/shaft is used in the vehicle, place a pry bar between the right side transaxle extension housing and the face of the tripod joint housing. Pry the joint housing outward (into the rubber boot). If the joint housing can be moved at least ½ inch from the extension housing, the driveshaft is a spring loaded model and does not have the circlip retainer.

— CAUTION —

Mishandling of the driveshaft assemblies, such as allowing the assemblies to dangle unsupported, pulling or pushing the ends can result in pinched rubber boots or damage to the CV joints. Boot sealing is vital to retaining special joint lubricants and to prevent contaminents from entering the joint areas.

10. Remove the speedometer pinion assembly from the right transaxle extension housing.

11. Remove the sway bar and the lower ball joint to steering knuckle bolts. Pry the ball joint stud from the steering knuckle. Push the steering knuckle outward and remove the driveshaft splined end from the wheel hub.

12. a. Vehicles with circlip driveshaft retainers—Turn the driveshafts to expose the ends of the circlips within the differential carrier case opening. Rotate the circlip to coincide with the flats of the driveshafts, squeeze the circlip ends together and remove the driveshaft/circlip as a unit from the differential side gears. Support the shaft and remove.

b. Vehicles with spring loaded driveshafts—Support the driveshaft at the CV joints and pull outward from the transaxle on the inner joint housing.

— CAUTION —

Do not pull on the driveshaft.

13. Remove the converter dust cover, mark the torque converter and drive plate relationship and remove the torque converter mounting bolts.

14. To rotate the engine, remove the access plug located in the right fender splash panel, and use a suitable socket/ratchet assembly to turn the engine crankshaft.

— CAUTION —

Dirt and sand can cause misalignment, resulting in speedometer pinion gear damage. Be certain all parts and mating surfaces are clean and free of foreign material.

4. Install the locking bolt assembly and torque to 60 in. lbs. (7N•m).

DRIVESHAFT TRANSAXLE OIL SEALS

Removal and Installation

1. Remove the drive shaft assembly from the transaxle.

NOTE: Refer to the transaxle Removal and Installation section for drive shaft removal, handling and installation information.

2. Remove the oil seal with a seal remover tool or its equivalent.

3. Inspect the seal seat and bore.

4. Lubricate the seal lip with transmission fluid or petroleum jelly, seat it squarely in its bore and install the seal to its seat with a seal installer tool.

5. Reinstall the drive shaft in the reverse order of its removal.

15. Remove the connector from the neutral starter switch. Certain models may require the removal of the lower cooler pipe at this time, if not accomplished earlier.

16. Remove the engine mount bracket from the front cross member.

17. Remove the front mount insulator through bolt and front engine mount bolts.

NOTE: It will be necessary to adjust the engine support to obtain the zero clearance needed to relieve the pressure from the mounts and bolts.

18. Place the removal jack under the transaxle, remove the left engine mount and the long bolt through the mount.

19. Remove the lower bell housing bolts. Pry against the engine and lower transaxle, being careful of the torque converter.

Installation of the transaxle is a reversal of the procedure but remember to fill the differential with Dexron® II automatic

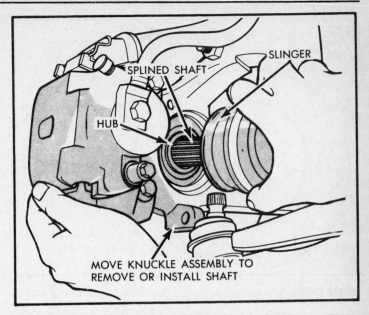

Separating or installing splined shaft into hub assembly (©Chrysler Corp.)

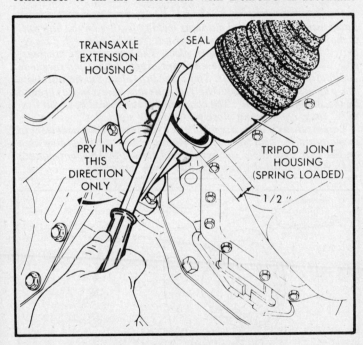

Identifying spring loaded drive shaft (©Chrysler Corp.)

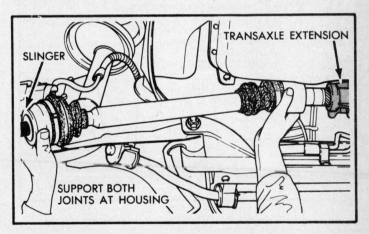

Supporting of drive shaft during removal or installation (©Chrysler Corp.)

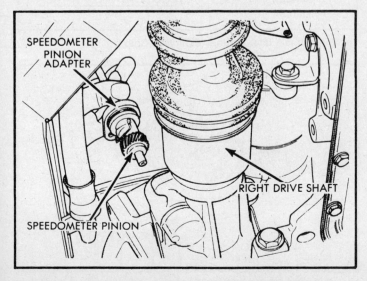

Speedometer drive pinion adapter removal (©Chrysler Corp.)

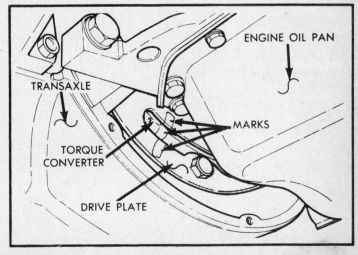

Mark torque converter and drive plate before separation (©Chrysler Corp.)

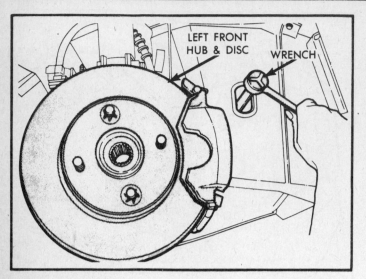

Rotate engine through fender panel access hole (©Chrysler Corp.)

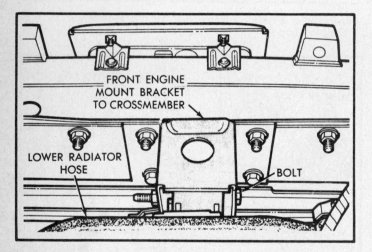

Location of front engine mount bracket to cross member (©Chrysler Corp.)

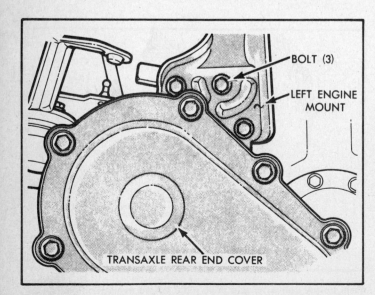

Left engine mount location (©Chrysler Corp.)

transmission fluid, if equipped with separate sump, before lowering the car. Also pay particular attention to the proper positioning of the "circlips" on the driveshaft inboard ends, with the "tangs" laying on the flattened end of the shaft. Holding the joint housing, a quick, firm push will complete the lock-up of the "circlips" on the axle side gear.

CAUTION
Make sure the clips are positioned correctly.

When reinstalling the lower ball joint to the steering knuckle, torque the clamp bolt to 50 foot-pounds (68N•m). The differential cover is not installed with a gasket, but with RTV sealant in a ribbon about ⅛" wide. The screws are torqued to 165 inch-pounds (19N•m). If the inner drive shaft boots appear collapsed or deformed, slip a small round rod under the boot to vent some air into it since a vacuum may have formed when it was pushed home.

CAUTION
Early transaxle units had a unique locking feature on the hub nuts to maintain preload and prevent the nut from backing off. This required that the nut be staked in place. The hub nuts are not reusable. Install washer and a new hub nut. Apply brakes and torque to 200 foot-pounds (271N•m). Stake nut into place but do not use a sharp chisel. The tool should be 7/16" wide and have a radius ground on the end of about 1/16". The completed stake should be about 3/16" to ¼" long, conforming closely to the axle shaft slot.

Later transaxle units use a more conventional lock and cotter pin to maintain the bearing preload. Again, a new nut should be used on the hub, and apply the brakes and torque to 180 foot-pounds (245N•m). Install the nut lock and a new cotter pin.

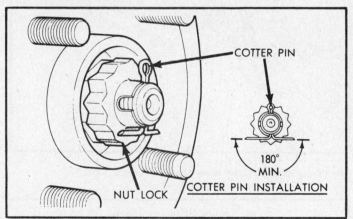

Locking hub nut, later models (©Chrysler Corp.)

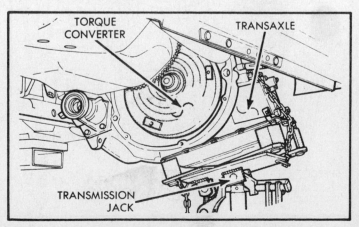

Lowering or raising transaxle assembly (©Chrysler Corp.)

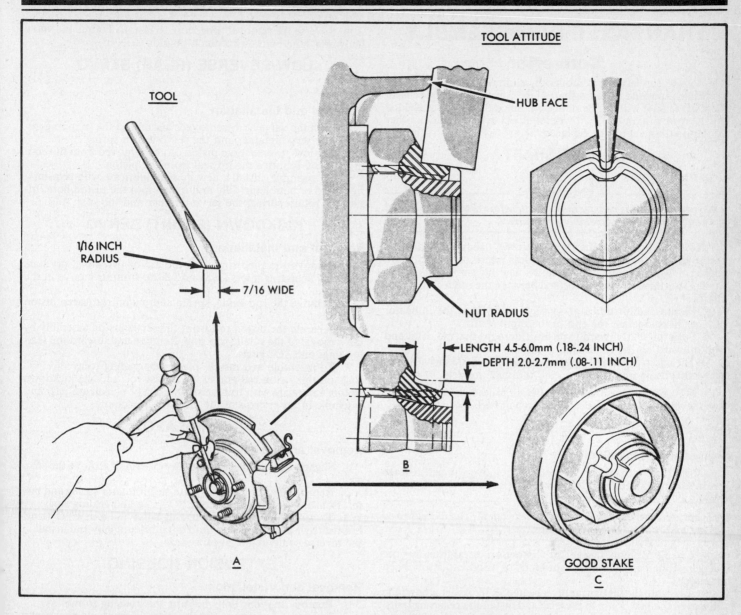

Staking hub nut, early models (©Chrysler Corp.)

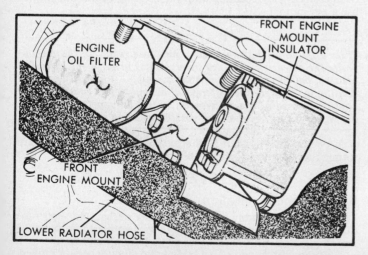

Engine mount bracket removal or installation (©Chrysler Corp.)

BENCH OVERHAUL

Before removing any of the transaxle subassemblies for bench overhaul, the unit should be cleaned. Cleanliness during disassembly and assembly is necessary to avoid further transaxle trouble after assembly. Before removing any of the transaxle subassemblies, plug all the openings and clean the outside of the transaxle thoroughly. Steam cleaning or car wash type high pressure equipment is preferable. Parts should be washed in a cleaning solvent, then dried with compressed air. *Do not wipe parts with shop towels.* The lint and fibers will find their way into the valve body and other parts and cause problems later. The case assembly was accurately machined and care must be used to avoid damage. Pay attention to the torque values to avoid case distortion.

121

TRANSAXLE DISASSEMBLY

Converter

The torque converter is removed by sliding the unit out of the transaxle input and reaction shaft. If the converter is to be reused, set it aside so it will not be damaged. Since the units are welded and have no drain plugs, converters subject to burnt fluid or other contamination should be replaced.

INPUT SHAFT

End Play Check

———————— CAUTION ————————

This measurement is considered critical, before disassembly and at the completion of the assembly procedures.

Measuring the input shaft end play will usually indicate if a thrust washer change is required, unless major components are replaced, which would then require new measurements to be made. This thrust washer is located between the input and output shafts.

1. Mount a dial indicator in such a way that the indicator plunger bears against the end of the input shaft.
2. Push the shaft inward to its limit, zero the dial indicator and pull outward on the input shaft.
3. The end play should be between 0.007 to 0.073 inch (0.18 to 1.85 mm) beginning with the 1980 transaxle models.

NOTE: Both removal and installation procedures are outlined together for easier reference by the repairman.

Oil Pan

Removal and Installation

1. With the transaxle held securely, remove the pan to case bolts. Gently tap the pan loose from the case.

———————— CAUTION ————————

It is not recommended to insert a tool between the pan and case as a prying tool. Case damage can result.

2. Check the pan flange for distortion, straightening the flanges of the pan with a straight block of wood and a soft faced hammer.
3. To install the oil pan, apply a bead of RTV sealer around the flanges of the pan, mate to the case and install the retaining bolts. Torque the bolts to 150 inch-pounds (16N•m) through 1980, and 165 inch-pounds (19N•m) 1981 and later.

Oil Filter

Removal and Installation

1. Three Torx R type screws are used to hold the filter to the valve body. The screws must be removed and replaced with the use of the proper tool bit.
2. When re-installing or replacing the filter assembly, torque the screws to 35 inch-pounds (4N•m) through 1980, and 40 inch-pounds (5N•m), 1981 and later.

Valve Body

Removal and Installation

1. After oil pan and filter removal, take the "E" clip off the park rod and pull the park rod free of its support.
2. Remove the seven valve body attaching bolts.
3. Remove the valve body along with the governor tubes being very careful not to bend or force the tubes. Place the valve body where it will be protected from damage if other transaxle work is to be done.

4. Reverse the removal procedure to install. Torque the valve body attaching bolts to 105 inch-pounds (12N•m).

LOW/REVERSE (REAR) SERVO

Removal and Installation

1. With the valve body removed, disconnect the snap ring, remove the servo retainer and the servo return spring.
2. The low/reverse servo piston can be removed from the bore in the case. Remove the lip seal from the piston.
3. To assemble, install a new lip seal, lubricate with transmission fluid or petroleum jelly and install into the piston bore. Install the return spring, the servo retainer and the snap ring.

KICKDOWN (FRONT) SERVO

Removal and Installation

1. Remove the snap ring with the aid of two small pry bars (1980) or snap ring pliers (1981 and later) from its groove in the case bore.
2. Remove the rod guide, spring and piston rod/servo piston assembly.
3. Separate the piston rod from the servo piston assembly by the removal of the small snap ring. Remove and discard the sealing rings and "O" rings.
4. To assemble and install, place new sealing rings and "O" rings on the piston rod guide, the piston rod and the kickdown piston. Lubricate with transmission fluid or petroleum jelly and assemble in the reverse of the removal procedure.

ACCUMULATOR

Removal and Installation

1. Slightly depress the accumulator plate and remove the snap ring.
2. Remove the accumulator plate, accumulator spring and piston from the case bore. Remove "O" ring and sealing rings.
3. To assemble, install new sealing rings and a new "O" ring. Lubricate with transmission fluid or petroleum jelly and install in the reverse of the removal procedure.

EXTENSION HOUSING

Removal and Installation

1. Remove the four bolts holding the housing to the case.
2. Twist the housing to break it free, turning clockwise and counterclockwise, repeating until the housing comes off. Do not use a prying tool.

———————— CAUTION ————————

If the differential bearing retainer had been removed (the unit opposite the extension, retained by six bolts) prior to the extension housing, hold on to the differential assembly. When the extension housing is removed, the differential assembly will roll out of the housing (providing the differential cover was removed) and fall, damaging the differential and possibly causing personal injury.

3. When reassembling, the extension housing bolts are torqued to 250 inch-pounds (28N•m).

GOVERNOR

Removal and Installation

The governor assembly is a special offset design. No shaft runs through it so it can be removed for service without removing the transfer gear cover, transfer gear or governor support.

1. If the oil pan and valve body have already been removed, just unbolt the governor from the governor support and remove.

NOTE: Since the transfer gears need pullers to remove them, and a special fixture to hold the gear when the transfer shaft nut is removed, (it is torqued to 200 foot-pounds or 270N•m) the above method is the best way to remove the governor for service if there is no need to open up the transfer gear end of the transaxle

2. At reassembly, the governor-to-support screws are torqued to 60 inch-pounds (7N•m).

NOTE: The following assemblies are outlined for removal only. The assembly is outlined during the unit re-assembly.

OIL PUMP

Removal

1. Tighten the front band adjusting screw until the band is tight on the front clutch retainer. This prevents the front clutch retainer from coming out with the pump, which might cause unnecessary damage to the clutches.
2. Remove the seven pump attaching bolts.

─────────────── CAUTION ───────────────

Because the oil pump bolts are metric, conventional non-metric threaded slide hammers cannot be used to pull the pump. Adapters are available to attach to the slide hammer threads, but in no case should non-metric tools be forced into the metric threads.

───

3. Pull oil pump, remove the gasket, and loosen the kickdown band adjusting screw.

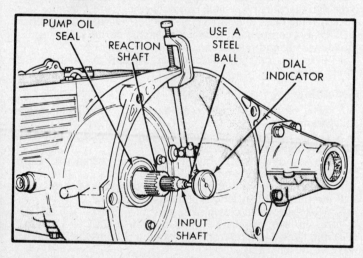

Measuring input shaft end play (©Chrysler Corp.)

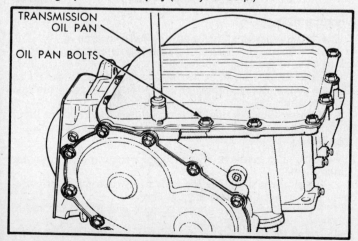

Removing oil pan retaining bolts (©Chrysler Corp.)

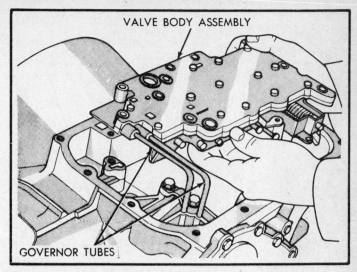

Removal of valve body and governor tubes (©Chrysler Corp.)

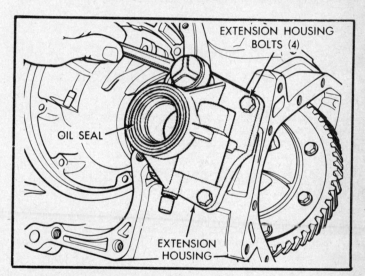

Removing retaining bolts from extension housing (©Chrysler Corp.)

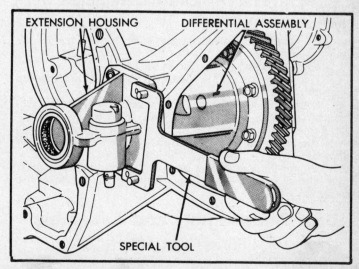

Using special tool to slowly rotate the extension housing during removal or installation (©Chrysler Corp.)

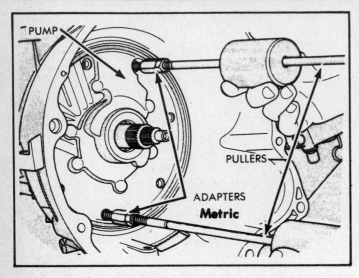

Removal of oil pump with metric pullers (©Chrysler Corp.)

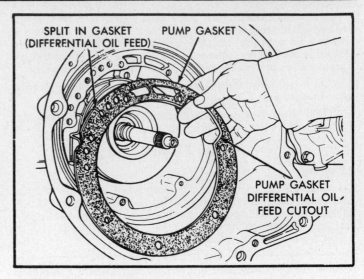

Oil pump gasket removal or installation (©Chrysler Corp.)

Front Unit

FRONT BAND AND CLUTCH

Removal

1. Make sure kickdown band adjusting screw has been loosened after pump removal.
2. Withdraw kickdown band and strut.
3. Slide front clutch assembly out of the case.

INPUT SHAFT AND REAR CLUTCH

Removal

1. Remove the number two thrust washer and grasp the input shaft, pulling it and the rear clutch assembly out of the case.
2. Remove the number three thrust washer from the output shaft.

Rear Unit

PLANETARY GEAR ASSEMBLIES

Removal

1. Remove the front planetary gear snap ring and remove the front planetary gear.
2. Remove the number six thrust washer.
3. Remove the sun gear driving shell and the numbers seven and eight thrust washers.
4. Remove the number nine thrust washer and the rear planetary gear assembly.
5. Remove the number ten thrust washers, the overrunning clutch cam and clutch rollers and springs. There should be eight rollers and eight springs.
6. Remove the low-reverse band and strut and the number eleven thrust washer. (A-413 and A-470—loosen low/reverse band.)

Unit Disassembly and Assembly

FRONT CLUTCH

Disassembly

1. Remove the large, waved snap ring and lift out the thick steel plate.

2. Take particular note of the order of the clutch plates. Through 1980, there are two driving discs and three clutch plates. Note that there are two clutch plates together. 1981 and later uses three driving discs and three clutch plates, stacked alternately.
3. With a compressor, relieve the tension on the snap ring, remove the ring and release the compressor.
4. Take out the spring retainer, spring and piston from the clutch retainer.

Assembly

1. After all parts have been cleaned, renew the seals on the clutch piston.
2. Install the piston; lube the seals with Dexron® II or petroleum jelly to keep from damaging them.
3. Reverse the disassembly procedure and install the return spring, retainer and snap ring.
4. Install the new clutches; make sure the order is correct. Install the thick steel (reaction) plate and snap ring.
5. Make sure front clutch plate clearance is .067-.106 in (1.7-2.7mm) through 1980, and 0.87 to 0.133 inch (2.22 to 3.37mm), 1981 and later. Measure from the reaction plate to the "farthest" wave of the snap ring.

REAR CLUTCH

Disassembly

1. Carefully pry the large snap ring from its groove.
2. Remove the thick steel (reaction) plate and the clutches, taking note of the order.
3. Carefully pry the large, waved snap ring from its groove so that the piston spring and piston can be removed from the rear clutch retainer.
4. Remove the snap ring in the rear clutch retainer if the input shaft is to be removed. The shaft will have to be pressed out.

Assembly

1. After all parts have been cleaned, renew the seals on the clutch piston.
2. Install the piston; lube the seals with Dexron® II or petroleum jelly to keep from damaging them.
3. Reverse the disassembly procedure and install the return spring, retainer and snap ring.
4. Install the new clutches; make sure the order is correct. Install the thick steel (reaction) plate and snap ring, selective. (Refer to specification.)

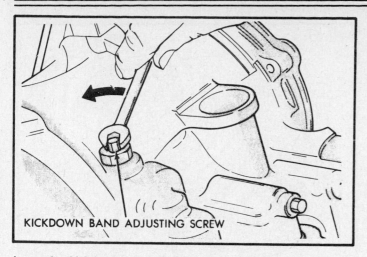

Loosening kickdown band adjusting screw (©Chrysler Corp.)

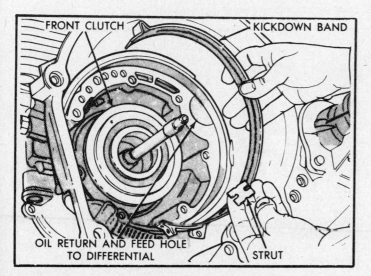

Removal of kickdown band and strut (©Chrysler Corp.)

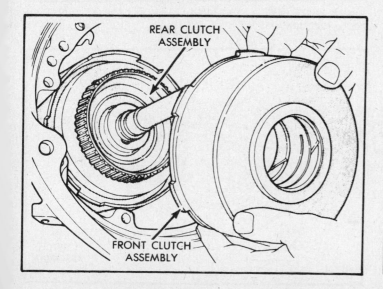

Removal of front clutch assembly (©Chrysler Corp.)

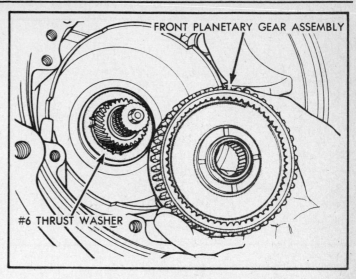

Removal of front planetary assembly (©Chrysler Corp.)

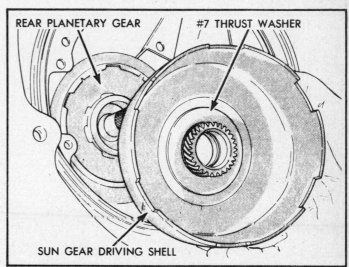

Removal of drive shell (©Chrysler Corp.)

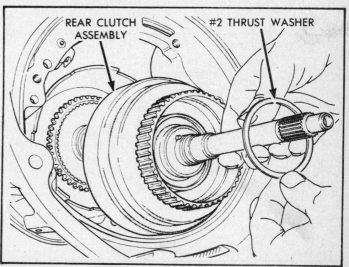

Removal of rear clutch assembly (©Chrysler Corp.)

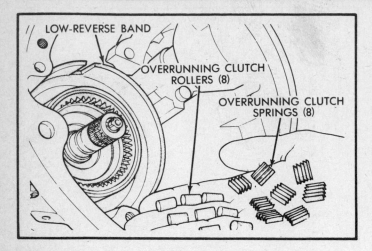

Removal of the overrunning clutch rollers and springs (©Chrysler Corp.)

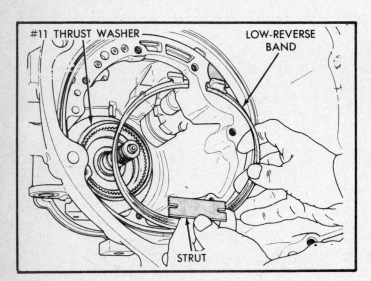

Low-reverse band and strut removal or installation (©Chrysler Corp.)

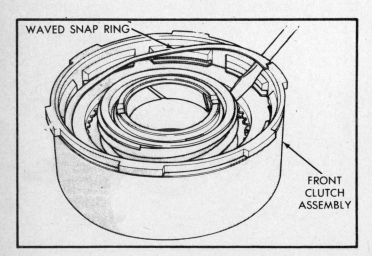

Removal of front clutch waved washer (©Chrysler Corp.)

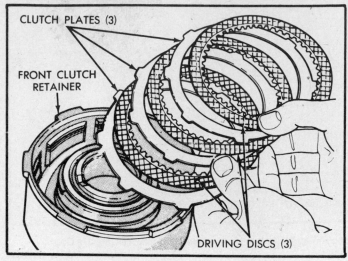

Front clutch disc and plate locations (©Chrysler Corp.)

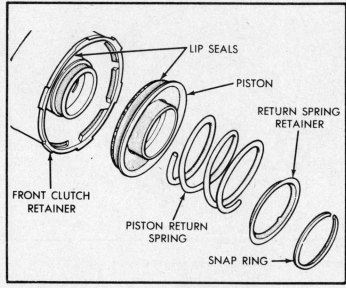

Exploded view of front clutch return spring and piston (©Chrysler Corp.)

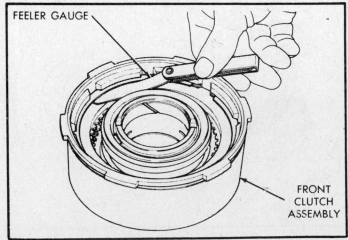

Measuring front clutch plate clearance (©Chrysler Corp.)

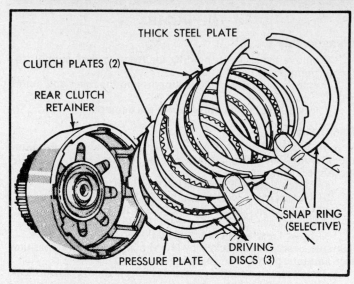

Rear clutch disc and plate location (©Chrysler Corp.)

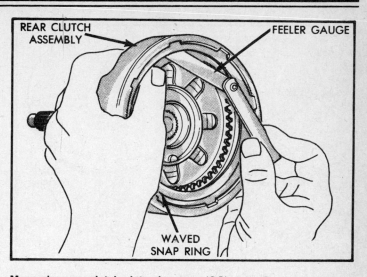

Measuring rear clutch plate clearance (©Chrysler Corp.)

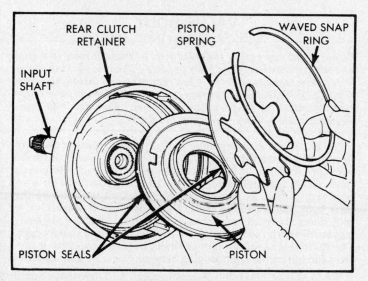

Removal of rear clutch waved snap ring, piston and spring (©Chrysler Corp.)

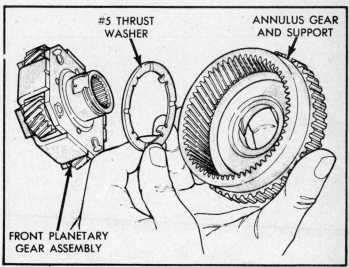

Separation of front planetary gear assembly (©Chrysler Corp.)

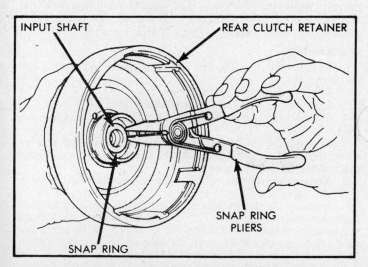

Removal of input shaft, if necessary (©Chrysler Corp.)

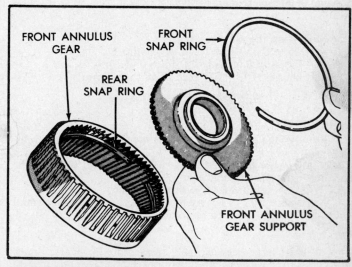

Separation of front annulus gear support from the front annulus gear (©Chrysler Corp.)

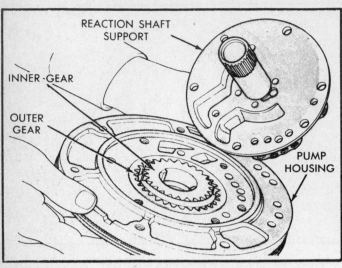

Separation of the reaction shaft support from the pump housing (©Chrysler Corp.)

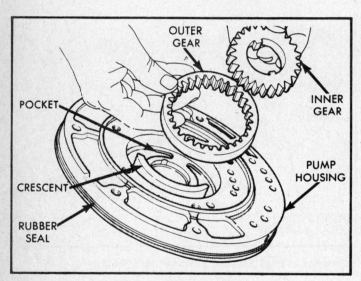

Removal of the pump gears (©Chrysler Corp.)

5. Make sure the plate clearance is:
1980—0.016 to 0.030 inch (0.40 to 0.94mm)
1981-82—0.018 to 0.037 inch (0.46 to 0.95mm)
1983 and later—0.023-0.037 inch (0.58 to 0.95mm)

FRONT PLANETARY

Disassembly

1. Remove the snap ring that holds the planetary to the annulus gear.
2. Remove the number four thrust washer and separate the planetary from the annulus gear.
3. Remove the number five thrust washer.
4. If it is necessary to service the annulus gear support, a small screwdriver can be used to remove the snap ring.

Assembly

After all parts have been cleaned, reassemble in reverse order. Check the thrust washers carefully for excessive wear and inspect the planetary gear carrier for cracks. Check the pinions for broken or worn teeth.

OIL PUMP

Disassembly

1. Remove the six bolts holding the reaction shaft support to the oil pump housing.
2. Remove the reaction shaft support and the inner and outer gears.
3. Clean all parts well and inspect for damage.

Assembly

1. If the inner and outer gears are still serviceable, reinstall in the oil pump body. The clearance must be checked and be with these specifications:
    a. Outer Gear to Pocket, 0.0018 to 0.0056 inch.
    b. Outer Gear I.D to Crescent, 0.0059 to 0.012 inch.
    c. Outer Gear Side Clearance, 0.001 to 0.002 inch.
    d. Inner Gear O.D. to Crescent, 0.0063 to 0.0124 inch.
    e. Inner Gear Side Clearance, 0.001 to 0.002 inch.
The side clearance is checked by laying a straight edge across the face and pump body and inserting a feeler gauge.
2. Install reaction shaft support and torque the six bolts to 250 inch-pounds (28N•m).
3. Renew seals.

VALVE BODY
— CAUTION —
Do not clamp any part of the valve body or transfer plate in a vise. Any slight distortion of the body or plate will cause sticking valves or excessive leakage or both. When removing and installing valves or plugs, slide them in or out very carefully. Do not use force to remove or install valve. Clean all parts well, blow dry with compressed air. Do not dry with shop towels.

NOTE: When disassembling the valve body, identify all valve springs with a tag for assembly reference later. Check parts for burns or nicks. Slight imperfections can be removed with crocus cloth. Using a straightedge, inspect all mating surfaces for warpage or distortion. Be sure all metering holes are open in both the valve body and separator plate. Use a penlight to inspect valve body bores for scratches, burrs, pits or scores. Remove slight irregularities with crocus cloth. Do not round off the sharp edges. The sharpness of these edges is vitally important because it prevents foreign matter from lodging between the valve and the bore.

When valves, plugs and bores are clean and dry, they should fall freely in the bores. Valve bodies and their bores do not change dimensionally with use. Therefore, a valve body that functioned properly when the vehicle was new, will operate properly if it is correctly and thoroughly cleaned. There should be no need to replace a valve body unless it is damaged in handling.

Disassembly

1. Remove the detent spring-attaching screw and remove the detent spring.
2. Remove the valve body screws.
3. Remove the transfer and separator plates.
4. Take note of the location of the 8 steel balls and remove them.
5. Remove the "E"-clip from the throttle valve shaft and remove the washer and oil seal. Lift the manual valve lever from the throttle valve lever assembly.
6. Remove the throttle valve lever and then the manual valve from the valve body.
7. Remove the screws holding the pressure regulator and adjuster assembly to the valve body. Use caution since the springs will be under tension. Do not alter the settings of the throttle pressure adjusting screws. Remove the line pressure valve, switch valve, and kickdown valves and their springs.
8. The governor plugs can be removed after removing their respective end covers.

9. Pressure regulator valve plugs, shift valves and shuttle valve can all be removed after their end covers have been removed. Be careful that the parts do not become mixed. Label parts if necessary.

Assembly

1. To reassemble, reverse the above sequence. Make certain parts are clean.

2. All screws on the valve body are to be torqued to 40 inch-pounds (4.5N•m) with the exception of the transfer plate-to-case screws. These are tightened to 105 inch-pounds (12N•m). Verify the correct position of the check balls.

Transfer and Output Shaft Service

To remove the output shaft, its bearing and select shim, it is recommended that the transfer shaft assembly be removed first. It should be noted that the planetary gear sets must be removed to accurately check the output shaft bearing turning torque. To remove the transfer shaft so that the output shaft can be serviced, follow this procedure.

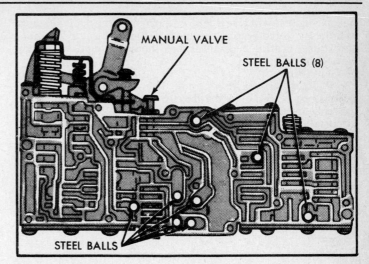

Check ball locations—1981 and later (©Chrysler Corp.)

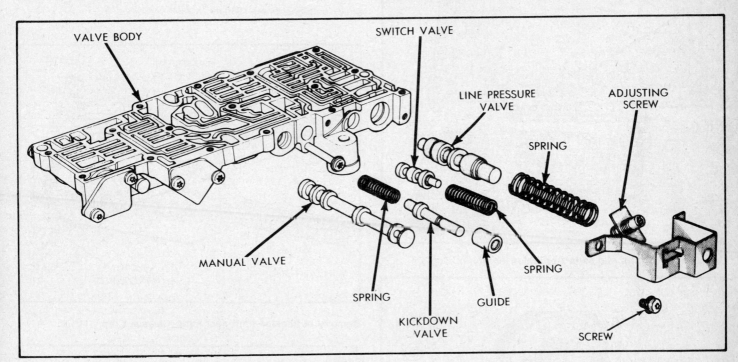

Pressure regulator and manual control valves—1980 (©Chrysler Corp.)

TRANSFER SHAFT

Disassembly

1. Remove the transfer gear cover. There are ten bolts. Note that RTV sealer is to be used on reassembly.

2. Because the nut on the transfer gear shaft has been torqued to 200 foot-pounds (270N•m) a special fixture is needed to hold the gear. A piece of plate or angle iron, drilled to suit the gear and bolted into place should hold the gear while sufficient force is applied to the 30mm socket and wrench to break free the nut. Remove it and the washer.

3. A gear puller is needed to pull the transfer shaft gear from its splined shaft. Note the select shim and bearing. Remove governor support retainer, the low/reverse band anchor pin and the governor assembly.

NOTE: Pullers and/or press will be required to change and in-

stall bearings or bearing cups. They are to be replaced in sets only.

4. With snap ring pliers, reach in alongside the transfer shaft and remove the snap ring at the head of the shaft. The transfer shaft may need the help of a slide hammer puller to help it out, due to a retainer with external seals.

5. Inspect bearings for excessive wear. Renew seals in the retainer.

Transfer Shaft, Output Shaft and Differential Bearing

PRECAUTIONS

Take extreme care when removing and installing bearing cups and cones. Use only an arbor press for installation, a hammer may not properly align the bearing cup or cone. Burrs or nicks on the bearing seat will give a false end play reading while gauging. Improperly seated bearing cup and cones are subject to low mileage failure. Bearing cups and cones should be replaced if they show signs of:

    a. Pitting

    b. Heat Distress

If distress is seen on either the cup or bearing rollers, both the cup and cone must be replaced. Bearing end play and drag torque specifications *must be maintained* to avoid premature bearing failures.

    a. All bearing adjustments, except transfer shaft bearing, must be made with no other gear train component interference or in gear mesh.

    b. Used (original) bearings may loose up to 50% of the original drag torque after break-in.

    c. When replacement of either the output or transfer gear is required, both gears should be replaced in a matched set.

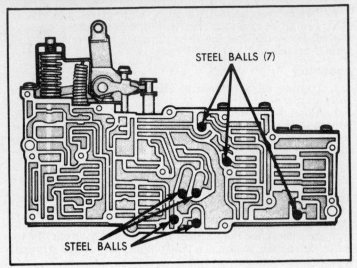

Check ball locations—1980 (©Chrysler Corp.)

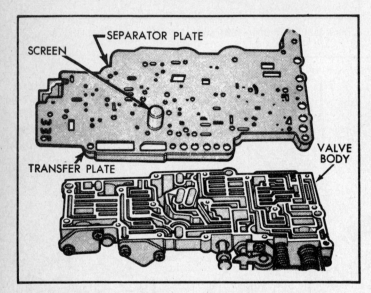

Removal of transfer and separator plates (©Chrysler Corp.)

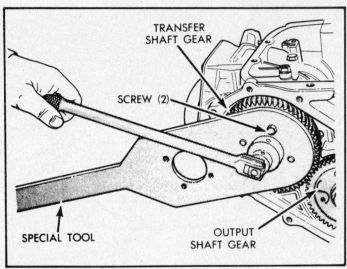

Removal of transfer shaft gear nut (©Chrysler Corp.)

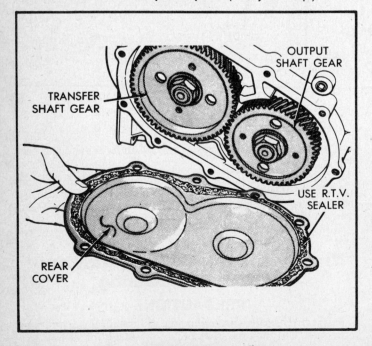

Rear cover removal or installation (©Chrysler Corp.)

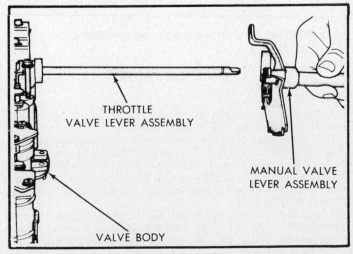

Separation of manual control lever from throttle valve lever after removal of "E" clip retainer (©Chrysler Corp.)

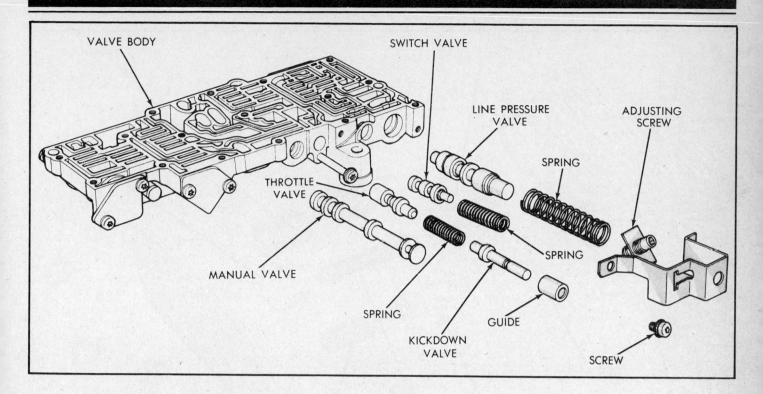

Pressure regulator and manual control valve—1981 and later (©Chrysler Corp.)

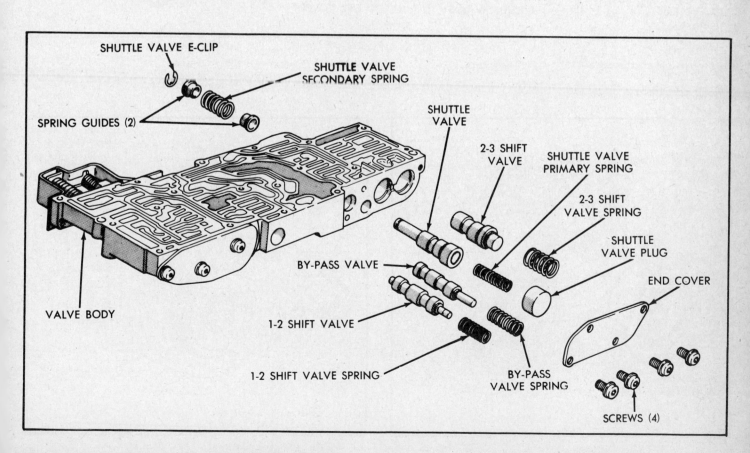

Shift valve and shuttle valve—1981 and later (©Chrysler Corp.)

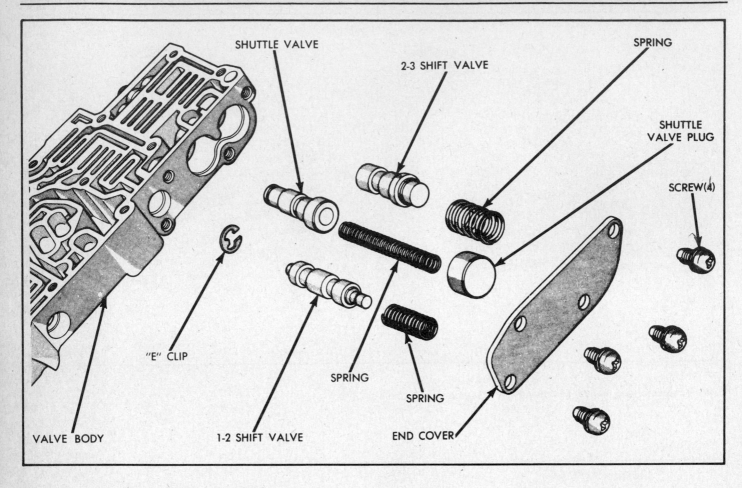

Shift valve and shuttle valve—1980 (©Chrysler Corp.)

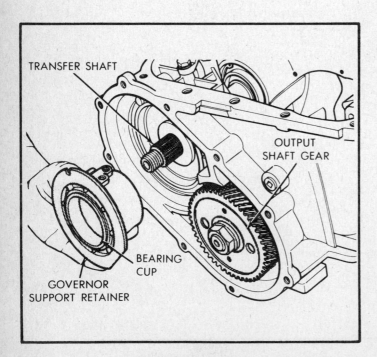

Removal of governor support retainer (©Chrysler Corp.)

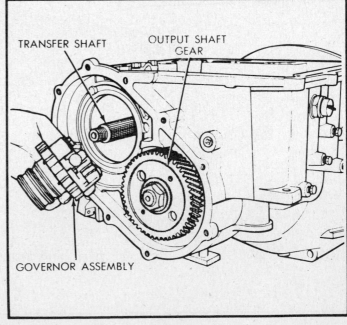

Removal of governor assembly (©Chrysler Corp.)

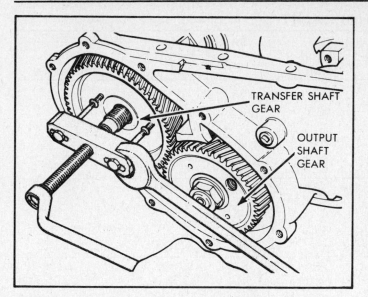

Use of puller to remove transfer shaft gear (©Chrysler Corp.)

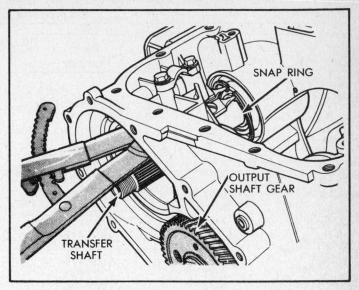

Removal of transfer shaft snap ring (©Chrysler Corp.)

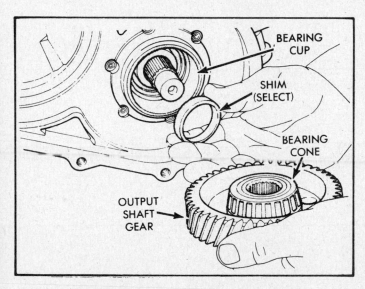

Output shaft gear and selective shims (©Chrysler Corp.)

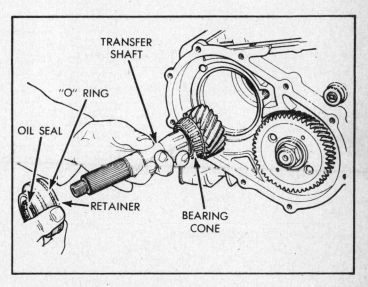

Removal of transfer shaft assembly (©Chrysler Corp.)

TRANSFER SHAFT BEARINGS

1. If the retaining nut and washer are to be removed, use the gear holding tool. Use a gear pulling tool to remove the gear from the shaft.

2. Install a 0.090 inch (2.29 mm) and 0.055 inch (1.39 mm) gauging shims on the transfer shaft behind the governor support.

3. Install transfer shaft gear and bearing assembly and torque nut to 200 foot-pounds (271 N•m).

NOTE: A few drops of Automatic Transmission Fluid applied to the bearing rollers will ensure proper seating and rolling resistance.

4. To measure bearing end play:
   a. Mount a steel ball with grease on the end of the transfer shaft.
   b. Push down on the gear while rotating back and forth to ensure proper seating of the bearing rollers.

   c. Using a dial indicator mounted to the transaxle case, measure transfer shaft end play by raising and lowering gear.

5. Refer to the Transfer Shaft Bearing Shim Chart for the required shim combination to obtain the proper bearing setting.

6. Use gear holding tool to remove the retaining nut and washer. Remove the transfer gear using a gear puller.

7. Remove the two gauging shims and install the correct shim combination. Install the transfer gear and bearing assembly.

8. Install the retaining nut and washer and torque to 200 foot-pounds (271 N•m).

9. Measure bearing end play as outlined in step 4. End play should be between 0.002 and 0.010 inch (0.05 mm and 0.25 mm).

NOTE: If end play is too high, install a 0.002 inch (0.05 mm) thinner shim combination. If end play is too low, install a 0.002 inch (0.05 mm) thicker shim combination. Repeat until the proper end play is obtained.

BEARING SHIM CHART

Shim Thickness			Bearing Usage		
mm	Inch	Part Number	Output Shaft	Transfer Shaft	Differential
0.94	.037	4207166	x	x	—
0.99	.039	4207167	x	x	—
1.04	.041	4207168	x	x	—
1.09	.043	4207169	x	x	—
1.14	.045	4207170	x	x	—
1.19	.047	4207171	x	x	—
1.14	.049	4207172	x	x	—
1.29	.051	4207173	x	x	—
1.34	.053	4207174	x①	x	—
1.39	.055	4207175	x	x①	—
1.84	.072	4207176	x	x	—
2.29	.090	4207177	x	x①	—
6.65	.262	4207159	x	—	—
7.15	.281	4207160	x	—	—
7.65	.301	4207161	x①	—	—
12.65	.498	4207162	x	—	—
13.15	.518	4207163	x	—	—
13.65	.537	4207164	x①	—	—
0.50	.020	4207134	—	—	x①
0.55	.022	4207135	—	—	x
0.60	.024	4207136	—	—	x
0.65	.026	4207137	—	—	x
0.70	.027	4207138	—	—	x
0.75	.029	4207139	—	—	x
0.80	.031	4207140	—	—	x
0.85	.033	4207141	—	—	x
0.90	.035	4207142	—	—	x
0.95	.037	4207143	—	—	x
1.00	.039	4207144	—	—	x
1.05	.041	4207145	—	—	x

①Also used as gauging shims

OUTPUT SHAFT

Disassembly

1. Using the same holding tool as was used on the transfer shaft gear, hold the output shaft gear securely and remove the nut and washer from the shaft.

2. With a puller, remove the output shaft gear from the shaft. Take note of the selective shim.

3. Remove the output shaft and annulus gear assembly. The shaft is a press fit in the annulus gear and must be pressed in and out.

SHIM THICKNESS

TRANSFER SHAFT

Shim thickness needs only to be determined if any of the following parts are replaced: (a) transaxle case, (b) transfer shaft, (c) transfer shaft gear, (d) transfer shaft bearings, (e) governor support retainer, (f) transfer shaft bearing retainer, (g) retainer snap ring and (h) governor support.

OUTPUT SHAFT

Shim thickness need only to be determined if any of the following parts are replaced: (a) transaxle case, (b) output shaft, (c) rear planetary annulus gear, (d) output shaft gear, (e) rear annulus and output shaft gear bearing cones, and (f) overrunning clutch race cups.

The output shaft bearing turning torque is 3 to 8 inch-pounds if the proper shim has been installed.

Differential Service

Disassembly

1. As described previously, remove the transfer shaft assembly.

2. Remove the ten differential cover bolts. Note that RTV sealer is to be used on reassembly.

3. With a 13mm socket, remove the six differential bearing retainer bolts.

4. Gently rotate the bearing retainer back and forth and pull out of the case.

TRANSFER BEARING SHIM CHART

End Play (with 2.29mm and 1.39mm gauging shims installed)		Required Shim Combination	Total Thickness	
mm	Inch	mm	mm	Inch
0	0	2.29+1.39	3.68	.145
.05	.002	2.29+1.39	3.68	.145
.10	.004	2.29+1.39	3.68	.145
.15	.006	2.29+1.39	3.68	.145
.20	.008	2.29+1.34	3.63	.143
.25	.010	2.29+1.29	3.58	.141
.30	.012	2.29+1.24	3.53	.139
.35	.014	2.29+1.19	3.48	.137
.40	.016	2.29+1.14	3.43	.135
.45	.018	2.29+1.09	3.38	.133
.50	.020	2.29+1.04	3.33	.131
.55	.022	2.29+ .99	3.28	.129
.60	.024	1.84+1.39	3.23	.127
.65	.026	1.84+1.34	3.18	.125
.70	.028	1.84+1.29	3.13	.123
.75	.030	1.84+1.24	3.08	.121
.80	.032	1.84+1.19	3.03	.119
.85	.034	1.84+1.14	2.98	.117
.90	.036	1.84+1.09	2.93	.115
.95	.038	1.84+1.04	2.88	.113
1.00	.040	1.84+ .99	2.83	.111
1.05	.042	1.39+1.39	2.78	.109
1.10	.044	1.39+1.34	2.73	.107
1.15	.046	1.39+1.29	2.68	.105
1.20	.048	1.39+1.24	2.63	.103
1.25	.049	1.39+1.19	2.58	.101
1.30	.050	1.39+1.14	2.53	.099
1.35	.052	1.39+1.09	2.48	.097
1.40	.055	1.39+1.04	2.43	.095
1.45	.057	1.39+ .99	2.38	.093
1.50	.059	.94+1.39	2.33	.091
1.55	.061	.94+1.34	2.28	.089
1.60	.063	.94+1.29	2.23	.087

5. With a 13mm socket, remove the four extension housing bolts.

6. Gently rotate the extension housing back and forth and pull out of the case.

—— CAUTION ——

When the extension housing is pulled out, the differential assembly will roll out of the case. To prevent damage, hold on to the differential assembly when removing extension housing.

NOTE: Pullers and/or press will be required to change and install bearings or bearing cups. They are to be replaced in sets only.

7. To remove pinion shaft, first withdraw the roll pin. Use a screw extractor like an "Easy-Out" and pull the pin from the case. Drive the pinion shaft out with a brass drift and hammer.

8. Remove the pinion gears and side gears as well as the four thrust washers by rotating the pinion gears to the opening in the differential case.

9. If the ring gear is to be removed, take note that a 10mm, 12 point socket will be required. There are eight bolts. Upon reassembly, they are to be torqued to 70 foot-pounds (95 N•m).

NOTE: Immerse the ring gear in boiling water for 15 minutes before installing ring gear onto the differential case.

10. Renew the seal in the differential bearing retainer.

NOTE: Shim thickness need only be determined if any of the following parts are replaced: a. transaxle case, b. differential carrier, c. differential bearing retainer, d. extension housing, or e. differential bearings.

Refer to the "Bearing Adjustment Outline" to determine the proper shim thickness for correct bearing preload and proper bearing turning torque.

Assembly

1. Reverse the above procedure to reassemble the differential. Torque the ring gear bolts to 70 foot-pounds (95 N•m). Be sure to install the pinion shaft with the proper end out to receive the roll pin. Inspect bearings and cups. Renew the seal in extension housing before assembling. Extension housing bolts are torqued to 250 inch-pounds (28 N•m), the bearing retainer bolts are also torqued to 250 inch-pounds (28 N•m).

NOTE: Install the differential cover without sealer, temporarily, since the axle (drive shaft) circlips should be checked after installation for proper seating. If the circlips fit satisfactorily, then the cover, with RTV sealer, can be fitted and the bolts torqued to 165 inch-pounds (19 N•m).

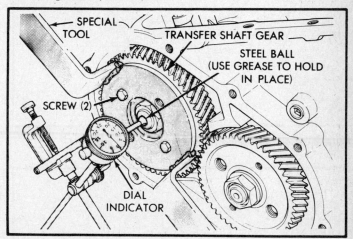

Checking transfer shaft end play (©Chrysler Corp.)

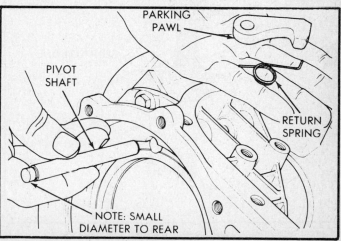

Parking pawl removal or installation (©Chrysler Corp.)

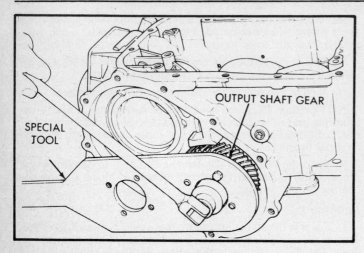

Removing output shaft retaining nut and washer (©Chrysler Corp.)

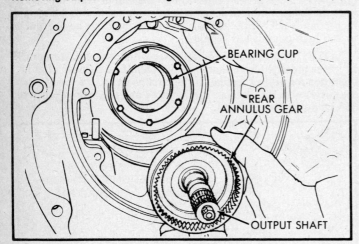

Removal of output shaft and rear annulus gear assembly (©Chrysler Corp.)

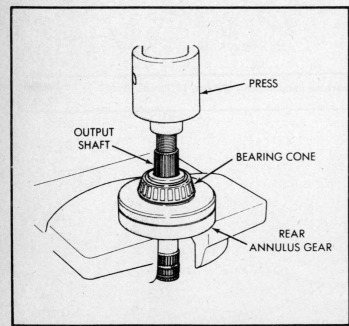

Removal of output shaft from rear planetary annulus gear (©Chrysler Corp.)

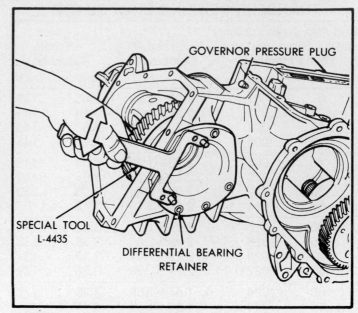

Rotate bearing retainer to remove (©Chrysler Corp.)

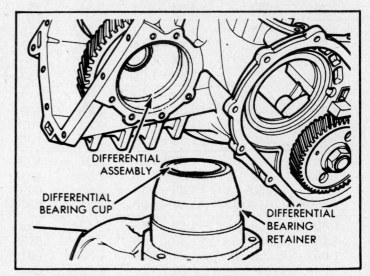

Differential bearing retainer (©Chrysler Corp.)

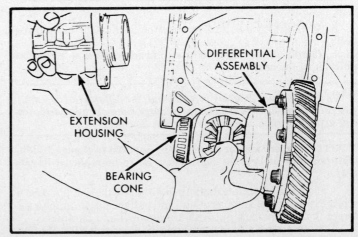

Holding differential carrier when removing the extension housing and bearing retainer (©Chrysler Corp.)

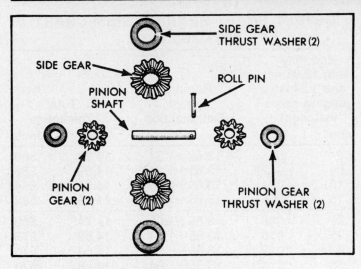

Exploded view of pinion gear set (©Chrysler Corp.)

OUTPUT SHAFT BEARINGS

1980

1. If the retaining nut and washer are to be removed, use the gear holding tool. Use a gear puller to remove the gear from the shaft.

2. With output shaft gear removed, install a 0.301 inch (7.65 mm) gauging shim on the planetary rear annulus gear hub and a 0.053 inch (1.34 mm) gauging shim on the output shaft using lubriplate to hold the shims in place. The 7.65 mm shim has a larger inside diameter and must be installed first. The 1.34 mm shim pilots on the output shaft.

3. Install output shaft gear and bearing assembly, torque the retaining nut to 200 foot-pounds (271 N•m).

NOTE: A few drops of Automatic Transmission Fluid applied to the bearing rollers will ensure proper seating and rolling resistance.

4. To measure bearing end play:
   a. Mount a steel ball with lubriplate on the end of the output shaft.
   b. Push down on the gear while rotating back and forth to ensure seating of the bearing rollers.
   c. Using a dial indicator, mounted to the transaxle case, measure output shaft end play by moving the gear up and down.

5. Once bearing end play has been determined, refer to the Output Shaft Bearing Shim Chart for the required shim combination to obtain proper bearing setting.

NOTE: a. The 6.65 mm (.262 inch) 7.15 mm (.281 inch) or 7.65 mm (.301 inch) shim is always installed first. These shims have a lubrication hole which is necessary for proper bearing lubrication.
   b. Shims thinner than 6.65 mm listed in the chart are common to both the transfer and output shaft bearings.

6. Remove the retaining nut and washer. Remove the output shaft gear.

7. Remove the two gauging shims and install the proper shim combination, making sure to install the 6.65, 7.15, or 7.65 mm shim first. Use lubriplate to hold the shims in place. Install the output gear and bearing assembly.

8. Install the retaining nut and washer and torque to 200 foot-pounds (271 N•m).

9. Using an inch-pound torque wrench, check the turning torque. The torque should be between 3 to 8 inch-pounds.

NOTE: If the turning torque is too high, install a 0.002 inch (0.050 mm) thicker shim. If the turning torque is too low, install a

0.002 inch (0.050 mm) thinner shim. Repeat until the proper turning torque of 3 to 8 inch-pounds is obtained.

OUTPUT SHAFT BEARING SHIM CHART 1980

End Play (with 7.65mm and 1.34mm gauging shims installed)		Required Shim Combination	Total Thickness	
mm	Inch	mm	mm	Inch
0	0	7.65 + 1.34	8.99	.354
.05	.002	7.65 + 1.24	8.89	.350
.10	.004	7.65 + 1.19	8.84	.348
.15	.006	7.65 + 1.14	8.79	.346
.20	.008	7.65 + 1.09	8.74	.344
.25	.010	7.65 + 1.04	8.69	.342
.30	.012	7.65 + .99	8.64	.340
.35	.014	7.65 + .94	8.59	.338
.40	.016	7.15 + 1.39	8.54	.336
.45	.018	7.15 + 1.34	8.49	.334
.50	.020	7.15 + 1.29	8.44	.332
.55	.022	7.15 + 1.24	8.39	.330
.60	.024	7.15 + 1.19	8.34	.328
.65	.026	7.15 + 1.14	8.29	.326
.70	.028	7.15 + 1.09	8.24	.324
.75	.030	7.15 + 1.04	8.19	.322
.80	.032	7.15 + .99	8.14	.320
.85	.034	7.15 + .94	8.09	.318
.90	.036	6.65 + 1.39	8.04	.316
.95	.038	6.65 + 1.34	7.99	.314
1.00	.040	6.65 + 1.29	7.94	.312
1.05	.042	6.65 + 1.24	7.89	.311
1.10	.044	6.65 + 1.19	7.84	.309
1.15	.046	6.65 + 1.14	7.79	.307
1.20	.048	6.65 + 1.09	7.74	.305
1.25	.049	6.65 + 1.04	7.69	.303
1.30	.051	6.65 + .99	7.64	.301
1.35	.053	6.65 + .94	7.59	.299

Note: Average Conversion .05mm = .002 inch

1981 AND LATER

With output shaft gear removed.

1. Install a 0.537 inch (13.65 mm) and a 0.053 inch (1.34 mm) gauging shims on the planetary rear annulus gear hub using grease to hold the shims in place. The 13.65 mm shim has a larger inside diameter and must be installed over the output shaft first. The 1.34 mm shim pilots on the output shaft.

2. Install output shaft gear and bearing assembly, torque to 200 ft. lbs. (271 N•m).

3. To measure bearing end play:
   a. Mount a steel ball with grease into the end of the output shaft.
   b. Push and pull the gear while rotating back and forth to insure seating of the bearing rollers.
   c. Using a dial indicator, mounted to the transaxle case, measure output shaft end play by raising and lowering gear.

4. Once bearing end play has been determined, refer to the output shaft bearing shim chart for the required shim combination to obtain proper bearing setting.

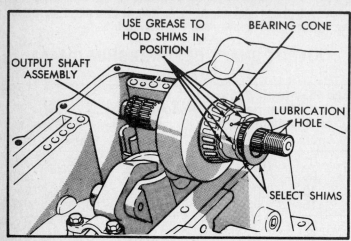

Installing output shaft assembly with selective shim held in place with grease (©Chrysler Corp.)

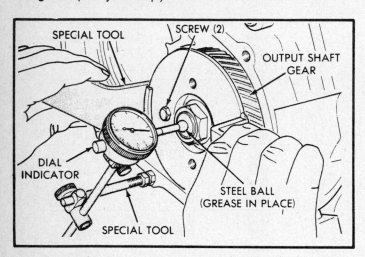

Checking output shaft and end play (©Chrysler Corp.)

a. The 0.498 inch (12.65 mm), 0.518 inch (13.15 mm), 0.537 inch (13.65 mm) shims are always installed first. These shims have lubrication slots which are necessary for proper bearing lubrication.

b. Shims thinner than 12.65 mm listed in the chart are common to both the transfer shaft and output shaft bearings.

5. Remove the retaining nut and washer. Remove the output shaft gear.

6. Remove the two gauging shims and install the proper shim combination, making sure to install the 12.65, 13.15, or 13.65 mm shim first. Use grease to hold the shims in place. Install the output shaft gear and bearing assembly.

7. Install the retaining nut and washer and torque to 200 ft. lbs. (271 N•m).

8. Using an inch-pound torque wrench, check the turning torque. The torque should be between 3 and 8 inch-pounds.

NOTE: If the turning torque is too high, install a 0.002 inch (0.050 mm) thicker shim. If the turning torque is too low, install a 0.002 inch (0.050 mm) thinner shim. Repeat until the proper turning torque is 3 to 8 inch pounds.

DIFFERENTIAL BEARINGS

NOTE: The use of special tools are noted in the outline and those that have been approved by Chrysler Corporation, or their equivalents, should be used when making the following critical measurements.

OUTPUT SHAFT BEARING SHIM CHART
1981 and Later

End Play (with 13.65mm and 1.34mm gauging shims installed)		Required Shim Combination	Total Thickness	
mm	Inch	mm	mm	Inch
.0	.0	13.65+1.34	14.99	.590
.05	.002	13.65+1.24	14.89	.586
.10	.004	13.65+1.19	14.84	.584
.15	.006	13.65+1.14	14.79	.582
.20	.008	13.65+1.09	14.74	.580
.25	.010	13.65+1.04	14.69	.578
.30	.012	13.65+ .99	14.64	.576
.35	.014	13.65+ .94	14.59	.574
.40	.016	13.15+1.39	14.54	.572
.45	.018	13.15+1.34	14.49	.570
.50	.020	13.15+1.29	14.44	.568
.55	.022	13.15+1.24	14.39	.566
.60	.024	13.15+1.19	14.34	.564
.65	.026	13.15+1.14	14.29	.562
.70	.028	13.15+1.09	14.24	.560
.75	.030	13.15+1.04	14.19	.558
.80	.032	13.15+ .99	14.14	.556
.85	.034	13.15+ .94	14.09	.554
.90	.036	12.65+1.39	14.04	.552
.95	.038	12.65+1.34	13.99	.550
1.00	.040	12.65+1.29	13.94	.548
1.05	.042	12.65+1.24	13.89	.547
1.10	.044	12.65+1.19	13.84	.545
1.15	.046	12.65+1.14	13.79	.543
1.20	.048	12.65+1.09	13.74	.541
1.25	.049	12.65+1.04	13.69	.539
1.30	.051	12.65+ .99	13.64	.537
1.35	.053	12.65+ .94	13.59	.535

Average Conversion .05mm = .002 inch

1. Remove the bearing cup from the differential bearing retainer and remove the existing shim, from under the cup. The original shim should not be re-used.

2. Install a 0.020 inch (0.50 mm) gauging shim, and reinstall the bearing cup into the retainer. Use an arbor press to install the cup.

NOTE: A few drops of Automatic Transmission Fluid applied to the bearing rollers will ensure proper seating and rolling resistance.

3. Install the bearing retainer into the case and the torque bolts to 250 inch-pounds (28 N•m).

4. Position the transaxle assembly vertically on the support stand and install Tool L-4436 or its equivalent, into the extension.

5. Rotate the differential assembly at least on full revolution to ensure the tapered roller bearings are fully seated.

6. Attach a dial indicator to the case and zero the indicator on the flat end of Tool L-4436 or its equivalent.

7. Place a large screwdriver to each side of the ring gear and

lift with enough force to take up the clearance between the bearings. Check the dial indicator for the amount of end play. Caution should be used not to damage the transmission case and/or differential cover sealing surface.

8. Once the end play has been determined, refer to the differential bearing shim chart for the required shim combination to obtain the proper bearing setting.

9. Remove the differential bearing retainer. Remove the bearing cup and the 0.020 inch (0.50 mm) gauging shim.

10. Install the proper shim combination under the bearing cup. Make sure the oil baffle is installed properly in the bearing retainer below the bearing shim and cup.

11. Install the differential retainer. Make sure to seal the retainer to the housing with RTV sealer and torque the bolts to 250 inch-pounds (28 N•m).

12. Using special Tool L-4436 or its equivalent, and an inch-pound torque wrench, check the turning torque of the differential. The turning torque should be between 5 and 18 inch-pounds.

NOTE: If the turning torque is too high, install a 0.002 inch (0.050 mm) thinner shim. If the turning torque is too low, install a 0.002 inch (0.050 mm) thicker shim. Repeat until 5 to 18 inch-pounds turning torque is obtained.

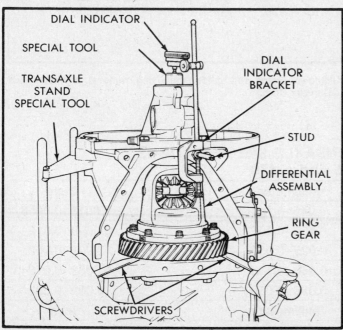

Checking differential bearing end play (©Chrysler Corp.)

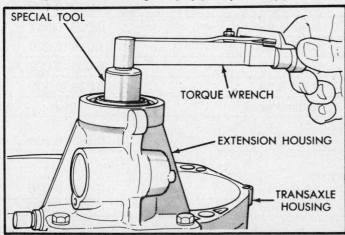

Checking differential bearing turning torque (©Chrysler Corp.)

DIFFERENTIAL BEARING SHIM CHART

End Play (with .50mm gauging shim installed)		Required Shim Combination		Total Thickness	
mm	Inch	mm		mm	Inch
0	0	.50		.50	.020
.05	.002	.75		.75	.030
.10	.004	.80		.80	.032
.15	.006	.85		.85	.034
.20	.008	.90		.90	.035
.25	.010	.95		.95	.037
.30	.012	1.00		1.00	.039
.35	.014	1.05		1.05	.041
.40	.016	.50 +	.60	1.10	.043
.45	.018	.50 +	.65	1.15	.045
.50	.020	.50 +	.70	1.20	.047
.55	.022	.50 +	.75	1.25	.049
.60	.024	.50 +	.80	1.30	.051
.65	.026	.50 +	.85	1.35	.053
.70	.027	.50 +	.90	1.40	.055
.75	.029	.50 +	.95	1.45	.057
.80	.031	.50 +	1.00	1.50	.059
.85	.033	.50 +	1.05	1.55	.061
.90	.035	1.00 +	.60	1.60	.063
.95	.037	1.00 +	.65	1.65	.065
1.00	.039	1.00 +	.70	1.70	.067
1.05	.041	1.00 +	.75	1.75	.069
1.10	.043	1.00 +	.80	1.80	.071
1.15	.045	1.00 +	.85	1.85	.073
1.20	.047	1.00 +	.90	1.90	.075
1.25	.049	1.00 +	.95	1.95	.077
1.30	.051	1.00 +	1.00	2.00	.079
1.35	.053	1.00 +	1.05	2.05	.081
1.40	.055	1.05 +	1.05	2.10	.083

Transaxle Assembly

NOTE: When assembling this unit, use only automatic transmission fluid or petroleum jelly to lubricate the transmission components.

With the transmission case thoroughly cleaned and the various sub assemblies overhauled and assembled, the assembly procedure is as follows:

1. Install the low-reverse band (rear) and strut assembly into the case along with the #11 thrust washer.

2. Install the overrunning clutch rollers and springs into the cam assembly and install into the case along with the #10 thrust washer.

3. Install the #9 thrust washer and the rear planetary gear assembly. Use petroleum jelly to retain the thrust washer if necessary.

4. Install the sun gear driving shell and the #7 thrust washer onto the rear planetary gear.

5. The #6 thrust washer is installed followed by the front planetary gear carrier and carefully set into the driving shell. Install the front planetary gear snap ring.

6. Install the #3 thrust washer. Install the #2 thrust washer onto the rear clutch assembly and install into the case.

7. Install the front clutch assembly onto the rear clutch assembly.

8. Install the kickdown band and strut assembly. Snug down the adjusting screw temporarily to help hold the band in place.

9. Lube the pump outer seal and install into the case. Use a new gasket. Torque the bolts to specifications.

10. Install the overhauled valve body along with the governor tubes into the case. Install the valve body attaching screws and torque to specifications. Adjust bands as required.

11. Install the parking rod and retain with the "E" clip.

12. Install a new oil filter

13. Install the oil pan using RTV sealer.

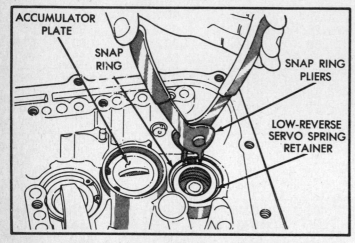

Removal or installation of low-reverse servo snap ring with location of accumulator assembly noted (©Chrysler Corp.)

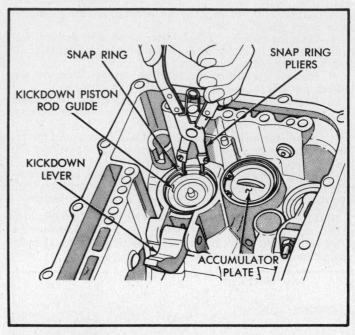

Kickdown piston rod guide snap ring removal or installation (©Chrysler Corp.)

TORQUEFLITE AUTOMATIC TRANSAXLE SPECIFICATIONS
A-404, A-413, A-415 and A-470

Pump clearances	Millimeter	Inch
Outer gear to pocket	0.045 -0.141	0.0018 -0.0056
Outer gear I.D. to crescent	0.150 -0.306	0.0059 -0.012
Outer gear side clearance	0.025 -0.050	0.001 -0.002
Inner gear O.D. to crescent	0.160 -0.316	0.0063 -0.0124
Inner gear side clearance	0.025 -0.050	0.001 -0.002
End play	**Millimeter**	**Inch**
Input shaft	0.18 -1.85	0.007 -0.073
Front clutch retainer	0.76 -2.69	0.030 -0.106
Front carrier	0.89 -1.45	0.007 -0.057
Front annulus gear	0.09 -0.50	0.0035 -0.020
Planet pinion	0.15 -0.59	0.006 -0.023
Reverse drum	0.76 -3.36	0.030 -0.132
Clutch clearance and selective snap rings	**Millimeter**	**Inch**
Front clutch (non-adjustable measured from reaction plate to "farthest" wave) (1980)	1.7 -2.7	0.067 -0.106
Front clutch (non-adjustable measured from reaction plate to "farthest" wave) (1981 and Later) three disc	1.14 -2.45	0.045 -0.096
two disc	0.86 -2.03	0.034 -0.080
Rear clutch (all are three disc) Adjustable	0.40-0.94	0.016-0.037

TORQUEFLITE AUTOMATIC TRANSAXLE SPECIFICATIONS
A-404, A-413, A-415 and A-470

Clutch clearance and selective snap rings		Millimeter	Inch
Sun gear drive shell, steel	Nos. 7, 8	0.85 -0.91	0.033 -0.036
1981 and later			
Front Carrier, Steel Backed Bronze	Nos. 5, 6	1.22 -1.28	0.048 -0.050
Sun Gear (Front)	No. 7	0.85 -0.91	0.033 -0.036
Sun Gear (Rear)	No. 8	0.85 -0.91	0.033 -0.036
Rear Carrier, Steel Backed Bronze	Nos. 9, 10	1.22 -1.28	0.048 -0.050
All			
Rev. drum, phenolic	No. 11	1.55 -1.60	0.061 -0.063

Tapered roller bearing settings		Millimeter	Inch
Output shaft		0.0-0.07 preload	0.0 -0.0028
Transfer shaft		0.05-0.25 end play	0.002-0.010
Differential		0.15-0.29 preload	0.006-0.012
Selective Snap Rings (3)		1.52-1.57	0.060-0.062
		1.93-1.98	0.076-0.078
		2.36-2.41	0.093-0.095

Band Adjustment:

Kickdown, Backed off from 8 N•m (72 in. lbs.)		A-404 3 Turns,
		A-413 & A-470
		1981 —2 turns
		1982 and later—2¾ turns
Low-Reverse	A-404	non-adjustable
	A-413 & A-470	3½ Turns backed off from 5 N•m (41 in. lbs.)

Thrust washers		Millimeter	Inch
All			
Reaction shaft support (phenolic)	No. 1	1.55 -1.60	0.061 -0.063
Rear clutch retainer (phenolic)	No. 2	1.55 -1.60	0.061 -0.063
Output shaft, steel backed bronze	No. 3	1.55 -1.65	0.061 -0.065
Front annulus, steel backed bronze	No. 4	2.95 -3.05	0.116 -0.120
1980			
Carrier, steel backed bronze	Nos. 5, 6, 9, 10	1.22 -1.28	0.048 -0.050

TORQUE SPECIFICATIONS
A-404, A-413, A-415 and A-470 Automatic Transaxle

		Torque	
	Qty	Newton-meters	Inch-Pounds
BOLT, SCREW OR NUT			
Bolt—Bell Housing Cover	3	12	105
Bolt—Flex Plate to Crank (A-404)	6	68	50 ① ② ③
Bolt—Flex Plate to Torque Converter (A-404)	3	54	40 ① ④
Screw Assy. Transaxle to Cyl. Block	3	95	70 ①
Screw Assy. Lower Bell Housing Cover	3	12	105
Screw Assy. Manual Control Lever	1	12	105
Screw Assy. Speedometer to Extension	1	7	60
Connector, Cooler Hose to Radiator	2	12	110
Bolt—Starter to Transaxle Bell Housing	3	54	40 ①

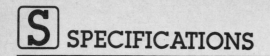

TORQUE SPECIFICATIONS
A-404, A-413, A-415 and A-470 Automatic Transaxle

	Qty	Torque Newton-meters	Torque Inch-Pounds
BOLT, SCREW OR NUT			
Bolt—Throttle Cable to Transaxle Case	1	12	105
Bolt—Throttle Lever to Transaxle Shaft	1	12	105
Bolt—Manual Cable to Transaxle Case	1	28	250
Bolt—Front Motor Mount	2	54	40①
Bolt—Left Motor Mount	3	54	40①
CASE			
Connector Assembly, Cooler Line	2	28	250
Plug, Pressure Check	7	5	45
Switch, Neutral Safety	1	34	25①
DIFFERENTIAL AREA			
Ring Gear Screw	8	95	70①
Bolt, Extension to Case	4	28	250
Bolt, Differential Bearing Retainer to Case	6	28	250
Screw Assy., Differential Cover to Case	10	19	165
TRANSFER & OUTPUT SHAFT AREAS			
Nut, Output Shaft	1	271	200①
Nut. Transfer Shaft	1	271	200①
Bolt, Gov to Support	2	7	60
Bolt, Gov to Support	1	7	60
Screw Assy., Governor Counterweight	1	28	250
Screw Assy., Rear Cover to Case	10	19	165
Plug, Reverse Band Shaft	1	7	60
PUMP & KICKDOWN BAND AREAS			
Bolt, Reaction Shaft Assembly	6	28	250
Bolt Assy., Pump to Case	7	31	275
Nut, Kickdown Band Adjustment Lock	1	47	35①
VALVE BODY & SPRAG AREAS			
Bolt, Sprag Retainer to Transfer Case	2	28	250
Screw Assy., Valve Body	16	5	40
Screw Assy., Transfer Plate	16	5	40
Screw Assy., Filter	2	5	40
Screw, Transfer Plate to Case	7	12	105
Screw Assy., Oil Pan to Case	14	19	165
Nut, Reverse Band Adjusting Lock	1	14	120

① Foot pounds
② A-413 = 88 N•m 65 ft. lbs.
③ A-470 = 136 N•m 100 ft. lbs.
④ A-413 and A-470 = 54 N•m 40 ft. lbs.

SPECIAL TOOLS

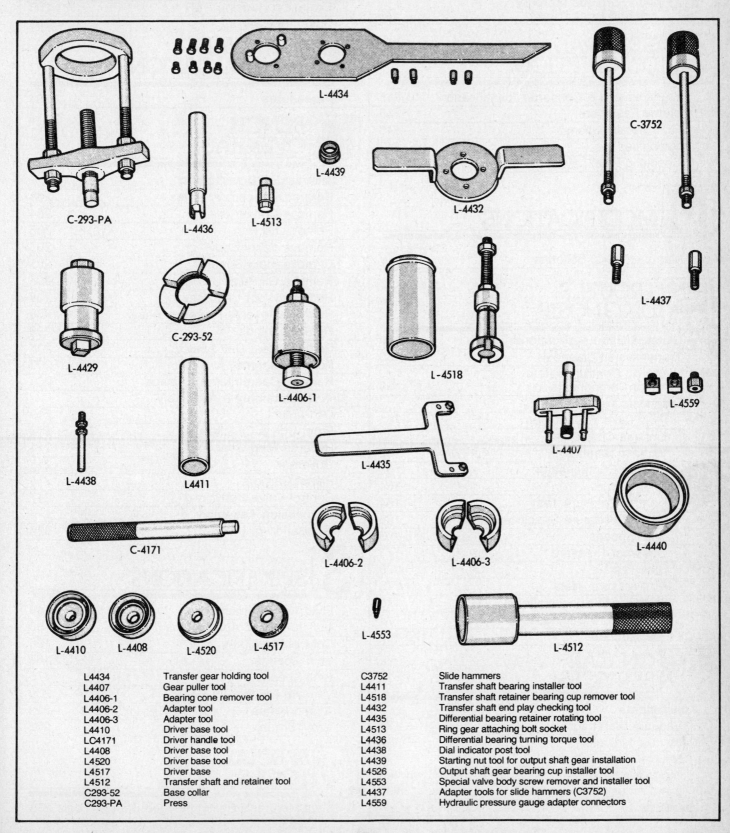

C-293-PA
L-4436
L-4513
L-4439
L-4434
L-4432
C-3752
L-4429
C-293-52
L-4406-1
L-4518
L-4437
L-4438
L4411
L-4435
L-4407
L-4559
C-4171
L-4406-2
L-4406-3
L-4440
L-4410
L-4408
L-4520
L-4517
L-4553
L-4512

L4434	Transfer gear holding tool		C3752	Slide hammers
L4407	Gear puller tool		L4411	Transfer shaft bearing installer tool
L4406-1	Bearing cone remover tool		L4518	Transfer shaft retainer bearing cup remover tool
L4406-2	Adapter tool		L4432	Transfer shaft end play checking tool
L4406-3	Adapter tool		L4435	Differential bearing retainer rotating tool
L4410	Driver base tool		L4513	Ring gear attaching bolt socket
LC4171	Driver handle tool		L4436	Differential bearing turning torque tool
L4408	Driver base tool		L4438	Dial indicator post tool
L4520	Driver base tool		L4439	Starting nut tool for output shaft gear installation
L4517	Driver base		L4526	Output shaft gear bearing cup installer tool
L4512	Transfer shaft and retainer tool		L4553	Special valve body screw remover and installer tool
C293-52	Base collar		L4437	Adapter tools for slide hammers (C3752)
C293-PA	Press		L4559	Hydraulic pressure gauge adapter connectors

INDEX

FORD MOTOR COMPANY
C-5

APPLICATIONS

C-5 AUTOMATIC TRANSMISSION (CODE C)

1982

Capri, Cougar, XR-7, Granada—200/232 CID Engines
Fairmont, Zephyr, Mustang—200/255 CID Engines
Thunderbird—200 CID Engine
F100

1983

Fairmont, Zephyr—200 CID Engine
Capri, Cougar, XR-7, Mustang, Thunderbird—232 CID Engine
LTD, Marquis—200/232 CID Engines
F100, Bronco II, Ranger

1984

LTD, Marquis, Cougar XR-7, Thunderbird, F150, Bronco II, Ranger

GENERAL DESCRIPTION

TRANSMISSION AND CONVERTER IDENTIFICATION

Transmission

The C-5 Automatic Transmission is a fully automatic unit with three forward and one reverse speeds. A lock-up converter is used in most models, to provide mechanical coupling of the engine to the rear wheels. Simpson type planetary gears are used for reduction.

The C-5 Automatic Transmission resembles the C-4 Automatic Transmission, both internally and externally. The C-5 unit has replaced the C-4 unit in production.

The major differences between the two units are in the hydraulic systems, where several new valves have been incorporated along with a new timing valve body. The converter relief valve has been moved from the pump assembly reactor support to the timing valve body, thereby causing the oil pump assemblies not to be interchangeable.

With the exception of an added tool to install the reverse and high clutch piston, most all special tools needed to service the C-4 unit will also service the C-5 unit.

The C-5 Automatic Transmission can be identified by the code letter C under the transmission section of the Vehicle Certification label, found on the driver's door lock post. A model identification tag is located under the lower intermediate servo cover bolt, with the transmission model, build date code and the assembly part number, containing the prefix and suffix.

The first line on the tag shows the transmission model prefix and suffix. A number appearing after the suffix indicates that internal parts have been changed after initial production start up. For example, a PEE-FL model transmission that has been changed internally would read PEE-FL1. Both transmissions are basically the same, but some service parts in the PEE-FL1 transmission are slightly different than the PEE-FL transmission.

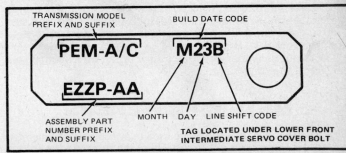

Identification plate explanation (©Ford Motor Company)

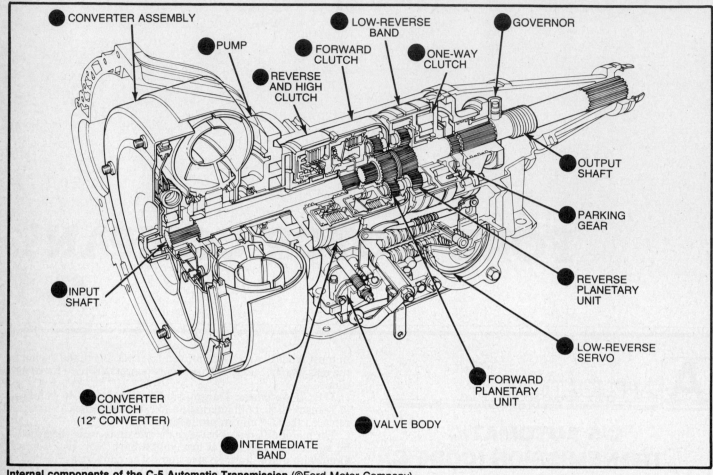

Internal components of the C-5 Automatic Transmission (©Ford Motor Company)

Therefore, it is important that the codes on the transmission identification tag be checked when ordering parts or making inquiries about the transmission.

Converter

A twelve inch torque converter is used in most models, incorporating a centrifugally operated lock-up clutch mechanism, negating the use of electrical or hydraulic lock-up components.

With the centrifugal lock-up feature, the torque converter is changed to a more efficient mechanical coupling as the speed of the input shaft is increased. The lock-up mechanism is designed to engage at various predetermined speeds of the converter, depending upon the vehicle model and driving conditions. With the centrifugal clutch lock-up, a mechanical connection exists between the engine and the rear wheels, resulting in improved driveline efficiency and fuel economy. The torque converter cannot be disassembled for field service. 1983—Fairmont Futura, Zephyr for altitude use and LTD, Marquis sedans (Calif) and station wagons use 10¼ inch non-lock-up converters, when equipped with 3.3L engines.

The torque converter can be identified by the letter stamped on the face of the converter.

METRIC FASTENERS

Metric bolts and fasteners may be used in attaching the transmission to the engine and also in attaching the transmission to the chassis crossmember mount.

The metric fastener dimensions are very close to the dimensions of the familiar inch system fasteners, and for this reason, replacement fasteners must have the same measurement and strength as those removed.

—WARNING—

Do not attempt to inter-change metric fasteners for inch system fasteners. Mismatched or incorrect fasteners can result in damage to the transmission unit through malfunctions or breakage and possible personal injury.

FLUID SPECIFICATIONS

Type H fluid, meeting Ford Motor Company's specifications ESP-M2C166-H, is used in the C-5 Automatic Transmission. To avoid filling or topping off the fluid level with the wrong type fluid, this information is stamped on the dipstick blade.

Checking the Fluid Level

The C-5 Automatic Transmission is designed to operate with the fluid level between the arrows at the hot low mark and the hot full mark.

TRANSMISSION AT NORMAL OPERATING TEMPERATURE (150°-170° F. DIPSTICK HOT TO THE TOUCH)

1. With the vehicle on a level surface, engine idling, wheels blocked, foot brakes applied, move the transmission gear selector

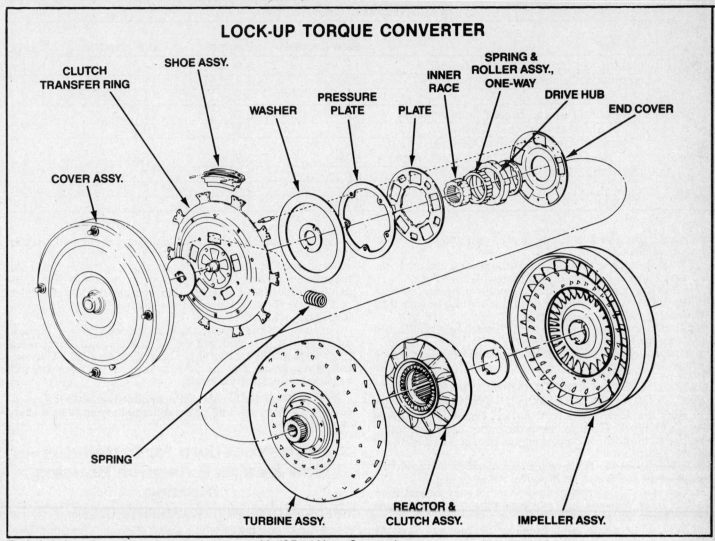

LOCK-UP TORQUE CONVERTER

CLUTCH TRANSFER RING

SHOE ASSY.

SPRING & ROLLER ASSY., ONE-WAY

INNER RACE

PRESSURE PLATE

WASHER

PLATE

DRIVE HUB

END COVER

COVER ASSY.

SPRING

TURBINE ASSY.

REACTOR & CLUTCH ASSY.

IMPELLER ASSY.

Exploded view of torque converter lock-up assembly (©Ford Motor Company)

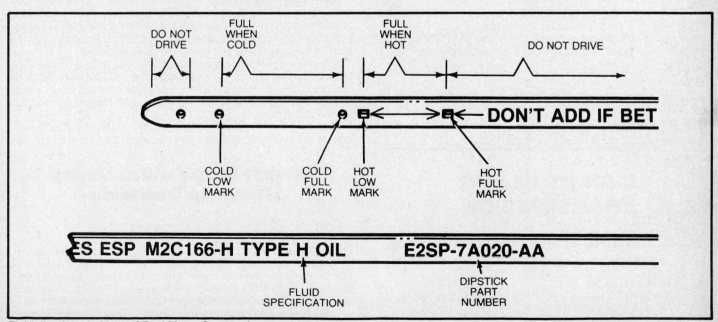

DO NOT DRIVE

FULL WHEN COLD

FULL WHEN HOT

DO NOT DRIVE

DON'T ADD IF BET

COLD LOW MARK

COLD FULL MARK

HOT LOW MARK

HOT FULL MARK

ES ESP M2C166-H TYPE H OIL

E2SP-7A020-AA

FLUID SPECIFICATION

DIPSTICK PART NUMBER

Fluid dipstick markings (©Ford Motor Company)

FLUID REFILL CAPACITY

Year	Model	Converter Size (inches)	Engine	U.S. Quarts	Liters
1982	Mustang, Capri, Fairmont, Zephyr	12	3.3, 4.2L	11	10.4
	Granada, Cougar, Thunderbird, XR-7	12	3.3, 3.8L	11	10.4
	F100, F150	12	3.8, 4.2L	11	10.4
1983-84	Fairmont, Futura, Zephyr (less Altitude)	12	3.3L	11	10.4
	LTD, Marquis (Sdn-less Calif.)	12	3.3L	10.3	9.8
	Fairmont Futura, Zephyr (Altitude), LTD, Marquis (Sdn-Calif.), (Stat. Wgn.)	10¼	3.3L	7.5	7.1
	Mustang, Capri, Thunderbird, XR-7	12	3.8L	11	10.4
	F100, F150	12	3.8L	11	10.4
	Ranger	10¼	2.3L	7.5	7.1

through the gear positions to engage each gear and to fill the oil passages with fluid.

2. Place the selector lever in the Park position and apply the parking brake. Do not turn off the engine. Allow to idle.

3. Clean the dipstick area of dirt and remove the dipstick from the filler tube. Wipe the dipstick clean, and reinsert it in the filler tube making sure it is seated firmly.

4. Remove the dipstick for the second time from the filler tube and check the fluid level.

5. If necessary adjust the fluid to its proper level and replace the dipstick firmly in the tube.

TRANSMISSION AT ROOM TEMPERATURE (70°-95° F. DIPSTICK COOL TO THE TOUCH)

1. With the vehicle on a level surface, engine idling, wheels blocked, foot brakes applied, move the transmission selector lever through the gear positions to engage each gear and to fill the oil passages with fluid.

2. Place the selector lever in the Park position and apply the parking brake. *Do not* turn off engine. Allow to idle.

3. Clean the dipstick area of dirt and remove the dipstick from the filler tube. Wipe the dipstick clean, reinsert it back into the filler tube and seat it firmly.

4. Again remove the dipstick from the filler tube and check the fluid level as indicated on the dipstick. The level should be between the middle and the top holes on the dipstick.

5. If necessary, add enough fluid to bring the level between the middle hole and the top hole on the dipstick.

6. When the fluid level is correct, fully seat the dipstick in the filler tube to avoid contamination of the fluid by entrance of dirt and water.

M MODIFICATIONS

C-5 AUTOMATIC TRANSMISSION

Rear Output Shaft Retaining Ring Deleted

1982 FORD MODELS, 1982 LINCOLN-MERCURY MODELS AND LIGHT TRUCKS EQUIPPED WITH THE C-5 AUTOMATIC TRANSMISSION

C-5 transmissions built after March 8, 1982 will not have a rear output shaft retaining ring. A design change to the parking gear (wider) and a shoulder will retain the governor collector body.

The deleted rear output shaft retaining ring was used to hold the governor collector body in position on the output shaft. Current production, after March 8, 1982, transmissions have a wider parking gear and a shoulder on the output shaft for governor collector body retention.

For both past and current model service replacement, the new output shaft will be used, and the old park gear and the retaining ring will be retained for service. The new output shaft has the retaining ring groove and the old park gear and retaining ring will be packaged together for service.

NOTE: When disassembling the transmission, hold the governor collector body when lifting the collector body and output shaft out of the case.

Service Procedure for Installation of New Design Extension Housing Bushing

1982 GRANADA, COUGAR AND 1983 RANGER

A new design bushing used on Rangers and some Granadas/Cougars.

Ranger applications with the C5 transmission have a new design extension housing bushing. The bushing is teflon/lead impregnated with no fluid drain-back hole. For service requiring replacement of the bushing, align the split line to the top of the extension housing when the new bushing is installed.

Some initial build Ranger C5 applications may have the passenger car type bronze bushing and some 1982½ Granada/Cougars may have the Ranger (teflon/lead) type bushing. In the event service is required, replace the bushing with the same type that has been removed.

If the extension and bushing assembly requires replacement, replace the assembly with the part cataloged for that application.

Upshift Irregularities During Warm-up Operation

ALL C-5 EQUIPPED VEHICLES (1982)

Some C-5 automatic transmissions, built prior to September 10, 1981 (transmission build date code-J10) may exhibit shift concerns caused by irregularities in the D2 valve. This condition results in a 1-3 shift or second gear starts, at all throttle openings. The condition may go away as the transmission warms up to normal operating temperatures and may return as the transmission cools down.

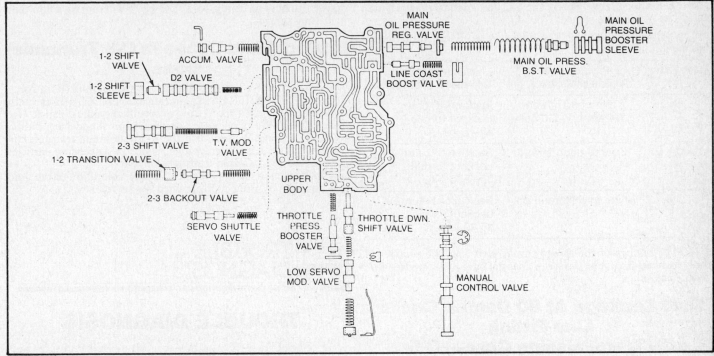

Exploded view of upper valve body (©Ford Motor Company)

Similar concerns, i.e., delayed shifts, no 1-2 upshift, second gear starts or 1-3 shifts may be also caused by chips, burrs in either the governor assembly or the main control. Service using the following procedures:

1. First determine whether there are metal particles or other material (such as clutch material, etc.) in the transmission fluid. If the fluid is found to have metal particles or materials, clean and service the transmission in the usual manner.

2. If the above fluid condition is not evident, road test the vehicle to determine if line pressure cutback is occuring. Attach a pressure gauge to the line pressure port of the case. Cutback should occur between 10 mph and 16 mph. If line pressure cutback is not observed, then the governor is not operating properly.

3. If line pressure cutback is observed, then the governor is operating properly and the main control is the probable source. Remove the main control and inspect the D2 valve and valve bore for observable causes (i.e., chips or burrs). If no obvious cause is observed, then D2 valve bore irregularity is the probable cause and the main control must be replaced.

Start-up Shudder and Vibration (10-15 MPH)

1983 T-BIRD, COUGAR W/3.8L ENGINE AND C-5 TRANSMISSION

This article outlines a procedure to service a start-up shudder condition at 10-15 mph on Thunderbird and Cougar vehicles built prior to January 20, 1983. The shudder may be felt in the steering column and is caused in part by the engine angle being near the high end of specification (3½° ± ½°).

To service this condition, use the following procedure:

1. Inspect for a spacer approximately ¼″ thick between the No. 3 crossmember and the rear engine mount.

2. If the spacer is not found, replace the No. 3 crossmember, color coded white, with crossmember (Part No. EOSZ-6A023-A) color coded purple.

Intermediate Band Adjustment Screw Change—C-4 and C-5 Transmissions

1981-82 FAIRMONT, GRANADA, MUSTANG, T-BIRD, ZEPHYR, COUGAR, XR-7, CAPRI, F-SERIES AND E-SERIES LIGHT TRUCKS

During 1981 model C4 transmission production, a change of intermediate band adjustment screw and nut was incorporated—from coarse to fine thread.

The adjustment specifications are **different** for the intermediate band on C4 transmissions depending on the thread of the adjustment screw and nut.

Prior to any intermediate band adjustment or service, always examine the threads of the adjustment screw to determine the type of threads—fine or coarse.

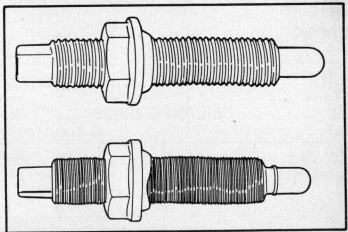

Comparison of coarse and fine threaded band adjusting bolts (©Ford Motor Company)

NOTE: This change affects the C-5 Automatic Transmission during its production stages.

The following chart denotes Intermediate Band Adjustment Specifications:

Transmission Type	Pitch on Thread Adjustment Screw & Nut	Intermediate Band Adjustment Specification
C4	Fine pitch thread (C4 trans W/C5 case)	Back-off 3 turns. Locknut torque 35-45 lbs.-ft.
C4	Coarse pitch thread	Back-off 1¾ turns. Locknut torque 35-45 lbs.-ft.
C5	Fine pitch thread only	Back-off 4¼ turns. Locknut torque 35-45 lbs.-ft.

NOTE: Enough of the thread can be seen from the outside of the transmission case so the screw does not have to be removed for visual inspection.

Fluid Leakage At 90 Degree Cooler Line Fitting To Transmission Case—C-5 Transmission

ALL 1982 MODELS SO EQUIPPED

Loss of transmission fluid at the cooler line fitting-to-case on units built prior to September 10, 1981 (transmission build date indicated by J-10) may be attributed to an undersize threaded fitting.

To service, the fitting must be inspected. If the 90 degree fitting does not appear tightly secured to the transmission case, the 90 degree fitting is to be replaced. DO NOT attempt to teflon tape the fitting threads.

Correct Fluid Usage in C-5 Transmissions

The C-5 Automatic Transmission uses a special fluid (Ford specification ESP-M2C166-H) Motorcraft part no. XT-4-H in quart cans only. Use only Type H fluid as specified on the dipstick. Use of any other fluid may cause a transmission shudder condition.

The H-type fluid used with the C-5 automatic transmission contains a special detergent which retains in suspension particles generated during normal transmission use.

This characteristic may result in a dark coloration of the fluid and does not by itself indicate need for service.

TROUBLE DIAGNOSIS

In order to properly diagnose transmission problems and avoid making second repairs for the same problem, all of the available information and knowledge must be used. Included is a knowledge of the components of the transmission and their function. Also, test procedures and their accompanying specifications charts aid in finding solutions to problems. Further answers are found by road testing vehicles and comparing all of the results of the above to the Ford C-5 Diagnostic Chart. The diagnostic chart gives condition, cause and correction for most possible trouble conditions in the Ford C-5 transmissions.

CLUTCH AND BAND APPLICATION CHART
C-5 Automatic Transmission

Gear/Range	Reverse and High Clutch	Forward Clutch	Intermediate Band	Low-Reverse Band	One-Way Clutch
Park/Neutral	—	—	—	—	—
Drive 1st	—	Applied	—	—	Holding
Drive 2nd	—	Applied	Applied	—	—
Drive 3rd	Applied	Applied	—	—	—
Manual 1	—	Applied	—	Applied	—
Manual 2	—	Applied	Applied	—	—
Reverse	Applied	—	—	Applied	—

CHILTON'S THREE "C's" TRANSMISSION DIAGNOSIS CHARTS
C-5 Automatic Transmission

Condition	Cause	Correction
Slow initial engagement	a) Improper fluid level b) Damaged or improperly adjusted linkage c) Contaminated fluid d) Improper clutch and band application, or oil control pressure	a) Add fluid as required b) Repair or adjust linkage c) Perform fluid level check d) Perform control pressure test

CHILTON'S THREE "C's" TRANSMISSION DIAGNOSIS CHARTS
C-5 Automatic Transmission

Condition	Cause	Correction
Rough initial engagement in either forward or reverse	a) Improper fluid level b) High engine idle c) Looseness in the driveshaft, U-joints or engine mounts d) Incorrect linkage adjustment e) Improper clutch or band application, or oil control pressure f) Sticking or dirty valve body	a) Perform fluid level check b) Adjust idle to specifications c) Repair as required d) Repair or adjust linkage e) Perform control pressure test f) Clean, repair or replace valve body
Harsh engagements—(warm engine)	a) Improper fluid level b) TV linkage misadjusted long disconnected/sticking/damaged return spring disconnected c) Engine curb idle too high d) Valve body bolts—loose/too tight e) Valve body dirty/sticking valves	a) Perform fluid level check b) Adjust linkage c) Check engine curb idle d) Tighten to specification e) Determine source of contamination. Service as required
No/delayed forward engagement (reverse OK)	a) Improper fluid level b) Manual linkage—misadjusted damaged c) Low main control pressure d) Forward clutch assembly burnt/damaged e) Valve body bolts—loose/too tight f) Valve body dirty/sticking valves g) Transmission filter plugged h) Pump damaged	a) Perform fluid level check b) Check and adjust or service as required c) Control pressure test, note results d) Perform air pressure test e) Tighten to specification f) Determine source of contamination. Service as required g) Replace filter h) Visually inspect pump gears. Replace pump if necessary
No/delayed reverse engagement (forward OK)	a) Improper fluid level b) Manual linkage misadjusted/damaged c) Low main control pressure in reverse d) Reverse clutch assembly burnt/worn e) Valve body bolts loose/too tight f) Valve body dirty/sticking valves g) Transmission filter plugged h) Pump damaged	a) Perform fluid level check b) Check and adjust or service as required c) Control pressure test d) Perform air pressure test e) Tighten to specification f) Determine source of contamination. Service as required g) Replace filter h) Visually inspect pump gears. Replace if necessary
No/delayed reverse engagement and/or no engine braking in manual low (1)	a) Improper fluid level b) Linkage out of adjustment c) Low reverse band servo piston burnt/worn d) Bands out of adjustment	a) Perform fluid level check b) Service or adjust linkage c) Perform air pressure test d) Adjust reverse band

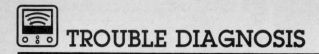

CHILTON'S THREE "C's" TRANSMISSION DIAGNOSIS CHARTS
C-5 Automatic Transmission

Condition	Cause	Correction
No/delayed reverse engagement and/or no engine braking in manual low (1)	e) Polished, glazed band of drum	e) Service or replace as required
	f) Planetary low one way clutch damaged	f) Replace
No engine braking in manual second gear	a) Improper fluid level	a) Perform fluid level check
	b) Linkage out of adjustment	b) Service or adjust linkage
	c) Intermediate band out of adjustment	c) Adjust intermediate band
	d) Improper band or clutch application, or oil pressure control system	d) Perform conrol pressure test
	e) Intermediate servo leaking	e) Perform air pressure test of intermediate service for leakage. Service as required
	f) Intermediate one way clutch damaged	f) Replace
	g) Polished or glazed band or drum	g) Service or replace as required
Forward engagement slips/shudders/chatters	a) Improper fluid level	a) Perform fluid level check
	b) Manual linkage misadjusted/damaged	b) Check and adjust or service as required
	c) Low main control pressure	c) Control pressure test
	d) Valve body bolts—loose/too tight	d) Tighten to specification
	e) Valve body dirty/sticking valves	e) Determine source of contamination. Service as required
	f) Forward clutch piston ball check not seating	f) Replace forward clutch cylinder. Service transmission as required
	g) Forward clutch piston seal cut/worn	g) Replace seal and service clutch as required
	h) Contamination blocking forward clutch feed hole	h) Determine source of contamination. Servicd as required
	i) Low one way clutch (planetary) damaged	i) Determine cause of condition. Service as required
No drive in any gear	a) Improper fluid level	a) Perform fluid level check
	b) Damaged or improperly adjusted linkage	b) Repair or adjust linkage
	c) Improper clutch or band application, or oil pressure	c) Perform control pressure test
	d) Internal leakage	d) Check and repair as required
	e) Valve body loose	e) Tighten to specification
	f) Damaged or worn clutches	f) Perform air pressure test
	g) Sticking or dirty valve body	g) Clean, repair or replace valve body
No drive forward, reverse OK	a) Improper fluid level	a) Perform fluid level check
	b) Damaged or improperly adjusted linkage	b) Repair or adjust linkage
	c) Improper clutch or band application, or oil pressure control system	c) Perform control pressure test
	d) Damaged or worn forward clutch or governor	d) Perform air pressure test

CHILTON'S THREE "C's" TRANSMISSION DIAGNOSIS CHARTS
C-5 Automatic Transmission

Condition	Cause	Correction
No drive forward, reverse OK	e) Valve body loose f) Dirty or sticking valve body	e) Tighten to specification f) Clean, repair or replace valve body
No drive, slips or chatters in first gear in D. All other gears normal	a) Damaged or worn (planetary) one-way clutch	a) Service or replace planetary one-way clutch
No drive, slips or chatters in second gear	a) Improper fluid level b) Damaged or improperly adjusted linkage c) Intermediate band out of adjustment d) Improper band or clutch application e) Damaged or worn servo and/or internal leaks f) Dirty or sticking valve body g) Polished, glazed intermediate band or drum	a) Perform fluid level check b) Service or adjust linkage c) Adjust intermediate band d) Perform control pressure test e) Perform air pressure test f) Clean, service or replace valve body g) Replace or service as required
Starts up in 2nd or 3rd	a) Improper fluid level b) Damaged or improperly adjusted linkage c) Improper band and/or clutch application, or oil pressure control system d) Damaged or worn governor. Sticking governor e) Valve body loose f) Dirty or sticking valve body g) Cross leaks between valve body and case mating surface	a) Perform fluid level check b) Service or adjust linkage c) Perform control pressure test d) Peform governor check. Replace or service governor, clean screen e) Tighten to specification f) Clean, service or replace valve body g) Service or replace valve body and/or case as required
Reverse shudders/chatters/slips	a) Improper fluid level Low main control pressure in reverse c) Reverse servo bore damaged d) Low (planetary) one-way clutch damaged e) Reverse clutch drum, bushing damaged f) Reverse clutch stator support seal rings, ring grooves worn/damaged g) Reverse clutch piston seal cut/worn h) Reverse band out of adjustment or damaged i) Looseness in the driveshaft, U-joints or engine mounts	a) Perform fluid level check b) Control pressure test c) Determine cause of condition. Service as required d) Determine cause of condition. Service as required e) Determine cause of condition. Service as required f) Determine cause of condition. Service as required g) Determine cause of condition. Service as required h) Adjust reverse band. Service as required i) Service as required
Shift points incorrect	a) Improper fluid level b) Improper vacuum hose routing or leaks c) Improper operation of EGR system	a) Perform fluid level check b) Correct hose routing c) Repair or replace as required

CHILTON'S THREE "C's" TRANSMISSION DIAGNOSIS CHARTS
C-5 Automatic Transmission

Condition	Cause	Correction
Shift points incorrect	d) Linkage out of adjustment	d) Repair or adjust linkage
	e) Improper speedometer gear installed	e) Replace gear
	f) Improper clutch or band application, or oil pressure control system	f) Perform shift test and control pressure test
	g) Damaged or worn governor	g) Repair or replace governor, clean screen
	f) Dirty or sticking valve body	f) Clean, repair or replace valve body
No upshift at any speed in D	a) Improper fluid level	a) Perform fluid level check
	b) Vacuum leak to diaphragm unit	b) Repair vacuum line or hose
	c) Linkage out of adjustment	c) Repair or adjust linkage
	d) Improper band or clutch application, or oil pressure control system	d) Perform control pressure test
	e) Damaged or worn governor	e) Repair or replace governor, clean screen
	f) Dirty or sticking valve body	f) Clean, repair or replace valve body
Shifts 1-3 in D, all upshifts harsh/delayed or no upshifts	a) Improper fluid level	a) Perform fluid level check
	b) Intermediate band out of adjustment	b) Adjust band
	c) Damaged intermediate servo and/or internal leaks	c) Perform air pressure test. Repair front servo and/or internal leaks
	d) Polished, glazed band or drum	d) Repair or replace band or drum
	e) Improper band or clutch application, or oil pressure control system	e) Perform control pressure test
	f) Dirty of sticking valve body	f) Clean, repair or replace valve body. (Refer to Modification Section)
	g) Manual linkage—misadjusted, damaged	g) Check and adjust or service as required
	h) Governor sticking	h) Perform governor test. Service as required
	i) Main control pressure too high	i) Control pressure test. Service as required
	j) TV control rod incorrect	j) Change TV control rod
	k) Valve body bolts—loose/too tight	k) Tighten to specification
	l) Vacuum leak to diaphragm unit	l) Check vacuum lines to diaphragm unit. Service as necessary. Perform vacuum supply and diaphragm tests.
	m) Vacuum diaphragm bent, sticking, leaks	m) Check diaphragm unit. Service as necessary
Mushy/early all upshifts pile up/upshifts	a) Improper fluid level	a) Perform fluid level check
	b) Low main control pressure	b) Control pressure test. Note results
	c) Valve body bolts loose/too tight	c) Tighten to specification
	d) Valve body valve or throttle control valve sticking	d) Determine source of contamination. Service as required

CHILTON'S THREE "C's" TRANSMISSION DIAGNOSIS CHARTS
C-5 Automatic Transmission

Condition	Cause	Correction
Mushy/early all upshifts pile up/ upshifts	e) Governor valve sticking	e) Perform governor test. Repair as required.
	f) TV control rod too short	f) Install correct TV control rod
No 1-2 upshift	a) Improper fluid level	a) Perform fluid level check
	b) Kickdown linkage misadjusted	b) Adjust linkage
	c) Manual linkage—misadjusted/ damaged	c) Check and adjust or service as required
	d) Governor valve sticking. Intermediate band out of adjustment	d) Perform governor test. Service as required. Adjust intermediate band
	e) Vacuum leak to diaphragm unit	e) Check vacuum lines to diaphragm unit. Service as required
	f) Vacuum diaphragm bent, sticking, leaks	f) Check diaphragm unit. Service as necessary
	g) Valve body bolts—loose/too tight	g) Tighten to specification
	h) Valve body dirty/sticking valves	h) Determine source of contamination. Service as required
	i) Intermediate clutch band and/or servo assembly burnt	i) Perform air pressure test
Rough/harsh/delayed 1-2 upshift	a) Improper fluid level.	a) Perform fluid level check
	b) Poor engine performance	b) Tune engine
	c) Intermediate band out of adjustment	c) Adjust intermediate band
	d) Main control pressure too high	d) Control pressure test. Note results
	e) Governor valve sticking	e) Perform governor test. Service as required.
	f) Damaged intermediate servo	f) Air pressure check intermediate servo
	g) Engine vacuum leak	g) Check engine vacuum lines. Service as necessary. Check vacuum diaphragm unit. Service as necessary. Perform vacuum supply and diaphragm tests
	h) Valve body bolts—loose/too tight	h) Tighten to specifications
	i) Valve body dirty/sticking valves	i) Determine source of contamination. Service as required
	j) Vacuum leak to diaphragm unit	j) Check vacuum lines to diaphragm unit. Service as required
	k) Vacuum diaphragm bent, sticking, leaks	k) Check diaphragm unit. Service as necessary
Mushy 1-2 shift	a) Improper fluid level	a) Perform fluid level check
	b) Incorrect engine performance	b) Tune adjust engine idle as required
	c) Improper linkage adjustment	c) Repair or adjust linkage
	d) Intermediate band out of adjustment	d) Adjust intermediate band

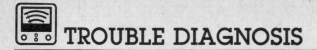

CHILTON'S THREE "C's" TRANSMISSION DIAGNOSIS CHARTS
C-5 Automatic Transmission

Condition	Cause	Correction
Mushy 1-2 shift	e) Improper band or clutch application, or oil pressure control system	e) Perform control pressure test
	f) Damaged high clutch and/or intermediate servo or band	f) Perform air pressure test. Repair as required
	g) Polished, glazed band or drum	g) Repair or replace as required
	h) Dirty or sticking valve body	h) Clean, repair or replace valve body
	i) Governor valve sticking	i) Test governor, clean or repair
No 2-3 upshift	a) Low fluid level	a) Perform fluid level check
	b) TV linkage misadjusted (long)/ sticking/damaged	b) Adjust linkage. Service as required
	c) Low main control pressure to direct clutch	c) Control pressure test. Note results
	d) Valve body bolts—loose/too tight.	d) Tighten to specification
	e) Valve body dirty/sticking valves	e) Determine source of contamination, then service as required
	f) Direct clutch or reverse/high clutch assembly burnt/worn	f) Stall test. Determine cause of condition. Service as required
Harsh/delayed 2-3 upshift	a) Low fluid level	a) Perform fluid level check
	b) Incorrect engine performance	b) Check engine tune-up
	c) Engine vacuum leak	c) Check engine vacuum lines. Service as necessary. Check vacuum diaphragm unit. Service as necessary. Perform vacuum supply and diaphragm tests
	d) Damaged or worn intermediate servo release and high clutch piston check ball	d) Air pressure test the intermediate servo. Apply and release the high clutch piston check ball. Service as required
	e) Valve body bolts—loose/too tight	e) Tighten to specification
	f) Valve body dirty/sticking valves	f) Determine source of condition. Service as required
	g) Vacuum diaphragm or TV control rod bent, sticking, leaks	g) Check diaphragm and rod. Replace as necessary
Soft/early/mushy 2-3 upshift	a) Improper fluid level	a) Perform fluid level check
	b) Valve body bolts loose/too tight	b) Tighten to specification.
	c) Valve body dirty/sticking valves	c) Determine source of contamination. Service as required
	d) Vacuum diaphragm or TV control rod bent, sticking, leaks.	d) Check diaphragm and rod. Replace as necessary
Engine over-speeds on 2-3 shift	a) Improper fluid level	a) Perform fluid level check
	b) Linkage out of adjustment	b) Service or adjust linkage
	c) Improper band or clutch application, or oil pressure control system	c) Perform control pressure test
	d) Damaged or worn high clutch and/or intermediate servo	d) Perform air pressure test. Service as required

CHILTON'S THREE "C's" TRANSMISSION DIAGNOSIS CHARTS
C-5 Automatic Transmission

Condition	Cause	Correction
Engine over-speeds on 2-3 shift	e) Dirty or sticking valve body	e) Clean, service or replace valve body
Erratic shifts	a) Improper fluid level b) Poor engine performance c) Valve body bolts—loose/too tight d) Valve body dirty/sticking valves e) Governor valve stuck f) Output shaft collector body seal ring damaged	a) Perform fluid level check b) Check engine tune-up c) Tighten to specification d) Line pressure test, note results. Determine source of contamination. Service as required e) Perform governor test. Service as required f) Service as required
Rough 3-1 shift at closed throttle in D	a) Improper fluid level b) Incorrect engine idle or performance c) Improper linkage adjustment d) Improper clutch or band application, or oil pressure control system e) Improper governor operation f) Dirty or sticking valve body	a) Perform fluid level check b) Tune, and adjust engine idle c) Repair or adjust linkage d) Perform control pressure test e) Perform governor test. Repair as required f) Clean, repair or replace valve body
No forced downshifts	a) Improper fluid level b) Linkage out of adjustment c) Improper clutch or band application, or oil pressure control system d) Damaged internal kickdown linkage e) Dirty or sticking valve body	a) Perform fluid level check b) Repair or adjust linkage c) Perform control pressure test d) Repair internal kickdown linkage e) Clean, repair or replace valve body
No 3-1 shift in D	a) Improper fluid level b) Incorrect engine idle or performance c) Damaged governor d) Dirty or sticking valve body	a) Perform fluid level check b) Tune, and adjust engine idle c) Perform governor check. Repair as required d) Clean, repair or replace valve body
Runaway engine on 3-2 downshift	a) Improper fluid level b) Linkage out of adjustment c) Intermediate band out of adjustment d) Improper band or clutch application, or oil pressure control system e) Damaged or worn intermediate servo f) Polished, glazed band or drum g) Dirty or sticking valve body	a) Perform fluid check b) Repair or adjust linkage c) Adjust intermediate band d) Perform control pressure test e) Air pressure test check the intermediate servo. Repair servo and/or seals f) Repair or replace as required g) Clean, repair or replae valve body

CHILTON'S THREE "C's" TRANSMISSION DIAGNOSIS CHARTS
C-5 Automatic Transmission

Condition	Cause	Correction
Engine over-speeds on 3-2 downshift	a) Improper fluid level	a) Perform fluid level check
	b) Linkage out of adjustment	b) Service or adjust linkage
	c) Intermediate band out of adjustment	c) Adjust intermediate band
	d) Improper band or clutch application, and one way clutch, or oil pressure control system	d) Perform control pressure test. Service clutch
	e) Damaged or worn intermediate servo	e) Air pressure test check the intermediate servo. Service servo and/or seals
	f) Polished, glazed band or drum	f) Service or replace as required
	g) Dirty of sticking valve body	g) Clean, service or replace valve body
Shift efforts high	a) Manual shift linkage damaged/misadjusted	a) Check and adjust or service as required
	b) Inner manual leve nut loose	b) Tighten nut to specification
	c) Manual lever retainer pin damaged	c) Adjust linkage and install new pin
Poor vehicle acceleration	a) Poor engine performance	a) Check engine tune-up
	b) Torque converter one-way clutch locked up	b) Replace torque converter
No engine braking in manual first gear	a) Improper fluid level	a) Perform fluid level check
	b) Linkage out of adjustment	b) Repair or adjust linkage
	c) Band out of adjustment	c) Adjust reverse band
	d) Oil pressure control system	d) Perform control pressure test
	e) Damaged or worn reverse servo	e) Perform air pressure test of reverse servo. Repair reverse clutch or rear servo as required
	f) Polished, glazed band or drum	f) Repair or replace as required
No engine braking in manual second gear	a) Improper fluid level	a) Perform fluid level check
	b) Linkage out of adjustment	b) Repair or adjust linkage
	c) Intermediate band out of adjustment	c) Adjust intermediate band
	d) Improper band or clutch application, or oil pressure control system	d) Perform control pressure test
	e) Intermediate servo leaking	e) Perform air pressure test of intermediate servo for leakage. Repair as required
	f) Polished or glazed band or drum	f) Repair or replace as required
Transmission noisy, valve resonance NOTE: Gauges may aggravate any hydraulic resonance. Remove gauge and check for resonance level	a) Improper fluid level	a) Perform fluid level check
	b) Linkage out of adjustment	b) Repair or adjust linkage
	c) Improper band or clutch application, or oil pressure control system	c) Perform control pressure test
	d) Cooler lines grounding	d) Free up cooler lines
	e) Dirty sticking valve body	e) Clean, repair or replace valve body
	f) Internal leakage or pump cavitation	f) Repair as required

CHILTON'S THREE "C's" TRANSMISSION DIAGNOSIS CHARTS
C-5 Automatic Transmission

Condition	Cause	Correction
Transmission overheats	a) Improper fluid level	a) Perform fluid level check
	b) Incorrect engine idle, or performance	b) Tune, or adjust engine idle
	c) Improper clutch or band application, or oil pressure control system	c) Perform control pressure test
	d) Restriction in cooler or lines	d) Repair restriction
	e) Seized one-way clutch	e) Replace one-way clutch
	f) Dirty or sticking valve body	f) Clean, repair or replace valve body
Transmission fluid leaks	a) Improper fluid level	a) Perform fluid level check
	b) Leakage at gasket, seals, etc.	b) Remove all traces of lube on exposed surfaces of transmission. Check the vent for free breathing. Operate transmission at normal temperatures and inspect for leakage. Repair as required
	c) Vacuum diaphragm unit leaking	c) Replace diaphragm

HYDRAULIC CONTROL SYSTEM

In order to diagnose transmission trouble the hydraulic control circuits must be traced. The main parts of the hydraulic control system are the oil pump, valve body, governor, and the servo systems togehter with the fluid passages connecting the units. The clutches and bands control the planetary gear units which determine the gear ratio of the transmission.

Major Components

The C-5 Automatic transmission oil pump operates constantly whenever the engine is operating and at engine speed, driven by the converter pump cover, which is attached to the engine flywheel or flex plate, providing fluid pressure to the hydraulic system.

The major components of the hydraulic control system are as follows:

1. Reservoir or sump—The oil pan containing a supply of automatic transmission fluid for use in the hydraulic control system.

2. Screens—Both a pan and a pump inlet screen protects the hydraulic system from dirt or other foreign material that maybe carried by the fluid.

3. Oil pump—Provides fluid pressure to the hydraulic system whenever the engine is operating.

4. Main line oil pressure regulator valve—Regulates the main control line pressure in the hydraulic system and also supplys converter, cooler and lubrication systems with pressured fluid.

5. Main pressure booster valve and sleeve—Causes fluid pressure to be boosted depending upon the range or gear and causes the line pressure to increase or decrease in relation to the engine load.

6. Fluid cooler—Located in the radiator and removes heat generated in the torque converter and transmission by having the fluid flow through the cooler core.

7. Intermediate servo accumulator—Cushions or smooths the 1-2 upshift.

8. Converter—Couples the engine to the transmission gear train input shaft.

9. Drain-back valve—Prevents the lubrication fluid from draining back into the sump after the engine is stopped.

10. Converter pressure relief valve—Prevents excessive pressure build-up in the converter unit during operation.

11. Reverse and High clutch—Applied by hydraulic pressure to couple the input shaft to the sun gear.

12. Forward clutch—Applied by hydraulic pressure to couple the input shaft to the forward ring gear.

13. Intermediate servo—Applies hydraulically to actuate the intermediate band.

14. Low-reverse servo—Applies hydraulically to actuate the low-reverse band.

15. Throttle valve—Regulates throttle pressure (T.V.) as an engine load signal to the hydraulic system.

16. Governor—Provides a road speed signal to the hydraulic control system.

17. 1-2/3-2 timing control valve—Routes servo release fluid to the accumulator on a 1-2 upshift and joins the servo release fluid pressure with the high clutch on a 3-2 downshift.

18. 3-2 timing valve—Regulates the reverse and high clutch pressure for a smooth 3-2 downshift.

19. Cutback valve—Provides a reduction or cut-back in line pressure as the road speed of the vehicle increases.

20. Manual valve—Directs the line pressure to the various passages to apply or block off passages during the application of clutches and band servos, depending upon the shift selector position in the valve body.

21. 1-2 shift valve and sleeve—Acted on by governor pressure to control the Drive 2 valve.

22. Drive 2 valve—Control the 1-2 upshift and the 3-1 or 2-1 downshift.

23. 2-3 Shift valve—Controls the 3-2 downshift and the 2-3 upshift.

24. Throttle pressure modulator—Modulates the T.V. or boosted T.V. pressure to cause a lower T.V. signal to the Drive 2 valve.

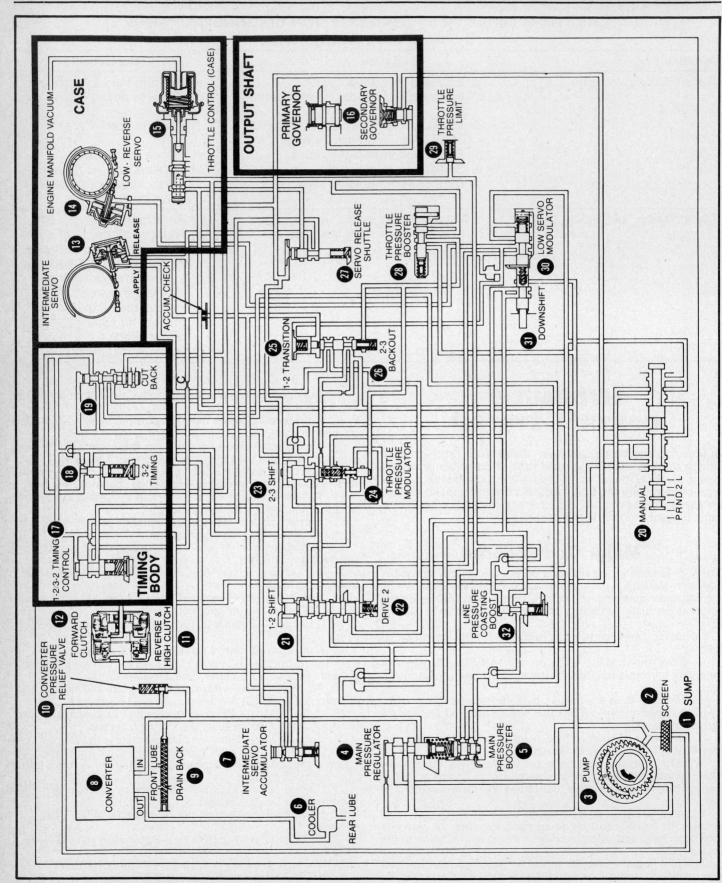

Hydraulic schematic of C-5 transmission (©Ford Motor Company)

25. 1-2 Transition valve—Prevents band to band tie-up on a manual 1-2 shift.

26. 2-3 Back-out valve—Prevents clutch to band tie-up on a closed throttle 2-3 upshift.

27. Servo release shuttle valve—Selects servo release orifices on a 3-2 downshift, depending upon road speed.

28. Throttle pressure booster valve—Provides a boosted T.V. pressure in a high engine load mode.

29. Throttle pressure limit valve—Regulates maximum T.V. pressures.

30. Low servo modulator valve—Modulates the reverse servo apply pressure in a manual shift to the first gear.

31. Downshift valve—Causes through detent kickdown shifts to occur at higher road speed than the torque demand downshifts. It also provides maximum delay on wide open throttle (WOT) upshifts.

32. Line pressure coasting boost valve—Causes a boost in the line pressure when in ranges 1 and 2.

Diagnosis Tests

GENERAL DIAGNOSTIC SEQUENCE

Before starting any test procedures, a selected sequence should be followed in the diagnosis of C-5 automatic transmission malfunctions. A suggested sequence is as follows;

1. Inspect the fluid level and correct as required.
2. Check the freedom of movement of the downshift linkage and adjust as required.
3. Check the manual linkage synchronization and adjust as required.

4. Inspect the vacuum routings to the modulator and be sure sufficient engine vacuum is available.

5. Install a 400 psi oil pressure gauge to the main line pressure port on the transmission case. Should this arrangement be used on a road test, route and secure the hose so as not to drag or be caught during the test.

Preform the pressure test in all gears and N/P positions. Record all results.

6. Perform the road test over a predetermined route to verify shift speeds and engine performance. Refer to the pressure gauge during all shifts for irregularities in the pressure readings. With the aid of a helper, record all readings for reference.

7. During the road test, governor operation can be noted and the shift speeds recorded as the throttle valves are moved through various positions. Should further testing of the governor system be needed, this can be accomplished when the vehicle is returned to the service center, by a shift test.

8. Should a verification of engine performance or initial gear engagement be needed, a stall test can be done to aid in pinpointing a malfunction.

9. Adjust transmission bands should the malfunction indicate loose or slipping bands.

10. Perform a case air pressure test, should the malfunction indicate internal transmission pressure leakage.

FLUID LEVEL AND CONDITION

The fluid level should be checked with the transmission at normal operating temperature, however, the cold fluid check can be made, if necessary (refer to the fluid level checking and fluid specification outline at the beginning of this section). Should top-

RANGE	CHECK FOR	CONDITION (OK OR NOT OK)
1	Engagement	
	Should be **no** 1-2 upshift	
	Engine braking in low gear	
	Shifts 3-2 and then 2-1 coming out of D at cruise	
	No slipping	
2	Engagement/Starts in second gear	
	Should be **no** 2-3 upshift	
	Shifts 3-2 coming out of D at cruise	
	No slipping	
D	Engagement/Starts in first gear	
	Upshifts not mushy or harsh	
	Upshifts and downshifts at specified speeds	
	● Minimum Throttle 1-2	
	● Minimum Throttle 2-3	
	● Minimum Throttle 3-2	
	● Minimum Throttle 2-1	
	● To-detent (heavy throttle) 1-2	
	● To-detent (heavy throttle) 2-3	
	● To-detent (heavy throttle) 3-2	
	● Through-detent (W.O.T.) 1-2	
	● Through-detent (W.O.T.) 2-3	
	● Through-detent (W.O.T.) 3-2	
	● Through-detent (W.O.T.) 3-1 or 2-1	
R	Engagement	
	Back up without slip	

Typical road test diagnosis sequence (©Ford Motor Company)

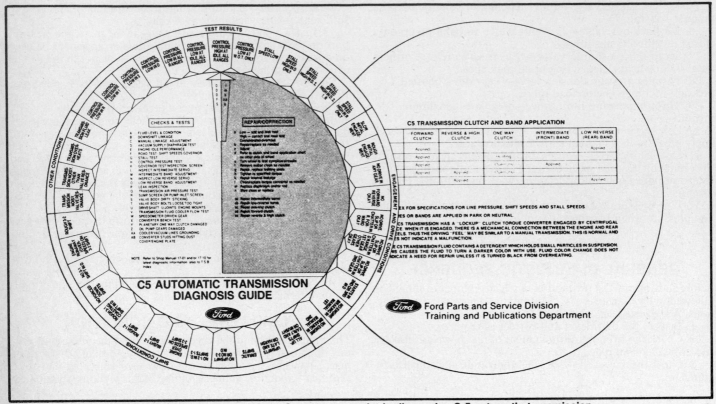

Slide wheel diagnostic tool, available from Ford Motor Company to assist in diagnosing C-5 automatic transmission (©Ford Motor Company)

ping off of the fluid level be necessary, add only type F automatic transmission fluid as specified on the dip stick. Should the fluid level be low, be sure to inspect the transmission for signs of leakage.

The fluid condition should be observed during the checking operation. The fluid should be clean and not discolored from contaminates.

NOTE: Type H fluid contains a detergent which retains particles in suspension, which are generated in normal automatic transmission operation. This characteristic does not in its self indicate a transmission malfunction, although the fluid may be dark in color.

By smelling the fluid, a burnt or rotten egg odor indicates a major transmission failure with overhaul required. Should burned flakes, solid residue or varnish in the fluid or on the dipstick be evident, overhaul of the unit is indicated.

DOWNSHIFT LINKAGE CHECK

Check the linkage for binding and for proper operation. The rod must not move until the throttle is almost wide open. With the throttle at the wide open position, the downshift linkage should have some slight travel (0.050-0.070 inch). Should binding of the rod, a sticking valve or rod misalignment be evident, the condition must be corrected before the vehicle is road tested.

NOTE: Refer to the "On-Car Adjustment" outline for proper adjustment procedures.

MANUAL LINKAGE CHECK

Before starting the engine, move the shift lever through each gear range, feeling the detents in the transmission. The detents and the shift selector should be syncronized. Place the shift selector in the D position and against its stop. Try to move the selector lever to the manual 2 position without raising the lever. If there is free movement to the D stop or if the lever stop is up on the manual 2 stop, an adjustment is required.

—— CAUTION ——

Do not roadtest the vehicle until the adjustments have been completed. Refer to the "On-Car Adjustment" outline for proper adjustment procedures.

Vacuum Diaphragm

The modulated throttle system, which adjusts throttle pressure for the control of the shift valves, is operated by engine manifold

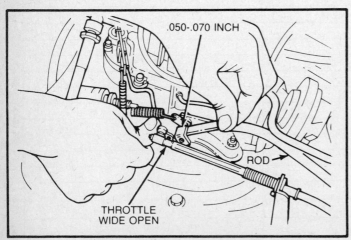

Downshift rod adjustment (©Ford Motor Company)

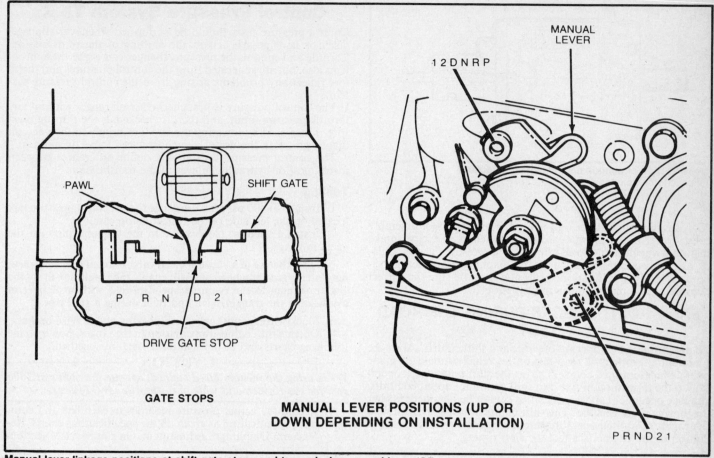

Manual lever linkage positions at shift gate stops and transmission manual lever (©Ford Motor Company)

vacuum through a vacuum diaphragm and must be inspected whenever a transmission defect is apparent.

MANIFOLD VACUUM

Testing

1. With the engine idling, remove the vacuum supply hose from the modulator nipple and check the hose end for the presence of engine vacuum with an appropriate gauge.

2. If vacuum is present, accelerate the engine and allow it to return to idle. A drop in vacuum should be noted during acceleration and a return to normal vacuum at idle.

3. If manifold vacuum is not present, check for breaks or restrictions in the vacuum lines and repair.

VACUUM DIAPHRAGM

Testing

1. Apply at least 18 in. Hg. to the modulator vacuum nipple and observe the vacuum reading. The vacuum should hold.

2. If the vacuum does not hold, the diaphragm is leaking and the modulator assembly must be replaced.

NOTE: A leaking diaphragm causes harsh gear engagements and delayed or no up-shifts due to maximum throttle pressure developed.

3. Remove the vacuum diaphragm from the transmission and attach it to a good vacuum source set at 18 in. of vacuum. If the vacuum holds at 18 in., then the diaphragm is not leaking.

4. Check for operation of the diaphragm return spring by holding a finger over the end of the control rod and removing the vac-

uum source. When the vacuum source is removed the spring should push out on the rod. If it does not push out, replace the diaphragm unit.

ALTITUDE COMPENSATING MODULATOR

To control shift spacing and shift timing where engine performance is greatly affected by changes in altitudes, and altitude

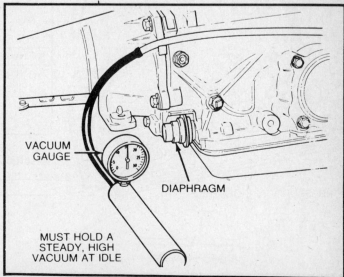

Checking manifold vacuum supply (©Ford Motor Company)

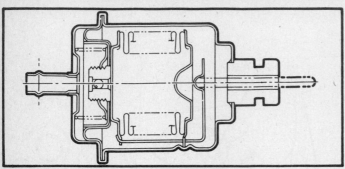

Cross-section of altitude compensating modulator
(©Ford Motor Company)

compensating modulator unit is used. The modulator assembly exerts force on the throttle valve as a function of engine intake manifold vacuum and local atmospheric pressure. The modulator assembly is composed of a flexible diaphragm, an aneroid bellows assembly, a calibration spring and case. Be sure the correct modulator is replaced in the transmission.

SHIFT POINT CHECKS DURING THE ROAD TEST

To determine if the governor pressure and shift control valves are functioning properly, a road test of the vehicle should be made over a predetermined course. During the shift point check operation, if the transmission does not shift within the specified limits, slippage occurs or certain gear ratios cannot be obtained, further diagnosing must be done. The shift points must be checked with the engine at normal operating temperature to avoid fast idle operation of the engine to affect the shift timing.

Control Pressure System Tests

Control pressure tests should be performed whenever slippage, delay or harshness is felt in the shifting of the transmission. Throttle and modulator pressure changes can cause these problems also, but are generated from the control pressures and therefore reflect any problems arising from the control pressure system.

The control pressure is first checked in all ranges without any throttle pressure input, and then is checked as the throttle pressure is increased by lowering the vacuum supply to the vacuum diaphragm, with the use of a vacuum bleed valve or stall test.

The control pressure tests should define differences between mechanical or hydraulic failures of the transmission.

Testing

1. Install a 0-400 psi pressure gauge to the control pressure tap, located on the left side of the transmission case.
2. Install a vacuum bleed valve in the vacuum line near the vacuum gauge.

NOTE: The use of a vacuum bleed valve or hand operated vacuum tester is recommended and will enable the repairman to set the engine vacuum to the required specifications without danger of overheating the transmission and fluid during a stall test.

3. Block wheels and apply both parking and service brakes.
4. Operate the engine/transmission in the ranges shown on the following charts and at the manifold vacuum specified.

—————————— CAUTION ——————————
When using the vacuum bleed method, operate the engine at 1000 rpm for the 10 inch and wide open throttle (WOT) tests.
————————————————————————————————

5. Record the actual pressure readings in each test and compare to the specification as given on the specifications charts. Refer to Vacuum Diaphragm Adjustment, On-Car Services section.

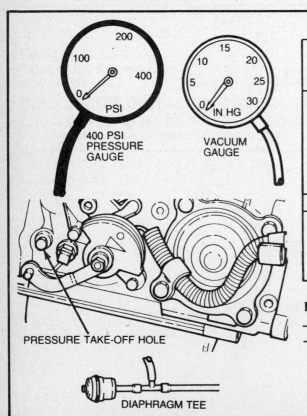

PRESSURE TAKE-OFF HOLE

DIAPHRAGM TEE

Control pressure test preparation (©Ford Motor Company)

Engine RPM	Manifold Vacuum In-Hg	Throttle	Range	PSI Record Actual	PSI Record Spec.
Idle	Above 12	Closed	P N D 2 1 R		
As Required	10	As Required	D, 2, 1		
As Required	Below 3	Wide Open	D 2 1 R		

Results: _____

_____

SPECIFICATIONS AND RESULTS

PRECAUTIONS BEFORE IDLE TESTS

1. Be sure manifold vacuum is above 15 in. Hg. If lower and unable to raise it, check for vacuum leaks and repair

2. Be sure the manifold vacuum changes with throttle plate opening. Check by accelerating quickly and releasing the accelerator and observing the vacuum reading.

PRECAUTIONS IF STALL TEST IS USED ON PRESSURE RISE TEST (REFER TO STALL TEST PROCEDURES)

1. Don't operate engine/transmission at stall for longer than 5 seconds per test.

2. Operate the engine between 1000 and 1200 rpm at the end of a test for approximately one to two minutes for cooling.

3. Release the accelerator immediately in case of slippage or spin-up of the transmission to avoid more damage to the unit.

CONTROL PRESSURE TESTS

Condition	Cause	Correction
Pressure low at idle in all ranges	a) Low transmission fluid level	a) Repair leaks and adjust fluid to proper level
	b) Restricted intake screen or filter	b) Change transmission fluid and screen
	c) Loose oil tubes	c) Re-install or replace tubes as needed
	d) Loose valve body or regulator to case bolts	d) Torque bolts or replace as needed
	e) Excessive leakage in front pump	e) Replace seals
	f) Leak in case	f) Replace case
	g) Control valves or regulator valve sticking	g) Clean valve body and replace fluid and screen
Pressure high at idle in all ranges	a) EGR system	a) Clean EGR system and replace valve if needed
	b) Improper operation of vacuum diaphragm (vacuum modulator)	b) Adjust or replace vacuum diaphragm
	c) Vacuum line	c) Repair or replace the vacuum line
	d) Throttle valves or control rod	d) Repair or replace as needed
	e) Regulator boost valves sticking	e) Clean or replace valve body
Pressure OK at idle in all ranges but low at 10 in. of vacuum	a) Vacuum diaphragm (modulator)	a) Adjust or replace vacuum diaphragm (modulator)
	b) Control rod or throttle valve sticking	b) Clean, repair or replace as needed
Pressure OK at 10 in. vacuum but low at 1 in. of vacuum	a) Excessive oil pressure leakage	a) Replace oil seals as needed
	b) Low oil pump capacity	b) Repair or replace oil pump
	c) Restricted oil pan screen	c) Change transmission fluid and screen
Pressure low in drive	a) Forward clutch	a) Replace forward clutch
Pressure low in 2	a) Forward clutch or intermediate servo	a) Replace forward clutch or intermediate servo
Pressure low in 1	a) Forward clutch and/reverse clutch or servo	a) Replace forward clutch or reverse clutch, and repair or replace servo
Pressure low in R	a) High clutch and/reverse clutch or servo	a) Replace high clutch or reverse clutch, and repair or replace servo
Pressure low in P/N	a) Valve body	a) Clean or replace valve body
Pressure high or low in all test conditions	a) Modulator assembly and/or diaphragm control rod	a) Replace modulator and/or diaphragm control rod

Automatic Shift Point Tests

Testing

The shift test can be performed in the repair shop to check the shift valve operation, governor operation, shift delay pressures, throttle boost and downshift valve action. The following procedure can be used for a guide.

1. Raise the vehicle and support safely so the drive wheels are clear of the floor. Install an oil pressure gauge.

2. Disconnect and plug the vacuum line to the modulator valve. Attach either a hand operated vacuum pump or an electrically operated vacuum pump hose to the nipple on the modulator valve.

3. Assuming the vacuum diaphragm is intact within the modulator valve, apply 18 inches of vacuum to the diaphragm. With the engine operating, place the transmission in the DRIVE mode and make minimum throttle shifts of the 1-2 and 2-3 gearing. As the shift is made, the speedometer needle and the oil pressure gauge needle will make a momentary movement, the speedometer needle moving up, while the oil pressure gauge needle moves downward. Both needles will stabilize as the shift is completed. As the shift is being made, the drive line will bump, due to the interruption of torque. If the shifts are within specifications, the 1-2, 2-3 and governor valves are operating satisfactory.

4. If the shift points are not in specifications, a governor test should be made to isolate the problem.

— CAUTION —
After each test, operate the engine in neutral at 1000 rpm to cool the transmission for a period of one to two minutes.

5. To check the shift delay pressures and the throttle boost, decrease the vacuum at the modulator diaphragm to 0-2 inches of vacuum and make the 1-2 shift. If the shift point raises to specifications, the throttle boost and shift delay valves are operating properly.

6. To check the downshift valve action, keep the vacuum at 0-2 inches at the modulator diaphragm. Position the downshift linkage in the wide open throttle position (WOD) and repeat the 1-2 shift test. The speed of the shift point should be higher.

— CAUTION —
Never exceed 60 mph speedometer speed during any of the above tests.

CONTROL PRESSURE SPECIFICATIONS—1982

Transmission Model*	Range	10" Vacuum
PEN-C, G, J, K,	D	90-101
PEM-AL, AM	2,1	123-136
	R	151-168
PEP-E, F, G, H, P, N	D	87-97
	2,1	119-132
	R	145-162
PEP-B, D	D	86-99
	2,1	120-132
	R	143-165

CONTROL PRESSURE SPECIFICATIONS—1983

Transmission Type	Transmission Model	Range	Idle 15" & Above	Idle 10"	WOT Stall Thru Detent
C5	PEN-G,P,S,U,Y,Z	D	55-70	94-107	162-174
		2,1	107-109	100-112	162-174
		R	91-117	156-178	271-291
		P,N	55-70	94-107	162-174
C5	PEN-AA,AB	D	54-72	92-109	161-176
		2,1	107-119	100-112	161-176
		R	90-121	154-182	268-293
		P,N	54-72	92-109	161-176
C5	PEP-V	D	64-68	86-97	160-169
		2,1	105-114	100-109	160-169
		R	76-96	144-162	267-281
		P,N	64-68	86-97	160-169
C5	PEP-R	D	67-80	99-110	157-165
		2,1	102-112	99-110	157-165
		R	113-133	166-184	261-275
		P,N	67-80	99-110	157-165
C5	PEP-B @	D	66-81	97-111	153-165
		2,1	102-112	103-111	153-165
		R	110-134	162-174	256-274
		P,N	66-81	97-111	153-165
C5	PEJ-AE,AG	D	60-64	83-94	157-165
		2,1	101-111	97-106	157-165
		R	70-90	139-156	262-275
		P,N	60-64	83-94	157-165

CONTROL PRESSURE SPECIFICATIONS—1983

Transmission Type	Transmission Model	Range	Idle 15" & Above	Idle 10"	WOT Stall Thru Detent
C5	PEJ-AF,AH @	D	60-64	82-96	155-167
		2,1	102-110	97-106	155-167
		R	69-94	137-160	259-278
		P,N	60-94	82-96	155-167
C5	PEJ-AJ	D	57-61	83-93	157-165
		2,1	101-111	97-106	157-165
		R	70-90	139-156	262-275
		P,N	57-61	83-93	157-165
C5	PEJ-AK @	D	57-61	82-96	155-167
		2,1	102-110	97-106	155-167
		R	69-94	137-147	259-279
		P,N	57-61	83-93	157-167
C5	PEA-CR	D	64-68	83-94	163-172
		2,1	109-117	104-114	163-172
		R	79-85	139-157	272-287
		P,N	64-68	83-94	163-172

@ Absolute barometric pressure (ABP) 29.25

SHIFT SPEEDS—ACTUAL M.P.H.
C5 Automatic Transmission

1983 3.8L MUSTANG/CAPRI/LTD/MARQUIS/THUNDERBIRD/COUGAR
PEP-R, PEP-W

Throttle	Range	Shift	OPS—R.P.M.	1	2	3
Closed (Above 17" Vacuum)	D	1-2	413-456	12-13	11-13	10-11
	D	2-3	580-761	17-22	15-20	14-18
	D	3-1	331-366	10-11	9-10	8-9
	1	2-1	1074-1271	31-37	29-34	25-30
To Detent (Torque Demand)	D	1-2	907-1187	26-35	24-32	21-28
	D	2-3	1600-1852	47-54	43-49	38-44
	D	3-2	1459-1614	43-47	39-43	34-38
Through Detent (W.O.T.)	D	1-2	1480-1718	43-50	39-46	35-40
	D	2-3	2621-2901	76-85	70-77	62-68
	D	3-2	2359-2516	69-73	63-67	56-59
	D	3-1 2-1	1061-1292	31-38	28-34	25-30

Axle Ratio	Tire Size	Use Column No.
2.47:1	P185/75R14	1
	P195/75R14	1
	205/70HR14	1
	220/55R390	1
2.73:1	P185/75R14	2
	P195/75R14	2
	205/70HR14	2
	220/55R390	2
3.08:1	P185/75R14	3
	P195/75R14	3

1983 3.8L MUSTANG/CAPRI—ALTITUDE
PEP-B1

Throttle	Range	Shift	OPS—R.P.M.	1
Closed (Above 17" Vacuum)	D	1-2	411-457	11-12
	D	2-3	580-761	15-20
	D	3-1	331-366	9-10
	1	2-1	1074-1269	28-33
To Detent (Torque Demand)	D	1-2	845-1185	22-31
	D	2-3	1527-1850	40-49
	D	3-2	1436-1610	38-42
Through Detent (W.O.T.)	D	1-2	1464-1716	39-45
	D	2-3	2600-2898	68-76
	D	3-2	2338-2513	62-66
	D	3-1 2-1	1046-1290	28-34

Axle Ratio	Tire Size	Use Column No.
2.73:1	P185/75R14	1
	P195/75R14	1
	205/70HR14	1
	220/55R390	1

1983 3.8L T'BIRD/COUGAR
PEP-V

Throttle	Range	Shift	OPS—R.P.M.	1	2
Closed (Above 17" Vacuum)	D	1-2	421-467	12-14	12-14
	D	2-3	586-807	17-23	17-24
	D	3-1	331-366	10-11	10-11
	1	2-1	1091-1313	32-38	32-39
To Detent (Torque Demand)	D	1-2	831-1193	24-35	25-35
	D	2-3	1496-1845	44-54	44-55
	D	3-2	1330-1542	39-45	40-46
Through Detent (W.O.T.)	D	1-2	1506-1769	44-51	45-53
	D	2-3	2655-2971	77-87	79-89
	D	3-2	2387-2582	69-75	71-77
	D	3-1 2-1	1080-1332	31-39	32-40

Axle Ratio	Tire Size	Use Column No.
2.47:1	P185/75R14	1
	P195/75R14	2
	P205/70R14	1
	220/55R390	1
	205/60R390	1

1983 3.3L FAIRMONT/ZEPHYR-SEDAN, POLICE, TAXI, LTD/MARQUIS
PEN-P, PEN-G, PEN-S, PEN-U, PEN-Y, PEN-Z, PEN-CA

Throttle	Range	Shift	OPS—R.P.M.	1	2
Closed (Above 17" Vacuum)	D	1-2	399-446	10-11	11-12
	D	2-3	585-847	15-22	15-22
	D	3-1	331-366	8-9	9-10
	1	2-1	1091-1317	28-34	29-35
To Detent (Torque Demand)	D	1-2	492-964	13-25	13-25
	D	2-3	1107-1551	29-40	29-41
	D	3-2	1040-1515	27-39	27-40
Through Detent (W.O.T.)	D	1-2	1514-1775	39-46	40-47
	D	2-3	2683-3008	69-78	71-80
	D	3-2	2426-2633	63-68	64-70
	D	3-1 2-1	1094-1344	28-35	29-35

Axle Ratio	Tire Size	Use Column No.
2.73	P175/75R14	1
	190/65R390	
2.73	P185/75R14	2
	P195/75R14	2
	P205/70R14	2
	195/70R14	2

1983 3.3L FAIRMONT/ZEPHYR-SEDAN, POLICE, TAXI
PEN-AA, AB, BA

Throttle	Range	Shift	OPS—R.P.M.	1	2
Closed (Above 17" Vacuum)	D	1-2	398-449	10-12	10-12
	D	2-3	582-854	15-22	15-23
	D	3-1	331-366	8-9	9-10
	1	2-1	1091-1317	28-34	29-35
To Detent (Torque Demand)	D	1-2	490-994	13-26	13-26
	D	2-3	1085-1589	28-41	29-42
	D	3-2	978-1545	35-40	26-41
Through Detent (W.O.T.)	D	1-2	1506-1781	39-46	40-47
	D	2-3	2673-3016	69-78	71-80
	D	3-2	2416-2641	62-68	64-70
	D	3-1 2-1	1087-1348	28-35	29-36

Axle Ratio	Tire Size	Use Column No.
2.73	P175/75R14 190/65R390	1
2.73	P185/75R14	2
	P195/75R14	2
	P205/70R14	2
	195/70HR14	2

1983 3.8L F100 4 x 2
PEA-CR1

Throttle	Range	Shift	OPS—R.P.M.	1	2	3
Closed (Above 17" Vacuum)	D	1-2	409-444	11-12	12-13	13-14
	D	2-3	655-864	19-24	19-25	20-27
	D	3-1	331-366	9-10	10-11	10-11
	1	2-1	1104-1303	31-37	32-38	34-40
To Detent (Torque Demand)	D	1-2	490-910	14-26	14-27	15-28
	D	2-3	1079-1489	30-42	31-45	33-46
	D	3-2	1017-1498	29-42	30-44	31-46
Through Detent (W.O.T.)	D	1-2	1513-1751	43-49	44-51	48-54
	D	2-3	2682-2975	76-84	78-87	82-91
	D	3-2	2435-2610	69-74	71-76	75-80
	D	3-1 2-1	1100-1329	31-38	32-39	34-41

Axle Ratio	Tire Size	Use Column No.
2.73:1	P195/75R15SL	1
	P215/75R15SL	2
	P235/75R15XL	3

1983 2.3L RANGER 4 x 2
PEJ-AE1

Throttle	Range	Shift	OPS—R.P.M.	1	2	3	4	5	6
Closed (Above 17" Vacuum)	D	1-2	405-440	8-9	8-9	8-9	8-9	8-9	8-9
	D	2-3	880-1116	18-23	18-24	19-24	17-21	17-22	18-22
	D	3-1	331-366	6-7	7-8	7-8	6-7	6-7	6-7
	1	2-1	1478-1724	30-35	31-37	32-37	28-33	29-34	30-35
To Detent (Torque Demand)	D	1-2	831-1441	17-30	18-30	18-31	16-28	16-28	17-29
	D	2-3	1477-2004	30-41	31-43	32-44	28-38	29-39	30-40
	D	3-2	1458-1740	30-36	31-37	32-38	28-33	29-34	29-35
Through Detent (W.O.T.)	D	1-2	1977-2283	40-47	42-49	43-50	38-44	39-45	40-46
	D	2-3	3071-3438	63-70	65-73	67-75	59-66	66-68	62-69
	D	3-2	2743-2965	56-60	58-63	60-65	53-57	54-58	55-60
	D	3-1 2-1	1485-1768	30-36	32-38	32-39	28-34	29-35	30-36

Axle Ratio	Tire Size	Use Column No.
3.45	185/75R14SL	1
	195/75R14SL	2
	P205/75R14SL	3
	P205/75R14XL	3
3.73	185/75R14SL	4
	195/75R14SL	5
	P205/75R14SL	6
	P205/75R14XL	

1984 3.8L LTD/MARQUIS—50 STATES

Throttle	Range	Shift	OPS—R.P.M.	1	2
Closed (Above 17" Vacuum)	D	1-2	421-467	11-12	11-13
	D	2-3	586-807	15-21	16-22
	D	3-1	331-366	9-10	9-10
	1	2-1	1091-1313	29-35	29-35
To Detent (Torque Demand)	D	1-2	612-1063	16-28	16-29
	D	2-3	1240-1659	33-44	33-45
	D	3-2	1139-1542	30-41	31-42
Through Detent (W.O.T.)	D	1-2	1506-1769	40-47	41-48
	D	2-3	2655-2971	70-78	72-80
	D	3-2	2387-2582	63-68	64-70
	D	3-1 2-1	1080-1332	28-35	29-36

Axle Ratio	Tire Size	Use Column No.
2.73:1	P185/75R14	1
	P195/75R14	2

1984 3.8L THUNDERBIRD/COUGAR—50 STATES

Throttle	Range	Shift	OPS—R.P.M.	1	2
Closed (Above 17" Vacuum)	D	1-2	421-467	11-13	11-12
	D	2-3	586-807	16-22	15-21
	D	3-1	331-366	9-10	9-10
	1	2-1	1091-1313	29-35	29-35
To Detent (Torque Demand)	D	1-2	831-1193	22-32	22-32
	D	2-3	1496-1845	40-50	40-49
	D	3-2	1330-1542	36-42	35-41
Through Detent (W.O.T.)	D	1-2	1506-1769	41-48	40-47
	D	2-3	2655-2971	72-80	70-78
	D	3-2	2387-2582	64-70	63-68
	D	3-1 2-1	1080-1332	29-36	28-35

Axle Ratio	Tire Size	Use Column No.
2.73:1	P195/75R14	1
	P205/70R14	1
	205/70HR14	1
	220/55R390	2

1984 3.8L LTD/MARQUIS, THUNDERBIRD/COUGAR—UNIQUE CANADA

Throttle	Range	Shift	OPS—R.P.M.	1	2
Closed (Above 17" Vacuum)	D	1-2	399-446	9-10	9-11
	D	2-3	500-744	12-17	12-18
	D	3-1	331-366	8-9	8-9
	1	2-1	1091-1317	25-31	26-31
To Detent (Torque Demand)	D	1-2	829-1192	19-28	20-28
	D	2-3	1493-1844	35-43	36-44
	D	3-2	1354-1564	32-36	32-37
Through Detent (W.O.T.)	D	1-2	1514-1775	35-41	36-42
	D	2-3	2666-2981	62-70	64-71
	D	3-2	2407-2602	56-61	57-62
	D	3-1 2-1	1094-1344	26-31	26-32

Axle Ratio	Tire Size	Use Column No.
3.08:1	P185/75R14	1
	P195/75R14	2
	P205/70R14	1
	205/70HR14	1
	220/55R390	1

1984 3.8L MUSTANG/CAPRI—50 STATES/ALTITUDE

Throttle	Range	Shift	OPS—R.P.M.	1	2
Closed (Above 17″ Vacuum)	D	1-2	413-456	11-12	11-12
	D	2-3	580-761	15-20	16-20
	D	3-1	331-366	9-10	9-10
	1	2-1	1074-1271	28-33	29-34
To Detent (Torque Demand)	D	1-2	907-1187	24-31	24-32
	D	2-3	1600-1852	42-49	43-50
	D	3-2	1459-1614	38-42	40-43
Through Detent (W.O.T.)	D	1-2	1480-1718	39-45	40-46
	D	2-3	2621-2901	69-76	71-78
	D	3-2	2359-2516	62-66	64-68
	D	3-1 2-1	1061-1292	28-34	29-35

Axle Ratio	Tire Size	Use Column No.
2.73:1	P185/75R14	1
	P195/75R14	2
	205/70HR14	2
	220/55R390	1

1984 3.8L MUSTANG/CAPRI—ALTITUDE

Throttle	Range	Shift	OPS—R.P.M.	1	2
Closed (Above 17″ Vacuum)	D	1-2	411-457	11-12	11-12
	D	2-3	580-761	15-20	16-20
	D	3-1	331-366	9-11	9-10
	1	2-1	1074-1269	28-33	29-34
To Detent (Torque Demand)	D	1-2	845-1185	22-31	23-32
	D	2-3	1527-1850	40-49	41-49
	D	3-2	1436-1610	38-42	39-43
Through Detent (W.O.T.)	D	1-2	1464-1716	38-45	39-46
	D	2-3	2600-2898	68-76	70-78
	D	3-2	2338-2513	61-66	63-68
	D	3-1 2-1	1046-1290	27-34	28-35

Axle Ratio	Tire Size	Use Column No.
2.73:1	P185/75R14	1
	P195/75R14	2
	205/70HR14	2
	220/55R390	1

1984 3.8L MUSTANG/CAPRI—CANADA

Throttle	Range	Shift	OPS—R.P.M.	1	2
Closed (Above 17″ Vacuum)	D	1-2	421-467	11-12	11-13
	D	2-3	586-807	15-21	16-22
	D	3-1	331-366	9-10	9-10
	1	2-1	1091-1313	29-35	29-35
To Detent (Torque Demand)	D	1-2	925-1193	24-31	25-32
	D	2-3	1613-1845	42-49	43-50
	D	3-2	1330-1542	35-41	36-41
Through Detent (W.O.T.)	D	1-2	1506-1764	40-47	41-48
	D	2-3	2655-2971	70-78	72-80
	D	3-2	2387-2582	63-68	64-70
	D	3-1 2-1	1080-1332	28-35	29-36

Axle Ratio	Tire Size	Use Column No.
2.73:1	P185/75R14	1
	P195/75R14	2
	205/70HR14	2
	220/55R390	1

1984 4.9L F-150—50 STATES
3.08 Axle Ratio

Throttle	Range	Shift	OPS—R.P.M.	1	2	3
Closed (Above 17" Vacuum)	D	1-2	405-449	10-12	11-12	10-11
	D	2-3	574-776	15-20	16-21	14-19
	D	3-1	331-366	8-9	9-10	8-9
	1	2-1	1004-1192	26-31	27-32	25-30
To Detent (Torque Demand)	D	1-2	724-995	19-26	20-27	18-25
	D	2-3	1341-1536	35-40	36-42	34-38
	D	3-2	1070-1259	28-33	29-34	27-31
Through Detent (W.O.T.)	D	1-2	1373-1598	35-41	37-43	34-40
	D	2-3	2413-2681	62-69	65-73	60-67
	D	3-2	2170-2324	56-60	59-63	54-58
	D	3-1 2-1	998-1218	26-31	27-33	25-30

Axle Ratio	Tire Size	Use Column No.
3.08:1	P215/75R15SL	1
	P235/75R15XL	2
	P195/75R15SL	3

1984 5.0L F-150—49 STATES/CANADA
3.55 Axle Ratio

Throttle	Range	Shift	OPS—R.P.M.	1	2	3
Closed (Above 17" Vacuum)	D	1-2	413-456	11-12	11-12	10-11
	D	2-3	580-761	15-22	16-21	15-19
	D	3-1	331-366	8-9	9-10	8-9
	1	2-1	1122-1320	29-34	30-36	28-33
To Detent (Torque Demand)	D	1-2	1031-1240	27-32	28-34	26-31
	D	2-3	1690-1852	44-48	46-50	42-46
	D	3-2	1459-1614	38-42	40-44	36-40
Through Detent (W.O.T.)	D	1-2	1516-1755	39-45	41-48	38-44
	D	2-3	2621-2901	68-75	71-79	66-73
	D	3-2	2359-2516	61-65	64-68	59-63
	D	3-1 2-1	1110-1341	29-35	30-36	28-34

Axle Ratio	Tire Size	Use Column No.
3.55:1	P215/75R15SL	1
	P235/75R15XL	2
	P195/75RSL	3

1984 3.8L BRONCO II/RANGER 4x4—50 STATES/CANADA

Throttle	Range	Shift	OPS—R.P.M.	1	2	3	4
Closed (Above 17" Vacuum)	D	1-2	399-446	9-10	9-10	8-9	8-9
	D	2-3	826-1120	18-25	19-25	17-23	17-23
	D	3-1	331-366	7-8	7-8	7-8	7-8
	1	2-1	1420-1695	32-38	32-38	29-35	30-36
To Detent (Torque Demand)	D	1-2	898-1435	20-32	20-33	18-30	19-30
	D	2-3	1660-2166	37-48	38-49	34-45	35-
	D	3-2	1595-1885	35-42	36-43	33-39	34-40
Through Detent (W.O.T.)	D	1-2	1921-2250	43-50	44-51	39-46	40-47
	D	2-3	3156-3564	70-79	72-81	65-73	66-75
	D	3-2	2817-3082	63-69	64-70	58-63	59-65
	D	3-1 2-1	1423-1727	32-38	32-39	29-36	30-36

Axle Ratio	Tire Size	Use Column No.
3.45:1	P195/75R15SL	1
	P205/75R15SL	2
3.73:1	P195/75R15SL	3
	P205/75R15SL	4

1984 2.8L BRONCO II/RANGER 4x4—ALTITUDE

Throttle	Range	Shift	OPS—R.P.M.	1	2
Closed (Above 17" Vacuum)	D	1-2	398-449	8-9	8-9
	D	2-3	823-1128	17-23	17-24
	D	3-1	331-366	7-8	7-8
	1	2-1	1420-1695	29-35	30-36
To Detent (Torque Demand)	D	1-2	848-1466	17-30	18-31
	D	2-3	1607-2207	33-45	34-46
	D	3-2	1559-1895	32-39	33-40
Through Detent (W.O.T.)	D	1-2	1912-2257	39-46	40-48
	D	2-3	3144-3577	65-74	66-75
	D	3-2	2805-3091	58-64	59-65
	D	3-1 2-1	1415-1733	29-36	30-36

Axle Ratio	Tire Size	Use Column No.
3.73:1	P195/75R15SL	1
	P205/75R15SL	2

GOVERNOR PRESSURE TEST

Testing

To perform a governor pressure test, use the following procedure as a guide.

1. Raise the vehicle and support safely so the drive wheels are clear of the floor. Install an oil pressure gauge.

2. Disconnect and plug the vacuum line to the modulator valve. Attach either a hand operated vacuum pump or an electrically operated vacuum pump hose to the nipple on the modulator valve.

3. With the engine operating, place the selector lever in the DRIVE position, with no load on the engine and apply 10 inches of vacuum to the modulator diaphragm.

4. Increase the engine speed slowly and watch the speedometer and the control pressure gauge.

5. The control pressure cutback should occur between 6-20 mph.

─────────── CAUTION ───────────

Do not exceed 60 mph speedometer speed and after each test, place the transmission in neutral and operate the engine at 1000 rpm to cool the transmission.

6. The governor is good if the cutback of the control pressure occurs within specifications. If the cutback does not occur within specifications, check the shift speeds to verify that it is the governor and not a stuck cutback valve. Service or replace the governor as required.

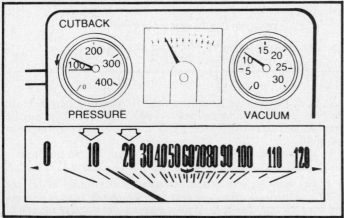

Checking shift points and governor light load tests (©Ford Motor Company)

STALL TEST

The stall test is used to check the maximum engine rpm (no more increase in engine rpm at wide open throttle) with the selector lever in the "D", "2", "1" and reverse positions and to determine if any slippage is occurring from the clutches, bands or torque converter. The engine operation is noted and a determination can be made as to its performance.

Performing the Stall Test

1. Check the engine oil level, start the engine and bring to normal operating temperature.

2. Check the transmission fluid level and correct as necessary. Attach a calibrated tachometer to the engine and a 0-400 psi oil pressure gauge to the transmission control pressure tap on the left side of the case.

3. Mark the specified maximum engine rpm on the tachometer cover plate with a grease pencil to immediately check if the stall speed is over or under specifications.

4. Apply the parking brake and block both front and rear wheels.

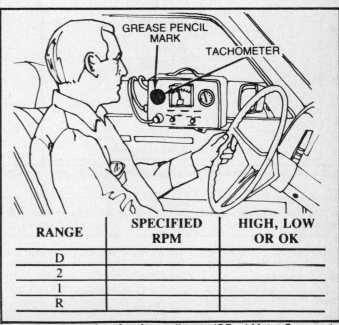

RANGE	SPECIFIED RPM	HIGH, LOW OR OK
D		
2		
1		
R		

Preparation for and performing stall tests (©Ford Motor Company)

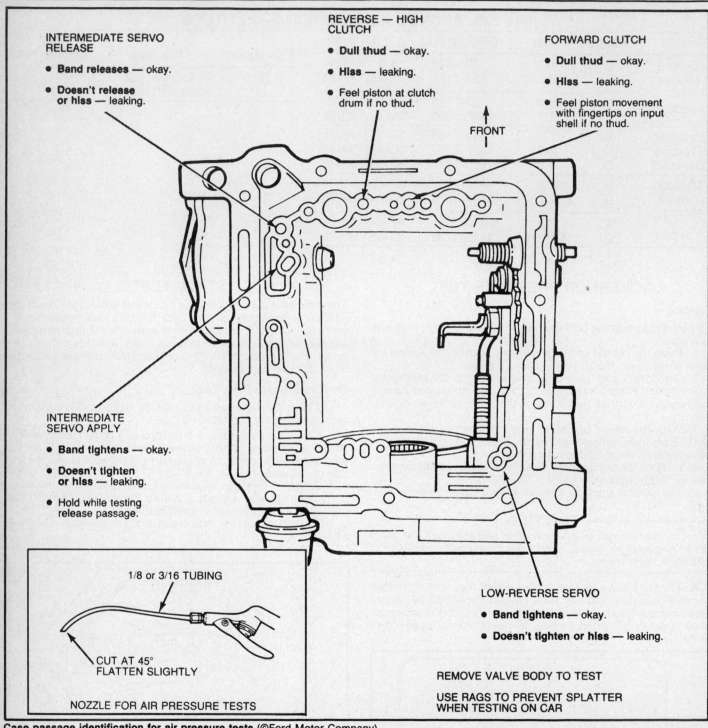

INTERMEDIATE SERVO RELEASE

- **Band releases** — okay.

- **Doesn't release or hiss** — leaking.

REVERSE — HIGH CLUTCH

- **Dull thud** — okay.

- **Hiss** — leaking.

- Feel piston at clutch drum if no thud.

FRONT

FORWARD CLUTCH

- **Dull thud** — okay.

- **Hiss** — leaking.

- Feel piston movement with fingertips on input shell if no thud.

INTERMEDIATE SERVO APPLY

- **Band tightens** — okay.

- **Doesn't tighten or hiss** — leaking.

- Hold while testing release passage.

1/8 or 3/16 TUBING

CUT AT 45° FLATTEN SLIGHTLY

NOZZLE FOR AIR PRESSURE TESTS

LOW-REVERSE SERVO

- **Band tightens** — okay.

- **Doesn't tighten or hiss** — leaking.

REMOVE VALVE BODY TO TEST

USE RAGS TO PREVENT SPLATTER WHEN TESTING ON CAR

Case passage identification for air pressure tests (©Ford Motor Company)

─────── CAUTION ───────

Do not allow anyone in front of the vehicle while performing the stall test.

5. While holding the brake pedal with the left foot, place the selector lever in "D" position and slowly depress the accelerator.

6. Read and record the engine rpm when the accelerator pedal is fully depressed and the engine rpm is stabilized. Read and record the oil pressure reading at the high engine rpm point.

─────── CAUTION ───────

The stall test must be made within five seconds.

7. Shift the selector lever into the "N" position and increase the engine rpm to approximately 1000-1200. Hold the engine speed for one to two minutes to cool the converter, transmission and fluid.

8. Make similar tests in the "2", "1" and reverse positions.

─────── CAUTION ───────

If at any time the engine rpm exceeds the maximum as per the specifications, indications are that a clutch unit or band is slipping and the stall test should be stopped before more damage is done to the internal parts.

9. Refer to the stall test results chart for further diagnostic information.

STALL SPEED SPECIFICATIONS—1982

Vehicle Application	Engine Disp.	Transmission Type	Converter Size	Stall Speed Min.	Max.
F-100	3.8L	C5	12″	1759	1961
F-100	4.2L	C5	12″	1869	2077

STALL SPEED SPECIFICATIONS—1983-84

Vehicle	Engine/Litre Displacement	Transmission Type	Converter Size (Inches)	ID	Stall Speed (RPM) Min.	Max.
Mustang/Capri/Fairmont/ Zephyr/LTD/Marquis	3.3L	C5	12″	FY	1527	1785
		C5	10¼″	GD	1503	1760
LTD/Marquis/Mustang/Capri/ Fairmont/Zephyr	3.8L	C5	12″	GB	1648	1911
Ranger 4x4, Bronco II	2.3L	C5	10¼″	BU①	2635③	3031③
F-100, F-150	3.8L	C5	12″	GB②	1737	2022

① 1984 GH   ③ 1984 Min. stall speed—2539
② 1984 GE   Max. stall speed—2988

STALL SPEED TEST RESULTS CHART

Selector Positions	Stall Speed(s) High (Slip)	Stall Speeds Low
D only	Low (Planetary) One-Way Clutch	
D, 2 and 1	Forward Clutch	1. Does engine misfire or bog down under load?
All Driving Ranges	Perform Control Pressure Test	Check Engine for Tune-Up. If OK . . .
R Only	Reverse and High Clutch or Low-Reverse Band or Servo	2. Remove torque converter and bench test for reactor one-way clutch slip.

AIR PRESSURE TESTS

Air pressure testing is helpful in locating leak points during disassembly, and in verifying that the fluid circuits are not leaking during build-up. If the road test disclosed which clutch or servo isn't holding, that is the circuit to be air tested. Use air pressure regulated to about 25 psi and check for air escaping to detect leakage. If the pressures are found to be low in a clutch, servo or passageway, a verification can be accomplished by removing the valve body and performing an air pressure test. This test can serve two purposes:

1. To determine if a malfunction of a clutch or band is caused by fluid leakage in the system or is the result of a mechanical failure.
2. To test the transmission for internal fluid leakage during rebuilding and before completing the assembly.

Air Pressure Test Procedure

1. Obtain an air nozzle and adjust for 25 psi.
2. Apply air pressure (25 psi) to the passages as listed in the accompanying chart.

AIR PRESSURE DIAGNOSIS CHART

Passage	Tests OK If	Leaking If
Reverse-and-high clutch	Dull thud or you can feel piston movement at the clutch drum	Hissing or no piston movement
Forward clutch	Dull thud or you can feel piston movement on the input shell	Hissing or no piston movement
Intermediate servo apply	Front band tightens	Hissing or no application
Intermediate servo release	Band releases while applying pressure to both passages 6 and 7	Hissing or no band release
Low-and-reverse servo apply	Rear band tightens	Hissing or no band apply

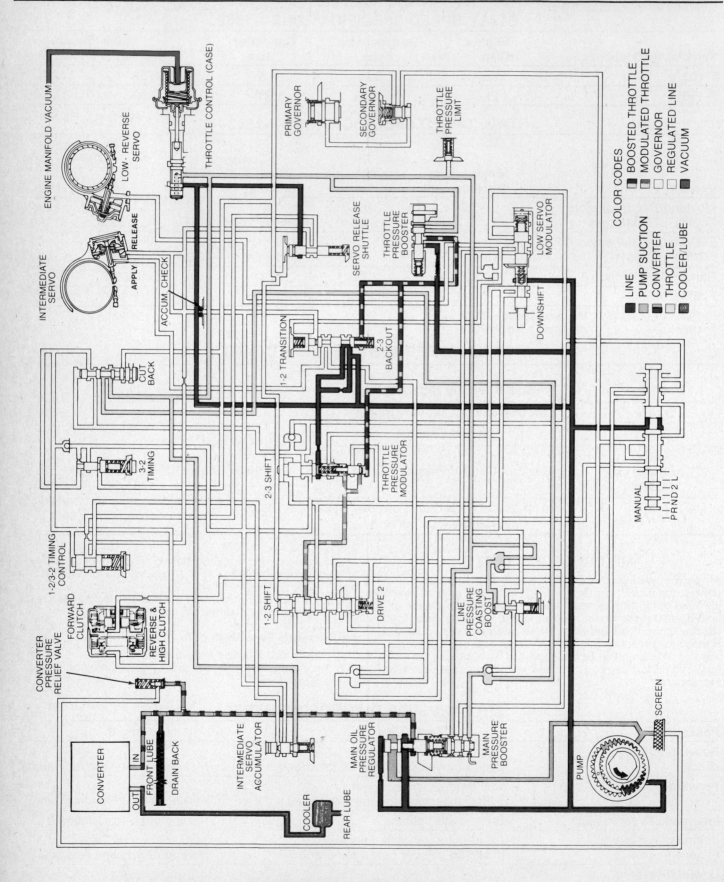

Neutral/Park Position (©Ford Motor Company)

NEUTRAL/PARK

Units Applied—None

The selector lever is in the Park or Neutral position and no torque is transmitted to the output shaft of the transmission. However, in the Park position, the output shaft is mechanically locked by the parking pawl and gear.

THE PRESSURE REGULATOR AND SUPPLY SYSTEM

The oil pump is supplying pressurized fluid to the pressure regulator and to the manual valve, the throttle pressure booster valve, throttle control valve, servo release shuttle valve and the 2-3 shift valve. Pressure is also routed to the torque converter passage, feeding the front lubrication system, the cooler system and the rear lubrication system. The regulator valve is controlling the main line pressure psi level and the converter pressure relief valve is limiting the converter pressure.

THE FLOW CONTROL SYSTEM

Throttle pressure is being directed to the main pressure booster valve, throttle pressure booster valve, cut-back valve, intermediate servo accumulator valve, line pressure coasting boost valve and to the throttle pressure limit valve, preventing excessive throttle pressure, should the throttle valve stick.

THE CLUTCHES, BAND SERVOS AND ACCUMULATOR SYSTEM

None of the applying members are receiving fluid pressure while the transmission is in the Park or Neutral position.

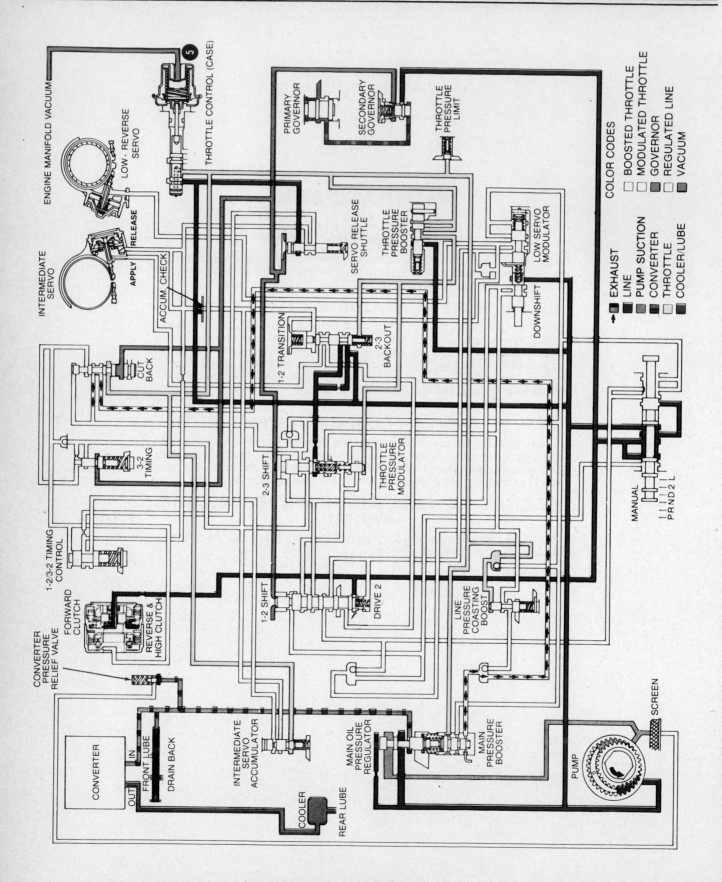

Drive, First Gear (©Ford Motor Company)

DRIVE—FIRST GEAR

Units Applied—Forward Clutch, One Way Clutch

The selector lever is in the Drive position and the vehicle is moving approximately 15-20 mph with the throttle half open.

THE PRESSURE REGULATOR AND SUPPLY SYSTEM

The oil pump is supplying pressurized fluid to the pressure regulator valve, which in turn directs regulated fluid pressure to the manual control valve, the converter, cooler and lubrication systems.

THE FLOW CONTROL SYSTEM

With the manual control valve in the Drive position, pressurized fluid is directed to the governor, the throttle valve assembly and to the forward clutch. The forward clutch is applied and because the throttle valve and governor assemblies are in operation, their respective circuits are opened. Throttle pressure is applied to the throttle pressure booster valve, the line pressure coasting boost valve, intermediate servo accumulator valve, throttle pressure modulator valve, 2-3 back-out valve and the throttle pressure limit valve. Manifold vaccum to the throttle valve diaphragm is approximately 4 Hg and a regulated throttle pressure of approximately 65 psi. The throttle pressure boost valve will not regulating T.V. pressure until the T.V. pressure reaches approximately 68 psi. The governor pressure is regulated from approximately 10 psi to about 80 psi, proportional to road speed. The governor pressure is used to operate the cutback valve, between 9-12 psi, preventing a rough upshift during the 1-2 shift. As the road speed of the vehicle increases, the upshifts automatically occur by movement of the shift and related valves, acted upon by the increase in governor pressure. The governor pressure is opposed by T.V. pressure and line pressure, assisted by spring tension.

THE CLUTCHES, BAND SERVOS AND ACCUMULATOR SYSTEMS

The forward clutch is applied and the one-way clutch is holding. The accumulator is not operating while in the 1st gear position.

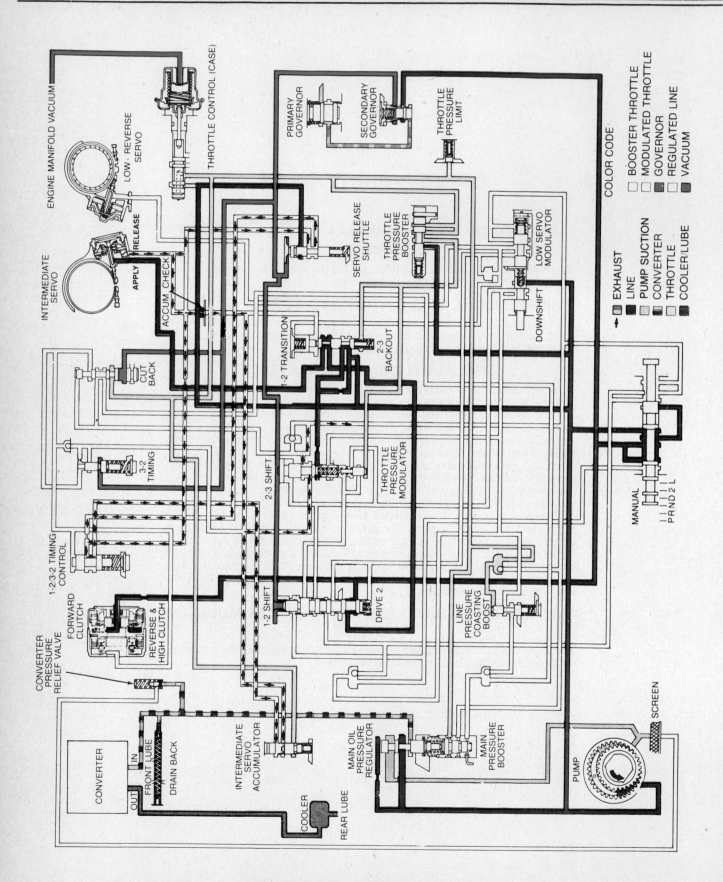

Drive, Second Gear (©Ford Motor Company)

DRIVE—SECOND GEAR

Units Applied—Forward Clutch, Intermediate Band

The selector lever is in the Drive position. The 1-2 shift has been completed and the transmission is now in the second speed. The vehicle is traveling approximately 20 mph and the throttle is one-half open.

PRESSURE REGULATOR AND SUPPLY SYSTEM

The oil pump is supplying pressurized fluid to the pressure regulator valve, which in turn, directs regulated fluid pressure to the manual control valve, the converter cooler and lubrication systems.

FLOW CONTROL SYSTEM

The line pressure is still directed to the forward clutch and the governor assembly. The governor pressure had shifted the control pressure cutback valve before the 1-2 upshift. Vacuum to the T.V. diaphragm is approximately 5 Hg and the regulated T.V. pressure is about 60 psi. The throttle pressure booster valve is in operation and as the speed of the vehicle increases, so does the governor pressure, in order to make the 2-3 upshift. This is accomplished by governor pressure overcoming the T.V. and main line pressure resistance.

THE CLUTCHES, BAND SERVOS AND ACCUMULATOR SYSTEM

The forward clutch remains engaged while the intermediate band has engaged during the 1-2 shift. The servo accumulator valve is used to control the 1-2 upshift feel by allowing the intermediate band to apply smoothly through the control of fluid (not-pressurized) exhausting from the servo release side.

Three exhaust paths are open for the exhausting procedure, one, with the vehicle below 30 mph, the servo release shuttle valve is held open by its spring and the fluid can exhaust around it to the 1-2/3-2 timing control valve. Secondly, at any road speed, the servo release fluid flows through the exhaust passage, to the high speed downshift orifice, to join the exhaust flow at the 1-2/3-2 timing control valve. The fluid then flows between the valve lands and the top of the accumulator valve. As the pressure builds up enough to overcome T.V. pressure, the accumulator moves down, causing a cushioning effect due to the pressure balance. The fluid then flows to the 2-3 shift valve, which is connected to the reverse pressure circuit, which is exhausted in all forward gears.

Third, the fluid can exhaust through the orifice in the accumulator check valve. This orifice causes a gradual bleed down of fluid, directing the fluid into the flow path from the accumulator exhaust.

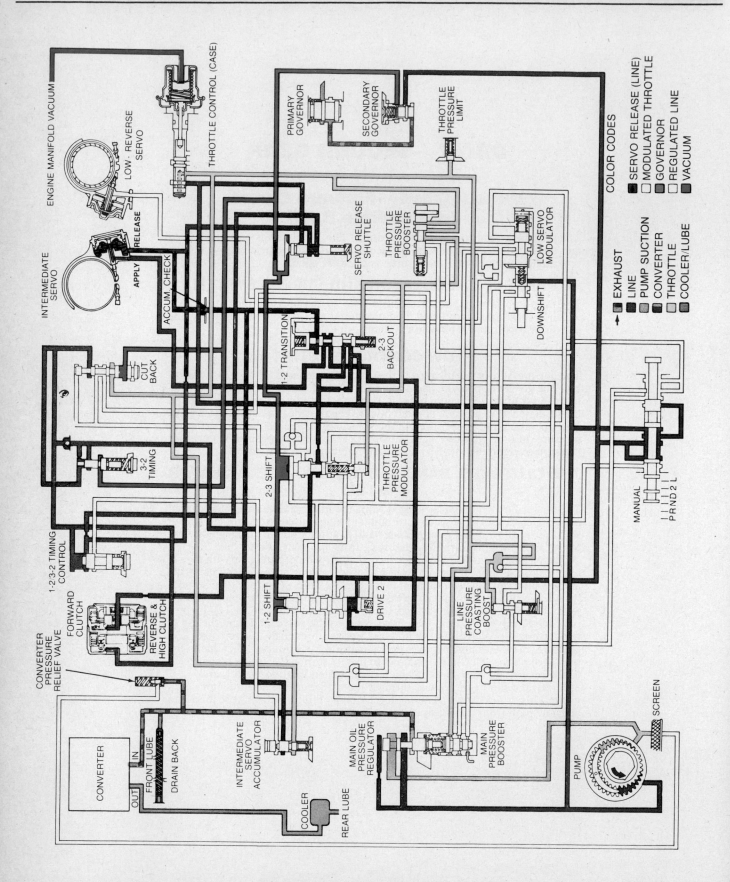

ENGINE MANIFOLD VACUUM

LOW · REVERSE SERVO

THROTTLE CONTROL (CASE)

PRIMARY GOVERNOR

SECONDARY GOVERNOR

THROTTLE PRESSURE LIMIT

COLOR CODES

SERVO RELEASE (LINE)
MODULATED THROTTLE
GOVERNOR
REGULATED LINE
VACUUM

INTERMEDIATE SERVO

APPLY   RELEASE

ACCUM. CHECK

SERVO RELEASE SHUTTLE

THROTTLE PRESSURE BOOSTER

LOW SERVO MODULATOR

EXHAUST
LINE
PUMP SUCTION
CONVERTER
THROTTLE
COOLER/LUBE

CUT BACK

1-2 TRANSITION

2-3 BACKOUT

DOWNSHIFT

3-2 TIMING

2-3 SHIFT

THROTTLE PRESSURE MODULATOR

MANUAL
P R N D 2 L

1-2-3-2 TIMING CONTROL

FORWARD CLUTCH

REVERSE & HIGH CLUTCH

1-2 SHIFT

DRIVE 2

LINE PRESSURE COASTING BOOST

CONVERTER PRESSURE RELIEF VALVE

SCREEN

CONVERTER

IN

OUT

FRONT LUBE

DRAIN BACK

INTERMEDIATE SERVO ACCUMULATOR

MAIN OIL PRESSURE REGULATOR

MAIN PRESSURE BOOSTER

PUMP

COOLER

REAR LUBE

Drive, Third Gear (©Ford Motor Company)

DRIVE—THIRD GEAR

Units Applied—Forward Clutch, Reverse/High Clutch

The selector lever is in the Drive position. The 2-3 up-shift has been completed and the transmission is now in the third speed and the vehicle traveling at 30 mph. During the 2-3 up shift, it is necessary to apply the reverse and high (direct) clutch and to release the intermediate band servo in such a manner as to avoid an engine overspeed. The timing of the band release and the clutch apply is controlled to provide a slight "tie-up", causing the clutch to slip momentarily until the band is fully released.

PRESSURE REGULATOR AND SUPPLY SYSTEM

The oil pump is supplying pressurized fluid to the pressure regulator valve, which in turn, directs regulated fluid pressure to the manual control valve, the converter and the lubrication systems. The line pressure is still directed to the forward clutch and to the governor assembly. The engine vacuum to the T.V. pressure modulator remains around 5 Hg, with the regulated T.V. pressure near 60 psi.

THE CLUTCHES, BAND SERVOS AND ACCUMULATOR SYSTEM

As the 2-3 upshift occurred, governor pressure overcame the T.V. pressure, the line pressure and the valve spring pressure, to move the 2-3 shift valve. As the 2-3 shift valve moved, the intermediate servo release exhaust path through the reverse circuit, was closed. The 2-3 shift valve has opened the direct clutch apply circuit, through the upshift orifice, which control the build-up of pressure to apply the clutch, until the servo is fully released.

Since the release side of the servo piston has a larger area than the apply side and is aided by the spring, the servo will release the band as soon as the release pressure builds up to equal the apply pressure. As the servo is released, a pressure "build-up" occurs, equalizing the entire servo release and direct clutch apply and stopping the slight slippage of the direct clutch. A unique feature is that release pressure is applied to the top of the 2-3 back-out valve, to prevent a clutch-band tie up, should the operator release the accelerator during the upshift.

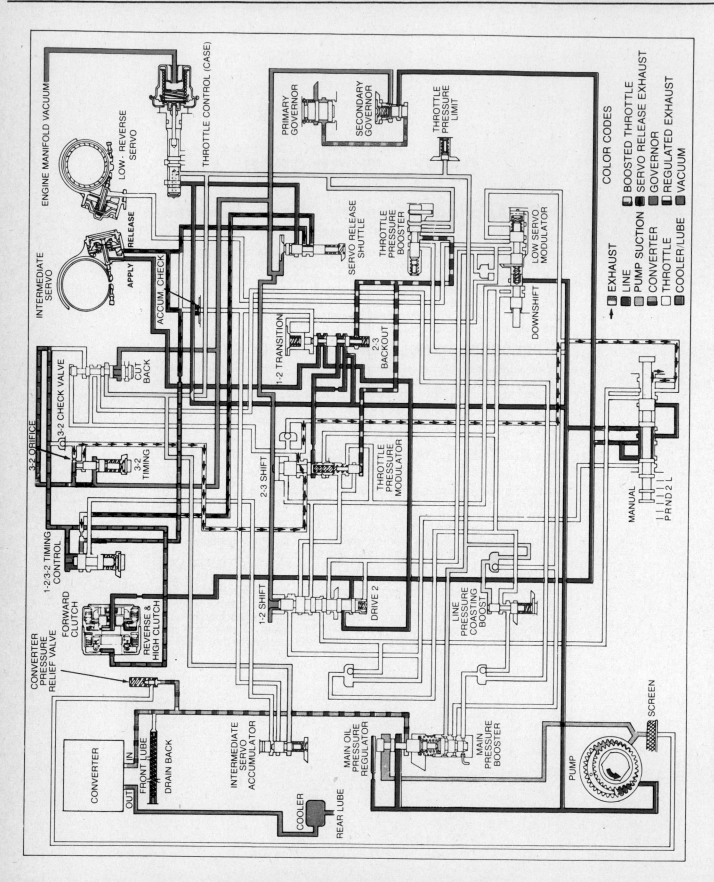

3-2 Downshift, Torque Demand (©Ford Motor Company)

3-2 DOWNSHIFT, TORQUE DEMAND

Units Applied—Forward Clutch, Intermediate Band

As the operator depresses the accelerator to nearly full open throttle without depressing the downshift rod, the transmission will downshift on what is known as a "Torque Demand" downshift. The 3-2 torque demand downshift requires careful timing to prevent roughness during the downshift. When the transmission assembly is equipped with a converter clutch and the vehicle is at cruising speed, the converter clutch is operating at high capacity lock-up and there is very little slip in the converter to cushion the shift. During the downshift, the reverse/high (direct) clutch must be released and the intermediate servo applied.

PRESSURE REGULATOR AND SUPPLY SYSTEM

The oil pump is supplying pressurized fluid to the pressure regulator valve, which in turn directs regulated fluid pressure to the manual control valve, the converter, cooler and to the lubrication systems.

THE CLUTCHES, BAND SERVOS AND ACCUMULATOR SYSTEMS

Main line pressure is directed to the forward clutch and governor system. While the transmission is in third gear, the forward and reverse/high (direct) clutches are engaged. With the 3-2 torque demand downshift, the forward clutch remains applied while the reverse/high (direct) clutch is released and the intermediate band is applied. As the throttle is depressed, the engine vacuum drops to approximately 2-3 Hg, causing the T.V. pressure to be regulated near maximum and causing the line pressure to be boosted. Modulated throttle pressure and spring force has forced the 2-3 shift valve up, causing the intermediate servo to apply and exhausting the servo release circuit to the reverse system. To properly time the downshift, the 3-2 check valve closes as soon as the reverse/high (direct) clutch apply circuit is forced to exhaust through the 3-2 timing valve or the 3-2 orifice. The 3-2 orifice is so small, causing the timing valve to be forced down by the back pressure in the clutch circuit. At the same time, the 1-2/3-2 timing valve is held down by the reverse and high clutch pressure. This permits the servo release exhaust flow to join the reverse and high clutch flow. However, the servo release in the servo is not the same as clutch pressure because of the high and low speed orifices. The 3-2 timing valve goes into regulation, maintaining a back pressure in the clutch apply circuit and back to the low speed and high speed orifices in the servo release circuit, until the servo piston has fully applied. This pressure controls the clutch release, allowing it to slip until the servo is fully on. As the release exhaust flow stops, the 3-2 timing valve moves back up and the clutch pressure then bleeds through the 3-2 orifice. As the clutch pressure drops below 13 psi, the 1-2/3-2 valve moves back up.

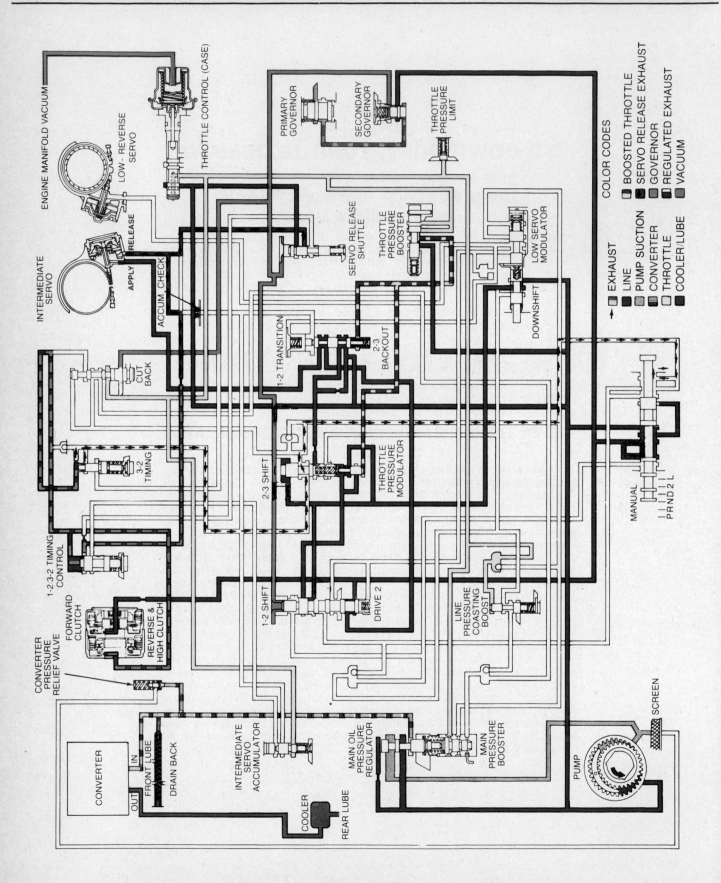

3-2 Downshift, Through Detent (©Ford Motor Company)

3-2 DOWNSHIFT, THROUGH DETENT

Units Applied—Forward Clutch, Intermediate Band

As the vehicle is being driven in the drive position, third gear mode, and the need to downshift into the second gear mode, the operator pushes the accelerator to the floor, actuating the downshift rod, which in turn, moves the downshift valve to open the kickdown circuit to main line pressure. This causes the 3-2 downshift at a higher road speed than a torque demand shift.

THE PRESSURE REGULATOR AND SUPPLY SYSTEMS

The oil pump is supplying pressurized fluid to the pressure regulator valve, which in turn directs regulated fluid pressure to the manual control valve, the converter, cooler and to the lubrication systems.

THE CLUTCHES, BAND SERVOS AND ACCUMULATOR SYSTEMS

Main line pressure is directed to the forward clutch and to the governor system. While the transmission is in the third gear, both the forward clutch and the reverse/high (direct) clutch are engaged,. With the 3-2 downshift, the forward clutch remains engaged while the reverse/high (direct) clutch is released and the intermediate band is applied. As the downshift valve is moved, pressure is directed to the spring end of the 2-3 shift valve and on a differential area at the other end, causing the valve to be shifted up. The reverse/high (direct) clutch, intermediate servo release system is exhausted around the 2-3 valve and to the reverse circuit. The intermediate servo is applied and the reverse/high (direct) clutch is released and the transmission is in the second speed. During the downshift, the manifold vacuum is close to zero, the throttle valve is regulating maximum T.V. pressure, along with the throttle pressure booster valve, which is regulating a boosted T.V. pressure in another circuit. It should be noted that the "kickdown" pressure is also effective on a differential area of the Drive two valve. At low road speed, this pressure may force the Drive two and the 1-2 shift valves up. Thus the intermediate servo apply would exhaust and the transmission would downshift to the first gear.

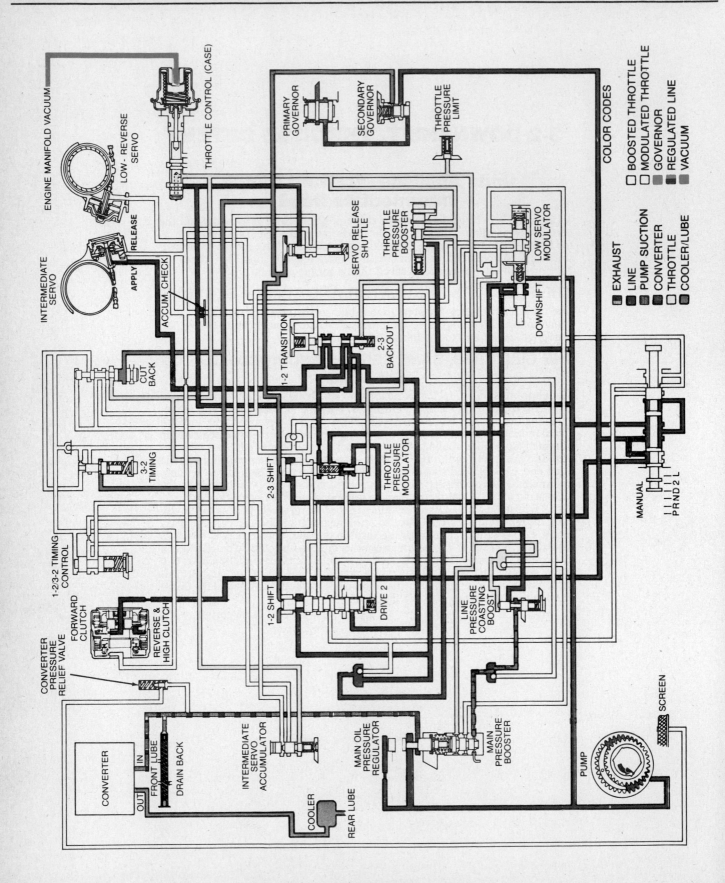

Manual Second Gear (©Ford Motor Company)

MANUAL SECOND GEAR

Units Applied—Forward Clutch, Intermediate Band

The selector lever is in the Manual Second gear position. The transmission will start out and remain in the second speed, without upshifting or downshifting. This locking out the 2-3 and 2-1 shifts is accomplished through the application of boosted line pressure to the shift valves so that governor pressure cannot overcome the increase in the pressure and make the shift.

PRESSURE REGULATOR AND SUPPLY SYSTEM

The oil pump is supplying pressurized fluid to the pressure regulator valve, which in turn directs regulated fluid pressure to the manual control valve, the converter, cooler and the lubrication systems. The line pressure is directed to the forward clutch, the governor assembly and the apply side of the intermediate band servo.

THE CLUTCHES, BAND SERVOS AND ACCUMULATOR SYSTEMS

The first gear lock-out is accomplished by having the fluid pressure applied between the 1-2 shift valve and the Drive Two valve. The Drive Two valve is forced down by the pressure and held down, thereby locking out the 2-1 downshift. The third gear lockout is accomplished by having main line pressure applied to the kickdown areas of the 2-3 shift valve. Because of the three differential areas and the valve spring end surface, the valve is subjected to the boosted main line pressure and the valve cannot be upshifted no matter how high the governor pressure becomes.

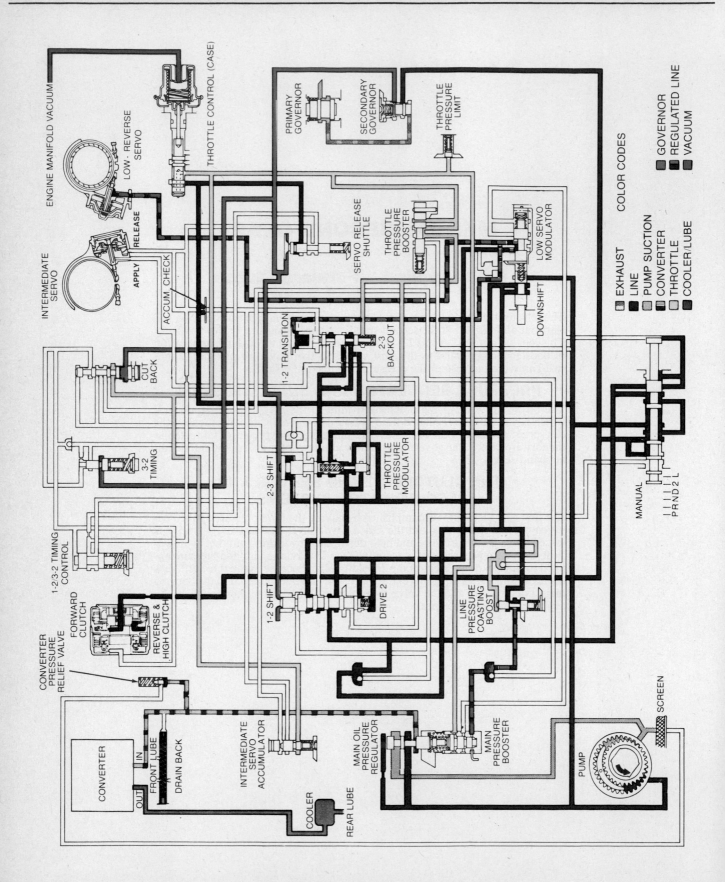

Manual Low Gear (©Ford Motor Company)

MANUAL LOW GEAR

Units Applied—Forward Clutch, Low/Reverse Band

The selector lever is in the Manual Low (First) gear position. The transmission will start out in first gear and will remain in first gear. The difference between Drive First Gear and Manual Low (First) Gear, is that the low/reverse band is engaged to provide an engine brake and both the second and third gear lockouts are engaged.

PRESSURE REGULATOR AND SUPPLY SYSTEM

The oil pump is supplying pressurized fluid to the pressure regulator valve, which in turn directs regulated pressure to the manual control valve, the converter, cooler and the lubrication systems. The line pressure is directed to the forward clutch and to the governor assembly. A regulated line pressure is directed to the low/reverse servo, applying the low/reverse band.

THE CLUTCHES, BAND SERVOS AND ACCUMULATOR SYSTEM

The low/reverse band servo is applied, the upshifts are locked out and the line pressure boost system is in operation. The line pressure coasting boost valve supplies a regulated pressure to the end of the main pressure boost valve, increasing the line pressure. This boosted line pressure is applied to the varied surfaces of the 2-3 shift valve, causing a combined force that governor pressure cannot overcome, thereby causing a high gear lockout. The second gear lockout is provided by combining fluid pressures on the Drive Two valve's varied surfaces, against which the governor pressure cannot overcome therefore preventing the 1-2 upshift.

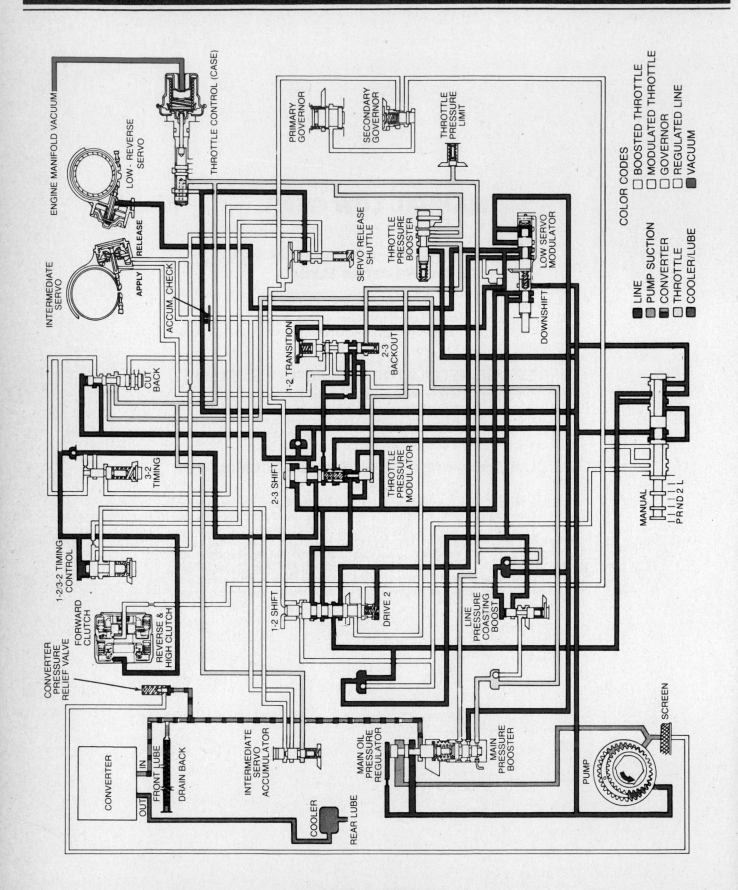

Reverse (©Ford Motor Company)

REVERSE

Units Applied—Reverse/High Clutch, Low/Reverse Band

With the selector lever in the Reverse position, the line pressure is boosted to the maximum to handle the high/reverse band torque. Governor pressure is not developed and the shift valves are held in the "downshifted" position by their springs and hydraulic pressure.

PRESSURE REGULATOR AND SUPPLY SYSTEM

The oil pump is supplying pressurized fluid to the pressure regulator valve, which in turn directs regulated pressure to the manual valve, the converter, cooler and the lubrication systems. With the throttle open moderately, the T.V. pressure is directed to the end of the main pressure booster valve to assist in the increase of main line pressure. It should be noted on the fluid schematic that main line pressure is routed in reverse position only, to assist the two T.V. pressures reacting on the main pressure booster valve, aiding in the increase psi in the main line pressure.

THE CLUTCHES, BAND SERVOS AND ACCUMULATOR SYSTEMS

As the manual valve is moved to the reverse position, line pressure is directed to the reverse/high clutch servo to apply the band, and routed to the end of the low servo modulator valve, to prevent regulated servo apply pressure. The line pressure is also directed to the low/reverse servo, which in turn applies the low/reverse band. Both the second and third gear lock-out systems are activated, although no governor pressure is developed to move the valves.

 ON CAR SERVICES

ADJUSTMENTS
Vacuum Diaphragm

Adjustment

The vacuum diaphragm units used on the C-5 transmissions are non-adjustable. When a replacement unit is installed, the control line pressure must be checked. If the pressure is not to specifications, a longer or shorter throttle valve rod must be installed to bring the pressure within the specified limits. Five selective rods are available to obtain the proper pressure.

Length (inch)	Color code
1.5925-1.5875	Green
1.6075-1.6025	Blue
1.6225-1.6175	Orange
1.6375-1.6325	Black
1.6585-1.6535	Pink/White

NOTE: If the length of the rod is not known, it should be measured with a micrometer. To determine if a change in the length of the throttle valve rod is needed, use the following procedure.

1. Attach a tachometer to the engine.
2. Attach a hand vacuum pump to the vacuum diaphragm unit.

NOTE: An air bleed valve can also be used.

3. Attach an oil pressure gauge to the control pressure port on the side of the transmission case.
4. Apply the parking brake and the service brakes. Chock the wheels to avoid movement of the vehicle.
5. Start the engine and allow it to reach normal operating temperature.
6. Adjust the engine idle speed to specifications of 1000 rpm and apply 10 inches of vacuum to the vacuum diaphragm unit.
7. With the brakes applied, move the selector lever through all detent positions. Read and record the pressure readings in all selector positions.
8. Compare the pressure readings to the specified pressure reading on the line pressure charts.
9. If the pressure is within specifications, no rod change is required.
10. If the pressure is below specifications, use the next longer rod and retest.
11. If the pressure is above specifications, use the next shorter rod and retest.

Manual Linkage
COLUMN SHIFT

Adjustment

1. Place the selector lever in the DRIVE position. An eight (8) pound weight should be hung from the selector lever to be sure the lever is definitely against the DRIVE position stop during the linkage adjustment.
2. Loosen the adjusting nut located on the slotted rod end.
3. Position the transmission lever in the drive position which is the third detent position from the full counterclockwise position.
4. Be sure the slotted rod end has the flats aligned with the flats on the mounting stud.
5. Making sure that the selector lever has not moved from the DRIVE position, tighten the nut to 10-20 ft. lbs.
6. Move the selector lever through all detents to be certain that adjustment is correct.

CONSOLE OR FLOOR SHIFT

Adjustment
SOLID LINK TYPE

1. Position the transmission selector lever in the DRIVE position against the rearward DRIVE stop. Hold the selector lever in this position during the adjustment.
2. Raise the vehicle and loosen the manual lever shift rod retaining nut and move the transmission manual lever to the DRIVE position, third detent position from the back of the transmission.
3. With the transmission selector lever and the manual selector lever in the DRIVE position, tighten the attaching nut to 10-15 ft. lbs.
4. Check the operation of the shift lever in each transmission detent.

CABLE TYPE

1. Position the transmission selector lever in the DRIVE position against the rearward DRIVE Stop. Hold the selector lever in this position during the adjustment.
2. Raise the vehicle and loosen the manual shift lever cable retaining nut. Move the transmission manual lever to the DRIVE position, third detent position from the rear of the transmission.
3. With both the manual lever and the selector levers in the DRIVE positions, tighten the attaching nut to 10-15 ft. lbs.

TRANSMISSION VACUUM DIAPHRAGM ASSEMBLY SPECIFICATIONS

Diaphragm Type	Diaphragm Part No.	Identification	Throttle Valve Rod* Part No. (7A380)	Length	Identification
S-HAD	D70P-7A377-AA	1 White Stripe	D3AP-JA	1.5925-1.5876	Green Daub
			D3AP-HA	1.6075-1.6025	Blue Daub
SAD	1983-E2DP-7A377-AA	No Identification	D3AP-KA	1.6225-1.6175	Orange Daub
	1982-E2DP-7A377-AA		D3AP-LA	1.6375-1.6325	Black Daub
S-SAD	D6AP-7A377-AA	1 Green Stripe	D3AP-MA	1.6585-1.6535	Pink/White Daub

*Selective Fit Rods
SAD—Single Area Diaphragm
S-SAD—Super Single Area Diaphragm
S-HAD—Super High Altitude Diaphragm

4. Check the operation of the selector lever in each detent position.

1983 RANGER

1. Position the selector lever in the DRIVE position and loosen the trunnion nut.

—————— CAUTION ——————

Be sure the selector lever is held against the rearward DRIVE detent stop during the linkage adjustment.

2. Position the transmission manual lever in the drive range by moving the bellcrank lever all the way rearward and then forward to the third detent position.

3. With the shift lever and the manual transmission lever in the DRIVE position, tighten the trunnion bolt to 13-23 ft. lbs. while holding a light forward pressure on the shift control tower arm.

NOTE: The forward pressure on the shifter arm will ensure correct positioning within the DRIVE detent.

4. After the adjustment, check for correct PARK engagement. The lever must move to the right when engaged in the PARK position. Operate the shift lever through all detents to assure proper transmission detent operation.

Shift Linkage Grommets

Urethane plastic grommets are used to connect the various rods and levers. It is most important to replace the old grommet with a new one whenever the rod is disconnected from a grommet. A special tool is needed to properly remove and replace the grommets from the levers. The proper procedure is as follows.

Replacement

1. Place the lower jaw of the tool between the lever and the rod. Position the stop pin against the end of the rod and force the rod out of the grommet.

2. Remove the grommet from the lever by cutting off the large shoulder with a sharp knife.

3. Adjust the tool stop to ½ inch and coat the outside of the grommet with lubricant. Place a new grommet on the stop pin and force it into the lever hole. Turn the grommet several times to be sure the grommet is properly seated.

4. Squeeze the rod into the bushing until the stop washer seats against the grommet.

Neutral Start Switch

Adjustment

1. After the selector lever is properly adjusted, loosen the two switch attaching bolts.

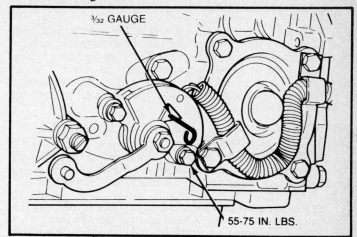

Neutral start switch adjustment (©Ford Motor Company)

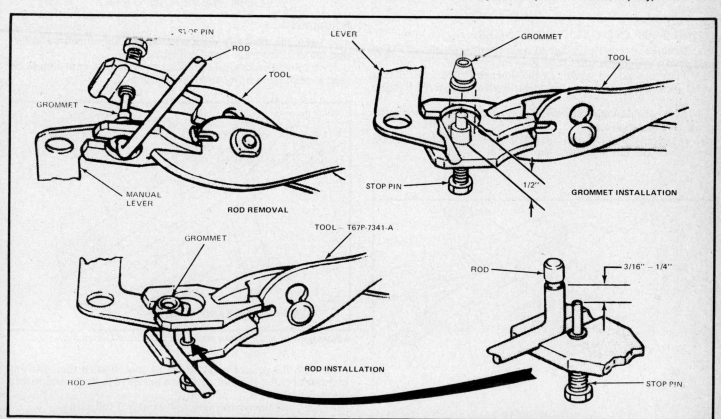

Removal and installation of shifting linkage grommets (©Ford Motor Company)

2. With the transmission selector lever in the NEUTRAL position, rotate the switch and insert a number 43 drill shank or a special gauge pin into the gauge pin holes of the switch. It is most important to install the drill or pin a full 31/64 inch into the three holes of the switch components.

3. Tighten the switch attaching screws to 55-75 in. lbs. and remove the pin or drill from the switch.

4. Check the operation of the switch. The engine should only start in the PARK and NEUTRAL positions.

Kickdown Linkage

Adjustment
1982 GRANADA/COUGAR AND FAIRMONT/ZEPHYR, 1982-83 MUSTANG/CAPRI, 1983 FAIRMONT FUTURA/ZEPHYR AND LTD/MARQUIS—ALL WITH 2.3L ENGINE

1. With the carburetor linkage held at the wide open throttle (WOT) position, have the downshift rod held downward with a 6 pound weight holding the rod against the "Through Detent" stop.

2. Adjust the kickdown adjusting screw to obtain a 0.010-0.080 inch clearance between the screw and the throttle arm.

3. Return the system to the idle position and reinstall the kickdown rod retracting spring.

1983 MUSTANG/CAPRI AND THUNDERBIRD/XR-7—ALL WITH 3.8L ENGINE

1. With the carburetor linkage held at the wide open throttle (WOT) position, have the downshift rod held downward with a 4½ pound weight holding the rod against the "through detent" stop.

2. Adjust the kickdown adjusting screw head to obtain 0.010-0.080 inch between the screw head and the throttle arm.

3. Return the carburetor and downshift rod to the idle position and secure all pivot points. Reinstall retracting spring, if removed.

1982-83 F-100 AND F-150, 1983 RANGER

1. Rotate the throttle linkage to wide open throttle (WOT) position with the engine off.

2. Place a 6 pound weight in the downshift rod and insert a 0.060 inch spacer between the throttle lever and the adjusting screw.

3. Move the adjusting screw until contact is made between the screw and the spacer.

4. Remove the spacer and a gap of 0.010-0.080 inch should exist between the screw and the throttle rod.

5. Remove the weight from the downshift rod and return both the rod and the carburetor linkage to the idle position.

1982 THUNDERBIRD/XR-7 AND GRANADA/COUGAR, 1982 FAIRMONT/ZEPHYR AND MUSTANG/CAPRI, 1983 FAIRMONT FUTURA/ZEPHYR AND LTD/MARQUIS—ALL WITH 3.3L ENGINE

1. With the carburetor linkage held at the wide open throttle (WOT) position, hold the downshift rod downward with a 4¼ pound weight, against the "Through Detent" stop.

2. Adjust the kickdown adjusting screw to obtain a clearance of 0.010-0.080 inch between the screw head and the throttle arm. Lock the screw in position with the locknut.

3. Release the carburetor and downshift linkage to their free position.

4. Reinstall the downshift retracting spring on the 1982 models, if removed during the adjustment.

Band Adjustment
INTERMEDIATE BAND

Adjustment

1. Raise the vehicle and support safely. Clean dirt and foreign material from the band adjusting screw area.

2. Remove the locknut and discard. A new locknut should be used at each band adjustment procedure.

3. With the proper band adjusting tool, tighten the adjusting screw until either the tool clicks at a preset 10 ft. lbs. or indicates a torque of 10 ft. lbs. (13.5 N•m).

4. Back the adjusting screw off exactly 4¼ turns.

5. While holding the adjusting screw from turning, install a new locknut and tighten to 40 ft. lbs. (54 N•m).

LOW-REVERSE BAND

Adjustment

1. Raise the vehicle and support safely. Clean the dirt and foreign material from the band adjusting area.

2. Remove the locknut and discard. A new locknut should be used at each band adjustment procedure.

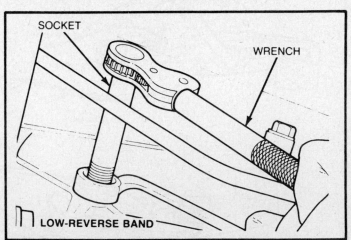

Adjustment of low/reverse band (©Ford Motor Company)

3. With the proper band adjusting tool, tighten the adjusting screw until either the tool clicks at a preset 10 ft. lbs. or indicates a torque of 10 ft. lbs. (13.5 N•m).

4. Back off the adjusting screw exactly 3 full turns.

5. While holding the adjusting screw from turning, install a new locknut and tighten to 40 ft. lbs. (54 N•m).

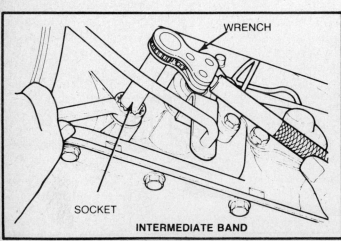

Adjustment of intermediate band (©Ford Motor Company)

SERVICES

Fluid Changes

Ford Motor Company does not recommend the periodic changing of the automatic transmission fluid, because of normal maintenance and lubrication requirements performed on the automatic transmissions by mileage or time intervals. However, if the vehicle is used in continous service or driven under severe conditions, the automatic transmission fluid must be changed every 22,500 miles. No time limit is given, but as a rule of thumb, between 18 and 20 months would be an average in comparison to the mileage limit.

Severe conditions are described as extensive idling, frequent short trips of 10 miles or less, vehicle operation when the temperature remains below +10°F. for 60 days or more, sustained high speed operation during hot weather (+90°F.), towing a trailer for a long distance or driving in severe dusty conditions. If fleet vehicles and vehicles accumulating 2000 miles or more per month are not equipped with an auxiliary transmission oil cooler, the severe condition rating applies.

NOTE: Each vehicle operated under severe conditions should be treated individually.

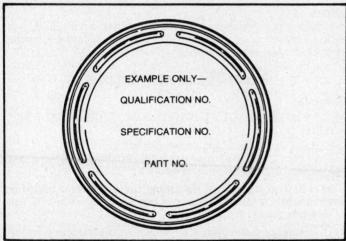

Fluid container identification locations (©Ford Motor Company)

Type H automatic transmission fluid, meeting Ford Motor Company's specifications (ESP-M2C166-H), should be used in the C-5 automatic transmission. Failure to use the proper grade and type fluid could result in internal transmission damage.

When the transmission has to be removed for major repairs, the unit should be drained completely. The converter, cooler and cooler lines must be flushed to remove any particles or dirt that may have entered the components as a result of the malfunction or failure.

Oil Pan

Removal

1. Raise the vehicle and support safely. Place a drain pan under the transmission.
2. On pan filled transmissions, remove the filler tube from the oil pan to drain the transmission fluid. On case filled transmissions, loosen the oil pan bolts to drain the fluid from the pan.

NOTE: If the same fluid is to be used again, filter it through a 100 mesh screen. Reuse the fluid only if it is in good condition.

3. Remove the transmission oil pan and bolts.

CAUTION
Care must be exercised when working with automatic transmission fluid while it is hot. Resulting burns can cause severe personal injury.

---

4. Remove the filter screen attaching bolt and the filter screen.
5. Thoroughly clean and remove all gasket material from the oil pan and the mating surface of the transmission.

NOTE: Remove and discard the nylon shipping plug from the oil pan, if remaining. This plug was used to retain fluid in the transmission during manufacture and has no further use.

Installation

1. Install a new gasket on the oil pan and install the filter screen and bolt. Torque the filter screen bolt to 25-40 in. lbs.
2. Install the oil pan to the transmission mating surface. Install the oil pan retaining bolts and torque to 13-16 ft. lbs. Install the filler tube and tighten the fitting securely, if equipped.
3. If the converter has not been drained, install three quarts of type H fluid. If the transmission is dry, install five quarts of type H fluid.
4. Start the engine and check the fluid level. Add enough fluid to bring the level to the cold level on the dipstick.
5. Check the fluid level when the engine/transmission assembly reaches normal operating temperature. Correct the level as necessary.
6. Final check is to move the shifting lever through all detents and recheck the fluid level.

CAUTION
Do not overspeed the engine during the warm-up period.

DRAINING OF TORQUE CONVERTER

1. Remove the lower engine dust cover.
2. Rotate the torque converter until the drain plug is in view.
3. Remove the drain plug and allow the converter to drain.

NOTE: Due to the length of time needed for the draining of the converter, it is suggested this procedure be performed prior to other operations.

4. Install the drain plug and the lower engine dust cover.
5. Remove the cooler lines and flush lines and cooler.
6. Reinstall cooler lines and fill transmission as required to bring fluid to its proper level.

NOTE: When leakage is found at the oil cooler, the cooler must be replaced. When one or more of the cooler lines must be replaced, each must be fabricated from the same size steel line as the original.

Vacuum Diaphragm

Removal

1. Raise the vehicle and support safely.
2. Disconnect the vacuum (modulator) diaphragm hose.
3. Remove the unit retaining bracket and bolt. Pull the modulator assembly from the transmission case.

NOTE: Do not pry or bend the bracket during the removal procedure.

4. Remove the vacuum unit control rod from the transmission case.

Installation

1. Place the correct vacuum unit control rod in the transmission case passage.
2. Install the vacuum modulator unit into the transmission case. Secure the unit with the bracket and retaining bolt. Torque the bolt to 28-40 ft. lbs.

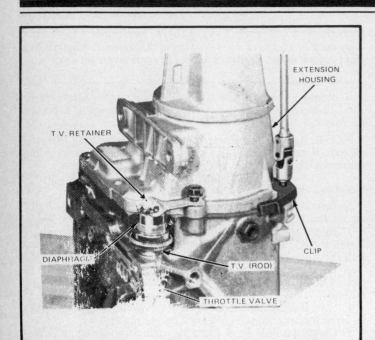

Removal or installation of diaphragm assembly and extension housing (©Ford Motor Company)

3. Install the vacuum hose to the modulator nipple, lower the vehicle and road test as required.

Control Valve Body

Removal

1. Raise the vehicle and support safely.
2. Drain the transmission oil pan as described in fluid change procedure.
3. Remove the transmission oil pan retaining bolts, oil pan and gasket.
4. Shift the transmission in the PARK position.
5. Remove the filter screen attaching bolt and the filter screen.
6. Remove the valve body to case attaching bolts. Hold the manual valve in the valve body and remove the valve body from the case.

─────────── CAUTION ───────────

Failure to hold the manual valve in the valve body during the removal could cause the manual valve to become bent or damaged.

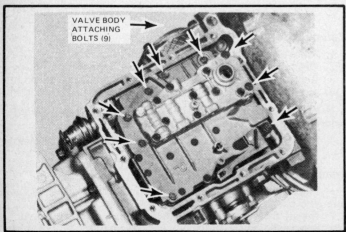

Location of valve body retaining bolts (©Ford Motor Company)

7. If the valve body is to be disassembled, refer to the appropriate outline in this section.

Installation

1. Thoroughly clean and remove all gasket material from the transmission pan mounting face and from the oil pan.

NOTE: Remove and discard the nylon plug from the oil pan. This was used to retain fluid in the transmission during manufacture and is no longer needed.

2. Position the transmission manual lever in the PARK detent. While holding the manual valve, position the valve body onto the transmission case. Be sure the inner downshift lever is between the downshift lever stop and the downshift valve and that the two lands on the end of the manual valve engage the actuating pin on the manual detent lever. Install the valve body retaining bolts (7) through the valve body and into the case. Do not tighten at this time.
3. Snug the valve body to case bolts evenly. Be sure all components are aligned. Torque the valve body to case bolts to 80-120 in. lbs.
4. Position the filter screen and install the bolt. Tighten the bolt to 25-40 in. lbs.
5. Install a new gasket on the oil pan and install in place on the transmission case. Install the retaining bolts and torque to 13-16 ft. lbs. If equipped with the pan filler tube, attach and securely tighten.
6. Lower the vehicle and fill the transmission with fluid, type H, to its proper level. Verify level at normal operating temperature. Check pan area for leakage.

Low-Reverse Servo

Removal

ALL MODELS, EXCEPT MUSTANG/CAPRI WITH 3.8L ENGINE

1. Raise the vehicle and support safely.
2. Loosen the low-reverse band adjusting screw locknut and tighten the band adjusting screw to 10 ft. lbs.

NOTE: The purpose of tightening the low-reverse adjusting screw is to insure the band strut will remain in place when the servo piston is removed.

3. Disengage the neutral start switch wiring harness from the routing clips. Note the position of the clips before removing.
4. Remove the servo cover retaining bolts. Remove the servo cover and seal from the case.
5. Remove the servo piston and return spring from the case. The piston seal cannot be replaced separately. The seal is bonded to the piston and both must be replaced as a unit.

Installation

1. Lubricate the piston/seal with transmission fluid and install in the case along with the return spring. Install a new seal on the cover and position the cover to the case with two longer bolts 180 degrees apart as installation bolts.
2. Install two cover retaining bolts, remove the two long bolts and install the remaining cover retaining bolts. Position the neutral start switch wiring harness routing clips on the proper cover bolts.
3. Torque the cover bolts to 13-20 ft. lbs.
4. Adjust the low-reverse band. Refer to the Band Adjusting procedure outline.

─────────── CAUTION ───────────

If the band cannot be adjusted properly, the low-reverse band struts have moved from their positions. It will be necessary to remove the oil pan, screen and valve body to properly install the struts and readjust the low-reverse band.

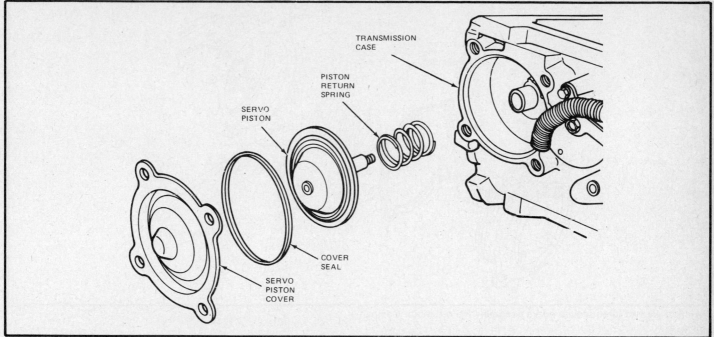

Exploded view of low/reverse servo assembly (©Ford Motor Company)

5. Lower the vehicle. If necessary, correct the fluid level.
6. Road test the vehicle as required.

Removal
MUSTANG/CAPRI WITH 3.8L ENGINE

1. Working from under the engine hood, remove the fan shroud attaching bolts and position the shroud back over the fan.
2. Raise the vehicle and support safely.
3. Support the transmission with and adjustable stand or a transmission jack.
4. Remove the number 3 crossmember to body bracket through bolts.
5. Carefully lower the transmission to obtain working clearance.
6. Loosen the low-reverse band adjusting screw locknut and adjust the band to 10 ft. lbs.

NOTE: The purpose of tightening the low-reverse band adjusting screw is to insure the band struts will remain in place when the servo piston is removed.

7. Disengage the neutral start switch wiring harness from the routing clips. Note the position of the routing clips on the servo cover bolts.
8. Remove the servo retaining bolts from the case and cover. Remove the servo cover and seal.
9. Remove the servo piston/seal and return spring. The piston seal is bonded to the piston and cannot be replace separately. Both must be replaced as a unit.

Installation

1. Install the piston return spring and piston assembly into the case bore. Install a new gasket on the cover.
2. Using two long bolts, 180 degrees apart to position the cover to the case, install two of the retaining bolts through the cover and into the case. Remove the two long bolts and install the remaining two bolts in their place. Position the wiring harness routing clips on their proper bolts and torque the cover bolts to 13-20 ft. lbs.
3. Install the neutral switch wiring in the routing clips.

4. Adjust the low-reverse band. Refer to the Band Adjusting procedure outline.

——— CAUTION ———
If the band cannot be adjusted properly, the low-reverse band struts have moved from their positions. It will be necessary to remove the oil pan, screen and valve body to properly install the struts and re-adjust the low-reverse band.

5. Raise the transmission back into position and install the crossmember through bolts. Remove the support from under the transmission.
6. Lower the vehicle, position the fan shroud and re-install the retaining bolts.
7. Inspect and correct as necessary, the transmission fluid level, check for leaks and road test as required.

Intermediate Servo

Removal

1. Working from underneath the engine hood, remove the fan shroud attaching bolts and position the shroud back over the fan.

NOTE: Not necessary on light trucks, steps 1, 2, 3, 4, 5, 6.

2. Raise and support the vehicle safely.
3. Support the transmission with an adjustable stand or a transmission jack.
4. Remove the number 3 crossmember to body bracket through bolts.
5. Carefully lower the transmission to obtain working clearance.
6. On vehicles equipped with the 3.8L engine, disconnect the transmission cooler lines using the correct special tool. Refer to "Cooling Line Removal and Installation" outline.
7. Remove the servo cover attaching bolts, along with the transmission I.D. tag. Note its position on cover.
8. Remove the servo cover and the piston assembly from the transmission case. Remove the piston return spring.

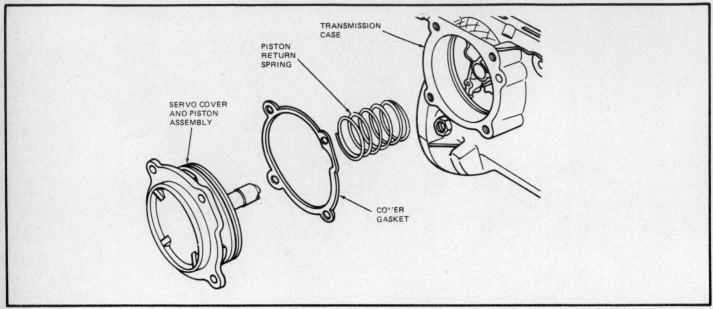

Exploded view of intermediate servo assembly (©Ford Motor Company)

9. Disassemble the servo as required and discard the cover gasket.

Installation

1. Position a new gasket on the servo cover. Align the notch in the gasket with a fluid passage in the case, during the installation.

2. Install the piston return spring, servo cover/piston assembly into the case. Using two long bolts 180 degrees apart, position the cover to the case. Install two retaining bolts and remove the two long bolts. Install the two remaining retaining bolts in the cover and torque to 16-22 ft. lbs. (12-20 ft. lbs. on light trucks).

3. Adjust the intermediate band as outlined in the Band Adjusting procedure outline.

NOTE: If the band cannot be adjusted properly, the band strut has dropped from it position. It is necessary to remove the oil pan, screen and valve body to reinstall the strut. Re-adjust the intermediate band.

Use the following procedures as applicable to the vehicle being serviced.

4. On models equipped with the 3.8L engine, connect the transmission cooler lines.

5. Raise the transmission and install the crossmember through bolts. Remove the transmission support.

6. Lower the vehicle and position the fan shroud. Install the shroud retaining bolts.

7. Inspect and correct as required, the transmission fluid level, check for leaks and road test, if necessary.

Extension Housing

Removal

1. Raise the vehicle and support safely.

2. Matchmark the drive shaft and remove from the vehicle.

3. Position an adjustable stand or transmission jack to support the transmission.

4. Remove the speedometer cable from the extension housing.

5. Remove the rear engine support to crossmember attaching nuts.

6. Raise the transmission and remove the rear support to body bracket through bolts. Remove the crossmember.

7. Loosen the extension housing attaching bolts and allow the unit to drain into a container. Remove vacuum tube clip with housing bolt.

8. Remove the extension housing attaching volts and remove the housing from the transmission. Discard the gasket.

Installation

1. Install a new gasket on the rear of the transmission case. Install the rear extension housing and install the retaining bolts. Install the vacuum tube clip with one bolt. Torque the bolts to 28-40 ft. lbs.

2. Position the crossmember and install the through bolts. Torque the nuts to 35-50 ft. lbs.

3. Lower the transmission and install the engine rear support to crossmember attaching nuts.

4. Remove the transmission support and install the speedometer cable in the extension housing.

5. Install the drive shaft in the same position following the matchmarks.

6. Lower the vehicle and fill the transmission with type H fluid to its proper level.

7. Check the extension housing for leakage, re-check the fluid level and road test, if required.

NOTE: The following operations can be accomplished with the rear extension housing on or off the transmission.

Seal

Removal and Installation

1. With the driveshaft removed, use a special puller tool to remove the seal assembly from the extension housing.

2. Using a seal installer tool, tap the seal into its seat in the extension housing. Lubricate the lip portion of the seal and install the driveshaft.

Bushing

Removal and Installation

1. Remove the extension housing seal with special puller tool. Using a special bushing remover tool, pull the bushing from the extension housing.

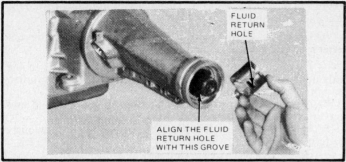

Installation of bushing in extension housing (©Ford Motor Company)

2. With a special bushing driver tool, tap the bushing into its seat in the extension housing. Install the seal in its seat in the housing by using the special seal driver tool.

NOTE: Be sure the fluid drain back hole in the bushing is aligned with the groove in the extension housing.

Governor

Removal

1. Remove the extension housing. Refer to the "Extension Housing Removal and Installation" procedure.
2. Remove the governor housing to governor distributor attaching bolts. Slide the governor away from the distributor body and off the shaft. Check governor screen.
3. The governor can be disassembled or replaced as required.

Installation

1. Slide the governor over the output shaft and position the governor on the governor distributor body. Install the retaining bolts and torque to 80–120 in. lbs. Be sure screen is in place.
2. Install the extension housing. Refer to the "Extension Housing Removal and Installation" procedure.

REMOVAL & INSTALLATION

C-5 AUTOMATIC TRANSMISSION

Removal
ALL CAR MODELS

1. Protect fender areas and disconnect the negative battery cable.
2. Remove the air cleaner assembly on vehicles equipped with the 3.8L engine.
3. After removing the attaching bolts, position the fan shroud back over the fan assembly.
4. Disconnect the thermactor air injection hose at the catalytic converter check valve on models equipped with the 3.8L engine and on the 1982 Mustang/Capri models equipped with the 4.2L engine.

NOTE: The check valve is located on the right side of the engine compartment, near the firewall.

5. Remove the two upper transmission to engine attaching bolts, accessible from the engine compartment, on vehicles equipped with the 3.8L engine.
6. Raise the vehicle and support safely.
7. Match-mark and remove the driveshaft.
8. While supporting the exhaust system, disconnect the muffler inlet pipe from the catalytic converter outlet pipe. Wire the exhaust system assembly to the vehicle's undercarriage.
9. Remove the exhaust pipe(s) from the manifold(s) and by pulling back on the converters, release the converter hangers from their mounting brackets. Lower the pipe assemblies and set aside.

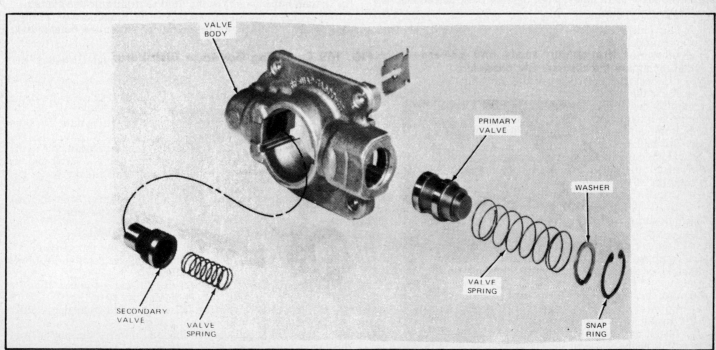

Exploded view of governor assembly (©Ford Motor Company)

10. Remove the speedometer driven gear from the extension housing.

11. Disconnect the neutral start switch wiring from the neutral start switch. Remove vacuum hose from modulator nipple.

12. Disconnect the downshift rod at the transmission manual lever. On floor mounted shift equipped vehicles, remove the shift cable routing bracket and disconnect the cable from the transmission manual lever.

13. Remove the converter housing dust shield and remove the converter to drive plate attaching nuts.

NOTE: The crankshaft must be turned to gain access to all the converter to drive plate attaching nuts.

14. Remove starter cable, remove starter attaching bolts and lower starter from the engine.

15. Loosen the attaching nuts from the rear support to the number three crossmember.

16. Position a transmission jack under the transmission and secure the transmission to the jack with a safety chain.

17. Remove the through bolts securing the number three crossmember to the body brackets.

18. Lower the transmission enough to gain working room and disconnect the oil cooler lines.

19. On vehicles equipped with the 3.8L engine and 1982 Cougar/Capri models, remove the four remaining transmission to engine attaching bolts. On all other models, remove the six remaining bolts.

20. Pull the transmission rearward to clear the converter studs from the drive plate and lower the transmission.

Installation

1. With the vehicle in the air and supported safely, raise the transmission on a transmission jack and into position to mate the converter studs with the drive plate holes and the transmission dowels on the rear of the engine to the transmission bell housing.

NOTE: It will be necessary to rotate the converter to align the converter studs and the converter drain plug to the holes in the drive plate. Be sure during the installation that the converter studs are in the drive plate holes before bolting the transmission bell housing to the engine.

2. On vehicles equipped with the 3.8L engine and 1982 Cougar/Capri models, install the four transmission to engine bolts. On all other models, install the six transmission to engine bolts. Tighten the attaching bolts to 40-50 ft. lbs.

3. Connect the cooler lines to the transmission.

4. Raise the transmission by the jack mechanism and install the number three crossmember through bolts. Install the attaching nuts and tighten to 20-30 ft. lbs.

5. Remove the safety chain and the transmission jack from under the vehicle.

6. Tighten the rear support attaching bolt nuts to 30-50 ft. lbs.

7. Install the starter assembly, tighten the bolts to 15-20 ft. lbs., and install the starter cable.

8. Install the converter to drive plate attaching nuts and torque to 20-30 ft. lbs. Install the dust shield and if previously removed, position the linkage bellcrank bracket and install the attaching bolts.

9. Connect the shift linkage to the transmission manual lever. If equipped with floor mounted shift, connect the cable to the manual lever and install the routing bracket with the attaching bolt.

10. Connect the downshift rod to the transmission lever.

11. Connect the neutral start switch wiring harness to the switch. Install vacuum hose to modulator nipple.

12. Install the speedometer driven gear assembly in the rear extension housing. Tighten the clamp bolt to 36-54 in. lbs.

13. Install the catalytic converters into their hanger brackets

and install the exhaust pipe(s) to the exhaust manifold. Install the attaching nuts, but do not tighten.

NOTE: If the exhaust pipe(s) were disconnected from the converters, install new gaskets or seals before connecting.

14. Disconnect the wire holding the exhaust system to the body undercarriage and connect the pipe to the converter outlet. Do not tighten the attaching nuts.

15. Align the exhaust system and tighten the manifold and converter outlet attaching nuts.

16. Install the driveshaft in the vehicle, aligning the previously made match-marks.

17. Check and if necessary, adjust the shift linkage.

18. Recheck undercarriage assembly and lower the vehicle.

19. On vehicles equipped with the 3.8L engine, install the two transmission to engine attaching bolts from the engine compartment.

20. On vehicles equipped with the 3.8L engine and 1982 Mustang/Capri models equipped with the 4.2L engine, connect the thermactor air injection hose to the converter check valve.

21. Position the fan shroud and install the retaining bolts.

22. Install the air cleaner on vehicles equipped with the 3.8L engine.

23. Connect the negative battery cable.

24. Add the correct type and amount of fluid to the transmission assembly as required.

25. Start the engine, being sure the starter will only operate in PARK or NEUTRAL positions.

26. Check and correct the transmission fluid level.

27. Raise the vehicle and inspect for leakage and correctness of assembly. Lower and road test as required.

Removal
LIGHT TRUCK AND RANGER MODELS

NOTE: Differences in the removal and installation procedures exist between models and model years. References are made to each throughout the removal and installation procedure outline.

1. Disconnect the negative battery cable. Raise the vehicle and support safely.

2. Place a drain pan under the transmission oil pan, loosen the oil pan bolts and allow the fluid to drain into the container. Carefully, lower the oil pan and allow the remainder of the fluid to drain from the pan. Reinstall the pan with a few bolts to hold the pan in place.

NOTE: Certain oil pans will have the filler tube installed. Remove to drain.

3. Remove the converter drain plug access cover from the bottom of the converter housing.

4. Remove the converter to flywheel attaching nuts. Turn the engine crankshaft to locate each nut.

5. Turn the converter to place the converter drain plug in the bottom position. Place a drain pan under the converter and remove the drain plug. Reinstall the plug after the converter has drained.

6. Matchmark the driveshaft and disconnect from the rear yoke. Pull the shaft from the rear of the transmission.

1982 LIGHT TRUCK AND RANGER MODELS

7. Disconnect the oil cooler lines from the transmission.

8. Disconnect the downshift and range selector control rods from the transmission manual levers.

9. Remove the speedometer driven gear assembly from the rear extension housing.

10. Remove the neutral start switch wires from the retainer clips and separate the connector assembly.

11. Disconnect the starter cable and remove the starter from the engine.

12. Remove the vacuum hose from the modulator nipple.

13. Position a transmission jack under the transmission and secure the unit with a safety chain.

14. Remove the two engine rear support crossmember-to-frame attaching bolts.

15. Remove the two engine rear support-to-extension housing attaching bolts.

1983 AND LATER LIGHT TRUCKS

16. Disconnect the starter cable and remove the starter from the engine.

17. Disconnect the neutral start switch wire at the connector.

18. Position a transmission jack under the transmission and remove the rear mount-to-crossmember insulator attaching nuts and the two crossmember-to-frame attaching bolts. Remove the right and left crossmember gussets.

19. Remove the two rear insulator-to-extension housing attaching bolts.

20. Disconnect the downshift and selector linkage from the transmission manual levers.

21. Remove the bellcrank bracket from the converter housing.

22. Raise the transmission assembly enough to gain clearance for removal of the crossmember. Remove the rear mount from the crossmember and remove the crossmember from the side supports.

23. Lower the transmission to gain access to the oil cooler lines and disconnect.

24. Disconnect the speedometer cable and remove the speedometer driven gear from the rear extension housing.

25. Remove the bolt holding the transmission filler tube to the engine block.

ALL MODELS

26. Be sure the safety chain is securing the transmission to the transmission jack. Remove the converter housing-to-engine bolts.

27. Pull the transmission to the rear while lowering the unit. Remove the transmission from under the vehicle.

Installation
ALL MODELS

1. Have the vehicle in the air and supported safely.

2. Position the transmission on the transmission jack and secure with the safety chain.

3. Move the transmission and jack assembly under the vehicle and position the transmission in-line with the engine block, having rotated the converter to align the attaching bolt holes in the flywheel with the attaching bolts of the converter. Push the assembly forward, mating the dowel pins on the engine with the holes in the converter housing.

4. Install the converter housing-to-engine attaching bolts. Torque to 40-50 ft. lbs.

—————————— CAUTION ——————————

Be sure drain plug is in place, tightened and positioned properly in the flywheel.

1983 AND LATER LIGHT TRUCKS

5. Install the bolt holding the filler tube to the engine block.

6. Install the speedometer driven gear assembly and speedometer cable to the rear extension housing.

7. Raise or lower the transmission to connect the oil cooler lines to the transmission case.

8. Raise the transmission assembly enough to install the crossmember to the side supports. Install the rear support to the crossmember.

9. Install the downshift and selector linkage to the transmission manual levers, while installing the bellcrank bracket to the converter housing.

10. Install the two rear insulator-to-extension housing attaching bolts.

11. Install the rear mount-to-crossmember insulator attaching nuts and install the left and right crossmember gussets. Remove the transmission jack.

12. Install the neutral start switch wiring connector and properly route the wiring through the retaining clips.

13. Install the starter assembly to the engine and install the starter cable.

1982 LIGHT TRUCK AND RANGER MODELS

14. Install the two engine rear support-to-extension housing attaching bolts. Install the crossmember to the frame and install the attaching bolts. Remove the transmission jack.

15. Install the vacuum hose to the nipple of the modulator.

16. Install the starter to the engine and install the starter cable.

17. Connect the neutral start wiring connector and route the wiring through the retainer clips as necessary.

18. Install the speedometer driven gear assembly and the speedometer cable to the rear extension housing.

19. Connect the downshift and range selector control rods to the transmission manual levers.

20. Connect the oil cooler lines at the transmission.

ALL MODELS

21. Install the drive shaft into the rear of the transmission and align the matchmarks at the yoke and secure.

22. Install the converter attaching nuts and tighten to 20-34 ft. lbs. Install the converter drain plug access cover.

23. Install the oil filler tube to the oil pan, if equipped. Otherwise, be sure a new gasket is on the oil pan and the retaining bolts are properly tightened.

24. Lower the vehicle, install the proper type and quantity of fluid into the transmission. Install the negative battery cable and start the engine. Recheck the fluid level and correct as required.

25. Raise the vehicle and check for leakage. Inspect the assembly for correct installation. Road test as required when lowered. Make any further adjustments.

C-5

AUTOMATIC TRANSMISSION

Before Disassembly

1. Clean the exterior of the transmission assembly before any attempt is made to disassemble the unit, to prevent the entrance of dirt or other foreign material from entering the transmission assembly or internal components during the disassembly and assembly phases.

NOTE: If steam cleaning is done to the exterior of the transmission assembly, immediate disassembly should be done to avoid rusting from condensation in the internal parts.

2. All screw, bolt and nut fasteners must be tightened to the torque indicated in the specification section, or as noted in the assembly outline.

3. When assembling the sub-assemblies, each component part should be lubricated with clean transmission fluid. Lubricate the sub-assemblies as they are installed in the transmission case.

4. Needle bearings, thrust washers and seals should be lightly coated with petroleum jelly during the assemble of the sub-assemblies and transmission.

5. During the assembly of the transmission and the sub-assemblies, always use new gaskets and seals.

6. Careful handling of the many components of the transmission is important to prevent the marring of the precision machined surfaces.

7. Whenever a seal is removed from a piston, shaft or servo, note the type of seal and the direction of the sealing lip. Look for modifications in seal or component application during the reassembly.

8. Keep the transmission service area clean and well organized. Provide a supply of lint-free shop clothes.

TRANSMISSION DISASSEMBLY

Converter

Removal

1. With the transmission secured on a work bench or in a transmission holding fixture, grasp the torque converter firmly and pull the assembly straight out of the transmission.

NOTE: The torque converter is a heavy unit and care must be exercised to be prepared to handle the weight.

Inspection
CHECKING CONVERTER END PLAY

1. Place the converter on a flat surface with the flywheel side down and the converter pump drive hub up.

2. Insert a special end play checking tool (Ford number T80L-7902-A or equivalent) into the drive hub opening of the converter pump, until the tool bottoms.

3. Tighten the threaded inner post of the tool, which will expand and lock the tool sleeve in the turbine spline.

4. Attach a dial indicator to the threaded post of the tool, with the indicator button resting on the converter pump housing. Set the dial indicator to zero.

5. Lift the tool and dial indicator assembly upward as far as possible and note the dial indicator reading. This reading is the total end play of the turbine and stator.

6. Replace the converter if the end play reading exceeds the specified limits of measurement.
End Play Specifications:
New or Rebuilt Converter—0.023 inch max.
Used Converter—0.050 inch max.

CHECKING CONVERTER ONE-WAY CLUTCH

1. The converter should be placed on a flat surface with the flywheel side down.

Checking one-way clutch operation (©Ford Motor Company)

2. Insert a one-way clutch holding tool (Ford number T77L-7902-A or equivalent) in one of the grooves of the stator thrust washer, located directly under the converter pump drive hub.

3. Insert the one-way clutch torquing tool (Ford number T76L-7902-C or equivalent) into the converter pump drive hub and engage the one-way clutch inner race.

4. Attach a torque wrench to the one-way clutch torquing tool, and with the one-way clutch holding tool held stationary, turn the torque wrench counterclockwise. The converter should lock-up and hold a ten pound force.

5. Turn the torque wrench in a clockwise direction and the one-way clutch should rotate freely.

6. Repeat the operation in at least five different locations around the converter.

7. If the one-way clutch fails to lock-up, replace the converter assembly.

CHECKING STATOR TO IMPELLER INTERFERENCE

1. Position the oil pump assembly on a flat surface with the splined end of the stator shaft pointing up.

2. Mount the converter on the pump with the splines of the stator shaft engaged with the splines of the one-way cluch inner race. The converter hub should then engage the pump drive gear.

3. Hold the oil pump body stationary and rotate the converter counterclockwise. The converter should rotate freely without any signs of interference or scraping within the converter assembly.

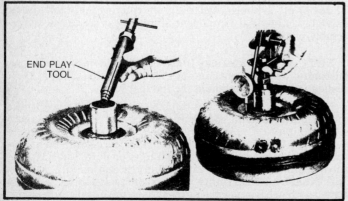

Checking converter end play (©Ford Motor Company)

Checking stator to impeller interference (©Ford Motor Company)

4. If any indication of scraping or interference is noted, the converter should be replaced.

CHECKING THE STATOR-TO-TURBINE INTERFERENCE

1. Position the converter on the bench, flywheel side down, or in a vise using a holding fixture (Ford Number T83L-7902-3A or equivalent). When using the holding fixture, clamp it tightly in a vise. Place the converter on the holding fixture, aligning the pilot hub and one stud in the appropriate holes.

2. Install the holding wire into one of the grooves provided in the reactor thrust washer.

3. With the holding wire in position, spline the torque adapter tool in the converter. Make sure the shaft splines engage the splines in the turbine hub.

4. Install the pilot guide tool over the shaft and onto the impeller hub.

5. Hold the converter assembly and turn the torque converter turbine by rotating both clockwise and counterclockwise, using a torque wrench and a ¾ socket.

6. Replace the converter if there is a loud scraping noise or if the input shaft will not turn with 5 ft. lbs. of torque.

NOTE: If scraping or interference exists, the stator front thrust washer may be worn, allowing the stator to contact the turbine. If such is the case, the converter must be replaced.

VISUAL INSPECTION OF THE CONVERTER

Before installation of the converter, the crankshaft pilot should be inspected for nicks or burrs that could prevent the pilot from entering the crankshaft. Remove as necessary.

Inspect the converter front pump drive hub for nicks or burrs that could damage the pump oil seal during installation.

Checking stator to turbine interference (©Ford Motor Company)

Disassembly of Transmission

1. Mount the transmission in a suitable transmission holding fixture, separately or on a work bench area.

2. Remove the input shaft from the transmission assembly.

NOTE The input shaft may come out of the transmission when the converter is removed.

3. With the transmission inverted, remove the oil pan retaining bolts. Remove the pan and discard the gasket.

NOTE: Remove and discard the oil filler tube shipping plug found in the oil pan.

4. Remove the screw retaining the screen assembly. Lift the screen assembly from the valve body. Remove rubber grommet.

5. Remove the nine valve body retaining bolts and lift the valve body from the transmission case.

6. Remove the screen from the oil pump inlet bore, in the transmission case.

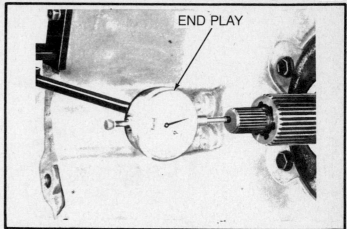

Checking end play of input shaft before disassembly (©Ford Motor Company)

7. Loosen the band adjusting locknuts on the adjusting screws. Remove the four band struts from inside the transmission.

8. In order to check the gear train end play bore disassembly, install the input shaft and force the gear train to the rear. Mount a dial indicator so that the indicator stem is touching the end of the input shaft and zero the indicator.

9. Using the rear brake drum for a fulcrum, not the aluminum planet carrier, pry the gear train forward. Read the indicated endplay on the dial indicator and record. The specified endplay is between 0.008 and 0.042 inch. If the endplay is incorrect, the thrust washer will have to be changed during the re-assembly. Remove the dial indicator.

10. Remove the input shaft and lay aside.

11. With the converter housing positioned so as not to cause a bind, remove the seven retaining bolts and remove the converter housing from the case assembly.

NOTE: On a car transmission, the converter housing bolts also hold the oil pump to the case. On truck transmissions, five bolts are used to retain the converter housing and seven bolts are used to retain the oil pump to the case.

12. Remove the oil pump assembly. If necessary, pry the gear assembly forward to loosen the pump assembly.

—————— CAUTION ——————
Pry on the rear drum, not on the aluminum planet carrier.

13. Remove the number one and number two thrust washers from the stator support. Remove and discard the gasket.

NOTE: Tag the thrust washers for assembly identification.

14. Reaching into the transmission case, align the intermedi-

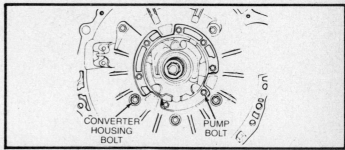

Converter housing and oil pump attachment on light truck transmission applications (©Ford Motor Company)

205

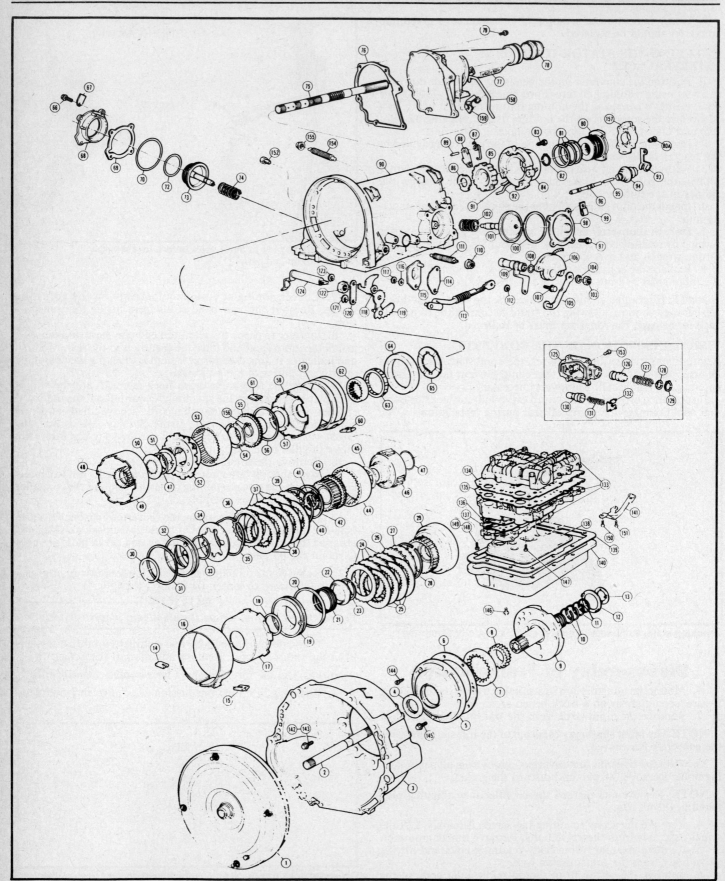

Exploded view of C-5 Automatic Transmission (©Ford Motor Company)

1. Converter Assembly
2. Shaft—Input
3. Housing Converter
4. Seal Assy.—Front Oil Pump
5. Body—Front Pump
6. Gasket—Front Oil Pump
7. Gear)—Frt. Oil Pump Driven
8. Gear—Frt. Oil Pump Drive
9. Stator Support—Frt. Oil Pump
10. Seal—Fwd. Cl. Cyl.
11. Seal—Rev. Cl. Cyl.
12. Washer—Frt. Pump Supt. Thrust (Sel.)—No. 1
13. Washer—Rev. Cl. Thrust—No. 2
14. Strut—Intermediate Brake
15. Strut—Intermediate Brake
16. Ban Assy.—Intermediate
17. Drum Assy.—Intermediate Brake
18. Seal—Rev. Cl. Inner
19. Piston Assy.—High Clutch
20. Seal—High Cl. Outer
21. Spring—High Cl. Piston
22. Retainer—Cl. Piston Spring
23. Ring
24. Plate—Cl. Ext. Spline—(Steel)
25. Plate Assy.—Cl. Int. Spline (Friction)
26. Plate—Clutch Pressure
27. Spring—Rev. Cl. Press. Plate Disc
28. Snap Ring (Selective)
29. Cylinder—Fwd. Clutch
30. O-Ring—Cl. Piston Oil
31. Seal—Fwd. Cl. Outer
32. Piston Assy.—Fwd. Clutch
33. Ring—Fwd. Cl. Pst. Spring Press
34. Spring—Fwd. Cl. Piston Disc
35. Ring)—Ret. Wave Int.
36. Plate—Fwd. Cl. Press
37. Plate—Cl. Ext. Spline (Steel)
38. Plate Assy. Cl. Int. Spline (Friction)
39. Plate—Clutch Press
40. Ring—Retaining Ext. (Sel.)
41. Washer—Fwd. Cl. Hub—Thrust—No. 3
42. Retainer
43. Hub & Bshg. Assy.—Fwd. Cl.
44. Gear—Output Shaft Ring
45. Washer—Rev. Planet Pinion—Thrust—No. 4
46. Planet Assy.—Fwd.
47. Retainer
48. Gear—Sun
49. Shell—Input
50. Washer—Input Shell Thrust—No. 5
51. Washer—Rev. Plt. Carrier—Thrust (Frt.)—No. 6
52. Planet Assy.—Reverse
53. Gear—Output Shaft Ring

54. Washer—Rev. Drum Thrust—No. 7
55. Hub—Output Shaft
56. Ring
57. Washer—Rev. Drum Thrust—No. 8
58. Drum Assy.—Rev. Brake
59. Band Assy.—Reverse
60. Strut—Rev. Brake
61. Strut—Rev. Band (Anchor)
62. Race—Overrun Clutch—Inner
63. Spring & Roller Assy.—OWC
64. Race—Overrun Clutch—Outer
65. Washer—Rev. Drum to Case—Thrust—No. 9.
66. Bolt
67. Tag—Service Identification
68. Cover—Interm. Band Servo
69. Gasket—Interm. Band Servo
70. Seal—Interm. Band Servo Cover—Large
71. Not Used
72. Seal—Interm. Band Servo Piston—Small
73. Piston Assy. Interm. Band Servo
74. Spring—Interm. Band Servo Piston
75. Shaft Assy.—Output
76. Gasket—Extension
77. Extension Assy.
78. Seal Assy.—Ext. Oil
79. Bolt
80. Body—Gov. Oil Collector
80A. Screen Assy.—Gov. Oil
81. Ring—Governor Seal
82. Ring (Not Used After Mid-1982 Production)
83. Bolt
84. Sleeve—Oil Distributor
85. Gear—Output Shaft Parking
86. Washer—Output Shaft Thrust—RR—No. 10
87. Spring—P.P. Return
88. Pawl Assy.—Parking
89. Pin
90. Case Assembly
91. Tube—Oil Distributor
92. Tube—Oil Distributor
93. Clip—Throt. Cntl. Valve Diaphragm
94. Diaphragm Assy.—T.V. Control
95. Rod—T.V. Control
96. Valve—Throttle Control
97. Bolt
98. Cover—Rev. Band Servo
99. Clip—Electrical Wiring Harness
100. Seal—Rev. Bnd. Servo Piston Cover
101. Piston Assy.—Rev. Band Servo
102. Spring—Rev. Servo Piston
103. Nut
104. Washer

105. Lever Assy.—Dwnshift Control—Outer
106. Switch Assy.—Neutral Start
107. Screw & Wshr. Assy.
108. Seal
109. Lever Assy.—Manual Control
110. Nut
111. Screw
112. Ring
113. Rod Assy.—Park Lever Actuating
114. Spacer—Parking Lever
115. Lever Assy.—Parking Actuating
116. Washer
117. Ring Retaining
118. Roller—Park Lever Actuating Rod
119. Lever Assy.—Man. Vlv. Detent—Inner
120. Link—P.P. Toggle Oper. Lever
121. Ring
122. Nut
123. Ring
124. Lever Assy.—Dwnshft. Detent—Inner
125. Body—Governor Valve
126. Valve—Governor Primary
127. Spring—Gov. Primary Valve
128. Washer
129. Retaining Ring—Internal
130. Valve—Gov. Secondary
131. Spring—Gov. Secondary Valve
132. Retainer—Gov. Sec. Valve Spring
133. Control Assy.—Main
134. Plate—Control Vlv. Body Sep.
135. Gasket—Control Vlv. Body Sep.
136. Plate—3-2 Timing Body Sep.
137. Gasket—3-2 Timing Body Sep.
138. Screen & Grommet Assy.—Oil Pan
139. Gasket—Oil Pan
140. Pan Assy.—Oil Pan
141. Spring Assy.—Main Vlv. Detent
142. Bolt
143. Bolt
144. Screw
145. Bolt
146. Bolt
147. Screw
148. Screw
149. Screw
150. Screw
151. Screw
152. Plug
153. Bolt
154. Screw
155. Nut
156. Ring
157. Body Assy. Governor
158. Tube—Vent
159. Clamp—Vent Tube

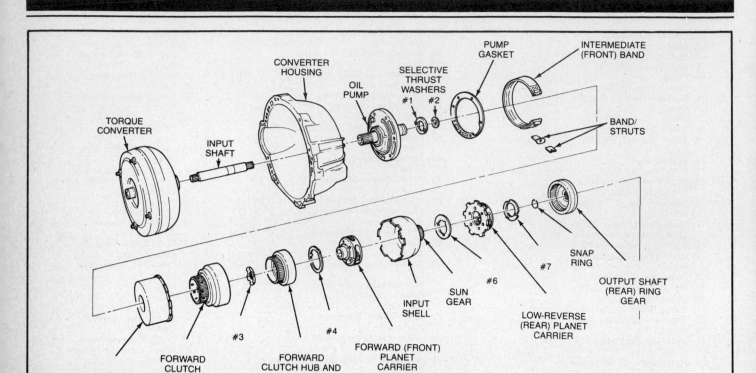

Exploded view of front internal components of transmission (©Ford Motor Company)

ate (front) band ends with the clearance hole in the case and remove the band.

15. Remove the clutch packs, front planetary and input shell as a unit from the transmission case. To prevent the assembly from rolling off bench, place the unit on the bench with the sun gear up.

16. Remove the reverse planet carier assembly. Remove the number six and number seven thrust washers from the carrier.

NOTE: Tag the thrust washers for assembly identification.

17. Align the low-reverse (rear) band ends with the clearance hole in the case and remove the band.

18. Place the transmission case face down on the bench or with the fixture.

19. Remove the extension housing bolts, the diaphragm retainer and tubing clip and the T.V. diaphragm with the diaphragm rod.

20. Using a magnet, remove the throttle valve from its bore in the case.

NOTE: If necessary, push the valve out from the inside of the case.

21. Lift the extension housing from the transmission case. Discard the gasket and remove the seal from the housing and discard.

NOTE: A spline seal may be found on the end of the output shaft. This is used for shipping only. Remove and discard.

22. Place the manual valve lever in the PARK position to lock the output shaft. Unbolt and remove the governor assembly.

23. Remove the governor screen and check for contamination.

24. Place the transmission in a horizontal position and remove the hub snapring retaining the reverse ring gear and hub assembly to the output shaft. Remove the reverse ring gear and hub assembly.

25. Remove the low-reverse drum. After removal, remove the number eight thrust washer from the low-reverse drum.

NOTE: Tag the thrust washer for assembly identification.

26. Place the transmission case face down. Lift the output shaft and governor collector body from the case (1982).

27. (Early 1982 models) Remove the snapring from the output shaft and separate the collector body from the output shaft. Remove the seals from the selector body.

NOTE: Mid 1982 and later output shafts do not use the retaining snapring holding the governor collector body to the shaft. The shaft can be lifted from the collector body separately and then the collector body can be removed.

28. Remove the four bolts holding the distributor sleeve and tubes. Remove the sleeve and tubes, being careful not to bend any of the tubes.

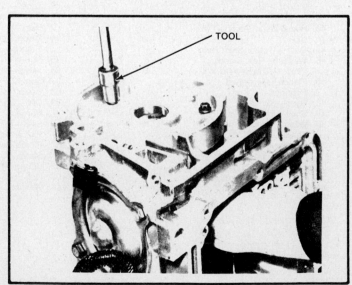

Removal of the one-way clutch retaining bolts with special socket (©Ford Motor Company)

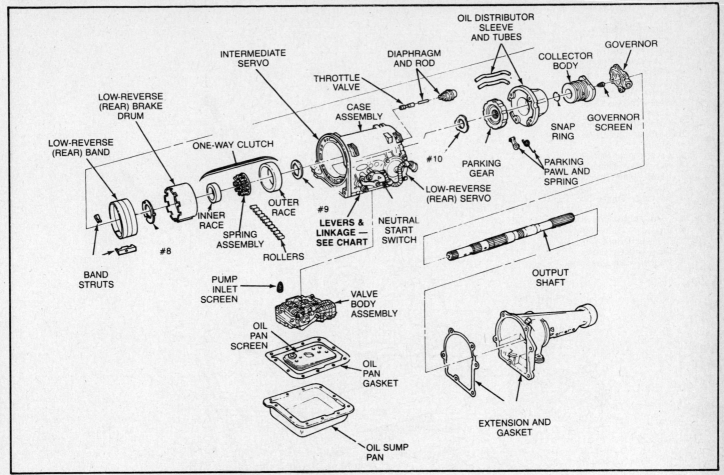

Exploded view of rear internal components (©Ford Motor Company)

29. Remove the parking gear and the number ten thrust washer.

NOTE: Tag the thrust washer for assembly identification.

30. Remove the spring, pawl and pivot pin.

31. With the transmission case still setting on its front area, reach into the rear of the transmission case and grasp the one-way clutch and keep it from falling, while removing the six special retaining bolts.

———— CAUTION ————

Use a special tool socket, Ford number T65P-7B456-B or its equivalent. A regular 5/16 inch socket may break due to the high torque necessary to remove the bolts.

32. Carefully, remove the one-way clutch assembly from the case. Remove the number nine thrust washer.

NOTE: Tag the thrust washer for assembly identification.

33. Remove the four bolts holding the intermediate servo and carefully remove the cover from the case. Remove the piston and spring from the cover. Remove and discard the gasket. Remove the piston seals.

34. Remove the low-reverse servo cover retaining bolts. Note the location of the wiring clips for installation purposes.

35. Remove the cover and discard the seal. Push the piston rod outward from inside the case. Remove the piston assembly and spring.

NOTE: The piston seal is bonded to the piston and cannot be removed.

36. Remove the cooler line fittings from the case. Remove the "O" rings and discard.

NOTE: This completes the usual disassembly of the C-5 Automatic Transmission case.

Case Internal Linkage

Removal

NOTE: The case internal linkage should only be disassembled if the components or case is damaged or the case must be replaced.

1. Position the downshift lever and note its relation to the case. Lubricate the outer lever nut with a penetrating oil and remove the nut, washer and the downshift lever.

2. Remove the "O" ring and inner downshift lever.

3. Remove the two retaining bolts and remove the neutral start and/or back-up lamp switch.

4. From inside the case, remove the hex nut from the inner manual lever and shaft. Push the manual lever out and remove the inner lever.

5. Noting the outer lever's position in relation to the case, remove the manual lever and shaft. Remove and discard the lever oil seal.

6. Remove the retainer and pull the manual lever link off the pin in the case.

7. At the rear of the case, remove the lower retainer and washer from the park pawl actuating lever. Remove the lever and link, attached to the actuating rod, through the rear of the case.

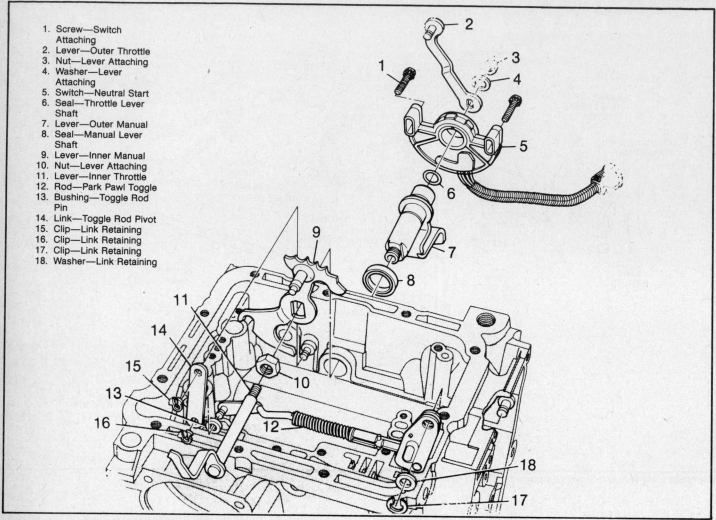

1. Screw—Switch Attaching
2. Lever—Outer Throttle
3. Nut—Lever Attaching
4. Washer—Lever Attaching
5. Switch—Neutral Start
6. Seal—Throttle Lever Shaft
7. Lever—Outer Manual
8. Seal—Manual Lever Shaft
9. Lever—Inner Manual
10. Nut—Lever Attaching
11. Lever—Inner Throttle
12. Rod—Park Pawl Toggle
13. Bushing—Toggle Rod Pin
14. Link—Toggle Rod Pivot
15. Clip—Link Retaining
16. Clip—Link Retaining
17. Clip—Link Retaining
18. Washer—Link Retaining

Manual and shift linkage components (©Ford Motor Company)

Inspections

1. No further disassembly is needed unless a part is damaged or bent. Replace as required.

Assembly

1. Lubricate the manual lever seal and install with the garter spring towards center of case. Install squarely into the seal bore with a seal installer tool.

2. Install the park actuating linkage. Install the retainer on the pin over the manual lever link.

3. Install the flat washer and the retainer over the park pawl actuating lever.

4. Install the outer manual lever and shaft in the original disassembled location.

5. Install the inner manual lever onto the flats of the outer manual lever shaft in its original position. Tighten the nut to 30-40 ft. lbs.

6. Install the neutral start and/or back-up lamp switch. Do not tighten the screws until the switch is adjusted.

7. Install the inner downshift lever assembly and shaft seal "O" ring. Install the outer downshift lever in its original position and install the nut and lockwasher. Tighten the nut to 12-16 ft. lbs.

UNIT DISASSEMBLY AND ASSEMBLY

Oil Pump

Disassembly

1. Remove the number one and two thrust washers from the stator support.

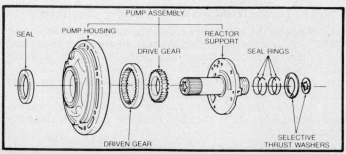

Exploded view of oil pump assembly (©Ford Motor Company)

2. Remove the teflon and cast iron rings from the stator support.

3. Remove the stator support to pump body attaching bolts and lift the stator support from the pump body.

4. Remove the pump gears from the pump body, noting their direction. The chamfer on the drive gear and the dot on the driven gear must face the pump body.

5. Remove the oil seal from the pump body, using a hammer and punch.

6. The bushing can be removed with the use of a bushing remover tool and a press.

Inspection

1. Inspect the mating surfaces of the pump body and cover for burrs.

2. Inspect the drive and driven gear bearing surfaces for scores and check the gear teeth for burrs.

3. Check all fluid passages for obstructions.

4. If any parts are scored deeply, worn or damaged, replace the pump assembly as a unit. Minor burrs and scores may be removed with crocus cloth.

Assembly

1. With the use of a bushing installer tool and press, install the bushing into the pump body. When the bushing is seated, stake the bushing to the pump body, using a chisel.

NOTE: Two notches are located in the bushing bore to be used as the stacking points.

2. Using a seal installer, install the oil seal in the front of the pump body.

=== CAUTION ===

The seal must be square in the bore. If the seal is not correct or the garter spring is out of place, replace the seal.

3. Lubricate the inside of the pump body with petroleum jelly and install the gears.

NOTE: The chamfered side of the drive gear and the dot on the driven gear must face the pump body.

4. Bolt the reactor support to the pump body with the five bolts. Torque the bolts to 12-20 ft. lbs.

5. Mount the pump on the converter hub and check the freeness of rotation of the pump gears.

6. Remove the pump from the converter and install the seals on the stator support. Place the iron seals in the lower grooves and the teflon seals in the upper grooves.

=== CAUTION ===

When installing the teflon rings, make sure the scarf ends overlap properly and when installing the cast iron rings, make sure the ends are securely interlocked.

7. Install the number one and number two thrust washers.

NOTE: These thrust washers are selective thicknesses and are used to limit the transmission end play to a specific tolerance. When installing, the thrust washers should be installed in pairs to obtain the desired end play of 0.008-0.042 inch (0.020-1.07 mm). Use petroleum jellly to lubricate.

8. If the end play is known, select the proper thrust washers from the chart and install.

9. If the end play is not known, install the original thrust washers. The end play will be checked and if necessary, corrected during the assembly of the transmission.

Identification of drive and driven oil pump gears
(©Ford Motor Company)

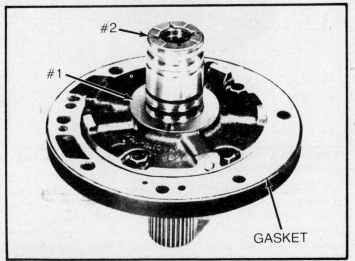

Location of numbers one and two thrust washers
(©Ford Motor Company)

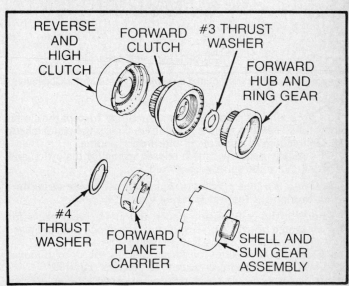

Exploded view of forward gear train and clutch assemblies
(©Ford Motor Company)

Forward (Front) Gear Train and Clutches

Disassembly

1. Lift the input shell and sun gear from the reverse-high clutch.
2. Remove the forward clutch hub and ring gear from the forward clutch. Separate and remove the front planet carrier and the number four thrust washer.

NOTE: The front planetary carrier is removed with the forward clutch hub.

3. Remove the number three thrust washer from the forward clutch. Separate the forward clutch from the direct (reverse-high) clutch.

NOTE: Assembly procedures for the Forward (Front) Gear Train and Clutches follow the disassembly and assembly of the sub-units.

Disassembly of Sub-Units

FORWARD CLUTCH

1. Remove the clutch pack retaining snapring and remove the clutch pack from forward clutch drum.
2. Using a pry tool, disengage the piston retaining ring from the clutch drum ring groove.
3. Remove the piston retaining ring, the Belleville piston return spring and the thrust ring from the forward clutch drum.
4. To remove the piston from the clutch drum, turn the piston clockwise or if necessary, blow the piston from the drum with air pressure.
5. Remove and discard the piston and the drum hub seals.

Inspection

1. Inspect the thrust surfaces, piston bore and clutch plate splines for scores and burrs. Replace the clutch cylinder if it is badly scored or damaged.

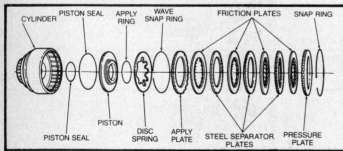

Exploded view of forward clutch assembly (©Ford Motor Company)

2. Check all fuid passages for obstructions. Inspect the clutch piston for scores and replace if required. Check the piston check ball for freedom of movement and proper seating.
3. Check the Belleville clutch release spring for distortion and cracks. Replace the spring if required.

NOTE: It is a good practice to replace the Belleville spring during an overhaul of the transmission unit.

4. Inspect the composition plates and steel clutch plates for worn or scored bearing surfaces. Inspect the clutch pressure place for worn or scored surface. Replace as required.
5. Check the steel plates for flatness and for freedom of movement on the clutch hub serrations. Replace as required.

NOTE: It is a good practice to replace the composition and steel clutch plates during an overhaul of the transmission unit.

6. Check the clutch hub thrust surfaces for scores and check the splines of the clutch hub and stator support for wear. Replace as required.
7. Inspect the bushing in the stator support for scores. Inspect the input shaft for damage or worn splines.

Assembly

1. Using petroleum jelly, lubricate and install a new seal on the clutch drum hub.
2. Using petroleum jelly, lubricate and install a new seal on the clutch piston. Note the direction of the sealing lip. The lip should face into the cylinder.

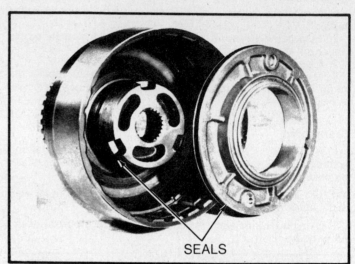

Installation of forward clutch piston and positioning of seals (©Ford Motor Company)

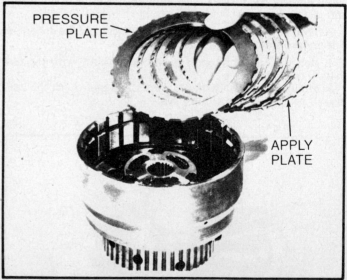

Installation of pressure plate and clutch pack into clutch housing (©Ford Motor Company)

3. Being sure both seals are lubricated, install the clutch piston into the clutch drum. To seat the piston properly into the drum, rotate the piston while pressing downward on it.

— **CAUTION** —

Be sure the seal lip is started into the clutch drum bore properly.

4. Install the thrust ring and Belleville piston return spring into the clutch drum.

NOTE: The dish of the Belleville spring must be down.

5. Install the wave snapring, working it firmly into the groove of the clutch drum. Be sure the ring is fully seated in the clutch drum groove.

6. Install the forward clutch pressure plate with the dished side of the plate facing the piston.

7. Install the clutch pack, starting with a friction plate and alternating with the steel plate until all plates are installed. The last plate to be installed is the rear pressure plate. The number of clutch plates vary with the transmission application.

NOTE: Before installing new clutch plates, soak in automatic transmission fluid at least 15 minutes.

8. Install the rear pressure plate and the clutch pack retaining ring. Be sure the retaining ring is properly seated in its groove on the forward clutch drum.

NOTE: The clutch pack retaining ring is a selective type snapring.

9. With the use of a feeler gauge, check the clearance between the pressure plate and the clutch pack retaining ring while holding the pressure plate downward. The clearance should be 0.025-0.050 inch (0.64-1.3 mm). If the clearance is not within the specified clearance, a selective snaprings must be used to obtain the correct clearance. The snaprings are available in the following thicknesses:
0.050-0.054 inch
0.064-0.068 inch
0.078-0.082 inch
0.092-0.096 inch
0.104-0.108 inch
Recheck the clutch pack clearance after installing the selective snapring.

Measuring clutch pack clearance on the forward clutch assembly (©Ford Motor Company)

10. Using air pressure, check the clutch assembly for operation. The clutch should be heard and felt, apply smoothly and have no leakage. As the air is stopped, the piston should return to the released position.

REVERSE-HIGH CLUTCH

Disassembly

1. Remove the clutch pack retaining snapring. Remove the clutch pack from the direct clutch drum, along with the Belleville disc spring and pressure plate.

2. Using a clutch spring compressor tool, compress the piston return spring and remove the spring retaining ring, using a set of external snapring pliers.

3. Remove the clutch piston from the clutch drum. If the piston is difficult to remove by turning it, air pressure can be used as required.

4. Remove the seal from the clutch piston and the seal from the clutch drum hub. Discard both.

Inspection

1. Inspect the drum band surface, bushings and thrust surfaces for scores. Badly scored parts must be replace. Minor scores can be removed with crocus cloth.

2. Inspect the clutch piston bore and the piston inner and outer bearing surfaces for scores. Check the air bleed valve for freeness, located in the clutch piston. Check the orifice to be sure it is not plugged.

3. Check all fluid passages for obstructions.

4. Inspect the clutch pressure plate for scores. Replace if necessary.

5. Inspect the composition and steel clutch plates. Check their fit on the splines of the clutch hub.

NOTE: It is a good practice to replace the composition and steel clutch plates during the overhaul of the transmission unit.

Assembly

1. Using petroleum jelly, lubricate and install a new seal on the clutch drum hub.

2. Using petroleum jelly, lubricate and install a new seal on the clutch piston, noting the direction of the seal lip.

NOTE: The seal lip should face into the clutch drum.

3. Being sure both seals are lubricated and the piston bore is lubricated with petroleum jelly, install the piston into the clutch drum bore with the use of a seal protector tool. Push the piston to the bottom of the bore with an even thumb pressure.

4. Position the piston return spring and the spring retainer on the clutch piston and compress the return spring, using the spring compressor tool. Install the spring retainer ring.

—————————— CAUTION ——————————
Be sure the retainer ring is in its groove properly before releasing the spring compressor tool.

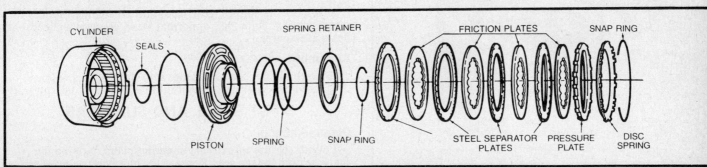

Exploded view of reverse-high clutch assembly (©Ford Motor Company)

CYLINDER SEALS SPRING RETAINER FRICTION PLATES SNAP RING PISTON SPRING SNAP RING STEEL SEPARATOR PLATES PRESSURE PLATE DISC SPRING

5. To check the clutch pack clearance, install the clutch pack in the following order;

NOTE: The order of clutch pack installation for the check is not the correct installation sequence. This is done only for the check procedure. After checking the pack clearance, remove the plates and install in their proper sequence.

    a. Install a metallic plate.
    b. Alternately install the composition and metallic plates until two composition plates remain.
    c. Install the two remaining composition plates together.
    d. Install the disc spring.
    e. Install the pressure plate.

6. Install the clutch pack retaining ring. Using a feeler gauge, check the clearance between the pressure plate and the clutch pack retaining ring, while holding the pressure plate downward as the clearance is checked. The proper clearance is 0.025-0.050 inch (0.64-1.35 mm). If the clearance is not correct, selective snaprings are available in the following thicknesses:

    0.050-0.054 inch
    0.064-0.068 inch
    0.078-0.082 inch
    0.092-0.096 inch

7. Remove the clutch pack retaining ring and lift the clutch pack from the clutch drum. The clutch pack can now be installed into the clutch drum in the proper sequence, as follows;

    a. Install a metallic plate.
    b. Alternately intall the composition and metallic plates.
    c. Install the pressure plate.

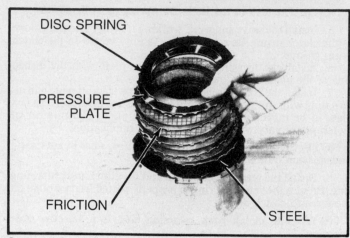

Correct order of clutch pack assembly after clutch pack clearance check (©Ford Motor Company)

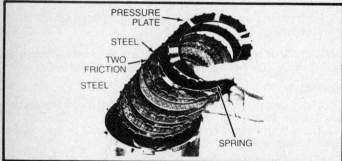

Temporary clutch pack assembly to make clearance check (©Ford Motor Company)

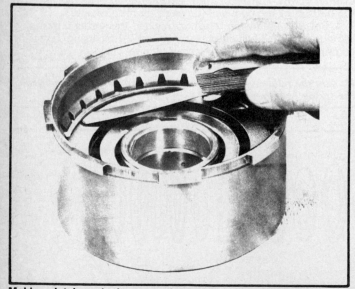

Making clutch pack clearance check (©Ford Motor Company)

    d. Install the disc spring with the splines facing the snapring.
    e. Install the clutch pack retaining ring into its groove in the clutch drum.

8. Using air pressure, check the operation of the clutch assembly. The clutch plates should be heard to engage and felt to apply smoothly and without leakage. When the air pressure is removed, the clutch pack should release smoothly and completely.

NOTE: During the air test, two holes must be blocked and the air pressure applied to the third.

FORWARD CLUTCH HUB AND RING GEAR

Disassembly

1. Remove the snapring retaining the hub to the ring gear.
2. Separate the hub from the ring gear.

Inspection

1. Inspect the splines, gear teeth and all mating surfaces for scores, pitting, chips and abnormal wear. Replace the components as required.

Assembly

1. Assemble the ring gear and forward clutch hub together.
2. Install the retaining snapring into its groove in the ring gear.

REVERSE RING GEAR AND HUB

Disassembly

1. Remove the snapring retaining the hub and flange to the ring gear.
2. Separate the hub and flange from the ring gear.

Inspection

1. Inspect the splines, gear teeth and all mating surfaces for scores, pitting, chips and abnormal wear. Replace the components as required.

Assembly

1. Assemble the hub and flange into the ring gear splines.
2. Install the snapring retainer into its groove in the ring gear.

INPUT SHELL AND SUN GEAR

Disassembly

1. With the use of external snapring pliers, remove the rear snapring from the sun gear. Remove the number five thrust washer.

2. Remove the sun gear from the input shell. If necessary, remove the snapring from the front of the sun gear.

Inspection

1. Inspect the splines, gear teeth and all mating surfaces for scores, pitting, chips and abnormal wear. Check the input shell for cracks and distortion. Replace the components as required.

Assembly

1. Install the front snapring on the sun gear. Install the sun gear into the input shell.

2. Install the number five thrust washer and the rear snapring retainer on the sun gear.

ONE-WAY CLUTCH

Disassembly

1. While pressing downward, rotate the inner race to separate it from the outer race spring retainer cage ring.

── **CAUTION** ──

Note position of components for assembly identification. Do not lose rollers or springs during the disassembly.

Inspection

1. Inspect the rollers and mating surfaces on the inner and outer races for scoring, indentations and other abnormal wear indicators.

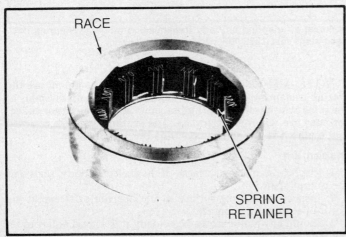

Position outer race with bolt holes down and install spring retainer
(©Ford Motor Company)

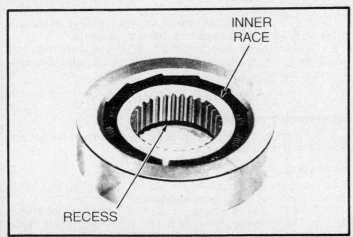

Install inner race with recessed spline down
(©Ford Motor Company)

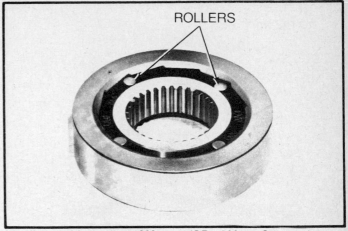

Installation of four rollers, 90° apart (©Ford Motor Company)

2. Inspect the spring and roller case for bent or damaged spring retainers.

Assembly

1. Position the one-way clutch outer race an the workbench with the bolt holes down.

2. Install the spring retainer with the cage ring down.

3. Install the inner race with the recessed end of the splines down.

4. Install four rollers spaced 90° apart between the inner and outer races. Install the remaining eight rollers and rotate the inner race to seat the components.

GOVERNOR

Disassembly

1. With the use of snapring pliers, remove the snapring from the governor bore containing the primary governor valve.

2. Remove the primary valve spring and the spring seat washer from the bore.

3. Remove the primary valve from the governor bore.

4. Remove the secondary valve spring retaining plate and pull the secondary valve and spring from the governor bore.

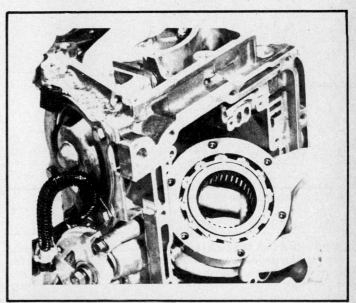

Installation of one-way clutch into transmission case
(©Ford Motor Company)

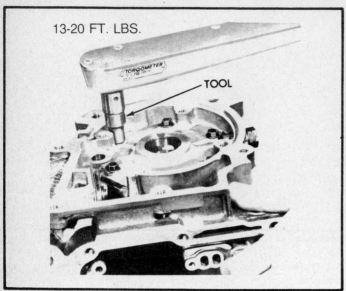

13-20 FT. LBS.

TOOL

Use of special socket and torque wrench to install bolts to the one-way clutch assembly (©Ford Motor Company)

Inspection

1. Inspect the governor valves and bores for scores, pitting or chips.
2. Inspect for free movement of the valves in their bores and fluid passages for cleanliness.
3. Inspect the springs for distortion.
4. Replace components as required.

Assembly

1. Install the secondary valve in the governor bore.
2. Position the secondary valve spring and depress, installing the spring retainer plate in its groove.

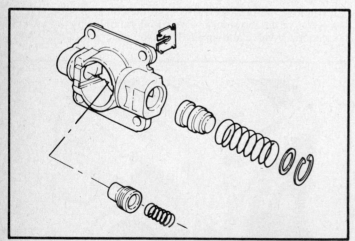

Exploded view of governor assembly (©Ford Motor Company)

─────── **CAUTION** ───────

Note the direction in which the plate is installed. The plate should be installed with the concave area facing the spring, thereby holding the spring in the correct position.

─────────────────────────

3. Install the primary valve in the governor bore, install the primary valve spring, the spring seat washer and the snapring.

OUTPUT SHAFT/GOVERNOR COLLECTOR BODY

Disassembly

1982

1. Remove the retaining snapring from the output shaft.
2. Separate the collector body from the output shaft.
3. Remove the three sealing rings from the collector body and discard.

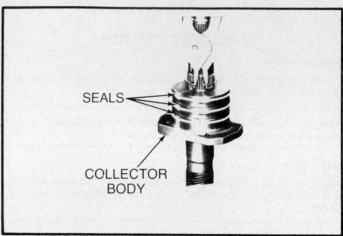

SEALS

COLLECTOR BODY

Removal of snapring on early transmission models. Snapring not used since mid-1982 (©Ford Motor Company)

NOTE: Mid-1982 and later C-5 transmissions do not use the retaining snapring on the output shaft. During the disassembly of the later transmissions, the output shaft and the governor collector body are removed separately. The sealing rings are removed and replaced in the same manner as the 1982 models.

Inspection

1. Inspect the mating surfaces of the collector body, seals and the output shaft.
2. Inspect the mating surface of the distributor sleeve at the point of sealing ring contact.
3. Should any major scores be evident, it is a good policy to replace the distributor sleeve and the collector body to prevent fluid pressure loss after reassembly.

Assembly

1. (All C-5 Transmissions) Install the sealing rings on the collector body with the tapered ends meeting properly.
2. (1982) Install the output shaft through the collector body and install the retaining snapring. Carefully lay aside until transmission unit assembly.

PLANET CARRIERS

Disassembly and Assembly

1. The individual components of the planet carriers are not serviceable and must be replaced as a unit.

Inspection

1. The pins and shafts in the planet assemblies should be checked for loose fits or poor engagement.
2. Check the shaft retaining pins should be checked for proper staking. The retaining pins must not be below the surface of the carrier more than 0.040 inch (1.0 mm).
3. Inspect the pinion gears for abnormal wear, chips and freeness of rotation.

Control Valve Body Assembly

Inspection

1. As each subsection of the control valve body assembly is disassembled, the internal components should be cleaned in solvent and blown dry with moisture free air pressure. The internal components should be inspected for any of the following conditions and immediately reassembled in the appropriate subsection to prevent the mixing of the internal components of one subsection to an other.

    a. Inspect all valve and plug bores of scores. Check all fluid passages for obstructions.

    b. Inspect the check valves for burrs and/or distortion

    c. Inspect the plugs and valves for burrs or scores.

    d. Inspect all springs for distortion or breakage.

    e. Check all valves and plugs for freedom of movement in their respective bores. When dry, they should fall from their own weight in their bores.

    f. Roll the manual valve on a flat surface to check for a bent condition.

    g. Replace the valve body to screen gasket during the assembly.

TIMING VALVE BODY

Disassembly

1. Prepare a clean area on a work bench with room to spread the valve body components onto during the disassembly. All valves, springs and check balls must be kept in their correct order for ease in the assembly procedure.

2. Remove the ten screws from the timing valve body to lower valve body (Nine 5/16 inch heads and one 3/8 inch head bolts). Note the location of the short screw.

3. Carefully lift the timing valve body off the lower valve body. Remove the converter relief valve and spring.

4. Invert the timing valve body and remove the screw, separator plate and gasket. Note the position of the check ball and orifice "puck" and remove both.

5. Remove the retainers, the 1-2/3-2 shift timing valve, the 3-2 timing valve and the cut back valve from the valve body. Keep the springs with each valve.

NOTE: As each section of the valve body is disassembled, cleaned and inspected, each should be reassembled in their correct sequence and set aside until the complete assembly of the valve body is required. This procedure prevents mixing of section components and improper valve body operation after the overhaul is completed.

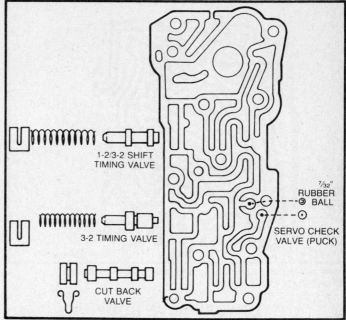

Exploded views of timing body component locations (©Ford Motor Company)

Assembly

1. Inspect the valve body and valves as indicated at the beginning of the valve body outline.

2. Install the valves, springs and retainers in their respective bores.

3. Install the check ball and check valve in the timing valve body.

NOTE: Depending upon vehicle application, there may be either a black or tan check valve (puck) used. During the reassembly, or when the puck replacement is required, be sure the correct colored puck is installed.

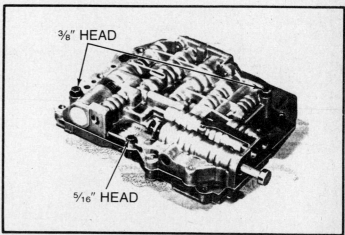

Remove three bolts, invert and remove the nine bolts to separate the upper and lower valve body (©Ford Motor Company)

4. Position the separator and gasket plate on the timing body and using either alignment pins or tapered punches, install the attaching screw and tighten to 25-40 in. lbs. (3-5 N•m).

5. Place the converter relief valve and the gasket with the timing valve body and lay aside until ready for complete valve body assembly.

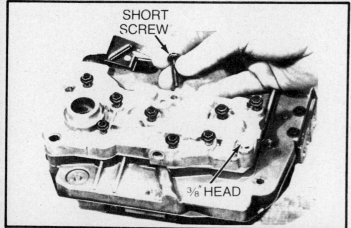

Removal of timing body attaching screws. Note location of short screw (©Ford Motor Company)

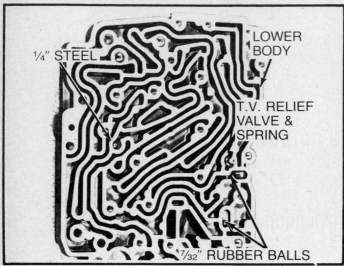

Lower valve body check balls and check valve locations
(©Ford Motor Company)

LOWER VALVE BODY

Disassembly

CAUTION

The lower valve body contains check balls which have to be held in position when the upper and lower valve body sections are separated. Follow this outline for the proper separation technique.

1. Remove the upper valve body to lower valve body attaching screws (three).

2. Turn the valve body assembly over and remove the nine lower body to upper body attaching screws. Remove the detent spring.

3. Carefully grip the separator plate and the lower valve body together and lift the body and plate away from the upper valve body. Turn the lower valve body and separator plate over with the separator plate facing up.

4. Remove the separator plate and the gasket. Discard the gasket.

5. **Important:** Identify the locations of the check balls in the lower valve body to aid in the reassembly. Remove the check balls and the throttle pressure limit valve and spring from the lower valve body.

6. **Important:** Identify the location of the check ball in the upper valve body to aid in the reassembly. Do not remove at this time. Set aside until the upper valve body is to be disassembled and assembled.

NOTE: A multi-channeled wooden block is a good holding tool for the disassembly of the valve bodies, holding the valves in a channel as they are removed from the valve body. This method keeps the valves in order of removal without fear of them rolling against each other and becoming mixed.

7. Clean, inspect and reinstall the throttle pressure limit valve and spring into its seat and position the black check balls in their seats in the lower valve body. Set the lower valve body aside until the complete assembly is done.

8. Noting the position of the checkball in the upper valve body, remove the ball and set aside.

9. A general removal procedure is given for the removal of the varied valves, retainers and springs. Lay the components of each bore out in order to prevent mixing them. After the complete removal of the components, the cleaning and inspection, of the

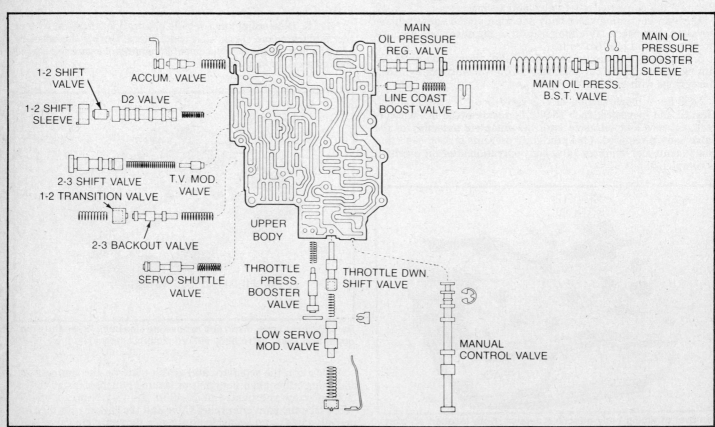

Exploded view of upper valve body components   (©Ford Motor Company)

components and valve body, reassemble the valves, springs and retainers back into the valve body, in the reverse order of their removal.

NOTE: A wooden dowel pin or an aluminum fabricated tool is useful to relieve spring pressure when attempting to remove the retainers in the valve body bores.

CAUTION

Added or deleted internal components are sometimes found in a valve body bore that do not coincide with the components shown in an illustration. This can occur as a production change by the manufacturer for many various reasons. Consequently, components of a valve body bore must be kept in their proper order for correct reassembly.

a. Manual Control Valve—Remove the "E" clip retainer with an appropriate tool and remove the manual valve from its bore.

b. Low Servo Modulator Valve—Push inward on the end of the bore plug with a small probe and release the valve retainer. Lift the retainer from the valve body. Remove the bore plug, the spring, and the low servo modulator valve from the bore.

c. Throttle Downshift Valve—Using a long spring tool, such as the wooden dowel, lightly push inward and with the use of a magnet, remove the valve spring retainer from the opening of the valve body. Remove the throttle downshift valve and spring.

d. Throttle Pressure Boost Valve—Holding the valve body in a stationary position, and covering the bore, pull the bore plug lock pin from the valve body to release the bore plug. Remove the bore plug, the throttle pressure boost valve and the spring.

NOTE: During reassembly, tap lock pin in with small hammer.

e. Intermediate Servo Accumulator Valve—Push inward on the bore plug and remove the bore plug retainer with a magnet. Remove the bore plug, the intermediate servo accumulator valve and spring from the valve body bore.

f. Drive 2 Valve, 1-2 Shift Valve—Remove the three cover plate screws and remove the cover plate. Taking each bore separately, remove the sleeve, 1-2 shift valve, drive 2 valve and spring. From the second bore, remove the 2-3 shift valve, spring and the T.V. modulator valve.

NOTE: During the installation of the cover plate screws, torque to 25-40 in. lbs. (3-4.5 N•m).

g. Manual Low Control Valve/2-3 Backout Valve/Servo Shuttle Valve—Remove the two cover plate attaching screws and remove the cover. Taking each bore separately, remove the spring, manual control valve, backout valve and the spring. From the second bore, remove the servo shuttle valve and spring.

NOTE: During the installation of the cover plate screws, torque to 25-40 in. lbs. (3-4.5 N•m).

h. Main Pressure Boost Valve/Oil Pressure Regulator Valve—Pushing inward on the bore plug, remove the retaining clip from the plug groove. Remove the main pressure booster sleeve, the main pressure boost valve, the spring, inner spring and spring seat and the main oil pressure regulator valve.

NOTE: Some models do not use an inner spring.

i. Line Pressure Coasting Valve—Pushing inward with a spring tool, remove the spring retainer plate with a magnet. Remove the spring and line pressure coasting boost valve.

10. With the valves back in their respective bores, position the lower valve body with the channelled side up. Place the check balls and the pressure limiting valve in the lower valve body using petroleum jelly to retain in place.

NOTE: The steel check ball is larger than the others and must be placed in its proper location as was noted upon removal.

11. Place the gasket on the valve body and install locating pins (¼ inch drill bits or special pins). Install the separator plate and temporarily attach the plate to the valve body with the oil filter screen screw and tighten. Remove the alignment pins or drill bits.

12. Install the check ball in the upper valve body, using petroleum jelly to retain it.

13. Grasp the lower valve body and the separator plate. While holding the separator plate against the body, turn the assembly over and position the lower valve body on the upper valve body.

14. Install aligning pins and install two screws. Tighten the screws to 80-100 in. lbs. (9-13.5 N•m). Install the 5/16 inch head screw and tighten to 40-60 in. lbs. (4-5.7 N•m). Remove the oil filter screen screw and the alignment pins from the separator plate.

15. Position the detent spring and roller on the lower valve body and install the screw. Tighten to 40-60 in. lbs. (4.5-6.7 N•m). Use a drift to hold the assembly in place while the attaching screw is being tightened. Install the nine remaining screws and tighten to 40-60 in. lbs. (4.5-6.7 N•m).

NOTE: Do not forget to tighten the screw in the suction passage under the valve body.

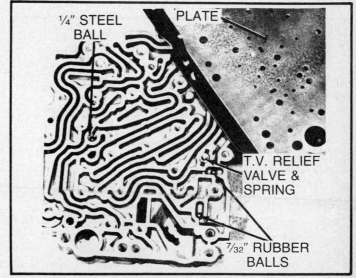

Lower valve body check balls and check valve locations before plate and gaskets are installed (©Ford Motor Company)

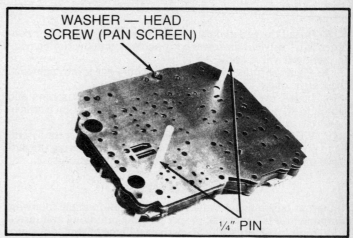

Alignment of separator plate during screw tightening (©Ford Motor Company)

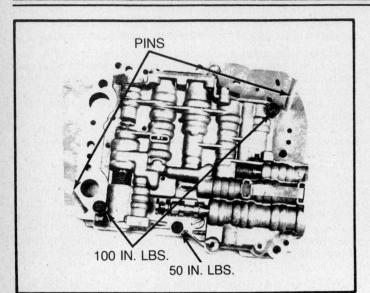

PINS

100 IN. LBS.

50 IN. LBS.

Alignment of torquing of bolts for lower and upper valve body assembly (©Ford Motor Company)

CONVERTER RELIEF VALVE & SPRING

TIMING BODY

Installation of converter relief valve and spring (©Ford Motor Company)

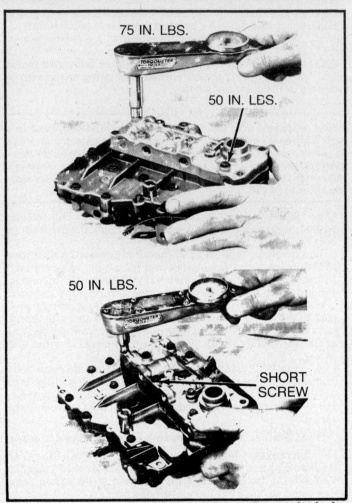

75 IN. LBS.

50 IN. LBS.

50 IN. LBS.

SHORT SCREW

Torquing of timing valve body bolts to the upper/lower valve body assembly (©Ford Motor Company)

16. Install the gasket on the lower valve body. Install the converter relief valve in the lower body and position the timing body on the lower valve body.

17. Align the timing valve body with only one screw, tightened finger tight only. Visually check the alignment.

18. Install the remaining timing body attaching screws and tighten to 40-60 in. lbs. (4.5-6.7 N•m). Tighten the ¼ inch attaching screw to 52-72 in. lbs. (5.9-8.1 N•m).

19. Place the assembled valve body aside and cover the assembly to prevent dirt or other foreign objects from entering the passages, until ready for installation on the transmission case.

Bushings

Numerous bushings are available for installation in the following components. However, the proper bushing removing and installation tools must be used to properly install the bushings in a professional manner. If the bushing bore is damaged during the removal procedure or the new bushing is scored, cocked in the bore or crimped on the ends, assembly and operation of the transmission components will be affected.

   a. Sun Gear Bushing
   b. Case Bushing
   c. Pump Housing Bushing
   d. Forward Clutch Hub Bushing
   e. Low and Reverse Brake Drum Bushing

ASSEMBLY OF TRANSMISSION

1. Inspect the transmission case for re-use. Check the installation and operation of the shift linkage.

2. With the sealing portion of the threads wrapped with teflon tape, install the oil cooler pipe fittings into their respective passages on the transmission case. Torque to 18-24 ft. lbs. (24-31 N•m).

NOTE: Be sure to use new "O" rings in each fitting.

3. Position the transmission case on its side with the low-reverse servo bore up. Lubricate and install the spring and piston assembly. Install cover with a new cover seal. Lubricate the seal with petroleum jelly.

4. Install the retaining bolts in the cover with the wiring harness hangers in its proper position. Tighten the bolts to 12-20 ft.

lbs. (17-27 N•m). Position the wiring harness from the neutral start switch/back-up lamp switch into the wiring harness clips.

5. Install new seals on the intermediate piston and position a new gasket on the servo cover.

NOTE: A lubricant can be used to hold the gasket in place on the servo cover. Align the gasket with the fluid port in the case.

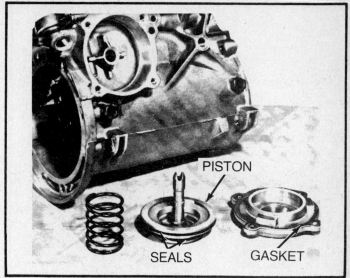

Installation of intermediate servo components (©Ford Motor Company)

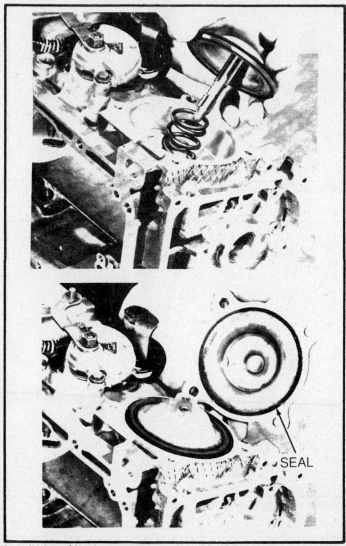

Installation of low/reverse servo assembly (©Ford Motor Company)

Installation of parking pawl and gear (©Ford Motor Company)

6. Install the piston into the cover and install the spring on the piston spring. Position the cover and piston in the case. Install the retaining bolts in the cover along with the transmission I.D. tag. Tighten the bolts to 16-22 ft. lbs. (22-30 N•m).

7. Lightly coat the number nine thrust washer with petroleum jelly and install in the transmission case at the rear.

8. Having previously assembled the one way clutch, position the transmission case front end down and install the one-way clutch over the number nine thrust washer. Install the one-way clutch retaining bolts and torque to 13-20 ft. lbs. (17-27 N•m), using the special socket available for this operation.

9. Check the parking pawl assembly for proper operation and install the number ten thrust washer and parking gear on the rear of the case. Spring load the parking pawl by looping the bend in the spring over the spring seat provided in the case. Check operation with manual lever.

10. Position the distributor sleeve on the case, making sure the oil tubes are fully seated in the case oil passages. During the installation of the distributor sleeve, be sure the parking pawl spring remains seated against the case. Torque the retaining bolts to 12-20 ft. lbs. (16-27 N•m).

11. Lubricate the oil seals and install the governor oil collector body into the distributor sleeve.

NOTE: On the 1982 model transmissions, the output shaft and the governor oil collector body must be assembled before the collector body is installed in the case. Both are then installed as a unit.

12. Position the transmission case on its top with the oil pan flange up. Lightly coat the number eight thrust washer with petroleum jelly and install in the low-reverse drum. Install the low-reverse drum into the transmission case and over the output shaft.

NOTE: Check the one-way clutch operation. The drum should turn free clockwise and lock up when turned counterclockwise.

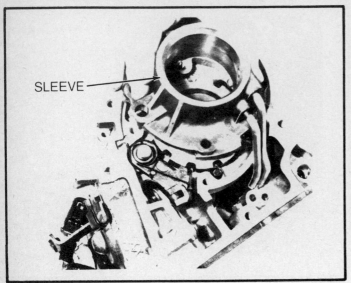

Installation of distributor sleeve on the transmission case
(©Ford Motor Company)

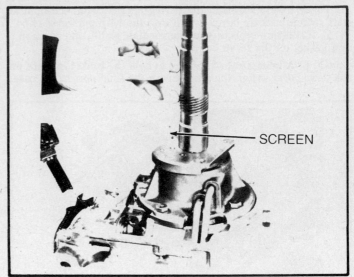

Installation of governor screen (©Ford Motor Company)

Installation of governor oil collector body and output shaft on early 1982 transmission models. Mid-1982 and later models can have the individual components installed separately because snapring is not used (©Ford Motor Company)

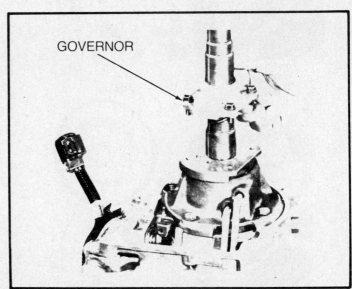

Installation of governor (©Ford Motor Company)

13. Install the reverse ring gear and hub assembly. Install the snapring to hold the reverse ring gear and hub in place on the output shaft.

NOTE: It may be necessary to push the output shaft forward to gain access to the snapring groove.

14. Install a new locknut on the rear band adjusting screw and start the screw into the case threads. Install the band strut stop into its passage in the case.

15. Align the band lugs with the relief clearance provided in the case and install the low-reverse band with the double lug of the band facing the adjusting screw.

16. Install the band struts and hand tighten the adjuster screw to hold the band in position.

17. Position the transmission case on its front flange. Install the governor screen into its passage in the governor distributor body. Position the governor assembly onto the governor distribu-

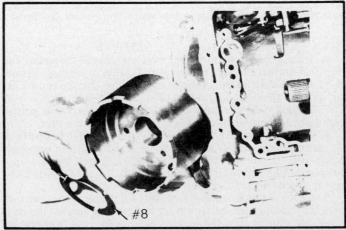

Installation of number eight thrust washer to the low/reverse drum
(©Ford Motor Company)

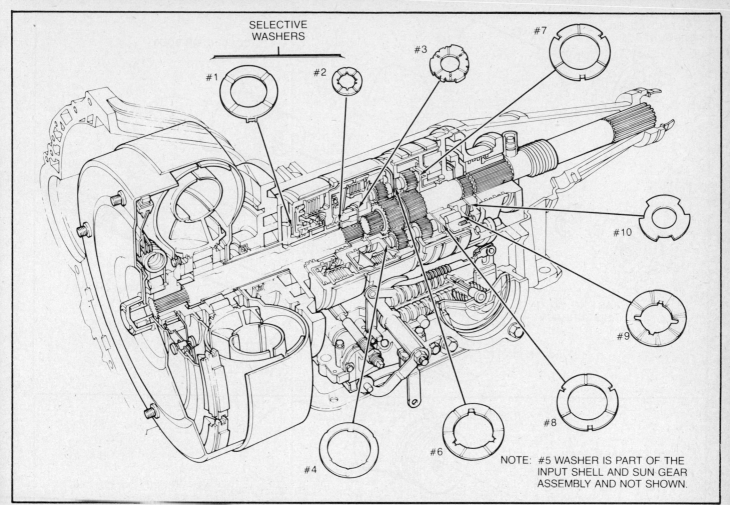

Location of thrust washers in the C-5 automatic transmission (©Ford Motor Company)

NOTE: #5 WASHER IS PART OF THE INPUT SHELL AND SUN GEAR ASSEMBLY AND NOT SHOWN.

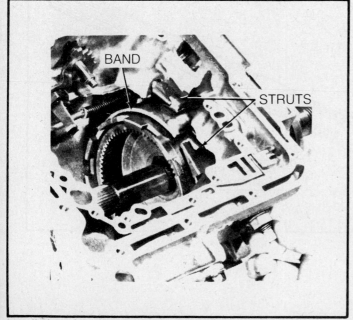

Installation of low/reverse band and struts
(©Ford Motor Company)

Installation of the hub and ring gear assembly
(©Ford Motor Company)

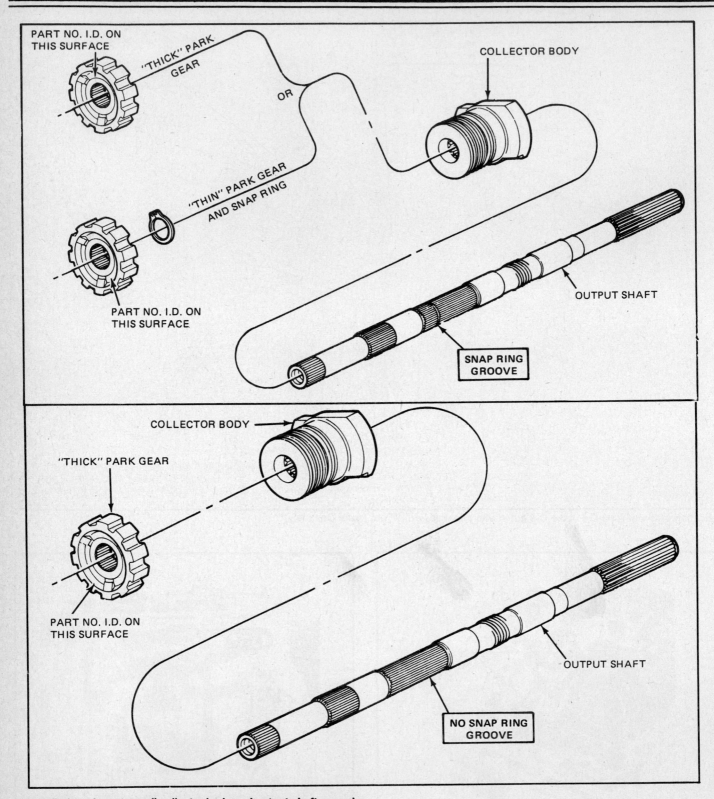

PART NO. I.D. ON THIS SURFACE

"THICK" PARK GEAR

OR

"THIN" PARK GEAR AND SNAP RING

PART NO. I.D. ON THIS SURFACE

COLLECTOR BODY

OUTPUT SHAFT

SNAP RING GROOVE

COLLECTOR BODY

"THICK" PARK GEAR

PART NO. I.D. ON THIS SURFACE

OUTPUT SHAFT

NO SNAP RING GROOVE

Installation of governor oil collector body and output shaft on early 1982 transmission models. Mid-1982 and later models can have the individual components installed separately because snapring is not used (©Ford Motor Company)

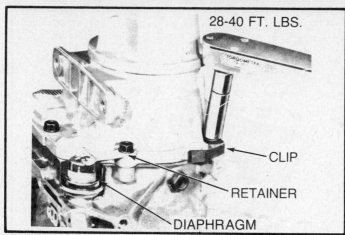

Installation of rear extension housing assembly
(©Ford Motor Company)

Installation of reverse planetary carrier (©Ford Motor Company)

tor body and install the attaching screws. Torque to 80-120 in. lbs. (9-13 N•m).

18. Position a new extension housing gasket on the case and position the extension housing without installing the attaching bolts.

19. Install the throttle valve and install the throttle valve rod and vacuum diaphragm.

20. Install the extension housing attaching bolts and torque to 28-40 ft. lbs. (38-54 N•m). Position the transmission identification tag and the modulator clamp in their proper locations.

21. Position the transmission with the oil pan flange up. Lightly lubricate the number six and seven thrust washers with petroleum jelly and position each on the reverse planetary gear assembly.

NOTE: The number seven thrust washer is placed on the gear side of the planetary gear assembly while the number six thrust washer is placed on the opposite side.

22. Install the planetary gear assembly into the transmission case, making sure the lugs are fully engaged in the low-reverse drum slots.

23. Install the forward clutch into the reverse-high clutch. Position the number three thrust washer on the forward clutch hub after lightly lubricating the washer with petroleum jelly.

24. Lightly lubricate the number four thrust washer and install on the front planetary assembly and install the front planetary

Installation of the front gear train (©Ford Motor Company)

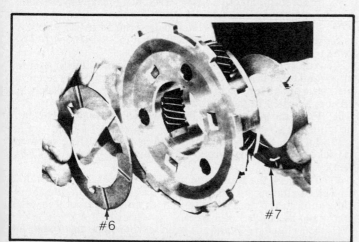

Installation of number six and seven thrust washers on the reverse planetary carrier (©Ford Motor Company)

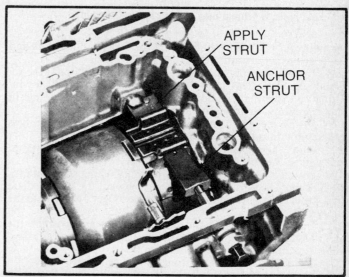

Installation of the intermediate band and struts
(©Ford Motor Company)

Preparation for installation of oil pump assembly
(©Ford Motor Company)

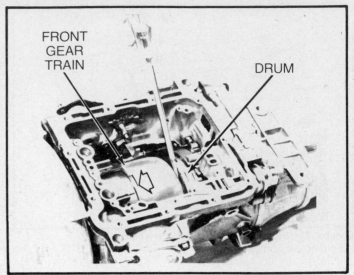

Gear train movement procedure for end play check
(©Ford Motor Company)

Checking input shaft end play (©Ford Motor Company)

unit in the forward clutch hub. Install the forward clutch hub and ring gear in the forward clutch.

25. Install the input shell and sun gear assembly onto the reverse-high clutch. Check the assembly for proper assembly by inserting and rotating the input shaft. The shaft should rotate in both directions. Remove the input shaft and lay aside.

26. Install the clutch packs, front planetary and input shell as an assembly into the transmission.

27. Align the intermediate band lugs with the relief clearance provided in the case and install the band.

28. Install a new locknut on the band adjusting screw and install the screw into its hole in the case. Install the intermediate band struts and tighten the adjusting screw finger tight to hold the band in place.

29. Install a new gasket on the front pump and position the pump assembly in the case and install two converter housing/pump attaching bolts. Snug the bolts.

30. Install the input shaft through the stator support. Position a dial indicator stylus against the end of the input shaft. Position a prying tool against a lug on the reverse-high clutch and push the gear train rearward.

31. Be sure the input shaft is fully seated and zero the indicator dial. Place the pry tool between the input shell and the reverse planetary gear assembly. Pry the input shell forward and read the dial indicator results.

32. If the end play is not within the specifications of 0.008 to 0.042 inch (0.20 to 1.07 mm), the number one and number two thrust washers must be changed. These thrust washers must be changed in pairs to obtain the specified clearances. After washer replacement, recheck end play. Check specification chart.

33. If the end play is within the specified limits, remove the dial indicator and the bolts holding the front pump assembly. Position the converter housing and install the attaching bolts. Tighten to 28-40 ft. lbs. (38-54 N•m).

NOTE: On the Truck models, the oil pump housing attaching bolts are installed and torqued to 28-38 ft. lbs. (38-51 N•m). Then position the converter housing on the transmission and bolt into place. Torque to 28-40 ft. lbs. (38-54 N•m).

34. Adjust the intermediate band by turning the adjusting screw out of the case several turns. Adjust the screw to 10 ft. lbs. (13.55 N•m) or with the use of an overrun or breakaway wrench, adjusted to the 10 ft. lbs. rating.

35. From the point of 10 ft. lbs. or wrench breakaway, back off the adjusting screw exactly 4¼ turns.

36. Tighten the locknut while holding the adjusting screw in its backed off position. Torque the locknut to 35-45 ft. lbs. (47-61 N•m).

37. Adjust the low-reverse band by turning the adjusting screw out several turns from its finger tight position. Adjust the screw to 10 ft. lbs. (13.55 N•m) or with the use of an overrun or breakaway wrench, adjusted to the 10 ft. lbs. rating.

38. From the point of 10 ft. lbs. or wrench breakaway, back off the adjusting screw exactly 3 turns.

39. Tighten the locknut while holding the adjusting screw in its backed off position. Torque the locknut to 35-45 ft. lbs. (47-61 N•m).

40. To check the transmission for proper assembly, install a slip yoke on the output shaft and turn the shaft in both directions. If the output shaft does not turn in both directions, the transmission is not assembled properly.

41. The clutch packs and the band servos can be checked by an air pressure check to each of the appropriate hydraulic passageways, using an air pressure of approximately 25 psi. The clutches should be heard and felt to apply smoothly and without leakage.

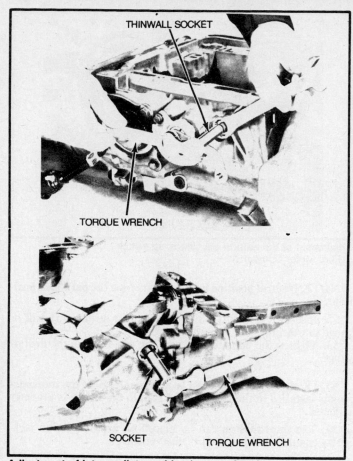

Adjustment of intermediate and low/reverse band
(©Ford Motor Company)

When the air pressure is released, the clutches should return to their released position.

42. When the air pressure is applied to the band servo passages, the band can be seen applying and releasing when the air pressure is removed.

43. Install the front oil pump inlet screen in the bore of the transmission.

44. Install the valve body carefully, making sure as the valve body is lowered into the case, the manual valve engages the manual lever and the downshift lever is positioned to engage the throttle downshift valve.

45. Install the valve body attaching bolts and torque to 80-120 in. lbs. (9-13 N•m).

NOTE: Place the two long bolts in their proper position at the left and right forward location on the timing valve body.

Installation of the valve body and filter screen
(©Ford Motor Company)

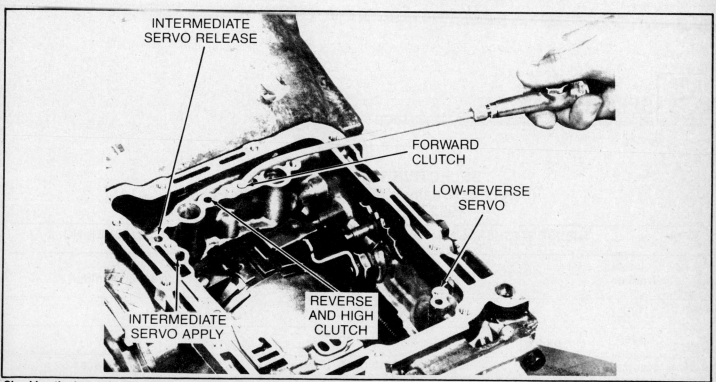

Checking the internal units with air pressure (©Ford Motor Company)

12-16 FT. LBS.

Installation of oil pan and torquing of the retaining bolts
(©Ford Motor Company)

3/32 IN.

Adjustment of the neutral start/back-up switch
(©Ford Motor Company)

46. Install the filter screen on the valve body and be sure the oil seal is in its proper position. Install the attaching screw and torque to 25-40 in. lbs. (3-4.5 N•m).

47. Position a new gasket on the oil pan and install the pan on the flange of the case.

48. Install the oil pan attaching bolts and torque to 12-16 ft. lbs. (16-22 N•m).

49. Install the input shaft and be sure it is fully seated.

50. Install the torque converter assembly, making sure the converter is fully seated, engaging the input shaft, stator support and the oil pump drive gear.

51. Place the transmission on its oil pan and place the manual lever in the neutral position and hold in place.

NOTE: Neutral position is two detents from the park lock position.

52. Insert a 3/32 inch (0.089 inch diameter minimum) drill or gauge pin through the hole in the switch.

53. Tighten the bolts to 55-75 in. lbs. and remove the drill or gauge.

NOTE: A continuity test can be performed before the transmission is installed in the vehicle to be certain the switch is properly adjusted.

54. The transmission can be placed on a transmission jack, safety chained and installed in the vehicle.

SPECIFICATIONS

SELECTIVE THRUST WASHERS
(Selective Washers Must Be Installed In Pairs)
1982 and Later—All Models

THRUST WASHER NO. 1		THRUST WASHER NO. 2
Color of Washer	Thickness	Washer Number
Red	0.053-0.0575	2
Green	0.070-0.0745	3
Neutral	0.087-0.0915	2 or 3 Plus Spacer①

① This is a selective spacer used with washer 2 or 3. When used, install next to stator support.

CLUTCH PLATES
1982—Car Models

Model	Forward Clutch			Reverse Clutch		
	External Spline (Steel)	Internal Spline (Comp.)	Free Pack Clear (Inches)	External Spline (Steel)	Internal Spline (Comp.)	Free Pack Clear (Inches)
PEN Fairmont/Zephyr, Thunderbird/XR7, Granada/Cougar, Mustang Capri	4	5		3	3	
PEP Granada/Cougar,	4	5		3	3	.030-.055
PEM Mustang/Capri Fairmont/Zephyr	4	5		4	4	

CLUTCH PLATES
1983—Car Models

Model	Forward Clutch			Reverse Clutch		
	External Spline (Steel)	Internal Spline (Comp.)	Free Pack Clear (Inches)	External Spline (Steel)	Internal Spline (Comp.)	Free Pack Clear (Inches)
PEN Fairmont, Futura/ Zephyr, Thunderbird/XR7, LTD/Marquis, Mustang Capri	4	5	—	3	3	0.025-0.050
PEP LTD/Marquis	4	5	—	3	3	0.025-0.050

CLUTCH PLATES
1982—F100, F150 Trucks

Engine	Forward Clutch			Reverse Clutch		
	External Spline (Steel)	Internal Spline (Comp.)	Free Pack Clear (Inches)	External Spline (Steel)	Internal Spline (Comp.)	Free Pack Clear (Inches)
3.8L	4	5	0.025-0.050	3	3	0.050-0.071
4.2L	4	5	0.025-0.050	4	4	0.050-0.071

CLUTCH PLATES
1983—F100 Truck

Engine	Forward Clutch			Reverse and High Clutch		
	External Spline (Steel)	Internal Spline (Comp.)	Free Pack Clear (Inches)	External Spline (Steel)	Internal Spline (Comp.)	Free Pack Clear (Inches)
3.8L	4	5	0.025-0.050	3	3	0.025-0.050

CLUTCH PLATES
1983 and Later—Ranger

Engine	Forward Clutch			Reverse Clutch		
	External Spline (Steel)	Internal Spline (Comp.)	Free Pack Clear (Inches)	External Spline (Steel)	Internal Spline (Comp.)	Free Pack Clear (Inches)
2.3L	3	4	0.025-0.050	3	3	0.0250-0.050

VACUUM DIAPHRAGM ASSEMBLY SPECIFICATIONS
1982—F100, F150

Diaphragm Type	Diaphragm Part No.	Identification	Throttle Valve Rod*		
			Part No. (7A380)	Length	Identification
S-SAD	D6AP-7A377-AA	1 Green Stripe	D3AP-JA	1.5925-1.5876	Green Daub
			D3AP-HA	1.6075-1.6025	Blue Daub
			D3AP-KA	1.6225-1.6175	Orange Daub
			D3AP-LA	1.6375-1.6325	Black Daub
			D3AP-MA	1.6585-1.6535	Pink/White Daub

*Selective Fit Rods
S-SAD—Super Single Area Diaphragm

CHECKS AND ADJUSTMENTS
1982—Car Models

Operation	Specification
Transmission End Play	0.008-0.042 inch (Selective Thrust Washers Available)
Torque Converter End Play	New or Rebuilt 0.023 maximum. Used 0.050 maximum.
(Intermediate) Band Adjustment Front	Remove and discard lock nut. Install new nut. Adjust screw to 13.55 N•m (10 lb-ft), then backoff 4¼ turns. Hold screw and tighten lock nut to 54.33 N•m (40 lb-ft).
(Reverse) Band Adjustment Rear	Remove and discard lock nut. Adjust screw to 13.55 N•m (10 lb-ft), then back off 3 turns. Install new lock nut and tighten to 54.33 N•m (40 lb-ft).
Selective Snap Ring Thickness (Fwd. or Rev. Clutch)	0.050-0.054, 0.064-0.068, 0.078-0.082, 0.092-0.096, 0.104-0.108

CHECKS AND ADJUSTMENTS
1983—Car Models

Operation	Specification
Transmission End Play	0.008-0.042 inch (Selective Thrust Washers Available)
Torque Converter End Play	New or Rebuilt 0.023 maximum. Used 0.050 maximum.
(Intermediate) Band Adjustment Front	Remove and discard locknut. Install new nut. Adjust screw to 13.55 N•m (10 lb-ft), then backoff 4¼ turns. Hold screw and tighten locknut to 54.33 N•m (40 lb-ft)
(Reverse) Band Adjustment Rear	Remove and discard locknut. Adjust screw to 13.55 N•m (10 lb-ft), then back off 3 turns. Install new locknut and tighten to 54.33 N•m (40 lb-ft).
Selective Snap Ring Thickness (Fwd. or Rev. Clutch)	0.050-0.054, 0.064-0.068, 0.078-0.082, 0.092-0.096, (0.104-0.108—Fwd Clutch Only).

CHECKS AND ADJUSTMENTS
1982—F100, F150

Operation	Specification
Transmission End Play	0.008-0.042 inch (Selective Thrust Washers Available)
Torque Converter End Play	New or Rebuilt 0.023 maximum. Used 0.050 maximum.
(Intermediate) Band Adjustment Front	Remove and discard lock nut. Install new nut. Adjust screw to 13.55 N•m (10 lb-ft), then backoff 4¼ turns. Hold screw and tighten lock nut to 54.33 N•m (40 lb-ft).
(Reverse) Band Adjustment Rear	Remove and discard lock nut. Adjust screw to 13.55 N•m (10 lb-ft), then back off 3 turns. Install new lock nut and tighten to 54.33 N•m (40 lb-ft).
Selective Snap Ring Thickness (Fwd. or Rev. Clutch)	0.050-0.054, 0.064-0.068, 0.078-0.082, 0.092-0.096, 0.104-0.108

CHECKS AND ADJUSTMENTS
1983—F100

Operation	Specification
Transmission End Play	0.008-0.042 inch (Selective Thrust Washers Available)
Torque Converter End Play	New or Rebuilt 0.023 Maximum. Used 0.050 Maximum.
(Intermediate) Band Adjustment Front	Remove and discard locknut. Install new nut. Adjust screw to 13.55 N•m (10 ft-lbs), then back off 4¼ turns. Hold screw and tighten locknut to 54.33 N•m (40 ft-lbs).
(Reverse) Band Adjustment Rear	Remove and discard locknut. Adjust screw to 13.55 N•m (10 ft-lbs), then back off 3 turns. Install new locknut and tighten to 54.33 N•m (40 ft-lbs).
Selective Snap Ring Thickness (Fwd. or Rev. Clutch)	0.050-0.054, 0.064-0.068, 0.078-0.082, 0.092-0.096, 0.104-0.108

CHECKS AND ADJUSTMENTS
Ranger 1983 and Later

Operation	Specification
Transmission End Play	0.008-0.042 inch (Selective Thrust Washers Available)
Torque Converter End Play	New or Rebuilt 0.023 maximum. Used 0.050 maximum.
(Intermediate) Band Adjustment Front	Remove and discard locknut. Install new nut. Adjust screw to 13.55 N•m (10 ft-lbs), then back off 4¼ turns. Hold screw and tighten locknut to 54.33 N•m (40 ft-lbs).
(Reverse) Band Adjustment Rear	Remove and discard locknut. Adjust screw to 13.55 N•m (10 ft-lbs), then back off 3 turns. Install new locknut and tighten to 54.33 N•m (40 ft-lbs).
Selective Snap Ring Thickness (Fwd. or Rev. Clutch)	0.050-0.054, 0.064-0.068, 0.078-0.082, 0.092-0.096, 0.104-0.108

VACUUM DIAPHRAGM ASSEMBLY SPECIFICATIONS
1982 and Later—Car Models

Diaphragm Type	Diaphragm Part No.	Identification	Throttle Valve Rod* Part No. (7A380)	Length	Identification
S-HAD	D70P-7A377-AA	1 White Stripe	D3AP-JA	1.5925-1.5876	Green Daub
			D3AP-HA	1.6075-1.6025	Blue Daub
SAD	EZDP-7A377-AA	No Identification	D3AP-KA	1.6225-1.6175	Orange Daub
			D3AP-LA	1.6375-1.6325	Black Daub
S-SAD	D6AP-7A377-AA	1 Green Stripe	D3AP-MA	1.6585-1.6535	Pink/White Daub

*Selective fit rods   SAD—Single Area Diaphragm   S-SAD—Super Single Area Diaphragm   S-HAD—Super High Altitude

VACUUM DIAPHRAGM ASSEMBLY SPECIFICATIONS
1983—F100

| Diaphragm Type | Diaphragm Part No. | Identification | Throttle Valve Rod* | | |
			Part No. (7A380)	Length	Identification
S-SAD	D6AP-7A377-AA	1 Green Stripe	D3AP-JA	1.5925-1.5876	Green Daub
			D3AP-HA	1.6075-1.6025	Blue Daub
			D3AP-KA	1.6225-1.6175	Orange Daub
			D3AP-LA	1.6375-1.6325	Black Daub
			D3AP-MA	1.6585-1.6535	Pink/White Daub

*Selective fit rods
S-SAD—Super Single Area Diaphragm

VACUUM DIAPHRAGM ASSEMBLY SPECIFICATIONS
Ranger 1983 and Later

| Diaphragm Type | Diaphragm Part No. | Identification | Throttle Valve Rod* | | |
			Part No. (7A380)	Length	Identification
S-SAD	D6AP-7A377-AA	1 Green Stripe	D3AP-JA	1.5925-1.5876	Green Daub
S-HAD	D70P-7A377-AA	No Color	D3AP-HA	1.6075-1.6025	Blue Daub
			D3AP-KA	1.6225-1.6175	Orange Daub
			D3AP-LA	1.6375-1.6325	Black Daub
			D3AP-MA	1.6585-1.6535	Pink/White Daub

*Selective fit rods
S-SAD—Super Single Area Diaphragm

TORQUE SPECIFICATIONS

Description	N•m	in. lbs.
End Plates To Valve Body	2.82-4.51	25-40
Separator Plate To Timing Valve Body	2.82-4.51	25-40
Lower Body To Upper Body (10-24)	4.51-6.77	40-60
Screen To Timing Valve Body	2.82-4.51	25-40
Governor To Governor Oil Collector Body	9.03-12.55	80-120
Pump Assembly To Case	2.25-3.95	20-38
Main Control To Case	9.03-13.55	80-120
Neutral Switch To Case	6.21-8.47	55-75

TORQUE SPECIFICATIONS

Description	N•m	in. lbs.
Upper Body To Lower Body (Long) (¼-20)	9.03-12.55	80-120
Upper Body To Lower Body (Short) (10-24)	4.51-6.77	40-60
3-2 Timing Valve Body To Upper Body (10-24)	4.51-6.77	40-60
3-2 Timing Valve Body To Lower Body (¼-20)	5.9-8.1	52-72
Detent Spring and Lower Body To Upper Body	4.51-6.77	40-60
Detent Spring and Main Control To Case	9.03-12.55	80-120
3-2 Timing Valve Body To Lower Body (10-24)	4.51-6.77	50-60
Speedometer Clamp Bolt	4-6	36-54

TORQUE SPECIFICATIONS

Description	N•m	ft. lbs.
Overrunning Clutch Race To Case	18-27	13-20
Push Connector To Transmission Case	24-31	18-23
Oil Pan To Case	16-22	12-16
Stator Support To Pump	17-27	12-20
Converter to Flywheel	27-46	20-34
Converter Housing Cover To Converter Housing	17-21	12-16
Converter Housing To Case	38-55	28-40
Engine Rear Cover Plate To Transmission	17-21	12-16
Rear Servo Cover To Case	17-27	12-20
Intermediate Servo Cover To Case	22-30	16-22
Oil Distributor Sleeve To Case	16-27	12-20

TORQUE SPECIFICATIONS

Description	N•m	ft. lbs.
Extension Housing To Case	38-54	28-40
Pump and Converter Housing To Case	38-51	28-38
Engine To Transmission (3.8L)	38-51	28-38
Transmission To Engine (3.3L, 4.2L)	55-67	40-50
Outer Throttle Lever To Shaft	17-21	12-16
Band Adjusting Screws To Case	13.5	10
Inner Manual Lever To Shaft	41-54	30-40
Pump Pressure Plug To Case	9-16	6-12
Intermediate Band and Reverse Band Adjusting Screw Locknut	47-61	35-45
Drain Plug To Converter Cover	20-24	15-18

SPECIAL TOOLS

SPECIAL SERVICE TOOLS

Description	Tool Number	Description	Tool Number
Impact Slide Hammer	T50T-100-A	Extension Housing Seal Installer	T61L-7657-A
Puller Attachment	T58L-101-A	Extension Housing Bushing Installer	T77L-7697-B
Bench Mounted Holding Fixture	T57L-500-B	Extension Housing Bushing Remover	T77L-7697-A
Air Nozzle Assembly	Tool-7000-DE	Lip Seal Protector—Reverse Clutch	T82L-77404-A
Shift Linkage Insulator Tool	T67P-7341-A	Converter Clutch Holding Tool	T77L-7902-A
Output Shaft Retainer Pliers	T73P-77060-A	Converter Clutch Torquing Tool	T76L-7902-C
Clutch Spring Compressor	T65L-77515-A	End Play Checking Tool	T80L-7920-A
Pressure Gauge 0-400 P.S.I.	T57L-77820-A	Band Adjustment Torque Wrench Set	T71P-77370-A
Pump Seal Remover	Tool-1175AC	Shift Lever Seal Installer	Tool-77288
Pump Seal Installer	T63L-77837-A	Case Bolt Socket 5/16 Hex	T65P-7B-456-B
Extension Housing Seal Remover	T74P-77248-A	Transmission Bushing Set	T66L-7003-B

VALVE BODY SPRING TOOL FABRICATION

When assembling a valve body, the tool shown below will ease installation of those springs retained by a flat, slotted plate. The tool is not available from a manufacturer and must, therefore, be fabricated in the shop. The tool is cut from a 3/8-inch aluminum rod to the dimensions shown on the illustration. To simplify cutting and measuring, the illustration is actual size and can be used to check the accuracy of the fabricated tool.

To use the tool, position the spring in the valve body bore and compress it with the tool. While holding the spring compressed install the retainer plate over the end of the tool. The shape of the tool allows the plate slot to fit over the end of the tool while it is holding the spring compressed against the valve.

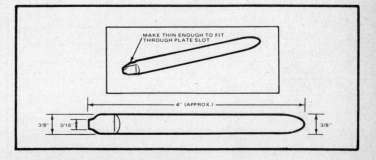

MAKE THIN ENOUGH TO FIT THROUGH PLATE SLOT

4" (APPROX.)

3/8" 3/16" 3/8"

INDEX

FORD MOTOR COMPANY
ATX
Automatic Transaxle

APPLICATIONS

1981-83
Escort/Lynx, EXP/LN-7

1984
Tempo/Topaz, Escort/Lynx, EXP

GENERAL DESCRIPTION

The ATX automatic transaxle is a front wheel drive unit, housing both an automatic transmission and a differential in a single housing, bolted to the engine and mounted transversely in the vehicle. The ATX unit uses three friction clutch units, one band and a single one-way clutch. A compound planetary gear set is used to transmit the engine torque through the unit as the varied internal units are applied and released, providing three forward and one reverse gear ratios. Unique features of the transaxle are:

1. The valve body is mounted on top of the transaxle case.
2. The oil pump is mounted opposite the torque converter.
3. The parking gear is installed on the final drive unit.
4. The torque converter contains a planetary gear set, which is used to split the input power between mechanical and hydraulic drive, in most gears.
5. Two input shafts are used from the converter to the gear train.

235

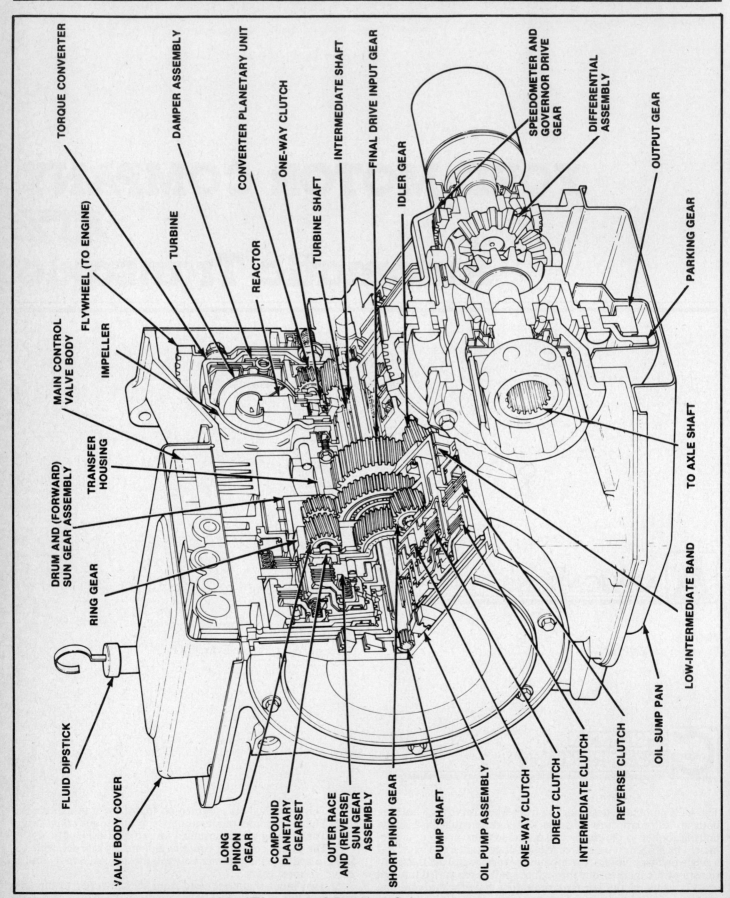

Sectional view of internal components of the ATX transaxle (© Ford Motor Co.)

Labels (clockwise/around diagram):

TORQUE CONVERTER · DAMPER ASSEMBLY · CONVERTER PLANETARY UNIT · ONE-WAY CLUTCH · INTERMEDIATE SHAFT · FINAL DRIVE INPUT GEAR · IDLER GEAR · SPEEDOMETER AND GOVERNOR DRIVE GEAR · DIFFERENTIAL ASSEMBLY · OUTPUT GEAR · PARKING GEAR · TURBINE · REACTOR · TURBINE SHAFT

FLYWHEEL (TO ENGINE) · MAIN CONTROL VALVE BODY · IMPELLER · DRUM AND (FORWARD) SUN GEAR ASSEMBLY · TRANSFER HOUSING · RING GEAR

TO AXLE SHAFT · LOW-INTERMEDIATE BAND · OIL SUMP PAN · REVERSE CLUTCH · INTERMEDIATE CLUTCH · DIRECT CLUTCH · ONE-WAY CLUTCH · OIL PUMP ASSEMBLY · PUMP SHAFT · SHORT PINION GEAR · OUTER RACE AND (REVERSE) SUN GEAR ASSEMBLY · COMPOUND PLANETARY GEARSET · LONG PINION GEAR

VALVE BODY COVER · FLUID DIPSTICK

TRANSAXLE AND CONVERTER IDENTIFICATION

Transaxle

The ATX automatic transaxle is identified by the letter "B" stamped on the vehicle certification label, mounted on the left driver's door body pillar post. The identification tag is located on one of the valve body pan retaining screws, above the oil pump location. The identification tag indicates the model code, the part number prefix and suffix, build code and transaxle serial number.

Converter

The ATX torque converter is identified by either a reference or part number stamped on the converter body and is matched to a specific engine. The torque converter is a welded unit and is not repairable. If internal problems exists, the torque converter must be replaced.

Transmission Fasteners

Metric bolts and nuts are used in the construction of the transaxle, along with the familiar inch system fasteners. The dimensions of both systems are very close and for this reason, replacement fasteners must have the same measurement and strength as those removed. Do not attempt to interchange metric fasteners for inch system fasteners. Mismatched or incorrect fasteners can result in damage to the transaxle unit through malfunctions, breakage or personal injury. Care should be exercised to replace the fasteners in the same locations as removed.

CAPACITIES

Year	Models	Quart	Liter
1981-82	All	10	9.46
1983-84	All	8.3	7.9

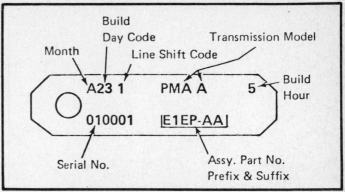

Typical ATX transaxle identification tag (© Ford Motor Co.)

Fluid Type Specifications

Only Motorcraft Dexron® II, Series D or CJ fluids, meeting Ford Motor Company's specifications ESP-M2C138-CJ, should be used in the ATX transaxle. Failure to use the proper fluid could result in internal transaxle damage.

Checking the ATX Transaxle Fluid Level

The ATX transaxle is designed to operate with the fluid level between the ADD and FULL mark on the dipstick, with the transaxle unit at normal operating temperature of 155 to 170 degrees Fahrenheit. If the fluid level is at or near the bottom indicator on the dip stick, either cold or hot, do not drive the vehicle until fluid has been added.

TRANSAXLE AT ROOM TEMPERATURE

70° to 95° F., Dipstick cool to the touch
1. With the vehicle on a level surface, engine idling, wheels blocked, foot brakes applied, move the selector lever through the gear positions to engage each gear and to fill the oil passages with fluid.

(ENGLISH) INCH SYSTEM Bolt, 1/2-13x1	METRIC SYSTEM Bolt M12-1.75x25
G- Grade Marking (bolt strength) L- Length, (inches)** T- Thread Pitch (thread/inch) D- Nominal Diameter (inches)	P- Property Class* (bolt strength) L- Length (millimeters)** T- Thread Pitch (thread width crest to crest mm) D- Nominal Diameter (millimeters)

*The property class is an Arabic numeral distinguishable from the slash SAE English grade system.

**The length of all bolts is measured from the underside of the head to the end.

Examples of differences between inch and metric bolts (© Ford Motor Co.)

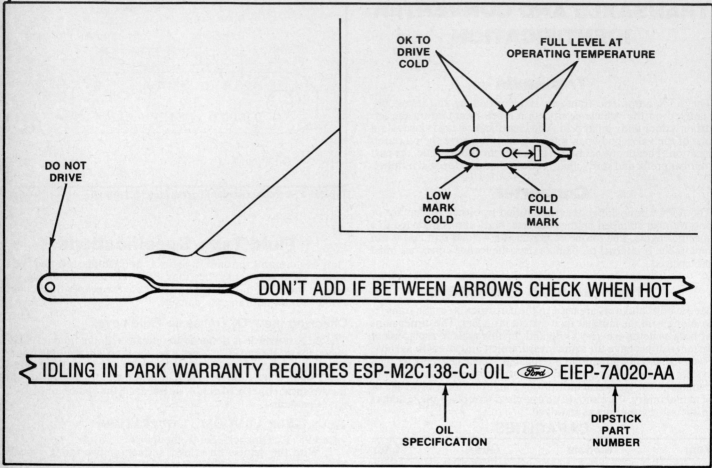

Fluid dipstick markings (© Ford Motor Co.)

2. Place the selector lever in the PARK position and apply the parking brakes, allowing the engine to idle.

3. Clean the dipstick area of dirt and remove the dipstick from the filler tube. Wipe the dipstick clean and re-insert it back into the filler tube and seat it firmly.

4. Remove the dipstick from the filler tube again and check the fluid level as indicated on the dipstick. The level should be between the cold low mark and the cold full mark on the dipstick indicator.

5. If necessary, add enough fluid to bring the level to its cold full mark. Re-install the dipstick and seat it firmly in the filler tube.

6. When the transaxle reaches normal operating temperature of 155° to 170° F., re-check the fluid level and correct as required to bring the fluid to its hot level mark.

TRANSAXLE AT NORMAL OPERATING TEMPERATURE

155° to 170° F., Dipstick Hot to the Touch

1. With the vehicle on a level surface, engine idling, wheels blocked, foot brake applied, move the selector lever through the gear positions to engage each gear and to fill the passageways with fluid.

2. Place the selector lever in the PARK position and apply the parking brake, allowing the engine to idle.

3. Clean the dipstick area of dirt and remove the dipstick from the filler tube. Wipe the dipstick clean, re-insert the dipstick into the filler tube and seat firmly.

4. Again remove the dipstick from the filler tube and check the fluid level as indicated on the dipstick. The level should be between the ADD and FULL marks. If necessary, add enough fluid to bring the fluid level to the full mark.

5. When the fluid level is correct, fully seat the dipstick in the filler tube.

NOTE: When the automatic transaxle fluid has become hotter than 155° to 170° F., the fluid should be allowed to cool before checking the level. Such causes of overheating are extended periods of high speed driving, trailer towing or stop and go traffic during periods of hot weather.

M MODIFICATIONS

FORD ATX TRANSAXLE MODIFICATIONS

Main Control Baffle Plate

1981 Escort/Lynx

Some ATX transaxles will be built with an oil baffle plate attached to the valve body. This baffle prevents fluid from spilling out of the breather vent in the oil pan. When servicing the transaxles equipped with this baffle plate, be sure to position the plate properly and do not discard.

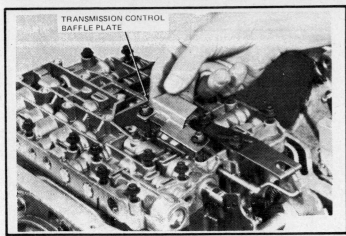

Transaxle control baffle plate location on valve body
(© Ford Motor Co.)

Valve Body To Case Attaching Bolt Torque Pattern

1981 Escort/Lynx

Proper torquing of the valve body attaching bolts will minimize the possibility of cross fluid leakage, sticking valves and erratic shifts. The bolt torque is 72-96 *inch pounds* (8-11 N•m).

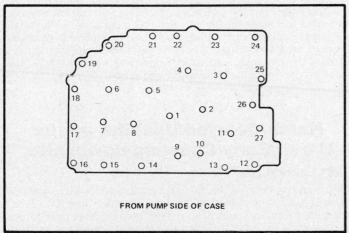

Valve body torque sequence (© Ford Motor Co.)

Cold Weather Cold Start/Shift

1981 Escort/Lynx

To improve cold starting and transaxle shifts on the ATX transaxle vehicles in sub-freezing weather, a new multi-viscosity automatic transaxle fluid should be used. The regular factory lubricant should be drained and the unit refilled with Motorcraft Ford Type MV automatic transaxle fluid, XT-3-MV, or equivalent, which meets Ford Specification number ESP-M2C164-A.

Drain and refill the transaxle as outlined in this transaxle section. In addition, have the vehicle in such a position as to be able to disconnect the cooler line return fitting, located at the pump end of the transaxle. With a routing hose into a container, start the engine and run for approximately 20-25 seconds, draining about three quarts of fluid from the transaxle, flushing the cooler and lines. Stop the engine and re-connect the fluid line and torque to 18-23 ft. lbs. Lower the vehicle and refill and transaxle with the multi-viscosity fluid to its correct level.

Shift Concerns

1981 Escort/Lynx

If concerns of shifting on new Escorts and Lynxs exists, this could be concerned to idle speeds and T.V. linkage. Verify and reset, if necessary, the idle speeds and T.V. linkage prior to performing any internal transaxle servicing.

Proper Seating of the Torque Converter

1981 Escort/Lynx

If the ATX torque converter is not properly engaged to the oil pump drive shaft, damage may occur to the oil pump. To determine whether the torque converter is fully seated, measure the distance between the converter stud face and the converter housing face. The dimension should read 1.205 to 1.126 inches (30.6 to 28.6 mm).

Powertrain Related Noise Transmitted Through Speedometer Cable and Engine Mounts

1981 Escort/Lynx

A transaxle gear noise, described as a buzzing, ticking or gear whine, can be transmitted into the passenger compartment via the speedometer cable conduit and/or by the engine mounts that can be grounded or bound up.

Prior to performing any service or repairs on the transaxle for gear noise, it must be determined that the noise is originating from the transaxle. To determine if the noise is coming from the transaxle, perform the following test;

1. Stop the vehicle.
2. Place the gear selector in neutral.
3. Increase the engine idle speed.
4. If the noise remains, the transaxle is not at fault. If the noise level changes or goes away, proceed with the following checks.

ENGINE MOUNTS

1. Verify the engine mounts are neutralized by loosening the bottom two retaining nuts on the left front engine mount. Loosen the bottom retaining nut on the left rear engine mount.
2. Position the engine mounts in the mounting brackets.
3. Maintain the correct engine mount alignment in the brackets with a prybar when tightening all the bottom retaining nuts to 55 ft. lbs.

SPEEDOMETER CABLE CONDUIT

1. Disconnect the speedometer cable at the transaxle and road test the vehicle. If the noise stops, the noise is being transmitted from the transaxle to the passenger compartment through the speedometer cable.
2. If noise is being transmitted through the speedometer cable, the installation of a 14 inch piece of ⅜ inch diameter fuel hose over the speedometer cable will reduce the noise.
3. Spirally cut the hose and position it between the speedometer head and the dash panel grommet. Position the hose so that it overlaps the metal portion of the disconnect ferrule assembly by ¼ inch. The hose can be installed from the interior of the vehicle without disconnecting either end of the speedometer cable.

Transfer Gear Housing Removal

1981 Escort/Lynx

Idler gear damage can be done during the transfer gear housing removal, if the technician prys down upon the idler gear while removing the housing. To remove the transfer gear housing correctly, the technician must pry upward, never downward.

Throttle Valve (T.V.) Linkage Adjustment Procedure

1981 Escort/Lynx and 1982 EXP/LN7

When ever curb idle speeds are adjusted to the specifications indicated on the Emission Control Decal and the engine RPM increase is more than 100 rpm, or for any decrease in rpm, the transaxle throttle valve linkage must be checked and readjusted as required. The adjustments must be made at the T.V. control rod assembly sliding trunnion block.

The following procedure must be followed:

1. After the curb idle set to specification, turn the engine off and insure that the carburetor throttle lever is against the hot engine curb idle stop (the choke must be OFF).

NOTE: The linkage cannot be properly set if the choke is allowed to cool and the throttle lever allowed to be on the choke fast idle cam.

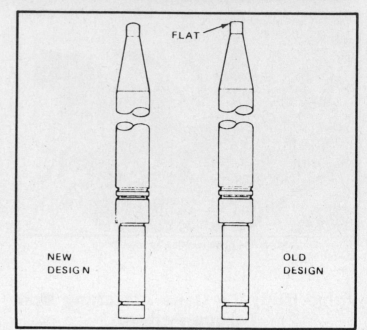

Difference in servo rod ends between old and new designs (© Ford Motor Co.)

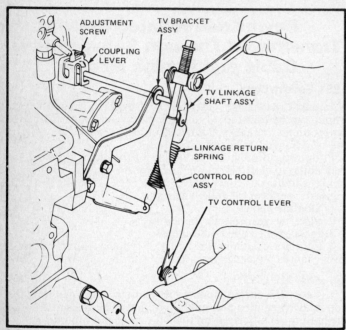

Adjustment procedure for T.V. linkage control (© Ford Motor Co.)

2. Set the coupling lever adjustment screw at its approximate midrange. Insure that the TV linkage shaft assembly is fully seated upward into the coupling lever.

3. Loosen the bolt on the sliding trunnion block on the TV control rod assembly one turn minimum.

4. Remove any corrosion from the control rod and free-up the trunnion block so that it slides freely on the control rod.

5. Rotate the transaxle TV control lever up using one finger and a light force, 2.2 Kg (approximately 5 pounds), to insure that the TV control lever is against its internal idle stop. Without relaxing the force on the TV control lever, tighten the bolt on the trunnion block to specification.

6. Verify that the carburetor throttle lever is still against the hot engine curb idle stop. If not, repeat Steps 1 through 6.

Revised Low-Intermediate Servo Rod and Band

1981 Escort/Lynx

The low-intermediate servo rod and band and seat has been changed to increase the ease of assembly. The new servo rod is round tipped while the old servo rod was flat tipped. The band

seat has been changed to accept the new rounded servo rod. The old and new servo rods are not interchangeable and car must be exercised to be sure the replacement rod is the same as the original used. Replacement of the low-intermediate band on transaxles built prior to February 17, 1981, will necessitate the replacement of the new design servo rod. The new servo rods will use the same grooved identification as the old design.

Harsh/Delayed Upshifts and/or Harsh/Early Coasting downshifts

1981 Escort/Lynx

Harsh and/or delayed upshifts and harsh and/or early coasting downshifts maybe caused by the outer throttle valve lever binding with the manual control lever shaft because of an over-torque condition on the outer throttle valve lever attaching nut and lock washer. The torque specifications should be revised from 12-15 *foot* pounds to 88-115 *inch* pounds.

To check for possible binding, disconnect the outer throttle valve lever from the throttle control rod and check the throttle valve lever for a binding or hanging up condition. Also, check for clearance between the outer throttle valve lever and the manual control lever (0.010-0.015 inches minimum). If the throttle valve lever is binding or there is insufficient end clearance between the levers, it will be necessary to remove and discard the old lever. Install a new outer throttle lever (E1FZ-7A394-A) on the inner throttle lever shat and torque the attaching nut and lock washer to 88-115 *inch* pounds.

If the lever is not binding, the following other components should be checked for proper operation:

1. Check the throttle linkage system for freedom of movement (i.e., throttle control rod and carburetor throttle shaft).

2. Check the throttle kicker for proper operation (A/C and/or Power Steering equipped vehicles—RPM increases at idle when A/C is turned on or by turning steering wheel either direction).

3. Check engine idle RPM.

4. Check the throttle linkage adjustment.

Powertrain Noise Transmitted Through The Transaxle Shift Cable

1981 Escort/Lynx and 1982 EXP/LN7

Should a powertrain noise remain after insulating the speedometer cable and neutralizing the engine mounts, proceed to the transaxle shift cable stand-off (control) bracket mounting attachment bolts.

1. Remove the two attachment bolts for the stand-off (control) bracket and examine the insulators for correct positioning in the bracket or evidence of grounding or overtorquing. Replace if damaged. If the insulators are to be reused or new ones installed, torque the attaching bolts to 15-25 ft. lbs.

—————————— CAUTION ——————————

Do not over-torque, as the overtorquing will eliminate the effectiveness of the insulators.

Governor Gear Damage

1981 Escort/Lynx

ATX governor driven gear will exhibit two major patterns of identified damage and to eliminate the possibility of repeat service, perform one of the following two procedures:

1. When all teeth on the governor driven gear are in an hour glass or apple core shape, it may have been caused by a nick and/or burr on the speedometer drive gear located on the differential.

   a. Remove the lower oil pan and inspect the speedometer drive gear for nicks and/or burrs by running a finger along each gear tooth. Since the drive gear is not a hardened gear, most nicks and/or burrs can be serviced b dressing with a file.

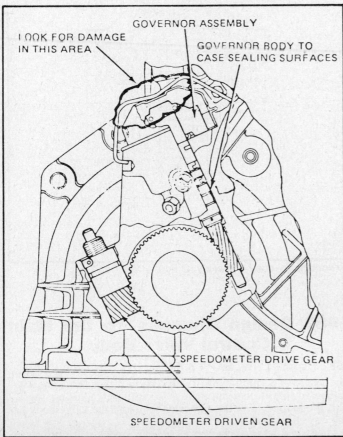

Governor gear damage appraisal (© Ford Motor Co.)

NOTE: Make sure that all fillings are cleaned from the transaxle and differential before assembling the lower oil pan to the case.

   b. If the damaged speedometer drive gear can be serviced, then replace the governor assembly. If the damaged speedometer drive gear cannot be serviced, then replace both the governor assembly and the speedometer drive gear.

   c. Because the speedometer drive gear is not a hardened gear, it can be easily damaged if struck or dropped. Care must be taken to not damage the drive gear during disassembly or assembly of the ATX transaxle.

   d. Since the drive gear turns both the governor assembly and the speedometer driven gear assembly, the speedometer driven gear assembly should be inspected for damage and replaced if necessary.

2. When only one or two teeth on the governor are affected, it is the result of the governor assembly being momentarily stopped while the speedometer drive gear continues to turn. When this occurs, the technician must determine the reason for the damage.

   a. Check for excessive metal and/or fiber debris in the transaxle fluid which could indicate bearing or clutch damage. Check the fluid level. Inspect the governor body to case sealing surfaces for gouging or distortions.

   b. Check to see if the governor screen was improperly installed or omitted. The governor screen prevents miscellaneous debris from entering the governor hydraulic circuit.

   c. Check the governor bore in the case for distortion in the areas of the no. 3 transaxle to engine mounting bolt hole. Some cases were found to have a shallow thread depth in the no. 3 bolt hole. When the attaching bolt is installed into a shallow hole, the bolt cuts into the case and causes the distortion in the case governor bore. When this happens, the case must be replaced, as well as the governor.

   d. Check for damage to the governor cover and/or governor top, i.e., flyweight cage. Replace if necessary.

Service Oil Pump Insert

1981 Escort/Lynx and 1982 EXP/LN7

In the vent of ATX oil pump insert damage, the pump insert is serviced separately from the complete oil pump assembly (part number E1FZ-7F402-A).

Water In Transaxle Fluid

1981 Escort/Lynx and 1982 EXP/LN7

Reports of water being found in the transaxle fluid of the ATX has been recorded. Under normal operating conditions, water entry is restricted by the valve located on the top of the valve body cover. However, if water is forcefully directed at the valve, the resulting splash from the cover may allow be allowed to enter the valve. When water is being used to clean or cool the engine, care must be taken to prevent the vent from becoming sprayed with water.

—————————— CAUTION ——————————

If water is found in the transaxle fluid, a total drain, flush and refill of the transaxle and converter assembly is required.

Engine Speed-up During The 2-3 Upshift

1981 Escort/Lynx and 1982 EXP/LN7

A complaint of engine speed-up during the 2-3 upshift can be serviced as follows:

1. Remove the main control valve assembly from the transaxle in the prescribed manner.
2. Remove the separator plate from the main control valve body.

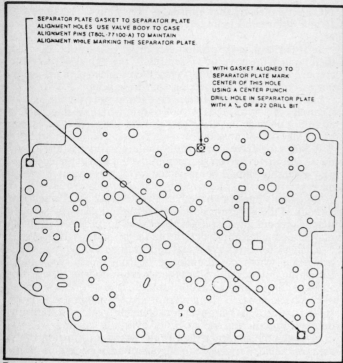

Reworking separator plate (© Ford Motor Co.)

6. Remove the production 2-1 scheduling valve spring and install the service replacement 2-1 scheduling valve spring (color-Purple).

7. Remove the production 3-2 shift control valve spring and install the service replacement 3-2 shift control valve spring (Size and color-Large Diameter, Purple).

8. Remove the production 2-3 shift T.V. modulator valve spring and install the service replacement 2-3 shift T.V. modulator valve spring (color-White).

9. Remove the production 1-2 shift valve accumulator valve spring and install the service replacement 1-2 shift accumulator valve spring (color-Dark Green).

10. Install the six check balls and relief valve in the main control valve body.

11. Assemble the separator plate and gasket to the main control valve body. Torque the bolts to 90 in. lbs.

12. Assemble the valve body to the transaxle in the prescribed manner.

GOVERNOR ASSEMBLY

1. Remove the governor assembly from the transaxle.

2. Remove and discard the two governor flyweight springs.

3. Install the service replacement governor spring (color-Brown) into either one of the governor spring positions. The other governor spring is not replaced.

4. Re-install the modified governor assembly into the transaxle assembly.

5. An authorized modification decal should be obtained and installed next to the Vehicle Emission Control Label.

3. Remove and discard the number two check ball.

4. Some main control valve body assemblies were manufactured without the number two check ball. In these instances, the separator plate must be reworked as shown in the accompanying illustration.

5. Assemble the reworked separator plate and new gasket to the main control valve body.

6. Install the main control valve body assemby in the transaxle and complete the assembly of the components.

Delay 1-2 upshift and/or 3-2 Coasting Downshift shudder (49 States Only)

1981 Escort/Lynx and 1982 EXP/LN7 (Transaxle Models PMA-A, A1, A2, K, and K1)

To correct delayed 1-2 upshifts and/or 3-2 coasting downshift shudder, a shift modification spring kit, part number E2FZ-7F415-A, is available to re-work the main control valve body assembly and the governor.

─────── **CAUTION** ───────

Before installing the shift modification spring kit, be sure the shifting problem is not being caused by binding/damaged/mis-adjusted transaxle throttle linkage and/or improper engine idle settings.

VALVE BODY RE-WORK

1. Remove the valve body from the transaxle.

2. Remove the separator plate and gasket from the main control valve body.

3. Note the position of the six check balls and the relief valve, then remove and set aside.

4. Remove the production 2-3 shift valve spring and install the service replacement spring (color-Black).

5. Remove the production 1-2 shift valve spring and the 1-2 shift T.V. modulator valve spring and install the service replacement 1-2 shift T.V. modulator valve spring (color-White). Discard the 1-2 shift valve spring.

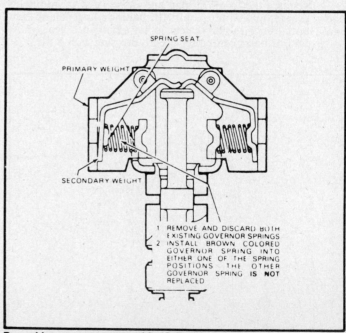

Reworking governor assembly (© Ford Motor Co.)

1982 Design Changes To the Main Control Valve Body

1982 Escort/Lynx, EXP/LN7

The 1982 ATX main control valve body differs from the 1981 models in that it does not have a 1-2 shift valve spring, the 1-2 T.V. modulator valve has a shorter stem and the valve body has one less check ball.

The manufacturing changes have been mistaken for improperly built main control valve body assemblies.

New Design ATX Flywheel

1982 EXP/LN7 Equipped w/1.6L H.O. Engines

The new designed flywheel can be identified by the following features:

    1. Reduced converter to flywheel attaching nut access hole diameters.

    2. Stamped "H.O." on the engine side of the flywheel and can be viewed when the lower engine dust cover is removed.

    3. Four daubs of green paint on the transaxle side of the flywheel between the spokes.

    4. Part number is E2FZ-6375-A (1.6L H.O. only)

——————— CAUTION ———————

The 1.6L H.O. engine cannot use the E1FZ-6375-C flywheel which is used on the standard 1.6L engines.

The new flywheel requires a 15mm-6 point-⅜ drive-thin walled socket with an O.D. of 20.55mm or less (Snap-on FSM 151 or equivalent). In some instances the flywheel-to-converter attaching nut access hole may be too small for the thin walled socket. If this occurs, find a socket with a smaller O.D., (20.5mm or less) or grind off some material on this present socket. A 15mm socket with an O.D. of 20.5mm will fit all cases. However, a new flywheel to converter fastener with a 13mm hex drive will be introduced into all ATX vehicle production and service in March 1982, that will permit the use of a standard wall socket-13mm 6 point.

Governor Drive Gear Service

1981 Escort/Lynx and 1982 EXP/LN7

A governor drive gear is now serviced separately, rather than the complete governor assembly replacement when the drive gear teeth have become damaged. The removal and installation procedures are outlined in the disassemby and assembly section.

New Design Plastic Speedometer Drive Gear

1981 Escort/Lynx and 1982 EXP/LN7

A new design plastic speedometer drive gear has replaced the present design steel gear for both production and service use.

——————— CAUTION ———————

The steel speedometer gear must not be used in an ATX transaxle that originally was manufactured with a plastic gear. Improper use of the steel speedometer gear may result in damage to the differential housing.

Misdiagnosis of Differential Seal Leakage

1981 Escort/Lynx and 1982 EXP/LN7

Field reports have indicated that fluid leaks from the transaxle input shaft seal, valve body cover gasket, engine main seal or oil pan gasket, will collect and give the appearance of being a differential seal leakage. In the event a transaxle exhibits a lubricant leak, clean off all traces of the fluid and allow the vehicle to stand, observing the location of the seepage. If no signs of a leak appear, run the engine in neutral and recheck the area again. if no leak occurs, drive the vehicle rechecking the area again. If seepage originates near the bottom of the bell housing, then the differential seals are not the cause of the leak.

If servicing the transaxle requires halfshaft removal, the halfshafts should be removed carefully and with the proper tools so that the differential seals are not damaged. The differential seals will then not need to be replaced when the transaxle is reinstalled.

Torque Converter Cleaning Procedure
All Converter Assemblies Without Drain Plugs

1981 Escort/Lynx and 1982 EXP/LN7

This article releases a revised service procedure for torque converter cleaning to be used in addition to the Rotunda Model No. 60081-A torque converter cleaner for all torque converter assemblies without a drain plug.

Elimination of the converter drain plug requires a revised cleaning procedure. The lack of this plug increases the amount of residual flushing solvent retained in the converter after cleaning. The internal design of the converter does not allow for the drilling of a service drain hole. The following procedure is to be used after removal of the torque converter from the cleaning equipment.

    1. Thoroughly drain remaining solvent through hub.

    2. Add one quart of clean transmission fluid to the converter and hand agitate.

    3. **THOROUGHLY** drain solution through converter hub.

Breakage of Gear Shift Lever

1981 Escort/Lynx and 1982 EXP/LN7

When a gear shift lever is replaced due to breakage failure, the shift cable should also be replaced. A new shift cable assembly has been released for production and service applications. The revised shift cable assembly can be identified by a white tie tag affixed to the cable housing assembly.

No 1-2 Upshift

1981-83 Escort/Lynx and 1981-83 EXP/LN7

Some vehicles may exhibit a no 1-2 upshift condition during acceleration. The 1-2 upshift can only be obtained by the release of the accelerator. This condition is also accompanied with an engine overrun (neutral feeling) during the partial throttle backout at speeds near 30 mph. The cause of this condition may be a stuck 1-2 T.V. modulator valve. Since the governor may cause a similar condition, it is important to verify the neutral interval condition during the release of the throttle at the 30 mph speed.

The stuck 1-2 T.V. modulator valve can only be verified by the valve body assembly removal. With the separator plate and gasket removed, check and verify the 1-2 T.V. modulator valve is either stuck or free. If the condition exists, clean up the valve body bore and install one of the following kits, depending upon the vehicle model year and valve body prefix. The kit contains one (1) 1-2 shift valve and one (1) 1-2 T.V. modulator valve. The applications for each kit are as follows:

1981-82 MODELS YEARS

Part Number E2FZ-7F417-A for models PMA-k, R
                        PMB-A with E2EP, E2GP

Part Number E3FZ-7F417-A for models PMA-K,R,Y
                        PMB-A1 with E3EP

A brinelling effect or bore deformation will be apparent on the bore surface where the 1-2 shift valve stops. It is this brinelling or deformation condition that causes the 1-2 T.V. modulator valve to stick at its most outward position.

Servicing Bearing Assembly For Transfer Housing

1981-83 Escort/Lynx and 1981-83 EXP/LN7

A revised service procedure and parts packaging method for the case and transfer housing assembly. The transfer housing bearing may be damaged when removed from the case and transfer housing assembly during the service. To avoid this condition in the future, the bearing will be included with the case and transfer housing assembly.

NOTE: The case and transfer housing are lined bored and matched during assembly. Therefore, neither are interchangeable with other cases or transfer housing.

Final Gear Set Individual Component Release

1981-83 Escort/Lynx and 1981-83 EXP/LN7

The final drive matched gear set has been revised to release the gears individually. The input gear, idler gear and bearing assembly, and the output gear may be serviced separately. Each gear as released, will service all current and past model applications. However, the final drive input gear will incorporate the use of a spacer for all 1.6L, 1.6L H.O. and 1.6L EFI units that contain the 25/32 inch long input gear bearing as opposed to the currently released 27/32 inch long bearing. It will be necessary to measure the bearing lengths to determine if the spacer is required for models built prior to March 31, 1983.

To install the spacer, turn the case 90° so the pump side is facing up and follow this procedure:
1. Install the thrust (needle) bearing number one (1) on the reactor support.
2. Install the cage needle bearing on the reactor support.
3. Install spacer on the reactor support.
4. Install the input gear over the spacer and cage bearing.

NOTE: For the 1983½ 2.3L applications, the spacer is not required.

Revised Procedure For Transaxle Halfshaft Removal

1981-83 Escort/Lynx and 1981-83 EXP/LN7

If extreme resistance is encountered using the current prybar method of removal of the halfshafts from the differential, use the following procedure to avoid damage or broken ATX transaxle cases and/or bent oil pans, resulting in fluid leaks.

In addition to the prescribed procedures for halfshaft removal, the following additions to the procedure are listed:
1. With the vehicle on a lift, remove the transaxle oil pan and discard the old gasket.
2. Insert a large bladed prybar between the differential pinion shaft and the inboard C.V. joint stub shaft.
3. Give a sharp tap to the handle of the prybar to dislodge the circlip from the sidegear, thus freeing the halfshaft from the differential.

Prior to the installation of the halfshaft into the differential, install a new circlip on the inboard stub shaft. In addition, a new transaxle oil pan gasket and transaxle fluid must be installed.

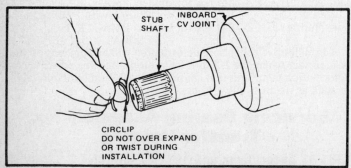

Installation of new circlip on stub axle shaft (© Ford Motor Co.)

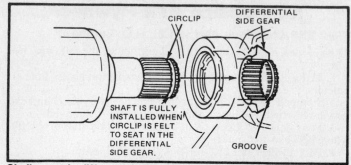

Circlip seat in differential gear groove (© Ford Motor Co.)

Torque the oil pan bolts to 15-19 ft. lbs. and fill the transaxle to its specified level.

NOTE: Use the dipstick to insure proper transaxle fluid level to avoid over or under filling of the transaxle.

Cooler Line Disconnect Tool Usage Push Connect Fittings— Transaxle End Only

To service (transaxle cooler lines, a Tool, Ford Number T82L-9500-AH or equivalent, is required. The illustration shows the tool end and its proper orientation for disassembly of tube from fitting. The purpose of the tool is to spread the "duck bill" retainer to disengage the tube bead. The following steps are necessary for use of the tool:

To facilitate use of the tool, clean the road dirt from the fitting before inserting the tool into the fitting. Also, it is important to avoid any contamination of the fitting and transaxle, dirt in the fitting could cause an O-ring leak.
1. Slide the tool over the tube.
2. Align the opening of the tool with one of the two tabs on the fitting "duck bill" retainer.
3. Firmly insert tool into fitting until it seats against the tube bead (a definite click should be heard).
4. With a thumb held against the tool, firmly pull back on the tube until it disengages from the fitting.

— **CAUTION** —

Do not attempt to separate the cooler line from the fitting by prying with another tool. This will break the plastic insert in fitting and bend the cooler lines at the junction to the fitting.

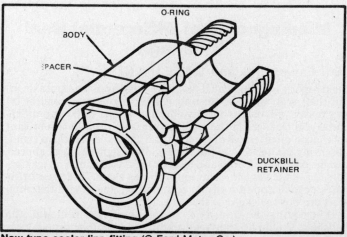

New type cooler line fitting (© Ford Motor Co.)

Before assembly of the lines in the fitting, visually inspect the plastic retainer in the fitting for a broken tab. If a tab is broken, the fitting must be replaced. Also visually inspect the cooler lines to make sure they are not bent at the junction of the fitting.

Tube assembly is accomplished by inserting the tube into the fitting until the retainer engages the tube head (a definite click should be heard). Pull back on the tube to ensure full engagement.

TROUBLE DIAGNOSIS

A logical and orderly diagnosis outline and charts are provided with clutch and band applications, shift speed and governor pressures, main control pressures and oil flow circuits to assist the repairman in diagnosing the problems, causes and the extent of repairs needed to bring the automatic transaxle back to its acceptable level of operation.

Preliminary checks and adjustments should be made to the manual valve linkage, accelerator and downshift linkages.

Transaxle oil level should be checked, both visually and by smell, to determine whether the fluid level is correct and to observe any foreign material in the fluid, if present. Smelling the fluid will indicate if any of the bands or clutches have been burned through excessive slippage or overheating of the trans.

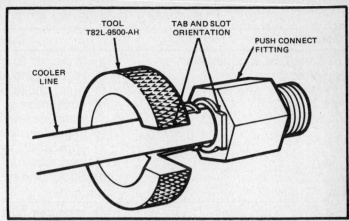

Cooler line disconnect tool usage (© Ford Motor Co.)

It is most important to locate the defect and its cause, and to properly repair them to avoid having the same problem reoccur.

In order to more fully understand the ATX automatic transaxle and to diagnose possible defects more easily, the clutch and band application chart and a general description of the hydraulic control system is given.

CLUTCH AND BAND APPLICATION CHART
ATX Automatic Transaxle

Range and Gear		Band	Direct Clutch	Intermediate Clutch	Reverse Clutch	One-Way Clutch
Park		—	—	—	—	Applied
Reverse		—	Applied	—	Applied	Applied
Neutral		—	—	—	—	Applied
D	1st	Applied	—	—	—	Applied
	2nd	Applied	—	Applied	—	—
	3rd	—	Applied	Applied	—	—
2	1st	Applied	—	—	—	Applied
	2nd	Applied	—	Applied	—	—
1	1st	Applied	Applied	—	—	Applied

CHILTON'S THREE "C's" TRANSAXLE DIAGNOSIS CHARTS

Condition	Cause	Correction
Slow initial engagement	a) Improper fluid level b) Damaged or improperly adjusted manual linkage c) Incorrect T.V. linkage adjustment d) Contaminated fluid e) Improper clutch and band application, or oil control pressure f) Dirty valve body	a) Add fluid as required b&c) Service or adjust linkage d) Change fluid and filter e) Perform control pressure test f) Clean, repair, or replace valve body

CHILTON'S THREE "C's" TRANSAXLE DIAGNOSIS CHARTS

Condition	Cause	Correction
Rough initial engagement in either forward or reverse	a) Improper fluid level b) High engine idle c) Auto. choke on (warm temp) d) Looseness in halfshafts, CV joints, or engine mounts e) Improper clutch or band application, or oil control pressure f) Incorrect T.V. linkage adjustment g) Sticky or dirty valve body	a) Perform fluid check b) Adjust idle to specs. c) Disengage choke d) Service as required e) Perform control pressure test f) Service or adjust linkage g) Clean, repair, or replace valve body
No drive in any gear	a) Improper fluid level b) Damaged or improperly adjusted manual linkage c) Improper clutch or band application, or oil control pressure d) Internal leakage e) Valve body loose f) Damaged or worn clutches or band g) Sticking or dirty valve body	a) Perform fluid check b) Service or adjust linkage c) Perform control pressure test d) Check and repair as required e) Tighten to specs. f) Perform air pressure test g) Clean, repair, or replace valve body
No forward drive— reverse OK	a) Improper fluid level b) Damaged or improperly adjusted manual linkage c) Improper one-way clutch, or band application, or oil pressure control system d) Damaged or worn band, servo or clutches e) Valve body loose f) Dirty or sticking valve body	a) Perform fluid level check b) Service or adjust linkage c) Perform control pressure test d) Perform air pressure test e) Tighten to specs. f) Clean, service or replace valve body
No drive, slips, or chatters in reverse— forward OK	a) Improper fluid level b) Damaged or improperly adjusted manual linkage c) Looseness in half shafts, CV joints, or engine mounts d) Improper oil pressure control e) Damaged or worn reverse clutch f) Valve body loose g) Dirty or sticking valve body	a) Perform fluid level check b) Service or adjust linkage c) Service as required d) Perform control pressure test e) Perform control pressure test f) Tighten to specs. g) Clean, service, or replace valve body
Car will not start in neutral or park	a) Neutral start switch improperly adjusted b) Neutral start wire disconnected/damaged c) Manual linkage improperly adjusted	a) Service or adjust neutral start switch b) Replace/repair c) Service or adjust linkage
No drive, slips or chatters in first gear in D	a) Damaged or worn one-way clutch b) Improper fluid level c) Damaged or worn band d) Incorrect T.V. linkage adjustment	a) Service or replace one-way clutch b) Perform fluid level check c) Service or replace band assembly d) Service or adjust linkage

CHILTON'S THREE "C's" TRANSAXLE DIAGNOSIS CHARTS

Condition	Cause	Correction
No drive, slips, or chatters in second gear	a) Improper fluid level b) Incorrect T.V. linkage adjustment c) Intermediate friction clutch d) Improper clutch application e) Internal leakage f) Dirty or sticking valve body g) Polished, glazed band or drum	a) Perform fluid level check b) Service or adjust linkage c) Service clutch d) Perform control pressure test e) Perform air pressure test f) Clean, service, or replace valve body g) Replace or service as required
Starts up in 2nd or 3rd	a) Improper fluid level b) Damaged or improperly adjusted manual linkage c) Improper band and/or clutch application, or oil pressure control system d) Damaged or worn governor e) Valve body loose f) Dirty or sticking valve body g) Cross leaks between valve body and case mating surface	a) Perform fluid level check b) Service or adjust linkage c) Perform control pressure test d) Perform governor check Replace or service governor and e) Tighten to specifications f) Clean, service, or replace valve body g) Replace valve body and/or case as required
Shifts points incorrect	a) Improper fluid level b) T.V. linkage out of adjustment c) Improper clutch or band application, or oil pressure system d) Damaged or worn governor e) Dirty or sticking valve body	a) Perform fluid level check b) Service or adjust linkage c) Perform shift test and control pressure test d) Service or replace governor and clean screen e) Clean, service, or replace valve body
No upshifts at any speed in D	a) Improper fluid level b) T.V. linkage out of adjustment c) Improper band or clutch application, or oil pressure control system d) Damaged or worn governor e) Dirty or sticking valve body	a) Perform fluid level check b) Service or adjust linkage c) Perform control pressure test d) Service or replace governor and clean screen e) Clean, service or replace valve body
Shifts 1-3 in D	a) Improper fluid level b) Intermediate friction clutch c) Improper clutch application, or oil pressure control system d) Dirty or sticking valve body	a) Perform fluid level check b) Service c) Perform control pressure test d) Clean, service or replace valve body

CHILTON'S THREE "C's" TRANSAXLE DIAGNOSIS CHARTS

Condition	Cause	Correction
Engine over-speeds on 2-3 shift	a) Improper fluid level	a) Perform fluid level check
	b) Improper band or clutch application, or oil pressure control system	b) Perform control pressure test
	c) Damaged or worn direct clutch and/or servo	c) Perform air pressure test and service as required
	d) Dirty or sticking valve body	d) Clean, service or replace valve body
Mushy 1-2 shift	a) Improper fluid level	a) Perform fluid level check
	b) Incorrect engine performance	b) Tune adjust engine idle ad required
	c) Improper T.V. linkage adjustment	c) Service or adjust
	d) Improper intermediate clutch application, or oil pressure control system	d) Perform control pressure test
	e) Damaged intermediate clutch	e) Perform air pressure test and service as required
	f) Dirty or sticking valve body	f) Clean, service or replace valve body
Rough 1-2 shift	a) Improper fluid level	a) Perform fluid level check
	b) Improper T.V. linkage adjustment	b) Service or adjust linkage
	c) Incorrect engine idle or performance	c) Tune and adjust engine idle
	d) Improper intermediate clutch application or oil pressure control system	d) Perform control pressure test
	e) Dirty or sticking valve body	e) Clean, service or replace valve body
Rough 2-3 shift	a) Improper fluid level	a) Perform fluid level check
	b) Incorrect engine performance	b) Tune and adjust engine idle
	c) Improper band release or direct clutch application, or oil control pressure system	c) Perform control pressure test
	d) Damaged or worn servo release and direct clutch piston check ball	d) Air pressure test the servo apply and release and the direct clutch piston check ball. Service as required
	e) Improper T.V. linkage adjustment	e) Service or adjust linkage
	f) Dirty or sticking valve body	f) Clean, service, or replace valve body
Rough 3-2 shift at closed throttle in D	a) Improper fluid level	a) Perform fluid level check
	b) Incorrect engine idle or performance	b) Tune and adjust engine idle
	c) Improper T.V. linkage adjustment	c) Service or adjust linkage
	d) Improper band or clutch application, or oil pressure control system	d) Perform control pressure test

CHILTON'S THREE "C's" TRANSAXLE DIAGNOSIS CHARTS

Condition	Cause	Correction
Rough 3-2 shift at closed throttle in D	e) Improper governor operation	e) Perform governor test. Service as required
	f) Dirty or sticking valve body	f) Clean, service or replace valve body
No forced downshifts	a) Improper fluid level	a) Perform fluid level check
	b) Improper clutch or band application, or oil pressure control system	b) Perform control pressure test
	c) Damaged internal kickdown linkage	c) Service internal kickdown linkage
	d) T.V. linkage out of adjustment	d) Service or adjust T.V. linkage
	e) Dirty or sticking valve body	e) Clean, service or replace valve body
	f) Dirty or sticking governor	f) Clean or replace governor
Runaway engine on 3-2 or 3-1 downshift	a) Improper fluid level	a) Perform fluid level check
	b) T.V. linkage out of adjustment	b) Service of adjust T.V. linkage
	c) Band out of adjustment	c) Check and adjust servo rod travel
	d) Improper band or clutch application, or oil pressure control system	d) Perform control pressure test
	e) Damaged or worn servo	e) Air pressure test check the servo. Service servo and/or seals
	f) Polished, glazed band or drum	f) Service or replace as required
	g) Dirty or sticking valve body	g) Clean, service or replace valve body
No engine braking in manual first gear	a) Improper fluid level	a) Perform fluid level check
	b) T.V. linkage out of adjustment	b&c) Service or adjust linkage
	c) Damaged or improperly adjusted manual linkage	
	d) Band or clutch out of adjustment	d) Check direct clutch and service as required and check servo rod travel
	e) Oil pressure control system	e) Perform control pressure test
	f) Polished, glazed band or drum	f) Service or replace as required
	g) Dirty or sticking valve body	g) Clean, service or replace valve body
No engine braking in manual second gear	a) Improper fluid level	a) Perform fluid level check
	b) T.V. linkage out of adjustment	b&c) Service or adjust linkage
	c) Damaged or improperly adjusted manual linkage	
	d) Improper band or clutch application, or oil pressure control system	d) Perform control pressure d) test
	e) Servo leaking	e) Perform air pressure test of servo for leakage and service as required

CHILTON'S THREE "C's" TRANSAXLE DIAGNOSIS CHARTS

Condition	Cause	Correction
No engine braking in manual second gear	f) Polished, glazed band or drum	f) Service or replace as required
Transaxle noisy—valve resonance	a) Improper fluid level	a) Perform fluid level check
	b) T.V. linkage out of adjustment	b) Service or adjust T.V. linkage
Note; Gauges may aggravate any hydraulic resonance. Remove gauge and check for resonance level	c) Improper band or clutch application, or oil pressure control system	c) Perform control pressure test
	d) Cooler lines grounding	d) Free cooler lines
	e) Dirty or sticking valve body	e) Clean, service or replace valve body
	f) Internal leakage or pump cavitation	f) Service as required
Transaxle overheats	a) Excessive tow loads	a) Check Owner's Manual for tow restriction
	b) Improper fluid level	b) Perform fluid level check
	c) Incorrect engine idle or performance	c) Tune or adjust engine idle
	d) Improper clutch or band application, or oil pressure control system	d) Perform control pressure test
	e) Restriction in cooler or lines	e) Service restriction
	f) Seized converter one-way clutch	f) Replace converter
	g) Dirty or sticking valve body	g) Clean, service or replace valve body
Transaxle fluid leaks	a) Improper fluid level	a) Perform fluid level check
	b) Leakage at gaskets, seals, etc.	b) Remove all traces of lube on exposed surfaces of transaxle. Check for free-breathing. Operate transaxle at normal temperatures and inspect for leakage. Service as required.

THE HYDRAULIC CONTROL SYSTEM

The hydraulic Control System of the ATX automatic transaxle is used to supply fluid for the torque converter operation, to direct fluid under pressure to apply the servo bands and clutches, to lubricate the transaxle parts and to remove heat generated by the internal components of the transaxle and the torque converter.

The Main Components

The main components are listed, along with a description of their function in the valve body and transaxle.

1. **SUMP**—The transmission oil pan contains a supply of hydraulic fluid for the system.

2. **SCREEN**—Protects the pump inlet from dirt and other foreign material that may cling to the fluid.

3. **OIL PUMP**—Pumps hydraulic fluid to the system when the engine is running.

4. **MAIN OIL PRESSURE BOOSTER VALVE**—Increases or decreases main control pressure in relation to throttle opening.

Also provides different main control pressures depending on range or gear ratio.

5. **MAIN OIL PRESSURE REGULATOR VALVE**—Regulates main (line) control pressure in the system.

6. **CONVERTER RELIEF VALVE**—Prevents excess pressure build-up in the torque converter.

7. **COOLER**—Removes heat generated in the torque converter and transmission.

NOTE: Cooler return fluid is used for lubrication before it returns to the sump.

8. **MANUAL VALVE**—Moves with the shift selector and directs control pressure to various passages to apply clutches and servos, and to provide automatic functions of the hydraulic system.

9. **THROTTLE PLUNGER**—Varies spring force on throttle valve with throttle opening. Also operates "kickdown" system at wide-open throttle.

10. **THROTTLE CONTROL VALVE**—Regulates throttle pressure as an engine load signal to the hydraulic system.

11. **T.V. LIMIT VALVE**—Regulates maximum T.V. (throttle) pressure in the throttle control circuit.

12. **1-2 ACCUMULATOR VALVE**—And . . .

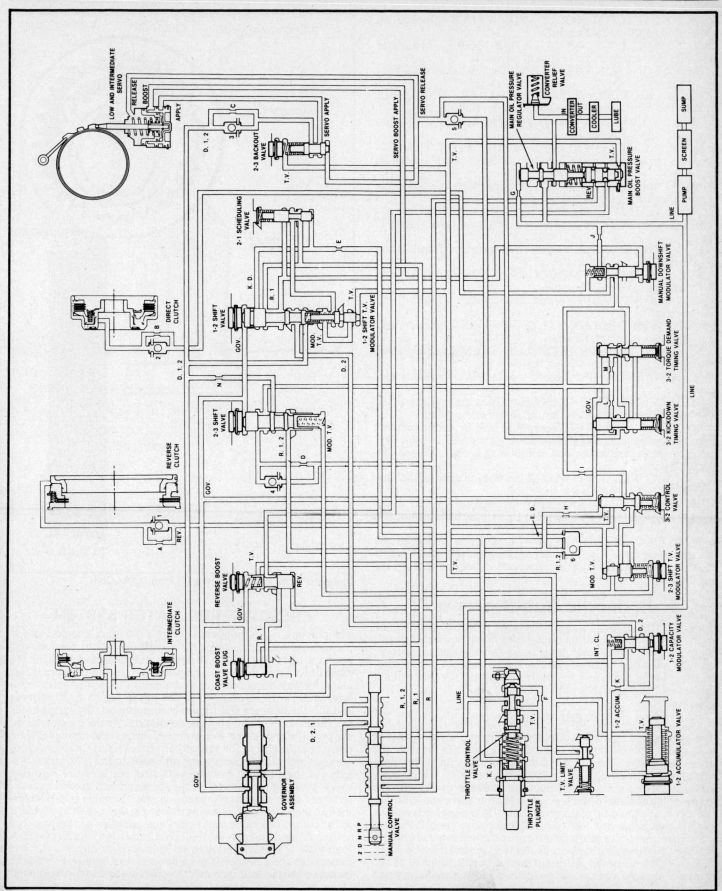

Schematic diagram of the ATX transaxle (© Ford Motor Co.)

13. **1-2 CAPACITY MODULATOR VALVE**—Operate together to smooth the 1-2 upshift.

14. **2-3 SHIFT T.V. MODULATOR VALVE**—Modulates T.V. pressure acting on the 2-3 shift valve.

15. **3-2 CONTROL VALVE**—Regulates 3-2 downshift timing.

16. **3-2 KICKDONW TIMING VALVE**—Operates to smooth the 3-2 downshift during kickdown (full throttle).

17. **3-2 TORQUE DEMAND TIMING VALVE**—Operates to smooth the 3-2 downshift at part throttle.

18. **MANUAL DOWNSHIFT MODULATOR VALVE**—Provides modulated line pressure to the direct clutch in Manual Low (1).

19. **2-3 BACKOUT VALVE**—Controls feed rate of apply pressure to low and intermediate servo.

20. **2-1 SCHEDULING VALVE**—Determines 2-1 downshift speed when the shift selector is moved to Manual Low (1) from D range.

21. **1-2 SHIFT VALVE**—Controls automatic 1-2 upshift and 2-1 downshift.

22. **1-2 SHIFT T.V. MODULATOR VALVE**—Modulates T.V. pressure on 1-2 shift valve.

23. **2-3 SHIFT VALVE**—Controls automatic 2-3 upshift and 3-2 downshift.

24. **REVERSE BOOST VALVE**—Provides increased main control pressure in reverse gear.

25. **COAST BOOST VALVE PLUG**—No hydraulic function except to plug a hole.

26. **GOVERNOR**—Road speed input signal to hydraulic system.

27. **INTERMEDIATE CLUTCH**—Locks the ring gear of the compound planetary gear set to the intermediate shaft.

28. **REVERSE CLUTCH**—is applied only in reverse gear. It's purpose is to hold the ring gear stationary, therefore, it is installed in the transaxle case rather than in a rotating cylinder like the other clutches.

29. **DIRECT CLUTCH**—Locks the turbine shaft to the low-reverse sun gear with no free-wheeling.

30. **LOW AND INTERMEDIATE SERVO**—When under fluid pressure, forces a piston rod to tighten the band around the drum and lock it stationary.

31. **TORQUE CONVERTER**—Couples the engine to the planetary gear train. Also provides torque multiplication which is equivalent to additional gear reduction during certain drving conditions.

Hydraulic Sub-Systems

Before the transaxle can transfer the input power from the engine to the drive wheels, hydraulic pressures must be developed and routed to the varied components to cause them to operate, through numerous internal systems and passages. A basic understanding of the components, fluid routings and systems, will aid in the trouble diagnosis of the transaxle.

OIL PUMP

The oil pump is a positive displacement pump, meaning that as long as the pump is turning and fluid is supplied to the inlet, the pump will deliver fluid in a volume proportionate to the input drive speed. The pump is in operation whenever the engine is operating, delivering more fluid than the transaxle needs, with the excess being bled off by the pressure regulator valve and routed to the sump. It should be remembered, the oil pump is driven by a shaft which is splined into the converter cover and through a drive gear insert. The gears, in turn, are installed in a body, which is bolted to the pump support at the rear of the transaxle case.

Should the oil pump fail, fluid would not be supplied to the transaxle to keep the converter filled, to lubricate the internal working parts and to operate the hydraulic controls.

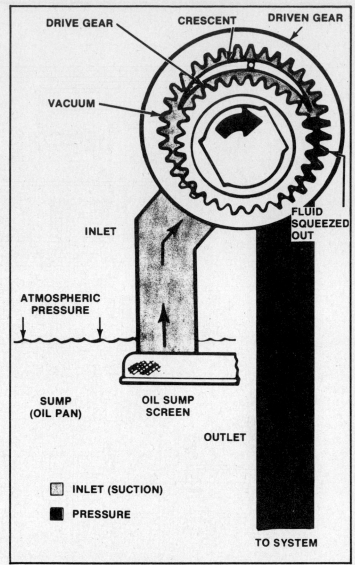

Operation of oil pump assembly (© Ford Motor Co.)

PRESSURE REGULATOR SYSTEM

The pressure regulator system controls the main line pressure at pre-determined levels during the vehicle operation. The main oil pressure regulator valve and spring determines the psi of the main line control pressure. The main line control pressure is regulated by balancing pressure at the end of the inner valve land, against the valve spring. When the pump begins fluid delivery and fills the passages and transaxle components, the spring holds the valve closed and there is no regulation. As the pressure rises, the pressure regulator valve is moved against the spring tension, opening a passage to the torque converter. Fluid then flows into the converter, the cooler system and back to the lubrication system. As the pressure continues its rise, the pressure regulator valve is moved further against the spring tension, and at a predetermined psi level and spring tension rate, the valve is moved further to open a passage, allowing excess pressurized fluid to return to the sump. The valve then opens and closes in a vibrating type action, dependent upon the fluid requirements of the transaxle. A main line ol pressure booster valve is used to increase the line pressure to meet the needs of higher pressure, required when the transaxle torque load increases, to operate the clutches and band servo.

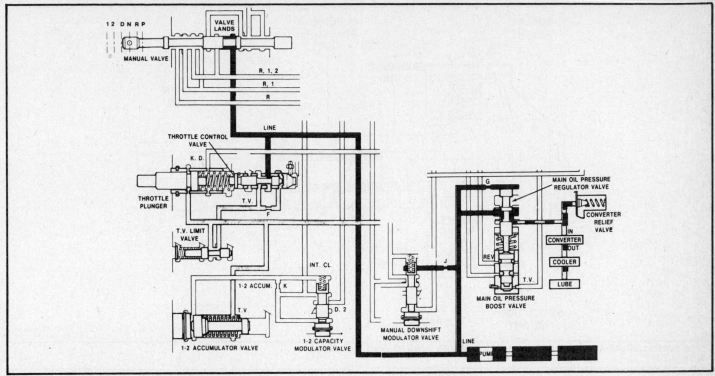

Main line control pressure routing (© Ford Motor Co.)

THE MANUAL CONTROL VALVE

Main line control pressure is always present at the manual control valve. Other than required passages, such as to the converter fill, the lubricating system and to certain valve assemblies, the manual valve must be moved to allow the pressurized fluid to flow to the desired components or to charge certain passages in order to engage the transaxle components in their applicable gear ratios.

GOVERNOR ASSEMBLY

The governor assembly reacts to vehicle road speed and provides a pressure signal to the control valves. This pressure signal causes automatic upshifts to occur as the road speed increases and permits downshifts as the road speed decreases. The governor has three hydraulic passages, an exhaust governor pressure out and line pressure in, controlled by springs and weights, with the weight position determined by centrifugal force as the governor assembly rotates.

THROTTLE VALVE

The ATX transaxle uses a manually controlled throttle valve to prvide the T.V. or throttle pressure signal that is proportional to the throttle opening of the carburetor. This throttle pressure signal is needed for the hydraulic control system to know what the engine load is, so the shifting from one ratio to another can be done at its proper time.

The T.V. system operates during closed throttle, light throttle and wide open throttle operations. The kickdown is actuated with the throttle in the wide open position.

NOTE: In case of the linkage becoming disconnected or other linkage failure, the system will go to full T.V. limit pressure to protect the clutches and band from slippage and burn-out.

T.V. pressure has several functions in the system, to delay upshifts and to boost line pressure when higher engine loads exist. Shift T.V. modulator valves convert T.V. pressure to lesser modulated pressure, necessary to match the requirements for balancing pressure and spring force against governor pressure. At closed

throttle and at light throttle, there may not be enough T.V. pressure to cause the modulator valves to modulate. In either case, the only delay forces will be from the line pressure on the differential areas plus, of course, spring force. Thus, upshifts can occur at minimum road speeds with the throttle closed or nearly closed. Two kinds of forced downshifts can be obtained, *torque demand* and *wide open throttle kickdown*. With our understanding that shift points depend upon the balance between governor pressure and downshift delay pressure, and should we change that balance to overcome governor presssure, downshifts will occur.

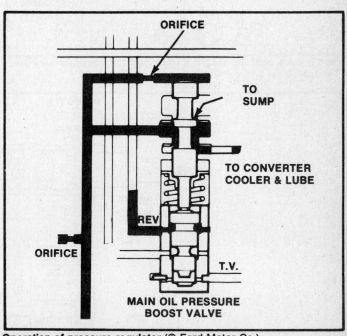

Operation of pressure regulator (© Ford Motor Co.)

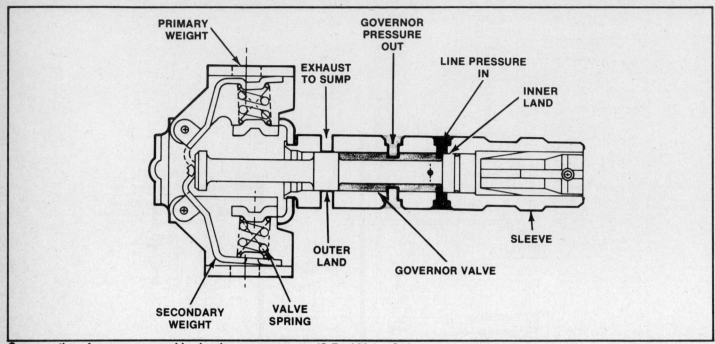

Cross section of governor assembly showing pressure ports (© Ford Motor Co.)

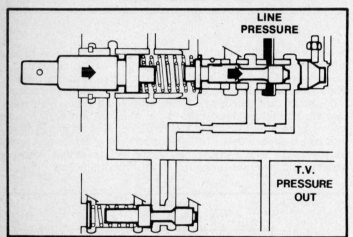

Throttle valve position at light throttle and T.V. pressure between 10-85 psi (© Ford Motor Co.)

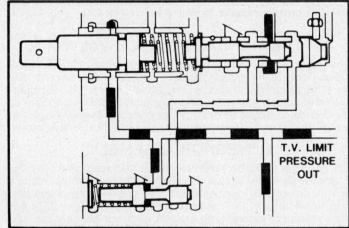

Throttle valve position at T.V. limit of 85 psi and up (© Ford Motor Co.)

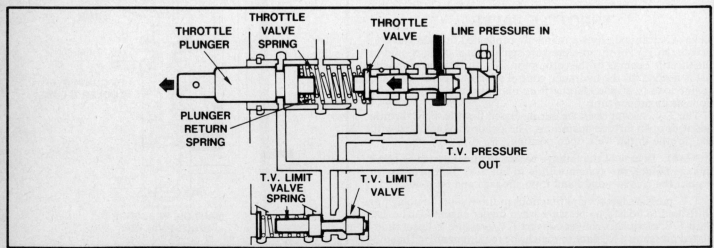

Throttle valve position at closed throttle and T.V. pressure approximately 10 psi (© Ford Motor Co.)

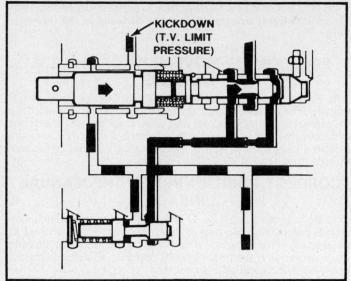

Throttle valve position at wide open throttle (W.O.T.) kickdown (© Ford Motor Co.)

DIAGNOSIS TESTS

General Diagnosis Sequence

A general diagnosis sequence should be followed to determine in what area of the transaxle a malfunction exists. The following sequence is suggested by Ford Motor Company to diagnose and test the operation of the ATX transaxle.

  1. Inspect fluid level and condition.

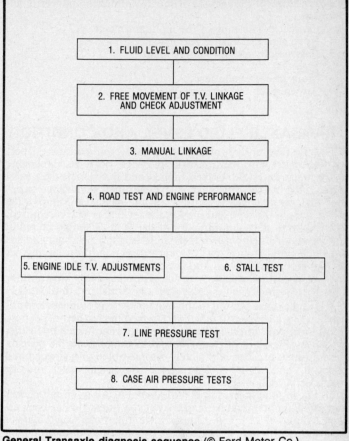

General Transaxle diagnosis sequence (© Ford Motor Co.)

HYDRAULIC SUB-SYSTEM FUNCTION IN RELATION TO GEARING

Sub-System	Function	Gear(s)
Fluid Supply	Pump oil to operate, lubricate, cool	All
Main Oil Pressure Regulator	Match line pressure to system pressure needs; charge converter-cooler-lube	All
Governor	Road speed signal to control valves	1,2,3
Throttle (T.V.)	Engine load signal to control valves	All
Modulated T.V.	Control automatic upshift road speeds	1,2
Kickdown	Force wide-open throttle downshifts	2,3
Shift Valve	Control automatic upshifts and downshifts	1,2,3
1-2 Lockout	Prevent 1-2 shift valve from "upshift" movement	R and Manual 1
2-3 Lockout	Prevent 2-3 shift valve from "upshift" movement	R and Manual 1,2
1-2 Accumulator and Intermediate Clutch Apply	Cushion 1-2 upshift	1 (Ranges D and 2)
Servo Apply	Cause servo to apply the band	1 and 2, R
Servo Boost	Increase apply force of servo.	R and Manual 1
Servo Release	Cause servo to release the band	R and 3
Direct Clutch	Cause direct clutch to apply	3 and R, Low
Reverse Clutch	Cause reverse clutch to apply	R
Reverse Pressure Boost	Cause maximum line pressure in reverse	R
3-2 Downshift	Control exhaust of direct clutch and servo apply	3

2. Freedom of movement of the T.V. linkage and verify adjustment.
3. Correct positioning of the manual linkage.
4. Road test and engine performance.
5. Engine idle and T.V. adjustment.
6. Stall test.
7. Main line pressure test.
8. Air pressure test of case.

TRANSAXLE FLUID LEVEL AND CONDITION

1. With the transaxle at normal operating temperature, inspect the fluid level with the transaxle in PARK position, the engine operating at curb idle, brakes applied and the vehicle on a level surface. Move the shift selector lever through each range to engage the transaxle gearing and to fill the passages. Remove the dipstick from the tube and inspect the level. Correct as required.

2. Observe the color and odor of the fluid. It should be red in color and not smell burned. If the fluid is black or brown and has a burned odor, indications of overheated condition having occurred, along with clutch and band failure are evident.

3. Inspect the fluid for evidence of specks of any kind and for anti-freeze, which would cause gum or varnish on th dipstick.

4. If specks are present in the fluid or there is evidence of anti-freeze, the transaxle pan must be removed for further inspection. If fluid contamination or transaxle failure is confirmed by further evidence of coolant or excessive specks or solids in the oil pan, the transaxle must be completely disassembled and cleaned and serviced. This includes cleaning the torque converter and the transaxle cooling sytem.

5. During the disassembly and assembly, all overhaul checks and adjustments must be made. After the transaxle has been assembled and re-installed in the vehicle, the remaining diagnosis tests should be made to confirm the problem and/or malfunction has been corrected.

NOTE: It would be a waste of time to perform any further tests should anti-freeze or excessive specks be found in the transaxle fluid.

FREEDOM OF MOVEMENT OF THE T.V. LINKAGE

1. Check for wide open carburetor and linkage travel at full throttle. The carburetor full throttle stop must be contacted by the carburetor throttle linkage and there must be a slight amount of movement left in the transaxle throttle linkage. Be sure the throttle linkage return spring is connected and the carburetor throttle lever returns to a closed position.

CORRECT POSITIONING OF THE MANUAL LINKAGE

1. Be sure the detent for D (DRIVE) in the transaxle corresponds exactly with the stop in the console, Hydraulic leakage at the manual valve can cause delay in engagement and/or slipping while operating if the linkage is not correctly adjusted. Remember: This is a critical adjustment.

ROAD TEST AND ENGINE PERFORMANCE

When making the road test, note the quality of the shift and its engagement. If soft or mushy shifts occur, or if initial engagement or shift engagement is too harsh, an inoperative or improperly adjusted T.V. linkage could be the cause. Correct the condition and road test again. During the road test, check the shift points with the engine at normal operating temperature to avoid fast idle operation of the engine, which would affect the shift timing. Perform the road test over a predetermined course, keeping traffic safety in mind. Evaluate engine performance during the road test.

Check the minimum throttle upshifts in Drive. The transaxle should start in first gear, shift to second and then shift to third, within the shift points of the Service Specifications.

ROAD TEST

Range		Check for	Condition (OK or Not OK)
1		Engagement	
		No 1-2 Upshift	
		Engine Braking in 1st Gear	
		Slipping	
2		Engagement and Shift Feel	
		Automatic 1-2 Upshift	
		Automatic 2-1 Downshift	
		Slipping	
D		Engagement and Shift Feel	
	Look Up Specs. For Shift Points	Minimum Throttle 1-2	
		Minimum Throttle 2-3	
		Minimum Throttle 3-2	
		Minimum Throttle 2-1	
		W.O.T. 1-2	
		W.O.T. 2-3	
		W.O.T. 3-2	
		W.O.T. 2-1	
		Slipping	
R		Engagement	
		Back-up Without Slip	

With transaxle in third gear, depress the accelerator pedal to the floor. The transaxle should shift from third to second or third to first, depending on vehicle speed.

Check the closed throttle downshifts from third to first by coasting down from about 30 mph (48 km/h), in third gear. The shifts should occur within the limits of the Service Specifications.

When the selector lever is at 2 (Second), the transaxle will operate in first and in second gears.

With the transaxle in third gear and road speed over approximately 30 mph (48 km/h), the transaxle shift to second gear when the selector lever is moved from Drive to 2 (Second), to 1 (First). The transaxle will shift into 1 (First) when road speeds are less than 30 mph (48 km/h).

When the selector lever is moved from drive (D) to second (2), the transaxle will shift into Second (2), regardless of vehicle speed.

This check will determine if the governor pressure and shift control valves are functioning properly. During the shift point check operation, if the transaxle does not shift within specifications, or certain gear ratios cannot be obtained, refer to the Diagnosis Guides to resolve the problem.

A shift test can be performed in the shop to check shift valve operation, governor circuits, shift delay pressures, throttle boost and downshift valve action.

— CAUTION —

Never exceed 60 mph (97 km/h) speedometer speed.

1. Raise the vehicle, place the transaxle in Drive and make a minimum throttle 1-2, 2-3 shift test. At this point of shift you will see the speedometer needle make a momentary surge and feel the driveline bump. If the shift points are within specification, the 1-2 and 2-3 shift valves and governor are OK. If the shift points are not within specification, perform a Governor Check to isolate the problem.

Governor Check

Accelerate vehicle to 30-40mph (48-64 km/h) then back off throttle completely. If the governor is functioning properly, the transaxle will shift to third gear.

ENGINE IDLE AND T.V. ADJUSTMENT

A condition of too high or too low engine idle could exist and be found during the road test. Should idle adjustment be necessary

by more than 50 rpm, the T.V. linkage must be re-checked for proper adjustment. Refer to the adjustment section for T.V. linkage adjustment procedures.

STALL TEST

The stall test can be made in Drive 2, 1 (First) or reverse at full throttle, to check engine performance converter operation and the holding abilities of the direct clutch, reverse clutch, the low-intermediate band and the gear train one-way clutch.

1. To perform the stall test, start the engine and allow it to come to normal operating temperature. Apply both the parking and service brakes during the test.

— CAUTION —

Do not allow any one to stand either in front of or behind the vehicle during the stall test. Personal injury could result.

2. Install a tachometer to the engine. Place the selector lever in the desired detent and depress the accelerator to the wide open position, noting the total rpm achieved.

— CAUTION —

Do not hold the throttle open for more than five (5) seconds at a time during the test.

3. After the test, move the selector lever to the Neutral position and increase the engine speed to 1000 rpm and hold approximately 15-30 seconds to cool the converter before making a second or third test.

4. During the test, if the engine rpm exceeds the maximum limits, release the accelerator immediately because clutch or band slippage is indicated and repairs to the transaxle should be done.

MAIN LINE PRESSURE TEST

1. Place the selector lever in the Park position and apply the parking brake.

2. Attach a 300 psi pressure gauge to the line port on the transaxle case with enough flexible hose to make the gauge accessible while operating the engine.

3. Start and operate the engine until normal operating temperature is reached.

4. With the selector lever in the desired position, refer to the pressure specifications chart and compare pressure reading with manufacturer's specifications.

STALL TEST

Range	Specified Stall Speed	Actual (High or Low)
D or 2		
1		
R		

Ranges(s)	Stall Speed(s) High (Slip)	Stall Speeds Low
D,2	Turbine Shaft One-Way Clutch	
D,2,1	Low-Intermediate Band or Servo	1. Check Engine for Tune-up. If OK . . .
R	Reverse Clutch	2. Remove Torque Converter and Bench Test for Reactor One-Way Clutch Slip
All Driving Ranges	1. Check T.V. Adjustment 2. Perform Control Pressure Test	

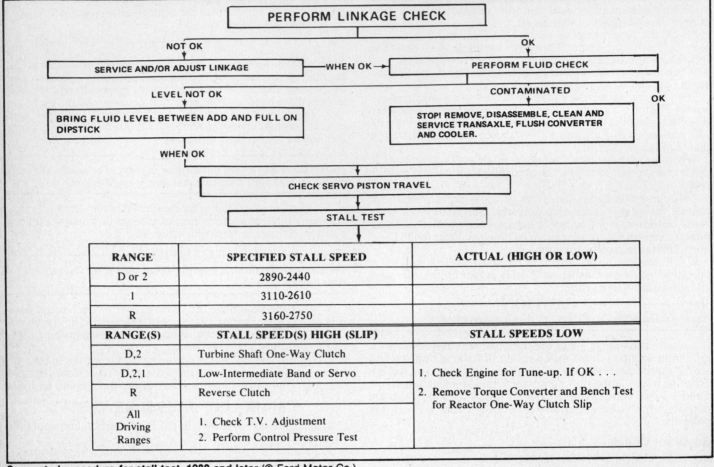

```
              PERFORM LINKAGE CHECK
         NOT OK                          OK
SERVICE AND/OR ADJUST LINKAGE  —WHEN OK→  PERFORM FLUID CHECK
         LEVEL NOT OK                     CONTAMINATED          OK
BRING FLUID LEVEL BETWEEN ADD AND FULL ON      STOP! REMOVE, DISASSEMBLE, CLEAN AND
DIPSTICK                                       SERVICE TRANSAXLE, FLUSH CONVERTER
         WHEN OK                               AND COOLER.

              CHECK SERVO PISTON TRAVEL

                   STALL TEST
```

RANGE	SPECIFIED STALL SPEED	ACTUAL (HIGH OR LOW)
D or 2	2890-2440	
1	3110-2610	
R	3160-2750	

RANGE(S)	STALL SPEED(S) HIGH (SLIP)	STALL SPEEDS LOW
D,2	Turbine Shaft One-Way Clutch	
D,2,1	Low-Intermediate Band or Servo	1. Check Engine for Tune-up. If OK . . .
R	Reverse Clutch	2. Remove Torque Converter and Bench Test for Reactor One-Way Clutch Slip
All Driving Ranges	1. Check T.V. Adjustment 2. Perform Control Pressure Test	

Suggested procedure for stall test, 1983 and later (© Ford Motor Co.)

NOTE: Wide open throttle (W.O.T.) readings are to be made at full stall. However, be sure to run the engine at fast idle in neutral for cooling between tests. To avoid operating at stall, have a helper manually force the T.V. linkage to the kickdown position, which will simulate W.O.T.

Keep in mind that clutch and servo leakage may or may not show up on the control pressure test. This is because (1) the pump has a high output volume and the leak may not be severe enough to cause a pressure drop; and (2) orifices between the pump and pressure chamber may maintain pressure at the source, even with a leak down-stream. Pressure loss caused by a less-than-major leak is more likely to show up at idle than at W.O.T. where the pump is delivering full volume.

Conversely, manipulating the T.V. linkage to simulate W.O.T., but actually testing at idle, the leak is more likely to cause a pressure loss in the W.O.T. position.

To further isolate leakage in a clutch or servo circuit, it is necessary to remove the oil pan (to drain the fluid) and the valve body; and to perform case air pressure tests.

5. To determine control pressure variation causes, refer to the Control Pressure Diagnosis chart.

AIR PRESSURE TEST OF CASE

A NO DRIVE condition can exist, even with the correct transaxle fluid pressure, because of inoperative clutches or band. Erratic shifts could be caused by a stuck governor valve. The inoperative units can be located through a series of checks by substituting air pressure for the fluid pressure to determine the location of the malfunction.

A NO DRIVE condition in Drive and 2 may be caused by an inoperative band or one-way clutch. When there is no drive in 1, the difficulty could be caused by improper functioning of the direct clutch or band and the one-way clutch. Failure to drive in re-

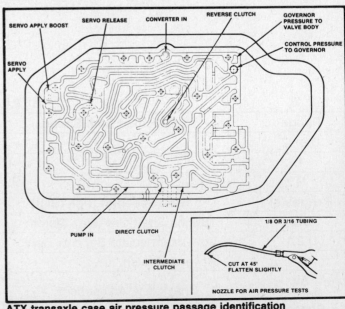

ATX transaxle case air pressure passage identification (© Ford Motor Co.)

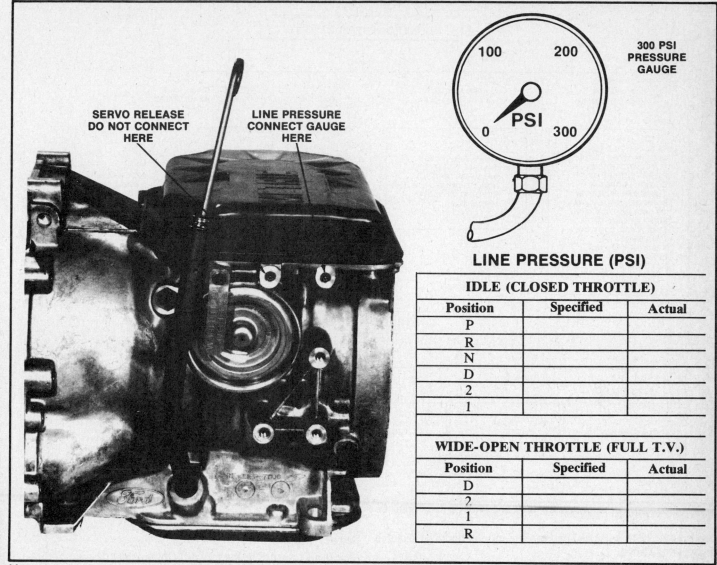

300 PSI PRESSURE GAUGE

SERVO RELEASE DO NOT CONNECT HERE

LINE PRESSURE CONNECT GAUGE HERE

LINE PRESSURE (PSI)

IDLE (CLOSED THROTTLE)		
Position	**Specified**	**Actual**
P		
R		
N		
D		
2		
1		

WIDE-OPEN THROTTLE (FULL T.V.)		
Position	**Specified**	**Actual**
D		
2		
1		
R		

Line pressure test ports, gauge and test results shown on typical chart (© Ford Motor Co.)

LINE PRESSURE TEST RESULTS
1981-82

Control Pressure Condition	Possible Cause(s)
Low in P	Valve body
Low in R	Direct clutch, reverse clutch, valve body
Low in N	Valve body
Low in D	Servo, valve body
Low in 2	Servo, valve body
Low in 1	Servo, direct clutch, valve body
Low at idle in all ranges	Low fluid level, restricted inlet screen, loose valve body bolts, pump leakage, case leakage, valve body, excessively low engine idle, fluid too hot.
High at idle in all ranges	T.V. linkage, valve body
Okay at idle but low at W.O.T.	Internal leakage, pump leakage, restricted inlet screen, T.V. linkage, valve body (T.V. or T.V. limit valve sticking)

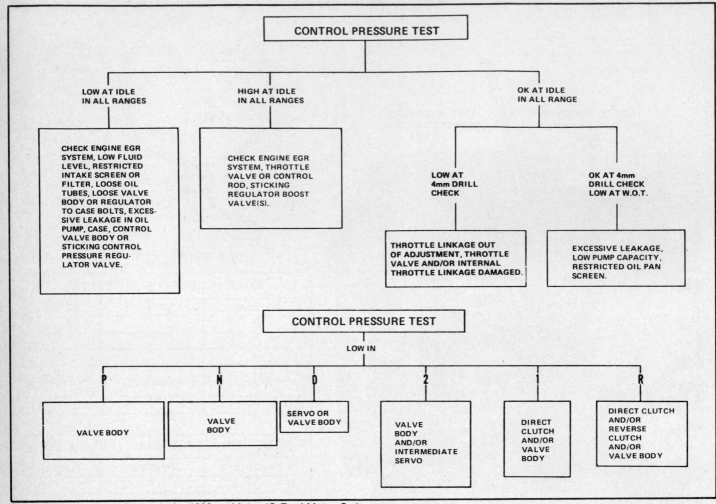

Control pressure test diagnosis for 1983 and later (© Ford Motor Co.)

verse range could be caused by a malfunction of the reverse clutch or one-way clutch.

When you have a slip problem but do not know whether it is in the valve body or in the hydraulic system beyond the valve body, the air pressure tests can be very valuable.

To properly air test the Automatic Transaxle a main control to case gasket and the following special service tools or equivalent will be required.

- Adapter Plate (Ford number, T82P-7006-B)
- Adapter Plate Attaching Screws (Ford number, T82L-7006-C)
- Air Nozzle TOOL (Ford number, 7000-DE)
- Air Nozzle Rubber Tip TOOL (Ford number, 7000-DD)

With the main control body removed, position the adapter plate and gasket on the transmission. Install the adapter plate attaching screws and tighten the screws to 80-100 in. lbs. (9-11 N•m) torque. Note that each passage is identified on the plate. Using the air nozzle equipped with the rubber tip, apply air pressure to each passage in the following order:

Band Apply Servo

Apply air pressure to the servo apply passage in the service tool plate. The band should apply, however, because of the cushioning effect of the servo release spring the application of the band may not be felt or heard. The servo should hold the air pressure without leakage and a dull thud should be heard when air pressure is removed allowing the servo piston to retrun to the release position.

Direct Clutch

Apply air pressure to the forward clutch apply passage in the service tool plate. A dull thud can be heard or movement of the piston can be felt on the case as the clutch piston is applied. If the clutch seal(s) are leaking a hissing sound will be heard.

Intermediate Clutch

Apply air pressure to the intermediate clutch apply passage in the service tool plate. A dull thud can be heard or movement of the piston can be felt on the case as the clutch piston is applied. If the clutch seal(s) are leaking a hissing sound will be heard.

Reverse Clutch

Apply air pressure to the reverse clutch apply passage in the service tool plate. A dull thud can be heard or movement of the piston can be felt on the case as the clutch piston is applied. If the clutch seal(s) are leaking a hissing sound will be heard.

Converter In

This passage can only be checked for blockage. If the passage holds air pressure remove the service tool plate and check for an obstruction or damage.

Control Pressure to Governor

Remove the governor cover and while applying air pressure to the passage in the service to plate watch for movement of the governor valve.

Governor to Control Pressure

This passage can only be checked for blockage. If the passage holds air pressure remove the service tool plate and check for an obstruction or damage.

Pump In (Bench Test)

With the transmission removed from the vehicle and the converter removed, the rotating pump gears should be heard when air pressure is applied to this passage. This check is normally performed during the assembly of an overhauled transmission.

TRANSAXLE FLUID COOLER

Flow Check

The linkage, fluid and control pressure must be within specifications before performing this flow check.

Remove the transaxle dipstick from the filler tube. Place a funnel in the transaxle filler tube. Raise the vehicle, remove the cooler return line from its fitting in the case. Attach a hose to the cooler return line and fasten the free end of the hose in the funnel installed in the fillr tube. Start the engine and set idle speed at 1000 rpm with the transaxle in Neutral.

Observe the fluid flow at the funnel. When the flow is "solid" (air bleeding has been completed), the flow should be liberal. If there is not a liberal flow at 1000 rpm in Neutral, low pump ca-pacity, main circuit system leakage, or cooler system restriction is indicated.

To separate transaxle trouble from cooler system trouble, observe the flow at the transaxle case converter-out fitting.

Transaxle Fluid Leakage

The transaxle assemblies present other than the usual fluid leakages found on the rear drive transmission assemblies. Again, as a rule of thumb, start at the top and work downward when attempting to correct transaxle fluid leaks. Some of the possible leakage areas are listed as follows:

1. Speedometer cable connection at the transaxle.
2. Oil pan gasket, pan flange or bolts.
3. Filler tube connection at transaxle case.
4. Fluid lines and fittings.
5. Transaxle fluid cooler.
6. Throttle control lever and/or manual lever shaft seals.
7. Converter drain plug, converter hub seal or defective welds.
8. Engine or power steering oil leaks, dropping on the transaxle, causing the appearance of transaxle fluid leakage.
9. Differential Bearing retainer "O" rings, gaskets and governor cover.
10. Oil pump gasket area.
11. Servo cover seal.

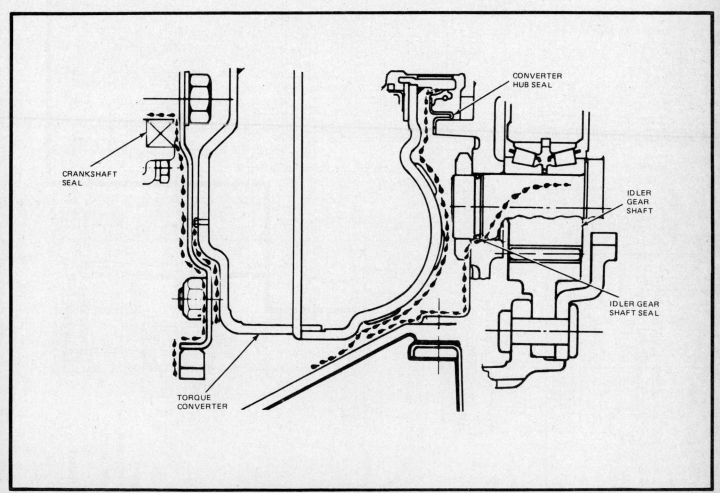

Possible fluid leakage around converter assembly (© Ford Motor Co.)

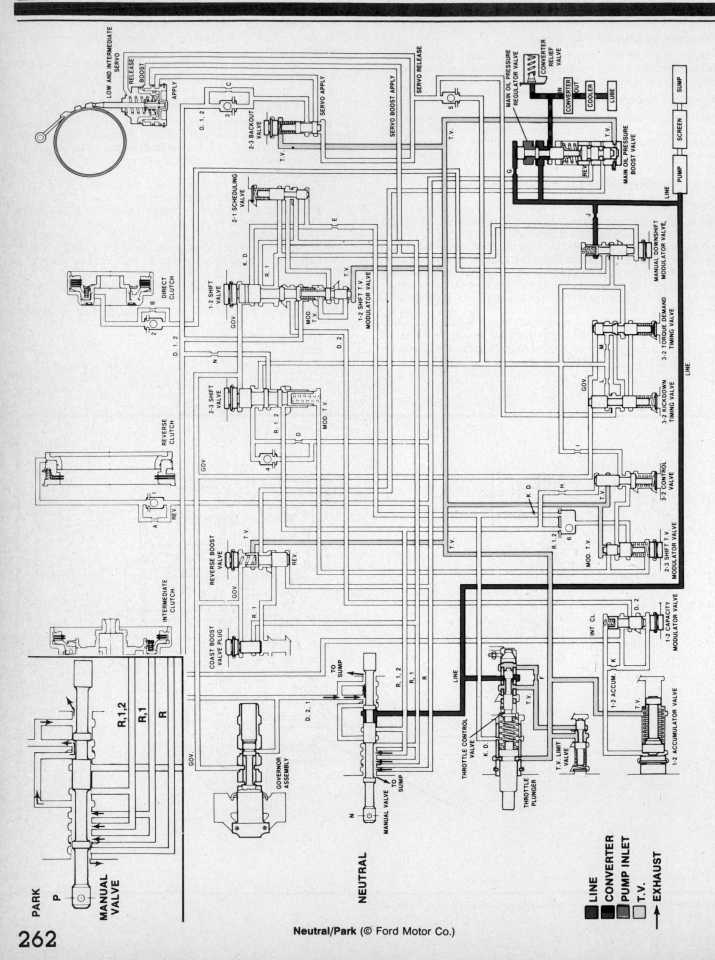

Neutral/Park (© Ford Motor Co.)

NEUTRAL/PARK

Units Applied—None

The selector lever is in the neutral or park position and no torque is being transmitted to the output shaft.

THE PRESSURE REGULATOR AND SUPPLY SYSTEM

The oil pump is delivering fluid to the main control system and the pressure regulator valve is regulating the line pressure and charging the converter-cooler-lubrication systems.

THE FLOW SYSTEM

The manual control valve has the fluid passages to the applying components blocked or the passage in an exhaust position. The throttle valve is regulating a minimum T.V. pressure with all the T.V. passages filled. Pressure is not directed to the governor assembly.

THE CLUTCHES, BAND SERVO AND ACCUMULATOR SYSTEM

There is no fluid pressure directed to the clutches, band servo or is there accumulator valve action.

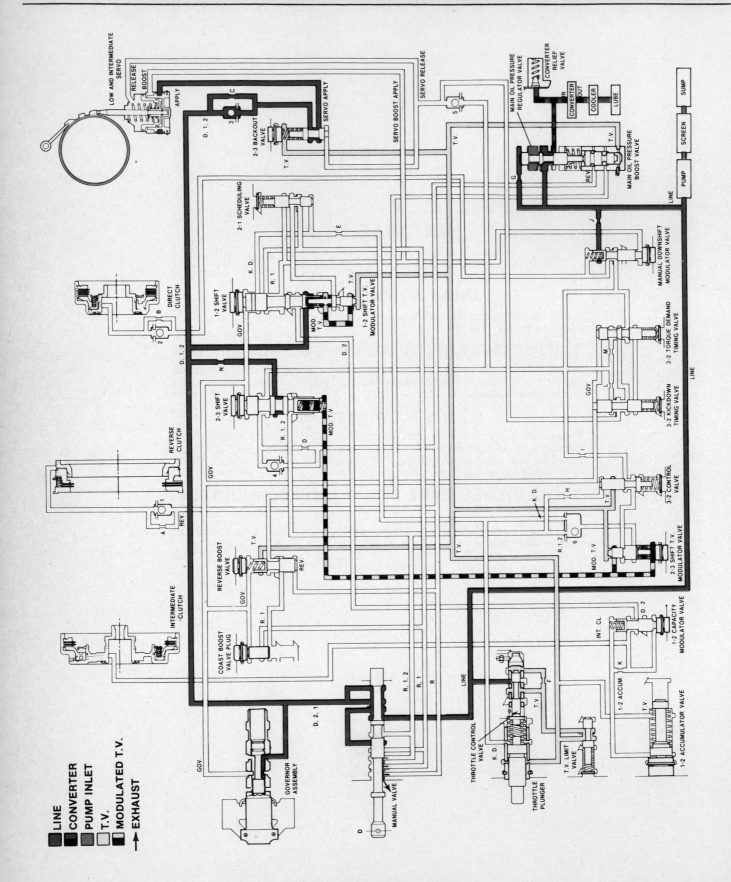

Drive, First Gear (© Ford Motor Co.)

DRIVE, FIRST GEAR

Units Applied—Band Servo, One-way Clutch Holding

The vehicle is in the Drive position and traveling at half-throttle.

PRESSURE REGULATOR AND SUPPLY SYSTEM

The oil pump is supplying fluid to the manual valve and pressure regulator valve. The torque converter, cooler and lubricating systems are charged.

THE FLOW SYSTEM

Main line pressure is directed to the governor and to the T.V. system. Main line pressure is also directed to the shift valves. The apply port of the low/intermediate servo is charged with line pressure. Governor pressure is generated as the vehicle starts to move, reacting on the varied valve load in opposition to the main line and T.V. pressures. The throttle valve is regulating moderate T.V. pressure to all T.V. passages. The T.V. limit valve is not regulating T.V. pressure. The T.V. pressure at the end of the oil pressure boost valve is causing line pressure to increase moderately, providing the band with greater holding power as the engine torque is increased. Shift delay pressure is also increased with the increase of line pressure. As the main line and T.V. pressures are equalled by the governor pressure, hydraulic and spring action cause valve movement and allow the upshift into second gear.

THE CLUTCHES, BAND SERVO AND ACCUMULATOR SYSTEM

With the apply port of the Low and Intermediate servo charged with line pressure, the Low and Intermediate band is applied. The one-way clutch is holding and the transaxle is in first gear.

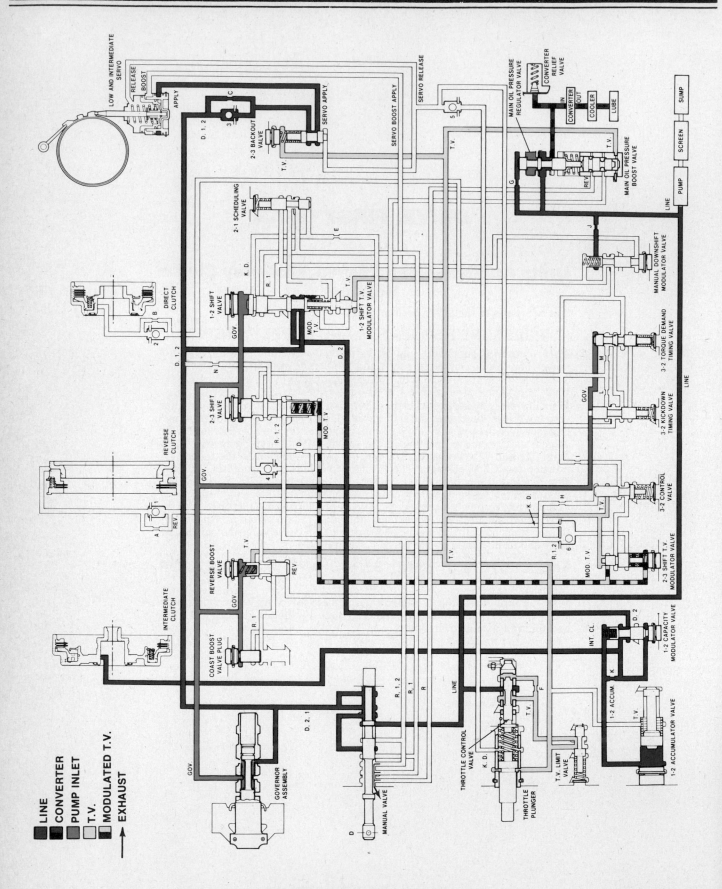

Drive, Second Gear (© Ford Motor Co.)

DRIVE, SECOND GEAR

Units Applied—Band Servo, Intermediate Clutch

The vehicle has shifted into second speed and is accelerating about 25 mph at half throttle or less.

THE PRESSURE REGULATOR AND SUPPLY SYSTEM

The pump is delivering fluid to the pressure regulator valve and manual valve. The torque converter, cooler and lubricating systems are charged.

THE FLOW SYSTEM

With the pressure regulator valve regulating line pressure, the pressure is directed to the governor, T.V. system, shift valves and band servo. The governor pressure has increased proportionate to the vehicle's road speed, which has caused the upshift from first to second speed, the passage to the intermediate clutch apply has opened. The T.V. pressure at the end of the main oil boost valve causes the line pressure to increase moderately. This increases the holding force against the band and clutch so as to handle engine torque and to increase the shift delay pressure. Should throttle pressure be increased, the shift to third speed would be delayed. As the governor pressure increases and overcomes main line and T.V. pressures, the 2-3 shift occurs.

THE CLUTCHES, BAND SERVO AND ACCUMULATOR SYSTEM

The low and Intermediate band remains applied and during the 1-2 shift, the intermediate clutch is applied, releasing the one-way clutch. The 1-2 accumulator valve and the 1-2 capacity modulator valve acts together to cushion the intermediate clutch application.

If the intermediate clutch were applied directly from the 1-2 shift valve, it would instantly be exposed to line pressure. This would cause a sudden application of the clutch and a harsh 1-2 upshift. The upshift is cushioned by controlling its rate of application. The 1-2 accumulator valve and 1-2 capacity modulator valve provide the cushioning effect.

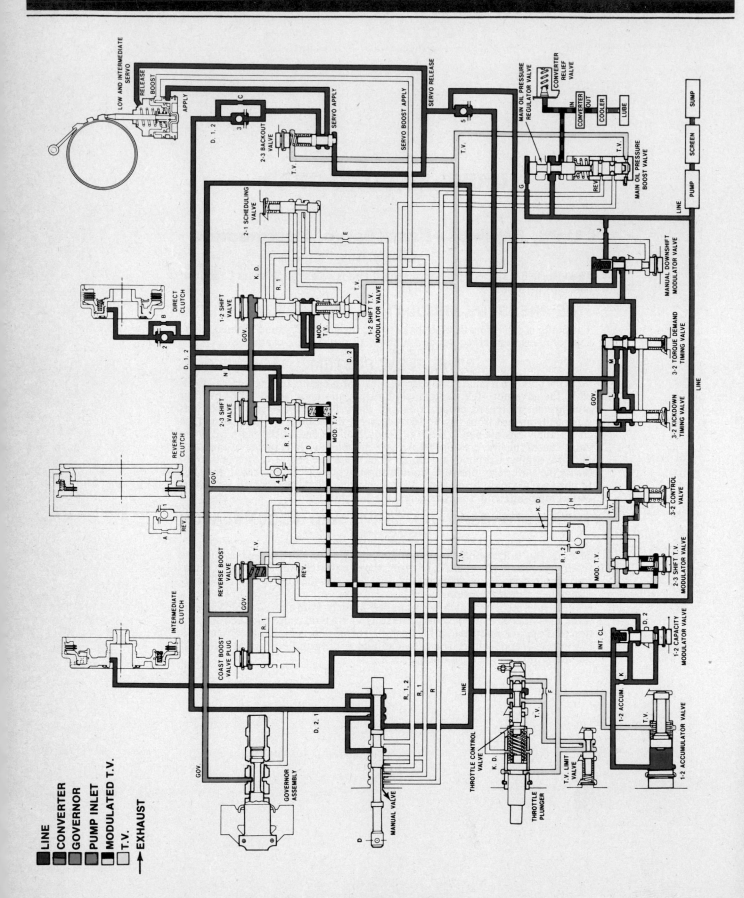

Drive, Third Gear (© Ford Motor Co.)

DRIVE, THIRD SPEED

Units Applied—Direct Clutch, Intermediate Clutch

The transaxle has shifted into third speed and the vehicle is traveling approximately 35 mph with less than one half throttle opening.

THE PRESSURE REGULATOR AND SUPPLY SYSTEM

The pump is delivering fluid to the pressure regulator and manual valves. The torque converter, cooler and lubricating systems are charged.

THE FLOW SYSTEM

The main line pressure is regulated by the pressure regulator valve and is routed to the governor, the shift valves, T.V. valve, intermediate clutch apply and with the shift to third speed, to the direct clutch apply. The governor pressure is proportional to the vehicle's road speed, having made the 2-3 upshift. The 2-3 shift T.V. modulator valve is producing modulating pressure, which is applied to the spring end of the 2-3 shift valve. Should an increase of throttle opening occur, this modulated pressure would increase and overcome the governor pressure, causing a 3-2 downshift. A higher regulated line pressure is controlled by T.V. pressure acting on the end of the main oil pressure boost valve.

THE CLUTCHES, BAND SERVO AND ACCUMULATOR SYSTEM

The intermediate clutch remains applied, while the band servo release pressure has overcome the apply pressure, releasing the band. As the band releases, the direct clutch apply passage is charged, causing the application of the direct clutch and placing the transaxle in third speed. The accumulator valve is ineffective during the shift.

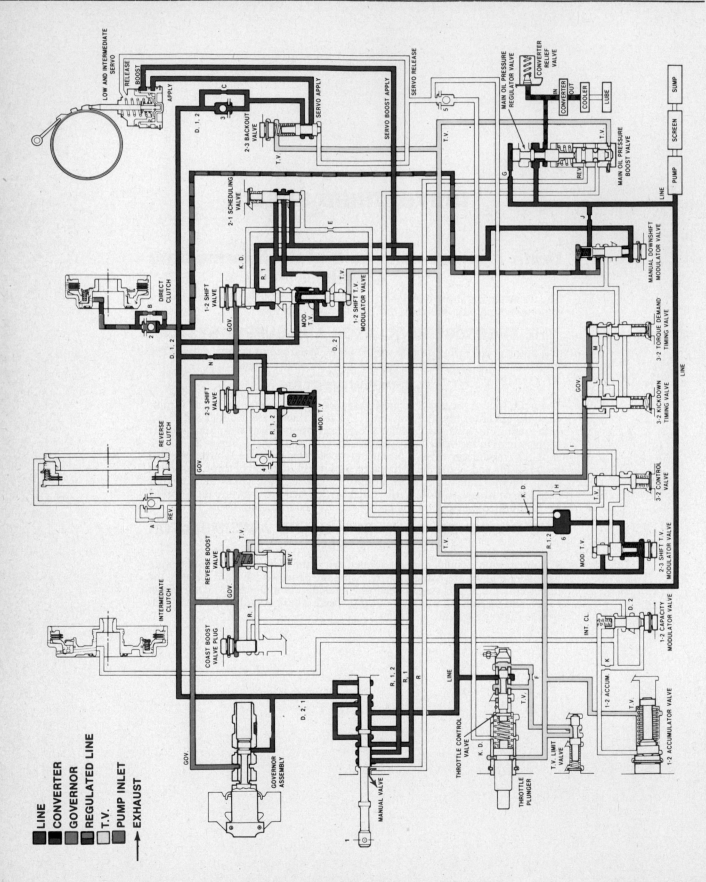

Manual Low, First Gear (© Ford Motor Co.)

MANUAL LOW, FIRST GEAR

Units Applied—Band Servo, Direct Clutch

The manual control valve is in Range 1, Manual Low, First Gear, with the vehicle accelerating at light throttle.

THE PRESSURE REGULATOR AND SUPPLY SYSTEM

The pump is delivering fluid to the pressure regulator and manual valve. The torque converter, cooler and lubricating systems are charged.

THE FLOW SYSTEM

With the manual valve positioned in the manual low detent, line pressure is directed to the governor, throttle valve, manual downshift modulator valve. The upshift lockout system is actuated to prevent governor pressure from causing an upshift, by having main line pressure available at more differential areas of the 1-2 and 2-3 shift valves. To aid in the increase of band holding pressure to handle the low gear torque, mainline pressure is directed to the servo boost port, along with the apply port. The T.V. system is directed to the main oil pressure boost valve, causing a slight increase to the regulated main line pressure. The regulated line pressure is routed to apply the direct clutch.

THE CLUTCHES, BAND SERVO AND ACCUMULATOR SYSTEM

The low/intermediate band is applied and with the direct clutch applied, there is engine braking in low gear on deceleration. The accumulator valve is inoperative with only T.V. pressure directed to it.

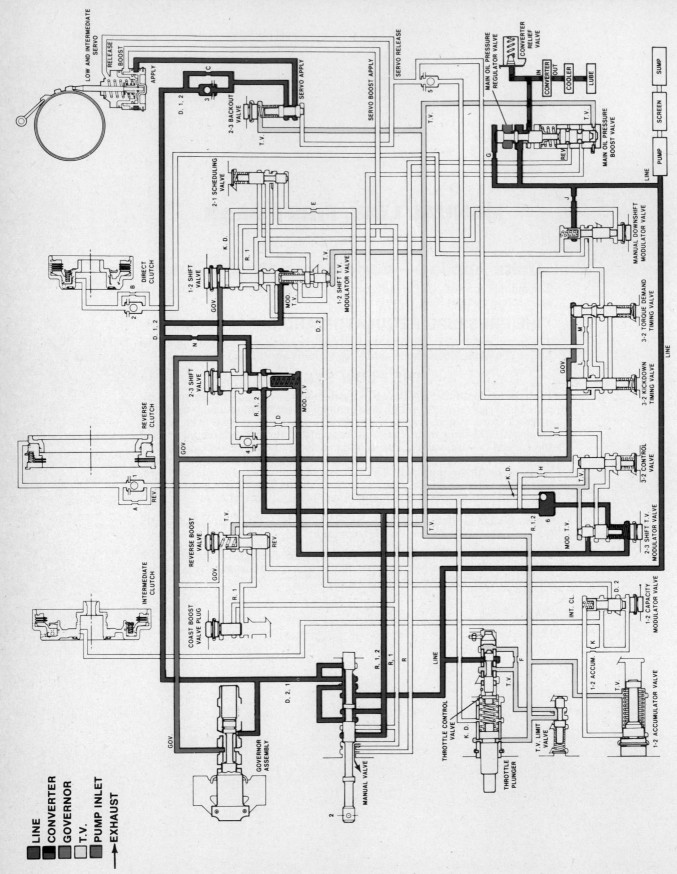

Manual Two, First Gear (© Ford Motor Co.)

LINE
CONVERTER
GOVERNOR
T.V.
PUMP INLET
→EXHAUST

MANUAL TWO, FIRST GEAR

Units Applied—Band Servo, One Way Clutch

The manual valve is positioned in the Manual Two detent and the transaxle is in the first gear. The difference between the Drive Range and the Manual Two range is that third gear is locked out in the Manual Two range. The vehicle is traveling at low speed and at light throttle.

THE PRESSURE REGULATOR AND SUPPLY SYSTEM

The pump is delivering fluid to the pressure regulator and manual valve. The torque converter, cooler and lubricating systems are charged.

THE FLOW SYSTEM

The manual valve, being positioned in the Manual Two position, charges the passages for the governor, shift valves, band servo apply port, T.V. system, the 2-3 shift modulator valve and an extra surface of the 2-3 shift valve (to lockout an upshift to the third speed). The governor system is charged with governor pressure proportional to the vehicle's road speed and is directed to both the 1-2 and 2-3 shift valves. However, with the more 2-3 shift valve surface exposed to the main line pressure, the 2-3 shift cannot be accomplished by the increase in governor pressure. The T.V. pressure is low and the 1-2 shift T.V. modulator valve has not moved and this causes only spring pressure and a small main line pressure area on the 1-2 shift valve to resist the gradual increase in governor pressure, hence, the 1-2 shift will occur at a low road speed. If the throttle would be opened more, modulated T.V. pressure would occur and the upshift would be delayed to a higher road speed.

THE CLUTCHES, BAND SERVO AND ACCUMULATOR SYSTEM

The Low/intermediate band servo is applied, along with the mechanical one-way clutch. The 1-2 accumulator valve has T.V. pressure directed to it and will modulate the intermediate clutch cushioning when the 1-2 shift occurs.

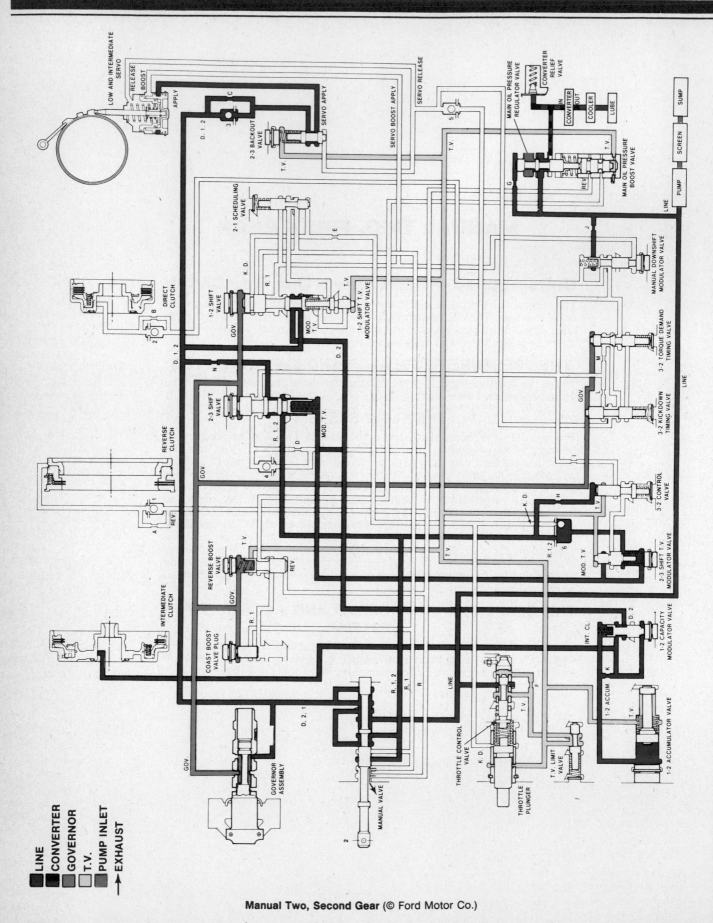

Manual Two, Second Gear (© Ford Motor Co.)

MANUAL TWO, SECOND GEAR

Units Applied—Band Servo, Intermediate Clutch

The manual valve is positioned in the Manual Two detent and the transaxle has just shifted into second speed. The third speed lock-out system is actuated to prevent a 2-3 upshift.

THE PRESSURE REGULATOR AND SUPPLY SYSTEM

The pump is delivering fluid to the pressure regulator valve and manual valve. The torque converter, cooler and lubricating systems are charged.

THE FLOW SYSTEM

With the pressure regulator valve regulating line pressure, the pressure is directed to the governor, T.V. system, shift valves and band servo. The governor pressure has increased proportionate to the vehicle's road speed, which has caused the upshift from first to second speed, the passage to the intermediate clutch apply has opened. The T.V. pressure at the end of the main oil boost valve causes the line pressure to increase moderately. This increases the holding force against the band and clutch so as to handle engine torque. Line pressure is directed to the 2-3 shift modulator valve, preventing it from going into regulation. The modulated T.V. passage is charged with line pressure instead of modulated T.V. pressure. With the increase of valve surface exposed to main line pressure and the spring tension, the governor pressure cannot overcome the resistance and therefore, the 2-3 upshift cannot occur. The throttle valve is regulating a moderate T.V. pressure and has assisted with cushioning the upshift and remains applied to the differential area of the 1-2 accumulator valve. The 1-2 shift valve has pushed the 1-2 shift modulator valve inward so that it cannot regulate, therefore, causing the modulated T.V. pressure not to be effective on the spring end of the shift valve. An increase of T.V. pressure on the modulator valve can force 2-1 downshift.

THE CLUTCHES, BAND SERVO AND ACCUMULATOR SYSTEMS

The shift from first speed to second speed has been accomplished by the application of the intermediate clutch upon the movement of the 1-2 shift valve. The low/intermediate band servo remains on. If the intermediate clutch were applied directly from the 1-2 shift valve, it would instantly be exposed to line pressure. This would cause a sudden application of the clutch and a harsh 1-2 upshift. The upshift is cushioned by controlling its rate of application. The 1-2 accumulator valve and 1-2 capacity modulator valve provide the cushioning effect.

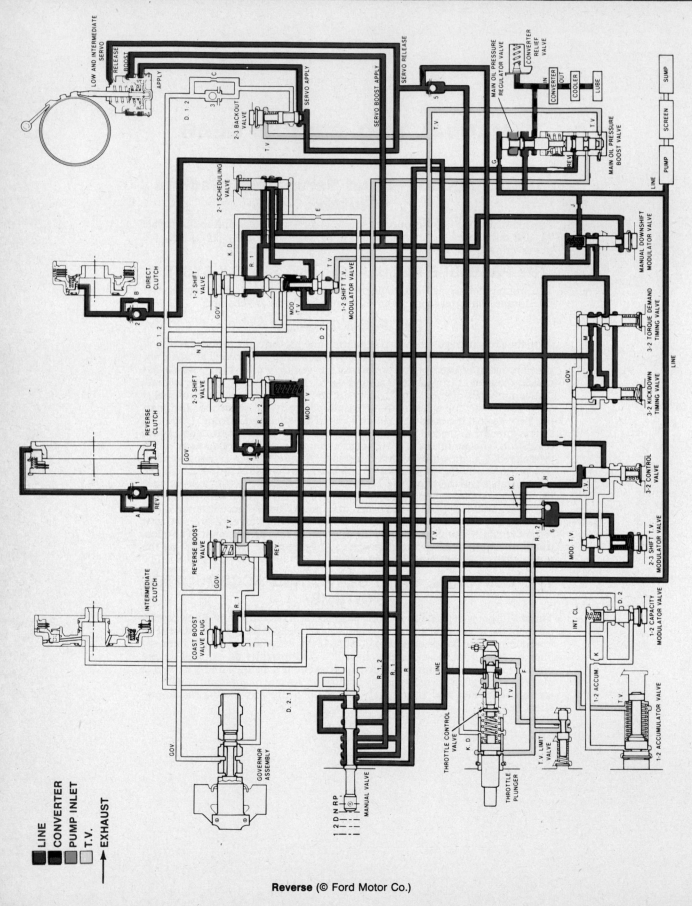

Reverse (© Ford Motor Co.)

REVERSE

Units Applied—Reverse Clutch, Direct Clutch, One-way Clutch

The manual valve is positioned in the reverse detent, the vehicle is slowly moving in reverse at a light throttle.

THE PRESSURE REGULATOR AND SUPPLY SYSTEM

The pump is delivering fluid to the pressure regulator valve and the manual valve. The torque converter, cooler and lubricating systems are charged.

THE FLOW SYSTEM

As the manual valve is moved into the reverse position, the main control pressure is cut-off to the governor, therefore preventing the build-up of governor pressure. The intermediate clutch is prevented from applying due to its apply passages cut off from the main line pressure. The low/intermediate servo has main line pressure directed to the apply, boost and release ports, and along with the strength of the servo return spring, the servo cannot be applied. Main line pressure is directed to the reverse clutch and direct clutch apply ports. Main line pressure must increase with the transaxle in the reverse gear, to hold the clutches from slipping, due to the high engine torque in reverse. To accomplish this, main line pressure moves the reverse boost valve outward, charging a second T.V. passage to the main oil pressure boost valve. Also, main line pressure is applied to a differential area of the main oil pressure boost valve. Both second and third gear lock-outs are applied. The 2-3 shift valve is moved enough to allow main line pressure to apply the direct clutch. T.V. pressure is applied to the end of the main line oil pressure boost valve, from the T.V. passage and to a differential area from the reverse boost valve, causing the line pressure to be at its maximum in the reverse gear.

THE CLUTCHES, BAND SERVO AND ACCUMULATOR SYSTEMS

Boosted main line pressure is directed to the reverse clutch and to the direct clutch. The one-way clutch is engaged when the transaxle is in the reverse gear mode. The accumulator valve has T.V. pressure directed to it, but is inactive.

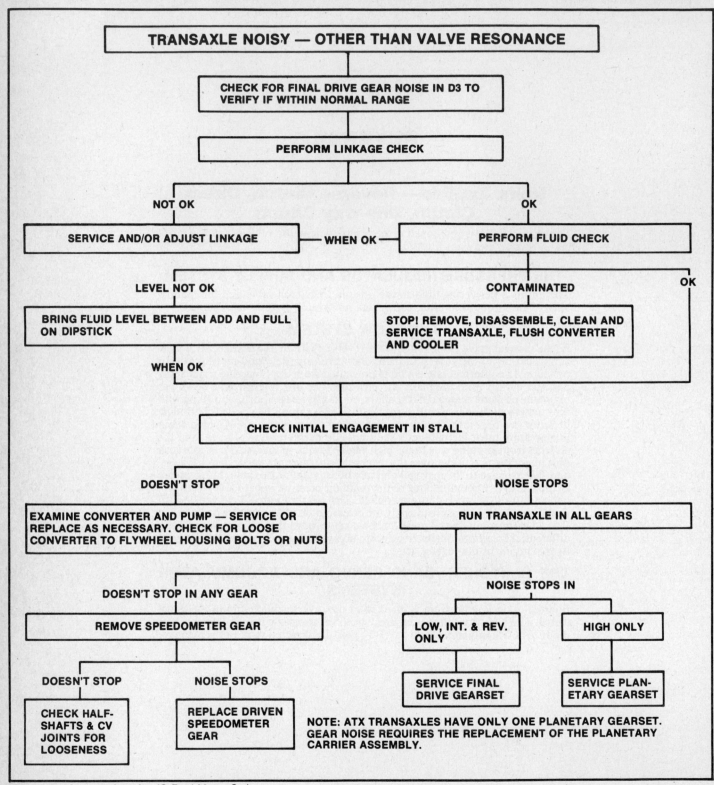

TRANSAXLE NOISY — OTHER THAN VALVE RESONANCE

CHECK FOR FINAL DRIVE GEAR NOISE IN D3 TO VERIFY IF WITHIN NORMAL RANGE

PERFORM LINKAGE CHECK

NOT OK — SERVICE AND/OR ADJUST LINKAGE — **WHEN OK**

OK — PERFORM FLUID CHECK

LEVEL NOT OK — BRING FLUID LEVEL BETWEEN ADD AND FULL ON DIPSTICK

CONTAMINATED — STOP! REMOVE, DISASSEMBLE, CLEAN AND SERVICE TRANSAXLE, FLUSH CONVERTER AND COOLER

OK

WHEN OK

CHECK INITIAL ENGAGEMENT IN STALL

DOESN'T STOP — EXAMINE CONVERTER AND PUMP — SERVICE OR REPLACE AS NECESSARY. CHECK FOR LOOSE CONVERTER TO FLYWHEEL HOUSING BOLTS OR NUTS

NOISE STOPS — RUN TRANSAXLE IN ALL GEARS

DOESN'T STOP IN ANY GEAR — REMOVE SPEEDOMETER GEAR

NOISE STOPS IN

DOESN'T STOP — CHECK HALF-SHAFTS & CV JOINTS FOR LOOSENESS

NOISE STOPS — REPLACE DRIVEN SPEEDOMETER GEAR

LOW, INT. & REV. ONLY — SERVICE FINAL DRIVE GEARSET

HIGH ONLY — SERVICE PLANETARY GEARSET

NOTE: ATX TRANSAXLES HAVE ONLY ONE PLANETARY GEARSET. GEAR NOISE REQUIRES THE REPLACEMENT OF THE PLANETARY CARRIER ASSEMBLY.

Diagnosis of transaxle noise (© Ford Motor Co.)

ON CAR SERVICES

ADJUSTMENTS
T.V. Linkage Adjustment

Two methods of T.V. linkage adjustment can be done. One method is by the manual adjustment of the linkage and the second method is the linkage adjustment using line pressure.

INFORMATION COMMON TO ALL THROTTLE LINKAGE SYSTEMS ON THE ATX

The control rod is adjusted to proper length during initial assembly. The external TV control lever actuates the internal TV control mechanism which regulates the TV control pressure. The external TV control lever motion is controlled by stops internal to the transaxle at idle and beyond wide open throttle (WOT). The linkage return spring must overcome the transaxle TV lever load (due to spring loading to WOT).

Adjustment of fine adjustment screw for T.V. linkage
(© Ford Motor Co.)

The TV control linkage is set to its proper length during initial assembly using the sliding trunnion block on the TV control rod assembly. Any required adjustment of the TV control linkage can normally be accomplished using this sliding trunnion block. Whenever it is necessary to set the TV linkage using a line pressure gauge, use the adjustment screw at the coupling lever at the carburetor, throttle body or bell-crank, depending on application.

When the linkage is within its adjustment range at a nominal setting, the TV control lever on the transaxle will just contact its internal idle stop position (lever up as far as it will travel when the carburetor throttle body is at its hot engine curb idle position with the A/C Off if so equipped).

At Wide-Open Throttle (WOT), the TV control lever on the transmission will not be at its wide-open stop. The wide-open throttle position must not be used as the reference point in adjusting linkage.

Linkage Adjustment
1.6L CARBURETED ENGINES

The TV control linkage must be adjusted at the TV control rod assembly sliding trunnion block using the following procedure

except in the case where a line pressure gauge is used for linkage adjustment.

1. Set the engine curb idle speed to specification. Refer to the Engine/Emissions Diagnosis manual.

2. After the curb idle check, turn the engine off and insure that the carburetor throttle lever is against the hot engine curb idle stop (the choke must be Off).

NOTE: The linkage cannot be properly set if the throttle lever allowed to be on the choke fast idle cam.

3. Set the coupling lever adjustment screw at its approximate midrange.

CAUTION

The following steps involve working in proximity to the EGR system. Allow the EGR system to cool before proceeding.

Adjusting linkage arm (© Ford Motor Co.)

4. Loosen the bolt on the sliding trunnion block on the TV control rod assembly one turn minimum.

Remove any corrosion from the control rod and free-up the trunnion block so that it slides freely on the control rod.

5. Rotate the transaxle TV control lever up using one finger and a light force, (approximately 5 pounds to insure that the TV control lever is against its internal idle stop. Without relaxing the force on the TV control lever, tighten the bolt on the trunnion block to specification.

6. Verify that the carburetor throttle lever is still against the hot engine curb idle stop. If not, repeat Steps 2 through 6.

Linkage Adjustment Using Line Pressure

The following procedure may be used to check and/or adjust the TV control linkage using a fine pressure gauge.

1. Place the shift selector lever in the Park position.

2. Apply the emergency brake.

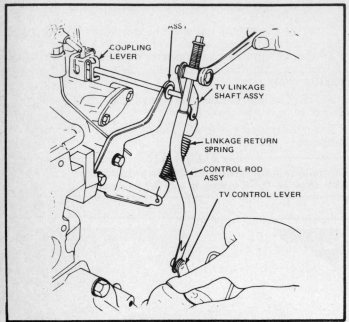

Adjusting T.V. control rod (© Ford Motor Co.)

3. Attach a 0-300 psi (0-2500 KPa) pressure gauge to the line press port on the transaxle with sufficient flexible hose to make gauge accessible while operating engine.

4. Operate engine until normal operating temperature is reached and throttle lever is against the hot engine curb idle stop (with A/C Off if so equipped).

5. Verify that the coupling lever adjusting screw is in contact with the TV linkage shaft assembly. If not, then the linkage must first be readjusted using the procedure under Linkage Adjustment procedure.

6. Verify that the carburetor throttle lever is against its hot engine curb idle stop. With engine operating at idle and in Park, line pressure must be 52-66 psi (357-455 KPa). If the line pressue is greater than 66 psi (455 KPa), the TV control linkage is set too long.

7. Place a 4mm drill (a 5/32 inch drill or 0.157 inch gauge pin) between the coupling lever adjustment screw and the TV linkage shaft. With the engine operating at idle and in park, the line pressure must be 72-88 psi (496-606 KPa). A low reading indicates linkage is set short. A high reading indicates linkage is set too long.

8. Correct a long setting by backing out (CCW) the coupling lever adjustment screw; turn in (CW) the adjustment screw for a short rod condition. This adjusting screw will change line pressure by approximately 2 psi per turn. If insufficient adjusting capacity is available, the TV control rod length must be reset using the Linkage Adjustment procedure.

Shift Trouble Diagnosis Related to Throttle Linkage Adjustment

If there is a complaint of poor transaxle shift quality, the following diagnostic procedure should be followed:

A. **Symptoms:** Excessively early and/or soft upshifts with or without slip-bump feel. No forced downshift (kickdown) function at appropriate speeds.
   Cause: TV control linkage is set too short.
   Remedy: Adjust linkage using Linkage Adjustment procedure.

B. **Symptoms:** Extremely delayed and harsh upshifts and harsh idle engagement.
   Cause: TV control linkage is set too long.

Remedy: Adjust linkage using Linkage Adjustment procedure.

C. **Symptoms:** Harsh idle engagement after engine warm up. Shift clunk when throttle is backed off after full or heavy throttle acceleration. Harsh coasting downshifts (automatic 3-2, 2-1 shifts in D range). Delayed upshifts at light acceleration.
   Cause: Interference due to hoses, wires, etc. prevents return of TV control rod or TV linkage shaft.
   Remedy: Correct interference area. Check or reset linkage using the Linkage Adjustment procedure.
   Cause: Excess friction due to binding of grommets prevents return of TV control linkage.
   Remedy: Check for bent or twisted rods or levers causing misalignment of grommets. Repair or replace defective components (replace grommets if damaged). Reset TV control linkage using the Linkage Adjustment procedure.

D. **Symptoms:** Erratic/delayed upshifts, possibly no kickdown, harsh engagements.
   Cause: Clamping bolt on trunnion at upper end of TV control rod is loose.
   Remedy; Reset TV control linkage using the Linkage Adjustment procedure.

E. **Symptoms:** No upshifts and harsh engagements.
   Cause: TV control rod disconnected. (Transaxle is at maximum TV pressure.)
   Remedy: Reconnect TV control rod. Replace grommet(s) if rod disconnect was due to defective grommet(s).
   Cause: Linkage return spring broken or disconnected.
   Remedy: Reconnect or replace spring.

Shift Linkage Adjustment

1. Move the selector lever into the "D" position and against the gate stop.

NOTE: Be sure to hold the lever against the stop during the adjustment.

2. Raise the vehicle and support safely. Loosen the nut retaining the control cable to the manual lever of the transaxle.

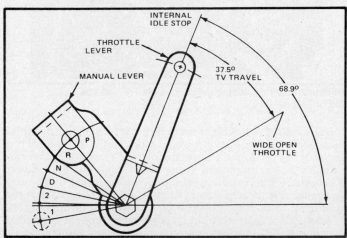

Throttle and manual linkage lever positions at the transaxle (© Ford Motor Co.)

3. Move the Transaxle lever rearward to the last detent, then forward *two* steps to the "D" detent.

4. Tighten the nut to 10-15 ft. lbs. torque.

5 Lower the vehicle and verify the adjustment.

Band Adjustment

The band servo piston rod is measured during the assembly of the transaxle and selected from a graduated group of rods to a specific length. No other adjustments are possible.

SERVICES

Oil Pan

Removal and Installation (including Fluid Drain and Refill)

1. Raise the vehicle and support safely. Place a drain pan under the oil pan and loosen the pan attaching bolts.

2. Allow the fluid to drain from the oil pan, to the level of the pan flange. Remove the pan attaching bolts in such a manner as to allow the oil pan to drop slowly, draining more of the fluid from the oil pan.

3. Remove the oil pan and drain the remaining fluid into the container. Discard the old gasket and clean the oil pan.

4. Clean or replace the oil filter screen. Install a new gasket on the oil pan and install the pan on the transaxle. Tighten the oil pan attaching bolt to 15-19 ft. lbs.

5. Lower the vehicle and fill the transaxle to the correct level with the specified fluid. Re-check the level as required, using the room temperature checking procedure.

——— CAUTION ———

Using fluid other than specified, could result in transaxle malfunction and/or failure.

NOTE: The A/T fluid should be changed every 30,000 miles (48,000 Km) if the vehicle accumulates 5,000 miles (8,045 Km) or more per month or is used in continuous stop and go service.

Converter Draining (When equipped with drain plug)

1. With the vehicle raised and supported safely, remove the converter drain access plate.

2. Rotate the engine in the normal direction of rotation until the converter drain plug is accessible.

3. Place a drain pan under the converter and remove the plug.

4. After the torque converter has drained, install the drain plug and torque to 8-12 ft. lbs. (10-16 N•m)

Valve Body

Removal

1. Position the vehicle, open the hood and set the parking brake.

2. Remove the battery and battery tray. Remove the ignition coil.

3. Remove the dipstick from the transaxle. Remove the supply hoses and the vacuum lines from the managed air valve. Remove the valve from the valve body cover.

4. Disconnect the neutral start switch connector and the fuel evaporator hose at the frame rail.

5. Disconnect the fan motor and water temperature sending unit wiring.

6. Remove the valve body cover retaining bolts and remove the valve body cover. Discard the gasket.

7. Remove the valve body attaching bolts and remove the valve body, with gasket, from the transaxle.

NOTE: Disassembly and assembly of the valve body can be found in the transaxle disassembly and assembly section.

Installation

1. Install two valve body alignment pins in the transaxle.

2. Install the valve body to case gasket.

3. Temporarily remove one of the alignment pins while positioning the valve body, to allow the attachment of the manual valve. After the manual linkage is attached to the manual valve, re-install the alignment pin.

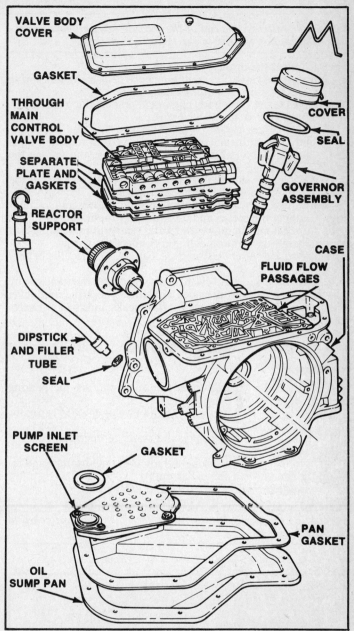

Arrangement of the hydraulic components (© Ford Motor Co.)

Valve body position on the transaxle case (© Ford Motor Co.)

4. Connect the throttle valve control spring.

5. Install the valve body retaining bolts (27), the detent spring and the oil pressure regulator exhaust plate.

6. Remove the valve body alignment pins. Tighten the attachment bolts to 6-8 ft. lbs. (8-11 N•m).

7. Install a new gasket on the transaxle case and install the valve body cover. Install the valve body cover retaining bolts (10), along with the transaxle identification tag, and tighten the attaching bolts to 7-9 ft. lbs. (9-12 N•m).

8. Attach the neutral start switch connector and install the managed air valve on the main control cover.

9. Connect the managed air valve supply hoses and vacuum lines. Connect the fuel evaporator hoses at the frame rail.

10. Connect the fan motor and water temperature sending unit wiring. Install the ignition coil and connect the wiring.

11. Install the battery tray and the battery. Connect the battery cables.

12. Start the engine and cycle the fluid through the transaxle by moving the shift lever through all detents. Check the fluid level and correct as required. Check for fluid leaks and road test vehicle, if necessary.

Servo Cover

Removal

1. Position the vehicle, open the hood and set the parking brake.

2. Disconnect the battery cables and unplug the FM capacitor wiring, if equipped.

3. Disconnect the fan motor and water temperature sending unit wire connectors.

4. Disconnect the fan shroud to radiator attaching nuts and remove the fan and fan shroud assembly.

5. Remove the filler tube to case attaching bolt.

6. Remove the filler tube and dipstick. Have container under transaxle to catch small amount of transaxle fluid that will drain from dipstick opening.

7. Remove the lower left mount to case attaching bolt from the left front (number 1) engine mount.

8. Remove the servo cover and snap ring with the use of the servo cover removing and installation tool, Ford number T81P-70027-A or its equivalent.

NOTE: Some fluid will leak from the case when the servo cover is removed.

Installation

1. Install new seals on the servo cover and install in place, using the servo installation and removal tool, Ford Number T81P-70027-A or its equivalent.

2. Install the mount to case attaching bolt in the left front engine mount.

3. With a new seal, install the filler tube and install the retaining bolt with the identification tag attached.

4. Install the fan and fan shroud assembly. Install the retaining nuts.

5. Connect the fan motor and temperature sending unit wiring connectors and connect the FM capacitor wiring, if equipped.

6. Connect the battery cables and start the engine. Cycle the transaxle fluid. Check the fluid level and correct as required.

7. Check the assembly for fluid leaks and road test the vehicle as required.

Governor

Removal

1. Position the vehicle and raise the hood. Set the parking brake.

2. Disconnect the battery cables and remove the two managed air valve supply rear hoses and all vacuum lines from the managed air valve.

3. Remove the attaching screw for the managed air valve supply hose band from the intermediate shift control bracket.

4. Remove the air cleaner.

5. With a long pry bar, remove the governor cover retaining clip and remove the governor cover. The governor can then be removed for service.

Installation

1. With the governor installed, install the governor cover with a new "O" ring seal in its bore of the transaxle housing.

2. With a long pry bar, position the governor cover retaining clip in its place on the cover.

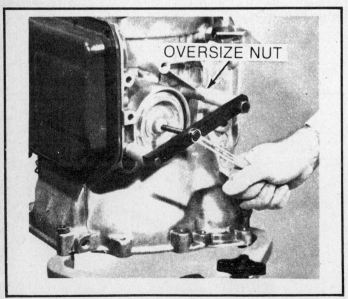

Removal or installation of the servo cover using special tool bar (© Ford Motor Co.)

OVERSIZE NUT

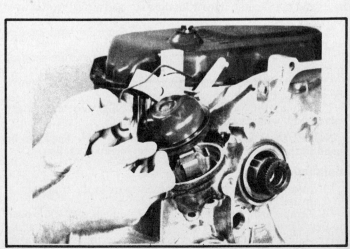

Removal or installation of governor cover (© Ford Motor Co.)

3. Install the managed air valve supply hose band to the intermediate shift control bracket attaching screw.

4. Connect the managed air valve supply hoses (2) to the rear of the valve and all vacuum lines to the valve.

5. Connect the battery cables and start the engine.

6. Cycle the transaxle fluid and check the level. Correct as required.

7. Check the transaxle for fluid leakage and road test the vehicle as required.

Neutral Start Switch

Removal

1. Position the vehicle and open the hood. Set the parking brake.

2. Disconnect the battery cables. Remove the managed air valve supply hoses from the rear of the valve and the vacuum lines from the valve. Remove the supply hose band retaining screw from the intermediate shift control bracket.

3. Remove the air cleaner assembly.

4. Disconnect the neutral start switch wire connector.

5. Remove the neutral start switch retaining bolts and remove the switch from the manual shaft.

Installation

1. Position the neutral start switch over the manual shaft and loosely install the two retaining bolts and washer through the switch and into the case.

2. Set the neutral start switch, using a number 43 drill (0.089 inch) and tighten the attaching bolts to 7-9 ft. lbs. (9-12 N•m).

3. Connect the neutral switch wiring connector.

4. Install the air cleaner assembly.

5. Install the supply hose band retaining screw into the intermediate shift control bracket.

6. Connect the two managed air valve supply hoses and all the vacuum lines to the managed air valve.

7. Connect the battery cables and start the engine. Cycle the fluid through the transaxle and check the operation of the neutral start switch. The engine should only start with the transaxle in either Park or Neutral shift positions.

REMOVAL & INSTALLATION

Transaxle Removal

ALL EXCEPT 1984 MODELS EQUIPPED WITH 2.3L H.S.C. ENGINE

NOTE: The 1984 ATX transaxle and the 2.3L H.S.C. engine must be removed and installed as a unit. Should any attempt be made to remove either component separately, damage to the ATX transaxle or to the lower engine compartment metal structure may result.

1. Position the vehicle on a lifting device, open the hood and protect the fender surfaces. Disconnect the negative battery cable.

2. Remove the bolts retaining the managed air valve to the valve body cover.

3. Disconnect the wiring harness from the neutral start switch.

4. Disconnect the throttle valve linkage and the manual valve lever cable at their respective levers.

5. Remove the two transaxle to engine upper bolts, located below and on either side of the distributor.

6. Raise the vehicle on the lifting device. Remove the nut from the control arm to steering knuckle attaching bolt, at the ball joint, both right and left sides.

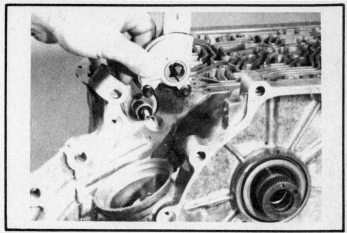

Neutral start switch assembly (© Ford Motor Co.)

7. With the use of a punch and hammer, drive the bolt out of the knuckle, both right and left sides.

NOTE: The bolt and nut from the right and left sides must be discarded and new ones used during the assembly.

8. With the use of a pry bar, disengage the control arm from the steering knuckle, on both the right and left sides.

——————— **CAUTION** ———————
Do not use a hammer on the knuckle to remove the ball joints.

NOTE: The plastic shield installed behind the rotor contains a molded pocket into which the lower control arm ball joint fits.

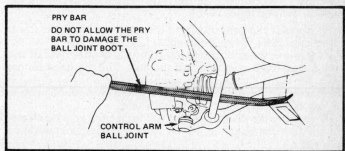

PRY BAR
DO NOT ALLOW THE PRY BAR TO DAMAGE THE BALL JOINT BOOT

CONTROL ARM BALL JOINT

Correct position of pry bar (© Ford Motor Co.)

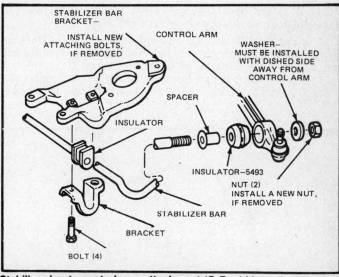

STABILIZER BAR BRACKET—

INSTALL NEW ATTACHING BOLTS, IF REMOVED

CONTROL ARM

WASHER— MUST BE INSTALLED WITH DISHED SIDE AWAY FROM CONTROL ARM

SPACER

INSULATOR

INSULATOR—5493

NUT (2) INSTALL A NEW NUT, IF REMOVED

STABILIZER BAR

BRACKET

BOLT (4)

Stabilizer bar to control arm attachment (© Ford Motor Co.)

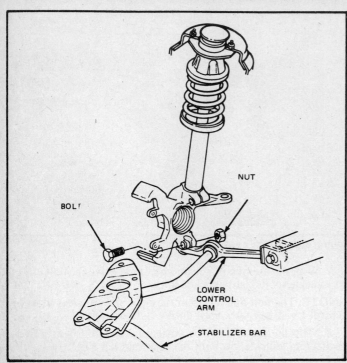

Steering knuckle pinch bolt and nut (© Ford Motor Co.)

When disengaging the control arm from the knuckle, clearance for the ball joint can be provided by bending the shield back towards the rotor. Failure to provide clearance for the ball joint can result in damage to the shield.

9. Remove the bolts attaching the stabilizer bar to the frame rail to both sides. Discard the bolts.

10. Remove the stabilizer bar to control arm attaching nut and washer from both sides. Discard the nuts. Pull the stabilizer bar out of the control arms.

11. Remove the bolt attaching the brake hose routing clip to the suspension strut bracket, on both sides.

12. Remove the steering gear tie rod to steering knuckle attaching nut and disengage the tie rod from the steering knuckle on both sides.

13. Pry the halfshaft from the right side of the transaxle. Position the halfshaft on the transaxle housing.

NOTE: Due to the configuration of the ATX transaxle case, the right halfshaft assembly must be removed first.

14. Insert the differential tool, Ford number T81P-4026-A or its equivalent into the right side halfshaft bore and drive the left halfshaft from the transaxle differential side gear.

15. Pull the left halfshaft from the transaxle and support the end of the shaft by wiring the shaft to the underbody of the vehicle.

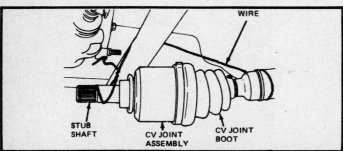

Support shaft and CV joint assembly with wire (© Ford Motor Co.)

CAUTION

Never allow the halfshaft to hang unsupported as damage to the outboard CV joint may result.

---

16. Install seal plugs into the bores of the left and right halfshafts.

17. Remove the starter support brackets and disconnect the starter cable. Remove the starter attaching bolts and remove the starter.

18. Remove the transaxle support bracket and the outer dust cover from the torque converter housing.

19. Remove the torque converter to flywheel retaining nuts. Matchmark torque converter to flywheel. Turn the crankshaft pulley bolt to bring the retaining nuts into an accessible position.

20. Remove the nuts attaching the left front (number 1) insulator mount to the body bracket.

21. Remove the bracket to body attaching bolts and remove the bracket.

22. Remove the left rear (number 4) insulator mount bracket attaching nut.

23. Disconnect the transaxle cooler lines and remove the bolts attaching the manual lever bracket to the transaxle case.

24. Position a transmission jack or other lifting device under the transaxle and remove the four remaining transaxle to engine attaching bolts.

25. Separate the transaxle from the engine enough for the torque converter studs to clear the flywheel and lower the transaxle approximately 2 to 3 inches.

26. Disconnect the speedometer cable and continue lowering the transaxle from the vehicle.

CAUTION

When moving the transaxle away from the engine, if the number one insulator mount contacts the body before the converter studs clear the flywheel, remove the insulator mount.

Installation

1. With the transaxle on a lifting device or transmission jack, position the assembly under the vehicle and slowly raise the unit into position to mate with the engine.

2. With the unit almost in position, attach the speedometer cable to the transaxle assembly. Rotate the converter or the flywheel until the matchmarks made during the removal, are in alignment. Raise the transaxle and position to the engine. Install the four lower transaxle to engine retaining bolts. Torque to 40-50 ft. lbs. (54-68 N•m).

3. Install the oil cooler lines and bolt the manual lever bracket to the transaxle case.

4. Install the left rear (number 4) insulator mount bracket attaching nut.

5. Install the left front insulator mount bracket attaching bolts and install the nuts attaching the left front (number 1) insulator mount to body bracket.

6. Install the torque converter to flywheel retaining nuts and torque to 17-29 ft. lbs. (23-39 N•m).

7. Install the transaxle support bracket and the dust cover to the torque converter housing.

8. Install the starter and retaining bolts. Attach the starter cable and install the starter support brackets.

9. Remove the left halfshaft bore seal plug, install a new circlip on the CV joint stub shaft and insert the stub shaft into the differential. Carefully align the splines of the stub axle with those of the differential gear. Push the CV joint until the circlip is felt to seat in the differential side gear.

CAUTION

Use care during the stub axle installation, not to damage the differential oil seal.

---

10. Using the same method, install the right side stub shaft into the differential side gear splines. Be sure the new circlip seats in the groove of the differential side gear.

11. Install the steering gear tie rod to steering knuckle attaching nut, after installing the tie rod stud in its bore on the steering knuckle, on both the right and left sides. Lock in place as required.

12. Install the brake hose routing clip retaining bolts on the left and right side suspension strut brackets.

13. Install the stabilizer bar into the control arms and install new nuts and washers.

14. Install new bolts and attach the stabilizer bar to the frame rails on both sides.

15. Install the lower control arm ball joints into the steering knuckle assemblies on the right and left sides. Using new bolts, install them into the steering knuckle, locking the ball joint stud to the steering knuckle. Torque to 37-44 ft. lbs. (50-60 N•m) by tightening the nut. Do not tighten the bolt.

16. Lower the vehicle and install the two upper engine to transaxle bolts, torquing them to 40-50 ft. lbs. (54-68 N•m).

17. Connect the two linkages, the throttle and manual controls, to their respective levers.

18. Connect the neutral start switch wire connector and install the bolts retaining the managed air valve to the valve body cover.

19. Connect the negative battery cable and verify the transaxle fluid level.

20. Start the engine and cycle the fluid through the transaxle by moving the manual valve control lever.

21. Re-check the assembly, the fluid level and road test as required.

Removal

2.3L HIGH SWIRL COMBUSTION (H.S.C.) ENGINE AND TRANSAXLE ASSEMBLY

1. Mark the position of the hood and remove the hood from the vehicle.

2. Disconnect the negative battery cable and remove the air cleaner.

3. Position a drain pan under the lower radiator hose and remove the lower hose. Allow the coolant to drain into the pan.

CAUTION

Do not drain the cooling system at this point if the coolant is at normal operation temperature. Personal injury can result, due to excessive heat of the coolant.

---

4. Remove the upper radiator hose from the engine.

5. Disconnect the oil cooler lines at the rubber hoses below the radiator.

6. Remove the coil assembly from the cylinder head.

7. Disconnect the coolant fan electrical connector, remove the radiator shroud and cooling fan as an assembly. Remove the radiator.

8. If equipped with air conditioning, discharge the system and remove the pressure and suction lines from the air conditioning compressor.

CAUTION

Refrigerant R-12 is contained in the air conditioning system under high pressure. Extreme care must be used when discharging the system.

---

9. Identify and disconnect all electrical and vacuum lines as necessary.

10. Disconnect the accelerator linkage, the fuel supply and return hoses on the engine and the thermactor pump discharge hose at the pump. Disconnect T.V. linkage at transaxle.

11. If equipped with power steering, disconnect the pressure and return lines at the power steering pump. Remove the power steering lines bracket at the cylinder head.

12. Install an engine holding or support tool device to the engine lifting eye. Raise the vehicle on a hoist or other lifting device.

13. Remove the starter cable from the starter.

14. Remove the hose from the catalytic converter.

15. Remove the bolt attaching the exhaust pipe bracket to the oil pan.

16. Remove the exhaust pipes to exhaust manifold retaining nuts. Pull the exhaust system from the rubber insulating grommets.

17. Remove the speedometer cable from the transaxle.

18. Position a coolant drain pan under the heater hoses and remove the heater hose from the water pump inlet tube. Remove the remaining heater hoses from the steel tube on the intake manifold.

19. Remove the water pump inlet tube clamp attaching bolt at the engine block and remove the two clamp attaching bolts at the underside of the oil pan. Remove the inlet tube.

20. Remove the bolts retaining the control arms to the body. Remove the stabilizer bar brackets retaining bolts and remove the brackets.

21. Remove the bolt retaining the brake hose routing clip to the suspension strut.

22. From the right and left sides, remove the nut from the ball joint to steering knuckle attaching bolt. Drive the bolt out of the steering knuckle with a punch and hammer.

CAUTION

Discard the bolt and nut. DO NOT re-use the bolt or nut.

---

23. Separate the ball joint from the steering knuckle by using a pry bar. Position the end of the pry bar outside of the bushing pocket to avoid damage to the bushing or ball joint boot.

NOTE: The lower control arm ball joint fits into a pocket formed in the plastic disc brake shield. This shield must be bent back, away from the ball joint while prying the ball joint out of the steering knuckle.

24. Due to the configuration of the ATX transaxle housing, the right side halfshaft must be removed first. Position the pry bar between the case and the shaft and pry outward.

CAUTION

Use extreme care to avoid damaging the differential oil seal or the CV joint boot.

---

25. Support the end of the shaft by suspending it from a convenient underbody component with a length of wire.

CAUTION

Do not allow the halfshaft to hand unsupported; damage to the outboard CV joint may occur.

---

26. Install a driver, Ford number T81P-4026-A or its equivalent, in the right halfshaft bore of the transaxle, and tap the left halfshaft from its circlip retaining groove in the differential side gear splines. Support the left halfshaft in the same manner as the right halfshaft. Install plugs in the left and right halfshaft bores.

27. Disconnect the manual shift cable clip from the lever on the transaxle. Remove the manual shift linkage bracket bolts from the transaxle and remove the bracket.

28. Remove the left hand rear (number 4) insulator mount bracket from the body bracket by removing the two nuts.

29. Remove the left hand front (number 1) insulator to transaxle mounting bolts.

30. Lower the vehicle and attach the lifting equipment to the two existing eyes on the engine. Remove the engine holding or support tool.

NOTE: Do not allow the front wheels to touch the floor.

31. Remove the right hand (number 3A) insulator intermediate bracket to engine bracket bolts, intermediate bracket to insu-

lator attaching nuts and the nut on the bottom of the double end- ed stud which attaches the intermediate bracket to the engine bracket. Remove the bracket.

32. Carefully lower the engine/transaxle assembly to the floor. Raise the vehicle from over the assembly. Separate the engine from the transaxle and do the necessary repair work to the trans- axle assembly.

Installation

1. Raise the vehicle on a hoist or other lifting device.
2. Position the assembled engine/transaxle assembly directly under the engine compartment.
3. Slowly and carefully, lower the vehicle over the engine/ transaxle assembly.

NOTE: Do not allow the front wheels to touch the floor.

4. With lifting equipment in place and attached to the two lifting eyes on the engine, raise the engine/transaxle assembly up through the engine compartment and position it to be bolted fast.
5. Install the right hand (number 3A) insulator intermediate attaching nuts and intermediate bracket to the engine bracket bolts. Install the nut on the bottom of the double ended stud that attaches intermediate bracket to the engine bracket. Tighten to 75-100 ft. lbs. (100-135 N•m).
6. Install an engine support fixture to an engine lifting eye to support the engine/transaxle assembly. Remove the lifting equip- ment.
7. Raise the vehicle and position a lifting device under the engine. Raise the engine and transaxle assembly into its operating position.
8. Install the insulator to bracket nut and tighten to 75-100 ft. lbs. (100-135 N•m).
9. Tighten the left hand rear (number 4) insulator bracket to body bracket nuts to 75-100 ft. lbs. (100-135 N•m).
10. Install the starter cable to the starter.
11. Install the lower radiator hose and install the retaining bracket and bolt. Tighten to specifications.
12. Install the manual shift linkage bracket bolts to the trans- axle. Install the cable clip to the lever on the transaxle.
13. Connect the lower radiator hose to the radiator. Install the thermactor pump discharge hose at the pump.
14. Install the speedometer cable to the transaxle.
15. Position the exhaust system up and into the insulating grommets, located at the rear of the vehicle.
16. Install the exhaust pipe to the exhaust manifold bolts and tighten to specifications.
17. Connect the gulp valve hose to the catalytic converter.
18. Position the stabilizer bar and the control arms assemblies in position and install the attaching bolts. Tighten all fasteners to specifications.
19. Install new circlips in the stub axle inboard spline grooves on both the left and right halfshafts. Carefully align the splines of the stub axle with the splines of the differential side gears and with some force, push the halfshafts into the differential unit until the circlips can be felt to seat in their grooves in the differential side gears.
20. Connect the control arm ball joint stud into its bore in the steering knuckle and install new bolts and nuts.

─────────── CAUTION ───────────
Do not use the old bolts and nuts. Their torque holding capacity is no longer of any value.

21. Tighten the new bolt and nut to 37-44 ft. lbs. (50-60 N•m).

NOTE: Tighten the nut only and hold the bolt from turning.

22. Position the brake hose routing clip on the suspension components and install their retaining bolts.
23. Lower the vehicle and remove the engine support tool.

24. Connect the vacuum and electrical lines that were discon- nected during the removal procedure.
25. Install the disconnected air conditioning components.
26. Connect the fuel supply and return lines to the engine and connect the accelerator cable.
27. Install the power steering pressure and return lines. Install the brackets.
28. Connect the T.V. linage at the transaxle.
29. Install the radiator shroud and the coolant fan assembly. Tighten the bolts to specifications.
30. Install the coil and connect the coolant fan electrical con- nector.
31. Install the upper radiator hose to the engine and connect the transaxle cooler lines to the rubber hoses under the radiator. Fill the radiator and engine with coolant.
32. Install the negative battery cable and the air cleaner assem- bly.
33. Install the hood in its original position.
34. Check all fluid levels and correct as required.
35. Start the engine and check for leakage. Correct any fluid levels as required.
36. Charge the air conditioning system and road test the vehi- cle as necessary.

BENCH OVERHAUL

GENERAL SERVICE PRECAUTIONS

When servicing this unit, it is recommended that as each part is disassembled, it is cleaned in solvent and dried with compressed air. All oil passages should be blown out and checked for obstruc- tions. Disassembly and reassembly of this unit and it parts must be done on a clean work bench. As is the case when repairing any hydraulically operated unit, cleanliness is of the utmost impor- tance. Keep bench, tools, parts, and hands clean at all times. Also, before installing bolts into aluminum parts, *always dip the threads into clean transmission oil.* Anti-seize compound can also be used to prevent bolts from galling the aluminum and seizing. Always use a torque wrench to keep from stripping the threads. Take care with the seals when installing them, especially the smaller O-rings. The slightest damage can cause leaks. Aluminum parts are very susceptible to damage so great care should be exer- cised when handling them. The internal snap rings should be ex- panded and the external snap rings compressed if they are to be re-used. This will help insure proper seating when installed. Be sure to replace any O-ring, gasket, or seal that is removed, al- though often the Teflon seal rings, when used, will not need to be removed unless damaged. Lubricate all parts with Dexron® II when assembling.

Transaxle Disassembly

1. Mount the transaxle in a fixture, if available to the repair- man. The fixture should be free to rotate as required.

NOTE: The following disassembly procedures will be outlined with the assumption that the transaxle is mounted to a fixture.

2. With the use of universal converter handles, lift the con- verter out of the transaxle assembly. Remove the handles and set aside.
3. Pull the oil pump drive shaft from the input shaft.
4. Rotate the assembly 180° and remove the differential end seal and allow the remaining transaxle fluid to drain into a con- tainer. Remove the dipstick from the case.

5. Remove the oil pan retaining bolts (13), remove the pan and discard the gasket.

6. Remove the oil filter retaining bolts (3), remove the filter and discard the gasket.

7. Remove the retaining bolts (6) from the differential retainer housing. Using small pry bars, wiggle the retainer to break it loose.

— **CAUTION** —

Do not damage the shims.

Lifting converter from transaxle (© Ford Motor Co.)

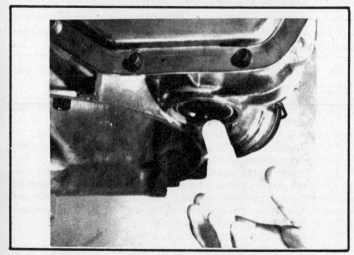

Installation of plastic plug in the differential opening
(© Ford Motor Co.)

8. Lift the differential assembly towards the retainer to free the retainer without damaging the shims.

9. Lift the differential retainer with the inner seal and the outer "O" ring, from the axle assembly.

10. Remove the selective shim and copper taper shim.

— **CAUTION** —

Note the position of the notch in the taper shim for correct installation during the assembly.

11. Remove the differential assembly by lifting up and out. Lay aside for later disassembly, if necessary.

12. Remove the valve body cover retaining bolts (10), remove the cover and gasket and discard the gasket.

13. Disconnect the throttle lever return spring and loosen the valve body attaching bolts (27).

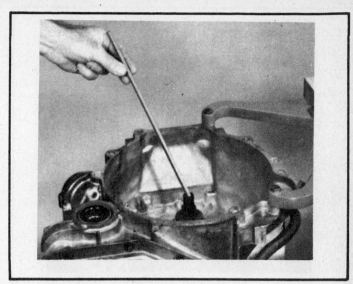

Removal of oil pump shaft (© Ford Motor Co.)

Removal of oil filter and gasket (© Ford Motor Co.)

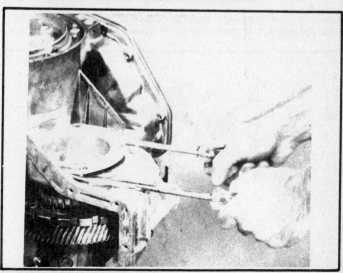

Breaking differential retainer loose after removal of retaining bolts
(© Ford Motor Co.)

287

Removal of differential retainer with two seals, one inner and one outer "O" ring (© Ford Motor Co.)

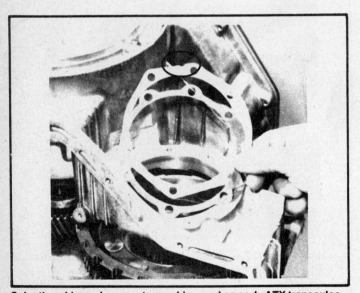

Selective shim and copper taper shim used on early ATX transaxles. Note the position of the notch for re-assembly (© Ford Motor Co.)

Removing baffle plate (© Ford Motor Co.)

Removal of the differential assembly (© Ford Motor Co.)

14. Remove the main oil pressure regulator and transaxle control baffle plate with the 7 special bolts.

NOTE: Because of their length, keep the 7 special bolts separate from the remaining valve body bolts.

15. Remove the detent spring and roller assembly, remove the remaining bolts and lift the valve body from the transaxle. Discard the assembly to case gasket.

─────── CAUTION ───────

Lift the valve body assembly carefully from the T.V. plunger cam and off the "Z" link on the rooster comb.

─────────────────────────

16. With a piece of wire, lift the governor filter from its bore in the transaxle case.

17. Remove the governor cover and remove the governor.

18. Remove the speedometer driven gear retaining pin. The use of a small pry bar to start the pin out and the use of side cutter type pliers to pull the pin out of the case, is recommended.

19. With the use of a wooden hammer handle, tap the driven gear from the transaxle case from the inside out.

20. Rotate the transaxle to place the pump assmbly on the top. Remove the pump attaching bolts (7) and with the use of a special slide hammer type tool, remove the pump assembly from the transaxle assembly. The selective thrust washer number 12 usually come out with the pump assembly.

21. Remove the pump to case gasket and discard.

22. Remove the needle thrust bearing, number 11, from the top of the intermediate clutch. Lift the intermediate clutch assembly from the case assembly.

23. Remove the number 10 thrust bearing from the top of the direct clutch. Lift out the ring gear assembly along with the direct clutch assembly.

─────── CAUTION ───────

The ring gear assembly and the direct clutch parts are loose and can separate during handling.

─────────────────────────

NOTE: During the disassembly, the ring gear and direct clutch can be removed separately.

24. Remove the number 7 thrust washer from the surface of the planetary assembly.

25. Remove the reverse clutch snap ring and remove the reverse clutch pack.

26. Remove the planetary assembly and the number 5 thrust washer.

113. Case & Hsg. Assy.
114. Screen Assy.—Gov. Oil
115. Gasket—Oil Filter
116. Filter Assy.—Oil
117. Bolt (3 Req'd.)
118. Gasket—Oil Pan
119. Pan—Oil
120. Bolt (13 Req'd.)
121. Strut—Low/Interm. Band Anchor
122. Shaft—Parking Pawl
123. Pawl—Parking Brake
124. Plug
125. Spring—Park Pawl Return
126. Pin—Parking Pawl Roller
127. Spring Assy.—Manual Valve Detent
128. Spring—Throttle Vlv. Control Lever
129. Shaft Assy.—TV Lever Actuating
130. Nut
131. Lever—Parking Pawl Actuating
132. Spring—Park Pawl Ratcheting
133. Actuator—Manual Lever
134. Washer
135. Lever—Manual Vlv. Detent—Inner
136. Nut—Stamped
137. Pin—Speedo Retaining
138. Support Assy.—Conv. Reactor
139. Seal Assy.—Conv. Imp. Hub
140. Converter Assembly
141. Governor Assembly
142. Seal
143. Cover—Governor
144. Clip—Gov. Cover Retaining
145. Gear—Speedo Driven
146. Pin
147. Seal
148. Retainer—Speedo Driven Gear
149. Seal—Manual Control Lever
150. Lever Assy.—Manual Control
151. Switch Assy.—Neutral Start
152. Bolt (2 Req'd.)
153. Lever Assy.—Throttle Vlv.—Outer
154. Washer
155. Nut
156. Bolt (5 Req'd.)
157. Washer—Transaxle Diff. Side Gr. Thrust
158. Gear—Transaxle Diff. Side
159. Pinion—Transaxle Diff. Pinion Thrust
160. Washer—Transaxle Diff. Pinion Thrust
161. Pin—4.75MM X 38.1MM
162. Shaft—Transaxle Diff. Pinion
163. Oil Pump Thrust Washer (Selective)
164. Washer (2 Req'd.)
165. Washer (2 Req'd.)
166. Shaft—Idler Gear
167. Seal
168. Nut

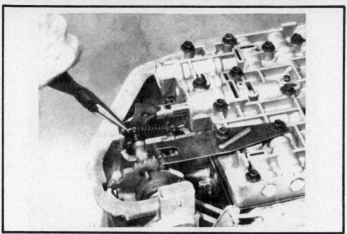

Disconnecting inner T.V. control spring (© Ford Motor Co.)

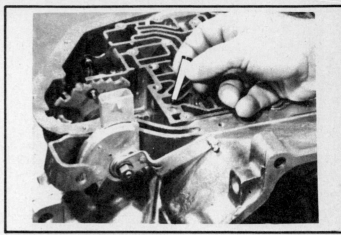

Location of governor filter screen (© Ford Motor Co.)

Removal of the detent spring (© Ford Motor Co.)

Removing speedometer gear retaining pin (© Ford Motor Co.)

Removal of pump from case with slide hammer type tools
(© Ford Motor Co.)

Lifting pump assembly from the case, exposing thrust washer number 11 (© Ford Motor Co.)

Removal of thrust washer number 11 (© Ford Motor Co.)

Removal of intermediate clutch assembly (© Ford Motor Co.)

Removal of ring gear and direct clutch assemblies
(© Ford Motor Co.)

Removal of the planetary assembly and number 5 thrust washer
(© Ford Motor Co.)

Removal of the reverse clutch pack (© Ford Motor Co.)

27. Remove the reverse clutch return springs and holder assembly. Remove the reverse clutch piston.

28. Pry the reverse clutch cylinder upward to loosen, and then remove from the case, along with the piston and seals.

29. Install a servo cover remover/installer tool, Ford number T81P-70027-A or its equivalent and remove the servo retaining snap ring. Back the tool off and allow the spring pressure to neutralize. Remove the cover, servo piston and tool.

30. Remove the low-intermediate band and the sun gear with the drum assembly.

NOTE: Lift the sun gear assembly and rotate clockwise to remove.

31. Remove the number 4 thrust washer from the transfer housing.

32. Remove the transfer housing attaching bolts (55), pry the transfer housing from the idler gear shaft and remove the transfer housing.

CAUTION

When prying against the transfer housing, lift upward against the housing only. Prying downward can result in damage to the transfer gear teeth.

33. Remove the number 3 thrust needle bearing from the input gear and remove the gear. Remove the caged needle bearing, number 2, from the hub of the case.

34. Lift out the number 1 thrust needle bearing.

35. Rotate the case as necessary. Install an allen wrench into the idler gear shaft, wedging the handle between the band anchor strut and the case. With a socket and breaker bar, remove the idler shaft locknut from the converter side of the case. Tap on the end of the shaft and remove the idler gear assembly from the case.

NOTE: Do not disassemble the gear assembly.

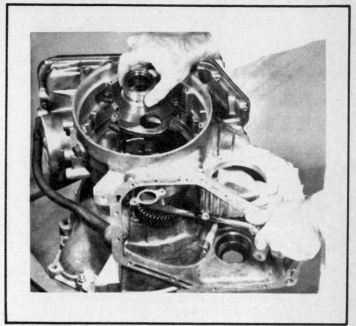

Remove the transfer housing (© Ford Motor Co.)

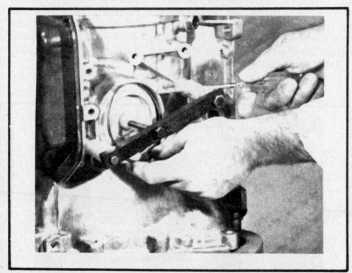

Removing the servo cover retaining snapring (© Ford Motor Co.)

Removal of the drum and sun gear assembly (© Ford Motor Co.)

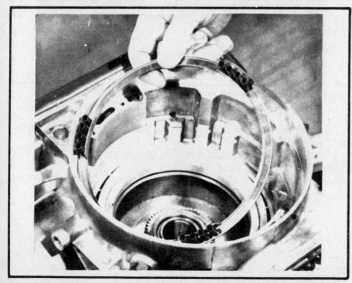

Removal of the reverse clutch return spring and damper assembly (© Ford Motor Co.)

Remove the low and intermediate band (© Ford Motor Co.)

Removal of the idler gear assembly (© Ford Motor Co.)

36. Inspect the reactor shaft for damage. Do not remove unless the shaft is considered unserviceable. Special puller tools are required, should this operation be needed. Proceed as follows:

a. Remove the reactor support retaining bolts (5).

b. With the special tool mounted in place, force the reactor support out of the case.

c. To install a new reactor support, place a guide pin in the new support and seat into the case with the special tools used as a press. Install the reactor support bolts and remove the guide pin. Torque the bolts to 6-8 ft. lbs. (8-11 N•m).

Sub Assemblies
MANUAL AND THROTTLE LINKAGE

Disassembly

NOTE: The manual and throttle linkage are normally not disassembled unless damaged linkage or leaking seals are encountered.

1. Remove the throttle valve outer lever retaining nut while holding the lever stationary.

— CAUTION —

Should the throttle lever be allowed to rotate, damage to the inner lever can result.

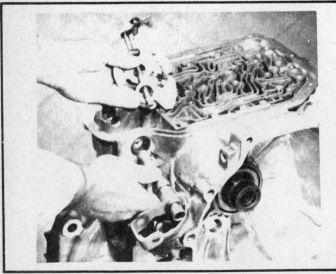

Manual and throttle linkage components (© Ford Motor Co.)

2. Remove the neutral start switch retaining screws and the neutral start switch.

3. Remove the manual lever retaining pin from the lever and shaft.

4. Remove the parking pawl ratcheting spring. Loosen and remove the inner manual lever (detent) and parking pawl actuating lever to manual shaft retaining nut.

5. Remove the manual lever and shaft assembly. With the manual lever out, the throttle valve lever and components can be removed.

6. Remove the parking pawl return spring. With the shaft out of the case, remove the manual lever shaft seal from the case. Remove the throttle valve lever shaft seal from the manual lever.

Assembly

1. Install the manual lever shaft seal in the case using a special seal installer, Ford Number T81P-70337-A or its equivalent.

2. Install the throttle lever shaft seal using an appropriate sized socket.

3. Install the parking pawl return spring.

4. Install the inner manual lever detent and parking pawl actuator attaching nut, the inner manual lever detent and the parking pawl actuator in the case, on the throttle shaft and insert the manual lever and shaft assembly into the case, over the throttle lever.

5. Position the parking pawl actuator and inner manual lever detent on the manual lever shaft and install the attaching nut. Tighten the nut securely.

6. Install the parking pawl ratcheting spring.

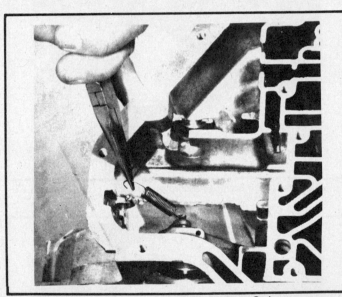

Installation of paking pawl spring (© Ford Motor Co.)

7. Install the manual lever retaining pin through the manual lever and into the shaft.

8. Install the neutral start switch and retaining screws. Do not tighten the retaining screws.

9. Install the outer throttle valve lever and adjust the neutral start switch, refering to the On-Car Adjustment section.

PUMP

Disassemby

1. Remove the number 12 thrust washer from the clutch support.

2. Remove the sealing rings from the clutch support.

3. Remove the pump to case seal from the outer circle of the pump. Matchmark the clutch support to the pump body.

Oil pump drive gear, driven gear and pump drive insert
(© Ford Motor Co.)

PUNCH MARK

Assembling driven gear to pump body with chamfered teeth and
center punch mark to the pump body (© Ford Motor Co.)

Seal locations on oil pump (© Ford Motor Co.)

GUIDE PINS

Use of guide pins to properly locate pump components during bolt
tightening (© Ford Motor Co.)

4. Remove the clutch support to pump body bolts (5) and separate the clutch support from the pump body.

5. Remove the insert from the pump drive gear and remove the pump driven gear. Remove the pump drive gear.

Inspection

1. Inspect the mating surfaces of the pump body and cover for burrs.

2. Inspect the drive and driven gear bearing surface for scores and check the gear teeth for burrs.

3. Check the fluid passages for obstructions.

4. If any of the parts are found to be worn or damaged, the pump should be replaced as a unit. Minor scores and burrs can be removed with crocus cloth.

Assembly

1. Install the pump drive and driven gears. Install the pump drive insert.

2. Position the clutch support on the pump body in its proper position. Use guide pins to align.

3. Install the clutch support to pump body retaining bolts (5) and torque to 6-8 ft. lbs. (8-11 N•m).

4. Install a new pump body to case seal in its groove on the pump body.

5. Install the seal rings on the clutch support. Overlap the scarf cuts properly.

6. Install the number 12 thrust washer on the clutch support.

INTERMEDIATE CLUTCH

Disassembly

1. Remove the intermediate shaft retaining snapring.

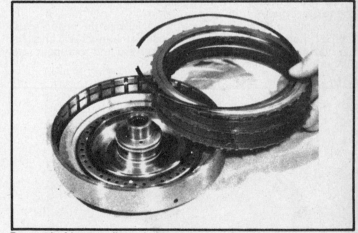

Removal of intermediate clutch pack (© Ford Motor Co.)

2. Remove the intermediate shaft from the intermediate clutch cylinder. Inspect the shaft stop ring and replace if damaged.

3. Remove the clutch pack retaining ring, remove the pressure plate and clutch pack. Remove the seal rings from the clutch cylinder hub.

4. With the use of a clutch spring compressor tool, Ford number T65L-77515-A or its equivalent, disengage the piston retaining snap ring. Slowly release the spring pressure and remove the tool from the clutch cylinder.

5. Remove the snapring and piston return spring retainer and remove the piston from the cylinder.

6. Remove the piston seal from the clutch cylinder and the seal from the clutch piston.

Removal or installation of the intermediate clutch return spring, using special spring removal tool (© Ford Motor Co.)

Inspection

1. Inspect the piston check ball. Be sure the ball is present and free in its cage.

2. Inspect the clutch piston bore and the piston inner and outer bearing surfaces for burrs or scores.

3. Check the clutch pressure plate for scores on the clutch plate bearing surfaces. Check the clutch release springs for distortion.

Assembly

1. Lubricate and install the seal, with the lip facing up, on the clutch piston.

2. Lubricate and install the seal, with the lip facing down, on the clutch cylinder hub.

3. Apply a light film of petroleum jelly to the piston seals, clutch cylinder seal area and the clutch piston inner seal area. Install the clutch piston by pushing downward and rotating it into its bore in the clutch cylinder.

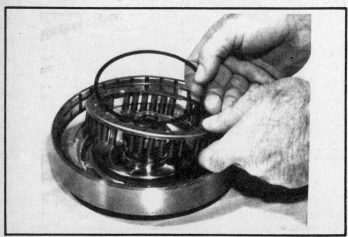

Installation of intermediate clutch return spring assembly into clutch cylinder (© Ford Motor Co.)

4. Position the piston return springs, retainer and piston retaining ring on the clutch cylinder.

5. Install the clutch spring compressor tool, depress the piston and return springs and install the piston retaining ring. Remove the clutch spring compressor tool carefully, being sure the retaining ring is in its groove.

6. Install the seal rings on the clutch cylinder hub. Be sure the scarf cut seals overlap at the bevel edge.

7. Soak the fiber clutch plates in transmission fluid and install the clutch plates in the following order:
    a. one steel plate next to piston
    b. one fiber plate
    c. one steel plate
    d. one fiber plate
    e. pressure plate
    f. selective snapring

8. Two methods of measuring clutch pack clearance of the intermediate clutch can be used.

Feeler Gauge Method—Measure the free play clearance between the pressure plate and the first fiber plate in two places, 180° apart, with a feeler gauge blade. If the feeler gauge reading is 0.020-0.035 inch (0.51-0.88 mm), the clearance is within specifications. If the reading is under 0.020 inch (0.51 mm), install a smaller selective snapring and re-measure. If the reading is over 0.035 inch (0.88 mm), install a thicker selective snapring and repeat the measurement procedure.

Measuring the clutch pack with the feeler gauge method (© Ford Motor Co.)

Install intermediate clutch shaft and retain with snapring (© Ford Motor Co.)

Dial Indicator Method—Position a dial indicator on the clutch cylinder hub with the stem touching the top of the pressure plate. Push downward on the clutch pack with at least 10 pounds of pressure. Release the pressure and zero the dial indicator. Lift the pressure plate with the thumbs of both hands and note the dial indicator reading. Take two readings, 180° apart and use the average of the two readings. The clearance should be 0.030-0.044 inch (0.75-1.22 mm) for three plates. If the clearance is not within limits, selective snaprings are available. Install the correct snapring and re-check the clearance.

9. The selective snaprings are available in the following thicknesses:

    0.049-0.053 inch (1.245-1.346 mm)
    0.059-0.063 inch (1.499-1.600 mm)
    0.070-0.074 inch (1.778-1.880 mm)

10. If removed, install the stop ring on the intermediate shaft and install the shaft into the clutch cylinder hub.

11. Install the intermediate shaft retaining ring.

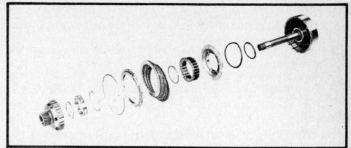

Exploded view of direct and one-way clutch assembly
(© Ford Motor Co.)

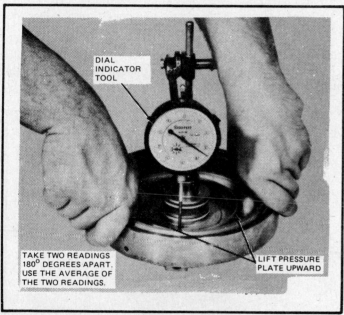

Measurement of the clutch pack with dial indicator method
(© Ford Motor Co.)

Use of special spring compression tool to remove and install the spring assembly and its retaining ring (© Ford Motor Co.)

DIRECT CLUTCH

Disassembly

1. Remove the ring gear off the one way clutch and direct clutch assembly, if not already off.

2. Lift the one way clutch outer race and the sun gear from the direct clutch.

3. Remove the number 8 thrust washer and the one way clutch.

4. Remove the clutch pack retaining snapring. Remove the pressure plate and clutch pack. Remove the number 9 brass thrust washer.

5. With the use of a clutch spring compressor tool, Ford number T81P-70235-A or its equivalent, remove the piston retaining snapring from the clutch cylinder.

6. Remove the piston return snapring retainer and remove the clutch piston.

NOTE: Snapring pliers can be used to aid in the piston removal.

7. Remove the piston seal and the clutch cylinder hub seal. Discard the seals.

Installation of the spring assembly and the retaining snapring in the clutch housing (© Ford Motor Co.)

Inspection

1. Inspect the piston check ball. Be sure the ball is present and free in its cage.

2. Inspect the clutch piston bore and the piston inner and outer bearing surfaces for burrs or scores.

3. Check the clutch pressure plate for scores on the clutch plate bearing surfaces. Check the clutch return springs for distortion.

Assembly

1. Lubricate and install the clutch cylinder hub seal with the lip facing downward.

2. Lubricate the install the seal on the piston with the seal lip facing upward.

3. Apply a light film of petroleum jelly to the piston and hub seals, the sealing areas and install the clutch piston into its bore in the clutch cylinder.

4. Position the piston return spring retainer and the piston retaining snapring in position on the clutch cylinder.

5. With the use of the clutch spring compressor tool, compress the clutch return springs and install the piston retaining snapring. Install the number 9 thrust washer.

6. Soak the fiber clutch plates in transaxle fluid. Install the clutch pack, starting with a steel plate, alterating the fiber and steel plates for a total of four fiber and four steel plates. Install the pressure plate and the selective retaining snapring.

7. Install the one way clutch and the number 8 thrust washer.

NOTE: When properly installed, the thrust washer tabs will be against the shoulder of the inner race.

8. Two methods of measuring the clutch pack clearance of the direct clutch can be used.
Feeler Gauge Method—Measure the free play clearance between the pressure plate and the first fiber plate, in two places, 180° apart, with a feeler gauge blade.

NOTE: If necessary, the one way clutch and the number 8 thrust washer can be removed until the measurements are completed.

If the feeler gauge reading is 0.031-0.047 inch (0.78-1.20 mm), the clearance is within specifications. If the reading is under 0.031 inch (0.78 mm), install a smaller selective snapring and remeasure. If the reading is over 0.047 inch (1.20 mm), install a thicker selective snapring and repeat the measurement procedure.

Dial Indicator Method—Position a dial indicator on the clutch cylinder hub with the stem touching the top of the pressure plate. Push downward on the clutch pack with at least a 10 pound pressure. Release the pressure and zero the dial indicator. Lift the pressure plate with the thumbs of both hands and note the dial indicator reading. Take two readings and average the results of the two readings, take 180° apart. The clearance, with four fiber friction plates, should be 0.040-0.056 inch (1.01-1.43 mm). If the clearance is not within specifications, selective snaprings are available. Install the correct snapring and re-check the clearance.

9. The selective snaprings are available in the following thicknesses:
   0.050-0.054 inch (1.26-1.36 mm)
   0.062-0.066 inch (1.58-1.68 mm)
   0.075-0.079 inch (1.90-2.00 mm)

10. If the one way clutch and the number 8 thrust washer was removed, install then into the clutch cylinder.

11. Install the sun gear/clutch race assembly into the clutch cylinder.

NOTE: The one way clutch allows the sun gear/clutch race to rotate in one direction only.

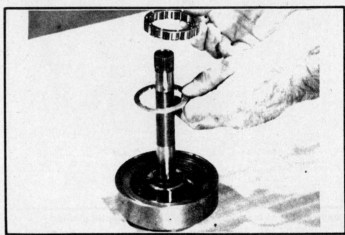

Assembling number 9 thrust washer and cage, roller and spring assembly with the smooth surface down (© Ford Motor Co.)

Installation of thrust washer number 8 and one-way clutch outer race and sun gear (© Ford Motor Co.)

Measurement of the direct clutch pack with the feeler gauge method (© Ford Motor Co.)

REVERSE CLUTCH

Disassembly

1. Remove the seals from the clutch cylinder and the clutch piston.

Inspection

1. Check the clutch cylinder and the clutch piston for scores or burrs.

Assembly

1. Install the new seal on the clutch piston with the lip facing upward.
2. Install the inner seal on the clutch cylinder with the lip facing down.
3. Install the outer clutch cylinder seal. The seal is square cut, making the direction of the seal unimportant.

BAND APPLY SERVO

Disassembly

1. Remove the piston spring and remove the servo piston from the cover.
2. Remove the piston rod retaining clip. Remove the rod, cushion spring and spring retainer washer from the piston.
3. Remove the seals from the servo cover. Remove the seals from the servo piston.

Inspection

1. Inspect the servo bore for cracks, burrs or scores.
2. Check the fluid passages for obstructions.
3. Inspect the servo spring and servo band struts for distortion or damage.
4. Check the servo piston for burrs or scores.

Assembly

1. Position the spring retainer washer and cushion spring on the servo rod. Install the spring and rod assembly in the servo piston.
2. Compress cushion spring and install the retaining clip.
3. Install the seals on the servo piston.
4. Install the seals on the servo cover.
5. Lubricate the piston seals with petroleum jelly and install the piston into the cover.
6. Install the piston return spring on the piston rod.

VALVE BODY

Disassembly

There is no definite disassembly procedure for the valve body components. When removing the valves and springs from the valve body, a channeled type holder should be be used to hold the valves and springs in their correct order, until their re-assembly. A general disassembly and assembly outline is suggested, but the step by step procedure will depend upon the discretion of the repairman.

─── **CAUTION** ───

During the disassembly or assembly of the valve body, do not turn the throttle valve adjusting screw. This adjustment is set during the manufacture of the valve body and must not be altered.

1. Remove the separator plate attaching screws, the separator plate and gasket.
2. Note the location of the check balls and the relief valve. Remove and set aside.

NOTE: 1981-82 transaxle models use six check balls in the valve body, while the 1983 and later models use only five check balls.

Installation of seals on the reverse clutch cylinder (© Ford Motor Co.)

Servo cover and piston seal locations (© Ford Motor Co.)

3. Remove the valve plug retainer, the valve plug, reverse boost valve and spring.
4. Remove the valve plug retainer, the valve plug, the 2-3 shift valve and valve spring.
5. Remove the valve plug retainer, the valve plug, the 1-2 shift valve, the 1-2 T. V. modulator valve and spring.
6. With the aid of a fabricated valve spring depressing tool, remove the valve spring retainer, the 2-1 scheduling valve and valve spring.
7. Remove the valve plug retainer, the valve plug, the 2-3 back-out valve and valve spring.
8. Remove the valve sleeve retainer, the main pressure boost sleeve, the main oil regulator valve, spring and spring retainer.
9. Remove the plug retainer, the valve plug, the manual low downshift valve and spring.
10. With the use of the fabricated valve spring depressing tool, remove the spring retainer, the 3-2 torque demand timing control valve and spring.
11. Depress the valve spring and remove the 3-2 kickdown timing valve and spring.
12. Depress the valve spring and remove the 3-2 control valve and spring.
13. Remove the plug retainer, the valve plug, the 2-3 shift T.V. modulator valve and spring.
14. Remove the plug retainer and remove the valve plug, the 1-2 capacity modulator valve and spring.

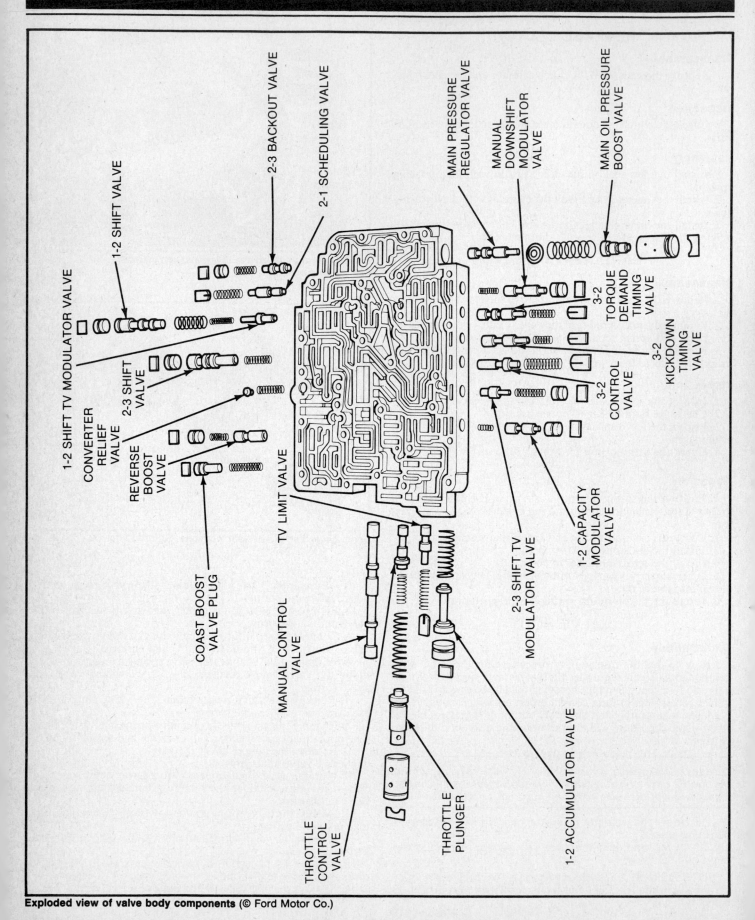

Exploded view of valve body components (© Ford Motor Co.)

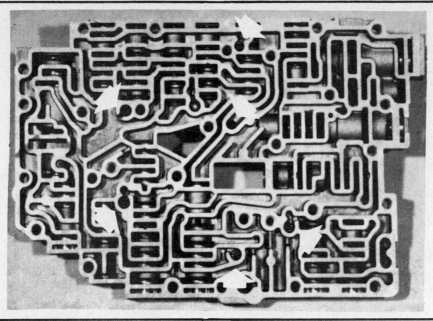

Position of the six check balls in the 1981-82 ATX transaxle models (© Ford Motor Co.)

15. Remove the valve plug retainer, the valve plug, the 1-2 accumulator valve and spring.

16. Depress the valve spring and remove the valve spring retainer, the T.V. limit valve and spring.

17. Remove the valve sleeve retainer, the throttle valve plunger sleeve, throttle pressure valve, throttle plunger return spring, throttle pressure valve and spring. Remove the washer and throttle pressure adjusting sleeve.

CAUTION

Do not turn the throttle valve adjusting screw. This adjustment is set during the manufacture and must not be altered.

---

18. Remove the manual control valve.

Inspection

1. Inspect all valves and plug bores for scores. Check all fluid passages for obstructions. Inspect the check valves for freedom of movement. Inspect all mating surfaces for burrs or distortion. If needed, polish the valves and plugs with crocus cloth to remove minor burrs or scores.

2. Inspect all springs for distortion.

3. Check all valves and plugs in their bores for freedom of movement. Valves and plugs, when dry, must fall from their own weight in their respective bores.

4. Roll the manual valve on a flat surface to check for a bent condition.

Assembly

The assembly of the valve body should follow, in principle, the disassembly procedure. However, the assembly will depend upon the discretion of the repairman. When the valves have all been installed, the completion of the assembly can be done as follows:

1. Install the check balls and relief valve in their proper seats in the valve body.

2. Install two alignment pins and the separator plate gasket.

3. Install the separator plate and attaching bolts. Torque the bolts to 80-90 *inch pounds* and remove the alignment pins.

TRANSFER HOUSING BEARING
Removal

1. Position the transfer housing in the case and install the attaching bolts to secure the housing.

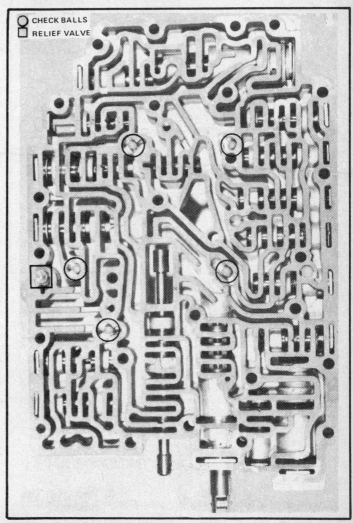

CHECK BALLS
RELIEF VALVE

Position of the five check balls in the 1983 and later ATX transaxle models (© Ford Motor Co.)

Temporarily install the transfer housing in the case to remove the bearing assembly (© Ford Motor Co.)

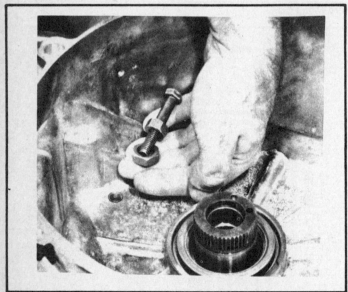

After threading the cup, install bolt and nut, along with an oversize nut as a spacer, to remove the cup from the case (© Ford Motor Co.)

2. Using a slide hammer type tool, remove the bearing from the transfer housing.

Installation

1. Remove the transfer housing from the case and support the housing from underneath.
2. Install the new bearing in the transfer housing with the use of a bearing installer tool.

NOTE: The transfer housing and the ATX transaxle case are matched parts. If one is damaged, both must be replaced.

PARKING PAWL AND BAND STRUT

Removal

1. Working in the converter housing, thread a ⅜ inch national coarse, bottoming type tap into the welsh plug, holding the parking pawl and band anchor pin in position.
2. Position a nut over the plug to act as a spacer.

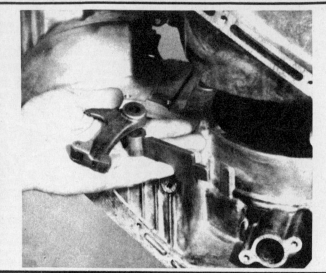

With the pin removed, the park pawl and band anchor strut can be removed (© Ford Motor Co.)

NOTE: The hole in the nut has to be larger than the diameter of the plug.

3. With the spacer nut in position, install a nut on a ⅜ inch—16 national coarse bolt and thread the bolt into the newly made threads of the plug.
4. Thread the nut on the bolt downward, against the spacer nut, causing the plug to move upward and out of the case.
5. With the use of a magnet, remove the parking pawl and band anchor pin from the case. Remove the parking pawl and band anchor from the case.

Installation

1. Position the parking pawl and band anchor in the case, with the band strut positioned closest to the pump housing end of the transaxle.
2. Install the parking pawl and band anchor pin in the transaxle case.
3. Position a new welsh plug in the case bore and seat with an appropriate tool.

NOTE: The threaded welsh plug can be re-used if necessary, if not damaged.

GOVERNOR DRIVEN GEAR

Removal

1. Support the governor assembly on a vise and remove the roll pin from the driven gear with a 3/32 inch drift.
2. Clamp the plastic driven gear in a vise, grip the governor body firmly, twist and pull the body at the same time, separating the driven gear from the governor drive shaft.

Installation

1. Align the driven gear to the governor drive shaft. Press the gear on the shaft as far as possible with hand pressure.
2. Be sure the governor gear is properly aligned with the governor drive shaft and tap the driven gear on the shaft with a soft faced hammer. The driven gear is in its proper position when the molded shoulder is seated against the governor body.
3. With the use of a drill press, if possible, drill a ⅛ inch hole through the plastic gear, in line with the hole in the governor drive shaft.
4. Supporting the governor assembly to protect the plastic driven gear, install a new roll pin through the gear and shaft.

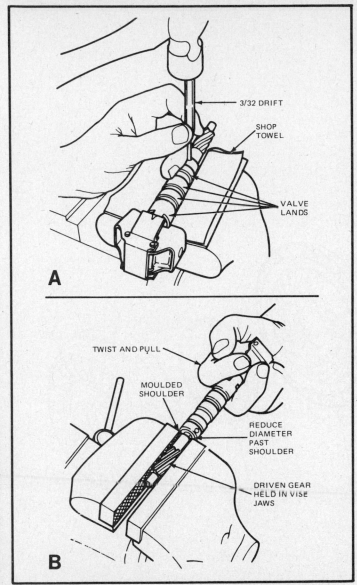

A—Removing the pin from the governor driven gear. B—Twisting the governor shaft from the driven gear (© Ford Motor Co.)

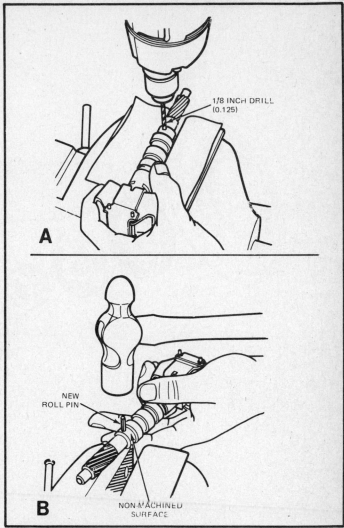

A—Drilling hole through the new governor driven gear. B—Installation of new roll pin (© Ford Motor Co.)

— CAUTION —

Do Not re-use the old roll pin.

CONVERTER ASSEMBLY

Reactor One-Way Clutch Check

NOTE: Special Tools are needed for this check.

1. Align the slot in the thrust washer with the slot in the holding lug.

NOTE: To align the slots, use tool, Ford number T81P-7902-B or its equivalent to turn the reactor.

2. Position the holding wire, Ford number T81P-7902-A or its equivalent, in the holding lug.

3. While holding the wire in position in the lug, install the one-way clutch torquing tool, Ford number T81P-7902-B or its equivalent, in the reactor spline.

4. Continue holding the wire and turn the torquing tool counterclockwise with a torque wrench. If the torquing tool begins to

Insert holding wire with tab and slot aligned in the converter, in order to lock the reactor (© Ford Motor Co.)

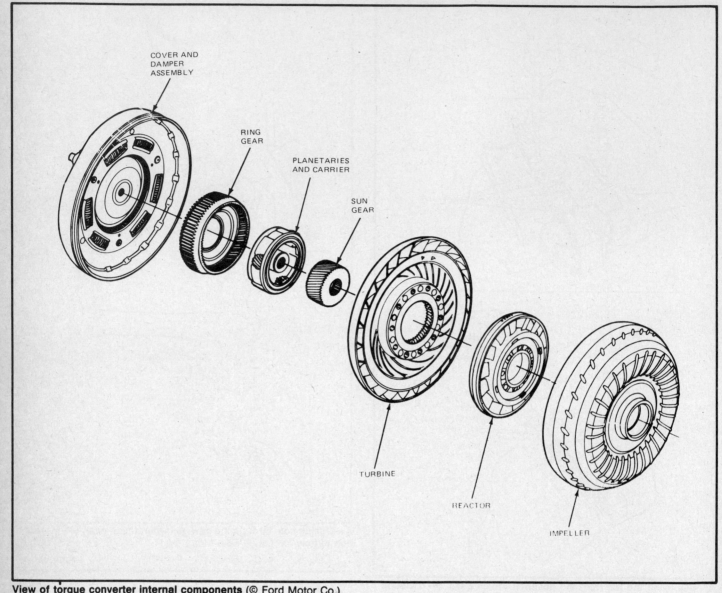

View of torque converter internal components (© Ford Motor Co.)

COVER AND
DAMPER
ASSEMBLY

RING
GEAR

PLANETARIES
AND CARRIER

SUN
GEAR

TURBINE

REACTOR

IMPELLER

Install one way clutch torquing tool into the converter hub
(© Ford Motor Co.)

With special end play checking tool in place, mount the dial indicator. Zero it and obtain the end play reading (© Ford Motor Co.)

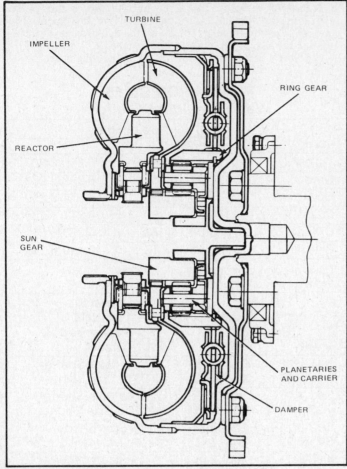

TURBINE

IMPELLER

RING GEAR

REACTOR

SUN GEAR

PLANETARIES AND CARRIER

DAMPER

Sectional view of torque converter (© Ford Motor Co.)

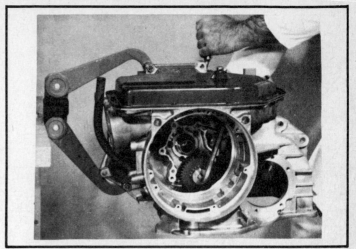

Holding the idler gear shaft with an Allen wrench (© Ford Motor Co.)

turn before the torque wrench reaches 10 ft. lbs. (13.5 N•m), replace the converter.

5. Remove the special tools.

Checking End Play of Converter

1. Insert the end play checking tool, T81P-7902-D or its equivalent, into the converter hub. Tighten the nut enough to permit lifting the converter by the handles of the tool.

2. Mount a dial indicator on the special mounting block and zero the dial indicator, with the stylus on the outer portion of the converter.

3. Lift the converter and observe the dial indicator reading. The reading should not exceed 0.023 inch (0.58 mm). If the reading is exceeded, replace the converter.

— CAUTION —

In cases where the end play is zero, the internal rotational friction must not exceed 5 ft. lbs. (6.7 N•m). Check by using torquing tool T81P-7902-B or its equivalent, but without using the holding wire.

TRANSAXLE ASSEMBLY

1. Place the transaxle case in the holding tool and position the case with the converter housing upright.

2. Install a new "O" ring on the idler gear shaft and install the shaft into the case. Position the idler gear on the shaft from the inside of the case.

3. Install an Allen wrench in the idler gear shaft and allow it to turn until the wrench catches on the band anchor strut. Install thread locking sealant to the attaching nut and tighten to 110-130 ft. lbs. (149-176 N•m) for the 1981-82 models, and 80-100 ft. lbs. (108-136 N•m) for 1983 and later models. Remove the Allen wrench.

4. Turn the transaxle case over and lock into position. Install the number 1 thrust bearing on the support assembly.

5. Install the input gear caged bearing on the support assembly. Install the input gear. Install the number 3 needle thrust bearing on the input gear.

6. Position the transfer housing in the case, making sure it is firmly seated on the alignment dowels. Install the transfer housing bolts and tighten to 15-19 ft. lbs. (20-26 N•m) for 1981-82 models and 18-23 ft. lbs. (24-32 N•m) for 1983 and later models.

— CAUTION —

Before installing the transfer housing, be sure the band strut is rotated to its operating position.

NOTE: The transaxle case and the housing are matched parts. If one is damaged, both must be replaced.

7. Install the number 4 thrust washer on the transfer housing.

8. Install the sun gear and the drum assembly. Install the intermediate band, making sure the band lug engages the strut.

Installing the drum and sun gear into position, within the band (© Ford Motor Co.)

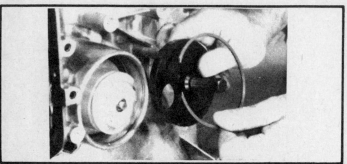

Install servo piston selection disc tool in place and retain with snap ring (© Ford Motor Co.)

Taking measurement with dial indicator and torque wrench (© Ford Motor Co.)

9. The servo travel check must be made at this time, if any of the following components have been changed during the overhaul.

NOTE: It is a good practice to do the servo travel check whenever the unit is disassembled and assembled.

a. Transaxle case
b. Band assembly
c. Drum and sun gear assembly
d. Servo piston
e. Servo piston rod
f. Band anchor strut

Special tools are required to perform the servo travel check. Ford Tool numbers are as follows;

a. Return spring—T81P-70027-A
b. Servo piston selector tool—T81P-70023-A
c. Dial indicator—TOOL-4201-C

These tools or their equivalents must be used to determine the length of the servo piston rod to be used.

Procedure

a. If necessary, clean and assemble the servo piston. Do not install the piston seals. This check is performed without the seals on the piston.

b. Install the return spring, Ford number T81P-70027-A or its equivalent, on the servo rod and position the rod in the servo bore of the case.

c. Install the servo piston selector tool, Ford number T81P-70023-A or its equivalent, in the servo bore and secure it with the servo cover snapring.

d. Tighten the gauge disc screw to 10 ft. lbs. (13.5 N•m).

e. Mount the dial indicator, Ford number TOOL-4201-C or its equivalent, to the transaxle case and position the indicator stylus through the hole in the gauge disc. Be sure the stylus has contacted the servo piston and zero the dial indicator.

f. Back off the gauge disc screw until the piston movement stops and read the dial indicator total piston movement. The amount of piston travel as shown on the dial indicator will determine the servo rod length to be installed.

g. Select a piston rod from the accompanying chart.

PISTON ROD SIZES
With Paint Identification

I.D. Color①	Rod Length②	
	MM	Inch
Yellow	160.52-160.22	6.319/6.307
Green	159.91-159.61	6.295/6.283
Red	159.30-159.00	6.271/6.259
Black	158.69-158.39	6.247/6.235
Orange	158.08-157.78	6.223/6.211
Blue	157.47-157.17	6.199/6.187

① Daub of paint on tip or rod.
② From far end of snap ring groove to end ot rod.

For This Dial Indicator Reading		Install A New Piston Rod That Is . . .
MM	Inch	
2.45-2.98	.096-.117	5th Size Shorter
3.05-3.58	.120-.141	4th Size Shorter
3.65-4.18	.144-.165	3rd Size Shorter
4.25-4.78	.167-.188	2nd Size Shorter
5.12-5.14	.202-.202	1 Size Shorter
5.15-6.28	.203-.247	NO CHANGE
6.29-6.31	.248-.248	1 Size Longer
6.65-7.18	.262-.283	2nd Size Longer
7.25-7.78	.285-.306	3rd Size Longer
7.85-8.38	.309-.330	4th Size Longer
8.45-8.98	.333-.353	5th Size Longer

NOTE: For readings not on Table, select nearest one and repeat measurement with the new rod.

PISTON ROD SIZES
With Groove Identification

I.D	Rod Length①	
	mm	Inch
0 Groove	160.22-160.52	6.313-6.324
1 Grooves	159.61-159.90	6.289-6.300
2 Grooves	159.00-159.30	6.265-6.276
3 Grooves	158.39-158.69	6.240-6.252
4 Grooves	157.78-158.08	6.216-6.189
5 Grooves	157.17-157.47	6.197-6.209

① From far end of snap ring groove to end of rod.

If the dial indicator reads:

Less than 5.15mm (used) Less than 5.15mm (new) (.203 in.) The piston rod is too long. A shorter rod (more grooves) will have to be installed.	More than 2.04mm (used) More than 6.28mm (new) (.247 in.) The piston rod is too short. A longer rod (less grooves) will have to be installed.	5.15-2.04mm (used) 5.15-6.28mm (new) (.203-.247 in.) The piston rod is the correct length and no change is required.

10. Install the piston seals on the piston and install it into its bore in the case. Using the servo piston remover/installing tool, Ford Number T81P-70027-A or its equivalent, compress the piston spring far enough to allow installation of the retaining ring. Remove the tool.

NOTE: Before removing the compressing tool, be sure the piston rod has engaged to band lug.

11. Position the reverse clutch cylinder in the case, tapping it in place with a hammer handle.

Measuring reverse clutch pack clearance (© Ford Motor Co.)

Preparing seals on the reverse clutch piston and cylinder (© Ford Motor Co.)

12. Install the reverse clutch piston in the clutch cylinder, using the seal protector, Ford Number T81P-70402-A or its equivalent. Apply even pressure when installing the piston in the drum.

13. Install the number 5 thrust washer on the planetary assembly, holding it in place with petroleum jelly. Install the planetary on the sun gear in the case.

14. Install the reverse clutch return spring and holder assembly.

15. To check the reverse clutch pack clearance, use the following procedure.

a. This check has to be made without the piston return spring and holder assembly in position and with the clutch pack installed. After the clutch pack clearance is made, the clutch pack is removed and the spring and retainer holder assembly installed.

b. Install the clutch pack wave spring, the clutch pack, starting with a steel plate, fiber plate, steel plate, fiber plate, pressure plate and the selective sized snapring.

c. Using a feeler gauge, measure the clearance between the snapring and the pressure plate in two places, 180° apart while holding a downward pressure of 10 pounds (40 N) on the clutch pack.

d. If the average reading is 0.018-0.039 inch (0.46-1.00 mm) for the 1981-82 models, and 0.030-0.053 inch (0.76-1.35 mm) for the 1983 and later models, the clutch pack clearance is within specifications.

e. If the reading is below 0.018 inch (0.46 mm) on the 1981-82 models, and below 0.030 (0.76 mm) for the 1983 and later models, install a thinner selective snapring and re-check the clearance.

f. If the measurement is more than 0.039 inch (1.00 mm) for the 1981-82 models, and more than 0.053 inch (1.35 mm) on the 1983 and later models, install a thicker selective snapring and re-check the clutch pack clearance.

g. Remove the retaining snapring and clutch pack assembly. Install the reverse clutch return spring and holder assembly, the clutch pack assembly and the retaining snapring.

16. Install the number 7 thrust needle bearing on the planetary gear assembly.

17. Install the intermediate clutch hub and ring gear assembly.

18. Install the direct clutch assembly and install the number 10 thrust needle bearing on the direct clutch housing.

19. Install the intermediate clutch with a rotating movement side to side, to engage the clutch plates with the hub.

REVERSE CLUTCH
Selective Snap Rings

Thickness	Part No.
1.89-1.94 mm (.074-.076 inch)	N800654
2.33-2.43 mm (.092-.096 inch)	N800655
2.77-2.87 mm (.109-.113 inch)	N800656
3.21-3.31 mm (.126-.130 inch)	N800657
For This Clearance Reading	**Install a New Ring That Is . . .**
0.12-0.46 mm (.005-.018 inch)	One Size THINNER
1.02-1.32 mm (.040-.052 inch)	One Size THICKER
1.45-1.75 mm (.057-.069 inch)	2nd Size THICKER
1.88-2.26 mm (.074-.089 inch)	3rd Size THICKER

Placement of measuring bar and depth micrometer for end play check (© Ford Motor Co.)

Measurement of end play in two places, necessary to obtain an average reading (© Ford Motor Co.)

20. To check the clutch for proper engagement, use the number 11 thrust bearing. Position the thrust bearing on one of the machined tabs and push it up against the case. If the thrust bearing is flush with or slightly below the machined pump housing surface, the clutch is fully engaged.

21. Install the number 11 thrust needle bearing. Install alignment pins, Ford number T80L-77100-A or their equivalent, into the transaxle case oil pump bolt holes, 180° apart. Install the pump housing gasket on the case.

22. Check the transaxle end play with the appropriate special tools, Ford numbers T81P-77389-A (end play alignment cup), T80L-77003-A (gauge bar) or their equivalents.

NOTE: The end play setting is critical. It must be properly checked to assure success in the rebuilding process.

   a. Position the assembled tools in the intermediate clutch center bore. Be sure the gauge bar rests on the pump to case gasket.

   b. Position a depth micrometer (0-1 inch) on the gauge bar and through the inner hole in the bar, to measure against the surface of the thrust washer bearing.

   c. Seat the micrometer and measur apart, and average the readings. Locate the accompanying chart and select the n er from the selection.

NOTE: If needed, refer to the accompa nesses of the number 12 thrust washer.

   d. Remove the tools from the transa

END PLAY ADJUSTMENT ME

For This Reading	W
.779-.796 inch (19.78-20.22 mm)	
.789-.804 inch (20.04-20.42 mm)	
.797-.812 inch (20.24-20.62 mm)	
.807-.825 inch (20.50-20.95 mm)	

WASHER THICKNE

Inch	MM
.055-.057	1.40-1.45
.063-.065	1.60-1.65
.071-.073	1.80-1.85
.081-.083	2.05-2.10

23. Install the correct number 12 thrust w body.

NOTE: The use of petroleum jelly will hold to the pump body during its installation.

24. Position the pump body in the case, us and tap into position. Start the retaining bol two guide pins. Torque the bolts to 7-9 ft. lbs

Installation of pump assembly over the two guide (© Ford Motor Co.)

NOTE: The washers on the pump retaining bolts provide the bolt seal and must not be substituted. Failure to use the sealing washers may result in a transaxle fluid leak.

25. Install the differential assembly by sliding the unit in and then down.

26. Differential Bearing End Play Check—The differential bearing end play is set during the manufacture and does not need to be checked or adjusted unless one or more of the following components have been replaced: transaxle case, differential case, differential bearings and differential bearing retainer.

Tapered roller differential bearings were used on early transaxle models and later changed to ball bearings. Both types could be encountered when overhauling numerous ATX transaxles. The end play adjustment is basically the same for both type bearings, but with different measurement specifications.

a. Remove the differential seal and bearing retainer "O" ring from the differential bearing retainer.

b. Position the differential assembly in place and install the differential retainer in the transaxle case.

c. Install the shim selector spacer tool, Ford number T81P-4451-A or its equivalent, in units equipped with tapered bearings and shim selector spacer tool, Ford number T83P-4451-BA or its equivalent, in units equipped with ball bearings. Place the shim selector spacer tool in the center of the differential seal bore of the differential retainer.

NOTE: The measurement of the T83P-4451-BA spacer or its equivalent must be 0.053 inch (1.35 mm) thick.

d. Position the gauge bar, Ford number T81P-4451-A or its equivalent, accross the differential bearing retainer and snugly hand tighten two attaching bolts to hold the gauge bar in place.

e. Tighten the center screw on the gauge bar and rotate the differential assembly several times to seat the bearings. Torque the center screw to 10 *inch pounds,* rotate the differential assembly and recheck the center screw torque.

f. With the use of feeler gauge blades, measure the clearance between the bearing retainer and the case.

NOTE: Be sure there are no burrs on the case mounting surfaces to hinder the blade measurement.

g. Obtain measurements from three positions around the bearing retainer to case gap. Take an average of the three clearance readings.

Example:

1st Reading	0.075 inch (1.91 mm)
2nd Reading	0.074 inch (1.88 mm)
3rd Reading	0.076 inch (1.91 mm)
Average of the three readings	0.075 inch (1.91 mm)

h. Tapered roller bearing type units—To determine the shim thickness needed, subtract the standard "Interference Factor" of 0.048 inch (1.22 mm), which includes 0.018 inch (0.46 mm) preload, plus the 0.030 inch (0.76 mm) tapered shim.

Example:

Average Reading	0.075 inch (1.91 mm)
Interference factor	0.048 inch (1.22 mm)
Shim size needed	0.027 inch (0.69 mm)

Select the proper shim from the accompanying chart. For odd numbered shim requirements, use the next *larger* shim.

i. Ball bearing type units—To determine the shim thickness needed, subtract the average reading from the thickness of the shim spacer tool, which is constant.

Example:

Constant reading	0.053 inch (1.35 mm)
Average reading	0.025 inch (0.63 mm)
Shim required	0.028 inch (0.72 mm)

Select the proper shim from the accompanying chart. For odd numbered shim requirements, use the next *smaller* shim.

Use of special tools to measure differential bearing end play (© Ford Motor Co.)

DIFFERENTIAL BEARING END PLAY SHIMS

Part No.	Inch	MM
E1FZ-4067-A	0.012	0.30
B	0.014	0.35
C	0.016	0.40
D	0.018	0.45
E	0.020	0.50
F	0.022	0.55
G	0.024	0.60
H	0.026	0.65
J	0.028	0.70
K	0.030	0.75
L	0.032	0.80
M	0.033	0.85
N	0.035	0.90
P	0.037	0.95
R	0.039	1.00
S	0.041	1.05
T	0.043	1.10
U	0.045	1.15
V	0.047	1.20
W	0.049	1.25
X	0.051	1.30

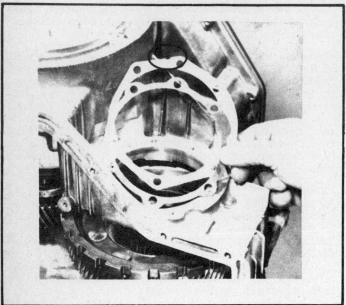

Position notch in proper position when using the copper colored tapered shim (© Ford Motor Co.)

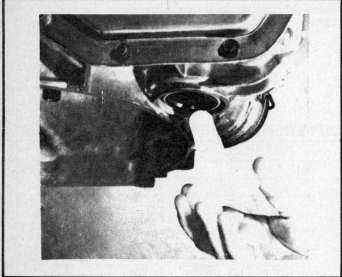

Installation of plastic plug in the differential opening (© Ford Motor Co.)

j. Remove the special tools and differential bearing retainer from the transaxle. Install the oil seal and the "O" ring on the bearing retainer for installation.

27. Position the differential shims, as required by model and install a new seal on the differential retainer and position the retainer in the case. It will be necessary to tap the retainer into the case to properly seat it.

28. Apply a hardening sealer to the threads of the retaining bolts and install. Torque to 15-19 ft. lbs. (20-26 N•m).

29. Install a new seal on the filter and install to the case. Install the retaining bolts and torque to 7-9 ft. lbs. (9-12 N•m).

30. Install the oil pan with a new gasket, torquing the pan bolts to 15-19 ft. lbs. (20-26 N•m). Rotate the transaxle housing assembly and install new differential end seals and the converter hub seal, using seal installer tools. Install the plastic plug in the differential opening.

Installation of governor assembly (© Ford Motor Co.)

31. Install a new seal on the speedometer gear retainer and install it in the case. Tap into position and install the retaining pin.

NOTE: Be sure the flat of the speedometer gear retainer is properly positioned to the case before installing the pin.

32. Install the governor in its bore of the case. Install a new governor cover seal and install the cover. Be sure the cover is properly seated and install the retaining wire clip.

33. Rotate the gear box as required and install the governor filter in the valve body channel of the case.

34. Using alignment pins, install the valve body gasket. Install the valve body. Connect the throttle valve control spring to the separator late and install the Z-link in the manual valve while positioning the valve body on the case. Be sure the roller on the end of the throttle valve plunger has engaged the cam on the end of the throttle lever shaft.

NOTE: One alignment pin has to be removed to allow the Z-link to be installed in the manual valve. When installed, replace the alignment pin.

35. Install the detent spring and roller assembly to the valve body. Install the main oil pressure regulator and transmission control baffle plates.

NOTE: The main oil pressure regulator plate uses longer bolts.

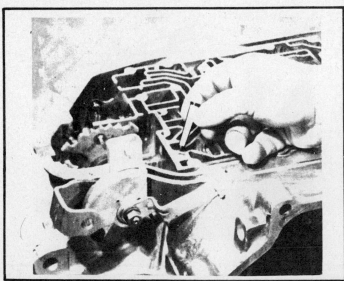

Installation of governor filter (© Ford Motor Co.)

36. Tighten the valve body attaching bolts in a specific sequence and to specifications of 72-96 *inch pounds* (8-11 N•m).

37. Install the throttle lever return spring to the spring anchor on the throttle lever.

NOTE: Be sure of installation of the spring as this spring applies T.V. if the T.V. linkage should disconnect or break.

38. Position the manual lever in the Neutral position and hold it there. Insert a 3/32 inch drill or pin through the aligning hole in the switch. Move the neutral switch until the drill or pin seats in the case. Torque the two retaining bolts to 7-9 ft. lbs. (9-12 N•m).

39. Using guide pins, install a new valve body cover gasket on the transaxle case. Install the valve body cover and install the retaining bolts. Torque the bolts to 7-9 ft. lbs. (9-12 N•m).

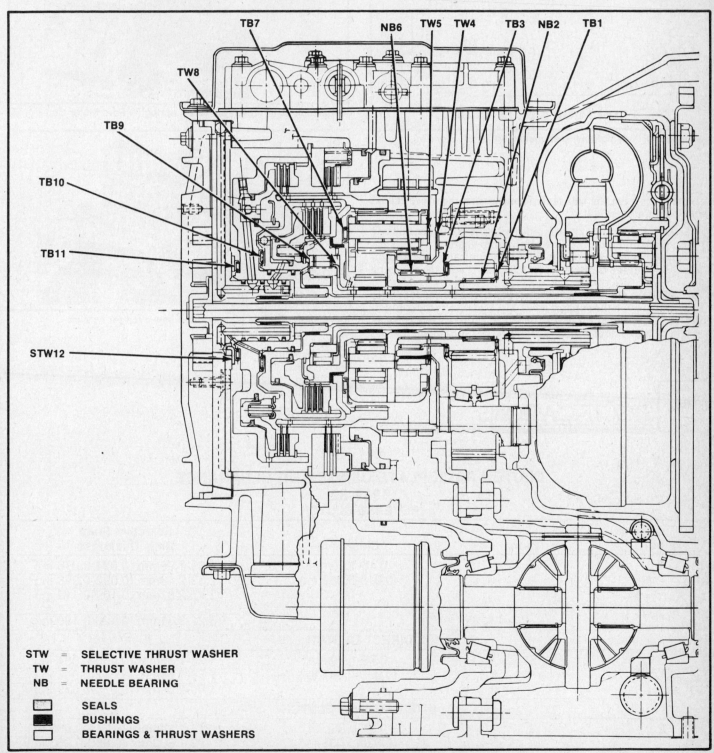

STW = SELECTIVE THRUST WASHER
TW = THRUST WASHER
NB = NEEDLE BEARING

SEALS
BUSHINGS
BEARINGS & THRUST WASHERS

Location of thrust washers, bushings and needle bearings in the ATX transaxle (© Ford Motor Co.)

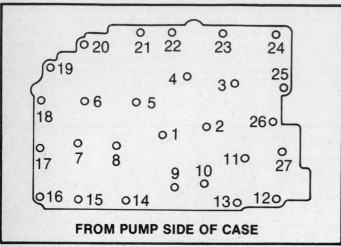

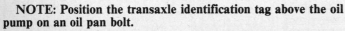

FROM PUMP SIDE OF CASE

Correct valve body tightening sequence (© Ford Motor Co.)

Installation of throttle lever return spring (© Ford Motor Co.)

Installation of baffle plate and the seven longer screws
(© Ford Motor Co.)

NOTE: Position the transaxle identification tag above the oil pump on an oil pan bolt.

40. Rotate the transaxle assembly with the converter housing in the up position and install the oil pump shaft.

41. Install a new seal on the fluid level indicator tube and install the tube in the transaxle case, retaining it with the attaching bolt.

42. With the aid of lifting handles, install the torque converter into its position on the support assembly. By twisting the converter during the installation, it will be felt to drop twice into place.

43. The transaxle assembly can now be installed in the vehicle.

SPECIFICATIONS

CLUTCH PACK PLATE USAGE AND CLEARANCE
1981-82
REVERSE CLUTCH

Steel	Friction	Clearance	Selective Snap Ring Thickness
2	2	0.46-1.00mm (0.018-0.039 in.)	1.89-1.99mm (0.074-0.078 in.)
			2.33-2.43mm (0.092-0.096 in.)
			2.77-2.87mm (0.109-0.113 in.)
			3.21-3.31mm (0.126-0.130 in.)
DIRECT CLUTCH			
3	3	0.78-1.20mm (0.031-0.047 in.)	1.26-1.36mm (0.050-0.054 in.)
			1.58-1.68mm (0.062-0.066 in.)
			1.90-2.00mm (0.075-0.079 in.)
INTERMEDIATE CLUTCH			
2	2	0.51-0.88mm (0.020-0.035 in.)	1.245-1.346mm (0.049-0.053 in.)
			1.499-1.600mm (0.060-0.063 in.)
			1.778-1.880mm (0.070-0.074 in.)

CLUTCH PACK PLATE USAGE AND CLEARANCE
1983

Steel	Friction	Clearance	Selective Snap Ring Thickness
		REVERSE CLUTCH	
2 or 3	2 or 3	0.76-1.40mm (0.030-0.055 in.)	1.89-1.99mm (0.074-0.078 in.)
			2.33-2.43mm (0.092-0.096 in.)
			2.77-2.87mm (0.109-0.113 in.)
			3.21-3.31mm (0.126-0.130 in.)
		DIRECT CLUTCH	
3	3	0.78-1.20mm (0.031-0.047 in.)	1.26-1.36mm (0.050-0.054 in.)
			1.58-1.68mm (0.062-0.066 in.)
4	4	1.01-1.43mm (0040-0.056 in.)	1.90-2.00mm (0.075-0.079 in.)
		INTERMEDIATE CLUTCH	
2	2	0.56-0.88mm (0.022-0.035 in.)	1.24-1.34mm (0.049-0.053 in.)
			1.51-1.61mm (0.060-0.064 in.)
3	3	0.75-1.12mm (0.030-0.044 in.)	1.78-1.88mm (0.071-0.075 in.)

1984

Steel	Friction	Clearance	Selective Snap Ring Thickness
		REVERSE CLUTCH	
3*	3*	0.76-1.40mm (0.030-0.055 in.)	1.89-1.99mm (0.074-0.078 in.)
			2.33-2.43mm (0.092-0.096 in.)
			2.77-2.87mm (0.109-0.113 in.)
			3.21-3.31mm (0.126-0.130 in.)

*With Cushion Spring

Steel	Friction	Clearance	Selective Snap Ring Thickness
		DIRECT CLUTCH	
4	4	1.01-1.43mm (0.040-0.056 in.)	1.26-1.36mm (0.050-0.054 in.)
			1.58-1.68mm (0.062-0.066 in.)
			1.90-2.00mm (0.075-0.079 in.)
		INTERMEDIATE CLUTCH	
3	3	0.75-11.12mm (0.030-0.044 in.)	1.24-1.34mm (0.049-0.053 in.)
			1.51-1.61mm (0.060-0.064 in.)
			1.78-1.88mm (0.071-0.075 in.)

SERVO PISTON TRAVEL

Year	Acceptable Travel①	Available Rod Lengths②	Identification
1981-82	5.5-6.28mm (0.203-0.247)	157.4-157.7mm (6.197-6.209 in.)	0 Groove
		156.8-157.1mm (6.173-6.185 in.)	1 Groove
		156.2-156.5mm (6.161-6.173 in.)	2 Groove
		155.6-155.9mm (6.125-6.138 in.)	3 Groove
		155.0-155.3mm (6.102-6.144 in.)	4 Groove
		154.4-154.7mm (6.079-6.091 in.)	5 Groove

311

SERVO PISTON TRAVEL

	Acceptable Travel①	Available Rod Lengths②	Identification
1983-84	5.15-7.04mm (0.203-0.277 inch)	160.22-160.52mm (6.313-6.324 inch)	0 Groove
		159.61-159.90mm (6.289-6.300 inch)	1 Groove
		159.00-159.30mm (6.265-6.276 inch)	2 Groove
		158.39-158.69mm (6.240-6.252 inch)	3 Groove
		157.78-158.08mm (6.216-6.189 inch)	4 Groove
		157.17-157.47mm (6.197-6.209 inch)	5 Groove

① Rod Stroke—not piston stroke
② Measured from far end of snap ring groove to end of rod

TRANSAXLE END PLAY
1981-84

Measured Depth	Thrust Washer Required	Identification Code
2.00-1.77mm (0.079-0.070 inch)	1.40-1.45mm (0.055-0.057 inch)	AA
2.20-2.00mm (0.087-0.079 inch)	1.60-1.65mm (0.063-0.065 inch)	BA
2.41-2.20mm (0.095-0.087 inch)	1.80-1.85mm (0.071-0.073 inch)	CA
1.77-1.46mm (0.070-0.057 inch)	1.15-1.20mm (0.045-0.047 inch)	EA

SHIFT POINTS
1983

		PMA-K3		PMA-P		PMA-R1	
		Base Engine		EFI Engine		HO Engine	
Drive Range		km/h	mph	km/h	mph	km/h	mph
Idle:	1-2	16-30	10-19	16-30	10-19	16-30	10-19
	2-3	24-50	15-31	24-50	15-31	24-50	15-31
	3-2	22-40	14-25	22-40	14-25	22-40	14-25
	2-1	16-24	10-15	16-24	10-15	16-24	10-15
Part Throttle:	1-2	18-27	11-17	18-27	11-17	18-27	11-17
	2-3	43-72	27-45	38-67	24-42	43-72	27-45
	3-2	38-67	24-42	32-61	20-38	38-67	24-42
WOT:	1-2	46-72	29-45	54-82	34-51	54-82	34-51
	2-3	94-118	59-74	98-125	61-78	98-125	61-78
	3-2	83-109	52-68	88-117	55-73	88-117	55-73
	2-1	35-61	22-38	45-70	28-44	45-70	28-44
Manual Low:	2-1	32-61	20-38	32-61	20-38	32-61	20-38

Axle Ratio: 3.3:1
Tire Size: P165/70R13, P165/80R13

SHIFT POINTS
1981-82

Drive Range		MPH
Idle:	1-2	10-17
	2-3	16-31
	3-2	14-22
	2-1	9-14
Part Throttle:	1-2	17-32
	2-3	29-46
	3-2	24-42
	2-1	13-20
WOT:	1-2	29-46
	2-3	58-75
	3-2	51-67
	2-1	19-35
Manual Low:	2-1	21-38

SHIFT POINTS
1984

		PMA-N	
		2.3L HSC Engine	
Drive Range		km/h	mph
Idle:	1-2	17-29	11-18
	2-3	25-50	16-31
	3-2	26-40	16-25
	2-1	15-23	9-14
Part Throttle:	1-2	19-44	12-27
	2-3	42-70	26-43
	3-2	36-45	22-41
WOT:	1-2	38-66	23-41
	2-3	84-112	52-69
	3-2	76-102	49-64
	2-1	24-51	15-32
Manual Low:	2-1	32-61	20-38

Axle Ratio: 3.3:1
Tire Size: P165/70R13, P165/80R13

LINE PRESSURE
1981-82

	Pressure (At Idle)		Pressure (WOT Stall)	
Range	kPa	PSI	kPa	PSI
D-2-1	296-400	43-58	724-875	105-127
R	483-724	70-105	1585-1965	230-285
P-N	296-400	43-58	NA	

NOTE: Governor Pressure is at zero (vehicle stationary). Transaxle is at operating temperature.

LINE PRESSURE
1983

	Pressure (At Idle)		Pressure (WOT Stall)			
	All Engines		Base		HO and EFI	
Range	kPa	PSI	kPa	PSI	kPa	PSI
D-2-1	377-455	54-66	669-779	97-113	731-841	106-122
R	531-765	77-111	1434-1793	208-260	1600-1958	232-284
P-N	377-455	54-66	669-779	97-113	731-841	106-122

NOTE: Governor Pressure is at zero (vehicle stationary). Transaxle is at operating temperature.

LINE PRESSURE
1984

Transaxle Model	Range	Pressure (At Idle)		Pressure (WOT Stall)	
		kPa	PSI	kPa	PSI
PMA-N	D-2-1-P-N	338-420	49-61	655-765	95-111
	R	455-689	66-100	1413-1772	205-257
PMA-U, V	D-2-1-P-N	—	54-66	—	106-122
PMB-C, D	R	—	77-111	—	232-284

NOTE: Governor Pressure is at zero (vehicle stationary). Transaxle is at operating temperature.

TORQUE CHART

Description	N•m	ft. lbs.
Reactor Support to Case	8-11	6-8
Separator Plate to Valve Body	8-11	6-8
Filler Tube Bracket to Case	9-12	7-9
Filter to Case	9-12	7-9
Valve Body Cover to Case	9-12	7-9
Pump Support to Pump Body	8-11	6-8
Natural Safety Switch to Case	9-12	7-9
Pump Assembly to Case	9-12	7-9
Valve Body to Case	8-11	72-96 (in. lbs.)
Oil Pan to Case	20-26	15-19
Lower Ball Joint to Steering Knuckle	50-60	37-44
Transfer Housing to Case ①	24-32	18-23
Differential Retainer to Case (with Sealant)	20-26	15-19
Pressure Test Port Plugs to Case ②	5-11	4-8
Cooler Tube Fitting to Case	24-31	18-23
Outer Throttle Lever to Shaft Nut ③	10-13	7.5-9.5
Inner Manual Lever to Shaft Nut	43-65	32-48
Idler Shaft Attaching ④	108-136	80-100
Converter Drain Plug	10-16	8-12
Valve Body Retaining Bolts	8-11	6-8
T.V. Adjuster Locknut	2.7-4.1	24-36 (in. lbs.)

① 1981-82—20-26 N•m, 15-19 ft. lbs.
② 1981-82—9-15 N•m, 7-11 ft. lbs.
③ 1981-82—16-20 N•m, 12-15 ft. lbs.
④ 1981-82—149-176 N•m, 110-130 ft. lbs.

PISTON ROD SIZES
With Paint Identification

I.D. Color ①	Rod Length ② MM	Rod Length ② Inch
Yellow	160.52-160.22	6.319/6.307
Green	159.91-159.61	6.295/6.283
Red	159.30-159.00	6.271/6.259
Black	158.69-158.39	6.247/6.235
Orange	158.08-157.78	6.223/6.211
Blue	157.47-157.17	6.199/6.187

① Daub of paint on tip or rod.
② From far end of snap ring groove to end of rod.

For This Dial Indicator Reading MM	For This Dial Indicator Reading Inch	Install A New Piston Rod That Is . . .
2.45-2.98	.096-.117	5th Size Shorter
3.05-3.58	.120-.141	4th Size Shorter
3.65-4.18	.144-.165	3rd Size Shorter
4.25-4.78	.167-.188	2nd Size Shorter
5.12-5.14	.202-.202	1 Size Shorter
5.15-6.28	.203-.247	NO CHANGE
6.29-6.31	.248-.248	1 Size Longer
6.65-7.18	.262-.283	2nd Size Longer
7.25-7.78	.285-.306	3rd Size Longer
7.85-8.38	.309-.330	4th Size Longer
8.45-8.98	.333-.353	5th Size Longer

NOTE: For readings not on Table, select nearest one and repeat measurement with the new rod.

STALL SPEED SPECIFICATIONS

Year and Vehicle	Engine/Litre Displacement	Transmission Type	Converter Size (Inches)	ID	Stall Speed (RPM) Min.	Stall Speed (RPM) Max.	K—Factor
1981-82							
Escort/Lynx	—	ATX	9.25	—	1850	2550	—
1983							
Escort/Lynx,	1.6L	ATX	9.25	B01	2440	2890	300
EXP/LN7	EFI 1.6L	ATX	9.25	D12	2750	3160	320
	HO 1.6L	ATX	9.25	D12	2610	3110	320
1984							
Tempo/Topaz	2.3L HSC	ATX	9.25	E05	2272	2664	320
Escort/Lynx, EXP	1.6L (EFI)	ATX	9.25	E04	2627	3095	—
	1.6L (HO)	ATX	9.25	E04	7655	3147	—

PISTON ROD SIZES
With Groove Identification

I.D	Rod Length①	
	mm	Inch
0 Groove	160.22-160.52	6.313-6.324
1 Grooves	159.61-159.90	6.289-6.300
2 Grooves	159.00-159.30	6.265-6.276
3 Grooves	158.39-158.69	6.240-6.252
4 Grooves	157.78-158.08	6.216-6.189
5 Grooves	157.17-157.47	6.197-6.209

① From far end of snap ring groove to end of rod.

If the dial indicator reads:

Less than 5.15mm (used) Less than 5.15mm (new) (.203 in.) The piston rod is too long. A shorter rod (more grooves) will have to be installed.	More than 2.04mm (used) More than 6.28mm (new) (.247 in.) The piston rod is too short. A longer rod (less grooves) will have to be installed.	5.15-2.04mm (used) 5.15-6.28mm (new) (.203-.247 in.) The piston rod is the correct length and no change is required.

DIFFERENTIAL BEARING END PLAY SHIMS

Part No.	Inch	MM
E1FZ-4067-A	0.012	0.30
B	0.014	0.35
C	0.016	0.40
D	0.018	0.45
E	0.020	0.50
F	0.022	0.55
G	0.024	0.60
H	0.026	0.65
J	0.028	0.70
K	0.030	0.75
L	0.032	0.80
M	0.033	0.85
N	0.035	0.90
P	0.037	0.95
R	0.039	1.00
S	0.041	1.05
T	0.043	1.10
U	0.045	1.15
V	0.047	1.20
W	0.049	1.25
X	0.051	1.30

REVERSE CLUTCH
Selective Snap Rings

Thickness	Part No.
1.89-1.94 mm (.074-.076 inch)	N800654
2.33-2.43 mm (.092-.096 inch)	N800655
2.77-2.87 mm (.109-.113 inch)	N800656
3.21-3.31 mm (.126-.130 inch)	N800657

For This Clearance Reading	Install a New Ring That Is . . .
0.12-0.46 mm (.005-.018 inch)	One Size THINNER
1.02-1.32 mm (.040-.052 inch)	One Size THICKER
1.45-1.75 mm (.057-.069 inch)	2nd Size THICKER
1.88-2.26 mm (.074-.089 inch)	3rd Size THICKER

END PLAY ADJUSTMENT MEASUREMENTS

For This Reading	Use This Washer Part ID
.779-.796 inch (19.78-20.22 mm)	AA
.789-.804 inch (20.04-20.42 mm)	BA
.797-.812 inch (20.24-20.62 mm)	CA
.807-.825 inch (20.50-20.95 mm)	CA

WASHER THICKNESS

Inch	MM	ID
.055-.057	1.40-1.45	AA
.063-.065	1.60-1.65	BA
.071-.073	1.80-1.85	CA
.081-.083	2.05-2.10	DA

1984 STALL SPEED SPECIFICATION
ATX Transaxle

Vehicle Application	Engine Disp.	Converter Size	Converter ID	Stall Speed Min.	Stall Speed Max.
Escort/Lynx/EXP/LN7	1.6L (EFI)	9¼"	E04	2627	3095
Tempo/Topaz	2.3L	9¼"	E05	2272	2664
Escort/Lynx/EXP/LN7	1.6L (HO)	9¼"	E04	2655	3147

1984 LINE PRESSURE SPECIFICATIONS
ATX Transaxle

Transmission Model	Range	Line Pressure at Idle	WOT Stall
PMA-U, V	D, 2, 1, P, N	54-66	106-122
PMB-C, D	R	77-111	232-284
PMA-N	D, 2, 1, P, N	49-61	95-111
	R	66-100	205-257

SPECIAL TOOLS

TOOL NO.	TOOL NAME	APPLICATION
T81P-77000-AB	Plastic Storage Case	New special tool storage
T57L-500-B	Bench Mounting Fixture	Hold and turn transmission
T81P-7902-C	Converter Handles	Lift Converter
T81P-78103-A	Remover Adapter	Remove Pump
T81P-78103-B	Adapter Bolts	Remove Pump
T50T-100-A	Slide Hammer (large)	Various
—	12 mm Allen	Idler Gear
—	32 mm, 12-point Socket	Idler Gear
—	Breaker Bar	Idler Gear
TOOL-1175-AC	Seal Remover	Various
T81P-70027-A	Servo Installer Tool	Servo snap ring
T71P-19703-C	O-Ring Pick	Various
—	30 mm End Wrench	Park mechanism

TOOL NO.	TOOL NAME	APPLICATION
T80L-77100-A	Guide Pins (2)	Various
T65L-77515-A	Spring Compressor	Intermediate & Direct
T81P-70222-A	Compressor Adapter	Inter. Clutch snap ring
TOOL-7000-DE	Air Nozzle	Various
D81L-4201-A	Feeler Gauge, Metric	Various
T80L-77515-A	Adapter Extension	Direct Clutch snap ring
T81P-70235-A	Spring Compressor	Direct Clutch snap ring
T73P-77060-A	Snap Ring Plier	Various
T81P-7902-A	Holding Wire	Converter clutch
T81P-7902-B	1-Way Clutch Torquing Tool	Converter
D81L-600-B	Ft. Lb. Torque Wrench	Various

SPECIAL TOOLS

TOOL NO.	TOOL NAME	APPLICATION
T81P-7902-D	End Play Checking Tool	Converter
TOOL-4201-C	Dial Indicator	Converter; Servo
T77F-1102-A	Bearing Puller	Remove bearing
T81P-77380-A	Housing Bearing Replacer	Transfer Bearing Housing
T77F-4220-B1	Differential Bearing Remover	Differential Bearing
T57L-4220-A	Bearing Cone Remover	Differential Bearing
T81P-4220-A	Step Plate	Differential Bearings
T81P-4221-A	Bearing Installer	Differential Bearings
T81P-4451-A	Shim Selection Tool	Differential Preload
D81L-600-D	In. Lb. Torque Wrench	Various
—	3/8" Natl. Coarse Bottom Tap	Park Pawl, Band Strut
—	Bar Magnet	Pin removal
T81P-70363-A	Spacer	Reactor Support
T81P-70363-A1	Receiver	Reactor Support
T81P-70363-A2	Sleeve	Reactor Support

TOOL NO.	TOOL NAME	APPLICATION
T81P-79363-A3	Collar	Reactor Support
T81P-70363-A4	Adapter	Reactor Support
T81P-70363-A5	Screw	Reactor Support
T81P-70363-A6	Guide Pins	Reactor Support
T81P-70023-A	Selection Tool	Servo Rod Travel
T81P-70402-A	Seal Protector	Reverse Clutch Piston
T80L-77003-A	Gauge Bar	End Play
T81P-77389-A	Align. Cup	End Play
D80P-4201-A	0-1" Depth Microm.	End Play
T81P-1177-A	Differential Seal Replacer	Differential Seals
T81P-1177-B	Plastic Plug	Differential Seal
T81P-70401-A	Converter Hub Seal Replacer	Converter Hub Seal
T81P-70337-A	TV Seal Replacer	Control Lever
—	3/32" Drill Bit	Neutral Adj.
T81P-4026-A	Differential Rotator	Differential
T80L-77030-B	Servo Piston Remover	Air Check Puck

INDEX

GENERAL MOTORS LOCK-UP TORQUE CONVERTERS

GENERAL MOTORS TRANSMISSION IDENTIFICATION
"Automatic"

Parts Book Code	Service Identity	Manufacturer	Function	Physical Identification
M34	125	Hydra-matic	FWD	I.D. Plate on Rear Section of Case
MD9	125C	Hydra-matic	FWD-TCC	I.D. Plate on Rear Section of Case
MD2	180C	Strasbourg	RWD-TCC	I.D. Plate on Case
M29	200	Hydra-matic	RWD	I.D. Plate on Rear Section of Case
MV9	200C	Hydra-matic	RWD-TCC	I.D. Plate on Rear Section of Case
MW9	200-4R	Hydra-matic (3-Rivers)	RWD-OD-TCC	I.D. Plate on Rear Section of Case
M-31	250C	Chevrolet	RWD-TCC	I.D. Stamping on Gov. Cover
M-57	325-4L	Hydra-matic	RWD-OD-TCC	I.D. Plate on Trans. Case
M-33	350	Buick	RWD	I.D. Stamping on Gov. Cover
M-38	350	Chevrolet & Canada	RWD	I.D. Stamping on Right Side of Pan
M-40	400	Hydra-matic	RWD	I.D. Plate on Case
MV4	350C	Chevrolet	RWD-TCC	I.D. Stamping on Right Side of Pan
MX2	350C	Buick	RWD-TCC	I.D. Stamping on Gov. Cover or 1-Z Acc. Cover
MX3	350C	Buick	RWD-TCC	I.D. Stamping on Gov. Cover or 1-Z Acc. Cover
MX5	350C	Buick	TCC	Forward Clutch Apply Switch
MD-8	700-R4	Chevrolet	RWD-OD-TCC	Stamped on Case Boss
ME-9	440-T4	Hydra-matic	FWD-OD-TCC	Stamped or Inked on Case

FWD—Front Wheel Drive
OD—Overdrive
TCC—Torque Converter Clutch
RWD—Rear Wheel Drive
I.D.—Identification

General Information

The computer command control is a system that controls emissions by close regulation of the air-fuel ratio and by the use of a three-way catalytic converter which lowers the level of oxides of nitrogen, hydrocarbons and carbon monoxide.

The essential components are an exhaust gas oxygen sensor (OS), an electronic control module (ECM), an electronically controlled air-fuel ratio carburetor and a three-way catalytic converter (ORC).

To maintain good idle and driveability under all conditions, input signals are used to modify the computer output signal. These input signals are supplied by the engine temperature sensor, the vacuum control switch(es), the throttle position switch (TPS), the distributor (engine speed), the manifold absolute pressure sensor (MAP) and the barometer pressure sensor (BARO).

Why should this system affect the Automatic Transmission repairman? With the use of the Torque Converter Clutch (TCC) to provide a direct mechanical link-up between the engine and the drive wheels, the means of applying its engagement and disengagement modes must be controlled, to provide the optimum advantage in operation and fuel economy. This control of the Torque Converter Clutch operation was included in the overall control of the engine and its components by the Electronic Control Module.

To aid the repairman in understanding the system operation, as it applies to transmission/transaxle converter clutch application, a brief outline is given. Should the need arise to diagnose and repair the system, refer to the appropriate Chilton's Professional Automotive Repair Manual.

The Computer Command Control System was used on certain vehicles sold in California, beginning in 1981 and is used on all 1982 and later General Motors vehicles except diesel engines and certain throttle body injection type carbureted engines, although the Electronic Control System is similar in appearance and operation.

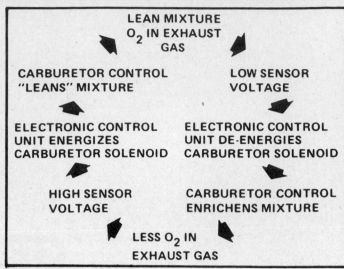

Computer Command Control (CCC) basic cycle of operation (©General Motors Corp.)

System Operation

There are two primary modes of operation for the Computer Command Control System:

1. Open Loop.
2. Closed Loop.

Open Loop Mode of Operation

In general terms, each system will be in the open loop mode of operation (or a variation of) whenever the engine operating conditions do not conform with the programmed criteria for closed loop operation, such as when the engine is first started through its reaching normal operating temperature mode.

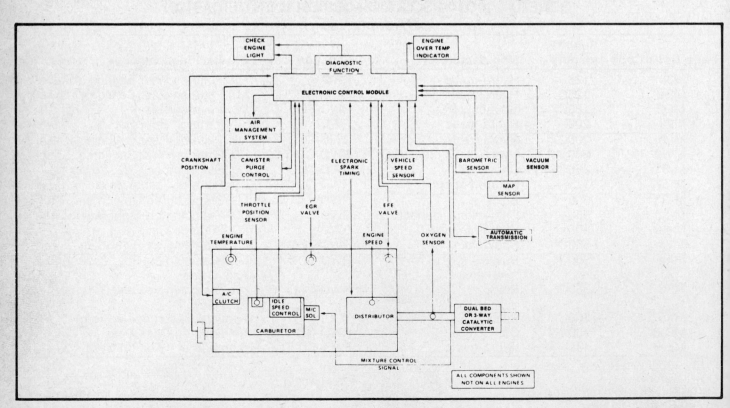

Computer Command Control system (©General Motors Corp.)

During open loop operation the air/fuel mixture is maintained at a programmed ratio that is dependent on the type of engine operation involved. The oxygen sensor data is not accepted by either system during this mode of operation. The following conditions involve open loop operation.

1. Engine Start-UP
2. Coolant or Air Temperature Too Low
3. Oxygen Sensor Temperature Too Low
4. Idle
5. Wide Open Throttle (WOT)
6. Battery Voltage Too Low

Closed Loop Mode of Operation

When all input data conforms with the programmed criteria for closed loop operation, the oxygen content output voltage from the oxygen sensor is accepted by the microprocessor. This results in an air/fuel mixture that will be optimum for the current engine operating condition and also will correct any pre-existing too lean or too rich mixture condition.

NOTE: A high oxygen content in the exhaust gas indicates a lean air/fuel mixture. A low oxygen content indicates a rich air/fuel mixture. The optimum air/fuel mixture ratio is 14.7:1.

System Components & Operation

ELECTRONIC CONTROL MODULE (ECM)

The electronic control module (ECM) monitors the voltage output of the oxygen sensor, along with information from other input signals, to generate a control signal to the carburetor solenoid. The control signal is continually cycling the solenoid between "ON" (lean command) and "OFF" (rich command). When the solenoid is on (energized), the solenoid pulls down a metering rod which reduces fuel flow. When the solenoid is off (deenergized), the spring-loaded metering rod returns to the up position and fuel flow increases. The amount of time on relative to time off is a function of the input voltage from the oxygen sensor.

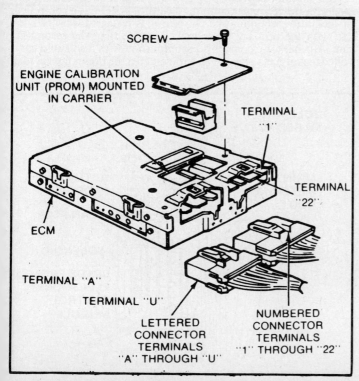

Location of PROM unit on the Electronic Control Module (ECM), CCC system (©General Motors Corp.)

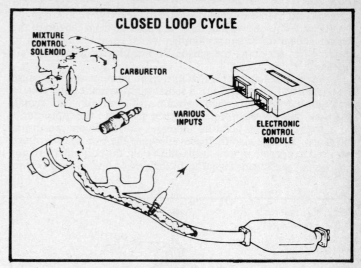

Typical Closed Loop cycle, CCC system (©General Motors Corp.)

On 3.8 liter V-6 engines, the ECM also controls the electronic spark timing system (EST). On 5.7 liter V-8 engines, the ECM also controls the electronic module retard (EMR) system. The EMR module has the capability of retarding the engine timing 10 degrees during certain engine operations to reduce the exhaust emissions.

During other engine operations, the module functions the same as a standard HEI module. The terminal "R" on the module is connected to the ECM and the retard is accomplished by an internal ground. The timing is retarded 10 degrees only when the engine coolant temperature is between 19°C (66°F) and 64°C (147°F), with the throttle opening position below 45% and the engine speed above 400 rpm.

NOTE: The ECMs are not the same, with PROMs being separately programmed for a specific vehicle/engine combination. Do not attempt to interchange.

Tachometer Signal to Computer

The computer monitors the engine crankshaft position signal in order to determine engine rpm. This signal is generated as a pulse from the HEI distributor.

The tachometer signal comes from the tach terminal of the distributor. A tachometer signal filter is located between the distributor and the computer to reduce radio noise.

A tachometer cannot be connected in the line between the tach filter and the computer, or the computer may not receive a tach signal. The presence of a tach signal from the distributor can be determined by connecting a tachometer to the distributor tach terminal.

ENGINE COOLANT SENSOR

The coolant temperature sensor in the engine block sends the ECM information on engine temperature which can be used to vary the air-fuel ratio as the engine coolant temperature varies with time during a cold start. It also accomplishes various switching functions at different temperatures (EGR, EFF, etc.), provides a switch point for hot temperature light indication and varies spark advance.

The coolant temperature sensor has a connector which lets the ground return lead surround the signal lead. This design provides an interference shield to prevent high voltage in the area (such as spark plug leads) from affecting the sensor signal to the computer.

NOTE: The ground return wire goes to the computer which internally grounds the wire.

EXHAUST OXYGEN SENSOR

The oxygen sensor located in the exhaust manifold compares the oxygen content in the exhaust stream to the oxygen content in the outside air. This shows that there is a passage from the top of the oxygen sensor to the inner chamber which permits outside air to enter. When servicing the sensor, do not plug or restrict the air passage.

A rich exhaust stream is low in oxygen content and will cause the oxygen sensor to send a rich signal, approximatley one volt, to the computer. A lean exhaust stream will result in a lean signal, less than half a volt, from the oxygen sensor to the computer.

As the sensor temperature increases during engine warm-up, the sensor voltage also increases. Because the minimum voltage required to operate this circuit is half a volt, the computer will not use the oxygen sensor signal until the sensor has reached 600°F.

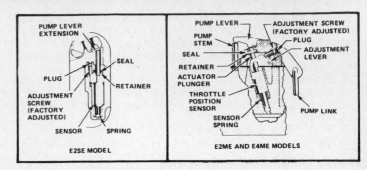

Throttle positioner sensor (TPS) (©General Motors Corp.)

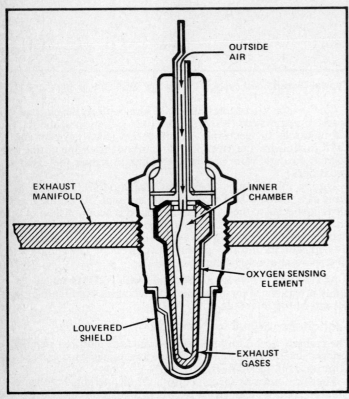

Typical oxygen sensor (©General Motors Corp.)

THROTTLE POSITION SENSOR (TPS)

This sensor is located in the carburetor body and is actuated by the accelerator pump lever. The stem of the sensor projects up through the air horn, contacting the underside of the lever. As the throttle valves are opened, the pump lever presses down proportionately on the sensor, thus indicating throttle position.

The throttle position sensor changes the voltage in circuit E (reference voltage) to G (voltage input to the computer) as the sensor shaft moves up or down. This is similar to the operation of the gas tank gauge sending unit, except that the throttle position sensor permits the computer to read throttle position.

BAROMETRIC PRESSURE SENSOR

The barometric pressure sensor provides a voltage to the computer to allow ambient pressure compensation of the controlled functions. This unit senses ambient barometric pressure and provides information to the computer on atmospheric pressure changes due to weather and/or altitude.

The computer uses this information to adjust the air-fuel ratio. The sensor is mounted under the instrument panel near the right-hand A/C outlet and is electronically connected to the computer. The atmospheric opening is covered by a foam filter.

MIXTURE CONTROL (M/C)

The mixture control solenoid actuates two spring-loaded rods, controlling fuel flow to the idle and main metering circuits of the carburetor. Energizing the solenoid lowers the metering rod into the main metering jet. This makes the air-fuel mixture in the Dualjet and Quadrajet carburetors leaner. The Varajet carburetor has a solenoid operated fuel control valve.

The mixture control solenoid changes the air-fuel ratio by allowing more or less fuel to flow through the carburetor. When no electrical signal is applied to the solenoid, maximum fuel flow to the idle and main metering circuits. When an electrical signal is applied to the solenoid, the mixture is leaned. (Leaning means reducing the amount of fuel mixed with the air.)

COMPUTER COMMAND CONTROL SYSTEM CARBURETORS

Three types of Rochester carburetors are used for system applications. The Varajet is a two barrel, staged opening carburetor. The Quadrajet is a four barrel staged opening carburetor. The Dualjet is a two barrel non-staged carburetor, essentially the primary side of a Quadrajet.

The metering rods and an idle bleed valve are connected to a 12 volt mixture control solenoid. The model E2SE carburetor, used with the computer command control system, is a controlled air-fuel ratio carburetor of a two barrel, two stage down-draft design with the primary bore smaller in size than the secondary bore. Air-fuel ratio control is accomplished with a solenoid controlled on/off fuel valve which supplements the preset flow of fuel

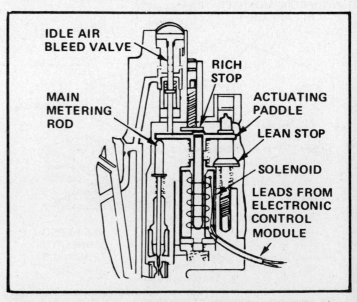

Typical mixture control solenoid used with E2ME and E4ME carburetors (©General Motors Corp.)

which supplies the idle and main metering systems. The solenoid on/off cycle is controlled by a 12 volt signal from the computer. The solenoid also controls the amount of air bled into the idle system. The air bleed valve and fuel control valve work together so that the fuel valve is closed when the air bleed valve is open, resulting in a leaner air-fuel mixture. Enrichment occurs when the fuel valve is open and air bleed valve closed.

The Quadrajet-Dualjet arrangement is such that the level of metering is dependent on the positioning of rods in the orifices. The Varajet system is different in that it features a non-moving-part main system for lean mixtures and a supplemental system to provide for rich mixture.

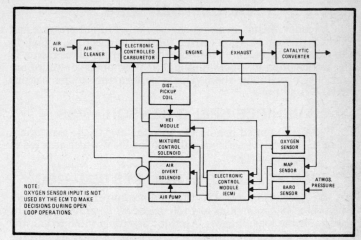

Typical CCC system functional block schematic, non turbo equipped (©General Motors Corp.)

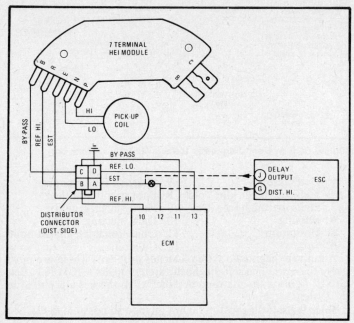

Electronic Spark Control schematic (©General Motors Corp.)

ELECTRONIC SPARK TIMING (EST)

Electronic spark timing is a computer controlled system that has all the engine spark timing information stored in memory. At various engine operating conditions as determined by rpm and manifold pressure, the system determines (from a table) the proper spark advance. It then produces the firing signal at the desired crankshaft position. Other parameters, such as coolant temperature and barometric pressure, can be sensed and this information used to modify, as appropriate, the spark advance number from the table. The system provides a much more flexible and accurate spark timing control than the conventional centrifugal and vacuum advance mechanisms in the distributor.

AIR FLOW CONTROL SYSTEMS

Two types of air systems are used on computer command control engines, the pulse air injection reactor (PAIR) and the belt-driven air pump (AIR). Both types are controlled by the computer through solenoid valves. The PAIR system uses an on/off solenoid which is open during cold operation and wide open throttle (WOT). Air is injected into the exhaust ports when the solenoid valves are open.

AIR MANAGEMENT SYSTEM

The computer controlled solenoid can divert air during any desired operating mode. The valves diverting and switching the air flow are the air diverter valve and the air select valve. With the air divert valve, a rapid increase of engine manifold vacuum diverts air to the air cleaner and high air system pressure is diverted to the air cleaner. The air select valve switches air between the catalytic converter and exhaust ports.

DISTRIBUTOR HEI MODULE

The computer will control the module above 200 rpm by applying a voltage to the by-pass line and signaling terminal E.

Current loss at terminals R or B will cause the distributor (HEI) module to take over. Loss of terminal E electronic spark timing will cause the engine to stop (assuming by-pass voltage is present).

If the engine is equipped with electronic spark control, the computer electronic spark timing line would go to the electronic spark control distributor high. The electronic spark control delay output would go to the HEI electronic spark timing input.

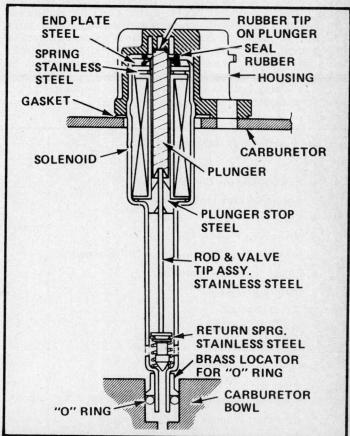

Typical mixture control solenoid used with E2SE carburetor (©General Motors Corp.)

VACUUM SENSORS

The vacuum sensors measure changes in manifold pressure and provide this information (in the form of an electrical signal) to the ECM. The pressure changes reflect need for adjustments in the air/fuel mixture, spark timing (EST) and other controlled operations to maintain good vehicle performance under various driving conditions.

VEHICLE SPEED SENSOR—VSS

The VSS is mounted behind the speedometer in the instrument cluster. It provides a series of pulses to the ECM which are used to determine vehicle speed.

IDLE SPEED CONTROL SYSTEM—ISC

An Idle Speed Control—ISC is used on some engines to control idle speed. ISC maintains low idle speed while preventing stalls due to engine load changes. A motor assembly mounted on the carburetor moves the throttle lever to open or close the throttle blades. The ECM monitors engine load to determine proper idle speed. To prevent stalling, the ECM monitors the air conditioning compressor switch, transmission, park/neutral switch and the ISC throttle switch. With this information the ECM will control the ISC motor and vary the engine idle as necessary.

Trouble Diagnosis

BUILT-IN DIAGNOSTIC SYSTEM

The computer command control system should be considered as a possible trouble source of engine performance, fuel economy and exhaust emissions complaints only after diagnostic checks, which apply to engines without the computer command control system, have been completed.

Before suspecting the computer command control system or any of its components as a trouble source, check the ignition system including the distributor, timing, spark plugs and wires. Check the air cleaner, evaporative emissions system, EFE system, PCV system, EGR valve and engine compression. Also inspect the intake manifold, vacuum hoses and hose connections for leaks. Inspect the carburetor mounting bolts.

The following symptoms could indicate a possible problem with the computer command control system.

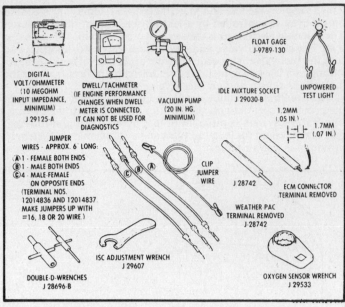

Typical CCC system diagnostic tools (©General Motors Corp.)

1. Detonation
2. Stalls or rough idle, cold
3. Stalls or rough idle, hot
4. Missing
5. Hesitation
6. Surges
7. Sluggish performance
8. Poor gasoline mileage
9. Hard starting, cold
10. Hard starting, hot
11. Objectionable exhaust odor
12. Cuts out

A built-in diagnostic system catches problems which are most likely to occur. The self-diagnostic system lights a "CHECK ENGINE" light on the instrument panel when there is a problem in the system.

Since the self-diagnostics do not include all possible faults, the absence of a code does not mean there is no problem with the system. To determine this, a system performance check is necessary. It is made when the "CHECK ENGINE" light does not indicate a problem but the computer command system is suspected because no other reason can be found for a complaint. By grounding a

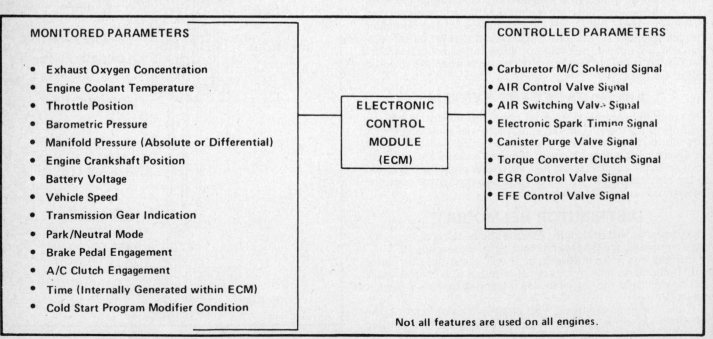

MONITORED PARAMETERS

- Exhaust Oxygen Concentration
- Engine Coolant Temperature
- Throttle Position
- Barometric Pressure
- Manifold Pressure (Absolute or Differential)
- Engine Crankshaft Position
- Battery Voltage
- Vehicle Speed
- Transmission Gear Indication
- Park/Neutral Mode
- Brake Pedal Engagement
- A/C Clutch Engagement
- Time (Internally Generated within ECM)
- Cold Start Program Modifier Condition

ELECTRONIC CONTROL MODULE (ECM)

CONTROLLED PARAMETERS

- Carburetor M/C Solenoid Signal
- AIR Control Valve Signal
- AIR Switching Valve Signal
- Electronic Spark Timing Signal
- Canister Purge Valve Signal
- Torque Converter Clutch Signal
- EGR Control Valve Signal
- EFE Control Valve Signal

Not all features are used on all engines.

CCC system monitored and controlled parameters (©General Motors Corp.)

"TROUBLE CODE" test lead under the instrument panel, the "CHECK ENGINE" light will flash a numerical code if the diagnostic system has detected a fault.

As a bulb and system check, the light will come on when the ignition is turned on with the engine stopped. The "CHECK ENGINE" light will remain on for a few seconds after the engine is started. If the "TROUBLE CODE" test lead is grounded with the ignition switch on and the engine stopped, the light will flash a code "12" which indicates the diagnostic system is working. This consists of one flash followed by a pause, and then two more flashes. After a long pause, the code will be repeated two more times. The cycle will then repeat itself until the engine is started or the ignition is turned off.

If the "TROUBLE CODE" test lead is grounded with the engine running and a fault has been detected by the system, the trouble code will flash three times. If more than one fault has been detected, its code will be flashed three times after the first code set. The series will then repeat itself.

A trouble code indicates a problem with a given circuit. For example, code 14 indicates a problem in the coolant sensor circuit. This includes the coolant sensor, harness and electronic control module (ECM).

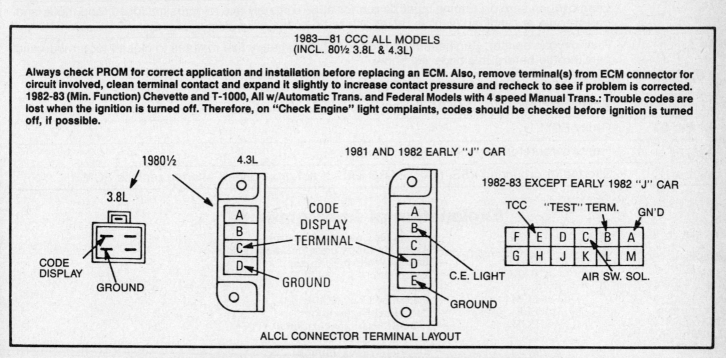

1983—81 CCC ALL MODELS
(INCL. 80½ 3.8L & 4.3L)

Always check PROM for correct application and installation before replacing an ECM. Also, remove terminal(s) from ECM connector for circuit involved, clean terminal contact and expand it slightly to increase contact pressure and recheck to see if problem is corrected. 1982-83 (Min. Function) Chevette and T-1000, All w/Automatic Trans. and Federal Models with 4 speed Manual Trans.: Trouble codes are lost when the ignition is turned off. Therefore, on "Check Engine" light complaints, codes should be checked before ignition is turned off, if possible.

ALCL CONNECTOR TERMINAL LAYOUT

Assembly Line Communication Link (ALCL) connector terminal arrangement, typical (©General Motors Corp.)

TROUBLE CODE IDENTIFICATION CHART CCC
All Except Chevette

Code #	Problem Indicated
12	No tachometer or reference signal to computer. This code will only be present while a fault exists, and will not be stored if the problem is intermittent.
13	Oxygen sensor circuit. The engine has to operate for about five minutes (eighteen minutes 3.8L V6) at part throttle before this code will show.
14	Shorted coolant sensor circuit. The engine has to run two minutes before this code will show.
15	Open coolant sensor circuit. The engine has to operate for about five minutes at part throttle before this code will show.
21	Shorted wide open throttle switch and/or open closed-throttle switch circuit (when used). Throttle position sensor circuit. (Must run 25 seconds below 800 rpm to set code.)
23	Open or grounded carburetor solenoid circuit.
24	Trouble in the Vehicle Speed Sensor (VSS) circuit—The vehicle must operate up to 5 minutes at road speed for this code to set.
32	Barometric pressure sensor (BARO) output low.
34	Manifold absolute pressure (MAP) sensor output high. (Engine must operate up to 5 minutes below 800 rpm to set code).

TROUBLE CODE IDENTIFICATION CHART CCC
All Except Chevette

Code #	Problem Indicated
35	Idle speed control (ISC) circuit shorted (operate engine over ½ throttle for over two seconds to set code.
42	Electronic Spark Timing (EST) bypass circuit grounded.
43	Throttle position sensor out of adjustment.
44	Lean oxygen sensor. Engine must be run for approximately five minutes in closed loop mode and part throttle at roadload (vehicle drive) before this code will show.
45	Rich oxygen sensor. Engine must be run for approximately five minutes in closed loop mode and part throttle before this code will show.
44 and 45	Faulty oxygen sensor or open sensor circuit.
51	Faulty calibration unit (PROM) or improper PROM installation.
52 and 53	Faulty ECM.
54	Faulty carburetor solenoid and/or computer.
55	Shorted or grounded VSS, MAP, BARO TPS. If not grounded or shorted replace ECM.

Explanation of Abbreviations

CCC	— Computer Command Control
ALCL	— Assembly Line Communication Link
BAT+	— Battery Positive Terminal
BARO.	— Barometric
Conv.	— Converter
ECM	— Electronic Control Module
EFE	— Early Fuel Evaporation
EGR	— Exhaust Gas Recirculation
ESC	— Electronic Spark Control
EST	— Electronic Spark Timing
HEI	— High Energy Ignition
ISC	— Idle Speed Control
MAP	— Manifold Absolute Pressure
M/C	— Mixture Control
OEM	— Original Equipment Manufacture
PCV	— Positive Crankcase Ventilation
P/N	— Park, Neutral
Port.	— Exhaust Ports
PROM	— Programmable Read Only Memory (engine calibration unit)
TCC	— Torque Converter Clutch
"Test" lead or terminal	— Lead or ALCL connector terminal which is grounded to obtain a trouble code
TPS	— Throttle Position Sensor (on carburetor)
Vac.	— Vacuum
VIN	Vehicle Identification Number
VSS	Vehicle Speed Sensor (signals load speed)
WOT	Wide Open Throttle

GENERAL MOTORS TORQUE CONVERTER CLUTCH DIAGNOSIS

Conventional Torque Converter System

Three basic components make up the conventional torque converter, a pump bolted to the engine's flywheel, a turbine connected to the automatic transmission's input shaft and a stator unit mounted between the pump and the turbine. When the engine is operating, the pump vanes directs hydraulic fluid to the vanes of the turbine, forcing the turbine to rotate. As the turbine rotates, the turbine vanes directs the fluid to the stator vanes, which in turn adds torque multiplication to the automatic transmission input shaft by redirecting the fluid back to the pump vanes. When the transmission is in first or second gear, the pump rotates faster than the turbine, 1.5 to 2 times for every rotation of the turbine. This difference in speed between the pump and the turbine, along with the action of the stator, multiplies the torque of the engine. As the transmission reaches third or top gear, the pump and the turbine are spinning at nearly the same speed, cancelling out the action of the stator since torque multiplication is not needed. The pump can now rotate approximately 1.1 times for every rotation of the turbine.

Torque Converter Clutch System

To eliminate the difference in speed between the converter pump and turbine in the top gear application, a mechanical type clutch was added between the turbine and the torque converter pump cover on the flywheel side. Additional components were added to complete the mechanical link-up between the engine and the transmission' planetary gear scts and their holding components. This mechanical link-up eliminates the difference in speed between the pump and turbine, resulting in greater fuel economy for the vehicle.

PRINCIPLES OF OPERATION

The additional components added to the converter unit are; the pressure plate, spring and dampener assembly and friction material. Transmission oil pressure is routed, at specific times, to apply or disengage the converter clutch unit. The friction material is bonded to the outer inch around the cover side of the plate and around the center at the spline area. The center friction material is not bonded in a full circle, since this friction area must supply support against the converter cover during the clutch apply so that the plate does not flex. It must also allow oil flow to the entire surface of the plate during the release phase. If this area was bonded in a complete circle, the release pressure area would not release the clutch. The turbine thrust spacer is located in the hub area of the pressure plate and contacts the turbine and the converter cover. The pressure plate moves in relation to the thrust spacer.

The thrust spacer has "O" ring seals that are important to the

shift feel of the clutch. The outer "O" ring seals the pressure plate hub. The inner "O" ring seal the inner area of the thrust spacer.

A firm clutch apply depends upon the releasing of all pressure on the engine side of the pressure plate. Damaged or missing "O" ring seals in the turbine thrust spacer can cause a pressure in the release side and cause the clutch to slip or intermittently apply and release. This condition can cause a vibration similar to a wheel balance problem should it happen during the clutch apply speeds.

It should be noted there are two types of pressure plates used. Both types have spring type torsional dampening components. The pressure plate used with the diesel engine has additional valves on the pressure plate. These valves are used to equalize the oil pressure on both sides of the pressure plate during a disengagement phase, because the diesel engine is compressing a full charge of air on every stroke, even during deceleration. This rapid slowing of the diesel engine causes a reverse rotation of the plate on the hub and opens two valves which allows the oil to movc to the front of the plate, effecting a quicker clutch release. This results in a smoother clutch release and less rpm drop. Other converter clutch units do not use the poppet valve in the pressure plate assembly.

Diesel engine converters are identified by code markings and by having either three or six nuts, each of which are welded halfway around the nut (180 degrees), while the gasoline engine converters have three nuts and are welded in one spot.

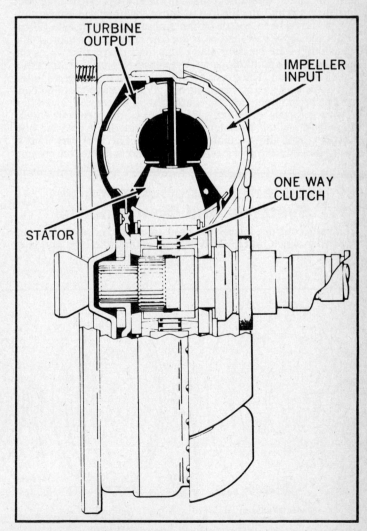

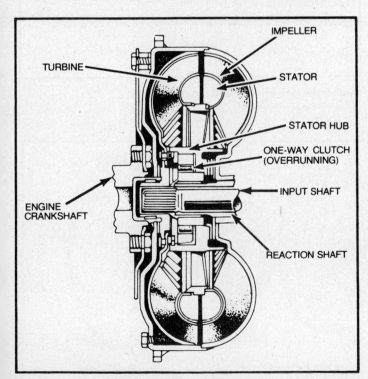

Cross section of typical torque converter assembly
(©General Motors Corp.)

Cut-away view of impeller input (pump), stator and turbine output
(©General Motors Corp.)

To aid in reducing torsional shock during converter clutch apply, a damper assembly is incorporated in the converter clutch pressure plate. The spring loaded damper is splined to the converter turbine assembly. The converter clutch pressure plate is attached to the pivoting mechanism of the damper assembly. This pivoting action allows the pressure plate to rotate independent of the damper assembly, up to approximately 45°. The rate of independent rotation is controlled by the pivoting mechanism acting on the springs in the damper assembly.

Converter Clutch Engagement and Disengagement

The converter clutch should engage when the engine is warm enough to handle the slight extra load and when the vehicle speed is high enough to allow operation to be smooth and the vehicle free of engine pulses. The converter clutch should release when the emissions would be affected as in a coast condition, torque multiplication is needed in the converter and when coming to a stop and a mechanical connection from engine to the rear wheels would be detrimental.

Clutch Operation Hydraulically

When a Torque converter clutch equipped vehicle is in the top speed (may apply in 2nd, 3rd or 4th speeds, depending upon the transmission/transaxle model) an apply valve directs converter feed oil pressure to the turbine side of the pressure plate. The fluid pressure forces the pressure plate against the housing cover to engage the clutch for a direct mechanical link-up, causing the converter pump and the turbine to move together as a single unit. When the vehicle coasts or the transmission/transaxle downshifts, the apply valve redirects the converter feed pressure to the front side of the pressure plate. This fluid movement forces the pressure plate and the housing cover apart to break the direct mechanical link-up. The converter clutch is then disengaged and the converter acts as any conventional torque converter. The converter clutch apply valve is controlled by a solenoid, and when activated, opens an oil pressure passage to the converter clutch, applying it. When the solenoid is deactivated, the pressure passage is closed and the clutch disengages. The apply solenoid is controlled by a series of electrical, electronic and vacuum components.

Converter Clutch Application Systems And Components

Different control systems are used to apply and disengage the converter clutch unit in the 1980 models and the 1981 and later models.

Basically, the torque converter clutch system has developed in two stages. The first stage, which started in the 1980 model year, used two electrical and vacuum switches to control the operation of the TCC. The second stage, introduced at the beginning of the 1981 model year, continues for 1982. It uses four sensors and the ECM of the Computer Command Control system to control the operation of the torque converter clutch.

The 1980 system typically uses a brake switch and low vacuum switch in the feed circuit to the TCC solenoid in the transmission.

As long as the brakes aren't applied and engine vacuum is above 5 in. Hg, the TCC solenoid receives a voltage feed. What it doesn't have is a ground, which it needs to operate. The ground for the system is controlled by the governor switch. When governor line pressure is high enough, which is relative to vehicle road speed, the contacts in the switch will close. This provides the TCC solenoid with a ground which, in turn, applies the TCC.

The system used on the 1980 diesel engines used this same system with one addition: a high vacuum switch was installed in the feed circuit to the TCC solenoid. This switch opens the feed circuit to the TCC solenoid during periods of high engine vacuum, as in a coastdown situation. This basic system is used up to the present time on diesel engines, except the high vacuum switch function is replaced by the poppet valves, in the torque converter.

Since 1981, the ECM on most Computer Command Control

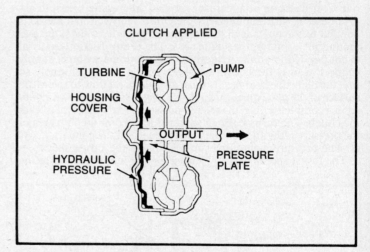

Mechanical lock-up of torque converter clutch (©General Motors Corp.)

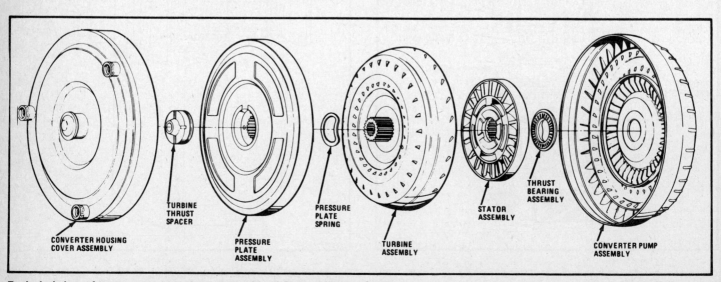

Exploded view of torque converter clutch assembly (©General Motors Corp.)

equipped vehicles has controlled the ground for the TCC solenoid, replacing the governor switch of the earlier system. Typically, in ECM controlled systems, a TCC brake switch is installed in the feed circuit to the TCC solenoid.

Provided the brakes aren't applied, voltage is fed to the TCC solenoid. But, again, the TCC solenoid needs a ground for operation. So, when the ECM has the proper input from four sensors (the coolant temperature sensor, throttle position sensor, vacuum sensor and vehicle speed sensor), it provides the TCC solenoid with a ground. In turn, that allows operation of the TCC. To prevent application of the TCC in lower gears, this system may also use hydraulically actuated electrical switches installed in the valve body.

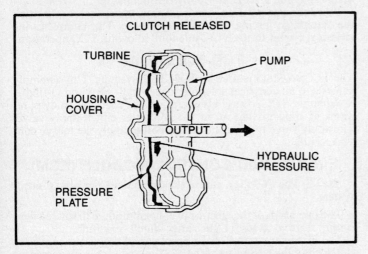

Torque converter clutch release, reverting converter to a conventional torque converter operation (©General Motors Corp.)

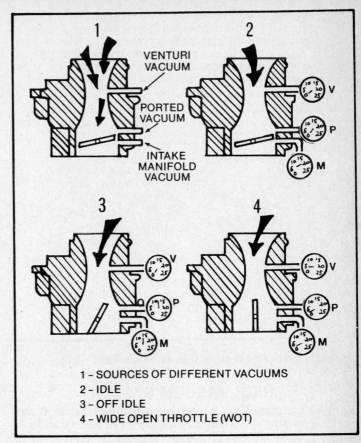

1 – SOURCES OF DIFFERENT VACUUMS
2 – IDLE
3 – OFF IDLE
4 – WIDE OPEN THROTTLE (WOT)

Sources of engine related vacuum (©General Motors Corp.)

Control Components

To control the application and release of the converter clutch during various driving conditions: vacuum, electrical and electronic controls are used. Most of the controls are external to the transmission/transaxle assemblies. It should be noted that all controlling components may not be on each vehicle equipped with the converter clutch.

PORTED VACUUM

Ported vacuum is used on the 1980 TCC system and it's simply a vacuum port positioned above the throttle plates. It provides the vacuum source for the engine vacuum switch. When the throttle plate is closed during deceleration, the vacuum signal to the engine vacuum switch drops to zero. This opens the contacts in the vacuum switch, releasing the torque converter clutch.

VACUUM DELAY VALVE

The vacuum delay valve is used on some of the 1980 TCC systems with gasoline engines. Its purpose is to delay the response of the vacuum switch to slight, momentary changes in engine vacuum. This helps avoid unnecessary disengagement and engagement of the torque converter clutch.

The vacuum delay valve is positioned in the vacuum line between the ported vacuum source on the carburetor and the vacuum switch.

LOW VACUUM SWITCH

The low vacuum switch is used in 1980 TCC systems. This normally open switch consists of a steel housing with a diaphragm and port on one end and a set of electrical contacts and blade terminals on the other. A hose from a ported vacuum source on the carburetor or throttle body is connected to the port on the vacuum switch. When ported vacuum is high, the diaphragm is pulled

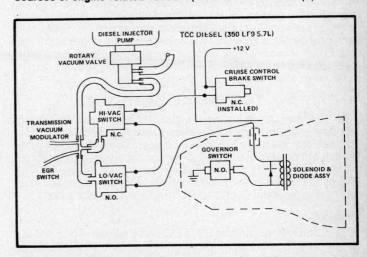

Typical converter clutch controls with diesel engine usage (©General Motors Corp.)

so that the electrical contacts touch each other. This provides the circuit for a voltage feed to the TCC solenoid. However, when ported vacuum is low, as during closed throttle deceleration, the diaphragm is released. This caused the contacts to separate, breaking the circuit to the TCC solenoid. Now the torque converter clutch is released.

Testing

The low vacuum switch can be tested with an ohmmeter and a vacuum pump. Connect the test leads from the ohmmeter to the blade terminals on the switch. Without any vacuum applied to the port on the switch, resistance will be infinite. Now, connect the hose from the vacuum pump to the vacuum port. Pump the vacuum pump until the gage reads between approximately 3 and 9 in. Hg. on gasoline engines and 5 to 6 in. Hg. on diesel engines. Now the resistance between the terminals will be zero. If the switch doesn't pass either of these tests, replace it.

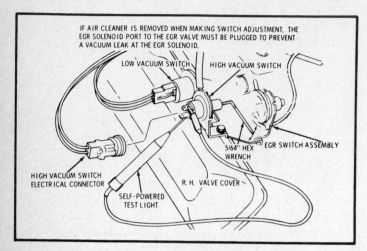

Testing and adjustment of the high vacuum switch
(©General Motors Corp.)

HIGH VACUUM SWITCH

The high vacuum switch is used only with diesel engines. It consists of a housing with a diaphragm and port on one end and a set of electrical contacts and blade terminals on the other.

A hose from the vacuum pump (via the injection pump-mounted vacuum regulator valve and low vacuum switch) is connected to the port on the high vacuum switch. The contacts in the switch are normally closed. However, during periods of high vacuum, as during a zero throttle coastdown, the diaphragm separates the contacts. This breaks the circuit to the torque converter clutch, thereby avoiding feeling the engine pulses during coastdown and reducing emissions.

TCC BRAKE SWITCH

The TCC brake switch is used with all TCC systems. This switch consists of a set of normally closed contacts housed in the brake light switch. When the brake pedal is depressed, the plunger in the switch opens the contacts, breaking the circuit to the torque converter clutch. This avoids stalling the engine during braking. When the brake pedal is released, the contacts close and once again complete the circuit to the torque converter clutch.

Testing

Use an ohmmeter to test the TCC brake switch. Place the test leads from the ohmmeter on each of the blade terminals at the rear of the switch.

With the plunger fully extended, resistance should be infinite. With the plunger pushed in, resistance should be zero. If the switch fails either one of those tests, it should be replaced.

Adjustments

The adjustment of the switch is important. If the switch is screwed in too far, the contacts that complete the circuit to the torque converter clutch will not open when the brakes are applied. This can cause the engine to stall at idle. The switch should be adjusted so that the plunger just contacts the brake lever when the brake pedal is in the released position.

GOVERNOR SWITCH

The governor switch is used on the 1980 TCC system and some

later diesel engine applications. This normally open switch consists of a housing, diaphragm, port, electrical contacts and terminals. The governor switch is positioned in the pressure line from the governor. As vehicle speed increases, so does the oil pressure from the governor. When the oil pressure reaches a predetermined level (which usually coincides with approximately 40 MPH) the normally open contacts in the governor switch close. This completes the circuit through the switch and gives the TCC solenoid a ground. In turn, this allows the application of the torque converter clutch.

THIRD GEAR SWITCH

The third gear switch consists of a switch body, blade terminals, diaphragm and a set of normally open contacts

When the transmission is in third gear, transmission oil acts on the diaphragm forcing the contacts to close. This completes the electrical circuit to the TCC solenoid, allowing TCC operation.

TCC SOLENOID

The TCC solenoid is used with all TCC systems. This assembly consists of an electrical solenoid, check ball, seat, and O-ring.

When the TCC solenoid is energized, the check ball moves, redirecting transmission oil to the converter clutch apply valve. The apply valve routes transmission oil to apply the torque converter clutch.

ELECTRONIC CONTROL MODULE (ECM)

NOTE: The ECM is a part of the Computer Command Control system.

The operation of the electronic control module discussed here is only relative to torque converter clutch operation.

The ECM has controlled the operation of the torque converter clutch since the beginning of the 1981 model year in all passenger cars equipped with gasoline engines.

The electronic control module provides a ground for the TCC solenoid in the transmission when four conditions are met:
1. Engine coolant temperature is above a predetermined value.
2. The throttle position sensor and vacuum sensor indicate the engine isn't under a heavy load.
3. The throttle isn't closed.
4. Vehicle speed is above a predetermined value.

COOLANT TEMPERATURE SENSOR

The coolant temperature sensor is a part of the Computer Command Control system and is positioned in the engine coolant stream. This sensor works on the principle of varying resistance.

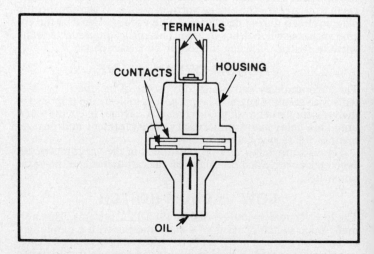

Typical governor switch—Note contact appearance
(©General Motors Corp.)

The ECM delivers a five-volt electrical signal to the coolant temperature sensor. Depending on the resistance offered by the coolant temperature sensor, an electrical signal is sensed by the ECM. The difference in voltage between the five-volt output signal from the ECM and the voltage at the coolant temperature sensor represents the coolant temperature to the ECM. The voltage at the coolant temperature sensor drops as coolant temperature increases.

A faulty sensor that indicates engine coolant is always below a predetermined temperature (usualy between 130°-150°F) will prevent the engagement of the TCC. If the sensor is improperly indicating that coolant temperature is always above the predetermined temperature, the TCC will engage before the engine is warmed up and can cause drivability problems.

When the coolant is cold, the sensor has a resistance of approximately 100,000 ohms. When the coolant is at normal operating temperature, the sensor has a resistance of less than 1,000 ohms.

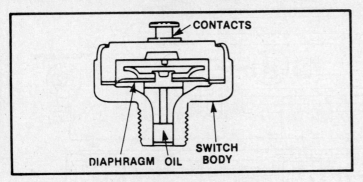

Typical top gear switch—Note contact appearance (©General Motors Corp.)

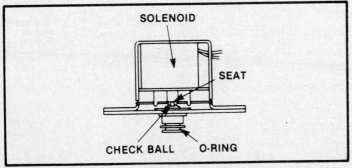

Typical torque converter clutch solenoid (©General Motors Corp.)

Testing

A faulty coolant temperature sensor is indicated by a Code 14 or 15 and can be tested by accessing the stored trouble codes in the ECM.

THROTTLE POSITION SENSOR (TPS)

The throttle position sensor (TPS) is a part of the Computer Command Control system. The TPS is a variable resistor that converts the degree of throttle plate opening to an electrical signal that the ECM uses.

The resistance between terminals A and B of the TPS ranges from about 10,000-15,000 ohms when the throttle is closed, to approximately 1,000 ohms when the throttle is wide open. The resulting voltages returned to the ECM vary from under one volt at closed throttle to nearly five volts at wide open throttle.

The degree of throttle opening, together with the amount of engine vacuum sensed by the vacuum sensor, provides the ECM with information directly relating to engine load. If the engine load is high enough, the ECM will break the circuit to the TCC. It does this by denying a ground for the TCC circuit.

The TPS is located in the carburetor on carbureted engines. In electronic fuel injection systems, the TPS is mounted on the throttle body. On EFI systems that use dual throttle bodies, the TPS is mounted on the outboard side of the left throttle body.

Testing

When testing for a malfunctioning TPS, keep in mind that it's part of the Computer Command Control system. If the TPS is malfunctioning, either a Code 21 or 22 will be stored in the memory of the ECM. To check for this, you'll have to access the memory of the ECM.

VACUUM SENSOR (VS)

The vacuum sensor (also known as a MAP sensor) is part of the Computer Command Control system. Its purpose is to sense changes in engine vacuum and supply a voltage to the ECM relative to the strength of the vacuum signal.

Testing

A vacuum sensor that's faulty is indicated by a Code 33 or 34 which can be determined by accessing the trouble code(s) stored in the ECM.

VEHICLE SPEED SENSOR (VSS)

The vehicle speed sensor is part of the Computer Command Control system and consists of a reflective blade, light emitting diode, photo cell and buffer/amplifier.

The reflective blade of the VSS is part of the speedometer cable/head assembly. When the vehicle starts moving, the speedometer cable starts rotating. Since the reflective blade is attached to the cable, it also begins to rotate. As the blade enters the light beam provided by the L.E.D., light is reflected back at the photo cell. The photo cell "sees" the light which causes a low power electrical signal to be sent to the buffer/amplifier. The buffer/amplifier conditions and amplifies the electrical signal and then sends it to the ECM. The number of electrical signals sent to the ECM in a fixed period of time indicates road speed.

The vehicle speed sensor is located in the speedometer head behind the instrument panel. To service the VSS, the instrument panel cluster must be removed.

Testing

Since the VSS is part of the Computer Command Control system, if it's faulty a Code 24 will be stored in the memory of the ECM. To verify a faulty VSS, access the memory of the ECM.

EGR BLEED SOLENOID

The EGR bleed solenoid is a normally closed switch that's used in some Computer Command and non-Computer Command Control applications. It controls an air bleed in the EGR control vacuum passage. This solenoid is used because less EGR is needed at TCC engagement speeds and helps avoid feeling engine pulsing during TCC engagement.

When the TCC solenoid is energized, so is the EGR bleed solenoid. With the EGR bleed solenoid energized, the air bleed in the EGR control vacuum passage is opened. This adds air to the EGR signal vacuum, reducing or eliminating EGR and allowing smoother engine operation.

THERMAL VACUUM VALVE

The thermal vacuum valve is used in the non-Computer Command Control system and consists of a body, two vacuum ports and a thermally activated valve. The end of the valve is immersed in engine coolant. When coolant temperature is below approximately 130°F, the valve blocks the vacuum from the ported vacuum source on the carburetor. When coolant temperature reaches 130°F, the valve moves, connecting carburetor ported vacuum to the vacuum switch. In turn, this allows operation of the TCC. The thermal vacuum valve prevents the application of the torque converter clutch at engine coolant temperatures below 130°F.

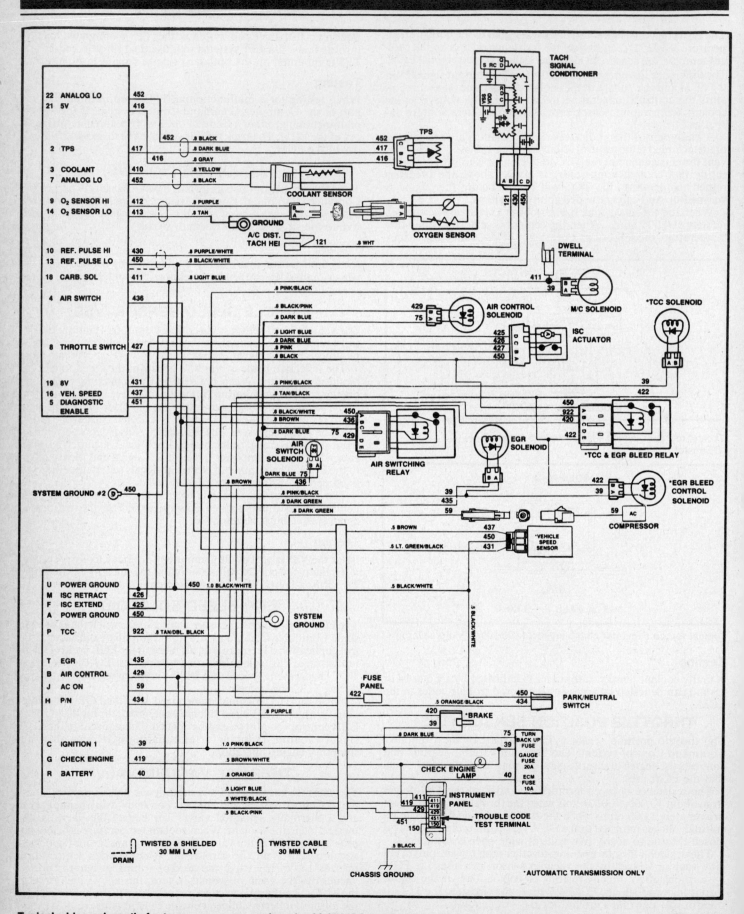

Typical wiring schematic for torque converter equipped vehicles (©General Motors Corp.)

VACUUM REGULATOR VALVE

The vacuum regulator valve replaced the rotary switch on 1982 diesel engines. This valve uses two sets of contacts wired in series. The first set of contacts are normally open when the engine is at or near idle speed. This prevents a voltage feed from reaching the TCC solenoid, which, in turn, doesn't activate the TCC. When the throttle is opened partway, the first set of contacts closes. This completes the feed circuit to the TCC solenoid and the TCC applies. The second set of contacts is normally closed. They open near and at full throttle, breaking the feed circuit to the TCC solenoid.

Adjustments

The adjustment of the vacuum regulator valve is critical to proper TCC operation. This procedure relies on using a carburetor angle gage and vacuum gage to properly test and adjust the VRV.

FOURTH GEAR SWITCH

The fourth gear switch operates in the same manner as the third gear switch, except that the contacts close when the transmission is in fourth gear. It looks exactly like the third gear switch.

4-3 PULSE SWITCH

The normally closed 4-3 pulse switch is a pressure-activated electrical switch that opens the circuit to the TCC momentarily on a 4-3 downshift. This allows the engine to receive torque multiplication from the torque converter and reduce downshift harshness.

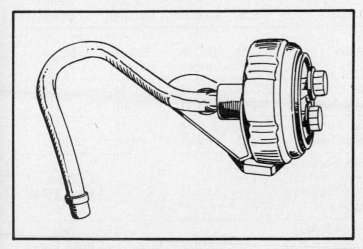

4-3 pulse switch (©General Motors Corp.)

TCC RELAY

The TCC relay is used on some Computer Command Control systems. This normally closed relay allows control of two solenoids without overloading the ECM. The two solenoids are used for the TCC and EGR bleed.

ROTARY SWITCH

The rotary switch is used on 1981 diesel engines with a TCC transmission. Two types of rotary switches are used. The first type contains one set of electrical contacts that are normally closed. When the accelerator is near or at full throttle, the contact points open, breaking the feed circuit to the TCC solenoid. In turn, this releases the TCC. The second type of rotary switch uses two sets of contacts wired in series. The first set of contacts are normally open when the engine is at or near idle speed. This prevents a voltage feed from reaching the TCC solenoid, which, in turn, doesn't activate the TCC. When the throttle is opened partway, the first set of contacts close. This completes the feed circuit

to the TCC solenoid and the TCC applies. The second set of contacts are normally closed. They open near and at full throttle, breaking the feed circuit to the TCC solenoid. The rotary switch was replaced by the vacuum regulator valve on 1982 diesel engines with a TCC transmission.

Testing

The rotary switch can be tested using an ohmmeter. Disconnect the electrical connectors and connect the test leads from the ohmmeter to the TCC terminals leading to the switch. The switch that uses one set of contacts should have no resistance until the throttle is at or near wide open. When the throttle is at this point, resistance should be infinite. The switch that uses two sets of contacts should show infinite resistance with the throttle at or near the closed position. When the throttle is opened halfway, resistance should be zero. And when the throttle is near or at wide open, resistance should be infinite once again. Replace the rotary switch if it doesn't pass these tests.

TCC COLD OVERRIDE SWITCH

The TCC cold override switch is in the TCC solenoid feed circuit on 1982 5.7L V-8 diesels. This normally open switch prevents TCC engine engagement when engine temperature is below 67° C (152° F).

Diagnosis of the Converter Clutch Systems

The diagnosing of the converter clutch system problems can be separated into four major catagories.
1. External electrical controls, less the CCC system.
2. Internal electrical controls.
3. Grounding circuit for the ECM, when equipped with the CCC system.
4. Internal hydraulic system.

PRELIMINARY INSPECTION AND ADJUSTMENT PROCEDURES

Before performing any diagnostic procedures on the converter clutch system, inspect and adjust the following components, as required.
1. Inspect all electrical and vacuum connections, wires and hoses.
2. Be certain the engine is properly turned. Can be diagnosed as a poorly operating transmission/transaxle.
3. Inspect the fluid level and correct as required. Inspect the fluid condition.
4. Inspect the manual linkage and throttle cable (TV) adjustments.
5. Road test the vehicle, with owner, if possible, to verify complaint.

CONVERTER CLUTCH DRIVING CHARACTERISTICS

The converter clutch units have a specific operational characteristics that should not be diagnosed as a transmission/transaxle malfunction. One characteristic, called vehicle "chuggle" is best described as a varying fore and aft motion of the vehicle while driving at a steady speed with the converter clutch engaged. This condition has been misdiagnosed as engine surge, engine miss and tire and wheel balance problems. Another driving characteristic is called a "bump," which occurs when the driver releases the accelerator quickly. The bump is the result from the reversal of the engine torque during deceleration. Both "chuggle" and "bump" characteristics are normal of a vehicle equipped with a converter clutch and repairs are not necessary.

GOVERNOR SWITCHES

If problem is encountered when coverter clutch engages, causing

CONVERTER CLUTCH ELECTRICAL AND HYDRAULIC CONTROLS
1980 Models

Engines	Transmission & Codes	Oil to Solenoid T.C.C. Valve	Switches			Vacuum Controls		Test Lead
			Not In Trans.	In Trans.			Source	
Gas	200-C	Direct	1. Brake N.C.	Gov. Press. SW-N.O.		1. TVS-EGR	EGR-Ported	Near Fuse Panel ①
	250-C	Clutch	2. Lo. Vac. N.O.			2. TVS-EFE		
	350-C					3. Relay Valve		
						4. Delay Valve		
Diesel	200-C	Direct	1. Brake-N.C.	Gov. Press. SW-N.O.		Rotary Valve At Inj. Pump	Vacuum Pump	Near Fuse Panel ①
	350-C	Clutch	2. Lo. Vac.-N.O.					
			3. Hi Vac-N.C.					

① Test lead in feed side of solenoid
② Test lead in ground side of circuit
N.O. = Normally open
N.C. = Normally closed

CONVERTER CLUTCH ELECTRICAL AND HYDRAULIC CONTROLS
1981 Models

Transmissions & Codes	Oil to Solenoid T.C.C. Valve	Switches		Sensors			Test Lead
		Not In Trans.	In Trans.	V.S.S.	Coolant	T.P.S.-Vacuum	
200-C 250-C 350-C MV-4	Direct Clutch	Brake N.C.	None	E.C.M. Input	E.C.M. Input	E.C.M. Input	In Fuse Panel ②
350-C MX-2	Forward Clutch	Brake N.C.	3rd Gear Switch Normally Open	E.C.M. Input	E.C.M. Input	E.C.M. Input	②
350-C MX-3	Forward Clutch	Brake N.C.	2rd Gear Switch Normally Open	E.C.M. Input	E.C.M. Input	E.C.M. Input	②
350-C Lt. Truck MV-4	Direct Clutch	1. Brake N.C. 2. Lo Vac-N.O. 3. 3rd Gear On Trans (EGR)	Gov. Press. Switch-Normally Open Speed & EGR Solenoid Ground				Near Fuse Panel ②
350-C Diesel	Forward Clutch	Brake & Rotary Valve	3rd Gear Switch-N.O. Gov. Press. Switch-N.O. (Speed & EGR Solenoid)				Near Fuse Panel ①
200-C Diesel	Direct Clutch	Brake & Rotary Valve	Gov. Pressure-Veh. Speed & E.C.R. Solenoid Ground-Normally Open				Near Fuse Panel ①
200-4R MW-9	2nd Clutch & T.C.C. Shift Valve	Brake N.C.	1-4th Gear N.C. 2-4-3 Pulse N.C.	E.C.M. Input	E.C.M. Input	E.C.M. Input	In Fuse Panel ②
125-C MD-9	Line	Brake N.C.	3rd Gear Switch Normally Open	E.C.M. Input	E.C.M. Input	E.C.M. Input	In Fuse Panel ②

① Test lead in feed side of solenoid
② Test lead in ground side of circuit
N.O. = Normally open
N.C. = Normally closed

CONVERTER CLUTCH ELECTRICAL AND HYDRAULIC CONTROLS
1982 Without CCC Systems

Transmission and Code	Oil to Solenoid & TCC Valve	Switches Not in Trans.	Switches In Trans.	Apply in Gear	Sensor Device Speed	Sensor Device Temp	Sensor Device Load	Test Lead
350C-MX2 5.7L Diesel	Forward Clutch	Ign-Brake VRV at Inj. Pump	3rd Gear- N.O. Gov.- N.O.	3	Gov. Sw. 40 mph	None	Sw. at Inj. Pump (Heavy Load)	In ALDL①
200-4R-MW9 5.7L Diesel	2nd Clutch Oil Thru TCC Shift Valve	Ign-Brake VRV at Inj. Pump (Open Near W.O.T.)	Gov.- N.O. (Used for EGR Bleed Only)	2-3-4	TCC Shift Valve (Hyd.)	None	Sw. at Inj. Pump (Heavy Load Open)	In ALDL①
325-4L-M57 5.7L Diesel	2nd Clutch Oil Thru TCC Shift Valve	Ign-Brake VRV at Inj. Pump (Open Near W.O.T.)	Gov.- N.O. (Used for EGR Bleed Only)	2-3-4	TCC Shift Valve (Hyd.)	None	Sw. at Inj. Pump (Heavy Load Open)	In ALDL①
700-R4-MD8 6.2L Diesel	2nd Clutch Oil Thru TCC Shift Valve	Ign-Brake TPS at Inj. Pump (Open at Light Throttle)	4-3 Pulse N.C.	2-3-4	TCC Shift Valve (Hyd.)	None	TPS at Inj. Pump (Light Load Open)	Wire Near① Fuse Panel 6″ Lt. Gn.
700-R4-MD8 6.2L Diesel	2nd Clutch Oil Thru TCC Shift Valve	Ign-Brake TPS at Inj. Pump (Open at Light Throttle) Relay-4 W.D. N.C. 4 W.D. Sw. at Transfer Case	4-3 Pulse- N.C. 4th Gear- N.O. (Bypasses Relay to Provide TCC in 4th Only When in 4 W.D.	2-3-4 (ex. 4 W.D.) 4th on 4 W.D.	TCC Shift Valve (Hyd.)	None	TPS at Inj. Pump (Light Load Open) Stays Applied at Heavy Throttle	Wire Near① Fuse Panel 6″ Lt. Gn.
700-R4-MD8 Gas-	2nd Clutch Oil Thru TCC Shift Valve	Ign-Brake Low VAC	4-3 Pulse- N.C. 4th Gear- N.O. (Bypass Lo VAC in 4th)	2-3-4	TCC Shift Valve (Hyd.)	Thermal Vacuum Valve to Lo VAC Sw.	Lo VAC Sw. and Ported VAC Sig. (Stays on in 4th)	Wire Near① Fuse Panel 6″ Lt. Gn.
			3rd Clutch- N.O. TCC Signal- N.O.	EGR Bleed Control				

①Test lead in feed side of solenoid.
N.O. = Normally open.
N.C. = Normally closed.
*Assembly line diagnostic link mounted under dash.

CONVERTER CLUTCH ELECTRICAL AND HYDRAULIC CONTROLS
1982 With CCC Fuel Systems—EMC Control

Transmissions and Codes	Oil to Solenoid & TCC Valve	Switches		Apply Possible Gear	ECM Input Sensors			Test Lead
		Not in Trans.	In Trans.		Speed	Temp.	Load	
125-C (MD9)	Line	Ign-Brake	3rd Gear- N.O.	3rd	Vehicle Speed Sensor	Coolant Sensor	TPS and Vacuum	Note ②③
200C-MV9 250C-M31	Direct Clutch	Ign-Brake	None	3rd	Vehicle Speed Sensor	Coolant Sensor	TPS and Vacuum	ALDL*
350C-MV4	Direct Clutch	Ign-Brake	None	3rd	Vehicle Speed Sensor	Coolant Sensor	TPS and Vacuum	ALDL*
350C-MX2	Forward Clutch	Ign-Brake	3rd Gear- N.O.	3rd	Vehicle Speed Sensor	Coolant Sensor	TPS and Vacuum	ALDL*
350C-MX3	Forward Clutch	Ign-Brake	2nd Gear- N.O.	2nd 3rd	Vehicle Speed Sensor	Coolant Sensor	TPS and Vacuum	ALDL*
350C-MX5	Forward Clutch	Ign-Brake	2nd Gear- N.C. 3rd Gear- N.C.	1st 2nd 3rd	Vehicle Speed Sensor	Coolant Sensor	TPS and Vacuum	ALDL*
200-4R MW9	2nd Clutch Thru TCC Shift Valve	Ign-Brake	4-3 Pulse- N.C. 4th Clutch- N.C.	2-3- 4	Vehicle Speed Sensor	Coolant Sensor	TPS and Vacuum	ALDL*
325-4L M57	2nd Clutch Thru TCC Shift Valve	Ign-Brake	4-3 Pulse- N.C. 4th Clutch- N.C.	2-3- 4	Vehicle Speed Sensor	Coolant Sensor	TPS and Vacuum	ALDL*
700-R4 MD8	2nd Clutch Thru TCC Shift Valve	Ign-Brake	4-3 Pulse N.C. 4th Clutch- N.C.	2-3- 4	Vehicle Speed Sensor	Coolant Sensor	TPS and Vacuum	ALDL*

① Test Lead in feed side of solenoid.
② Test Lead in ground side of solenoid.
③ J-Car in fuse panel—others in ALCL.

N.O.=Normally open.
N.C.=Normally closed.
*Assembly line diagnostic link mounted under dash.

TORQUE CONVERTER CLUTCH

Number Code	Part Number	Color Code	On/Off Psi	Transmission
33	8641197	Green	33-30	350C
34	8633398	Green	34-31	200C
36	8630740	Tan	36-33	350C
38	8633363	White	38-35	350C
40	8641265	Violet	40-36	350C
42	8630819	Yellow	42-38	350C
44	8633361	Pink	44-40	350C
46	8633362	Silver	46-42	200C
48	8633359	Orange	48-44	200C
50	8633397	White	50-46	200C
52	8633360	Yellow	52-50	200C
54	8633364	Lt. Brown	54-50	200C

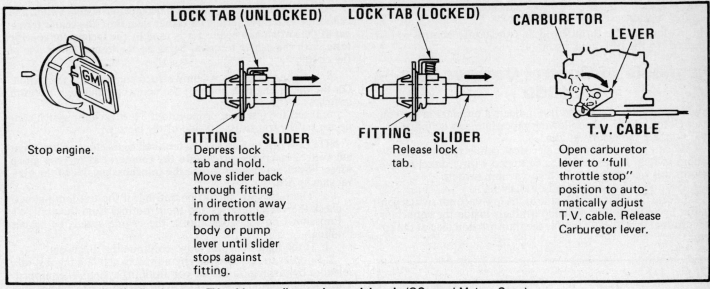

LOCK TAB (UNLOCKED)   **LOCK TAB (LOCKED)**   **CARBURETOR LEVER**

Stop engine.

FITTING   **SLIDER**
Depress lock tab and hold. Move slider back through fitting in direction away from throttle body or pump lever until slider stops against fitting.

FITTING   **SLIDER**
Release lock tab.

T.V. CABLE
Open carburetor lever to "full throttle stop" position to automatically adjust T.V. cable. Release Carburetor lever.

Initial adjustment of self-adjusting type TV cable, gasoline engine models only (©General Motors Corp.)

a torsional vibration or chuggle, an improved coverter clutch engagement can be attained by changing the Governor switch, which is located on the valve body of the 350C-250C transmissions, or on the case next to the valve body on the 200C Transmissions.

Use this procedure: First road test the vehicle and see what road speed the clutch engages (check speedometer). Then remove governor switch and check number that is stamped on switch. Add eight to the number on switch and select the switch closest to the sum of those numbers. Example: 36 is on switch you remove, add 8, then replace with a number 44 (8633361). Re-road test.

Throttle Valve (T.V.) Cable Adjustment

GASOLINE ENGINE WITH MANUAL CABLE

1. Engine must be stopped.
2. Unlock the T.V. cable snap lock by pushing upon the snap lock button.
3. Rotate the carburetor lever by hand to the wide open throttle position.
4. Lock the T.V. cable by pressing down on the cable snap button.

GASOLINE ENGINES WITH SELF-ADJUSTING CABLE

1. Engine must be stopped.
2. Depress the T.V. cable lock tab. With the lock tab depressed, move the cable slider back through the cable fitting in a direction away from the carburetor throttle body or accelerator pump lever.
3. Release the lock tab to lock the cable slider in its position.

4. Rotate the carburetor lever by hand to the wide open throttle position to automatically adjust the T.V. cable.

DIESEL ENGINES WITH MANUAL T.V. CABLE

1. The engine must be stopped.
2. Remove the cruise control rod, if equipped.
3. Unlock the T.V. cable snap lock by pushing up on the snap lock button.
4. Remove the T.V. cable from the bell crank.
5. Remove the throttle rod from the bell crank by moving it away from its attaching pin on the bell crank.
6. Rotate the bell crank to the wide open throttle stop position and hold it in this position.

NOTE: If the bell crank cannot be placed in the wide open throttle stop position when the accelerator pedal is depressed, all wide open throttle stop adjustments must be made with the accelerator in the completely depressed position, instead of rotating the bell crank by hand.

7. Push the throttle rod and pump lever to the wide open throttle stop position. Adjust the throttle rod to meet the bell crank pin at the wide open throttle stop position.

NOTE: Do not connect the throttle rod to the bell crank at this time.

8. Release the bell crank and reconnect the T.V. cable to the bell crank.
9. Rotate the bell crank to the wide open throttle stop position and hold in place.

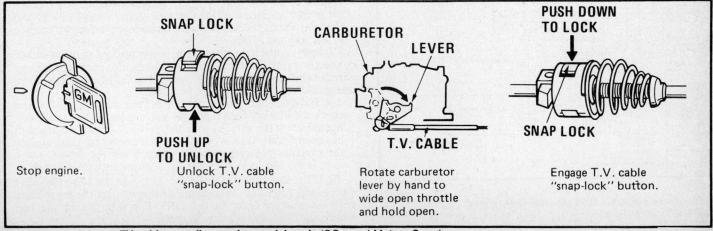

SNAP LOCK   **CARBURETOR LEVER**   **PUSH DOWN TO LOCK**

Stop engine.

PUSH UP TO UNLOCK
Unlock T.V. cable "snap-lock" button.

T.V. CABLE
Rotate carburetor lever by hand to wide open throttle and hold open.

SNAP LOCK
Engage T.V. cable "snap-lock" button.

Adjusting manual type TV cable, gasoline engine models only (©General Motors Corp.)

10. Lock the T.V. cable snap lock by pushing down on the cable snap lock button. Release the bell crank.

11. Reconnect the throttle rod and the cruise control rod (if equipped) to the bell crank assembly.

Diagnosis of Control Components— 1980

Should the results of the road test indicate a problem in the converter clutch system, the following procedure can be followed.

1. Operate the engine at idle.

2. Locate and remove the electrical connection on the low vacuum switch. If the vehicle is equipped with a diesel engine, perform this operation on the high vacuum switch.

3. Ground the negative lead of a test light.

4. Locate the transmission side of the low vacuum switch connection by probing both female terminals inside the connector. The terminal that doesn't light is the transmission side of the circuit.

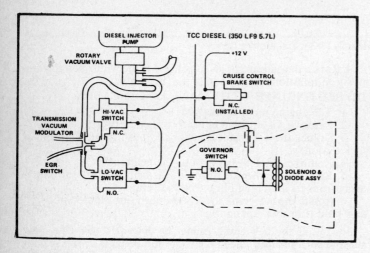

Electrical schematic for gasoline engines with vacuum delay valve
(©General Motors Corp.)

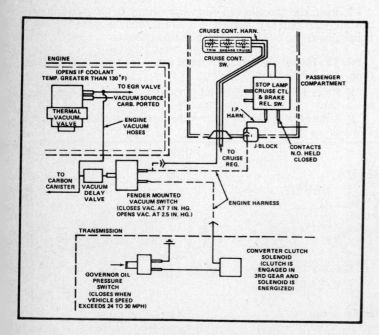

Electrical schematic for 1980 diesel engine, typical
(©General Motors Corp.)

NOTE: Certain vehicle models have the low vacuum switch and connector with three terminals rather than two. The center terminal of the switch and connector is used by the factory for specific tests, with the center terminal being on the transmission side of the circuit.

5. Reconnect the low vacuum switch connector to the switch. On the diesel engines, connect the connector the high vacuum switch.

6. Insert the test light probe into the low vacuum switch connector on the transmission side of the circuit.

NOTE: When testing a three terminal connector and low vacuum switch, insert the probe into the connector at the two green wires. For diesel engines, probe the transmission side of the high vacuum switch.

a. The test lamp should be out, but if the test lamp glows, check the vacuum hoses and their routings from the vehicle's Emission Control label. Check the engine speed for proper idling.

b. If the light does not glow, continue the diagnosis.

7. In order to increase the engine speed, activate the fast idle solenoid by turning on the air conditioning system, if equipped. The test light should remain off. On diesel equipped vehicles, disconnect the pink and green wire connector from the engine coolant switch to activate the fast idle solenoid. The test light at the high vacuum switch should remain off.

a. Should the test light glow, adjust the fast idle speed to proper specifications. On diesel engines, it is necessary to adjust the fast idle speed and the high vacuum switch (procedures follow this testing outline).

NOTE: Should the test light continue to glow at the transmission/transaxle side of the electrical circuit, on the low vacuum or high vacuum switches after a fast idle speed or high vacuum switch adjustment, check the operation of the low vacuum switch and double check the vacuum hose routings against the vehicle's Emission Control label.

b. If the test light remains off with the engine at idle, with the fast idle solenoid activated, continue the diagnosis.

8. With the test light still in place on either the low or high vacuum switch, slowly raise the engine speed. The test light should glow when the engine speed is increased and go out when the engine speed is decreased back to idle. With the engine idle speed above idle and the light glowing, depress the brake pedal and the light should go out.

a. If the test lamp indicates the vacuum switches are operating properly, continue the diagnosis.

b. Should the test light glow above engine idle speed, but not go out when the brake pedal is depressed, check the brake switch for proper operation.

c. If the test light does not glow at any engine speed, check for a blown fuse in the fuse panel, broken or loose wires and connectors in the converter clutch control circuit or check the operation of the low and/or high vacuum switches. Also, check for proper operation of the thermal vacuum valve (TVV) and the relay valve, if equipped, and recheck for the proper routing of the vacuum hoses.

9. Insert a test light in series between the low vacuum switch connector terminals. On the diesel models, also connect a jumper wire between the high vacuum switch connector terminals. Turn the ignition switch to the ON position.

a. If the test light glows, remove the transmission oil pan and check the wire between the apply valve solenoid and the governor switch. If the wire is grounded, pinched or cut, the problem has been found. However, should this not be the case, replace the governor pressure switch and again test the circuit.

b. If the test light does not glow, continue with the test.

10. If the test light did not glow, as in test 9b, raise the drive wheels and blocking the remaining wheels, start the engine and with the selector lever in the DRIVE position, spin the rear wheels up to approximately 50 mph.

11. The test light between the low vacuum switch electrical connector terminals should begin to glow between approximately 35 to 50 mph and should stop glowing at speed below 30 mph.

a. If the test light does not glow as stated, check the wire between the low vacuum switch and the transmission electrical connector for an open circuit. If this is found, repair or replace the wire as required.

b. If the circuit is without defect, remove the transmission oil pan and check for a loose, disconnected or cut wire. Check for a defective solenoid. If the solenoid is defective, replace it. If the solenoid is good, replace the governor pressure switch.

c. If the test light between the low vacuum switch connector terminals begins to glow between 35 and 50 mph and shuts off at speeds below 30 mph, the electrical circuits and components are operating properly. Remove the test lamp and jumper wire. Re-connect the wire connectors as required.

12. If a vacuum or electrical malfunction has not been found, to correct the problem with the converter clutch unit, an internal hydraulic/mechanical controls check will have to be done.

NOTE: Refer to diagnostic pages for 1980 procedures.

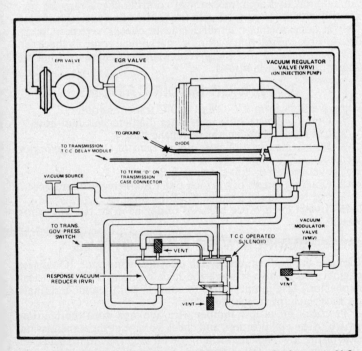

Typical diesel engine EGR system. Differences exist between V-6 and V-8 engines and from year to year (©General Motors Corp.)

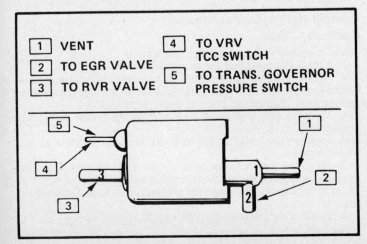

1	VENT	
2	TO EGR VALVE	
3	TO RVR VALVE	
4	TO VRV TCC SWITCH	
5	TO TRANS. GOVERNOR PRESSURE SWITCH	

TCC solenoid assembly (©General Motors Corp.)

Engine Idle and Fast Idle Adjustments
GASOLINE AND DIESEL ENGINE—1980

Refer to the appropriate Chilton Automotive Service manual and/or to the vehicle's Emission Control Information label for the proper engine idle and fast idle adjusting procedures for the particular vehicle being serviced. Adjust to specifications as listed on the Emission Control Information label.

High Vacuum Switch Adjustment
5.7L DIESEL ENGINES

1. Using a self-powered test light, connect the test light lead to either terminal at the high vacuum switch. Connect the test probe to the other switch terminal.

2. With the engine at high idle speed, energize the fast idle solenoid by disconnecting the pink and green wire connector from the coolant temperature switch, normally located on the intake manifold at the rear of the engine.

3. Remove the seal cap on the rear of the high vacuum switch.

— CAUTION —

If the air cleaner assembly is removed when making the switch adjustment, the EGR solenoid port to the EGR valve must be plugged to prevent a vacuum leak at the EGR solenoid.

4. Check the test lamp. If the light glows, this indicates the high vacuum switch has a closing circuit. If the test light is off, turn the switch adjustment screw clockwise until the test light begins to glow. An Allen type hex wrench is needed, sized to 5/16 inch.

5. Adjust the vacuum switch by slowly turning the adjustment screw counterclockwise until the light goes off.

6. With the wrench and screw at just the light off position, turn the wrench clockwise an additionmal 1/8 to 3/16 inch to properly adjust the high vacuum switch.

High Vacuum Switch Check
5.7 L DIESEL ENGINE

1. Disconnect the vacuum hose and electrical connector from the high vacuum switch (if they're not already disconnected).

2. Attach one lead of a test light to either of the two high vacuum switch terminals.

3. Ground the remaining high vacuum switch terminal.

4. Attach the remaining test light lead to the **hot** side of the battery.

5. Attach a hand vacuum pump with a gauge to the high vacuum switch vacuum port.

6. Work the hand vacuum pump.

a. The test light should remain glowing until the vacuum reading on the hand pump gauge reaches 11.5 to 13 inches and then goes out.

b. Slowly let air back into the hand pump. The test light should go on when vacuum drops below 11.5 to 13 inches.

7. If the test light does not turn on and off at the specified vacuum values, the high vacuum switch is inoperative and must be replaced.

Low Vacuum Switch Check

1. Disconnect the vacuum hose and electrical connector from the low vacuum switch (if not already disconnected).

2. Attach one lead of a test light to either of the two low vacuum switch terminals.

3. Ground the remaining low vacuum switch terminal.

4. Attach the remaining test light lead to the hot side of the low vacuum switch connector.

5. Attach a hand vacuum pump with a gauge to the vacuum port of the low vacuum switch.

6. Turn the ignition switch to the ON position.

7. Work the hand vacuum pump.

a. The test light should remain off until the hand vacuum pump gauge reads between:

- 5.5 and 6.5 inches for the 3.8 Liter engine
- 6.5 and 7.5 inches for the 4.9 Liter engine
- 7.5 and 8.5 inches for the 5.7 Liter engine
- 5.0 and 6.0 inches for the 5.7 Liter diesel engine

b. The test light should begin glowing between the vacuum values given above.

8. Slowly let air into the vacuum pump.

a. The test light should remain on until the hand vacuum pump gauge drops to between:

- .3 and 1.3 inches for the 3.8 Liter engine
- 1.2 and 2.2 inches for the 4.9 Liter engine
- 1.5 and 2.5 inches for the 5.7 Liter engine
- 3.5 and 4.5 inches for the 5.7 Liter diesel engine

b. The test light should go out between the values given above.

9. If the low vacuum switch does not turn the test light on and off at the vacuum values given above, the switch must be replaced.

NOTE: The high vacuum limit (the point at which the test light begins glowing) and the low vacuum limit (the point at which the test light turns off) must have at least 4 inches of difference for all gasoline engines. On diesel engines, the low vacuum switch will turn the test light on and off at the same vacuum level.

Brake Switch Check

NOTE: Make sure that the brake switch is properly adjusted before performing the following check.

1. Disconnect the electrical connector from the rear of the brake switch. (The exposed terminals are for converter clutch release and cruise control, if so equipped.)
2. Turn the ignition switch to the ON position.
3. Check for current at the connector. (Current should flow from only one terminal; otherwise, the switch is defective and must be replaced.)
4. Ground one of the terminals of the brake release switch with a jumper wire.
5. Connect one test light lead to the remaining brake release switch terminal.
6. Attach the remaining test light lead to the brake switch connector wire. The test light should now glow.
7. Depress brake pedal.
   a. If the test light goes out, the brake switch is okay.
   b. If the test light is off before brake application, or if the test light does not go off during brake application, the brake switch is inoperative and must be replaced.

Thermal Vacuum Valve (TVV) Check

1. Disconnect the vacuum hose at the thermal vacuum valve EFE port.
2. Attach a vacuum gauge to the EFE port.

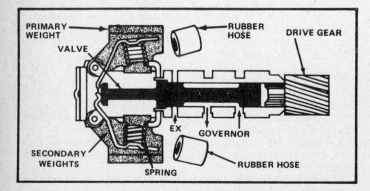

PRIMARY WEIGHT — VALVE — RUBBER HOSE — DRIVE GEAR — EX — GOVERNOR — SECONDARY WEIGHTS — SPRING — RUBBER HOSE

Rubber hose location on governor assembly to test TCC operation, typical (©General Motors Corp.)

3. Start the engine and check the vacuum gauge reading.
   a. With a cold engine, the vacuum gauge should read a minimum of 10 inches vacuum.
   b. With a warm engine (approximately 5 minutes running at fast idle), the vacuum reading should be zero.
4. If these readings are **not** obtained, the TVV switch is inoperative and must be replaced.

NOTE: An engine is cold when engine coolant temperature is below 150 degrees Fahrenheit for 4.9 Liter engines, and below 120 degrees Fahrenheit for 3.8 and 5.7 Liter engines. Conversely, an engine is considered warm when engine coolant temperature is above 150 degrees Fahrenheit for 4.9 Liter engines, and above 120 degrees Fahrenheit for 3.8 and 5.7 Liter engines.

Diagnosis of Internal Hydraulic/ Mechanical Controls—1980 Models

GENERAL INFORMATION

An internal hydraulic/mechanical controls check may be performed with the transmission in the vehicle; however, this should only be done after all external diagnostic checks have been made. In addition, the internal hydraulic/mechanical controls check can only be performed after the governor has been removed from the transmission and modified.

GOVERNOR MODIFICATIONS

For governors from 250 C and 350 C transmissions:
1. Obtain a length of ½ inch outer diameter vacuum hose.
2. Cut two ¾ inch lengths off of the hose.
3. Insert one piece of hose under each of the two governor weights.

For governors from 200 C transmissions:
1. Obtain a length of 5/16 inch outer diameter vacuum hose.
2. Cut two ⅜ inch lengths off of the hose.
3. Insert each piece of hose under each of the governor weights.

JUMPER WIRE CONNECTIONS

Remove the low vacuum switch electrical connector. (On diesel engine models, also remove the high vacuum switch electrical connector.) Use jumper wires to connect both female terminals on each vacuum switch connector.

To check for proper jumper wire hookups, turn the ignition switch to the ON position, and check voltage at the transmission side of the low vacuum switch, (or the high vacuum switch on diesel engine models)—a twelve volt reading should be obtained. If not, doublecheck the jumper wire connections and check the voltage again.

Internal Hydraulic/Mechanical Controls Check

When a proper voltage reading is obtained:
1. Install the modified test governor.
2. Make sure that the vehicle's rear wheels are several inches off the ground, and apply the parking brake so that the rear wheels cannot turn. (Adjust the parking brake if necessary.)
3. With the gear selector in PARK, start the engine and run it at idle.
4. Step on the brake pedal to break the current flow to the transmission.
5. Place the gear selector lever in the DRIVE position. The modified test governor, with its weights held out by the strips of vacuum tubing, should cause the transmission to shift into third gear.
6. Release the brake pedal; the engine should stall.

IF ENGINE STALLS . . .

If the engine stalls, the transmission converter clutch's internal hydraulic and mechanical controls are working properly. The diagnosis is complete.

Remove the modified test governor from the transmission and take out the piece of vacuum tubing under each of the governor weights.

It is also extremely important to make sure that the governor weight springs are seated in their proper locations before reinstall the governor.

Also, be sure to remove the jumper wire at the low vacuum switch electrical connector and reconnect the connector to the switch. (On diesel engine models, also do the same at the high vacuum switch.)

IF THE ENGINE DOES NOT STALL . . .

If the engine does **not** stall during the internal controls check, check for loose solenoid mounting bolts.

1. On 250 C and 350 C transmissions, also check for a missing check ball in the solenoid.

2. For 200 C transmissions, check for a missing check ball or "O" ring.

CONVERTER CLUTCH SOLENOID LOCATIONS

THM 180C	On valve body
THM 200C	On oil pump
THM 200-4R	Through case and into oil pump
THM 250C	Valve body
THM 350C	Valve body
THM 700-R4	Through case and into oil pump
THM 125C	Valve body
THM 325-4L	On accumulator housing
THM 440	Valve body

Solenoid Checks

WITH REMOVABLE CHECK BALL ASSEMBLY

1. Remove the solenoid from the transmission/transaxle assembly.

2. Press on the bottom of the solenoid to remove the plastic check ball assembly.

3. Disassemble the check ball assembly and check for scores, nicks or scratches on the check ball and ball seat. If necessary, replace the solenoid assembly.

4. When reassembling the check ball assembly, check for the ball seat being offset and the check ball positioned directly under the ball seat.

5. Reinstall the check ball assembly into the solenoid and reinstall the solenoid into the transmission/transaxle assembly.

WITH NON-REMOVABLE CHECK BALL ASSEMBLY

1. Remove the solenoid from the transmission/transaxle assembly.

2. Hold the solenoid up to a light and visually inspect the check ball and the "O" ring.

3. If either the ball or the "O" ring seems scratched, nicked or scored, replace the solenoid.

4. Replace the solenoid into the transmission/transaxle.

Other Possible Problems

Other possible problems that can effect the converter clutch system, as well as other major assemblies in the transmission/transaxle units include:

1. An apply valve which is sticking, binding or damaged.

2. A turbine shaft "O" ring which is missing or damaged.

3. Direct clutch oil passages which are blocked, restricted or interconnected.

Having completed all diagnostic and servicing procedures, be sure to road test the vehicle a second time to make sure the problem is resolved.

Diagnosis of Control Components—1981 and Later With and Without Electronic Control Module (ECM)

GENERAL INFORMATION

Tachometers and Ohmmeters are used to test the varied circuits in the 1981 and later converter clutch systems. Because of the many transmission/transaxle applications, it is important to identify the unit and its controlling components, in order to properly test and diagnose the converter clutch operation.

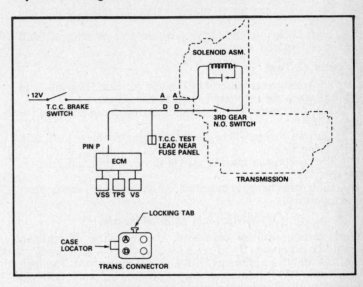

1981 and later TCC wiring schematic when equipped with Computer Command Control, typical (©General Motors Corp.)

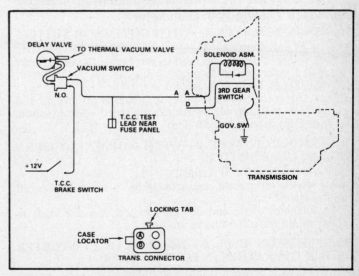

1981 and later TCC wiring schematic except with Computer Command Control, typical (©General Motors Corp.)

TACHOMETER DIAGNOSIS

The tachometer is used to verify the converter clutch operation during a road test with the vehicle weight and resistance acting upon the converter. An on-hoist test is inconclusive because the rpm changes in light load conditions are hard to detect.

The tachometer to be used should be one of the following;

1. Equipped with a primary pick-up lead.

2. Equipped with a secondary pick-up lead.

3. Balancer mag-tach type.

The tachometer that is used should be mounted in the passenger compartment, with the leads routed and taped to prevent damage. Place the tachometer in a position that it is easily readable. Observe all driving safety regulations.

Testing With the Tachometer
1. Verify the tachometer is operating properly.
2. Road test the vehicle, using the drive position.
3. Allow the transmission/transaxle to shift into the top gear.
4. Hold the road speed steady and read the tachometer.
5. While holding the speed steady, depress the brake pedal just enough to open the converter clutch circuit and read the tachometer.
6. Shift to the next lowest manual range and repeat steps 4 and 5.
7. Shift back into the Drive position and monitor all shift points, as required.

Results of Test

1. The rpm change is step 4 to 5 should increase. This indicates slippage when the converter clutch is disengaged.
2. The rpm change will be greater if the top gear is an overdrive gear.
3. The rpm change will be greater with greater engine load, such as on an incline.
4. The tachometer must be read at the same mph indicated on the speedometer.
5. If no rpm change is indicated, converter clutch engagement is not occurring.

OHMMETER DIAGNOSIS

When testing with an ohmmeter, the following information should be observed;
1. Use only an ohmmeter with a needle movement. The high impedance DVOM does not operate because the small miliamp current passing through the solenoid coil, reacts as though the resistance was zero.
2. Disconnect the wire harness at the transmission/transaxle.

Resistance Testing With Ohmmeter

TRANSMISSION TYPE A—WITH GOVERNOR SWITCH
Meter A—Leads Term A—D.
  Check solenoid diode—no need to run engine. Reverse meter leads and make 2nd check.
Meter B—Leads Term D to ground.
  Check Governor Switch requires rear wheels off ground and run vehicle to Governor Switch closing speed—Meter should change from infinity to near zero.

TRANSMISSION TYPE B—WITH NORMALLY OPEN (N.O.) 3rd GEAR SWITCH
Meter A—Leads to Term A and D.
  Rear wheels off ground, engine running to make 2-3 upshift and complete circuit.
  Test solenoid, diode and 3rd gear switch. Reverse leads to check diode while holding in 3rd gear.

TRANSMISSION TYPE C—200-4R WITH CONVERTER CLUTCH OPERATION IN FOURTH GEAR
Meter A—Leads between Conn. A and ground.
  Engine stopped, check continuity of solenoid and diode. Reverse leads and check diode.
Meter B—Leads Term D to ground.
  Check Governor Switch requires rear wheels off ground and run vehicle to Governor Switch closing speed—Meter should change from infinity to near zero.

TRANSMISSION TYPE D—
WITH NORMALLY CLOSED (N.C.) 4-3 PULSE SWITCH
WITH NORMALLY OPEN (N.O.) 4TH GEAR SWITCH
WITH NORMALLY OPEN (N.O.) 3RD GEAR SWITCH
AND NORMALLY
OPEN (N.O.) CONVERTER CLUTCH SIGNAL SWITCH

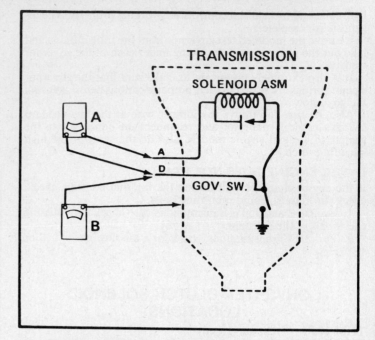

Transmission type A (©General Motors Corp.)

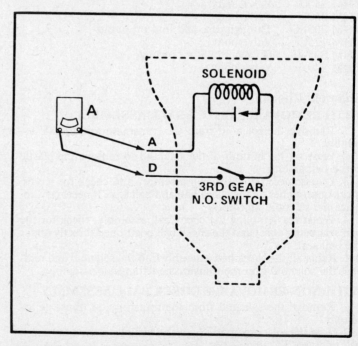

Transmission type B (©General Motors Corp.)

Meter A—Leads between Conn. A and ground.
  Step 1—Engine stopped, check continuity of solenoid, diode and 4-3 sw. Reverse leads and check diode.
  Step 2—Run engine with rear wheels off ground and make downshift to check operation of 4-3 sw.
Meter B—Leads between Conn. and A & B.
  Check 4th clutch switch requires rear wheels off ground. Run engine to make 3-4 upshift—Meter should change from infinite to zero.
Meter C—Leads Term D to ground.
  Requires rear wheels off ground. Run engine and vehicle to close 3rd clutch and TCC signal switches. Meter change from infinite to near zero.

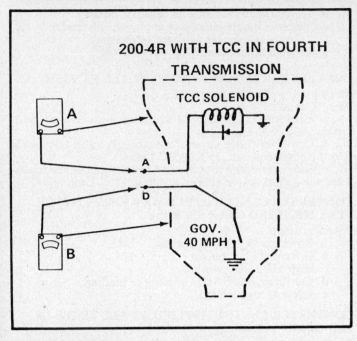

Transmission type C (©General Motors Corp.)

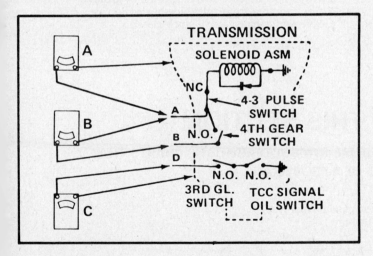

Transmission type D (©General Motors Corp.)

TRANSAXLE TYPE A—
WITH NORMALLY CLOSED (N.C.) 4-3 DOWNSHIFT SWITCH
WITH NORMALLY CLOSED (N.C.) 4TH CLUTCH SWITCH
WITH THREE WIRE CONNECTOR

Meter A—Leads between Conn. A and B.
    Step 1—Engine stopped, check continuity of solenoid, diode and 4-3 sw. Reverse leads and check diode.
    Step 2—Run engine with rear wheels off ground and make downshift to check operation of 4-3 sw.
Meter B—Check 4th clutch switch requires rear wheels off ground. Run engine to make 3-4 upshift—Meter should change from zero to infinite.

TRANSAXLE TYPE B—
WITH NORMALLY CLOSED (N.C.) 4-3 DOWNSHIFT SWITCH
WITH NORMALLY OPEN (N.O.) GOVERNOR SWITCH
WITH TWO WIRE CONNECTOR

Meter A—Leads between Conn. A and ground.
    Step 1—Engine stopped, check continuity of solenoid, diode and 4-3 switch. Reverse leads and check diode.
    Step 2—Rear wheels off ground, run engine and make downshift to. check operation of 4-3 pulse switch.
Meter B—Leads Term D to ground.
    Requires rear wheels off ground. Run engine and vehicle to Governor Switch closing speed—Meter change from infinite to near zero.

Solenoid Diode Check

The transmission/transaxle solenoids should not be bench tested by touching the leads to an automobile battery. The internal diode will be destroyed by touching the negative terminal (black, marked with a −) to the positive battery terminal and the positive terminal (red, marked with a +) to the negative battery terminal. The diodes used in the solenoids must only be checked using a meter reading or scale type ohmmeters, set on the X1 scale. Electronic or digital type meters canot be used because of false indications being obtained.

Testing Procedure

1. Set the ohmmeter on the X1 scale and zero the needle.
2. Connect the positive meter and solenoid leads together and the negative meter and solenoid leads together.
3. If the meter reading is 20 to 40 ohms (depending upon solenoid temperature), the diode and/or coil is not shorted.
4. If the meter reading is 0 ohms, the diode or coil is shorted.
5. If the meter reading indicates an open circuit reading, the coil is open.

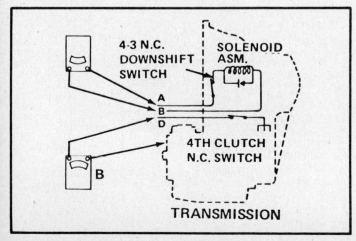

Transaxle type A (©General Motors Corp.)

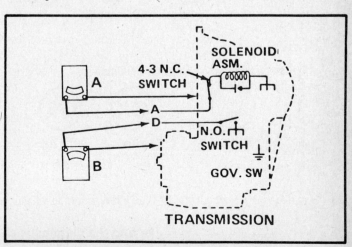

Transaxle type B (©General Motors Corp.)

6. When the ohmmeter leads are reversed, the solenoid is operative if the reading is 2 to 15 ohms less than those in step 3.

7. If the meter reading is zero, the diode is open.

Converter Clutch Diagnose When Equipped with C.C.C., E.C.M. or Governor Switch Control

Preliminary Checks

1. Check transmission/transaxle oil level and correct as required.

2. Check manual linkage and throttle cable adjustments as required.

3. Road test vehicle to verify complaint at normal operating temperature.

NOTE: If the engine performance indicates the need for an engine tune-up, this should be done before further testing or diagnosing of the unit is made. Poor engine performance can result in rough shifting or other malfunctions.

Road Test Results

CONVERTER CLUTCH APPLIES ERRATICALLY
(This may be described as a shudder, jerking, jumping or rocking sensation).

Possible causes:
  a. Vacuum hose leakage.
  b. Vacuum switch malfunction.
  c. Release oil exhaust orifice at pump blocked or restricted.

  d. Turbine shaft "O" ring damaged or missing.
  e. Converter malfunction, such as pressure plate warped, etc.
  f. "O" ring at solenoid damaged or missing.
  g. Solenoid bolts loose, 200C, 200-4R, 125C

CONVERTER CLUTCH APPLIED IN ALL RANGES
(Engine will stall when put in gear).
Possible causes:
  a. Converter clutch valve in pump stuck in the apply position. 200C, 200-4R.
  b. Converter clutch valve in the auxiliary valve body stuck in the apply position. 250C, 350C Units.
  c. Converter clutch control valve or converter clutch regulator valve stuck in the applied position. 125C Unit.

CONVERTER CLUTCH APPLIES AT VERY LOW OR VERY HIGH 3RD GEAR SPEEDS
Possible causes:
  a. Governor switch malfunction.
  b. Governor Malfunction.
  c. High Main line pressure.
  d. Converter clutch valve sticking or binding.
  e. Solenoid malfunction.

CONVERTER CLUTCH APPLIED AT ALL TIMES IN 3RD GEAR
Possible causes:
  a. Governor pressure switch shorted to ground.
  b. Ground wire from solenoid shorted to case.
  c. Solenoid exhaust valve stuck closed.

HOW TO USE THIS SECTION

THIS SECTION CONTAINS A SERIES OF PICTURE/SYMBOL DIAGNOSTIC CHARTS THAT WILL HELP YOU QUICKLY FIND THE CAUSE OF A PROBLEM.

The charts use symbols, like those used on highway signs. For example, you may be told to:

 Connect

 Disconnect

 Check

 Repair Replace Or Adjust

 Stop

Or, you may be told that a particular condition is:

 Light

 No Limit

 OK

 Not OK

In addition, the charts use pictures like these:

 Ignition On

 Dwell Meter

 Voltmeter

 Digital Voltmeter

Plus a few words to tell you what to do.

To find the diagnostic chart you need:

● Perform Diagnostic Circuit Check

TORQUE CONVERTER CLUTCH DIAGNOSIS

DIAGNOSIS CIRCUIT CHECK
1981-83 CCC System, All Models
(incl. 1980½ 3.8L and 4.3L Engines)

Step/Sequence   **Result**

Always check PROM for correct application and installation before replacing an ECM. Also, remove terminal(s) from ECM connector for circuit involved, clean terminal contact and expand it slightly to increase contact pressure and recheck to see if problem is corrected.

1982-83 (Min. Function) Chevette and T-1000, All w/Automatic Trans. and Federal Models with 4 speed Manual Trans.: Trouble codes are lost when the ignition is turned off. Therefore, on "Check Engine" light complaints, codes should be checked before ignition is turned off, if possible.

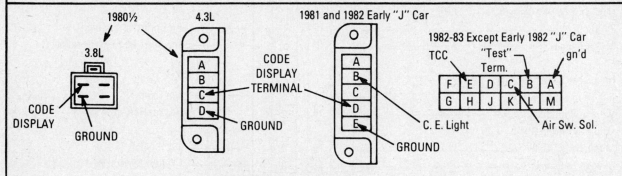

ALCL CONNECTOR TERMINAL LAYOUT

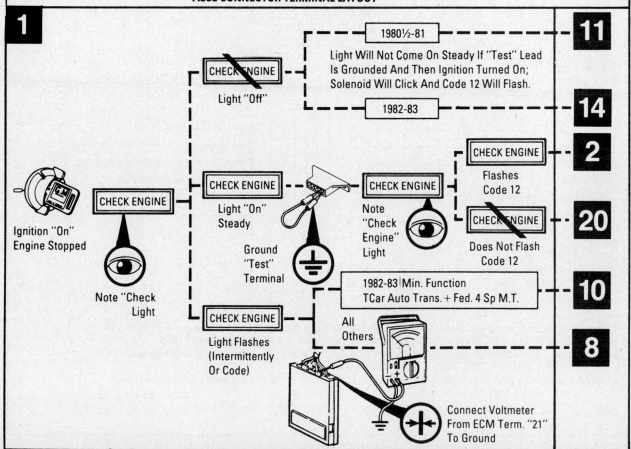

ECM TERMINAL IDENTIFICATION
1981 CCC System Production
(Note: Not all terminals used on all engine applications)

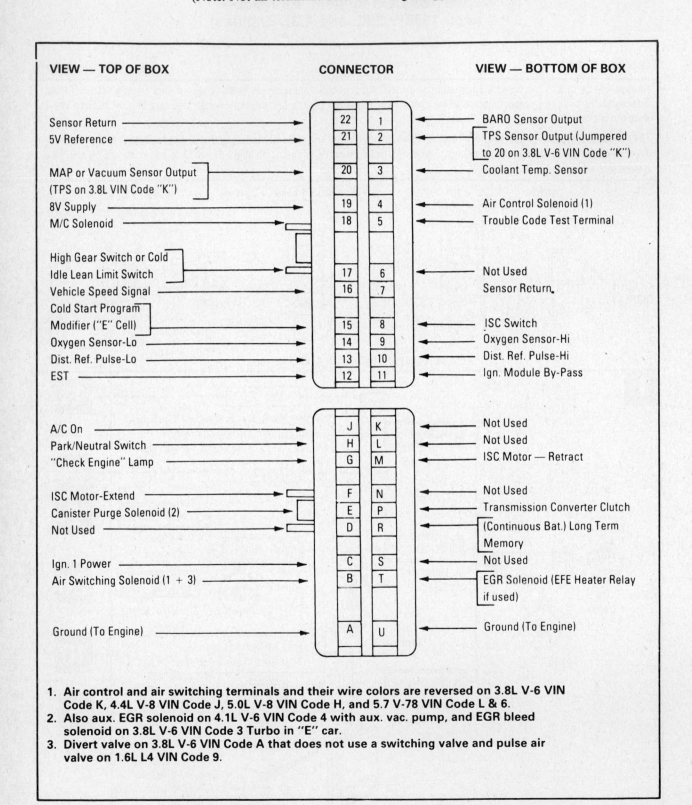

VIEW — TOP OF BOX   CONNECTOR   VIEW — BOTTOM OF BOX

Top of Box	Terminal	Terminal	Bottom of Box
Sensor Return	22	1	BARO Sensor Output
5V Reference	21	2	TPS Sensor Output (Jumpered to 20 on 3.8L V-6 VIN Code "K")
MAP or Vacuum Sensor Output (TPS on 3.8L VIN Code "K")	20	3	Coolant Temp. Sensor
8V Supply	19	4	Air Control Solenoid (1)
M/C Solenoid	18	5	Trouble Code Test Terminal
High Gear Switch or Cold Idle Lean Limit Switch	17	6	Not Used
Vehicle Speed Signal	16	7	Sensor Return.
Cold Start Program Modifier ("E" Cell)	15	8	ISC Switch
Oxygen Sensor-Lo	14	9	Oxygen Sensor-Hi
Dist. Ref. Pulse-Lo	13	10	Dist. Ref. Pulse-Hi
EST	12	11	Ign. Module By-Pass

Top of Box	Terminal	Terminal	Bottom of Box
A/C On	J	K	Not Used
Park/Neutral Switch	H	L	Not Used
"Check Engine" Lamp	G	M	ISC Motor — Retract
ISC Motor-Extend	F	N	Not Used
Canister Purge Solenoid (2)	E	P	Transmission Converter Clutch
Not Used	D	R	(Continuous Bat.) Long Term Memory
Ign. 1 Power	C	S	Not Used
Air Switching Solenoid (1 + 3)	B	T	EGR Solenoid (EFE Heater Relay if used)
Ground (To Engine)	A	U	Ground (To Engine)

1. **Air control and air switching terminals and their wire colors are reversed on 3.8L V-6 VIN Code K, 4.4L V-8 VIN Code J, 5.0L V-8 VIN Code H, and 5.7 V-78 VIN Code L & 6.**
2. **Also aux. EGR solenoid on 4.1L V-6 VIN Code 4 with aux. vac. pump, and EGR bleed solenoid on 3.8L V-6 VIN Code 3 Turbo in "E" car.**
3. **Divert valve on 3.8L V-6 VIN Code A that does not use a switching valve and pulse air valve on 1.6L L4 VIN Code 9.**

ECM TERMINAL IDENTIFICATION
1982 CCC System
(Note: Not all terminals used on all engine applications)

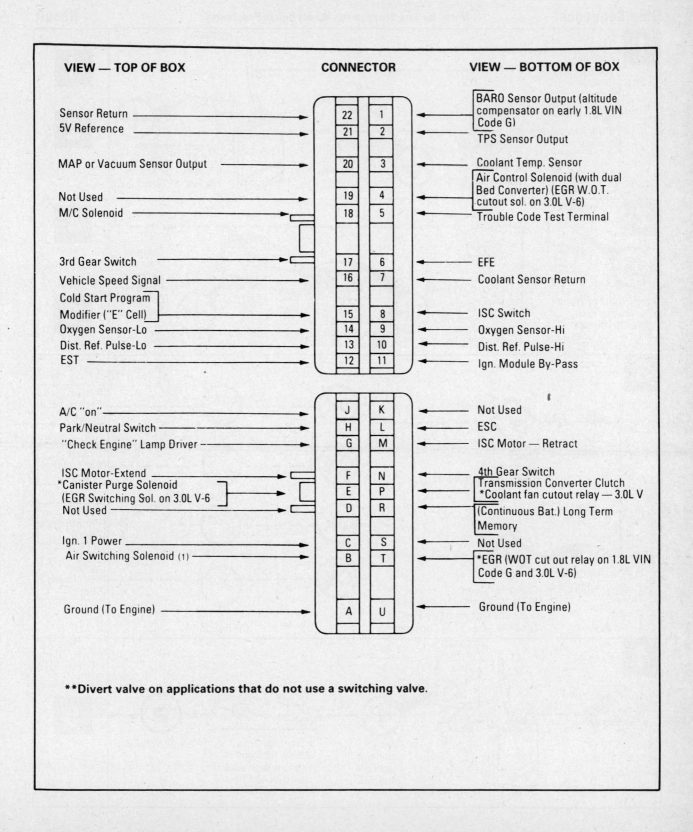

VIEW — TOP OF BOX

- Sensor Return — 22
- 5V Reference — 21
- MAP or Vacuum Sensor Output — 20
- Not Used — 19
- M/C Solenoid — 18
- 3rd Gear Switch — 17
- Vehicle Speed Signal — 16
- Cold Start Program Modifier ("E" Cell) — 15
- Oxygen Sensor-Lo — 14
- Dist. Ref. Pulse-Lo — 13
- EST — 12

CONNECTOR

VIEW — BOTTOM OF BOX

- 1 — BARO Sensor Output (altitude compensator on early 1.8L VIN Code G)
- 2 — TPS Sensor Output
- 3 — Coolant Temp. Sensor
- 4 — Air Control Solenoid (with dual Bed Converter) (EGR W.O.T. cutout sol. on 3.0L V-6)
- 5 — Trouble Code Test Terminal
- 6 — EFE
- 7 — Coolant Sensor Return
- 8 — ISC Switch
- 9 — Oxygen Sensor-Hi
- 10 — Dist. Ref. Pulse-Hi
- 11 — Ign. Module By-Pass

- A/C "on" — J
- Park/Neutral Switch — H
- "Check Engine" Lamp Driver — G
- ISC Motor-Extend — F
- *Canister Purge Solenoid (EGR Switching Sol. on 3.0L V-6) — E
- Not Used — D
- Ign. 1 Power — C
- Air Switching Solenoid (1) — B
- Ground (To Engine) — A

- K — Not Used
- L — ESC
- M — ISC Motor — Retract
- N — 4th Gear Switch
- P — Transmission Converter Clutch *Coolant fan cutout relay — 3.0L V
- R — (Continuous Bat.) Long Term Memory
- S — Not Used
- T — *EGR (WOT cut out relay on 1.8L VIN Code G and 3.0L V-6)
- U — Ground (To Engine)

**Divert valve on applications that do not use a switching valve.

TROUBLE CODE 24—VEHICLE SPEED SENSOR
Carbureted Engines

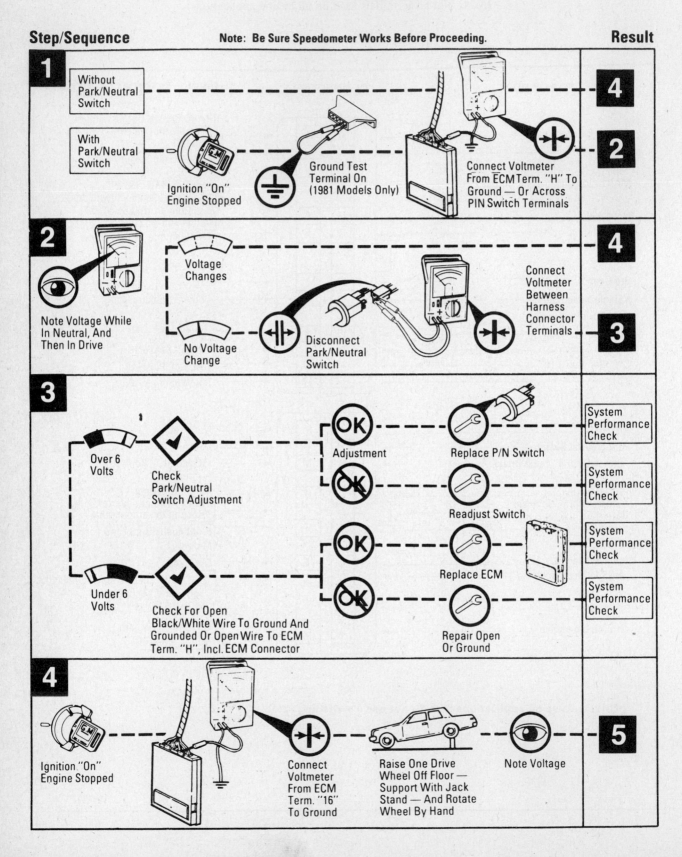

Step/Sequence   Note: Be Sure Speedometer Works Before Proceeding.   **Result**

1

Without Park/Neutral Switch — **4**

With Park/Neutral Switch

Ignition "On" Engine Stopped

Ground Test Terminal On (1981 Models Only)

Connect Voltmeter From ECM Term. "H" To Ground — Or Across PIN Switch Terminals — **2**

2

Note Voltage While In Neutral, And Then In Drive

Voltage Changes — **4**

No Voltage Change

Disconnect Park/Neutral Switch

Connect Voltmeter Between Harness Connector Terminals — **3**

3

Over 6 Volts — Check Park/Neutral Switch Adjustment

OK — Adjustment — Replace P/N Switch — System Performance Check

Not OK — Readjust Switch — System Performance Check

Under 6 Volts — Check For Open Black/White Wire To Ground And Grounded Or Open Wire To ECM Term. "H", Incl. ECM Connector

OK — Replace ECM — System Performance Check

Not OK — Repair Open Or Ground — System Performance Check

4

Ignition "On" Engine Stopped

Connect Voltmeter From ECM Term. "16" To Ground

Raise One Drive Wheel Off Floor — Support With Jack Stand — And Rotate Wheel By Hand

Note Voltage — **5**

TROUBLE CODE 24—VEHICLE SPEED SENSOR (Cont.)
Carbureted Engines

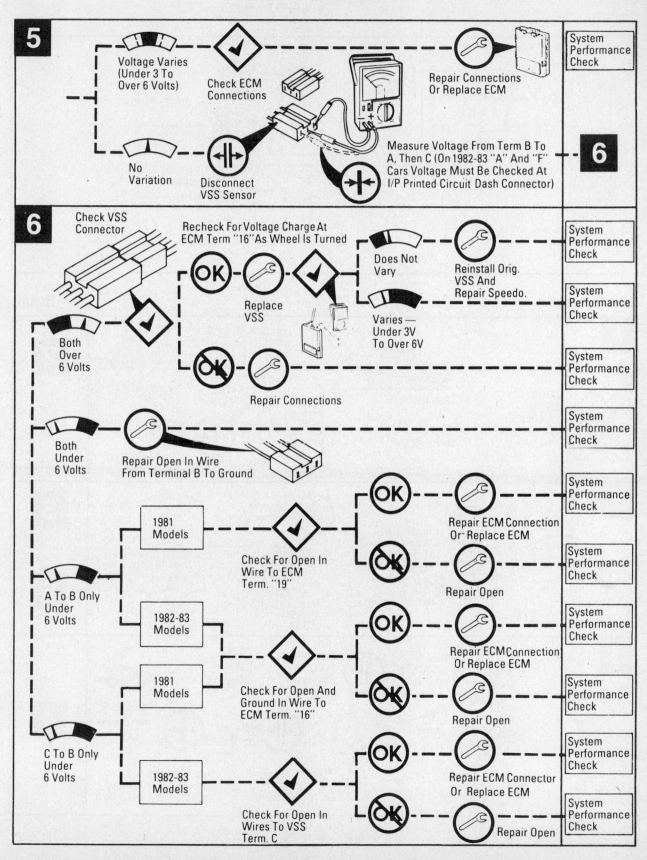

TROUBLE CODE 24—VEHICLE SPEED SENSOR
Throttle Bore Injected Engines

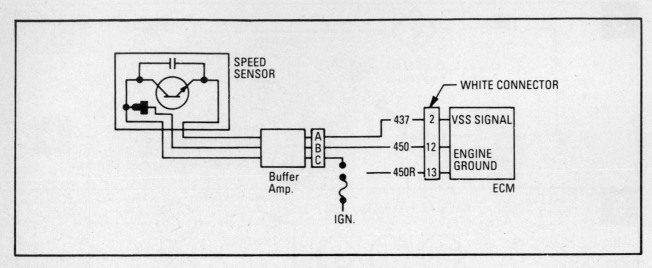

Step/Sequence   **Result**

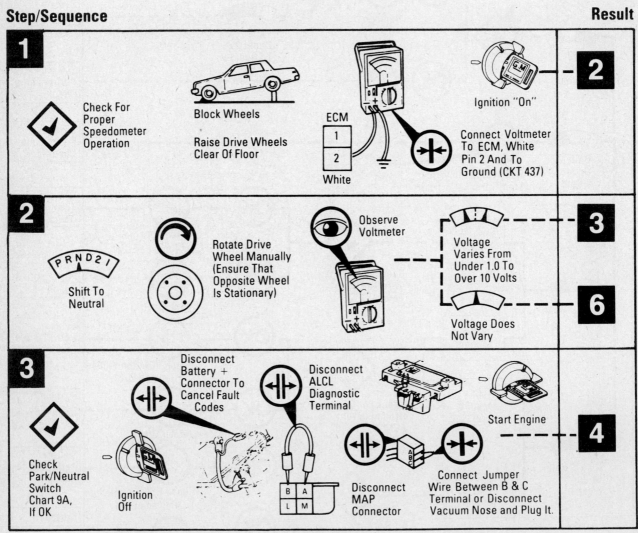

TROUBLE CODE 24—VEHICLE SPEED SENSOR (Cont.)
Throttle Bore Injected Engines

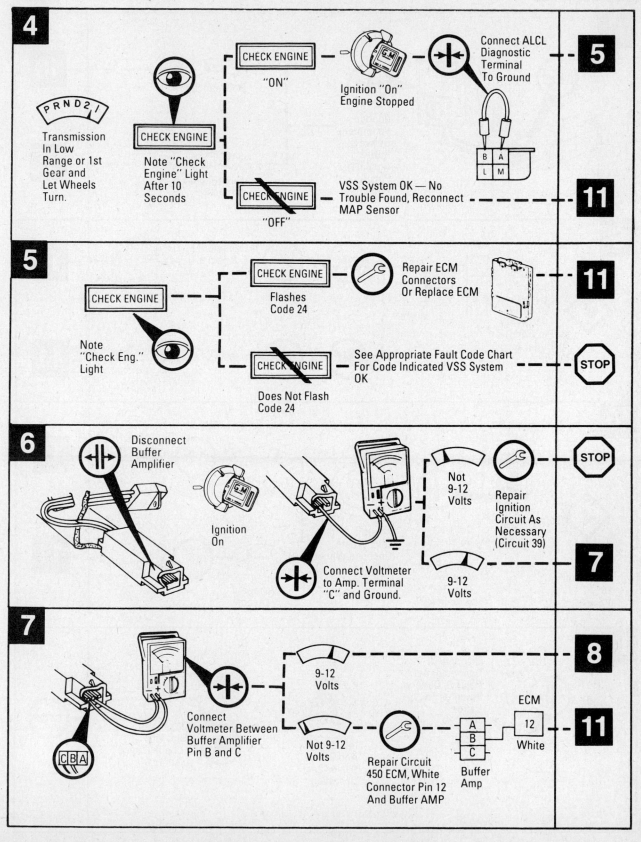

4

PRND21

Transmission In Low Range or 1st Gear and Let Wheels Turn.

CHECK ENGINE

Note "Check Engine" Light After 10 Seconds

CHECK ENGINE "ON"

Ignition "On" Engine Stopped

Connect ALCL Diagnostic Terminal To Ground — **5**

B A / L M

CHECK ENGINE "OFF"

VSS System OK — No Trouble Found, Reconnect MAP Sensor — **11**

5

CHECK ENGINE

Note "Check Eng." Light

CHECK ENGINE / Flashes Code 24

Repair ECM Connectors Or Replace ECM — **11**

CHECK ENGINE / Does Not Flash Code 24

See Appropriate Fault Code Chart For Code Indicated VSS System OK — STOP

6

Disconnect Buffer Amplifier

Ignition On

Connect Voltmeter to Amp. Terminal "C" and Ground.

Not 9-12 Volts

Repair Ignition Circuit As Necessary (Circuit 39) — STOP

9-12 Volts — **7**

7

CBA

Connect Voltmeter Between Buffer Amplifier Pin B and C

9-12 Volts — **8**

Not 9-12 Volts

Repair Circuit 450 ECM, White Connector Pin 12 And Buffer AMP

A B C Buffer Amp

ECM 12 White — **11**

TROUBLE CODE 24—VEHICLE SPEED SENSOR (Cont.)
Throttle Bore Injected Engines

Step/Sequence   **Result**

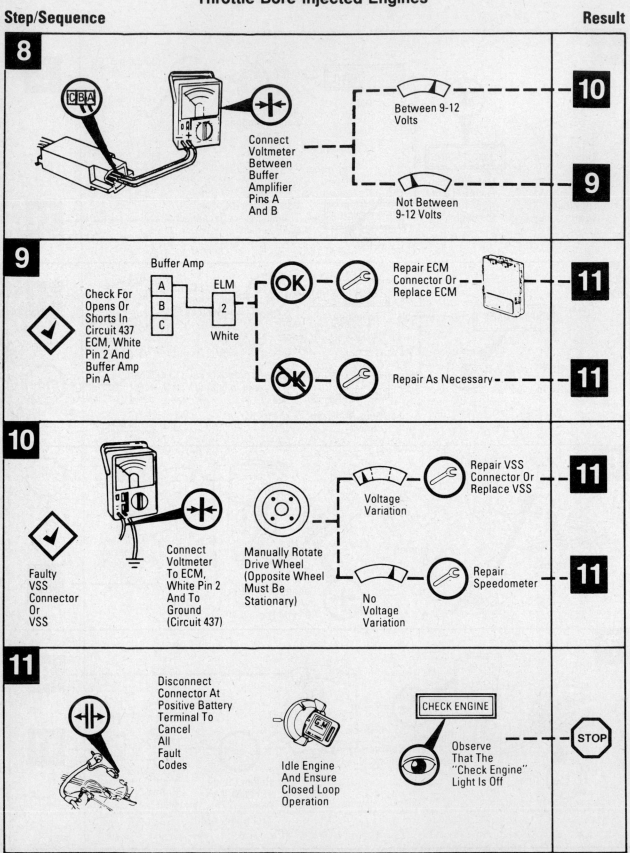

TORQUE CONVERTER CLUTCH (TCC) ELECTRICAL DIAGNOSIS
Fuel Injected Engines

Note: Mechanical checks, such as linkage, oil level, etc., should be performed prior to using this diagnostic procedure.

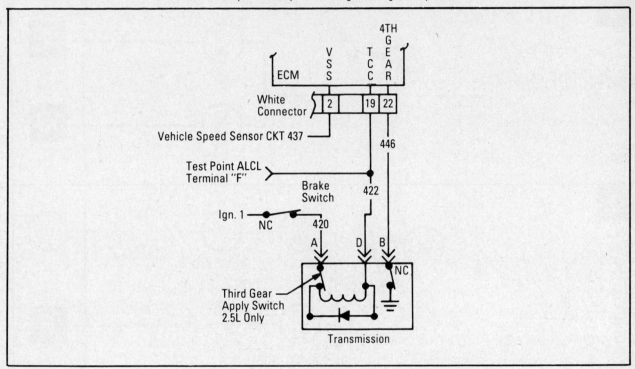

Step/Sequence | **Result**

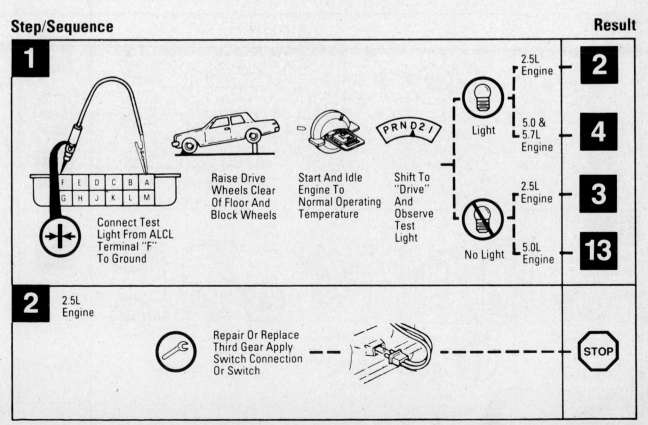

TORQUE CONVERTER CLUTCH (TCC) ELECTRICAL DIAGNOSIS (Cont.)
Fuel Injected Engines

Step/Sequence   **Result**

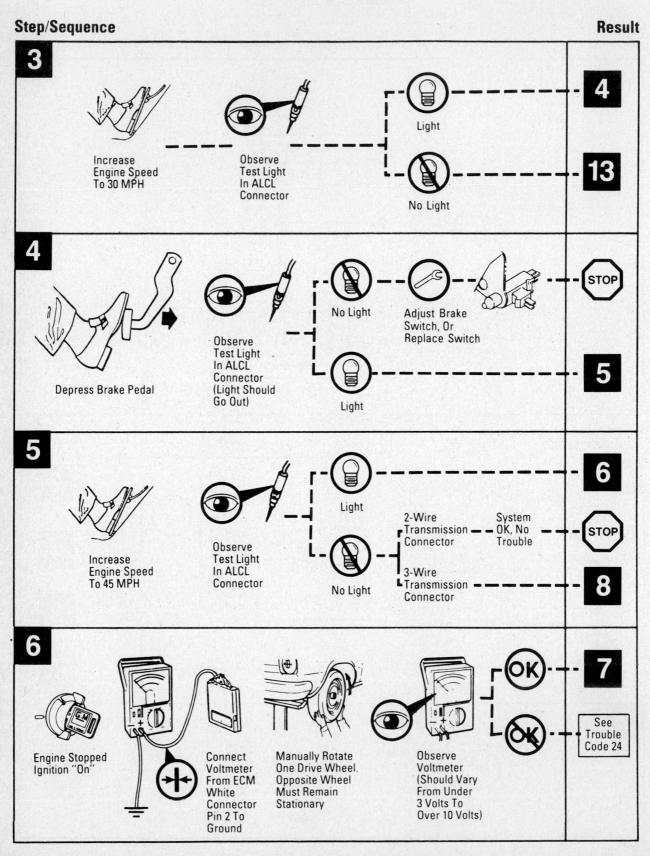

3 — Increase Engine Speed To 30 MPH → Observe Test Light In ALCL Connector
- Light → **4**
- No Light → **13**

4 — Depress Brake Pedal → Observe Test Light In ALCL Connector (Light Should Go Out)
- No Light → Adjust Brake Switch, Or Replace Switch → **STOP**
- Light → **5**

5 — Increase Engine Speed To 45 MPH → Observe Test Light In ALCL Connector
- Light → **6**
- No Light:
  - 2-Wire Transmission Connector → System OK, No Trouble → **STOP**
  - 3-Wire Transmission Connector → **8**

6 — Engine Stopped Ignition "On" → Connect Voltmeter From ECM White Connector Pin 2 To Ground → Manually Rotate One Drive Wheel. Opposite Wheel Must Remain Stationary → Observe Voltmeter (Should Vary From Under 3 Volts To Over 10 Volts)
- OK → **7**
- Not OK → See Trouble Code 24

TORQUE CONVERTER CLUTCH (TCC) ELECTRICAL DIAGNOSIS (Cont.)
Fuel Injected Engines

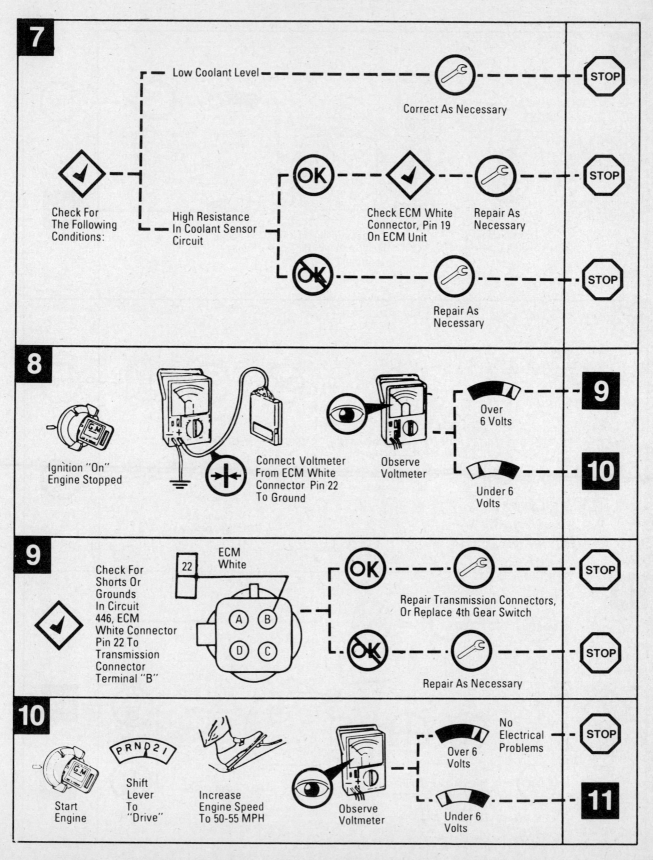

7

Low Coolant Level — Correct As Necessary — STOP

Check For The Following Conditions:

High Resistance In Coolant Sensor Circuit

OK — Check ECM White Connector, Pin 19 On ECM Unit — Repair As Necessary — STOP

OK (not) — Repair As Necessary — STOP

8

Ignition "On" Engine Stopped

Connect Voltmeter From ECM White Connector Pin 22 To Ground

Observe Voltmeter

Over 6 Volts — **9**

Under 6 Volts — **10**

9

Check For Shorts Or Grounds In Circuit 446, ECM White Connector Pin 22 To Transmission Connector Terminal "B"

22 ECM White

OK — Repair Transmission Connectors, Or Replace 4th Gear Switch — STOP

OK (not) — Repair As Necessary — STOP

10

Start Engine

PRND21 Shift Lever To "Drive"

Increase Engine Speed To 50-55 MPH

Observe Voltmeter

Over 6 Volts — No Electrical Problems — STOP

Under 6 Volts — **11**

TORQUE CONVERTER CLUTCH (TCC) ELECTRICAL DIAGNOSIS (Cont.)
Fuel Injected Engines

Step/Sequence   **Result**

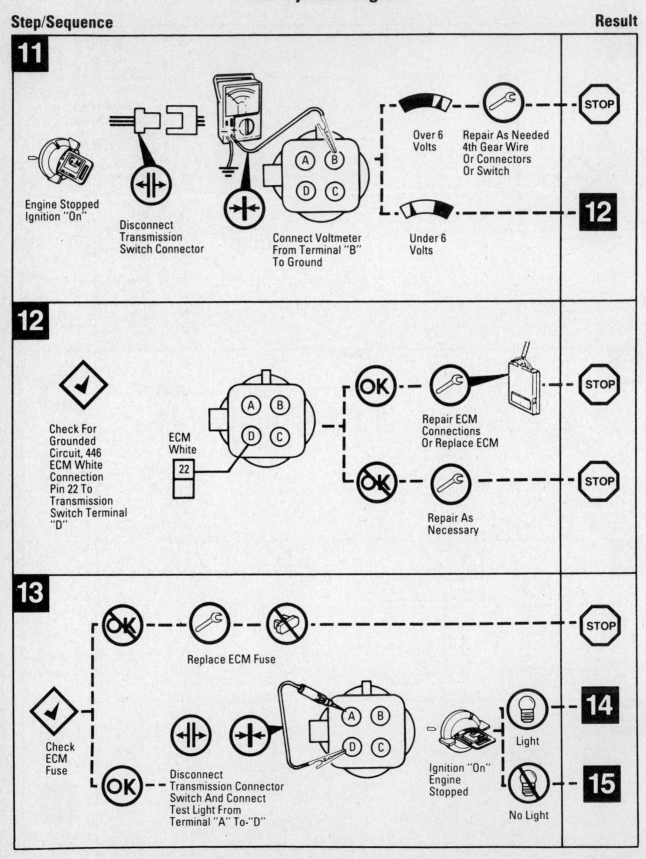

11

Engine Stopped Ignition "On"

Disconnect Transmission Switch Connector

Connect Voltmeter From Terminal "B" To Ground

Over 6 Volts — Repair As Needed 4th Gear Wire Or Connectors Or Switch — STOP

Under 6 Volts — **12**

12

Check For Grounded Circuit, 446 ECM White Connection Pin 22 To Transmission Switch Terminal "D"

ECM White 22

OK — Repair ECM Connections Or Replace ECM — STOP

OK (crossed out) — Repair As Necessary — STOP

13

OK (crossed out) — Replace ECM Fuse — STOP

Check ECM Fuse

OK — Disconnect Transmission Connector Switch And Connect Test Light From Terminal "A" To-"D"

Ignition "On" Engine Stopped

Light — **14**

No Light — **15**

TORQUE CONVERTER CLUTCH (TCC) ELECTRICAL DIAGNOSIS (Cont.)
Fuel Injected Engines

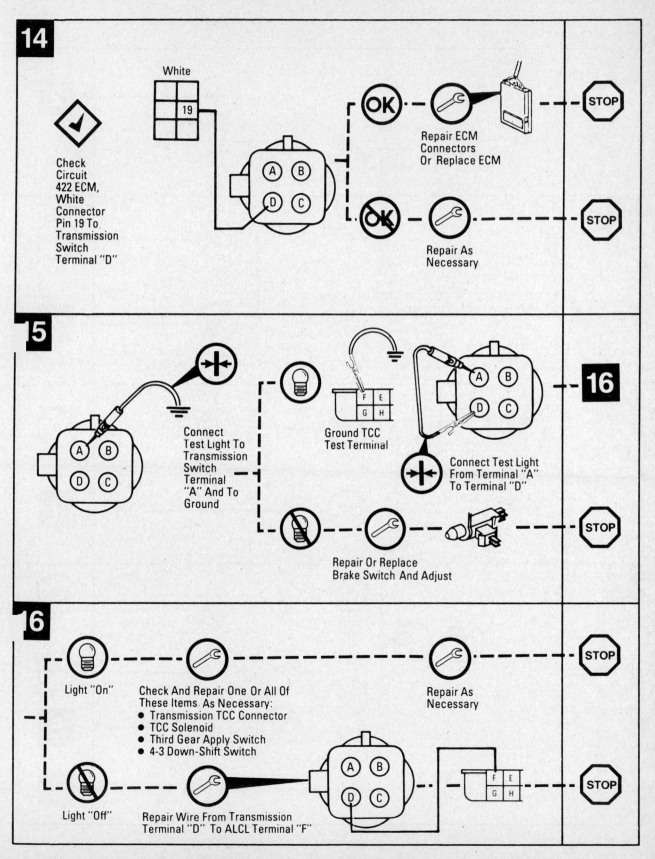

14

White

19

Check Circuit 422 ECM, White Connector Pin 19 To Transmission Switch Terminal "D"

Repair ECM Connectors Or Replace ECM

STOP

Repair As Necessary

STOP

15

Connect Test Light To Transmission Switch Terminal "A" And To Ground

Ground TCC Test Terminal

16

Connect Test Light From Terminal "A" To Terminal "D"

Repair Or Replace Brake Switch And Adjust

STOP

16

Light "On"

Check And Repair One Or All Of These Items As Necessary:
- Transmission TCC Connector
- TCC Solenoid
- Third Gear Apply Switch
- 4-3 Down-Shift Switch

Repair As Necessary

STOP

Light "Off"

Repair Wire From Transmission Terminal "D" To ALCL Terminal "F"

STOP

TORQUE CONVERTER CLUTCH DOES NOT APPLY
1980 Gasoline and Diesel Engine Applications

Step/Sequence   **Result**

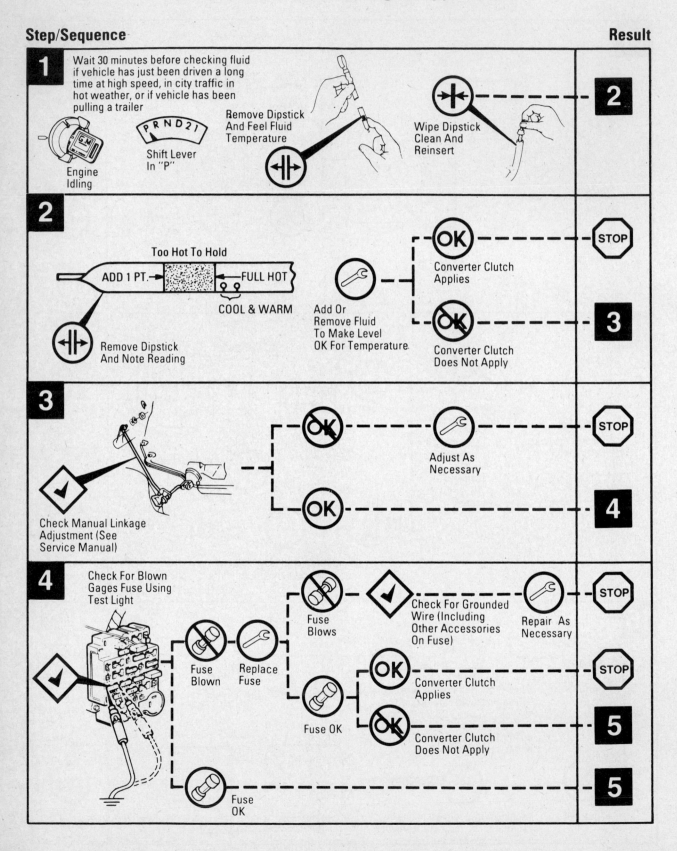

TORQUE CONVERTER CLUTCH DOES NOT APPLY (Cont.)
1980 Gasoline and Diesel Engine Applications

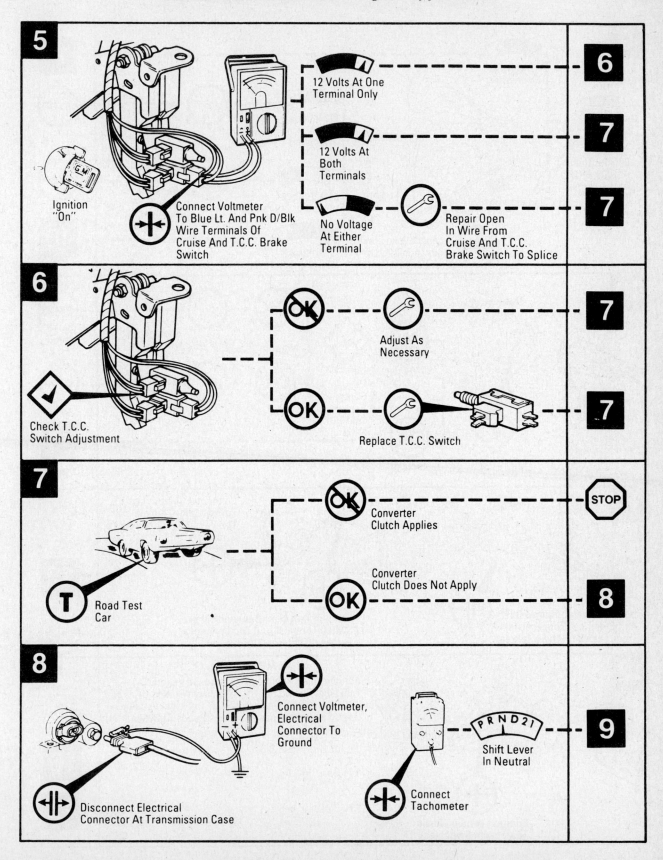

5 Ignition "On"

Connect Voltmeter To Blue Lt. And Pnk D/Blk Wire Terminals Of Cruise And T.C.C. Brake Switch

12 Volts At One Terminal Only → **6**

12 Volts At Both Terminals → **7**

No Voltage At Either Terminal → Repair Open In Wire From Cruise And T.C.C. Brake Switch To Splice → **7**

6 Check T.C.C. Switch Adjustment

Adjust As Necessary → **7**

Replace T.C.C. Switch → **7**

7 Road Test Car

Converter Clutch Applies → STOP

Converter Clutch Does Not Apply → **8**

8 Disconnect Electrical Connector At Transmission Case

Connect Voltmeter, Electrical Connector To Ground

Connect Tachometer

Shift Lever In Neutral → **9**

TORQUE CONVERTER CLUTCH DOES NOT APPLY (Cont.)
1980 Gasoline and Diesel Engine Applications

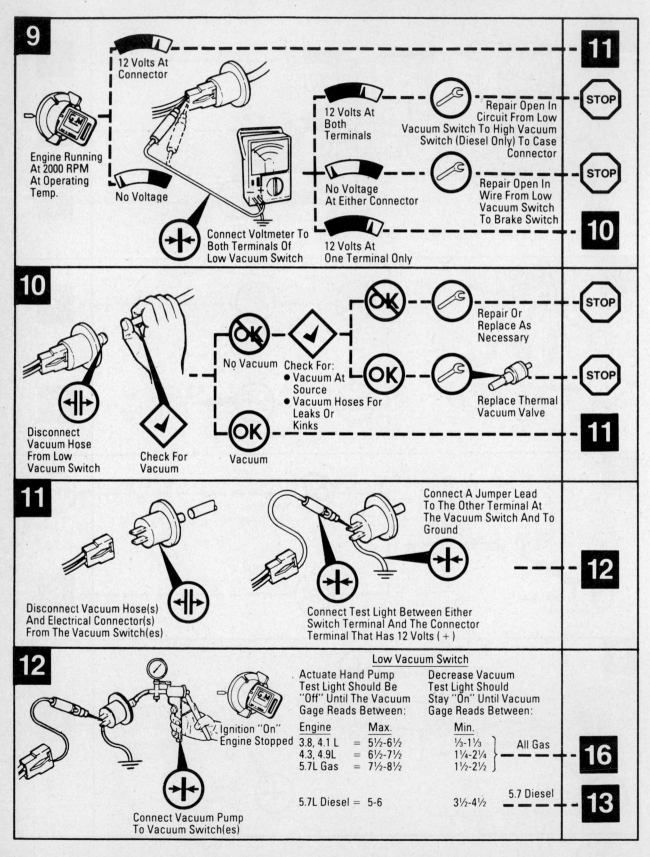

9

12 Volts At Connector

Engine Running At 2000 RPM At Operating Temp.

No Voltage

Connect Voltmeter To Both Terminals Of Low Vacuum Switch

12 Volts At Both Terminals

No Voltage At Either Connector

12 Volts At One Terminal Only

Repair Open In Circuit From Low Vacuum Switch To High Vacuum Switch (Diesel Only) To Case Connector — STOP

Repair Open In Wire From Low Vacuum Switch To Brake Switch — STOP

11

10

10

Disconnect Vacuum Hose From Low Vacuum Switch

Check For Vacuum

No Vacuum

Vacuum

Check For:
- Vacuum At Source
- Vacuum Hoses For Leaks Or Kinks

OK — Repair Or Replace As Necessary — STOP

OK — Replace Thermal Vacuum Valve — STOP

11

11

Disconnect Vacuum Hose(s) And Electrical Connector(s) From The Vacuum Switch(es)

Connect A Jumper Lead To The Other Terminal At The Vacuum Switch And To Ground

Connect Test Light Between Either Switch Terminal And The Connector Terminal That Has 12 Volts (+)

12

12

Ignition "On" Engine Stopped

Connect Vacuum Pump To Vacuum Switch(es)

Low Vacuum Switch

Actuate Hand Pump Test Light Should Be "Off" Until The Vacuum Gage Reads Between:

Decrease Vacuum Test Light Should Stay "On" Until Vacuum Gage Reads Between:

Engine	Max.	Min.	
3.8, 4.1 L	= 5½–6½	⅓–1⅓	All Gas
4.3, 4.9L	= 6½–7½	1¼–2¼	
5.7L Gas	= 7½–8½	1½–2½	
5.7L Diesel	= 5–6	3½–4½	5.7 Diesel

16

13

TORQUE CONVERTER CLUTCH DOES NOT APPLY (Cont.)
1980 Gasoline and Diesel Engine Applications

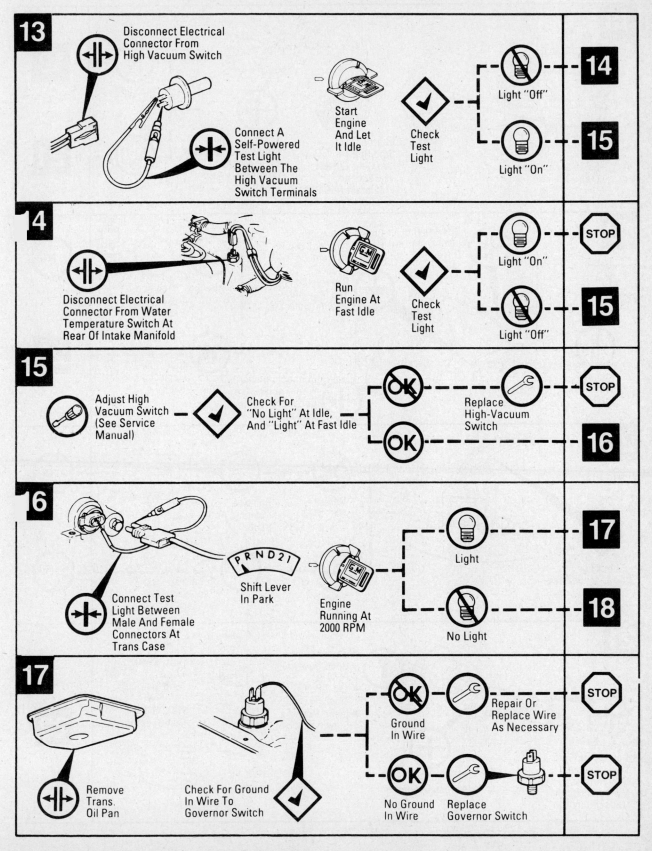

13 Disconnect Electrical Connector From High Vacuum Switch — Connect A Self-Powered Test Light Between The High Vacuum Switch Terminals — Start Engine And Let It Idle — Check Test Light — Light "Off" → **14** / Light "On" → **15**

14 Disconnect Electrical Connector From Water Temperature Switch At Rear Of Intake Manifold — Run Engine At Fast Idle — Check Test Light — Light "On" → **STOP** / Light "Off" → **15**

15 Adjust High Vacuum Switch (See Service Manual) — Check For "No Light" At Idle, And "Light" At Fast Idle — OK → Replace High-Vacuum Switch → **STOP** / OK → **16**

16 Connect Test Light Between Male And Female Connectors At Trans Case — Shift Lever In Park — Engine Running At 2000 RPM — Light → **17** / No Light → **18**

17 Remove Trans. Oil Pan — Check For Ground In Wire To Governor Switch — Ground In Wire → Repair Or Replace Wire As Necessary → **STOP** / No Ground In Wire → Replace Governor Switch → **STOP**

TORQUE CONVERTER CLUTCH DOES NOT APPLY (Cont.)
1980 Gasoline and Diesel Engine Applications

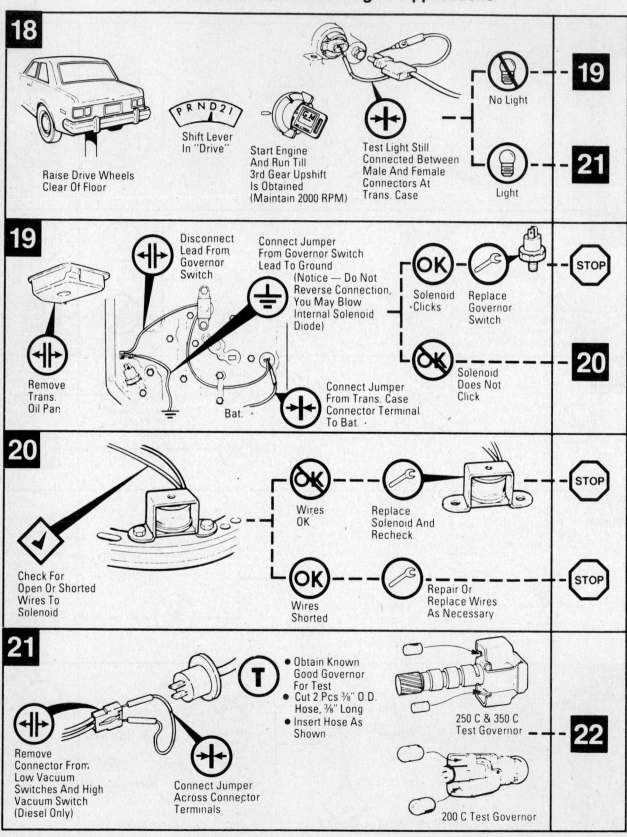

TORQUE CONVERTER CLUTCH DOES NOT APPLY (Cont.)
1980 Gasoline and Diesel Engine Applications

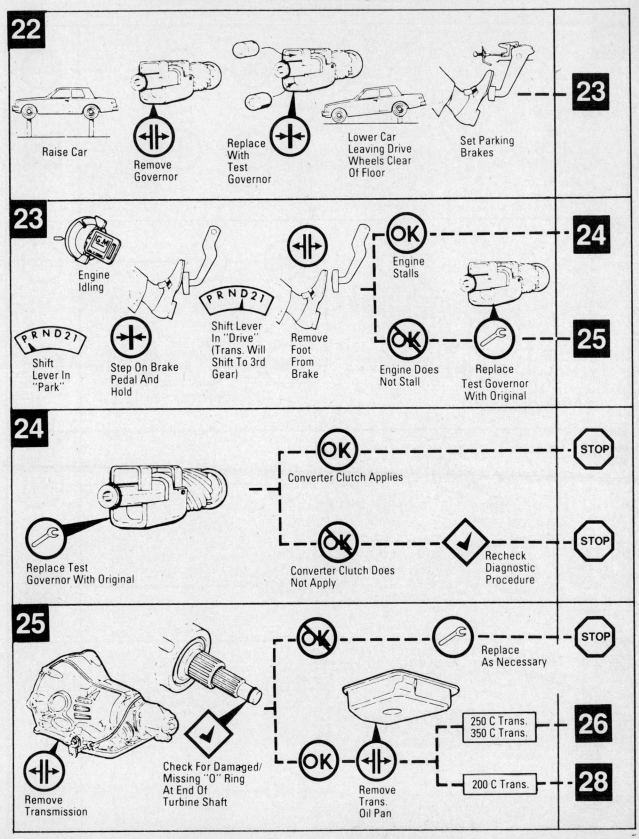

22
- Raise Car
- Remove Governor
- Replace With Test Governor
- Lower Car Leaving Drive Wheels Clear Of Floor
- Set Parking Brakes → **23**

23
- Engine Idling
- Shift Lever In "Park" (PRND21)
- Step On Brake Pedal And Hold
- Shift Lever In "Drive" (Trans. Will Shift To 3rd Gear) (PRND21)
- Remove Foot From Brake
- Engine Stalls OK → **24**
- Engine Does Not Stall → Replace Test Governor With Original → **25**

24
- Replace Test Governor With Original
- Converter Clutch Applies → STOP
- Converter Clutch Does Not Apply → Recheck Diagnostic Procedure → STOP

25
- Remove Transmission
- Check For Damaged/ Missing "O" Ring At End Of Turbine Shaft
- Replace As Necessary → STOP
- Remove Trans. Oil Pan → 250 C Trans. / 350 C Trans. → **26**
- 200 C Trans. → **28**

TORQUE CONVERTER CLUTCH DOES NOT APPLY (Cont.)
1980 Gasoline and Diesel Engine Applications

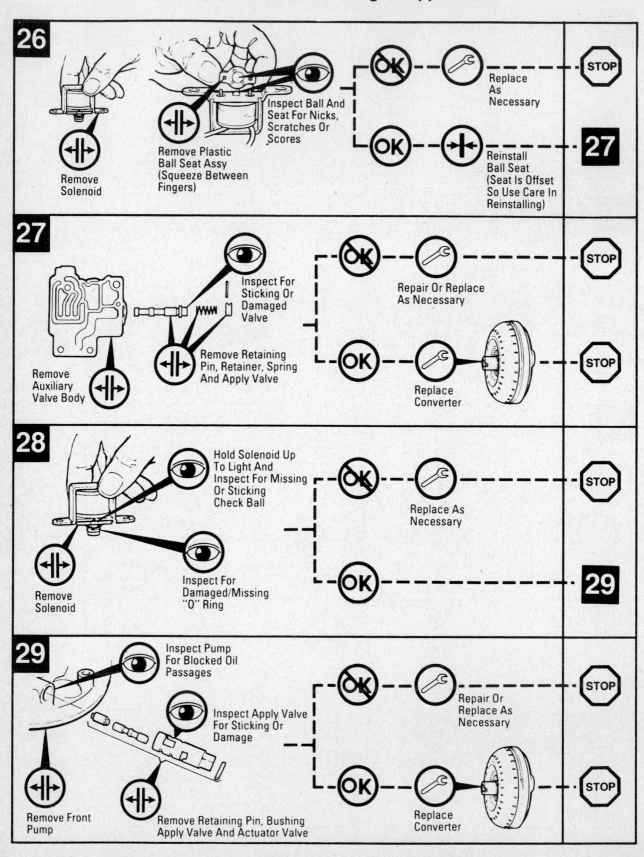

26

Remove Solenoid

Remove Plastic Ball Seat Assy (Squeeze Between Fingers)

Inspect Ball And Seat For Nicks, Scratches Or Scores

OK — Replace As Necessary — STOP

OK — Reinstall Ball Seat (Seat Is Offset So Use Care In Reinstalling) — **27**

27

Remove Auxiliary Valve Body

Remove Retaining Pin, Retainer, Spring And Apply Valve

Inspect For Sticking Or Damaged Valve

OK — Repair Or Replace As Necessary — STOP

OK — Replace Converter — STOP

28

Remove Solenoid

Hold Solenoid Up To Light And Inspect For Missing Or Sticking Check Ball

Inspect For Damaged/Missing "O" Ring

OK — Replace As Necessary — STOP

OK — **29**

29

Remove Front Pump

Remove Retaining Pin, Bushing Apply Valve And Actuator Valve

Inspect Pump For Blocked Oil Passages

Inspect Apply Valve For Sticking Or Damage

OK — Repair Or Replace As Necessary — STOP

OK — Replace Converter — STOP

TORQUE CONVERTER CLUTCH DOES NOT APPLY
1981 and later TCC Diagnosis without EGR Bleed Solenoid

Step/Sequence   **Result**

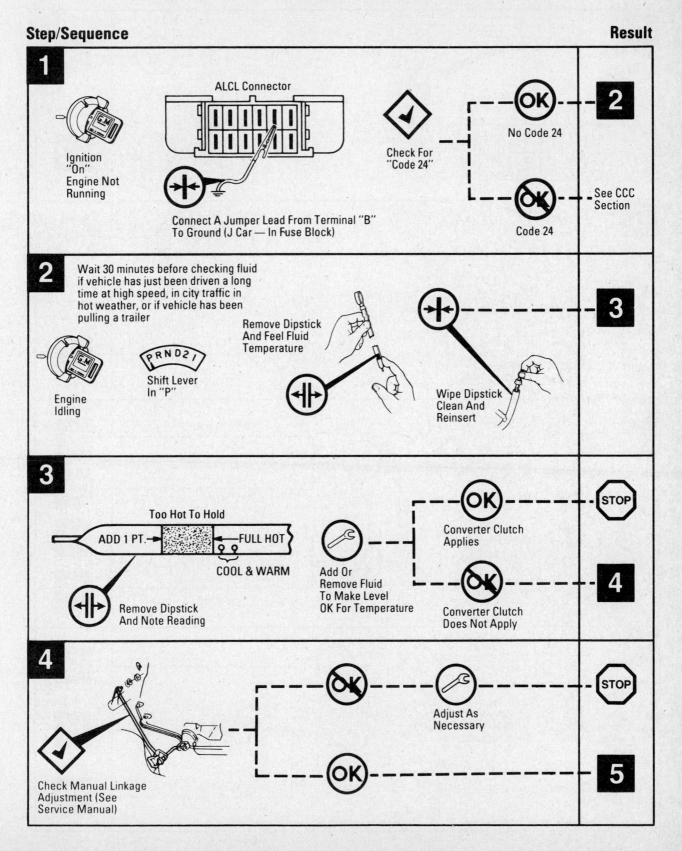

1

Ignition "On"
Engine Not
Running

ALCL Connector

Connect A Jumper Lead From Terminal "B"
To Ground (J Car — In Fuse Block)

Check For "Code 24"

No Code 24 — **2**

Code 24 — See CCC Section

2

Wait 30 minutes before checking fluid
if vehicle has just been driven a long
time at high speed, in city traffic in
hot weather, or if vehicle has been
pulling a trailer

Engine Idling

PRND21
Shift Lever In "P"

Remove Dipstick And Feel Fluid Temperature

Wipe Dipstick Clean And Reinsert

3

3

Too Hot To Hold

ADD 1 PT.   FULL HOT

COOL & WARM

Remove Dipstick And Note Reading

Add Or Remove Fluid To Make Level OK For Temperature

Converter Clutch Applies — STOP

Converter Clutch Does Not Apply — **4**

4

Check Manual Linkage Adjustment (See Service Manual)

Adjust As Necessary — STOP

OK — **5**

TORQUE CONVERTER CLUTCH DOES NOT APPLY (Cont.)
1981 and Later TCC Diagnosis Without EGR Bleed Solenoid

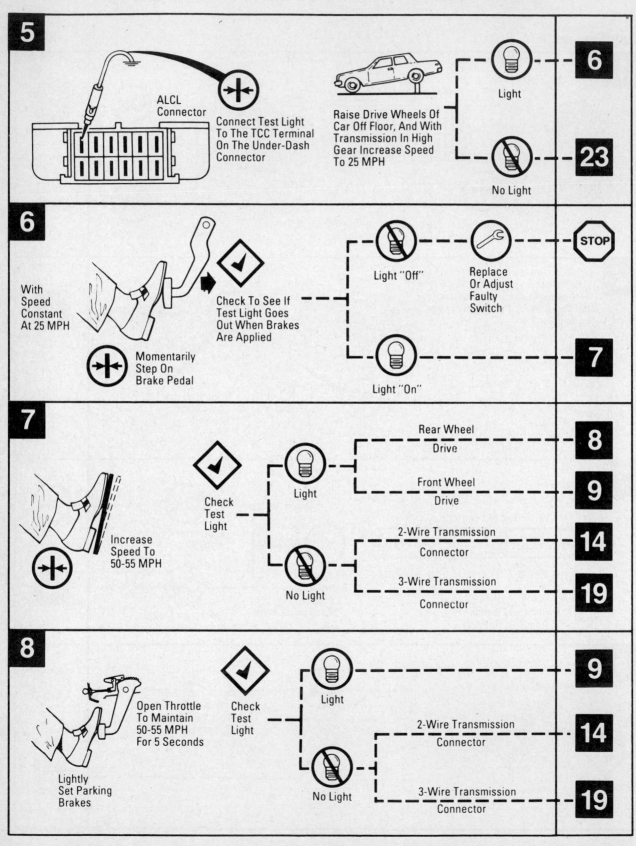

5 — ALCL Connector — Connect Test Light To The TCC Terminal On The Under-Dash Connector — Raise Drive Wheels Of Car Off Floor, And With Transmission In High Gear Increase Speed To 25 MPH — Light → **6** — No Light → **23**

6 — With Speed Constant At 25 MPH — Momentarily Step On Brake Pedal — Check To See If Test Light Goes Out When Brakes Are Applied — Light "Off" → Replace Or Adjust Faulty Switch → **STOP** — Light "On" → **7**

7 — Increase Speed To 50-55 MPH — Check Test Light — Light → Rear Wheel Drive → **8** / Front Wheel Drive → **9** — No Light → 2-Wire Transmission Connector → **14** / 3-Wire Transmission Connector → **19**

8 — Open Throttle To Maintain 50-55 MPH For 5 Seconds — Lightly Set Parking Brakes — Check Test Light — Light → **9** — No Light → 2-Wire Transmission Connector → **14** / 3-Wire Transmission Connector → **19**

TORQUE CONVERTER CLUTCH DOES NOT APPLY (Cont.)
1981 and Later TCC Diagnosis Without EGR Bleed Solenoid

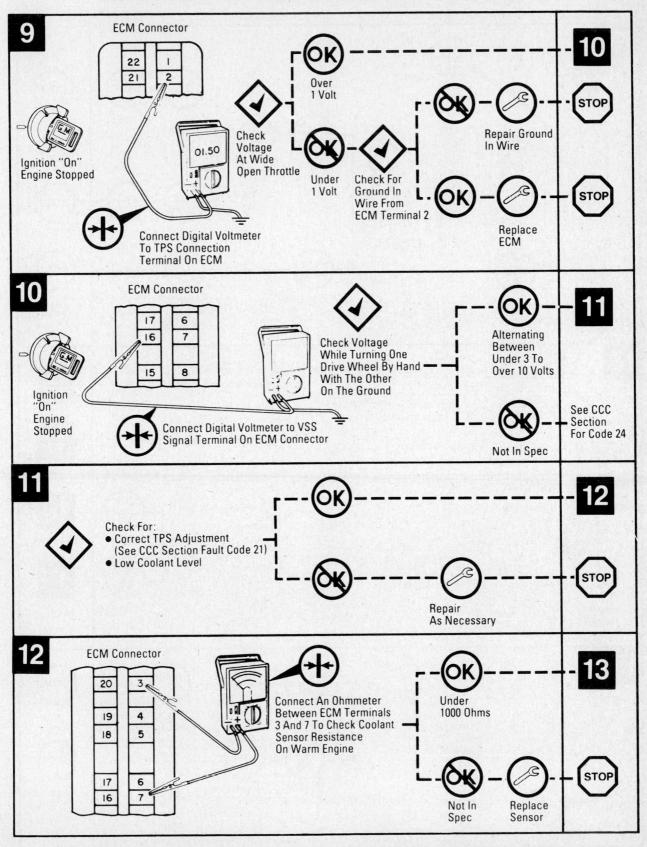

TORQUE CONVERTER CLUTCH DOES NOT APPLY (Cont.)
1981 and Later TCC Diagnosis Without EGR Bleed Solenoid

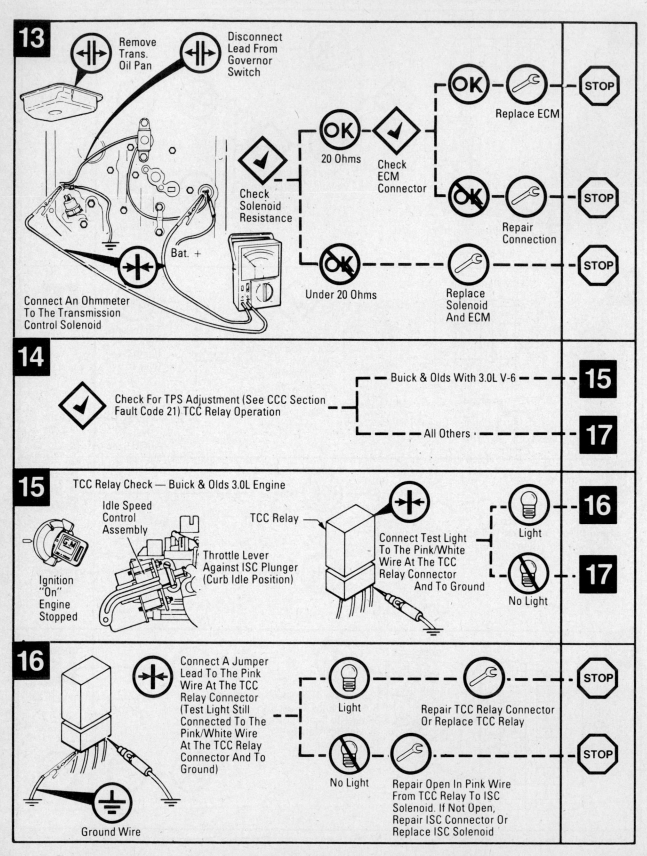

13 Remove Trans. Oil Pan — Disconnect Lead From Governor Switch — Check Solenoid Resistance — 20 Ohms — Check ECM Connector — OK — Replace ECM — STOP — Not OK — Repair Connection — STOP — Under 20 Ohms — Replace Solenoid And ECM — STOP — Connect An Ohmmeter To The Transmission Control Solenoid — Bat. +

14 Check For TPS Adjustment (See CCC Section Fault Code 21) TCC Relay Operation — Buick & Olds With 3.0L V-6 — **15** — All Others — **17**

15 TCC Relay Check — Buick & Olds 3.0L Engine — Idle Speed Control Assembly — Throttle Lever Against ISC Plunger (Curb Idle Position) — Ignition "On" Engine Stopped — TCC Relay — Connect Test Light To The Pink/White Wire At The TCC Relay Connector And To Ground — Light — **16** — No Light — **17**

16 Connect A Jumper Lead To The Pink Wire At The TCC Relay Connector (Test Light Still Connected To The Pink/White Wire At The TCC Relay Connector And To Ground) — Light — Repair TCC Relay Connector Or Replace TCC Relay — STOP — No Light — Repair Open In Pink Wire From TCC Relay To ISC Solenoid. If Not Open, Repair ISC Connector Or Replace ISC Solenoid — STOP — Ground Wire

TORQUE CONVERTER CLUTCH DOES NOT APPLY (Cont.)
1981 and Later TCC Diagnosis Without EGR Bleed Solenoid

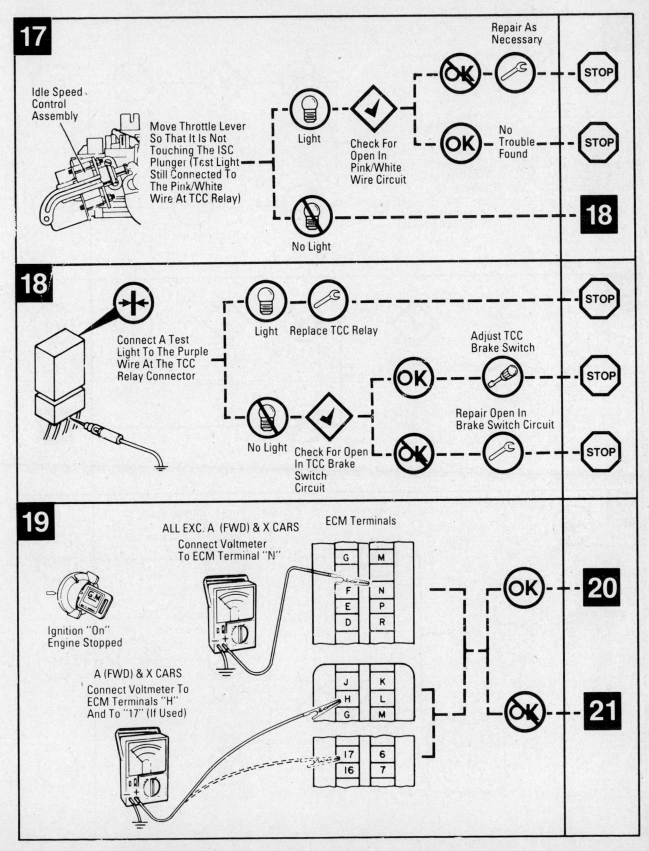

17

Idle Speed Control Assembly

Move Throttle Lever So That It Is Not Touching The ISC Plunger (Test Light Still Connected To The Pink/White Wire At TCC Relay)

Light

Check For Open In Pink/White Wire Circuit

No Light

Repair As Necessary

OK — STOP

OK — No Trouble Found — STOP

18

18

Connect A Test Light To The Purple Wire At The TCC Relay Connector

Light — Replace TCC Relay — STOP

No Light

Check For Open In TCC Brake Switch Circuit

Adjust TCC Brake Switch

OK — STOP

Repair Open In Brake Switch Circuit

OK — STOP

19

ALL EXC. A (FWD) & X CARS
Connect Voltmeter To ECM Terminal "N"

ECM Terminals

G	M
F	N
E	P
D	R

Ignition "On" Engine Stopped

A (FWD) & X CARS
Connect Voltmeter To ECM Terminals "H" And To "17" (If Used)

J	K
H	L
G	M

| 17 | 6 |
| 16 | 7 |

OK — **20**

OK — **21**

TORQUE CONVERTER CLUTCH DOES NOT APPLY (Cont.)
1981 and Later TCC Diagnosis Without EGR Bleed Solenoid

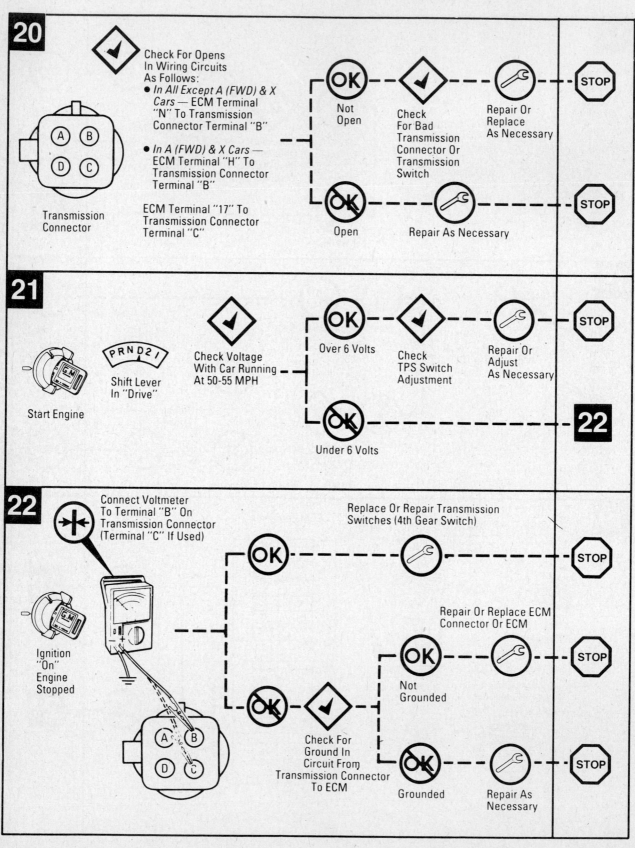

20

Transmission Connector

Check For Opens In Wiring Circuits As Follows:
- In All Except A (FWD) & X Cars — ECM Terminal "N" To Transmission Connector Terminal "B"
- In A (FWD) & X Cars — ECM Terminal "H" To Transmission Connector Terminal "B"

ECM Terminal "17" To Transmission Connector Terminal "C"

Not Open → Check For Bad Transmission Connector Or Transmission Switch → Repair Or Replace As Necessary → STOP

Open → Repair As Necessary → STOP

21

Start Engine

PRND21 Shift Lever In "Drive"

Check Voltage With Car Running At 50-55 MPH

Over 6 Volts → Check TPS Switch Adjustment → Repair Or Adjust As Necessary → STOP

Under 6 Volts → **22**

22

Connect Voltmeter To Terminal "B" On Transmission Connector (Terminal "C" If Used)

Ignition "On" Engine Stopped

Replace Or Repair Transmission Switches (4th Gear Switch)

OK → Replace Or Repair Transmission Switches → STOP

Check For Ground In Circuit From Transmission Connector To ECM

Not Grounded → Repair Or Replace ECM Connector Or ECM → STOP

Grounded → Repair As Necessary → STOP

TORQUE CONVERTER CLUTCH DOES NOT APPLY (Cont.)
1981 and Later TCC Diagnosis Without EGR Bleed Solenoid

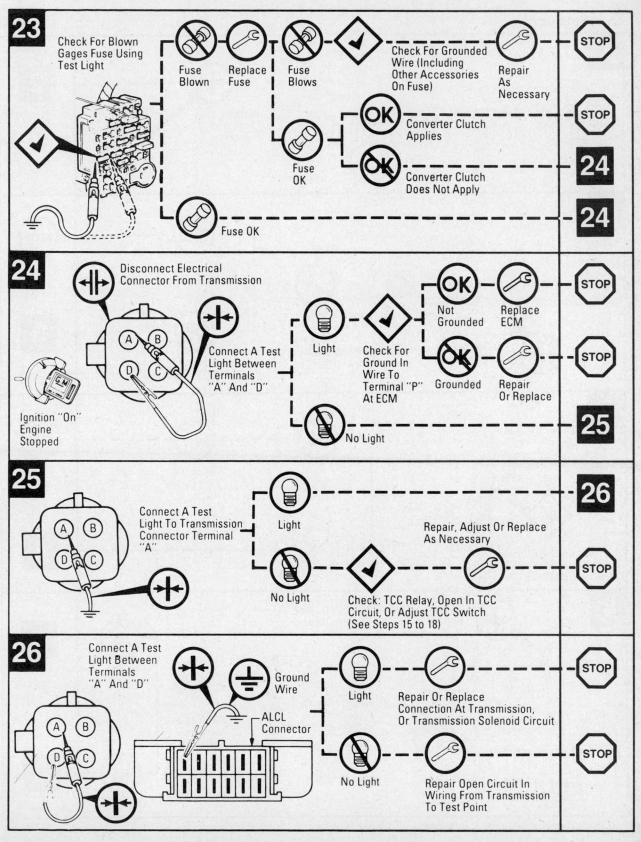

23 Check For Blown Gages Fuse Using Test Light

Fuse Blown — Replace Fuse — Fuse Blows — ✓ Check For Grounded Wire (Including Other Accessories On Fuse) — Repair As Necessary — STOP

Fuse OK — Converter Clutch Applies — STOP

Fuse OK — Converter Clutch Does Not Apply — **24**

Fuse OK — **24**

24 Disconnect Electrical Connector From Transmission

Connect A Test Light Between Terminals "A" And "D"

Ignition "On" Engine Stopped

Light — Check For Ground In Wire To Terminal "P" At ECM — Not Grounded — Replace ECM — STOP

Grounded — Repair Or Replace — STOP

No Light — **25**

25 Connect A Test Light To Transmission Connector Terminal "A"

Light — **26**

No Light — ✓ Check: TCC Relay, Open In TCC Circuit, Or Adjust TCC Switch (See Steps 15 to 18) — Repair, Adjust Or Replace As Necessary — STOP

26 Connect A Test Light Between Terminals "A" And "D"

Ground Wire

ALCL Connector

Light — Repair Or Replace Connection At Transmission, Or Transmission Solenoid Circuit — STOP

No Light — Repair Open Circuit In Wiring From Transmission To Test Point — STOP

TORQUE CONVERTER CLUTCH DOES NOT APPLY
1981 and Later TCC w/5.7L Diesel Engine

Step/Sequence

Result

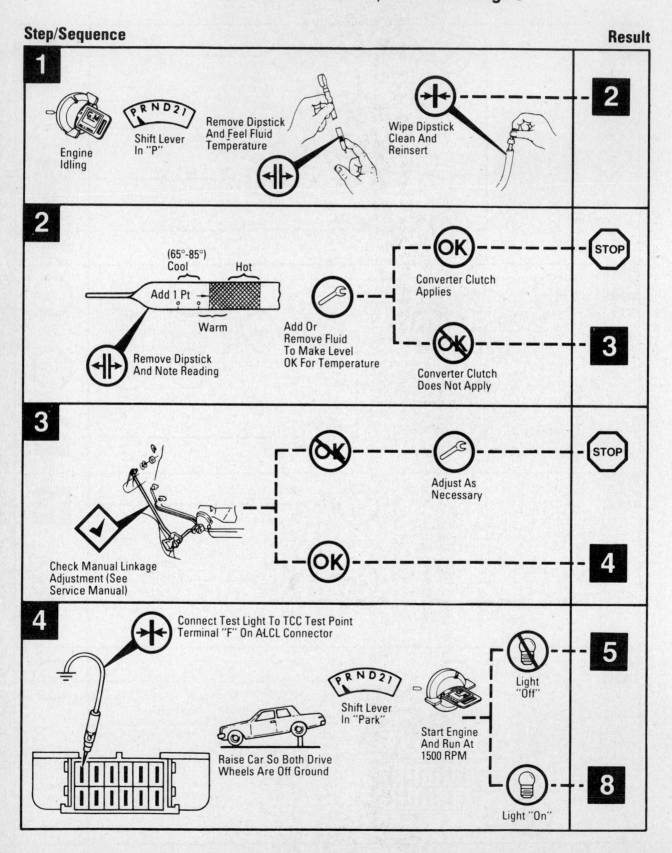

1

Engine Idling

Shift Lever In "P"

Remove Dipstick And Feel Fluid Temperature

Wipe Dipstick Clean And Reinsert

→ **2**

2

(65°–85°) Cool | Warm | Hot

Add 1 Pt

Remove Dipstick And Note Reading

Add Or Remove Fluid To Make Level OK For Temperature

Converter Clutch Applies → **STOP**

Converter Clutch Does Not Apply → **3**

3

Check Manual Linkage Adjustment (See Service Manual)

Adjust As Necessary → **STOP**

→ **4**

4

Connect Test Light To TCC Test Point Terminal "F" On ALCL Connector

Raise Car So Both Drive Wheels Are Off Ground

Shift Lever In "Park"

Start Engine And Run At 1500 RPM

Light "Off" → **5**

Light "On" → **8**

TORQUE CONVERTER CLUTCH DOES NOT APPLY (Cont.)
1981 and Later TCC w/5.7L Diesel Engine

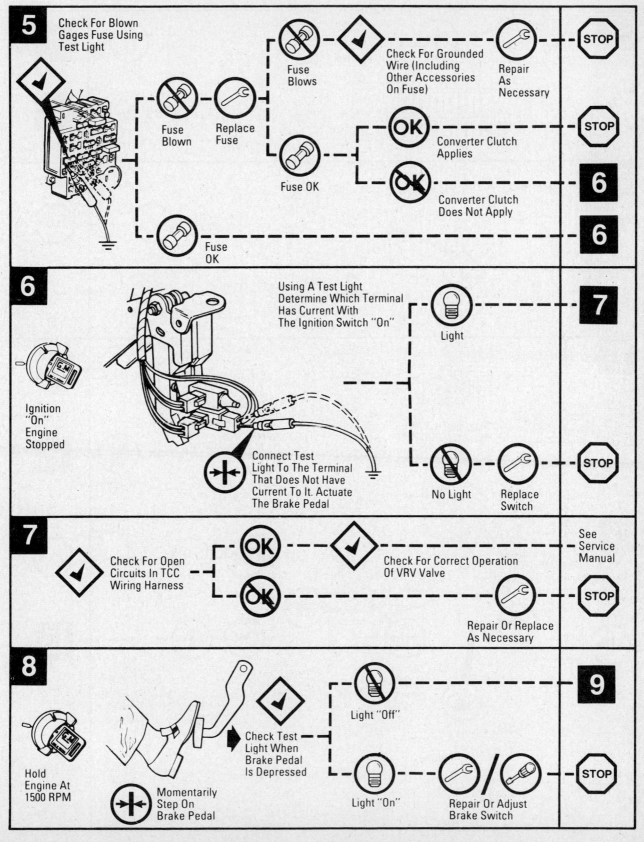

5 Check For Blown Gages Fuse Using Test Light

Fuse Blown — Replace Fuse

Fuse Blows — Check For Grounded Wire (Including Other Accessories On Fuse) — Repair As Necessary — STOP

Fuse OK — OK Converter Clutch Applies — STOP

OK Converter Clutch Does Not Apply — **6**

Fuse OK — **6**

6 Ignition "On" Engine Stopped

Connect Test Light To The Terminal That Does Not Have Current To It. Actuate The Brake Pedal

Using A Test Light Determine Which Terminal Has Current With The Ignition Switch "On"

Light — **7**

No Light — Replace Switch — STOP

7 Check For Open Circuits In TCC Wiring Harness

OK — Check For Correct Operation Of VRV Valve — See Service Manual

OK — Repair Or Replace As Necessary — STOP

8 Hold Engine At 1500 RPM

Momentarily Step On Brake Pedal

Check Test Light When Brake Pedal Is Depressed

Light "Off" — **9**

Light "On" — Repair Or Adjust Brake Switch — STOP

TORQUE CONVERTER CLUTCH DOES NOT APPLY (Cont.)
1981 and Later TCC w/5.7L Diesel Engine

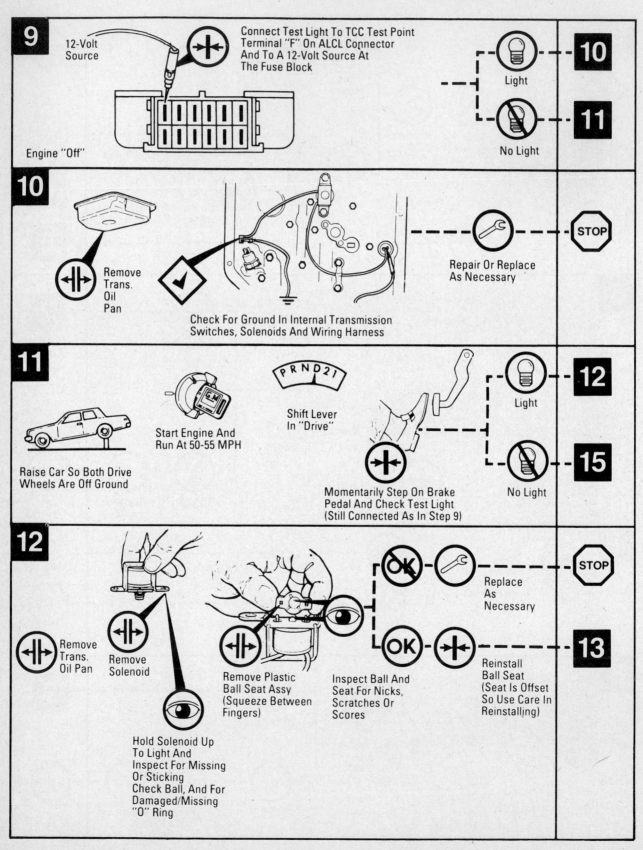

9 12-Volt Source — Connect Test Light To TCC Test Point Terminal "F" On ALCL Connector And To A 12-Volt Source At The Fuse Block — Engine "Off"

10 Light

11 No Light

10 Remove Trans. Oil Pan — Check For Ground In Internal Transmission Switches, Solenoids And Wiring Harness — Repair Or Replace As Necessary — STOP

11 Raise Car So Both Drive Wheels Are Off Ground — Start Engine And Run At 50-55 MPH — PRND21 Shift Lever In "Drive" — Momentarily Step On Brake Pedal And Check Test Light (Still Connected As In Step 9)

12 Light

15 No Light

12 Remove Trans. Oil Pan — Remove Solenoid — Hold Solenoid Up To Light And Inspect For Missing Or Sticking Check Ball, And For Damaged/Missing "O" Ring — Remove Plastic Ball Seat Assy (Squeeze Between Fingers) — Inspect Ball And Seat For Nicks, Scratches Or Scores

OK — Replace As Necessary — STOP

OK — Reinstall Ball Seat (Seat Is Offset So Use Care In Reinstalling) — **13**

TORQUE CONVERTER CLUTCH DOES NOT APPLY (Cont.)
1981 and Later TCC w/5.7L Diesel Engine

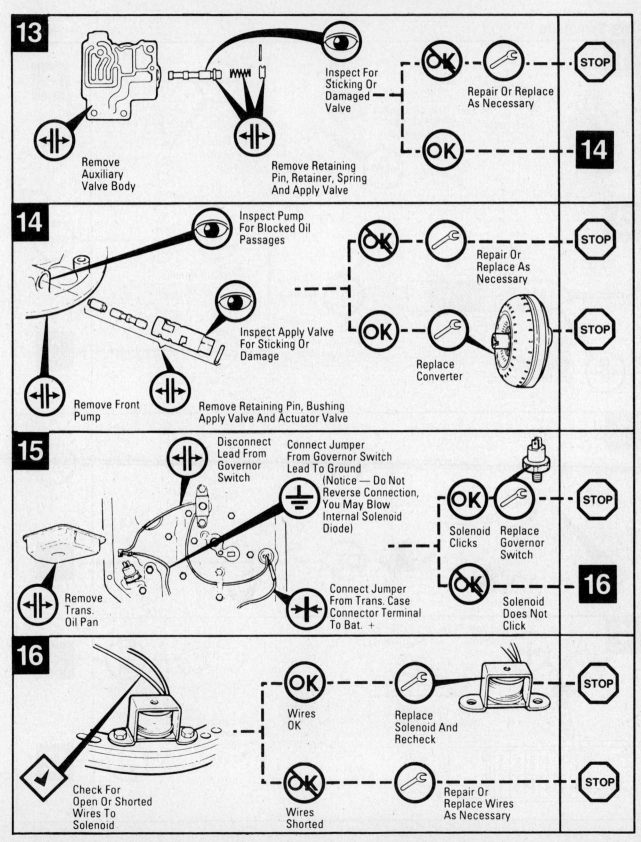

13 Remove Auxiliary Valve Body

Remove Retaining Pin, Retainer, Spring And Apply Valve

Inspect For Sticking Or Damaged Valve

Repair Or Replace As Necessary — STOP

OK → **14**

14 Inspect Pump For Blocked Oil Passages

Remove Front Pump

Inspect Apply Valve For Sticking Or Damage

Remove Retaining Pin, Bushing Apply Valve And Actuator Valve

Repair Or Replace As Necessary — STOP

Replace Converter — STOP

15 Remove Trans. Oil Pan

Disconnect Lead From Governor Switch

Connect Jumper From Governor Switch Lead To Ground (Notice — Do Not Reverse Connection, You May Blow Internal Solenoid Diode)

Connect Jumper From Trans. Case Connector Terminal To Bat. +

Solenoid Clicks — Replace Governor Switch — STOP

Solenoid Does Not Click — **16**

16 Check For Open Or Shorted Wires To Solenoid

Wires OK — Replace Solenoid And Recheck — STOP

Wires Shorted — Repair Or Replace Wires As Necessary — STOP

TORQUE CONVERTER CLUTCH DOES NOT APPLY
1982 and Later TCC w/4.3L Engine

Step/Sequence   **Result**

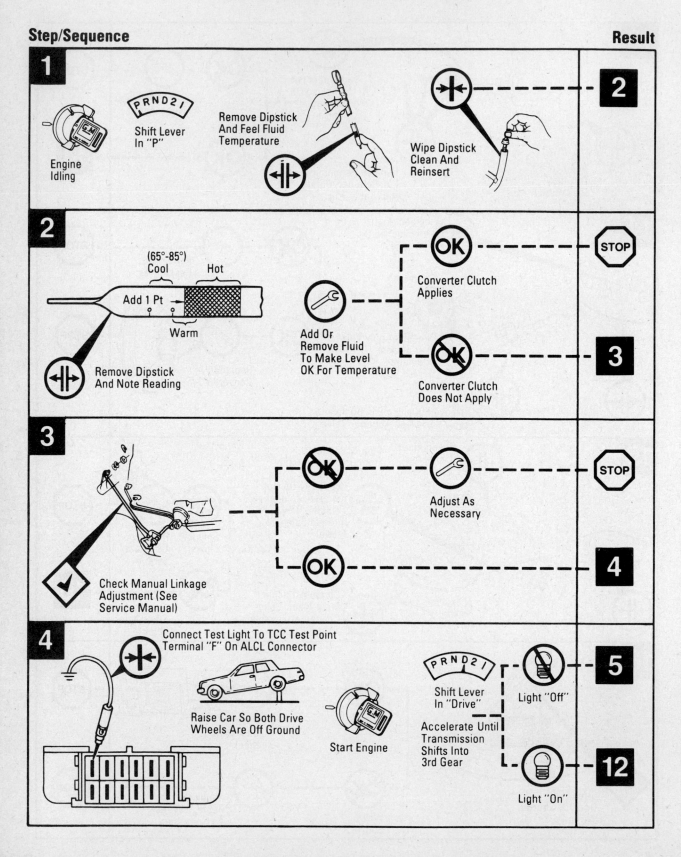

TORQUE CONVERTER CLUTCH DOES NOT APPLY (Cont.)
1982 and Later TCC w/4.3L Engine

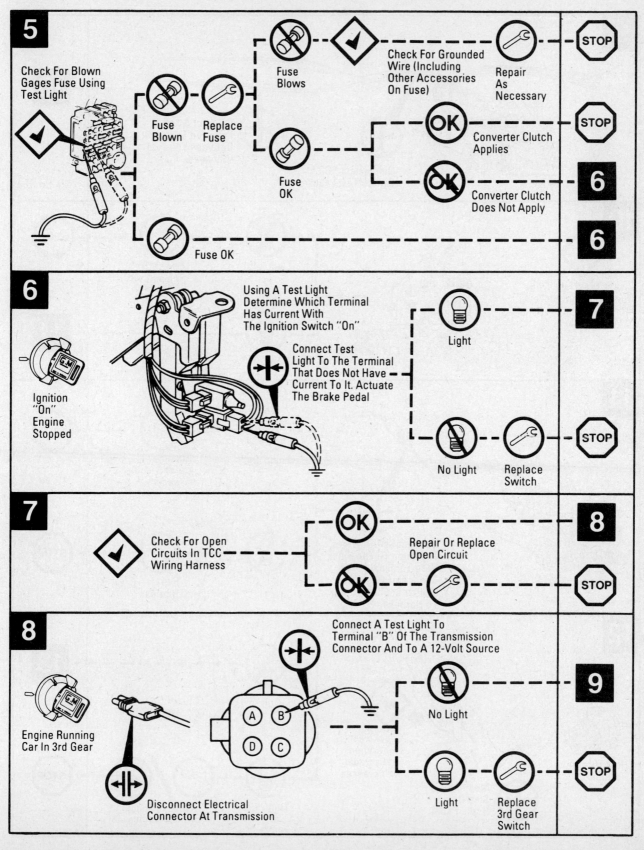

5 Check For Blown Gages Fuse Using Test Light

Fuse Blown — Replace Fuse — Fuse Blows — Check For Grounded Wire (Including Other Accessories On Fuse) — Repair As Necessary — STOP

Fuse OK — Converter Clutch Applies — STOP

Converter Clutch Does Not Apply — **6**

Fuse OK — **6**

6 Ignition "On" Engine Stopped

Using A Test Light Determine Which Terminal Has Current With The Ignition Switch "On"

Connect Test Light To The Terminal That Does Not Have Current To It. Actuate The Brake Pedal

Light — **7**

No Light — Replace Switch — STOP

7 Check For Open Circuits In TCC Wiring Harness

OK — **8**

Not OK — Repair Or Replace Open Circuit — STOP

8 Engine Running Car In 3rd Gear

Disconnect Electrical Connector At Transmission

Connect A Test Light To Terminal "B" Of The Transmission Connector And To A 12-Volt Source

No Light — **9**

Light — Replace 3rd Gear Switch — STOP

TORQUE CONVERTER CLUTCH DOES NOT APPLY (Cont.)
1982 and Later TCC w/4.3L Engine

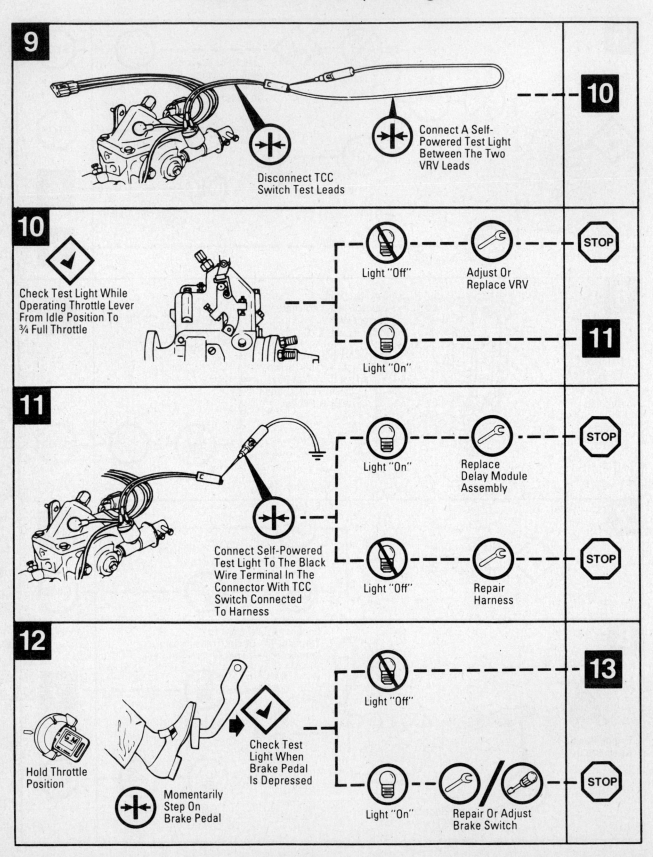

9 Disconnect TCC Switch Test Leads

Connect A Self-Powered Test Light Between The Two VRV Leads → **10**

10 Check Test Light While Operating Throttle Lever From Idle Position To ¾ Full Throttle

Light "Off" — Adjust Or Replace VRV — **STOP**

Light "On" — **11**

11 Connect Self-Powered Test Light To The Black Wire Terminal In The Connector With TCC Switch Connected To Harness

Light "On" — Replace Delay Module Assembly — **STOP**

Light "Off" — Repair Harness — **STOP**

12 Hold Throttle Position

Momentarily Step On Brake Pedal

Check Test Light When Brake Pedal Is Depressed

Light "Off" — **13**

Light "On" — Repair Or Adjust Brake Switch — **STOP**

TORQUE CONVERTER CLUTCH DOES NOT APPLY (Cont.)
1982 and Later TCC w/4.3L Engine

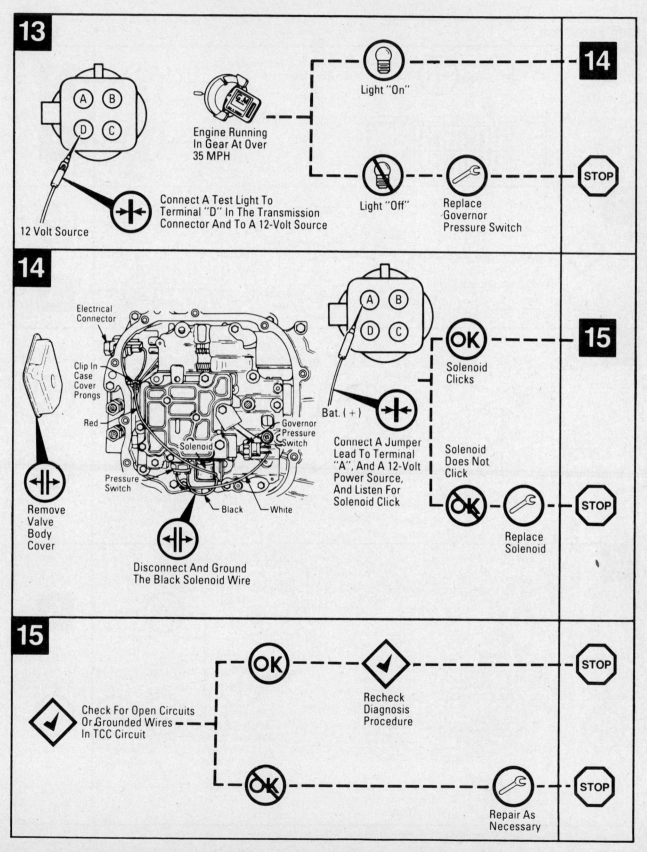

13

A B
D C

12 Volt Source

Engine Running
In Gear At Over
35 MPH

Connect A Test Light To
Terminal "D" In The Transmission
Connector And To A 12-Volt Source

Light "On" — **14**

Light "Off" — Replace
Governor
Pressure Switch — **STOP**

14

Electrical
Connector

Clip In
Case
Cover Prongs

Red

Solenoid

Governor
Pressure
Switch

Pressure
Switch

Black   White

Remove
Valve
Body
Cover

Disconnect And Ground
The Black Solenoid Wire

A B
D C

Bat. (+)

Connect A Jumper
Lead To Terminal
"A", And A 12-Volt
Power Source,
And Listen For
Solenoid Click

Solenoid
Clicks — **15**

Solenoid
Does Not
Click

Replace
Solenoid — **STOP**

15

Check For Open Circuits
Or Grounded Wires
In TCC Circuit

OK — Recheck
Diagnosis
Procedure — **STOP**

Repair As
Necessary — **STOP**

TORQUE CONVERTER CLUTCH OPERATION IN SECOND GEAR AS WELL AS IN THIRD GEAR
1982 and Later TCC w/4.3L Diesel Engine

Step/Sequence   **Result**

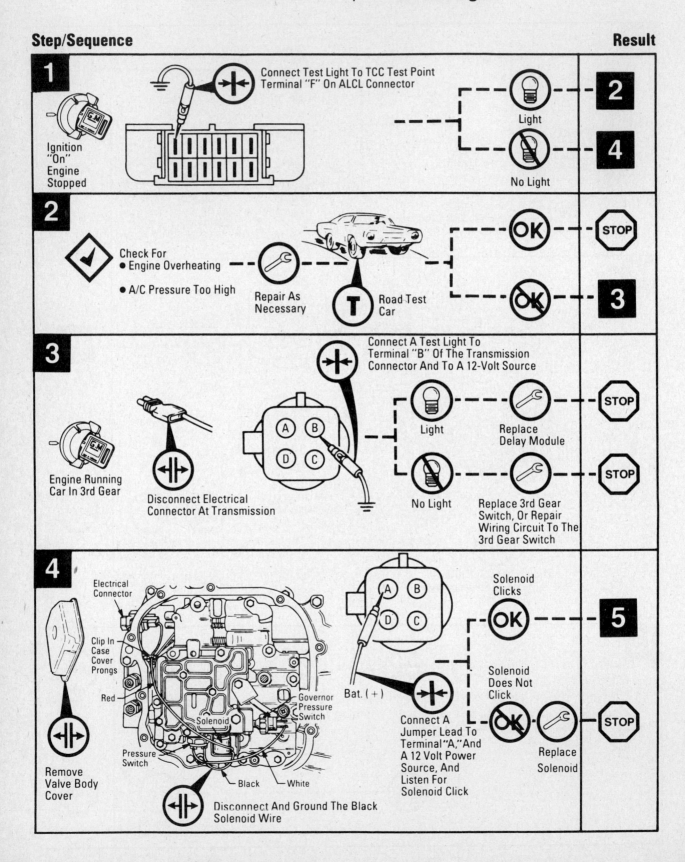

1 Ignition "On" Engine Stopped

Connect Test Light To TCC Test Point Terminal "F" On ALCL Connector

Light → **2**

No Light → **4**

2 Check For
- Engine Overheating
- A/C Pressure Too High

Repair As Necessary

Road Test Car

OK → STOP

OK (no) → **3**

3 Engine Running Car In 3rd Gear

Disconnect Electrical Connector At Transmission

Connect A Test Light To Terminal "B" Of The Transmission Connector And To A 12-Volt Source

Light → Replace Delay Module → STOP

No Light → Replace 3rd Gear Switch, Or Repair Wiring Circuit To The 3rd Gear Switch → STOP

4 Remove Valve Body Cover

Electrical Connector
Clip In Case Cover Prongs
Red
Governor Pressure Switch
Solenoid
Pressure Switch
Black — White

Disconnect And Ground The Black Solenoid Wire

Bat. (+)

Connect A Jumper Lead To Terminal "A," And A 12 Volt Power Source, And Listen For Solenoid Click

Solenoid Clicks OK → **5**

Solenoid Does Not Click OK (no) → Replace Solenoid → STOP

TORQUE CONVERTER CLUTCH OPERATION IN SECOND GEAR AS WELL AS IN THIRD GEAR
(Cont.)
1982 and Later TCC w/4.3L Diesel Engine

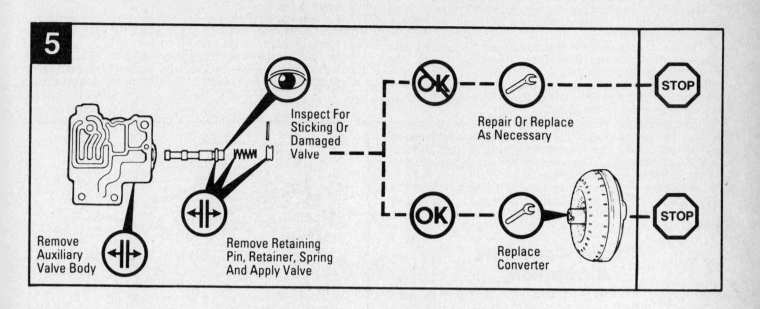

Verification Of Converter Clutch Valve Operation—1980

1. Using a tee fitting, install an oil pressure gauge to the cooler out line at the radiator.
2. Remove the vacuum line from the vacuum switch.
3. Raise the wheels and run the vehicle in DRIVE range until the 3rd gear upshift is obtained. Maintain 2000 rpm and note the oil pressure reading.
4. While maintaining 2000 rpm, re-connect the vacuum hose to the vacuum switch and observe the oil pressure reading. The pressure should drop 5 to 15 psi. This indicates the converter clutch valve is operating and if the converter clutch is inoperative, a missing "O" ring at the end of the turbine shaft or a defective converter could be the cause.
5. If the pressure does not drop, check the solenoid for a missing check ball or "O" ring, loose solenoid bolts, defective solenoid ball seat or ball. The converter clutch valve could be sticking, binding or damaged, or the direct clutch oil passages could be blocked, restricted or interconnected.
6. Should the oil pressure drop to zero, the cooler feed orifice in the converter clutch valve bushing is blocked, restricted or missing. Transmission failure could result due to lack of lubricating fluid.

Torque Converter Evaluation

Before a torque converter is replaced, verify that all of the other external and internal component checks have been made. A torque converter should only be replaced if one of the following conditions exists:
1. Front oil pump or body are badly scored. When these components become scored, cast-iron grindings enter the torque converter and oil circuit. This scoring is usually the result of the drive gear in the pump wearing into the crescent, or down into the pocket, or the outer gear wearing against the pocket. A cracked flexplate can also cause the drive lugs on the pump drive gear to become badly damaged.

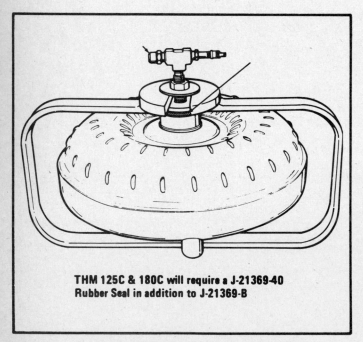

THM 125C & 180C will require a J-21369-40 Rubber Seal in addition to J-21369-B

Air pressure checking tools installed on torque converter
(©General Motors Corp.)

2. An internal converter failure, such as the converter clutch not engaging. However, all the external checks and internal checks must be made before condemning the converter. Some other types of internal converter failure are: the stator overrun clutch not locking or a thrust bearing that's failed. These types of failures are usually associated with aluminized oil present in the converter.
3. An external leak is apparent, such as at the hub weld area. However, a converter that's been in service for some time and didn't leak, probably never will.
4. End play in the converter exceeds .050 inch. This measurement can't be estimated, but must be made with Kent Moore tools J-21371, J-21371-8, J-25020, J-29060 or their equivalent.

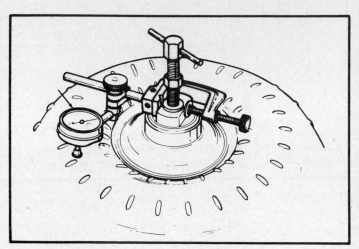

Checking end play of torque converter components
(©General Motors Corp.)

5. A scored or otherwise damaged hub. A damaged hub can cause a front seal failure or front pump housing failure.
6. A broken, damaged or poorly fitting converter pilot. This can cause the converter to not fit into the crankshaft bore properly or to be misaligned with the crankshaft centerline.
7. The converter has an imbalance problem which cannot be corrected. Most converter imbalance problems are minor and can be corrected by following the converter vibration procedure. Also, check for missing balance weights on the converter and flexplate. Replace the converter if the balance weights are missing. If these checks and test don't solve the problem, try balancing the flexplate.

A torque converter should NOT be replaced if it displays any of the following conditions:

1. The transmission oil has an odor or is discolored but there is no evidence of metallic particles. This is not an indication of converter or front pump damage. However, if the oil is discolored with engine coolant, the converter with a converter clutch must be replaced, as well as the friction materials and seals in the transmission.
2. Fretting wear on the hub where the oil pump drive gear locates. A small amount of wear is normal and does not require the replacement of the converter or front pump.
3. A defective oil cooler which allowed engine coolant to mix with the transmission oil. Conventional torque converters should be drilled, drained and repaired.

NOTE: A TCC torque converter must be replaced if engine coolant is found in the transmission oil.

4. Damaged threads in the torque converter attaching lugs. Repair the threads using a reputable thread repair kit.

Diagnosis of Converter Clutch Internal Control Components On Specific Transmission/Transaxle Assemblies

1980 THM 200C, 250C, 350C CHEVROLET BUILT TRANSMISSION—ALL GAS ENGINES WITHOUT DELAY VALVE

1. Direct clutch oil is fed to the TCC apply valve via the TCC solenoid.
2. The ignition switch, brake switch and low vacuum switch control the feed voltage to the TCC solenoid.
3. The governor switch acts as a speed sensor for TCC operation and provides the ground for the TCC solenoid.
2. The ignition switch, brake switch and low vacuum switch control the feed voltage to the TCC solenoid.
3. The governor switch acts as a speed sensor for TCC operation and provides the ground for the TCC solenoid.
4. The delay valve slows the response of the low vacuum switch.

1980 THM 200C, 350C with 5.7L DIESEL

1. Direct clutch oil is fed to the TCC apply valve via the TCC solenoid.
2. The ignition switch, brake switch, low vacuum switch and high vacuum switch control the feed voltage to the TCC solenoid.
3. The governor switch acts as a speed sensor for TCC operation and provides a ground for the TCC solenoid.

1981 THM 200C 5.7L DIESEL WITH EGR BLEED. TCC APPLYS IN 3RD SPEED ONLY

1. The direct clutch oil is fed to the TCC apply valve via the TCC solenoid.
2. The ignition switch, brake switch and rotary vacuum switch control the feed voltage to the TCC and EGR bleed solenoids.
3. The governor switch acts as a speed sensor for TCC operation and controls the ground for the EGR bleed solenoid.

Diagnosis:

A. Test light between test lead and ground.
1. Test light lights when all of the following are met:
   a. Ignition on.
   b. Brake switch closed.
   c. Rotary switch at specifications.

1980 THM 200C, 250C, 350C CHEVROLET BUILT TRANSMISSION—ALL GAS ENGINES WITH DELAY VALVE

1. Direct clutch oil is fed to the TCC apply valve via the TCC solenoid.
2. Test light will not go out when TCC engages.
3. Test light does not monitor EGR solenoid.
4. Test light at transmission side of EGR solenoid can test governor switch without pan removal. Disconnect EGR solenoid &

connect test light. Light should be on until governor switch closes & TCC engages.

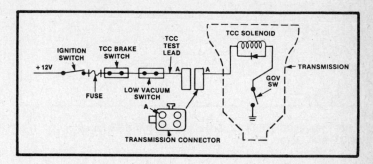

1980 THM 200C, 250C, 350C Chevrolet built, with gasoline engine less vacuum delay valve (©General Motors Corp.)

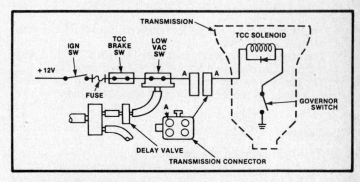

1980 THM 200C, 250C, 350C Chevrolet built, with gasoline engine and vacuum delay valve (©General Motors Corp.)

B. Jumper Wire Diagnosis—
NOTE: Do not use jumper wire between test lead and ground.
1. Connect jumper wire between EGR bleed solenoid transmission side and ground.
2. Ignition on—
   a. Listen for EGR solenoid click.
   b. Disconnect EGR solenoid connector, maintain test ground and listen for TCC solenoid click.
1. No click—TCC solenoid problem.
2. Clicks—verify TCC engagement in 3rd gear by driving.
   a. Engages—governor switch problem.
   b. No engage—TCC solenoid seal or ball seat.

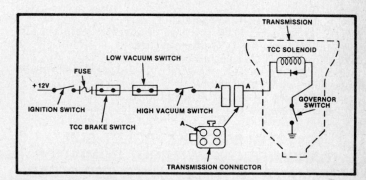

1980 THM 200C, 350C with 5.7L diesel engine (©General Motors Corp.)

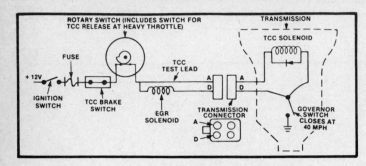

1981 THM 200C with 5.7L diesel engine and EGR bleed (©General Motors Corp.)

THM 350C-5.7L DIESEL WITH EGR BLEED. TCC APPLIES IN 3RD SPEED ONLY

1. The forward clutch oil is fed to the TCC apply valve via the TCC solenoid.
2. The third gear switch is necessary to restrict TCC operations to third gear.
3. The governor switch acts as a speed sensor for TCC operation and provides a ground for the EGR bleed solenoid.
4. The ignition switch, brake switch and rotary switch control the feed voltage to the TCC and EGR bleed solenoids.

Diagnosis:

A. Test light between test lead and ground.
1. Test light lights when all of the following are met:
   a. Ignition on.
   b. Brake switch closed.
   c. Rotary switch at specifications.

2. Test light will not go out when TCC engages.
3. Test light does not monitor EGR solenoid.
4. Test light at transmission side of EGR solenoid and ground can be used to test operation or failure of 3rd gear switch and governor switch but cannot isolate which is at fault if test shows failure.
   a. Disconnect EGR solenoid connector & connect test light. Light should be on until 3rd gear switch & governor switch close and TCC engages.
B. Jumper wire diagnosis—

NOTE: Do not use jumper wire between test and 2nd ground.

1. Connect jumper wire between EGR bleed solenoid transmission side and ground.
2. Ignition on—
   a. Listen for EGR solenoid click.
   b. Disconnect EGR solenoid connector, maintain test ground & listen for TCC solenoid click.
   1. No click—TCC solenoid problem.
   2. Clicks—Verify TCC engagement in 3rd gear by driving on hoist with jumper wire still on.
      a. Engages—governor switch problem.
      b. No engage—TCC solenoid seal or ball seat.

1981 THM 350C CHEVROLET-BUILT TRANSMISSION—WITHOUT COMPUTER COMMAND CONTROL—WITH EGR BLEED

1. Direct clutch oil is fed to the TCC apply valve via the TCC solenoid.

2. The governor switch acts as a speed sensor for TCC operation and provides the ground for the TCC and EGR bleed solenoids.
3. The ignition switch, brake switch and low vacuum switch control the feed voltage to both the TCC and EGR bleed solenoids.
4. The high gear switch only controls the EGR solenoid. The high gear switch is mounted externally on the transmission.

Diagnosis:

A. Test light between test lead and ground.

NOTE—Test lead is in TCC solenoid feed circuit.

1. Test light will light when all the following are met:
   a. Ignition on.
   b. Brake switch closed.
   c. Vacuum switch closed (vac. over spec.)

2. Test light will not go out when TCC engages.
3. Test light does not monitor EGR bleed solenoid.
4. Test light between EGR solenoid high gear switch terminal and ground will test EGR solenoid circuit. This means we can test governor switch without removing the oil pan if TCC does not work:

   a. Install test light at EGR solenoid.
   b. If needed, bypass high gear switch with a wire.
   c. Operate vehicle to 45-50 MPH—light going off means governor switch is OK since light is in ground side of EGR solenoid circuit.
B. Jumper wire diagnosis.

NOTE: Do not use jumper between test lead and ground.

1. Jumper wire between transmission terminal D and ground.
   a. Ignition on-listen for solenoid click.
   1. No click—TCC solenoid problem.
   2. Click—drive on hoist to verify TCC engage in 3rd gear
   a. No engage—TCC solenoid seal or ball seat.
   b. Engages—disconnect ground wire & verify.
   a. No engage—governor switch problem.
   b. Engage—no problem found.

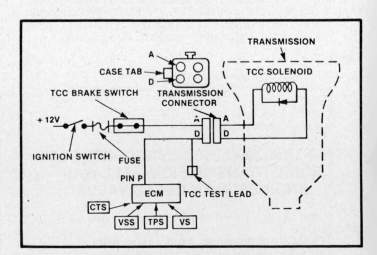

1981-82 THM 200C, 250C, 350C Chevrolet built with CCC system, without EGR bleed (©General Motors Corp.)

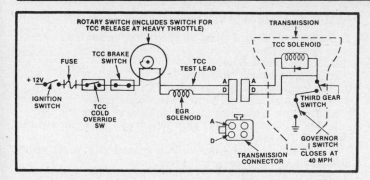

THM 350C with 5.7L diesel engine and EGR bleed. TCC applies in third speed only (©General Motors Corp.)

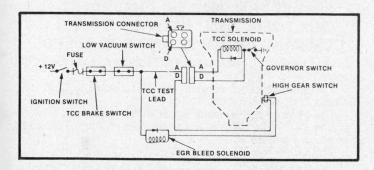

1981 THM 350C Chevrolet built without CCC system and with EGR bleed (©General Motors Corp.)

1981-82 THM 200C, 250C, 350C CHEVROLET-BUILT WITH COMPUTER COMMAND CONTROL—WITHOUT EGR BLEED

1. Direct clutch oil is fed to the TCC apply valve via the TCC solenoid.
2. No internal electrical switches are used.
3. The ignition and brake switches control the feed voltage to the TCC solenoid.
4. The ECM controls the TCC solenoid ground.

Diagnosis:

A. Test light between test lead and ground.
1. Ignition switch on—test light goes on (if not, check at brake switch).
2. Tap brake pedal—test light goes off and on.
3. Start engine—light stays on at all times until the following are met:

    a. Coolant temperature up to specifications.
    b. Vehicle speed to specifications.
    c. Throttle position/vacuum switch signal to specifications.
Note that solenoid can be energized even before third gear is achieved—TCC then comes on with 2-3 shift.
4. When vehicle TCC is on, test light is off.

    a. Goes on with change in throttle position, then back off with slight delay.
    b. Tap brake pedal—light stays off—ECM keeps ground.
    c. Downshift causes light to go on via TPS sensor and vacuum.

B. Jumper wire between test lead and ground.

NOTE: Use jumper wire if test light stays on at all times in A-3 above. Jumper wire bypasses ECM & causes full time solenoid on.

1. Ignition on engine off—Touch wire between test lead and ground and listen for solenoid click.
2. Road test or drive wheels on rack to verify TCC coming on as trans. shifts to 3rd gear. If TCC comes on, refer to CCC charts for ECM & input diagnosis.

THM 200C OR CHEVROLET BUILT 250C, 350C WITH E.G.R BLEED

1. Direct clutch oil to solenoid and apply valve.
2. Ignition switch controls solenoid feed (both).
3. TCC relay controls ground for both solenoids.
4. Brake switch controls TCC relay coil feed.
5. ECM controls TCC relay coil ground.

Diagnosis:

A. Test light between test lead and ground, EGR bleed solenoid disconnected.
1. Ignition on—test light on—no brake switch effect.
2. Start engine-drive position—light stays on until:
    a. Coolant temperature to specifications.
    b. Vehicle speed to specifications.
    c. TPS-VAC signal to specifications.
Note that TCC relay maybe energized before 3rd gear is reached in transmission.
3. When TCC is on, TCC relay is energized and light is off.
    a. Goes on with throttle changes and out with slight delay.
    b. Tap brake pedal—light goes on and off—no delay. (tests relay operation).

B. Jumper wire between test light & ground.

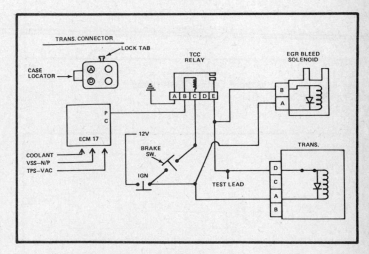

THM 200C, 250C, 350C with EGR bleed (©General Motors Corp.)

NOTE: Use only if test light stays on any time ignition switch is on. Jumper wire by-passes TCC relay points (EGR solenoid disconnected).

1. Turn ignition on—listen for TCC solenoid click.
    a. No click—problems in transmission.
    b. Does click—road test or test on hoist to verify TCC engagement.

1. No engagement—check TCC solenoid seal & ball seat.
2. Engages—check TCC relay operation by moving jumper wire to TCC relay terminal B.
   a. TCC relay should click & TCC solenoid should click.
   b. No click—ground TCC relay terminal E—TCC solenoid should click.

1981-82 THM 125C WITHOUT COMPUTER COMMAND CONTROL OR EGR BLEED

1. Line oil is fed to the TCC apply valve via the TCC solenoid.
2. The ignition switch, brake switch and low vacuum switch control the feed voltage to the TCC solenoid.
3. The governor switch acts as a speed sensor for TCC operation and provides the ground for the TCC solenoid.

Test Light Diagnosis—

Test light between test lead and ground.

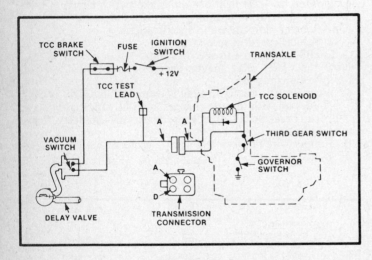

1981-82 THM 125C without CCC or EGR bleed
(©General Motors Corp.)

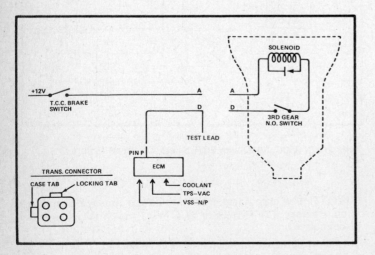

1981-82 THM 350C, Model MX-2, Buick built
(©General Motors Corp.)

NOTE: Test lead is in TCC solenoid feed circuit.

1. Test light will light when all the following are met:
   a. Ignition on.
   b. Brake switch closed.
   c. Vacuum switch closed.
2. Test light will not go out when TCC engages.
3. Test light at terminal D in transaxle connector.
   a. Test one conditions met cause light to go on.
   b. Light goes out as 3rd gear switch and governor switch close and TCC engages.
   c. The vehicle drive wheels off the ground to drive the vehicle and allow TCC engagement test.
4. Jumper wire—Do not use jumper wire on this system.
   a. Do not use wire at test lead—electrical damage may result.
   b. Do not use wire at transmission terminal D since TCC may engage any time.

1981-82 THM 200C OR CHEVROLET-BUILT 250C-350C WITH COMPUTER COMMAND CONTROL AND EGR BLEED

1. Direct clutch oil is fed to the TCC apply valve via the TCC solenoid.
2. The ignition switch controls the feed voltage to both the TCC and EGR bleed solenoids.
3. The brake switch controls the TCC relay coil feed.
4. The TCC relay controls the ground for both the TCC and EGR bleed solenoids.
5. The ECM controls the ground of the TCC relay coil.

1981-82 THM 350C WITH MX-2 VALVE BODY—BUICK BUILT

1. Forward clutch oil to solenoid and apply valve.
2. Requires 3rd clutch oil switch.
3. ECM controls solenoid ground.
4. Brake Switch— Ignition Switch controls solenoid feed.

Diagnosis:

A. Test light between test lead and ground.
1. Test light does not go on until transmission reaches 3rd gear to complete circuit to test lead (18-20 mph) (if not-test at brake switch).
2. Test light will then come on until the following are met:
   a. Coolant up to specifications.
   b. TPS-VAC to specifications.
   c. VSS to speed.

Note that all ECM requirements may be met before 3rd gear is reached—light may not come on.
3. When TCC is on, test light is off. While in 3rd gear.
   a. Tap brake pedal causes light to stay out— ECM keeps ground.

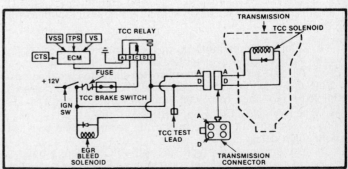

1981-82 THM 200C or Chevrolet built 250C, 350C with CCC and EGR bleed (©General Motors Corp.)

b. Throttle position change causes light to go on and off with slight delay.

c. Downshift causes light to stay out because internal switch goes open.

B. Jumper wire between test lead and ground.

NOTE: Use jumper wire if light stays on at all times in A-2 above. Jumper wire by-passes ECM and causes TCC engage in 3rd at all loads.

1981-82 THM (MX-3)—BUICK BUILT

1. Forward clutch oil to solenoid and apply valve.
2. Requires 3rd or 2nd clutch oil switch.
3. ECM controls solenoid ground.
4. Brake Switch—Ignition Switch controls solenoid feed.

Diagnosis:

A. Test light between test lead and ground.

1. Test light does not go on until transmission reaches 2nd gear to complete circuit to test lead (18-20 mph) (if not-test at brake switch).

2. Test light will then come on until the following are met:
   a. Coolant up to specifications.
   b. TPS-VAC to specifications.
   c. VSS to speed.

Note that all ECM requirements may be met before 3rd gear is reached—light may not come on.

3. When TCC is on, test light is off. While in 2nd gear.
   a. Tap brake pedal causes light to stay out—ECM keeps ground.
   b. Throttle position change causes light to go on and off with slight delay.
   c. Downshift causes light to stay out because internal switch goes open.

B. Jumper wire between test lead and ground.

NOTE: Use jumper wire if light stays on at all time in A-2 above. Jumper wire by-passes ECM and causes TCC engage in 3rd at all loads.

1981-82 THM 125C WITH COMPUTER COMMAND CONTROL—WITHOUT EGR BLEED

1. Line oil is fed to the TCC apply valve via the TCC solenoid.
2. The third gear switch is required to prevent TCC application in lower gears.
3. The ignition and brake switches control the feed voltage to the TCC solenoid.
4. The ECM controls the solenoid ground.

Diagnosis:

A. Test light between test lead and ground.

1. Test light does not go on until transmission reaches third gear to complete circuit to test lead (18-20 mph).

2. Test light will then come on until the following are met:
   a. Coolant up to specifications.
   b. TPS-VAC to specifications.
   c. VSS to speed.

Note that all ECM may be met before 3rd gear is reached—light may not come on.

3. When TCC is on, test light is off. While in 3rd gear:
   a. Tap brake pedal causes light to stay out—ECM keeps ground.
   b. Throttle position change causes light to go on and off with slight delay.
   c. Downshift causes light to stay out because internal switch goes open.

B. Jumper wire between test lead and ground.

NOTE: Use jumper wire if light stays on at all times in A-2 above. Jumper wire by-passes ECM & causes TCC engage in 3rd at all leads.

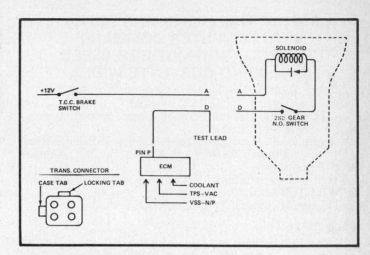

1981-82 THM 350C, Model MX-3, Buick built
(©General Motors Corp.)

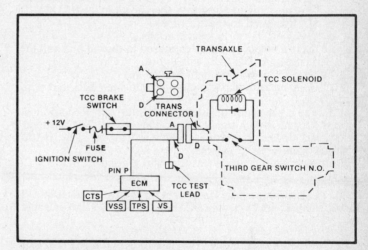

1981-82 THM 125C with CCC, less EGR bleed
(©General Motors Corp.)

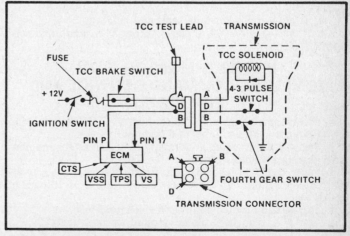

1981-82 THM 200-4R, 700-R4 with CCC system, less EGR bleed. Includes Corvette with EFI (©General Motors Corp.)

a. Vehicle on hoist or on road test—accelerate to 25 mph & listen for solenoid click as transmission shifts 3rd gear.

b. Feel for engine pulsations on coast until trans. shifts out of 3rd.

1981-82 THM 200-4R AND 700-R4 WITH COMPUTER COMMAND CONTROL—WITHOUT EGR BLEED (INCLUDING CORVETTE W/EFI)

1. Second gear clutch oil is fed through the TCC shift valve to the TCC apply valve via the TCC solenoid.

2. The 4-3 pulse switch is normally closed. It opens momentarily during a 4-3 downshift.

3. When the ECM recognizes the fourth gear switch is activated, it provides more TPS movement before the TCC is disengaged in fourth gear.

4. The ignition switch and brake switch control the feed voltage to the TCC solenoid.

5. The ECM controls the TCC solenoid ground.

Diagnosis:

A. Test light between test lead and ground.

1. Ignition on-brake off—test light comes on.

2. Tap brake pedal—test light goes off and on.

3. Start engine and drive—light stays on until the following:

a. Coolant temperature up to specifications.

b. Vehicle speed to specifications.

c. TPS-VAC signal to specifications.

Note that the solenoid can be energized in second gear and the TCC can come on. The light will go out.

4. When TCC is on, test light will be out.

a. Goes on with throttle changes and then back out with slight delay.

b. Tap brake pedal—light stays out since only feed affected.

c. 4th gear switch signals larger TPS change TCC affected.

d. 4-3 downshift may leave light off as 4-3 pulse switch pulses open for TCC pulses.

B. Jumper wire between test lead and ground.

NOTE: Use jumper wire if test light stays on at all times in A-3 above. Jumper wire by-passes ECM and causes full time solenoid on.

1. Ignition on engine off—Touch wire between test lead and ground and listen for solenoid click.

2. Road test or drive wheels—drive to verify that TCC does engage after 1-2 shift and holds engaged in 3rd and 4th at all loads.

a. If not—check solenoid seals and ball seat.

b. If yes—refer to CCC diagnosis for ECM and input sensors.

1981-82 THM 200-4R WITH COMPUTER COMMAND CONTROL AND EGR BLEED

1. Second gear clutch oil is fed through the TCC shift valve to the TCC apply valve via the TCC solenoid.

2. The 4-3 pulse switch is normally closed. It opens momentarily during a 4-3 downshift.

3. When the ECM recognizes the fourth gear switch is activated, it provides more TPS movement before the TCC is engaged in fourth gear.

4. The ignition switch controls the solenoid feed.

5. The TCC relay controls the ground for both the TCC and EGR bleed solenoids.

6. The brake switch controls the TCC relay coil feed.

7. The ECM controls the ground of the TCC relay coil.

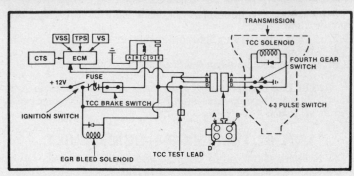

1981-82 THM 200-4R with CCC system and EGR bleed
(©General Motors Corp.)

Diagnosis:

A. Test light between test lead and ground.

1. Ignition on—test light on—no brake pedal effect.

2. Start engine and drive—light stays on until:

a. Coolant temperature to specifications.

b. Vehicle speed to specifications.

c. TPS-VAC signal to specifications.

Note that the relay and both solenoids can be energized in second gear and TCC can come on. Test light goes off as relay closes.

3. When TCC is on, relay is energized and test light is off.

a. Goes on with throttle changes and goes out with slight delay.

b. Tap brake pedal and light goes on and off—no delay.

c. 4-3 downshift leaves light out as relay may stay on, but full throttle downshift may use TPS to affect ECM and light goes on.

d. 4th gear switch causes wide throttle movement before TCC is affected in 4th gear.

B. Jumper wire between test lead and ground.

NOTE: Use jumper wire if test light stays on at all times in A-3 above. Jumper wire by-passes ECM and causes full time solenoid on.

1. Turn ignition on—listen for TCC solenoid click.

a. No click—problem in transmission.

b. Does click—road test or test on hoist to verify TCC engage.

1. No engage—check TCC solenoid seal and ball seat.

2. Engages—check TCC relay operation by moving jumper wire to TCC relay terminal B.

a. TCC relay should click and TCC solenoid should click.

b. No click—ground TCC relay terminal E—TCC solenoid should click.

1982 THM 700-R4 CORVETTE CCC OR EFI

1. 2nd clutch oil through TCC shift valve to solenoid and apply valve.

2. 4-3 pulse switch is normally closed. Opens only momentarily on 4-3 downshifts.

3. 4th gear switch is input to ECM (N.C.) provides wider TPS movement before TCC is affected while in 4th

4. Ignition switch and brake switch control feed to solenoid.

5. ECM controls solenoid ground.

Diagnosis:

A. Test light between test lead and ground.

1. Ignition on-brake off—test light comes on.

2. Tap brake pedal—test light goes off and on.

3. Start engine and drive—light stays on until the following.

a. Coolant temperature up to specifications.

b. Vehicle speed to specifications.

c. TPS-VAC signal to specifications.

Note that the solenoid can be energized in second gear and the TCC can come on. The light will go out.

4. When TCC is on, test light will be out.

   a. Goes on with throttle changes and then back on with slight delay.

   b. Tap brake pedal—light stays out since only feed affected.

   c. 4th gear switch signals larger TPS change before TCC affected.

   d. 4-3 downshift may leave light off as 4-3 pulse switch pulses open for TCC pulses.

B. Jumper wire between test lead and grounds.

NOTE: Use jumper wire if light stays on at all times in A-3 above. Jumper wire by-passes ECM & causes full time solenoid on.

1. Ignition on engine off—touch wire between test lead and ground and listen for solenoid click.

2. Road test or drive wheels—drive to verify that TCC does engage after 1-2 shift and holds engaged in 3rd and 4th at all loads.

   a. If not—check solenoid seals and ball seat.

   b. If yes—refer to CCC diagnosis for ECM and input sensors.

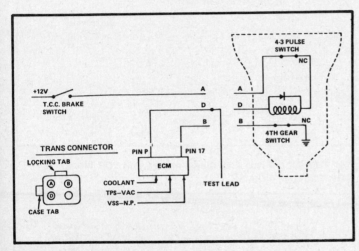

1982 THM 700-R4—Corvette equipped with CCC or EFI (©General Motors Corp.)

1982 THM 325-4L—5.7L DIESEL

1. 2nd clutch oil through TCC shift valve to solenoid—apply valve area.

2. Solenoid has constant ground—and will be energized when key is turned "on" unless throttle switch is open.

3. TCC will engage as soon as signal oil from TCC shift valve is available.

4. Load control at heavy throttle switch on injector pump.

Diagnosis—

A—test light at test lead monitors feed circuit.

B—DO NOT use jumper wire at test lead.

1982 THM 350-C (MX-5)—BUICK BUILT

1. Forward clutch oil to solenoid and apply valve.

2. ECM controls solenoid ground.

3. Brake switch—Ignition switch controls solenoid feed.

4. 2nd and 3rd clutch oil switches used to match engagement load with gear used.

Diagnosis—

A. Test light between test lead and ground.

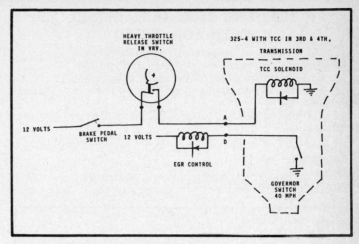

1982 THM 325-4L with 5.7L Diesel engine (©General Motors Corp.)

1. Ignition switch on—test light goes on (if not check at brake switch).

2. Tap brake pedal—test light goes off and on.

3. Start engine—light stays on at all time until the following are met:

   a. Coolant temperature up to specifications.

   b. Vehicle speed to specifications.

   c. Throttle position/vacuum switch signal to specifications.

Note that solenoid can be energized even before 2nd gear is achieved—TCC then comes on in first.

4. When vehicle TCC is on, test light is off.

   a. Goes on with change in throttle position, then back off with slight delay.

   b. Tap brake pedal—light stays off—ECM keeps ground.

   c. Downshift causes light to go on via TPS sensor and vacuum.

B. Jumper wire between test lead and ground.

NOTE: Use jumper wire if test light stays on at all times in A-3 above. Jumper wire bypasses ECM and causes full time solenoid on.

1. Ignition on engine off—Touch wire between test lead and ground and listen for solenoid click.

NOTE: The jumper wire at test lead will apply TCC as soon as shift lever is moved to any forward gear. An idling engine will stall.

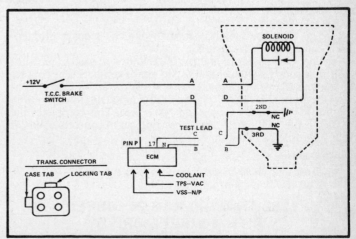

1982 THM 350C, Model MX-5, Buick built (©General Motors Corp.)

1982 THM-350C—5.7L DIESEL WITH EGR BLEED

Forward clutch oil to solenoid and apply valve.
1. Requires 3rd gear switch to keep apply to 3rd.
2. Governor switch for vehicle speed information.
3. Release switch at injection pump for Heavy Throttle Release.
4. EGR bleed controlled through 3rd clutch and governor switches.
5. TCC remains engaged on coast until 3-2 downshift.

Diagnosis—

A—Test light at test lead monitors feed circuit.
B—DO NOT use jumper wire at test lead.

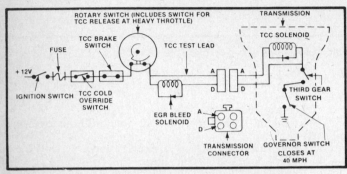

1982 THM 350C with 5.7L diesel engine with EGR bleed
(©General Motors Corp.)

1982 THM 200-4R 5.7L DIESEL WITH EGR BLEED

1. Second gear clutch oil is fed through the TCC shift valve to the TCC apply valve via the TCC solenoid.
2. The TCC solenoid has a constant ground. It is energized when the ignition switch is turned "ON," unless the throttle switch in the rotary switch is open.
3. The TCC will engage as soon as the signal oil from the TCC apply valve is available.

Diagnosis—

A—Test light at test lead monitors feed circuit.
B—DO NOT use jumper wire at test lead.

1982 THM 700-R4 6.2L DIESEL 2-WHEEL DRIVE

1. Second gear clutch oil is fed through the TCC shift valve via the TCC solenoid.
2. The 4-3 pulse switch is normally closed. It opens momentarily during a 4-3 downshift.
3. The TCC solenoid is directly grounded at case mounting.
4. The rotary switch contains two sets of contacts. The first set of contacts is open at light throttle, while the second set of contacts are normally closed. The first set of contacts closes anytime the throttle is opened more than 10 percent. This completes the circuit to the TCC solenoid. The second set of contacts opens at heavy throttle to release the TCC.

Diagnosis—

A—Test light at test lead monitors feed circuit.
B—DO NOT use jumper wire at test lead.

1982 THM 700-R4 6.2L DIESEL WITH 4-WHEEL DRIVE

1. Second gear clutch oil is fed through the TCC shift valve to the TCC apply valve via the TCC solenoid.

2. The 4-3 pulse switch is normally closed. It opens momentarily during a 4-3 downshift.
3. The TCC solenoid is directly grounded to the transmission case.
4. The rotary switch contains two sets of contacts.
5. When in 2-wheel drive, the feed to the TCC solenoid is through the ignition switch, brake switch, rotary switch and 4-wheel drive relay.
6. When in 4-wheel drive, the contacts in the 4-wheel drive relay open and the fourth gear switch must close to feed the TCC solenoid.
7. A switch in the transfer case closes when the vehicle is in 4-wheel drive. In turn, this energizes the 4-wheel drive relay, opening the contacts. This opens the circuit and provides the ground for the 4-wheel drive indicator light. The transfer case switch also prevents TCC operation in second and third gears when in 4-wheel drive.

Diagnosis—

A—test light at test lead monitors feed circuit
B—DO NOT use jumper wire at test lead

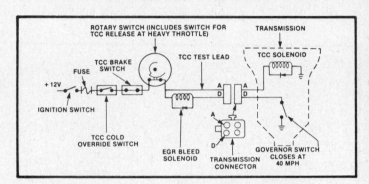

1982 THM 200-4R with 5.7L diesel engine with EGR bleed
(©General Motors Corp.)

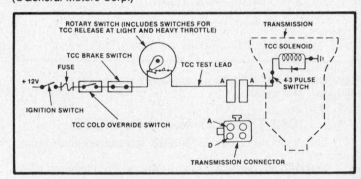

1982 THM 700-R4 with 6.2L diesel engine, Two wheel drive
(©General Motors Corp.)

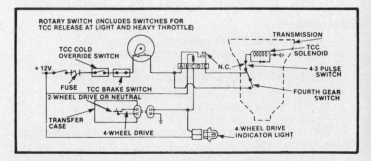

1982 THM 700-R4 with 6.2L diesel engine, Four wheel drive
(©General Motors Corp.)

1982 THM 700-R4 LIGHT TRUCK WITH GAS ENGINE 2- OR 4-WHEEL DRIVE

1. Second gear clutch oil is fed through the TCC shift valve to the TCC apply valve via the TCC solenoid.

2. The 4-3 pulse switch is normally closed. It opens momentarily during a 4-3 downshift.

3. The fourth gear switch is used to bypass the vacuum switch when the transmission is in fourth gear. This keeps the TCC engaged at all throttle openings in fourth gear.

4. The vacuum switch opens when vacuum drops to approximately 1-3 in. Hg near wide open throttle. The switch is also open at idle.

5. The EGR bleed solenoid is energized when the transmission is in third or fourth gear and both the third clutch and TCC signal switches close.

Diagnosis—

A—test light at test lead monitors feed circuit
B—DO NOT use jumper wire at test lead

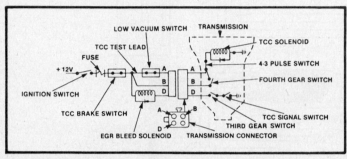

1982 THM 700-R4, light truck with gasoline engine, two or four wheel drive (©General Motors Corp.)

1982 THM 350C 5.7L DIESEL WITHOUT EGR BLEED

1. Direct clutch oil is fed to the TCC apply valve via the TCC solenoid.

2. The third gear switch is necessary to restrict TCC operation to third gear.

3. The governor switch acts as a speed sensor for TCC operation and provides the ground for the third gear switch and TCC solenoid.

4. A release switch is included in the rotary switch on the injection pump to release the TCC during heavy throttle applications.

5. The TCC solenoid remains energized during coastdown until the governor switch opens. The TCC clutch is released by the poppet valves inside the converter.

Diagnosis—

A—test light at test lead monitors feed circuit
B—DO NOT use jumper wire at test lead

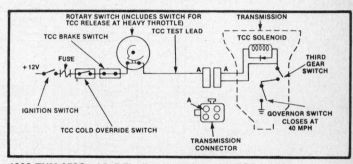

1982 THM 350C with 5.7L diesel engine with EGR bleed (©General Motors Corp.)

TORQUE CONVERTER CLUTCH OIL FLOW

1983 And Later Wiring Information Refer To Individual Automatic Transmission Sections.

GENERAL INFORMATION

In all converter clutches, fluid pressure delivered to the stator side of the pressure plate applies the clutch, while fluid pressure applied to the engine side of the pressure plate releases the clutch.

REAR DRIVE VEHICLES

In the automatic transmissions installed in the rear drive vehicles, the release fluid is delivered through a drilled passage in the turbine shaft. The release fluid is fed between the stator shaft bushing and the front oil delivery ring on the turbine shaft. The bushing acts as the front seal as fluid is directed to the drilled turbine shaft and to the engine side of the pressure plate.

Apply fluid is delivered between the converter hub and the stator shaft. Apply fluid is delivered between the converter hub and the stator shaft. Apply fluid moves the pressure plate against the converter cover to apply the clutch. Fluid is sealed at the oil pump drive gear, the pressure plate friction area and at the turbine thrust spacer "O" rings in both areas.

FRONT DRIVE VEHICLES

In the Automatic transaxles installed in the front drive vehicles, release fluid is delivered through a hollow turbine shaft around the pump shaft to the engine side of the pressure plate. Apply fluid is delivered through the turbine shaft by way of a sleeve pressed in the shaft. The sleeve allows apply fluid to be routed around the sprocket area in the link cavity without losing pressure. There are two teflon rings at the valve body end of the turbine shaft sleeve and one at the converter end of the sleeve on the turbine shaft. Missing and/or damaged seals could cause improper clutch apply.

Hydraulic Converter Clutch Controls

A converter clutch apply (control) valve is used to control the direction of oil flow throughout the torque converter and therefore the apply or release of the converter clutch.

All apply valves are moved to the apply position by oil pressure through an orifice to an area between the valve and a bleed (TCC) Solenoid. The restriction is smaller than the bleed in the solenoid so no pressure is available to move the valve when the solenoid is not energized electrically.

The 200-C apply valve train (2-piece) is located in the oil pump. Line oil on the small end holds the valve in the release position. Direct clutch oil (in 3rd gear) acts on the large end of the valve train when the solenoid is energized.

The 250-C—350-C apply valve is a one piece valve located in an auxiliary valve body on the front of the separator plate. The valve is held in the release position by spring pressure. 2-3 clutch oil, acting on the ring land difference, moves the valve to the apply position. In the Chevrolet built units (M-31 & M-38). Buick built units (MX2, MX3, MX5) use forward clutch oil to move the

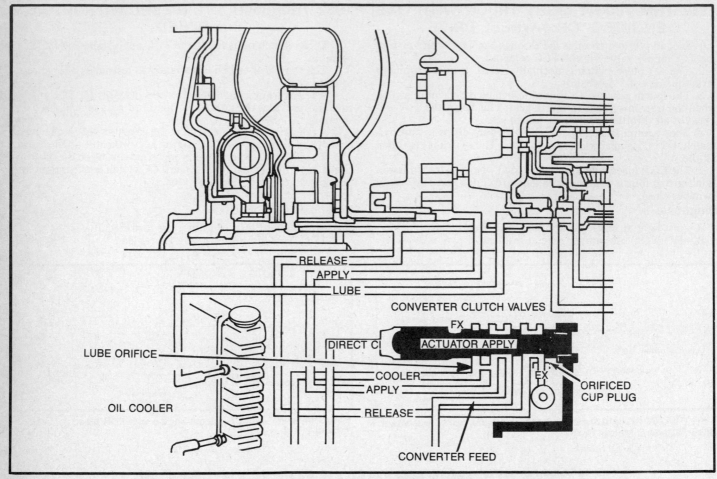

THM 200C oil flow schematic to apply Torque Converter Clutch (©General Motors Corp.)

valve to the apply position. This allows the clutch to be applied in a lower gear than 3rd.

The overdrive transmissions use a one piece valve spring loaded to the release position. Oil to move it to the apply position is controlled by a TCC shift valve that operates like any shift valve. Governor pressure must rise to move the shift valve before oil called signal can move the apply valve. The 1-2 shift must also be made to supply 2nd clutch oil to the TCC shift valve. The screen in the signal oil passages helps to keep the apply valve and the solenoid bleed clean.

The 125-C apply valve is a one piece valve held released by line oil pressure. Line oil controlled by the solenoid is used to move the valve to the apply position. A TCC regulator valve is used to regulate line oil to the converter during clutch apply. This limits converter oil pressure much like the converter feed orifice does in the other transmissions and in release position in the 125-C.

In all cases, oil returning from the converter during the release operation is routed to the oil cooler, then to the lube passages.

SOURCE OF CONVERTER CLUTCH OIL SUPPLY

Oil to the solenoid-apply valve area to move the valve to the apply position is different on different transmissions.
1. 200-C, 250-C and Chev. built 350-C—direct clutch oil.
2. 350-C Buick built—forward clutch oil.
3. 125-C—line oil
4. Overdrive Trans.—2nd. clutch oil through a TCC shift valve.

ACTION OF RELEASE OIL DURING CONVERTER CLUTCH APPLY

In all cases oil from the converter release passage during the apply:
1. Passes through an orifice to slow the oil allowing a timing-dampening action during the apply. The orifice may be
   a. A scallop in a check ball seat (in turbine shaft)
   b. A hole near the converter valve in transfer plate, valve body, or pump assy.
2. Is exhausted without going through cooler and lube passages. Lube oil is passed to the cooler and lube passages through another orifice.

The direction of oil flow to the converter is reversed when the apply valve is moved. The valve is held in the release position by spring pressure or by line oil pressure.

BLOCKED SOLENOID VALVE CONDITIONS

With the various pressure sources of fluid to the apply valve, a stuck closed solenoid valve can cause the following conditions:
1. Direct clutch oil operated will have TCC apply whenever 3rd gear is achieved even at an 18 mph light throttle shift. This can cause rough engine and stalling. It could also cause vehicle jerk on coast down before a 3-2 or 3-1 downshift.
2. The 350-C with forward clutch oil operated TCC apply, will cause the engine to stall as the shift lever is moved to any forward gear.
3. The overdrive transmissions would have TCC shift valve shifts to direct signal oil to the apply valve. We could also feel the coast jerkiness.

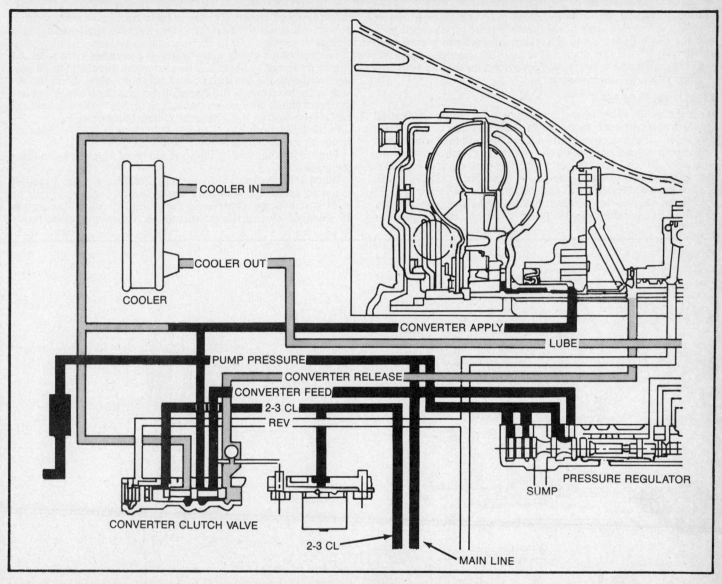

THM 250C, 350C oil flow schematic to apply Torque Converter Clutch (©General Motors Corp.)

4. The 125-C uses line oil to the apply valve and we could expect engine stall in a shift to any gear (forward or reverse) when the driveline connection is made to the drive wheels.

NOTE: If the apply valve is stuck in the apply position, the transmission will react in the same manner as the 125-C in step four. If the apply valve is stuck in the released position, the converter clutch will not apply at any time.

OIL FLOW—CONVERTER CLUTCH

THM 200-C

In Park, Neutral, Reverse, and First gear, the converter clutch apply valve, located in the pump, is held in the release position by line pressure. That is, the apply valve in this position takes converter feed oil, coming from the pressure regulator valve, and sends it into the release passage, through the turbine shaft, and into the cavity between the converter clutch pressure plate and the converter cover. This moves the clutch pressure plate away from the converter cover, releasing the converter clutch.

After the oil releases the converter clutch, it flows from behind the pressure plate and through the converter. From the converter, the oil flows backwards through the apply passage to the apply

valve. The apply valve then sends oil returning from the converter to the transmission cooler in the radiator. Oil, returning from the cooler, is then directed to the transmission lubrication system.

The converter clutch apply valve is controlled by a solenoid operated exhaust valve that is located in the direct clutch oil passage leading to the converter clutch actuator valve. When the vehicle is in drive range, third gear, direct clutch oil which applies the direct clutch also passes through an orifice to the solenoid exhaust valve and to the converter clutch actuator valve.

When vehicle speed in drive range, 3rd gear, reaches a predetermined speed, (35-45 mph), the governor pressure switch or ECM switch closes, completing the ground circuit and energizes the solenoid closing the exhaust valve. This allows direct clutch oil to move the converter clutch valve or apply valve to the apply position.

With the converter clutch valve in the apply position, converter feed oil is redirected from the release passage to the apply passage. Converter feed oil then flows from the apply passage to the converter by flowing between the converter hub and stator shaft. The converter is now being charged with oil from the apply side of the converter clutch pressure plate.

As the pressure plate begins to move to its applied position, release oil on the front side of the pressure plate is redirected back into the turbine shaft down the release passage and is exhausted at the converter clutch apply valve orifice to dampen apply.

Oil to cooler and lube system is provided through an orifice in the apply line to cooler passage.

THM 250-C and 350-C

With the apply valve in the release position, converter feed oil flows through the open apply valve to the converter clutch release passage in the pump cover. It then flows through the turbine shaft to the front or release side of the converter clutch, between the converter clutch pressure plate and the converter cover. This moves the clutch pressure plate away from the converter cover, releasing the converter clutch and charging the converter with oil. The oil then leaves the converter by flowing between the converter hub and stator shaft into the pump cover and to the converter

clutch apply oil circuit. The apply oil circuit is now being used in a reverse direction. The oil then flows from the apply passage into the cooler passage and to the lubrication system.

The converter clutch apply valve is controlled by a solenoid operated exhaust valve that is located in the direct clutch oil passage leading to the converter clutch actuator valve. When the vehicle is in drive range, third gear, direct clutch oil which applies the direct clutch also passes through an orifice to the solenoid exhaust valve and to the converter clutch acutator valve.

In the Buick built 350-C, forward clutch oil is supplied past the orifice to the apply valve—solenoid area.

This oil is exhausted by the solenoid bleed until the solenoid is energized.

When vehicle speed in drive range, 3rd gear, reaches a pre-determined speed, (35-45 mph), the governor pressure switch or ECM switch closes, completing the ground circuit and energizes the solenoid, closing the exhaust valve. This allows oil to move

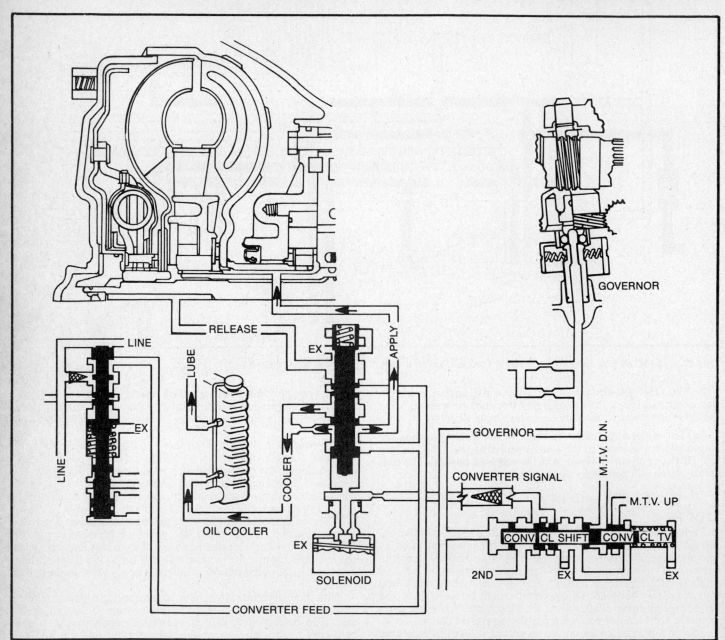

THM 200-4R, 325-4L, 700-R4 oil flow schematic to apply Torque Converter Clutch (©General Motors Corp.)

the converter clutch valve or apply valve to the apply position.

With the converter clutch valve in the apply position, converter feed oil is redirected from the release passage to the apply passage. Converter feed oil then flows from the apply pasage to the converter hub and stator shaft. The converter is now being charged with oil from the apply side of the converter clutch pressure plate.

As the pressure plate begins to move to its applied position, release oil on the front side of the pressure plate is redirected back into the turbine shaft down the release passage and is exhausted at the converter clutch apply valve. Check ball orifice to dampen appy.

Oil to cooler and lube system is provided through an orifice in the apply line to cooler passage.

OVERDRIVE UNITS

In Park, Neutral, Reverse, and First gear, the converter clutch apply valve located in the pump, is held in the release position by the converter clutch apply valve spring. The apply valve in this position takes converter feed oil, coming from the pressure regulator valve, and sends it into the release passage, through the turbine shaft, and into the release passage, through the turbine shaft, and into the cavity between the converter clutch pressure plate and the converter cover. This moves the clutch pressure plate away from the converter cover, releasing the converter clutch.

After the oil releases the converter clutch, it flows from behind the pressure plate and through the converter. From the converter, the oil flows backwards throughout the apply passage to the apply valve. The apply valve then sends oil returning from the converter, to the transmission cooler in the radiator. Oil, returning from the cooler, is then directed to the transmission lubrication system.

The apply valve is controlled by the converter clutch shift valve and will stay in the release position until it receives converter clutch signal oil from the converter clutch shift valve in the valve body.

It should be noted that the converter clutch apply valve can shift to apply the converter only when the converter clutch solenoid is energized electrically. When the solenoid is not energized, the converter clutch signal oil is exhausted and the converter will stay in the release position. The converter clutch solenoid would be off under conditions such as: high engine vacuum (idle), low engine vacuum (full throttle), braking, or cold engine operation.

In the hydraulic system as described thus far, the 1-2. 2-3. 3-4. and converter clutch shifts will always take place at the same vehicle speeds: that is, whenever the governor pressure overcomes the force of the springs on the shift valves. When accelerating under a heavy load or for maximum performance, it is desirable to have the shifts occur at higher vehicle speeds.

As the pressure plate begins to move to its applied position, release oil on the front side of the pressure plate is redirected back into the turbine shaft past the scallop in the check ball seat, then down the release passage and is exhausted at the converter clutch apply valve to dampen the apply.

Oil to cooler and lube system is provided through an orifice in the apply line to cooler passage.

THM 125-C

The apply or release of the converter clutch is determined by the direction that the converter feed oil is routed to the converter. The converter feed oil from the pressure regulator valve flows to the converter clutch control valve. The position of the converter clutch control valve controls which direction converter feed oil flows to the converter.

The converter clutch control valve is held in the release position in park, neutral, reverse, drive range 1st gear and 2nd gear, by line pressure acting on the end of the converter clutch apply valve. With the converter clutch control valve in the release position, converter feed oil flows into the converter clutch release passages. It then flows between the pump drive shaft and turbine shaft to the front or release side of the converter clutch, between the converter clutch pressure plate and the converter cover. This

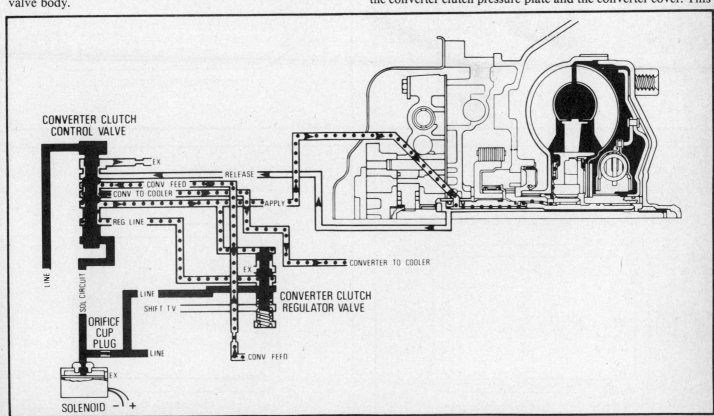

THM 125C oil flow schematic to apply Torque Converter Clutch (©General Motors Corp.)

moves the converter clutch pressure plate away from the converter cover, releasing the converter clutch and charging the converter with oil. The oil then leaves the converter by flowing through the turbine shaft into the converter clutch apply oil circuit. The apply oil circuit is now being used in a reverse direction. The oil then flows from the apply passage into the cooler passage and to the lubrication system.

To prevent the converter clutch from applying in drive range 3rd gear, at car speeds below converter clutch engagement speeds, the C3 or governor pressure switch (depending on system) will break the circuit to the solenoid exhaust valve. This de-energizes the solenoid and opens the exhaust valve to the exhaust the solenoid circuit oil at the converter clutch control valve. Line pressure then holds the converter clutch control valve in the release position.

When car speed in drive range 3rd gear, reaches converter clutch engagement speed, the C3 or governor pressure switch (de-pending on system) will activate the solenoid, closing the exhaust valve. This allows solenoid circuit to move the converter clutch control valve against line pressure. With the converter clutch control valve in the apply position, regulated line oil, from the converter clutch regulator valve, is allowed to pass into the converter apply passage. It then flows through the turbine shaft to the apply side of the converter clutch. The regulated line oil from the converter clutch regulator valve, controls the apply feel of the pressure plate.

As the pressure plate begins to move to its applied position, release oil on the front side of the pressure plate is redirected back between the turbine shaft and pump drive shaft and exhausted at the converter clutch control valve through an orifice, to time the clutch apply. When the converter clutch control valve moved to the apply position, orificed converter feed oil entered the converter to cooler passage to provide oil to the lubrication system.

TRANSMISSION/TRANSAXLE OIL PAN IDENTIFICATION

Parts Book Code	Service Identity	Parts Book Code	Service Identity	Parts Book Code	Service Identity
MD9	125C	M-31	250C	MX3	350C
MD2	180C	M-57	325-4L	MX5	350C
MV9	200C	MV4	350C	MD-8	700-R4
MW9	200-4R	MX2	350C	ME-9	400-T4

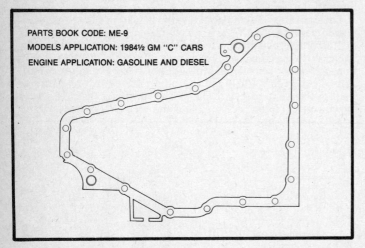

PARTS BOOK CODE: ME-9

MODELS APPLICATION: 1984½ GM "C" CARS

ENGINE APPLICATION: GASOLINE AND DIESEL

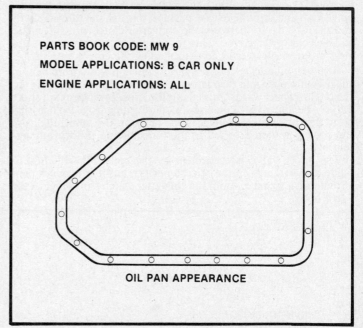

PARTS BOOK CODE: MW 9

MODEL APPLICATIONS: B CAR ONLY

ENGINE APPLICATIONS: ALL

OIL PAN APPEARANCE

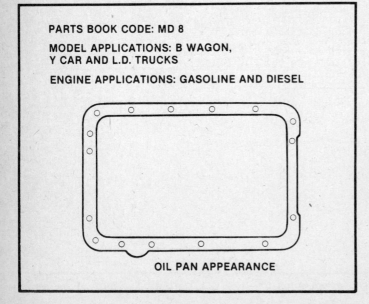

PARTS BOOK CODE: MD 8

MODEL APPLICATIONS: B WAGON, Y CAR AND L.D. TRUCKS

ENGINE APPLICATIONS: GASOLINE AND DIESEL

OIL PAN APPEARANCE

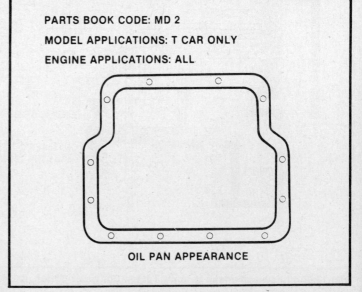

PARTS BOOK CODE: MD 2

MODEL APPLICATIONS: T CAR ONLY

ENGINE APPLICATIONS: ALL

OIL PAN APPEARANCE

ENGINE TRANSMISSION MARRIAGE I. D. CODE

(I. D. Plate or Ink Stamp on Bell)

Engine Mfg.	Hydramatic Built Transmission	Buick Built 350-350C Transmission	Chevrolet & Canadian Built 350-350C Transmission
Chevrolet	C-	J-	W-T-X M- 1980-83 350C Comp. V- 350C
Buick	B-	K-	—
Oldsmobile	O-	L-	—
Pontiac	P-	M- THRU 1979	—
Cadillac	A-	—	—
Jaguar	Z-	—	—
Non ECM Export 1981 Chevrolet 5.0	E-	—	—
Non ECM Export 1982-83 Chevrolet 5.0	H-	W-	—

PARTS BOOK CODE: MV 4

MODEL APPLICATIONS: '81 A, B, G, Y, L.D. TRUCKS

ENGINE APPLICATIONS: GASOLINE AND DIESEL

ID LOCATION: STAMPED ON RIGHT SIDE OF OIL PAN

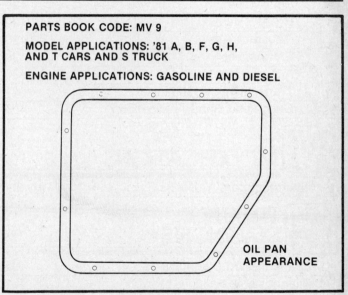

OIL PAN APPEARANCE

PARTS BOOK CODE: MV 9

MODEL APPLICATIONS: '81 A, B, F, G, H, AND T CARS AND S TRUCK

ENGINE APPLICATIONS: GASOLINE AND DIESEL

OIL PAN APPEARANCE

PARTS BOOK CODE: M 31

MODEL APPLICATIONS: '81 A, B AND G CARS

ENGINE APPLICATIONS: ALL

ID LOCATION: STAMPED ON GOV COVER

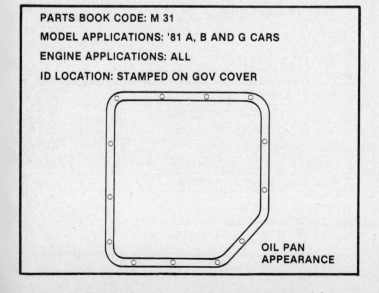

OIL PAN APPEARANCE

PARTS BOOK CODE: MD 9

MODEL APPLICATIONS: X, J AND '82 A CARS

ENGINE APPLICATIONS: ALL

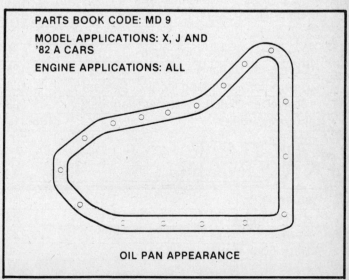

OIL PAN APPEARANCE

INDEX

GENERAL MOTORS TURBO HYDRA-MATIC 125C Automatic Transaxle

GENERAL MOTORS THM-125C AUTOMATIC TRANSAXLE APPLICATION CHART

Year	Make	Model
1982 and Later	Buick	Skylark (X body)
	Buick	Century (A body)
	Buick	Skyhawk (J body)
1982 and Later	Chevrolet	Citation (X body)
	Chevrolet	Celebrity (A body)
	Chevrolet	Cavalier (J body)
1982 and Later	Oldsmobile	Omega (X body)
	Oldsmobile	Ciera (A body)
	Oldsmobile	Firenza (J body)
1982 and Later	Pontiac	Phoenix (X body)
	Pontiac	6000 (A body)
	Pontiac	2000 (J body)

GENERAL MOTORS 125C AUTOMATIC TRANSAXLE APPLICATION CHART

Year	Make	Model
1982 and Later	Cadillac	Cimarron (J body)

The General Motors THM 125C automatic transaxle is a fully automatic transaxle consisting of a compound planetary gear set and dual sprocket, drive link assembly and a four element hydraulic torque converter. Also contained in the transaxle assembly are the differential and final drive gear set.

The friction elements required to obtain the desired function of the planetary gear sets are provided for by three multiple disc clutches, a roller clutch and a band.

The hydraulic system is pressurized by a vane type pump which provides the working pressure required to operate the automatic controls and the friction elements.

Contained in the four element torque converter assembly are a pump, a pressure plate splined to the turbine, the turbine and a stator assembly. The pressure plate provides a mechanical direct drive coupling of the engine to the planetary gear, when applied.

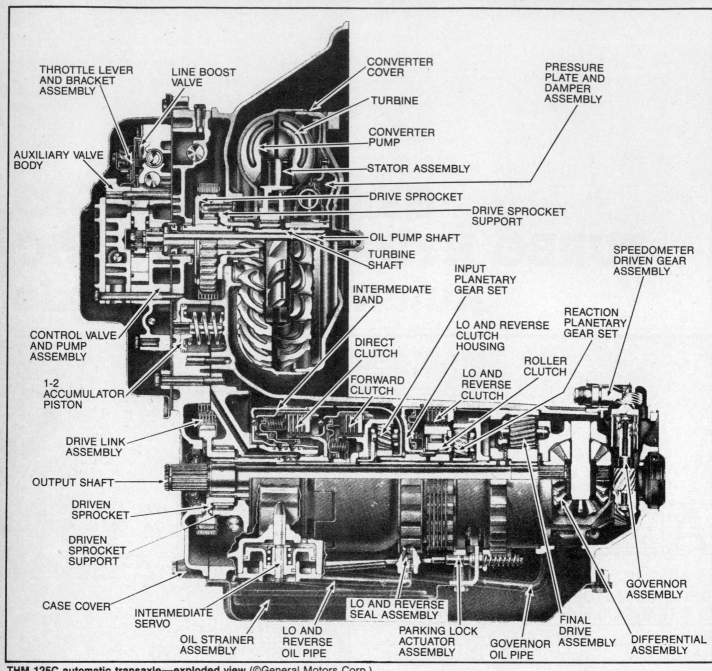

THM 125C automatic transaxle—exploded view (©General Motors Corp.)

TRANSAXLE AND CONVERTER IDENTIFICATION

Transaxle

The model identification code is located on top of the transaxle, near the manual control lever shaft. The serial number is stamped on the oil pan flange pad, to the right of the oil dipstick.

Torque Converter

The torque converter is a welded unit and cannot be disassembled for repairs. Should this unit need to be replaced, both new and rebuilt units are available.

Metric Fasteners

The THM 125C automatic transaxle uses metric fasteners. Metric fastener dimensions are very close to the dimensions of the inch system fasteners, and for that reason, replacement fasteners must have the same measurement and strength as those removed. Do not attempt to interchange metric fasteners for inch fasteners. Mismatched or incorrect fasteners can result in damage to the transaxle unit through malfunctions or breakage, or even personal injury. Care should be taken to reuse the fasteners in the same location as removed.

Fluid Capacities

The THM 125C automatic transaxle has a fluid capacity of 9

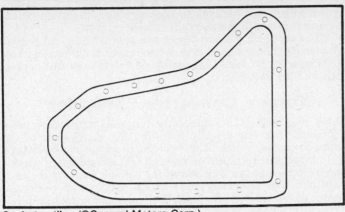

Gasket outline (©General Motors Corp.)

quarts including the torque converter. If the torque converter has not been drained the fluid capacity is 4 quarts. Be sure to use Dextron® II automatic transmission fluid in the THM 125C transaxle. Always bring the transaxle up to operating temperature and recheck the fluid level. Never overfill the unit.

Check fluid Levels.

1. Position the selector lever in "P."
2. Apply brakes and start engine.
3. Move the selector lever through each of the selector ranges.
4. Check the oil level on the dipstick. Add fluid as required.
5. The fluid level at room temperature should be ½ inch above the full mark or between the two dimples on the transaxle dipstick.
6. At normal operating temperature the fluid level should be between the add and full marks on the transaxle dipstick.

NOTE: Due to the shape of the filler tube, oil level readings may be misleading. Look carefully for a full oil ring on both sides of the dipstick. If there is any doubt, recheck the level. Remember that in this unit the cold level will be higher than the hot level. Do not overfill this unit or foaming, loss of fluid and possible overheating may occur.

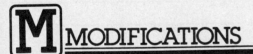 **MODIFICATIONS**

Solenoid And Clip Assembly

After August 1981, all THM 125C automatic transaxles are being built with a new design solenoid and clip assembly. This new design solenoid and clip assembly includes a plastic tubular clip to prevent the wire from moving off its location on the valve body during assembly of the unit. The new design solenoid and clip assembly and the old design assembly, which uses a metal retainer, can be interchanged. However, due to the difference of the wire length, the plastic clip, which is available for service separately, cannot be used with the old design solenoid assembly. When installing a new design solenoid assembly be sure to remove and discard the metal clip from the old design solenoid assembly.

Torque Converter Change

Starting in 1982, all THM 125C automatic transaxles will be built with a new design 245 millimeter torque converter. This new torque converter will replace the present 254 millimeter torque converter.

Turbine Shaft Design Change

Starting in 1982, all THM 125C automatic transaxles will be built using a new design turbine shaft. The spline of the new shaft will be 5.1 millimeters longer than the old style turbine shaft, and will incorporate an O-ring seal groove.

Redesigned Oil Pump Drive Shaft

Beginning in January 1982, a new style oil pump drive shaft will be used in all THM 125C automatic transaxles. The new shaft is 23.7 millimenters longer and has 15 teeth on the oil pump spline rather than the old shaft which has 20 teeth on the oil pump spline and is 23.7 millimeters shorter in length.

New Design Torque Converter Housing Oil Seal

Due to the usage of a new turbine shaft and oil pump drive shaft a new design torque converter housing oil seal is being used in all units produced after December 1981. The new oil seal can be identified by the part number 8637420 stamped on the front face of the seal. The old design seal will have either the part number 8631158 stamped on it or no part identifcation at all.

Oil Weir Usage

During the month of September 1981 all THM 125C automatic transaxles were assembled with a new part called an oil weir. This part was used by General Motors for one month as a production trial run. The oil weir is located in the rear case oil pan area. It's function is to revise the lubrication flow around the differential

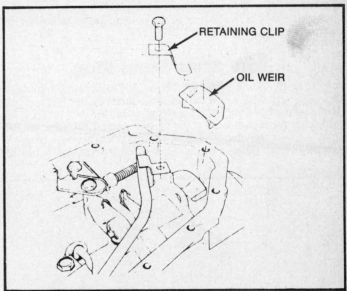

Oil weir location 125C automatic transaxle (©General Motors Corp.)

assembly. The oil weir part number is 8637836 and is held in position by a retaining clip, part number 8637837. Both of these parts are available for service. Automatic transaxles built without an oil weir do not require the addition of the part during service.

Intermediate Band and Direct Clutch Assembly

In late August 1981 some 1982 automobiles built with the THM 125C automatic transaxle used a new wide design intermediate band assembly, part number 8637623 and a new type direct clutch housing and drum assembly, part number 8637976. This new design direct clutch housing has a wider surface finish area on the drum outside diameter in order to accommodate the new wider intermediate band assembly.

401

The narrow design direct clutch housing assembly, part number 8631928 can only be used with the narrow design intermediate band assembly, part number 8631030. Do not use the narrow design direct clutch housing assembly with the wider design intermediate band assembly or interference will result.

The narrow design intermediate band is 1.49 inch in width and the new design intermediate band is 1.74 inch in width.

The following is a list of automatic transaxle models incorporating this design change; BE, BL, PL, PK, PI, CT, CL, CV, CS, LE, OP, HM, HW, HS.

Pressure Regulator Valve Retaining Pin

When diagnosing the 125C automatic transaxle for no drive or harsh shifts (high line pressure), check the control valve assembly for a worn or missing pressure regulator valve retaining pin.

If, after checking the pressure regulator valve retaining pin, it is found to be either missing or worn, the following repair must be performed.

1. Position the control valve and oil pump assembly with the machined portion face down. Be certain that the machined face is protected in order to prevent damage to its surface.

2. Using a ⅜ drift punch and hammer, close the pressure regulator valve retaining pin hole. Close the pin hole only enough to hold the new retaining pin in place after assembly.

3. Reassemble the pressure regulator and reverse boost valve train assembly.

4. Retain the valve train with a new steel retaining pin, part number 112496. Be sure that the new pin is inserted from and flush with the machined face of the control valve and oil pump assembly.

New Style Band Plug

Beginning mid-June 1981, all THM 125C automatic transaxles are being built with a new design band anchor plug. This new design band anchor plug has a tab which holds the part in place. All automatic transaxles built prior to mid June 1981 have the old design style band anchor plug. A staking operation was required to hold the old plug in place. This staking operation is not re-

quired with the new design band anchor plug as due to the tab extension it is held in place by the reverse oil pipe.

When replacing the new design band anchor plug, the reverse oil pipe must be removed first. When repairing automatic transaxles prior to mid June 1981 use the new style band anchor plug, part number 8637640.

Torque Converter "Shudder"

Some 1982 THM 125C automatic transaxles may experience a "shudder" feel immediately following the engagement of the torque converter clutch. If this occurs, check for the following:

1. Inspect the turbine shaft seal and O-ring for damage. The O-ring is located at the long end of the turbine shaft (spline end) with one large diameter yellow teflon seal located below the torque converter feed lube holes. Two other teflon seals both yellow with green speckles are located at the short end of the turbine shaft. Replace the damaged seals as required.

2. Inspect the pump shaft seal for damage. Replace as required.

3. Check the torque converter clutch control regulator valve in the auxiliary control valve assembly for freeness. Replace as required.

In the Spring of 1982 a new governor pressure switch went into production for diesel equipped vehicles. In order to correct the "shudder" the new governor pressure switch raises the torque converter clutch apply speed. In servicing automatic transaxles equipped with a diesel engine, refer to the following chart for the proper governor pressure switch usage.

GOVERNOR PRESSURE SWITCH APPLICATION CHART THM-125C

Automatic Transaxle Model	Governor Pressure Switch Number
OP, HU, HY, H6, HR	8643369
HW	8637296
HS	8643368
CD, HI, HC	8643367

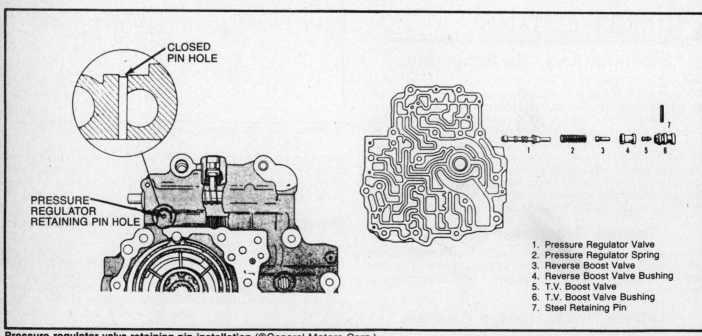

CLOSED PIN HOLE

PRESSURE REGULATOR RETAINING PIN HOLE

1. Pressure Regulator Valve
2. Pressure Regulator Spring
3. Reverse Boost Valve
4. Reverse Boost Valve Bushing
5. T.V. Boost Valve
6. T.V. Boost Valve Bushing
7. Steel Retaining Pin

Pressure regulator valve retaining pin installation (©General Motors Corp.)

No Torque Converter Clutch Release

Some 1982 THM 125C automatic transaxles may experience a no-torque converter clutch release condition. If this is the case, check the auxiliary control valve assembly for the proper location of the solenoid orifice cup plug. After checking the solenoid orifice cup plug, the following conditions could occur:

1. The solenoid orifice cup plug could be missing or damaged with a hole in it. This will cause the no-torque converter clutch release condition. Repair or replace as required.

2. The solenoid orifice cup plug could be installed too far into the bore past the third land in the auxiliary control valve assembly. Correct as required.

Service Case Packages With Missing Plugs

Some 1982 THM 125C automatic transaxle service case packages, part number 8631916 may have been assembled without three cup plugs and one pipe plug. If you encounter a service case package without these four parts, see the list below for the correct part and number.

Parking pawl shaft cup plug—part number 8631016.
Third oil cup plug—part number 8611710.
Case servo orifice cup plug—part number 8628864.
Governor pressure pipe plug—part number 0444612 or part number 044613.

Service Package For Intermediate Band/Direct Clutch Housing Assembly

A new intermediate band and direct clutch housing service package has been assembled and released to repair all THM 125C automatic transaxles. This new service package, part number 8643941 consists of a direct clutch housing, drum assembly, and an intermediate band assembly. These parts must be used together as a complete unit. These items are no longer available individually and can only be obtained as a set.

New Design Oil Pump Shaft Seal

At the start of production, all 1982 "A" and "X" body vehicles equipped with the THM 125C automatic transaxle are being built with a new design oil pump shaft seal. This new seal will assure adequate torque converter clutch apply oil pressure. Also included in this seal design change are the 1982 "J" body vehicles built after July 31, 1981.

When replacing the control valve oil pump assembly, be sure that the oil pump shaft is completely seated in the control valve oil pump assembly. The new design oil pump shaft seal may be used on all 125C automatic transaxles.

Design Change Low—Reverse Clutch Assembly

Beginning around the middle of July 1981, some 1982 vehicles produced with the THM 125C automatic transaxle were assembled with a new design low and reverse clutch assembly. This design change produces a more desirable neutral to reverse shift. The new design assembly consists of a modified low and reverse piston which eliminates the need for an apply ring. A smaller low and reverse clutch housing feed orifice is also used, as is a waved steel clutch plate, located next to the low and reverse piston. The new waved steel clutch plate eliminates the one flat steel clutch plate.

Burnt Band and Direct Clutch Assembly Condition

Some THM 125C automatic transaxle equipped vehicles may experience a burnt band and direct clutch condition. A possible cause of the burnt band and direct drive condition might be the third accumulator check valve not seating properly. This condition allows the intermediate band to drag while the direct clutch is applied, causing excessive friction. If the third accumulator is found to be defective, order service package part number 8643964, which contains a new dual land third accumulator check valve and conical spring. Refer to the following procedure to replace the accumulator assembly.

1. Remove the intermediate servo cover and gasket.

2. Remove the third accumulator check valve and spring. Inspect the third accumulator valve bore for wear and damage to the valve seat and also for the presence of the valve seat.

3. Plug both the feed and exhaust holes in the bore using petroleum jelly.

4. Replace the third accumulator check valve with the new dual land check valve. Center the valve to be sure that it is seated properly.

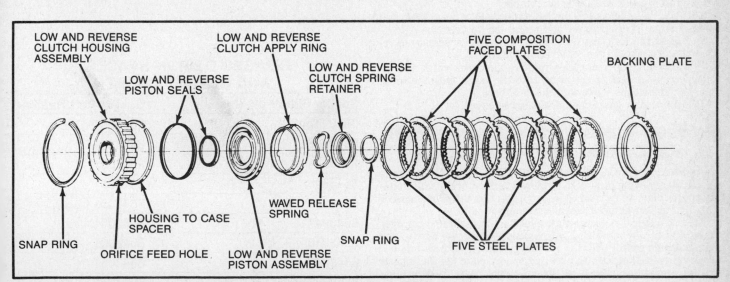

Old design Low and Reverse clutch housing and piston assembly (©General Motors Corp.)

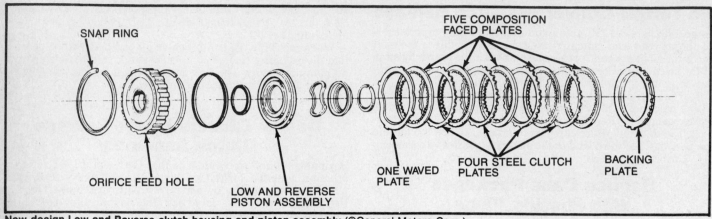

New design Low and Reverse clutch housing and piston assembly (©General Motors Corp.)

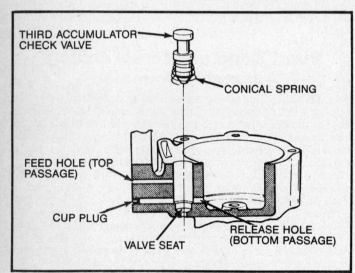

Third accumulator check valve replacement
(©General Motors Corp.)

5. Leak test the valve seat by pouring solvent into the accumulator check valve bore. Check for a leak on the inside of the case. A small amount of leakage is acceptable.

6. If the valve leaks tap the assembly with a brass drift and rubber mallet in order to try and reseat the valve.

7. Repeat the leak test procedure. It may be necessary to replace the case should the valve continue to leak.

8. If the valve does not leak, remove the check valve and install the new conical valve spring onto the valve, with the small end first. Install the valve into the case bore.

9. Using a new gasket install the servo cover.

Revised Valve Control Spacer Plate and Gasket Service Package

Starting with the month of March 1982, all THM 125C automatic transaxles are being built with a revised version of the valve control spacer plate and gasket. It is important that the proper spacer plate and gasket be used when servicing the unit.

The revised design spacer plate package will include the proper gasket and can be identified with a yellow stripe. Be sure to use the old design gasket with the old design spacer plate and the revised design gasket with the revised spacer plate, as these parts are not interchangeable. Use the following chart to determine proper usage.

OLD DESIGN SPACER AND GASKET CHART

Spacer Plate Part Number	Gasket Part Number
8637119	8637096
8637121	8637096
8637122	8637096
8637123	8637096
8637124	8637096
8637125	8637096
8637127	8637096
8637128	8637096
8637129	8637096
8637130	8637096
8637815	8637096
8637816	8637096
8637817	8637096
8637818	8637096

REVISED DESIGN SPACER AND GASKET CHART

Spacer Plate Part Number	Gasket Part Number
8643942	8643051
8643943	8643051
8643944	8643051
8643945	8643051
8643946	8643051
8643947	8643051
8643948	8643051
8643949	8643051
8643950	8643051

TROUBLE DIAGNOSIS

CLUTCH AND BAND APPLICATION CHART
THM 125C

Range	Gear	Direct Clutch	Intermediate Band	Forward Clutch	Roller Clutch	Low-Reverse Clutch
Park—Neut.	—	—	—	—	—	—
Drive	First	—	—	Applied	Holding	—
	Second	—	Applied	Applied	—	—
	Third	Applied	—	Applied	—	—
Int.	First	—	—	Applied	Holding	—
	Second	—	Applied	Applied	—	—
Low	First	—	—	Applied	Holding	Applied
	Second	—	Applied	Applied	—	—
Rev.	—	Applied	—	—	—	Applied

CHILTON'S THREE "C'''s" TRANSMISSION DIAGNOSIS CHART

Condition	Cause	Correction
No drive in Drive range	a) Low fluid level	a) Add as required
	b) Manual linkage	b) Adjust as required
	c) Clogged oil stainer	c) Change screen and fluid
	d) Pressure regulator stuck	d) Clean valve and bore
	e) Faulty oil pump	e) Overhaul pump
	f) Manual valve disconnected	f) Repair link
	g) Faulty forward clutch	g) Overhaul
	h) Faulty roller clutch	h) Overhaul or replace
Oil pressure too high or too low	a) Throttle valve cable broken or not adjusted	a) Adjust or replace as required
	b) Throttle valve bracket bent or broken	b) Repair or replace
	c) Line boost valve binding	c) Clean valve body
	d) Throttle valve boost valve binding	d) Clean valve body
	e) Reverse boost valve binding	e) Clean valve body
	f) Pressure regulator binding	f) Clean valve and bore
	g) Pressure relief valve spring damaged	g) Replace
	h) Manual valve disconnected	h) Repair link
	i) Faulty oil pump	i) Overhaul pump
No drive or slipping in reverse	a) Throttle valve cable broken or not adjusted	a) Adjust or replace as required
	b) Manual linkage	b) Adjust as required
	c) Throttle valve binding	c) Clean valve body
	d) Reverse boost valve binding	d) Clean valve body
	e) Malfunction in Low/Reverse clutch assembly	e) Overhaul

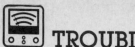

CHILTON'S THREE "C"s TRANSMISSION DIAGNOSIS CHART

Condition	Cause	Correction
No drive or slipping in reverse	f) Reverse oil pipe plugged or out of place	f) Remove, clean, replace seal
	g) Check ball #4 out of place	g) Restore to proper location
	h) Malfunction in direct clutch assembly	h) Overhaul
	i) Spacer plate clogged	i) Clean valve body
No engine braking in L2	a) Faulty intermediate servo	a) Replace seal or assembly
	b) Faulty intermediate band	b) Replace band
No engine braking in L1 Note: No reverse would be a complaint with this condition	a) Malfunction in Low/Reverse clutch assembly	a) Overhaul
No part throttle or detent downshifts	a) Throttle valve cable broken or not adjusted	a) Adjust or replace as required
	b) Throttle valve binding	b) Clean valve body
	c) Shift T.V. valve binding	c) Clean valve body
	d) Spacer plate clogged	d) Clean valve body
	e) 2-3 T.V. bushing passages clogged	e) Clean valve body
	f) Throttle plunger bushing passages clogged	f) Clean valve body
Low or high shift points	a) Throttle valve cable broken or not adjusted	a) Adjust or replace as required
	b) Throttle valve binding	b) Clean valve body
	c) Shift T.V. valve binding	c) Clean valve body
	d) Line boost valve binding	d) Clean valve body
	e) 1-2 or 2-3 Throttle valve binding	e) Clean valve body
	f) Spacer plate or gasket out of position	f) Replace gaskets, align plate
	g) Throttle valve bracket bent or broken	g) Repair or replace
Note: Look for external leak	h) Governor seal or cover worn or damaged	h) Replace affected parts
First speed only—no 1-2 shift	a) Malfunction in governor assembly or feed circuits	a) Service or replace governor, clean passages
	b) 1-2 Shift train binding	b) Clean valve body
	c) Faulty intermediate servo	c) Replace seal or assembly
First and second speed only—no 2-3 shift	a) Malfunction in pump or control valve assembly	a) Overhaul pump, clean valve body as required
	b) 2-3 Valve train binding	b) Clean valve body
	c) Case and cover leakage	c) Check for missing 3rd oil cup plug, direct clutch accumulator check valve or servo bleed cup plug
	d) Oil seals leaking on driven sprocket support	d) Replace seals, check for clogged passages
	e) Malfunction in direct clutch assembly	e) Overhaul
	f) Faulty intermediate servo	f) Replace seal or assembly
	g) Governor seal or cover work or damaged	g) Replace affected parts
Third speed only	a) 2-3 Shift valve binding in upshift position	a) Clean valve body
	b) Malfunction in governor assembly or feed circuits	b) Service or replace governor, clean passages

CHILTON'S THREE "C"s TRANSMISSION DIAGNOSIS CHART

Condition	Cause	Correction
Drive in Neutral	a) Manual linkage b) Forward clutch will not release c) Cross leakage in case	a) Adjust as required b) Overhaul c) Clean valve body mating surfaces, replace gaskets
Won't hold in Park	a) Manual linkage b) Broken internal linkage c) Loose parts on internal linkage, detent roller	a) Adjust as required b) Replace affected parts c) Adjust or replace as required
Slips on 1-2 shift	a) Low fluid level b) Throttle valve cable broken or not adjusted c) Spacer or gasket out of position d) 1-2 Accumulator valve binding e) Faulty 1-2 accumulator assembly f) Faulty intermediate servo g) T.V. valve or shift T.V. valve binding h) Faulty intermediate band	a) Add as required b) Adjust or replace as required c) Replace gaskets, align plate d) Clean valve body e) Replace seal or piston as required f) Replace seal or assembly g) Clean valve body h) Replace band
Slips on 2-3 shift	a) Low fluid level b) Throttle valve cable broken or not adjusted c) Throttle valve binding d) Spacer plate or gasket out of position e) Faulty intermediate servo f) Malfunction in direct clutch assembly	a) Add as required b) Adjust or replace as required c) Clean valve body d) Replace gaskets, align plate e) Replace seal or assembly f) Overhaul
Rough 1-2 shift	a) Throttle valve cable broken or not adjusted b) Throttle valve, T.V. plunger or shift T.V. valve binding c) 1-2 accumulator valve binding d) Faulty 1-2 accumulator assembly e) Faulty intermediate servo	a) Adjust or replace as required b) Clean valve body c) Clean valve body d) Replace seal or piston as e) Replace seal or assembly
Rough 2-3 shift	a) Throttle valve cable broken or not adjusted b) Throttle valve, T.V. plunger or shift T.V. valve binding	a) Adjust or replace as required b) Clean valve body
Transaxle noisy	a) Pump noise due to low fluid level, cavication b) Pump noise due to damage c) Gear noise	a) Add as required b) Overhaul pump c) Check for grounding to body, worn roller bearings

Note: If noisy in 3rd gear or on turns only, check differential and final drive unit

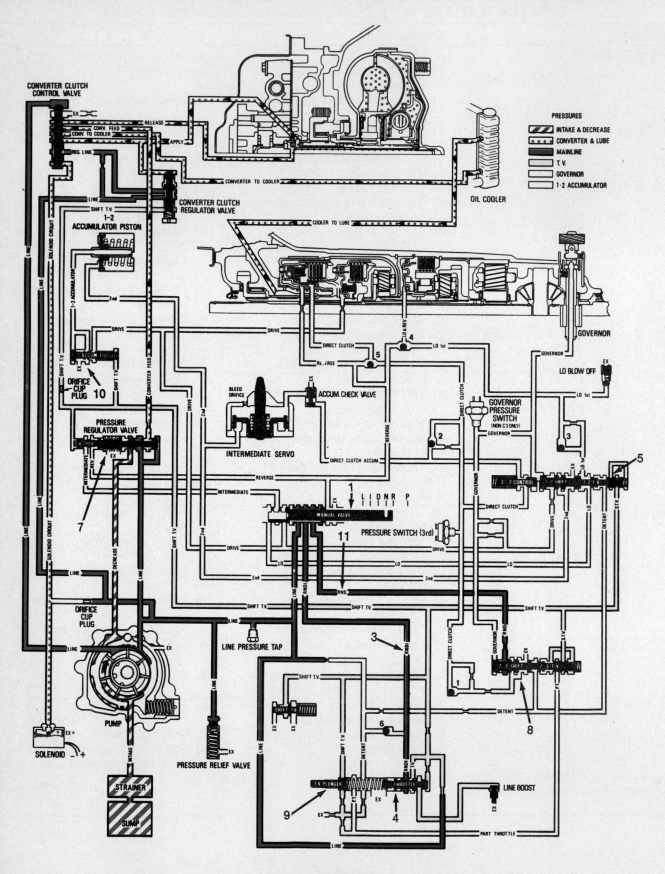

Neutral—engine running

Neutral—Engine Running

DIRECT CLUTCH—RELEASED
INTERMEDIATE BAND—RELEASED
FORWARD CLUTCH—RELEASED
LOW AND REVERSE CLUTCH—RELEASED
ROLLER CLUTCH—RELEASED

HYDRAULIC CONTROL

When the selector lever is moved to the Neutral (N) position, the manual valve ①, is positioned to allow line pressure to enter two passages as follows:

First it enters the reverse, neutral, drive, intermediate (RNDI) passage ③. RNDI oil is directed to the seat RNDI and detent check ball 6, and to the throttle valve ④, where it is regulated to a variable pressure called throttle valve (T.V.) pressure. T.V. pressure increases with carburetor opening and is directed to the shift throttle valve. This valve limits shift T.V. oil pressure from going above 620 kPa (90 psi).

Shift T.V. oil is then directed to the 1-2 ⑤ and 2-3 ⑧ throttle valves, T.V. boost valve ⑦, T.V. plunger ⑨ and the 1-2 accumulator valve ⑩.

Shift T.V. oil acting on the T.V. boost valve will boost line pressure according to throttle opening.

Second, line pressure enters the reverse, neutral, drive (RND) ⑪ passage and is directed to a land on the 2-3 shift valve.

CHECK VALVE BALLS

1—Direct clutch exhaust check valve ball
2—Direct clutch accumulator check valve ball
3—Low 1st check valve ball
4—Low and reverse check valve ball
5—Direct clutch and reverse check valve ball
6—RNDI and detent check valve ball

SUMMARY

The converter is filled, all the clutches and the band are released, the transmission is in Neutral (N).

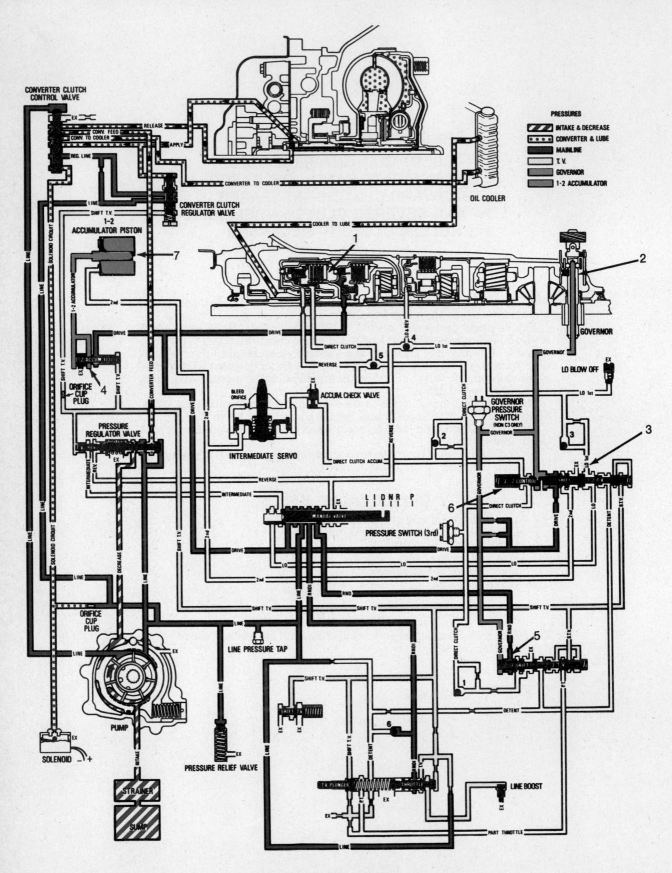

Drive range—first gear

Drive Range—First Gear
FORWARD CLUTCH—APPLIED
ROLLER CLUTCH—HOLDING

HYDRAULIC CONTROL

When the selector lever is moved to Drive (D) position, the manual valve is repositioned to allow line pressure to enter the drive passage. Drive oil then flows to the following: forward clutch ①, governor assembly ②, 1-2 shift valve ③ and 1-2 accumulator valve ④.

BASIC CONTROL

Drive oil is directed to the forward clutch through an orifice where it acts on the clutch piston to apply the forward clutch.

Drive oil is directed to the 1-2 shift valve.

Drive oil is directed to the 1-2 accumulator valve and is regulated to a pressure called 1-2 accumulator pressure; this pressure is directed to the 1-2 accumulator piston ⑦ to act as a cushion for the band apply on 1-2 shift.

Drive oil at the governor assembly is regulated to another variable pressure called governor pressure. Governor pressure increases with vehicle speed and acts against the 1-2 and 2-3 ⑤ shift valves and the 3-2 control valve.

CHECK VALVE BALLS

1—Direct clutch exhaust check valve ball
2—Direct clutch accumulator check valve ball
3—Low 1st check valve ball
4—Low and reverse check valve ball
5—Direct clutch and reverse check valve ball
6—RNDI and detent check valve ball

SUMMARY

The converter is filled; the forward clutch is applied; the transmission is in Drive (D) range—first gear.

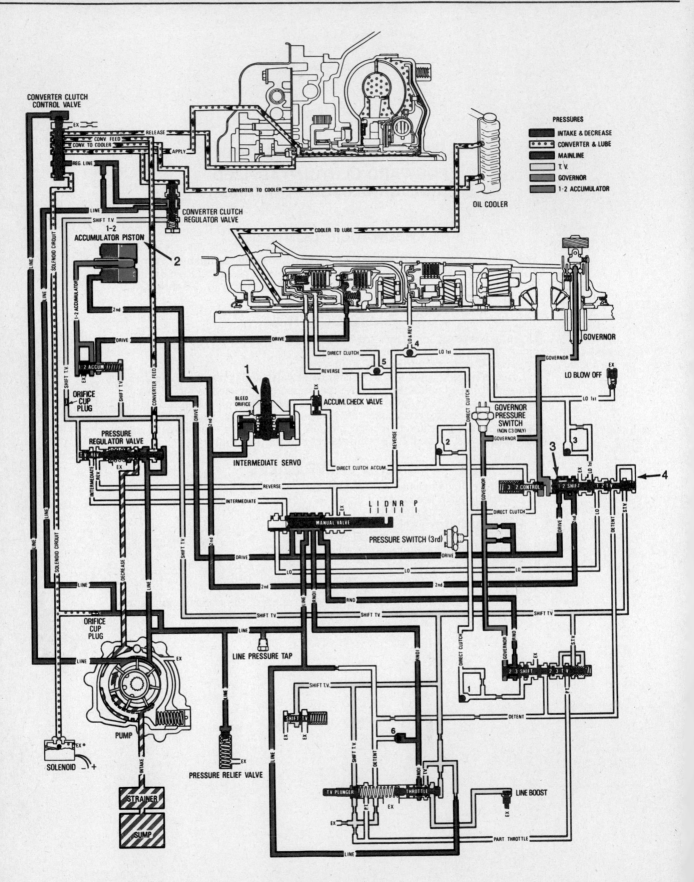

Drive range—second gear

Drive Range—Second Gear
FORWARD CLUTCH—APPLIED
INTERMEDIATE APPLIED

HYDRAULIC CONTROL

As both vehicle speed and governor pressure increase, the force of governor oil acting on the 1-2 shift valve ③ overcomes the pressure of shift T.V. oil and the force of the 1-2 T.V. spring ④. This allows the 1-2 valve to open and drive oil to enter the second (2nd) oil passage. This oil is called second (2nd) oil.

Second oil from the 1-2 shift valve is directed to the following: intermediate servo ① and 1-2 accumulator piston ②.

BASIC CONTROL

Second oil from the 1-2 shift valve is directed to the intermediate servo to apply the intermediate band. At the same time, 2nd oil moves the 1-2 accumulator piston against 1-2 accumulator pressure and the accumulator spring to maintain a controlled buildup of pressure on the intermediate servo during the 1-2 shift for a smooth band apply.

CHECK VALVE BALLS

1—Direct clutch exhaust check valve ball
2—Direct clutch accumulator check valve ball
3—Low 1st check valve ball
4—Low and reverse check valve ball
5—Direct clutch and reverse check valve ball
6—RNDI and detent check valve ball

SUMMARY

The forward clutch and intermediate band are applied; the transmission is in Drive (D) range—second gear.

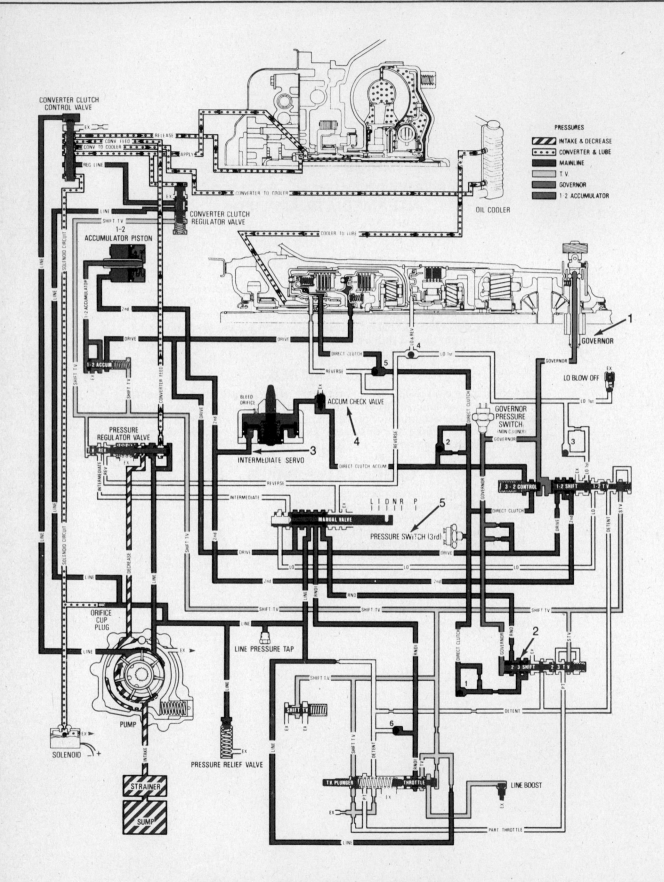

Drive range—third gear (converter clutch released)

Drive Range—Third Gear
(Torque Converter Clutch Released)

FORWARD CLUTCH—APPLIED
DIRECT CLUTCH—APPLIED
CONVERTER CLUTCH—RELEASED

HYDRAULIC CONTROL

As both vehicle speed and governor pressure increase ①, the force of governor oil acting on the 2-3 shift valve ② overcomes the force of the 2-3 T.V. spring and shift T.V. oil. This allows the 2-3 shift valve to open and RND oil enters the direct clutch oil passage. This oil is called direct clutch oil. Dirext clutch oil from the 2-3 shift valve is directed to the following: direct clutch exhaust check ball ①, 3-2 control valve, direct clutch and reverse check ball ⑤, direct clutch accumulator check ball ②, accumulator check valve ④, intermediate servo ③, and the third clutch pressure switch ⑤.

BASIC CONTROL

Direct clutch oil from the 2-3 shift valve flows past the direct clutch exhaust check ball ①, past the 3rd clutch pressure switch, to the direct clutch and reverse check ball ⑤, seating it in the reverse passage, and to the inner area of the direct clutch piston, applying the direct clutch, accumulator check ball ② into the direct clutch accumulator passage, where it is called direct clutch accumulator oil, to the dircct clutch accumulator check valve, seating it; and to the release side of the intermediate servo. The pressure of the direct clutch accumulator oil combined with the servo cushion spring, moves the servo piston against 2nd oil and acts as an accumulator for a smooth intermediate band release and direct clutch apply. Direct clutch oil also flows through the 3-2 control valve to the direct clutch accumulator passage.

CHECK VALVE BALLS

1—Direct clutch exhaust check valve ball
2—Direct clutch accumulator check valve ball
3—Low 1st check valve ball
4—Low and reverse check valve ball
5—Direct clutch and reverse check valve ball
6—RNDI and detent check valve ball

SUMMARY

The forward and direct clutches are applied and the intermediate band is released; the transmission is in Drive (D) range — third gear (direct drive).

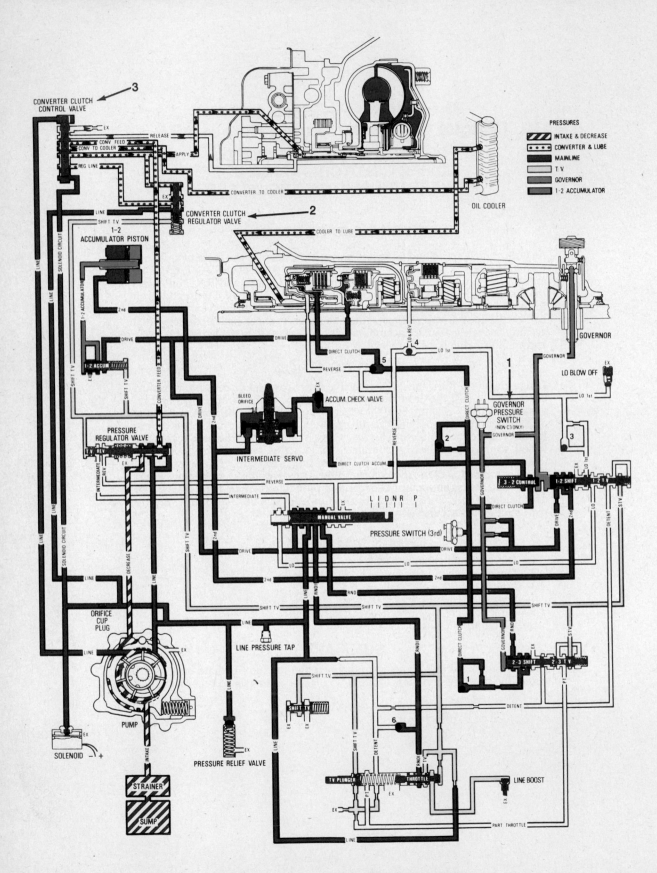

Drive range—third gear (converter clutch applied)

Drive Range—Third Gear
(Torque Converter Clutch Applied)

FORWARD CLUTCH—APPLIED
DIRECT CLUTCH—APPLIED
CONVERTER CLUTCH—APPLIED

HYDRAULIC CONTROL

When car speed in drive range 3rd gear, reaches converter clutch engagement speed, the C3 or governor pressure switch (depending on system) ① will activate the solenoid, closing the exhaust valve. This allows solenoid circuit oil to move the converter clutch control valve ③ against line pressure. With the converter clutch control valve in the apply position, regulated line oil, from the converter clutch regulator valve, ② is allowed to pass into the converter apply passage. It then flows through the turbine shaft to the apply side of the converter clutch. The regulated line oil, from the converter clutch regulator valve, controls the apply feel of the pressure plate.

As the pressure plate begins to move to its applied position, release oil on the front side of the pressure plate is redirected back between the turbine shaft and pump drive shaft and exhausted at the converter clutch control valve through an orifice, to time the clutch apply. When the converter clutch control valve moved to the apply position, orificed converter feed oil entered the converter to cooler passage to provide oil to the lubrication system.

CHECK VALVE BALLS

1—Direct clutch exhaust check valve ball
2—Direct clutch accumulator check valve ball
3—Low 1st check valve ball
4—Low and reverse check valve ball
5—Direct clutch and reverse check valve ball
6—RNDI and detent check valve ball

SUMMARY

The forward and direct clutches are applied, the converter clutch is applied and the intermediate band is released; the transmission is in Drive (D) range — third gear (direct drive).

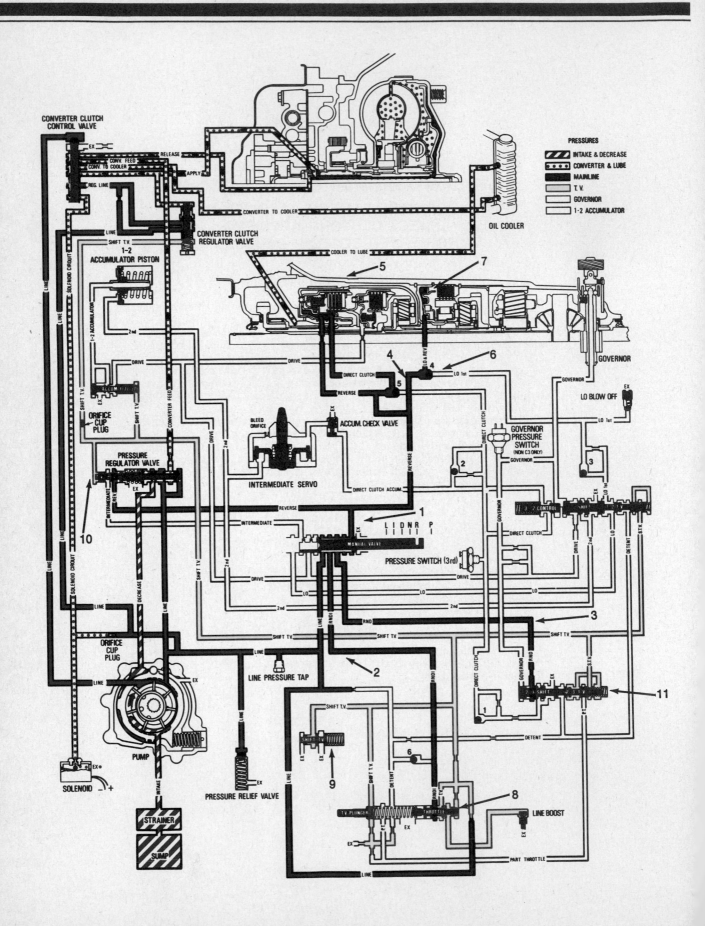

Reverse
DIRECT CLUTCH—APPLIED
LOW AND REVERSE CLUTCH—APPLIED

HYDRAULIC CONTROL

When the selector lever is moved to the Reverse (R) position, the manual valve is repositioned to allow line pressure to enter three (3) passages, as follows: reverse ①, RNDI (Reverse, Neutral, Drive and Interediate) ② and RND (Reverse, Neutral, and Drive) ③.

First, reverse oil from the manual valve seats direct clutch and reverse check ball (5) ④ in the direct clutch passage and flows to both the inner and outer areas of the clutch piston, applying the direct clutch ⑤. Reverse oil also seats the low and reverse check ball (4) ⑥ in the low 1st passage and applies the low and reverse clutch ⑦. Reverse oil flows to the reverse boost valve and will boost reverse line pressure to about 827 kPa (120 psi).

Second, RNDI oil from the manual valve flows to the throttle valve ⑧ and is regulated to T.V. pressure. T.V. oil flows through the shift T.V. valve ⑨ and is limited by it to approximately 620 kPa (90 psi).

Oil from the shift T.V. valve is directed to the T.V. boost valve ⑩. Shift T.V. oil acting on the T.V. boost valve will boost reverse line pressure to approximately 1447 kPa (210 psi).

Third, RND oil from the manual valve is directed to the 2-3 shift valve ⑪, but this has no function in Reverse.

CHECK VALVE BALLS

1—Direct clutch exhaust check valve ball
2—Direct clutch accumulator check valve ball
3—Low 1st check valve ball
4—Low and reverse check valve ball
5—Direct clutch and reverse check valve ball
6—RNDI and detent check valve ball

SUMMARY

The direct clutch is applied. The low and reverse clutch is applied. The transmission is in Reverse (R).

HYDRAULIC CONTROL SYSTEM

Major Components

FLUID RESERVOIRS

The hydraulic control system requires a supply of transmission fluid. Due to the low profile of the transaxle, a reservoir other than the oil pan is required to maintain a specific fluid level during hot and cold transaxle operation, so that the oil pump can provide pressured fluid to the hydraulic control system. This added reservoir, located in the lower section of the valve body cover, is controlled by a thermostatic element, operating by opening and closing according to the temperature of the fluid that is trapped in the reservoir portion of the valve body cover. As the temperature of the fluid in the valve body reservoir increases, the volume of the fluid increases. As the temperature decreases, the thermostatic element opens and allows the fluid to drain into the lower sump reservoir or oil pan.

OIL PUMP ASSEMBLY

The oil pump is a variable capacity vane-type pump, driven by the engine. The pump is located within the control valve assembly. A slide is incorporated in the pump that automatically regulates the pump output according to the needs of the transaxle. Maximum pump output is attained when the priming spring has been fully extended and has the slide held against the side of the pump body. As the slide moves towards the center, the pump output is reduced until the minimum pump output is reached.

PRESSURE REGULATOR VALVE

Movement of the pump slide is accomplished by directing fluid from the pressure regulator to the pump side opposite the priming spring. When the engine is stopped, the slide is held in the maximum output position by the priming spring. As the engine is started and the pump rotor is operated, its fluid output is directed to the pressure regulator valve. When the fluid output is below the desired pressure, the regulator valve is held in its bore by the pressure regulator spring. With the pressure regulator valve held in this position, the pump slide is held by the priming spring for maximum pressure output. As the pump output and the control pressure increases, the pressure regulator valve is moved against the pressure regulator spring. This allows fluid to be directed to the slide and causes the slide to move against the priming spring, decreasing the pump output. Fluid is also directed from the pressure regulator valve to fill the converter. When filled, the fluid is directed to the transaxle fluid cooler, located in the radiator. The fluid returning from the cooler is then directed to the lubrication system.

THROTTLE VALVE

The requirements of the transaxle for the apply of the band and clutches will vary with the engine torque and throttle opening. Under heavy throttle operation, the control pressure (approximately 70 psi) is not sufficient to hold the band or clutches in the applied mode without slipping. To provide a higher control (line) pressure when the throttle is opened, a throttle valve, relating to the throttle opening and engine torque, is provided in the valve body. As the accelerator pedal is depressed and the throttle plates are opened, the mechanical linkage (T.V. cable) relays the movement to the throttle plunger and increases the force on the T.V. spring and throttle valve, increasing T.V. pressure.

NOTE: T.V. pressure can be regulated from 0 to 105 psi, approximately.

SHIFT T.V. VALVE

A shift T.V. valve is used to control the T.V. pressure to a maximum of 90 psi for shift control, by exhausting the excess pressure.

T.V. BOOST VALVE

The T.V. boost valve is used to boost line pressure from 70 to 140 psi as the throttle opening directs.

LINE BOOST VALVE

A feature has been included in the T.V. system that will prevent the transaxle from being operated with low or minimum line pressure in the event that the T.V. cable becomes broken or disconnected. This feature is the line boost valve, which is located in the control valve and oil pump assembly at the T.V. regulating exhaust port. The line boost valve is held off its seat by the throttle lever and bracket assembly, allowing the T.V. pressure to regulate normally when the T.V. cable is properly adjusted. Should the T.V. cable become broken, disconnected or not adjusted properly, the line boost valve will close the T.V. exhaust port and keep the T.V. and line pressure at full line pressure psi.

GOVERNOR ASSEMBLY

The governor is driven by the differential and final drive carrier and, dependent upon vehicle speed, signals the valve body to make the shifts by increasing the governor pressure to oppose the main control and throttle pressure until the pressure forces are equal. This allows the valve springs to move the shifting valve and causes the transaxle to shift into another gear ratio. The governor pressure is developed from drive pressure, which is metered through two orifices and directed through the governor shaft to primary and secondary check balls, seated opposite of each other, and tends to exhaust through the check ball seats. The governor weights are so arranged that the primary weight, assisted by the primary spring, acts on one check ball, while the secondary weight, assisted by the secondary spring, acts on the other check ball. As the governor turns, the weights are moved outward by centrifugal force. This force is relayed to the check balls and seats them to control the governor pressure being exhausted. As the speed of the governor increases, so does the force relayed to the check balls. The heavier or primary weight and spring are more sensitive to changes in differential and final drive carrier speeds at lower rpm than the secondary weight. At greater vehicle speeds, as centrifugal force increases on the primary weight, the primary ball check is held tighter to its seat and cannot exhaust any fluid. From this point on, the secondary weight and spring are used to apply force to the secondary check ball and regulates the exhausting of the governor oil pressure.

1-2 AND 2-3 SHIFT VALVES

The 1-2 and 2-3 shift valves are used to change the gear ratios at predetermined speeds, fluid pressures and engine torque demands.

1-2 ACCUMULATOR VALVE

Controlling of the intermediate band apply pressure is accomplished by the 1-2 accumulator valve which provides a variable accumulator pressure to cushion the band apply in relation to throttle opening. At light throttle operation, the engine develops a small amount of torque, and as a result, the band requires less apply force to hold the direct clutch housing. At heavy throttle, the engine develops a large amount of torque which requires a greater apply pressure to lock the band on the direct clutch housing. If the band locks too slowly, it will slip excessively and burn due to the heat created by the slippage.

2-3 SHIFT ACCUMULATION

The 2-3 shift accumulation system operates in the same manner as the 1-2 accumulator valve operation, only to soften the direct clutch application during the 2-3 shift, by acting upon the release side of the intermediate servo piston.

TRANSAXLE DOWNSHIFTING

Transaxle downshifting is accomplished at part throttle and full throttle openings. Throttle, governor and control pressures are used in relation to each other, to provide the downshifting and movement of the necessary valves. An examination of the flow circuits for downshifting will show the operation of the various valves during the downshifting procedure. The transaxle will automatically downshift during the coast down with the throttle closed.

Diagnosis Tests

Automatic transaxle malfunctions may be caused by three major operating conditions. These conditions are improper transaxle adjustments, poor engine performance and hydraulic or mechanical malfunctions.

The suggested sequence for transaxle diagnosis is:
1. Check and adjust transaxle fluid level as required.
2. Check and adjust T.V. cable as required.
3. Check, correct and adjust manual linkage as necessary.
4. Check vehicle engine performance.
5. Install an oil pressure gauge and tachometer and check the transaxle control pressure.
6. Road test in all transaxle shift selector ranges and note any changes in operation and oil pressure.
7. Attempt to isolate the unit that is involved in the malfunction.
8. If the road test indicates that the engine is in need of a tune up, it should be performed before any corrective action is taken to repair the transaxle.

Control Pressure Test

To test the control pressure on the THM 125C automatic transaxle, connect the oil pressure gauge to the transaxle control pressure port. This port is located on top of the transaxle above the valve body oil pan. Install a tachometer to the engine and verify that the manual control linkage and the throttle control linkage are correct. Be sure that both the engine and the automatic transaxle are at operating temperature. Check the transaxle fluid level and adjust as required, before testing.

Minimum T. V. Line Pressure Test

1. Adjust the T.V. cable to specifications.
2. Be sure that the brakes are applied.
3. Install the oil pressure gauge to the transaxle.
4. Take and record the line pressure readings in the ranges and at the engine RPM as indicated in the Line Pressure Specification Chart.
5. Total testing time must not exceed two minutes for all combinations.

Maximum T. V. Line Pressure Test

1. Tie or hold the T.V. cable to the full extent of its travel.
2. Be sure that the brakes are applied.
3. Install the oil pressure gauge to the transaxle.
4. Take and record the line pressure readings in the ranges and at the engine RPM as indicated in the Line Pressure Specification Chart.
5. Total testing time must not exceed two minutes for all combinations.

LINE PRESSURE SPECIFICATIONS
1982 Model THM-125C Automatic Transaxle

Range	Model	Normal Oil Pressure At Maximum T.V.	Normal Oil Pressure At Minimum T.V.
Park at 1000 RPM	CI, HY, HC, CJ, EF, EA, EB, EQ, EC, EK	No T.V. pressure in Park. Line pressure is equal to Park at minimum T.V.	50-70
	PO, PL, PZ, HX, PK, PI, EL		60-80
	CL, CE, CD, CV, HM, HS, HW, OP, BL, BF		70-90
Reverse at 2000 RPM	EF, EA, EB, EQ, EC	234-254	95-115
	CI, CJ, HC, HY, EK	199-219	95-115
	PO, PL, PZ, PI, PK, HX, EL	216-236	112-132
	CL, CE, CD, CV, HM, HS, HW, OP, BL, BF	267-287	128-148
Neutral at 1000 RPM	EF, EA, EB, EQ, EC	130-150	50-70
	CI, CJ, HC, HY, EK	110-130	50-70
	PO, PL, PZ, PI, PK, HX, EL	120-140	60-80
	CL, CE, CD, CV, HM, HS, HW, OP, BL, BF	150-170	70-90
Drive at 1000 RPM	EF, EA, EB, EQ, EC	130-150	50-70
	CI, CJ, HC, HY, EK	110-130	50-70
	PO, PL, PZ, PI, PK, HX, EL	120-140	60-80
	CL, CE, CD, CV, HM, HS, HW, OP, BL, BF	150-170	70-90
Inter. at 1000 RPM	CI, HY, HC, CJ, EF, EA, EB, EQ, EC, EK	92-113	93-113
	PO, PL, PZ, HX, PK, PI, EL	110-130	110-130
	CL, CE, CD, CV, HM, HS, HW, OP, BL, BF	125-145	125-145
Low at 1000 RPM	CI, HY, HC, CJ, EF, EA, EB, EQ, EC, EK	No T.V. pressure in Low. Line pressure is equal to interrange at minimum T.V.	93-113
	PO, PL, PZ, HX, PK, PI, EL		110-130
	CL, CE, CD, CV, HM, HS, HW, OP, BL, BF		125-145

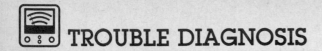

LINE PRESSURE SPECIFICATIONS
1983 Model THM-125C Automatic Transaxle

Range	Model	Normal Oil Pressure At Maximum T.V.	Normal Oil Pressure At Minimum T.V.
Park at 1000 RPM	EM, EN, EI, EF, EK, EB, EQ	No T.V. pressure in Park. Line pressure is equal to Park at minimum T.V.	58-62
	CA, CB, CF, HC, HY, PG, PW, EL, HW		67-75
	CE, CL, CT, HM, HS, CK, OP, HD, HV, BF, BL		75-85
	EP		75-85
Reverse at 1000 RPM	EM, EN	200-220	100-107
	EI	220-240	100-107
	EF, EK	235-255	100-107
	EB, EQ	240-280	110-117
	CA, CB, CF, HC, HY, PG, PW, EL, HW	217-240	118-130
	CE, CL, CT, HM, HS, CK, OP, HD, HV	240-295	130-150
	BF, BL	240-285	140-160
	EP	230-260	133-147
Neutral at 1000 RPM	EM, EN	115-125	58-62
	EI	125-135	58-62
	EF, EK, EB, EQ	135-145	58-62
	CA, CB, CF, EL, HC, HY, HW, PG, PW	123-140	67-75
	CE, CK, CL, CT, HD, HM, HS, HV, OP	150-170	75-85
	BF, BL	130-147	75-85
	EP	132-147	75-85
Drive at 1000 RPM	EM, EN	115-125	58-62
	EI	125-135	58-62
	EF, EK, EB, EQ	135-145	58-62
	CA, CB, CF, EL, HC, HY, HW, PG, PW	123-140	67-75
	CE, CK, CL, CT, HD, HM, HS, HV, OP	150-170	75-85
	BF, BL	130-147	75-85
	EP	132-147	75-85
Inter. at 1000 RPM	EM, EN, EI, EF, EK	No T.V. pressure in Inter. Line pressure is equal to Interrange at minimum T.V.	105-110
	EB, EQ		125-130
	CA, CB, CF, EL, HC, HY, HW, PG, PW		115-132
	CE, CK, CL, CT, HD, HM, HS, HV, OP		130-150
	BF, BL		160-183
	EP		135-150
Low at 1000 RPM	EM, EN, EI, EF, EK	No T.V. pressure in Low. Line pressure is equal to Low Range at minimum T.V.	105-110
	EB, EQ		125-130
	CA, CB, CF, EL, HC, HY, HW, HW, PG, PW		115-132
	CE, CK, CL, CT, HD, HM, HS, HV, OP		130-150
	BF, BL		160-183
	EP		135-150

Air Pressure Test

The positioning of the THM 125C transaxle in the vehicle and the valve body location will cause the air pressure tests to be very difficult. It is advisable to make any air pressure tests during the disassembly and assembly of the transaxle to ascertain if a unit is operating.

Stall Speed Test

General Motors Corporation does not recommend performing a stall test because of the excessive heat that is generated within the transaxle by the converter during the tests.

Recommendations are to perform the control pressure test and road test to determine and localize any transaxle malfunctions.

Road Test

Drive Range

Position selector lever in Drive range and accelerate the vehicle. A 1-2 and 2-3 shift should occur at throttle openings. (The shift points will vary with the throttle openings). Check part throttle 3-2 downshift at 30 MPH by quickly opening throttle approximately three-fourths. The transmission should downshift at 50 MPH, by depressing the accelerator fully.

Intermediate Range

Position the selector lever in Intermediate range and accelerate the vehicle. A 1-2 shift should occur at all throttle openings. (No 2-3 shift can be obtained in this range.) The 1-2 shift point will vary with the throttle opening. Check detent 2-1 downshift at 20 MPH the transaxle should downshift 2-1. The 1-2 shift in Intermediate range is somewhat firmer than in Drive range. This is normal.

Low Range

Position the selector level in the Low range and accelerate the vehicle. No upshift should occur in this range.

Intermediate Range (Overrun Braking)

Position the selector lever in Drive range, and with the vehicle speed at approximately 50 MPH, with closed or zero throttle, move the selector lever to Intermediate range. The transmission should downshift to 2nd. An increase in engine rpm and an engine braking effect should be noticed.

Low Range (Overrun Braking)

At 40 MPH, with throttle closed, move the selector lever to Low. A 2-1 downshift should occur in the speed range of approximately 40 to 25 MPH, depending on valve body calibration. The 2-1 downshift at closed throttle will be accompanied by increased engine rpm and an engine braking effect should be noticed. Stop vehicle.

Reverse Range

Position the selector lever in Reverse position and check for reverse operation.

Torque Converter Stator Operation Diagnosis

The torque converter stator assembly and its related roller clutch can possibly have one of two different type malfunctions.
1. The stator assembly freewheels in both directions
2. The stator assembly remains locked up at all times

Malfunction Type One

If the stator roller clutch becomes ineffective, the stator assembly freewheels at all times in both directions. With this condition, the vehicle will tend to have poor acceleration from a standstill. At speeds above 30-35 MPH, the vehicle may act normal. If poor acceleration problems are noted, it should first be determined that the exhaust system is not blocked, the engine is in good tune and the transmission is in 1st gear when starting out.

If the engine will freely accelerate to high rpm in Neutral, it can be assumed that the engine and exhaust system are normal. Driving the vehicle in Reverse and checking for poor performance will help determine if the stator is freewheeling at all times.

Malfunction Type Two

If the stator assembly remains locked up at all times, the engine rpm and vehicle speed will tend to be limited or restricted at high speeds. The vehicle performance when accelerating from a standstill will be normal. Engine over-heating may be noted. Visual examination of the converter may reveal a blue color from the overheating that will result.

CONVERTER CLUTCH OPERATION AND DIAGNOSIS

Converter Clutch Operation

The "apply" or "release" of the torque converter clutch assembly is determined by the direction that the feed oil is distributed to the torque converter. When transmission oil is routed to the cov-

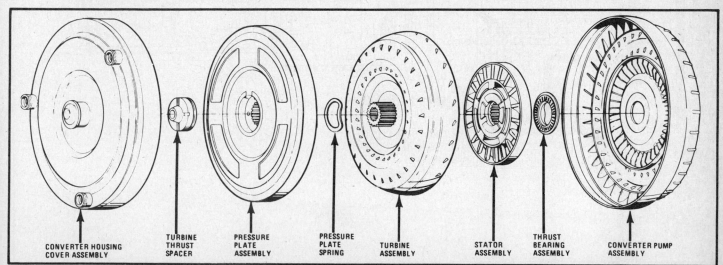

Torque converter clutch assembly—exlpoded view (©General Motors Corp.)

CONVERTER HOUSING COVER ASSEMBLY | TURBINE THRUST SPACER | PRESSURE PLATE ASSEMBLY | PRESSURE PLATE SPRING | TURBINE ASSEMBLY | STATOR ASSEMBLY | THRUST BEARING ASSEMBLY | CONVERTER PUMP ASSEMBLY

er assembly and the clutch plate the torque converter clutch is in the released position. When transmission oil is routed to the turbine side of the clutch plate the torque converter clutch is in the applied position.

To assist in the reduction of torsional shock during torque converter clutch "apply" a damper assembly has been installed in the torque converter clutch pressure plate. The spring loaded damper assembly is splined to the torque converter turbine assembly. The torque converter clutch pressure plate is attached to the pivoting mechanism, which is incorporated within the damper assembly. The pivoting action allows the clutch pressure plate to rotate independently of the damper assembly up to about forty-five degrees. The rate of this independent rotation is controlled by a pivoting mechanism acting on the springs that are assembled in the damper assembly. The spring cushioning effect of the damper assembly aids in the reduction of the engagement feel of the torque converter clutch "apply" function. To further aid in the "apply" and "release" function of the torque converter clutch during various driving situations other types of controls have been incorporated in the electrical system.

Torque Converter Clutch (T.C.C.)— Released Position

The release of the torque converter clutch is determined by the direction that the torque converter feed oil is routed to the torque converter. The torque converter feed oil from the pressure regulator flows to the torque converter clutch control valve. The position of the torque converter clutch control valve controls the direction that the torque converter feed oil flows to the torque converter.

The torque converter clutch control valve is held in the release position in "Park," "Neutral," "Reverse," "Drive," "First" and "Second," by line pressure acting on the end of the torque converter clutch apply valve. With the torque converter clutch control valve in the released state, the converter feed oil flows into the torque converter clutch release passages. The oil then flows between the pump driveshaft and the turbine shaft to the front or release side of the torque converter clutch. The oil flow then continues between the torque converter clutch pressure plate and the torque converter cover. This operation moves the converter clutch pressure plate away from the converter cover, releasing the converter clutch and charging the converter with oil. The oil then leaves the converter by flowing through the turbine shaft into the converter clutch apply oil circuit. The apply oil circuit is now being used in a reverse direction. The oil then flows from the apply passage into the cooler passage and to the lubrication system.

Torque Converter Clutch (T.C.C.)— Applied Position

At vehicle speeds below torque converter clutch engagement speed, the C3 or governor pressure switch, depending on the system, will break the circuit to the solenoid exhaust valve. This operation is done in order to prevent the torque converter clutch from applying in the drive- third gear mode. This de-energizes the solenoid and opens the exhaust valve to exhaust the solenoid circuit oil at the converter clutch control valve. Line pressure then holds the converter clutch control valve in the release position.

When the vehicle speed in the drive range- third gear reaches torque converter clutch engagement speed, the C3 or governor pressure switch, depending on the system, will activate the solenoid, closing the exhaust valve. This allows solenoid circuit oil to move the converter clutch control valve against line pressure. With the converter clutch control valve in the apply position, regulated line oil, from the converter clutch regulator valve, is allowed to pass into the converter apply passage. It then flows through the turbine shaft to the apply side of the converter clutch.

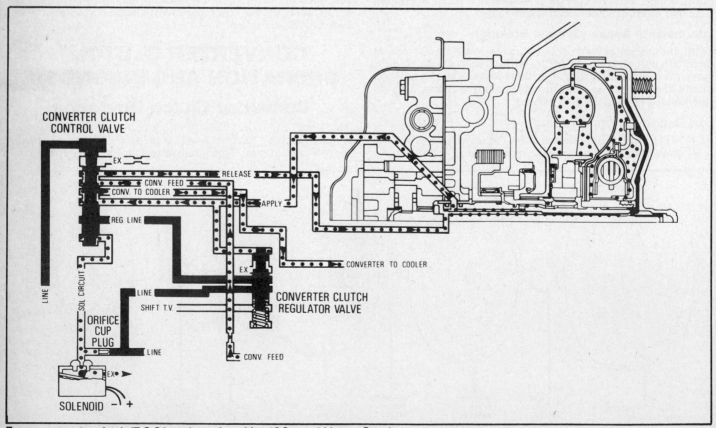

Torque converter clutch (T.C.C.)—released position (©General Motors Corp.)

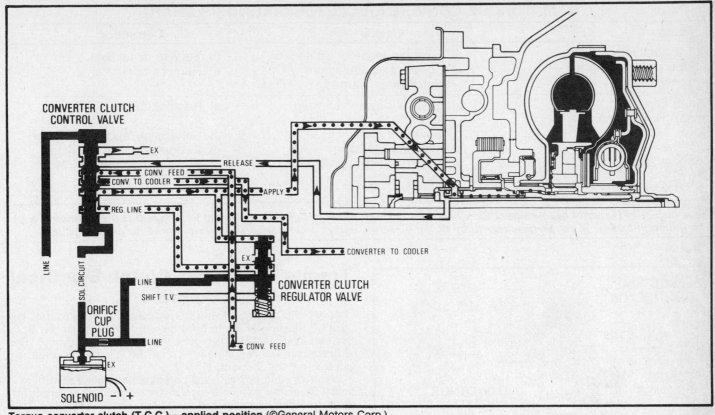

Torque converter clutch (T.C.C.)—applied position (©General Motors Corp.)

The regulated line oil, from the converter clutch regulator valve, controls the apply feel of pressure plate. As the pressure plate begins to move to its applied position, release oil in the front side of the pressure plate is redirected back between the turbine shaft and pump drive shaft and exhausted at the converter clutch control valve through an orifice, to time the clutch apply. When the converter clutch control valve moves to the apply position, orificed converter feed oil enters the torque converter to cooler passage in order to provide oil to the lubrication system.

Troubleshooting the Torque Converter Clutch

Before diagnosing the torque converter clutch system as being at fault in the case of rough shifting or other malfunctions, make sure that the engine is in at least a reasonable state of tune. Also, the following points should be checked:

1. Check the transmission fluid level and correct as necessary.
2. Check the manual linkage adjustment and correct as necessary.
3. Road test the vehicle to verify the complaint. Make sure that the vehicle is at normal operating temperature.
4. If the problem has been traced to the torque converter clutch system, refer to the G.M. Torque Converter Clutch Diagnosis Chart.

NOTE: When diagnosing a torque converter clutch problem on the 1983 Oldsmobile Ciera equipped with a 3.0 liter engine, disconnect the engine cooling fan relay.

G. M. TORQUE CONVERTER CLUTCH DIAGNOSIS CHART

Condition	Cause	Correction
Clutch applied in all ranges (engine stalls when put in gear)	a) Converter clutch valve stuck in apply position	a) R&R oil pump and clean valve—R&R auxiliary valve body and clean valve
Clutch does not apply: applies erratically or at wrong speeds	a) Electrical malfunction in most instances	a) Follow troubleshooting procedure to determine if problem is internal or external to isolate defect.
Clutch applies erratically; shudder and jerking felt	a) Vacuum hose leak b) Vacuum switch faulty c) Governor pressure malfunction	a) Repair hose as needed b) Replace switch c) Replace switch

G. M. TORQUE CONVERTER CLUTCH DIAGNOSIS CHART

Condition	Cause	Correction
Clutch applies erratically; shudder and jerking felt	d) Solenoid loose or damaged e) Converter malfunction; clutch plate warped	d) Service or replace e) Replace converter
Clutch applies at a very low or high 3rd gear	a) Governor switch shorted to ground b) Governor malfunction c) High line pressure d) Solenoid inoperative or shorted to case	a) Replace switch b) Service or replace governor c) Sevice pressure regulator d) Replace solenoid

—— **CAUTION** ——

When inspecting the stator and turbine of the torque converter clutch unit, a slight drag is normal when turned in the direction of free-wheel rotation because of the pressure exerted by the waved spring washer, located between the turbine and the pressure plate.

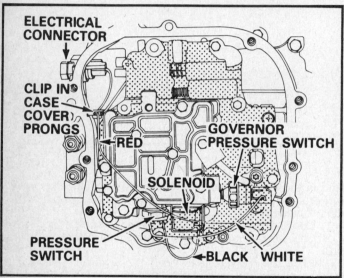

ELECTRICAL CONNECTOR
CLIP IN CASE COVER PRONGS
RED
GOVERNOR PRESSURE SWITCH
SOLENOID
PRESSURE SWITCH
BLACK WHITE

Non computer command control system component location inside the auxiliary valve body (©General Motors Corp.)

Torque Converter Clutch-Electrical Controls

Two types of electrical control systems are used to control the "apply" function of the torque converter clutch assembly. Both systems use the third clutch pressure switch and a solenoid. The difference in the two systems is that the vehicle speed sensing controls are not the same.

Vehicles equipped with the computer command control system (C3) use this system to energize the solenoid when certain vehicle speed has been reached.

Vehicles that are not equipped with the computer command system (C3) use a governor pressure switch to energize the solenoid when certain vehicle speed has been reached.

Computer Command Control System

Vehicles equipped with the computer command control system utilize the following components to accomplish the "apply" function of the torque converter clutch assembly.

1. Vacuum sensor—which sends engine vacuum information to the electronic control module.

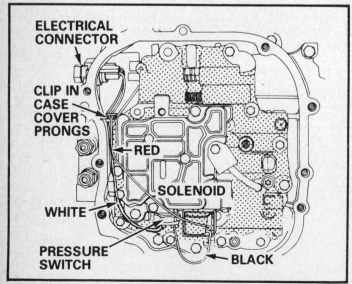

ELECTRICAL CONNECTOR
CLIP IN CASE COVER PRONGS
RED
SOLENOID
WHITE
PRESSURE SWITCH
BLACK

Computer command control system component location inside the auxiliary valve body (©General Motors Corp.)

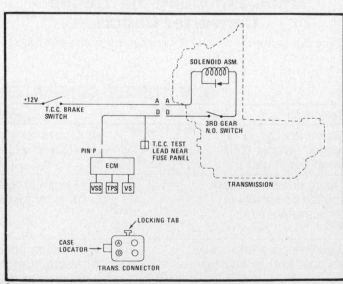

Computer command control system wiring diagram (©General Motors Corp.)

2. Throttle position sensor—which sends throttle position information to the electronic control module.

3. Vehicle speed sensor—which sends vehicle speed information to the electronic control module.

4. Electronic control module—which energizes and grounds the transaxle electrical system.

5. Brake release switch—which avoids stalling the engine when braking. Any time that the brakes are applied the torque converter clutch is released.

6. Third gear switch—which prevents operation until third gear speed is obtained.

Non Computer Command Control System—Diesel Engines

Vehicles not equipped with the computer command control system utilize the following components to accomplish the "apply" function of the torque converter clutch assembly.

1. Engine coolant fan temperature switch—which is a two position switch that closes when engine coolant temperature is about 246 degrees F. This causes the cooling fan to operate at high speed and bypass the delay feature in the torque converter clutch delay module. The torque converter clutch will operate when the governor pressure switch is closed.

2. Air condition high pressure switch—which closes when the air conditioner high pressure side reaches 370 psi. It performs the same functions as the engine coolant fan temperature switch.

3. Vacuum regulator valve—which opens at about ¾ or more throttle and disengages the torque converter clutch on heavy acceleration.

4. Governor pressure switch—which completes the ground circuit for the torque converter clutch and EGR solenoids when the vehicle reaches about 35 mph.

5. Third gear switch—which signals the torque converter clutch assembly when the transaxle is operating in third gear. This switch also prevents the torque converter clutch from operating in first or second gear unless the engine coolant fan temperature switch is closed, or the air condition high pressure switch is closed.

6. Torque converter control module—which delays the torque converter control "apply" function to keep the torque converter clutch and the direct clutch from applying at the same time. This

would cause an objectionable thump. The delay feature is overridden when either the air condition high pressure switch or the dual temp high switch is closed. When either switch is closed, the torque converter clutch assembly will "apply" as soon as the governor pressure switch closes.

7. Brake release switch—which avoids stalling the engine when braking. Any time that the brakes are applied, the torque converter clutch is released.

Non Computer Command Control System—Gas Engines

Vehicles not equipped with the computer command control system utilize the following components to accomplish the "apply" function of the torque converter clutch assembly.

1. Ported vacuum—which opens the vacuum switch to release the clutch during a closed throttle coast down.

2. Vacuum delay valve—which slows the vacuum switch response to vacuum changes.

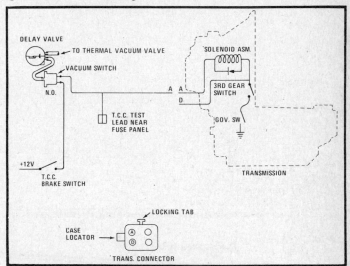

Non computer command control system wiring diagram—gas engines (©General Motors Corp.)

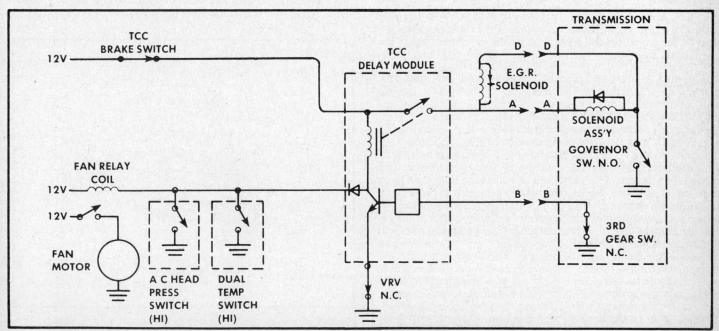

Non computer command control system wiring diagram—diesel engines (©General Motors Corp.)

3. Engine vacuum switch—which releases the torque converter clutch when the engine vacuum drops to approximately 1.5-3.0 inches during moderate acceleration, prior to a part throttle or detent downshift.

4. Thermal vacuum valve—which prevents the torque converter clutch from applying until the engine coolant temperature reaches 130 degrees F.

5. Brake release switch—which avoids stalling the engine when braking. Any time that the brakes are applied, the torque converter clutch is released.

Torque Converter Clutch Electrical Diagnosis

NOTE: When diagnosing a torque converter clutch problem on the 1983 Oldsmobile Ciera equipped with a 3.0 liter engine, be sure to disconnect the engine cooling fan relay.

Before making any electrical checks on the THM 125C automatic transaxle, the following points should be checked in order.
1. Check and adjust transaxle fluid level.
2. Check and adjust manual linkage.
3. Road test the vehicle and verify the complaint.
4. If the problem has been traced to the electrical function of the torque converter clutch assembly, refer to the proper Transaxle Converter Clutch Electrical Diagnosis Chart.

NOTE: When using the torque converter clutch electrical diagnosis chart for vehicles equipped with the computer command control system be sure to check for the presence of code 24 before performing the torque converter electrical diagnosis checks outlined in the chart. Refer to the proper Chilton Manual for the correct procedure to determine the presence of code 24.

ON CAR SERVICES

Adjustments

THROTTLE LINKAGE

Adjustment

The T.V. cable controls line pressure, shift points, part throttle downshifts and detent downshifts. The T.V. cable operates the throttle lever and bracket assembly, which is located within the valve body assembly.

The throttle lever and bracket assembly have two functions. The primary function of this assembly is to transfer throttle movement to the T.V. plunger in the control valve pump assembly as related by the T.V. cable and linkage. This causes T.V. pressure and line pressure to increase according to throttle opening; it also controls part throttle and detent downshifts. The proper adjustment of the T.V. cable is based on the T.V. plunger being fully depressed (flush with the T.V. bushing) at wide open throttle. The secondary function of this assembly involves the line boost lever and line boost valve. The function of this system is to prevent the transmission from operating at low (idle position) pressures, if the T.V. cable should become broken or disconnected. If the cable is connected (not broken or stretched), the line boost lever will not move from its normal spring-loaded "up" position which holds the line boost valve off its seat. The line boost lever will drop down to allow the line boost valve to seat only if the cable is broken, disconnected or extremely out of adjustment. With the valve body cover removed, it should be possible to pull down on the line boost lever and, when released, the lever spring should return the lever to the normal "up" position. If the throttle lever

and bracket assembly binds or sticks so the line boost lever cannot lift the line boost valve off its seat, high line pressures and delayed upshifts will result.

The cable should be checked for freeness by pulling out on the upper end of the cable. The cable should travel a short distance with slight spring resistance. This light resistance is caused by the

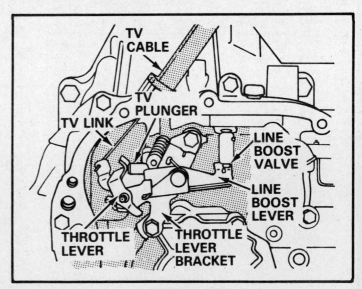

Throttle lever and bracket assembly (©General Motors Corp.)

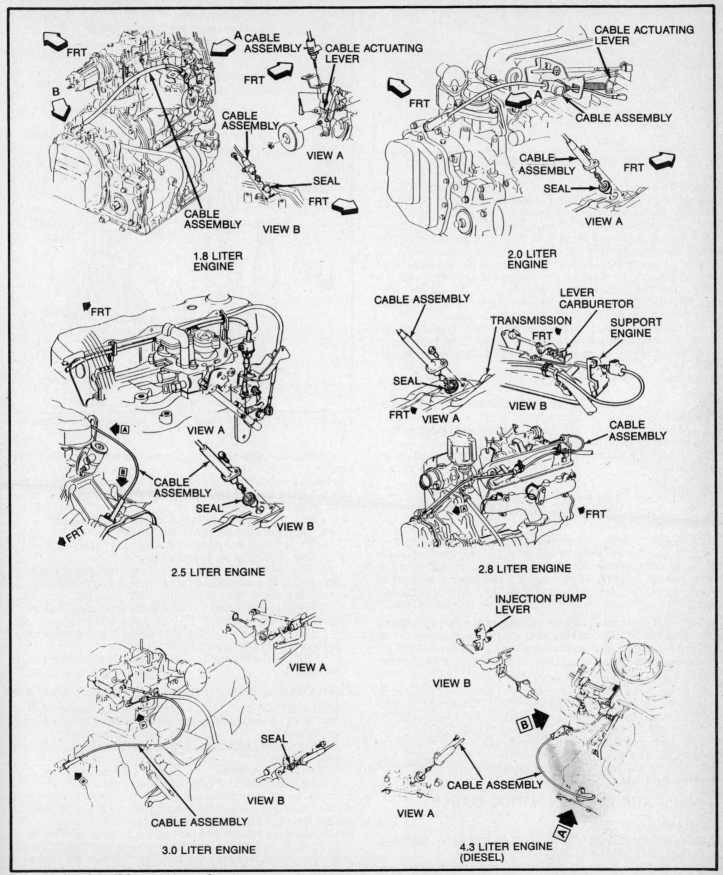

1.8 LITER ENGINE

2.0 LITER ENGINE

2.5 LITER ENGINE

2.8 LITER ENGINE

3.0 LITER ENGINE

4.3 LITER ENGINE (DIESEL)

T.V. cable locations (©General Motors Corp.)

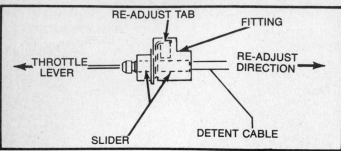

T.V. cable adjuster (©General Motors Corp.)

small coiled return spring on the T.V. lever and bracket that returns the lever to zero T.V., or closed throttle position. Pulling the cable farther out moves the lever to contact the T.V. plunger which compresses the T.V. spring which has more resistance. By releasing the upper end of the T.V. cable, it should return to the zero T.V. position. This test checks the cable in its housing, the T.V. lever and bracket, and the throttle valve plunger in its bushing for freeness. To check on the adjustment and verify that it is correct, use the following procedure:

1. Install line pressure gauge. Adjust engine speed to 1000 rpm with the selector in Park, and check line pressure.
2. Check line pressure in Neutral at 1000 rpm. Pressure should be in the same as or no more than 10 psi higher than in Park.
3. Adjust engine speed to 1400 rpm and make sure that there is an increase in line pressure.

If readjustment is necessary, the following procedure is suggested:

1. Depress and hold the metal lock tab that will be found on the cable adjuster by the idler lever.
2. Move the slider through the fitting away from the idler lever until the slider stops against the fitting.
3. Release the metal lock tab. As a double check, repeat the adjustment.

MANUAL LINKAGE

Adjustment

The THM 125C automatic transaxle manual linkage must be adjusted so that the shift selector indicator and stops correspond to the automatic transaxle detent positions. If the manual linkage is not adjusted correctly, an internal transaxle leak could develop. This could cause a clutch or band to slip. The following procedure should be used when adjusting the transaxle manual linkage.

NOTE: If the manual linkage adjustment is made with the selector lever in "P", the parking pawl should freely engage the reaction internal gear in order to keep the vehicle from rolling. If not properly adjusted, transaxle, vehicle or personal injury may occur.

1. Position the selector lever in "N".
2. Position the transaxle lever in "N". Obtain "N" position by turning the transaxle lever clockwise from "P" through "R" into "N". Or, turn the lever counterclockwise from "L" through "S" ("1" through "2" on some vehicles) and "D" to "N".
3. Loosely assemble the pin part of the shift cable through the transaxle lever slotted hole.
4. Tighten the nut. The lever must be held out of "P" when tightening the nut.

PARK LOCK CONTROL CABLE

Adjustment
CENTURY, SKYLARK, CITATION, CELEBRITY, OMEGA, CIERA, PHOENIX AND 6000

1. Position the selector lever in "P". Lock the steering column.
2. Position the transaxle lever into the "P" position.

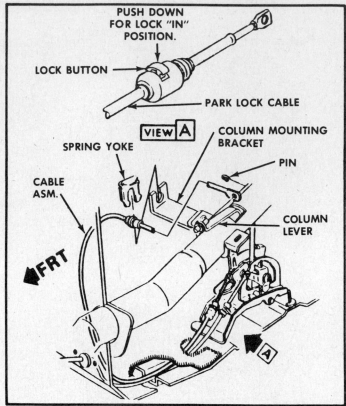

Park/lock cable routing—A and X series (©General Motors Corp.)

3. Install the cable-to-shifter mounting bracket with the spring yoke.
4. Install the cable-to-park lock pin on the shifter. Install the lock pin. Push the lock button on the cable housing in to set the cable length.
5. Check the cable operation in the following manner:
   a. Turn the ignition key to the "Lock" position.
   b. Press the detent release button in the shifter handle.
   c. Pull the shifter lever rearward.
   d. The shifter lock-hook must engage into the shifter base slot, within 2° maximum movement of the shifter lever.
   e. Turn the ignition key to the "Off" position.
   f. Repeat steps b and c. The selector lever must be able to move rearward to the "L" ("1" on some vehicles) position.
   g. Repeat Steps a through d to assure that the adjustment nut has not slipped during check.
   h. Return the key to the "Lock" position and check key removal.

SKYHAWK, CAVALIER, FIRENZA, CIMARRON AND 2000

1. The ignition lock cylinder on the steering column must be in the "Lock" position. Snap the park lock cable-to-steering column sliding pin.
2. Snap the park lock cable column end fitting into the steering column bracket.
3. Position the selector lever in the "P" position.
4. Install the park lock cable terminal to the shifter park lock lever pin. Install the retainer pin. Install the park lock cable to the shifter mounting bracket by pushing the lock button housing against the adjusting spring, dropping the cable through the slot in the mounting bracket and seating the housing to the shifter.
5. Push the lock adjustment button down to complete the adjustment procedure. Check the cable operation in the following manner:
   a. With the ignition in the "Lock" position, try to push the

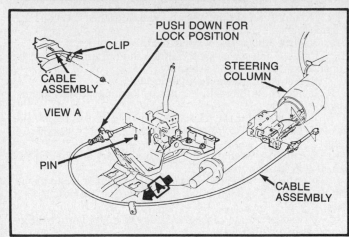

Park/lock cable routing— J series (©General Motors Corp.)

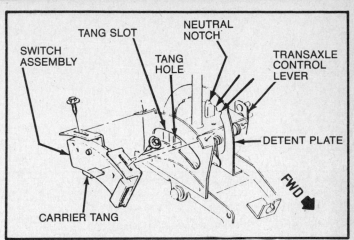

Floor shift switch assembly (©General Motors Corp.)

button on the shift handle. Button travel must not be enough to let the shifter move out of "P".

b. Turn the ignition key to the "Run" position. The shifter should select the gears when the handle turns rearward.

c. With the shifter in neutral, the ignition lock cylinder should not return to "Lock".

d. Return the shifter to "P" then return the ignition key to the "Lock" position.

NEUTRAL SAFETY AND REVERSE LIGHT SWITCH

Adjustment

FLOOR SHIFT MODELS

1. Remove center console and all related components in order to service the switch assembly.
2. Position the automatic transaxle control shifter assembly in "N".
3. Loosen the switch attaching screws.
4. Turn the switch on the shifter assembly to align the service adjustment hole with the carrier tang hole.
5. Install a .90 inch diameter gauge pin to a depth of about .060 inch.
6. Tighten the switch adjusting screws.
7. Remove the gauge pin. Check for correct adjustment.

COLUMN SHIFT MODELS

1. Locate the neutral safety switch at the bottom of the steering column.
2. With the switch installed move the housing all the way down toward the low gear position.
3. Adjust the switch by positioning the selector lever in "P". The main housing and the housing back should ratchet, providing proper switch adjustment.

SERVICES

FLUID CHANGES

The conditions under which the vehicle is operated is the main consideration in determining how often the transaxle fluid should be changed. Different driving conditions result in different transaxle fluid temperatures. These temperatures affect change intervals.

If the vehicle is driven under severe service conditions, change the fluid and filter every 15,000 miles. If the vehicle is not used under severe service conditions, change the fluid and replace the filter every 100,000 miles.

Do not overfill the transaxle. It only takes one pint of fluid to change the level from add to full on the transaxle dipstick. Overfilling the unit can cause damage to the internal components of the automatic transaxle.

OIL PAN

Removal and Installation

Some THM 125C automatic transaxles may be built using RTV silicone sealant in place of the usual oil pan gasket. RTV sealant is an effective substitute for this application, but its usage depends on the type of oil pan being used in the transaxle assembly. If RTV sealant is used on an oil pan, the flange surface must be either flat or have depressed stiffening ribs. Do not use RTV sealant on transaxle oil pans which have raised stiffening ribs.

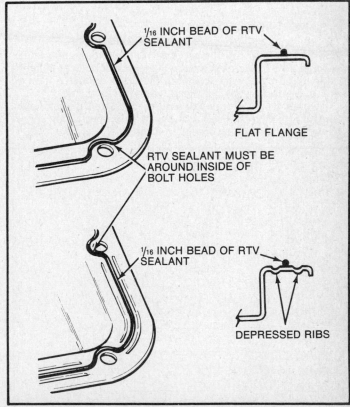

Oil pan design using RTV sealant (©General Motors Corp.)

431

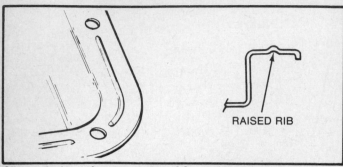

RAISED RIB

Oil pan design using pan gasket (©General Motors Corp.)

OIL PANS USING REGULAR PAN GASKET

1. Raise the vehicle and support it safely.
2. With a drain pan under the transaxle assembly, remove the oil pan attaching bolts from the front and side of the oil pan.
3. Loosen the rear pan bolts approximately four turns.
4. Carefully pry the transaxle oil pan loose with a suitable tool allowing the fluid to drain into the drain pan.
5. Remove the remaining bolts from the assembly. Remove both the oil pan and gasket from the vehicle.
6. Remove the transaxle filter and O-ring seal.
7. Install a new filter and O-ring seal locating the filter against the dipstick stop.
8. Install a new transaxle pan gasket on the oil pan. Install the oil pan to the transaxle assembly and tighten the bolts to 12 ft. lbs.
9. Lower the vehicle. Add about four quarts of the proper grade and type automatic transmission fluid.
10. With the selector lever in "P" apply the parking brake and block the wheels. Start the engine and let it idle. Do not race the engine.
11. Move the selector lever through all the ranges. With the selector lever in "P" check for proper fluid level and correct as required.

OIL PANS USING RTV SEALANT

1. Raise the vehicle and support it safely.
2. A special bolt will be necessary to remove the oil pan because of the RTV assembly process. This special bolt can be fabricated by grinding down a section of the shank diameter of an oil pan bolt, just below the bolt head, to about 3/16 inch.
3. Remove all of the oil pan bolts except A and B as indicated in illustration. Remove bolt A and install the special bolt, finger tight. Loosen bolt B four complete turns.

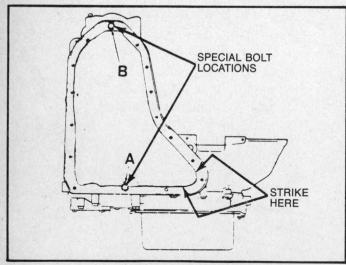

SPECIAL BOLT LOCATIONS

B

A

STRIKE HERE

Oil pan removal procedure (©General Motors Corp.)

4. Do not try to pry the oil pan loose from the transaxle case, as damage may occur.
5. Using a rubber mallet strike the oil pan corner.
6. Remove the special bolt. Let the fluid drain. Remove the oil pan from the transaxle assembly.
7. Remove the transaxle filter and O-ring.
8. Install a new filter and O-ring seal locating the filter against the dipstick stop.
9. When installing the transaxle oil pan be sure to remove all the old RTV sealant from both the oil pan and the transaxle case flange.
10. Be sure that both of these surfaces are dry and free of any film. If not, leakage may result.
11. Install a 1/16 inch bead of RTV sealant on the oil pan flange. The bead of RTV sealant must also be applied around the bolt holes.
12. Install the oil pan to the transaxle assembly. Torque the attaching bolts to 12 ft. lbs.
13. Lower the vehicle. Add about four quarts of the proper grade and type automatic transmission fluid.
14. With the selector lever in "P" apply the parking brake and block the wheels. Start the engine and let it idle. Do not race the engine.
15. Move the selector lever through all of the ranges. With the selector lever in "P", check for proper fluid level. Correct as required.

LOW AND REVERSE PIPES

Removal and Installation

1. Raise the vehicle and support it safely.
2. Remove the transaxle fluid pan. Remove the fluid filter and O-ring seal.
3. Remove the reverse oil pipe, seal back-up ring and the O-ring.
4. Remove the low and reverse cup plug assembly.
5. To install, position the low and reverse cup plug assembly in its proper place.
6. Position the reverse oil pipe, seal back-up ring and O-ring in its proper place.
7. Install a new fluid filter and O-ring seal. Install the transaxle oil pan.
8. Lower the vehicle and fill with the proper grade and type automatic transmission fluid. Road test and correct as required.

PARKING PAWL SHAFT

Removal and Installation

1. Raise the vehicle and support it safely.
2. Remove the transaxle fluid pan. Remove the fluid filter and the O-ring.
3. Remove the dipstick stop, rod retainer and parking lock bracket.
4. Remove the clip, rod, pin and spring.
5. To install, position the clip, rod, pin and spring assembly to its proper mounting spot within the transaxle assembly.
6. Install the dipstick stop, rod retainer and parking lock bracket.
7. Install a new fluid filter and O-ring seal. Install the transaxle fluid pan.
8. Lower the vehicle. Fill the transaxle with the proper grade and type automatic transmission fluid. Road test and correct as required.

INTERMEDIATE SERVO ASSEMBLY

Removal and Installation

1. Raise the vehicle and support it safely.

6. Position the intermediate servo assembly to the transaxle. Intsall the servo cover.
7. Install the reverse oil pipe retaining brackets.
8. Install a new fluid filter and O-ring seal. Install the transaxle fluid pan.
9. Lower the vehicle from the hoist. Fill the transaxle with the proper grade and type automatic transmission fluid. Road test and correct as required.

ACCUMULATOR CHECK VALVE

Removal and Installation

1. Raise the vehicle and support it safely.
2. Remove the transaxle fluid pan. Remove the fluid filter and O-ring seal.
3. Remove the reverse oil pipe retaining brackets. Remove the intermediate servo cover and gasket.
4. Remove the intermediate servo assembly from the transaxle assembly.
5. Remove the third accumulator check valve and spring from its mounting place inside the transaxle.

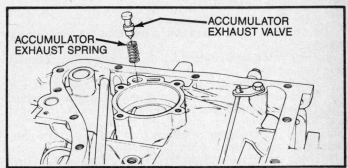

Accumulator check valve location (©General Motors Corp.)

6. Install the third accumulator valve and spring in its proper place.
7. Install the intermediate servo assembly in the automatic transaxle.
8. Install the intermediate servo cover and gasket. Install the reverse oil pipe brackets.
9. Install a new fluid filter and O-ring seal. Install the transaxle fluid pan.
10. Lower the vehicle. Fill the automatic transaxle with the proper grade and type automatic transmission fluid. Road test and correct as required.

SPEEDOMETER DRIVE GEAR

Removal and Installation

1. Raise the vehicle and support it safely.
2. Disconnect the speedometer cable from the transaxle assembly.
3. Remove the speedometer driven gear and the sleeve assembly from its mounting place.
4. Remove the transaxle governor cover and O-ring.
5. Remove the speedometer drive gear assembly from the automatic transaxle.
6. To install, position the speedometer drive gear assembly into the transaxle. Install the transaxle governor cover using a new O-ring.
7. Install the speedometer driven gear and sleeve assembly. Connect the speedometer cable to the transaxle case.
8. Lower the vehicle. Check the fluid level and correct as necessary. Road test the vehicle.

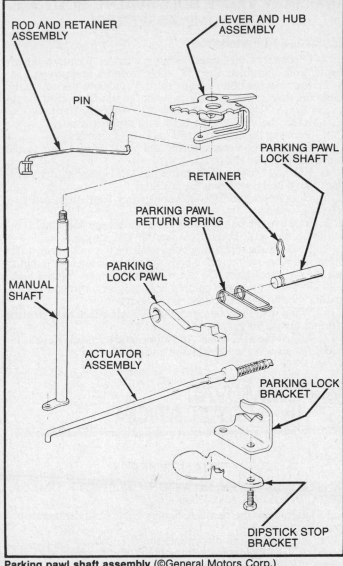

Parking pawl shaft assembly (©General Motors Corp.)

2. Remove the transaxle fluid pan. Remove the fluid filter and O-ring seal.
3. Remove the reverse oil pipe retaining brackets.
4. Remove the intermediate servo cover and gasket.
5. Remove the intermediate servo assembly from the automatic transaxle.

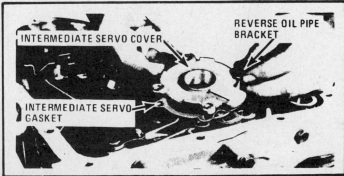

Intermediate servo assembly location (©General Motors Corp.)

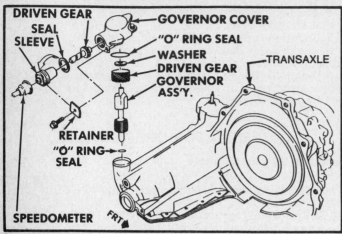

Speedometer drive and governor assembly—exploded view (©General Motors Corp.)

GOVERNOR ASSEMBLY

Removal and Installation

1. Raise the vehicle and support it safely.
2. Disconnect the speedometer cable from the transaxle assembly.
3. Remove the speedometer driven gear and sleeve assembly from the transaxle.
4. Remove the transaxle governor cover and O-ring. Carefully remove the governor assembly from its mounting in the transaxle.
5. To install, position the governor assembly in the transaxle. Install the governor cover using a new O-ring.
6. Install the speedometer driven gear and sleeve assembly. Connect the speedometer cable to the transaxle case.
7. Lower the vehicle. Adjust the transaxle fluid level as required. Road test the vehicle.

T.V. CABLE

Removal and Installation

1. Remove the air cleaner from the engine.
2. Disconnect the T.V. cable from the throttle lever.
3. Remove the bolt securing the T.V. cable to the transaxle assembly. Pull up on the cable cover at the transaxle until the cable is seen.
4. Disconnect the T.V. cable from the transaxle rod.
5. To install, reverse the removal procedure.
6. Check and adjust as required.

AUXILIARY VALVE BODY, VALVE BODY AND OIL PUMP ASSEMBLY

Removal and Installation

1. Disconnect the negative battery cable. Remove the air cleaner and disconnect the T.V. cable from its mounting place.
2. Remove the bolt securing the T.V. cable to the automatic transaxle. Pull up on the cable cover at the transaxle until the cable can be seen. Disconnect the T.V. cable from the transaxle rod.
3. Raise the vehicle on a hoist and support it safely.
4. Remove the left front tire and wheel assembly.
5. Remove the bolts securing the valve body cover to the transaxle. Remove the cover.
6. Remove the bolt that secures the TCC solenoid to the auxiliary valve body. Remove the solenoid.
7. Disconnect the TCC solenoid wires from the third gear pressure switch.
8. Remove the bolt securing the T.V. linkage and bracket assembly to the valve body. Remove the T.V. linkage.
9. Remove the remaining bolts securing the valve body to its mounting. Remove the valve body assembly, being careful not to lose the six check balls. Do not remove the green colored bolt.
10. Remove the green colored bolt only when separating the auxiliary valve body from the valve body.
11. When installing, be sure to hold the six check balls in place with petroleum jelly.
12. Adjust the T.V. cable. Add automatic transaxle fluid as required. Road test the vehicle and correct as required.

TRANSAXLE

CENTURY, SKYLARK, CITATION, CELEBRITY, OMEGA, CIERA, PHOENIX AND 6000

1. Disconnect the negative battery cable at the transaxle.
2. Remove:
   a. Air cleaner and disconnect the T.V. cable.
   b. T.V. cable lower attaching bolt and disconnect the cable from the transaxle.
   c. Strut shock bracket bolts from the transaxle.
   d. Oil cooler lines from the strut bracket.
   e. Transaxle-to-engine bolts, leaving the bolt near the starter installed loosely.

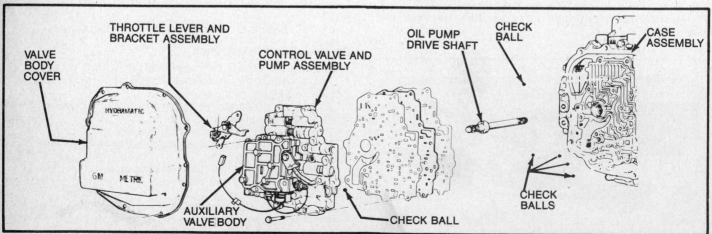

Auxiliary valve body, valve body and oil pump assembly (©General Motors Corp.)

f. Shift linkage retaining clip and washer at the transaxle.

g. Shift linkage bracket bolts.

3. Disconnect the speedometer drive cable at the upper and lower couplings (at the transducer if equipped with cruise control).

4. Disconnect the oil cooler lines at the transaxle.

5. Install the engine support fixture, locating it at the center of the cowl for four cylinder engines and on the strut towers for six cylinder engines.

NOTE: When installing a lift chain onto the aluminum cylinder head of the 4.3 liter V6 diesel engine, be sure that the bolt is tight or damage to the cylinder head may occur.

6. Rotate the steering wheel to position the steering gear stub shaft bolt in the upward position. Remove the bolt.

7. Raise the vehicle and place a jack under the engine to act as a support during removal and installation.

8. Remove the left front tire and wheel assembly.

9. Remove the power steering line brackets, remove the mounting bolts for the steering rack assembly, and support the assembly.

10. Disconnect the driveline vibration absorber, if so equipped.

11. Disconnect the left side lower ball joint at the steering knuckle.

12. Remove the front stabilizer bar reinforcements and bushings from the right and left cradle side members.

13. Using a drill with a ½ in. bit, drill through the spot weld located between the rear holes of the left side front stabilizer bar mounting.

14. Disconnect the engine and transaxle mounts from the cradle.

15. Remove the sidemember-to-cross-member bolts.

16. Remove the bolts from the left side body mounts.

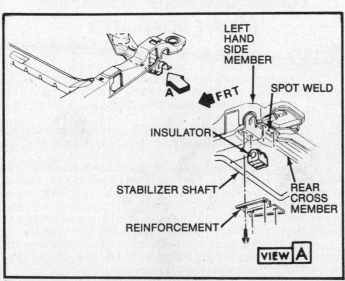

Spot weld location (©General Motors Corp.)

17. Remove the left side and front crossmember assembly. It may be necessary to carefully pry the crossmember loose.

18. Install axle shaft boot protectors, and using the appropriate special tools, pull the axle shaft cones out and away from the transaxle.

19. Pull the left axle shaft out of the transaxle.

20. Rotate the strut assembly so that the axle shaft is out of the way.

21. Remove:

a. Starter and converter shields.

b. Flywheel-to-converter bolts.

c. Two transaxle extension bolts from the engine-to-transaxle bracket.

d. Rear transaxle mount bracket assembly. It may be necessary to raise the transaxle assembly.

22. Securely attach a transaxle jack to the transaxle assembly.

23. Remove the two braces to the right end of the transaxle bolts.

24. Remove the remaining transaxle-to-engine bolt.

25. Remove the transaxle by moving it towards the driver's side, away from the engine.

26. Installation is performed in the reverse of the previous steps. Note the following:

a. When raising the transaxle into place, guide the right side axle shaft into the transaxle.

b. Check and adjust all front end alignment settings after the installation is complete.

c. Adjust the transmission detent cable.

SKYHAWK, CAVALIER, FIRENZA, CIMARRON, AND 2000

1. Disconnect the negative battery cable where it attaches to the transaxle.

2. Insert a ¼ x 2 in. bolt into the hole in the right front motor mount to prevent any mislocation during the transaxle removal.

3. Remove the air cleaner. Disconnect the T.V. cable.

4. Unscrew the bolt securing the T.V. cable to the transaxle. Pull up on the cable cover at the transaxle until the cable can be seen. Disconnect the cable from the transaxle rod.

5. Remove the wiring harness retaining bolt at the top of the transaxle.

6. Remove the hose from the air management valve and then pull the wiring harness up and out of the way.

7. Install an engine support bar. Raise the engine high enough to take the pressure off the motor mounts.

NOTE: The engine support bar must be located in the center of the cowl and the bolts must be tightened before attempting to support the engine.

8. Remove the transaxle mount and bracket assembly. It may be necessary to raise the engine slightly to aid in removal.

9. Disconnect the shift control linkage from the transaxle.

10. Remove the top transaxle-to-engine mounting bolts. Loosen, but do not remove, the transaxle-to-engine bolt nearest to the starter.

11. Unlock the steering column. Raise and support the front of the car. Remove the front wheels.

12. Pull out the cotter pin and loosen the castellated ball joint nut until the ball joint separates from the control arm. Repeat on the other side of the car.

13. Disconnect the stabilizer bar from the left lower control arm.

14. Remove the six bolts that secure the left front suspension support assembly.

15. Connect an axle shaft removal tool to a slide hammer.

16. Position the tool behind the axle shaft cones and then pull the cones out and away from the transaxle. Remove the axle shafts and plug the transaxle bores to reduce fluid leakage.

17. Remove the nut that secures the transaxle control cable bracket to the transaxle, then remove the engine-to-transaxle stud.

18. Disconnect the speedometer cable at the transaxle.

19. Disconnect the transaxle strut (stabilizer) at the transaxle.

20. Remove the four retaining screws and remove the torque converter shield.

21. Remove the three bolts securing the torque converter to the flex plate.

22. Disconnect and plug the oil cooler lines at the transaxle. Remove the starter.

23. Remove the screws that hold the brake and fuel line brack-

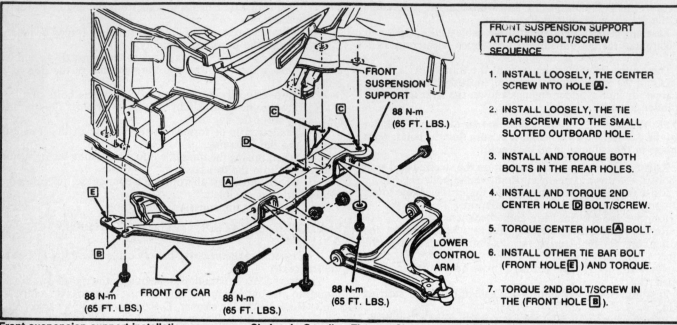

Front suspension support installation sequence—Skyhawk, Cavalier, Firenza, Cimarron and 2000 (©General Motors Corp.)

Within the illustration:

FRONT SUSPENSION SUPPORT

88 N·m (65 FT. LBS.)

LOWER CONTROL ARM

FRONT OF CAR

88 N·m (65 FT. LBS.)

88 N·m (65 FT. LBS.)

88 N·m (65 FT. LBS.)

FRONT SUSPENSION SUPPORT ATTACHING BOLT/SCREW SEQUENCE

1. INSTALL LOOSELY, THE CENTER SCREW INTO HOLE **A**.

2. INSTALL LOOSELY, THE TIE BAR SCREW INTO THE SMALL SLOTTED OUTBOARD HOLE.

3. INSTALL AND TORQUE BOTH BOLTS IN THE REAR HOLES.

4. INSTALL AND TORQUE 2ND CENTER HOLE **D** BOLT/SCREW.

5. TORQUE CENTER HOLE **A** BOLT.

6. INSTALL OTHER TIE BAR BOLT (FRONT HOLE **E**) AND TORQUE.

7. TORQUE 2ND BOLT/SCREW IN THE (FRONT HOLE **B**).

ets to the left side of the underbody. This will allow the lines to be moved slightly for clearance during transaxle removal.

24. Remove the bolt that was loosened in Step 10.

25. Remove the transaxle to the left.

Installation is in the reverse order of removal. Please note the following:

a. Reinstall both axle shafts AFTER the transaxle is in position.

b. When installing the front suspension support assembly you must follow the tightening sequence shown in the illustration.

c. Check alignment when installation is complete.

BENCH OVERHAUL

Before Disassembly

Cleanliness is an important factor in the overhaul of the 125C automatic transaxle. Before opening up this unit, the entire outside of the transaxle assembly should be cleaned, preferably with a high pressure washer such as a car wash spray unit. Dirt entering the transaxle internal parts will negate all the time and effort spent on the overhaul. During inspection and reassembly all parts should be thoroughly cleaned with solvent then dried with compressed air. Wiping cloths and rags should not be used to dry parts since lint will find its way in to the valve body passages.

Wheel bearing grease, long used to hold thrust washers and lube parts, should not be used. Lube seals with Dexron® II and use ordinary unmedicated petroleum jelly to hold the thrust washers and to ease the assembly of seals, since it will not leave a harmful residue as grease often will. Do *not* use solvent on neoprene seals, friction plates if they are to be reused, or thrust washers. Be wary of nylon parts if the transaxle failure was due to failure of the cooling system. Nylon parts exposed to water or antifreeze solutions can swell and distort and must be replaced.

Before installing bolts into aluminum parts, always dip the threads into clean transmission oil. Anti-seize compound can also be used to prevent bolts from galling the aluminum and seiz-

ing. Always use a torque wrench to keep from stripping the threads. Take care with the seals when installing them, especially the smaller "O"-rings. The internal snap rings should be expanded and the external rings should be compressed, if they are to be reused. This will help insure proper seating when installed.

Torque Converter Inspection

TORQUE CONVERTER

Removal

1. Make certain that the transaxle is held securely.

2. The converter pulls out of the transaxle. Be careful since the converter contains a large amount of oil. There is no drain plug on the converter so the converter should be drained through the hub.

3. Place the transaxle in a holding fixture if possible. Turn the transaxle so that the right-hand axle opening is down so that the unit can drain.

4. If the oil in the converter is discolored but does not contain metal bits or particles, the converter is not damaged and need not be replaced. Remember that color is no longer a good indicator of transmission fluid condition. In the past, dark color was associated with overheated transmission fluid. It is not a positive sign of transmission failure with the newer fluids like Dexron® II.

5. If the oil in the converter contains metal particles, the converter is damaged internally and must be replaced. The oil may have an "aluminum paint" appearance.

6. If the cause of oil contamination was burned clutch plates or overheated oil, the converter is contaminated and should be replaced.

TORQUE CONVERTER INSPECTION

After the converter is removed from the transaxle, the stator roller clutch can be checked by inserting a finger into the splined inner race of the roller clutch and trying to turn the race in both directions. The inner race should turn freely in the clockwise direction, but not turn in the counterclockwise direction. The inner race may tend to turn in the counterclockwise direction, but with great difficulty, this is to be considered normal. Do not use such items as the driven sprocket support or the shafts to turn the race, as the results may be misleading. Inspect the outer hub lip and the inner bushing for burrs or jagged edges to avoid injury to your fingers when testing the torque converter.

Transaxle Disassembly

EXTERNAL COMPONENTS

1. Remove the speedometer driven gear and the sleeve assembly from the transaxle case.

2. Remove the governor cover O-ring. Discard the O-ring.

3. Remove the governor cover to speedometer drive gear thrust bearing assembly. Remove the speedometer drive gear assembly.

4. Remove the transaxle oil pan. If RTV sealant was used do not pry the oil pan loose from the transaxle case as damage to the pan flange or case will occur. Use a rubber mallet and strike the edge of the oil pan to shear the RTV seal.

5. Remove and discard the fluid filter and O-ring seal.

6. Remove the reverse oil pipe retaining brackets. Remove the intermediate servo cover and gasket. Discard the gasket.

7. Remove the intermediate servo assembly from its mounting in the transaxle.

8. Check for the proper intermediate band apply pin by installing special tool J-28535 or an equivalent intermediate band apply pin gauge. Hold the tool in place using the two intermediate servo cover screws. Remove the band apply pin from the intermediate servo assembly. Install special tool J-28535-4 or equivalent on the band apply pin. Position this assembly into the apply pin gauge. To check, compress the band apply 100 inch pounds torque. If any part of the white line appears in the window, the pin is the correct length. If the white line connot be seen, change the band apply pin and recheck. Replace parts as required.

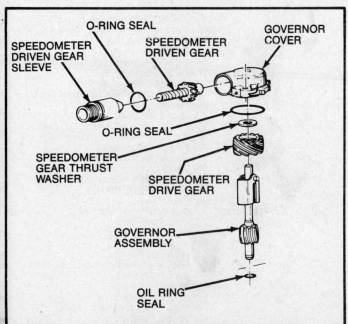

Speedometer drive and governor assembly—exploded view (©General Motors Corp.)

9. Remove the third accumulator check valve and spring assembly.

10. Remove the reverse oil pipe, seal back up ring and O-ring seal.

11. Remove the low and reverse cup plug assembly by grinding about ¾ inch from the end of a number four easy out. Using the modified tool, remove the seal assembly.

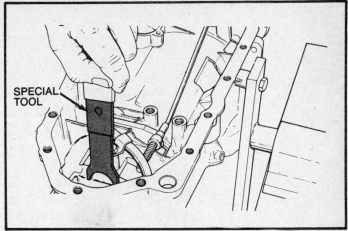

"C" ring removal (©General Motors Corp.)

12. Remove the dipstick stop and the parking lock bracket.

13. If equipped, remove the oil weir clip and remove the oil weir assembly.

14. Position the final drive unit so that the "C" ring is visible. Position the "C" ring so that the open side is facing the access window. Using special tool J-28583 or equivalent push the "C" ring partially off of the output shaft.

15. Carefully turn the output shaft so that the "C" ring is up. Remove the "C" ring by pulling it out with a needle nose pliers.

16. Remove the output shaft from the transaxle assembly.

VALVE BODY, CASE COVER AND SPROCKET LINK ASSEMBLY

1. Remove the valve body cover. If RTV sealant was used, do not pry the transaxle oil pan loose from the transaxle case as damage to the transaxle case or oil pan flange will occur.

2. Remove the two bolts retaining the throttle lever and bracket assembly.

3. Remove the throttle lever and bracket assembly with the T.V. cable link.

4. Remove the auxiliary valve body bolts except for the green colored bolt. Do not remove the green colored bolt unless it is necessary to separate the valve body from the auxiliary valve body.

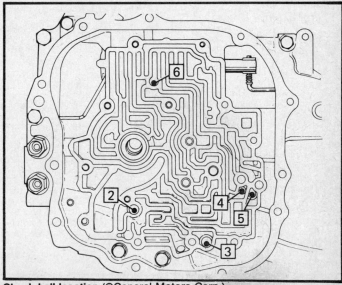

Check ball location (©General Motors Corp.)

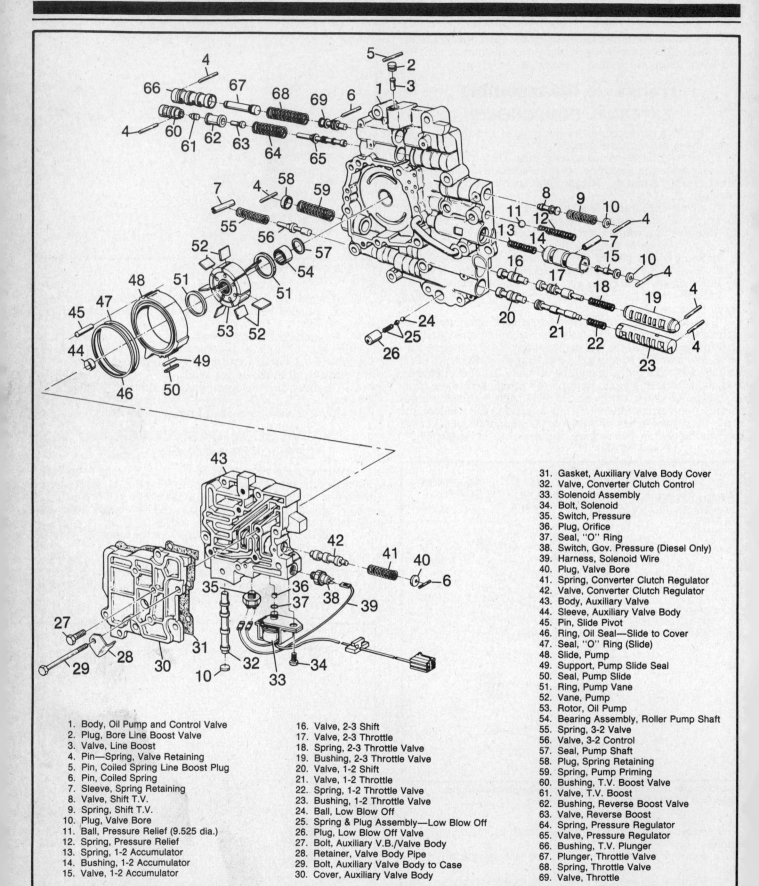

1. Body, Oil Pump and Control Valve
2. Plug, Bore Line Boost Valve
3. Valve, Line Boost
4. Pin—Spring, Valve Retaining
5. Pin, Coiled Spring Line Boost Plug
6. Pin, Coiled Spring
7. Sleeve, Spring Retaining
8. Valve, Shift T.V.
9. Spring, Shift T.V.
10. Plug, Valve Bore
11. Ball, Pressure Relief (9.525 dia.)
12. Spring, Pressure Relief
13. Spring, 1-2 Accumulator
14. Bushing, 1-2 Accumulator
15. Valve, 1-2 Accumulator

16. Valve, 2-3 Shift
17. Valve, 2-3 Throttle
18. Spring, 2-3 Throttle Valve
19. Bushing, 2-3 Throttle Valve
20. Valve, 1-2 Shift
21. Valve, 1-2 Throttle
22. Spring, 1-2 Throttle Valve
23. Bushing, 1-2 Throttle Valve
24. Ball, Low Blow Off
25. Spring & Plug Assembly—Low Blow Off
26. Plug, Low Blow Off Valve
27. Bolt, Auxiliary V.B./Valve Body
28. Retainer, Valve Body Pipe
29. Bolt, Auxiliary Valve Body to Case
30. Cover, Auxiliary Valve Body

31. Gasket, Auxiliary Valve Body Cover
32. Valve, Converter Clutch Control
33. Solenoid Assembly
34. Bolt, Solenoid
35. Switch, Pressure
36. Plug, Orifice
37. Seal, "O" Ring
38. Switch, Gov. Pressure (Diesel Only)
39. Harness, Solenoid Wire
40. Plug, Valve Bore
41. Spring, Converter Clutch Regulator
42. Valve, Converter Clutch Regulator
43. Body, Auxiliary Valve
44. Sleeve, Auxiliary Valve Body
45. Pin, Slide Pivot
46. Ring, Oil Seal—Slide to Cover
47. Seal, "O" Ring (Slide)
48. Slide, Pump
49. Support, Pump Slide Seal
50. Seal, Pump Slide
51. Ring, Pump Vane
52. Vane, Pump
53. Rotor, Oil Pump
54. Bearing Assembly, Roller Pump Shaft
55. Spring, 3-2 Valve
56. Valve, 3-2 Control
57. Seal, Pump Shaft
58. Plug, Spring Retaining
59. Spring, Pump Priming
60. Bushing, T.V. Boost Valve
61. Valve, T.V. Boost
62. Bushing, Reverse Boost Valve
63. Valve, Reverse Boost
64. Spring, Pressure Regulator
65. Valve, Pressure Regulator
66. Bushing, T.V. Plunger
67. Plunger, Throttle Valve
68. Spring, Throttle Valve
69. Valve, Throttle

Valve body assembly—exploded view (©General Motors Corp.)

5. Remove the remaining control valve body retaining bolts.

6. Remove the control valve and oil pump assembly. Place it on a clean work bench with the machined surface up.

7. Remove the number one check ball from the spacer plate. Remove the oil pump shaft. Remove the spacer plate and the gaskets.

8. Remove the five check balls which are located in the transaxle case cover.

9. Check the input shaft to case cover end play for the proper selective snap ring thickness.

10. To do this, rotate the transaxle assembly so that the right axle end is up. Install tool J-26958-10 or equivalent into the right hand axle end. Install an output shaft loading tool and bracket to the right hand axle end. Adjust the loading tool by turning the handle in until the knob bottoms. This is the correct load.

11. Rotate the transaxle assembly so that the transaxle case cover is up. Install an an input shaft lifter tool into the input shaft bore. Secure by turning the handle. Install the dial indicator and the dial indicator post on the transaxle assembly. Place the dial indicator extension on the end play tool. Press down on the lifting tool and zero in the dial indicator.

12. Pull up on the end play tool and take the end play reading. The end play should be 0.10-0.84 mm (.004"-.033"). The selective snap ring controlling the end play is located on the input shaft. If the end play is not in the proper range, select the proper snap ring from the input shaft selective snap ring chart. Measure the thickness for positive identification.

INPUT SHAFT SELECTIVE SNAP RING CHART

Thickness (inches)	Identification
.071-.076	White
.078-.084	Blue
.088-.092	Brown
.095-.099	Yellow
.103-.107	Green

13. Disconnect the manual valve rod from the manual valve.

14. Remove the remaining transaxle case cover bolts.

15. Install two bolts about two inches long into the transaxle case cover dowel pin holes. These bolts will self tap, bottom out on the dowel pins and separate the transaxle case cover from the transaxle case. Do not pry the case cover from the case, as damage to the mating surfaces will result.

16. Remove the transaxle case cover. Place the case cover on the work bench with the 1-2 accumulator side up. The 1-2 accumulator pin may fall out.

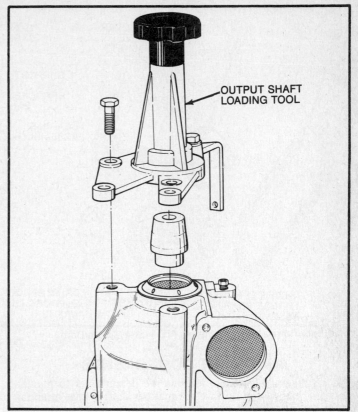

Output shaft loading tool installation (©General Motors Corp.)

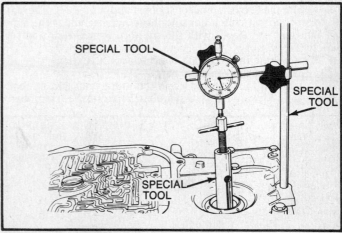

Checking input shaft to case cover end play (©General Motors Corp.)

NOTE: To remove the gasket, spray gasket remover on the transaxle case and case cover gasket surface. Use a plastic edged gasket scraper to avoid damaging the machined surfaces.

17. Remove the 1-2 accumulator spring and the center case to case cover gasket.

18. Remove the case cover to drive sprocket thrust washer and the driven sprocket thrust bearing assembly. The case cover to drive sprocket thrust washer may be on the case cover.

19. Remove the turbine shaft "O" ring.

20. Remove the drive sprocket, driven sprocket and link assembly.

21. Remove the drive and driven sprocket to support thrust washers. These thrust washers may have come off with the sprockets.

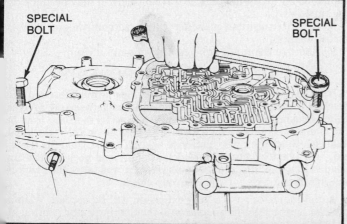

Transaxle case removal using special bolts (©General Motors Corp.)

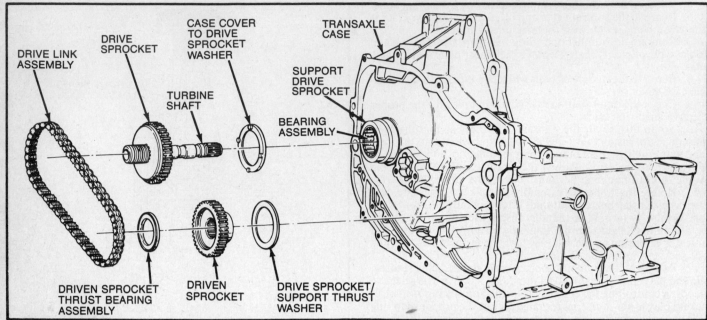

Drive link and related components (©General Motors Corp.)

INPUT UNIT COMPONENTS

1. Using a small punch, remove the detent lever to manual shaft pin. Locate and remove the manual shaft to case retaining pin by prying up on it with a suitable tool.

2. Remove the detent lever, manual shaft, and parking lock rod.

3. Locate the driven sprocket support and remove it. There is a support-to-direct clutch housing thrust washer under the support that may come out with the support. Remove it, and set aside for inspection.

4. Remove the intermediate band anchor hole plug.

5. Remove the intermediate band.

6. Reach into the case and grasp the input shaft and remove the direct and forward clutch assemblies. Separate the assemblies.

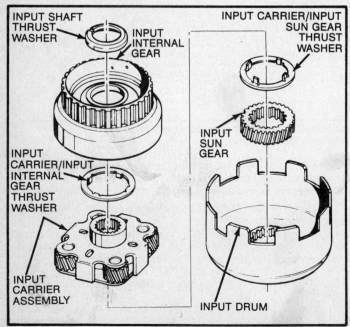

Input unit—exploded view (©General Motors Corp.)

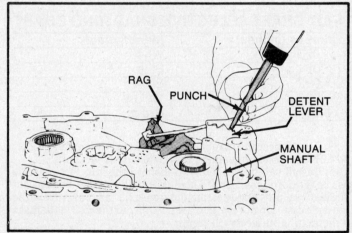

Retaining pin removal (©General Motors Corp.)

7. Remove the input internal gear and the thrust washer that should be on top of the gear. If it is not there, it may be stuck on the input shaft.

8. Remove the input planetary carrier assembly along with its thrust washers.

9. Remove the input sun gear and the input drum.

REACTION UNIT COMPONENTS

NOTE: There are selective fit snap rings located between the reaction sun gear and the input drum and also between the reverse clutch housing and the low roller clutch. Special tools are used in the factory procedure which involves a preload on the right hand axle end. Since the right hand axle was taken out when the transaxle was removed from the vehicle, the preload goes against an adapter plug that fits into the transaxle case and takes the place of the right hand axle for the end play check.

A dial indicator with a long extension will be needed. With a preload on the right-hand axle end, the dial indicator is brought to bear on the reaction sub gear, between the ends of the snap ring. Press down on the sun gear to make sure that it is seated, and

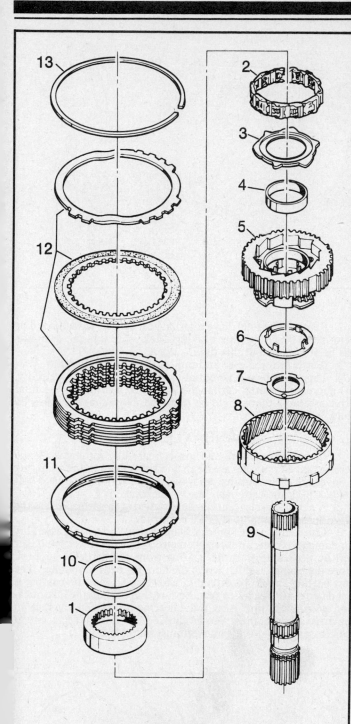

1. Race, Low Roller Clutch
2. Roller Assembly, Low Clutch
3. Washer, Reaction Carr./Int. Gr. Thrust
4. Bushing, Reaction Carrier
5. Carrier Assembly, Reaction
6. Washer, Reaction Carr./Int. Gr. Thrust
7. Bearing, Reaction Sun/Int. Gr. Thrust
8. Gear, Reaction Internal
9. Shaft, Final Drive Sun Gear
10. Spacer, Reverse Housing/Low Race Selective
11. Plate, Low & Reverse Clutch Backing
12. Plate, Low & Reverse Clutch
13. Snap Ring

Reaction Components—exploded view (©General Motors Corp.)

zero the indicator. Rotate the selective fit snap ring under the indicator and read the reaction sun gear to input drum play. It should be from 0.013 to −0.005". If more or less snap ring thickness is required, select one that will bring the clearance into specification. They are available from the factory in sizes from 0.089-0.093" up to 0.136-0.140" in increments of 0.004".

REACTION GEAR TO INPUT DRUM SELECTIVE SNAP RING CHART

Thickness (Inches)	Identification
.089-.093	Pink
.096-.100	Brown
.103-.107	Light Blue
.109-.113	White
.116-.120	Yellow
.123-.127	Light Green
.129-,133	Orange
.136-.140	No Color

In a similar manner, the reverse clutch housing to the Low roller clutch selective fit snap ring should be checked. A preload on the output shaft (right hand axle end) is again used and the dial indicator is set up as before, and zeroed. Place a suitable tool through the opening in the case next to the parking pawl and lift the reaction internal gear to check the low and reverse selective end play. The end play should be 0.003-0.046". If more or less selective washer clearance is required, select one that will bring the clearance into specification. They are available from the factory in sizes from 0.039-0.043" to 0.122-0.126" in increments of 0.004".

REVERSE CLUTCH HOUSING TO LOW RACE SELECTIVE WASHER CHART

Thickness (Inches)	Identification
.039-.043	One
.056-.060	Two
.072-.076	Three
.089-.093	Four
.105-.109	Five
.122-.126	Six

To continue with the disassembly of the reaction unit parts, proceed as follows:
1. Remove the reaction sun gear.
2. Locate and remove the low and reverse clutch housing-to-case snap ring, which is 0.092" thick.
3. Remove the low and reverse clutch housing.
4. Remove the low and reverse clutch housing-to-case spacer ring which is 0.042" thick.
5. Reach into the case and grasp the final drive sun gear shaft and pull out the reaction gear set.
6. Separate the parts by removing the roller clutch and reaction carrier assembly from off the final drive sun gear shaft.
7. Remove the four-tanged thrust washer from the end of the reaction carrier (or the inside of the internal gear if it has stuck there).
8. Remove the low and reverse clutch plates, taking note of their number and order.

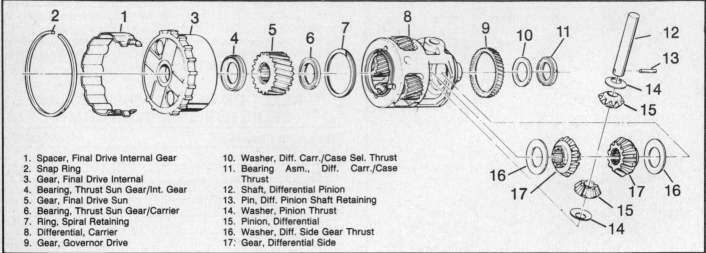

1. Spacer, Final Drive Internal Gear
2. Snap Ring
3. Gear, Final Drive Internal
4. Bearing, Thrust Sun Gear/Int. Gear
5. Gear, Final Drive Sun
6. Bearing, Thrust Sun Gear/Carrier
7. Ring, Spiral Retaining
8. Differential, Carrier
9. Gear, Governor Drive
10. Washer, Diff. Carr./Case Sel. Thrust
11. Bearing Asm., Diff. Carr./Case Thrust
12. Shaft, Differential Pinion
13. Pin, Diff. Pinion Shaft Retaining
14. Washer, Pinion Thrust
15. Pinion, Differential
16. Washer, Diff. Side Gear Thrust
17. Gear, Differential Side

Final drive—exploded view (©General Motors Corp.)

9. Remove the internal gear to sun gear thrust bearing from the reaction gear, and remove the internal gear from the final drive sun gear.

FINAL DRIVE COMPONENTS

The end play of the final drive to case should be checked before further disassembly. Again mount the dial indicator to the transaxle by first rotating the transaxle in the holding fixture so that the right-hand axle opening is facing up. No preload is needed for this check. Position the indicator to bear on the axle shaft and push down on the shaft before setting the indicator to zero. Using a suitable tool, position it in the governor bore and lift on the governor drive gear to read the final drive to case end play. The end play should be from 0.005-0.032″.

The selective fit washer that controls this end play is located between the differential carrier and the differential carrier case thrust bearing assembly. If the washer needs to be changed to bring the end play reading within the specifications, they are available in sizes from 0.055-0.59″ to 0.091-0.095″ in increments of 0.004″. After checking the end play, proceed as follows:

FINAL DRIVE TO CASE SELECTIVE WASHER CHART

Thickness (Inches)	Identification
.055-.059	Zero
.059-.062	One
.062-.066	Two
.066-.070	Three
.070-.074	Four
.074-.078	Five
.078-.082	Six
.082-.086	Seven
.086-.091	Eight
.091-.095	Nine

1. Rotate the transaxle so that the case cover side up as before and locate and remove the final drive internal gear spacer snap ring, which is 0.092″ thick.

2. Remove the final drive internal gear spacer. Do not bend or deform the spacer when removing. Make sure that the governor has been removed at this time.
3. Reach into the case and pull out the final drive unit.
4. There will be a differential-to-case thrust washer (selective fit) and a differential carrier-to-case roller bearing on the final drive assembly that should be removed. Note that they may be stuck in the case.

TRANSAXLE CASE

1. Clean the case well and inspect carefully for cracks. Make certain that all passages are clean and that all bores and snap ring grooves are clean and free from damage. Check for stripped bolt holes. Check the case bushings for damage.
2. A new converter seal can be installed at this time, unless the drive sprocket support is to be removed.
3. Check the drive sprocket support roller bearing assembly for damage. If it requires replacement, a slide hammer type puller will be needed to pull the bearing from the sprocket support. Once the bearing is out, inspect the bore for wear or damage. The new bearing should be driven in with care so that the bearing is not damaged and is in straight. Be sure that the bearing identification is installed "up." Also, if the bearing is replaced, the race on the drive sprocket must also be checked carefully. If replacement is necessary, the drive sprocket must be replaced.

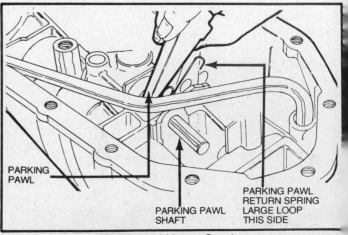

PARKING PAWL
PARKING PAWL SHAFT
PARKING PAWL RETURN SPRING LARGE LOOP THIS SIDE

Parking pawl removal (©General Motors Corp.)

4. If it proves necessary to remove the drive sprocket, rotate the transaxle so that the right-hand axle side is up. The converter seal must be removed. When removing the retaining bolts place one hand under the support. To reinstall the support, use a hardening type compound on the bolt threads and torque to 18 footpounds. Renew the converter seal.

5. If the parking pawl and related parts are to be removed, begin by turning the transaxle to the oil pan side up. Use a punch to remove the cup plug. Remove the parking pawl shaft retainer, then the shaft, pawl and return spring. Check the pawl carefully for cracks.

6. If it is necessary to remove the governor oil pipe, note that the pipe is held firmly in place with Loctite® and may require a great amount of force to remove. A large pry bar may be used to remove the pipe from its mounting in the transaxle case. Use Loctite® or equivalent on both ends of the pipe when reinstalling.

7. If the manual shaft oil seal is to be replaced, pry out the old seal and drive in the new seal at this time. Be sure that the seal is installed with the lip up.

8. Check the axle seal for damage. Replace as required.

Component Disassembly and Assembly

DIFFERENTIAL AND FINAL DRIVE

1. Remove the final drive internal gear from the differential carrier and also the thrust bearing from between the internal gear and the sun gear.

2. Remove the final drive sun gear and also the thrust bearing from between the sun gear and differential carrier.

3. Examine the governor drive gear. It is not necessary to remove it unless it is to be replaced. If removal is necessary, a gear puller will be required and a soft hammer will be needed to drive the gear back on.

4. Inspect the differential side gears and pinions for excessive wear or damage. If the differential side gears are to be replaced, a lock pin that is installed through the pinion shaft will have to be removed.

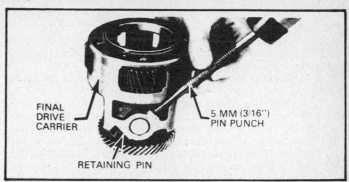

Differential shaft retaining pin removal (©General Motors Corp.)

NOTE: This pin can only be removed one way. A 3/16″ pin punch can be used to drive out the pin. Drive from the carrier side to the governor gear side. When reinstalling the pin, turn the carrier assembly over and drive the pin in from the governor gear side.

5. With the lock pin removed, the pinion shaft can be removed, along with the pinion gears and thrust washers. Do this by rotating the gears until they are in the access "window" in the carrier where they can be removed. If any pinion does not have a thrust washer with it, then it has fallen off and needs to be removed from the carrier.

6. Remove the differential side gears. The gears should slide out. Be sure that the thrust washers are also removed with the differential side gears.

7. Carefully examine the pinion gears and the differential side gears along with their thrust washers. Look for excessive wear or scoring. If it is determined that all parts are useable, begin assembly by coating the thrust washers with petroleum jelly and install the differential gears and their thrust washers into the case. Coat the pinion gear thrust washers in the same way and install them on their gears and then carefully install the pinion gears through each "window."

8. Align the pinion gears by sliding the pinion shaft through the gears. With the gears in line, remove the pinion shaft. Rotate the pinions to seat them in place and insall the pinion shaft.

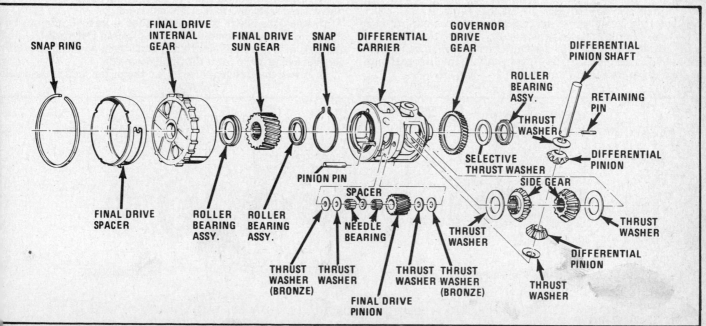

Differential and final drive assembly (©General Motors Corp.)

9. Install the "one way" lock pin by inserting it from the governor gear side and driving it into place with a ⅜" drift pin.

10. Final drive pinion end play should be checked at this time. The end play should be from .009 to .025 inch. If pinions must be removed, do the following.

    a. Locate and remove the snap ring which retains the pinion pins.

    b. Remove the pinion pins.

    c. Remove the final drive pinions. Caution should be used since each pinion and thrust washer assembly contains 36 needle bearings. Try to hold the pinion and thrust washer assembly from the ends to prevent dropping the needle bearings. There are four of these pinion assemblies.

    d. The pinion assemblies should be cleaned and the rollers carefully examined. Check the pinion for wear or damaged teeth. Make sure that the spacer between the two rows of roller bearings and the thrust washers is not scored or damaged.

11. Reassemble the final drive pinions and their related pieces by installing a thrust washer on a pinion pin. Retain it with petroleum jelly.

12. Apply a thin coat of petroleum jelly on the pin and carefully lay 18 needle rollers on the pinion shaft.

13. Install the needle spacer on the shaft again, with petroleum jelly to hold it in place. Carefully lay 18 more rollers on the shaft using the petroleum jelly as necessary to retain these parts. Add the other thrust washer.

14. Carefully insert the pinion shaft and its rollers into the pinion. Install a bronze thrust washer on both ends of the pinion, on top of the steel thrust washers.

15. Carefully pull out the pinion shaft.

16. Install the pinion assembly into the carrier and, hold the pinion from the end, so that all the pieces will stay together.

17. As each pinion assembly is installed, carefully install the pinion shaft, stepped end last. Align the step so that the step is on the outside.

18. Repeat the installation procedure for the remaining pinions and then install the snap ring.

19. Inspect the final drive sun gear to carrier case thrust bearing. If it is reusable, install it with the outer race against the carrier.

20. Inspect the sun gear, especially around the splines and gear teeth for excessive wear or damage. It is installed with the step side up.

21. Install the internal gear to sun gear thrust washer roller bearing into the final drive internal gear, with the cupped race side on the internal gear. Use petroleum jelly to retain it.

22. Carefully turn the final drive internal gear over, being careful not to disturb the thrust bearing. Install the internal gear onto the final drive carrier.

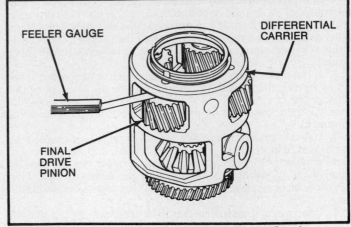

Differential pinion end play check (©General Motors Corp.)

23. Inspect the differential selective thrust washer for scored, rough or pitted surfaces. Also check the differential roller bearing thrust washer for damage. If these parts are serviceable, install first the selective washer, and then the thrust bearing assembly, with the inner race against the selective thrust washer.

FORWARD CLUTCH

1. Position the forward clutch assembly so that it is situated with the input shaft facing down. Remove the clutch pack snap ring.

2. Remove the backing plate, the clutch plates, and then compress the spring pack to remove the snap ring. Remove the retainer and spring assembly.

3. Remove the piston and discard the seals.

4. Clean all parts and check for damage or excessive wear. Make sure that the check ball is free and not sticking in its capsule. Check the piston for burrs or cracks and the housing for damaged snap ring grooves.

5. Inspect the input shaft splines and journals for damage. Check the shaft sleeve. The sleeve must not turn. The slot in the sleeve must be aligned with the hole in the input shaft.

6. Inspect the Teflon seals on the shaft for damage. Do not remove these seals unless they are damaged.

7. Allow the clutch plates to soak for at least 20 minutes before using them in assembly. Soak the plates in Dexron® II. Lube the seals with petroleum jelly and install them on the piston with the lips facing away from the apply ring side.

8. Install the clutch apply ring on the piston, and then install

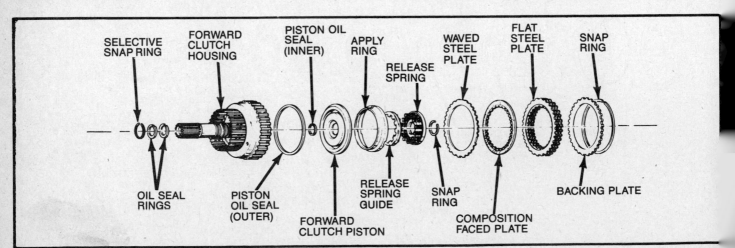

Forward clutch assembly—exploded view (©General Motors Corp.)

the piston into the forward clutch housing. Use care and plenty of lubricant to protect the seals.

9. Install the spring guide and then the spring and spring retainer. Compress the assembly and install the snap ring.

10. Install the clutch plates starting with a waved steel plate, then a friction plate, and alternate with steel plates until the clutch pack is installed. Install the backing plate with the flat side "up."

11. Install the snap ring and make certain that the friction plates turn freely.

12. Inspect the input shaft to driven sprocket snap ring for wear. Do not remove this snap ring unless replacement is necessary, as this is a selective fit snap ring.

DIRECT CLUTCH

1. Remove the large outer snap ring from the direct clutch housing. Remove the backing plate and clutch plates.

2. Remove the snap ring that holds the apply ring and the release spring assembly. Remove the two components.

3. Remove the direct clutch piston. Discard the seals. Remove the center seal from the housing.

4. Clean all parts and check for damage or excessive wear. Make sure that the check ball is free and not sticking in its capsule. Check the piston for burrs or cracks and the housing for damaged snap rings.

5. Allow the clutch plates to soak for at least 20 minutes before using them in assembly. Soak the plates in Dexron® II. Lube the seals with petroleum jelly and install them on the piston with the lips facing away from the clutch apply ring side.

6. Install the center seal on the housing with the lip facing "up."

7. Coat the seals with petroleum jelly and slide the piston into the housing. Be very careful since the sharp snap ring grooves could damage the seals.

8. An installation tool can be made from wire to ease the installation process. Once the piston is in place, rotate the piston to help seat the seals.

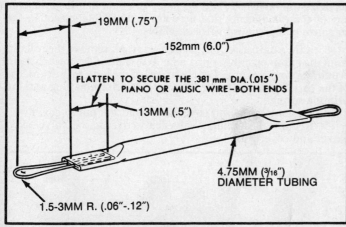

Piston installation tool (©General Motors Corp.)

19MM (.75")
152mm (6.0")
FLATTEN TO SECURE THE .381 mm DIA.(.015") PIANO OR MUSIC WIRE–BOTH ENDS
13MM (.5")
4.75MM (³/₁₆") DIAMETER TUBING
1.5-3MM R. (.06"-.12")

9. Install the apply ring, retainer and springs and the snap ring.

10. Install the clutch plates, starting with the steel plate and alternating with the friction plates until they are all in place.

11. Install the backing plate making sure that the flat side is "up." Install the snap ring.

CONTROL VALVE AND PUMP ASSEMBLY

NOTE: As each part of the valve train is removed, place the pieces in order and in a position that is relative to the position on

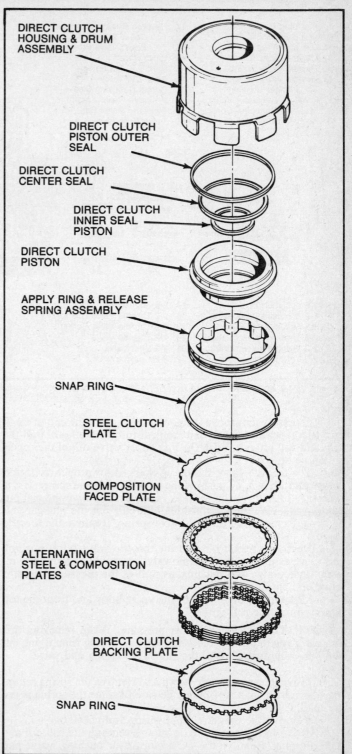

DIRECT CLUTCH HOUSING & DRUM ASSEMBLY

DIRECT CLUTCH PISTON OUTER SEAL

DIRECT CLUTCH CENTER SEAL

DIRECT CLUTCH INNER SEAL PISTON

DIRECT CLUTCH PISTON

APPLY RING & RELEASE SPRING ASSEMBLY

SNAP RING

STEEL CLUTCH PLATE

COMPOSITION FACED PLATE

ALTERNATING STEEL & COMPOSITION PLATES

DIRECT CLUTCH BACKING PLATE

SNAP RING

Front direct clutch—exploded view (©General Motors Corp.)

the valve body to lessen chances for error in assembly. None of the valves, springs or bushings are interchangeable.

1. Remove the roll pins by pushing through from the rough casting side of the control valve body, except, of course, the blind hole roll pins.

2. Lay the valve body on a clean work bench with the machined side up and the line boost valve at the top. The line boost valve should be checked for proper operation before removing it.

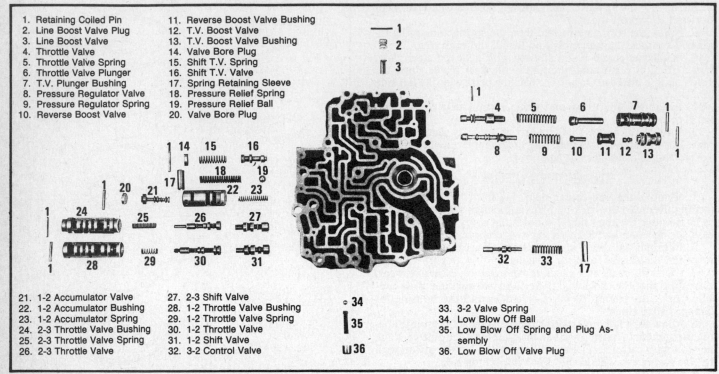

1. Retaining Coiled Pin
2. Line Boost Valve Plug
3. Line Boost Valve
4. Throttle Valve
5. Throttle Valve Spring
6. Throttle Valve Plunger
7. T.V. Plunger Bushing
8. Pressure Regulator Valve
9. Pressure Regulator Spring
10. Reverse Boost Valve
11. Reverse Boost Valve Bushing
12. T.V. Boost Valve
13. T.V. Boost Valve Bushing
14. Valve Bore Plug
15. Shift T.V. Spring
16. Shift T.V. Valve
17. Spring Retaining Sleeve
18. Pressure Relief Spring
19. Pressure Relief Ball
20. Valve Bore Plug

21. 1-2 Accumulator Valve
22. 1-2 Accumulator Bushing
23. 1-2 Accumulator Spring
24. 2-3 Throttle Valve Bushing
25. 2-3 Throttle Valve Spring
26. 2-3 Throttle Valve
27. 2-3 Shift Valve
28. 1-2 Throttle Valve Bushing
29. 1-2 Throttle Valve Spring
30. 1-2 Throttle Valve
31. 1-2 Shift Valve
32. 3-2 Control Valve
33. 3-2 Valve Spring
34. Low Blow Off Ball
35. Low Blow Off Spring and Plug Assembly
36. Low Blow Off Valve Plug

Control valve body and related components (©General Motors Corp.)

If it is necessary to remove the boost valve, grind the end of a #49 drill to a taper and lightly tap the drill into the roll pin. Pull the drill and roll pin out. Push the line boost valve out of the top of the valve body.

3. The throttle valve should be checked for proper operation before removing it, by pushing the valve against the spring. If it is necessary to remove the throttle valve, first remove the roll pin holding the T.V. plunger bushing and pull out the plunger and bushing. Remove the throttle valve spring. Remove the throttle valve.

4. Remove the roll pin and the throttle valve boost bushing and valve assembly. In the same valve train will be found the reverse boost valve and bushing, as well as the pressure regulator valve and spring.

5. Move to the other side of the valve body and from the top bore, remove the roll pin.

NOTE: This roll pin is under pressure. When removing this pin, use a rag to prevent the bore plug and spring from flying out and becoming lost. This is the shift T.V. spring and valve.

6. Move to the next bore down and remove the spring retaining sleeve with snap ring pliers. Be careful since the spring is under load.

7. Remove the pressure relief spring and check ball.

8. Move to the next bore down and remove the roll pin and the bore plug. Remove the 1-2 accumulator bushing, valve and spring.

9. At the next bore down, remove the roll pin and 2-3 throttle valve. Behind the 2-3 throttle valve will be the 2-3 shift valve.

10. At the next bore down, remove the roll pin and 1-2 throttle bushing, valve and spring. Behind the valve will be the 1-2 shift valve which is also removed.

11. At the opposite side of the valve body there is a spring retaining sleeve that holds the 3-2 control valve and spring. This sleeve is under load. Cover the open end of the bore when removing the sleeve to prevent loss of the spring. Remove the 3-2 control valve and the spring.

12. Use a ¼" punch to remove the low blowoff valve plug. Remove the valve spring, spring plug and ball.

NOTE: The low blowoff assembly must be removed and replaced if the control valve pump body is washed in solvent. These are some of the few parts that are serviced separately in the valve body. The technician should, therefore, use great caution when servicing the valve body and the pump so as not to lose or damage any of the components that may not be available except in the complete pump/control valve assembly.

13. If the pump assembly is to be serviced, remove the roll pin from the pump priming spring bore. Use caution because this pin is under spring pressure. Cover the end of the bore to prevent loss of the parts inside. Remove the priming spring cup plug and the priming spring.

14. Remove the pump cover screw and the pump cover.

15. Remove the auxiliary valve body cover screw, valve body, gasket and cover.

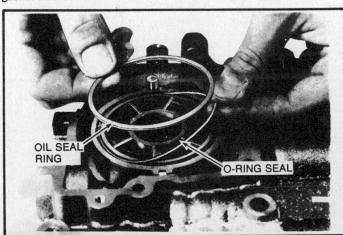

Oil seal and O-ring installation (©General Motors Corp.)

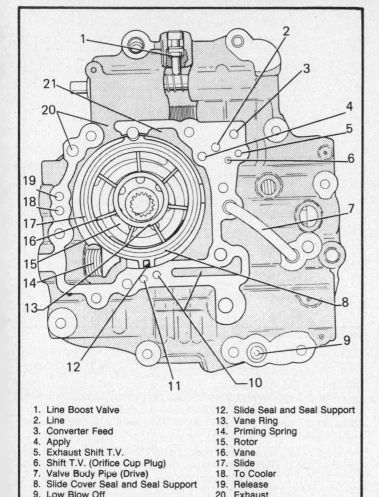

Variable capacity vane oil pump (©General Motors Corp.)

1. Line Boost Valve
2. Line
3. Converter Feed
4. Apply
5. Exhaust Shift T.V.
6. Shift T.V. (Orifice Cup Plug)
7. Valve Body Pipe (Drive)
8. Slide Cover Seal and Seal Support
9. Low Blow Off
10. Governor
11. Third Clutch
12. Slide Seal and Seal Support
13. Vane Ring
14. Priming Spring
15. Rotor
16. Vane
17. Slide
18. To Cooler
19. Release
20. Exhaust
21. Decrease

16. Remove the pump slide, rotor, the seven vanes and the two vane seal rings.

17. Clean all pump components as foreign matter in the pump can cause damage and be circulated to other transaxle components. Pump seals should not be washed in solvent.

18. If the pump shaft bearing is to be replaced, drive it out toward the pump pocket. The new bearing would then be driven in from the pump pocket side.

19. Install until the bearing cup is .017-.005 inch below the pump pocket face. Inspect all parts for wear or damage.

20. Turn the valve assembly so that the pump pocket side is up.

21. Install the pump slide and the pump slide seal support into the pocket. Install the pump slide seal. Retain with petroleum jelly. Make sure that the seal is located properly.

22. Position the pump slide with the pump slide pivot hole. Install the pump slide pivot pin.

23. Install a vane ring in the pocket and then the rotor. Install the seven vanes into the pump and make sure that each vane is seated flush with the rotor. Install the top vane ring.

24. Lube and install the O-ring into the pump slide. Over the O-ring, install the oil seal ring.

25. Check the auxiliary valve body sleeve for damage. Install the auxiliary valve body, gasket and cover.

26. Align the pump rotor step with the auxiliary valve body

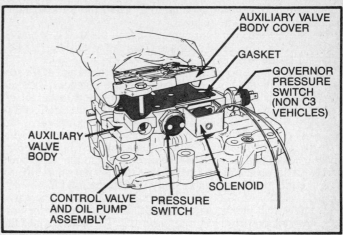

Auxiliary valve body cover alignment (©General Motors Corp.)

sleeve. Install and torque the auxiliary valve body screw to 9 foot pounds.

27. Install the pump primary spring and cup plug, flat side out. Compress the cup plug and install the roll pin.

28. Position the control valve and pump assembly so that the machined side is up and the pump pocket is on the right-hand side. All parts must be clean before assembly.

29. Starting at the lower right-hand side, install the 3-2 control valve, large end first, the spring and the spring retainer. Make sure that the retainer is level with or below the machined surface.

30. Move to the opposite side to the lower left-hand bore, and install the 1-2 shift valve large end first. Place the 1-2 T.V. spring in the 1-2 T.V. bushing and install the 1-2 T.V. valve and bushing assembly into the bore, making sure that the pin slot is aligned with the pin hole in the valve body. Install the roll pin.

31. Still on the left-hand side, move to the next bore up and install the 2-3 shift valve, large end first. Install the 2-3 T.V. spring into the bushing and install the 2-3 T.V. valve into the bushing with the larger end toward the valve body and insert the assembly into the bore. Make sure that the pin slot is aligned with the pin hole in the valve body. Install the roll pin.

32. Move to the next bore up and install the 1-2 accumulator spring. Install the 1-2 accumulator valve into the bushing, small end first. Install the bore plug with the flat side first. Install the assembly into the bore. Make sure that the pin slot is aligned with the pin hole in the valve body. Push in on the plug and install the roll pin.

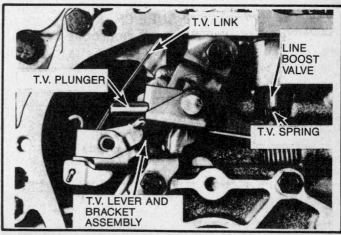

Throttle lever and bracket assembly installation (©General Motors Corp.)

33. Move to the next bore up and install the pressure relief ball, the spring and the retainer.

34. Move to the next bore up and install the shift T.V. valve, small end first. Install the spring and bore plug with the flat side first and install the roll pin.

35. Move to the opposite side of the valve body and at the second bore from the top, install the pressure regulator with the small end to the outside, and follow with the spring. Install the reverse boost valve into the bushing and see that the small end is toward the outside of the valve body. Insert the boost valve and bushing assembly into the bore with the open end first. Now install the T.V. boost valve, small (stem) end first into the T.V. boost bushing and then install the assembly into the valve body bore with the open end first. Make sure that the pin slot is aligned with the pin hole in the valve body. Install the roll pin.

36. Move to the top bore on the right-hand side of the valve body and install the throttle valve with the stem end to the outside, and follow with the spring. Insert the T.V. plunger into the T.V. bushing, small end first. Install the T.V. plunger assembly into the bore with the open end first. Make sure that the pin slot that is in the T.V. plunger bushing is aligned with the pin hole in the valve body. Install the roll pin for the bushing, as well as the roll pin that belongs in the throttle valve pin hole.

37. At the top of the valve body, install the line boost valve with the stem end first into the bore. Install the bore plug with the ring end first, and insert the roll pin. Make certain that the line boost valve moves freely.

38. Install the low blowoff ball in the lower right-hand corner of the rough casting side of the valve body. Assemble the blowoff spring and the spring plug. Install the spring and plug assembly with the plug end first, and then install the outer plug with the cupped end first, using a plastic hammer until it seats in its bore.

Transaxle Assembly

1. If the parking pawl or its shaft has been removed, inspect the pawl for cracks before installing it. Place the return spring on the pawl and place into the case. Slide the shaft through the case into the pawl and check for free movement of the pawl. Install the parking pawl shaft retainer clip. With a ⅜" rod, install the shaft cup plug.

2. If the governor pipe had been removed, coat both ends with Loctite® or its equivalent and install. Install the governor pipe retainer strap and its bolt.

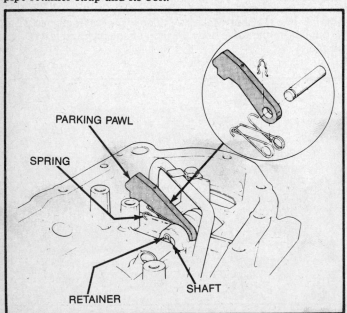

Parking pawl and related components (©General Motors Corp.)

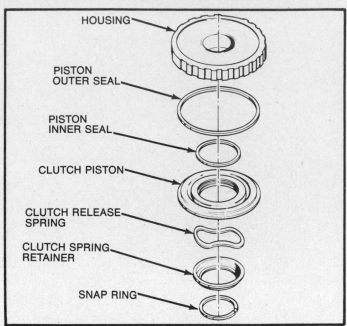

Low/reverse clutch—exploded view (©General Motors Corp.)

3. Reinstall the cup plug if so equipped.

4. The manual shaft seal and the axle seal should be checked and replaced as required.

6. Install the differential and final drive unit. Carefully lower the final drive unit into the transaxle case. Install the final drive internal gear spacer with the cupped side against the final drive internal gear.

NOTE: The spacer has an opening for the parking pawl. Make sure that the parking pawl passes through the spacer freely.

7. Install the final drive spacer snap ring into the case. Install the snap ring in such a way that the snap ring opening is away from the spacer ring gap. The snap ring is .092 inch thick.

8. Install the reaction gear set. Turn the transaxle case so that the case cover side is up.

9. Inspect the final drive sun gear shaft and journals for damage or wear. If the sun gear shaft and its reaction internal gear are usable, install the internal gear on the sun gear shaft.

10. Install the internal gear to sun gear roller thrust bearing so that the inner race goes against the internal gear.

11. The low roller clutch should be disassembled if necessary to inspect the rollers and also to check the planetary pinions for end play. To do this follow these steps:

a. Remove the Reverse clutch-to-low race selective washer. Remove the low roller clutch race and then the clutch cage assembly.

b. Remove the thrust washer that will be found in the reaction carrier. Inspect for excessive wear.

c. Check the planetary pinion end play with feeler gauges. End play should be 0.009"-0.027".

d. If any of the clutch rollers have come out of the cage, install them by compressing the spring and inserting the roller from the outside. Install the clutch cage assembly into the reaction carrier.

e. Install the roller clutch inner race with the splined side up. It may have to be rotated clockwise to allow it to drop in.

f. Install the four-tanged internal gear thrust washer, using petroleum jelly to hold it in place.

g. Assemble the reaction carrier and clutch assembly onto the internal gear.

12. With the low roller clutch assembled the next item to be installed is the low/reverse clutch housing-to-roller clutch selective washer.

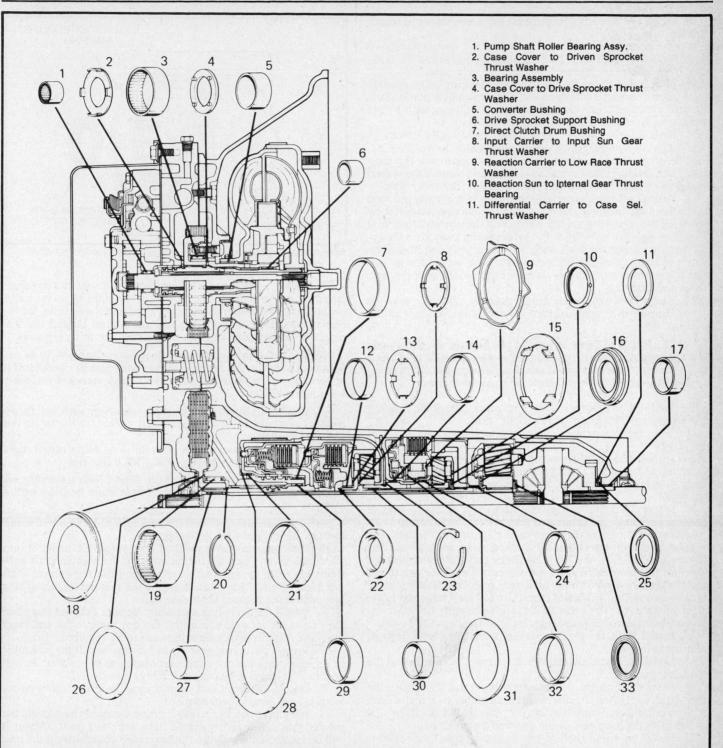

1. Pump Shaft Roller Bearing Assy.
2. Case Cover to Driven Sprocket Thrust Washer
3. Bearing Assembly
4. Case Cover to Drive Sprocket Thrust Washer
5. Converter Bushing
6. Drive Sprocket Support Bushing
7. Direct Clutch Drum Bushing
8. Input Carrier to Input Sun Gear Thrust Washer
9. Reaction Carrier to Low Race Thrust Washer
10. Reaction Sun to Internal Gear Thrust Bearing
11. Differential Carrier to Case Sel. Thrust Washer

12. Input Internal Gear Bushing
13. Input Carrier to Input Int. Gear Thrust Washer
14. Low and Reverse Clutch Housing Bushing
15. Reaction Carrier to Int. Gear Thrust Washer
16. Sun Gear to Internal Gear Thrust Bearing
17. Case Bushing

18. Driven Sprocket Thrust Bearing Assembly
19. Bearing Assembly
20. Selective Snap Ring
21. Direct Clutch Bushing
22. Input Shaft Thrust Washer
23. Selective Snap Ring
24. Final Drive Internal Gear Bushing
25. Differential Carrier to Case Thrust Brg. Assy.

26. Driven Sprocket Support Thrust Washer
27. Input Shaft Bushing
28. Thrust Washer
29. Driven Sprocket Support Bushing
30. Reaction Sun Gear Bushing
31. Reverse Housing to Low Race Selective Washer
32. Reaction Carrier Bushing
33. Sun Gear to Carrier Thrust Bearing

Thrust washer and bushing locations (©General Motors Corp.)

13. Grasp the assembly by the final drive sun shaft and install into the case.

14. The components making up the low and reverse clutch are assembled next. Inspect the backing plate for cracks and if it is usable, install into the case with the stepped side down.

15. New clutch plates should have been soaking in Dexron® II for at least 20 minutes before installation. Install the plates starting with a friction (composition) plate and following with a steel plate until the clutch pack has been installed.

16. Install the low and reverse spacer ring (0.0042" thick).

17. The low/reverse clutch piston seals should be replaced. Begin by compressing the spring retainer and removing the snap ring. Then disassemble the spring retainer and remove the waved spring and piston. Discard the seals. Remove the apply ring.

18. Inspect all parts especially the housing for a plugged feed hole. Check the bushing and the piston for damage. Assemble by installing the apply ring on the piston and then by installing new seals. The seals are installed with the lips facing away from the apply ring side. Lube the seals with petroleum jelly and install the piston carefully into the housing. Install the waved spring and then the retainer, cupped side down. Compress the assembly and install the snap ring.

19. Lower the low/reverse clutch assembly into the case. Be sure to line up the clutch oil feed hole with the feed hole in the case.

NOTE: If it is difficult to get the low/reverse clutch housing past the snap ring groove, install the reaction sun gear to use as a tool. Rotate the sun gear while pushing down on the clutch housing until the housing drops below the snap ring groove.

20. With the low/reverse clutch in place, install the housing case snap ring. This snap ring is 0.092" thick.

21. With the reaction sun gear in place, install the selective snap ring.

22. Inspect the input drum for damage. Note that there is an angle on the roll pins. This is normal and no attempt should be made to straighten them. Install the input drum on the reaction sun gear.

23. Inspect the input sun gear for damage or excessive wear. If it is usable, install the input sun gear into the input drum.

24. Inspect the input planetary carrier for wear or damage. The end play of the pinions should be checked with a feeler gauge. End play should be 0.009"-0.027". Also check that the pinion pins are tight and that the pinion gears rotate freely. Check the two thrust washers that are used with the planetary gear. One is the input internal gear-to-input planetary carrier (it has four tangs and is the larger of the two). The other is the input planetary carrier-to-input sun gear (also has four tangs, but the smaller of the two).

25. Install both the thrust washers using petroleum jelly to hold them in place.

26. Install the input planetary carrier into the case. Install the input internal gear.

27. Place the forward clutch assembly on the bench with the input shaft up. Install the direct clutch assembly over it and onto the forward clutch. When they are properly seated, it will be $1^7/_{32}$ inches from the tang end of the forward clutch drum.

28. Install the input shaft-to-input internal gear thrust washer with the rounded side against the input shaft, and the stepped side facing out. Petroleum jelly will hold it in place.

29. Install the direct and forward clutch assemblies into the case. It may prove helpful to rotate the unit when installing rather than pushing down on the unit. To make sure that the assembly is properly installed, measure with a steel rule from the case face to the direct clutch housing. It should be approximately $1^{11}/_{16}$" (42mm).

30. Install the intermediate band. Make sure that the eye end is located in the case and that the lug end is aligned with the apply pin bore, otherwise the band will not operate.

31. Install the band anchor hole plug.

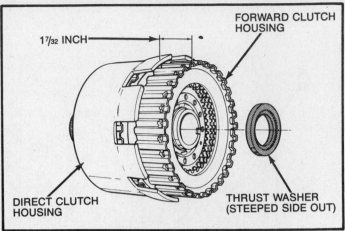

Assembled height of clutch assemblies (©General Motors Corp.)

32. Inspect the driven sprocket support for wear and pay close attention to the support sleeve. It must be tight in its bore and aligned with the holes in the support. Inspect the bushing for excessive wear as well as the bearing assemblies. Inspect the seal rings but do not remove them unless they are to be replaced.

NOTE: If the driven sprocket bearing assembly is to be replaced, the race on the driven sprocket must also be checked. If it is necessary to replace the race, the driven sprocket assembly must be replaced.

33. Install the direct clutch drum-to-driven sprocket thrust washer with plenty of lubricant and then install the driven sprocket support.

34. Inspect the manual shaft parts for wear. Slight raised edges on the detent lever can be removed with a fine file.

NOTE: The manual shaft and the detent lever assembly are made as a matched set. Any replacement must be done with a matched set.

Install the manual shaft and the park lock rod into the case and through the driven sprocket support.

35. If the manual valve rod had been removed, install it into the detent lever. Place the detent lever on the manual shaft hub-side away from the sprocket support and push the manual shaft into place. With a small punch, install the manual shaft retaining pin. Install the manual shaft case nail.

36. Install the drive link assembly. Be sure that the gears and their parts are in good condition. Do not remove the seal rings from the turbine shaft unless they are to be replaced.

37. Inspect the driven gear thrust bearing race. If the race must be replaced, then the drive sprocket must also be replaced, as well as the drive support bearing assembly.

38. Install the drive and driven thrust washers using petroleum jelly to retain them in place.

39. Install the sprockets into the link assembly and locate the colored guide link which should have numbers on it, so that it will be assembled facing the transaxle case cover. Install the unit into the transaxle case.

40. Install the roller bearing thrust washer on the driven sprocket with the outer race against the sprocket.

41. Inspect the case cover for cracks or any damage. Check the bolt holes for damaged threads and see that the vent assembly is not damaged. If the vent must be replaced, use Loctite® or its equivalent on the replacement vent and tap into place with a plastic hammer. Coolant line connectors need not be removed unless they are to be replaced. Coat the threads of any replacement connector with thread sealer.

42. Install the manual detent spring and roller assembly and torque the retaining screw to 8 foot-pounds.

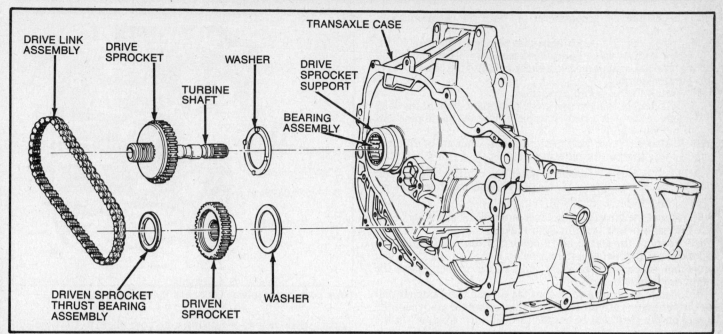

Drive link assembly and related components (©General Motors Corp.)

43. Inspect the axle oil seal and replace if necessary.

44. Inspect the case cover sleeve. Make sure that the hole in the sleeve aligns with the case cover passages that intersect the case cover pump shaft bore.

45. Inspect the manual valve. If it needs to be replaced, the cup plug will have to be removed so that the valve can be slid out. When installing a manual valve, be sure that the small end goes in first. Coat the cup plug with sealant before installing and tap it in until just below the surface.

NOTE: For a brief period, a production trial run was made using a steel manual valve instead of aluminum. The steel valve has an extra locating land on the shaft. If service replacement is required of the manual valve, the present design aluminum valve should be used.

46. Renew the seal in the 1-2 accumulator piston. Otherwise the seal should not be removed. Install the accumulator piston and make sure that it is installed with the flat side down.

47. Inspect the thermo-element valve and plate. If the valve has to be replaced, be sure that the roll pin and washers are installed to their specific heights. Carefully measure the pins, their height should be .21 inch.

48. To remove the valve use a pair of long nosed pliers and pry off the washer from the spring pin. Remove the element. Inspect the element and replace as required.

49. Install the original thermo-element and plate. The roll pin washers are to be installed to a specification height of exactly 5.24mm (0.21″).

50. Install the tanged thrust washer on the case cover, and retain with petroleum jelly. This thrust washer protects the driven sprocket. If the two dowel pins were removed from the case cover, they should now be installed.

51. Install the 1-2 accumulator spring into the case. Install the center gasket on the case, using petroleum jelly to retain it.

52. Using a new gasket, install the case-to-case cover. All screws are torqued to 18 foot-pounds,

53. There are two screws that are installed from the torque converter side and they should be installed, with new washers, and torqued to 18 foot-pounds.

54. Install the manual valve rod into the manual valve and install the clip. The rod may have to be pulled up in place with long nose pliers.

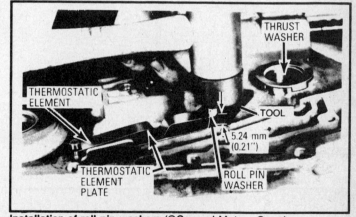

Installation of roll pin washers (©General Motors Corp.)

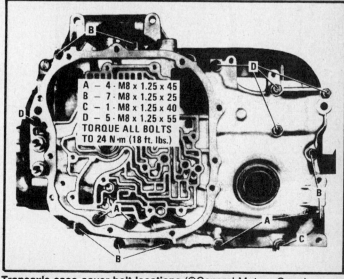

A — 4 - M8 x 1.25 x 45
B — 7 - M8 x 1.25 x 25
C — 1 - M8 x 1.25 x 40
D — 5 - M8 x 1.25 x 55
TORQUE ALL BOLTS
TO 24 N·m (18 ft. lbs.)

Transaxle case cover bolt locations (©General Motors Corp.)

55. Install the 1-2 accumulator pin with the chamfered end first.

56. Install the five check balls that belong in the case cover. Lay a new control valve pump body gasket in place, and install the spacer plate. Install the sixth check ball into the control valve and pump assembly.

57. Install the oil pump drive shaft.

58. It is helpful to have two guide pins made from 6mm bolts to help guide the valve body into place. Use the guide pins and install the valve body.

59. Install the valve body retaining bolts. They are of different lengths and different torque specifications.

NOTE: There is a capped roll pin in the center of the two roll pins by the element plate. If this pin is removed, it must be installed to a height of .24 inch.

60. Install the throttle valve lever and bracket assembly to the T.V. link and install the unit onto the case.

61. Inspect the valve body cover for damage, especially around the gasket flange and bolt holes. If the flange is distorted, straighten with a block of wood and a rubber mallet. Install the pan, using a new gasket.

62. Rotate the transaxle so that the oil pan side is up. Install the output shaft. Turn the shaft carefully so that the groove for the C-ring on the shaft will be visible through the "window" in the

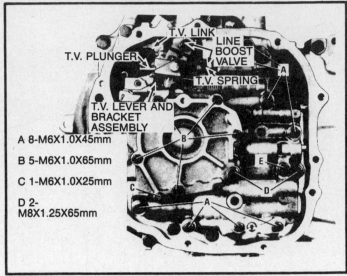

Valve body bolt locations (©General Motors Corp.)

A 8-M6X1.0X45mm

B 5-M6X1.0X65mm

C 1-M6X1.0X25mm

D 2-M8X1.25X65mm

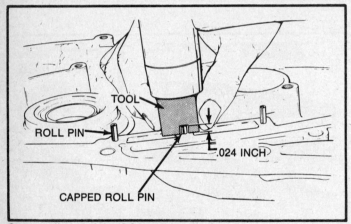

Center roll pin height (©General Motors Corp.)

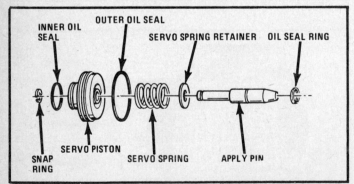

Intermediate servo—exploded view (©General Motors Corp.)

case. Install a new C-clip, using long nose pliers to start the clip and then a long tool to push the clip home. Make sure that it is seated in the groove.

63. Install the parking lock bracket and dipstick stop. Make sure that the parking actuator rod is positioned over the pawl and out of the park range. Torque the two retaining screws to 18 foot-pounds. Check the assembly for proper operation.

64. Install a new low/reverse seal assembly, using a piece of 3/8 inch rod as a driver.

65. Renew the O-ring seal in the reverse oil pipe and install the pipe with the plain end first, then the end with the seal.

66. Install the intermediate servo assembly. The seals should not be removed unless they are to be replaced. Make sure that the seals are seated in their grooves.

67. Install the servo cover with a new gasket, and install the three cover screws. Position the reverse oil pipe bracket and torque the screws to 8 foot-pounds.

68. Install a new oil strainer and O-ring seal. The screen should be positioned against the dipstick stop.

69. Install the pan using a new gasket or RTV sealant depending on which was used upon assembly.

70. Install the governor assembly. Install the speedometer drive gear and thrust washer on the governor. Renew the O-ring seal in the governor cover, lube with petroleum jelly and install the cover and retaining bolts.

NOTE: Make certain that the governor shaft is centered in the cover and not misaligned before tightening the bolts.

71. Install the speedometer driven gear assembly and retainer. Torque the screw to 75 inch-pounds.

72. Place the transaxle onto the jack and secure. Install the torque converter and see that it is fully seated and that all shafts are engaged.

73. Install the transaxle into the vehicle. Fill with the proper grade and type automatic transmission fluid. Adjust linkage as required. Roadtest the vehicle.

SPECIFICATIONS

1982 THM 125C AUTOMATIC CLUTCH PLATE AND APPLY RING CHART
Cimarron, Cavalier and 2000

Direct Clutch			Forward Clutch				Low & Reverse Clutch		
Flat Steel Plate	Comp. Faced Plate	Apply Ring	Waved Plate	Flat Steel Plate	Comp. Faced Plate	Apply Ring	Flat Steel	Comp. Faced Plate	Apply Ring
No. 4 Thickness 2.3mm (0.09")	No. 4	I.D.①7 Width 19mm (0.75")	No. 1 Thickness 1.6mm (0.06")	No.3 Thickness 1.9mm (0.08")	No. 4	I.D.①O Width 12mm (0.47")	No. 5	No.5	I.D.①O or A Width 15.4mm (0.61")

① Measure the width of the clutch apply ring for positive identification.

NOTE: The direct and forward clutch flat steel clutch plates and the forward clutch waved steel plate should be identified by their thickness. The direction of the forward production installed composition faced plates must not be interchanged. For service, the direct and forward clutch use the same composition faced plates.

1982 THM 125C AUTOMATIC TRANSAXLE CLUTCH PLATE AND APPLY RING CHART
Firenza and Skyhawk

Direct Clutch				Forward Clutch			Low & Reverse Clutch		
Flat Steel Plate	Comp. Faced Plate	Apply Ring	Waved Plate	Flat Steel Plate	Comp. Faced Plate	Backing Plate	Waved Plate	Flat Steel Plate	Comp. Faced Plate
No. 4 Thickness 2.3mm (0.09")	No. 4	I.D.①7 Width 19mm (0.75")	No. 1 Thickness 1.6mm (0.06")	No. 3 Thickness 1.9mm (0.08")	No. 4	I.D.② Width ②	No.1	No.4	No. 5

① Measure the width of the clutch apply ring for positive identification.
② Backing plates are selective. Code 1 is .24-.23
    Code 2 is .21-.20
    Code 3 is .19-.18

NOTE: The direct and forward clutch flat steel clutch plates and the forward clutch waved steel plate should be identified by their thickness. The direction of the forward production installed composition faced plates must not be interchanged. For service, the direct and forward clutch use the same composition faced plates.

1982 THM 125C AUTOMATIC TRANSAXLE CLUTCH PLATE AND APPLY RING CHART
Century, Skylark, Citation, Celebrity, Omega, Ciera, Phoenix and 6000

Direct Clutch			Forward Clutch				Low & Reverse Clutch			
Flat Steel Plate	Comp. Faced Plate	Apply Ring	Waved Plate	Flat Steel Plate	Comp. Faced Plate	Backing Plate	Waved Plate	Flat Steel Plate	Comp. Faced Plate	Apply Ring
No. 4 Thickness 2.3mm (0.09")	No. 4	I.D.①7 Width 19mm (0.75")	No. 1 Thickness 1.6mm (0.06")	No. 3 Thickness 1.9mm (0.08")	No. 4	I.D.② Width ②	No.1	No. 4	No. 5	I.D.①O or A Width 15.4mm (0.61")

① Measure the width of the clutch apply ring for positive identification.
② Backing plates are selective. Code 1 is .24-.23
    Code 2 is .21-.20
    Code 3 is .19-.18

NOTE: The direct and forward clutch flat steel clutch plates and the forward clutch waved steel plate should be identified by their thickness. The direction of the forward production installed composition faced plates must not be interchanged. For service, the direct and forward clutch use the same composition faced plates.

1983 and Later THM 125C AUTOMATIC TRANSAXLE CLUTCH PLATE AND APPLY RING
All Models

Clutch	Flat Steel Plate No.	Flat Steel Plate Thickness	Comp. Faced Plate No.	Waved Plate No.	Waved Plate Thickness	Backing Plate I.D.①	Backing Plate Width
Direct EF, EK, EP	3	2.3mm (0.09")	3	—	—	—	9.25mm (0.36")
All Others	4	2.3mm (0.09")	4	—	—	—	4.92mm (0.19")
Forward All	3	1.9mm (0.08")	4	1	1.6mm (0.06")	—	②
Low and Reverse All	4	—	5	1	1.94mm (0.08")	—	—

① Measure the width of the clutch apply ring for positive identification.
② Backing plates are selective. Code 1 is .24-.23
                       Code 2 is .21-.20
                       Code 3 is .19-.18

NOTE: The direct and forward clutch flat steel clutch plates and the forward clutch waved steel plate should be identified by their thickness. The direction of the forward production installed composition faced plates must not be interchanged. For service, the direct and forward clutch use the same composition faced plates.

TORQUE SPECIFICATION CHART

Description	Quantity	Torque Specification
Valve body to Case Cover	2	8 ft. lbs. (11 N•m)
Pump Cover to Case Cover	1	18 ft. lbs. (24 N•m)
Pump Cover to Valve Body	4	8 ft. lbs. (11 N•m)
Pump Cover to Valve Body	3	8 ft. lbs. (11 N•m)
Solenoid to Valve Body	1	8 ft. lbs. (11 N•m)
Valve Body to Case Cover	9	8 ft. lbs. (11 N•m)
Valve Body to Case	1	18 ft. lbs. (24 N•m)
Valve Body to Driven Sprocket Support	1	18 ft. lbs. (24 N•m)
Case Cover to Case	4	18 ft. lbs. (24 N•m)
Case Cover to Case	4	18 ft. lbs. (24 N•m)
Case Cover to Case	1	18 ft. lbs. (24 N•m)
Case Cover to Case	7	18 ft. lbs. (24 N•m)
Case Cover to Case	2	18 ft. lbs. (24 N•m)
Case to Drive Sprocket Support	4	18 ft. lbs. (24 N•m)
Oil Pan and Valve Body Cover	27	12 ft. lbs. (16 N•m)
Manual Detent Spring Assembly to Case	1	8 ft. lbs. (11 N•m)
Cooler Connector	2	23 ft. lbs. (38 N•m)
Line Pressure Take-Off	1	8 ft. lbs. (11 N•m)
Intermediate Servo Cover	4	8 ft. lbs. (11 N•m)
Parking Lock Bracket to Case	2	18 ft. lbs. (24 N•m)
Pipe Retainer to Case	2	18 ft. lbs. (24 N•m)
Governor Cover to Case	2	8 ft. lbs. (11 N•m)
Speedometer Driven Gear to Governor Cover	1	75 in. lbs. (9 N•m)
T.V. Cable to Case	1	75 in. lbs. (9 N•m)
Pressure Switch	2	8 ft. lbs. (11 N•m)

SPECIAL TOOLS

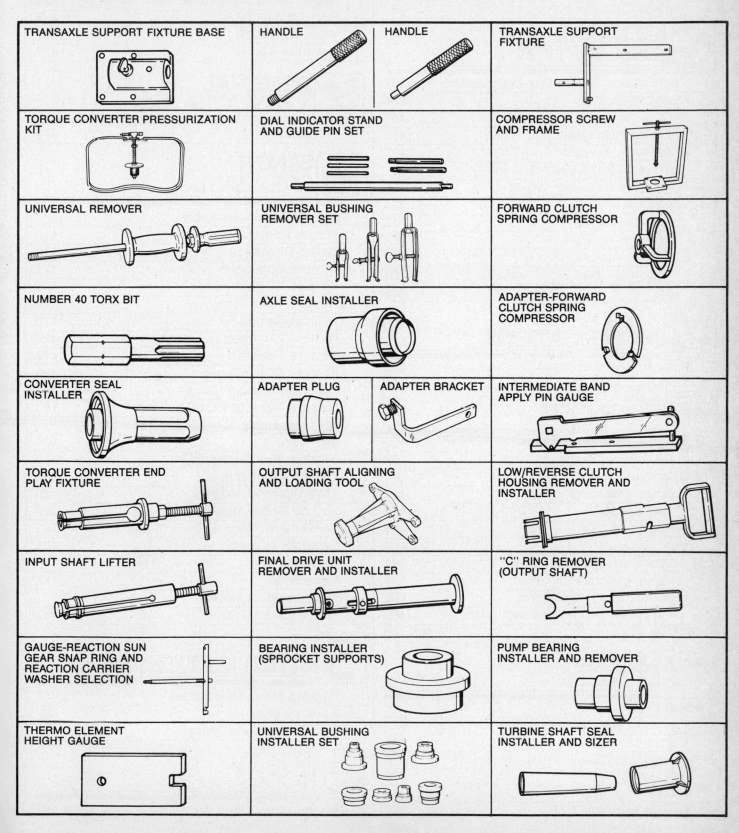

TRANSAXLE SUPPORT FIXTURE BASE	HANDLE	HANDLE	TRANSAXLE SUPPORT FIXTURE
TORQUE CONVERTER PRESSURIZATION KIT	DIAL INDICATOR STAND AND GUIDE PIN SET		COMPRESSOR SCREW AND FRAME
UNIVERSAL REMOVER	UNIVERSAL BUSHING REMOVER SET		FORWARD CLUTCH SPRING COMPRESSOR
NUMBER 40 TORX BIT	AXLE SEAL INSTALLER		ADAPTER-FORWARD CLUTCH SPRING COMPRESSOR
CONVERTER SEAL INSTALLER	ADAPTER PLUG	ADAPTER BRACKET	INTERMEDIATE BAND APPLY PIN GAUGE
TORQUE CONVERTER END PLAY FIXTURE	OUTPUT SHAFT ALIGNING AND LOADING TOOL		LOW/REVERSE CLUTCH HOUSING REMOVER AND INSTALLER
INPUT SHAFT LIFTER	FINAL DRIVE UNIT REMOVER AND INSTALLER		"C" RING REMOVER (OUTPUT SHAFT)
GAUGE-REACTION SUN GEAR SNAP RING AND REACTION CARRIER WASHER SELECTION	BEARING INSTALLER (SPROCKET SUPPORTS)		PUMP BEARING INSTALLER AND REMOVER
THERMO ELEMENT HEIGHT GAUGE	UNIVERSAL BUSHING INSTALLER SET		TURBINE SHAFT SEAL INSTALLER AND SIZER

INDEX

GENERAL MOTORS TURBO HYDRA-MATIC 180C

APPLICATIONS

GENERAL MOTORS 180C AUTOMATIC TRANSMISSION APPLICATION CHART

Year	Make	Model
1982	Chevrolet	Chevette
	Pontiac	T-1000
1983-84	Chevrolet	Chevette
	Pontiac	1000

GENERAL DESCRIPTION

Transmission and Torque Converter Identification

The THM 180C automatic transmission is a fully automatic unit consisting mainly of a four element hydraulic torque converter and a compound planetary gear set. Three multiple disc clutches, a roller clutch, and a band provide the friction elements required to obtain the desired function of the compound planetary gear set. The THM 180C automatic transmission also utilizes a hydraulic system pressurized by a gear type pump which provides the working pressure required to operate the friction elements and the automatic controls.

Transmission Identification

The THM 180C automatic transmission can be identified by the Vin Location Tag, which is positioned on the right side of the automatic transmission case. This tag incorporates the model and year of the unit, the serial number of the transmission and the transmission part number. There is also an I.D. Location Tag, which is positioned on the left side of the assembly, just after the torque converter housing.

Torque Converter Identification

The torque converter is a welded unit and cannot be disassembled. No specific data is given for quick identification by the repairman. Should the torque converter require repair, order a replacement unit from the information given on the transmission identification tag.

Metric Fasteners

Metric tools will be required to service this unit. Due to the large number of alloy parts used, torque specifications should be strictly observed. Before installing capscrews into aluminum parts, always dip the screws into oil to prevent the screws from galling the aluminum threads and to prevent seizing. Aluminum castings and valve body parts are very susceptible to nicks and burrs.

The metric fastener dimensions are very close to the dimensions of the familiar inch system fasteners, and for this reason, replacement fasteners must have the same measurement and strength as those removed.

Do not attempt to inter-change metric fasteners for inch system fasteners. Mismatched or incorrect fasteners can result in damage to the transmission unit through malfunctions, breakage or possible personal injury.

Care should be taken to re-use the fasteners in the same locations as removed.

Fluid Capacities

To refill the THM 180C automatic transmission after complete overhaul, add five quarts of Dexron® II automatic transmission

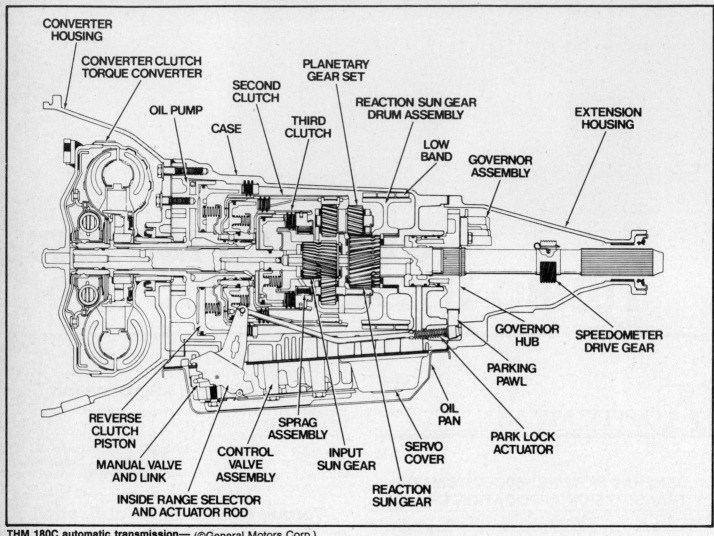

CONVERTER
HOUSING

CONVERTER CLUTCH
TORQUE CONVERTER

OIL PUMP

CASE

SECOND
CLUTCH

THIRD
CLUTCH

PLANETARY
GEAR SET

REACTION SUN GEAR
DRUM ASSEMBLY

LOW
BAND

GOVERNOR
ASSEMBLY

EXTENSION
HOUSING

GOVERNOR
HUB

SPEEDOMETER
DRIVE GEAR

PARKING
PAWL

PARK LOCK
ACTUATOR

OIL
PAN

SERVO
COVER

REACTION
SUN GEAR

INPUT
SUN GEAR

CONTROL
VALVE
ASSEMBLY

SPRAG
ASSEMBLY

MANUAL VALVE
AND LINK

REVERSE
CLUTCH
PISTON

INSIDE RANGE SELECTOR
AND ACTUATOR ROD

THM 180C automatic transmission— (©General Motors Corp.)

fluid. To refill the 180C automatic transmission after the pan has been removed and replaced, add three quarts of Dexron® II automatic transmission fluid. Recheck and correct level after starting engine.

Checking Fluid Level

TRANSMISSION AT OPERATING TEMPERATURE (HOT)

The THM 180C automatic transmission is designed to operate at the "FULL HOT" mark on the dipstick, at normal operating temperature. Normal operating temperature is obtained after at

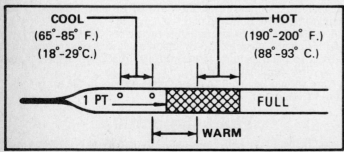

COOL
(65°-85° F.)
(18°-29°C.)

HOT
(190°-200° F.)
(88°-93° C.)

1 PT   FULL

WARM

Transmission dipstick markings (©General Motors Corp.)

least fifteen miles of highway type driving. To determine the proper fluid level, proceed as follows.
1. Make sure vehicle is parked level.
2. Apply parking brake and move selector lever to Park.
3. Start engine but do not race. Allow to idle.
4. Move selector through each range, back to Park, then check level. The fluid should read "FULL HOT".
5. Correct the fluid level as required.

TRANSMISSION AT ROOM TEMPERATURE (COLD)

Automatic transmissions are frequently overfilled because the fluid level is checked when the fluid is cold and the dipstick indicates fluid should be added. However, the low reading is normal since the level will rise as the fluid temperature increases. To determine the proper fluid level, proceed as follows.
1. Make sure that the vehicle is parked level.
2. Apply the parking brake. Move the selector lever into the park position.
3. With the engine running, remove the dipstick, wipe it clean and reinsert it until the cap seats.
4. Remove the dipstick and note the reading. It should be between the two dimples below the "ADD" mark.
5. Adjust the fluid level as required.

Fluid Drain Intervals

The transmission operating temperature resulting from the type of driving conditions under which the car is used is the main consideration in establishing the proper frequency of transmission fluid changes.

Change the transmission fluid and service the screen every 15,000 miles (24 000 km) if the car is usually driven under one or more of the following conditions.

1. In heavy city traffic.
2. Where the outside temperature regularly reaches 90°F. (32°C).
3. In very hilly or mountainous areas.
4. Commercial use, such as taxi, police car, or delivery service.

If you do not use your car under any of these conditions, change the fluid and service screen every 100,000 miles (160 000 km).

NOTE: DO NOT OVERFILL. It takes only one pint to raise lever from "ADD" to "FULL" with a hot transmission.

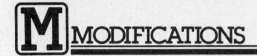

Information regarding any modifications to the THM 180C automatic transmission is not available at the time of publication.

CLUTCH AND BAND APPLICATION CHART

Range	Reverse Clutch	Second Clutch	Third Clutch	Low Band	Sprag
Park/Neutral	Released	Released	Released	Released	Locked
Drive range—first gear	Released	Released	Released	Applied	Locked
Drive range—second gear	Released	Applied	Released	Applied	Overrunning
Drive range—third gear	Released	Applied	Applied	Released	Locked
L₁ range	Released	Released	Applied	Applied	Locked
L₂ range	Released	Applied	Released	Applied	Overrunning
Reverse range	Applied	Released	Applied	Released	Locked

CHILTON'S THREE "C's" TRANSMISSION DIAGNOSIS CHART
THM 180C

Condition	Cause	Correction
Won't move in any range	a) Low fluid level b) Clogged filter screen c) Manual valve disconnected d) Input shaft broken e) Pressure regulator valve stuck open f) Faulty oil pump	a) Add as required b) Replace screen c) Repair link d) Replace affected parts e) Clean valve and bore f) Repair or replace
Must "jiggle" selector to move	a) Manual linkage adjustment b) Selector shaft retaining pin broken c) Manual valve link loose d) Selector shaft nut loose	a) Adjust as required b) Replace pin c) Repair or replace link d) Tighten or replace
Sudden start after RPM increase	a) Servo piston binding b) Low fluid level c) Faulty oil pump d) Check ball in valve body out of place	a) Repair or replace servo b) Add as required c) Repair or replace d) Remove valve body and check for proper locations of check balls

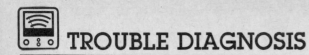

CHILTON'S THREE "C's" TRANSMISSION DIAGNOSIS CHART
THM 180C

Condition	Cause	Correction
Heavy jerking when starting out	a) Low oil pressure	a) Check fluid level, clogged oil screen. Replace if necessary
	b) Pressure regulator valve stuck	b) Clean valve and bore
	c) Check ball in valve body out of place	c) Remove valve body and check for proper location of check balls
Won't move in "D" or "L2". OK in "L1" and "R"	a) Input sprag failure	a) Replace affected parts
Won't move in "D", "L2" or "L1". OK in "R"	a) Faulty band	a) Replace band
	b) Servo piston binding	b) Repair or replace servo
	c) Parking pawl did not disengage	c) Repair faulty parking lock parts
Won't move in "R". OK in other ranges	a) Reverse clutch failure	a) Overhaul
Car moves in "N"	a) Manual linkage adjustment	a) Adjust as required
	b) Planetary gear set broken	b) Replace planetary and other parts if affected
	c) Faulty band	c) Check for proper position and adjustment
No 1-2 upshift (Stays in 1st gear)	a) Governor valves stuck	a) Service or replace governor
	b) 1-2 Shift valve stuck	b) Clean valve body
	c) Faulty oil pump hub seals	c) Replace hub seals
	d) Governor screen clogged	d) Remove and clean screen
No 2-3 upshift (Stays in 2nd gear)	a) 2-3 Shift valve stuck	a) Clean valve body
	b) Governor circuit leaking	b) Check governor seals
Upshifts at full throttle only	a) Faulty vacuum modulator	a) Replace modulator
	b) Vacuum leak	b) Check engine and accessories for vacuum leak
	c) Detent cable broken	c) Replace cable
	d) Detent valve stuck	d) Clean valve and bore
Upshifts only at part throttle	a) Detent pressure regulator valve stuck	a) Clean valve body
	b) Detent cable broken or out of adjustment	b) Repair or replace as necessary
Transmission keeps slipping to a lower gear	a) Manual linkage broken	a) Replace affected parts
	b) Pressure loss at governor	b) Replace governor seals
Slips during 1-2 upshift	a) Low oil pressure	a) Check fluid level, clogged oil screen. Replace if necessary
	b) Second clutch seals leak	b) Overhaul
	c) Faulty oil pump hub seals	c) Replace hub seals
Slips during 2-3 upshift	a) Low oil pressure	a) Check fluid level, clogged oil screen. Replace if necesary
	b) Faulty band	b) Adjust or replace
	c) Third clutch leaking	c) Replace seals
	d) Input shaft bushing worn	d) Replace bushing
	e) Check ball in valve body out of place	e) Remove valve body and check for proper locations of check balls

CHILTON'S THREE "C's" TRANSMISSION DIAGNOSIS CHART
THM 180C

Condition	Cause	Correction
Abrupt 1-2 upshift	a) High oil pressure	a) Check for stuck pressure regulator-Clean bore
	b) 1-2 Accumulator stuck	b) Clean valve and bore
	c) Second clutch spring broken	c) Overhaul clutch-Replace affected parts
Abrupt 2-3 upshift	a) High oil pressure	a) Check for stuck pressure regulator-Clean bore
	b) Faulty band	b) Adjust or replace
No engine braking in "L1"	a) Manual linkage adjustment	a) Adjust as required
	b) Manual low control valve stuck	b) Clean valve body
No engine braking in "L2"	a) Manual linkage adjustment	a) Adjust as required
Screeching noise when starting	a) Converter failure	a) Replace converter

HYDRAULIC CONTROL SYSTEM

The THM 180C automatic transmission uses a gear type pump to draw fluid through the filter screen in order to supply fluid to the different hydraulic units and valves. The pump drive gear is keyed to the converter pump hub. Since the converter is attached to the engine by means of a flex-plate, whenever the engine is turning, the oil pump in the automatic transmission is turning.

The hydraulic control system can be divided into four major types of elements.

1. Pressure regulating valves. These would include the main pressure regulating valve, the modulator valve, the detent pressure regulator valve, the 1-2 accumulator valve and the governor.

2. Selector valves (both manually and hydraulically controlled). These would include the manual valve, detent valve, 1-2 shift valve, 2-3 shift valve, 3-2 downshift control valve, the manual low and reverse control valve and the boost control valve.

3. Timing valves. These would include the low speed downshift timing valve, the high speed downshift timing valve and the second clutch orifice valve.

4. The accumulators. These would be the 1-2 accumulator and the low servo piston.

Main Pressure Regulator Valve

Transmission fluid under pressure from the oil pump is delivered to the line port of the main pressure regulator valve. This port is connected through a damping orifice to the regulator port at the end of the pressure regulator valve. As the pressure in this port increases, it moves the valve against the spring force until the second spool of the valve just opens to the line port. This allows the pump pressure to be bypassed into the pump suction passage. In this way, the valve will regulate at a fixed minimum pressure as determined by the spring force, and all excess pump delivery oil will be bypassed back into the pump suction passage. By moving from its "bottomed" position to the pressure regulating position, the valve also opens line pressure to the converter feed passage. This oil is then directed through the converter, through the oil cooler, to the gear box lubrication system, and then back to the oil sump.

It is desirable to have a variable line pressure for the clutches and band that will increase with engine torque. This is done by introducing a "modulator" pressure on the end of the boost valve. The force of the boost valve acts against the end of the regulator valve and increases the line pressure above the base pressure as established by the spring force. By allowing this line pressure to come into the stepped area between the spools of the boost valve, an additional pressure increase, over and above that previously described, is obtained. The regulated line pressure is then fed to the manual valve, the modulator valve and the detent pressure regulator valve.

Vacuum Modulator And Modulator Valve

Line pressure is brought to the second port of the modulator valve. This pressure passes between the spools of the valve and into the modulator port. The modulator port is connected to the regulating port at the end of the valve through a damping orifice. As the pressure in the regulating port increases, it moves the valve outward against the spring force of the modulator assembly until the end spool of the valve just closes the line port. If there is excess pressure building up in the regulator port, the valve will continue to move until the second spool just opens to the exhaust port. In this way, the valve tends to regulate between the line and exhaust ports.

Since the modulator spring force is a constant, thereby causing the modulator valve to regulate at a fixed pressure, as the car speed increases, the pressure requirements decrease. It is for this reason that governor pressure, which is a function of car speed, is directed to the area between the two different diameter spools at the outboard end of the valve. As the pressure increases, it creates an outward force on the modulator valve and in effect reduces the spring force of the modulator assembly. In addition, higher car speeds will produce a somewhat lower modulator and line pressure for any given vacuum, by virtue of the governor pressure acting on the modulator valve. Modulator pressure is then directd to the pressure regulator boost valve, the 1-2 shift control valve, the 2-3 shift control valve by way of the 3-2 control valve, the detent valve, the 1-2 acccumulator valve and the low speed downshift timing valve.

Accumulator Valve

The accumulator valve is used to establish a desired pressure to eventually control the rate of apply of the second clutch during the 1-2 upshift. Again, the regulating action is esentially the same as for the modulator valve or detent pressure regulating valve. The ports and spools operate in the same way. However, for increased engine torque, it is necessary to increase the accumulator pressure. This is done by introducing modulator pressure to the small end of the accumulator valve. As the modulator pressure increases, it adds to the spring force and increases the accumulator pressure. The accumulator pressure is fed to the bottom, spring-loaded side, of the accumulator piston.

Governor

The governor assembly is mounted on the output shaft. It contains two interconnected regulating valves. Its purpose is to supply an oil pressure that is a function of the output shaft speed and therefore, a function of the vehicle speed. Line pressure is supplied to the governor from the manual valve. The governor operates on the principle of centrifugal force. Line pressure is directed to the outer-most port of the secondary valve. The secondary spring holds the valve in an outward position so that the outer spool of the valve is open to line pressure. As the line pressure builds up between the spools, it exerts a force on the larger diameter inner spool to start counteracting the spring. When the hydraulic force is large enough, it moves the valve inward against the spring force until the outer spool closes the line port. If the pressure between the spools still creates a force larger than the spring force, the valve will continue to move inward until the excess pressure opens to the exhaust port. The valve then regulates between the line and the exhaust port. A fixed governor pressure in the secondary valve has now been established with no rotation of the output shaft. As the governor begins to rotate, the outward force (due to the weight of the secondary valve) is added to the force of the spring. Therefore, as the speed increases, the outward force and, in turn, the secondary valve pressure increases. The secondary valve pressure is directed to the feed port of the primary valve. With no rotation of the governor, the pressure acts against the large inner spool and forces it to open to the exhaust port. Since there is no spring force on the primary valve, it will continue to keep the feed port closed and the exhaust port open. The final governor pressure is then zero. As the governor begins to rotate, the weight of the primary valve creates an outward force working against the oil pressure. The pressure in the primary valve port now increases as a function of speed. This continues up to the speed where the outward force finally holds the primary valve outward, keeping the feed port open.

In summary, at zero speed, the governor pressure is zero. As the speed increases, the governor pressure will increase as dictated by the primary valve until the speed is great enough to hold the primary valve all the way out. At speeds above this point, governor pressure is established by the secondary valve. Governor pressure is then directed to the modulator valve, the 1-2 shift valve, the 2-3 shift valve, and the high speed downshift timing valve.

Manual Valve

The manual valve has a direct mechanical hook-up to the shift linkage. Its purpose is to direct the hydraulic pressure to the various circuits to establish the base hydraulic range of the transmission. Line pressure is fed to the manual valve. In the Park and Neutral positions, the valve seals line pressure from entering any of the circuits. At the same time all circuits are open to exhaust, so that the transmission remains in a neutral condition. In the Reverse position, line pressure is directed to the reverse clutch piston, the boost control valve and the reverse and manual control valves. All of the other manual control circuits are open to ex-

haust. In the Drive position, the manual valve directs oil to the governor, the 1-2 shift valve, the 1-2 acccumulator valve and also to the apply side of the low servo piston by way of the high speed downshift timing valve. The Reverse, Second or Intermediate, and Low ports are exhausted. In Second or Intermediate, the Drive circuits remain pressurized. In addition, pressure is supplied to the boost control valve and to the 2-3 shift valve. The Reverse and Low ports are exhausted. In Low, the pressure is supplied to the 1-2 shift valve and to the reverse and manual control valve, in addition to the circuits already pressurized in Drive and Second. The Reverse port is exhausted.

Detent Valve

The purpose of the detent valve is to cause the transmission to shift to a lower gear for additional performance when the accelerator is depressed all the way down. The detent valve is connected to the throttle linkage mechanically. A spring holds the detent valve in the retracted position. Two pressures, "detent regulator" and "modulator" are supplied to the detent valve. In the retracted or part-throttle position, the detent valve directs modulator pressure to the 1-2 and the 2-3 shift control valves and to the 3-2 control valve. In the full throttle position, modulator pressure is blocked and the passages that were receiving modulator pressure now receive detent regulator pressure. In this position, detent regulator pressure is also supplied to additional ports of the 1-2 and 2-3 shift control valves and the 3-2 control valve.

1-2 Shift Valve

The 1-2 shift valve and the shift control valve both have the job of determining whether the transmission is in First or Second gear. With the shift valve bottomed in its bore, the valve blocks the Drive or line pressure and the second clutch is open to exhaust. The valve is held in this position by a spring as well as any modulator pressure that may be acting against the two spools of the 1-2 shift control valve. As the vehicle speed and the governor pressure increase, a force is developed on the end of the shift valve. When this force is great enough to overcome the spring and the force of the 1-2 shift control valve, the shift valve closes the exhaust and opens the line pressure port to the second clutch port.

To prevent a "hunting" condition of the shift valve, the modulator pressure supply to the second spool of the control valve is cut off as the shift valve opens line pressure to the second clutch. The oil in this pocket is exhausted out through the detent passage. An additional force keeping the valve in the upshifted position is obtained by line pressure acting on the larger diameter second spool of the shift valve. Because of this, even though the governor pressure might be maintained at a constant pressure after the valve upshifts, a higher modulator pressure is required to cause the valve to downshift. If the accelerator is depressed to the point where the detent spring force is felt, the vacuum will drop and the modulator pressure will increase. If the spring force plus the modulator pressure acting against the end spool of the shift valve are great enough to overcome the governor and line pressure acting on the shfit valve, a "part throttle" forced downshift will occur. If not, the transmission will remain in the higher gear.

If the accelerator is pressed through the detent, the detent valve supplies detent regualtor pressure to all three spools of the shift control valve, and a higher downshifting force is obtained as compared to the part throttle condition. Because of this, a through detent forced downshfit can be obtained at a speed higher than for the part throttle condition. However, there is still a limiting speed at which a through detent forced downshift will occur. If the selector lever is placed in the Manual Low position, line pressure is supplied directly to the spring pocket between the valves. Since line pressure can never be less than governor pressure, the force established by the line pressure on the shift valve plus the spring force will move the shift valve to a downshifted position regardless of vehicle speed.

2-3 Shift Valve and 3-2 Control Valve

The function and operation of the 2-3 shift valve and the shift control valves are the same as that described above for the 1-2 shift valve, with the following exceptions. The downshifted position establishes Second or Intermediate gear, and the upshifted position establishes Third or High gear. Modulator pressure is supplied to the end spool of the 2-3 control valve through the 3-2 control valve. When the control valve moves to the upshifted position, line pressure is introduced to the third clutch circuit. The third clutch circuit also directs pressure to the end spool of the 3-2 control vlave. During light throttle conditions, third clutch pressure acting on the end of the 3-2 control valve moves the valve against the spring and the force established by the modulator pressure. This exhausts the modulator pressure from behind the end spool of the 2-3 control valve, and the spring is the only remaining force acting on the shift valve to produce a downshift. In this condition, it is not possible to obtain a "part throttle" forced downshift. If the accelerator is depressed far enough to cause a substantial drop in vacuum the increased modulator pressure on the 3-2 control valve plus the spring will overcome the force of the third clutch pressure. This feeds the modulator pressure back to the 2-3 control valve and a "part throttle" forced downshift will occur. As with the 1-2 shift valve, there is a limiting speed at which this can occur. When the selector lever is placed in Second or Intermediate, the line pressure is directed to the spring pocket between the 2-3 shift and shift control valves and the shift valve will be held in the downshifted or Second gear, regardless of the vehicle speed.

Manual Low and Reverse Control Valve

The third clutch is applied in the manual Low position as well as the Reverse range to prevent a free wheeling condition. In Drive or Third gear, third clutch pressure is also directed to the release side of the Low servo. This is the pressure which causes the Low band to release during a 2-3 upshift. However, in manual Low the band must remain applied even though the third clutch is on. These conditions are achieved by routing third clutch pressure to the release side of the Low servo through the manual low and reverse control valve. In the Drive range, the spring holds the valve in its "bottomed" position and permits the third clutch pressure to be directed to the servo release circuit. When the selector lever is placed in the manual Low position, line pressure is introuced between the manual low and reverse control valves. This forces the low control valve over against the spring. In this position, third clutch pressure is cut off from the servo release and the servo release is opened to exhaust. The third clutch exhaust passage is now open to detent regulator pressure which applies the third clutch since the shift valve is in the downshifted position. Because the servo release passage is open to exhaust, the low band will remain applied. When the selector is placed in the Reverse position, the line pressure acts on the end of the reverse control valve and forces the low control valve into the same position as in the manual Low. This causes the third clutch to be applied.

Low Band Servo

The low band servo applies the band to provide engine braking in Second gear in the Low range. It is also used as an accumulator for the apply of the direct clutch and is used in conjunction with a series of check balls and the controlling orifices as a part of the timing for the release of the direct clutch. To keep from applying the front band in Neutral, Drive or Reverse the fluid is directed from the manual valve to the release side of the servo piston.

Planetary Gears

In this transmission, planetary gears are used as the basic means of multiplying the torque from the engine. Power flow through the planetary gear set is accomplished by applying power to one member, holding another member, thereby making it a reaction member, and obtaining the transmitted power from the third member. This results in any one of the following conditions.

1. The torque is increased along with a proportional decrease in output speed.
2. Speed can be increased with a proportional decrease of output torque.
3. It can act as a direct connection for direct drive.
4. It can reverse the direction of rotation.

The type of gear set that is used in the planetary utilizes two sets of planetary pinions in one carrier, two sun gears and one ring gear. The short pinions are in constant mesh with both the input (front) sun gear and the long pinions. The long pinions are in constant mesh with the reaction (rear) sun gear, the short pinions and the ring gear.

First Gear

In first gear, the reaction sun gear is held stationary. The input sun gear rotates in a clockwise direction (viewed from the front), turning the short pinions counterclockwise and the long planet pinions clockwise. The long planet pinions turn the ring gear clockwise and walk around the held reaction sun gear, driving the planet carrier and output shaft assembly in a clockwise direction.

Second Gear

In second gear, the reaction sun gear is again held stationary. The ring gear is the input and is driven in a clockwise direction turning the long planet pinions clockwise which walk around the stationary reaction sun gear, driving the planet carrier assembly and output shaft in a clockwise direction. The sprag allows the input sun gear to overrun.

Third Gear

In third gear, the ring gear is driven in a clockwise direction and the input sun gear is also driven in the same direction. The long and short planetary pinions cannot rotate on their shafts in this situation, thus causing the planetary carrier, output shaft and gears to rotate clockwise as a solid unit to provide direct drive.

Reverse

In reverse gear, the ring is held and the input sun gear is driven in a clockwise direction. This causes the short planet pinions to turn counterclockwise, turning the long planet pinions clockwise. The long planet pinions then walk around the inside of the stationary ring gear, driving the planet carrier assembly and output shaft in a counterclockwise direction.

DIAGNOSIS TESTS

Automatic transmission malfunctions may be caused by four general conditions: poor engine performance, improper adjustments, hydraulic malfunctions, or mechanical malfunctions.

The suggested sequence for diagnosis is as follows
1. Check and correct oil level
2. Check and adjust T.V. cable
3. Check and correct manual linkage
4. Check engine tune
5. Install oil pressure gauge and tachometer and check control pressure

6. Road test in all ranges, noting changes in operation and oil pressure

7. Attempt to isolate the unit involved in the malfunction

8. If road test indicates that the engine needs to be tuned up, do so before any corrective action is taken on the automatic transmission.

CONTROL PRESSURE TEST

1. Using a suitable transmission jack or support, take the weight off of the transmission crossmember.

2. Remove the crossmember bolts.

3. Carefully lower the transmission just enough to remove the pressure tap plug which is located on the left side of the transmission.

4. Install the pressure gauge and hose.

5. Install the crossmember.

6. Perform the pressure test.

NOTE: The pressures on the gauge are supplied by the servo apply pressure.

Test One

With the vehicle "coasting" at 30 MPH, the vacuum line still connected, and the accelerator closed (foot off throttle), minimum pressures should be:

Drive	65 psi.
L2	65 psi.
L1	80 psi.

Test Two

With the output shaft speed at zero, the vacuum line disconnected from the modulator and the engine speed adjusted to 1500 rpm, the maximum pressures should be:

Drive	120 psi.
L2	120 psi.
L1	160 psi.

NOTE: On replacing the pressure tap plug, torque to 5 to 7 foot-pounds.

STALL SPEED TEST

General Motors Corporation does not recommend the use of a stall speed test to determine whether a malfunction exists in the THM 180C automatic transmission. Excessive heat is generated by this test and could cause more transmission problems if not controlled.

ROAD TEST

When road testing a vehicle equipped with a THM 180C automatic transmission, be sure that the transmission is at the proper operating temperature. Operate the transmission in each position to check for slipping and any variation in the shifting pattern. Note whether the shifts are harsh or spongy. By utilizing the clutch and band application chart with any malfunctions noted, the defective unit or circuit can be found.

AIR PRESSURE TEST

The air pressure test can be used to determine if cross passages are present within the transmission case or the valve body of the THM 180C automatic transmission. Also, this test is used to determine if the clutch passages are open.

TORQUE CONVERTER STATOR OPERATION TEST

The torque converter stator assembly and its related roller clutch can possibly have one of two different type malfunctions.

1. The stator assembly freewheels in both directions.

2. The stator assembly remains locked up at all times.

CONDITION A

If the stator roller clutch becomes ineffective, the stator assembly freewheels at all times in both directions. With this condition, the vehicle will tend to have poor acceleration from a standstill. At speeds above 30-35 MPH, the vehicle may act normal. If poor acceleration problems are noted, it should first be determined that the exhaust system is not blocked, the engine is in good tune and the transmission is in gear when starting out.

If the engine will freely accelerate to high rpm in Neutral, it can be assumed that the engine and exhaust system are normal. Driving the vehicle in Reverse and checking for poor performance in forward gears will help determine if the stator is freewheeling at all times.

CONDITION B

If the stator assembly remains locked up at all times, the engine rpm and vehicle speed will tend to be limited or restricted at high speeds. The vehicle performance when accelerating from a standstill will be normal. Engine over-heating may be noted. Visual examination of the converter may reveal a blue color from the over-heating that will result.

Under conditions A or B above, if the converter has been removed from the transmission, the stator roller clutch can be checked by inserting a finger into the splined inner race of the roller clutch and trying to turn the race in both directions. The inner race should turn freely in the clockwise direction, but not turn or be very difficult to turn in the counterclockwise direction.

VACUUM MODULATOR TESTING

A defective vacuum modulator can cause one or more of the following conditions:

    a. Soft up and down transmission shifts

    b. Harsh upshifts

    c. Engine burning automatic transmission fluid

    d. Automatic transmission overheating

    e. Delayed upshifts

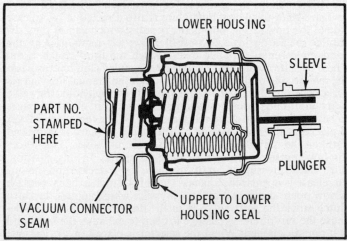

Modulator assembly—cross section (©General Motors Corp.)

Whenever a vacuum modulator is suspected of malfunctioning, a vacuum check should be made of the vacuum supply. If, the vacuum supply is found to be in proper order the vacuum modulator must be inspected. This inspection can be performed with the modulator either on or off the vehicle transmission.

Modulator Test (Modulator Installed In Vehicle)

1. Remove the vacuum line and attach a vacuum pump to the modulator connector pipe.

2. Apply 18 inches of vacuum to the modulator assembly. The vacuum should remain at 18 inches without leaking down.

3. If the vacuum reading drops sharply or will not remain at 18 inches, the diaphragm is leaking and the unit must be replaced.

4. If transmission fluid is present on the vacuum side of the diaphragm or in the vacuum hose, the diaphragm is leaking and the unit must be replaced.

NOTE: Gasoline or water vapors may settle on the vacuum side of the diaphragm. Do not diagnose as transmission fluid.

Modulator Test (Modulator Removed From Vehicle)

1. Remove the modulator assembly from the automatic transmission.

2. Attach a vacuum pump to the modulator connector pipe and apply 18 inches of vacuum.

3. The vacuum should hold at 18 inches, if the diaphragm is good and will drop to zero if the diaphram is leaking.

4. With the control rod in the transmission side of the vacuum modulator, apply vacuum to the connector pipe. The rod should move inward with light finger pressure applied to the end of the rod. When the vacuum is released, the rod will move outward by pressure from the internal spring.

Internal Spring Load Comparison Test

1. Install the known good vacuum modulator in one end of the gauge. Place the unit to be tested into the other end of the gauge.

2. While holding the assembly horizontally, force both vacuum modulator towards the center of the gauge, until one sleeve end touches the center line scribed on the gauge. The distance between the center line and the sleeve end on the opposite vacuum modulator should not exceed 1/16.

NOTE: Certain comparison gauges may use the control rod that is used with the vacuum modulator or a special rod. Follow the manufacturer's instructions.

3. Inspect the control rod for straightness and the vacuum modulator stem for being concentric to the can.

TORQUE CONVERTER CLUTCH

Converter Clutch Operation and Diagnosis

The THM 180C automatic transmission uses a torque converter clutch (TCC), which incorporates a unit inside the torque converter with a friction material attached to a pressure plate and splined to the turbine assembly. When the clutch is applied, it presses against the converter cover. The result is a mechanical direct drive of the engine to the transmission. This eliminates slippage and improves fuel economy as well as reducing fluid temperature.

There are a number of controls to operate the torque converter clutch, all of which are determined by drive range selection. For example, the clutch is applied in direct drive above a certain preset minimum speed. At wider throttle openings the converter clutch will apply after the 2-3 shift. When the vehicle slows, or the transmission shifts out of direct drive, the fluid pressure is released, the converter clutch releases and the converter operates in the conventional manner.

The engaging of the converter clutch as well as the release is determined by the direction of the converter feed oil. The converter feed oil from the pressure regulator valve flows to the converter clutch apply valve. The position of the converter clutch apply valve controls the direction in which the converter feed oil flows to the converter.

A spring-loaded damper assembly is splined to the converter turbine assembly while the clutch pressure plate is attached to a pivoting unit on the damper assembly. The result is that the pressure plate is allowed to rotate independently of the damper assembly up to about 45 degrees. This rotation is controlled by springs in the damper assembly. The spring cushioning aids in reducing the effects felt when the converter clutch applies.

To help insure that the converter clutch applies and releases at the proper times, controls have been incorporated into the electrical system.

Troubleshooting The Torque Converter Clutch

Before diagnosing the torque converter clutch system as being at fault in the case of rough shifting or other transmission malfunctions, make sure that the engine is in at least a reasonable state of tune. Also, the following points should be checked:

1. Check the transmission fluid level and correct as necessary.

2. Check the manual linkage adjustment and correct as necessary.

3. Road test the vehicle to verify the complaint. Make sure that the vehicle is at normal operating temperature.

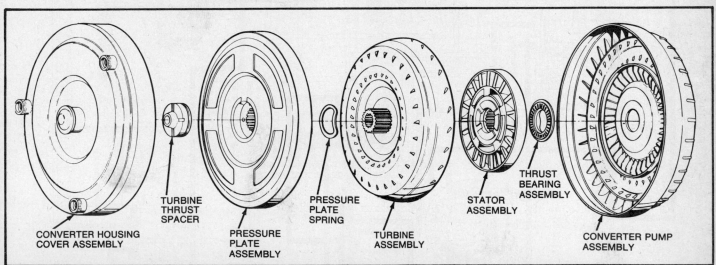

Torque converter clutch assembly—exploded view (©General Motors Corp.)

CONVERTER HOUSING COVER ASSEMBLY

TURBINE THRUST SPACER

PRESSURE PLATE ASSEMBLY

PRESSURE PLATE SPRING

TURBINE ASSEMBLY

STATOR ASSEMBLY

THRUST BEARING ASSEMBLY

CONVERTER PUMP ASSEMBLY

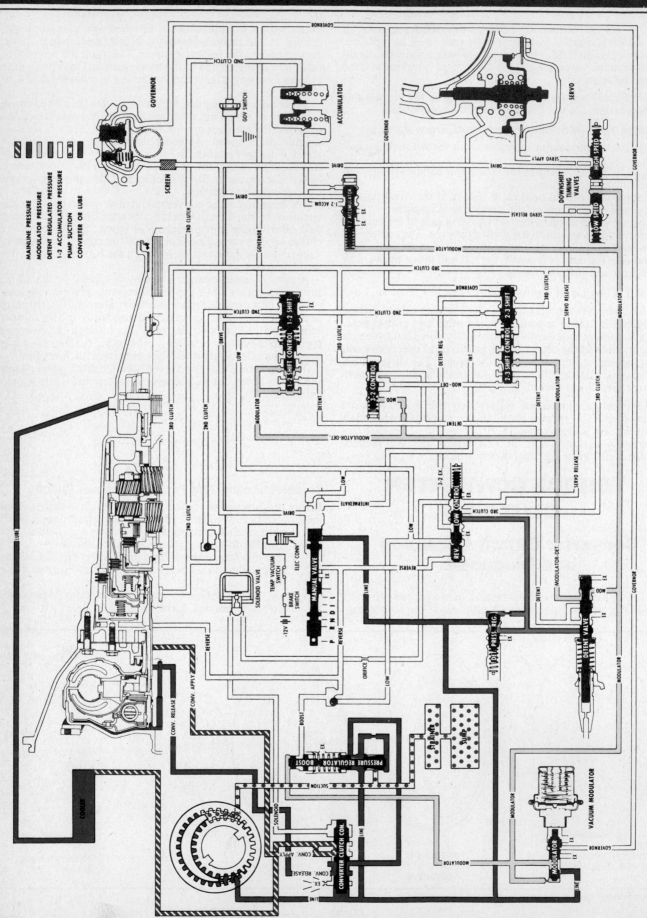

Neutral and Park—Engine Running

NEUTRAL AND PARK—ENGINE RUNNING

Units Applied or Released

REVERSE CLUTCH—RELEASED
SECOND CLUTCH—RELEASED
THIRD CLUTCH—RELEASED
LOW BAND—RELEASED
SPRAG—LOCKED

HYDRAULIC CONTROL

Whenever the engine is running with the selector in Neutral, oil is pulled from the sump into the oil pump and is dispensed from the pump under pressure. Line oil is directed to the vacuum modulator valve, to the pressure regulator valve to the manual valve. The converter is fed through the pressure regulator valve, the return oil from the converter being directed through the cooler and back into the transmission's lubricating system.

Line oil directed to the vacuum modulator valve becomes regulated to modulator oil and acts on the pressure regulator boost valve, the low speed downshift timing valve, the 1-2 accumulator valve, and the detent valve. The modulator oil passes through the detent valve to act on the 1-2 shift control valve, the 3-2 control valve and the 2-3 shift control valve. Line oil passes through the manual valve, and is regulated at the detent pressure regulator valve before being directed to the Reverse and Low control valve.

SUMMARY

The converter is filled, the clutches and low band are released. The transmission is in Neutral.

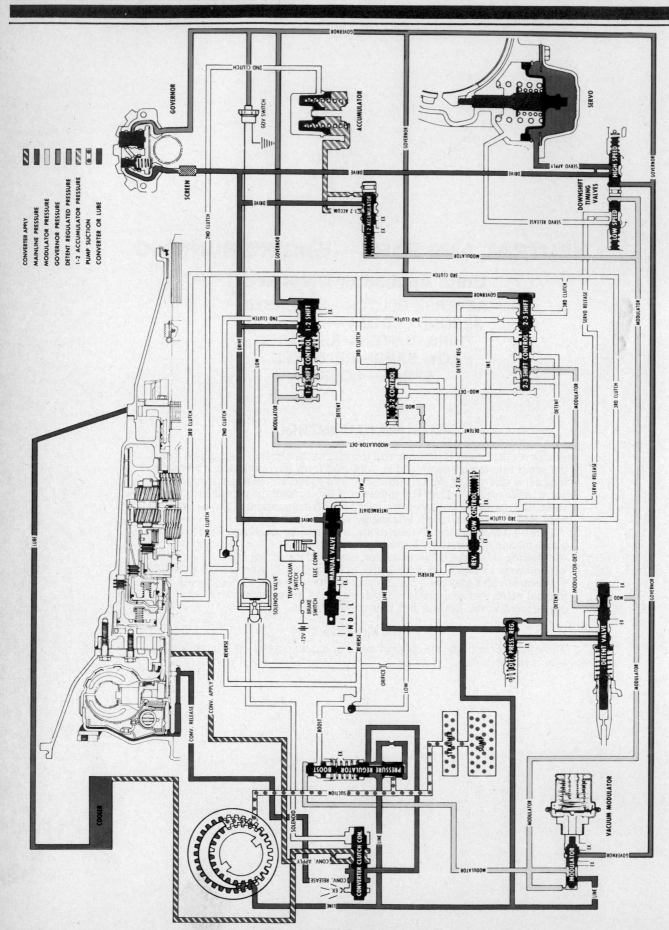

Drive Range—First Gear

DRIVE RANGE—FIRST GEAR

Units Applied or Released

REVERSE CLUTCH—RELEASED
SECOND CLUTCH—RELEASED
THIRD CLUTCH—RELEASED
LOW BAND—APPLIED
SPRAG—LOCKED

HYDRAULIC CONTROL

When the selector lever is moved to the "Drive" position on the quadrant, the manual valve is positioned to allow line oil to enter the drive circuit and is directed to the 1-2 shift valve, the governor, the 1-2 accumulator valve and the high speed downshift timing valve.

The drive oil directed to the 1-2 accumulator valve is regulated and directed to fill the bottom portion of the accumulator. The drive oil also passes through an orifice at the high speed downshift timing valve and passes through the valve to apply the low band servo.

Drive oil at the governor is regulated to a variable pressure which increases with vehicle speed and acts on the ends of the 1-2, 2-3 shift valves, high speed downshift timing valve, and the vacuum modulator valve.

SUMMARY

The clutches are off, the low band is applied, the transmission is in drive range—first gear.

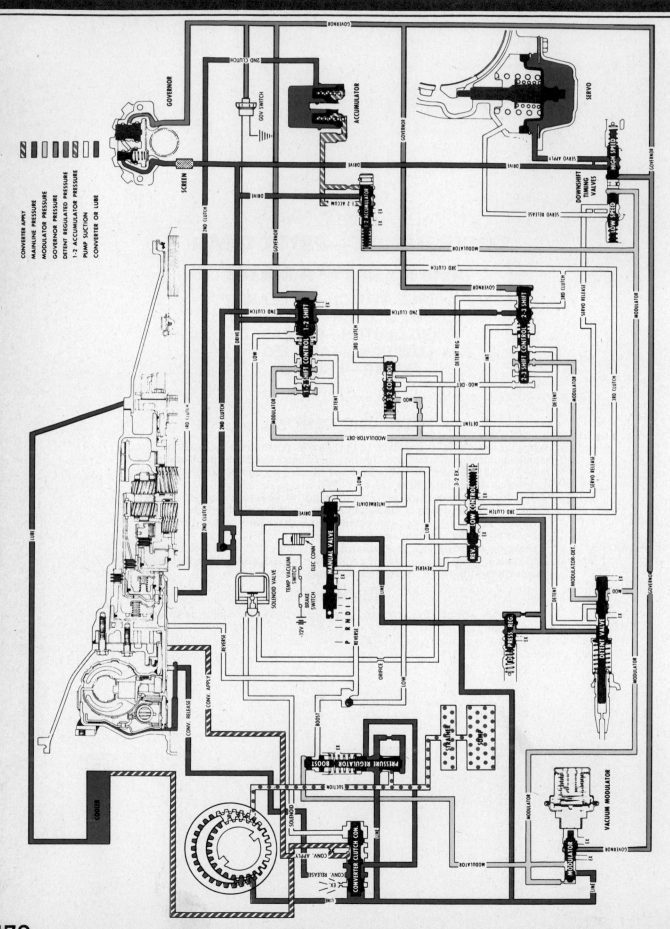

CONVERTER APPLY
MAINLINE PRESSURE
MODULATOR PRESSURE
GOVERNOR PRESSURE
DETENT REGULATED PRESSURE
1-2 ACCUMULATOR PRESSURE
PUMP SUCTION
CONVERTER OR LUBE

Drive Range—Second Gear

DRIVE RANGE—SECOND GEAR

Units Applied or Released

REVERSE CLUTCH—RELEASED
SECOND CLUTCH—APPLIED
THIRD CLUTCH—RELEASED
LOW BAND—APPLIED
SPRAG—OVERRUNNING

HYDRAULIC CONTROL

As the vehicle increases speed, the governor allows more drive oil to pass through, and this increased pressure, acting on the end of the 1-2 shift valve, overcomes, the 1-2 shift valve spring pressure and allows drive oil to pass through the valve to feed the second clutch oil passages.

Second clutch oil passes through the second clutch orifice control valve, seating the ball, and is metered to the second clutch piston to begin to apply the second clutch, while a portion of the oil is directed to the accumulator. As the upper portion of the accumulator fills with second clutch oil, it overcomes the lesser pressure of 1-2 accumulator oil and spring at the bottom of the accumulator piston, forcing the piston downward. The upper portion of the accumulator is now filled, allowing full oil pressure to the second clutch piston for the final apply. The accumulator, therefore, acts as a reservoir to produce a damping effect for a smooth second clutch apply and the 1-2 shift.

Second clutch oil from the 1-2 shift valve is simultaneously directed to the 2-3 shift valve to be used as the oil source for the 2-3 shift.

SUMMARY

The second clutch is on, the band is on, the transmission is in drive range—second gear.

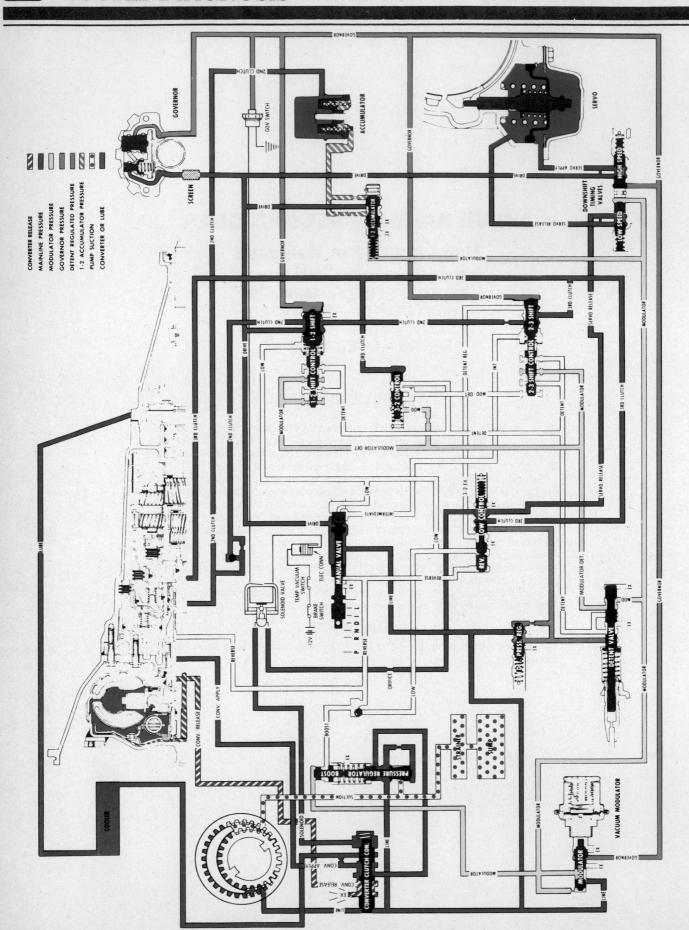

Drive Range—Third Gear

DRIVE RANGE—THIRD GEAR

Units Applied or Released

REVERSE CLUTCH—RELEASED
SECOND CLUTCH—APPLIED
THIRD CLUTCH—APPLIED
LOW BAND—RELEASED
SPRAG—LOCKED

HYDRAULIC CONTROL

As vehicle speed increases, the governor allows more oil to pass through to act against the spring at the 2-3 shift valve. This allows the second clutch oil at the 2-3 shift valve to be released and pass through the valve as third clutch oil, directed to the third clutch piston to apply third clutch. At the same time, third clutch oil is directed to the 3-2 control valve, acting against the spring and modulator oil, cutting off modulator oil pressure to the 2-3 shift control valve. Third control oil also is directed to the Reverse and Low control valve and passes through the valve as servo release oil to the low speed downshift timing valve. The low speed downshift timing valve is held open against the spring by increased modulator oil pressure. The oil passes through the valve and is directed to the top of the low band servo, to act with the servo piston spring and force the servo piston downward, releasing the low band.

Servo release oil is also directed from near the low reverse control valve through an orifice to the converter clutch control valve and the solenoid area. Oil will bleed out through the solenoid until the governor pressure (and vehicle speed) closes the governor switch. The solenoid is then energized to close the bleed and oil pressure can now move the converter clutch valve to apply the TCC.

SUMMARY

The second clutch is on, the third clutch is on, the band is released. The transmission is in drive range—third gear—as speed increases the TCC is applied.

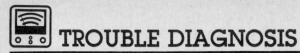

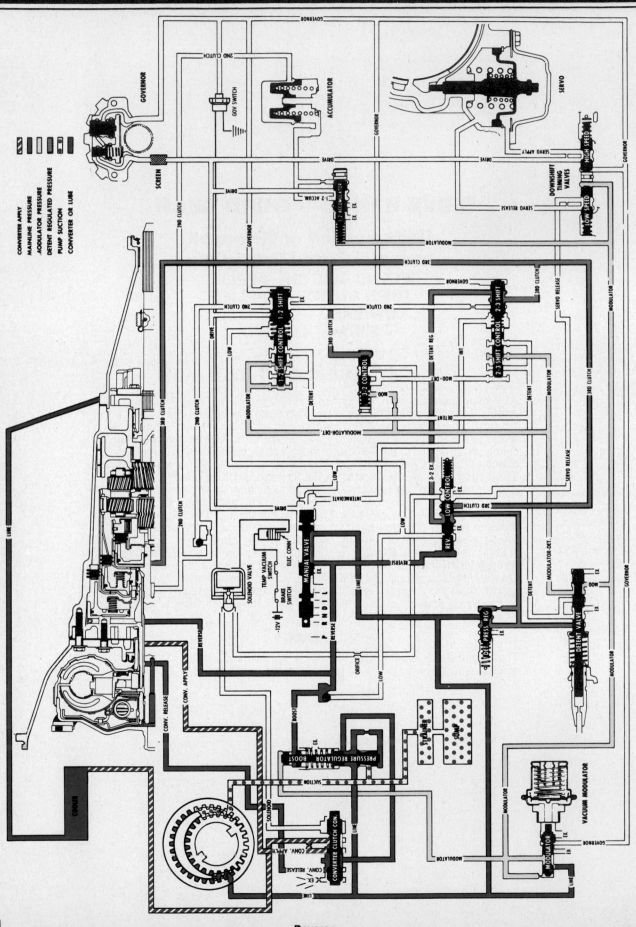

Reverse

REVERSE

Units Applied or Released

REVERSE CLUTCH—APPLIED
SECOND CLUTCH—RELEASED
THIRD CLUTCH—APPLIED
LOW BAND—RELEASED
SPRAG—LOCKED

HYDRAULIC CONTROL

When the selector lever is moved to the Reverse position on the quadrant, the manual valve is positioned to allow Reverse oil to pass through the manual valve into the Reverse oil passage. The reverse oil applies the reverse clutch. At the same time, reverse oil is directed to the pressure regulator boost control valve cavity to seat the check ball and prevent reverse oil passing into the intermediate oil passage. It is then directed to the pressure regulator boost valve forcing the pressure regulator valve downward to increase oil pressure in the circuit.

Reverse oil is also directed to act on the end of the Reverse and Low control valve against the spring to allow detent regulated oil to pass through the valve to the 2-3 shift valve. The detent regulated oil passes through the 2-3 shift valve and into the third clutch oil passages to apply the third clutch. The third clutch oil also acts on the end of the 3-2 control valve against the spring and modulator oil pressure, closing off the supply of modulator oil to the 2-3 shift control valve. Third clutch oil at the reverse and low control valve is closed off from passing through the valve, and into the servo release passage.

SUMMARY

The reverse clutch is on and the third clutch is on. The transmission is in Reverse Range.

 ON CAR SERVICES

Adjustments

T.V. AND DETENT CABLE

Adjustment

Before adjusting the cable the following steps should be taken:

a. Check transmission fluid and correct as required.

b. Be sure that the engine is operating and that the brakes are not dragging.

c. Be sure that the correct cable has been installed in the vehicle that you are servicing.

d. Check that the cable is connected at both ends.

1. To adjust, depress the re-adjust tab. Move the slider back through the fitting in the direction away from the throttle body until the slider stops against the fitting.

2. Release the re-adjust tab.

3. Open the carburetor or pump lever to the full stop throttle position to automatically adjust the cable. Release the carburetor or pump lever.

4. Check the cable for sticking or binding. Road test the vehicle as required.

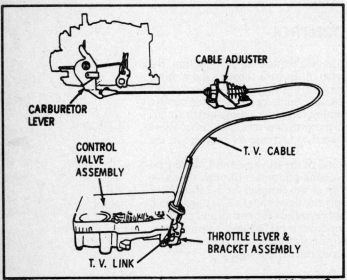

Throttle valve cable and related components (©General Motors Corp.)

MANUAL LINKAGE

Adjustment

1. Position the selector lever in the Neutral position.

2. With the connecting link of the shift rod loosened from the shifter, put the transmission in Park by moving the lever on the transmission clockwise. Then turn the lever counter-clockwise, two detents. This will be Neutral. Make sure neither the transmission lever nor the shifter lever moves. Then adjust the link so that the hole aligns with the shifter pin without preload or forcing.

3. Install the link, add the shimwasher and retainer.

NEUTRAL SAFETY SWITCH

Adjustment

1. New switches come with a small plastic alignment pin installed. Leave this pin in place. Position the shifter assembly in Neutral.

2. Remove the old switch and install the replacement, align the pin on the shifter with the slot in the switch, and fasten with the two screws.

3. Move the shifter from Neutral position. This shears the plastic alignment pin and frees the switch.

If the switch is to be adjusted, not replaced, insert a 3/32″ drill bit or similar size pin and align the hole and switch. Position switch, adjust as necessary. Remove the pin before shifting from Neutral.

LOW BAND

Adjustment

1. Raise the vehicle and support safely.

2. Remove the oil pan and valve body from the transmission.

3. Loosen the locknut and tighten the servo adjusting bolt to 40 in. lbs.

4. Back the adjusting bolt off exactly five turns and tighten the locknut while holding the adjusting bolt to prevent turning.

5. Reinstall the valve body and oil pan. Fill the transmission with fluid to specifications. Start the engine and recheck the level. Check for leakage. Lower the vehicle and roadtest.

Services

OIL PAN AND FILTER

Removal and Installation

1. Raise the vehicle and support it safely.

2. Remove the pan bolts from the transmission pan, and allow the fluid to drain.

3. Remove the transmission oil filter and discard the gasket.

4. Clean all gasket surfaces. Using a new gasket, install a new transmission filter to its mounting on the valve body assembly.

5. Install the transmission oil pan, using a new gasket, torque the retaining bolts to 7-10 ft. lbs.

6. Lower the vehicle, fill the transmission and check as required.

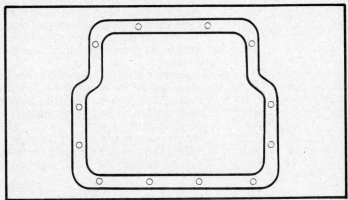

180C transmission pan identification (©General Motors Corp.)

VACUUM MODULATOR

Removal and Installation

1. Raise the vehicle and support it safely.

2. Disconnect the vacuum line from the modulator.

3. Remove the modulator assembly from the vehicle, using the proper tool.

4. Install the modulator into the transmission case after coating the O-ring with transmission fluid.

5. Connect the vacuum line. Lower the vehicle and check for proper operation of the modulator.

T.V./DETENT CABLE

Removal and Installation

1. If necessary, remove the air cleaner assembly from the vehicle.

2. Push in on the re-adjust tab and move the slider back through the fitting in the direction away from the throttle lever.

3. Disconnect the cable terminal from the throttle lever.

4. Compress the locking tabs and disconnect the cable assembly from the bracket.

5. Remove the routing clips or straps. Remove the screw and washer securing the cable to the automatic transmission assembly.

6. Disconnect the cable from the link and remove the cable from the vehicle.

7. Install a new seal into the automatic transmission case hole.

8. Connect and secure the transmission end of the cable to the transmission case using the bolt and washer. Torque the bolt to 8 ft. lbs.

9. Route the cable as removed and connect the straps or clips.

10. Position the cable through the bracket and engage the locking tabs of the cable on the bracket.

11. Connect the cable terminal to the throttle lever. Adjust the throttle cable as required.

12. If removed, install the air cleaner.

SERVO ASSEMBLY

Removal and Installation

1. Raise the vehicle and support it safely.

2. Remove the transmission oil pan, pan gasket and filter.

3. Remove the screw and the retainer securing the detent cable to the transmission. Disconnect the detent cable.

4. Remove the throttle lever and the bracket assembly.

5. Remove the manual detent roller and the spring assembly.

6. Remove the transfer plate reinforcement from the valve body assembly.

7. Remove the servo cover.

8. Remove the valve body attaching bolts and remove the valve body from the transmission.

9. Compress the servo piston, using the proper tool.

10. Remove the servo piston snap ring. Slowly loosen the servo piston compression tool and remove the servo piston, return spring and apply rod.

11. Installation is the reverse of removal. Be sure to adjust the apply rod by tightening the bolt to 40 in. lbs. Then back off the bolt exactly five turns. Tighten the locknut while holding the adjusting bolt firmly.

12. Lower the vehicle, fill the transmission with the proper grade and type automatic transmission fluid and road test as required.

SPEEDOMETER DRIVEN GEAR

Removal and Installation

1. Raise the vehicle and support it safely.

2. Disconnect the speedometer cable.

3. Remove the retainer bolt, retainer, speedometer driven gear and the O-ring seal.

4. Install the speedometer driven gear using a new O-ring seal coated with transmission fluid.

5. Continue the installation in the reverse order of removal. Adjust the transmission fluid level as required.

REAR OIL SEAL

Removal and Installation

1. Raise the vehicle and support it safely.

2. Remove the driveshaft. If equipped, remove the tunnel strap.

3. Pry the seal from the rear extension housing, using the proper tool.

4. Coat the new seal with transmission oil and drive it into place using a rear transmission seal installer tool, or equivalent.

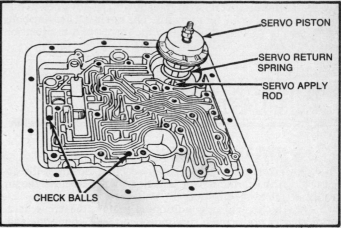

Servo and related components (©General Motors Corp.)

5. Continue the installation in the reverse order of the removal. Correct the transmission fluid level as required. Lower the vehicle and check for transmission fluid leaks.

VALVE BODY

Removal and Installation

1. Raise the vehicle and support it safely. Drain the transmission fluid.

2. Remove the oil screen and disconnect the detent cable by removing the capscrew and retainer on the outside of the case.

3. Remove the two bolts holding the manual detent roller and spring and remove the spring.

4. Remove the bolts from the transfer plate reinforcement and remove the reinforcement.

5. Remove the throttle lever and bracket assembly, being careful not to bend the throttle lever link.

6. Remove the servo cover and gasket.

7. Remove the remaining bolts attaching the valve body to the case. Remove valve body and transfer plate.

NOTE: The two check balls in the case may drop out when removing the valve body. Be careful that they do not become lost and, at reassembly, make sure they are installed in the proper position. Also, be careful that the manual valve and link are not dropped and damaged or lost.

8. Installation is the reverse of removal. Be sure to fill the automatic transmission with the proper grade and type transmission fluid. Lower the vehicle, and check for leaks. Correct as required.

GOVERNOR

Removal and Installation

1. Raise the vehicle and support it safely. Remove the driveshaft.

2. Support transmission with a suitable jack and remove the transmission mount. If necessary, remove the crossmember for clearance.

3. Remove the speedometer driven gear.

4. Remove the extension housing bolts and remove the housing and gasket.

5. Push down on the speedometer drive gear retaining clip and remove the speedometer drive gear.

6. Remove the four bolts from the governor body and remove governor and gasket.

7. If it is necessary to remove the governor hub use lock-ring pliers to remove the snap ring and slide governor hub off the shaft.

8. Installation is a reverse of the above. The governor-to-hub bolts are torqued to 6-7 foot-pounds. The extension housing bolts are torqued to 20-25 foot-pounds while the support-to-extension bolts are torqued to 29-36 foot-pounds.

REMOVAL & INSTALLATION

TRANSMISSION REMOVAL

1. Disconnect the negative battery cable. Disconnect the detent cable at the carburetor or injection pump. Remove the air cleaner. Remove the dipstick.

2. On vehicles with air conditioning, remove the screws holding the heater core cover, disconnect the wire connector and, leaving the hoses attached, place the heater core cover out of the way.

3. Raise the vehicle on a hoist and support it safely. Drain the transmission fluid. Remove the driveshaft.

4. Remove speedometer cable and the cooler tubes from the transmission.

5. Disconnect the shift control linkages.

6. Raise the transmission slightly with a jack and remove the support bolts and converter bracket.

7. Disconnect the exhaust pipe at the rear of the catalytic converter and at the manifold and remove exhaust as an assembly.

8. Remove the pan under the torque converter and remove the three flexplate bolts. Mark the converter and flexplate so that they can be reassembled in the same manner.

9. Lower the transmission until there is access to the engine mounting bolts and remove them.

10. Raise the transmission to its normal position and support the engine with a jack. Slide transmission back and down.

NOTE: Hold on to the converter and/or keep the rear of the transmission lower than the front so it won't fall from the bell housing.

INSTALLATION

1. Transmission installation is the reverse of the removal procedure.

2. Make sure that the converter pump hub keyway is seated into the oil pump drive lugs. The distance from the face of the bell housing to the end of the hub should be .200 to .280 inches. Check that the converter has free movement.

3. Start all bolts in the converter finger tight so that the flexplate will not be distorted, and align the marks made at disassembly. Then torque the bolts to 20-30 foot-pounds. The transmission support-to-extension should be torqued to 29-36 foot-pounds and the exhaust system parts to 35 foot-pounds.

4. Lower the vehicle from the hoist. Fill the transmission with the proper grade and type automatic transmission fluid.

5. Make linkage and cable adjustments as required. Road test the vehicle as required.

BENCH OVERHAUL

Torque Converter Inspection

1. Make certain that the transmission is held securely.

2. The converter pulls out of the transmission. Be careful since the converter contains a large amount of oil. There is no drain plug on the converter so the converter should be drained through the hub.

3. If the oil in the converter is discolored but does not contain metal bits or particles, the converter is not damaged and need not be replaced. Remember that color is not longer a good indicator of transmission fluid condition.

4. If the oil in the converter contains metal particles, the converter is damaged internally and must be replaced. The oil may have an "aluminum paint" appearance.

5. If the cause of oil contamination was burned clutch plates or overheated oil, the converter is contaminated and should be replaced.

6. If the pump gears or cover show signs of damage, the converter will contain metal particles and must be replaced.

Before Disassembly

Before opening up the transmission, the outside of the unit should be thoroughly cleaned, preferably with high-pressure cleaning equipment. Dirt entering the transmission internal parts will negate all the effort and time spent on the overhaul. During inspection and reassembly, all parts should be thoroughly cleaned with solvent then dried with compressed air. Wiping cloths and rags should not be used to dry parts since lint will find its way into valve body passages. Lube the seals with Dexron® II and use ordinary unmedicated petroleum jelly to hold the thrust washers and to ease the assembly of seals. Do not use solvent on neoprene seals, friction plates or thrust washers. Be wary of nylon parts if the transmission failure was due to the cooling system. Nylon parts exposed to antifreeze solutions can swell and distort, so they must be replaced. Before installing bolts into aluminum parts dip the threads in clean oil. Anti-seize compound is also a good way to prevent the bolts from galling the aluminum and seizing.

Transmission Disassembly
EXTERNAL COMPONENTS

Removal

1. Remove the torque converter assembly from the transmission housing.

2. Mount the transmission assembly in the holding fixture.

3. Drain the automatic transmission through the rear extension housing.

4. Remove the oil pan retaining bolts. Remove the oil pan and discard the gasket.

5. Remove the manual detent roller and spring assembly. Remove the transmission filter and discard the filter gasket.

6. Disconnect the governor pressure switch electrical connector and the solenoid wiring harness.

7. Disconnect the governor pressure switch. Disconnect the torque converter clutch solenoid and the solenoid pipes. Be sure not to bend the solenoid pipes when removing them from their mounting place.

8. Remove the transfer plate reinforcment. Remove the servo cover and gasket.

9. Remove the valve body with its gasket and transfer plate. Care must be taken so that the manual valve and manual valve link are not damaged or lost during valve body removal. To prevent the manual link from falling into the transmission case, place a piece of paper toweling in the case void below it, before removing the valve body.

10. Compress the servo piston using the servo piston compressor tool. The offset of the tool must be positioned toward the rear of the transmission case.

11. Using needle nose pliers, remove the servo piston to transmission case snap ring.

12. Before removing the installation bolts on the tool, loosen the compression screw to relieve the tension on the servo spring.

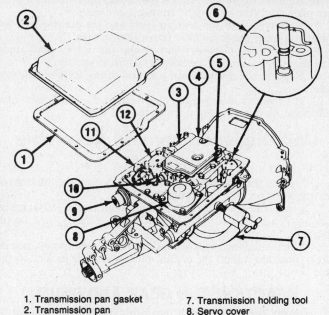

1. Transmission pan gasket
2. Transmission pan
3. Valve body and transfer plate
4. Filter
5. Manual detent spring
6. Manual valve and link
7. Transmission holding tool
8. Servo cover
9. Modulator assembly
10. Governor pressure switch
11. Solenoid valve
12. Transfer plate reinforcement

External components—exploded view (©General Motors Corp.)

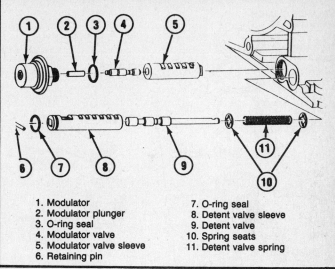

1. Modulator
2. Modulator plunger
3. O-ring seal
4. Modulator valve
5. Modulator valve sleeve
6. Retaining pin
7. O-ring seal
8. Detent valve sleeve
9. Detent valve
10. Spring seats
11. Detent valve spring

Modulator and detent valve with their related components (©General Motors Corp.)

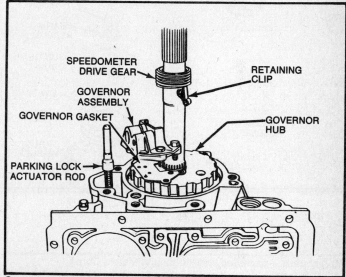

Governor assembly and related components (©General Motors Corp.)

Remove the tool, the servo piston assembly, the return spring and the servo apply rod.

13. Remove the two check balls, which are located in the oil passage of the transmission case.

14. Remove the selector inner lever hex nut from the selector lever shaft. Place a piece of paper in the transmission case under the hex nut before removing it, this will catch the nut, should it drop.

15. Remove the selector inner lever from the selector lever shaft. Remove the selector lever shaft pin by pulling upwards with pliers. To prevent the spring from collapsing, insert a wire into the middle of the spring pin.

16. Install the outside attaching nut on the selector lever shaft. Place a suitable driver on the face of the nut and drive the selector lever shaft out of the transmission case.

17. Remove the selector lever shaft oil seal. Remove the electrical connector from the transmission case.

18. Remove the vacuum modulator and O-ring, using the proper tool. Care should be taken not to lose the modulator plug. Remove the modulator valve and sleeve from the transmission case.

19. Remove the detent valve retaining spring pin by pulling upward with pointed nose diagonal pliers. To prevent collapse of the spring pin, insert a wire into the middle of the spring pin. Remove the detent sleeve, valve, spring and spring seats.

EXTENSION HOUSING, SPEEDOMETER DRIVE GEAR AND GOVERNOR

Disassembly

1. Remove the speedometer driven gear housing retainer. Remove the gear assembly from the extension housing.

2. Remove the rear extension housing oil seal, using the proper seal removal tool. Remove the extension housing and gasket from the transmission.

3. Depress the speedometer drive gear retaining clip and remove the gear by sliding it off the output shaft.

4. Remove the governor body and gasket. Remove the governor hub snap ring from the output shaft.

5. Slide the governor hub from the output shaft, be sure not to lose the governor hub oil screen.

INTERNAL COMPONENTS

Removal

1. Remove the torque converter housing oil seal, using the proper removal tool.

2. Remove the seven outer torque converter housing bolts. Loosen, but do not remove the five inner torque converter housing bolts.

3. Remove the O-ring seal from the input shaft.

NOTE: If the rubber seal is not removed, the second clutch and third clutch will come out with the converter housing. The rubber seal may shear, while you are holdng the parts, allowing the second clutch and third clutch to fall possibly causing personal injury.

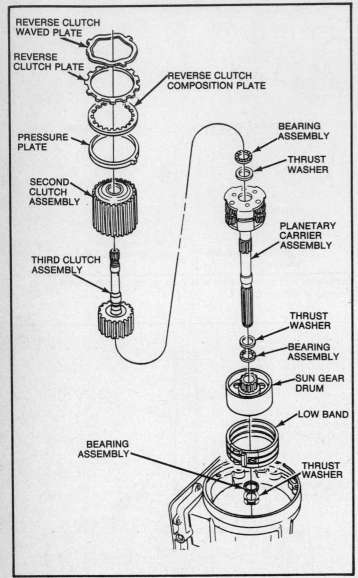

Internal parts—exploded view (©General Motors Corp.)

4. Remove the torque converter housing with the oil pump, oil pump flange gasket and the reverse clutch assemblies. Be sure not to loose the selective thrust washer between the oil pump hub and the second clutch drum.

5. Lift up on the input shaft and remove both the second and third clutch assemblies. Separate the assemblies from one another.

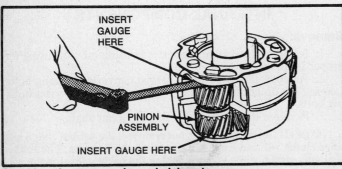

Checking planetary carrier and pinion clearance
(©General Motors Corp.)

6. Remove the reverse clutch plates and the aluminum pressure plate from the automatic transmission case.

7. Remove the inside selector lever and the parking lock actuator rod from the automatic transmission case.

8. Remove the planetary carrier and the output shaft along with the two Torrington Bearings and thrust washer.

9. Remove the reaction sun gear and drum. Remove the low band.

10. If necessary, remove the case vent and install a new case vent upon reassembly. Do not use the old vent.

Unit Disassembly and Assembly

LOW BAND

1. Position the automatic transmission case so that the front of the transmission case is upward.

2. Inspect the low band for cracks, flaking, wear, looseness or burring. If any of these conditions exist the band must be replaced.

3. When installing the low band into the transmission case be sure to position it onto the anchor pins, which are located in the case.

REACTION SUN GEAR AND DRUM

1. Inspect the reaction gear assembly. Check for chipped or nicked teeth. Inspect the sun gear drum for scoring. Replace these components as required.

2. Check the reaction sun gear drum bushing. If necessary, replace.

3. When installing, place the thrust washer and the bearing into the transmission case. Use petroleum jelly to retain the thrust washer in place. The transmission case bushing acts as a guide to center the bearing.

4. Position the reaction sun gear and drum assembly into the transmission case. Be sure that the sun gear is facing upward.

5. Install the bearing and thrust washer onto the sun gear. Retain the thrust washer using petroleum jelly.

PLANETARY CARRIER

1. Inspect both the planetary carrier and the planetary pinions for excessive wear, damage or distortion. Replace as required.

2. Check the clearance of all planetary pinions using a feeler gauge. The clearance should be between .005-.035 inch. Replace the entire assembly if damage is evident.

3. When installing, insert the output shaft and the planetary carrier assembly from the front of the transmission case to spline with the reaction sun gear.

4. Install the thrust washer, then install the Torrington Bearing into the planetary carrier. Be sure to use petroleum jelly as a retainer.

THIRD CLUTCH ASSEMBLY

Disassembly

1. Position the third clutch assembly in a vise. Install special tool J-29351 or equivalent onto the third clutch drum. Position the five pins of the tool in the elongated slots. Do not put a pin into a slot, if the internal ring is not visible in the slot. Slide the compressing ring over the pin cage.

2. Pull on the pin cage handle or input sun gear. If the ring is hanging up on one side causing the clutch hub to cock, insert a punch into the slot, to compress the ring.

NOTE: Mounting the clutch pack at a ninety degree angle will prevent the ring from sliding back into its groove, during tool removal.

3. After the retaining ring has been pressed out of the clutch drum groove, remove the sprag assembly.

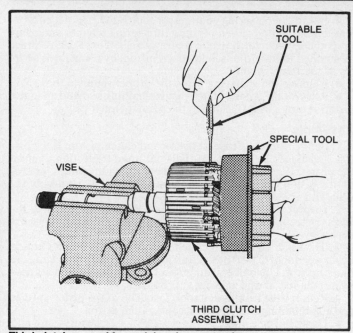

Third clutch assembly retaining ring removal
(©General Motors Corp.)

4. Remove the input shaft-to-input sun gear thrust washer and Torrington Bearing. This bearing and thrust washer may be staked together.

5. Remove the third clutch plates from the third clutch drum. The plates should be kept in the same sequence as they were installed in the clutch.

6. Remove the input sprag race and retainer assembly from the third clutch hub and input sun gear assembly.

7. Push the sprag assembly and retaining rings from the sprag race and retainer.

8. Using compressor tool J-23075 or equivalent, on the third clutch piston retaining seat, compress the third clutch piston return springs using an arbor press. Remove the snap ring. Use care not to let the retaining seat catch the snap ring groove. Remove the compressor tool.

9. Remove the retaining seat and the twelve return springs. Remove the third clutch piston from the third clutch drum.

Assembly

1. Before assembly, inspect all of the third clutch piston return springs for wear and defects. Inspect the check ball in the third clutch piston. Shake the piston and listen for movement of the check ball, which will indicate proper operation. If the ball is missing, falls out upon inspection or piston is damaged, replace the piston. Install a new lip seal on the piston, if necessary.

2. Remove the oil lip seal from the input shaft inside of the third clutch drum and install a new lip seal, if necessary, with the lip pointing downward.

3. Inspect, and if necessary replace the steel thrust washer on the front face of the third clutch drum. Air check the oil passages in the input shaft.

4. Install the third clutch piston into the third clutch drum. Use transmission fluid so that the seal is not damaged upon installation.

5. Install all of the third clutch piston return springs onto the piston. Install the retaining seat.

6. Use compressor tool J-23075 or equivalent, on the retaining seat and compress the piston return springs. Care must be taken so that the retaining seat does not catch in the snap ring groove and damage the retainer.

7. Install the snap ring. Remove the compressor tool. Inspect and replace, if necessary, the thick thrust washer and bearing.

8. Install the thrust washer and bearing onto the input shaft. The bearing will face the input sun gear if properly installed. Secure with petroleum jelly.

9. Inspect the sprag assembly for wear, damage, or sprags that freely fall out of the cage. Inspect the input sub gear for chipped or nicked teeth or abnormal wear. Replace parts as required.

10. Install the sprag cage and two retaining rings on the third clutch hub with the flared shoulder on the sprag cage outer diameter toward the input sun gear.

11. Install the outer sprag race and retainer assembly over the sprag assembly. Holding the input sun gear with the left hand, the sprag race and retainer assembly should hold firm when turned with your right hand in a clockwise direction and should rotate freely when turned counterclockwise.

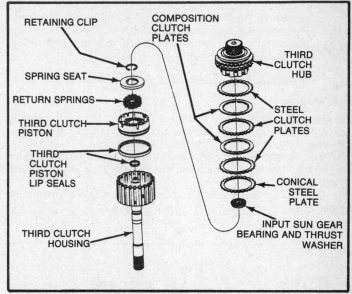

Third clutch assembly—exploded view (©General Motors Corp.)

NOTE: This procedure must be followed exactly, to be sure that the sprag has not been installed wrong.

12. Inspect the condition of the third clutch composition and steel plates, replace as required.

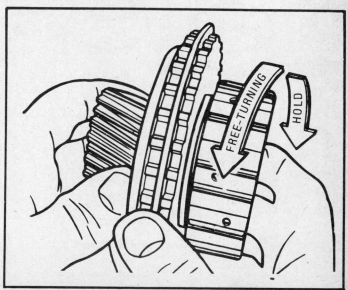

Correct sprag assembly test (©General Motors Corp.)

13. Install the third clutch plates on the third clutch hub in the following order: steel plate, composition plate, steel plate, composition plate, steel plate, conical steel plate. When installed correctly, the I.D. of the conical plate will touch the steel plate below it but, the O.D. will not.

14. Mount the clutch housing in a vise. Install the third clutch hub and sprag assembly into the third clutch housing until the sprag race rests on the third clutch drum.

15. Install tool J-29351 or equivalent, on the sprag race so that the pins in the tool fingers compress the retaining ring.

16. Slide the sprag assembly into the third clutch drum until the retaining ring is inside the drum.

NOTE: Do not push on the input sun gear while installing the sprag assembly or the clutch plates will slip off of their location and prevent assembly.

17. Remove the tool. Slide the sprag assembly into the third clutch drum until the retaining ring catches in the retaining ring groove. If necessary, use a small suitable tool to help compress the retaining ring while installing the sprag assembly.

SECOND CLUTCH ASSEMBLY

Disassembly

1. Remove the ring gear retaining ring from the second clutch drum. Remove the ring gear. Remove the second clutch spacer retaining ring. Remove the second clutch spacer.

2. Remove the second clutch steel and composition plates. The plates should be kept in the same sequence as they were installed in the clutch.

3. Remove the second clutch assembly to third clutch assembly thrust washer.

4. Install clutch spring compressor tool J-23327 or its equivalent, on the second clutch piston return spring retainer and compress the second clutch piston return springs. Tool J-23327 must be adapted to fit in the second clutch piston, by using three sockets of the same height.

5. Remove the snap ring using the proper removal tool.

6. Remove the second clutch piston retaining seat and all of the piston return springs. Remove the second clutch piston.

Assembly

1. Before assembly, inspect the second clutch piston. If the piston is damaged or if the check falls out upon inspection, replace the piston. If necessary, install two new piston lip seals. One seal on the piston O.D. and one on the second clutch drum hub. Install with lips down.

2. Inspect the piston return springs. Replace as required. Inspect the second clutch hub bushing for wear or scoring, replace if necessary.

3. To install the second clutch piston into the second clutch drum, use tool J-23080 or its equivalent, to prevent damaging the outer lip seal. Use a liberal amount of transmission fluid for ease of installation and to prevent seal damage.

4. Remove the installation tool. Install all of the piston springs and the retaining seat on the second clutch piston.

5. Using spring compressor tool J-23327 or its equivalent, and three sockets on the retaining seat, compress the second clutch piston return springs. Care should be taken so that the retainer does not catch in the snap ring groove and damage the retainer.

6. Install the snap ring using the proper tool. Install the second to third clutch thrust washer so that the tang seats in the slot of the second clutch hub. Secure the assembly using petroleum jelly. Inspect the condition of the composition and steel plates, replace as required.

7. Install the second clutch plates into the second clutch drum with the waved clutch plate first, then a steel plate, a composition plate, a steel plate, etc. Use a liberal amount of transmission fluid.

8. Install the second clutch spacer plate into the second clutch drum with the wavy end toward the clutch plates.

9. Install the second clutch spacer retaining ring. Install the ring gear into the second clutch drum. Be sure that the grooved edge is facing up. Install the ring gear and the retaining ring.

SECOND AND THIRD CLUTCH ASSEMBLIES

1. When installing these two assemblies, align the tangs of the second clutch drive plates in the second clutch drum.

2. Align the tangs of the second clutch drive plates in the second clutch drum. Insert the third clutch drum and the input shaft through the top of the second clutch drum, seating the third clutch drum splines into the second clutch plate splines. Holding the second and third clutch assemblies by the input shaft, lower into the transmission case, indexing the ring gear in the second clutch drum with the long planetary pinion gear teeth.

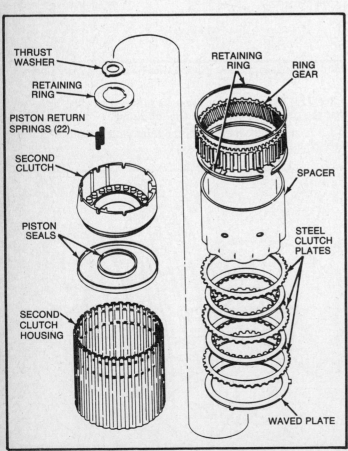

Second clutch assembly (©General Motors Corp.)

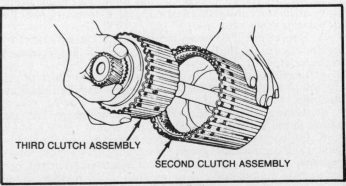

Third clutch into second clutch installation
(©General Motors Corp.)

SELECTIVE WASHER THICKNESS DETERMINATION

1. Install tool J-23085 or equivalent, on the transmission case flange and against the input shaft.

2. Loosen the thumb screw on the tool to allow the inner shaft of the tool to drop on the second clutch housing thrust face.

3. Tighten the thumb screw, then remove tool.

4. Compare the thickness of the selective washer removed earlier from the transmission to the protruding portion of the inner shaft of tool J-23085. The selective washer used in reassembly should be the thickest washer available without exceeding the dimension of the shaft protruding from tool J-23085. The dimension of the washer selected should be equal to or slightly less than the inner shaft for correct end play in the transmission.

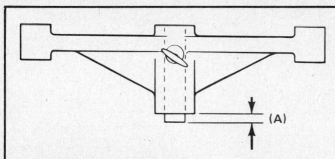

WHEN MEASURED GAP (A) IS:

INCHES	mm	USE WASHER PART NUMBER
.069 – .074	1.78 – 1.88	5258202
.075 – .079	1.93 – 2.03	5258203
.080 – .084	2.06 – 2.16	5258204
.085 – .089	2.18 – 2.29	5258205
.090 – .094	2.31 – 2.41	5258206
.095 – .100	2.46 – 2.57	5258207

FOLLOWING THE PROCEDURE SHOULD RESULT IN FINAL END-PLAY FROM 0.36 mm TO 0.79 mm (.014 in. TO .031 in.)

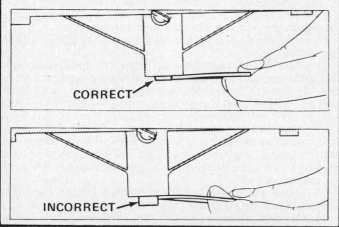

Selective washer selection chart (©General Motors Corp.)

TORQUE CONVERTER HOUSING, OIL PUMP AND REVERSE CLUTCH ASSEMBLY

Dissembly

1. If not already removed, remove the selective washer from the oil pump shaft.

2. Remove the oil pump outer seal. Observe the position of the square cut seal.

3. Remove the bolts holding the torque converter housing to the oil pump. Separate the two assemblies. Remove the oil pump wear plate.

4. Check the torque converter pump hub for nicks, burrs or damage. Correct as required.

5. Mark the relative location of the oil pump gears and remove them.

6. Using compressor tool J-23327, or its equivalent, on the reverse clutch retaining seat, compress the clutch return springs. Remove the snap ring, using the proper removal tool.

7. Loosen compressor tool and remove the reverse clutch retaining ring and all of the reverse clutch springs. Use care not to let the spring retainer catch in the ring groove.

8. Remove the reverse clutch piston. The reverse clutch piston may be removed by blowing compressed air into the piston apply passage of the oil pump.

9. The valves, located in the oil pump, may be removed by using a pair of needle nose pliers to remove the retaining pin. However, it is not recommended that these valves be disassembled during overhaul, unless they were determined by oil pressure checks to have been malfunctioning.

NOTE: Use care when disassembling the valves as they are under spring pressure.

10. Remove from the pressure regulator bore the retaining pin, the pressure regulator boost valve sleeve, boost valve, the pressure regulator spring, the two spring seats, and the pressure regulator valve.

11. Remove from the converter clutch actuator bore the retaining pin, bore plug, spring and the converter clutch actuator valve.

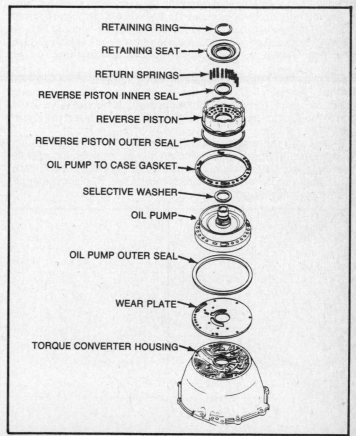

Reverse clutch assembly—exploded view (©General Motors Corp.)

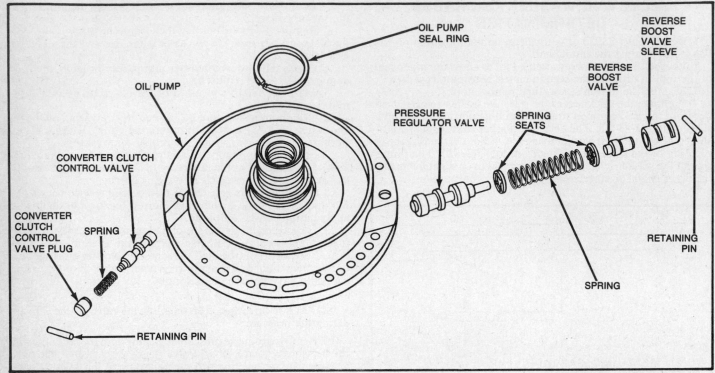

Oil pump—exploded view (©General Motors Corp.)

Assembly

1. Before assembly, inspect the pressure regulator boost valve, the pressure regulator valve and the torque converter clutch actuator valve for nicks or damage. Replace components as required.

2. Thoroughly clean the pressure regulator boost valve, the pressure regulator valve, and the converter clutch actuator valve. Immerse valves in transmission fluid before installing in their bores.

3. Install the pressure regulator valve, the two spring seats, the spring, the boost valve and the sleeve in the oil pump pressure regulator bore. Depress the pressure regulator boost valve sleeve until the back end lines up with the pin hole and insert the retaining pin to secure.

4. Install the converter clutch actuator valve, spring and bore plug in the oil pump converter clutch actuator bore. Depress the bore plug past the pinhole and insert the retaining pin to secure.

5. Inspect the oil pump hub oil seal rings. Replace if damage or side wear is found.

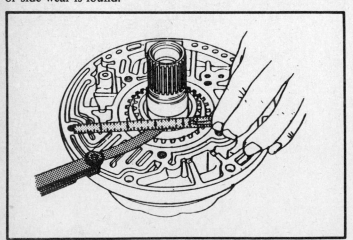

Oil pump clearance check (©General Motors Corp.)

6. Inspect the reverse clutch piston for damage. Replace as required. If necessary, install the two new oil seals on the reverse clutch piston. Install the reverse clutch piston onto the rear face of the oil pump. Be sure to use transmission fluid to aid in the installation.

7. Inspect the reverse clutch piston springs. Replace parts as required. Install all of the reverse clutch piston return springs. Set the retaining seat and the snap ring in place.

8. Compress the return springs using compressor tool J-23327 or equivalent. Care should be taken not to damage the retainer, should it catch in snap ring groove.

9. Install the snap ring using the proper tool. Do not air check the reverse clutch at this time, as the clutch is not complete and damage to the return spring retaining seat may occur.

10. Install the oil pump gears using the location mark made before disassembly.

11. Check the end clearance of both gears to the oil pump face. Be sure to measure between the face of the gears and the pump face, not between the crescent and the pump face. Use a straight edge and a feeler gage. Clearance should be between .0127-.0839 mm or .0005 to .00325 inch.

12. Install the oil pump wear plate onto the oil pump. Insert guide pins into the oil pump for alignment with the torque converter housing. Inspect the front face of the torque converter housing for oil leaks. Install a new converter housing oil seal, using the proper tool.

13. Install the torque converter housing on the oil pump. Loosely install the oil pump bolts into the converter housing.

14. Use the torque converter housing to oil pump aligning tool to align the two units. The tool should bottom on the oil pump gear.

NOTE: Failure to use this tool will cause pump damage when the transmission is operated after assembly.

15. Tighten the five inner torque converter housing bolts to 14 ft. lbs. Rotate the alignment tool to check for freeness. Remove the tool.

16. Install a new pump flange gasket and rubber seal.

17. Position the proper size selective thrust washer onto the oil pump shaft. Retain the washer using petroleum jelly.

18. Install the two guide pins in the transmission case and lower the torque converter housing and oil pump into the transmission case. Bolt the two units together and torque the retaining bolts to 25 ft. lbs.

19. Check for correct assembly by turning the input shaft. Install a new O-ring seal on the input shaft.

GOVERNOR HUB

Disassembly

1. Using the proper tool, remove the snap ring from the output shaft.

2. Remove the governor hub from the output shaft.

Assembly

1. Before installation, inspect the three seal rings on the governor hub. Replace as required.

2. Remove the governor hub oil screen. Use care not to damage or lose the oil screen. Inspect the screen, clean it with solvent and air dry. Replace, if necessary.

3. Install the oil screen flush with the governor hub.

4. Inspect the governor hub splines for cracks or chipped teeth. Replace the governor hub if required.

5. Turn the case so that the bottom of the transmission is facing upward.

6. Slide the governor hub along the output shaft and seat it into the case. Use a liberal amount of transmission fluid on the oil seal rings.

7. Install the snap ring over the output shaft, using the proper installation tool.

GOVERNOR BODY AND SPEEDOMETER DRIVE GEAR

Disassembly

1. Depress the secondary valve spring, using the proper tool. Remove the secondary valve spring retainer.

2. Remove the secondary valve spring, secondary valve and primary valve from the governor body.

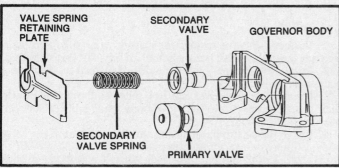

VALVE SPRING RETAINING PLATE • SECONDARY VALVE • GOVERNOR BODY • SECONDARY VALVE SPRING • PRIMARY VALVE

Governor assembly—exploded view (©General Motors Corp.)

3. Inspect the primary and secondary valve for nicks, burrs, etc. If necessary, use crocus cloth to remove any small burrs. Do not remove the sharp edges of the valve since these edges perform a cleaning action with the valve bore.

4. Inspect the secondary valve spring for breakage and distortion. Replace as required. Clean the assembly in solvent, air dry and blow out all oil passages. Inspect all oil passages and valve bores for nicks, burrs or varnish build up. Replace as necessary.

Assembly

1. Install the primary valve in the governor placing the small portion of the valve in first. Use a liberal amount of transmission fluid. There is no spring for the primary valve.

2. Install the secondary valve in the governor with the small spool portion of the valve first. Install the secondary valve spring.

3. Depress the secondary valve spring and install the retainer. Install a new governor body gasket.

4. Bolt the governor body to the governor hub. Torque to 6 ft. lbs. The two governor valves should move freely after the governor body is torqued.

5. Install the speedometer drive gear retaining clip onto the output shaft.

6. While depressing the retaining clip, slide the speedometer gear over the output shaft and install the gear and retaining clip.

SERVO PISTON

Disassembly

1. Remove the servo piston return spring and apply rod.

2. Hold the servo piston sleeve at the flat portion of the sleeve with a wrench, loosen the adjusting bolt locknut and remove.

3. Use an arbor press to depress the servo piston sleeve and remove the piston sleeve retaining ring.

4. Push the sleeve through the piston and remove the cushion spring and spring retainer.

5. Remove the servo piston ring.

6. Inspect the cushion spring, adjusting bolt and piston sleeve for damage. Inspect the piston for damage and the piston ring for side wear, replace if necessary.

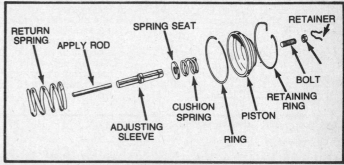

RETURN SPRING • APPLY ROD • SPRING SEAT • RETAINER • BOLT • RETAINING RING • PISTON • RING • CUSHION SPRING • ADJUSTING SLEEVE

Servo piston and related components (©General Motors Corp.)

Assembly

1. Assemble the servo piston by reversing the disassembly procedure.

2. Install the servo apply rod, spring and piston into the case, using a liberal amount of transmission fluid.

3. Compress the servo piston spring using the piston compressor tool. Tap the servo piston with a rubber mallet while compressing, until the piston is seated, to avoid damage to the oil seal ring or case.

4. Install the servo retaining ring. Remove the tool.

5. Use a 3/16″ hex head wrench on the servo adjusting bolt and adjust the servo apply rod by tightening the adjusting bolt 40 in. lbs. Be certain that the locknut remains loose. Back off the bolt exactly five turns. Tighten the nut, holding the adjusting bolt and sleeve firmly.

VALVE BODY

Disassembly

1. Remove the manual valve and manual valve link from the valve body, then turn the unit over so that the transfer plate is facing upward. Remove the two bolts and take off the transfer plate and gasket.

2. Using caution to avoid damage to the valve body, use a small "C"-clamp to compress the accumulator piston.

3. Using the proper tool, remove the retaining ring.

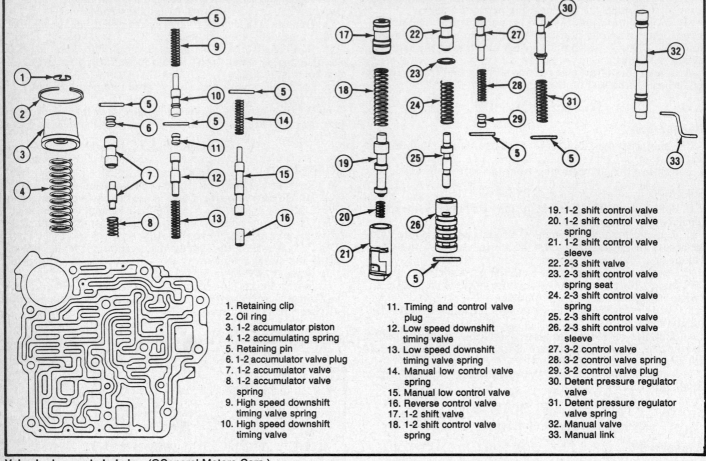

Valve body—exploded view (©General Motors Corp.)

1. Retaining clip
2. Oil ring
3. 1-2 accumulator piston
4. 1-2 accumulating spring
5. Retaining pin
6. 1-2 accumulator valve plug
7. 1-2 accumulator valve
8. 1-2 accumulator valve spring
9. High speed downshift timing valve spring
10. High speed downshift timing valve
11. Timing and control valve plug
12. Low speed downshift timing valve
13. Low speed downshift timing valve spring
14. Manual low control valve spring
15. Manual low control valve
16. Reverse control valve
17. 1-2 shift valve
18. 1-2 shift control valve spring
19. 1-2 shift control valve
20. 1-2 shift control valve spring
21. 1-2 shift control valve sleeve
22. 2-3 shift valve
23. 2-3 shift control valve spring seat
24. 2-3 shift control valve spring
25. 2-3 shift control valve
26. 2-3 shift control valve sleeve
27. 3-2 control valve
28. 3-2 control valve spring
29. 3-2 control valve plug
30. Detent pressure regulator valve
31. Detent pressure regulator valve spring
32. Manual valve
33. Manual link

4. Carefully loosen the "C"-clamp so that the spring pressure is gradually released.

5. Remove the accumulator piston, oil ring and spring.

6. Remove the 1-2 shift control valve retaining pin, valve sleeve, control valve, spring and valve. Check for burrs in the valve body bore made by the retaining pin before the other parts can be removed.

7. Similarly, remove the 2-3 shift control valve retaining pin and its related parts.

8. Remove the 3-2 control valve retaining pin and plug and its related parts.

9. Remove the detent pressure regulator valve retaining pin, its spring and detent pressure regulator valve.

10. Remove the high downshift timing valve retaining pins and its related parts.

11. Remove the manual low and reverse control valve retaining pin and its related parts.

12. Remove the manual low and reverse control valve retaining pin and its related parts.

13. Remove the 1-2 accumulator valve retaining pin and its related parts.

NOTE: It is extremely important to have a clean work area. Handle all parts carefully with clean hands. Tools should also be rinsed off since many valve failures are caused initially by dirt and other foreign matter preventing a valve from functioning properly. Use compressed air to blow out valve body passages. Check each valve for free movement in its bore. Crocus cloth may be used to remove small burrs. _DO NOT REMOVE THE SHARP EDGES OF THE VALVES. THESE SHARP EDGES ARE NECESSARY TO KEEP DIRT FROM STICKING IN THE BORE._

The entire valve body should be inspected carefully and if any parts are damaged, the entire valve body should be replaced. Inspect the spring for distortion or collapsed coils.

Assembly

1. Inspect the valve springs for distortion or collapsed coils. Replace the entire valve body assembly if any parts are damaged.

2. Inspect the transfer plate for dents or distortion. Replace, if necessary.

3. Reassemble the valves, springs, plugs and retaining pins in their proper location into the valve body using a liberal amount of transmission fluid.

4. Install the accumulator spring and the piston into the valve body. Compress the accumulator piston using tool J-22269-01 or equivalent. Install the retaining ring. Install a new valve body gasket and transfer plate.

5. Bolt the transfer plate and gasket to the valve body. Torque the assembly to 7 ft. lbs. Install the steel check balls into the transmission case. Install a new transmission case to transfer plate gasket on the transmission case.

6. Install a guide pin in the transmission case for correct alignment of the valve body and transfer plate.

7. Install the manual valve into the valve body bore using liberal amount of transmission fluid. Install the long side of the manual valve link pin into manual valve and position the manual valve in its proper location.

8. Install the valve body onto the transmission case. Position the short side of the link pin into the inside selector lever.

9. Torque the valve body bolts to 14 ft. lbs. Start in the center of the valve body and work outward.

Transmission Assembly

If the automatic transmission was completely overhauled, rather than a specific component, follow the assembly procedure below.

1. Install a new seal for the selector lever shaft and carefully install the shaft from the outside. Be careful not to damage the seal. Lube with DEXRON® II.

2. Insert the spring pin to secure the selector lever shaft.

3. Install selector lever on shaft and tighten nut.

4. Insert the parking pawl actuating rod retaining ring.

5. With the transmission rotated so that the front of the case is upward, place the low band in the case and locate the band onto the anchor pins in the case.

6. Place the torrington bearing (reaction sun gear-to-case) into the case.

7. Install the reaction sun gear and drum into the band so that the reaction sun gear is facing upward. Then install the torrington bearing (output shaft-to-output sun gear) onto the sun gear. Petroleum jelly will help hold it in place.

8. Install the torrington bearing (sun gear-to-output shaft) and thrust washer (sun gear-to-output shaft) and planetary carrier assembly into the case so that it splines with the reaction sun gear.

9. Make sure the second clutch drive plates are aligned. Then, insert the third clutch drum, seating the third clutch drum splines into the second clutch spline plates.

10. Holding the assemblies together by grasping the input shafts, lower into the transmission case, indexing the ring gear in the second clutch drum with the long planetary pinion gear teeth.

11. Install the reverse clutch pressure plate with the flat side up. Make certain that the lug on the pressure plate fits into one of the narrow notches in the case. Then install a reverse clutch steel plate, composition plate, steel, composition, etc. into the case using plenty of DEXRON® II on the clutch surfaces.

12. Install the reverse clutch cushion plate (wave washer) making sure that all three of its lugs are engaged in the narrow notches in the case.

NOTE: At this point the end play must be measured. Jig up a dial indicator to index on the second clutch drum hub. Desired end play is .014 to .031 inch (0.36 mm to 0.79 mm). Compare the thickness of the selective washer (washer number 1, oil pump hub-to-second clutch). If this washer, in conjunction with the measured end play will not produce the desired end play, select a different washer from the chart.

SELECTIVE WASHER APPLICATION CHART
180C Automatic Transmission

Part Number	Thickness (inches)
5258202	.069-.074
5258203	.075-.079
5258204	.080-.084
5258205	.085-.089
5258206	.090-.094
5258207	.095-.100

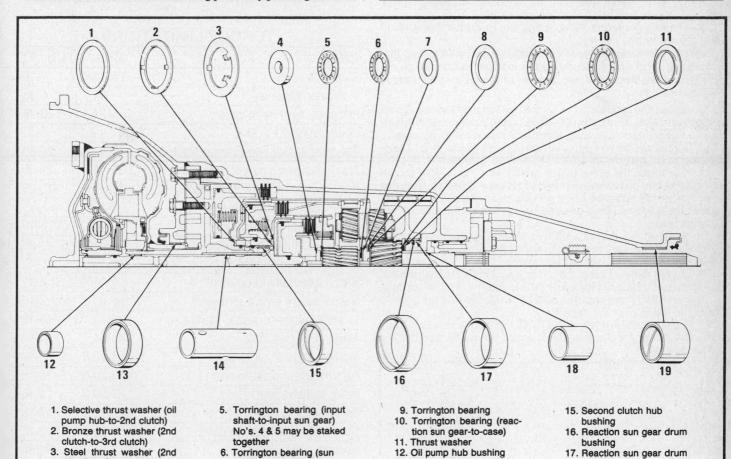

1. Selective thrust washer (oil pump hub-to-2nd clutch)
2. Bronze thrust washer (2nd clutch-to-3rd clutch)
3. Steel thrust washer (2nd clutch-to-3rd clutch)
4. Thrust washer (input shaft-to-input sun gear)
5. Torrington bearing (input shaft-to-input sun gear) No's. 4 & 5 may be staked together
6. Torrington bearing (sun gear-to-output shaft)
7. Thrust washer
8. Thrust washer (output shaft-to-reaction sun gear)
9. Torrington bearing
10. Torrington bearing (reaction sun gear-to-case)
11. Thrust washer
12. Oil pump hub bushing (front)
13. Converter housing bushing
14. Oil pump body bushing (rear)
15. Second clutch hub bushing
16. Reaction sun gear drum bushing
17. Reaction sun gear drum bushing sleeve
18. case bushing
19. Extension bushing

Thrust washer and bearing location guide (©General Motors Corp.)

13. After determining the proper selective washers, install on the oil pump shaft with petroleum jelly. Use two headless bolts as guide pins in the case to help guide the pump in place. After installing the guide pins, with a new pump flange gasket installed, lower the converter housing and oil pump assembly into the case.

14. Remove the guide pins; bolt the converter housing to the case. The bolts should be torqued to 22-26 foot-pounds. Make sure the input shaft turns as a check for correct assembly.

15. For governor installation, it is beneficial to turn the transmission so that the bottom (oil pan flange) is facing upward. Then slide the governor hub onto the output shaft and seat it in the case. Protect the seals on the hub with a liberal amount of DEXRON® II.

16. Install the snap ring over the output shaft.

17. Using a new governor body gasket, bolt the governor body to the hub; torque to 6-8 foot-pounds. The governor valves should move freely.

18. Install the speedometer drive gear retaining clip on the output shaft, then slide the gear on. Depress the clip and snap the gear into place.

19. With a new gasket, install the extension housing, making sure the parking pawl shaft will align. Torque the bolts to 20-30 foot-pounds.

20. Install the speedometer driven gear and the retainer into the slot in the speedometer housing. Torque the retainer bolt to 6-8 foot-pounds.

Install the detent valve, using a new seal and plenty of DEXRON® II. Make sure that the detent valve, sleeve, spring and spring seat are installed in proper order.

21. Depress the detent valve spring and insert the spring pin to hold the assembly.

NOTE: The detent valve sleeve contains slots which must face the oil pan. Make sure the spring pin is inserted into the groove provided in the sleeve and not into one of the oil passage slots in the sleeve.

22. Install the modulator valve and sleeve into the case, small end of valve first. Use a new "O-Ring" on the vacuum modulator and install plunger, and then thread modulator into the case.

23. Install the servo apply rod, spring and piston in the transmission case, again with DEXRON® II as lubricant.

24. Compress the servo piston spring being careful of the oil seal ring as the piston moves inward. Install the servo retaining ring. Adjust the servo by using a 3/16" hex wrench on a socket to tighten the bolt to 40 inch-pounds, being certain that the lock nut remains loose.

25. Back off the bolt *exactly* five turns. Tighten the lock nut.

26. Install the steel check balls in the oil passages of the case. Make sure they are in the proper places

27. Install a new gasket onto the case. Before installing the transfer plate. Use bolts for guide pins to aid in correct alignment of the valve body and transfer plate. Remember that the bolts to make the guide pins are metric.

28. Lube manual valve with DEXRON® II and install in its bore. Install the *long side* of the manual valve link pin into the manual valve.

29. Install the *short end* of the manual valve link into the selector lever. Install the valve body and transfer plate assembly over the guide pins; make sure valve link does not come off.

30. Install the selector lever roller spring and retainer. These bolts are torqued to 13-15 foot-pounds. The valve body bolts should be troqued starting from the center and working outward. These too should be torqued to 13-15 foot-pounds, as well as the reinforcement plate bolts which can be installed at this point.

31. Replacement of the oil strainer is recommended, as well as using a new gasket. Torque the screws to 13-15 foot-pounds.

32. With a new gasket, install the servo cover and torque the screws to 17-19 foot-pounds.

33. Install a new pan gasket and pan; torque the screws to 7-9 foot-pounds.

34. Slide the torque converter in place, making sure that the pump hub keyway is seated in the oil pump drive lugs. Check the distance from the case flange to the converter hub. It should be .83 to .91 inch. Turn the converter to check for free movement.

TORQUE LIMITATIONS

Item	N•m	Lb. Ft.
Oil pan-to-case	9.8-12.8	7-10
Modulator assembly	52	38
Extension housing-to-case	27.5-34.3	20-25
Oil pressure check plug	6.4-9.8	5-7
Converter housing-to-cylinder block	27-41	20-30
Transmission support-to-extension	39-48	29-36
Shift lever-to-selector lever shaft	20-34	15-25
Detent cable, retainer-to-case	7-10	5-7
Oil cooler fittings-to-case	11-16	8-12
Oil cooler fittings-to-radiator	20-34	15-25
Oil cooler hose clamps-to-cooler lines	0.8-1.2	.6-.9
Shifter assembly-to-console	8.5-11	6-8
Neutral safety switch-to-bracket	1.6-2.2	1.2-1.6
Lower cover-to-converter housing	18-22	13-16
Flexplate-to-converter	41-54	30-40
Transfer plate-to-valve body	7.8-10.8	6-8
Reinforcement plate-to-case	17.7-20.6	13-15
Valve body-to-case	17.7-20.6	13-15
Servo cover-to-case	22.6-25.5	17-19
Converter housing-to-oil pump	17.7-20.6	13-15
Converter housing-to-case	32.4-35.3	24-26
Selector lever locknut	10.8-14.7	8-11
Governor body-to-governor hub	7.8-9.8	6-7
Servo adjusting bolt locknut	16.7-20.6	12-15
Planetary carrier lock plate	27-48	20-35

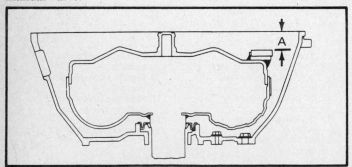

Torque converter installation (©General Motors Corp.)

SPECIAL TOOLS

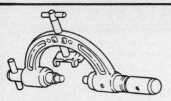

TRANSMISSION HOLDING FIXTURE

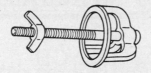

CLUTCH PISTON COMPRESSOR

CONVERTER HOUSING BUSHING REMOVER/ INSTALLER

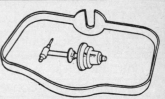

CONVERTER LEAK TEST FIXTURE

REACTION SUN GEAR DRUM BUSHING SLEEVE INSTALLER

2ND CLUTCH PISTON SEAL INSTALLER

CAPE CHISEL

BUSHING REMOVER

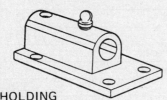

HOLDING FIXTURE BASE

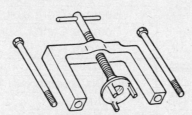

SERVO/3RD CLUTCH PISTON SPRING COMPRESSOR

REACTION SUN GEAR DRUM BUSHING INSTALLER

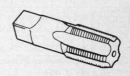

OIL PUMP BUSHING REMOVER (3/4 - 14 NPT)

REAR CASE BUSHING REMOVER/INSTALLER

CONVERTER-TO-OIL PUMP ALIGNMENT TOOL

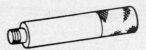

DRIVER HANDLE

2ND CLUTCH DRUM BUSHING REMOVER/ INSTALLER

CONVERTER HOUSING OIL SEAL INSTALLER

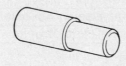

OIL PUMP BUSHING INSTALLER

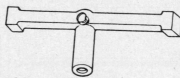

OIL PUMP-TO-2ND CLUTCH DRUM GAGING TOOL

SLIDE HAMMER

VACUUM MODULATOR WRENCH

EXTENSION HOUSING OIL SEAL INSTALLER

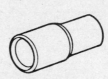

EXTENSION HOUSING BUSHING REMOVER/ INSTALLER

CONVERTER HOUSING SEAL REMOVER

INDEX

GENERAL MOTORS
TURBO HYDRA-MATIC 200-4R

TRANSMISSION APPLICATION CHART

Year	Division	Transmission Model
1981 and Later	Buick	200-4R
1981 and Later	Cadillac	200-4R
1981 and Later	Oldsmobile	200-4R
1981 and Later	Pontiac	200-4R
1981 and Later	Chevrolet	200-4R

The T.H.M. 200-4R automatic transmission is a fully automatic unit consisting primarily of a three element hydraulic torque converter with a converter clutch, a compound planetary gear set and an overdrive unit. Five multiple-disc clutches, two roller clutches, and a band provide the friction elements required to obtain the desired function of the compound planetary gear set and the overdrive unit.

The torque converter couples the engine to the planetary gears and overdrive unit through oil and hydraulically provides additional torque multiplication when required. The combination of the compound planetary gear set and the overdrive unit provides four forward ratios and one reverse.

The torque converter consists of a converter clutch, a driving member, driven member and a reaction member known as the pressure plate and damper assembly, pump, turbine and stator.

Changing of the gear ratios is fully automatic in relation to vehicle speed and engine torque. Vehicle speed and engine torque signals are constantly fed to the automatic transmission to provide the proper gear ratio for maximum efficiency and performance at all throttle openings.

The shift quadrant has seven positions, which are indicated in the following order: P, R, N, D, 3, 2, 1.

Transmission and Torque Converter Identification

TRANSMISSION

The THM 200-4R automatic transmission can be identified by the serial number plate which is located on the right side of the transmission case. This identification tag contains information that is important when servicing the unit.

TORQUE CONVERTER

The torque converter is a welded unit and cannot be disassembled for service. Any internal malfunctions require the replacement of the converter assembly. The replacement converter must be matched to the model transmission through parts identification. No specific identification is available for matching the converter to the transmission for the average repair shop.

DIESEL ENGINES

Vehicles equipped with diesel engines use a different torque converter. To identify these units, examine the weld nuts. Most gas engine converters have their weld nuts spot welded onto the converter housing, usually in two spots. The diesel converters have the weld nuts completely welded around their entire circumference.

TURBOCHARGED V6 ENGINES

Vehicles equipped with turbocharged V6 engines use a different torque converter. These units have a high stall speed converter, allowing a stall speed of about 2800 rpm. These converters must not be replaced with a standard converter, otherwise performance will be sluggish and unsatisfactory. When ordering replacements for the turbocharged units, make certain to specify that the vehicle has turbocharging in order to obtain the proper replacement.

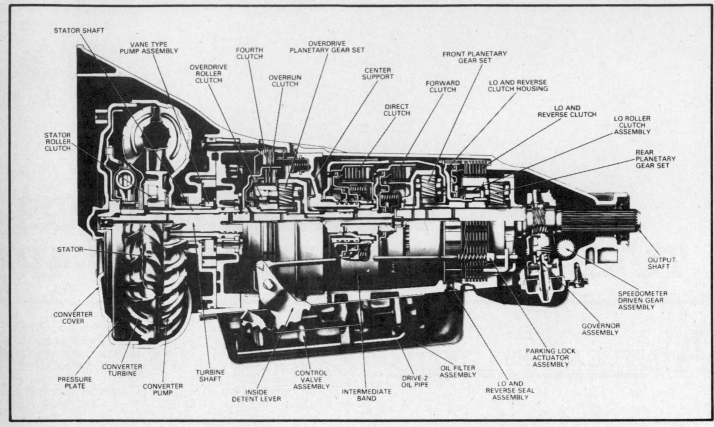

THM 200-4R automatic transmission—exploded view (© General Motors Corp.)

Metric Fasteners

Metric bolt sizes and thread pitches are used for all fasteners on the THM 200-4R automatic transmission. The use of metric tools is mandatory in the service of this transmission.

Do not attempt to interchange metric fasteners for inch system fasteners. Mismatched or incorrect fasteners can result in damage to the transmission unit through malfunctions, breakage or possible personal injury. Care should be taken to reuse the fasteners in the same locations as removed, whenever possible. Due to the large number of alloy parts used, torque specifications should be strictly observed. Before installing capscrews into aluminum parts, always dip screws into oil to prevent the screws from galling the aluminumn threads and to prevent seizing.

Fluid Capacities

The fluid capacities are approximate and the correct fluid level should be determined by the dipstick indicator. Use only Dexron® II automatic transmission fluid when adding or servicing the THM 200-4R automatic transmission.

FLUID CAPACITIES THM 200-4R

Division	Fluid Change (Pints)	Overhaul (Pints)
Buick	7	22①
Cadillac	7②	22
Oldsmobile	7	22
Pontiac	7	22
Chevrolet	7	22

① 1983 models use 23 pints   ② 1983 models use 10.6 pints

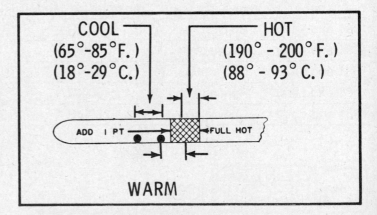

Automatic transmission dipstick (© General Motors Corp.)

Checking Fluid Level

The THM 200-4R transmission is designed to operate at the "FULL HOT" mark on the dipstick at normal operating temperatures, which range from 190° to 200° F. Automatic transmissions are frequently overfilled because the fluid level is checked when cold and the dipstick level reads low. However, as the fluid warms up, the level will rise, as much as ¾ of an inch. Note that if the transmission fluid is too hot, as it might be when operating under city traffic conditions, trailer towing or extended high speed driving, again an accurate fluid level cannot be determined until the fluid has cooled somewhat, perhaps 30 minutes after shutdown.

To determine proper fluid level under normal operating temperatures, proceed as follows:

1. Make sure vehicle is parked level.
2. Apply parking brake; move selector to Park.
3. Start engine but do not race engine. Allow to idle.
4. Move selector through each range, back to PARK, then check level. The fluid should read "FULL HOT" (transmission end of dipstick too hot to hold comfortably).

Do not overfill the transmission. Overfilling can cause foaming and loss of fluid from the vent. Overheating can also be a result of overfilling since heat will not transfer as readily. Notice the condition of the fluid and whether there seems to be a burnt smell or metal particles on the end of the dipstick. A milky appearance is a sign of water contamination, possibly from a damaged cooling system. All this can be a help in determining transmission problems and their source.

Fluid Drain Intervals

The main considerations in establishing fluid change intervals are the type of driving that is done and the heat levels that are generated by such driving. Normally, the fluid and strainer would be changed at 100,000 miles. However, the following conditions may be considered severe transmission service.

1. Heavy city traffic
2. Hot climates regularly reaching 90° F. or more
3. Mountainous areas
4. Frequent trailer pulling
5. Commercial use such as delivery service, taxi or police car use

If the vehicle is operated under any of these conditions, it is recommended that the fluid be changed and the filter screen serviced at 15,000 mile intervals. Again, be sure not to overfill the unit. Only one pint of fluid is required to bring the level from "ADD" to "FULL" when the transmission is hot.

MODIFICATIONS

Torque Converter Clutch Inoperative

Some 1983 vehicles equipped with the 200-4R automatic transmission may experience a condition of an inoperative torque converter clutch. On DFI equipped vehicles, a code 39 would also be present. This condition may be caused by the torque converter clutch harness locating clip grounding the wiring to the automatic transmission control valve body assembly.

For identification purposes, the automatic transmission serial number tag is located on the right rear of the transmission case. All 200-4R automatic transmissions with a date build code prior to 245 may have been assembled with the TCC harness locating clip positioned incorrectly.

To correct the inoperative TCC condition, replace the applicable torque converter clutch solenoid and harness assembly (P/N 8634960 for AA model transmissions and P/N 8634961 for OM model transmissions). Correctly position the clip by rotating it as far rearward as possible; then, bend it toward the depression in the control valve body assembly (approximately 60° clockwise from its original position.

HARSH AUTOMATIC TRANSMISSION UPSHIFTS

Some 1982 and 1983 "C" body vehicles, equipped with the HT4100 engine may experience delayed and/or harsher than normal automatic transmission upshifts, especially the 1-2 shift. This condition may be caused by a misrouted transmission TV cable, that results in an incorrect adjustment between the cable actuating lever on the throttle linkage and the TV link in the automatic transmission.

When diagnosing a vehicle exhibiting this condition, inspect the TV cable housing at the locator clip for any indication of the housing having been moved ¾ to 1 inch from its original mounting. If the cable has been moved, it will be necessary to reroute the cable to its correct position, before re-adjusting the TV cable. Replacement of the cable assembly is necessary only if the cable binds or sticks because of being kinked in the locator clip area. Be sure that the cable is routed around the oil pressure switch wiring harness, HEI distributor, air pipes and the manifold vacuum pipes.

"BUZZ" CONDITION ELIMINATION DUE TO NEW PUMP DESIGN

New design pump assemblies were introduced late in the 1982 model year. This new design eliminates a buzz condition that is caused by the pressure regulator valve. The design changes involve a new pump body, pump cover and the pressure regulator valve with its orifice.

When servicing these components on all 1981 and 1982 automatic transmissions, a complete pump assembly must be installed. See the pump assembly chart for the required part ordering information.

When replacing the pump, be sure not to mix the old pump halves (body and cover) with the new design pump halves as this may create a "no drive" condition, or may not eliminate the buzz condition at all.

AUTOMATIC TRANSMISSION OIL LEAK

Early production 1983 vehicles equipped with the TH4100 engine may experience an automatic transmission oil leak at the front edge of the automatic transmission oil pan. This condition can be caused by interference between the back edge of the flywheel cover and the front edge of the automatic transmission oil pan flange. A new design flywheel cover, part number 1627822, has been put into production to eliminate this interference.

Vehicles with this condition can be corrected by removing about 1/16-1/8 inch of material from the top, rear edge of the two radii and the back edge of the flywheel cover with a file. Before resealing the automatic transmission oil pan with RTV sealant make certain its flange is not deformed.

SHIFT BUSINESS WHILE IN CRUISE CONTROL—MODEL BY

Some 1982 vehicles equipped with the 4.1 Liter V6 engine may experience a transmission shift busyness at highway speeds with the cruise control engaged. This problem refers to the cycling of the automatic transmission between fourth and third gears. The condition is most noticeable while driving up inclines. To correct this condition, install transmission service package 8634987 into the control valve body assembly. This service package contains a 3-4 throttle valve, bushing and spring and a steel coiled pin.

PUMP ASSEMBLY CHART

Model Year	Transmission Model	Pump Assembly	Pressure Regulator
1981-82	BY,AA,AD	8639077	8637546
1982	OM	8639135	8637546
1982	AH	8639079	8637546

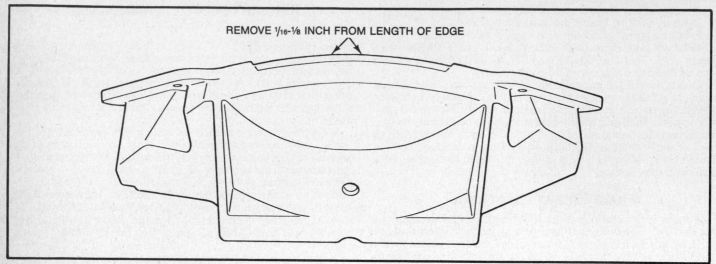

REMOVE ¹/₁₆-¹/₈ INCH FROM LENGTH OF EDGE

Grinding points on back edge of flywheel cover
(© General Motors Corp.)

PARKING LOCK ASSEMBLY—DESIGN CHANGE

Starting in October, 1982, the parking lock rod assembly in the 1983 model year automatic transmission was changed from a two piece unit to a one piece assembly.

When servicing the parking rod mechanism, it is important that the correct parts be used. The detent levers and rod assemblies are not interchangeable between the two designs. The two piece design part numbers are 8639110 and 8634184. The one piece design part number is 8634991.

NO FOURTH GEAR

Some 1982 and 1983 vehicles equipped with the THM 200-4R automatic transmission may experience a no fourth gear engagement condition. On DFI equipped vehicles, codes 29 and/or 39 could also be present. The no fourth gear condition may be caused by a broken hub weld on the overrun clutch housing.

When diagnosing vehicles exhibiting this condition, test drive the unit applying a light throttle in the drive range to about 30-35 MPH (third gear). Move the selector lever into manual second and release the throttle. The transmission should downshift and coastdown overrun braking should occur.

If this does not happen, remove the automatic transmission from the vehicle. Inspect the overrun clutch housing for a brake at the hub weld. If the hub weld is broken, the cause is due to misaligned pinions in the overdrive carrier. In all cases where the hub weld is broken on the overrun clutch housing, both the overrun clutch housing and the overdrive carrier must be replaced. Use part numbers 8634107 (overrun clutch housing) and 8634117 (overdrive carrier).

SELECTIVE WASHER—NEW DESIGN

Any time internal repairs are performed to the 200-4R automatic transmission, inspect the selective washer used to establish front (input) unit end play for wear or damage.

Beginning in late March 1983, a new design selective washer went into production and is now available for service on the forward clutch shaft to output shaft units. This new service part is made from a different material and can be identified by a raised portion on it's identification tab.

When servicing a transmission that necessitates the replacement of the front (input) unit selective washer due to wear or damage, use the following procedure:

1. Inspect both shafts for wear or damage on the selective washer mating surfaces. If damage or wear is found, replace the necessary components.

2. Select the proper selective washer from the selective washer chart.

3. Check the front end play to verify the proper washer selection. Front end play should be 0.022-0.051 in.

SELECTIVE WASHER CHART

ID Number	Color	Part Number	Thickness (inches)
1	—	8639291	0.065-0.070
2	—	8639292	0.070-0.075
3	Black	8639293	0.076-0.080
4	Light Green	8639294	0.081-0.085
5	Scarlet	8639295	0.086-0.090
6	Purple	8639296	0.091-0.095
7	Cocoa Brown	8639297	0.096-0.100
8	Orange	8639298	0.101-0.106
9	Yellow	8639299	0.106-0.111
10	Light Blue	8639300	0.111-0.116
11	Blue	8639301	0.117-0.121
12	—	8639302	0.122-0.126
13	Pink	8639303	0.127-0.131
14	Green	8639304	0.132-0.136
15	Gray	8639305	0.137-0.141

CLUTCH AND BAND APPLICATION CHART
Turbo Hydra-matic 200-4R

Selector	Converter Clutch	Overrun Clutch	Intermediate Band	Overdrive Roller Clutch	Direct Clutch	Low Reverse Clutch	Forward Clutch	Fourth Clutch	Low and Reverse Clutch
Park	Released	Released	Released	Holding	Released	Not Holding	Released	Released	Released
Neutral	Released	Released	Released	Holding	Released	Not Holding	Released	Released	Released
Drive (1st gear)	—	Holding	—	—	—	Holding	Applied	—	—
Drive (2nd gear)	Released	—	Applied	Holding	—	—	Applied	—	—
Drive (converter clutch applied)	Applied	—	Applied	Holding	—	—	Applied	—	—
Drive (3rd gear)	Applied	—	—	Holding	Applied	—	Applied	—	—
Drive (4th gear)	Applied	—	—	—	Applied	—	Applied	Applied	—
Reverse	—	—	—	Holding	Applied	Applied	—	—	—

CHILTONS THREE "C's" TRANSMISSION DIAGNOSIS CHART
Turbo Hydra-matic 200-4R

Condition	Cause	Correction
Transmission oil leak	a) Attaching pan bolts loose	a) Retorque pan bolts
	b) Filler pipe seal damaged	b) Replace filler pipe seal
	c) T.V. cable seal damaged, missing or improperly positioned.	c) Replace T.V. cable seal as required.
	d) Real transmission seal damaged	d) Replace rear transmission seal
	e) Speedometer drive O-ring damaged	e) Replace speedometer drive O-ring seal
	f) Line pressure tap plug	f) Replace or repair as necessary
	g) Fourth clutch pressure tap plug	g) Replace or repair as necessary
	h) Porous casting	h) Replace transmission case as required
	i) Intermediate servo O-ring damaged	i) Replace intermediate servo O-ring
	j) Front pump seal damaged or bolts loose	j) Replace pump seal or tighten pump bolts

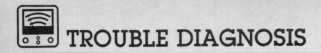

CHILTONS THREE "C's" TRANSMISSION DIAGNOSIS CHART

Condition	Cause	Correction
No drive in drive range	a) Low oil level b) Manual linkage misadjusted c) Low oil pressure due to plugged oil filter d) Pump assembly pressure regulator valve stuck e) Pump rotor tangs damaged by torque converter f) Overdrive unit springs missing in the roller clutch or rollers galled g) Forward clutch does not apply h) Cup plug leaking or missing in the rear of the forward clutch shaft i) Low and reverse roller clutch springs missing or rollers galled	a) Adjust oil level b) Adjust manual linkage c) Replace transmission oil filter d) Repair as required e) Correct the problem as required f) Repair or replace defective components as required g) Repair forward clutch assembly h) Replace cup plug i) Repair or replace low and reverse roller clutch assembly
High or low oil pressure	a) Throttle valve cable misadjusted, broken, binding or wrong part b) Throttle valve or plunger valve binding c) Pressure regulator valve binding d) T.V. boost valve binding e) T.V. boost valve not the right part number—low pressure only f) Reverse boost valve binding g) Manual valve unhooked or mispositioned h) Pressure relief valve ball or spring missing i) Pump slide seal stuck or seal damaged or missing j) Pump air bleed orifice missing or damaged k) T.V. limit valve binding l) Line bias valve binding in open position—high pressure only m) Line bias valve binding in closed position—low pressure only	a) Repair or replace throttle valve cable as required b) Repair or replace defective component as required c) Free binding pressure regulator valve as required d) Free binding T.V. boost valve e) Install the correct T.V. boost valve f) Free binding reverse boost valve g) Repair or replace manual valve as required h) Repair or replace pressure relief valve components i) Replace seal as required j) Replace as required k) Correct T.V. limit valve as required l) Repair or replace valve as required m) Repair or replace valve as required
1-2 shift—full throttle only	a) Throttle valve cable stuck, unhooked or broken b) Throttle valve cable misadjusted c) T.V. exhaust ball lifter or number 5 ball binding or mispositioned d) Throttle valve and plunger binding	a) Repair or replace cable as required b) Adjust cable as required c) Replace or reposition T.V. exhaust ball number 5 as required d) Correct as required

CHILTONS THREE "C's" TRANSMISSION DIAGNOSIS CHART

Condition	Cause	Correction
1-2 Shift—Full throttle only	e) Valve body assembly gaskets leaking, damaged or incorrectly installed	e) Replace gaskets as necessary
	f) Transmission case porosity	f) Replace transmission case
First speed only—no 1-2 shift	a) Governor and governor feed passages plugged	a) Free blockage as necessary
	b) Governor ball or balls missing in governor assembly	b) Replace ball or balls as required
	c) Inner governor cover rubber O-ring seal missing or leaking	c) Replace rubber O-ring seal
	d) Governor seal shaft seal missing or damaged	d) Replace governor shaft seal
	e) Governor driven gear stripped	e) Replace governor driven gear
	f) Governor weights binding on pin	f) Correct problem as required
	g) Governor driven gear not engaged with governor shaft	g) Correct problem as necessary
	h) Control valve assembly 1-2 shift, Low 1st detent, or 1-2 throttle valve stuck in downshift position	h) Free stuck valve as required
	i) Control valve assembly spacer plate gaskets in wrong position	i) Replace spacer plate gaskets as required
	j) Intermediate band anchor pin missing or unhooked from band	j) Repair or replace band anchor pin
	k) Intermediate servo cover oil seal ring missing	k) Check and replace ring as required
	l) Wrong intermediate cover and piston	l) Check part and replace as necessary
	m) 1-2 accumulator housing bolts loose or housing face damaged	m) Repair or replace parts as required
	n) 1-2 accumulator plate missing or damaged	n) Replace spacer plate as required
Drive in Neutral	a) Manual linkage misadjusted	a) Adjust linkage
	b) Forward clutch does not release	b) Correct as necessary
	c) Forward clutch exhaust ball sticking	c) Free sticking exhaust ball as required
	d) Forward clutch plates burned together	d) Replace forward clutch assembly
	e) Case leakage at forward clutch passage (D4)	e) Correct case as required
First and second speed only—no 2-3 shift	a) 2-3 shift valve or 2-3 throttle valve stuck in the downshift position	a) Free the stuck valve or valves as required
	b) Valve body gaskets leaking mispositioned or incorrectly installed	b) Replace valve body spacer gaskets as required
	c) Reverse/3rd check ball not seating or damaged	c) Properly seat check ball or replace
	d) Transmission case porosity	d) Replace transmission case as needed

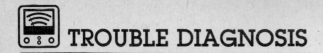

CHILTONS THREE "C's" TRANSMISSION DIAGNOSIS CHART
Turbo Hydra-matic 200-4R

Condition	Cause	Correction
First and second speeds only, no 2-3 shifts	e) Direct clutch feed passage in the center support plugged or not drilled through	e) Free blockage or drill passage through
	f) Direct clutch inner seal ring missing or damaged	f) Replace or install inner seal ring
	g) Center oil seal ring missing or damaged on direct clutch	g) Replace or install seal ring
	h) Check ball or retainer missing or damaged from direct clutch piston	h) Replace direct clutch ball
	i) Direct clutch plates damaged or missing	i) Replace damaged or missing plates as required
	j) Direct clutch backing plate snap ring out of groove	j) Correct as required
	k) Release spring guide mislocated, preventing piston check ball from seating in retainer	k) Correct as required
	l) Servo to case oil seal broken or missing on intermediate servo piston	l) Replace seal on piston
	m) Intermediate servo or capsule missing or damaged	m) Correct as required
	n) Exhaust hole in case between servo piston seal rings plugged or not drilled	n) Free blockage or drill passage
	o) Bleed orifice cup plug missing from intermediate servo pocket in case	o) Install orifice cup plug
Slips on 1-2 shift	a) Low fluid level	a) Correct fluid level
	b) Spacer plate and gaskets damaged or not installed properly	b) Correct as required
	c) Accumulator valve sticking in valve body or weak or missing spring	c) Free sticking valve or replace spring as required
	d) 1-2 accumulator piston seal leaking, spring missing or broken	d) Replace seal or spring as required
	e) Leak between 1-2 accumulator piston and pin	e) Correct as required
	f) 1-2 accumulator piston binding or piston bore damaged	f) Replace or repair accumulator piston as required
	g) Wrong intermediate band apply pin	g) Install correct pin
	h) Leakage between pin and case	h) Correct as required
	i) Apply pin feed hole not drilled completely	i) Drill hole through
	j) Porosity in intermediate servo piston	j) Replace piston
	k) Cover to intermediate servo seal ring missing or damaged	k) Replace seal ring
	l) Leak between intermediate servo apply pin and case	l) Find and correct leak
	m) T.V. cable not adjusted	m) Adjust T.V. cable
	n) T.V. limit valve binding	n) Correct as required

CHILTONS THREE "C's" TRANSMISSION DIAGNOSIS CHART
Turbo Hydra-matic 200-4R

Condition	Cause	Correction
Slips on 1-2 shift	o) Intermediate band worn or burned	o) Replace intermediate band
	p) Case porosity in 2nd clutch passage	p) Replace transmission case as required
Rough 1-2 shift	a) T.V. cable not adjusted or binding	a) Adjust T.V. cable or free binding as required
	b) Throttle valve or T.V. plunger binding	b) Correct binding as required
	c) T.V. limit valve, accumulator and line bias valve binding	c) Correct binding problem as required
	d) Wrong intermediate servo supply pin	d) Install correct pin
	e) Intermediate servo to case oil seal ring missing or damaged	e) Replace oil seal ring
	f) Bleed cup plug missing in case	f) Install bleed cup plug as required
	g) 1-2 accumulator oil ring damaged or piston stuck	g) Replace oil ring or free stuck piston
	h) 1-2 accumulator broken, spring missing or bore damaged	h) Repair or replace as required
	i) 1-2 shift check ball #8 missing or stuck	i) Free or replace check ball as required
Slips 2-3 shift	a) Low fluid level	a) Correct fluid level
	b) T.V. cable not adjusted	b) Adjust T.V. cable
	c) Throttle valve binding	c) Free binding throttle valve
	d) Direct clutch orifice partially blocked in spacer plate	d) Free blockage as required
	e) Intermediate servo to case oil seal ring missing or damaged	e) Replace or install new ring
	f) Intermediate servo or piston bore damaged	f) Replace intermediate servo
	g) Intermediate servo orifice bleed cup plug missing in case	g) Install cup plug as required
	h) Direct clutch piston or housing cracked	h) Replace piston or housing as required
	i) Direct clutch piston seals cut or missing	i) Replace or install new seals
	j) Check ball or capsule damaged in direct clutch	j) Correct as required
	k) Center support seal rings damaged or missing	k) Replace or install new center support seal rings
Rough 2-3 shift	a) T.V. cable mispositioned	a) Reposition T.V. cable
	b) Throttle valve and plunger binding	b) Correct binding as required
	c) T.V. limit valve binding	c) Correct T.V. limit valve binding
	d) Exhaust hole undrilled or plugged between intermediate servo piston seals, not allowing the servo piston to complete its stroke	d) Unplug or drill hole as required

CHILTONS THREE "C's" TRANSMISSION DIAGNOSIS CHART
Turbo Hydra-matic 200-4R

Condition	Cause	Correction
Rough 2-3 shift	e) 3rd accumulator check ball number 2 missing or stuck	e) Free blockage or replace ball as required
	f) 3-2 exhaust check ball number 4 missing or stuck	f) Free blockage or replace ball as required
Slips 3-4 shift	a) Low fluid level	a) Correct fluid level
	b) Control valve assembly spacer plate or gasket mispositioned or damaged	b) Correct gasket or spacer plate as required
	c) Accumulator valve sticking causing low 3-4 accumulator pressure	c) Free sticking accumulator valve as required
	d) Weak or missing accumulator valve spring	d) Install or replace spring
	e) 3-4 accumulator piston stuck, bore damaged or oil ring damaged	e) Replace defective component as required
	f) Center support bolts loose	f) Tighten bolts
	g) Fourth clutch piston surface damaged or seals damaged	g) Replace piston or seals as required
	h) Improper clutch plate usage	h) Check and replace plates as needed
	i) Fourth clutch plates burned	i) Replace fourth clutch plates
Rough 3-4 shift	a) T.V. cable mispositioned	a) Reposition cable as required
	b) Throttle valve and plunger binding	b) Free binding problem as required
	c) T.V. limit valve binding	c) Free binding T.V. limit valve
	d) 3-4 accumulator piston stuck or bore damaged	c) Free piston or correct bore damage as required
	e) Fourth clutch piston stuck	d) Free fourth clutch piston
First, second and third speed only—no 3-4 shift	a) 3-4 shift valve or 3-4 throttle valve stuck	a) Free stuck valve as required
	b) Orifice in spacer plate blocked	b) Free blockage as required
	c) Center support oil passages plugged or not drilled	c) Correct as required
	d) Center support bolts loose	d) Tighten bolts
	e) Fourth clutch piston cracked or damaged	e) Replace piston as required
	f) Fourth clutch piston seals damaged, missing or not installed properly	f) Correct as required
	g) Fourth clutch burned	g) Replace fourth clutch
	h) Overrun clutch plates burned	h) Replace clutch plates
No engine braking in manual low—first gear	a) Manual linkage misadjusted	a) Adjust manual linkage
	b) D-3 orifice in spacer plate plugged	b) Free blockage in spacer plate
	c) Valve body gaskets leaking, damaged or installed wrong	c) Correct as required
	d) D-2 oil pipe leaking or out of position	d) Correct leaking as required
	e) Low overrun clutch valve binding in valve body	e) Free binding valve

No engine braking in manual low—first gear	f) Low/reverse check ball number 10 missing or defective	f) Install or replace check ball
	g) Low/detent check ball number 9 missing or defective	g) Install or replace check ball
	h) Low/reverse overrun clutch orifice in spacer plate plugged	h) Unplug or replace spacer plate as required
	i) PT/D-3 check ball number 3 check ball missing or defective	i) Install or replace check ball
	j) D-3 oil passage plugged or not drilled in turbine shaft or overrun clutch	j) Drill or unplug oil passage
	k) Oil seals missing or damaged in the overrun clutch piston	k) Replace seals as required
	l) Overrun clutch seals burned	l) Replace as required
	m) Overrun clutch backing plate snap ring out of groove	m) Replace as required
	n) Low reverse clutch piston seals missing or damaged	n) Replace seals as required
	o) Cup plug or seal missing or damaged	o) Install or replace cup plug
No engine braking in manual 2nd—2nd gear	a) Manual linkage misadjusted	a) Adjust manual linkage
	b) Valve body gaskets leaking or damaged	b) Replace gaskets as required
	c) D-2 oil pipe leaking or out of position	c) Reposition or replace pipe
	d) D-3 orifice in spacer plate plugged	d) Unplug orifice in spacer plate
	e) PT/D-3 check ball number 3 missing or defective	c) Install or replace check ball as required
	f) Intermediate servo cover to case oil seal ring missing or damaged	f) Install or replace ring as required
	g) Intermediate band off its anchor pin, broken or burned	g) Repair as required
	h) D-3 oil passage not drilled through in overrun clutch or turbine shaft	h) Drill passage through
	i) Oil seals missing or damaged in overrun clutch piston	i) Replace or install seals
	j) Overrun clutches burned	j) Replace overrun clutch
	k) Overrun clutch backing plate snap ring out of groove	k) Replace components as required
No engine braking in manual 3rd—3rd gear	a) Valve body gaskets leaking or damaged	a) Replace gaskets as required
	b) D-2 oil pipe leaking or out of position	b) Reposition or replace pipe
	c) D-3 orifice in spacer plate plugged	c) Unplug orifice in spacer plate
	d) PT/D-3 check ball number 3/ missing or defective	d) Install or replace check ball as required
	e) D-3 oil passage not drilled through in overrun clutch or turbine shaft	e) Drill passage through
	f) Oil seals missing or damaged in overrun clutch piston	f) Replace or install seals
	g) Overrun clutches burned	g) Replace overrun clutch
	h) Overrun clutch backing plate snap ring out of groove	h) Replace components as required

CHILTONS THREE "C's" TRANSMISSION DIAGNOSIS CHART
Turbo Hydra-matic 200-4R

Condition	Cause	Correction
Will not hold in park	a) Manual linkage misadjusted	a) Adjust manual linkage
	b) Parking pawl binding in case	b) Correct binding as required
	c) Actuator rod, spring, or plunger damaged	c) Correct as required
	d) Parking pawl broken, loose or damaged	d) Correct as required
	e) Manual shaft to case pin missing or loose	e) Correct as required
	f) Inside detent lever and pin nut loose	f) Replace or repair as required
	g) Manual detent roller and spring assembly bolt loose	g) Tighten bolt as required
	h) Manual detent pin or roller damaged, mispositioned or missing	h) Correct as required

Hydraulic Control System

THROTTLE VALVE SYSTEM

The THM 200-4R automatic transmission uses a throttle valve (T.V.) cable between the carburetor and the control valve assembly. The T.V. cable controls automatic transmission line pressure, shift points, shift feel, part throttle downshift and detent downshifts. The cable operates the throttle lever and the bracket assembly. This cable and bracket assembly serve two basic functions.

1. The first duty of this assembly is to transfer the movement of the carburetor throttle plate to the T.V. plunger in the control valve assembly. Thus the T.V. pressure and line pressure can increase according to throttle opening; it also controls part throttle and detent downshifts. The proper adjustment of the T.V. cable is therefore critical, and is based on the T.V. plunger being fully depressed to flush with the T.V. bushing at wide open throttle.

2. The second function of the assembly involves the T.V. exhaust valve lifter rod, spring and T.V. exhaust ball. The function of this system is to prevent the transmission from operating at low (idle position) pressures, should the cable break or become disconnected. As long as the cable is properly connected, not broken or stretched, the T.V. lifter rod will not move from its normal, spring-loaded "up" position which holds the T.V. exhaust check ball off its seat. The T.V. lifter rod will drop down to allow the T.V. exhaust ball to seat only if the cable breaks or becomes disconnected and out of adjustment. With the transmission pan removed, it should be possible to pull down on the T.V. exhaust valve lifter rod and the spring should return the rod to its normal "up" position. If the throttle lever and bracket assembly and/or lifter rod binds or sticks so that the T.V. lifter rod cannot lift the exhaust ball off its seat, high line pressures and delayed upshifts will result. The shape of the throttle valve lifter rod is critical, especially the 90° (right angle) bend. *It must not be bent to any other angle or it will not work properly.*

The importance of the throttle valve cable and its associated parts becomes clear since, if the T.V. cable is broken, sticky, misadjusted or if an incorrect part for the car model is fitted, the car may exhibit various malfunctions which could be attributed to internal component failure. Sticking or binding T.V. linkage can result in delayed or full throttle shifts. The T.V. cable must be free to travel to the full throttle position and return to the closed throttle position without binding or sticking.

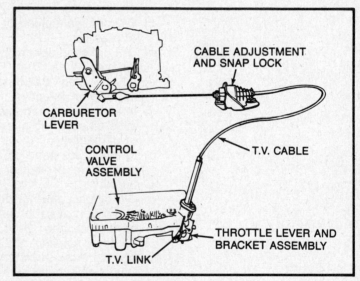

T.V. cable and related components (© General Motors Corp.)

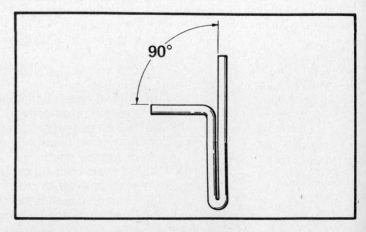

Throttle valve lifter rod (© General Motors Corp.)

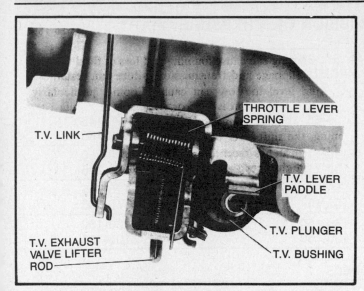

Throttle valve and bracket assembly (© General Motors Corp.)

Labels: T.V. LINK, THROTTLE LEVER SPRING, T.V. LEVER PADDLE, T.V. PLUNGER, T.V. BUSHING, T.V. EXHAUST VALVE LIFTER ROD

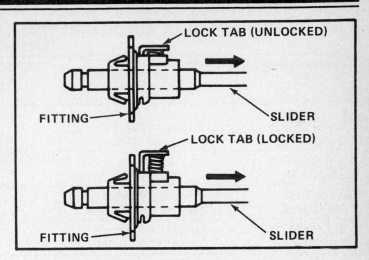

Labels: LOCK TAB (UNLOCKED), FITTING, SLIDER, LOCK TAB (LOCKED), FITTING, SLIDER

T.V. cable adjustment—typical (© General Motors Corp.)

Checking the throttle valve linkage for sticking or binding should be done with the engine running at idle, the selector in Neutral and the brakes set. The reason for this is that some binding or sticking may occur only when the engine is running and may not be noted or obtained with the engine turned off.

Checking T.V. Cable

To check the T.V. cable with the engine running, pull the cable to full travel beyond the carburetor lever pin that it attaches to and then release the cable. It should return to the closed throttle position against the carburetor lever pin.

If the T.V. cable sticks, it will remian ahead of the carburetor lever pin.

Sticking or Incorrectly Adjusted Cable Problems

NOTE: Check the throttle valve cable with the engine running in Neutral, not Park. Adjust the cable with the engine off.

A stuck T.V. cable could be caused by one or more of the following problems:
1. A damaged cable housing or a housing with a kink or sharp bend. Re-route or replace if required.
2. A sharp burr on the T.V. link dragging in the cable housing. Correct with a fine file, smoothing the end.
3. The T.V. link could be bent. Straighten or replace.
4. Misalignment of the throttle lever and bracket assembly, at the coiled pin in the control valve assembly.
5. The throttle lever and bracket assembly could possibly be binding or damaged or the throttle lever spring unhooked. Correct as necessary.

Length adjustment is also important to the T.V. cable. If it is adjusted too long, it may result in:
1. Early shifts or slipping shifts and/or no detent downshifts.
2. Delayed or full throttle shifts caused by forcing the transmission to operate in the high pressure mode. The complaint could be described as no upshifts and the closed throttle 3-2 shift may automatically occur as high as 45 mph. The transmission senses a malfunction and to prevent burning the clutches and band because of low line pressures, it will go into the high pressure mode. Line pressures and test procedures are described below. If, on the other hand, the T.V. cable is adjusted too short or not adjusted at all, it will result in raising the line pressure and shift points. Also, the carburetor will not be able to reach full throttle opening.

Diagnosis Tests

CONTROL PRESSURE TEST

NOTE: Before making the control pressure test, check the transmission fluid level, adjust the T.V. cable, check and adjust the manual linkage and be sure that the engine is not at fault, rather than the automatic transmission.

1. Install the oil pressure gauge to the automatic transmission. Connect a tachometer to the engine.
2. Raise and support the vehicle safely. Be sure that the brakes are applied at all times.
3. Total running time must not exceed two minutes.
4. Minimum line pressure check: set the T.V. cable to specification. Apply the brakes and take the reading in the ranges and rpm's that are indicated in the automatic transmission oil pressure chart.
5. Full line pressure check: hold the T.V. cable to the full extent of its travel. Apply the brakes and take the reading in the ranges and rpm's that are indicated in the automatic transmission oil pressure chart.
6. Record all readings and compare them with the data in the chart.

AIR PRESSURE TEST

Air pressure testing should be done in moderation to avoid excessive fluid spray and damage to the internal parts during disassembly and assembly, through partial retention of units.

STALL SPEED TEST

Stall speed testing is not recommended by General Motors Transmission Division. Extreme overheating of the transmission unit can occur, causing further internal damages. By pressure testing and road testing, the malfunction can be determined and by consulting the diagnosis chart, the cause and correction can normally be found.

ROAD TEST

1. Road test using all selective ranges, noting when discrepancies in operation or oil pressure occur.
2. Attempt to isolate the unit or circuit involved in the malfunction.
3. If engine performance indicates an engine tune-up is required, this should be performed before road testing is completed or transmission correction attempted. Poor engine performance can result in rough shifting or other malfunctions.

THM 200-4R AUTOMATIC TRANSMISSION OIL PRESSURE CHART

1981 MODELS

Transmission	Selector Lever	NORMAL OIL PRESSURE AT MINIMUM T.V. (P.S.I.)	NORMAL OIL PRESSURE AT FULL T.V. (P.S.I.)
BM,BY,EG, OG,CU,PH,	Park and Neutral at 1000 RPM	55-65 55-65	120-145 140-165
BM,BY,EG, OG,CU,PH,	Reverse at 1000 RPM	100-110 100-110	210-250 240-285
BM,BY,EG, OG,CU,PH,	Drive and Manual Third at 1000 RPM	55-65 55-65	120-145 140-165
BM,BY,EG, OG,CU,PH,	Manual Second and Low at 1000 RPM	130-150 130-150	130-150 130-150

1982 MODELS

Transmission	Selector Lever	NORMAL OIL PRESSURE AT MINIMUM T.V. (P.S.I.)	NORMAL OIL PRESSURE AT FULL T.V. (P.S.I.)
CQ,AA,HG,OG BY,CR	Park and Neutral at 1000 RPM	55-65 55-65	120-145 130-155
CQ,AA,HG,OG BY,CR	Reverse at 1000 RPM	100-110 100-110	210-250 215-260
CQ,AA,HG,OG BY,CR,	Drive and Manual Third at 1000 RPM	55-65 55-65	120-145 130-155
CQ,AA,HG,OG BY,CR	Manual Second and Low at 1000 RPM	130-150 130-150	130-150 130-150

1983 MODELS

Transmission	Selector Lever	NORMAL OIL PRESSURE AT MINIMUM T.V. (P.S.I.)	NORMAL OIL PRESSURE AT FULL T.V. (P.S.I.)
OM OG,AA,AP,BY,HE AH BR ZR	Park and Neutral at 1000 RPM	55-65 55-65 55-65 55-65 65-75	110-127 123-140 140-160 145-170 160-190
OM OG,AA,AP,BY,HE AH BR ZR	Reverse at 1000 RPM	105-120 105-120 105-120 105-120 120-140	220-235 230-260 260-297 275-315 293-350
OM OG,AA,AP,BY,HE AH BR ZR	Drive and Manual Third at 1000 RPM	55-65 55-65 55-65 55-65 65-75	110-127 123-140 140-160 145-170 160-190
OM OG,AA,AP,BY,HE AH BR ZR	Manual Second and Low at 1000 RPM	122-140 122-140 122-140 122-140 140-160	122-140 122-140 122-140 122-140 140-160

1984 MODELS

Transmission	Selector Lever	NORMAL OIL PRESSURE AT MINIMUM T.V. (P.S.I.)	NORMAL OIL PRESSURE AT FULL T.V. (P.S.I.)
AA,AP BQ BT,BY,CH,CR,OG,OJ CQ HE,HG OF OZ OM	PARK & NEUTRAL @ 1000 RPM	50-60 55-65 55-65 55-62 55-65 55-65 70-90 55-65	120-135 155-175 117-132 165-190 125-140 105-122 175-210 110-127

THM 200-4R AUTOMATIC TRANSMISSION OIL PRESSURE CHART
1981 MODELS

Transmission	Selector Lever	NORMAL OIL PRESSURE AT MINIMUM T.V. (P.S.I.)	NORMAL OIL PRESSURE AT FULL T.V. (P.S.I.)
		1984 MODELS	
AA,AP		95-110	220-250
BQ		105-120	285-325
BT,BY,CH,CR,OG,OJ		105-120	220-245
CQ	REVERSE	80-90	235-265
HE,HG	@ 1000 RPM	105-120	230-260
OF		105-120	200-225
OZ		130-167	325-392
OM		105-120	207-235
AA,AP		50-60	120-135
BQ		55-65	155-175
BT,BY,CH,CR,OG,OJ	DRIVE (D4)	55-65	117-132
CQ	& MANUAL	55-62	165-190
HE,HG	THIRD (D3)	55-65	125-140
OF	@ 1000 RPM	55-65	105-122
OZ		70-90	175-210
OM		55-65	110-127
AA,AP	*MANUAL	112-127	112-127
BQ,BT,BY,CH,CR, HG,HE,OG,OF,OJ, OM	SECOND (D2) & LOW (D1) @ 1000 RPM	122-137	122-137
CQ		115-130	115-130
OZ		152-196	152-196

CONVERTER STATOR OPERATION

The torque converter stator assembly and its related roller clutch can possibly have one of two different type malfunctions.
  A. The stator assembly freewheels in both directions.
  B. The stator assembly remains locked up at all times.

Condition A

If the stator roller clutch becomes ineffective, the stator assembly freewheels at all times in both directions. With this condition, the vehicle will tend to have poor acceleration from a standstill. At speeds above 30-35 MPH, the vehicle may act normal. If poor acceleration problems are noted, it should first be determined that the exhaust system is not blocked, the engine is in good tune and the transmission is in gear when starting out.

If the engine will freely accelerate to high rpm in netural, it can be assumed that the engine and exhaust system are normal. Driving the vehicle in reverse and checking for poor performance will help determine if the stator is freewheeling at all times.

Condition B

If the stator assembly remains locked up at all times, the engine rpm and vehicle speed will tend to be limited or restricted at high speeds. The vehicle performance when accelerating from a standstill will be normal. Engine over-heating may be noted. Visual examination of the converter may reveal a blue color from the overheating that will result.

Under conditions A or B above, if the converter has been removed from the transmission, the stator roller clutch can be checked by inserting a finger into the splined inner race of the roller clutch and trying to turn the race in both directions. The inner race should turn freely in the clockwise direction, but not turn or be very difficult to turn in the counterclockwise direction.

Converter Clutch Operation and Diagnosis

TORQUE CONVERTER CLUTCH

The GM Torque Converter Clutch (TCC) incorporates a unit inside the torque converter with a friction material attached to a pressure plate and splined to the turbine assembly. When the clutch is applied, it presses against the converter cover. The result is a mechanical direct drive of the engine to the transmission. This eliminates slippage and improves fuel economy as well as reducing fluid temperature.

There are a number of controls to operate the torque converter clutch, all determined by drive range selection. For example, the clutch is applied in direct drive above a certain preset minimum speed. At wider throttle openings the converter clutch will apply after the 2-3 shift. When the vehicle slows, or the transmission shifts out of direct drive, the fluid pressure is released, the converter clutch releases and the converter operates in the conventional manner.

The engaging of the converter clutch as well as the release is determined by the direction of the converter feed oil. The converter feed oil from the pressure regulator valve flows to the converter clutch apply valve. The position of the converter clutch apply valve controls the direction in which the converter feed oil flows to the converter.

A spring-loaded damper assembly is splined to the converter turbine assembly while the clutch pressure plate is attached to a pivoting unit on the damper assembly. The result is that the pressure plate is allowed to rotate independently of the damper assembly up to about 45 degrees. This rotation is controlled by springs in the damper assembly. The spring cushioning aids in reducing the effects felt when the converter clutch applies.

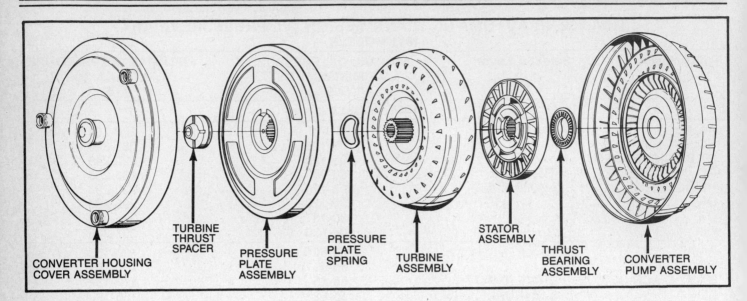

Torque converter clutch—exploded view (© General Motors Corp.)

To help insure that the converter clutch applies and releases at the proper times, controls have been incorporated into the electrical system. The converter clutch is applied when all of the conditions listed below exist:

1. The brake pedal is released.
2. The engine vacuum is above 2.5 inches of vacuum.
3. The engine coolant is above 130°F.
4. The vehicle speed is above 24 to 30 mph.
5. The transmission is in 3rd gear.

Converter clutch units are different for V6 or V8 engine applications and should not be interchanged. Poor engine and/or transmission operation will occur.

TROUBLESHOOTING THE TORQUE CONVERTER CLUTCH

Before diagnosing the TCC system as being at fault in the case of rough shifting or other malfunctions, make sure that the engine is in at least a reasonable state of tune. Also, the following points should be checked:

1. Check the transmission fluid level and correct as necessary.
2. Check the manual linkage adjustment and correct as necessary.
3. Road test the vehicle to verify the complaint. Make sure that the vehicle is at normal operating temperature.

G.M. TORQUE CONVERTER CLUTCH (TCCC)

Condition	Cause	Correction
Clutch applied in all ranges (engine stalls when put in gear)	a) Converter clutch valve stuck in apply position	a) Free stuck valve as required
Clutch does not apply: applies erratically or at at wrong speeds	a) Electrical malfunction in most instances	a) Follow troubleshooting procedure to determine if problem is internal or external to isolate defect
Clutch applies erratically; shudder and jerking felt	a) Vacuum hose leak b) Vacuum switch faulty c) Governor pressure switch malfunction d) Solenoid loose or damaged e) Converter malfunction; clutch plate warped	a) Repair hose as needed b) Replace switch c) Replace switch d) Service or replace e) Replace converter
Clutch applies at a very low or high 3rd gear	a) Governor switch shorted to ground b) Governor malfunction c) High line pressure d) Solenoid inoperative or shorted to case	a) Replace switch b) Service or replace governor c) Service pressure regulator d) Replace solenoid

CAUTION: When inspecting the stator and turbine of the torque converter clutch unit, a slight drag is normal when turned in the direction of freewheel rotation because of the pressure exerted by the waved spring washer, located between the turbine and the pressure plate.

If it has been determined that there is a problem with the TCC system, the next step is to determine if the problem is internal or external. The following procedure can be used:

1. Disconnect the electrical connector at the transmission case.
2. Raise and safely support vehicle.
3. Start engine and adjust the speed to 2000 rpm, gear selector in Neutral.
4. Test for 12 volts at the connector using a volt/ohm meter or a test light. If 12 volts are present, the problem is internal. If no voltage (or low voltage according to the meter) is present at the connector, the problem is external.

If the problem is internal (12 volts at the connector) the following steps can be taken:

1. With the wire to the transmission case disconnected, take a 12 volt test light and connect it to the female connector and ground to the male transmission connector.
2. Start the engine and adjust the speed to 2000 rpm, gear selector in park.
3. If the test light comes on, the governor switch or the internal wiring is shorted to ground. The oil pan will have to be removed, the wiring checked and/or the governor switch replaced.
4. If the test light does not light, make sure that the vehicle is off the ground, and run in Drive until the transmission shifts to 3rd gear. Keep the engine speed to 2000 rpm.

5. If the test light now comes on, the internal hydraulic/mechanical controls will have to be checked.
6. If the test light still does not light, there is a problem with the solenoid or governor switch.

To test for solenoid or governor switch electrical malfunction, the following steps can be used:

1. Drain the transmission fluid and remove the oil pan.
2. Using an external 12 volt source, (self-powered test light or small lantern battery, etc.) connect a positive lead to the case connector. Remove the lead wire from the governor pressure switch and connect it to the ground lead of the external 12 volt source.

CAUTION

Do not reverse the leads or the solenoid diode will be destroyed by the reverse voltage. Do not use an automobile battery for this test. A self-powered test light is best for these tests.

---

3. If the solenoid clicks, it can be considered serviceable; replace the governor switch.
4. If the solenoid does not click, check the wiring. If the wiring appears to be good, replace the solenoid and recheck.
5. For more information refer to the section on torque converter clutch operation, which is located in the front of this manual.

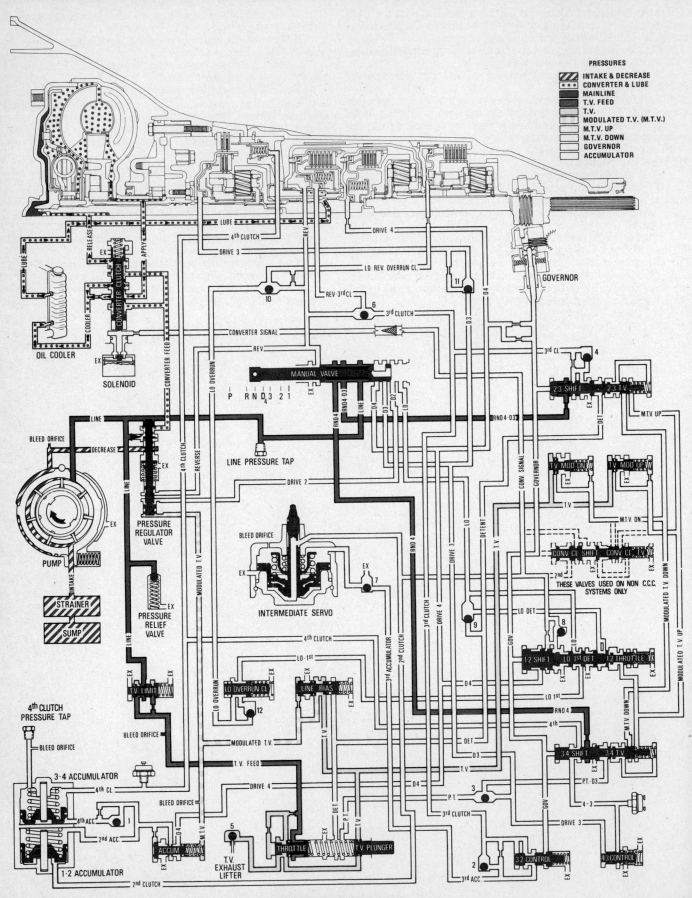

Neutral—Engine Running

NEUTRAL—ENGINE RUNNING

Units Applied or Released
CONVERTER CLUTCH—RELEASED
OVERRUN CLUTCH—RELEASED
INTERMEDIATE BAND—RELEASED
OVERDRIVE ROLLER CLUTCH—HOLDING
DIRECT CLUTCH—RELEASED
LOW & REVERSE CLUTCH—NOT HOLDING
FOURTH CLUTCH—RELEASED
FORWARD CLUTCH—RELEASED
LOW & REVERSE CLUTCH—RELEASED

Basic Control
When the selector lever is moved to the Neutral (N) position, the manual valve is positioned to allow line pressure to enter two (2) passages as follows:

FIRST: Line pressure enters the Reverse, Neutral, Drive 4 (RND4) passage and is directed to a land on the 3-4 shift valve.

SECOND: Line pressure enters the Reverse, Neutral, Drive 4, Drive 3 (RND4D3) passage and is directed to a land on the 2-3 shift valve.

Summary
The converter is filled; all the clutches, except the overdrive roller clutch, and the band are released; the transmission is in Neutral (N).

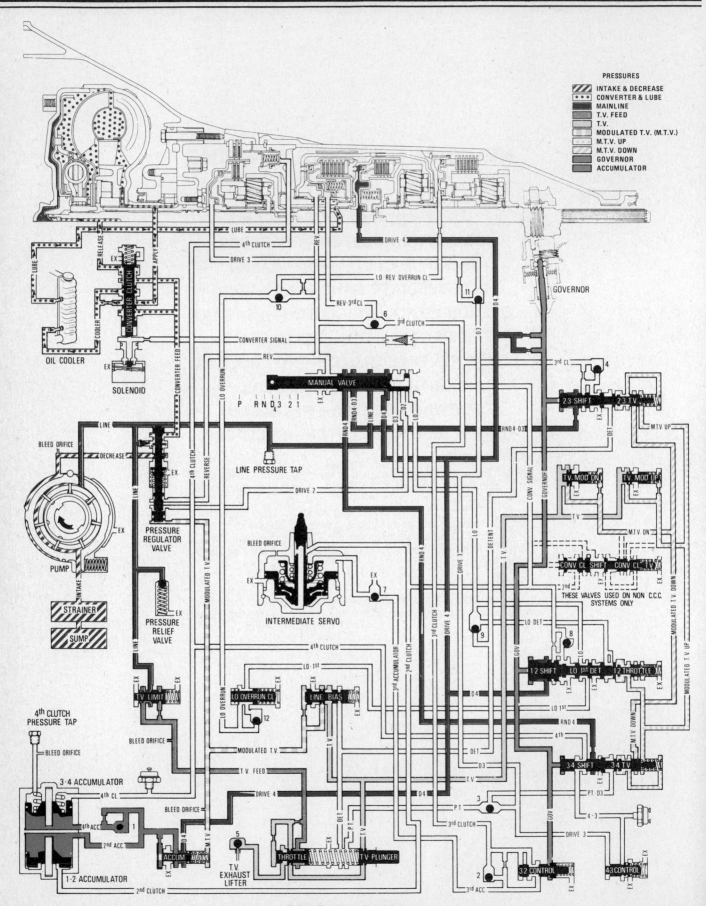

Drive Range—First Gear

DRIVE RANGE—FIRST GEAR

Units Applied or Released

OVERDRIVE ROLLER CLUTCH—HOLDING

FORWARD CLUTCH—APPLIED

LOW ROLLER CLUTCH—HOLDING

When the selector lever is moved to the Drive (D) position, the manual valve is repositioned to allow line pressure to enter the Drive 4 (D4) passage. Drive 4 oil then flows to the forward clutch, governor assembly, 1-2 shift valve and the accumulator valve.

Basic Control

Drive 4 oil is directed to the forward clutch where it acts on the clutch piston to apply the forward clutch.

Drive 4 oil is directed to the 1-2 shift valve. Drive 4 oil is directed to the accumulator valve and is regulated to a pressure called accumulator pressure; this pressure is directed to the 1-2 and 3-4 accumulator pistons to act as a cushion for the band and fourth clutch apply.

Drive 4 oil is orificed into the governor passage, and is regulated to a variable pressure called governor pressure. Governor pressure increases with vehicle speed and acts against the 1-2, 2-3, 3-4, converter clutch shift valves, and the 3-2 control valve.

In first gear, there could be sufficient throttle valve plunger travel to increase T.V. pressure enough to open the M.T.V. up and the M.T.V. down valves. In first gear, M.T.V. up exerts pressure against governor pressure at the 1-2, 2-3, 3-4, and converter clutch throttle valves. M.T.V. down pressure is stopped by a land at each of the throttle valves.

Summary

The converter clutch is released, the overdrive roller clutch is holding, the forward clutch is applied; the transmission is in Drive (D) range—first gear.

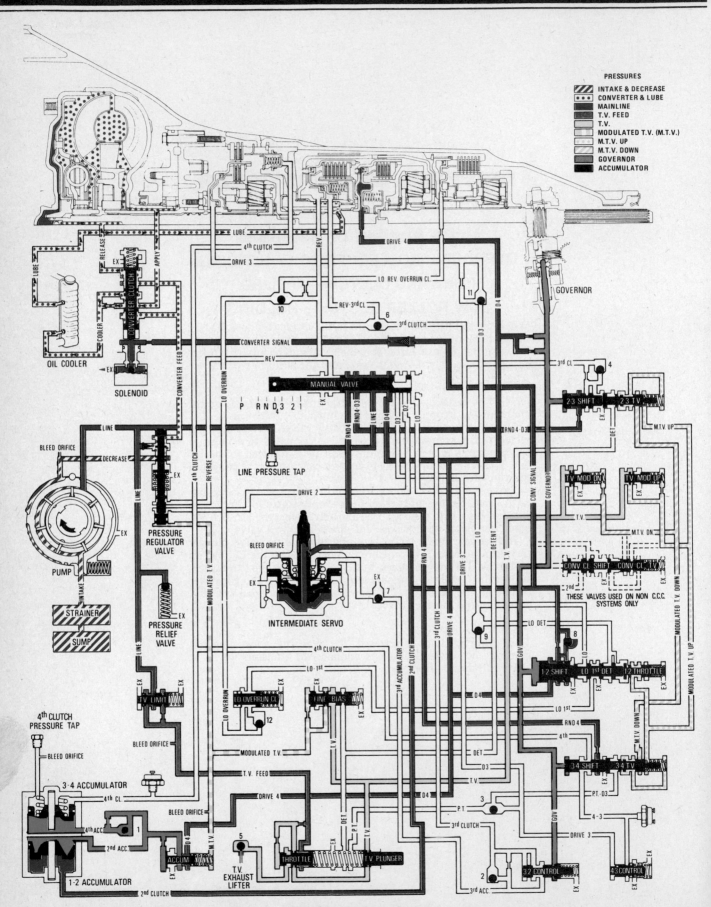

Drive Range—Second Gear

DRIVE RANGE—SECOND GEAR

Units Applied or Released

CONVERTER CLUTCH—RELEASED

FORWARD CLUTCH—APPLIED

OVERDRIVE ROLLER CLUTCH—HOLDING

INTERMEDIATE BAND—APPLIED

As both vehicle speed and governor pressure increase, the force of the governor oil acting on the 1-2 shift valve overcomes the pressure of M.T.V. up oil and the force of the 1-2 throttle valve spring. This allows the 1-2 shift valve to open and Drive 4 (D4) oil to enter the second (2nd) oil passage. This oil is called second (2nd) oil. Second oil from the 1-2 shift valve is directed to the 1-2 shift check ball (8), intermediate servo, 1-2 accumulator piston and the converter clutch shift valve.

Basic Control

Second oil from the 1-2 shift valve will seat the 1-2 shift check ball forcing 2nd oil through an orifice. Second oil is then directed to the intermediate servo to apply the intermediate band. At the same time, 2nd oil moves the 1-2 accumulator piston against accumulator pressure and the accumulator spring to maintain a controlled build-up of pressure on the intermediate servo during the 1-2 shift for a smooth band apply.

Summary

The converter clutch is released, the overdrive roller clutch is holding, the forward clutch is applied, and the intermediate band is applied; the transmission is in Drive (D) range—second gear.

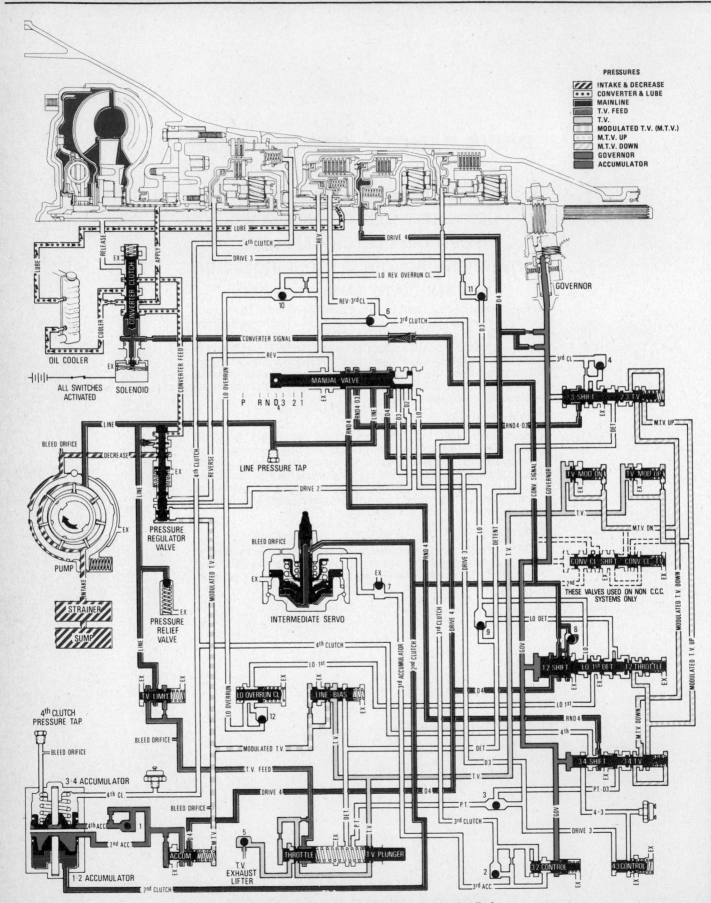

PRESSURES

- ▨ INTAKE & DECREASE
- ∴ CONVERTER & LUBE
- ■ MAINLINE
- T.V. FEED
- T.V.
- MODULATED T.V. (M.T.V.)
- M.T.V. UP
- M.T.V. DOWN
- GOVERNOR
- ACCUMULATOR

Drive Range—Second Gear Converter Clutch Applied

DRIVE RANGE—SECOND GEAR
CONVERTER CLUTCH APPLIED

Units Applied or Released

CONVERTER CLUTCH—APPLIED
FORWARD CLUTCH—APPLIED
OVERDRIVE ROLLER CLUTCH—HOLDING
INTERMEDIATE BAND—APPLIED

As vehicle speed and governor pressure increase, the force of governor oil acting on the converter clutch shift valve overcomes the pressure of M.T.V. up oil and the force of the converter clutch T.V. spring. This allows the converter shift valve to open and 2nd oil to enter the converter clutch signal passage. Providing the converter clutch solenoid is on, converter clutch signal oil will shift the converter clutch apply valve, and redirect converter feed oil into the apply passage. The apply oil flows between the stator shaft and converter hub to charge the converter with oil and push the converter pressure plate against the converter cover, causing a mechanical link between the engine and the turbine shaft. The rate of apply is controlled by the orifice check ball capsule in the end of the turbine shaft.

At the same time the converter clutch apply valve will direct converter feed oil through an orifice to the transmission cooler. Cooler oil is directed to the transmission lubrication system.

Summary

The converter clutch is applied, the overdrive roller clutch is holding, the forward clutch is applied, and the intermediate band is applied; the transmission is in Drive (D) range—second gear. The converter clutch is shown applied in 2nd gear. In some models, the converter clutch shift valve will not shift until the transmission is in 3rd gear.

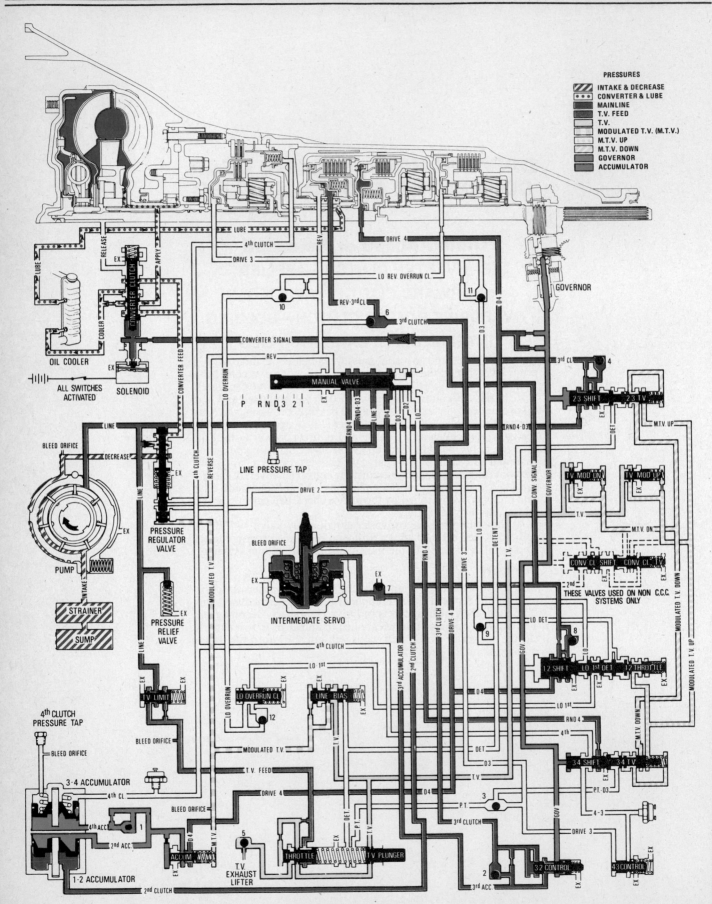

Drive Range—Third Gear

DRIVE RANGE-THIRD GEAR

Units applied or released

CONVERTER CLUTCH-APPLIED①
DIRECT CLUTCH-APPLIED
OVERDRIVE ROLLER CLUTCH-HOLDING
FORWARD CLUTCH-APPLIED

As both vehicle speed and governor pressure increase, the force of governor oil acting on the 2-3 shift valve overcomes the force of the 2-3 T.V. spring and M.T.V. up oil. This allows the 2-3 shift valve to open and allows RND4D3 oil to enter the 3rd clutch passage. Third clutch oil from the 2-3 shift valve is directed to the 3-2 exhaust check ball (4), third clutch and reverse check ball (6), inner piston of the direct clutch, third clutch accumulator check ball (2), intermediate servo assembly and the 3-2 control valve.

Basic Control

Third clutch oil from the 2-3 shift valve flows past the 3-2 exhaust check ball (4), to the 3rd/reverse check ball (6), seating it in the reverse passage. Third clutch oil then flows to the inner area of the direct clutch piston, applying the direct clutch. At the same time, 3rd clutch oil is directed past the 3rd clutch accumulator check ball (2), seats the 3rd accumulator exhaust check ball (7), and then into the release side of the intermediate servo. This 3rd clutch accumulator pressure combined with the servo cushion spring, moves the servo piston against second oil and acts as an accumulator for a smooth intermediate band release and direct clutch apply.

Third clutch oil flows through the 3-2 control valve to the 3rd clutch accumulator passage.

Summary

The converter clutch is applied①, the overdrive roller clutch is holding, the forward clutch is applied, the direct clutch is applied, and the intermediate band is released; the transmission is in Drive (D) range—third gear (direct drive).

① The converter clutch may or may not be applied, depending on shift calibration and solenoid operation.

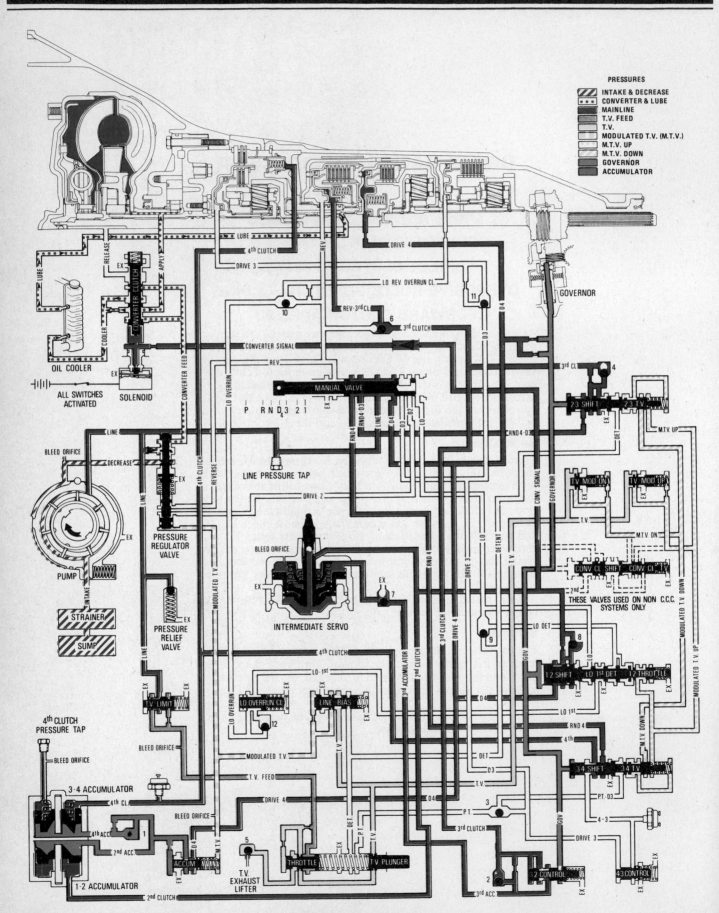

Drive Range—Overdrive

DRIVE RANGE-OVERDRIVE

Units applied or released

CONVERTER CLUTCH-APPLIED①

DIRECT CLUTCH-APPLIED

FOURTH CLUTCH-APPLIED

FORWARD CLUTCH-APPLIED

As both vehicle speed and governor pressure increase, the force of governor oil acting on the 3-4 shift valve overcomes the force of the 3-4 T.V. spring and M.T.V. up oil. This allows the 3-4 shift valve to open and RND4 oil enters the 4th clutch passage. Fourth clutch oil from the 3-4 shift valve is directed to the fourth clutch apply piston and the 3-4 accumulator piston.

Basic Control

Fourth oil from the 3-4 shift valve is directed to the 4th clutch piston to apply the 4th clutch. At the same time, fourth clutch oil moves the 3-4 accumulator piston against accumulator pressure and the accumulator spring to maintain a controlled build-up of pressure on the 4th clutch during the 3-4 shift, for a smooth 3-4 shift.

Summary

The converter clutch①, 4th clutch, direct clutch, and forward clutch are applied; the transmission is in Drive (D) range—overdrive.

①The converter clutch may or may not be applied, depending on solenoid operation.

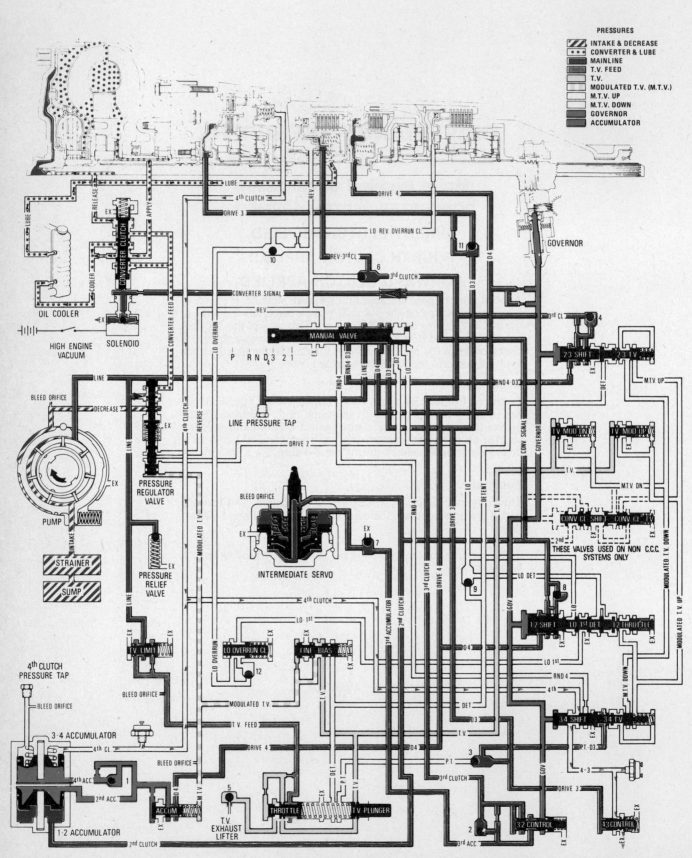

PRESSURES

▨	INTAKE & DECREASE
⋯	CONVERTER & LUBE
▰	MAINLINE
	T.V. FEED
	T.V.
	MODULATED T.V. (M.T.V.)
	M.T.V. UP
	M.T.V. DOWN
	GOVERNOR
	ACCUMULATOR

Manual Third

MANUAL THIRD

Units Applied or Released

CONVERTER CLUTCH—RELEASED①
FORWARD CLUTCH—APPLIED
OVERRUN CLUTCH—APPLIED
DIRECT CLUTCH—APPLIED

Basic Control

A forced 4-3 downshift can be accomplished by moving the selector lever from Drive (D) range to third (3rd) gear.

When the selector lever is moved to the third (3rd) gear position, line pressure is blocked from the RND4 passage, and D3 oil from the manual valve is directed to the overrun clutch check ball (11), overrun clutch, 4-3 control valve, part throttle and drive 3 (D3) check ball (3) and the 3-4 shift valve. D3 oil will open the 4-3 control valve and close the 3-4 shift valve to allow 4th clutch and 4th accumulator oil to pass back through the 3-4 shift valve and exhaust at the 4-3 control valve. D3 oil will also pass through an orifice and apply the overrun clutch to keep the overdrive roller clutch from overrunning when engine braking is needed.

Summary

The forward and direct clutches are applied. The 4th clutch is released. The transmission is in manual 3rd, direct valve drive. The overrun clutch is applied to allow engine braking.

①In manual 3rd, the converter clutch is shown released by the engine vacuum switch and there is no M.T.V. up or M.T.V. down pressure. This is assuming the throttle is released. If the throttle is opened sufficiently, the converter clutch could engage and the M.T.V. up and M.T.V. down valves could open.

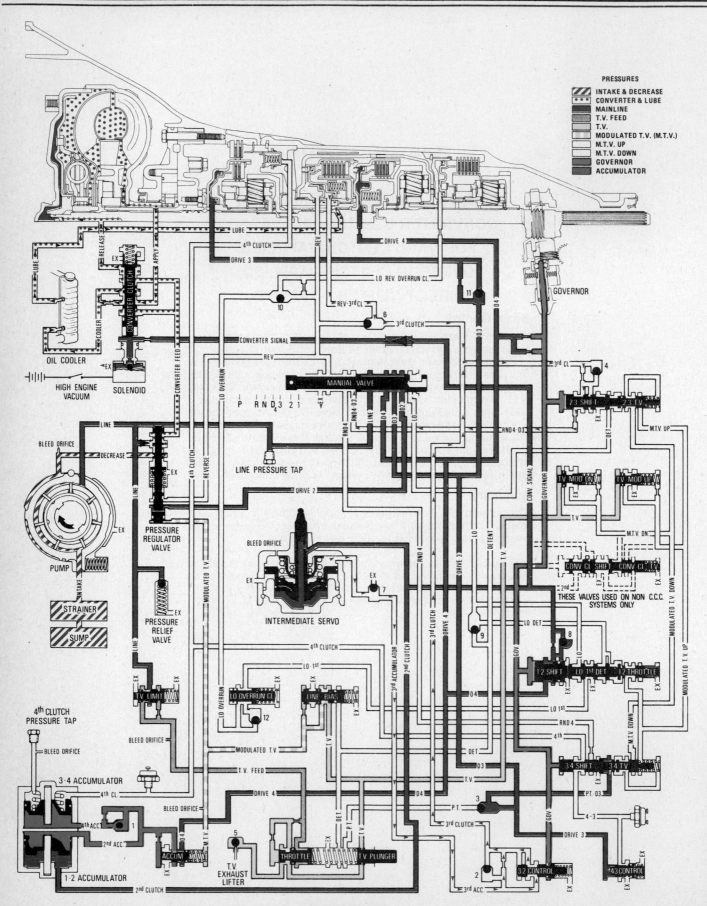

Manual Second

MANUAL SECOND

Units Applied or Released

CONVERTER CLUTCH—RELEASED①
FORWARD CLUTCH—APPLIED
OVERRUN CLUTCH—APPLIED
INTERMEDIATE BAND—APPLIED

Basic Control

A forced 3-2 downshift can be accomplished by moving the selector lever from third (3rd) gear to the second (2nd) gear position.

When the selector lever is moved to the second (2nd) gear position, RND4D3, 3rd clutch, and 3rd accumulator oil will exhaust at the manual valve. With no pressure to apply the 3rd clutch, or release the intermediate band, the transmission will shift to second gear.

The manual valve will also direct line pressure into the D2 passage. Drive 2 (D2) oil will act on the reverse boost valve to boost line pressure to 965 kPa (140 psi) which is required to prevent the intermediate band and forward clutch from slipping.

Summary

The forward clutch and intermediate band are applied. The transmission is in second gear. Also, the overrun clutch is still applied to allow engine braking when needed.

① In manual 2nd, the converter clutch is shown released by the engine vacuum switch and there is no M.T.V. up or M.T.V. down pressure. This is assuming the throttle is released. If the throttle is opened sufficiently, the converter clutch could engage and the M.T.V. up and M.T.V. down valves could open.

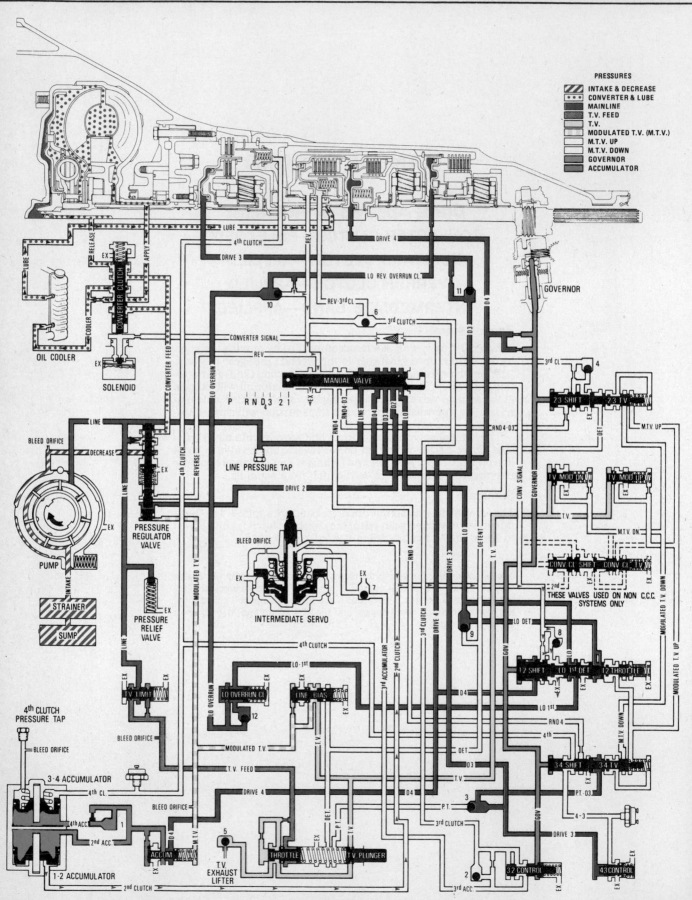

Manual Low

MANUAL LOW

Units Applied or Released

CONVERTER CLUTCH—RELEASED

FORWARD CLUTCH—APPLIED

OVERRUN CLUTCH—APPLIED

LOW AND REVERSE CLUTCH—APPLIED

Basic Control

Maximum downhill braking can be obtained at speeds below 30 mph (48 km/h), with the selector in Low (1st) range. Low (1st) oil pressure which is 965 kPa (140 psi) is the same as second (2nd) oil pressure because second (D2) oil is still present. Low oil from the manual valve is directed to the low and detent check ball (9), 1-2 shift valve train, low and reverse check ball (10) and the low and reverse overrun clutch.

Low oil at the low 1st/detent valve combined with M.T.V. down and 1-2 throttle valve spring force will close the 1-2 shift valve at speeds below approximately 30 mph (48 km/h). This allows 2nd oil to exhaust, releasing the intermediate band, and low oil to travel to the low overrun clutch valve. The low overrun clutch valve regulates low oil pressure down to approximately 205 kPa (30 psi) and then directs this regulated oil to the low/reverse overrun clutch and applies it.

Summary

The forward clutch is applied. The low and reverse, and the overrun clutch are applied to allow engine braking. The intermediate band is released, the transmission is in Low range—first gear.

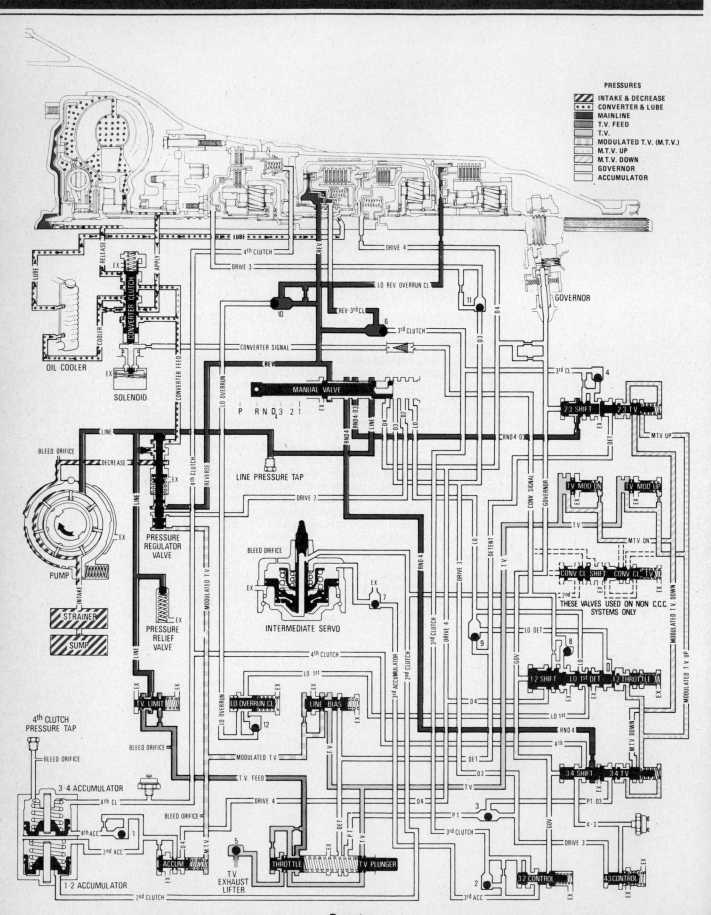

Reverse

REVERSE

Units Applied or Released

OVERDRIVE ROLLER CLUTCH—HOLDING

DIRECT CLUTCH—APPLIED

LOW AND REVERSE CLUTCH—APPLIED

Basic Control

When the selector lever is moved to the Reverse (R) position, the manual valve is repositioned to allow line pressure to enter the reverse passage which directs oil to the low and reverse check ball (10), low and reverse overrun clutch, third clutch and reverse check ball (6), inner area of the direct clutch and the outer area of the direct clutch.

Reverse oil seats the low/reverse check ball (10) in the low overrun clutch passage and flows to the low/reverse overrun clutch piston, applying the low/reverse overrun clutch. Reverse oil also seats the 3rd/reverse check ball (6) in the 3rd clutch passage and flows to the inner area of the direct clutch piston. In addition, reverse oil is directed to the outer area of the direct clutch piston thus both the inner and the outer areas of the direct clutch piston combine to apply the direct clutch.

Reverse oil acting on the reverse boost valve in the pressure regulator will boost line pressure to approximately 725 kPa (105 psi). M.T.V. oil from the line bias valve acting on the T.V. boost valve, in the pressure regulator, will further boost line pressure from 725 kPa (105 psi) at idle to 1725 kPa (250 psi) at full throttle.

Summary

The overdrive roller clutch is holding. The direct clutch is applied. The low and reverse clutch is applied. The transmission is in Reverse (R).

ON CAR SERVICES

Adjustments

SHIFT INDICATOR

1. With the engine off, position the selector lever in neutral.
2. If the pointer does not align with the "N" indicator position, move the clip on the shift bowl until alignment has been achieved.

NOTE: The manual linkage must be adjusted correctly before this adjustment can be made properly.

NEUTRAL SAFETY SWITCH

The neutral safety switch is not adjustable on vehicles equipped with this type of automatic transmission. The switch is located in the steering column, and can be serviced only after removing the steering wheel.

T.V. AND DETENT CABLE

NOTE: Before any adjustment is made to the T.V. or detent cable be sure that the engine is operating properly, the transmission fluid level is correct, the brakes are not dragging, the correct cable has been installed and that the cable is connected at both ends.

Diesel Engine

1. Stop the engine. If equipped, remove the cruise control rod.
2. Disconnect the transmission T.V. cable terminal from the cable actuating lever.
3. Loosen the lock nut on the pump rod and shorten it several turns.
4. Rotate the lever assembly to the full throttle position. Hold this position.
5. Lengthen pump rod until the injection pump lever contacts the full throttle stop.
6. Release the lever assembly and tighten pump rod lock nut. Remove the pump rod from the lever assembly.
7. Reconnect the transmission T.V. cable terminal to cable actuating lever.
8. Depress and hold the metal re-adjust tab on the cable upper end. Move the slider through the fitting in the direction away from the lever assembly until the slider stops against the fitting.
9. Release the re-adjust tab. Rotate the cable actuating lever assembly to the full throttle stop and release the cable actuating lever assembly. The cable slider should adjust out of the cable fitting toward the cable actuating lever.
10. Reconnect the pump rod and cruise control throttle rod if so equipped.
11. If equipped with cruise control, adjust the servo throttle rod to minimum slack (engine off) then put clip in first free hole closest to the bellcrank but within the servo bail.

Gas Engine

1. Stop engine.
2. Depress and hold the metal re-adjust tab on the cable upper end. Move the slider through the fitting in the direction away from the lever assembly until the slider stops against the fitting. Release re-adjust tab.
3. Rotate the cable actuating lever assembly to the full throttle stop and release the cable actuating lever assembly. The cable slider should adjust out of the cable fitting toward the cable actuating lever. Check cable for sticking and binding.
4. Road test the vehicle. If the condition still exists, remove the transmission oil pan and inspect the throttle lever and bracket assembly on the valve body.

5. Check to see that the T.V. exhaust valve lifter rod is not distorted or binding in the valve body assembly or spacer plate.
6. The T.V. exhaust check ball must move up and down as the lifter does. Be sure that the lifter spring holds the lifter rod up against the bottom of the valve body.
7. Make sure that the T.V. plunger is not stuck. Inspect the transmission for correct throttle lever to cable link.

MANUAL LINKAGE

There are many variations of the manual linkage used with the THM 200-4R, due to its wide vehicle application. A general adjustment procedure is outlined for the convenience of the repairman.

Loosen the shift rod adjusting swivel clamp at the cross shaft. Place the transmission detent in the neutral position and the column selector in the neutral position. Tighten the adjustment swivel clamp and shift the selector lever through all ranges, confirming the transmission detent corresponds to the shift lever positions and the vehicle will only start in the park or neutral positions.

INTERMEDIATE BAND

The intermediate band is adjusted by a selective intermediate servo apply pin. Because of possible inaccessibility to the intermediate servo piston assembly on the transmission/vehicle application, due to the clearance restrictions, the special tools needed for the pin selection cannot be installed and used. Should the band adjustment be necessary and the adjusting clearance is not available, the transmission would have to be removed from the vehicle.

The servo apply pin selection procedure is as follows.

1. Remove the servo cover and retaining ring from the transmission case with a special depressing tool.
2. Pull the servo cover from the case and remove the seal.
3. Remove the intermediate servo piston and band apply pin assembly.
4. Install the special tool into the intermediate servo bore and retain with the servo cover retaining ring.
5. Install the special pin, (part of the special tool), into the tool base, making sure the tapered pin end is properly positioned against the band apply lug. Be sure the band anchor pin is properly located in the case and the band anchor lug.
6. Install a dial indicator gauge on top of the special tool zero post and adjust the gauge to zero.

NOTE: The special tool base should be squarely against the servo cover retaining ring.

7. Align the special tool and the special indicator pin. The band selection pin should register between the high and low limits as marked on the tool. If not, possible trouble can exist with the intermediate band, direct clutch or the transmission case.
8. If the band selection pin registers in its proper zone, apply 100 in. lbs. of torque to the hex nut on the special tool. Measure the amount of travel on the dial indicator gauge. Remove the special tools.
9. Using the accompanying chart, install the proper band apply pin into the transmission and reassemble the intermediate servo into the transmission case.

INTERMEDIATE BAND APPLY PIN SELECTION CHART

Dial Indicator Travel	Apply Pin Identification
0.0-0.029 inch	one ring
0.029-0.057 inch	two rings
0.057-0.086 inch	three rings
0.086-0.114 inch	wide ring

NOTE: The apply pin identification ring is located on the band end of the pin.

Services

FLUID CHANGE AND OIL PAN

Removal

1. Raise and safely support car.
2. Place drain pan under transmission oil pan. Remove the oil pan attaching bolts from the front and side of the pan.
3. Loosen, but do not remove the rear pan bolts, then bump the pan loose and allow fluid to drain.
4. Remove the remaining bolts and remove pan.
5. Clean pan in solvent and dry with compressed air.
6. Remove the two bolts holding the filter screen to the valve body. Discard gasket.

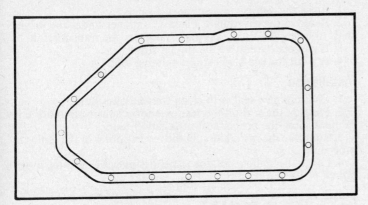

Transmission pan identification (© General Motors Corp.)

Installation

1. Clean screen in solvent and blow dry, or replace as required.
2. Install screen with new gasket; torque bolts to 6-10 foot-pounds.
3. Install new gasket on pan and torque bolts to 10-13 foot-pounds.
4. Lower car and add 3 quarts of Dexron® II.
5. With selector in Park start engine and idle. Apply parking brake. *Do not race engine.*
6. Moe selector through all ranges and end in Park. Check fluid level. Add if necessary to bring the level between the dimples on the dipstick.

VALVE BODY

Removal

1. Raise the vehicle on a hoist and support it safely.
2. Drain the transmission fluid. Remove the fluid pan. Discard the gasket or R.T.V. sealant.
3. Remove the two bolts retaining the filter. Remove the filter from the valve body.
4. Remove bolt and washer securing T.V. cable to transmission and disconnect T.V. cable.
5. Remove throttle lever and bracket assembly. Do not bend throttle lever link.
6. Disconnect the wire leads on the electrical connector at the transmission case. Remove the connectors at the 4-3 pressure switch and the fourth clutch pressure switch. Remove the solenoid attaching bolts, clips and solenoid assembly.
7. Remove the manual detent roller and spring assembly.
8. Support the valve body assembly. Remove the valve body retaining bolts.

9. Holding the manual valve, remove the valve body assembly. Be sure to use care in order to prevent loss of the three check balls located in the valve body assembly.
10. Position the valve body assembly down with the spacer plate side up.

Installation

1. Using new gaskets, as required, position the valve body assembly against the transmission. Install the valve body retaining bolts and torque them 7-10 ft. lbs.
2. Continue the installation in the reverse order of the removal procedure.
3. Use a new gasket when installing the oil pan. If the transmission uses R.T.V. sealant be sure that both mating surfaces are clean before applying new sealant.
4. Lower the vehicle. Fill the transmission to specification using the proper grade and type automatic transmission fluid.
5. Start the engine and check for leaks. Check to see that the transmission is properly filled once the vehicle has reached operating temperature.

INTERMEDIATE SERVO

Removal

1. Raise the vehicle and support it safely.
2. Remove the four catalytic converter heat shield bolts. Slide the heat shield away from the catalytic converter.
3. Using the special intermediate servo removal tool, depress the servo cover and remove the retaining ring.
4. Remove the cover and the seal ring. The seal ring may be in the transmission case.
5. Remove the intermediate servo piston and bore apply pin assembly.

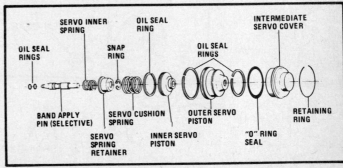

Intermediate servo—exploded view (© General Motors Corp.)

Installation

1. Position the bore apply pin assembly and the intermediate servo piston to its mounting in the transmission case.
2. Using a new seal ring install the servo cover. Depress the servo cover and install the retainer ring.
3. Continue the installation in the reverse order of the removal procedure.
4. Lower the vehicle. Check the fluid level and correct as required.
5. Start the engine and check for leaks. Once the vehicle has reached operating temperature recheck the fluid level.

ACCUMULATOR

Removal

1. Raise the vehicle and support it safely.
2. Drain the transmission fluid. Remove the fluid pan, gasket and filter.

3. Remove the valve body assembly.

4. Support the 1-2 accumulator housing. Remove the four 1-2 accumulator housing retaining bolts, housing and gasket.

5. Lay the 1-2 accumulator housing down with the plate side facing upward.

6. Support the valve body spacer plate, gaskets and accumulator plate to prevent dropping the eight check balls and the 3-4 accumulator spring, piston and pin which are located in the transmission case.

7. Remove the remaining retaining bolt on the accumulator plate. After the removal of the spacer plate and gaskets the band anchor pin may come out of its bore.

Installation

NOTE: The intermediate band anchor pin must be located on the intermediate band or damage to the transmission will result.

1. Installation is the reverse of the removal procedure.

2. Be sure to retain the eight check balls, using petroleum jelly or equivalent.

3. Replace all gaskets as required. Lower the vehicle. Fill with the proper grade and type transmission fluid. Start the engine and check for leaks.

GOVERNOR

Removal

1. Raise the vehicle and support it safely.

2. Drain the transmission fluid. Remove the fluid pan. Discard the gasket and screen.

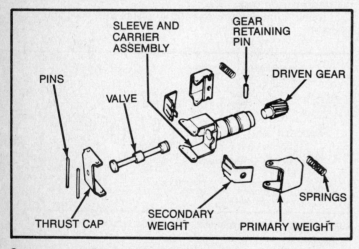

Governor assembly (© General Motors Corp.)

3. Remove the governor cover attaching bolts.

4. Remove the governor cover and gasket. Discard the gasket.

5. The governor assembly may come out along with the cover. It may also be necessary to rotate the output shaft counterclockwise while removing the governor. Do not use any type of pliers to remove the governor from its bore.

Installation

1. To install, position the governor assembly in its bore within the transmission case.

2. Install the governor cover using a new gasket. Torque the retaining bolts to 18 ft. lbs.

3. Continue the installation in the reverse order of the removal procedure.

4. Lower the vehicle. Fill the transmission with the proper grade and type automatic transmission fluid.

5. Start the engine and check for leaks. Once the engine has reached operating temperature recheck the fluid.

SPEEDOMETER DRIVEN GEAR

Removal

1. Raise the vehicle and support it safely.

2. Disconnect the speedometer cable.

3. Remove the retainer bolt, retainer, speedometer driven gear and O-ring seal.

Installation

1. Coat the new O-ring seal with transmission fluid and install it along with the other components.

2. Install the speedometer cable.

3. Lower the vehicle. Replace any transmission that may have been lost.

REAR OIL SEAL

Removal

1. Raise the vehicle and support it safely.

2. Remove the driveshaft. Place a container under the driveshaft to catch any fluid that may leak from the transmission.

3. If equipped, remove the tunnel strap.

4. Pry out the old seal using a suitable tool.

Installation

1. Coat the new seal with clean transmission fluid.

2. Position the seal on the rear extension housing and drive it in place using the proper seal installation tools.

3. Continue the installation in the reverse order of the removal procedure.

4. Lower the vehicle. Fill the transmission with clean oil, as required.

REMOVAL & INSTALLATION

REMOVAL

1. Disconnect the negative battery cable.

2. Remove the air cleaner assembly. Disconnect the T.V./detent cable at its upper end.

3. Remove the transmission dipstick. Remove the bolt holding the dipstick tube, if accessible.

4. Raise the vehicle and support it safely.

5. Drain the transmission. Remove the driveshaft. Matchmark the driveshaft to aid in installation.

6. Disconnect the speedometer cable at the transmission. Disconnect the shift linkage at the transmission.

7. Disconnect all electrical leads at the transmission. Disconnect any clips that retain these leads.

8. Remove the inspection cover. Mark the flexplate and torque converter, to aid in installation.

9. Remove the torque converter to flex plate retaining bolts. Remove the catalytic converter support bracket, if necessary.

10. Position the transmission jack under the transmission and remove the rear transmission mount.

11. Remove the floor pan reinforcement. Remove the crossmember retaining bolts. Move the crossmember out of the way.

12. Remove the transmission to engine bolt on the left side. This is the bolt that retains the ground strap.

13. Disconnect and plug the transmission oil cooler lines. It may be necessary to lower the transmission in order to gain access to the cooler lines.

14. With the transmission still lowered, disconnect the T.V. cable.

15. Support the engine, using the proper tools and remove the remaining engine to transmission bolts.

16. Carefully disengage the transmission assembly from the engine. Lower the transmission from the transmission jack.

Installation

1. To install, reverse the removal procedures.
2. Before installing the flexplate to torque converter bolts, make sure that the weld nuts on the converter are flush with the flexplate and that the torque converter rotates freely by hand in this position.
3. Be sure that the flexplate and torque converter marks made during the removal procedure line up with each other.
4. Adjust the shift linkage and the T.V. cable as required.
5. Lower the vehicle and fill the transmission with the proper grade and type automatic transmission fluid.
6. Start the engine and check for leaks. Once the vehicle has reached operating temperature, recheck the fluid level.

BENCH OVERHAUL

Before Disassembly

Clean the exterior of the transmission assembly before any attempt is made to disassemble, to prevent dirt or other foreign materials from entering the transmission assembly or its internal parts.

NOTE: If steam cleaning is done to the exterior of the transmission, immediate disassembly should be done to avoid rusting from condensation of the internal parts.

Take note of thrust washer locations. It is most important that thrust washers and bearings be installed in their original positions. Handle all transmission parts carefully to avoid damage.

Ring groove wear on governor supports, input shaft, pump housings and other internal parts should be checked using new rings installed in the grooves.

Converter Inspection

The converter cannot be disassembled for service.

CHECKING CONVERTER END PLAY

1. Place the converter on a flat surface with the flywheel side down.
2. Attach a dial indicator so that the end play can be determined by moving the turbine shaft in relation to the converter hub. End play for the Turbo Hydra-Matic 200-4R should be no more than .0-.050 of an inch. If the clearance is greater than this, replace the converter.

CHECKING CONVERTER ONE-WAY CLUTCH

1. If the one-way clutch fails, then the stator assembly freewheels at all times in both directions. The car will have poor low speed acceleration.
2. If the stator assembly remains locked up at all times, the car speed will be limited or restricted at high speeds. The low speed operation may appear normal, although engine overheating may occur.
3. To check one-way clutch operation, insert a finger into the splined inner race of the roller clutch and try to turn the race in both the directions. The inner race should turn freely in the clockwise direction, but it should not turn in the counterclockwise direction.

NOTE: Inspect the converter hub for burrs or jagged metal to avoid personal injury.

4. If the one-way clutch does not operate properly, the converter must be replaced.

VISUAL INSPECTION OF THE CONVERTER

Before installation of the converter, check it carefully for damage, stripped bolt holes or signs of heat damage. Check for loose or missing balance weights, broken converter pilot, or leaks, all of which are cause for replacement. Inspect the converter pump drive hub for nicks or burrs that could damage the pump oil seal during installation.

Transmission Disassembly

TORQUE CONVERTER AND OIL PAN

1. Remove the torque converter from the transmission by pulling it straight out of the transmission housing.
2. Position the transmission assembly in a suitable holding fixture.
3. Remove the transmission fluid pan bolts. Discard the pan gasket, or R.T.V. sealant. Remove and discard the fluid screen.

VALVE BODY

1. Disconnect the wire leads at the electrical connector, which is located in the transmission case and the pressure switches on the valve body assembly.
2. Remove the electrical connector and O-ring seal from the transmission case.
3. Remove the solenoid assembly attaching bolts. Remove the clips and the solenoid.
4. Remove the throttle lever and bracket assembly. Do not bend the throttle lever link. The T.V. exhaust valve lifter and spring may separate from the throttle lever and bracket assembly.
5. Remove the manual detent roller and spring assembly, the signal pipe retaining clip and the signal pipe.
6. On non-C3 models, remove the 4-3 pressure switch retaining bolt.
7. Remove the remaining valve body retaining bolts. Do not drop the manual valve, as damage to the valve may occur.
8. Hold the manual valve in its bore. Remove the valve body assembly. Care must be taken as three check balls will be exposed on top of the spacer plate to valve body gasket. Remove the exposed check balls.
9. Lay the valve body assembly down with the spacer plate gasket side up.

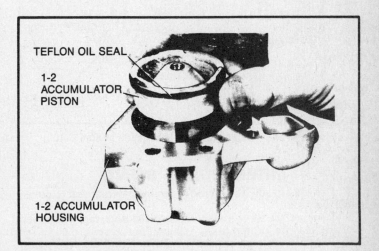

TEFLON OIL SEAL

1-2 ACCUMULATOR PISTON

1-2 ACCUMULATOR HOUSING

Accumulator housing and related components
(© General Motors Corp.)

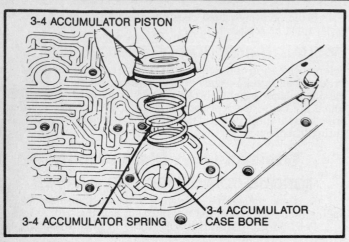

3-4 ACCUMULATOR PISTON

3-4 ACCUMULATOR SPRING

3-4 ACCUMULATOR CASE BORE

3-4 accumulator assembly removal (© General Motors Corp.)

1-2 ACCUMULATOR

1. Remove the 1-2 accumulator housing retaining bolts. Remove the accumulator housing, spring, plate and gasket.

2. Remove the 1-2 accumulator piston from the housing. It may be necessary to apply low air pressure (about 3 PSI) to the orifice in the accumulator housing passage in order to remove the 1-2 accumulator piston.

3. Remove the valve body gaskets and spacer plate. Remove the 3-4 accumulator spring, piston and pin from the transmission case. Remove the eight check balls from the core passages in the transmission case.

GOVERNOR

1. Remove the governor cover attaching bolts. Remove the governor cover and gasket.

2. Remove the governor assembly from the transmission case.

3. It may be necessary to rotate the output shaft counterclockwise while removing the governor. Do not use any type of pliers to remove the governor from its bore in the transmission case.

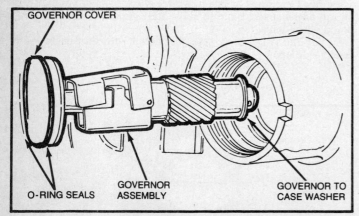

GOVERNOR COVER

O-RING SEALS

GOVERNOR ASSEMBLY

GOVERNOR TO CASE WASHER

Governor assembly—exploded view (© General Motors Corp.)

INTERMEDIATE SERVO

1. Using a suitable tool, remove the intermediate servo cover retaining ring.

2. Remove the servo cover. Discard the seal ring. The cover seal ring may be located in the transmission case.

3. Remove the intermediate servo piston and the band apply pin assembly.

4. Install the special tool into the intermediate servo bore and retain with the servo cover retaining ring.

5. Install the special pin, (part of the special tool), into the tool base, making sure the tapered pin end is properly positioned against the band apply lug. Be sure the band anchor pin is properly located in the case and the band anchor lug.

6. Install a dial indicator gauge on top of the special tool zero post and adjust the gauge to zero.

NOTE: The special tool base should be squarely against the servo cover retaining ring.

7. Align the special tool and the special indicator pin. The band selection pin should register between the high and low limits as marked on the tool. If not, possible trouble can exist with the intermediate band, direct clutch or the transmission case.

8. If the band selection pin registers in its proper zone, apply 100 in. lbs. of torque to the hex nut on the special tool. Measure and record the amount of travel on the dial indicator gauge. Select a new apply pin as required. Remove the special tools.

INTERMEDIATE BAND APPLY PIN SELECTION CHART

Dial Indicator Travel	Apply Pin Identification
0.0-0.029 inch	one ring
0.029-0.057 inch	two rings
0.057-0.086 inch	three rings
0.086-0.114 inch	wide ring

3-4 ACCUMULATOR

1. Inspect the 3rd accumulator check valve for missing check ball, check ball binding or stuck in the tube, oil feed slot in tube missing or restricted, improperly assembled, loose fitting or not fully seated in the case and damaged or missing.

2. If the 3rd accumulator check valve assembly requires replacement, use a 6.3 mm (#4) easy out and remove the check valve assembly from the case by turning and pulling straight out.

3. Install new check valve assembly, small end first, into the case. Position the oil feed slot in tube so it faces the servo cover.

4. Using a ⅜″ diameter metal rod and hammer, drive the check valve assembly until it is seated in the 3rd accumulator case hole.

FRONT OIL PUMP

1. Remove the front pump seal.

2. Remove the front pump retaining bolts and washers.

3. Using a suitable tool, remove the front pump assembly and gasket from the transmission case.

4. Remove the front pump oil deflector plate.

OVERDRIVE UNIT

1. Check the overdrive unit end play by installing the rear unit support tool (J-25013-1) on the sleeve of the output shaft. Then bolt the output shaft loading fixture adapter tool (J-29332) to the end of the transmission case.

2. Position the transmission accordingly and remove the pump-to-case bolt and washer. Install an eleven inch long bolt and locking nut.

3. Install the oil pump end play checking fixture adapter (J-25022) on to the oil pump remover tool (J-24773-5) and secure both tools on the end of the turbine shaft.

4. Position the dial indicator gauge and clamp the assembly on the bolt positioning indicator point cap nut on top of the oil pump removal tool.

5. Lift up on the oil pump removal tool with approximately three lbs. of upward force and while holding the upward force, set the indicator to zero.

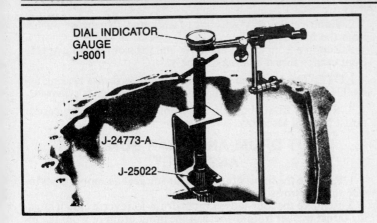

Overdrive unit end play check (© General Motors Corp.)

NOTE: The above procedure must be performed to eliminate the tolerance difference between the turbine shaft snap ring and the overdrive carrier.

6. With the indicator gauge set at zero, increase the force to about twenty lbs. Read the dial indicator and record the reading. Overdrive unit end play should be .004-.027 in.

7. The selective washer controlling this end play is located between the pump cover and the overrun clutch housing. Replace the thrust washer as required to bring the end play within specification.

8. Remove the dial indicator gauge and the special tools once the washer has been replaced.

OVERDRIVE UNIT END PLAY SELECTIVE WASHER CHART

Identification	Thickness (inches)
Zero—Scarlet	0.167-0.171
One—White	0.172-0.176
Two—Cocoa Brown	0.177-0.180
Three—Gray	0.181-0.185
Four—Yellow	0.186-0.190
Five—Light Blue	0.191-0.195
Six—Purple	0.196-0.200
Seven—Orange	0.201-0.204
Eight—Green	0.205-0.209

FOURTH CLUTCH ASSEMBLY

1. Remove the front pump using the required pump removal tool.

2. Remove the fourth clutch plate-to-transmission case snap ring.

3. Grasp the turbine shaft and lift out the overdrive unit assembly and the fourth clutch plate assembly.

4. Remove the fourth clutch plate assembly from the overdrive unit assembly. Be sure to remove the one remaining steel plate from the inside of the transmission case.

5. Remove the overdrive internal gear-to-carrier thrust washer. Remove the overdrive internal gear. Remove the internal gear-to-support thrust washer.

6. Install the fourth clutch compressor and center support tool (J-29334-1) on the fourth clutch spring and retainer assembly. Install the rest of the tool to the transmission case housing using two governor cover bolts.

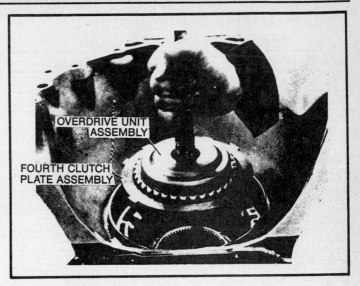

Overdrive assembly and fourth clutch plate assembly (© General Motors Corp.)

7. Compress fourth clutch spring and retainer assembly; then remove support to fourth clutch spring snap ring and spring and retainer assembly.

8. Remove the fourth clutch compressor and center support tool.

9. Remove the fourth clutch piston from inside the transmission assembly.

FRONT UNIT PARTS

1. To check the front unit end play, push the forward clutch shaft downward. Install the forward and direct clutch unit fixture tool (J-29337) in the end of the forward clutch shaft.

2. Mount the dial indicator gauge and clamp the assembly on the bolt positioning indicator point on top of the forward and direct clutch unit fixture tool.

3. Move the output shaft upward by turning the adjusting screw on the output shaft loading fixture adapter tool (J-29332) until the white line on the sleeve of the rear unit support tool (J-25013-1) begins to disappear. Set the dial indicator gauge to zero.

4. Pull the forward and direct clutch unit fixture tool upward and read the end play. Record the result. The end play should be .022-.051 in. If the end play is not within the specification given, replace the front unit end play selective washer. The selective washer controlling this end play is located between the forward clutch shaft and the output shaft.

5. Remove the dial indicator and clamp assembly. Do not remove the output shaft loading fixture adapter tool or the rear unit support tool.

CENTER SUPPORT

1. Remove the two center support-to-transmission case bolts.

2. Remove the center support-to-transmission case beveled snap ring.

3. Install the fourth clutch compressor and center support remover tool (J-29334-1) on the center support. Retain the tool in place using the center support-to-fourth clutch spring snap ring.

4. Using the fourth clutch compressor and center support removal tool and a slide hammer, remove the center support. Be sure that the center support bolts located on the valve body assembly have been removed.

5. Remove the support-to-direct clutch thrust washer. The thrust washer may be stuck on the back of the direct clutch.

FRONT UNIT END PLAY SELECTIVE WASHER CHART

Identification	Thickness (inches)
One— —	0.065-0.070
Two— —	0.070-0.075
Three—Black	0.076-0.080
Four—Light Green	0.081-0.085
Five—Scarlet	0.086-0.090
Six—Purple	0.091-0.095
Seven—Cocoa Brown	0.096-0.100
Eight—Orange	0.101-0.106
Nine—Yellow	0.106-0.111
Ten—Light Blue	0.111-0.116
Eleven— —	0.117-0.121
Twelve— —	0.122-0.126
Thirteen—Pink	0.127-0.131
Fourteen—Green	0.132-0.136
Fifteen—Gray	0.137-0.141

FORWARD AND DIRECT CLUTCH ASSEMBLY

1. Install the forward and direct clutch unit fixture tool (J-29337) in the end of the forward clutch shaft. Grasp the tool and remove the direct and forward clutch assemblies.
2. Lift the direct clutch assembly off of the forward clutch assembly.

NOTE: The direct forward clutch thrust washer may stick to the end of the direct clutch housing when it is removed from the forward clutch housing.

3. Remove the intermediate band assembly.
4. Remove the band anchor pin.

FRONT GEAR PARTS

1. Remove the output shaft-to-forward clutch shaft front selective washer. The washer may be stuck to the end of the forward clutch shaft.
2. To check the rear unit end play, loosen the output shaft loading fixture adapter tool (J-29332) adjusting screw on the output shaft. Push the output shaft downward.
3. Install the dial indicator gauge and plunger extension (J-7057). Position the extension end against the output shaft and set the dial indicator gauge to zero.
4. Move the output shaft upward by turning the adjusting screw on the tool until the white line on the sleeve of the tool begins to disappear. Read and record the rear unit end play. It should be .004-.025 in. If the end play is not within specification, replace the rear unit selective washer. The selective washer is located between the front internal gear thrust washer and the output shaft snap ring.
5. Remove the dial indicator and clamp assembly. Do not remove the rear unit support tool or the output shaft loading fixture adapter tool.
6. Using snapring pliers, remove the output shaft-to-selective washer snap ring.

FRONT INTERNAL GEAR

1. Remove the front internal gear, rear selective washer and the thrust washer from inside the transmission case.

2. Remove the rear selective washer and the thrust washer from the internal gear.
3. Remove front carrier assembly and the front internal gear to front carrier thrust bearing assembly.

NOTE: The front sun gear to front carrier thrust bearing assembly and race may come out as the front carrier is removed.

4. Remove front sun gear and front sun gear to front carrier thrust bearing assembly.

INPUT DRUM AND REAR SUN GEAR ASSEMBLY

1. Remove the input drum and rear sun gear assembly from inside the transmission case.
2. Remove the four-tanged input drum-to-reverse clutch housing thrust washer from the rear of the input drum or from the reverse clutch housing.

LOW AND REVERSE CLUTCH HOUSING ASSEMBLY

1. Grind approximately ¾ in. from end of 6.3 mm (#4) easy out to remove cup plug. Remove the housing to case cup plug assembly by turning the easy out 2 or 3 turns and pulling it straight out. Do not reuse the plug and seal assembly.
2. Remove the low and reverse clutch housing-to-transmission case beveled snap ring.

NOTE: The flat side of the snap ring should have been against the low and reverse clutch housing with the beveled side up.

3. Using the reverse clutch housing installer and remover tool (J-28542), remove the low and reverse clutch housing assembly.
4. Remove the low and reverse clutch housing-to-transmission case spacer ring.

REAR GEAR PARTS

1. Be sure that the governor assembly has been removed from the transmission case.
2. Grasp the output shaft and lift out the remainder of the rear unit gear parts. Lay the assembly down in a horizontal position.

ROLLER CLUTCH AND REAR CARRIER ASSEMBLY

1. Remove the roller clutch and rear carrier assembly from the output shaft.
2. Remove the four-tanged rear carrier-to-rear internal gear thrust washer from the end of the rear carrier, or from the inside of the rear internal gear.
3. Remove the low and reverse clutch plates from the output shaft.

REAR INTERNAL GEAR

1. Remove the rear internal gear-to-rear sun gear thrust bearing assembly from the rear internal gear.
2. Remove the rear internal gear from the output shaft.
3. Position the transmission so that the rear unit support tool and the output shaft loading fixture adapter tool can be removed from the transmission case.
4. If necessary, remove the rear oil seal.

MANUAL SHAFT AND PARKING PAWL PARTS

1. Position the transmission with the oil pan side up.
2. Remove the hex nut which holds the inside detent lever to the manual shaft.
3. Remove the parking lock actuator rod and the inside detent lever assembly.
4. Remove the manual shaft retaining pin from the transmission case and slide the manual shaft out of the case.

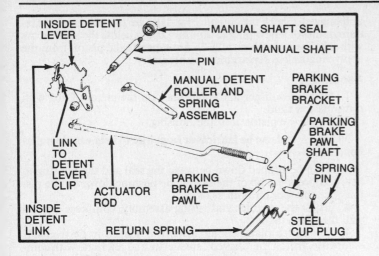

Manual shaft and parking pawl components
(© General Motors Corp.)

5. Inspect the manual shaft to case oil seal for damage, replace as required.

6. Remove the parking lock bracket. Remove the parking lock pawl shaft retaining pin.

7. Using a 6.3 mm (#4) Easy-Out®, remove the parking lock pawl cup plug. You will have to grind about ¾ inch from the end of the Easy-Out in order to remove the cup plug.

8. Using a 4 mm (#3) Easy-Out®, remove the parking pawl shaft. Remove the parking pawl and the return spring.

Unit Disassembly and Assembly
FRONT UNIT

Disassembly

1. Disassemble the front unit (direct clutch) by removing the snap ring that fits into the circumference of the direct clutch housing.

2. Take out the backing plate and the clutch plates.

NOTE: The number of clutch plates to be found will vary depending on the model of the unit. Take care when disassembling the clutch packs so that the right number of clutches will be installed and will be in their proper order. Also, due to differences in their composition material, do not mix the plates of the direct clutch with those of the forward clutch.

3. With a suitable spring compressor, compress the retainer and spring assembly and then remove the snap ring.

4. Remove the retainer and spring assembly.

5. Remove the release spring guide and the clutch piston.

NOTE: It is not necessary to remove the clutch apply ring from the piston unless the piston or apply ring requires replacement. These apply rings will vary between models. There will be an identifying number on the apply ring which will be needed if replacement is required.

Inspection

Clean and inspect all parts. Look for cracks, wear, burrs or any damage. Blow parts dry with compressed air. Discard all seals that are removed. Do not overlook the center seal in the direct clutch housing. Check for free operation of the check balls and see that the snap ring grooves are not damaged.

Assembly

1. If the clutch apply ring has been removed, install it back on the piston.

2. Install the inner and outer seals on the piston. Lube them with Dexron® II.

NOTE: The lips on the seals should face away from the clutch apply ring side.

3. Install the new center seal in the clutch housing, again with the lip in the proper position and well lubricated.

4. Install the piston into the housing. The seals should be well lubricated with transmission fluid.

NOTE: A tool can be fabricated from wire to help ease installation. This can be slipped down between the seal and the housing to help compress the lip of the seal while pushing down on the piston.

5. Install the release spring guide onto the piston, indexing the guide notch onto the check ball assembly. Install the retainer and spring assembly.

6. Compress the assembly and install the snap ring.

7. New clutch plates should always be soaked in Dexron® II for at least thirty minutes before use. Install a flat steel plate and alternate with composition plates, following the sequence of disassembly.

8. Install the backing plate, chamfered side up, and the snap ring.

9. Double-check to make sure that the composition plates turn freely.

10. Set the unit aside until the transmission is ready for assembly.

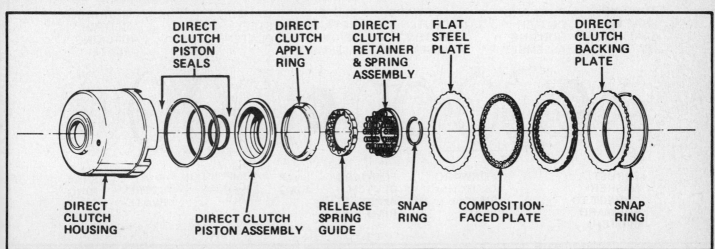

Direct clutch assembly—exploded view (© General Motors Corp.)

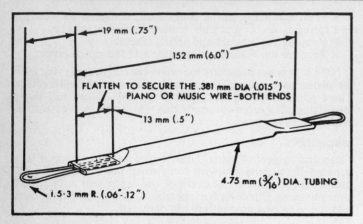

Piston installation tool (© General Motors Corp.)

INTERMEDIATE UNIT

Disassembly

1. Inspect the teflon seals on the shaft of the forward clutch assembly. They should not be removed unless they are going to be replaced. Original equipment seals will be teflon while service replacements are usually cast iron. Test the teflon seals to see that they rotate freely in the grooves. If they are to be replaced, cut them off with a sharp knife, then check the grooves for nicks or burrs. Lubricate any new seals with petroleum jelly.

2. Remove the thrust washer from the forward clutch and check it for wear or damage.

3. Turn the clutch over with the shaft facing down. Remove the snap ring and the clutch backing plate.

4. Remove the clutch plates, taking note of the number of plates and their order so that they can be reassembled properly. With a compressor, push against the retainer and remove the snap ring. Remove the retainer and spring assembly from the housing.

5. Remove the forward clutch piston.

Inspection

Clean and inspect all parts well. Look for cracks, wear, burrs or any damage. Blow parts dry with compressed air. Discard all seals that are removed. Check the housing for cracks and see that the lube hole is open, the check ball is free and the snap ring groove is undamaged. Check the cup plug for damage. If replacement is required, install a new plug to 1.0mm (.039") below the surface. As with the direct clutch piston, do not separate the piston from the apply ring unless replacement is necessary.

Assembly

1. Install new inner and other seals on the piston. Lube with transmission fluid.

2. Install the piston into the housing.

NOTE: A tool can be fabricated from wire to help ease installation.

This can be slipped down between the seal and the housing to help compress the lip of the seal while pushing down on the piston. Use the tool on both seals.

3. Install the retainer and spring assembly, compress and install the snap ring.

4. New clutch plates should always be soaked in Dexron® II before use. Install the "waved" steel plate and alternate with composition plates referring to the proper sequence at disassembly.

5. Install the backing plate, with the chamfered side up, then the snap ring.

NOTE: Double-check to make certain that the composition plates turn freely.

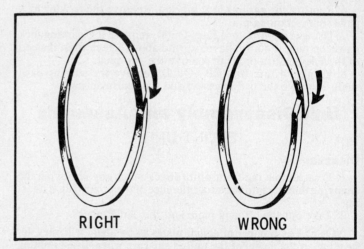

Teflon seal installation (© General Motors Corp.)

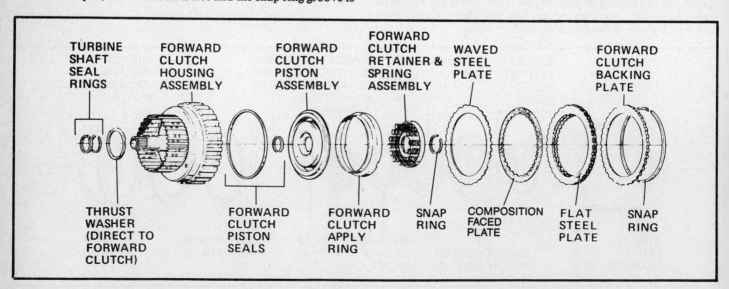

Forward clutch assembly—exploded view (© General Motors Corp.)

6. If the teflon rings on the the turbine are to be replaced, cut off the original rings and install new ones, well lubricated with transmission fluid.

NOTE: Service replacement rings may be teflon or cast iron. If they are teflon, make certain that they are installed properly, and that the ends do not overlap. Also, new teflon rings may sometimes look like they are distorted after they have been installed. However, once they have been exposed to the oil and the normal operating temperatures of the transmission, the new seals will regain their proper shape and fit freely in their grooves. A free fit of a used teflon ring does not indicate leakage in operation.

7. Install the thrust washer onto the turbine shaft.
8. Set the unit aside until the transmission is ready for assembly.

REAR UNIT

Disassembly

1. The low/reverse clutch pack is removed after the low/reverse clutch housing is withdrawn from the case.
2. Disassemble the clutch housing by compressing the clutch spring retainer and removing the snap ring. Remove the retainer.
3. Remove the wave release spring and then the piston.

Inspection

Clean and inspect all parts well. Look for cracks, wear, burrs or any damage. Blow parts dry with compressed air. Discard all seals that are removed. Check the housing for cracks and see that the oil feed hole is clear. Check the bushing for excessive wear.

Assembly

1. Install new inner and outer seals on the piston. Lube with transmission fluid.
2. Be certain that the lips of the seals are away from the clutch apply ring side. Install the piston into the housing. The seals should be well lubricated with transmission fluid.
3. Install the waved release spring, then the retainer with the cupped side down.
4. Compress the assembly and install the snap ring.
5. Set the unit aside until the transmission is ready for assembly.

CENTER SUPPORT

Disassembly

1. Remove the fourth clutch inner and outer seals.
2. Check the condition of the cast iron oil rings. Remove them from the center support if necessary.

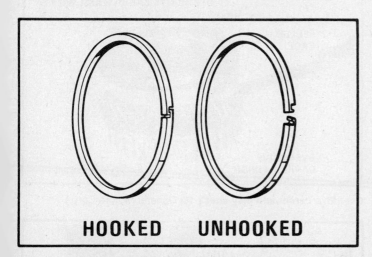

HOOKED   UNHOOKED

Cast iron seal ring installation (© General Motors Corp.)

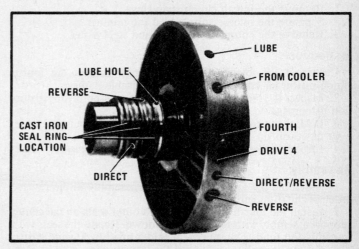

Center support and seal rings (© General Motors Corp.)

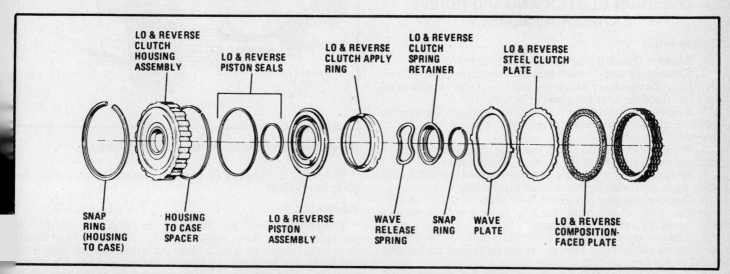

Low and reverse clutch piston assembly—exploded view (© General Motors Corp.)

537

Inspection

1. Inspect the bushings for scoring, wear or galling. Check the oil ring grooves and the oil rings for nicks and other damage.
2. Air check the oil passages to be sure that they are open and not interconnected.
3. Inspect the piston sealing surfaces for scoring and scratches.
4. Inspect the center support for cracks or porosity.
5. Inspect the center support for burrs or raised edges. If present, remove them with fine abrasive paper.

Assembly

1. If removed, install the cast iron oil seal rings on the center support.

NOTE: When installing cast iron oil seal rings, make sure the ends overlap and interlock. Make sure ends are flush with each other when interlocked, and oil seal rings are seated in ring grooves to prevent damage to rings during reassembly of mating parts over rings. Coat the rings with clean transmission fluid.

2. Set the assembly aside until the transmission is ready to be assembled.

FOURTH CLUTCH ASSEMBLY

Disassembly

1. Remove the fourth clutch snap rings.
2. Separate the release springs and the retainer.
3. Remove the composition faced and steel plates.

Inspection

1. Inspect the fourth clutch snap rings. Inspect the fourth clutch piston for cracks, wear or other visable damage.
2. Inspect the release springs and retainer assembly for distortion or damage.
3. Inspect the composition faced and steel plates for damage, wear or burning.
4. Inspect the backing plate for scratches or damage.

Assembly

1. Assemble the fourth clutch piston assembly in the reverse order of the disassembly procedure.
2. Install the fourth clutch inner and outer seals on the center support assembly with the lips facing down. Retain the seals with transmission fluid. The inner seal is identified by a white stripe.
3. Set the assembly aside until the transmission is to be reassembled.

OVERRUN CLUTCH AND OVERDRIVE CARRIER ASSEMBLY

Disassembly

1. Remove the snap ring from the turbine shaft.
2. Remove the turbine shaft from the overdrive carrier assembly. It may be necessary to tap the end of the shaft to disengage the shaft from the overdrive carrier splines.
3. Remove the overdrive carrier assembly from the overrun clutch assembly. Remove the overdrive sun gear from the overrun clutch assembly.
4. Remove the overrun clutch snap ring. Remove the overrun clutch backing plate from the overrun clutch housing.
5. Remove the clutch plates from the overrun clutch housing. Keep them separated from the other plate assemblies.
6. Remove the overrun clutch hub snap ring. Remove the overdrive roller clutch cam assembly. Inspect the roller clutch cam ramps for any signs of damage.
7. Remove the roller clutch assembly. Inspect it for damage. Remove the retainer and wave spring assembly from the housing. Remove the overrun clutch piston assembly.
8. Remove the inner and outer seal from the overrun clutch piston. Inspect the piston for damage.

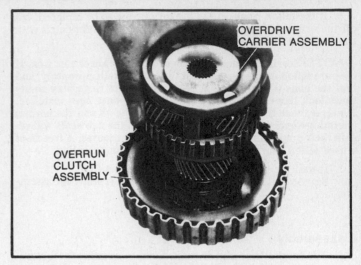

Overrun clutch and overdrive carrier assembly
(© General Motors Corp.)

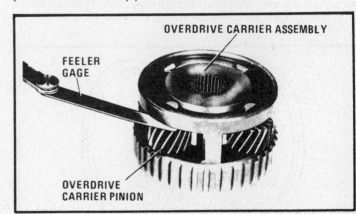

Overdrive carrier end play check (© General Motors Corp.)

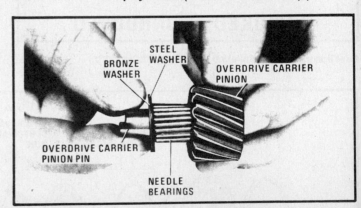

Needle bearing installation (© General Motors Corp.)

9. Inspect the housing for damage. Inspect the snap rings, replace as required.

Assembly

1. Install new inner and outer seals on the piston with the lips facing away from clutch apply ring side. Oil the seals and install the overrun clutch piston. To make the piston easier to install, insert the piston installing tool between the seal and housing; rotate tool around the housing to compress the lip of the seal, while pushing down slightly on the piston.

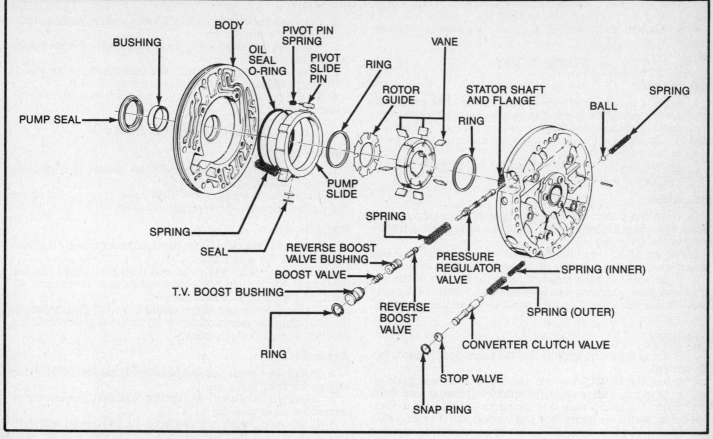

Front pump—exploded view (© General Motors Corp.)

2. Install the overrun clutch waved release spring. Install the overrun clutch waved spring retainer with the cupped face down.

3. Install the roller clutch cam on the roller clutch assembly. The locating tangs on the roller clutch must set on the roller clutch cam.

4. Install the roller clutch assembly on the overrun clutch hub.

5. Compress the retainer by pushing down on the roller clutch assembly. Install the narrow snap ring.

6. Oil and install the overrun clutch plates into the overrun clutch housing, starting with a flat steel and alternating composition-faced and flat steel clutch plates.

7. Install the backing plate with the chamfered side up. Install the snap ring. Be sure that the composition faced plates turn freely.

8. Set the unit aside until you are ready to reassemble the transmission.

OVERDRIVE CARRIER ASSEMBLY

Disassembly

1. Before disassembly, inspect the locating splines for damage. Inspect the roller clutch race for damage, scratches or wear. Inspect the carrier housing for cracks or wear. Inspect the pinions for damage, rough bearings or tilt.

2. Check the pinion end play. It should be .009-.024 in. If it is not within specification, repair or replace the defective component as required.

3. Remove the overdrive carrier snap ring. Remove the overdrive carrier pinions. Remove the pinions, thrust washer and roller needle bearings.

4. Inspect the pinion pocket thrust faces for burrs. Remove them if they are present.

5. Remove the overdrive sun gear to overdrive carrier thrust bearing assembly. Inspect the unit.

Assembly

1. Install thrust bearing assembly by placing the small diameter race down. Hold in place with transmission fluid.

2. Install 19 needle bearings into each pinion, thumb lock needle bearings to hold them in place.

3. Place a bronze and steel thrust washer on each side so steel washer is against pinion. Hold them in place with transmission fluid.

4. Place the pinion assembly in position in the carrier and use a pilot shaft to align parts in place.

5. Push the pinion pin in place while rotating the pinion from side to side. Install the overdrive carrier snap ring to retain the pinion pins.

6. Set the assembly aside until you are ready to assemble the transmission.

FRONT PUMP

Disassembly

1. Remove the front pump-to-transmission case seal ring. Inspect the ring, replace as required.

2. Position the pump so that the front pump cover side is up.

3. Remove the pump cover-to-pump body attaching bolts. Separate the front pump cover from the front pump body.

4. Remove the stator shaft to overrun selective thrust washer. Inspect the components for damage and replace as required.

Assembly

1. Assemble the pump cover to the pump body. Retain the components in place using the attaching bolts.

539

2. Align the cover and body using tool #J-25015 or equivalent.

3. Torque the retaining bolts to 18 ft. lbs.

4. Set the unit aside until you are ready to assemble the transmission.

PUMP BODY

Disassembly

1. Using a suitable tool, remove the pump slide spring. Be careful when removing this spring as it is under high pressure.

2. Remove the pump slide, slide to wear plate oil seal and the back O-ring seal. Remove the rotor, rotor guide, the seven vanes and the two vane rings.

3. Remove the pump slide seal and the seal support. Remove the pivot slide pin and spring.

Inspection.

1. Wash the pump body, springs, pump slide, pump rotor, vanes, vane rings and rotor guide in suitable solvent. Do not wash the pump seals in the solvent.

2. Inspect all of the components for damage, wear, cracking and scoring. Replace defective parts and components as required.

3. If the seal has been removed, coat the outside of the seal body with non-hardening sealing compound. Position the pump body oil seal side up and install a new pump seal using a seal installation tool.

Assembly

1. Position the pump body so that the pump pocket side is facing upward.

2. Install the slide O-ring seal and the slide-to-wear plate oil seal in the pump. Retain the parts with clean transmission fluid.

3. Install the pump slide into the pump pocket with the seal side down. Install the pump slide seal support and the pump slide seal. Retain the parts using clean transmission fluid. Be sure that this seal is installed correctly.

4. Install the pivot pin spring and the pivot slide pin. Install the vane ring in the pump pocket. Install the rotor guide in the pump rotor.

5. Install the pump rotor into the pump pocket. Center and seat the pump rotor on the rotor guide so that the rotor is flush with the pump slide.

6. Install the seven vanes into the pump. Be sure that the vane pattern is installed against the vane ring. Install the top vane ring. Install the pump slide spring.

PUMP COVER

Disassembly

1. Using a suitable tool, remove the converter clutch valve from the pump cover.

2. Using a punch, remove the pressure relief spring retaining sleeve. Remove the pressure relief valve assembly.

Inspection

1. Inspect both the converter clutch valve and the pressure relief valve for damage. Replace defective components as required.

2. Inspect the pump cover to be sure that all the oil passages are open.

3. Inspect the four cup plugs. If a plug is missing, install a new cup plug to $1/32$ in. below the top of the hole. Use a $9/32$ in. rod on the two smaller cup plugs a $5/16$ in. rod on the line to case plug and a $7/16$ in. rod on the larger plug when installing new plugs.

4. Inspect the orifice plugs. If they require replacement, position the new plug, orifice end first, into the plug hole from the rough casting side.

5. Drive the plug flush to 0.10 in. below the top of the hole. Stake the top of the hole in two places to retain the plug.

Assembly

1. Assemble the converter clutch valve and the pressure relief valve into the pump cover.

2. Assemble the pump cover to the pump body. Finger tighten the attaching bolts.

3. Align the pump cover with the pump body using tool J-25015 or equivalent. Torque the pump bolts to 18 ft. lbs.

4. Set the assembly aside until you are ready to reassemble the transmission.

INTERMEDIATE SERVO

Disassembly

1. Compress the servo assembly and remove the retaining ring.

2. Remove and separate the band apply pin, and the spring and washer from the servo piston assembly.

Inspection

1. Inspect the pin oil seals for damage. Inspect the pin for damage and fit to the case bore.

2. Inspect the inner and outer seal rings for damage and free movement. Do not remove unless replacement is required. Inspect the spring, replace as required.

3. To check for proper intermediate servo band apply pin; see the procedure for intermediate servo removal and installation which is located in this section.

Assembly

1. Install the retainer on the band apply pin. Install the snap ring on the band apply pin.

2. Install the band apply pin, retainer end first, through the intermediate servo pistons.

3. If removed, install new intermediate servo inner and outer seal rings. Be sure that the cut ends are assembled in the same manner as they were cut. Be sure that the rings are seated in the grooves to prevent damage to them. Retain the rings using transmission fluid.

4. Install a new seal ring on the servo cover.

5. Set the unit aside until you are ready to reassemble the transmission.

VALVE BODY

Disassembly

NOTE: As each valve train component is removed, place the individual valve train in the order that it is removed and in a separate location relative to its position in the valve body. None of the valves, bushings or springs are interchangeable; some roll pins are interchangeable. Remove all roll pins and spring retaining sleeve by pushing through from the rough case surface side of the control valve pump assembly, except for the blind hole roll pins.

1. Lay the control valve assembly machined face up, with the manual valve at the top.

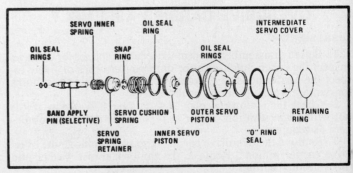

Intermediate servo assembly—exploded view
(© General Motors Corp.)

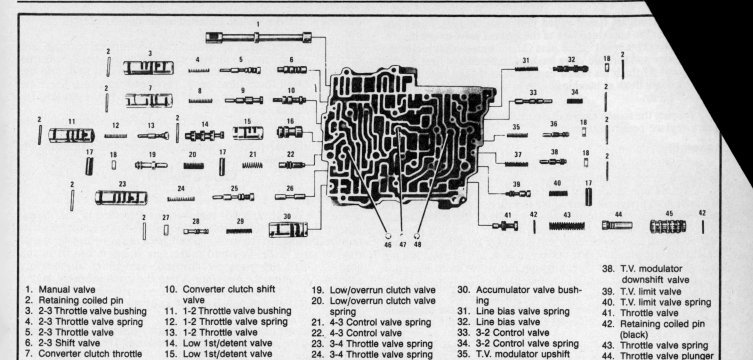

Valve body assembly—exploded view (© General Motors Corp.)

1. Manual valve
2. Retaining coiled pin
3. 2-3 Throttle valve bushing
4. 2-3 Throttle valve spring
5. 2-3 Throttle valve
6. 2-3 Shift valve
7. Converter clutch throttle bushing
8. Converter clutch throttle valve spring
9. Converter clutch throttle valve
10. Converter clutch shift valve
11. 1-2 Throttle valve bushing
12. 1-2 Throttle valve spring
13. 1-2 Throttle valve
14. Low 1st/detent valve
15. Low 1st/detent valve bushing
16. 1-2 Shift valve
17. Spring retaining sleeve
18. Valve bore plug [12.50mm (.500 in.)]
19. Low/overrun clutch valve
20. Low/overrun clutch valve spring
21. 4-3 Control valve spring
22. 4-3 Control valve
23. 3-4 Throttle valve spring
24. 3-4 Throttle valve spring
25. 3-4 Throttle valve spring
26. 3-4 Shift valve
27. Valve bore plug
28. Accumulator valve
29. Accumulator valve spring
30. Accumulator valve bushing
31. Line bias valve spring
32. Line bias valve
33. 3-2 Control valve
34. 3-2 Control valve spring
35. T.V. modulator upshift valve spring
36. T.V. modulator upshift valve
37. T.V. modulator downshift valve spring
38. T.V. modulator downshift valve
39. T.V. limit valve
40. T.V. limit valve spring
41. Throttle valve
42. Retaining coiled pin (black)
43. Throttle valve spring
44. Throttle valve plunger
45. Throttle valve plunger bushing
46. #11 D3
47. #8 1-2 shift valve
48. #1-2 low 1st

2. Remove the 3 check balls if still intact.
3. Remove manual valve from upper bore.

NOTE: Some of the roll pins in the valve body assembly have pressure against them. Hold a shop towel over the bore while removing the pin, to help prevent possibly losing a bore plug, spring, etc.

4. Remove roll pin from upper left bore. Remove 2-3 throttle valve bushing, 2-3 throttle valve spring, 2-3 throttle valve and 2-3 shift valve. The 2-3 throttle valve spring and 2-3 throttle valve may be inside the 2-3 throttle valve bushing.

5. From the next bore down, remove the roll pin. Remove the converter clutch throttle bushing, converter clutch throttle valve spring, converter clutch throttle valve, and converter clutch shift valve. The converter clutch throttle valve spring and the converter clutch throttle valve may be inside the converter clutch throttle bushing.

6. From the next bore down, remove the outer roll pin. Remove the 1-2 throttle valve bushing, 1-2 throttle valve spring, 1-2 throttle valve and low 1st/detent valve: The 1-2 throttle valve spring and the 1-2 throttle valve may be inside the 1-2 throttle valve bushing. Remove the inner roll pin. Remove the low 1st/detent valve bushing and 1-2 shift valve.

7. From the next bore down, remove the outer spring retaining sleeve. This spring is under load so be careful when removing it. Remove the bore plug, 4-3 control valve and spring. This spring is also under extreme pressure. Remove the low overrun clutch valve spring and the low overrun clutch valve.

8. From the next bore down, remove the roll pin. Remove the 3-4 throttle valve bushing, 3-4 throttle valve spring, 3-4 throttle valve and 3-4 shift valve. The 3-4 throttle valve and spring may be inside the 3-4 throttle valve bushing.

9. From the last bore down, remove the roll pin and bore plug. Remove the accumulator valve bushing, accumulator valve and accumulator spring. The accumulator spring and accumulator valve may be inside the accumulator bushing.

10. From the upper right bore, remove roll pin, valve bore plug, line bias valve and line bias valve spring.

11. From the next bore down, remove the roll pin, 3-2 control valve spring and 3-2 control valve.

12. From the next bore down, remove the roll pin, valve bore plug, T.V. modulator upshift valve and T.V. modulator upshift valve spring.

13. From the next bore down, remove the roll pin, valve bore plug, T.V. modulator downshift valve and T.V. modulator downshift valve spring.

14. From the next bore down, remove spring retaining sleeve, T.V. limit valve spring and T.V. limit valve.

NOTE: This sleeve is under a load. Cover the open end of the bore to prevent loss of spring.

15. From the last bore, remove the outer roll pin from the rough casting side, the throttle valve plunger bushing, throttle valve plunger and throttle valve spring. Remove the inner roll pin as follows:
   a. Grind a taper to one end of a #49 drill.
   b. Lightly tap the tapered end into the roll pin.
   c. Pull the drill and coil pin out.
   d. Remove the throttle valve.

Inspection

1. Wash control valve body, valves, springs, and other parts in clean solvent and air dry.
2. Inspect valves for scoring, cracks and free movement in their bores.
3. Inspect bushings for cracks or scored bores.
4. Inspect valve body for cracks, damage or scored bores.
5. Inspect springs for distortion or collapsed coils.
6. Inspect bore plugs for damage.

pins (zinc coated), flared end
control valve assembly. In-
ack finish) that retain the
g, tapered end first. Coiled
sting face. Make sure that all
ed face or damage to the transmis-

rth clutch pressure switch for damage. If nec-
pressure switch.

bly

1. Position the valve body assembly so that you can install the fourth clutch pressure switch.

2. Install into lower right bore, throttle valve, smaller outside diameter land first, make sure valve is seated at the bottom of the bore. Install inner roll pin between the lands of this valve. Install the T.V. spring into the bore. Install the throttle valve plunger, stem end first, into the throttle valve plunger bushing and install these two parts into the bore, valve end first. Install outer roll pin from rough cast surface side, aligning pin with slot in bushing.

3. In the next bore up, install T.V. limit valve, stem end first. Install the T.V. limit valve spring. Compress the T.V. limit valve spring and install the spring retaining sleeve from the machined face. Make sure the sleeve is level with or below the machined surface.

4. In the next bore up, install T.V. modulator downshift valve spring then install the T.V. modulator downshift valve, smaller chamfered stem end first. Install bore plug, hole out, and roll pin.

5. In the next bore up, install the T.V. modulator upshift valve spring then install the T.V. modulator upshift valve, smaller chamfered stem end first. Install bore plug, hole out, and roll pin.

6. In the next bore up, install 3-2 control valve, smaller stem end out. Install 3-2 control valve spring and roll pin.

7. In the next bore up, install line bias valve spring then install the line bias valve, smaller stem end first. Install bore plug, hole out, and roll pin.

8. In the lower left bore, install accumulator bushing into bore, aligning the pin slot in line with the pin hole in control valve assembly. Install accumulator spring then accumulator valve, smaller end first. Next, install bore plug, hole out, and roll pin.

9. In the next bore up, install 3-4 shift valve, chamfered end first. Install the 3-4 throttle valve spring into the 3-4 throttle valve bushing. Next, install the 3-4 throttle valve, stem end first into the 3-4 bushing. Install the 3-4 throttle valve and bushing into the bore, making sure the pin slot is aligned with the pin hole in the control valve assembly. Install the roll pin.

10. In the next bore up, install low/overrun clutch valve, smaller end first. Next, install the low/overrun clutch valve spring; compress the spring and install the spring retaining sleeve from the machined face. Make sure the sleeve is level with or below the machined surface. Install the 4-3 control valve spring and 4-3 control valve smaller stemmed end first. Install bore plug, hole out and retaining sleeve from the machined face. Make sure the sleeve is level with or below the machined surface.

11. In the next bore up, install the 1-2 shift valve, small stem outward. Install the 1-2 shift valve bushing, small I.D. first and aligning pin hole in bushing with the inner pin hole in the control valve assembly. Install the inner roll pin. Next, install low 1st/detent valve long stem end out. Install the 1-2 throttle valve spring into the 1-2 throttle valve bushing and the 1-2 throttle valve, stem end first, into the bushing. Install these three parts, valve end first, into the bore, aligning the bushing so the outer pin can be installed in the pin slot. Install the outer roll pin.

12. In the next bore up, install the converter clutch shift valve, short stemmed end first. Next, install the converter clutch throttle valve spring into the converter clutch throttle bushing and the converter clutch throttle valve, stem end first, into the bushing. Install these three parts, valve end first, into the bore, aligning the

bushing so the pin can be installed in the pin slot. Install the roll pin.

13. In the next bore up, install the 2-3 shift valve, large end first. Next, install the 2-3 throttle valve spring into the 2-3 throttle valve bushing and the 2-3 throttle valve, stem end first, into the bushing. Install these three parts, valve end first, into the bore, aligning the bushing so the pin can be installed in the pin slot. Install the roll pin.

14. Install manual valve with the inside detent lever pin hole first.

15. Set the valve body assembly aside, until the transmission is ready to be reassembled.

GOVERNOR

Inspection

1. Once the governor is removed (as described in the Transmission Disassembly section), inspect it carefully. Look for nicks or other damage to the driven gear. Check the governor shaft seal ring for cuts or damage and make sure it has a free fit in the groove. Often the gears are stripped, sometimes all the way around. Assuming the governor is free and turns properly, take a very close look at the edges of the worm gear teeth that drive the governor. If they look rough, polish away the roughness or a new output gear and/or governor assembly will promptly be ruined too. Sometimes the factory heat treating process leaves a scale build up on the output worm gear oversize and excessively wears the governor gear or even strips it.

2. Note that different transmission models will use different numbers of springs, some one, some two.

NOTE: The governor with one spring must use the secondary spring. The secondary spring is located between the governor weight and the governor shaft, while the primary spring is located between the governor weight and the governor gear.

3. Make sure the two check balls are in place and that the washer is not worn excessively.

4. Renew the seals as necessary and remember to lube them with Dexron® II or petroleum jelly.

5. Set the governor aside until the transmission is ready for assembly.

Transmission Assembly

After all parts have been cleaned and the subassemblies checked and overhauled as necessary, begin reassembly.

1. Install a new manual shaft seal. Make sure the lip is facing inward, toward the transmission.

2. Install the parking pawl and return spring, with the "tooth" on the pawl toward the inside of the case and the spring under the tooth. Make sure the spring ends push against the case pad and slide the pawl shaft in. The tapered end goes in first. Do not forget to install a new shaft cup plug, open end out, driving it in with a rod ⅜ in. in diameter, past the retaining pin hole. Finally install the retaining pin, by positioning with pliers, then gently tapping the pin in place.

3. Install the parking lock bracket. The pawl will probably have to be held toward the center of the transmission while the bracket is put into place. Torque the bolts to 20 ft. lbs.

4. Take the parking actuator rod and slip the end with the 90° bend into the detent plate assembly, on the "pin side," and slip the opposite end between the parking pawl and lock bracket.

5. Carefully examine the manual shaft for any burrs or rough edges that might damage the seal. Apply some Dexron® II to the shaft and seal and slide the shaft, threaded end first, into place. There is a small retaining pin that is installed. It retains the shaft in the larger of the two grooves. Install the detent lever on the shaft by turning the shaft until the flats line up. Install the hex nut, and tighten to 20-25 ft. lbs.

6. Prior to installing the output shaft, carefully examine it for damage or wear. The speedometer gear should be examined for wear.

7. If the output shaft is determined to be re-usable, install the rear internal gear onto the shaft, hub end first, if it has not been assembled yet. The roller clutch and rear pinion carrier should have already been assembled. See the section "Unit Disassembly and Assembly." Slide the rear carrier into the rear internal gear, and, holding the output shaft from its front end, lower the assembly into the case, until the parking pawl lugs on the rear gear align flush with the parking pawl tooth. At this point, install the speedometer driven gear as a double check that the drive gear is positioned on the proper journal. The attaching bolt is torqued to 6-10 ft. lbs.

8. Make certain that the low/reverse clutch selective washer is in place, then install the clutches, well oiled with Dexron® II, alternating friction and steel plates in the order determined at disassembly. Install the housing-case spacer ring. The low-reverse clutch housing assembly is installed next. Note that there is a feed hole in the housing that must be aligned with the feed hole to the reverse clutch case feed passage. Make sure that the low-reverse clutch housing assembly is fully seated past the case snap ring groove.

9. Install the snap ring, flat side against the housing, beveled side up. Position the ring gap 180° from the parking rod.

10. Install the rear sun gear and input drum. Double-check for chipped teeth, damaged splines or other damage. Install the four-tanged thrust washer on the input drum. Retain the components in place using transmission fluid.

11. Inspect the front sun gear for damage or wear. Note that there is an identification mark (either a groove or a drill spot) which goes against the input drum snap ring. Follow this with the thrust bearing and race assembly. The needle bearings go against the gear.

12. The front planetary carrier should have been cleaned, inspected and end play checked. If the planetary is within specifications, install in the case. The thrust bearing which goes on the front of the corner is installed with its small diameter race against the carrier. Transmission fluid will hold it in place.

INPUT DRUM

REAR SUN GEAR

SNAP RING (INPUT DRUM TO REAR SUN GEAR)

THRUST WASHER (DRUM TO HOUSING)

Rear sun gear and input drum (© General Motors Corp.)

13. After the front internal gear has been inspected, install along with tanged thrust washer, using transmission fluid to hold it. If the *rear* selective washer had been determined to give proper end play, reuse it. Then install the snap ring, making sure it is seated in its groove.

NOTE: The rear selective thrust washer must be installed with the identification number toward the front of the transmission.

14. Install the *front* selective washer, using transmission fluid and with the identification number to the front.

15. Install a new intermediate band with the apply lug and anchor pin lug located in the case slot. Install the band anchor, pin stem end first, seating the stem in the band hole lug.

16. The direct clutch and forward clutch assemblies are now ready for installation. It would be convenient to have a hole in the work bench or other arrangement to receive the turbine shaft. First position the direct clutch assembly over the hole, clutch plate end up. It will help if the clutch plate teeth are aligned to make the forward clutch assembly easier to install.

17. Install the forward clutch assembly, shaft first into the direct clutch; rotate back and forth until the forward clutch is seated.

18. To check that the forward clutch is in fact, seated, measure with a steel ruler from the tang end of the direct clutch housing to the end of the forward clutch drum. It should be approximately ⅝ in.

19. Holding both clutch assemblies so that they do not separate, lower into the case. The direct clutch housing will be approximately 4⅛ in. from the pump face in the case if it is correctly seated.

20. Install the overdrive unit assembly at this time. As you are installing the overdrive unit assembly, it may be necessary to rotate the assembly in order to get the assembly seat properly.

21. Install the front pump assembly. One suggestion is to take two 8mm x 1.25 bolts several inches long and by sawing the heads off, make two guide pins to help with the pump assembly. Before installing the pump, confirm that the intermediate band anchor pin lug is aligned with the band anchor pin hole in the case and that the stem of the anchor pin locates in the hole of the band lug. Apply transmission fluid to the direct clutch thrust washer, install on the back of the pump and turn the pump over. With a new gasket and the outer seal well lubricated, lower the pump gently onto the guide pins and into the case.

22. Use new washers on the pump bolts and torque them 15-20 ft. lbs. Try the turbine shaft to make sure that it can be rotated as the pump is being tightened. If not, the forward and direct clutch housings have not been properly installed, and are not indexing with all the clutch plates. This must be corrected before the pump can be installed completely. The turbine shaft must rotate freely.

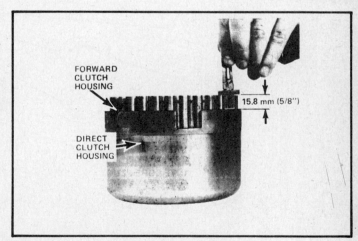

FORWARD CLUTCH HOUSING

15.8 mm (5/8")

DIRECT CLUTCH HOUSING

Forward clutch installation (© General Motors Corp.)

23. Front unit end play should have been checked at disassembly to determine if a thrust washer change is necessary. It can be rechecked by mounting a dial indicator to rest on the turbine shaft. This end play is controlled by the selective washer between the output shaft and turbine shaft. At this point, the transmission fixture, if used, should be rotated so that the transmission is horizontal, oil pan side up.

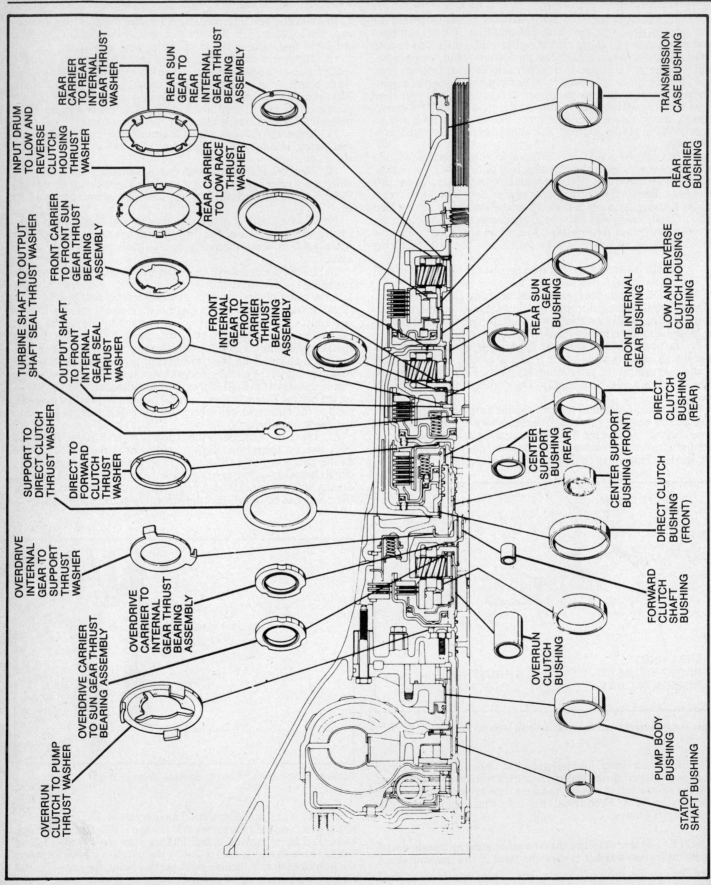

Automatic transmission bushing locations (© General Motors Corp.)

CLUTCH PLATE AND APPLY RING USAGE CHART

Overrun Clutch				Fourth Clutch				Direct Clutch					
Flat Steel Plate		Composition Faced Plate		Flat Steel Plate		Composition Faced Plate		Flat Steel Plate		Composition Faced Plate		Apply Ring	
No.	Thickness	No.		No.	Thickness	No.		No.	Thickness	No.		ID.	Width
2	0.077 in.	2		3	0.077 in	2		6	0.091 in	6		9	0.429 in.

CLUTCH PLATE AND APPLY RING USAGE CHART

Forward Clutch							Low and Reverse Clutch						
Wave Plate		Flat Steel Plate		Composition Faced Plate	Apply Ring		Wave Plate		Flat Steel Plate		Composition Faced Plate	Apply Ring	
No.	Thickness	No.	Thickness	No.	ID.	Width	No.	Thickness	No.	Thickness	No.	ID.	Width
1	0.062 in.	3	0.077 in.	4	8	0.0492 in.	1	0.077 in.	7	0.077 in.	6	0	0.0516 in.

24. Take the clean and already inspected governor assembly and place the governor to case washer on the end, holding it with transmission fluid. Install the governor cover onto the governor, making certain that the small seal on the end has been renewed.

NOTE: If the seal is slightly damaged, a pressure leak will result. For the same reason, examine carefully the governor cover. A seal that had previously leaked or that deteriorated would have allowed enough end play to develop to have badly worn the governor cover. If in doubt, replace the governor cover.

CAUTION

Do not use any type of hammer to install the governor assembly into the case. Lube the seals with Dexron II® to help ease installation. Expect the last 1/16 in. of travel to be a tight fit as the governor cover end seal is being compressed, but do not hammer on the governor cover.

25. Install the intermediate servo piston into its cover and install the assembly into the case, tapping lightly if necessary. Make sure the tapered end of the band apply pin is properly located against the band apply lug. Install the retaining ring.

26. The low and reverse clutch housing to case cup plug and seal is installed next. Make sure the seal seats against the housing. Use a ⅜" rod to drive the plug in until it seats against the seal.

27. Install the valve body. Note the check balls that belong in the valve body and case. There should be four in the valve body and one in the case. Begin by installing the 5th check ball in the case. It is the throttle valve exhaust check ball.

28. It would be helpful to make two guide pins from some 6.3 x 1.0 metric bolts. Screw these into the case on each side of the valve body location. Install four check balls into the ball seat pockets in the control valve body and retain with transmission fluid. Install the valve body spacer plate gasket.

29. Put the spacer plate on the gasket and then the spacer plate to case gasket.

30. Put two of the attaching bolts through the assembly, then install using a finger to position the manual valve into the detent lever pin.

31. Hold the assembly tightly as it is lowered onto the guide pins so that the check balls, 1-2 accumulator piston and manual valve do not fall out. Remove the guide pins and start the bolts into place. Replace the manual detent roller and spring assembly.

32. Install the throttle lever and bracket assembly seeing that the slot fits into the roll pin, aligning the lifter through the valve body bore and link through the T.V. linkage case bore. Install the bolt, then torque all control valve assembly bolts to 12 ft. lbs.

33. Install the oil screen using a new gasket and torque to 12 ft. lbs.

34. Install the oil pan with a new gasket and torque the retaining bolts evenly to 10-13 ft. lbs. The transmission is now ready for the torque converter and then to be moved to the transmission jack for installation.

SPECIFICATIONS

TORQUE SPECIFICATIONS—THM 200-4R

Item	Ft. Lbs.	N•m
Pump cover bolts	18	24
Pump to case attaching bolts	18	24
Parking pawl bracket bolts	18	24
Control valve body bolts	11	15
Oil screen retaining bolts	11	15
Bottom pan attaching bolts	12	16
Converter to flywheel bolts	35	48

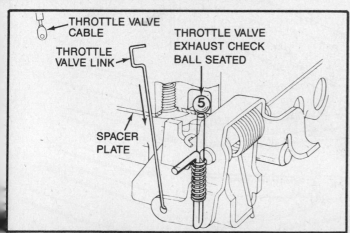

THROTTLE VALVE CABLE
THROTTLE VALVE LINK
THROTTLE VALVE EXHAUST CHECK BALL SEATED
⑤
SPACER PLATE

Throttle lever assembly (© General Motors Corp.)

TORQUE SPECIFICATIONS—THM 200-4R

Item	Ft. Lbs.	N•m
Transmission to engine mounting bolts	25	34
Converter dust shield screws	8	11
Manual shaft nut	23	31
Speedometer driven gear attaching bolts	8	11
Detent cable attaching screw	6	9
Oil cooler line to transmission connector	25	37
Oil cooler line to radiator connector	20	27
Linkage swivel clamp nut	30	41

TORQUE SPECIFICATIONS—THM 200-4R

Item	Ft. Lbs.	N•m
Shifter assembly to sheet metal screws	8	10
Converter bracket to adapter nuts	13	17
Catalytic converter to rear exhaust pipe nuts	17	23
Exhaust pipe to manifold nuts	12	16
Rear transmission support bolts	40	54
Mounting assembly to support nuts	21	29
Mounting assembly to support center nut	33	44
Adapter to transmission bolts	33	44

SPECIAL TOOLS

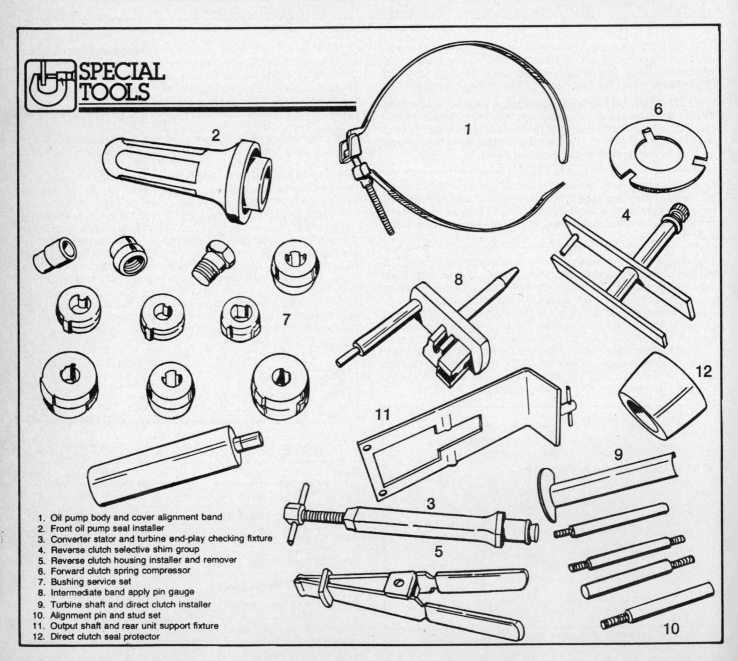

1. Oil pump body and cover alignment band
2. Front oil pump seal installer
3. Converter stator and turbine end-play checking fixture
4. Reverse clutch selective shim group
5. Reverse clutch housing installer and remover
6. Forward clutch spring compressor
7. Bushing service set
8. Intermediate band apply pin gauge
9. Turbine shaft and direct clutch installer
10. Alignment pin and stud set
11. Output shaft and rear unit support fixture
12. Direct clutch seal protector

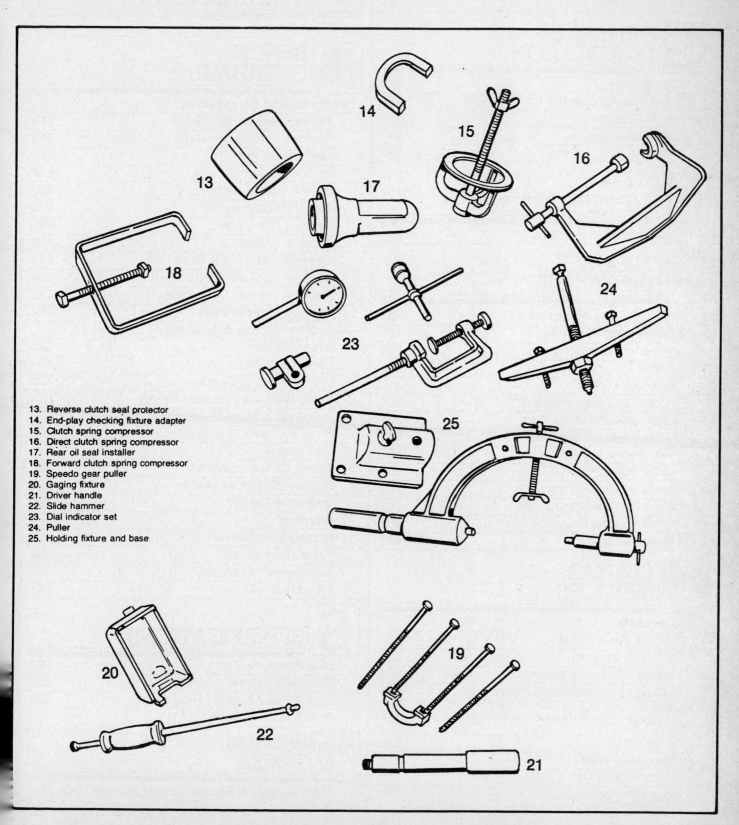

13. Reverse clutch seal protector
14. End-play checking fixture adapter
15. Clutch spring compressor
16. Direct clutch spring compressor
17. Rear oil seal installer
18. Forward clutch spring compressor
19. Speedo gear puller
20. Gaging fixture
21. Driver handle
22. Slide hammer
23. Dial indicator set
24. Puller
25. Holding fixture and base

INDEX

GENERAL MOTORS
TURBO HYDRA-MATIC 325-4L
Automatic Transaxle

APPLICATIONS

TRANSAXLE APPLICATION CHART

Year	Transmission Type	Model Identification
1982 and Later	325-4L	Riviera
1982 and Later	325-4L	Seville, Eldorado
1982 and Later	325-4L	Toronado

GENERAL DESCRIPTION

The THM 325-4L automatic transaxle is a fully automatic front wheel drive transaxle. This unit, consists primarily of a four element hydraulic torque converter with a torque converter clutch, three compound planetry gear sets and an overdrive unit. Five multiple-disc clutches, two roller clutches and a band provide the friction elements required to obtain the desired function of the compound planetary gear set and the overdrive unit.

The torque converter smoothly couples the engine to the overdrive unit and planetary gears through oil and hydraulically provides additional torque multiplication as required. The combination of the compound planetary gear set and the overdrive unit provides four forward ratios and one reverse. Changing of the gear ratios is fully automatic in relation to vehicle speed and engine torque. Vehicle speed and engine torque signals are constantly fed to the automatic transaxle to provide the proper gear ratios for maximum efficiency and performance at all throttle openings.

A hydraulic system, pressurized by a gear type pump, provides the working pressure required to operate the friction elements and automatic controls.

Transaxle and Torque Converter Identification

TRANSAXLE

The THM 325-4L automatic transaxle can be identified by locating the unit number plate, which is positioned on the left side of the torque converter housing.

TORQUE CONVERTER

Torque converter usage differs with the type engine and the area in which the vehicle is to be operated. No specific physical markings are designated so that the repairman can identify the converter. It is most important to obtain the transaxle model and serial number, know the specific operating area and the vehicle VIN number before replacement of the converter unit is attempted.

Metric Fasteners

Metric bolts sizes and thread pitches are used for the THM 325-4L. The metric fastener dimensions are very close to the dimensions of the familiar inch system fasteners.

For this reason, replacement fasteners must have the same measurement and strength as those removed.

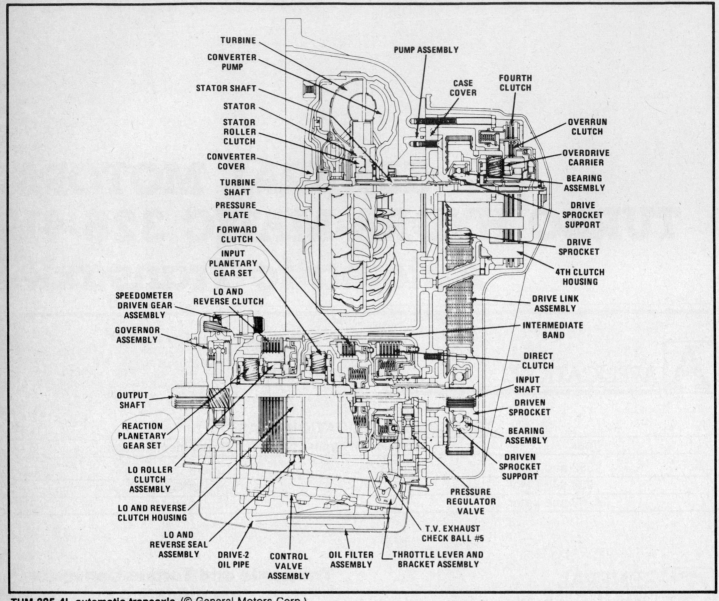

THM 325-4L automatic transaxle (© General Motors Corp.)

Do not attempt to interchange metric fasteners for inch system fasteners. Mismatched or incorrect fasteners can result in damage to the unit through malfunctions, breakage or possible personal injury.

Care should be taken to re-use the fasteners in the same locations as removed, whenever possible.

Fluid Capacities

The fluid level should be checked at each engine oil change. Use only Dexron® II or equivalent transmission fluid. Under normal operating conditions, the fluid may be expected to last 100,000 miles. However, if the vehicle is used in what is considered severe service, then the automatic transaxle fluid and filter should be changed every 18,000-24,000 miles or a time interval of 18-24 months. Severe service would include heavy city traffic, high temperature areas (regularly over 90°F), mountainous areas or frequent trailer towing. Commercial service is also to be considered severe service, so more frequent service to the automatic transaxle will be required.

If any service work is performed on the transaxle, the following capacities should be followed.

a) pan removal—five quarts of fluid
b) overhaul—twelve quarts of fluid

The fluid level should be established by the dipstick rather than by using a specific number of quarts.

Checking Fluid Levels

1. Verify that the transaxle is at normal operating temperature. At this temperature, the end of the dipstick will be too hot to hold in the hand. Make sure that the vehicle is level.

2. With the selector in Park, allow the engine to idle. *Do not race engine.* Move the selector through each range and back to Park.

3. Immediately check the fluid level, engine still running. Fluid level on the dipstick should be at the "FULL HOT" mark.

4. If the fluid level is low, add fluid as required. One pint will bring the fluid level from "ADD" to "FULL."

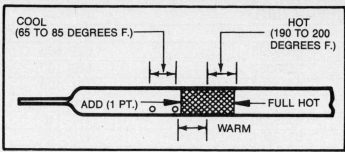

COOL
(65 TO 85 DEGREES F.)

HOT
(190 TO 200 DEGREES F.)

ADD (1 PT.) — FULL HOT

WARM

THM 325-4L automatic transaxle dipstick (© General Motors Corp.)

Often it is necessary to check the fluid level when there is no time or opportunity to run the vehicle to warm the fluid to operating temperature. In this case, the fluid should be around room temperature (70°). The following steps can be used:

1. Place the selector in Park and start engine. *Do not race engine.* Move the selector through each range and back to Park.

2. Immediately check the fluid level, engine still running, off fast idle. Fluid level should be between the two dimples on the dipstick, approximately ¼" *below* the "ADD" mark on the dipstick.

3. If the fluid level is low, add fluid as required, to bring the fluid level to between the two dimples on the dipstick. *Do not overfill.*

M MODIFICATIONS

Automatic Transaxle Fluid Leak in Final Drive Area

Some 1982 vehicles equipped with the THM 325-4L automatic transaxle may experience a transaxle oil leak in the final drive to transaxle case mating area and/or an erratic upshift caused by a loose or missing governor cup plug in the transaxle case passage.

Automatic transaxle with the fluid leak problem are, model AJ serial number 58856, model AL serial number 8327 and model AM serial number 5587. These identification numbers are located on the transaxle identification tag, which is mounted on the left side of the bell housing.

In order to correct an automatic transaxle with this problem the following procedure must be followed.

1. Remove the final drive assembly.

2. Remove the original governor cup plug.

3. Install a new governor cup plug, part number 8620318. Use Loctite 240® or equivalent to seal the cup plug to the transaxle case. Staking the plug cup into the transaxle case will not assure an adequate seal.

4. Install the final drive assembly. Be sure to use a new gasket.

Hydraulic Noise in Park and/or Neutral

Some vehicles equipped with the THM 325-4L automatic transaxle may experience a hydraulic buzzing sound in the park and/or neutral shift selector positions. This condition may be caused by an orifice cup plug missing from the pressure regulator valve.

In order to correct this condition, the following procedure must be performed.

1. Remove the automatic transaxle fluid pan. Discard the pan gasket. Remove the pressure regulator valve.

2. Inspect the valve for a missing orifice cup plug, which is located at the end of the valve.

3. If the cup plug is missing, inspect the pressure regulator valve bushing as well as the transaxle case for the original plug. If found, remove and discard.

4. Install the new pressure regulator valve, part number 8623422. Be sure that the new valve is equipped with an orifice cup plug.

5. Install the transaxle oil pan, using a new pan gasket. Fill the transaxle as required with the proper grade and type automatic transmission fluid.

No Drive or Slipping

Some 1983 vehicles may experience a no drive or slipping condition. This condition, while not noticed in reverse, could be caused by a loose or missing solid cup plug in the input shaft of the forward clutch assembly.

When servicing any 1983 THM 325-4L automatic transaxle for this condition, and the forward clutch assembly shows signs of burning, inspect the housing end of the input shaft which is part of the forward clutch assembly. If the solid cup plug is loose or missing, apply pressure to the forward clutch piston will be lost. This pressure loss will cause the no drive or slipping condition. If the solid cup plug is missing from the feed passage, it must be located before the transaxle is reassembled. It could possibly be in the open end of the output shaft. Tap the end of the output shaft on a table and remove the solid cup plug.

The solid cup plug, part number 8628145, is serviced separately. To install the cup plug, use a 5/16 inch punch. Apply loctite 290® or equivalent to the plug before installation. Drive the plug into the larger of the two holes until it is .039 inch below the surface.

New Style Selective Washer for Input to Output Shaft

Beginning at the end of March, 1983, a new style selective washer went into production. This new style selective washer is now available when servicing the input to output shaft assemblies.

This new style selective washer is made from a different material and can be identified by a raised portion on the identification tab.

When servicing an automatic transaxle that necessitates the replacement of this selective washer due to wear or damage, the following procedure must be followed.

1. Inspect the two shafts for wear or damage on the selective

SELECTIVE WASHER CHART

Identification Number	Color	Part Number	Thickness (inches)
1	----	8639291	.065-.070
2	----	8639292	.070-.075
3	Black	8639293	.076-.080
4	Light Green	8639294	.081-.085
5	Scarlet	8639295	.086-.090

SELECTIVE WASHER CHART

Identification Number	Color	Part Number	Thickness (inches)
6	Purple	8639296	.091-.095
7	Cocoa Brown	8639297	.096-.100
8	Orange	8639298	.101-.106
9	Yellow	8639299	.106-.111
10	Light Blue	8639300	.111-.116
11	Blue	8639301	.117-.121
12	----	8639302	.122-.126
13	Pink	8639303	.127-.131
14	Green	8639304	.132-.136
15	Gray	8639305	.137-.141

washer mating surfaces. If wear or damage is found, replace the components.

2. Use the proper selective washer from the selective washer chart.

3. Check the front end play to verify the proper selective washer selection. Front end play for the THM 325-4L automatic transaxle should be .022 to .051 inch.

Automatic Transaxle Bottom Oil Pan Leak

Some 1982 and 1983 vehicles equipped with the THM 325-4L automatic transaxle may exhibit a transaxle oil pan leak. This leak is caused by an interference between the 1-2 and 3-4 accumulator housing and the bottom oil pan.

Starting in April, 1983, all THM 325-4L automatic transaxles are being produced using a new design accumulator housing. This new design housing will correct the interference problem.

When servicing any THM 325-4L transaxle for a bottom oil leak problem, be sure to inspect for interference with the accumulator housing when the oil pan is removed. If evidence of interfer-

ence exists, remove the housing and grind off a portion of the casting boss. When performing this operation use caution to avoid damaging the cup plug.

4-2 Downshift Hitch (Model AJ)

Some vehicles equipped with transaxle model AJ, may experience a 4-2 downshift as a two shift feel with a slight hesitation and a bump in between. This condition is most noticeable during a full throttle detent downshift.

Starting in February, 1983, all automatic transaxles beginning with transaxle serial number 83-AJ-30723 are being built using a new control valve assembly. This new control valve assembly will correct the 2-4 downshift condition.

When servicing any 1983 model AJ transaxle for this condition use service package 8635949, which contains the proper components to correct the problem.

No Fourth Gear Engagement

Some 1982 and 1983 vehicles equipped with the THM 325-4L automatic transaxle may not engage into fourth gear (overdrive).

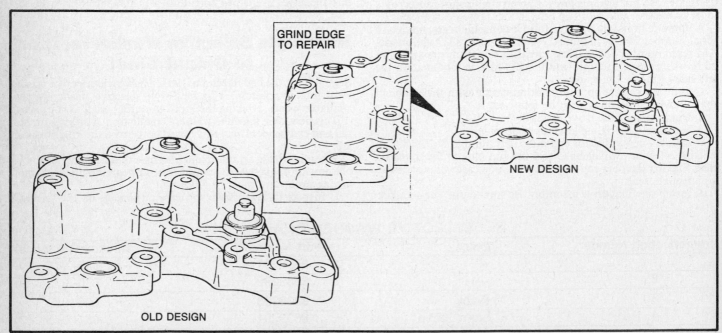

GRIND EDGE TO REPAIR

NEW DESIGN

OLD DESIGN

THM 325-4L accumulator housing (© General Motors Corp.)

If this condition exists, the following diagnostic procedure will aid in correction of the problem.

Test drive the vehicle applying light throttle in drive range (third gear) to about 30-35 mph. Move the selector lever into manual second "2" and release the throttle. The automatic transaxle should downshift and coastdown overrun braking should occur.

If coastdown overrun braking does not occur, remove the transaxle from the vehicle. Inspect the overrun clutch housing for a break in the hub weld. If the hub weld is broken, the cause may be due to misaligned pinions in the overdrive carrier.

In all instances where the weld is broken on the overrun clutch housing, both the overrun clutch housing, part number 8635941, and the overdrive carrier, part number 8635036, must be replaced.

Shift Busyness, Cruise Control Engaged

Some 1981 and 1982 vehicles equipped with the THM 325-4L automatic transaxle model AM and the 4.1 Liter engine, may experience a transaxle shift busyness at highway speeds with the cruise control engaged. Shift busyness refers to the cycling of the transaxle between fourth and third gears. This condition is noticeable while driving up inclines. In order to correct this problem, install service package 8635944 into the control valve assembly.

Delayed Engagement and/or Loss of Engine Power

Some 1982 and 1983 vehicles equipped with the THM 325-4L automatic transaxle may exhibit either delayed engagement when moving the selector lever from Park to Reverse or an apparent loss of engine power resulting from improper low and reverse clutch operation.

Delayed engagement (hot or cold) when moving the automatic

TROUBLE DIAGNOSIS

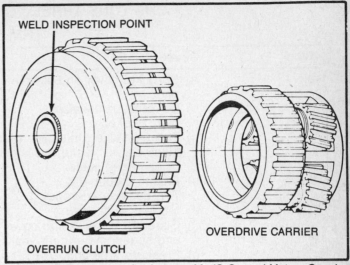

Weld location—overrun clutch assembly (© General Motors Corp.)

transaxle selector lever from Park to Reverse after a complete overhaul can be caused by an insufficient number of flat steel plates installed in the low and reverse clutch assembly. The low and reverse clutch assembly should have one waved steel plate, seven flat steel plates and six composition faced plates installed in it.

An apparent loss of engine power or automatic transaxle operation in two gears at one time on any THM 325-4L automatic transaxle can be caused by the incorrect application of the low and reverse clutch assembly. The incorrect apply of the low and reverse clutch can be caused by a missing locator pin securing the low first detent valve bushing in the control valve assembly. This missing pin will permit the bushing to rotate in its control valve bore and apply the low and reverse clutch through the use of "detent" fluid. Whenever the throttle angle is above sixty degrees of travel, "detent" fluid is available.

To correct this condition, reroute the valve body, orient the bushing correctly in its bore and install a locator pin, part number 8628400.

CLUTCH AND BAND APPLICATION CHART
THM 325-4L

Range/Gear		Low-Reverse Clutch	Low-Roller Clutch	Forward Clutch	Intermediate Band	Direct Clutch	Fourth Clutch	Overrun Clutch	Overdrive Roller Clutch
Park		—	—	—	—	—	—	—	—
Reverse		Applied	—	—	—	Applied	—	—	Holding
Neutral		—	—	—	—	—	—	—	Holding
Drive 4	First	—	Holding	Applied	—	—	—	—	—
	Second	—	—	Applied	Applied	—	—	—	Holding
	Third	—	—	Applied	—	Applied	—	—	Holding
	Fourth	—	—	Applied	—	Applied	Applied	—	—
Drive 3	First	—	Holding	Applied	—	—	—	Applied	—
	Second	—	—	Applied	Applied	—	—	Applied	—
	Third	—	—	Applied	—	Applied	—	Applied	—
Drive 2	First	—	Holding	Applied	—	—	—	Applied	—
	Second	—	—	Applied	Applied	—	—	Applied	—
Low	First	Applied	—	Applied	—	—	—	Applied	—

CHILTONS THREE "C's" DIAGNOSIS CHART
THM 325-4L

Condition	Cause	Correction
Oil leak	a) Sprocket cover and bottom oil pan	a) Retorque attaching bolts
	b) Cover to pan sealant bead broken	b) Reseal assemblies as required
	c) Throttle valve cable, filler pipe, electrical connector missing or damaged seals.	c) Replace missing or damaged seal, as required
	d) Engine mount and T.V. cable interference	d) Correct interference between T.V. cable and engine mount
	e) Manual shaft seal	e) Seal assembly damaged, replace as required
	f) Governor cover, servo cover and speedometer gear seal	f) Repair damaged O-ring seal
	g) Pressure taps and cooler fittings	g) Retorque fittings
	h) Transaxle case at final drive	h) Repair damaged gasket Retorque attaching bolts
	i) Torque converter	i) Weld seam leaking, repair or replace
	j) Pump seal damaged	j) Repair as required Retorque attaching bolts
	k) Governor oil cup plug not seated properly	k) Repair or replace as required
Oil out the vent	a) Oil level too high	a) Correct as required
	b) Drive sprocket support holes blocked	b) Clear blockage
	c) Water in transaxle fluid	c) Correct as required
High or low oil pressure	a) Oil level high or low	a) Correct as required
	b) T.V. cable broken or misadjusted	b) Repair cable or replace as required
	c) T.V. lever and bracket assembly roll pin binding	c) Correct as required
	d) Throttle valve plunger stuck or binding	d) Repair or replace as required
	e) Pressure regulator valve stuck, binding or misassembled	e) Repair or replace as required
	f) Reverse boost valve and bushing stuck or binding	f) Repair or replace as required
	g) M.T.V. valve and bushing stuck or binding	g) Repair or replace as required
	h) Pressure relief valve ball missing or spring distorted	h) Repair or replace as required
	i) T.V. limit valve or line bias valve stuck or mising	i) Repair or replace as required
	j) Oil filter plugged, pick up tube cracked, O-ring damaged	j) Replace filter, replace pick up tube replace damaged O-ring
	k) Oil pump gears damaged	k) Replace oil pump assembly
No drive in drive range	a) Low oil level	a) Correct oil level
	b) Low oil pressure	b) Correct as required
	c) Manual linkage misadjusted	c) Adjust
	d) Torque converter stator roller clutch broken	d) Replace components as required
	e) Overdrive roller clutch springs or rollers damaged	e) Repair or replace roller clutch assembly

CHILTONS THREE "C's" DIAGNOSIS CHART
THM 325-4L

Condition	Cause	Correction
No Drive in drive range	f) Overdrive carrier assembly pinions, sun gear or internal gear damage	f) Repair or replace components as required
	g) Damaged oil pump gears	g) Replace pump
	h) Broken drive link assembly sprockets or sprocket bearings	h) Replace components as required
	i) Forward clutch assembly damaged, or components within the unit defective	i) Repair or replace assembly or components as required
	j) Damaged low roller clutch springs or rollers	j) Repair or replace components as necessary
	k) Forward clutch input shaft broken	k) Replace components as required
No engine braking in manual ranges	a) Manual linkage misadjusted	a) Adjust linkage
	b) Spacer plate or gaskets misadjusted, damaged or plugged	b) Replace defective components as required
	c) 4-3 control valve-manual third only binding or stuck	c) Replace 4-3 control valve
	d) D2 signal pipe-manual second only leaking	d) Repair as required
	e) Number three check ball leaking or missing	e) Replace check ball
	f) Number nine check ball leaking or missing	f) Replace check ball as required
	g) Overrun clutch assembly damaged piston seals or clutch plates	g) Replace or repair damaged components
	h) Blocked turbine shaft oil passages	h) Remove blockage
No part throttle	a) T.V. valve or plunger stuck or binding	a) Repair or replace valve or plunger
	b) Spacer plate or gaskets mispositioned or blocked	b) Replace components as required or remove blockage
	c) T.V. cable misadjusted	c) Readjust cable
	d) T.V. downshift modulator valve	d) Correct as required
Won't hold in park	a) Manual linkage misadjusted	a) Adjust linkage
	b) Internal linkage damaged, mispositioned or mis-assembled	b) Correct as required
Shifts points high or low	a) T.V. cable misadjusted or damaged	a) correct as required
	b) T.V. limit valve stuck or binding	b) Correct as required
	c) Throttle valve or plunger stuck or binding	c) Repair or replace as required
	d) T.V. modulator upshift or downshift valves stuck or binding	d) Repair or replace valves as needed

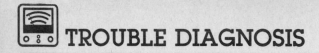

CHILTONS THREE "C's" DIAGNOSIS CHART
THM 325-4L

Condition	Cause	Correction
Shifts points high or low	e) Mispositioned or binding spacer plate or gaskets	e) Replace spacer plate or gasket
	f) T.V. lever and bracket assembly unhooked, mispositioned or mis-assembled	f) Correct as required
	g) Governor assembly or cover damaged or leaking	g) Repair or replace as required
First speed only, no 1-2 shift	a) Internal governor assembly damaged	a) Repair or replace unit, as required
	b) Control valve assembly 1-2 shift, low/first detent or 1-2 throttle valve stuck	b) Repair or replace defective components as necessary
	c) Intermediate band assembly burned or damaged.	c) Replace band assembly
	d) Intermediate band assembly band anchor plug missing	d) Install band anchor plug
	e) Intermediate servo assembly band apply pin too short, wrong piston cover combination or seal damage	e) Correct defective component as necessary
	f) 1-2, 3-4 accumulator housing spacer plate blocked or mis-positioned, gasket damage or housing porosity	f) Correct the problem as required
1-2 Shift—full throttle only	a) T.V. cable misadjusted, bent or disconnected	a) Readjust, connect or replace as required
	b) T.V. lever and bracket assembly roll pin wedged against the valve body casting	b) Correct as required
	c) Throttle valve or plunger stuck or binding	c) Free component as required
	d) Spacer plate or gaskets blocked or mispositioned	d) Free blockage or reposition components
First and second speeds only—no 2-3 shift	a) Control valve assembly 2-3 shift valve or throttle valve stuck or binding	a) Correct components as necessary
	b) Spacer plate and gaskets blocked or mispositioned	b) Free blockage or reposition spacer plate and gaskets
	c) Transaxle case interconnected passages or porosity	c) Replace transaxle case
	d) Transaxle case cover number 7 pellet and spring not seating	d) Replace number 7 pellet and spring
	e) Transaxle case cover third/reverse cup plug leaking	e) Replace third/reverse cup plug
	f) Transaxle case cover gasket damaged	f) Replace case cover gasket
	g) Transaxle case cover porosity or interconnected passages	g) replace transaxle case cover
	h) Driven sprocket support oil seal rings leaking or sprocket support gasket damaged	h) Replace oil seal rings or sprocket support gasket
	i) Number 6 check ball missing or leaking	i) Replace number 6 check ball

CHILTONS THREE "C's" DIAGNOSIS CHART
THM 325-4L

Condition	Cause	Correction
First and second speeds only—no 2-3 shift	j) Direct clutch assembly piston seals or ball capsule damaged k) Internal governor assembly malfunction	j) Replace components or assembly as required k) Repair or replace governor assembly as required
No reverse or slips in reverse	a) Manual linkage misadjusted b) Low and reverse clutch piston, seals or cup plug seal assembly damaged c) Direct clutch misassembled, piston or seals or ball capsule damaged d) Reverse boost valve binding or stuck e) Reverse oil pipe leaking f) Number 6 check ball missing or leaking g) Number 10 check ball missing or leaking h) Spacer plate mispositioned or damaged i) Transaxle case cover, case or valve body reverse passage leak	a) Adjust linkage b) Replace piston, seals or cup plug seal assembly as required c) replace defective component d) Repair or replace reverse boost valve e) Replace reverse oil pipe f) Replace number 6 check ball g) Replace number 10 check ball h) Replace spacer plate i) Replace defective component as necessary
Drive in neutral range	a) Manual linkage misadjusted b) Transaxle case or case cover leak into D4 oil passage c) Forward clutch plates fused or ball capsule won't release	a) Adjust linkage b) Replace defective component as required c) Replace forward clutch plates or free ball capsule
Slipping 1-2 shift	a) Low fluid level b) Mispositioned or blocked spacer plate/gaskets c) Accumulator housing bolts loose or housing porosity d) 1-2 accumulator piston or seal damaged, stuck or binding e) Intermediate band damaged or burnt lining f) Intermediate servo assembly porosity, damaged piston or seal or wrong apply pin g) Pressure regulator valve sticking or binding h) Line bias valve, throttle valve or plunger binding or stuck i) T.V. cable misadjusted j) Transaxle case or case cover leak in second oil passage	a) Correct as required b) Correct as required c) Tighten bolts or replace housing d) Correct as required e) Replace intermediate band or lining f) Repair or replace defective component as required g) Repair or replace pressure regulator valve h) Correct the required component as necessary i) Adjust cable j) Replace component as required
Rough 1-2 shift	a) T.V. cable misadjusted b) Throttle valve or plunger binding or stuck	a) Adjust cable b) Correct as required

CHILTONS THREE "C's" DIAGNOSIS CHART
THM 325-4L

Condition	Cause	Correction
Rough 1-2 shift	c) T.V. limit valve, line bias valve or accumulator stuck or binding	c) Repair or replace components as required
	d) Intermediate servo assembly piston bleed orifice missing or wrong apply pin	d) Correct as required
	e) 1-2 accumulator piston or seal damaged, binding or stuck	e) Repair or replace defective components as required
	f) Number 8 check ball missing or blocked	f) Free blockage or install number 8 check ball
	g) Servo bleed orifice missing or blocked	g) Repair as required
Slipping 2-3 shift	a) Low fluid level	a) Correct as required
	b) T.V. cable misadjusted	b) Adjust cable
	c) Mispositioned or blocked spacer plate/gaskets	c) Free blockage or replace spacer plate/gaskets
	d) Leaking number 7 pellet and spring	d) Replace number 7 pellet and spring
	e) Servo piston seal rings damaged	e) Replace servo piston or seal rings
	f) Servo bleed orifice missing or damaged	f) Correct as required
	g) Driven sprocket support case, case cover leak in the third clutch passage	g) Correct the defective component as required
	h) Direct clutch damaged ball capsule, piston or housing	h) Repair or replace defective component
	i) Direct clutch piston or seal damaged	i) Repair or replace component as necessary
Rough 2-3 shift	a) T.V. cable misadjusted	a) Adjust cable
	b) Throttle valve or plunger binding or stuck	b) Correct defective parts as necessary
	c) T.V. limit or bias valve stuck or binding	c) Correct defective component as required
	d) M.T.V up valve stuck or binding	d) Correct defective component as required
No 3-4 shift	a) Shift valve or 3-4 throttle valve stuck or binding	a) Repair or replace defective parts as necessary
	b) Fourth clutch assembly piston or seal damaged	b) Replace piston or seals
	c) Fourth clutch assembly fourth feed O-ring seal missing or damaged	c) Replace O-ring seal
	d) Accumulator housing leak in the 3-4 accumulator circuit	d) Repair or replace as required
	e) Mispositioned or blocked spacer plate/gaskets	e) Free blockage or replace spacer plate/ gaskets
Slipping 3-4 shift	a) Accumulator housing piston or seal damaged	a) Replace or repair piston or seal
	b) Accumulator valve binding or stuck	b) Replace component as required

CHILTONS THREE "C's" DIAGNOSIS CHART
THM 325-4L

Condition	Cause	Correction
Slipping 3-4 shift	c) Fourth clutch internal leak, damaged piston seal, housing bolts loose or feed O-ring damaged	c) Correct and replace components as necessary
Rough 3-4 shift	a) T.V. cable misadjusted b) Throttle valve or plunger binding or stuck c) 3-4 accumulator piston and seal damaged, stuck or spring weak or missing	a) Adjust cable b) Correct as necessary c) Repair or replace defective component

Hydraulic Control System

The major components incorporated within the hydraulic control system are: Oil pump assembly, Pressure regulator assembly, Throttle valve, T.V. limit valve, T.V. exhaust check ball, Line bias valve and governor assembly.

OIL PUMP ASSEMBLY

The hydraulic pressure system requires a supply of transmission fluid and a pump to pressurize the fluid. This Transaxle uses an internal-external gear type pump with its oil intake connected to a screen assembly. The screen intake draws oil from the transaxle bottom pan or sump. The pump drive gear is keyed to the converter pump hub and therefore turns whenever the engine is operating. As the drive gear turns, it also turns the driven gear, causing oil to be lifted from the sump. As the gears turn, the oil is carried past the crescent section of the pump. Beyond the crescent, the gear teeth begin to come together causing the oil to be pressurized as it is squeezed from between the gear teeth. At this point, the oil is delivered through the pump outlet to the pressure regulator.

PRESSURE REGULATOR

Oil pressure is controlled by the pressure regulator valve. Oil is directed to the line passage and through an orifice to the top of the pressure regulator valve. When the desired line pressure is reached, the line pressure at the top of the valve moves the valve against the pressure regulator spring, thus opening a passage to feed the torque converter.

THROTTLE VALVE

Throttle valve pressure is related to carburetor opening which is related to engine torque. The system is a mechanical type with a fixed, direct relation between the carburetor throttle plate opening and the transaxle throttle plunger movement. As the accelerator pedal is depressed and the carburetor opened, the mechanical linkage (T.V. cable) relays the movement to the throttle plunger and increases the force of the T.V. spring against the throttle valve, increasing T.V. pressure which can regulate from 0 to 90 psi. T.V. oil is directed through the T.V. plunger to provide a hydraulic assist reducing the pedal effort necessary to actuate the plunger.

THROTTLE VALVE LIMIT VALVE

The pressure requirements of the transaxle for apply of the band and clutches vary with engine torque and throttle opening. Under heavy throttle operation, the 60 psi line pressure is not sufficient to hold the band and clutches on without slipping. To provide higher line pressure with greater throttle opening, a variable oil pressure related to throttle opening is desired. The throttle valve regulates line pressure in relation to carburetor opening. The T.V. limit valve limits this variable pressure to avoid excessive line pressure. The T.V. limit valve feeds the throttle valve and receives oil directly from the oil pump. As the pressure in the line leading from the T.V. limit valve and feeding the T.V. valve exceeds 90 psi, the pressure will push against the T.V. limit valve spring, bleeding off excess pressure. This limits T.V. feed pressure to a maximum of approximately 90 psi.

THROTTLE VALVE EXHAUST CHECK BALL

The throttle valve exhaust check ball feature has been included in the T.V. system. This feature will prevent the transaxle from becoming burned or damaged due to low line pressure in the event the T.V. cable becomes disconnected or broken. This check ball is located in the transaxle case pad at the T.V. regulating exhaust port. This check ball (5) is held off its seat by the T.V. exhaust lifter rod, when the T.V. cable is properly connected. This allows T.V. pressure to regulate normally. If the cable becomes disconnected, or is not properly adjusted, the T.V. exhaust lifter rod will drop down and allow the ball to close the exhaust port. This will block the T.V. exhaust port and keep T.V. pressure at 90 psi and line pressure at approximately 140 psi to prevent operating the transaxle with 60 psi line pressure at increased throttle openings.

LINE BIAS VALVE

The capacity of a band or clutch to resist slipping is directly related to the pressure supplied to its apply piston. In order to prevent the band or clutches from slipping when an increase in engine torque is applied, oil pressure supplied to the apply piston must be increased. However, excessive pressure will cause a harsh shift. It is then desirable to vary the pressure supplied to each apply piston at the same rate at which engine torque is varied.

The line bias valve is fed by throttle valve fluid and performs the function of regulating throttle valve pressure as engine torque varies. This oil pressure, called modulated throttle valve oil (M.T.V.), is fed to the T.V. boost valve in the bottom of the pres-

559

sure regulator valve, to increase line pressure as throttle opening or engine torque increases.

In summary, the T.V. plunger controls T.V. pressure which becomes M.T.V. pressure at the line bias valve, and the line bias valve regulates line pressure at the pressure regulator valve. It is this line pressure the manual valve routes to the shift valves and to the band and clutches. Line pressure is varied in relation to engine torque in such a manner as to apply the band or clutch with just enough pressure to hold against engine torque plus a safety factor, but not so much pressure that the shifts are harsh.

GOVERNOR ASSEMBLY

The vehicle speed signal for the shift is supplied by the transaxle governor which is driven by the output shaft. The governor assembly consists of a governor shaft, a driven gear, two check balls, a primary weight, a secondary weight, primary and secondary spring, one governor weight pin and an oil seal ring. The check balls seat in two pockets directly opposite each other in the governor shaft. The weights are so arranged that the primary weight, assisted by the primary spring, acts on one check ball and the secondary weight, assisted by the secondary spring, act on the other ball. As the governor turns, the weights are moved outward by the centrifugal force. This force is relayed to the check balls, seating them; and as the speed of the governor increases, so does the force acting on the check balls, which tends to keep them closed.

THROTTLE VALVE SYSTEM

The T H M 325-4L transaxle makes use of a throttle valve cable system, rather than the vacuum modulator system. This cable system controls line pressure, shift points, shift feel, part throttle downshifts, and detent downshifts. Do not think of the T.V. cable in the same way as a conventional detent cable. The function of the T.V. cable system more closely resembles the combined functions of both a detent cable and a vacuum modulator system. Since so many functions of the transaxle are dependent on the T.V. system, it can be seen that proper adjustment is critical to the satisfactory performance of the unit. Many transaxle problems or malfunctions could be solved by careful attention to, and adjustment of, the T.V. system.

The throttle valve cable operates the throttle lever and bracket assembly. This lever and bracket assembly serves two basic functions:

1. The first duty of this assembly is to transfer the movement of the carburetor throttle plate to the T.V. plunger in the control valve assembly. Thus, the T.V. pressure and line pressure can increase according to the throttle opening. It also controls part throttle and detent downshifts. The proper adjustment of the T.V. cable is, then, very important and is based on the T.V. plunger being fully depressed to flush with the T.V. bushing at wide open throttle.

2. The second function of the assembly involves the T.V. exhaust valve lifter rod, spring and T.V. exhaust ball. The function of this system is to prevent the transmission from operating at low (idle position) pressures, should the cable break or become disconnected. As long as the cable is properly connected, not broken or stretched, the T.V. lifter rod will not move from its normal, spring loaded "UP" position which holds the T.V. exhaust check ball off its seat. The T.V. lifter rod will drop down to allow the exhaust ball to seat only if the cable breaks or becomes disconnected or out of adjustment. With the transaxle pan removed, it should be possible to pull down on the T.V. exhaust valve lifter rod and the spring should return the rod to its normal "UP" position. If the throttle lever and the bracket assembly and/or the lifter rod binds or sticks so that the T.V. lifter rod cannot lift the exhaust ball off its seat, high line pressures and delayed upshifts will be the result. The shape of the throttle valve lifter rod is critical, especially the 90° bend.

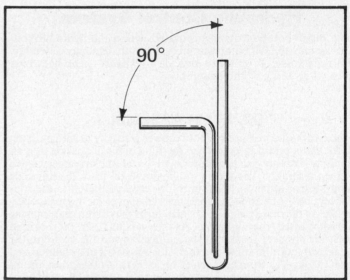

Throttle valve lifter rod (© General Motors Corp.)

If the T.V. cable is broken, sticky, mis-adjusted or if an incorrect part for the model is fitted, the vehicle may exhibit various malfunctions which could be attributed to internal component failure. Sticking or binding T.V. linkage can result in delayed or full throttle shifts. The T.V. cable must be free to travel to the full throttle position and return to the closed throttle position without binding or sticking.

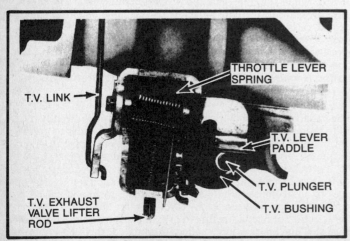

Throttle valve lever (© General Motors Corp.)

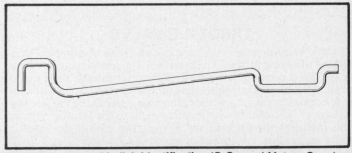

Throttle lever to cable link identification (© General Motors Corp.)

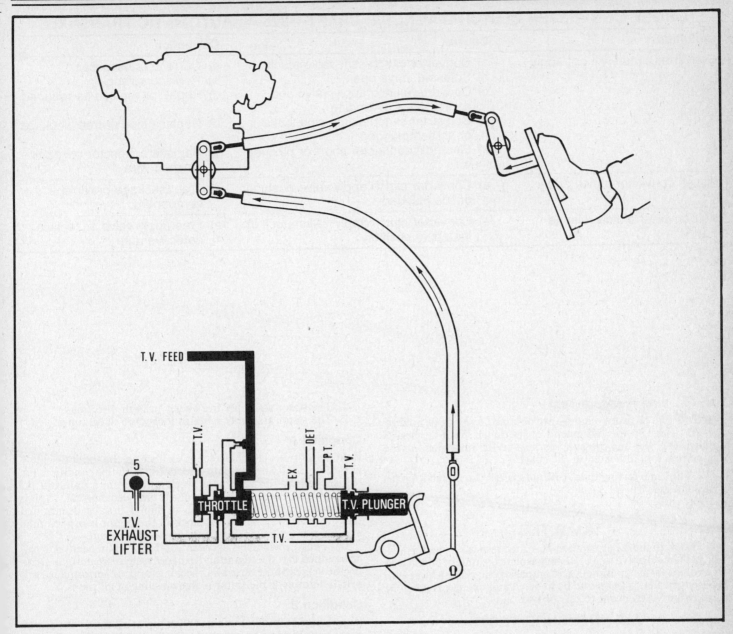

Accelerator, carburetor and T.V. linkage. (General Motors Co.)

Labels in figure: T.V. FEED, T.V., EX, DET, P.T., T.V., 5, THROTTLE, T.V. PLUNGER, T.V. EXHAUST LIFTER, T.V.

Diagnosis Tests

Automatic transaxle malfunctions may be caused by four general conditions: poor engine performance, improper adjustments, hydraulic malfunctions, or mechanical malfunctions.

The suggested sequence for diagnosis is as follows:

1. Check and correct oil level.
2. Check and adjust T.V. cable.
3. Check and correct manual linkage.
4. Check engine tune.
5. Install oil pressure gauge and tachometer and check control pressure.
6. Road test in all ranges, noting change in operation and oil pressure.
7. Attempt to isolate the unit involved in the malfunction.

CONTROL PRESSURE TEST

1. Check transaxle oil level and correct as required. Check and adjust T.V. cable. Check and correct outside manual linkage. Check engine tune.
2. Install an oil pressure gauge to line pressure and fourth clutch pressure taps.
3. Connect the tachometer to the engine.
4. Perform the control pressure test in the following manner.

Minimum T.V. Line Pressure Test

Adjust the T.V. cable to specifications. With the brakes applied, take the line pressure readings in the ranges and at the engine rpm's indicated in the chart.

TORQUE CONVERTER CLUTCH DIAGNOSIS CHART—325-4L AUTOMATIC TRANSAXLE

Condition	Cause	Correction
Converter clutch will not apply	a) Converter clutch shift valve stuck b) Solenoid stays open c) Converter clutch apply valve and spring stuck or binding d) Converter clutch signal pipe leaks or screen plugged e) Electrical connector short or pinched wire	a) Correct as necessary b) Replace solenoid c) Repair or replace as required d) Replace pipe or free blockage e) Replace connector or repair pinched wire
Rough converter clutch apply	a) Converter clutch apply valve bushing orifice plugged	a) Free blockage or replace component
No converter clutch release	a) Converter clutch apply valve stuck in the apply position	a) Free apply valve or replace defective unit

Full T.V. Line Pressure Test

Full T.V. line pressure readings are obtained by tying or holding the T.V. cable to the full extend of its travel. With the brakes applied, take the line pressure readings in the ranges and at the engine rpm's as indicated in the chart.

NOTE: Total testing time must not exceed two minutes for the combinations.

ROAD TEST

In addition to the oil pressure tests, a road test can be performed, using all the selective ranges, to help isolate the unit or circuit that is involved in the malfunction. Comparing the malfunction with the element that is known to be in use, the problem can often be quickly narrowed down to one or two units.

AIR PRESSURE TESTS

The positioning of the transaxle in the vehicle and the valve body location will cause the air pressure tests to be very difficult. It is advisable to make any air pressure tests during the disassembly and assembly of the transaxle to ascertain if a unit is operating.

STALL SPEED TEST

General Motors Corporation does not recommend performing a stall test because of the excessive heat that is generated within the transaxle by the converter during the tests.

Recommendations are to perform the control pressure test and road test to determine and localize any transaxle malfunctions.

CONVERTER STATOR OPERATION DIAGNOSIS

The torque converter stator assembly and its related roller clutch can possibly have one of two different type malfunctions.

1. The stator assembly freewheels in both directions.
2. The stator assembly remains locked up at all times.

Condition A

If the stator roller clutch becomes ineffective, the stator assembly freewheels at all times in both directions. With this condition, the vehicle will tend to have poor acceleration from a standstill. At speeds above 30-35 mph, the vehicle may act normal. If poor acceleration problems are noted, it should first be determined that the exhaust system is not blocked, the engine is in good tune and the transaxle is in First gear when starting out.

If the engine will freely accelerate to high rpm in Neutral, it can be assumed that the engine and exhaust system are normal. Driving the vehicle in Reverse and checking for poor performance will help determine if the stator is freewheeling at all times.

Condition B

If the stator assembly remains locked up at all times, the engine rpm and vehicle speed will tend to be limited or restricted at high speeds. The vehicle performance when accelerating from a standstill will be normal. Engine over-heating may be noted. Visual examination of the converter may reveal a blue color from the over-heating that will result.

Torque Converter Clutch Operation and Diagnosis

TORQUE CONVERTER CLUTCH

The GM Torque Converter Clutch (TCC) incorporates a unit inside the torque converter with a friction material attached to a pressure plate and splined to the turbine assembly. When the clutch is applied, it presses against the converter cover. The result is a mechanical direct drive of the engine to the transaxle. This eliminates slippage and improves fuel economy as well as reducing fluid temperature.

There are a number of controls to operate the torque converter clutch, all determined by drive range selection. When the vehicle slows, or the transaxle shifts out of direct drive, the fluid pressure

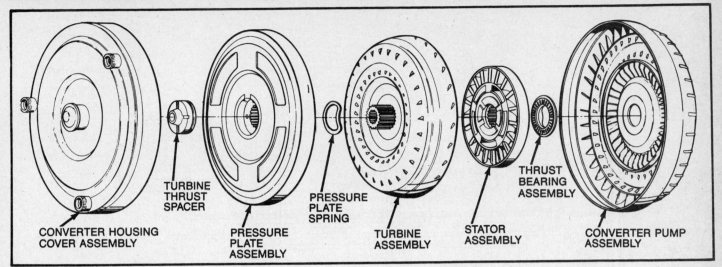

Torque converter clutch assembly (© General Motors Corp.)

Labels:
CONVERTER HOUSING COVER ASSEMBLY — TURBINE THRUST SPACER — PRESSURE PLATE ASSEMBLY — PRESSURE PLATE SPRING — TURBINE ASSEMBLY — STATOR ASSEMBLY — THRUST BEARING ASSEMBLY — CONVERTER PUMP ASSEMBLY

is released, the converter clutch releases and the converter operates in the conventional manner.

The engaging of the converter clutch as well as the release is determined by the direction of the converter feed oil. The converter feed oil from the pressure regulator valve flows to the converter clutch apply valve. The position of the converter clutch apply valve controls the direction in which the converter feed oil flows to the converter.

A spring-loaded damper assembly is splined to the converter turbine assembly while the clutch pressure plate is attached to a pivoting unit on the damper assembly. The result is that the pressure plate is allowed to rotate independently of the damper as-

sembly up to about 45 degrees. This rotation is controlled by springs in the damper assembly. The spring cushioning aids in reducing the effects felt when the converter clutch applies.

To help insure that the converter clutch applies and releases at the proper times, controls have been incorporated into the electrical system. The converter clutch is applied when all of the conditions listed below exist:

1. The brake pedal is released.
2. The engine vacuum is above 2.5 inches of vacuum.
3. The engine coolant is above 130°F.
4. The vehicle speed is above 24 to 30 mph.
5. The transaxle is in High gear.

TRANSAXLE LINE PRESSURE CHART
THM 325-4L

Model	Range-Zero Throttle (1000 RPM's)			Range-Full Throttle		
	N, D4, D3	D2, D1	Reverse	N, D4, D3	D2, D1	Reverse
AJ	64-77	126-153	91-109	129-155	126-153	184-220
AL, OK	64-77	126-153	91-109	129-155	126-153	184-220
AM, BE	64-77	148-179	126-152	113-135	148-179	224-268
OE	55-65	128-152	109-129	121-130	128-152	239-284
BJ	55-65	128-152	109-129	108-129	128-152	229-254

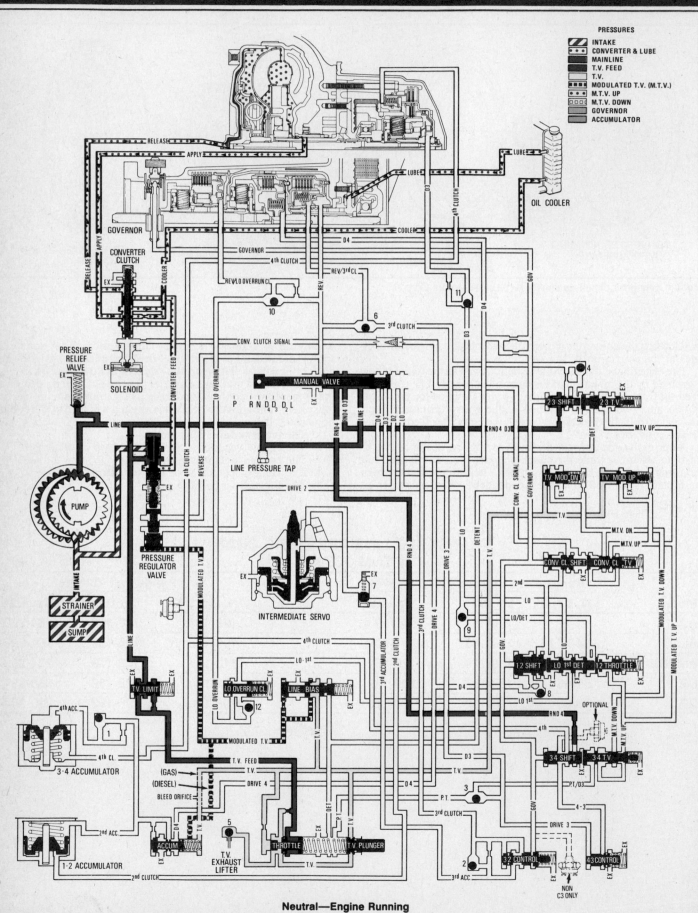

Neutral—Engine Running

NEUTRAL-ENGINE RUNNING

Converter Clutch—Released
Overrun Clutch—Released
Intermediate Band—Released
Overdrive Roller Clutch—Holding
Direct Clutch—Released
Low Roller Clutch-Not Holding
Fourth Clutch—Released
Forward Clutch—Released
Low and Reverse Clutch—Released

When the selector lever is moved to the Neutral position, the manual valve is positioned to allow line pressure to enter two passages as follows:

FIRST:

Line pressure enters the Reverse, Neutral, Drive 4 (RND4) passage and is directed to a land on the 3-4 shift valve.

SECOND:

Line pressure enters the Reverse, Neutral, Drive 4, Drive 3 (RND4D3) passage and is directed to a land on the 2-3 shift valve.

SUMMARY

The converter is filled; all the clutches, except the overdrive roller clutch, and the band are released; the transaxle is in Neutral.

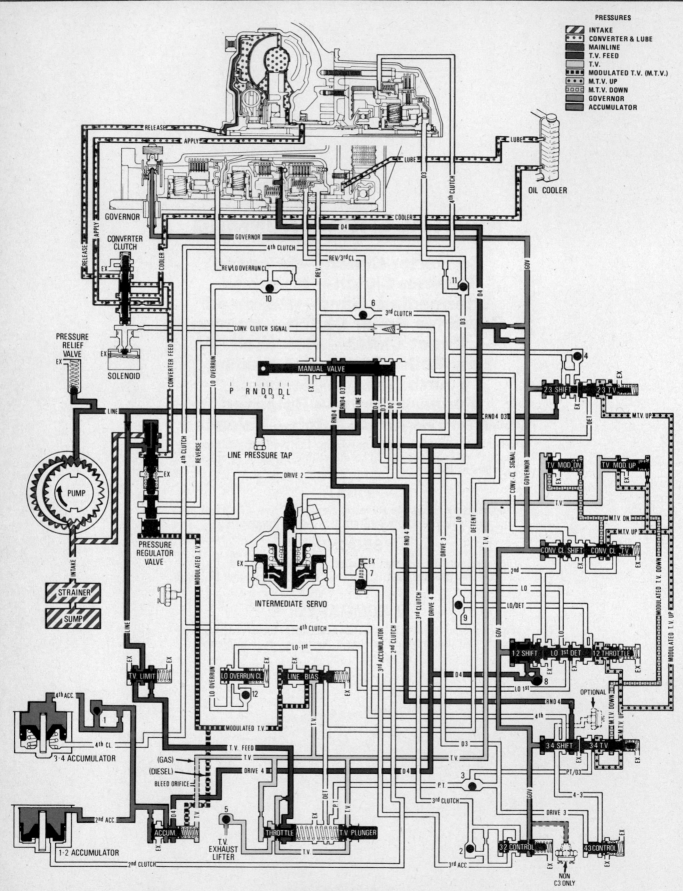

Drive Range—First Gear

DRIVE RANGE-FIRST GEAR

Overdrive Roller Clutch—Holding
Forward Clutch—Applied
Low Roller Clutch—Holding

When the selector lever is moved to the Drive position, the manual valve is positioned to allow line pressure to enter the Drive 4 passage. Drive 4 oil then flows to the 1-2 shift check ball, forward clutch, governor assembly, 1-2 shift valve and the accumulator valve.

Drive 4 oil is directed to the forward clutch were it acts on the clutch piston to apply the forward clutch.

Drive 4 oil is also directed to the 1-2 shift valve where it seats the check ball and is directed through an orifice before acting on the 1-2 shift valve. Drive 4 oil is directed to the accumulator valve and is regulated to a pressure called accumulator pressure; this pressure is directed to the 1-2 and 3-4 accumulator pistons to act as a cushion for the band and fourth clutch apply.

Drive 4 oil is orificed into the governor passage, and is regulated to a variable pressure called governor pressure. Governor pressure increases with vehicle speed and acts against the 1-2, 2-3, 3-4, converter clutch shift valves, and the 3-2 control valve.

In first gear, there could be sufficient throttle valve plunger travel to increase T.V. pressure enough to open the M.T.V. up and the M.T.V. down valves. In first gear, M.T.V. up exerts pressure against governor pressure at the 1-2, 2-3, 3-4, and converter clutch throttle valves. M.T.V. down pressure is stopped by a land at each of the throttle valves.

SUMMARY

The converter clutch is released, the overdrive roller clutch is holding, the forward clutch is applied; the transaxle is in Drive range—First gear.

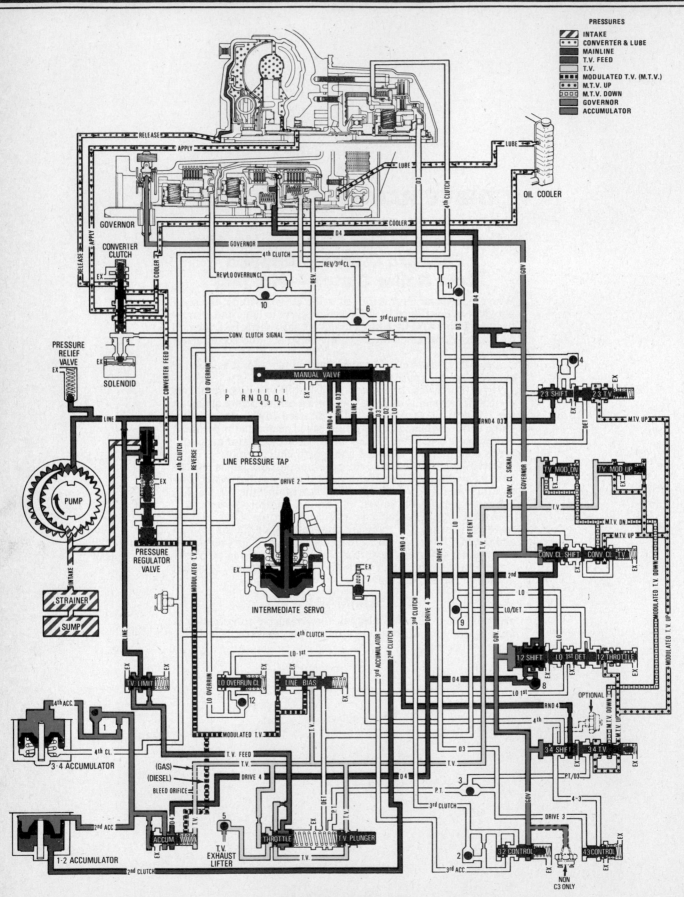

Drive Range—Second Gear

DRIVE RANGE—SECOND GEAR

Converter Clutch—Released
Forward Clutch—Applied
Overdrive Roller Clutch—Holding
Intermediate Band—Applied

As both vehicle speed and governor pressure increase, the force of the governor oil acting on the 1-2 shift valve overcomes the pressure of M.T.V. up oil and the force of the 1-2 throttle valve spring. This allows the 1-2 shift valve to open and Drive 4 oil to enter the second (2nd) oil passage. This oil is called second (2nd) oil. Second oil from the 1-2 shift valve is directed to the intermediate servo, 1-2 accumulator piston and the converter clutch shift valve. Second oil from the 1-2 shift valve is directed to the intermediate servo to apply the intermediate band. At the same time, 2nd oil moves the 1-2 accumulator piston against accumulator pressure and the accumulator spring to maintain a controlled build-up of pressure on the intermediate servo during the 1-2 shift for a smooth band apply.

SUMMARY

The converter clutch is released, the overdrive roller clutch is holding, the forward clutch is applied, and the intermediate band is applied; the transaxle is in Drive range—Second rear.

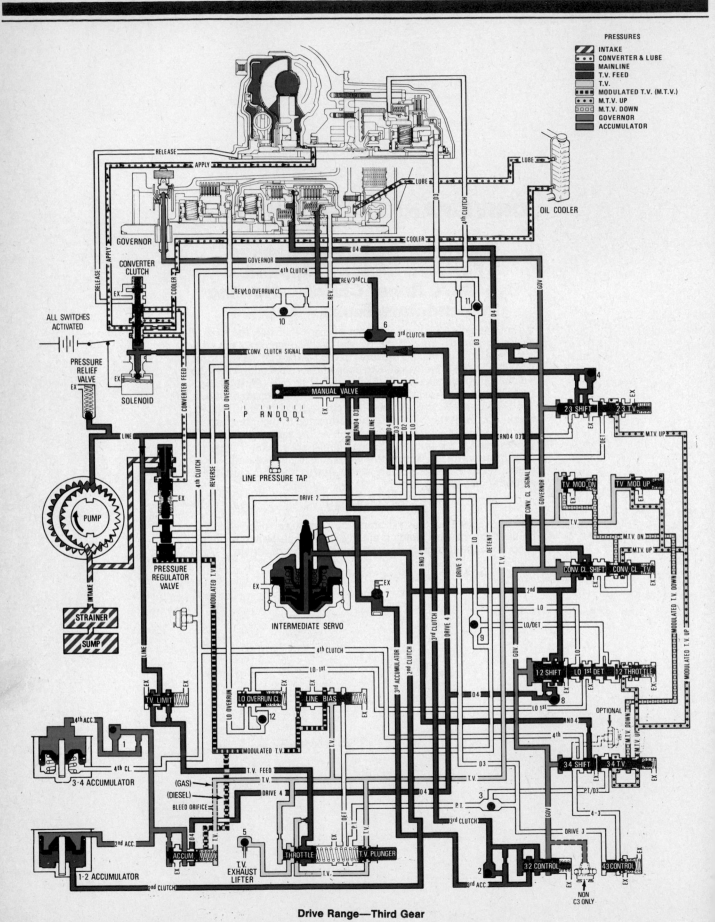

Drive Range—Third Gear

DRIVE RANGE—THIRD GEAR

Converter Clutch

The converter clutch may or may not be applied, depending on shift calibration and solenoid operation.

Direct Clutch—Applied
Overdrive Roller Clutch—Holding
Forward Clutch—Applied

As both vehicle speed and governor pressure increase, the force of governor oil acting on the 2-3 shift valve overcomes the force of the 2-3 T.V. spring and M.T.V. up oil. This allows the 2-3 shift valve to open allows RND4D3 oil to enter the 3rd clutch passage. Third Clutch oil form the 2-3 shift valve is directed to the 3-2 exhaust check ball (4), third clutch and reverse check ball (6), inner area of the direct clutch piston, third clutch accumulator check ball (2), third accumulator pellet and spring, intermediate servo and the 3-2 control valve.

Third clutch oil form the 2-3 shift valve flows past the 3-2 exhaust check ball (4), to the 3rd/reverse check ball (6), scating it in the reverse passage. Third clutch oil then flows to the inner area of the direct clutch piston, applying the direct clutch. At the same time, third clutch oil is directed past the 3rd clutch accumulator and check ball (2), seats the 3rd accumulator exhaust pellet and spring (7), and then into the release side of the intermediate servo. This 3rd clutch accumulator pressure, combined with the servo cushion spring, moves the servo piston against second oil and acts as an accumulator for a smooth intermediate band release and direct clutch apply.

Third clutch oil flows through 3-2 control valve to the 3rd clutch accumulator passage.

SUMMARY

The converter clutch is applied[1], the overdrive roller clutch is holding, the forward clutch is applied, the direct clutch is applied, and the intermediate band is released; the transaxle is in Drive range—Third gear (direct drive).

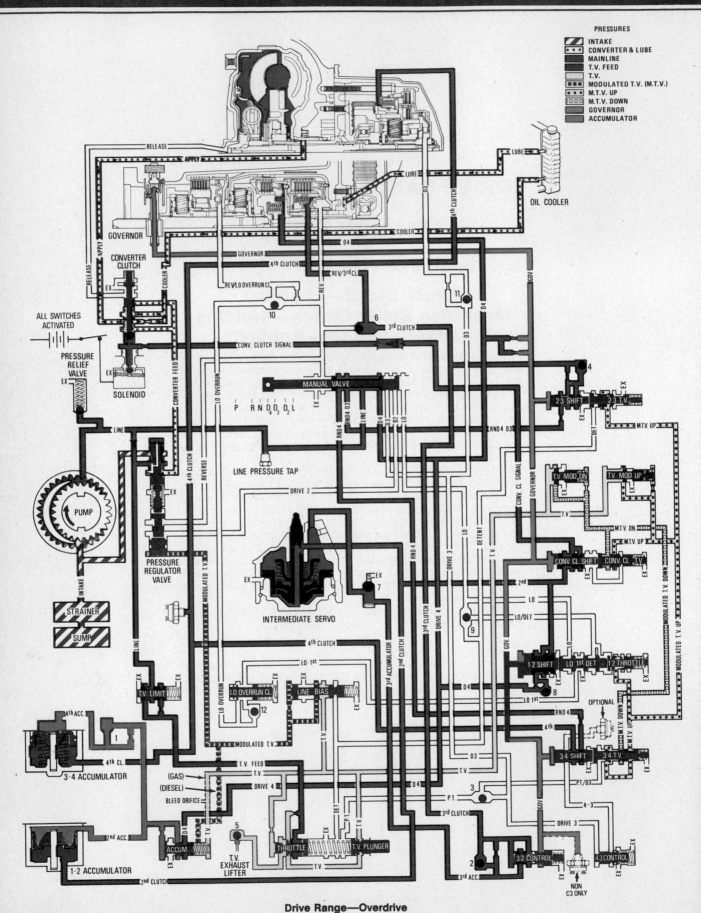

Drive Range—Overdrive

DRIVE RANGE—OVERDRIVE

Converter Clutch

The converter clutch may or may not be applied depending on solenoid operation.

Direct Clutch—Applied
Fourth Clutch—Applied
Forward Clutch—Applied

As both vehicle speed and governor pressure increase, the force of governor oil acting on the 3-4 shift valve overcomes the force of the 3-4 T.V. spring and M.T.V. up oil. This allows the 3-4 shift valve to open and RND4 oil enters the 4th clutch passage. Fourth clutch oil from the 3-4 shift valve is directed to the fourth clutch apply piston and the 3-4 accumulator piston.

Fourth oil from the 3-4 shift valve is directed to the 4th clutch piston to apply the 4th clutch. At the same time, fourth clutch oil moves the 3-4 accumulator piston against accumulator pressure and the accumulator spring to maintain a controlled build-up of pressure on the 4th clutch during the 3-4 shift, for a smooth 3-4 shift.

SUMMARY

The converter clutch, 4th clutch, direct clutch, and forward clutch are applied; the transaxle is in Drive range—overdrive.

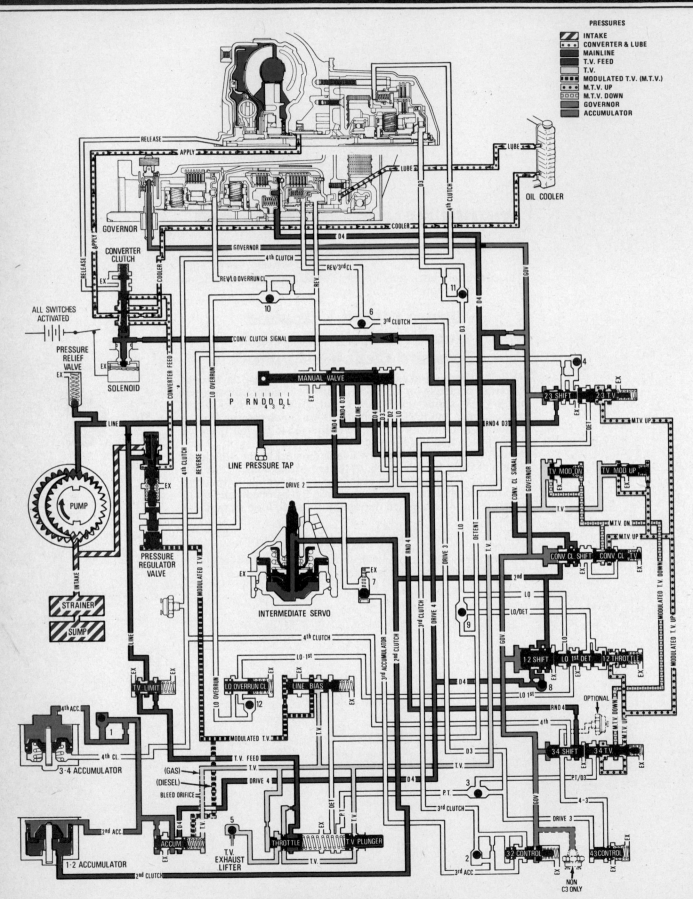

Drive Range—Converter Clutch Applied

DRIVE RANGE—CONVERTER CLUTCH APPLIED

Converter Clutch—Applied
Forward Clutch—Applied
Overdrive Roller Clutch—Holding
Intermediate Band—Applied

As vehicle speed and governor pressure increase, the force of governor oil acting on the converter clutch shift valve overcomes the pressure of M.T.V. up oil and the force of the converter clutch T.V. spring. This allows the converter clutch shift valve to open and second oil to enter the converter clutch signal passage. Providing the converter clutch solenoid is on, converter clutch signal oil will shift the converter clutch apply valve, and redirect converter feed oil into the apply passage. The apply oil flows between the stator shaft and converter hub to charge the converter with oil and push the converter pressure plate against the converter cover, causing a mechanical link between the engine and the turbine shaft. The rate of apply is controlled by an orifice check ball capsule in the end of the turbine shaft.

At the same time the converter clutch apply valve will direct converter feed oil through an orifice to the transaxle cooler. Cooler oil is directed to the lubrication system.

SUMMARY

The converter clutch is applied, the overdrive roller clutch is holding, the forward clutch is applied, and the intermediate band is applied; the transmission is in Drive range—Second gear. The converter clutch is shown applied in Second gear. In some models, the converter clutch shift valve will not shift until the transaxle is in Third gear.

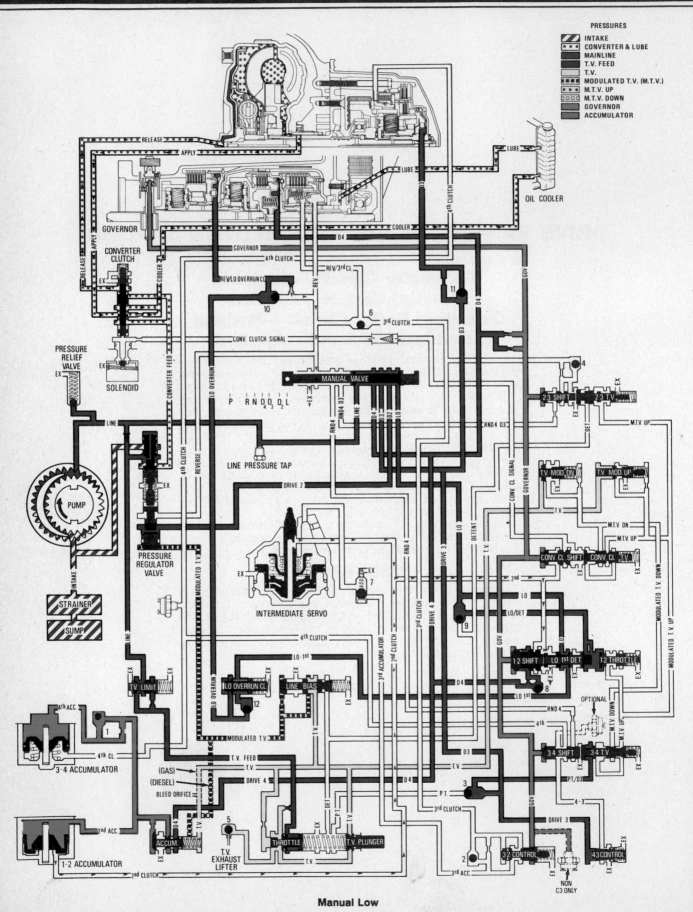

Manual Low

MANUAL LOW

Converter Clutch—Released
Forward Clutch—Applied
Overrun Clutch—Applied
Low and Reverse Clutch—Applied

Maximum downhill braking can be obtained at speeds below 30 mph, with the selector in Low range. Low oil pressure which is 140 psi is the same as second (2nd) oil pressure because second (D2) oil is still present.

Low oil from the manual valve is directed to the low and detent check ball, 1-2 shift valve train, low and reverse check ball (10), and the low and reverse overrun clutch.

Low oil at the low 1st/detent valve combined with M.T.V. down and 1-2 throttle valve spring force will close the 1-2 shift valve at speeds below approximately 30 mph. This allows second oil to exhaust, releasing the intermediate band, and low oil to travel to the low overrun clutch valve. The low overrun clutch valve regulates low oil pressure down to approximately 30 psi and then directs this regulated oil to the low/reverse overrun clutch and applies it.

SUMMARY

The forward clutch is applied. The low and reverse, and the overrun clutch are applied to allow engine braking. The intermediate band is released, the transaxle is in Low range—First gear.

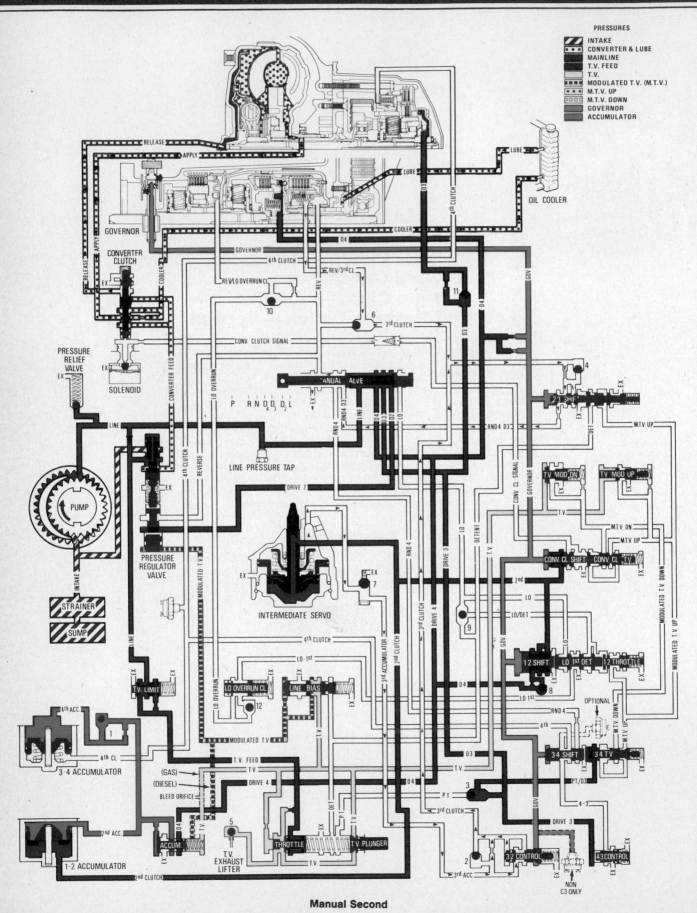

Manual Second

MANUAL SECOND

Converter Clutch—Released

In manual 2nd, the converter clutch is shown released by the engine vacuum switch and there is no M.T.V. up or M.T.V. down pressure. This is assuming the throttle is released. If the throttle is opened sufficiently, the converter clutch could engage and the M.T.V. up and M.T.V. down valves could open.

Forward Clutch—Applied
Overrun Clutch—Applied
Intermediate Band—Applied

A forced 3-2 downshift can be accomplished by moving the selector lever from Third gear to the Second gear position.

When the selector lever is moved to the Second gear position, RND4D3, 3rd clutch, and 3rd accumulator oil will exhaust at the manual valve. With no pressure to apply the 3rd clutch, or release the intermediate band, the transaxle will shift to second gear.

The manual valve will also direct line pressure into the D2 passage. Drive 2 oil will act on the reverse boost valve to boost line pressure to 140 psi which is required to prevent the intermediate band and forward clutch from slipping.

SUMMARY

The forward clutch and intermediate band are applied. The transaxle is in second gear. Also, the overrun clutch is still applied to allow engine braking when needed.

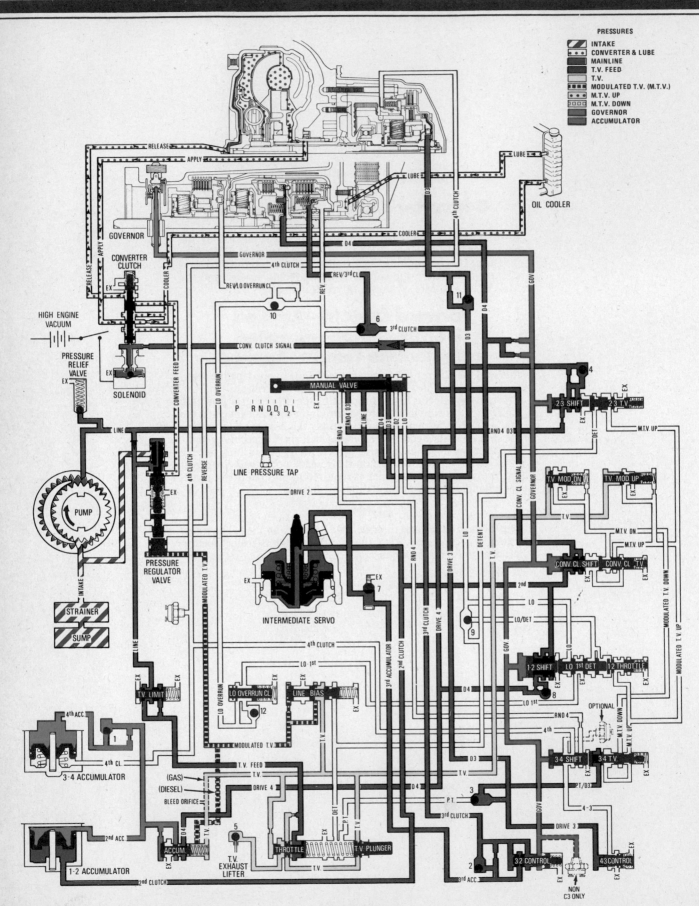

Manual Third

MANUAL THIRD

Converter Clutch—Released

In manual 3rd, the converter clutch is shown released by the engine vacuum switch and there is no M.T.V. up or M.T.V. down pressure. This is assuming the throttle is released. If the throttle is opened sufficiently, the converter clutch could engage and the M.T.V. up and M.T.V. down valves could open.

Forward Clutch—Applied
Overrun Clutch—Applied
Direct Clutch—Applied

A forced 4-3 downshift can be accomplished by moving the selector lever from Drive range to Third gear.

When the selector lever is moved to the Third gear position, line pressure is blocked from the RND4 passage, and D3 oil from the manual valve is directed to the overrun clutch check ball (1), overrun clutch, 4-3 control valve, part throttle and drive 3 check ball (3), and the 3-4 shift valve.

D3 oil will open the 4-3 control valve and close the 3-4 shift valve to allow 4th clutch and 4th accumulator oil to pass back through the 3-4 shift valve and exhaust at the 4-3 control valve. D3 oil will also pass through an orifice and apply the overrun clutch to keep the overdrive roller clutch from overrunning when e n g i n e braking is needed.

SUMMARY

The forward and direct clutches are applied. The 4th clutch is released. The transaxle is in manual 3rd, direct drive. The overrun clutch is applied to allow engine braking.

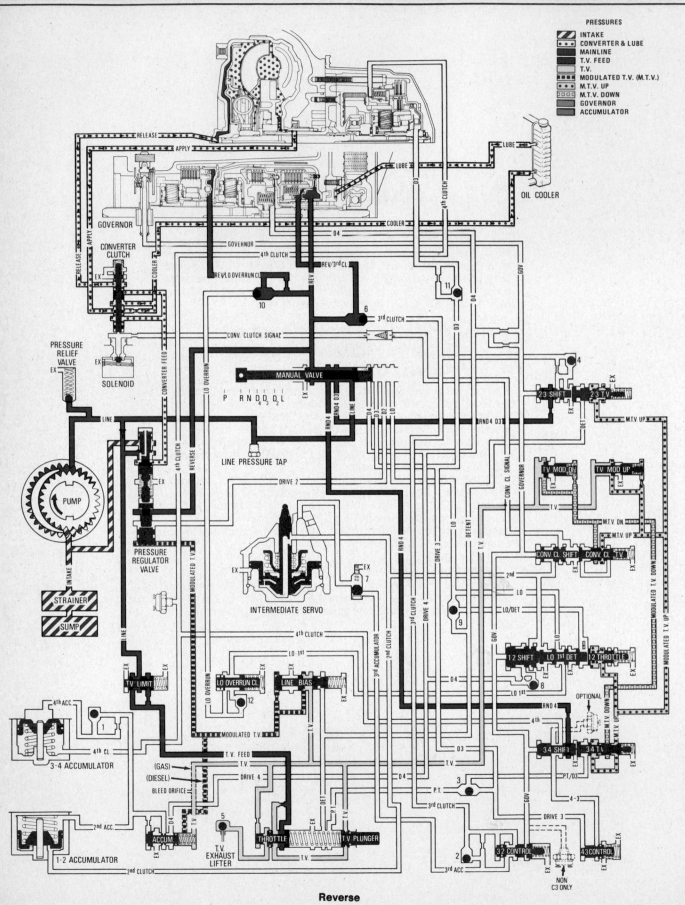

Reverse

REVERSE

Overdrive Roller Clutch—Holding
Direct Clutch—Applied
Low and Reverse Clutch—Applied

When the selector lever is moved to the Reverse position, the manual valve is repositioned to allow line pressure to enter the reverse passage which directs oil to the low and reverse check ball (10), low and reverse clutch, third clutch and reverse check ball (6), inner area of the direct clutch, outer area of the direct clutch and the reverse boost valve.

Reverse oil seats the low/reverse check ball (10) in the low overrun clutch passage and flows to the low/reverse clutch position, applying the low/reverse overrun clutch. Reverse oil also seats the 3rd/reverse check ball (6) in the 3rd clutch passage and flows to the inner area of the direct clutch piston. In addition, reverse oil is directed to the outer area of the direct clutch piston, thus both the inner and the outer areas of the direct clutch piston combine to apply the direct clutch.

Reverse oil acting on the reverse boost valve in the pressure regulator will boost line pressure to approximately 105 psi. M.T.V. oil form the line bias valve acting on the T.V. boost valve, in the pressure regulator, will further boost line pressure from 105 psi at idle to 250 psi at full throttle.

SUMMARY

The overdrive roller clutch is holding. The direct clutch is applied. The low and reverse clutch is applied. The transaxle is in Reverse.

ON CAR SERVICES

Adjustments

THROTTLE VALVE CABLE

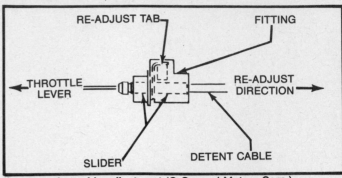

Throttle valve cable adjustment (© General Motors Corp.)

Before making any adjustments to the throttle valve cable, check the following:

a) Check and correct transaxle oil level

b) Be sure that the engine is operating properly, and that the brakes are not dragging.

c) Check that the correct cable has been installed in the vehicle.

d) Check that the cable is connected at both ends.

If the above checks are in order, proceed as follows.

DIESEL ENGINE

1. Stop engine. If equipped, remove cruise control rod.

2. Disconnect the transaxle T.V. cable terminal from the cable actuating lever.

3. Loosen the lock nut on the pump rod and shorten it several turns.

4. Rotate the lever assembly to the full throttle position and hold.

5. Lengthen the pump rod until the injection pump lever contacts the full throttle stop.

6. Release the lever assembly and tighten the pump rod lock nut. Remove the pump rod from the lever assembly.

7. Reconnect the transaxle T.V. cable terminal to the cable actuating lever.

8. Depress and hold the metal re-adjust tab on the cable upper end. Move the slider through the fitting in the direction away from the lever assembly until the slider stops against the fitting.

9. Release the re-adjust tab. Rotate the cable actuating lever assembly to the full throttle stop and release the cable actuating lever assembly. The cable slider should adjust (or ratchet) out of the cable fitting toward the cable actuating lever.

10. Reconnect the pump rod, and cruise control throttle rod if so equipped.

11. If equipped with cruise control, adjust the servo throttle rod to minimum slack (engine off) then put clip in first free hole closest to the bellcrank but within the servo bail.

12. Road test the vehicle.

13. If delayed or only full throttle shifts still occur, remove the oil pan and inspect the throttle lever and bracket assembly which is located on the control valve assembly.

14. Check that the T.V. exhaust valve lifter rod is not distorted or binding in the control valve assembly or spacer plate. The T.V. exhaust check ball must move up and down the same way that the lifter does.

15. Be sure that the lifter spring holds the lifter rod up against the bottom of the control valve assembly. Make sure that the T.V. plunger is not stuck. Inspect the transaxle for correct throttle lever to cable link positioning.

GAS ENGINE

1. Stop engine.

2. Depress and hold the metal re-adjust tab on the cable upper end. Move the slider through the fitting in the direction away from the lever assembly until the slider stops against the fitting.

3. Release re-adjust tab.

4. Rotate the cable actuating lever assembly to the full throttle stop and release the cable actuating lever assembly. The cable slider should adjust (or ratchet) out of the cable fitting toward the cable actuating lever.

5. Check cable for sticking and binding.

6. Road test the vehicle.

7. If delayed or only full throttle shifts still occur, remove the oil pan and inspect the throttle lever and bracket assembly which is located on the control valve assembly.

8. Check that the T.V. exhaust valve lifter rod is not distorted or binding in the control valve assembly or spacer plate. The T.V. exhaust check ball must move up and down the same way that the lifter does.

9. Be sure that the lifter spring holds the lifter rod up against the bottom of the control valve assembly. Make sure that the T.V. plunger is not stuck. Inspect the transaxle for correct throttle lever to cable link positioning.

BAND ADJUSTMENT

The THM 325-4L automatic transaxle uses an intermediate band and intermediate servo assembly with a selective band apply pin. The use of special tools are needed to select the proper length apply pin and because of the transaxle location in the vehicle body, only the servo cover and piston assembly removal should be attempted. Band apply pin measurements should be accomplished with the transaxle removed from the vehicle.

MANUAL LINKAGE ADJUSTMENT

The THM 325-4L does not use a vacuum modulator system. In addition to the T.V. cable, the manual linkage is the only other major adjustment that can be made with the transaxle in the vehicle. This will vary somewhat with the vehicle. However, the following steps should be applicable to all.

1. Place the selector in Park.

2. Check that the selector pointer on the indicator quadrant lines up properly with the range indicator in Park.

3. Apply the brakes and start the vehicle. If the vehicle starts in Park, shut the engine off and place the selector in Neutral. Again, the pointer should line up with the range indicator. Try to start the vehicle. If it starts in Neutral as well as Park, then the manual linkage should be in proper adjustment.

4. A further check can be made by verifying that the back-up lamps only come on in Reverse. Also, set the parking brake, apply the service brakes firmly and attempt to start the vehicle in gear. The engine must not start in any range except Park and Neutral.

5. If adjustment is needed, begin by loosening the clamp screw on the transaxle control shift rod. See that the rod is free to slide through the clamp. Lubricate if necessary.

6. Place the upper shift lever against the Neutral stop in the steering column. A detent will hold it there.

7. Set the transaxle outer lever in the Neutral position. Tighten the clamp screw to 20 foot-pounds torque.

8. Check the operation by the above tests. In addition, be sure that the key cannot be removed when the steering wheel is not locked, and the key in the Run position. With the key in Lock and the shift lever in Park, be sure that the key can be removed. When

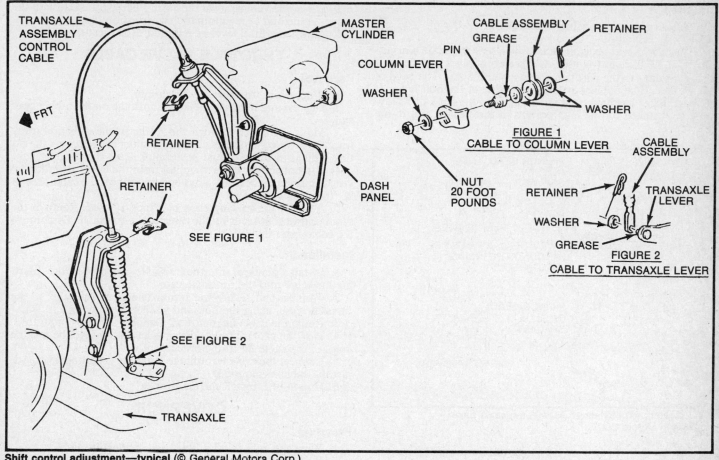

Shift control adjustment—typical (© General Motors Corp.)

the steering wheel is locked, verify that the shift lever cannot be moved from Park. Check for proper operation of the back-up lamps.

SHIFT CONTROL CABLE ADJUSTMENT

1. Position the steering column shift lever in the neutral position.
2. Set the transaxle lever in the neutral position.
3. Assemble the transaxle control cable. Install the pin, washer and retainer to the cable.
4. Properly install the shift cable. Do not hammer on the retainers.
5. Be sure that the shoulder on the pin is engaged in the column lever. Move the pin to give a free pin fit in the column lever. Tighten the attaching nut to the proper torque.

Services

FLUID CHANGE

General Motors does not recommend periodic fluid changes because of normal maintenance and lubrication requirements performed on the automatic transmission by mileage or time intervals.

If the vehicle is used in continuous service or driven under severe conditions (police or taxi type operation), the transaxle should be drained and refilled at mileage intervals of 18,000 to 24,000 miles or a time interval of 18 to 24 months.

NOTE: The miles or time intervals given are average. Each vehicle operated under severe conditions should be treated individually.

Automatic transmission fluids, (Dexron® II), meeting General Motors specifications, should be used in the THM 325-4L automatic transaxle. Failure to use the proper grade and type automatic transmission fluid could result in internal transaxle damage.

When the transaxle has to be removed for major repairs, the unit should be drained completely. The converter, cooler and cooler lines should be flushed to remove any particles or dirt that may have entered the components as a result of the malfunction or failure.

OIL PAN

Removal

1. Raise the vehicle on a hoist and support it safely.
2. With a drain pan placed under the transaxle oil pan, remove the pan attaching bolts from the front and side of the transaxle pan.
3. Loosen the rear pan attaching bolts approximately four turns.
4. Carefully pry the transaxle oil pan loose, using a suitable tool. Allow the transaxle fluid to drain.
5. Remove the remaining pan bolts and remove the pan from the vehicle.
6. Discard the pan gasket. If R.T.V. sealant has been used in place of the pan gasket, be sure to properly clean the pan in order to remove the old sealant.
7. If required, remove the screen to valve body bolts. Remove the screen from the valve body. Replace or clean the screen as necessary.

Installation

1. Install the screen using a new gasket or O-ring onto the valve body assembly.

2. Install the transaxle oil pan, using a new transaxle pan gasket. If, R.T.V. sealant is used as a sealer, apply a 1/16″ bead of R.T.V. Sealant to the part flange and assemble wet. The bead of R.T.V. should be applied around the inside of the bolt holes. If the part flange has depressed stiffening ribs, the bead of R.T.V. must be installed on the high portion of the surface, not in the groove.

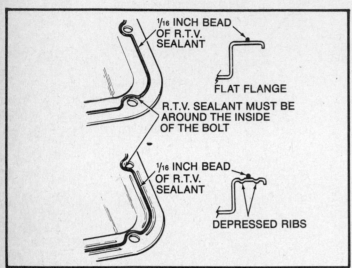

R.T.V. sealant application on special transaxle pans
(© General Motors Corp.)

3. Lower the vehicle from the hoist. Add the proper amount of automatic transmission fluid.

4. With selector lever in PARK position, apply parking brake, start engine and let idle. DO NOT RACE ENGINE.

5. Move selector lever through each range and, with selector lever in PARK range, check fluid level.

6. Correct the fluid level as required to bring the level between the dimples on the dipstick (transaxle cool).

VALVE BODY

Removal

1. Raise the vehicle on a hoist and support it safely. Drain the fluid.

2. Remove the transaxle oil pan and gasket. If R.T.V. sealant has been used, properly clean the mating surfaces.

3. Remove the oil screen and rubber O-ring.

4. Remove the screw and washer holding the cable to the transaxle and disconnect the T.V. cable.

5. Remove the throttle lever and bracket assembly. Do not bend the throttle lever link.

6. Disconnect the torque converter clutch electrical wiring.

7. Remove the oil transfer pipes and hold down brackets.

8. Support the valve body assembly. Remove the valve body retaining bolts.

9. Position the valve body assembly down and note the location of the check ball in the valve body.

NOTE: If the accumulator housing is to be removed, support the spacer plate during removal. Note the location of the check balls and then remove the spacer plate. Also, note the location of the check ball in the accumulator housing.

Installation

1. Installation is the reverse of removal. Be sure to torque the valve body retaining bolts to 8 ft. lbs.

2. Lower the vehicle from the hoist. Fill the transaxle with the proper grade and type automatic transmission fluid.

3. Adjust the fluid level as required. Road test the vehicle.

THROTTLE VALVE CABLE

Removal

1. If necessary, remove the air cleaner.

2. Depress and hold the metal re-adjust tab on the cable upper end.

3. Move the slider through the fitting in the direction away from the cable actuating lever until the slider stops against the fitting. This is in the re-adjust position. Release the re-adjust tab.

4. Disconnect the cable terminal from the cable actuating lever. Compress the locking tangs and disconnect the cable assembly from the bracket.

5. Remove the routing clips or straps, if used. Remove the screw and washer securing the cable to the transaxle. Disconnect the cable from the link.

Installation

1. Install a new seal into the transaxle case hole before inserting the cable into the transaxle case.

2. Connect and secure the transaxle end of the cable to the transaxle case, using the bolt and washer. Torque to 8 ft. lbs.

3. Route the cable as removed. Connect the clips or straps.

4. Pass the cable through the bracket and engage the locking tangs of the cable on to the bracket.

5. Connect the cable terminal to the cable actuating lever. Adjust the cable as required.

6. If removed, install the air cleaner.

GOVERNOR

Removal

1. Raise the vehicle on a hoist and support it safely.

2. Remove the speedometer cable at the transaxle. Be sure to catch fluid in a drain pan.

3. Remove the screws securing the governor cover. Remove the cover.

4. Remove the drive gear and the governor assembly from the transaxle case.

Installation

1. Install the drive gear and governor assembly into the transaxle case.

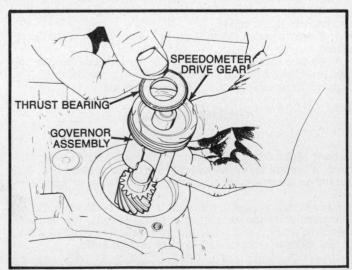

Governor assembly and related components
(© General Motors Corp.)

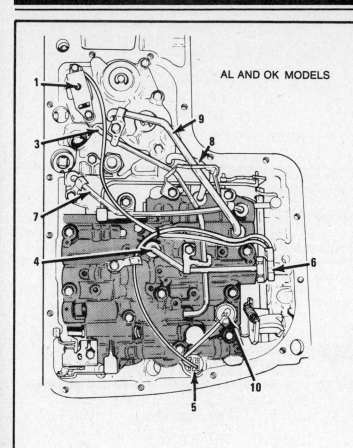

AL AND OK MODELS

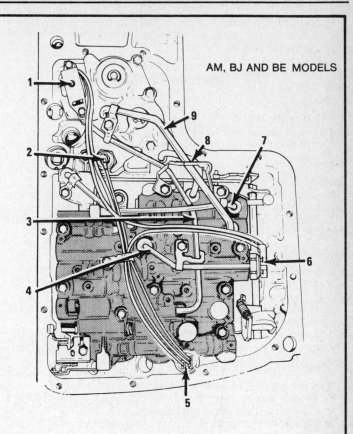

AM, BJ AND BE MODELS

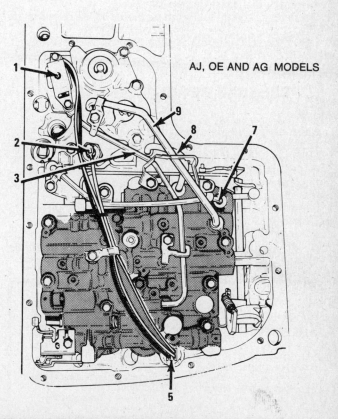

AJ, OE AND AG MODELS

1. Solenoid assembly
2. Fourth clutch pressure switch
3. Converter clutch signal pipe
4. 4-3 switch pipe
5. Connector assembly
6. 4-3 pressure switch
7. D2 signal pipe
8. Reverse signal pipe
9. Overrun clutch pipe
10. Governor pressure switch

Torque converter clutch electrical control connections (© General Motors Corp.)

2. Install the governor cover. Install the speedometer cable.

3. Lower the vehicle from the hoist. Correct the fluid level as required. Road test the vehicle.

INTERMEDIATE SERVO

Removal

1. Raise the vehicle on a hoist and support it safely.

2. Install special tool J-28493 or equivalent, on to the transaxle case. Tighten the bolt to remove the intermediate servo cover bolt.

3. Using a suitable tool, remove the intermediate servo cover retaining ring. Remove the special tool.

4. Remove the intermediate servo cover. Be sure to catch any excess fluid in a drain pan.

5. Remove the servo piston and the band apply pin assembly from the transaxle case.

Installation

1. Install the new inner and outer servo piston, seal rings and/or apply pin seal rings. Make sure that the rings are seated in the grooves to prevent damage to the rings.

2. Install the intermediate servo piston assembly into the intermediate servo cover.

3. Lubricate and install a new seal ring on the intermediate servo cover. This seal ring must be well lubricated to prevent damage or cutting of the ring.

4. Install the intermediate servo assembly into the transaxle case. If necessary, tap lightly with a non metal hammer.

5. Be sure that the tapered end of the band apply pin is properly located against the band apply lug.

6. Install the special tool on to the transaxle case. Tighten the bolt to depress the servo cover.

7. Install the servo retaining ring. Align the ring gap with an end showing in the transaxle case slot.

8. Remove the special tool from its mounting on the transaxle assembly.

9. Lower the vehicle from the hoist. Replace fluid as required. Road test the vehicle.

PRESSURE REGULATOR VALVE

Removal

1. Raise the vehicle on a hoist and support it safely.

2. Drain the fluid from the transaxle. Remove the oil pan. Discard the gasket. If R.T.V. sealant has been used, be sure to properly clean the mating surfaces of the transaxle case and the pan.

3. Pushing on the pressure regulator valve with a suitable tool, compress the pressure regulator spring.

4. Remove the retaining ring and slowly withdraw the tool to release spring tension.

5. Remove the drive to boost valve and bushing, reverse boost plunger and bushing, spacer, and the pressure regulator spring and valve.

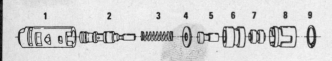

1. Pressure regulator bushing
2. Pressure regulator valve
3. Pressure regulator spring
4. Valve bushing spacer
5. Reverse boost valve
6. Reverse boost valve bushing
7. MTV boost valve
8. MTV boost valve bushing
9. Snap ring

Pressure regulator valve—exploded view (© General Motors Corp.)

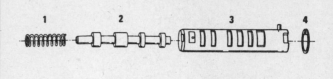

1. Converter clutch valve spring
2. Converter clutch valve
3. Converter clutch valve bushing
4. Snap ring

Torque converter clutch valve—exploded view (© General Motors Corp.)

Installation

1. Installation is the reverse of removal. Be sure to push the sleeve assembly past the retaining ring groove by compressing the pressure regulator valve spring, using tool J-24684 or equivalent.

2. Install the retaining ring.

3. Lower the vehicle from the hoist. Fill the transaxle, using the proper grade and type fluid. Road test as required.

Transaxle

REMOVAL

1. Disconnect the negative battery cable. Remove the air cleaner.

2. If the vehicle is equipped with a diesel engine, install tool J-26996-1 or equivalent.

3. Disconnect the speedometer cable at the transaxle.

4. Disconnect the T.V. cable from the bellcrank, diesel equipped, or the throttle lever, gasoline equipped, at its upper end. Disconnect the T.V. cable from its bracket by depressing both retainers and sliding the cable out.

5. Remove the center final drive bolt from the assembly.

6. Remove the two nuts on the left exhaust pipe to manifold connection. Remove the transaxle to engine bolts and stud from the top of the assembly.

7. Remove the fuel line to transaxle bracket.

8. Raise the vehicle on a hoist and support it safely.

9. Remove the starter. Remove the TCC electrical connector.

10. Disconnect the transaxle oil cooler lines. Plug the openings.

11. Remove the transaxle inspection cover.

12. Remove the two bolts on the left exhaust pipe. Remove the exhaust pipe.

13. Remove the three nuts on the right exhaust pipe. Remove the two bolts from the catalytic coverter hanger.

14. Remove the four bolts from the torque box cross-member, and the two bolts from the fuel lines.

15. Remove the torque converter to flexplate bolts. Be sure to mark the position of the flexplate to the torque converter for proper reassembly.

16. Disconnect the shift linkage at the transaxle. Remove the right hand transaxle mount.

17. Position the transmission jack under the transaxle.

18. Remove the left transaxle mount through bolt. Remove the lower bracket to transaxle bolt. Raise the transaxle assembly about two inches in order to gain access to the remaining upper bracket to transaxle bolts.

19. Remove the remaining engine to transaxle bolt and bracket.

20. Lower the transaxle carefully while disengaging the final drive unit.

21. Install a torque converter holding tool and remove the automatic transaxle from the vehicle.

INSTALLATION

1. Installation is the reverse of removal. The following points should be observed. Always replace the final drive to transaxle gasket.

2. Use care to see that the final drive splines engage the transaxle and then loosely install two final drive to transaxle lower attaching bolts.

3. After the final drive and transaxle are mated, align the bellhousing with the engine and install the remaining attaching bolts.

4. Before installing the converter to flywheel bolts, make sure that the weld nuts on the torque converter are flush with the flywheel and that the converter rotates freely in this position. Hand start the bolts and tighten all three finger tight so that the converter and flywheel will be in the proper alignment. Then torque the bolts evenly to specification.

5. Be sure to adjust the T.V. cable.

6. Refill the transaxle to the proper level with Dexron® II.

BENCH OVERHAUL

Before Disassembly

Before opening up the transaxle, the outside of the unit should be thoroughly cleaned, preferably with high-pressure cleaning equipment such as a car wash spray unit. Dirt entering the transaxle internal parts will negate all the effort and time spent on the overhaul. During inspection and reassembly, all parts should be thoroughly cleaned with solvent, then dried with compressed air. Wiping cloths and rags should not be used to dry parts since lint will find its way into valve body passages. Lube seals with Dexron® II and use ordinary unmedicated petroleum jelly to hold thrust washers to ease assembly of seals, since it will not leave a harmful residue as grease often will. Do not use solvent on neoprene seals, friction plates or thrust washers. Be wary of nylon parts if the transaxle failure was due to a failure of the cooling system. Nylon parts exposed to antifreeze solutions can swell and distort and so must be replaced. Before installing bolts into aluminum parts, always dip the threads into clean oil. Anti-seize compound is also a good way to prevent the bolts from galling the aluminum and seizing. Always use a torque wrench to keep from stripping the threads. Take care of the seals when installing them, especially the smaller O-rings. The internal snap rings should be expanded and the external snap rings should be compressed, if they are to be reused. This will help insure proper seating when installed.

Torque Converter

Removal and Inspection

1. Make certain that the transaxle is held securely.

2. The converter pulls out of the transaxle. Be careful since the converter contains a large amount of oil. There is no drain plug on the converter so the converter should be draind through the hub.

The fluid drained from the torque converter can help diagnose transaxle problems.

1. If the oil in the converter is discolored but does not contain metal bits or particles, the converter is not damaged and need not be replaced. Remember that color is no longer a good indicator of transmission fluid condition. In the past, dark color was associated with overheated transmission fluid. It is not a positive sign of transaxle failure with the newer fluids like Dexron® II.

2. If the oil in the converter contains metal particles, the converter is damaged internally and must be replaced. The oil may have an "aluminum paint" appearance.

3. If the cause of oil contamination was due to burned clutch plates or overheated oil, the converter is contaminated and should be replaced.

Transaxle Disassembly

OIL PAN AND FILTER

Removal

1. Remove the oil pan attaching bolts.

2. Separate the pan from the transaxle assembly.

3. Discard the pan gasket. If R.T.V. sealant has been used, properly clean both mating surfaces.

4. Remove the transaxle oil filter and O-ring.

EXTERNAL PARTS

Removal

1. Disconnect the wire leads at the transaxle case electrical connector and the pressure switches.

2. Remove the electrical connector and the O-ring seal from the transaxle case. Using a suitable tool, depress the connector tangs while pushing out on the connector.

3. Remove the solenoid assembly retaining bolts. Remove the solenoid and the O-ring seal.

4. Remove the pressure regulator assembly retaining snap ring.

5. Remove the T.V. boost valve bushing and valve, reverse boost valve bushing and valve, pressure regulator spring and the pressure regulator bushing and valve.

NOTE: If replacement of the valve bushing is necessary, you will have to determine if the bushings are oversized. The bushings and the transaxle case will both be stamped with "O.S", if in fact they are oversized.

6. Remove the torque converter clutch apply valve retaining snap ring.

7. Remove the torque converter clutch valve bushing, valve and spring.

8. Remove the D2 signal pipe, reverse signal pipe and the overrun pipe retainers. Remove the remaining oil pipes and solenoid assembly.

VALVE BODY

Removal

1. Remove the throttle lever and bracket assembly.

2. Remove the valve body assembly attaching bolts. Disconnect the manual valve.

3. Do not drop the manual valve, as damage to this component may result.

4. Remove the valve body assembly from its mounting in the transaxle. Note the location of the check ball on the spacer plate. Remove the check ball.

1-2, 3-4 ACCUMULATOR ASSEMBLY

Removal

1. Remove the 1-2, 3-4 accumulator housing attaching bolts. Remove the accumulator housing, and 1-2 spring.

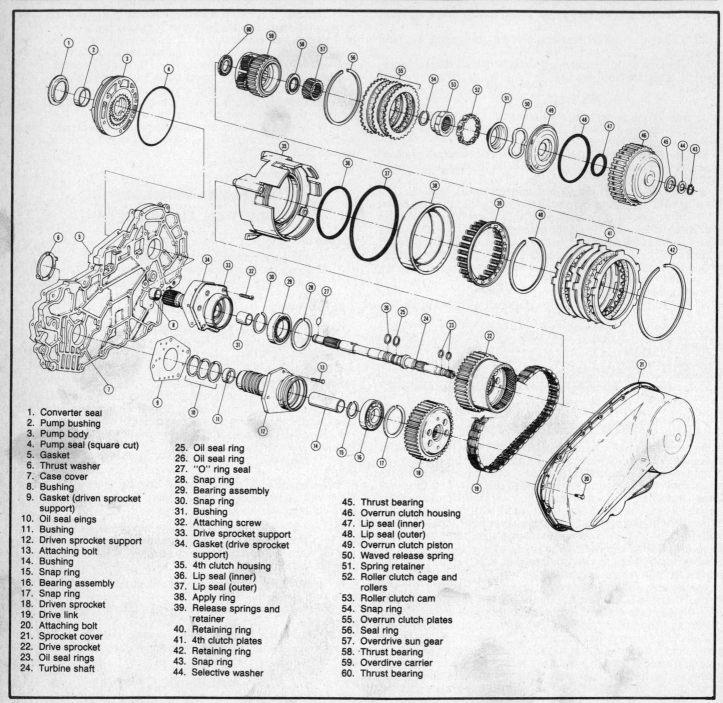

1. Converter seal
2. Pump bushing
3. Pump body
4. Pump seal (square cut)
5. Gasket
6. Thrust washer
7. Case cover
8. Bushing
9. Gasket (driven sprocket support)
10. Oil seal eings
11. Bushing
12. Driven sprocket support
13. Attaching bolt
14. Bushing
15. Snap ring
16. Bearing assembly
17. Snap ring
18. Driven sprocket
19. Drive link
20. Attaching bolt
21. Sprocket cover
22. Drive sprocket
23. Oil seal rings
24. Turbine shaft

25. Oil seal ring
26. Oil seal ring
27. "O" ring seal
28. Snap ring
29. Bearing assembly
30. Snap ring
31. Bushing
32. Attaching screw
33. Drive sprocket support
34. Gasket (drive sprocket support)
35. 4th clutch housing
36. Lip seal (inner)
37. Lip seal (outer)
38. Apply ring
39. Release springs and retainer
40. Retaining ring
41. 4th clutch plates
42. Retaining ring
43. Snap ring
44. Selective washer

45. Thrust bearing
46. Overrun clutch housing
47. Lip seal (inner)
48. Lip seal (outer)
49. Overrun clutch piston
50. Waved release spring
51. Spring retainer
52. Roller clutch cage and rollers
53. Roller clutch cam
54. Snap ring
55. Overrun clutch plates
56. Seal ring
57. Overdrive sun gear
58. Thrust bearing
59. Overdirve carrier
60. Thrust bearing

THM 325-4L automatic transaxle—exploded view (© General Motors Corp.)

2. One check ball will be exposed on top of the spacer plate to valve body gasket, remove it.

3. Remove the accumulator housing assembly gasket and spacer plate.

4. Remove the nine check balls from the transaxle case passages.

GOVERNOR AND SPEEDOMETER DRIVE GEAR ASSEMBLY

Removal

1. Remove the speedometer driven gear retaining bolt and retainer clip.

2. Remove the speedometer driven gear assembly from the governor cover. Remove the "O" ring seal from the speedometer driven gear assembly.

3. Remove the governor cover bolts.

4. Remove the governor cover and the "O" ring seal.

5. Remove the governor, bearing assembly and speedometer drive gear assembly from the transaxle case. The governor bearing assembly may be in the governor cover.

INTERMEDIATE SERVO ASSEMBLY

Removal

1. Install tool J-28493, or equivalent on to the transaxle case.

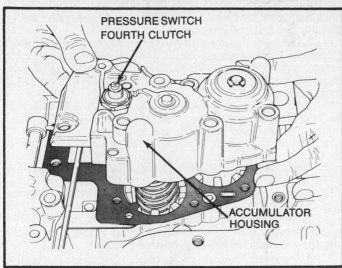

1-2, 3-4 accumulator housing (© General Motors Corp.)

Tighten the bolt to depress the servo cover.

2. Using a suitable tool, remove the intermediate servo cover retaining ring. Remove tool J-28493.

3. Using a pliers, remove the intermediate servo cover and O-ring seal. The cover O-ring seal may be located in the transaxle case bore.

4. If the intermediate servo cover and seal assembly can not be removed easily, apply air pressure into the intermediate servo exhaust port.

5. Remove the intermediate servo piston and band apply pin assembly.

OVERDRIVE UNIT AND DRIVE LINK ASSEMBLY

Removal

1. Rotate the transaxle to the sprocket cover side up.

2. Remove the sprocket cover retaining bolts.

3. Remove the cover and the R.T.V. sealant. Clean the excess sealant from the cover. Do not hit the cover to remove it, use a putty knife to break the transaxle case to case cover seal.

4. Check the overdrive end play by mounting a dial indicator gauge against the end of the turbine shaft. Set the dial indicator to zero.

5. Move the turbine shaft upward by pushing up from the converter side. The overdrive unit end play should be .004"-.029".

6. The selective washer controlling this end play is located between the turbine shaft retaining ring and the thrust bearing assembly. If more or less washer thickness is required to bring the end play within specifications, select the proper washer.

7. Remove the fourth clutch snap ring. Remove the fourth clutch plates. Remove the turbine shaft snap ring.

8. Remove the turbine shaft thrust washer, thrust bearing, and overdrive unit. The overdrive carrier may have to be removed separately.

9. Remove the overdrive carrier to drive sprocket thrust bearing assembly.

10. Remove the fourth clutch housing retaining bolts. Remove the housing.

11. Remove the fourth clutch housing to case cover O-ring seal. The O-ring seal may be located in the fourth clutch housing.

12. Using a snap ring pliers, remove the sprocket bearing retaining snap rings which are located under the drive and driven sprockets. The snap ring grooves are located in the sprocket supports.

13. To remove the drive and driven sprockets, drive link bearings and turbine shaft pull alternately on the drive and driven sprockets.

NOTE: If the sprockets are difficult to remove, place a small piece of fiberboard between the sprocket and a pry bar and alternately pry under each sprocket.

14. Remove the drive link from the drive and driven sprockets. Remove the turbine shaft.

15. Remove the oil pump by first removing the two opposite pump attaching flat head screws from the drive sprocket support using tool J-25359-5.

16. Install two 5/16x4 inch guide pins into the assembly. Remove the remaining pump flat head screws from the drive sprocket support.

17. Steady the pump from underneath with one hand then gently tap the guide pins until the pump is removed from the transaxle case.

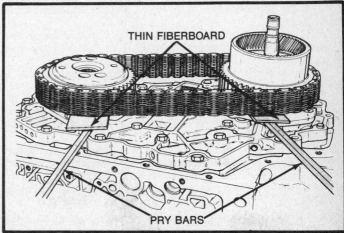

Sprocket removal (© General Motors Corp.)

18. To check the input end play, install tool J-26958 to the output end of the transaxle.

19. Remove the driven sprocket support to case bolt and install the dial indicator gauge.

20. Push the input shaft down. Raise the input shaft by pushing the handle down on the dial indicator gauge. The input unit end play should be .022-.051 inch.

21. The selective washer controlling this end play is located between the output shaft and the input shaft. If a different washer thickness is required to bring the end play within specifications, refer to the selective washer chart for the proper washer.

22. Remove the dial indicator gauge and tool J-25025-7. Do not remove tool J-26958.

23. To remove the case cover, remove the cover retaining bolts. Do not remove the driven sprocket support bolts. Remove the case cover and gasket.

24. Remove the thrust washer from the hub of the driven sprocket support. The thrust washer may be on the direct clutch housing.

25. Remove the pressure regulator screen from the case cover side of the case.

FORWARD AND DIRECT CLUTCH

Removal

1. Remove the forward and direct clutch assemblies from the transaxle case, using tool J-26959 or equivalent.

2. Remove the intermediate band.

3. Remove the direct clutch assembly from the forward clutch assembly.

4. The direct clutch to the forward clutch thrust washer may be on the end of the direct clutch housing when it is removed from the forward clutch housing.

INTERNAL GEAR PARTS

Removal

1. Remove the output shaft to the input shaft selective washer.

2. Check the reaction unit end play by loosening the adjusting screw on tool J-26958, which should still be installed on the output shaft. Push the output shaft downward.

3. Install the dial indicator gauge onto the transaxle case. Position the extension, of the tool, against the end of the output shaft. Set the dial indicator to zero.

4. Move the output shaft upward by turning the adjusting screw on tool J-26958 until it stops. Read and record the end play. The reaction unit end play should be .004-.025 inches.

5. The selective washer controlling this end play is located between the input internal gear thrust washer and the output shaft snap ring.

6. If more or less washer thickness is required, select the proper thrust washer from the reaction unit end play selective washer chart.

7. Remove the dial indicator gauge. Do not remove tool J-26958.

8. Using a snap ring pliers, remove the output shaft to the selective washer snap ring. Tighten the adjusting screw on tool J-26958, which is still located on the output shaft, to remove the snap ring.

9. Remove the input internal gear, reaction selective washer, and tanged thrust washer. Remove the reaction selective washer, and thrust washer from the input internal gear.

10. Remove the input carrier assembly. Remove the input internal gear to the input carrier thrust bearing assembly.

NOTE: The input sun gear, to the input carrier, thrust bearing assembly and race may come out as the input carrier is removed.

11. Remove the input sun gear to the input carrier thrust bearing assembly, and input sun gear. This thrust bearing requires only one thrust race.

12. Remove the input drum and the reaction sun gear assembly.

13. Remove the four tanged input drum to the low and reverse clutch housing thrust washer from the rear of the input drum or from the low and reverse clutch housing.

14. To remove the low and reverse clutch housing assembly, grind about ¾ inch from the end of a 6.3mm (#4) screw extractor to remove the cup plug. Remove the low and reverse cup plug assembly by turning the easy out two or three turns and pulling it straight out.

15. Remove the low and reverse clutch housing to transaxle case beveled snap ring. Using tool J-28542, remove the low and reverse clutch housing assembly and spacer ring.

16. Be sure that the governor assembly has been removed at this time.

17. Grasp the output shaft and lift out the rest of the reaction unit parts.

18. Remove the roller clutch and reaction assembly from the output shaft.

19. Remove the four tanged reaction carrier to reaction internal gear thrust washer, from the end of the reaction carrier or from the inside of the reaction internal gear.

20. Remove the low and reverse clutch plates from the output shaft. Take note that the top clutch plate is waved.

21. Remove the reaction internal gear to reaction sun gear thrust bearing assembly from the reaction internal gear. Remove the reaction internal gear from the output shaft.

22. Remove the governor assembly drive gear.

MANUAL SHAFT AND PARKING PAWL

Removal

1. Position the transaxle so that the oil pan is facing upward. Remove tool J-26958 from the transaxle case.

2. Remove the manual detent roller and spring assembly. Remove the parking strut shaft retaining ring.

3. Use a 6.3mm (#4) screw extractor to remove the parking lock cup plug by grinding about ¾ inch from the end of the Easy Out.

4. Use a 4mm (#4) screw extractor to remove the parking strut shaft. Remove the parking lock spring, strut and lever.

5. Remove the parking lock cam. Remove the inside detent lever retaining nut.

6. Remove the manual shaft and the inside detent lever assembly.

7. Inspect the manual shaft and seal for damage. If necessary, pry out the manual shaft seal using the proper seal removal tool.

8. Using a 4mm (#3) screw extractor, remove the parking pawl shaft.

9. Remove the parking pawl and the return spring.

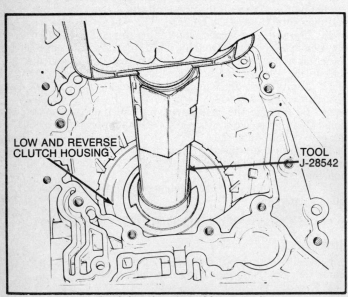

Low and reverse clutch housing assembly removal
(© General Motors Corp.)

LOW AND REVERSE CLUTCH HOUSING

TOOL J-28542

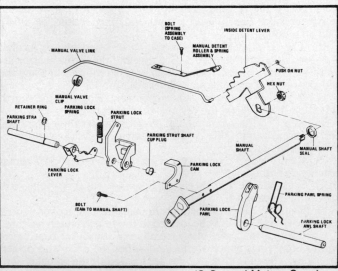

Manual shaft and related components (© General Motors Corp.)

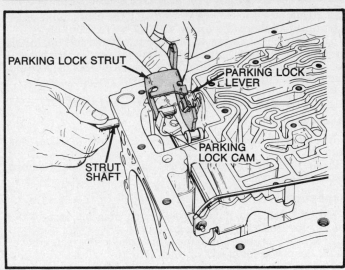

Parking strut shaft and related components
(© General Motors Corp.)

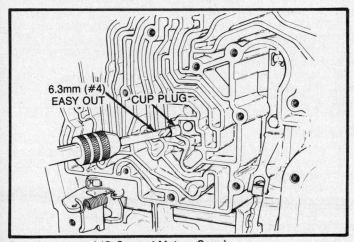

Cup plug removal (© General Motors Corp.)

Unit Disassembly and Assembly
DIRECT CLUTCH

Disassembly

1. Pry the snap ring from the direct clutch housing and remove the snap ring along with the backing plate.
2. Remove the clutch pack from the housing. Take note of the number of clutch plates and the order in which they are removed. Be sure to keep the direct clutch plates separate from the forward clutch plates.
3. Compress the assembly so that the spring retainer snap ring can be removed. Remove the retainer and spring assembly from the clutch housing.
4. Remove the release spring guide and the clutch piston. The seals should be discarded. Do not remove the apply ring from the piston unless the piston is damaged and replacement is required.

Inspection

1. Clean all parts thoroughly in solvent and blow dry with compressed air.
2. Check the piston for cracks or damage. See that the check ball is free.

Assembly

1. With all parts clean and dry, carefully install new seals on the piston. The seals should be lubricated with Dexron® II or petroleum jelly.
2. Install a new center seal in the clutch housing. Lubricate the seal to ease installation.
3. With the seals well lubricated, install the piston into the clutch housing using care so the seal will not be torn or damaged by the sharp edge on the snap ring groove. Rotate the piston to help with the installation. A tool made from wire can be fabricated to help ease the lip of the seal into place.
4. Install the spring guide making sure that the notch, or omitted rib, is aligned with the check ball in the piston. Then install the spring and retainer assembly. Compress the unit and install the snap ring.
5. Install the clutch pack. The composition plates should be well-oiled with Dexron® II preferably soaking in the oil for at least 20 minutes prior to assembly. Install the plates in the order determined at removal, staring with a steel plate.

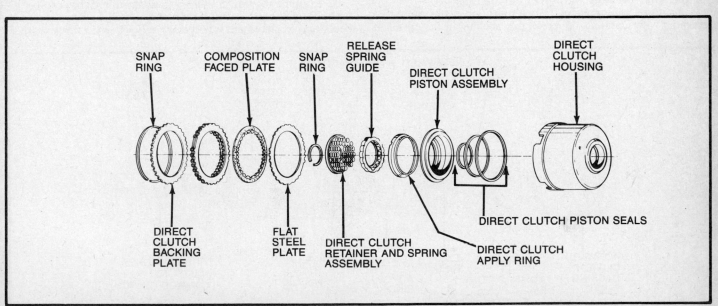

Direct clutch assembly—exploded view (© General Motors Corp.)

6. Install the backing plate with the chamfered side up. Install the snap ring and check the clutch pack for proper assembly by verifying that the composition plates turn freely. Set the direct clutch aside until the transaxle is ready for assembly.

FORWARD CLUTCH

Disassembly

1. Pry the snap ring from the forward clutch housing and remove the snap ring along with the backing plate.
2. Remove the clutch pack from the housing. Take note of the number of clutch plates and the order in which they are removed. Be sure to keep the forward clutch plates separate from the direct clutch plates.
3. Compress the assembly so that the spring retainer snap ring can be removed. Remove the retainer and spring assembly from the clutch housing.
4. Remove the forward clutch piston. The seals should be discarded. Do not remove the apply ring from the piston unless the piston is damaged and requires replacement.

Inspection

1. Clean all parts thoroughly in solvent and blow dry with compressed air.
2. Check the piston for cracks or damage. See that the check ball is free.
3. Inspect the housing snap-ring groove for burrs or damage. Check the input shaft for open and clean oil passages on both ends of the shaft. Inspect the cup plug for damage. If it needs to be replaced, a #4 Easy-Out can be used for removal. Install the replacement cup plug to 1mm (.039") below the surface.

Assembly

1. With all parts clean and dry, carefully install new seals on the piston. The seals should be lubricated with Dexron® II or petroleum jelly.
2. Install a new center seal in the clutch housing. Lubricate the seal to ease installation.
3. With the seals well lubricated, install the piston into the clutch housing using care so the seal will not be torn or damaged by the sharp edge on the snap ring groove. Rotate the piston to help with the installation.
4. Install the spring retainer assembly. Be careful that the retainer does not hang-up in the groove for the snap ring. Compress the assembly and install the snap ring.
5. Install the clutch pack. The composition plates should be well-oiled with Dexron® II, preferably soaking in the oil for at least 20 minutes prior to assembly. Install the plates in the order determined at removal, starting with the waved steel plate.
6. Install the backing plate with the chamfered side up. Install the snap ring and check the clutch pack for proper assembly by verifying that the composition plates turn freely. Set the forward clutch aside until the transaxle is ready for assembly.

LOW AND REVERSE CLUTCH

Disassembly

1. Compress the spring retainer and remove the snap ring from the clutch housing.
2. Remove the waved spring and the clutch piston. Remove the seals and discard.

Inspection

1. Check the feed holes in the clutch housing. Inspect the housing for scoring or other damage.
2. Remove any burrs from the splines on the snap ring groove. Check the piston for cracks or other damage.

Assembly

1. Replace the seals on the piston. The seals should be lubricated with Dexron® II or petroleum jelly. Make sure that the seal lips are installed facing away from the clutch apply ring side.
2. Install the piston into the clutch housing using care to protect the seal.
3. Install the waved spring, followed by the retainer, which is installed cupped face down.
4. Compress the assembly and install the snap ring. Set the unit aside until the transaxle is ready for assembly.

ROLLER CLUTCH AND REACTION CARRIER

Disassembly

1. Remove the roller clutch race from the reaction carrier.
2. Remove the roller clutch assembly. Be careful of the rollers and energizing springs.
3. Remove the thrust bearing from the inside of the reaction carrier and inspect carefully for wear or damage.
4. Remove the four-tanged reaction carrier-to-rear internal gear thrust washer.

Inspection

1. Examine the thrust washers to determine if they can be reused. If slight scoring or scuff marks are noted, replacement is not necessary. Replacement is necessary only when the thrust washer

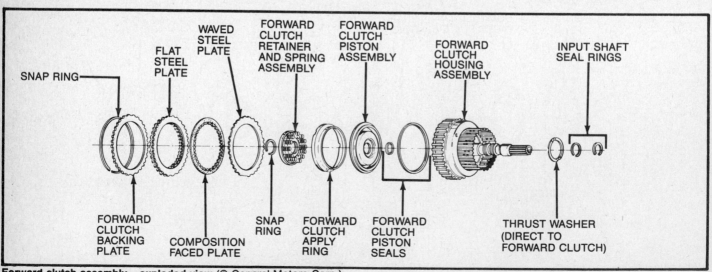

Forward clutch assembly—exploded view (© General Motors Corp.)

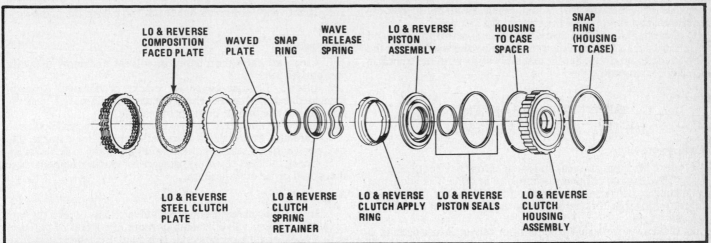

Low and reverse clutch assembly—exploded view (© General Motors Corp.)

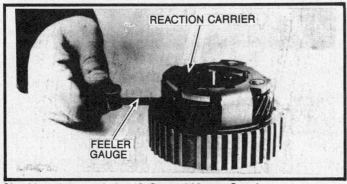

Checking pinion end play (© General Motors Corp.)

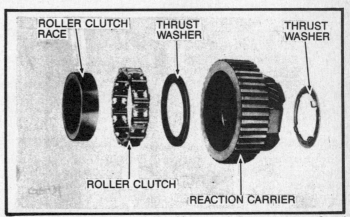

Roller clutch and reaction carrier assembly (© General Motors Corp.)

indicates material pick-up on the thrust surface or when the surface that the washer protects is deeply cut or scored.

2. Check the rollers for wear or damage. If a roller should come out of the cage assembly, the roller should be replaced from the outside of the cage to keep from damaging the energizing spring.

3. The pinion end-play on the planetary carrier should be checked. A feeler gauge can be used. End-play should be between .009" to .027".

Assembly

1. Install the roller clutch-to-reaction carrier thrust washer into the reaction carrier.

2. Install the roller clutch cage into the reaction carrier.

3. Install the roller clutch race into the roller clutch cage, spline side out, turning as needed to get the race into position.

4. Install the four-tanged thrust washer onto the reaction carrier on the pinion end. Align the slots on the carrier with the tangs on the washer. Use petroleum jelly to hold the washers in place.

5. The reaction internal gear should still be on the output shaft. If the output shaft does not need to be disassembled, that is, the governor gear does not have to be removed and the shaft is not damaged, then install the reaction carrier assembly onto the output shaft and into the reaction internal gear. Set the unit aside until the transaxle is ready for assembly.

REACTION SUN GEAR AND INPUT DRUM

Disassembly

1. Remove the input drum-to-reaction sun gear snap-ring.
2. Remove the reaction sun gear from the input drum.
3. Remove the four-tanged thrust washer from the end of the reaction sun gear. This thrust washer protects the input drum and the low and reverse clutch housing.

Inspection

1. Clean all parts well in solvent and blow dry.
2. Carefully inspect the reaction sun gear for broken teeth, splits, or cracks. Check that the lubrication holes are not plugged. Inspect the bushing for scoring or damage.
3. Make sure that the snap ring is not distorted or bent. If necessary, replace this snap ring. Carefully examine the four-tanged thrust washer for excessive wear. Expect some light marks or polishing of the surface, but deep gouges or signs of metal transfer means that the washer must be replaced.

Assembly

1. Insert the reaction sun gear into the input drum, making

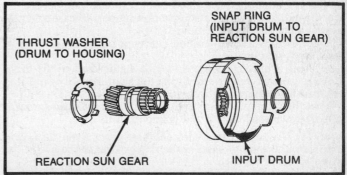

Reaction sun gear and input drum assembly
(© General Motors Corp.)

sure that the spline side goes in first. Being careful not to over-expand the snap ring, install the ring on the sun gear.

2. Coat the four-tanged thrust washer with petroleum jelly and install it on the sun gear. Align the tangs on the washer with the slots in the input drum. Set the assembly aside until the transaxle is ready for assembly.

INPUT SUN GEAR AND INPUT CARRIER ASSEMBLY

Disassembly

1. Once the input sun gear and input carrier have both been removed, there is no further disassembly to be done. Take note that the planetary carrier is a stamped unit and that the pinion pins are not removable. If there is damage to the carrier, it must be replaced.

2. If the input internal gear-to-input carrier thrust bearing is still on the carrier, remove it for cleaning. Also, the input sun gear-to-front carrier thrust bearing should be removed.

Inspection

1. Clean all parts thoroughly in solvent and blow dry with compressed air.

2. Thoroughly clean the input sun gear-to-input carrier thrust bearing for pitted or rough surfaces.

3. Inspect the input carrier for chipped teeth on the pinions, or excessive play. The pinion end-play should be checked. A feeler gauge can be used to check this clearance. Pinion end-play should be between .009" and .027".

Assembly

1. Install the input carrier-to-input internal gear thrust bearing onto the input carrier. Make sure that the smaller diameter race goes against the carrier. A liberal amount of petroleum jelly will help hold the bearing in place.

2. The input sun gear will be installed at the time of assembly, along with the input carrier, transaxle input internal gear and the selective thrust washer. Set these components aside until the transaxle is ready for assembly.

CASE COVER, DRIVE AND DRIVEN SPROCKETS

Disassembly

1. Normally, the drive and driven sprocket support assemblies are not to be removed. The support assemblies are pressed into the case cover and special care is needed to remove them. The case cover and the sprocket supports should be carefully examined for damage or any sign of leakage. The drive sprocket support stator shaft splines should be checked carefully *before* they are disassembled. Generally, unless the transaxle has seen abuse or is otherwise heavily damaged, the supports should not be removed. If it has been determined that the sprocket supports must be removed, first verify that all sprocket support-to-case cover attaching bolts have been removed.

2. Set the cover on two wood blocks or otherwise support it, stator shaft side up.

3. Using a plastic mallet, drive the stator shaft of the drive sprocket support downward. Strike the shaft carefully until it is removed from the case cover.

4. In the same manner, strike the hub of the driven sprocket support downward until it too is free from its bore.

NOTE: Use care when driving out these parts. Avoid damaging or distorting the stator shaft or the ring grooves in the hub of the driven sprocket support.

5. Discard the gaskets that will be found between the support and case cover.

6. Remove the converter out check valve from the pump cover.

Inspection

1. Clean all parts thoroughly in solvent and blow dry with compressed air.

2. Inspect the case cover for cracks or damage. A metal straightedge can be used to check the cover for flatness. Check the cup plugs for tightness, or signs of leakage.

3. Check for the presence of a check ball in the case cover.

4. Carefully examine the sprocket supports for damage. Do not remove the oil seal rings unless they are going to be replaced.

5. Check the case cover oil passages for cracks or any damage that could cause cross-leakage.

Assembly

1. Install the converter out check valve into its bore in the case cover. This check valve is actually more like a coil of flat steel with a hook or tang on one end. It is installed tanged end first, into the oil passages. Then coil the remainder of the valve within itself.

2. Install the drive sprocket support gasket. Two guide pins should be made to help keep the sprocket support straight. Carefully install the drive sprocket support and use a plastic mallet as needed to seat the support in the housing. Remove the guide pins and install the support bolts. These are to be torqued to 18 foot-pounds.

3. In the same manner, install the driven support gasket and support.

4. Install the thrust washer on the hub of the driven sprocket support. Note that there is a tab on the bearing that must be located in the case cover locating hole. Use petroleum jelly to hold it in place.

5. Replace the oil seal rings on the hub of the driven sprocket. Set the unit aside until the transaxle is ready for assembly.

OIL PUMP

Disassembly

1. Remove the drive gear from the oil pump body.
2. Remove the driven gear from the oil pump body.
3. Remove and discard the oil pump body to case O-ring seal.

Inspection

1. Clean all parts thoroughly in solvent and blow dry with compressed air.

2. Check the gear pocket for wear, nicks, burrs or other damage.

3. Check the gears in the same manner for any damage or excessive wear.

4. Pry out the front seal and check the bore for damage.

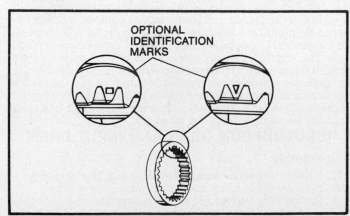

OPTIONAL
IDENTIFICATION
MARKS

Oil pump gear identification marks (© General Motors Corp.)

5. The pump body can be installed on the torque converter hub to check for an out-of-round condition or excessive play.

6. Gear clearance should also be checked. Put the gears in the pocket of the pump aligning the match-marks made earlier. With a feeler gauge, check the pump body face-to-gear clearance. The clearance should be from .0013" to .0035". Note that the larger, driven gear should have a factory identification mark on it. This mark must be down when the gear is installed. The pump drive gear, which is the smaller of the two and has the square tang on the inside diameter, has its identification mark on the tang and it must be installed with the mark facing up.

Assembly

1. Apply a thin coat of non-hardening sealer to the outer edge of the pump seal and install the seal to the pump.

2. With all parts clean and dry, install the pump gears into the pump pocket matching up the marks made at disassembly. Be sure that the driven gear's identification mark is down and the drive gear's mark on the tang faces up.

3. Lubricate the large outer O-ring that goes around the circumference of the pump with petroleum jelly and install the seal. The pump spacer plate and the pump can be set aside until the transaxle is ready for assembly.

FOURTH CLUTCH ASSEMBLY

Disassembly

1. Using a press and tool J-29334-1, or equivalent, compress the fourth clutch spring and retainer assembly. Remove the snap ring and the retainer assembly.

2. Remove the fourth clutch piston. Remove the fourth clutch inner and outer seals and discard them.

Inspection

1. Inspect the fourth clutch housing for cracks, or porosity. Also inspect for burrs or raised edges. If present, remove them with a fine stone or fine abrasive paper.

2. Inspect the piston sealing surface for scratches.

3. Air check the fourth clutch oil passage making certain it is open and not interconnected.

4. Inspect the snap ring for damage.

5. Inspect the release spring, and retainer assembly for distortion or damage.

6. Inspect the composition-faced and steel clutch plates for signs for wear or burning.

7. Inspect the backing plate for scratches or damage.

Assembly

1. Install the fourth clutch outer and inner seals on the fourth clutch housing with the seal lips facing downward. Use petroleum jelly to aid in the installation of the seals. The fourth clutch housing inner seal is identified by a white stripe.

2. Install the fourth clutch piston assembly into the fourth clutch piston housing.

3. Install the fourth clutch spring and retainer assembly. Using the press and tool J-29334-1, compress the spring and retainer assembly and install the fourth clutch housing to spring assembly snap ring.

4. Set the assembly aside until the transaxle is ready for reassembly.

OVERRUN CLUTCH ASSEMBLY

Disassembly

1. Separate the overdrive carrier assembly from the overrun clutch assembly. Remove the overdrive sun gear from the overrun clutch assembly.

2. Remove the overrun clutch snap ring using the proper tool. Remove the overrun clutch backing plate from the overrun clutch housing.

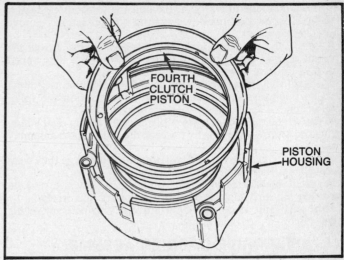

Fourth clutch piston assembly (© General Motors Corp.)

3. Remove the clutch plates from the overrun clutch housing. Be sure to keep them separated from the other plate assemblies.

4. Remove the overrun clutch hub snap ring, using a snap ring pliers.

5. Remove the overdrive roller clutch cam assembly. Remove the roller clutch assembly.

6. Remove the retainer and wave spring assembly from the housing. Remove the overrun clutch piston assembly.

7. Remove both the inner and outer seal from the overrun clutch piston.

Inspection

1. Inspect both the composition plates and the steel plates for wear and heat damage. Replace as required.

2. Inspect both the overrun clutch and the clutch housing for scoring, distortion, cracks, damage, wear and open oil passages. Replace components as required.

Assembly

1. Install new inner and outer seals on the piston with the lips facing away from the clutch apply ring side.

2. Install seal protector tool J-29335. Lubricate the seals and install the overrun clutch piston. To make the piston easier to install, insert the piston installing tool between the seal and the

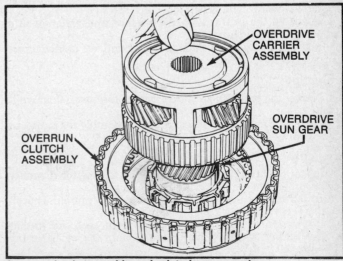

Overrun clutch assembly and related components (© General Motors Corp.)

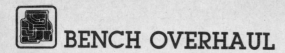
housing. Rotate the tool around the housing to compress the lip of the seal, while pushing down slightly on the piston. Remove tool J-29335.

3. Install the overrun clutch waved release spring. Install the overrun clutch waved spring retainer. Be sure that the cupped face is positioned downward.

4. Install the roller clutch cam on the roller clutch assembly. The locating tangs on the roller clutch must set on the roller clutch cam.

5. Install the roller clutch assembly on the overrun clutch hub. Install the narrow snap ring by pushing the roller clutch assembly down.

6. Lubricate and install the overrun clutch plates as they were removed, starting with a flat steel plate.

7. Install the backing plate, micro finish side down. Install the snap ring. Be sure that the composition plates turn freely.

8. Set the unit aside until you are ready to reassemble the transaxle.

OVERDRIVE CARRIER ASSEMBLY

Disassembly

1. Before disassembly, inspect the locating splines for damage, the roller clutch race for scratches or wear and the carrier housing for cracks and wear. Also, inspect the pinions for damage, rough bearings or tilt.

2. Check the pinion end play, it should be .009"-.024".

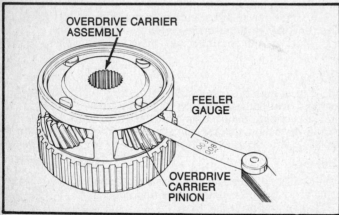

Overdrive carrier pinion end play check (© General Motors Corp.)

3. Remove the overdrive carrier snap ring. Using pliers, remove the overdrive pinion pins.

4. Remove the pinions, thrust washer and roller needle bearings.

5. Remove the overdrive sun gear to overdrive carrier thrust bearing assembly.

Inspection

1. Inspect the pinion pocket thrust faces for burrs. Remove if present.

2. Clean and inspect the thrust bearing assembly for pitting or rough conditions.

Assembly

1. Install the thrust bearing assembly by placing the diameter race down. Retain the part with petroleum jelly.

2. Install nineteen needle bearings into each pinion. Thumb lock the needle bearings to hold them in place.

3. Place a bronze and steel thrust washer on each side so that the steel washer is against the pinion. Retain the washer using petroleum jelly.

4. Place the pinion assembly in position inside the carrier. Use a pilot shaft to align the parts in place.

5. Push the on pin into place while rotating the pinion from the side.

6. Install the overdrive carrier snap ring in order to retain the pinion pins. Set the assembly aside until the transaxle is ready for assembly.

INTERMEDIATE SERVO PISTON

Disassembly

1. Once the intermediate servo assembly is out of the case, there is little to disassemble on the unit. It should be noted that there is an inner and an outer servo piston. These will separate by pulling them apart.

2. Be careful of the oil seal rings on the servo pistons, both inner and outer. They should not be removed unless they are to be replaced.

3. If the apply pin is to be removed, pry the snap ring from its groove and separate the apply pin from the retainer.

Inspection

1. Check the pin carefully for wear or damage, as well as the fit in the case bore. Do not remove the small oil seal rings from the apply pin unless they are to be replaced.

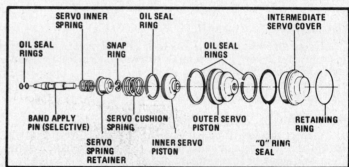

Intermediate servo—exploded view (© General Motors Corp.)

2. Inspect the inner and outer piston seal rings. These too should not be removed unless they are to be replaced.

3. Checking for proper pin application, since the pin is a selective fit, requires special tools that, in the case of the factory type units, only give relative readings. That is, dial indicator readings are valid only when used in conjunction with these special tools. However, in nearly all cases, the apply pin will not have to be changed unless the case itself is defective and needs to be replaced. In the course of a normal rebuild or seal job, the pin would not have to be replaced or even removed from the rest of the servo parts.

Assembly

1. If any of the oil seal rings have been removed, lubricate the replacement rings with Dexron® II or petroleum jelly. Make certain that the rings are fully seated in their grooves so that they will not be damaged on assembly.

2. Install the intermediate servo inner piston into the outer piston taking care to see that the seals are not torn or displaced as the inner servo goes into place.

3. Again using plenty of lubricant, replace the O-ring on the servo cover.

4. Assemble the apply pin retainer and the apply pin. Install the snap-ring to secure the assembly. Install this assembly into the servo inner piston along with the cushion spring. Set the unit aside until the transaxle is ready for assembly.

GOVERNOR

Disassembly

1. Remove the speedometer drive gear from the top of the

governor. There should be a thrust washer on the top of the drive gear to protect the assembly from the governor cover. This too should be removed.

2. Remove and discard the O-ring seal from the governor cover.

Inspection

1. Clean all parts in solvent and dry with compressed air.

2. Inspect the governor cover for wear or damage. Inspect the governor shaft seal ring for cuts or other signs of damage. If this seal is removed, it must be replaced.

3. Make sure that the two check balls are in place and that the weight springs are not mispositioned or damaged.

Assembly

1. If the shaft seal is to be replaced, it can be cut from the shaft. Be careful not to damage the groove. Lubricate the replacement seal with Dexron® II or petroleum jelly. Install the seal on the shaft and then carefully place the seal end of the shaft into the pilot hole in the case to size the seal to the shaft.

2. Install the speedometer drive gear onto the governor shaft on the weight end and make sure that the slot on the gear aligns with the pin in the shaft. Install the thrust washer on top of the drive gear.

3. Lubricate the replacement O-ring seal for the governor cover and install it into the groove in the cover. Set these parts aside until the transaxle is ready for assembly.

PRESSURE REGULATOR

Disassembly

1. The pressure regulator can be found in the transaxle case. It sits in a bore next to the hole for the oil pipe. With snap ring pliers, remove the internal snap ring.

2. Remove the pressure regulator bushing. Ordinary slip-joint pliers can be used to carefully graps the regulator bushing and pull it from the case.

3. Compress the regulator valve into the bushing and remove the inner roll pin. *Be careful* since the valve is under strong spring pressure. Release the valve slowly.

4. Remove the pressure regulator valve, the guide, and the spring from the bushing.

Inspection

1. Clean all parts well in solvent and blow dry with compressed air.

2. Check the fit of the pressure regulator valve in the bushing. It must move freely in the bore of the bushing.

3. Check the spring for distortion.

4. Examine the outer pin in the bushing for damage, such as being bent. This roll pin should not be removed unless it is to be replaced.

Assembly

1. With all parts clean and dry, begin by installing the spring and guide into the bushing.

2. Install the regulator valve into the bushing, stem end last. Retain with the roll pin.

3. If the outer roll pin has been removed, replace it with a new one. Set these parts aside until the transaxle is ready for reassembly.

VALVE BODY

Disassembly

NOTE: As each valve train is removed, place the individual valve train in the order that it is removed and in a separate location relative to its position in the valve body assembly. None of the valves, bushings or springs are interchangeable; some roll pins

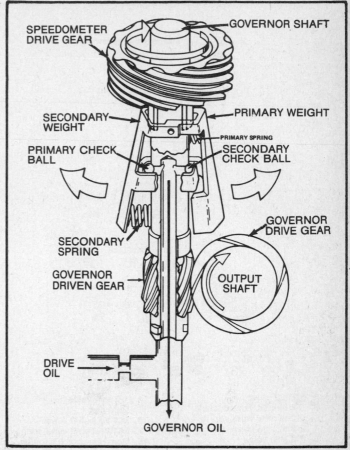

Governor assembly—cross section (© General Motors Corp.)

are interchangeable. Remove all the roll pins and spring retaining sleeves by pushing through from the rough case surface side of the control valve pump assembly, except for the blind hole pins.

1. Lay the control valve assembly machined face up, with the manual valve at the top.

2. If, the number one check ball is still in place remove it.

3. Some of the roll pins in the control valve assembly have pressure against them. Hold a towel over the bore while removing the pin to help prevent possibly losing a bore plug, spring, etc.

4. Remove the roll pin from the upper left bore. Remove the 2-3 throttle valve bushing, 2-3 throttle valve spring, 2-3 throttle valve and the 2-3 shift valve. The 2-3 throttle valve spring and 2-3 throttle valve may be inside the 2-3 throttle valve bushing.

5. From the next bore down, remove the spring retaining sleeve, valve bore plug, T.V. modulator downshift valve and the T.V. modulator downshift valve spring.

6. From the next bore down, remove the outer roll pin. Remove the 1-2 throttle valve bushing, 1-2 throttle valve spring, 1-2 throttle valve and the low 1st/detent valve: The 1-2 throttle valve spring and the 1-2 throttle valve may be inside the 1-2 throttle valve bushing. Remove the inner roll pin. Remove the low 1st/detent valve bushing and 1-2 shift valve.

7. From the next bore down, remove the spring retaining sleeve, valve bore plug, T.V. modulator upshift valve and the T.V. modulator upshift valve spring.

8. From the next bore down, remove the roll pin. Remove the converter clutch throttle bushing, converter clutch throttle valve spring, converter clutch throttle valve, and the converter clutch shift valve. The converter clutch throttle valve spring and the converter clutch throttle valve may be inside the converter clutch throttle bushing.

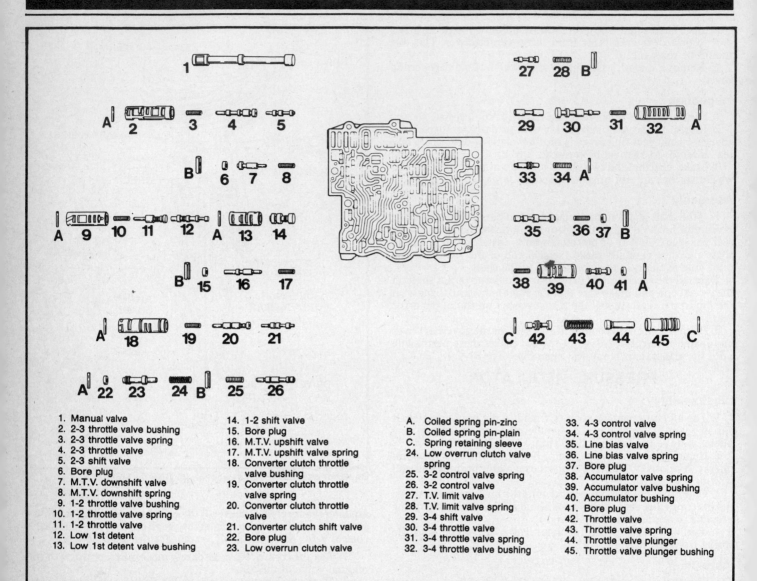

Valve body assembly—exploded view (© General Motors Corp.)

1.	Manual valve	14.	1-2 shift valve
2.	2-3 throttle valve bushing	15.	Bore plug
3.	2-3 throttle valve spring	16.	M.T.V. upshift valve
4.	2-3 throttle valve	17.	M.T.V. upshift valve spring
5.	2-3 shift valve	18.	Converter clutch throttle valve bushing
6.	Bore plug	19.	Converter clutch throttle valve spring
7.	M.T.V. downshift valve	20.	Converter clutch throttle valve
8.	M.T.V. downshift spring	21.	Converter clutch shift valve
9.	1-2 throttle valve bushing	22.	Bore plug
10.	1-2 throttle valve spring	23.	Low overrun clutch valve
11.	1-2 throttle valve		
12.	Low 1st detent		
13.	Low 1st detent valve bushing		

A.	Coiled spring pin-zinc	33.	4-3 control valve
B.	Coiled spring pin-plain	34.	4-3 control valve spring
C.	Spring retaining sleeve	35.	Line bias valve
24.	Low overrun clutch valve spring	36.	Line bias valve spring
25.	3-2 control valve spring	37.	Bore plug
26.	3-2 control valve	38.	Accumulator valve spring
27.	T.V. limit valve	39.	Accumulator valve bushing
28.	T.V. limit valve spring	40.	Accumulator bushing
29.	3-4 shift valve	41.	Bore plug
30.	3-4 throttle valve	42.	Throttle valve
31.	3-4 throttle valve spring	43.	Throttle valve spring
32.	3-4 throttle valve bushing	44.	Throttle valve plunger
		45.	Throttle valve plunger bushing

9. From the last bore down, remove the roll pin. Remove the bore plug, low/overrun clutch valve and the low/overrun clutch valve spring. From the same bore, remove the inner spring retaining sleeve. Remove the 3-2 control valve spring and valve.

10. From the upper right bore, remove the spring retaining sleeve. Remove the T.V. limit spring and valve.

11. From the next bore down, remove the roll pin. Remove the 3-4 throttle valve bushing, 3-4 throttle valve spring, 3-4 throttle valve and the 3-4 shift valve. The 3-4 throttle valve and spring may be inside the 3-4 throttle valve bushing.

12. From the next bore down, remove the roll pin. Remove the 4-3 control valve spring and 4-3 control valve.

13. From the next bore down remove the spring retaining sleeve, valve bore plug, line bias valve and the line bias valve spring.

14. From the next bore down, remove the roll pin and the bore plug. Remove the accumulator valve bushing, accumulator valve and the accumulator spring. The accumulator spring and accumulator valve may be inside the accumulator bushing.

15. From the last bore, remove the outer roll pin from the rough casting side, the throttle valve plunger bushing, throttle valve plunger and the throttle valve spring.

16. Remove the inner roll pin by grinding a taper to one end of

a #49 drill bit. Insert the tapered end into the roll pin. Pull the drill bit and the coil retaining pin out. Remove the throttle valve.

Inspection

1. Wash the control valve body, valves, springs, and other parts in clean solvent and air dry.

2. Inspect the valves for scoring, cracks and free movement in their bores.

3. Inspect the bushings for cracks or scored bores.

4. Inspect the valve body for cracks, damaged or scored bores.

5. Inspect the springs for distortion or collapsed coils.

6. Inspect the bore plugs for damage.

7. Install all of the flared coiled pins (zinc coated), flared end out, and from the machined face of the valve body assembly.

8. Install the two tapered coiled pins (black finish) that retain the throttle valve and throttle bushing, tapered end first.

9. The coiled pins do not fit flush on the rough casting face. Make sure that all of the coiled pins are flush against the machined face or damage to the transaxle will occur.

Assembly

1. Be sure that the control valve body is clean before starting the assembly procedure.

2. Install into the lower right bore, throttle valve, the smaller outside diameter land first, make sure the valve is seated at the bottom of the bore. Install the inner roll pin between the lands of this valve. Install the T.V. spring into the bore. Install the throttle valve plunger, stem end first, into the throttle valve plunger bushing. Install these two parts into the bore, valve end first. Install the outer roll pin from the rough cast surface side, aligning the pin with the slot in the bushing.

3. In the next bore up, install the accumulator bushing into the bore. Align the pin slot in line with the pin hole in the control valve assembly. Install the accumulator spring, then accumulator valve, the smaller end first. Next, install the bore plug, hole out, and roll pin.

4. In the next bore up, install the line bias valve spring, then install the line bias valve, smaller stem end first. Install the bore plug, the hole out, and the spring retaining sleeve.

5. In the next bore up, install the 4-3 control valve, the smaller end first, then the 4-3 control valve spring. Compress the spring and install the roll pin.

6. In the next bore up, install the 3-4 shift valve, chamfered end first. Install the 3-4 throttle valve spring into the 3-4 throttle valve bushing. Next, install the 3-4 throttle valve, the stem end first into the 3-4 bushing. Install the 3-4 throttle valve and bushing into the bore, making sure the pin slot is aligned with the pin hole in the control valve assembly. Install the roll pin.

7. In the last bore up, install the T.V. limit valve, the stem end first. Install the T.V. limit valve spring. Compress the T.V. limit valve spring and install the spring retaining sleeve from the machined face side. Make sure the sleeve is level with the machined surface.

8. In the lower left bore, install the 3-2 control valve, the smaller stem end out. Install the 3-2 control valve spring. Compress the spring and install the spring retaining sleeve. Be sure that the spring retaining sleeve does not damage the coiled spring. In the same bore install the low/overrun clutch valve spring and then the low/overrun clutch valve, the smaller end first. Next, install the bore plug, the hole out, and the roll pin.

9. In the next bore up, install the converter clutch shift valve, the short stemmed end first. Next, install the converter clutch throttle valve spring into the converter clutch throttle bushing and the converter clutch throttle valve, the stem end first, into the bushing. Install these three parts, the valve end first, into the bore, aligning the bushing so the pin can be installed in the pin slot. Install the roll pin.

10. In the next bore up, install the T.V. modulator upshift valve spring then install the T.V. modulator upshift valve, the smaller chamfered stem end first. Install the bore plug, the hole out and the spring retaining sleeve. Make sure the sleeve is level with or below the machined surface.

11. In the next bore up, install the 1-2 shift valve, the small stem outward. Install the 1-2 shift valve, the small stem outward. Install the 1-2 shift valve bushing, the small I.D. first, and align pin hole in bushing with the inner pin hole in the control valve assembly. Install the inner roll pin. Next, install the low 1st/detent valve, the long stem end out. Install the low 1st/detent valve, the long stem end out. Install the 1-2 throttle valve spring into the 1-2 throttle valve bushing and the 1-2 throttle valve, the stem end first, into the bushing. Install these three parts, the valve end first, into the bore, aligning the bushing so the outer pin can be installed in the pin slot. Install the outer roll pin.

12. In the next bore up, install the T.V. modulator downshift valve spring then install the T.V. modulator downshift valve, the smaller chamfered stem end first. Install the bore plug, the hole out, and the spring retaining sleeve. Make sure the sleeve is level with or below the machined surface.

13. In the next bore up, install the 2-3 shift valve, the large end first. Next, install the 2-3 throttle valve spring into the 2-3 throttle valve bushing, the 2-3 throttle valve stem end first, into the bushing. Install these three parts, the valve end first, into the bore,

aligning the bushing so the pin can be installed in the pin slot. Install the roll pin.

14. Install the manual valve with the inside detent lever rod slot first.

15. Set the control valve body aside, until ready to reassemble the transaxle.

Transaxle Assembly

1. Verify that the transaxle case has been thoroughly cleaned and that all bolt holes have been checked for damage or stripped threads. The vent should not be remove unless it is broken and must be replaced. It should be retained with Loctite®. Any cooler line connectors that may have been removed should have their threads coated with a good sealer. They should be torqued to 28 foot-pounds.

2. After it has been determined that all of the parking linkage is serviceable and that the manual linkage is not excessively worn, begin assembly by installing a new manual shift seal. Make sure that the lip of the seal faces inward toward the transaxle case.

3. Install the parking pawl and the return spring with the tooth of the pawl toward the center of the case and the spring under the tooth of the pawl. The ends of the spring should be toward the inside of the case, with the ends located in the slots in the case.

4. Install the parking pawl shaft with the tapered end going in first.

5. install the manual shaft and inside detent lever assembly making certain that the shaft fits into the flats in the hole in the detent lever. If the manual link (long thin rod) was disassembled from the detent lever, install the end back into the lever and retain with a new push nut.

6. Install the hex nut on the manual shaft and with a 15mm socket, torque to 23 foot-pounds.

7. Install the park lock cam onto the side of the manual shaft and with an 8mm socket, tighten to a torque of 8 foot-pounds.

8. Install the parking strut shaft (different from the parking pawl shaft) into the case while aligning the lock strut and lock lever. See that the lower strut arm is positioned between the lever tangs. Some units may have a washer that belongs between the parking lock lever and the case. Install the washer if so equipped. Finally, install the retaining ring.

9. Install the parking lock spring.

10. Using a piece of ⅜" rod for a driver, install a new parking strut shaft cup plug with the open end out. Drive the cup in until it is flush with the face of the case.

11. Install the manual lever detent roller and spring assembly. With a 10mm socket torque the retaining bolt to 11 foot-pounds. Check the operation of the park lock by working the linkage by hand.

12. The output shaft should be inspected for plugged lubrication passages and the splines checked for damage. Some early production output shafts were made with a snap ring while others have a shoulder against which the governor drive gear rests. If the output shaft has a shoulder, *do not* try to use a snap ring on this shaft. Install the reaction internal gear on the output shaft hub end first.

13. Install the reaction internal gear-to-reaction sun gear thrust bearing on the output shaft with the small diameter race first. This will place the inside diameter of the race toward the carrier assembly.

14. The roller clutch should have been installed at this point, into the reaction planetary carrier, and the thrust washers should be in place. Install the roller clutch and reaction carrier assembly into the reaction internal gear.

15 A special fitting is normally used to align the output shaft and aid in the installation of the reaction unit parts. The purpose of this assembly tool is also to help adjust the height of the reaction internal gear parking pawl lugs to align flush with the top of the parking pawl tooth. The main point is to make sure the parking pawl lugs align with the top of the pawl tool and to hold the

assembly in this relationship while the transaxle is being assembled. Sight through the parking pawl slot to line things up. With the reaction unit installed and aligned properly, the low and reverse clutch components are installed next.

16. The low and reverse clutch plates should be well-oiled with Dextron® II before use. It is normally recommended that clutch plates be soaked for at least 20 minutes before assembly. Install this clutch pack by starting with a flat steel plate and then alternate with the composition plates. Install the low and reverse clutch housing-to-case spacer into the transaxle case. The low and reverse clutch housing and piston should already be overhauled at this point, and it should be installed in the case aligning the feed hole to the clutch and the case passage. A large spring-loaded plier-like tool is used to lower the low and reverse clutch housing since it would be difficult to handle the clutch housing. Make sure that the clutch housing is seated past the case snap ring groove. If the clutch housing does not seat past the snap ring groove, take the reaction sun gear and input drum assembly, and using them as a tool, install them into the transaxle case. Rotate the reaction sun gear and drum back and forth tapping lightly to align the roller clutch race and the low and reverse clutch hub splines. Remove the sun gear and drum and check to see if the low and reverse clutch housing is now seated below the snap ring groove. If not, repeat the above process. Install the housing-to-case snap ring with the flat side against the housing which puts the ring's beveled side up.

17. Check to make sure that the four-tanged thrust washer is properly installed on the input drum. Petroleum jelly will help hold it in place. Install the reaction gear and input drum assembly.

18. Install the input sun gear with the identification mark on the gear against the input drum. These identification marks could be either a groove or a drill spot depending on the gear.

19. Lubricate and install the input sun gear-to-front carrier thrust bearing and race assembly. Install it so that the needle bearings are against the input sun gear.

20. Install the input carrier-to-input internal gear thrust bearing assembly on the input carrier. Make sure that the inside diameter race goes against the gear. Use plenty of petroleum jelly to hold it in place. Install the input carrier assembly onto the input sun gear.

21. Install the reaction selective washer and thrust washer on the input internal gear and use petroleum jelly to hold them in place. The selective washer must be installed with the identification number facing the snap-ring side.

22. Install the input internal gear.

23. Install the snap ring on the output shaft, making certain that it is fully seated in the groove. When completed, the output end-play can be checked with a dial indicator. End-play should be from .004″ to .025″.

24. Install the output shaft-to-input shaft selective thrust washer, indexing it into the output shaft with plenty of petroleum jelly to hold it in place.

25. Install the intermediate band into the case making sure that the anchor pin lug on the band as well as the apply lug is properly located in the case slot.

26. Position the direct clutch assembly with the clutch plate end up, over a hole in the workbench. Align the composition clutch plates so that the teeth in the plates are lined up with one another. This will make installation of the forward clutch easier. Install the forward clutch assembly with the input end first into the direct clutch. It may be helpful to hold the direct clutch housing and rotate the forward clutch until it is seated. As a check to make sure that the forward clutch is fully seated, it will be approximately ⅝″ from the tang end of the direct clutch housing to the end of the forward clutch drum. Grasp the direct and forward clutch assemblies together so that they will not separate and turn them so that the input shaft is facing up. Install these assemblies into the transaxle case, turning them as necessary to get them to seat. As a check to make sure that the clutches are fully seated, it will be approximately ⁷⁄₁₆″ from the case cover face to the direct clutch housing when the clutches are fully installed, and correctly seated.

27. Install a new case cover gasket and carefully lay the case cover on the transaxle. Install the retaining bolts and with a 13mm socket, snug down the bolts. Make sure the bolts are in their proper locations. While the bolts are being tightened, rotate the input shaft. If the shaft cannot be rotated, then the forward or direct clutch housings have not been installed properly and the clutch plates are not indexed. At this point, the condition must be corrected before the case cover can be fully installed.

28. Install the overhauled oil pump next with plenty of lubricant on the outer O-ring. It will be helpful to make two guide pins. These particular screws are not metric, but a standard ⁵⁄₁₆-18 thread. The guide pins should be about 4 inches long. First install the two guide pins in the pump attaching screw holes. Then install the pump spacer plate onto the oil pump face, taking care to align it properly. Align the guide pins with matching holes in the case cover and insert the flat-head screws into the open holes in the pump body. Tighten the flat-head screws, remove the guide pins and put in the last two screws. Tighten all of the screws to 18 foot-pounds.

29. Place the drive link chain around the drive and driven sprockets so that the links engage the teeth of the sprockets. Look for one of the links to be of a different color and to have etched numbers on it. This side should face the sprocket cover. Place the drive link chain and sprockets in position on the sprocket supports at the same time. A plastic mallet will probably be needed to gently seat the sprocket bearings into the sprocket supports.

30. Reach through the access holes in the sprockets with a pair of snap ring pliers and install the snap rings. Make sure that they are seated in their grooves.

31. Install a new sprocket cover gasket and then install the cover. The attaching bolts are torqued to 8 foot-pounds.

32. Install the overdrive carrier assembly and the overrun clutch unit.

33. Install the governor assembly into the transaxle case. Lubricate the O-ring and install the cover. Torque the retaining bolts to 8 ft. lbs. Install the speedometer driven gear assembly, retainer clip and bolt.

34. Install the intermediate servo piston assembly. Take care when the rings enter the transaxle case so that they will not be torn or damaged. The servo cover ring must also be well lubricated to prevent damage or cutting of the ring. A plastic hammer may be needed to gently tap the assembly into the case. Be sure that the tapered end of the apply pin is properly located against the band apply lug. Depress the cover and install the retaining ring. Align the ring gap of the ring with the slot in the case to aid future removal.

35. Position the transaxle with the oil pan side up. Install a new low and reverse clutch housing-to-case cup plug. The rubber end goes in first, into the hole in the case. A ⅜″ diameter rod can be used as a driver. Tap gently with a plastic mallet on the rod until the plug seats against the low and reverse clutch housing.

36. Install the 1-2 accumulator spring into the transaxle case.

37. Install the #5 and the #6 check balls into their proper locations in the case. Two guide pins should be made up to aid with the installation of the control valve body. These guide pins should be made from metric bolts, 6mm in diameter and several inches in length. Install the remaining four check balls in their proper locations in the valve body. Since the valve body will be inverted to install it, use some petroleum jelly to hold them in place.

38. Place the valve body-to-spacer plate gasket in place on the valve body. The two gaskets that are used in valve body assembly are usually very similar. They are often marked to help prevent confusion. Look for a "VB" either printed or stamped into the gasket. Install the spacer plate on top of this gasket. Place the spacer plate-to-case gasket on spacer plate. This gasket should be marked with a "CB".

39. Install two of the valve body attaching screws through the assembly. Carefully grasp the entire assembly and invert, and install on the case. Be very careful to hold all these parts together so that the check balls and the accumulator parts do not fall out of place. Also, hold one finger on the manual valve so that it will not fall from the valve body. Take note that two of the valve body bolts are ⅜" longer than the rest and must not be interchanged. Start the valve body bolts into the case with the exception of the throttle lever and bracket assembly and the oil screen retainer bolts. Remove the guide pins and replace with bolts.

40. Install the link onto the manual valve and install the valve clip.

41. Install the throttle lever and bracket assembly, making sure to locate the slot in the bracket with the roll pin, and aligning the lifter through the valve body opening and the link through the T.V. linkage case bore. Install the retaining bolt. Carefully torque all the control valve assembly bolts to 11 foot-pounds.

42. The pressure regulator can be installed next. Its bore is next to the opening for the oil suction pipe. Install the assembly into the case, and carefully fit the snap ring into the groove.

43. The oil screen should have been carefully and thoroughly cleaned in solvent and blown dry with compressed air. A new O-ring seal should be installed on the intake pipe. Lubricate this ring well with petroleum jelly, and install the screen assembly.

44. The oil pan should also have been cleaned well and all traces of debris removed. Check the pan for straightness and make sure that none of the bolt holes have been dished in from over-torque. A block of wood and a rubber mallet can be used to straighten the gasket flanges on the pan. Install the pan with a new gasket. The oil pan bolts are to be tightened to 12 foot-pounds of torque.

NOTE: One particular point to watch when installing the oil pan is a possible interference between the oil pan and the sprocket cover, resulting in oil leaks. Due to this interference, the pan will not seat tightly against the gasket and leaks will result. The interference is caused by the outside diameter of the washer head bolts squeezing the outer pan flange against the sprocket cover. A second design bolt with a smaller washer head has been used in later models. The smaller washer head will prevent this interference. The part number for the new bolt is GM #11502670.

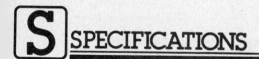

SPECIFICATIONS

OVERDRIVE UNIT END PLAY
SELECTIVE WASHER CHART

Identification Number	Color	Thickness (inches)
One	Gray	.063-.067
Two	Dark Green	.070-.074
Three	Pink	.077-.081
Four	Brown	.084-.088
Five	Light Blue	.091-.095
Six	White	.098-.102
Seven	Yellow	.105-.109
Eight	Light Green	.112-.116
Nine	Orange	.119-.123
Ten	Violet	.126-.130
Eleven	Red	.133-.137
Twelve	Dark Blue	.140-.144

INPUT UNIT END PLAY
SELECTIVE WASHER CHART

Identification Number	Color	Thickness (inches)
One	—	.065-.070
Two	—	.070-.075
Three	Black	.076-.080
Four	Light Green	.081-.085
Five	Scarlet	.086-.090
Six	Purple	.091-.095
Seven	Cocoa Brown	.096-.100
Eight	Orange	.101-.206
Nine	Yellow	.106-.111
Ten	Light Blue	.111-.116
Eleven	—	.117-.121
Twelve	—	.122-.126
Thirteen	Pink	.127-.131
Fourteen	Green	.132-.136
Fifteen	Gray	.137-.141

REACTION UNIT END PLAY
SELECTIVE WASHER CHART

Identification Number	Color	Thickness (inches)
One	Orange	.114-.119
Two	White	.021-.126
Three	Yellow	.128-.133
Four	Blue	.135-.140
Five	Red	.143-.147
Six	Brown	.150-.154
Seven	Green	.157-.161
Eight	Black	.164-.168
Nine	Purple	.171-.175

FORWARD CLUTCH PLATE AND APPLY
RING USAGE CHART

	Wave Plate	Flat Steel Plate	Composition Faced Plate	Apply Ring
Number	One	Three	Four	—
Thickness	.062 Inch	.077 Inch	—	—
Identification	—	—	—	Eight
Width	—	—	—	.492 Inch

S SPECIFICATIONS

DIRECT CLUTCH PLATE AND APPLY RING USAGE CHART

	Flat Steel Plate	Composition Faced Plate	Apply Ring
Number	Six	Six	—
Thickness	.91 Inch	—	—
Identification	—	—	Nine
Width	—	—	.492 Inch

LOW AND REVERSE CLUTCH PLATE AND APPLY RING USAGE CHART

	Wave Plate	Flat Steel Plate	Composition Faced Plate	Apply Ring
Number	One	Seven	Six	—
Thickness	.077 Inch	.077 Inch	—	—
Identification	—	—	—	Zero
Width	—	—	—	.516 Inch

TORQUE SPECIFICATIONS

Description of Usage	Torque
Valve Body Assembly to Case	9-12 ft.-lbs.
Accumulator Housing to Case	9-12 ft.-lbs.
Manual Detent Spring Assembly to Case	9-12 ft.-lbs.
Governor Cover to Case	6-10 ft.-lbs.
Sprocket Cover to Case	9 ft.-lbs.
Case Cover to Pump Body (Flat Head)	15-20 ft.-lbs.
Driven Support to Case Cover	15-20 ft.-lbs.
Case Cover to Case	15-20 ft.-lbs.
Fourth Clutch Housing to Case	15-20 ft.-lbs.
Oil Pan to Case	7-10 ft.-lbs.
Cam to Manual Shaft	6-9 ft.-lbs.
Manual Shaft to Inside Detent Lever (Nut)	20-25 ft.-lbs.
Cooler Connector	26-30 ft.-lbs.
Line Pressure Take-Off	5-10 ft.-lbs.
Third Accumulator Take-Off	5-10 ft.-lbs.
Governor Pressure Take-Off	5-10 ft.-lbs.
Fourth Pressure Take-Off	5-10 ft.-lbs.
Pressure Switch	5-10 ft.-lbs.

SPECIAL TOOLS

Tool	Number	Description
	J 21369-B	Converter Leak Test Fixture
	J 21465-17	Pump Bushing Remover and Installer
	J 21465-3	Drive Sprocket Support Bushing Installer
	J 21465-15	Drive Sprocket Support Bushing Remover
	J 23327	Direct & Forward Clutch Spring Compressor
	J 23456	Clutch Pack Compressor
	J 26744	Clutch Seal Installer
	J 26900-9	Thickness Gauge Set
	J 26900-27	Flexible Steel Scale (150mm)
	J 26958	Output Shaft Alignment and Loading Tool
	J 28492	Holding Fixture
	J 28493	Servo Cover Depressor

	J 25010	**Direct Clutch Seal Protector**
	J 25011	**Reverse Clutch Seal Protector**
	J 25014	**Intermediate Band Apply Pin Gauge**
	J 25018-A	**Adapter Forward Clutch Spring Compressor**
	J 25019	**Bushing Service Set**
	J 25025-A	**Pump and Valve Guide Pin and Indicator Stand Set**
	J 25359-5 #40	**Drive Bit**
	J 28494	**Input Shaft Lifter**
	J 28542	**Low & Reverse Clutch Housing Installer & Remover**
	J 28585	**Snap Ring Remover and Installer**
	J 28667	**Dial Indicator Extension**
	J 29060	**Converter End Play Checking Fixture**
	J 29334-1	**Fourth Clutch Spring Compressor**
	J 29846	**Turbine Shaft Seal Installer**

INDEX

GENERAL MOTORS TURBO HYDRA-MATIC 440 T4 Automatic Transaxle

APPLICATIONS

1984½ General Motors "C" Cars

GENERAL DESCRIPTION

Transmission and Converter Identification

TRANSMISSION

The THM 440-T4 (ME9) automatic transaxle is a fully automatic unit, consisting of four multiple disc clutches, a roller clutch, a sprag and two bands, requiring hydraulic and mechanical applications to obtain the desired gear ratios from the compound planetary gears. The transaxle identification can be located on one of three areas of the unit. An identification plate on the side of the case, a stamped number on the governor housing or an ink stamp on the bell housing.

CONVERTER

Two types of converters are used in the varied vehicle applications. The first type is the three element torque converter combined with a lock-up converter clutch. The second type is the three element torque converter combined with a viscous lock-up converter clutch that has silicone fluid sealed between the cover and the body of the clutch assembly. Identification of the torque converters are either ink stamp marks or a stamped number on the shell of the converter.

Metric Fasteners

The metric fastener dimensions are very close to the dimensions of the familiar inch system fasteners, and for this reason, replacement fasteners must have the same measurement and strength as those removed.

Do not attempt to inter-change metric fasteners for inch system fasteners. Mismatched or incorrect fasteners can result in damage to the transmission unit through malfunctions, breakage or possible personal injury.

Care should be taken to re-use the fasteners in the same locations as removed.

Capacities

Fluid Checking Procedure

1. Verify that the transmission is at normal operating temperature. At this temperature, the end of the dipstick will be too hot to hold in the hand. Make sure that the vehicle is level.
2. With the selector in Park, allow the engine to idle. *Do not race engine.* Move the selector through each range and back to Park.
3. Immediately check the fluid level, engine still running. Fluid level on the dipstick should be at the "FULL HOT" mark.
4. If the fluid level is low, add fluid as required, remembering that only one pint will bring the fluid level from "ADD" to "FULL".

Often it is necessary to check the fluid level when there is no time or opportunity to run the vehicle to warm the fluid to operating temperature. In this case, the fluid should be around room temperature (70°). The following steps can be used:

1. Place the selector in Park and start engine. *Do not race engine.* Move the selector through each range and back to Park.
2. Immediately check the fluid level, engine still running, off fast idle. Fluid level should be between the two dimples on the dipstick, approximately ¼ in. *below* the "ADD" mark on the dipstick.
3. If the fluid level is low, add fluid as required, to bring the fluid level to between the two dimples on the dipstick. *Do not overfill.* The reason for maintaining the low fluid level at room tem-

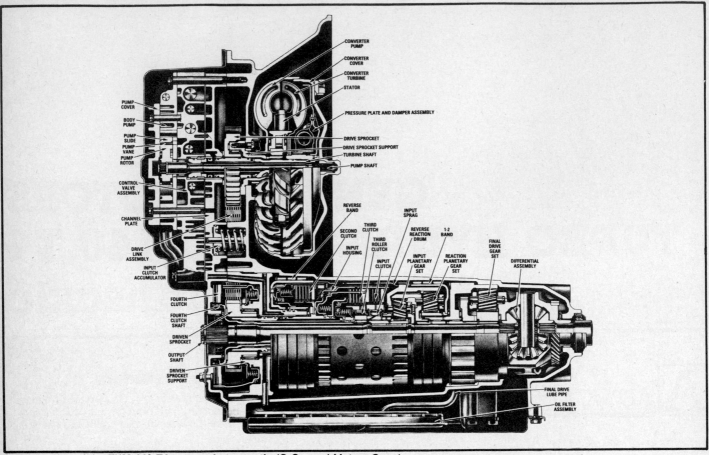

Cross section of the THM 440-T4 automatic transaxle (© General Motors Corp.)

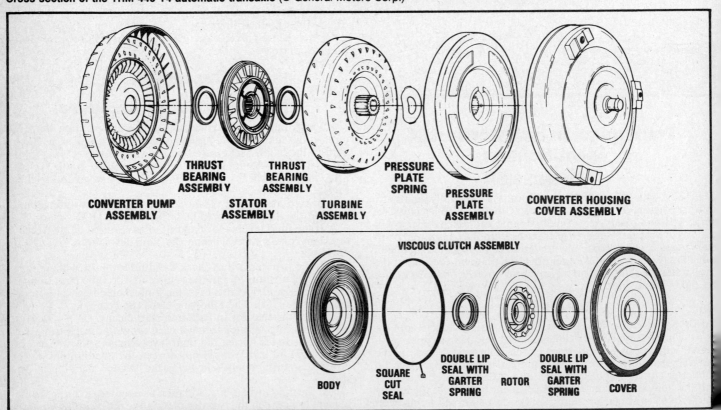

Two types of converters used with the THM 440-T4 transaxle (© General Motors Corp.)

perature is that the transmission fluid level will rise as the unit heats up. If too much fluid is added when cold, then the fluid will rise to the point where it will be forced out of the vent and overheating can occur.

If the fluid level is *correctly* established at 70°F as outlined above, it will appear at the "FULL" mark when the transmission reaches operating temperature.

When checking the fluid level it is a good idea to notice the condition of the fluid. If there is a burnt smell, or if there are metal particles on the end of the dipstick, these signs can help in diagnosing transmission problems. A milky appearance is a sign of water contamination, possibly from a damaged cooling system. Note if there are any air bubbles on the end of the dipstick. Oil with air bubbles indicates that there is an air leak in the suction lines which can cause erratic operation and slippage. All of these signs can help in determining transmission problems and their source.

FLUID SPECIFICATIONS

Dexron® II automatic transmission fluid or its equivalent is the only recommended automatic transmission fluid to be used in this unit. Make certain that only good quality, clean fluid is used when servicing this transmission. The use of any other grade of fluid can lead to unsatisfactory performance or complete unit failure.

MODIFICATIONS

Modification publications not available at time of printing.

TROUBLE DIAGNOSIS

CLUTCH AND BAND APPLICATION CHART
THM 440-T4 Automatic Transaxle

Range		4th Clutch	Reverse Band	2nd Clutch	3rd Clutch	3rd Roller Clutch	Input Sprag	Input Clutch	1-2 Band
NEUTRAL PARK							①	①	
DRIVE	1						HOLD	ON	ON
	2			ON			OVER-RUNNING	①	ON
	3			ON	ON	HOLD			
	4	ON		ON	①	OVER-RUNNING			
MANUAL	3			ON	ON	HOLD	HOLD	ON	
	2			ON			OVER-RUNNING	①	ON
	1			ON		HOLD	HOLD	ON	ON
REVERSE		ON					HOLD	ON	

①APPLIED BUT NOT EFFECTIVE

CHILTON'S THREE "C's" DIAGNOSIS CHART
THM 440-T4 Automatic Transaxle

Condition	Cause	Correction
Oil Leakage	a) Side cover, bottom pan and gaskets, loose bolts	a) Repair or replace cover, gasket and torque bolts
	b) Damaged seal at T.V. cable, fill tube or electrical connector	b) Replace seal as required
	c) Damaged seal assembly on manual shaft	c) Replace seal assembly as required

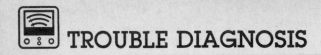

CHILTON'S THREE "C's" DIAGNOSIS CHART
THM 440-T4 Automatic Transaxle

Condition	Cause	Correction
Oil Leakage	d) Leakage at governor cover, servo covers, modulator, parking plunger guide, speedometer driven gear sleeve	d) Replace damaged "O" ring seals as required
	e) Converter or converter seal leaking	e) Replace converter and seal as required
	f) Axle seals leaking	f) Remove axles and replace seals as required
	g) Pressure ports or cooler line fittings leaking	g) Tighten or repair stripped threads
Fluid foaming or blowing out the vent	a) Fluid level high	a) Correct fluid level
	b) Fluid foaming due to contaminates or over-heating of fluid	b) Determine cause of contamination or overheating and repair
	c) Drive sprocket support has plugged drain back holes	c) Open drain back holes in sprocket support
	d) Thermo element not closing when hot	d) Replace thermo element
	e) Fluid filter "O" ring damaged	e) Replace fluid filter "O" ring
High or low fluid pressure, verified by pressure gauge	a) Fluid level high or low	a) Correct fluid level as required
	b) Vacuum modulator or hose leaking	b) Repair or replace hose or modulator
	c) Modulator valve, pressure regulator valve, pressure relief valve nicked, scored or damaged. Spring or ball checks missing or damaged	c) Repair or replace necessary components
	d) Oil pump or components damaged, parts missing	d) Repair or replace oil pump assembly
No drive in DRIVE range	a) Fluid level low	a) Correct fluid level
	b) Fluid pressure low	b) Refer to low fluid pressure causes
	c) Manual linkage mis-adjusted or disconnected	c) Repair or adjust manual linkage
	d) Torque converter loose on flex plate or internal con-verter damage	d) Verify malfunction and repair as required
	e) Oil pump or drive shaft damaged	e) Repair or replace oil pump and/or drive shaft
	f) Number 13 check ball mis-assembled or missing	f) Correct or install number 13 check ball in its proper location
	g) Damaged drive link chain, sprocket or bearings	g) Replace damaged components
	h) Burned or missing clutch plates, damaged piston seals or piston, Housing check ball damaged, input shaft seals or feed passages blocked or damaged	h) Repair and/or replace damaged input clutch assembly components

CHILTON'S THREE "C's" DIAGNOSIS CHART
THM 440-T4 Automatic Transaxle

Condition	Cause	Correction
No drive in DRIVE range	i) Input sprag and/or input sun gear assembly improperly assembled or sprag damaged	i) Correctly assemble or replace input sprag and input sun gear assembly
	j) Pinions, sun gear or internal gears damaged on input and reaction carrier assemblies	j) Repair or replace carrier assemblies as required
	k) 1-2 band or servo burned or damaged. Band apply pin incorrect in length	k) Repair or replace band and/or servo components as required
	l) 1-2 servo oil pipes leaking fluid	l) Correct oil tubes to prevent leakage
	m) Final drive assembly broken or damaged	m) Repair or replace necessary components of final drive
	n) Parking pawl spring broken	n) Replace parking pawl spring
	o) Output shaft damage, broken or misassembled	o) Repair, replace or re-assemble output shaft
First speed only, no 1-2 shift	a) Governor assembly defective	a) Repair or replace governor
	b) Number 14 check ball missing	b) Install number 14 check ball
	c) 1-2 shift valve sticking or binding	c) Repair or clean valve and bore
	d) Accumulator and/or pipes	d) Repair/renew components
	e) 2nd clutch assembly damaged	e) Repair/renew components
	f) Oil seal rings damaged on driven sprocket support	f) Replace oil seal rings
	g) Splines damaged or parts missing from reverse reaction drum	g) Repair or replace damaged components
Harsh or soft 1-2 shift	a) Fluid pressure	a) Check pressure and correct
	b) Defective accumulator assembly	b) Repair or replace accumulator assembly
	c) Accumulator valve stuck	c) Repair or clean valve and bore
	d) Missing or mislocated number 8 check ball	d) Install or re-locate number 8 check ball
High or low 1-2 shift speed	a) Disconnected or misadjusted T.V. cable	a) Connect and/or adjust T.V. cable
	b) Bent or damaged T.V. link, lever and bracket assembly	b) Repair or replace damaged components
	c) Stuck or binding T.V. valve and plunger	c) Correct binding condition or remove stuck valve and plunger
	d) Incorrect governor pressure	d) Correct governor pressure
No 2-3 upshift, 1st and 2nd speeds only	a) Defective 1-2 servo or components	a) Repair or replace 1-2 servo assembly
	b) Defective number 7 check ball and capsule assembly	b) Check, repair or replace check ball and capsule
	c) Number 11 check ball not seating	c) Check, repair or replace check ball
	d) 2-3 shift valve stuck in control valve assembly	d) Remove stuck 1-2 shift valve and repair
	e) Seals damaged or blocked passages on input shaft	e) Replace seals and open passages
	f) Defective third clutch assembly	f) Overhaul third clutch assembly

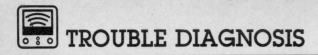

CHILTON'S THREE "C's" DIAGNOSIS CHART
THM 440-T4 Automatic Transaxle

Condition	Cause	Correction
No 2-3 upshift, 1st and 2nd speeds only	g) Defective third roller clutch assembly h) Numbers 5, 6 and/or accumulator valve stuck	g) Inspect, repair or replace necessary components h) Repair as required
Harsh or soft 2-3 shift	a) Fluid pressure b) Mislocated number 12 check ball	a) Test and correct fluid pressure b) Correct check ball location
High or low 2-3 shift speed	a) Disconnected or misadjusted T.V. cable b) Bent or damaged T.V. link, lever and bracket assembly c) Stuck or binding T.V. valve and plunger d) Incorrect governor pressure	a) Connect and/or adjust T.V. cable b) Repair or replace damaged components c) Correct binding condition or remove stuck valve and plunger d) Correct governor pressure
No 3-4 shift	a) Incorrect governor pressure b) 3-4 shift valve stuck in control valve assembly c) Defective 4th clutch assembly d) Spline damage to 4th clutch shaft	a) Correct governor pressure b) Free 3-4 shift valve and repair control valve assembly c) Overhaul 4th clutch assembly d) Replace 4th clutch shaft
Harsh or soft 3-4 shift	a) Fluid pressure b) Defective accumulator assembly c) Mislocated number 1 check ball	a) Test and correct fluid pressure b) Repair or replace accumulator assembly c) Correct check ball location
High or low 3-4 shift	a) Disconnected or misadjusted T.V. cable b) Bent or damaged T.V. link, lever and bracket assembly c) Stuck or binding T.V. valve and plunger d) Incorrect governor pressure	a) Connect and/or adjust T.V. cable b) Repair or replace damaged components c) Correct binding condition or remove stuck valve and plunger d) Correct governor pressure
No converter clutch apply (Vehicles equipped with E.C.M.)	a) Improper E.C.M. operation b) Electrical system of transaxle malfunctioning c) Converter clutch apply valve stuck d) Number 10 check ball missing e) Converter clutch blow-off check ball not seating or damaged f) Seals damaged on turbine shaft g) Damaged seal on oil pump drive shaft	a) Verify proper E.C.M. operation b) Test and correct electrical malfunction c) Free converter clutch apply valve and repair d) Install missing check ball e) Inspect channel plate and check ball. Repair as required f) Replace seals and inspect shaft g) Replace seal on oil pump drive shaft
No converter clutch apply (vehicles not equipped with E.C.M.)	a) Electrical system of transaxle malfunctioning b) Converter clutch shift and/or apply valves stuck c) Number 10 check ball missing	a) Test and correct electrical malfunction b) Free converter clutch shift and/or apply valves c) Install missing check ball

CHILTON'S THREE "C's" DIAGNOSIS CHART
THM 440-T4 Automatic Transaxle

Condition	Cause	Correction
No converter clutch apply (vehicles not equipped with E.C.M.)	d) Converter clutch blow-off check ball not seated or damaged	d) Inspect channel plate and check ball. Repair as required
	e) Seals damaged on turbine shaft	e) Replace seals and inspect shaft
	f) Damaged oil seal on seal pump drive shaft	f) Replace seal on oil pump drive shaft
Converter clutch does not release	a) Converter clutch apply valve stuck in the apply position	a) Free apply valve for converter clutch and repair as required
Rough converter clutch apply	a) Converter clutch regulator valve stuck	a) Free converter clutch regulator valve and repair as required
	b) Converter clutch accumulator piston or seal damaged	b) Replace seal or piston as required Check accumulator spring
	c) Seals damaged on turbine shaft	c) Replace seals on turbine shaft
Harsh 4-3 downshift	a) Number 1 check ball missing in control valve assembly	a) Install number 1 check ball in control valve assembly
Harsh 3-2 downshift	a) 1-2 servo control valve stuck	a) Free 1-2 servo control valve
	b) Number 12 check ball missing	b) Install number 12 check ball
	c) 3-2 control valve stuck	c) Free 3-2 control valve
	d) Number 4 check ball missing	d) Install number 4 check ball
	e) 3-2 coast valve stuck	e) Free 3-2 coast valve
	f) Input clutch accumulator piston or seal damaged	f) Replace input clutch accumulator piston and/or seal
Harsh 2-1 downshift	a) Number 8 check ball missing	a) Install number 8 check ball
No reverse	a) Fluid pressure	a) Test and correct fluid pressure
	b) Defective oil pump	b) Test and correct oil pump malfunction
	c) Broken, stripped or defective drive link assembly	c) Repair, replace as required
	d) Reverse band burned or damaged	d) Replace rear band as required
	e) Defective input clutch	e) Repair, replace defective input clutch components
	f) Defective input sprag	f) Replace defective sprag
	g) Piston or seal damaged, pin selection incorrect for rear servo assembly	g) Repair rear servo as required and install correct pin if needed
	h) Defective input and reaction carriers	h) Replace input and reaction carriers as required
No park range	a) Parking pawl, spring or parking gear damaged	a) Repair as required
	b) Manual linkage broken or out of adjustment	b) Repair linkage or adjust as required
Harsh shift from Neutral to Drive or from Neutral to Reverse	a) Number 9 check ball missing	a) Install number 9 check ball
	b) Number 12 check ball missing	b) Install number 12 check ball
	c) Thermal elements not closing when warm	c) Replace thermal elements
No viscous clutch apply (Vehicles with E.C.M.)	a) Improper E.C.M. operation	a) Verify E.C.M. operation and repair as required
	b) Damaged thermister	b) Replace thermister
	c) Damaged temperature switch	c) Replace temperature switch

PRELIMINARY CHECK PROCEDURE

CHECK TRANSMISSION OIL LEVEL
CHECK AND ADJUST T.V. CABLE
CHECK OUTSIDE MANUAL LINKAGE AND CORRECT
CHECK ENGINE TUNE
INSTALL OIL PRESSURE GAGE*
CONNECT TACHOMETER TO ENGINE

CHECK OIL PRESSURES IN THE FOLLOWING MANNER:

Minimum T.V. Line Pressure Check
Set the T.V. cable to specification; and with the brakes applied, take the line pressure readings in the ranges and at the engine r.p.m.'s indicated in the chart below.

Full T.V. Line Pressure Check
Full T.V. line pressure readings are obtained by tying or holding the T.V. cable to the full extent of its travel; and with the brakes applied, take the line pressure readings in the ranges and at the engine r.p.m.'s indicated in the chart below.

NOTICE	Total running time for this combination not to exceed 2 minutes.
CAUTION	Brakes must be applied at all times.

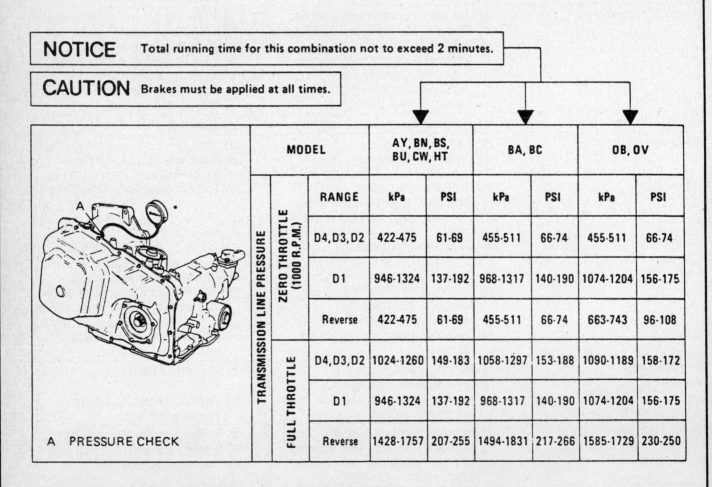

		MODEL	AY, BN, BS, BU, CW, HT		BA, BC		OB, OV	
		RANGE	kPa	PSI	kPa	PSI	kPa	PSI
TRANSMISSION LINE PRESSURE	ZERO THROTTLE (1000 R.P.M.)	D4, D3, D2	422-475	61-69	455-511	66-74	455-511	66-74
		D1	946-1324	137-192	968-1317	140-190	1074-1204	156-175
		Reverse	422-475	61-69	455-511	66-74	663-743	96-108
	FULL THROTTLE	D4, D3, D2	1024-1260	149-183	1058-1297	153-188	1090-1189	158-172
		D1	946-1324	137-192	968-1317	140-190	1074-1204	156-175
		Reverse	1428-1757	207-255	1494-1831	217-266	1585-1729	230-250

A   PRESSURE CHECK

Line pressure is basically controlled by pump output and the pressure regulator valve. In addition, line pressure is boosted in Reverse, Intermediate and Lo by the reverse boost valve.

Also, in the Neutral, Drive and Reverse positions of the selector lever, the line pressure should increase with throttle opening because of the T.V. system. The T.V. system is controlled by the T.V. cable, the throttle lever and bracket assembly and the T.V. link, as well as the control valve pump assembly.

Operation Principles

The torque converter smoothly couples the engine to the planetary gears and the overdrive unit through fluid and hydraulically/mechanically provides additional torque multiplication when required. The combination of the compound planetary gear set provides four forward gear ratios and one reverse. The changing of the gear ratios is fully automatic in relation to the vehicle speed and engine torque. Signals of vehicle speed and engine torque are constantly being directed to the transaxle control valve assembly to provide the proper gear ratio for maximum engine efficiency and performance at all throttle openings.

Quadrant Positions

The quadrant has seven positions indicated in the following order: P, R, N, Ⓓ, D, 2, 1.

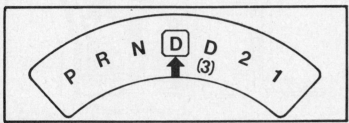

Quadrant for shift selector (© General Motors Corp.)

P—Park position enables the transaxle output shaft to be held, thus preventing the vehicle from rolling either forward or backward. (For safety reasons, the vehicle parking brake should be used in addition to the transaxle "Park" position). Because the output shaft is mechanically locked, the park position should not be selected until the vehicle has come to a stop. The engine may be started in the Park position.

R—Reverse enables the vehicle to be operated in a rearward direction.

N—Neutral position enables the engine to be started and operated without driving the vehicle. If necessary, this position must be selected if the engine has to be restarted while the vehicle is moving.

Ⓓ—Drive Range is used for most highway driving conditions and maximum economy. Drive Range has four gear ratios, from the starting ratio, through direct drive to overdrive. Downshifts to a higher ratio are available for safe passing by depressing the accelerator.

D—Manual Third can be used for conditions where it is desired to use only three gears. This range is also useful for braking when descending slight grades. Upshifts and downshifts are the same as in Drive Range for first, second and third gears, but the transaxle will not shift to fourth gear.

2—Manual Second adds more performance. It has the same starting ratio as Manual Third Range, but prevents the transaxle from shifting above second gear, thus retaining second gear for acceleration or engine braking as desired. Manual Second can be selected at any vehicle speed. If the transaxle is in third or fourth gear it will immediately shift to Second Gear.

1—Manual Lo can be selected at any vehicle speed. The transaxle will shift to second gear if it is in third or fourth gear, until it slows below approximately 40 mph. (64 km/h), at which time it will downshift to first gear. This is particularly beneficial for maintaining maximum engine braking when descending steep grades.

Torque Converter

The torque converter assembly serves three primary functions. First, it acts as a fluid coupling to smoothly connect engine power through oil to the transaxle gear train. Second, it multiplies the torque or twisting effort from the engine when additional performance is desired. Thirdly, it provides direct drive through the torque converter.

The torque converter assembly consists of a three-element torque converter combined with a friction clutch. The three elements are the pump (driving member), the turbine (driven or output member), and the stator (reaction member). The converter cover is welded to the pump to seal all three members in an oil filled housing. The converter cover is bolted to the engine flexplate which is bolted directly to the engine crankshaft. The converter pump is therefore mechanically connected to the engine and turns at engine speed whenever the engine is operating.

The stator is located between the pump and turbine and is mounted on a one-way roller clutch which allows it to rotate clockwise but not counterclockwise.

The purpose of the stator is to redirect the oil returning from the turbine and change its direction of rotation back to that of the pump member. The energy in the oil is then used to assist the engine in turning the pump. This increases the force of the oil driving the turbine; and as a result, multiples the torque or twisting force of the engine.

The force of the oil flowing from the turbine to the blades of the stator tends to rotate the stator counterclockwise, but the roller clutch prevents it from turning.

With the engine operating at full throttle, transaxle in gear, and the vehicle standing still, the converter is capable of multiplying engine torque by approximately 2.0:1.

As turbine speed and vehicle speed increases, the direction of the oil leaving the turbine changes. The oil flows against the rear side of the stator vanes in a clockwise direction. Since the stator is now impeding the smooth flow of oil in the clockwise direction, its roller clutch automatically releases and the stator revolves freely on its shaft.

CONVERTER CLUTCH

The converter clutch mechanically connects the engine to the drive train and eliminates the hydraulic slip between the pump and turbine. When accelerating, the stator gives the converter the capability to multiply engine torque (maximum torque multiplication is 2.0:1) and improve vehicle acceleration. At this time the converter clutch is released. When the vehicle reaches cruising speed, the stator becomes inactive and there is no multiplication of engine torque (torque multiplication is 1.0:1). At this time the converter is a fluid coupling with the turbine turning at almost the same speed as the converter pump. The converter clutch can now be applied to eliminate the hydraulic slip between the pump and turbine and improve fuel economy.

The converter clutch cannot apply in Park, Reverse, Neutral, and Drive Range—First Gear.

On those vehicles equipped with computer command control, converter clutch operation is controlled by the solenoid. The solenoid is controlled by the brake switch, third clutch pressure switch, and the computer command control system.

On those vehicles not equipped with computer command control, converter clutch operation is controlled by the converter clutch shift valve and the solenoid together. When the converter clutch shift valve is used, it is used in place of the converter clutch plug.

Converter Clutch Applied

The converter clutch is applied when oil pressure is exhausted between the converter pressure plate and the converter cover and pressure is applied to push the pressure plate against the converter cover.

When the solenoid is energized converter signal oil, from the converter clutch plug, pushes the converter clutch apply valve to the left. Converter clutch release oil then exhausts, and converter clutch apply oil from the converter clutch regulator valve pushes the converter pressure plate against the converter cover to apply the converter clutch.

Converter Clutch Released

The converter clutch is released when oil pressure is applied between the converter cover and the converter pressure plate.

Converter feed pressure from the pressure regulator valve passes through the converter clutch apply valve into the release passage. The release oil feeds between the pump shaft and the turbine shaft to push the pressure plate away from the converter cover to release the converter clutch.

Converter Clutch Apply Feel

Converter clutch apply feel is controlled by the converter clutch regulator valve and the converter cutch accumulator.

The converter clutch regulator valve is controlled by T.V. and controls the pressure that applies the converter clutch. The converter clutch accumulator absorbs converter feed oil as converter release oil is exhausting. Less oil is then fed to the converter clutch regulator valve and the apply side of the converter clutch. This gives a cushion to the converter clutch apply (Figure 53).

VISCOUS CONVERTER CLUTCH

Viscous Converter Clutch Applied

The viscous converter clutch performs the same function as the torque converter clutch that is explained in this section. The primary difference between the converter clutch and the viscous converter clutch is the silicone fluid that is sealed between the cover and the body of the clutch assembly. The viscous silicone fluid provides a smooth apply of the clutch assembly when it engages with the converter cover.

When the viscous clutch is applied there is a constant but minimal amount of slippage between the rotor and the body. Despite this slippage (approx. 40 rpm @ 60 mph) good fuel economy is attained at highway torque. The viscous converter clutch is controlled by the solenoid and through the ECM which monitors: vehicle speed; throttle angle; transmission gear; transmission fluid temperature; engine coolant temperature; outside temperature and barometric pressure.

Viscous Converter Clutch Apply

The viscous converter clutch is capable of applying at approximately 25 mph providing that the transmission is in second gear and the transmission oil temperature is below 93.3° C (200° F). (This temperature is monitored by the ECM through the thermistor.) When transmission oil temperatures are above 93.3° C (200° F) but below 157° C (315° F) the viscous clutch will not apply until approximately 38 mph. If transmission oil temperature exceeds 157° C (315° F) a temperature switch located in the channel plate will open and release the viscous clutch to protect the transmission from overheating.

Description of Hydraulic Components

MANUAL VALVE: Mechanically connected to the shift selector. It is fed by line pressure from the pump and directs pressure according to which range the driver has selected.

1-2 SERVO: A hydraulic piston and pin that mechanically applies the 1-2 band in first and second gear. Also absorbs third clutch oil to act as an accumulator for the 2-3 shift.

REVERSE SERVO: A hydraulic piston and pin that mechanically applies the reverse band when reverse range is selected by the driver.

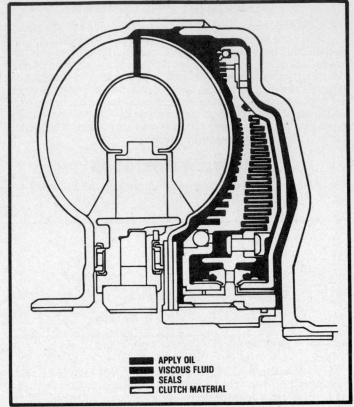

APPLY OIL
VISCOUS FLUID
SEALS
CLUTCH MATERIAL

Viscous converter clutch applied (© General Motors Corp.)

MODULATOR VALVE: Is controlled by the vacuum modulator assembly and regulates line pressure, into a modulator pressure that is proportional to engine vacuum (engine torque).

MODULATOR ASSEMBLY: By sensing engine vacuum, it causes the modulator valve to regulate modulator pressure that is proportional to engine torque (inversely proportional to engine vacuum).

1-2 ACCUMULATOR PISTON: Absorbs second clutch oil to provide a cushion for the second clutch apply. The firmness of the cushion is controlled by the 1-2 accumulator valve.

3-4 ACCUMULATOR PISTON: Absorbs fourth clutch oil to provide a cushion for the fourth clutch apply. The firmness of the cushion is controlled by the 1-2 accumulator valve.

1-2 SERVO THERMO ELEMENTS: When cold, it opens another orifice to the servo, to provide less of a restriction for a quick servo apply. When warm, it blocks one of the two orifices to the servo and slow the flow of oil and provide a good neutral/drive shift feel.

INPUT CLUTCH ACCUMULATOR: Absorbs input clutch apply oil to cushion the input clutch apply.

CONVERTER CLUTCH ACCUMULATOR: Cushions the converter clutch apply by absorbing converter clutch feed oil and slowing the amount of oil feeding into the converter clutch apply passage.

3-2 DOWNSHIFT VALVE: Controlled by 2nd clutch oil that opens the valve when line pressure exceeds 110 psi and allows T.V. oil to enter the 3-2 downshift passage.

THERMO ELEMENT: Maintains a level of transmission fluid in the side cover that is needed for the operation of the hydraulic pressure system. The thermo element allows fluid levels to increase or decrease with the increase or decrease of fluid temperature.

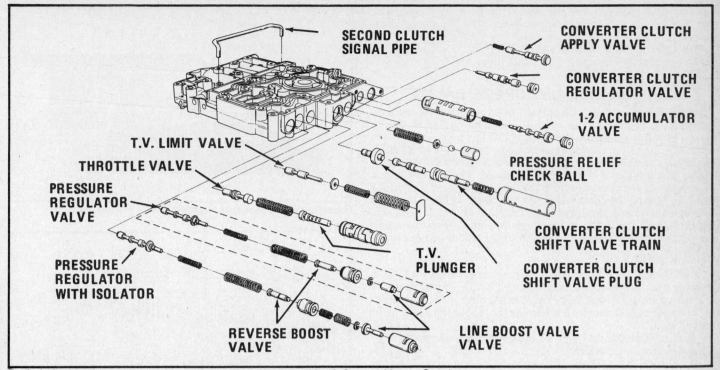

Exploded view of the second side of the valve body assembly (© General Motors Corp.)

1-2 SHIFT VALVE TRAIN: Shifts the transaxle from 1st to 2nd gear or 2nd to 1st gear, depending on governor, T.V., detent, or low oil pressures.

3-4 M.T.V. VALVE: Modulates T.V. pressure going to the 3-4 throttle valve to a lower pressure so that a light throttle 3-4 upshift will not be delayed.

2-3 ACCUMULATOR VALVE: Receives line pressure from the manual valve and controlled by modulator pressure. The 2-3 accumulator valve, in third gear and overdrive, varies 1-2 servo. Apply (2-3 accumulator) oil pressure in proportion to changes in modulator pressure (engine torque).

3-2 CONTROL VALVE: Controlled by governor oil, it controls the 3-2 downshift timing by regulating the rate at which the third clutch releases and the 1-2 band applies.

2-3 SHIFT VALVE TRAIN: Shifts the transaxle from 2nd to 3rd gear or 3rd to 1st gear, depending on governor T.V., detent or drive 2 oil pressures.

3-4 SHIFT VALVE TRAIN: Shifts the transaxle from 3rd to 4th gear or 4th to 3rd gear, depending on governor, 3-4 M.T.V., 4-3 M.T.V., part throttle, or drive 3 oil pressures.

4-3 M.T.V. VALVE: Modulates T.V. pressure going to the 3-4 throttle valve to a lower pressure to prevent an early downshift at light to medium throttle.

REVERSE SERVO BOOST VALVE: Under hard acceleration the higher line pressure will open the valve to provide a quick feed to the reverse servo and prevent the reverse band from slipping during application.

1-2 SERVO CONTROL VALVE: Closed by second oil during a drive range 3-2 downshift, it slows down the 1-2 servo apply.

1-2 SERVO BOOST VALVE: Under hard acceleration the higher line pressure will open the valve to provide a quick feed to the 1-2 servo and prevent the 1-2 band from slipping during application.

CONVERTER CLUTCH APPLY VALVE: Controlled by the converter clutch solenoid, it directs oil to either the release or the apply side of the converter clutch.

CONVERTER CLUTCH REGULATOR VALVE: Controlled by T.V. pressure and fed by converter clutch feed pressure it regulates converter clutch apply pressure.

1-2 ACCUMULATOR VALVE: Receives line pressure from the manual valve and controlled by modulator pressure. It varies 1-2 and 3-4 accumulator pressure in proportion to changes in modulator pressure (engine torque).

PRESSURE RELIEF CHECK BALL: Prevents line pressure from exceeding 245-360 psi.

CONVERTER CLUTCH SHIFT VALVE PLUG: Allows second oil to feed into the converter clutch signal passage. The plug is used on models with vehicles equipped with computer command control.

CONVERTER CLUTCH SHIFT VALVE TRAIN (NON C3 SYSTEMS): Sends signal oil to the converter clutch apply valve and together with the converter clutch solenoid determines whether the converter clutch should be released or applied. It is controlled by governor, T.V. and detent oil.

T.V. LIMIT VALVE: Limits the line pressure fed to the throttle valve to 90 psi.

THROTTLE VALVE: A regulating valve that increases T.V. pressure as the accelerator pedal is depressed and is controlled by T.V. plunger movement.

T.V. PLUNGER: Controlled by the throttle lever and bracket assembly and linked to the accelerator pedal. When accelerating, this valve compresses the throttle valve spring causing the throttle valve to increase T.V. pressure. It also controls the opening of the part throttle and detent ports.

PRESSURE REGULATOR VALVE: Controls line pressure by regulating pump output and is controlled by the pressure regulator spring, the reverse boost valve, and the line boost valve.

PRESSURE REGULATOR VALVE WITH ISOLATOR: Same function as pressure regulator valve except isolator system assists in stabilizing the pressure regulator system.

REVERSE BOOST VALVE: Boosts line pressure by pushing the pressure regulator valve up when acted on by Park, Reverse, Neutral (PRN) oil or lo oil pressure.

LINE BOOST VALVE: Boosts line pressure by pushing the pressure regulator valve up when acted on by modulator oil pressure.

SECOND CLUTCH SIGNAL PIPE: Directs second clutch oil to apply or release the 1-2 control valve.

CLUTCH EXHAUST CHECK BALLS

To complete the exhaust of apply oil when the input, second, or third clutch is released, an exhaust check ball assembly is installed near the outer diameter of the clutch housings. Centrifugal force, resulting from the spinning clutch housings, working on the residual oil in the clutch piston cavity would give a partial apply of the clutch plates if it were not exhausted. The exhaust check ball assembly is designed to close the exhaust port by clutch apply pressure seating the check ball when the clutch is being applied.

When the clutch is released and clutch apply oil is being exhausted, centrifugl force on the check ball unseats it and opens the port to exhaust the residual oil from the clutch piston cavity.

CHECK BALLS

1. Fourth Clutch Check Ball: Forces fourth clutch oil to feed through one orifice and exhaust through a different orifice.

2. 3-2 Control Check Ball: Forces exhausting 1-2 servo release oil to either flow through an orifice or the regulating 3-2 control valve.

3. Part Throttle and Drive 3 Check Ball: Separates part throttle and drive 3 oil passages to the 3-4 shift valve.

4. Third Clutch Check Ball: Forces third clutch oil to feed through one orifice and exhaust through a different orifice.

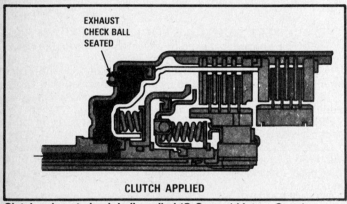

Clutch exhaust check ball applied (© General Motors Corp.)

5. 2-3 Accumulator Feed Check Ball: In third gear and fourth gear forces D4 oil to be orificed into the 1-2 servo (2-3 accumulator).

6. 2-3 Accumulator Exhaust Check Ball: In first gear, allows the 2-3 accumulator exhaust passage to feed and apply the 1-2 servo unrestricted. In third gear, forces exhausting 1-2 servo oil to either flow through an orifice or the regulating 2-3 accumulator valve.

7. Third Clutch Accumulator Ball and Spring: In third gear, it closes the 1-2 servo release passage exhaust. On a 3-2 down shift after 1-2 servo release oil has dropped to a low pressure, the spring will unseat the check ball and allow the oil to exhaust completely.

8. Second Clutch Check Ball: Forces second clutch oil to feed through one orifice and exhaust through a different orifice.

9. Reverse Servo Feed Check Ball: Forces oil feeding the reverse servo to orifice, but allows the oil to exhaust freely.

10. Converter Clutch Release/Apply Check Ball: Separates converter clutch release and converter clutch apply passages to the converter clutch blow-off ball.

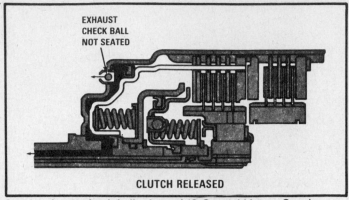

Clutch exhaust check ball released (© General Motors Corp.)

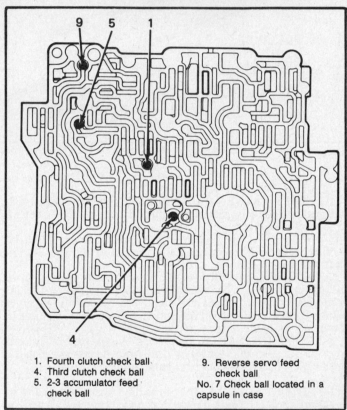

1. Fourth clutch check ball
4. Third clutch check ball
5. 2-3 accumulator feed check ball
9. Reverse servo feed check ball
No. 7 Check ball located in a capsule in case

Check ball location in valve body (© General Motors Corp.)

11. Third/Lo-1st Check Ball: Separates the third clutch and lo-1st passages to the third clutch.

12. 1-2 Servo Feed Check Ball: Forces oil feeding the apply side of the 1-2 servo to orifice but allows the oil to exhaust unrestricted.

13. Input Clutch/Reverse Check Ball: Minimizes neutral—drive and neutral—reverse apply time by allowing the park, reverse, neutral (PRN) circuit to feed and apply the input clutch quicker.

14. Detent/Modulator Check Ball: Allows detent oil to apply force to the pressure regulator system during part or full throttle detent and when driving at high altitude.

15. Converter Clutch Blow Off Check Ball: Prevents converter clutch release or apply pressure from exceeding 100 psi.

16. Low Blow Off Check Ball: Prevent lo-1st pressure to the third clutch from exceeding 70 psi in manual lo.

17. Cooler Check Ball: When the engine is shut off the spring seats the ball to prevent converter drainback.

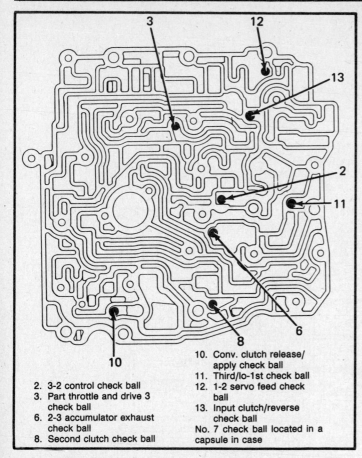

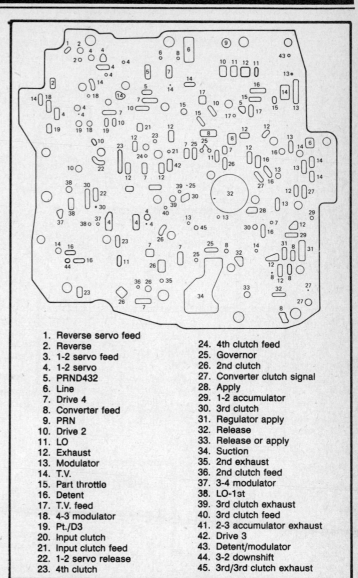

2. 3-2 control check ball
3. Part throttle and drive 3 check ball
6. 2-3 accumulator exhaust check ball
8. Second clutch check ball

10. Conv. clutch release/ apply check ball
11. Third/lo-1st check ball
12. 1-2 servo feed check ball
13. Input clutch/reverse check ball
No. 7 check ball located in a capsule in case

Check ball location in valve body channel plate
(© General Motors Corp.)

1. Reverse servo feed
2. Reverse
3. 1-2 servo feed
4. 1-2 servo
5. PRND432
6. Line
7. Drive 4
8. Converter feed
9. PRN
10. Drive 2
11. LO
12. Exhaust
13. Modulator
14. T.V.
15. Part throttle
16. Detent
17. T.V. feed
18. 4-3 modulator
19. Pt./D3
20. Input clutch
21. Input clutch feed
22. 1-2 servo release
23. 4th clutch

24. 4th clutch feed
25. Governor
26. 2nd clutch
27. Converter clutch signal
28. Apply
29. 1-2 accumulator
30. 3rd clutch
31. Regulator apply
32. Release
33. Release or apply
34. Suction
35. 2nd exhaust
36. 2nd clutch feed
37. 3-4 modulator
38. LO-1st
39. 3rd clutch exhaust
40. 3rd clutch feed
41. 2-3 accumulator exhaust
42. Drive 3
43. Detent/modulator
44. 3-2 downshift
45. 3rd/3rd clutch exhaust

Identification of spacer plate passages (© General Motors Corp.)

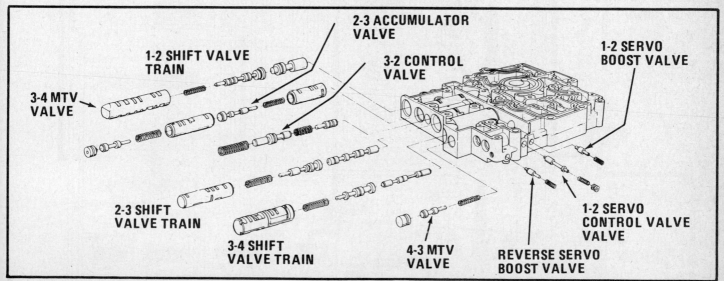

3-4 MTV VALVE

1-2 SHIFT VALVE TRAIN

2-3 ACCUMULATOR VALVE

3-2 CONTROL VALVE

1-2 SERVO BOOST VALVE

2-3 SHIFT VALVE TRAIN

3-4 SHIFT VALVE TRAIN

4-3 MTV VALVE

REVERSE SERVO BOOST VALVE

1-2 SERVO CONTROL VALVE VALVE

Exploded view one side of the valve body assembly (© General Motors Corp.)

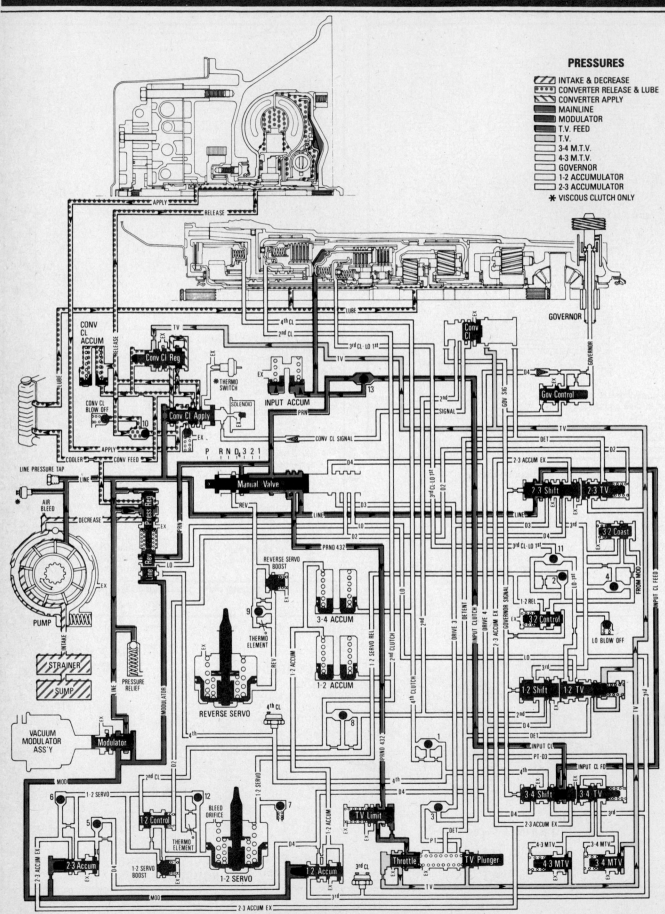

Park—Engine Running (© General Motors Corp.)

PARK—ENGINE RUNNING

Units Applied:

Input Clutch
Parking pawl
Input Sprag holding

BASIC OPERATION

With the selector lever in the Park (P) position, oil from the pump is directed to the following:

1. Pressure Regulator Valve: Regulates pump output based on modulator, Drive 2, Reverse, and pressure regulator valve spring pressure. As line pressure increases, the pressure regulator valve directs oil into the converter feed passage.

2. Converter Clutch Apply Valve: Held to the right by line pressure and directs converter feed pressure to the release side of the converter clutch.

3. Converter Clutch Regulator Valve: Regulates converter feed pressure into converter apply pressure which is used to apply the converter clutch in other ranges.

4. Modulator Valve: Controlled by the modulator, it regulates modulator pressure inversely to engine vacuum. Modulator pressure controls line pressure and accumulator pressure for proper shift feel.

5. Manual Valve: Controlled by the shift selector in Park, the manual valve directs oil to the following:

   a. Input Clutch: The input clutch is applied and drives the input sun gear.

   b. Reverse Boost Valve: Works with modulator pressure to boost line pressure from a minimum of 65 psi to a maximum of 230 psi in Park, Reverse, and Neutral.

   c. T.V. Limit Valve: Limits the feed to the throttle valve to a maximum of 90 psi.

   d. Throttle Valve and Plunger: Regulates T.V. pressure in proportion to accelerator pedal movement from 0-90 psi. T.V. pressure pushes against governor pressure on each of the shift valves to change shift points according to road demands.

6. 2-3 Shift Valve: Directs line pressure through the 3-4 shift valve to the input clutch.

SUMMARY

The converter clutch is released; the input clutch is applied; the input sprag is driving the input sun gear; the modulator and T.V. circuits are filled, and the parking pawl is engaged.

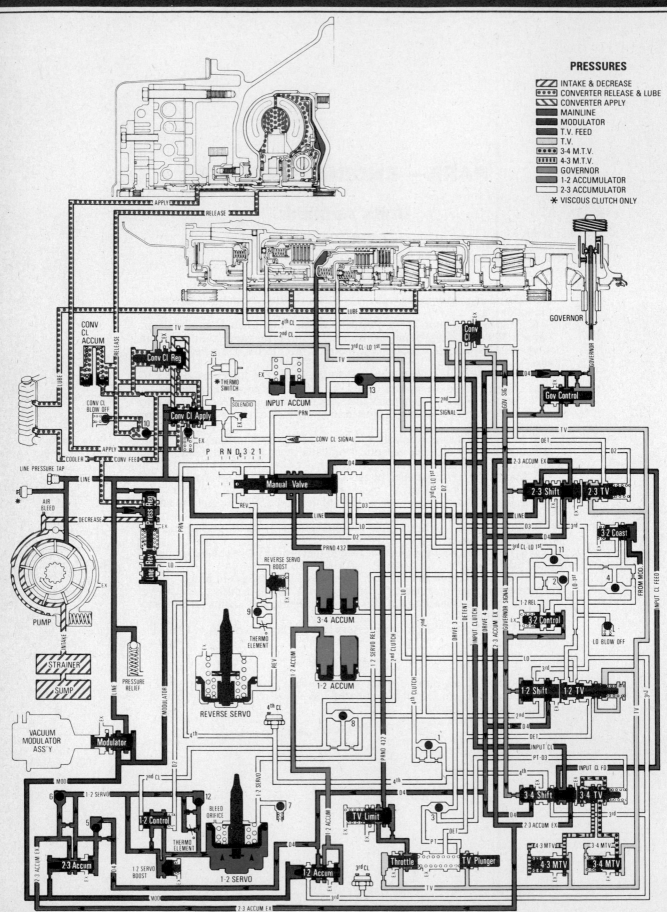

PRESSURES

- INTAKE & DECREASE
- CONVERTER RELEASE & LUBE
- CONVERTER APPLY
- MAINLINE
- MODULATOR
- T.V. FEED
- T.V.
- 3-4 M.T.V.
- 4-3 M.T.V.
- GOVERNOR
- 1-2 ACCUMULATOR
- 2-3 ACCUMULATOR
- ✱ VISCOUS CLUTCH ONLY

Drive Range—First Gear (© General Motors Corp.)

DRIVE RANGE—FIRST GEAR

Units Applied:

Input Sprag Holding
Input Clutch
1-2 Band

BASIC OPERATION

When the selector lever is moved to the Drive (D) position, the manual valve directs line pressure into the Drive 4 (D4) passage. Drive 4 oil flows to the following:

　1. 2-3 Shift Valve: Feeds line pressure through the orifices at the 1-2 servo control valve and check ball No. 12 to the 1-2 servo. The 1-2 servo applies the 1-2 band.

　2. Governor: Governor pressure increases with vehicle speed. The governor signal pressure pushes against the 1-2, 2-3 and 3-4 throttle valve springs to upshift the transaxle when sufficient vehicle speed is attained.

　3. 1-2 Shift Valve: Drive 4 oil at the 1-2 shift valve is the feed oil for the second clutch when the transaxle makes a 1-2 shift.

　4. 1-2 Accumulator Valve: 1-2 Accumulator oil pressure is controlled by modulator pressure. Accumulator pressure at the 1-2 and 3-4 accumulator pistons controls the 1-2 and 3-4 shift feel.

SUMMARY

The converter clutch is released, the input clutch is driving the input sprag, the input sprag is driving the input sun gear and the 1-2 band is holding the reaction sun gear.

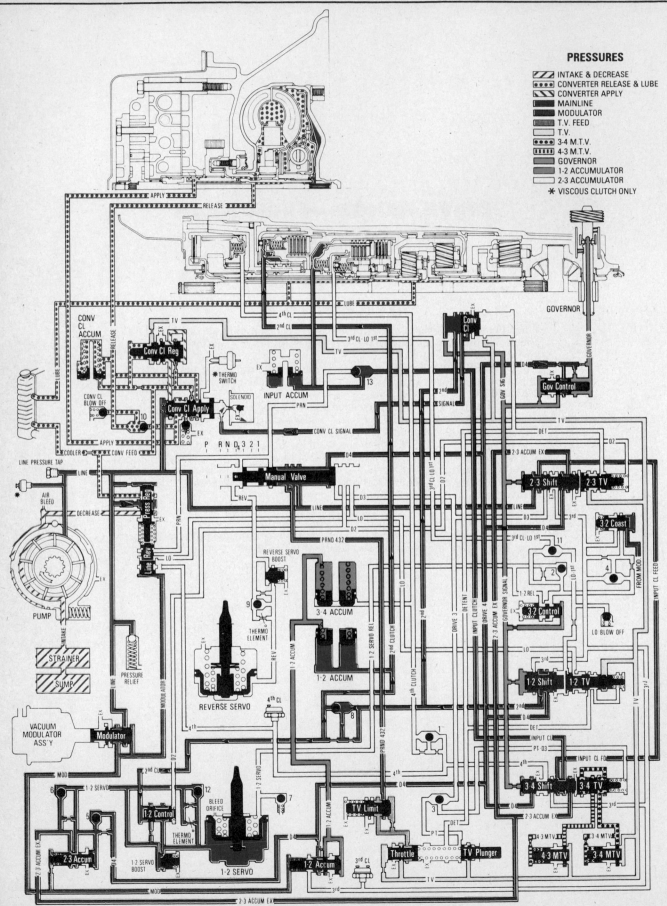

PRESSURES

- ▨ INTAKE & DECREASE
- ▦ CONVERTER RELEASE & LUBE
- ▨ CONVERTER APPLY
- ▮ MAINLINE
- ▮ MODULATOR
- ▨ T.V. FEED
- ▯ T.V.
- ▦ 3-4 M.T.V.
- ▥ 4-3 M.T.V.
- ▨ GOVERNOR
- ▨ 1-2 ACCUMULATOR
- ▯ 2-3 ACCUMULATOR
- ✱ VISCOUS CLUTCH ONLY

624

Drive Range—Second Gear (© General Motors Corp.)

DRIVE RANGE—SECOND GEAR

Units Applied:

Second Clutch
Input Clutch
1-2 Band

BASIC OPERATION

As vehicle speed increases, governor pressure overcomes T.V. pressure and 1-2 throttle valve spring pressure and opens the 1-2 shift valve. The 1-2 shift valve allows line pressure to fill the second clutch passage which is directed to the following:

1. Converter Clutch Apply Valve: When the solenoid is not electrically activated, the converter clutch is released. When the solenoid is electrically activated, converter clutch signal oil shifts the converter clutch apply valve and applies the converter clutch. The oil circuit shown is for a vehicle equipped with computer command control. Vehicles not equipped with computer command control have a converter clutch shift valve in place of the converter clutch plug.

2. 1-2 Servo Control Valve: Closes one orifice in the 1-2 servo apply passage to provide proper shift feel during a 3-2 downshift.

3. Second Clutch Check Ball (8): Orifices the feed to the second clutch.

4. 1-2 Accumulator: Cushions the second clutch apply by absorbing second clutch oil. The amount of cushion is controlled by the accumulator pressure.

5. Second Clutch Piston: Applies the second clutch.

SUMMARY

The converter clutch is released, the second clutch is driving the input carrier/reaction internal gear, the 1-2 band is holding the reaction sun gear and the input sun gear is overrunning the input sprag.

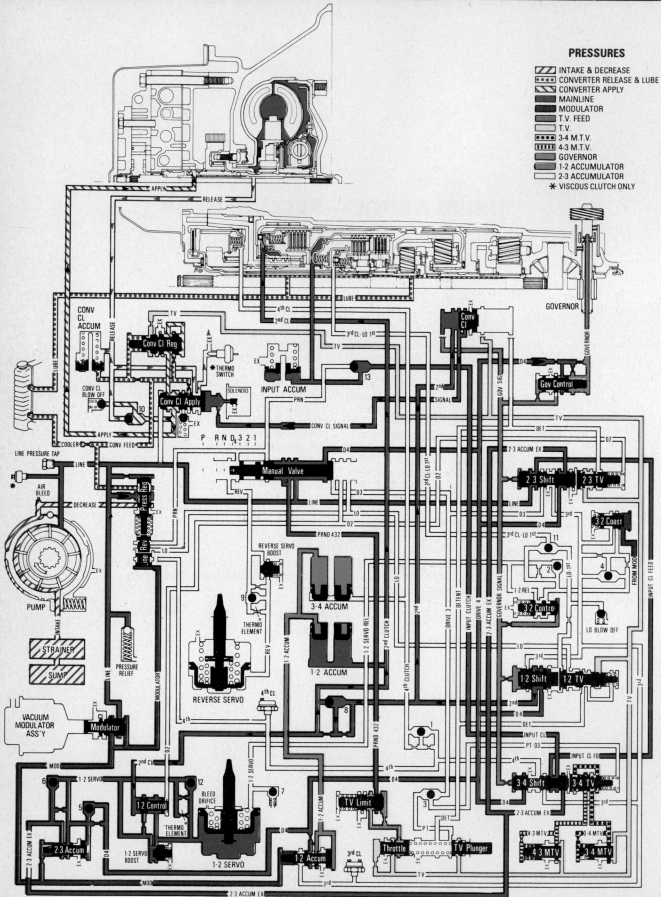

626

Drive Range—Converter Clutch Applied (© General Motors Corp.)

DRIVE RANGE—CONVERTER CLUTCH APPLIED

BASIC OPERATION

On vehicles equipped with computer command control, converter clutch operation is controlled by the solenoid (converter clutch apply for vehicles not equipped with computer command control is discussed below). The timing of the converter clutch apply is determined by the computer command control calibration. The oil flow diagram to the left shows the converter clutch applied in second gear, but it may not apply until third or fourth gear, depending on calibration.

When the solenoid is electronically activated, the converter clutch apply valve moves to the left and redirects converter feed oil as follows:

1. Converter clutch release oil is exhausted.

2. Converter clutch apply oil from the converter clutch regulator valve is directed into the apply passage. Apply oil pushes the converter pressure plate against the converter cover.

3. Converter Clutch Accumulator: As converter clutch release oil is exhausted, the converter clutch accumulator absorbs converter feed oil, sends less oil to the apply passage and cushions the converter clutch apply.

4. Converter Clutch Shift Valve: Vehicles not equipped with computer command control use the converter clutch shift valve in place of the converter clutch plug. The converter clutch shift valve is controlled by governor, T.V., and detent oil. It works with the converter clutch solenoid to apply or release the converter clutch.

5. Converter Clutch Blow-Off Check Ball: Prevents converter clutch apply pressure from exceeding 100 psi.

SUMMARY

The converter clutch can be applied in second, third, or fourth gear. Converter clutch apply oil pressure is regulated by the converter clutch regulator valve; the converter clutch accumulator gives proper apply feel; the converter clutch blow off check ball protects the converter from high pressures.

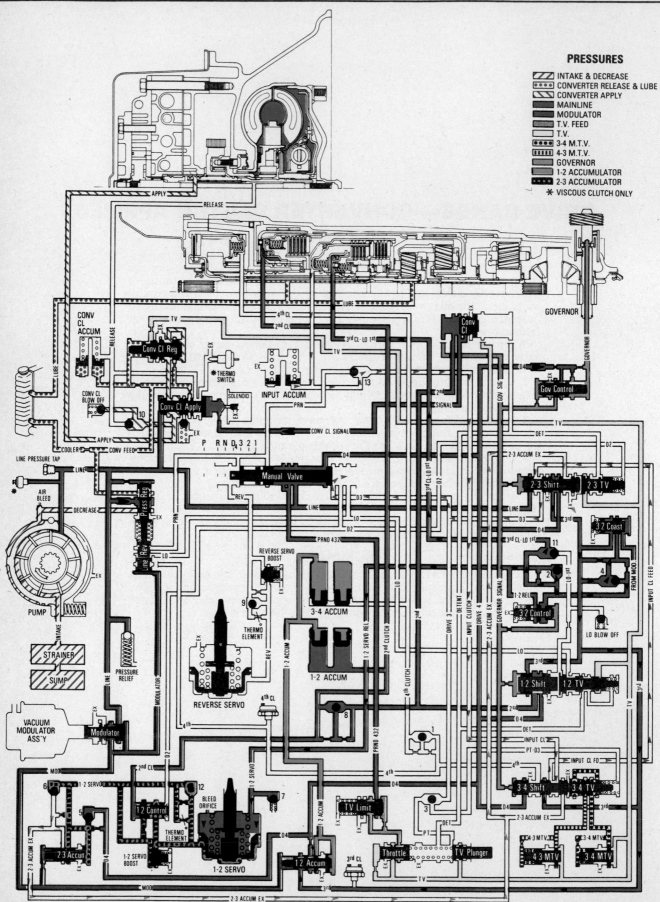

PRESSURES

- INTAKE & DECREASE
- CONVERTER RELEASE & LUBE
- CONVERTER APPLY
- MAINLINE
- MODULATOR
- T.V. FEED
- T.V.
- 3-4 M.T.V.
- 4-3 M.T.V.
- GOVERNOR
- 1-2 ACCUMULATOR
- 2-3 ACCUMULATOR
- ✱ VISCOUS CLUTCH ONLY

Drive Range—Third Gear (© General Motors Corp.)

DRIVE RANGE—THIRD GEAR

Units Applied:

Converter Clutch ①
Third Clutch
Second Clutch
Third Roller Clutch Holding

BASIC OPERATION

As vehicle speed increases, governor pressure overcomes T.V. pressure and 2-3 throttle valve spring pressure and opens the 2-3 shift valve. The 2-3 shift valve causes the following changes in the hydraulic circuit:

1. Releases the Input Clutch: Line pressure is blocked from entering the input clutch passage and input clutch oil pressure is exhausted.

2. Releases the 1-2 Servo: Drive 4 pressure is blocked from entering the 2-3 accumulator exhaust passage and the 2-3 accumulator exhaust passage is opened to exhaust. This causes check ball No. 5 and No. 6 to seat and the 2-3 accumulator valve to regulate the oil on the apply side of the 1-2 servo into an accumulator oil pressure that is proportional to modulator pressure.

3. Applies the Third Clutch: Third clutch oil is directed to the following:

  a. Third Clutch Check Ball (4): Orifices the feed to the third clutch.

  b. Release Side of the 1-2 Servo: Releases the 1-2 servo by pushing the 1-2 servo piston down against the accumulator oil pressure on the apply side of the 1-2 servo. This also acts as an accumulator for the third clutch.

  c. Third Clutch Piston: Applies the third clutch.

  d. 3-4 Shift Valve: Feeds the fourth clutch when in fourth gear.

  e. 1-2 Accumulator: Boosts accumulator pressure slightly for the 3-4 shift.

SUMMARY

The input clutch and the 1-2 band are released. The second clutch is driving the input carrier, the third clutch prevents the input sun gear from turning faster than turbine speed and the input sun gear and input carrier together drive the input internal gear in direct drive.

① The converter clutch may or may not be applied, depending on shift calibration and solenoid operation.

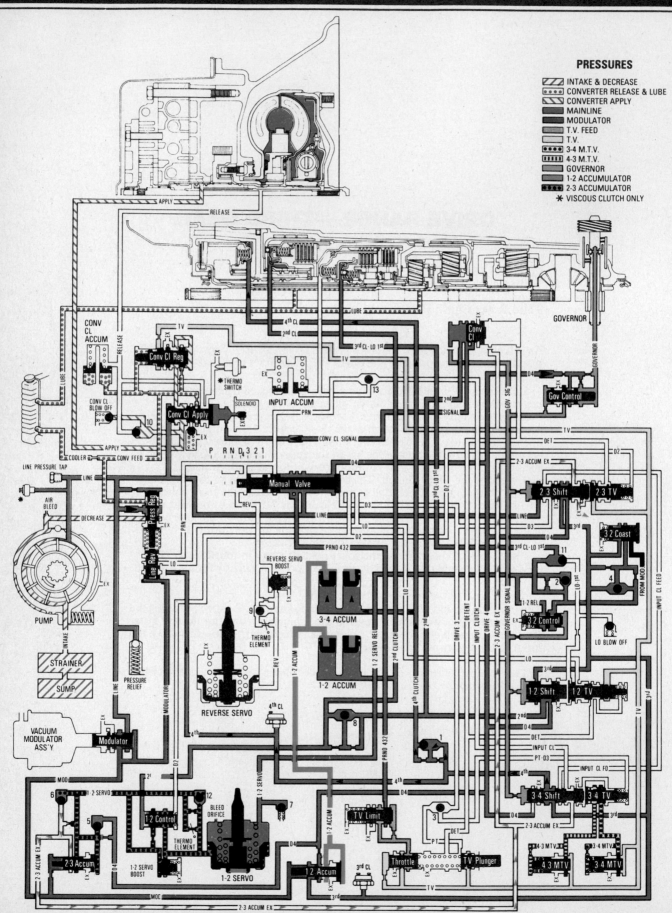

PRESSURES

- INTAKE & DECREASE
- CONVERTER RELEASE & LUBE
- CONVERTER APPLY
- MAINLINE
- MODULATOR
- T.V. FEED
- T.V.
- 3-4 M.T.V.
- 4-3 M.T.V.
- GOVERNOR
- 1-2 ACCUMULATOR
- 2-3 ACCUMULATOR
- * VISCOUS CLUTCH ONLY

Drive Range—Fourth Gear (© General Motors Corp.)

DRIVE RANGE—FOURTH GEAR

Units Applied:

Converter Clutch ①
Third Clutch
Fourth Clutch
Second Clutch
Third Roller Clutch

BASIC OPERATION

As vehicle speed increases, governor pressure overcomes 3-4 M.T.V. and 3-4 throttle valve spring pressure and opens the 3-4 shift valve. The 3-4 shift valve then allows third pressure to fill the fourth clutch passage which is directed to the following:

1. Fourth Clutch Check Ball (1): Orifices the feed to the fourth clutch.
2. 3-4 Accumulator: Cushions the fourth clutch apply by absorbing fourth clutch oil. The amount of cushion is controlled by the accumulator pressure.
3. Fourth Clutch Piston: Applies the fourth clutch.

SUMMARY

The fourth clutch hold the input sun gear, the second clutch drives the input carrier around the stationary sun gear, and the input internal gear is driven in overdrive.

① The converter clutch may or may not be applied, depending on shift calibration and solenoid operation.

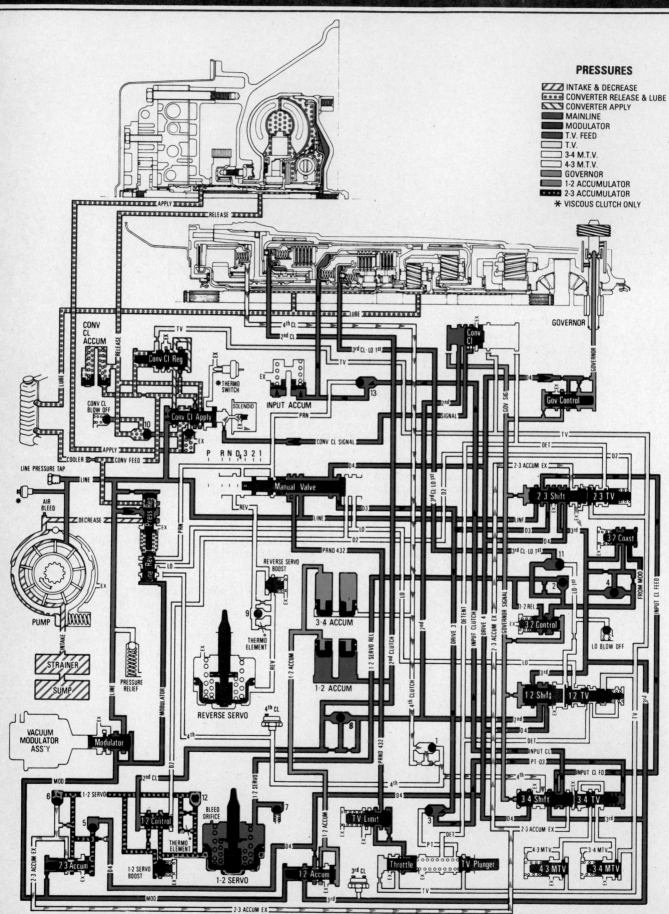

PRESSURES

INTAKE & DECREASE
CONVERTER RELEASE & LUBE
CONVERTER APPLY
MAINLINE
MODULATOR
T.V. FEED
T.V.
3-4 M.T.V.
4-3 M.T.V.
GOVERNOR
1-2 ACCUMULATOR
2-3 ACCUMULATOR
* VISCOUS CLUTCH ONLY

Manual Third (© General Motors Corp.)

MANUAL THIRD

Units Applied:

Third Roller Clutch Holding
Second Clutch
Input Clutch
Third Clutch
Input Sprag Holding

BASIC OPERATION

When the selector lever is moved to the Manual Third (3) position, the manual valve directs line pressure into the Drive 3 (D3) passage. Drive 3 oil flows to the following:

1. 3-4 Shift Valve: Drive 3 pressure pushes the 3-4 shift valve closed. Fourth clutch oil exhausts and fourth clutch releases.

2. 2-3 Shift Valve: Drive 3 pressure feeds into the input clutch passage, applying the input clutch.

SUMMARY

The transaxle can shift between first, second, and third gears as in Drive Range, but is prevented from shifting to fourth gear. The input clutch is applied to give engine braking. Line pressure is the same as in Drive Range.

NOTE: In Manual Third, the converter clutch is shown released and there is no 3-4 M.T.V. or 4-3 M.T.V. as shown. This is assuming the throttle is released. If the throttle is opened enough, the converter clutch could engage and the 3-4 M.T.V. and 4-3 M.T.V. valves could open.

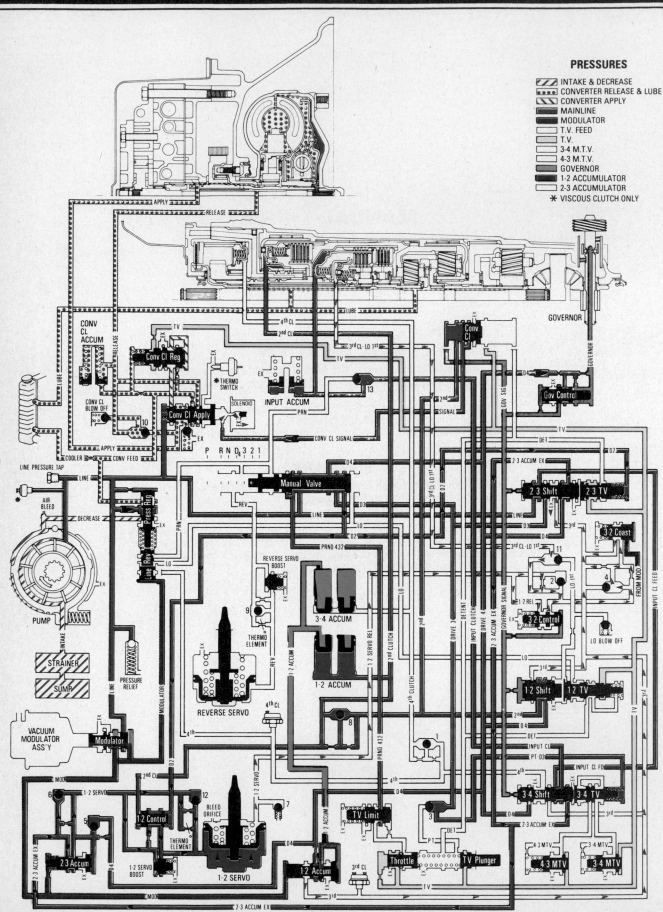

MANUAL SECOND

Units Applied:

Second Clutch
Input Clutch
1-2 Band

BASIC OPERATION

When the selector lever is moved to the Manual Second (2) position, the manual valve directs line pressure into the Drive 2 (D2) passage. Drive 2 oil flows to the following:

    1. 1-2 Servo Control Valve: Shifts to provide a quick feed and apply of the 1-2 servo.

    2. 2-3 Shift Valve: The 2-3 shift valve closes and directs oil pressure to the following:

        a. Third clutch and 1-2 servo release oil exhausts at a rate controlled by the 3-2 control valve and the 3-2 coast valve for proper shift timing of the third clutch exhaust and the 1-2 servo apply.

        b. Drive 4 oil fills the 2-3 accumulator exhaust passage and applies the 1-2 servo.

        c. Line pressure keeps the input clutch applied.

SUMMARY

The transaxle can shift between first and second gear as in Drive Range, but is prevented from shifting to third gear. Line pressure is the same as in Drive Range.

NOTE: In Manual Second, the converter clutch is shown released and there is no 3-4 M.T.V. or 4-3 M.T.V. as shown. This is assuming the throttle is released. If the throttle is opened enough, the converter clutch could engage and the 3-4 M.T.V. and 4-3 M.T.V. valve could open.

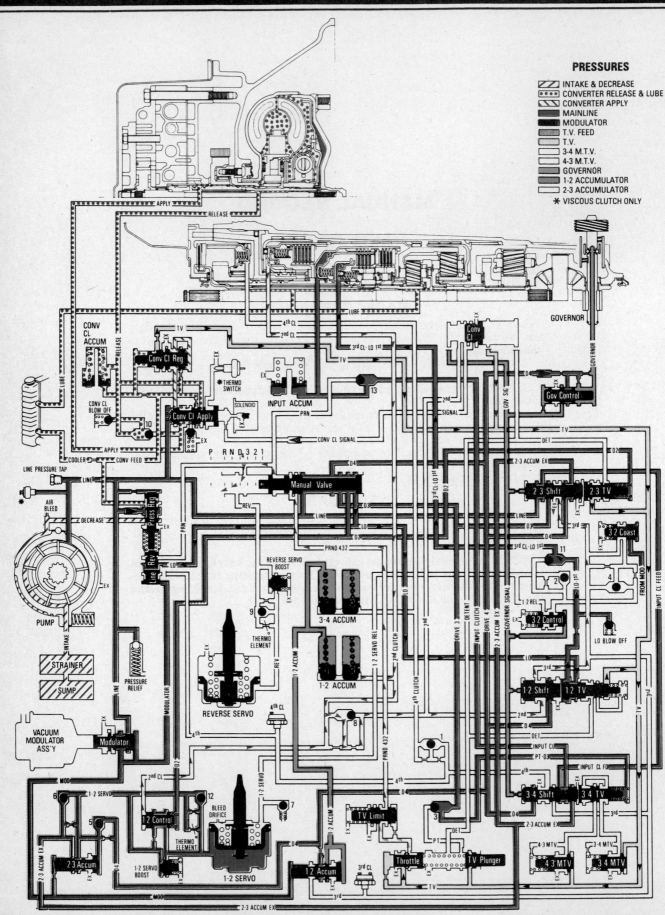

PRESSURES

- ▨ INTAKE & DECREASE
- CONVERTER RELEASE & LUBE
- CONVERTER APPLY
- MAINLINE
- MODULATOR
- T.V. FEED
- T.V.
- 3-4 M.T.V.
- 4-3 M.T.V.
- GOVERNOR
- 1-2 ACCUMULATOR
- 2-3 ACCUMULATOR
- ✱ VISCOUS CLUTCH ONLY

Manual Low (© General Motors Corp.)

MANUAL LOW

Units Applied:

Input Clutch
Third Clutch
Input Sprag Holding
Third Roller Clutch Holding
1-2 Band

BASIC OPERATION

When the selector lever is moved to the Manual Lo (1) position, the manual valve exhausts oil pressure in the Park Reverse Neutral Drive 4 Drive 3 Drive 2 (PRND432) passage. The manual valve also directs line pressure into the lo passage. Lo oil flows to the following:

1. Pressure Regulator Valve: Boosts line pressure to a steady 165 psi to prevent the clutches from slipping during hard engine braking.

2. 1-2 Shift Valve: At speeds below 40 mph (64 km/hr), the 1-2 shift valve closes and directs oil pressure to the following:

   a. Second clutch oil exhausts and the second clutch releases.
   b. Lo oil fills the Lo-1st passage. Lo-1st oil applies the third clutch.

3. T.V. Limit Valve: Lo oil forces the T.V. limit valve to open and exhaust T.V. feed oil resulting in no T.V. pressure in Manual Lo.

SUMMARY

The input clutch and sprag drive the input sun gear. The third clutch and third roller clutch provide engine braking by preventing the input sprag from over-running. The 1-2 band holds the reaction sun gear stationary and line pressure is boosted to prevent the clutches from slipping.

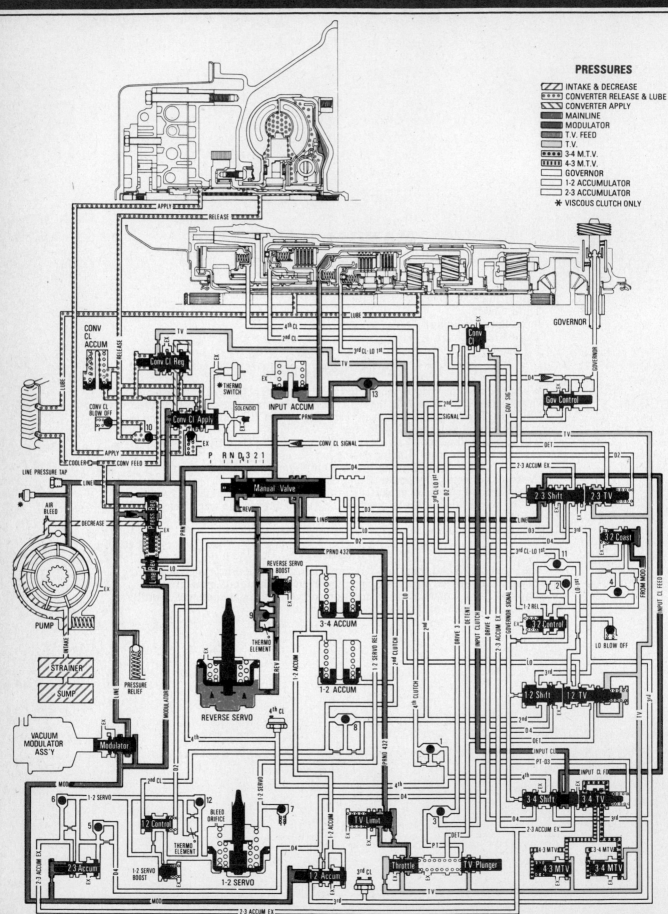

PRESSURES

- ▨ INTAKE & DECREASE
- ▨ CONVERTER RELEASE & LUBE
- ▨ CONVERTER APPLY
- ■ MAINLINE
- ■ MODULATOR
- ▨ T.V. FEED
- □ T.V.
- ▨ 3-4 M.T.V.
- ▨ 4-3 M.T.V.
- □ GOVERNOR
- □ 1-2 ACCUMULATOR
- □ 2-3 ACCUMULATOR
- ✱ VISCOUS CLUTCH ONLY

Reverse (© General Motors Corp.)

REVERSE

Units Applied:

Input Clutch
Reverse Band
Input Sprag Holding

BASIC OPERATION

When the selector lever is moved to the Reverse (R) position, the manual valve directs line pressure to the following:

1. Line pressure passes through the 2-3 shift valve and 3-4 shift valve to the input clutch. The input clutch is applied and drives the input sun gear.

2. Park Reverse Neutral (PRN) Passage: The PRN passage provides an alternate passage to apply the input clutch. At the reverse boost valve, PRN pressure boosts line pressure from a minimum of 65 psi to a maximum of 230 psi at full throttle.

3. Reverse Servo: Line pressure feed to the reverse servo is controlled by the reverse servo boost valve for good reverse servo apply feel. The reverse servo applies the reverse band which holds the input carrier stationary.

SUMMARY

Line pressure is boosted to prevent the clutches from slipping. The input clutch drives the input sun gear. The reverse band holds the input carrier stationary and the input internal gear is driven in reverse.

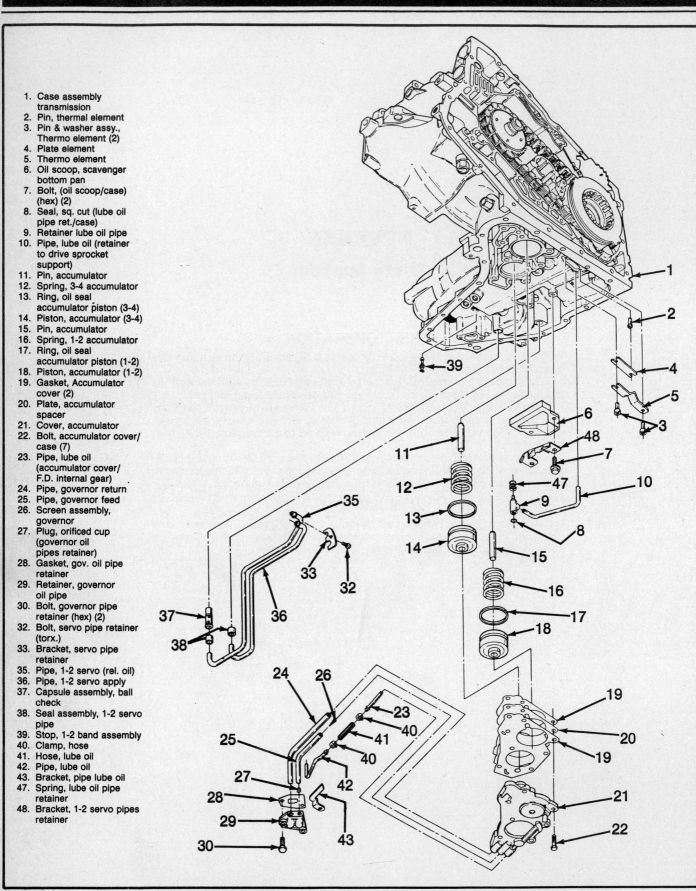

1. Case assembly transmission
2. Pin, thermal element
3. Pin & washer assy., Thermo element (2)
4. Plate element
5. Thermo element
6. Oil scoop, scavenger bottom pan
7. Bolt, (oil scoop/case) (hex) (2)
8. Seal, sq. cut (lube oil pipe ret./case)
9. Retainer lube oil pipe
10. Pipe, lube oil (retainer to drive sprocket support)
11. Pin, accumulator
12. Spring, 3-4 accumulator
13. Ring, oil seal accumulator piston (3-4)
14. Piston, accumulator (3-4)
15. Pin, accumulator
16. Spring, 1-2 accumulator
17. Ring, oil seal accumulator piston (1-2)
18. Piston, accumulator (1-2)
19. Gasket, Accumulator cover (2)
20. Plate, accumulator spacer
21. Cover, accumulator
22. Bolt, accumulator cover/ case (7)
23. Pipe, lube oil (accumulator cover/ F.D. internal gear)
24. Pipe, governor return
25. Pipe, governor feed
26. Screen assembly, governor
27. Plug, orificed cup (governor oil pipes retainer)
28. Gasket, gov. oil pipe retainer
29. Retainer, governor oil pipe
30. Bolt, governor pipe retainer (hex) (2)
32. Bolt, servo pipe retainer (torx.)
33. Bracket, servo pipe retainer
35. Pipe, 1-2 servo (rel. oil)
36. Pipe, 1-2 servo apply
37. Capsule assembly, ball check
38. Seal assembly, 1-2 servo pipe
39. Stop, 1-2 band assembly
40. Clamp, hose
41. Hose, lube oil
42. Pipe, lube oil
43. Bracket, pipe lube oil
47. Spring, lube oil pipe retainer
48. Bracket, 1-2 servo pipes retainer

Exploded view of the governor control body, accumulator cover, pistons and component parts (© General Motors Corp.)

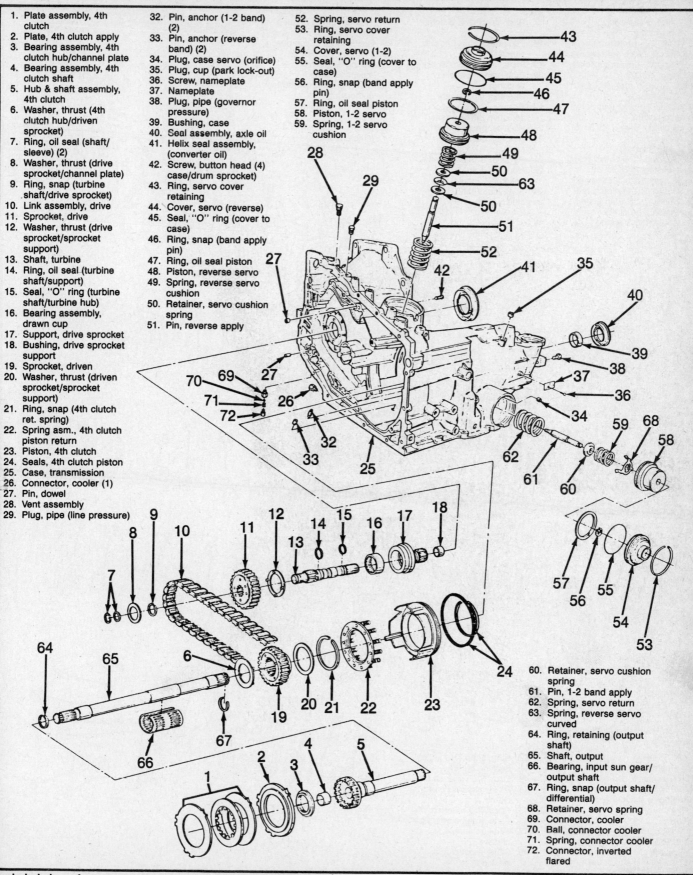

1. Plate assembly, 4th clutch
2. Plate, 4th clutch apply
3. Bearing assembly, 4th clutch hub/channel plate
4. Bearing assembly, 4th clutch shaft
5. Hub & shaft assembly, 4th clutch
6. Washer, thrust (4th clutch hub/driven sprocket)
7. Ring, oil seal (shaft/sleeve) (2)
8. Washer, thrust (drive sprocket/channel plate)
9. Ring, snap (turbine shaft/drive sprocket)
10. Link assembly, drive
11. Sprocket, drive
12. Washer, thrust (drive sprocket/sprocket support)
13. Shaft, turbine
14. Ring, oil seal (turbine shaft/support)
15. Seal, "O" ring (turbine shaft/turbine hub)
16. Bearing assembly, drawn cup
17. Support, drive sprocket
18. Bushing, drive sprocket support
19. Sprocket, driven
20. Washer, thrust (driven sprocket/sprocket support)
21. Ring, snap (4th clutch ret. spring)
22. Spring asm., 4th clutch piston return
23. Piston, 4th clutch
24. Seals, 4th clutch piston
25. Case, transmission
26. Connector, cooler (1)
27. Pin, dowel
28. Vent assembly
29. Plug, pipe (line pressure)

32. Pin, anchor (1-2 band) (2)
33. Pin, anchor (reverse band) (2)
34. Plug, case servo (orifice)
35. Plug, cup (park lock-out)
36. Screw, nameplate
37. Nameplate
38. Plug, pipe (governor pressure)
39. Bushing, case
40. Seal assembly, axle oil
41. Helix seal assembly, (converter oil)
42. Screw, button head (4) case/drum sprocket
43. Ring, servo cover retaining
44. Cover, servo (reverse)
45. Seal, "O" ring (cover to case)
46. Ring, snap (band apply pin)
47. Ring, oil seal piston
48. Piston, reverse servo
49. Spring, reverse servo cushion
50. Retainer, servo cushion spring
51. Pin, reverse apply

52. Spring, servo return
53. Ring, servo cover retaining
54. Cover, servo (1-2)
55. Seal, "O" ring (cover to case)
56. Ring, snap (band apply pin)
57. Ring, oil seal piston
58. Piston, 1-2 servo
59. Spring, 1-2 servo cushion

60. Retainer, servo cushion spring
61. Pin, 1-2 band apply
62. Spring, servo return
63. Spring, reverse servo curved
64. Ring, retaining (output shaft)
65. Shaft, output
66. Bearing, input sun gear/output shaft
67. Ring, snap (output shaft/differential)
68. Retainer, servo spring
69. Connector, cooler
70. Ball, connector cooler
71. Spring, connector cooler
72. Connector, inverted flared

Exploded view of case assembly drive link and sprocket (© General Motors Corp.)

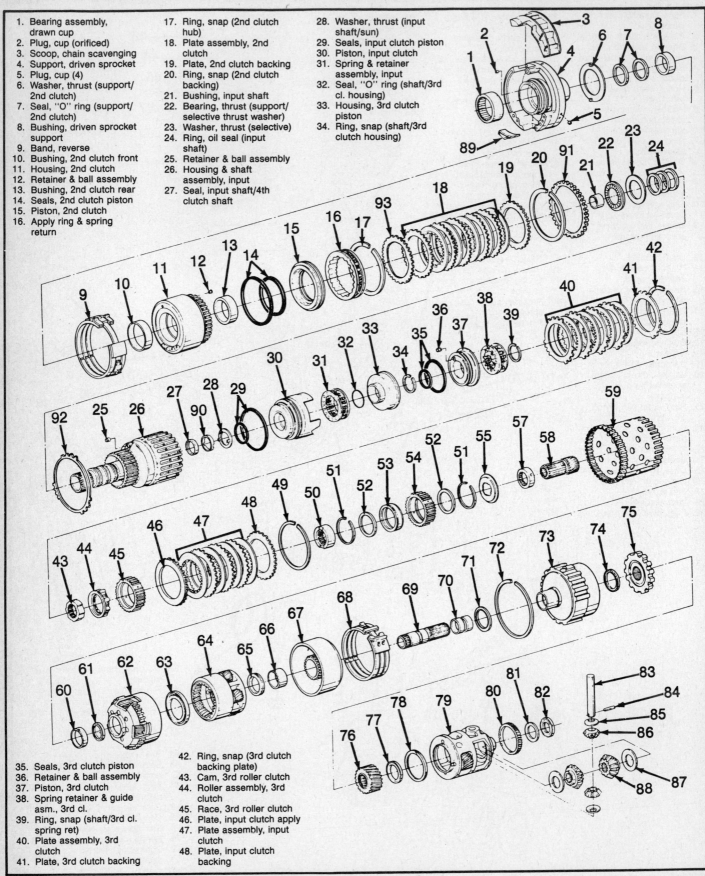

1. Bearing assembly, drawn cup
2. Plug, cup (orificed)
3. Scoop, chain scavenging
4. Support, driven sprocket
5. Plug, cup (4)
6. Washer, thrust (support/2nd clutch)
7. Seal, "O" ring (support/2nd clutch)
8. Bushing, driven sprocket support
9. Band, reverse
10. Bushing, 2nd clutch front
11. Housing, 2nd clutch
12. Retainer & ball assembly
13. Bushing, 2nd clutch rear
14. Seals, 2nd clutch piston
15. Piston, 2nd clutch
16. Apply ring & spring return

17. Ring, snap (2nd clutch hub)
18. Plate assembly, 2nd clutch
19. Plate, 2nd clutch backing
20. Ring, snap (2nd clutch backing)
21. Bushing, input shaft
22. Bearing, thrust (support/selective thrust washer)
23. Washer, thrust (selective)
24. Ring, oil seal (input shaft)
25. Retainer & ball assembly
26. Housing & shaft assembly, input
27. Seal, input shaft/4th clutch shaft

28. Washer, thrust (input shaft/sun)
29. Seals, input clutch piston
30. Piston, input clutch
31. Spring & retainer assembly, input
32. Seal, "O" ring (shaft/3rd cl. housing)
33. Housing, 3rd clutch piston
34. Ring, snap (shaft/3rd clutch housing)

35. Seals, 3rd clutch piston
36. Retainer & ball assembly
37. Piston, 3rd clutch
38. Spring retainer & guide asm., 3rd cl.
39. Ring, snap (shaft/3rd cl. spring ret)
40. Plate assembly, 3rd clutch
41. Plate, 3rd clutch backing

42. Ring, snap (3rd clutch backing plate)
43. Cam, 3rd roller clutch
44. Roller assembly, 3rd clutch
45. Race, 3rd roller clutch
46. Plate, input clutch apply
47. Plate assembly, input clutch
48. Plate, input clutch backing

Exploded view of THM 440-T4 transaxle internal components (© General Motors Corp.)

49. Ring, snap (input clutch backing plate)
50. Race, input sprag inner
51. Ring, snap (sprag)
52. Wear plate, input sprag
53. Sprag assembly, input clutch
54. Race, input sprag outer
55. Retainer, input sprag
57. Spacer, input sun gear
58. Gear, input sun
59. Drum, reverse reaction
60. Bushing, reaction internal gear
61. Bearing assembly, (input sun/carrier)
62. Carrier assemby, input
63. Bearing asm., (input/ reaction carrier)
64. Carrier assembly, reaction
65. Bearing assembly, (reaction carrier/sun gear)

66. Bushing, reaction sun
67. Gear & drum asm., reaction sun
68. Band, 1-2
69. Shaft, final drive sun gear
70. Bushing, final drive internal
71. Bearing assembly, reaction sun gear/ internal gear
72. Ring, snap (internal gear/case)
73. Gear, final drive internal
74. Bearing asm., (int. gear/ park gear)
75. Gear parking
76. Gear, final drive sun
77. Bearing, thrust (sun gear/carrier)
78. Ring, snap (final drive carrier)

79. Carrier, final drive
80. Gear, governor drive
81. Washer, carrier/case selective
82. Bearing asm., (selective washer/case)
83. Shaft, differential pinion
84. Pinion, differential pinion shaft ret.
85. Washer, pinion thrust
86. Pinion, differential
87. Washer, differential side gear thrust
88. Gear, differential side
89. Weir, oil reservoir
90. Sleeve, lock up
91. Support, 2nd clutch housing
92. Plate, reverse reaction drum
93. Plate, 2nd clutch waved

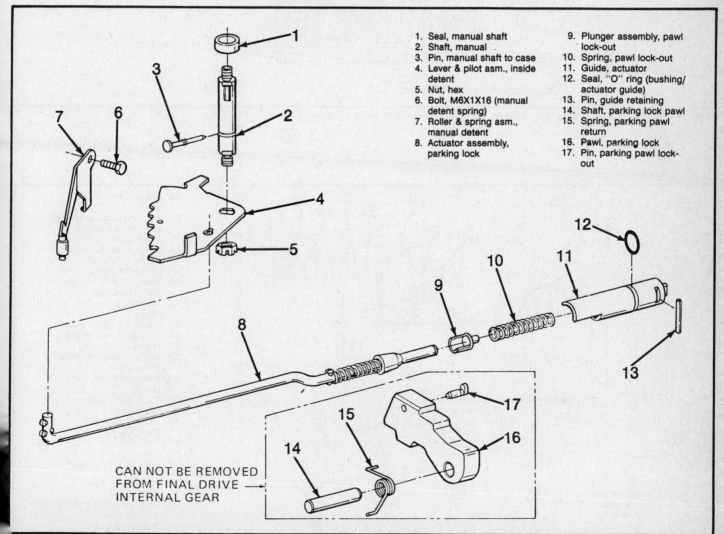

1. Seal, manual shaft
2. Shaft, manual
3. Pin, manual shaft to case
4. Lever & pilot asm., inside detent
5. Nut, hex
6. Bolt, M6X1X16 (manual detent spring)
7. Roller & spring asm., manual detent
8. Actuator assembly, parking lock
9. Plunger assembly, pawl lock-out
10. Spring, pawl lock-out
11. Guide, actuator
12. Seal, "O" ring (bushing/ actuator guide)
13. Pin, guide retaining
14. Shaft, parking lock pawl
15. Spring, parking pawl return
16. Pawl, parking lock
17. Pin, parking pawl lock-out

CAN NOT BE REMOVED FROM FINAL DRIVE INTERNAL GEAR

Exploded view of manual linkage assembly (© General Motors Corp.)

643

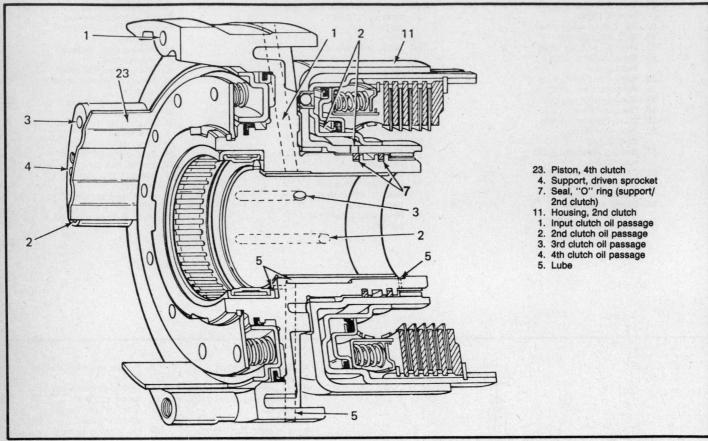

23. Piston, 4th clutch
4. Support, driven sprocket
7. Seal, "O" ring (support/ 2nd clutch)
11. Housing, 2nd clutch
1. Input clutch oil passage
2. 2nd clutch oil passage
3. 3rd clutch oil passage
4. 4th clutch oil passage
5. Lube

Cross section of the driven sprocket support assembly (© General Motors Corp.)

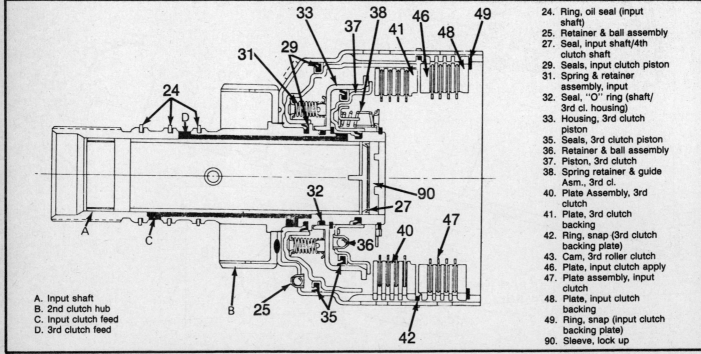

24. Ring, oil seal (input shaft)
25. Retainer & ball assembly
27. Seal, input shaft/4th clutch shaft
29. Seals, input clutch piston
31. Spring & retainer assembly, input
32. Seal, "O" ring (shaft/ 3rd cl. housing)
33. Housing, 3rd clutch piston
35. Seals, 3rd clutch piston
36. Retainer & ball assembly
37. Piston, 3rd clutch
38. Spring retainer & guide Asm., 3rd cl.
40. Plate Assembly, 3rd clutch
41. Plate, 3rd clutch backing
42. Ring, snap (3rd clutch backing plate)
43. Cam, 3rd roller clutch
46. Plate, input clutch apply
47. Plate assembly, input clutch
48. Plate, input clutch backing
49. Ring, snap (input clutch backing plate)
90. Sleeve, lock up

A. Input shaft
B. 2nd clutch hub
C. Input clutch feed
D. 3rd clutch feed

Cross section of the input clutch assembly (© General Motors Corp.)

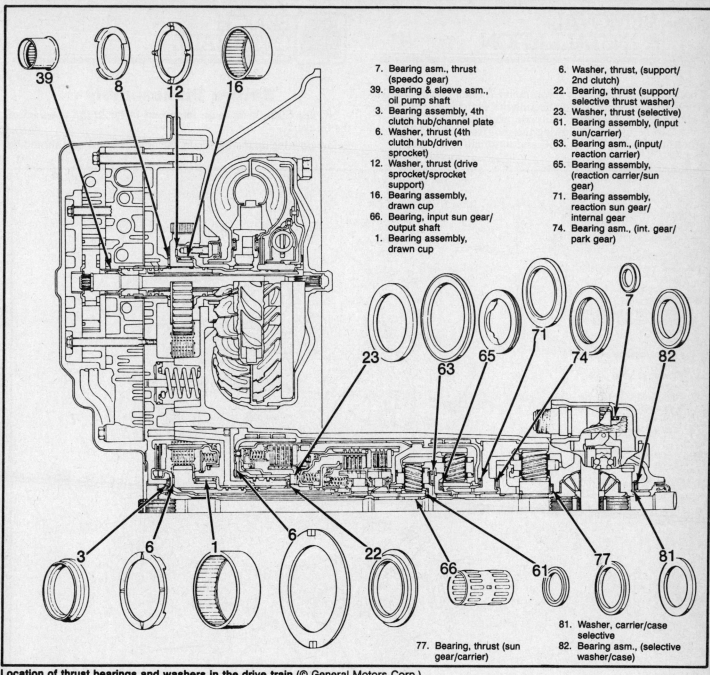

7. Bearing asm., thrust (speedo gear)
39. Bearing & sleeve asm., oil pump shaft
3. Bearing assembly, 4th clutch hub/channel plate
6. Washer, thrust (4th clutch hub/driven sprocket)
12. Washer, thrust (drive sprocket/sprocket support)
16. Bearing assembly, drawn cup
66. Bearing, input sun gear/output shaft
1. Bearing assembly, drawn cup

6. Washer, thrust, (support/2nd clutch)
22. Bearing, thrust (support/selective thrust washer)
23. Washer, thrust (selective)
61. Bearing assembly, (input sun/carrier)
63. Bearing asm., (input/reaction carrier)
65. Bearing assembly, (reaction carrier/sun gear)
71. Bearing assembly, reaction sun gear/internal gear
74. Bearing asm., (int. gear/park gear)

77. Bearing, thrust (sun gear/carrier)

81. Washer, carrier/case selective
82. Bearing asm., (selective washer/case)

Location of thrust bearings and washers in the drive train (© General Motors Corp.)

 **REMOVAL & INSTALLATION**

BENCH OVERHAUL

There has been no factory recommended removal and installation procedure published affecting the vehicles in which the THM 440-T4 automatic transaxle are installed. A general guide can be used by following the removal and installation procedures for the THM 125C and automatic transaxle.

Before Disassembly

NOTE: Cleanliness is an important factor in the overhaul of the transaxle.

Before opening up the transaxle, the outside of the unit should be

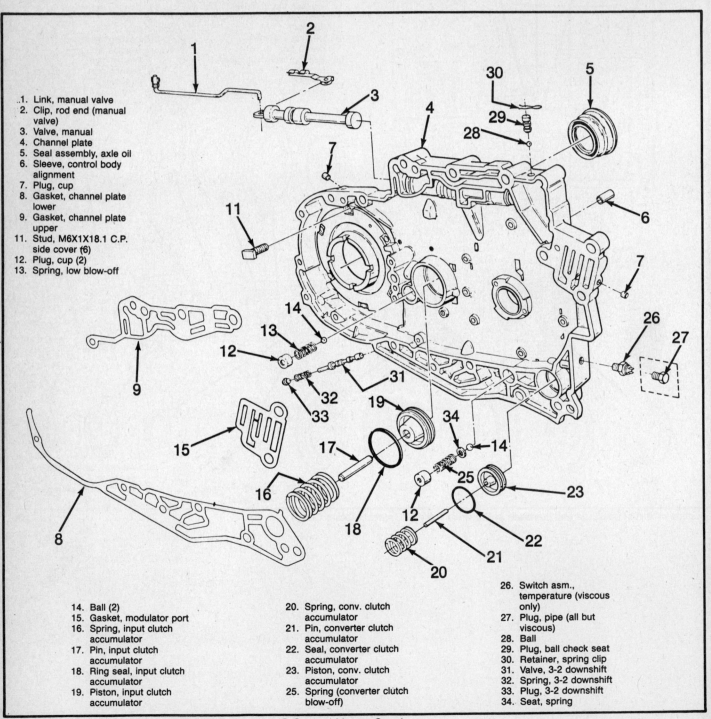

1. Link, manual valve
2. Clip, rod end (manual valve)
3. Valve, manual
4. Channel plate
5. Seal assembly, axle oil
6. Sleeve, control body alignment
7. Plug, cup
8. Gasket, channel plate lower
9. Gasket, channel plate upper
11. Stud, M6X1X18.1 C.P. side cover (6)
12. Plug, cup (2)
13. Spring, low blow-off

14. Ball (2)
15. Gasket, modulator port
16. Spring, input clutch accumulator
17. Pin, input clutch accumulator
18. Ring seal, input clutch accumulator
19. Piston, input clutch accumulator

20. Spring, conv. clutch accumulator
21. Pin, converter clutch accumulator
22. Seal, converter clutch accumulator
23. Piston, conv. clutch accumulator
25. Spring (converter clutch blow-off)

26. Switch asm., temperature (viscous only)
27. Plug, pipe (all but viscous)
28. Ball
29. Plug, ball check seat
30. Retainer, spring clip
31. Valve, 3-2 downshift
32. Spring, 3-2 downshift
33. Plug, 3-2 downshift
34. Seat, spring

Exploded view of channel plate and component parts (© General Motors Corp.)

1. Converter assembly
2. Bushing, converter pump
3. Sleeve, governor shaft
4. Ring, oil seal (governor shaft)
5. Governor assembly
6. Gear, speedometer drive
7. Bearing asm., thrust (speedo gear)
8. Seal, "O" ring (governor cover)
9. Cover, governor
10. Screw, governor cover/case
11. Gear, speedo driven
12. Seal, "O" ring
13. Sleeve, speedo driven gear
14. Retainer, speedo driven gear
15. Bolt, speedo gear retaining
16. Case assembly
17. Valve, modulator
18. Seal, "O" ring
19. Modulator assembly
20. Retainer, modulator
21. Bolt, (modulator)
23. Electrical connector
24. Channel, plate assembly
25. Ball, check valve (7)
26. Bolt, channel plate to case (5)
27. Bolt, channel plate to driven support (6)
28. Ring, oil seal (oil pump)
29. Shaft, oil pump drive
30. Gasket, spacer plate/channel plate
31. Plate, valve body spacer
32. Gasket, spacer plate/valve body
33. Screen asm., conv. clutch solenoid
34. Ball, check valve (5)
35. Valve assembly, control
38. Screen assembly, oil pump pressure
39. Bearing & sleeve asm., oil pump shaft
40. Bolt, V.B. to C.P. (torque head) (6)
41. Bolt, valve body to C.P. (hex) (1)
42. Bolt, V.B. to driven support (torque) (2)
43. Bolt, valve body to case (hex) (3)
44. Pump assembly
45. Bolt, pump body to case (hex) (2)
46. Bolt, pump cover to C.P. (hex) (10)
47. Bolt, pump cover to valve body (hex) (1)
48. Harness, wiring
49. Link throttle lever to cable
50. Lever & bracket assembly, throttle
51. Pan, case side cover
52. Screw, special M8x1.25x16.0
53. Nut, flanged hex (M6x1.0)
54. Bolt, M6x1.0x35 LG. P.B./C.P. hex (1)
55. Bolt, M6x1.0x45 LG. V.B./C.P. (2)
56. Washer, conical

57. Seal assembly, oil filter
58. Filter assembly, oil
59. Pan, transmission oil
60. Screw, special M8x1.25x16.0)
61. Wire conduit
62. Clip, two wire

63. Gasket, transmission oil pan
64. Gasket, side cover to case
65. Gasket, side cover to channel plate
66. Magnet, chip collector

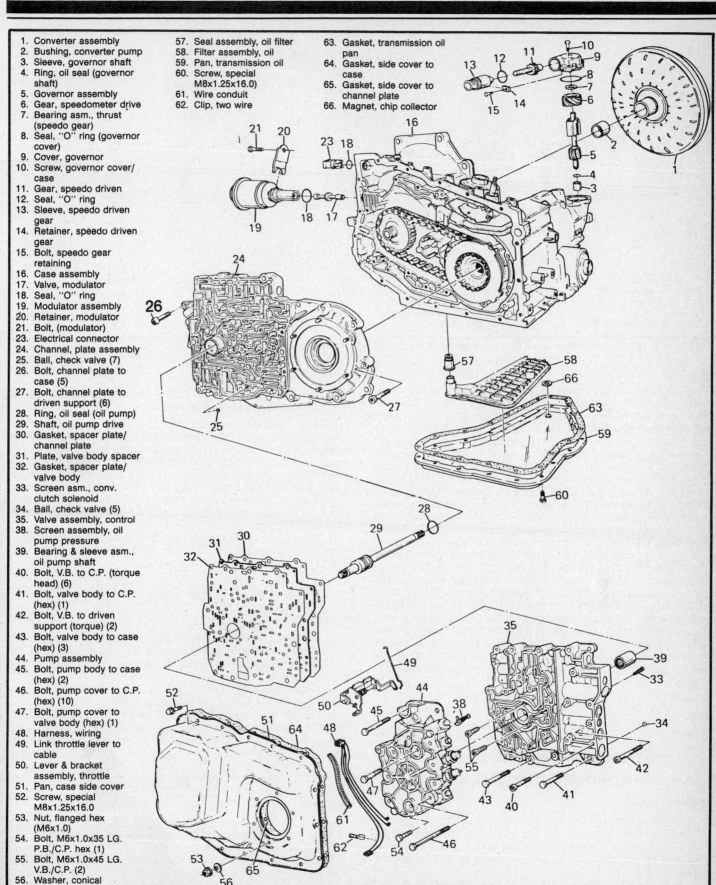

Exploded view of the THM 440-T4 automatic transaxle (© General Motors Corp.)

647

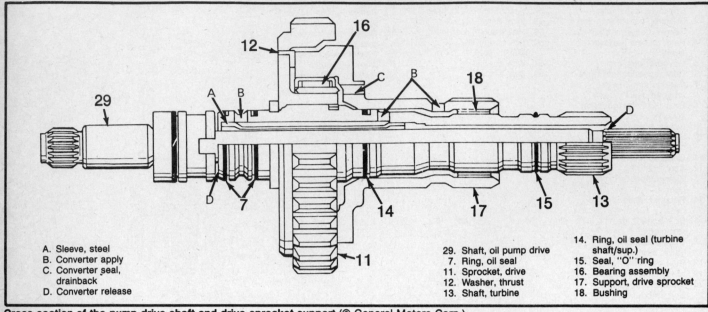

A. Sleeve, steel
B. Converter apply
C. Converter seal, drainback
D. Converter release

29. Shaft, oil pump drive
7. Ring, oil seal
11. Sprocket, drive
12. Washer, thrust
13. Shaft, turbine

14. Ring, oil seal (turbine shaft/sup.)
15. Seal, "O" ring
16. Bearing assembly
17. Support, drive sprocket
18. Bushing

Cross section of the pump drive shaft and drive sprocket support (© General Motors Corp.)

thoroughly cleaned, preferably with high-pressure cleaning equipment such as a car wash spray unit. Dirt entering the transaxle internal parts will negate all the effort and time spent on the overhaul. During inspection and reassembly, all parts should be thoroughly cleaned with solvent, then dried with compressed air. Wiping cloths and rags should not be used to dry parts since lint will find its way into valve body passages. Wheel bearing grease, long used to secure thrust washers and to lube parts should not be used. Lube seals with Dexron® II and use ordinary unmedicated petroleum jelly to hold thrust washers to ease assembly of seals, since it will not leave a harmful residue as grease often will. DO NOT use solvent on neoprene seals, friction plates or thrust washers. Be wary of nylon parts if the transaxle failure was due to a failure of the cooling system. Nylon parts exposed to antifreeze solutions can swell and distort and so must be replaced (Speedo gears, some thrust washers, etc.). Before installing bolts into aluminum parts, always dip the threads into clean oil. Anti-seize compound is also a good way to prevent the bolts from galling the aluminum and seizing. Always use a torque wrench to keep from stripping the threads. Take care of the seals when installing them, especially the smaller O-rings. The internal snap rings should be expanded and the external snap rings should be compressed, if they are to be reused. This will help insure proper seating when installed.

Transaxle Disassembly
TORQUE CONVERTER

Removal

1. Make certain that the transaxle is held securely.
2. Pull the converter straight out of the transaxle. Be careful since the converter contains a large amount of oil. There is no drain plug on the converter so the converter should be drained through the hub.

NOTE: The transaxle fluid that is drained from the converter can help diagnose transaxle problems.

1. If the oil in the converter is discolored but does not contain metal bits or particles, the converter is not damaged and need not be replaced. Remember that color is no longer a good indicator of transaxle fluid condition. In the past, dark color was associated with overheated transaxle fluid. It is not a positive sign of transaxle failure with the newer fluids like Dexron® II.
2. If the oil in the converter contains metal particles, the converter is damaged internally and must be replaced. The oil may have an "aluminum paint" appearance.
3. If the cause of oil contamination was due to burned clutch plates or overheated oil, the converter is contaminated and should be replaced.

OIL PAN

Removal

1. Remove the oil pan attaching bolts. Carefully bump the pan with a rubber mallet to free the pan. If the pan is pried loose instead, be very careful not to damage the gasket surfaces. Discard the pan gasket.
2. Inspect the bottom of the pan for debris that can give an indication of the nature of the transaxle failure.
3. Check the pan for distorted gasket flanges, especially around the bolt holes, since these are often dished-in due to overtorque. They can be straightened with a block of wood and a rubber mallet if necessary.

OIL FILTER

Removal

1. The oil filter is retained by a clip as well as the interference fit of the oil intake tube and O-ring. Move the clip out of the way and pull the filter from the case.
2. Discard the O-ring from the intake pipe. Often the O-ring will stick to its bore in the case.

3. The oil pressure regulator is in the bore next to the oil filter intake pipe opening. If it is to be removed, use snap ring pliers to remove the retaining ring and then pull the pressure regulator bushing assembly from the case.

GOVERNOR

Removal

1. Since the speedometer drive gear is attached to the governor assembly, first remove the speedometer driven gear attaching bolt and the retaining clip.

2. Remove the speedometer driven gear from the governor cover. Remove the governor cover and discard the O-ring.

3. Remove the governor assembly along with the speedometer drive gear thrust bearing.

4. Remove the modulator retainer and lift out the modulator. Discard the O-ring. Lift out the modulator valve using a magnet.

Governor and modulator assemblies—exploded view
(© General Motors Corporation)

INTERMEDIATE SERVO

Removal

1. To remove the intermediate servo assembly, the cover will have to be depressed to relieve the spring pressure on the snap ring that retains the cover. The factory type tool for this is similar to a clamp that hooks to the case and applies with a screw operated arm. The object is to release the spring holding pressure the cover has on the snap ring.

2. Pliers can be used to grasp the servo cover to remove it. Discard the seals. Make sure that the cover seal ring is not stuck in the case groove where it might be overlooked.

3. Remove the servo assembly and the servo return springs. Remove the apply pin from the servo assembly.

NOTE: The servo assemblies are not interchangeable due to the reverse servo pin being longer than the 1-2 pin. Keep the servo assemblies separate.

OIL PUMP

Removal

1. Disconnect the side cover attaching nuts and bolts and remove the side cover. Discard the gaskets.

2. Detach the solenoid wiring harness from the case connector and pressure switch. Remove the throttle valve assembly from the valve body.

3. Remove the oil pump bolts and lift the oil pump assembly from the valve body.

VALVE BODY

Removal

1. Remove the valve body retaining bolts. Remove the valve body from the channel plate.

2. Remove the check balls from the spacer plate. Detach the spacer plate and discard the gaskets.

3. Remove the check balls from the channel plate.

OIL PUMP SHAFT AND CHANNEL PLATE

Removal

1. Remove the oil pump shaft by sliding it out of the channel plate assembly. Place the detent lever in the park position and remove the manual valve clip.

2. Remove the channel plate attaching bolts and lift the channel plate from the transaxle case.

3. Remove the accumulator piston and the converter clutch accumulator piston and spring. Discard all gaskets.

FOURTH CLUTCH (C4) AND OUTPUT SHAFT

Removal

1. Remove the three (3) clutch plates along with the apply plate. Remove the thrust bearing.

NOTE: The thrust bearing may still be on the case cover from earlier disassembly.

2. Remove the front clutch hub and shaft assembly. This will expose the output shaft.

3. Rotate the output shaft until the output shaft C ring is visible. Remove the C-ring.

4. Pull the output shaft from the transaxle being careful not to damage it.

DRIVE LINK ASSEMBLY

Removal

1. Remove the turbine shaft O-ring located at the front of the unit.

2. Reach through the access holes in the sprockets and slip the snap rings from their grooves.

3. Remove the sprockets and the chain as an assembly. It will require alternately pulling on the sprockets until the bearings come out of their support housings.

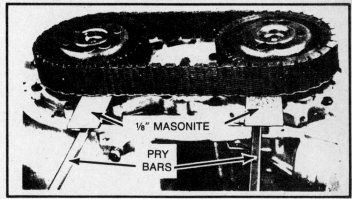

Removing tight sprockets (© General Motors Corporation)

NOTE: If the sprockets are difficult to remove, use two small pieces of masonite or similar material to act both as wedges and as pads for a pry bar. Do not pry on the chain or the case.

4. After removing the drivelink assembly, take note as to the position of the colored link on the chain. It should be facing out. Remove the thrust washers.

5. Lift out the drive sprocket support and remove the thrust washer located on the casing.

CHECK INPUT UNIT END-PLAY

The factory tools for checking the end-play on this unit are somewhat elaborate and it is unlikely that every shop will be equipped in the same manner. However, the object is to pre-load the output shaft to remove the clearance. The factory tool mounts on the output end of the transaxle and a knob and screw arrangement can be tightened, forcing the output shaft upwards. A dial indicator is mounted on the end of the input shaft. By raising the input shaft with a suitable bar (again, the factory tool is special and grips the input shaft splines) the input unit end-play can be measured. Input shaft end-play should be 0.020–0.042 in.

INPUT HOUSING AND SHAFT ASSEMBLY

Removal

1. Clamp the clutch and final drive tool to the second clutch housing. Lift the second clutch housing and the input shaft assembly out of the unit.
2. Remove the reverse band and the reverse reaction drum. Remove the input carrier assembly.

NOTE: The reverse band assembly may lift out with the second clutch housing.

3. Remove the thrust bearing and the reaction carrier. The thrust bearing is located at one end of the reaction carrier.
4. Remove the thrust bearing which may be stuck to the reaction carrier.
5. Remove the reaction sun gear and the drum assembly. Remove the 1-2 band.

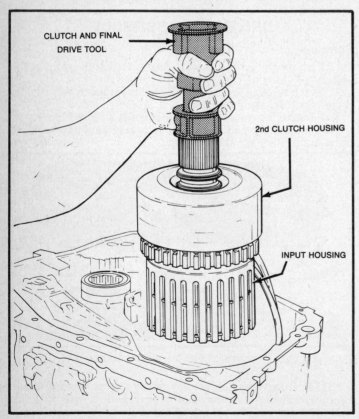

Input housing and shaft removal (© General Motors Corporation)

NOTE: The 1-2 band assembly should not be cleaned in cleaning solvent.

6. Remove the bearing ring and the sun gear shaft. A final drive internal bushing will be found on the sun gear shaft.

FINAL DRIVE ASSEMBLY

Removal

1. With a suitable tool, remove the snap ring at the head of the internal final drive gear.
2. Clamp the clutch and final drive tool to the final drive internal gear and lift it out.
3. The final drive carrier will be removed with the final drive internal gear.

MANUAL SHAFT/DETENT LEVER AND ACTUATOR ROD

Removal

1. It is not necessary to disassemble the manual shaft, detent lever or the actuator rod unless replacement is needed.
2. Remove the manual shaft and detent lever retaining bolts and remove the shaft and lever.
3. Remove the actuator rod assembly and check for wear or damage.
4. Remove the actuator guide assembly and check for damage.

MANUAL LINKAGE/ACTUATOR REPLACEMENT

Removal

1. Remove the manual shaft lock nut and pin and lift out the manual shaft with the detent lever.
2. Remove the retaining pin from the case and detach the actuator guide assembly.
3. Remove the O-ring from the actuator guide and discard the O-ring.

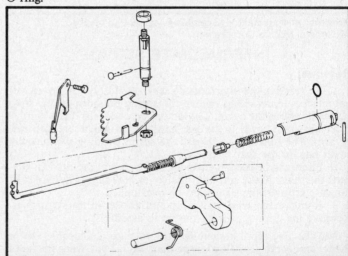

Manual linkage—exploded view (© General Motors Corporation)

4. The parking lock pawl assembly cannot be removed from the final drive internal gear.

NOTE: If the manual shaft seal is needed to be replaced, remove the axle oil seal along with the converter seal and then remove the manual shaft seal from its mounting in the transaxle case.

Unit Disassembly and Assembly
CASE

1. Clean the case well and inspect carefully for cracks. Make certain that all passages are clean and that all bores and snap ring

grooves are clean and free from damage. Check for stripped bolt holes. Check the case bushings for damage.

2. A new manual shaft seal can be installed at this time, along with a new axle oil seal and converter seal. Tap the seals into place with a suitable tool. The seal lips must face into the case.

3. Check the drive sprocket support assembly for damage. If it requires replacement, a slide hammer type puller can be used to pull the bearing from the sprocket support. Once the bearing is out, inspect the bore for wear or damage. The new bearing should be drive in straight and with care so as not to damage it.

4. If the parking pawl and related parts are to be removed, begin by turning the transaxle to the oil pan side up. Use a punch to remove the cup plug. Remove the parking pawl shaft retainer, then the shaft, pawl and return spring. Check the pawl for cracks.

FINAL DRIVE UNIT

Disassembly

1. Remove the final drive gear snap ring and lift out the final drive gear unit. Lift out the bearing assembly and the parking gear.

2. Remove the final drive sun gear along with the final drive carrier and the governor drive gear.

3. Remove the carrier washer and the bearing assembly.

4. Place the final drive carrier on its side and remove the differential pinion shaft by tapping out the pinion shaft retaining pin.

5. Remove the pinion thrust washer and the differential pinion. Remove the two side gear thrust washers and the two differential side gears.

Inspection

1. Clean all parts well and check for damage or excessive wear. Check the gears for burrs and cracks.

2. Inspect the washers and replace any that appear damaged or warped.

3. Check the bearing assemblies for any mutilation and replace as needed.

Assembly

1. Install the differential side gears and washers into the final drive carrier.

2. Install the pinion thrust washers onto the differential pinions. A small amount of petroleum jelly can be used to hold the washers in place.

3. Place the pinions and washers into the final drive carrier.

4. Insert the differential pinion shaft into the final drive carrier to check alignment of the pinions, then remove.

5. If the pinions are out of alignment, correct and reinstall the differential pinion shaft. Tap the pinion shaft retaining pin into position.

6. Assemble the sun gear into the final drive carrier with the stepped side facing out. Install the parking gear onto the sun gear.

7. Install the thrust bearing assembly into the final drive internal gear and place the unit onto the final drive carrier.

8. Install the thrust washer and the thrust bearing onto the carrier hub. Install the snap ring making sure it seats properly in its groove.

FINAL DRIVE SUN GEAR SHAFT

Disassembly

1. Lift off the reverse reaction drum and the input carrier assembly.

2. Remove the reaction carrier bearing, which may be stuck to the input carrier assembly.

3. Remove the internal gear bearing and the final drive sun gear.

4. Lift out the 1-2 band from the reaction sun gear and drum assembly.

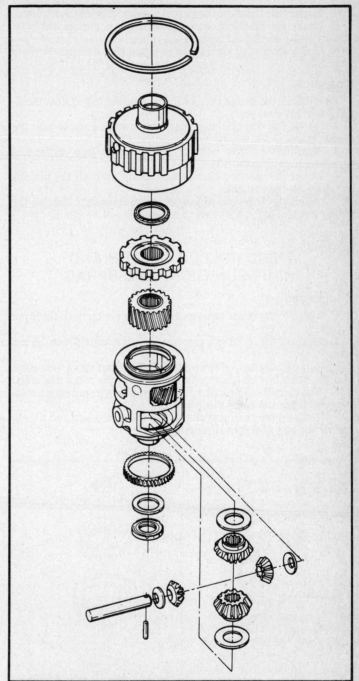

Final drive assembly—exploded view
(© General Motors Corporation)

5. Remove the bearing assembly from the reaction sun gear and drum assembly.

Inspection

1. Inspect the final drive sun gear shaft for damaged splines. Replace if necessary.

2. Inspect the 1-2 band assembly for damage from heat or excessive wear. Check the band assembly for lining separation or lining cracks.

NOTE: The 1-2 band assembly is presoaked in a friction solution and should not be washed in a cleaning solvent.

3. Inspect the sun gear/drum assembly for any scoring or damaged teeth.

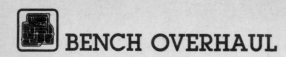

4. Inspect the thrust bearings for damage. Replace as required.

5. Check the reaction carrier assembly for pinion end play. Pinion end play should be 0.23-0.61mm.

6. Check for pinion damage or internal gear damage. Replace as needed.

Assembly

1. Position the inside race of the thrust bearing against the final drive internal gear.

2. Install the reaction sun gear and drum assembly into the case.

3. Position the thrust bearing inside the reaction carrier and retain with petroleum jelly.

4. Install the reaction carrier and rotate until all the pinions engage with the sun gear.

5. Install the reverse reaction drum making sure that all the spline teeth engage with the input carrier.

THIRD ROLLER CLUTCH AND INPUT SUN GEAR AND SPRAG

Disassembly

1. Remove the input sprag and 3rd roller clutch from the input sun gear.

2. Remove the input sun gear spacer and retainer from the sun gear.

3. Remove the snap ring and lift off the input sprag wear plate and the 3rd roller clutch race and cam from the roller assembly.

4. Disassemble the input sprag assembly by removing the inner race from the sprag assembly.

5. Remove the snap ring that holds the wear plate and lift out the wear plate and sprag assembly.

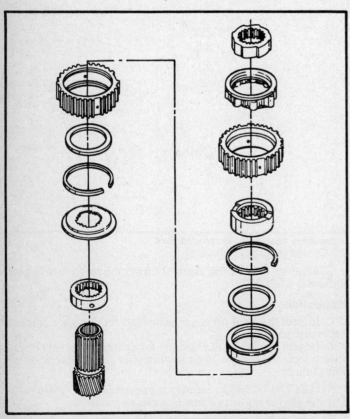

Third roller clutch assembly (© General Motors Corporation)

Inspection

1. Clean all parts in cleaning solvent and blow dry using compressed air.

2. Inspect the outer race and roller cam for any cracks or scoring. Replace as required.

3. Inspect the roller assembly for damaged rollers and springs. Replace any loose rollers by depressing the spring and inserting the roller.

4. Inspect the sprag assembly for damaged sprags or cages and replace as required.

5. Inspect the inner race and wear plates for any scoring or damage. Replace as required.

Assembly

1. Position one wear plate against the snap ring and hold in position with petroleum jelly.

2. Insert the wear plate with the snap ring against the sprag assembly.

3. Install the spacer on the input sun gear and place the sprag retainer over the spacer.

4. Install the sprag snap ring. Make sure the snap ring seats properly.

5. Install the sprag assembly and the roller clutch onto the sun gear.

INPUT CLUTCH ASSEMBLY

Disassembly

1. Remove the input clutch snap ring and remove the input clutch backing plate.

2. Remove the steel and compostion clutch plates, along with the input clutch apply plate.

3. Remove the third clutch snap ring and remove the third clutch backing plate.

4. Remove the steel and composition clutch plates, along with the third clutch waved plate.

5 Remove the snap ring from the spring retainer, and lift out the third clutch piston from its housing.

6. Remove the third clutch piston inner seal from the shaft.

7. Compress the third clutch piston housing and remove the snap ring. Remove the third clutch piston housing.

8. Remove the O-ring seal and take out the spring retainer. Remove the input clutch piston and inner seal.

Inspection

1. Wash all parts in cleaning solvent and blow dry using compressed air.

2. Inspect all parts for scoring, wear or damage.

3. Inspect the input clutch housing for damaged or worn bushings.

4. Check the fourth clutch shaft seal and replace if damaged or cut.

5. Repair or replace any parts found to be defective.

Assembly

1. Lubricate all parts with automatic transmission fluid prior to assembling.

2. Install the input clutch piston seal with the piston seal protector. Position the input piston in the housing.

3. Install the O-ring on the input shaft making sure it seats properly. Install the spring retainer in the piston.

4. Install the third clutch piston housing into the input housing. Compress the third clutch housing with a clutch spring compressor and install the snap ring.

5. Install the third clutch inner seal on the third clutch piston and install the third clutch piston.

6. Install the third clutch spring retainer and compress the spring retainer using the clutch spring compressor and install the snap ring.

7. Install the third clutch plates and the third clutch backing plate. Install the snap ring.

NOTE: When installing the third clutch plates, start with a steel plate and alternate between composition and steel plates. When installing the third clutch backing plate, make sure that the stepped side is facing up.

8. Install the input clutch apply plate with the notched side facing the snap ring. Install the input clutch plates.

NOTE: When installing the input clutch plates, start with a composition plate and alternate between steel and composition plates.

9. Install the input clutch backing plate and secure with a snap ring.

RETAINER AND BALL ASSEMBLY

Replacement (optional)

1. Remove the retainer and ball assembly from the housing with a ⅜ in. (9.5mm) drift.
2. Tap in a new retainer using a ⅜ in. (9.5mm) drift.

PISTON SEAL

Replacement (optional)

1. Remove the input clutch piston seal and the third clutch piston seal.
2. Inspect the clutch piston for any remaining seals and remove.
3. Install a new input clutch piston seal and a new third clutch piston seal. Lubricate with transmission fluid.

FOURTH CLUTCH SHAFT SEAL

Replacement (optional)

1. Remove the lock up sleeve using a suitable tool and remove the oil seal.
2. Install the new oil seal into the input shaft making sure that the seal tab aligns with the slot in the shaft.
3. Install the lock up sleeve in the shaft using a bench press.

INPUT SHAFT SEAL

Replacement (optional)

1. Remove the seal rings from the input shaft with a suitable tool.
2. Adjust the seal protector so that the bottom matches the seal ring groove.
3. Lubricate the oil seal ring and place it on the seal protector.
4. Slide the seal into position with the seal pusher over the seal protector.
5. Size the seal with a seal sizer and gently work the tool over the seal with a twisting motion.

SECOND CLUTCH HOUSING

Disassembly

1. Remove the second clutch hub snap ring and lift out the second clutch wave plate.
2. Remove the second clutch plate assembly and the second clutch backing plate.
3. Remove the next snap ring and remove the second clutch housing support.
4. Remove the thrust bearing and thrust washer. Remove the reverse band.
5. Remove the second clutch housing. Remove the second clutch piston seals which may be stuck on the second clutch housing.

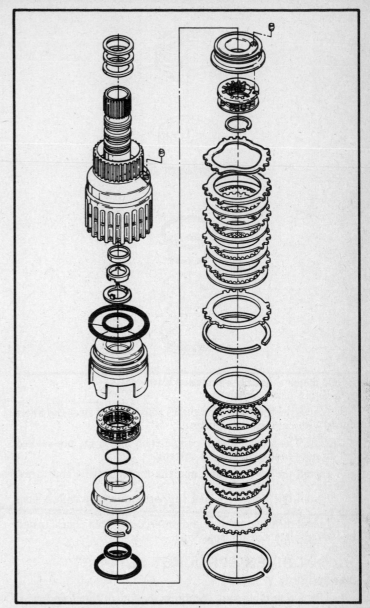

Input clutch assembly (© General Motors Corporation)

6. Remove the second clutch piston and the spring return apply ring.

Inspection

1. Wash all parts in cleaning solvent and blow dry using compressed air.
2. Inspect all parts for scoring, wear or damage.
3. Inspect the second clutch piston and seal for damage or warping.
4. Repair or replace damaged parts as required.

Assembly

1. Lubricate a new piston seal with automatic transmission fluid and install in the second clutch piston.
2. Install a new retainer and ball assembly into the second clutch housing using a ⅜ in. (9.5mm) drift.
3. Install the second clutch piston into the second clutch housing. Make sure the seals are not damaged.
4. Install the spring return apply ring into the second clutch housing. Using a spring compressor, compress the spring return apply ring and insert the snap ring.

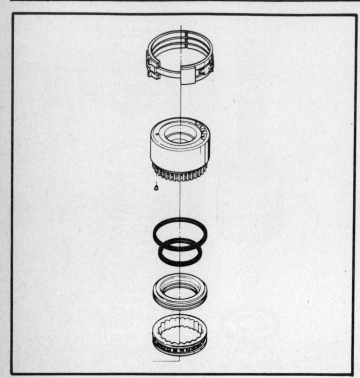

Second clutch assembly—exploded view
(© General Motors Corporation)

5. Install the second clutch plates starting with steel and alternating with composition plates.

NOTE: The second clutch composition plates are pre-soaked and do not require soaking in solvent.

6. Install the reverse band and the thrust bearing and thrust washers.

7. Install the clutch housing support and secure with a snap ring.

8. Install the backing plate and the second clutch plates. Install the waved plate and the snap ring.

DRIVEN SPROCKET SUPPORT

Disassembly

1. Using a suitable tool, compress the fourth clutch spring assembly and remove the snap ring.

2. Remove the fourth clutch piston and the piston seals. Discard the piston seals.

3. Remove the bearing assembly from the driven sprocket support.

4. Remove the chain scavening scoop and the oil reservoir weir.

5. Remove the thrust washer and the O-ring seals.

Inspection

1. Clean all parts thoroughly in solvent and blow dry using compressed air.

2. Inspect the driven sprocket support for cracks or damage.

3. Inspect the seals and pistons for damage. Replace as necessary.

4. Check the spring retainer for distorted or damaged springs.

5. Inspect the oil reservoir weir and the chain scavenging scoop for cracks or damage.

6. Repair or replace any damaged parts as required.

Assembly

1. Lubricate new O-rings and install them behind the thrust washer on the driven sprocket support.

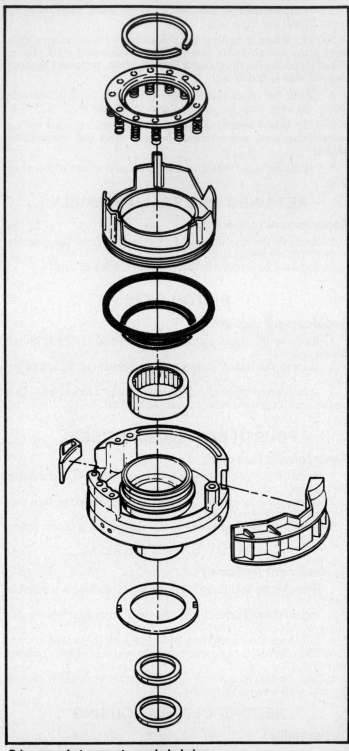

Drive sprocket support—exploded view
(© General Motors Corporation)

2. Install the oil reservoir weir and the chain scavenging scoop on the driven sprocket support.

3. Install the bearing assembly on the driven sprocket support, between the oil reservoir weir and the chain scavenging scoop.

4. Install new seals on the fourth clutch piston and install the fourth clutch piston.

5. Install the fourth clutch spring assembly and using a suitable tool, compress the springs and insert the snap ring.

OIL PUMP

Disassembly

1. Remove the pump bolts from the cover. Lift off the pump cover. Remove the pump cover sleeve and the vane ring.
2. Remove the pump rotor and the bottom vane ring. Remove the oil seal ring and the O-ring from the oil pump slide.
3. Remove the oil pump slide. Enclosed in the oil pump slide are the pump slide seal and support along with the inner and outer pump priming springs.

NOTE: The pump rotor, vane rings and oil pump slide are factory matched units. Therefore, if any parts need replacing, all parts must be replaced.

4. Remove the pivot pin and the roll pin from the oil pump body.
5. Remove the 3-2 coast down valve, spring and bore plug from the oil pump body. Remove the oil pressure switches.

Inspection

1. Clean all parts thoroughly in solvent and blow dry using compressed air.
2. Check the pump body for warping or cracks. Make sure that the oil passages are free of debris.
3. Check the oil pump slide and springs for excessive wear.
4. Check the rotor and vanes for any damage. Inspect the pump slide seal and support for any cracks.
5. Repair or replace damaged parts as needed.

Assembly

1. Install the 3-2 coast down valve along with the spring and bore plug into the oil pump body.
2. Install the lower vane ring into the pump pocket. Install the pump slide into the pump pocket being careful not to dislodge the lower vane ring.
3. Install the pump slide seal and support into the oil pump slide. Install the pump slide seal and support into the pump slide.
4. Insert the inner priming spring into the outer priming spring. Press the springs into the pump body.
5. Install the O-ring seal onto the oil pump slide. Install the oil seal ring onto the oil pump slide.
6. Install the oil pump rotor onto the oil pump body. Insert the pump vanes into the oil pump rotor. Install the upper vane ring onto the oil pump rotor.

NOTE: The pump vanes must be installed flush with the top of the oil pump rotor.

7. Install the pump cover onto the oil pump body. Install the cover bolts.
8. Install the oil pressure switches into the oil pump body.

CONTROL VALVE

Disassembly

NOTE: As each part of the valve train is removed, place the pieces in order and in a position that is relative to the position on the valve body to lessen the chances for error in assembly. None of the valves, springs or bushings are interchangeable.

1. Lay the valve body on a clean work bench with the machined side up and the line boost valve at the top. The line boost valve should be checked for proper operation before its removal. If it is necessary to remove the boost valve, grind the end of a #49 drill to a taper (a small Allen wrench can sometimes be substituted) and lightly tap the drill into the roll pin. Push the line boost valve out of the top of the valve body.
2. The throttle valve should be checked for proper operation before removing it, by pushing the valve against the spring. If it is necessary to remove the throttle valve, first remove the roll pin holding the T.V. plunger bushing and pull out the plunger and

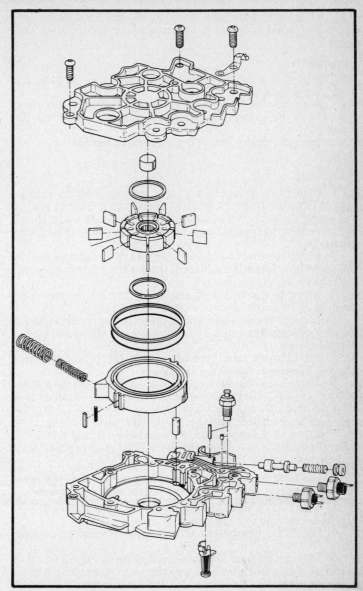

Oil pump—exploded view (© General Motors Corporation)

bushing. Remove the throttle valve spring. Remove the blind hole roll pin using the drill method described earlier.

3. On the same side of the valve body, move to the next bore down. Remove the straight pin and remove the reverse boost valve and bushing, as well as reverse boost spring and the pressure regulator assembly.

NOTE: Models equipped with a diesel engine will not have a reverse boost spring or a pressure regulator modulator spring.

4. Move to the other side of the valve body and from the top bore remove the 1-2 throttle valve bushing retainer and lift out the throttle valve bushing and the 1-2 shift valve assembly.
5. Move to the next bore and remove the spring pin and lift out the 2-3 accumulator bushing assembly.
6. At the next bore down, remove the 3-2 control sleeve and the 3-2 control valve assembly.
7. Move to the next bore and remove the spring pin. Remove the 2-3 throttle valve bushing and its components.
8. Move to the next bore and remove the coiled spring pin. Remove the 3-4 throttle valve assembly.
9. The two remaining bores contain the 1-2 servo pipe lip seals, which are removed.

10. At the side of the valve body, are the servo assemblies. Remove the coiled spring pins and detach the servo valves and springs.

Inspection

1. Wash all bushings, springs and valves in solvent. Blow dry using compressed air.
2. Inspect all valves and bushings for any scoring or scratches.
3. Check the springs for collapsed coils and bore plugs for damage.
4. Repair or replace any defective parts as needed.

Assembly

1. Install the reverse servo boost valve and spring into its proper location in the valve body. Install the 1-2 servo control valve and the 1-2 servo boost valve into the valve body. Install the correct springs behind each valve and insert the coiled spring pins.
2. Install new servo pipe lip seals. Move to the bore next to the servo pipe lip seals, and install the 3-4 throttle assembly. Install the coiled spring pin.
3. Move to the next bore and install the 2-3 throttle valve bushing and its components. Install the spring pin.
4. Move to the next bore and in the following order install 3-2 isolator valve and spring, 3-2 control valve and spring and the 3-2 control sleeve.
5. Move to the next bore and install the 2-3 accumulator bushing assembly. Install the spring pin.
6. Move to the last bore on the side and install in the following order the 1-2 shift valve and throttle valve, the throttle valve spring and the 1-2 throttle valve bushing. Insert the 1-2 throttle valve bushing retainer into the 1-2 throttle valve bushing.
7. Move to the other side of the valve body and install the pressure regulator valve assembly. Install the reverse boost valve and bushing. Install the straight pin.

NOTE: The reverse boost spring and a pressure regulator modulator spring will only be found on models with a gas engine.

8. Install in the next bore the throttle valve assembly. Secure the assembly with the spring pin.
9. Install the line boost valve assembly. Insert the retainer clip.
10. Move to the next bore and install throttle valve feed valve assembly. Make sure the valve stop plate is in its proper position.
11. Move to the next bore and install the converter clutch shift valve assembly securing it with the bushing and a coiled spring pin.
12. The next bore is the pump pressure valve and bushing locations. Secure these units with a spring pin.
13. Moving to the next bore, install the 1-2 accumulator assembly. Make sure that the valve bore plug is in place over the 1-2 accumulator valve.
14. Assemble the converter clutch valves into the next two bore holes.
15. Install the second clutch pipes in the top of the valve body. Install the release cover plate gasket and cover.

CHANNEL PLATE

Disassembly

1. Remove the modulator port gasket and the upper channel plate gasket. Remove the lower channel plate gasket and discard all gaskets.
2. Remove the input clutch accumulator piston and spring. Discard the input clutch ring seal.
3. Remove the converter clutch accumulator piston and the converter clutch spring. Discard the converter clutch seal. Remove the axle oil seal.
4. Remove the manual valve assembly. Detach the manual valve clip. Remove the channel plate stud from the case side of the channel plate.

Inspection

1. Wash all parts in solvent and blow dry using compressed air.
2. Check all parts for excessive wear or damage. Check the channel plate for cracks or warping.
3. Repair or replace any defective parts as required.

Assembly

1. Install the channel plate stud to the channel plate. Attach the manual valve clip to the manual valve assembly. Install the manual valve assembly into the channel plate.
2. Press in a new axle oil seal using a suitable tool. Install a new converter clutch seal. Place the converter clutch piston on its shaft with a new seal. Install the converter clutch spring.
3. Install the input clutch piston with a new input clutch seal. Install the input clutch spring.

Transaxle Assembly

Before the assembly of the transaxle begins, make certain that the case and all other parts are clean that all parts are serviceable or have been overhauled. Inspect the case carefully for cracks or any signs of porosity. Inspect the vents to make sure that they are open. Check the case lugs, the intermediate servo bore and snap ring grooves for damage. Check the bearings that are in the case and replace if they appear to be worn.

NOTE: If the bearings are replaced, they must be installed with the bearing identification facing up.

The converter seal should be replaced. After all these preliminary checks have been made, begin the reassembly of the transaxle. Make certain that the transaxle is held securely in the proper support fixture.

1. If the manual shaft seals were removed during disassembly, replace as required. Install a new O-ring on the actuator guide assembly and install the actuator rod onto the detent lever.
2. Install the manual shaft into the transaxle case and insert the detent lever onto the manual shaft. Install the lock nut and torque to 25 ft. lbs. (34 N•m). Insert the retaining pin into the case.
3. Turn the case so it faces up and using the clutch and final drive tool, install the final drive internal gear assembly. Install the final drive snap ring.

NOTE: The clutch and final drive tool will clamp to the end of the final drive internal gear assembly.

4. The input housing and shaft assembly should be installed at this point. It should be overhauled as outlined earlier in the section "Unit Disassembly and Assembly". Carefully lower the input housing into the case.
5. Clamp the clutch and final drive tool to the second clutch housing. Lower the second clutch housing into the transaxle case, on top of the input housing and shaft assembly.
6. Install the already assembled driven sprocket support onto the input shaft. Install the drawn cup bearing assembly to the front of the driven sprocket.
7. The drive link assembly is to be installed next. Make sure that the gears and related parts are in satisfactory condition. Install the thrust washers using petroleum jelly to hold them in place.
8. Install the sprockets into the link assembly and locate the colored guide link so that it will be assembled facing the case cover. With the assembly oriented properly, install into the case.
9. Install the thrust washer on the driven sprocket with the outer race against the sprocket.
10. The output shaft should be installed next. Insert the output shaft into the driven sprocket and install the output shaft differ-

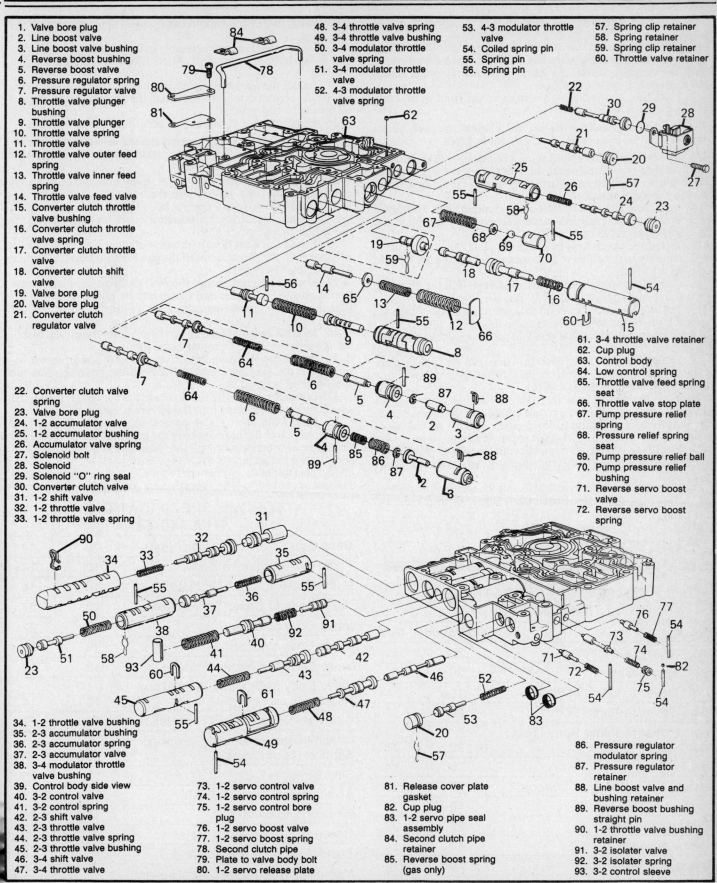

1. Valve bore plug
2. Line boost valve
3. Line boost valve bushing
4. Reverse boost bushing
5. Reverse boost valve
6. Pressure regulator spring
7. Pressure regulator valve
8. Throttle valve plunger bushing
9. Throttle valve plunger
10. Throttle valve spring
11. Throttle valve
12. Throttle valve outer feed spring
13. Throttle valve inner feed spring
14. Throttle valve feed valve
15. Converter clutch throttle valve bushing
16. Converter clutch throttle valve spring
17. Converter clutch throttle valve
18. Converter clutch shift valve
19. Valve bore plug
20. Valve bore plug
21. Converter clutch regulator valve

22. Converter clutch valve spring
23. Valve bore plug
24. 1-2 accumulator valve
25. 1-2 accumulator bushing
26. Accumulator valve spring
27. Solenoid bolt
28. Solenoid
29. Solenoid "O" ring seal
30. Converter clutch valve
31. 1-2 shift valve
32. 1-2 throttle valve
33. 1-2 throttle valve spring

34. 1-2 throttle valve bushing
35. 2-3 accumulator bushing
36. 2-3 accumulator spring
37. 2-3 accumulator valve
38. 3-4 modulator throttle valve bushing
39. Control body side view
40. 3-2 control valve
41. 3-2 control spring
42. 2-3 shift valve
43. 2-3 throttle valve
44. 2-3 throttle valve spring
45. 2-3 throttle valve bushing
46. 3-4 shift valve
47. 3-4 throttle valve

48. 3-4 throttle valve spring
49. 3-4 throttle valve bushing
50. 3-4 modulator throttle valve spring
51. 3-4 modulator throttle valve
52. 4-3 modulator throttle valve spring
53. 4-3 modulator throttle valve
54. Coiled spring pin
55. Spring pin
56. Spring pin

57. Spring clip retainer
58. Spring retainer
59. Spring clip retainer
60. Throttle valve retainer
61. 3-4 throttle valve retainer
62. Cup plug
63. Control body
64. Low control spring
65. Throttle valve feed spring seat
66. Throttle valve stop plate
67. Pump pressure relief spring
68. Pressure relief spring seat
69. Pump pressure relief ball
70. Pump pressure relief bushing
71. Reverse servo boost valve
72. Reverse servo boost spring

73. 1-2 servo control valve
74. 1-2 servo control spring
75. 1-2 servo control bore plug
76. 1-2 servo boost valve
77. 1-2 servo boost spring
78. Second clutch pipe
79. Plate to valve body bolt
80. 1-2 servo release plate

81. Release cover plate gasket
82. Cup plug
83. 1-2 servo pipe seal assembly
84. Second clutch pipe retainer
85. Reverse boost spring (gas only)

86. Pressure regulator modulator spring
87. Pressure regulator retainer
88. Line boost valve and bushing retainer
89. Reverse boost bushing straight pin
90. 1-2 throttle valve bushing retainer
91. 3-2 isolater valve
92. 3-2 isolater spring
93. 3-2 control sleeve

Valve body assembly (© General Motors Corporation)

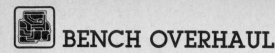

ential snap ring. The snap ring location is at the opposite end of the case.

11. Install the fourth clutch shaft onto the output shaft. Insert the fourth clutch bearing assembly into the exposed end of the fourth clutch shaft. Install the fourth clutch apply plate. Install the fourth clutch plate assembly.

12. Install the channel plate assembly to the front of the case. Torque the bolts to 10 ft. lbs. (14 N•m).

NOTE: When installing the channel plate to the case, petroleum jelly can be used to hold the gaskets in place.

13. The oil pump drive shaft should be installed next. Install a new oil seal ring on the oil pump drive shaft. Insert the drive shaft into its proper position and rotate to be sure of the spline engagement in the drive sprocket.

14. Install the eight check balls in the channel plate. Install the spacer plate/channel plate gasket, the valve body spacer plate and the spacer plate/valve body gasket.

15. Install the check balls in the spacer plate. Attach the valve body assembly to the channel plate assembly. Torque the bolts to 10 ft. lbs. (14 N•m).

16. The oil pump assembly is installed next. Bolt the oil pump to the valve body. Torque to 10 ft. lbs. (14 N•m).

17. Install the throttle lever on the pump assembly. Attach the throttle lever to the throttle lever cable link.

18. Position the wiring harness and secure using the two wire clip and the five wire clip.

19. Install the side cover gaskets. These can be held in place with a small amount of petroleum jelly. Install the side cover case pan. Torque to 10 ft. lbs. (14 N•m).

20. Turn the transaxle in its fixture so as that the top of the unit faces up. Install the servo return spring and the reverse apply pin. Slide the servo cushion spring retainer with the reverse servo spring and the other retainer onto the reverse apply pin.

21. Install the reverse servo piston with the oil seal ring and secure with the snap ring. Install the reverse servo cover and retaining ring.

22. On the side of the transaxle install the servo return spring and the 1-2 band apply pin. Install the retainer. Assemble the 1-2 servo piston and install behind the 1-2 band apply pin. Install the snap ring.

23. Rotate the transaxle assembly in its fixture so as to gain access to the bottom of the unit. Attach the scavenging scoop and bolts.

24. Install the accumulator assemblies making sure not to intermix the accumulator springs. Install the drive sprocket support oil lube pipe and retainer.

25. Install the cover gasket and accumulator spacer plate.

NOTE: At this point the thermo element assembly can be installed, if removed earlier. Make certain that the element plates are not bent during installation.

26. Assemble the oil pipes, cover, body and gasket as a unit and install with their gaskets into the transaxle.

27. Install the governor control body bolts and torque to 20 ft. lbs. (27 N•m). Install the accumulator cover bolts. No torque is needed on these bolts.

28. Install a new oil filter with a new oil filter seal. Install a new pan gasket on the pan and install the pan on the transaxle. Torque to 10 ft. lbs. (14 N•m).

29. Using a magnet, install the modulator valve. Place a new O-ring on the modulator and insert into its proper position. Install the modulator retainer and bolt. Torque to 20 ft. lbs. (27 N•m).

30. Install a new oil seal ring on the governor assembly. Install the governor into the transaxle case.

31. Install the speedometer drive gear onto the governor assembly. Install the speedometer gear thrust bearing onto the speedometer gear.

32. Install a new O-ring seal in the governor cover. Install the speedometer driven gear into the governor cover.

33. Install the O-ring seal on the speedometer driven gear sleeve. Assemble the gear sleeve to the governor cover. Install the unit to the case and secure with the speedometer gear retainer and bolt. Install the governor cover case screw.

34. The transaxle is now ready for the torque converter and then to be moved to the transaxle jack for installation.

TORQUE SPECIFICATIONS
THM 440-T4

Item	Foot Pounds	N•m
Cooler Fitting Connector	30	41
Modulator to Case	20	27
Pump Cover to Channel Plate	10	14
Pump Cover to Pump Body	20	27
Pump Cover to Pump Body (Torx Head)	20	27
Pipe Plug	10	14
Case to Drive Sprocket Support	20	27
Manifold to Valve Body	10	14
Governor to Case	20	27
Pressure Switch	10	14
Solenoid to Valve Body	10	14
Detent Spring to Valve Body	10	14

TORQUE SPECIFICATIONS
THM 440-T4

Item	Foot Pounds	N•m
Case Side Cover to Channel Plate	10	14
Pump Cover to Valve Body	10	14
Pump Cover to Channel Plate	10	14
Valve Body to Case (Torx Head)	20	27
Valve Body to Case	20	27
Pump Body to Case	20	27
Valve Body to Channel Plate	10	14
Valve Body to Channel Plate (Torx Head)	10	14
Channel Plate to Case (Torx Head)	20	27
Channel Plate to Driven Sprocket Support (Torx Head)	20	27
Side Cover to Case	10	14
Accumulator Cover to Case	20	27
Oil Scoop to Case	10	14
Governor Control Body Retainer	20	27
Transmission Oil Pan to Case	10	14
Manual Shaft to Inside Detent Lever (Nut)	25	34

THRUST WASHER GUIDE
THM 440-T4

I.D. Number	Dimension (in.)	Color
1	2.90-3.00	Orange/Green
2	3.05-3.15	Orange/Black
3	3.20-3.30	Orange
4	3.35-3.45	White
5	3.50-3.60	Blue
6	3.65-3.75	Pink
7	3.80-3.90	Brown
8	3.95-4.05	Green
9	4.10-4.20	Black
10	4.25-4.35	Purple
11	4.40-4.50	Purple/White
12	4.55-4.65	Purple/Blue

THRUST WASHER GUIDE
THM 440-T4

I.D. Number	Dimension (in.)	Color
13	4.70-4.80	Purple/Pink
14	4.85-4.95	Purple/Brown
15	5.00-5.10	Purple/Green

FINAL DRIVE END PLAY
THM 440-T4

I.D. Number	Thickness
1	0.059-0.062 inches (1.50-1.60mm)
2	0.062-0.066 inches (1.60-1.70mm)
3	0.066-0.070 inches (1.70-1.80mm)
4	0.070-0.074 inches (1.80-1.90mm)
5	0.074-0.078 inches (1.90-2.00mm)
6	0.078-0.082 inches (2.00-2.10mm)

SPECIAL TOOLS

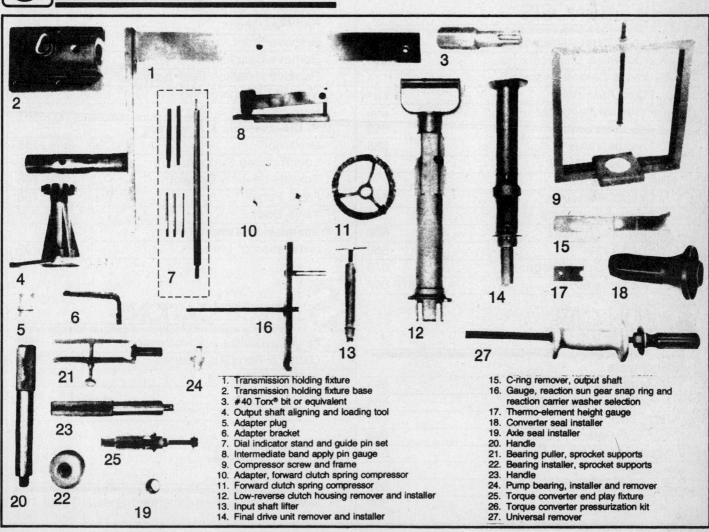

1. Transmission holding fixture
2. Transmission holding fixture base
3. #40 Torx® bit or equivalent
4. Output shaft aligning and loading tool
5. Adapter plug
6. Adapter bracket
7. Dial indicator stand and guide pin set
8. Intermediate band apply pin gauge
9. Compressor screw and frame
10. Adapter, forward clutch spring compressor
11. Forward clutch spring compressor
12. Low-reverse clutch housing remover and installer
13. Input shaft lifter
14. Final drive unit remover and installer
15. C-ring remover, output shaft
16. Gauge, reaction sun gear snap ring and reaction carrier washer selection
17. Thermo-element height gauge
18. Converter seal installer
19. Axle seal installer
20. Handle
21. Bearing puller, sprocket supports
22. Bearing installer, sprocket supports
23. Handle
24. Pump bearing, installer and remover
25. Torque converter end play fixture
26. Torque converter pressurization kit
27. Universal remover

INDEX

GENERAL MOTORS
TURBO HYDRA-MATIC 700-R4

APPLICATIONS

TRANSMISSION APPLICATION CHART

Year	Model	Transmission Model
1982 and later	Corvette	700-R4
1982 and later	Impala, Caprice	700-R4
1983 and later	Camaro, Firebird	700-R4
1983 and later	Parisienne	700-R4
1982 and later	Chevrolet and GMC	700-R4

GENERAL DESCRIPTION

The T.H.M. 700-R4 is a fully automatic transmission consisting of a three element hydraulic torque converter with the addition of a torque converter clutch.

This automatic transmission also consists of two planetary gear sets, five multiple disc type clutches, two roller or one way clutches and a band which are used in order to provide the friction elements to produce four forward speeds, the last of which is an overdrive speed.

The torque converter, through oil, couples the engine power to the gear sets and hydraulically provides additional torque multiplication when required. Also, through the converter clutch, the converter drive and driven members operate as one unit when applied providing mechanical drive from the engine through the transmission.

The gear ratio changes are fully automatic in relation to vehicle speed and engine torque. Vehicle speed and engine torque are directed to the transmission providing the proper gear ratios for maximum efficiency and performance at all throttle openings.

A hydraulic system pressurized by a variable capacity vane type pump provides the operating pressure required for the operation of the friction elements and automatic controls.

Transmission and Torque Converter Identification

TRANSMISSION

The THM 700-R4 automatic transmission can be identified by the serial number plate which is located on the right side of the transmission case. This identification tag contains information that is important when servicing the unit.

TORQUE CONVERTER

The torque converter is a welded unit and cannot be disassembled for service. Any internal malfunctions require the replacement of the converter assembly. The replacement converter must be matched to the model transmission through parts identification. No specific identification is available for matching the converter to the transmission for the average repair shop.

DIESEL ENGINE

Vehicles equipped with diesel engines use a different torque converter. To identify these units, examine the weld nuts. Most gas engine converters have their weld nuts spot welded onto the converter housing, usually in two spots. The diesel converters have the weld nuts completely welded around their entire circumference.

TURBOCHARGED V-6 ENGINE

Vehicles equipped with turbo-charged V-6 engines use a different torque converter. These units have a high stall speed converter, allowing a stall speed of about 2800 rpm. These converters must not be replaced with a standard converter, otherwise performance will be sluggish and unsatisfactory. When ordering replacements for the turbo-charged units, make certain to specify that the vehicle has turbo-charging in order to obtain the proper replacement.

Metric Fasteners

Metric fasteners are very close to the dimensions of the familiar

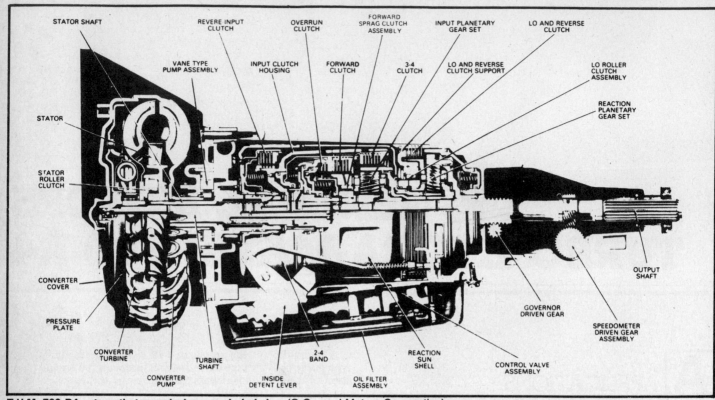

T.H.M. 700-R4 automatic transmission—exploded view (© General Motors Corporation)

inch system fasteners. For this reason, replacement fasteners must have the same measurement and strength as those removed.

NOTE: Do not attempt to interchange metric fasteners for inch system fasteners. Mismatched or incorrect fasteners can result in damage to the transmission unit through malfunctions or breakage, or possible personal injury.

Care should be taken to reuse the fasteners in the same locations as removed. Keep them in a safe place when removed, for if lost, replacement could be inconvenient. The following locations could have metric fasteners.

Fluid Capacities

The fluid capacities are approximate and the correct fluid level should be determined by the dipstick indicator. Use only Dexron® II automatic transmission fluid when adding, or servicing the THM 700-R4 automatic transmission.

When a complete transmission overhaul is done the transmission will take about 23 pints of transmission fluid. When a fluid change is done the transmission will take about 10 pints of transmission fluid.

Checking Fluid Level

The THM 700-R4 transmission is designed to operate at the "FULL HOT" mark on the dipstick at normal operating temperatures, which range from 190° to 200° F. Automatic transmissions are frequently overfilled because the fluid level is checked when cold and the dipstick level reads low. However as the fluid warms up the level will rise, as much as ¾ of an inch. Note that if the transmission fluid is too hot, as it might be when operating under city traffic conditions, trailer towing or extended high speed driving, again an accurate fluid level cannot be determined until the fluid has cooled somewhat, perhaps 30 minutes after shutdown.

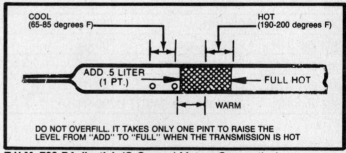

T.H.M. 700-R4 dipstick (© General Motors Corporation)

To determine proper fluid level under normal operating temperatures, proceed as follows:
1. Make sure vehicle is parked level.
2. Apply parking brake; move selector to Park.
3. Start engine but do not race engine. Allow to idle.
4. Move selector through each range, back to PARK, then check level. The fluid should read "FULL HOT" (transmission end of dipstick too hot to hold comfortably.)

Do not overfill the transmission. Overfilling can cause foaming and loss of fluid from the vent. Overheating can also be a result of overfilling since heat will not transfer as readily. Notice the condition of the fluid and whether there seems to be a burnt smell or metal particles on the end of the dipstick. A milky appearance is a sign of water contamination, possibly from a damaged cooling system. All this can be a help in determining transmission problems and their source.

Fluid Drain Intervals

The main considerations in establishing fluid change intervals are the type of driving that is done and the heat levels that are generated by such driving. Normally, the fluid and strainer would be changed at 100,000 miles. However, the following conditions may be considered severe transmission service.

1. Heavy city traffic
2. Hot climates regularly reaching 90°F. or more
3. Mountainous areas
4. Frequent trailer pulling
5. Commercial use such as delivery service, taxi or police car use

If the vehicle is operated under any of these conditions, it is recommended that the fluid be changed and the filter screen serviced at 15,000 mile intervals. Again, be sure not to overfill the unit. Only one pint of fluid is required to bring the level from "ADD" to "FULL" when the transmission is hot.

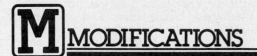

MODIFICATIONS

VALVE BODY SPACER PLATE HOLE MISSING

On some early T.H.M. 700-R4 automatic transmissions the valve body spacer plate gasket may be missing a passage hole. If this is the case replace the valve body spacer gasket with part number 8647065.

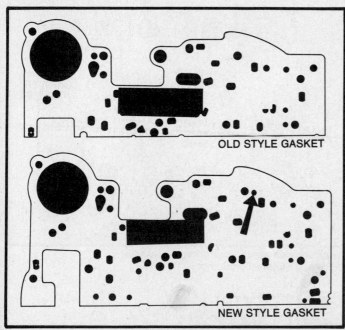

OLD STYLE GASKET

NEW STYLE GASKET

Spacer plate gasket design change (© General Motors Corporation)

TRANSMISSION OIL FILTER INSTALLATION

When installing the oil filter assembly to the valve body of the T.H.M. 700-R4 automatic transmission, be very careful not to cut the O-ring. Press the O-ring into its bore with firmness, but do not strike the filter. A cut O-ring will show up as a valve buzz, low line pressure, soft shifts or a converter clutch chatter.

FRONT TORRINGTON BEARING INSTALLATION

On some T.H.M. 700-R4 transmissions, when installing the front Torrington bearing that goes between the pump and the input housing, be sure that the black surface of the bearing is against the pump. If the black surface is not against the pump damage to the unit can occur.

VALVE BODY BORE PLUGS

Valve body bore plugs that have a recess on one side should always be assembled with the recess towards the outside of the valve body. Failure to do so can result in mispositioning of the valves and springs.

R.T.V. SEALANT—TRANSMISSION OIL PAN

Do not use R.T.V. sealant on the fluid pan of the T.H.M. 700-R4 automatic transmission. Use of this sealant could cause a possible block to the servo exhaust port. Use only a fluid pan gasket, when servicing this transmission.

LATE OR ERRATIC UPSHIFTS

On some T.H.M. 700-R4 automatic transmissions late or erratic upshifts may occur, if this happens, especially with changes in the temperature, remove the valve body and inspect the T.V. sleeve. The sleeve can rotate in the valve body and cause the passages to become blocked. To correct the problem, remove the sleeve and the valve and clean thoroughly. When reinstalling the sleeve, align it so that all of the ports are open and not restricted. Insert the pin and make sure it is seated all the way down to help prevent rotation of the sleeve.

TORQUE CONVERTER RATTLE— DIESEL ENGINE

On some vehicles equipped with a diesel engine, a rattle may exist coming from the torque converter area when the torque converter clutch is applied. If this problem exists, you should check the clutch throttle line up. If it is found to be defective, it should be replaced with part number 8642970. The new part will raise the lock up torque converter function to forty miles per hour, which is in fourth gear only. If the rattle still persists, the torque converter should be checked and replaced with part number 8647323 or 8642964.

BURNT 3-4 CLUTCH AND BAND ASSEMBLY

If, when servicing a T.H.M. 700-R4 automatic transmission you encounter a burnt 3-4 clutch and band, inspect the third accumulator check valve. The accumulator valve is located behind servo assembly, which is located in the transmission case. To inspect the third accumulator, pour some solvent into the capsule. The solvent should only go into the servo area. If there is any trace of solvent inside the case barrel the capsule assembly should be replaced. Follow the procedure outlined below when making this repair.

1. Remove the old capsule using a #4 easy-out.
2. Install new capsule, small end first so that one of the four holes will align with the passage into the servo when the capsule is fully installed.
3. Use a 3/8 in. rod to drive the capsule into the case, far enough that the feed hole in the capsule is completely open into the servo bore. This can be approximated by marking the rod at 1 5/8 in. from the end that goes into the case. Again recheck with solvent.

ACCUMULATOR HOUSING PLATE ELIMINATION

In 1982 a change was made to eliminate the plate that was located under the accumulator housing in all T.H.M. 700-R4 automatic transmissions. To do this the accumulator housing and gaskets have been changed.

If you are rebuilding the old style unit, update it by ordering service kit 8642967. This kit contains all the necessary parts to eliminate the accumulator housing plate.

PARK TO REVERSE—HARSH SHIFT

Changes have been made to the T.H.M. 700-R4 automatic transmission to improve the park to reverse shift feel. If a park to reverse harsh shift feel exists, it can be corrected by installing a new style valve body spacer gasket, case gasket and spacer plate. Also a new style oil pump cover and waved reverse clutch plate must be installed.

The new design parts are being used beginning with transmission serial number 9M6184D. All earlier units can be updated by using these new parts. Refer to the park/reverse change chart for the proper information when ordering the required parts.

PARK/REVERSE CHANGE CHART

Component	Old Part Number	New Part Number
Valve body to spacer gasket	8642920	8642952
Spacer-to-case gasket	8642920	8642952
Spacer plate	8642655-A	8647066-B
Oil pump cover (TN,TP,M6,MH units)	8647043	8647190
Oil pump cover (all other units)	8647042	8647189
Waved reverse clutch plate	8642060	8647067

DETENT LEVER TO MANUAL VALVE LINK CHANGE

Beginning July 1983 all T.H.M. 700-R4 automatic transmissions are being built with a new detent lever to manual valve link. This design change provides a new retention of the detent lever to the manual valve link without the retaining clip.

When servicing a transmission using the old style assembly, replace it with the new design components. The new design component is part number 8654113. The old design part numbers are 8642244 and 8654037.

BURNED THREE-FOUR CLUTCH DIAGNOSIS-MODEL 3YH

When diagnosing a 700-R4 transmission for a burned three-four clutch check the spacer plate for correct identification. If the plate is identified by the letter "C" change the plate. Use part number 8654083 which is identified with the letter "E". The new spacer plate has a larger third clutch feed hole.

NEW DESIGN OIL PUMP COVER

Beginning in the middle of July 1983, all transmissions are being fitted with a new oil pump cover and a new oil pump to transmission case gasket. This new design prevents the transmission oil from exhausting out of the breather during harsh deceleration or on sharp turns.

When servicing any 1983 and later automatic transmissions be sure to use the new design components. The new pump to case gasket cannot be used with the past oil pump cover. The past pump to case gasket can be used with the new oil pump cover, but will continue to exhaust oil out of the breather.

GRINDING NOISE IN ALL RANGES

Starting in January, 1984, all transmissions are being built using a new reaction internal gear. This new gear has a change in the parking lugs and internal gear teeth area. The new gear is the same dimensionally as the old gear. Identification marks have been added to the new gear. Two types of identifying marks are being used. The first is an ink stamp on the top chamfer of the gear. The second is a broached line on three parking lugs equally spaced around the internal reaction gear. When replacing the internal reaction gear order part number 8654161.

NEW STYLE SERVO COVER AND SEAL

Starting in the middle of April 1983, transmissions are being built using a new style 2-4 servo cover and seal. This design change provides a tighter fit between the case bore and the 2-4 servo cover.

The new servo cover seal is part number 8647351 and can be identified with a green stripe. The old servo cover seal is part number 8642112 which is still used on the second apply piston. The old servo seal cannot be used on the new design servo cover. If it is used the cover will leak transmission oil.

Forward Sprag Clutch Modification

During the 1982 model year, a new front sprag was introduced in the T.H.M. 700-R4 automatic transmission. This new design front sprag assembly is replacing the front roller clutch assembly. To update the older units to the new design sprag assembly, order service kit 8642947.

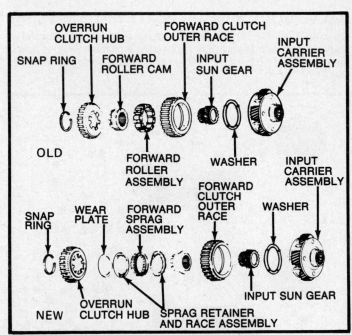

Forward clutch sprag assemblies—exploded view
(© General Motors Corporation)

 # TROUBLE DIAGNOSIS

Hydraulic Control System

To provide the working pressure within the transmission, a gear-type pump is used to operate the elements to provide the friction function as well as the automatic controls.

The hydraulic control system directs the path and pressure of the fluid so that the proper element can be applied as needed. The valve body directs the pressure to the proper clutch or band servo.

PUMP ASSEMBLY

A hydraulic pressure system requires a source of clean hydraulic fluid and a pump to pressurize the fluid. The THM 700-R4 uses a variable capacity vane type pump. The pump rotor is keyed to the converter pump hub and therefore turns whenever the engine is

CLUTCH AND BAND APPLICATION CHART

Selector Range	2-4 Band	Reverse Input Clutch	Overrun Clutch	Forward Clutch	Forward Sprag Clutch Assembly	3-4 Clutch	Low Roller Clutch	Low Reverse Clutch
First DR4				Applied	Applied		Applied	
Second DR4	Applied			Applied	Applied			
Third DR4				Applied	Applied	Applied		
Fourth DR4	Applied				Applied	Applied		
Third DR3			Applied	Applied	Applied	Applied		
Second DR2	Applied		Applied	Applied	Applied			
First Low			Applied	Applied	Applied		Applied	Applied
Reverse		Applied						Applied

CHILTON'S THREE "C's" AUTOMATIC TRANSMISSION DIAGNOSIS CHART

Condition	Cause	Correction
High or low shift points	a) T.V. cable binding or out of adjustment b) Improper external linkage travel c) Binding throttle valve or plunger in valve body d) T.V. modulator up or down valve sticking in valve body e) Valve body gaskets or spacer plate damaged f) T.V. limit valve sticking in valve body g) Pressure regulator valve to T.V. boost valve sticking in pump assembly h) Front pump slide sticking	a) Correct as required b) Correct linkage as required c) Free binding as required d) Free sticking modulator valve e) Replace gaskets or spacer plate as required f) Free sticking T.V. limit valve g) Repair or replace defective component as required h) Correct as required
First speed only— no upshift	a) Governor valve sticking b) Governor driven gear damaged, retaining pin missing, wrong retaining pin, weights and springs damaged c) Burrs on governor output shaft, sleeve or case d) 1-2 shift valve sticking in valve body e) Valve body gaskets or spacer plate damaged f) Case porosity or restricted fluid passages g) 2-4 servo apply passages blocked, damaged servo piston seals or damaged apply pin h) 2-4 band assembly burned, band anchor pin missing	a) Correct as required b) Repair or replace defective component as necessary c) Correct defective part as required d) Correct 1-2 shift valve as required e) Replace gaskets or spacer plate required f) Correct as required g) Repair or replace defective component as required h) Repair or replace defective component as required

TROUBLE DIAGNOSIS

CHILTON'S THREE "C's" AUTOMATIC TRANSMISSION DIAGNOSIS CHART

Condition	Cause	Correction
Slips in first gear	a) Forward clutch plates burned	a) Replace forward clutch plates as required
	b) Forward clutch piston seals cut or damaged	b) Replace piston seals as required
	c) Damaged forward clutch housing or check ball	c) Replace defective part as required
	d) Forward clutch low oil or oil pressure	d) Correct as required
	e) Valve body accumulator valve sticking	e) Free sticking valve
	f) Valve body gaskets or spacer plate damaged	f) Replace gaskets or spacer plate as required
	g) Internal T.V. linkage binding	g) Correct internal linkage problem as required
	h) 1-2 accumulator piston seals cut or damaged	h) Replace damaged seals as required
	i) Leak between 1-2 accumulator piston and pin	i) Repair or replace as required
	j) Missing or broken 1-2 accumulator spring	j) Replace spring as required
1-2 full throttle shifts only	a) T.V. cable not adjusted	a) Adjust cable as required
	b) Throttle lever and bracket assembly missing, damaged or missing exhaust check ball	b) Repair or replace defective component as required
	c) Throttle link not connected, damaged or hanging on upper sleeve	c) Repair throttle link as required
	d) Throttle valve or plunger sticking in open position	d) Free sticking plunger as required
	e) Blockage of case interconnecting passages	e) Free blockage as required
1-2 slip or rough shift	a) Throttle lever and bracket assembly damaged or not installed properly	a) Correct lever and bracket assembly as required
	b) Valve body throttle valve or bushing sticking	b) Correct as required
	c) Sticking 1-2 shift valve in valve body	c) Free sticking valve
	d) Valve body gaskets or spacer plate damaged	d) Replace damaged gaskets or spacer plate as required
	e) Sticking line bias valve, accumulator valve or T.V. limit valve in valve body	e) Repair or replace defective component as required
	f) 2-4 servo incorrect apply pin	f) Install proper apply pin
	g) Damaged 2-4 servo oil seal rings, bore or restricted oil passages	g) Repair or replace as required
	h) Damaged second accumulator piston seal, bore or porus piston	h) Replace defective part as required
	i) Missing second accumulator spring or restricted oil passages	i) Replace missing spring or free restricted oil passages
	j) Burned 2-4 band	j) Replace 2-4 band
2-3 slip or rough shift	a) 2-3 shift valve sticking in valve body	a) Free sticking valve
	b) Accumulator valve sticking in valve body	b) Free sticking accumulator valve
	c) Valve body gaskets or spacer plate damaged	c) Replace spacer plate or gaskets
	d) Throttle valve sticking or T.V. limit valve sticking in valve body	d) Free sticking valve as required

CHILTON'S THREE "C's" AUTOMATIC TRANSMISSION DIAGNOSIS CHART

Condition	Cause	Correction
2-3 slip or rough shift	e) 3-4 clutch plates burned, piston seals damaged, case porosity, exhaust ball open, restricted apply passages	e) Repair or replace defective component as required
	f) 3-4 clutch check ball #7 damaged, excessive clutch plate travel	f) Repair or replace defective component as required
3-4 slip or rough shift	a) 2-3 shift valve sticking in valve body	a) Free sticking valve
	b) Accumulator valve sticking in valve body	b) Free sticking accumulator valve
	c) Valve body gaskets or spacer plate damaged	c) Replace spacer plate or gaskets
	d) Throttle valve sticking or T.V. limit valve sticking in valve body	d) Free sticking valve as required
	e) Servo damaged or missing piston seals, piston bores, piston porosity or incorrect band apply pin	e) Repair or replace defective component as required
	f) 3-4 clutch burned	f) Replace defective clutch as required
	g) 2-4 band burned	g) Replace defective band as required
	h) 3-4 accumulator spring missing, piston porosity, bore damaged, restricted feed passage or broken oil seal ring	h) Repair or replace defective component as required
No reverse, or slips in reverse	a) Forward clutch will not release	a) Correct
	b) Manual linkage out of adjustment	b) Adjust manual linkage as required
	c) Reverse boost valve sticking in front pump assembly	c) Correct stuck valve as required
	d) Valve body spacer plate or gaskets damaged	d) Replace defective gaskets or spacer plate as required
	e) Low reverse clutch piston seals damaged, plates burned, restricted apply passages, or cover plate loose or gasket damaged	e) Repair or replace defective component as required
	f) Reverse input clutch plates burned, seals damaged or restricted apply passages	f) Repair or replace defective component as required
	g) Reverse input housing exhaust ball and capsule damaged	g) Repair or replace as required
No part throttle downshifts	a) Binding external or internal linkage	a) Adjust linkage as required
	b) T.V. modulator downshift valve or throttle valve binding in valve body	b) Replace defective component as required
	c) Throttle valve bushing or feed hole restricted	c) Correct as required
	d) Check ball #3 mispositioned in valve body	d) Replace or reposition check ball as required
No overrun braking— manual 3-2-1	a) External manual linkage not adjusted	a) Adjust linkage as required
	b) Overrun clutch plates burned or piston seals damaged	b) Replace clutch plates or seals as required
	c) Overrun clutch piston exhaust check ball sticks	c) Free sticking ball as required
	d) Valve body gaskets or spacer plate damaged	d) Replace damaged gaskets or spacer plate as required
	e) 4-3 sequence valve sticking in valve body	e) Free sticking valve as required

CHILTON'S THREE "C's" AUTOMATIC TRANSMISSION DIAGNOSIS CHART

Condition	Cause	Correction
No overrun braking— manual 3-2-1	f) Valve body check balls 3, 9 or 10 mispositioned g) Turbine shaft oil feed passage restricted, teflon seal rings damaged or plug missing	f) Replace or reposition check balls as required g) Repair or replace components as required
Drive in neutral	a) Forward clutch burned b) Manual linkage or manual valve disconnected or out of adjustment	a) Replace forward clutch as required b) Connect or adjust components as required
Second speed start— drive range	a) Governor assembly b) T.V. cable	a) Repair as required b) Adjust or repair as required
No park or will not hold in park	a) Actuator rod assembly bent or damaged b) Parking lock pawl return spring damaged c) Parking brake bracket, detent roller or parking pawl damaged d) Parking lock pawl interference with low reverse piston	a) Repair or replace parts as needed b) Correct as required c) Replace parts as required d) Correct interference

operating. A slide is fitted around the rotor and vane which automatically regulates pump output, according to the needs of the transmission. Maximum pump output is obtained when the priming spring has been fully extended and has the slide held against the side of the body. As the slide moves toward the center, the pump output is reduced until minimum output is reached.

PRESSURE REGULATOR

As the pump rotor rotates, the pump output is directed to the pressure regulator valve. The pressure regulator valve is held closed by the pressure regulator valve spring. As the pump pressure increases, the pressure regulator valve is opened, directing oil from the pressure regulator to a cavity on the side of the pump opposite the priming spring. This oil pressure acts against the priming spring and moves the slide, decreasing the pump output to a steady 65 psi. With the engine off, the slide is held in a maximum output position by the priming spring.

T.V. LIMIT VALVE

The pressure requirements of the transmission for apply of the band and clutches vary with engine torque and throttle opening. Under heavy throttle operation, 65 psi line pressure is not sufficient to hold the band and clutches on without slipping. To provide higher line pressure with greater throttle opening, a variable oil pressure related to throttle opening is desired. The throttle valve regulates line pressure in relation to carburetor opening. The T.V. limit valve limits this variable pressure to avoid excessive line pressure. The T.V. limit valve feeds the throttle valve and receives oil directly from the oil pump. As the pressure in the line leading from the T.V. limit valve and feeding the T.V. valve exceeds 90 psi, the pressure will push against the T.V. limit valve spring, bleeding off excess pressure. This limits T.V. feed pressure to a maximum of approximately 90 psi.

THROTTLE VALVE

Throttle valve pressure is related to carburetor opening which is related to engine torque. The system is a mechanical type with a direct, straight line relation between the carburetor throttle plate opening and the transmission throttle plunger movement.

As the accelerator pedal is depressed and the carburetor

opened, the mechanical linkage (T.V. Cable) relays the movement to the throttle plunger and increases the force of the T.V. spring against the throttle valve, increasing T.V. pressure which can regulate to 90 psi. T.V. oil is directed through the T.V. plunger to provide a hydraulic assist reducing the pedal effort necessary to actuate the plunger.

LINE BOOST VALVE

A feature has been included in the T.V. system that will prevent the transmission from being operated with low or minimum line pressure in the event the T.V. cable is disconnected or broken. This feature is the line boost valve which is located in the control valve and pump assembly at the T.V. regulating exhaust port.

The line boost valve is held off its seat by the throttle lever and bracket assembly (this allows T.V. oil to regulate normally) when the T.V. cable is properly adjusted. If the T.V. cable becomes disconnected or is not adjusted properly, the line boost valve will close the T.V. exhaust port and keep T.V. and line pressure at full line pressure.

Diagnosis Tests

CONTROL PRESSURE TEST

NOTE: Before making the control pressure test, check the transmission fluid level, adjust the T.V. cable, check and adjust the manual linkage and be sure that the engine is not at fault, rather that the automatic transmission.

1. Install the oil pressure gauge to the automatic transmission. Connect a tachometer to the engine.
2. Raise and support the vehicle safely. Be sure that the brakes are applied at all times.
3. Total running time must not exceed two minutes.
4. Minimum line pressure check: set the T.V. cable to specification. Apply the brakes and take the reading in the ranges and rpm's that are indicated in the automatic transmission oil pressure chart.
5. Full line pressure check; hold the T.V. cable the full extent of its travel. Apply the brakes and take the reading in the ranges and rpm's that are indicated in the automatic transmission oil pressure chart.
6. Record all readings and compare them with the data in the chart.

AUTOMATIC TRANSMISSION OIL PRESSURES

Range	Model	Normal Oil Pressure At Minimum T.V. psi	Normal Oil Pressure At Full T.V. psi
Park & Neutral @ 1000 rpm	TC, MB, MC, MJ, VN	55–65	130–170
	TE, TH, TK, MD, ME, MK, MW, VH	55–65	130–170
	VA, ML, T7, MP, MS, PQ, YN, YK, YP, YG, YF, T2	55–65	130–170
	T8, TZ, TP, TS, MH, VJ, TL	65–75	130–170
	YH	65–75	140–180
	Y9	55–65	140–180
Reverse @ 1000 rpm	TC, MB, MC, MJ, VN	90–105	210–285
	TE, TH, TK, MD, ME, MK, MW, VH	90–105	210–285
	VA, ML, T7, MP, MS, PQ, YN, YK, YP, YG, YF, T2	90–105	210–285
	T8, TZ, TP, TS, MH, VJ, TL	110–120	210–285
	YH	110–120	225–300
	Y9	90–105	225–300
Drive & Manual Third @ 1000 rpm	TC, MB, MC, MJ, VN	55–65	130–170
	TE, TH, TK, MD, ME, MK, MW, VH	55–65	130–170
	VA, ML, T7, MP, MS, PQ, YN, YK, YP, YG, YF, T2	55–65	130–170
	T8, TZ, TP, TS, MH, VJ, TL	65–75	130–170
	YH	65–75	140–180
	Y9	55–65	140–180
Manual Second & LO @ 1000 rpm	TC, MB, MC, MJ, VN	100–120	100–120
	TE, TH, TK, MD, ME, MK, MW, VH	100–120	100–120
	VA, ML, T7, MP, MS, PQ, YN, YK, YP, YG, YF, T2	100–120	100–120
	T8, TZ, TP, TS, MH, VJ, TL	100–120	100–120
	YH	100–120	100–120
	Y9	100–120	100–120

AIR PRESSURE TEST

Air pressure testing should be done in moderation to avoid excessive fluid spray and damage to the internal parts during disassembly and assembly, through partial retention of units.

STALL SPEED TEST

Stall speed testing is not recommended by General Motors Transmission Division. Extreme overheating of the transmission unit can occur, causing further internal damages. By pressure testing and road testing, the malfunction can be determined and by consulting the diagnosis chart, the cause and correction can normally be found.

ROAD TEST

1. Road test using all selective ranges, noting when discrepancies in operation or oil pressure occur.
2. Attempt to isolate the unit or circuit involved in the malfunction.
3. If engine performance indicates and engine tune-up is required, this should be performed before road testing is completed or transmission correction attempted. Poor engine performance can result in rough shifting or other malfunctions.

Converter Stator Operation

The torque converter stator assembly and its related roller clutch can possibly have one of two different type malfunctions.
1. The stator assembly freewheels in both directions.
2. The stator assembly remains locked up at all times.

CONDITION A

If the stator roller clutch becomes ineffective, the stator assembly freewheels at all times in both directions. With this condition, the vehicle will tend to have poor acceleration from a standstill. At speeds above 30-35 mph, the vehicle may act normal. If poor acceleration problems are noted, it should first be determined that the exhaust system is not blocked, the engine is in good tune and the transmission is in gear when starting out.

If the engine will freely accelerate to high rpm in neutral, it can be assumed that the engine and exhaust system are normal. Driving the vehicle in reverse and checking for poor performance will help determine if the stator is freewheeling at all times.

CONDITION B

If the stator assembly remains locked up at all times, the engine rpm and vehicle speed will tend to be limited or restricted at high speeds. The vehicle performance when accelerating from a standstill will be normal. Engine over-heating may be noted. Visual examination of the converter may reveal a blue color form the overheating that will result.

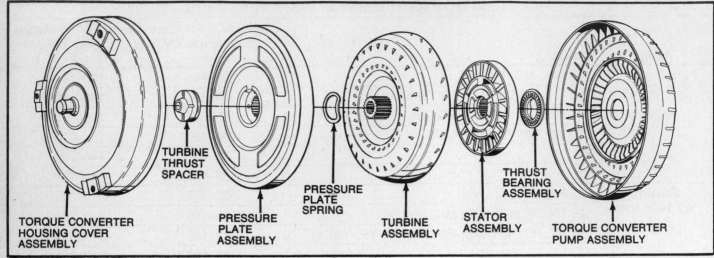

TURBINE THRUST SPACER

PRESSURE PLATE SPRING

THRUST BEARING ASSEMBLY

TORQUE CONVERTER HOUSING COVER ASSEMBLY

PRESSURE PLATE ASSEMBLY

TURBINE ASSEMBLY

STATOR ASSEMBLY

TORQUE CONVERTER PUMP ASSEMBLY

Torque converter assembly—exploded view (© General Motors Corporation)

Under conditions A or B above, if the converter has been removed from the transmission, the stator roller clutch can be checked by inserting a finger into the splined inner race of the roller clutch and trying to turn the race in both directions. The inner race should turn freely in the clockwise direction, bu not turn or be very difficult to turn in the counterclockwise direction.

Converter Clutch Operation and Diagnosis

TORQUE CONVERTER CLUTCH

The torque converter clutch assembly consists of a three-element

torque converter with the addition of a converter clutch. The converter clutch is splined to the turbine assembly, and when operated, applies against the converter cover providing a mechanical direct drive coupling of the engine to the planetary gears.

Converter clutch operation is determined by a series of controls and by drive range selection. The transmission must be in drive range, and the car must have obtained a preset speed depending on engine and transmission combination.

For more detailed information regarding the torque converter clutch, refer to the general section in this manual.

CHILTON'S THREE "C's" TRANSMISSION DIAGNOSIS CHART— G.M. TORQUE CONVERTER CLUTCH (TCCC)

Condition	Cause	Correction
Clutch applied in all ranges (engine stalls when put in gear)	a) Converter clutch valve stuck in apply position	a) R&R oil pump and clean valve
Clutch does not apply: applies erratically or at wrong speeds	a) Electrical malfunction in most instances	a) Follow troubleshooting procedure to determine if problem is internal or external to isolate defect
Clutch applies erratically; shudder and jerking felt	a) Vacuum hose leak b) Vacuum switch faulty c) Governor pressure switch malfunction d) Solenoid loose or damaged e) Converter malfunction; clutch plate warped	a) Repair hose as needed b) Replace switch c) Replace switch d) Service or replace e) Replace converter
Clutch applies at a very low or high 3rd gear	a) Governor switch shorted to ground b) Governor malfunction c) High line pressure d) Solenoid inoperative or shorted to case	a) Replace switch b) Service or replace governor c) Service pressure regulator d) Replace solenoid

CAUTION: When inspecting the stator and turbine of the torque converter clutch unit, a slight drag is normal when turned in the direction of freewheel rotation because of the pressure exerted by the waved spring washer, located between the turbine and the pressure plate.

TORQUE CONVERTER CLUTCH ELECTRICAL DIAGNOSIS TEST

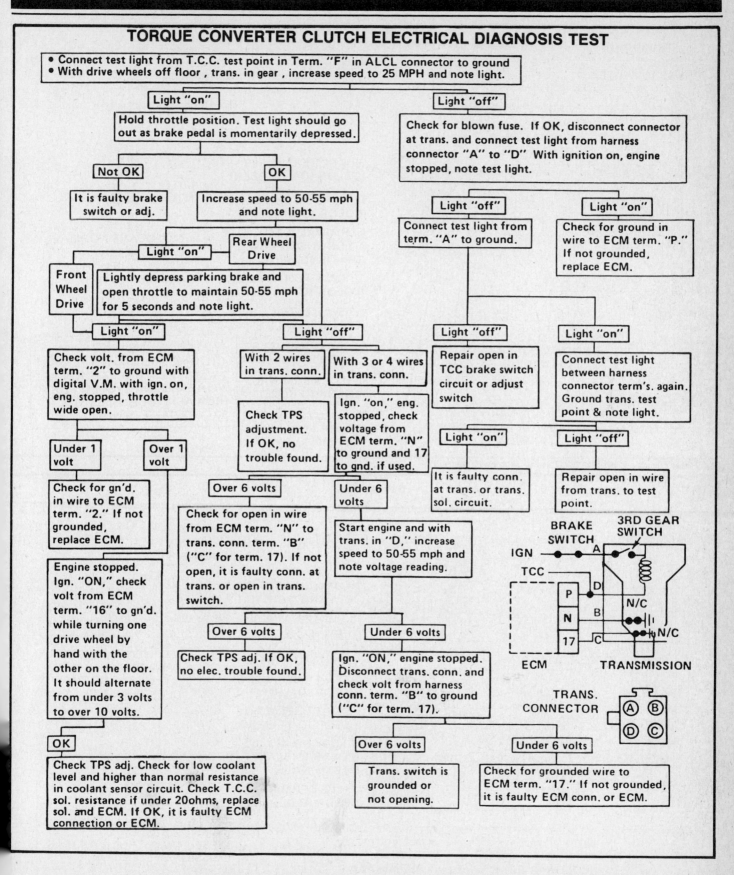

- Connect test light from T.C.C. test point in Term. "F" in ALCL connector to ground
- With drive wheels off floor , trans. in gear , increase speed to 25 MPH and note light.

Light "on"

Hold throttle position. Test light should go out as brake pedal is momentarily depressed.

Not OK

It is faulty brake switch or adj.

OK

Increase speed to 50-55 mph and note light.

Light "on"

Rear Wheel Drive

Front Wheel Drive

Lightly depress parking brake and open throttle to maintain 50-55 mph for 5 seconds and note light.

Light "on"

Check volt. from ECM term. "2" to ground with digital V.M. with ign. on, eng. stopped, throttle wide open.

Under 1 volt

Over 1 volt

Check for gn'd. in wire to ECM term. "2." If not grounded, replace ECM.

Engine stopped. Ign. "ON," check volt from ECM term. "16" to gn'd. while turning one drive wheel by hand with the other on the floor. It should alternate from under 3 volts to over 10 volts.

OK

Check TPS adj. Check for low coolant level and higher than normal resistance in coolant sensor circuit. Check T.C.C. sol. resistance if under 20ohms, replace sol. and ECM. If OK, it is faulty ECM connection or ECM.

Light "off"

With 2 wires in trans. conn.

Check TPS adjustment. If OK, no trouble found.

With 3 or 4 wires in trans. conn.

Ign. "on," eng. stopped, check voltage from ECM term. "N" to ground and 17 to gnd. if used.

Over 6 volts

Check for open in wire from ECM term. "N" to trans. conn. term. "B" ("C" for term. 17). If not open, it is faulty conn. at trans. or open in trans. switch.

Over 6 volts

Check TPS adj. If OK, no elec. trouble found.

Under 6 volts

Start engine and with trans. in "D," increase speed to 50-55 mph and note voltage reading.

Under 6 volts

Ign. "ON," engine stopped. Disconnect trans. conn. and check volt from harness conn. term. "B" to ground ("C" for term. 17).

Over 6 volts

Trans. switch is grounded or not opening.

Under 6 volts

Check for grounded wire to ECM term. "17." If not grounded, it is faulty ECM conn. or ECM.

Light "off"

Check for blown fuse. If OK, disconnect connector at trans. and connect test light from harness connector "A" to "D" With ignition on, engine stopped, note test light.

Light "off"

Connect test light from term. "A" to ground.

Light "on"

Check for ground in wire to ECM term. "P." If not grounded, replace ECM.

Light "off"

Repair open in TCC brake switch circuit or adjust switch

Light "on"

Connect test light between harness connector term's. again. Ground trans. test point & note light.

Light "on"

It is faulty conn. at trans. or trans. sol. circuit.

Light "off"

Repair open in wire from trans. to test point.

BRAKE SWITCH

3RD GEAR SWITCH

IGN

TCC

P

N

17

ECM

A

D

B

C

N/C

N/C

TRANSMISSION

TRANS. CONNECTOR

A B
D C

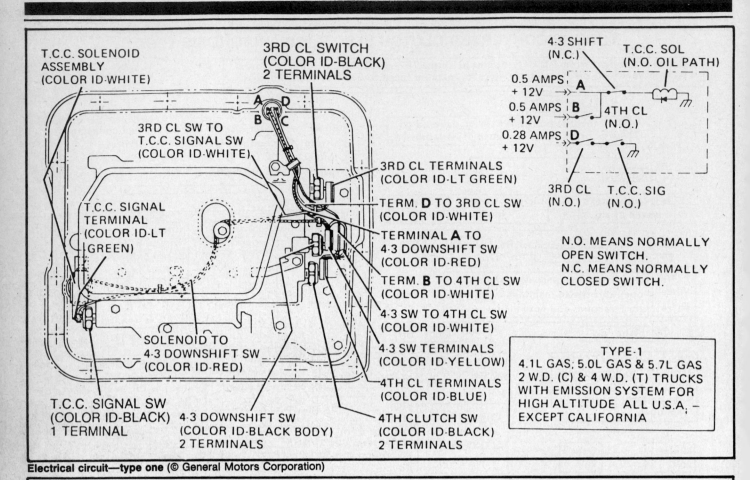

T.C.C. SOLENOID ASSEMBLY (COLOR ID-WHITE)

3RD CL SWITCH (COLOR ID-BLACK) 2 TERMINALS

3RD CL SW TO T.C.C. SIGNAL SW (COLOR ID-WHITE)

T.C.C. SIGNAL TERMINAL (COLOR ID-LT GREEN)

SOLENOID TO 4-3 DOWNSHIFT SW (COLOR ID-RED)

T.C.C. SIGNAL SW (COLOR ID-BLACK) 1 TERMINAL

4-3 DOWNSHIFT SW (COLOR ID-BLACK BODY) 2 TERMINALS

3RD CL TERMINALS (COLOR ID-LT GREEN)

TERM. D TO 3RD CL SW (COLOR ID-WHITE)

TERMINAL A TO 4-3 DOWNSHIFT SW (COLOR ID-RED)

TERM. B TO 4TH CL SW (COLOR ID-WHITE)

4-3 SW TO 4TH CL SW (COLOR ID-WHITE)

4-3 SW TERMINALS (COLOR ID-YELLOW)

4TH CL TERMINALS (COLOR ID-BLUE)

4TH CLUTCH SW (COLOR ID-BLACK) 2 TERMINALS

4-3 SHIFT (N.C.)   T.C.C. SOL (N.O. OIL PATH)

0.5 AMPS + 12V → A

0.5 AMPS + 12V → B   4TH CL (N.O.)

0.28 AMPS + 12V → D

3RD CL (N.O.)   T.C.C. SIG (N.O.)

N.O. MEANS NORMALLY OPEN SWITCH.
N.C. MEANS NORMALLY CLOSED SWITCH.

TYPE-1
4.1L GAS; 5.0L GAS & 5.7L GAS 2 W.D. (C) & 4 W.D. (T) TRUCKS WITH EMISSION SYSTEM FOR HIGH ALTITUDE ALL U.S.A. – EXCEPT CALIFORNIA

Electrical circuit—type one (© General Motors Corporation)

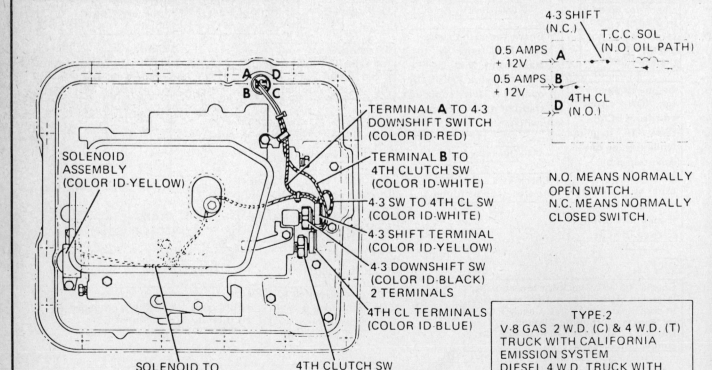

SOLENOID ASSEMBLY (COLOR ID-YELLOW)

SOLENOID TO 4-3 DOWNSHIFT SW (COLOR ID-RED)

TERMINAL A TO 4-3 DOWNSHIFT SWITCH (COLOR ID-RED)

TERMINAL B TO 4TH CLUTCH SW (COLOR ID-WHITE)

4-3 SW TO 4TH CL SW (COLOR ID-WHITE)

4-3 SHIFT TERMINAL (COLOR ID-YELLOW)

4-3 DOWNSHIFT SW (COLOR ID-BLACK) 2 TERMINALS

4TH CL TERMINALS (COLOR ID-BLUE)

4TH CLUTCH SW (COLOR ID-BLACK) 2 TERMINALS

4-3 SHIFT (N.C.)   T.C.C. SOL (N.O. OIL PATH)

0.5 AMPS + 12V → A

0.5 AMPS + 12V → B

D   4TH CL (N.O.)

N.O. MEANS NORMALLY OPEN SWITCH.
N.C. MEANS NORMALLY CLOSED SWITCH.

TYPE-2
V-8 GAS 2 W.D. (C) & 4 W.D. (T) TRUCK WITH CALIFORNIA EMISSION SYSTEM DIESEL 4 W.D. TRUCK WITH EMISSION SYSTEM FOR ALL U.S.A.

Electrical circuit—type two (© General Motors Corporation)

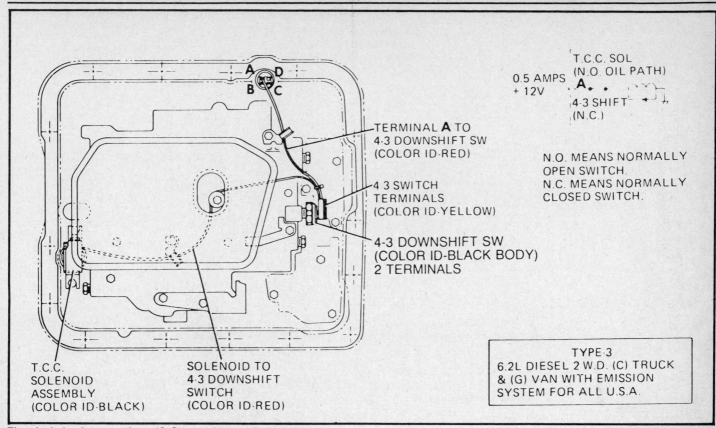

TERMINAL **A** TO
4·3 DOWNSHIFT SW
(COLOR ID·RED)

4·3 SWITCH
TERMINALS
(COLOR ID·YELLOW)

4·3 DOWNSHIFT SW
(COLOR ID·BLACK BODY)
2 TERMINALS

T.C.C. SOL
(N.O. OIL PATH)
A
4·3 SHIFT
(N.C.)

0.5 AMPS
+ 12V

N.O. MEANS NORMALLY
OPEN SWITCH.
N.C. MEANS NORMALLY
CLOSED SWITCH.

T.C.C.
SOLENOID
ASSEMBLY
(COLOR ID·BLACK)

SOLENOID TO
4·3 DOWNSHIFT
SWITCH
(COLOR ID·RED)

TYPE·3
6.2L DIESEL 2 W.D. (C) TRUCK
& (G) VAN WITH EMISSION
SYSTEM FOR ALL U.S.A.

Electrical circuit—type three (© General Motors Corporation)

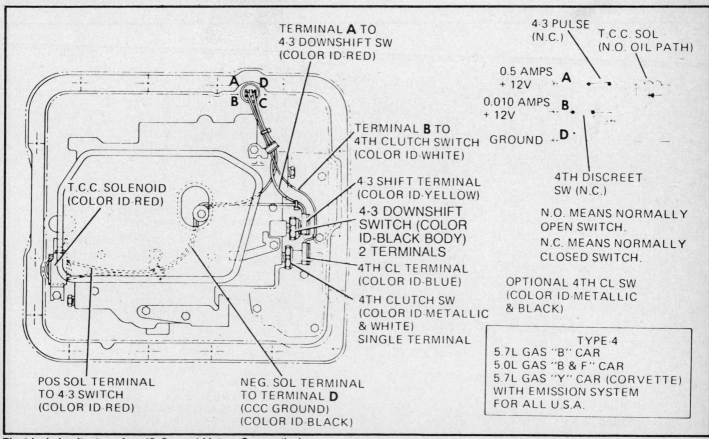

TERMINAL **A** TO
4·3 DOWNSHIFT SW
(COLOR ID·RED)

TERMINAL **B** TO
4TH CLUTCH SWITCH
(COLOR ID·WHITE)

4·3 SHIFT TERMINAL
(COLOR ID·YELLOW)

4·3 DOWNSHIFT
SWITCH (COLOR
ID·BLACK BODY)
2 TERMINALS

4TH CL TERMINAL
(COLOR ID·BLUE)

4TH CLUTCH SW
(COLOR ID·METALLIC
& WHITE)
SINGLE TERMINAL

4·3 PULSE
(N.C.)
T.C.C. SOL
(N.O. OIL PATH)

0.5 AMPS
+ 12V
A

0.010 AMPS
+ 12V
B

GROUND
D

4TH DISCREET
SW (N.C.)

N.O. MEANS NORMALLY
OPEN SWITCH.
N.C. MEANS NORMALLY
CLOSED SWITCH.

OPTIONAL 4TH CL SW
(COLOR ID·METALLIC
& BLACK)

T.C.C. SOLENOID
(COLOR ID·RED)

POS SOL TERMINAL
TO 4·3 SWITCH
(COLOR ID·RED)

NEG. SOL TERMINAL
TO TERMINAL **D**
(CCC GROUND)
(COLOR ID·BLACK)

TYPE·4
5.7L GAS "B" CAR
5.0L GAS "B & F" CAR
5.7L GAS "Y" CAR (CORVETTE)
WITH EMISSION SYSTEM
FOR ALL U.S.A.

Electrical circuit—type four (© General Motors Corporation)

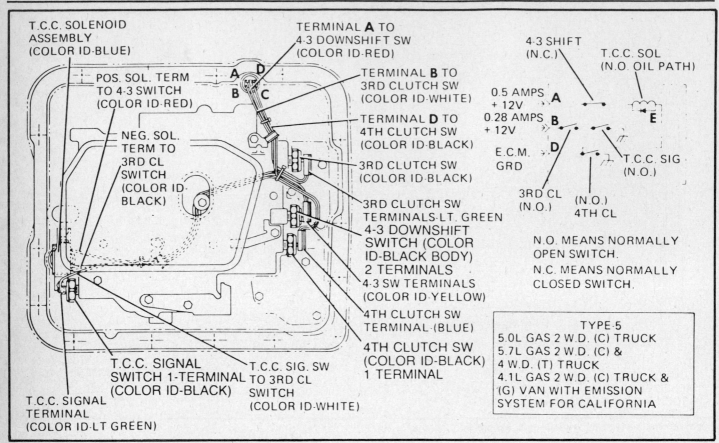

T.C.C. SOLENOID
ASSEMBLY
(COLOR ID-BLUE)

TERMINAL **A** TO
4-3 DOWNSHIFT SW
(COLOR ID-RED)

4-3 SHIFT
(N.C.)

T.C.C. SOL
(N.O. OIL PATH)

POS. SOL. TERM
TO 4-3 SWITCH
(COLOR ID-RED)

TERMINAL **B** TO
3RD CLUTCH SW
(COLOR ID-WHITE)

0.5 AMPS
+ 12V

0.28 AMPS
+ 12V

E.C.M.
GRD

TERMINAL **D** TO
4TH CLUTCH SW
(COLOR ID-BLACK)

NEG. SOL.
TERM TO
3RD CL
SWITCH
(COLOR ID-
BLACK)

3RD CLUTCH SW
(COLOR ID-BLACK)

3RD CLUTCH SW
TERMINALS-LT. GREEN

4-3 DOWNSHIFT
SWITCH (COLOR
ID-BLACK BODY)
2 TERMINALS

T.C.C. SIG
(N.O.)

3RD CL
(N.O.)

(N.O.)
4TH CL

4-3 SW TERMINALS
(COLOR ID-YELLOW)

4TH CLUTCH SW
TERMINAL-(BLUE)

N.O. MEANS NORMALLY
OPEN SWITCH.

N.C. MEANS NORMALLY
CLOSED SWITCH.

4TH CLUTCH SW
(COLOR ID-BLACK)
1 TERMINAL

T.C.C. SIGNAL
SWITCH 1-TERMINAL
(COLOR ID-BLACK)

T.C.C. SIG. SW
TO 3RD CL
SWITCH
(COLOR ID-WHITE)

TYPE-5
5.0L GAS 2 W.D. (C) TRUCK
5.7L GAS 2 W.D. (C) &
4 W.D. (T) TRUCK
4.1L GAS 2 W.D. (C) TRUCK &
(G) VAN WITH EMISSION
SYSTEM FOR CALIFORNIA

T.C.C. SIGNAL
TERMINAL
(COLOR ID-LT GREEN)

Electrical circuit—type five (© General Motors Corporation)

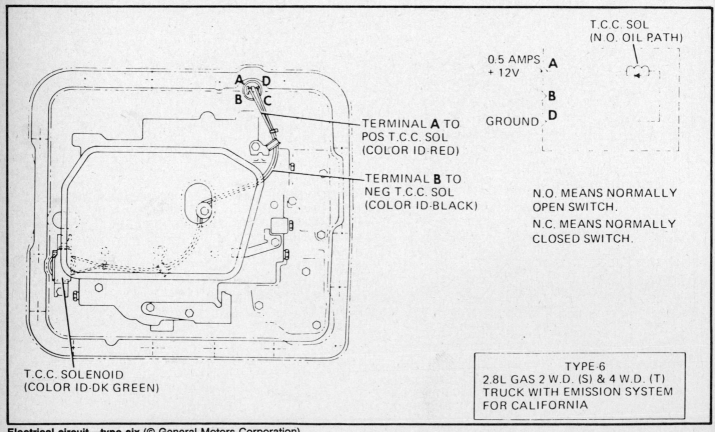

T.C.C. SOL
(N.O. OIL PATH)

0.5 AMPS
+ 12V

GROUND

TERMINAL **A** TO
POS T.C.C. SOL
(COLOR ID-RED)

TERMINAL **B** TO
NEG T.C.C. SOL
(COLOR ID-BLACK)

N.O. MEANS NORMALLY
OPEN SWITCH.

N.C. MEANS NORMALLY
CLOSED SWITCH.

T.C.C. SOLENOID
(COLOR ID-DK GREEN)

TYPE-6
2.8L GAS 2 W.D. (S) & 4 W.D. (T)
TRUCK WITH EMISSION SYSTEM
FOR CALIFORNIA

Electrical circuit—type six (© General Motors Corporation)

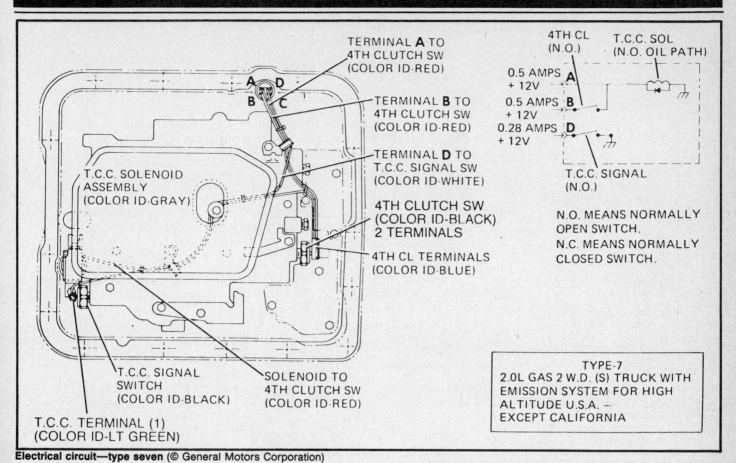

TERMINAL **A** TO
4TH CLUTCH SW
(COLOR ID-RED)

TERMINAL **B** TO
4TH CLUTCH SW
(COLOR ID-RED)

TERMINAL **D** TO
T.C.C. SIGNAL SW
(COLOR ID-WHITE)

4TH CLUTCH SW
(COLOR ID-BLACK)
2 TERMINALS

4TH CL TERMINALS
(COLOR ID-BLUE)

T.C.C. SOLENOID
ASSEMBLY
(COLOR ID-GRAY)

T.C.C. SIGNAL
SWITCH
(COLOR ID-BLACK)

T.C.C. TERMINAL (1)
(COLOR ID-LT GREEN)

SOLENOID TO
4TH CLUTCH SW
(COLOR ID-RED)

4TH CL
(N.O.)

T.C.C. SOL
(N.O. OIL PATH)

0.5 AMPS
+ 12V   **A**

0.5 AMPS
+ 12V   **B**

0.28 AMPS
+ 12V   **D**

T.C.C. SIGNAL
(N.O.)

N.O. MEANS NORMALLY
OPEN SWITCH.

N.C. MEANS NORMALLY
CLOSED SWITCH.

TYPE-7
2.0L GAS 2 W.D. (S) TRUCK WITH
EMISSION SYSTEM FOR HIGH
ALTITUDE U.S.A. —
EXCEPT CALIFORNIA

Electrical circuit—type seven (© General Motors Corporation)

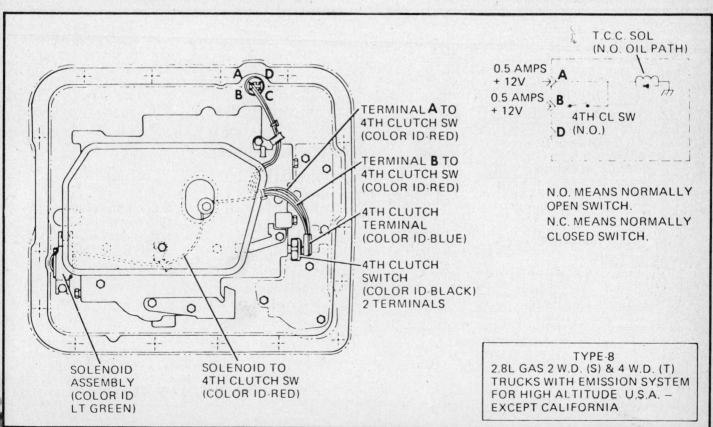

TERMINAL **A** TO
4TH CLUTCH SW
(COLOR ID-RED)

TERMINAL **B** TO
4TH CLUTCH SW
(COLOR ID-RED)

4TH CLUTCH
TERMINAL
(COLOR ID-BLUE)

4TH CLUTCH
SWITCH
(COLOR ID-BLACK)
2 TERMINALS

T.C.C. SOL
(N.O. OIL PATH)

0.5 AMPS
+ 12V   **A**

0.5 AMPS
+ 12V   **B**

4TH CL SW
(N.O.)

D

N.O. MEANS NORMALLY
OPEN SWITCH.

N.C. MEANS NORMALLY
CLOSED SWITCH.

SOLENOID
ASSEMBLY
(COLOR ID
LT GREEN)

SOLENOID TO
4TH CLUTCH SW
(COLOR ID-RED)

TYPE-8
2.8L GAS 2 W.D. (S) & 4 W.D. (T)
TRUCKS WITH EMISSION SYSTEM
FOR HIGH ALTITUDE U.S.A. —
EXCEPT CALIFORNIA

Electrical circuit—type eight (© General Motors Corporation)

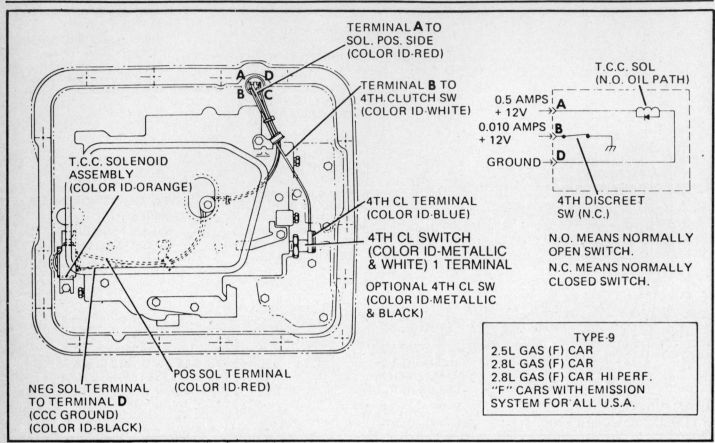

TERMINAL A TO
SOL. POS. SIDE
(COLOR ID-RED)

TERMINAL B TO
4TH. CLUTCH SW
(COLOR ID-WHITE)

A D
B C

T.C.C. SOLENOID
ASSEMBLY
(COLOR ID-ORANGE)

4TH CL TERMINAL
(COLOR ID-BLUE)

4TH CL SWITCH
(COLOR ID-METALLIC
& WHITE) 1 TERMINAL

OPTIONAL 4TH CL SW
(COLOR ID-METALLIC
& BLACK)

POS SOL TERMINAL
(COLOR ID-RED)

NEG SOL TERMINAL
TO TERMINAL D
(CCC GROUND)
(COLOR ID-BLACK)

T.C.C. SOL
(N.O. OIL PATH)

0.5 AMPS
+ 12V   A

0.010 AMPS   B
+ 12V

GROUND   D

4TH DISCREET
SW (N.C.)

N.O. MEANS NORMALLY
OPEN SWITCH.

N.C. MEANS NORMALLY
CLOSED SWITCH.

TYPE-9
2.5L GAS (F) CAR
2.8L GAS (F) CAR
2.8L GAS (F) CAR HI PERF.
"F" CARS WITH EMISSION
SYSTEM FOR ALL U.S.A.

Electrical circuit—type nine (© General Motors Corporation)

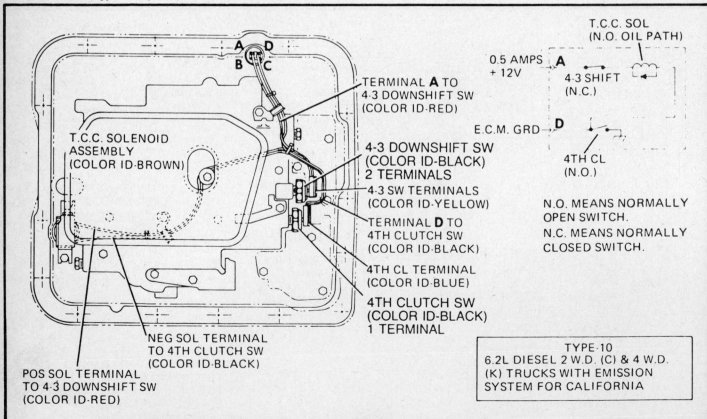

A D
B C

TERMINAL A TO
4-3 DOWNSHIFT SW
(COLOR ID-RED)

T.C.C. SOLENOID
ASSEMBLY
(COLOR ID-BROWN)

4-3 DOWNSHIFT SW
(COLOR ID-BLACK)
2 TERMINALS

4-3 SW TERMINALS
(COLOR ID-YELLOW)

TERMINAL D TO
4TH CLUTCH SW
(COLOR ID-BLACK)

4TH CL TERMINAL
(COLOR ID-BLUE)

4TH CLUTCH SW
(COLOR ID-BLACK)
1 TERMINAL

NEG SOL TERMINAL
TO 4TH CLUTCH SW
(COLOR ID-BLACK)

POS SOL TERMINAL
TO 4-3 DOWNSHIFT SW
(COLOR ID-RED)

T.C.C. SOL
(N.O. OIL PATH)

0.5 AMPS
+ 12V   A

4-3 SHIFT
(N.C.)

E.C.M. GRD   D

4TH CL
(N.O.)

N.O. MEANS NORMALLY
OPEN SWITCH.

N.C. MEANS NORMALLY
CLOSED SWITCH.

TYPE-10
6.2L DIESEL 2 W.D. (C) & 4 W.D.
(K) TRUCKS WITH EMISSION
SYSTEM FOR CALIFORNIA

Electrical circuit—type ten (© General Motors Corporation)

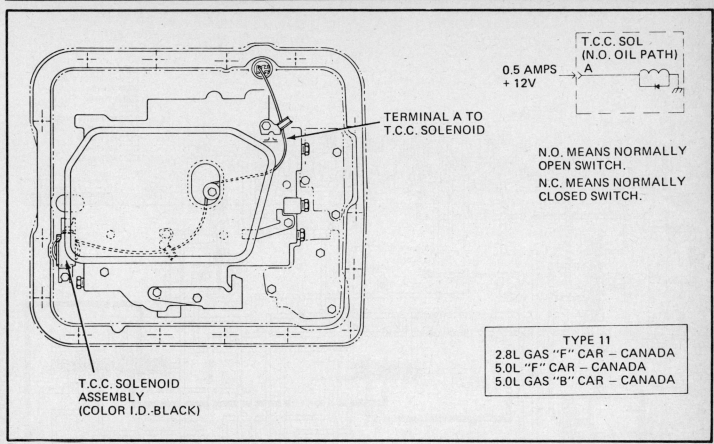

TERMINAL A TO
T.C.C. SOLENOID

N.O. MEANS NORMALLY
OPEN SWITCH.

N.C. MEANS NORMALLY
CLOSED SWITCH.

TYPE 11
2.8L GAS "F" CAR — CANADA
5.0L "F" CAR — CANADA
5.0L GAS "B" CAR — CANADA

T.C.C. SOLENOID
ASSEMBLY
(COLOR I.D.-BLACK)

Electrical circuit—type eleven (© General Motors Corporation)

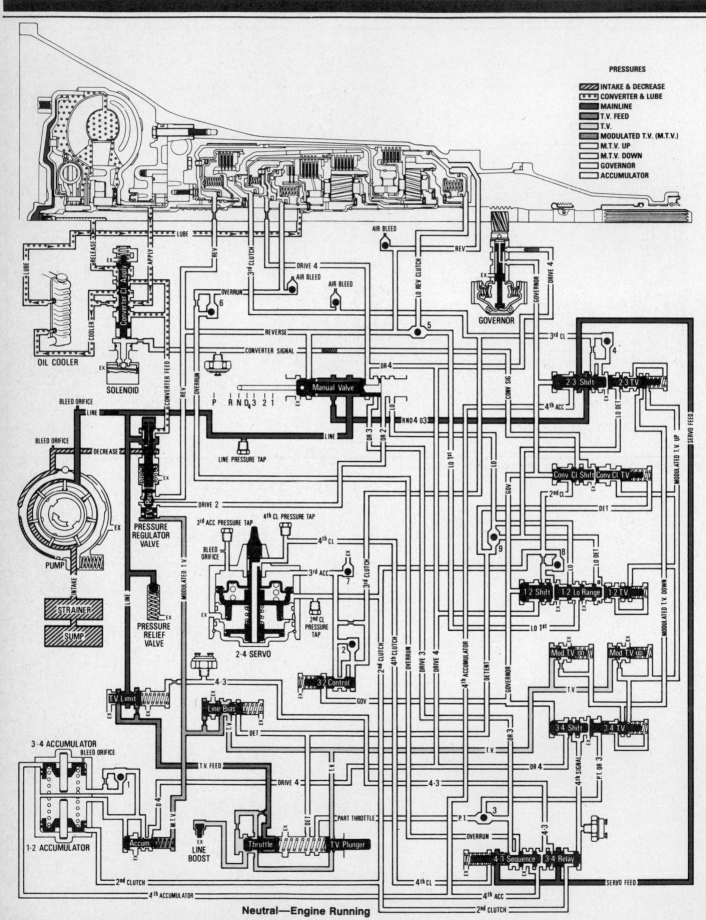

Neutral—Engine Running

NEUTRAL—ENGINE RUNNING

UNITS APPLIED OR RELEASED

Converter clutch—released

Reverse input clutch—released

Forward clutch—released

3-4 clutch—released

Low and reverse clutch—released

Low roller clutch—not holding

2-4 band—released

Overrun clutch—released

Input roller clutch—not holding

BASIC CONTROL

When the selector lever is moved to the neutral (N) position, the line pressure is directed to the same areas as in park, except in neutral (N) the manual valve directs oil into the reverse, neutral, drive 4, drive 3 (RND4D3) oil is directed to the 2-3 shift valve which directs RND4D3 oil to the 3-4 relay valve through the servo feed passage. Oil at these valves is available for use in other ranges.

SUMMARY

The converter is filled from the release side; all clutches and the band are released. At idle, there is not sufficient T.V. pressure to open the M.T.V. up or M.T.V. down valves.

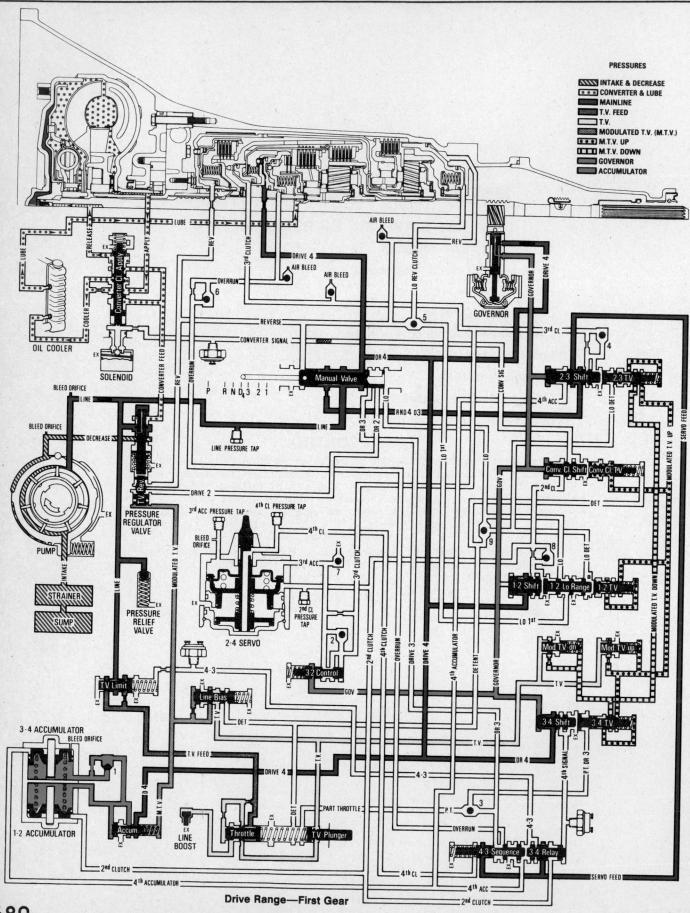

Drive Range—First Gear

DRIVE RANGE—FIRST GEAR

UNITS APPLIED OR RELEASED

Forward clutch—applied

Low reverse clutch—holding

Input roller clutch—holding

When the selector lever is in the drive (D) position, the manual valve is repositioned to allow line pressure to enter the drive (D4) passage. Drive (D4) oil then flows to the forward clutch, governor valve, 1-2 shift valve, accumulator valve and the 3-4 shift valve.

BASIC CONTROL

Drive 4 oil is directed to the forward clutch where it acts on the clutch piston to apply the forward clutch.

Drive 4 oil is directed to the 1-2 and 3-4 shift valves. Drive 4 oil is directed to the accumulator valve and is regulated to a pressure called accumulator pressure; this pressure is directed to the 1-2 and 3-4 accumulator pistons to act as a cushion for the band apply in second gear and overdrive.

Drive 4 oil is orificed into the governor passage, and is regulated to a variable pressure called governor pressure. Governor pressure increases with vehicle speed and acts against the 1-2, 2-3, 3-4, converter clutch and the 3-2 control valve springs.

In first gear, there could be sufficient throttle valve plunger travel to increase T.V. pressure enough to open the M.T.V. up and the M.T.V. down valves. In first gear, M.T.V. up exerts pressure against governor pressure at the 1-2, 2-3, 3-4, and converter clutch throttle valves. M.T.V. down pressure is stopped by a land at the 2-3 and 3-4 throttle valves.

SUMMARY

The converter clutch is released, the input roller clutch is holding, the forward clutch is applied; the transmission is in drive (D) range—first gear.

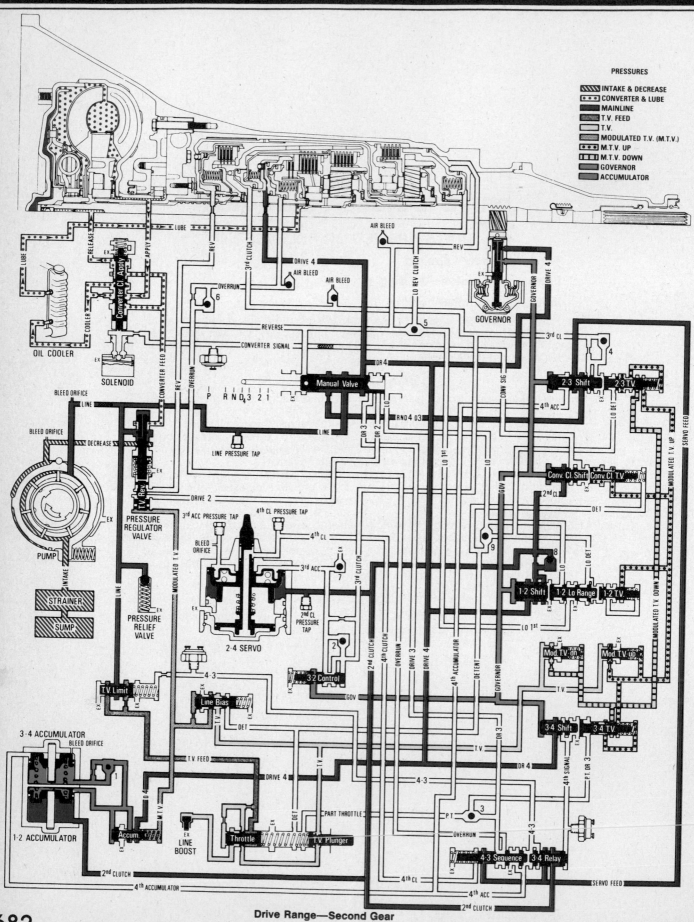

PRESSURES

- INTAKE & DECREASE
- CONVERTER & LUBE
- MAINLINE
- T.V. FEED
- T.V.
- MODULATED T.V. (M.T.V.)
- M.T.V. UP
- M.T.V. DOWN
- GOVERNOR
- ACCUMULATOR

Drive Range—Second Gear

DRIVE RANGE—SECOND GEAR

UNITS APPLIED OR RELEASED

2-4 band—applied

Input roller clutch—holding

Forward clutch—applied

As both vehicle speed and governor pressure increase, the force of the governor oil acting on the 1-2 shift valve overcomes the pressure of M.T.V. up oil and the force of the 1-2 throttle valve spring. This allows the 1-2 shift valve to open and drive 4 (D4) oil to enter the second (2nd) oil passage. This oil is called second (2nd) oil. Second oil from the 1-2 shift valve is directed to the 1-2 shift check ball (8), 2-4 servo, 1-2 accumulator piston, converter clutch shift valve and the 3-4 relay valve.

BASIC CONTROL

Second oil from the 1-2 shift valve will seat the 1-2 shift check ball (8) forcing 2nd oil through an orifice. Second oil is then directed to the 2-4 servo to apply the 2-4 band. At the same time, 2nd oil moves the 1-2 accumulator piston against accumulator pressure and the accumulator spring to maintain a controlled build-up of pressure on the servo during the 1-2 shift for a smooth band apply. 2nd oil at the converter clutch shift valve and the 3-4 relay valve is available for use in other ranges.

SUMMARY

The converter clutch is released, the 2-4 band is applied, the forward clutch is applied, and the input roller clutch is holding; the transmission is in drive (D) range—second gear.

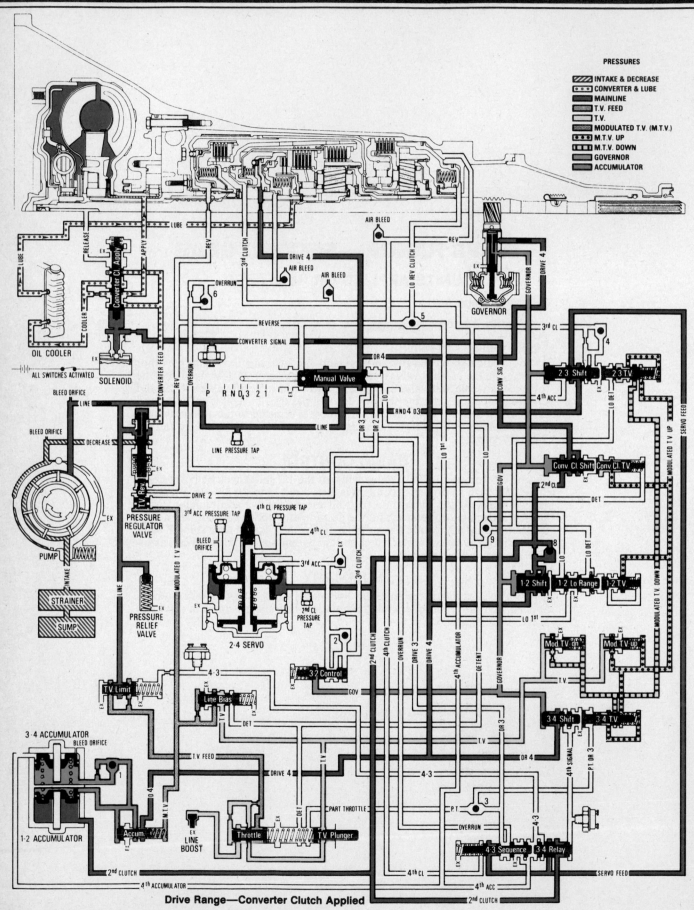

Drive Range—Converter Clutch Applied

DRIVE RANGE—CONVERTER CLUTCH APPLIED

UNITS APPLIED OR RELEASED

Converter clutch—applied

Forward clutch—applied

2-4 band—applied

Input roller clutch—holding

BASIC CONTROL

As vehicle speed and governor pressure increase, the force of governor oil acting on the converter clutch shift valve overcomes the pressure of M.T.V. up oil and the force of the converter clutch T.V. spring. This allows the converter clutch shift valve to open and 2nd oil to enter the converter clutch signal passage. Providing the converter clutch solenoid is on, converter clutch signal oil will shift the converter clutch apply valve, and redirect converter feed oil into the apply passage. The apply oil flows between the stator shaft and converter hub to charge the converter with oil and push the converter pressure plate against the converter cover, causing a mechanical link between the engine and the turbine shaft. The rate of apply is controlled by the orifice check ball capsule in the end of the turbine shaft.

At the same time the converter clutch apply valve will direct converter feed oil through an orifice to the transmission cooler. Cooler oil is directed to the transmission lubrication system.

SUMMARY

The converter clutch is applied, the 2-4 band is applied, the forward clutch is applied, and the input roller clutch is holding; the transmission is in drive (D) range—second gear. The converter clutch is shown applied in 2nd gear. In some models, the converter clutch shift valve will not shift until the transmission is in 3rd gear.

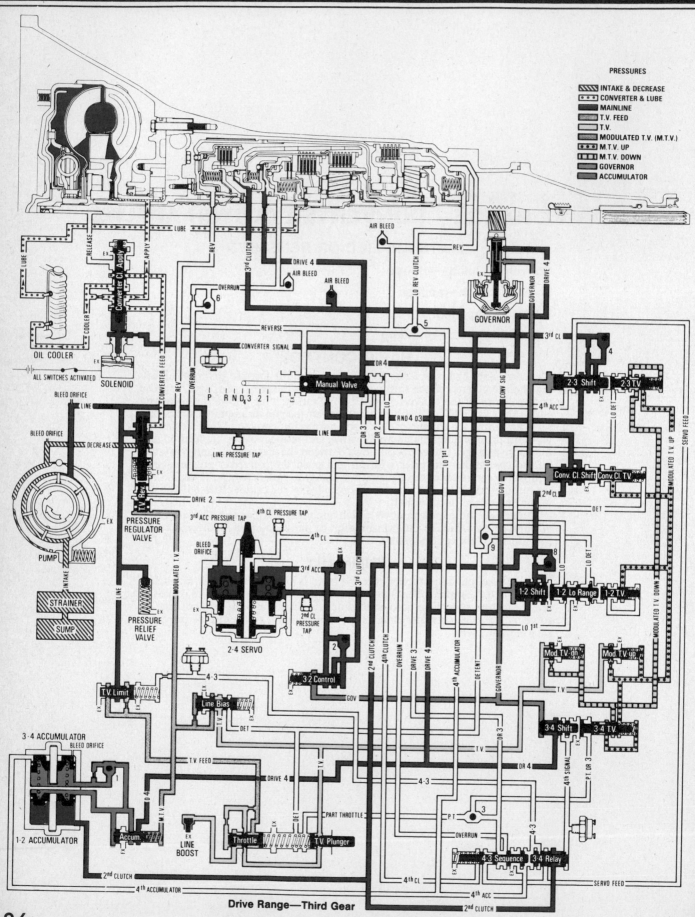

PRESSURES

- INTAKE & DECREASE
- CONVERTER & LUBE
- MAINLINE
- T.V. FEED
- T.V.
- MODULATED T.V. (M.T.V.)
- M.T.V. UP
- M.T.V. DOWN
- GOVERNOR
- ACCUMULATOR

Drive Range—Third Gear

DRIVE RANGE—THIRD GEAR

UNITS APPLIED OR RELEASED

Converter clutch—applied①

Input roller clutch—holding

Forward clutch—applied

3-4 clutch—applied

BASIC CONTROL

As both vehicle speed and governor pressure increase, the force of governor oil acting on the 2-3 shift valve overcomes the force of the 2-3 T.V. spring and M.T.V. up oil. This allows the 2-3 shift valve to open and allows RND4D3 oil to enter the 3rd clutch passage. Third clutch oil from the 1-2 shift valve is directed to the 3-2 exhaust check ball (2), the third accumulator check ball (4), third accumulator exhaust check ball (7), 2-4 servo (release side) and the 3-2 control valve.

Third clutch oil from the 2-3 shift valve flows past the 3-2 exhaust check ball (4), to the 3-4 clutch piston. At the same time, 3rd clutch oil is directed past the 3rd clutch accumulator check ball (2), seats the 3rd accumulator exhaust check ball (7), and then into the release side of the 2-4 servo. This 3rd clutch accumulator pressure combined with the servo cushion spring, moves the 2nd apply piston, in the 2-4 servo, against 2nd clutch oil and acts as an accumulator for a smooth 2-4 band release and 3-4 clutch apply.

Third clutch oil is present at the 3-2 control valve in preparation of a third gear to second gear shift.

SUMMARY

The converter clutch is applied①, the forward clutch is applied, the input roller clutch is holding, the 3-4 clutch is applied and the 2-4 band is released; the transmission is in drive (D) range—third gear (direct drive).

① The converter clutch may or may not be applied, depending on shift calibration and solenoid operation.

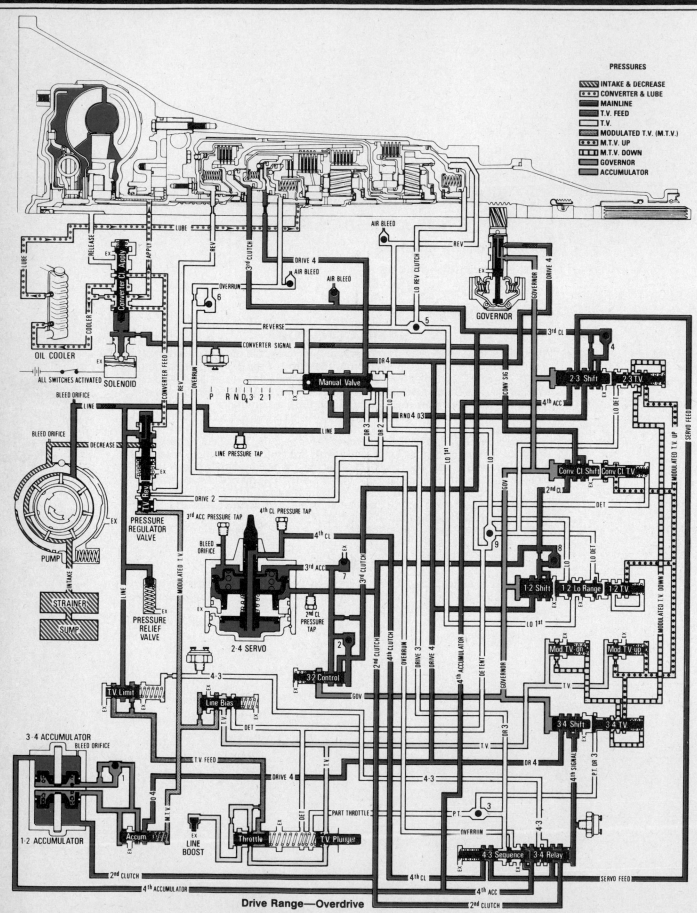

Drive Range—Overdrive

DRIVE RANGE—OVERDRIVE

UNITS APPLIED OR RELEASED

Converter clutch—applied①

Forward clutch—applied

3-4 clutch—applied

2-4 band—applied

Input roller clutch—not holding

BASIC CONTROL

As both vehicle speed and governor pressure increase, the force of governor oil acting on the 3-4 shift valve overcomes the force of the 3-4 T.V. Spring and M.T.V. up oil. This opens the 3-4 shift valve sending drive 4 (D4) into the 4th signal passage. 4th signal oil will overcome the 4-3 sequence valve spring and open the 3-4 relay and the 4-3 sequence valves, allowing 2nd clutch oil to enter the servo feed passage. Servo feed oil is directed to the 2-3 shift valve which in turn directs oil to the 3-4 accumulator and 4-3 sequence valve. Servo feed oil is also directed to the 4-3 sequence valve which in turn directs oil to the fourth apply piston in the 2-3 servo.

Servo feed oil passes through the 4-3 sequence valve and becomes 4th clutch oil. 4th clutch oil then enters the 2-4 servo, applies pressure on the 4th apply piston, and applies the 2-4 band.

SUMMARY

The converter clutch, 2-4 band, forward clutch, the 3-4 clutch are applied, and the input roller clutch is overrunning; the transmission is in drive (D) range—overdrive.

① The converter clutch may or may not be applied depending on solenoid operation.

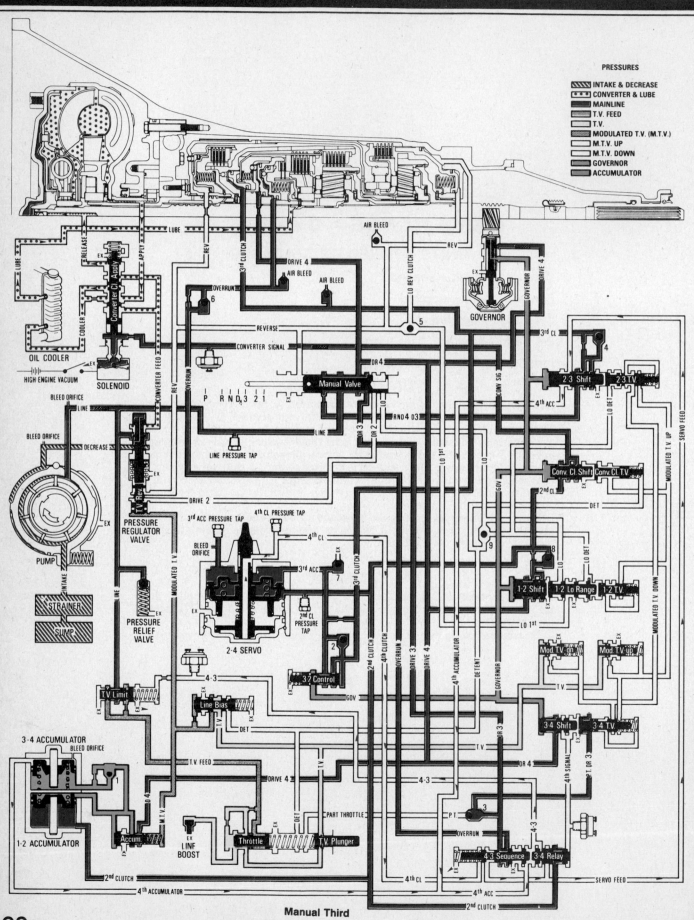

Manual Third

MANUAL THIRD

UNITS APPLIED OR RELEASED

Converter clutch—released①

Forward clutch—applied

Overrun clutch—applied

3-4 clutch—applied

BASIC CONTROL

The forced 4-3 downshift can be accomplished by moving the selector lever from drive range to third gear. When the selector lever is moved to the third gear position, D3 oil from the manual valve is directed to the 4-3 sequence valve, part throttle and drive 3 check ball (3) and the 3-4 shift valve. D3 oil will close the 3-4 shift valve and allow the fourth signal oil to exhaust.

D3 oil combined with the 4-3 sequence valve spring force will close the 4-3 sequence valve to allow the 4th clutch and 4th accumulator oil to exhaust and release the band. D3 oil then flows into the overrun clutch passage where it applies the overrun clutch to keep the input roller clutch from overrunning when engine braking is needed.

SUMMARY

The forward and 3-4 clutches are applied. The 2-4 band is released. The transmission is in manual third, direct drive. The overrun clutch is applied to allow engine braking.

①In manual 3rd, the converter is shown released by the engine vacuum switch and there is no M.T.V. up or M.T.V. down pressure. This is assuming the throttle is released. If the throttle is opened sufficiently, the converter clutch could engage and the M.T.V. up and M.T.V. down valves could open.

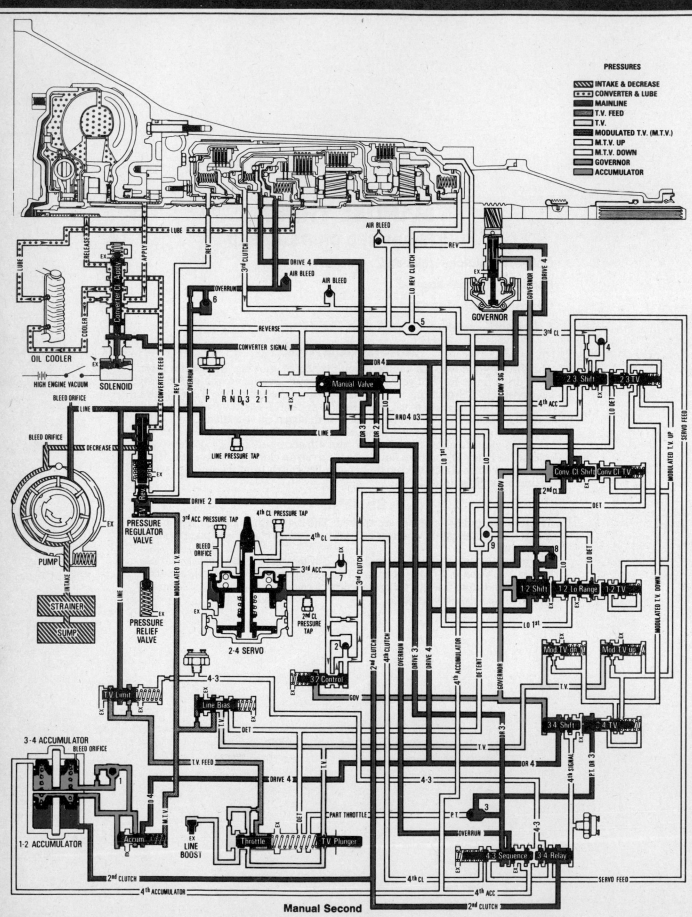

Manual Second

MANUAL SECOND

UNITS APPLIED OR RELEASED

Converter clutch—released①

Overrun clutch—applied

2-4 band—applied

Forward clutch—applied

BASIC CONTROL

A forced 3-2 downshift can be accomplished by moving the selector lever from third (3rd) gear to the second (2nd) gear position.

When the selector lever is moved to the second (2nd) gear position, RND4D3, 3rd clutch, and 3rd accumulator oil will exhaust at the manual valve. With no pressure to apply the 3-4 clutch, or release the 2-4 band, the transmission will shift to second gear.

The manual valve will also direct line pressure into the D2 passage. Drive 2 (D2) oil will act on the reverse boost valve to boost line pressure to 110 psi which is required to prevent the 2-4 band and forward clutch from slipping.

SUMMARY

The forward clutch and 2-4 band are applied. The transmission is in second gear. Also, the overrun clutch is still applied to allow engine braking when needed.

① In manual 2nd, the converter clutch is shown released by the engine vacuum switch and there is no M.T.V. up or M.T.V. down pressure. This is assuming the throttle is released. If the throttle is opened sufficiently, the converter clutch could engage and the M.T.V. up and M.T.V. down valves could open.

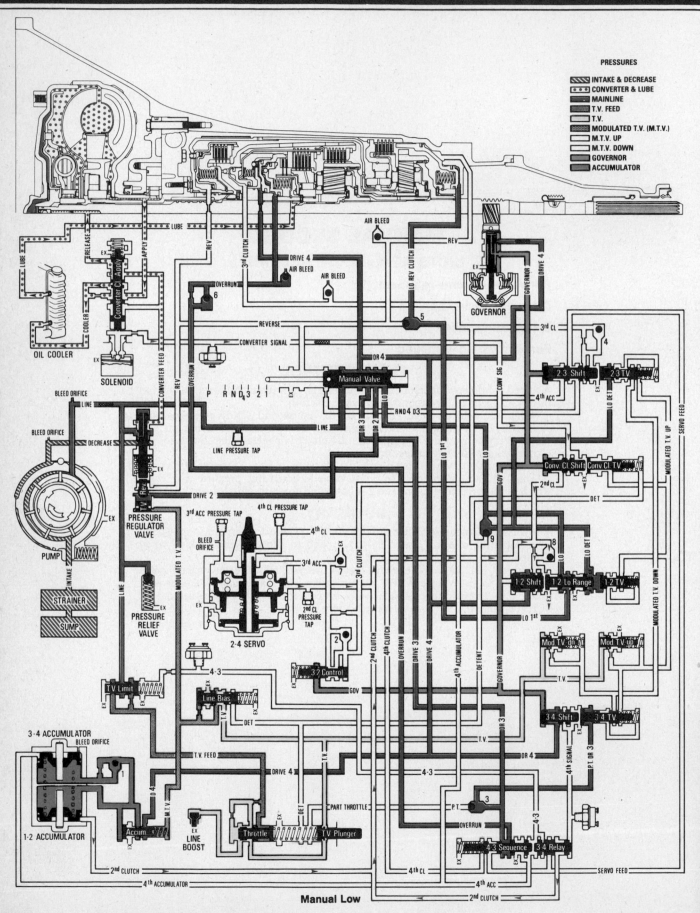

Manual Low

MANUAL LOW

UNITS APPLIED OR RELEASED

Converter clutch—released

Forward clutch—applied

Overrun clutch—applied

Low roller clutch—applied

BASIC CONTROL

Maximum downhill braking can be obtained at speeds below 30 mph with the selector in low (1st) range. Low 1st oil pressure, which is 110 psi, is the same as second (2nd) oil pressure because second (D2) oil is still present.

Low oil from the manual valve is directed to the low and detent check ball (9), 1-2 shift valve train, low and reverse check ball (10) and the low and reverse clutch assembly.

Low oil at the low 1st detent valve combined with M.T.V. down and 1-2 throttle valve spring force will close the 1-2 shift valve at speeds below approximately 30 mph. This allows 2nd oil to exhaust, releasing the 2-4 band, and low oil to travel to the low and reverse clutch and applies it.

SUMMARY

The forward clutch is applied. The low and reverse, and the overrun clutch are applied to allow engine braking. The 2-4 band is released, the transmission is in low range—first gear.

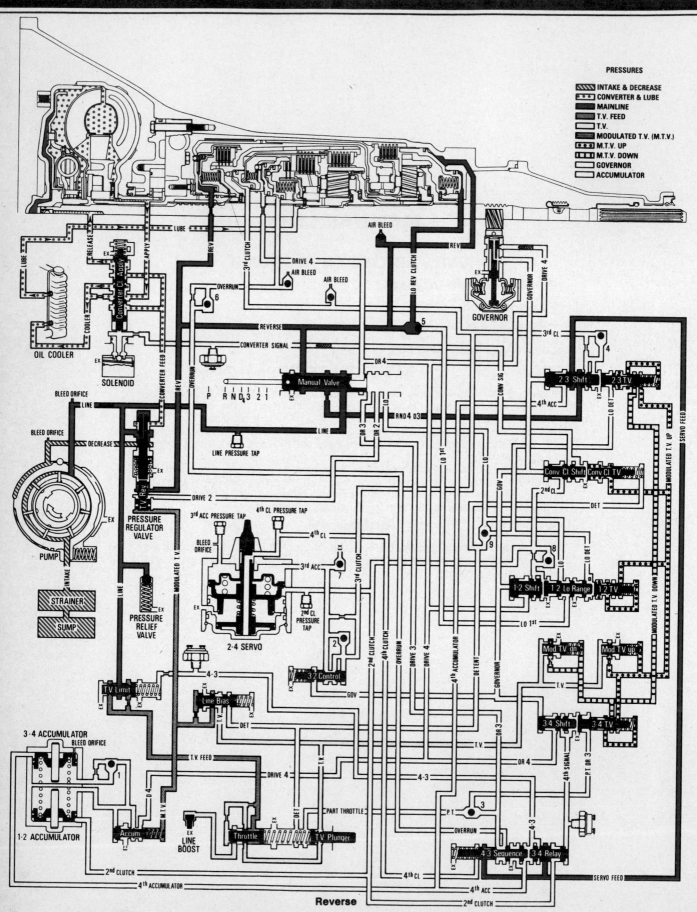

Reverse

REVERSE

UNITS APPLIED OR RELEASED

Reverse input clutch—applied

Low and reverse clutch—applied

BASIC CONTROL

When the selctor lever is moved into the reverse position, the manual valve is repositioned to allow line pressure to enter the reverse passage which directs oil to the low and reverse check ball (5), low and reverse clutch, reverse input clutch and the reverse boost valve.

Reverse oil seats the low and reverse check ball (5) in the low 1st passage and flows to the low and reverse clutch piston, applying the low and reverse clutch.

Reverse oil is orificed into the reverse input clutch piston and applies the reverse input clutch.

Reverse oil acting on the reverse boost valve in the pressure regulator will boost line pressure to approximately 100 psi. M.T.V. oil from the line bias valve acting on the T.V. boost valve, in the pressure regulator, will further boost line pressure from 100 psi at idle to 245 psi at full throttle.

SUMMARY

The reverse input clutch is applied. The low and reverse clutch is applied. The transmission is in reverse (R).

ON CAR SERVICES

Adjustments

SHIFT INDICATOR

COLUMN MOUNTED SHIFTER

1. With the engine off, position the selector lever in the neutral position.
2. If the pointer does not align with the "N" indicator position, move the clip on the shift bowl until alignment has been achieved.

NOTE: The manual linkage must be adjusted correctly before this adjustment can be made properly.

NEUTRAL SAFETY SWITCH

FLOOR MOUNTED SHIFTER

1. New switches comes with a small plastic alignment pin installed. Leave this pin in place. Position the shifter assembly in neutral.
2. Remove the old switch and install the replacement, align the pin on the shifter with the slot in the switch, and fasten with the two screws.
3. Move the shifter from the neutral position. This shears the plastic alignment pin and frees the switch.

If the switch is to be adjusted, not replaced, insert a 3/32 in. drill bit or similar size pin and align the hole and switch. Position switch, adjust as necessary. Remove the pin before shifting from neutral.

COLUMN MOUNTED SHIFTER

1. Remove wire connectors from the combination back-up and neutral safety switch.
2. Remove two screws attaching the switch to the steering column.
3. Installation is the reverse of removal. To adjust a new switch:
   a. Position the shift lever in neutral.
   b. Loosen the attaching screws. Install a 0.090 in. gauge pin into the outer hole in the switch cover.
   c. Rotate the switch until the pin goes into the alignment hole in the inner plastic slide.
   d. Tighten the switch to column attaching screws and remove the gauge pin. Torque the screws to 20 in. lbs. maximum.
   c. Make sure that the engine starts only in the park and neutral positions.

MECHANICAL NEUTRAL START SYSTEM

Vehicles with this system use a mechanical block rather than an electrical neutral start system. The system only allows the lock cylinder to rotate to the start position when the shift lever is in neutral or park.

PARK LOCK CABLE

FLOOR MOUNTED SHIFTER

1. Remove the floor shift knob. Remove the console trim panel. Remove the hush panel.
2. Snap the park lock cable (column end) into the steering column bracket.
3. Snap the cable to the steering column sliding pin. The steering column sliding pin must have the ignition lock cylinder in the lock position.
4. Position the selector lever in the park position.
5. Install the park lock cable terminal to the shifter park lock

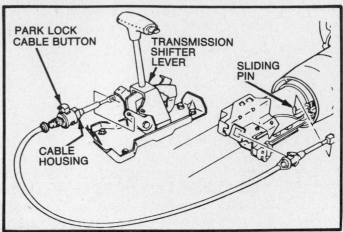

Park lock cable—floor shift models (© General Motors Corporation)

lever pin. Install the retainer pin. Install the park lock cable to the shifter mounting bracket by pushing the lock button housing against the adjusting spring. Drop the cable through the slot in the mounting bracket and seat the housing to shifter.

6. Push the lock button down to complete the adjustment.
7. With the ignition key in the lock position, depress the button on the shift handle. Button travel must not be sufficient to move the shifter lever out of the park position.
8. Move the ignition key to the run position. The shifter should select the gears by the handle rotating rearward. Check and be sure that the ignition lock cylinder cannot be turned to lock.
9. Return the shifter lever to the park position. Return the ignition key to the lock position. Check that the ignition key can be removed from the ignition switch.
10. If the ignition key is difficult to remove, pry up on the park lock cable button. Pull the cable housing rearward one notch and push the lock button down.
11. If the ignition key is still difficult to remove repeat the above step.

NOTE: If the park lock cable housing is moved to far rearward, the shift lever may come out of the park position when the ignition is locked with the key removed.

T.V. AND DETENT CABLE

NOTE: Before any adjustment is made to the T.V. or detent cable be sure that the engine is operating properly, the transmission fluid level is correct, the brakes are not dragging, the correct cable has been installed and that the cable is connected at both ends.

DIESEL ENGINE

1. Stop the engine. If equipped, remove the cruise control rod.
2. Disconnect the transmission T.V. cable terminal from the cable actuating lever.
3. Loosen the lock nut on the pump rod and shorten it several turns.
4. Rotate the lever assembly to the full throttle position. Hold this position.
5. Lengthen pump rod until the injection pump lever contacts the full throttle stop.
6. Release the lever assembly and tighten pump rod lock nut. Remove the pump rod from the lever assembly.
7. Reconnect the transmission T.V. cable terminal to cable actuating lever.
8. Depress and hold the metal re-adjust tab on the cable upper end. Move the slider through the fitting in the direction away from the lever assembly until the slider stops against the fitting.

9. Release the re-adjust tab. Rotate the cable actuating lever assembly to the full throttle stop and release the cable actuating lever assembly. The cable slider should adjust out of the cable fitting toward the cable actuating lever.

10. Reconnect the pump rod and cruise control throttle rod if so equipped.

11. If equipped with cruise control, adjust the servo throttle rod to minimum slack (engine off) then put clip in first free hole closest to the bellcrank but within the servo bail.

GAS ENGINE

1. Stop engine.

2. Depress and hold the metal re-adjust tab on the cable upper end. Move the slider through the fitting in the direction away from the lever assembly until the slider stops against the fitting. Release readjust tab.

3. Rotate the cable actuating lever assembly to the full throttle stop and release the cable actuating lever assembly. The cable slider should adjust out of the cable fitting toward the cable actuating lever. Check cable for sticking and binding.

4. Road test the vehicle. If the condition still exists, remove the transmission oil pan and inspect the throttle lever and bracket assembly on the valve body.

5. Check to see that the T.V. exhaust valve lifter rod is not distorted or binding in the valve body assembly or spacer plate.

6. The T.V. exhaust check ball must move up and down as the lifter does. Be sure that the lifter spring holds the lifter rod up against the bottom of the valve body.

7. Make sure that the T.V. plunger is not stuck. Inspect the transmission for correct throttle lever to cable link.

MANUAL LINKAGE

There are many variations of the manual linkage used with the THM 700-R4 due to its wide vehicle application. A general adjustment procedure is outlined for the convenience of the repairman.

Loosen the shift rod adjusting swivel clamp at the cross shaft. Place the transmission detent in the neutral position and the column selector in the neutral position. Tighten the adjustment swivel clamp and shift the selector lever through all ranges, confirming the transmission detent corresponds to the shift lever positions and the vehicle will only start in the park or neutral positions.

Services

DETENT CABLE

Removal

1. If required, remove the air cleaner.

2. Push in on the readjust tab and move the slider back through the fitting in the direction away from the throttle lever.

3. Disconnect the cable terminal from the throttle lever. Compress the locking tab and disconnect the cable assembly from the bracket.

4. Remove the routing clips or straps. Remove the screw and washer securing the cable to the transmission and disconnect the cable from the link.

Installation

1. Install a new oil seal in the transmission case hole. Position and install the cable at the transmission case. Torque the retaining bolt to 8 ft. lbs.

2. Route the cable as removed and connect the clip or strap. Pass the cable through the bracket and engage the locking tabs of the cable on the bracket.

3. Connect the cable terminal to the throttle lever. Adjust the cable as required.

4. Install the air cleaner, if removed.

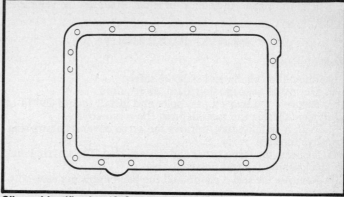

Oil pan identification (© General Motors Corporation)

FLUID CHANGE AND OIL PAN

Removal

1. Raise and safely support the vehicle.

2. Place drain pan under transmission oil pan. Remove the oil pan attaching bolts from the front and side of the pan.

3. Loosen, but do not remove the rear pan bolts, then bump the pan loose and allow fluid to drain.

4. Remove the remaining bolts and remove pan.

5. Clean pan in solvent and dry with compressed air.

6. Remove the two bolts holding the filter screen to the valve body. Discard gasket.

Installation

1. Install the filter assembly using a new gasket. Torque the retaining bolts to 6-10 ft. lbs.

2. Install new gasket on pan and torque bolts to 10-13 ft. lbs.

3. Lower the vehicle and add 3 quarts of Dexron® II.

4. With selector in park start engine and idle. Apply parking brake. *Do not race engine.*

Move selector through all ranges and end in park. Check fluid level. Add if necessary to bring the level between the dimples on the dipstick.

VALVE BODY

Removal

1. Raise the vehicle on a hoist and support it safely.

2. Drain the transmission fluid. Remove the fluid pan. Discard the gasket.

3. Remove the two bolts retaining the filter. Remove the filter from the valve body.

4. Disconnect the electrical connectors at the valve body assembly.

5. Remove the detent spring and roller assembly from the valve body. Remove the valve body to transmission case retaining bolts.

6. Remove the valve body assembly while disconnecting the manual control valve link from the range selector inner lever. Remove the throttle lever bracket from the T.V. link.

7. Position the valve body assembly down, with the spacer plate side up.

Installation

1. Using new gaskets, as required, position the valve body assembly against the transmission. Install the valve body retaining bolts and torque them 7-10 ft. lbs.

2. Continue the installation in the reverse order of the removal procedure.

3. Use a new gasket when installing the oil pan.

4. Lower the vehicle. Fill the transmission to specification using the proper grade and type automatic transmission fluid.

5. Start the engine and check for leaks. Road test the vehicle as required.

SERVO ASSEMBLY

Removal

1. Raise the vehicle and support safely.
2. Drain the transmission fluid, as required.
3. Remove the two oil pan bolts and install tool #J-29714 or equivalent. Using the tool, depress the servo cover.
4. With a suitable tool, remove the servo cover retaining ring. Remove the tool.
5. Remove the servo cover and the seal ring. The seal ring may be stuck inside the transmission case.
6. Remove the servo piston and the band apply pin assembly.

Installation

1. Position the band apply pin assembly and the servo piston in its mounting within the transmission case.
2. Using a new seal ring install the servo cover.
3. Continue the installation in the reverse order of the removal procedure.
4. Lower the vehicle. Check and correct the fluid level, as required. Start the engine and check for leaks.

SPEEDOMETER DRIVEN GEAR

Removal

1. Raise the vehicle and support it safely.
2. Disconnect the speedometer cable.
3. Remove the retainer bolt, retainer, speedometer driven gear and O-ring seal.

Installation

1. Coat the new O-ring seal with transmission fluid and install it along with the other components.
2. Install the speedometer cable.
3. Lower the vehicle. Replace any transmission that may have been lost.

REAR OIL SEAL

Removal

1. Raise the vehicle and support it safely.
2. Remove the driveshaft. Place a container under the driveshaft to catch any fluid that may leak from the transmission.
3. If equipped, remove the tunnel strap.
4. Pry out the old seal using a suitable tool.

Installation

1. Coat the new seal with clean transmission fluid.
2. Position the seal on the rear extension housing and drive it in place using the proper seal installation tools.
3. Continue the installation in the reverse order of the removal procedure.
4. Lower the vehicle. Fill the transmission with clean oil, as required.

GOVERNOR

Removal

1. Raise the vehicle and support it safely. Drain the transmission fluid as required.
2. If the vehicle is equipped with four wheel drive, disconnect the shift rod at the shifter. Remove the transfer case shifter bolts at the transmission case and move the unit aside.
3. Remove the governor cover from the side of the transmission case. Be sure not to damage the cover.
4. Remove the governor from its mounting inside the transmission case.

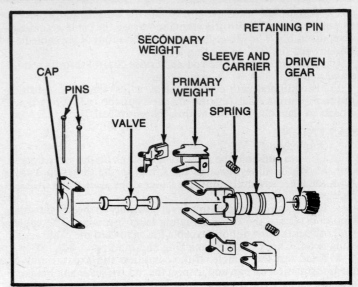

Governor assembly—exploded view
(© General Motors Corporation)

Installation

1. Position the governor-assembly inside the transmission case.
2. Install the governor cover using a new O-ring coated with clean transmission fluid.
3. Lower the vehicle. Check and correct the transmission fluid level as required. Start the engine and check for leaks.

REMOVAL & INSTALLATION

ALL EXCEPT TRUCKS

Removal

1. Disconnect the negative battery cable.
2. Remove the air cleaner assembly. Disconnect the T.V./detent cable at its upper end.
3. Remove the transmission dipstick. Remove the bolt holding the dipstick tube, if accessible.
4. Raise the vehicle and support it safely. Remove the torque arm to transmission retaining bolts, on F Series vehicles.

NOTE: Rear spring force will cause torque arm to move toward floor pan when arm is disconnected from transmission. Carefully place a piece of wood between the floor pan and torque arm when disconnecting the arm to avoid possible damage to floor pan and to avoid possible injury to hand or fingers.

5. Drain the transmission. Remove the driveshaft. Matchmark the driveshaft to aid in installation.
6. Disconnect the speedometer cable at the transmission. Disconnect the shift linkage at the transmission.
7. Disconnect all electrical leads at the transmission. Disconnect any clips that retain these leads.
8. Remove the inspection cover. Mark the flexplate and torque converter, to aid in installation.
9. Remove the torque converter to flexplate retaining bolts. Remove the catalytic converter support bracket, if necessary.
10. Position the transmission jack under the transmission and remove the rear transmission mount.
11. Remove the floor pan reinforcement. Remove the crossmember retaining bolts. Move the crossmember out of the way
12. Remove the transmission to engine bolt on the left side

This is the bolt that retains the ground strap.

13. Disconnect and plug the transmission oil cooler lines. It may be necessary to lower the transmission in order to gain access to the cooler lines.

14. With the transmission still lowered, disconnect the T.V. cable.

15. Support the engine, using the proper tools and remove the remaining engine to transmission bolts.

16. Carefully disengage the transmission assembly from the engine. Lower the transmission from the transmission jack.

Installation

1. To install, reverse the removal procedures.
2. Before installing the flexplate to torque converter bolts, make sure that the weld nuts on the converter are flush with the flexplate and that the torque converter rotates freely by hand in this position.
3. Be sure that the flexplate and torque converter marks made during the removal procedure line up with each other.
4. Adjust the shift linkage and the T.V. cable as required.
5. Lower the vehicle and fill the transmission with the proper grade and type automatic transmission fluid.
6. Start the engine and check for leaks. Once the vehicle has reached operating temperature recheck the fluid level.

TRANSMISSION REMOVAL

Removal
TRUCK MODELS

NOTE: If the vehicle is equipped with four wheel drive the transfer case must first be removed.

1. Disconnect the negative battery cable. Remove the air cleaner assembly.
2. Disconnect the T.V. cable at the upper end. Raise the vehicle and support it safely.
3. Remove the driveshaft. Match mark the assembly to aid in installation.
4. Disconnect the speedometer cable at the transmission. Disconnect the shift linkage at the transmission.
5. Disconnect all electrical leads at the transmission and remove any clips that retain the leads to the transmission.
6. Remove the brake line to crossmember clips and remove the crossmember, four wheel drive vehicles only.
7. Remove the transmission support brace attaching bolts at the torque converter, if equipped.
8. Remove the exhaust crossover pipe and catalytic converter attaching bolts. Remove the components as an assembly.
9. Remove the inspection cover and mark the torque converter in relation to the flywheel. This will assure proper line up on installation.
10. Remove the torque converter to flywheel retaining bolts. Disconnect the catalytic converter support bracket.
11. Position the transmission jack under the transmission and raise the unit slightly.
12. Remove the transmission support retaining bolts.
13. Remove the left body mounting bolts and loosen the radiator support mounting bolt.
14. Raise the vehicle on the left side to gain the necessary clearance to remove the upper attaching bolt. Support the vehicle by placing a block of wood between the frame and the first body mount.
15. Slide the transmission support toward the rear of the vehicle.
16. Lower the transmission jack in order to gain access to the oil cooler lines. Disconnect and plug the oil cooler lines.
17. Support the engine using the proper tool and remove the transmission to engine retaining bolts.
18. Slide the transmission back and lower it from the vehicle. Install the torque converter retaining tool as required.

Installation

1. To install, reverse the removal procedures.
2. Before installing the flexplate to torque converter bolts, make sure that the weld nuts on the converter are flush with the flexplate and that the torque converter rotates freely by hand in this position.
3. Be sure that the flexplate and torque converter marks made during the removal procedure line up with each other.
4. Adjust the shift linkage and the T.V. cable as required.
5. Lower the vehicle and fill the transmission with the proper grade and type automatic transmission fluid.
6. Start the engine and check for leaks. Once the vehicle has reached operating temperature recheck the fluid level.

TRANSFER CASE

Removal

1. Shift the transfer case into the 4HI position.
2. Disconnect the negative battery cable. Raise the vehicle and support it safely.
3. Drain the transfer case.
4. Match mark the transfer case driveshafts to aid in reinstallation. Remove and match mark the rear driveshaft.
5. Disconnect the speedometer cable and the vacuum harness at the transfer case.
6. Remove the catalytic converter hanger bolts at the converter.
7. Raise the transmission and transfer case and remove the transmission mount retaining bolts. Remove the mount and the catalytic converter hanger. Lower the transmission and the transfer case.
8. Support the transfer case and remove the case attaching bolts. Remove the shift lever mounting bolts, in order to remove the upper left transfer case retaining bolt.
9. Separate the transfer case from the adapter plate and remove the assembly from the vehicle.

Installation

1. Installation is the reverse of the removal procedure.
2. Fill the transfer case with the proper grade and type fluid.
3. Lower the vehicle. Start the engine and check for leaks. Roadtest as required.

Before Disassembly

Clean the exterior of the transmission assembly before any attempt is made to disassemble, to prevent dirt or other foreign materials from entering the transmission assembly or its internal parts.

NOTE: If steam cleaning is done to the exterior of the transmission, immediate disassembly should be done to avoid rusting from condensation of the internal parts.

Take note of thrust washer locations. It is most important that thrust washers and bearings be installed in their original positions. Handle all transmission parts carefully to avoid damage.

Ring groove wear on governor supports, input shaft, pump housings and other internal parts should be checked using new rings installed in the grooves.

Converter Inspection

The converter cannot be disassembled for service.

Checking Converter End Play

1. Place the converter on a flat surface with the flywheel side down.

2. Atttach a dial indicator so that the end play can be determined by moving the turbine shaft in relation to the converter hub. End play for the Turbo Hydra-Matic 700-R4 should be no more than 0.0-0.050 of an inch. If the clearance is greater than this, replace the converter.

Checking Converter One-Way Clutch

1. If the one-way clutch fails, then the stator assembly freewheels at all times in both directions. The car will have poor low speed acceleration.

2. If the stator assembly remains locked up at all times, the car speed will be limited or restricted at high speeds. The low speed operation may appear normal, although engine overheating may occur.

3. To check one-way clutch operation, insert a finger into the splined inner race of the roller clutch and try to turn the race in both directions. The inner race should turn freely in the clockwise direction, but it should not turn in the counterclockwise direction.

NOTE: Inspect the converter hub for burrs or jagged metal to avoid personal injury.

4. If the one-way clutch does not operate properly, the converter must be replaced.

Visual Inspection of the Converter

Before installation of the converter, check it carefully for damage, stripped bolt holes or signs of heat damage. Check for loose or missing balance weights, broken converter pilot, or leaks, all of which are cause for replacement. Inspect the converter pump drive hub for nicks or burrs that could damage the pump oil seal during installation.

Transmission Disassembly

TORQUE CONVERTER AND OIL PAN

1. Remove the torque converter from the transmission by pulling it straight out of the transmission housing.

2. Position the transmission assembly in a suitable holding fixture.

3. Remove the transmission fluid pan bolts. Discard the pan gasket, or R.T.V. sealant. Remove and discard the fluid screen.

VALVE BODY

1. Remove the transmission fluid pan retaining bolts. Remove the transmission pan from the transmission assembly.

2. Remove and discard the pan gasket. Remove the fluid filter and O-ring. Discard these components.

3. Disconnect the inner harness connector at the outside connector located in the transmission case, by bending the locking tab outward and pulling the connector upwards.

4. Remove the outside electrical connector and O-ring seal from the transmission case by bending the inner tab inward with a suitable tool and pushing downward.

5. Remove the solenoid and attaching bolts, and O-ring from the case and pump. If the solenoid is not free, gently pry up with a suitable tool.

6. Disconnect all wire leads at the pressure switches and remove the complete wiring harness and solenoid assembly.

7. Remove the 1-2 accumulator housing, attaching bolts, 1-2 accumulator spring, and piston, gasket and plate.

8. Remove the oil passage cover retaining bolts from the transmission case. Remove the cover.

9. Remove the manual detent roller assembly. Remove the harness wire retaining clips and retaining bolts.

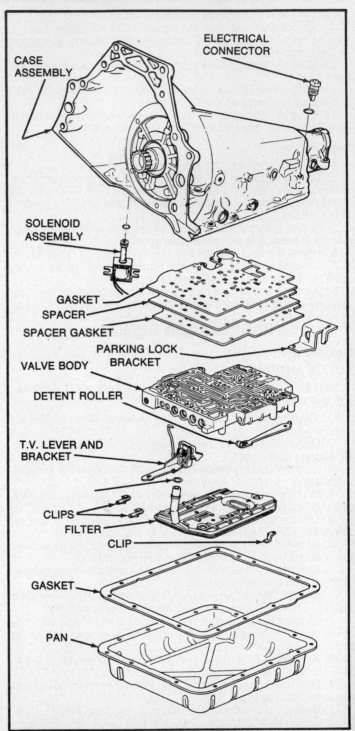

Valve body component location (© General Motors Corporation)

10. Remove the throttle lever bracket assembly and the T.V. link.

11. Remove the remaining valve body retaining bolts.

12. Unhook the manual valve retaining clip at the inside detent lever and remove the valve body, spacer plate and gaskets.

13. Be sure not to loose the three check balls located in the valve body.

14. Remove the 3-4 accumulator spring, piston and pin from the transmission case.

15. Remove the five check balls and the check valve from the transmission case passages.

16. Remove the converter clutch and governor screens from the transmission case.

GOVERNOR

1. Position the transmission assembly in a suitable holding fixture.

2. Remove the governor cover from the side of the transmission case. Be sure not to damage the cover.

3. Remove and discard the governor cover seal ring.

SECOND AND FOURTH SERVO

1. Install the servo removal tool on the servo cover. Depress the cover and remove the snap ring using a suitable tool.

2. Remove the servo cover and the O-ring. Remove the fourth gear apply piston and its O-ring.

3. Remove the second servo piston assembly.

4. Remove the inner servo piston assembly and the oil seal ring. Release the spring.

5. To check the 2-4 servo apply pin, proceed as follows.

6. Install the servo apply pin checking tool into the servo bore and secure it in place using a snap ring.

7. Disassemble the 2-4 servo using the proper tools and insert the servo pin into the tool, locating the end of the pin on the band anchor lug.

8. Apply 100 inch lbs. of torque using a torque wrench.

9. If any part of the white line appears in the window, the pin is the correct length. If the white line does not appear select another pin until the line does appear.

SERVO PIN SELECTION CHART

Pin Identification	Pin Length (inches)
Two rings	2.61-2.62
Three rings	2.67-2.68
Wide band	2.72-2.73

END PLAY CHECK

1. Position the transmission vertically, with the front pump side upward.

2. Remove the front pump to transmission case bolt and washer. Install an eleven inch bolt and locking nut.

3. Install the transmission end play checking tool on the end of the turbine shaft. Mount the dial indicator gauge on the bolt positioning the indicator point cap nut on top of the tool. With the dial indicator set at zero, pull upwards. The end play should be 0.005-0.036 inch. The selective washer controlling transmission end play is located between the input housing and the roller bearing on the pump hub. If more or less end clearance is required to bring the transmission within specifications, select the proper washer.

TRANSMISSION END PLAY— SELECTIVE WASHER CHART

Identification	Thickness (inches)
7	0.074–0.078
8	0.080–0.084
9	0.087–0.091
0	0.094–0.098
1	0.100–0.104
2	0.107–0.111
3	0.113–0.118
4	0.120–0.124

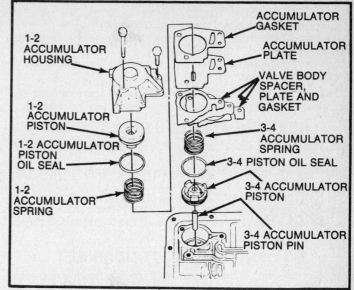

1-2 and 3-4 accumulator assembly—exploded view
(© General Motors Corporation)

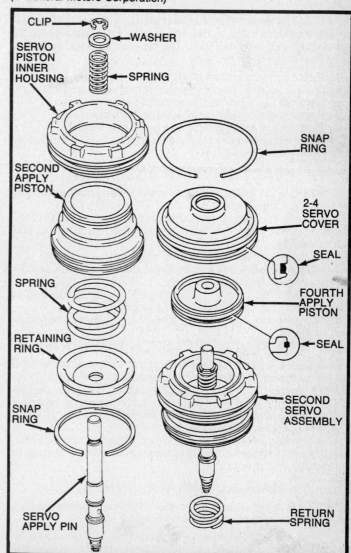

2-4 servo assembly—exploded view (© General Motors Corporation)

FRONT PUMP

1. Remove and discard the front pump seal.
2. Remove the front pump to transmission case retaining bolts and washers.
3. Using the pump removal tool, remove the front pump from the transmission case.

NOTE: The filter and the solenoid must be removed from the transmission assembly before the front pump can be removed.

REVERSE AND INPUT CLUTCHES

1. Remove the front pump assembly from the transmission case.
2. Remove the reverse input drum washer from the pump assembly.
3. Remove the reverse and input clutch assemblies from the transmission by lifting them out with the turbine shaft.
4. Do not remove the teflon seals on the turbine shaft unless required.

2-4 BAND AND INPUT GEAR SET

1. Remove the 2-4 band assembly from the transmission case. Remove the band anchor pin from the transmission case.
2. Remove the input gear assembly from the transmission case.

NOTE: The output shaft and the reaction internal gear assembly are assembled using loctite, which holds the parts together as one unit to aid in installation. During transmission operation these parts may separate.

3. Install the output shaft holding tool to the rear of the transmission case in order to prevent the output shaft from falling.
4. Remove the input carrier to output shaft snap ring.
5. Remove the output shaft tool and the output shaft.
6. Remove the input carrier and the thrust washer.
7. Remove the reaction shaft thrust bearing from the input internal gear assembly.

REACTION GEAR ASSEMBLY

1. Remove the reaction shaft to reaction sun gear washer. Remove the reaction shell.
2. Remove the reaction shell to inner race washer. Remove the low and reverse support to transmission case retaining ring and support spring.
3. Remove the reaction sun gear assembly.
4. Remove the low and reverse clutch plate assemblies and the low and reverse clutch plates.
5. Remove the reaction internal gear. Remove the output shaft if not removed and the bearing assembly.
6. Remove the support bearing assembly from the transmission case hub.

LOW AND REVERSE CLUTCH COMPONENTS

1. Remove the parking lock bracket and the retaining bolts, if not yet removed. Position the parking lock pawl inwards.
2. Using the clutch spring compressor tool, compress the low and reverse clutch spring retainer. Remove the spring retaining ring and the low and reverse spring assembly.
3. Remove the special tools.
4. Remove the low and reverse clutch piston. It may be necessary to apply compressed air to the transmission case passage to remove the component.

MANUAL LINKAGE (INNER)

NOTE: It is not necessary to remove the inner manual linkage unless service to these components is required.

1. Rotate the transmission to the horizontal position and loosen the manual shaft retaining nut and move inboard on the manual shaft.

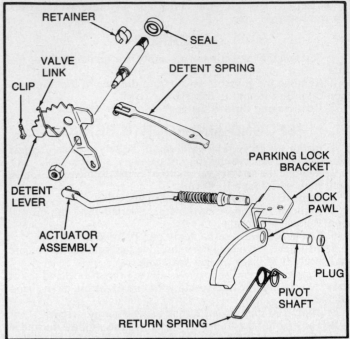

Parking lock linkage—exploded view (© General Motors Corporation)

2. Move the inner detent lever and connected actuator rod assembly and manual shaft retainer inboard.
3. Gently tap the manual shaft outboard until the retaining nut is free. If necessary install a retaining nut on the outside end of the manual shaft. With a suitable tool remove the manual shaft retainer and connect inner detent lever and actuator rod.
4. Remove the manual shaft and nut.
5. If necessary remove the inside detent lever from the actuator rod assembly by rotating the rod and indexing notches in the rod with the hole in the lever.
6. Inspect the manual shaft seal in the case for damage, and proper location and if necessary replace the seal.
7. Be sure that the new seal is bottomed square against the bottom of the transmission case bore and with the opened or sealing surface facing inward.
8. Inspect all components for wear, scoring or damage. Repair or replace defective components as required.

PARKING PAWL AND RETURN SPRING

1. Using an easy out, remove the parking lock shaft retaining plug from the outside of the transmission case.
2. Remove the parking lock shaft, pawl and return spring.
3. Inspect all components for wear, damage or scoring. Repair or replace defective components as required.

TRANSMISSION CASE AND RELATED COMPONENTS

1. Inspect the case for damage, cracks, porosity or interconnected oil passages.
2. Inspect the valve body case pad for flatness or land damage. The oil passage lands are considered acceptable if a void exists and is not in excess of fifty percent of the land. The condition of the valve body pad can also be checked by inspecting the mating face of the spacer plate to the case gasket for a proper case land impression.
3. Air check the case passages for restrictions or blockage.
4. Inspect the case internal clutch plate lugs for damage, or wear.
5. Inspect the speedometer, servo and accumulator bores for damage and clearance relative to the mating parts.

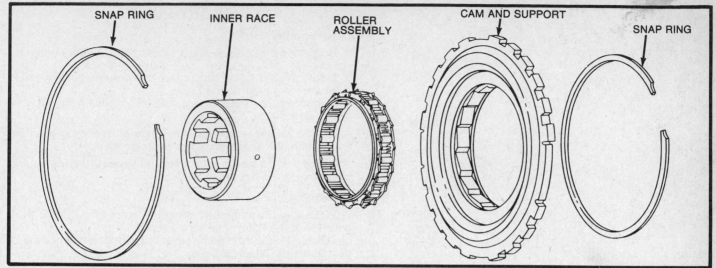

Low reverse clutch support assembly—exploded view (© General Motors Corporation)

6. Inspect all bolt holes for damaged threads. Helo-coils® can be used for repair.

7. Inspect the cooler line connectors for damage and proper torque.

8. Inspect all snap ring grooves for damage.

9. Inspect the governor locating pin for proper length. A incorrect length results in a damaged governor gear.

10. Inspect the third accumulator check valve, if replacement is needed, use a number four easy out and remove the check valve assembly from the transmission case.

11. Install a new check valve assembly into transmission case with the small end first. Position the oil feed slot in the sleeve so that it aligns with the servo passage.

12. Seat the check valve assembly using a ⅜ in. metal rod. Drive the check valve assembly into the case approximately 42.0mm.

Unit Disassembly and Assembly

GOVERNOR

Disassembly

1. Cut off the end of the governor weight pin. Remove the pins, outer weight and the secondary weight.

2. Remove the governor valve from the governor sleeve.

3. To replace the governor drive gear, remove the governor gear retaining pin.

4. Support the governor assembly on plates installed in the exhaust slots of the governor sleeve. Position the assembly in a press. Press the gear out of the sleeve.

5. Clean and inspect all parts of the governor assembly. Repair or replace defective components as required.

Assembly

1. Support the governor assembly on the plates which are installed in the exhaust slots of the sleeve.

2. Position a new gear on the sleeve and press it in place until it is seated against the shoulder.

3. A new pin hole must be drilled through the sleeve and gear. Locate the new hole position 90 degrees from the existing hole. While supporting the governor in press, center punch and drill a new hole through the sleeve and gear using a standard ⅛ in. drill.

4. Install the retaining pin. Stake the assembly in two locations.

5. Set the assembly aside until the transmission is ready to be reassembled.

LOW REVERSE SUPPORT ASSEMBLY

Disassembly

1. Remove the low reverse inner race.

2. Remove the snap ring retaining the roller assembly to the low reverse support.

3. Remove the roller assembly from its mounting.

4. Clean and inspect all components for wear, damage or scoring. Repair or replace defective components as required.

Assembly

1. Position the low reverse support on the bench so that the chamfered side is up.

2. Install the low reverse roller assembly into the support with the oil lube hole down or rearward.

NOTE: Care should be taken to insure that the rollers and spring are not damaged and that the rollers do not become dislodged.

3. Install the low reverse inner race into the roller assembly by rotating clockwise.

4. When installed, the inner race should rotate in the clockwise direction and lock up in the counterclockwise direction.

5. Set the assembly aside until the transmission is ready to be reassembled.

THROTTLE LEVER AND BRACKET ASSEMBLY

Disassembly

1. Unhook and remove the line boost spring. Remove the retaining nut from the pin.

2. Remove the pin, torsion lever spring, line boost lever, throttle lever and the bracket.

3. Clean and inspect all parts for wear, damage or scoring. Repair or replace defective components as required.

Assembly

1. Assembly of the throttle lever and bracket is the reverse of the disassembly procedure.

2. Set the assembly aside until you are ready to reassemble the transmission.

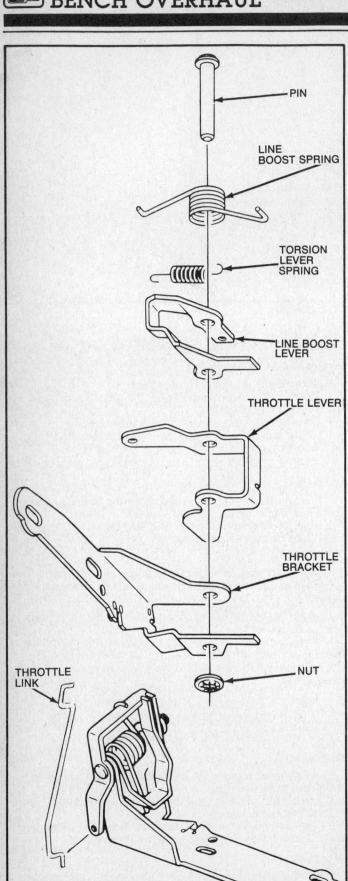

PIN

LINE BOOST SPRING

TORSION LEVER SPRING

LINE BOOST LEVER

THROTTLE LEVER

THROTTLE BRACKET

THROTTLE LINK

NUT

Throttle lever and bracket assembly (© General Motors Corporation)

FRONT PUMP

Disassembly

1. Remove the pump to drum washer from the front pump assembly.

2. Remove the front pump cover to transmission case gasket from the front pump cover.

3. Remove the front pump to case oil seal ring from the front pump assembly.

NOTE: Do not remove the two teflon oil seal rings from the front pump hub unless they require replacement.

4. Remove the front pump cover and separate the front pump cover from the front pump body.

Assembly

1. Position the pump body assembly over a hole in the work bench with the stator shaft facing down.

2. Assemble the front pump cover to the front pump body. Finger tighten the retaining bolts.

3. Position the pump cover and the pump body using tool J-21368 or equivalent. Place a holding bolt or a suitable tool through a pump to transmission case bolt hole and the bench hole.

4. Remove the tool and torque the retaining cover bolts to 18 ft. lbs.

5. Install a new pump to case gasket on the pump, use transmission fluid to retain the gasket in place.

6. If removed install the teflon oil seal rings on the stator hub.

7. Install the pump to case oil seal on the pump cover. Be sure not to twist the seal and make certain that the seal is seated properly.

8. Install the front pump cover to transmission case gasket aligning holes. Retain them using clean transmission fluid.

9. Install the front pump to drum thrust washer.

FRONT PUMP BODY

Disassembly

1. Remove the pump slide spring by compressing the spring and pulling it straight out.

NOTE: The spring is retained under pressure. Before removing it place a covering over the assembly to prevent injury.

2. From the pump pocket remove the pump guide rings, the pump vanes, the pump rotor and the rotor guide.

3. Remove the slide from the pump pocket. Remove the slide seal and support seal from the pump body pocket or slide.

4. Remove the pivot slide pin and spring from the pocket.

5. Remove the slide seal ring. Remove the slide backup seal from the slide pump pocket.

6. Clean and inspect all parts for wear, damage or scoring. Repair or replace defective components as required.

Assembly

1. Install the pump slide O-ring and flat steel ring into the groove on the back side of the slide.

2. Install the small pivot pin and spring into the small hole located in the pump pocket.

3. Install the pump slide into the pump, position the assembly so that the notch in the slide is indexed with the pivot pin hole and the flat oil seal ring facing downward into the pocket.

4. Install the pump slide seal and support into the slide adjacent to the rotor.

NOTE: The pump slide seal (composition) must be positioned against the other diameter of the pump pocket.

5. Install a vane ring into the pump pocket centering on the stator hole.

6. Install the composition rotor guide into the deep pocket of

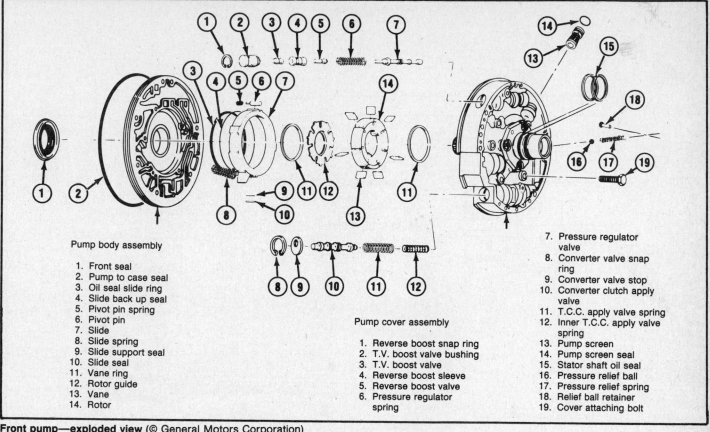

Front pump—exploded view (© General Motors Corporation)

Pump body assembly

1. Front seal
2. Pump to case seal
3. Oil seal slide ring
4. Slide back up seal
5. Pivot pin spring
6. Pivot pin
7. Slide
8. Slide spring
9. Slide support seal
10. Slide seal
11. Vane ring
12. Rotor guide
13. Vane
14. Rotor

Pump cover assembly

1. Reverse boost snap ring
2. T.V. boost valve bushing
3. T.V. boost valve
4. Reverse boost sleeve
5. Reverse boost valve
6. Pressure regulator spring
7. Pressure regulator valve
8. Converter valve snap ring
9. Converter valve stop
10. Converter clutch apply valve
11. T.C.C. apply valve spring
12. Inner T.C.C. apply valve spring
13. Pump screen
14. Pump screen seal
15. Stator shaft oil seal
16. Pressure relief ball
17. Pressure relief spring
18. Relief ball retainer
19. Cover attaching bolt

the rotor indexing the notches, and retain with transmission fluid.

7. Install the rotor and guide into the pump pocket with the guide positioned downward.

8. Install the vanes into the rotor positioning so they are flush with the rotor and with the full wear pattern against the slide.

9. Install the vane guide ring into the rotor.

10. Compress the pump slide spring and install into pump pocket.

FRONT PUMP COVER

Disassembly

1. Using a suitable tool, push on the retainer to compress the converter clutch apply valve spring and remove the snap ring. Release the valve spring tension. Remove the retainer and the converter clutch apply valve and spring.

2. Remove the pressure relief spring retaining rivet. The rivet is under strong spring pressure. Remove the pressure relief spring and ball. If required, apply air pressure to remove the ball.

3. Remove the oil screen and O-ring from the pump cover.

4. Position the pump assembly with the stator shaft facing downward. Secure the assembly to the work bench using a pump holding bolt.

5. Clean and inspect all components for wear, scoring and damage. Repair or replace defective components as required.

Assembly

1. Position the O-ring on the oil pump screen and install it in the bore of the front pump with the seal end last.

2. Install the pressure relief ball and spring. Be sure to install the ball first. Install the retaining rivet.

3. Install the converter clutch apply valve spring on the long

end of the converter clutch apply valve. Retain the components in place using transmission fluid.

4. Install the converter clutch apply valve and spring into the bore of the front pump. Install the retainer and the snap ring.

5. Position the pump cover so that the pressure regulator bore is located in the vertical position.

6. Install the pressure regulator valve into the bore of the pump cover with the large land and the orifice hole first, positioning with a magnet into the bottom of the bore.

7. Install the pressure regulator valve spring into the bore.

8. Install the T.V. boost valve into the T.V. bushing. Long land of valve into the large hole of the bushing—retain the valve with transmission fluid.

9. Install the reverse boost valve into the reverse sleeve, small end of valve first. Retain with transmission fluid.

10. Using a small magnet install the T.V. boost valve and bushing into the cover with the small hole in the bushing rearward.

11. With the T.V. boost valve and bushing compressed and with the snap ring groove visible, install the snap ring.

VALVE BODY

Disassembly

As each part of the valve train is removed, place the individual part in the order that it was removed and in the same relative location as its true position in the valve body. All parts must be reassembled in the same location as they were removed.

Remove all outside roll pins by pushing them through from the rough casting side of the valve body assembly. Removal of the inner roll pins can be accomplished by grinding a taper to one end of a number 49 (1/16 in.) drill bit. Lightly tap the tapered end of the drill bit into the roll pin and then pull the drill bit and the pin out of its bore.

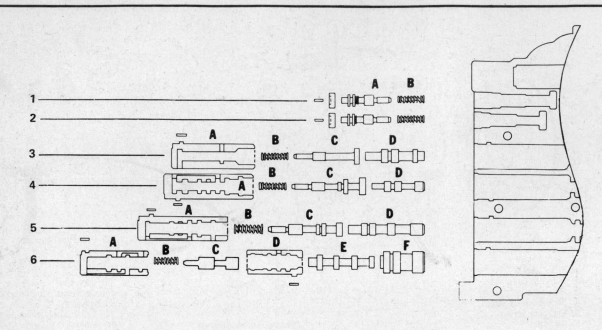

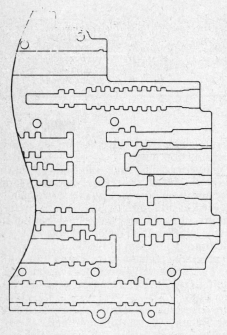

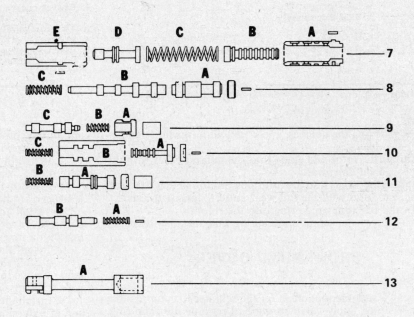

1. (A) T.V. modulator.
   (B) T.V. modulator
   downshift valve spring.
2. (A) T.V. modulator upshift
   valve.
   (B) T.V. modulator upshift
   valve spring.
3. (A) Converter clutch valve
   sleeve.
   (B) Converter clutch
   throttle valve spring.
   (C) Converter clutch
   throttle valve.

(D) Converter clutch shift
   valve.
4. (A) 3-4 throttle valve
   sleeve.
   (B) 3-4 throttle valve
   spring.
   (C) 3-4 throttle valve.
   (E) 3-4 shift valve.
5. (A) 2-3 throttle valve
   sleeve.
   (B) 2-3 throttle valve
   spring.
   (C) 2-3 throttle valve.

(D) 2-3 shift valve.
6. (A) 1-2 throttle valve
   sleeve.
   (B) 1-2 throttle valve
   spring.
   (C) 1-2 throttle valve.
   (D) Lo range sleeve.
   (E) 1-2 lo range valve.
   (F) 1-2 shift valve.
7. (A) Throttle valve plunger
   sleeve.
   (B) Throttle valve plunger.
   (C) Throttle valve spring.

(D) Throttle valve.
   (E) Throttle valve sleeve.
8. (A) 3-4 relay valve.
   (B) 4-3 sequence valve.
   (C) 4-3 sequence valve
   spring.
9. (A) T.V. limit plug.
   (B) T.V. limit valve spring.
   (C) T.V. limit valve.
10. (A) Accumulator valve.
    (B) Accumulator sleeve.
    (C) Accumulator spring.

11. (A) Line bias valve.
    (B) Line bias spring.
12. (A) 3-2 control valve
    spring.
    (B) 3-2 control valve.
13. (A) Manual valve.

Valve body assembly—bore location (© General Motors Corporation)

The spring retaining sleeves can be removed by compressing with needle-nose pliers and moving upward through the exposed hole.

Some of the roll pins have applied pressure against them. When removing, care should be taken to prevent the possible loss of parts.

Do not remove the pressure switches unless they require replacement.

Remove the three check balls from the passage side of the body—if present.

Position the valve body machined side up: positioning the manual valve lower right and remove the link and retaining clip, if attached.

1. From the No. 1 bore, remove the retaining pin, valve bore plug, T.V. modulator downshift valve and T.V. modulator downshift valve spring.

2. From bore No. 2, remove the retaining pin, valve bore sleeve, T.V. modulator upshift valve and T.V. modulator upshift valve spring.

3. From bore No. 3, remove the retaining pin. Remove the converter clutch throttle sleeve, converter clutch throttle valve spring and valve, and the converter clutch shift valve.

4. From bore No. 4, remove the retaining pin, 3-4 throttle valve sleeve, 3-4 throttle valve spring, 3-4 throttle valve and 3-4 shift valve.

5. From bore No. 5, remove the retaining pin. Remove the 2-3 throttle valve sleeve and 2-3 throttle valve spring, 2-3 throttle valve and 2-3 shift valve.

6. From bore No. 6, remove the outer roll pin. Remove the 1-2 throttle valve sleeve, 1-2 throttle valve spring, 1-2 throttle valve and lo range valve. Remove the inner retaining pin and remove the lo range valve sleeve and 1-2 shift valve.

7. From bore No. 7, remove the outer roll pin from the rough casting side, the throttle valve plunger sleeve, throttle valve plunger and throttle valve spring. Remove the inner roll pin and valve.

8. From bore No. 8, remove the retaining roll pin and plug. Remove the 3-4 relay valve, 4-3 sequence valve and spring.

9. From bore No. 9, using needle nose pliers, compress and remove the spring retainer. Remove the T.V. limit plug and spring valve.

10. From bore No. 10, remove the retaining roll pin and plug. Remove the 1-2 accumulator valve, spring and sleeve.

11. From bore No. 11, using needle nose pliers, compress the line bias valve spring retainer and remove the plug, line bias and spring.

12. From bore No. 12, remove the roll pin, 3-2 control valve spring and 3-2 control valve.

13. Remove the manual valve from bore No. 13.

14. Clean and inspect all components for wear, scoring and damage. Repair or replace defective components as required.

Assembly

Install all parts in the reverse order as they were removed. Assemble all bore plugs against the retaining pins with the recessed holes outboard. All the roll pins must be installed so they do not extend above the flat machined face of the valve body pad. Install all flared coiled pins with the flared end out.

Make certain all retaining or roll pins are installed into the proper locating slots in the sleeves, not in the oil passage holes. The bushing for the 1-2 accumulator valve train must be assembled with the small hole for the roll pin facing the rough casting side of the valve body.

Transmission Assembly

NOTE: Some assembly and disassembly of components will be done as the transmission is being assembled.

1. Position the transmission on the transmission stand in the vertical position. The parking pawl must be removed from the case before installing the low reverse clutch piston.

2. Lubricate and install the inner, center, and outer seals on the low reverse clutch piston if removed. (Large aluminum).

3. Install the low reverse clutch piston in the transmission case indexing the piston with the notch at the bottom of the case with the hub facing downward, making certain the piston is fully seated in the downward position and the parking pawl will index into the opening in the piston wall.

4. Install the low reverse clutch spring retainer assembly into the case with the flat side of the retainer upwards.

5. Install tool J-23327 or equivalent and compress the springs, indexing the tool retaining plate so that the tool is free to slide over the case hub.

6. Install the low reverse clutch snap ring. Remove all of the tools.

7. Install the reaction internal gear support bearing on the case hub so that the longer inside "L" race is positioned downward.

8. Install the reaction internal gear and output shaft on the bearing assembly in the case. When the gear is properly seated it will be centered with the long open slot in the case and the parking lock pawl can be engaged with the external teeth of the internal gear.

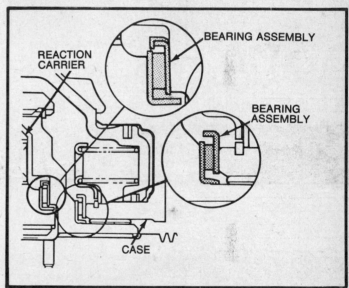

Reaction internal gear—"L" race positioning
(© General Motors Corporation)

NOTE: If the reaction internal gear and output shaft were removed as one unit, install them into the case at this time, otherwise assemble only the reaction internal gear.

9. Install the reaction carrier to support thrust bearing on the internal gear support so that the longer outside "L" race is positioned downwards.

10. Install the reaction carrier (with large outside hub) locating the reverse hub upwards.

11. Install the low and reverse clutch plates, starting with steel and alternating with composition indexing with the splines of the reaction carrier and case, aligning the steel plates.

NOTE: Some low reverse clutch assemblies are equipped with four composition and four steel plates, while others are equipped with five steel and five composition plates. The thickness for the composition faced plates is 0.088 in. The thickness for the steel plates is 0.069 in.

12. Remove the low reverse inner race and install the low reverse support and roller assembly with the chamfered side up in the case, indexing with the case splines.

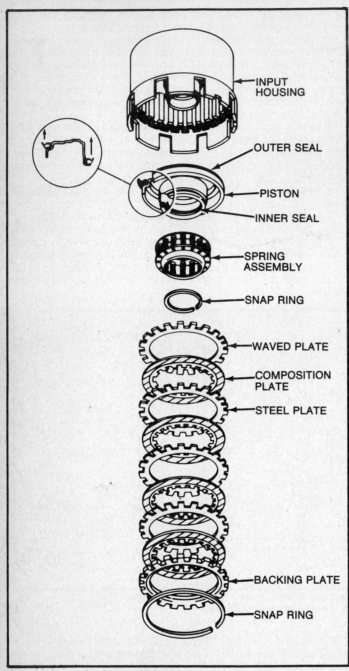

Reverse input clutch—exploded view
(© General Motors Corporation)

Labels for exploded view:
- INPUT HOUSING
- OUTER SEAL
- PISTON
- INNER SEAL
- SPRING ASSEMBLY
- SNAP RING
- WAVED PLATE
- COMPOSITION PLATE
- STEEL PLATE
- BACKING PLATE
- SNAP RING

13. Install the low reverse inner race into the roller assembly and rotate until the internal splines are engaged, then push downward for full engagement. The bottom tanges will be flush with the reaction hub when seated.

14. Install the low reverse snap ring and support spring into the transmission case.

REACTION AND INPUT GEAR SETS

1. Install the snap ring on the reaction sun gear if removed, and install into the reaction carrier indexing the pinions.

2. Install the nylon low reverse thrust washer with 4 locating ears on the low reverse inner race.

3. Install the reaction sun gear shell (large housing with end slots and holes) engaging the splines of the shell onto the sun gear.

4. Install the reaction shaft to shell thrust washer indexing.

the tangs in the shell. (Bronze thrust washer with wide thrust face).

5. Install the input internal gear and shaft positioning the shaft end first.

NOTE: If the output shaft and the reaction gear were removed as separate parts during disassembly position the output shaft into the transmission with all components. Install the output shaft support tool J-29837 or equivalent and adjust it so that the output shaft is positioned up as far as possible.

6. Install the input carrier to reaction shaft thrust bearing with the "L" race on the outside.

7. Install the input carrier assembly, with the hub end down.

8. Install a new snap ring on the output shaft.

9. Install the input sun gear, indexing the gear end with the input carrier pinions.

10. Install the input carrier thrust washer on the input carrier.

REVERSE INPUT CLUTCH

1. Separate the reverse input clutch from the input clutch assembly. Remove the stator bearing and the selective washer from the input housing.

2. Remove the snap ring from the reverse input housing. Remove the reverse input clutch backing plate.

3. Remove the reverse input steel and composition clutch plates.

4. Using tool J-23327 or equivalent compress the reverse input spring assembly and remove the snap ring.

5. Remove all tools.

6. Remove the reverse input clutch release spring assembly.

7. Remove the reverse input clutch piston. Remove both the inner and outer seals.

8. Clean and inspect all components for wear, damage and scoring. Repair or replace defective components as required.

9. Lubricate and install the inner and outer seals on the reverse input clutch piston with the seal lips facing away from the hub.

10. Install the reverse clutch piston into the reverse input housing with the hub facing up. Use a feeler gauge to position the seal.

11. Install the reverse input clutch spring assembly with the large opening first.

12. Install tools J-23327 and J-25018-A or equivalent on the spring retainer. Compress the spring retainer and install the retaining snap ring. Remove all tools. Install the waved steel reverse plate. The waved plate is thinner and will show some high burnished spots. No indexing or alignment is required. Install a composition plate, then install the balance of the plates, alternating composition faced and flat steel. The reverse clutch plates are the largest plates with equally spaced tangs.

13. Install the reverse input backing plate with the chamfered side facing upward.

14. Install the backing plate snap ring.

INPUT CLUTCH ASSEMBLY

1. Position the input clutch assembly on the bench with the turbine shaft located in a bench hole and resting on the turbine shaft housing.

2. Remove the snap ring retaining the 3-4 clutch backing plate.

3. Remove the 3-4 clutch backing plate.

4. Remove the 3-4 clutch plates (composition and steel).

5. Remove the 3-4 clutch apply plate.

6. Remove the 3-4 clutch retaining apply ring.

7. Remove the forward clutch backing plate snap ring.

8. Remove the forward clutch backing plate.

9. Remove the forward clutch cam assembly and outer race by pulling up.

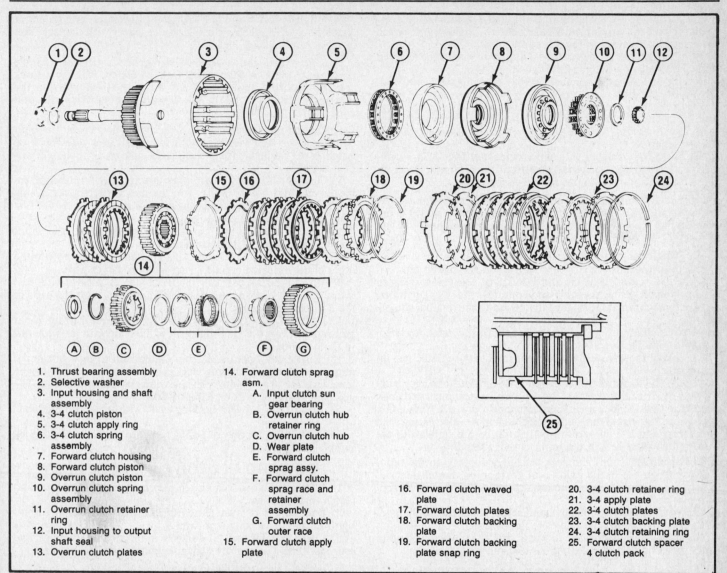

1. Thrust bearing assembly
2. Selective washer
3. Input housing and shaft assembly
4. 3-4 clutch piston
5. 3-4 clutch apply ring
6. 3-4 clutch spring assembly
7. Forward clutch housing
8. Forward clutch piston
9. Overrun clutch piston
10. Overrun clutch spring assembly
11. Overrun clutch retainer ring
12. Input housing to output shaft seal
13. Overrun clutch plates
14. Forward clutch sprag asm.
  A. Input clutch sun gear bearing
  B. Overrun clutch hub retainer ring
  C. Overrun clutch hub
  D. Wear plate
  E. Forward clutch sprag assy.
  F. Forward clutch sprag race and retainer assembly
  G. Forward clutch outer race
15. Forward clutch apply plate
16. Forward clutch waved plate
17. Forward clutch plates
18. Forward clutch backing plate
19. Forward clutch backing plate snap ring
20. 3-4 clutch retainer ring
21. 3-4 apply plate
22. 3-4 clutch plates
23. 3-4 clutch backing plate
24. 3-4 clutch retaining ring
25. Forward clutch spacer 4 clutch pack

Input clutch—exploded view (© General Motors Corporation)

10. Remove the input sun gear bearing (it can be located on the back side of the input inner race).

11. Remove the input housing to output shaft nylon seal.

12. Remove the forward clutch plates (steel and composition).

13. Remove the forward clutch apply plate and spacer if used.

14. Remove the overrun clutch plates (2 steel and 2 composition).

15. Install tools J-23456 and J-25018 or equivalent and compress the overrun clutch spring retainer.

16. Remove the overrun clutch retaining snap ring.

17. Remove all tools.

18. Remove the overrun clutch spring assembly.

19. Remove the overrun clutch piston assembly.

20. Remove the inner and outer seals from the overrun clutch piston.

21. Remove the forward clutch piston assembly.

22. Remove the inner and outer seals from the forward clutch piston assembly.

NOTE: Apply air pressure to the 3-4 feed hole in the turbine shaft—3rd hole from the shaft end. If unable to remove parts strike housing on a soft surface squarely on the open end.

23. Remove the forward clutch housing assembly.

24. Remove the 3-4 clutch spring assembly.

25. Remove the 3-4 apply ring and piston.

26. Remove the O-ring from the input housing assembly.

27. Inspect the four teflon oil seal rings on the turbine shaft for damage or distortion. Replace only if necessary.

28. Clean and inspect all components for wear, damage and scoring.

29. Repair or replace defective components as required. Do not replace the teflon seals unless required.

30. If removed, install the four teflon oil seal rings on the turbine shaft. Assemble with a long edge to a long edge and the large O-ring on the inside of the housing.

31. If removed, install the small O-ring on the end of the turbine shaft.

32. Position the input clutch housing over the bench hole with the turbine shaft in a hole pointing downwards.

33. Install the inner and outer seals on the 3-4 piston (smallest aluminum piston) with the lips facing away from the hub.

34. Install the 3-4 piston in the input housing, rotate and gently push downward making certain the piston is properly seated.

35. Install the inner and outer seals on the forward clutch piston (largest aluminum) with the lips facing away from the tangs.

36. Lubricate and install the forward clutch piston (largest remaining aluminum) into the forward clutch housing (large steel).

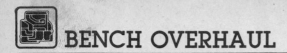

37. Install the 3-4 spring retainer into the 3-4 clutch apply ring.

38. Install the assembled forward clutch housing and piston on the spring retainer in the 3-4 apply ring.

39. The notches of the forward clutch piston must be indexed with the long apply tangs of the 3-4 apply ring.

40. Install seal protector tool J-29883 or equivalent on the input housing shaft.

41. Hold the 3-4 apply ring and assembled parts by the tangs and install into the input clutch housing and firmly seat the forward clutch piston. Remove tools. Use care to insure the pistons do not separate.

42. Install overrun clutch seal protector tool J-29882 or equivalent on the input housing shaft and install the overrun clutch piston with the hub facing upward and remove tool.

NOTE: When properly positioned the overrun piston will be approximately 3/16 inch below the snap ring groove on the input housing hub if not seated install the clutch spring compressor tool and gently tap until all parts are fully seated.

43. Install the overrun clutch spring retainer on the overrun clutch piston locating the release springs on the piston tabs.

44. Position tools J-23456 and J-25018 or equivalent overrun on the overrun spring assembly and compress the spring retainer. Do not over compress springs as distortion to the retainer can occur.

45. With the springs compressed, install the retaining snap ring and remove all tools.

46. Install the splined nylon output shaft seal, with the seal lip facing up.

47. On the forward clutch piston in the input housing, install the four overrun clutch plates. Starting with a steel plate and positioning so that the long recessed slot is indexed with a wide notch in the housing, install the remaining clutch plates alternating steel and composition. The overrun plates will be the smallest of the three clutch plate sets in the input clutch assembly.

48. Install the input sun gear bearing assembly on the input clutch hub on top of the nylon seal positioning the outside "L" race in the downward position. Make certain the bearing is properly centered.

49. With a suitable tool, align and center the inside drive tangs of the two overrun clutch plates (composition).

50. Install the assembled forward clutch cam assembly and outer race clutch hub indexing the overrun clutch plates.

51. Install the forward clutch spacer (thick steel) into the input clutch housing, indexing the lug on the spacer with the large slot in the input housing.

NOTE: A five clutch plate forward clutch, will use a single thick apply plate. A four clutch forward clutch, will use a thick spacer and a thin apply plate, and must be assembled with the thin apply plate first and the spacer with the holes facing the thin apply plate.

52. Install the waved steel forward clutch plate into the input housing. Index the wide slot with two small ears with the wide notch in the housing. The waved steel plate will show high burnish marks.

53. Install a forward clutch plate assembly (composition) on the forward clutch hub. In the same manner, install the remaining forward clutch plates alternating composition and steel. The last plate installed will be composition.

54. Install the forward clutch backing plate into the input housing, with the chamfered side up.

55. Install the forward clutch backing plate snap ring into the input clutch housing (smaller ring with the larger gap).

56. Install the 3-4 gear ring retaining plate (flat plate with legs) into the clutch housing indexing each apply lug with the ends of the 3-4 gear apply ring.

57. Install the 3-4 gear apply plate (thick steel) into the input housing indexing the long wide gear of the plate with the wide slot in the housing.

58. Install a 3-4 plate assembly (composition) then install the remaining plates alternating steel and composition indexing the long wide ear of the plate with the wide slot in the housing. The last plate installed will be composition.

59. Install the 3-4 gear backing plate with the chamfered side up.

60. Install the 3-4 gear retaining ring into the input housing assembly.

FORWARD CLUTCH CAM ASSEMBLY

1. Remove the overrun clutch hub snap ring, clutch hub and clutch thrust washer.

2. Remove the forward clutch sprag cam and the sprag assembly from the forward clutch cam.

3. Clean and inspect all components for wear, damage and scoring. Repair or replace defective components as required.

THIRD AND FOURTH CLUTCH INFORMATION CHART

Model	Flat Steel		Composition Faced		Apply Plate		Backing Plate		Apply Ring	
	No.	Thickness	No.	Thickness	No.	Thickness	No.	Thickness	No.	Length
TC, MB, MC, MJ, VN, T2, VA, ML, MP, MS, T7, YF, PQ	4	0.077 in. (1.97mm)	5	0.079 in. (2.03mm)	1	0.128 in. (3.30mm)	1	selective	1	3.71 in. (94.13mm)
All Others	5	0.077 in. (1.97mm)	6	0.079 in. (2.03mm)	1	0.128 in. (3.30mm)	1	selective	1	3.71 in. (94.13mm)

FORWARD CLUTCH INFORMATION CHART

Model	Flat Steel		Composition Faced		Apply Plate		Spacer		Waved Steel	
	No.	Thickness	No.	Thickness	No.	Thickness	No.	Thickness	No.	Thickness
TC, MB, MC, MJ, VN, T2, VA, ML, MP, MS, T7, YH, YF, PQ	3	0.077 in. (1.97mm)	4	0.079 in. (2.03mm)	1	0.251 in. (6.44mm)	1	0.330 in. (0.835mm)	1	0.079 in. (2.03mm)
All Others	4	0.077 in. (1.97mm)	5	0.079 in. (2.03mm)	1	0.251 in. (6.44mm)	none	—	1	0.079 in. (2.03mm)

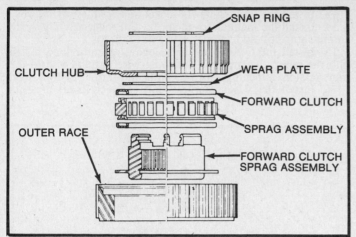

Forward clutch cam—exploded view
(© General Motors Corporation)

Labels: SNAP RING, WEAR PLATE, FORWARD CLUTCH, SPRAG ASSEMBLY, FORWARD CLUTCH SPRAG ASSEMBLY, CLUTCH HUB, OUTER RACE

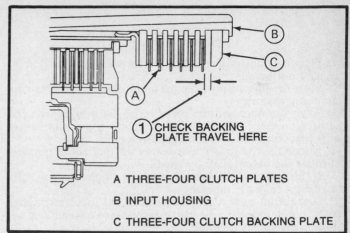

Checking Backing Plate Travel (© General Motors Corporation)

Labels: B, C, A, ① CHECK BACKING PLATE TRAVEL HERE

A THREE-FOUR CLUTCH PLATES

B INPUT HOUSING

C THREE-FOUR CLUTCH BACKING PLATE

4. Position the forward clutch cam with the retainer side down.

5. Install the sprag assembly with the two retainer rings over the cam hub. The lipped edge of the sprag must face the cam retainer.

6. Place the overrun hub thrust washer on the overrun hub and place this unit over the forward clutch cam. Install the overrun clutch hub snap ring in the I.D. of the cam.

7. Install the assembled hub, cam and sprag inner race assembly into the forward clutch outer race by rotating clockwise. When holding the outer race in your left hand, the overrun clutch hub must rotate freely, in a clockwise direction and must hold in a counterclockwise direction.

THREE-FOUR CLUTCH PISTON TRAVEL CHECK

1. Using a feeler gauge measure the end clearance between the backing plate and the first composition plate.

2. If the clearance is not within specification, select the proper backing plate from the three-four backing plate court.

INTERNAL COMPONENTS

1. Install the reverse and input clutch assemblies as a complete unit into the transmission case indexing the 3-4 clutch plates of the input assembly with the input internal gear. The complete assembly will be properly seated when the reverse housing is located just below the pump face of the case. Be sure that all clutch plates are fully seated.

2. Install the 2-4 band into the case indexing the band anchor pin end with the case pin hole. Install the band anchor pin in the case, indexing with the 2-4 band end.

SERVO ASSEMBLY

1. Remove the fourth apply piston from the second apply piston assembly.

2. Remove the servo apply pin spring from the servo apply pin.

3. Disassemble the second servo apply piston assembly using J-22269-01 and separate the second apply piston, spring and retainer.

4. Remove the retaining 'E' ring washer and spring from the servo apply pin, and remove the pin.

5. Remove all oil seal rings.

6. Clean and inspect all components for wear, scoring and damage. Repair or replace defective components as required.

7. Assemble the components in the reverse order of disassembly. Assemble all flat edged seals with the flat edge to the flat edge and coat them with clean transmission fluid.

8. Install the complete 2-4 servo assembly into the case indexing the servo apply pin on the 2-4 band end and check for proper engagements.

9. Recheck for the correct apply pin length if any of the servo parts, the 2-4 band or the input housing have been replaced.

10. Install the servo cover and O-Ring into the case.

11. Install the servo compressing tool and compress the servo cover.

THREE—FOUR BACKING PLATE SELECTION CHART

Model	Backing Plate Travel	Backing Plate ①	
		DIM	I.D.
TC, MB, MC, MJ, VN, T2, VA, ML, MP, MS, T7, YF, PQ	0.055-0.109 in. (1.39-2.78mm)	0.278 in. (7.125mm)	1
		0.239 in. (6.125mm)	2
All Others	0.049-0.113 in. (1.25-2.87mm)	0.200 in. (5.125mm)	3
		0.161 in. (4.125mm)	4

① Use backing plate which gives correct travel

12. Install the servo retaining ring, indexing the ring ends with the slot in the case.

FRONT PUMP

1. Place the transmission in the vertical position in order to install the front pump.

2. Place the aligning pins into the transmission case. Install the front pump assembly.

3. Align the filter and the pressure regulator holes with the transmission case holes. Retain the pump in place using the pump attaching bolts. Torque the bolts to 18 ft. lbs.

4. Rotate the transmission assembly to a horizontal position and rotate the output shaft by hand.

5. If the shaft will not rotate, loosen the pump retaining bolts and attempt to rotate the shaft.

6. If the shaft now turns, the reverse and input assemblies have not been indexed properly or some other transmission assembly problem has occurred.

7. Rotate the transmission vertically and correct the problem before proceeding.

VALVE BODY AND RELATED COMPONENTS

1. Install the 1-2 accumulator pin into the transmission case. Install the accumulator piston and seal over the pin with the lug end up. Install the spring on the piston.

2. Install the governor and the converter clutch oil screens into the transmission case.

3. Install the five check balls into the transmission case. Install the valve body alignment pins.

4. Install the spacer plate to case gasket with the small "C" on the transmission case.

5. Install the valve body spacer on the guide pins. Align the holes as required.

6. Install the valve body to spacer gasket with the "V" on the spacer plate.

7. Install the three exhaust balls and check valve into the valve body. Retain the components using transmission fluid.

8. Install the valve body and connect the link to the inside detent lever.

9. Remove the aligning pins. Install the valve body retaining bolts. Torque the bolts to 8 ft. lbs.

10. Attach the retaining clip to the link and the inside detent lever.

11. Install the throttle lever and bracket, and T.V. link locating the slot in the bracket with the roll pin on the valve body top face, aligning the link through the T.V. linkage case bore. Attach with two valve body to case bolts and torque to 8 ft. lbs.

12. Install the valve body attaching bolt and harness clip and torque to 8 ft. lbs.

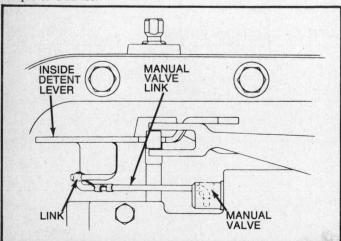

Manual valve link and clips (© General Motors Corporation)

13. Install the parking pawl bracket and torque to 18 ft. lbs.

14. Install the manual detent spring and roller assembly with an attaching bolt and torque to 11 N•m (8ft. lbs.).

15. Install the O-Ring on the solenoid assembly and install into the pump, locating the attaching wire harness toward the transmission, attaching with two bolts and torque to 18 ft. lbs.

16. Install the wiring harness and connect to all pressure switches.

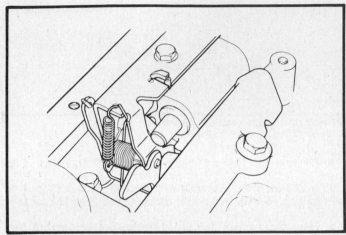

T.V. bracket and lever assembly (© General Motors Corporation)

NOTE: Each pressure switch will be color coded for switch and wire connector identification. When connecting the wire connectors to the pressure switches, always connect the same colors. It is not necessary to connect the same wire connector to the same pressure switch terminals as they are reversible.

17. Install the O-Ring on the outside electrical connector and install into the case by compressing the inside tang or gently taping in board, locating the tab with the case notch.

18. Attach the inside electrical connector to the outside electrical connector.

19. Install the oil passage cover to the transmission with the three attaching bolts. Torque the component to 8 ft. lbs.

20. Install the 3-4 accumulator piston into the accumulator housing with the lug end up. Install the piston spring into the housing on the piston.

21. Position the 3-4 accumulator plate and gasket on the transmission with the gasket on top. Install the housing, spring and piston on the transmission case. Secure the assembly in place with the retaining bolts. Torque the bolts 8 ft. lbs.

22. Install the speedo gear and retaining clip on the output shaft, positioning the large notch on the speedo gear rearward. On shafts with 2 speedo clip holes, use the hole nearest the yoke end of the shaft for Corvettes only.

23. Install the output shaft seal in the output shaft sleeve and install on the output shaft with J25016 or equivalent. Install the oil seal ring on the case extension and install on case. Positioning so the speedo hole is located on the same side as the governor. Torque bolts to 23 ft. lbs.

24. Install the governor assembly. Apply a sealant to the edge of the cover, then install cover.

25. Install the O-Ring on the filter and install in the transmission.

26. Install a new oil pan gasket on the transmission case and install the attaching bolts and torque to 8 ft. lbs.

27. Install all remaining outside connectors such as driven speedo gear and adaptor, outside manual lever and nut.

28. Remove the transmission from the holding fixture and install the torque converter.

S SPECIFICATIONS

TORQUE SPECIFICATIONS

Location	Quantity	Size	Torque
Accumulator cover to case	2	1.0x30.3	11 N•m (8 ft. lb.)
Accumulator cover to case	1	1.0x60.0	11 N•m (8 ft. lb.)
Detent spring to valve body	1	1.75x20.0	22 N•m (18 ft. lb.)
Valve body to case	15	1.0x50.0	11 N•m (8 ft. lb.)
Oil passage cover to case	3	1.0x16.0	11 N•m (8 ft. lb.)
Solenoid assembly to pump	2	1.0x12.0	11 N•m (8 ft. lb.)
Transmission oil pan to case	16	1.25x16	24 N•m (18 ft. lb.)
Pressure switches	1-3	1/8-27	11 N•m (8 ft. lb.)
Park brake bracket to case	2	1.25-20.00	41 N•m (31 ft. lb.)
Pump cover to body	5	1.25-40.00	22 N•m (18 ft. lb.)
Pump assembly to case	7	1.25-60	22 N•m (18 ft. lb.)
Case extension to case	4	1.50-30.0	31 N•m (23 ft. lb.)
Manual shaft to inside det. lever	1	1.50 Nut	31 N•m (23 ft. lb.)
Pressure plugs	3	1/8-27	11 N•m (8 ft. lb.)
Connector cooler pipe	2	1/4-18	38 N•m (28 ft. lb.)

SPECIAL TOOLS

Holding Fixture & Base

Oil Pump Body & Cover Alignment Band
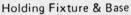

Rear Seal Installer

Pump Oil Seal Installer

Piston Compressor

Bushing Remover
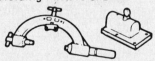

Clutch Spring Compressor
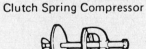

Clutch Spring Compressor Adaptor

Clutch Spring Compressor Press

Universal Remover

Oil Pump Remover & End Play Checking Fixture
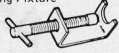

End Play Checking Fixture Adaptor

Bushing & Universal Remover Set

Bushing Remover

Servo Cover Compressor

Output Shaft Support Fixture

Inner Overrun Clutch Seal Protector

Inner Forward Clutch Seal Protector

2-4 Band Apply Pin Tools

INDEX

ALLISON MT SERIES
640•643•644•650•653•654 CR

APPLICATIONS

Medium and heavy duty vehicles, domestic and import

MT 640, 643, 650, 653

One or two drive axle vehicles .... up to 73,280 lb (33,240 kg)

MT 644, 654CR

Vehicle application:

	MT 644	MT 654CR
Truck (GVW or GCW)	55,000 lb (24948 kg)	80,000 lb (36288 kg)
Emergency equipment (GVW)	55,000 lb (24948 kg)	80,000 lb (36288 kg)
Transit bus (GVW)	42,000 lb (19051 kg)	52,000 lb (23587 kg)
Inter-city bus (GVW)	42,000 lb (19051 kg)	52,000 lb (23587 kg)

Horsepower Application

	MT 644	MT 654CR
Truck	250 hp (186 kW)	300 hp (224 kW)
Emergency equipment .	300 hp (224 kW)	300 hp (224 kW)
Transit bus	230 hp (172 kW)	250 hp (186 kW)
Inter-city bus	300 hp (224 kW)	300 hp (224 kW)

G GENERAL DESCRIPTION

General Description

The models MT 640, 643 and 644 have four forward speeds and one reverse. The models MT 650, 653, and 654CR have five forward speeds and one reverse. Shifting in all forward ranges, selected by the operator, is fully automatic, except certain MT 644 and 654CR models, which have a second gear start in all forward ranges except the "First" position.

The four speed units use three planetary gear sets, actuated by five hydraulic clutches, while the five speed units use four planetary gear sets, actuated by six hydraulic clutches. All automatic transmission models are designed to be operated by either gasoline or diesel engines and all are equipped with lock-up torque converters, controlled by hydraulic pressure, dependent upon the rotational speed of the output shaft.

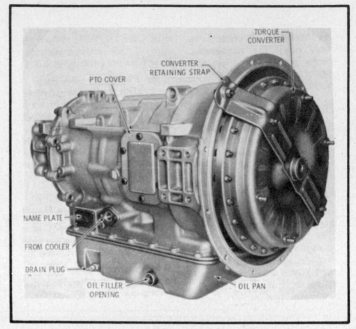

Right front view of MT 640, 643 models (©General Motors Corp.)

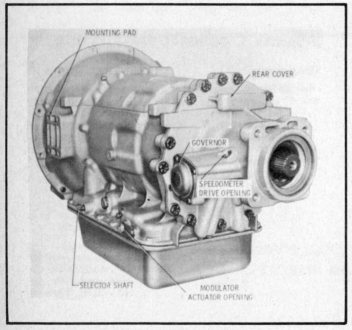

Left rear view of MT 640, 643 models (©General Motors Corp.)

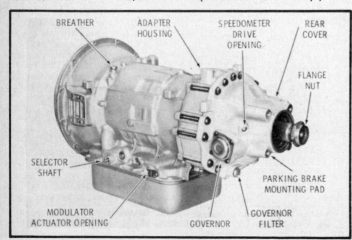

Left rear view MT 650, 653 models (©General Motors Corp.)

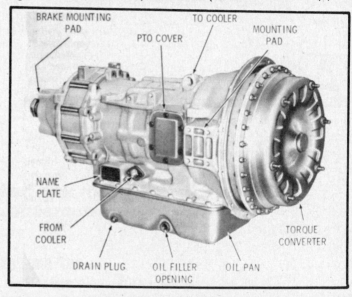

Right front view MT 650, 653 models (©General Motors Corp.)

Transmission and Converter Identification

TRANSMISSION

The transmission nameplate, located on the right rear side of the transmission, includes the transmission serial number, assembly number, and the model designation. All three of these numbers must be supplied when ordering parts or requesting service information.

TORQUE CONVERTER

The torque converter serves as both a fluid coupling and a torque multiplier during its operational phases. A hydraulic operated lock-up clutch is used to lock the turbine element of the coverter to the engine driven flywheel. When the lock-up is applied, the engine to transmission gearing is a 1:1 speed ratio. The converter is a serviceable unit on all MT models.

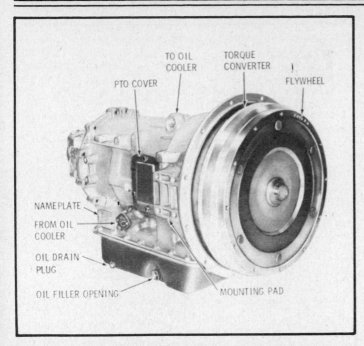

Right front view MT 644 models (©General Motors Corp.)

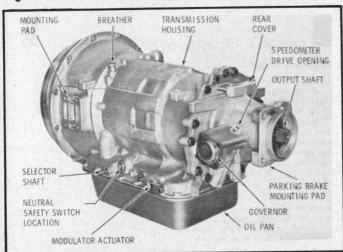

Left rear view MT 644 models (©General Motors Corp.)

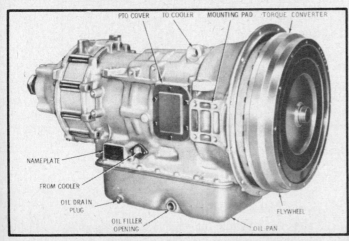

Right front view MT 654CR models (©General Motors Corp.)

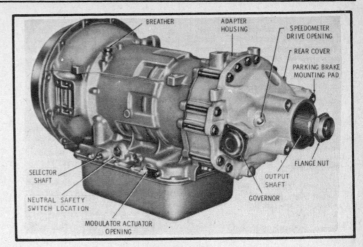

Left rear view MT 654CR models (©General Motors Corp.)

Metric Fasteners

The metric fastener dimensions are very close to the dimensions of the familiar inch system fasteners, and for this reason, replacement fasteners must have the same measurement and strength as those removed.

Do not attempt to inter-change metric fasteners for inch system fasteners. Mismatched or incorrect fasteners can result in damage to the transmission unit through malfunctions, breakage or possible personal injury.

Care should be taken to re-use the fasteners in the same locations as removed.

Fluid Specifications

Dexron II or Dexron transmission fluids are the only fluids recommended for use in on-highway automatic transmission. Type C-3 oil is recommended for use in automatic transmissions used in off-highway applications, and must conform to the ambient temperature, (see chart below), fluid viscosity grade and dealer recommended specifications for the area.

When the ambient temperature for transmissions using Dexron oil is below −30°F (−34°C), an auxiliary preheat is required. Raise the sump temperature above −30°F (−34°C) before operating the transmission. The minimum ambient temperature for preheat requirements on transmissions using C-3 oil is shown below.

Viscosity Grade	Ambient Temperature Requiring Preheat
SAE 30	30°F (−1°C) and below
SAE 15W-40	5°F (−15°C) and below
SAE 10W SAE 10W-30	−10°F (−23°C) and below
SAE 5W-20	−30°F (−35°C) and below

CHECKING OIL LEVEL

Maintaining the proper oil level is very important. The transmission oil is used to apply clutches and lubricate and cool the components. If the oil level is too low the result can be poor performance (clutches will not receive adequate oil supply). If the oil level is too high, overheating results from the oil being churned and aerated. Drain any excess oil to restore the proper level.

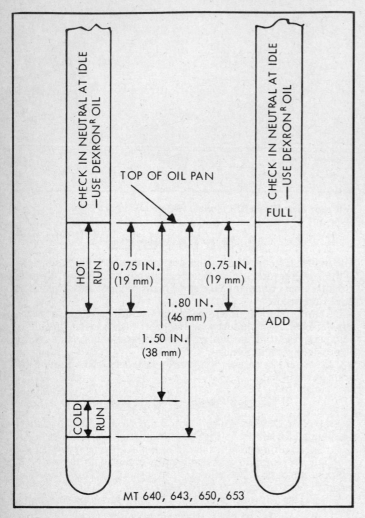

Dipstick markings for models MT 640, 643, 650, 653 (©General Motors Corp.)

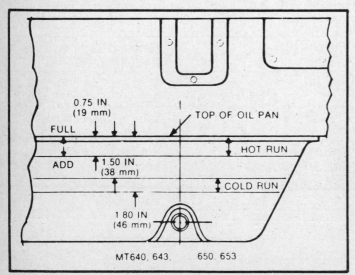

Correct fluid levels in the automatic transmission oil pan, MT 640, 643, 650, 653 (©General Motors Corp.)

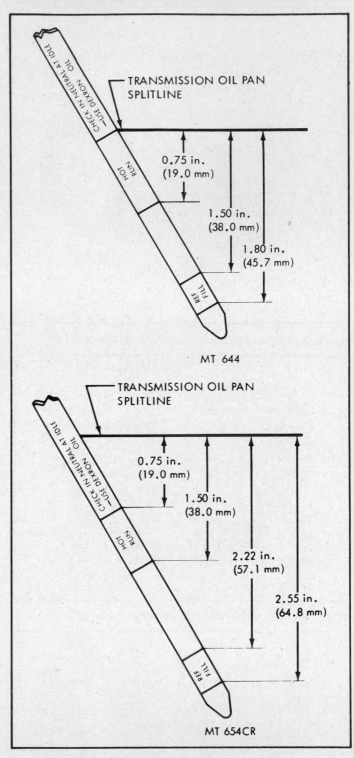

Dipstick markings for models MT 644, 654CR (©General Motors Corp.)

Oil Level Check Procedure

1. Check the oil while the vehicle is on level ground and the parking brake applied. Start the engine and shift the transmission through all drive ranges to fill the clutch cavities and oil passages, then shift to neutral.

2. Run the engine for at least one minute at 1000-1200 rpm to clear the system of air.

3. When adding oil or checking the oil level, dirt or foreign material must not be allowed to enter the fill pipe.

4. Clean around the end of the fill pipe before removing the dipstick.

5. **Cold Oil Check (COLD RUN Band).** A cold oil check should be performed with the engine idling and the oil temperature at 60 to 120°F (16-49°C). Remove the dipstick from the oil filler tube and check the oil level. If the oil level registers in the COLD RUN band, the transmission may be safely operated. If it registers at or below the bottom line of the COLD RUN band add oil to bring the oil level to the middle of the COLD RUN band. A hot oil check may be made after the transmission reaches operating temperature.

6. **Hot Oil Check. (HOT RUN Band).** A hot oil check should be performed with the engine idling and the oil temperature at 160° to 200°F (71° to 93°C). Remove the dipstick from the oil filler tube and check the oil level. If the oil level registers in the HOT RUN band, the transmission may be safely operated. If it registers at or below the bottom line of the HOT RUN band, add oil to bring the level to the middle of the HOT RUN band.

7. **Hot Oil Check (ADD and FULL).** A hot oil check should be performed with the engine idling and the oil temperature at 160° to 200°F (71° to 93°C). Remove the dipstick from the oil filler tube and check the oil level. If the oil level registers between the FULL and ADD lines, the transmission may be safely operated. If it registers on or below the Add line, add oil to bring the oil level to the midpoint between the FULL or ADD lines.

8. **Adjusting Oil Level.** Approximately one U.S. quart (0.946 litre) of oil is required to raise the level from the bottom of the Hot Run band to the top of the band (or from Add to Full). Drain oil to the top of the Hot Run band (or to Full) if a hot oil check shows the level is above that point. The oil level should never be above the top of the Cold Run band in a cold oil check. Drain to reduce the level if necessary.

9. **Safe Level.** The safe operating level is from the Add mark to the Full mark on the dipstick.

MODIFICATIONS

No major modifications made to units prior to the publishing date of this manual. Any modifications needed during the disassembly, inspection and assembly of the transmission units are given in the appropriate text.

TROUBLE DIAGNOSIS

A logical and orderly diagnosis outline and charts are provided with clutch and band applications, shift speed and governor pressures, main control pressures and oil flow circuits to assist the repairman in diagnosing the problems, causes and the extent of repairs needed to bring the automatic transmission back to its acceptable level of operation.

Preliminary checks and adjustments should be made to the manual valve linkage, accelerator and downshift linkages.

Transmission oil level should be checked, both visually and by smell, to determine whether the fluid level is correct and to observe any foreign material in the fluid, if present. Smelling the fluid will indicate if any of the bands or clutches have been burned through excessive slippage or overheating of the transmission.

It is most important to locate the defect and its cause, and to properly repair it to avoid having the same problem recur.

CLUTCH APPLICATION CHART

Range	Clutches Engaged	Ratio
	MT 640, 643, 644 MODELS	
Neutral	First	0:0
First	Forward and First	3.58:1
Second	Forward and Second	2.09:1
Third	Forward and Third	1.39:1
Fourth	Forward and Fourth	1.00:1
Reverse	Fourth and First	5.67:1
	MT 650, 653 MODELS	
Neutral	First	0:0
First	Forward and Low	8.05:1
Second	Forward and First	3.58:1
Third	Forward and Second	2.09:1
Fourth	Forward and Third	1.39:1
Fifth	Forward and Fourth	1.00:1
Reverse	Fourth and First	5.67:1

CLUTCH APPLICATION CHART

Range	Clutches Engaged	Ratio
	MT 654CR MODELS	
Neutral	Low	0:0
First	Forward and Low	4.17:1
Second	Forward and First	2.21:1
Third	Forward and Second	1.66:1
Fourth	Forward and Third	1.27:1
Fifth	Forward and Fourth	1.00:1
Reverse	Fourth and Low	10.76:1

CHILTON'S THREE "C" TRANSMISSION DIAGNOSIS CHART
Models MT 640, 643, 644, 650, 653, 654CR

Condition	Cause	Correction
No response to shift lever movement	1. Range selector linkage disconnected. 2. Range selector linkage defective or broken. 3. Main pressure low. 4. Range selector not engaged at control valve.	1. Connect linkage. 2. Repair or replace linkage 3. Refer to "Low Main Pressure." 4. Install or replace parts involved (inside oil pan).
Rough shifting	1. Manual selector linkage out of adjustment. 2. Control valves sticking. 3. Modulator valve sticking; spring adjustment. 4. Modulator actuator cable kinked or out of adjustment.	1. Adjust linkage. 2. Replace or rebuild control valve assembly. 3. Repair or replace valves; adjust spring. 4. Replace or adjust actuator cable.
Dirty oil	1. Failure to change oil at proper interval. 2. Heat excessive. 3. Clutch failure. 4. Damaged oil filter.	1. Change oil, install new filter. 2. Refer to "Transmission Overheats." 3. Overhaul transmission. 4. Replace filter.
Oil leaking at output shaft	1. Oil seal at output flange worn or damaged. 2. Flange worn at seal surface.	1. Replace seal. 2. Replace flange.
High stall speed	1. Oil level low. 2. Clutch pressure low. 3. Forward clutch slipping (forward). 4. First clutch slipping.	1. Add oil to proper level. 2. Refer to "Low Main Pressure." 3. Rebuild forward clutch. 4. Rebuild first clutch.
Low stall speed	1. Engine not performing efficiently (may be due to high altitude). 2. Broken converter parts.	1. Refer to engine manufacturer's specifications. 2. Replace or rebuild converter assembly.
Clutch slippage in all forward gears	1. Oil level low. 2. Clutch (main) pressure low. 3. Forward clutch slipping. 4. Seal rings on front support hub worn or broken.	1. Add oil to proper level. 2. Refer to "Low Main Pressure." 3. Rebuild forward clutch and replace piston seal rings. 4. Replace seal rings.

CHILTON'S THREE "C" TRANSMISSION DIAGNOSIS CHART
Models MT 640, 643, 644, 650, 653, 654CR

Condition	Cause	Correction
Clutch slippage in first and reverse only	1. First clutch slipping. 2. Low clutch slipping (MT-654CR)	1. Rebuild clutch and replace piston seal rings. 2. Rebuild clutch and replace piston seal rings.
Clutch slippage in second or third (MT 640, 643, 644) or third or fourth (MT 650, 653, 654CR) only	1. Clutch for particular range slipping.	1. Rebuild clutch and replace piston seal rings.
Automatic shifts occur at too high speed	1. Governor valve stuck. 2. Shift signal valve spring adjustment too tight. 3. Valves sticking. 4. Shift points not properly adjusted.	1. Clean or replace governor. 2. Back off spring adjusting ring. 3. Overhaul valve body assembly. 4. Adjust shift points.
Automatic shifts occur at too low speed	1. Governor valve stuck. 2. Governor spring weak. 3. Shift signal valve spring adjustment too loose. 4. Modulator valve stuck. 5. Shift points not properly adjusted.	1. Clean or replace governor. 2. Replace governor. 3. Tighten spring adjusting ring. 4. Clean or replace modulator valve. 5. Adjust shift points.
Low main pressure in all ranges	1. Low oil level. 2. Oil filter element clogged. 3. Seal ring at oil filter tube (filter output) leaking or missing. 4. Main-pressure regulator valve spring weak. 5. Control valve body leakage. 6. Valves stuck (trimmers, relays, and main-pressure regulator). 7. Oil pump, worn or damaged.	1. Add oil to proper level. 2. Replace filter. 3. Replace seal ring. 4. Replace spring. 5. Replace or rebuild valve body assembly. 6. Overhaul valve body assembly, main-pressure regulator valve. 7. Replace or rebuild oil pump.
Low main pressure in one operating range, normal in other ranges	1. Leakage in clutch apply circuits for specific range. 2. Excessive leakage at clutch piston seals for specific range.	1. Replace or rebuild valve body assembly. 2. Overhaul transmission and replace piston seals.
Excessive creep in first and reverse gears	1. Idle throttle setting too high.	1. Adjust throttle setting.
Low lubrication pressure	1. Oil level low. 2. Excessive internal oil leakage. 3. Cooler lines restricted. 4. Lubrication valve spring weak.	1. Add oil to proper level. 2. Check the valve body mounting bolts; lubrication valve seat and spring; low main pressure. 3. Reroute or replace as necessary. 4. Replace valve spring.
Oil leaking into converter housing	1. Converter pump hub seal worn. 2. Converter pump hub worn at seal area. 3. Engine rear seal worn. 4. Converter cover-to-pump seal ring damaged or missing.	1. Replace seal. 2. Replace pump hub. 3. Replace rear seal. 4. Remove converter, replace pump seal ring.

CHILTON'S THREE "C" TRANSMISSION DIAGNOSIS CHART
Models MT 640, 643, 644, 650, 653, 654CR

Condition	Cause	Correction
Transmission overheats	1. Oil level low. 2. Oil level high. 3. Cooler restricted (oil or coolant side).	1. Add oil to proper level. 2. Drain oil to proper level. 3. Remove restrictions.
Clutch slippage in fourth and reverse only (MT 640, 643, 644)	1. Fourth clutch slipping. 2. Seal rings on center support hub worn or broken.	1. Rebuild clutch and replace piston seal rings. 2. Replace seal rings.
Clutch slips in first only (MT 650, 653, 654CR)	1. Low clutch slipping.	1. Rebuild clutch and replace piston seal rings.
Vehicle moves in neutral	1. Range selector linkage out of adjustment.	1. Adjust linkage properly. Refer to "ON VEHICLE SERVICE"
Oil thrown from filler tube	1. Dipstick loose. 2. Oil level too high. 3. Breather clogged. 4. Dipstick gasket worn.	1. Tighten cap; replace if necessary. 2. Drain oil to proper level. 3. Clean or replace breather. 4. Replace gasket or dipstick.
Clutch slippage in first only (MT 640, 643, 644)	1. First clutch slipping.	1. Rebuild clutch and replace piston seal rings.
Clutch slipping in second only MT 650, 653, 654CR	1. First clutch slipping.	1. Rebuild clutch and replace piston seal rings.

SHIFTING SEQUENCE

Number of Speeds

The MT 640, 643 and 644 units have four speeds forward and one reverse, while the MT 650, 653, and 654CR units have five forward speeds and one reverse. Shifting occurs automatically when any of the forward drive ranges are selected by the operator, except LOW range on some MT 644 and 654CR models, which have a second gear start feature, when the range selected is any forward range except first.

Neutral (N)-Place the shift lever in neutral position before starting the engine. A neutral start switch (on the transmission or in the selector linkage) prevents starting the engine when the selector lever is not in neutral. Apply the vehicle brakes and shift to neutral any time the engine is running and operator is not at the vehicle controls.

FORWARD DRIVE RANGES

MT 640, 643

Shift From Neutral-The engine should be at idle speed when any shift is made from neutral to any drive range.

Drive (D)-This range is the most commonly used forward range. It includes all four forward gears. To drive in this range, simply depress the accelerator. The transmission will start in first gear, and automatically upshift at the proper speeds through second, third and fourth gears. Transmissions having the second gear start option will start in second gear and automatically upshift at the proper speeds through third and fourth gears. Downshift also will occur automatically, in relation to vehicle speed and throttle position.

Drive 3 (D3)-In this range, the transmission will start in first gear and automatically upshift, at the proper speeds, to second gear and then to third gear. Second gear start units will start in second gear and automatically upshift to third gear at the proper speed.

Drive 2 (D2)-In this range, the transmission will start in first gear, and automatically upshift, at the proper speed, to second gear. Second gear units will stay and operate in this gear only.

Drive 1 (D1)-In this range, the transmission will start and remain in first gear.

MT 650, 653

Shift From Neutral-The engine should be at idle speed when any shift is made from neutral to a drive range.

Drive (D)-This range is the most commonly used forward range. It includes four gears (2-3-4-5). To drive in this range, simply depress the accelerator. The transmission will start in second gear, and automatically upshift at the proper speeds through third, fourth and fifth gears. Downshifts will also occur automatically in relation to the speed and throttle position.

Drive 3 (D3)-This range includes three gears (2-3-4). The transmission will start in second gear and automatically upshift to third and fourth gears at the proper speed.

Drive 2 (D2)-This range, in transmissions prior to S/N 13801, includes two gears (2-3). The transmission will start in second gear and automatically upshift to third at the proper speed. After S/N 13800 (MT 650), and in all MT 653 models, this range is restricted to second gear.

Drive 1 (D1)-In this range the transmission will operate in first gear only.

MT 644,654CR

NOTE: Some MT 644 and MT 654CR models have a second gear start feature. By selecting any range except first, the vehicle will start in second gear.

Shift from neutral-The engine should be at idle speed when any shift is made from neutral to a drive range.

Drive-This range is the most commonly used forward range. To drve in this range, simply depress the accelerator. The transmission will start in first gear (except second gear start) and automatically upshift at the proper speeds through each of the four (MT 644) or five (MT 654CR) gears. Transmissions with second gear start, when gear and automatically upshift through each gear. Downshfits will also occur automatically in relation to the speed and throttle position.

Drive 4 (MT 654CR)-The range included four gears (1-2-3-4). The transmission will start in first gear and automatically upshift to second, third, and fourth gears at the proper speed. Second gear start units will start in second gear and automatically upshift to third and fourth gears at the proper speed.

Drive 3-This range includes three gears (1-2-3). The transmission will start in first gear and automatically upshift to second and third gears at the proper speed. Second gear start units will start in second gear and automatically upshift to third gear at the proper speed.

Drive 2-This range includes two gears (1-2). The transmission will start in first gear and automatically upshift to second at the proper gear. Second gear start units will stay in this gear.

Drive 1-In this range the transmission will operate in first gear only

ALL MODELS

Reverse (R)-To move the vehicle backward, idle the engine, move the selector to the reverse position and depress the accelerator.

ALL MODELS

Towing-All lubrication and clutch apply oil is provided by the engine-driven oil pump. Because of the pump location ahead of the transmission gearing and clutches, the oil pump cannot be operated by towing or pushing the vehicle. Therefore, any time the vehicle must be towed or pushed for more than a half mile, the driveline must be disconnected or the driving wheels raised from the ground.

Range Selection-Drive (D) range should be selected for normal loads, grades and traffic conditions with an open road ahead. Drive 3 (D3) should be selected for moderate grades, areas with restrictive speed limits, and moderately heavy traffic. Drive 2 (D2) should be selected for very heavy traffic, steep grades, or rough terrain. Drive 1 (D1) is the creeper gear. It is restricted to starting heavy loads, operating on extreme grades, or in mud and dcep snow. Do not attempt full-power upshifts from, or downshifts to, this range.

Lockup Clutch-The lockup clutch automatically locks the converter output and input elements together. When the vehicle attains sufficient speed, hydraulic pressure automatically applies the clutch. When the transmission does not include modulated lockup, the lockup clutch is engaged in only the two highest gears. When modulated lockup is included, closed throttle downshifting will hold lockup engagement until shortly before the 2-1 shift (MT 640, 643) or 3-2 shift (MT 650, 653). When the lockup clutch is applied, the engine output is directed to the transmission gearing at a 1:1 speed ratio.

HYDRAULIC SYSTEM

The hydraulic system generates, directs and controls the flow of hydraulic fluid with-in the automatic transmission, during its various speed ratios. The transmission fluid is drawn from the

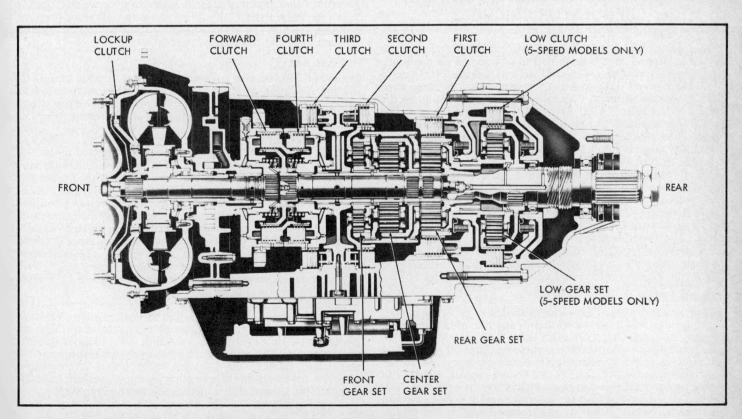

Location of clutches and gearing, typical of all models (©General Motors Corp.)

sump, through a filter by the oil pump and discharged into the bore of the main pressure regulator valve, where main line pressure is regulated by the valve. The pressure regulator valve directs main line pressure to other regulator valves and control valves in the system.

The converter, cooler and lubrication systems are charged from the pressure regulator valve regulated pressure. The converter-in fluid flows through the lock-up relay valve to the torque converter. The converter-in circuit keeps the torque converter lubricated, cooled and filled with fluid. The excess fluid is exhausted back into the sump by the converter pressure regulator valve. The converter-out fluid flows to an external cooler where either a flow of air or water moves over or through the cooler to remove the heat from the transmission fluid. Lubricating fluid is directed through the transmission to the components requiring continuous lubrication and cooling. Excess fluid is routed to the sump through the lubrication regulator valve.

In the MT 640 (prior to S/N 13801), main pressure is directed to eight points in the hydraulic system. Later models (after S/N 13800) and all MT 643 models have main pressure directed to nine points. These are; 3-4, 2-3, 1-2 shift signal valves, 1-2 relay valve, range selector valve, modulator pressure regulator valve, governor valve and the lockup valve. The addition of the trimmer regulator valve is the ninth main pressure point.

In the MT 650 (prior to S/N 13801), main pressure is directed to eight points in the hydraulic system. Later models (after S/N 13800) and all MT 653 models have pressure directed to nine points. These are; 4-5, 3-4, 2-3 shift signal valves, the 2-3 relay valve, range selector valve, modulator pressure regulator valve, governor valve and the lockup valve. The addition of the trimmer regulator valve was the ninth main pressure point.

Hydraulic Circuits

RANGE SELECTOR VALVE, FORWARD REGULATOR CIRCUIT

MT 640, 643

The range selector valve is manually shifted to select the operating range desired. It can be shifted to any one of six positions. These are: neutral (N), reverse (R), drive (D), drive 3 (D3), drive 2 (D2) and drive 1 (D1). At each of these positions the range selector valve establishes the hydraulic circuit for operation in the condition indicated. D, D3, D2 and D1 are forward ranges. The lowest gear attainable is first gear. Anytime the vehicle starts off in any one of these four ranges, it is in first gear. Shifting within any range is automatic, depending upon vehicle speed and throttle position.

The forward regulator pressure is directed from the range selector valve to the main-pressure regulator valve when the range selector valve is in any position except reverse. In neutral, and all forward ranges, this regulator pressure assists pump pressure acting downward on the main-pressure regulator valve. In reverse, the forward regualtor pressure is absent. This allows the main pressure regulator valve to ride higher in its bore, and increases main pressure. The increase in pressure is necessary to handle the higher torque produced in reverse operation.

MT 650, 653

The range selector valve is manually shifted to select the operating range desired. It can be shifted to any one of six positions. These are: neutral (N), reverse (R), drive (D), drive 3 (D3), drive 2 (D2) and drive 1 (D1). At each of these positions the range selector valve establishes the hydraulic circuit for operation in the condition indicated. D, D3, D2 and D1 are forward ranges. The lowest gear attainable is first gear which is present in D1 only. D2, D3 or D position will start the transmission in second gear and automatically shift within its range, depending on the vehicle speed and throttle position. Later MT 650 (after S/N 13800) and

all MT 653 transmissions do not upshift in D2 position under normal operating conditions.

The forward regulator pressure directed from the selector valve to the main-pressure regulator valve when the range selector valve is in any position except reverse. In neutral, and all forward ranges, this regulator pressure assists pump pressure acting downward on the main-pressure regulator valve. In reverse, the forward regulator pressure is absent. This allows the main pressure regulator valve to ride higher in its bore, and increases main pressure. The increase in pressure is necessary to handle the higher torque produced in reverse operation. In earlier MT 650 models, forward regulator pressure was effective in only third, fourth and fifth gears. It originated at the line that connects the 2-3 and 3-4 relay valves.

MT 644, 654CR

The range selector valve is manually shifted to select the desired operating range. It can be shifted to any one of six (MT 644) or seven (MT 654CR) positions. At each of these positions, the selector valve establishes the hydraulic circuit for operation. D or D5, D4, D3, D2 and D1 are forward ranges. In each of these positions, the transmission will start in first gear (except on second gear start), and automatically shift through the gears in that range (no upshift from D1). Upshifts and downshifts are controlled by vehicle speed and throttle position.

The forward regulator circuit originates at the manual selector valve, and terminates at the main pressure regulator valve. In every forward range the circuit is pressurized. This pressure pushes the main pressure regulator valve downward slightly and reduces main pressure.

GOVERNOR CIRCUIT

A centrifugal-type governor, driven by the transmission output, controls the position of the governor valve. The position of the governor valve determines the pressure in the governor circuit. When the transmission output is not rotating, governor pressure is absent. When the transmission output rotates, governor pressure varies with the speed of rotation.

MT 640, 643

In the MT 640 and 643, governor pressure is directed to the 1-2, 2-3 and 3-4 shift signal valves, and modulated lockup valve. In earlier models, that do not include the modulated lockup valve, governor pressure is directed to the top of the lockup valve.

MT 650, 653

In the MT 650 and 653, governor pressure is directed to the 2-3, 3-4 and 4-5 shift signal valves, 2-1 inhibitor valve, and the modulated lockup valve. In models that do not include the modulated lockup valve, governor pressure is directed to the top of the lockup valve. At the 2-1 inhibitor valve, governor pressure acts upon the top of the valve. When governor pressure is sufficient to push the valve downward, road speed is too high to permit a downshift to first gear. Thus a 2-1 shift cannot occur until governor pressure (and road speed) is reduced. Thus, DR1 pressure is blocked from reaching the top of the 1-2 shift valve until road speed (and governor pressure) is decreased to a value that will allow the inhibitor valve to move upward.

In second gear start units, the presence of governor pressure at the bottom of the 1-2 shift valve and forward regulator pressure on the 1-2 modulator valve, plus the assistance of spring force under the 1-2 shift valve, causes the shift valve to move upward against its stop. This allows main pressure to pass through the 1-2 shift signal valve to the 1-2 relay valve. The 1-2 relay valve is forced downward in its bore allowing apply pressure to be directed to the second clutch, permitting second gear start.

MT 644, 654CR

Governor pressure is directed to the shift signal valves, 1-2 shift valve (MT 654CR), modulated lockup shift valve, and to the governor accumulator valve. (The governor accumulator valve is not included in the MT 644 system.) The governor accumulator valve (MT 654CR) is a spring-loaded valve that absorbs pressure surges and provides a more uniform governor pressure.

MODULATOR PRESSURE CIRCUIT

NOTE: A vacuum modulator actuator may be used on gasoline engine installations. The vacuum actuator controls modulator pressure levels to essentially the same values as does the mechanical control. In addition to mechanical and vacuum actuators, an air pressure actuator may be used (either diesel or gasoline installations) to control modulator pressure. The air pressure in the actuator varies with throttle position.

The modulator valve produces a regulated pressure which is derived from main pressure. The valve is moved rightward by a spring at the left end of the valve when the throttle is closed. The valve is moved leftward by the cam and spring action when the throttle is opened. When the spring force at the left of the valve is in balance with the spring force and modulator pressure at the right of the valve, modulator pressure is regulated. When the throttle setting is increased, the movement of the actuator cam forces the modulator valve to the left. This leftward movement reduces modulator pressure. When the throttle setting is reduced, the downward movement of the actuator cam allows this spring at the left to push the valve to another regulating position. Because the throttle setting varies with load and engine speed, modulator pressure also varies. This varying pressure is directed to the 1-2, 2-3 and 3-4 shift signal valves (MT 640, 643), 2-3, 3-4 and 4-5 shift signal valves (MT 650, 653), trimmer regulator valve, and modulated lockup valve. Earlier models do not include the modulated lockup valve.

At the shift signal valves, modulator pressure acts on calibrated areas to assist the upshift of the valves against spring pressure. Each one of the shift valves and springs is so calibrated that the valves will shift in the proper sequence and at the proper time. At a given governor pressure, an increase in modulator pressure will upshift a signal valve. A decrease in modulator pressure will cause a downshift if governor pressure alone will not hold the valve upward. At the trimmer regulator valve, modulator pressure assists in regulating the trimmer regulator pressure.

At the lockup modulated shift valve, modulator pressure assists governor pressure in moving (or holding) the valve downward. The variation in modulator pressure will vary the timing of lockup clutch engagement and release. The primary purpose of lockup modulation is to prolong the engagement of the lockup clutch (at closed throttle) in lower ranges to provide greater engine-braking. All modulated lockup valves are adjustable, but not all transmissions have modulated lockup. Models with adjustable lockup may be adjusted by rotating the adjusting ring at the bottom of the valve until the desired shift point is attained.

TRIMMER VALVES

The purpose of the trimmer valves is to avoid shift shock. The valves reduce pressure to the clutch apply circuit during initial application, then gradually return the pressure to operating maximum. This applies the clutch gently and harsh shifts are prevented. Although each trimmer is calibrated for the clutch it serves, all four trimmers function in the same manner. Each trimmer includes (top to bottom) an orificed trimmer valve, trimmer valve plug, two trimmer springs, and a stop pin.

When any clutch (except forward) is applied, apply pressure is sent to the top end of the valve. Initially, the plug and valve are forced downward against the spring until oil escapes to exhaust. The escape of oil, as long as it continues, reduces clutch apply pressure. However, oil flows through an orifice in the trimmer valve to the cavity between the trimmer valve and the trimmer

valve plug. Pressure in this cavity forces the plug farther downward to the stop. The plug stops, but the flow through the orifice continues. The pressure below the trimmer valve, because it is acting upon a greater diameter than at the upper end, pushes the trimmer valve to the upper end of the valve bore. This stops the escape of oil to the exhaust. When the escape of oil is stopped, clutch pressure rises, and clutch pressure is at the maximum. The plug remains downward until the clutch is released. Upon release of the clutch, the spring pushes the trimmer components to the top of the valve bore. In this position the trimmer is reset and ready to repeat the action upon the next clutch application.

A trim boost accumulator valve (MT 654CR only) is connected to the trimmer regulator pressure circuit. The accumulator will absorb surges in the trimmer regulator pressure and provide a more uniform regulator pressure.

TRIMMER REGULATOR VALVE

The trimmer regulator valve reduces main pressure to a regulated pressure. The regulated pressure is raised or lowered by changes in modulator pressure.

MT 640, 643, 650, 653
AFTER SERIAL NUMBER 13800
Trimmer regulator pressure is directed to the lower sides of the first and second trimmer plugs on some models, or to the lower sides of the first, second, third and fourth trimmer plugs on models equipped with smooth shift. This varies the clutch apply pressure pattern of the trimmer valves. A higher modulator pressure (closed throttle) will reduce trimmer regulator pressure. This results in a lower initial clutch pressure. Conversely, a lower modulator pressure (open throttle) results in higher regulator pressure and a higher initial clutch pressure.

MT 644, 654CR
Trimmer regulator pressure is directed to the lower side(s) of the low- (MT 654CR), first-, and second-clutch trimmer regulator plug(s), (MT 644), first, second, third-and-fourth-clutch trimmer regulator plug(s) (later MT 644), to vary the clutch apply pressure pattern of the trimmer valves. A higher modulator pressure (closed throttle) will reduce trimmer regulator pressure. This results in lower initial clutch pressure. Conversely, a lower modulator pressure (open throttle) results in higher regulator pressure and a higher initial clutch pressure.

LOCKUP CLUTCH OPERATION

Lockup clutch engagement and release are controlled by the modulated lockup valve and the lockup valve. The modulated lockup valve is actuated by a combination of governor and modulator pressures. Governor pressure alone will not move (or hold) the valve downward at a given road speed. Modulator pressure, assisting governor pressure, will move (or hold) the valve downward at a lower road speed. The purpose of the modulated lockup valve is to prolong lockup clutch engagement while vehicle speed decreases (closed throttle). This feature provides engine braking action at speeds lower than the normal lockup disengagement point when the valve is not in the system.

In its downward position, the modulated lockup valve directs main pressure to the top of the lockup valve. Main pressure pushes the lockup valve downward. In its downward position, the valve directs main pressure to the lockup clutch. This engages the clutch. The position of the lockup valve affects the volume of oil flowing to the torque converter. When the valve is upward (lockup clutch released), there is maximum flow to the converter. When the valve is downward (clutch engaged), converter-in flow is restricted by an orifice, and flow is reduced. When the lockup clutch is engaged, a signal pressure is sent to the main pressure regulator valve. This signal pressure moves the regulator valve downward slightly, and main pressure decreases.

On models with adjustable lockup, modulator assistance at the

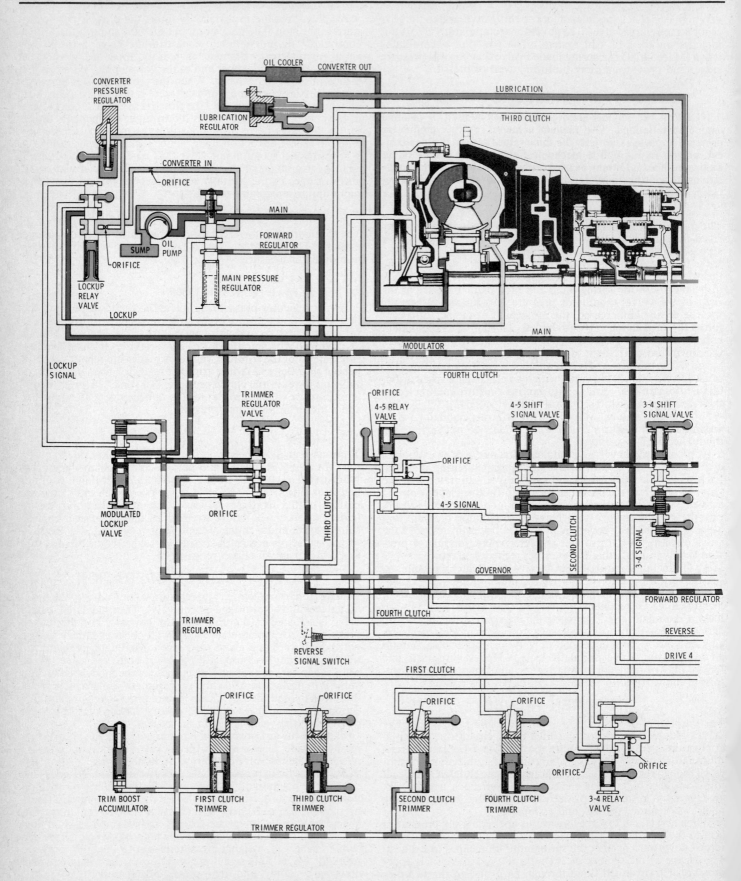

Oil flow schematics, MT 654CR models (©General Motors Corp.)

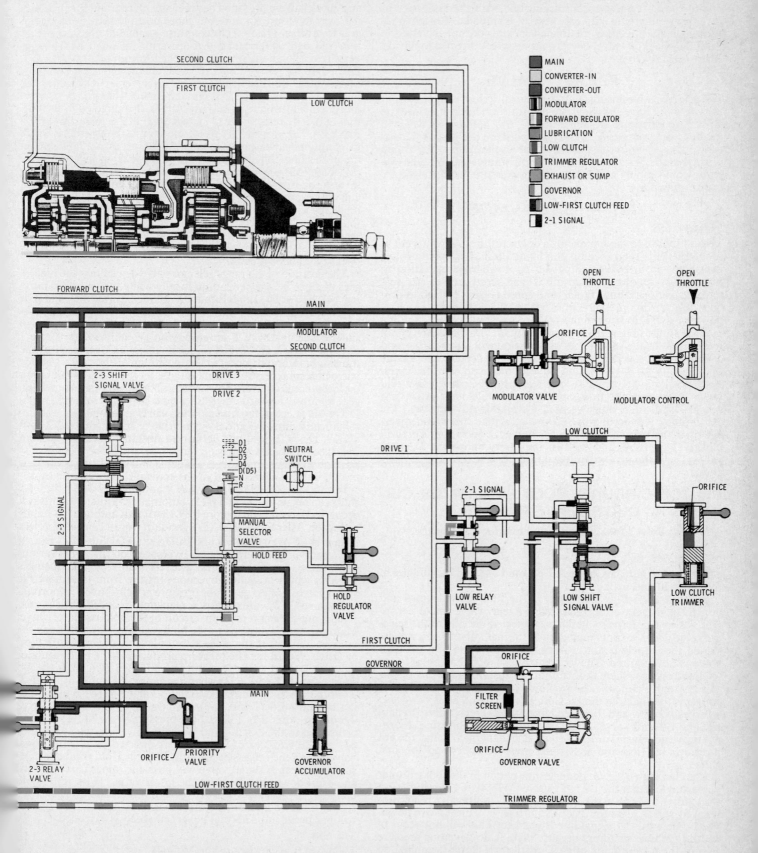

SECOND CLUTCH

FIRST CLUTCH

LOW CLUTCH

MAIN — CONVERTER-IN — CONVERTER-OUT — MODULATOR — FORWARD REGULATOR — LUBRICATION — LOW CLUTCH — TRIMMER REGULATOR — EXHAUST OR SUMP — GOVERNOR — LOW-FIRST CLUTCH FEED — 2-1 SIGNAL

OPEN THROTTLE   OPEN THROTTLE

FORWARD CLUTCH

MAIN

MODULATOR

SECOND CLUTCH

ORIFICE

MODULATOR VALVE   MODULATOR CONTROL

2-3 SHIFT SIGNAL VALVE   DRIVE 3

DRIVE 2

LOW CLUTCH

D1 D2 D3 D4 D(D5) N R

NEUTRAL SWITCH   DRIVE 1

ORIFICE

2-1 SIGNAL

2-3 SIGNAL

MANUAL SELECTOR VALVE   HOLD FEED

HOLD REGULATOR VALVE

LOW RELAY VALVE   LOW SHIFT SIGNAL VALVE   LOW CLUTCH TRIMMER

FIRST CLUTCH

GOVERNOR   ORIFICE

FILTER SCREEN

MAIN

ORIFICE   PRIORITY VALVE   GOVERNOR ACCUMULATOR   ORIFICE   GOVERNOR VALVE

2-3 RELAY VALVE

LOW-FIRST CLUTCH FEED

TRIMMER REGULATOR

modulated lockup valve is not present. By setting the adjusting ring to the shift point specifications and with the assistance of governor pressure, lockup engagement is initiated. Earlier models, which do not have modulated lockup, do not include the modulated lockup valve. Governor pressure is directed to the top of the lockup valve.

PRIORITY VALVE

The priority valve ensures that the control system upstream from the valve will have sufficient pressure during shifts to perform its automatic functions. In later MT 644, MT 650 and all MT 653 models, while in reverse, first clutch pressure can bypass the priority valve. Without the priority valve, the filling of a clutch might require a greater volume of oil (momentarily) than the pump could supply and still maintain pressure for the necessary control functions.

2-1 INHIBITOR VALVE

MT 650, 653

The 2-1 inhibitor valve prevents a downshift from second gear to first gear while road speed is too high. Similarly, it will protect the engine from overspeeding during downgrade operation in first gear by making a 1-2 upshift if road speed exceeds that safe for first gear operation. When road speed is great enough to produce a governor pressure that pushes the 2-1 inhibitor valve downward, D1 pressure to the 1-2 shift valve is blocked, thus, if a manual shift to Drive 1 (first gear) is made, D1 pressure cannot reach the 1-2 shift valve. The transmission will remain in second gear until road speed (and governor pressure) decreases to a value that permits the 2-1 inhibitor valve to move upward. In its upward position, D1 pressure can reach the 1-2 shift valve and move it downward to first gear position. While operating in first gear (1-2 shift valve downwards; 2-1 inhibitor valve upward), the 2-1 inhibitor valve will move downward if road speed (and governor pressure) exceeds that safe for first-gear operation. This will block D1 pressure, and exhaust the cavity above the 1-2 shift valve. The shift valve will move upward to give second gear operation.

CLUTCH CIRCUITS, HOLD REGULATOR CIRCUITS, DRIVE RANGES

NOTE: Refer to the appropriate Fluid Flow Schematic.

MT 640, 643, 650, 653

There are five clutches in the MT 640 and 643 and six clutches in the MT 650 and 653.

Each clutch has its own circuit. The first, second, third and fourth clutches are each connected to a relay valve and to a trimmer valve. The forward clutch is connected directly to the selector valve and does not connect to a trimmer valve. Since it is assumed the vehicle is not moving, the application of a trimmer valve is not required. The low clutch (MT 650, 653 only) is not trimmed because there is no automatic upshifting from or downshifting to this clutch. The low clutch circuit (MT 650, 653 only) connects the clutch to the 1-2 shift valve. The 1-2 shift valve also receives 1-2 (low-and- first) feed from the 2-3 relay valve. In neutral, the 1-2 shift valve is held upward by spring pressure. It cannot move downward unless Drive 1 line is charged. In the upward position, 1-2 (low-and first) feed pressure is sent to the first clutch.

The first clutch circuit connects the clutch to the first trimmer valve and to either the 1-2 relay valve (MT 640, 643) or to the 1-2 shift valve (MT 650, 653). In neutral the 1-2 shift valve is held upward by spring pressure. The 1-2 shift valve cannot move downward unless the 2-1 signal line is charged. This will not occur in neutral (vehicle standing) because there is no governor pressure to shift the 2-1 inhibitor valve. Only the first clutch is applied, so the transmission output cannot rotate. On MT 643 models

equipped with 2nd-gear start and on MT 653 models, a bypass and check ball are provided between the reverse and first trimmer passages to ensure a rapid and more positive shift from second gear to reverse. The first clutch is also applied in first gear operation (MT 640, 643), second gear operation (MT 650, 653) and reverse gear operation. Shifting the selector from neutral to D, D3, D2 or D1 charges the forward clutch circuit and applies the forward clutch. Shifting from neutral to reverse (R) charges the fourth clutch, while the first clutch remains charged. In reverse, fourth clutch (reverse signal) pressure is also directed to the bottom of the 1-2 relay valve (MT 640, 643) or 2-3 relay valve (MT 650, 653). The pressure at this location prevents either relay valve from moving downward. On later models, to ensure rapid charging of the first clutch when a shift is made from low to reverse (MT 650, 653), a bypass and check ball are provided between the reverse and first trimmer passages. When the circuits are charged, and the selector valve is at D, the MT 640 or 643 model will automatically shift from first to second, second to third and third to fourth. The MT 650 or 653 model will automatically shift from second to third, third to fourth and fourth to fifth. These shifts occur as a result of governor pressure, and (if throttle is not fully open) modulator pressure.

The position of the range selector valve determines the highest gear that can be reached automatically while the vehicle is moving. MT 640 or 643 models that do not incorporate a second gear start will automatically shift 1-2, 2-3 and 3-4 when the range selector valve is in Drive 4 position. In Drive 3, automatic 1-2, 2-3 shifts occur. In Drive 2, an automatic 1-2 shift occurs. Drive 1 does not permit an upshift to occur unless an overspeed of the transmission output occurs. The positions of the range selector valve in second gear start units is the same; only the transmission performance is affected. The transmission always starts in second gear when any forward range other than Drive 1 is selected. When Drive 4 is selected, the transmission starts in second gear and automatically shifts 2-3 and 3-4. In Drive 3, an automatic 2-3 shift occurs. Drive 2 does not permit an upshift to occur unless an overspeed of the transmission output occurs. Drive 1 is the only position in which first gear is available and upshifting is not permitted unless an overspeed of the transmission output occurs.

In the MT 650 or 653, Drive (D) automatic 2-3, 3-4 and 4-5 shifts can occur. In Drive 3 (D3), automatic 2-3 and 3-4 shifts can occur. In Drive 2 (D2) (before S/N 13801), an automatic 2-3 shift can occur. After S/N 13800, (D2), no shift from 2 can occur unless output shaft overspeed occurs. In Drive 1 (D1) no shift from 1 can occur unless output shaft overspeed occurs. The various drive ranges limit the highest gear attainable by introducing a pressure which prevents governor pressure from upshifting the signal valves (unless governor pressure is well above that normally attained). This pressure is a regulated, reduced pressure derived from the main pressure circuit at the hold regulator valve. Main pressure is directed to the hold regulator valve through the hold feed line when the range selector lever is in Drive 1, Drive 2 or Drive 3 position. The pressure produced in the hold regulator valve is directed to the 3-4 shift valve (MT 640, 643) or the 4-5 shift valve (MT 650, 653) when the range selector is in Drive 3. The hold pressure is directed to the 2-3 and 3-4 (MT 640, 643) or the 3-4 and 4-5 (MT 650, 653) when the range selector is in Drive 2 position. After S/N 13800, hold pressure in the MT 650 or 653 is directed to the 2-3, 3-4 and 4-5 shift valves. In the MT 640 or 643 and MT 650 or 653, pressure is directed to all shift signal valves when the range selector is in Drive 1. Hold regulator pressure at each shift signal valve will push the upper valve upward and exert downward force on the lower valve. Thus, when hold pressure is present, a greater governor pressure (higher road speed) must be attained before the upshift occurs. The upshift will not occur until normal governed speed is exceeded.

MT 644

There are five clutches in the MT 644.

Each clutch has its own circuit. The first, second, third, and fourth clutches are each connected to a relay valve and to a trimmer valve. The forward clutch is connected directly to the selector valve and does not connect to a trimmer valve. Since it is assumed the vehicle is not moving, the application of a trimmer valve is not required. The first clutch circuit (neutral, reverse, and first gear) connects the first clutch to the first clutch trimmer valve and the 1-2 relay valve. On later models, to ensure rapid charging of the first clutch when a shift is made from first to reverse, a bypass and check ball are provided between the reverse and first trimmer passages. The second clutch circuit (second gear) connects the second clutch to the second clutch trimmer and the 2-3 relay valve. The third clutch circuit (third gear) connects the third clutch to the third clutch trimmer and the 3-4 relay valve. The fourth clutch circuit (fourth or reverse gear) connects the fourth clutch to the fourth clutch trimmer and the 3-4 relay valve. The forward clutch circuit (first through fourth gears) connects the forward clutch to only the range valve. No clutches except the first clutch (for neutral and first), the first and fourth clutches (for reverse), and the forward clutch (for any forward range) can be engaged unless the transmission output is rotating to provide governor pressure. The position of the range selector valve determines which of these clutches will be engaged when the vehicle is not moving.

In second gear start models, forward regulator and Drive 1 pressures at the 1-2 shift signal modulator valve plus the spring force against the 1-2 shift signal valve cause the shift valve and modulator valve to move against the stop. In this position main pressure passes through the signal valve to the 1-2 relay valve. The 1-2 relay valve moves downward. In this position the relay valve exhausts the low clutch and directs apply pressure through the 2-3 relay valve to the second clutch. The applied second clutch permits second gear start. When reverse operation is selected, forward regulator and Drive 1 pressures are not present at the 1-2 shift signal valve. Therefore, the 1-2 relay valve is held upward by spring force. The relay valve in this position directs apply pressure to the low clutch. (Low and fourth combine to produce reverse operation.) The position of the range selector valve determines the highest gear that will be reached automatically while the vehicle is moving. Models that do not incorporate a second gear start can automatically shift 1-2, 2-3, and 3-4 when the range selector valve is in Drive 4 position. In Drive 3, automatic 1-2, 2-3 shifts can occur. In Drive 2, an automatic 1-2 shift can occur. Drive 1 will not permit an upshift to occur. In the lower ranges (Drive 1, 2, and 3), the transmission will not upshift above the highest gear selected unless the engine governed speed is exceeded. The positions of the range selector valve in second gear start units is the same; only the transmission performance is affected. Selecting Drive 4, automatically starts the transmission in second gear. Drive 1 is the only position in which first gear is available. The various drive ranges limit the highest gear attainable by introducing a pressure which prevents governor pressure from upshifting the signal valves (unless governor pressure is well above that normally attained). This pressure is a regulated, reduced pressure derived from the main pressure circuit at the hold regulator valve. Main pressure is directed to the hold regulator valve through the hold feed line when the range selector lever is in Drive 1, Drive 2, or Drive 3 position. The pressure produced in the hold regulator valve is directed to the 3-4 shift signal valve when the range selector is at D3. Hold pressure is directed to the 2-3 and 3-4 shift signal valves when the range selector is at D2. Hold pressure is directed to the 1-2, 2-3, and 3-4 shift signal valves when the range selector is at D1. Hold regulator pressure at each shift signal valve will push the upper valve upward, and raise the pressure at which the lower valve will be pushed upward by governor pressure. Thus, when hold regulator pressure is present, an upshift can occur at that shift signal valve, but only at an elevated speed.

MT 654CR
There are six clutches in the MT 654CR. Each clutch has its own

circuit. The low, first, second, third, and fourth clutches are each connected to a relay valve and to a trimmer valve. The forward clutch is connected directly to the selector valve and does not connect to a trimmer valve. Since it is assumed the vehicle is not moving, the application of a trimmer valve is not required. The low clutch circuit connects the clutch to the low relay valve and the low trimmer valve. In neutral, reverse, and first gear, low-first clutch feed pressure is directed from the 2-3 relay valve to the low relay valve. The 1-2 shift valve remains in an upward position, directing 2-1 signal pressure to the top of the 1-2 relay valve. The 1-2 relay valve is held downward by 2-1 signal pressure. In this position, the 1-2 relay valve directs low-first clutch feed pressure to the low clutch circuit.

Because only the low clutch is applied with the range selector valve in neutral, the transmission output does not rotate. The low clutch is also applied in first and reverse gear operation.

The first clutch circuit (second gear) connects the first clutch to the first clutch trimmer valve and the 1-2 relay valve. In second gear, governor pressure forces the 1-2 shift valve downward, blocking 2-1 signal pressure to the 1-2 relay valve. With the absence of 2-1 signal pressure, the 1-2 relay valve spring moves the valve to the top of its bore, directing 1-2 feed pressure to the first clutch and first trimmer valve. Shifting the range selector from neutral to D, D4, D3, D2, or D1 charges the forward clutch circuit and applies the forward clutch. Shifting from neutral to reverse (R) charges the fourth clutch, while the low clutch remains charged. In reverse, fourth clutch (reverse signal) pressure is also directed to the bottom of 2-3 relay valve. The pressure at this location prevents the relay valve from moving downward. When the circuits are charged and the range selector valve is at D, the transmission will automatically shift from first to second, second to third, third to fourth, and fourth to fifth. These shifts occur as a result of governor pressure, and (if throttle is not fully open) modulator pressure.

The position of the range selector valve determines the highest gear which will be reached automatically. In Drive (D), automatic 1-2, 2-3, 3-4, and 4-5 shifts can occur. In Drive 4 (D4), automatic 1-2, 2-3, and 3-4 shifts can occur. In Drive 3 (D3), automatic 1-2 and 2-3 shifts can occur. In Drive 2 (D2), an automatic 1-2 shift can occur. In Drive 1 (D1) no shift from 1 will occur. In the lower ranges (D1, D2, D3, and D4), the transmission will not upshift above the highest gear selected unless the engine governed speed is exceeded. The various drive ranges limit the highest gear attainable by introducing a pressure which prevents governor pressure from upshifting the signal valves (unless governor pressure is well above that normally attained). This pressure is a regulated, reduced pressure derived from the main pressure circuit at the hold regulator valve. Main pressure is directed to the hold regulator valve through the hold feed line when the selector lever is in Drive 1, Drive 2, Drive 3, or Drive 4 position. The pressure produced in the hold regulator valve is directed to the 4-5 shift signal valve when the selector is at D4. Hold pressure is directed to the 3-4 and 4-5 shift signal valves when the selector is at D3. Hold pressure is directed to the 2-3, 3-4, and 4-5 shift signal valves when the selector is at D2. Hold pressure is directed to the 2-3, 3-4, and 4-5 shift signal valves and to the 1-2 shift valve when the selector is at D1. Hold regulator pressure at each shift signal valve will push the upper valve upward, and raise the pressure at which the lower valve will be pushed upward by governor pressure. Thus, when hold regulator pressure is present, an upshift can occur at that shift signal valve, but only at an elevated speed.

AUTOMATIC UPSHIFTS
MT 640, 643, 650, 653
When the transmission is operating in first gear (MT 640, 643) or second gear (MT 650, 653), with the range selector valve at Drive (D), a combination of governor pressure and modulator pressure, or governor pressure alone, will upshift the transmission to second (MT 640, 643) or third (MT 650, 653) gear. At closed or part

throttle, modulator pressure exists and will assist governor pressure. At full throttle, there is no modulator pressure. Thus, upshifts occur at a lower road speed when the throttle is closed; but are delayed until higher speed (greater governor pressure) is attained when the throttle is open.

Governor pressure is dependent upon rotation speed of the transmission output. The greater the vehicle speed, the greater the governor pressure. When governor pressure is sufficient, the first upshift (1-2 for MT 640, 643 or 2-3 for MT 650, 653) will occur. With a further increase in governor pressure (and vehicle speed) the second upshift (2-3 for MT 640 and 643 or 3-4 for MT 650 and 653) will occur. A still further increase will cause a third upshift (3-4 for MT 640 and 643 or 4-5 for MT 650 and 653). Not that each of these shifts will be delayed or hastened by the decrease or increase, respectively, of modulator pressure. In other drive ranges, the same upshift sequence occurs until the highest gear attainable in that range selection is reached. In any automatic upshift, the shift signal valve acts first. This directs a shift pressure to the relay valve. The relay valve shifts, exhausting the applied clutch and applying a clutch for a higher gear.

MT 644

When the transmission is operating in first gear, with the range selector valve at drive (D), a combination of governor pressure and modulator pressure, or governor pressure alone, will upshift the transmission to second gear. At closed, or part throttle, modulator pressure exists and will assist governor pressure. At full throttle, there is no modulator pressure. Thus, upshifts occur at a lower vehicle speed when the throttle is closed and are delayed by opening the throttle.

Governor pressure is dependent upon rotation speed of the transmission output shaft. The greater the vehicle speed, the greater the governor pressure. When governor pressure is sufficient, the first upshift (1-2) will occur. With a further increase in governor pressure (and vehicle speed) the second upshift (2-3) will occur. A still further increase will cause a third upshift (3-4). Each of these shifts will be delayed or hastened by the decrease or increase, respectively, of modulator pressure. In other drive ranges, the same upshift sequence occurs until the highest gear attainable in that range selection is reached. In any automatic upshift, the shift signal valve acts first. This directs a shift pressure to the relay valve. The relay valve shifts, exhausting the applied clutch and applying a clutch for a higher gear.

MT 654CR

When the transmission is operating in first gear, with the range selector valve at drive (D), a combination of governor pressure alone will upshift the transmission to second gear. At closed, or part throttle, modulator pressure exists and will assist governor pressure. At full throttle, there is no modulator pressure. Thus, upshifts occur sooner when the throttle is closed, and they are delayed when the throttle is opened.

Governor pressure is dependent upon rotation speed of the transmission output. The greater the output speed (vehicle speed), the greater the governor pressure. When governor pressure is sufficient, the first upshift (1-2) will occur. With a further increase in governor pressure (and vehicle speed), the greater the governor pressure. When governor pressure is sufficient, the first upshift (1-2) will occur. With a further increase in governor pressure (and vehicle speed), the second upshift (2-3) will occur. A still further increase will cause a third upshift (3-4) and a fourth upshift (4-5) to occur. Note that each of these shifts will be delayed or hastened by the decrease or increase, respectively, of modulator pressure.

In other drive ranges, the same upshift sequence occurs until the highest gear attainable in that range selection is reached. In any automatic upshift, the shift signal valve acts first. This directs a shift pressure to the relay valve. The relay valve shifts, exhausting the applied clutch and applying a clutch for a higher gear.

AUTOMATIC DOWNSHIFTS

Automatic downshifts, like upshifts, are controlled by governor and modulator pressures. Downshifts occur in sequence as governor pressure and/or modulator pressure decrease. Low modulator pressure (open throttle) will hasten the downshift; high modulator pressure (closed throttle) will delay downshifts. In any automatic downshift, the shift signal valve acts first. This exhausts the shift signal pressure holding the relay valve downward. The relay valve then moves upward, exhausting the applied clutch and applying the clutch for the next lower gear.

DOWNSHIFT AND REVERSE INHIBITING

It is inherent in the system, as a result of calibrations of valve areas and spring forces, to prevent downshifts at too rapid a rate or to prevent a shift to reverse while moving forward. For example, if the vehicle is traveling at a high speed in fourth gear (4) and the selector valve is inadvertently moved to D1, the transmission will not immediately shift to first gear (MT 640, 644, 643). Instead it will shift 4-3-2-1 as speed decreases (it will remain in fourth gear if speed is not decreased sufficiently to require an automatic downshift).

A second example is, if the vehicle is traveling at a high speed in Fifth gear (MT 654CR) and the selector valve is inadvertently moved to D1, the transmisison will not immediately shift to first gear. Instead it will shift 5-4-3-2-1 as speed decreases.

The progressive downshift occurs because the regulator hold pressure is calibrated, along with the valve areas to shift the signal valves downward against governor pressure only when governor pressure decreases to a value corresponding to a safe downshift speed. Thus, if speed is too great, governor pressure is sufficient to hold the shift signal valve upward against drive 3, drive 2 or drive 1 pressure (all of which are the regulated holding pressure originating in the hold regulator valve). As governor pressure decreases, all shift signal valves move downward in sequence.

Diagnosis Tests

The engine and the transmission must be regarded as a single unit during the troubleshooting or diagnostic phase. Because of the numerous engine-transmission applications available, the particular engine specifications must be obtained through the engine manufacturer or representative. The engine must be maintained in a good state of tune. A thorough understanding of the transmission operation and its components, is a definite asset to the diagnostician during the diagnosing/troubleshooting phase.

Oil pressure ports are located on the sides of the transmission and capped with pipe plugs. Remove the necessary pipe plug, install an oil pressure gauge hose to the port and oil pressure diagnosis can be made.

Test stands are available for both the transmission and valve body, to make tests, repairs and/or adjustments.

Pressure Tests

Pressure ports are provided for main line pressure, governor pressure, Reverse signal pressure and converter lock-up signal pressure. Refer to the transmission illustrations for the correct pressure port locations. Refer to the specifications in the specifications section for the correct fluid pressure.

Transmission Stall Test

A stall test should be conducted when the power package (engine and transmission) is not performing satisfactorily. The purpose of the test is to determine if the transmission is the malfunctioning component.

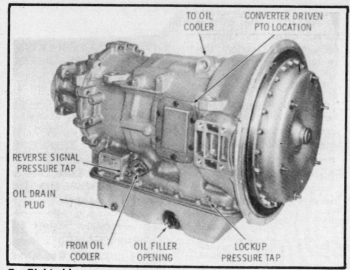

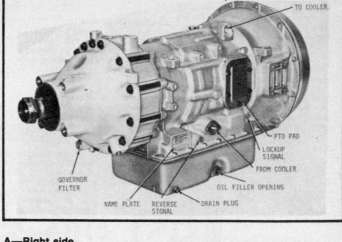

A—Right side

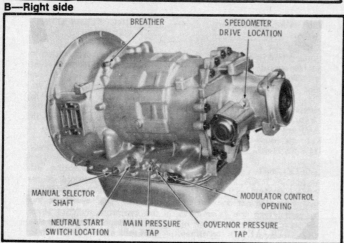

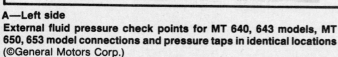

A—Left side
External fluid pressure check points for MT 640, 643 models, MT 650, 653 model connections and pressure taps in identical locations (©General Motors Corp.)

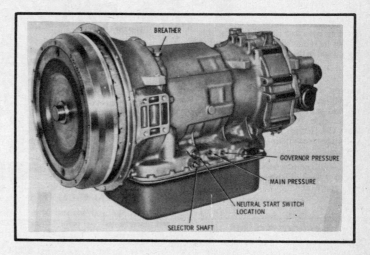

B—Left side
External fluid pressure check points, MT 644, 654CR models (©General Motors Corp.)

CAUTION

When conducting a converter stall test, the vehicle must be positively prevented from moving. Both the parking and service brakes must be applied and, if necessary, the vehicle should be blocked to prevent movement forward or in reverse. Do not maintain the stalled condition longer than 30 seconds due to rapid heating of the transmission oil. With the transmission in Neutral, run the engine at 1200 to 1500 rpm for two minutes to cool the oil between tests. Do not allow the converter-out temperature to exceed 300°F. Keep close check to prevent the engine cooling system from overheating.

Procedure

1. A torque converter stall test is performed by locking the transmission output, putting the transmission in gear, accelerating the engine to full throttle, and noting the maximum rpm the engine will attain. The speed attained is then compared to the speed specified as normal for those conditions by the vehicle manufacturer. An engine speed above or below the specified range may indicate a malfunction in the engine or transmission.

NOTE: Engine power will decrease with an increase in elevation (altitude), becoming more pronounced at greater elevation. This will result in a lower engine speed under converter-stall conditions.

2. After making allowances for elevation, a low engine speed may indicate the engine is not delivering full power. If low engine speed persists after engine is tuned, refer to the "Troubleshooting" procedures and chart.

3. If high engine speed is noted, refer to the "troubleshooting" chart.

Air Pressure Test

Upon the removal of the control valve assembly, the various passages can be used with reduced air pressure to determine if the clutch units are operating or if piston seals have developed leakages. The interconnecting passages can be checked for leakages or damage.

Vacuum Diaphragm Test

The vacuum diaphragm can be inspected for leakage with the use of an outside vacuum source. Apply vacuum to the diaphragm nipple and the vacuum should not leak away. Should a loss of vacuum occur, the diaphragm is defective and the unit should be replaced.

Inspect the vacuum supply line at the diaphragm with the engine operating to be assured a vacuum supply is present.

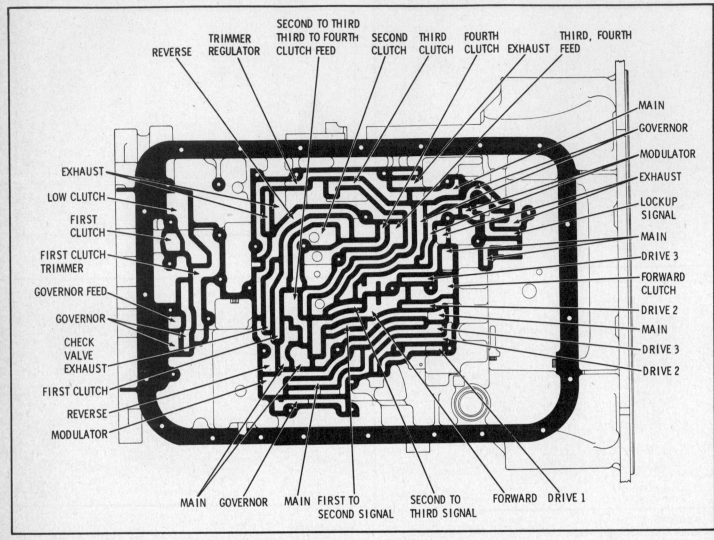

REVERSE · TRIMMER REGULATOR · SECOND TO THIRD THIRD TO FOURTH CLUTCH FEED · SECOND CLUTCH · THIRD CLUTCH · FOURTH CLUTCH · EXHAUST · THIRD, FOURTH FEED

MAIN · GOVERNOR · MODULATOR · EXHAUST · LOCKUP SIGNAL · MAIN · DRIVE 3 · FORWARD CLUTCH · DRIVE 2 · MAIN · DRIVE 3 · DRIVE 2

EXHAUST · LOW CLUTCH · FIRST CLUTCH · FIRST CLUTCH TRIMMER · GOVERNOR FEED · GOVERNOR · CHECK VALVE EXHAUST · FIRST CLUTCH · REVERSE · MODULATOR

MAIN · GOVERNOR · MAIN · FIRST TO SECOND SIGNAL · SECOND TO THIRD SIGNAL · FORWARD · DRIVE 1

Transmission case component port identification, MT 640, 643, 650, 653 models (©General Motors Corp.)

ON CAR SERVICES

ADJUSTMENTS

Proper adjustment of the manual selector valve linkage is important as the shift tower detents must correspond exactly to those in the transmission. Periodic inspections should be made for bent or worn parts, loose threaded connections, loose bolts and an accumulation of grease and dirt. All moving joints must be kept clean and well lubricated.

The following general procedures are applicable to most vehicles:

1. The manual selector lever should move easily and give a crisp feel in each position. The linkage should be adjusted so that the stops in the shift tower match the detents in the transmission.
2. When the linkage is correctly adjusted, the pin which engages the shift lever linkage at the transmission can be moved freely in each range.

SHIFT LINKAGE

Adjustment

1. Place the range selector lever against the stop in "R" (Reverse) position.
2. Disconnect the clevis from the transmission shift lever.
3. Place the transmission shift lever in "R" (Reverse) position.

NOTE: The reverse position is full counterclockwise movement of the lever.

4. Loosen the jam nut at the clevis. Turn the clevis clockwise or counterclockwise on the threaded cable core until the holes in the clevis align with the hole in the shift lever. Install the clevis pin into the clevis and shift lever holes.

NOTE: The pin should enter the holes freely, and if not, adjust the clevis slightly by one-half turn in each direction until the pin does enter freely.

5. Turn the clevis on full turn clockwise to allow for cable backlash and install the pin permanently.
6. Move the range selector through all the drive ranges. The transmission detent should fully engage just before the range selector lever hits the stops in the shift control cover.

7. Spread the cotter pin, if not previously done and tighten the lock nut against the clevis.

CAUTION

Do not use pliers on the cable core when tightening the lock nut after positioning the clevis and pin. The cable core finish may be damaged, resulting in cable core seal failure.

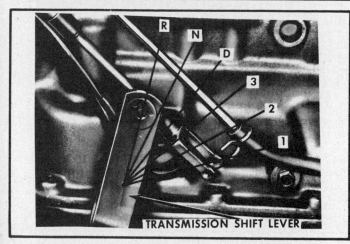

Selector lever detent positions (©General Motors Corp.)

SHIFT LINKAGE CABLE

Removal

1. Disconnect the clevis from the transmission shift lever.
2. Disconnect the cable from the bracket at the side of the transmission and remove cable clips attaching the cable to the chassis and cab.
3. Remove the four cross-recess screws attaching the range selector assembly to the tower or bracket, depending on the model.
4. Remove the range selector assembly with the attached cable from the tower and disconnect the shift indicator light wire harness if equipped.
5. Disconnect the cable from the range selector as follows:
6. Remove the U-bolt or clamp that attaches the cable to the hanger on all models.

TELEFLEX CONTROL

1. Loosen the jam nut on the cable core beneath the trunnion and turn the trunnion adjusting nut until it releases the cable core.

CAUTION

Trunnion has been placed in proper hole at factory. If its location is changed in any way, operation of the vehicle could result in personal injury.

MORSE CONTROL

1. First remove the trunnion and cable assembly from the range selector, then loosen the setscrew and remove the threaded cable core from the trunnion.

QUADCO CONTROL

1. Remove the cotter pin securing the trunnion to the range selector lever. Then loosen the jam nut and remove the trunnion from the cable core.

Installation

NOTICE: Do not use pliers on the cable core when tightening the jam nut after positioning the trunnion on the new cable core. The cable core finish may be damaged resulting in cable core seal failure.

Assemble the new cable core to the range selector as follows:

TELEFLEX CONTROL

1. Position the threaded end of the cable core to the trunnion adjusting nut.
2. Turn the adjusting nut to obtain 25 mm (1-inch) dimension.
3. Tighten the jam nut against the adjuster nut and secure the cable core housing to the hanger with a U-bolt.

MORSE CONTROL

1. Adjust the setscrew to the dimension 1/16 inch (1.6 mm) to flush.
2. Thread the trunnion onto the cable core up against the setscrew. Tighten the setscrew to 3 N•m (23 in. lbs.) torque.

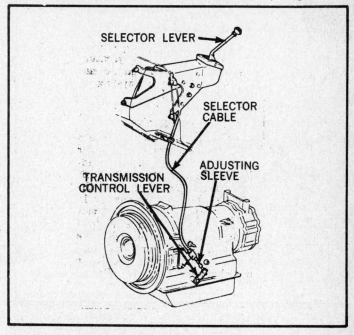

Typical cable routing, MT 650, 653 models (©General Motors Corp.)

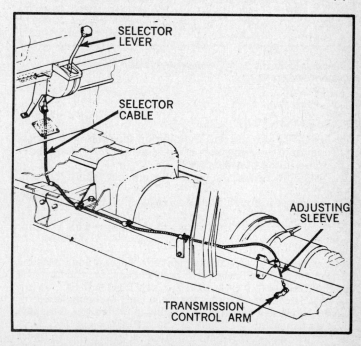

Typical cable routing, MT 640, 643 models (©General Motors Corp.)

735

3. Install the trunnion in its original hole and secure the cable core housing to the hanger with a clamp.

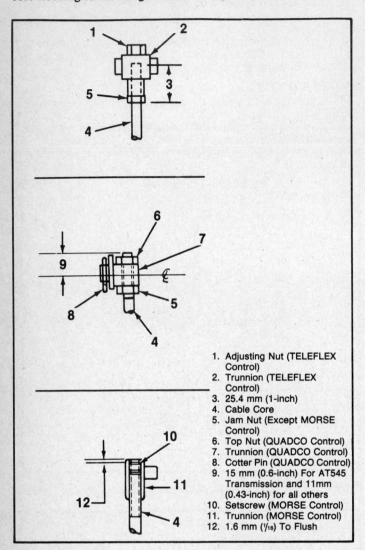

1. Adjusting Nut (TELEFLEX Control)
2. Trunnion (TELEFLEX Control)
3. 25.4 mm (1-inch)
4. Cable Core
5. Jam Nut (Except MORSE Control)
6. Top Nut (QUADCO Control)
7. Trunnion (QUADCO Control)
8. Cotter Pin (QUADCO Control)
9. 15 mm (0.6-inch) For AT545 Transmission and 11mm (0.43-inch) for all others
10. Setscrew (MORSE Control)
11. Trunnion (MORSE Control)
12. 1.6 mm (1/16) To Flush

Trunnion adjustment for MT models and later AT models
(©General Motors Corp.)

QUADCO CONTROL

1. Install the jam nut and trunnion on the cable core. Adjust the trunnion to the dimension of 0.43 inch (11 mm) from center of trunnion to top of cable core.

2. Install the top nut and tighten the jam nut against the trunnion.

3. Install the trunnion in its original hole and secure it with a new cotter pin.

4. Secure the cable core housing to the hanger with a clamp.

ALL MODELS

1. Connect the shift indicator light wire harness and install the shift control cover in the tower or bracket depending on the truck model. Install the four cross-recess screws. Tighten the screws to 5 N•m (4 ft. lbs.) torque. Install the cable clips to the underside of the cab and chassis, and attach the cable to the bracket at the side of the transmission.

2. Adjust the linkage as described earlier in this section under "Shift Linkage Adjustment."

T.V. THROTTLE VALVE LINKAGE

Adjustment

Prior to making any checks or adjustments to the throttle valve transmission control linkage, check engine performance and the accelerator linkage for proper readjustment.

3208-CATERPILLAR AND 8.2 LITER DIESEL ENGINES

1. Secure the cable hub to the mounting bracket and transmission case.
2. Disconnect the clevis return spring.
3. Disconnect the clevis from the fuel lever by removing the cotter pin and washers.
4. Rotate the fuel control lever to Wide Open Throttle position (Not Over-Ride) and hold.
5. Pull the cable all the way out (to built-in stop).
6. Adjust the clevis so the hole in the fuel lever (or fuel lever pin) is aligned with the forward end of clevis slot.
7. Tighten the jam nuts at the clevis.
8. Connect the clevis to the fuel lever by installing the washers and a new cotter pin.
9. Install the clevis return spring and check for free return to idle position.

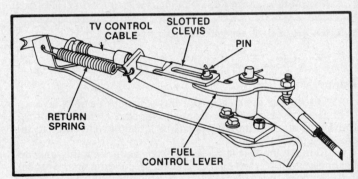

Throttle valve linkage used with the 8.2 Liter diesel engine
(©General Motors Corp.)

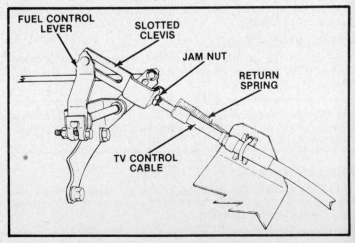

Throttle valve linkage used with the Caterpillar 3208 diesel engine
(©General Motors Corp.)

Shift Speed Adjustments

NOTE: Transmission shift point cannot be satisfactorily adjusted if the transmission has the wrong governor installed. Check the two- or three-digit code on the head of the governor.

MT 640, 643, 650, 653

If the letter "M" follows the two-digit code, the governor is a service replacement assembly. If the "M" is not included, the governor was installed at original factory build.

MT 644, 654CR

Check the three digit code on the head of the governor against that listed for serial numbered transmission being worked on, in an appropriate parts manual.

CALIBRATED ON TEST STAND OR IN VEHICLE.

Proper timing of shift speed points is necessary for maximum transmission performance. Shifts may be adjusted on the test stand when the transmission is rebuilt or overhauled, or during road testing of the vehicle.

Test stand equipment differs among rebuild or overhaul facilities. Some shops may have equipment to drive and load the transmission, with instrumentation for observing performance. Other shops may have test stands on which the valve body and governor can be calibrated before installation into the transmission. If test stand equipment is not available, satisfactory calibrations of shift point may be made after road testing the vehicle.

Location of Adjusting Components.

Shift speeds are changed by changing the positions of adjusting rings that determine the retaining force of certain valve springs in the valve body.

A special tool (J24314—see special tools table) is used to depress and rotate the adjusting rings to the proper positions. Clockwise rotation increases spring force and will raise the shift point. Counterclockwise rotation will reduce spring force, and lower the shift point.

NOTE: Each notch of adjustment will alter the shift point approximately 40 rpm.

Checks Before Adjusting Shift Points

When calibration is to be made during a road test, or on a test stand that simulates road operation, certain preparations must be made.

1. Warm up the transmission or test stand setup to normal operating temperature (160° to 220° F for road test).
2. Check the engine no-load governor setting, and adjust if required, to conform to the transmission's engine speed requirements.
3. Check the engine for satisfactory performance before checking shift points.
4. Check the linkage that controls the mechanical modulator valve actuator in the transmission (diesel) for proper travel, routing and operation. Check condition and routing of vacuum line, hoses and connections for the vacuum modulator use with most gasoline engines.
5. Check the shift selector linkage for proper range selection.
6. Provide accurate instrumentation required for observing speeds, temperatures, pressures, vacuum, etc.

CALIBRATION BY ROAD TEST METHOD

1. Note the no-load governed speed of the engine. This is the base speed from which checks and adjustments are made.
2. Automatic upshifts should occur as follows.
   a. MT 640, 643, 650, 653—Subtract 200 rpm from the no-load governed speed recorded, and record the remainder as the desired speed for all automatic upshifts, except the 1-2 shift of the MT 640, 643 and the 2-3 shift of the MT 650, 653. The latter two shifts should occur at no-load governed speed, less 600 rpm.
   b. MT 644, 654CR—Subtract 100 rpm from the no-load governed speed recorded, and record the remainder as the desired speed for all automatic upshifts, except the 1-2 shift. The

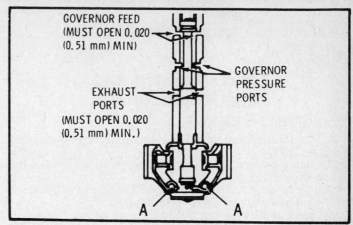

Cross section of the governor assembly (©General Motors Corp.)

latter shift should occur at no-load governed speed less 200 rpm. It is also required that second gear lockup release must occur prior to the 2-1 downshift.

NOTE: Before road test, determine the vehicle tachometer error with a test tachometer. Make corrections for error, as required, in subsequent tests.

3. Drive the vehicle and check the engine speed (at full throttle) at which each upshift occurs. Each upshift should occur at the speed specified above.
4. If an upshift speed does not reach that specified, the shift point may be raised by adjusting (increasing) the spring force on the 1-2, 2-3, 3-4 or 4-5 shift signal valve. If the upshift speed exceeds the specified rpm, or if upshift does not occur at all, the spring force must be reduced. Adjust the force on only the springs for valves that do not upshift at the proper speed.

NOTE: If more than one shift signal valve spring requires adjustment, it may be necessary to adjust the modulator valve one position in the same direction as for the signal valves. If all upshift points are either too high or too low, by approximately the same amount, only the modulator valve should be adjusted.

ALTERNATE METHOD USING SPEEDOMETER READINGS

When a tachometer is not available for checking shift points, the vehicle speedometer can be used. Proceed as outlined below.

1. Check the top speed of the vehicle in each selector hold position (first, second, third gears). Record the top speed for each.
2. For checking the shift points, place the selector at DRIVE (D) so that all automatic shifts can occur. Drive the vehicle at full throttle from a standing start until the 3-4 or 4-5 upshift occurs, recording the mph at which each upshift occurs.
3. **MT 640, 643, 650, 653**—Compare the upshift speeds with the hold speeds recorded in step 2. The 2-3 upshift in the MT 640, 643 should occur at approximately two mph below the top speed for second gear; the 3-4 upshift two mph below top speed for third gear. The 3-4 and 4-5 upshifts for the MT 650, 653 should occur approximately two mph below the top speeds of third and fourth gear, respectively. The 1-2 (MT 640, 643) and 2-3 (MT 650, 653) upshifts are not to be adjusted relative to hold speeds. Instead, the 2-1 downshift (MT 640, 643) or 3-2 downshift (MT 650, 653) should occur, with closed throttle, at 3 to 5 mph.
4. **MT 644, 654CR**—Compare the upshift speeds with the hold speeds recorded in step 2. The 2-3 upshift should occur at approximately 2 mph below the top speed for second gear; the 3-4 upshift 2 mph below top speed for third gear; the 4-5 upshift 2 mph below the top speed for fourth gear. The 1-2 upshift is not to be adjusted relative to hold speeds. Instead, the 2-1 downshift should occur, with closed throttle, at 3 to 5 mph.

737

SERVICES

Fluid Changes and Filter Replacement

Removal and Installation

1. The transmission should be at operating temperature of no less than 160°F.

2. Shift the selector lever in the neutral position and block the vehicle from moving.

3. Place a waste oil container under the oil pan and remove the fluid drain plug and gasket from the pan.

4. Remove the retaining bolts for the oil pan and remove.

5. Remove the bolt holding the filter and remove the filter and discard. Remove the oil suction tube from the transmission and discard the seal ring from the upper end of the suction tube.

6. MT 640, 643, 650, 653 models up to Serial Number 58071 and the early MT 644 models, have a secondary governor oil screen, located in the rear cover and retained by a pipe plug. Remove the pipe plug and filter. If the filter is undamaged, clean it and re-install. If the filter is damaged, replace the filter with a new one. Install the filter in its bore with the open end first and retain it with the pipe plug. Tighten the pipe plug to 4-5 ft. lbs. (5.5-6.7 N•m).

7. MT 640, 643, 650, 653 models after Serial Number 58071, later MT 644 models and MT 654CR models, use a round governor secondary filter, retained by a hex headed plug and sealed with an "O" ring seal to the rear cover. Replace the filter with a new one, install a new "O" ring seal on the hex headed plug and tighten the plug to 50-70 ft. lbs. (68-95 N•m).

8. Install a new seal on the filter tube and either install the tube separately or with the oil filter. Install the retaining screw and tighten to 10-15 ft. lbs. (14-20 N•m).

9. Place the oil pan gasket onto the oil pan. A sealer or cement may be applied only to the area of the oil pan flange that is outside the raised bead of the flange.

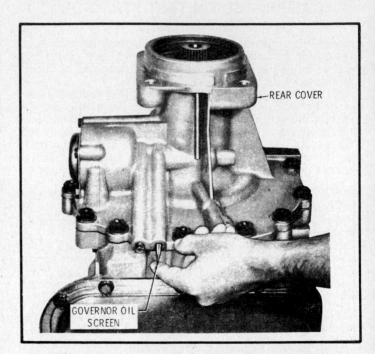

Governor filter screen used prior to serial number 58071 and on all MT 640, 643, 650, 653 and early 644 models (©General Motors Corp.)

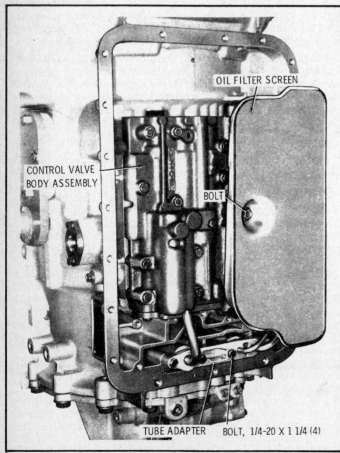

Oil filters used on early model transmissions (©General Motors Corp.)

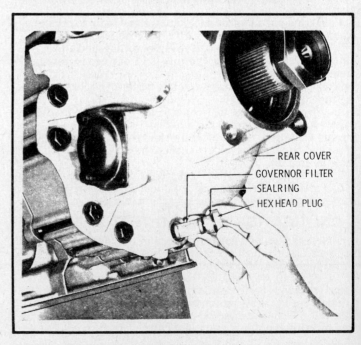

Governor filter screen used after serial number 58070 and on all MT 640, 643, 653, 654CR and later 644 models (©General Motors Corp.)

10. Install the oil pan and gasket to the transmission and retain in place with four retaining bolts, one at each corner. Install the remaining bolts and bottom out before tightening any of the bolts.

11. Alternately tighten the bolts 180° apart to 5 ft. lbs. (6.7 N•m). Repeat the procedure, tightening the bolts to 10-15 ft. lbs. (14-20 N•m).

12. Install the filler tube to the side of the oil pan, if required. Install the drain plug and tighten to 15-20 ft. lbs. (20-27 N•m).

13. Remove the dipstick and install approximately 15 quarts of transmission fluid into the transmission filler tube. Adjust the fluid level accordingly for the transmission model and vehicle combination.

14. Start the engine and allow the transmission to reach normal operating temperature. Recheck and verify the fluid level. Correct as required.

FLUID CONTAMINATION

Examination of fluid

EXAMINE AT OIL CHANGE.

At each oil change, examine the oil which is drained for evidence of dirt or water. A normal amount of condensation will emulsify in the oil during operation of the transmission. However, if there is evidence of water, check the cooler (heat exchanger) for leakage between the water and oil areas. Oil in the water side of the cooler (or vehicle radiator) is another sign of leakage. This, however, may indicate leakage from the engine oil system. Any accumulation of sludge or soft dirt in the sump should be removed.

METAL PARTICLES.

Metal particles in the oil (except for the minute particles normally trapped in the oil filter) indicate damage has occurred in the transmission. When these particles are found in the sump, or on the magnetic plate in the bottom of the oil pan, the transmission must be disassembled and closely inspected to find the source. Metal contamination will require complete disassembly of the transmission and cleaning of all internal and external circuits, cooler, and all other areas where the particles could lodge.

COOLANT LEAKAGE

1. If engine coolant leaks into the transmission oil system, immediate action must be taken to prevent malfunction and possible serious damage. The transmission must be completely disassembled, inspected, and cleaned. All traces of the coolant, and varnish deposits resulting from coolant contamination, must be removed.

2. A Gly-Tek test kit to detect glycol in transmission oil can be obtained from Nelco Company, 1047 McKnight Road South, St. Paul, Minnesota 55119.

NOTE: Some transmission oils will give a positive indication because of "additives" in the oil. When test results are questionable, test a clean (unused) sample of the same type or brand to confirm results.

FOAMING AND AERATING

1. Transmission performance will be affected when the oil foams or aerates. The primary causes of aeration are low oil in the sump, too much oil in the sump, or a defective or missing seal ring on the intake pipe.

2. A low oil level (denoted on the dipstick) will not completely envelope the oil filter. Therefore oil and air are drawn by the input pump and are directed to the clutches and converter, causing converter cavitational noises and irregular shifting. The aeration also changes the viscosity and color to a thin milky liquid.

3. At the normal oil level ("FULL" mark on the dipstick) the oil is slightly below the planetary gear units. If additional oil is added bringing the oil level above the "FULL" mark, the planetary units will run in the oil, foaming and aerating the oil. Overheating and irregular shift patterns can occur when the oil is aerated.

4. A defective seal ring on the filter intake pipe will also cause the input pump to draw air and oil from the sump, causing the same problems as in step 2.

AUXILIARY FILTER

Some vehicles have an auxiliary filter installed in the oil return line (between the oil cooler and transmission) to prevent debris from being flushed into the transmission. If the vehicle does not have an auxiliary filter installed and a debris causing failure occurs, debris can be flushed into the transmission and cause a repeat failure. It is recommended that an auxiliary filter be installed before the vehicle is placed back in service. This recommendation applies whether the failed transmission is overhauled or replaced with a new or rebuilt unit.

Approved filter assemblies, such as the AC type PM 13-7, PF 132W, or PM 16-1, can be used satisfactorily. The filter must have a 40 micron filtering ability. Maximum pressure drop across the filter must not exceed 3 psi (20 kPa) at 8 gpm (30 liters/minute) flow and at 180°F (82°C). Filter burst pressure must be 200 psi (1378 kPa) minimum.

FLUSHING THE OIL COOLER AND LINES

The oil cooler and lines must be flushed following a transmission breakdown. This will help prevent more trouble after the transmission is repaired.

1. Disconnect oil cooler lines at the transmission case. If an auxiliary filter has been previously installed, disconnect the cooler return line at the filter instead of at the transmission. (Change the auxiliary filter element.)

2. Back-flush the oil cooler and lines using clean solvent and compressed air.

NOTICE: DO NOT exceed 689 kPa (100 psi) air pressure or damage may result to oil cooler.

3. Remove all remaining cleaning solvent from the system with compressed air.

4. Flush the cooling system again with transmission fluid. After the final flush, test the oil cooler for free flow of oil. If the flow is restricted, the radiator bottom, tank and cooler assembly must be replaced.

Components

VACUUM MODULATOR

Removal

1. Disconnect the vacuum line from modulator.
2. Remove retaining bolt and retainer.
3. Remove modulator and valve actuating rod from transmission case. Remove the seal ring from the modulator.

Installation

1. Install the valve actuating rod in case, larger diameter end inserted first.
2. Place a new seal ring on modulator. Lubricate the seal ring with oil-soluble grease and install modulator in case.
3. Position the modulator so that vacuum connector pipe faces directly forward. Place retainer on modulator with the bent tabs against transmission and secure with bolt. Reconnect vacuum line.

SELECTOR SHAFT SEAL

Removal

MT 644, 654CR

1. Remove the control linkage from the selector shaft.

2. Place the seal remover tool, Kent Moore J-26401 or its equivalent, over the end of the selector shaft.

3. Drive the seal remover into the oil seal to cause the seal to engage the tool.

4. Screw the seal remover tool center bolt inward to remove the seal from its bore.

Installation

1. Clean the seal bore in the transmission housing.
2. Install the new seal, lip first onto the selector shaft.
3. Using seal installer tool, Kent Moore J-26282-1 or its equivalent, install the seal into its bore.

NOTE: The seal is positioned properly when its outer surface is clear of the lead chamfer in the seal bore.

4. Install the control linkage to the selector shaft.

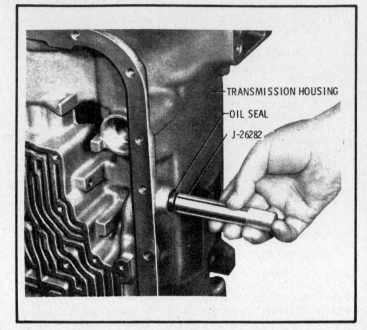

Installation of selector shaft oil seal (©General Motors Corp.)

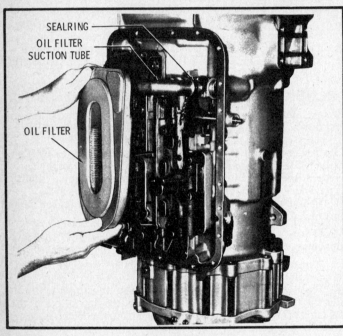

Oil filters used on later model transmissions (©General Motors Corp.)

NEUTRAL START SWITCH

Different types of neutral start switches are used with this type of automatic transmission. On one type, the switch is mounted on the gear box housing and no adjustment is needed or provided for. Another type, the switch is mounted on the steering housing and must be adjusted by loosening the attaching screws and moving the switch either right or left, and retightening the attaching screws. A third type can be mounted on the manual control lever at the transmission and normally, no adjustment is provided for, and replacement of the switch is necessary if a defect occurs in the neutral switch contacts.

CONTROL VALVE BODY

Removal

1. Drain transmission. Remove oil pan, transmission oil filter and oil intake pipe. With the use of a rubber band, secure the range selector valve so as not to lose it.

2. Remove the bolt that retains the detent spring and roller assembly. Remove the assembly.

3. Loosen the two bolts and allow them to remain as guide bolts while removing the other sixteen bolts.

4. Hold the valve body firmly and remove the two guide bolts. Move the control valve body in a downward and outward movement to clear the actuator pin in the housing bore.

5. Remove the check ball from the governor pressure channel recess.

Installation

1. Install the check ball into the governor pressure channel recess.

2. With the selector lever secured, install the valve body so that the actuator pin enters the housing bore.

3. Position the valve body to the transmission case and install the eighteen bolts.

NOTE: Do not tighten at this time.

4. Install the governor oil screen into the bore of the valve body.

5. Install the oil transfer plate and the attached tubes.

6. Engage the selector valve with the detent lever pin. Install the detent spring and lever and install the bolt.

7. Torque the detent lever bolt and the eighteen bolts to 8 to 12 ft. lbs.

8. Install the transmission oil pan and gasket. Install the oil pan bolts and torque to 10 to 15 ft. lbs.

GOVERNOR

Removal

Remove governor cover and gasket from case. Rotate the governor clockwise to disengage drive gears. Remove governor.

Installation

Install governor in case, replace gasket and cover.

EXTENSION HOUSING REAR OIL SEAL

Removal

1. Disconnect drive shaft. Remove the output flange components and the parking brake linkage.
2. Remove parking brake drum.
3. Remove seal with proper tool.

Installation

1. Lubricate the oil seal lip with a high temperature grease. Coat the outer edge of oil seal with a non-hardening sealer.

2. Place the oil seal, lip first, squarely into rear of transmission case. Using a seal installer, drive the oil seal into case until driver contacts against case.

NOTE: The oil seal should be .51 to .55 inch forward of brake mounting surface on case.

3. Install output flange components. Tighten retaining bolts to 83 to 100 foot pounds torque. Stake the tab washer into the flange washer and bend the tab washer against a flat of the bolt head.

4. Install the parking brake drum, parking brake linkage and drive shaft.

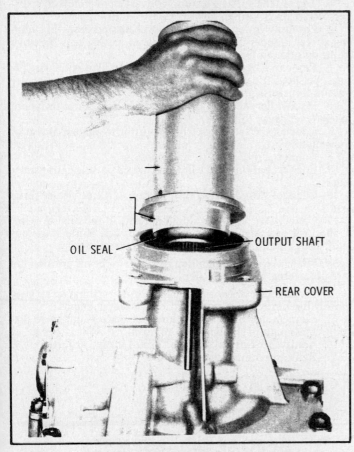

Installing rear cover oil seal typical (©General Motors Corp.)

RETAINING OUTPUT FLANGE

Thrust washer failures at the rear planetary carrier are due to the flange retaining bolt not being properly tightened, or loosening during operation.

MT 640, 643

1. Install a new ½-20 x 1½ inch bolt (181431 or 9409060 or equivalent) and a ½-inch special lockwasher (6752556 or equivalent) to retain the output flange. Be sure the threads of the bolt and mating threads in the output shaft are clean and not damaged.

2. If bolt 181431 (or equivalent) is used, tighten the bolt to 83-100 ft. lbs. (113-136 N•m). If bolt 9409060 (or equivalent) is used, tighten the bolt to 96-115 ft. lbs. (130-156 N•m). Stake the edge of the washer into the hole in the retainer washer, and bend the other side against a flat of the retaining bolt head.

MT 644 BOLT AND WASHER

1. If the new bolt has a nylon patch, install the flat washer and bolt into the output shaft. Tighten the bolt to 102-121 ft. lbs. (138-164 N•m).

2. If the new bolt is plain (without nylon patch) install the bent washer and bolt into the output shaft. Tighten the bolt to 96-115 ft. lbs. (130-156 N•m). Then stake the washer into the hole in the retainer washer and bend the bent part against a flat of the bolt head.

MT 650, 653, 654CR

1. The output flange retainer nut is self-locking. It may be reused up to a maximum of five times if minimum removal torque limits are met.

2. Before removing the nut, clean the output shaft threads to remove dirt, contamination. Remove any burrs or thread damage that may be present.

3. The first time the retaining nut is removed from the shaft, it must take a minimum of 400 in. lbs. (45 N•m) to rotate the nut from the shaft; each subsequent time the nut must require at least 300 in. lbs. (34 N•m) to remove it from the shaft. (The torque values must be measured after the initial breakaway torque required to loosen the output flange nut from the output flange is achieved.)

4. Each time the nut is reused, deeply scribe one of the flats on the nut; this will allow field service personnel to determine how many times the nut has been reused and prevent the nut from being used more than the maximum limit of five times.

5. Before installing the output flange retainer nut onto the output shaft, be sure the output shaft and retainer nut threads are clean and free from damage.

NOTE: Installation of the output shaft flange nut requires 600-800 ft. lbs. (814-1085 N•m). To prevent thread galling and inaccurate torque readings due to increased friction, lubricate the threads of the output shaft and flange retainer nut prior to installation.

6. Lubricate the threads of the output shaft and retainer nut with transmission fluid or Molykote type G (or equivalent). Install the nut and tighten to 600-800 ft. lbs. (814-1085 N•m).

—————— CAUTION ——————

The use of an impact wrench requires a means to hold the flange. Failure to hold the flange can cause internal damage to the transmission.

REMOVAL & INSTALLATION

NOTE: Since applications will differ from model to model it must be understood that the following general procedures apply to all vehicles. It may be necessary to remove the air tanks, fuel tanks, special equipment, etc. on some vehicles to provide clearance for removal.

Transmission Removal

1. Block vehicle so that it cannot move. Disconnect ground strap from battery negative (—) post. Remove the spark plugs so the engine can be turned over manually, if equipped with gasoline engine.

2. Remove the level gauge (dipstick). Drain transmission. disconnecting filler tube at right side of transmission pan. Remove bracket holding filler tube to transmission and remove filler tube from vehicle. Replace dipstick in tube and cover the pan opening to prevent entry of foreign material.

Transmission mounted on low transmission jack assembly for removal or installation. Note the safety chain (©General Motors Corp.)

3. Disconnect cooler lines from fittings on side of transmission case. Plug line ends and case openings with lint-free material.

4. Disconnect the range selector cable from shift lever at left side of transmission.

5. Disconnect vacuum modulator line from modulator, if equipped. Also, on conventional cab models, disconnect wiring from neutral safety and back-up lamp switches. On diesel engine models, disconnect the modulator and modulator control valve from the transmission.

6. Disconnect the speedometer shaft fitting from adapter at rear of transmission.

7. Disconnect the propeller shaft from transmission.

8. Disconnect the mechanical parking brake linkage at the right side of the transmission (if used).

9. Through the opening in the flywheel housing, use a pry-bar, as necessary to manually turn the flywheel. As the flywheel is rotated, remove the six bolts retaining flywheel flex plate assembly to converter cover.

NOTE: The oil filter may have to be removed on gasoline V-8 engines to gain access to converter attaching bolts.

10. Support the transmission with a 500-pound (minimum) transmission floor jack. The jack must be positioned so transmission oil pan will not support the weight of transmission. Fasten a safety chain over top of transmission and to both sides of jack.

11. Place a support under rear of engine and remove transmission case-to-crossmember support bolts. Raise the engine to remove weight from the engine rear mounts.

12. Remove the transmission case-to-flywheel housing bolts and washers.

13. Carefully inspect transmission and surrounding area to be sure no lines, hoses, or wires will interfere with transmission removal.

NOTE: When removing transmission, keep rear of transmission lower than the front so as not to lose converter.

14. Move transmission assembly from the engine, lower the assembly carefully and move it out from the vehicle.

15. Install converter holding tool, if necessary.

Transmission Installation

1. Raise vehicle sufficiently to allow installation of transmission. With transmission assembly mounted on transmission jack move transmission into position aligning converter with flywheel. Check for and clean away any foreign material in flywheel pilot hole, flex-plate assembly, and front face of transmission case. Rotate flywheel as necessary so that the six studs in converter cover are aligned with holes in flex plate. Carefully move transmission assembly toward engine so flex-plate-to-converter cover nuts can be loosely installed and so that pilot on transmission converter enters pilot hole in center of flywheel.

2. Install bolts and washers that attach transmission case-to-flywheel housing. Tighten bolts to specified foot-pounds torque.

3. Tighten the six flex-plate-to-converter cover nuts to specified foot-pounds torque.

4. Carefully lower engine and transmission assembly onto engine rear mounts. Tighten engine rear mounting nuts. Remove lifting equipment from beneath vehicle.

5. Remove plugs from cooler lines and transmission case fittings. Be sure fittings are clean and lint-free, then connect cooler lines-to-transmission.

6. Install filler tube and bracket on right side of transmission. Install level gauge (dipstick).

7. Connect the speedometer shaft fitting to adapter at rear of transmission.

8. Connect drive shaft to transmission.

9. Connect parking brake linkage (if used) at side of transmission.

10. Connect shift cable to shift lever at left side of transmission.

11. Connect the vacuum modulator line to modulator. Also, connect wiring to neutral safety switch (left side of transmission) and back-up lamp switch (right side of transmission).

NOTE: Make sure the ignition switch is in the off position before proceeding to the next step.

12. Install spark plugs and connect battery ground strap, previously disconnected. If equipped with gasoline engine.

13. Connect any other lines, hoses, or wires which were disconnected to aid in transmission removal.

14. Adjust the shift linkage (see "Shift Linkage Adjustment").

15. Refill the transmission.

BENCH OVERHAUL

BEFORE DISASSEMBLY

A transmission overhaul stand should be used to mount the transmission, in order to have the front, rear and bottom of the unit freely accessible for removal and installation of the internal components. The fixture holding plate is attached to the PTO opening on the side of the transmission case. It should be noted, not to allow the fixture holding plate attaching bolts to project into the inside of the transmission case, preventing the removal and installation of the internal components. Because of the weight factor of the complete unit and its internal components, a lifting device should be available and used as required during the disassembly and assembly of the unit to prevent personal injury or damage to the unit.

Disassembly

1. With the transmission installed in a holding device and in a vertical position, remove the converter from the transmission with a lifting tool.

2. Remove the modulator, if equipped, the oil pan and oil filter.

3. a. **MT 640, 643, 644 models**—Remove the tubes from the valve body, marking them for reassembly. Remove the modulated lock-up valve body, the tube adapter and control valve body assembly. Secure the range selector valve with a rubber band to prevent the valve from falling from the valve body during the removal. Remove governor check ball, if equipped.

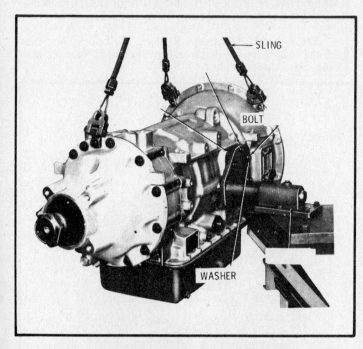

Transmission assembly mounted in a holding fixture with lifting device attached (©General Motors Corp.)

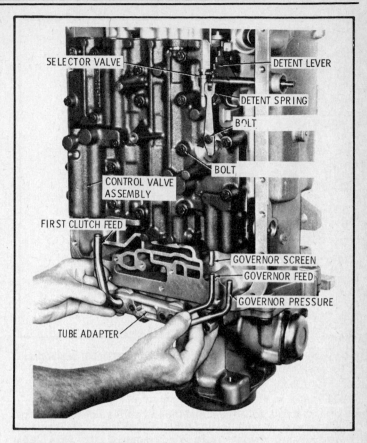

Removing tubes from MT 640, 643, 644 models after the modulated lock-up valve body has been removed (©General Motors Corp.)

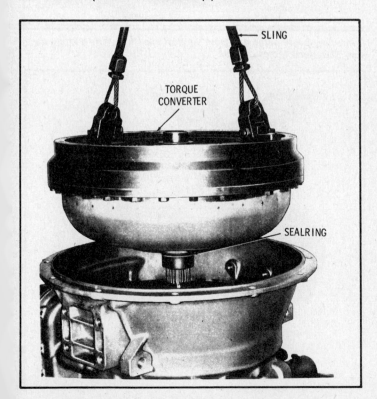

Removing torque converter assembly (©General Motors Corp.)

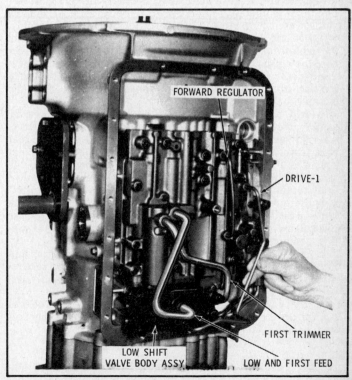

Removing oil tubes from the valve body components, MT 650, 653 models (©General Motors Corp.)

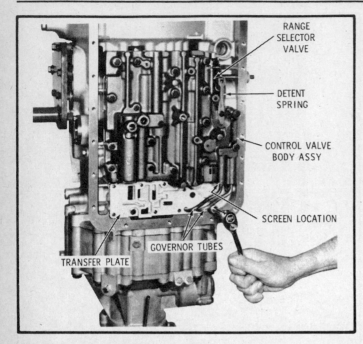

Removing the low shift valve oil transfer plate, MT 650, 653 models (©General Motors Corp.)

b. **MT 650, 653**—Remove the low shift valve assembly by first removing the following tubes; Drive-1, forward regulator (The forward regulator tube is not required after SN 47284), low and first feed and the first trimmer. If the tubes are fastened to the control valve body with bolts, remove the bolts and the tubes. Remove the low shift valve assembly and the separator plate that is directly behind the valve body. Remove the low shift oil transfer plate and two governor tubes as an assembly. Remove the filter screen from the tube bore in the control valve assembly and discard the filter. Using a rubber band, secure the range control valve in the valve body. Remove the retaining bolts from the valve body and remove it from the transmission housing. Remove the governor check ball from the housing.

c. **MT 654CR**—Remove the modulated lock-up valve assembly, the low trimmer valve assembly and the low shift signal valve assembly. On models equipped with the second gear start feature, remove the separator plate. Remove the detent spring and roller assembly, and attach a rubber band to the range selector valve to hold in position. Remove the valve body retaining bolts and remove the control valve assembly.

6. Remove the twelve bolts and rubber covered washers holding the front support and oil pump assembly. With the use of a collar type lifting tool, remove the oil pump and front support assembly from the transmission housing.

d. **MT 640, 643, 650, 653 models**—Remove the bearing and one race at the rear of the support assembly (the second race remains on the support hub). Remove the support assembly gasket.

e. **MT 644, 654CR**—Remove the bearing and the two races from the rear of the support assembly. Remove the support assembly gasket.

NOTE: The front support and pump assembly are fitted into the transmission with very little clearance. If the housing is cold, the unit may bind. If so, heat the housing with a sun lamp or stream of warm air. Never use a torch to heat the transmission case.

4. Grasp the turbine shaft and lift the forward clutch and attached P.T.O. gear, along with the fourth clutch hub from the housing. Remove the bearing and two races from the rear of the clutch.

NOTE: The P.T.O. gear is not present in all models.

5. Remove the fourth clutch assembly from the transmission by grasping the spring retainer and lifting the assembly from the housing.

a. **MT 640, 643, 650, 653**—Remove the bearing and race from the rear of the clutch assembly (the second race remains on the center support hub).

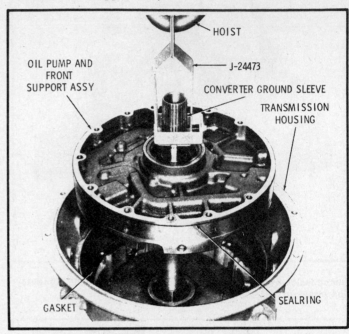

Removing the oil pump and front support assembly with a lifting device (©General Motors Corp.)

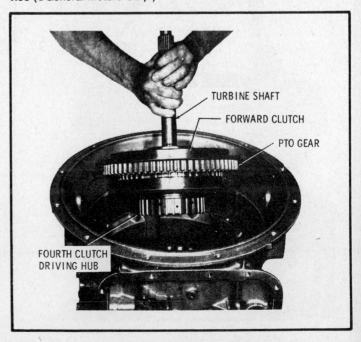

Removing the forward clutch and turbine shaft assembly (©General Motors Corp.)

b. **MT 644, 654CR**—Remove the bearing race from the rear of the clutch assembly.

6. Remove the snap ring retaining the back plate for the third clutch and remove the back plate and the six clutch plates.

7. Remove the center support anchor bolt from the case and remove the snap ring retaining the center support to the case.

8. With the use of a grasping tool, lift the center support from the transmission.

a. **MT 644, 654CR**—Remove the two seal rings and roller bearing assembly from the center support hub.

NOTE: Due to very little clearance between the center support and the case, a binding condition may exist. Heat the case with a heat lamp or direct a stream of warm air over the case. Do not use a torch to heat the case.

9. a. **MT 650, 653, 654CR**—Use a grasping tool and lift the gear unit from the transmission housing.

b. **MT 640, 643, 644**—Remove the governor cover and remove the governor assembly from the case. Using a grasping tool, lift the gear unit and mainshaft assembly from the housing. Remove the governor drive gear, the speedometer drive gear and then the sleeve spacer.

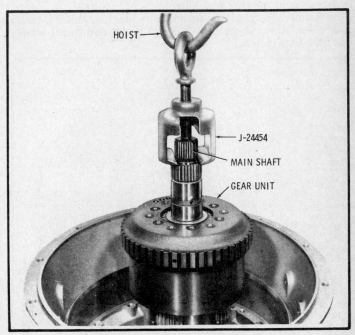

Removing the gear unit from the transmission case, typical of all models (©General Motors Corp.)

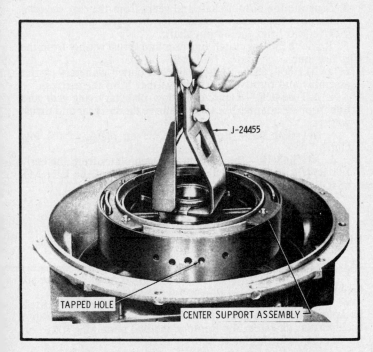

Removing the center support assembly (©General Motors Corp.)

Removal of the fourth clutch assembly (©General Motors Corp.)

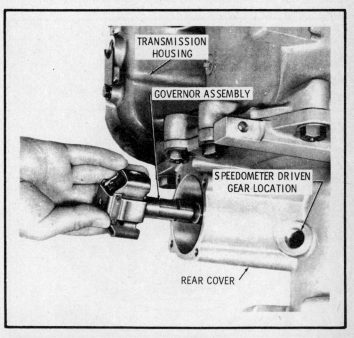

Removing the first clutch plate and ring gear (©General Motors Corp.)

745

SECOND AND FIRST CLUTCHES

Disassembly

MT 650, 653, 654CR

1. Remove the positioning snap ring for the center support assembly. Remove the six plates (eight plates—MT 654CR models) of the second clutch and remove the backing plate.

2. Remove the first clutch ring gear and hub assembly from the housing. Remove the snap ring and separate the first clutch ring gear from the ring gear hub.

3. Remove the retaining snap ring and remove the first clutch back plate. Remove the twelve clutch plates and thrust washer from the first clutch.

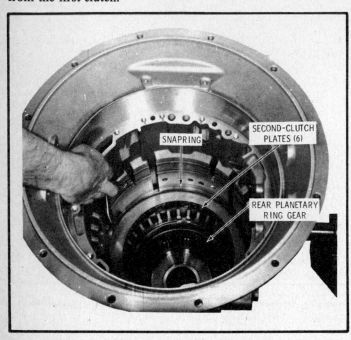

Removing the second clutch snap ring (©General Motors Corp.)

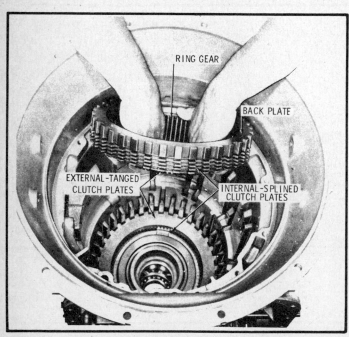

Removing the back plate, first clutch plates and the rear planetary ring gear, MT 640, 643 models (©General Motors Corp.)

REAR COVER, LOW CLUTCH COMPONENTS

Disassembly

MT 650, 653, 654CR

NOTE: MT 650 transmission models having serial numbers 49996 through 55402 may include a spacer between the output flange and the output shaft rear bearing. This spacer should be used at re-assembly except when the output shaft is replaced. If the letter "F" is not stamped after the serial number within the above range, a spacer, part number 6883908 should be installed, unless the output shaft is being replaced.

1. Remove the governor cover and gasket. Remove the governor from its bore and remove the rear cover bolts.

2. Attach a lifting sling to the output shaft and with an upward movement, raise the output shaft and rear cover from the adapter housing.

3. Separate the output shaft and gears from the rear cover.

4. Remove the spacer, speedometer drive gear and the governor drive gear from the output shaft.

5. Remove the low clutch ring gear and thrust washer from the ring gear hub.

6. a. **MT 650, 653**—Remove the low clutch planetary carrier assembly and remove the thrust washer from the carrier.

   b. **MT 654CR**—Remove the low planetary ring gear and hub from the adapter housing. Remove the sun gear and thrust washer.

   c. **MT 650, 653**—Remove the eleven plates of the low clutch.

   d. **MT 654CR**—Remove the thirteen plates from the early MT 654CR models and the fifteen plates from the later MT 654CR models.

SECOND AND FIRST CLUTCHES, REAR COVER

Disassembly

MT 640, 643, 644

1. Remove the positioning center support snap ring, the six (eight on MT 644) clutch plates and the backing plate.

2. Remove the retaining snap ring for the first clutch backplate, ten clutch plates (nine on the MT 644), ring gear and back plate as an assembly. Remove the two remaining (three on the MT 644) clutch plates.

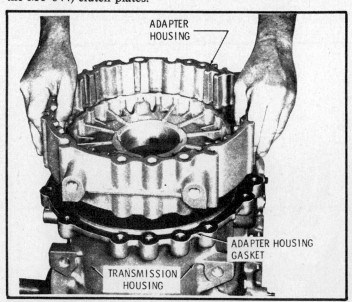

Removal of the adapter housing, MT 654CR models (©General Motors Corp.)

NOTE: The lock-up valve and main pressure regulator valve snap rings can be removed at the same time with the use of a special compression tool for the valve springs.

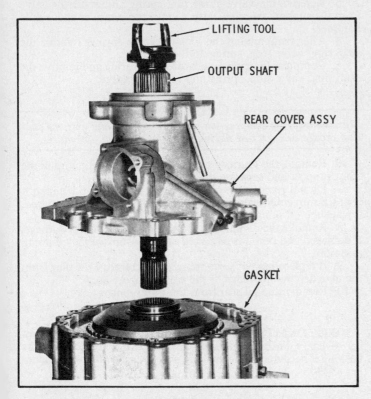

Lifting the rear cover assembly from the transmission, MT 650, 653 models (©General Motors Corp.)

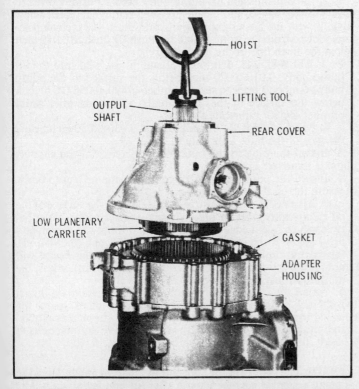

Lifting the rear cover assembly from the transmission, MT 654CR models (©General Motors Corp.)

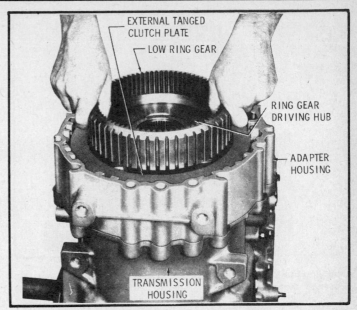

Removing the low planetary ring gear and hub assembly, MT 654CR models (©General Motors Corp.)

Removing the low planetary ring gear, MT 650, 653 models (©General Motors Corp.)

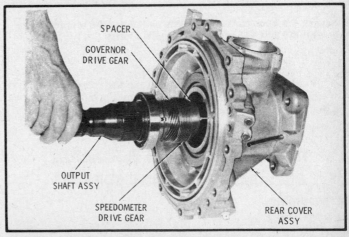

Removal of the output shaft assembly from the rear cover, MT 650, 653 models (©General Motors Corp.)

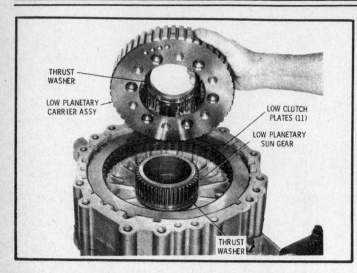

Removing the low planetary carrier assembly, MT 650, 653 models (©General Motors Corp.)

Labels on image: THRUST WASHER, LOW PLANETARY CARRIER ASSY, LOW CLUTCH PLATES (11), LOW PLANETARY SUN GEAR, THRUST WASHER

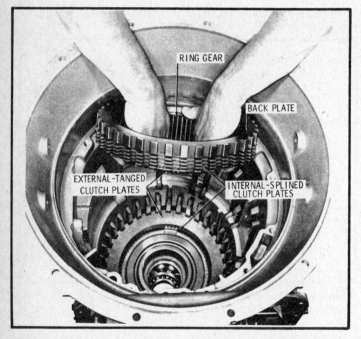

Removing the back plate, first clutch plates and the rear planetary ring gear, MT 640, 643 models (©General Motors Corp.)

Labels on image: RING GEAR, BACK PLATE, EXTERNAL-TANGED CLUTCH PLATES, INTERNAL-SPLINED CLUTCH PLATES

3. Invert the transmission and remove the speedometer driven gear. Remove the rear cover to case retaining bolts and remove the rear cover and gasket.

Individual Unit
Disassembly and Assembly
OIL PUMP AND FRONT SUPPORT

Disassembly

ALL MODELS

1. Remove the two hook type seal rings (all Models), needle bearings and bearing race from the hub of the front support (MT 640, 643, 650, 653 models).

2. Remove the oil pump seal ring from the hub and the needle bearing from the inside diameter of the converter ground sleeve, if replacement is necessary.

3. Remove the valve guide pin, spring and regulator valve from the support assembly with a valve pin remover and a slide hammer.

4. After compressing the lock-up valve spring, remove the snap ring, valve stop, spring and valve.

5. Compress the main regulator valve spring and remove the snap ring, valve stop, spring and regulator valve.

----------- CAUTION -----------

Maximum spring compression measures 65 lbs. and extreme caution should be exercised during the valve removal procedures.

6. Remove the fourteen bolts that retain the oil pump to the front support and separate the two units.

7. Do not remove the ground sleeve from the front support. If much movement is apparent or the ground sleeve is damaged, replace the oil pump assembly.

8. Remove the oil pump gears and inspect them for damage. If damaged and pump is damaged or worn, replace the oil pump assembly.

9. If replacement of parts are required, remove the plug from the outside circumference of the front support body.

10. Remove the oil seal from the pump body.

NOTE: On MT 640, 643, 650, 653 models prior to serial number 49490, a bushing was used in the pump body. Replace the bushing if necessary. The bushing was not used after serial number 49490.

Assembly

1. If the transmission oil pump body used a bushing prior to serial number 49490, and the bushing was removed, install a new bushing with the bushing splitline within the 10-12 o'clock position, viewed from the front. Install the bushing flush to 0.010 inch below the flush line of the pump body.

2. a. **MT 640, 643, 650, 653**—Install a new seal into the oil pump body, 0.010-0.020 inch below the surface of the pump body on models prior to serial number 49490, 0.050-0.070 inch below the surface of the pump body on models after serial number 49490. Lubricate the seal.

   b. **MT 644, 654CR**—Install the seal 0.030-0.050 inch below the face of the hub. Lubricate the seal.

3. Install the plug in the outer circumference of the support body, if removed.

4. Install the pump gears in place within the oil pump body. Measure the clearance as follows:

   a. **All models**—Place a straight edge across the surface of the oil pump with gears in place. Insert a feeler gauge blade between the straight edge and the surface of both the driven and drive gears. If the clearance exceeds 0.0024 inch (0.061 mm), the gears and/or the pump body are worn. If the new gears will not reduce the clearance to 0.0024 inch (0.061 mm) or less, the oil pump must be replaced.

5. Install the front support on the oil pump assembly, install two 5/16 inch bolts 180° apart and tighten a few threads. Install the entering band around the oil pump and front support assembly. Install the remaining bolts and torque the twelve 5/16 inch bolts to 17-20 ft. lbs. and the two 3/8 inch bolts to 36-43 ft. lbs.

NOTE: The surface of the split line of the front support and the oil pump assembly must be smooth after the bolt installation. The tolerance between this surface and the transmission housing is critical.

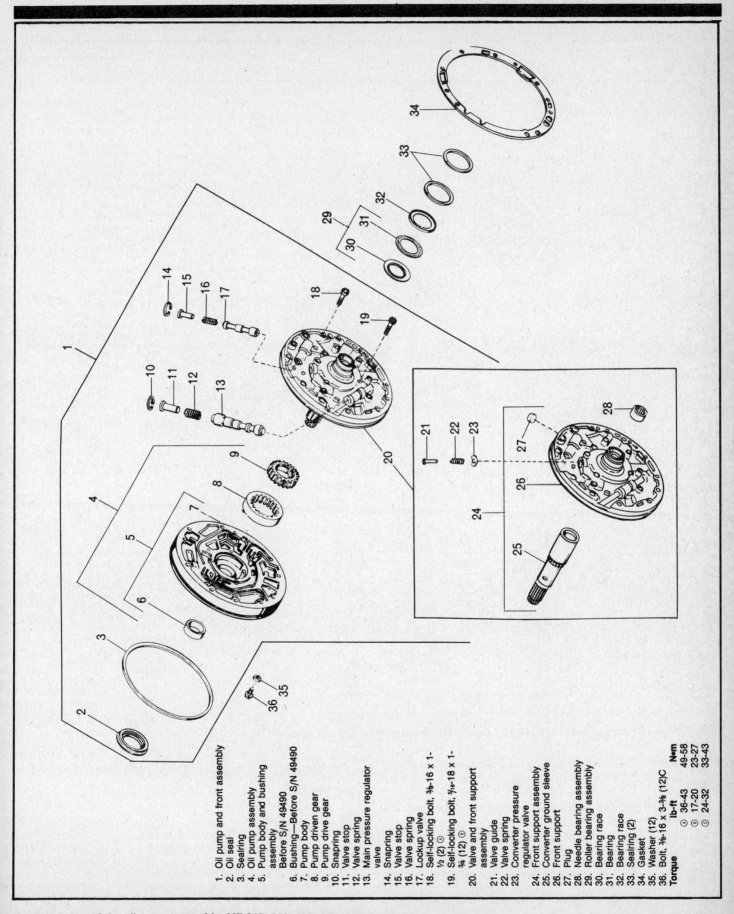

1. Oil pump and front assembly
2. Oil seal
3. Sealring
4. Oil pump assembly
5. Pump body and bushing assembly
6. Bushing—Before S/N 49490
   Before S/N 49490
7. Pump body
8. Pump driven gear
9. Pump drive gear
10. Snapring
11. Valve stop
12. Valve spring
13. Main pressure regulator valve
14. Snapring
15. Valve stop
16. Valve spring
17. Lockup valve
18. Self-locking bolt, ⅜-16 x 1-½ (2) ⓐ
19. Self-locking bolt, ⁵/₁₆-18 x 1-¾ (12) ⓑ
20. Valve and front support assembly
21. Valve guide
22. Valve spring
23. Converter pressure regulator valve
24. Front support assembly
25. Converter ground sleeve
26. Front support
27. Plug
28. Needle bearing assembly
29. Roller bearing assembly
30. Bearing race
31. Bearing
32. Bearing race
33. Sealring (2)
34. Gasket
35. Washer (12)
36. Bolt, ⅜-16 x 3-⅜ (12)C

Torque	lb-ft	N•m
ⓐ	36-43	49-58
ⓑ	17-20	23-27
ⓒ	24-32	33-43

Exploded view of the oil pump assembly, MT 640, 643, 650, 653 models (©General Motors Corp.)

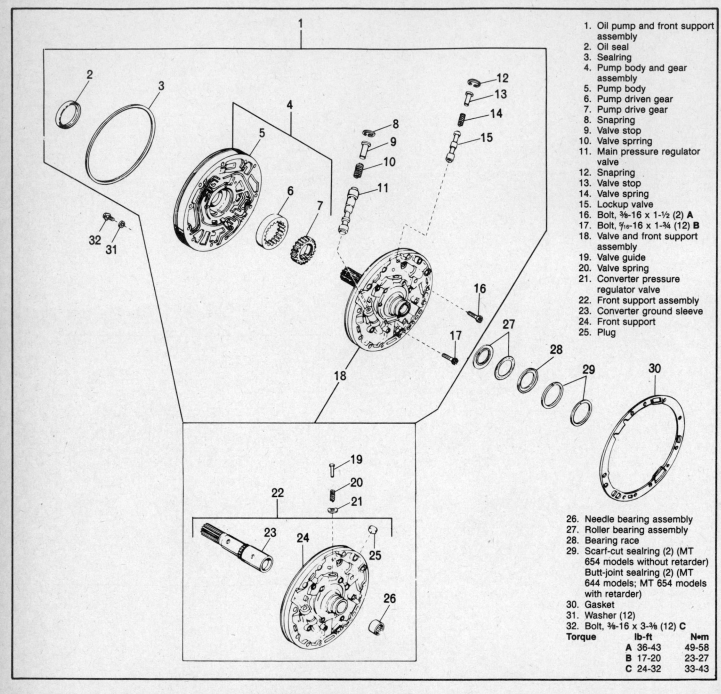

1. Oil pump and front support assembly
2. Oil seal
3. Sealring
4. Pump body and gear assembly
5. Pump body
6. Pump driven gear
7. Pump drive gear
8. Snapring
9. Valve stop
10. Valve sprring
11. Main pressure regulator valve
12. Snapring
13. Valve stop
14. Valve spring
15. Lockup valve
16. Bolt, ⅜-16 x 1-½ (2) **A**
17. Bolt, ⁵⁄₁₆-16 x 1-¾ (12) **B**
18. Valve and front support assembly
19. Valve guide
20. Valve spring
21. Converter pressure regulator valve
22. Front support assembly
23. Converter ground sleeve
24. Front support
25. Plug
26. Needle bearing assembly
27. Roller bearing assembly
28. Bearing race
29. Scarf-cut sealring (2) (MT 654 models without retarder)
    Butt-joint sealring (2) (MT 644 models; MT 654 models with retarder)
30. Gasket
31. Washer (12)
32. Bolt, ⅜-16 x 3-⅜ (12) **C**

Torque	lb-ft	N•m
A	36-43	49-58
B	17-20	23-27
C	24-32	33-43

Exploded view of the oil pump assembly, MT 644, 654CR models (©General Motors Corp.)

6. Install the needle bearing into the front support gound sleeve with appropriate tools, until the bearing is 1.240-1.260 inch (31.50-32.00 mm) from the face of the hub.

NOTE: The installed bearing must be able to withstand a 200 pound load without moving in the hub.

7. Install the lock-up valve, spring, valve stop and snap ring. Install the main regulator valve, spring, valve stop and snap ring.

8. Install the pressure regulator valve and the spring on the valve guide pin. Press the assembly into the support housing. The guide pin must extend 1.16-1.20 inch above the finished surface.

9. Lubricate the seal rings and install them into the slot on the oil pump body.

FORWARD CLUTCH AND TURBINE SHAFT
Disassembly

MT 640, 643, 650, 653

1. Remove the seal rings from the housing.

2. If the centrifugal valve components are located in the clutch housing assembly (after serial number 49489), the assembly must be positioned with the turbine shaft downward.

3. Remove the P.T.O. gear (if equipped) by compressing the snap ring. Located within the gear, to allow the gear to slide from the clutch housing.

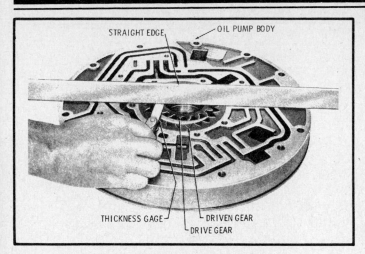

Measuring driven gear end clearance (©General Motors Corp.)

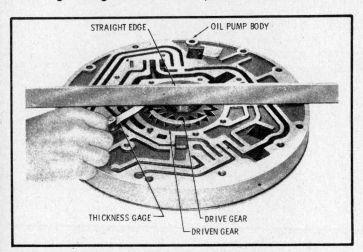

Measuring driven gear end clearance (©General Motors Corp.)

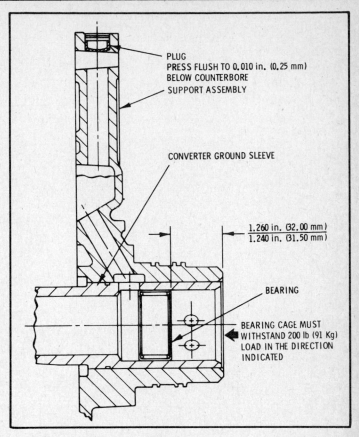

PLUG
PRESS FLUSH TO 0.010 in. (0.25 mm)
BELOW COUNTERBORE
SUPPORT ASSEMBLY

CONVERTER GROUND SLEEVE

1.260 in. (32.00 mm)
1.240 in. (31.50 mm)

BEARING

BEARING CAGE MUST
WITHSTAND 200 lb (91 Kg)
LOAD IN THE DIRECTION
INDICATED

Installation of the outer plug and needle bearing assembly, typical
(©General Motors Corp.)

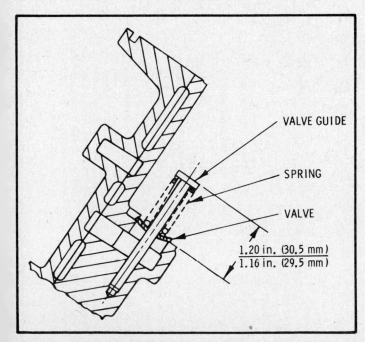

VALVE GUIDE

SPRING

VALVE

1.20 in. (30.5 mm)
1.16 in. (29.5 mm)

Installation of the converter pressure regulator valve
(©General Motors Corp.)

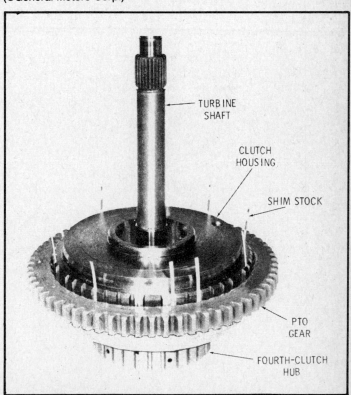

TURBINE
SHAFT

CLUTCH
HOUSING

SHIM STOCK

PTO
GEAR

FOURTH-CLUTCH
HUB

Use of shim stock to compress the snap ring during the removal of the P.T.O. gear (©General Motors Corp.)

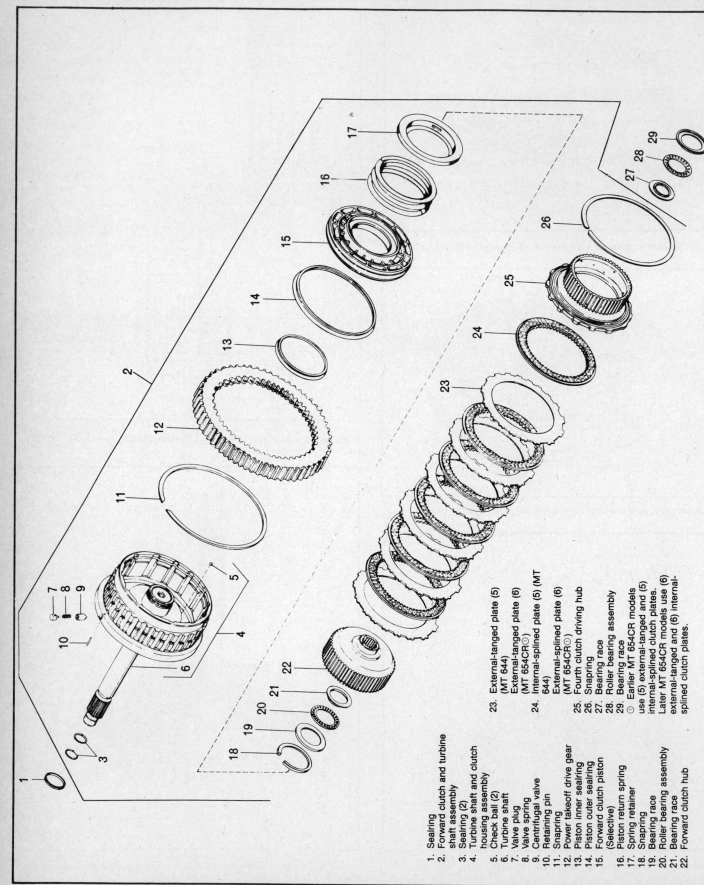

1. Sealring
2. Forward clutch and turbine shaft assembly
3. Sealring (2)
4. Turbine shaft and clutch housing assembly
5. Check ball (2)
6. Turbine shaft
7. Valve plug
8. Valve spring
9. Centrifugal valve
10. Retaining pin
11. Snapring
12. Power takeoff drive gear
13. Piston inner sealring
14. Piston outer sealring
15. Forward clutch piston (Selective)
16. Piston return spring
17. Spring retainer
18. Snapring
19. Bearing race
20. Roller bearing assembly
21. Bearing race
22. Forward clutch hub
23. External-tanged plate (5) (MT 644)
    External-tanged plate (6) (MT 654CR⊙)
24. Internal-splined plate (5) (MT 644)
    External-splined plate (6) (MT 654CR⊙)
25. Fourth clutch driving hub
26. Snapring
27. Bearing race
28. Roller bearing assembly
29. Bearing race
⊙ Earlier MT 654CR models use (5) external-tanged and (5) internal-splined clutch plates. Later MT 654CR models use (6) external-tanged and (6) internal-splined clutch plates.

Exploded view of the forward clutch and turbine shaft assembly, MT 644, 654CR models (©General Motors Corp.)

9. Press turbine shaft from housing only if replacement is necessary. To press the shaft from the housing, place the assembly, shaft downward, in a press. Support the assembly at the front hub of the housing.

Assembly

1. If the turbine shaft was removed, press a new one in place against the housing. To insure a satisfactory fit, a minimum of 250 pounds press out force is required.

2. Install the centrifugal valve, conical end first, into its bore in the forward clutch housing. Install the spring and plug. Retain the plug with the pin. Press the pin into the bore until it protrudes 0.080-0.100 inch (2.03-2.54 mm) above the front surface of the clutch housing.

3. If the balls were removed, install them in their bore and stake in three places around each bore to retain the balls. Each ball must have at least 0.020 inch (0.51 mm) axial movement and each stake must be able to withstand a 30 pound load applied against the ball.

4. Position the clutch housing and shaft assembly downward and lubricate and install the piston seal rings in their grooves in the housing hub and piston.

NOTE: Be sure the seal ring lips face towards the oil pressure side of the piston. If the seal rings are installed incorrectly, the forward clutch will not operate.

5. Install the piston into the housing, being careful not to damage the seal rings.

NOTE: Either the direct measurement method or the stack dimension computation method can be used to deteremine clutch clearance which must be established during the assembly. The stack dimension computation method is normally used when quantity or assembly line overhaul practices are used, requiring the use of new clutch plates.

6. **Direct measurement method**—Alternately install the five external tanged plates and the five internal splined plates, starting with an external tanged plate. Install the fourth clutch drive hub and retain it with a snap ring.

NOTE: Later MT 654CR models use six internal splined clutch plates and six external tanged clutch plates.

7. Hold the fourth clutch drive hub firmly against the snap ring and using a go, no go gauge or feeler gauge blade, check the clearance between the fourth clutch drive hub and the internal splined clutch plate. The correct clearance for the ten plate forward clutch is 0.079-0.130 inch (2.00-3.30 mm). The correct clearance for the twelve plate forward clutch is 0.094-0.148 inch (2.39-3.75 mm). When the clearance is obtained, and a go, no-go gauge is used, the smaller end will fit between the hub and the plate and the larger end will not. If needed, new clutch plates, thicker or thinner pistons would have to be obtained.

8. Upon completion of the direct measurement method procedure, remove the snap ring that retains the fourth clutch drive hub and remove the hub. Remove the clutch plates, both internal and external.

NOTE: Soak the internal splined clutch plates in transmission fluid for at least two minutes before reassembly into the clutch housing.

9. **Stack Method**—Stack the clutch plates on a hard surface and place the forward clutch hub on the top of the clutch plate stack. With a press, apply a 980-1020 pound pressure on the clutch pack and clutch hub. Measure the distance from the inner top of the clutch hub to the hard surface of the support. Refer to the accompanying chart for stack dimensions for the ten and twelve clutch packs, and select the correct piston.

10. Place the clutch housing and shaft assembly and assembled piston on a press bed and install the piston return spring, spring retainer and position the snap ring on the hub. Using a

compressor or the press, depress the spring retainer sufficiently to install the snap ring in its groove in the housing hub.

11. Install the bearing race, outer lip first, onto the hub of the forward clutch housing. Apply oil soluble grease to the bearing and the bearing race before installing them into the forward clutch hub. Install the bearing, flat side first, into the inner hub. Install the bearing onto the race.

12. Position the clutch housing and shift downward and place the forward clutch hub, splined OD first, into the hub of the forward clutch housing. Re-install the clutch plates, starting with an external tanged clutch plate. Install the fourth clutch drive hub and retain it with a snap ring.

13. If the model is equipped with a P.T.O. gear, invert the assembly and install the snap ring into the forward clutch housing. Heat the P.T.O. gear to 375° F. (190° C) maximum, and install the gear, chamfered end of splines first. Be sure the retaining snap ring springs outward into the groove in the splines.

14. Install two hook type seal rings at the base of the shaft and one near the end of the shaft. Retain with oil soluble grease. Install the bearing race, outer lip first, onto the hub of the clutch housing. Retain with oil soluble grease.

FOURTH CLUTCH

Disassembly
ALL MODELS

1. Remove the bearing race from the front hub housing (MT 640, 643, 650, 653) and the bearing race from the rear hub of the fourth clutch housing.

2. With the aid of a compressor tool, depress the spring retainer so that the snap ring can be removed. Remove the snap ring that retains the backing plate and remove the plate from the housing.

NOTE: On later MT 654CR models, a spacer is used directly under the spring.

3. Remove the eight clutch plates and the piston. Remove the seal rings from the piston and from the fourth clutch housing.

NOTE: Later MT 654CR models use ten clutch plates.

4. If necessary, remove the check balls from the housing.

Assembly

1. If the check balls were removed, replace them and stake at three equally spaced places on the housing and piston.

NOTE: Each ball must have at least 0.200 inch (0.51 mm) axial movement and each stake must be able to withstand a 30 pound load applied against the ball.

2. Lubricate and install the piston seal rings in the piston and housing hub. Face the seal ring lips towards the oil pressure side of the piston.

NOTE: Either the direct measurement method or the stack dimension computation method can be used to determine clutch clearance which must be established during the assembly. The stack dimension computation method is normally used when quantity or assembly line overhaul poractices are used, requiring the use of new clutch plates.

3. **Direct Measurement Method**—Install the piston into the fourth clutch housing. Alternately install the four external tanged clutch plates and the four internal splined clutch plates. Install the backing plate and retain it with a snap ring.

4. Using either a go, no-go or a feeler gauge blade, measure the clearance between the backing plate and the first internal splined clutch plate. The correct clearance is 0.064-0.125 inch (1.625-3.175 mm). If the clearance is not correct, and new clutch plates are used, a thicker or thinner piston will have to be selected.

NOTE: The correct clearance for the ten plate fourth clutch is 0.068-0.127 inch (1.73-3.22 mm).

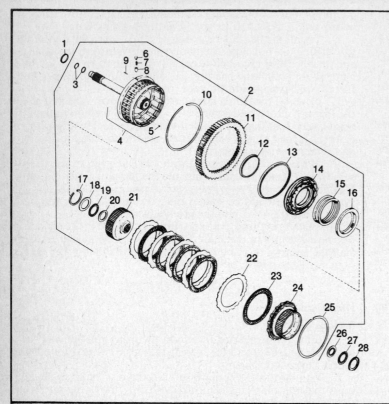

1. Sealring
2. Forward clutch and turbine shaft assembly
3. Sealring (2)
4. Turbine shaft and clutch housing assembly
5. Check ball (2)
6. Valve plug After S/N 49489
7. Valve spring After S/N 49489
8. Centrifugal valve After S/N 49489
9. Retainer pin After S/N 49489
10. Snapring
11. PTO drive gear
12. Housing sealring
13. Piston sealring
14. Forward clutch piston (ar):
    0.995—1.005 inch (25.27-25-53 mm) thk (A)
    1.020—1.030 inch (25.91-26.16 mm) thk (B)
    1.045—1.055 inch (26.54-26.80 mm) thk (C)
15. Forward clutch piston ring
16. Spring retainer
17. Snapring
18. Bearing race
19. Roller bearing assembly
20. Bearing race
21. Forward clutch hub
22. External-tanged plate (5)
23. Internal-splined plate (5)
24. Fourth-clutch driving hub
25. Snapring
26. Bearing race
27. Roller bearing assembly
28. Bearing race

Exploded view of the forward clutch and turbine shaft assembly, MT 640, 643, 650, 653 models (©General Motors Corp.)

NOTE: To compress the snap ring evenly, insert ten pieces of steel shim stock (3/32 x 0.020 x 3 inch) between the snap ring and the P.T.O gear evenly and equally in the 360 degree circle and push the gear from the housing.

4. Remove the snap ring retaining the fourth clutch hub in the forward clutch housing and remove the fourth clutch hub and the forward clutch hub from the housing.

5. Remove the bearing and bearing race(s) from the forward clutch hub.

6. Remove the five internal splined plates and the five external tanged plates from the forward clutch housing.

7. With the aid of a compression tool, depress the spring retainer and remove the snap ring. Remove the retainer, piston return spring and piston. Remove the seal rings from the piston and housing.

8. Remove the balls from the housing and shaft assemblies, only if replacement is necessary.

9. On models after serial number 49489, remove the pin plug, valve spring and the centrifugal valve from the outer circumference of the forward clutch housing.

NOTE: The centrifugal valve may have been incorporated in some models prior to serial number 49489 through field service repairs. These transmissions so modified should have the letter "M" stamped on the name plate.

Assembly

1. On models with the centrifugal valve assembly, reassemble the components into the outer circumference of the forward clutch housing.

NOTE: Be sure the color code of any new parts are the same as the parts replaced and each new part must be identically coded.

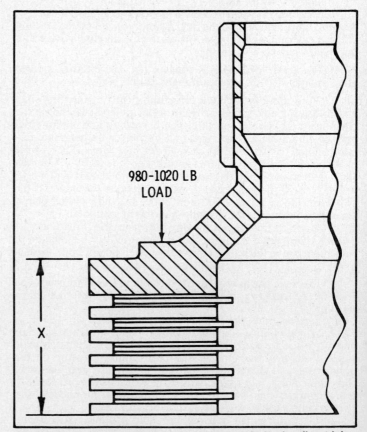

980-1020 LB LOAD

X

Stack method of measurement for the forward clutch, all models (©General Motors Corp.)

2. Replace the balls into the housing and shaft assembly, if removed. Stake in three equal places to retain the balls.

NOTE: The balls should have at least a 0.020 inch axial movement and be retained by the stakes when a 30 pound load is applied against the balls.

3. Lubricate and install the piston seal rings into their grooves in the housing hub and piston.

NOTE: Make sure the seal ring lips face towards the oil side of the piston, otherwise the forward clutch will not operate properly.

4. Install the piston into the forward clutch housing carefully, so as not to cut the seal ring.

NOTE: Either the direct measurement method or the stack dimension computation can be used to determine clutch clearance which must be established during the assembly. The stack dimension computation method is normally used when quantity or assembly line overhaul practices are used, requiring the use of new clutch plates.

5. **Direct Measurement Method**—Alternately install the five external tanged plates and the five internal splined plates. Install the fourth clutch drive hub and retain it with a snap ring.

6. Measure the running clearance of the forward clutch by holding the fourth clutch driving hub firmly against the snap ring and using a go, no-go gauge or a feeler gauge blade, measure the clearance between the fourth clutch driving hub and the internal splined plates. The operating clearance should be 0.079-0.130 inch (2.01-3.30 mm). If needed, new clutch plates, thicker or thinner piston would have to be installed to gain the proper operating clearance of the unit.

7. Upon completion of the direct measurement method procedure, remove the snap ring that retains the fourth clutch driving hub and remove the hub with the clutch plates.

8. **Stack Method**—Stack the forward clutch plates on a hard surface and place the fourth clutch hub on the top of the stack. With a press, apply a 980-1020 pound load on the clutch pack and clutch hub. Measure the distance from the inner top of the clutch hub to the hard surface of the support. Refer to the accompanying chart for stack dimensions and select the correct piston.

9. Place the clutch housing and shaft assembly with the assembled piston on a press or a compression tool and compress the spring retainer enough to install the snap ring into its groove in the housing hub.

10. Install the bearing race, outlip first, into the hub of the forward clutch housing.

NOTE: Use oil soluble grease to hold the races and bearings in place to prevent the dislocation of either race or bearing assembly during the assembly procedure.

11. Install the other bearing race, flat side first, into the inner hub of the forward clutch hub and install the bearing onto the race. Retain with oil soluble grease.

12. Place the forward clutch hub, splined OD first, onto the hub of the forward clutch housing. Reinstall the ten clutch plates, starting with an external tanged plate.

13. Install the fourth clutch drive hub and retain it with the snap ring.

14. Install the P.T.O. gear snap ring onto the forward clutch housing. Install the P.T.O. gear, chamfered side first, from the rear of the housing, forward until the snap ring engages its mating groove in the gear.

15. Install the bearing race, flat side last, and bearing into the hub of the forward clutch. Retain the bearing components with oil soluble grease.

16. Install the two seal rings at the base of the shaft and one near the end of the shaft. Install the bearing race, outer lip first, onto the hub of the clutch housing and retain the seal rings and bearings with oil soluble grease.

FORWARD CLUTCH AND TURBINE SHAFT ASSEMBLY

Disassembly

MT 644, 654CR

1. Remove the hook type seal rings from the forward clutch and turbine shaft.

2. Remove the snap ring. Remove the fourth clutch hub and forward clutch hub from the housing.

3. Remove the bearing races and bearing from the clutch or housing hubs. Remove the clutch plates from the forward clutch housing.

4. With the use of a press or a compression type tool, depress the spring retainer and remove the retainer snapring. Remove the retainer, piston return spring and piston. Remove the seal rings from the piston and housing assembly.

5. Remove the balls from the housing, only if replacement is necessary.

6. Remove the pin plug, centrifugal valve, valve spring and plug from the outer circumference of the housing assembly.

7. If the transmission is equipped with a P.T.O. gear, remove the gear by compressing the snap ring and pressing the gear from the housing.

8. To compress the snap ring, locate the opening (missing spline) nearest the snap ring gap. Insert a small screwdriver into the opening and press the snap ring into its groove in the housing. Then slip a piece of shim stock that is 3/32 x 0.020 x 3-in. (2.36 x 0.50 x 76 mm) between the snap ring and the inner ends of the gear splines. Repeat the operation at the other side of the snap ring gap. Then, working at each missing spline opening, insert strips of shim stock at approximately 3-in. (72 mm) increments. With all shims in place, position the assembly, shaft downward, in a press. Support the PTO gear and press the housing from the gear. Remove the snap ring.

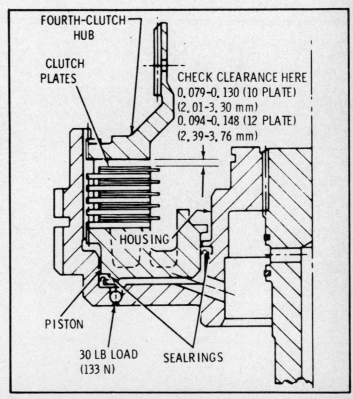

Direct measurement of the forward clutch running clearance, MT 644, 654CR models (©General Motors Corp.)

755

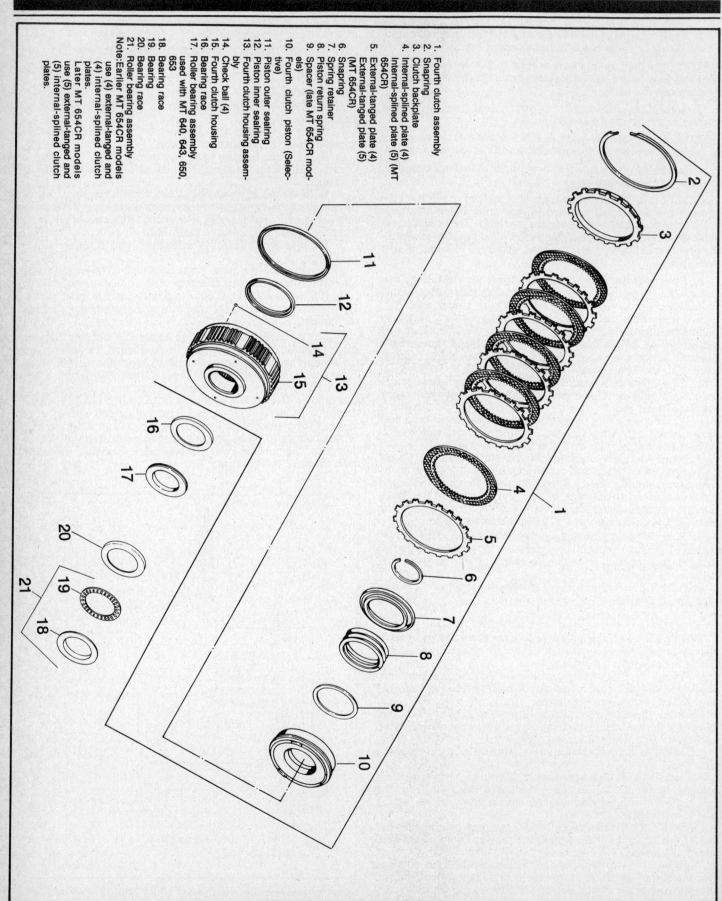

1. Fourth clutch assembly
2. Snapring
3. Clutch backplate
4. Internal-splined plate (4)
   Internal-splined plate (5) (MT 654CR)
5. External-tanged plate (4)
   External-tanged plate (5) (MT 654CR)
6. Snapring
7. Spring retainer
8. Piston return spring
9. Spacer (late MT 654CR models)
10. Fourth clutch piston (Selective)
11. Piston outer sealring
12. Piston inner sealring
13. Fourth clutch housing assembly
14. Check ball (4)
15. Fourth clutch housing
16. Bearing race
17. Roller bearing assembly
    used with MT 640, 643, 650, 653
18. Bearing race
19. Bearing
20. Bearing race
21. Roller bearing assembly

Note: Earlier MT 654CR models use (4) external-tanged and (4) internal-splined clutch plates.
Later MT 654CR models use (5) external-tanged and (5) internal-splined clutch plates.

Exploded view of the fourth clutch assembly (©General Motors Corp.)

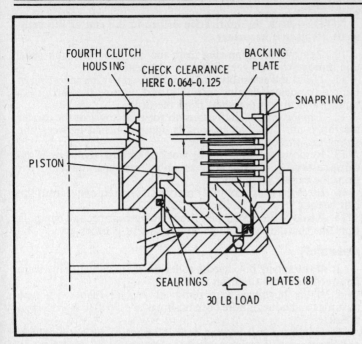

Direct measurement of the fourth clutch running clearance, all models (©General Motors Corp.)

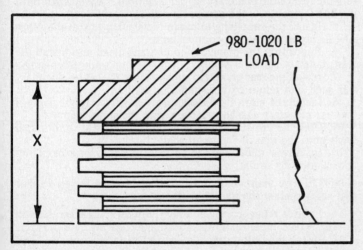

Stack method of measurement for the fourth clutch, all models (©General Motors Corp.)

5. **The Stack Method**—Stack the clutch plates on a hard surface and place the backing plate on the top of the clutch plate stack. With a press, apply a 920-1020 pound pressure on the clutch pack and the backing plate. Measure the distance from the inner top of the backing plate to the hard surface of the support. Refer to the accompanying chart for the stack dimensions for the eight and ten plate clutch pack, and select the correct piston.

6. Install the piston return spring and spring retainer. Using a compressor tool, depress the spring retainer and install the snap ring to retain the spring retainer.

7. With the clutch pack removed from the housing, soak the internal splined clutch plates for approximately two minutes in transmission fluid and install in the housing. Install the backing plate and the snap ring.

8. Install the bearing race, outer lip first, onto the hub of the clutch housing. Use an oil soluble grease to retain the race during the assembly.

CENTER SUPPORT

Disassembly
ALL MODELS

1. Remove and discard the fourth clutch filter screen and seal ring, located in the fourth clutch pressure passage (MT 644, 654CR models). Remove the pistons with their attached parts.

NOTE: Earlier MT 644, 654CR models may not be equipped with the filter screen and seal ring.

2. Remove the inner and outer seal rings from each piston.
3. Disassemble the piston assemblies. Cut the self-locking retainer rings to prevent damage to the piston projections.
4. Remove the four self-locking retainer rings, the retainer and the twenty springs from each piston.
5. Remove the two step joint seal rings and a roller bearing assembly from the hub of the center support assembly.
6. Remove the bushing from the support assembly, if worn or damaged. Remove the check ball that is freed during the bushing removal.

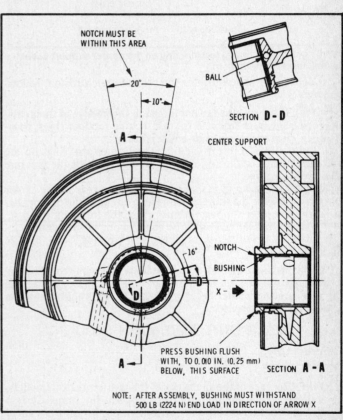

Installation of bushing in the center support. Note the position of the check ball (©General Motors Corp.)

Assembly

1. Replace the bushing and ball in the center support, if removed.
2. Place the third clutch piston, temporarily, into the front piston cavity of the center support assembly.
3. Install the springs into the pocket of the piston and align the spring retainer of the four ejector pin bosses of the piston. Compress the springs by forcing the retainers into the recess at the outer edge of the center support, when the self locking retainer rings are installed.
4. Install a new self locking retainer ring on each of the ejector pins of each piston. Remove the piston from the center support.

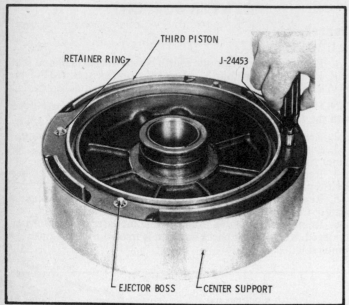

RETAINER RING THIRD PISTON J-24453

EJECTOR BOSS CENTER SUPPORT

Installing the self-locking retainer ring on the center support assembly (©General Motors Corp.)

5. Repeat the procedure for the second clutch piston, following steps 2 to 4.

NOTE: If the pistons are not forced to the bottom of their cavities during the installation of the self locking retainer rings, proper clutch clearance cannot be established.

6. Lubricate and install the inner and outer seal rings on the pistons. The lips of the seal rings must face towards the pressure side of the pistons.

7. Install the second clutch piston into the rear of the center support, but leave the third clutch piston out until the final installation of the center support assembly into the transmission case.

8. Install the seal ring into the center bore of the center support. Install a new filter through the seal ring (MT 644, 654CR models).

NOTE: Earlier MT 644, 654CR models will require machining of the fourth clutch pressure port to permit installation of the seal ring and screen. Counter bore tool, J-29032 or its equivalent, can be used for this purpose.

GEAR UNIT AND MAIN SHAFT

Disassembly
ALL MODELS

NOTE: Because of the similarity of the gear units in all models, the majority of the rebuilding procedures are the same. Certain changes in the disassembly and assembly procedures will be noted as the rebuilding process is being accomplished.

1. Remove the thrust washer from the front of the gear unit. Remove the front sun gear and the thrust washer from the gear.

2. Lift off the front planetary carrier assembly. Remove the thrust washer from the assembly.

3. Remove the center sun gear shaft assembly.

4. Remove the bearing assembly and race from the sun gear shaft assembly.

5. Remove the snap-ring that retains the front planetary ring gear and remove the ring gear.

6. Remove the center planetary carrier assembly.

7. Remove the main shaft and attaching parts from the planetary connecting drum.

8. Remove the thrust washers from the front of the shaft.

9. Remove the spiral snap-ring that retains the rear planetary sun gear on the main shaft and remove the main shaft.

NOTE: Check the lubrication orifice in the end of the main shaft. Replace if necessary.

10. Remove the snap-ring from the rear planetary sun gear, and remove the sun gear from the ring gear.

11. Invert the assembly and remove the retaining snap-ring of the rear planetary carrier assembly, and remove the carrier assembly and the output shaft from the drum.

12. Tap the output shaft assembly forward, towards the carrier assembly, until the ball bearing is lightly pinched between the spring pin and carrier assembly.

13. Remove the snap-ring by working through the front of the carrier assembly. Tap the shaft assembly rearward, and remove it from the carrier assembly.

14. Press the shaft assembly rearward, and remove it from the ball bearing.

15. Remove the spring pin, needle roller bearing, and cup plug from the shaft, only if the part replacement is necessary.

Assembly

1. If the spring pin, needle roller bearing, and cup plug were removed, reinstall them on the shaft.

2. If the bushings were removed, replace them with new bushings and hone or bore both bushings to 1.5640 to 1.5655 inch diameter.

3. Install the ball bearing onto the front of the output shaft, and position the bearing against the spring pin.

4. Install the shaft assembly with the bearings front end first, into the rear of the planetary carrier assembly. Tap the shaft until the bearing contacts the carrier rear hub.

5. Install the snap-ring to retain the shaft, and seat the snap-ring firmly in the carrier counter bore.

6. Reposition the planetary connecting drum and install the rear planetary carrier assembly. Install the retaining snap-ring.

7. Install the rear planetary sun gear into the center planetary ring gear, and retain with a snap-ring.

8. Install the main shaft assembly, rear first, into the front of the rear planetary sun gear. Retain with the spiral snap-ring.

9. Coat the thrust washers with oil soluble grease and install them onto the rear of the main shaft.

10. Install the main shaft and attaching parts, into the planetary connecting drum.

NOTE: The main shaft must seat against the thrust washer that seats against the output shaft.

11. Lubricate the bearing and race with oil soluble grease, and install the race, inner lip upward. Install the bearing onto the race.

12. Install the center planetary carrier assembly, pinions first, into the center planetary ring gear, and retain it with a snap-ring.

13. Install the center sun gear shaft assembly to seat on the bearing assembly.

14. Lubricate the thrust bearings and install into the rear hub of the front planetary carrier assembly and install the carrier assembly.

15. Install a lubricated thrust washer into the rear of the front sun gear. Install the missing internal spline tooth with the spring pin in the center sun gear shaft assembly.

16. Install a lubricated thrust washer onto the center sun gear shaft.

NOTE: In later assemblies, the thrust washers may be replaced with thrust bearing assemblies.

OUTPUT SHAFT

Removal
MT 650, 653

1. Remove the spring pin, shaft and place the shaft into a press and remove the ball bearing.

2. Remove the needle bearing and core plug, only if necessary.

1. Gear unit and shaft assembly
2. Thrust washer
3. Front sun gear
4. Thrust washer
5. Front planetary carrier assembly
6. Pinion pin (6)
7. Bronze thrust washer (12)
8. Steel thrust washer (12)
9. Pinion (6)
10. Roller bearing (12)
11. Front planetary carrier assembly
12. Bushing
13. Thrust washer
14. Snapring
15. Front planetary ring gear
16. Center planetary carrier assembly
17. Pinion pin (4)
18. Center planetary carrier
19. Bronze thrust washer (8)
20. Steel thrust washer (8)
21. Pinion (400)
22. Roller bearing (72)
23. Sun gear shaft assembly
24. Spring pin (2)
25. Shaft and bushing assembly
26. Bushing (2)
27. Shaft
28. Needle roller bearing assembly
29. Bearing race
30. Planetary connecting drum
31. Snapring
32. Center planetary ring gear
33. Main shaft assembly
34. Lubrication orifice plug
35. Main shaft
36. Rear planetary sun gear
37. Rear planetary carrier assembly
38. Needle roller bearing assembly
39. Roller bearing assembly
40. Rear planetary carrier
41. Bronze thrust washer (8)
42. Steel thrust washer (8)
43. Pinion (40)
44. Bearing roller (72)
45. Pinion pin (4)
46. Needle roller bearing
47. Snapring
48. Low sun gear
49. Snapring

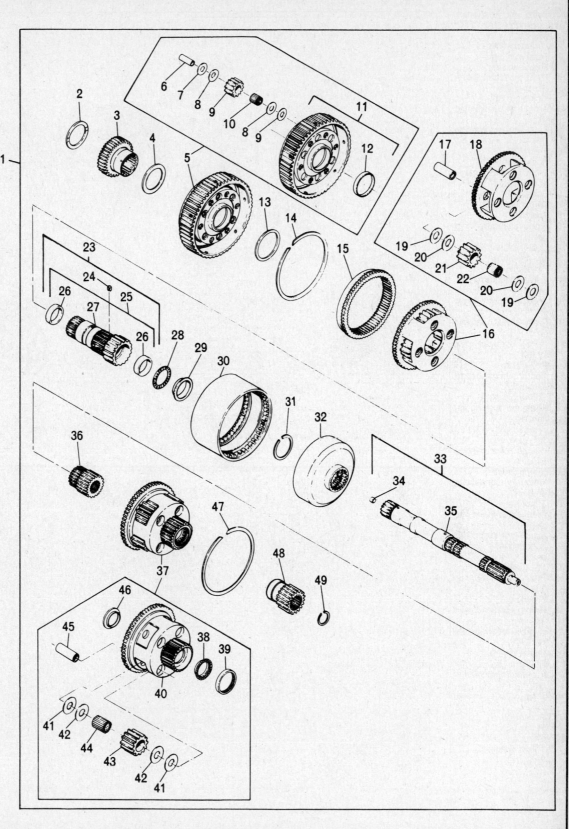

Exploded view of gear unit assembly, MT 654CR models (©General Motors Corp.)

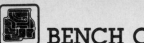

1. Gear unit and shaft assembly (MT 650, 653)
2. Thrust washer
3. Front sun gear
4. Thrust washer
5. Front planetary carrier assembly
6. Pinion pin (6)
7. Bronze thrust washer (12)
8. Steel thrust washer (12)
9. Pinion (6)
10. Roller (120)
11. Front planetary carrier assembly
12. Bushing
13. Thrust washer
14. Snapring
15. Front planetary ring gear
16. Center planetary carrier assembly
17. Pinion pin (4)
18. Center planetary carrier
19. Bronze thrust washer (8)
20. Steel thrust washer (8)
21. Center planetary pinion (4)
22. Roller (72)
23. Center sun gear shaft assembly
24. Spring pin (2)
25. Shaft and bushing assembly
26. Sleeve bushing (2)
27. Sun gear shaft
28. Needle roller bearing assembly
29. Bearing race
30. Planetary connecting drum
31. Snapring
32. Center planetary ring gear
33. Main shaft assembly
34. Lubrication orifice plug
35. Main shaft
36. Rear planetary sun gear
37. Snapring
38. Rear planetary carrier assembly
39. Needle bearing assembly
40. Pinion pin (4)
41. Rear planetary carrier
42. Bronze thrust washer (8)
43. Steel thrust washer (8)
44. Roller (72)
45. Pinion (4)
46. Snapring
47. Thrust washer

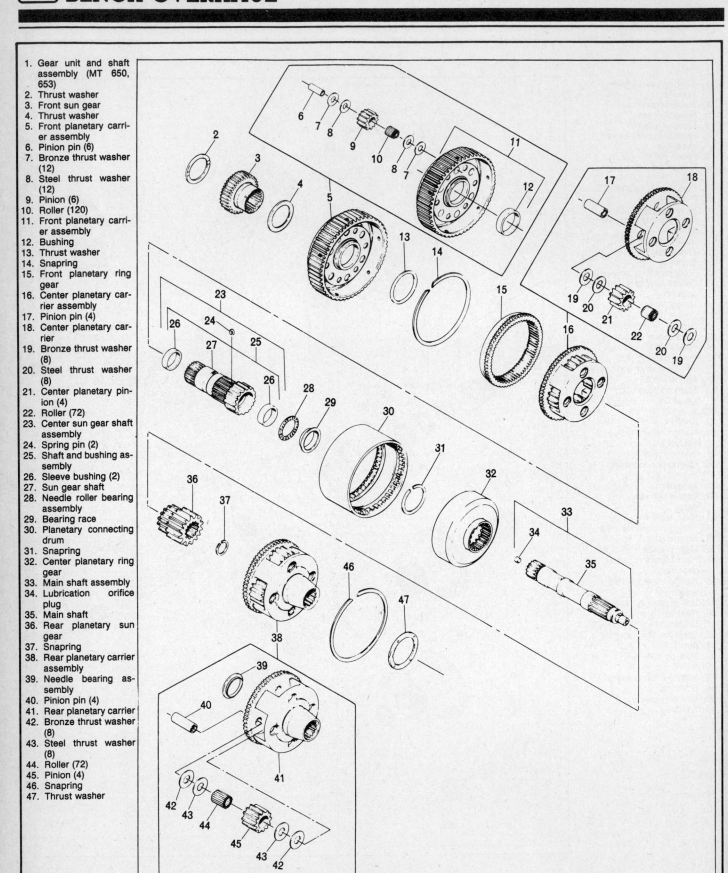

Exploded view of gear unit assembly, MT 650, 653 models (©General Motors Corp.)

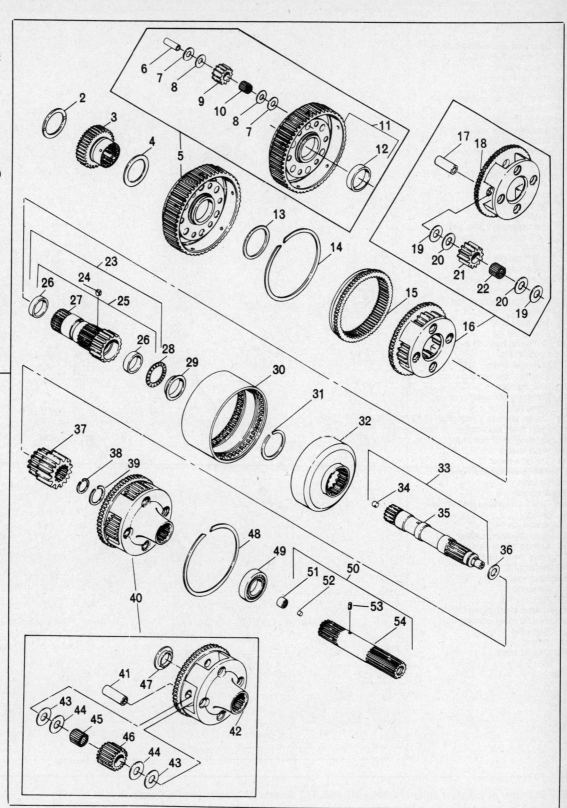

1. Gear unit and main shaft assembly
2. Thrust washer
3. Front sun gear
4. Thrust washer
5. Front planetary carrier assembly
6. Pinion pin (6)
7. Bronze thrust washer (12)
8. Steel thrust washer (12)
9. Front planetary pinion (6)
10. Roller (120)
11. Front planetary carrier assembly
12. Bushing
13. Thrust washer
14. Snapring
15. Front planetary ring gear
16. Center planetary carrier assembly
17. Pinion pin (4)
18. Center planetary carrier
19. Bronze thrust washer (8)
20. Steel thrust washer (8)
21. Center planetary pinion (4)
22. Roller (72)
23. Sun gear shaft assembly
24. Spring pin (2)
25. Shaft and bushing assembly
26. Bushing (2)
27. Shaft
28. Needle roller bearing
29. Bearing race
30. Planetary connecting drum
31. Snapring
32. Center planetary ring gear
33. Main shaft assemblly
34. Lubrication orifice plug
35. Main shaft
36. Thrust washer①
37. Rear planetary sun gear
38. Snapring
39. Snapring①
40. Rear planetary carrier assembly
41. Pinion pin (4)
42. Rear planetary carrier
43. Bronze thrust washer (8)
44. Steel thrust washer (8)
45. Roller (72)
46. Pinion (4)
47. Needle roller bearing assembly①
48. Snapring①
49. Ball bearing①
50. Output shaft assembly①
51. Needle roller bearing①
52. Cup plug①
53. Spring pin①
54. Output shaft①
① Not used with models equipped with a retarder

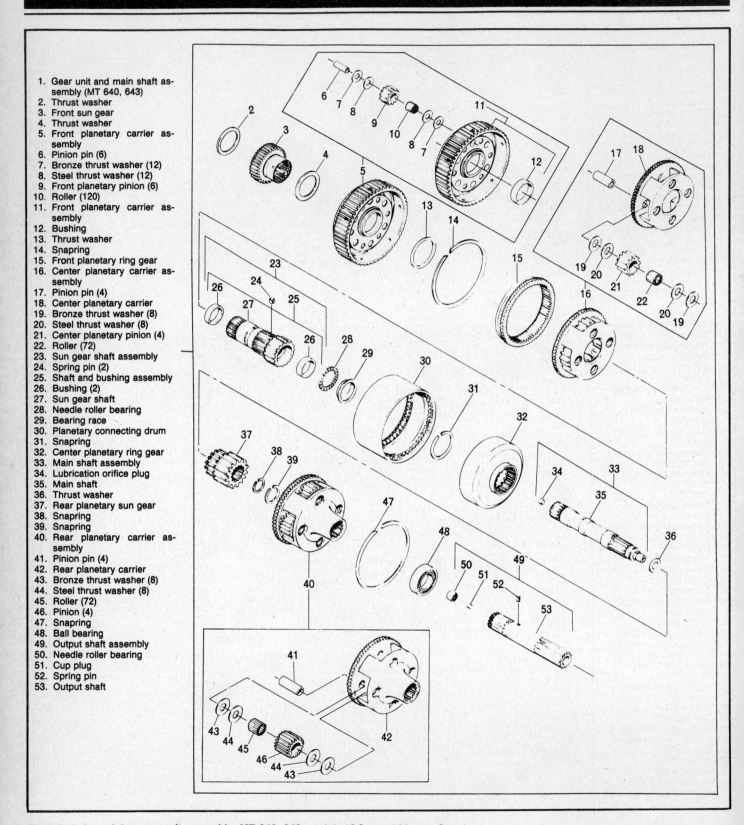

1. Gear unit and main shaft assembly (MT 640, 643)
2. Thrust washer
3. Front sun gear
4. Thrust washer
5. Front planetary carrier assembly
6. Pinion pin (6)
7. Bronze thrust washer (12)
8. Steel thrust washer (12)
9. Front planetary pinion (6)
10. Roller (120)
11. Front planetary carrier assembly
12. Bushing
13. Thrust washer
14. Snapring
15. Front planetary ring gear
16. Center planetary carrier assembly
17. Pinion pin (4)
18. Center planetary carrier
19. Bronze thrust washer (8)
20. Steel thrust washer (8)
21. Center planetary pinion (4)
22. Roller (72)
23. Sun gear shaft assembly
24. Spring pin (2)
25. Shaft and bushing assembly
26. Bushing (2)
27. Sun gear shaft
28. Needle roller bearing
29. Bearing race
30. Planetary connecting drum
31. Snapring
32. Center planetary ring gear
33. Main shaft assembly
34. Lubrication orifice plug
35. Main shaft
36. Thrust washer
37. Rear planetary sun gear
38. Snapring
39. Snapring
40. Rear planetary carrier assembly
41. Pinion pin (4)
42. Rear planetary carrier
43. Bronze thrust washer (8)
44. Steel thrust washer (8)
45. Roller (72)
46. Pinion (4)
47. Snapring
48. Ball bearing
49. Output shaft assembly
50. Needle roller bearing
51. Cup plug
52. Spring pin
53. Output shaft

Exploded view of the gear unit assembly, MT 640, 643 models (©General Motors Corp.)

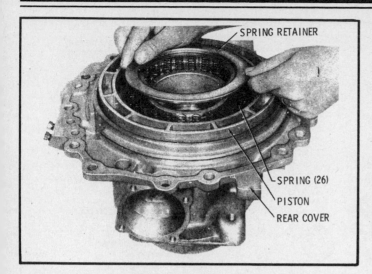

Removing or installing the first clutch piston snap ring retainer in the rear cover, MT 640, 643, 644 models (©General Motors Corp.)

Assembly

Install the new ball bearing onto the output shaft, and a new spring pin.

REAR COVER AND FIRST CLUTCH PISTON

Disassembly

MT 640, 643, 644

1. Remove the dust cover from the rear cover.
2. With the aid of a suitable tool, remove the output shaft oil seal from the rear cover.
3. Remove the snap-ring on the rear bearing and remove the rear bearing from the output shaft.

NOTE: Do not remove the inner snap-ring unless replacement is necessary.

4. Compress the spring retainer and springs, with a spring compressor tool, and remove the retainer snap-ring.
5. Remove the retainer and the twenty-six springs.
6. Remove the clutch piston and the inner and outer seal rings from the pistons.
7. Remove all remaining parts from the rear cover (tubes, snap-rings, governor support pin, and plugs).

Assembly

1. Install the governor support pin, if removed, to between 5.896 to 5.886 inches (149.50-149.75 mm), from the face of the housing to the face of the pin. Press the metal drain tube into the rear cover 0.050-0.100 inch (1.27-2.54 mm) from the chamfer in the cover on the early models and on the late models, press the rubber tube into the rear cover 0.020-0.150 inch (0.50-3.80 mm) below the surface of the cover.

2. Install the other small parts into the rear cover, listed under step 7 of the disassembly procedure.

3. Lubricate the sealrings and install them into the grooves of the piston.

NOTE: The lips of the sealrings must face to the rear of the pistons.

4. Install the piston into the rear cover, using extreme care to prevent the lip of the seal from being damaged.
5. Install the twenty-six springs into the piston pockets and install the springs retainer, cupped side first, onto the springs.
6. Compress the springs and retainer with a compressor tool, and retain with a snapring.

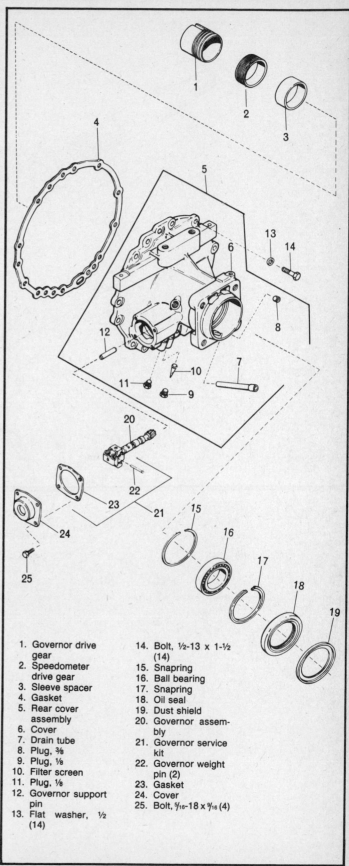

1. Governor drive gear
2. Speedometer drive gear
3. Sleeve spacer
4. Gasket
5. Rear cover assembly
6. Cover
7. Drain tube
8. Plug, ⅜
9. Plug, ⅛
10. Filter screen
11. Plug, ⅛
12. Governor support pin
13. Flat washer, ½ (14)
14. Bolt, ½-13 x 1-½ (14)
15. Snapring
16. Ball bearing
17. Snapring
18. Oil seal
19. Dust shield
20. Governor assembly
21. Governor service kit
22. Governor weight pin (2)
23. Gasket
24. Cover
25. Bolt, ⁹/₁₆-18 x ⁹/₁₆ (4)

Exploded view of the rear cover assembly, MT 640, 643 models (©General Motors Corp.)

763

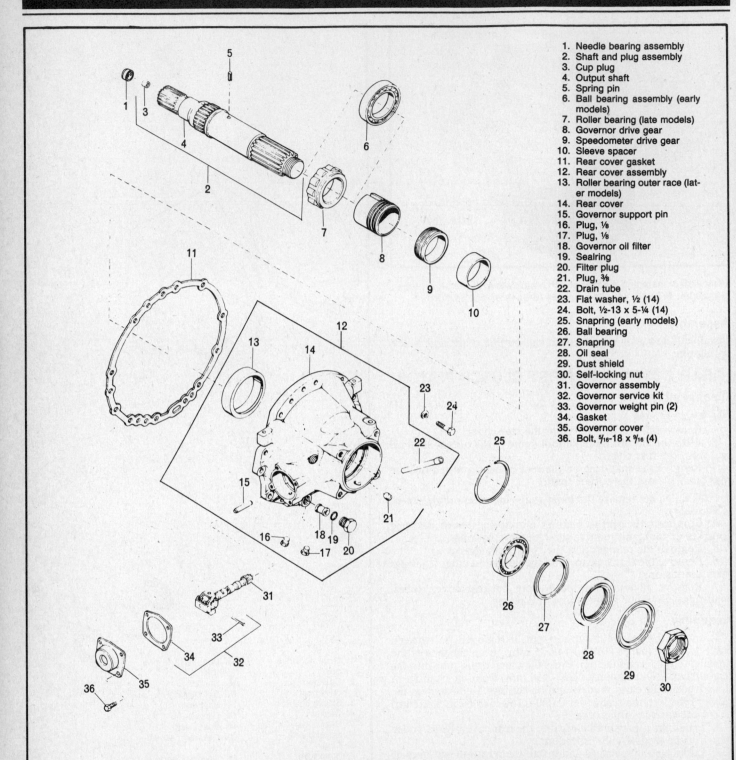

1. Needle bearing assembly
2. Shaft and plug assembly
3. Cup plug
4. Output shaft
5. Spring pin
6. Ball bearing assembly (early models)
7. Roller bearing (late models)
8. Governor drive gear
9. Speedometer drive gear
10. Sleeve spacer
11. Rear cover gasket
12. Rear cover assembly
13. Roller bearing outer race (later models)
14. Rear cover
15. Governor support pin
16. Plug, ⅛
17. Plug, ⅛
18. Governor oil filter
19. Sealring
20. Filter plug
21. Plug, ⅜
22. Drain tube
23. Flat washer, ½ (14)
24. Bolt, ½-13 x 5-¼ (14)
25. Snapring (early models)
26. Ball bearing
27. Snapring
28. Oil seal
29. Dust shield
30. Self-locking nut
31. Governor assembly
32. Governor service kit
33. Governor weight pin (2)
34. Gasket
35. Governor cover
36. Bolt, 5/16-18 x 9/16 (4)

Exploded view of the rear cover assembly, MT 650, 653 models (©General Motors Corp.)

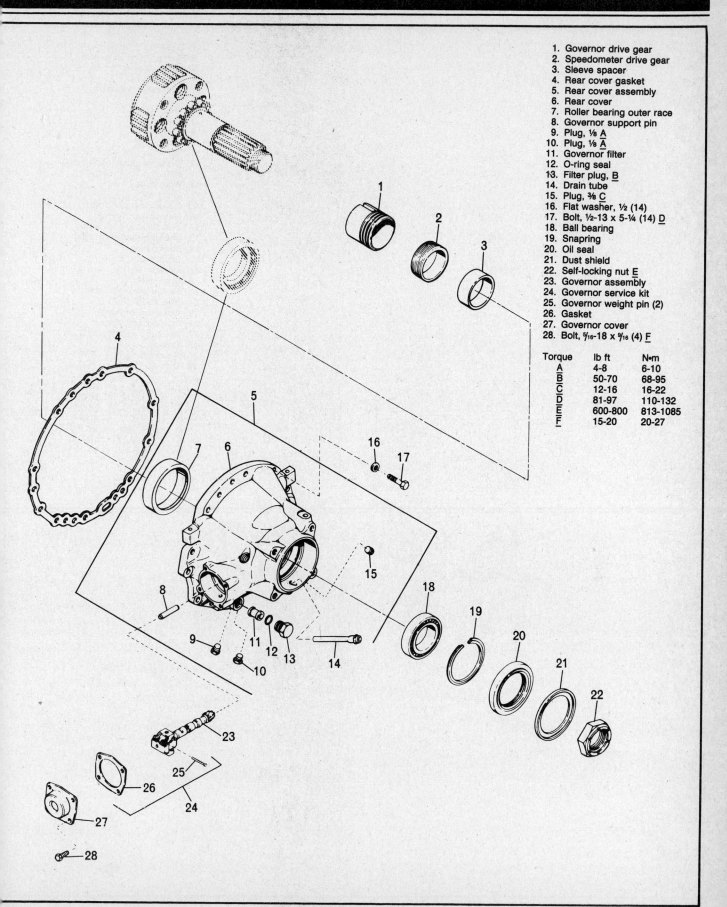

1. Governor drive gear
2. Speedometer drive gear
3. Sleeve spacer
4. Rear cover gasket
5. Rear cover assembly
6. Rear cover
7. Roller bearing outer race
8. Governor support pin
9. Plug, ⅛ A
10. Plug, ⅛ A
11. Governor filter
12. O-ring seal
13. Filter plug, B
14. Drain tube
15. Plug, ⅜ C
16. Flat washer, ½ (14)
17. Bolt, ½-13 x 5-¼ (14) D
18. Ball bearing
19. Snapring
20. Oil seal
21. Dust shield
22. Self-locking nut E
23. Governor assembly
24. Governor service kit
25. Governor weight pin (2)
26. Gasket
27. Governor cover
28. Bolt, ⁵⁄₁₆-18 x ⁹⁄₁₆ (4) F

Torque	lb ft	N•m
A	4-8	6-10
B	50-70	68-95
C	12-16	16-22
D	81-97	110-132
E	600-800	813-1085
F	15-20	20-27

Exploded view of the rear cover assembly, MT 654CR models (©General Motors Corp.)

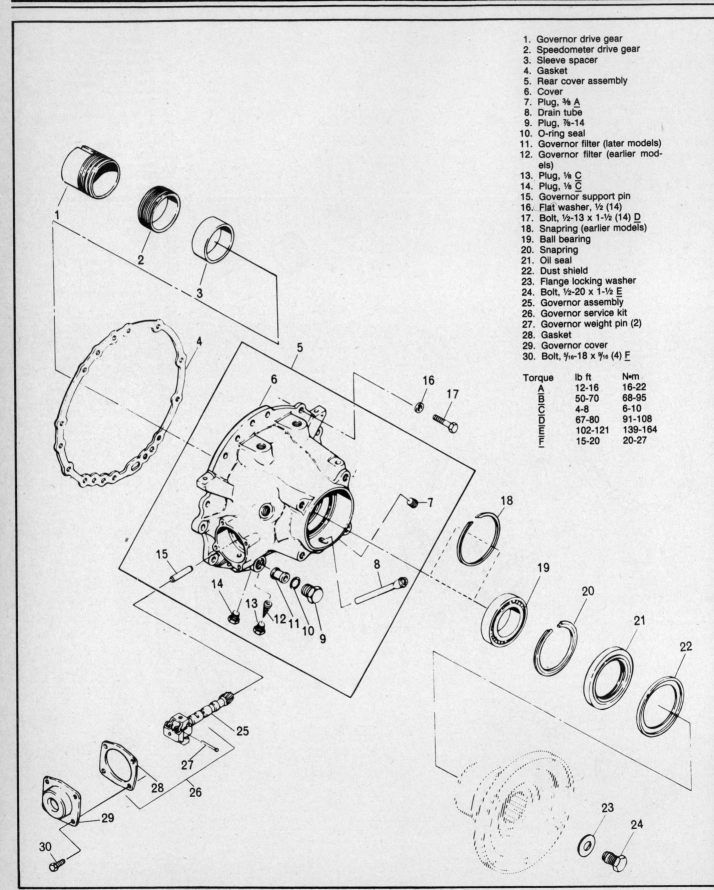

1. Governor drive gear
2. Speedometer drive gear
3. Sleeve spacer
4. Gasket
5. Rear cover assembly
6. Cover
7. Plug, ⅜ A
8. Drain tube
9. Plug, ⅞-14
10. O-ring seal
11. Governor filter (later models)
12. Governor filter (earlier models)
13. Plug, ⅛ C
14. Plug, ⅛ C
15. Governor support pin
16. Flat washer, ½ (14)
17. Bolt, ½-13 x 1-½ (14) D
18. Snapring (earlier models)
19. Ball bearing
20. Snapring
21. Oil seal
22. Dust shield
23. Flange locking washer
24. Bolt, ½-20 x 1-½ E
25. Governor assembly
26. Governor service kit
27. Governor weight pin (2)
28. Gasket
29. Governor cover
30. Bolt, ⁵⁄₁₆-18 x ⁹⁄₁₆ (4) F

Torque	lb ft	N•m
A	12-16	16-22
B	50-70	68-95
C	4-8	6-10
D	67-80	91-108
E	102-121	139-164
F	15-20	20-27

Exploded view of the rear cover assembly, MT 644 models (©General Motors Corp.)

766

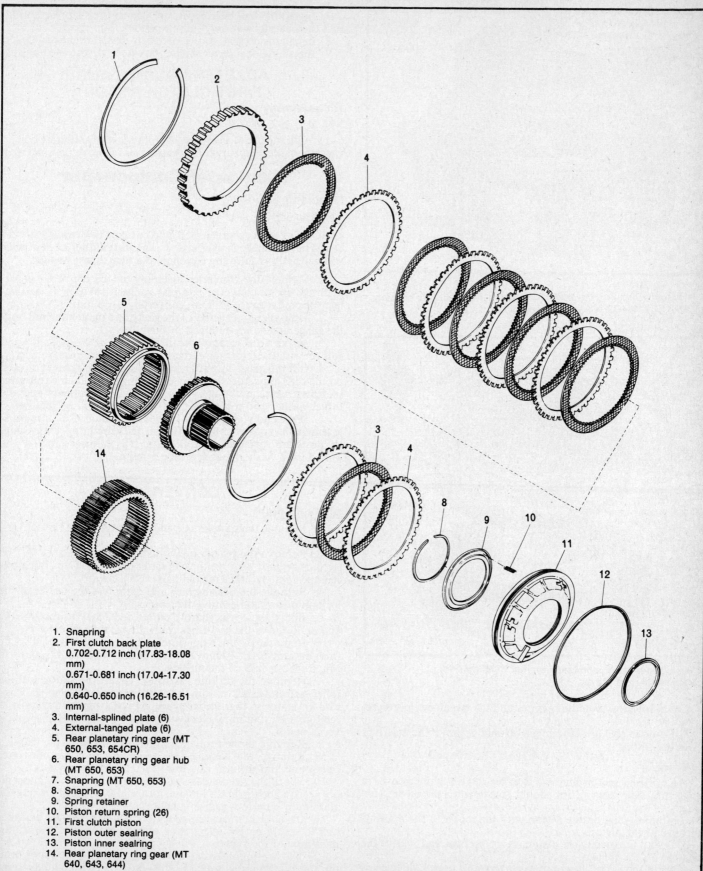

1. Snapring
2. First clutch back plate
   0.702-0.712 inch (17.83-18.08 mm)
   0.671-0.681 inch (17.04-17.30 mm)
   0.640-0.650 inch (16.26-16.51 mm)
3. Internal-splined plate (6)
4. External-tanged plate (6)
5. Rear planetary ring gear (MT 650, 653, 654CR)
6. Rear planetary ring gear hub (MT 650, 653)
7. Snapring (MT 650, 653)
8. Snapring
9. Spring retainer
10. Piston return spring (26)
11. First clutch piston
12. Piston outer sealring
13. Piston inner sealring
14. Rear planetary ring gear (MT 640, 643, 644)

Exploded view of the first clutch and rear planetary gears (©General Motors Corp.)

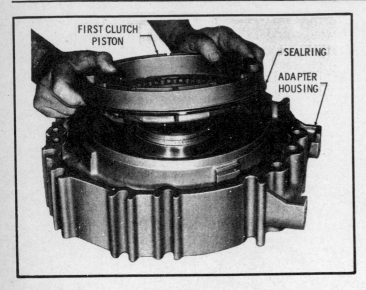

Removing or installing the first clutch piston in the adapter housing, MT 650, 653, 654CR models (©General Motors Corp.)

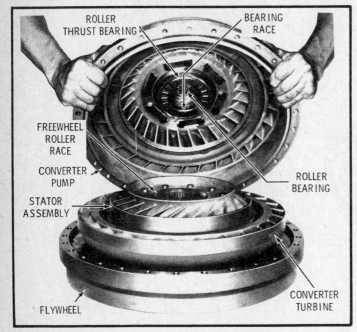

Torque converter components, typical of all models (©General Motors Corp.)

2. Remove the tool, the retainer and the twenty-six piston release springs.

3. Remove the low-clutch piston and remove the sealrings from the piston.

Assembly

1. Lubricate and install the piston sealrings into the grooves of the piston. The sealring lips should face towards the oil pressure side.

2. Align the lug on the piston with the recess in the housing, and install the piston.

3. Install the twenty-six piston return springs, and replace the retainer on the springs.

4. With the aid of the compressor tool and draw bolt, depress the springs bend install the snap-ring. Remove the tool.

7. Install the ball bearing firmly, against the snapring and install the bearing snapring, fully expanded, into its groove.

8. Install the oil seal, spring loaded lip first, into the rear cover.

9. Install the dust cover shield, flat side first, into the housing.

ADAPTER HOUSING AND FIRST-CLUTCH PISTON

Disassembly

MT 650, 653, 654CR

1. With the use of a suitable compressor tool and draw bolt arrangement, depress the spring retainer and remove the snap ring.

Converter Components

Checking End Play

MT 650, 653

NOTE: This measurement should be taken before and after the converter assembly is overhauled. The installation of new parts will normally require the selection of a new thrust washer.

1. Support the converter assembly on the converter cover. With the use of converter end play gauge J-24470 or its equivalent, place the gauge into the converter pump hub.

2. Hold the center screw of the gauge and tighten the nut until the gauge is securely retained in the hub.

3. Install a dial indicator so that the stem of the indicator is in contact with the top of the end play gauge. Zero the dial indicator.

4. Lift the gauge upward and record the reading as indicated on the dial indicator. End play exceeding 0.025 inch (0.64 mm) indicates wear on the converter internal components and the thrust washer and replacement of worn parts will be required.

5. If the end play does not exceed 0.025 inch (0.64 mm), disassemble the converter for inspection and rebuilding. Unless major parts are replaced while the converter is disassembled, the same thrust washer/spacer can be re-used.

CONVERTER

Disassembly

1. Remove the six retainers and six spacers from the converter cover.

2. Remove the twenty-four nuts from the cover.

3. As a unit, remove the converter cover, lock-up clutch piston and remove other related parts.

4. Remove the bearing race and compress the center of the lock-up piston and remove the snap-ring.

5. Bump the cover sharply on a wood block to remove the piston. Remove the seal rings from the piston and cover.

6. Remove the lock-up clutch plate and clutch back plate from the converter. Remove the roller bearing assembly and seal ring from the hub of the turbine.

7. Remove the turbine assembly. Grasp the stator and the roller race and remove from the converter pump assembly. Position the stator so that the freewheeling roller race is upward and remove it by rotating it clockwise while lifting it out of the converter stator.

8. Remove the ten rollers and ten springs from the stator.

9. Remove the bearing race assembly from the converter pump hub and the seal ring from the converter pump.

10. Check the needle bearing assembly. If the bearing assembly needs to be replaced, remove it carefully to avoid nicking the aluminum bore in which it is held.

11. Install a new bearing assembly, using a bearing installer tool to insure proper installation of the bearing into the aluminum bore of the stator.

12. The bearing assembly must be driven into the stator until the top of the outer shell is 0.025-0.035 inch (0.64-0.89 mm) above the shoulder in the side plate.

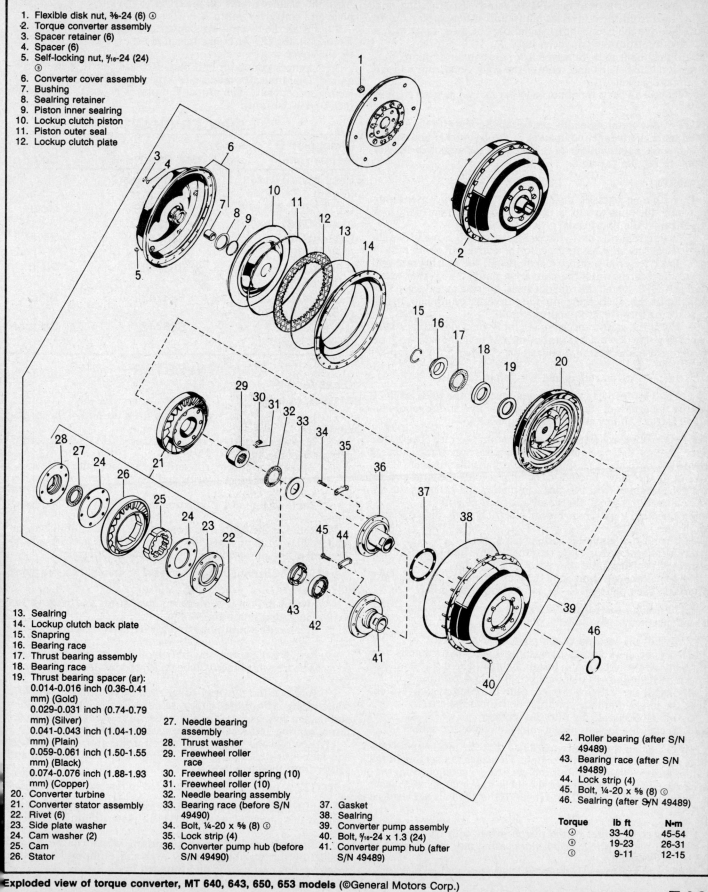

1. Flexible disk nut, ⅜-24 (6) Ⓐ
2. Torque converter assembly
3. Spacer retainer (6)
4. Spacer (6)
5. Self-locking nut, ⁵⁄₁₆-24 (24) Ⓑ
6. Converter cover assembly
7. Bushing
8. Sealring retainer
9. Piston inner sealring
10. Lockup clutch piston
11. Piston outer seal
12. Lockup clutch plate

13. Sealring
14. Lockup clutch back plate
15. Snapring
16. Bearing race
17. Thrust bearing assembly
18. Bearing race
19. Thrust bearing spacer (ar):
    0.014-0.016 inch (0.36-0.41 mm) (Gold)
    0.029-0.031 inch (0.74-0.79 mm) (Silver)
    0.041-0.043 inch (1.04-1.09 mm) (Plain)
    0.059-0.061 inch (1.50-1.55 mm) (Black)
    0.074-0.076 inch (1.88-1.93 mm) (Copper)
20. Converter turbine
21. Converter stator assembly
22. Rivet (6)
23. Side plate washer
24. Cam washer (2)
25. Cam
26. Stator

27. Needle bearing assembly
28. Thrust washer
29. Freewheel roller race
30. Freewheel roller spring (10)
31. Freewheel roller (10)
32. Needle bearing assembly
33. Bearing race (before S/N 49490)
34. Bolt, ¼-20 x ⅝ (8) Ⓒ
35. Lock strip (4)
36. Converter pump hub (before S/N 49490)
37. Gasket
38. Sealring
39. Converter pump assembly
40. Bolt, ⁵⁄₁₆-24 x 1.3 (24)
41. Converter pump hub (after S/N 49489)

42. Roller bearing (after S/N 49489)
43. Bearing race (after S/N 49489)
44. Lock strip (4)
45. Bolt, ¼-20 x ⅝ (8) Ⓒ
46. Sealring (after S/N 49489)

Torque	lb ft	N•m
Ⓐ	33-40	45-54
Ⓑ	19-23	26-31
Ⓒ	9-11	12-15

Exploded view of torque converter, MT 640, 643, 650, 653 models (©General Motors Corp.)

13. Prior to serial number 49490, remove the bearing and bearing race from the converter pump hub. After serial number 49490, remove the needle bearing and bearing race, along with a roller bearing from the converter hub.

14. If the hub is to be removed from the converter pump, flatten the four lock strips and remove the eight bolts, and remove the hub and gasket.

15. Inspect all parts for abnormal wear and replace the parts as necessary.

NOTE: The stator assembly can be rebuilt, but with the need of special tools and balance equipment. It can be quicker and cheaper for the average rebuilder to replace a stator assembly then to attempt to rebuild the unit.

Assembly

1. With a new gasket, install the hub on the converter pump and torque the bolts to 9 to 11 ft. lbs. Bend the corners of the lock strips against the bolt heads.

2. Install seal ring on to the converter pump along with a lubricated bearing race assembly into the converter pump hub.

3. Prior to serial number 49490, install the bearing race and the needle bearing into the converter pump hub. After serial number 49490, install the roller bearing, bearing race (lugged side first) and the needle bearing into the converter pump hub. Install the seal ring into the groove of the hub.

4. Place the stator and cam assembly on a flat surface with the bearing side down. Coat the bottom of the stator cams with oil soluble grease and install a collapsible retainer with a cord attached.

5. Install the ten rollers and ten springs.

NOTE: The open end of the spring touching the roller must be towards the center of the stator cam assembly and the rollers installed in the shallow end of the cam pockets.

6. Install the free wheel roller race until the race engages the roller. Rotate the race in a clockwise direction while pressing downward until the race touches the collapsible retainer.

7. Lift the stator enough to be able to pull the cord and remove the retainer. Seat the race completely and rotate in the opposite direction to lock the stator and cam assembly.

8. Install the stator and cam assembly into the converter pump hub.

9. Install the converter turbine assembly.

10. Install the bearing race into the turbine hub and install the lubricated bearings onto the race.

11. Install the seal ring on to the lock-up clutch back plate and install the back plate on to the torque converter pump.

NOTE: Align the balance marks on the converter pump with the balance marks on the back plate.

12. Install the lock-up clutch plate on to the plate.

13. If a new converter cover bushing is needed in the converter hub, remove the old one and install the new. The inside diameter should be 0.9990 to 1.0010 inch. (25.375-25.425 mm).

14. Install the seal ring retainer onto the converter cover hub. Place the larger diameter towards the rear of the cover.

15. Install the seal ring into the retainer.

16. Install the lockup piston into the converter cover.

NOTE: Align the balance marks so that the piston guide pins enter the nearest hole in the piston. To insure the seating of the piston, measure the distance from the pump cover mounting surface to the piston. The distance should be approximately 1½ inches. The lock-up clutch will not release if the piston is not engaged with the pins.

17. Force the center of the piston down with hand pressure and install the snapring. Install the bearing race into the hub of the converter pump.

18. Install the cover, lock-up clutch piston, and related parts.

Align the balance marks on the cover to the lock-up clutch back plate and converter pump.

19. Install the twenty-four converter cover nuts and torque to 19 to 23 ft. lbs. (23-31 N•m). Install the six spacers and retainers on the cover.

20. Recheck converter end play. Replace thrust spacer as required. Dial indicator reading is dimension "B" as listed in following spacer chart. The proper end play is between 0.001-0.025 inch (0.03-0.64 mm).

SPACER CHART

Dimension B inches (mm)	Use Part No.	Color
Less than 0.0177 (0.449)	Use no spacer	
0.0177-0.034 (0.449-0.86)	6837429	Gold
0.034-0.049 (0.86-1.24)	6837430	Silver
0.049-0.062 (1.24-1.57)	6837431	Plain
0.062-0.079 (1.57-2.00)	6837432	Black
0.079-0.093 (2.00-2.369)	6837433	Copper

CONVERTER

Disassembly

MT 644, 654CR

1. Remove the hook type seal ring from the hub of the torque converter.

2. Remove the thirty bolts and washers that retain the torque converter pump to the flywheel.

3. Separate the torque converter pump from the flywheel.

4. Remove the roller bearing and the race from the converter pump assembly.

5. Remove the seal ring from the flange of the converter pump.

6. Remove the snap ring from the converter pump hub on models after serial number 743. Remove the roller bearing from the bore of the pump hub, if replacement is necessary.

NOTE: The bearing must be pressed or driven from the pump hub.

7. Flatten the corners of the six lock strips and remove the twelve bolts that retain the pump hub.

8. Remove the pump hub and gasket from the pump assembly.

9. Remove the stator assembly by lifting it from the turbine cover. The freewheel race will be removed with the stator assembly.

10. Remove the flywheel roller race by twisting it clockwise while lifting it from the stator assembly. Remove the ten rollers and the ten springs from the stator assembly. Remove the needle thrust bearing and race from the stator assembly.

11. Remove the torque converter turbine from the flywheel and lock-up clutch components. Remove the ball bearings and spacer from the turbine hub.

NOTE: A bearing puller is required to remove the bearing.

12. Lifting on the internal splines of the lock-up clutch plate, remove the clutch plate and the back plate. Remove the back plate key.

13. Remove the lock-up clutch piston, which can be accomplished by turning the assembly over and bumping the piston from the flywheel cavity, on a wooden block.

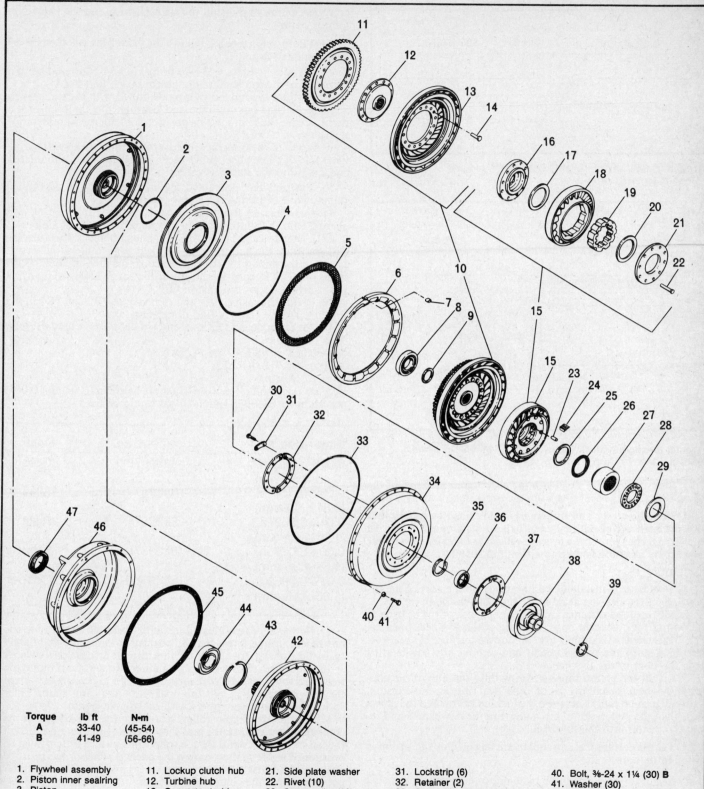

Torque	lb ft	N·m
A	33-40	(45-54)
B	41-49	(56-66)

1. Flywheel assembly
2. Piston inner sealring
3. Piston
4. Piston outer sealring
5. Lockup clutch plate
6. Lockup clutch backplate
7. Key
8. Ball bearing
9. Spacer (selective)
10. Turbine assembly

11. Lockup clutch hub
12. Turbine hub
13. Converter turbine
14. Rivet (16)
15. Stator assembly
16. Stator thrust washer
17. Stator cam washer
18. Stator
19. Cam
20. Stator cam washer

21. Side plate washer
22. Rivet (10)
23. Stator roller (10)
24. Stator roller spring (10)
25. Bearing race
26. Thrust bearing
27. Freewheel roller race
28. Thrust bearing
29. Thrust bearing race
30. Bolt, ⅜-16 x 1¼ (12) **A**

31. Lockstrip (6)
32. Retainer (2)
33. Converter pump sealring
34. Converter pump
35. Internal snapring (later models)
36. Roller bearing
37. Converter pump hub gasket
38. Converter pump hub
39. Hook-type sealring

40. Bolt, ⅜-24 x 1¼ (30) **B**
41. Washer (30) Remote Mount
42. Converter drive housing assembly
43. Internal snapring
44. Ball bearing assembly
45. Gasket
46. Converter cover
47. Oil seal

Exploded view of torque converter, MT 644, 654CR models (©General Motors Corp.)

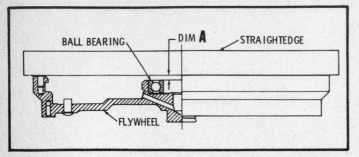

Locating measurement "A", MT 644, 654CR models
(©General Motors Corp.)

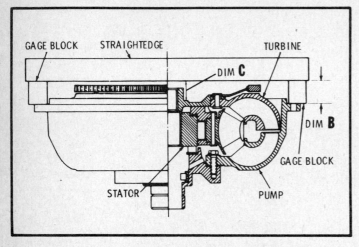

Locating measurement "B" and "C", MT 644, 654CR models
(©General Motors Corp.)

14. Remove the seal ring from the outer circumference of the piston. Remove the seal ring from the inner hub of the flywheel.

NOTE: The stator and turbine assemblies can be rebuilt, but with the need of special tools and balance equipment. It can be quicker and cheaper for the average rebuilder to replace the stator and turbine assemblies then to attempt to rebuild them.

Assembly

1. Temporarily install the ball bearing into the bore of the flywheel. Seat the bearing against the shoulder in the bore.

2. Measure the distance from the inner race of the bearing to the bottom of a straight edge, laid across the flywheel opening. This measurement is dimension "A" for the purpose of spacer selection. Record the measurement and remove the ball bearing from the bore of the flywheel.

3. Install the piston inner seal ring onto the hub of the converter flywheel. Install the piston outer seal ring on to the piston. Using alignment marks between the lock-up piston and the dowel pins, align the piston dowel pin holes with the dowel pins and install the piston into the flywheel.

NOTE: Be certain the dowel pins are engaged as the piston is seated in its bore.

4. Install the lock-up clutch plate on to the piston and install the back plate lock key into the bore of the flywheel. Install the back plate, flat side first, and engage the notch in the plate with the lock key in the flywheel.

5. If the roller bearing was removed from the pump hub, press a new bearing in place. On models after serial number 743, install the snapring.

6. Install two guide bolts into the pump huband install the gasket over the guide bolts. Install the hub and gasket into the

converter pump and install the six lockstrips and the twelve retaining bolts.

NOTE: Install ten bolts, remove the guide pins and then install the remaining two.

7. Torque the bolts to 33-40 ft. lbs. (45-54 N•m) and bend a corner of each strip against the head of each bolt head.

8. With the assembled pump positioned with the hub downward, install the bearing race and bearing into the bore of the pump. Leave the pump in this position for later measurement for the spacer.

9. Install the bearing race, needle roller thrust bearing (bearing first) into the freewheel roller race. Install the race, shouldered end first, into the stator assembly.

10. Position the assembled stator parts into the assembled pump, while centering the stator carefully.

11. Position the converter turbine, without the bearing and spacer, onto the stator assembly while centering it carefully.

12. Using a straight edge and equal height blocks, measure the distance from the bottom of the straight edge to the shoulder adjacent to the hub of the turbine. Record this measurement as dimension "C." Record the height of the gauge blocks supporting the straight edge as dimension "B."

13. Using dimension "A" and dimensions "B" and "C" in the formula $X = A - (B-C)$, find dimension "X."

14. An example is as follows and should only be used as such.

$X = A - (B-C)$
$X = 0.064 - (0.094 - 0.084)$ inch
$X = 0.064 - 0.010$ inch
$X = 0.054$ inch

Because the result ($X = 0.054$ inch) is between 0.044 and 0.062, part number 6839978 (plain color) would be used.

Dimension X	Use Part No.	Color
0.018-0.032 in. (0.46-0.81 mm)	6839976	Gold
0.032-0.044 in. (0.81-1.11 mm)	6839977	Silver
0.044-0.062 in. (1.11-1.57 mm)	6839978	Plain
0.062-0.077 in. (1.57-1.95 mm)	6839979	Black
0.077-0.0963 in. (1.96-2.45 mm)	6839980	Copper

15. Remove the turbine and install the selected spacer onto the hub of the turbine. Press the ball bearing onto the hub and firmly against the spacer. Install the turbine into the assembled flywheel.

16. Place the stator assembly on a flat surface and remove the freewheel roller race. Be sure the lower race and bearing remain in the stator assembly. Coat the pockets of the cam, stator roller springs and the stator rollers with oil soluble grease.

17. Install the stator roller retaining ring, J-24218-2 or its equivalent, into the stator and seat it against the bearing. Install the ten stator rollers and the ten roller springs. The rollers must be positioned in the shallow end of the pockets. The springs must be positioned so that the end of the spring that touches the roller points towards the center of the stator.

NOTE: The curved end of the B type spring fits against the roller.

18. Rotate the roller race clockwise while pushing it into the stator. When the roller race touches the retaining ring, remove the retaining ring by pulling on the attached cord. Continue to rotate and push the roller race until it seats against the bearing.

19. Rotate the roller race counterclockwise and install the assembled stator onto the converter turbine. Carefully center the assembly.

20. Check to be sure the roller bearing and race are in place in the converter pump. User oil soluble grease to retain the bearing and race. Install the seal ring into the converter pump flange and install the converter pump onto the flywheel.

21. Install the thirty bolts and nuts with washers. Evenly turn the bolts and nuts to tighten. Torque to 41-49 ft. lbs. (56-66 N•m) and install the hook type seal ring on the hub of the converter pump assembly.

Hydraulic Control Components

MODULATED LOCK-UP VALVE BODY ASSEMBLY

Disassembly

ALL MODELS

1. Mark the adjusting ring to indicate its position in relation to the retaining pin.
2. Depress the ring against the spring pressure and remove the retaining pin.
3. Remove the adjusting ring, valve stop, spring and valve from the valve body.

Assembly

1. Install the valve with the small diameter first, into the valve body bore.
2. Install the spring, the valve stop (undrilled end first), into the spring.
3. Install the adjusting ring, flat side first, over the valve stop. Align the adjusting ring to the previously made alignment marks, prior to disassembly.
4. Depress the spring with the adjusting ring and install the retaining pin through the holes in the valve body and the valve stop.

NOTE: Be sure the adjusting ring is aligned with the pin as it was before its removal.

LOW SHIFT VALVE ASSEMBLY

Disassembly

MT 650, 653

1. Mark the location of the adjusting ring in respect to the retaining pin. Depress the adjusting ring against the spring pressure and remove the retaining pin.
2. Remove the adjusting ring, washer, valve stop, valve spring and low shift signal valve from the valve body.
3. Remove the valve stop, spring and low shift relay valve.

Assembly

1. Install the low shift relay valve into the longer bore of the valve body. Install the spring and valve stop into the same bore. Depress the stop and install the pin into the valve body.
2. Install the low shift signal valve, stem end first, into the remaining valve bore. Install the spring, stop, washer and adjusting ring, flat side first, into the valve body bore. Align the hole in the valve stop and the slot in the adjusting ring with the hole in the valve body.
3. Install the retainer pin, being sure the adjusting ring is aligned as it was prior to its removal.

CONTROL VALVE ASSEMBLY

MT 640, 643, 650, 653

Disassembly

The valve body disassembly and assembly is usually left to the discretion of the rebuilder, to formulate a procedure that is both

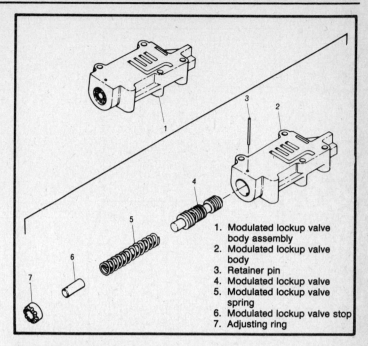

1. Modulated lockup valve body assembly
2. Modulated lockup valve body
3. Retainer pin
4. Modulated lockup valve
5. Modulated lockup valve spring
6. Modulated lockup valve stop
7. Adjusting ring

Exploded view of the modulated lock-up valve assembly, typical (©General Motors Corp.)

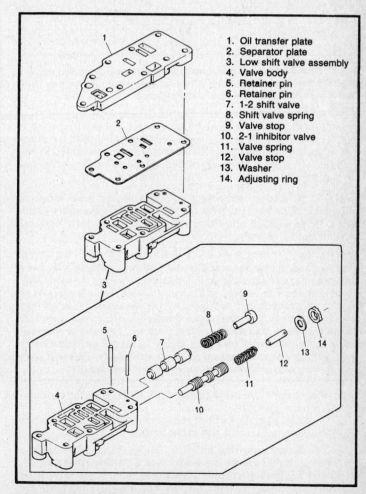

1. Oil transfer plate
2. Separator plate
3. Low shift valve assembly
4. Valve body
5. Retainer pin
6. Retainer pin
7. 1-2 shift valve
8. Shift valve spring
9. Valve stop
10. 2-1 inhibitor valve
11. Valve spring
12. Valve stop
13. Washer
14. Adjusting ring

Exploded view of the low shift valve assembly, MT 650, 653 models (©General Motors Corp.)

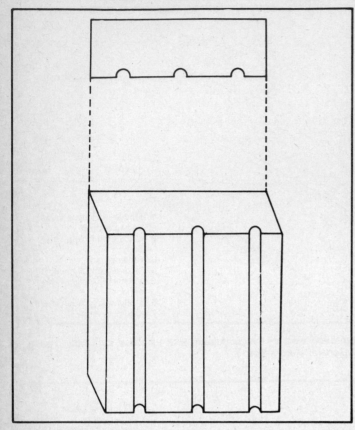

Typical multi-channeled hardwood or steel block used for valve body disassembly, to lay the valves and springs in channels to retain their sequence. (©General Motors Corp.)

3. Remove retaining pin (55) from modulator body (54) while applying pressure to adjusting ring (53). Remove the adjusting ring.

4. Remove valve stop (52), washer (51), spring (50), modulator valve (49) and actuator pin (48).

NOTE: Only those models equipped with modulated lock-up use separator plate (46). All others use plate (45).

5. Remove separator plate (45), or (46). Later MT 650, 653 models include a slot in the separator plate, that engages the flared end of retaining pin (40). The separator plate must be slid lengthwise to disengage it from pin (40).

6. Remove priority valve (4), spring (3) and stop (2). On later MT 650, 653 models, a ¼-inch (6.35 mm) ball (56) is used. Note the location of the ball in the valve body before removal.

7. Place the control valve body on the work table, flat side down.

logical and practical. Because of the complexity and importance of the valve body calibration being retained, reference by numbers in the text, coded on key lists accompanying exploded views of the valve bodies, are used to identify the valve body components during the disassembly and assembly procedure.

NOTE: It is suggested that a multi-channelled wood block or its equivalent, be used to retain the sequence of disassembly of the valves, valve springs and other components from their original bores in the valve body.

CAUTION

The valve body assembly contains many springs, some of which are similar and can be interchanged by mistake. Because the valve bodies are similar, the springs will vary in the different models as to length and strength, but will appear to be the same. If the springs are not re-installed in their same locations from which removed, the calibration of the valve body functions will be lost. For this reason, it is recommended that each spring be tagged or identified in some manner upon its removal from the valve body. This will simplify correct reassembly of the valve body components.

1. Place valve assembly on the work table, with the modulator valve body upward.

2. Remove three bolts from the modulator body and remove the modulator body from the valve body.

NOTE: Before removing pins (12, 24, 30, 36, and 55), make a note or sketch that shows the position of adjusting rings (10, 23, 29, 35 and 53) in respect to their retaining pins. If the valve body is reassembled with the same springs, and the adjusting rings are in their original positions, the original calibration of the valve body is maintained.

1. Control valve assembly	52. Valve stop
2. Valve stop pin	53. Adjusting ring
3. Priority valve spring	54. Modulator valve body
4. Priority valve	55. Retainer pin
5. Hold regulator valve	56. Check ball (after S/N 47284, MT 650, 653 only)
6. Regulator valve spring	57. Control valve body
7. Valve stop pin	58. Third clutch trimmer valve
8. Valve plug (prior to S/N 66940)	59. Trimmer plug
9. Washer (after S/N 66939)	60. Valve outer spring
10. Adjusting ring (after S/N 66939)	61. Valve inner spring (after S/N 13800)
11. Selector valve	62. Valve stop
12. Retainer pin	63. First clutch trimmer valve
13. 1-2 shift valve return spring	64. Trimmer plug
14. 1-2 shift valve	65. Valve outer spring
15. 1-2 modulator valve	66. Valve inner spring (after S/N 13800-MT 650, 653; all 640, 643)
16. 1-2 shift valve spring	
17. Valve stop	67. Valve stop
18. 1-2 shift valve bore washer	68. Second clutch trimmer valve
19. 2-3 shift valve (MT 650, 653) 1-2 shift valve (MT 640, 643)	69. Trimmer plug
20. Shift modulator valve	70. Valve outer spring
21. Shift valve spring	71. Valve inner spring (after S/N 13800-MT 650, 653; all 640, 643)
22. Valve stop	
23. Adjusting ring	72. Valve stop
24. Retainer ring	73. Fourth clutch trimmer valve
25. 3-4 shift valve (MT 650, 653) 2-3 shift valve (MT 640, 643)	74. Trimmer plug
26. Shift modulator valve	75. Valve outer spring
27. Shift valve spring	76. Valve inner spring (after S/N 13800)
28. Valve stop	77. Valve stop
29. Adjusting ring	78. Trimmer valve cover
30. Retainer ring	79. Bolt, ¼-20 x ⅝ (8) ⊕
31. 4-5 shift valve (MT 650, 653) 3-4 shift valve (MT 640, 643)	80. Retainer pin (2)
32. Modulator valve	81. 3-4 relay valve (MT 650, 653) 2-3 relay valve (MT 640, 643)
33. Valve spring	
34. Valve stop	82. Valve spring
35. Adjusting ring	83. Valve stop (later models)
36. Retainer ring	84. 2-3 relay valve (MT 650, 653) 1-2 relay valve (MT 640, 643)
37. 4-5 relay valve (MT 650, 653) 3-4 relay valve (MT 640, 643)	
	85. Valve spring
38. Valve spring	86. Spacer
39. Valve stop (later models)	87. First clutch tube (MT 640, 643)
40. Retainer pin	
41. Trimmer regulator valve	88. Governor tube (2)
42. Trimmer regulator spring	89. Governor screen assembly
43. Trimmer regulator valve stop	90. Trimmer tube (MT 650, 653)
44. Retainer pin	91. Low and first feed tube (MT 650, 653)
45. Separator plate (non-modulated lockup)	
46. Separator plate (modulated lockup)	92. Drive-1 tube (MT 650, 653)
47. Bolt, ¼-20 x 1-¾ (3) ⊕	93. Forward regulator tube (MT 650, 653)
48. Modulator valve actuator pin	
49. Modulator valve	
50. Valve spring	Torque
51. Washer	

	lb ft	N•m
⊕	9-11	12-15

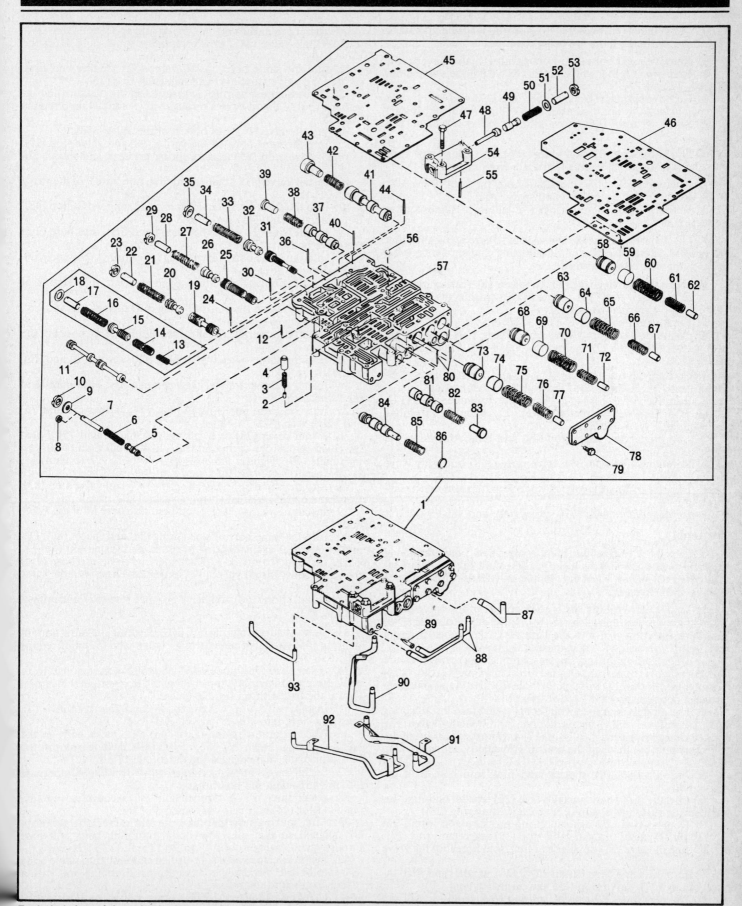

Exploded view of the valve body assembly, MT 640, 643, 650, 653 models (©General Motors Corp.)

NOTE: Trimmer valve cover (78) is spring loaded and must be restrained while the bolts are being removed.

8. Remove eight bolts (79) from trimmer valve cover (78).

9. Remove trimmer valve cover (78). Remove valve stops (62, 67, 72 and 77).

10. Remove springs (60, 61, 65, 66, 70, 71, 75 and 76). Springs (61, 66, 71 and 76) are used after S/N 13800. Remove trimmer plugs (59, 64, 69 and 74). Remove trimmer valves (58, 63, 68 and 73).

NOTE: Valve stop (83) and spacer (86) are spring loaded and must be restrained while pins (80) are being removed.

11. Remove two retainer pins (80) from the control valve.

12. Remove valve stop (83) and spacer (86).

13. Remove relay valve springs (82 and 85). Remove relay valve (81 and 84).

NOTE: Adjusting ring (10) and washer (9) are applicable after S/N 66939. Record location of the adjusting ring in relation to retaining pin (12) before removal.

14. Depress adjusting ring (10) or spacer (8), (earlier models). Remove pin (12), ring (10) or spacer (8), washer (9) (if used), valve stop (7), spring (6) and valve (5).

15. Remove selector valve (11).

16. On models equipped with second gear start, remove pin (24) washer (18), pin (17), spring (16), valve (15), valve (14) and spring (13).

17. Compress adjusting rings (23, 29 and 35) and remove retainer pins (24, 30, and 36). Remove the adjusting rings.

18. Remove valve stops (22, 28 and 34). Remove springs (21, 27 and 33). Remove modulator valves (20, 26 and 32). Remove shift valves (19, 25 and 31).

19. Compress relay valve stop (39) and remove retainer pin (40).

20. Remove valve stop (39), valve spring (38), and relay valve (37).

21. Depress trimmer regulator valve stop (43) and remove retainer pin (44).

22. Remove valve stop (43), spring (42), and valve (41).

Assembly

NOTE: Check the position of all components, configuration of all valves and plugs and the identification of all springs before installation. All valves, when dry, should move freely, by their own weight, in their bores.

1. Install valve (5) into its bore in bore A of the valve body.

2. Late models: install spring (6), valve stop (7), washer (9) and adjusting ring (10) into the bore A. Earlier models: install spring (6), valve stop (7) and spacer (8) into the bore A.

3. Depress the adjusting ring or spacer against spring pressure and install pin (12). Record original location of pin (12) during assembly. Install pin (12) through the hole in valve stop (7). Earlier models, depress spacer (8) and install pin (12).

4. For models equipped with second gear start, install spring (13), 1-2 shift valve (14), open end first, 1-2 modulator valve (15), longer land first, spring (16), stop (17) and washer (18) into bore B. Insert pin (24) through the hole in valve body and valve stop (17).

5. Install valve (19), shorter land first, into bore B of the valve body.

6. Into the same bore, install valve (20) smaller end first. Install spring (21), valve stop (22) and adjusting ring (23).

7. Depress ring (23) against spring pressure and install pin (24) so that it passes through valve stop (22) and retains ring (23).

8. Install valve (25), smaller end first, into bore C of the valve body.

9. Into the same bore, install valve (26), smaller end first. Install spring (27), valve stop (28) and adjusting ring (29).

10. Depress ring (29) against spring pressure and install pin (30) so that it passes through valve stop (28) and retains ring (29).

11. Install valve (31), smaller end first, into bore D of the valve body.

12. Into the same bore, install valve (32), smaller end first, spring (33), valve stop, (34) and adjusting ring (35).

13. Depress adjusting ring (35) against spring pressure and install pin (36) so that it passes through valve stop (34) and retains ring (35).

14. Install valve (37) into bore E of the valve body.

15. Into the same bore, install spring (38) and valve stop (39). Depress valve stop (39) against spring pressure and install pin (40).

16. Install valve (41), smaller end first, into bore F of the valve body.

17. Into the same bore, install spring (42) and valve stop (43). Depress valve stop (43) and install pin (44).

18. Install trimmer valve (58), open end first, into bore G of the valve body.

19. Into the same bore, install plug (59), springs (60) and (61), and valve stop (62).

20. Install trimmer valve (63), open end first, into bore H of the valve body.

21. Into the same bore, install plug (64) springs (65 and 66), and valve stop (67).

22. Install trimmer valve (68), open end first, into bore I of the valve body.

23. Into the same bore, install plug (69), spring (70 and 71), and valve stop (72).

24. Install trimmer valve (73), open end first, into bore K of the valve body.

25. Into the same bore, install plug, (74) springs (75 and 76) and valve stop (77).

26. Install cover (78) over springs (60, 65, 70 and 75). Force the cover against the spring pressure, and install eight ¼-20 x ⅝-inch bolts (79). Tighten the bolts to 9-11 lb. ft. (12-15 N•m).

27. Install valve (81) into bore L of the valve body.

28. Into the same bore, install spring (82) and valve stop (83). Depress stop (83) against spring pressure, and install pin (80).

29. Install valve (84), larger end first, into bore M of the valve body.

30. Into the same bore, install spring (85) and spacer (86). Depress the spacer against spring pressure, and install pin (80).

31. Install actuator rod (48), smaller end first, into bore N, of the valve body. Install valve (49), longer land first, into the same bore.

32. Install spring (50), washer (51), valve stop (52), and adjusting ring (53).

33. Depress adjusting ring (53) against spring pressure, and install pin (55) so that it pass through valve stop (52) and retains ring (53).

34. If steel ball (56) models MT 650, 653, was removed from body during disassembly, replace the ball in its original location. Retain the ball with oil soluble grease.

35. Install valve stop (2), spring (3) and priority valve (4), open end first, into valve body bore C.

36. Place separator plate (45) or (46) onto valve body so the bolt holes align. Later MT 650, 653 models include a slot in the separator plate, that engages the flared end of pin (40).

37. Install the assembled modulator valve onto separator plate (45) or (46). Align the bolt holes.

38. Install three ¼-20 x 1¾-inch bolts (47) through valve body, plate (45) or (46) and into valve body.

39. After making sure that the plate and valve body are properly aligned so that all valve body mounting bolts will pass through them, tighten bolts 47 to 9-11 lb. ft. (12-15 N•m).

40. Install selector valve (11), drilled end first, into valve body bore P. Secure the valve against dropping out, with a rubber band, cord, or soft wire.

41. Using adjusting tool J-24314 or its equivalent. Position the

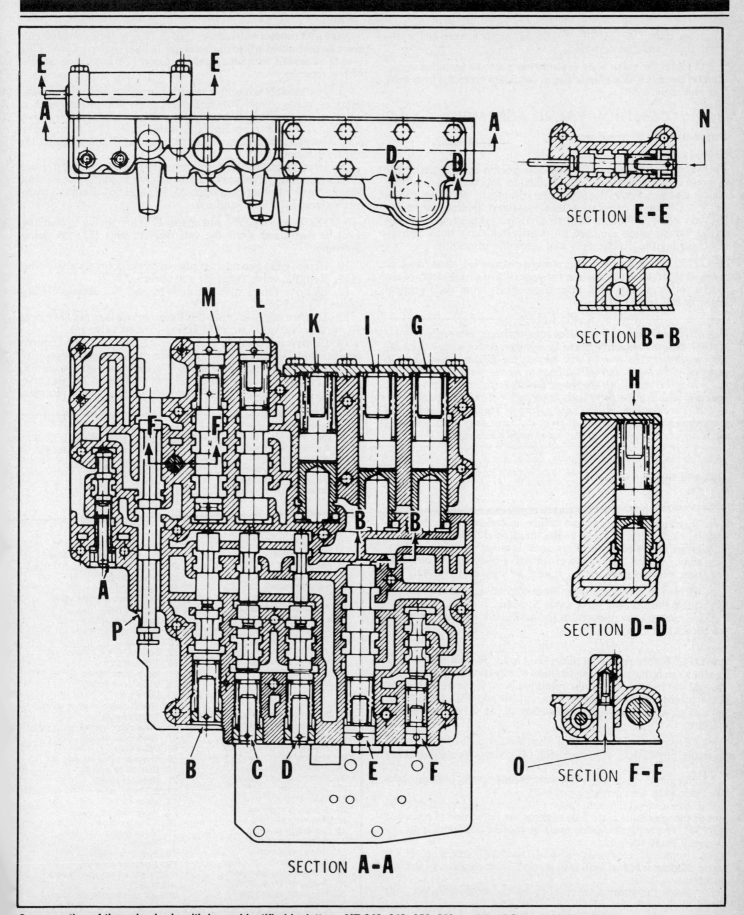

SECTION **E-E**

SECTION **B-B**

SECTION **D-D**

SECTION **F-F**

SECTION **A-A**

Cross section of the valve body with bores identified by letters, MT 640, 643, 650, 653 models (©General Motors Corp.)

adjusting rings (10, 23, 29, 35 and 53) as they were before the valve body was disassembled.

NOTE: If the valve body assembly is not to be installed immediately, cover it with a plastic bag or wrap it to protect it from dust, dirt and moisture.

CONTROL VALVE ASSEMBLY

Disassembly Procedure

MT 644, 654CR

The valve body disassembly and assembly is usually left to the discretion of the rebuilder, to formulate a procedure that is both logical and practical. Because of the complexity and importance of the valve body calibration being retained, reference by numbers in the text, coded on key lists accompanying exploded views of the valve bodies, are used to identify the valve body components during the disassembly and assembly procedure.

NOTE: It is suggested that a multi-channelled wood block or its equivalent, be used to retain the sequence of disassembly of the valves, valve springs and other components from their original bores in the valve body.

--------- CAUTION ---------

The valve body assembly contains many springs, some of which are similar and can be interchanged by mistake. Because the valve bodies are similar, the springs will vary in the different models as to length and strength, but will appear to be the same. If the springs are not re-installed in their same locations from which removed, the calibration of the valve body functions will be lost. For this reason, it is recommended that each spring be tagged or identified in some manner upon its removal from the valve body. This will simplify correct reassembly of the valve body components.

Disassembly

MT 644

NOTE: The valve body assembly contains a number of springs, some of which are similar and can be mistakenly interchanged. Also, springs vary in valve bodies used on different models. If springs are not reinstalled in the same locations from which they were removed, the calibration of the valve body will be affected. For these reasons each spring should be tagged at removal.

1. Remove selector valve. Place the valve assembly on the work table, modulator valve body upward.

2. Remove three bolts from the modulator body and remove the modulator body.

NOTE: Before removing pins (11, 17, 23, 30, and 48), make a note or sketch that shows the position of adjusting rings (9, 16, 22, 29, and 46) in respect to their retaining pins. If the valve body is reassembled with the same springs, but the adjusting rings not in their original positions, the calibration of the valve body will be affected.

3. Remove retainer pin (48) from modulator body (47) while applying pressure to adjusting ring (46). Remove the adjusting ring.

4. Remove valve stop (45), washer (44), spring (43), modulator valve (42), and actuator pin (41).

5. Remove oil separator plate (39). Some models include a T-slot in the separator plate that engages the flared end of retaining pin (34). The separator plate must be moved horizontally to disengage it from the pin.

6. Remove the priority valve (4), spring (3), and stop (2). On some models, a 1/4-in. ball (49) is used. Note location of the ball and remove it.

7. Place the control valve body on the work table, flat side down.

NOTE: Trimmer valve cover (70) or (79) is spring loaded and must be restrained while the bolts are being removed. Cover (70) is used on models without a retarder. Cover (79) is used on models with a retarder.

8. For models without a retarder, remove eight bolts from trimmer valve cover (70). Remove cover. For models with a retarder, remove four bolts and four bolts from trimmer valve cover (79). Remove accumulator valve body (84) from cover (79). Remove accumulator valve (81), spring (82), and stop (83) from valve body (84).

9. For all models, remove springs (53, 57, 58, 62, 63, 67, and 68) from control valve body. Remove valve stops (54, 59, 64, and 69). Remove trimmer plugs (52, 56, 61, and 66). Remove trimmer valves (51, 55, 60, and 65).

NOTE: Valve stop (75) and spacer (78) are spring loaded and must be restrained while the two retainer pins (72) are being removed.

10. Remove the two retainer pins from the control valve body.
11. Remove valve stop (75) and spacer (78).
12. Remove relay valve springs (74 and 77). Remove relay valves (73 and 76).
13. Depress adjusting ring (9). Remove retainer pin (11), ring (9), washer (8), valve stop (7), spring (6) and valve (5).
14. Compress adjusting rings (16, 22, and 29) and remove retainer pins (17, 23, and 30). Remove the adjusting rings.
15. Remove springs (14, 20, and 27). Remove valve stops (15, 21, and 28). Remove modulator valves (13, 19, and 26). Remove shift valves (12, 18, and 25). If model is equipped with a retarder, remove sleeve (24).

1. Control valve assembly	38. Separator plate
2. Valve stop pin	39. Bolt, 1/4-20 x 1¾ (3)
3. Priority valve spring	40. Modulator valve actuator pin
4. Priority valve	41. Modulator valve
5. Hold regulator valve	42. Valve spring
6. Regulator valve spring	43. Washer
7. Valve stop pin (used after S/N 846) ①	44. Valve stop
	45. Adjusting ring
8. Washer (used after S/N 846) ①	46. Modulator valve body
	47. Retainer pin
9. Adjusting ring (used after S/N 846) ①	48. Ball 1/4
	49. Control valve body
10. Selector valve	50. Third clutch trimmer valve
11. Retainer pin	51. Trimmer plug
F. Return spring ②	52. Valve spring
12. 1-2 shift valve	53. Valve stop
E. 1-2 shift valve ②	54. First clutch trimmer valve
13. Shift modulator valve	55. Trimmer plug
D. Shift modulator valve ②	56. Valve outer spring
14. Shift valve spring	57. Valve inner spring
C. Shift valve spring ②	58. Valve stop
15. Valve stop	59. Second clutch trimmer valve
B. Valve stop ②	60. Trimmer plug
16. Adjusting ring	61. Valve outer spring
A. Washer	62. Valve inner spring
17. Retainer pin	63. Valve stop
18. 2-3 shift valve	64. Fourth clutch trimmer valve
19. Shift modulator valve	65. Trimmer plug
20. Shift valve spring	66. Valve outer spring
21. Valve stop	67. Valve inner spring
22. Adjusting ring	68. Valve stop
23. Retainer pin	69. Trimmer valve cover
24. 3-4 shift valve	70. Bolt, 1/4-20 x ⅝ (8)
25. Shift modulator valve	71. Retainer pin (2)
26. Valve spring	72. 2-3 relay valve
27. Valve stop	73. Valve spring
28. Adjusting ring	74. Valve stop
29. Retainer pin	75. 1-2 relay valve
30. 3-4 relay valve	76. Valve spring
31. Relay valve spring	77. Spacer
32. Relay valve stop	78. First clutch tube
33. Retainer pin	79. Governor tube (2)
34. Trimmer regulator valve	① One piece stop used before S/N 847
35. Regulator valve spring	
36. Regulator valve stop	② Used on second gear start only
37. Retainer pin	

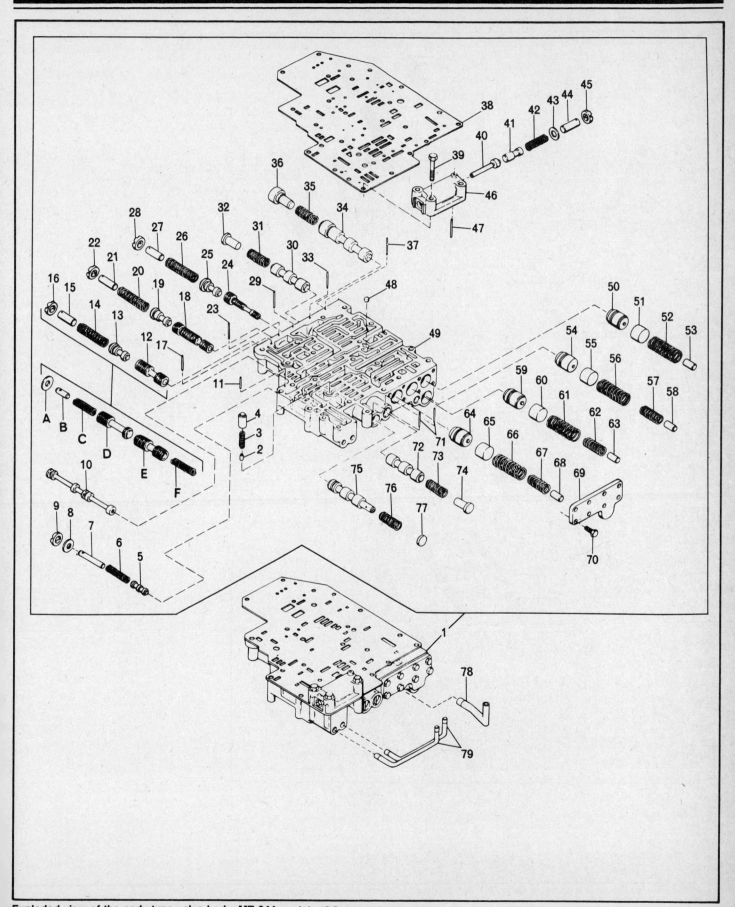

Exploded view of the early type valve body, MT 644 models (©General Motors Corp.)

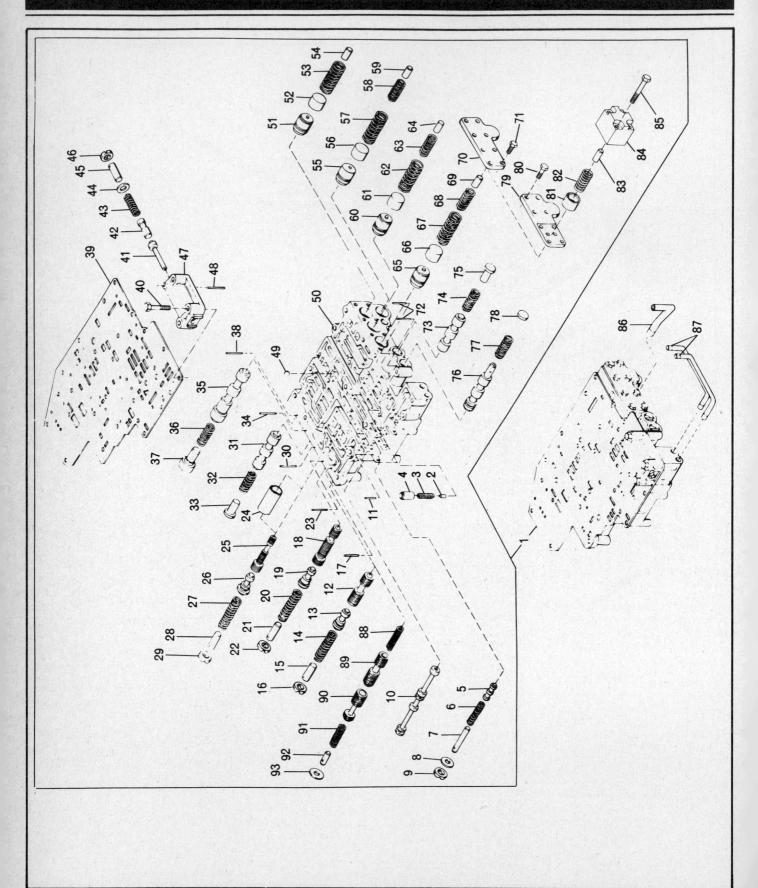

Exploded view of the later type valve body, MT 644 models (©General Motors Corp.)

1. Control valve assembly
2. Valve stop pin
3. Priority valve spring
4. Priority valve
5. Hold regulator valve
6. Regulator valve spring
7. Valve stop pin (used after S/N 846) ①
8. Washer (used after S/N 846) ①
9. Adjusting ring (used after S/N 846) ①
10. Selector valve
11. Retainer pin
12. 1-2 shift valve
13. Shift modulator valve
14. Shift valve spring
15. Valve stop
16. Adjusting ring
17. Retainer pin
18. 2-3 shift valve
19. Shift modulator valve
20. Shift valve spring
21. Valve stop
22. Adjusting ring
23. Retainer pin
24. 3-4 valve sleeve
25. 3-4 shift valve
26. Shift modulator valve
27. Valve spring
28. Valve stop
29. Adjusting ring
30. Retainer pin
31. 3-4 relay valve
32. Relay valve spring
33. Relay valve stop
34. Retainer pin
35. Trimmer regulator valve
36. Regulator valve spring
37. Regulator valve stop
38. Retainer pin
39. Separator plate
40. Bolt, ¼-20 x 1¾ (3) **A**
41. Modulator valve actuator pin
42. Modulator valve
43. Valve spring
44. Washer
45. Valve stop
46. Adjusting ring
47. Modulator valve body
48. Retainer pin
49. Ball ¼
50. Control valve body
51. Third clutch trimmer valve

52. Trimmer plug
53. Valve spring
54. Valve stop
55. First clutch trimmer valve
56. Trimmer plug
57. Valve outer spring
58. Valve inner spring
59. Valve stop
60. Second clutch trimmer valve
61. Trimmer plug
62. Valve outer spring
63. Valve inner spring
64. Valve stop
65. Fourth clutch trimmer valve
66. Trimmer plug
67. Valve outer spring
68. Valve inner spring
69. Valve stop
70. Trimmer valve cover
71. Bolt, ¼-20 x ¾ (8) **A**
72. Retainer pin (2)
73. 2-3 relay valve
74. Valve spring
75. Valve stop
76. 1-2 relay valve
77. Valve spring
78. Spacer
79. Trimmer valve cover ③
80. Bolt, ¼-20 x ¾ (4) **A** ③
81. Accumulator valve ③
82. Valve spring ③
83. Valve stop ③
84. Accumulator valve body ③
85. Bolt, ¼-20 x 2½ (4) **A** ③
86. First clutch tube ③
87. Governor tube (2) ③
88. Return spring ②
89. 1-2 shift valve ②
90. Shift modulator valve ②
91. Shift valve spring ②
92. Valve stop ②
93. Washer ②

Torque	lb ft	N·m
A	9-11	13-14

① One piece stop used before S/N 847
② Used on second gear start only
③ Used with retarder

NOTE: For models equipped with second gear start, remove pin (17), washer (93), stop (92), spring (91), modulator valve (90), 1-2 shift valve (89), and spring (88).

16. Compress relay valve stop (33) and remove retainer pin (34).

17. Remove valve stop (33), valve spring (32), and relay valve (31).

18. Remove retainer pin (38), stop (37), spring (36), and valve (35).

Assembly

NOTE: Check the position of all components, configuration of all valves and plugs, and the identification of all springs before installation. All valves, when dry, should move freely by their own weight in their bores.

1. Install valve (5) into bore A in valve body.

2. Install spring (6), valve stop (7), washer (8), and adjusting ring (9), into the same bore.

3. Depress the adjusting ring against spring force and install pin (11) so that it passes through valve stop and retains the adjusting ring.

4. If model is not equipped with second gear start, install valve (12), shorter land first, into bore B in valve body into the same bore, install valve (13), smaller end first. Install spring (4), valve stop (15), and adjusting ring (16). Depress ring (16) against spring force and install pin (17) so that it passes through valve stop and retains the adjusting ring.

5. If model is equipped with second gear start, install spring (88), valve (89) (open end first), valve (90) (longer land first), spring (91), stop (92), and washer (93) into bore B. Depress washer (93) against spring force and install pin (17) so that it passes through stop (92) and retains the washer (93).

6. For all models, install valve (18), smaller end first, into bore C in valve body.

7. Into the same bore, install valve (19), smaller end first. Install spring (20), valve stop (21), and adjusting ring (22).

8. Depress ring (22) against spring force and install pin (23) so that it passes through valve stop (21) and retains the adjusting ring.

9. Install valve (25), smaller end first, into bore D in valve body.

10. Into the same bore, install valve (26), smaller end first, spring (27), valve stop (28), and adjusting ring (29).

11. Depress adjusting ring (29) against spring force and install pin (30) so that it passes through valve stop (28) and retains the adjusting ring.

12. Install valve (31) into bore E in valve body.

13. Install spring (32) and valve stop (33). Depress valve stop (33) against spring force and install pin (34).

14. Install valve (35), smaller end first, into bore F in valve body.

15. Into the same bore, install spring (36) and valve stop (37). Depress valve stop (36) and install pin (38).

16. Install trimmer valve (51), open end first, into bore G in valve body.

17. Into the same bore, install plug (52), spring (53), and valve stop (54).

18. Install trimmer valve (55), open end first, into bore H in valve body.

19. Into the same bore, install plug (56), springs (57 and 58), and valve stop (59).

20. Install trimmer valve (60), open end first, into bore I in valve body.

21. Into the same bore, install plug (61), springs (62 and 63), and valve stop (64).

22. Install trimmer valve (65), open end first, into bore K in valve body.

23. Into the same bore, install plug (66), springs (67 and 68), and valve stop (69).

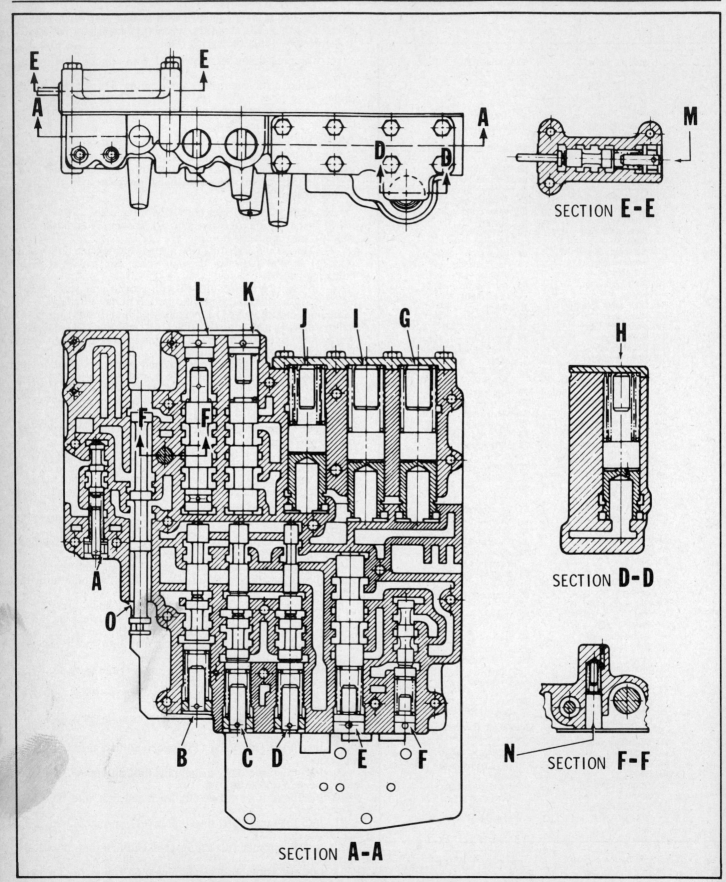

SECTION **E-E**

SECTION **D-D**

SECTION **F-F**

SECTION **A-A**

Cross section of the control valve assembly with bores identified with letters, MT 644 models (©General Motors Corp.)

24. For models without a retarder, install cover (70). Push the cover against the spring force, and install eight ¼-20 x ¾-in. bolts. Tighten the bolts to 9-11 lb. ft. (13-14 N•m).

25. For models with a retarder, install cover (79). Push the cover against the spring force, and install four ¼-20 x ¾-in. bolts. Install spring (82) and stop (83) into accumulator valve body (84). Install accumulator valve (81), open end first, onto spring (82). Install assembled accumulator parts onto cover (79). Install four ¼-20 x 2-½-in. bolts. Tighten bolts 80 and 85 to 9-11 lb. ft. (13-14 N•m).

26. For all models, install valve (73) into bore L in valve body.

27. Into the same bore, install spring (74) and valve stop (75). Depress valve stop against spring force, and install pin (72).

28. Install valve (76), larger end first, into bore M in valve body.

29. Into the same bore, install spring (77) and spacer (78). Depress the spacer against spring force, and install pin (72).

30. Install actuator pin (41), smaller end first, into bore N in valve body. Install valve (42), longer land first, into the same bore.

31. Install spring (43), washer (44), valve stop (45), and adjusting ring (46).

32. Depress adjusting ring (46) against spring force, and install pin (48) so that it passes through valve stop and retains the adjusting ring.

33. If ball (49) was removed from valve body during disassembly, replace the ball in its original location. Retain the ball with oil-soluble grease.

34. Install valve stop (2), spring (3), and priority valve (4), open end first, into bore O in valve body.

35. Place separator plate (39) onto the valve body 40 so the bolt holes align. Some models include a T-slot in the separator plate that engages the flared end of pin (34).

36. Install the assembled modulator valve onto oil separator plate (39). Align the bolts holes.

37. Install three ¼-20 x 1-¾-in. bolts (40) through valve body (47), plate (39), and into valve body (50).

38. After making sure that the plate and valve body are properly aligned, tighten bolts 40 to 9-11 lb. ft. (13-14 N•m).

39. Using adjusting tool J-24314 or equivalent, position adjusting rings (9, 16, 22, 29, and 46), as they were before the valve body was disassembled.

40. Install selector valve (10), drilled end first, into bore P in valve body. Secure the valve with a rubber band, cord, or soft wire.

NOTE: If the valve body assembly is not to be installed immediately, cover it with a plastic bag or wrap it to protect it from dust, dirt, and moisture.

LOW TRIMMER VALVE ASSEMBLY

Disassembly

MT 654CR

1. While depressing plug (30) against spring force, remove retainer pin (24).
2. Release plug (30) and remove it.
3. Remove springs (27) and (28), and valve stop (29). Remove trimmer plug (26) and trimmer valve (25).

Assembly

1. Install trimmer valve (25), open end first, into valve body (23). Install plug (26).
2. Install spring (27), spring (28), and valve stop (29).
3. Install plug (30). Depress plug (30) against spring force, and install pin (24). Pin (24) must be flush with, to 0.020 in. (0.50mm) below, the mounting face of the valve body.

LOW SHIFT SIGNAL VALVE ASSEMBLY

Disassembly

MT 654CR

1. Mark adjusting ring (15) to indicate its position in relation to pin (11).
2. Depress plug (21) against spring force sufficiently to remove pin (19). Remove pin (19), plug (21), valve (20), and spring (18).
3. Remove pin (11), adjusting ring (15), washer (66), and valve stop (17).
4. Depress valve stop (14) against spring force. Remove pin (10), valve stop (14), spring (13), and valve (12).

Assembly

1. Install valve (20), smaller diameter end first, into bore of valve body (9). Install plug (21). Install pin (19) to retain the plug.
2. Install spring (18) into the opposite end of the bore. Install valve stop (17), washer (16), and adjusting ring (15).
3. Depress adjusting ring (15) against spring force, and install pin (11) so that it passes through valve stop and retains the adjusting ring.
4. Install valve (12), spring (13), and valve stop (14).
5. Depress valve stop against spring force, and install the retaining pin.

CONTROL VALVE ASSEMBLY

Disassembly

MT 654CR

NOTE: The valve body assembly contains a number of springs, some of which are similar and can be mistakenly interchanged. Also, springs vary in valve bodies used on different models. If springs are not reinstalled in the same locations from which they were removed, the calibration of the valve body will be affected. For these reasons each spring should be tagged, at removal.

1. Remove selector valve (10). Place valve assembly on the work table, modulator valve body (49) upward.
2. Remove three bolts (42) from the modulator body and remove the modulator body.

NOTE: Before removing retaining pins (11, 17, 23, 29, and 50), make a note or sketch that shows the position of adjusting rings (9, 16, 22, 28, and 48) in relation to their retaining pins. If the valve body is reassembled with the same springs, but the adjusting rings are not in their original positions, the calibration of the valve body will be affected.

3. Remove retaining pin (50) from modulator body (49) while applying pressure to adjusting ring (48). Remove the adjusting ring.
4. Remove valve stop (47), washer (46), spring (45), modulator valve (44), and actuator pin (43).
5. Remove oil transfer plate (38) and separator plate (51) while holding them firmly together to prevent losing balls (39, 40, and 41).
6. Invert the plates and place them on the bench.
7. Remove separator plate (51), and balls (39, 40, and 41).
8. Remove priority valve (4), spring (3), and stop (2).

NOTE: Trimmer valve cover (77) is spring loaded and must be restrained while the bolts are being removed.

9. Place control valve body (52) on the work table, flat side down. Remove eight bolts (78) from trimmer valve cover (77).
10. Remove trimmer valve (77). Remove valve stops (57, 62, 67, and 76).
11. Remove accumulator valve (70), spring (69), and valve stop (68).

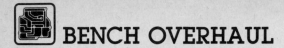

1. Modulated lockup valve assembly
2. Modulated lockup valve body
3. Retainer pin
4. Modulating lockup valve
5. Modulating lockup valve spring
6. Modulating lockup valve stop
7. Adjusting ring MT654CR
8. Low shift signal valve assembly
9. Low shift signal valve body
10. Retainer pin
11. Retainer pin
12. Relay valve
13. Relay valve spring
14. Relay valve stop
15. Adjusting ring
16. Spacer washer
17. Low shift signal valve stop
18. Low shift signal valve spring
19. Retainer pin
20. Low shift signal valve
21. Low shift signal valve plug
22. Low trimmer valve assembly
23. Low trimmer valve body
24. Retainer pin
25. Trimmer valve
26. Trimmer plug valve
27. Primary trimmer valve spring
28. Secondary trimmer valve spring
29. Trimmer valve stop
30. Plug
31. Separator plate (2nd gear start)

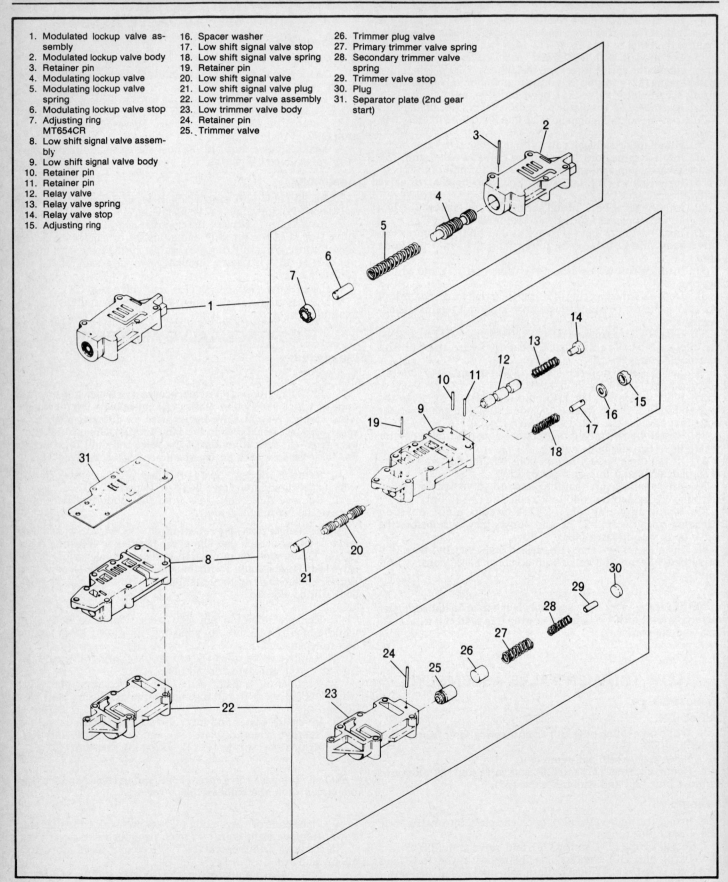

Exploded view of the modulated lock-up, low shift and low trimmer valve body assemblies, MT 654CR models (©General Motors Corp.)

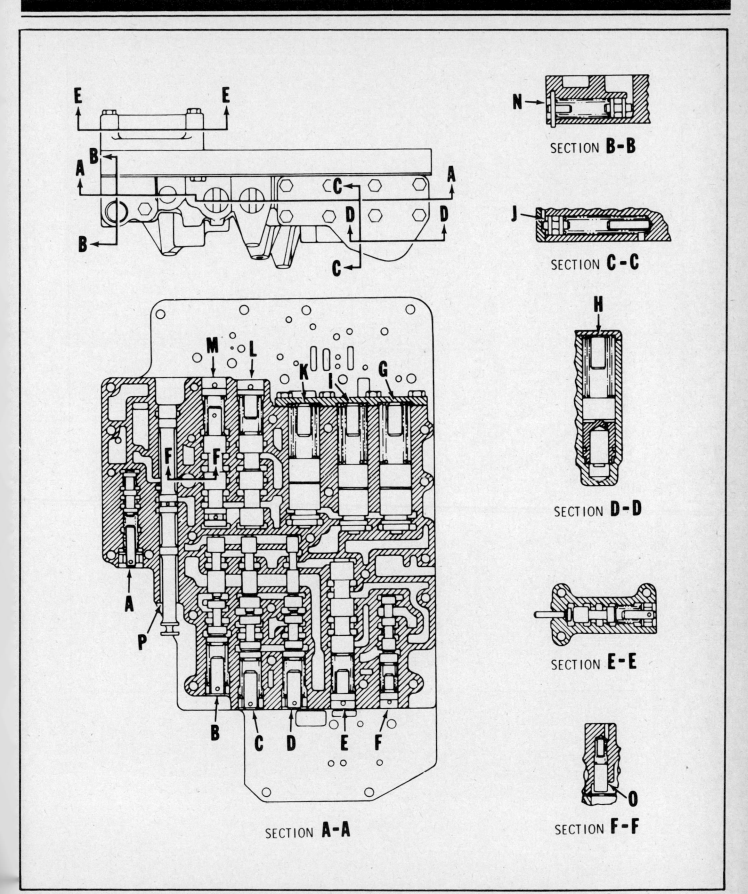

SECTION **B-B**

SECTION **C-C**

SECTION **D-D**

SECTION **E-E**

SECTION **F-F**

SECTION **A-A**

Cross section of the control valve assembly with bores identified with letters, MT 654CR models (©General Motors Corp.)

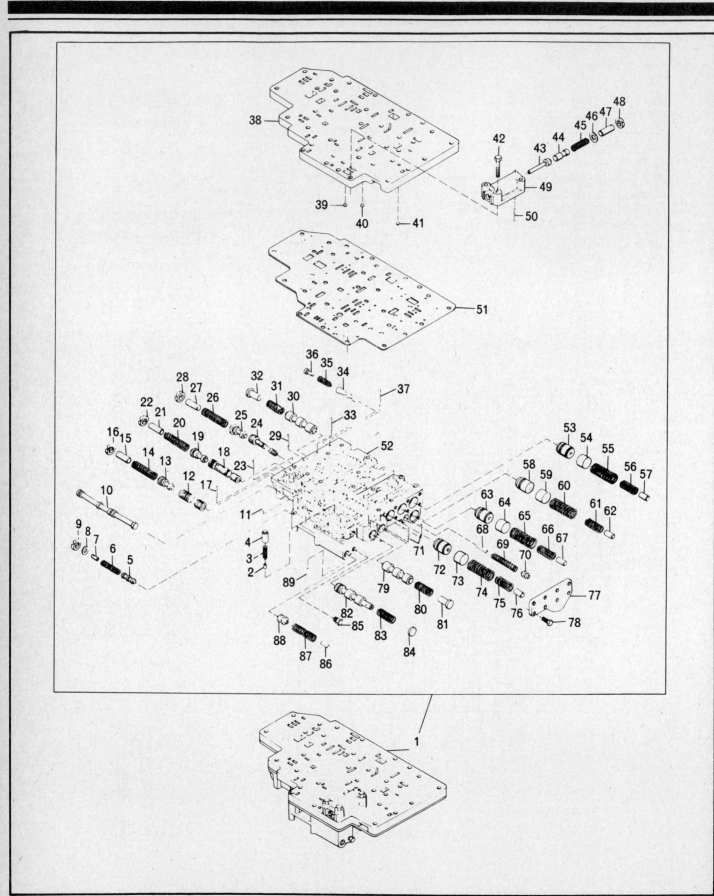

Exploded view of valve body assembly, MT 654CR models (©General Motors Corp.)

12. Remove springs (55, 56, 60, 61, 65, 66, 74, and 75). Remove trimmer plugs (54, 59, 64, and 73). Remove trimmer valves (53, 58, 63, and 72).

NOTE: Valve stop (81) and spacer (84) are spring loaded and must be restrained while two retainer pins (71) are being removed.

13. Remove two retainer pins (71) from the control valve body.

14. Remove valve stop (81) and spacer (84).

15. Remove relay valve springs (80) and (83). Remove relay valves (79 and 82).

16. Depress adjusting ring (9). Remove pin (11), ring (9), washer (8), valve stop (7), spring (6), and valve (5).

17. Depress adjusting rings (16, 22, and 28) and remove retainer pins (17, 23, and 29). Remove the adjusting rings.

18. Remove valve stops (15, 21, and 27). Remove springs (14, 20, and 26). Remove modulator valves (13, 19, and 25). Remove shift valves (12, 18, and 24).

19. Depress relay valve stop (32) and remove retainer pin (33).

20. Remove valve stop (32), valve spring (31), and relay valve (30).

21. Remove pin (37), valve (34), spring (35), and valve stop (36).

22. Remove plug (85). Remove, if present, the conical screen from the plug bore. Discard the screen. Do not install a screen at reassembly.

23. Depress spring (87) and remove pin (89). Remove valve stop (86), spring (87), and valve (88).

Assembly

NOTE: Check the position of all components, configuration of all valves and plugs, and identification of all springs before installation. All valves when dry, should move freely by their own weight in their bores.

1. Install valve (5) into bore A of the valve body.

2. Into the same bore, install spring (6), valve stop (7), washer (8), and adjusting ring (9).

3. Depress the adjusting ring against spring force and install pin (11) so that it passes through valve stop (7) and retains adjusting ring (9).

4. Install valve (12), shorter land first, into bore B in valve body.

5. Into the same bore, install valve (13), smaller end first. Install spring (14), valve stop (15), and adjusting ring (16).

6. Depress the adjusting ring against spring force and install pin (17) so that it passes through valve stop and retains the adjusting ring.

7. Install valve (18) shorter land end first, into bore C in valve body.

8. Into the same bore, install valve (19), smaller end first. Install spring (20), valve stop (21), and adjusting ring (22).

9. Depress ring (22) against spring force and install pin (23) so that it passes through valve stop and retains the adjusting ring.

10. Install valve (24), shorter land end first, into bore D in valve body.

11. Into the same bore install valve (25), smaller end first, spring (26), valve stop (27), and adjusting ring (28).

12. Depress adjusting ring (28) against spring force and install pin (29) so that it passes through valve stop and retains the adjusting ring.

13. Install valve (30) into bore E in valve body.

14. Install spring (31) and valve stop (32). Depress valve stop (32) against spring pressure and install pin (33).

15. Install valve (34), smaller end first, into bore F in valve body (52).

16. Into the same bore, install spring (35) and valve stop (36). Depress valve stop (36) and install pin (37).

17. Install trimmer valve (53), open end first, into bore G in valve body (52).

18. Into the same bore, install plug (54), springs (55 and 56), and valve stop (57).

19. Install trimmer valve (58), open end first, into bore H in valve body (52).

20. Into the same bore, install plug (59), springs (60 and 61), and valve stop (62).

21. Install trimmer valve (63), open end first, into bore I in valve body (52).

22. Into the same bore, install plug (64), spring (65), spring (66), and valve stop (67).

23. Install spring (69) into bore J in valve body (52).

24. Into the same bore, install stop 68. Install accumulator valve (70) against spring (69).

25. Install trimmer valve (72), open end first, into bore K in valve body (52).

26. Into the same bore, install plug (73), springs (74 and 75), and valve stop (76).

27. Install cover (77). Push the cover against the spring force, and install eight ¼-20 x ¾-in. bolts (78). Tighten the bolts to 9-11 lb. ft. (13-14 N•m).

28. Install valve (79) into bore L in valve body.

29. Into the same bore, install spring (80) and valve stop (81). Depress stop (81) against spring force, and install pin (71).

30. Install valve (82), larger end first, into bore M in valve body.

1. Control valve assembly	47. Valve stop
2. Valve stop pin	48. Adjusting ring
3. Priority valve spring	49. Modulator valve body
4. Priority valve spring	50. Retainer pin
5. Hold regulator valve	51. Separator plate
6. Regulator valve spring	52. Control valve body
7. Valve stop pin	53. Third clutch trimmer valve
8. Washer	54. Trimmer plug
9. Adjusting ring	55. Valve outer spring
10. Selector valve	56. Valve inner spring
11. Retainer pin	57. Valve stop
12. 2-3 shift valve	58. First clutch trimmer valve
13. Shift modulator valve	59. Trimmer plug
14. Shift valve spring	60. Valve outer spring
15. Valve stop	61. Valve inner spring
16. Adjusting ring	62. Valve stop
17. Retainer pin	63. Second clutch trimmer valve
18. 3-4 shift valve	64. Trimmer plug
19. Shift modulator valve	65. Valve outer spring
20. Shift valve spring	66. Valve inner spring
21. Valve stop	67. Valve top
22. Adjusting ring	68. Valve stop
23. Retainer pin	69. Valve spring
24. 4-5 shift valve	70. Trimmer boost valve
25. Shift modulator valve	71. Retainer pin (2)
26. Valve spring	72. Fourth clutch trimmer valve
27. Valve stop	73. Trimmer plug
28. Adjusting ring	74. Valve outer spring
29. Retainer pin	75. Valve inner spring
30. 4-5 relay valve	76. Valve stop
31. Relay valve spring	77. Trimmer valve cover
32. Relay valve stop	78. Bolt, ¼-20 x ¾ (8) A
33. Retainer pin	79. 3-4 relay valve
34. Trimmer regulator or valve	80. Valve spring
35. Regulator valve spring	81. Valve stop
36. Regulator valve stop	82. 2-3 relay valve
37. Retainer pin	83. Valve spring
38. Oil transfer plate	84. Spacer
39. Check ball, ¼	85. Plug B
40. Check ball, ¼	86. Valve stop
41. Check ball, ¼	87. Valve spring
42. Bolt, ¼-20 x 2-½ (3) A	88. Governor accumulator valve
43. Modulator valve actuator pin	89. Retainer pin
44. Modulator valve	
45. Valve spring	
46. Washer	

Torque	lb ft	N•m
A	9-11	13-14
B	4-5	6-7

31. Into the same bore, install spring (83) and spacer (84). Depress the spacer against spring force, and install pin (71).

32. Install accumulator valve (88) into bore N in valve body.

33. Into the same bore, install spring (87) and valve stop (86). Depress spring (87) and install pin (89) so that it passes through valve stop (86) and retains spring (87).

34. Install plug (85) into the valve body. Tighten the plug to 4-5 lb. ft. (6.7 N•m).

35. Install actuator rod (43), smaller end first, into valve body. Install valve (44), longer land first, into the same bore.

36. Install spring (45), washer (46), valve stop (47), and adjusting ring (48).

37. Depress adjusting ring (48) against spring pressure, and install pin (50) so that it passes through valve stop and retains the adjusting ring.

38. Install valve stop (2), spring (3), and priority valve (4), open end first, into bore O in the valve body.

39. Position oil transfer plate (38) on the bench so that the oil channels (bottom) are upward. Install balls (39, 40, and 41) into their locations. Retain the balls with oil-soluble grease.

40. Place separator plate (51) onto transfer plate (38) so that bolt holes align.

41. Invert the assembled oil transfer plate (38) and separator plate (51). Install these onto the valve body so that the bolt holes align.

42. Install the assembled modulator valve onto oil transfer plate (38). Align the bolt holes.

43. Force the separator plate, oil transfer plate, and modulator valve, against the valve body to compress spring (3).

44. Install three ¼-20 x 2-½-in. bolts (42) through valve body plates (38 and 51), and into the valve body.

45. After making sure that the plates and valve body are properly aligned, tighten the bolts 42 to 9-11 lb. ft. (12-15 N•m).

46. Install selector valve (10), drilled end first, into bore P in valve body. Secure the valve with a rubber band, cord, or soft wire.

47. Using adjusting tool J-24314 or its equivalent, position adjusting rings (9, 16, 22, 28, and 48) as they were before the valve body was disassembled.

NOTE: If the valve body assembly is not to be installed immediately, cover it with a plastic bag or wrap it to protect it from dust, dirt, and moisture.

Transmission Assembly
CLUTCH CLEARANCES

Correct running clearances of the clutch packs are required during the assembly of the transmission. The clearances for the low, first, second and third clutches are established by direct measurement on all transmission models, but also can be measured by the stack method. Both methods are defined through the transmission assembly procedure.

SECOND CLUTCH CLEARANCE WHILE SELECTING THE CENTER SUPPORT SNAP RING

1. Position the transmission housing with the converter end upward. Install the second clutch back plate into the transmission.

2. Alternately install three internally splined clutch plates and three externally tanged clutch plates, beginning with an internally splined plate, into the transmission of the MT 640, 643, 650, 653 models. On the MT 644 and 654CR models, beginning with an internally splined clutch plate, install four of the internally splined clutch plates and four of the externally tanged clutch plates, into the transmission. Retain the clutch plates with a snap ring.

3. Remove the third clutch piston from the center support assembly, if equipped. Attach the center support lifting bracket, J-24455 or its equivalent, into the recess between the seal rings on the support hub.

4. Align the tapped hole in the center support assembly with the anchor bolt hole in the transmission housing, at the valve body attachment area. Lower the center support assembly into the transmission housing, seating it firmly against the second clutch retaining snap ring. Remove the lifting device from the center support and install the anchor bolt and washer through the case and into the support. Tighten finger tight.

5. With the use of a compressor bar and components, such as tools J-24475-2, J-24475-2 and J-23717-1 or their equivalent, compress the center support by applying a torque of five (5) ft. lbs. to the center tool screw.

6. With the use of special tool J-24208-4 or its equivalent, measure the clearance between the top edge of the center support and the top of the snap ring groove in the housing. Select the proper size snap ring from the following chart.

Measured Clearance in. (mm)	Snap ring Thickness in. (mm)	Snap ring Color
0.150-0.154 (3.81-3.91)	0.148-0.150 (3.76-3.81)	Blue/White
0.154-0.157 (3.91-3.99)	0.152-0.154 (3.86-3.91)	Yellow
0.157-0.160 (3.99-4.06)	0.155-0.157 (3.94-3.99)	Green
0.160-0.164 (4.06-4.17)	0.158-0.160 (4.01-4.06)	Red

NOTE: White is used with the MT 644 and 654CR models. The Blue is used with the MT 640, 643, 650, 653 models.

7. Install the selected snap ring and remove the compressor tools from the transmission.

8. Invert the transmission housing, output end upward.

9. Using the gauge J-26918 or its equivalent, check the second plate clearance by inserting the gauge between the back plate and the transmission housing. The prescribed clearance for the models MT 640, 643, 650, 653 is 0.049-0.111 inch (1.24-2.82 mm) and for the models MT 644, 654CR, 0.059-0.129 inch (1.50-3.27 mm).

10. If the clearance is too great, remove the clutch plates and measure the thickness of each internal splined plate. Replace the plates as necessary to obtain the prescribed clearance. If new internal splined plates will not give the proper clearance, the back plate may be replaced by a thicker or thinner plate.

Installing the Rear Cover and First Clutch
REAR COVER

Installation

MT 640, 643, 644

1. Place the rear cover gasket on the transmission and install the rear cover assembly, carefully aligning the holes in the gasket and the cover, to the holes in the transmission case.

2. Install the pre-assembled rear cover onto the transmission housing. Install the fourteen retaining bolts.

3. Tighten two bolts that are 180° apart to 33 ft. lbs. (45 N•m). Repeat the entire procedure for sets of two bolts 180° apart until all are tightened evenly. Repeat the procedure, tightening each of the fourteen bolts to 67-80 ft. lbs. (91-108 N•m).

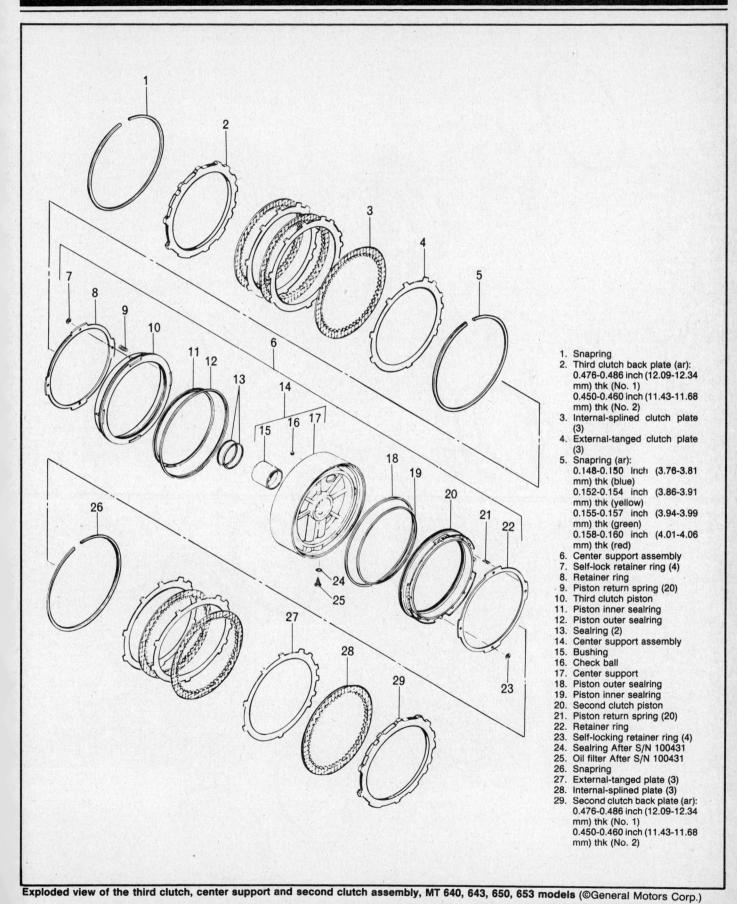

1. Snapring
2. Third clutch back plate (ar):
   0.476-0.486 inch (12.09-12.34 mm) thk (No. 1)
   0.450-0.460 inch (11.43-11.68 mm) thk (No. 2)
3. Internal-splined clutch plate (3)
4. External-tanged clutch plate (3)
5. Snapring (ar):
   0.148-0.150 inch (3.76-3.81 mm) thk (blue)
   0.152-0.154 inch (3.86-3.91 mm) thk (yellow)
   0.155-0.157 inch (3.94-3.99 mm) thk (green)
   0.158-0.160 inch (4.01-4.06 mm) thk (red)
6. Center support assembly
7. Self-lock retainer ring (4)
8. Retainer ring
9. Piston return spring (20)
10. Third clutch piston
11. Piston inner sealring
12. Piston outer sealring
13. Sealring (2)
14. Center support assembly
15. Bushing
16. Check ball
17. Center support
18. Piston outer sealring
19. Piston inner sealring
20. Second clutch piston
21. Piston return spring (20)
22. Retainer ring
23. Self-locking retainer ring (4)
24. Sealring After S/N 100431
25. Oil filter After S/N 100431
26. Snapring
27. External-tanged plate (3)
28. Internal-splined plate (3)
29. Second clutch back plate (ar):
    0.476-0.486 inch (12.09-12.34 mm) thk (No. 1)
    0.450-0.460 inch (11.43-11.68 mm) thk (No. 2)

Exploded view of the third clutch, center support and second clutch assembly, MT 640, 643, 650, 653 models (©General Motors Corp.)

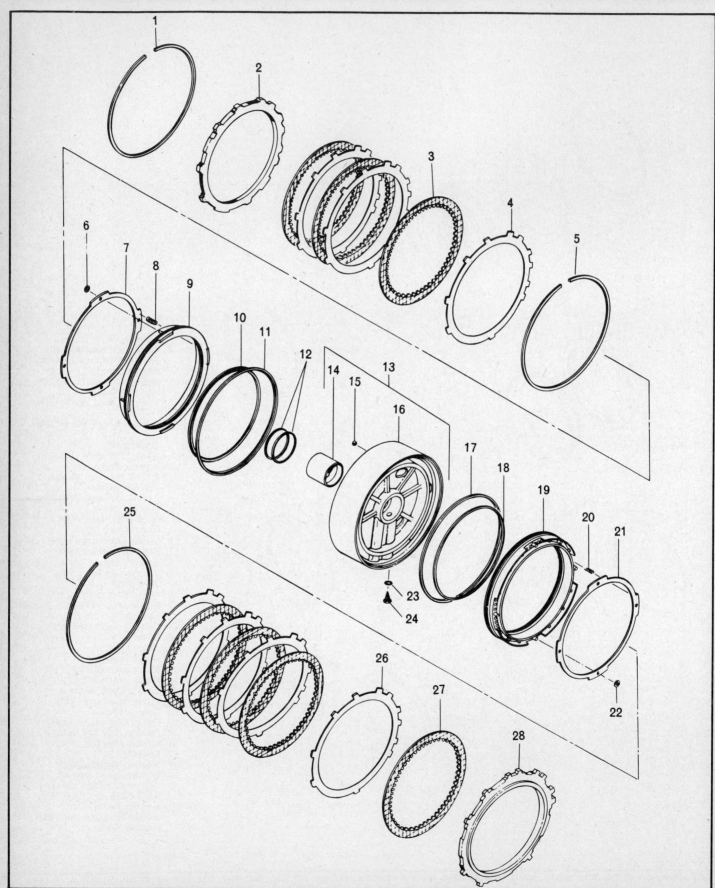

Exploded view of the third clutch, center support and second clutch assembly, MT 644, 654CR models (©General Motors Corp.)

1. Snapring
2. Third clutch backplate (selective)
3. Internal-splined clutch plate (3)
4. External-tanged clutch plate (3)
5. Snapring (selective)
6. Self-locking retainer ring (4)
7. Retaining ring
8. Piston return spring (20)
9. Third clutch piston
10. Piston inner sealring
11. Piston outer sealring
12. Scarf-cut sealring (2) (MT 654 models without retarder)
    Butt-joint sealring (2) (MT 644 models; MT 654 models with retarder)
13. Center support assembly
14. Bushing
15. Check ball
16. Center support
17. Piston outer sealring
18. Piston inner sealring
19. Second clutch piston
20. Piston return spring (20)
21. Retaining ring
22. Self-locking retainer ring (4)
23. Sealring
24. Filter screen
25. Snapring
26. External-tanged plate (4)
27. Internal-splined plate (4)
28. Second clutch backplate (marked):
    3—0.234-0.244 in. (5.94-6.19 mm)
    4—0.208-0.218 in. (5.28-5.53 mm)

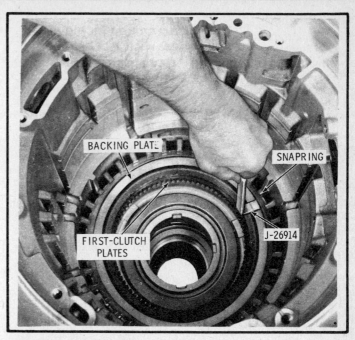

Checking first clutch clearance, MT 640, 643, 644 models
(©General Motors Corp.)

FIRST CLUTCH

Direct Measurement Method

MT 640, 643, 644

1. Invert the transmission, front side up.
2. Remove the snap ring retaining the center support assembly. Remove the center support anchor bolt and washer. Attach a lifting device to the center support and remove the center support from the transmission.
3. Remove the second clutch snap ring and remove the clutch plates and backing plate from the transmission. Retain the second clutch plates in a pack and do not mix them with other clutch plates.
4. Install one external tanged, one internal splined and then one external tanged first clutch plates into the transmission.
5. Place the rear planetary ring gear (extended tooth side down on the MT 640, 643 and the separator ring down on the MT 644 model) on a work table area. Beginning with an internal splined clutch plate, install five internal splined and four external tanged clutch plates, along with the back plate (flat side first) onto the ring gear. Install the ring gear and plates, as an assemby, into the transmission housing.
6. Retain the first clutch pack with a snap ring.
7. Using the first clutch clearance gauge, J-26914 or its equivalent, measure the clearance between the snap ring and the back plate. The prescribed clearance is 0.074-0.147 inch (1.88-3.73 mm) for all models.
8. If the clearance is too great, remove the plates and measure the thickness of each internal splined clutch plate. Replace as necessary to obtain the prescribed clearance. If new clutch plates will not provide the correct clearance, a thicker or thinner back plate can be obtained to achieve the desired measurement.

Stack Method

1. Stack the desired number of clutch plates and piston in a press that can provide 980 to 1020 pounds of pressure on the clutch plate pack.
2. Measure the distance from the top outer edge of the clutch piston to the flat surface that the clutch pack is setting upon.
3. Refer to the accompanying chart to select the first clutch back plate.

LOW CLUTCH RUNNING CLEARANCE

Direct Measurement Method

MT 650, 653, 654CR

1. Position the adapter housing and the assembled first clutch piston on a work bench with the piston downward. Install the six external tanged clutch plates and the five internal splined clutch plates, for a total of eleven clutch plates on the MT 650, 653 models. MT 654CR early models use a total of thirteen clutch plates, seven external tanged clutch plates and six internal splined clutch plates. Later model MT 654CR units use eight external tanged clutch plates and seven internal splined clutch plates for a total of fifteen.
2. Position the rear cover, piston upward, and install the rear cover gasket.
3. With the use of a depth micrometer, measure and record the dimension (A), from the top of the housing to the top of the clutch plate. Use hand pressure only to hold the plates in place at point of measurement.
4. Using the depth micrometer, measure and record the dimension (B), from the top of the piston to the gasket on the mounting flange.
5. Subtract dimension B from dimension A to obtain the running clearance for the low clutch. The clearance is acceptable if within 0.081-0.139 inch (2.06-3.53 mm) for the MT 650, 653 models. Keep the clearance closer to 0.081 (2.06 mm) for longer clutch pack life. The clearance for the MT 654CR models should be within 0.073-0.145 inch (1.85-3.68 mm) for the thirteen plate clutch pack and 0.073-0.141 inch (1.85-3.58 mm) for the fifteen plate clutch pack.
6. To obtain the desired clearance, new clutch plates and/or a piston with a different thickness would have to be used.

Stack Method

1. Stack the desired number of clutch plates in the rear of the adapter housing.

2. With a pressure load of 980 to 1020 pounds on the clutch plate pack, measure the distance between the top of the adapter housing and the top of the clutch pack. From the accompanying chart, select the low clutch piston to be used with the clutch pack. Use the clutch pack and the selected piston when the transmission is assembled.

LOW-CLUTCH COMPONENTS MODELS

Installation

MT 650, 653

1. Install the gasket, the adapter housing, and the first-clutch piston to the transmission case, using two six inch guide bolts for alignment.

NOTE: Thrust washers can be retained with oil soluble grease.

2. Install the tanged thrust washer and the low planetary sun gear into the housing.

3. Install the thrust washer into the low planetary unit and install the planetary assembly into the sun gear.

4. Install the thrust washer onto the hub of the low ring gear. Center the thrust washer within the planetary assembly and install the ring gear.

5. Beginning with an externally tanged clutch plate, install six externally tanged plates and five internally splined plates, alternately.

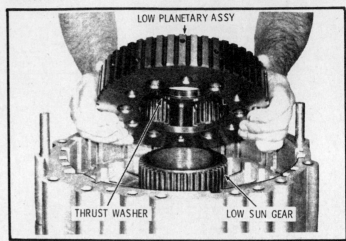

Installing the low planetary carrier assembly, MT 650, 653 models (©General Motors Corp.)

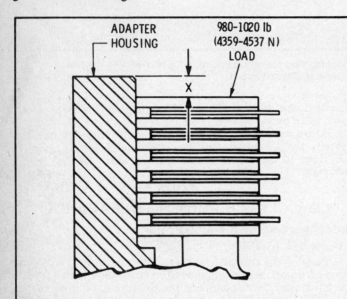

THIRTEEN PLATE CLUTCH	
DIM. X =	USE PISTON MARKED
0.3957-0.4325 in. (10.050-10.985 mm)	A
0.4325-0.4615 in. (10.985-11.722 mm)	B
0.4615-0.4967 in. (11.722-12.616 mm)	C

FIFTEEN PLATE CLUTCH	
DIM. X =	USE PISTON MARKED
0.2749-0.3133 in. (6.982-7.957 mm)	C
0.3133-0.3516 in. (7.957-8.930 mm)	B
0.3516-0.3899 in. (8.930-9.903 mm)	A

Stack method of measurement for the low clutch, MT 650, 653, 654CR models (©General Motors Corp.)

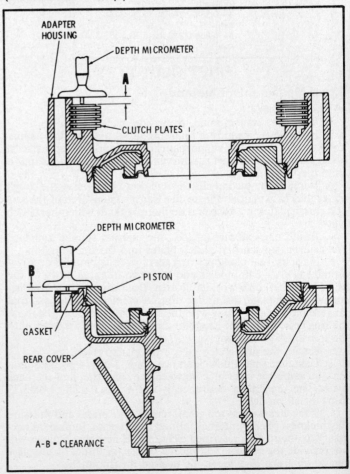

Direct method of measurement for the low clutch running clearance, MT 650, 653, 654CR models (©General Motors Corp.)

NOTE: Position the three sets of double tanged lugs, located on the external tanged plates, into the double tanged notches of the adapter housing. If not positioned properly, movement of the stationary plates will occur.

6. Install the output shaft assembly into the low ring gear.

7. Install the governor drive gear and engage the spring pin with the slot in the drive gear. Install the speedometer drive gear and spacer on the output shaft, also.

LOW CLUTCH AND PLANETARY COMPONENTS

Installation
MT 654CR

1. Install the two six inch guide bolts into the rear of the transmission housing. Install the adapter housing gasket, the adapter housing and the first piston assembly, using the guide bolts.

2. If the low planetary ring gear and the driving hub have been separated, place the ring gear on a work bench with the internal snap ring groove up. Install the drive hub, external splines first, into the ring gear and install the snap ring to retain the hub.

3. Install the low planetary ring gear and hub into the adapter housing.

--- CAUTION ---

Be sure the three sets of double tangs engage the three sets of double grooves in the adapter housing.

4. Re-install the low clutch pack, previously removed, into the adapter housing. Beginning with an external tanged plate, alternately install seven (eight on later models) external tanged and six (seven on later models) internal splined clutch plates. Install the thrust washer onto the front hub of the low planetary carrier assembly and retain with oil soluble grease.

5. Install the low planetary carrier assembly into the low ring gear.

6. Install the speedometer drive gear and then the spacer onto the output shaft.

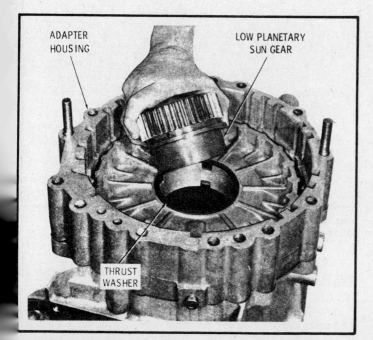

Installing the low planetary sun gear, MT 650, 653 models
(©General Motors Corp.)

REAR COVER

Installation
MT 650, 653, 654CR

1. Install the rear cover gasket onto the adapter housing and install the rear cover assembly onto the two guide bolts.

2. Install twelve of the fourteen bolts and washers through the rear cover and adapter housing, into the transmission housing. Snug the bolts and remove the two guide bolts. Replace with the two remaining hex headed bolts. Tighten two bolts that are 180° apart to 30-33 ft. lbs. (41-45 N•m). Move around the bolt circle and tighten each bolt in turn, in the same manner. Repeat the procedure, tightening all bolts to 67-80 ft. lbs. (91-108 N•m) on the MT 650, 653 models, and 81-97 ft. lbs. (110-132 N•m) on the MT 654CR models.

3. Install the governor into the rear cover. Install the governor cover gasket and the cover. Tighten the governor retaining bolts to 15-20 ft. lbs. (20-27 N•m).

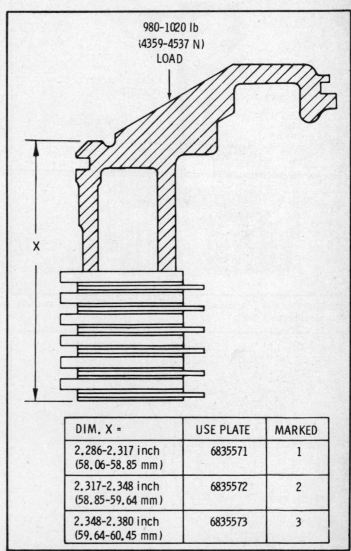

DIM. X =	USE PLATE	MARKED
2.286-2.317 inch (58.06-58.85 mm)	6835571	1
2.317-2.348 inch (58.85-59.64 mm)	6835572	2
2.348-2.380 inch (59.64-60.45 mm)	6835573	3

Stack method of measurement for the first clutch, all models
(©General Motors Corp.)

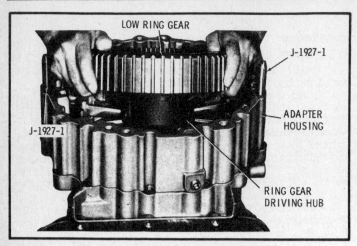

Installing the low ring gear and hub, MT 654CR models (©General Motors Corp.)

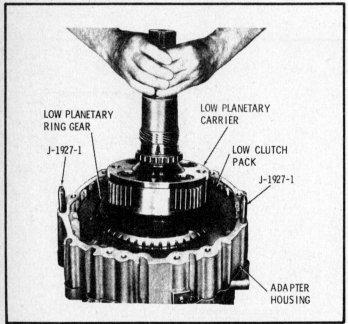

Installing the low planetary carrier assembly, MT 654CR models (©General Motors Corp.)

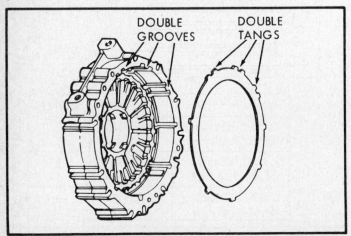

Correct positioning of the external tanged clutch plates in the adapter housing (©General Motors Corp.)

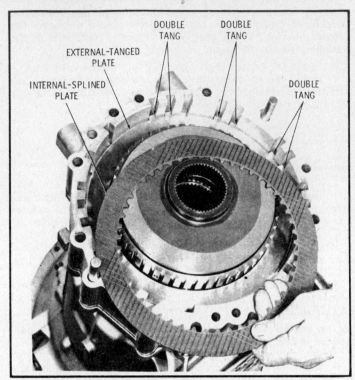

Installing the low clutch plates, typical (©General Motors Corp.)

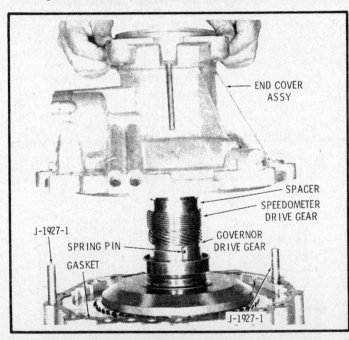

Installation of the end cover assembly, typical (©General Motors Corp.)

FIRST CLUTCH CLEARANCE

Direct Measurement Method

MT 650, 653, 654CR

1. Invert the transmission, front side upward. Remove the center support anchor bolt that were temporarily installed previously.

2. Remove the snap ring that retains the center support assembly.

NOTE: It may be necessary to compress the center support to remove the retaining snap ring.

3. Attach a lifting device to the center support assembly and remove from the transmission. Keep the snap ring and center support assembly together.

4. Remove the second clutch plate retaining snap ring. Remove the six second clutch plates and the back plate from the MT models 650, 653, while removing the eight second clutch plates and the back plate from the transmission housing on the MT 654CR models.

— CAUTION —

Maintain the second clutch pack and back plate as a unit. Do not mix with other clutch packs.

5. **MT 650, 653 Models**—Install the ring gear hub into the ring gear and retain it with a snap ring. Install the tanged thrust washer into the hub of the adapter housing. Install the rear planetary ring gear and hub assembly.

6. Starting with an external tanged clutch plate, alternately install six external tanged and six internal splined clutch plates. Install the back plate, flat side first and retain it with a snap ring.

7. Using the first clutch gauge, J-26914 or its equivalent, measure the clearance between the snap ring and the back plate. The clearance should be 0.074-0.147 inch (1.88-3.73 mm).

8. If the clearance is not correct, measure the total plate thickness and replace the plates as required to obtain the desired clearance. If necessary, the back plate can be replaced with a thinner or thicker unit.

9. **MT 654CR Models**—Install one external tanged and one internal splined clutch plate into the transmission housing.

10. Place the rear planetary ring gear, with the separator ring down, on a work table. Beginning with an internal splined clutch plate, install five internal splined clutch plates and four external tanged clutch plates, along with the back plate, flat side first, on to the ring gear. Install the ring gear and plates, as an assembly, into the transmission housing.

11. Retain the first clutch pack with a snap ring. Using the first clutch pack gauge, or its equivalent, measure the clearance between the snap ring and the back plate. The prescribed clearance is 0.074-0.147 inch (1.88-3.73 mm).

12. If the clearance is not correct, remove the plates and measure the thickness of each internal splined clutch plate. Replace as required to achieve the prescribed clearance. If the new plates do not produce the correct clearance, the back plate may have to be replaced with either a thicker or thinner one.

Stack Method

1. Stack the desired number of clutch plates and piston in a press that can provide 980-1020 pounds of pressure on the clutch pack.

2. Measure the distance from the top outer edge of the clutch piston to the flat surface that the clutch pack is setting upon.

3. Refer to the accompanying chart to select the first clutch back plate.

GEAR UNIT

Installation
MT 640, 643, 644

1. Using a lifting tool, raise the gear unit assembly and guide it into the transmission housing.

2. Engage the pinion teeth of the rear planetary carrier assembly with the teeth of the rear planetary ring gear.

MT 650, 653

1. Retain the thrust washer to the rear planetary carrier assembly. With the aid of a lifting tool, lift the unit and lower it into the transmission case.

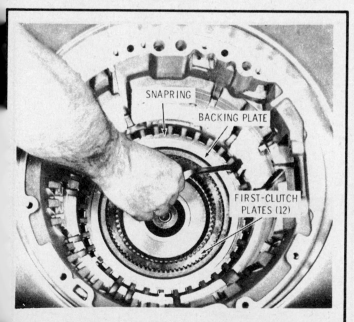

Installation of the first clutch plates and snap ring, typical
(©General Motors Corp.)

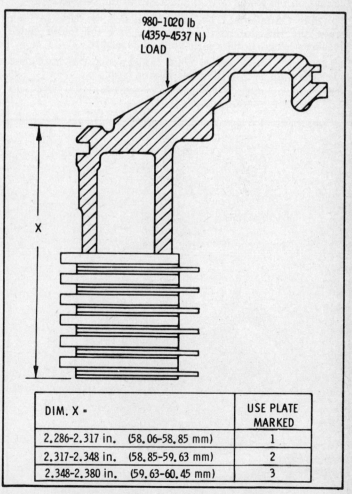

DIM. X =		USE PLATE MARKED
2.286-2.317 in.	(58.06-58.85 mm)	1
2.317-2.348 in.	(58.85-59.63 mm)	2
2.348-2.380 in.	(59.63-60.45 mm)	3

Stack method of measurement for the first clutch, all models
(©General Motors Corp.)

2. Engage the internal splines of the rear planetary carrier assembly hub with the splines of the output shaft, and the pinions of the rear carrier assembly with the teeth of the rear planetary ring gear.

MT 654CR

1. Attach a gear lifting device to the splines of the main shaft and carefully lower the assembled gear unit into the transmission housing.

2. Engage the pinion teeth of the low planetary carrier with those of the low sun gear, and the pinion teeth of the rear planetary carrier with those of its ring gear. Align the splines on the rear carrier with those of the low ring gear hub.

SECOND CLUTCH

Installation

1. Install the previously selected second clutch backing plate and clutch pack. Alternately install the internal splined clutch plates and the external tanged clutch plates, starting with an internal splined clutch plate.

2. Install the retaining snap ring for the second clutch.

3. Be sure the thrust washer is in place on the front sun gear.

CENTER SUPPORT

Installation

1. Install the third clutch piston into the center support. Align the lugs on the piston with the recesses in the support.

NOTE: On later MT 644, 654CR models, be sure the filter screen and the seal ring are installed into the fourth clutch pressure passage in the center support assembly.

2. Attach a lifting device to the center support assembly and lower the support into the transmission case.

3. Align the center support bolt holes and seat the support firmly against the second clutch snap ring.

NOTE: Insure that the gap of the second clutch snap ring is between any two of the four tangs of the second clutch spring retainer ring.

4. Align the tapped hole in the support with the anchor bolt hole in the transmission case and install a new locking bolt to secure the center support assembly. Torque the bolt to 39-46 ft. lbs. (53-62 N•m).

5. Install the previously selected snap ring to hold the center support and piston assembly.

NOTE: Position the gap of the snap ring between any two retaining ring tabs.

6. Install the needle roller bearing assembly with the rollers up, into the center support hub.

7. Install the step joint seal rings onto the hub and retain them with oil soluble grease.

FOURTH CLUTCH

Installation

NOTE: Fourth clutch assembly procedures differ between the MT 640, 643, 650, 653 models and the MT 644, 654CR models. The fourth clutch is installed BEFORE the third clutch plate and/or pack is selected and installed on the MT 644, 654CR models and on the MT 640, 643, 650, 653 models, the fourth clutch is installed AFTER the third clutch plate pack is selected and installed.

1. Having previously selected the clutch pack, insure that the needle bearing race is in place on the rearward hub of the fourth clutch housing.

2. Grasp the unit by the spring retainer and install it onto the center support hub.

THIRD CLUTCH

Selection of Clutch Pack and Installation
Direct Measurement Method

1. Beginning with an external tanged clutch plate, alternately

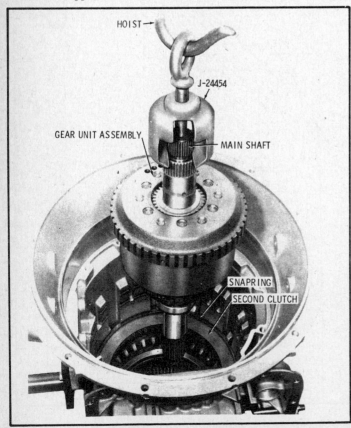

Installation of gear unit, typical (©General Motors Corp.)

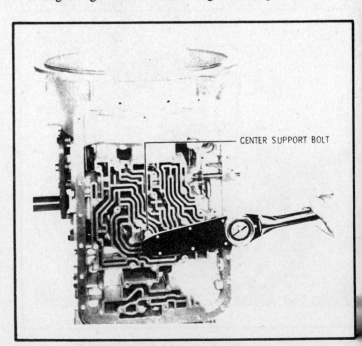

Tightening center support anchor bolt (©General Motors Corp.)

install three internal splined clutch plates and the three external tanged clutch plates. Be sure to position the external tanged clutch plates in their double tanged grooves in the transmission case.

2. Install the backing plate and the retaining snap ring.

3. By using a third clutch clearance gauge, J-26916 or its equivalent, measure the clearance between the snap ring and the backing plate. The running clearance should be 0.050-0.114 inch (1.27-2.89 mm)

4. If needed, new clutch plates should be installed to obtain the desired clearance. A thicker or thinner backing plate can be used, if the desired clearance is not obtained by changing the clutch plates.

Stack Method

1. Stack the desired number of clutch plates and the third clutch piston in a press that can provide 980-1020 pounds of pressure on the clutch plate stack.

2. Measure the distance from the top outer edge of the clutch piston to the flat surface of the press table, that the clutch pack is setting on.

3. Refer to the accompanying chart to select the third clutch backplate.

FORWARD CLUTCH

Installation

1. Align the internal splined plates of the fourth clutch and direct air pressure to the apply port for the fourth clutch.

NOTE: The air applying the fourth clutch prevents movement of the clutch plates during the forward clutch installation.

2. Secure the needle bearing and race on the forward clutch hub with oil soluble grease.

3. Install the forward clutch assembly while engaging the fourth clutch hub within the internal splined plates of the fourth clutch.

4. The forward clutch should be properly seated when the front surface of the forward clutch housing is approximately ½ inch (12.7 mm) behind the forward edge of the P.T.O. opening in the transmission case.

5. A second check is to apply short bursts of air to the fourth clutch and if the forward clutch remains stationary, it is positioned properly.

OIL PUMP AND FRONT SUPPORT ASSEMBLY

Installation

1. Install the oil pump and front support gasket. Be sure the two seal rings are in place on the base of the turbine shaft.

2. Install the bearing and race assemblies, race first, into the hub of the support assembly. Be sure the race is present on the front of the forward clutch housing.

3. Install the step joint seal rings onto the hub. Retain with oil soluble grease.

4. Install two guide bolts on the case and with the aid of a collar type lifting device, lower the oil pump and front support assembly into the case.

5. Install ten of the retaining bolts in the front support assembly. Snug the bolts securely. Remove the two guide bolts and install the remaining two bolts. Tighten the first two bolts, 180° apart, to 15 ft. lbs. (20 N•m). Move approximately 90° around the bolt pattern and repeat the procedure. Tighten the bolts at 180° spacing. Repeat the entire process, tightening all twelve bolts to 24-32 ft. lbs. (33-43 N•m).

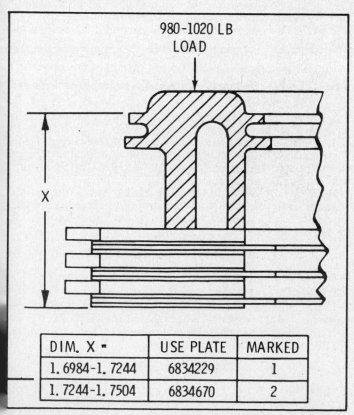

DIM. X =	USE PLATE	MARKED
1.6984-1.7244	6834229	1
1.7244-1.7504	6834670	2

Stack method of measurement for the third clutch, all models
(©General Motors Corp.)

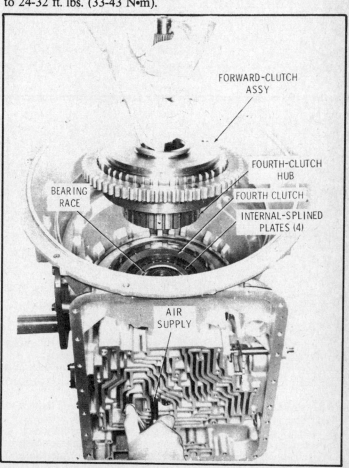

Installing the forward clutch assembly, typical
(©General Motors Corp.)

Hydraulic Control Units

NOTE: The transmissions are grouped and procedures outlined for each, to install the valve body assembly and its components in their sequence of assembly.

CONTROL VALVE ASSEMBLY

Installation

MT 640, 643

1. Install the governor check ball into the deep pocket end of the governor pressure recess.
2. With the range selector valve secured to avoid dropping out of the valve body, position the valve body so that the actuator pin enters the housing bore. Install the valve body and install the eighteen retaining bolts. Do not tighten at this time.

NOTE: Early transmission units had seventeen short bolts and one ½ inch longer bolt.

3. If the governor oil screen is present, discard it, as later models discontinued its use.

Installing the control valve assembly, typical. Note position of governor check ball (©General Motors Corp.)

CONTROL VALVE ASSEMBLY

Installation

MT 650, 653

1. Install the governor check ball into the deep pocket end of the governor pressure recess of the transmission case.
2. Secure the range selector valve to prevent it falling from the valve body. Position the control valve assembly so the actuator pin enters the housing bore. Install the control valve assembly and install the retaining bolts. Do not tighten at this time.

NOTE: Early transmission units had seventeen short bolts and one ½ inch longer bolt.

3. If a governor oil screen is present, discard it, as later models do not use the screen.
4. Retain the oil transfer plate with two retaining bolts. Temporarily install seven bolts to align the transfer plate. Torque the two oil transfer retaining bolts to 9-11 ft. lbs. (12-15 N•m) and then remove the seven bolts.
5. Engage the groove in the range selector valve with the pin on the detent lever. Position the detent spring to engage a notch in the detent lever and install one bolt. Torque the bolt to 9-12 ft. lbs. (12-15 N•m).

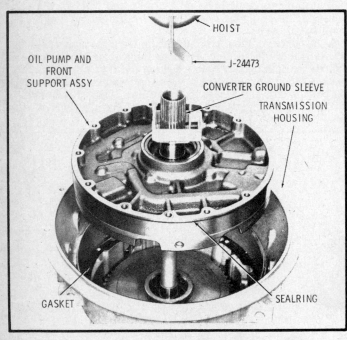

Installing the oil pump and front support assembly, typical (©General Motors Corp.)

TUBE ADAPTER

Installation

MT 640, 643

1. Place the tube adapter and tubes in position so the tubes can be inserted into their respective bores in the valve body.
2. Insert the three tubes, first clutch feed, governor feed and governor pressure, into the valve body, being sure each is properly seated.
3. Install the retaining bolts for the tube adapter and tighten to 9-11 ft. lbs. (12-15 N•m).
4. Engage the notch in the range selector valve with the pin on the detent lever. Position the detent spring to engage a notch in the detent lever and install the retaining bolt. Torque the bolt 9-11 ft. lbs. (12-15 N•m).
5. Starting from the center, tighten the valve body retaining bolts to 9-11 ft. lbs. (12-15 N•m).

LOW SHIFT VALVE BODY

Installation

MT 650, 653

1. If the jumper tubes have bolt brackets attached, install the separator and low shift valve onto the oil transfer plate.
2. Install the seven retaining bolts to retain the low shift valve, but do not tighten the bolts as yet.

VALVE TUBING

Installation

MT 650, 653

NOTE: Loose jumper tubes were used on earlier models. Current models use jumper tubes with bolt brackets permanently attached.

1. Install the valve jumper tubes in the following sequence by inserting the tube ends into the bores in the valve bodies, drive— 1, forward regulator, first trimmer and low and first feed tube. The forward regulator tube is required on some transmissions prior to serial number 47285. Fully seat each tube in its bore.

2. Position each of the bracketed jumper tubes in their proper positions. Install the retaining bolts but do not tighten.

3. Starting from the center, tighten the control valve body bolts and low shift valve body bolts to 9-11 ft. lbs. (12-15 N•m).

─────────────── CAUTION ───────────────
Do not allow the bracketed jumper tubes to move during the torquing of the retaining bolts.

CONTROL VALVE ASSEMBLY
Installation
MT 644

1. Install the ¼ inch governor check ball into the deep pocketed recess in the governor pressure valley in the transmission case.

2. Secure the range selector valve to prevent its loss and position the valve body assembly so the actuator pin enters the housing bore. Install the eighteen retaining bolts but do not tighten at this time.

NOTE: Leave the valve body bolts loose to permit moving the valve body for engagement of the selector valve with the shift pin.

3. Engage the notch in the range selector valve with the pin on the detent lever. Position the detent spring to engage a notch in the detent lever. Install the one bolt to retain the detent spring.

TUBE ADAPTER
Installation
MT 644

1. Place the tube adapter and the tubes in position so that the tubes can be inserted into their bores in the valve body (First clutch feed, governor feed and governor pressure). Be sure each tube is seated securely in the valve body.

2. Install the four retaining bolts in the tube adapter.

3. Snug all the bolts, eighteen valve body bolts, four tube adapter bolts and the detent spring bolt.

4. Tighten the eighteen valve body bolts in a pattern from the center to the outside to 9-11 ft. lbs. (12-15 N•m).

5. Tighten the four adapter bolts and the detent spring bolts to 9-11 ft. lbs. (12-15 N•m).

MODULATED LOCK-UP VALVE ASSEMBLY
Installation
MT 644

1. Install the modulated lock-up valve assembly and retain with the three bolts. Tighten the bolts to 9-11 ft. lbs. (12-15 N•m).

NOTE: Earlier model transmissions use four bolts to retain the modulated lock-up valve assembly. Later models use only three bolts. If the bolt holes in the earlier models have been reworked to accept bolts two inches long, install the assembly with three of the two inch long bolts. If the bolt holes have not been reworked, use three of the 1¾ inch bolts.

CONTROL VALVE ASSEMBLY
Installation
MT 654CR

1. Secure the range selector valve to prevent its loss. Position the valve body assembly so the modulator actuator pin enters the housing bore. Engage the groove in the range selector valve with the pin on the detent lever.

2. Secure the control valve assembly to the transmission with

fifteen three inch long bolts, three bolts, three and one half inches long and one bolt, one and one-half inch long.

3. Position the detent spring to engage a notch in the detent lever and install the retaining bolt. Tighten to 9-11 ft. lbs. (12-15 N•m). Tighten the valve body retaining bolts to 9-11 ft. lbs. (12-15 N•m).

MODULATED LOCK-UP VALVE ASSEMBLY
Installation
MT 654 CR

1. Install the modulated lock-up valve assembly and retain it with the three retaining bolts.

2. Tighten the bolts to 9-11 ft. lbs. (12-15 N•m).

NOTE: Earlier models used four bolts to retain the modulated lock-up valve assembly. If four bolts were removed during the disassembly, use only three bolts for the valve body installation.

LOW SHIFT SIGNAL VALVE ASSEMBLY
Installation
MT 654CR

NOTE: The separator plate is used only on model with the second gear start feature.

1. Install the low shift signal valve assembly. If equipped, install the separator plate. Install the two retaining bolts. Snug, but do not tighten.

LOW TRIMMER VALVE ASSEMBLY
Installation
MT 654CR

1. Install the low trimmer valve assembly onto the low shift valve assembly. Retain the assembly with the six retaining bolts.

2. Tighten the two bolts that retain the low shift signal valve assembly and the six bolts that retain the low trimmer valve assembly to 9-11 ft. lbs. (12-15 N•m).

OIL PAN
Installation
ALL MODELS

1. Install the suction tube and the new seal ring. Install the oil filter/screen and tighten the retaining bolt to 10-15 ft. lbs. (14-20 N•m).

2. Install two guide pins on the transmission pan flange area. Install the oil pan gasket.

3. Install the washer headed bolts to retain the oil pan. Remove the guide pins and install the remaining two bolts.

4. Torque the bolts to 10-13 ft. lbs. (14-18 N•m). After the gasket sets, apply 5 ft. lbs. (7 N•m) torque to each bolt to insure a proper seal.

TORQUE CONVERTER ASSEMBLY
Installation
ALL MODELS

1. After serial number 49489, be sure the seal ring is installed and lubricated in its groove in the pump hub.

2. Attach a lifting device to the converter, and with the transmission in the upward position, lower the converter into the transmission.

3. Gently rotate the converter to engage the flats on the pump hub with the flats in the transmission oil pump. Also, the splines of the turbine hub, within the converter, must engage the splines of the turbine shaft.

4. On transmission models, MT 640, 643, 650, 653, measure the distance from the transmission mounting flange to the converter cover, when the converter is seated. The distance should be

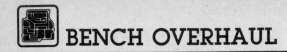
approximately 9/16 inch (14.29 mm). If the measurement is greater than the allowable distance, raise the converter assembly slightly, rotate it and reseat the unit.

5. Remove the lifting device and install a restraining strap to prevent the converter from dropping out of position before transmission installation into the vehicle.

OUTPUT SHAFT COMPONENTS AND GOVERNOR

Installation
MT 640, 643, 644

1. Install the governor drive gear, slot first, onto the output shaft. Engage the slot in the drive gear with the protruding pin in the output shaft. Install the speedometer drive gear and sleeve spacer onto the output shaft.

2. Install the ball bearing assembly into the rear cover, seating it firmly against the snap ring in the rear cover.

NOTE: The inner snap ring is not used in later MT 644 Transmission models.

3. Install the retaining snap ring with the beveled side of the snap ring facing the rear of the transmission and fully expanded in its groove of the housing.

4. Install the oil seal into the rear of the rear cover. Drive the seal into the rear cover bore until its rearward surface is 1.03-1.07 inch (26.2-27.2 mm) below the rear face of the rear cover.

5. Place the dust shield in place and drive it into the rear cover until it is flush with to 0.040 inch below the rear face of the rear cover.

6. Install the governor assembly, gasket and cover. Install the four retaining bolts and tighten to 15-20 ft. lbs. (20-27 N•m).

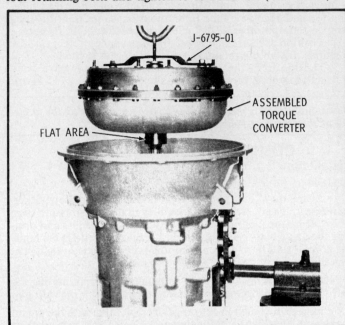

Installing the torque converter assembly (©General Motors Corp.)

SPECIFICATIONS

SPECIFICATIONS
MT 640, 643, 650, 653, 644, 654CR Models

RATING

MT 640, 643, 650, 653
Input torque .... 585 lb ft (793 N•m)
Input speed .... 4000 rpm (max)
Input power (Actual, installed, SAE 500 ft, 85°F) .... 250 hp (186 kW) (max)

MT 644, 654CR
Input torque
  MT 644 .... 780 lb ft (1056 N•m)
  MT 654CR (early models) .... 780 lb ft (1056 N•m)
  MT 654CR (late models) .... 950 lb ft (1287 N•m)
Input speed .... 3000 rpm max
Input horsepower (max)

DRIVE

Direct mount (All) .... Flex disk
Remote mount (MT 644, 654CR) .... Shaft, universal joints

ROTATION (VIEWED FROM INPUT)

Input .... clockwise
Output (in forward ranges) .... clockwise

SPECIFICATIONS
MT 640, 643, 650, 653, 644, 654CR Models

TORQUE CONVERTER

MT 644, 654CR

Type .... Single stage, poly-phase, 3 element
Converter model .... TC 430 TC 470 TC 494 TC 495 TC 496 TC 497
Torque multiplication
   ratio (at stall) 3.59:1 3.04:1 1.92:1 2.21:1 1.83:1 2.70:1
Lockup clutch .... Automatic in selected ranges

MT 640, 643, 650, 653

Type .... Single stage, poly-phase, 3-element
Converter model .... TC 350 TC 360 TC 370 TC 380
Torque multiplication ratio (at stall) 3.1:1 2.96:1 2.4:1 1.8:1
Lockup clutch .... Automatic in selected ranges

DRIVE RANGE AND SEQUENCES

MT 644 .... Reverse, neutral, 1-2-3-4, 1-2-3, 1-2, 1
MT 644 with 2nd gear start .... Reverse, neutral, 2-3-4, 2-3, 2, 1
MT 654CR .... Reverse, neutral, 1-2-3-4-5, 1-2-3-4, 1-2-3, 1-2, 1
MT 654CR with 2nd gear start .... Reverse, neutral, 2-3-4-5, 2-3-4, 2-3, 2, 1
MT 640, 643 .... Reverse, neutral, 1-2-3-4, 1-2-3, 1-2, 1
MT 650 .... (Before S/N 13801) Reverse, neutral, 2-3-4-5, 2-3-4, 2-3, 1
MT 650, 653 .... (After S/N 13800) Reverse, neutral, 2-3-4-5, 2-3-4, 2, 1
Drive range and shift control .... Mechanical (external)
Shift mechanism .... Hydraulic (internal control)
Shift modulation:
   Diesel models .... Mechanical
   Gasoline models .... Vacuum or mechanical
Clutches .... Oil cooled, hydraulically actuated, spring released, self-compensating for wear
Gearing .... Planetary, straight-cup spur, constant mesh

OIL CAPACITY (LESS EXTERNAL CIRCUITS)

MT 640, 643, 650, 653 .... 4 US gal (15 liters) (approx)
MT 644, 654CR .... Rebuild 23 US qt (22 liters), Refill-17 US qt (16 liters)
Filter (All) .... Integral (in sump)
Sump (All) .... Integral
Input pressure pump .... Engine driven, positive displacement
Oil type .... Dexron® or Dexron® II
Oil temperature:
   Converter out .... 300°F (148°C) (max)
   Sump .... 250°F (121°C) (max)

OIL PRESSURES

MT 640, 643, 650, 653

Main pressure (in forward drive range, vehicle brakes applied)

	MT 640 (prior to S/N 47020)	MT 640, 643 (eff. with S/N 47020)	MT 650 (prior to S/N 47285)	MT 650, 653 (eff. with S/N 47285)
At idle (600 rpm)	125 psi min. (861 kPa)	125 psi min. (861 kPa)	125 psi min. (861 kPa)	125 psi min. (861 kPa)
At 1200 rpm	137-167 psi (945-1151 kPa)	165-190 psi (1138-1310 kPa)	187-217 psi (1289-1496 kPa)	165-190 psi (1138-1310 kPa)

Lubrication pressure (2000 rpm) .... 23-30 psi (159-207 kPa)
Converter-out pressure (2000 rpm) .... 32-52 psi (221-359 kPa)

MT 644, 654CR

Main pressure—

   At idle (600 rpm) .... 160 psi (1103 kPa) min
   At stall (1200 rpm) .... 180-205 psi (1240-1413 kPa)
Lubrication pressure (at governed speed) .... 15 psi (103 kPa) min

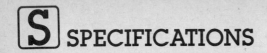

SPECIFICATIONS
MT 640, 643, 650, 653, 644, 654CR Models

OIL PRESSURES

MT 640, 643, 650, 653
Main pressure (in forward drive range, vehicle brakes applied)

Converter-out pressure (1650 rpm) ....30-50 psi (206-344 kPa)

GOVERNOR PRESSURE

MT 640, 643

Engine governed speed range (rpm)	Governor pressure, psi (kPa)	At rpm①
2400-2800	63 to 71 (434-490)	1500
3000-3400	54 to 61 (372-421)	1500
3600-4000	59 to 65 (407-448)	2200

①Transmission output speed. May be read from engine tachometer during lockup in highest gear.

MT 650, 653

Engine governed speed range (rpm)	Governor pressure, psi (kPa)	At rpm①
2400-2600	74 to 82 (510-565)	1500
2800	54 to 58 (372-400)	1500
3000	54 to 58 (372-400)	1500
3200-3400	58 to 65 (400-448)	1650 (before S/N 26911)
3200-3400	82 to 91 (565-627)	2200 (after S/N 26910)
3600-4000	43 to 48 (296-331)	1650 (before S/N 26911)
3600-4000	59 to 65 (407-448)	2200 (after S/N 26910)

MT 644, 654CR

Engine governed speed range (rpm)	Governor pressure psi	kPa	At rpm*	Code No.**
MT 644 1950-2600	63-71	434-490	1500	461
MT 654CR 1950-2200	82-91	(565-627)	1650	462
MT 654CR 2300-2600	59-65	(407-448)	1650	463

*Transmission output speed. May be read from engine tachometer during lockup in highest gear.
**Code number is stamped on end of governor.

GEAR RATIOS (MECHANICAL)

MT 644

Gear	Clutch(es) Applied	Ratio
Neutral	First	
First	Forward and first	3.58:1
Second	Forward and second	2.09:1
Third	Forward and third	1.39:1
Fourth	Forward and fourth	1.00:1
Reverse	Fourth and first	5.67:1

MT 654CR

Gear	Clutch(es) Applied	Ratio
Neutral	Low	
First	Forward and low	4.17:1
Second	Forward and first	2.21:1

SPECIFICATIONS
MT 640, 643, 650, 653, 644, 654CR Models

MT 654CR

Gear	Clutch(es) Applied	Ratio
Third	Forward and second	1.66:1
Fourth	Forward and third	1.27:1
Fifth	Forward and fourth	1.00:1
Reverse	Fourth and low	10.76:1

MT 640, 643

Gear	Clutch(es) Applied	Ratio
Neutral	First	
First	Forward and first	3.58:1
Second	Forward and second	2.09:1
Third	Forward and third	1.39:1
Fourth	Forward and fourth	1.00:1
Reverse	Fourth and first	5.67:1

MT 650, 653

Gear	Clutch(es) Applied	Ratio
Neutral	First	
First	Forward and low	8.05:1
Second	Forward and first	3.58:1
Third	Forward and second	2.09:1
Fourth	Forward and third	1.39:1
Fifth	Forward and fourth	1.00:1
Reverse	Fourth and first	5.67:1

SPEEDOMETER DRIVE

Type .... Spiral gear
MT 640, 643 drive gear data .... 5 tooth lh helix angle
MT 650, 653 drive gear data .... 7 tooth lh helix angle
MT 644 .... 8 teeth, LH helix
MT 654CR .... 11 teeth, LH helix
Driven gear .... Supplied by customer

POWER TAKE-OFF

Type .... Converter driven
Mounting flange .... One opening—SAE 6 bolt
Gear data .... 6 pitch, 64 teeth, 20° pressure angle
Location .... Right side

PARKING BRAKE PROVISION

Drum type .... 12 x 3 in. (304 x 76 mm) or 12 x 4 in. (304 x 101 mm)
Weight .... 50 lb (22.7 Kg)

DRY WEIGHT (LESS PARKING BRAKE)

MT 640, 643 .... 510 lb (231 kg)
MT 650, 653 .... 540 lb (245 kg)
MT 644 .... 562 lb (255 kg)
MT 654CR (early models) .... 625 lb (283 kg)
MT 654CR (late models) .... 640 lb (290 kg)

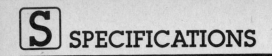

WEAR LIMITS SPECIFICATIONS
MT 640, 643, 650, 653, 644, 654 CR

Description	Wear Limit in.	mm
TORQUE CONVERTER, LOCKUP CLUTCH		
MT 644, 654CR		
Piston face wear	No scoring permissible	
Clutch plate thickness	0.190	4.32
Backplate face wear	No scoring permissible	
Stator assembly:		
front thrust washer ID	4.016	102.00
front thrust washer thickness	0.460	11.68
rear thrust washer ID	4.018	102.05
Thrust bearing race thickness	0.029	0.74
Roller race OD	No scoring permissible	
MT 640, 643, 650, 653		
Bushing—clearance on turbine shaft (A, foldout 6)	0.0045	0.114
Piston—face wear	No scoring permissible	
Clutch plate—thickness	0.175	4.45
Back plates—face wear	No scoring permissible	
Side plates—inside diameter of	2.857	72.57
Stator thrust washer in stator—thickness (Measure across thrust face and needle bearing with bearing installed)	0.435	11.05
Roller race—diameter	No scoring permissible	
OIL PUMP, FRONT SUPPORT ASSY		
MT 644, 654CR		
Driven gear end clearance (axial)	0.0024	0.061
Drive gear end clearance (axial)	0.0024	0.061
MT 640, 643, 650, 653		
Bushing—clearance on pump hub	0.005	0.140
Driven gear:		
Side clearance	0.0024	0.061
Diametral clearance	0.0084	0.213
Drive gear—side clearance	0.0024	0.061
FORWARD CLUTCH, TURBINE SHAFT		
MT 644, 654CR		
Turbine shaft and clutch housing—area contacted by seals	No wear or scoring permissible	
External-tanged clutch plate:		
minimum thickness	0.0955	2.425
minimum oil groove depth	0.008	0.20
maximum cone	0.010	0.24
Internal-splined clutch plate minimum thickness	0.090	2.29
Fourth-clutch driving hub:		
minimum thickness at clutch plate contact area	0.248	6.30
minimum oil groove depth	0.008	0.20
maximum cone	0.010	0.25

WEAR LIMITS SPECIFICATIONS
MT 640, 643, 650, 653, 644, 654 CR

Description	in.	Wear Limit	mm
FORWARD CLUTCH, TURBINE SHAFT			
MT 640, 643, 650, 653			
External-tanged clutch plate			
Thickness	0.0955		2.426
Cone	0.010		0.25
Internal-splined clutch plate:	0.090		2.29
Thickness	0.010		0.25
Cone			
Fourth clutch driving hub—step			
wear at clutch plate contact area	0.252		6.40
FOURTH CLUTCH			
MT 644, 654CR			
Clutch backplate—minimum thickness at clutch			
plate contact area	0.248		6.29
Internal-splined plate:			
minimum thickness	0.090		2.29
minimum oil groove depth	0.008		0.20
maximum cone	0.010		0.25
External-tanged plate:			
minimum thickness	0.0955		2.425
minimum oil groove depth	0.008		0.20
maximum cone	0.010		0.25
MT 640, 643, 650, 653			
Clutch back plate—step wear at clutch			
plate contact area	0.252		6.40
Internal-splined plate:			
Thickness	0.090		2.29
Cone	0.010		0.25
External-tanged plate:			
Thickness	0.0955		2.426
Cone	0.010		0.25
THIRD CLUTCH, CENTER SUPPORT, SECOND CLUTCH			
MT 644, 654CR			
Backplate (ident 1) minimum thickness	0.476		12.09
Backplate (ident 2) minimum thickness	0.450		11.43
Internal-splined plate:			
minimum thickness	0.117		2.97
minimum oil groove depth	0.008		0.20
maximum cone	0.010		0.25
External-tanged plate:			
minimum thickness	0.0955		2.4
minimum oil groove depth	0.008		0.20
maximum cone	0.010		0.25
Backplate (ident 3) minimum thickness	0.234		5.94
Backplate (ident 4) minimum thickness	0.208		5.28

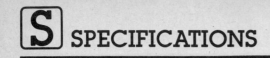
WEAR LIMITS SPECIFICATIONS
MT 640, 643, 650, 653, 644, 654 CR

Description	Wear Limit	
	in.	mm
MT 640, 643, 650, 653		
Back plate (ident 1):		
Thickness	0.476	12.09
Cone	0.010	0.25
Back plate (ident 2):		
Thickness	0.450	11.43
Cone	0.010	0.25
Internal-splined plate:		
Thickness	0.117	2.97
Cone	0.010	0.25
External-tanged plate:		
Thickness	0.0955	2.426
Cone	0.010	0.25
Bushing—clearance on sun gear shaft	0.0061	0.155
REAR COVER COMPONENTS (All)		
Governor—clearance in rear cover bore	0.0035	0.089
GEAR UNIT, MAIN SHAFT		
MT 650, 653		
Thrust washer—thickness	0.092	2.34
Thrust washer—thickness	0.091	2.31
Front carrier bushing—clearance on sun gear	0.0049	0.124
Thrust washer—thickness	0.091	2.31
Sun gear shaft bushing—clearance on main shaft	0.0061	0.154
Sun gear shaft—clearance in support bushing	0.0061	0.154
MT 640, 643		
Thrust washer—thickness	0.092	2.34
Thrust washer—thickness	0.091	2.31
Front carrier bushing—clearance on sun gear shaft	0.0049	0.124
Thrust washer—thickness	0.091	2.31
Sun gear shaft bushing—clearance on main shaft	0.0061	0.154
Sun gear shaft—clearance in support bushing	0.0061	0.154
Thrust washer—thickness	0.091	2.31
MT 644		
Thrust washer thickness	0.092	2.34
Pinion end play	0.031	0.79
Front carrier bushing clearance on sun gear	0.0049	0.124
Sun gear shaft bushing clearance on main shaft	0.0061	0.153
Sun gear shaft clearance in support bushing	0.0061	0.153
MT 654CR		
Thrust washer thickness	0.092	2.34
Pinion end play	0.031	0.79
Front carrier bushing clearance on sun gear	0.0049	0.124
Sun gear shaft bushing clearance on main shaft	0.0061	0.153
Sun gear shaft clearance in support bushing	0.0061	0.153

WEAR LIMITS SPECIFICATIONS
MT 640, 643, 650, 653, 644, 654 CR

Description	in.	Wear Limit	mm
FIRST CLUTCH, REAR PLANETARY RING GEARS			
MT 644, 654CR			
Backplate (ident 1) thickness	0.702		17.83
Backplate (ident 2) thickness	0.671		17.04
Backplate (ident 3) thickness	0.640		16.26
Internal-splined plate:			
minimum thickness	0.090		2.29
minimum oil groove depth	0.008		0.020
maximum cone	0.010		0.25
External-tanged plate:			
minimum thickness	0.0955		2.425
minimum oil groove depth	0.008		0.020
maximum cone	0.010		0.25
MT 640, 643, 650, 653			
Back plate (ident 1)—thickness	0.702		17.83
Back plate (indent 2)—thickness	0.671		17.04
Back plate (indent 3)—thickness	0.640		16.26
Internal-splined plate:			
Thickness	0.090		2.29
Cone	0.010		0.25
External-tanged plate:			
Thickness	0.0955		2.426
Cone	0.010		0.25
LOW CLUTCH PLANETARY, ADAPTER HOUSING			
654CR			
Thrust washer thickness	0.091		2.31
Internal-splined plate:			
minimum thickness	0.117		2.97
minimum oil groove depth	0.008		0.020
maximum cone	0.010		0.25
External-tanged plate:			
minimum thickness	0.0955		2.425
minimum oil groove depth	0.008		0.020
maximum cone	0.010		0.25
Pinion end play	0.031		0.79
MT 650, 653			
Thrust washer—thickness	0.091		2.31
Thrust washer—thickness	0.123		3.12
Carrier bushing—clearance on ring gear hub	0.0049		0.124
External-tanged plate—thickness	0.0955		2.426
Internal-splined plate thickness	0.117		4.50

SPECIFICATIONS

EIGHT PLATE CLUTCH

Dim. X =		Use Piston Marked
1.0140-1.0450 in.	(25.756-26.543 mm)	B
1.0450-1.0760 in.	(26.543-27.330 mm)	A

TEN PLATE CLUTCH

Dim. X =		Use Piston Marked
1.2552-1.2804 in.	(31.882-32.522 mm)	A
1.2300-1.2552 in.	(31.242-31.882 mm)	B
1.2045-1.2299 in.	(30.594-31.239 mm)	C

TEN PLATE CLUTCH

Dim. X =		Use Piston Marked
1.2045-1.2305 in.	(30.594-31.254 mm)	C
1.2305-1.2565 in.	(31.254-31.915 mm)	B
1.2565-1.2820 in.	(31.915-32.562 mm)	A

TWELVE PLATE CLUTCH

Dim. X =		Use Piston Marked
1.4550-1.4850 in.	(36.957-37.719 mm)	A
1.4250-1.4550 in.	(36.195-36.957 mm)	B
1.3950-1.4250 in.	(35.433-36.195 mm)	C

SPECIAL TOOLS

Tool No. ①	Description
J-6438-01	Forward and fourth clutch spring compressor. (Used with J-24204-2 on fourth clutch only.)
J-24204-2	Clutch spring compressor base for the low, first, and fourth clutches
J-24452	Low and first spring compressor (Used with J-24204-2)
J-24475-A	Selective snapring fixture
	Hex head bolt, ⅜-16x1-¼
J-24475-1	Compressor base
J-24475-2	Compressor bar
J-23717-1	Center bolt
J-24208-4	Snapring gage
J-24420	Universal puller (Used with J-24534 or J-24463-2)
J-24463-2	Puller leg assembly—MT 644. (Used with J-24420)
J-24534	Puller leg assembly—MT 654CR. (Used with J-24420)
J-24218-2	Stator roller retainer ring (4-inch O.D.)
J-24454	Gear unit lifter
J-24462	Transmission holding fixture adapter set. (Used with J-3289-20, J-23642)
J-24462-1	Holding plate

Tool No. ①	Description
	Hex head bolt, ⅜-16x1-¾ (6)
	Standard flat washer, ⅜ (6)
J-23642-01	Transmission holding fixture. (Used with J-3289-20, J-24462)
J-3289-20	Holding fixture base (used with J-23642, J-24462)
J-24458	Valve pin installer
J-6125-1	Slide hammer assembly
J-24412-2	Valve pin remover (Used with J-6125-1)
J-24453	Lock-ring installer
J-24459	Main regulator and lockup valve spring compressor
J-24171	Output shaft seal and dust shield remover assembly
J-24171-1	Jaw attachment
J-24171-2	Rod assembly
J-24171-3	Hose adapter
J-24171-4	Slide hammer
J-24171-5	Hook
J-24461	Oil pump body and front support centering band
J-24473	Front-support lifter assembly
J-29146	Forward clutch gage, 0.094-0.148 in. (2.38 or 3.75 mm)

Tool No. ①	Description
J-26913	Forward clutch 0.079-0.130 in. (2.00-3.30 mm)
J-26914	First clutch gage, 0.074-0.147 in. (1.88-3.73 mm)
J-26916	Third clutch gage, 0.050-0.114 in. (1.27-2.89 mm)
J-29156	Fourth clucth gage, 0.068-0.127 in. (1.72-3.22 mm) or
J-26917	Fourth clutch gage, 0.064-0.125 in. (1.62-3.17 mm)
J-26918	Second clutch gage, 0.059-0.129 in. (1.49-3.27 mm)
J-24455	Center support lifter
J-24369	Output shaft orifice plug installer
J-26282	Shift lever seal installer
J-24314	Valve body adjusting ring tool
J-1927-1	Adapter housing guide bolts, ½-13x6—MT 654CR
J-24315-1	Pump body and front support guide bolts, ⅜-16x6
J-3387-2	Oil pan guide screws, ⁵/₁₆-18x3
J-24448	Output shaft oil seal installer—MT 644 (Used with J-24202-4)
J-24620	Output shaft oil seal installer—MT 654CR. (Used with J-24202-4)
J-26912	Oil pump seal installer. (Used with J-24202-4)
J-24447	Rear bearing installer—MT 654CR (Used with J-24202-4)
J-24198	Dust shield installer (used with J-24202-4)
J-24202-4	Driver handle
J-24468	Sun gear shaft bushing installer
J-24446	Rear bearing installer
J-24457	Front support bearing installer. (Used with J-8092)
J-24451	Output shaft bearing installer (Used with J-8092)
J-8092	Driver handle

Tool No. ①	Item	Description
J-34016		Output shaft bearing installer (used with J-8092)
J-25393		Rear cover bearing race installer—MT 654CR
J-24474		Oil pump bushing installer
J-25587-01		Planetary carrier rebuild tool kit
J-25587-1		Removing, installing and swaging fixture
J-25587-2		Pin remover and installer adapter
J-25587-3		Support block
J-25587-4		Support block
J-25587-6		Pin remover and nstaller spacer
J-25587-8		Pin installer
J-25587-11		Pin installer
J-25587-12		Pin installer
J-25587-13		Pin installer
J-25587-16		Pin remover
J-25587-17		Bottom swaging tool holder
J-25587-18		¾" loading pin
J-25587-20		⅝" loading pin
J-25587-22		½" loading pin
J-25587-23		Swaging tool
J-25587-25		Swaging tool
J-25587-27		Swaging tool
J-25587-48		¾" guide pin
J-25587-49		⅝" guide pin
J-25587-50		½" guide pin
J-29121-1		Rivet punch
J-29121-3		Rivet removing pin
J-29521		Stator rivet set
J-29521-1		Stator rivet base
J-29521-2		Top plate
		Bolt ⅝-71x3.25

① Items J-25587-1 through J-25587-65 are contained in J-25587-01 kit to service MT 644 and MT 654CR planetary carrier assemblies. Components to service other models are also included in the kit.

Note: Tools may be ordered from Kent-Moore Tool Division, 1501 S. Jackson St., Jackson, Michigan 49203

INDEX

AUDI/VOLKSWAGEN TRANSAXLE TYPE 089 • 090

A APPLICATIONS

Application

Audi 4000, 5000
Volkswagen Rabbit, Scirocco, Jetta, Dasher, Quantom, Vanagon
Fiat Strada

G GENERAL DESCRIPTION

The series 010, types 089, 090 automatic transaxle is a fully automatic three speed unit, containing a three piece torque converter, forward and reverse planetary gear sets, three multiple disc clutches, and one band. The final drive unit is part of the transaxle assembly, containing the differential assembly. Shift control is by manually operated linkage.

Transmission and Converter Identification

TRANSMISSION

Code letters and numbers are stamped on the top of the transmission case, as well as on a pad on the front of the converter housing by the dipstick handle. These code letters and numbers denote the series of the transmission, the model code, and the date of manufacture. These numbers are important when ordering service replacement parts.

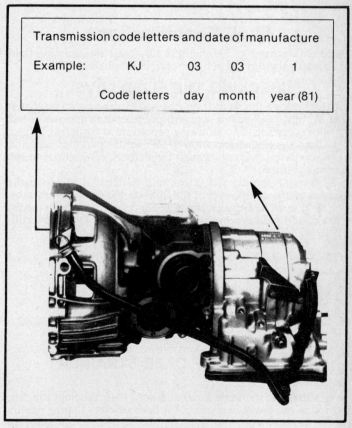

Transmission code letters and date of manufacture			
Example: KJ	03	03	1
Code letters	day	month	year (81)

Typical transaxle identification marking locations
(©Volkswagen of America, Inc.)

CONVERTER

The torque converter will have a letter stamped on the outside of one of the lugs. It is important to make note of the letter for parts ordering.

Transmission Metric Fasteners

These transmissions are of metric design, and metric bolt sizes and thread pitches are used for all fasteners on these transmissions.

The metric fastener dimensions are very close to the dimensions of the familiar inch system fasteners, and for this reason, replacement fasteners must have the same measurement and strength as those removed.

Do not attempt to interchange metric fasteners for inch system fasteners. Mismatched or incorrect fasteners can result in damage to the transmission unit through malfunctions, breakage or possible personal injury.

Care should be taken to reuse the fasteners in the same locations as removed, whenever possible.

NOTE: All threaded case holes must be checked for quality of their threads, especially the bolt holes for the mount brackets. It is virtually impossible to rethread these bolt holes after the transaxle has been installed in the vehicle.

Capacities

The fluid quantities are approximate and the correct fluid level should be determined by the dipstick indicator for the correct level.

Dry fill—6.4 U.S. quarts (6 Liters).
Refill—3.2 U.S. quarts (3 Liters).

Fluid Specifications

Use only Dexron® or Dexron® II automatic transmission fluid or its equivalent to fill, refill or correct the fluid level.

CHECKING THE FLUID LEVEL

When checking the fluid level, the vehicle engine/transaxle assembly must be at normal operating temperature and positioned on a level surface. The following procedure is suggested.

1. Start the engine and allow to idle, set the parking brake and move the selector lever through the detents, returning it to the Neutral position.

2. Remove the dipstick, clean and re-insert it. Remove the dipstick and note the level of the fluid on the dipstick indicator. The level must be between the upper and lower marks on the indicator. Add fluid as required to correct the level. Do not overfill.

M MODIFICATIONS

DELETION OF CASE STRAINER

SERIES 010

As of automatic transaxle serial number 21040, the fluid strainer, located in the pressure channel has been deleted. During repairs on the transaxles prior to serial number 21040, do not re-install the fluid strainer in the pressure channel.

DELETION OF GOVERNOR STRAINER

TYPE 089

As of automatic transaxle serial number 09040, the fluid strainer, located in the governor assembly, has been deleted. During repairs on the transaxles prior to transmission serial number 08040, do not re-install the fluid strainer in the governor assembly.

Location of Converter code letter (©Volkswagen of America, Inc.)

OIL PUMP SHAFT SPLINE CHANGE

TYPES 090, 089

To aid in the assembly, the oil pump shaft splines have been lengthened and tapered for easier insertion into the converter. New pump shafts can be installed in earlier transaxles. Part numbers remain unchanged.

Type 090—Old Shaft
Measured between the inner shoulder edges
Part number 090323561—20.047 inches (509.2 mm).
Type 090—New Shaft
Overall length measurement
Part number 090323561—21.523 inches (546.7 mm).
Type 089—Old Shaft
Measured between the inner shoulder edges
Part number 089323561—17.838 inches (453.1 mm).
Type 089—New Shaft
Overall length measurement
Part number 089323561—19.315 inches (490.6 mm).

LEFT AND RIGHT DRIVE FLANGE REPLACEMENT

TYPE 089

The drive flange oil seal contact surface has been widened and the shaft shortened. The new shaft can be installed in older transaxles without determining the end play and inserting adjusting shims. Measurement is made from the forward edge of the seal surface to the inner end of the shaft.

New Shaft Dimensions
Right—Part number 089409356—1.931 inches (49.05 mm).
Left—Part number 089409355—2.894 inches (73.5 mm).
Old Shaft Dimensions
Right—Part number 082409356—1.970 inches (50.05 mm).
Left—Part number 082409355—2.933 inches (74.5 mm).

SPRING IDENTIFICATION TABLE— VALVE BODY ASSEMBLIES

TYPE 089—AUDI, VANAGON

These tables allows identification of the springs by their dimensions. Coil diameter and free length can vary between new and used springs, due to settling, so check the spring wire thickness and number of coils first, as a means of spring identification. Use the inner coil diameter and free length, if necessary.

——— CAUTION ———
Several springs of the valve body may have the same dimensions. However, do not interchange them because the tolerances of each spring is different.

NOTE: The part numbers are listed for identification only and the springs are available by special order only.

VALVE BODY SPRING IDENTIFICATION TABLE
Audi—Transaxle Type 089

	Description	Coils	Wire thickness mm (in.)	Free length[1] mm (in.)	Inner diameter[2] of coil mm (in.)	As of transm. No.
1	Spring/throttle pressure limiting valve	14.5	1.1 (0.042)	35.3 (1.388)	7.7 (0.302)	
2	Spring/main pressure limiting valve	11.0	1.2 (0.472)	32.4 (1.274)	7.7 (0.302)	
3	Spring/main pressure valve	16.5 16.5	1.5 (0.059) 1.5 (0.059)	71.6 (2.818) 77.0 (3.031)	11.9 (0.468) 11.9 (0.468)	23 079
4	Spring/control valve 3—2	12.5	1.0 (0.039)	32.4 (1.274)	7.7 (0.302)	
5	Spring/throttle pressure valve	16.0	1.25 (0.048)	43.3 (1.703)	7.75 (0.304)	
6	Spring/shift valve 1—2	6.5 9.5	0.9 (0.035) 0.8 (0.031)	19.9 (0.783) 26.0 (1.024)	8.1 (0.317) 8.2 (0.323)	alternative
7	Spring/converter pressure valve	12.5 8.5	1.0 (0.039) 1.25 (0.049)	32.4 (1.274) 22.2 (0.874)	7.7 (0.302) 7.7 (0.302)	gradual
8	Spring/modulator pressure valve	12.0 11.5	0.7 (0.027) 0.8 (0.031)	18.7 (0.736) 28.6 (1.125)	5.3 (0.208) 7.75 (0.305)	11 098[3]
9	Spring/shift valve 2—3	6.5 9.5	0.9 (0.035) 0.8 (0.031)	19.9 (0.783) 26.0 (1.024)	8.1 (0.317) 8.2 (0.323)	alternative
10	Spring/kickdown control valve 3—2	11.5	0.9 (0.035)	28.4 (1.118)	8.1 (0.317)	
11	Spring/apply valve 1st/reverse gear brake	11.5	0.9 (0.035)	28.4 (1.118)	8.1 (0.317)	

[1] Free length can vary due to tolerances and settling
[2] Inner coil diameter is within tolerance of ±0.3 mm (0.012 in.)
[3] Valve changed from 8 mm (0.315 in.) to 11 mm (0.433 in.)

VALVE BODY SPRING IDENTIFICATION TABLE
Vanagon—Transaxle Type 089, 090

Description	Coils	Wire thickness mm (in.)	Free length[1] mm (in.)	Inner diameter[2] of coil mm (in.)
1. Spring/throttle pressure limiting valve	14.5	1.1 (0.042)	37.9 (1.492)	7.7 (0.302)
2. Spring/main pressure limiting valve	12.5	1.2 (0.047)	27.5 (1.083)	7.6 (0.299)
3. Spring/main pressure valve	16.5	1.4 (0.055)	69.2 (2.724)	11.9 (0.468)
4. Spring/control valve 3-2	16.5	1.1 (0.042)	44 (1.732)	7.75 (0.304)
5. Spring/throttle pressure valve	11.5	0.8 (0.032)	28.6 (1.126)	7.75 (0.304)
6. Spring/shift valve 1-2	6.5	0.9 (0.035)	19.9 (0.783)	8.1 (0.317)
7. Spring/shift valve 2-3	8.5	0.8 (0.032)	17.4 (0.685)	6.95 (0.274)
8. Spring/modulator pressure valve	12.5	1.0 (0.039)	32.4 (1.274)	7.7 (0.302)
9. Spring/converter pressure valve	8.5	1.25 (0.049)	22.2 (0.874)	7.7 (0.302)
10. Spring/kickdown control valve 3-2	11.5	0.9 (0.035)	28.4 (1.118)	8.1 (0.317)
11. Spring/apply valve 1st/reverse gear brake	10.5	0.63 (0.025)	36.3 (1.429)	9.0 (0.354)

[1] Free length can vary due to tolerances and settling
[2] Inner coil diameter is within tolerance of ± 0.3 mm

OPERATING LEVER, PARK LOCK, MANUAL VALVE AND OPERATING LEVER MODIFICATION

SERIES 10 TRANSAXLE

Three versions of the modifications have been made. The manual valves have been modified with necessary changes made to the operating levers. The operating lever parking lock assembly has been modified with necessary changes made to the operating rod assembly. The modified parts must be installed in their proper combination of either of the three versions.

THRUST WASHER MODIFICATION

SERIES 10 TRANSAXLE

Earlier thrust washer for the direct reverse clutch to oil pump was steel/bronze and plastic and the thrust washer for the forward clutch was steel/bronze. A new plastic thrust washer with three outer lugs has been released for use between the direct reverse clutch and the oil pump, and between the forward clutch and the direct reverse clutch. The new plastic thrust washer can be installed in earlier transaxle assemblies.

OIL PUMP AND FORWARD CLUTCH MODIFICATIONS

SERIES 10 TRANSAXLES

The in-service oil pump used a locating lug type thrust washer between the oil pump and the forward clutch. The forward clutch housing used a drilled area, 180° apart, to seat the thrust washer and the contact area of the oil pump was machined. The new oil pump thrust washer contact area is not machined and a three piece thrust bearing assemlby is now used in place of the single thrust washer. The forward clutch housing is not drilled, since it

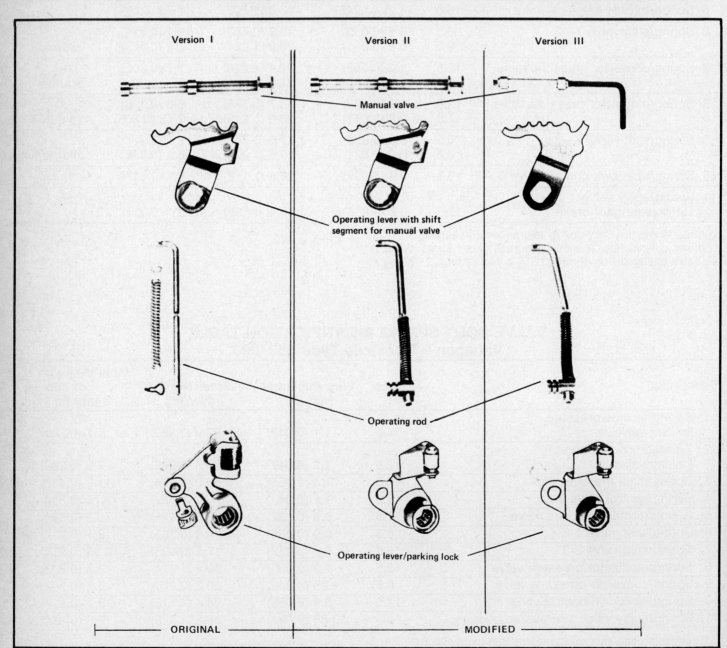

Operating lever modifications (©Volkswagen of America, Inc.)

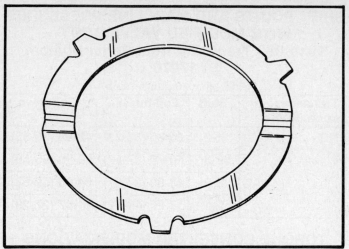

New style thrust washers (©Volkswagen of America, Inc.)

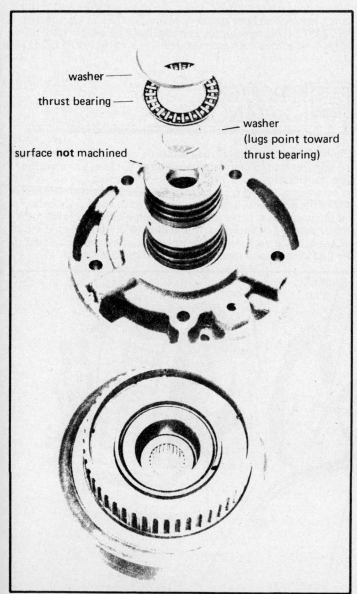

washer

thrust bearing

washer
(lugs point toward
thrust bearing)

surface **not** machined

New oil pump and forward clutch modifications
(©Volkswagen of America, Inc.)

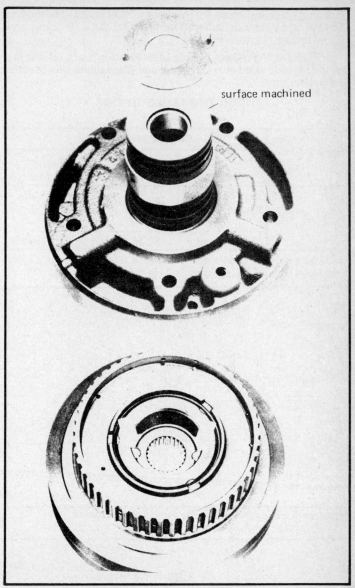

surface machined

Old style oil pump and forward clutch modifications
(©Volkswagen of America, Inc.)

is not necessary to locate the lugs of the bearing in the clutch housing. Care must be exercised during the assembly of the units, not to interchange any of the components, new to old or old to new, as transaxle failure will result.

TURBINE SHAFT MODIFICATION

Series 10 Transaxle

The turbine shaft splines have been modified from the forward clutch/oil pump assembly that uses a thrust washer, to a turbine shaft grooved for a circlip on the end of the splines, used with the forward clutch/oil pump using the new thrust bearing modification. The new shaft must always be installed with a circlip, never without. The new shaft and circlip can be installed in the transaxle using the forward clutch/oil pump and thrust washer.

VALVE BODY MODIFICATION

**TYPE 090 FROM SERIAL NUMBER 17070
TRANSAXLE CODE-NG, VALVE BODY CODE-BH**

The new valve body can be installed in transaxles from serial number 01068. Modifications have been made to the separation

815

plate markings and check ball locations. New springs are used in the shift and operation calibration, affecting the shift points and the main line pressure settings.

NOTE: For Valve Body Spring Identification chart, refer to the Spring Identification chart for Audi and Vanagon in this Modification Section.

Main pressure in bar
(psi)

Transmission code letters	Selector lever position		
	Drive idle speed ①	Drive full throttle	Reverse idle speed
NG	speed higher than 50 km/h (32 mph)	—	car stationary
	2.9-3.0 (41-42)	5.85-5.95 (83-84)	9.1-9.7 (129-138)

*Carry out this test on dynamometer:
—accelerate up to 50 km (32 mph)
—release accelerator pedal (idle speed)
—check pressure on gauge

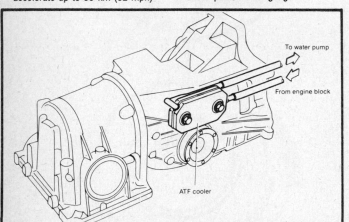

Location of transaxle fluid cooler on varied transaxles (©Volkswagen of America, Inc.)

SHIFT POINTS AND MAIN LINE PRESSURES WITH MODIFIED VALVE BODY
Type 090 Transaxle from Serial Number 17070
Shift points in km/h (mph)

Transmission code letters	Shift	Full throttle	Kickdown
NG	1-2	25-36 (16-22)	49-52 (30-32)
	2-3	60-76 (37-47)	89-90 (55-56)
	3-2	43-60 (27-37)	84-86 (52-53)
	2-1	17-20 (11-12)	44-47 (27-29)

TORQUE CONVERTER MODIFICATIONS

TYPE 090 TRANSAXLE

Torque converters coded Z, using modified impeller and turbine vanes, are used in later transaxle assemblies. The part number is 090323571. This new torque converter can be used in earlier vehicles with torque converters coded D, part number 033325571-D.

📟 TROUBLE DIAGNOSIS

The VW/Audi and Fiat Strada transaxle assemblies are basically the same, except in their configuration of the final drive housing. The transmission units are the same, both using the Series 010 transmissions. However, the major difference is the nomenclature of the internal components by VW/Audi and Fiat Strada. To aid the repairman, separate transmission band and clutch application charts, diagnosis charts and double keyed exploded views are used, along with component nomenclature changes noted in the disassembly and assembly text as required.

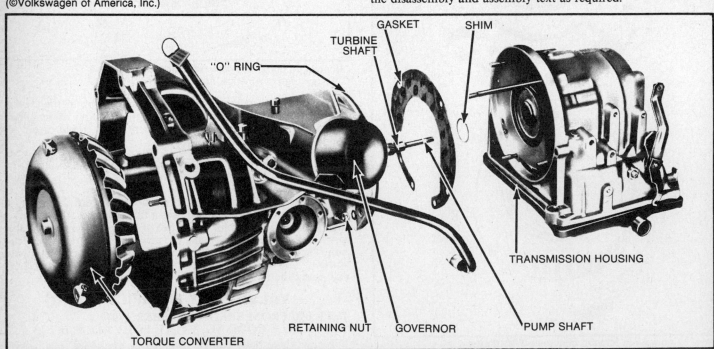

Transaxle type used with Audi models, Jetta and Vanagon. Note final drive configuration (©Volkswagen of America, Inc.)

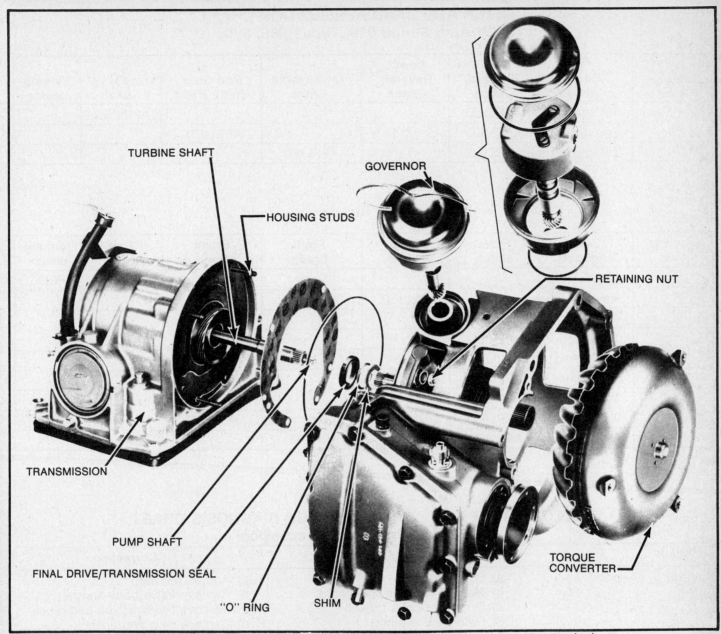

TURBINE SHAFT

HOUSING STUDS

GOVERNOR

RETAINING NUT

TRANSMISSION

PUMP SHAFT

FINAL DRIVE/TRANSMISSION SEAL

"O" RING

SHIM

TORQUE CONVERTER

Transaxle type used with Rabbit, Scirocco, Fiat Strada. Note final drive configuration (©Volkswagen of America, Inc.)

CLUTCH AND BAND APPLICATION CHART
VW/Audi Series 010, Types 089, 090

Selector lever	Gear engaged	Forward Clutch	Direct Reverse Clutch	1st/Reverse Brake	2nd Gear Brake Band	One-way Clutch	Parking device
P	Park						APPLIED
R	Reverse		APPLIED	APPLIED			
N	Neutral						
D	1st speed	APPLIED				APPLIED	
	2nd speed	APPLIED			APPLIED		
	3rd speed	APPLIED	APPLIED				

CLUTCH AND BAND APPLICATION CHART
VW/Audi Series 010, Types 089, 090

Selector lever	Gear engaged	Forward Clutch	Direct Reverse Clutch	1st/Reverse Brake	2nd Gear Brake Band	One-way Clutch	Parking device
2	1st speed	APPLIED				APPLIED	
	2nd speed	APPLIED			APPLIED		
1	1st speed	APPLIED		APPLIED			

Fiat Strada

Selector lever	Gear engaged	Front clutch	Rear clutch	Front brake	Brake Band	Free wheel	Parking device
P	Park						APPLIED
R	Reverse		APPLIED	APPLIED			
N	Neutral						
D	1st speed	APPLIED				APPLIED	
	2nd speed	APPLIED			APPLIED		
	3rd speed	APPLIED	APPLIED				
2	1st speed	APPLIED				APPLIED	
	2nd speed	APPLIED			APPLIED		
1	1st speed	APPLIED		APPLIED			

CHILTON'S THREE "C's" TRANSMISSION DIAGNOSIS CHART
Audi/VW Automatic Transmission

Condition	Cause	Correction
No drive in all gears	a) Low fluid level b) Manual valve disconnected c) Converter bolts broken d) Defective oil pump	a) Add as required b) Remove valve body and repair c) Remove transmission and repair d) Replace oil pump/drive
No drive in forward gears	a) Defective oil pump b) Forward planetary failed	a) Overhaul clutch b) Replace planetary
No drive in 1st gear	a) One-way clutch failed b) Defective forward clutch	a) Replace clutch b) Overhaul clutch
No drive in 2nd gear	a) 2nd gear brake band failed	a) Overhaul transmission replace band
No drive in 3rd gear	a) Direct and reverse clutch failed	a) Overhaul clutch
No drive in Reverse	a) 1st and reverse clutch failure b) Direct and reverse clutch failed c) Defective forward clutch	a) Overhaul transmission replace clutch components b) Overhaul clutch c) Overhaul clutch
Drive in Neutral	a) Forward clutch seized	a) Overhaul clutch

CHILTON'S THREE "C's" TRANSMISSION DIAGNOSIS CHART
Audi/VW Automatic Transmission

Condition	Cause	Correction
No 2nd gear upshift	a) Defective governor	a) Overhaul or replace
	b) Accumulator cover loose	b) Check accumulator, cover and seals
	c) Valve body dirty	c) Clean, change filter and fluid
	d) 2nd gear brake band failed	d) Overhaul transmission and replace band
No 3rd gear upshift	a) Governor dirty	a) Remove, disassemble and clean
	b) Valve body dirty	b) Clean, change filter and fluid
	c) 2-3 Shift valve sticking	c) Clean valve body
	d) Check balls out of place	d) Remove valve body, replace check balls as required
Noisy in Drive during start	a) 1st gear one-way clutch failed	a) Replace clutch and affected parts
Shift speed above or below normal speed	a) Governor dirty	a) Remove, disassemble and clean
	b) Valve body dirty	b) Clean, change filter and fluid
No kickdown	a) Accelerator cable out of adjustment	a) Adjust cable to specifications

CHILTON'S THREE "C's" TRANSMISSION DIAGNOSIS CHART
Fiat Strada

Condition	Cause	Correction
Low oil level	a) Oil leaking from inlet	a) Correct inlet leakage
	b) Oil leaking from seals	b) Replace seals
Oil escaping from inlet piping	a) High oil level	a) Correct oil level
	b) Clogged transmission vent valve	b) Clean vent valve
	c) Leak in oil pump suction line	c) Correct oil pump suction leakage
Oil leakage at transmission bell housing	a) Oil leaking from converter	a) Replace or repair converter
	b) Transmission bell housing seal	b) Replace bell housing seal
	c) Capscrew securing housing to transmission case	c) Reseal capscrew and torque properly
Oil leakage near transmission case	a) Selector valve sealing ring	a) Replace selector valve sealing ring
	b) Oil sump gasket	b) Replace oil pan gasket
	c) Sealing ring on oil inlet piping	c) Replace sealing ring
	d) Oil pressure point connector	d) Tighten port plug
Low oil pressure	a) Low oil level	a) Correct fluid level
	b) Clogged oil filter	b) Replace oil filter
	c) Leak in oil pump suction line	c) Repair suction line leakage
	d) Leak in hydraulic circuit	d) Locate hydraulic circuit leakage and repair
	e) Oil pressure regulator valve spring out of adjustment	e) Adjust or replace regulator valve spring
High oil pressure	a) Main pressure regulator valve spring out of adjustment	a) Adjust or replace regulator valve spring

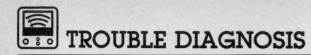

CHILTON'S THREE "C's" TRANSMISSION DIAGNOSIS CHART
Fiat Strada

Condition	Cause	Correction
"P" difficult to disengage	a) Selector lever linkage jammed	a) Correct binding or jammed condition
No take off with selector lever at "D", "2", "1" or "R"	a) Low oil level b) Oil filter clogged c) Selector lever linkage disconnected d) Input shaft failed e) Oil pressure regulator valve stuck open f) Defective oil pump	a) Correct oil level b) Replace oil filter c) Reconnect selector lever linkage d) Install new input shaft e) Correct pressure regulator valve operation f) Replace oil pump
Take off only after repeated movement of selector lever	Selector valve not aligned with valve body ports: a) Distorted or badly adjusted connecting cable b) Nut securing sector to shaft loose	a) Adjust or replace the connecting cable b) Tighten the retaining nut
No take off after shift from "P" to "D", "2" or "1"	a) Parking device stuck in engagement position	a) Correct binding or jammed condition
Sudden take off at high engine rpm	a) Front clutch piston seized b) Low oil level c) Defective oil pump d) Oil filter missing	a) Overhaul unit as required b) Correct fluid level c) Replace oil pump d) Install oil filter
Bumpy take off Smooth only in "R"	a) Low oil pressure b) Pressure regulator valve stuck	a) Correct oil pressure b) Correct pressure regulator valve operation
No take off in "D" or "2", only in "1" and "R"	a) Defective free wheel	a) Overhaul unit as required
No take off in "D", "2" and "1" ("R" only)	a) Defective front clutch	a) Overhaul unit as required
No take off in "R"	a) Defective front brake b) Defective rear clutch	a) Overhaul unit as required b) Overhaul unit as required
Take off in "N"	a) Selector lever linkage incorrectly adjusted	a) Adjust linkage correctly
No) 1-2 upshift with selector lever at "D" or "2" (transmission locked in 1st)	a) Centrifugal speed governor valve sticking b) 1-2 shift valve stuck in 1st c) Leaking seals on oil pump hub d) Leaking governor hydraulic circuit e) Clogged governor filter f) Worn brake hand	a) Free up governor valve b) Free up 1-2 shift valve c) Replace seals on oil pump hub d) Locate and repair leaking governor hydraulic circuit e) Remove or replace governor filter f) Replace brake band
No 2-3 upshift with selector lever at "D" (transmission locked in 2nd)	a) 2-3 shift valve stuck in 2nd b) Leaking governor hydraulic circuit	a) Free up 2-3 shift valve b) Locate and repair leaking governor hydraulic circuit
Upshifts in "D" and "2" only with throttle valve completely open	a) Modulator and relief valves stuck b) Kick-down valve or control cable stuck	a) Free up modulator and relief valves b) Free up or replace valve or cable
Upshifts in "D" and "2" only with throttle valve partially open	a) Kick-down valve cable incorrectly adjusted b) Kick-down valve cable failed	a) Correct kick-down cable adjustment b) Replace kick-down cable or adjust

CHILTON'S THREE "C's" TRANSMISSION DIAGNOSIS CHART
Fiat Strada

Condition	Cause	Correction
No downshift with kick-down actuated	a) Kick-down valve cable failed b) Kick-down valve cable incorrectly adjusted	a) Replace kick-down cable and adjust b) Correct kick-down cable adjustment
Downshift at high speeds	a) Loss of pressure in governor	a) Correct governor oil pressure loss
Rough 3-2 downshift with kick-down actuated and at high speed	a) Rear brake incorrectly adjusted b) 3-2 shift valve seized or defective spring	a) Correct rear brake adjustment b) Free up 3-2 shift valve or replace spring
During downshift with kick-down actuated, engine idles and revs up	a) Low oil pressure b) Excessive band brake play or loose adjusting screw	a) Correct low oil pressure malfunction b) Adjust band
Engine braking minimal with lever at "1"	a) Selector lever linkage incorrectly adjusted b) Front clutch piston and front brake stuck	a) Adjust selector lever linkage b) Overhaul unit as required
Engine braking minimal with lever at "2"	a) Selector lever linkage incorrectly adjusted b) Front clutch piston and front brake stuck	a) Adjust selector lever linkage b) Overhaul unit as required
Car not restrained with lever at "P"	a) Selector lever linkage incorrectly adjusted b) Parking release spring failed c) Parking pawl stop failed	a) Adjust selector lever linkage b) Replace parking release spring c) Replace parking pawl stop
Excessive noise in all gears	a) Excessive play between sun and planet gears b) Defective thrust bearings c) Worn bushings d) Excessive end float e) Parking release spring unhooked or incorrectly installed f) Nuts securing bell housing to transmission case	a) Replace necessary gears b) Replace thrust bearings c) Replace bushings d) Correct end play e) Connect parking release spring or install correctly f) Tighten nuts securely
Screech on starting	a) Converter defective	a) Replace converter assembly
Excessive quantity of ferrous deposits in oil	a) Oil pump b) Clutch hub worn	a) Replace oil pump, clean and examine unit for wear b) Replace clutch hub, clean and examine unit for wear
Excessive quantity of aluminum deposits in oil	a) End float adjustment thrust washer	a) Replace thrust washer, clean and examine unit for wear)

"E" Mode Transaxles

Condition	Cause	Correction
Transmission does not disengage from engine with closed throttle and selector lever in position E	a) Accelerator cable incorrectly adjusted b) Selector lever cable incorrectly adjusted c) Main pressure too high d) Declutching valve in valve body sticking	a) Adjust accelerator cable b) Adjust selector lever cable c) Adjust accelerator cable d) Disassemble valve body and check declutch valve

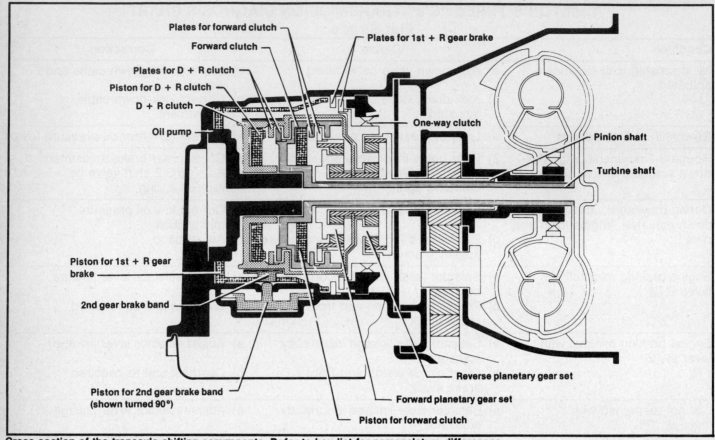

Plates for forward clutch
Forward clutch
Plates for D + R clutch
Piston for D + R clutch
D + R clutch
Oil pump
Plates for 1st + R gear brake
One-way clutch
Pinion shaft
Turbine shaft
Piston for 1st + R gear brake
2nd gear brake band
Piston for 2nd gear brake band (shown turned 90°)
Reverse planetary gear set
Forward planetary gear set
Piston for forward clutch

Cross section of the transaxle shifting components. Refer to key list for nomenclature differences (©Volkswagen of America, Inc.)

HYDRAULIC CONTROL SYSTEM

The power flow from the torque converter flows to the planetary gears by means of the the turbine shaft, through the hollow drive pinion. All three forward gears and reverse are obtained by driving or holding either the sun gear, planetary gear carrier or annulus (internal ring) gear.

The hydraulic control system directs the path and pressure of the fluid so that the proper element can be applied as needed. The valve body directs the pressure to the proper clutch or band servo. There are three ways in which these control valves are operated.

1. The manual valve is connected to the selector lever by a cable. Shifting the lever moves the manual valve to change the range of the transaxle.

2. The kick down valve and the modulated pressure valves are operated and controlled by a mechanical cable, connected to the accelerator linkage.

3. The governor controls the pressure relative to speed and so makes the transaxle sensitive to changes in vehicle speed.

With the engine running, the oil pump supplies the torque converter with fluid. The fluid is passed through the impeller, and at low speeds, the oil is redirected by the stator to the converter turbine in such a manner that it actually assists in delivering power or mulitplying engine torque. As the impeller speed increases, the direction of the oil leaving the turbine changes and flows against the stator vanes in such a manner that the stator is now impeding the flow of oil. At this point, the roller clutch in the converter re-

leases and the stator revolves freely on its shaft. Once the stator becomes inactive, there is no further multiplication of torque within the converter. At this point, the converter is merely acting as a fluid coupling at approximately a one-to-one ratio.

The converter is attached to planetary gears by the turbine shaft, so that a smooth gear change can be made without interrupting the flow of power from the engine. Various ratios (3 forward and 1 reverse) can be obtained by holding, releasing or driving different parts of the planetary gear set.

To accomplish this, three multiple disc clutches, one band and a one-way clutch are used. The clutches and the band are applied and released by oil pressure, while the one-way clutch mechanically prevents the rotation of the front brake/front planetary hub assembly when the transaxle is in the DRIVE position, first speed ratio and under an application of torque from the engine.

The valve body controls the shifting of the transmission, dependent upon the engine load and the road speed.

Major Components

CLUTCHES

Multiple disc clutches are used with-in the rear clutch drum and the front clutch drum. A third multiple disc clutch is used as a brake clutch, between the front brake/front planet hub and the case. This brake clutch replaces the low/reverse band, as used in the Series 003 transaxle models.

BAND

The second gear brake band is used to stop the rotation of the direct/reverse clutch drum by hydraulic application, providing a second speed ratio. The band is applied in the second gear when

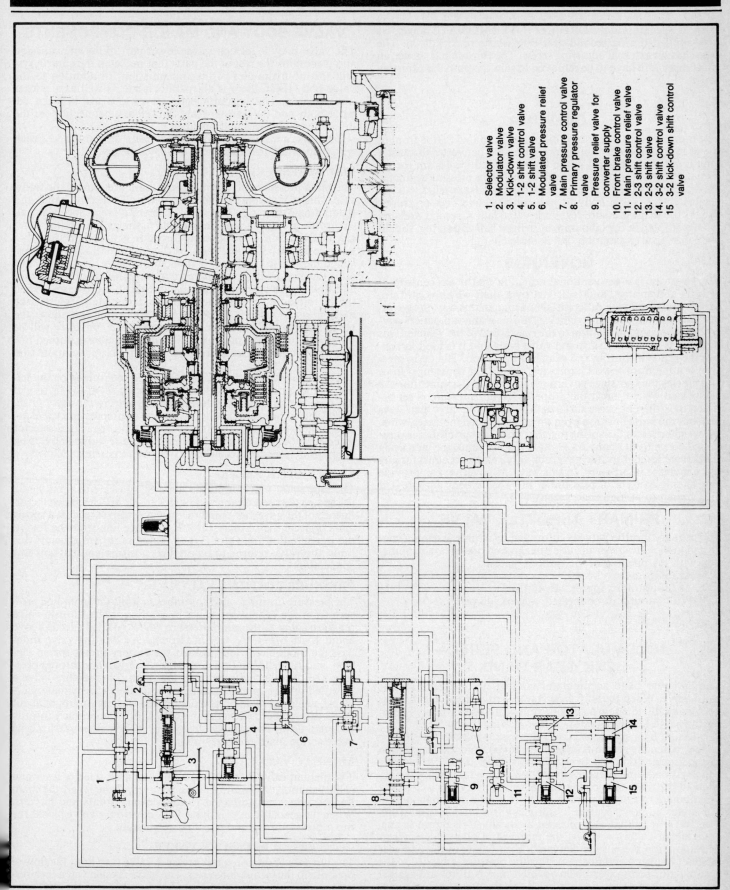

1. Selector valve
2. Modulator valve
3. Kick-down valve
4. 1-2 shift control valve
5. 1-2 shift valve
6. Modulated pressure relief valve
7. Main pressure control valve
8. Primary pressure regulator valve
9. Pressure relief valve for converter supply
10. Front brake control valve
11. Main pressure relief valve
12. 2-3 shift control valve
13. 2-3 shift valve
14. 3-2 shift control valve
15. 3-2 kick-down shift control valve

Hydraulic system schematic, typical of series 010 transaxles (©Volkswagen of America, Inc.)

the gear selector is in the DRIVE or INTERMEDIATE range. It is also applied during second gear downshifts or kickdown. The band has an external adjusting screw. The throttle relay lever, in most cases, will have to be removed to gain access to the adjusting screw.

OIL PUMP

The transaxle uses a gear type oil pump, mounted on the front of the gear box assembly and is driven by the converter through a long input shaft. The oil pump draws filtered fluid from the oil pan and sends it, under pressure, to the main pressure regulator valve, located in the valve body. A main pressure relief valve is located in the valve body to prevent excessive high pressures, should the main pressure regulator valve fail. A second pressure relief is located in the oil pump, utilizing a ball and spring, should the control valve assembly fail completely.

GOVERNOR

The governor is a conventional design in that it has centrifugal weights and springs, and is driven by a shaft which is, in turn, driven by a gear in the differential housing. In this way, the governor only rotates when the vehicle is moving, and it produces governor oil pressure in relation to the road speed of the vehicle. This pressure is then directed to the valve body and it is used to control the gearshift timing and gearshift operation. The main pressure coming from the oil pump acts against the centrifugal force and presses the two-stage governor valve and at the same time the centrifugal weight, until the proper governor pressure is set between the different valve surfaces. The governor valve then stays at about the same position even though the speed increases, while the weight presses the spring together until the spring disc is positioned correctly at about 20-22 mph. At this point, the increasing centrifugal force from the governor valve alone accounts for any more increase in pressure. In this way, the governor can provide an exacting amount of pressure at low road speeds and prevent high pressures at high road speeds.

PRIMARY THROTTLE VALVE

The primary throttle valve is controlled by a cable assembly connected to the carburetor throttle linkage, and operates in conjunction with the opening of the throttle plates.
1. At idle, approx. 5-6 psi
2. At full throttle, approx. 45-48 psi
3. With vaccum disconnected, approx. 48 psi

ACCUMULATOR AND SERVO— 2ND GEAR BAND

The 2nd gear band accumulator controls the pressure for the band apply. When the shift from 1st to 2nd is made, the drum is held gradually to allow a smooth shift and to keep the shift from feeling harsh to the operator. A free-moving piston which is under tension by a spring receives oil pressure to both sides of the piston. When the gearshift selector is moved from the 1st position to the 2nd position, oil from the shift valve in the valve body which is main line pressure, regulated by a jet or orifice is supplied to the underside of the 2nd gear band servo as well as the accumulator. At the beginning of the shift, the accumulator piston is pressed down against its spring by this main line pressure. The 2nd gear band is also released by means of its return spring, being pressed downward. At the moment of gear change, throttled main line pressure is delivered from below to the 2nd gear band servo piston and this same throttle pressure is applied to the accumulator piston from below which moves it upward against the main line pressure. By thus balancing the pressures and forces involved, a smooth shift is obtained.

VALVE BODY AND MAJOR COMPONENTS

The valve body is located in the lower part of the transmission and it contains the rest of the parts that make up the control system for the hydraulics of the transmission. In addition to the valve body itself, there is a separator plate as well as a thicker transfer plate. The separator plate serves as a seal between the valve body and the transfer plate, as well as a connection for the different oil passages and openings.

There are a number of different valves in the valve body, each with a specific function. These are listed below.

MAIN PRESSURE VALVE

The main pressure valve controls the main pressure of the transaxle. This oil controls the operation of the clutches and bands and the transaxle operation in general. There is a preset spring as well as throttle pressure acting on one side of the spring. On the other side and working in the opposite direction is the oil pressure that is to be regulated, and it acts on two different sized surfaces. When the gearshift selector is in Neutral, Drive, 2nd or 1st, this oil is directed by the manual valve to a second area on the valve and thus works against the spring and throttle pressures. When the oil pressure exceeds the spring and throttle pressures, the main pressure valve is pushed against the spring and allows the oil to flow to the converter valve so that the converter will be filled with oil. As the pressure builds up, the valve is pushed further and allows the excess pressure to return to the pump suction circuit.

The oil pressure with a closed throttle is determined by the setting of the spring tension which is originally set at the factory at the time the governor is calibrated. *This setting must not be altered.* The oil pressures acting against the main pressure valve depend on engine speed, throttle position, road speed and selector lever position. In this way, the main pressure valve delivers an appropriate pressure according to the requirements.

MODULATOR VALVE

The modulator valve limits the main oil pressure to about 86-88 psi at a road speed of approximately 16-18 MPH. Under the influence of the governor pressure, the valve moves against a spring and connects the primary throttle pressure line with the line to the pressure limiting valve. When the pressure drops below this limit, the valve returns to its original position and cuts off this connection.

PRESSURE LIMITING VALVE

The pressure limiting valve continues to limit the main line pressure from the modulator valve by restricting the throttle valve pressure going to the main pressure valve. At road speeds above about 15-18 MPH, the face of the pressure limiting valve slides past the modulator valve against the factory preset spring tension, and restricts the flow from a second primary throttle pressure line. Another passage feeds the main line pressure valve a throttled primary pressure which is limited to approximately 27-29 psi, while the main pressure is limited to a maximum of about 86-88 psi. At speeds lower than 16-18 MPH, the primary throttle pressure flows unrestricted by means of the pressure limiting valve to the main pressure valve.

MANUAL VALVE

The manual valve is connected to the gear shift selector lever and cable assembly. According to the position of the lever, the main line oil pressure is directed to the various points and circuits. When the gearshift lever is in the Park position, a valve blocks the main pressure inlet and the flow of pressure.

CONVERTER PRESSURE VALVE

The purpose of the converter pressure valve is to limit the flow of pressure to the torque converter. The valve is open when the pressure reads below about 60-62 psi. The flow of oil to the converter will then be unrestricted. However, when the pressure rises above this limit, the valve is pushed against a spring and the flow of oil is then restricted so that the converter will not be subjected to a pressure above 62-65 psi.

KICK-DOWN VALVE

The kick-down valve is used to provide added fluid pressure to the shift valves, causing either a downshift from third to second, second to first or a delay in the upshift when added acceleration is needed. The kick-down valve is operated by a mechanical cable, connected between the carburetor throttle linkage and the transaxle valve body. The kick-down and throttle valves work in conjunction with each other, since both are controlled by the mechanical cable.

1-2 SHIFT VALVE

The 1-2 shift valve engages 1st and 2nd gear according to the amount of governor pressure by either relieving oil pressure or applying oil pressure to the feed end of the 2nd gear servo.

When starting out in Drive or 2nd, the valve spring and the throttle pressure oil push the valve into the 1st position. The line pressure to the valve is then closed and the feed to the 2nd band servo receives no oil pressure. As the speed increases, the governor pressure overcomes the spring force and the throttle pressure, and the valve is pushed against the spring into the 2nd gear position.

At this point the main line pressure opens up and the feed side of the 2nd gear servo, as well as the underside of the accumulator, receive oil pressure. The band is applied and 2nd gear is engaged. The governor pressure is reinforced by the main line pressure which acts on the area between the valve diameters. In this way, the valve is held in the 2nd gear position even at speeds which are below the upshift speed. This prevents the continuous up and down shifting which might occur in this range when the speed remains almost constant. When starting off in 1st gear position, both surfaces of this valve are under main line pressure.

2-3 SHIFT VALVE

The 2-3 shift valve shifts the transaxle from 2nd gear to 3rd according to the governor pressure, the secondary throttle pressure and the position of the kickdown valve. It can also shift back from 3rd to 2nd by exhausting the oil from the release side of the 2nd gear servo and the direct and reverse clutch piston. At low speeds, the valve spring and the throttle pressure hold the valve in the 2nd gear position. The main oil line from the manual valve is then closed. As the speed increases, and the governor pressure becomes greater than the spring force and the throttle pressure, the valve snaps to the 3rd gear position. The main line pressure opens and oil is supplied to the release side of the 2nd gear band as well as to the direct and reverse clutch. As soon as main line pressure enters, it acts against the valve and prevents the valve from moving to an off position. The main pressure holds the valve in the 3rd gear position unitl the road speed drops below the upshift speed. This gives a speed difference between upshifting and downshifting which should fit in with normal driving practice and prevent continuous up and downshifting.

2-3 CONTROL VALVE

The purpose of this valve is to vary the restriction of the main line pressure as it is fed from the 1-2 shift valve to the feed side of the 2nd gear band, according to the road speed and engine load. This smooths out the 3-2 downshift under all driving conditions. When kickdowns are made at high speed, as well as shifts made at low speeds without throttle, the governor pressure takes over to hold the valve against the stop against primary throttle pressure. The pressure from the 1-2 shift valve to the 2nd gear band is then restricted by a small jet that is near the 2-3 valve. This causes a delay in the band apply after the direct clutch is released and gives the engine time to accelerate to its new speed. When downshifts are made with throttle at medium speeds, the primary throttle pressure predominates and the result is that the valve is pressed to its stop against regulator pressure. The pressure line from the 1-2 shift valve is then connected to the feed side of the band by an additional large jet, and since the engine needs less time to change speed, the band is applied quicker.

E-MODE
AUTOMATIC TRANSAXLE

A modified version of the Series 010 (Types 089, 090) transaxles has been released and is used in 1982 and later selected vehicles. When the transaxle is placed in the "E" position, the drive between the transaxle and the differential is disengaged when ever the accelerator pedal is released. The vehicle will "freewheel" on deceleration and at idle because the transaxle is then in the Neutral mode. If the selector lever is placed in any other position, the transaxle will operate in its normal manner.

In order to obtain the freewheeling mode, the forward clutch and the valve body were modified. To control the operation of the forward clutch, two new valves were added to the valve body and several other valves were modified.

The new valves are the forward clutch release valve and the forward clutch engagement valve with a separate plate clutch.

The modification of existing valves affects the manual valve and the transfer plate. In addition, a de-clutching valve has been added to the kickdown valve.

Manual Valve Modification

The manual valve has an additional position "E" along with the valve body channels being redesigned.

DECLUTCHING VALVE

The declutching valve was added to the kickdown valve and opens as soon as the accelerator pedal is released.

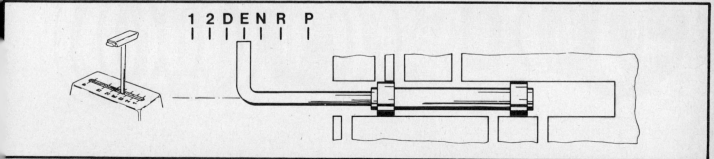

Manual valve in "E" position (©Volkswagen of America, Inc.)

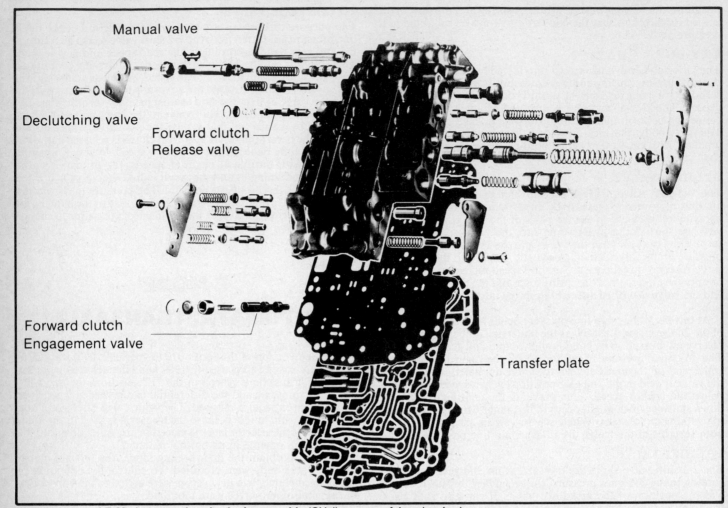

Manual valve

Declutching valve

Forward clutch
Release valve

Forward clutch
Engagement valve

Transfer plate

Exploded view of E-Mode transaxle valve body assembly (©Volkswagen of America, Inc.)

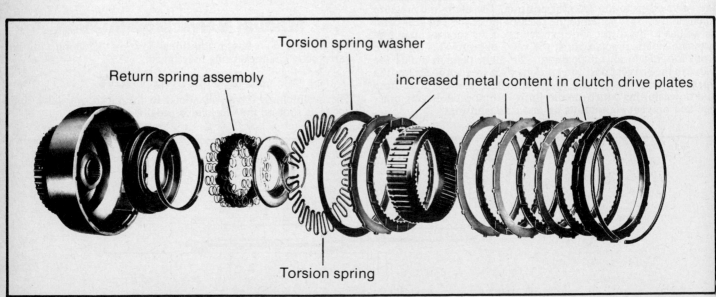

Return spring assembly

Torsion spring washer

Increased metal content in clutch drive plates

Torsion spring

Exploded view of "E" mode forward clutch components (©Volkswagen of America, Inc.)

FORWARD CLUTCH VALVE

The release valve controls the main pressure for the forward clutch in conjunction with the throttle pressure.

FORWARD CLUTCH ENGAGEMENT VALVE

In conjunction with the plate valve, the engagement valve ensures that the forward clutch engages quickly and smoothly.

Operation

SELECTOR LEVER IN "E" POSITION FORWARD CLUTCH RELEASED

1. As the accelerator pedal is released, throttle pressure on the forward clutch release valve is reduced by the mechanical opening of the declutching valve.

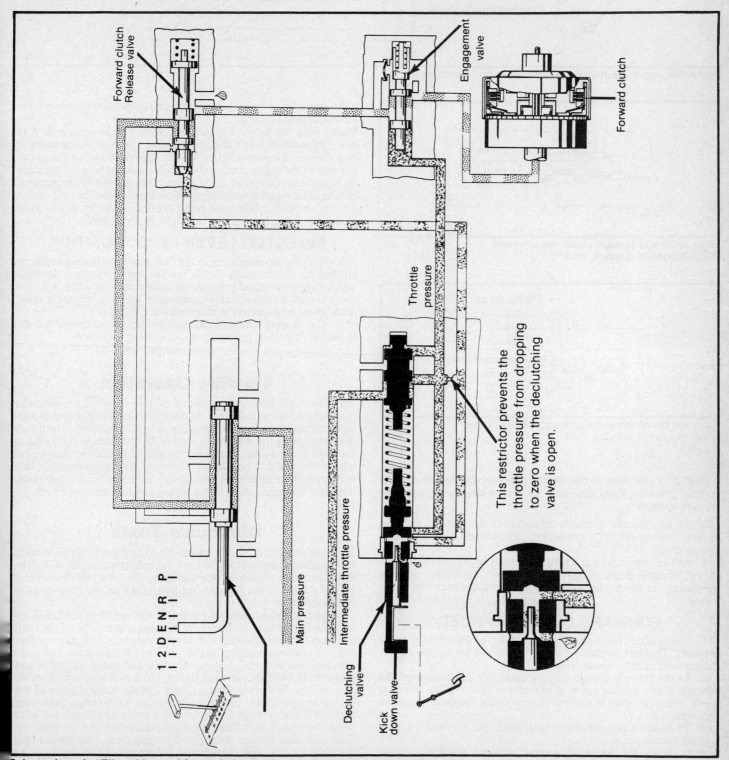

Selector lever in "E" position and forward clutch released (©Volkswagen of America, Inc.)

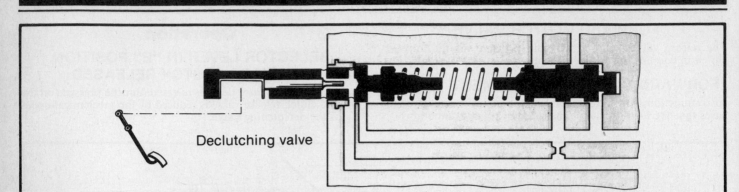

Declutching valve mechanism (©Volkswagen of America, Inc.)

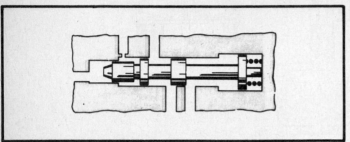

Cross section of forward clutch release valve
(©Volkswagen of America, Inc.)

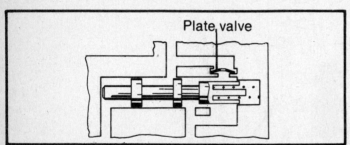

Cross section of forward clutch engagement valve
(©Volkswagen of America, Inc.)

NOTE: A restrictor in the throttle pressure circuit prevents the throttle pressure from dropping to zero when the declutching valve is opened.

2. As the throttle pressure is reduced, the release valve is moved, cutting off main pressure to the forward clutch engagement valve.

3. As the pressure to the forward clutch engagement valve is cut off, throttle pressure moves the engagement valve, opening the passage to the release valve, so the forward clutch can be released.

FORWARD CLUTCH APPLIED

1. As the accelerator pedal is depressed, the declutching valve is closed. Throttle pressure is allowed to build up on one side of the forward clutch release valve.

2. As the throttle pressure is increased, spring tension on the forward clutch release valve is overcome, allowing the valve to move. Main pressure is allowed to flow to the forward clutch engagement valve.

3. To insure a fast, smooth engagement, the forward clutch is applied in two steps.

Step 1—When the declutching valve is closed, throttle pressure builds up and moves the forward clutch release valve, allowing main pressure to flow through the engagement valve to quickly fill the forward clutch.

Step 2—As the forward clutch begins to engage from a flow of main pressure through the engagement valve, main pressure is also directed through a restrictor, filling a chamber on the opposite side of the engagement valve land and equalizing the pressure on both sides of the land. Spring tension forces the valve to move, closing off the direct route of main pressure to the forward clutch and only allowing restricted main pressure to apply the forward clutch, resulting in a quick, but smooth application.

SELECTOR LEVER IN "D" POSITION

1. With the selector lever in the "D" position, main pressure is applied to the forward clutch release valve via two passages which direct the main pressure in such a manner as to hold the forward clutch release valve in the open position, allowing main pressure to be supplied to the forward clutch.

2. The forward clutch remains applied on deceleration and the transaxle functions in its normal operating sequence.

Throttle Operation

To insure smooth engagement of the forward clutch, the declutching valve must first be closed before any throttle movement occurs. A two stage operation is used to accomplish this. A delaying spring mechanism is located in the throttle cable end at the throttle plate area. This delaying spring mechanism allows the accelerator pedal to be slightly depressed before the throttle plate is moved, assuring the operating lever, mounted on the transaxle, will close the declutching valve before any throttle movement occurs.

Diagnosis Tests

To troubleshoot automatic transaxles, it is important that several basic points be understood to save the technician's time as well as the customer's money. Understanding what the problem is and how it started is the best beginning to finding the transmission malfunction.

A road test should be performed if the vehicle's condition allows for it. Use care so that more damage is not done on the road test than has already occurred. Inspect carefully for leaks or other signs of obvious damage. Make sure that all the cable and linkages are attached. Pull out the dipstick and check the color and smell of the fluid. Be sure that the engine is in at least a reasonable state of tune. When road testing, pick a route that will show all the transaxle operations, and try the unit in each range, including kickdown and reverse. If the trouble cannot be pinpointed after using the Clutch and Band Application in conjunction with the road test, then further testing will be required. This means that the shift points, stall speed and oil pressure will have to be checked.

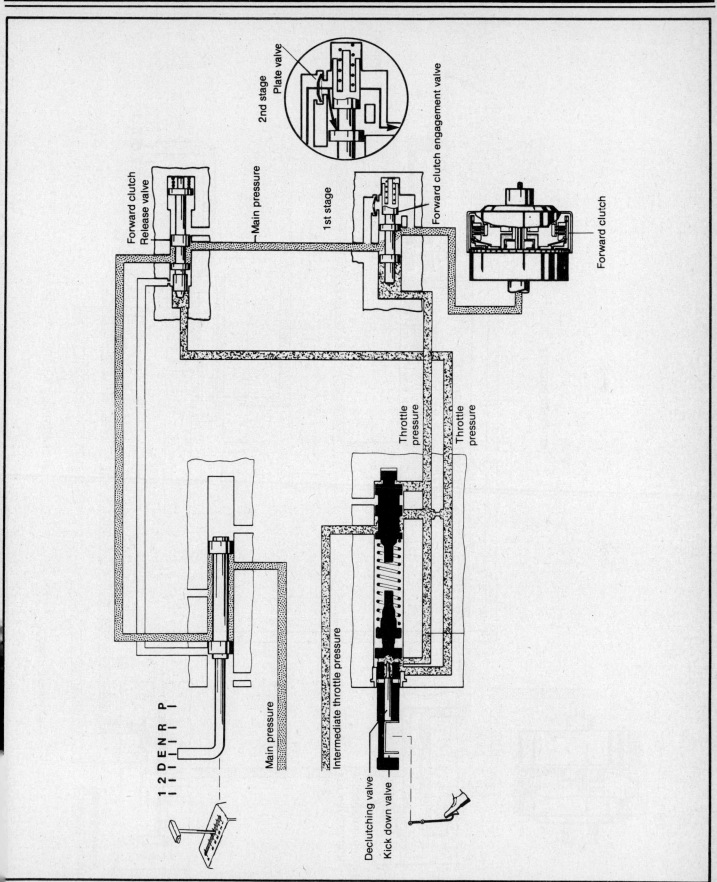

2nd stage

Plate valve

Forward clutch engagement valve

Forward clutch Release valve

Main pressure

1st stage

Forward clutch

Throttle pressure

Throttle pressure

Main pressure

Intermediate throttle pressure

1 2 D E N R P

Declutching valve

Kick down valve

Selector lever in "E" position and forward clutch applied (©Volkswagen of America, Inc.)

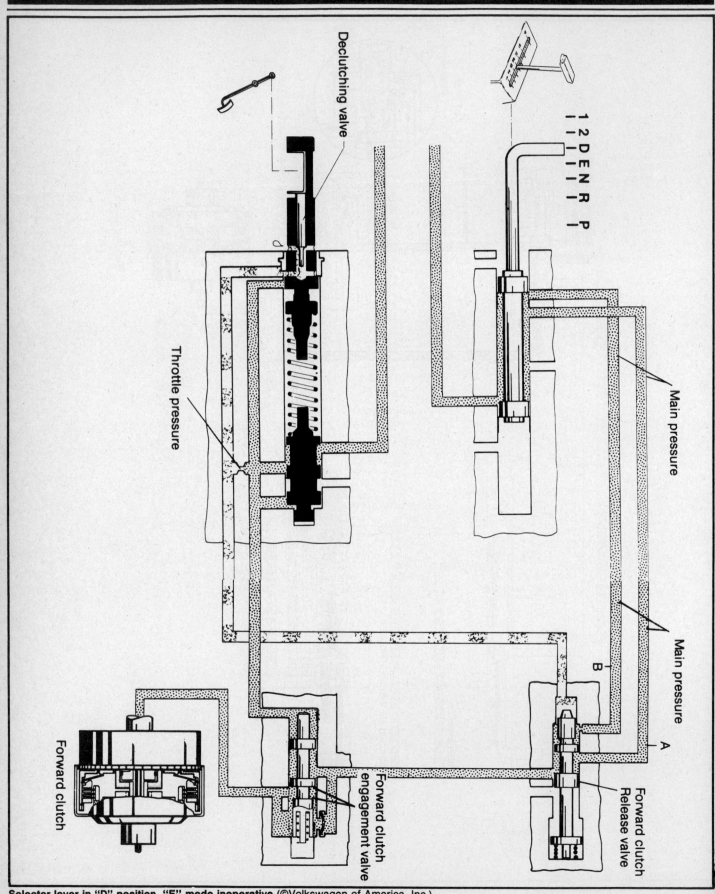

Declutching valve

Throttle pressure

Forward clutch

Forward clutch engagement valve

Forward clutch Release valve

Main pressure

Main pressure

A

B

1 2 D E N R P

Selector lever in "D" position, "E" mode inoperative (©Volkswagen of America, Inc.)

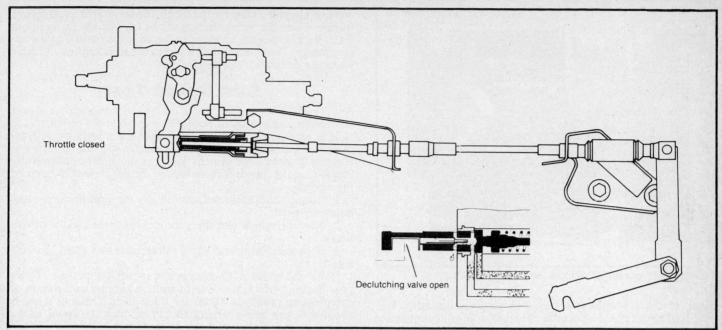

Throttle closed and declutching valve open (©Volkswagen of America, Inc.)

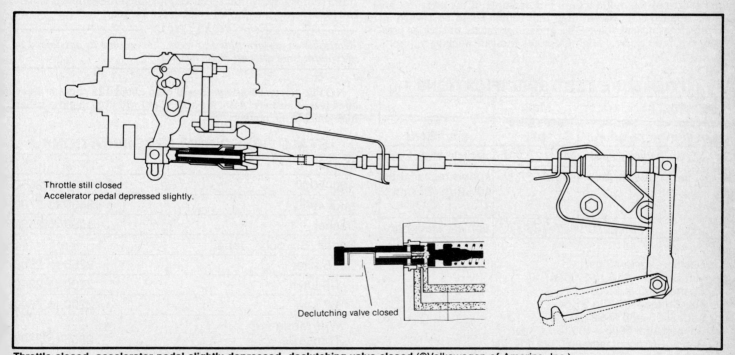

Throttle closed, accelerator pedal slightly depressed, declutching valve closed (©Volkswagen of America, Inc.)

Pressure Test

The pressure test port is located near the mid-section of the transaxle housing, next to the band servo. The pressure gauge to be used should have at least a 150 psi capacity.

1. Connect the pressure gauge hose to the pressure port and route the hose so that the gauge can be read from the drivers position.

2. Start the engine and apply the brakes. The engine/transaxle assembly must be at normal operating temperature.

3. Place the selector lever in the "D" position and allow the engine to idle. Observe the pressure reading and refer to the pressure specifications for the specific pressure required for the vehicle.

4. Place the selector lever in reverse and allow the engine to idle. Observe the pressure reading and refer to the pressure specifications for the specified pressure required for the vehicle.

5. For the full throttle pressure test, the manufacturer recommends the test be done on a dynamometer. However, if the test is done on the road, the pressure hose must be protected from drag-

Pressure port location (©Volkswagen of America, Inc.)

ging. Vehicle and traffic safety must be observed during the test.

6. Establish a speed of 25 mph or higher, apply full throttle and observe the pressure gauge reading. Refer to the pressure specifications for the specified pressure required for the vehicle.

The pressure tests should be carefully reviewed to help locate the source of the malfunction. For example, if the pressures are lower than specifications, then the trouble could be a worn oil pump, internal leaks past worn or damaged seals, or sticking pressure regulator valves. High pressures indicate sticking valves.

PRESSURE TEST SPECIFICATIONS

Selector lever position	Accelerator pedal position	Main pressure psi	Test conditions
D	idle speed*	41-42 ① ⑤	vehicle stationary
	full throttle	83-84 ② ⑥	speed higher than 40 km/h (25 mph). ④
R	idle speed	129-138 ③ ⑦	vehicle stationary

① Dasher—41 to 43 psi
Fiat Strada—55.5 to 57 psi
② Dasher—83 to 85 psi
Fiat Strada—89.6 to 91 psi
Audi 5000—80 to 82 psi
③ Dasher/Audi 5000—108 to 117 psi
Rabbit/Scirocco/Jetta—109 to 117 psi
(Model EQ to S/N 16079—100 to 109 psi)
Fiat Strada—104 to 105.3 psi
④ For safety reasons, the manufacturer recommends the test be made on a dynamometer.
⑤ "E" mode transaxle—42-44 psi
⑥ "E" mode transaxle—85-86 psi
⑦ "E" mode transaxle—131-145 psi

Air Pressure Test

Air can be applied to appropriate passages so that the operation of the bands and clutches can be checked. Use a reduced amount of air pressure and make certain that the air is relatively free from dirt and moisture. Observe the clutch and servo area for excessive leakage. Often the clutch housing can be felt with the finger tips to feel if the clutches are applying as the air is introduced to the apply passage. The bands should move as the air is applied and relax when the pressure is removed.

Stall Speed Test

A stall speed test is a quick test of the torque converter but since it is a demanding test on the transaxle, it should only be done if the vehicle accelerates poorly or if it fails to reach high speed. A tachometer will be required that is compatible with the ignition system that is used on the vehicle. Again, never perform this test any longer than the time it takes to look at the tachometer and record the reading.

1. Install the tachometer according to the manufacturer's recommendations.

2. Start the vehicle and apply the parking brake and the service brake.

3. Shift into Drive and apply full throttle and check the stall speed.

If the stall speed is 200 rpm below specification, then suspect poor engine performance due to ignition timing, carburetion or compression problems. If, on the other hand, the stall speed is about 400 rpm below what it should be, then the stator in the torque converter is bad. If the stall speed is too high, then the fault is in the forward clutch or the one-way clutch for 1st gear. As a further double check, run the test again in 1st gear on the selector. If the rpm is now within specifications, then the problem is narrowed down to the one-way clutch for 1st gear.

—————— CAUTION ——————
Remember to perform this test in as short a time as possible. The maximum time allowed is 20 seconds.

NOTE: Normal stall speed will drop about 125 rpm for every 4000 feet of altitude. Also, the stall speed will drop slightly under high outside air temperature.

STALL SPEED RPM SPECIFICATIONS

Model	RPM
Audi 5000	2400 to 2650
Audi 4000	2450 to 2700
Dasher	1950 to 2550
Rabbit, Scirocco, Jetta	
1.5 Liter	2250 to 2500
1.6 Liter	2100 to 2350
1.7 Liter	2200 to 2500
W/E Mode Transaxle	2555 to 2805
Fiat Strada	2260

Road Test

If the transaxle is operative, the vehicle should be road tested in each gear range and under all possible road conditions. The shift points should be noted and recorded, checked against specifications and malfunction probabilities listed. The shifts should be smooth and take place quickly, without a lag in the acceleration. Listen for any signs of engine flare-up during the shifts, which would indicate a slipping brake band or clutches. Check the transaxle for abnormal fluid leakages.

If the shift point are incorrect or the transaxle does not have a kick-down, check and verify the accelerator cable for proper adjustment.

SHIFT POINTS AT VARIED VEHICLE SPEEDS

(Shift points in mph)

AUDI 4000

Shift	Full throttle	Kickdown
1-2	20-28	34-37
2-3	48-61	66-67
3-2	35-48	62-64
2-1	14-16	29-31

AUDI 5000

1-2	24-30	42-46
2-3	58-62	75-77
3-2	36-43	72-74
2-1	16-18	39-43

DASHER, QUANTUM

1-2	19-24	35-39
2-3	49-53	64-66
3-2	30-36	61-63
2-1	14-17	31-35

RABBIT/SCIROCCO/JETTA

1-2	20-23	36-39
2-3	51-54	68-69
3-2	31-36	64-65
2-1	15-17	32-35

Trans. TB

1-2	32-46	55-59
2-3	78-98	105-107
3-2	56-77	99-101
2-1	23-26	47-51

Trans. EQ up to 17 07 0

1-2	32-43	53-57
2-3	78-94	103-104
3-2	57-73	96-99
2-1	22-25	46-50

Trans. EQ up to 16 07 0

1-2	32-37	58-63
2-3	82-87	109-111
3-2	50-58	103-105
2-1	24-27	52-56

FIAT STRADA

D to 2	——	Below 70
D or 2 to 1	——	Below 40
1 to 2	40	
2 to 3	70	
3 to 2	——	Below 64 (Manual)
2 to 1	——	Below 32 (Manual)

ON CAR SERVICES

ADJUSTMENTS

Throttle Linkages

The 010 Series (Type 089, 090) transaxles, use a mechanical throttle valve system, controlled by cables from the acccelerator pedal, to the transaxle and back to the carburetor or fuel injection throttle plate(s). It is most important the cable assemblies be free of kinks, bends or high operating resistance and the choke plate off, with the fast idle cam in the off position on carbureted models. The accelerator pedal height is an important factor in the adjustment of the cables and where dimensions are available, will be noted for the specific applications.

Adjustments
QUANTUM, AUDI 4000

1. Verify the throttle valve is closed and operating lever has freedom of movement.
2. Loosen the lock nuts on the throttle cable bracket, located on the cylinder head.
3. Pull the sleeve of the throttle cable in the direction of the throttle plates. Turn the rear adjusting nut against the bracket and lock into position with the front adjusting nut.

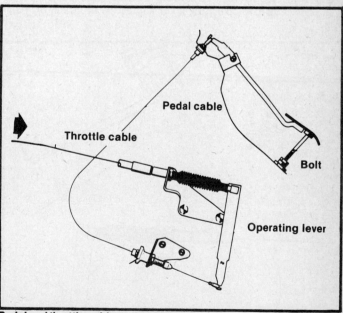

Pedal and throttle cable arrangement, Quantum and Audi 4000 models (©Volkswagen of America, Inc.)

4. From inside the vehicle, remove the accelerator pedal stop. On vehicles equipped with air conditioning, remove the switch.
5. Using a metric bolt, M8 x 135 mm, thread two nuts on the bolts, with the bottom of the last nut to the top of the bolt head, giving a dimension of 4⅞ inch (124 mm). Lock the inner nut against the lower outer bolt to maintain this dimension.
6. Install this bolt in place of the accelerator pedal stop, being sure the bolt head touches the pedal plate only, not the pedal rod.
7. Adjust the pedal cable so the accelerator pedal touches the substituted pedal stop, while the operating lever on the transaxle housing is in the closed throttle position.

8. Remove the substituted bolt from under the accelerator pedal, install the original pedal stop and if equipped with air conditioning, install the switch.

Verifying Adjustment

1. Depress the accelerator pedal until resistance is felt at the full throttle position, without going to the kick-down position.
2. The throttle lever must contact its stop.
3. Depress the accelerator pedal to its full stop and note the cable attaching trunnion at the throttle plate lever. The spring coils at the trunnion must be pressed together.
4. The operating lever on the transaxle housing must be in contact with its kick-down stop.

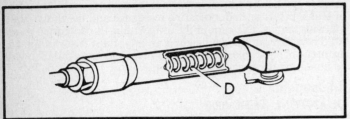

Spring coils (D) within cable trunnion (©Volkswagen of America, Inc.)

Adjustments

RABBIT, SCIROCCO, JETTA

1. Verify the throttle plates are fully closed, the choke is off and the fast idle cam is in the off position on carbureted engines. On fuel injected models, be sure the throttle plate is fully closed.
2. The transaxle operating lever should be in its full off position.

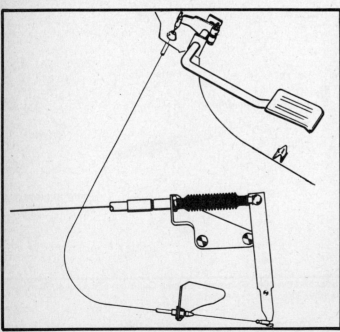

Pedal and accelerator cable arrangement, Rabbit, Scirocco, Jetta, Dasher similar (©Volkswagen of America, Inc.)

3. Check to ascertain if the ball socket on the end of the cable can be install without tension, on the ball stud of the operating lever. If so, the cable is properly adjusted.
4. If necessary to adjust, turn the adjusting nut until the correct tension is obtained. Tighten any lock nuts that were loosened.

Verifying Adjustment

1. Press the accelerator to the floor, against its stop, which would be the kick-down position. Hold pedal down.
2. Be sure all play has been removed from the operating lever. If necessary, loosen the adjusting nut on the transaxle bracket and adjust to eliminate all free play. Recheck this adjustment several times to make sure it is correct. Tighten lock nut and recheck again. Readjust, if necessary.

Adjustment

FIAT STRADA

1. Check to verify accelerator pedal travel is four inches. If applicable, include the floor mat thickness measurement in the adjustment. Bend the accelerator pedal rod as required.
2. With the accelerator pedal fully depressed, including the kick down position, be sure the linkage is at its full travel. Adjust as required.
3. Be sure the carburetor pedal and throttle plates close properly after adjustment.

Adjustment

AUDI 5000

1. On this application there is to be found two sections of linkage as well as a cable. One linkage is the connection between the throttle body and the rocker lever, or bellcrank. The other linkage is the one that connects the transmission operating lever to the bellcrank. It has, on its lower end, an adjustable sliding plate. The cable runs from the accelerator pedal to the transaxle. Begin adjustment by setting the throttle valve to the idle position. Press the rocker lever (bellcrank) back to the stop.
2. Remove the adjustable ball joint from its stud on the rocker lever and adjust as necessary. Again, the object is to obtain a free fit without forcing anything, and without any free-play.
3. Down at the transaxle, loosen the bolt holding the sliding adjusting plate to the linkage, and adjust for a free fit without play or tension.
4. To adjust the accelerator cable, make sure that the pedal is in the idle position. Carefully measure the distance from the stop on the floor to the pedal plate. It should be 80mm (3¼ inch). Adjust the cable end on the transmission to correct this figure if necessary. Double-check that the throttle is fully open when the accelerator pedal is pressed before the kickdown position. On the linkage that runs to the transmission, on the upper end at the ball joint, there is a kickdown take-up spring incorporated into the linkage. This spring must not be compressed after making this adjustment.

DASHER

1. Check that the throttle valve on the injection system is closed, that is, at the idle position. Remove the ball socket from the transaxle operating lever.
2. Push the transaxle lever to the zero-throttle position. If the ball end on the cable can be installed without placing the cable in tension, then the adjustment is correct. If the ball end will not fit properly, loosen the locknut on the bracket in the engine compartment that holds the cable. Turn the adjusting nut until the ball end can be attached without forcing.
3. Double-check that the transaxle lever is still in the zero-throttle position and then tighten the locknut.
4. The accelerator cable from the pedal to the transaxle operating lever must also be checked. Remove the cover under the dashboard to provide access to the top of the accelerator linkage.
5. Locate the arm on the end of the accelerator pedal and the clamping bolt. Loosen this bolt, but do not remove.
6. From a piece of stiff wire such as welding rod or brazing rod, make a support for the accelerator pedal that is 105mm (4¼ inch) from the pedal stop on the floor to the deepest part of the curve under the pedal. Double-check that the transaxle operating lever has not moved from its zero throttle position.

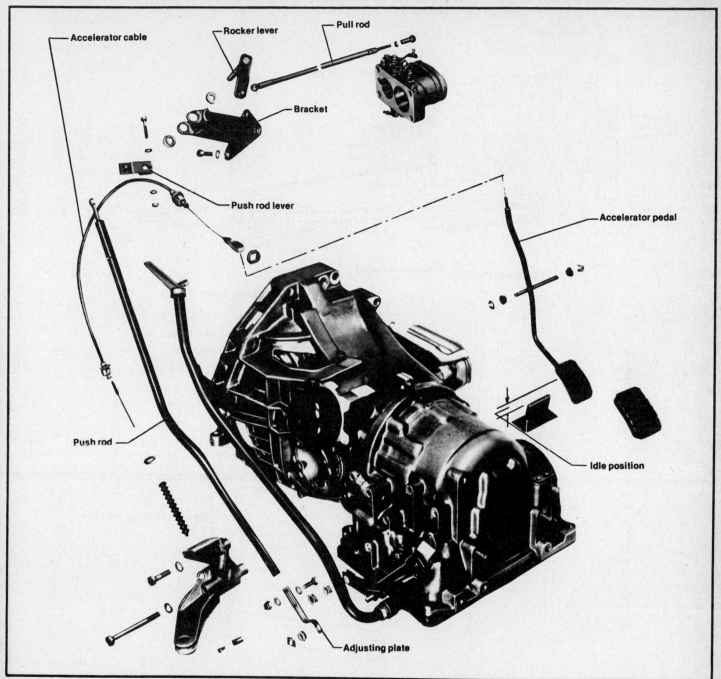

Accelerator cable — **Rocker lever** — **Pull rod**

Bracket

Push rod lever

Accelerator pedal

Push rod

Idle position

Adjusting plate

Pedal and accelerator cable arrangement, Audi 5000 models (©Volkswagen of America, Inc.)

7. Pull the relay bracket or lever slowly to take up the slack in the cable. Tighten the clamp bolt. Remove the wire support and push the accelerator pedal down to the stop. The operating lever on the transaxle must be on the kickdown stop without any play.

─── CAUTION ───

On all of the above adjustments, it is of the utmost importance that when assembling the different pieces of linkage to their pivots and brackets, that none of the pieces are under tension or pressure or being forced to fit in any way. Many problems that appear to be transaxle malfunctions are caused by improper throttle linkage adjustments.

Adjustment
RABBIT, JETTA
WITH DIESEL ENGINE AND "E" MODE TRANSAXLE
─── CAUTION ───
When adjusting the accelerator linkage and the pedal cable, always place the selector lever in the "P" position and set the parking brake when the engine is running.

NOTE: The throttle controls must be readjusted whenever the idle or full throttle stop screws have been turned.

1. Set the parking brake and place the selector lever in the "P" position.

835

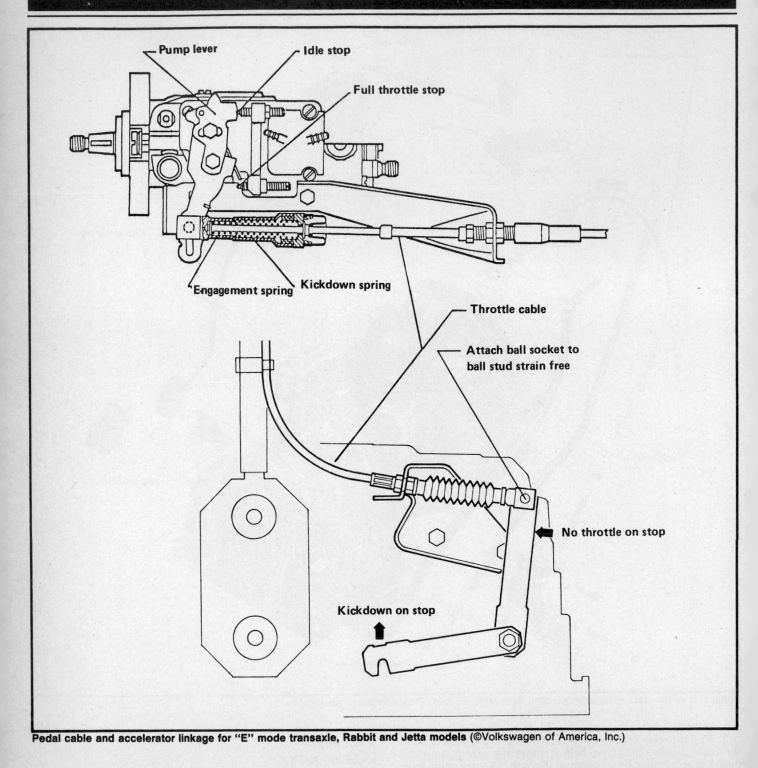

Pedal cable and accelerator linkage for "E" mode transaxle, Rabbit and Jetta models (©Volkswagen of America, Inc.)

2. Remove the plastic injection pump cover and check the idle and maximum engine speeds. Adjust as required.

3. Loosen the accelerator pedal cable adjuster at the bracket before the operating lever. Disconnect the cable at the operating lever.

4. Remove the circlip and ball socket on the pump lever.

5. Adjust the ball stud travel from the idle stop to the full throttle stop by moving the ball stud in the pump lever slot. The travel should be 1.259 ± 0.040 inch (32 ± 1 mm).

6. Remove the rubber boot from the delay spring mechanism and loosen the adjusting nuts on the throttle cable.

7. Push the transaxle lever to the closed throttle position and pull the cable housing away from the delay spring mechanism.

NOTE: Be sure the delay spring is not compressed.

8. With the cable housing in this position, tighten the adjusting nuts, attach the ball socket to the ball stud and install the circlip.

9. Connect the accelerator cable to the lever.

10. Press the accelerator cable into the kick-down position. With the aid of a helper, adjust the accelerator cable adjuster so that the transaxle lever contacts the stop.

NOTE: Be sure the accelerator kick-down spring (delay spring mechanism) is compressed.

11. Lock the accelerator cable adjusting nut.

12. Operate the cable and be sure the accelerator pedal cable is at stop and the cable is free of any tension.

Checking Accelerator Cable

1. Push the pump lever against the idle stop. The delay spring mechanism must not be compressed.

2. Move the transaxle operating lever to the closed throttle position, and press the accelerator pedal into the full throttle position. Push the pump lever against the full throttle stop.

NOTE: The kick-down spring must not be compressed.

3. Press the accelerator pedal past the full throttle point to the stop. The transaxle lever must be against the stop and the kick-down spring (delay spring mechanism) compressed.

Band Adjustment

The adjuster for the band is on the side of the case. The adjustment procedure is;

1. Center the band by first torquing the adjusting screw to 87 in. lbs. (10 N•m). Loosen the screw and then retighten to a torque of 43 in. lbs (5 N•m).

2. Carefully loosen the adjuster screw exactly 2½ turns. Hold the screw so that it does not turn, and tighten the locknut.

--- CAUTION ---

Loc-Tite® or similar substance is used on the band adjusting bolt to case threads. If the bolt cannot be easily turned, it should be heated to break the seal prior to turning the bolt in the case to prevent damage to the case threads.

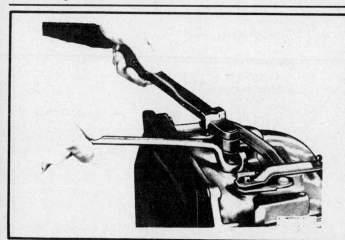

Adjustment of Band, typical. Shift or operating lever may have to be repositioned (©Volkswagen of America, Inc.)

Manual Linkage

Depending on the vehicle, the adjustment is done either at the transaxle or at the selector lever. If the adjustment calls for the removal of the console, the following points may prove helpful.

1. The shifter handle is usually retained by a set screw. Remove the set screw and the handle should pull up and off.

2. The shifter pattern indicator can be removed by prying off in most cases. It is held on by plastic clips. "Brush type" covers may be held on by screws. Check carefully.

3. The console itself is held on by a few Phillips-head screws.

It is extremely important that the selector lever cable be carefully adjusted to avoid burned clutches. Adjust the selector cable as follows:

1. Place the selector lever in Neutral and start the engine. Allow to idle.

2. Apply the parking brake and the service brakes, and then place the selector lever in Reverse. Take note of any reduction in engine speed. There should be a noticeable reduction in speed as the clutch applies. Speed up the engine slightly with the accelerator pedal to increase the idle speed.

3. Keep the accelerator pedal in this position and place the selector lever in Park. The engine speed must increase, indicating that the direct and reverse clutch is disengaged. The engine speed should increase, not drop. If the engine speed does not increase, when placing the lever in Park, or if it drops when pulling the lever against the stop (NOT actually shifting into Reverse) thus indicating a partial apply of the clutch, then the setting is incorrect and must be adjusted. Operating the transaxle with the controls not in complete travel will result in the unit burning up in only a few miles of operation. This is an important point to watch with the 010 series transmissions. The detent gate that is normally found in the transmission shifter assembly, in the driver's compartment, has been eliminated on late model units so that the detents that are felt are in the transmission only.

Adjustment

QUANTAM, AUDI 5000, 4000, FIAT STRADA

1. Remove the console.

2. Shift the selector lever ino Park.

3. Loosen the clamp nut under the shifter selector lever.

4. Press the selector lever to the rear stop to remove cable slack.

5. Tighten the clamp nut.

6. Check operation. Install console.

RABBIT, SCIROCCO

1. Place the selector lever in Park. Make sure that it is fully engaged.

2. Loosen the clamp screw nut on the transaxle lever.

3. Move the transaxle operating lever all the way counter-clockwise, and tighten the clamp nut.

4. Check operation.

DASHER

1. Remove the console. Shift the selector lever into park.

2. Loosen the cable clamp nut. This nut is located directly under the shifter lever, and retains the swivel and washers to the forward end of the cable.

3. Move the lever on the transaxle into Park, and push fully

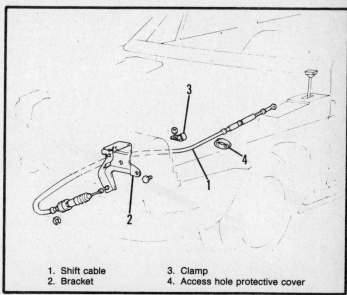

1. Shift cable   3. Clamp
2. Bracket   4. Access hole protective cover

Typical cable routing from shift lever to transaxle (©Volkswagen of America, Inc.)

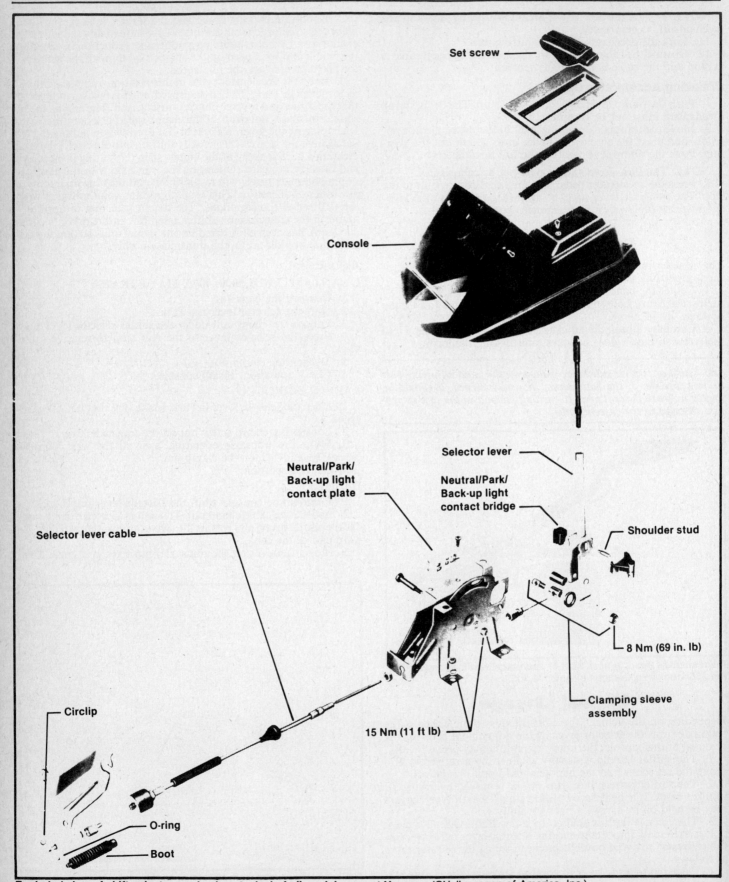

Exploded view of shift selector mechanism, typical of all models except Vanagon (©Volkswagen of America, Inc.)

against the stop. This removes all slack from the cable and the linkage.

4. Tighten the clamp nut and replace the console.
5. Check operation.

VANAGON

1. Loosen the shift rod bolt.
2. Shift the selector lever into the "P" position.
3. Push the transaxle operating lever to the rear and into the "P" position.
4. Push the shift rod to the rear and tighten the shift rod bolt.
5. Check shifting detents for proper operation. The engine must not start unless the shift lever is in the "P" or "N" positions.

Neutral Safety Switch

The neutral safety switch used on these applications is mounted on the transaxle selector lever in the driver's compartment. In each case, the switch can be found working off a portion of the selector lever. Removal of the lever cover or console will be required to adjust the switch. Note that there are elongated holes in the switch for the mounting screws. The mouting screws are loosened and the switch moved as necessary so that the starter will operate in Park and Neutral only. This adjustment is important since a dangerous situation can occur if the transaxle were allowed to start in gear.

SERVICES
Fluid Change

1. Raise and safely support vehicle.
2. Place a large drain pan under the transaxle. If the unit has a drain plug, remove it and allow to drain. If the unit does not have a drain plug, the filler tube connection can be loosened to allow most of the fluid to drain. It is often advantageous to drain the fluid when hot, when many of the contaminates are in suspension. However, be carefull since transaxle fluid temperatures often reach 300°F.

3. After the fluid has drained, install the drain plug, or filler tube connection if removed. Lower the vehicle and add 2 quarts of Dexron® type automatic transmission fluid.

Oil Pan

Removal and Installation

The oil pan can be removed while the transaxle is in the vehicle. Along with the pan, the valve body and other internal components can be inspected, and serviced. The following procedure can be used.

1. Raise and safely support vehicle.
2. Place a large drain pan under the transaxle. If the unit has a drain plug, remove it and allow to drain. If the unit does not have a drain plug, the filler tube connection can be loosened to allow most of the fluid to drain. In any case, the filler tube will have to be removed to allow pan removal.
3. Remove the oil pan retaining screws. Remove the oil pan. If the pan is stuck, tap gently with a rubber mallet. Prying the pan off is not recommended since the gasket surfaces can be damaged. Inspect the oil pan carefully for debris to help get an indication of the condition of the transaxle internal components. Remove the fluid strainer and clean or replace as required.
4. Install the strainer and make sure that the oil pan is thoroughly clean. See that there are no traces of gasket material on either the pan flange or the transaxle gasket rail. Install the pan, taking care to see that the new gasket on the pan is smooth and straight. The pan bolts are only snugged down. Working diagonally, torque the screws to only 7 foot-pounds. Allow the gasket to "set" for about five minutes and retorque to 14 foot-pounds.
5. Lower the vehicle and, following the information in the section "Fluid Change," refill the transaxle and check the fluid level carefully.

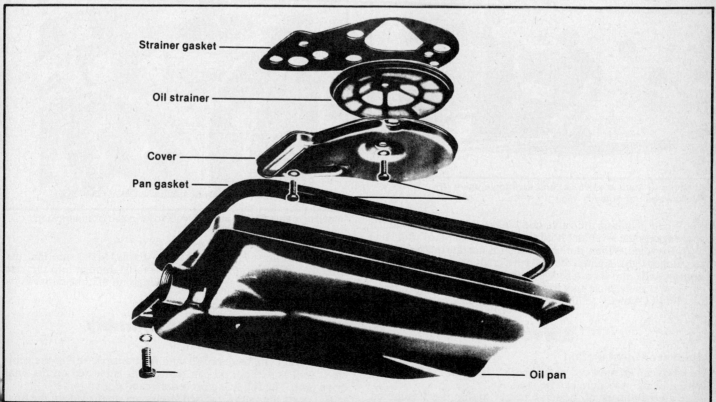

Strainer gasket

Oil strainer

Cover

Pan gasket

Oil pan

Oil pan and filter assembly—later models (©Volkswagen of America, Inc.)

Valve Body

Removal and Installation

The valve body can be removed on these units with the transaxle still in the vehicle. The following procedure can be used.

1. Following the information given above, drain the oil and remove the oil pan.

2. Remove all but one of the retaining bolts. This is important because otherwise the valve body, separator plate and transfer plate will come apart and the check balls will fall out of place. After all but the last bolt is removed, carefully remove this last bolt while holding these valve body components together. Carefully lower the assembly, holding it firmly to keep the parts intact. The factory does not recommend that the valve body be disassembled or even the three major parts separated (since the check valves may become lost) unless the fluid was extremely dirty. The valve body components are very fragile and easily damaged.

Removing servo piston retaining clip (©Volkswagen of America, Inc.)

Locations of manual valve (A) and Kickdown valve (B) (©Volkswagen of America, Inc.)

3. When installing the valve body make sure that the manual valve engages the lever and hold the assembly in place as the one bolt is installed. When the unit is secure, install the rest of the bolts, finger-tight. Tighten the bolts in a cross pattern, first to only 2 foot-pounds and then 4 foot-pounds.

4. Lower the vehicle and, following the information in the section "Fluid Change," refill the transaxle and check the fluid level carefully.

Servos

Removal and Installation

The servo can be removed with the transaxle still in the vehicle. The following procedure can be used.

1. Tap the outside of the servo piston so that the pressure on the circlip will be released. Remove the circlip.

Installing servo piston assembly (©Volkswagen of America, Inc.)

2. Remove the servo assembly.

3. Installation is a reversal of the above. Make sure that the seals are well lubricated. Press the servo far enough into the case that the circlip can be installed. Make certain that the clip is in its proper place.

Governor Assembly

Removal and Installation

The governor can be removed with the transaxle still in the vehicle as well as without oil pan removal. It is located on the final drive unit. The following procedure can be used.

1. Locate the round, pressed steel cover on the side of the final drive unit. Note that the governor usually will need only cleaning.

Governor assembly location on transaxle
(©Volkswagen of America, Inc.)

If, however, the valve body is replaced, then the governor will have to be replaced regardless of the condition of the original governor. This is because the valve body and the governor have been calibrated to work together. With the cover removed from the final drive, pull the governor from the case.

2. Check the drive gear and the thrust plate for wear. Again, because the governor affects the pressure and thereby the operation of the valve body, and replacement of the governor will affect pressure. For this reason, replacement governor shafts are available, so that the valve portion can remain with the unit for which it was calibrated.

3. Installation is a reversal of the above procedure. Be sure to check the seal at the innermost end of the governor shaft bore in the final drive housing. This is especially important if the hypoid oil in the final drive has been contaminated by the automatic transmission fluid. Pry out any defective seals and replace them. Install the new seal with the lip outward, toward the governor body. Note too that the design of the governor changed with the 010 series, serial number ET 27 016. Operation and removal is the same. For overhaul information, see the section "Unit Disassembly and Assembly."

REMOVAL & INSTALLATION

AUDI 5000

Removal

1. Disconnect the battery ground strap and remove the windshield washer reservoir.

2. Note that this model uses a cooler for the transmission. Remove the hoses at the cooler and clamp them shut.

3. Unsnap the ball connection at the upper end of the accelerator linkage rod, remove the speedometer cable and remove the upper engine to transaxle mounting bolts.

4. The engine will have to be supported since mounts will be removed. The factory tool is a bar-like arrangement that is placed across the engine compartment, supported by the inner flanges on the top of the fenders. A hook is attached and is fitted to the lifting ring on the engine. Once this lifting fixture is in place, take the weight off the engine by lifting with the hook slightly.

5. Locate the guard plate that is under the subframe. Remove this plate as well as the exhaust pipe bracket from the transaxle. Remove the front exhaust pipe.

6. Remove the guard plate that should be found on the right driveshaft (axle). Unbolt the driveshafts at the transaxle end of the shaft. Remove the starter motor.

7. Remove the shifter cable holder from the transaxle, and disconnect the cable from the operating lever on the the transaxle. Remove the accelerator linkage rod from the transaxle by removing the retaining clip. Also, disconnect the accelerator cable from the lever.

8. Remove the right side guard plate from the subframe. Remove the transaxle mounts from the subframe.

9. Working through the starter opening, remove the torque converter bolts.

10. Support the transaxle with a suitable jack and raise slightly to take the weight off the remaining mounting bolts. Remove the lower engine to transaxle bolts. Remove the rear subframe mounting bolts.

11. Move the driveshafts to the rear and carefully separate the engine and transaxle. Lower the transaxle carefully and remove from the vehicle. Be careful that the torque converter does not fall from the case. Run a length of wire across the opening to hold the converter in place.

Installation

1. The installation is basically a reversal of the above sequence, with the following points to watch. Use care to see that the transaxle and final drive assembly is balanced on the jack. Lift the transaxle assembly and install to the engine.

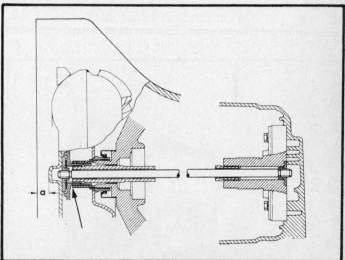

Correct installation of oil pump drive shaft during transaxle installation (©Volkswagen of America, Inc.)

—————— CAUTION ——————

It is very important that the torque converter be fully seated. The distance from the face of the transmission case to the pilot or hub of the converter must be 10mm or 0.393 inch. The torque converter must move freely by hand. If the torque converter should slip off the one-way clutch support, the converter will probably pull the oil pump shaft out of the oil pump. This will result in severe damage to the transmission when the transaxle is bolted into place. It is important to check the distance mentioned above very carefully.

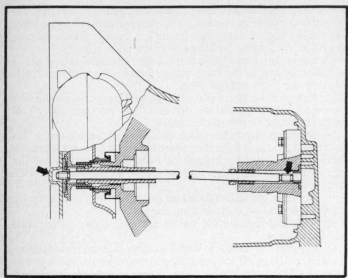

Incorrect installation of oil pump drive shaft, should converter slip off the one-way clutch support. Internal damage will result (©Volkswagen of America, Inc.)

2. Install the lower engine to transaxle bolts, install the subframe and install the transaxle mounts on the subframe. Converter bolts are torqued to 22 foot-pounds.

3. It is absolutely necessary that, once the transaxle is installed, the accelerator cable and the accelerator linkage rod be adjusted. Refer to the section "On Car Services" for specific instructions. Also, check the accelerator pedal adjustment. Press the pedal to the full throttle position, but not into the kick-down position. Make sure that the kick-down take-up spring on the linkage is not compressed. The throttle valve on the fuel injection should be fully open. The "On Car Services" section also has instructions on adjusting the selector cable. This too must be adjusted. Refill the unit with Dexron® II type fluid only.

Typical removal and installation of transaxle on a lifting device tool (©Volkswagen of America, Inc.)

RABBIT, SCIROCCO, JETTA

Removal

1. Remove both the battery ground strap and the positive cable at the battery.

2. Remove the speedometer cable at the transaxle.

3. Remove the two upper engine to transaxle bolts. Loosen the left transaxle mount, which is the one near the battery. The weight will have to be taken off the engine. The factory tool for this consists of a bar that spans the engine compartment and rests on the fender ledge, or inner flange. A threaded rod from the bar with a hook arrangement is designed to fit into the lifting ring on the engine. By taking the weight of the mounts with the threaded hook, the mounts can be disconnected as needed and the engine will still be secure.

4. Remove the rear transaxle mount.

5. Disconnect the driveshafts (axles) at the transaxle.

6. Remove the starter motor. Do not overlook the third bolt that is between the engine and starter.

7. Remove the converter plate and transaxle shield.

8. Remove the torque converter from the drive plate. Install transmission jack.

9. Place the selector lever in Park and remove the cable connection. Remove the cable bracket, disconnect the accelerator cable and the pedal cable.

10. Remove the left transaxle carrier, or mount. Remove the lower bolt and nut holding the transaxle. Check for any missed bolts and then move the transmission and jack away from the engine. Carefully lower the transaxle away from the car. Make sure that the torque converter does not fall. A length of wire across the opening of the case will hold converter in place until the transaxle can be secured in the disassembly fixture and the torque converter removed.

Installation

1. Installation is basically a reversal of the above sequence, with the following points to watch. Use care to see that the transaxle and final drive assembly is balanced on the jack.

2. Check the torque converter by turning as a check that it is not out of position. It is possible to install the unit with the converter out of alignment so that it will jam when the transaxle is tightened.

3. Be sure to torque the engine to transaxle bolts 40 foot-pounds.

4. Check the engine to transaxle alignment. The left mount must be in the center of the space provided for it in the mount on the body.

5. Torque the driveshaft bolts to 30 ft. lbs. and the converter bolts to 22 foot-pounds.

6. See the section "On Car Services" for information on the selector cable and accelerator/pedal cable adjustments. Refill the unit with Dexron® type fluid.

DASHER

Removal

1. Remove the battery ground strap and disconnect the speedometer cable from the final drive. Remove the two upper transaxle to engine bolts. Support the engine with support tool.

2. Remove the nuts from the exhaust manifold and disconnect the head pipe.

3. Remove the converter cover plate.

4. Remove the starter motor.

5. Working through the starter opening, remove the torque converter bolts. Remove exhaust pipe bracket and cable bracket. Disconnect cable from transaxle lever.

6. Remove the bolts holding the driveshafts (axles) at the final drive and position them out of the way. Mechanic's wire can be used to tie the shafts out of the way.

7. The left ball joint is held on by two bolts. Mark the position of the left ball joint so that it can be reinstalled in the same place to avoid the need for a front end alignment. Remove the bolts and then reassemble with the ball joint moved out for clearance.

8. Remove the through bolt from the mount and remove the mount from the body.

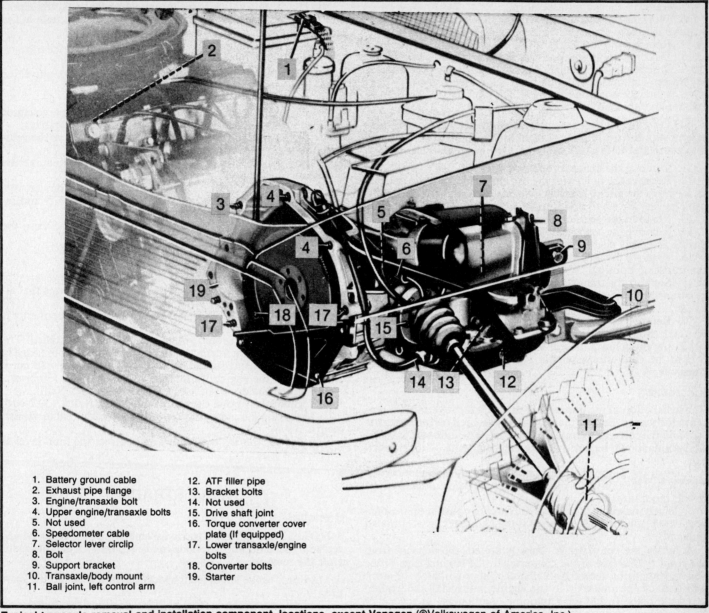

1. Battery ground cable
2. Exhaust pipe flange
3. Engine/transaxle bolt
4. Upper engine/transaxle bolts
5. Not used
6. Speedometer cable
7. Selector lever circlip
8. Bolt
9. Support bracket
10. Transaxle/body mount
11. Ball joint, left control arm
12. ATF filler pipe
13. Bracket bolts
14. Not used
15. Drive shaft joint
16. Torque converter cover plate (if equipped)
17. Lower transaxle/engine bolts
18. Converter bolts
19. Starter

Typical transaxle removal and installation component, locations, except Vanagon (©Volkswagen of America, Inc.)

9. Remove the third upper engine to transaxle bolt.

10. Loosen the two lower engine to transmission bolts. Support the transaxle with a jack and lift slightly. Remove the bolts and move the transaxle to the rear and carefuly lower. Be careful that the torque converter does not fall from the case. Run a length of wire across the opening to hold the converter in place.

Installation

1. The installation is basically the reversal of the above sequence, with the following points to watch. Use care to see that the transmisison and final drive assembly is balanced on the jack. Lift the transaxle assembly and install to the engine.

--- CAUTION ---

It is very important that the torque converter be fully seated. The distance from the face of the transaxle case to the pilot or hub of the converter must be 30mm or 1³/₁₆ inch. The torque converter must move freely by hand. If the torque converter should slip off the one-way clutch support, the converter will pull the oil pump shaft out of the oil pump. This will result in severe damage to the transaxle

when the transaxle is bolted to the engine. The transaxle to engine bolts should be torqued to 40 foot-pounds.

2. Install the mounts and crossmember making sure that everything lines up.

3. Return the ball joint to its original position, and torque the nuts to 47 ft. lbs. The driveshaft bolts get torqued to 30 foot-pounds, the converter bolts to 22 foot-pounds.

4. Attach the selector lever cable to the transaxle. Install the exhaust system components as required.

AUDI 4000, QUANTUM

Removal

1. Disconnect the battery ground strap.

2. Remove the coolant hose and the upper engine/transaxle bolts.

3. Install the engine support tool and raise the vehicle.

4. Remove both front stop bolts.

5. Remove the starter assembly.

6. Working through the starter hole in the converter housing, remove the three converter bolts.

7. Remove the coolant hoses at the transaxle fluid cooler.

8. Disconnect the speedometer cable from the transaxle.

9. Disconnect the left and right drive shafts from the transaxle flanges. Tie the shafts to the body with wire.

10. Mark the position of the left ball joint on the control arm and remove the ball joint/control arm bolts.

NOTE: The ball joint assembly can be held away from the lower arm with the use of a six to eight inch metal bar, bolted to the lower arm and to the ball joint and used as an extension.

11. Remove the exhaust pipe brackets.

12. Remove the holder for the selector cable from the transaxle. Remove the circlip from the selector cable and disconnect the cable.

13. Remove the selector cable bracket on the transaxle.

14. Remove the center bolt from the engine mount and lift the engine assembly slightly with the engine support tool.

15. Remove the bracket for the throttle and the pedal cable on the transaxle housing.

16. Support the transaxle assembly with a lifting device, such as a transmission jack or its equivalent. Raise the assembly slightly.

17. Remove the lower engine/transaxle bolts and separate the transaxle from the engine.

18. Carefully lower the transaxle from underneath the vehicle. Secure the converter assembly to prevent its falling from the transaxle.

Installation

The installation of the transaxle is basically the reversal of the removal sequence. Be sure the transaxle is secured on the lifting device and the converter is retained in place. The following installation points should be noted during the installation of the transaxle.

1. Push the pump shaft fully into the pump splines.

2. Install the converter into the transaxle before attempting to install the transaxle.

3. When installing the converter, carefully push it on the one-way clutch support. Check to see if the converter can be rotated by hand.

4. When the converter is properly seated, the distance from the front flat surface of the converter to the leading edge of the converter housing should be 0.393 inch (approximately 10 mm).

5. Attach the transaxle to the engine and install the engine/transaxle bolts. Install the remaining components in reverse of their removal. Align the engine/transaxle mounts before tightening bolts.

6. Adjust the throttle cable and selector lever cable as necessary.

7. Install transmission fluid and correct the level as required.

8. Check the camber setting of the left wheel to verify the correct replacement of the ball joint and bolts.

9. The tightening torques are as follows;

Drive shaft/flange bolts	33 ft. lbs. (45 N•m)
Torque converter bolts	22 ft. lbs. (30 N•m)
Transaxle/engine bolts	40 ft. lbs. (55 N•m)
Ball joint/control arm	48 ft. lbs. (65 N•m)
Mount to body	30 ft. lbs. (40 N•m)
Mount to transaxle	40 ft. lbs. (55 N•m)

VANAGON

Removal

1. Remove the battery ground strap and the fan housing grille.

2. Remove the three torque converter bolts through the hole on top of the transaxle housing.

NOTE: To gain access to the torque converter bolts, the crankshaft must be rotated until each bolt appears in the hole in the transaxle housing.

3. Disconnect the left and right drive shafts from the transaxle.

4. Disconnect the wiring from the starter and remove the starter assembly.

5. Loosen the bracket for the dipstick tube.

6. Disconnect the accelerator linkage. Pry off the accelerator cable and remove the circlip from the selector lever cable.

7. Install an engine support tool from the bottom of the vehicle body to the engine.

8. Remove the engine/transaxle ground strap. Remove the mounting bracket and the selector lever cable.

9. Support the transaxle assembly with a lifting device.

10. Remove the rear transaxle mount from the body and remove the engine/transaxle bolts.

11. Lower the transaxle from under the vehicle. Secure the converter to prevent its falling from the transaxle.

Installation

1. The installation of the transaxle is basically the reversal of the removal sequence. However, there are certain points that attention should be given during the installation.

2. Be sure the pump shaft is fully seated before the converter is installed.

3. The converter should rotate by hand when installed. The proper distance from the flat of the converter front to the edge of the converter housing should be ⅜ inch (approximately 10 mm).

4. Tighten the engine/transaxle bolts to 22 ft. lbs. (30 N•m).

5. Tighten the drive shaft bolts to 33 ft. lbs. (45 N•m).

6. Tighten the torque converter bolts to 22 ft. lbs. (30 N•m).

7. Make the necessary accelerator and pedal cable adjustments.

8. Refill the transaxle assembly and correct the fluid level as required.

FIAT STRADA

Removal

NOTE: The engine/transaxle assembly must be removed and replaced as a unit. The transaxle can be separated from the engine after the removal.

1. Remove the hood, (scribe location), the jack and the spare tire.

2. Disconnect the battery negative and positive battery cables.

3. Drain the cooling system completely.

4. If equipped with A/C, slowly bleed the freon from the system.

—————— CAUTION ——————

Wear protective gloves and clothing. Do not discharge the freon near an open flame, as a toxic gas may result.

5. Remove the air cleaner assembly and its connecting hoses. Plug the openings on the engine to prevent dirt from entering.

6. Mark the electrical wiring to identify during assembly, and remove from the electrical components.

7. Remove the fuel system hoses from the carburetor and vapor cannister. Mark hoses for identification during assembly.

8. Remove the accelerator cable. Disconnect the A/C compressor delivery hose and the compressor return hose, if equipped with A/C.

9. Disconnect the heater hoses and the top on bottom radiator hoses.

10. Raise the vehicle and support safely.

11. Remove the front wheel assemblies. Remove the left and

right splash shields from the fender wells and from the front center.

12. Separate the strut assemblies from the hub carriers by the removal of the retaining bolts.

13. Remove the tie rod end retaining nuts and separate the end from the hub carrier.

14. Remove the Allen headed cap screws from the drive axle flanges, along with the retaining plates. Discard the Allen headed cap screws. New ones must be used during the installation.

15. Remove the catalytic converter (all models), and the front exhaust pipe from the vehicle on air pump equipped models.

─────────────── CAUTION ───────────────
Allow the catalytic converter to cool before attempting to remove.

16. Disconnect the speedometer cable from the transaxle.

17. Place the selector lever in the "1" position and remove the "E" clip and washer. Slide the shift cable eyelet off the pin on the transaxle lever. Remove the nut to free the clamp and lay the shift cable to one side.

18. Attach a lifting sling to the engine/transaxle assembly and place a jack under the center engine mount.

19. Remove the bolts to separate the engine mount from the body.

NOTE: Do not remove the bolt unless the mount is damaged.

20. Remove two bolts attaching the right engine mount to the mounting bracket. Do not remove the right engine mount from the engine.

21. Remove the two upper bolts while only loosening the lower bolts and remove the right mount mounting bracket.

22. Remove the bolt and washer from the left engine mount.

23. Separate the sway bar from the mounting bracket. Remove the mounting bracket from the body.

24. Slowly remove the jack supporting the center engine mount. Lower the engine/transaxle assembly from the engine compartment.

25. Support the engine transaxle/assembly and remove the bolts to separate the flywheel from the converter. Remove accelerator cable from transaxle.

26. Remove the bolts from the converter housing to engine and separate the transaxle from the engine. Prevent the torque converter from falling from the assembly during the separation sequence.

Installation

1. The installation of the engine transaxle assembly is basically the reversal of the removal sequence. The engine/transaxle must be joined before the unit is raised into position in the engine compartment.

Note: The torque converter coupled to the engine of the Fiat Strada, utilizes a four lug flywheel-to-converter attachment instead of the usual three lug attachment, although three lug unit maybe encountered. The final drive unit configuration is different from the Audi/VW model usage.

2. Using new Allen headed cap screws, torque to 31 ft. lbs. when installing the drive shafts to the transaxle flanges.

3. Torque the engine/transaxle bolts to 21.7 ft. lbs.

 **BENCH OVERHAUL**

Before Disassembly

When servicing the series 10 transaxles it is recommended that the technician be aware of the importance of cleanliness. Cleanliness is an important factor in the overhaul of the transaxle. Be-

fore opening up the transaxle the outside of the unit should be thoroughly cleaned, preferably with high-pressure cleaning equipment such as a car wash spray unit. Dirt entering the transaxle internal parts will negate all the effort and time spent on the overhaul.

During the inspection and reassembly, all parts should be cleaned with solvent then dried with compressed air. Wiping cloths and rags should not be used to dry parts since lint will find its way into the valve body passages. Lube seals with Dexron® II and use ordinary unmedicated petroleum jelly to hold the thrust washers and ease the assembly of seals, since it will not leave a harmful residue as grease often will. Do not use solvent on neoprene seals, friction plates or composition thrust washers if they are to be re-used.

Before installing bolts into aluminum parts, always dip the threads into clean transmission fluid. Anti-scize compound can also be used to prevent bolts from galling the aluminum and seizing. Always use a torque wrench to keep from stripping the threads. Take care with the seals when installing them, especially the smaller O-rings. The slightest damage can cause leaks. Aluminum parts are very susceptible to damage and so great care should be used when handling them. The internal snap rings should be expanded and the external snap rings compressed if they are to be re-used. This will help insure proper seating when installed.

Converter Inspection

The torque converter that is used on these units is of conventional design. It is a sealed, welded unit and so it cannot be disassembled for service or repair. There are, however, a few checks that should be made on the torque converter.

The torque converter contains approximately 2 quarts of transmission fluid. The fluid can be drained through the hub, since there is no drain plug on these units. The factory recommends a plastic tube and container arrangement to siphon the fluid from the converter. However, the converter can be inverted and the

Measuring converter bushing for wear
(©Volkswagen of America, Inc.)

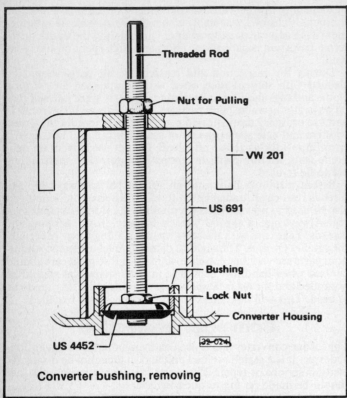

Converter bushing, removing

Suggested tool and method for converter bushing removal
(©Volkswagen of America, Inc.)

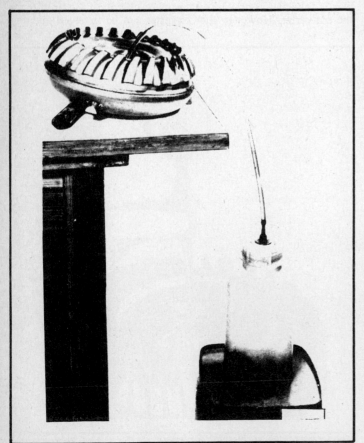

Method used to drain converter (©Volkswagen of America, Inc.)

fluid drained into a pan. The fluid that is drained from the torque converter can help in diagnosing the condition of the converter.

1. If the oil in the converter is discolored but does not contain metal bits or particles, the converter is not damaged and need not be replaced. Remember that fluid color is no longer a good indicator of transmission fluid condition. In the past, dark color was associated with overheated transmission fluid. It is not a positive sign of transaxle failure with the newer fluids.

2. If the oil in the converter contains metal particles, the converter is damaged internally and must be replaced. The oil may have an "aluminum paint" appearance.

3. If the cause of the oil contamination was due to burned clutch plates or overheated oil, the converter is contaminated and should be cleaned or replaced.

The converter should be checked carefully for damage, especially around the seal area. The bushing can be collapsed to remove it since the design of the hub prevents it from being driven all the way through. Remove any sharp edges or burrs from the seal surface. A silicone type seal is used on these transaxles and it is driven into place in the front housing. Since this type of seal is soft, a great amount of care is needed to see that the seal surface on the converter is smooth and clean. Also, the seal itself should not be exposed to any type of solvent. If the case is to be washed with solvent, the seal must be replaced, usually as the last item before installation of the converter at the completion of the overhaul.

The converter bushing can also be checked for wear with an internal dial indicator. The wear limit is 34.25mm or 1.348 inch. The maximum out of round is 0.03mm or 0.001 inch. The bushing can be replaced. The inside diameter must be 1.340 to 1.341 inch (34.03 to 34.05mm).

The most important point to remember when working with the converter actually involves the oil pump. Since the drive shaft for the oil pump extends into the converter area, the technician must make absolutely certain that the pump shaft is installed all the way into the pump drive splines. Also, when the converter is installed on the one-way clutch support, make certain that the converter is not tilted or misaligned. If the converter slips off of the clutch housing, remove it and check the oil pump shaft again. The converter can pull the shaft forward and disengage the shaft from the pump. The shaft then drops down on the pump end, unseen, and when the transmission is installed and tightened down, the shaft will cause a great amount of internal damage as it is pushed through the pump castings. The importance of checking this oil pump shaft and the proper handling of the converter cannot be over-emphasized.

Transaxle Separation and Transmission Disassembly

NOTE: To aid the repairman in identifying the internal transmission components, the VW/Audi nomenclature will be used with the Fiat Strada nomenclature in parenthesis, with the abbreviation F/S preceding it.

1. Remove the converter assembly. Drain all fluid and oil from both the transmission and final drive units.

NOTE: When the transmission and final drive units are assembled as a unit assembly, it is known as a "Transaxle assembly". Otherwise, each is known by its unit name, transmission or final drive.

2. Mount the transaxle assembly on a holding fixture, if available.

3. Remove the oil pump shaft, the governor and the oil filler pipe with dipstick.

4. Remove the retaining nuts and separate the transmission unit from the final drive. Remove the turbine (input) shaft.

5. Remove the capscrews retaining the flange and remove the flange and gasket. Remove the oil pan.

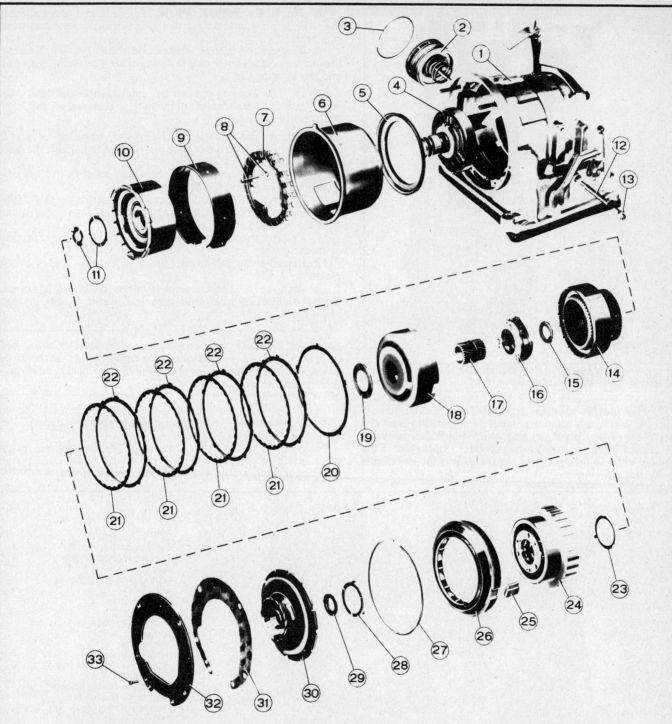

1. Transmission case
2. Cover and brake band piston (rear brake)
3. Retaining ring
4. Oil pump
5. Front brake
6. Front brake bell housing
7. Spring cover with springs
8. Cap screws
9. Rear brake band
10. Rear clutch
11. Friction washer
12. Push rod
13. Brake band adjusting screw and lock nut
14. Front clutch
15. Thrust bearing
16. Rear planetary gears
17. Sun gear
18. Drive housing
19. Friction washer
20. Front brake corrugated plate
21. Front brake plates with facing
22. Front brake steel plates
23. Friction washer
24. Front brake-front planet hub
25. Free wheel location pin
26. Free wheel
27. Free wheel retaining ring
28. Friction washer
29. Thrust bearing
30. Parking plate/front ring gear/governor drive gear
31. Flange gasket
32. Flange
33. Flange cap screw

Exploded view of internal transaxle components (©Volkswagen of America, Inc.)

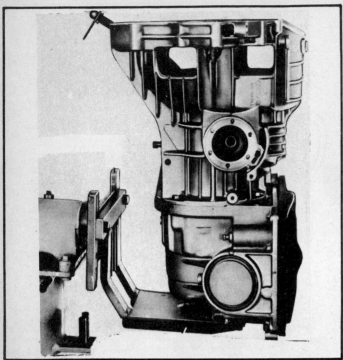

Preparing to separate final drive from the transmission with unit on a holding fixture (©Volkswagen of America, Inc.)

NOTE: End play between the transmission and final drive is controlled by a selective shim and must be adjusted to limit the end play of the reverse planetary ring gear. Should this measurement be needed for any reason by the rebuilder at this point in the disassembly, refer to the assembly sequence, near the end of this section for the procedures.

6. Check that the parking pawl is not engaged and withdraw the parking plate, containing the governor drive gear and front ring gear.

7. Remove the friction washer and thrust bearing. Remove the one way clutch outer race (F/S-free wheel) retaining snap ring and the locating pin.

NOTE: The locating pin can be removed after the outer one-way clutch (F/S-free wheel) outer race is removed on the VW/ Audi transmissions.

8. Remove the one-way clutch (F/S-free wheel) outer race. If necessary, two stiff pieces of wire can be used to help lift the race, if required.

9. Remove the reverse planetary gear set (F/S-front brake-front planet hub) and the thrust washer.

10. Remove the forward planetary gear set/drive shell (F/S-rear planet assembly/drive housing) from the transmission, along with the thrust bearing.

11. Remove the forward clutch (F/S-front clutch) and friction or thrust washer.

12. Remove the 1st/reverse brake (F/S-front brake) clutch plates.

13. Remove the direct/reverse (F/S-rear clutch) unit. Loosen the band adjusting screw and push rod. Remove the 2nd gear brake band.

CAUTION

Loc-Tite® or similar substance is used on the band adjusting bolt to case threads. If the bolt cannot be easily turned, it should be heated to break the seal prior to turning the bolt in the case to prevent damage to the case threads.

---

14. Remove the bolts holding the spring holder and the oil pump. Remove the spring plate with the springs attached. Remove the oil pump assembly.

15. Remove the 2nd gear brake band (F/S-rear brake) piston cover retaining ring. Remove the cover and remove the piston and ring assembly. Remove the piston return spring.

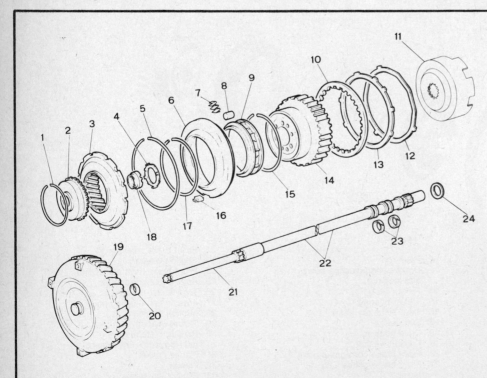

1. Retaining ring
2. Centrifugal governor drive gear
3. Parking plate and front ring gear
4. Friction washer
5. Retaining ring
6. Free wheel outer race
7. Spring
8. Needle roller
9. Needle roller cage
10. Front brake plate with facing
11. Drive housing
12. Front brake corrugated plate
13. Front brake steel plate
14. Front brake-front planet hub
15. Retaining ring
16. Free wheel locating pin
17. Retaining ring
18. Thrust bearing
19. Torque converter
20. Converter hub housing
21. Oil pump drive shaft
22. Input shaft
23. Sealing rings
24. Thrust washer

Exploded view of front section of transmission with Fiat nomenclature (©Volkswagen of America, Inc.)

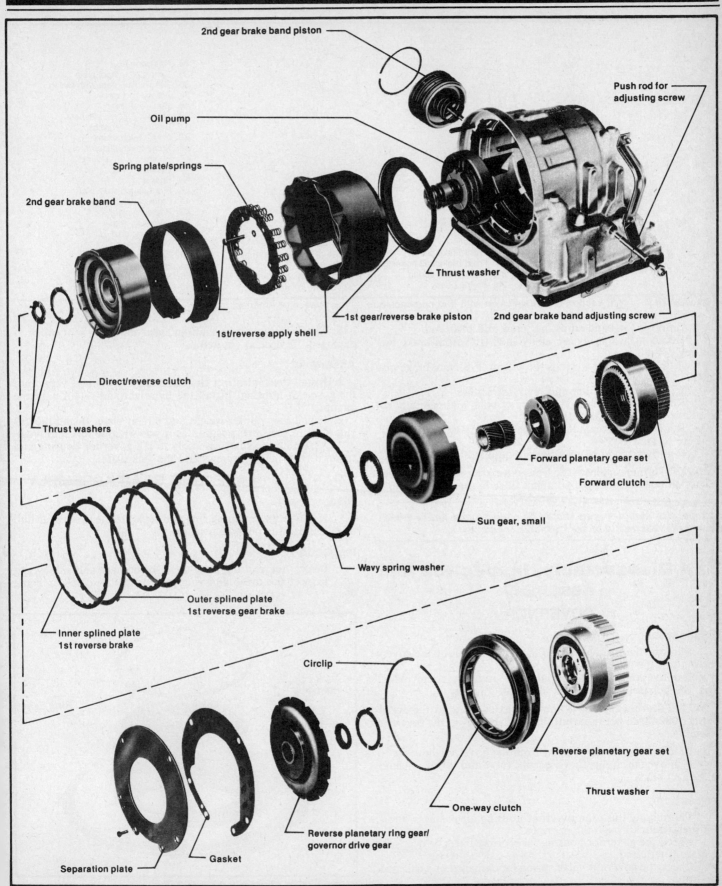

2nd gear brake band piston

Push rod for adjusting screw

Oil pump

Spring plate/springs

2nd gear brake band

Thrust washer

Direct/reverse clutch

1st gear/reverse brake piston

2nd gear brake band adjusting screw

1st/reverse apply shell

Thrust washers

Forward planetary gear set

Forward clutch

Sun gear, small

Outer splined plate 1st reverse gear brake

Wavy spring washer

Inner splined plate 1st reverse brake

Circlip

Reverse planetary gear set

Thrust washer

One-way clutch

Reverse planetary ring gear/governor drive gear

Separation plate

Gasket

Exploded view of transmission components with Audi/VW nomenclature (©Volkswagen of America, Inc.)

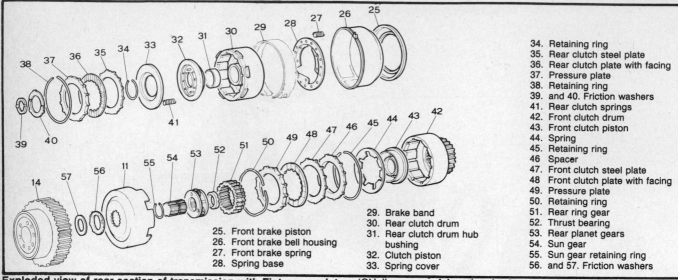

34.	Retaining ring
35.	Rear clutch steel plate
36.	Rear clutch plate with facing
37.	Pressure plate
38.	Retaining ring
39. and 40.	Friction washers
41.	Rear clutch springs
42.	Front clutch drum
43.	Front clutch piston
44.	Spring
45.	Retaining ring
46.	Spacer
47.	Front clutch steel plate
48.	Front clutch plate with facing
49.	Pressure plate
50.	Retaining ring
51.	Rear ring gear
52.	Thrust bearing
53.	Rear planet gears
54.	Sun gear
55.	Sun gear retaining ring
56. and 57.	Friction washers

25. Front brake piston
26. Front brake bell housing
27. Front brake spring
28. Spring base

29. Brake band
30. Rear clutch drum
31. Rear clutch drum hub bushing
32. Clutch piston
33. Spring cover

Exploded view of rear section of transmission with Fiat nomenclature (©Volkswagen of America, Inc.)

16. Remove the band adjusting screw and push rod.
17. Remove the 1st/reverse apply shell (F/S-front brake bell housing).
18. Remove the 1st reverse brake piston (F/S-front brake piston).
19. Remove the oil filter and retaining screws
20. Remove the valve body retaining bolts and carefully remove the valve body from the case.
21. Remove the accumulator piston spring and piston from the bore in the case.
22. Remove the oil pump filter, if equipped.

NOTE: During repairs to the transaxles prior to serial number 21040, do not re-install the oil pump filter in the pressure bore.

─────── CAUTION ───────
Pistons with moulded seals should be replaced and not be reused during the reassembly of the transaxle components.
───────────────────────

Unit Disassembly, Inspection and Assembly
GOVERNOR

Disassembly

1. Remove the two screws and lock plate retaining the governor shaft to the governor body.
2. Remove and discard the oil filter from the circuit plate. Note the position of the circuit plate and remove.

NOTE: During repairs to the transaxles prior to the serial number 08040, do not re-install the fluid strainer in the governor assembly.

3. Remove the counter weight from the governor housing.
4. Remove the circlip, the flyweight, valve and spring, cap and centralizer shaft.

Inspection

1. Thoroughly flush the governor housing oil passages. Blow compressed air through the passages.
2. Check the governor housing for scoring, burrs or deposits. Replace if required.
3. Check the governor valve spring for damaged or weakened condition.
4. Check the valve for scores or burrs.

5. Check the governor shaft and gear for being bent, worn or damaged. Replace as rquired.

Assembly

1. Install the centralizer shaft and cup, spring and valve into the governor housing. Install the flyweight and retain with the circlip.
2. Install the counter weight and circuit plate. Install the circuit plate in the same position as it was when it was removed.
3. Assemble the shaft assembly to the governor housing and retain it with the two screws and the lock plate.

PARKING PLATE/RING GEAR ASSEMBLY

Disassembly

1. Remove the retaining ring and separate the drive gear hub from the parking plate/ring gear.

Inspection

1. Inspect the parking plate teeth for damage and side wear.
2. Inspect the drive and ring gear teeth for scores or being worn.

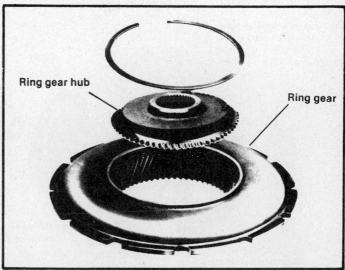

Ring gear hub

Ring gear

Exploded view of parking plate/ring gear
(©Volkswagen of America, Inc.)

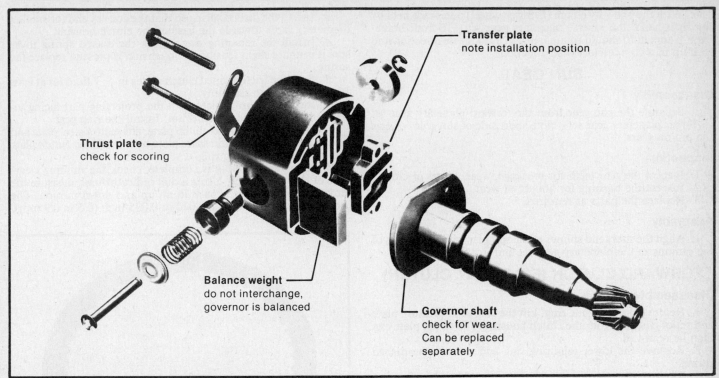

Thrust plate
check for scoring

Transfer plate
note installation position

Balance weight
do not interchange,
governor is balanced

Governor shaft
check for wear.
Can be replaced
separately

Exploded view of governor assembly (©Volkswagen of America, Inc.)

3. Replace the components as required.

Assembly

1. Mate the splines of the drive gear hub and parking plate/ring gear. Install the retaining ring.

ONE-WAY CLUTCH (F/S-FREE WHEEL)

Disassembly

1. Mark the position of the cage to the outer race.
2. Remove the retaining rings, top and bottom.
3. Tap the cage lightly and remove the cage from the outer ring.
4. Disassemble the rollers and the springs, noting their direction for assembly.

Inspection

1. Inspect the springs for distortion or breakage.
2. Inspect the rollers and outer race for wear, galling or brinnelling.
3. Replace the worn or damaged parts.

Assembly

1. Position the lower retaining ring in the outer ring.
2. Heat the outer ring to 300°F. (150°C.) on a hot plate.
3. Using gloves and two sets of pliers, place the cage on top of the outer ring, aligning the previously made marks, and install the cage into the outer ring quickly. Be sure the cage "dogs" are securely positioned in the appropriate outer ring grooves. Rotate the cage slightly immediately after installation, if necessary.

NOTE: The cage quickly absorbs the heat from the outer ring and will lock-up. If the cage is not correctly positioned, do not force it, but remove it and repeat the operation.

4. When the unit has cooled down, install the springs and rollers in the cage. Install the top retaining ring.
5. Install the one-way clutch (F/S-free wheel) on the reverse planetary gear set (F/S-front brake/front planet hub).

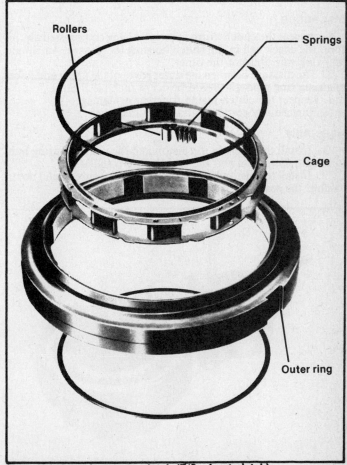

Rollers

Springs

Cage

Outer ring

Exploded view of one-way clutch (F/S - front clutch)
(©Volkswagen of America, Inc.)

6. With the one-way clutch (F/S-free wheel) outer race held by the right hand, the reverse planetary gear set (F/S-front brake/front planet hub) should rotate freely in a clockwise direction and lock-up in a counterclockwise direction.

SUN GEAR

Disassembly

1. Separate the sun gear from the forward planetary gear set (F/S-rear planetary gear set). Note short side of sun gear engages the pinion gears.

Inspection

1. Inspect the gear teeth for breakage, wear, scores or chips.
2. Inspect the bushing for abnormal wear.
3. Replace the parts as required.

Assembly

1. Align the short end splines of the sun gear with the splines of the pinions in the planetary gear set and install in place.

FORWARD CLUTCH (F/S-FRONT CLUTCH)

Disassembly

1. Remove the retaining ring. Lift the ring gear, pressure plate and set of clutches from the clutch housing. The thrust plate can then be removed.
2. Remove the lower retaining ring and remove the dished spring.
3. Remove the piston assembly from the clutch housing.
4. Remove the seals from the clutch housing hub and the piston.

Inspection

1. Inspect the clutch drum for wear. Using compressed air, inspect the check ball in the clutch housing for leakage. Air should flow one way, but not the other.
2. The distance between the outer edges of the upper and lower retaining ring grooves should be 1.173 inch (29.8 mm).
3. Inspect the clutch piston for wear or damage.
4. Replace any components as required.

Assembly

1. Install the seals on the piston and the clutch housing hub. Lubricate the piston and the seals before installation.
2. Install the piston in the clutch housing, being careful not to damage the seals.

Measuring end play of forward clutch pack
(©Volkswagen of America, Inc.)

3. Install the dished spring so that the convex end (or smaller diameter), faces towards the base of the clutch housing.
4. Install the retaining ring. Check the dished spring to be sure it is under slight tension. If no tension is present, replace the spring.
5. Soak the friction lined clutch plates in A/T fluid for at least 15 minutes before assembly.
6. Install the thrust plate with the projecting part facing towards the base of the clutch drum. Install the ring gear.
7. Starting with a lined clutch plate, alternate a steel plate and a lined plate. Install the pressure plate next to a lined clutch plate and install the retaining ring.
8. After the assembly is complete, check the running clearance of the clutch pack. Using a dial indicator tool, measure the movement of the clutch pack in an up and down motion. The proper clearance should be 0.020 to 0.035 inch (0.5 to 0.9 mm).

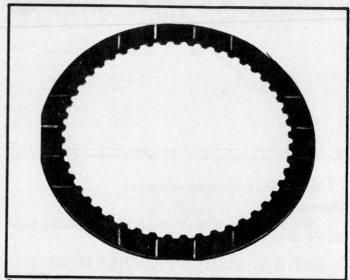

Grooved plates used in forward clutch assembly
(©Volkswagen of America, Inc.)

9. Should the measurement be out of specifications, pressure plates of different thicknesses are available to allow clearance adjustment.
10. To test the assembly, install the forward clutch (F/S-front clutch) and the direct/reverse (F/S-rear clutch) with the thrust washers, on the oil pump.
11. Apply compressed air to the "A" port as illustrated.
12. The piston must compress the clutch plates under air pressure and release them when the air pressure is removed.

DIRECT/REVERSE CLUTCH (F/S-REAR CLUTCH)

Disassembly

1. Remove the clutch pack retaining snap ring and remove the clutch pack assembly.
2. Install a special spring compressor tool and compress the spring cover in the clutch housing. Remove the retaining ring, release the compressor tool and remove. Remove the spring cover, the springs and the piston.

Inspection

1. Inspect the clutch drum bushing. The bushing can be replaced, if required. The old bushing can be used to press the new bushing into a measurement of 0.067 inch (1.7 mm) below the top edge.
2. Inspect the clutch drum for wear or damage.

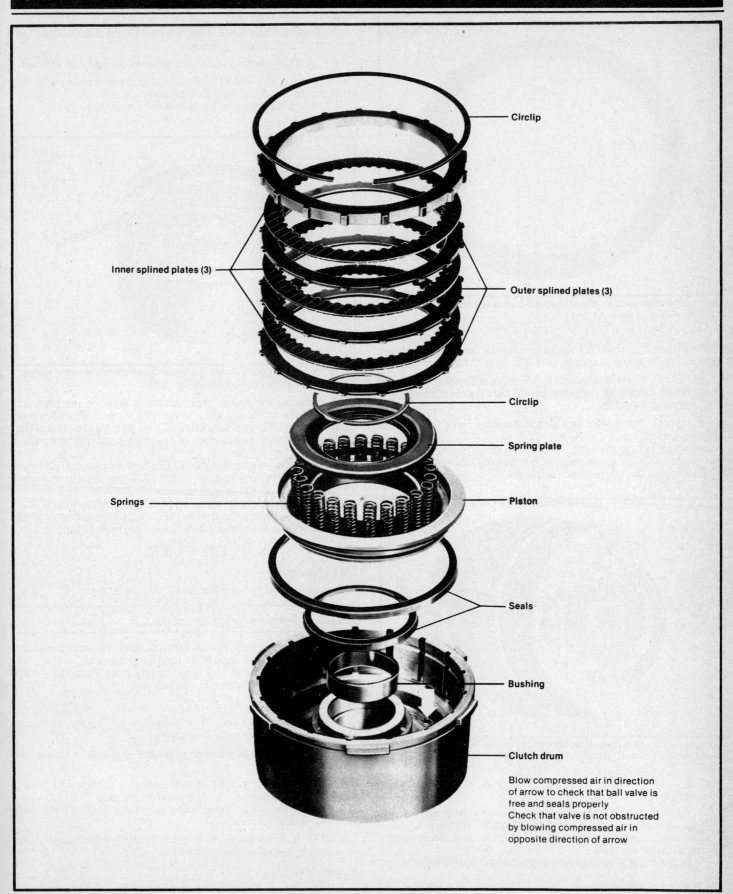

Circlip

Inner splined plates (3)

Outer splined plates (3)

Circlip

Spring plate

Springs

Piston

Seals

Bushing

Clutch drum

Blow compressed air in direction
of arrow to check that ball valve is
free and seals properly
Check that valve is not obstructed
by blowing compressed air in
opposite direction of arrow

Exploded view of forward clutch (F/S - rear clutch) (©Volkswagen of America, Inc.)

Grooved plates used in direct/reverse clutch assembly
(©Volkswagen of America, Inc.)

3. The distance between the outer edges of the upper and lower retaining ring grooves should be 1.230 inch (31.25 mm).

NOTE: If the measurement is out of specifications, different sized clutch drums are available. Install only the clutch drum with the correct dimensions.

4. Inspect the piston and clutch housing bore for wear or damaged surfaces.

5. Using compressed air, inspect the check ball for leakage. Air should flow in one direction, but not the other.

6. Replace the components as required.

Air pressure ports to check clutch operation. A - forward clutch, B - direct/reverse clutch (©Volkswagen of America, Inc.)

Assembly

1. Install the seals on the clutch housing hub and on the piston. Lubricate the piston and seals before installation.

2. Install the piston in the clutch housing bore, being careful not to damage the seals.

3. Install the 24 springs on the piston and position the spring cover.

4. Install the compresing tool. Compress the springs and install the spring cover retaining ring. Remove the tool.

5. Soak the new lined clutches in A/T fluid for at least 15 minutes before installing them.

NOTE: Only clutch plates with grooved facings can be used.

6. Starting with a steel plate, alternate the steel plates with the lined plates, finishing with a lined plate.

7. Install the pressure plate and the retaining ring.

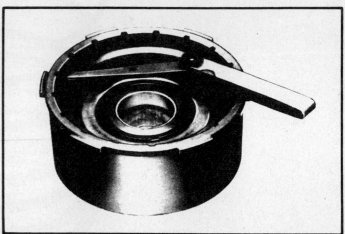

Measuring clutch pack running clearance on direct/reverse clutch assembly (©Volkswagen of America, Inc.)

8. Measure the clutch pack clearance between the pressure plate and the retaining snap ring. The correct measurement should be 0.0807 to 0.0984 inch (2.05 to 2.50 mm). To correct the clearance, different thicknesses of retaining snap rings are available.

9. To test the assembly, install the forward clutch (F/S-front clutch) and the direct/reverse clutch (F/S-rear clutch) with the thrust washers, on the oil pump.

10. Apply compressed air to the "B" port as illustrated.

11. The piston must compress the clutch plates under air pressure and release the plates when the air pressure is removed.

OIL PUMP

Disassembly

1. Remove the cover plate and retaining screws.

—————— CAUTION ——————
The cover plate is under spring tension.

2. Remove the check ball and spring. Remove the drive plate, drive gear and driven gear from the pump housing.

3. Remove the small and large sealing rings from the pump body hub. Remove the thrust washer.

Inspection

1. Inspect the drive and driven gears, the drive plate, and cover plate for abnormal wear or damage.

NOTE: The drive and driven gears are supplied as an assembly.

2. Inspect the pump housing hub sealing ring grooves for wear.

3. Inspect the pump body for wear or damage.

4. Inspect the thrust washer and oil pump body mating surfaces for abnormal wear.

NOTE: It is advisable to replace thrust washers indicating wear during the rebuilding process.

Assembly

1. Lubricate and install the drive gear, driven gears and the drive plate.

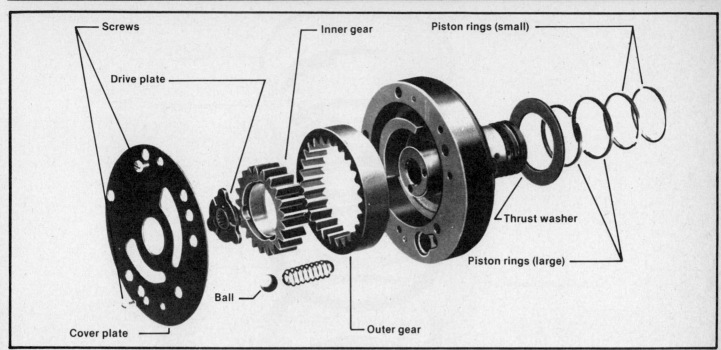

Exploded view of oil pump assembly (©Volkswagen of America, Inc.)

NOTE: Install the driven gear with the code letter facing towards the cover plate.

2. Install the spring and check ball in the pump housing.

3. Install the cover plate and retain with the retaining capscrews.

4. Install the thrust washer, the large seal rings and the small seal rings. Be sure the seal rings are hooked together at their ends.

5. After the assembly, insert the oil pump drive shaft and check that the gear rotate freely.

2ND GEAR BRAKE BAND PISTON (F/S-REAR BRAKE)

Disassembly

1. The piston assembly can be disassembled by removing the circlip from the piston shaft.

—————— **CAUTION** ——————

The piston shaft is under spring tension. Upon disassembly, do not lose the shim from between the piston and the accumulator spring.

2. Remove the seals from the piston and cover.

NOTE: "O" ring seals are used on the cover, while lip seals are used on the piston. Note the positioning of the lip seals.

Inspection

1. Inspect the springs for distortion or being broken.

2. Inspect the piston and cover assemblies for wear or damage. Inspect the piston diameter.

Assembly

1. Install the piston shaft, shim and spring into the piston and retain with the circlip.

NOTE: If the piston is replaced, the unit is pre-assembled and adjusted.

2. Lubricate and install the "O" ring seals in the cover assembly.

3. Lubricate and install the lip seals on the piston with the small seal lip facing the bottom of the cover and the large seal lip facing the open end of the cover.

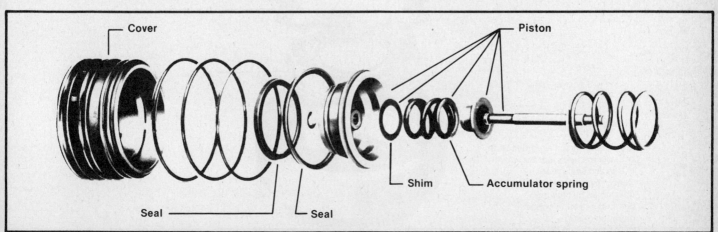

Exploded view of brake band piston (©Volkswagen of America, Inc.)

855

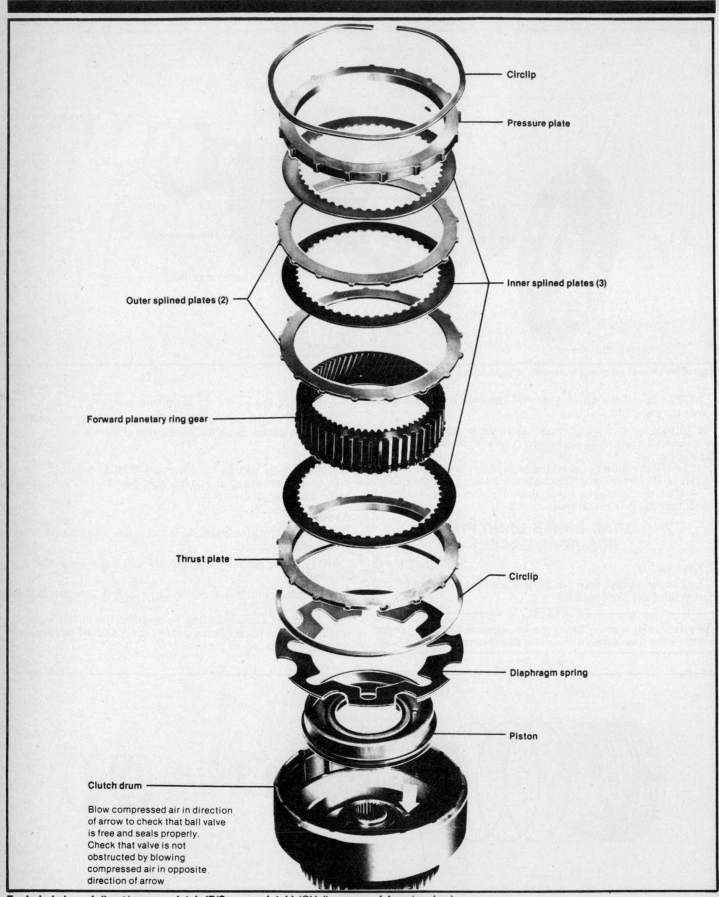

Circlip

Pressure plate

Inner splined plates (3)

Outer splined plates (2)

Forward planetary ring gear

Thrust plate

Circlip

Diaphragm spring

Piston

Clutch drum

Blow compressed air in direction
of arrow to check that ball valve
is free and seals properly.
Check that valve is not
obstructed by blowing
compressed air in opposite
direction of arrow

Exploded view of direct/reverse clutch (F/S - rear clutch) (©Volkswagen of America, Inc.)

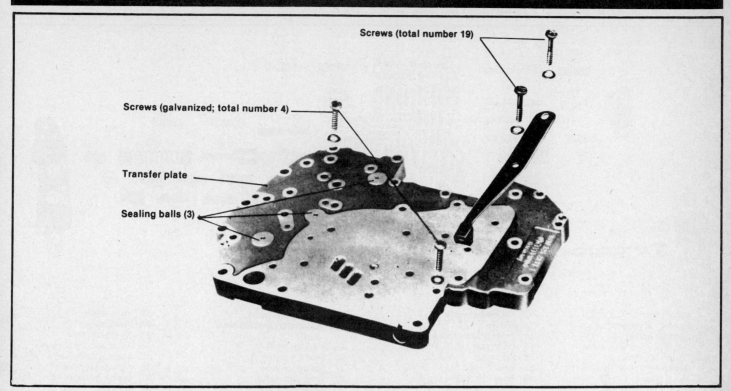

transfer plate used with Rabbit, Jetta diesel engine models (©Volkswagen of America, Inc.)

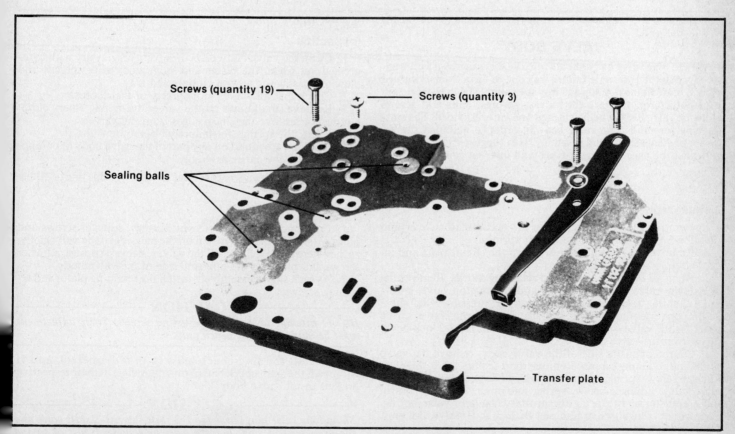

separation plate and transfer plate. Note location of three sealing balls in transfer plate
(©Volkswagen of America, Inc.)

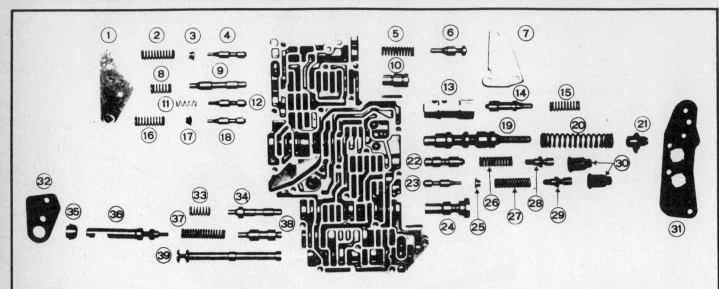

Exploded view of Fiat Strada valve body components (©Volkswagen of America, Inc.)

1. Valve plate
2. Spring for valve
3. Seat for spring
4. 3-2 kick-down shift valve
5. Spring for valve
6. 3-2 shift valve
7. Valve plate
8. Spring for valve
9. 2-3 shift control valve
10. 2-3 shift valve
11. Spring for valve
12. Main relief valve
13. Sleeve
14. Front brake control valve
15. Spring for valve
16. Spring for valve
17. Seat for spring
18. Pressure relief valve for converter supply
19. Primary regulator valve
20. Spring for valve
21. Adjuster screw for valve
22. Main control valve
23. Modulated pressure relief valve
24. 1-2 shift valve
25. Seat for spring
26. Spring for valve
27. Spring for valve
28. Adjuster screw for valve
29. Adjuster screw for valve
30. Plugs for adjuster screws
31. Valve plate
32. Valve plate
33. Spring for valve
34. 1-2 shift control valve
35. Bushing for valve
36. Kick-down valve
37. Spring for valve
38. Modulator valve
39. Selector valve

VALVE BODY

NOTE: The valve body should only be disassembled for cleaning or when the transaxle failure was due to dirty fluid or burned friction plate linings. A storage tray is available from the transaxle manufacturer, to store the valves, springs, balls and screws while the valve body is being cleaned and/or overhauled. The storage tray resembles the valve body in order to maintian the sequence of disassembly and assembly. It is suggested the tray or its equivalent be used. Different types and internal components are used.

Disassembly

1. Remove the screws retaining the accumulator cover and kick-down valve control lever detent spring.
2. Remove the retaining screws from the circuit plate and intermediate plate to valve body.
3. Remove the valve plates and retaining screws. Remove the kick-down valve, bushing, spring and modulator valve, spring and 1-2 shift valve, spring seat and spring, pressure relief valve for the converter fluid supply, spring and main relief valve, spring and 2-3 shift valve, spring and spring seat and the 3-2 kick-down valve from the valve body.
4. On the opposite side of the valve body, remove the valve plates and retaining screws. Remove the 1-2 shift valve, the plug, adjuster screw, spring, spring seat and modulated pressure relief valve, plug, adjuster screw, spring and main pressure control valve, adjuster screw, spring and primary regulator valve, spring, front brake control valve and sleeve, 2-3 shift valve, 3-2 shift valve and spring.
5. Remove the five (6 mm diameter) check balls, and if equipped, the sixth ball, (3 mm diameter). Mark the locations of each ball for reference during the assembly

Inspection

1. Clean the valve body parts in solvent and air dry with compressed air. Clean the plates and valve body with solvent and blow the passages dry with compressed air.
2. Check that all valves move freely in their bores.
3. Remove small burrs on the valves, using fine emery cloth, but do not remove the sharp edges from the valves.
4. Check the springs for failure or lack of tension.
5. If defects are found on any part of the valve body or components, replace the entire assembly.

NOTE: The valve springs are not interchangeable due to different tension values.

Assembly

1. Lubricate the valves, sleeves, springs, adjuster screws and plugs with A/T fluid and install on the one side of the valve body, as they were removed. Install the valves, sleeves, springs, adjuster screws and plugs on the opposite side of the valve body.
2. As each side is assembled, install the retaining plates and retaining screws.

—————————— CAUTION ——————————

Do not attempt to turn the adjusting screws. Their adjustment must be made on a test bench only.

3. Install the five check balls (6 mm diameter), and if equipped, the sixth check ball (3 mm diameter) in their respective pockets in the valve body.

—————————— CAUTION ——————————

Should the valve plugs over the 1-2 shift valve, 2-3 shift valve and converter control valve become loose or dislodged, loss of second gear or third gear and the lack of proper converter charging can occur.

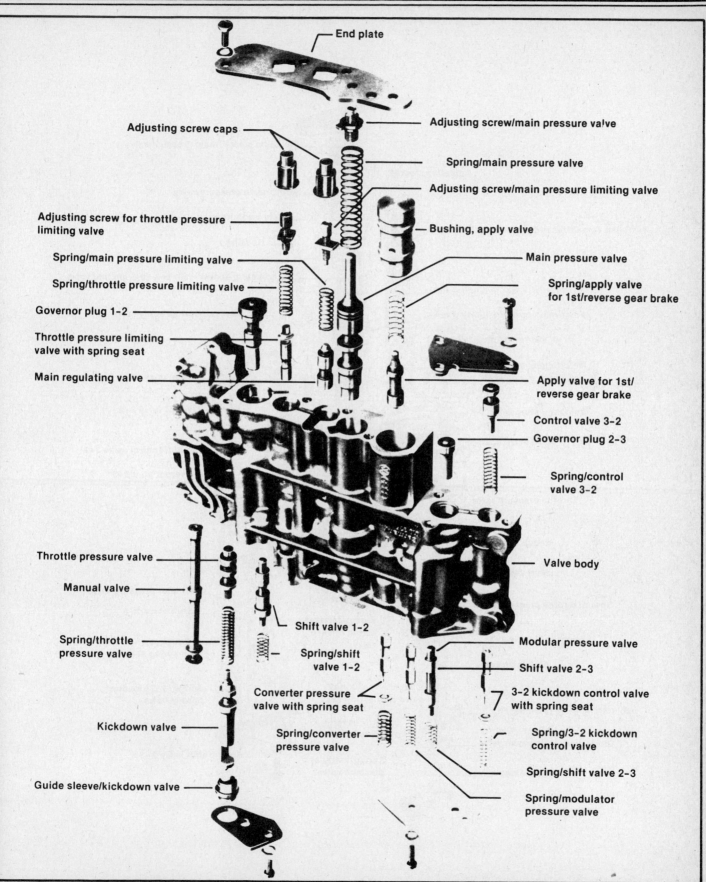

End plate

Adjusting screw caps

Adjusting screw/main pressure valve

Spring/main pressure valve

Adjusting screw/main pressure limiting valve

Adjusting screw for throttle pressure limiting valve

Bushing, apply valve

Spring/main pressure limiting valve

Main pressure valve

Spring/throttle pressure limiting valve

Spring/apply valve for 1st/reverse gear brake

Governor plug 1-2

Throttle pressure limiting valve with spring seat

Main regulating valve

Apply valve for 1st/reverse gear brake

Control valve 3-2

Governor plug 2-3

Spring/control valve 3-2

Valve body

Throttle pressure valve

Manual valve

Spring/throttle pressure valve

Shift valve 1-2

Modular pressure valve

Spring/shift valve 1-2

Shift valve 2-3

Converter pressure valve with spring seat

3-2 kickdown control valve with spring seat

Kickdown valve

Spring/converter pressure valve

Spring/3-2 kickdown control valve

Guide sleeve/kickdown valve

Spring/shift valve 2-3

Spring/modulator pressure valve

Exploded view of valve body components of one type of Audi/VW transaxle models (©Volkswagen of America, Inc.)

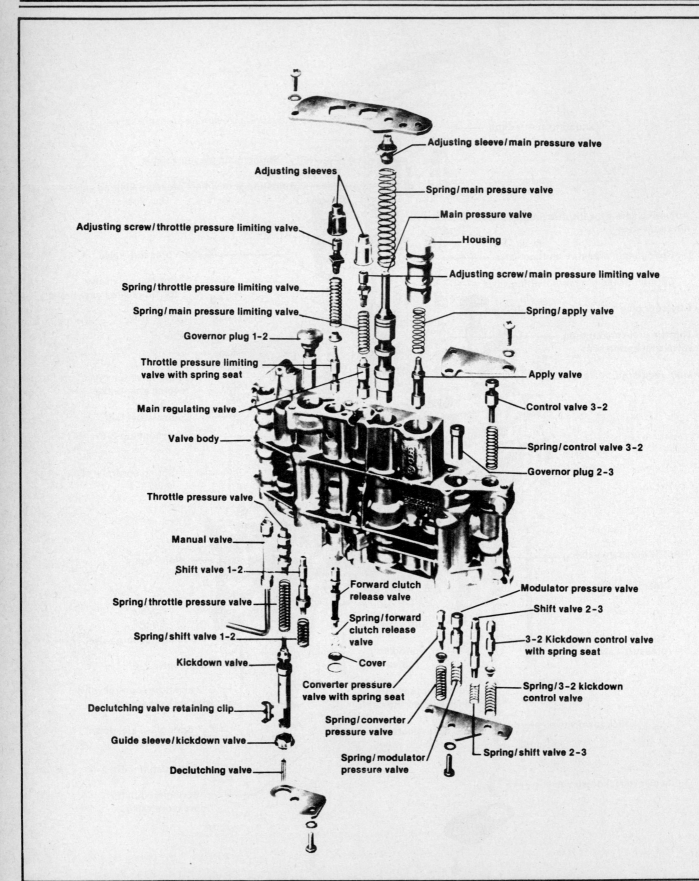

Adjusting sleeve/main pressure valve

Adjusting sleeves

Spring/main pressure valve

Main pressure valve

Adjusting screw/throttle pressure limiting valve

Housing

Adjusting screw/main pressure limiting valve

Spring/throttle pressure limiting valve

Spring/main pressure limiting valve

Spring/apply valve

Governor plug 1-2

Throttle pressure limiting valve with spring seat

Apply valve

Main regulating valve

Control valve 3-2

Valve body

Spring/control valve 3-2

Governor plug 2-3

Throttle pressure valve

Manual valve

Shift valve 1-2

Forward clutch release valve

Modulator pressure valve

Spring/throttle pressure valve

Shift valve 2-3

Spring/forward clutch release valve

3-2 Kickdown control valve with spring seat

Spring/shift valve 1-2

Kickdown valve

Cover

Spring/3-2 kickdown control valve

Converter pressure valve with spring seat

Declutching valve retaining clip

Spring/converter pressure valve

Guide sleeve/kickdown valve

Spring/shift valve 2-3

Declutching valve

Spring/modulator pressure valve

Exploded view of "E" mode valve body used with Rabbit, Jetta diesel engine models (©Volkswagen of America, Inc.)

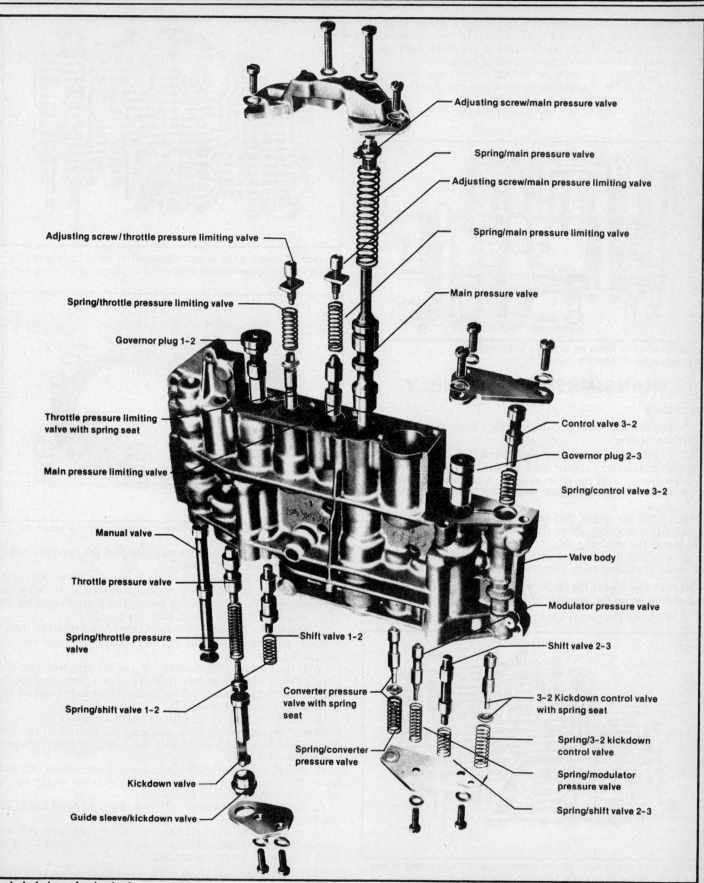

Adjusting screw/main pressure valve

Spring/main pressure valve

Adjusting screw/main pressure limiting valve

Spring/main pressure limiting valve

Adjusting screw / throttle pressure limiting valve

Spring/throttle pressure limiting valve

Main pressure valve

Governor plug 1-2

Throttle pressure limiting valve with spring seat

Control valve 3-2

Governor plug 2-3

Main pressure limiting valve

Spring/control valve 3-2

Manual valve

Throttle pressure valve

Valve body

Modulator pressure valve

Spring/throttle pressure valve

Shift valve 1-2

Shift valve 2-3

Converter pressure valve with spring seat

3-2 Kickdown control valve with spring seat

Spring/shift valve 1-2

Spring/3-2 kickdown control valve

Spring/converter pressure valve

Spring/modulator pressure valve

Kickdown valve

Spring/shift valve 2-3

Guide sleeve/kickdown valve

Exploded view of valve body components for second type of Audi/VW transaxle models (©Volkswagen of America, Inc.)

4. Install the intermediate plate on the valve body and check to see if three balls are visible through ports in the upper section of the circuit plate. If not, check to see if the check balls are in their proper location, or replace the valve body.

5. Install the circuit plate on the valve body and torque the screws to 2.9 ft. lbs. Fasten the accumulator cover to the circuit plate and torque the screws to 2.2 ft. lbs.

6. Fasten the kick-down valve control lever detent spring to the valve body.

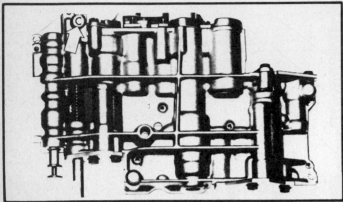

Location of code letter on typical valve body (©Volkswagen of America, Inc.)

TRANSMISSION ASSEMBLY

Procedure

1. Install 1st/reverse (F/S-front brake) brake piston into the transmission case.

2. Position the 1st/reverse apply shell (F/S-front brake bell housing) in the transmission case so that the lugs on the shell/housing line up with the grooves in the transmission case.

3. Install the band actuator rod until it touches the band adjuster screw.

4. Install the spring, 2nd gear brake piston and cover in the transmission housing. Press the cover/piston assembly inward and install the retaining ring.

5. Position the oil pump into the transmission case with the oil pump rib facing away from the band actuator rod.

NOTE: The lugs of the thrust washer straddle the oil pump rib and should be on the opposite or top side of the transmission.

6. Position the twenty springs on the spring plate and attach

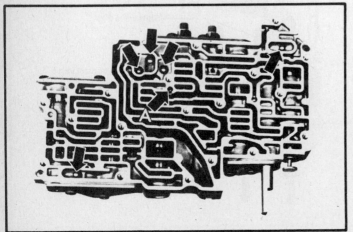

Location of 5 check balls (6 mm diameter) and 1 check ball (3 mm diameter - arrow A) in valve body used by Vanagon (©Volkswagen of America, Inc.)

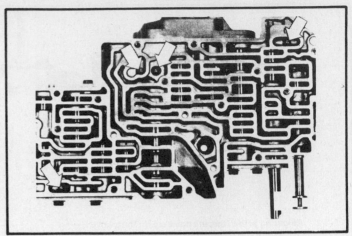

Location of check balls (6 mm diameter) in valve body used by Dasher models, other models similar (©Volkswagen of America, Inc.)

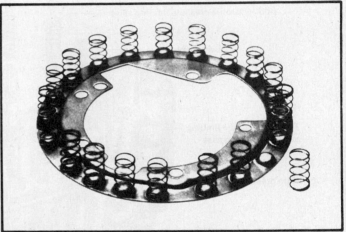

Installing springs on the spring plate (©Volkswagen of America, Inc.)

the spring plate assembly to the oil pump with the retaining bolts. Torque to 61 *inch* lbs. (7 N•m).

7. Insert the oil pump drive shaft into the oil pump drive plate and rotate the shaft in a clockwise direction, checking for any binding from the oil pump gears. The gears should rotate freely. Remove the drive shaft from the pump.

8. Install the 2nd gear (F/S-rear) brake band into the transmission case making sure the actuator rods engage with the two lugs on the band.

9. If the forward (F/S-rear) clutch and the direct/reverse (F/S-rear) clutch assemblies have not previously been assembled, coat the two thrust washers with petroleum jelly and install on the forward (F/S-front) clutch drum.

10. Insert the forward (F/S-front) clutch drum into the direct/reverse (F/S-rear) clutch drum, engaging the grooves of the forward (F/S-front) clutch drum with the direct/reverse (F/S-rear) clutch assembly.

11. Install the input shaft into the clutch assemblies, lift and install the clutch assemblies into the transmission, engaging the two clutch units to the oil pump collar.

12. Coat the thrust washer with petroleum jelly and install on the forward (F/S-front) clutch hub.

13. Install the forward planetary (F/S-rear planetary) gear set into the forward (F/S-front) clutch drum until the planetary gear teeth mesh with the ring gear teeth.

NOTE: The sun gear short splined end must be engaged with the planetary gear teeth when the planetary gear set is installed.

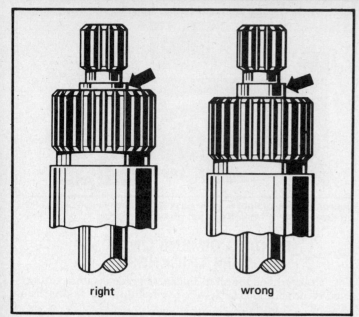

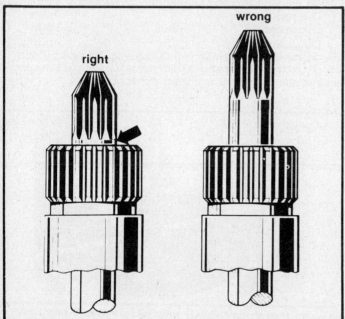

Checking pump shaft for full engagement, both old style (A), and new style (B) (©Volkswagen of America, Inc.)

14. Install the drive shell/housing, along with the thrust washer, on the sun gear.

15. Install the reverse-planetary gear set (F/S-front brake-front planet hub) into the transmission case until the sun gear meshes with the planet gear teeth. Install the thrust washer, coated with petroleum jelly, on the planet carrier hub.

16. Install the 1st/reverse (F/S-front) brake plates, starting with the wavy spring washer (F/S-front brake corrugated plate), a steel plate, followed by a lined plate. Alternate the clutch plates, steel to lined, until all are installed.

17. Coat the thrust washer with petroleum jelly and install. Install the one-way clutch (F/S-free wheel) into the transmission case. Rotate the reverse planetary gear set (F/S-front brake-front planet hub) in a clockwise direction while pressing the one-way clutch (F/S-free wheel) into operating position.

NOTE: To verify the correct operation of the one-way clutch (F/S-free wheel), position the transmission in the upright position and while holding the one-way clutch (F/S-free wheel) outer race stationary, the reverse planetary gear set (F/S-front brake-front planet hub) should rotate freely in a clockwise direction and lock-up in a counterclockwise direction.

18. Install the one-way clutch (F/S-free wheel) outer race locating pin in the housing of the transmission case.

19. An indicator of correct assembly of the transmission components, is the installation of the outer race retaining snap ring without interference from the assembly.

NOTE: The snap ring opening must be opposite the locating pin.

20. Position the transmission horizontally. Loosen the band adjusting lock nut and tighten the adjusting screw to 87 *inch* lbs. (10 N•m). Loosen and retighten the adjusting screw to 43 *inch* lbs. (5 N•m). Loosen the adjusting screw exactly 2½ turns and tighten the lock nut.

21. Install the reverse planetary ring gear/governor drive gear (F/S-parking plate/front ring gear/governor drive gear) on the reverse planetary gear set (F/S-front brake-front planet hub).

22. Install the flange with the two gaskets. Install the retaining cap screws.

23. Install the valve body and accumulator piston and spring into its bore in the transmisssion case. Install the valve body to the transmission housing, connecting the manual valve and the kick-down valve. Tighten all bolts diagonally and to a torque of 35 *inch* lbs. (4 N•m).

24. Install the gasket, oil strainer, cover and attach with the retaining screws. Torque to 26 *inch* lbs. (3 N•m).

25. Using a new gasket, install the oil pan and install the retaining bolts. Torque to 14 ft. lbs. (20 N•m).

Assembly of Transmission and Final Drive

End play between the transmission and final drive must be measured and adjusted as required to limit the end play movement of the reverse planetary ring gear (F/S-front brake-front planet hub), before the two units are assembled.

Measuring from straight edge to final drive housing, finding dimension "A" (©Volkswagen of America, Inc.)

FINDING DIMENSION "A"—
FINAL DRIVE UNIT

1. Have the final drive unit in an upright position with the seal, sealing ring and thrust washer removed.

2. Using a straight edge laid across the face of the final drive unit, measure the distance from the top face of the straight edge to the top of the oil sleeve bushing, with a depth measuring tool. Record the reading.

3. Measure the distance from the straight edge to the face of the final drive housing and record the measurement.

NOTE: This measurement is the thickness of the straight edge tool.

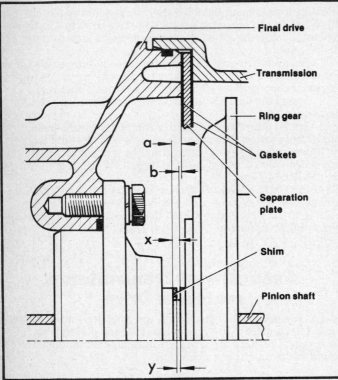

Adjustment of transmission/final drive end play
(©Volkswagen of America, Inc.)

4. An example of the measurements and results would be as follows;

From the straight edge to oil sleeve bushing	18.7 mm
From straight edge to final drive surface	−8.0 mm
Represents Dimension "A"	10.7 mm

FINDING DIMENSION "B"—
TRANSMISSION UNIT

1. Position the transmission with its attaching studs upright.

2. Lay the straight edge tool across the face of the housing and measure the distance from the straight edge to the gasket on the plate.

3. Measure the distance from the straight edge to the shoulder for the shim on the plate.

4. An example of the measurements and results would be as follows;

From the straight edge to plate	19.2 mm
From the straight edge to shoulder	−10.0 mm
Represents dimension "B"	9.2 mm

Measuring from straight edge to gasket on transmission plate, finding dimension "B" (©Volkswagen of America, Inc.)

FINDING DIMENSION "X"—
SHIM THICKNESS

1. To determine the shim thickness needed, subtract dimension "B" from dimension "A". The result would be dimension "X".

2. An example of finding dimension "X" would be as follows;

Dimension "A"		10.7 mm
Dimension "B"	(Subtract)	− 9.2 mm
Dimension "X"		1.5 mm

3. Shims are available in two thicknesses, 0.4 and 1.2 mm.

4. From the following chart, determine the shim or shim combination and to be used to correct dimension "X."

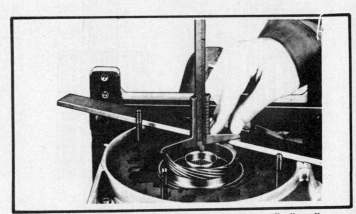

Measuring from straight edge to shoulder for shims, finding dimension "B" (©Volkswagen of America, Inc.)

Measuring from straight edge to pinion bearing spacer on pinion shaft, finding dimension "A" (©Volkswagen of America, Inc.)

ALLOWABLE END PLAY—DIMENSION "Y"

An allowable end play clearance, described as dimension "Y", is constant and should be between 0.23 to 0.84 mm or 0.009 to 0.033 inch. This measurement must be included in the stacking of the proposed thrust washer(s), as determined in the preceding steps. An example of the inclusion of the end play clearance is as follows;

1. As the previous examples explained how to find dimensions "A" and "B", resulting in dimension "X", the theoretical use of thrust washers to this dimension would be the use of two 0.4 mm washers, for a total of 0.8 mm. Using the dimension "X" of 1.5 mm and subtracting 0.8 mm from it, the result is 0.7 mm which falls within the 0.23 to 0.84 mm allowable end play.

Dimension "X"	1.5 mm
2 x 0.4 mm shim	− 0.8 mm
Dimension "Y"	0.7 mm

JOINING OF UNITS

1. Install the oil seal, thrust washer and turbine shaft with "O" ring seals.
2. Install final drive outer "O" ring seal and lubricate.
3. Have the transmission in an upright position and carefully set the final drive unit onto the transmission mating surface and studs. Install the retaining nuts and torque to 22 ft. lbs. (30 N•m).
4. Place the assembled transaxle horizontal and install the oil pump shaft. Be sure the shaft engages the oil pump drive plate correctly.
5. Install the converter assembly and retain it with a holding bar.

SPECIFICATIONS

CAPACITIES

Dry fill	6.4 US Quarts (6 Liters)
Refill	3.2 US Quarts (3 Liters)

BAND ADJUSTMENT

1st torque—87 in. lbs. and release
2nd torque—43 in. lbs.
Loosen adjuster screw exactly 2½ turn
Tighten adjusting screw nut 14 ft. lbs. (18 N•m)

PRESSURE TEST SPECIFICATIONS

Selector lever position	Accelerator pedal position	Main pressure psi	Test conditions
D	idle speed*	41-42①⑤	vehicle stationary
	full throttle	83-84②⑥	speed higher than 40 km/h (25 mph). ④
R	idle speed	129-138③⑦	vehicle stationary

① Dasher—41 to 43 psi
  Fiat Strada—55.5 to 57 psi
② Dasher—83 to 85 psi
  Fiat Strada—89.6 to 91 psi
  Audi 5000—80 to 82 psi
③ Dasher/Audi 5000—108 to 117 psi
  Rabbit/Scirocco/Jetta—109 to 117 psi
  (Model EQ to S/N 16079—100 to 109 psi)
  Fiat Strada—104 to 105.3 psi
④ For safety reasons, the manufacturer recommends the test be made on a dynamometer.
⑤ "E" mode transaxle—42-44 psi
⑥ "E" mode transaxle—85-86 psi
⑦ "E" mode transaxle—131-145 psi

STALL SPEED RPM SPECIFICATIONS

Model	RPM
Audi 5000	2400 to 2650
Audi 4000	2450 to 2700
Dasher	1950 to 2550
Rabbit, Scirocco, Jetta	
1.5 Liter	2250 to 2500
1.6 Liter	2100 to 2350
1.7 Liter	2200 to 2500
W/E Mode Transaxle	2555 to 2805
Fiat Strada	2260

END PLAY SHIM CHART

Measured End Play mm (in.)	Number and Size of Shims
0.23-0.84 (.009-.033)	No shim
0.85-1.24 (.034-.049)	One 0.4mm shim
1.25-1.64 (.050-.065)	Two 0.4mm shims
1.65-2.04 (.066-.081)	One 1.2mm shim
2.05-2.44 (.082-.097)	One 0.4mm and one 1.2mm shim
2.45-2.84 (.098-.113)	Two 0.4mm and one 1.2mm shim
2.85-3.24 (.114-.129)	Two 1.2mm shims
3.25-3.64 (.130-.145)	One 0.4mm and two 1.2mm shims
3.65-3.88 (.146-.155)	Two 0.4mm and two 1.2mm shims

NOTE: Shims are available in two sizes: 0.4mm, part no. 010 323 345 A and 1.2mm, part no. 010 323 346 A

SPECIAL TOOLS

ASSORTED DRIVERS

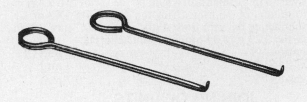

HOOKS FOR REMOVING ONE-WAY CLUTCH

DIAL INDICATOR

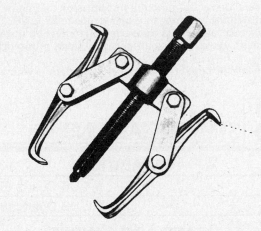

GEAR PULLER

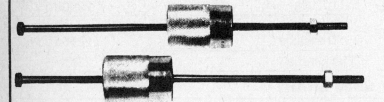

SLIDE HAMMERS

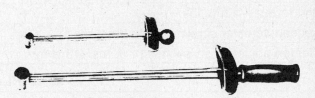

TORQUE WRENCHES

CROSS POINT BLADE SOCKET

CROSS POINT BLADE

PULLER FOR REAR CLUTCH DRUM HUB BUSHING

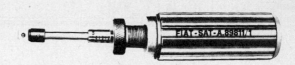

TORQUE SCREWDRIVER

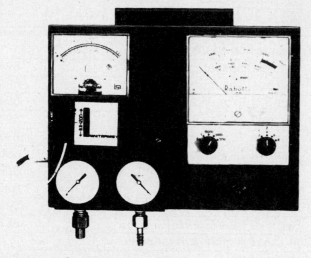

ROAD PERFORMANCE TESTER

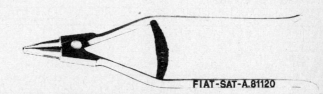

SNAP RING PLIERS

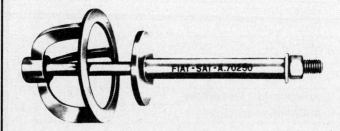

CLUTCH SPRING COMPRESSOR

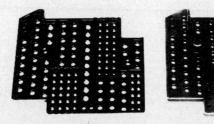

VALVE AND SPRING WASHING CONTAINER

TORQUE SPECIFICATIONS

Drive shaft/flange bolts	33 ft. lbs. (45 N•m)
Torque converter bolts	22 ft. lbs. (30 N•m)
Transaxle/engine bolts	40 ft. lbs. (55 N•m)
Ball joint/control arm	48 ft. lbs. (65 N•m)
Mount to body	30 ft. lbs. (40 N•m)
Mount to transaxle	40 ft. lbs. (55 N•m)
Oil Pan	14 ft. lbs. (18 N•m)
Valve Body	35 In. lbs. (4 N•m)

INDEX

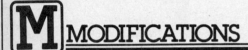

BORG WARNER MODEL 66

APPLICATIONS

BORG WARNER MODEL 66 APPLICATION CHART

Type	Model	Transmission Identification
Jaguar	XJ6 4.2	6066
	XJ6 3.4	6067
Rover	3500 Series	——

GENERAL DESCRIPTION

The Borg Warner Model 66 automatic transmission is a three speed unit consisting of a planetary gear set, hydraulic control system, oil pump, clutches and bands and a torque converter.

The planetary gear set provides three forward speeds and reverse. It consists of two sun gears, two sets of pinions, a pinion (planet) carrier and a ring gear. There are six selector lever positions (P,R,N,D,2, and 1) with provision for manually holding the low and 2nd gears and for kickdown shifts.

The hydraulic control system includes the governor, throttle cable, manual linkage and the valve body all affecting the application or release of the clutches and bands. Governor pressure varies in direct relation to vehicle speed. The throttle cable controls throttle pressure in relation to engine speed. The valve body controls the application of the bands and clutches to hold the planetary gear set.

The oil pump is located directly behind the torque converter and is mechanically connected to engine output. This means that pressure is always supplied while the engine is running.

Mechanical torque multiplication is increased hydraulically by the torque converter. The converter provides a continuous range of torque multiplication from 1:1 to 2.3:1

TRANSMISSION AND CONVERTER IDENTIFICATION

Transmission

The Borg Warner Model 66 automatic transmission is identified by a yellow name plate which will have Model 66 and the number "6606" stamped on the name plate, this automatic transmission is used in all XJ6 4.2 models. All automatic transmissions used in the XJ6 3.4 model will have a golden brown name plate which will have Model 66 and the number "6067" stamped on the name plate.

Converter

The torque converter is a welded unit and cannot be disassembled for service by the average repair shop. New and rebuilt units are available.

Transmission Metric Fasteners

The metric fastener dimensions are very close to the dimensions of the familiar inch system fasteners, and for this reason, replacement fasteners must have the same measurement and strength as those removed.

Do not attempt to interchange metric fasteners for inch system fasteners. Mismatched or incorrect fasteners can result in damage to the transmission unit through malfunctions, breakage or possible personal injury.

Care should be taken to reuse the fasteners in the same locations as removed.

Fluid Capacities

The Jaguar XJ6 4.2 has an automatic transmission fluid capacity of 8.7 quarts. The Jaguar XJ6 3.4 has a fluid capacity of 7.6 quarts. These figures include the torque converter, if the converter has not been drained use between 2.5 and 3.0 quarts of automatic transmission fluid. Always bring the transmission up to operating temperature and recheck the fluid level. Never overfill the transmission.

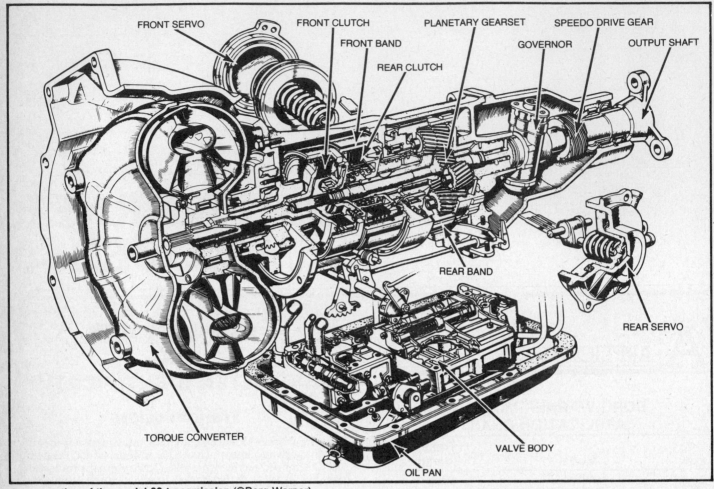

FRONT SERVO · FRONT CLUTCH · PLANETARY GEARSET · SPEEDO DRIVE GEAR

FRONT BAND · GOVERNOR · OUTPUT SHAFT

REAR CLUTCH

REAR BAND

REAR SERVO

TORQUE CONVERTER

OIL PAN · VALVE BODY

Cross section of the model 66 transmission (©Borg Warner)

Checking Fluid Level

The automatic transmission, when at normal operating temeprature, is designed to operate with its fluid level between the MIN and MAX mark on the transmission dipstick.

1. With the vehicle on a level surface, foot brakes applied and the engine running at idle, move the selector lever through each range. Allow time in each range for the transmission to engage. Return the lever to Park.

2. With the engine still running remove the dipstick, wipe it clean and replace it.

3. Once again remove the dipstick and note the reading on the HOT side of the stick. Add the proper amount of transmission fluid to bring the fluid level to the MAX mark on the dipstick.

4. The difference between the MAX and MIN marks on the dipstick represent approximately 1 quart of automatic transmission fluid.

Ⓜ MODIFICATIONS

Transmission Oil Pump Assembly

A groove has been added to the oil pump/converter bush to improve lubrication of the bush. This groove stops short of the front edge of the bush to prevent the oil seal from being swamped. A tin/aluminum pump drive gear bush is also being used. The new stator support will have an increased diameter bush to accommodate the increased diameter input shaft. A large pump suction tube is being used to ensure that the end of the tube is immersed in transmission fluid at all times.

Input Shaft and Front Clutch Assembly

An input shaft of larger diameter is being used on all later Borg Warner model 66 automatic transmissions.

Rear Clutch and Front Drum Assembly

To improve the lubrication path to the rear clutch and the front band the following changes were made to the rear clutch and front drum assembly:

1. The rear clutch piston face (clutch plate side) now has four slots at right angles to one another to improve the oil flow from the inside diameter of the clutch pack.

2. The four wide grooves on the inside diameter of the front drum (steel clutch late splines area) have been deepened to enable more oil flow around the plates.

3. Between the outside and inside diameter of the front drum, so that they line up with the four deepened grooves, four holes have been drilled to enable an oil feed to the front band to be maintained.

4. The rearmost lubrication groove between the three sealing ring grooves of the front drum has also been deepened and the

holes size increased in order to improve the oil flow.

5. The lubrication feed hole in the reverse sun gear has been increased in diameter

One-Way Clutch Assembly

An upgraded first gear one-way clutch assembly has been introduced which has 30 sprags instead of the 24 sprags on earlier assemblies. The center support of the transmission now has increased diameter rear clutch and lubrication drillings.

Carrier Assembly

An improved lubrication oil flow has been achieved by introducing a wider bush into the carrier cover which has opposing helical oil grooves. Non-crowned shaved short pinions have also been introduced. These pinions have no identification groove in order to improve their durability.

Output Shaft Lubrication Hole

The lubrication hole in the output shaft has been increased in diameter to allow a better flow of automatic transmission fluid.

Maincase and Servos

The front clutch and governor feed hole in the rear of the maincase has been increased 5.0 mm. The rear servo piston and cover have been strengthened for increased service life.

Transmission Oil Pan

A new deeper oil pan is now being used in order to ensure that the oil pump suction pipe is at all times below the fluid level. An oil filter spacer is now being used on the transmission because of the deep oil pan.

Transmission Cooler and Line Cleaning

It is important that the cooler lines and the cooler are thoroughly flushed to remove any contaminated automatic transmission fluid before being completely re-connected to the transmission. If this precaution is not taken the transmission overhaul could be completely wasted. A small amount of thrust washer debris or burnt friction material will very rapidly spread throughout a transmission and torque converter.

Manual Level Cross Shaft Greasing

It is advisable to grease the manual valve lever cross shaft when installing the front servo cover. This is done to eliminate the possibility of the cross shaft corroding in the bore of the servo cover due to the ingress of salt and other foreign matter. It is essential that lithium based grease BB NO. 3 be used, as this type of grease is compatible with the rubber O-ring. Also it is important that the following procedure be used to apply the grease, in order to reduce the possibility of grease being forced past the O-ring and into the transmission.

1. Remove the front servo cover. After cleaning the cross shaft bore in the servo cover apply a small amount of grease into the cross shaft bore hole of the front servo cover.

2. Wipe off any excess grease from the front servo cover gasket face, it is important that this face be clean.

3. Install the gasket and replace the cover. Torque the front servo cover bolts 13 to 18 ft. lbs.

4. Remove any excess grease on the protruding end of the cross shaft.

Dimpled Thrust Washers in Torque Converter Assembly

In order to improve durability and stop the spinning of the bearing thrust race, all in service 11 inch torque converters are now using a dimpled bearing thrust race. The following is a list of improved torque converters incorporating this design change together with the old style torque converter that it replaces.

Torque Converter Modification

The torque converter has an increased spline size to accommodate the larger input shaft. The stator one-way clutch inner race has a revised profile adding to its increase in hardness. A Torrington race has been introduced into the impeller side of the stator, the impeller blades also have a rib formed in them giving them added strength. Six impeller blades are welded in two equally spaced places at the impeller shell to strengthen the assembly. The blower ring has been deleted and the converter mounting bosses are welded to the front cover.

Should this unit require repair, new and rebuilt units are available from parts supplier outlets.

Pressure Take Off Plug Improvement

In order to aid in the removal and installation of the pressure take off plug a new hexagon headed plug has been introduced which will replace the hexagon allen key head plug that is currently being used. The new plug can be installed in service if required in place of the old plug. When installing the new plug be sure that the torque is 6 to 8 ft. lbs. when the transmission is cold.

Kickdown 3-2 Flare Up Model 66 4.2 Series

Some model 66 automatic transmissions installed in the 4.2 series have a kickdown 3-2 flare up condition occurring at about 50 miles per hour. To correct this problem the front band adjustment must be checked and set to the correct setting. This adjustment is very important as misadjustment can cause this kickdown 3-2 problem. The procedure is as follows.

1. Loosen the locknut.
2. Adjust the square ended adjusting screw to 5 foot pounds.
3. Back off the adjusting screw ⅝ ths. of a turn.
4. Retighten the locknut to 35 ft. lbs. This will ensure that the adjusting screw will not turn.

If correct adjustment of the front band does not cure the problem, a modification in the form of a change to the servo orifice control valve spring should be done. The valve body assembly should be installed with a new spring Part Number 35-296 in place of the old spring Part Number 04-66-156-018F. The difference being that the new spring is 27.5 mm long and the old spring is 32.0 mm long.

REVISED TORQUE CONVERTER ASSEMBLIES

Old Style Torque Converter	Improved Torque Converter	Automatic Transmission
0466-511-049X (Ident. 6049)	0466-511-061C (Ident. 6061)	Model 66 4.2 Series
0466-511-055M (Ident. 6055)	0466-511-067H (Ident. 6067)	Model 66 3.4 Series

Automatic Transmission Fluid

Model 66 automatic transmissions are filled at the factory with type "G" automatic transmission fluid. The type "G" automatic transmission fluid is an improvement to the type "F" automatic tranmsmission fluid in that it has the capability of reducing oxi- dation at elevated temperatures. When transmissions are filled with type "G" automatic transmission fluid type "F" automatic transmission fluid can be used for topping off. The more type "F" automatic transmission fluid is used in the system, the more temperature will be reduced.

TROUBLE DIAGNOSIS

CLUTCH AND BAND APPLICATION CHART
Borg Warner Model 66

	Front Clutch	Rear Clutch	Front Band	Rear Band	One-Way Clutch
Drive 1st gear	Applied	—	—	—	Holding
Drive 2nd gear	Applied	—	Applied	—	—
Drive 3rd gear	Applied	Applied	—	—	—
1—Low gear	Applied	—	—	Applied	—
2—1st gear	Applied	—	—	—	Holding
2—2nd gear	Applied	—	Applied	—	—
Reverse gear	—	Applied	—	Applied	—

NOTE: Rear band is released in "N", but applied in "P" for constructional reasons only.

CHILTON'S THREE "C's" TRANSMISSION DIAGNOSIS CHART
Borg Warner Model 66

Condition	Cause	Correction
No starter action in "P" or "N"; Starter motor action in all other selector lever positions; Back-up lights inoperative.	a) Neutral safety switch out of adjustment or defective	a) Replace or adjust switch as needed
Excessive thump into "D", "1" or "R"	a) Engine idle too high b) Throttle cable out of adjustment c) Valves sticking in control valve body	a) Adjust idle speed b) Adjust or replace throttle cable c) Clean control valve body or replace it necessary
Vehicle moves with selector lever in "N"	a) Manual linkage out of adjustment b) Fault in front clutch support housing c) Fault in stator support shaft bearing d) Fault in forward sun gear shaft seals	a) Adjust manual linkage b) Replace front clutch support housing c) Replace stator support shaft bearing d) Replace forward sun gear shaft seals
Stall speed above specification and transmission grabs in selector lever position "1" and "R"	a) Throttle cable out of adjustment b) Filter clogged c) Valve body sticking d) Oil pump defect	a) Adjust or replace throttle cable b) Replace fluid and filter c) Clean valve body and replace fluid and filter d) Repair or replace oil pump

CHILTON'S THREE "C's" TRANSMISSION DIAGNOSIS CHART
Borg Warner Model 66

Condition	Cause	Correction
Grabs in position "1" only	a) Front clutch	a) Repair or replace front clutch
	b) Stator support shaft bearing	b) Replace stator support shaft bearing
Grabs in position "R" only	a) Rear band out of adjustment	a) Adjust rear band
	b) Rear servo gasket	b) Replace rear servo gasket
	c) Rear clutch	c) Repair or replace rear clutch
	d) Defect in rear brake band	d) Replace rear brake band
Stall speed below 1150 rpm	a) Torque converter bad	a) Replace torque converter
Heavy engagement of all selector lever positions except park	a) Manual linkage out of adjustment	a) Adjust manual linkage
Parking pawl does not hold vehicle	a) Manual linkage out of adjustment	a) Adjust manual linkage
	b) Parking lock linkage, pawl or gear faulty	b) Replace as needed
No drive in "D", "2", "1" or "R"	a) Fluid level low	a) Adjust fluid to proper level
	b) Manual linkage out of adjustment	b) Adjust manual linkage
	c) Throttle cable out of adjustment	c) Adjust throttle cable
No drive in selector position "D", "2" or "1"	a) Output shaft oil seals	a) Replace oil seals
	b) Governor pressure tube loose	b) Repair or replace tube
	c) Front clutch faulty	c) Replace front clutch
	d) Stator support shaft bearing faulty	d) Replace stator support shaft bearing
	e) Sun gear shaft seals	e) Replace sun gear shaft seals
No drive in "D" 1st gear	a) One-way clutch faulty	a) Replace one-way clutch
No drive in "D" 1st gear but moves in "1"	a) One-way clutch installed backwards	a) Install one-way clutch properly
No 2nd gear in position "D" or "2"	a) Front band out of adjustment	a) Adjust front band
	b) Front servo gasket	b) Replace front servo gasket
	c) Front servo tubes loose	c) Tighten or replace tubes
	d) Valve body sticking	d) Clean or replace valve body
No 3rd gear in position "D", "R" normal	a) Valve body sticking	a) Clean or replace valve body
	b) Governor sticking	b) Clean or replace governor
Slips in "D" 2nd gear	a) Front band out of adjustment	a) Adjust front band

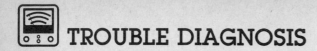

CHILTON'S THREE "C's" TRANSMISSION DIAGNOSIS CHART
Borg Warner Model 66

Condition	Cause	Correction
Slips in "D" of "1" 1st gear and "R"	a) Rear band out of adjustment	a) Adjust rear band
No engine braking in "1" and no movement in "R"	a) Rear band worn out or not adjusted b) Rear servo gasket faulty c) Rear servo pressure tubes loose	a) Adjust or replace rear band b) Replace rear servo gasket c) Repair or replace tubes
Faulty or sticky kickdown; faulty part-throttle shifts points	a) Throttle cable out of adjustment b) Filter clogged c) Oil pump and/or O-ring faulty d) Valves sticking e) Governor sticking f) Output shaft oil seals faulty g) Governor pressure tube leaks	a) Adjust throttle cable b) Replace fluid and filter c) Repair and/or replace pump or O-ring d) Clean or replace valve body e) Clean or replace governor f) Replace oil seals g) Repair or replace tube
Improper or hesitant kickdown and improper part throttle shift points	a) Throttle cable out of adjustment b) Valves sticking c) Oil pump faulty d) Vacuum leak at intake manifold e) Governor sticking g) Governor pressure tube loose	a) Adjust throttle cable b) Clean or replace valve body c) Repair or replace oil pump d) Replace intake manifold gasket e) Clean or replace governor g) Repair or replace tube
Improper 1-2 shift	a) Valves sticking	a) Clean or replace valve body
Improper 2-3 shift	a) Valves sticking	a) Clean or replace valve body
No upshift	a) Governor sticking b) Output shaft seals faulty c) Governor pressure tube loose	a) Clean or replace governor b) Replace seals c) Repair or replace tube
No "D" 3rd gear and "R" inoperative	a) Valves sticking b) Rear clutch pressure tube loose c) Faulty piston rings in intermediate shaft hub	a) Clean or replace valve body b) Repair or replace tube c) Replace piston rings
Reduced maximum speed in all gears and transmission is overheating	a) Torque converter one-way clutch locked, will not free wheel	a) Replace converter

CHILTON'S THREE "C's" TRANSMISSION DIAGNOSIS CHART
Borg Warner Model 66

Condition	Cause	Correction
Rough and delayed shifts	a) Throttle cable out of adjustment b) Sticking regulator valve c) Fluid intake filter clogged d) Oil pump faulty e) O-ring on pump pick-up pipe faulty	a) Adjust or replace throttle cable b) Clean or replace valve body c) Replace filter d) Repair or replace oil pump e) Replace O-ring
Engine races into and out of 2nd gear	a) Front brake band out of adjustment b) Front servo seals faulty or front servo tube loose c) Front brake band worn d) Valves sticking	a) Adjust front brake band b) Replace front servo seal and/or repair tube c) Replace band d) Clean valve body
Engine races as 2-3 and 3-2 shifts are occuring	a) Rear clutch feed tube leaks b) Rear clutch worn c) Rear clutch seal rings d) Valves sticking	a) Tighten or replace tube b) Replace rear clutch c) Replace seal rings d) Clean valve body
Whining when engine is running	a) Oil pump gears and/or converter bushing	a) Replace pump gears and/or converter bushing
Irregular noises from the gearbox but not in "D" 3rd gear	a) Planetary gearset broken	a) Replace broken parts
Whine for short time after starting vehicle, only when vehicle has sat 12 hours or more	a) Converter valve faulty—will not affect performance	a) Replace converter valve

DIAGNOSTIC TEST RESULTS CHART

Condition	Cause	Correction
Low control pressure	a) Low fluid level b) Manual valve out of adjustment c) Downshift cable out of adjustment d) Filter clogged e) Oil suction tube or O-ring faulty f) Oil pump faulty	a) Correct fluid level b) Adjust manual linkage c) Adjust cable d) Replace filter e) Replace pipe or O-ring f) Overhaul pump
High control pressure	a) Downshift cable out of adjustment b) Throttle or regulator valve sticking	a) Adjust cable b) Clean valve body

DIAGNOSTIC TEST RESULTS CHART

Condition	Cause	Correction
Stall rpm high in "1" and "R"	a) Downshift cable out of adjustment b) Valve sticking c) Filter clogged d) Suction or O-ring leaks e) Oil pump faulty	a) Adjust cable b) Clean the valve body c) Replace the filter d) Replace O-ring or suction tube e) Overhaul oil pump
Stall rpm high in "1" only	a) Front clutch support housing seals b) Forward sun gear shaft seals	a) Replace seals b) Replace seals
Stall rpm high in "R" only	a) Rear band worn or out of adjustment b) Rear servo piston seal or rear servo tube fit c) Rear clutch feed tube leaks d) Rear clutches worn or faulty sealing rings	a) Adjust band and/or replace if needed b) Replce seal or tube as needed c) Repair fit or replace tube d) Replace rear clutches or seal rings as needed
Stall rpms under 1,300 Road test vehicle		
Poor acceleration all speeds	a) Engine condition	a) Repair engine
Poor acceleration under 30 mph and normal over 30 mph	a) Converter one-way clutch slips	a) Replace converter
Shift speed off specification at kickdown	a) Downshift cable out of adjustment b) Governor valve sticking c) Output shaft rings or governor tube seals faulty	a) Adjust cable b) Clean or replace valve c) Replace as needed
Shift speed off 1-2 shift only	a) Valves sticking	a) Clean valve body
Shift speed off 2-3 shift only	a) Valves sticking	a) Clean valve body
No upshifts	a) Valves sticking b) Output shaft seal rings or governor shaft seal faulty	a) Clean valve body b) Replace as needed
No upshift and no reverse	a) Valves sticking	a) Clean valve body
Reduces maximum shift in all ratios and converter overheats reduced top speed to approximately 50 MPH	a) Converter one-way clutch seized	a) Replace converter

Hydraulic Control System

In diagnosing automatic transmission problems it is helpful to have a better understanding of the hydraulic control system. The hydraulic control system consists of a valve body, oil pump, clutch and band apply passages and pistons, and the governor. The gear ratio of the automatic transmission is determined by the planetary gear units which are controlled by the clutches and bands.

Major components

PUMP

The impeller of the torque converter drives the oil pump, which is an internal/external gear type unit, whenever the engine is running. The pump takes transmission fluid from the oil pan, through a strainer, and delivers it under pressure to the hydraulic system.

GOVERNOR

The governor is mounted on the output (driven) shaft and revolves with the output shaft whenever the vehicle is in motion. Governor movement speed varies directly with the speed of the vehicle. The centrifugal force of the governor rotation controls the two governor valve ports. These ports are connected to the system by passages drilled into the shaft. Automatic transmission fluid enters one port, at line pressure, from the manual valve and returns to the shift valves at governor pressure through the second port. The governor pressure increases as the speed of the vehicle increases.

VALVE BODY

The valve body incorporates the pressure regulator system, the flow control system and check valves. This unit controls the automatic up and down shifting, kickdown shifts and manual shifts.

Contained in the valve body are the secondary regulator valve, downshift valve, primary regulator valve, manual valve, both the 1-2 and 2-3 shift valves, servo orifice control valve, throttle valve and the modulator plug and valve.

CONTROL PRESSURE

Test

Before pressure testing check the fluid and adjust to the proper level. Also, check and adjust the throttle linkage.
1. Attach a tachometer to the engine.
2. Raise the vehicle and support it safely.
3. Connect a pressure gauge to the main control pressure port.
4. Check the pressure in "D" and at idle speed.
5. Leave the gauges connected and lower the vehicle.
6. While operating the vehicle on level ground, check the main control pressure at kickdown.
7. Road test and record shift speed points and compare to specifications.

DIAGNOSIS TESTS

Stall Test

With all four wheels blocked, both foot and hand brake applied, and test gauges attached, place the selector lever in "D" and depress the accelerator to the floor. Record the highest rpm and compare the results to the figures below.

RPM	Condition
Under 1300	Stator free wheel spin
1950 to 2100	Normal
Over 2500	Clutch slip

Repeat the stall test in "1" and "R" and record the results for comparison with the above information. Be sure not to exceed ten seconds per stall test and always run the engine at approximately 1000 rpm in "N" between tests to cool the transmission.

Air Pressure Test

If internal fluid pressure leakage or clutch and band problems are indicated, the problems can be pinpointed by air pressure testing.
1. Raise the vehicle and support it safely.
2. Drain the transmission fluid and remove the pan.
3. Remove the fluid pressure tubes and using reduced com-

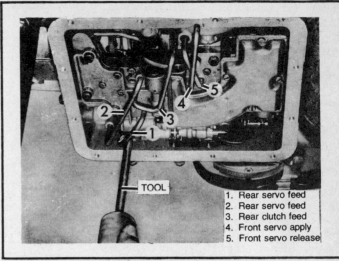

1.	Rear servo feed
2.	Rear servo feed
3.	Rear clutch feed
4.	Front servo apply
5.	Front servo release

Oil delivery tube removal with pulling tool (©Borg Warner)

pressed air (approximately 25 psi) apply the air at the pressure holes and listen for leakage and the movement of the elements.
4. Remove the extension housing and air test at the 3 holes in the rear transmission cover.

Road Test

Road testing should follow the complete procedure detailed below. The automatic transmission should be at normal working operative temperature. Refer to the Gear Change Speeds chart for any appropriate testing information.
1. With the brakes applied and the engine idling, move the automatic transmission selector lever from "N" to "R", then from "N" to "D", then from "N" to "2" and finally, from "N" to "1". Be sure that engagement is felt with each gear selection.
2. Check the stall speed.
3. Place the selector lever in "D" and accelerate with minimum throttle opening to check the speed of the first gear to second gear shift.
4. Continue with minimum throttle and check the speed of the second gear to third gear shift.
5. Once again, place the selector lever in "D" and accelerate with maximum throttle opening (kickdown) to check the speed of the first gear to second gear shift.
6. Continue with maximum throttle and check the speed of the second gear to the third gear shift.
7. Check for kickdown shift from third gear to second gear.
8. Check for kickdown shift from second gear to first gear.
9. Check for kickdown shift from third gear to first gear.
10. Check for (roll-out) downshift with minimum throttle from second gear to first gear.
11. Check for part throttle downshift from third gear to second gear.

Should a problem be apparent during the road test, refer to Chiltons three C's Diagnosis Chart.

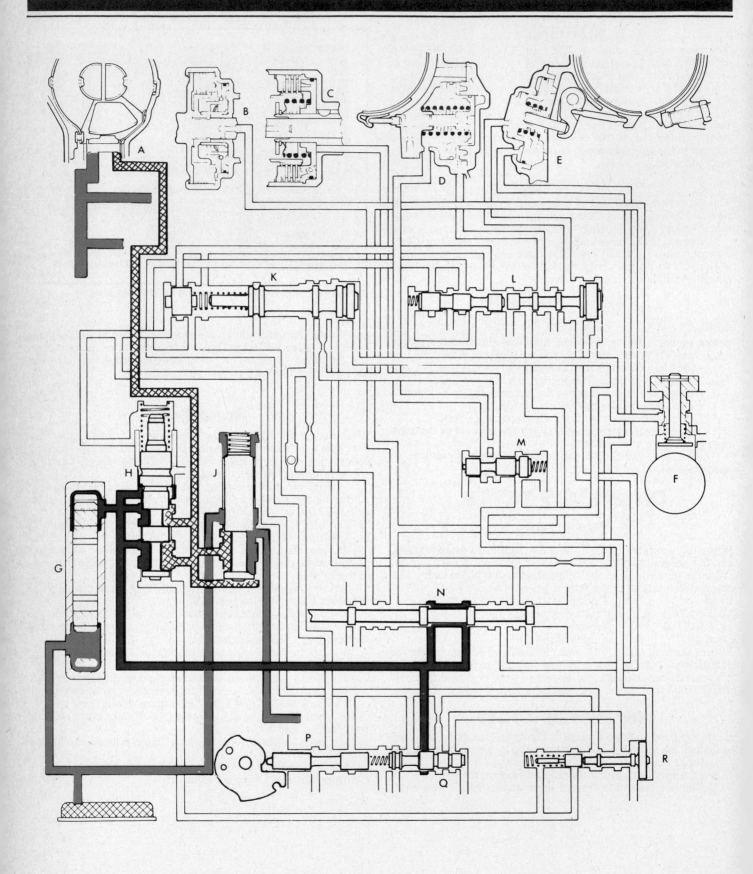

Neutral

Neutral

UNITS APPLIED—NONE

The selector lever is in Neutral and the engine speed is at idle. The foot brake is applied and the vehicle is at rest.

PRESSURE SUPPLY SYSTEM

The oil pump (G) is supplying fluid pressure to the primary regulator valve (H), the manual valve (N) and the throttle valve (Q).

PRESSURE REGULATING SYSTEM

The primary regulator valve (H) is controlling the pressure valve of line pressure and supplying the secondary regulator valve (J). The secondary regulator valve (J) is directing pressure to the converter (A) and the lubrication circuits. The secondary regulator valve (J) also acts as a high pressure relief valve for the system.

FLOW CONTROL SYSTEM

None of the flow control valves are operating in Neutral.

CLUTCH AND BAND SERVO SYSTEM

No clutches or bands are applied in Neutral.

A. Torque converter
B. Front clutch
C. Rear clutch
D. Front servo
E. Rear servo
F. Governor
G. Pump
H. Primary regulator valve

J. Secondary regulator valve
K. 2-3 shift valve
L. 1-2 shift valve
M. Servo orifice control valve
N. Manual valve
P. Downshift valve
Q. Throttle valve
R. Modulator valve

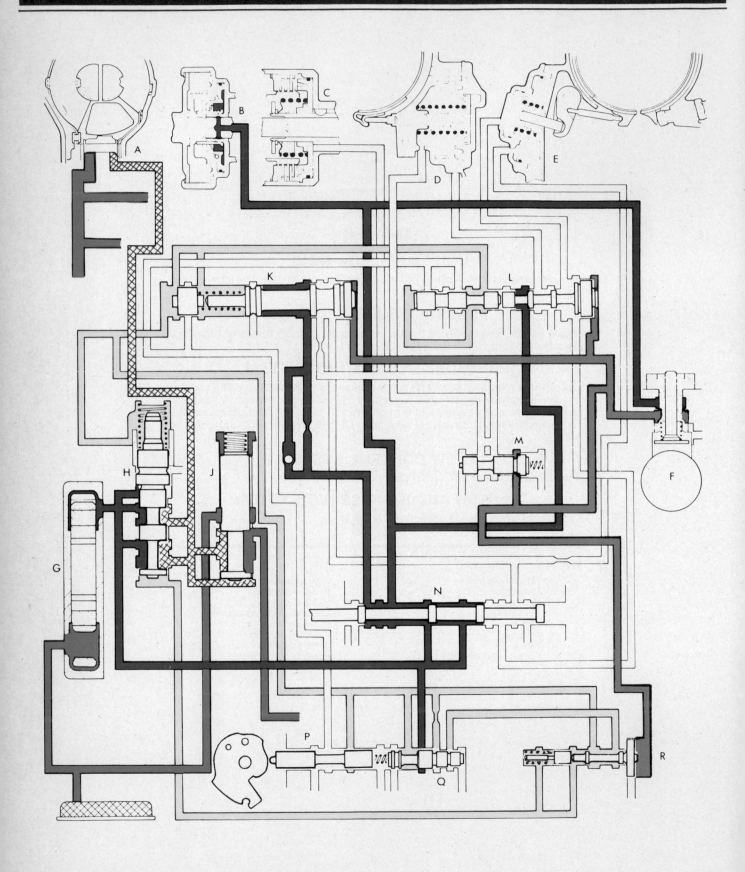

Drive—First Gear

Drive—1st Gear

Units Applied—Front Clutch, One-Way Clutch

The selector lever is in "D", the vehicle speed is less than 8 mph and engine speed is at half throttle.

PRESSURE SUPPLY SYSTEM

The oil pump (G) is supplying fluid pressure to the primary regulator valve (H) and the manual valve (N). The oil pump (G) also supplies fluid directly the throttle valve (Q).

PRESSURE REGULATING SYSTEM

The primary regulator valve (H) is controlling line pressure and supplying pressure to the secondary regulator valve (J). The secondary regulator valve (J) acts as a pressure relief valve and supplies pressure to the converter (A) and lubrication circuits.

FLOW CONTROL SYSTEM

The manual valve (N) is supplying pressure to the 1-2 shift valve (L), the 2-3 shift valve, the front clutch (B) and the governor (F).

The governor (F) is supplying pressure to the 1-2 shift valve (L), the 2-3 shift valve (K), the servo orifice control valve (M) and the modulator valve (R).

The throttle valve (Q) is directing pressure to the modulator valve (R), the primary regulator valve (H), the 1-2 shift valve (L) and the 2-3 shift valve (K).

The throttle and governor pressures are acting on the shift valves to control subsequent upshifts and downshifts.

CLUTCH AND BAND SERVO SYSTEM

In Drive 1st gear, the front clutch (D) is applied by the manual valve and the one-way clutch is holding.

A. Torque converter
B. Front clutch
C. Rear clutch
D. Front servo
E. Rear servo
F. Governor
G. Pump
H. Primary regulator valve

J. Secondary regulator valve
K. 2-3 shift valve
L. 1-2 shift valve
M. Servo orifice control valve
N. Manual valve
P. Downshift valve
Q. Throttle valve
R. Modulator valve

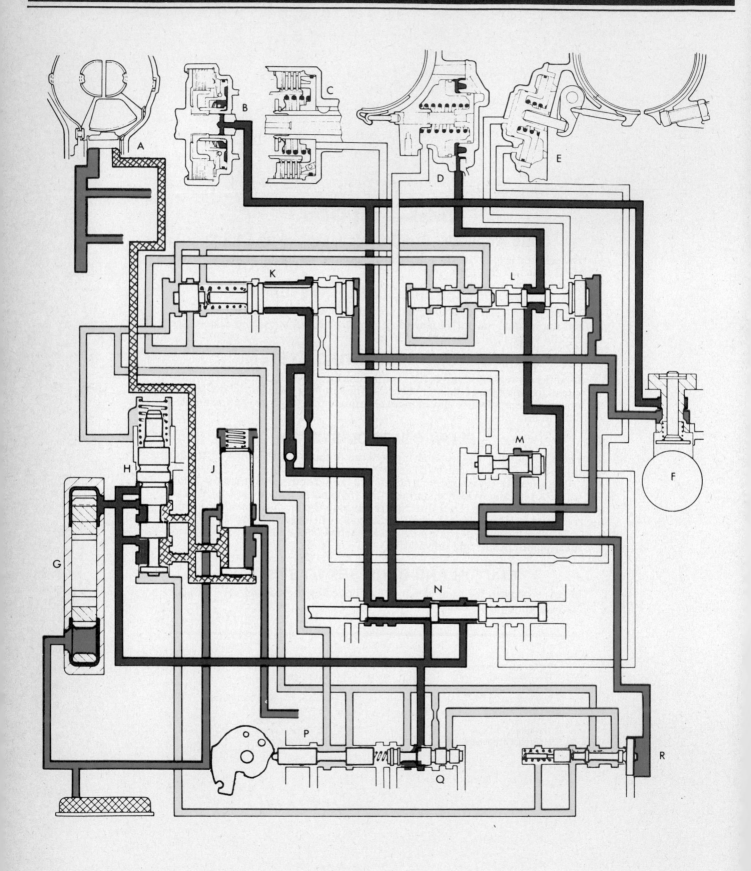

Drive—Second Gear

Drive—2nd Gear

UNITS APPLIED—FRONT CLUTCH, FRONT BAND

The selector lever is in Drive and the vehicle is traveling between 25-34 MPH with engine speed at half throttle.

PRESSURE SUPPLY SYSTEM

The oil pump (G) is supplying fluid pressure to the primary regulator valve (H) and the manual valve (N). The oil pump (G) is also supplying fluid directly to the throttle valve (Q).

PRESSURE REGULATING SYSTEM

The primary regulator valve (H) is controlling line pressure and supplying pressure to the secondary regulator valve (J). The secondary regulator valve also acts as a pressure relief valve and supplies fluid to the torque converter (A) and the lubrication circuits.

FLOW CONTROL SYSTEM

The manual valve (N) is directing pressure to the 2-3 shift valve (K). Also, the manual valve (N) is directing pressure to the 1-2 shift valve (L), the front clutch (B) and the governor (F). Governor pressure is present at the modulator valve (R), the servo orifice control valve (M), 1-2 shift valve (L), and the 2-3 shift valve (K). Throttle pressure is present at the modulator valve (R), both ends of the primary regulator valve (H), the downshift valve (P), the 1-2 shift valve (L) and the 2-3 shift valve (K). The governor pressure has overcome throttle pressure at the 1-2 shift valve (L) and moved it to open a passage to the apply side of the front servo (E).

CLUTCH AND BAND SERVO SYSTEM

The transmission is in Drive 2nd gear with the front clutch (B) and the front band (D) applied.

A. Torque converter
B. Front clutch
C. Rear clutch
D. Front servo
E. Rear servo
F. Governor
G. Pump
H. Primary regulator valve

J. Secondary regulator valve
K. 2-3 shift valve
L. 1-2 shift valve
M. Servo orifice control valve
N. Manual valve
P. Downshift valve
Q. Throttle valve
R. Modulator valve

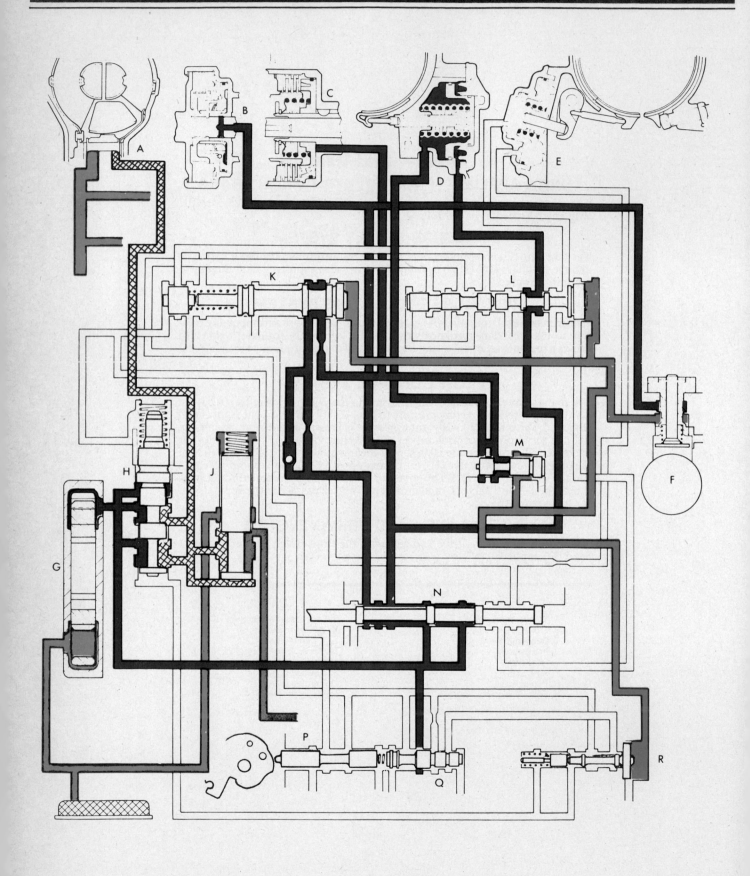

Drive—Third Gear

Drive-3rd Gear

UNITS APPLIED—FRONT CLUTCH, REAR CLUTCH

The selector lever is in "D" position and the vehicle speed is between 33-49 MPH. Also, the engine speed is at half throttle.

PRESSURE SUPPLY SYSTEM

The oil pump (G) is supplying fluid pressure to the primary regulator valve (H) and the manual valve (N). The oil pump (G) also supplies fluid to the throttle valve (Q).

PRESSURE REGULATING SYSTEM

The primary regulator valve (H) is controlling line pressure and supplying pressure to the secondary regulator valve (J). The secondary regulator valve (J) acts as a pressure relief valve and supplies pressure to the converter (A) and the lubrication circuits.

FLOW CONTROL SYSTEM

The manual valve (N) is directing pressure to the 1-2 shift valve (L), the 2-3 shift valve (K), the front clutch (B) and the governor (F).

Governor pressure is present at the modulator valve (R), the servo orifice control valve (M), the 1-2 shift valve (L) and the 2-3 shift valve (K).

Although throttle pressure is not shown in this drawing, it is present at both ends of the primary regulator valve (H), the modulator valve (R), the downshift valve (P), the 1-2 shift valve (L) and the 2-3 shift valve (K). Throttle pressure is at a minimum and has been overcome by governor pressure at the 2-3 shift valve (K). This opens a passage from the 2-3 shift valve (K) to the orifice control valve (M) and the rear clutch (C). The filling of the large release cavity on the front servo (D) occurs before and times the application of the rear clutch (C) after the release of the front band (D) to avoid tie-up of both 2nd and 3rd gears. The orifice restricts the pressure build-up for a few seconds to soften the release and application of the front band (D) and rear clutch (C).

CLUTCH AND BAND SERVO SYSTEM

The front clutch (B) and the rear clutch (C) are applied in drive 3rd gear. There are no accumulator pistons in the Model 66; however, the release cavity on the front servo (D) is used in connection with the servo orifice control valve for the same purpose as an accumulator.

A. Torque converter
B. Front clutch
C. Rear clutch
D. Front servo
E. Rear servo
F. Governor
G. Pump
H. Primary regulator valve

J. Secondary regulator valve
K. 2-3 shift valve
L. 1-2 shift valve
M. Servo orifice control valve
N. Manual valve
P. Downshift valve
Q. Throttle valve
R. Modulator valve

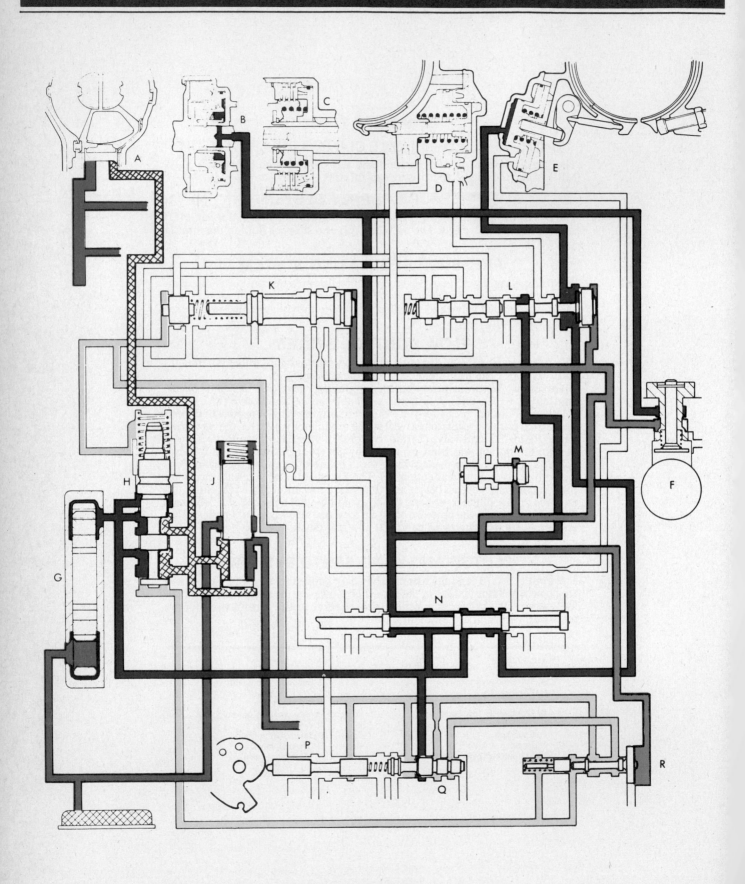

Manual 1—First Gear

Manual 1—1st Gear

UNITS APPLIED—FRONT CLUTCH, REAR BAND

The selector lever is in "1" position and the vehicle is starting to move.

PRESSURE SUPPLY SYSTEM

The oil pump (G) is supplying fluid pressure to the primary regulator valve (H), the manual valve (N) and the throttle valve (Q).

PRESSURE REGULATING SYSTEM

The primary regulator valve (H) is supplying pressure to the secondary regulator valve (J) and the secondary regulator valve (J) is directing pressure to the torque converter (A) and lubrication circuits. The secondary regulator valve (J) also acts as a high pressure relief valve for the system.

FLOW CONTROL SYSTEM

The manual valve (N) is directing pressure to the 1-2 shift valve (L). The manual valve (N) is also supplying pressure to the front clutch (B), the governor (F) and another land on the 1-2 shift valve (L). The two pressures on the 1-2 shift valve (L) including pressure on the wider land opposing governor pressure, lock out upshifts. The 1-2 shift valve (L) has an apply passage open to the rear servo (E).

CLUTCH AND BAND SERVO SYSTEM

With the front clutch (B) and rear servo (E) applied the transmission is in "1"—low gear.

A. Torque converter	J. Secondary regulator valve
B. Front clutch	K. 2-3 shift valve
C. Rear clutch	L. 1-2 shift valve
D. Front servo	M. Servo orifice control valve
E. Rear servo	N. Manual valve
F. Governor	P. Downshift valve
G. Pump	Q. Throttle valve
H. Primary regulator valve	R. Modulator valve

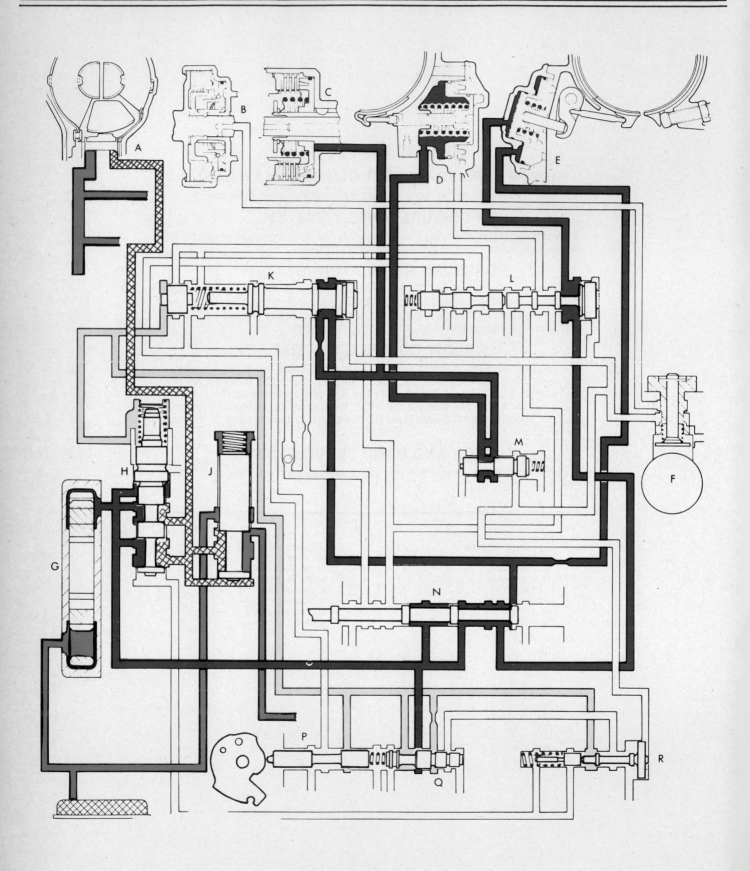

Reverse

Reverse

UNITS APPLIED—REAR CLUTCH, FRONT BAND

The selector lever is in Reverse and the engine speed is at idle. It is assumed that the foot brake is applied.

PRESSURE SUPPLY SYSTEM

The oil pump (G) is supplying fluid pressure to the primary regulator valve (H), the manual valve (N) and the throttle valve (Q).

PRESSURE REGULATING SYSTEM

The primary regulator valve (H) is controlling line pressure and supplying the secondary regulator valve (J). The secondary regulator valve (J) is directing pressure to the torque converter (A) and the lubrication circuits. The secondary regulator valve also acts as a high pressure relief valve for the system.

FLOW CONTROL SYSTEM

The manual valve (N) is directing pressure ot the 2-3 shift valve (K), the release side of the rear servo (E) and the 1-2 shift valve (L). The 2-3 shift valve (K) is supplying pressure to the orifice control valve (M) and the rear clutch (C). The servo orifice control valve (M) is supplying pressure to the front servo apply (D). There is no governor pressure in Reverse. Throttle pressure is directed to the modulator valve (R), the 2-3 shift valve (K) and the increase end of the primary regulator valve (H). This means that the primary regulator valve (H) is controlling line pressure to a higher level to compensate for the greater torque in Reverse.

CLUTCH AND BAND SERVO SYSTEM

The rear servo is not applied since both the apply and release side of the servo are pressurized. The front servo is applying the band and the rear clutch is applied. This means that the transmission is in Reverse gear.

A. Torque converter
B. Front clutch
C. Rear clutch
D. Front servo
E. Rear servo
F. Governor
G. Pump
H. Primary regulator valve

J. Secondary regulator valve
K. 2-3 shift valve
L. 1-2 shift valve
M. Servo orifice control valve
N. Manual valve
P. Downshift valve
Q. Throttle valve
R. Modulator valve

PRND ON CAR SERVICES

ADJUSTMENTS
Throttle Linkage

Adjustment

Install a pressure gauge to the control pressure port on the automatic transmission case. It may be necessary to lift the carpet and remove the access plate in order to remove the plug from the transmission case. There is a bracket between the transmission case and the rear mount. Do not remove this bracket, use the hole in the bracket to reach the port.

1. Bring the engine to normal operating temperature.
2. Block all four wheels. Apply the hand and foot brakes.
3. Move the selector into the "D" position and check the pressure to 60-75 psi at idle.
4. Increase the engine speed to 1200 rpm and check the pressure to 75-115 psi.

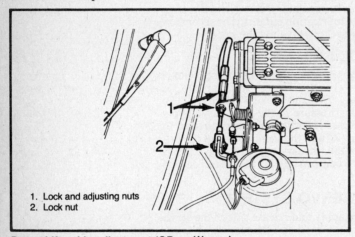

1. Lock and adjusting nuts
2. Lock nut

Downshift cable adjustment (©Borg Warner)

5. If the pressures do not agree with the specifications above, adjust the downshift cable as follows.
6. Shut the engine off and put the selector lever in "N".
7. Loosen the locknut on the downshift cable.
8. Using the adjuster nut on the outer cable, adjust the length of the cable to alter the pressure. Increase the cable length to increase the pressure and decrease the cable length to decrease the pressure.
9. The ferrule on the inner cable should be .010 inch from the threaded end of the outer cable. Lock the locknut.
10. Remove the pressure gauge and replace the plug.
11. Replace the access plate and carpeting as required.
12. Check the fluid level and road test the vehicle.

Front and Rear Band

Adjustment

Both the front and rear band adjustment should be checked and adjusted after 1,000 miles on a new vehicle and every 15,000 miles thereafter. It may be necessary to remove the access plate in the left footwell in order to reach the front band.

1. Loosen the locknut on the adjuster screw.
2. Back off the adjuster screw 2 or 3 turns.
3. Torque the adjuster screw to 5 ft. lbs. and back off ¾ of a turn.
4. Hold the adjuster screw and torque the locknut to 35 ft. lbs.

Manual Linkage

Adjustment

1. Remove the console cover.
2. Take off the split pin and washer securing the cable to the lever and detach the cable.
3. Place the selector lever in "1" and the lever on the transmission in the "1" position.
4. Adjust the lock nuts on the holding bracket at the console until the cable can be connected to the selector lever without moving the lever.
5. Tighten the lock nuts and secure the cable with a new split pin.
6. Replace the console cover.

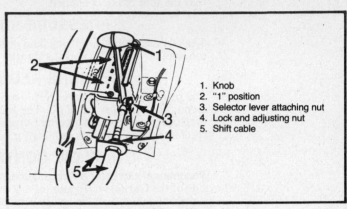

1. Knob
2. "1" position
3. Selector lever attaching nut
4. Lock and adjusting nut
5. Shift cable

Manual linkage adjustment (©Borg Warner)

Neutral Safety Switch

Adjustment

1. Disconnect the battery.
2. Remove the gearshift knob.
3. Pry the electric window switch from the center console. Do not disconnect the window switches.
4. Remove the 2 screws and lift the lettered selector panel to gain access to the cigar lighter and door switch terminals.
5. Disconnect the door lock and cigar lighter terminals and remove the selector panel.
6. Remove the positive connector from the safety switch.

NOTE: The safety switch is grounded.

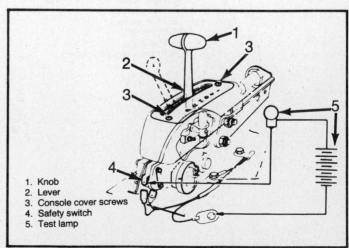

1. Knob
2. Lever
3. Console cover screws
4. Safety switch
5. Test lamp

Neutral safety switch adjustment (©Borg Warner)

7. Connect a test lamp in series with a battery and the safety switch.

8. Place the selector lever in "N" and loosen the lock nut on the safety switch.

9. Move the switch until the test lamp lights.

10. Tighten the lock nut and check to see if the light is on in "P" and off in the other positions.

11. Disconnect the test lamp, and connect the position wire to the switch.

12. Connect the cigar lighter and door lock switches.

13. Refit the selector cover panel.

14. Install the window switch and gearshift knob.

15. Connect the battery cable.

16. Check the operation of the windows, cigar lighter and door locks.

SERVICES

Throttle Linkage

Removal and Installation

1. Remove the automatic transmission pan from the transmission assembly. Disconnect the cable from the downshift cam.

2. Position cable removal tool CWB-62 or equivalent on the plastic ferrule, push upwards until ferrule, together with cable, is pressed out of the transmission case.

3. Remove the split pin, washer and clevis pin securing clevis to throttle linkage; discard the split pin.

4. Loosen the lock nut and withdraw the downshift cable.

5. Place new O-ring on plastic ferrule.

6. Lubricate the ferrule with fresh transmission fluid.

—————————— CAUTION ——————————
Do not lubricate inner cable.

7. Press the ferrule into the case and connect the cable to the cam.

8. Connect the clevis to the throttle linkage; use a new split pin.

9. With accelerator pedal released and throttle levers resting on idle screws adjust cable until heel of downshift cam just makes contact with downshift valve.

10. With accelerator pedal depressed check that the lobe of the cam fully depresses the downshift valve.

11. Install pan and gasket on case.

12. Refill transmission with fluid.

13. Check and adjust throttle pressure if necessary.

Fluid Change Interval

For normal service vehicles every 24,000 miles is sufficient for changing the automatic transmission fluid and filter. For severe service vehicles a shorter service interval should be used.

1. Raise and support the vehicle safely.

2. Drain the automatic transmission fluid.

3. Remove the automatic transmission pan.

4. Remove the oil filter attaching bolts and remove the filter from the transmission assembly.

5. After cleaning the pan to transmission mating surfaces install a new oil filter.

6. Using a new transmission pan gasket install the transmission pan.

7. Fill the automatic transmission with three quarts of the proper type of automatic transmission fluid. Be sure to check the fluid level on the dipstick.

8. Start the engine and bring the transmission to normal operating temperature, then check the fluid level and correct as required.

Valve Body

Removal and Installation

1. Move the selector lever to the "P" position. Raise and support the vehicle on a hoist.

2. Drain the automatic transmission and remove the pan.

3. Disconnect the downshift cable from the cam.

4. Using a suitable and safe tool, pry the tubes from the transmission. Be careful not to damage these tubes.

5. Take note of the placement of the magnet and remove it.

6. Remove the valve body to casing bolts.

7. Remove the valve body using care not to drop the manual valve.

NOTE: Extreme care must be taken to be sure that the removal of the valve body does not damage the torque converter feed, pump feed or pump outlet pipes.

8. When installing the valve body in the transmission case be sure that the tubes are correctly located in the valve body. The valve body may be tapped gently with a soft mallet to be sure that correct location is obtained.

9. Align the pin on the detent lever so that it engages with the groove machined in the manual valve.

10. Install the valve body retaining bolts. Be sure that the shortest bolt is installed in front.

11. Reconnect the kickdown cable to the cam.

12. Install the transmission oil pan using a new pan gasket.

13. Fill the transmission with the proper type transmission fluid to the "MAX" mark on the transmission dipstick. Run the engine until it reaches normal operating temperature and adjust the fluid level as required.

14. Lower the vehicle and road test.

Front Servo

Removal and Installation

1. Drain the automatic transmission and remove the pan.

2. Remove the valve body.

3. Remove the servo assembly along with the push rod and spring. Discard the servo cover gasket.

4. The brake band strut may fall out, if so, recover it.

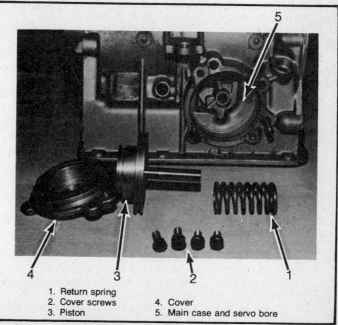

1. Return spring
2. Cover screws
3. Piston
4. Cover
5. Main case and servo bore

Front servo exploded view (©Borg Warner)

5. Using petroleum jelly, install a new gasket on the servo body. Set the strut in position on the brake band.

6. Insert the push rod and spring into the case and make sure that the strut is in the slot in the end of the push rod.

7. Install the servo cover bolts and torque them to 19 ft. lbs.

8. Install the valve body and adjust the brake band.

9. Install the transmission pan. Fill the transmission with the proper type of automatic transmission fluid. Road test and adjust as required.

Rear Servo

Removal and Installation

1. Drain the automatic transmission and remove the transmission oil pan. Remove the valve body assembly.

2. Remove the nuts and bolts securing the intermediate exhaust pipe to the front pipe.

3. Separate intermediate pipe from front pipe and remove and discard the gasket.

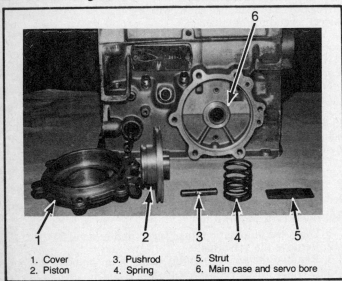

| 1. Cover | 3. Pushrod | 5. Strut |
| 2. Piston | 4. Spring | 6. Main case and servo bore |

Rear servo exploded view (©Borg Warner)

4. Remove screws and special washers securing left hand heat shield to vehicle body; withdraw the heat shield.

5. Remove the bolt and spring washer securing the gear shift cable connecting block to the mounting bracket.

6. Remove the self-locking nut holding the selector lever to the selector shaft. Withdraw the lever and selector cable assembly.

7. Mark the position of the rear servo to the transmission case.

8. Remove the rear servo attaching bolts and withdraw the servo, push rod and spring. Recover the brake band strut, should it fall out.

9. To install, position a new gasket on the rear servo body with petroleum jelly.

10. Position the brake band strut in the case.

11. Install the rear servo attaching bolts and torque them to 19 ft. lbs.

12. Install the selector cable and attach the cable to the lever with the self locking nut.

13. Attach the shift cable connecting block to the mounting bracket with bolt and spring washer.

14. Install the heat shield on the left-hand side of the body.

15. Position the front exhaust pipe into the intermediate pipe using heat resistant sealer on the gasket.

16. Install the bolts and nuts on the exhaust and tighten them.

17. Install the valve body and pan with new gasket.

18. Adjust the rear band and fill the transmission with fluid.

Governor

Removal and Installation

1. Remove rear extension housing.

2. Slide speedometer drive gear off output shaft.

3. Move selector lever to "N".

4. Rotate the output shaft to a position from which the governor securing plug can be removed.

5. Note the fitted position of the governor and remove the plug.

6. Slide the governor off the output shaft.

7. Depress the governor weight and remove the snap ring.

8. Take the stem, spring and valve from the governor body.

9. Replace parts as needed.

10. Install the valve, spring and stem into the governor body.

11. Depress the governor weight and install the snap ring.

12. Slide the governor on the output shaft, aligning the blind hole on the shaft.

13. Install the securing plug and spring washer. Make sure that the end of the plug enters the blind hole in the output shaft.

14. Torque the plug to 16.5 ft. lbs.

15. Slide the speedometer drive gear on the output shaft.

16. Install the extension housing and check the fluid level.

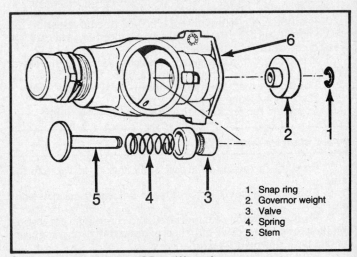

1. Snap ring
2. Governor weight
3. Valve
4. Spring
5. Stem

Governor exploded view (©Borg Warner)

Rear Extension Housing

Removal and Installation

1. Disconnect the battery cables.

2. Set the engine lifting hook tool through the engine support bracket and the rear engine lifting eyelet.

3. Remove the center mounting nut from the rear support. Take off the nuts and washers from the front end of the strengthening plate.

4. Unfasten the heat shield.

5. Position a jack to support the engine mounting and remove the bolts.

6. Lower the jack and remove the mounting.

7. Remove the bolts securing the support plate to the floor pan.

8. Remove the bolts and nuts fastening the drive shaft to output flange.

9. Lower the engine slightly. Be careful not to damage the heater control valve.

10. Place the transmission selector lever in "P".

11. Remove the output flange center bolt and take off the output flange.

12. Disconnect the speedometer right angle drive. Remove the driven gear plate and the driven gear.

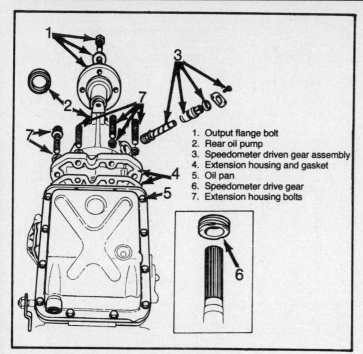

1. Output flange bolt
2. Rear oil pump
3. Speedometer driven gear assembly
4. Extension housing and gasket
5. Oil pan
6. Speedometer drive gear
7. Extension housing bolts

Rear extension housing exploded view (©Borg Warner)

13. Remove the selector cable mounting bracket.

14. Note the location of the stud type bolts and then remove all of the extension housing to case bolts.

15. Withdraw the extension housing and remove the gasket.

16. Pry the rear oil seal out of the extension housing and install a new one.

17. Using a new gasket install the extension housing and the selector cable mounting bracket on the transmission case.

18. Torque the extension to case bolts to 42.5 ft. lbs.

19. Secure the selector cable connect block to the mounting bracket.

20. Replace the speedometer driven gear O-ring and install the driven gear and plate.

21. Connect the speedometer cable and right angle drive.

22. Install the output flange and torque the center bolt to 40-50 ft. lbs.

23. Raise the engine slightly on the support tool.

24. Refasten the drive shaft to the output flange.

25. Fasten rear engine mounting support to transmission tunnel.

26. Use the bolts and special washers to secure the rear engine mounting support plate to the floor pan.

27. Position a jack to support the rear engine mount in place and install the attaching bolts.

28. Install the center mounting nut on the rear engine mount.

29. Remove the engine lifting tool from the engine compartment.

30. Connect the battery.

31. Check the fluid level.

REMOVAL & INSTALLATION

Transmission Assembly

Removal

1. Position the vehicle on a hoist and support it safely. Disconnect the battery.

2. Remove the dipstick from the dipstick tube and remove the bolt holding the dipstick tube to the manifold.

3. Remove the bolts holding the upper fan cowl to the lower fan cowl. Slacken the bolts securing the cowl bracket to the radiator in order to facilitate the removal of the top cowl.

4. Remove and discard the split pin securing the kickdown cable to the throttle bellcrank, withdraw the clevis pin and washer; slacken the locknut and disconnect the cable.

5. Remove the union nut holding the dipstick tube to the transmission oil pan. Remove the dipstick tube. Drain the transmission fluid.

6. Disconnect the exhaust system. Remove the exhaust heat shields from the floor pan.

7. Position the transmission jack to the automatic transmission.

8. Remove the bolts securing the crash plate to the automatic transmission case studs. Remove the nut securing the crash plate to the rear mounting bolt.

9. Remove the bolts, spacers and washers securing the rear engine mounting to the floor pan.

10. Remove the bolts holding the driveshaft tunnel spreader plate to the floor pan.

11. Position the engine support bracket and locate the hook at the engine rear lifting eye. Turn the adjusting nut to take the weight of the engine. Be sure not to damage the heater control valve.

12. Remove the rubber pad from the top of the transmission.

13. Remove the nut holding the selector lever bellcrank to the cross shaft and remove the bellcrank.

14. Remove the bolt securing the selector cable trunnion to the mounting bracket.

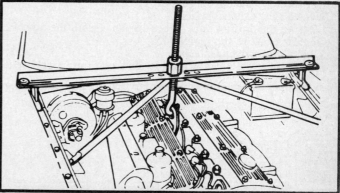

Engine support tool (©Borg Warner)

15. Remove the bolts securing the tie plate to the engine oil pan and transmission converter housing front cover plate. Remove the cover plate.

16. Rotate the engine until a torque converter securing bolt is accessible; knock back the lock tab and remove the bolt; repeat this procedure for the three remaining torque converter securing bolts.

17. Remove and discard the tab washers.

18. Remove the bolt and washer securing the breather pipe clip.

19. Remove the screw securing the oil cooler pipe clamp plate to the sump bracket.

20. Disconnect the transmission oil lines and breather pipes from the transmission case.

21. Disconnect the speedometer cable from the drive pinion. Disconnect the electrical wires from the starter and solenoid.

22. Be sure that the transmission is secured to the transmission jack.

23. Remove the nut, bolts and washers securing the torque converter housing to the engine block. Remove the starter and spacer.

24. Lower the transmission jack and carefully remove the auto-

matic transmission from the vehicle.

25. Remove the torque converter from the input shaft.

Installation

1. Install the torque converter to the input shaft. Be sure that the torque converter is correctly engaged on the input shaft spline.

2. Position and secure the automatic transmission on the transmission jack.

3. Install the rubber pad on top of the transmission unit. Raise the transmission unit and install it in its proper place. Install the bolts securing the torque converter housing to the engine. Do not tighten these bolts until the starter and spacer have been installed.

4. Align the torque converter to drive plate holes with new tab washers. Do not tighten until all four bolts are installed. Be sure to bend over the tab washers.

5. Reconnect the electrical connections to the starter and solenoid. Install the oil cooler lines to the transmission. Install the breather pipe.

6. Install the torque converter front cover, and the tie plate between the engine oil pan and the torque converter housing.

7. Install the driveshaft.

8. Install the gear selector bellcrank to the cross shaft. Secure and align the gear selector lever trunnion to the mounting plate.

9. Reconnect the speedometer cable to the drive pinion.

10. Install the driveshaft tunnel spreader plate, exhaust heat shield and the rear engine mounting.

11. Install the crash plate and secure the bolts to the transmission case studs.

12. Remove the transmission jack from the transmission assembly. Remove the engine support bracket.

13. Install the exhaust system.

14. Install the dipstick tube to the oil pan. Install the dipstick tube securing bolt to the manifold.

15. Install the upper fan cowl.

16. Reconnect the kickdown cable. Be sure to use a new split pin and adjust as required.

17. Refill the automatic transmission with the proper type automatic transmission fluid. Road test and adjust as required.

BENCH OVERHAUL

Before Disassembly

Thoroughly clean the transmission before teardown and maintain a high standard of cleanliness during all transmission repair work. Use lint free rags. Install new gaskets and O-rings. Clean all metal parts with industrial solvent and lubricate them with transmission fluid before installation.

Soak new clutches in clean transmission fluid before installing them.

Converter Inspection

Check the converter by doing the stall test and road test on the vehicle.

The converter is a sealed unit and must be replaced as a unit.

Transmission

Disassembly

1. Remove the torque converter housing bolts. Lift the converter housing from the transmission.

2. Remove the dipstick tube and drain the transmission fluid,

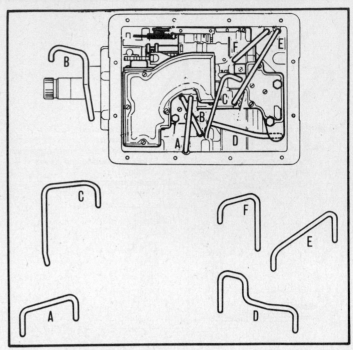

Oil pressure tube location (©Borg Warner)

if not previously done.

3. Invert the automatic transmission and position the selector in the "P" mode.

4. Remove the speedometer driven gear housing and the driven gear.

5. Take off the bolt securing the output flange and remove the flange.

6. Remove the extension housing bolts.

NOTE: Record the position of the regular bolts, stud type bolts and spacers for installation.

7. Withdraw the extension housing and remove the gasket.

8. Replace the rear oil seal.

9. Slide the speedometer drive off the output shaft.

10. Remove the oil pan bolts and pan from the case. Discard the gasket.

11. Take the magnet from the valve body.

12. Note the position of the oil tubes and without damaging them pry the tubes out. Do not pry out the tube under the valve body until after the valve body is removed.

13. Disconnect the throttle cable from the cam.

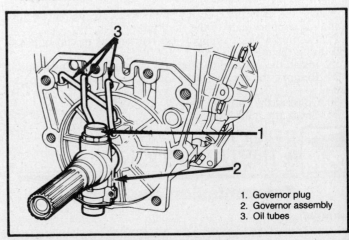

1. Governor plug
2. Governor assembly
3. Oil tubes

Governor assembly location (©Borg Warner)

14. Remove the valve body and then remove the final fluid tube.

15. Carefully pry or pull the oil cooler tube out of the case, without damaging it.

16. Remove the oil tube retaining plate.

17. Using suitable long-nosed pliers, withdraw the pump inlet tube.

18. Take out the pump outlet pipe.

19. Withdraw the converter feed tube.

20. Scribe alignment marks on the oil pump and transmission case.

21. Remove the oil pump to transmission case bolts and washers.

22. Support the stator tube and withdraw the oil pump.

23. Discard the gasket and the bronze thrust washer.

24. Remove the plug and spring washer securing the governor on the output shaft.

25. Slide the governor off the shaft. Note the position of the governor for installation.

26. Carefully pry the governor feed, governor return and lubrication tubes from the case.

27. Loosen the locknut and unscrew the front brake band adjuster. If the strut falls, recover it.

28. Loosen the locknut and unscrew the rear brake band adjuster. If the strut falls recover it.

29. Remove the front clutch assembly together with the input shaft.

30. Remove one steel and one bronze washer. Discard the bronze washer.

31. Take out the rear clutch assembly. Remove and discard the sealing rings.

32. Note the fitted position of the front brake band; compress and withdraw the brake band.

33. Withdraw the forward sun gear shaft.

34. Remove the small needle roller bearing from the input end of the forward sun gear shaft.

35. Take the flange backing washer and large needle bearing from the output end of the forward sun gear shaft.

36. Remove the metal sealing rings from the input end of the shaft and discard them.

37. Remove the fiber sealing ring from the output end of the shaft and discard it.

38. Remove the bolts and lockwashers securing the center support.

39. Push the output shaft forward to displace the center support and sun gear assembly.

40. Withdraw the center support and sun gear assembly from the case and remove the needle bearing from the input end of the sun gear assembly.

41. Separate the center support from the sun gear assembly.

42. Pull the output shaft towards the rear of the transmission.

43. Note the installed position of the rear brake band. Compress and remove the rear brake band.

44. Withdraw the output shaft and ring gear assembly.

45. Remove the bronze thrust washer and discard it.

46. Remove the front servo to case attaching bolts.

47. Take out the front servo, operating rod and spring; remove and discard the gasket.

48. Scribe alignment marks on the rear servo and transmission case.

49. Remove the rear servo to case attaching bolts.

50. Withdraw the rear servo, operating rod and spring; remove and discard the O-rings and gasket.

51. Remove the plate securing the parking pawl and the rear servo lever pivot pin.

52. Take out the rear servo pivot pin and operating lever.

53. Remove the parking pawl pivot pin, pawl and torsion spring.

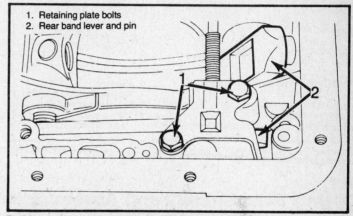

1. Retaining plate bolts
2. Rear band lever and pin

Parking brake pawl retaining plate (©Borg Warner)

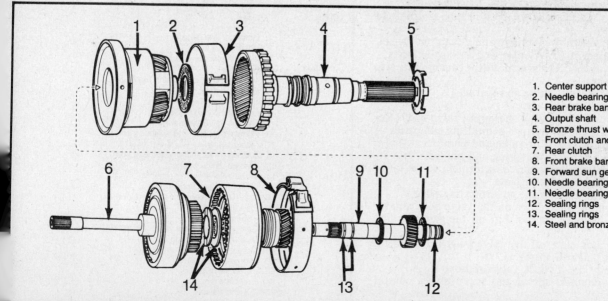

1. Center support and sun gear
2. Needle bearing
3. Rear brake band
4. Output shaft
5. Bronze thrust washer
6. Front clutch and input shaft
7. Rear clutch
8. Front brake band
9. Forward sun gear shaft
10. Needle bearing
11. Needle bearing
12. Sealing rings
13. Sealing rings
14. Steel and bronze thrust washers

Exploded view of the model 66 gear train (©Borg Warner)

54. Release the clip and remove the pin locating the manual valve lever.

55. Take out the detent shaft, manual lever, spacer and washers. Remove and discard the O-ring and oil seal.

56. Remove the parking brake rod from the parking pawl.

57. Remove the torsion spring from the parking brake rod operating lever.

58. Using a punch, drive out the operating lever pivot pin; withdraw the lever and spring.

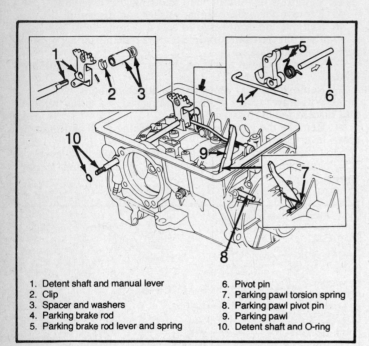

1. Detent shaft and manual lever
2. Clip
3. Spacer and washers
4. Parking brake rod
5. Parking brake rod lever and spring
6. Pivot pin
7. Parking pawl torsion spring
8. Parking pawl pivot pin
9. Parking pawl
10. Detent shaft and O-ring

Internal linkage removal (©Borg Warner)

Unit Disassembly and Assembly

VALVE BODY

1. Remove the manual valve from the valve body.

2. Remove the screws securing the suction tube assembly to the lower valve body.

3. Lift off the tube assembly. Remove and discard the gasket.

4. Remove the upper to lower valve body attaching bolts.

5. Turn over the valve body and remove the cam mounting to upper valve body bolts.

6. Take out the downshift valve and spring.

7. Lift off the upper valve body.

8. Remove both end plates from the upper valve body. Release the tension slowly on the springs behind the end plates.

9. Remove the spring, 1-2 shift valve and plunger.

10. Take out the 2-3 shift valve, spring and plunger.

11. Remove the screws holding the collector plate to the lower valve body and lift off the collector plate.

12. Loosen the screws holding the governor line plate.

13. Hold the separating plate down on the valve body and remove the governor line plate screws. Lift off the governor line plate.

14. Slide the separator plate off the valve body being careful not to lose the check ball and spring.

15. If the valve body has a check valve, remove it.

16. Take out the retainer, spring and servo orifice control valve.

17. Withdraw the retaining pin, plug, modulator valve and spring.

18. Remove the throttle valve spring retainer and the throttle valve retainer.

19. Take out the throttle valve and spring.

20. Remove the screw, spacer and detent spring.

21. If the roller arm is peened to the valve body, swing the arm clear to remove the regulator valve retaining plate.

22. Release the spring tension slowly when removing the regulator valve retaining plate.

23. Remove the spring, sleeve and primary regulator valve.

24. Take out the spring and secondary regulator valve.

25. Check all springs to specification.

26. Check all valves for free movement and the bores for dam-

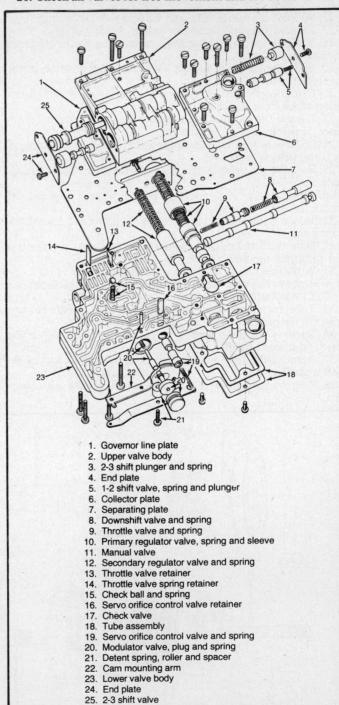

1. Governor line plate
2. Upper valve body
3. 2-3 shift plunger and spring
4. End plate
5. 1-2 shift valve, spring and plunger
6. Collector plate
7. Separating plate
8. Downshift valve and spring
9. Throttle valve and spring
10. Primary regulator valve, spring and sleeve
11. Manual valve
12. Secondary regulator valve and spring
13. Throttle valve retainer
14. Throttle valve spring retainer
15. Check ball and spring
16. Servo orifice control valve retainer
17. Check valve
18. Tube assembly
19. Servo orifice control valve and spring
20. Modulator valve, plug and spring
21. Detent spring, roller and spacer
22. Cam mounting arm
23. Lower valve body
24. End plate
25. 2-3 shift valve

Exploded view of the valve body assembly (©Borg Warner)

age. If the valves or the valve body is damaged, replace the component.

27. Install the secondary regulator valve and spring.

28. Insert the primary regulator valve, sleeve and spring.

29. Install the regulator valve retaining plate.

30. Attach the detent roller spring and assembly with a screw and spacer.

31. Insert the throttle valve, spring, spring retainer and valve retainer.

32. Install the spring, modulator valve, plug and retaining pin.

33. Insert the servo orifice control valve, spring and retainer.

34. Set in the check valve, if equipped.

35. Install the spring and the check ball.

36. Set the separator plate and while holding the plate down attach the governor line plate with the attaching bolts.

37. Insert the plunger, spring and 2-3 shift valve.

38. install the plunger, 1-2 shift valve and spring.

39. Install the two end plates on the upper valve body.

40. Set the upper valve body on the lower valve body.

41. Insert the spring and downshift valve.

42. Install the cam mounting arm on the valve body with the attaching screws.

43. Turn the valve body over and install the upper to lower valve body attaching screws.

44. Using a new gasket install the suction tube assembly on the lower valve body.

45. Set in the manual valve.

ONE-WAY CLUTCH

NOTE: No overhaul of this assembly is possible. In the event of defects, the unit must be replaced.

1. Remove the assembly from the transmission after taking note of its installed position.

2. Check the sprag faces for flat spots.

3. Install the one-way clutch assembly in the planet carrier. Be sure that the lip faces out and that the clutch is fully seated in the recess.

FORWARD SUN GEAR SHAFT

1. Check the shaft for any obstructions in its passages. If any obstructions are encountered, clear them with compressed air.

2. Check the splines, sealing rings and the sealing ring grooves for burrs or damage.

3. Check the large and small needle roller bearings for wear and damage.

REAR CLUTCH ASSEMBLY

1. Compress the piston return spring and remove the snap ring.

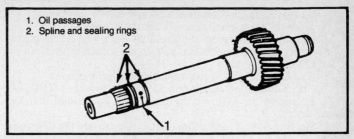

1. Oil passages
2. Spline and sealing rings

Forward sun gear shaft (©Borg Warner)

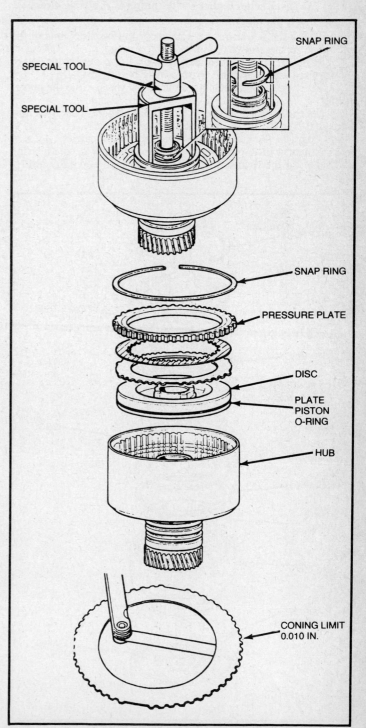

SNAP RING

SPECIAL TOOL

SPECIAL TOOL

SNAP RING

PRESSURE PLATE

DISC

PLATE
PISTON
O-RING

HUB

CONING LIMIT
0.010 IN.

Exploded view of the rear clutch assembly (©Borg Warner)

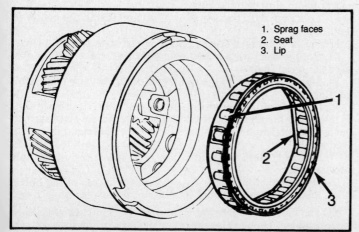

1. Sprag faces
2. Seat
3. Lip

One-way clutch assembly (©Borg Warner)

2. Remove the tool, retainer and spring.

3. Take the large snap ring off the pressure plate.

4. Remove the pressure plate, clutch discs and clutch plates.

5. Apply air pressure to the hole in the clutch housing to remove the clutch piston.

6. Remove the piston seal and install a new one.

7. Check the outer clutch coning for not less than 0.010 in.

8. Lubricate the piston with clean fluid and install it in the clutch drum.

9. Starting with a steel plate, install alternately the discs and plates.

NOTE: Install clutch plates with coning in the same direction.

10. Install the pressure plate.

11. Using the piston return spring compressor tool, install the snap ring in the spring retainer.

12. Hold the large needle bearing in place, on the output end of the forward sun gear shaft, with a little petroleum jelly.

13. Position the flanged end of the thrust washer into the planet carrier.

14. Set the forward sun gear shaft in the planet carrier; fit a new fiber seal ring on the output end of the shaft.

15. Position the center support in the planet carrier.

16. Smear a little petroleum jelly on the small needle bearing and set it on the thrust washer on the forward sun gear shaft.

17. Install the rear clutch on the forward sun gear shaft and put new seal rings on the input end of the shaft.

18. Stagger the gaps in the seal rings when installing them.

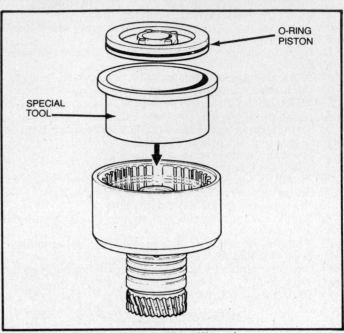

Front clutch piston installation (©Borg Warner)

FRONT CLUTCH ASSEMBLY

1. Remove the snap ring and take out the turbine shaft.

2. Remove and discard the bronze thrust washer.

3. Remove the clutch hub, four plates and five discs.

4. Take off the snap ring and return spring.

5. Apply compressed air in the clutch housing to remove the piston.

6. Remove the plain or Belleville washers from under the piston.

7. Take the O-ring off the piston.

8. Coat a new O-ring with clean transmission fluid and install it on the piston.

9. Place the plain and Belleville washers in the housing.

NOTE: Some later transmissions have all Belleville and no plain washers. Install the Belleville washers in three opposing pairs.

10. Soak a new oil seal in transmission fluid and insert it, open end outward, into the housing.

11. Lubricate with transmission fluid and install the piston in the housing.

12. Set in the return spring and secure it with the snap ring.

13. Put the steel washer and a new bronze washer on the forward sun gear shaft.

14. Stagger the gaps on the input end of the sun gear shaft sealing rings.

15. Install the front clutch hub on the rear clutch hub and shaft.

16. Install the clutch plates and discs alternately starting with the heavier plate with no notches in it. Five plates and five discs are installed.

17. Align the teeth inside the discs and insert the clutch hub into the discs.

18. Set a new bronze thrust washer in the recess of the hub.

19. Install the turbine shaft and secure it with the snap ring.

NOTE: Never separate the front and rear clutches after they are assembled. Doing this will cause damage to the forward sun gear sealing rings.

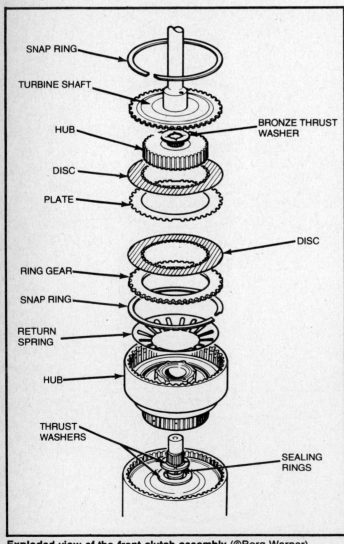

Exploded view of the front clutch assembly (©Borg Warner)

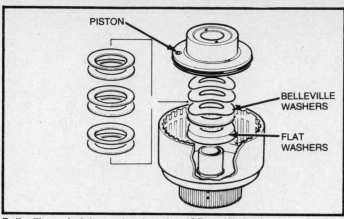

Belleville and plain washer location (©Borg Warner)

OIL PUMP ASSEMBLY

1. Remove the pump body to pump adaptor bolts.
2. If it is necessary to tap the adaptor to separate it from the body, use a hide or hard rubber mallet.
3. Mark the gears with die marker before removing them.
4. Remove the gears and inspect the pump body and gears for wear or damage.
5. Replace the O-ring and oil seal with new parts.
6. Soak new parts and seals in transmission fluid.
7. Set the gears into the pump body using the alignment marks to position them.
8. Install the pump body to adaptor bolts and torque them alternately a little at a time to 2.5 ft. lbs.

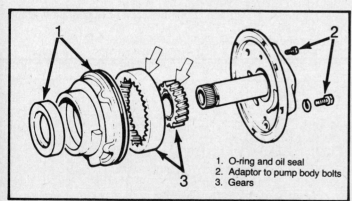

1. O-ring and oil seal
2. Adaptor to pump body bolts
3. Gears

Exploded view of the oil pump (©Borg Warner)

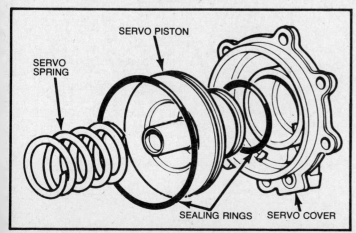

Exploded view of the rear servo (©Borg Warner)

FRONT SERVO ASSEMBLY

1. Remove the piston and the return spring from the front servo assembly.
2. Check the spring and the fluid passages. Replace parts as required.
3. When installing the spring and piston coat the new O-rings with automatic transmission fluid.

REAR SERVO ASSEMBLY

1. Remove the piston and the return spring from the rear servo assembly.
2. Replace parts as required.
3. When installing the piston and spring coat the new O-rings with automatic transmission fluid.

GOVERNOR ASSEMBLY

1. Depress the governor stem and remove the snap ring.
2. Take the govenor weight, spring, stem and valve from the governor body.
3. Replace parts or entire assembly as needed.
4. Install the valve, spring, stem and weight. Secure the stem with a new snap ring.

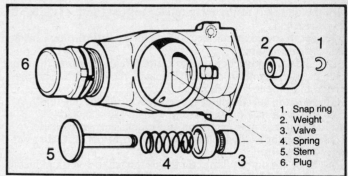

1. Snap ring
2. Weight
3. Valve
4. Spring
5. Stem
6. Plug

Exploded view of the governor assembly (©Borg Warner)

Transmission

Assembly

1. Smear the large bronze thrust washer with petroleum jelly and position it lug side into the case.
2. Set the output shaft into the case.
3. Postion the front and rear brake bands in the case.
4. Align the oil holes in the center support with the oil holes in the case and insert the clutch assemblies as a unit into the case.
5. Make sure that the planet gears are fully engaged with the ring gear.
6. Install the center support bolts and finger tighten only at this time.
7. Put a new bronze washer on the oil pump, with the lugs facing the pump.

NOTE: The oil pump thrust washer is selective to obtain proper end play. Two washer thicknesses are available. It is recommended that the thinner thrust washer be used, since it almost always gives proper end play.

8. Install the oil pump, with a new gasket, on the case.
9. Coat a new O-ring with transmission fluid and set it in the oil pump inlet tube.
10. Install the oil pump inlet and outlet tubes and secure them with the retaining plate. Torque the retaining plate bolts to 1.75 ft. lbs.
11. Torque the oil pump bolts in a diagonal pattern to 19 ft. lbs.
12. Tighten the center support bolts in small amounts, starting

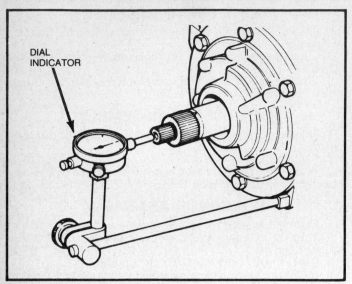

DIAL
INDICATOR

Checking total end play (©Borg Warner)

with the one next to the accumulator pistons, until 17.3-20.3 ft. lbs. is reached.

13. Set in the governor feed and governor return tubes. Install the lubrication tube.

14. Slide the governor on the output shaft, aligning the plug with the blind hole in the shaft. Install the spring washer and torque the plug to 16.5 ft. lbs.

15. Side the speedometer drive gear on the output shaft.

16. Install a new oil seal in the transmission housing.

17. Position a new extension housing gasket on the case.

18. Install the extension housing and torque the bolts alternately to 42.5 ft. lbs.

19. Slide the output flange on the output shaft and hand install the washer and bolt.

20. Move the selector lever until the parking pawl engages with the gear.

21. Torque the output flange bolt to 40-50 ft. lbs.

22. Install a dial runout gauge on the end of the turbine shaft.

23. Insert a suitable lever between the front clutch and the front of the case. Ease the gear train to the rear of the case and zero the dial indicator.

24. Insert a lever between the ring gear and rear clutch, and ease the gear train forward. End play should read between .008 and 0.29 in. If end play exceeds .029 in. install the proper selective thrust washers to correct it.

25. Remove the dial indicator gauge.

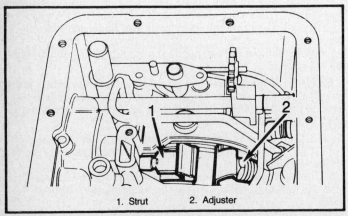

1. Strut   2. Adjuster

Front band strut location (©Borg Warner)

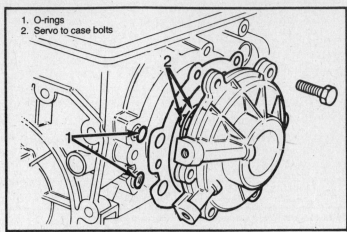

1. O-rings
2. Servo to case bolts

Rear servo O-ring installation (©Borg Warner)

26. Lubricate and install a new O-ring on the speedometer driven gear shaft.

27. Insert the driven gear shaft and secure it with it's cover and two bolts.

28. Using a new gasket, install the front servo. Torque the bolts alternately to 19 ft. lbs.

29. Set the front brake band strut in the case. Insert the proper end of the strut in the slot on the servo rod.

30. Tighten the front band adjusting screw until contact is made with the brake band.

31. Install a new O-ring in the rear servo body oil holes.

32. Using a new gasket, install the servo assembly. Make sure that the operating rod is in the detent of the operating lever.

33. Install the rear band strut in the case.

34. Tighten the rear band adjusting screw until contact is made with the band.

35. Torque the rear servo to case bolts to 19 ft. lbs.

36. Insert the oil tube that extends under the valve body.

37. Install the valve body and torque the bolts to 6.75 ft. lbs.

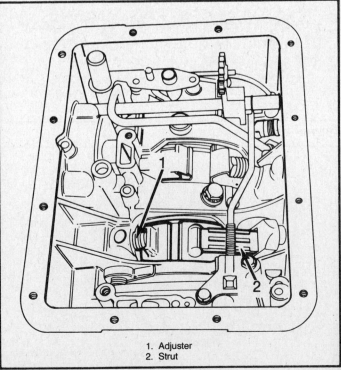

1. Adjuster
2. Strut

Rear brake band strut location (©Borg Warner)

38. Connect the throttle cable to the cam.
39. Fit in the remaining oil tubes.
40. Install the magnet on the valve body.
41. Install the transmission oil pan, using a new gasket. Torque the bolts to 5.75 ft. lbs.
42. Fasten the dipstick and the breather to the transmission case.

43. Install the converter housing. Torque the bolts at the top of the housing 20 to 30 ft. lbs. Torque the bolts at the bottom of the housing 30 to 50 ft. lbs.
44. Tighten the front and rear band adjusting screws to 5 ft. lbs., and then back them off ¾ of a turn.
45. Tighten both band adjusting lock nuts to 35 ft. lbs. Hold the adjusting screws from turning while tightening the lock nuts.

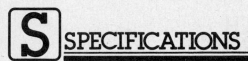

SPECIFICATIONS

VALVE SPRING IDENTIFICATION

Description	Length	Diameter	Number of Coils	Color
Secondary regulator valve	2.593 in.	.480-.490 in.	23	Blue
Primary regulator valve	2.94 in.	.604-.610 in.	14	Blue
Servo orifice control valve	1.08 in.	.198-.208 in.	17	Yellow
2-3 shift valve	1.59 in.	.275-.285 in.	22.5	Yellow
1-2 shift valve	1.094 in.	.230-.240 in.	13	Plain
Throttle return valve	.807 in.	.136-.146 in.	28	Yellow
Modulator valve	1.069 in.	.150-.160 in.	19	Plain
Throttle valve	1.175-1.185 in.	.230-.240 in.	18	Green
Dump ball valve	.70 in.	.210-.230 in.	16	Plain or white

SPECIAL TOOLS

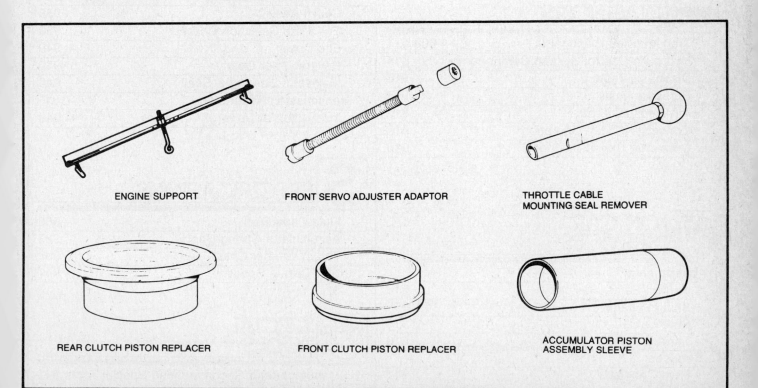

ENGINE SUPPORT

FRONT SERVO ADJUSTER ADAPTOR

THROTTLE CABLE MOUNTING SEAL REMOVER

REAR CLUTCH PISTON REPLACER

FRONT CLUTCH PISTON REPLACER

ACCUMULATOR PISTON ASSEMBLY SLEEVE

INDEX

HONDA
3 SPEED • 4 SPEED
Automatic Transaxle

 APPLICATIONS

HONDA AUTOMATIC TRANSAXLE APPLICATION CHART

Year	Model	Transaxle Type
1981 and Later	Civic	3 speed unit
1981-82	Accord	3 speed unit
1983 and Later	Accord	4 speed unit
1981-82	Prelude	3 speed unit
1983 and Later	Prelude	4 speed unit

 GENERAL DESCRIPTION

Three Speed Transaxle

The three speed Honda automatic transaxle is a combination of a three element torque converter and a dual shaft automatic transaxle which provides three forward speeds and one reverse speed. The entire unit is placed in line with the engine assembly.

Later Civic's are equipped with a lock up torque converter. The lock up mechanism engages above thirty miles per hour in drive. Lock up of the torque converter is prevented by a servo valve, which unless the throttle is opened sufficiently, the converter will not engage.

Four Speed Transaxle

The four speed Honda automatic transaxle is a combination of a three element torque converter and a dual shaft automatic transaxle which provides four forward speeds and one reverse speed.

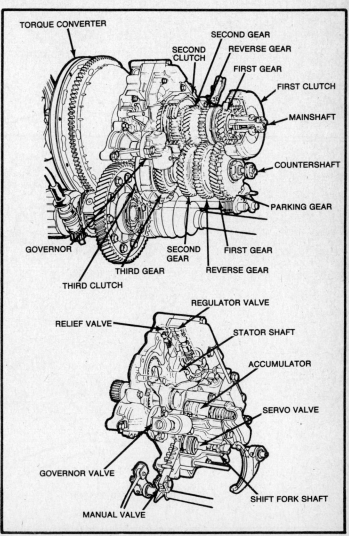

Three speed automatic transaxle—exploded view

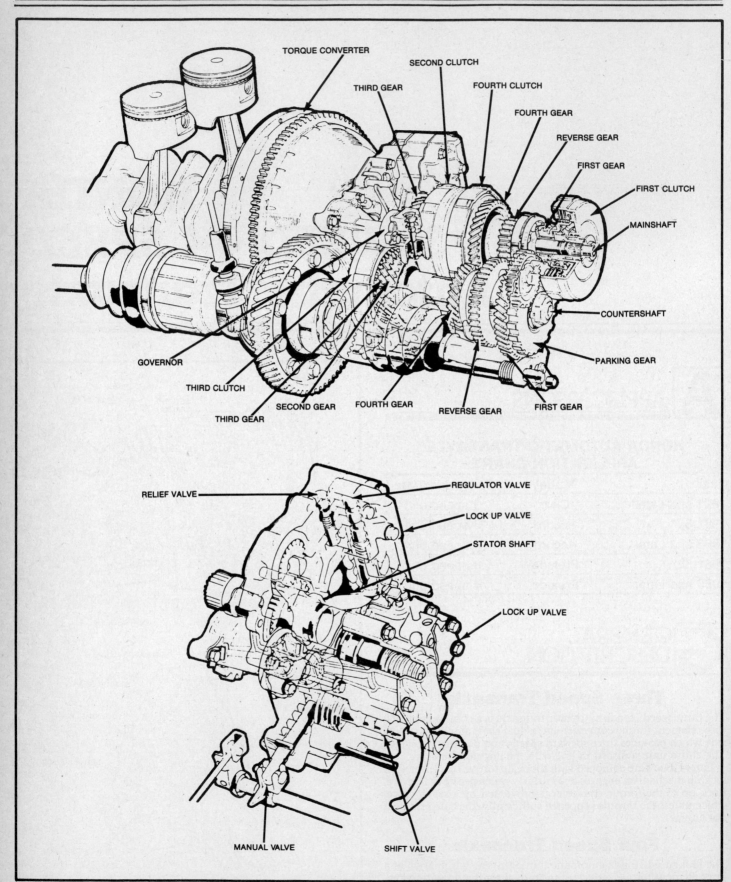

TORQUE CONVERTER

SECOND CLUTCH

THIRD GEAR

FOURTH CLUTCH

FOURTH GEAR

REVERSE GEAR

FIRST GEAR

FIRST CLUTCH

MAINSHAFT

COUNTERSHAFT

PARKING GEAR

FIRST GEAR

REVERSE GEAR

FOURTH GEAR

SECOND GEAR

THIRD GEAR

THIRD CLUTCH

GOVERNOR

RELIEF VALVE

REGULATOR VALVE

LOCK UP VALVE

STATOR SHAFT

LOCK UP VALVE

MANUAL VALVE

SHIFT VALVE

Four speed automatic transaxle—exploded view

The entire unit is placed in line with the engine assembly.

The Honda four speed automatic transaxle is equipped with a lock up torque converter. When the transaxle is in D4 and at speeds above forty three miles per hour, the torque converter will utilize the lock up function. Lock up of the torque converter is prevented by a servo valve, which unless the throttle is opened sufficiently, the torque converter will not engage.

Transaxle and Torque Converter Identification

TRANSAXLE

Both the three speed automatic transaxle and the four speed automatic transaxle identification numbers are stamped on a plate, which is located on top of the automatic transaxle assembly. This plate can be viewed from the top the engine compartment.

TORQUE CONVERTER

Torque converter usage differs with the type of engine and the type of vehicle that the automatic transaxle is being used in. Some early model three speed Honda torque converters can be disassembled. However, should problems exist within the torque converter replacement of the unit is recommended.

Metric Fasteners

Metric bolt sizes and thread pitches are used for all fasteners in both the Honda three speed and the Honda four speed automatic transaxles.

The metric fasteners have dimensions that are very close to the dimensions of the familiar inch system fasteners, and for this reason, replacement fasteners must have the same measurement and strength as those removed.

The fasteners should be reused in the same locations as removed. Do not interchange metric fasteners for the inch system fasteners, as mismatched or incorrect fasteners can result in damages to the transmission unit through malfunctions, breakage or possible personal injury.

Checking Transaxle Fluid Level

The transaxle fluid should be at normal operating temperature, the engine stopped and the vehicle on a level surface.

NOTE: The dipstick is screwed into the transaxle case.

1. Unscrew the dipstick and remove if from the transaxle.
2. Wipe the dipstick clean and reinsert into the transaxle.

IMPORTANT Do not screw the dipstick in.

3. Remove the dipstick and read the fluid level as indicated on the dipstick.
4. Correct the fluid level, as required. Use the proper grade and type automatic transmission fluid.

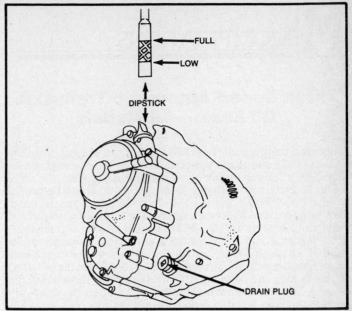

Three speed transaxle dipstick location

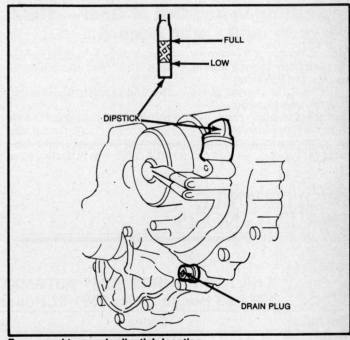

Four speed transaxle dipstick location

FLUID CAPACITIES
Honda Three Speed and Four Speed Automatic Transmissions

Year	Transmission	Model	Oil Drain (refil)	Dry Refil
1981-83	Three speed	Civic	2.6 quarts	5.2 quarts
1984 and Later	Three speed	Civic	2.9 quarts	5.6 quarts
1981-82	Three speed	Accord	2.6 quarts	5.2 quarts
1983 and Later	Four speed	Accord	3.0 quarts	6.0 quarts
1981-82	Three speed	Prelude	2.6 quarts	5.2 quarts
1983 and Later	Four speed	Prelude	3.0 quarts	6.0 quarts

MODIFICATIONS

Three Speed Automatic Transaxle Oil Leak—All Models

Automatic transmission fluid leaking, not just seeping, from the bottom of the automatic transaxle between the housings can be caused by a leaking torque converter housing gasket.

On Accords and Preludes from automatic transaxle model number AK-3000001 through AK-3056816 the torque converter housing gasket and both housings must be replaced to correct the problem. Use parts kit H/C-123152 when making this repair.

On Accords and Preludes from automatic transaxle model number AK-3056817 on, and all Civics, replace the torque converter housing gasket. Use parts kit H/C-106589 for the two dowel pin housing and parts kit H/C-106883 for the three dowel pin housing. If either kit comes equipped with a black two dowel pin torque converter housing gasket, do not use it.

Lock Up Torque Converter Slipping or Shifting In and Out of Gear—1983 and Later Accord

The lock up torque converter may cause a surge or shifting feeling by continually locking and unlocking. To correct this problem, perform the following;

1. Check the throttle control cable and bracket. If necessary, adjust to specification.
2. Road test the vehicle at 55 mph on a level road and observe the tachometer for signs of torque converter surging. Do not use the cruise control when road testing the vehicle. If the torque converter still surges, shorten the throttle cable one turn clockwise and try the road test again. If the problem still exists shorten the cable again. The cable can be shortened approximately three millimeters shorter than specification.

NOTE: Adjusting the cable more than three millimeters cause harsh shifting on part throttle upshifts and closed throttle downshifts.

3. Retest the vehicle at 55 mph with the cruise control engaged. If the torque converter surges with the cruise control engaged, but is okay with it disengaged, adjust the cruise control cable at the actuator to its minimum specification.

Mainshaft Bushing Seizure—1983 and Later Accord and Prelude

On some Accords and Preludes, insufficient clearance between the automatic transaxle bushing and the fourth clutch feed pipe can result in inadequate lubrication of the bushing. In extreme cases the bushing will overheat and seize itself onto the clutch feed pipe. When this happens, some of the transmission fluid will be diverted, resulting in clutch slippage in D3 and D4, or transaxle lock up when the unit is shifted into reverse.

In order to correct the problem the automatic transaxle must be removed from the vehicle. Disassemble the transaxle and inspect all parts for wear, damage and contamination. Clean and replace all damaged parts as required. In all cases, replace the mainshaft and end cover, including the first and fourth clutch feed pipes.

When replacing the fourth clutch feed pipe, follow the procedure below;

1. Install the O-ring in the fourth clutch feed pipe guide. Slip the guide onto the pipe.
2. Install the feed pipe in the end cover so that the tabs on the end of the feed pipe fit into the slots in the end cover.
3. Use a long metal tube, which is longer and smaller in diameter than the feed pipe, to tap the feed pipe down until it bottoms in the end cover.
4. Use a center punch to stake the feed pipe in place.
5. Install the end cover on the transaxle.

TROUBLE DIAGNOSIS

CHILTON'S THREE "C's" AUTOMATIC TRANSAXLE DIAGNOSIS CHART
1981-83 Honda Civic, 1981-82 Honda Accord and Prelude—Three speed

Condition	Cause	Correction
Vehicle will not move	a) Low fluid level	a) Correct fluid level as required
	b) Stuck regulator valve or damaged spring	b) Free stuck regulator valve or replace damaged spring
	c) Stuck servo shaft	c) Correct as required
	d) Damaged mainshaft	d) Replace mainshaft as required
	e) Manual shift out of adjustment	e) Adjust manual shift
	f) Damaged final gear	f) Replace final gear as required
	g) Broken flex plate	g) Replace flex plate
	h) Filter clogged	h) Replace filter
Vehicle does not move in D1 but will move in 2, D2 and D3	a) Manual shift out of adjustment	a) Adjust manual shift as required
	b) Worn or damaged one way clutch	b) Repair or replace one way clutch
	c) Damaged low gear	c) Replace low gear as required
	d) First clutch piston stuck or O-ring	d) Repair or replace piston or O-ring seal as required

CHILTON'S THREE "C's" AUTOMATIC TRANSAXLE DIAGNOSIS CHART
1981-83 Honda Civic, 1981-82 Honda Accord and Prelude—Three speed

Condition	Cause	Correction
Vehicle does not move in D1 but will move in 2, D2 and D3	e) First clutch feed pipe or O-ring damaged f) Worn or burnt first clutch disc g) First clutch check ball stuck	e) Repair or replace component as required f) Replace first clutch disc as required g) Free stuck check ball as required
Vehicle does not move in 2, but okay in drive	a) Manual shift out of adjustment	a) Adjust manual shift as required
Vehicle does not move in reverse, but okay in drive and 2	a) Stuck servo shaft b) Damaged reverse gear	a) Correct servo shaft blockage as required b) Replace reverse gear as required
Engine vibrates at idle	a) Lack of engine power	a) Correct engine as required
Up shift speed too high	a) Faulty governor valve b) Throttle control cable out of adjustment c) Defective throttle valve "A" d) Defective modulator valve	a) Repair or replace governor valve b) Adjust throttle control cable as required c) Replace defective part as required d) Replace modulator valve as required
Jumps from D1 to D3 while selector is in drive	a) Defective 2-3 shift valve	a) Replace defective shift valve as required
All up shift points too early	a) Throttle cable out of adjustment b) Defective throttle valve "A" c) Defective modulator valve	a) Adjust throttle cable b) Replace defective valve as required c) Replace modulator valve as required
D1 and D2 upshift point too early	a) Faulty 1-2 shift valve	a) Repair or replace shift valve as required
D2 and D3 upshift point too early	a) Defective 2-3 shift valve	a) Repair or replace shift valve as required
Harsh shift from D1 to D2	a) Faulty second clutch piston b) Damaged second clutch piston O-ring c) Worn or damaged second clutch sealing rings d) Worn or burnt second clutch disc e) Second clutch check ball stuck f) Defective second accumulator g) No second ball check valve	a) Repair or replace piston b) Replace O-ring c) Replace sealing srings as required d) Replace disc as required e) Correct as required f) Repair or replace accumulator as required g) Install second ball check valve
Engine races in shifting from D2 into D3	a) Defective throttle valve "B" b) Defective third accumulator c) Defective orifice control valve d) Foreign matter stuck in main orifice e) Defective third clutch piston f) Damaged third clutch piston O-ring g) Damaged third clutch feed pipe or O-ring h) Worn or burnt third clutch disc	a) Repair or replace defective part b) Repair or replace as required c) Replace orifice control valve d) Correct as required e) Repair or replace as required f) Replace O-ring g) Repair or replace defective part as required h) Correct defective part as required
Engine vibrates when shifting from D2 into D3	a) Faulty second clutch piston or damaged O-ring seal b) Second clutch check ball stuck	a) Repair or replace defective component as required b) Correct as required

CHILTON'S THREE "C's" AUTOMATIC TRANSAXLE DIAGNOSIS CHART
1981-83 Honda Civic, 1981-82 Honda Accord and Prelude—Three speed

Condition	Cause	Correction
Engine vibrates when shifting from D2 into D3	c) Worn or damaged second clutch sealing rings	c) Correct as required
	d) Worn or burned second clutch disc	d) Replace second clutch disc as required
	e) Foreign matter stuck in second orifice	e) Correct as required
	f) Foreign matter stuck in separator port orifice	f) Correct as required
Vehicle creeps forward in neutral	a) Shift cable out of adjustment	a) Adjust shift cable as required
	b) Faulty first clutch piston or damaged O-ring	b) Repair or replace defective part as required
	c) Damaged first clutch feed pipe or O-ring	c) Repair or replace defective part as necessary
	d) Faulty matter stuck in first clutch check valve	d) Correct as required
	e) Worn or burnt first clutch disc	e) Replace first clutch disc
	f) Fluid level too high	f) Check fluid level
	g) Burnt needle bearings	g) Correct as required
	h) Burnt thrust washer	h) Correct as required
	i) Improper clutch clearance	i) Correct as required
	j) Faulty second clutch piston or damaged O-ring seal	j) Repair or replace defective component as required
	k) Foreign matter stuck in second clutch check valve	k) Correct as required
	l) Worn or damaged second clutch sealing ring	l) Replace sealing ring
	m) Worn or burnt second clutch disc	m) Replace clutch disc
	n) Defective third clutch piston or stuck O-ring	n) Replace piston or O-ring as required
	o) Foreign matter stuck in third clutch check valve	o) Correct as required
	p) Damaged third clutch feed pipe or O-ring	p) Repair or replace components as required
	q) Worn or burnt third clutch disc	q) Replace third clutch disc
Excessive time lag from neutral to drive	a) Faulty first clutch piston or O-ring seal	a) Repair or replace first clutch piston or O-ring seal
	b) Foreign matter stuck in first clutch piston check valve	b) Correct as required
	c) Damaged first clutch feed pipe or O-ring seal	c) Replace feed pipe or O-ring seal
	d) Worn or damaged first clutch sealing rings	d) Replace components as required
	e) Worn or burnt first clutch disc	e) Repair or replace as required
	f) Foreign matter stuck in low orifice	f) Correct as required
Excessive time lag from neutral to reverse	a) Stuck servo shaft	a) Correct as required
	b) Faulty second clutch piston or O-ring seal	b) Repair or replace second clutch piston or O-ring
	c) Foreign matter stuck in second clutch check ball valve	c) Correct as required
	d) Damaged second clutch feed pipe or O-ring	d) Replace feed pipe or O-ring as required
	e) Worn or burnt second clutch disc	e) Replace second clutch disc as required

CHILTON'S THREE "C's" AUTOMATIC TRANSAXLE DIAGNOSIS CHART
1984 and Later Honda Civic—Three speed

Condition	Cause	Correction
Vehicle runs but does not move	a) Fluid level low b) Stuck regulator valve or damaged spring c) Stuck servo shaft d) Damaged mainshaft e) Damaged final gear f) Broken flex plate	a) Correct fluid level b) Replace regulator valve or spring as required c) Repair as required d) Replace mainshaft e) Repair or replace as required f) Replace flex plate
Vehicle does not move in D1 but does move in D3 and D3	a) Manual shift out of adjustment b) Worn or damaged one way clutch c) Damaged low gear d) First clutch piston stuck or O-ring damaged e) Foreign matter stuck in first clutch check valve f) Damaged first clutch feed pipe or O-ring g) Worn or damaged first clutch sealing rings h) Worn or damaged first clutch disc	a) Adjust manual shift b) Repair or replace one way clutch c) Repair or replace low gear as needed d) Repair or replace first clutch piston or O-ring e) Correct as required f) Repair or replace feed pipe and O-ring as required g) Replace sealing rings as required h) Replace clutch disc as required
Vehicle does not move in 2, but is movable in D	a) Manual shift out of adjustment b) Damaged second gear c) Second clutch piston stuck or O-ring d) Foreign matter stuck in second clutch check valve e) Worn or damaged second clutch sealing rings f) Worn or damaged second clutch disc	a) Adjust manual shift as required b) Repair or replace second gear as required c) Repair or replace components as required d) Correct as required e) Replace sealing rings as required f) Replace clutch disc as required
Engine vibrates at idle	a) Lack of engine power b) Broken flex plate	a) Correct as required b) Correct as required
Selector lever jumps from D1 into D3 from drive	a) Defective 2-3 shift valve	a) Correct defective shift valve as required
Up shift points too early	a) Faulty governor valve b) Throttle cable out of adjustment c) Defective throttle valve "A" d) Cable housing damaged	a) Repair or replace as required b) Adjust cable at transmission c) Replace as required d) Repair or replace as required
D1 and D2 up shift point too early	a) Faulty governor valve b) Defective 1-2 shift valve	a) Repair or replace as required b) Repair or replace shift valve as required
D2 and D3 up shift point too early	a) Faulty governor valve b) Defective 2-3 shift valve	a) Repair or replace as required b) Repair or replace shift valve as required
Harsh shift from D1 to D2 or from D2 to D3	a) Second clutch piston stuck or O-ring damaged b) Foreign matter stuck in second clutch check valve c) Worn or damaged second clutch sealing rings	a) Repair or replace piston or O-ring as required b) Correct as required c) Repair or replace as required

CHILTON'S THREE "C's" AUTOMATIC TRANSAXLE DIAGNOSIS CHART
1984 and Later Honda Civic—Three speed

Condition	Cause	Correction
Harsh shift from D1 to D2 or from D2 to D3	d) Worn or burnt second clutch disc e) Defective throttle valve "R" f) Defective second accumulator	d) Replace second clutch disc as needed e) Correct as required f) Repair or replace as required
Harsh shift from D2 to D1	a) Defective throttle valve "B" b) Defective third accumulator c) Defective clutch pressure control valve d) Defective third orifice control valve e) Foreign matter stuck in third ball check valve	a) Correct as required b) Repair or replace as required c) Repair or replace pressure control valve as required d) Replace defective third clutch orifice valve e) Correct as required
Harsh shift from D3 to D2	a) Defective throttle valve "B" b) Defective second accumulator c) Foreign matter stuck in third ball check valve	a) Correct as required b) Replace or repair as required c) Correct as required
Engine races in shifting from D2 into D3	a) Defective throttle valve "B" b) Defective third accumulator c) Defective second orifice control valve d) Foreign matter stuck in third orifice e) Defective third clutch piston f) Damaged third clutch piston O-ring g) Damaged third clutch feed pipe or O-ring h) Worn or burnt third clutch disc i) Defective clutch pressure control valve	a) Repair or replace defective part b) Repair or replace as required c) Replace orifice control valve d) Correct as required e) Repair or replace as required f) Replace O-ring g) Repair or replace defective part as required h) Correct defective part as required i) Replace clutch pressure control valve as required
Engine vibrates when shifting from D2 to D3	a) Faulty second clutch piston or damaged O-ring seal b) Second clutch check ball stuck c) Worn or damaged second clutch sealing rings d) Worn or burned second clutch disc e) Foreign matter stuck in second orifice f) Foreign matter stuck in separator port orifice g) Defective throttle valve "B" h) Defective third accumulator i) Foreign matter stuck in third ball check valve	a) Repair or replace defective components as required b) Correct as required c) Correct as required d) Replace second clutch disc as required e) Correct as required f) Correct as required g) Correct as required h) Repair or replace accumulator i) Correct as required
Vehicle creeps forward in neutral	a) Shift cable out of adjustment b) Faulty first clutch piston or damaged O-ring c) Damaged first clutch feed pipe or O-ring d) Faulty matter stuck in first clutch check valve e) Worn or burnt first clutch disc f) Fluid level too high	a) Adjust shift cable as required b) Repair or replace defective part as required c) Repair or replace defective part as necessary d) Correct as required e) Replace first clutch disc f) Check fluid level

910

CHILTON'S THREE "C's" AUTOMATIC TRANSAXLE DIAGNOSIS CHART
1984 and Later Honda Civic—Three speed

Condition	Cause	Correction
Vehicle creeps forward in neutral	g) Burnt needle bearings	g) Correct as required
	h) Burnt thrust washer	h) Correct as required
	i) Improper clutch clearance	i) Correct as required
	j) Faulty second clutch piston or damaged O-ring seal	j) Repair or replace defective component as required
	k) Foreign matter stuck in second clutch check valve	k) Correct as required
	l) Worn or damaged second clutch sealing ring	l) Replace sealing ring
	m) Worn or burnt second clutch disc	m) Replace clutch disc
	n) Defective third clutch piston or stuck O-ring	n) Replace piston or O-ring as required
	o) Foreign matter stuck in third clutch check valve	o) Correct as required
	p) Damaged third clutch feed pipe or O-ring	p) Repair or replace components as required
	q) Worn or burnt third clutch disc	q) Replace third clutch disc
Excessive time lag from neutral	a) Faulty first clutch piston or O-ring seal	a) Repair or replace first clutch piston or O-ring seal
	b) Foreign matter stuck in first clutch piston check valve	b) Correct as required
	c) Damaged first clutch feed pipe or O-ring seal	c) Replace feed pipe or O-ring seal
	d) Worn or damaged first clutch sealing rings	d) Replace components as required
	e) Worn or burnt first clutch disc	e) Repair or replace as required
	f) Foreign matter stuck in first orifice	f) Correct as required
Excessive time lag from neutral to reverse	a) Shift cable out of adjustment	a) Adjust as required
	b) Servo shaft stuck	b) Correct as required
	c) Defective 2-3 shift valve	c) Repair or replace shift valve

CHILTON'S THREE "C's" AUTOMATIC TRANSAXLE DIAGNOSIS CHART
1983 and Later Honda Accord and Prelude—Four Speed

Condition	Cause	Correction
Engine runs but vehicle does not move	a) Low fluid level	a) Correct fluid level
	b) Stuck regulator valve or damaged spring	b) Correct regulator valve or spring as required
	c) Damaged mainshaft	c) Replace mainshaft as required
	d) Damaged final gear	d) Repair or replace as required
	e) Damaged flex plate	e) Replace flex plate
Vehicle does not move in D3 or D4, but does move in D2	a) Manual shift out of adjustment	a) Adjust manual shift as required
	b) Worn or damaged one way clutch	b) Repair or replace as required
	c) Stuck first clutch piston or damaged O-ring seal	c) Repair or replace defective components as required
	d) Damaged first clutch feed pipe or O-ring	d) Repair or replace parts as required
	e) Foreign matter stuck in first clutch check valve	e) Correct as required
	f) Worn or burnt first clutch disc	f) Replace clutch disc as required
	g) Defective CPC valve	g) Repair or replace valve as required

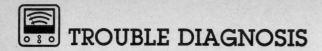

CHILTON'S THREE "C's" AUTOMATIC TRANSAXLE DIAGNOSIS CHART
1983 and Later Honda Accord and Prelude—Four Speed

Condition	Cause	Correction
Vehicle does not move in D2, but does move in D3 and D4	a) Manual shift out of adjustment b) Damaged second gear c) Stuck second clutch piston or damaged O-ring d) Foreign matter stuck in second clutch check valve e) Worn or damaged second clutch sealing rings f) Worn or burnt second clutch disc	a) Adjust manual shift as required b) Repair or replace second gear as needed c) Repair or replace defective components as required d) Correct as required e) Replace second clutch sealing rings as required f) Replace clutch disc as required
Vehicle does not move in reverse, but okay in D3, D4 and D2	a) Stuck servo shaft b) Manual shift out of adjustment c) Damaged reverse gear d) Defective 2-3 shift valve e) Stuck fourth clutch piston or damaged O-ring f) Foreign matter stuck in fourth clutch check valve g) Worn or damaged fourth clutch sealing rings h) Worn or burnt fourth clutch disc	a) Correct as required b) Adjust shift linkage as required c) Repair or replace gear as required d) Repair or replace defective shift valve e) Repair or replace defective components as required f) Correct as required g) Correct as required h) Replace clutch disc as required
Engine vibrates at idle	a) Lack of engine power b) Improper clutch clearance	a) Correct as required b) Correct clutch clearance as required
Up shift speed too high	a) Faulty governor valve b) Throttle control cable out of adjustment c) Defective throttle valve "A" d) Defective modulator valve	a) Repair or replace governor valve as required b) Adjust cable as required at transmission case c) Repair or replace throttle valve d) Repair or replace valve as required
Jumps from first to third in D3	a) Defective 2-3 shift valve	a) Repair or replace defective 2-3 shift valve as required
Jumps from first to fourth in D4	a) Defective 2-3 shift valve b) Defective 3-4 shift valve	a) Repair or replace defective shift valve as required b) Repair or replace defective valve as required
Up shift points are too early or late	a) Faulty governor valve b) Throttle cable out of adjustment c) Defective throttle valve "A" d) Defective modulator valve	a) Repair or replace governor valve b) Adjust throttle cable c) Repair or replace valve as required d) Repair or replace valve as required
Early or late up shift point— first to second	a) Faulty governor valve b) Defective 1-2 shift valve	a) Repair or replace valve as required b) Repair or replace shift valve as required
Early or late shift point— second to third	a) Faulty governor valve b) Defective 2-3 shift valve	a) Repair or replace valve b) Repair or replace valve
Early or late up shift point— third to fourth	a) Faulty governor valve b) Defective 3-4 shift valve	a) Repair or replace valve b) Repair or replace valve

CHILTON'S THREE "C's" AUTOMATIC TRANSAXLE DIAGNOSIS CHART
1983 and Later Honda Accord and Prelude—Four Speed

Condition	Cause	Correction
Harsh shift from first to second	a) Stuck second clutch piston or damaged O-ring b) Foreign matter stuck in second clutch check valve c) Worn or damaged second clutch sealing rings d) Worn or burnt second clutch disc e) Defective throttle valve "B" f) Defective second accumulator	a) Repair or replace defective component as required b) Correct as required c) Replace second clutch sealing rings as required d) Replace clutch disc as required e) Repair or replace valve f) Repair or replace accumulator
Harsh shift from second to third	a) Defective throttle valve "B" b) Defective third accumulator c) Defective second orifice control valve d) Stuck third clutch piston or damaged O-ring e) Foreign matter stuck in third clutch check valve f) Damaged third clutch feed pipe or O-ring g) Worn or burnt third clutch disc	a) Repair or replace defective valve b) Repair or replace accumulator c) Replace defective orifice control valve d) Repair or replace defective components as required e) Correct as required f) Repair or replace defective component as required g) Replace clutch disc as required
Harsh shift from third to fourth	a) Defective throttle valve "B" b) Defective fourth accumulator c) Stuck fourth clutch piston or damaged O-ring d) Foreign matter stuck in fourth clutch check valve e) Worn or damaged fourth clutch sealing rings f) Worn or burnt fourth clutch disc g) Lack of engine power	a) Repair or replace valve b) Repair or replace accumulator c) Repair or replace defective components as required d) Correct as required e) Correct as required f) Replace clutch as required g) Correct as required
Vehicle creeps forward in neutral	a) Shift cable out of adjustment b) Fluid level too high c) Burnt needle bearings d) Burnt thrust washer e) Improper clutch clearance f) Stuck first clutch piston or damaged O-ring seal g) Damaged first clutch feed pipe or O-ring h) Foreign matter stuck in first clutch check valve i) Worn or burnt first clutch disc j) Stuck second clutch piston or damaged O-ring k) Foreign matter stuck in second clutch check valve l) Worn or damaged second clutch sealing rings m) Worn or burnt second clutch disc n) Stuck third clutch piston or damaged O-ring o) Foreign matter stuck in third clutch check valve	a) Adjust shift cable b) Adjust fluid level c) Correct as required d) Replace thrust washer e) Correct clutch clearance f) Repair or replace defective components as required g) Repair or replace parts as required h) Correct as required i) Replace clutch disc as required j) Repair or replace defective component as required k) Correct as required l) Replace second clutch sealing rings as required m) Replace clutch disc as required n) Repair or replace defective components as required o) Correct as required

CHILTON'S THREE "C's" AUTOMATIC TRANSAXLE DIAGNOSIS CHART
1983 and Later Honda Accord and Prelude—Four Speed

Condition	Cause	Correction
Vehicle creeps forward in neutral	p) Damaged third clutch feed pipe or O-ring	p) Repair or replace defective component as required
	q) Worn or burnt third clutch disc	q) Replace clutch disc as required
	r) Stuck fourth clutch piston or damaged O-ring	r) Repair or replace defective components as required
	s) Foreign matter stuck in fourth clutch check valve	s) Correct as required
	t) Worn or damaged fourth clutch sealing rings	t) Correct as required
	u) Worn or burnt fourth clutch disc	u) Replace clutch disc as required
Excessive time lag from neutral to D3 and D4	a) Foreign matter stuck in first orifice	a) Correct as required
	b) Stuck first clutch piston or damaged O-ring seal	b) Repair or replace defective components as required
	c) Damaged first clutch feed pipe or O-ring	c) Repair or replace parts as required
	d) Foreign matter stuck in first clutch check valve	d) Correct as required
	e) Worn or burnt first clutch disc	a) Replace clutch disc as required
Excessive time lag from neutral to reverse	a) Stuck servo shaft	a) Repair or replace as required
	b) Defective 2-3 shift valve	b) Repair or replace valve as required
	c) Stuck fourth clutch piston or damaged O-ring	c) Repair or replace defective components as required
	d) Foreign matter stuck in fourth clutch check valve	d) Correct as required
	e) Worn or damaged fourth clutch sealing rings	e) Correct as required
	f) Worn or burnt fourth clutch disc	a) Replace clutch disc as required

Hydraulic Control System

THREE SPEED TRANSAXLE

The Honda three speed automatic transaxle hydraulic control system incorporates the valve body assembly, which includes a main valve body and regulator valve. This assembly is bolted to the torque converter case through a separator plate.

The main valve body contains a manual valve, 1-2 shift valve, 2-3 shift valve, pressure relief valve, orifice control valve, torque converter check valve and the oil pump gear.

The servo valve body includes the shift fork shaft, throttle control valves, throttle modulator valve, and the accumulator pistons.

The regulator valve regulates the fluid pressure within the hydraulic control system. Fluid from the regulator passes through the manual valve to the various control valves.

The first and third clutches receive fluid from the valves through their respective feed pipes.

FOUR SPEED TRANSAXLE

The Honda four speed automatic transaxle hydraulic control system incorporates the valve body assembly, which includes a main valve body and regulator valve. This assembly is bolted to the torque converter case through a separator plate.

The main valve body contains a manual valve, 1-2 shift valve, 2-3 shift valve, 3-4 shift valve, pressure relief valve, orifice control valve, torque converter check valve and the oil pump gear.

The servo valve body includes the shift fork shaft, throttle control valves, throttle modulator valve, and the accumulator pistons.

The regulator valve regulates the fluid pressure within the hydraulic control system. Fluid from the regulator passes through the manual valve to the various control valves.

The first, third and fourth clutches receive fluid from the valves through their respective feed pipes.

Diagnosis Tests

CONTROL PRESSURE TEST

Control pressure tests should be performed whenever slippage, delay or harshness is felt in the shifting of the automatic transaxle. These tests can pinpoint the differences between mechanical and hydraulic failures within the transaxle. Before making any tests be sure that the transaxle is full of fluid, the engine is in tune, the transaxle is up to operating temperature and that all external linkage is adjusted properly.

Line Pressure Test

1. Raise the vehicle and support it safely.
2. Install the gauge set to the proper transaxle pressure test ports.
3. Start the engine and run at 2000 rpm.
4. With the selector lever in neutral or park the specification should be 107-114 psi.

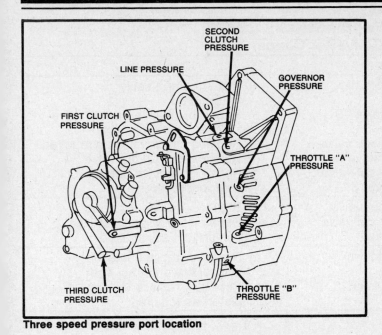

Three speed pressure port location

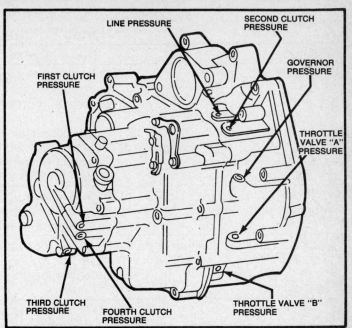

Four speed pressure port location

5. If the vehicle is equipped with a three speed transaxle the specification should be 100-114 psi for the rest of the gear selections.

6. If the vehicle is equipped with a four speed transaxle the specification should be 100-114 psi in D3 or D4 and 71-114 psi for the rest of the gear selections.

7. When reinstalling the pressure port plugs, do not reuse the aluminum washers.

Throttle Pressure Test

1. Raise the vehicle and support it safely.
2. Install the gauge set to the proper transaxle pressure test ports.
3. Start the engine and run at 1000 rpm. Disconnect the throttle control cable at the throttle lever.
4. Read the pressure with the lever released it should be zero.
5. Manually push the lever up to simulate full throttle. Read and record the specification on the gauge. For the three speed transaxles before 1984 the specification should be 90-93 psi. For three speed transaxles beginning with 1984 the specification should be 78-82 psi. For all four speed transaxles the specification should be 86-88 psi.
6. When reinstalling the pressure port plugs, do not reuse the aluminum washers.

Governor Pressure Test

1. Raise the vehicle and support it safely.
2. Install the gauge set to the proper transaxle pressure test ports.
3. Start the engine and run the vehicle at a speed of 38 mph.
4. With the selector lever in drive (D3 if vehicle is equipped with a four speed transaxle) record the pressure reading.
5. For 1981-83 three speed transaxles, the specification should be 46-49 psi. For 1984 and later three speed transaxles and all four speed transaxles, the specification should be 31-33 psi.
6. When reinstalling the pressure port plugs, do not reuse the aluminum washers.

Stall Speed Test

1. Raise the vehicle and support it safely.
2. Connect an engine tachometer and start the engine.
3. Once the engine has reached normal operating temperature, position the selector lever in drive (D3 if the vehicle is equipped with a four speed transaxle).

4. Fully depress the gas pedal for six to eight seconds, and note the engine speed.

NOTE: To prevent damage to the automatic transaxle, do not test stall speed for more than ten seconds at a time.

5. Allow two minutes for the transaxle to cool and then repeat the test in 2 (D4 and 2 if the vehicle is equipped with a four speed transaxle) and reverse.
6. All stall speed readings must be the same in all selector positions.
7. For 1981-83 three speed transaxles the specification should be 2400-2500 rpm. For all 1984 and later three speed transaxles the specification should be 2700 rpm. For all four speed transaxles the specification should be 2400 rpm.

AIR PRESSURE TEST

Air pressure testing should be done in moderation to avoid excessive fluid spray and damage to the internal parts during disassembly and assembly, through partial retention of units.

ROAD TEST

1. Road test using all selective ranges, noting when discrepancies in operation or oil pressure occur.
2. Attempt to isolate the unit or circuit involved in the malfunction.
3. If engine performance indicates an engine tune-up is required, this should be performed before road testing is completed or transaxle correction attempted. Poor engine performance can result in rough shifting or other malfunctions.

Converter Clutch Operation and Diagnosis

TORQUE CONVERTER CLUTCH

Three Speed Transaxle

When the Honda three speed automatic transaxle is in drive and at speeds above thirty miles per hour, pressurized fluid is bled off from the back of the torque converter through an oil passage causing the lock up function of the torque converter to take place. As

CHILTON'S THREE "C's" DIAGNOSIS CHART
Honda Torque Converter Clutch

Condition	Cause	Correction
Harsh shift into lock up	a) Throttle control cable out of adjustment	a) Adjust control cable as required
	b) Defective throttle valve "B"	b) Repair or replace throttle valve "B" as required
	c) Faulty converter check valve	c) Replace check valve as required
	d) Defective lock up cut valve	d) Replace lock up cut valve
	e) Defective governor cut valve or lock up shift valve	e) Repair or replace defective component as required
Lock up clutch does not disengage at low speed	a) Defective lock up cut valve	a) Replace lock up cut valve
	b) Defective governor cut valve or lock up shift valve	b) Repair or replace defective component as required
Vibration in lock up position	a) Defective lock up control valve	a) Repair or replace lock up control valve as required
	b) Defective lock up piston	b) Repair or replace lock up piston as required

this function occurs the mainshaft rotates at the same speed as the engine crankshaft.

The lock up valve body is bolted to the top of the regulator body, and includes the lock up shift valve. The lock up shift valve controls the engagement of the lock up function according to vehicle speed and throttle pressure.

The lock up control is integrated with the regulator valve body and regulates the torque converter oil pressure in relation to vehicle speed and throttle opening. The lock up cut out valve is the servo valve. It prevents the lock up function from taking place when the throttle is not opened sufficiently.

Four Speed Transaxle

When the Honda four speed automatic transaxle is in drive and at speeds above forty three miles per hour, pressurized fluid is drained from the back of the torque converter through an oil passage causing the lock up function of the torque converter to occur. As this takes place the mainshaft rotates at the same speed as the engine crankshaft.

The pressure control valve body is bolted to the top of the regulator body and includes the pressure control shift valve and pressure control timing valve. The pressure control shift valve controls the range of lock-up according to vehicle speed and throttle pressure. The timing valve senses when the transaxle is in fourth gear.

The clutch pressure control valve is bolted to the top of the servo valve and prevents the lock up function from taking place when the throttle is not opened sufficiently.

Adjustments
NEUTRAL SAFETY SWITCH

Adjustment

1. Move the selector lever through park, reverse and neutral to check the continuity of the switch.
2. Replace the switch if there is not continuity between the terminals.

3. To replace the switch, remove the console. Remove the switch retaining bolts and electrical connections. Remove the switch from its mounting.
4. When installing, position the slider on the switch in the neutral position.
5. Shift the selector lever in the neutral position. Align the switch lug with the actuator rod.
6. Continue the installation in the reverse order of the removal position.

SHIFT INDICATOR

Adjustment

1. Check that the index mark of the indicator aligns with the N mark of the shift indicator panel when the transaxle is in neutral.
2. If not aligned, remove panel mounting screws and adjust by moving panel.

SHIFT CABLE ADJUSTMENT

Adjustment

1. Remove the console assembly.
2. Shift the selector lever into drive. Remove the lock pin from the cable adjuster.
3. Check that the hole in the adjuster is in line with the hole in the shift cable.

NOTE: There are two holes in end of the shift cable. They are positioned 90° apart to allow cable adjustments in ¼ turn increments.

4. If not perfectly aligned, loosen locknut on shift cable and adjust as required.
5. Tighten the locknuts. Install lock pin on adjuster.

NOTE: If the lock pin binding as you reinstall it, the cable is still out of adjustment and must be readjusted.

6. Start engine and check shift lever in all gears.

THROTTLE CONTROL CABLE BRACKET

Adjustment

1. Disconnect the throttle control cable from the throttle control lever.
2. Bend down the lock tabs of the lock plate and remove the two bolts to free the bracket.

3. Loosely install a new lock plate.

4. Position the special tool between the throttle control lever and the bracket.

NOTE: The special tool is designed so that the distance between the lever and the bracket is 3.287 in. when it is installed.

5. Position the bracket so that there is no binding between the bracket and the special tool. Then tighten the two bolts, bend up the lock plate tabs against the bolts heads.

NOTE: Make sure the control lever doesn't get pulled toward the bracket side as you tighten the bolts.

THROTTLE CONTROL CABLE

Adjustment

1. Check that the carburetor throttle cable play is correct.

2. Be sure that the engine has reached operating temperature. The electric fan should come on twice.

3. Be sure that the idle speed is within specification. Check that the choke is functioning properly.

4. Be sure that the distance between the throttle control lever and the throttle control bracket is correct.

5. With the engine off, disconnect the throttle control cable from the throttle control lever.

6. Disconnect the vacuum tube from the dash pot and connect the vacuum pump and keep vacuum applied.

7. Attach a weight of about 2.6 lbs to the accelerator pedal. Raise the pedal, then release it, this will allow the weight to remove the normal free play from the throttle cable. Secure the cable.

8. Lay the end of the throttle control cable on the battery.

9. Adjust the distance between the throttle control cable end and the locknut to 3.3 inch.

10. Insert the end of throttle control cable in the groove of the throttle control lever.

11. Insert the throttle control cable in the bracket and secure it with the locknut. Be sure that the cable is not kinked or twisted.

12. Check that the cable moves freely by depressing the accelerator.

13. Remove the weight on the accelerator pedal and push the pedal to make sure that there is the specified play at the throttle control lever.

14. Start the engine and check the synchronization between the carburetor and the throttle control cable.

NOTE: The throttle control lever should start to move as engine speed increases.

15. If the throttle control lever moves before engine speed increases, turn the cable lock nut counter clockwise and re-tighten the other lock nut.

16. If the throttle control lever moves after engine speed increases, turn the lock nut clockwise and re-tighten the other lock nut.

Services

FLUID CHANGE

1. Raise the vehicle and support safely.

2. Remove the transmission drain plug and allow the fluid to drain into a waste container. Remove the dipstick to aid in the draining.

3. When the fluid draining is complete, install the drain plug and tighten securely.

4. Fill with new fluid through the dipstick opening.

NOTE: The fluid refill may be less because of the fluid remaining in the units and the recesses of the case.

REMOVAL & INSTALLATION

Removal
1981-83 CIVIC

1. Disconnect the negative battery cable.

2. Position the selector lever in neutral.

3. Disconnect the battery cable from the starter. Disconnect the water temperature sending unit wiring and the ignition timing thermosensor wiring.

4. Disconnect and plug the transaxle oil cooler lines at the transaxle.

5. Remove the starter mounting bolt on the transaxle side and the top transaxle mounting bolt.

6. Loosen the front wheel nuts. Raise the vehicle and support it safely.

7. Drain the transaxle and reinstall the drain plug.

8. Remove the throttle control cable.

9. Remove the cable clip and then pull the speedometer cable out of the holder.

10. Do not remove the holder or the speedometer gear may fall into the transaxle housing.

11. Remove the nut and washer from each end of the stabilizer bar. Remove both mounting brackets and then remove the bar.

12. Disconnect right and left lower arm ball joints and tie-rod end ball joints using ball joint remover tool, or you can remove pivot bolts from lower control arms instead.

13. Turn the right steering knuckle outward as far as it will go. Position a suitable tool against inboard CV joint, pry right axle out of transaxle housing approximately ½ inch (to force its spring clip out of groove inside differential gear splines), then pull it out the rest of the way. Repeat on opposite side.

14. Place a jack under engine oil pan and raise engine just enough to take weight off mounts.

15. Remove engine damper from center beam.

16. Remove front and rear torque rods, and rear torque rod brackets.

17. Remove rear engine mount and its bracket.

18. Cut a block of wood, 1" x 2" x 4", and place between the center beam and the oil pan, then lower the jack and let engine rest on center beam.

19. Remove engine damper bracket and torque converter cover plate from the transaxle.

20. Remove engine-side starter mounting bolt, then remove starter.

21. Raise transmission jack securely against the transaxle.

22. Remove center console and shift indicator.

23. Remove lock pin from adjuster and shift cable.

24. Remove both bolts and pull shift cable out of housing.

25. Unbolt torque converter from drive plate by rotating crank and removing eight bolts.

26. Remove two remaining the transaxle mounting bolts.

27. Roll the transaxle away from engine to clear the two dowel pins, then lower the jack.

28. Reinstall center beam, then remove hoist.

1984 AND LATER CIVIC

1. Disconnect the negative battery cable.

2. Position the selector lever in the neutral position.

3. Disconnect the battery cable from the starter. Disconnect the transaxle ground cable.

4. Disconnect and plug the transaxle oil cooler lines at the transaxle.

5. Remove the two starter mounting bolts. Remove the top three transaxle mounting bolts.

6. Loosen the front wheel nuts. Raise the vehicle and support it safely.

7. Drain the transaxle and reinstall the drain plug.

8. Remove the throttle control cable.

9. Remove the cable clip and then pull the speedometer cable out of the holder.

10. Do not remove the holder or the speedometer gear will fall into the transaxle housing.

11. Remove the engine and wheelwell splash shields from the front end of the frame.

12. Remove the exhaust header pipe.

13. Disconnect the right and left lower arm ball joints and tie rod end ball joints using the ball joint remover.

NOTE: Make sure the floor jack is positioned securely under the lower control arm, at the ball joint. Otherwise torsion bar tension on the lower control arm may cause the arm to jump suddenly away from the steering knuckle as the ball joint is being removed.

14. Turn the right steering knuckle outward as far as it will go. Position a suitable tool against the inboard CV joint, pry right axle out of the transaxle housing approximately ½ inch (to force its spring clip out of groove inside deferential gear splines), then pull it out the rest of the way. Repeat on opposite side.

15. Attach a chain hoist to the bolt near the distributor, then lift the engine slightly to unload the mounts.

16. Raise the transmission jack and secure it against the transaxle assembly.

17. Remove the bolts from the front transaxle mount.

18. Remove the transaxle housing bolts from the engine torque bracket.

19. Remove the torque converter housing bolts from the rear transaxle mount.

20. Remove the torque converter cover plate.

21. Remove the drive plate bolts.

22. Remove the cotter pin from the shift cable control pin, then pull out the control pin.

23. Remove the cable holder and carefully remove the shift cable.

NOTE: Be careful not to lose the shift cable bushing.

24. Remove the one remaining transaxle mounting bolt from the engine side.

25. Pull the transaxle away from engine to clear the two dowel pins, then lower the jack.

26. Remove torque converter from the transaxle.

1981 AND LATER ACCORD AND PRELUDE

1. Disconnect the negative battery cable.

2. Position the selector lever in neutral.

3. Disconnect the battery cable from the starter. Disconnect the wire from the solenoid.

4. Disconnect and plug the transaxle oil cooler lines at the transaxle.

5. Remove the starter mounting bolt on the transaxle side and the top transaxle mounting bolt.

6. Loosen the front wheel nut. Raise the vehicle and support it safely.

7. Drain the transaxle. Reinstall the transaxle drain plug.

8. Remove the throttle control cable.

9. On some vehicles it may be necessary to remove the right front wheel well fender shield.

10. If the vehicle is not equipped with power steering, remove the cable clip and pull the speedometer cable out of the housing. Do not remove the holder because the speedometer gear may fall into the transaxle housing.

11. If the vehicle is equipped with power steering, remove the speed sensor along with the speedometer cable and hoses.

12. Remove the transaxle-side starter motor mounting bolt and two upper transaxle mounting bolts.

13. Place transmission jack securely beneath transaxle, and hook hanger plate with hoist; make sure hoist chain is tight.

14. Remove subframe center beam.

15. Remove the ball joint pinch bolt from the right side lower control arm, then use a lead or brass hammer to tap the control arm free of the knuckle.

16. Remove the right side radius rod.

17. Disconnect the stabilizer bar at the right side lower control arm.

18. Detach stabilizer spring from radius rods.

19. Remove front self-locking nuts from radius rods on each side.

20. Remove lower arm bolt from both sides of sub frame.

21. Turn right side steering knuckle to its most outboard position. Pry CV joint out approximately ½ in., then pull CV joint out of transaxle housing.

NOTE: Do not pull on the driveshaft or knuckle since this may cause the inboard CV joint to separate; pull on the inboard CV joint.

22. Remove engine-side starter motor bolt. Detach starter motor and lower through chassis.

23. Remove the transaxle damper bracket located in front of torque converter cover plate.

24. Remove torque converter cover plate.

25. Disconnect the shift cable from transaxle.

26. Wire the shift cable away from the transaxle assembly.

27. Remove both bolts and pull shift cable out of housing.

28. Unbolt torque converter assembly from drive plate by removing eight bolts.

29. Remove the three rear engine mounting bolts from the transaxle housing. Remove the rear engine mount.

30. Remove the lower transaxle mounting bolt.

31. Pull the transaxle assembly away from the engine in order to clear the two dowel pins.

32. Pry the left side CV joint out about ½ in. Pull the transaxle out and lower the assembly on the transmission jack.

33. Remove the torque converter assembly from the transaxle.

Installation
1981-83 CIVIC

1. Slide torque converter onto mainshaft.

2. Position the transaxle on the transmission jack, and raise to engine level.

3. Check that the two dowel pins are installed in torque converter housing.

4. Align dowel pins with holes in block; align torque converter bolt heads with holes in drive plate.

5. If you left the front end connected on driver's side, insert left axle (with new spring clip on the end) into differential as you roll the transaxle up to the engine.

6. Secure the transaxle to engine with two lower mounting bolts.

7. Attach the torque converter to the drive plate with the eight bolts, and torque to 9 ft. lbs. Rotate crank as necessary to tighten bolts to ½ torque, then final torque, in a criss-cross pattern. Check for free rotation after tightening last bolt.

8. Secure cable retainer to guide (below shift console).

9. Remove transmission jack.

10. Install the torque converter cover plate and damper bracket.

11. Place a jack under engine oil pan and raise engine only enough to align bolt holes for rear motor mount bracket.

NOTE: Place a flat piece of wood on the jack lifting pad, to prevent damage to oil pan.

12. Install rear engine mount and bracket.

13. Install starter with engine-side mounting bolt and torque to 33 ft. lbs.

14. Install front and rear torque rods and brackets.

15. Install new 26mm spring clip on end of each axle.

16. Turn right steering knuckle fully outward, and slide axle into differential until you feel its spring clip engage side gear. Repeat on left side or, if left axle is already in, check to be sure spring clip has engaged side gear.

17. Reconnect lower arm and tie rod end ball joints. Torque lower arm nuts to 25 ft. lbs. and the tie rod nuts to 32 ft. lbs.

18. Install stabilizer bar. Torque end nuts and bracket bolts to 31 ft. lbs.

19. Install the front wheels. Lower the vehicle from the lift.

20. Insert the speedometer cable into the gear holder and secure the cable with the clip. Install the boot.

21. Install the transaxle side starter mounting bolt. Install the top transaxle mounting bolt. Torque all bolts to 33 ft. lbs.

22. Connect the transaxle oil cooler lines.

23. Install the forward bolt for the rear torque rod bracket. Attach the shift control cable to the shift lever with the pin and clip. Install the center console as required.

24. Connect all necessary electrical wiring.

25. Connect the negative battery cable. Fill the transaxle with the proper grade and type automatic transmission fluid. Adjust the shift cable.

26. Install and adjust throttle control cable as required. Road test the vehicle.

1984 AND LATER CIVIC

1. Slide the torque converter onto mainshaft.

2. Position the transaxle on the transmission jack, and raise to engine level.

3. Check that the two dowel pins are installed in torque converter housing.

4. Align dowel pins with holes in block; align torque converter bolt heads with holes in drive plate.

5. If you left the front end connected on driver's side, insert left axle (with new spring clip on the end) into differential as you roll the transaxle up to the engine.

NOTE: New 26mm spring clips must be used on both axles.

6. Secure the transaxle to engine with engine side mounting bolt and torque to 50 ft. lbs.

7. Attach torque converter to drive plate with eight bolts, and torque to 9 ft. lbs. Rotate crank as necessary to tighten bolts to ½ torque, then final torque, in a criss-cross pattern. Check for free rotation after tightening last bolt.

8. Install the shift cable.

9. Remove the transmission jack.

10. Install the torque converter cover plate.

11. Install the rear transmission mount and torque its bolts to 47 ft. lbs.

12. Install the engine torque bracket and torque the retaining bolts to 33 ft. lbs.

13. Loosely install the front transaxle mounting bolts.

14. Install the starter mounting bolts and torque to 33 ft. lbs.

15. Install a new 26mm spring clip on end of each axle.

16. Turn right steering knuckle fully outward, and slide axle into differential until you feel its spring clip engage side gear. Repeat on left side or, if left axle is already in, check to be sure spring clip has engaged side gear.

17. Reconnect the lower arm ball joints and torque to 33 ft. lbs.

18. Reconnect the tie-rod end ball joints and torque to 33 ft. lbs.

19. Install the splash shields and exhaust header pipe.

20. Install the front wheels. Lower the vehicle.

21. Remove the chain hoist.

22. Insert the speedometer cable into the gear holder and secure it with the clip. Install the boot.

23. Install the three top transaxle mounting bolts. Torque them to 42 ft. lbs.

24. Connect the transaxle oil cooler lines.

25. Attach the shift control cable to the shift lever with the retaining pin and clip. Intall the center console as required.

26. Connect all electrical wiring.

27. Connect the negative battery cable. Fill the transaxle with the proper grade and type automatic transmission fluid.

28. Start the engine and check for proper shift cable adjustment. Adjust the cable as required.

29. Install and set the throttle control cable as required.

30. Road test the vehicle and check for leaks.

1981 and Later Accord and Prelude

1. Attach the shift cable to the shift arm with the retaining pin. Secure the cable to the edge of the transaxle housing with the cable holder and bolt. Torque the bolt to 9 ft. lbs.

2. Install torque converter on the transaxle.

3. Place the transaxle on transmission jack, and raise to engine level.

4. Hook hanger plate with hoist and make hoist chain tight.

5. Check that the two dowel pins are installed in the transaxle housing.

6. Install new 26mm spring clips on the end of each axle.

7. Align dowel pins with holes in block; align torque converter bolt head with holes in drive plate.

8. Fit the left axle into the differential as you raise the transaxle up to the engine.

9. Secure the transaxle to engine with the two lower mounting bolts.

10. Install rear and front engine mounts on the transaxle housing, torque to 28 ft. lbs.

11. Install the front transaxle mount bolts and torque them to 28 ft. lbs.

12. Attach torque converter to drive plate with eight bolts, and torque to 9 ft. lbs. Rotate crank as necessary to tighten bolts to ½ torque, then the final torque, in a crisscross pattern. Check for free rotation after tightening the last bolts.

13. Remove the transmission jack.

14. Install torque converter cover plate, torque two bolts (in oil pan flange). Torque bolts to 9 ft. lbs.

15. Install damper bracket, torque two nuts to 40 ft. lbs. and three bolts to 22 ft. lbs.

16. Remove the hoist from the transaxle assembly.

17. Install the starter mount bolts, and troque them to 33 ft. lbs.

18. Install the rear torque rod and brackets.

19. Turn right steering knuckle fully outward, and slide axle into differential until you feel its spring clip engage side the gear. Check that the left axle spring clip is engaged in its side gear.

20. Reconnect ball joint to knuckle, then torque its bolt to 40 ft. lbs. Reinstall the damper fork and torque its bolt to 32 ft. lbs.

21. Install the speedometer cable. Align the tab on the cable end with the slot in the holder. Install the clip so the bent leg is on the groove. After installation pull the cable to be sure that its secure.

22. Install the front tires and wheels. Lower the vehicle to the ground.

23. Install the transaxle side starter mounting bolts. Torque to 33 ft. lbs. Install the top transaxle mounting bolt and torque to 33 ft. lbs.

24. Connect the transaxle oil cooler lines to the transaxle assembly.

25. Connect all necessary wiring and electrical connectors.

26. Connect the negative battery cable. Fill the transaxle with the proper grade and type automatic transmission fluid.

27. Install and connect the shift cable. Install the console assembly as required.

28. Start the engine and shift the transaxle through all the gears. If the shift cable is out of adjustment correct it.

29. Install the throttle cable and adjust it as required. Road test the vehicle.

BENCH OVERHAUL

Before Disassembly

1. Clean the exterior of the automatic transaxle before any attempt is made to disassemble the unit. This procedure is done to prevent dirt or other foreign material from entering the transaxle and damaging the internal parts.

CAUTION

If steam cleaning is done to the exterior of the automatic transaxle immediate disassembly should be done to avoid rust from condensation, which will form on the internal parts of the transaxle.

---

2. Handle all automatic transaxle parts carefully to avoid nicking or burring the bearing or mating surface.
3. Lubricate all internal parts with automatic transmission fluid before assembling.
4. Do not use other lubricants except on gaskets and thrust washers, as may be indicated. Gaskets and thrust washers may be coated with petroleum jelly in place of other lubricants.
5. Always use new gaskets and seals during the assembly.
6. Tighten all nuts and bolts to the specified torque.

Torque Converter Inspection

Some three speed automatic transaxles are equipped with a torque converter that can be disassembled. Only qualified repair shops that have special equipment should attempt disassembly and reassembly of the torque converter.

THREE SPEED TRANSAXLE

Disassembly

1. Locate alignment marks on the converter cover and converter pump. If not visible, scribe marks so that the converter cover and pump may be reassembled in the same position.
2. Remove the retaining bolts holding the converter cover to the starter ring gear.
3. Separate the converter cover from the pump body with the use of a plastic or rawhide hammer.
4. Remove the turbine thrust washer and remove the turbine from the converter pump.
5. Remove the serrated thrust washer from between the turbine and the stator.
6. Remove the stator from the pump body, along with the thrust washer.
7. Remove the snap rings from the stator and remove the front and rear side plates. Push the one-way clutch assembly from the stator body.

CAUTION

As the one-way clutch assembly is removed from the stator, the rollers and springs may become disengaged and fall from the assembly. Do not lose the rollers or springs.

Inspection

1. Inspect the cover for cracks, nicks and burrs on the sealing surfaces.
2. Inspect the thrust washers for overheating indications, extreme wear and a galling condition.
3. Inspect the turbine and converter pump cover for broken or damaged vanes, nicks and burrs, and thrust washer wear surfaces for scores.

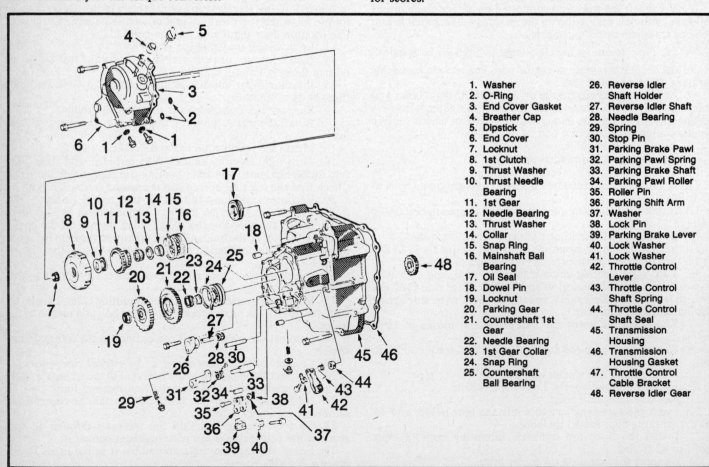

1. Washer
2. O-Ring
3. End Cover Gasket
4. Breather Cap
5. Dipstick
6. End Cover
7. Locknut
8. 1st Clutch
9. Thrust Washer
10. Thrust Needle Bearing
11. 1st Gear
12. Needle Bearing
13. Thrust Washer
14. Collar
15. Snap Ring
16. Mainshaft Ball Bearing
17. Oil Seal
18. Dowel Pin
19. Locknut
20. Parking Gear
21. Countershaft 1st Gear
22. Needle Bearing
23. 1st Gear Collar
24. Snap Ring
25. Countershaft Ball Bearing
26. Reverse Idler Shaft Holder
27. Reverse Idler Shaft
28. Needle Bearing
29. Spring
30. Stop Pin
31. Parking Brake Pawl
32. Parking Pawl Spring
33. Parking Brake Shaft
34. Parking Pawl Roller
35. Roller Pin
36. Parking Shift Arm
37. Washer
38. Lock Pin
39. Parking Brake Lever
40. Lock Washer
41. Lock Washer
42. Throttle Control Lever
43. Throttle Control Shaft Spring
44. Throttle Control Shaft Seal
45. Transmission Housing
46. Transmission Housing Gasket
47. Throttle Control Cable Bracket
48. Reverse Idler Gear

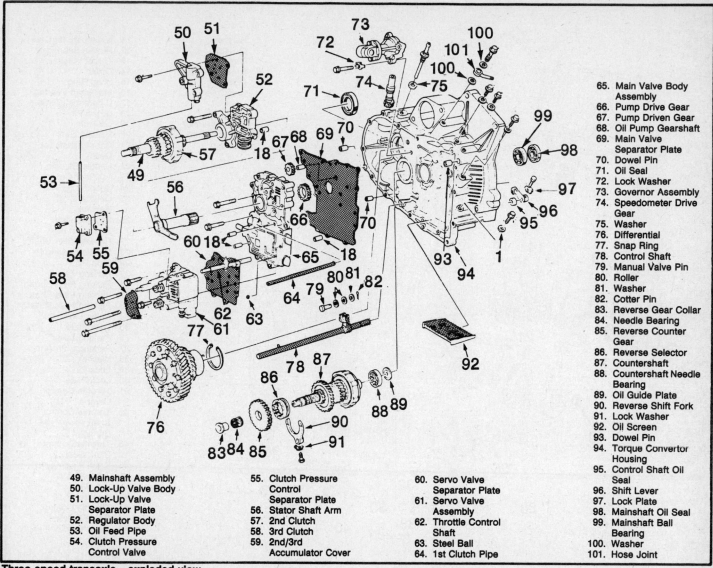

65.	Main Valve Body Assembly
66.	Pump Drive Gear
67.	Pump Driven Gear
68.	Oil Pump Gearshaft
69.	Main Valve Separator Plate
70.	Dowel Pin
71.	Oil Seal
72.	Lock Washer
73.	Governor Assembly
74.	Speedometer Drive Gear
75.	Washer
76.	Differential
77.	Snap Ring
78.	Control Shaft
79.	Manual Valve Pin
80.	Roller
81.	Washer
82.	Cotter Pin
83.	Reverse Gear Collar
84.	Needle Bearing
85.	Reverse Counter Gear
86.	Reverse Selector
87.	Countershaft
88.	Countershaft Needle Bearing
89.	Oil Guide Plate
90.	Reverse Shift Fork
91.	Lock Washer
92.	Oil Screen
93.	Dowel Pin
94.	Torque Convertor Housing
95.	Control Shaft Oil Seal
96.	Shift Lever
97.	Lock Plate
98.	Mainshaft Oil Seal
99.	Mainshaft Ball Bearing
100.	Washer
101.	Hose Joint

49. Mainshaft Assembly	55. Clutch Pressure Control Separator Plate	60. Servo Valve Separator Plate	
50. Lock-Up Valve Body		61. Servo Valve Assembly	
51. Lock-Up Valve Separator Plate	56. Stator Shaft Arm	62. Throttle Control Shaft	
52. Regulator Body	57. 2nd Clutch	63. Steel Ball	
53. Oil Feed Pipe	58. 3rd Clutch	64. 1st Clutch Pipe	
54. Clutch Pressure Control Valve	59. 2nd/3rd Accumulator Cover		

Three speed transaxle—exploded view

4. Inspect the stator for broken vanes and the operation of the one-way clutch. Using the stator torque converter shaft, installed in the one-way clutch from the pump side (thinner vanes up), the one-way clutch should turn in a counterclockwise direction and lock-up in a clockwise direction.

5. Inspect the one-way clutch springs and rollers for breakage, distortion, galling and indentations on the stator cam.

6. Inspect the converter hub surface and serrations for damage. Inspect the O-ring groove for burrs.

Assembly

1. Hold the stator with the thinner vanes up and place the stator cam with the wide shoulder upward, into the stator body. Place a roller into the opening between the stator cam and the stator ring. Insert a spring on the deep side of the roller pocket and continue the roller/spring installation, with the center of the spring against the roller.

2. Install the stator side plates and the snap rings and lock into place. Install side plates with grooved side out.

3. Inspect the one-way clutch operation. With the thinner vane side up (converter pump side), the one-way clutch should free-wheel in a counterclockwise rotation and lock up in a clockwise rotation.

4. Place the converter pump body on a flat surface with the vanes up. Install the thrust washer in the converter pump.

5. Place the stator assembly in the pump body, with the thicker vanes up and the stator resting on the thrust washer.

6. Place the serrated thrust washer in the stator, being sure the washer is flush with the stator surface.

7. Install the large O-ring on the pump body and set the turbine in place over the stator assembly.

8. Install the thrust washer in the turbine center and install the converter cover, aligning the match marks.

9. Slide the starter ring gear up over the pump cover and install the bolts through the converter cover and into the starter ring gear. The flat side of the ring gear should be towards the torque converter cover.

Transaxle Disassembly

TRANSAXLE HOUSING

Disassembly

THREE AND FOUR SPEED TRANSAXLES

1. Remove the transaxle dipstick. Remove the end cover retaining bolts. Remove the end cover.

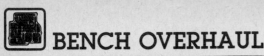

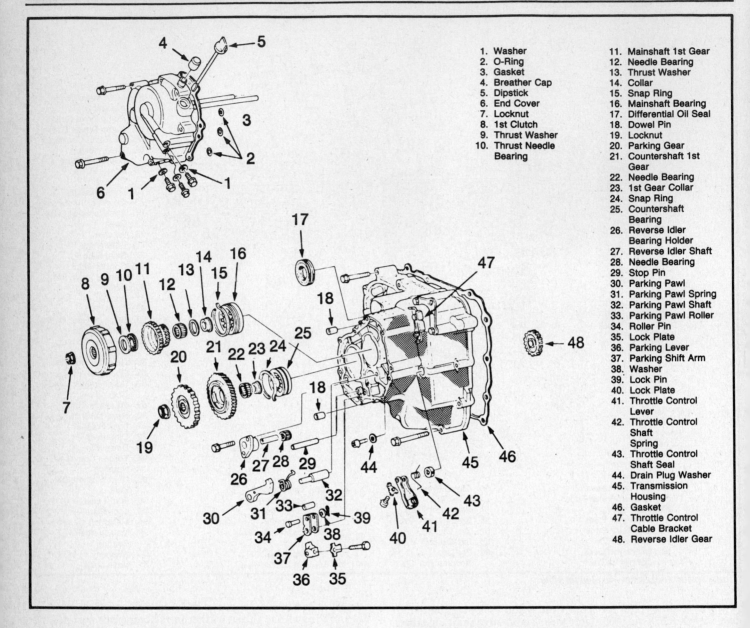

1. Washer
2. O-Ring
3. Gasket
4. Breather Cap
5. Dipstick
6. End Cover
7. Locknut
8. 1st Clutch
9. Thrust Washer
10. Thrust Needle Bearing
11. Mainshaft 1st Gear
12. Needle Bearing
13. Thrust Washer
14. Collar
15. Snap Ring
16. Mainshaft Bearing
17. Differential Oil Seal
18. Dowel Pin
19. Locknut
20. Parking Gear
21. Countershaft 1st Gear
22. Needle Bearing
23. 1st Gear Collar
24. Snap Ring
25. Countershaft Bearing
26. Reverse Idler Bearing Holder
27. Reverse Idler Shaft
28. Needle Bearing
29. Stop Pin
30. Parking Pawl
31. Parking Pawl Spring
32. Parking Pawl Shaft
33. Parking Pawl Roller
34. Roller Pin
35. Lock Plate
36. Parking Lever
37. Parking Shift Arm
38. Washer
39. Lock Pin
40. Lock Plate
41. Throttle Control Lever
42. Throttle Control Shaft Spring
43. Throttle Control Shaft Seal
44. Drain Plug Washer
45. Transmission Housing
46. Gasket
47. Throttle Control Cable Bracket
48. Reverse Idler Gear

2. Shift the transaxle into the park position. Lock the mainshaft in place by using the mainshaft holder.

3. Remove the end cover gasket, dowel pins and O-rings.

4. Pry the staked edge of the locknut flange out of the notch in the first clutch.

5. Remove the mainshaft locknut. Be careful as the mainshaft locknut is left hand threaded.

6. Remove the first clutch assembly. Remove the thrust washer, needle bearing and the first gear from the transaxle.

7. Remove the needle bearing and the thrust washer from the mainshaft.

8. Pry the staked edge of the locknut out of the notch in the parking gear. Remove the countershaft locknut and the parking pawl stop pin.

9. Remove the parking pawl, shaft and spring from the transaxle case.

10. Remove the parking gear and first gear countershaft as a complete unit.

11. From the countershaft, remove the needle bearing and the first gear collar. From the mainshaft, remove the O-ring and the first gear collar.

12. Remove the reverse idler bearing holder.

13. Bend down the tab on the lock plate which is under the parking shift arm bolt. Remove the bolt. Remove the parking shift arm spring.

14. Bend down the tab on the throttle control lever bolt lock plate, then remove the bolt. Remove the throttle control lever and spring from throttle valve shaft.

15. Remove the retaining bolts as indicated in the retaining bolt illustration.

NOTE: Retaining bolt number one will not come all the way out of the transaxle housing because the throttle control cable bracket is in the way. Just unscrew the bracket so that it is free of the threads in the converter housing and leave it in place. If you remove the bracket you will have to readjust it upon installation.

16. Align the control shaft spring pin with the cutout in the transaxle housing.

17. Install the transaxle housing puller. Screw in the puller and separate the transaxle housing from the rest of the transaxle assembly.

18. Remove the puller from the transaxle housing.

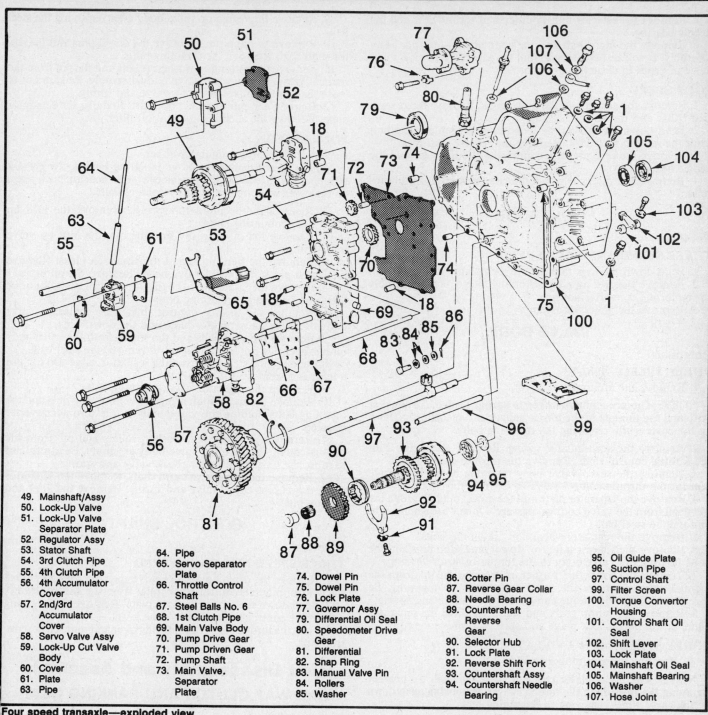

49. Mainshaft/Assy
50. Lock-Up Valve
51. Lock-Up Valve Separator Plate
52. Regulator Assy
53. Stator Shaft
54. 3rd Clutch Pipe
55. 4th Clutch Pipe
56. 4th Accumulator Cover
57. 2nd/3rd Accumulator Cover
58. Servo Valve Assy
59. Lock-Up Cut Valve Body
60. Cover
61. Plate
63. Pipe

64. Pipe
65. Servo Separator Plate
66. Throttle Control Shaft
67. Steel Balls No. 6
68. 1st Clutch Pipe
69. Main Valve Body
70. Pump Drive Gear
71. Pump Driven Gear
72. Pump Shaft
73. Main Valve. Separator Plate

74. Dowel Pin
75. Dowel Pin
76. Lock Plate
77. Governor Assy
79. Differential Oil Seal
80. Speedometer Drive Gear
81. Differential
82. Snap Ring
83. Manual Valve Pin
84. Rollers
85. Washer

86. Cotter Pin
87. Reverse Gear Collar
88. Needle Bearing
89. Countershaft Reverse Gear
90. Selector Hub
91. Lock Plate
92. Reverse Shift Fork
93. Countershaft Assy
94. Countershaft Needle Bearing

95. Oil Guide Plate
96. Suction Pipe
97. Control Shaft
99. Filter Screen
100. Torque Convertor Housing
101. Control Shaft Oil Seal
102. Shift Lever
103. Lock Plate
104. Mainshaft Oil Seal
105. Mainshaft Bearing
106. Washer
107. Hose Joint

Four speed transaxle—exploded view

MAINSHAFT AND COUNTERSHAFT

Removal

THREE SPEED—1981-83

1. Remove the gasket, dowel pins and the first and third oil feed pipes.

2. Remove the reverse idler gear collar, needle bearing and the countershaft reverse gear.

3. Bend down the tab on the lock plate and remove the bolt on the reverse shift fork.

4. Remove the reverse shift fork and the selector sleeve as a complete unit.

5. Remove the countershaft second gear. Remove the mainshaft and the countershaft together. It will be necessary to pull the assembly up on a slight angle in order to clear the governor.

THREE SPEED—1984 AND LATER

1. Remove the gasket and the dowel pins. Remove and clean the magnet.

2. Remove the reverse gear collar, needle bearing and the countershaft reverse gear.

3. Bend down the tab on the lock plate and remove the reverse shift retaining bolt.

4. Remove the reverse shift fork and the selector sleeve as a unit.

5. Remove the selector hub, countershaft second gear and the needle bearing.

6. Remove the mainshaft and the countershaft together as an assembly. It will be necessary to pull the assembly up on a slight angle in order to clear the governor.

FOUR SPEED

1. Remove the gasket and the dowel pins. Remove the reverse gear collar and the needle bearing.

2. Bend down the tab on the lock plate and remove the bolt from the reverse shift fork. Remove the reverse shift fork.

3. Remove the selector hub, countershaft fourth gear and the needle bearing.

4. Remove the mainshaft and the countershaft assembly together.

GOVERNOR

Removal

THREE SPEED AND FOUR SPEED

1. Bend down the lock tabs on the lock plate.

2. Remove the retaining bolts holding the governor assembly to the torque converter housing.

3. Remove the governor assembly.

VALVE BODY

Removal

THREE SPEED—1981-83

1. Remove the accumulator cover.

NOTE: The accumulator cover is spring loaded. To prevent stripping the threads in the torque converter housing press down on the cover while removing the retaining bolts.

2. Remove the accumulator spring. Remove the E-clip from the throttle control shaft. Remove the throttle control shaft.

3. Remove the servo valve body retaining bolts. The inside bolt for the throttle control valve cover may stay in place.

4. Remove the separator plate and the dowel pins. Remove the steel ball from the valve body oil passage. Do not use a magnet to remove the steel ball.

5. Remove the regulator valve body retaining bolts.

6. Remove the stator shaft arm, dowel pins, stop pins and the bolts holding the valve body to the torque coverter housing.

7. Remove the cotter pin, washer, rollers and the pin from the manual valve. Remove the valve body from its mounting. Be sure not to loose the torque converter check valve and spring.

8. Remove the pump gears and shaft. Remove the separator plate, dowel pins, check valve and spring. Remove the filter.

THREE SPEED—1984 AND LATER

1. Remove the accumulator cover.

NOTE: The accumulator cover is spring loaded. To prevent stripping the threads in the torque converter housing push down on the cover while removing the retaining bolts.

2. Remove the accumulator springs. Remove the lock up valve body mounting bolts.

3. Slide up on the lock up valve body. Remove the oil feed pipe and the lock up valve body.

4. Remove the first and third clutch pipes. Remove the clutch pressure control valve and the clutch pressure control valve separator plate.

5. Remove the servo valve body retaining bolts and remove the servo valve body.

6. Remove the E-clip from the throttle control shaft. Remove the throttle control shaft.

7. Remove the servo valve separator plate and dowel pins.

8. Remove the steel balls from the valve body oil passage. Do not use a magnet to remove the balls.

9. Remove the regulator valve body after removing the steel ball.

10. Remove the stop pin. Remove the dowel pins and the stator shaft arm. Remove the retaining bolts.

11. Remove the cotter pin, washer, rollers and the pin from the manual valve. Remove the valve body assembly. Be sure not to loose the torque converter check valve and spring.

12. Remove the pump gears and shaft. Remove the separator plate. Remove the suction pipe and oil filter.

FOUR SPEED

1. Remove the accumulator cover.

NOTE: The accumulator cover is spring loaded. To prevent stripping the threads in the torque converter housing push down on the cover while removing the retaining bolts.

2. Remove the accumulator springs. Remove the lock up valve body mounting bolts.

3. Remove the oil pipes by first moving the lock up valve body upward.

4. Remove the first, third and fourth clutch pipes. Remove the clutch pressure control valve body. Remove the oil pipes.

5. Remove the E-clip from the throttle control shaft. Remove the servo valve body retaining bolts.

6. Remove the throttle control shaft from the servo valve body. Remove the separator plate and the dowel pins.

7. Remove the steel balls and the spring from the valve body oil passages. Do not use a magnet to remove the steel balls.

8. Remove the steel ball from the regulator valve. Do not use a magnet to remove the steel ball.

9. Remove the regulator valve retaining bolts.

10. Remove the stator shaft arm, dowel pins, stop pins and the retaining bolts holding the valve body to the torque converter housing.

11. Remove the cotter pin, washer, rollers and pin from the manual valve. Remove the valve body assembly. Be careful not to loose the torque converter check valve and spring.

12. Remove the pump gears and shaft. Remove the separator plate, dowel pins check valve and spring. Remove the filter and suction pipe.

CONTROL SHAFT

Removal

THREE SPEED AND FOUR SPEED

1. Remove the cable holder. Remove the cotter pin. Remove the control pin and control lever roller from the control lever.

2. Bend down the tab on the lock plate. Remove the retaining bolt in the control lever. Remove the lever.

3. Turn the torque converter housing over and remove the control rod.

Unit Disassembly and Assembly
ONE WAY CLUTCH AND PARKING GEAR

Disassembly

1. Separate the countershaft first gear from the parking gear by turning the parking gear assembly counterclockwise.

2. Remove the one way clutch assembly by prying it upward using a suitable tool.

3. Inspect all parts for wear, scoring or damage. Replace defective components as required.

Assembly

1. Assemble the components in the reverse order of the disassembly procedure.

2. Once the components are assembled, hold the countershaft first gear and turn the parking gear in a counterclockwise direction, it must turn freely.

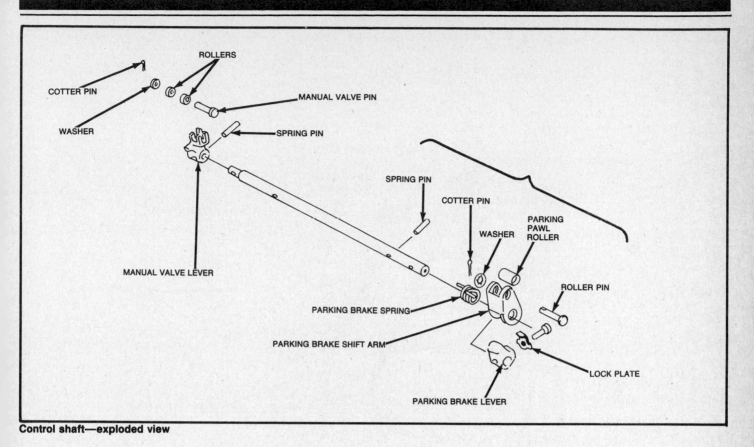

Control shaft—exploded view

VALVE BODY

Disassembly

1. Position the valve body assembly in a suitable holding fixture.
2. Remove the retaining bolts securing the shift valve covers.
3. Remove the internal components from inside the valve body after removing each of the shift valve covers.
4. Remove the torque converter check spring and valve from the top of the valve body.
5. Remove the pump driven gear and the drive gear from the valve body.
6. Remove the valve spring cap, relief valve spring and the valve.
7. Remove the orifice control spring seat, spring and the second gear orifice control valve.
8. Remove the detent spring, rollers and manual valve from the valve body assembly.
9. Inspect all parts for wear, damage and scoring. Repair or replace defective components as required.

Assembly

1. Before reassembly coat all parts with clean automatic transmission fluid.
2. Slide the spring into the hole in the big end of the shift valve. While holding the steel balls in place, position the sleeve over the valve.
3. Position the shift spring in the valve. Install the assembly into the valve body and retain it in place with the valve cover.
4. Position the relief spring into the relief valve. Install the assembly into the valve body. Be sure to install the relief valve first.
5. Compress the relief valve spring and then slip the check valve cap into place with the recessed side facing the spring.

6. Install the manual valve, detent rollers and spring into the valve body.
7. Install the pump gears and shaft into the valve body. Measure the thrust clearance of the driven gear to the valve body. It should be 0.001-0.002 in. The service limit specification is 0.003 in.
8. Measure the side clearance of the drive and driven gears. It should be 0.004-0.006 in. for 1981-83 three speed transaxles and 0.008-0.010 in. for all other transaxles. The service limit specification is 0.002-0.004 in.
9. Lay the valve body assembly aside until the transaxle is ready to be reassembled.

REGULATOR VALVE BODY

Disassembly

1. Hold the retainer in place while removing the lock bolt. Once the lock bolt is removed, slowly release the retainer.
2. On 1984 and later three speed transaxles, hold the lock up valve cover in place and remove the screws. Remove the spring and the control valve.
3. On four speed transaxles it may also be necessary to hold the lock up valve in place and remove the screws, while removing the spring and the control valve.
4. Clean all parts and check for wear, damage or scoring. Repair or replace defective components as required. Coat all parts with transmission fluid.

Assembly

1. Install the pressure regulator valve along with the inner and outer springs.
2. Install the reaction spring, spring seat and the retainer.
3. Align the hole in the retainer with the hole in the valve body. Press the retainer into the valve body and tighten the lock bolt.

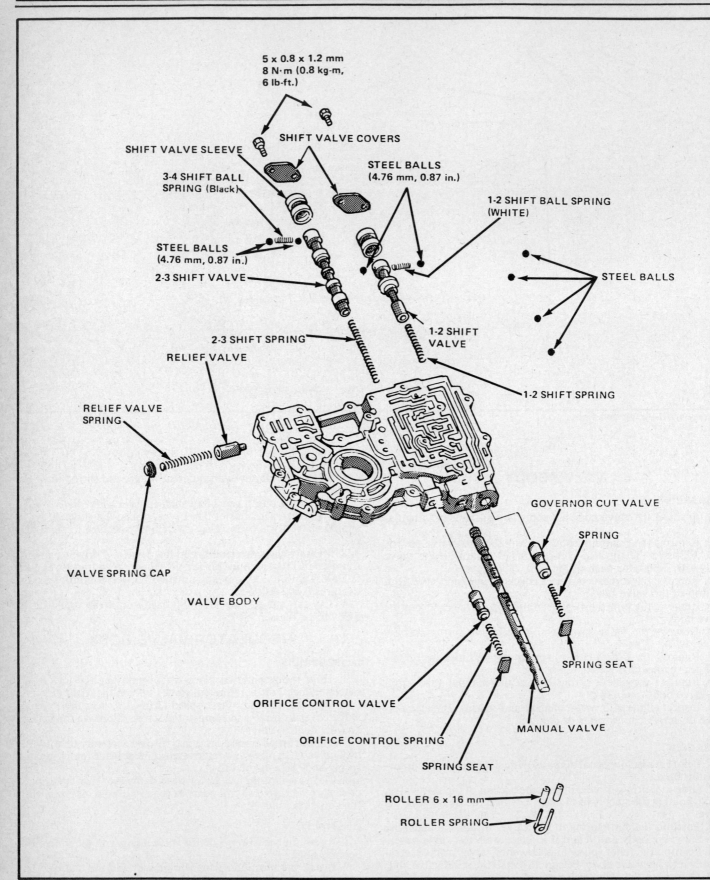

5 x 0.8 x 1.2 mm
8 N·m (0.8 kg-m,
6 lb-ft.)

SHIFT VALVE COVERS

SHIFT VALVE SLEEVE

3-4 SHIFT BALL
SPRING (Black)

STEEL BALLS
(4.76 mm, 0.87 in.)

1-2 SHIFT BALL SPRING
(WHITE)

STEEL BALLS
(4.76 mm, 0.87 in.)

2-3 SHIFT VALVE

STEEL BALLS

2-3 SHIFT SPRING

RELIEF VALVE

1-2 SHIFT VALVE

1-2 SHIFT SPRING

RELIEF VALVE
SPRING

VALVE SPRING CAP

VALVE BODY

GOVERNOR CUT VALVE

SPRING

SPRING SEAT

ORIFICE CONTROL VALVE

ORIFICE CONTROL SPRING

MANUAL VALVE

SPRING SEAT

ROLLER 6 x 16 mm

ROLLER SPRING

Three speed valve body—exploded view

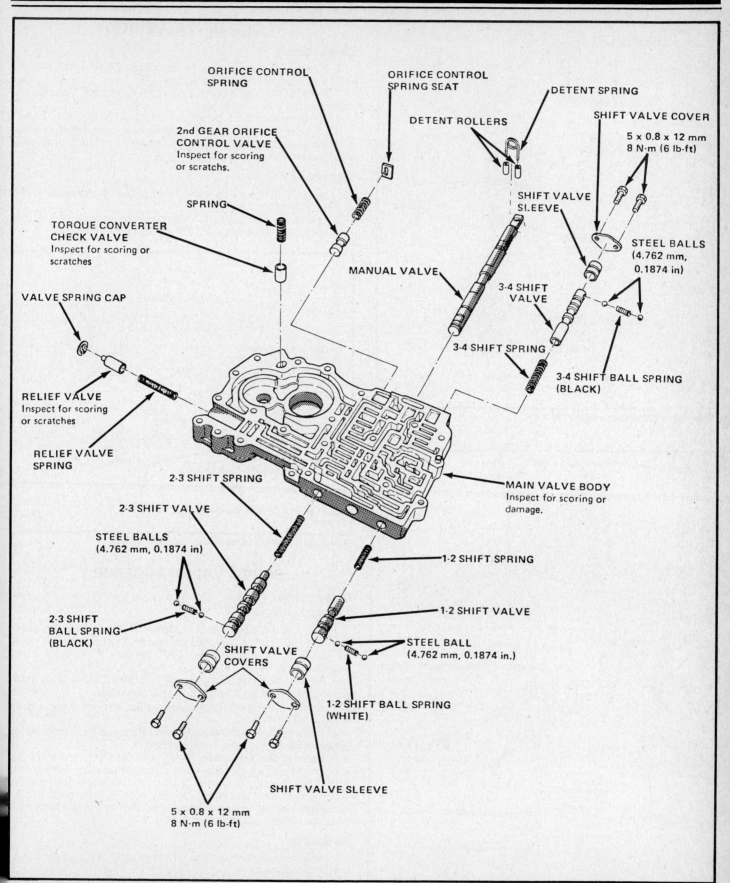

ORIFICE CONTROL SPRING

ORIFICE CONTROL SPRING SEAT

DETENT SPRING

DETENT ROLLERS

SHIFT VALVE COVER
5 x 0.8 x 12 mm
8 N·m (6 lb-ft)

2nd GEAR ORIFICE CONTROL VALVE
Inspect for scoring or scratchs.

SPRING

TORQUE CONVERTER CHECK VALVE
Inspect for scoring or scratches

SHIFT VALVE SLEEVE

MANUAL VALVE

3-4 SHIFT VALVE

STEEL BALLS
(4.762 mm, 0.1874 in)

VALVE SPRING CAP

3-4 SHIFT SPRING

RELIEF VALVE
Inspect for scoring or scratches

3-4 SHIFT BALL SPRING (BLACK)

RELIEF VALVE SPRING

2-3 SHIFT SPRING

MAIN VALVE BODY
Inspect for scoring or damage.

2-3 SHIFT VALVE

STEEL BALLS
(4.762 mm, 0.1874 in)

1-2 SHIFT SPRING

2-3 SHIFT BALL SPRING (BLACK)

1-2 SHIFT VALVE

SHIFT VALVE COVERS

STEEL BALL
(4.762 mm, 0.1874 in.)

1-2 SHIFT BALL SPRING (WHITE)

SHIFT VALVE SLEEVE

5 x 0.8 x 12 mm
8 N·m (6 lb-ft)

Four speed valve body—exploded view

927

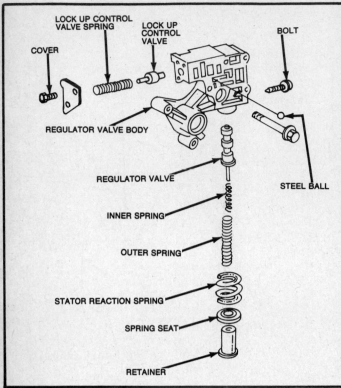

Regulator valve body—exploded view

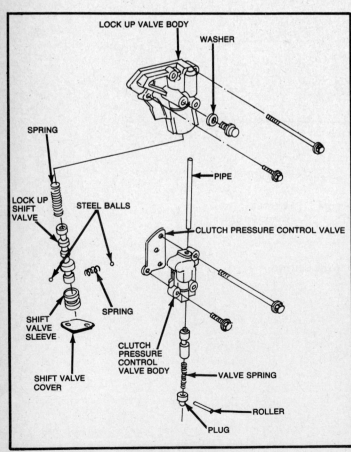

Three speed lock up valve body—exploded view

LOCK UP VALVE BODY

Disassembly

1. Remove the shift valve cover retaining bolts. Remove the shift valve sleeve, valve and spring.

2. Remove the clutch pressure control valve plug. Remove the roller, spring and control valve.

3. Remove the clutch pressure control valve separator plate.

4. Clean and inspect all parts. Repair or replace defective components as required. Coat all parts in clean automatic transmission fluid before installation.

Assembly

1. Assemble the lock up valve body in the reverse order of the disassembly procedure.

2. Install the assembly onto the regulator valve body. Set the unit aside unti the transaxle is ready to be reassembled.

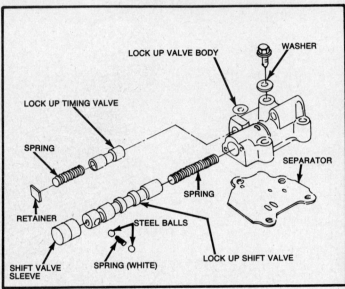

Four speed lock up valve body—exploded view

SERVO VALVE ASSEMBLY

Disassembly

THREE SPEED

1. Remove the throttle valve retainer. Remove the outer throttle valve "B", spring "B" and the inner throttle valve "B". Remove the outer throttle valve "A", spring "A" and the inner throttle valve "A".

2. Remove the lock up valve seat, spring and valve, if the vehicle is equipped with a lock up torque converter.

3. Remove the modulator valve spring retainer plate, spring and modulator valve.

4. Remove the accumulator cover. Remove the accumulator pistons and their related components.

5. Remove the servo valve along with the servo return spring.

6. Do not adjust or remove the throttle pressure adjustment bolt, it has been pre set at the factory for the proper shift points.

7. Clean all parts and check for wear, scoring or damage. Repair or replace parts as required. Before installation coat all parts with clean automatic transmission fluid.

Assembly

1. Assemble the servo valve in the reverse order of the disassembly procedure.

2. Once the component has been assembled, set it aside until the automatic transaxle is ready to be reassembled.

ACCUMULATOR SPRING SELECTION CHART

Component	Three Speed (81-83)	Three Speed (84- Later)	Four Speed
Servo valve return spring	1.20 inch	1.44 inch	1.59 inch
Second accumulator spring	3.70 inch	3.91 inch	3.28 inch
Third accumulator spring	3.70 inch	3.70 inch	4.21 inch
Fourth accumulator spring	—	—	3.72 inch

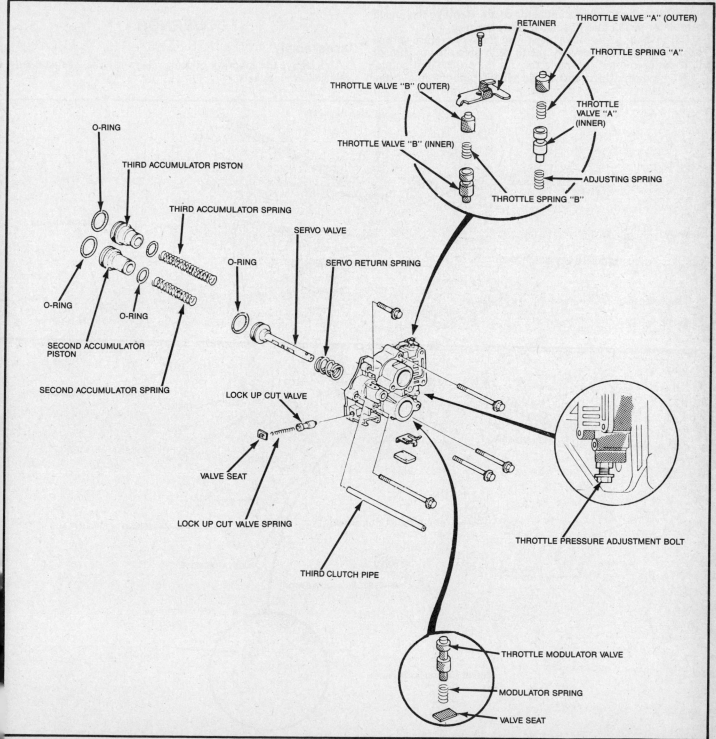

Three speed servo valve assembly—exploded view

Disassembly
FOUR SPEED

1. Remove the throttle valve retainer. Remove the outer throttle valve "B", spring "B" and the inner throttle valve "B". Remove the outer throttle valve "A", spring "A" and the inner throttle valve "A".

2. Remove the modulator valve spring, retainer plate and spring and the modulator valve.

3. Remove the second and third accumulator cover. Remove the pistons and their related components.

4. Remove the fourth accumulator cover. Remove the fourth accumulator piston and its related components.

5. Remove the servo valve along with the servo return spring.

6. Do not adjust or remove the throttle pressure adjustment bolt, it has been pre set at the factory for the proper shift points.

7. Remove the third and fourth clutch pipes. Remove the clutch pressure control valve body and its related components.

8. Clean all parts and check for wear, scoring or damage. Repair or replace parts as required. Before installation coat all parts with clean automatic transmission fluid.

Assembly

1. Assemble the servo valve in the reverse order of the disassembly procedure.

2. Once the component has been assembled, set it aside until the automatic transaxle is ready to be reassembled.

GOVERNOR

Disassembly

1. Remove the governor housing retaining bolts, by first bending back the lock tabs.

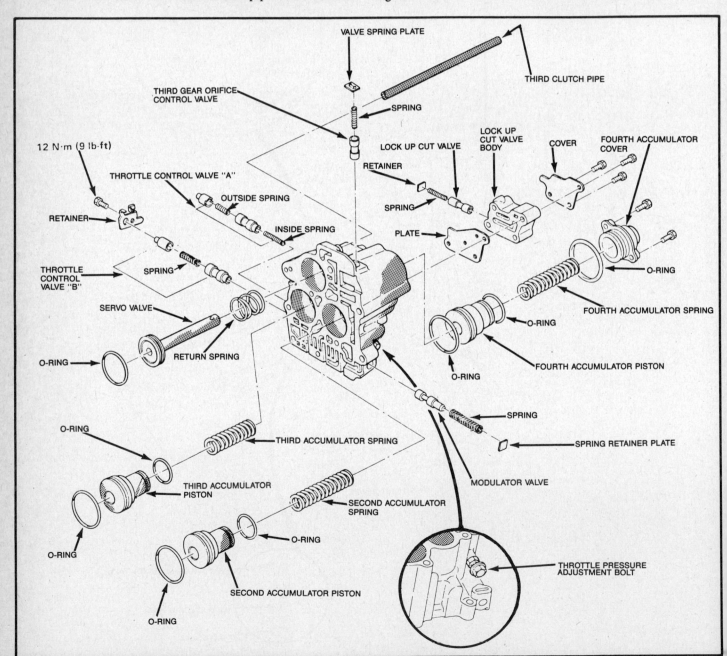

Four speed servo valve assembly—exploded view

2. Remove the governor housing E-clip and remove the governor housing internal components.

3. Remove the snap ring and gear from the governor holder. Remove the key and the dowel pins along with the pipe from the governor assembly shaft.

4. Clean and inspect all parts for wear, scoring or damage. Repair or replace components as required.

Assembly

1. Inspect the inside of the governor housing where the secondary weight sits for smoothness, correct as required.

2. Assemble the governor in the reverse order of the disassembly procedure. Be sure to use new lock tabs.

3. Set the governor aside until the transaxle is ready for reassembly.

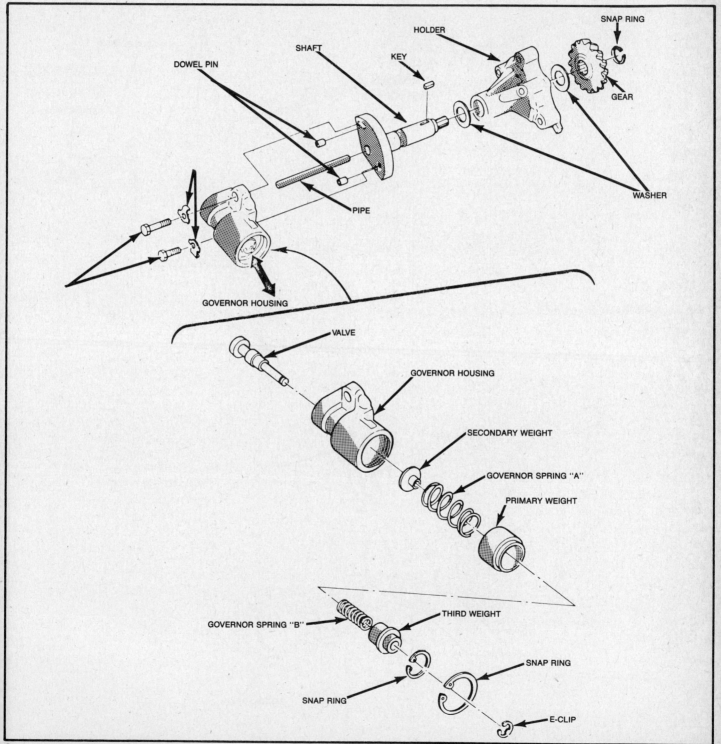

Governor assembly—exploded view

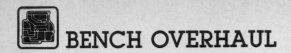

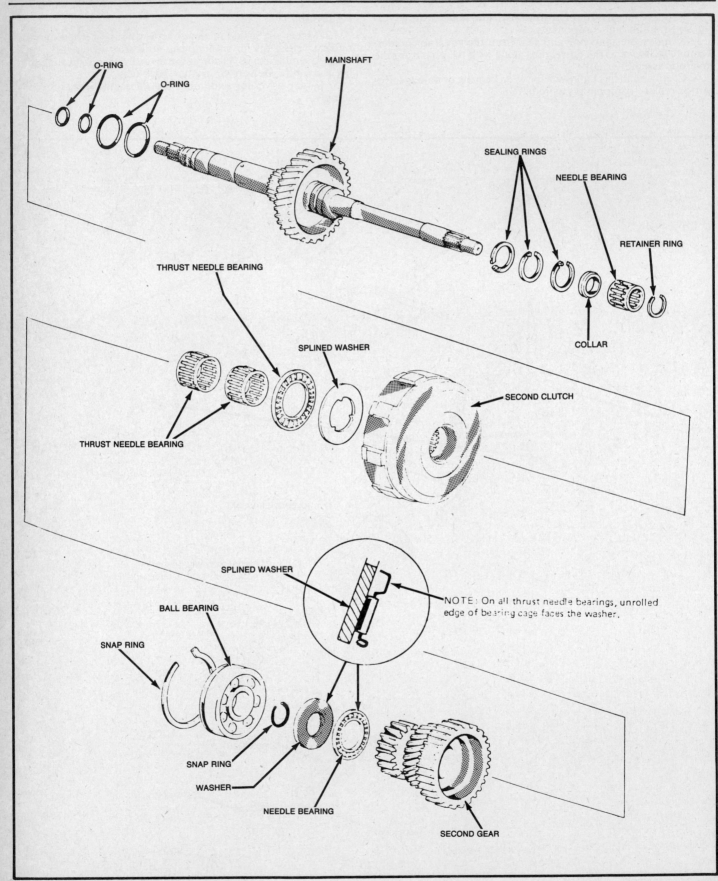

Three speed mainshaft assembly—exploded view

MAINSHAFT

Disassembly
THREE SPEED—1981-83

1. Remove the snap ring from the rear of the mainshaft assembly. Remove the needle bearing, spacer collar and the metal sealing rings. Discard the metal sealing rings.
2. Remove the snap ring from the front of the mainshaft assembly.
3. Remove and discard the O-ring seals. Remove the thrust washer, thrust needle bearing, and needle bearing.
4. Lift the second gear assembly from the mainshaft.
5. Separate the second gear assembly from the second clutch unit. Be sure not to lose the thrust needle bearing and the splined washer.
6. Clean and inspect all parts for wear, damage or scoring. Repair or replace defective components as required.
7. Coat all parts with clean automatic transmission fluid before reassembly.

Assembly

1. Assemble the mainshaft assembly in the reverse order of the disassembly procedure.
2. Check the mainshaft clearance measurement and replace the thrust washers as required.
3. Set the mainshaft assembly aside until the automatic transaxle is ready for reassembly.

THREE SPEED—1984 AND LATER

1. Remove the snap ring from the rear of the mainshaft assembly. Remove the needle bearing, spacer collar and the metal sealing rings. Discard the metal sealing rings.
2. Remove the snap ring from the front of the mainshaft assembly.
3. Remove the ball bearing, snap ring, washer, needle bearing and the second gear assembly.
4. Remove the second clutch assembly and separate it from the thrust needle bearing and splined washer.
5. Remove and discard the O-rings from the mainshaft assembly.
6. Clean and inspect all parts for wear, damage or scoring. Repair or replace defective components as required.
7. Coat all parts with clean automatic transmission fluid before reassembly.

Assembly

1. Assemble the mainshaft assembly in the reverse order of the disassembly procedure.
2. Check the mainshaft clearance measurement and replace the thrust washers as required.
3. Set the mainshaft assembly aside until the automatic transaxle is ready for reassembly.

FOUR SPEED

1. Remove the snap ring from the rear of the mainshaft assembly. Remove the needle bearing, spacer collar and the metal sealing rings. Discard the metal sealing rings.
2. Remove the snap ring from the front of the mainshaft assembly.
3. Remove the ball bearings, thrust needle bearing, snap ring, washer and the fourth gear assembly.
4. Remove the needle bearings, thrust needle bearing, fourth gear collar, thrust washer and the second and fourth clutch assembly.
5. Remove the remaining washers, gears, bearings and O-rings from the mainshaft assembly. Discard the O-rings.
6. Clean and inspect all parts for wear, damage or scoring. Repair or replace defective components as required.
7. Coat all parts with clean automatic transmission fluid before reassembly.

Assembly

1. Assemble the mainshaft assembly in the reverse order of the disassembly procedure.
2. Check the mainshaft clearance measurement and replace the thrust washers as required.
3. Set the mainshaft assembly aside until the automatic transaxle is ready for reassembly.

COUNTERSHAFT

Disassembly
THREE SPEED—1981-83

1. Remove the locknut. Remove the needle bearing, second gear, spacer collar, thrust washer and the needle bearing.
2. Remove the third gear assembly, thrust needle bearing, splined thrust washer and the third clutch assembly from the countershaft. Remove and discard the O-rings.
3. Clean and inspect all parts for wear, damage and scoring. Repair or replace defective components as required.
4. Coat all parts with clean automatic transmission fluid before reassembly.

Assembly

1. Assemble the countershaft in the reverse order of the disassembly procedure.
2. Check the countershaft clearance measurement and replace thrust washers as required.
3. Set the countershaft assembly aside until the automatic transaxle is ready to be reassembled.

Disassembly
THREE SPEED—1984 AND LATER

1. Remove the lock ring. Remove the reverse collar and needle bearing. Remove the reverse gear along with the reverse gear selector and the selector hub.
2. Remove the second gear assembly, needle bearing, and the splined thrust washer from the countershaft.
3. Remove the third gear assembly, needle bearing and the splined thrust washer from the countershaft assembly.
4. Remove the third clutch assembly and discard the O-ring seals.
5. Clean and inspect all parts for wear, damage and scoring. Repair or replace defective components as required.
6. Coat all parts with clean automatic transmission fluid before reassembly.

Assembly

1. Assemble the countershaft in the reverse order of the disassembly procedure.
2. Check the countershaft clearance measurement and replace thrust washers as required.
3. Set the countershaft assembly aside until the automatic transaxle is ready to be reassembled.

Disassembly
FOUR SPEED

1. Remove the snap ring. Remove the roller bearing, reverse gear collar and the needle bearing.
2. Remove the reverse gear, reverse gear selector and the selector hub from the countershaft.
3. Remove the fourth gear, needle bearing, spacer collar and second gear.
4. Remove the cotter washers, thrust needle bearing and the third gear assembly.
5. Remove the third clutch assembly, by first removing the thrust needle bearing, needle bearing and the splined thrust washer.
6. Remove and discard the O-rings from the countershaft assembly.

933

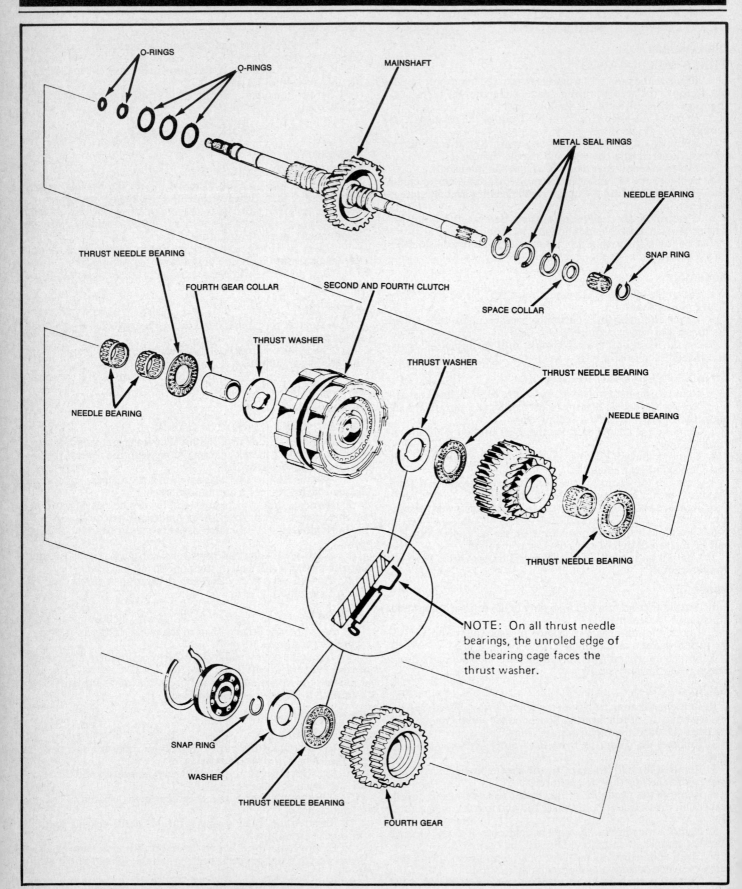

Four speed mainshaft assembly—exploded view

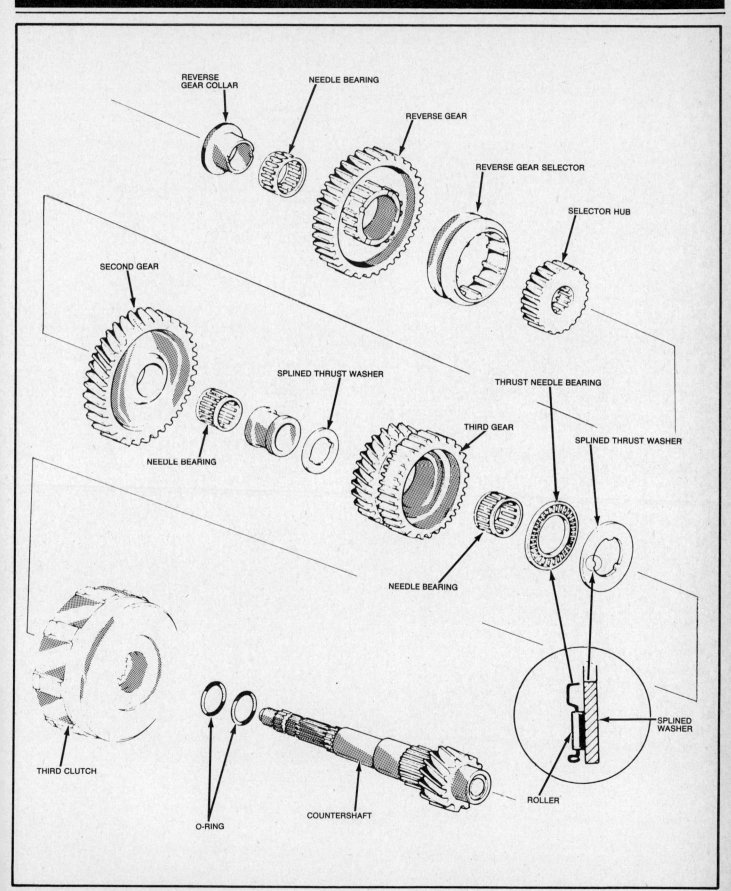

REVERSE GEAR COLLAR

NEEDLE BEARING

REVERSE GEAR

REVERSE GEAR SELECTOR

SELECTOR HUB

SECOND GEAR

SPLINED THRUST WASHER

THRUST NEEDLE BEARING

NEEDLE BEARING

THIRD GEAR

SPLINED THRUST WASHER

NEEDLE BEARING

THIRD CLUTCH

SPLINED WASHER

O-RING

COUNTERSHAFT

ROLLER

Three speed countershaft assembly—exploded view

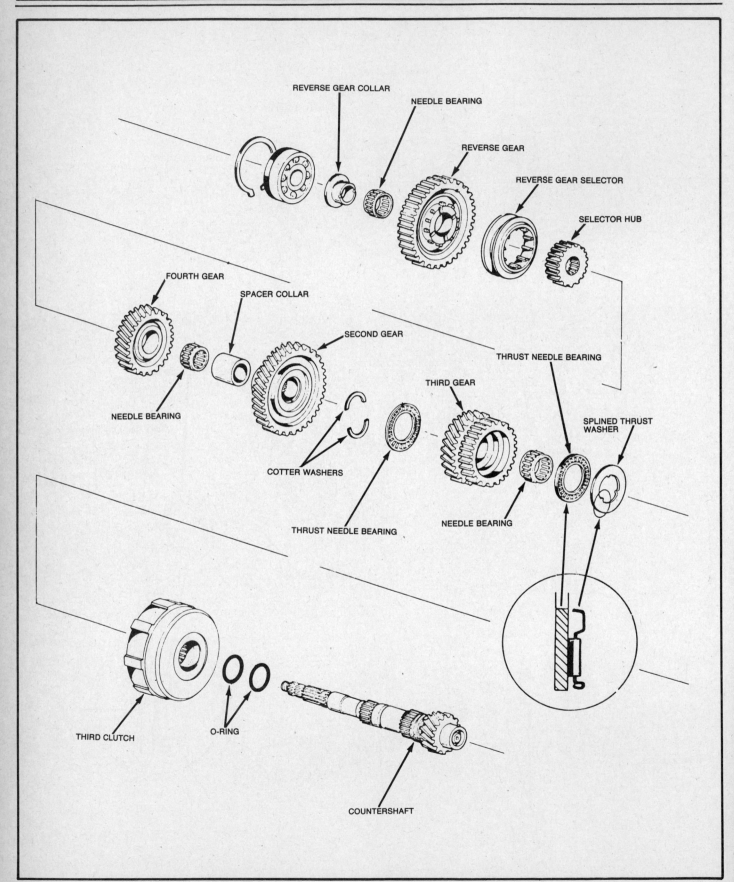

Four speed countershaft assembly—exploded view

7. Clean and inspect all parts for wear, damage and scoring. Repair or replace defective components as required.

8. Coat all parts with clean automatic transmission fluid before reassembly.

Assembly

1. Assemble the countershaft in the reverse order of the disassembly procedure.

2. Check the countershaft clearance measurement and replace thrust washers as required.

3. Set the countershaft assembly aside until the automatic transaxle is ready to be reassembled.

THRUST WASHER SELECTION CHART— ALL TRANSAXLES

Type	Part Number	Thickness (inches)
A	90411-PA9-010	0.117-0.118
B	90412-PA9-010	0.119-0.120
C	90413-PA9-010	0.121-0.122
D	90414-PA9-010	0.123-0.124
E	90415-PA9-010	0.125-0.126
F	90418-PA9-010	0.127-0.128
G	90419-PA9-010	0.129-0.130
H	90420-PA9-010	0.131-0.132
I	90421-PA9-010	0.133-0.134

MAINSHAFT/COUNTERSHAFT CLEARANCE MEASUREMENTS

THREE SPEED

1. Remove the mainshaft and the countershaft bearings from the transaxle housing.

2. Assemble the mainshaft and the countershaft together. On all thrust needle bearings the unrolled edge of the bearing cage faces the thrust washer.

3. Install the mainshaft assembly into the torque converter housing. Install the mainshaft holder to prevent the shafts from turning. Torque the locknut to 25 ft. lbs.

4. Hold the parking gear on the countershaft and torque the retaining nut to 25 ft. lbs.

5. Measure the thrust washer clearances using the proper feeler gauge. Make all measurements before changing the thrust washers.

6. On the mainshaft, measure the clearance between the shoulder on the washer and the thrust needle bearing.

7. If the clearance is not within specification, measure the thickness of the second clutch splined thrust washer (third gear thrust needle bearing on three speed transaxles 1984 and later) and select the correct washer to give correct clearance.

8. The correct specification is 0.003-0.006 in.

9. On the countershaft, measure the clearance between the shoulder on the selector hub and the shoulder on the second gear.

10. The correct clearance should be 0.003-0.006 in. If the correct clearance is not obtained, select a new washer to give the correct clearance.

11. Leave the feeler gauge in place while measuring the clearance for third gear. Measure the clearance between the thrust washer and third gear.

12. The clearance should be 0.003-0.006 in. If the correct clearance is not obtained, select a replacement thrust washer to obtain correct clearance.

THRUST WASHER SELECTION CHART— THREE SPEED TRANSAXLES

Type	Part Number	Thickness (inches)
A	90401-PA9-010	0.089-0.091
B	90402-PA9-010	0.091-0.093
C	90403-PA9-010	0.093-0.094
D	90404-PA9-010	0.095-0.096
E	90407-PA9-000	0.097-0.098
F	90408-PA9-000	0.099-0.100
G	90409-PA9-000	0.101-0.102

FOUR SPEED

1. Remove the mainshaft and the countershaft bearings from the transaxle housing.

2. Assemble the mainshaft and the countershaft together. On all thrust needle bearings the unrolled edge of the bearing cage faces the thrust washer.

3. Install the mainshaft assembly into the torque converter housing. Install the mainshaft holder to prevent the shafts from turning. Torque the locknut to 25 ft. lbs.

4. Hold the parking gear on the countershaft and torque the retaining nut to 35 ft. lbs.

5. Measure the thrust washer clearances using the proper feeler gauge. Make all measurements before changing the thrust washers.

6. On the countershaft, measure the clearance between the shoulder on the selector hub and the shoulder on fourth gear.

7. The clearance should be 0.003-0.006 in. If the clearance is not within the specification given, select the proper thrust washer to bring the clearance to within specification.

8. Leave the feeler gauge in the fourth gear measurement position while measuring second gear.

9. Second gear clearance should be 0.003-0.006 in. If clearance is not within specification select the proper thrust washer to bring the clearance within specification.

SPACER COLLAR SELECTION CHART— FOUR SPEED TRANSAXLES

Type	Part Number	Thickness (inches)
A	90503-PC9-000	1.534-1.535
B	90508-PC9-000	1.536-1.537
C	90504-PC9-000	1.538-1.539
D	90509-PC9-000	1.540-1.541
E	90505-PC9-000	1.542-1.543
F	90510-PC9-000	1.544-1.545
G	90507-PC9-000	1.546-1.547

10. Slide out the third gear. Measure and record the clearance between second and third gears. Slide third gear in and again measure the clearance between second and third gears. Be sure to leave the feeler gauge in the fourth gear measuring slot while measuring second gear clearance. Calculate the difference between the two readings to determine the actual clearance between the two gears.

11. On the mainshaft, measure the clearance between the shoulder of the second gear and third gear.

12. The correct clearance should be 0.003-0.006 in. If the clearance is not within the specification given, select the proper thrust washer to bring the clearance within specification.

CLUTCH ASSEMBLY

Disassembly
THREE SPEED

NOTE: The first, second and third clutch assemblies are all the same.

1. Remove the snap ring. Remove the end plate, clutch discs and clutch plates from the clutch assembly.
2. Install the clutch spring compressor tool and compress the assembly in order to remove the snap ring.
3. Remove the tool. Remove the snap ring, spring retainer and the spring.
4. Apply compressed air to the clutch drum and remove the clutch piston assembly. Remove and discard the O-ring seals.
5. Clean and inspect all parts for wear, damage and scoring. Replace defective parts, clutch discs and plates as required.
6. Before reassembly soak the clutch discs in clean automatic transmission fluid for about thirty minutes. Coat all parts with transmission fluid.

Assembly

1. Install a new O-ring on the clutch piston. Make sure that the spring washer is properly positioned.
2. Install the piston in the clutch drum. Apply pressure and rotate the assembly to ensure proper seating.
3. Install the return spring and the retainer. Position the snap ring on the spring retainer.
4. Assemble the spring compressor tool on the clutch assembly. Compress the unit until the snap ring is seated in its retaining groove. Remove the tool.
5. Starting with a clutch plate, alternately install the clutch discs and plates. Install the clutch end plate with the flat side toward the disc. Install the snap ring.
6. Measure the clearance between the clutch end plate and the top clutch disc. It should be 0.016-0.028 in. for the first clutch, 0.026-0.031 in. for the second clutch and 0.016-0.024 in. for the third clutch.

END PLATE SELECTION CHART

Part Number	Plate Number	Thickness (inches)
22551-PA9-010	one	0.091-0.094
22552-PA9-010	two	0.094-0.098
22553-PA9-010	three	0.098-0.102
22554-PA9-010	four	0.102-0.106
22555-PA9-010	five	0.106-0.110
22556-PA9-010	six	0.110-0.114
22557-PA9-010	seven	0.114-0.118
22558-PA9-010	eight	0.118-0.122
22559-PA9-010	nine	0.122-0.126
22560-PA9-010	ten	0.126-0.130

7. If the reading is not within specification select a new clutch end plate as required.
8. Check for clutch engagement by blowing compressed air into the oil passage of the clutch drum hub. Remove air pressure and check that the clutch releases.
9. Set the clutch assembly aside until you are ready to reassemble the automatic transaxle.

Disassembly
FOUR SPEED

NOTE: The first and third clutches are identical but are not interchangeable. The second and fourth clutches are also identical but not interchangeable.

1. Remove the snap ring. Remove the end plate, clutch discs and clutch plates from the clutch assembly.
2. Install the clutch spring compressor tool and compress the assembly in order to remove the snap ring.
3. Remove the tool. Remove the snap ring, spring retainer and the spring.
4. Apply compressed air to the clutch drum and remove the clutch piston assembly. Remove and discard the O-ring seals.
5. Clean and inspect all parts for wear, damage and scoring. Replace defective parts, clutch discs and plates as required.
6. Before reassembly soak the clutch discs in clean automatic transmission fluid for about thirty minutes. Coat all parts with transmission fluid.

Assembly

1. Install a new O-ring on the clutch piston. Make sure that the spring washer is properly positioned.
2. Install the piston in the clutch drum. Apply pressure and rotate the assembly to ensure proper seating.
3. Install the return spring and the retainer. Position the snap ring on the spring retainer.
4. Assemble the spring compressor tool on the clutch assembly. Compress the unit until the snap ring is seated in its retaining groove. Remove the tool.
5. Starting with a clutch plate, alternately install the clutch discs and plates. Install the clutch end plate with the flat side toward the disc. Install the snap ring.
6. Measure the clearance between the clutch end plate and the top clutch disc. It should be 0.016-0.028 in. for the first clutch, 0.026-0.031 in. for the second clutch and 0.016-0.023 in. for the third and fourth clutch.

END PLATE SELECTION CHART

Part Number	Plate Number	Thickness (inches)
22551-PC9-000	one	0.094
22552-PC9-000	two	0.098
22553-PC9-000	three	0.102
22554-PC9-000	four	0.106
22555-PC9-000	five	0.110
22556-PC9-000	six	0.114
22557-PC9-000	seven	0.118
22558-PC9-000	eight	0.122
22559-PC9-000	nine	0.126
22560-PC9-000	ten	0.130

7. If the reading is not within specification select a new clutch end plate as required.
8. Check for clutch engagement by blowing compressed air into the oil passage of the clutch drum hub. Remove air pressure and check that the clutch releases.
9. Set the clutch assembly aside until you are ready to reassemble the automatic transaxle.

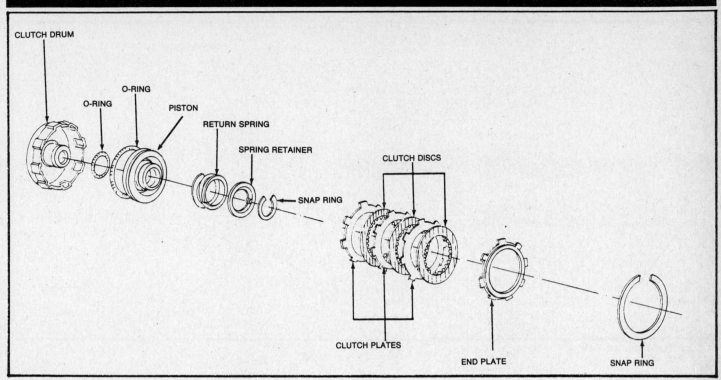

First and third clutch assemblies—exploded view

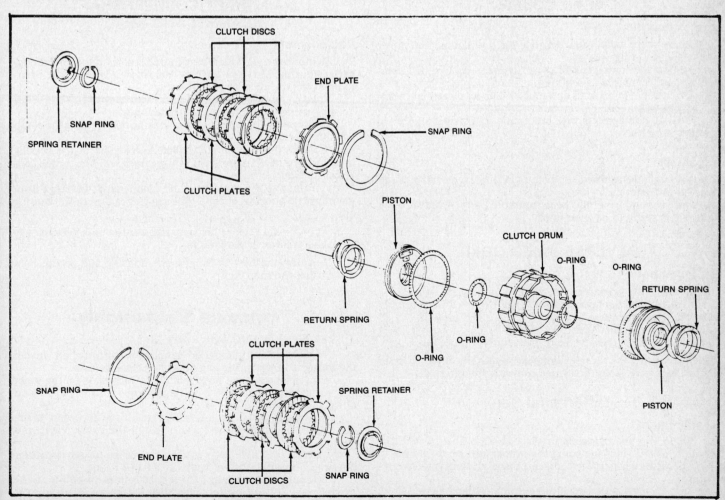

Second and fourth clutch assemblies—exploded view

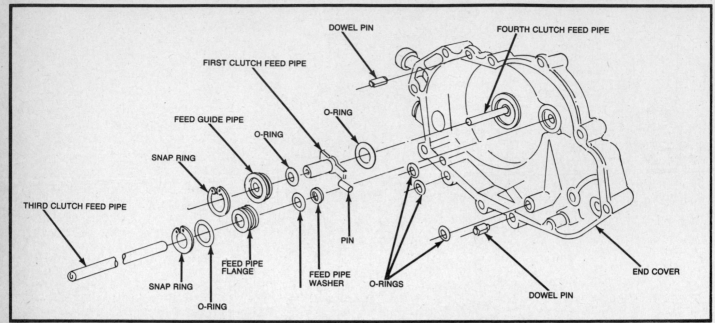

End cover—exploded view

END COVER

Disassembly

1. Remove the snap rings. Remove the dowel pins, feed pipes, washers and O-rings.
2. Inspect the transaxle end cover for wear, scoring and damage. Repair or replace as required.
3. Discard all O-ring seals and replace defective parts and components as required.
4. Coat all components with automatic transmission fluid before reassembly.

Assembly

1. Assemble the transaxle end cover in the reverse order of the removal procedure.
2. Once the end cover has been assembled set it aside until the transaxle is ready to be assembled.

REVERSE IDLER GEAR

Replacement

1. Remove the retaining bolt, washers and spring, if used.
2. Remove the idler bearing holder, shaft and bearing assembly from the transaxle case.
3. Remove the idler gear.
4. Installation is the reverse of the removal procedure.

NOTE: Install the reverse idler gear so that the larger chamfer on the shaft bore faces the torque converter housing.

Differential Seal

Replacement

1. Drive out the old seals in the transaxle housing and the torque converter housing using the proper seal removal tools.
2. Check the seal surface for wear, burrs or damage correct as required.
3. Coat the new seals with clean automatic transmission fluid. Install the seals using the proper seal installation tools.

MAINSHAFT/COUNTERSHAFT BEARING AND SEAL

Replacement

1. Remove the mainshaft bearing and seal from the torque converter housing. Drive in the new mainshaft bearing until it bottoms in the torque converter housing.
2. Install the mainshaft seal flush with the torque converter housing using the proper seal installation tool.
3. Position the torque converter housing and remove the countershaft bearing.
4. Be sure that the oil guide plate is installed in the bearing hole. Install a new countershaft bearing flush with the torque converter housing.
5. To remove the mainshaft and countershaft bearings from the transaxle housing, expand the snap ring and push the bearing out.

NOTE: Do not remove the snap rings unless it is necessary to clean the grooves in the housing.

6. Position the new bearing in the housing and secure it in place using the snap ring.

Transaxle Reassembly

THREE SPEED AND FOUR SPEED

1. Assemble the manual lever onto the control shaft. Install the torque converter housing onto the transaxle case.
2. Install the control lever and a new lock plate on the other end of the shaft. Tighten the bolt and torque it to 9 ft. lbs. Bend down the lock tab.
3. Install a new filter assembly. Install the separator plate, dowel pin, pump gears and shaft. Install the check valve and spring.
4. Install the valve body assembly onto the torque converter housing. Torque the valve body bolts to 12 ft. lbs.
5. Be sure that the pump drive gear rotates smoothly in the normal operating direction and that the pump shaft moves smoothly in both axial and normal operating directions.

6. Install the stator shaft arm, stop pin and the dowel pins. Install the regulator valve and torque the retaining bolts to 9 ft. lbs.

7. Install the steel ball or balls into the valve body oil passage or passages.

8. Install the separator plate. Install the throttle control shaft and the dowel pins.

9. Install the servo assembly. Be sure to use the proper retaining bolts in the proper retaining holes. Torque the retaining bolts to 9 ft. lbs.

10. Put the roller on each side of the manual valve stem. Attach the valve to the lever with the pin. Secure the assembly in place using the lock pin.

11. On 1984 and later three speed transaxles, install the first and third clutch feed pipes. Install the clutch pressure control separator plate onto the servo body and then install the clutch pressure control body. Install the lock up separator plate onto the regulator body. Install the oil feed pipe into the clutch pressure control body.

12. On all four speed transaxles, install the clutch pressure control valve body, cover, and separator plate onto the servo body. Install and torque the clutch pressure control valve body bolts to 9 ft. lbs. Install the first, third and fourth clutch feed pipes. Install the separator plate. Position the oil pass pipes between the pressure control valve and the clutch pressure control valve body and slide the assembly into place. Install the pressure control valve body bolts and torque them to 9 ft. lbs.

13. Install the accumulator springs. Install the accumulator cover and torque the retaining bolts to 9 ft. lbs., in a criss cross method. On the four speed transaxle, install the fourth accumulator cover and torque the retaining bolts to 9 ft. lbs.

14. Install the governor valve using new lock plates. Torque the retaining bolts to 9 ft. lbs. and bend the lock tabs.

15. Position the countershaft in place. Position the mainshaft in place. Do not tap on the shafts with a hammer to drive them in place.

16. Install the countershaft second gear. On all four speed transaxles, install the countershaft fourth gear and the needle bearing.

17. Assemble the reverse shift fork and the selector sleeve. Install these two components as an assembly on the·countershaft.

NOTE: Install the sleeve with the grooved side down and the unmarked side up. Check for wear on the surface of the sleeve and the shift fork.

18. Install the reverse shift fork over the servo valve stem. Align the hole in the stem with the hole in the fork. Install the bolt and the lock plate. Torque the bolt to 10 ft. lbs. and bend down the lock tab.

19. Install the countershaft reverse gear, needle bearing and reverse gear collar.

20. On 1984 and later three speed transaxles install the magnet.

21. Install a new gasket, the dowel pins and the oil feed pipes into the torque converter housing.

22. Position the automatic transaxle housing on the torque converter housing.

NOTE: Be sure main valve control shaft lines up with hole in housing and that reverse idler gear meshes with mainshaft and countershaft, or housing will not go on.

23. Install the retaining bolts and torque them in two steps. First to 20 ft. lbs. and then to 28 ft. lbs.

NOTE: When tightening the transaxle housing bolts, take care that you do not distort or damage the throttle control bracket; distortion or damage to bracket will change the transaxle shift points.

24. Install the throttle control lever and spring on the throttle control shaft. Install the bolt and a new lock plate. Torque the retaining bolt to 6 ft. lbs. and bend down the lock plate.

25. Install the parking shift arm and spring on the shift shaft with the retaining bolt and a new lock plate. Torque the bolt to 10 ft. lbs. and bend down the lock tab.

NOTE: The spring should put clockwise tension on the shift arm and force it against the stop pin.

26. Install the first gear collar and needle bearing on the countershaft. Install the collar on the mainshaft.

27. Install the reverse idler bearing holder. Install the O-rings on the mainshaft assembly.

28. Install the countershaft first gear and the parking gear on the countershaft.

29. Install the stop pin, parking pawl shaft and the pawl release spring.

NOTE: The end of the parking pawl release spring fits into the hole in the parking pawl. The release spring should put clockwise tension on the pawl which will force it away from the parking gear.

30. Shift the transaxle into the park position. Install the countershaft lock nut. Stake the lock nut flange into the gear groove.

31. Install the needle bearing and the thrust washer onto the mainshaft. Install the first gear, needle bearing and thrust washer onto the mainshaft.

32. Install the first clutch assembly on the mainshaft. Install the mainshaft lock nut. This nut has left hand threads. Stake the lock nut flange into the groove of the first clutch.

33. Install the gasket, dowel pins and O-rings on the transaxle housing. Install the end cover and torque the retaining bolts to 9 ft. lbs.

34. Install the transaxle cooler line fittings on the transaxle assembly.

35. Install the torque converter on the mainshaft assembly.

TORQUE SPECIFICATIONS

Item	Torque (ft. lbs.)
Drive plate to crankshaft bolts	34-38
Converter to drive plate bolts	7 -10
Control cable mounting bolts	7 -10
Center crossmember mounting bolts	14-18
Center mount bracket bolts	14-18
Starter retaining bolts	29-36

# SPECIAL TOOLS

Special tools needed for the disassembly and assembly of the Honda three and four speed transaxles are listed below.

1. Oil pressure gauge or gauge set with the installation attachments
2. Mainshaft holder
3. Clutch drum return spring compressor
4. Mainshaft locknut wrench
5. Transaxle case puller, slide hammer type
6. Ball joint remover
7. Lifting cable for engine and/or transaxle
8. Mechanics tool kit
9. Torque wrench, ft. lbs.
10. Bearing remover, slide hammer type
11. Hand operated air nozzle
12. Feeler gauge and straight edge
13. Bearing driver
14. Seal driver

INDEX

JATCO
L3N71B•4N71B•L4N71B•E4N71B•JM600

APPLICATIONS

Datsun	1982 810 Maxima, 200SX, 210	L3N71B
Nissan	1983-84 810 Maxima	L4N71B
	1983-84 720 Pick-up W/2WD	L3N71B
	1984 300ZX	E4N71B
Chrysler	(Mitsubishi) 1984 Conquest	L4N71B
		(JM600)

GENERAL DESCRIPTION

The L3N71B transmission is a three speed, fully automatic unit, consisting of two multiple disc clutches, a multiple disc brake, a brake band, a one way clutch, two planetary gear sets and a three element torque converter, housing hydraulically operated lock-up converter components.

The L4N71B Chrysler/Mitsubishi JM600 transmissions are four speed, fully automatic unit, consisting of three multiple disc clutches, a multiple disc brake, two brake bands, a one way clutch, three planetary gear sets and a three element torque converter, housing hydraulically operated lock-up converter compo-

nents. The fourth speed has an overdrive ratio of 0.686.

A hydraulic control system operates the friction elements and the automatic up and down shifts.

The E4N71B automatic transmission is based on the L4N71B model and can provide lock-up in all forward speeds (1 through 4) by electronic control, through a microcomputer. Either a standard or power shifting pattern is automatically selected by programs set in the lock-up control unit, depending upon the position of the accelerator and the vehicle speed.

Transmission and Converter Identification

TRANSMISSION

The transmission can be identified by a plate attached to the right side of the case. The plate contains the model and serial numbers. An identification of the number arrangements can be determined from the serial number in the following manner;
Example: 2601234

1. The first digit, in this case, 2, denotes the year, 1982.

2. The second digit or letter, in this case, 6, denotes the month of production. 6 = June
1 = January, 2 = February, 3 = March, 4 = April, 5 = May, 6 = June, 7 = July, 8 = August, 9 = September, X = October, Y = November, Z = December.

3. The next five digits represents the serial number for the month of transmission production.

AUTOMATIC TRANSMISSION MODEL CODE DESIGNATION

Year	Engine Model	Transmission Model Code	Transmission Model
1982	L24E	X6701	L3N71B
	LD28	X6700	L3N71B
1983-84	L24E	X8708	L4N71B
	LD28	X8707	L4N71B
1984	VG30E	X8075	E4N71B
	VG30E w/Turbo	X8006	4N71B (Non-Lockup)
1984	—	JM600	L4N71B

CONVERTER

The torque converters are identified by a letter or letters, stamped on the unit.

1982   Gasoline engine model L24E—converter code GC
        Diesel engine model LD28—converter code GB
1983-84 Gasoline engine model L24E—converter code GL
        Diesel engine model LD28—converter code GD
1984   Engine model VG30E-less turbo—converter code GK
        Engine model VG30E-with turbo—converter code GC
1984   Conquest (Chrysler/Mitsubishi) converter Code GKA

Transmission Metric Fasteners

Metric bolt sizes and thread pitches are used for all fasteners on the Jatco transmissions. The metric fastener dimensions are close to the dimensions of the familiar inch system fasteners, and for this reason, replacement fasteners must have the same measurement and strength as those removed.

--- CAUTION ---

Do not attempt to interchange metric fasteners for inch system fasteners. Mismatched or incorrect fasteners can result in damage to the transmission unit through malfunctions, breakage or possible personal injury.

Care should be taken to re-use the fasteners in the same locations as removed, whenever possible.

Transmission Fluid Capacity

L4N71B, E4N71B, JM600—7⅜ US quarts (7.0 Liters)
L3N71B—6½ US quarts (6.1 Liters)

TRANSMISSION FLUID LEVEL CHECK

The automatic transmissions are designed to operate with the oil level between the "L" and the "F" or "H" markings on the dipstick. The "L" mark on the dipstick indicates the transmission is approximately ⅞ US pint (0.4 liter) low. Only Dexron® transmission fluid or its equivalent can be used.

Checking Fluid Level

1. Operate the vehicle to bring the transmission to its normal operating temperature of between 122°-176° F. (50°-80° C.).
2. Park the vehicle on a level surface, apply the brakes and leave the engine running with the selector lever in the PARK position.
3. Slowly move the selector lever through the entire shift detent pattern and return it to the PARK position.
4. Remove the dipstick from the transmission tube, clean it and replace it back into the tube. Seat it fully to the tube.
5. Remove the dipstick and read the level as indicated.
6. Correct the level as required and recheck.

NOTE: Overfilling of the transmission can cause fluid loss during vehicle operation. Underfilling can cause lack of fluid pressure to the internal components, resulting in transmission failure.

M MODIFICATIONS

No known modifications were made to the L3N71B, L4N71B, JM600 or E4N71B automatic transmissions at time of printing.

TROUBLE DIAGNOSIS

NOTE: The nomenclature of the various applying members differ in varied applications, although each perform the same function. Where required, both names will be given to a specific unit for easier identification. Examples are as follows;

1. **The rear clutch is the same as the forward clutch.**
2. **The front clutch is the same as the reverse and high clutch.**
3. **The rear band is the same as the intermediate band.**

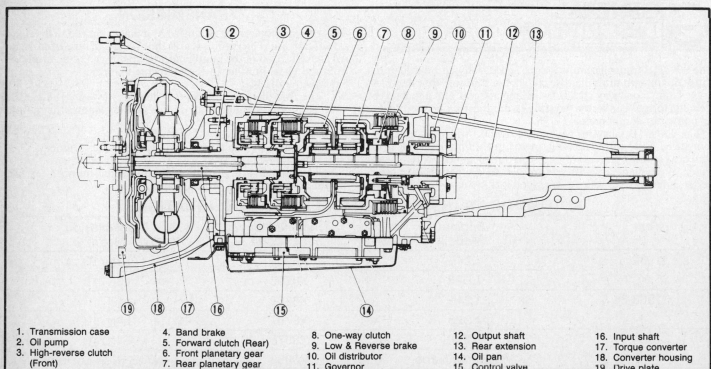

1. Transmission case
2. Oil pump
3. High-reverse clutch (Front)
4. Band brake
5. Forward clutch (Rear)
6. Front planetary gear
7. Rear planetary gear
8. One-way clutch
9. Low & Reverse brake
10. Oil distributor
11. Governor
12. Output shaft
13. Rear extension
14. Oil pan
15. Control valve
16. Input shaft
17. Torque converter
18. Converter housing
19. Drive plate

Cross section of L3N71B automatic transmission (© Nissan Motor Co. of USA)

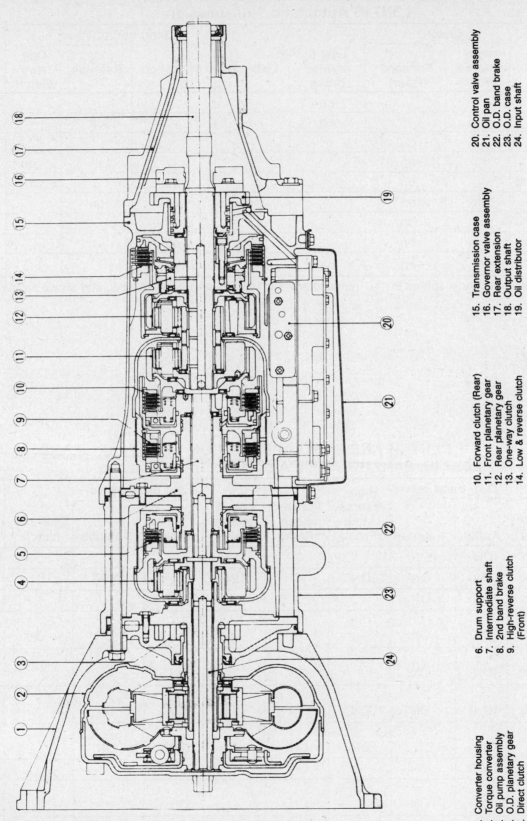

1. Converter housing
2. Torque converter
3. Oil pump assembly
4. O.D. planetary gear
5. Direct clutch

6. Drum support
7. Intermediate shaft
8. 2nd band brake
9. High-reverse clutch (Front)

10. Forward clutch (Rear)
11. Front planetary gear
12. Rear planetary gear
13. One-way clutch
14. Low & reverse clutch

15. Transmission case
16. Governor valve assembly
17. Rear extension
18. Output shaft
19. Oil distributor

20. Control valve assembly
21. Oil pan
22. O.D. band brake
23. O.D. case
24. Input shaft

Cross section of L4N71B, E4N71B, JM600 automatic transmission (© Nissan Motor Co. of USA)

CLUTCH AND BAND APPLICATION CHART
L3N71B Automatic Transmission

Range		High-reverse (Front)	Forward (Rear)	Low & reverse brake	Lock-up	Operation	Release	One way clutch	Parking pawl
		Clutch				**Band servo**			
Park				on					on
Reverse		on		on			on		
Neutral									
Drive	D1 Low		on					on	
	D2 Second		on			on			
	D3 Top	on	on		on	(on)	on		
2	Second		on			on			
1	1₂ Second		on			on			
	1₁ Low		on	on					

NOTE: The low & reverse brake is applied in "1₁" range to prevent free wheeling when coasting and allows engine braking.

CLUTCH AND BAND APPLICATION CHART
L4N71B, E4N71B, JM600 Automatic Transmissions

Range		Direct clutch	Apply	Release	High-reverse clutch (Front)	Forward clutch (Rear)	Low & reverse brake	Apply	Release	One-way clutch	Parking pawl
			O.D. band servo					**2nd band servo**			
Park		ON	(ON)	ON			ON				ON
Reverse		ON	(ON)	ON	ON		ON		ON		
Neutral		ON	(ON)	ON							
D	D₁ (Low)	ON	(ON)	ON		ON				ON	
	D₂ (Second)	ON	(ON)	ON		ON		ON			
	D₃ (Top)	ON	(ON)	ON	ON	ON		(ON)	ON		
	D₄ (O.D.)		ON		ON	ON		(ON)	ON		
2	Second	ON	(ON)	ON		ON		ON			
1	1₂ (Second)	ON	(ON)	ON		ON		ON			
	1₁ (Low)	ON	(ON)	ON		ON	ON			ON	

NOTE: The low & reverse brake is applied in "1₁" range to prevent free wheeling when coasting and allows engine braking.

CHILTON'S THREE "C's" AUTOMATIC TRANSMISSION DIAGNOSIS CHART
L3N71B, L4N71B, JM600 and E4N71B Automatic Transmission Models

Condition	Cause	Correction
Engine does not start in "N", "P" ranges	a) Range select linkage b) Neutral safety switch c) Ignition switch and starter motor d) Lock-up solenoid e) Lock-up control unit and/or sensors	a) Adjust linkage b) Adjust or replace c) Repair or replace d) Test, repair or replace solenoid e) Test repair or replace lock-up control unit and or sensors
Engine starts in range other than "N" and "P"	a) Range select linkage b) Neutral safety switch	a) Adjust linkage b) Adjust or replace
Vehicle moves in "N" range	a) Range select linkage b) Manual control valve c) Rear clutch d) Fluid quality not to specifications	a) Adjust linkage b) Adjust range select linkage/renew valve c) Renew rear clutch d) Drain and replace fluid
Vehicle will not move in "D" range (but moves in "2", "1" and "R" ranges)	a) Range select linkage b) Throttle valve pressure c) Manual control valve d) One way clutch of transmission	a) Adjust linkage b) Correct throttle valve or passage per air test c) Adjust range select linkage/renew valve d) Renew clutch
Vehicle will not move in "D", "1" or "2" ranges but moves in "R" range Clutch slips, very poor acceleration	a) Oil level b) Range select linkage c) Throttle valve pressure d) Manual control valve e) Leakage of fluid passage f) Engine adjustment and brake defects g) Rear clutch h) Front Clutch	a) Add if needed b) Adjust linkage c) Correct throttle valve or passage per air test d) Adjust range select linkage/renew valve e) Correct as per air test f) Repair as needed g) Renew rear clutch h) Renew front clutch
Sharp shock shifting from "N" to "D" range	a) Vacuum diaphragm and hoses b) Engine idle rpm c) Throttle valve pressure d) Rear clutch e) Control Valve	a) Renew diaphragm and hoses b) Set engine idle rpm c) Correct throttle valve or passage per air test d) Renew rear clutch e) Clean, repair or replace control valve assembly

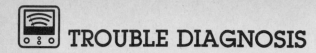

CHILTON'S THREE "C's" AUTOMATIC TRANSMISSION DIAGNOSIS CHART
L3N71B, L4N71B, JM600 and E4N71B Automatic Transmission Models

Condition	Cause	Correction
Vehicle will not move in "R" range (but moves in "D", "2" and "1" ranges). Clutch slips, very poor acceleration.	a) Oil level b) Range select linkage c) Throttle valve pressure d) Manual control valve assembly e) Leakage of passage f) Rear clutch g) Front clutch h) Low and reverse brake i) Front clutch check ball	a) Add if needed b) Adjust linkage c) Correct throttle valve or passage per air test d) Adjust range select linkage/renew valve assembly e) Correct as per air test f) Renew rear clutch g) Renew front clutch h) Renew low and reverse brake i) Repair or renew
Vehicle will not move in any range	a) Oil level b) Range select linkage c) Throttle valve pressure d) Manual control valve e) Leakage of fluid passage f) Oil pump g) Parking linkage h) Lock-up control i) Lock-up system sensors j) Lock-up solenoid	a) Add if needed b) Adjust linkage c) Correct throttle valve or passage per air test d) Adjust range select linkage/renew valve e) Correct as per air test f) Repair or renew g) Repair or renew h) Test, repair or replace lock-up control i) Test, repair or replace system sensors j) Test, repair or replace lock-up solenoid
Clutches or brakes slip When starting to move	a) Oil level b) Range select linkage c) Throttle valve pressure d) Manual control valve e) Leakage of fluid passage f) Oil pump g) Vacuum modulator and/or hoses	a) Add if needed b) Adjust linkage c) Correct throttle valve or passage per air test d) Adjust range select linkage/renew valve e) Correct as per air test f) Repair or renew g) Repair or renew
Excessive creep	a) High engine idle rpm	a) Adjust idle rpm
Vehicle braked in "R" range	a) Band servo b) Leakage of fluid passage c) Rear clutch d) Band brake e) Parking linkage	a) Renew band servo b) Correct as per air test c) Renew rear clutch d) Renew band brake e) Repair/renew linkage

CHILTON'S THREE "C's" AUTOMATIC TRANSMISSION DIAGNOSIS CHART
L3N71B, L4N71B, JM600 and E4N71B Automatic Transmission Models

Condition	Cause	Correction
No creep at all	a) Oil level b) range select linkage c) Low engine idle rpm d) Manual control valve e) Rear clutch f) Front clutch g) Oil pump h) Leakage of fluid passage i) Direct Clutch	a) Add if needed b) Adjust linkage c) Adjust idle rpm d) Adjust range select linkage/renew valve e) Renew rear clutch f) Renew front clutch g) Repair or renew oil pump h) Correct as per air test i) Renew direct clutch
Failure to change gear from "1st" to "2nd"	a) Range linkage b) Vacuum diaphragm and hoses c) Downshift solenoid kickdown switch and wiring d) Manual control valve e) Band servo f) Leakage of fluid passage g) Front clutch h) Front clutch check ball i) Governor valve	a) Adjust linkage b) Renew diaphragm/hoses c) Repair wiring and adjust or renew the solenoid downshift kickdown switch d) Adjust range select linkage/renew valve e) Renew band servo f) Correct as per air test g) Renew front clutch h) Renew front clutch check ball i) Repair or replace governor assembly
Failure to change gear from "2nd" to "3rd"	a) Range select linkage b) Vacuum diaphragm and hoses c) Downshift solenoid kickdown switch and wiring d) Manual control valve e) Governor valve f) Band servo g) Leakage of fluid passage h) Band brake i) Front clutch	a) Adjust linkage b) Renew diaphragm/hoses c) Repair wiring and adjust or renew the downshift solenoid kickdown switch d) Adjust range select linkage/renew valve e) Overhaul governor/ renew governor f) Renew band servo g) Correct as per air test h) Renew band brake i) Renew front clutch

CHILTON'S THREE "C's" AUTOMATIC TRANSMISSION DIAGNOSIS CHART
L3N71B, L4N71B, JM600 and E4N71B Automatic Transmission Models

Condition	Cause	Correction
Failure to Change gear from "3rd" to "4th"	a) Range selector linkage b) Vacuum diaphragm or hoses c) Kickdown solenoid, switch or wiring d) Oil quality e) Control valve assembly f) Governor g) Band servo h) Component or oil passage leakage i) O.D. band	a) Adjust range selector linkage b) Renew diaphragm/hoses c) Repair or renew solenoid, switch or wiring d) Correct oil quality e) Clean or renew control valve Assembly f) Clean or renew governor assembly g) Repair or renew band servo components h) Air test passages for case and components i) Adjust or renew O.D. band
Too high gear change point from "1st" to "2nd" and from "2nd" to "3rd"	a) Vacuum diaphragm and hoses b) Downshift solenoid kickdown switch and wiring c) Manual control valve d) Governor valve e) Leakage of fluid passage	a) Renew diaphragm/hoses b) Repair wiring and adjust or renew the downshift solenoid kickdown switch c) Adjust range select linkage/renew valve d) Overhaul governor/renew governor e) Correct as per air test
Too high a gear change point from "1st" to "2nd", from "2nd" to "3rd", from "3rd" to "4th"	a) Vacuum diaphragm or hoses b) Kickdown solenoid, switch or wiring c) Line pressure d) Oil quality e) Control valve assembly f) Governor g) Oil passage leakage	a) Renew diaphragm/hoses b) Repair or renew solenoid, switch or wiring c) Test line pressure with gauge and correct as required d) Correct oil quality e) Clean or renew control valve assembly f) Clean or renew governor assembly g) Air test passages for case and components
Gear change directly from "1st" to "3rd" occurs	a) Manual control valve b) Governor valve c) Leakage of fluid passage d) Band brake	a) Adjust range select linkage/renew valve b) Overhaul governor/renew governor c) Correct as per air test d) Renew band brake
Gear change directly from "2nd" to "4th" occurs	a) Oil quality b) Control valve assembly c) Oil passage leakage d) Governor e) Forward clutch (rear) f) Front clutch	a) Correct oil quality b) Clean or renew control valve assembly c) Air test passages for case and component leakage d) Clean or renew governor assembly e) Renew forward clutch (rear) f) Renew front clutch

CHILTON'S THREE "C's" AUTOMATIC TRANSMISSION DIAGNOSIS CHART
L3N71B, L4N71B, JM600 and E4N71B Automatic Transmission Models

Condition	Cause	Correction
Too sharp shock in change from "1st" to "2nd"	a) Vacuum diaphragm and hoses	a) Renew diaphragm/hoses
	b) Manual control valve	b) Adjust range select linkage/renew valve
	c) Band servo	c) Renew band servo
	d) Band brake	d) Renew band brake
	e) Torque converter	e) Renew torque converter
	f) Lock-up control unit and sensors	f) Test, repair or replace lock-up control unit and/or sensors
	g) Lock-up control solenoid	g) Test/repair or replace lock-up control solenoid
Too sharp shock in change from "2nd" to "3rd"	a) Vacuum diaphragm and hoses	a) Renew diaphragm/hoses
	b) Downshift solenoid kickdown switch and wiring	b) Repair wiring and adjust or renew the downshift solenoid kickdown switch
	c) Throttle valve pressure	c) Correct throttle valve or passage per air test
	d) Manual control valve	d) Adjust range select linkage/renew valve
	e) Band servo	e) Renew band servo
	f) Front clutch	f) Renew front clutch
	g) Torque converter	g) Renew torque converter
	h) Lock-up control unit and sensors	h) Test, repair or replace lock-up control unit and/or sensors
	i) Lock-up control solenoid	i) Test, repair or replace lock-up control solenoid
Too sharp shock in change from "3rd" to "4th"	a) Vacuum diaphragm and hoses	a) Renew diaphragm/hoses
	b) Line pressure	b) Test line pressure with gauge and correct as required
	c) Control valve assembly	c) Clean or renew control valve assembly
	d) Oil passage leakage	d) Air test passages for case and component leakage
	e) Band servo	e) Renew band servo components
	f) O.D. band or servo	f) Renew O.D. band or servo
	g) Lock-up solenoid	g) Test, repair or renew lock-up solenoid
	h) Lock-up control unit and/or sensors	h) Test, repair or renew lock-up control unit and/or sensors
	i) Torque converter	i) Renew torque converter
	j) Lock-up control valve	j) Repair or renew lock-up control valve

CHILTON'S THREE "C's" AUTOMATIC TRANSMISSION DIAGNOSIS CHART
L3N71B, L4N71B, JM600 and E4N71B Automatic Transmission Models

Condition	Cause	Correction
Almost no shock or slipping in change from "1st" to "2nd"	a) Oil level b) Range select linkage c) Vacuum diaphragm and hoses d) Throttle valve pressure e) Manual control valve f) Band servo g) Leakage of fluid passage h) Band brake	a) Add if needed b) Adjust linkage c) Renew diaphragm/hoses d) Correct throttle valve or passage per air test e) Adjust range select linkage/renew valve f) Renew band servo g) Correct as per air test h) Renew band brake
Almost no shock or engine runaway on "2nd" to "3rd" shift	a) Oil level b) Range select linkage c) Vacuum diaphragm and hoses d) Throttle valve pressure e) Manual control valve f) Band servo g) Leakage of fluid passage h) Front clutch i) Front clutch check ball	a) Add if needed b) Adjust linkage c) Renew diaphragm/hoses d) Correct throttle valve or passage per air test e) Adjust range select linkage/renew valve f) Renew band servo g) Correct as per air test h) Renew front clutch i) Renew front clutch check ball
Almost no shock or slipping in change from "3rd" to "4th"	a) Oil level b) range select linkage c) Vacuum diaphragm and hoses d) Line pressure e) Oil quality f) Control valve g) Oil passage leakage h) Band servo i) O.D. band	a) Correct oil level b) Adjust range select linkage c) Renew diaphragm/hoses d) Test line pressure with gauge and correct as required e) Correct oil quality f) Clean or renew control valve assembly g) Air test passages for case and component leakage h) Renew band servo components i) Renew O.D. band
Vehicle braked by gear change from "1st" to "2nd"	a) Manual control valve b) Front clutch c) Low and reverse brake d) One-way clutch of transmission	a) Adjust range select linkage/renew valve b) Renew front clutch c) Renew low and reverse brake d) Renew one-way clutch of transmission
Vehicle braked by gear change from "2nd" to "3rd"	a) Manual control valve b) Band servo c) Brake band	a) Adjust range select linkage b) Renew band servo c) Renew brake band

CHILTON'S THREE "C's" AUTOMATIC TRANSMISSION DIAGNOSIS CHART
L3N71B, L4N71B, JM600 and E4N71B Automatic Transmission Models

Condition	Cause	Correction
Vehicle braked by gear change from "3rd" to "4th"	a) Oil quality	a) Correct oil quality
	b) Direct clutch	b) Renew direct clutch components
	c) Control valve assembly	c) Clean or renew control valve assembly
	d) High-reverse clutch (front)	d) Renew high-reverse (front) clutch components
Maximum speed not attained, acceleration poor	a) Oil level	a) Add if needed
	b) Range select linkage	b) Adjust linkage
	c) Throttle valve pressure	c) Correct throttle valve or passage per air test
	d) High stall rpm	d) Renew torque converter
	e) Manual control valve	e) Adjust range select linkage/renew valve
	f) Band servo	f) Repair/renew band servo
	g) Rear clutch	g) Renew rear clutch
	h) Front clutch	h) Renew front clutch
	i) Band brake	i) Renew band brake
	j) Low and reverse brake	j) Renew low and reverse brake
	k) Oil pump	k) Repair or renew oil pump
Failure to change from "4th" to "3rd"	a) Vacuum diaphragm and hoses	a) Renew diaphragm/hoses
	b) Control valve assembly	b) Clean or renew control valve assembly
	c) Governor	c) Clean or renew governor assembly
	d) Oil passage leakage	d) Air test passages for case and component leakage
	e) Oil quality	e) Correct oil quality
	f) Direct clutch	f) Renew direct clutch components
	g) High-reverse clutch (front)	g) Renew high-reverse (front) clutch components
	h) O.D. band	h) Renew O.D. band
	i) O.D. cancel switch	i) Test, repair or replace O.D. cancel switch
	j) O.D. cancel solenoid	j) Test, repair or replace O.D. cancel solenoid
	k) Lock-up solenoid	k) Test, repair or replace lock-up solenoid
	l) O.D. cancel valve	l) Repair or replace O.D. cancel valve
Failure to change gear from "2nd" to "1st" or from "3rd" to "1st"	a) Vacuum diaphragm and hoses	a) Renew diaphragm/hoses
	b) Manual control valve	b) Adjust range select linkage/renew valve
	c) Governor valve	c) Overhaul governor/renew governor
	d) Band servo	d) Renew band servo
	e) Band brake	e) Renew band brake
	f) Leakage of fluid pressure passage	f) Correct as per air test
	g) One-way clutch of transmission	g) Renew one-way clutch of transmission

CHILTON'S THREE "C's" AUTOMATIC TRANSMISSION DIAGNOSIS CHART
L3N71B, L4N71B, JM600 and E4N71B Automatic Transmission Models

Condition	Cause	Correction
Failure to change from "3rd" to "2nd" and from "4th" to "2nd"	a) Vacuum diaphragm and hoses b) Control valve assembly c) Governor d) band servo (2nd and O.D.) e) Oil passage leakage f) Oil quality g) High-reverse (front) clutch h) O.D. band i) 2nd band brake	a) Renew vacuum diaphragm/hoses b) Clean or renew vacuum diaphragm/hoses c) Clean or renew governor assembly d) Renew band servo components e) Air test passages for case and component leakage f) Correct oil quality g) Renew high-reverse (front) clutch components h) Renew O.D. band components i) Renew 2nd band brake
Gear change shock felt during deceleration by releasing accelerator pedal	a) Range select linkage b) Vacuum diaphragm and hoses c) Downshift solenoid kickdown switch and wiring d) Throttle valve pressure e) Manual control valve f) Governor valve g) Leakage of fluid pressure passage h) Accumulor	a) Adjust linkage b) Renew diaphragm/hoses c) Repair wiring and adjust or renew the downshift solenoid kickdown switch d) Correct throttle valve or passage per air test e) Adjust range select linkage/renew valve f) Overhaul governor/renew governor g) Correct as per air test h) Repair accumulor
Too high change point from "3rd" to "2nd" and from "2nd" to "1st"	a) Range select linkage b) Vacuum diaphragm and hoses c) Downshift solenoid kickdown switch and wiring d) Throttle valve pressure e) Manual control valve f) Governor valve g) Leakage at fluid passage	a) Adjust linkage b) Renew diaphragm/hoses c) Repair wiring and adjust or renew the downshift solenoid kickdown switch d) Correct throttle valve or passage per air test e) Adjust range select linkage/renew valve f) Overhaul governor/renew governor g) Correct per air test

CHILTON'S THREE "C's" AUTOMATIC TRANSMISSION DIAGNOSIS CHART
L3N71B, L4N71B, JM600 and E4N71B Automatic Transmission Models

Condition	Cause	Correction
Too high a change point from "4th" to "3rd", from "3rd" to "2nd", from "2nd" to "1st"	a) Range selector linkage b) Vacuum diaphragm and hoses c) Kickdown solenoid, switches wiring d) Line pressure e) Control valve assembly f) Governor g) Oil passage leakage h) Lock-up control unit and sensors	a) Adjust range selector linkage b) Renew diaphragm/hoses c) Repair or renew solenoid, switches, wiring d) Test line pressure with gauge and correct as required e) Clean or renew control valve assembly f) Clean or renew governor assembly g) Air test passages for case and component leakage h) Test, repair or replace lock-up control and/or sensors
Failure to change from "3rd" to "2nd"	a) Vacuum diaphragm and hoses b) Manual control valve c) Governor valve d) Band servo e) Leakage of fluid pressure passage f) Front clutch g) Band brake	a) Renew diaphragm/hoses b) Adjust range select linkage/renew valve c) Overhaul governor/ renew governor d) Renew band servo e) Correct as per air test f) Renew front clutch g) Renew band brake
Kickdown operates or engine overruns when depressing pedal in "3rd" beyond kickdown speed limit	a) Range select linkage b) Vacuum diaphragm and hoses c) Main line pressure d) Manual control valve e) Governor valve f) Leakage of fluid pressure passage g) Front clutch	a) Adjust linkage b) Renew diaphragm/hoses c) Correct main line or passage per air test d) Adjust range select linkage/renew valve assembly e) Overhaul governor/ renew governor f) Correct as per air test g) Renew front clutch
No kickdown by depressing pedal in "3rd" within kickdown speed	a) Vacuum diaphragm and hoses b) Downshift solenoid kickdown switch and wiring c) Manual control valve d) Governor valve e) Band brake f) Leakage at fluid passage	a) Renew diaphragm/hoses b) Repair wiring and adjust or renew the solenoid downshift kickdown switch c) Adjust range select linkage/renew valve assembly d) Overhaul governor/ renew governor e) Renew band brake f) Correct per air test

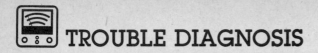

CHILTON'S THREE "C's" AUTOMATIC TRANSMISSION DIAGNOSIS CHART
L3N71B, L4N71B, JM600 and E4N71B Automatic Transmission Models

Condition	Cause	Correction
Engine Races extremely fast or slips in changing from "4th" to "3rd" when depressing pedal	a) Vacuum diaphragm and hoses	a) Renew vacuum diaphragm/hoses
	b) Main line pressure	b) Test line pressure with gauge and correct as required
	c) Control valve assembly	c) Clean or renew control valve assembly
	d) Band servo	d) Renew band servo components
	e) Oil passage leakage	e) Air test passages for case or component leakage
	f) Oil quality	f) Correct oil quality
	g) Direct clutch	g) Renew direct clutch components
	h) High-reverse (front) clutch and/or check ball	h) Renew high-reverse (front) clutch components and check ball for sealing
	i) O.D. band	i) Renew O.D. band
Kickdown does not operate with pedal depressed in "4th" within kickdown speed	a) Kickdown solenoid, switch and wire	a) Test, repair or renew as required
	b) Vacuum diaphragm and hoses	b) Renew diaphragm/hoses
	c) Fluid Quality	c) Drain and refill with new fluid
	d) Control valve assembly	d) Clean or replace control valve assembly
	e) Governor	e) Clean or replace governor
	f) High-reverse clutch (front)	f) Renew clutch assembly
	g) Direct clutch	g) Renew clutch assembly
	h) Leakage of fluid in pressure	h) Correct as per air test
Kickdown operates or engine overruns when depressing pedal in "4th" beyond kick-down vehicle speed limit	a) Range selector linkage	a) Adjust linkage
	b) Vacuum diaphragm and hoses	b) Renew diaphragm/hoses
	c) Line pressure	c) Correct line-pressure
	d) Fluid quality	d) Drain and refill with new fluid
	e) Control valve assembly	e) Clean or replace control valve assembly
	f) Governor	f) Clean or replace governor
	g) Leakage of fluid in pressure passage	g) Correct as per air test
	h) O.D. band brake	h) Correct O.D. band as required
Shift pattern does not change	a) Vacuum diaphragm or hoses	a) Renew diaphragm/hoses
	b) O.D. cancel switch	b) Test, repair or renew O.D. cancel switch
	c) Kickdown switch, solenoid, or wires	c) Test, repair or renew kickdown switch, solenoid or wires
	d) O.D. cancel solenoid	d) Test, repair or renew O.D. cancel solenoid
	e) Engine lack of power or braking problem	e) Adjust engine components as required. Check brake drag
	f) Lock-up control unit or sensors	f) Test, repair or renew lock-up unit or sensors

CHILTON'S THREE "C's" AUTOMATIC TRANSMISSION DIAGNOSIS CHART
L3N71B, L4N71B, JM600 and E4N71B Automatic Transmission Models

Condition	Cause	Correction
Engine races extremely or slips in changing from "3rd" to "2nd" when depressing pedal	a) Vacuum diaphragm and hoses b) Main line pressure c) Manual control valve d) Band servo e) Leakage of fluid pressure passage f) Front clutch	a) Renew diaphragm/hoses b) Correct main line or passage as per air test c) Adjust range select linkage/renew valve assembly d) Renew band servo e) Correct as per air test f) Renew front clutch
Failure to change from "3rd" to "2nd" when changing lever into "2" range	a) Range select linkage b) Main line pressure c) Manual control valve d) Band servo e) Band brake f) Leakage of fluid pressure passage	a) Adjust linkage b) Correct main line or passage per air test c) Adjust range select linkage/renew valve assembly d) Renew band servo e) Renew band brake f) Correct as per air test
Gear change from "2nd" to "1st" or from "2nd" to "3rd" in "2" range	a) Range select linkage b) Main line pressure c) Manual control valve	a) Adjust linkage b) Correct main line or passage per air test c) Adjust range select linkage/renew valve assembly
No shock on change from "1" range to "2" range or engine races extremely	a) Oil level b) Range select linkage c) Vacuum diaphragm and hoses d) Engine idle rpm e) High stall speed f) Manual control valve g) Transmission air check to determine if band servo is working h) Oil pump	a) Add if needed b) Adjust linkage c) Renew diaphragm/hoses d) Set idle rpm e) Renew band brake f) Adjust range select linkage/renew valve assembly g) Repair or renew servo h) Repair or renew
Failure to shift from "3rd" to "2nd" when shifting lever into "1" range	a) Range select linkage b) Main line pressure c) Manual control valve d) Governor valve e) Band servo f) Leakage of fluid pressure passage g) Low and reverse brake bands	a) Adjust linkage b) Correct main line or passage per air test c) Adjust range select linkage/renew valve assembly d) Overhaul governor/renew governor e) Renew band servo f) Correct as per air test g) Renew low and reverse brake bands

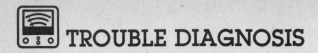

CHILTON'S THREE "C's" AUTOMATIC TRANSMISSION DIAGNOSIS CHART
L3N71B, L4N71B, JM600 and E4N71B Automatic Transmission Models

Condition	Cause	Correction
No engine braking in range "1"	a) Range select linkage b) Main line pressure c) Manual control valve d) Leakage of fluid pressure passage e) Low and reverse brake bands	a) Adjust linkage b) Correct main line or passage per air test c) Adjust range select linkage/renew valve assembly d) Correct as per air test e) Renew low and reverse brake bands
Gear change from "1st" to "2nd" or from "2nd" to "3rd" in "1" range	a) Range select linkage b) Manual control valve c) Leakage of fluid pressure passage	a) Adjust linkage b) Adjust range select linkage/renew valve assembly c) Correct as per air test
Does not change from "2nd" to "1st" in "1" range	a) Oil level b) Range select linkage c) Manual control valve d) Governor valve e) Band servo f) Leakage of fluid pressure passage g) Low and reverse brake	a) Add if needed b) Adjust linkage c) Adjust range select linkage/renew valve assembly d) Overhaul governor/renew governor e) Renew band servo f) Correct as per air test g) Renew low and reverse brake
Large shock in changing from "2nd" to "1st" in "1" range	a) Vacuum diaphragm and hoses b) High engine stall rpm c) Manual control valve	a) Renew diaphragm/hoses b) Renew low and reverse brake c) Adjust range select linkage/renew valve assembly
Transmission overheats	a) Oil level b) Band servo c) Cooler fluid pressure d) Restricted or no rear lubrication e) Manual control valve f) Leakage of fluid pressure passage g) Front clutch h) Band brake i) Low and reverse brake j) Line pressure k) "O" ring in input shaft l) Torque converter m) Lock-up orifice in oil pump cover n) Oil pump	a) Add if needed b) Renew band servo c) Correct cooler fluid or passage per air test d) Check passages e) Adjust range select linkage/renew valve assembly f) Correct as per air test g) Renew front clutch h) Renew band brake i) Renew low and reverse brake j) Test line pressure with gauge and correct as required k) Renew "O" ring in input shaft l) Renew torque converter m) Inspect orifice, clean or renew plate or oil pump assembly n) Renew oil pump assembly

CHILTON'S THREE "C's" AUTOMATIC TRANSMISSION DIAGNOSIS CHART
L3N71B, L4N71B, JM600 and E4N71B Automatic Transmission Models

Condition	Cause	Correction
Vehicle moves changing into "P" range or parking gear does not disengage when shifted out of "P" range	a) Range select linkage	a) Adjust linkage
Oil shoots out during operation. White smoke from exhaust during operation	a) Oil level b) Vacuum diaphragm and hoses c) Main line pressure d) Restricted or no rear lubrication e) Manual control valve f) Leakage of fluid pressure passage g) Rear clutch h) Band brake i) Low and reverse brake j) Oil pump k) One-way clutch torque converter l) Planetary gear	a) Add if needed b) Renew vacuum diaphragm/hoses c) Correct main line or passage per air test d) Check passages e) Adjust range select linkage/renew valve assembly f) Correct as per air test g) Renew rear clutch h) Renew band brake i) Renew low and reverse brake j) Renew oil pump k) Renew one-way clutch torque converter l) Renew planetary gear
Offensive smell at fluid fill pipe	a) Oil level b) Rear clutch c) Front clutch d) Band brake e) Low and reverse brake f) Oil pump g) Leakage of fluid pressure passage h) One-way clutch torque converter	a) Add if needed b) Renew rear clutch c) Renew front clutch d) Renew band brake e) Renew low and reverse brake f) Renew oil pump g) Correct as per air test h) Renew one-way clutch torque converter
Transmission noise in "P" and "N" ranges	a) Oil level b) Main line pressure c) Oil pump	a) Add if needed b) Correct main line or passage per air test c) Renew oil pump
Transmission noise in "D", "2", "1" and "R" ranges	a) Oil level b) Main line pressure c) Rear clutch d) Oil pump e) One-way clutch of transmission f) Planetary gear g) Torque converter	a) Add if needed b) Correct main line or passage per air test c) Renew rear clutch d) Renew oil pump e) Renew one-way clutch of transmission f) Renew planetary gear g) Renew torque converter

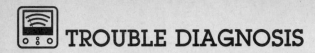

CHILTON'S THREE "C's" AUTOMATIC TRANSMISSION DIAGNOSIS CHART
L3N71B, L4N71B, JM600 and E4N71B Automatic Transmission Models

Condition	Cause	Correction
Transmission shifts to O.D. even if O.D. cancel switch is turned to "ON"	a) O.D. cancel switch and/or wiring b) O.D. cancel solenoid c) O.D. cancel valve d) Lock-up control unit and sensors	a) Inspect, renew cancel switch if necessary and/or repair wiring b) Renew O.D. cancel solenoid c) Clean or renew O.D. cancel valve d) Test, repair or renew lock-up control unit and sensors
Lamp inside O.D. cancel switch does not glow, even if ignition switch is turned to "ON" (engine not started)	a) O.D. cancel switch and/or wiring b) Lock-up control unit and sensors	a) Inspect, renew cancel switch or components, as required. Repair wiring as required b) Test repair or renew lock-up control unit and sensors
Lamp inside O.D. cancel switch does not glow, even if transmission is shifted to O.D.	a) O.D. cancel switch and/or wiring b) O.D. indicator switch	a) Inspect, renew cancel switch or components, as required. Repair wiring as required b) Repair or renew O.D. indicator switch
Lamp inside power shift switch does not glow even if shift pattern is turned to "power" pattern	a) O.D. cancel switch b) Lock-up control unit and sensors	a) Test, repair or renew O.D. cancel switch b) Test, repair or renew lock-up control unit or sensors
Lock-up does not occur in any range (E4N71B)	a) Lock-up solenoid b) Lock-up control unit and sensors c) Torque converter d) Lock-up control valve	a) Test, repair or renew lock-up solenoid b) Test, repair or renew lock-up control unit or sensors c) Renew torque converter d) Renew lock-up control valve
Lock-up does not occur in "4th" gear (L4N71B)	a) Governor b) O.D. band servo c) Lock-up control valve d) O.D. brake band	a) Clean or renew governor b) Repair O.D. band servo c) Clean or renew lock-up control valve d) Renew O.D. brake band
Large jolt changing from lock-up "OFF" to "ON"	a) Fluid quality b) Line pressure c) Governor d) Lock-up control unit and sensors e) Lock-up control valve f) O.D. brake band	a) Drain and replace fluid b) Correct line pressure to specs. c) Clean or renew governor d) Test, repair or renew lock-up control unit or sensors e) Clean or renew lock-up control valve f) Renew O.D. brake band
Torque converter not locked-up	a) Governor tube b) Governor c) Line pressure d) "O" ring in input shaft e) Torque converter f) Lock-up control valve g) Lock-up orifice in oil pump cover h) Oil pump	a) Repair or renew governor tube b) Clean or renew governor c) Test line pressure with gauge and correct as required d) Renew "O" ring in input shaft e) Renew torque converter f) Clean or renew lock-up control valve g) Inspect orifice, clean or renew plate or oil pump assembly h) Renew oil pump assembly

CHILTON'S THREE "C's" AUTOMATIC TRANSMISSION DIAGNOSIS CHART
L3N71B, L4N71B, JM600 and E4N71B Automatic Transmission Models

Condition	Cause	Correction
Lock-up piston slips	a) Line pressure	a) Test line pressure with gauge and correct as required
	b) "O" ring in input shaft	b) Renew "O" ring in input shaft
	c) Torque converter	c) Renew torque converter
	d) Lock-up orifice in oil pump cover	d) Inspect orifice, clean or renew plate or oil pump assembly
	e) Oil pump	e) Renew oil pump assembly
Lock-up points extremely high or low	a) Governor tube	a) Repair or renew governor tube
	b) Governor	b) Clean or renew governor
	c) Lock-up control valve	c) Clean or renew lock-up control valve
Engine stalls in R, D, 2, and 1 ranges	a) Torque converter	a) Renew torque converter
	b) Lock-up valve	b) Clean or renew lock-up valve

Preparation for Trouble Diagnosis

A logical and orderly diagnosis outline, with charts, is provided with clutch and band application charts, shift speed and governor pressures, main control pressures and a basic oil flow schematic to assist the repairman in diagnosing the problems, causes and extent of repairs needed to bring the automatic transmission back to its acceptable level of operation.

Preliminary checks and adjustments should be made to the manual linkage, accelerator and downshift switch control. Transmission oil level must be checked, both visually and by smell, to determine if the fluid level is correct and to observe the condition of the fluid, should any foreign material be present in the fluid. Smelling the fluid will indicate if internal damage has been done to the bands and/or clutches, through excessive slippage or overheating of the transmission.

It is most important to locate the defects and their causes and to properly repair them, avoiding a reoccurrence of the same problem which results in costly and time consuming repairs for a second time.

Hydraulic Control System

Hydraulic pressure, clutch and band applications control the changing of the gear ratios in the automatic transmissions. The clutches and bands are applied or released by the force of the fluid pressure, controlled by a system of valves and control mechanisms.

1. Screen or filter cleans foreign material from the fluid supply before entering the oil pump.
2. The oil pump supplies the oil pressure to the transmission and its components.
3. Converter pressure relief valve prevents excessive pressure build-up in the converter.
4. The torque converter is a fluid coupler, torque multiplier and a lock-up unit.
5. The rear (forward) clutch is applied in all forward gears.
6. The high-reverse (front) clutch is applied in reverse and high gears.
7. The low and reverse clutch brake is applied in Park, Reverse and range "1" low gear.
8. The rear lubrication passages lubricate the rear transmission components.
9. The front lubrication passages lubricate the front transmission components.
10. The oil cooler system removes heat from the transmission fluid as it flows through a cooler in the engine's cooling system.

11. Drain back valve prevents loss of fluid in the hydraulic circuits when the engine is stopped.
12. Throttle control valve regulates the throttle pressure in relation to the engine manifold vacuum through vacuum diaphragm assembly.

NOTE: A vacuum pump is used on the diesel engine to control the vacuum supply to the vacuum diaphragm.

13. The brake band servo is applied in the "2" speed and pressure released when the transmission is in "3" gear.
14. Pressure modifier valve uses throttle pressure, controlled by governor pressure, to modify the main line pressure from the regulator valve. It also modifies harsh shifting caused by excessive pump pressure.
15. Vacuum diaphragm moves the throttle valve in relation to the engine vacuum changes or controlled vacuum from the diesel engine installed vacuum pump.
16. Throttle back-up valve increases throttle pressure output to increase line pressure when the manual valve is shifted to either "2" or "1" range.
17. Governor provides road speed signals to the transmission control valve assembly and causes either up or down shifting.
18. Oil pressure regulator valve is used to control main line pressure.
19. Throttle solenoid downshift valve overrides normal upshifts to provide forced downshifts on full acceleration.
20. Manual selector valve moves with the shift selector and direct main line pressure to the various oil passages, applying units to provide the necessary gear ratios.
21. 1-2 shift valve controls the upshifts from "1st" to "2nd" and downshifts from "2nd" to "1st"
22. The 2-3 shift valve controls the upshift from "2nd" to "3rd" and downshifts from "3rd" to "2nd".
23. The 3-4 shift valve controls the upshift from "3rd" to "4th" and downshifts from "4th" to "3rd".
24. Second lock-up valve applies the brake band servo in "D", 1, and 2 ranges. The second lock-up valve locks out the 1-2 shift valve in the "2" range.
25. The speed cut valve controls the opening and closing of the line pressure passage to the high-reverse (front) clutch, dependent upon the governor pressure which is generated in proportion to car road speed.
26. When in operation, the lock-up control valve drains fluid from the front of the lock-up piston, located in the torque converter. As the fluid is drained, the turbine runner is coupled to the pump impeller, giving mechanical lock-up, rather than a fluid coupling effect.

27. The overdrive cancel solenoid and switch allow or prevent engagement of the overdrive unit, on demand of the operator.

28. Overdrive cancel valve works in conjunction with the overdrive cancel solenoid to allow or prevent the engagement of the overdrive unit.

29. The shift valve train system applies and exhausts the fluid pressures to the servos and clutch assemblies for upshifts and downshifts automatically on demand.

30. The Kickdown system forces downshifts by overriding the governor/throttle valve control of the shift valves.

Diagnosis Tests

OIL PRESSURE CIRCUITS

To utilize the oil flow charts for diagnosing transmission problems, the repairman must have an understanding of the oil pressure circuits and how each circuit affects the operation of the transmission, by the use of controlled oil pressure.

Control (line) pressure is a regulated main line pressure, developed by the operation of the front pump. It is directed to the main regulator valve, where predetermined spring pressure automatically moves the regulator valve to control the pressure of the oil at a predetermined rate, by opening the valve and exhausting excessive pressured oil back into the sump and holding the valve closed to build up pressure when needed.

Therefore, it is most important during the diagnosis phase to test main line control pressure to determine if high or low pressure exists. Do not attempt to adjust a pressure regulator valve spring to obtain more or less control pressure. Internal transmission damage may result.

The manual valve is the controlling agent of the automatic transmission. It is manually operated to a specific range, which in turn directs fluid pressure to the varied applying units, providing the necessary gear ratios to operate the vehicle under different road conditions and engine loads.

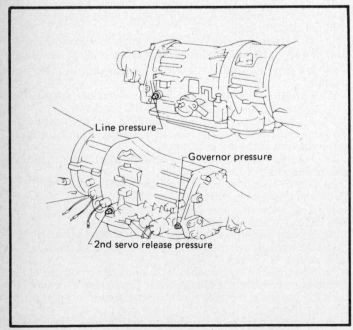

Pressure test port locations on the four speed automatic transmissions. The L4N71B, JM600 models utilize a pipe to the converter from the governor pressure port (© Nissan Motor Co. of USA)

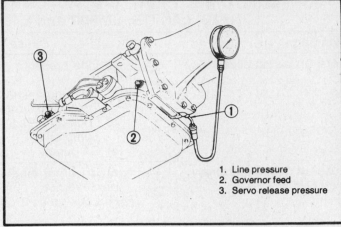

1. Line pressure
2. Governor feed
3. Servo release pressure

Installation of pressure gauge to line pressure port—L3N71B models illustrated (© Nissan Motor Co. of USA)

PRELIMINARY CHECKS

Verifying Malfunctions

1. Obtain as much information from the vehicle operator as to the nature of the malfunction.

2. Determine when the condition exists, only when first started, during the engine/transmission warm up period, after the assemblies have reached normal operating temperature of 122-176° F. (50-80° C.) or during all driving phases.

3. Verify fluid level and fluid condition, noting its color, texture and odor. Some common forms of contaminations are as follows;

 a. Dark or black fluid with a burned odor can indicate worn or burned friction material.

 b. Dark or black fluid without a burned odor can indicate a slight engine coolant leakage or addition of various types of additives.

 c. Milky white color of the fluid would indicate water contamination from the cooling system or from an outside source, such as road water or from a flood.

 d. Varnished fluid, light to dark brown and tacky, can indicate over or under filling, which in turn can cause overheating of the fluid and cause the fluid to oxidize.

4. Verify the engine idle of the vehicle is set to specifications.

5. Verify the shift linkage detents align with the detents in the transmission. In many cases, failure of the transmission can be traced to improperly adjusted manual control valve linkage.

ROAD TEST

A road test can be made to determine the condition of the transmission internal components through their applications and releases during the gear ratio changes, which occur automatically. Spin-up, dragging or harshness is normally produced during the shifting, either up or down. By referring to the clutch and band application chart for the components engaged during a particular gear range, the malfunctioning component can normally be pinpointed.

It is suggested by the manufacturer that an oil pressure gauge (0-400 psi) be installed on the transmission at the main line pressure port before any road-test is performed. A tachometer and vacuum gauge should also be install in such a manner that all hoses from the gauges be routed to avoid ground contact while the vehicle is in motion.

CAUTION

Road safety must be paramount with the gauges read and the results recorded by one person, while a second person operates the vehicle.

A road test sequence should be followed. It may be necessary to repeat a sequence under different throttle conditions, such as light, medium, full or wide open throttle. Each sequence should have its results recorded.

Before The Road Test

1. Check that engine can only be started in the "P" and "N" ranges and that the vehicle is locked in position with the selector lever in the "P" range. Record the results.

2. Shift the selector lever into the "R" (Reverse) range. Note the initial engagement. Drive the vehicle in the reverse range to detect slippage or other malfunctions. Record the results.

3. Move the selector lever to the "N" range. There should be no forward or rearward movement. Record the results.

4. Shift the selector lever to the "D" range and note the engagement of the internal components, note the results.

5. Shift the gear selector lever to the "2" range and note the gear engagement. Record the results.

6. Shift the selector lever to the "1" range and note the gear engagement. Record the results.

7. Record the line pressure and vacuum readings at each range position.

During Road Test

1. Using a pre-selected road test course, drive the vehicle through all automatic shifts and in all gear ranges.

2. Note the shift timing and check that the torque converter locks up at its speed of approximately 42 mph.

NOTE: Because the shock of the torque converter lock-up is very slight, it is advisable to have a tachometer connected to the engine, to determine the loss of rpm (200-400 rpm) as the converter locks up. Certa in vehicle/transmission applications have a lock-up light indicator mounted either on the console or the dash, to alert the operator of the converter clutch lock-up.

3. During the road test, note the shift quality and timing, check for slippage or hesitation during the shifts, harshness, overlapping of unit application during the shift, noise or other malfunctions.

ROAD TEST GUIDE FOR L3N71B MODELS

"D" RANGE

1. Check the vehicle speeds and the engine rpm as the automatic transmission upshifts from "1st" to "2nd", from "2nd" to "3rd" and when the torque converter has locked up, on a light acceleration with engine vacuum approximately at 4 inches.

2. On quick acceleration, check the shifts as was done in step one. The engine vacuum would be at zero inches.

3. Running at speeds of 19, 25, 31, 37 and 43 mph in "D" range, check the kick down operation from "3rd" to "2nd" and from "2nd" to "1st".

4. With the accelerator pedal released and engine vacuum approximately 18 inches or more, check the downshifting from "3rd" to "2nd" and from "2nd" to "1st".

5. With the accelerator pedal released and engine vacuum at 18 inches or more while driving at 30 mph, manually move the gear selector lever from the "D" position to the "1" position. The transmission should automatically shift to the "2nd" gear of the "1" position and engine braking should occur. As the vehicle slows, the transmission will downshift from the "2nd" gear to the "1st" gear while in the "1" position. Again, engine braking should occur.

6. With the accelerator pedal released, quick shift the selector lever into the "2" position while driving at 30 mph. A downshift from "3rd" to "2nd" should take place and engine braking should occur. Verify that the transmission remains in the "2nd" gear, regardless of vehicle speed.

"1" RANGE

1. Check for proper upshifting of the transmission from "1st" to "2nd" while in the "1" range. "3rd" gear is not attainable.

"2" RANGE

1. Check the transmisison for being locked into the "2nd" gear and not upshifting or downshifting, regardless of vehicle speed.

ROAD TEST GUIDE FOR L4N71B AND TM600 MODELS

"D" RANGE

1. On a light acceleration and with engine vacuum at approximately 4 inches, check the vehicle speeds and the engine rpm as the automatic transmission upshifts from "1st" to "2nd", from "2nd" to "3rd" and from "3rd" to "4th", with the O.D. cancel switch in the off position. Verify the torque converter lock-up with either the indicator light or with a tachometer attached to the engine.

2. On quick acceleration, check the upshifts as was done in step one. The engine vacuum would be at zero inches.

3. Running at speeds of 19, 25, 31, 37, 43 and 62 mph in the "D" range, check the kickdown operation from "4th" to "3rd" and from "3rd" to "2nd", both in and out of the O.D. mode.

4. With the accelerator pedal released and the engine vacuum approximately 18 inches or more, check the down shifting from the "4th" to "3rd", "3rd" to "2nd" and "2nd" to "1st" with the transmission in the O.D. mode. Check the down shifting with the transmission out of the O.D. mode from "3rd" to "2nd" and from "2nd" to "1st".

5. With the accelerator pedal released and the engine vacuum at 18 inches or more, traveling at a speed of 30 mph, manually move the gear selector lever from the "D" position to the "1" position. The transmission should automatically shift to the "2nd" gear of the "1" position and engine braking should occur. As the vehicle slows, the transmission will downshift from the "2nd" gear to the "1st" gear while in the "1" position. Again, engine braking should occur.

6. Quick shift the selector lever into the "2" position while releasing the accelerator pedal. Have the vehicle traveling at a road speed of 30 mph. A downshift from the "3rd" to "2nd" should take place and engine braking should occur. Verify that the transmission remains in the "2nd" gear, regardless of vehicle speed.

"1" RANGE

1. Check for proper transmission upshifting from "1st" to "2nd" while in the "1" range. The transmission should not shift into "3rd" gear.

"2" RANGE

1. Check the transmission for being locked into the "2nd" gear and not upshifting or downshifting, regardless of vehicle speed.

O.D. CANCEL SWITCH OPERATION

1. Verify that the transmission will not shift into the overdrive mode while the O.D. cancel switch is in the "ON" position.

O.D. INDICATOR LAMP

1. With the ignition switch in the "ON" position, without the engine operating, the O.D. indicator lamp should glow and go out as soon as the engine is started.

2. Verify the indicator lamp glows when the transmission is shifted into O.D. with the O.D. cancel switch in the "OFF" position.

ROAD TEST GUIDE FOR E4N71B MODELS

"P" RANGE

1. Place the control lever in "P" range and start the engine. Stop the engine and repeat the procedure in all other ranges and neutral.

2. Stop vehicle on a slight upgrade and place control lever in "P" range. Release parking brake to make sure vehicle remains locked.

"R" RANGE

1. Manually shift the control lever from "P" to "R", and note shift quality.

2. Drive the vehicle in reverse long enough to detect slippage or other abnormalities.

"N" RANGE

1. Manually shift the control lever from "R" and "D" to "N" and note quality.

2. Release parking brake with control lever in "N" range. Lightly depress accelerator pedal to make sure vehicle does not move. (When vehicle is new or soon after clutches have been replaced, vehicle may move slightly. This is not a problem.)

"D" RANGE

1. Manually shift the gear selector from "N" to "D" range, and note shift quality.

2. Drive the vehicle in "D" range. Record, on the symptom chart, respective vehicle speeds at which upshifting and downshifting occur. These speeds are to be read at several different intake manifold vacuum levels. Also, determine the timing at which shocks are encountered during shifting and which clutches are engaged.

3. Check to determine if shifting speed changes when accelerator pedal is depressed slowly and when it is depressed quickly.

4. Check to determine if shifting to overdrive gear cannot be made while power shift switch is "ON."

5. When vehicle is being driven in the 40-53 mph (65-85 km/h) speed range in "D₃" at half to light throttle position, fully depress accelerator pedal to make sure it downshifts from 3rd to 2nd gear.

6. When vehicle is being driven in the 16-22 mph (25-35 km/h) speed range in "D " range at half to light throttle position, fully depress accelerator pedal to make sure it downshifts from 2nd to 1st gear.

"2" RANGE

1. While vehicle is being driven in "2" range, make sure that it does not shift into 1st or 3rd gear, despite speed changes.

2. Shift control lever to "D" range and allow vehicle to operate at 25-31 mph (40-50 km/h). Then, shift to "2" range to make sure it downshifts to 2nd gear.

"1" RANGE

1. Shift control lever to "1" range and allow vehicle to run. Ensure that it does not upshift from 1st to 2nd gear although vehicle speed increases.

2. While vehicle is being driven in "1" range, release accelerator pedal to make sure that engine compression acts as a brake.

3. Shift control lever to "D" or "2" range and allow vehicle to run at 12-19 mph (20-30 km/h). Then, shift control lever to "1" range to make sure the downshift to 1st gear is made.

CONTROL PRESSURE SYSTEM TESTS

Control pressure tests should be performed whenever slippage, delay or harshness is felt in the shifting of the transmission. Throttle and modulator pressure changes can cause these problems also, but are generated from the control pressures and therefore reflect any problems arising from the control pressure system.

The control pressure is first checked in all ranges without any throttle pressure input, and then checked as the throttle pressure is increased by lowering the vacuum supply to the vacuum diaphragm with the use of the stall test.

The control pressure tests should define differences between mechanical or hydraulic failures of the transmission.

The transmissions are provided with three pressure test ports, line pressure, governor pressure and servo release pressure. Only the main line pressure test ports on the transmissions and the governor pressure test ports are of any value to the diagnostician in determining transmission malfunctions.

Testing

1. Install pressure gauges to the main line pressure test port and if equipped, to the governor pressure test port.

2. Install a tachometer and vacuum gauge to the engine.

3. Block the wheels and apply the parking brake.

4. Operate the engine/transmission in the ranges as listed on the accompanying charts and at the engine vacuum as specified.

5. Record the actual pressure readings in each test and compare them with specifications.

NOTE: Look for a steady rise in pressure as the vehicle speed increases under a light load and pressure should not drop between shifts more than 14 psi. Excessive pressure drop could indicate internal leakages.

Precautions Before Idle Tests

1. Be sure manifold vacuum is above 15 in. Hg. If lower, check for engine conditions and/or vacuum leaks and repair.

2. Make sure the manifold vacuum changes with throttle plate opening. Check by accelerating quickly and observing the vacuum reading.

Possible Malfunctions Due to Low Line Pressure

If line pressure does not rise, first check to make sure that vacuum hose is connected properly.

1. When line pressure is low at all positions, the problem may be due to:

    a. Wear on interior of oil pump

    b. Oil leakage at or around oil pump, control valve body, transmission case or governor

    c. Sticking pressure regulator valve

    d. Sticking pressure modifier valve

2. When line pressure is low at a particular position, the problem may be due to the following:

    a. If oil leaks at or around forward clutch (rear) or governor, line pressure is low in "D", "2" or "1" range but is normal in "R" range.

    b. If oil leaks at or around low and reverse brake circuit, line pressure becomes low in "R" or "P" range but is normal in "D", "2" or "1" range.

3. When line pressure is high, pressure regulator valve may have stuck.

LINE PRESSURE
At Stall Point

Range	Line Pressure (psi)
L24E ENGINE MODEL WITH L4N71B TRANSMISSION	
R	203-230
D	141-158
2	145-166
1	141-158
LD28 ENGINE MODEL WITH L4N71B TRANSMISSION	
R	242-270
D	134-156
2	142-171
1	134-156

NOTE: For the LD28 Engine models, set the engine vacuum at 5.91 in. Hg to measure line pressure.

LINE PRESSURE
At Idle

Range	Line Pressure (psi)
L24E ENGINE MODEL WITH L4N71B TRANSMISSION	
R	60-80
D	46-54
2	85-166
1	46-54
LD28 ENGINE MODEL WITH L4N71B TRANSMISSION	
R	43-100
D	43-57
2	85-171
1	43-57

NOTE: For the LD28 Engine models, set the engine vacuum at 23.62 in. Hg to measure line pressure.

Possible Malfunctions Due to Cut-down Pressure

1. When cut-down point disappears, the problem may be due to:

    a. Sticking pressure modifier valve
    b. Sticking governor valve
    c. Oil leaks at oil passage

2. When cut-down point is too low or too high, the problem may be due to:

    a. Incorrect springs (at pressure modifier valve or governor valve)
    b. Oil leaks at oil passage

LINE PRESSURE
E4N71B Automatic Transmission

Engine	Range	Line Pressure (psi)
	AT IDLE	
VG30E	R	65-85
W/O Turbo	D	40-54
	2	114-156
	1	40-54
VG30E	R	44-64
W/Turbo	D	40-54
	2	114-164
	1	40-54
	AT STALL TEST	
VG30E	R	284-347
W/O Turbo	D	156-178
	2	156-185
	1	156-178
VG30E	R	284-341
W/Turbo	D	242-273
	2	242-273
	1	242-273

LINE PRESSURE
At Stall Point

Range	Line Pressure (psi)
L24E ENGINE MODEL WITH L3N71B TRANSMISSION	
R	203-230
D	141-158
2	145-166
1	141-158
LD28 ENGINE MODEL WITH L3N71B TRANSMISSION	
R	279-301
D	148-173
2	142-171
1	148-173

NOTE: For the LD 28 Engine models, set the engine vacuum at 5.91 in. Hg to measure line pressure.

MAIN LINE PRESSURE CUT BACK POINT
L4N71B Transmission

Intake Manifold Vacuum (in.-Hg)	Vehicle Speed (mph)	Propeller Shaft Rotation (rpm)
L24E ENGINE MODELS		
0	22-27	1190-1440
3.94	11-16	600-850
LD28 ENGINE MODEL		
5.91	14-19	730-1030
13.78	9-12	470-670

NOTE: This indication of line pressure change from high to low values occurs as the output shaft rotation is gradually increased from a "stall point." The cut down point should occur at the above speeds.

LINE PRESSURE
At Idle

Range	Line Pressure (psi)
L24E ENGINE MODEL WITH L3N71B TRANSMISSION	
R	60-80
D	46-54
2	85-166
1	46-54
LD28 ENGINE MODEL WITH L3N71B TRANSMISSION	
R	105-119
D	55-70
2	85-171
1	55-70

NOTE: For the LD28 engine models, set the engine vacuum to 23.62 in. Hg to measure line pressure.

LINE PRESSURE AND VEHICLE SPEED AT SHIFT POINTS
L4N71B Transmission

Intake Manifold Vacuum① (in. Hg)	Shift	Vehicle Speed (mph)	Propeller Shaft Revolutions (rpm)	Line Pressure (psi)
		L24 ENGINE (GASOLINE)		
0 (Kickdown)	D-1 to 2	34-39	1790-2040	77-100
	D-2 to 3	60-65	3170-3420	77-100
	D-3 to 4	—	—	—
	D-4 to 3	—	—	—
	D-3 to 2	60-55	3130-2880	77-100
	D-2 to 1	30-25	1580-1330	77-100
3.94	D-1 to 2	13-17	680-930	64-87
	D-2 to 3	35-40	1860-2110	64-87
	D-3 to 4	58-63	3050-3300	64-87
	D-4 to 3	37-33	1970-1720	64-87
	D-3 to 2	22-18	1190-940	64-87
	D-2 to 1	11-7	600-350	64-87
0 (Full throttle)	1-2 to 1	30-25	1600-1350	80-102
11.81	1-2 to 1	30-25	1600-1350	80-102
		LD28 ENGINE (DIESEL)		
5.91 (Kickdown)	D-1 to 2	25-30	1320-1570	82-100
	D-2 to 3	50-55	2640-2890	82-100
	D-3 to 4	—	—	—
	D-4 to 3	—	—	—
	D-3 to 2	50-45	2630-2380	82-100
	D-2 to 1	25-21	1320-1070	82-100
13.78	D-1 to 2	9-14	470-720	68-82
	D-2 to 3	32-36	1650-1900	68-82
	D-3 to 4	44-49	2330-2580	68-82
	D-4 to 3	35-30	1860-1610	68-82
	D-3 to 2	24-19	1280-1030	68-82
	D-2 to 1	11-7	600-350	68-82
5.91 (Full Throttle)	1-2 to 1	25-21	1320-1070	80-102
23.62	1-2 to 1	25-21	1320-1070	80-102

① LD28 Diesel engine uses a vacuum pump and regulator instead of engine manifold vacuum.

LINE PRESSURE AND VEHICLE SPEED AT SHIFT POINTS
L3N71B Transmission

Intake Manifold Vacuum① (in. Hg)	Shift	Vehicle Speed (mph)	Propeller Shaft Revolutions (rpm)	Line Pressure (psi)
L24 ENGINE (GASOLINE)				
0 (Kickdown)	D-1 to 2	36-41	1790-2040	77-100
	D-2 to 3	63-68	3170-3420	77-100
	D-3 to 2	62-57	3130-2880	77-100
	D-2 to 1	31-26	1580-1330	77-100
3.94	D-1 to 2	14-18	680-930	64-87
	D-2 to 3	37-42	1860-2110	64-87
	D-3 to 2	24-19	1190-940	64-87
	D-2 to 1	12-7	600-350	64-87
0 (Full Throttle)	1-2 to 1	32-27	1600-1350	80-102
11.81	1-2 to 1	32-27	1600-1350	80-102
LD28 ENGINE (DIESEL)				
5.91 (Kickdown)	D-1 to 2	28-34	1320-1570	82-100
	D-2 to 3	56-62	2640-2890	82-100
	D-3 to 2	56-51	2630-2380	82-100
	D-2 to 1	28-23	1320-1070	82-100
13.78	D-1 to 2	10-15	470- 720	68-82
	D-2 to 3	35-41	1650-1900	68-82
	D-3 to 2	27-22	1280-1030	68-82
	D-2 to 1	13-7	600-350	68-82
5.91 (Full Throttle)	1-2 to 1	28-23	1320-1070	80-102
23.62	1-2 to 1	28-23	1320-1070	80-102

① LD28 Diesel engine uses a vacuum pump and regulator instead of engine manifold vacuum.

LINE PRESSURE
JM600 Automatic Transmission

Range	Line pressure (psi)
LINE PRESSURE AT IDLE	
R	44- 64
D	40- 54
2	114-164
1	40- 54
LINE PRESSURE AT STALL POINT	
R	284-341
D	242-273
2	242-259
1	249-273

MAIN LINE PRESSURE CUT BACK POINT
L3N71B Transmission

Intake Manifold Vacuum (in.-Hg)	Vehicle Speed (mph)	Propeller Shaft Rotation (rpm)
L24E ENGINE MODELS		
0	24-29	1190-1440
3.94	12-17	600-850
LD28 ENGINE MODEL		
5.91	16-22	730-1030
13.78	13-17	590-790

NOTE: This indication of line pressure change from high to low values occurs as the output shaft rotation is gradually increased from a "stall point." The cut down point should occur at the above speeds.

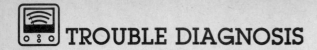

LINE PRESSURE AND VEHICLE SPEEDS AT SHIFT POINTS
E4N71B Automatic Transmission

Engine	Intake Manifold Vacuum (in. Hg)	Gearshift	Vehicle Speed (mph)	Propeller Shaft Revolution (rpm)	Line Pressure (psi)
VG30E W/O Turbo	1. Disconnect harness from lock-up control unit. Road test the vehicle to determine if all items listed in the → chart are within their specified values.		2. Reconnect harness to lock-up control unit. Road test the vehicle to see if shifting corresponds to the specified shift schedule pattern.		
	0 (Kickdown)	$D_1 \rightarrow D_2$	37-42	1900-2150	114-137
		$D_2 \rightarrow D_3$	63-68	3250-3500	114-137
		$D_3 \rightarrow D_4$	—	—	—
		$D_4 \rightarrow D_3$	—	—	—
		$D_3 \rightarrow D_2$	55-60	2850-3100	108-131
		$D_2 \rightarrow D_1$	26-31	1350-1600	108-131
	3.94	$D_1 \rightarrow D_2$	7-14	400- 700	80-102
		$D_2 \rightarrow D_3$	29-37	1500-1900	80-102
		$D_3 \rightarrow D_4$	42-52	2150-2650	80-102
		$D_4 \rightarrow D_3$	16-25	800-1300	71- 94
		$D_3 \rightarrow D_2$	9-19	450- 950	71- 94
		$D_2 \rightarrow D_1$	7-12	350- 600	71-131
	0 (Full throttle)	$1_2 \rightarrow 1_1$	26-31	1350-1600	105-128
	11.81	$1_2 \rightarrow 1_1$	24-29	1250-1500	92-114
VG30E W/Turbo	13.78 (Kickdown)	$D_1 \rightarrow D_2$	37-43	1850-2150	92-125
		$D_2 \rightarrow D_3$	64-70	3150-3450	92-125
		$D_3 \rightarrow D_4$	—	—	—
		$D_4 \rightarrow D_3$	—	—	—
		$D_3 \rightarrow D_2$	53-58	2600-2900	92-125
		$D_2 \rightarrow D_1$	29-34	1400-1700	92-125
	7.87	$D_1 \rightarrow D_2$	10-16	500- 800	46- 68
		$D_2 \rightarrow D_3$	13-21	650-1050	46- 68
		$D_3 \rightarrow D_4$	25-35	1250-1750	46- 68
		$D_4 \rightarrow D_3$	13-23	650-1150	46- 68
		$D_3 \rightarrow D_2$	7-17	350- 850	46- 68
		$D_3 \rightarrow D_1$	7-12	350- 600	46- 77
	13.78 (Full throttle)	$1_2 \rightarrow 1_1$	29-34	1400-1700	85-108
	17.72	$1_2 \rightarrow 1_1$	27-34	1350-1650	85-108

VEHICLE SPEED AT SHIFT POINTS
JM600 Automatic Transmission

Intake Manifold Vacuum (in. Hg)	Gearshift	Car speed (mph)	Output shaft speed (rpm)
13.8	$D_1 \to D_2$	37-42	1,800-2,100
	$D_2 \to D_3$	63-69	3,100-3,400
	$D_3 \to D_4$	—	—
	$D_4 \to D_3$	—	—
	$D_3 \to D_2$	52-58	2,550-2,850
	$D_2 \to D_1$	27-34	1,350-1,650
0	$D_1 \to D_2$	14-21	700-1,000
	$D_2 \to D_3$	42-50	2,050-2,450
	$D_3 \to D_4$	61-71	3,020-3,520
	$D_4 \to D_3$	34-44	1,670-2,170
	$D_3 \to D_2$	21-31	1,050-1,550
	$D_2 \to D_1$	7-12	350- 600
7.9	$D_1 \to D_2$	10-16	500- 800
	$D_2 \to D_3$	12-21	600-1,000
	$D_3 \to D_4$	25-35	1,260-1,760
	$D_4 \to D_3$	11-21	560-1,060
	$D_3 \to D_2$ or $D_3 \to D_1$	7-17	350- 850
	$D_2 \to D_1$	7-12	350- 600
13.8	$1_2 \to 1_1$	27-34	1,350-1,650
17.8	$1_2 \to 1_1$	26-32	1,300-1,600

LINE PRESSURE CUT-DOWN POINT
E4N71B Automatic Transmission

Engine	Intake Manifold Vacuum (in. Hg)	Vehicle Speed (mph)	Propeller Shaft Revolutions (rpm)
VG30E	0	17-23	900-1200
W/O Turbo	3.94	7-14	400-700
VG30E	13.78	18-24	1200-1600
W/Turbo	7.87	8-14	400-800

NOTE: The cut-down point indicates a point where line pressure changes from a high to a low value.

STALL TEST

The stall test is an application of engine torque, through the transmission and drive train to locked-up wheels, held by the vehicle's brakes. The engine's speed is increased until the rpms are stabilized. Given ideal engine operating conditions and no slippage from transmission clutches, bands or torque converter, the engine will stabilize at a specified test rpm.

Performing the Stall Test

1. Check the engine oil level and start the engine bringing it up to operating temperature.

2. Check the transmission fluid level and correct as necessary. Attach a calibrated tachometer to the engine and a 0-400 psi oil pressure gauge to the transmission control pressure tap on the right side of the case.

3. Mark the specified maximum engine rpm on the tachometer cover plate with a grease pencil to easily check if the stall speed is over or under specifications.

4. Apply the parking brake and block both front and rear wheels.

—— CAUTION ——

Do not allow anyone in front of the vehicle while performing the stall test.

5. While holding the brake pedal with the left foot, place the selector lever in "D" position and slowly depress the accelerator.

6. Read and record the engine rpm when the accelertor pedal is fully depressed and the engine rpm is stabilized. Read and record the oil pressure reading at the high engine rpm point.

NOTE: The stall test must be made within five seconds.

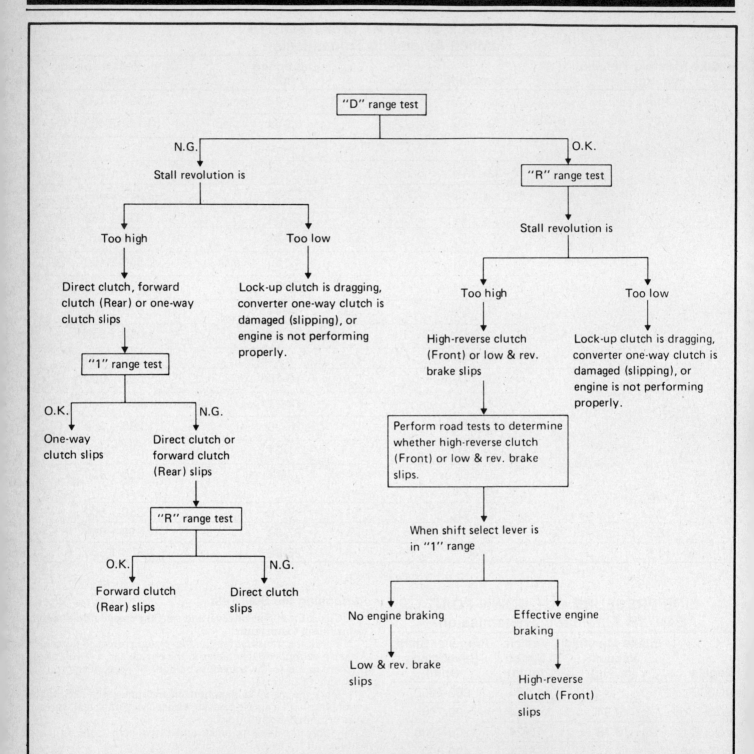

"D" range test

N.G. / O.K.

Stall revolution is → "R" range test

Too high / Too low

Too high: Direct clutch, forward clutch (Rear) or one-way clutch slips

Too low: Lock-up clutch is dragging, converter one-way clutch is damaged (slipping), or engine is not performing properly.

"1" range test

O.K. / N.G.

One-way clutch slips

Direct clutch or forward clutch (Rear) slips

"R" range test

O.K. / N.G.

Forward clutch (Rear) slips

Direct clutch slips

Stall revolution is

Too high / Too low

Too high: High-reverse clutch (Front) or low & rev. brake slips

Too low: Lock-up clutch is dragging, converter one-way clutch is damaged (slipping), or engine is not performing properly.

Perform road tests to determine whether high-reverse clutch (Front) or low & rev. brake slips.

When shift select lever is in "1" range

No engine braking

Low & rev. brake slips

Effective engine braking

High-reverse clutch (Front) slips

If converter one-way clutch is frozen, vehicle will have poor high speed performance. If converter one-way clutch is slipping, vehicle will be sluggish up to 50 or 60 km/h (30 or 40 MPH).

Stall test analysis (© Nissan Motor Co. of USA)

7. Shift the selector lever into the "N" position and increase the engine rpm to approximately 1000-1200 rpms. Hold this engine speed for one to two minutes to cool the transmission and fluid.

8. Make similar tests in the "2", "1" and "R" positions.

NOTE: If at any time the engine rpm races above the maximum as per specifications, indications are that a clutch unit or band is slipping and the stall test should be stopped before more damage is done to the internal parts.

Results of Stall Test
HIGH ENGINE RPM

If a slipping condition occurs during the stall test, indicated by high engine rpm, the selector lever position at the time of slippage provides an indication as to what holding member of the transmission is defective.

By determining the holding member involved, several possible causes of slippage can be diagnosed.
1. Slips in all ranges, control pressure low
2. Slips in "D", "1" or "2", rear clutch
3. Slips in 1st gear only, one-way clutch
4. Slips in "R" only, front clutch or low and reverse brake
Perform a road test to confirm these conditions.

LOW ENGINE RPM

When low stall speed is indicated, the converter one-way clutch is not holding, lock-up clutch is dragging or the engine is in need of a major tune-up. To determine which is at fault, perform a road test and observe the operation of the transmission and the engine. If the converter one-way clutch does not lock the stator, acceleration will be poor up to approximately 30 MPH. Above 30 MPH acceleration will be normal. With poor engine performance acceleration will be poor at all speeds. When the one-way clutch is seized and locks the stator from turning either way, the stall test rpm will bc normal. However, on a road test the vehicle will not go any faster than 50-55 MPH because of the 2:1 reduction ratio in the converter.

If slippage was indicated by high engine rpm, the road test will help identify the problem area observing the transmission operation during upshifts, both automatic and manual.

STALL SPEEDS

1982 and later L3N71B Transmission Model	1800 to 2100 rpm
1983 and later L4N71B Transmission Model	
With L24E Engine	1800 to 2100 rpm
With LD28 Engine	1650 to 1950 rpm
1984 E4N71B Transmission Model	
With VG30E w/o Turbo	2150 to 2450 rpm
With VG30E Turbo	2500 to 2800 rpm
1984 Conquest (L4N71B/JM600)	2350 to 2650 rpm

Precautions If Stall Test is Used
On Pressure Rise Test

(Refer to stall test procedures.)
1. Do not operate engine/transmission at stall for longer than 5 seconds per test.
2. Operate the engine between 1000 and 1200 rpm at the end of a test for approximately one to two minutes for cooling (in neutral).
3. Release the accelerator immediately in case of slippage or spin-up of the transmission to avoid more damage to the unit.

AIR PRESSURE TESTS

The control pressure test results and causes of abnormal pressures are to be used as a guide. Further testing or inspection could be necessary before repairs are made. If the pressures are found to be low in a clutch, servo or passageway, a verfication can be accomplished by removing the valve body and performing an air pressure test. This test can serve two purposes:

1. To determine if a malfunction of a clutch or band is caused by fluid leakage in the system or is the result of a mechanical failure.
2. To test the transmission for internal fluid leakage during the rebuilding and before completing the assembly.

Procedure
1. Obtain an air nozzle and adjust for 25 psi.
2. Apply air pressure (25 psi) to the passages as illustrated.

Vacuum Diaphragm

The modulated throttle system, which adjusts throttle pressure for the control of the shift valves, is operated by engine manifold vacuum through a vacuum diaphragm and must be inspected whenever a transmission defect is apparent.

Preparation of Vacuum Test

Before the vacuum diaphragm test is performed, check the engine vacuum supply and the condition and routing of the supply lines.

With the engine idling, remove the vacuum line at the vacuum diaphragm and install a vacuum gauge. There must be a steady, acceptable vacuum reading for the altitude at which the test is being performed.

If the vacuum is low, check for a vacuum leak or poor engine performance. If the vacuum is steady and acceptable, acclerate the engine sharply and observe the vacuum gauge reading. The vacuum should drop off rapidly at acceleration and return to the original reading immediately upon release of the accelerator.

If the vacuum reading does not change or changes slowly, check the vacuum supply lines for being plugged, restricted or connected to a vacuum reservoir supply. Repair the system as required.

MANIFOLD VACUUM TESTS
GASOLINE ENGINE

1. With the engine idling, remove the vacuum supply hose from the modulator nipple and check the hose end for the presence of engine vacuum with an appropriate gauge.
2. If vacuum is present, accelerate the engine and allow it to return to idle. A drop in vacuum should be noted during acceleration and a return to normal vacuum at idle.
3. If manifold vacuum is not present, check for breaks or restrictions in the vacuum lines and repair.

DIESEL ENGINE (LD28 ENGINE MODEL)

An engine operated vacuum pump is used to supply the vacuum needed to operate the transmission diaphragm and other vehicle vacuum operated components.

Vacuum Pump Inspection

1. Install a vacuum gauge between the vacuum pump and the vacuum diaphragm.
2. Start the engine and run it at idle speed of 600-750 rpm.
3. With the vacuum diaphragm not operating, the vacuum reading on the gauge should be 22.44-24.80 in. Hg.

VACUUM DIAPHRAGM TESTS

1. Apply at least 18 in. Hg. to the modulator vacuum nipple and observe the vacuum reading. The vacuum should hold.
2. If the vacuum does not hold, the diaphragm is leaking and the modulator assembly must be replaced.

NOTE: A leaking diaphragm causes harsh gear engagements and delayed or no up-shifts due to maximum throttle pressure developcd.

Additional Vacuum Diaphragm Testing
ON THE CAR TEST

The vacuum diaphragm is tested on the vehicle with the aid of an outside vacuum source, which can be adjusted to maintain a certain amount of vacuum. Apply 18 inches Hg. to the vaccum diaphragm vacuum nipple, through a hose connected to the outside vacuum source. The vacuum should hold at the applied level without any leakdown. If the vacuum level drops off, the vacuum diaphragm is leaking and must be replaced.

OFF CAR TEST

With the vacuum diaphragm removed from the automatic transmission, apply 18 inches Hg. to the diaphragm vacuum nipple.

The vacuum level should remain and not drop off. If the vacuum level drops, the diaphragm is leaking and the unit should be replaced.

A second test can be made with the diaphragm removed from the transmission. Insert the control rod into the valve end of the diaphragm and apply vacuum to the nipple. Hold a finger over the control rod and release the vacuum supply hose. The control rod should be moved outward by the pressure of the internal return spring. If the control rod does not move outward, a broken return spring is indicated.

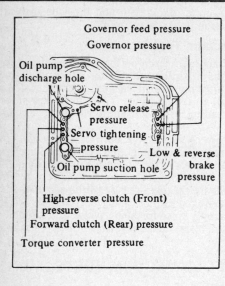

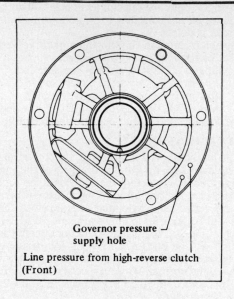

Governor pressure supply hole

Line pressure from high-reverse clutch (Front)

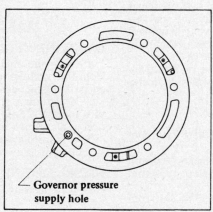

Governor pressure supply hole

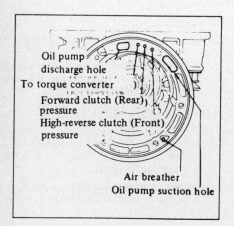

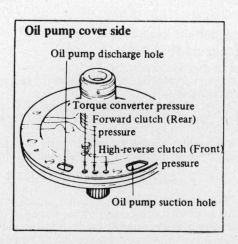

Fluid passage identification—L3N71B models (© Nissan Motor Co. of USA)

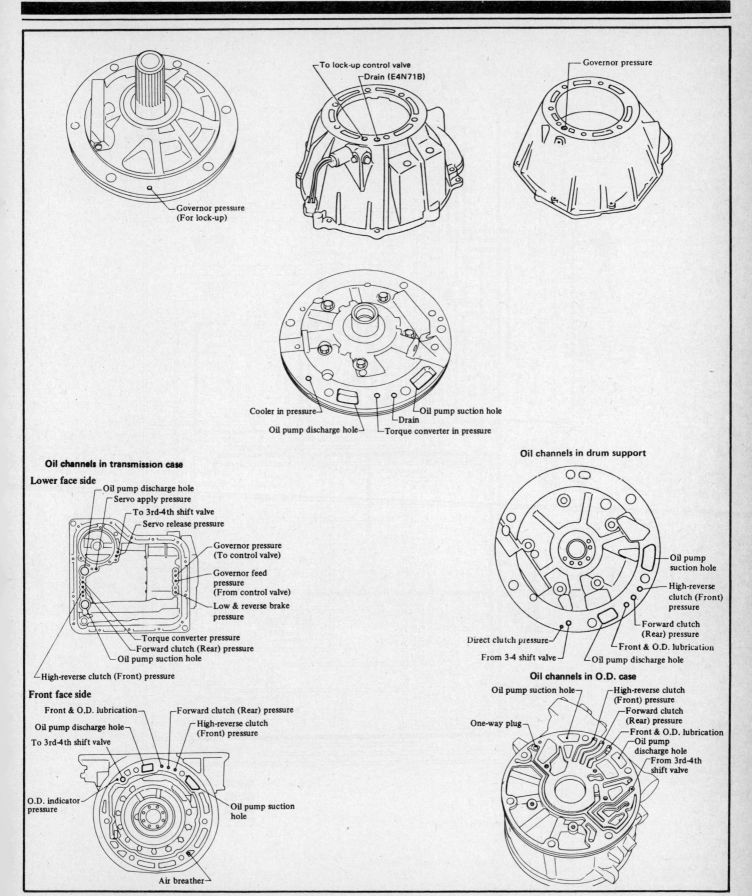

Fluid passage identification—L4N71B, E4N71B and JM600 models (© Nissan Motor Co. of USA)

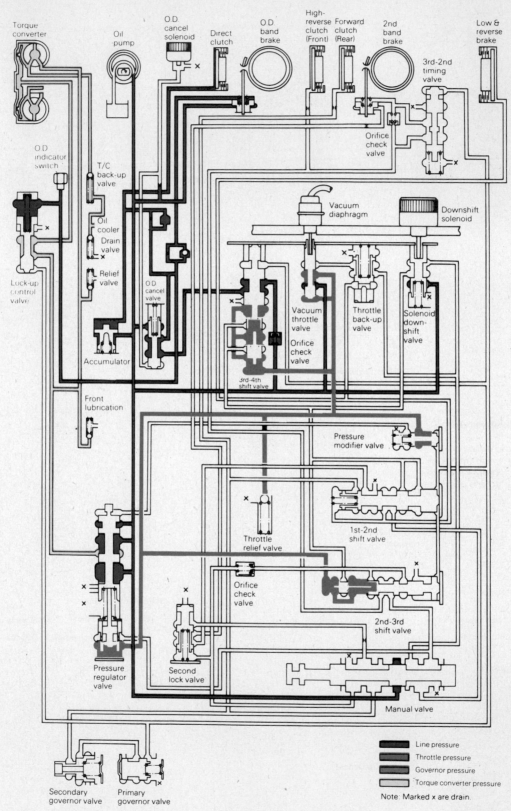

Torque converter

Oil pump

O.D. cancel solenoid

Direct clutch

O.D. band brake

High-reverse clutch (Front)

Forward clutch (Rear)

2nd band brake

Low & reverse brake

3rd-2nd timing valve

Orifice check valve

O.D. indicator switch

T/C back-up valve

Oil cooler

Drain valve

Relief valve

Lock-up control valve

O.D. cancel valve

Accumulator

Front lubrication

Vacuum diaphragm

Downshift solenoid

Vacuum throttle valve

Orifice check valve

Throttle back-up valve

Solenoid down-shift valve

3rd-4th shift valve

Pressure modifier valve

Throttle relief valve

Orifice check valve

1st-2nd shift valve

2nd-3rd shift valve

Pressure regulator valve

Second lock valve

Manual valve

Secondary governor valve

Primary governor valve

	Line pressure
	Throttle pressure
	Governor pressure
	Torque converter pressure

Note: Marked x are drain.

Units Applied
Direct clutch
O.D. band servo
(Apply and release)

Neutral (© Chrysler Corp.)

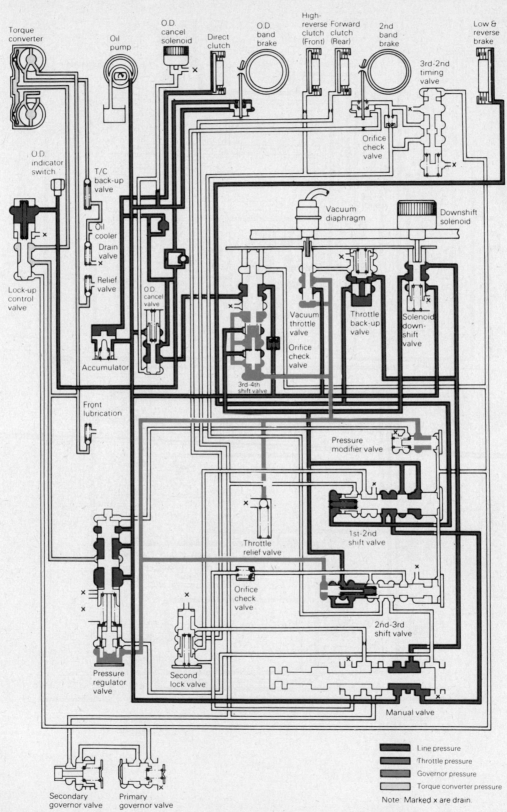

Torque converter

Oil pump

O.D. cancel solenoid

Direct clutch

O.D. band brake

High-reverse clutch (Front)

Forward clutch (Rear)

2nd band brake

Low & reverse brake

3rd-2nd timing valve

O.D. indicator switch

T/C back-up valve

Oil cooler

Drain valve

Relief valve

Lock-up control valve

O.D. cancel valve

Accumulator

Front lubrication

Orifice check valve

Vacuum diaphragm

Downshift solenoid

Vacuum throttle valve

Orifice check valve

Throttle back-up valve

Solenoid downshift valve

3rd-4th shift valve

Pressure modifier valve

1st-2nd shift valve

Throttle relief valve

Orifice check valve

2nd-3rd shift valve

Pressure regulator valve

Second lock valve

Manual valve

Secondary governor valve

Primary governor valve

	Line pressure
	Throttle pressure
	Governor pressure
	Torque converter pressure

Note: Marked x are drain.

Units Applied
Direct clutch
O.D. band servo
(Apply and release)
Low and reverse brake
Parking pawl

Park (© Chrysler Corp.)

975

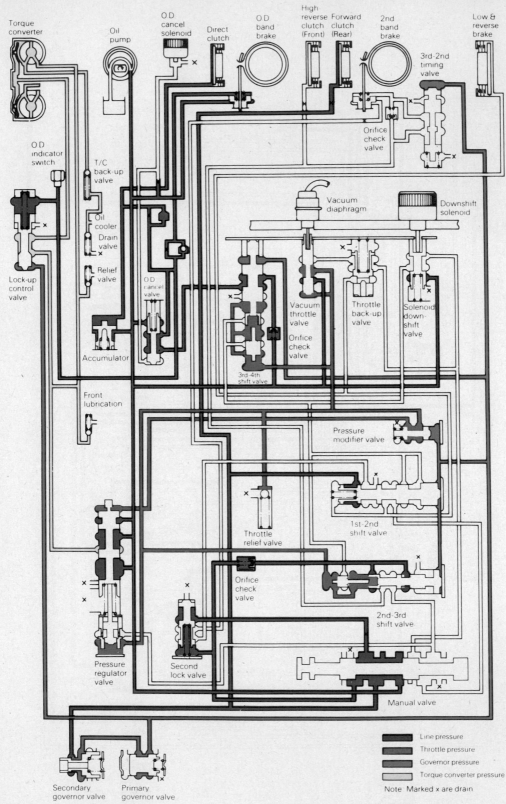

Torque converter

Oil pump

O.D. cancel solenoid

Direct clutch

O.D. band brake

High reverse clutch (Front)

Forward clutch (Rear)

2nd band brake

Low & reverse brake

O.D indicator switch

T/C back-up valve

Oil cooler

Drain valve

Relief valve

3rd-2nd timing valve

Orifice check valve

Lock-up control valve

O.D cancel valve

Accumulator

Front lubrication

Vacuum diaphragm

Downshift solenoid

Vacuum throttle valve

Orifice check valve

Throttle back-up valve

Solenoid down-shift valve

3rd-4th shift valve

Pressure modifier valve

Throttle relief valve

1st-2nd shift valve

Orifice check valve

2nd-3rd shift valve

Pressure regulator valve

Second lock valve

Manual valve

Secondary governor valve

Primary governor valve

Line pressure
Throttle pressure
Governor pressure
Torque converter pressure

Note: Marked x are drain

Units Applied
Direct clutch
O.D. band servo
(Apply and release)
Forward (rear) clutch
One-way clutch

Drive—First Gear (© Chrysler Corp.)

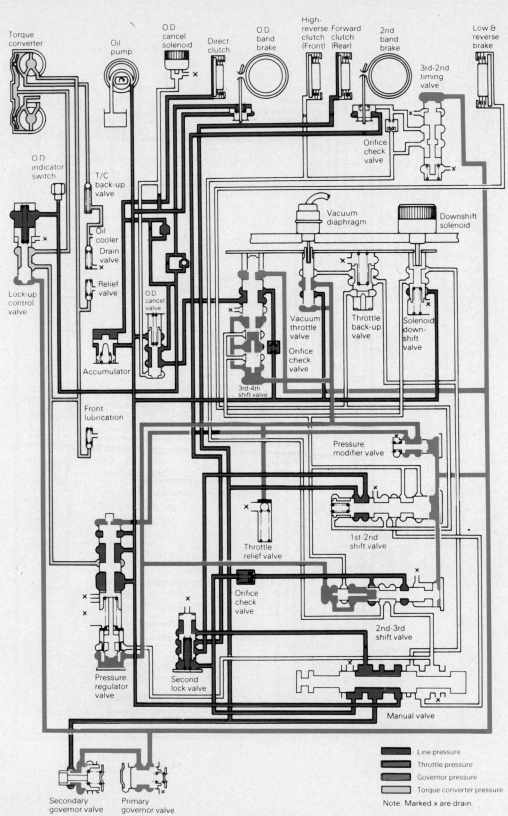

Torque converter

Oil pump

O.D. cancel solenoid

Direct clutch

O.D. band brake

High-reverse clutch (Front)

Forward clutch (Rear)

2nd band brake

Low & reverse brake

3rd-2nd timing valve

O.D. indicator switch

T/C back-up valve

Oil cooler

Drain valve

Relief valve

O.D. cancel valve

Lock-up control valve

Accumulator

Front lubrication

Orifice check valve

Vacuum diaphragm

Downshift solenoid

Vacuum throttle valve

Orifice check valve

3rd-4th shift valve

Throttle back-up valve

Solenoid down-shift valve

Pressure modifier valve

Throttle relief valve

Orifice check valve

1st-2nd shift valve

2nd-3rd shift valve

Pressure regulator valve

Second lock valve

Manual valve

Secondary governor valve

Primary governor valve

- Line pressure
- Throttle pressure
- Governor pressure
- Torque converter pressure

Note: Marked x are drain.

Units Applied
Direct clutch
O.D. band servo
(Apply and release)
Forward (rear) clutch
2nd band servo

Drive—Second Gear (© Chrysler Corp.)

977

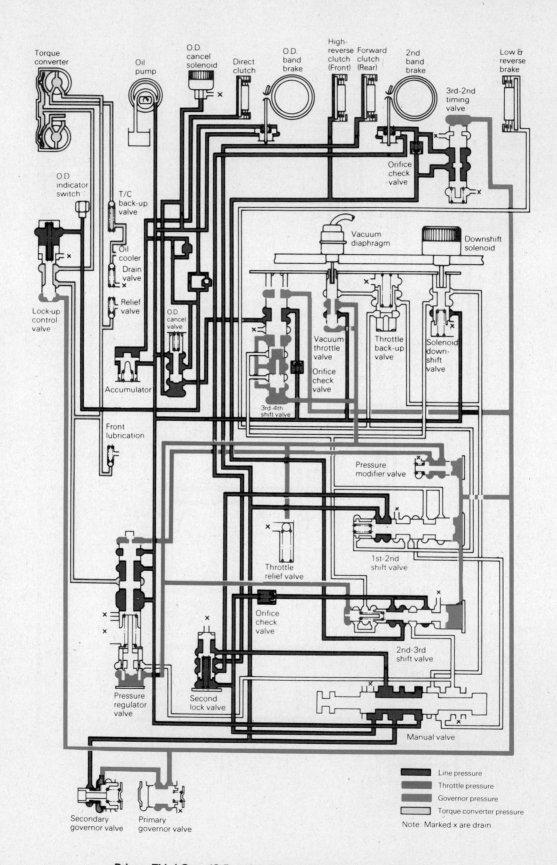

Drive—Third Gear (O.D. solenoid in operation) (© Chrysler Corp.)

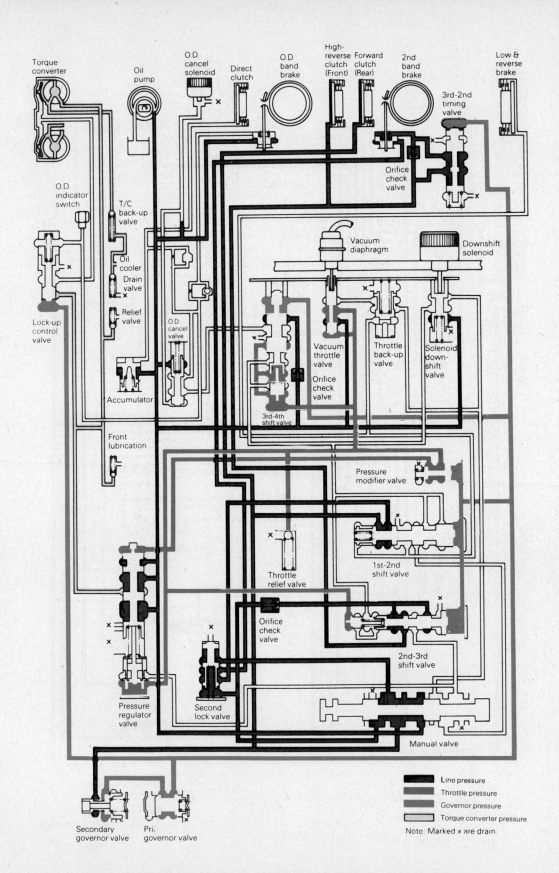

Drive—Fourth Gear (torque converter locked-up) (© Chrysler Corp.)

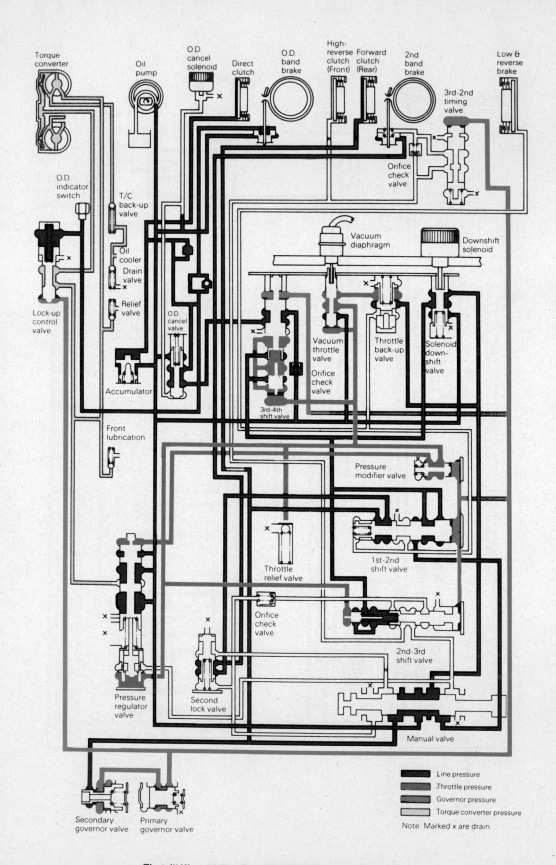

First ("1" or "L")—Second Gear (© Chrysler Corp.)

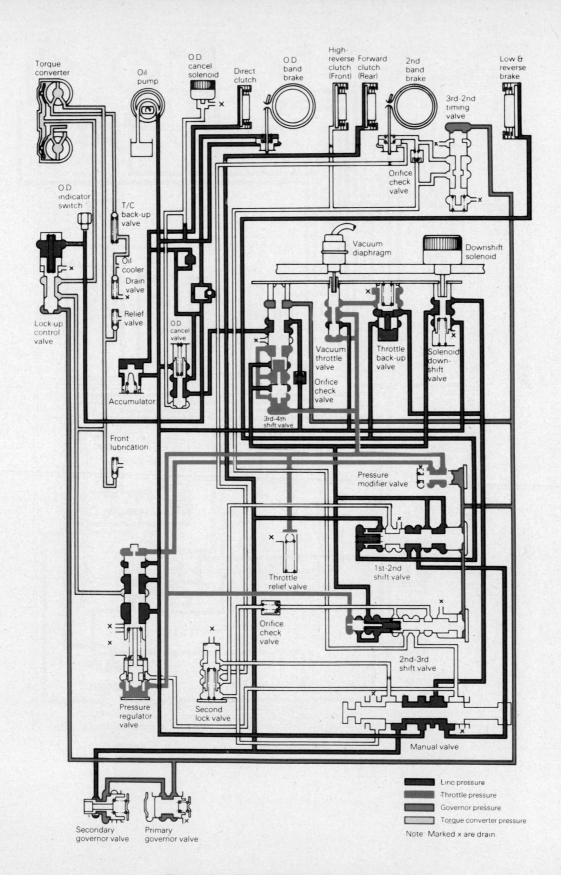

Torque converter

Oil pump

O.D. cancel solenoid

Direct clutch

O.D. band brake

High-reverse clutch (Front)

Forward clutch (Rear)

2nd band brake

Low & reverse brake

3rd-2nd timing valve

Orifice check valve

O.D. indicator switch

T/C back-up valve

Oil cooler

Drain valve

Relief valve

Lock-up control valve

O.D. cancel valve

Accumulator

Front lubrication

Vacuum diaphragm

Downshift solenoid

Vacuum throttle valve

Orifice check valve

Throttle back-up valve

Solenoid down-shift valve

3rd-4th shift valve

Pressure modifier valve

Throttle relief valve

Orifice check valve

1st-2nd shift valve

2nd-3rd shift valve

Pressure regulator valve

Second lock valve

Manual valve

Secondary governor valve

Primary governor valve

Line pressure
Throttle pressure
Governor pressure
Torque converter pressure

Note: Marked x are drain

First ("1" or "L")—First Gear (© Chrysler Corp.)

981

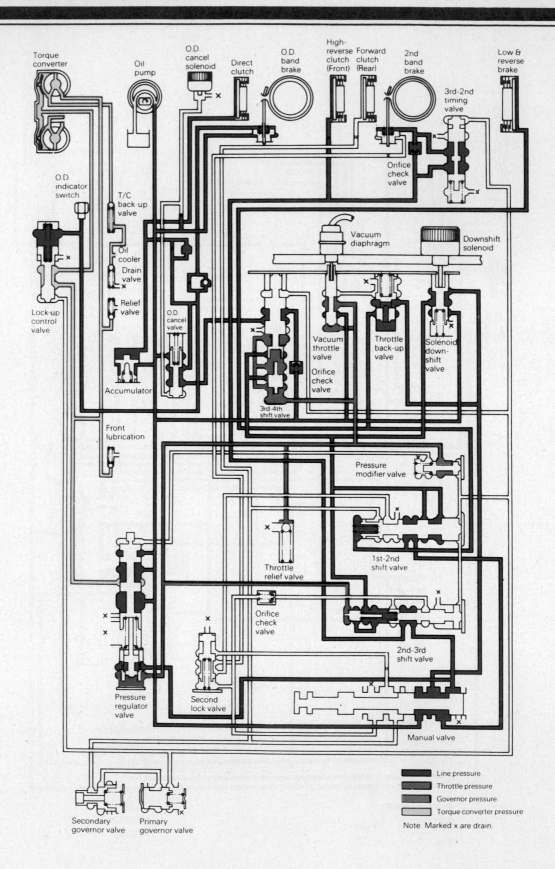

Torque converter

Oil pump

O.D. cancel solenoid

Direct clutch

O.D. band brake

High-reverse clutch (Front)

Forward clutch (Rear)

2nd band brake

Low & reverse brake

3rd-2nd timing valve

Orifice check valve

O.D. indicator switch

T/C back-up valve

Oil cooler

Drain valve

Relief valve

Lock-up control valve

O.D. cancel valve

Accumulator

Front lubrication

Vacuum diaphragm

Downshift solenoid

Vacuum throttle valve

Orifice check valve

Throttle back-up valve

Solenoid down-shift valve

3rd-4th shift valve

Pressure modifier valve

1st-2nd shift valve

Throttle relief valve

Orifice check valve

2nd-3rd shift valve

Pressure regulator valve

Second lock valve

Manual valve

Secondary governor valve

Primary governor valve

Line pressure
Throttle pressure
Governor pressure
Torque converter pressure

Note: Marked x are drain

Reverse (© Chrysler Corp.)

ON CAR SERVICES

Adjustments

Varied adjustments can be made and certain internal components can be removed and/or replaced with the transmission assembly remaining in the vehicle. A list of the serviceable components are as follows:

Manual linkage
Inhibitor (safety start) switch
Vacuum diaphragm and/or rod
Downshift solenoid
Kick down switch
Vacuum diaphragm (modulator) adjustment—LD28 Diesel Engine models
O.D. cancel switch and O.D. indicator light
Band Adjustment—
    Internal
    O.D. band
Control valve assembly
Extension oil seal
Parking linkage components
Governor valve assembly

MANUAL LINKAGE

Adjustment

1. Move the shift linkage through all detents with the selector lever. If the detents cannot be felt or the pointer indicating the gear range is improperly aligned, the linkage needs to be adjustment.
2. Place the gear selector lever in the Range "1" or "D" position.
3. Loosen the locknuts at the bottom of the gear selector lever to rod trunnion. Move the rod through the trunnion until the "D" or Range "1" is properly aligned and the transmission is in the "D" or Range "1" position.
4. Tighten the lock nuts to hold the trunnion in place.
5. Recheck the "P" and range "1" positions. Be sure the full detent can be felt when in the "P" position.
6. If the adjustment cannot be properly made, inspect the levers and rod for damage or worn grommets. Repair as necessary.

INHIBITOR (SAFETY START) SWITCH

Adjustment

1. The two major functions of the inhibitor switch are to illuminate the back-up lights when the selector lever is in the "R" position and to allow the engine to start when the transmission is in the "P" or "N" detents.
2. With the manual linkage properly adjusted, place the transmission manual lever in the "N" position, vertical position and third detent from the rear of the transmission.
3. Remove the screw from the alignment pin hole at the bottom of the switch. Loosen the two switch retaining screws.
4. Insert a 0.079 inch diameter alignment pin in the alignment pin hole, and inward through the hole in the inner switch rotor.
5. Tighten the switch attaching bolts 3.6-5.1 ft. lbs. and remove the alignment pin.
6. The switch can be tested, using a continuity tester or by checking the starting of the engine in the "P" and "N" positions only.

VACUUM DIAPHRAGM

Adjustment

The vacuum diaphragms used in production are non-adjustable.

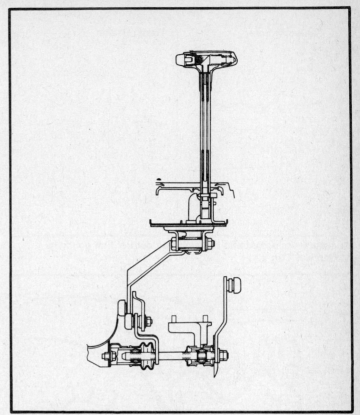

Shift linkage arrangement—JM600 models (© Chrysler Corp.)

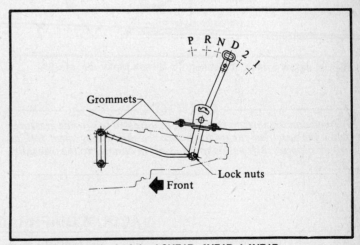

Shift linkage—typical of the L3N71B, 4N71B, L4N71B transmissions (© Nissan Motor Co. of USA)

However, adjustable diaphragms are sometimes available through the aftermarket supply. Should the transmission be equipped with the adjustable type, the following method of adjustment can be accomplished.

1. Remove the vacuum supply hose from the diaphragm's vacuum nipple.
2. Using a small screwdriver, turn the adjusting screw, located in the vacuum nipple, clockwise to increase the throttle pressure and counterclockwise to decrease the throttle pressure. One complete turn of the adjusting screw will change the throttle pressure approximately 2-3 psi.
3. After the adjustments are made, reinstall the vacuum supply hose and make the necessary pressure tests as required.

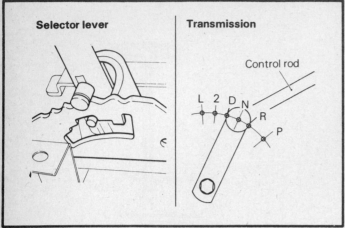

Selector lever detent and transmission control arm positions
(© Chrysler Corp.)

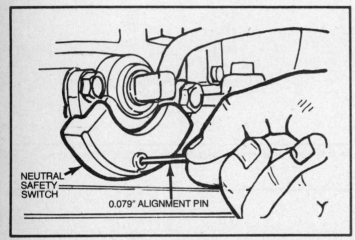

NEUTRAL SAFETY SWITCH

0.079" ALIGNMENT PIN

Neutral safety switch adjustment (© Nissan Motor Co. of USA)

── **CAUTION** ──

The vacuum diaphragm should not be adjusted to provide pressures below the specified ranges to change the shift engagement feel, as soft or slipping shift points could result in damage to the transmission.

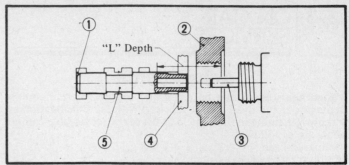

"L" Depth

Measurement for correct vacuum modulator rod
(© Nissan Motor Co. of USA)

VACUUM DIAPHRAGM ROD

Adjustment

The manufacturer's recommended adjustment of the vacuum diaphragm is the select the correct rod length between the diaphragm and the throttle valve in the valve body assembly. When the correct rod length is selected, the shift pattern of the transmission should be within specifications.

1. Disconnect the vacuum supply hose from the diaphragm and remove the diaphragm from the transmission case.
2. Using a depth gauge, measure the distance between the rod seat in the throttle valve when fully seated in the valve body, and the surface of the indented diaphragm seat on the transmission case. This distance is considered "L" depth.
3. From the accompanying chart, select the proper length diaphragm rod and install.
4. Install the diaphragm and seat properly with its sealing ring. Install the vacuum hose to the diaphragm nipple.
5. Road test for proper operation or perform the pressure test as previously outlined.

VACUUM MODULATOR

Adjustment

LD28 DIESEL ENGINE MODELS

1. Install a vacuum gauge between the vacuum pump and the vacuum modulator.
2. Start the engine and operate at 600-750 rpm.
3. Be sure the vacuum pump is operating properly. With the vacuum modulator not operating, the vacuum should read 22.44-24.80 in. Hg.
4. With the engine at 600-750 rpm, adjust the vacuum modula-

VACUUM DIAPHRAGM ROD SELECTION

Measured depth "L" mm (in)	Rod length mm (in)	Part number Nissan	Chrysler
Under 25.55 (1.0059)	29.0 (1.142)	31932-X0103	MD610614
25.65-26.05 (1.0098-1.0256)	29.5 (1.161)	31932-X0104	MD610615
26.15-26.55 (1.0295-1.0453)	30.0 (1.181)	31932-X0100	MD610616
26.65-27.05 (1.0492-1.0650)	30.5 (1.201)	31932-X0102	MD610617
Over 27.15 (1.0689)	31.0 (1.220)	31932-X0101	MD610618

tor to attain a vacuum of 23.62 ± 1.18 in. Hg. Vacuum at full throttle state should be 7.09 ± 1.18 in. Hg at 5000 rpm.

5. Adjustments would be made at the throttle lever adjusting rod to modulator assembly.

CAUTION

Do not attempt to adjust the modulator assembly with the engine at no load and operating at 5000 rpm. This adjustment should only be done on the road, through a trial and error method or on a chassis dynamometer.

KICKDOWN SWITCH

Adjustment

1. Fully depress the accelerator pedal. A click should be heard just before the pedal bottoms out.
2. If the switch requires adjustment, loosen the locknut and extend the switch until the pedal lever makes contact with the switch and the switch clicks.

CAUTION

Do not allow the switch to make contact too soon. This would cause the transmission to downshift on part throttle.

NOTE: If the switch is internally shorted, continuity is present through the switch in any position. Check with a continuity tester.

Band Adjustment
SECOND BAND SERVO

Adjustment

1. Remove the fluid and the oil pan from the transmission.
2. Loosen the locknut.
3. Torque the band servo piston stem 9-11 ft. lbs.
4. Back off the band adjusting servo piston stem two complete turns.

CAUTION

Do not back off the adjusting stem excessively as the anchor block could fall out of place.

5. While holding the adjusting stem, tighten the locknut to 11-29 ft. lbs. torque.
6. Using a new gasket, install the oil pan and fill the transmission with Dexron® fluid.

OVERDRIVE BAND

Adjustment

1. Remove the O.D. servo cover and gasket.

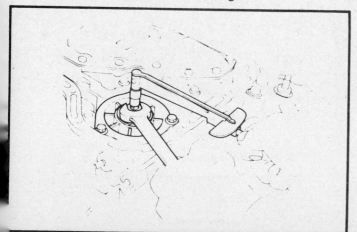

Adjustment of 2nd band (© Chrysler Corp.)

2. Loosen the servo piston stem locknut.
3. Tighten the servo piston stem 5.1-7.2 ft. lbs. Back off the stem two complete turns.
4. While holding the servo piston stem, tighten the locknut 11-29 ft. lbs.
5. Install the servo cover and gasket. Check the fluid level of the transmission and correct.

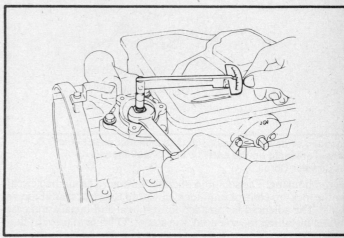

Adjustment of O.D. band (© Chrysler Corp.)

Service
DOWNSHIFT SOLENOID

Removal and Installation

1. Disconnect the solenoid wiring harness.
2. Place a pan underneath the downshift solenoid and remove it and its "O" ring seal. Fluid will drain into the pan.
3. Install a new solenoid with a lubricated "O" ring into its bore in the case. Tighten securely.
4. Connect the downshift solenoid wiring harness and refill the transmission with Dexron® II fluid.

O.D. CANCEL SWITCH AND
O.D. INDICATOR LIGHT

Removal and Installation
E4N71B, JM600 and L4N71B TRANSMISSIONS

The cancel switch and the indicator light are located on the center console box and can be replaced, if necessary, by the removal of the switch.

O.D. CANCEL SOLENOID

Removal and Installation
E4N71B, JM600 and L4N71B TRANSMISSIONS

The O.D. Cancel switch is located on the left side of the overdrive unit of the transmission assembly. Confirm that a clicking noise is heard when power is applied. The switch is replaced by unscrewing the switch from the case and installing a new switch and "O" ring in its place. Correct the transmission level.

NOTE: Have a drain pan placed under the cancel switch area, before removal, to catch the fluid that will drain from the switch bore.

LOCK-UP CONTROL SOLENOID

Removal and Installation
E4N71B TRANSMISSION

The lock-up control solenoid is located on the left side of the con-

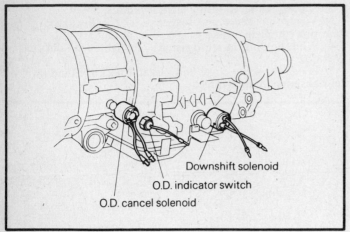

Downshift solenoid

O.D. indicator switch

O.D. cancel solenoid

Location of downshift solenoid, O.D. indicator switch and O.D. cancel solenoid on the L4N71B and JM600 models (© Chrysler Corp.)

verter housing. The solenoid operates through a grounding circuit in the lock-up control unit, located within the right rear of the vehicle. The solenoid is threaded for removal and installation ease. When installing the solenoid, use a new "O" ring to prevent fluid leakage.

LOW TEMPERATURE SENSOR

Removal and Installation
E4N71B TRANSMISSION

A sensor is mounted within the transmission and its function is to prevent converter lock-up if the transmission fluid temperature is below 68°F. (20°C.) by being inter-connected to the Lock-up Con-

trol Unit. A supplied voltage from the Lock-up Control Unit of 5 volts is required to activate this portion of the Low Temperature Sensor/Lock-up Control Unit operation when the fluid temperature is above the minimum requirements for converter clutch lock-up.

Troubleshooting and Diagnosis
E4N71B TRANSMISSIONS

CONTROL VALVE ASSEMBLY

Removal

1. Drain the fluid and remove the oil pan from the transmission.
2. Remove the kickdown solenoid, the vacuum diaphragm and rod.
3. Remove the retaining bolts from the control valve assembly. Three different lengths are used.
4. Carefully lower the valve body from the transmission. Remove the manual valve from the control valve assembly to avoid having it drop from the assembly.

Installation

1. Install the manual valve into the control valve assembly and position to the bottom of the transmission case.
2. With the manual control valve in the neutral position and the selector lever in the neutral position, align the groove in the valve with the control lug on the linkage.
3. Install the retaining bolts, placing the three different length bolts in their proper locations.
4. Torque the bolts 4.0-5.4 ft. lbs.
5. Operate the controls to be certain the manual valve can be moved in each detent.

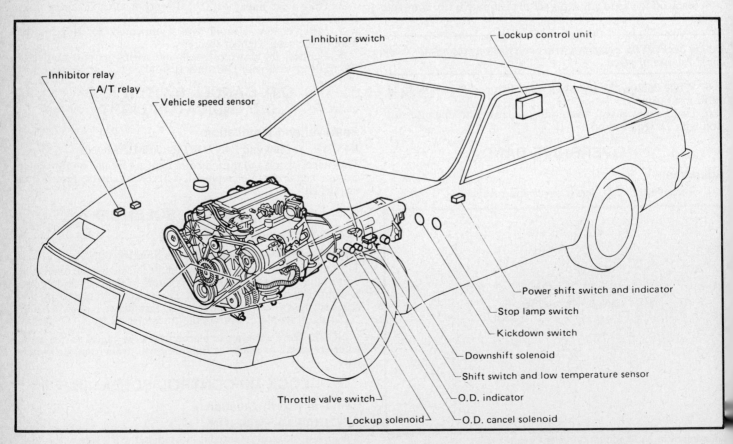

Inhibitor switch

Lockup control unit

Inhibitor relay

A/T relay

Vehicle speed sensor

Power shift switch and indicator

Stop lamp switch

Kickdown switch

Downshift solenoid

Shift switch and low temperature sensor

O.D. indicator

Throttle valve switch

O.D. cancel solenoid

Lockup solenoid

LOCK-UP CONTROL UNIT
E4N71B Transmissions
Check Voltage between No. 22 terminal (Ground) and each terminal

Terminal No.	Input/Output Signal Source	Test Procedure	Desired Results
1	Downshift solenoid	Measure when depressing and releasing accelerator pedal.	0V if turned on 12V if turned off
2	Lock-up solenoid	Measure while driving vehicle in "D" range.	0V if turned on 12V if turned off
3	Throttle sensor (power source)	Connect tester to terminals 3 and 5.	5V at all times
4	Throttle sensor	Measure while operating accelerator pedal.	Full-close throttle: 0.4V Full-open throttle: 4V
5	Throttle sensor (ground)	—	—
6	O.D. cancel solenoid	Measure while operating O.D. cancel switch.	0V if turned on 12V if turned off
7	Power shift indicator lamp	Measure while depressing accelerator pedal in "D" range with driving.	0V if turned on 12V if turned off
8	Idle contact switch	Measure while operating accelerator pedal.	Full-close throttle: 12V Part-open throttle: 0V
9	Full throttle contact switch		Throttle opening Over ½: 12V Below ¼: 0V
10	Inhibitor "2" range switch	Measure with control lever set to "2" range or other ranges.	12V if set to "2" range 0V if set to other ranges
11	Vehicle speed sensor	Check voltage variation while running vehicle over 1 m (3 ft) at very low speed	Voltage must vary from 0V to more than 5V
12	1-2 shift switch	Jack up rear wheels, set lever to D range, and measure while accelerating with a slightly open throttle.	D1 range: 0V D2, D3, and D4 ranges: 5V
13	A.S.C.D. cruise signal	Measure by repeatedly releasing vehicle speed setting during A.S.C.D. driving.	12V if A.S.C.D. is set 0V if A.S.C.D. is released
14	Brake switch	Measure while operating brake pedal	Braking condition: 12V Non-braking condition: 0V
15	A.S.C.D. O.D. cut signal	Measure by turning on and off accelerator switch during A.S.C.D. driving at D4 speed.	0V if accelerator switch is on 5V if accelerator switch is off
	3-4 shift switch	Jack up rear wheels, set lever to D range, and measure while accelerating with a slightly open throttle.	D1, D2, and D3 ranges: 0V D4 range: 5V
16	2-3 shift switch		D1 and D2 ranges: 0V D3 and D4 ranges: 5V
17	Power source	Make ground connection.	12V at all times
18	Power shift switch	Measure while operation power shift switch.	0V if turned on 12V if turned off

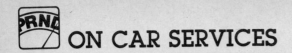
LOCK-UP CONTROL UNIT
E4N71B Transmissions
Check Voltage between No. 22 terminal (Ground) and each terminal

Terminal No.	Input/Output Signal Source	Test Procedure	Desired Results
19	Low-temperature sensor	When checking in installed state, refer to the items on the right. Remove sensor from transmission and make continuity test.	Continuity test Zero continuity at 20°C (68°F) or higher Continuity at 10°C (50°F) or lower (Reference) 5V if oil temp. is over 20°C (68°F) 0V if oil temp. is below 10°C (50°F)
20	—	—	—
21	Kickdown switch	Measure while operating accelerator pedal.	Full-open accelerator: 0V Less than full open: 5V
22	Ground	—	—

A.S.C.D.: Automatic Speed Control Device
O.D.: Overdrive

LOCK-UP CONTROL RUNNING TEST
E4N71B Transmissions

Order of Inspection	Test Items	Test Procedure

1	Lock-up signals	• Connect tester to control unit connector terminals, Nos. 2 and 22 and check lock-up signals while running vehicle.
		  Proper indication:
		    0V if lock-up solenoid is on.
		    12V if lock-up solenoid is off.

2	Wires for output signals	Check if connector between control unit and lock-up solenoid is properly connected. Also, check connector for continuity.
3	Lock-up solenoid	• Check if O-ring is installed to tip of solenoid. • Check operation of solenoid by applying 12V voltage.
4	Wires for input signals	Check if connections are properly made between control unit and following sensors. Also, check connectors for conduction. • Throttle sensor (Idle, high-throttle side) • Inhibitor switch (2 range) • Shift switches (1-2, 2-3 and 3-4) • Low-temperature sensor • Kickdown switch • Vehicle speed sensor • O.D. switch
5	Input signals	Check item given on inspection-4

OVERDRIVE CONTROL RUNNING TEST
E4N71B Transmissions

Order of Inspection	Test Item	Test Procedure
1	O.D. solenoid	Turn on key and set O.D. switch to "O.D. release" position to see if O.D. solenoid clicks.
2	Input signals	Inspect following items • Shift switches (1-2, 2-3 and 3-4) • Vehicle speed sensor • Low-temperature sensor • Full throttle contact switch • Kickdown switch

POWER SHIFT INDICATOR DIAGNOSIS
E4N71B Transmissions

Order of Inspection	Test Item	Test Procedure

1	Vehicle speed sensor	1. Connect tester to connector terminals, Nos. 11 and 22, of lock-up control unit.
		2. Check voltage variation by running vehicle over 1 m (3 ft) at very slow speed.
		    Proper indication:
		    Voltage must vary from 0V to over 5V.

2	Throttle sensor	1. Connect tester to connector terminals, Nos. 4 and 22, of lock-up control unit.
		2. Measure voltage while operating accelerator pedal.
		    Proper indication:
		    Accelerator pedal in full-close throttle position: 0V
		    Accelerator pedal in full-open throttle position: 4V

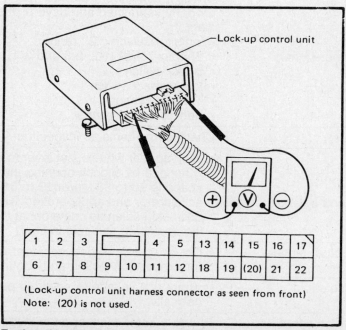

(Lock-up control unit harness connector as seen from front)
Note: (20) is not used.

Testing of lock-up control unit and harness connection terminal location (© Nissan Motor Co. of USA)

AUTOMATIC SPEED CONTROL DEVICE RUNNING TEST
E4N71B Transmissions

Order of Inspection	Test Item	Test Procedure
1	O.D. cancel solenoid signals	Jack up rear wheels, set lever to D range, and accelerate up to D4 speed by slightly opening throttle. Then, when vehicle speed is 30 to 80 km/h (19 to 50 mph), completely close accelerator and apply brakes over 0.7 second. To check if signals to turn on O.D. cancel solenoid come out at this time, check item "O.D. cancel solenoid" in chart.

2	A.S.C.D. cruise signals	1. Connect tester to connector terminals, Nos. 13 and 22, of lock-up control unit.
		2. Measure by repeatedly releasing vehicle speed setting during A.S.C.D. driving.
		Proper indication:
		  A.S.C.D. is set: 12V
		  A.S.C.D. is released: OV

DOWNSHIFT CONTROL RUNNING TEST
E4N71B Transmissions

Order of Inspection	Test Items	Test Procedure
1	O.D. cancel solenoid signals	• Jack up rear wheels, set lever to D range, and accelerate up to D4 speed by slightly opening throttle. Then, when vehicle speed is 30 to 80 km/h (19 to 50 MPH), completely close accelerator and apply brakes over 0.7 second. To check if signals to turn on O.D. cancel solenoid come out at this time, check item "O.D. cancel solenoid" in chart
2	Wires for output signals	• Check connector between control unit and O.D. cancel solenoid for proper connection and continuity.
3	O.D. cancel solenoid	• Apply 12V voltage to solenoid proper to see if it operates normally.
4	Wires for input signals	Check if connectors between control unit and sensors are properly connected and have proper continuity. Refer to circuit diagram • Inhibitor switch ("2" range) • Shift switches (1-2, 2-3 and 3-4) • Brake switch • Idle contact switch • Throttle sensor • Vehicle speed sensor
5	Input signals	Check same items as inspection-4 in chart
6	Downshift and solenoid signals	• Jack up rear wheels, set lever to D range, and accelerate up to D3 speed by slightly opening throttle. Then, when vehicle speed is 30 to 50 km/h (19 to 31 MPH), completely close accelerator and apply brakes. To check if signals to turn on downshift solenoid come out at this time, check items concerning downshift solenoid in chart
7	Wires for output signals	• Check connector between control unit and downshift solenoid for proper connection and continuity.
8	Downshift solenoid	• Apply 12V voltage to solenoid proper to see if it operates normally.
9	3-4 shift switch wires	Check in same manner as in inspection-4, above.
10	3-4 shift switch signals	Check in same manner as in inspection-5, above.

KICKDOWN CONTROL RUNNING TEST
E4N71B Transmissions

Order of Inspection	Test Item	Test Procedure
1	Downshift solenoid signals	Listen for a "click" to be emitted by downshift solenoid when accelerator pedal is fully depressed and ignition switch is "ON".
2	Kickdown switch signals	Connect tester to connector terminals, Nos. 21 and 22, of lock-up control unit. Measure while operating accelerator pedal. Full-open accelerator: 0V Less than full open: 5V
3	Wires for kickdown switch	Check connector between kickdown switch and control unit for proper connection and continuity.
4	Input signal wiring	Check connector between downshift solenoid and control unit for proper connection and continuity.
5	Downshift solenoid	Apply 12V voltage to solenoid proper to see if it functions normally.

SHIFT PATTERN CHANGE CONTROL RUNNING TEST
E4N71B Transmissions

Order of Inspection	Test Item	Test Procedure
1	Power shift indicator lamp signals	• Jack up rear wheels and accelerate in D range. When vehicle speed goes over 13 km/h (8 MPH), turn on power shift switch. • Jack up rear wheels and quickly depress accelerator pedal while in D range. To confirm if signals come out to turn on power shift indicator lamp in the above condition, check power shift indicator lamp
2	Power shift indicator lamp wirings	• Check connector between control unit and power shift indicator lamp for proper connection and continuity.
3	Input wiring	Check connectors between control unit and following sensors for proper connections and continuity. • Power shift switch • Throttle sensor • Vehicle speed sensor
4	Input signals	Check same items as inspection-3.
5	Input wiring	Check connectors between control unit and following sensors for proper connections and continuity. • Inhibitor switch ("2" range) • Shift switches (1-2, 2-3, and 3-4)
6	Input signals	Check same items as inspection-5.
7	Output wiring	Check connector between control unit and downshift solenoid for proper connections and continuity.
8	Downshift solenoid	• Apply 12V voltage to solenoid proper to see if it functions normally.
9	Input wiring	• Check connector between control unit and 3-4 shift switch for proper connections and continuity.
10	Input signals	Check item "3-4 shift switch" in chart.
11	Output wiring	Check connector between control unit and O.D. cancel solenoid for connections and continuity.
12	O.D. cancel solenoid	Apply 12V voltage to solenoid proper to see if it functions normally.

AUTOMATIC SPEED CONTROL DEVICE RUNNING TEST
E4N71B Transmissions

Order of Inspection	Test Item	Test Procedure
3	A.S.C.D. wiring harness	Refer to A.S.C.D. Electrical diagram.
4	A.S.C.D. controller	Refer to A.S.C.D. Electrical diagram.
5	A.S.C.D. O.D. cut signals	1. Connect tester to connector terminals, Nos. 15 and 22, of lock-up control unit. 2. Measure by repeatedly releasing vehicle speed setting during A.S.C.D. driving in D4 speed. Proper indication: Accelerator pedal is depressed: OV Accelerator pedal is released: 5V
6	A.S.C.D wiring harness	Refer to A.S.C.D. Electrical diagram.
7	Output signal wiring	Check connector between control unit and O.D. cancel solenoid for connections and continuity.
8	O.D. cancel solenoid	Apply 12V voltage to solenoid proper to see if it operates normally.

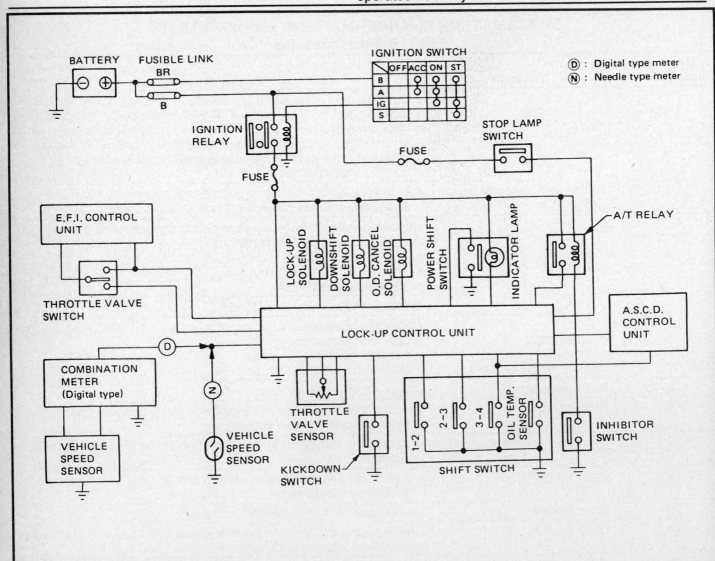

Lock-up control system electrical schematic—E4N71B models (© Nissan Motor Co. of USA)

6. With new "O" rings, install the kickdown solenoid and the vacuum diaphragm with its rod.

7. Using a new gasket, install the oil pan and torque the retaining bolts 3.6-5.1 ft. lbs.

8. Complete any other assembly and refill the transmission with the correct fluid. Correct the level as required.

EXTENSION OIL SEAL

Replacement

1. Remove the propeller shaft assembly.

2. With a seal removing tool, remove the seal from the extension housing.

3. Apply a coat of transmission fluid to the oil seal surface and drive the seal into the bore of the extension housing with a seal driver tool.

4. Coat the yoke of the drive shaft with vaseline and install in place.

5. Correct the fluid level of the transmission.

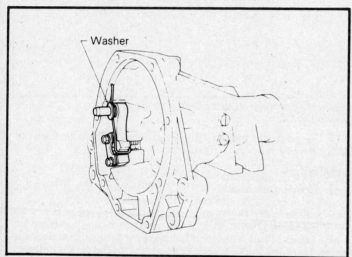

Parking mechanism in the extension housing (© Chrysler Corp.)

PARKING MECHANISM COMPONENTS

Removal

1. Drain the fluid by removing the oil pan assembly.

2. Remove the propeller shaft from the transmission.

3. Remove the speedometer cable and speedometer pinion.

4. Support the transmission with a wood block and a jack-type support. Remove the rear support mounting bolts.

5. Remove the rear extension housing bolts and remove the extension housing with the rear mount attached.

6. Remove the control valve assembly as previously outlined.

7. Inspect and repair the parking mechanism components as required.

Installation

1. After the necessary repairs to the parking mechanism components have been done, install the control valve assembly as previously outlined.

2. Install the rear extension housing with the rear mount attached. Torque the retaining bolts 14-18 ft. lbs.

3. Install the rear mount bolts and torque 43-58 ft. lbs.

4. Install the speedometer pinion and cable.

5. Install the propeller shaft.

6. Using a new gasket, install the oil pan and torque the retaining bolts 3.6-5.1 ft. lbs.

7. Refill the transmission to its correct level with Dexron® II fluid.

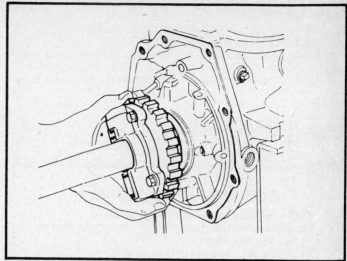

Removing or installing the governor and oil distributor body (© Chrysler Corp.)

GOVERNOR VALVE ASSEMBLY

Removal and Installation

1. Remove the propeller shaft and the rear extension housing as previously outlined.

2. Remove the governor assembly from the output shaft oil distributor.

3. Inspect and repair the governor assembly as required.

4. Install the governor assembly on the output shaft oil distributor body.

5. Torque the retaining bolts 3.6-5.1 ft. lbs.

6. Complete the assembly as outlined previously in the Parking Mechanism Component Removal and Installation section.

7. Correct the transmission fluid level as required.

TRANSMISSION FLUID CHANGE

The L3N71B, L4N71B, 4N71B, JM600 and E4N71B transmissions do not have a specific or periodic fluid change interval for normal maintenance, only the checking of the fluid and correcting the level as required. However, at the time of any major repairs or if the vehicle is used in continuous service or driven under severe conditions, the transmission fluid should be changed every 30,000 miles or 24 months.

NOTE: The time and mileage intervals are average. Each vehicle operated under severe conditions should be treated individually.

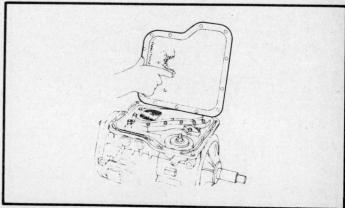

Inspection of debris in oil pan with the transmission out of the vehicle (© Nissan Motor Co. of USA)

Replacing the fluid

1. Drain the fluid by removing the oil pan.
2. Replace the screen as required.
3. Using a new gasket, install the oil pan and torque the retaining bolts, 3.6-5.1 ft. lbs.
4. Using Dexron® II fluid, fill the transmission to its proper level.

REMOVAL FROM VEHICLE

1. Disconnect the negative battery cable.
2. On gasoline engine models, disconnect the torsion shaft from the accelerator linkage.
3. Raise the vehicle and support safely.
4. Remove the propeller shaft from the transmission and plug the opening in the rear extension to prevent fluid leakage.
5. Disconnect the front exhaust pipe.
6. Disconnect the wiring connections at the inhibitor switch, the downshift solenoid, O.D. solenoid, lock-up control solenoid and the O.D. indicator switch.
7. Disconnect the selector range lever from the manual control shaft.
8. Disconnect the speedometer from the rear extension and remove the vacuum hose from the vacuum diaphragm nipple.
9. Disconnect the fluid filler tube and remove the fluid cooler lines from the transmission case. Remove governor tube between converter housing and transmission case.

NOTE: Plug all openings into the transmission to prevent foreign material to enter.

10. Support the engine under the oil pan, using a wooden block and jack type tool. Support the transmission by means of a transmission jack or equivalent.
11. Remove the gussets between the engine and the transmission bell assemblies. Remove the converter housing dust cover.
12. Remove the bolts securing the drive plate to the converter assembly.

NOTE: It is advisable to matchmark the converter and the drive plate to aid in the re-assembly.

13. Remove the rear engine mount securing bolts and the crossmember mounting bolts.

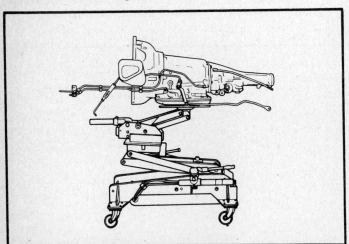

Typical jack assembly for removal or installation of the transmission (© Chrysler Corp.)

14. Remove the starter motor assembly.
15. Remove the bolts securing the transmission to the engine. Have the transmission secured on the jack assembly and slowly lower the assembly from the vehicle.
16. As the converter becomes accessible, retain it in the bell housing to avoid its dropping from the transmission.

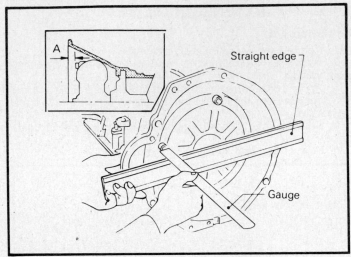

Measuring converter-to-bell housing flange distance
(© Chrysler Corp.)

17. Remove the transmission assembly from under the vehicle for necessary service operations.

Installation

1. Before installation of the transmission, the drive plate should be checked for run-out. The run-out, in one revolution of the crankshaft, should be no more than 0.020 inch.
2. The torque converter can be charged with approximately 2⅛ US quart of fluid and then installed on the transmission, lining up the notch in the torque converter with the notch in the oil pump.
3. The distance from the leading edge of the transmission bell housing and the leading edge of the bolt lugs of the converter should be no less than 1.38 inches, if the converter lugs and the oil pump lugs are correctly assembled.
4. With the converter properly installed, place the transmission on the jack and secure with a safety chain.
5. Raise the transmission into position and install the converter housing to engine attaching bolts. Torque the bolts to 29-36 ft. lbs.

NOTE: The converter and the drive plate matchmarks should be aligned as the converter housing and the engine are joined.

6. Install the starter assembly.
7. Install the rear engine mount securing bolts and the crossmember securing bolts.
8. Install the drive plate to converter bolts. Torque to 29-36 ft. lbs.
9. Install the converter dust cover and the engine to transmission gussets.
10. Remove the transmission jack from under the transmission and the support from under the engine.
11. Install the fluid cooler lines and the fluid filler tube. Install governor tube.
12. Install the speedometer cable to the rear extension housing and install the vacuum hose to the the vacuum diaphragm.
13. Connect the selector range lever to the manual control shaft.
14. Connect the wiring connectors and connections at the inhibitor switch, the downshift solenoid, O.D. solenoid, lock-up control solenoid and the O.D. indicator switch.

15. Connect the front exhaust pipe.

16. Install the propeller shaft and secure.

17. Recheck the assembly on the undercarriage and lower the vehicle.

18. On gasoline engines, connect the torsion shaft to the accelerator linkage.

19. Connect the negative battery cable.

20. Fill the transmission with Dexron® II fluid, start the engine, move the selector lever through all detents and re-check the fluid level. Correct as required.

21. Verify that no leakage is present and all components are operating properly. Re-check the fluid level and correct as necessary. Road test the vehicle.

BENCH OVERHAUL

Before Disassembly

Before removing the subassemblies from the transmission, thoroughly clean the outside of the case to prevent dirt from entering the mechanical parts during the overhaul and repair operation. If steam cleaning is used to remove the outside grime from the case, immediate disassembly of the transmission must be done to avoid internal rusting.

During the disassembly of the transmission and subassemblies, handle all the parts carefully to avoid nicking or burring the bearings or mating surfaces. Lubricate all internal parts of the transmission before assembly with either transmission fluid or petroleum jelly. Always use new gaskets and seals when assembling the transmission. Torque all bolts and nuts to their recommended torque.

Converter Inspection

The welded construction of the torque converter prohibits the disassembly or service unless highly specialized converter equipment is available. If the transmission has been diagnosed as having a defective lock-up unit or defective stator overrunning clutch, through road test and/or stall test procedures, torque converter replacement is mandatory.

It is advisable to replace the torque converter, should the transmission be contaminated with clutch and band debris, unless a commercial torque converter cleaner and flushing unit is available.

Transmission Disassembly

L3N71B TRANSMISSION

1. Remove the torque converter and drain the transmission fluid through the end of the rear extension housing.

2. Place the transmission on a holding tool, if available, with the oil pan upright.

3. If not previously removed, remove the governor tube between the case and converter housing. Remove the converter housing from the front of the transmission.

4. Remove the downshift solenoid, the vacuum diaphragm and rod from the transmission case. Remove "O" rings.

5. Remove the lock plate retaining bolt and remove the speedometer pinion.

6. Remove the oil pan and inspect the residue on the inside of the pan.

NOTE: An analysis of the residue can indicate the types of internal problems that will be encountered.

7. Remove the control valve assembly, noting the position of the different length bolts. Remove the manual valve from the valve body to avoid dropping it during the control valve assembly removal.

8. Loosen the band servo stem locknut and tighten the piston stem to avoid the high-reverse (front) drum from dropping out when the front pump is removed.

9. Note the positioning of the input shaft in the front pump and remove it.

——————— CAUTION ———————
During the assembly, do not install the shaft backwards.

10. Remove the front pump retaining bolts. Install slide hammer type tools in the pump body and carefully pull the pump from the case.

——————— CAUTION ———————
Do not allow the high-reverse (front) pump to drop.

11. Remove the high-reverse (front) thrust washer and bearing race. Back off the band servo piston stem to release the band. Remove the brake band strut, then remove the brake band, high reverse (front) and forward (rear) clutch assemblies as a unit.

NOTE: To avoid stretching the brake band unnecessarily, a clip is available to hold the open ends of the band in one position.

12. Remove the pump thrust bearings and the forward (rear) clutch thrust washers.

13. Remove the forward (rear) clutch hub, front planetary carrier and connecting shell, the rear clutch thrust bearing, front planetary carrier thrust washer and thrust bearing.

14. Loosen the band servo cover bolts approximately one-half their lengths. With the use of an air gun, carefully apply air pressure to loosen the band servo. Remove the band servo cover retaining bolts and remove the band servo piston assembly.

15. Remove the rear planetary carrier retaining snap ring and remove the rear planetary carrier from the case.

16. Remove the output shaft snap ring and remove the rear connecting drum with the internal (annulus) gear.

17. Remove the snap ring from inside the transmission case, holding the low and reverse brake assembly. Tilt the rear of the transmission upward and remove the low and reverse brake assembly.

18. Remove the rear extension from the transmission case.

NOTE: Do not lose the parking pawl, spring and retainer washer.

19. Remove the output shaft with the governor assembly attached. Remove the governor thrust washer and needle bearing.

20. Remove the one-way clutch inner race attaching bolts. Remove the one-way clutch inner race, return thrust washer, low and reverse return spring and the spring thrust ring.

21. With the use of an air gun, apply air pressure to the proper port and remove the low and reverse piston.

22. Should the manual control and parking mechanism need to be removed, the snap rings must be removed from both ends of the parking brake lever in order to remove the lever. Back off the manual shaft locknut and remove the manual plate and parking rod. The inhibitor switch and the manual shaft can be removed by loosening the two securing bolts.

L4N71B, E4N71B AND JM600 TRANSMISSIONS

1. Remove the torque converter and drain the transmission fluid through the end of the rear extension housing.

2. Place the transmission on a holding tool, if available, with the oil pan upright.

3. (L4N71B and JM600) remove the governor tube between the case and the converter housing. (E4N71B) remove the lock-up solenoid. Remove the converter housing from either model.

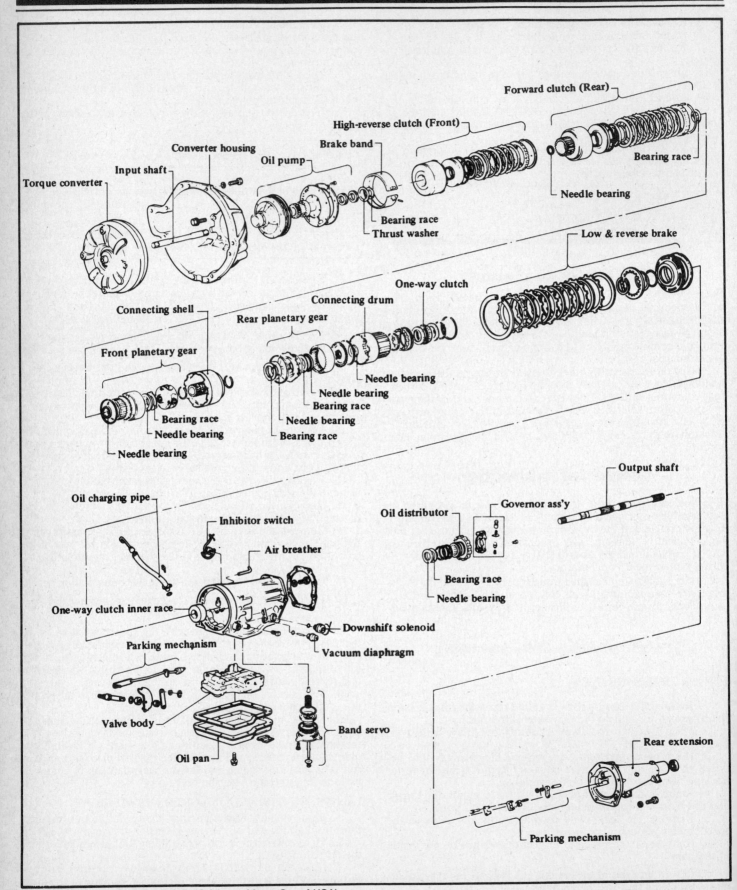

Torque converter

Input shaft

Converter housing

Oil pump

Brake band

High-reverse clutch (Front)

Forward clutch (Rear)

Bearing race

Needle bearing

Bearing race
Thrust washer

Low & reverse brake

Connecting shell

Rear planetary gear

Connecting drum

One-way clutch

Front planetary gear

Needle bearing
Needle bearing
Bearing race
Needle bearing
Bearing race

Bearing race
Needle bearing
Needle bearing

Oil charging pipe

Inhibitor switch

Air breather

Output shaft

Oil distributor

Governor ass'y

Bearing race
Needle bearing

One-way clutch inner race

Downshift solenoid

Parking mechanism

Vacuum diaphragm

Valve body

Band servo

Oil pan

Rear extension

Parking mechanism

Exploded view of L3N71B models (© Nissan Motor Co. of USA)

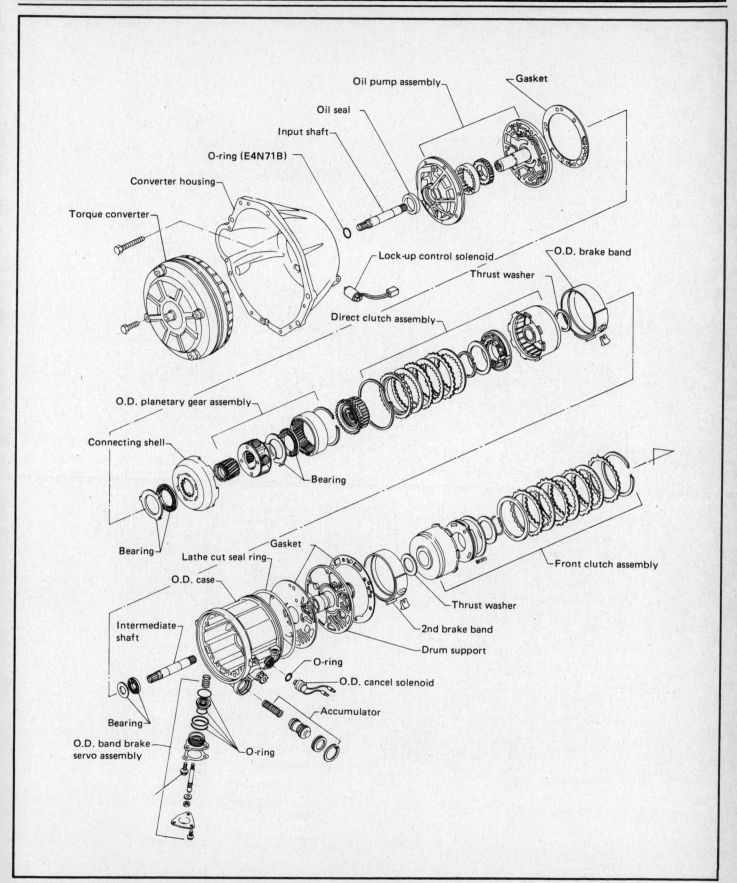

Oil pump assembly

Gasket

Oil seal

Input shaft

O-ring (E4N71B)

Converter housing

Torque converter

Lock-up control solenoid

O.D. brake band

Thrust washer

Direct clutch assembly

O.D. planetary gear assembly

Connecting shell

Bearing

Bearing

Gasket

Lathe cut seal ring

O.D. case

Intermediate shaft

Front clutch assembly

Thrust washer

2nd brake band

Drum support

O-ring

O.D. cancel solenoid

Accumulator

Bearing

O.D. band brake servo assembly

O-ring

Exploded view of L4N71B, E4N71B , JM600 models (© Nissan Motor Co. of USA)

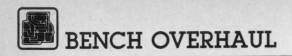

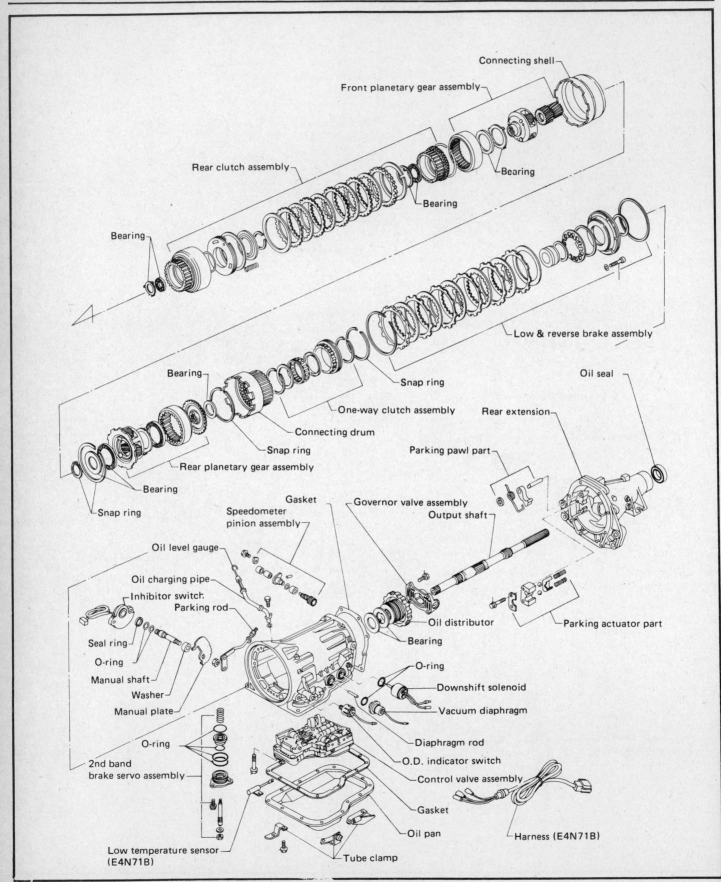

Exploded view of L4N71B, E4N71B, JM600 models (© Nissan Motor Co. of USA)

4. Remove the overdrive component assembly. Remove the high-reverse (front) clutch thrust washer and needle bearing with race. Remove input and intermediate shafts. Put overdrive component assembly aside.

5. Remove the downshift solenoid, vacuum diaphragm with rod and the "O" rings.

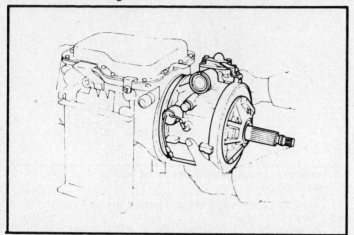

Removing the O.D. case assembly (© Chrysler Corp.)

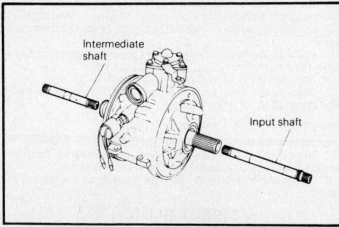

Removing the intermediate and input shafts (© Chrysler Corp.)

6. Remove the speedometer pinion.

7. Remove the oil pan and inspect the residue on the inside of the oil pan.

NOTE: An analysis of the residue can indicate the types of internal problems that will be encountered.

8. Remove the control valve assembly, noting the position of the three different length bolts. Remove the manual valve from the valve body to prevent its dropping during the control valve assembly removal.

9. Loosen the second band locknut and tighten the piston stem up to a maximum of two turns. If the stem can be turned more than two turns, the band is worn out. Back off the stem adjuster to release the band.

10. Remove the band strut. Remove the brake band, High-reverse (front) clutch, forward (rear) clutch and the front planetary gear assembly as a unit.

NOTE: To avoid stretching the band unnecessarily, a clip is available to hold the open ends of the band in one position.

11. Loosen the servo cover retaining bolts approximately one-half their length. Using an air gun, apply air into the servo apply port and raise the servo piston assembly. Remove the retaining bolts from the cover and remove the servo piston assembly from the case.

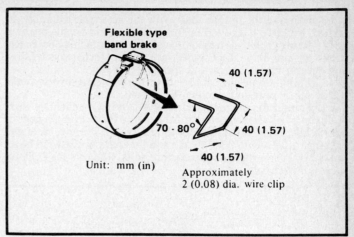

Installation of the wire clip to the band
(© Nissan Motor Co. of USA)

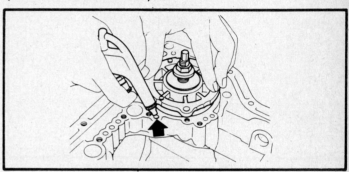

Removing the servo assembly with air pressure
(© Nissan Motor Co. of USA)

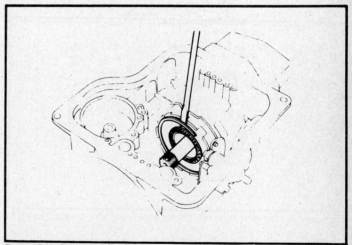

Removing the rear planetary carrier snapring and rear planetary carrier (© Chrysler Corp.)

12. Remove the rear planetary carrier snap ring and rear planetary carrier from the case.

13. Remove the output shaft snap ring and remove the connecting drum with the internal gear.

14. Remove the snap ring and tilt the transmission case upward in the rear and remove the low and reverse brake clutch assembly.

15. Remove the rear extension assembly.

─────────── **CAUTION** ───────────
Do not lose the parking pawl spring and retainer washer from the rear extension.

16. Remove the output shaft with the governor assembly attached. Remove the governor thrust washer and needle bearing.

17. Remove the one-way clutch inner race attaching bolts. Remove the one-way clutch inner race, return thrust washer, low and reverse return spring and spring thrust ring.

18. Using an air gun, apply air to the low and reverse brake piston apply port and remove the piston.

19. Should the manual control and parking mechanism need to be removed, the snap rings must be removed from both ends of the parking brake lever in order to remove the manual plate and parking rod. The inhibitor switch and the manual shaft can be removed by loosening the two securing bolts. Remove the O.D. indicator switch and "O" ring.

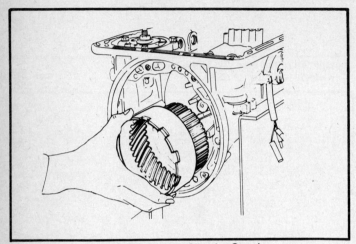

Removing the connecting drum (© Chrysler Corp.)

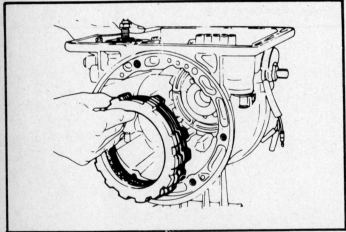

Remove the Low and Reverse brake assembly (© Chrysler Corp.)

Unit Disassembly, Inspection and Assembly

L4N71B, E4N71B, JM600 TRANSMISSIONS

OVERDRIVE COMPONENT UNIT

Disassembly

1. Remove the input and output shafts from the assembly, if not previously removed.

NOTE: Mark and note the position of the shafts before removal for easier installation.

2. Attach slide hammer type tool to the oil pump body and carefully remove the oil pump from the O.D. housing.

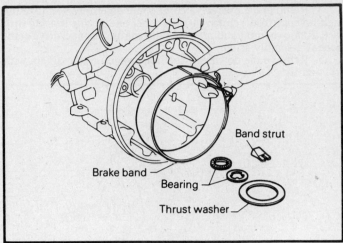

O.D. brake band, strut, bearing and thrust washer
(© Chrysler Corp.)

3. Remove the servo cover and loosen the servo piston stem and lock nut.

4. Remove the O.D. planetary gear set and the direct clutch assembly.

5. Remove the needle bearing with race and the direct clutch thrust washer. Remove the O.D. brake band and band strut.

6. Lightly tap the servo retainer and remove the O.D. servo assembly.

7. Remove the accumulator snap ring, apply pressure to remove the accumulator plug, piston and spring.

8. Remove the O.D. cancel solenoid and its "O" ring.

9. Remove the drum support from the O.D. component body, after removal of its retaining bolts.

Inspection of O.D. Component Units

1. Inspect the input and output shafts for abnormal wear.

2. Inspect the O.D. housing for wear points, cracks, damaged threads, blocked or damaged oil channels in the case.

3. Check one way plug in the O.D. housing and replace if required.

DIRECT CLUTCH

Disassembly

1. Remove the large clutch retaining plate snap ring.

2. Remove the clutch plate assembly from the drum.

3. Using a spring compressor tool, compress the clutch

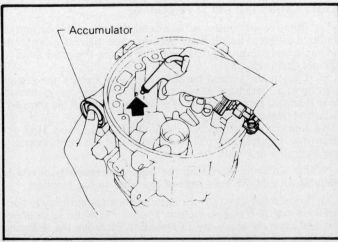

Removing the accumulator with air pressure (© Chrysler Corp.)

springs, remove the snap ring from the spring retainer.

4. Remove the compressing tool, the spring retainer and the springs (10).

5. Install the drum into the drum support and using an air gun, apply air into the apply port of the drum support to loosen the piston. Remove the piston from the drum.

6. Remove the clutch hub seal and the piston seal.

Inspection

1. Inspect the clutch drive plates for wear. If the drive plates are to be used again, standard drive plate thickness must be 0.0591-0.065 inch (1.50-1.65 mm), with a service minimum thickness of 0.055 inch (1.4 mm).

2. Inspect the degree of wear of the snap rings and retaining grooves. Check all springs for being worn or having broken coils. Inspect the driven clutch plates for scores, burrs or being burned.

3. Check the operation of the check ball in the apply piston with air pressure. Air should pass freely in one direction and be blocked in the other.

Assembly

1. With the clutch drum on a flat surface, lubricate the clutch hub and piston sealing surfaces. Install the seals on the clutch hub and on the piston. Use either transmission fluid or petroleum jelly as a lubricant.

— CAUTION —
Do not stretch the seals during their installation.

2. Install the piston into the clutch drum, being careful not to damage or kink the seal during the piston installation. After the piston installation, turn the piston by hand to ensure that no binding exists.

3. Install the springs (10) and the spring retainer into position. Install the spring compressing tool and carefully compress the

springs and retainer. Install the snap ring and be sure it is secured. Remove the compressing tool.

4. Install the two dished plates next to the piston with the first dished plate facing away from the piston, the second dished plate facing the first dished plate with the outer circumferences touching each other.

5. Install a driven steel plate, a drive plate, a steel plate and finish with a driven plate. Install the retaining or pressure plate and retain it with the large snap ring.

NOTE: Three driven and three drive plates are used when equipped with VG30E turbo engine.

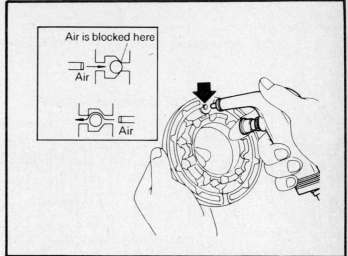

Checking the apply piston check ball with air pressure
(© Chrysler Corp.)

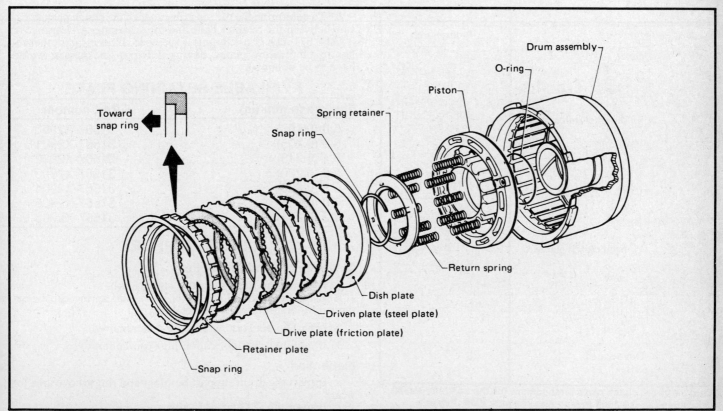

Typical exploded view of direct and front clutch assemblies (© Nissan Motor Co. of USA)

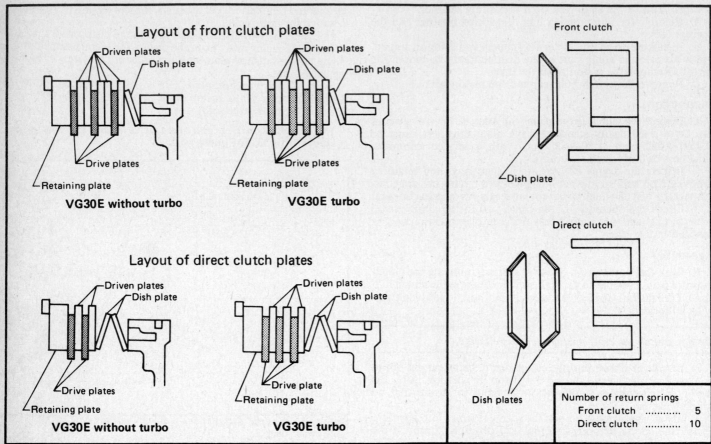

Direct and front clutch plate arrangement for E4N71B models used in the 1984 Nissan 300ZX (© Nissan Motor Co. of USA)

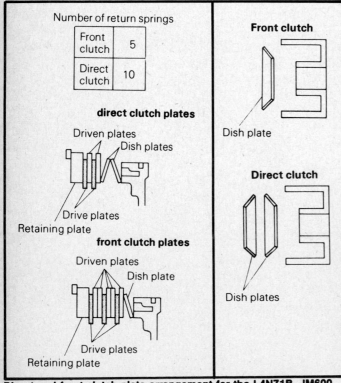

Direct and front clutch plate arrangement for the L4N71B, JM600 models used in the 1984 Nissan Maxima and 1984 Chrysler Conquest (© Nissan Motor Co. of USA)

6. To determine the running clearance of the clutch pack, measure between the retainer plate and the snap ring. A clearance of 0.063-0.071 inch (1.6-1.8 mm) is specified. If necessary, other retaining or pressure plates, having different thicknesses, would have to be obtained.

AVAILABLE RETAINING PLATE

Thickness mm (in)	Part number
5.0 (0.197)	31567-X2900
5.2 (0.205)	31567-X2901
5.4 (0.213)	31567-X2902
5.6 (0.220)	31567-X2903
5.8 (0.228)	31567-X2904
6.0 (0.236)	31567-X2905
6.2 (0.244)	31567-X2906

DRUM SUPPORT

Disassembly and Inspection

1. Remove the rings from the support hub.
2. If required, the O.D. cancel valve and spring can be removed by first removing the retaining pin.

NOTE: The pin staking must first be removed.

3. If required, the lubrication plug can be removed.

Inspection

1. Inspect the drum support bushings and ring groove area for wear.
2. Inspect the O.D. cancel valve and spring.
3. Inspect the internal surfaces for visible wear or damage.

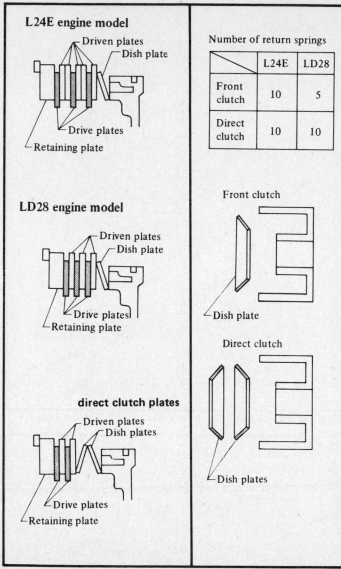

L24E engine model

Driven plates
Dish plate
Drive plates
Retaining plate

Number of return springs		
	L24E	LD28
Front clutch	10	5
Direct clutch	10	10

LD28 engine model

Driven plates
Dish plate
Drive plates
Retaining plate

direct clutch plates

Driven plates
Dish plates
Drive plates
Retaining plate

Front clutch

Dish plate

Direct clutch

Dish plates

Direct and front clutch plate arrangement for the L4N71B model used in 1983 Nissan Maxima (© Nissan Motor Co. of USA)

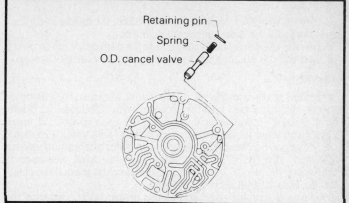

Location of O.D. cancel valve assembly (© Chrysler Corp.)

Retaining pin
Spring
O.D. cancel valve

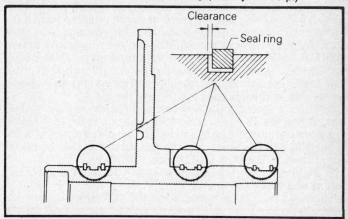

Clearance check between the ring groove and the seal rings (© Chrysler Corp.)

Clearance
Seal ring

4. Measure the clearance between the ring grooves and a new ring. The specified clearance should be 0.0020-0.0079 inch (0.05-0.20 mm). Replace the drum support if the clearance exceeds 0.0079 inch (0.20 mm).

Assembly

1. If removed, install the O.D. cancel valve and spring. Tap in the retaining pin. Secure the pin.
2. If removed, install the fiber lubrication plug.
3. Install the sealing rings on the support hub.

OIL PUMP

Disassembly

L4N71B, E4N71B, JM600 TRANSMISSIONS

1. Remove the front pump gasket and the "O" ring.
2. Remove the pump cover from the pump body.
3. Remove the retaining pin, the lock-up control valve and spring.
4. Remove the drive and driven oil pump gears from the housing. Note the direction and location of the gears. Mark the gears as required.

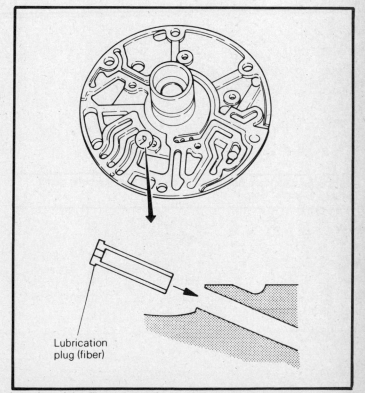

Lubrication plug (fiber)

Location of the fiber lubrication plug in the drum support (© Chrysler Corp.)

Inspection

1. Inspect the gears, lock-up control valve, the spring and all internal surfaces for damage, wear, or burrs.
2. Inspect the pump body and cover for damage, wear or burrs.
3. Inspect the bushing and pump shaft for wear or damage.

Assembly

1. Install gears into the oil pump body. Measure the clearance between the outer gear and the crescent with a feeler gauge blade. The standard clearance is 0.0055-0.0083 inch (0.14-0.21 mm). Replace the gears if the clearance exceeds 0.0098 inch (0.25 mm).
2. Measure the clearance between the outer gear and the pump body with the feeler gauge blade. The standard clearance is 0.0020-0.0079 inch (0.05-0.20 mm). Replace the gears if the clearance exceeds 0.0098 inch (0.25 mm).
3. Using a straight edge across the pump body, measure the clearance between the gears and the pump body cover with a feeler gauge blade. The standard clearance is 0.0008-0.0016 inch (0.02-0.04 mm). Replace the gears, or cover, or pump body if the measurement exceeds 0.0031 inch (0.08 mm) clearance. The standard clearance between the seal ring and the ring groove for the L4N71B, JM600 and the E4N71B transmissions is 0.0020-0.0079 inch (0.05-0.20 mm) with a wear limit of 0.0079 inch (0.20 mm).
4. Install the lock-up control valve and spring into the oil pump cover. Tap in the retaining pin. Secure the pin.
5. Using a special mounting tool and spacer, or their equivalent, mount the oil pump body with the gears in the tool. Install the cover on the pump body and lightly install the retaining bolts.
6. Using a dial indicator, set the run-out of the cover on the oil pump body to less than 0.0028 inch (0.07 mm).
7. Tighten the cover retaining bolts to 4.3-5.8 ft. lbs. (6-8 N•m) torque and check the runout.
8. Install the oil pump gasket and the "O" ring.

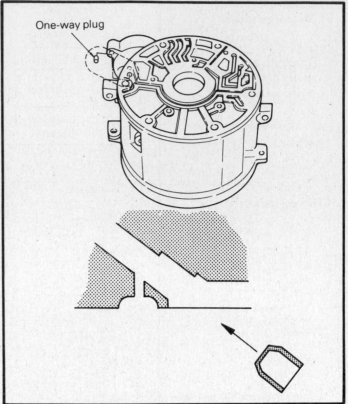

Installing the one way plug in the O.D. case (© Chrysler Corp.)

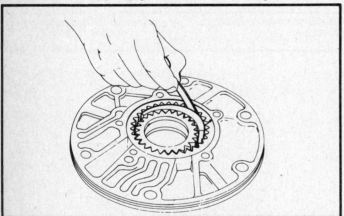

Measuring clearance between the cresent and the outer pump gear (© Chrysler Corp.)

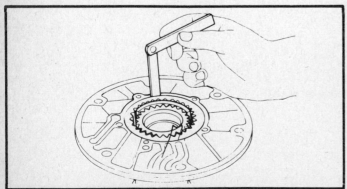

Measuring the clearance between the outer gear and the pump body (© Chrysler Corp.)

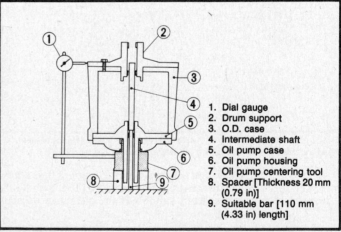

1. Dial gauge
2. Drum support
3. O.D. case
4. Intermediate shaft
5. Oil pump case
6. Oil pump housing
7. Oil pump centering tool
8. Spacer [Thickness 20 mm (0.79 in)]
9. Suitable bar [110 mm (4.33 in) length]

Checking drum support runout (© Nissan Motor Co. of USA)

DRUM SUPPORT HUB TO O.D. CASE

Assembly

1. Install the one way plug in the O.D. case, if it had been removed.
2. Mount the assembled oil pump into the special mounting tool and spacer, or their equivalent.
3. Mount the O.D. case, drum support and gasket in the oil pump assembly and temporarily assemble the drum support.

CAUTION

Be sure the O.D. case is seated in the oil pump body properly.

4. Install a 4.33 inch (110 mm) bar into the oil pump at the shaft location and install the intermediate shaft to set upon the top of the bar.

5. Using a dial indicator, set the run out of the drum support on the O.D. case to less than 0.0020 inch (0.05 mm).

6. Tighten the drum support bolts to 5.1-6.5 ft. lbs. (7-9 N•m).

7. Recheck the drum support run out. Correct as required.

8. Install the "O" ring and gasket.

9. Remove the assembly from the special tool and spacer.

10. Set the O.D. unit aside until the transmission is to be re-assembled.

OIL PUMP

Disassembly

L3N71B TRANSMISSIONS

1. Remove the "O" ring and the pump gasket.

2. Remove the pump body cover.

3. Remove the speed cut valve and the lock-up control valve from the pump body.

4. Remove the drive and driven gears from the pump body. Note the location and direction of the gears. Mark the gears as required.

Inspection

1. Inspect the gears, speed cut control valve and the lock-up control valve, the springs and all internal surfaces for damage, wear or burrs.

2. Inspect the pump body and cover for damage, wear or burrs.

3. Inspect the bushing and pump shaft for wear or damage.

Assembly

1. Install the drive and driven gears into the oil pump body. Measure the clearance between the outer gear and the crescent with a feeler gauge blade. The standard clearance is 0.0055-0.0083 inch (0.14-0.21 mm). Replace the gears if the clearance exceeds 0.0098 inch (0.25 mm).

2. Measure the clearance between the outer gear and the pump body with a feeler gauge blade. The standard clearance is 0.0020-0.0079 inch (0.05-0.20 mm). Replace the gears if the clearance exceeds 0.0098 inch (0.25 mm).

3. Using a straight edge across the pump body, measure the

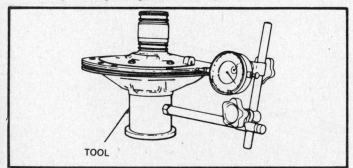

Checking oil pump body runout—L3N71B models

clearance between the gears and the pump body cover with a feeler gauge blade. The standard clearance is 0.0008-0.0016 inch (0.02-0.04 mm). Replace the gears, or cover or pump body if the measurements exceeds 0.0031 inch (0.08 mm) clearance.

4. Measure the clearance between the seal ring and the ring groove with a feeler gauge blade. The standard clearance for the L3N71B transmission is 0.0016-0.0063 inch (0.04-0.16 mm). Replace the oil pump body if the measurements exceed 0.0063 inch (0.16 mm) with the use of new rings as a measuring guide.

5. Install the speed cut control valve, the lock-up control valve and their springs. Install the retaining pins and secure.

6. Set the pump housing into a special holding tool, or its equivalent. With the use of a dial indicator, set the run out of the pump body cover to less than 0.0028 inch (0.07 mm).

7. Tighten the securing cover to body bolt to 4.3-5.8 ft. lbs. (6-8 N•m) torque. Recheck the cover run out. Re-set as required.

Remaining Disassembly, Inspection and Assembly of Components

The remaining disassembly, inspection and assembly procedures of the L3N71B, E4N71B, JM600 and L4N71B transmission components are basically the same. Differences in assembly procedures will again be encountered during the re-assembly of the transmission components into the case. Each difference will be noted accordingly as the assembly procedure progresses.

HIGH-REVERSE (FRONT) CLUTCH AND FORWARD (REAR) CLUTCH

Disassembly

1. Remove the large snap ring from the clutch housing, retaining the clutch pack.

2. Remove the clutch pack assembly from the clutch housing.

3. Using a compressing tool, compress the clutch springs and remove the snap ring from the spring retainer. Release the compressing tool and remove.

4. Remove the spring retainer and the springs.

5. Mount clutch housing on the front pump assembly and using an air gun, direct air to the piston apply port of the front pump and loosen the piston. Remove the piston from the clutch hub.

6. Remove the clutch housing hub seal and the piston seal.

Inspection

1. Inspect the clutch drive plates for wear. If the drive plates are to be used again, standard drive plate thickness must be 0.0591-0.0650 inch (1.50-1.65 mm), with a service thickness at a minimum of 0.055 inch (1.4 mm).

2. Inspect for the degree of wear of the snap rings and retaining grooves. Check all springs for being worn or having broken coils. Inspect the driven clutch plates for scores, burrs or being burned.

3. Check the operation of the check ball in the apply piston with air pressure. Air should pass freely in one direction and be blocked in the other.

CLUTCH PISTON RETURN SPRINGS

Trans-mission	Type	Quantity
L3N71B	High-Reverse (Front) Clutch	10 coil springs
	Forward (Rear) Clutch	10 coil springs
	Low & Reverse Brake	Bellville type spring
L4N71B, JM600①	Direct Clutch	10 coil springs
	High-Reverse (Front) Clutch W/L24E Engine	10 coil springs
	W/LD28 Engine	5 coil springs
	Forward (Rear) Clutch	8 coil springs
	Low & Reverse Brake	Bellville type spring
E4N71B	Direct Clutch	10 coil springs
	High-Reverse (Front) Clutch	5 coil springs
	Forward (Rear) Clutch	8 coil springs
	Low & Reverse Brake	Bellville type spring

① JM600: No specifications

1005

Assembly

1. With the clutch drum on a flat surface, lubricate the clutch hub and piston sealing surfaces. Install the seals on the clutch hub and piston. Use either transmission fluid or petroleum jelly as a lubricant.

CAUTION

Do not stretch the seals during their installation.

---

2. Install the piston into the clutch housing, being careful not to damage or kink the seals during the piston installation. After the piston is installed, turn it by hand to ensure that no binding exists.

3. Install either the 10 or 5 return springs, depending upon engine model, and postion the spring retainer. Install the spring compressing tool and carefully compress the springs and retainer. Install the snap ring and be sure it is secured. Remove the compressing tool.

4. Install the dished plate with the dish facing outward.

5. Install a steel driven clutch plate, and then a drive friction plate. Repeat this order until the correct number of clutch plates have been installed.

NOTE: Refer to the Specifications for correct number of clutch plates.

CAUTION

The L24E and VG30E engine models use two sets of driven steel clutch plates together in the high-reverse (front) clutch assembly in the following manner; the dished plate, a steel driven clutch plate, a drive friction clutch plate, two steel driven clutch plates, a drive friction clutch plate, two steel driven clutch plates and one drive friction clutch plate, followed by the retaining plate. The VG30E Turbo engine models only use one set of driven steel plates.

---

6. Install the retainer or pressure plate and the snap ring.

7. Measure the clutch pack running clearance with a feeler gauge blade. The clearance between the retainer plate and snap ring should be 0.063-0.079 inch (1.6-2.0 mm) on the high-reverse (front) clutch and 0.031-0.059 inch (0.8-1.5 mm) on the high-reverse (front) clutch and 0.031-0.059 inch (0.8-1.5 mm) on the forward (rear) clutch. If necessary to correct the clearance, different thicknesses of retainer plates are available.

8. To test the high-reverse (front) or forward (rear) clutch, assemble the clutch onto the oil pump assembly. Direct a jet of air into the apply port of the oil pump and listen or feel the clutch action, under air pressure and when released.

Control Valve Body Assembly

It is suggested that a valve and spring holding rack be available to the repairman during the disassembly, cleaning and re-assembly of the control valve body assembly, to maintain its sequence of assembly. Do not interchange valves, springs, sleeves or other internal parts, but return each component back to its original position to maintain the calibration of the control valve body assembly. There is no set sequence of control valve disassembly and assembly, but a general procedure is suggested.

HIGH-REVERSE (FRONT) CLUTCH
L4N71B, E4N71B, JM600 Transmissions

Thickness mm (in)	Part number Nissan	Part number Chrysler
5.0 (0.197)	31567-X2900	MD610366
5.2 (0.205)	31567-X2901	MD610367
5.4 (0.213)	31567-X2902	MD610368
5.6 (0.220)	31567-X2903	MD610369
5.8 (0.228)	31567-X2904	MD610370
6.0 (0.236)	31567-X2905	MD610371
6.0 (0.244)	31567-X2906	MD610372

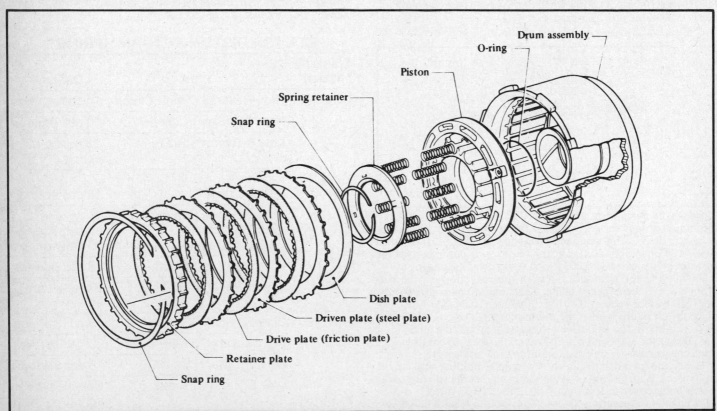

Exploded view of high-reverse (front) clutch assembly—typical (© Nissan Motor Co. of USA)

DIRECT CLUTCH
E4N71B Transmission

Thickness mm (in)	Part number Nissan
5.8 (0.228)	31567-X2904
6.0 (0.236)	31567-X2905
6.2 (0.244)	31567-X2906
6.4 (0.252)	31507-X8600
6.6 (0.260)	31507-X8601
6.8 (0.268)	31537-X2800
7.0 (0.276)	31537-X2801
7.2 (0.283)	31537-X0900 VG30E turbo
7.4 (0.291)	31537-X0901 only

L4N71B, JM600 Transmissions

Thickness mm (in)	Part number Nissan	Part number Chrysler
5.6 (0.220)	31567-X2903	MD610252
5.8 (0.228)	31567-X2904	MD610253
6.0 (0.236)	31567-X2905	MD610254
6.2 (0.244)	31567-X2906	MD610255
6.4 (0.252)	31567-X8600	MD610256
6.6 (0.260)	31567-X8601	MD610257
6.8 (0.268)	31567-X2800	MD610258
7.0 (0.276)	31567-X2801	MD610259

LOCK-UP VALVE BODY

Disassembly
L3N71B

1. Remove the oil strainer and its attaching screws, nuts and bolts.

2. Disassemble the valve body to separate the lower body, separation plate and the upper body.

3. During the separation of the components, do not lose the orifice check valve, servo orifice check valve, throttle relief check ball and the related springs.

4. Remove the side plate (A) retaining the pressure regulator valve, spring, spring seat, sleeve and plug, the second lock valve and spring. Maintain the correct sequence of the components.

5. Remove the side plate (B) retaining the vacuum throttle valve, throttle back-up valve and spring, the kickdown valve and its spring. Maintain the correct sequence of the components.

6. Remove the side plate (C) retaining the pressure modifier valve and spring, 2nd-3rd shift valve, spring and plug, 1st-2nd shift valve and spring. Maintain the correct sequence of the components.

Inspection

1. Because of the close tolerances between the valves and the valve body bores, clearances greater than 0.0012 inch (0.03 mm) between the valves and the bores necessitates the replacement of the valve body assembly.

2. Always use crocus cloth to clean the valves and valve body bores, never sandpaper or emery cloth.

3. Do not remove the sharp edges of the valves during the clean-up.

4. The valves can be cleaned with alcohol or lacquer thinner.

5. The valve body can be dip-cleaned with carburetor cleaner or lacquer thinner.

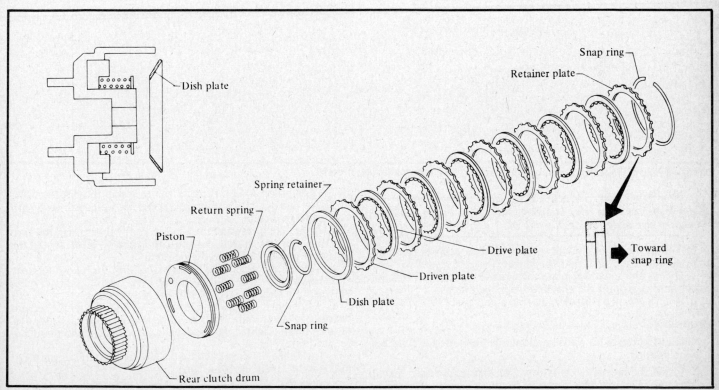

Exploded view of forward (rear) clutch—typical (© Nissan Motor Co. of USA)

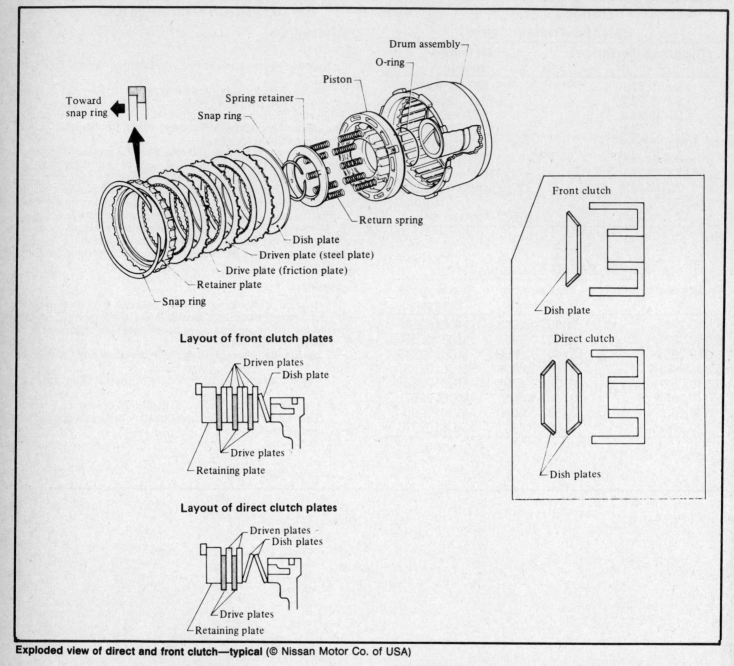

Toward snap ring

Drum assembly
O-ring
Piston
Spring retainer
Snap ring
Return spring
Dish plate
Driven plate (steel plate)
Drive plate (friction plate)
Retainer plate
Snap ring

Front clutch
Dish plate

Direct clutch
Dish plates

Layout of front clutch plates

Driven plates
Dish plate
Drive plates
Retaining plate

Layout of direct clutch plates

Driven plates
Dish plates
Drive plates
Retaining plate

Exploded view of direct and front clutch—typical (© Nissan Motor Co. of USA)

--- CAUTION ---

Do not leave the valve body submerged longer than five minutes. Rinse the valve body thoroughly and blow dry.

6. Check the fit of the valves in the valve body bores. The valves should drop of their own weight.

7. Check the separator plate for wear or damage. Check for scratch marks around the check valve or ball areas.

8. Check the oil passages in the upper and lower valve bodies.

Assembly

NOTE: **Lubricate all parts in automatic transmission fluid before installation.**

1. Install the pressure regulator valve, spring and seat. Install the pressure regulator plug, pressure regulator sleeve and the side plate "A".

2. Install the vacuum throttle valve. Install the throttle back-up valve and spring. Install the spring, the solenoid downshift valve and side plate "B".

3. Install the spring and the 1st-2nd shift valve. Install the 2nd-3rd shift plug, the spring and the 2nd-3rd shift valve. Install the pressure modifier valve and side plate "C".

4. Tighten the side plate screws 1.8-2.5 ft. lbs. (2.5-3.4 Nm).

5. Install the orifice check valve, valve spring, throttle relief valve spring and the steel ball in the valve body.

6. Assemble the upper and lower valve bodies with the separator plate in the middle. Tighten the retaining bolts 1.8-2.5 ft. lbs. (2.5-3.4 Nm). Tighten the nut for the valve body reamer bolt 3.6-5.1 ft. lbs. (5-7 Nm).

7. Install the oil screen assembly. Tighten the retaining bolts or nuts 1.8-2.5 ft. lbs. (2.5-3.4 Nm).

NOTE: **The manual valve is installed in the valve body when the valve body is attached to the transmission case.**

OVERDRIVE/LOCK-UP VALVE BODY

Disassembly

L4N71B, E4N71B, JM600

1. Remove the oil strainer with its retaining bolts, nuts and screws.

2. Remove the retaining nuts and bolts to separate the upper and lower valve bodies. Remove the separator plate, noting the position of the orifice check valve, servo orifice check valve and the throttle relief check ball with spring.

3. Remove side plate "A" retaining screws and carefully remove the cover. Remove the pressure regulator valve, spring and spring seat. Remove the sleeve and plug, the second lock valve with spring. Place in a rack or tray to maintain the correct sequence.

4. Remove the side plate "B" carefully. Remove the 3rd-4th shift valve, the vacuum throttle valve, throttle back-up valve with spring and the kickdown valve with spring. Maintain the correct sequence.

5. Remove side plate "C" carefully. Remove the pressure modifier valve with spring, the 2nd-3rd shift valve, spring and plug, along with the 1st-2nd shift valve with spring. Maintain the sequence of assembly.

NOTE: The manual valve was removed during the removal of the valve body from the transmission case.

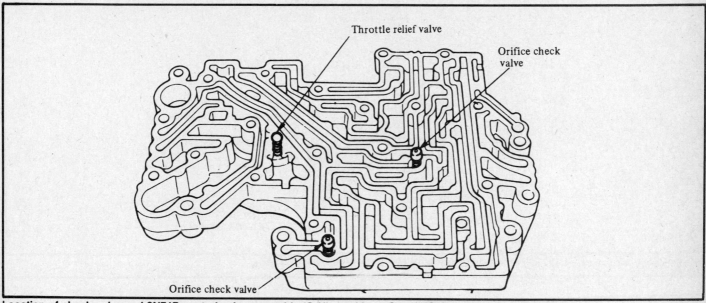

Location of check valves—L3N71B control valve assembly (© Nissan Motor Co. of USA)

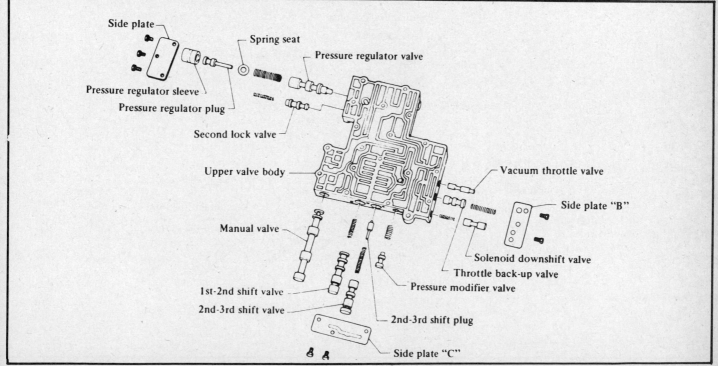

Exploded view of L3N71B control valve assembly (© Nissan Motor Co. of USA)

Inspection

1. Because of the close tolerances between the valves and the valve body bores, clearances greater than 0.0012 inch (0.03 mm) between the valves and the bores necessitates the replacement of the valve body assembly.

2. Always use crocus cloth to clean the valves and valve body bores, never sandpaper or emery cloth.

3. Do not remove the sharp edges of the valves during the clean-up.

4. The valves can be cleaned with alcohol or lacquer thinner.

5. The valve body can be dip-cleaned with carburetor cleaner or lacquer thinner.

— CAUTION —

Do not leave the valve body submerged longer than five minutes. Rinse the valve body thoroughly and blow dry.

6. Check the fit of the valves in the valve body bores. The

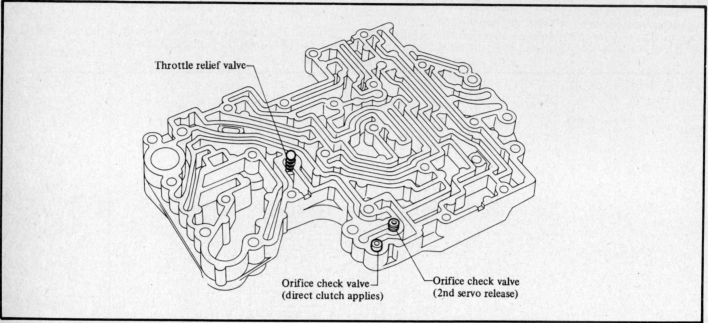

Location of check valves—L4N71B control valve assembly (© Nissan Motor Co. of USA)

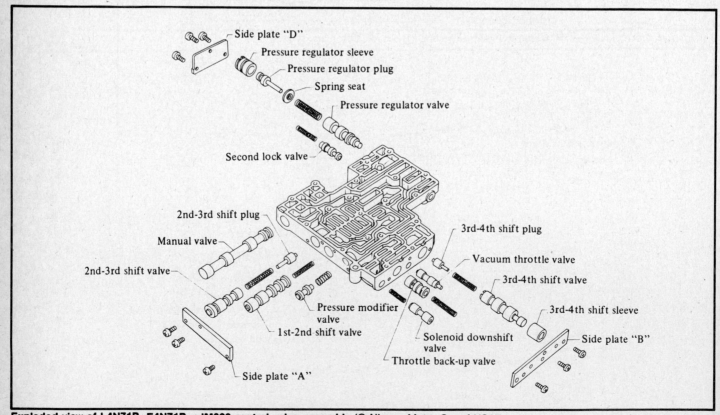

Exploded view of L4N71B, E4N71B JM600 control valve assembly (© Nissan Motor Co. of USA)

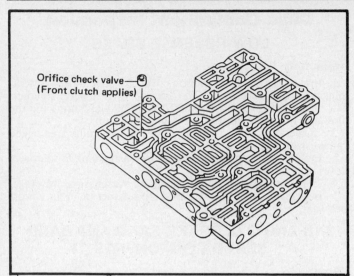

Location of check valves in the upper control valve assembly— E4N71B models (© Nissan Motor Co. of USA)

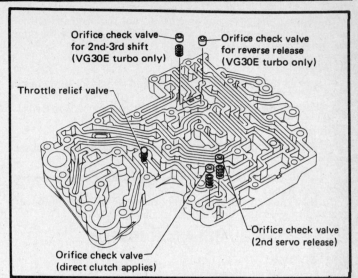

Location of check valves in the lower control valve body— E4N71B models (© Nissan Motor Co. of USA)

valves should drop of their own weight.

7. Check the separator plate for wear or damage. Check for scratch marks around the check valve or ball areas.

8. Check the oil passages in the upper and lower valve bodies.

9. Check the valve springs for weakened load conditions.

Assembly

NOTE: Lubricate all parts in automatic transmission fluid before installation.

1. Install the 2nd-3rd shift plug, the spring and the 2nd-3rd shift valve, the spring and the 1st-2nd shift valve, the spring and the pressure modifier valve. Install the side plate "A" and its retaining screws.

2. Install the spring and the solenoid downshift valve, the throttle back-up valve with its spring. Install the 3rd-4th shift plug, the spring, the 3rd-4th shift valve, the 3rd-4th shift sleeve and install the side plate "B" and its retaining screws.

3. Install the second lock valve and spring. Install the pressure regulator valve with spring, the spring seat, the pressure regulator plug, the pressure regulator sleeve and install the side plate "C" with its retaining screws.

4. Tighten the side plate retaining screws on "A", "B", and "C" plates 1.8-2.5 ft. lbs. (2.5-3.4 N•m).

5. Install the orifice check valve, the 2nd servo check valve and the throttle relief ball with spring, into the valve body channels. Install the separator plate and assemble the valve bodies together. Tighten the retaining bolts, nuts or screws 1.8-2.5 ft. lbs. (2.5-3.4 N•m). Tighten the nut for the reamer-bolt 3.6-5.1 ft. lbs. (5-7 N•m).

6. Install the oil strainer and retain it with its bolts, nuts or screws. Tighten to 1.8-2.5 ft. lbs. (2.5-3.4 N•m).

NOTE: The manual valve is installed in the valve body when the valve body is installed on the transmission case.

GOVERNOR

Disassembly

NOTE: The governor assemblies from the L3N71B and the L4N71B/E4N71B/JM600 transmissions are basically the same in appearances, but differences do exist. Do not attempt to interchange any of the components.

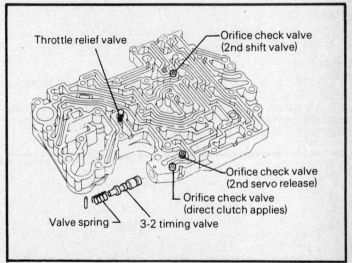

Location of the check valves—JM600 control valve assembly (© Chrysler Corp.)

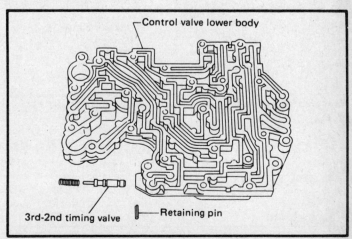

Lower control valve assembly—E4N71B models (© Nissan Motor Co. of USA)

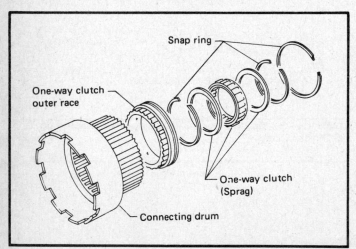

BENCH OVERHAUL

1. Remove the governor assembly from the oil distributor.
2. Carefully, disassemble the governor body, keeping the internal components in their sequence of assembly.

Inspection

1. Inspect the governor body bores and valves for scratches or scores.
2. Inspect the springs for weakness or having broken coils.

Assembly

NOTE: Do not interchange components of the primary and secondary governor valves.

1. Install the proper springs and valves into their respective bores and retain.
2. Install the governor assembly onto the oil distributor and tighten the retaining bolts 3.6-5.1 ft. lbs. (5-7 N•m).

ACCUMULATOR PISTON

Disassembly

L4N71B, E4N71B, JM600

1. Remove the accumulator plug snap ring and apply air pressure to the apply port within the O.D. housing.
2. Remove the accumulator plug, piston with seals, spring and the spacer.

Inspection

1. Inspect the piston and bore for scratches and scores.
2. Inspect the coil spring for weakness or being broken.

Assembly

1. Install new seals on the accumulator piston and lubricate with automatic transmission fluid.
2. Install the spacer, spring, piston with seals and plug into the accumulator bore of the O.D. housing.
3. Install the snap ring to retain the assembly.

Case Component Inspection

LOW-REVERSE BRAKE

Inspection

1. Inspect the steel and friction covered clutch plates for wear, being damaged or burned. The friction (drive) plate standard thickness is between 0.0748-0.0807 inch (1.90-2.05 mm) and the allowable thickness limit is 0.071 inch (1.8 mm).
2. Inspect the snap ring and groove in the clutch area of the transmission case for wear.
3. Inspect the piston and the clutch housing bore for damage, scores or scratches.
4. Inspect the piston return spring for weakness or breakage.
5. Inspect the thrust washer and the retainer plate for abnormal wear.

2ND AND O.D. BRAKE BAND AND BAND SERVO COMPONENTS

Inspection

1. Inspect the brake band friction surface for wear, cracked areas, chipped or burned.
2. Inspect the pistons and the piston bores for wear, scores or scratches.
3. Inspect the servo piston return spring for weakness or breakage.

NOTE: There is no band servo return spring in the O.D. band servo on the LD28 diesel engine models.

PLANETARY GEAR CARRIER ASSEMBLIES

Inspection

1. Inspect the planetary gear set for damage or worn gears.
2. Inspect the clearance between the pinion washer and the

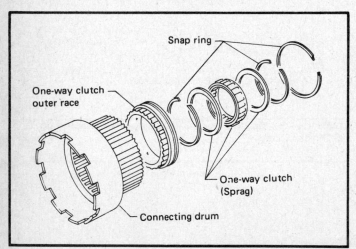

Exploded view of connecting drum (© Nissan Motor Co. of USA)

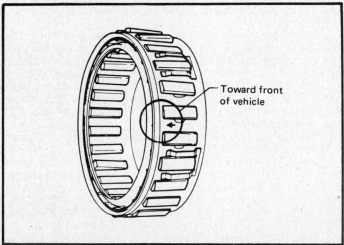

Correct direction of sprag assembly during installation
(© Nissan Motor Co. of USA)

ACCUMULATOR SPRING SPECIFICATIONS
L4N71B, E4N71B Transmissions

Valve spring	Wire dia. mm (in)	Outer coil dia. mm (in)	No. of active coil	Free length mm (in)	Installed	
					Length mm (in)	Load N (kg, lb)
Accumulator spring	1.8 (0.071)	14.85 (0.5846)	7.3	39.7 (1.563)	30.5 (1.201)	58.8 (6.0, 13.2)

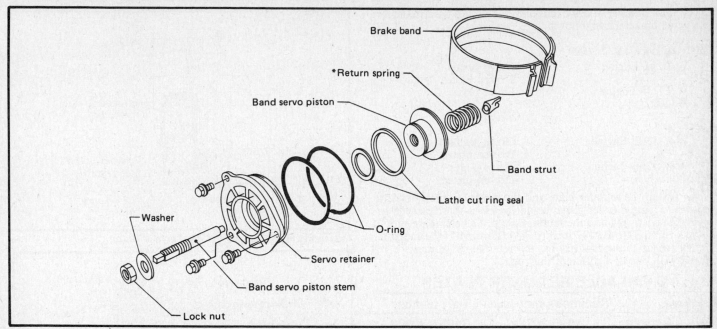

Typical 2nd and O.D. brake band and band servo assembly (© Nissan Motor Co. of USA)

planetary carrier, with a feeler gauge blade. The standard clearance is 0.0079-0.0276 inch (0.20-0.70 mm), with the maximum clearance of 0.0315 inch (0.80 mm).

NOTE: Since the planetary gear carrier assemblies cannot be disassembled to replace worn parts, the entire assembly must be replaced, should damaged or worn parts require replacement.

CONNECTING DRUM ASSEMBLY

Inspection

1. Remove the snap ring and remove the one-way clutch inner and outer races.
2. Inspect the one-way sprag and mating surfaces on the races for damage or wear. Replace the parts as required.
3. During the re-assembly of the one-way clutch, the arrow mark, located between two sprag segments, should be pointing towards the front of the vehicle and the one-way clutch should be free to rotate in a clockwise direction only.

Transmission Assembly

L3N71B, L4N71B, E4N71B, JM600

NOTE: Before assembling the transmission components, verify that all internal parts and case are clean and ready for assembly. Use transmission fluid to lubricate seals and necessary parts before installation. Petroleum jelly (vaseline) should be used to secure thrust washers and bearings for assembly purposes.

1. Lubricate the seals and components of the low & reverse brake piston and carefully install the piston into the case.
2. Install the thrust ring, piston return spring, thrust washer and one-way clutch inner race into the case.
3. Install the hex head bolts into the inner one-way clutch race from the rear of the case. Torque the bolts 9-13 ft. lbs. (13-18 N•m).

CAUTION

Be sure the return spring is centered on the race before the bolts are tightened.

4. Install the low & reverse brake clutches into position within the case, starting with the steel dished plate (no external lugs or internal splines), followed by a steel plate and a friction plate, alternating, until the total plates have been installed.

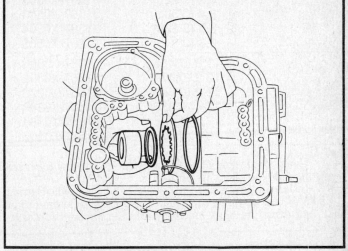

Installation of one-way clutch race components
(© Nissan Motor Co. of USA)

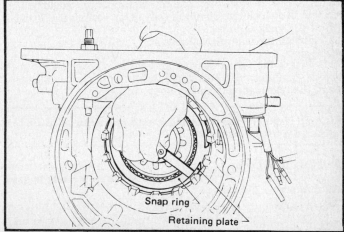

Measuring low and reverse brake clearance
(© Nissan Motor Co. of USA)

The total number of drive and driven clutches used in the low & reverse brake are as follows:

L3N71B, L4N71B, JM600

W/L24E Engine	Drive plates	5
	Driven plates	5
W/LD28 Engine, JM600	Drive plates	6
	Driven plates	6

E4N71B

W/VG30E Engine	Drive plates	6
	Driven plates	6
W/VG30E Turbo	Drive plates	7
	Driven plates	7

5. Install the retainer plate and the retaining snap ring into the case. Using a feeler gauge blade, measure the clearance between the snap ring and the retainer plate. The clearance should be between 0.0315-0.0492 inch (0.80-1.25 mm). If the measurement exceeds the specifications, the retainer plate must be replaced with one of a different thickness.

AVAILABLE RETAINER PLATES

Engines	Thickness mm (in)	Part number
L24E VG30E Turbo	7.8 (0.307)	31667-X0500
	8.0 (0.315)	31667-X0501
	8.2 (0.323)	31667-X0502
	8.4 (0.331)	31667-X0503
	8.6 (0.339)	31667-X0504
	8.8 (0.346)	31667-X0505
LD28 VG30E	11.8 (0.465)	31667-X0300
	12.0 (0.472)	31667-X0301
	12.2 (0.480)	31667-X0302
	12.4 (0.488)	31667-X0303
	12.6 (0.496)	31667-X0304
	12.8 (0.504)	31667-X0305

6. Using an air gun, apply air pressure to the low & reverse brake assembly to check its operation.

7. Install the governor thrust washer and the needle bearing.

8. Slide the governor distributor assembly onto the output shaft and install the shaft assembly into the transmission case.

—— CAUTION ——

Do not damage the governor distributor sealing rings.

9. Install the connecting drum with the sprag into the case, by rotating the drum clockwise. The connecting drum should be free to rotate in a clockwise direction only. This verifies the installation of the sprag is correct.

10. Install the rear internal gear and retain with the snap ring on the shaft.

11. Install the thrust bearing and thrust washer on the rear planetary gear assembly and install the unit into place in the case. Install the rear planetary carrier snap ring.

—— CAUTION ——

This snap ring is thinner than those used in a drum to retain the clutches. Do not interchange.

NOTE: If difficulty is experienced when installing the snap ring, pull the connecting drum forward as far as possible to gain sufficient groove clearance.

12. Assemble the high-reverse (front) clutch and the forward (rear) clutch, the front internal gear, front planetary carrier and the connecting shell. Secure all thrust bearings with petroleum jelly.

1014

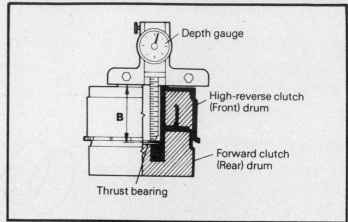

Measuring for dimension "B" (© Chrysler Corp.)

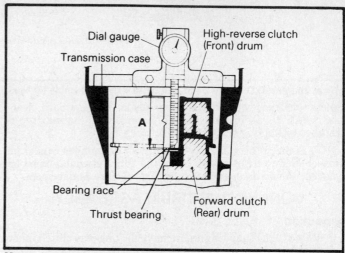

Measuring for dimension "A" (© Chrysler Corp.)

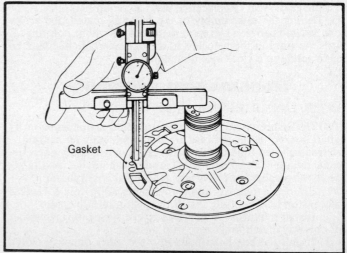

Measuring for dimension "C" (© Chrysler Corp.)

13. Lay the assembled high-reverse (front) clutch and the forward (rear) clutch flat on a level surface, with the high-reverse (front) clutch drum upward. With the rear hub thrust bearing properly seated, measure the distance from the face of the clutch drum to the top of the thrust bearing race, using a dial indicator gauge or a depth caliper with a seven inch post. This measurement is considered dimension "B".

14. Install the clutch drum assembly into the transmission

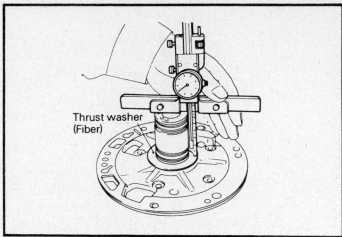

Measuring for dimension "D" (© Chrysler Corp.)

case, being sure all parts are properly seated.

15. Place the transmission in an upright position and measure from the rear hub thrust bearing race to the case oil pump flange. This measurement is considered dimension "A".

NOTE: The measuring procedure sequence to find the "A" and "B" dimensions can be reversed, depending upon the repairmans professional judgement.

16. Place the oil pump assembly flat on a level surface and install the gasket so as to include it in the measurement. Measure from the top of the drum support shaft (front clutch and rear clutch side) to the installed gasket. This measurement is considered dimension "C".

17. Install the fiber thrust washer over the drum support shaft and on to the oil pump body. Measure from the top of the drum support shaft to the top surface of the thrust washer. This dimension is considered dimension "D".

18. The difference between dimension "A" 0.004 inch or 0.1 mm) and dimension "C" minus dimension "D" is the front end play and must be within the specified of between 0.020-0.031 inch (0.5-0.8 mm). The front end-play can be adjusted with the high-reverse (front) clutch thrust washers of different sizes.

AVAILABLE HIGH-REVERSE CLUTCH (FRONT) THRUST WASHER

Thickness mm (in)	Part number
1.3 (0.051)	31528-X0107
1.5 (0.059)	31528-X0106
1.7 (0.067)	31528-X0105
1.9 (0.075)	31528-X0100
2.1 (0.083)	31528-X0101
2.3 (0.091)	31528-X0102
2.5 (0.098)	31528-X0103
2.7 (0.106)	31528-X0104

NOTE: To properly handle the L3N71B transmission oil pump body for measurement of dimension "C" and "D", the stator support must be held stationary and level.

19. To adjust total end play, measure dimension "A" as previously outlined. Measure dimension "C" as previously outlined. The difference between dimension "A" (-0.004 inch or, 0.1 mm) and dimension "C" is considered total end play.

20. The specific value of total end play is 0.0098-0.0197 inch (0.25-0.50 mm).

21. If the difference between dimension "A" and dimension "C" is not within specifications, the proper sized oil pump cover bearing race can be selected from the following chart.

AVAILABLE OIL PUMP COVER BEARING RACE

Thickness mm (in)	Part number
1.2 (0.047)	31556-X0100
1.4 (0.055)	31556-X0101
1.6 (0.063)	31556-X0102
1.8 (0.071)	31556-X0103
2.0 (0.079)	31556-X0104
2.2 (0.087)	31556-X0105

22. (L4N71B, E4N71B, JM600 Models)—Install the brake band, the band strut and the servo assembly. Pre-lubricate the servo seals before installation.

— **CAUTION** —

Do not damage the servo "O" rings during their installation.

23. Install the servo cover and torque the retaining bolts 3.6-5.1 ft. lbs. (5-7 N•m).

24. Finger tighten the servo piston stem enough to prevent the band and strut from dropping out of place.

NOTE: Do not adjust the band as yet.

25. Lubricate the bearing race and thrust washer, place them onto the drum support, if not previously done.

26. (L3N71B models)—Install the gasket on the oil pump and retain it with petroleum jelly. Align the pump to the transmission case and install two retaining bolts temporarily.

27. Adjust the brake band by torquing the piston stem to the specified torque of 9-11 ft. lbs. (12-15 N•m). Back the piston stem off two complete turns and secure the stem with the lock nut. Torque the nut to 11-29 ft. lbs. (15-39 N•m).

NOTE: Perform a final air check of the assembled components to verify tightness of bolts and to check against seal damage during the assembly.

28. (L4N71B, E4N71B, JM600 models)—Coat the drum support gasket with petroleum jelly and install on the drum support. Coat the drum support "O" ring with A/T fluid. Align the drum support with the O.D. case to the transmission case and install.

— **CAUTION** —

Be sure the drum support and O.D. case has been centered properly before installation.

29. Install two converter housing retaining bolts temporarily to hold O.D. case.

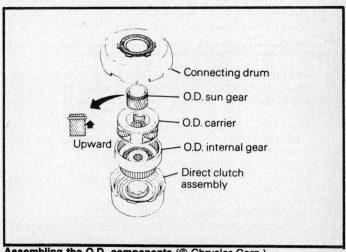

Assembling the O.D. components (© Chrysler Corp.)

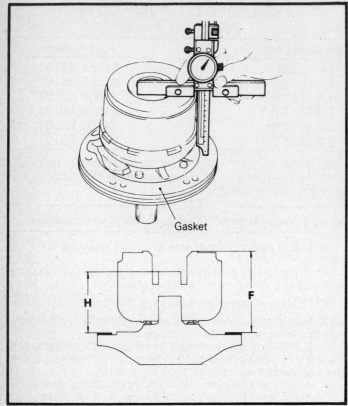

Measuring for dimension "H" and "F" (© Chrysler Corp.)

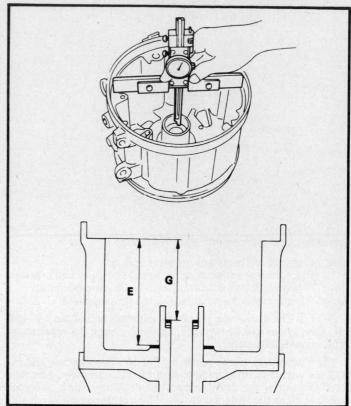

Measuring for dimension "E" and "G" (© Chrysler Corp.)

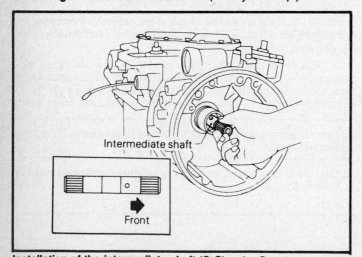

Installation of the intermediate shaft (© Chrysler Corp.)

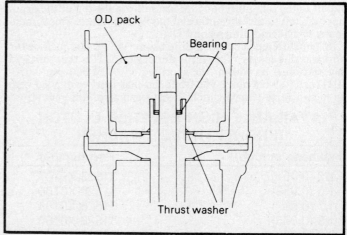

Location of the thrust bearing and washer on the O.D. pack
(© Chrysler Corp.)

30. Install the intermediate shaft, being careful of its proper direction into the transmission. The front end would have the oil hole closest to the splines, with the other end going into the transmission.

31. Adjust the O.D. pack end play as follows;

a. Assemble the direct clutch assembly, O.D. planetary gear set and the connecting drum. Install them on the O.D. pack.

b. Install the oil pump bearing, gasket and the O.D. pack on the oil pump and measure the distance from the top of the gasket on the pump flange to the installed bearing surface on the inside of the hub of the O.D. planetary gear and direct clutch assembly. This measurement is considered "H".

c. Measure the distance from the top of the oil pump gasket to the middle stop on the top of the O.D. planetary gear and direct clutch assembly. This measurement is considered "F".

d. Position the drum support so the front is upward and attach the thrust washer and needle bearing to the drum support and O.D. case.

e. Measure the distance from the outer flange surface of the O.D. case to the top of the O.D. case. This distance is considered "E".

f. Measure the distance from the outer flange surface of the O.D. case to the top of the needle bearing in the drum support. This measurement is considered "G".

g. The difference between the dimension "E" (0.004 inch or 0.1 mm) and "F" is the O.D. pack end play and must be between 0.020–0.031 inch (0.5–0.8 mm).

h. The O.D. pack end play can be adjusted with selective thrust washers, which are identified in the following chart.

AVAILABLE O.D. THRUST WASHER

Thickness mm (in)	Part number
1.5 (0.059)	31528-X0106
1.7 (0.067)	31528-X0105
1.9 (0.075)	31528-X0100
2.1 (0.083)	31528-X0101
2.3 (0.091)	31528-X0102
2.5 (0.098)	31528-X0103
2.7 (0.106)	31528-X0104

NOTE: The O.D. pack selective washers are the same as used in the front clutch assembly.

32. The O.D. total end play dimension is found by determining the difference between "G" (0.004 or 0.1 mm) and the "H" dimensions. The total end play must be between 0.0098-0.0197 inch (0.25-0.50 mm).

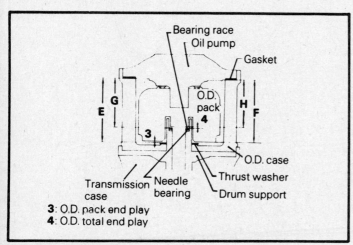

3: O.D. pack end play
4: O.D. total end play

O.D. pack end play (© Chrysler Corp.)

33. Should the resulting measured tolerance not be within specifications, selected bearing races can be determined for use from the following chart.

AVAILABLE O.D. BEARING RACES

Thickness mm (in)	Part number
1.2 (0.047)	31556-X0100
1.4 (0.055)	31556-X0101
1.6 (0.063)	31556-X0102
1.8 (0.071)	31556-X0103
2.0 (0.079)	31556-X0104
2.2 (0.087)	31556-X0105

34. Adjust the front band, making sure the band strut is positioned correctly. Torque the piston stem to 9-11 ft. lbs. (12-15 N•m). Back off the stem two full turns and tighten the stem lock nut to 11-29 ft. lbs. (15-39 N•m).

35. Lubricate the O.D. servo "O" rings with AT fluid and install the brake band, band strut and the O.D. band servo assembly.

36. Lubricate the seal ring of the direct clutch and install the O.D. bearing and race. Install the O.D. thrust washer and the O.D. pack on the drum support. Be sure the brake band strut is correctly installed.

37. Lubricate the "O" ring of the oil pump. Install the needle bearing and race. Position the oil pump and install.

38. Adjust the O.D. brake band, making sure the band strut is properly positioned. Torque the piston stem to 5.1-7.2 ft. lbs. (7-10 N•m). Back off the piston stem two full turns and tighten the lock nut to 11-29 ft. lbs. (15-39 N•m).

39. Using an air gun, test the operation of the O.D. band servo.

40. Install the accumulator spring, piston, plug and the snap ring.

41. Remove the two bolts used to temporarily tighten the O.D. case. Apply sealant to the sealing surfaces of the converter housing at the bolt locations and install the converter housing on the O.D. case. Tighten the converter housing retaining bolts to specifications.

42. Install the input shaft into position.

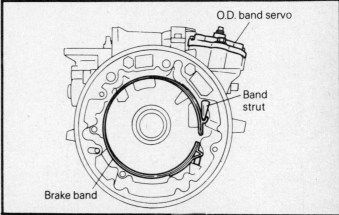

O.D. band and servo assembly (© Chrysler Corp.)

43. Perform an air check of the transmission assembled components before the installation of the valve body. Be sure the parking pawl, pin, spring and washer are correctly assembled.

44. Install the rear extension assembly and torque the retaining bolts to specifications.

45. Align the manual valve with the selector pin and install the valve body. Install the three sized retaining bolts in their proper locations. Torque the valve body retaining bolts to 4.0-5.4 ft. lbs. (5.4-7.4 N•m).

NOTE: Be sure the manual control valve can be moved in all its positions.

46. (L3N71B models) Check the pump to transmission case alignment and install the converter housing. Torque the retaining bolts 33-40 ft. lbs. (44-54 N•m).

47. (All Models) Before installing the vacuum diaphragm, measure the depth of the hole into which it is to be inserted. This measurement determines the correct rod length to be used with the diaphragm unit to ensure proper performance.

VACUUM DIAPHRAGM ROD SELECTION

Measured depth "L" mm (in)	Rod length mm (in)	Part number
Under 25.55 (1.0059)	29.0 (1.142)	31932 X0103
25.65-26.05 (1.0098-1.0256)	29.5 (1.161)	31932 X0104
26.15-26.55 (1.0295-1.0453)	30.0 (1.181)	31932 X0100
26.65-27.05 (1.0492-1.0650)	30.5 (1.201)	31932 X0102
Over 27.15 (1.0689)	31.0 (1.220)	31932 X0101

48. Install the vacuum diaphragm with the correct length rod.

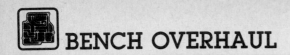

49. Install the downshift solenoid, being sure of its operation.

50. (L4N71B, E4N71B, JM600 models) Install the O.D. solenoid, the O.D. cancel solenoid, the lock-up solenoid, temperature sensing unit and the O.D. indicator switch.

51. (All models) Install the inhibitor switch and check for its proper operation in each gear position.

52. Install the oil pan using a new gasket. Tighten the retaining bolts to 3.6-5.1 ft. lbs. (5-7 N•m).

53. (L4N71B models) Install the governor tube and secure properly to the transmission case.

54. Install the converter, being sure the converter lugs are engaged with the oil pump drive gear.

NOTE: The converter can be filled with fluid before installation.

55. The transmission is ready for installation into the vehicle.

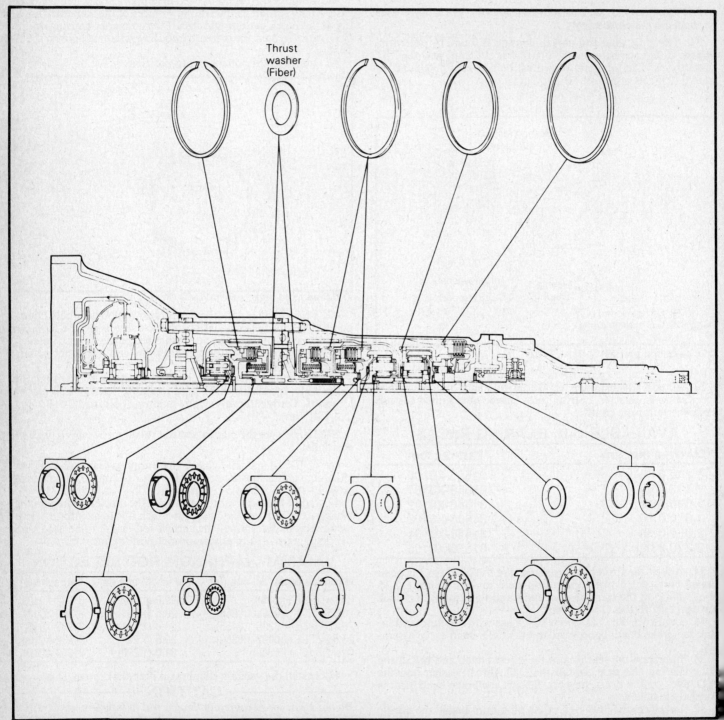

Location of thrust bearings and washers—L4N71B, E4N71B and JM600 models (© Chrysler Corp.)

 **SPECIFICATIONS**

TORQUE SPECIFICATIONS

Component part	N•m	kg-m	ft-lb
Transmission case to converter housing	44-54	4.5-5.5	33-40
Transmission case to rear extension	20-25	2.0-2.5	14-18
Oil pan to transmission case	5-7	0.5-0.7	3.6-5.1
2nd servo piston retainer to transmission case	7-9	0.7-0.9	5.1-6.5
2nd piston stem (when adjusting band brake) ①	12-15	1.2-1.5	9-11
2nd piston stem lock nut	15-39	1.5-4.0	11-29
Control valve body to transmission case	5.4-7.4	0.55-0.75	4.0-5.4
Lower valve body to upper valve body	2.5-3.4	0.25-0.35	1.8-2.5
O.D. servo piston retainer to O.D. case	10-15	1.0-1.5	7-11
O.D. stem (when adjusting band brake)	7-10	0.7-1.0	5.1-7.2
O.D. stem lock nut	15-39	1.5-4.0	11-29
Side plate to control valve body	2.5-3.4	0.25-0.35	1.8-2.5
Nut for control valve reamer bolt	5-7	0.5-0.7	3.6-5.1
Oil strainer to lower valve body	3-4	0.3-0.4	2.2-2.9

Component part	N•m	kg-m	ft-lb
Governor valve body to oil distributor	5-7	0.5-0.7	3.6-5.1
Oil pump housing to oil pump cover	6-8	0.6-0.8	4.3-5.8
Inhibitor switch to transmission case	5-7	0.5-0.7	3.6-5.1
Drive plate to Crankshaft	137-157	14.0-16.0	101-116
Drive plate to torque converter	39-49	4.0-5.0	29-36
Converter housing to engine	39-49	4.0-5.0	29-36
Rear mounting bracket to transmission	31-42	3.2-4.3	23-31
Rear mounting bracket to rear insulator	31-42	3.2-4.3	23-31
Rear mounting member	59-78	6.0-8.0	43-58
Gussets to transmission and engine	25-35	2.6-3.6	19-26
Manual shaft lock nut	29-39	3.0-4.0	22-29
Oil cooler pipe to transmission case	29-49	3.0-5.0	22-36
Drum support to O.D. case	7-9	0.7-0.9	5.1-6.5

① Turn back two turns after tightening.

 **SPECIAL TOOLS**

Tool number (Kent-Moore No.)	Tool name	
ST25420001 (J26063) (ST25420000) (J26063)	Clutch spring compressor	
ST25580001 (J25719)	Oil pump assembling gauge	
ST2505S001 (J25695)	Oil pressure gauge set	

INDEX

JATCO
RN3F01A • RL3F01A
Automatic Transaxle

APPLICATIONS

RN3F01A
1982 Datsun 310

RL3F01A
1983-84 Nissan Stanza
1982-83 Nissan Sentra
1983-84 Nissan Pulsar, NX

GENERAL DESCRIPTION

Both the RL3F01A and RN3F01A transaxle models are fully automatic units, consisting of two planetary gear sets, two multiple disc clutches, multiple disc brake, brake band and a one-way clutch. The RL3F01A transaxle model utilizes a lock-up clutch along with the usual three element torque converter used in both models. A hydraulic control system is used to operate the friction elements and automatic shift controls.

Transaxle and Converter Identification

TRANSAXLE

The identification label is attached to the transaxle on the upper right face of the transaxle case. The first figure denotes the transaxle model with "O" representing "automatic". The second figure represents the month of production. 1 through 9 represents

January through September respectively, while X, Y, and Z represent the months of October, November and December respectively. The following five digits of the number designation representing the serial production number for the month of assembly.

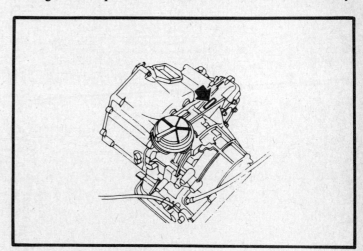

Location of transaxle identification number label
(© Nissan Motor Co. of USA)

TORQUE CONVERTER

The torque converters are coded by the manufacturer and sold through varied parts networks. Specific part numbers are used to identify the converters and to allow proper match-up to the transaxle assembly. When replacing a converter, verify the replacement unit is the same as the one originally used with the engine/transaxle combination. Lock-up and non-lock-up torque converters cannot be interchanged.

Transmission Metric Fasteners

Metric bolt sizes and thread pitches are used for all fasteners on the Jatco transaxles. The metric fastener dimensions are close to the dimensions of the familiar inch system fasteners, and for this reason, replacement fasteners must have the same measurement and strength as those removed.

1021

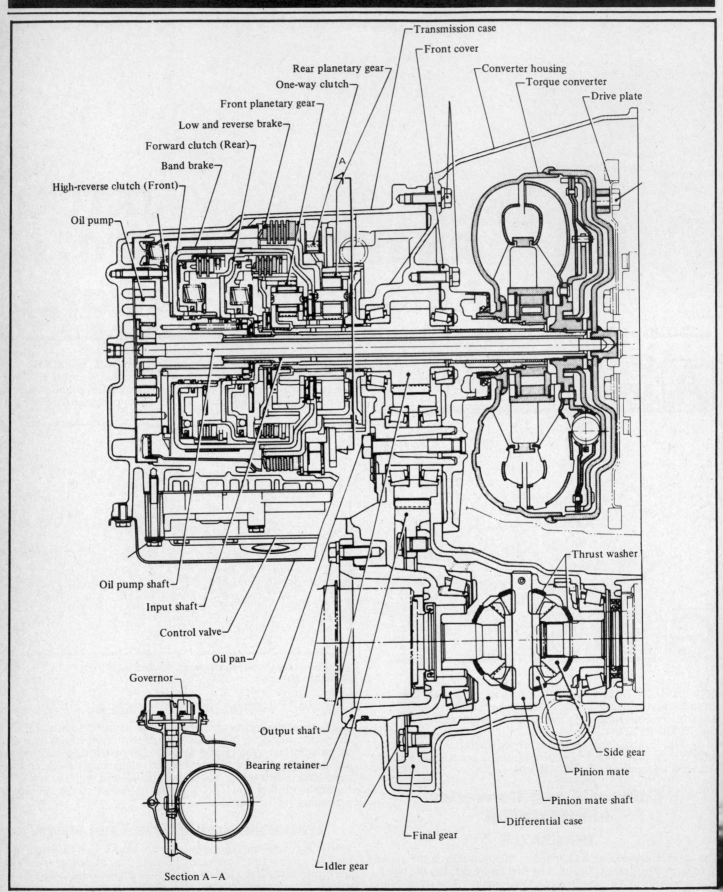

Section A–A

Cross section of Jatco automatic transaxle RL3F01A model with lock-up torque converter (© Nissan Motor Co. of USA)

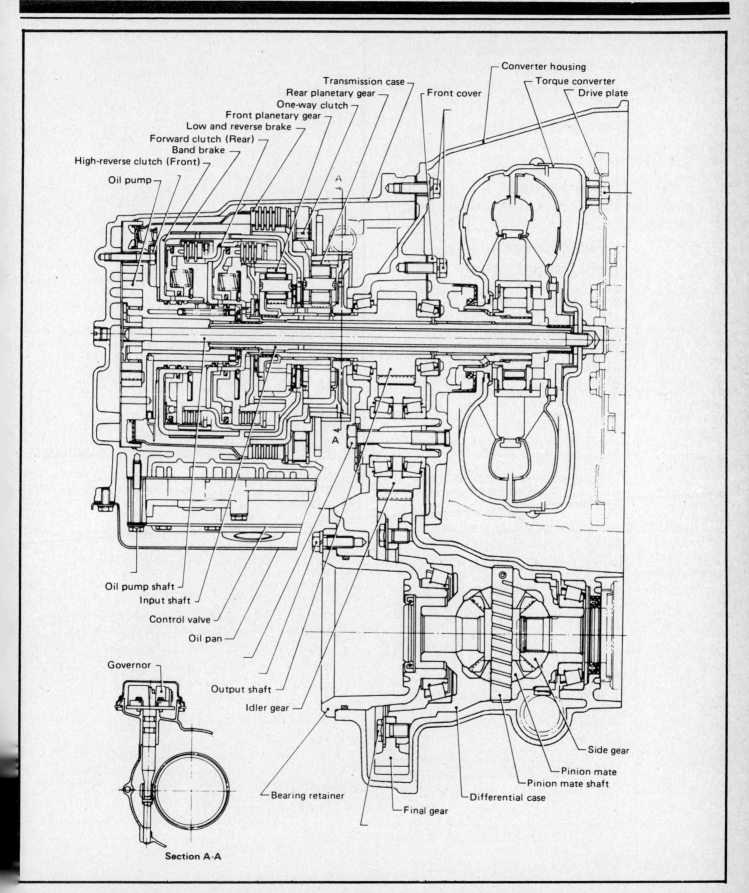

Transmission case
Rear planetary gear
One-way clutch
Front planetary gear
Low and reverse brake
Forward clutch (Rear)
Band brake
High-reverse clutch (Front)
Oil pump

Converter housing
Torque converter
Drive plate
Front cover

A

A

Oil pump shaft
Input shaft
Control valve
Oil pan

Governor

Output shaft
Idler gear

Bearing retainer
Final gear
Differential case

Side gear
Pinion mate
Pinion mate shaft

Section A-A

Cross section of Jatco automatic transaxle RN3F01A model without lock-up torque converter (© Nissan Motor Co. of USA)

Do not attempt to interchange metric fasteners for inch system fasteners. Mismatched or incorrect fasteners can result in damage to the transmission unit through malfunctions, breakage or possible personal injury.

Care should be taken to re-use the fasteners in the same locations as removed, whenever possible.

Fluid Specification

The use of Dexron®, or Dexron® II or its equivalent is recommended for use in the Jatco transaxle models.

Capacities

The capacity of the RL3F01A and RN3F01A transaxle models is 6⅜ US quarts (5¼ Imp. Quart, 6.0 Liter).

Fluid Level

CHECKING FLUID LEVEL

The transaxle fluid level is correct, if, after the engine start and with the engine operating at idle, the fluid level is within the values described.

1. Have the vehicle parked on a level surface and have the parking brake applied.

2. Allow the engine to operate for ten minutes and then move the gear selector through all the detent positions.

3. Position the gear selector in the "P" position and remove the dipstick indicator. Wipe clean and re-insert the dipstick indicator back into the transaxle.

4. Again, remove the dipstick and note the fluid indication on the dipstick indicator.

5. An illustration accompanies this outline, depicting effects of temperature upon the fluid level and what the correct fluid level would be.

6. Keep the fluid at the correct level. Overfilling can cause loss of fluid during high speed driving and underfilling may cause the internal friction elements to slip and burn.

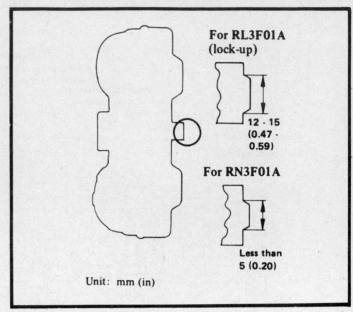

Unit: mm (in)

Identification differences between lock-up torque converter and non-lock-up torque converter (© Nissan Motor Co. of USA)

M MODIFICATIONS

No known transaxle modifications for the RL3F01A and RN3F01A transaxles were available at time of the printing of this publication.

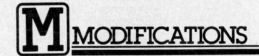

Ambient temperature	Fluid level	Ambient temperature	Fluid level
30 - 50°C (86 - 122°F)	Type 1. / Type 2. — L H, 2 (0.08), 2 (0.08), O.K. / COLD HOT	−10 - 10°C (14 - 50°F)	L H, O.K. 5 (0.20), 20 (0.79) / COLD HOT
10 - 30°C (50 - 86°F)	L H, 10 (0.39), 5 (0.20), O.K. / COLD HOT	−30 - −10°C (−22 - 14°F)	L H, O.K. 15 (0.59), O.K. / COLD HOT

Temperature affect on fluid level readings (© Nissan Motor Co. of USA)

TROUBLE DIAGNOSIS

CLUTCH AND BAND APPLICATION CHART
RL3F01A and RN4F01A Automatic Transaxles

Range		High-reverse clutch (Front)	Forward clutch (Rear)	Low & reverse brake	Lock-up	Band servo Operation	Band servo Release	One-way clutch	Parking pawl
Park									on
Reverse		on		on					
Neutral									
Drive	D_1 Low		on					on	
	D_2 Second		on			on			
	D_3 Top (3rd)	on	on		on	(on)	on		
2	2_1 Low		on					on	
	2_2 Second		on			on			
1	1_1 Low		on	on				on	
	1_1 Second		on			on			

The low & reverse brake is applied in "1_1" range to prevent free wheeling when coasting and allow engine braking.

CHILTON'S THREE "C's" TRANSAXLE DIAGNOSIS CHART
RL3F01A, RN3F01A Jatco Transaxles

Condition	Cause	Correction
Engine does not start in "N", "P" ranges	a) Range select cable b) Neutral safety switch c) Ignition switch and starter motor	a) Adjust cable b) Adjust or replace c) Repair or replace
Engine starts in range other than "N" and "P"	a) Range select cable b) Neutral safety switch	a) Adjust cable b) Adjust or replace
Sharp shock shifting from "N" to "D" range	a) Misadjusted throttle cable b) High engine idle c) High line pressure control d) Manual valve e) Forward (rear) clutch	a) Adjust throttle linkage b) Adjust the engine idle c) Adjust or locate malfunction causing high line pressure d) Adjust selector cable or renew manual control valve e) Renew clutch as required
Vehicle will not move in "D" range (but moves in "2", "1" and "R" ranges)	a) Range select cable b) Main line pressure c) Manual control valve d) One way clutch of transmission	a) Adjust cable b) Correct main line pressure or passage per air test c) Adjust range select renew valve d) Renew clutch

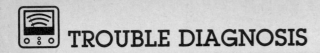

CHILTON'S THREE "C's" TRANSAXLE DIAGNOSIS CHART
RL3F01A, RN3F01A Jatco Transaxles

Condition	Cause	Correction
Vehicle will not move in "D", "1" or "2" ranges but moves in "R" range Clutch slips, very poor acceleration	a) Oil level b) Range select cable c) Main line pressure d) Manual control valve. e) Leakage at fluid passage f) Engine adjustment and brake defects g) Forward (rear) Clutch h) High-reverse (front) clutch	a) Add if needed b) Adjust cable c) Correct main line pressure or passage per air test d) Adjust range select cable/renew valve e) Correct as per air test f) Repair as needed g) Renew clutch as required h) Renew clutch as required
Vehicle will not move in "R" range (but moves in "D", "2" and "1" ranges). Clutch slips, very poor acceleration	a) Oil level b) Range select cable c) Throttle valve pressure d) Manual control valve e) Leakage of passage f) Forward (rear) clutch g) High-reverse (front) clutch h) Low and Reverse brake i) High-reverse (front) clutch check ball	a) Add if needed b) Adjust cable c) Correct throttle valve or passage per air test d) Adjust range select cable/renew valve e) Correct as per air test f) Renew clutch as required g) Renew clutch as required h) Renew low and reverse brake as required i) Test and replace check ball as required
Vehicle will not move in any range	a) Oil level b) Range select cable c) Main line pressure or pressure loss d) Manual control valve e) Leakage of fluid passage f) Oil pump g) Parking linkage h) Forward (rear) clutch	a) Add if needed b) Adjust cable c) Correct main line pressure or passage per air test d) Adjust range select cable/renew valve e) Correct as per air test f) Repair or renew g) Repair or renew h) Renew clutch as required
Clutches or brakes slip somewhat in starting to move	a) Oil level b) Range select cable c) Throttle valve cable pressure d) Manual control valve e) Leakage of fluid passage f) Oil pump g) Main line pressure	a) Add if needed b) Adjust cable c) Correct throttle valve or passage per air test d) Adjust range select cable/renew valve e) Correct as per air test f) Repair or renew g) Correct main line pressure
Vehicle moves in "N" range	a) Range select cable b) Manual control valve c) Forward (rear) clutch	a) Adjust cable b) Adjust range select cable/ renew valve c) Renew clutch as required
Excessive creep	a) High engine idle rpm	a) Adjust cable
Failure to change gear from "1st" to "2nd"	a) Range cable b) Throttle cable misadjusted c) Detent valve	a) Adjust cable b) Adjust throttle cable c) Repair or renew detent valve

CHILTON'S THREE "C's" TRANSAXLE DIAGNOSIS CHART
RL3F01A, RN3F01A Jatco Transaxles

Condition	Cause	Correction
Failure to change gear from "1st" to "2nd"	d) Manual control valve	d) Adjust range select cable/renew valve
	e) Band servo	e) Renew band servo
	f) Leakage of fluid passage	f) Correct as per air test
	g) High-reverse (front) clutch	g) Renew clutch as required
	h) Front clutch check (high-reverse) ball	h) Renew clutch check ball
	i) band brake	i) Replace band brake
	j) Governor valve	j) Governor overhaul or replace as required
Failure to change gear from "2nd" to "3rd"	a) Range select cable	a) Adjust cable
	b) Throttle cable misadjusted	b) Adjust throttle cable
	c) Detent valve	c) Repair or renew detent valve
	d) Manual control valve	d) Adjust range select cable/renew valve
	e) Governor valve	e) Overhaul governor/renew governor
	f) Band servo	f) Renew band servo
	g) Leakage of fluid passage	g) Correct as per air test
	h) Band brake	h) Renew band brake
	i) High-reverse (front) clutch	i) Renew clutch as required
	j) High-reverse (front) clutch check ball	j) Renew clutch check ball
Gear change directly from "1st" to "3rd" occurs	a) Manual control valve	a) Adjust range select cable/renew valve
	b) Governor valve	b) Overhaul governor/renew governor
	c) Leakage of fluid passage	c) Correct as per air test
	d) Band brake	d) Renew band brake
Too sharp shock in change from "1st" to "2nd"	a) Misadjusted throttle cable	a) Adjust throttle cable
	b) Manual control valve	b) Adjust range select cable/renew valve
	c) Band servo	c) Renew band servo
	d) Band brake	d) Renew band brake
	e) Engine stall rpm	e) Perform stall test
Too sharp shock in change from "2nd" to "3rd"	a) Misadjusted throttle cable	a) Adjust throttle cable
	b) Detent valve	b) Repair or renew detent valve
	c) Throttle valve pressure	c) Correct throttle valve or passage per air test
	d) Manual control valve	d) Adjust range select cable/renew valve
	e) Band servo	e) Renew band servo
	f) High-reverse (front) clutch	f) Renew clutch as required
Almost no shock or slipping in change from "1st" to "2nd"	a) Oil level	a) Add if needed
	b) Range select cable	b) Adjust cable
	c) Misadjusted throttle cable	c) Adjust throttle cable
	d) Low main line pressure	d) Correct main line pressure or passage per air test
	e) Manual control valve	e) Adjust range select cable/renew valve
	f) Band servo	f) Renew band servo

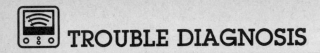

CHILTON'S THREE "C's" TRANSAXLE DIAGNOSIS CHART
RL3F01A, RN3F01A Jatco Transaxles

Condition	Cause	Correction
Almost no shock or engine runaway on "2nd" to "3rd" shift	g) Leakage of fluid passage h) Band brake	g) Correct as per air test h) Renew band brake
Almost no shock or engine runaway on "2nd" to "3rd" shift	a) Oil level b) Range select cable c) Misadjusted throttle cable d) Low main line pressure e) Manual control valve f) Band servo g) Leakage of fluid passage h) High-reverse (front) clutch i) Front clutch check (high-reverse) ball	a) Add if needed b) Adjust cable c) Adjust throttle cable d) Correct main line pressure or passage per air test e) Adjust range select cable/ renew valve f) Renew band servo g) Correct as per air test h) Renew clutch as required i) Renew front clutch check ball
Vehicle braked by gear change from "1st" to "2nd"	a) Manual control valve b) Front clutch (high-reverse) c) Low and reverse brake d) One-way clutch of transaxle	a) Adjust range select cable/renew valve b) Renew front clutch c) Renew low and reverse brake d) Renew one-way clutch of transaxle
Vehicle braked by gear change from "2nd" to "3rd"	a) Manual control valve b) Band servo c) Brake band	a) Adjust range select cable b) Renew band servo c) Renew brake band
Failure to change from "3rd" to "2nd"	a) Misadjusted throttle cable b) Manual control valve c) Governor valve d) Band servo e) Leakage of fluid pressure passage f) Front clutch (high-reverse) g) Band brake	a) Adjust throttle cable b) Adjust range select cable/renew valve c) Overhaul governor/ renew governor d) Renew band servo e) Correct as per air test f) Renew front clutch g) Renew band brake
Transaxle overheats	a) Oil level b) Band servo c) Main line pressure d) Restricted or no rear lubrication e) Manual control valve f) Leakage of fluid pressure passage g) Front clutch (high-reverse) h) Band brake i) Low and reverse brake j) Engine stall rpm	a) Add if needed b) Renew band servo c) Correct main line pressure or passage per air test d) Check passages e) Adjust range select cable/renew valve f) Correct as per air test g) Renew front clutch h) Renew band brake i) Renew low and reverse brake j) Locate malfunction and correct

CHILTON'S THREE "C's" TRANSAXLE DIAGNOSIS CHART
RL3F01A, RN3F01A Jatco Transaxles

Condition	Cause	Correction
Transaxle overheats	k) Oil Pump l) Torque converter m) Planetary gears	k) Renew oil pump l) Renew torque converter m) Renew planetary gears
Transaxle noise in "P" and "N" ranges	a) Oil level b) Main line pressure c) Oil pump	a) Add if needed b) Correct main line pressure or passage per air test test c) Renew oil pump
Transaxle noise in "D", "2", "1" and "R" ranges	a) Oil level b) Main line pressure c) Rear clutch (forward) d) Oil pump e) One-way clutch of transaxle f) Planetary gear	a) Add if needed b) Correct main line pressure or passage per air test test c) Renew rear clutch d) Renew oil pump e) Renew one-way clutch of transaxle f) Renew planetary gear
Failure to change gear from "2nd" to "1st" or from "3rd" to "1st"	a) Misadjusted throttle cable b) Manual control valve c) Governor valve d) Band servo e) Band brake f) Leakage of fluid pressure passage g) One-way clutch of transaxle	a) Adjust throttle cable b) Adjust range select cable/renew valve c) Overhaul governor/ renew governor d) Renew band servo e) Renew band brake f) Correct as per air test g) Renew one-way clutch of transaxle
Races extremely or slips in changing from "3rd" to "2nd"	a) Misadjusted throttle cable b) Main line pressure c) Manual control valve d) Band servo e) Leakage of fluid pressure passage f) Front clutch (high-reverse)	a) Adjust throttle cable b) Correct main line pressure or passage as per air test c) Adjust range select cable/renew valve d) Renew band servo e) Correct as per air test f) Renew front clutch
Failure to change from "3rd" to "2nd" when changing lever into "2" range	a) Range select cable b) Main line pressure c) Manual control valve d) Band servo e) Band brake f) Leakage of fluid pressure passage	a) Adjust cable b) Correct main line pressure or passage per air test c) Adjust range select cable/renew valve d) Renew band servo e) Renew band brake f) Correct as per air test
No shock on change from "1" range to "2nd" range or engine races extremely	a) Oil level b) Range select cable c) Misadjusted throttle cable d) Engine idle rpm e) High stall speed	a) Add if needed b) Adjust cable c) Adjust throttle cable d) Set idle rpm e) Renew band brake

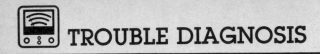
CHILTON'S THREE "C's" TRANSAXLE DIAGNOSIS CHART
RL3F01A, RN3F01A Jatco Transaxles

Condition	Cause	Correction
No shock on change from "1" range to "2nd" range or engine races extremely	f) Manual control valve	f) Adjust range select cable/renew valve
	g) Transmission air check to determine if band servo is working	g) Repair or renew servo
	h) Oil pump	h) Repair or renew
Failure to shift from "3rd" to "2nd" when shifting lever into "1" range	a) Range select cable	a) Adjust cable
	b) Main line pressure	b) Correct main line pressure or passage per air test
	c) Manual control valve	c) Adjust range select cable/renew valve
	d) Governor valve	d) Overhaul governor/renew governor
	e) Band servo	e) Renew band servo
	f) Leakage of fluid pressure passage	f) Correct as per air test
	g) High-reverse (front) clutch	g) Renew clutch as required
No engine braking in range "1"	a) Range select cable	a) Adjust cable
	b) Main line pressure	b) Correct main line pressure or passage per air test
	c) Manual control valve	c) Adjust range select cable/renew valve
	d) Leakage of fluid pressure passage	d) Correct as per air test
	e) Low and reverse brake	e) Renew low and reverse brake
Gear change from 2nd to 3rd in "2" range	a) Range select cable	a) Adjust cable
	b) Main line pressure	b) Correct main line pressure
	c) Manual valve	c) Adjust range select linkage/renew valve
	d) Band servo	d) Renew band servo
	e) Fluid quality	e) Correct fluid quality and refill transaxle
	f) Band brake	f) Correct or renew band brake
	g) Leakage fluid pressure passage	g) Correct as per air test
Gear change from "1st" to "2nd" or from "2nd" to "3rd" in "1" range	a) Range select cable	a) Adjust cable
	b) Manual control valve	b) Adjust range select linkage/renew valve
	c) Leakage of fluid pressure passage	c) Correct as per air test
Does not change from "2nd" to "1st" in "1" range	a) Oil level	a) Add if needed
	b) Range select cable	b) Adjust cable
	c) Manual control valve	c) Adjust range select cable/renew valve
	d) Governor valve	d) Overhaul governor/renew governor
	e) Band servo	e) Renew band servo
	f) Leakage of fluid pressure passage	f) Correct as per air test
	g) Low and reverse brake	g) Renew low and reverse brake

CHILTON'S THREE "C's" TRANSAXLE DIAGNOSIS CHART
RL3F01A, RN3F01A Jatco Transaxles

Condition	Cause	Correction
Large shock in changing from "2nd" to "1st" in "1" range	a) Misadjusted throttle cable b) High engine stall rpm c) Manual control valve d) Low and reverse brake	a) Adjust throttle cable b) Locate malfunction and correct c) Adjust range select cable/renew valve d) Renew low and reverse brake
Oil shoots out during operation. While smoke from exhaust during operation	a) Oil level b) Misadjusted throttle cable c) Main line pressure d) Restricted or no rear lubrication e) Manual control valve f) Leakage of fluid pressure passage g) Engine stall rpm h) Band brake i) Low and reverse brake j) Oil pump k) One-way clutch torque converter l) Planetary gear	a) Add if needed b) Adjust throttle cable c) Correct main line pressure or passage per air test d) Check passages e) Adjust range select cable/renew valve f) Correct as per air test g) Locate malfunction and correct h) Renew band brake i) Renew low and reverse brake j) Renew oil pump k) Renew one-way clutch torque converter l) Renew planetary gear
Vehicle moves changing into "P" range or parking gear does not disengage when shifted out of "P" range	a) Range select linkage b) Parking linkage	a) Adjust linkage b) Repair parking linkage

CHILTON'S THREE "C's" DIAGNOSIS CHART
Jatco RL3F01A With Lock-up Torque Converter

Condition	Cause	Correction
Torque converter not locked-up	a) Governor b) Line pressure malfunctions c) "O"-ring on input shaft d) Torque converter e) Speed cut valve f) Lock-up control valve g) Oil pump	a) Repair or renew governor b) Locate malfunction and adjust line pressure c) Renew "O" ring d) Renew torque converter e) Repair or renew speed cut valve f) Repair or renew lock-up control valve g) Repair or renew oil pump
Lock-up Piston slips	a) Line pressure malfunction b) "O" ring on input shaft c) Torque converter d) Oil pump	a) Locate malfunction and adjust line pressure b) Renew "O" ring c) Renew torque converter d) Repair of renew oil pump

CHILTON'S THREE "C's" DIAGNOSIS CHART
Jatco RL3F01A With Lock-up Torque Converter

Condition	Cause	Correction
Lock-up point is extremely high or low	a) Governor b) Speed cut valve c) Lock-up control valve	a) Repair or renew governor b) Repair or renew speed cut valve c) Repair or renew lock-up control valve
Engine is stopped in "R", "D", "2" and "L" range	a) Torque converter b) Lock-up control valve	a) Renew torque converter b) Repair or renew lock-up control valve
Transmission overheats	a) Line pressure malfunction b) "O" ring on input shaft c) Torque converter d) Oil pump	a) Locate malfunction and adjust line pressure b) Renew "O" ring c) Renew torque converter d) Repair or renew oil pump

Hydraulic Control System

Hydraulic pressure, clutch and band applications control the changing of gear ratios in the automatic transaxle. The clutches and the band are applied by the force of the fluid pressure, controlled by a system of valves, springs and other control mechanisms. Some of the controlling mechanisms and components are as follows:

1. Screen or filter to clean foreign material from the fluid supply before the fluid is drawn into the pump.

2. The oil pump supplies fluid pressure to the transaxle components.

3. Fluid pressure regulator valve is used to control main line pressure to the transaxle components.

4. A converter pressure relief valve is used to prevent fluid pressure build up in the torque converter.

5. The torque converter is used as a fluid coupling and torque multiplier between the engine and the transaxle gearing.

6. The forward (rear) clutch is applied in all forward gears.

7. The Low and reverse brake is applied in Reverse, and range "1" low gear.

8. The High-reverse (front) clutch is applied in reverse and the high gears.

9. The rear lubrication passages lubricate the rear transaxle components.

10. The front lubrication passages lubricate the front transaxle components.

11. The cooler system removes heat from the A/T fluid by having the fluid routed through a cooler unit within the vehicle's cooling system radiator and back into the transaxle.

12. Varied anti-drain back valves are used to prevent loss of fluid in the hydraulic circuits when the engine is stopped.

13. A throttle control valve regulates throttle pressure in relation to the position of the accelerator pedal through the use of a cable assembly.

14. The brake band is applied in the second speed, with the selector lever in the "D", "2" or "1" position. The brake hand is pressure released when the transmission is in the third speed, "D" position.

15. Pressure modifier valve uses throttle pressure, controlled by governor pressure, to modify the main line pressure from the regulator valve. This modifies the harsh shifting caused by excessive pump pressure.

16. Timing valves are used to control shifting under heavy load conditions.

17. The governor circuit provides road speed signals to the transaxle hydraulic control system.

18. Throttle cable is connected to the valve body and along with controlling the T.V. pressure, upon wide open throttle position of the accelerator, the detent valve is moved to control forced downshifting of the transaxle.

19. The manual control valve is used to direct fluid pressure to the varied units to control the range selection of gearing. The control valve is connected mechanically to the shift lever, located within the drivers compartment.

20. The shift valves control the up and down shifting of the transaxle, from one ratio to another.

21. When the transaxle is equipped with the lock-up torque converter, Lock-up control valve, speed cut valve and fail safe valves are used to control the on and off of the converter clutch.

MAJOR HYDRAULIC COMPONENTS

1. The main line control pressure system supplies fluid pressure to the transaxle and converter when the engine is operating.

2. Converter and lubrication systems regulates the converter fluid pressure, provides gear train lubrication and fluid cooling while the transaxle is operating.

3. Forward clutch pressure and governor pressure systems applies the forward clutch, which is applied in all forward speeds and applies pressure to the governor valve. The governor valve supplies regulated pressure to the rear side of the shift valves, dependent upon the road speed of the vehicle.

4. The low and reverse brake system applies the low and reverse brake in the "L" and "R" selector lever positions and locks out the second and third speed gears by directing pressure to the appropriate valves to prevent them from shifting.

5. The first gear lockout system allows the transaxle valve body to shift directly to the second speed and locks out the 1st and 3rd gears.

6. The brake band servo apply system applies the servo to hold the band to the surface of the reverse and high clutch cylinder.

7. Reverse pressure booster system increased the control or line pressure and applies the reverse and high clutch in the reverse range.

8. The shift valve train system applies and exhausts the fluid pressures to the servo and clutch assemblies for upshifts and downshifts automatically on demand.

9. The kickdown system forces downshift by overriding the governor/throttle valve control of the shift valves.

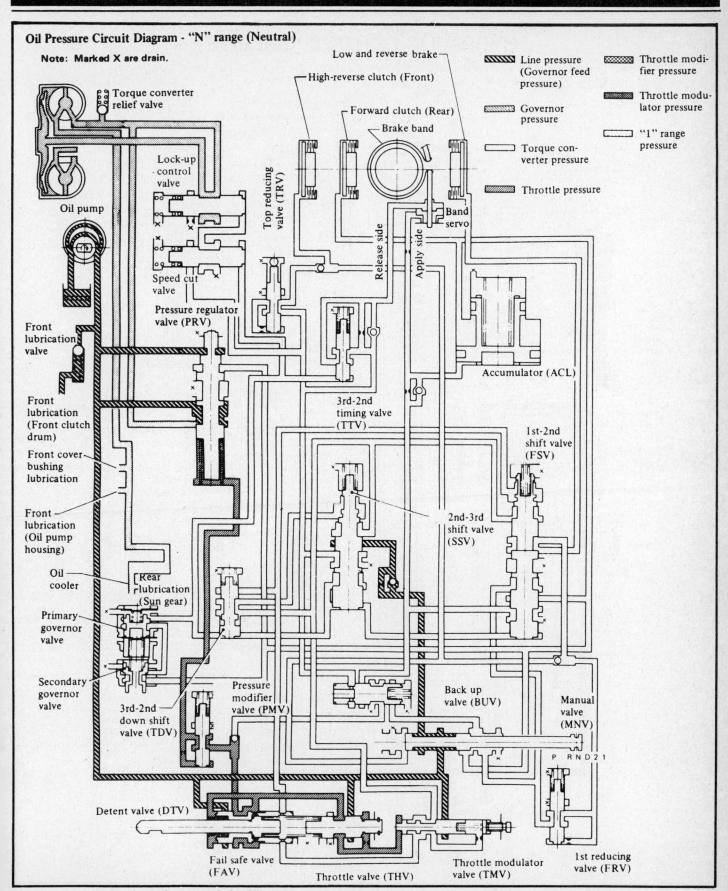

Oil Pressure Circuit Diagram - "N" range (Neutral)

Note: Marked X are drain.

Fluid pressure circuit schematic, transaxle in "N" position and equipped with lock-up torque converter (© Nissan Motor Co. of USA)

HYDRAULIC CONTROL CIRCUITS

Oil Pressure Circuit Diagram - "N" range (Neutral)

Note: Marked X are drain.

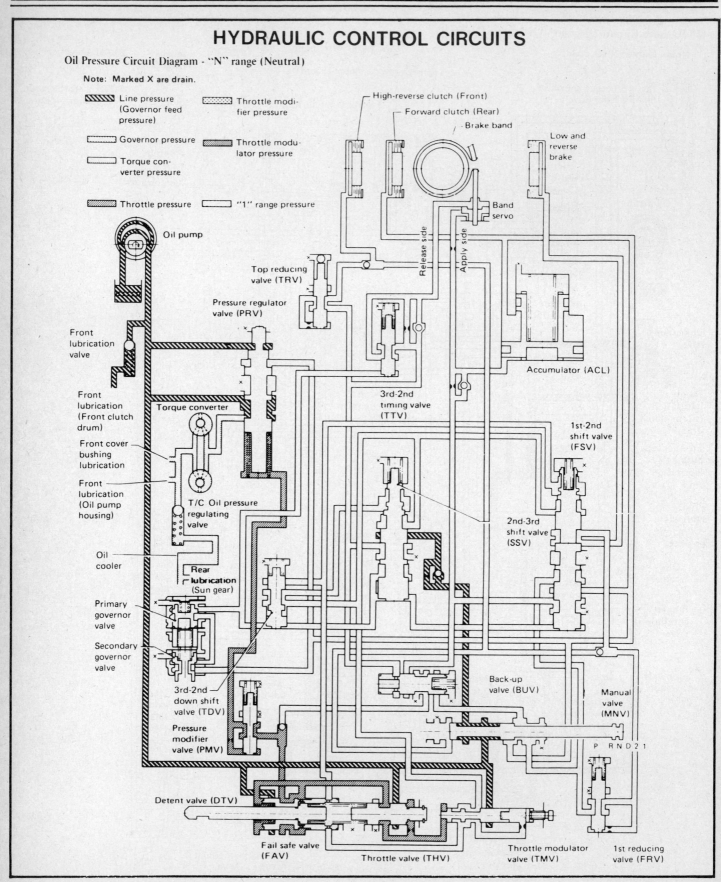

Fluid pressure circuit schematic, transaxle in "N" position and not equipped with lock-up torque converter (© Nissan Motor Co. of USA)

10. The governor system provides a varying pressure proportional to the vehicle speed and throttle opening to help control the timing qualities of the transaxle shifts.

11. The throttle pressure (T.V.) system provides a varying pressure proportional to throttle opening and engine load to help control the timing qualities of the transaxle shifts.

12. The throttle modifier system and the pressure modifier systems compensates and adjust control pressure to insure smoother shifting under the various loads and throttle openings of the engine.

Diagnosis Testing

OIL PRESSURE CIRCUITS

Control (line) pressure is a regulated main line pressure, developed by the operation of the front pump. It is directed to the main regulator valve, where predetermined spring pressure automatically moves the regulator valve to control the pressure of the oil at a predetermined rate, by opening the valve and exhausting excessive pressured oil back into the sump and holding the valve closed to build up pressure when needed.

Therefore, it is most important during the diagnosis phase to test main line control pressure to determine if high or low pressure exists. Do not attempt to adjust a pressure regulator valve spring to obtain more or less control pressure. Internal transmission damage may result.

The main valve is the controlling agent of the transmission, which directs oil pressure to separate passages used to control the valve train.

CONTROL PRESSURE SYSTEM TESTS

Control pressure tests should be performed whenever slippage, delay or harshness is felt in the shifting of the transmission. Throttle pressure changes can cause these problems also, but are generated from the control pressures and therefore reflect any problems arising from the control pressure system.

The control pressure is first checked in all ranges without any throttle pressure input, and then checked as the throttle pressure is increased.

The control pressure tests should define differences between mechanical or hydraulic failures of the transmission.

PRESSURE PORTS

RN3F01A

The non-converter lock-up equipped transaxles are provided with three pressure ports on the transaxle case. The port identification is as follows:
1. Line pressure, high-reverse (front) clutch
2. Line pressure, forward (rear) clutch
3. Governor pressure

RL3F01A

The lock-up converter equipped transaxles are provided with four pressure ports on the transaxle case. The port identification is as follows:
1. Line pressure, high-reverse (front) clutch
2. Line pressure, forward (rear) clutch
3. Governor pressure
4. Torque converter lock-up pressure

Testing Line Pressure

1. Install a pressure gauge to the line pressure port as follows:
   a. When the selector lever is in the "D", "2" or "1" range, install the pressure gauge to the Forward (rear) clutch pressure port.
   b. When the selector lever is in the "R" range, install the pressure gauge to the high-reverse (front) clutch pressure port.
2. Locate the pressure gauge so it can be seen by the operator.

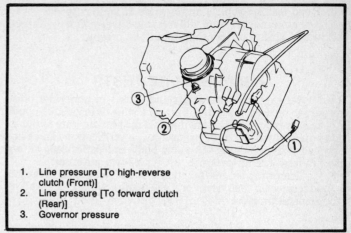

1. Line pressure [To high-reverse clutch (Front)]
2. Line pressure [To forward clutch (Rear)]
3. Governor pressure

Pressure port locations—RN3F01A transaxle
(© Nissan Motor Co. of USA)

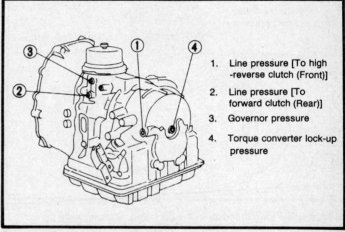

1. Line pressure [To high-reverse clutch (Front)]
2. Line pressure [To forward clutch (Rear)]
3. Governor pressure
4. Torque converter lock-up pressure

Pressure port locations—RL3F01A transaxle
(© Nissan Motor Co. of USA)

3. Measure line pressure at idle and at stall test speeds.

4. Road test the vehicle and note the pressure under different throttle and engine load conditions.

5. The key points of pressure testing are as follows:
   a. Look for a steady rise in line pressure as the car speed increases under light engine load.
   b. Pressure drop between shifts should not exceed 14 psi. Excessive leakage could be caused by an internal leak at a servo or clutch seal.
   c. Line pressure should be measured when the fluid temperature is 109-135°F. (43-57°C).

Lock-up Pressure Test

1. Install the pressure gauge to the lock-up pressure port on the transaxle case.

2. Shift the selector lever to the "D" position and operate the vehicle to allow the lock-up converter to operate.

3. With the lock-up converter not applied, a pressure reading of 28 psi or more, should be registered.

4. With the lock-up converter applied, a pressure reading of 7 psi or less, should be registered.

Governor Pressure Test

1. Install the pressure gauge to the governor pressure port on the transaxle case. Locate the gauge so it can be seen by the operator.

2. Road test the vehicle and operate at various speeds.

3. The governor pressure will increase directly with road speed and should always be less than main line pressure.

AIR PRESSURE TESTS

The control pressure test results and causes of abnormal pressures are to be used as a guide. Further testing or inspection could be necessary before repairs are made. If the pressures are found to be low in a clutch, servo or passageway, a verification can be accomplished by removing the valve body and performing an air pressure test. The air pressure test serves two purposes:

1. To determine if a malfunction of a clutch or band is caused by fluid leakage in the system or if the malfunction is the result of a mechanical problem.

2. To test the transaxle for internal fluid leakage during the rebuilding process and to verify operation of the units before completing the assembly.

Procedure

1. Obtain an air nozzle rated for 25-30 psi. Apply air pressure to the passages as illustrated.

STALL TEST

The stall test is an application of the engine torque, through the transaxle and drive train to locked-up road wheels, held by the vehicle's service brakes. The engine speed is increased until the rpms are stabilized. Given ideal engine operating conditions and no abnormal slippage from the transaxle clutches, bands or torque converter, the engine speed will stabilize at a specific test rpm.

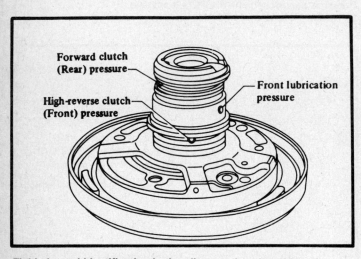

Fluid channel identification in the oil pump, housing side
(© Nissan Motor Co. of USA)

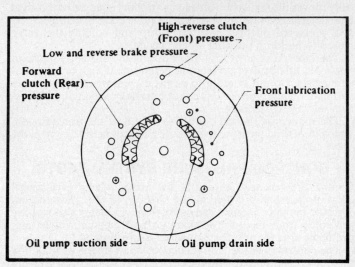

Fluid channel identification in the oil pump, plate side
(© Nissan Motor Co. of USA)

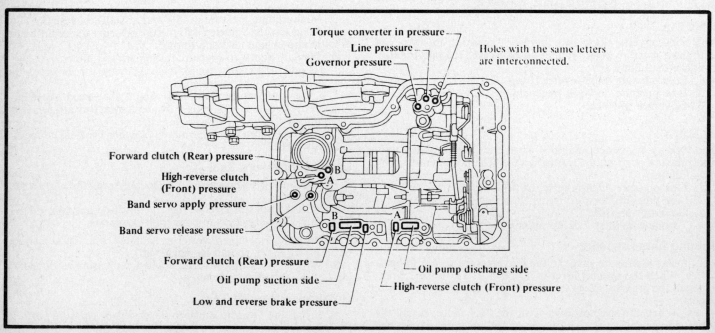

Fluid passage identification in RN3F01A transaxle case (© Nissan Motor Co. of USA)

Performing the Stall Test

1. Check the engine oil level and start the engine, bringing it up to normal operating temperature.

2. Check the transaxle fluid level and correct as required.

3. Attach a calibrated tachometer to the engine and a pressure gauge to the transaxle main line pressure port.

4. Mark the specified maximum engine rpm on the tachometer cover plate with a grease pencil to easily check if the stall speed is over or under the specifications.

5. Apply the parking brake and block the front and rear wheels.

CAUTION

Do not allow anyone to stand in front of the vehicle while performing the stall test.

6. Apply the foot service brakes and accelerate to wide open throttle.

CAUTION

Do not hold the throttle open for longer than five seconds.

7. Quickly note the engine stall speed and the pressure reading. Release the accelerator.

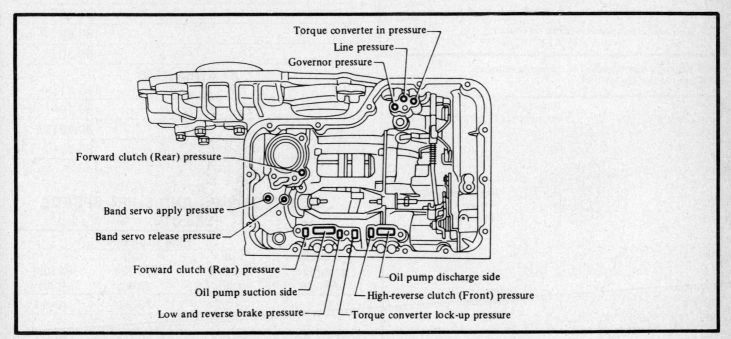

Fluid passage identification in RL3F01A transaxle case (© Nissan Motor Co. of USA)

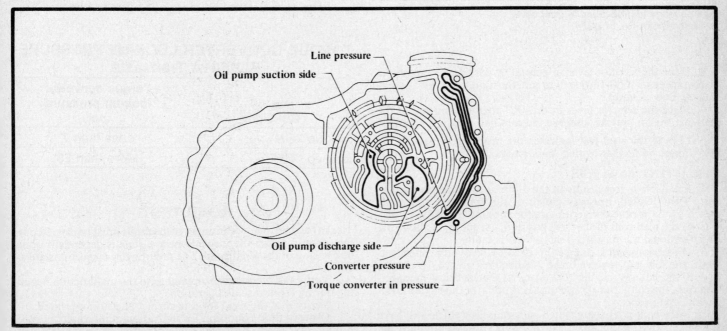

Fluid passage identification in converter housing side of case (© Nissan Motor Co. of USA)

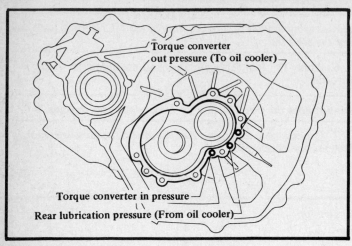

Fluid passage identification in converter housing
(© Nissan Motor Co. of USA)

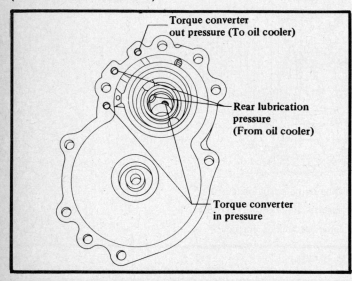

Fluid passage identification in front cover
(© Nissan Motor Co. of USA)

8. Place the selector lever in neutral or park and increase the engine speed to 1000-1500 rpm to cool the fluid. Hold for approximately two minutes.

9. Place the selector lever in the "R" position and repeat the stall test. Again, quickly observe the rpm and pressure readings.

NOTE: If the stall test indicates the proper stall rpm in the "D" range, no further testing is required.

STALL TEST ANALYSIS

1. Satisfactory test results in the "D" range indicates the forward (rear) clutch, one-way clutch of the transaxle and sprag clutch of the torque converter, are functioning properly.

2. If the stall rpm in the "D" position, 1st speed, is above the specifications, the forward (rear) clutch is faulty.

3. If the stall rpm in the "R" position is above the specifications, the low and reverse brake is defective.

4. If the stall rpm, in the "D" range, 1st gear, is below the specified rpm, the converter sprag clutch is slipping or the engine is not performing properly.

5. If the converter sprag clutch is frozen, the vehicle will have poor high speed performance. If the sprag clutch is slipping, the vehicle will be sluggish up to 30-40 mph.

STALL SPEED SPECIFICATIONS

1982 Datsun 310	1650-1950 RPM
1983-84 Nissan Stanza	2000-2300 RPM
1982-84 Nissan Sentra	1800-2100 RPM
1983-84 Nissan Pulsar, NX	1800-2100 RPM

LINE PRESSURE SPECIFICATIONS
1983-84 Pulsar and Stanza, 1982-84 Sentra

Range	Line Pressure (psi)
AT IDLING	
R	91-112
D	36-50
2	36-50
1	36-50
AT STALL TEST	
R	185-213
D	80-101
2	80-101
1	80-101

LINE PRESSURES AND SHIFT SPEEDS
1982 310

Throttle position Range	Full throttle (psi)	Half throttle (psi)	At idle (psi)
	Line Pressure		
D, 1	78-92	78-92	40-50
2 ($D_1 \rightarrow 2_2$)	80-92	80-92	78-92
R	192-206	192-206	85-107

TORQUE CONVERTER LOCK-UP PRESSURE
RL3F01A Transaxle

Condition	Torque converter lock-up pressure psi
Lock-up "ON"	Less than 7
Lock-up "OFF"	More than 28

ROAD TEST

Prior to road testing, preliminary inspections must be carried out. The order in which the inspections are done is dependent upon the decision of the repairman. The preliminary inspections are as follows:

1. Verify the customer complaint as to the malfunction occurring during the transaxle operation.

2. Verify that the fluid level is correct and not overfilled.

3. Observe fluid condition for indication of internally burned components, water or coolant contamination, or an internal varnish condition.

4. Verify engine operation. Verify cooling and oiling systems are operating normally and that all levels are correct.

5. Verify selector lever positioning is correct and properly aligned.

6. Verify transaxle throttle valve control cable is free and properly adjusted.

7. Install a tachometer to the engine and a oil pressure gauge to the transaxle.

8. The road test should be performed on a pre-selected course that has been used in the diagnosis of other transmission/transaxle malfunctions.

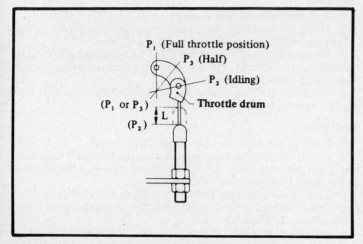

Throttle cable positioning at varied throttle openings
(© Nissan Motor Co. of USA)

Road Testing Procedure

1. **Park**—Place the control lever in "P" range and start the engine. Stop the engine and repeat the procedure in all other ranges and neutral. In Park, the car should be locked in position, unable to roll or move. Note all results on the Symptom Chart.

2. **Reverse**—Manually shift the control lever from "P" to "R", and note shift quality. Drive the car in reverse long enough to detect slippage or other abnormalities. Note results.

3. **Neutral**—Manually shift the control lever from "P" to "N" and note quality. In neutral no clutches or bands are applied, and there should be no movement. Note results.

4. **Drive**—Manually shift the control lever to range "D", and note shift quality. Drive the car through all automatic shifts and in all gear ranges. Note shift quality and timing [km/h (MPH)], check for slippage, noise, or other abnormal conditions. If necessary, drive the test sequence under different throttle openings (e.g. light, medium or full throttle).

5. **Range "2"**—Manually shift the control lever to range "2". Check for slippage, hesitation or abnormal condition. When the lever is set at this position, the transaxle will be automatically shifted between 1st and 2nd gears in response to the depression of the accelerator pedal. However, the transaxle is not shifted to 3rd gear. When the car is slowing down, the transaxle will automatically down-shift.

6. **Range "1"**—Manually shift the control lever to range "1". Note shift quality. It should, however, downshift immediately to 2nd gear and downshift again to 1st gear as road speed decreases. Accelerate and decelerate in 1st gear to determine engine braking. Note results.

The transaxle should not shift into 1st gear from "D" range if the car road speed is above approximately 65 km/h (40 MPH).

7. Record line pressure and governor pressure at each range and at each throttle valve opening.

LOCK-UP TORQUE CONVERTER

The lock-up of the clutch assembly to the torque converter occurs when the transaxle shifts into the third speed and the road speed is approximately 39-46 mph. During the transaxle downshifting, the lock-up will release at speeds of 44-37 mph.

Hydraulic fluid pressure is applied to both sides of the clutch plate assembly when in the released position and when applied, the pressure is exhausted from between the clutch and the converter front plate, allowing the clutch to lock-up mechanically.

ON CAR SERVICES

Adjustments
THROTTLE CABLE

Adjustment

To adjust the throttle cable, double nuts are provided and are located on the carburetor side of the cable.

1. Loosen the throttle cable double nuts.

2. With the throttle positioned in the wide open mode, move the cable fitting towards the transaxle completely while adjusting the two locknuts.

3. Loosen the locknut on the transaxle side, between one and one-half turns. Tighten the locknut on the carburetor side securely to 5.8-7.2 ft. lbs.

4. Ensure the throttle cable stroke is within the specified range of 1.079-1.236 in. (27.4-31.4mm) during the idle and wide open throttle operations.

NOTE: The throttle cable will be pulled outward when at wide open throttle position.

CONTROL CABLE

Adjustment

1. Place the selector lever in the "P" range.

2. Move the selector lever to the "1" range, feeling the detents in each position or range.

3. If the detents cannot be felt or the indicator is not properly aligned, the cable must be adjusted.

4. With the selector lever in the "P" position and the transaxle in the "P" position, adjust the control cable to the trunnion by loosening the locknuts on each side of the trunnion.

5. Center the trunnion in the transaxle lever and tighten the locknuts.

6. Move the selector lever from "P" position to the "1" position and check for detent feel and ease of cable operation.

7. Readjust as required. Lubricate the spring washer on the transaxle lever.

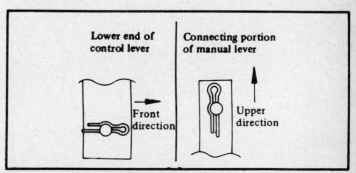

Proper positioning of spring retaining clip
(© Nissan Motor Co. of USA)

NEUTRAL SAFETY (INHIBITOR) SWITCH

Adjustment

1. Loosen the adjusting screws.
2. Position the selector lever in the "N" position.
3. Install a 0.098 in. (2.5mm) diameter pin into the adjusting holes in both the switch and the operating lever.
4. Tighten the adjusting screws to 1.4-1.9 ft. lbs. (2.0-2.5 N•m).
5. Check the operation of the switch in the "P" and "N" positions to allow the engine to start and the back-up lights to operate in the "R" position.

NOTE: An Ohmmeter can be used to check the continuity of the switch in the varied positions, if so desired.

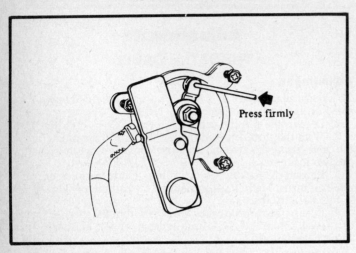

Installation of pin in adjustment holes of switch
(© Nissan Motor Co. of USA)

BRAKE BAND

Adjustment

1. Raise the vehicle and support safely. Drain the transaxle and remove the oil pan.
2. Remove the valve body and screen assembly from the transaxle.

NOTE: Refer to the valve body removal and installation procedure in the Service section of On Car Services.

3. Loosen the locknut.
4. Torque the anchor end pin to 2.9-4.3 ft. lbs. (4-6 N•m).
5. Back off the anchor end pin 2.5 complete turns.
6. While holding the anchor end pin, tighten the locknut to 12-16 ft. lbs. (16-22 N•m).

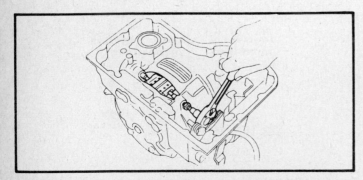

Adjustment location of brake band (© Nissan Motor Co. of USA)

7. Reinstall the valve body and screen assembly as per instructions in the Valve Body Removal and Installation section.
8. Install the oil pan, using a new gasket. Tighten the pan bolts to 3.6-5.1 ft. lbs. (5-7 N•m).
9. Fill the transaxle with fluid and verifty level after the units reach normal operating temperature.

Services
CONTROL VALVE ASSEMBLY

Removal

1. Raise the vehicle and support safely.
2. Drain the fluid from the transaxle assembly and remove the oil pan guard, the retaining bolts and the oil pan.
3. Remove the fluid screen, the valve body retaining bolts and the control valve body. Do not allow the manual valve to fall from the control valve assembly.
4. The control valve assembly can then be disassembled, inspected and assembled as required.

Installation

1. Position the selector lever in the "N" detent.
2. Install the control valve assembly to the transaxle case and install the retaining bolts. Align the manual plate with the groove in the manual valve during the installation.
3. Torque the retaining bolts to 5.1-6.5 ft. lbs. (7-9 N•m). Be sure the manual valve and control lever can be moved to all positions. Install the fluid screen.
4. Install a new gasket on the oil pan and attach to the transaxle case. Tighten the oil pan bolts to 3.6-5.1 ft. lbs. (5-7 N•m). Install the oil pan guard.
5. Install the drain plug if not previously installed. Tighten to 5.1-9.4 ft. lbs. (7-13 N•m).
6. Refill the transaxle, start the engine, move the selector lever through all detent positions and recheck the fluid level. Correct as required.

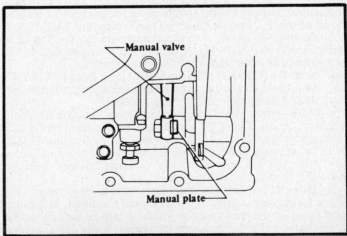

Aligning manual valve and manual plate
(© Nissan Motor Co. of USA)

THROTTLE CONTROL CABLE

Removal

1. Remove the control valve assembly as previously outlined.
2. Disconnect the throttle cable from the carburetor throttle lever and from the cable bracket.
3. Disconnect the transaxle end from the throttle lever in the case. Remove the cable assembly from the case.

Installation

1. Install the cable in the reverse of its removal procedure.
2. Bend the locking plate within the case, after tightening the lock nut.
3. Adjust the cable as outlined in the adjustment section.

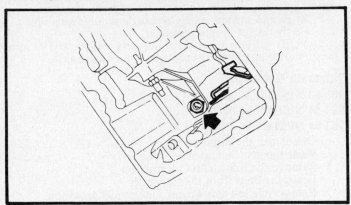

Location of bendable lockwasher on the throttle cable within the case (© Nissan Motor Co. of USA)

GOVERNOR ASSEMBLY

Removal

1. Disconnect the battery cables.
2. Remove the radiator reserve tank and remove the battery along with its support bracket.
3. Remove the snap retainer, governor cap with breather hose and the seal ring.
4. Remove the governor shaft retaining bolt.
5. Remove the governor shaft assembly from the transaxle.
6. The governor can now be replaced or repaired, as required.

Installation

1. Install the governor shaft assembly into the transaxle case. Secure with the retaining bolts.
2. Install the O-ring, the governor cap with the breather hose and secure it with the snap.

NOTE: Install the cap in the same direction as was removed.

3. Install the battery support, the battery, the radiator reserve tank and connect the battery cables.

NEUTRAL START (INHIBITOR) SWITCH

Removal

1. Remove the lower panel.
2. Remove the control cable from the transaxle manual lever.
3. Disconnect the electrical harness from the switch and remove the retaining screws.
4. Remove the switch.

Installation

1. Install the switch into position and install the retaining screws. Adjust the switch as described in the Adjustment section.
2. Tighten the screws to 1.4-1.8 ft. lbs. (2-2.5 N•m).
3. Install the wiring connector and the manual lever cable.
4. Test the switch for proper operation and movement.

DRIVE AXLE OIL SEALS

The left and right transaxle drive shaft oil seals can be replaced with the drive shafts removed from the unit. Special seal pulling tools are used to remove the seals while special installation tools are used to install the seals into the case components.

NOTE: Do not scratch the seal surface during the axle installation.

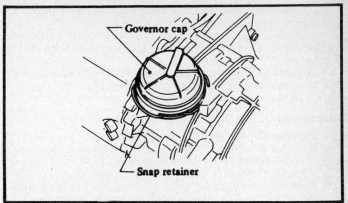

Governor snap retainer location. Note the position of the cap direction before removal (© Nissan Motor Co. of USA)

REMOVAL & INSTALLATION

TRANSAXLE ASSEMBLY

The transaxle assembly can be removed from the vehicle separately, except for the 1982 310 models, from which the engine and transaxle must be removed as a unit. When removing or installing the transaxle assembly, extreme care must be exercised to prevent damage to the unit or personal injury.

Removal

1982 310 MODELS

1. Remove the hood, after marking its location on the hinges.
2. Remove the battery and support bracket.
3. Remove the air cleaner assembly and plug the carburetor air horn to prevent entrance of unwanted material.
4. Drain the cooling system, remove the radiator and cooling fan.
5. If equipped, remove the power steering oil pump. Do not disconnect the lines, but lay aside safely.
6. Without disconnecting the air conditioning lines, remove the compressor and support within the engine compartment to prevent its dropping.
7. Disconnect the exhaust front pipe from the exhaust manifold.
8. Disconnect the selector lever control cable at the transaxle.
9. Remove the speedometer cable with the driven gear attached. Plug the hole to prevent entrance of unwanted material.
10. Disconnect the throttle control cable from the carburetor.
11. Remove the vacuum and electrical wiring/hoses from the engine. Mark each wire and hose to prevent mix-up during assembly.
12. Disconnect the fuel hose from the fuel pump assembly.
13. Disconnect the right and left drive shafts from the transaxle in the following manner:
   a. Raise the vehicle and support safely.
   b. Remove the wheel assembly.
   c. Remove the retaining bolts holding the lower ball joint to the transverse link (lower control arm).
   d. Drain the fluid from the transaxle.
   e. Disconnect the tie rod end from each side of the steering linkage.
   f. Pulling outward on the wheel assembly while holding the drive shaft, remove the shaft from the transaxle.

g. Install a suitable bar into the transaxle to hold the differential side gears from falling out of position.

14. Attach lifting eyes to the rear of the engine and to the front of the cylinder head. Attach a lifting chain or equivalent to the lifting eyes.

15. Disconnect the engine and transaxle mounts from the right side, the front and the rear side of the assembly.

16. Lift the engine/transaxle assembly from the vehicle.

Separation of the Engine/transaxle assembly

1. Remove the converter housing dust cover.
2. Remove the bolts retaining the drive plate to the torque converter. Mark converter to drive plate position.
3. Remove the starter motor from the assembly.
4. Remove the attaching bolts, securing the transaxle to the engine. Lift the transaxle away from the engine assembly.

Assembly of Transaxle to the Engine

1. Measure the drive plate runout with a dial indicator. Runout should not exceed 0.020 in. (0.5mm).
2. Measure the distance from the edge of the converter housing to the attaching lug face on the converter. The distance should not be less than 0.831 in. (21.1mm).
3. When joining the converter to the drive plate, align the previously made marks if the same parts are used.
4. After the converter is installed and tightened, rotate the engine crankshaft several times to be sure the converter/transaxle is free to rotate without binding.

Engine/Transaxle Installation

1. The installation of the engine/transaxle assembly is in the reverse order of its removal.
2. The following installation notes should be observed:
   a. When installing the assembly, ensure that brake tubes, master cylinder, etc., do not interfere with the installation.
   b. Align and tighten engine/transaxle mounts securely.
   c. Verify rubber mount clearance.
   d. Verify selector lever, neutral safety switch, starter and throttle cable operate properly before moving vehicle.

Transaxle Removal
1983-84 NISSAN STANZA
1982-84 NISSAN SENTRA
1983-84 NISSAN PULSAR, NX

1. Disconnect the negative battery cable.
2. Raise the vehicle and support safely.
3. Remove the front wheel assemblies.
4. Drain the fluid from the transaxle.
5. Remove the left side fender inner panel protector.
6. Disconnect the drive axles in the following manner:
   a. Remove the brake caliper assembly from each side and hang from the body with wire.
   b. Remove the steering tie rod end stud from the steering arm on each side.
   c. Remove the retaining bolts from the lower ball joints to lower control arms on each side.

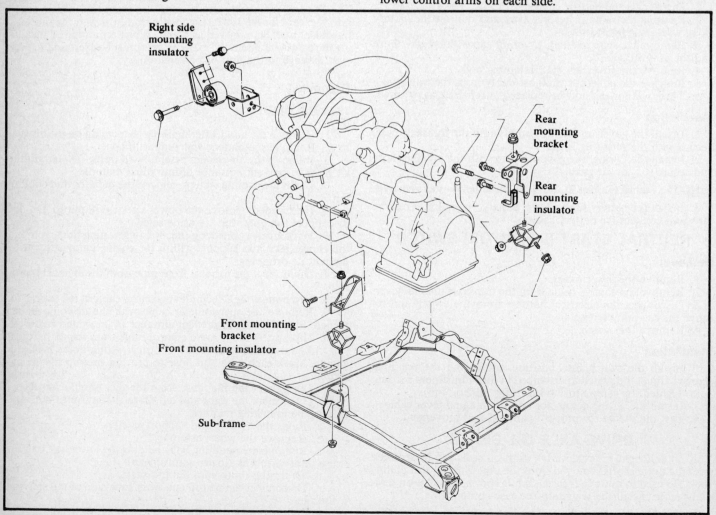

Engine/transaxle mount locations—1982 310 models (© Nissan Motor Co. of USA)

NOTE: Use new nuts upon installation.

   d. Pulling outward on the wheel assemblies while holding the drive shafts, remove the shafts from the transaxle.

NOTE: It may be necessary to pry the axle from the transaxle, along with the outward pressure applied to the wheel assemblies.

   e. With the drive shafts out of the transaxle, discard the circlips and install new ones before axle installation.

   7. Remove the speedometer cable.

   8. Disconnect the throttle control cable at the carburetor.

   9. Remove the selector cable from the transaxle control lever.

   10. Remove the dipstick tube assembly.

   11. Support the transaxle with a transmission type jack unit.

— **CAUTION** —

Do not place the support tool under the oil pan drain plug.

   12. Disconnect the oil cooler lines at the hose ends.

   13. Matchmark the torque converter to the drive plate and remove the retaining bolts from the drive plate to converter.

   14. Remove the engine mount securing bolts.

   15. Remove the starter assembly.

   16. Remove the engine to transaxle retaining bolts.

   17. Gradually move the support tool to loosen the transaxle from the engine, lower sufficiently and remove the transaxle through the vehicle's wheel opening on the left side.

Installation

   1. The installation of the transaxle is in the reverse order of removal. The following installation notes must be adhered to:

   a. Measure the drive plate runout with a dial indicator. The runout should not exceed 0.020 in. (0.5mm).

   b. Measure the distance from the edge of the converter housing to the attaching lug face on the converter. The distance should not be less than 0.831 in. (21.1mm).

   c. When joining the converter to the drive plate, align the previously made marks, if the same parts are used.

   d. After the converter has been bolted to the drive plate, rotate the engine crankshaft several times to be sure the converter/transaxle is free to rotate without binding.

   e. Upon assembly of the lower ball joints to the control arms, new nuts must be used to assure proper bolt torque retention.

   f. Be sure of selector lever, neutral safety switch, starter and throttle cable operation before moving vehicle.

BENCH OVERHAUL

Before Disassembly

With the openings on the transaxle plugged to prevent contamination, clean the outside of the unit thoroughly. If a steam cleaning unit is used for cleaning, the transaxle must be disassembled as soon as possible to avoid internal rusting of components.

   Disassembly must be done in a clean work area and the use of nylon cloth or paper towels to wipe parts, is recommended.

Disassembly

   1. Remove the converter assembly from the transaxle.

   2. If the transaxle has not been drained, remove the oil pan plug and drain the unit. Re-install the plug into the oil pan when drained.

   3. Remove the oil pump shaft and the input shaft.

   4. Remove the snap retainer, governor cap with breather hose and the O-ring.

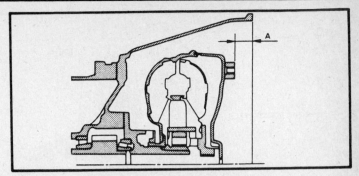

Positioning of converter within the converter housing
(© Nissan Motor Co. of USA)

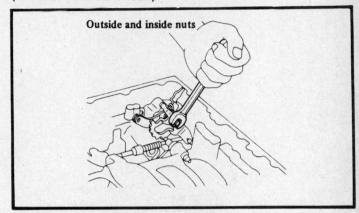

Removing the manual shaft securing nuts
(© Nissan Motor Co. of USA)

Outside and inside nuts

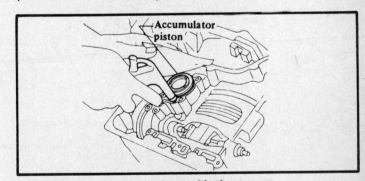

Accumulator piston

Removing the accumulator piston with air pressure
(© Nissan Motor Co. of USA)

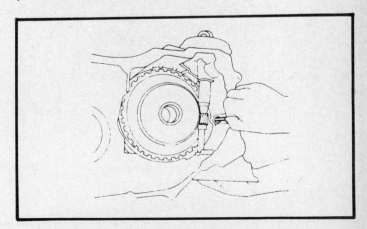

Removing parking pawl shaft (© Nissan Motor Co. of USA)

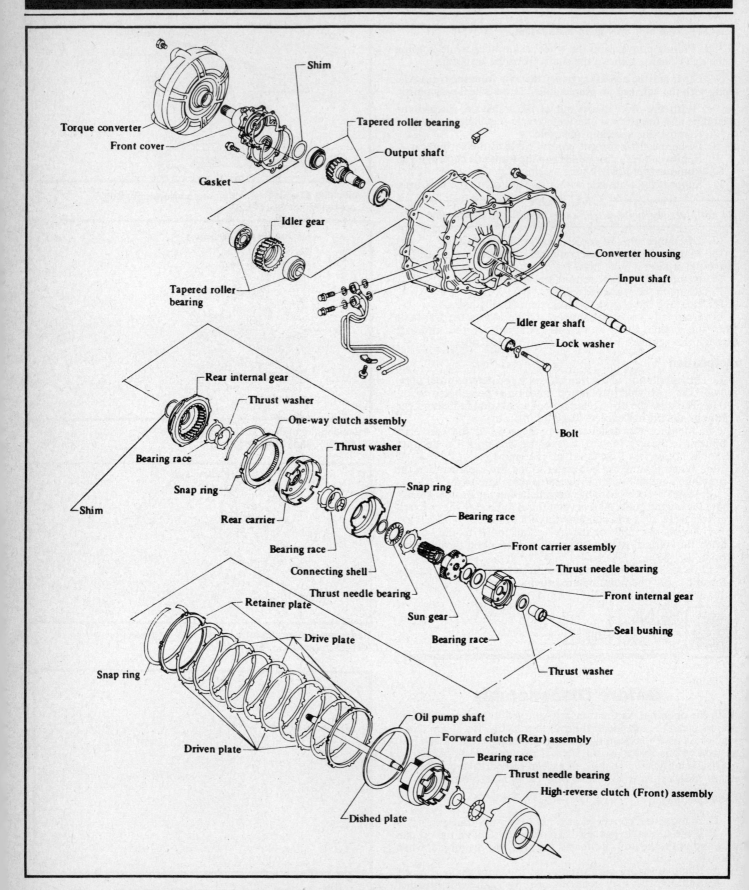

Exploded view of the forward section of the transaxle assembly (© Nissan Motor Co. of USA)

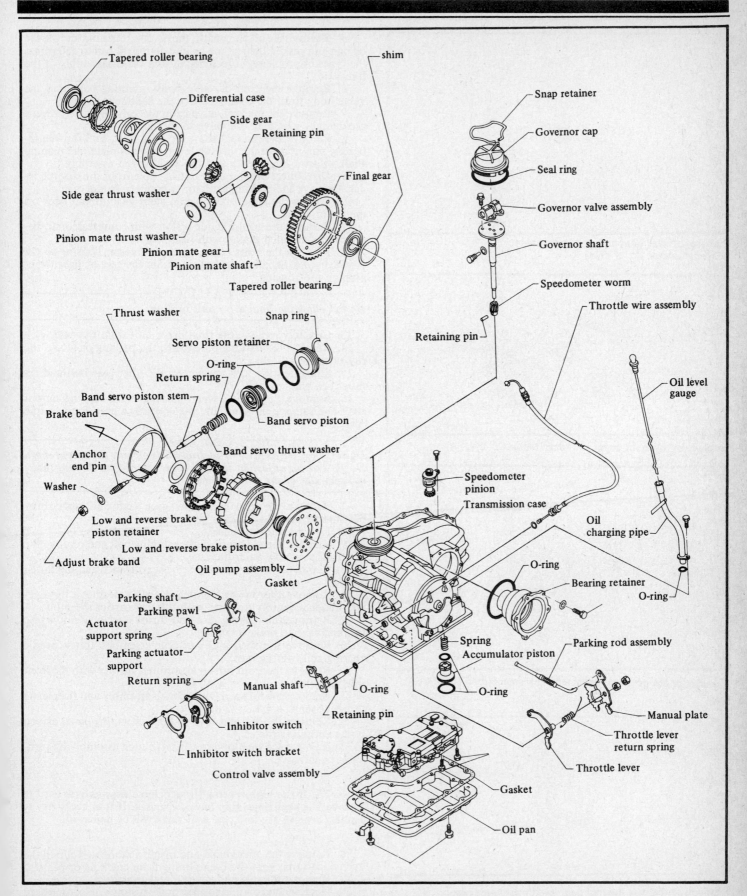

Exploded view of the rear section of the transaxle assembly (© Nissan Motor Co. of USA)

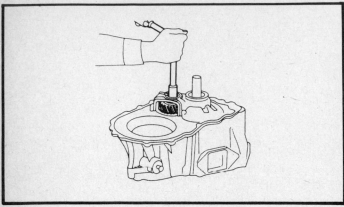

Removal of idler gear bolt and lockwasher
(© Nissan Motor Co. of USA)

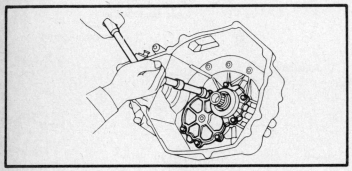

Removal of the front cover (© Nissan Motor Co. of USA)

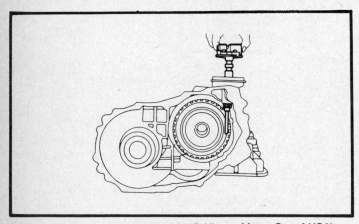

Removal of the governor assembly (© Nissan Motor Co. of USA)

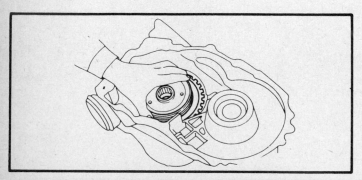

Removal of the rear internal gear and thrust components
(© Nissan Motor Co. of USA)

5. Remove the oil pan guard, the oil pan retaining screws, the oil pan and gasket. Inspect the residue in the oil pan to determine the types of problems to look for during the disassembly of the transaxle.

6. Remove the control valve body retaining bolts and the valve body from the case. Remove the sediment magnet.

7. Remove the manual valve from the valve body to prevent accidentally dropping the valve to the floor.

8. Remove the manual shaft securing nuts. Pull out the retaining pin, remove the throttle lever, manual plate, the manual shaft, selector range lever and the parking rod assembly.

9. Disconnect the throttle control cable from the throttle lever. Remove the parking actuator support from the case.

10. Loosen the band brake piston stem locknut and back off the piston stem.

11. Remove the accumulator piston with compressed air, being careful to catch piston with shop rag.

12. Remove the bolts retaining the converter housing to the transaxle case. Separate the housing from the case by lightly tapping on the housing.

— CAUTION —

Do not allow the final drive unit to drop.

13. Carefully remove the final drive unit from the case.

14. Remove the parking pawl shaft, the parking pawl and the return spring.

15. Straighten the lock washer on the idler gear bolt and remove the bolt.

16. Remove the front cover retaining bolts, tap the output shaft and remove the shaft and the cover as a unit. Remove the gasket.

— CAUTION —

Do not allow the front cover to drop while tapping the output shaft. Do not lose the adjusting shim which is attached to the rear internal gear side of the output shaft.

17. Remove the idler gear, idler gear shaft and taper roller bearings by tapping the idler gear shaft.

18. Remove the seal bushing.

19. Remove the governor shaft retaining bolt and remove the governor assembly from the case.

20. Remove the rear internal gear, bearing race and the thrust washer.

21. Remove the one-way clutch snapring. Remove the one-way clutch assembly together with the rear carrier assembly.

22. Remove the bearing race and thrust washer. Remove the low and reverse brake snapring.

23. Remove the shell and sun gear assembly, thrust needle bearing and bearing race.

24. Remove the front carrier assembly, together with the front internal gear.

25. Remove the forward (rear) clutch assembly and the plastic thrust washer.

26. Remove the low and reverse brake retaining plate, driven plates and drive plates.

27. Remove the high-reverse (front) clutch assembly by turning it in the case.

NOTE: If the high-reverse (front) clutch assembly is hard to remove, the seal rings may have expanded. If it is necessary to forcibly remove the unit, the seal rings will be damaged.

28. Remove the brake band and install a fabricated clip in the open ends to prevent the brake lining from cracking or peeling.

29. Remove the low and reverse brake retainer.

30. Remove the low and reverse brake piston with compressed air while holding a shop cloth to catch the piston.

31. Remove the oil pump assembly, the thrust washer and thrust needle bearing by lifting the assembly straight out of the case.

32. Remove the neutral safety switch and the band servo piston and return spring.

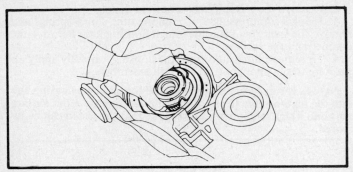

Removal of the one-way clutch assembly
(© Nissan Motor Co. of USA)

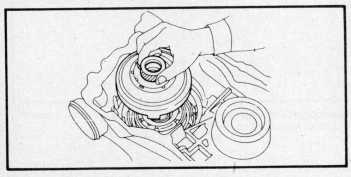

Removal of the shell and sungear assembly
(© Nissan Motor Co. of USA)

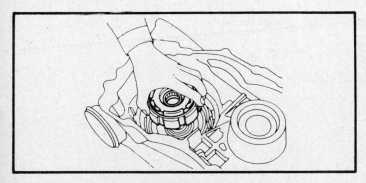

Removal of the front carrier and front internal gear
(© Nissan Motor Co. of USA)

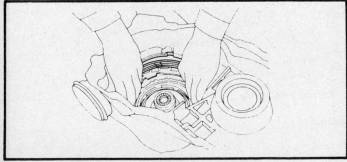

Removal of the low and reverse brake assembly
(© Nissan Motor Co. of USA)

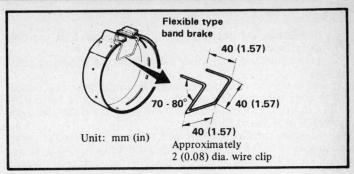

Flexible type band brake

40 (1.57)

70 - 80° 40 (1.57)

40 (1.57)

Unit: mm (in)

Approximately 2 (0.08) dia. wire clip

Installation of the fabricated band holding clip
(© Nissan Motor Co. of USA)

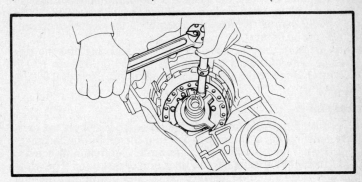

Removal of the low and reverse brake retainer
(© Nissan Motor Co. of USA)

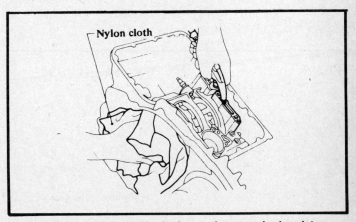

Nylon cloth

Using air pressure to remove the low and reverse brake piston
(© Nissan Motor Co. of USA)

Disassembly, Inspection and Assembly of Internal Components
OIL PUMP

Disassembly

1. Remove the oil pump plate retaining screws and remove the plate.

2. Remove the oil pump gear hub, the pressure relief spring and the steel ball from the housing.

3. Remove the driven and drive gears from the oil pump housing.

Inspection

1. Inspect the oil pump body, oil pump shaft and the ring grooves for wear.

2. Inspect the gears and internal surfaces for wear and damages.

3. Measure the clearance between the outer gear and the oil pump body crescent. The standard clearance should be 0.0079-0.0118 in. (0.20-0.30mm). Replace the assembly if the clearance exceeds 0.0138 in. (0.35mm).

4. Measure the clearance between the outer gear and the pump housing. The standard clearance should be 0.0079-0.0118 in. (0.20-0.30mm). Replace the assembly if the clearance exceeds 0.0138 in. (0.35mm).

5. Using a feeler gauge blade and a straightedge tool, measure the clearance between the gears and the pump body surface for the pump plate. The standard clearance should be 0.0008-0.0016 in. (0.02-0.04mm). Replace the assembly if the clearance exceeds 0.0031 in. (0.08mm).

6. Measure the clearance between the seal ring and the ring groove. The standard clearance is 0.0039-0.0098 in. (0.10-0.25mm). Replace the assembly if the clearance exceeds 0.098 in. (0.25mm).

Assembly

1. Install the oil pump gears, the oil pump gear hub, the pressure relief spring and the steel ball into the oil pump housing.

2. Install the oil pump plate and install the retaining screws.

3. Install the sealing rings in their proper positions. The white marked rings are to be installed on the top position of the hub while the rings with no marks are to be installed on the lower part of the hub.

HIGH-REVERSE (FRONT) CLUTCH

Disassembly

1. Remove the large retaining snapring and the retainer plate from the clutch drum.

2. Remove the clutch plates from the drum.

3. Using a compressing tool, compress the clutch springs and remove the snap ring from the clutch housing hub. Remove the retainer and the springs.

4. To remove the piston from the housing, carefully apply air pressure to the apply port in the hub assembly.

NOTE: It may be necessary to install the oil pump housing hub into the high-reverse (front) drum in order to have a flat surface port into which to apply air pressure so that the piston can be removed.

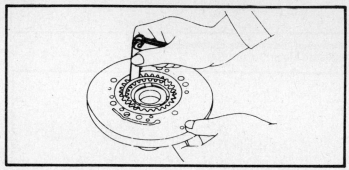

Measuring the clearance between the outer gear and the cresent (© Nissan Motor Co. of USA)

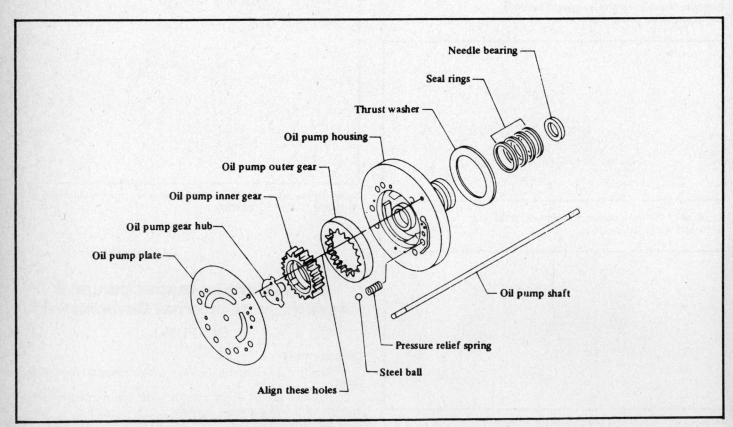

Exploded view of the oil pump assembly (© Nissan Motor Co. of USA)

Inspection

1. Inspect the clutch plates for wear or damage. The standard plate thickness for the drive plate is 0.0591-0.0650 in. (1.50-1.65mm). The plate thickness must not be less than 0.055 in. (1.4mm).

NOTE: It is good practice to install both the drive and driven clutch plates during the rebuilding process.

2. Inspect the snap rings and springs for being broken, weak or twisted. Inspect the spring retainer for being warped.
3. Check the clutch housing for damage, wear or broken areas.
4. Check the piston for damage, wear or broken seal ring grooves. If equipped with a ball check, be sure ball seats properly and is free in its bore.

Assembly

1. Install the piston lip seal and the clutch housing hub seal. Lubricate each seal with transmission fluid.

2. Install the piston into the clutch drum carefully, to avoid damaging the seals. Rotate the piston after it has been seated to be sure no binding exists.

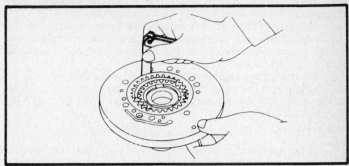

Measuring the clearance between the outer gear and the pump housing (© Nissan Motor Co. of USA)

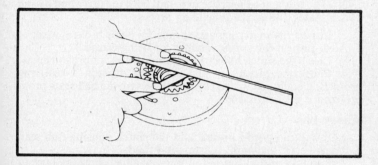

Measuring the clearance between the gears and the pump body plate (© Nissan Motor Co. of USA)

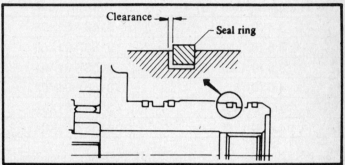

Measuring the clearance between the seal ring and the pump body hub grooves (© Nissan Motor Co. of USA)

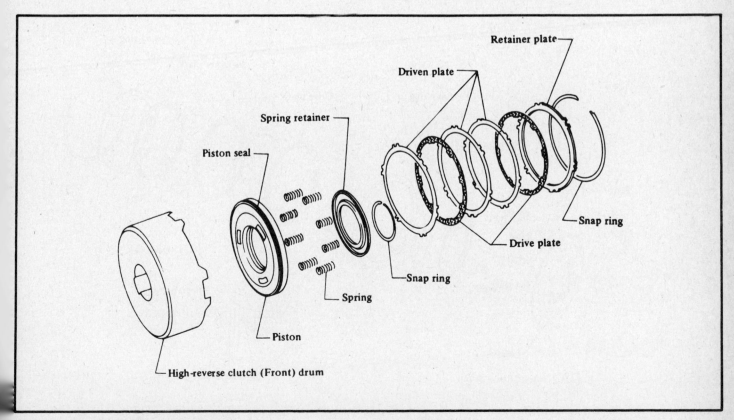

Exploded view of the high-reverse (front) clutch assembly (© Nissan Motor Co. of USA)

3. Install the springs, retainer and with the spring compressing tool installed, compress the springs and install the snap ring into its groove. Be sure the ring is properly seated.

4. Soak the drive (lined) plates in A/T fluid for approximately 15 minutes before installation into the clutch drum.

5. Install the drive (lined) and driven (steel) plates into the clutch drum, starting with one driven plate, one drive plate, two driven plates, one drive plate, the retainer plate and install the snap ring into its groove.

6. Measure the existing minimum clearance between the retainer plate and the snap ring. The standard clearance is 0.039-0.055 in. (1.0-1.4mm) with an allowable limit of 0.087 in. (2.2mm).

NOTE: The retaining snap ring is of the wave type.

7. If the specified measurement cannot be obtained, another retaining plate will have to be installed of the correct thickness. Retainer plates are available in the following thicknesses.

Thickness mm (in)	Part number
3.4 (0.134)	31537-01X05
3.6 (0.142)	31537-01X00
3.8 (0.150)	31537-01X01
4.0 (0.157)	31537-01X02
4.2 (0.165)	31537-01X03
4.4 (0.173)	31537-01X04

8. With the high-reverse (front) clutch assembly mounted on the oil pump housing, apply a jet of compressed air into the apply hole in the pump body to operate the clutch assembly.

FORWARD (REAR) CLUTCH

Disassembly

1. Remove the large retaining snap ring and the retainer plate from the clutch drum.

2. Remove the clutch pack assembly from the drum.

3. With the use of a compressing tool, remove the snap ring from the clutch drum hub, after compressing the springs.

4. Remove the retainer and springs.

5. The piston can be removed from the clutch drum with the use of air pressure, if required.

6. Discard the piston seals.

Inspection

1. Inspect the clutch plates for wear or damage. The standard plate thickness for the drive plate is 0.0591-0.0650 in. (1.50-1.65mm). The plate thickness must not be less than 0.055 in. (1.4mm).

NOTE: It is a good practice to install both the drive and driven clutch plates during the rebuilding process.

2. Inspect the snap rings and springs for being broken, weak or twisted. Inspect the spring retainer for being warped.

3. Check the clutch housing for damage, wear or broken areas.

4. Check the piston for damage, wear or broken seal ring grooves. If equipped with a check ball, be sure the ball seats properly and is free in its bore.

Assembly

1. Install the piston lip seal and the clutch housing hub seal. Lubricate each seal with transmission fluid.

2. Carefully install the piston into the clutch housing bore to avoid damaging the seals. Rotate the piston after it has been seated to be sure no binding exists.

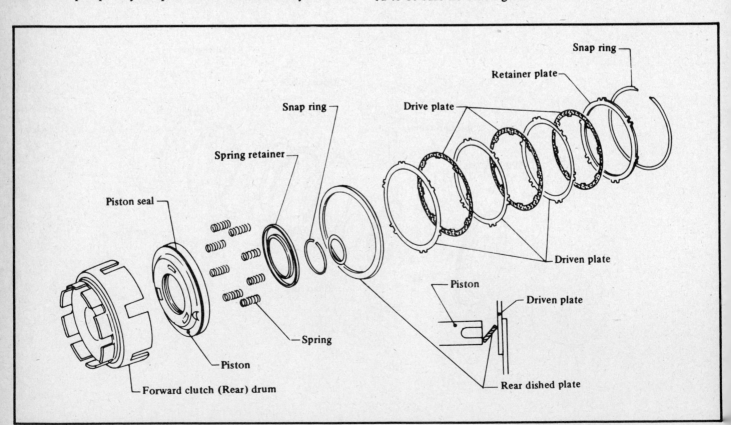

Exploded view of the forward (rear) clutch assembly (© Nissan Motor Co. of USA)

JATCO RN3F01A · RL3F01A SECTION 4

3. Install the springs and retainer. With the spring compressor tool installed, compress the springs and install the snap ring into its groove. Be sure the ring is properly seated.

4. Soak the lined drive plates in A/T fluid for approximately 15 minutes before installing into the clutch drum.

5. Install the drive (lined) plates and the driven (steel) plates into the clutch drum, starting with one driven plate, one drive plate, alternating with the remaining plates until a total of three driven (steel) and three drive (lined) plates have been installed. Position the retaining plate next to the last drive plate and install the snap ring. Be sure the ring is fully seated in its groove.

6. Measure the existing minimum clearance between the retainer plate and the snap ring. The standard clearance is 0.020-0.031 in. (0.5-0.8mm). The allowable limit is 0.094 in. (2.4mm).

NOTE: The retaining snap ring is of the wave type.

7. If the specified measurement cannot be obtained, another retaining plate will have to be used. Retainer plates are available in the following thicknesses:

Thickness mm (in)	Part Number
3.4 (0.134)	31537-01X05
3.6 (0.142)	31537-01X00
3.8 (0.150)	31537-01X01
4.0 (0.157)	31537-01X02
4.2 (0.165)	31537-01X03
4.4 (0.173)	31537-01X04

8. With the forward (rear) clutch mounted on the oil pump housing hub, apply a jet of compressed air into the apply hole for the forward (rear) clutch, testing its operation.

LOW AND REVERSE BRAKE ASSEMBLY

Disassembly

1. The low and reverse brake assembly is disassembled during the removal of the internal components of the transaxle.

Inspection

1. Inspect the low and reverse brake for damaged clutch drive plate facings and worn snap ring. Replace the components as required.

2. Test the piston return spring for weakness or being broken.

3. The drive plate thickness should be between 0.0748-0.0807 in. (1.90-2.05mm). The allowable limit is 0.071 in. (1.8mm).

NOTE: It is a good practice to replace the driving plates during the rebuilding process.

Assembly

1. The assembly of the low and reverse brake assembly will be outlined during the assembly of the transaxle.

BRAKE BAND

Disassembly and Assembly

1. The brake band is removed and replaced during the disassembly and assembly of the transaxle.

Inspection

1. Inspect the band friction material for wear, cracks, chips or burned spots. Replace as required.

2. Inspect the band strut and the band apply pin for damage or wear. Replace as required.

CONTROL VALVE ASSEMBLY

Disassembly

1. Remove the oil filter and magnet.

2. Disassemble the valve body and its remaining attaching bolts and nuts. Carefully separate the lower body, separator plate and upper body.

3. During the separation, do not lose the six steel balls on the valve body upper section.

4. Using a stiff piece of wire, remove the parallel pins form the valve body bores. Remove the plugs, 3rd-2nd downshift valves, 2nd-3rd shift valve, 1st-2nd shift valve, 1st-2nd control valve and the respective springs.

NOTE: Place each internal component on a rack to retain the correct sequence of assembly.

5. Remove the parallel pins with wire, remove the plugs, fail-safe valve, throttle valve, detent valve, throttle valve modulator valve with the spring guide, pressure modifier valve, 1st reducing valve, top reducing valve, 3rd-2nd timing valve and the respective springs.

6. Remove the back-up valve retaining plate by pressing its spring with a small probe. Remove the parallel pin, the plug, pressure regulator valve and its spring.

NOTE: Place each internal component on a rack to retain the correct sequence of assembly.

Inspection

1. If the inspection reveals excessive clearance between the valves and the bores in the valve body of over 0.0012 in. (0.03mm), replace the entire valve body rather than attempt a rework of the unit.

2. Clean the valves with alcohol or lacquer thinner. Clean the valve body with carburetor cleaner or lacquer thinner.

—————————— CAUTION ——————————
Do not allow the parts to be submerged longer than five to ten minutes. Rinse thoroughly and dry.

3. Check the valves for signs of burning. Clean with crocus cloth, but do not remove the sharp edges of the valve lands.

4. Check the separator plate for scratches or damage.

5. Check the bolt holes for damage or stripped threads.

6. Check the springs for distortion or being broken. Refer to the spring chart for specifications.

7. Check the worm tracks in the valve bodies for damage or sides broken, which would allow fluid pressure to cross into another channel.

Assembly

1. Assemble all the internal components in the reverse order of their removal.

2. Install the six steel balls in the upper valve body as illustrated.

3. Assemble the separator plate and lower valve body on to the upper valve body. Install the bolts and tighten as follows.

   a. Lower valve body to upper valve body securing bolts. 5.1-6.5 ft. lbs. (7-9 N•m).

   b. Accumulator support plate securing bolt, 2.5-3.3 ft. lbs. (3.4-4.4 N•m).

4. Install the oil filter and magnet. Tighten the filter bolts to 1.8-2.5 ft. lbs. (2.5-3.4 N•m).

NOTE: The manual valve is installed into the valve body during the valve body installation onto the transaxle case.

1051

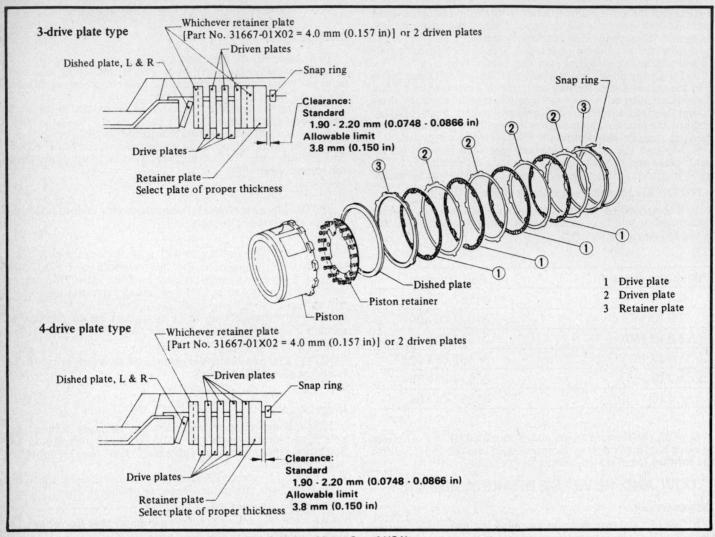

3-drive plate type

Whichever retainer plate
[Part No. 31667-01X02 = 4.0 mm (0.157 in)] or 2 driven plates

Driven plates

Dished plate, L & R

Snap ring

Snap ring

Clearance:
Standard
1.90 - 2.20 mm (0.0748 - 0.0866 in)
Allowable limit
3.8 mm (0.150 in)

Drive plates

Retainer plate
Select plate of proper thickness

Dished plate

Piston retainer

Piston

1 Drive plate
2 Driven plate
3 Retainer plate

4-drive plate type

Whichever retainer plate
[Part No. 31667-01X02 = 4.0 mm (0.157 in)] or 2 driven plates

Driven plates

Dished plate, L & R

Snap ring

Drive plates

Retainer plate
Select plate of proper thickness

Clearance:
Standard
1.90 - 2.20 mm (0.0748 - 0.0866 in)
Allowable limit
3.8 mm (0.150 in)

Exploded view of low and reverse brake assembly (© Nissan Motor Co. of USA)

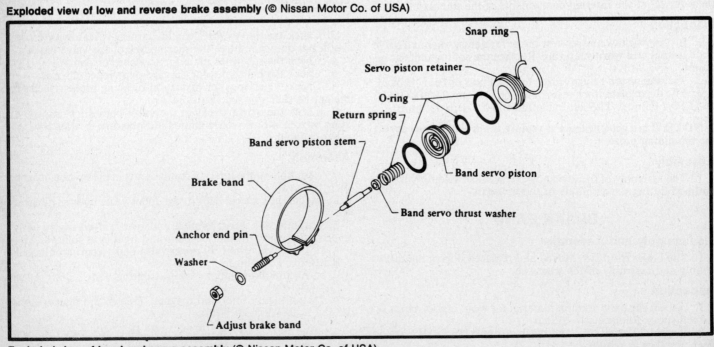

Snap ring

Servo piston retainer

O-ring

Return spring

Band servo piston stem

Brake band

Band servo piston

Band servo thrust washer

Anchor end pin

Washer

Adjust brake band

Exploded view of band and servo assembly (© Nissan Motor Co. of USA)

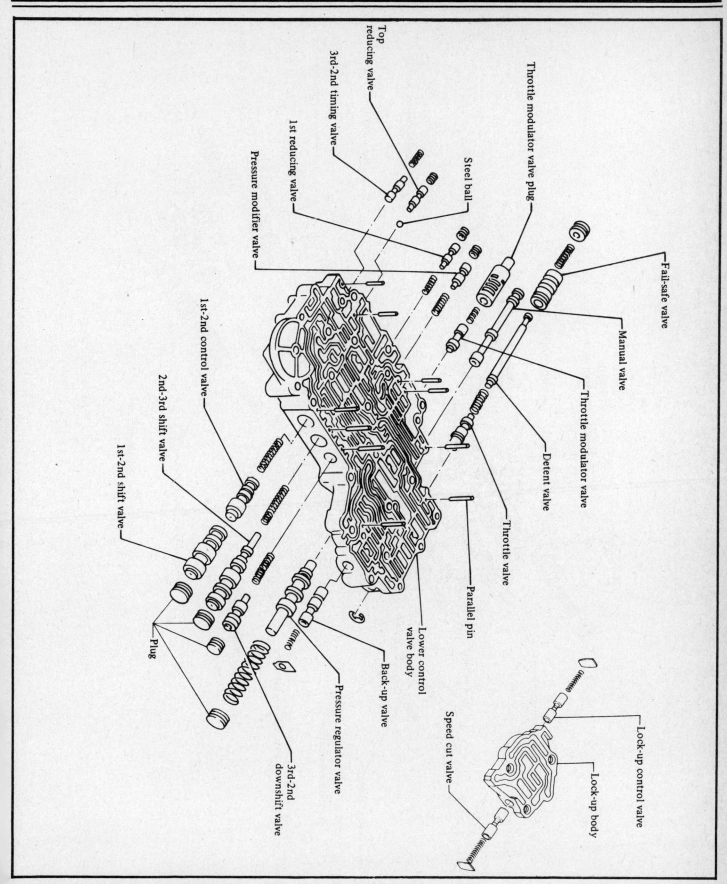

Exploded view of control valve assembly with lock-up controls (© Nissan Motor Co. of USA)

Labels (top to bottom, left group):
- Top reducing valve
- 3rd-2nd timing valve
- 1st reducing valve
- Pressure modifier valve
- Steel ball
- Throttle modulator valve plug
- Fail-safe valve
- Manual valve
- Throttle modulator valve
- Detent valve
- Throttle valve
- Parallel pin
- Lower control valve body
- Speed cut valve
- Back-up valve
- Pressure regulator valve
- 3rd-2nd downshift valve
- 1st-2nd shift valve
- 2nd-3rd shift valve
- 1st-2nd control valve
- Plug
- Lock-up control valve
- Lock-up body

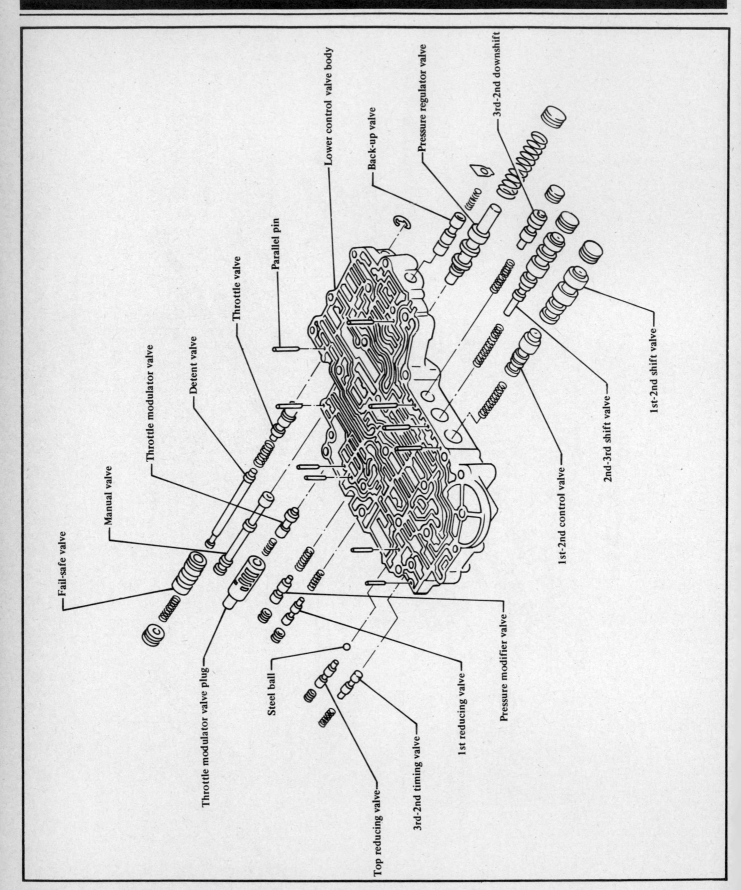

Exploded view of control valve assembly without lock-up controls (© Nissan Motor Co. of USA)

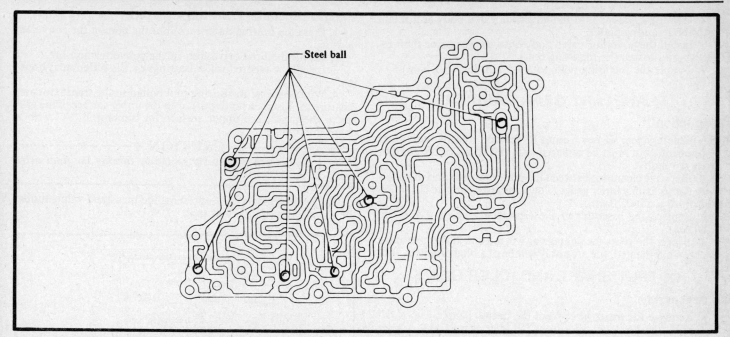

Location of check balls in the valve body, with or without lock-up controls (© Nissan Motor Co. of USA)

FINE ADJUSTING SCREW

A fine adjusting screw is located on the end of the throttle modulator sleeve and provides a maximum fine adjustment of approximately 3 mph. Tightening of the screw causes the shift point to occur at a lower point (mph) and if loosened, would allow the shift point to occur at a higher point (mph), except when in the kickdown mode.

The standard position of the adjusting screw between the top of the screw and the top of the locknut is 0.492-0.512 in. (12.5-13.0mm). The locknut is secured with a torque of 2.5-3.3 ft. lbs. (3.4-4.4 N•m).

BAND SERVE PISTON

Disassembly

1. The O-rings can be removed from the servo piston and the piston separated from the piston retainer.

Inspection

1. Inspect the piston assembly and case bore for wear and/or scoring. If damages are present on the piston assembly, replace the unit. Inspect the return spring.
2. If the case bore is scored to the extent of being nonusable, the case would have to be replaced.

Assembly

1. Assemble the piston to the piston retainer.
2. Lubricate and install the O-rings on the piston.

GOVERNOR

Disassemble

1. Remove the governor body from the governor shaft by removing the four retaining bolts.
2. Disassemble the governor valve body by removing the governor retaining plates. Matchmark valve positions.
3. If the governor gear is to be removed from the shaft, the roll pin must be driven from the gear/shaft assembly.

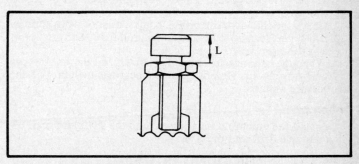

Standard position (L) of fine adjusting screw on valve body (© Nissan Motor Co. of USA)

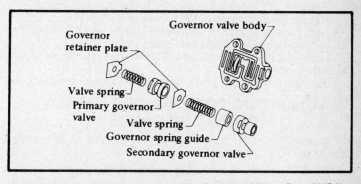

Exploded view of governor assembly (© Nissan Motor Co. of USA)

Inspection

1. Check the valves for indications of burning or scratches. Inspect the springs for weakness or burning.
2. Replace the parts as required or if necessary, replace the complete governor assembly.

Assembly

1. Install the governor gear on the shaft and align the roll pin holes. Install the roll pin.

2. Install the valves into the governor valve body and retain with the retaining plates.

3. Install the governor valve body onto the governor shaft assembly and install the retaining bolts.

4. Torque the retaining bolts to 3.6-5.1 ft. lbs. (5-7 N•m).

PLANETARY GEAR CARRIERS

Inspection

The planetary gear carrier cannot be divided into its individual components, but must be replaced as a unit if any of the components are faulty.

1. Check the clearance between the pinion washer and the planetary carrier with a feeler gauge. The standard clearance is 0.0079-0.0276 in. (0.20-0.70mm).

2. Replace the assembly if the clearance exceeds 0.0315 in. (0.80mm).

3. Inspect the gears for damage or worn teeth. If the gear train has been overheated, the assembly will be of a blue discoloration.

OUTPUT SHAFT AND IDLER GEAR

Disassembly

1. Remove the inner races from the output shaft.
2. Remove the outer races from the idler gear.

Inspection

1. Inspect all gears for excessive wear, chips, cracks or breakage.

2. Check the shafts for distortion, cracks, wear or worn splines.

3. Check the bearing to be sure all will roll freely and are free of cracks, pitting or wear.

4. When the bearings are cleaned in solvent, air dry or blow dry with compressed air. Do not allow the bearings to spin with the air pressure applied.

Assembly

1. Install the outer and inner races onto the shaft and gear, using a suitable drift and press.

BEARING HOUSING

Disassembly and Assembly

1. Remove the bearing housing from the transaxle case.
2. Remove the inner race, the oil seal and "O" ring.
3. Apply a coat of gear oil to the seal surface and "O" ring. Install the new seal and O-ring into place.
4. Install the inner race and install the bearing housing onto the transaxle case.
5. Tighten the bolts to 14-18 ft. lbs. (19-25 N•m) torque.

ADJUSTING PRELOAD OF TAPERED ROLLER BEARINGS

Before assembly of the transaxle unit, the tapered roller bearing preload must be adjusted.

NOTE: Tapered roller bearing preload is the same as rotary frictional force adjustment.

If the transaxle case, bearing housing, tapered roller bearings, differential case or converter housing is replaced, the final drive unit must be adjusted. This adjustment is accomplished with the use of selected shims of varied thickness.

Adjusting Procedure

Two types of adjusting procedures have been established by the manufacturer. It is the decision of the repair-person as to which procedure to follow.

TYPE ONE ADJUSTING PROCEDURE

1. Press the bearing outer race into the bore of the converter housing.

2. Install the final drive unit in the converter housing.

3. Install the tapered roller bearings on the differential housing.

4. With a special measuring tool bolted to the transaxle case, measure the distance (or depth) from the upper surface of the gasket to the inner race upper surface for dimension "A" with a depth micrometer.

─── CAUTION ───

Be sure the bearing is properly seated by turning the final drive gear.

5. The dimension "A" represents the measured value, minus the thickness of the special tool.

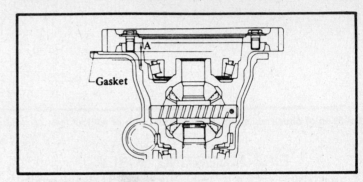

Dimension "A" measurement (© Nissan Motor Co. of USA)

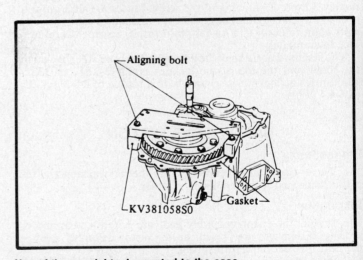

Use of the special tool mounted to the case
(© Nissan Motor Co. of USA)

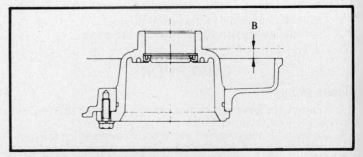

Measurement location to find dimension "B"
(© Nissan Motor Co. of USA)

6. Install the housing to the transaxle case.

7. Ensure the bearing is properly seated by turning the outer race while pushing on it.

8. The distance between the bearing seal on the bearing housing and the top surface of the transaxle case is considered dimension "B". The special tool is used to span the transaxle case surface and when used as a measuring tool, dimension "B" = thickness of the special tool, minus (-) the measured value.

9. Height "H" is the selective shim thickness needed to provide the proper preload. "H" is found by the following equation. H = A-B. The correct shim is selected from the charts in the specification section.

10. Remove the bearing retainer from the case and install the selected shim on the bearing housing. Seat the bearing assembly on the housing.

11. Lubricate the O-ring with vaseline and install it on the bearing housing.

12. Install the bearing housing to the transaxle case assembly.

13. Attach the converter housing gasket to the case. Install the retaining bolts and torque 10-13 ft. lbs. (14-18 N•m).

14. Turn the final drive assembly at least ten times and using a torque wrench, measure the preload (rotary frictional force) of the final drive tapered roller bearings. The torque should be 52-65 *inch* lbs. (5.9-7.4 N•m).

15. If the preload (rotary frictional force) is correct, disassemble the case, remove the final drive assembly and prepare for complete case reassembly.

NOTE: Changes in the rotary frictional force of the final drive assembly should be within 8.7 inch lbs. (1.0 N•m) per revolution, without binding.

TYPE TWO ADJUSTING PROCEDURE

1. With the bearing housing removed from the transaxle case, remove the bearing and shim from the housing. Reinstall the bearing *without* the shim onto the housing.

2. Install the final drive assembly into the transaxle case.

3. Install the gasket, the converter housing and the retaining bolts. Torque the retaining bolts 10-13 ft. lbs. (14-18 N•m) in a criss-cross pattern.

4. Attach a dial indicator to the case assembly with the indicator stem through the bearing housing and touching the differential side gear.

5. Using a special preload adapter tool or its equivalent, position the tool into the side gear and move the tool and gear up and down, while observing the dial indicator deflection. This deflection indicates the size of the shim needed for the bearing housing to bearing distance.

6. Select the desired thickness shim from the chart in the specification section.

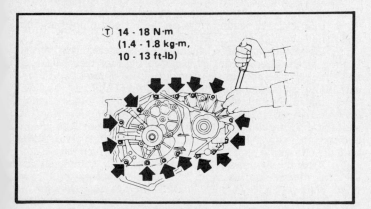

Installation of converter housing for test
(© Nissan Motor Co. of USA)

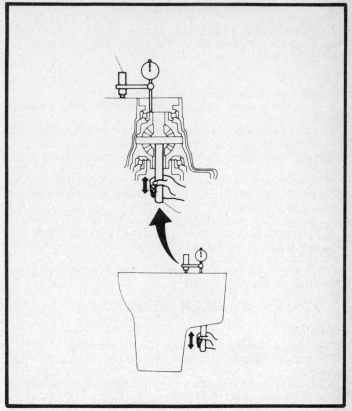

Use of special tool and dial indicator to determine the proper sized shim to be used (© Nissan Motor Co. of USA)

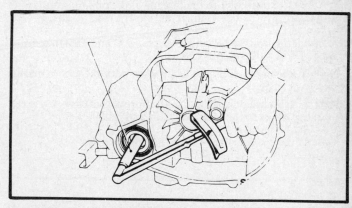

Use of special tool and torque wrench to determine the preload (rotary frictional force) of the differential side bearing
(© Nissan Motor Co. of USA)

7. Disassemble the bearing housing and remove the bearing from the housing. Install the shim and the bearing onto the bearing housing. Be sure both are properly seated.

8. With the use of the special turning tool and a torque wrench, turn the differential final drive unit and measure the preload (rotary frictional force) on the bearings.

9. The final drive unit must be turned at least ten times before measuring the preload. The changes in the reading of the preload per revolution should be within 8.7 *inch* lbs. (1.0 N•m) without binding.

10. The specified preload (rotary frictional force) for the bearings is 52-65 *inch* lbs. (5.9-7.4 N•m). If the measurement is outside the specifications, the unit will have to be disassembled, rechecked and reassembled.

OUTPUT SHAFT

If the transaxle case, output shaft, tapered roller bearing or front cover has been replaced, the output shaft must be adjusted by means of shims.

Adjustment

1. Lubricate the roller bearing with A/T fluid.
2. Press the bearing outer race into the bore of the transaxle case.
3. Install two or three shims on the front cover and press the bearing outer race into the bore of the front cover.
4. Install the gasket and the front cover on the converter housing.
5. Turn the output shaft at least ten times before measuring the preload (rotary frictional force) and be sure the output shaft turns freely without binding.
6. The specified preload is 3.1-4.2 *inch* lbs. (0.35-0.47 N•m).
7. If the preload is outside the specified range, the shims will have to be replaced with either thicker or thinner units. Refer to the specification section.
8. When preload has been corrected, remove the front cover and withdraw the output shaft.

IDLER GEAR

Assembly

1. Press the bearing outer races onto the idler gear.
2. Assemble the bearing inner races and idler shaft to the idler gear.
3. Attach the idler gear assembly and output shaft assembly to the converter housing.
4. Install the gasket and the front cover onto the converter housing. Before installing the bolts, clean the threads and the converter housing with solvent.
5. Apply locking sealer to the threads of the retaining bolts and install them into place. Tighten the bolts 10-13 ft. lbs. (14-18 N•m) torque.
6. Install the lockwasher and idler gear bolt and tighten temporarily to 20-27 ft. lbs. (26-36 N•m).

NOTE: Be sure to align the lockwasher with the groove on the converter housing.

7. After tightening the bolt, turn the output shaft five complete revolutions. Loosen the idler gear bolt and retighten it to 2.2-2.9 ft. lbs. (3-4 N•m).
8. Bend the lockwasher to lock the bolt in place.

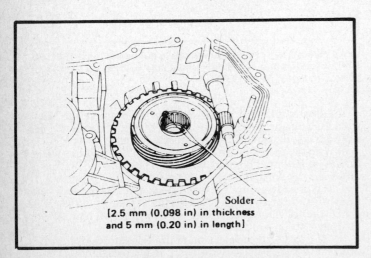

Use of solder strip or solder plate to measure end play
(© Nissan Motor Co. of USA)

END PLAY OF OUTPUT SHAFT

Adjusting

After the adjustment of the preload on the output shaft tapered roller bearing, the end play of the output shaft must be checked. A strip of solder or a solder plate can be used to check the end play clearance.

1. Using a strip of solder or solder plate, at least 0.098 in. (2.5mm) in diameter or thickness and 0.200 in. (5.0mm) in length, as the maximum gear clearance is 0.091 in. (2.3mm). If the diameter or thickness of the test solder is smaller than 0.098 in. (2.5mm), also use shims.

NOTE: Always use two strips or plates of solder, one on each side of the gear.

2. With the solder strip or plate in place, install the converter housing and output shaft assembly as a unit on the transaxle case.
3. Torque the retaining bolts to 10-13 ft. lbs. (14-18 N•m).
4. Remove the retaining bolts and housing assembly.
5. Measure the thickness of the solder strips or plates and if necessary, select shims of appropriate thickness so that the end play of the output shaft is within the specified range of 0.0098-0.0217 in. (0.25-0.55mm).

ASSEMBLY OF THE TRANSAXLE COMPONENTS

Before Assembly

1. Before proceeding with the final assembly of the transaxle, verify the case housing and all parts are free of dirt dust and other foreign material. Lubricate the parts in clean A/T fluid. Petroleum jelly (vaseline) can be used to secure thrust washers and bearings during the assembly.
2. All new seals and rings should have been installed on the individual components before the final assembly. If not, install them as the components are readied for assembly into the case.

Assembly

1. Lubricate the oil pump assembly and install it, along with the nylon washer and thrust bearing. Align the five bolt holes.
2. Lubricate the low and reverse brake piston seal. Install the piston into the case by lightly tapping upon it evenly.
3. Install the low and reverse piston retainer and springs. Align the holes and install the retaining bolts. Tighten to 5.1-6.5 ft. lbs. (7-9 N•m).
4. Apply air pressure to test the low and reverse brake piston. If the piston moves smoothly, the seal has not turned and is installed properly.
5. Install the brake band, the servo piston and "O" ring, the return spring and the snapring. Hold the piston into its bore with a small C-clamp until the snapring is installed into its groove.
6. Lubricate the sealing rings on the oil pump housing hub and install the high-reverse (front) clutch.
7. Install the forward (rear) clutch, front internal gear, thrust bearing, bearing race, front carrier, bearing race thrust bearing and sun gear assembly in their reverse order of removal. Lubricate the thrust washers and bearings with A/T fluid or vaseline.
8. Install the low and reverse brake dished retainer plate, drive and driven clutch plates, retainer plate and the snapring. Install the dished plate with the inner concave against the piston and the outer concave against the first driven (steel) plate. Alternate the remaining plates with a drive (lined), driven (steel), etc.
9. After the low and reverse brake has been completely assembled, measure the clearance between the snapring and the retainer plate with a feeler gauge blade. If the clearance exceeds the allowable limit of 0.150 in. (3.8mm), a different sized retainer plate must be installed. The preferred or standard clearance is 0.0748-0.0866 in. (1.90-2.20mm). The available plates are as follows:

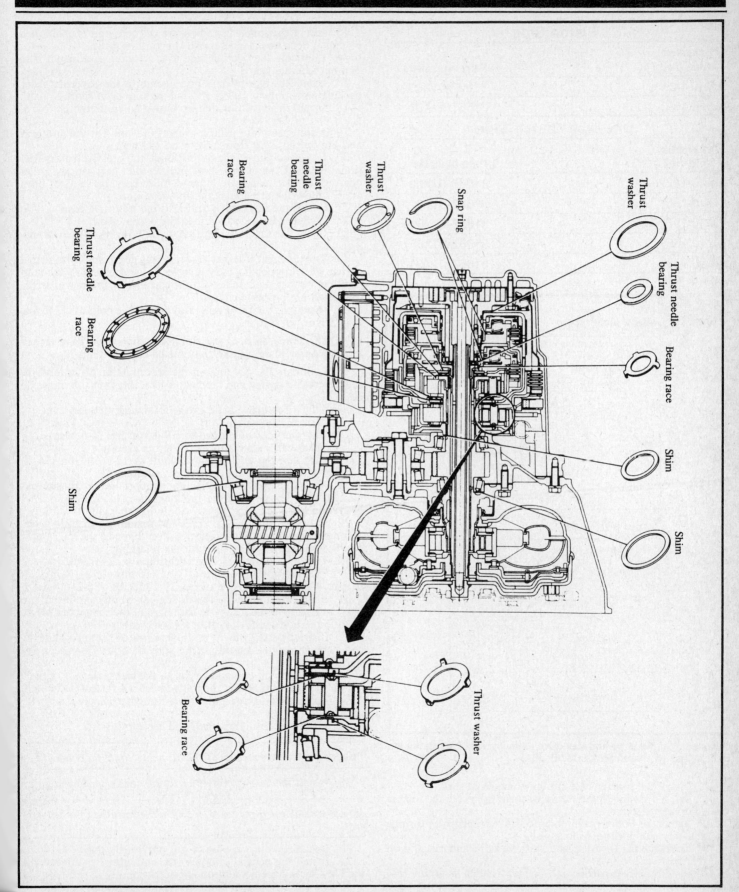

Location of thrust bearings and washers within the drive train (© Nissan Motor Co. of USA)

Piston Side

Thickness mm (in)	Part Number
3.6 (0.142)	31667-01X00
3.8 (0.150)	31667-01X01

One-way Clutch Side

Thickness mm (in)	Part Number
3.6 (0.142)	31667-01X00
3.8 (0.150)	31667-01X01
4.0 (0.157)	31667-01X02
4.2 (0.165)	31667-01X03
4.4 (0.173)	31667-01X04

4-drive plate type

Whichever retaining plate (Part No. 31667 01X02) or 2 driven plates
Driven plate
Retainer plate
Drive plate
Dished plate
Pay attention to its direction

3-drive plate type

Dished plate, L & R Pay attention to its direction.
Whichever retainer plate (Part No. 31667-01X02) or 2 driven plates
Driven plates
Drive plates
Retainer plate

Installation of the three and four drive plate low and reverse brake clutch pack (© Nissan Motor Co. of USA)

10. Install the bearing race on the connecting shell.
11. Apply vaseline to the thrust washer and install the washer onto the rear carrier.
12. Install the one-way clutch onto the rear carrier by turning the one-way clutch counterclockwise.
13. Lubricate the thrust washer with vaseline and install it on the rear carrier.
14. Install the rear carrier and one-way clutch assembly into the case by turning the one-way clutch/carrier assembly in a clockwise direction.

15. Install the snapring and ensure the bent end is positioned so that it does not interfere with the parking pawl.
16. Lubricate the bearing race with vaseline and install it to the rear internal gear.
17. Install the rear internal gear, assemble the governor shaft, parking pawl, return spring and the parking pawl shaft.
18. Install the governor shaft retaining bolt and tighten to 2.5-5.1 ft. lbs. (3.4-6.9 N•m).
19. Install the seal bushing properly to prevent the sun gear and the output shaft from becoming jammed.
20. If the end play of the output shaft, the preload (rotary frictional force) of the output shaft and the idler gear tapered roller bearings or the final drive tapered roller bearings has not been done, follow the previously outline procedure.
21. Install the final drive unit into the transaxle case.
22. Install the selected shim to the output shaft.
23. Install the gasket and the converter housing onto the transaxle case.
24. Turn the rear internal gear (parking gear) clockwise with a prybar while supporting the converter housing assembly by hand until the output shaft splines, front carrier and the rear internal gear teeth are properly engaged.
25. Install the retaining bolts and tighten the bolts 10-13 ft. lbs. (14-18 N•m) of torque.

NOTE: Three bolts as per the illustration must have thread locking sealer installed and the case be cleaned properly.

26. Lubricate the cut ring on the accumulator piston and install the return spring and the piston assembly into the transaxle case.
27. Adjust the brake band in the following manner:
    a. Loosen the locknut.
    b. Torque the anchor pin to 2.9-4.3 ft. lbs. (4-6 N•m).
    c. Back off the anchor pin 2.5 turns exactly.
    d. Tighten the anchor pin locknut to 12-16 ft. lbs. (16-22 N•m) while holding the anchor pin stationary.
28. Assemble the parking actuator support and the throttle cable to transaxle case. Tighten the locknut to 1.4-2.2 ft. lbs. (2-3 N•m) and bend the lock plate securely to the locknut.
29. Lubricate the manual shaft and install the throttle lever, manual plate, manual shaft, selector lever and parking rod assembly. Secure them to the case with the retaining pin.
30. Tighten the manual shift securing nut as follows:
    a. Tighten the inside nut to 19-23 ft. lbs. (25-31 N•m).
    b. Tighten the outside nut to 19-23 ft. lbs. (25-31 N•m).
31. Install the manual valve into the valve body and install the body assembly to the transaxle case. Install the magnet in place. Torque the bolts to 5.1-6.5 ft. lbs. (7-9 N•m).
32. Inspect the alignment and operation of the manual lever and parking pawl engagement. Be sure all bolts have been installed.
33. Install the oil pan and gasket to the transaxle case. Install the oil pan guard. Tighten the bolts to 3.6-5.1 ft. lbs. (5-7 N•m).
34. Install the seal ring and the governor cap. Secure it with the snap retainer.
35. Install the oil pump shaft and the input shaft.

CAUTION
Be sure the concave section of the oil pump shaft faces inward.

36. Install the torque converter to the converter housing.

CAUTION
Do not scratch the front cover oil seal while installing the converter.

37. Install the oil pan plug, if not previously done.
38. Install the neutral safety switch and adjust as outlined in the On-Car Service Section under Adjustments.
39. Verify the manual control lever is operating properly.
40. Prepare the transaxle for installation into the vehicle.

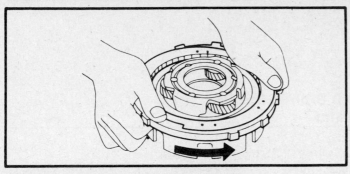

Installation of one-way clutch into the rear carrier
(© Nissan Motor Co. of USA)

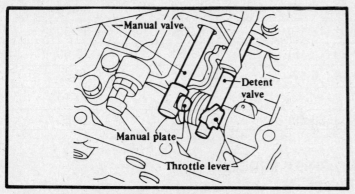

Alignment of manual valve and manual plate, along with the alignment of the throttle lever and the detent valve during the valve body installation (© Nissan Motor Co. of USA)

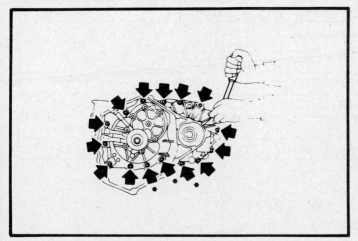

Use of a sealer is recommended on the star indicated bolts during the converter housing final assembly (© Nissan Motor Co. of USA)

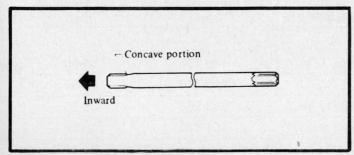

Direction of assembly for oil pump shaft
(© Nissan Motor Co. of USA)

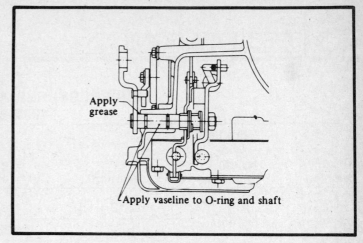

Installation of manual shaft assembly (© Nissan Motor Co. of USA)

Installation of the one-way clutch/rear carrier assembly into the case (© Nissan Motor Co. of USA)

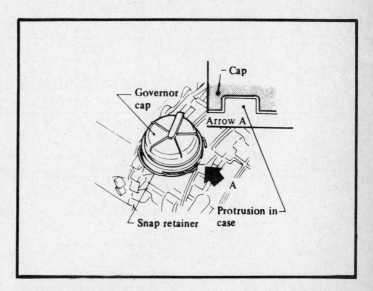

Installation of the governor cap. Note the direction of cap during the installation (© Nissan Motor Co. of USA)

S SPECIFICATIONS

LINE PRESSURES AND SHIFT SPEEDS
1982 Sentra

Throttle position	Throttle Wire length L mm (in)	Gearshift	Vehicle speed km/h (MPH)	Drive shaft revolutions (rpm)	Line pressure (psi)
Light throttle	3.7 (0.146)	$D_1 \rightarrow D_2$ ($2_1 \rightarrow 2_2$)	12-20 (7-12)	111-194	36-50
		$D_2 \rightarrow D_3$	22-31 (14-19)	211-295	36-50
		$D_3 \rightarrow D_2$	19-26 (12-16)	181-250	36-50
		$D_2 \rightarrow D_1$ ($2_2 \rightarrow 2_1$)	10-19 (6-12)	97-181	36-50
		$D_3 \rightarrow 2_2$ ($D_3 \rightarrow 1_2$)	—	—	80-101
		$1_2 \rightarrow 1_1$	49-63 (30-39)	470-610	36-50

LINE PRESSURES AND SHIFT SPEEDS
1983-84 Pulsar

Throttle position	Throttle Wire length L mm (in)	Gearshift	Vehicle speed km/h (MPH)	Drive shaft revolutions (rpm)	Line pressure (psi)
Light throttle (1/8 open)	3.7 (0.146)	$D_1 \rightarrow D_2$ ($2_1 \rightarrow 2_2$)	12-21 (7-13)	115-201	36-50
		$D_2 \rightarrow D_3$	23-32 (14-20)	219-306	36-50
		$D_3 \rightarrow D_2$	19-27 (12-17)	187-259	36-50
		$D_2 \rightarrow D_1$ ($2_2 \rightarrow 2_1$)	11-19 (7-12)	101-188	36-50
		$D_3 \rightarrow 2_2$ ($D_3 \rightarrow 1_2$)	—	—	80-101
		$1_2 \rightarrow 1_1$	50-66 (31-41)	487-632	36-50

LINE PRESSURES AND SHIFT SPEEDS
1983-84 Stanza

Throttle position	Throttle Wire length L mm (in)	Gearshift	Vehicle speed km/h (MPH)	Drive shaft revolutions (rpm)	Line pressure (psi)
Light throttle	3.7 (0.146)	$D_1 \rightarrow D_2$ ($2_1 \rightarrow 2_2$)	13-22 (8-14)	119-208	36-50
		$D_2 \rightarrow D_3$	24-34 (15-21)	226-316	36-50
		$D_3 \rightarrow D_2$	21-29 (13-18)	193-268	36-50
		$D_2 \rightarrow D_1$ ($2_2 \rightarrow 2_1$)	11-21 (7-13)	104-194	36-50
		$D_3 \rightarrow 2_2$ ($D_3 \rightarrow 1_2$)	—	—	80-101
		$1_2 \rightarrow 1_1$	54-71 (34-44)	503-653	36-50

LINE PRESSURES AND SHIFT SPEEDS
1983-84 Sentra w/engine E16
Transaxle Model 11X03

Throttle position	Throttle Wire length L mm (in)	Gearshift	Vehicle speed km/h (MPH)	Drive shaft revolutions (rpm)	Line pressure (psi)
Light throttle	3.7 (0.146)	$D_1 \to D_2$ ($2_1 \to 2_2$)	12-21 (7-13)	115-201	36-50
		$D_2 \to D_3$	23-32 (14-20)	219-306	36-50
		$D_3 \to D_2$	19-27 (12-17)	187-259	36-50
		$D_2 \to D_1$ ($2_2 \to 2_1$)	11-19 (7-12)	101-188	36-50
		$D_3 \to 2_2$ ($D_3 \to 1_2$)	—	—	80-101
		$1_2 \to 1_1$	50-66 (31-41)	487-632	36-50

LINE PRESSURES AND SHIFT SPEEDS
1983-84 Sentra w/engine CD17
Transaxle Model 03X17

Throttle position	Throttle Wire length L mm (in)	Gearshift	Vehicle speed km/h (MPH)	Drive shaft revolutions (rpm)	Line pressure (psi)
Light throttle	3.7 (0.146)	$D_1 \to D_2$ ($2_1 \to 2_2$)	13-22 (8-14)	119-208	36-50
		$D_2 \to D_3$	21-30 (13-19)	198-288	36-50
		$D_3 \to D_2$	18-26 (11-16)	170-245	36-50
		$D_2 \to D_1$ ($2_2 \to 2_1$)	11-21 (7-13)	104-194	36-50
		$D_3 \to 2_2$ ($D_3 \to 1_2$)	—	—	80-101
		$1_2 \to 1_1$	46-62 (29-39)	435-585	36-50

STALL SPEED SPECIFICATIONS

MODEL	RPM
1982 Datsun 310	1650-1950
1983-84 Nissan Stanza	2000-2300
1982-84 Nissan Sentra	1800-2100 ①
1983-84 Nissan Pulsar, NX	1800-2100

① 1500-1800 RPM w/CD17 engine

SPECIFICATIONS FOR INTERNAL COMPONENTS
Codes

Year/Model	Transaxle Code
1982 310	01X05
1983-84 Stanza	13X07
1983-84 Pulsar	11X03
1982 Sentra	11X00
1983-84 Sentra W/E16 engine	11X03
W/CD17 engine	03X17

SPECIFICATIONS FOR INTERNAL COMPONENTS

High-Reverse (Front) Clutch
TRANSAXLE MODEL CODES—01X05, 11X00, 13X07, 11X03, 03X17

Number of drive plates		2	
Number of driven plates		3	
Clearance mm (in.)	Standard	1.0-1.4 (0.039-0.055)	
	Allowable limit	2.2 (0.087)	
Drive plate thickness mm (in.)	Standard	1.80 (0.0709)	
	Allowable limit	1.6 (0.063)	
Thickness for retaining plate		Thickness mm (in)	Part number
		3.4 (0.134)	31537-01X05
		3.6 (0.142)	31537-01X00
		3.8 (0.150)	31537-01X01
		4.0 (0.157)	31537-01X02
		4.2 (0.165)	31537-01X03
		4.4 (0.173)	31537-01X04

Forward (Rear) Clutch
TRANSAXLE MODEL CODES—01X05, 11X00, 13X07, 11X03, 03X17

Number of drive plates		3 ①	
Number of driven plates		3 ②	
Clearance mm (in.)	Standard	0.8-1.2 (0.031-0.047) ③	
	Allowable limit	2.8 (0.110) ④	
Drive plate thickness mm (in.)	Standard	1.80 (0.0709)	
	Allowable limit	1.6 (0.063)	
Thickness for retaining plate		Thickness mm (in)	Part number
		3.4 (0.134)	31537-01X05
		3.6 (0.142)	31537-01X00
		3.8 (0.150)	31537-01X01
		4.0 (0.157)	31537-01X02
		4.2 (0.165)	31537-01X03
		4.4 (0.173)	31537-01X04

① Code 11X00—Four drive plates
② Code 11X00—Four Driven plates
③ Code 13X07—0.5-0.8mm (0.020-0.031 inch)
④ Code 13X07—2.4mm (0.094 inch)

Low and Reverse Brake
TRANSAXLE MODEL CODES—01X05

Number of drive plates	4
Number of driven plates	5
Clearance mm (in)	0.8-1.1 (0.031-0.043)

TRANSAXLE MODEL CODE—13X07

Number of drive plates		5
Number of driven plates		5
Clearance mm (in.)	Standard	1.90-2.20 (0.0748-0.0866)
	Allowable limit	3.8 (0.150)
Drive plate thickness mm (in.)	Standard	2.00 (0.0787)
	Allowable limit	1.8 (0.071)

TRANSAXLE MODEL CODE—11X00, 11X03

Number of drive plates		4
Number of driven plates		4 (6) ①
Clearance mm (in.)	Standard	1.90-2.20 (0.0748-0.0866)
	Allowable limit	3.8 (0.150)
Drive plate thickness mm (in.)	Standard	2.00 (0.0787)
	Allowable limit	1.8 (0.071)

TRANSAXLE MODEL CODE—03X17

Number of drive plates		3
Number of driven plates		3 (7) ①
Clearance mm (in.)	Standard	1.90-2.20 (0.0748-0.0866)
	Allowable limit	3.8 (0.150)
Drive plate thickness mm (in.)	Standard	2.00 (0.0787)
	Allowable limit	1.8 (0.071)

① In the case where two driven plates are used instead of the retaining plate.

SPECIFICATIONS FOR INTERNAL COMPONENTS

Oil Pump Clearance
ALL TRANSAXLE MODEL CODES
mm (in.)

Outer gear-pump housing	Standard	0.20-0.30 (0.0079-0.0118)
	Allowable limit	0.35 (0.0138)
Outer gear-crescent	Standard	0.20-0.30 (0.0079-0.0118)
	Allowable limit	0.35 (0.0138)
Gears-pump plate	Standard	0.02-0.04 (0.0008-0.0016)
	Allowable limit	0.08 (0.0031)
Seal ring-ring groove	Standard	0.10-0.25 (0.0039-0.0098)
	Allowable limit	0.25 (0.0098)

Planetary Carrier Clearance
ALL TRANSAXLE MODEL CODES
mm (in.)

Clearance between pinion washer and planetary carrier	Standard	0.20-0.70 (0.0079-0.0276)
	Allowable limit	0.80 (0.0315)

Identification marks on separator plate
Code 11X00 - U
Code 11X03 - W
Code 03X17 - R
Code 13X07 - AG

PreLoad (Rotary Frictional Force)
ALL MODEL CODES

	N•m	(in.-lb)
Output shaft	0.35-0.47	(3.1-4.2)
Final drive	5.9-7.4	(52-65)

Output Shaft End Play
ALL MODEL CODES

0.25-0.55 mm (0.0098-0.0217 in.)

Output Shaft End Play Adjusting Shims
ALL MODEL CODES

Thickness of soldering plate −0.05mm (0.0020 in)① mm (in)	Thickness mm (in)	Part number
0.55-0.85 (0.0217-0.0335)	0.3 (0.012)	31484-01x00
0.75-1.05 (0.0295-0.0413)	0.5 (0.020)	31484-01x01
0.95-1.25 (0.0374-0.0492)	0.7 (0.028)	31484-01x02
1.15-1.45 (0.0453-0.0571)	0.9 (0.035)	31484-01x03
1.35-1.65 (0.0531-0.0650)	1.1 (0.043)	31484-01x04
1.55-1.85 (0.0610-0.0728)	1.3 (0.051)	31484-01x05
1.75-2.05 (0.0689-0.0807)	1.5 (0.059)	31484-01x06
1.95-2.25 (0.0768-0.0886)	1.7 (0.067)	31484-01x07

① 0.05 mm (0.0020 in.) is the amount the soldering plate recovers due to its elasticity, and it must be subtracted from the thickness of soldering plate.

Final Drive Adjusting Shims
ALL MODEL CODES

H = A − B mm (in)	Thickness mm (in)	Part number
0-0.07 (0-0.0028)	0.38 (0.0150)	38453-01X00
0.07-0.15 (0.0028-0.0059)	0.46 (0.0181)	38453-01X01
0.15-0.23 (0.0059-0.0091)	0.54 (0.0213)	38453-01X02
0.23-0.31 (0.0091-0.0122)	0.62 (0.0244)	38453-01X03
0.31-0.39 (0.0122-0.0154)	0.70 (0.0276)	38453-01X04
0.39-0.47 (0.0154-0.0185)	0.78 (0.0307)	38453-01X05
0.47-0.55 (0.0185-0.0217)	0.86 (0.0339)	38453-01X06
0.55-0.63 (0.0217-0.0248)	0.94 (0.0370)	38453-01X07

S SPECIFICATIONS

SPECIFICATIONS FOR INTERNAL COMPONENTS

Final Drive Adjusting Shims
ALL MODEL CODES

H = A − B mm (in)	Thickness mm (in)	Part number
0.63-0.71 (0.0248-0.0280)	1.02 (0.0402)	38453-01X08
0.71-0.79 (0.0280-0.0311)	1.10 (0.0433)	38453-01X09
0.79-0.87 (0.0311-0.0343)	1.18 (0.0465)	38453-01X10
0.87-0.95 (0.0343-0.0374)	1.26 (0.0496)	38453-01X11
0.95-1.03 (0.0374-0.0406)	1.34 (0.0528)	38453-01X12
1.03-1.11 (0.0406-0.0437)	1.42 (0.0559)	38453-01X13
1.11-1.19 (0.0437-0.0469)	1.50 (0.0591)	38453-01X14
1.19-1.27 (0.0469-0.0500)	1.58 (0.0622)	38453-01X15
1.27-1.35 (0.0500-0.0531)	1.66 (0.0654)	38453-01X16

TORQUE SPECIFICATIONS

Unit		N•m	ft-lb
Drive plate to torque converter		49-69	36-51
Converter housing to engine	M8	16-22	12-16
	M10	39-49	29-36
Engine gusset to cylinder block (CD17 engine model)		30-40	22-30
Transaxle case to converter housing		14-18	10-13
Transaxle case to front cover		14-18	10-13
Oil pan to transaxle case		5-7	3.6-5.1
Bearing retainer to transaxle case		19-25	14-18
Piston stem (when adjusting band brake)①		4-5	2.9-3.6
Piston stem lock nut		16-22	12-16

TORQUE SPECIFICATIONS

Unit	N•m	ft-lb
Low and reverse brake piston retainer	7-9	5.1-6.5
Control valve body to transaxle case	7-9	5.1-6.5
Lower valve body to upper valve body	7-9	5.1-6.5
Final gear bolt	69-78	51-58
Oil strainer to lower valve body	5-7	3.6-5.1
Governor valve body to governor shaft	5-7	3.6-5.1
Governor shaft securing nut	3.4-6.9	2.5-5.1
Idler gear when adjusting turning frictional force)	26-36	20-27
Idler gear lock nut②	—	—
Throttle wire securing nut	5-7	3.6-5.1
Control cable securing nut	8-11	5.8-8.0
Inhibitor switch to transaxle case	2.0-2.5	1.4-1.9
Manual shaft lock nut	31-42	23-31
Oil cooler pipe to transaxle case	29-49	22-36
Test plug (oil pressure inspection hole)	5-10	3.6-7.2
Support actuator (parking rod inserting position) to rear extension	8-11	5.8-8.0
Engine to gusset	30-40	22-30
Gusset to converter housing	16-21	12-15

① Turn back 2.5 turns after tightening.
② Refer to Adjusting Turning Frictional Force of Tapered Roller Bearing.

SPECIAL TOOLS

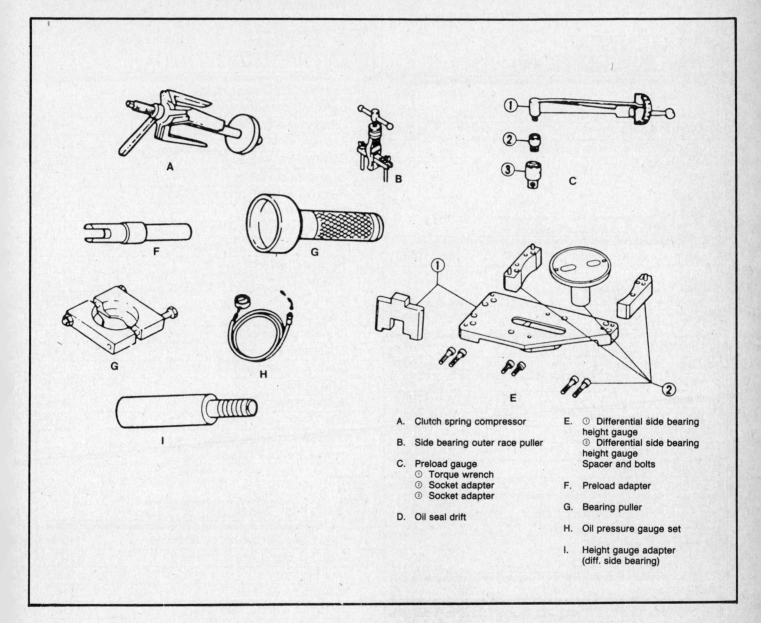

A. Clutch spring compressor

B. Side bearing outer race puller

C. Preload gauge
  ① Torque wrench
  ② Socket adapter
  ③ Socket adapter

D. Oil seal drift

E. ① Differential side bearing height gauge
  ② Differential side bearing height gauge
  Spacer and bolts

F. Preload adapter

G. Bearing puller

H. Oil pressure gauge set

I. Height gauge adapter (diff. side bearing)

INDEX

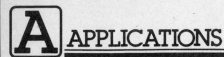

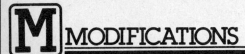

JATCO F3A (MAZDA) Automatic Transaxle

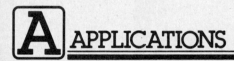

APPLICATIONS

Mazda 626
Mazda 323/GLC

GENERAL DESCRIPTION

The Jatco F3A transaxle is a fully automatic unit, consisting of three forward speeds and one reverse speed. The internal components are similar to the 3N71B and R3A automatic transmissions. Some of the differences are as follows:

1. The torque converter is located on the engine side and the oil pump is located on the other end of the transaxle. The front clutch, the rear clutch, front planetary and rear planetary gears are arranged in the respective order from the front, or oil pump end of the transaxle. During the section outline, the oil pump end will be referred to as the front and the converter end, or engine end, will be referred to as the rear of the transaxle.

2. The control valve is located under the front clutch and the rear clutch assemblies.

3. The governor is located on the outside of the case and responds to the speed of the output shaft to control operating oil pressure.

4. The low and reverse brake band is located on the outside of the rear planetary gears to shorten the total length of the transaxle.

5. The three shafts that are contained within the case are the oil pump driveshaft which transmit engine speed directly to the oil pump via a quill shaft inside the input shaft, the input shaft which transmits power from the torque converter turbine and drives the front clutch cover. The third shaft is the output shaft which transmits power from the front planetary gear carrier and the rear planetary gear annulus, through the main drive idler gear to the differential drive gear.

6. Both the transaxle and the differential use a commond sump with ATF fluid as the lubricant.

Transaxle and Converter Identification

TRANSAXLE

Identification tags are located on the front of the transaxle, under the oil cooler lines and identify the transaxle type and model. It is most important to obtain the tag information when ordering parts for a rebuild operation, since different models are used with different engines.

CONVERTER

The torque converter is a welded unit and cannot be disassembled unless special tools are available for that purpose. Identification codes are used by the manufacturer, but are not listed for general usage by the trade, other than type 12.

Transaxle Metric Fasteners

Metric bolt sizes and thread pitches are used for all fasteners on the Jatco transaxles. The metric fastener dimensions are close to the dimensions of the familiar inch system fasteners, and for this reason, replacement fasteners must have the same measurement and strength as those removed. Do not attempt to interchange metric fasteners for inch system fasteners. Mismatched or incorrect fasteners can result in damage to the transmission unit through malfunctions, breakage or possible personal injury. Care should be taken to reuse the fasteners in the same locations as removed whenever possible.

Fluid Specification

The use of type F automatic transmission fluid or its equivalent, is recommended for use in the F3A automatic transaxle models.

CAPACITIES

The capacity of the F3A transaxle is 6.0 US quarts, 5.7 Liters, or 5.0 Imp. quarts.

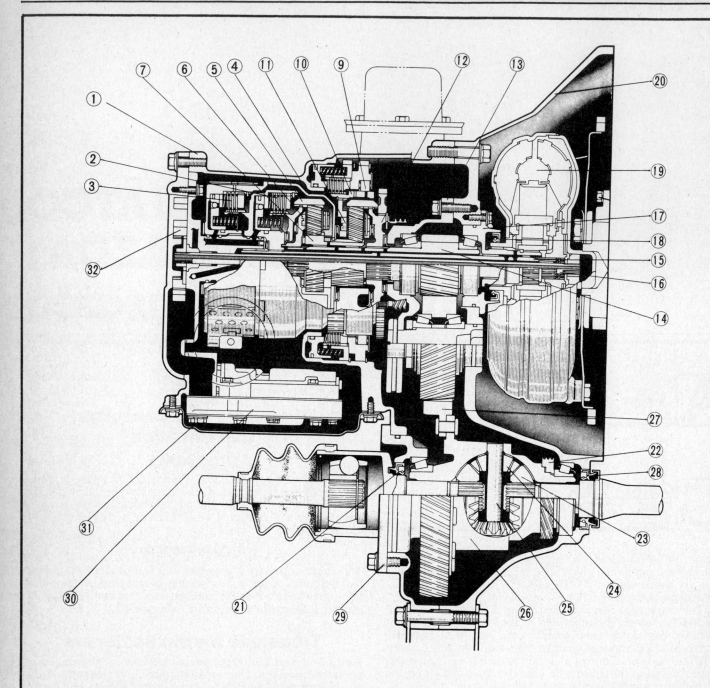

1. Transmission
2. Rear clutch
3. Front clutch
4. Connection shell
5. Rear clutch hub assembly
6. Planetary carrier
7. Sun gear
8. Low and reverse brake
9. One-way clutch

10. One-way clutch inner race
11. Planetary carrier
12. Drum hub assembly
13. Bearing housing
14. Output gear
15. Turbine shaft
16. Oil pump shaft
17. Bearing cover

18. Oil seal
19. Torque converter
20. Converter housing
21. Oil seal
22. Speedometer drive gear
23. Side gear
24. Pinion gear
25. Pinion shaft

26. Differential gear case
27. Ring gear
28. Oil seal
29. Side bearing housing
30. Control valve
31. Oil pan
32. Oil pump

Cross section of the F3A transaxle (©Toyo Kogyo Co. Ltd.)

Location of identification tags (©Toyo Kogyo Co. Ltd.)

FLUID LEVEL

Check the Fluid Level

With the engine/transaxle assemblies up to normal operating temperature, move the quadrant through all the selector positions and finish in the "P" position. The correct level is between the "F" and "L" marks on the dipstick. It is important to keep the level at, or slightly below, the "F" mark on the dipstick. Do not overfill the assembly.

Transaxle oil level should be checked, both visually and by smell, to determine that the fluid level is correct and to observe any foreign material in the fluid. Smelling the fluid will indicate if any of the bands or clutches have been burned through excessive slippage or overheating of the trans.

It is most important to locate the defect and its cause, and to properly repair them to avoid having the same problem recur.

In order to more fully understand the Jatco automatic transaxle and to diagnose possible defects more easily, the clutch and band applications chart and a general description of the hydraulic control system is given.

M MODIFICATIONS

Transaxle Modifications

No known transaxle modifications for the F3A units were available at the time of printing of this publication.

TROUBLE DIAGNOSIS

A logical and orderly diagnosis outline and charts are provided with clutch and band applications, shift speed and governor pressures, main control pressures and oil flow circuits to assist the repairman in diagnosing the problems, causes and extent of repairs needed to bring the automatic transaxle back to its acceptable level of operation.

Preliminary checks and adjustments should be made to the manual valve linkage, accelerator and downshift linkage.

CLUTCH AND BAND APPLICATION CHART
Jatco F3A Automatic Transaxle

Range		Front Clutch ①	Rear Clutch ②	Low & Reverse Brake Clutch	Brake Band Servo ③ Operation	Release	One-Way Clutch	Parking Pawl
Park		—	—	On	—	—	—	On
Reverse		On	—	On	—	On	—	—
Neutral		—	—	—	—	—	—	—
Drive	Low D1	—	On	—	—	—	On	—
	Second D2	—	On	—	On	—	—	—
	Top D3	On	On	—	(On)	On	—	—
2	Second	—	On	—	On	—	—	—
1	Second 1₂	—	On	—	On	—	—	—
	Low 1₁	—	On	On	—	—	—	—

① Reverse and high clutch
② Forward clutch
③ Intermediate band

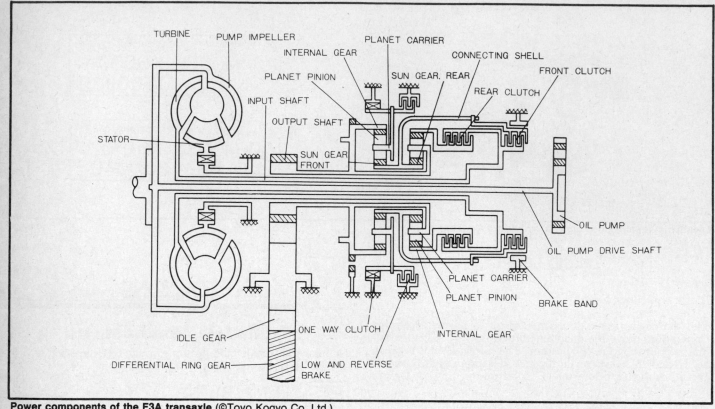

Power components of the F3A transaxle (©Toyo Kogyo Co. Ltd.)

CHILTON'S THREE "C's" DIAGNOSIS CHART
Jatco F3A Automatic Transaxle

Condition	Cause	Correction
Engine does not start in "N", "P" ranges	a) Range select linkage b) Neutral safety switch c) Ignition switch and starter motor	a) Adjust linkage b) Adjust or replace c) Repair or replace
Engine starts in range other than "N" and "P"	a) Range select linkage b) Neutral safety switch	a) Adjust linkage b) Adjust or replace
Sharp shock shifting from "N" to "D" range	a) Vacuum diaphragm and hoses b) Engine idle rpm c) Throttle valve pressure d) Manual control valve e) Rear clutch	a) Renew diaphragm and hoses b) Set engine idle rpm c) Correct throttle valve or passage per air test d) Repair or replace valve e) Renew rear clutch
Vehicle will not move in "D" range (but moves in "2", "1" and "R" ranges)	a) Range select linkage b) Throttle valve pressure c) Manual control valve d) One way clutch of transmission	a) Adjust linkage b) Correct throttle valve or passage per air test c) Adjust range select linkage/renew valve d) Renew clutch

CHILTON'S THREE "C's" DIAGNOSIS CHART
Jatco F3A Automatic Transaxle

Condition	Cause	Correction
Vehicle will not move in "D", "1" or "2" ranges but moves in "R" range Clutch slips, very poor acceleration	a) Oil level b) Range select linkage c) Throttle valve pressure d) Manual control valve e) Leakage of fluid passage f) Engine adjustment and brake defects g) Rear clutch	a) Add if necessary b) Adjust linkage c) Correct throttle valve or passage per air test d) Adjust range select linkage/renew valve e) Correct as per air test f) Repair as needed g) Renew rear clutch
Vehicle will not move in "R" range (but moves in "D", "2" and "1" ranges). Clutch slips, very poor acceleration.	a) Oil level b) Range select linkage c) Throttle valve pressure d) Manual control valve e) Leakage of passage f) Rear clutch g) Front clutch h) Low and reverse brake i) Front clutch check ball	a) Add if needed b) Adjust linkage c) Correct throttle valve or passage per air test d) Adjust range select linkage/renew valve e) Correct as per air test f) Renew rear clutch g) Renew front clutch h) Renew low and reverse brake i) Repair or renew
Vehicle will not move in any range	a) Oil level b) Range select linkage c) Throttle valve pressure d) Manual control valve e) Leakage of fluid passage f) Oil pump g) Parking linkage	a) Add if needed b) Adjust linkage c) Correct throttle valve or passage per air test d) Adjust range select linkage/renew valve e) Correct as per air test f) Repair or renew g) Repair or renew
Clutches or brakes slip somewhat in starting to move	a) Oil level b) Range select linkage c) Throttle valve pressure d) Vacuum diaphragm and hoses e) Manual control valve f) Leakage of fluid passage g) Oil pump	a) Add if needed b) Adjust linkage c) Correct throttle valve or passage per air test d) Renew as required e) Adjust range select linkage/renew valve f) Correct as per air test g) Repair or renew
Vehicle moves in "N" range	a) Range select linkage b) Manual control valve c) Rear clutch	a) Adjust linkage b) Adjust range select linkage/renew valve c) Renew rear clutch
Maximum speed not attained, acceleration poor	a) Oil level b) Range select linkage c) Throttle valve pressure d) High stall rpm e) Manual control valve	a) Add if needed b) Adjust linkage c) Correct throttle valve or passage per air test d) Renew torque converter e) Adjust range select linkage/renew valve

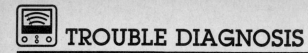

CHILTON'S THREE "C's" DIAGNOSIS CHART
Jatco F3A Automatic Transaxle

Condition	Cause	Correction
Maximum speed not attained, acceleration poor	f) Band servo	f) Repair/renew band servo
	g) Rear clutch	g) Renew rear clutch
	h) Front clutch	h) Renew front clutch
	i) Band brake	i) Renew band brake
	j) Low and reverse brake	j) Renew low and reverse brake
	k) Oil pump	k) Repair or renew oil pump
Vehicle braked in "R" range	a) Band servo	a) Renew band servo
	b) Leakage of fluid passage	b) Correct as per air test
	c) Rear clutch	c) Renew rear clutch
	d) Band brake	d) Renew band brake
	e) Parking linkage	e) Repair/renew linkage
No creep at all	a) Oil level	a) Add if needed
	b) Range select linkage	b) Adjust linkage
	c) Low engine idle rpm	c) Adjust idle rpm
	d) Manual control valve	d) Adjust range select linkage/renew valve
	e) Rear clutch	e) Renew rear clutch
	f) Front clutch	f) Renew front clutch
	g) Oil pump	g) Repair or renew oil pump
	h) Leakage of fluid passage	h) Correct as per air test
Excessive creep	a) High engine idle rpm	a) Adjust idle rpm
Failure to change gear from "2nd" to "3rd"	a) Range select linkage	a) Adjust linkage
	b) Vacuum diaphragm and hoses	b) Renew diaphragm/hoses
	c) Downshift solenoid kickdown switch and wiring	c) Repair wiring and adjust or renew the downshift solenoid
	d) Manual control valve	d) Adjust range select linkage/renew valve
	e) Governor valve	e) Overhaul governor/renew governor
	f) Band servo	f) Renew band servo
	g) Leakage of fluid passage	g) Correct as per air test
	h) Band brake	h) Renew band brake
Failure to change gear from "1st" to "2nd"	a) Range linkage	a) Adjust linkage
	b) Vacuum diaphragm and hoses	b) Renew diaphragm/hoses
	c) Downshift solenoid kickdown switch and wiring	c) Repair wiring and adjust or renew the solenoid downshift kickdown switch
	d) Manual control valve	d) Adjust range select linkage/renew valve
	e) Band servo	e) Renew band servo
	f) Leakage of fluid passage	f) Correct as per air test
	g) Front clutch	g) Renew front clutch
	h) Front clutch check ball	h) Renew front clutch check ball

CHILTON'S THREE "C's" DIAGNOSIS CHART
Jatco F3A Automatic Transaxle

Condition	Cause	Correction
Too high gear change point from "1st" to "2nd" and from "2nd" to "3rd"	a) Vacuum diaphragm and hoses b) Downshift solenoid kickdown switch and wiring c) Manual control valve d) Governor valve e) Leakage of fluid passage	a) Renew diaphragm/hoses b) Repair wiring and adjust or renew the downshift solenoid kickdown switch c) Adjust range select linkage/renew valve d) Overhaul governor/ renew governor e) Correct as per air test
Gear change directly from "1st" to "3rd" occurs	a) Manual control valve b) Governor valve c) Leakage of fluid passage d) Band brake	a) Adjust range select linkage/renew valve b) Overhaul governor/ renew governor c) Correct as per air test d) Renew band brake
Too sharp shock in change from "1st" to "2nd"	a) Vacuum diaphragm and hoses b) Manual control valve c) Band servo d) Band brake	a) Renew diaphragm/hoses b) Adjust range select linkage/renew valve c) Renew band servo d) Renew band brake
Too sharp shock in change from "2nd" to "3rd"	a) Vacuum diaphragm and hoses b) Downshift solenoid kickdown switch and wiring c) Throttle valve pressure d) Manual control valve e) Band servo f) Front clutch	a) Renew diaphragm/hoses b) Repair wiring and adjust or renew the downshift solenoid kickdown switch c) Correct throttle valve or passage per air test d) Adjust range select linkage/renew valve e) Renew band servo f) Renew front clutch
Almost no shock or slipping in change from "1st" to "2nd"	a) Oil level b) Range select linkage c) Vacuum diaphragm and hoses d) Throttle valve pressure e) Manual control valve f) Band servo g) Leakage of fluid passage h) Band brake	a) Add if needed b) Adjust linkage c) Renew diaphragm/hoses d) Correct throttle valve or passage per air test e) Adjust range select linkage/renew valve f) Renew band servo g) Correct as per air test h) Renew band brake
Almost no shock or engine runaway on "2nd" to "3rd" shift	a) Oil level b) Range select linkage c) Vacuum diaphragm and hoses	a) Add if needed b) Adjust linkage c) Renew diaphragm/hoses

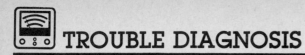

CHILTON'S THREE "C's" DIAGNOSIS CHART
Jatco F3A Automatic Transaxle

Condition	Cause	Correction
Almost no shock or engine runaway on "2nd" to "3rd" shift	d) Throttle valve pressure	d) Correct throttle valve or passage per air test
	e) Manual control valve	e) Adjust range select linkage/renew valve
	f) Band servo	f) Renew band servo
	g) Leakage of fluid passage	g) Correct as per air test
	h) Front clutch	h) Renew front clutch
	i) Front clutch check ball	i) Renew front clutch check ball
Vehicle braked by gear change from "1st" to "2nd"	a) Manual control valve	a) Adjust range select linkage/renew valve
	b) Front clutch	b) Renew front clutch
	c) Low and reverse brake	c) Renew low and reverse brake
	d) One-way clutch of transmission	d) Renew one-way clutch of transmission
Vehicle braked by gear change from "2nd" to "3rd"	a) Manual control valve	a) Adjust range select linkage
	b) Band servo	b) Renew band servo
	c) Brake band	c) Renew brake band
Failure to change from "3rd" to "2nd"	a) Vacuum diaphragm and hoses	a) Renew diaphragm/hoses
	b) Manual control valve	b) Adjust range select linkage/renew valve
	c) Governor valve	c) Overhaul governor/renew governor
	d) Band servo	d) Renew band servo
	e) Leakage of fluid pressure passage	e) Correct as per air test
	f) Front clutch	f) Renew front clutch
	g) Band brake	g) Renew band brake
Failure to change gear from "2nd" to "1st" or from "3rd" to "1st"	a) Vacuum diaphragm and hoses	a) Renew diaphragm/hoses
	b) Manual control valve	b) Adjust range select linkage/renew valve
	c) Governor valve	c) Overhaul governor/renew governor
	d) Band servo	d) Renew band servo
	e) Band brake	e) Renew band brake
	f) Leakage of fluid pressure passage	f) Correct as per air test
	g) One-way clutch of transmission	g) Renew one-way clutch of transmission
Gear change shock felt during deceleration by releasing accelerator pedal	a) Range select linkage	a) Adjust linkage
	b) Vacuum diaphragm and hoses	b) Renew diaphragm/hoses
	c) Downshift solenoid kickdown switch and wiring	c) Repair wiring and adjust or renew the downshift solenoid kickdown switch
	d) Throttle valve pressure	d) Correct throttle valve or passage per air test

CHILTON'S THREE "C's" DIAGNOSIS CHART
Jatco F3A Automatic Transaxle

Condition	Cause	Correction
Gear change shock felt during deceleration by releasing accelerator pedal	e) Manual control valve	e) Adjust range select linkage/renew valve
	f) Governor valve	f) Overhaul governor/renew governor
	g) Leakage of fluid pressure passage	g) Correct as per air test
Too high change point from "3rd" to "2nd" and from "2nd" to "1st"	a) Range select linkage	a) Adjust linkage
	b) Vacuum diaphragm and hoses	b) Renew diaphragm/hoses
	c) Downshift solenoid kickdown switch and wiring	c) Repair wiring and adjust or renew the downshift solenoid kickdown switch
	d) Throttle valve pressure	d) Correct throttle valve or passage per air test
	e) Manual control valve	e) Adjust range select linkage/renew valve
	f) Governor valve	f) Overhaul governor/renew governor
	g) Leakage at fluid passage	g) Correct per air test
No kickdown by depressing pedal in "3rd" within kickdown speed	a) Vacuum diaphragm and hoses	a) Renew diaphragm/hoses
	b) Downshift solenoid kickdown switch and wiring	b) Repair wiring and adjust or renew the solenoid downshift kickdown switch
	c) Manual control valve	c) Adjust range select linkage/renew valve
	d) Governor valve	d) Overhaul governor/renew governor
	e) Band brake	e) Renew band brake
	f) Leakage at fluid passage	f) Correct per air test
Kickdown operates or engine overruns when depressing pedal in "3rd" beyond kickdown speed limit	a) Range select linkage	a) Adjust linkage
	b) Vacuum diaphragm and hoses	b) Renew diaphragm/hoses
	c) Throttle valve pressure	c) Correct throttle valve or passage per air test
	d) Manual control valve	d) Adjust range select linkage/renew valve
	e) Governor valve	e) Overhaul governor/renew governor
	f) Leakage of fluid pressure passage	f) Correct as per air test
	g) Front clutch	g) Renew front clutch
Races extremely or slips in changing from "3rd" to "2nd"	a) Vacuum diaphragm and hoses	a) Renew diaphragm/hoses
	b) Throttle valve pressure	b) Correct throttle valve or passage as per air test
	c) Manual control valve	c) Adjust range select linkage/renew valve
	d) Band servo	d) Renew band servo

CHILTON'S THREE "C's" DIAGNOSIS CHART
Jatco F3A Automatic Transaxle

Condition	Cause	Correction
Races extremely or slips in changing from "3rd" to "2nd"	e) Leakage of fluid pressure passage f) Front clutch	e) Correct as per air test f) Renew front clutch
Failure to change from "3rd" to "2nd" when changing lever into "2" range	a) Range select linkage b) Throttle valve pressure c) Manual control valve d) Band servo e) Band brake f) Leakage of fluid pressure passage	a) Adjust linkage b) Correct throttle valve or passage per air test c) Adjust range select linkage/renew valve d) Renew band servo e) Renew band brake f) Correct as per air test
Gear change from "2nd" to "1st" or from "3rd" to "2nd"	a) Range select linkage b) Throttle valve pressure c) Manual control valve	a) Adjust linkage b) Correct throttle valve or passage per air test c) Adjust range select linkage/renew valve
No shock on change from "1" range to "2" range or engine races extremely	a) Oil level b) Range select linkage c) Vacuum diaphragm and hoses d) Engine idle rpm e) High stall speed f) Manual control valve g) Transmission air check to determine if band servo is working h) Oil pump	a) Add if needed b) Adjust linkage c) Renew diaphragm/hoses d) Set idle rpm e) Renew band brake f) Adjust range select linkage/renew valve g) Repair or renew servo h) Repair or renew
Failure to shift from "3rd" to "2nd" when shifting lever into "1" range	a) Range select linkage b) Throttle valve pressure c) Manual control valve d) Governor valve e) Band servo f) Leakage of fluid pressure passage g) Low and reverse brake	a) Adjust linkage b) Correct throttle valve or passage per air test c) Adjust range select linkage/renew valve d) Overhaul governor/renew governor e) Renew band servo f) Correct as per air test g) Renew low and reverse brake
No engine braking in range "1"	a) Range select linkage b) Throttle valve pressure c) Manual control valve d) Leakage of fluid pressure passage e) Low and reverse brake	a) Adjust linkage b) Correct throttle valve or passage per air test c) Adjust range select linkage/renew valve d) Correct as per air test e) Renew low and reverse brake

CHILTON'S THREE "C's" DIAGNOSIS CHART
Jatco F3A Automatic Transaxle

Condition	Cause	Correction
Gear change from "1st" to "2nd" or from "2nd" to "3rd" in "1" range	a) Range select linkage b) Manual control valve c) Leakage of fluid pressure passage	a) Adjust linkage b) Adjust range select linkage/renew valve c) Correct as per air test
Does not change from "2nd" to "1st" in "1" range	a) Oil level b) Range select linkage c) Manual control valve d) Governor valve e) Band servo f) Leakage of fluid pressure passage g) Low and reverse brake	a) Add if needed b) Adjust linkage c) Adjust range select linkage/renew valve d) Overhaul governor/renew governor e) Renew band servo f) Correct as per air test g) Renew low and reverse brake
Large shock in changing from "2nd" to "1st" in "1" range	a) Vacuum diaphragm and hoses b) High engine stall rpm c) Manual control valve	a) Renew diaphragm/hoses b) Renew low and reverse brake c) Adjust range select linkage/renew valve
Vehicle moves changing into "P" range or parking gear does not disengage when shifted out of "P" range	a) Range select linkage	a) Adjust linkage
Transmission overheats	a) Oil level b) Band servo c) Throttle valve pressure d) Restricted or no rear lubrication e) Manual control valve f) Leakage of fluid pressure passage g) Front clutch h) Band brake i) Low and reverse brake	a) Add if needed b) Renew band servo c) Correct throttle valve or passage per air test d) Check passages e) Adjust range select linkage/renew valve f) Correct as per air test g) Renew front clutch h) Renew band brake i) Renew low and reverse brake
Oil shoots out during operation. White smoke from exhaust during operation	a) Oil level b) Vacuum diaphragm and hoses c) Throttle valve pressure d) Restricted or no rear lubrication e) Manual control valve f) Leakage of fluid pressure passage g) Rear clutch	a) Add if needed b) Renew vacuum diaphragm/hoses c) Correct throttle valve or passage per air test d) Check passages e) Adjust range select linkage/renew valve f) Correct as per air test g) Renew rear clutch

CHILTON'S THREE "C's" DIAGNOSIS CHART
Jatco F3A Automatic Transaxle

Condition	Cause	Correction
Oil shoots out during operation. White smoke from exhaust during operation	h) Band brake i) Low and reverse brake j) Oil pump k) One-way clutch torque converter l) Planetary gear	h) Renew band brake i) Renew low and reverse brake j) Renew oil pump k) Renew one-way clutch torque converter l) Renew planetary gear
Offensive smell at fluid fill pipe	a) Oil level b) Rear clutch c) Front clutch d) Band brake e) Low and reverse brake f) Oil pump g) Leakage of fluid pressure passage h) One-way clutch torque converter	a) Add if needed b) Renew rear clutch c) Renew front clutch d) Renew band brake e) Renew low and reverse brake f) Renew oil pump g) Correct as per air test h) Renew one-way clutch torque converter
Transmission noise in "P" and "N" ranges	a) Oil level b) Throttle valve pressure c) Oil pump	a) Add if needed b) Correct throttle valve or passage per air test c) Renew oil pump
Transmission noise in "D", "2", "1" and "R" ranges	a) Oil level b) Throttle valve pressure c) Rear clutch d) Oil pump e) One-way clutch of transmission f) Planetary gear	a) Add if needed b) Correct throttle valve or passage per air test c) Renew rear clutch d) Renew oil pump e) Renew one-way clutch of transmission f) Renew planetary gear

HYDRAULIC CONTROL SYSTEM

Hydraulic pressure, clutch and band applications control the changing of gear ratios in the automatic transaxle. The clutches and bands are applied by the force of fluid pressure controlled by a system of values and control mechanisms.

1. Screen or filter cleans foreign material from the oil supply before entering the oil pump.

2. Oil pump supplies oil pressure to trans.

3. Converter pressure relief valve prevents converter pressure build up.

4. Torque converter is a fluid coupler and torque multiplier.

5. Rear clutch is applied in all forward gears.

6. Front clutch is applied in reverse and high gears.

7. Low and reverse brake (clutch) is applied in Park, Reverse and range "1" low gear.

8. Rear lubrication passages lubricate the rear transaxle components.

9. Front lubrication passages lubricate the front transaxle components.

10. Cooler system removes heat from converter by sending the transmission fluid through a cooler in the engine cooling system.

11. Drain back valve prevents loss of fluid in hydraulic circuits when engine is stopped.

12. Throttle control valve regulates throttle pressure in relation to the engine manifold vacuum through vacuum diaphragm (modulator).

13. Brake band servo is applied in 2nd gear and pressure released in high gear.

14. Pressure modifier valve uses throttle pressure, controlled by governor pressure, to modify the main line pressure from the regulator valve. Modifies harsh shifting caused by excessive pump pressure.

15. 2-3 timing valve slows down 2-3 shifts under heavy load condition.

16. Vacuum diaphragm (modulator) moves the throttle valve in relation to engine manifold vacuum changes.

17. Throttle backup valve increases throttle pressure output to delay the upshift at higher engine loads with engine vacuum low.

18. Governor provides road speed signal to the transaxle hydraulic control system.

19. Oil pressure regulator valve is used to control main line control pressure.

20. Throttle solenoid downshift valve overrides normal upshifts to provide forced downshifts on full acceleration.

21. Manual control valve moves with the shift selector and directs the line control pressure to the various oil passages.

22. 1-2 shift valve controls the upshift from first to second and the downshift from second to first.

23. 2-3 shift valve controls the upshift from second to third and downshift from third to second.

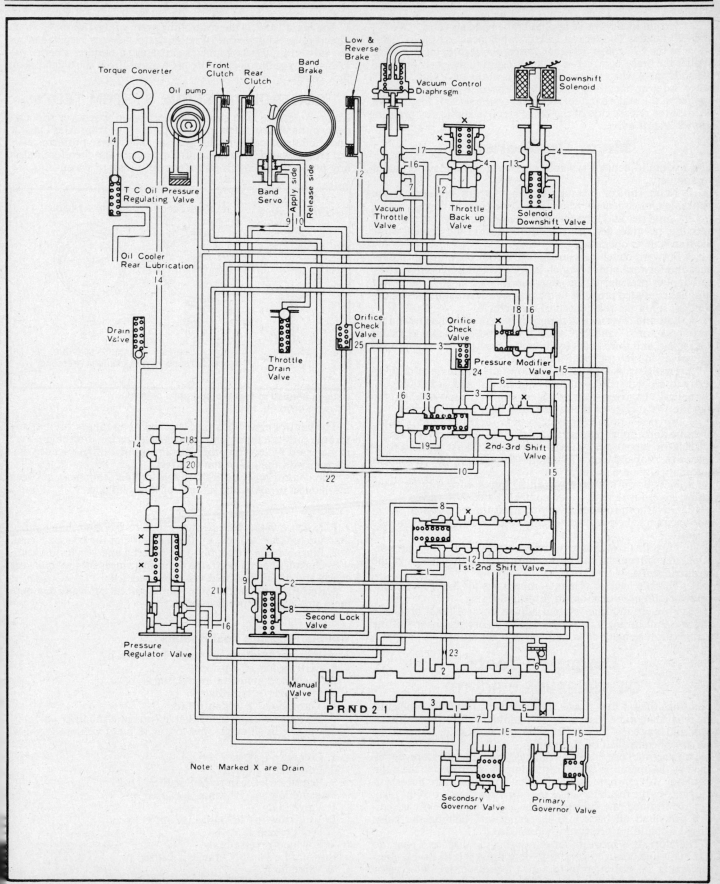

Hydraulic control schematic (©Toyo Kogyo Co. Ltd.)

24. Second lockup valve applies brake band servo in "D", "1" and "2" ranges. The second lockup valve locks out the 1-2 shift valve in the "2" range. In other words, the second lockup valve applies the brake band servo without regard to the position of the 1-2 shift valve when the manual lever is in the "2" range. In "D" range 3rd gear operation second lock up valve pressure remains applied at the brake band servo; however, the servo is inoperative because the release side of the brake servo is applied by pressure from 2-3 shift valve.

Major Components

The hydraulic control system consists of the following major components.

1. Main control pressure system supplies pressure to the transaxle and converter when the engine is operating.

2. Converter and lubrication system regulates converter fluid pressure, provides gear train lubrication and fluid cooling while the transaxle is operating.

3. Forward clutch pressure and governor pressure system applies the forward clutch, which is applied in all forward speeds, and applies pressure to the governor valve. The governor valve supplies regulated pressure to the rear side of the shift valves, dependent upon the road speed of the vehicle.

4. Low and reverse brake apply system applies the low and reverse brake in "1" and "R" selector lever positions and locks out the second and third gears by directing pressure to the appropriate valves to prevent them from shifting.

5. First gear lock out system allows the transaxle to shift directly to second speed and locks out the 1st and 3rd gears.

6. Brake band servo apply system applies the servo to hold the band to the surface of the reverse and high clutch cylinder.

7. Reverse pressure booster system increases control (line) pressure and applies reverse and high clutch in the reverse range.

8. Shift valve train system applies and exhaust the fluid pressures to servos and clutch assemblies for upshifts and downshifts automatically on demand.

9. Kick-down system (downshift) forces downshift by overriding governor/throttle valve control of the shift valves.

10. Governor provides a varying pressure proportional to engine vacuum to help control the timing and quality of the transaxle shifts.

11. Throttle (TV) system provides a varying pressure proportional to engine vacuum to help control the timing quality of the transaxle shifts.

12. Throttle backup system compensates for lower rate of engine vacuum at ½ or more of throttle opening.

13. Pressure modifier system adjusts control (line) pressures and 2-3 shift timing valve operation to insure smoother shifting under various engine load and vacuum conditions.

Diagnosis Tests

OIL PRESSURE CIRCUITS

To utilize the oil flow charts for diagnosing transaxle problems, the repairman must have an understanding of the oil pressure circuits and how each circuit affects the operation of the transaxle by the use of controlled oil pressure.

Control (line) pressure is a regulated main line pressure, developed by the operation of the front pump. It is directed to the main regulator valve, where predetermined spring pressure automatically moves the regulator valve to control the pressure of the oil at a predetermined rate, by opening the valve and exhausting excessive pressured oil back into the sump and holding the valve closed to build up pressure when needed.

Therefore, it is most important during the diagnosis phase to test main line control pressure to determine if high or low pressure exits. Do not attempt to adjust a pressure regulator valve spring to obtain more or less control pressure. Internal transaxle damage may result.

The main valve is the controlling agent of the transaxle which directs oil pressure to one of six separate passages used to control the valve train. By assigning each passage a number a better understanding of the oil circuits can be gained from the diagnosis oil flow charts.

CONTROL PRESSURE SYSTEM TESTS

Control pressure tests should be performed whenever slippage, delay or harshness is felt in the shifting of the transaxle. Throttle and modulator pressure changes can cause these problems also, but are generated from the control pressures and therefore reflect any problems arising from the control pressure system.

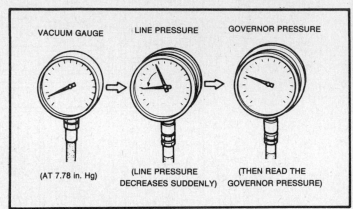

VACUUM GAUGE · LINE PRESSURE · GOVERNOR PRESSURE

(AT 7.78 in. Hg) · (LINE PRESSURE DECREASES SUDDENLY) · (THEN READ THE GOVERNOR PRESSURE)

Gauges needed to test the hydraulic circuits
(©Toyo Kogyo Co. Ltd.)

The control pressure is first checked in all ranges without any throttle pressure input, and then checked as the throttle pressure is increased by lowering the vacuum supply to the vacuum diaphragm with the use of the stall test.

The control pressure tests should define differences between mechanical or hydraulic failures of the transaxle.

Testing

1. Install a 0-400 psi pressure gauge to the main line control pressure tap, marked ML on the right side of the transaxle case.

2. Block wheels and apply both parking and service brakes.

3. Operate the engine/transaxle in the ranges on the following charts and at the manifold vacuum specified.

4. Record the actual pressure readings in each test and compare them to the given specifications.

Control Pressure Test Results

Low pressure at idle in all ranges is caused by
1. EGR system, if equipped
2. Vacuum diaphragm modulator
3. Manifold vacuum line
4. Throttle valve or control rod
5. Sticking regulator boost valve (pressure modifier valve)

OK at idle in all ranges, but low at 10 in. of vacuum is caused by
1. Excessive leakage
2. Low pump capacity
3. Restricted oil pan screen or filter

Pressure low in "P" range is caused by
1. Valve body

Pressure low in "R" range is caused by
1. Front clutch
2. Low and reverse brake

Pressure Low in "N" range is caused by
1. Valve body

Pressure low in "D" range is caused by
1. Rear clutch

Pressure low in "2" range is caused by
1. Rear Clutch
2. Brake band servo
Pressure low in "1" range is caused by
1. Rear clutch
2. Low and reverse brake
High or low pressure in all test conditions is caused by
1. Modulator control rod broken or missing
2. Stuck throttle valve
3. Pressure modifier valve or regulator valve

Precautions Before Idle Tests

1. Be sure manifold vacuum is above 15 in. Hg. If lower, check for engine conditions and/or vacuum leaks and repair.
2. Make sure the manifold vacuum changes with throttle plate opening. Check by accelerating quickly and observing the vacuum reading.

Precautions If Stall Test Is Used
On Pressure Rise Test

(Refer to stall test procedures.)
1. Do not operate engine/transaxle at stall for longer than 5 seconds per test.

2. Operate the engine between 1000 and 1200 rpm at the end of a test for approximately one to two minutes for cooling (in neutral).

3. Release the accelerator immediately in case of slippage or spin-up of the transaxle to avoid more damage to the unit.

AIR PRESSURE TESTS

The control pressure test results and causes of abnormal pressures are to be used as a guide. Further testing or inspection could be necessary before repairs are made. If the pressures are found to be low in a clutch, servo or passageway, a verification can be accomplished by removing the valve body and performing an air pressure test. This test can serve two purposes:

1. To determine if a malfunction of a clutch or band is caused by fluid leakage in the system or is the result of a mechanical failure.

2. To test the transaxle for internal fluid leakage during the rebuilding and before completing the assembly.

Procedure

1. Obtain an air nozzle and adjust for 25 psi.
2. Apply air pressure (25 psi) to the passages as listed.

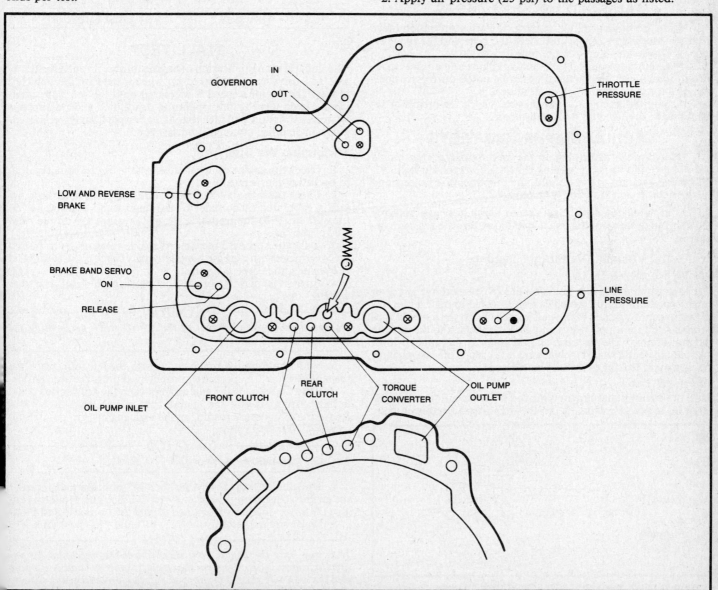

Identification of the fluid passages in the transaxle case (©Toyo Kogyo Co. Ltd.)

Vacuum Diaphragm

The modulated throttle system, which adjusts throttle pressure for the control of the shift valves, is operated by engine manifold vacuum through a vacuum diaphragm and must be inspected whenever a transaxle defect is apparent.

Preparation of Vacuum Test

Before the vacuum diaphragm test is performed, check the engine vacuum supply and the condition and routing of the supply lines.

With the engine idling, remove the vacuum line at the vacuum diaphragm and install a vacuum gauge. There must be a steady, acceptable vacuum reading for the altitude at which the test is being performed.

If the vacuum is low, check for a vacuum leak or poor engine performance. If the vacuum is steady and acceptable, accelerate the engine sharply and observe the vacuum gauge reading. The vacuum should drop off rapidly at acceleration and return to the original reading immediately upon release of the accelerator.

If the vacuum reading does not change or changes slowly, check the vacuum supply lines for being plugged, restricted or connected to a vacuum reservoir supply. Repair the system as required.

MANIFOLD VACUUM TESTS

1. With the engine idling, remove the vacuum supply hose from the modulator nipple and check the hose end for the presence of engine vacuum with an appropriate gauge.
2. If vacuum is present, accelerate the engine and allow it to return to idle. A drop in vacuum should be noted during acceleration and a return to normal vacuum at idle.
3. If manifold vacuum is not present, check for breaks or restrictions in the vacuum lines and repair.

VACUUM DIAPHRAGM TESTS

1. Apply at least 18 in. Hg. to the modulator vacuum nipple and observe the vacuum reading. The vacuum should hold.
2. If the vacuum does not hold, the diaphragm is leaking and the modulator assembly must be replaced.

NOTE: A leaking diaphragm causes harsh gear engagements and delayed or no up-shifts due to maximum throttle pressure developed.

Additional Vacuum Diaphragm Testing

ON THE CAR TEST

The vacuum diaphragm is tested on the vehicle with the aid of an outside vacuum source, which can be adjusted to maintain a certain amount of vacuum. Apply 18 inches Hg. to the vacuum diaphragm vacuum nipple, through a hose connected to the outside vacuum source. The vacuum should hold at the applied level without any leakdown. If the vacuum level drops off, the vacuum diaphragm is leaking and must be replaced.

OFF CAR TEST

With the vacuum diaphragm removed from the automatic transmission, apply 18 inches Hg. to the diaphragm vacuum nipple.

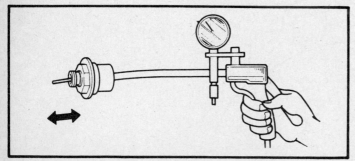

Testing vacuum modulator with a hand vacuum pump
(©Toyo Kogyo Co. Ltd.)

The vacuum level should remain and not drop off. If the vacuum level drops, the diaphragm is leaking and the unit should be replaced.

A second test can be made with the diaphragm removed from the transaxle. Insert the control rod into the valve end of the diaphragm and apply vacuum to the nipple. Hold a finger over the control rod and release the vacuum supply hose. The control rod should be moved outward by the pressure of the internal return spring. If the control rod does not move outward, a broken return spring is indicated.

VACUUM MODULATOR DIAPHRAGM ROD SPECIFICATIONS

Part No.			Diaphragm rod
0338	19	828	29.0mm (1.140 in)
0338	19	829	29.5mm (1.160 in)
0338	19	830	30.0mm (1.180 in)
0338	19	831	30.5mm (1.200 in)
0338	19	832	31.0mm (1.220 in)

STALL TEST

The stall test is an application of engine torque, through the transaxle and drive train to locked-up wheels, held by the vehicle's brakes. The engine's speed is increased until the rpms are stabilized. Given ideal engine operating conditions and no slippage from transmission clutches, bands or torque converter, the engine will stabilize at a specified test rpm.

Performing the Stall Test

1. Check the engine oil level and start the engine bringing it up to operating temperature.
2. Check the transaxle fluid level and correct as necessary. Attach a calibrated tachometer to the engine and a 0-400 psi oil pressure gauge to the transaxle control pressure tap on the right side of the case.
3. Mark the specified maximum engine rpm on the tachometer cover plate with a grease pencil to easily check if the stall speed is over or under specifications.
4. Apply the parking brake and block both front and rear wheels.

—— CAUTION ——

Do not allow anyone in front of the vehicle while performing the stall test.

5. While holding the brake pedal with the left foot, place the selector lever in "D" position and slowly depress the accelerator.
6. Read and record the engine rpm when the accelerator pedal is fully depressed and the engine rpm is stabilized. Read and record the oil pressure reading at the high engine rpm point. Stall speed—2200-2450 rpm.

—— CAUTION ——

The stall test must be made within five seconds.

7. Shift the selector lever into the "N" position and increase the engine speed to approximately 1000-1200 rpm. Hold this engine speed for one to two minutes to cool the transaxle and fluid.
8. Make similar tests in the "2", "1" and "R" positions.

—— CAUTION ——

If at any time the engine rpm races above the maximum as per specifications, indications are that a clutch unit or band is slipping and the stall test should be stopped before more damage is done to the internal parts.

Results of Stall Test

HIGH ENGINE RPM

If a slipping condition occurs during the stall test, indicated by high engine rpm, the selector lever position at the time of slippage provides an indication as to what holding member of the transaxle is defective.

By determining the holding member involved, several possible causes of slippage can be diagnosed.

1. Slips in all ranges, control pressure low
2. Slips in "D", "1" or "2", rear clutch
3. Slips in "D1" only, one-way clutch
4. Slips in "R" only, front clutch or low and reverse brake

Perform a road test to confirm these conditions.

LOW ENGINE RPM

When low stall speed is indicated, the converter one-way clutch is not holding or the engine is in need of a major tune-up. To determine which is at fault, perform a road test and observe the operation of the transaxle and the engine. If the converter one-way clutch does not lock the stator, acceleration will be poor up to approximately 30 mph. Above 30 mph acceleration will be normal. With poor engine performance acceleration will be poor at all speeds. When the one-way clutch is seized and locks the stator from turning either way, the stall test rpm will be normal. However, on a road test the vehicle will not go any faster than 50-55 mph because of the 2:1 reduction ratio in the converter.

If slippage was indicated by high engine rpm, the road test will help identify the problem area observing the transaxle operation during upshifts, both automatic and manual.

POSSIBLE LOCATIONS OF PROBLEMS DUE TO LINE PRESSURE

Malfunctions

1. Low pressure when in "D", "2", or "R" positions could be the result of a worn oil pump, fluid leaking from the oil pump, control valve or transaxle case, or the pressure regulator valve sticking.

STALL TEST HOLDING MEMBER CHART

Selector Lever Position	Holding Member Applied
"D" 1st Gear	Rear clutch One-way clutch
"1" Manual	Rear clutch Low and reverse brake clutch
"2" Manual	Rear clutch Rear band
Reverse	Front clutch Low and reverse brake clutch

Line Pressure At Stall Speed

"D" Range	128 to 156 psi
"2" Range	114 to 171 psi
"R" Range	228 to 270 psi

Line Pressure Before Stall Test—At Idle

"D" Range	43 to 57 psi
"2" Range	114 to 171 psi
"R" Range	57 to 110 psi

2. Low pressure when in "D" and "2" only could result from fluid leakage from the hydraulic circuit of the two ranges selected. Refer to the hydraulic fluid schematics.

3. Low fluid pressure when in the "R" position could result from a fluid leakage in the reverse fluid circuit. Refer to the hydraulic fluid schematic.

4. High pressure when idling could be the result of a broken or disconnected vacuum hose to the modulator or a defective vacuum modulator assembly.

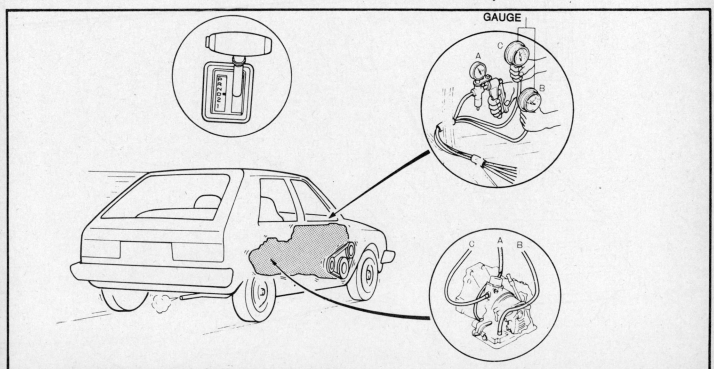

Line pressure cut back point (©Toyo Kogyo Co. Ltd.)

Main Line Pressure Cut-Back Point Test

1. Connect the fluid pressure test gauge to the line pressure test port outlet of the transaxle case.

2. Connect a fluid pressure test gauge to the governor pressure test port on the transaxle case.

3. Position the gauges so that each can be seen from the driver's seat.

4. Disconnect the vacuum hose to the vacuum modulator and plug the hose.

5. Connect a vacuum pump to the vacuum modulator and position the pump so it can be operated from the driver's seat.

6. If the line pressure drops abruptly when the engine rpm is increased gradually while the selector lever is in the "D" position. Measure the governor pressure.

7. Measure the governor pressure when the vacuum is at 0 in. Hg and at 7.78 in. Hg. The specifications are as follows:

   0 in. Hg—14-23 psi
   7.78 in. Hg— 6-14 psi

8. If the specifications are not met, check to see that the diaphragm rod has been installed or that it is more than standard. Check for a sticking valve inside the control valve assemble if the rod is correct.

Governor Pressure Test

1. Connect the fluid pressure gauge to the governor test port on the transaxle case. Position the gauge so that it is accessible to the operator.

2. Drive the vehicle with the selector lever in the "D" position.

3. Measure the governor pressure at the following speeds:

   20 mph—11.9-17.1 psi
   35 mph—19.9-28.4 psi
   55 mph—38.4-48.3 psi

4. If the test results do not meet the specifications, the following should be checked:

   a. Fluid leakage from the line pressure hydraulic circuit.
   b. Fluid leakage from the governor pressure hydraulic circuit.
   c. Governor malfunctions.

ROAD TEST

The road test is used to confirm malfunctions do exist within the transaxle unit, or that repairs have been accomplished and the transaxle unit is either operating properly or will require additional adjustments or repairs. The road test must be performed over a pre-determined drive course that has been used before to evaluate transmission and/or transaxle operations.

Should malfunctions occur during the road test, the selector range and road speed should be noted, along with the particular gear or shift point. By applying the point of malfunction in the operation of the transaxle, to the Clutch and Band Application Chart and the Chilton's Three "C's" diagnosis chart, the probable causes can be pinpointed.

Some of the points to be evaluated during the road test are as follows:

1. The shift point should be smooth and have a positive engagement.

2. The shifts speed are within specifications.

3. All shifts occur during the upshifts and downshifts when in the selector lever detents, as required.

4. All downshifts occur when a forced downshift is demanded.

5. No upshift to third when the selector lever is in the "2" position and the transaxle is in the second speed.

6. Only one upshift from the first speed when the selector lever is in the "1" position.

7. The vehicle is firmly locked when the lever is in the "P" position.

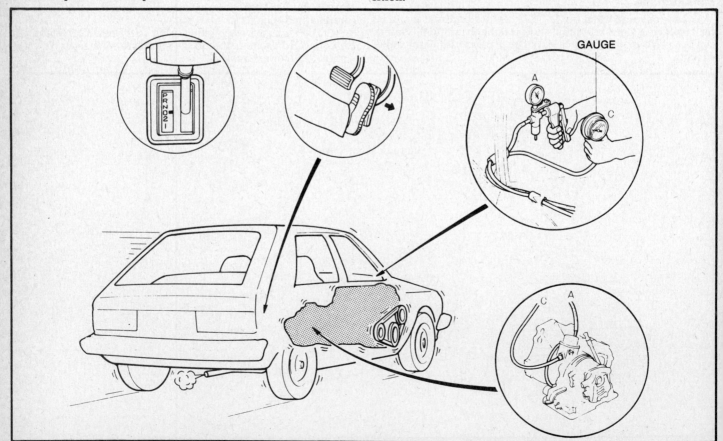

Governor pressure check (©Toyo Kogyo Co. Ltd.)

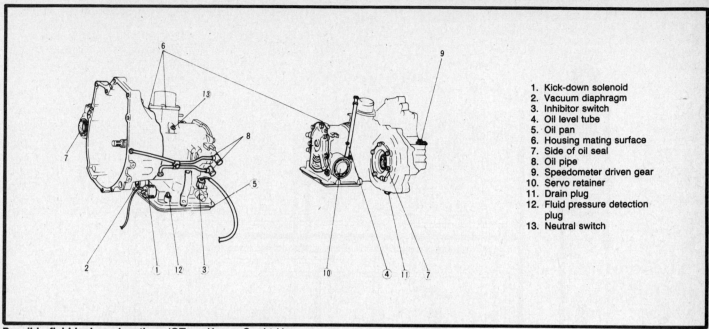

1. Kick-down solenoid
2. Vacuum diaphragm
3. Inhibitor switch
4. Oil level tube
5. Oil pan
6. Housing mating surface
7. Side of oil seal
8. Oil pipe
9. Speedometer driven gear
10. Servo retainer
11. Drain plug
12. Fluid pressure detection plug
13. Neutral switch

Possible fluid leakage locations (©Toyo Kogyo Co. Ltd.)

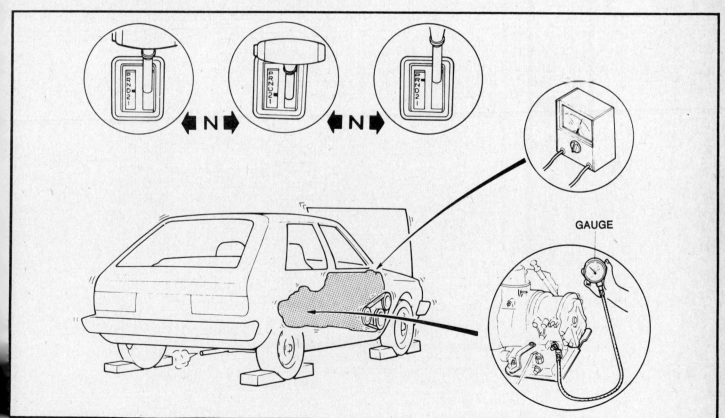

GAUGE

Line pressure test (©Toyo Kogyo Co. Ltd.)

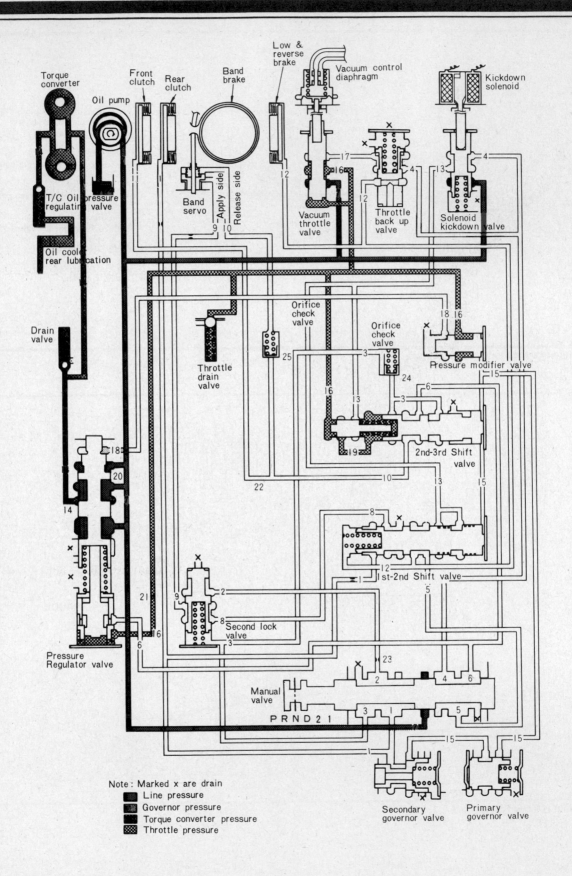

Torque converter

Oil pump

Front clutch

Rear clutch

Band brake

Low & reverse brake

Vacuum control diaphragm

Kickdown solenoid

T/C Oil pressure regulating valve

Oil cooler rear lubrication

Drain valve

Band servo

Apply side

Release side

Vacuum throttle valve

Throttle back up valve

Solenoid kickdown valve

Orifice check valve

Orifice check valve

Pressure modifier valve

Throttle drain valve

2nd-3rd Shift valve

18

14

20

21

1st-2nd Shift valve

Second lock valve

Pressure Regulator valve

Manual valve

P R N D 2 1

Secondary governor valve

Primary governor valve

Note : Marked x are drain

▪ Line pressure
▪ Governor pressure
▪ Torque converter pressure
▪ Throttle pressure

Neutral

Neutral

Units Applied

NONE

The transaxle is not transmitting torque to output shaft in Neutral range.

The oil pump is operating and has charged the main line control pressure system. Pressure is regulated.

The converter and cooler systems are charged. Control pressure is also routed to the vacuum throttle valve and the solenoid downshift valve.

The manual control valve is in the Neutral position and control pressure ⑦ is stopped at the manual valve.

Vacuum throttle valve pressure ⑯ is directed to the pressure modifier valve, 2-3 shift valve, 2-3 timing valve and the bottom of the pressure regulator valve. The pressure pushing up on the pressure regulator valve increases regulated line pressure. Since no clutches or bands are engaged, the transaxle is in Neutral.

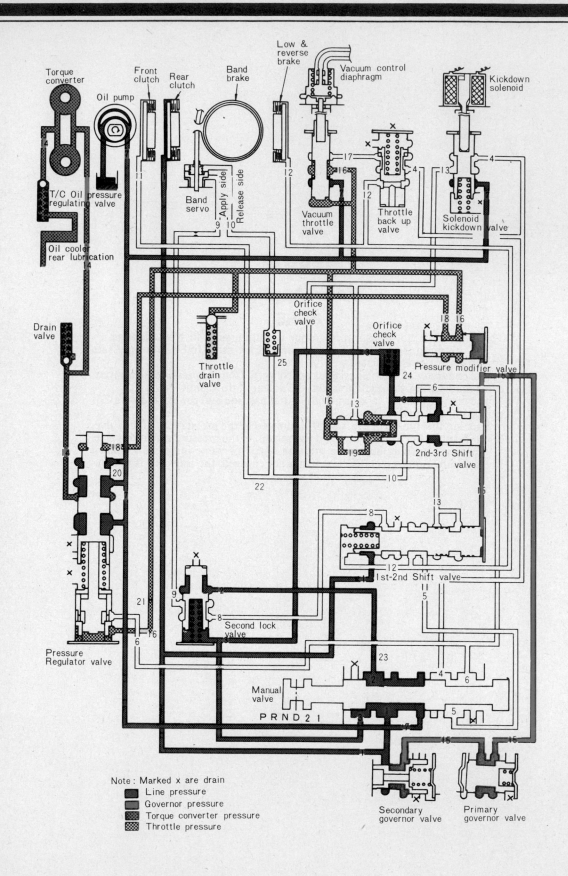

D₁ range, first gear

DRIVE—1ST GEAR

Units Applied

REAR CLUTCH, ONE-WAY CLUTCH

It is assumed the vehicle is moving at low speed (10-15 mph) and at a light throttle opening.

The oil pump is operating and has charged the main control pressure circuit. The fluid is being regulated.

The converter and cooler systems are charged with control pressure, which is also routed to the vacuum throttle valve and solenoid downshift valve.

The manual valve has been positioned to open passage ① leading to the governor secondary valve, the rear of the 1-2 shift valve and to apply the rear clutch.

The manual valve is positioned so that fluid pressure ② is directed to the second lock valve.

Passage ③ is charged. Fluid pressure is directed to the opposite end of the second lock valve, opposing and equalizing pressure ②.

Passage ③ fluid pressure is directed through the orifice check valve and to the 2-3 shift valve, where it is stopped by the valve lands and grooves.

Throttle valve pressure ⑯ is directed to the pressure modifier valve, 2-3 shift valve, 2-3 timing valve and the pressure regulator valve.

Governor pressure, generated in proportion to vehicle speed, is transmitted to the end of the 1-2 shift valve, 2-3 shift valve, 2-3 timing valve and the pressure modifier valve.

After initial start up and under hard acceleration, the oil pump output ⑦ may be high. The higher pump pressure causes higher line pressure ⑦ and harsh application of bands and clutches. The pressure modifier valve is designed to reduce line pressure ⑦ under these conditions. When governor pressure ⑮ overcomes throttle pressure ⑯ and spring force in the pressure modifier valve, then throttle pressure ⑱ is allowed to flow to the top of the pressure regulator valve. This new pressure pushing down on the pressure regulator valve reduces line pressure.

The 1-2 shift valve is not modulated by vacuum throttle valve pressure in the Jatco transaxle. Therefore, the 1-2 shift depends on governor pressure opposing spring and line pressure to regulate the 1-2 shift.

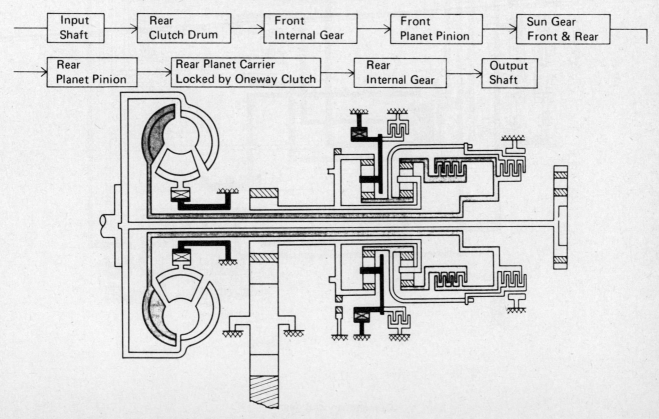

| Input Shaft | → | Rear Clutch Drum | → | Front Internal Gear | → | Front Planet Pinion | → | Sun Gear Front & Rear |

| Rear Planet Pinion | → | Rear Planet Carrier Locked by Oneway Clutch | → | Rear Internal Gear | → | Output Shaft |

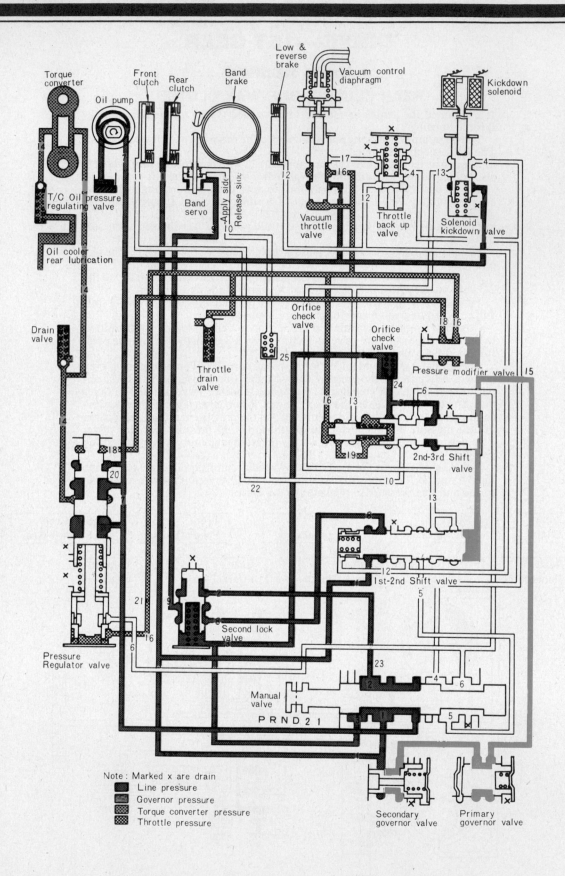

D₂ range, second gear

DRIVE—2ND GEAR
Units Applied
REAR CLUTCH, BAND SERVO

The transaxle is now in 2nd speed and the vehicle is moving approximately 35 mph at light throttle.

The oil pump is charging the main control system and pressure is regulated.

The converter and cooler systems are charged. Control pressure is routed to the vacuum throttle valve and the downshift solenoid valve.

The manual valve has been positioned to open passage ① to the secondary governor valve, the rear of the 1-2 shift valve and the apply side of the rear clutch.

Passage ② is charged and fluid pressure is directed to the end of the second lock valve.

Passage ③ is directed to the other end of the second lock valve. Fluid pressure ③ opposes and equalizes fluid pressure ② at the second lock valve.

Fluid pressure ③ is also directed through orifice check valve to the 2-3 shift valve where it is stopped by the valves lands and grooves.

Vacuum throttle valve pressure ⑯ is directed to the pressure modifier valve, 2-3 shift valve, 2-3 timing valve and pressure regulator valve.

Governor pressure ⑮, generated in proportion to vehicle speed, is transmitted to the end of the 1-2 shift valve, 2-3 shift valve and the pressure modifier valve.

After initial start up and under hard acceleration, the oil pump output ⑦ may be higher. The higher pump pressure causes harsh application of clutches and bands. The pressure modifier valve is designed to reduce regulated pressure ⑦ under these conditions. When governor pressure ⑮ overcomes throttle pressure ⑯ and spring pressure in the pressure modifier valve, then throttle pressure ⑱ is allowed to flow to the top of the pressure regulator valve. This new pressure pushing down on the pressure regulator valve reduces line pressure, thereby modulating the harsh shift.

As the governor pressure increases on the 1-2 shift valve, passage ⑧ opens and is directed through the center of the second lock valve ⑨ and to the apply side of the brake band servo. The brake band is applied and the transaxle is in 2nd speed.

| Input Shaft | → | Rear Clutch Drum | → | Front Internal Gear | → | Front Sun Gear Locked by Brake Band | → | Front Planet Pinion |

| Front Planet Carrier | → | Output Shaft |

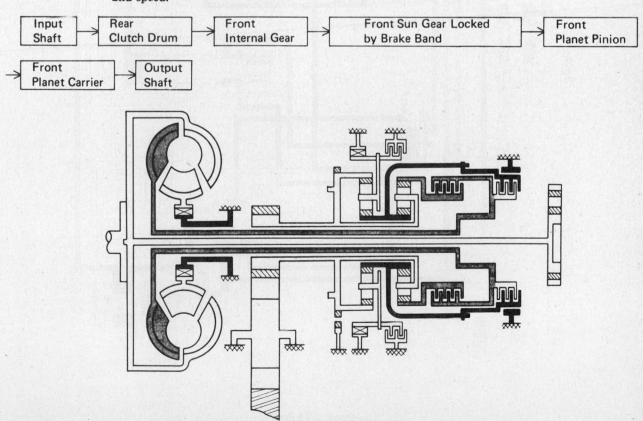

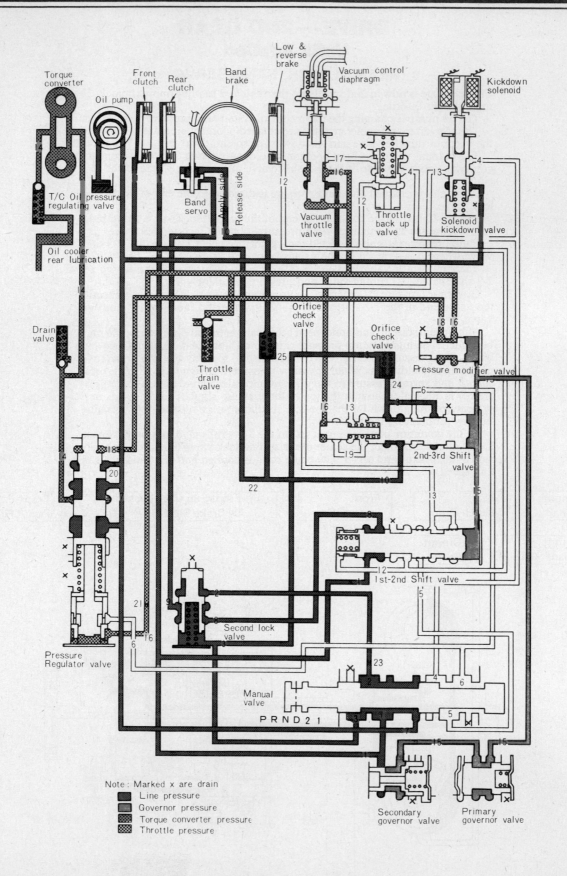

D₃ range, third gear

DRIVE—3RD GEAR
Units Applied
FRONT CLUTCH, REAR CLUTCH

The transaxle has shifted to 3rd speed and the vehicle is moving approximately 50 mph at ½ throttle.

The oil pump is charging the main control system and pressure is regulated.

The converter and cooler systems are charged. Control pressure is also routed to the vacuum throttle valve and the downshift solenoid valve.

The manual valve has been positioned to open passage ① to the secondary governor valve, the rear of the 1-2 shift valve and the apply side of the rear clutch.

Passage ② is charged and fluid pressure is directed to the end of second lock valve.

Passage ③ is directed to the other end of the second lock valve. Fluid pressure ③ opposes and equalizes fluid pressure ② at the second lock valve.

Fluid pressure ③ is also directed through the orifice check valve to the 2-3 shift valve where it is stopped by the valve lands and grooves.

Vacuum throttle valve pressure ⑯ is directed to the pressure modifier valve, 2-3 shift valve, 2-3 timing valve and pressure regulator valve.

Governor pressure ⑮, generated in proportion to vehicle speed, is transmitted to the end of the 1-2 shift valve, 2-3 shift valve and the pressure modifier valve.

After initial start up and under hard acceleration, the oil pump output ⑦ may be higher. The pressure modifier valve is designed to reduce regulated pressure ⑦ under these conditions. When governor pressure ⑮ overcomes throttle pressure ⑯ and spring pressure, the pressure modifier valve allows throttle pressure ⑱ to flow to the top of the pressure regulator valve. This new pressure pushing down on the pressure regulator valve reduces line pressure and modulates the harsh shift.

As vehicle speed increases, so does governor pressure on the 2-3 shift valve. When the valve is pushed to the left, passage ⑩ opens, directing fluid pressure to the release side of the brake band servo. At the same time that the second speed brake band is being released, the third speed ⑪ front clutch is being applied. Thus, the transaxle is shifted into 3rd speed.

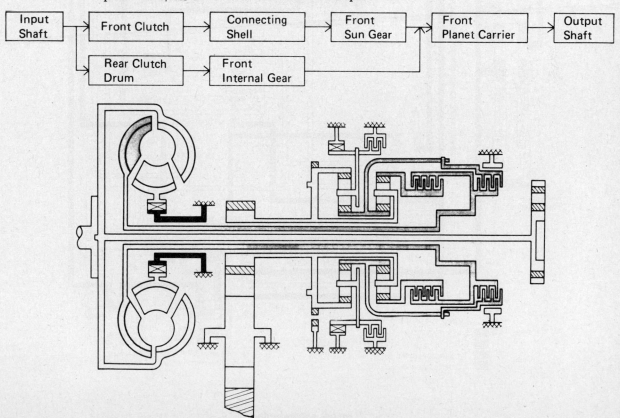

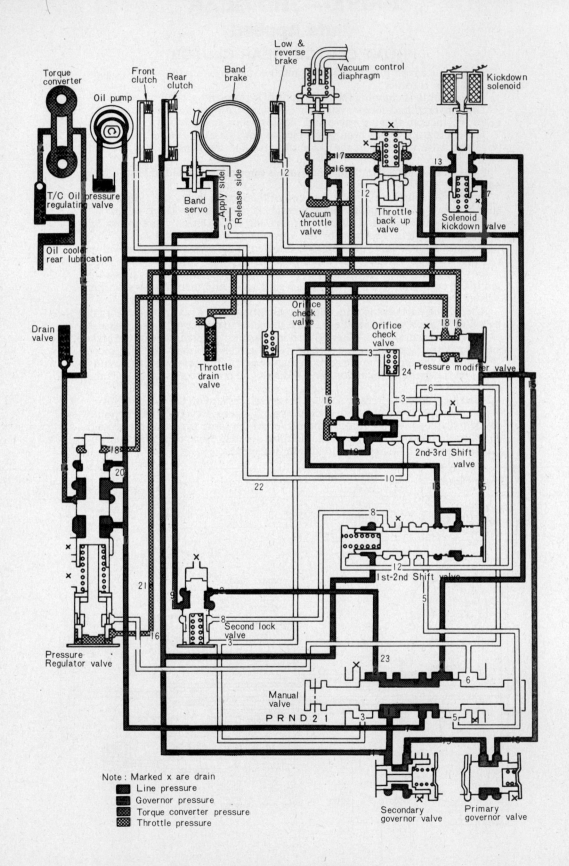

Torque converter

Oil pump

Front clutch

Rear clutch

Band brake

Low & reverse brake

Vacuum control diaphragm

Kickdown solenoid

T/C Oil pressure regulating valve

Band servo

Apply side

Release side

Vacuum throttle valve

Throttle back up valve

Solenoid kickdown valve

Oil cooler rear lubrication

Drain valve

Throttle drain valve

Orifice check valve

Orifice check valve

Pressure modifier valve

2nd-3rd Shift valve

1st-2nd Shift valve

Pressure Regulator valve

Second lock valve

Manual valve

P R N D 2 1

Secondary governor valve

Primary governor valve

Note : Marked x are drain
Line pressure
Governor pressure
Torque converter pressure
Throttle pressure

"2" range, second gear

MANUAL "2"—2ND GEAR

Units Applied

REAR CLUTCH, BAND SERVO

The "2" range means that the transaxle is locked in 2nd gear, regardless of the engine and vehicle speed conditions. This is accomplished totally by fluid pressure from manual valve passages opened in the "2" range position of the manual valve.

The oil pump is supplying pressure and pressure is regulated.

The converter and cooling systems are charged. Main line control pressure is also directed to the vacuum throttle valve and the solenoid downshift valve.

Manual valve passage① supplies the secondary governor valve.

Passage① directs fluid pressure to the rear clutch.

Passage① also supplies fluid pressure to the 1-2 shift valve.

The manual valve passage② directs fluid pressure to the upper end of the second lock valve. The downward fluid pressure locks the transmission in 2nd speed since it also allows passage② pressure to flow through to passage⑨, which is the apply side of the brake band servo. With the rear clutch and brake band applied, without regard to the position of the 1-2 shift valve, the transaxle is locked-up out of 1st and into 2nd gear. However, there is also provision for preventing upshifts into 3rd gear. The "2" range provides 2-3 upshift lock-out.

In the "2" range, two pressures combine to provide 2-3 upshift lockout. Passage④ supplies fluid pressure to the solenoid downshift valve and the throttle backup valve.

Through passage⑦, the throttle backup valve boosts the pressure in the throttle vacuum valve passage⑯.

Vacuum throttle valve pressure⑯, and solenoid downshift valve pressure⑬ both oppose the governor upshift pressure⑮ at the 2-3 shift valve. The two fluid pressures combine with spring pressure to lock out the 2-3 upshift. The transaxle is locked in 2nd speed.

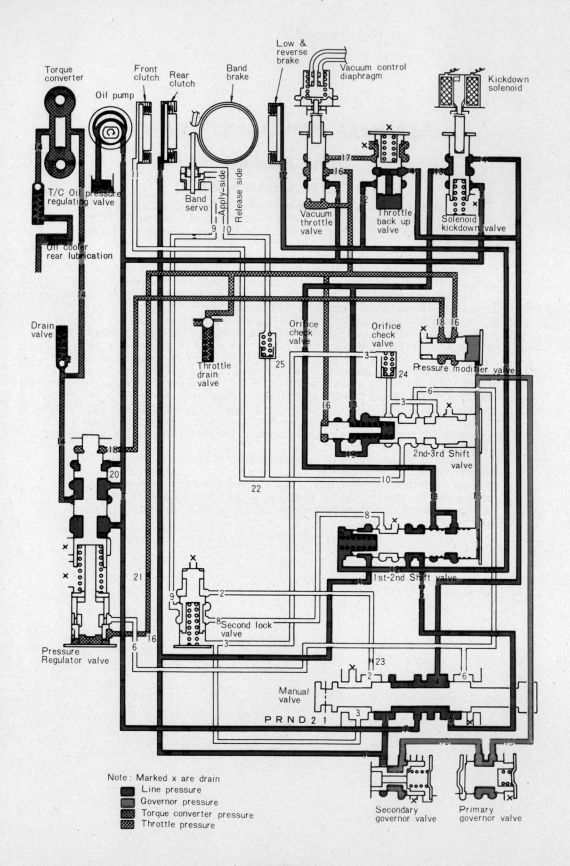

1₁ range, first gear

MANUAL "1"—1ST GEAR

Units Applied

REAR CLUTCH, LOW-REVERSE BRAKE

It is assumed the vehicle speed is less than 16 mph at light throttle. The shift lever is moved to the "1" range position and the transaxle is locked in Low gear.

The oil pump pressure is present and pressure is regulated.

Converter and cooler systems are charged. Main line control pressure is supplied to the throttle back up valve and the solenoid downshift valve.

The manual valve supplies passage①. Passage directs fluid pressure to the secondary governor valve, the rear clutch and the 1-2 shift valve.

Passage④ routes fluid pressure to the solenoid downshift valve and the throttle back up valve.

In "1" range, the manual valve applies fluid pressure to passage⑤. Passage⑤ directs fluid pressure to the 1-2 shift valve.

Passage⑫ routes fluid pressure from the 1-2 shift valve to the other end of the 1-2 shift valve. This pressure, plus solenoid downshift pressure⑬, is overcome to provide the upshift to 2nd speed.

Passage⑫ also directs fluid pressure to the throttle backup valve and the low and reverse brake.

Two pressures combined with spring pressure to lock out 2-3 upshifts in the "1" range. Solenoid downshift valve pressure⑬ is applied to the 2-3 and 1-2 shift valves.

Vacuum throttle valve pressure⑯ combined with throttle back-up valve pressure⑰ are applied to the 2-3 shift valve.

The rear clutch and the low and reverse brake are applied. The transaxle is locked in Low (1st) gear.

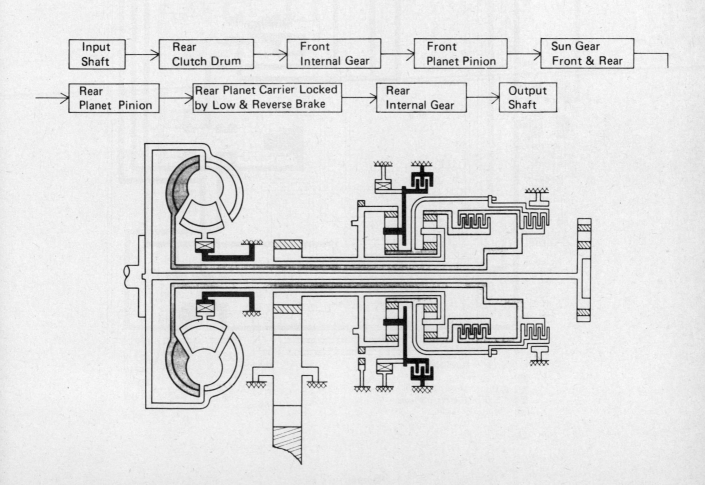

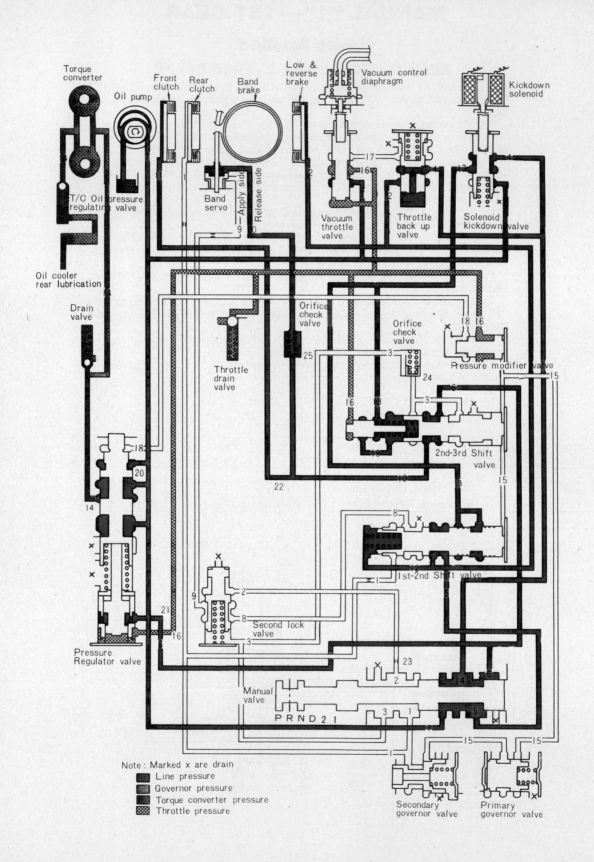

Torque converter

Oil pump

Front clutch

Rear clutch

Band brake

Low & reverse brake

Vacuum control diaphragm

Kickdown solenoid

T/C Oil pressure regulating valve

Band servo

Apply side

Release side

Vacuum throttle valve

Throttle back up valve

Solenoid kickdown valve

Oil cooler rear lubrication

Drain valve

Throttle drain valve

Orifice check valve

Orifice check valve

Pressure modifier valve

2nd-3rd Shift valve

1st-2nd Shift valve

Pressure Regulator valve

Second lock valve

Manual valve

P R N D 2 1

Secondary governor valve

Primary governor valve

Note : Marked x are drain
- Line pressure
- Governor pressure
- Torque converter pressure
- Throttle pressure

Reverse

REVERSE

Units Applied

FRONT CLUTCH, LOW-REVERSE BRAKE

The pump is supplying mainline control pressure and the pressure is being regulated.

The converter and cooler systems are charged.

The manual valve is in the Reverse position, and passages④, ⑤ and ⑥ are charged.

Passage④ supplies control line pressure to the throttle backup valve and the solenoid downshift valve.

Passage⑤ supplies control pressure to the 1-2 shift valve. The 1-2 shift valve routes the fluid pressure to passage⑫, which supplies pressure to the throttle backup valve and the low and reverse brake.

Passage⑥ supplies pressure to the 2-3 shift valve, the front clutch⑪ and the release side of the brake band servo⑩.

Passage⑥ also supplies pressure to one end of the regulator valve, thus increasing control pressure. More control pressure is needed in Reverse because of increased torque on the output shaft.

The application of pressure to the release side of the brake band servo serves only to ensure the release of the brake band. The front clutch and the low and reverse brake are the operating members of the power train in this gear.

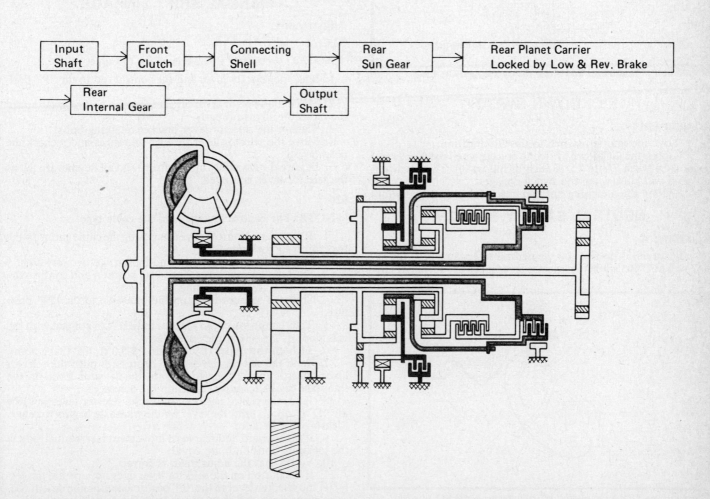

 ON CAR SERVICES

Adjustments

VACUUM MODULATOR

Adjustment

The vacuum modulator has no adjustments other than the replacement of the diaphragm rod. The rods are available in varied lengths as follows:

1.160 in. or 29.5mm
1.180 in. or 30.0mm
1.200 in. or 30.5mm
1.220 in. or 31.0mm
1.240 in. or 31.5mm

NOTE: The transaxle will have to be drained down before the vacuum modulator is removed. Add the necessary fluid and correct the level as required.

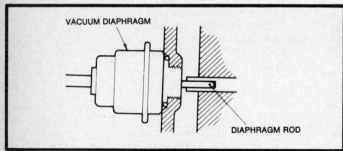

Installation of modulator assembly (©Toyo Kogyo Co. Ltd.)

KICKDOWN SWITCH

Adjustment

1. Move the ignition switch to the ON position.
2. Loosen the kickdown switch to engage when the accelerator pedal is between 7/8 to 15/16 inch of full travel. The downshift solenoid will click when the switch engages.
3. Tighten the attaching nut and check for proper operation.

NEUTRAL SAFETY SWITCH

Adjustment

No adjustment is possible on the neutral safety switch. If the engine will not start while the selector lever is in the "P" or "N" po-

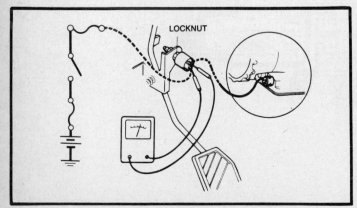

Checking the kickdown switch (©Toyo Kogyo Co. Ltd.)

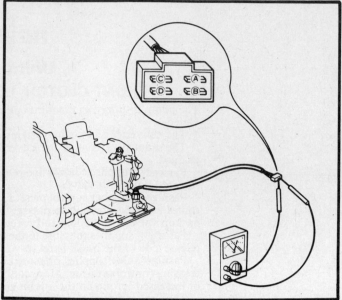

Checking the neutral starting switch (©Toyo Kogyo Co. Ltd.)

sitions and the back-up lamps do not operate, the switch is defective and must be replaced.

MANUAL SHIFT LINKAGE

Adjustment

GLC

NOTE: The control linkage is of the rod type.

1. Shift the selector lever and the control rod to the "P" position.
2. Move the selector lever bracket forward and rearward until the indicator aligns properly.
3. Tighten the selector lever bracket retaining bolts.
4. Move the selector lever through all ranges and recheck the positioning.
5. Be sure the assembly moves freely and all detents are felt as the selector lever is moved.

626

NOTE: The control linkage is of the cable type.

1. Remove the console cover, exposing the cable end with the two adjusting locknuts.
2. Engage the parking brake and loosen the two locknuts.
3. Shift the selector lever to the "N" position and confirm the detent roller is in the "N" range.
4. Shift the selector lever on the transaxle to the "N" position.
5. Tighten the lower (A) locknut until it is in contact with the trunnion on the selector lever linkage.
6. Tighten the upper (B) locknut 5.8-8.0 ft. lbs. (8-11 N•m).
7. With the selector lever knob depressed, push the selector lever towards the "P" position until the selector lever on the transaxle begins to move. Measure the distance.
8. From the center position, move the selector lever towards the "D" position until the lever on the transaxle begins to move. Measure the distance.
9. If the forward and rearward movement is not equal, adjust the locknuts until both are equal.
10. Verify that the adjustment is correct.
11. If the button on the selector lever does not operate properly, set the selector lever to the "P" position, loosen the detent roller mounting nut and then adjust by moving the detent roller.

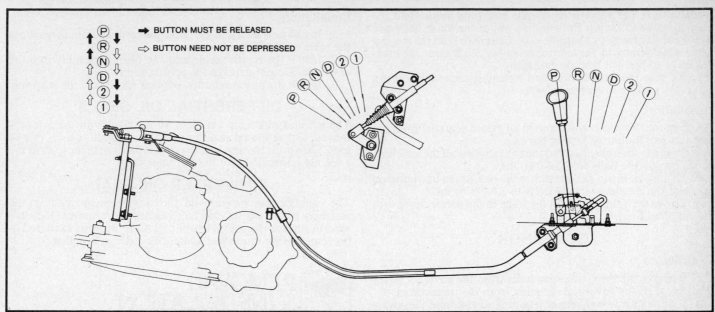

↑ ⓟ ↓
↑ ⓡ ⇓
↑ ⓝ ⇓
↑ ⓓ ⇓
↑ ② ⇓
↑ ① ⇓

→ BUTTON MUST BE RELEASED
⇨ BUTTON NEED NOT BE DEPRESSED

Manual shift linkage used with the Mazda 626 models (©Toyo Kogyo Co. Ltd.)

Services

TRANSAXLE FLUID CHANGE

The Jatco transaxle do not have a specific or periodic fluid change interval for the normal maintenance of the units. However, at the time of any major repairs or when the fluid has been contaminated, the converter, cooler and lines must be flushed to remove any debris and contaminated fluid. If the vehicle is used in continuous service or driven under severe conditions (police or taxi type operations), the transaxle should be drained, flushed and refilled at mileage intervals of 18,000-24,000 or at time intervals of 18-24 months.

NOTE: The time or mileage intervals given are average. Each vehicle operated under severe conditions should be treated individually.

Procedure

1. Remove the speedometer cable and driven gear from the transaxle case.
2. Remove the drain plug at the bottom of the transaxle case.
3. Allow the fluid to drain completely and reinstall the drain plug.
4. Add type F fluid to the transaxle through the speedometer gear opening in the case until the desired level is reached.
5. Reinstall the speedometer cable and driven gear into the transaxle case.

VACUUM DIAPHRAGM

NOTE: Drain the transaxle before removing the vacuum modulator.

Removal

1. Raise the vehicle and support safely. Disconnect the vacuum hose from the diaphragm unit.
2. Turn the threaded diaphragm unit to remove it from the transmission case.
3. Pull the actuating pin and the throttle valve from the transmission case.
4. Remove the O-ring from the assembly.

Installation

1. Install a new O-ring on the diaphragm unit.

2. Install the throttle valve, the actuating pin and the vacuum diaphragm tubes toward the transmission case and install the assembly into the case.
3. Tighten the vacuum diaphragm unit securely.

OIL PAN

Draining and Removal

1. Raise the vehicle and support safely.
2. Position a drain pan beneath the transaxle oil pan and starting at the rear, loosen, but do not remove the pan bolts.
3. Loosen the pan from the transaxle case and allow the fluid to drain gradually.
4. Remove all pan bolts except two at the front of the pan and allow the fluid to continue draining.
5. Remove the pan. Clean the remains of the old gasket from the pan and transaxle case.

Installation

1. Install a new gasket on the pan and install it to the transaxle case.
2. Install all pan bolts and torque to 3.6-5.8 ft. lbs.
3. Install three quarts of transmission fluid, type F into the filler tube (converter not drained).
4. Start the engine and operate the engine at idle speed for approximately two minutes. Then raise the engine speed to approximately 1200 rpm until the engine and transaxle reach operating temperature.

───── CAUTION ─────
Do not overspeed the engine during warm-up.

5. Check the fluid level after moving the gear selector through all ranges. Correct the fluid level as necessary.

VALVE BODY

Removal

1. Raise the vehicle so the transaxle oil pan is accessible.
2. Drain the transmission fluid by loosening the pan attaching bolts and allowing the fluid to drain.
3. Remove the pan attaching bolts, pan and gasket.
4. Remove the downshift solenoid, vacuum diaphragm, vacuum diaphragm rod and O-rings.

5. Remove the valve body-to-case attaching bolts. Hold the manual valve to keep it from sliding out of the valve body and remove the valve body from the case. Failure to hold the manual valve while removing the control assembly could cause the manual valve to become bent or damaged.

6. Refer to the Disassembly and Assembly section for control valve body repair operations.

Installation

1. Thoroughly clean and remove all gasket material from the pan and pan mounting face of the case.

2. Position the valve body to the case and install the attaching bolts. Torque the bolts to 5.8-8.0 ft. lbs.

3. Using a new pan gasket, secure the pan to the transmission case and torque the attaching bolts to 3.6-5.8 ft. lbs.

4. Lower the vehicle and fill the trans to the correct level with the specified fluid.

GOVERNOR

Removal

1. Remove the three retaining bolts from the governor cover assembly. Lift the governor assembly from the transaxle case.

2. Remove the two governor retaining screws from the governor sleeve. Remove the governor valve body.

3. Disassemble the governor valve body as required.

Installation

1. Reassemble the governor valve body.

2. Install the governor valve body to the governor sleeve.

3. Mount the governor to the transaxle case so that the sleeve projection is aligned with the mating mark on the transaxle case.

4. Install the three cover/governor retaining bolts and tighten to 3.6-5.8 ft. lbs. of torque.

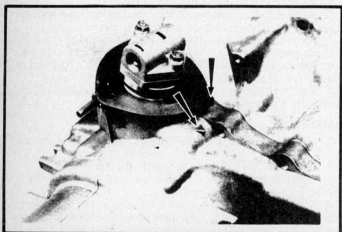

Governor to transaxle mating marks (©Toyo Kogyo Co. Ltd.)

SERVO

Removal

NOTE: Depending upon the configurations of the varied vehicle applications, the removal of the servo could require excessive movement of the engine/transaxle assembly. Perform this procedure as required.

1. With a pushing type tool, move the piston retainer inward and remove the snapring.

2. Remove the piston assembly from the case bore. Remove the return spring.

3. The seals can be removed and the piston assembly separated.

Installation

1. Install new seals and assemble the piston components. Coat the seals with A/T fluid or vaseline.

2. Install the return spring and the piston assembly into the case bore. Do not damage the sealing rings.

3. Install the piston retainer, depress and install the snapring.

DIFFERENTIAL OIL SEALS

The left and right axle seals can be installed with the axles removed. Conventional seal removing and installing tools can be used. Care must be exercised to prevent damage to the seals as the axles are reinstalled into the transaxle case.

CONVERTER OIL SEAL

The transaxle must be removed, the converter removed from the assembly before the seal can be replaced. Conventional tools are used to replace the converter oil seal. Care must be exercised to prevent damage to the seal as the converter is installed.

REMOVAL & INSTALLATION

Removal of Transaxle
MAZDA 626 MODELS

1. Disconnect the negative battery cable and the speedometer cable.

2. Disconnect the selector control cable from the transaxle. Disconnect the ground wire from the transaxle.

3. Disconnect the neutral start (inhibitor) switch from the transaxle.

4. Remove the starter assembly.

5. Attach engine support assembly to the engine hanger eyelets and suspend the engine within the compartment.

6. Remove the vacuum line to the modulator.

7. Remove the upper bolts retaining the transaxle to the engine.

8. Loosen the pipe clip and disconnect the oil hose from the oil pipe.

9. Raise the vehicle and support safely at the desired working height. Drain the transaxle fluid from the unit.

10. Remove the front wheels and the left and right splash pans (shields).

11. Remove the control link of the stabilizer bar and remove the under cover pan.

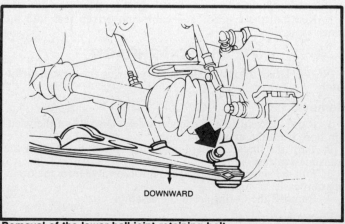

DOWNWARD

Removal of the lower ball joint retaining bolt (©Toyo Kogyo Co. Ltd.)

12. Remove the retaining bolts and nuts from the left and right lower arm ball joints to the steering knuckles. Pull the lower arms downward to separate them from the knuckles.

NOTE: Do not damage the ball joint dust covers.

13. Remove the left driveshaft from the transaxle in the following manner:

   a. Pull the front hub outward the move the drive shaft in the direction away from the transaxle, by tapping on it so that the coupling with the differential side gear is disconnected.

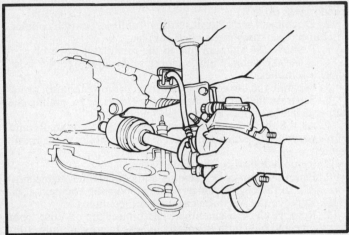

Removing the drive shaft from the transaxle (©Toyo Kogyo Co. Ltd.)

— CAUTION —

Do not strike the drive shaft with a hard force to begin with, but tap on it with increasing force.

   b. Pull the front hub outward and pull the drive shaft out from the transaxle and set aside.

— CAUTION —

To avoid damaging the oil seal, hold the joint with one hand while pulling the shaft straight out.

14. Remove the right drive shaft from the transaxle in the following manner:

   a. Insert a prybar between the driveshaft and the joint shaft. Pry the shaft assembly out of the joint shaft to start its movement.

   b. Pull the front hub outward and carefully remove the shaft from the joint shaft and set aside.

15. Remove the joint shaft bracket mounting bolts and pull the joint bracket from the transaxle as a complete assembly.

16. Remove the transaxle under cover pan.

17. Remove the retaining bolts between the torque converter and the drive plate.

18. Remove the crossmember and the left side lower arm to-

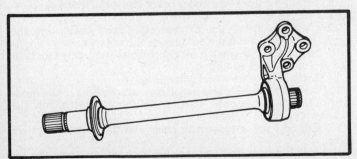

Joint shaft and bracket assembly (©Toyo Kogyo Co. Ltd.)

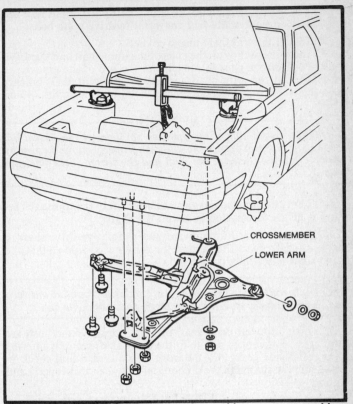

CROSSMEMBER

LOWER ARM

Removal or installation of crossmember and lower arm assembly (©Toyo Kogyo Co. Ltd.)

gether as an assembly after removing the nuts from the engine and transaxle.

19. It is suggested to attach a safety chain or rope to the transaxle during its removal from the vehicle, along with the use of a transmission type jack assembly.

— CAUTION —

The added safety measure is suggested because of the unbalanced weight of the assembly.

20. Remove the two lower bolts retaining the transaxle to the engine.

21. Remove the transaxle from the vehicle, being careful not to disengage the converter as the unit is being removed.

22. After the transaxle has been removed, disconnect and remove the axle mount bracket from the transaxle.

Installation

1. Install the transaxle mount bracket to the transaxle.

2. Position the transaxle on the jacking tool and secure with a safety chain or rope. Place the transaxle under the vehicle and carefully raise the assembly into place.

— CAUTION —

Because the transaxle is not well balanced, be sure the assembly is properly secured to the lifting device and the converter assembly is held in place.

3. Install and tighten the two mounting bolts between the transaxle and the engine. Tighten to 66-86 ft. lbs. (91-119 N•m).

4. Remove the jacking device from under the transaxle while maintaining the rope or chain support.

5. Install the crossmember and transaxle mount nuts. Tighten the M10 nuts to 31.8-40 ft. lbs. (40-55 N•m) and the M12 nuts to 69-85 ft. lbs. (95-118 N•m).

6. Tighten the converter to drive plate bolts 25-36 ft. lbs. (35-50 N•m).

NOTE: With a wrench on the crankshaft pulley bolt, turn the crankshaft to tighten the four converter to drive plate bolts.

7. Install the transaxle under cover.
8. Install new clips on the ends of the joint shaft and the drive shaft. Position the gaps in the clips to the top of the groove.
9. Mount the joint shaft and install the joint shaft bracket onto the engine. Tighten the bracket bolts 31.1-46 ft. lbs. (43-63 N•m).

─────── CAUTION ───────
During the installation of the shaft, do not damage the oil seal lip. If the shaft does not engage the side gear properly, move the gear by hand so that the center of the shaft and the center of the side gear meet.

NOTE: If the preload adapter has been left in the transaxle, remove it before attempting to install the shaft.

10. Pull the front hub outward and couple the drive shaft to the joint shaft. Push the joint at the differential side so that the drive shaft is securely coupled to the joint shaft.

─────── CAUTION ───────
After the installation of the drive shaft, pull the front hub outward and check to make sure the drive shaft does not come out.

11. Install the left drive shaft into the transaxle and push the joint at the differential side to fit the drive shaft securely into the differential side gear. Pull the front hub outward and check to make sure the shaft and the differential side gear are properly and securely positioned.

─────── CAUTION ───────
Be careful not to damage the oil seal.

12. Attach the left and right lower ball joints to the knuckle and tighten the clinch bolts and nuts 32-40 ft. lbs. (44-55 N•m).
13. Attach the stabilizer bar control link. The bolt should protrude approximately 1 inch (25.5mm) from the top of the nut.
14. Install the left and right splash shields.
15. Install the left and right wheel assemblies.
16. Lower the vehicle and connect the oil hose to the pipe and tighten the hose clamp.
17. Install and tighten the five bolts retaining the transaxle to the engine to 66-86 ft. lbs. (91-119 N•m).
18. Install the vacuum line to the modulator and connect the wiring to the kickdown solenoid and the neutral safety (inhibitor) switch.
19. Connect the transaxle ground wire.
20. Connect the selector control cable to the transaxle.

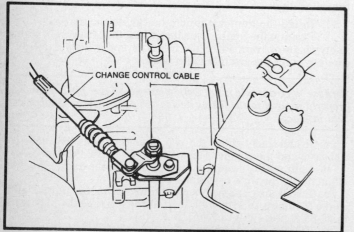

Installing the change control cable (©Toyo Kogyo Co. Ltd.)

21. Connect the speedometer cable to the transaxle.
22. Connect the battery cable and install the proper fluid into the transaxle.
23. Start the engine and correct the fluid level as required.
24. Adjust the manual linkage, the neutral starter switch and conduct a road test.
25. Verify correct operation and lack of fluid leakages.

Removal
GLC MODELS

1. Disconnect the negative battery cable. Disconnect the speedometer cable.
2. Disconnect the neutral starting (inhibitor) switch coupler. Disconnect the kickdown switch coupler.
3. Remove the vacuum line to the modulator assembly.
4. Raise the vehicle and support safely. Remove the front wheel assemblies.
5. Separate the lower ball joints from the lower control arms.
6. Separate the driveshaft from the transaxle by pulling the caliper assemblies outward in a jerking motion.
7. As the driveshafts are removed, support the shafts and joint assemblies to avoid damage. Tie the assemblies to the frame securely.
8. Remove the transaxle undercover.
9. Drain the transaxle assembly and connect the engine support chain to the engine hangers and support the engine.
10. Remove the front selector rod and counter rod.
11. Remove the crossmember. Disconnect the oil hose from the oil pipe and plug both the pipe and hose to prevent fluid from leaking.
12. Remove the upper front rubber mount from the left side of the transaxle.
13. Remove the starter motor from the engine assembly.
14. Remove the converter housing end cover and remove the bolts retaining the converter to the drive plates.
15. Support the transaxle with a jacking tool and secure the transaxle to the tool.
16. Remove the bell housing retaining bolts and remove the transaxle by slowly lowering the assembly from under the vehicle.
17. Do not allow the converter to drop from the assembly as it is being lowered from the vehicle.

Installation

1. The installation of the transaxle is in the reverse procedure of its removal.
2. Raise the transaxle into position, being careful not to drop the converter as the transaxle is raised into position. Install the retaining bolts into the bell housing and tighten to 26.8-39.8 ft. lbs. (3.7-5.5 M-kg).
3. Install the bolts retaining the converter to the drive plate. Tighten to 25.3-36.2 ft. lbs. (3.5-5.0 M-kg). Install the end cover.
4. Install the starter assembly to the engine.
5. Install the front left upper rubber mount to the transaxle.
6. Install the cross member and connect the oil hose to the oil pipe.
7. Install the front selector rod and the counter rod.
8. Install the transaxle under cover and remove the supporting engine chain.
9. Carefully install the left and right drive shafts into the transaxle, being careful not to damage the oil seals.
10. Install the lower ball joint clinch bolts and tighten to 32.5-39.8 ft. lbs. (4.4-5.5 M-kg).
11. Install the front wheel assemblies.
12. Lower the vehicle and install the vacuum hose to the modulator. Install the neutral starting (inhibitor) switch and the kickdown switch couplers.
13. Connect the speedometer cable and the battery negative cable.
14. Install the proper fluid into the transaxle and start the engine. Verify that the fluid level is correct as the engine warms up.

15. Inspect the transaxle assembly for fluid leakage and correct, if necessary.

16. Road test the vehicle. Verify the manual linkage and the neutral starting switch operates properly.

BENCH OVERHAUL

Before Disassembly

Before removing any of the subassemblies, thoroughly clean the outside of the transaxle to prevent dirt from entering the mechanical parts during the repair operation.

During the repair of the subassemblies, certain general instructions which apply to all units of the transaxle must be followed. These instructions are given here to avoid unnecessary repetition.

Handle all transaxle parts carefully to avoid nicking or burring the bearing or mating surfaces.

Lubricate all internal parts of the transaxle before assembly with clean automatic transmission fluid. Do not use any other lubricants except on gaskets and thrust washers which may be coated with petroleum jelly to facilitate assembly. Always install new gaskets when assembling the transaxle.

Tighten all bolts and screws to the recommended torque.

Transaxle Disassembly

Disassembly

1. Remove the converter assembly. Do not spill the fluid within the unit.

2. Mount the transaxle on a stand assembly or on a clean work bench area.

3. Remove the neutral starter switch, the kickdown solenoid and the vacuum modulator.

4. Remove the oil level gauge (dipstick) and the tube.

5. Remove the speedometer driven gear and pull the oil pump shaft from the turbine shaft. Remove the turbine shaft.

6. Remove the oil pan and control valve assembly.

7. Remove the steel ball and spring from the transaxle case.

8. Remove the oil pump assembly from the end of the transaxle, after Steps 9 and 10.

9. Measure the front clutch drum end play before any further disassembly is made. Push the front drum towards the oil pump position with a pry bar. Measure the distance (clearance) between the front clutch drum and the connecting shell. This clearance is the front clutch drum end play. The standard clearance is 0.020-0.031 in. (0.5-0.8mm).

10. If the clearance is not within specifications, the proper sized shim must be selected for the assembly.

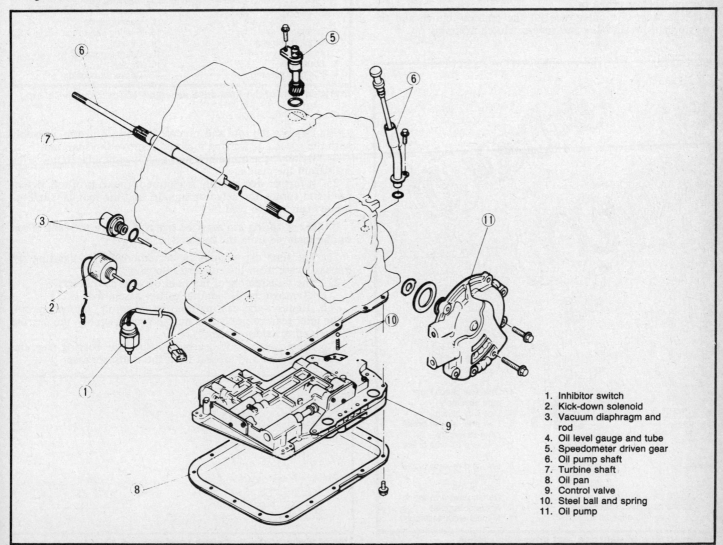

1. Inhibitor switch
2. Kick-down solenoid
3. Vacuum diaphragm and rod
4. Oil level gauge and tube
5. Speedometer driven gear
6. Oil pump shaft
7. Turbine shaft
8. Oil pan
9. Control valve
10. Steel ball and spring
11. Oil pump

Removal of exterior components of the transaxle (©Toyo Kogyo Co. Ltd.)

NOTE: A bearing race shim chart is included in the assembly procedure outline.

11. Should the oil pump be difficult to remove, tighten the brake band to anchor the front clutch. Slowly remove the oil pump.

12. The total end play will be checked during the assembly procedure.

13. Remove the brake band strut bolt and locknut.

14. Remove the brake band, the front clutch, the rear clutch and the hub assembly of the rear clutch, along with the thrust bearings and washers.

15. Remove the front planetary gear carrier assembly, the sun gear and spacer. Remove the connecting shell.

16. Remove the servo retaining snapring and remove the servo piston assembly.

17. Remove the governor retaining bolts and lift the governor from the transaxle case. Lift the cover from the governor assembly.

18. Remove the oil pipes from the case.

19. Remove the parking pawl assembly.

20. Remove the drum hub assembly from the case. Remove the one-way clutch assembly. Note the locations of the thrust bearings and washers.

21. Depress the low and reverse brake assembly with the use of a special type depressing tool. Remove the snapring from the snapring groove in the case.

22. Remove the outer race for the one-way clutch and the clutch plates for the low and reverse clutch assembly.

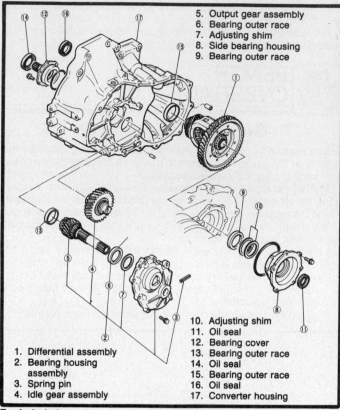

5. Output gear assembly
6. Bearing outer race
7. Adjusting shim
8. Side bearing housing
9. Bearing outer race

1. Differential assembly
2. Bearing housing assembly
3. Spring pin
4. Idle gear assembly
10. Adjusting shim
11. Oil seal
12. Bearing cover
13. Bearing outer race
14. Oil seal
15. Bearing outer race
16. Oil seal
17. Converter housing

Exploded view of the final drive assembly (©Toyo Kogyo Co. Ltd.)

23. Depress the low and reverse brake hub/piston assembly with the special depressing tool and remove the snapring.

24. Remove the brake hub and piston assembly. Remove the seals from the piston.

25. If further disassembly is required, the control rod, detent pawl and spring, the actuator support and the manual shaft assembly can be removed.

NOTE: A spring pin must be removed before the control rod can be removed from the transaxle.

26. The final drive unit can be removed by separating the transaxle case from the converter housing.

27. The disassembly of the final drive is as follows;
  a. Remove the differential carrier assembly.
  b. Remove the bearing housing assembly, the spring pin, the idler gear assembly, the output gear assembly, the bearing race and the shim assembly.
  c. Remove the side bearing housing, the bearing race, the adjusting shim and oil seal from the transaxle case.

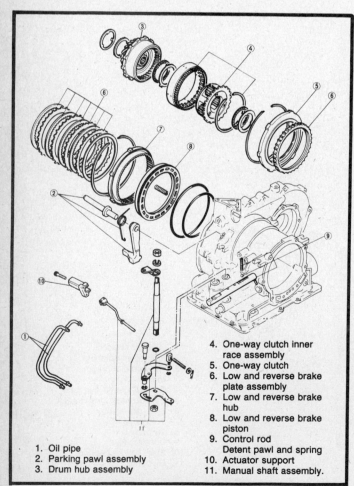

4. One-way clutch inner race assembly
5. One-way clutch
6. Low and reverse brake plate assembly
7. Low and reverse brake hub
8. Low and reverse brake piston
9. Control rod Detent pawl and spring
10. Actuator support
11. Manual shaft assembly.

1. Oil pipe
2. Parking pawl assembly
3. Drum hub assembly

Exploded view of transaxle rear drive train section (©Toyo Kogyo Co. Ltd.)

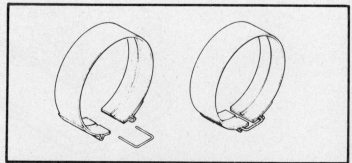

Use of a wire holder to prevent band damage (©Toyo Kogyo Co. Ltd.)

d. Remove the bearing cover, the bearing outer race, the oil seal, and the differential side bearing outer race from the converter housing.

NOTE: The oil seals and bearing outer races are included in the bearing housings and must be pressed from the housings for removal.

Transaxle Component Disassembly, Inspection and Reassembly

TORQUE CONVERTER

Disassembly

1. The torque converter is welded together and cannot be disassembled.

NOTE: Remanufacturing of torque converters is possible by specialty shops equipped to perform the necessary procedures.

Inspection

1. If the converter is to be reused, inspect the outer area of the converter for crack, inspect the bushing and seal surfaces for worn areas, scores, nicks or grooves.

2. The converter must be cleaned on the inside with cleaning solvent, dried, flushed with A/T fluid and drained until ready for installation.

OIL PUMP

Disassembly

1. Remove the pump cover and the drive flange. Mark the inner and outer gears.
2. Remove the inner and outer gears from the pump housing.
3. Remove the oil seals from the pump cover hub.

Identifying marks on the inner and outer oil pump gears (©Toyo Kogyo Co. Ltd.)

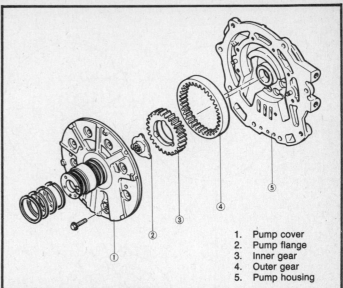

1. Pump cover
2. Pump flange
3. Inner gear
4. Outer gear
5. Pump housing

Exploded view of the oil pump (©Toyo Kogyo Co. Ltd.)

Inspection

1. Check the housing and cover for cracks or worn areas.
2. Check the gears for wear, broken or damaged gear teeth.
3. Check the inner gear bushing of the pump housing sleeve for being worn or damaged.
4. Check the clearance of the inner gear to the pump cover and the outer gear to the pump cover. Refer to the specifications chart.
5. Check the clearance of the outer gear teeth head to the crescent dam. Refer to the specifications chart.
6. Check the clearance between the outer gear to the housing. Refer to the specifications chart.
7. Check the clearance between the new seal rings and the seal ring groove in the pump cover hub. Refer to the specifications chart.

Assembly

1. The assembly of the oil pump is the reverse of the removal procedure.
2. Be sure the marks on the inner and outer gears are on the pump cover side.
3. Tighten the pump cover bolts 7.96-10.13 ft. lbs. (11-14 N•m).
4. After the assembly is complete, install the oil pump shaft and make sure the gears turn easily.

FRONT CLUTCH

Disassembly

1. Remove the retaining snapring from the drum.
2. Remove the retaining plate and the clutch plate assembly.

CLEARANCE FOR OIL PUMP COMPONENTS

Illustration	Measured location	Standard value	Limit
1	Inner gear to pump cover. Outer gear to pump cover	0.02-0.04mm (0.001-0.002 in)	0.08mm (0.003 in)
2	Head of outer gear teeth to Crescent dam	0.14-0.21mm (0.006-0.008 in)	0.25mm (0.010 in)
3	Outer gear to Housing	0.05-0.20mm (0.002-0.008 in)	0.25mm (0.010 in)
4	Seal ring to seal ring groove	0.04-0.16mm (0.002-0.006 in)	0.40mm (0.016 in)

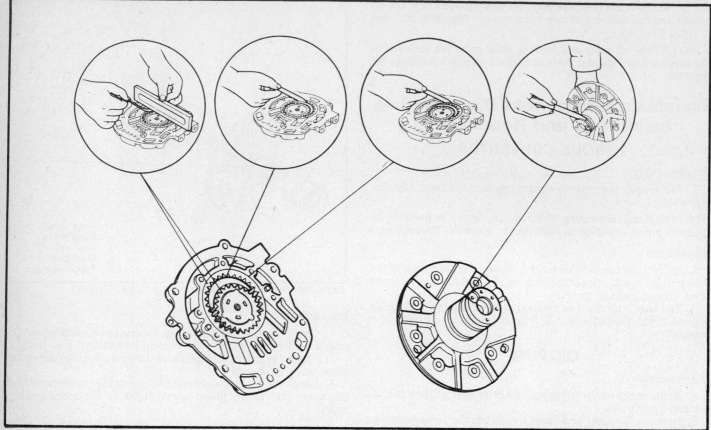

Measuring the oil pump gear clearance (©Toyo Kogyo Co. Ltd.)

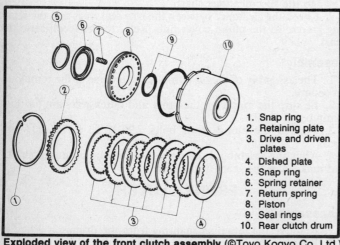

1. Snap ring
2. Retaining plate
3. Drive and driven plates
4. Dished plate
5. Snap ring
6. Spring retainer
7. Return spring
8. Piston
9. Seal rings
10. Rear clutch drum

Exploded view of the front clutch assembly (©Toyo Kogyo Co. Ltd.)

3. Remove the dished plate, noting the direction of the dish.

4. Remove the snapring from the drum hub with the use of a compressing tool.

5. Remove the piston from the drum by blowing compressed air into the apply hole in the drum. Remove the oil seals from the piston and drum hub.

Inspection

1. Inspect for damaged or worn drive plates, broken or worn snaprings, deformed spring retainer, or weakened return springs.

NOTE: The free length of the return springs is 0.992-1.071 in. (25.2-27.2mm).

2. Inspect the drum bushing for being worn.

Assembly

1. It is good practice to install new clutch plates, both drive and driven, during the overhaul of a transmission/transaxle unit, and not reuse the original plates.

2. Install the oil seals on the piston and the clutch drum hub. Lubricate the seals and grooves with vaseline or A/T fluid.

3. Install the piston into the drum, being careful not to cut or damage the seals.

4. Install the compressing tool and install the snapring holding the springs and spring retainer.

5. Install the dished plate with the protruding side facing the piston. Starting with a steel plate next to the dished plate, alternate with the lined plate and steel plate until three of each are installed.

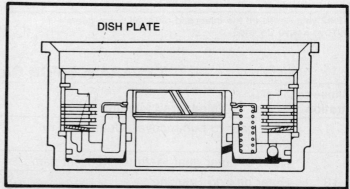

DISH PLATE

Direction of the dished plate in the front clutch (©Toyo Kogyo Co. Ltd.)

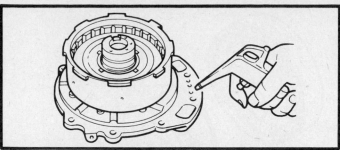

Checking the front clutch piston with air pressure
(©Toyo Kogyo Co. Ltd.)

6. Install the retaining plate and the retaining snapring.

7. Measure the front clutch clearance between the retaining plate and the snap ring. The standard clearance is 0.063-0.071 in. (1.6-1.8mm). If the clearance is not correct, adjust it with the proper sized retaining plate.

FRONT CLUTCH RETAINER PLATE SPECIFICATIONS

Part Number	Thickness of Retaining Plate
3959 19 504	5.2mm (0.2047 in)
3959 19 505	5.4mm (0.2126 in)
3959 19 506	5.6mm (0.2205 in)
3959 19 507	5.8mm (0.2284 in)
3959 19 508	6.0mm (0.2362 in)
3959 19 509	6.2mm (0.2441 in)

REAR CLUTCH

Disassembly

1. The disassembly of the rear clutch is in the same manner and procedure as the disassembly of the front clutch.

Inspection

1. Inspect the rear clutch components as was done for the front clutch components.

Assembly

1. Install the oil seals on the piston and the clutch drum hub. Lubricate the seals and grooves with vaseline or A/T fluid.

2. Install the piston into the drum, being careful not to cut or damage the oil seals.

3. Continue the assembly of the rear clutch in the same manner and procedure as was done for the front clutch.

4. A total of four steel and four lined clutch plates are used in the rear clutch assembly. (3 plates each for 1,300 cc engine equipped vehicles).

5. Measure the clutch clearance in the same manner as was done for the front clutch. The standard clearance is 0.031-0.059 in. (0.8-1.5mm).

6. If the clearance is not correct select the correct sized retaining plate for installation into the drum.

DRUM HUB

Disassembly

1. Remove the parking gear spring.

2. Remove the parking gear by pushing the two pins which project from the drive hub.

3. Remove the snapring, the internal gear and the drive hub.

Inspection

1. Inspect the components for broken or worn snaprings, damaged or worn gears, or broken teeth.

Assembly

1. Assembly of the drum hub is in the reverse of its disassembly procedure.

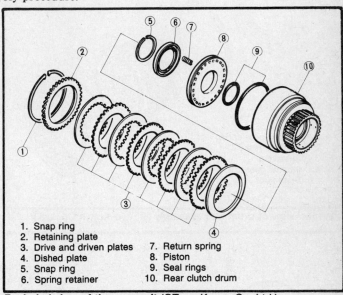

1. Snap ring
2. Retaining plate
3. Drive and driven plates
4. Dished plate
5. Snap ring
6. Spring retainer
7. Return spring
8. Piston
9. Seal rings
10. Rear clutch drum

Exploded view of the rear unit (©Toyo Kogyo Co. Ltd.)

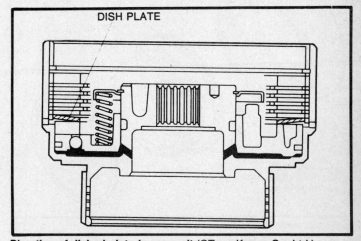

DISH PLATE

Direction of dished plate in rear unit (©Toyo Kogyo Co. Ltd.)

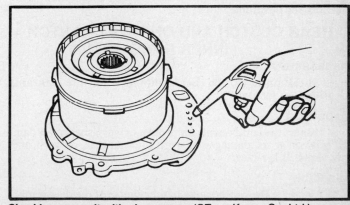

Checking rear unit with air pressure (©Toyo Kogyo Co. Ltd.)

1111

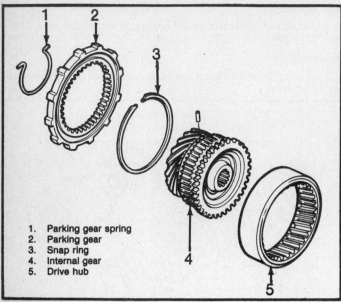

1. Parking gear spring
2. Parking gear
3. Snap ring
4. Internal gear
5. Drive hub

Exploded view of drum hub assembly (©Toyo Kogyo Co. Ltd.)

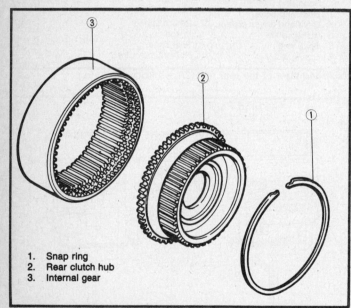

1. Snap ring
2. Rear clutch hub
3. Internal gear

Exploded view of rear clutch hub assembly (©Toyo Kogyo Co. Ltd.)

2. Make certain the snapring and parking gear spring are in their proper positions.

REAR CLUTCH AND ONE-WAY CLUTCH INNER RACE

Disassembly

1. These units can be disassembled when the retaining snaprings are removed.

Inspection

1. Inspect the components for broken or worn snaprings, damage or worn gears, damaged or worn internal gear, or worn one-way clutch inner race.

Assembly

1. Assemble the components in the reverse of the disassembly procedure.

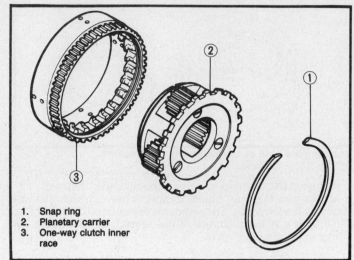

1. Snap ring
2. Planetary carrier
3. One-way clutch inner race

Exploded view of clutch inner race and planetary gear carrier (©Toyo Kogyo Co. Ltd.)

PLANETARY CARRIER

Inspection

1. Inspect the rotation of the gears and the clearance between the pinion washer and the planetary carrier.
2. The standard clearance is 0.031 in. (0.8mm).

GOVERNOR

Disassembly

1. The governor can be completely disassembled, with the removal of the shaft and gear, if required.
2. Remove the valve assembly from the governor shaft platform. Disassemble the valves from the body.
3. Should the shaft and gear need to be removed, drive the retaining pin from the gear-to-shaft and pull the gear from the shaft. Do not lose the shims, bearing and sleeve.

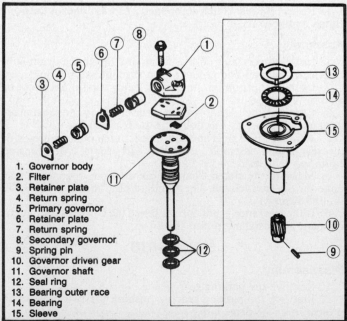

1. Governor body
2. Filter
3. Retainer plate
4. Return spring
5. Primary governor
6. Retainer plate
7. Return spring
8. Secondary governor
9. Spring pin
10. Governor driven gear
11. Governor shaft
12. Seal ring
13. Bearing outer race
14. Bearing
15. Sleeve

Exploded view of governor assembly (©Toyo Kogyo Co. Ltd.)

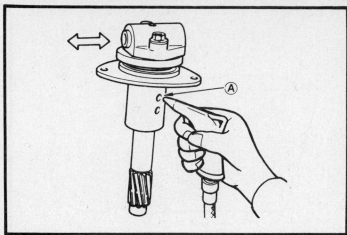

Testing governor valves with air pressure (©Toyo Kogyo Co. Ltd.)

Inspection

1. Inspect the governor assembly for damaged or worn valves, clogged filter, weakened return spring and the sliding condition of the valve.

Assembly.

1. The assembly of the governor assembly is in the reverse of the removal procedure.
2. Tighten the governor valve body-to-governor shaft platform to 5.79-7.96 ft. lbs. (8-11 N•m).

GOVERNOR SPRING TENSION SPECIFICATIONS

Spring	Outer diameter	Free length
Primary spring	8.7-9.3mm (0.350-0.366 in)	12.5-14.5mm (0.492-0.728 in)
Secondary spring	9.2-9.8mm (0.362-0.386 in)	12-14mm (0.472-0.551 in)

CONTROL VALVE ASSEMBLY

Disassembly

1. The valve body is a precision unit within the transaxle and must be handled with extreme care. It must not be disassembled unless a reason exists to perform the procedure.
2. No specific order of disassembly is outline, but the repairman must rely upon his the professional expertise and judgement that dictates such repairs.
3. The valves and springs should be arranged in a channeled block or tray, in their disassembled order, to provide an assembly sequence.
4. Note the position of the check balls and the worm tracks that each were removed.

Inspection

1. Inspect the valve body assembly for damaged or worn valves, damaged oil passages, cracked or damaged valve body, weakened springs and the operation of each valve in its bore of the valve body.

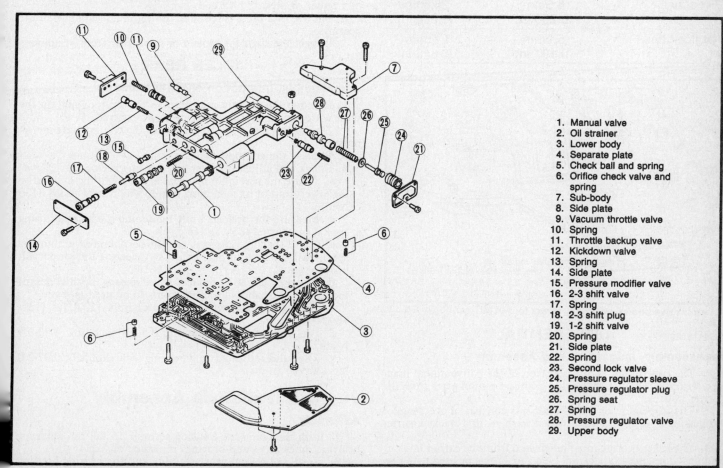

1. Manual valve
2. Oil strainer
3. Lower body
4. Separate plate
5. Check ball and spring
6. Orifice check valve and spring
7. Sub-body
8. Side plate
9. Vacuum throttle valve
10. Spring
11. Throttle backup valve
12. Kickdown valve
13. Spring
14. Side plate
15. Pressure modifier valve
16. 2-3 shift valve
17. Spring
18. 2-3 shift plug
19. 1-2 shift valve
20. Spring
21. Side plate
22. Spring
23. Second lock valve
24. Pressure regulator sleeve
25. Pressure regulator plug
26. Spring seat
27. Spring
28. Pressure regulator valve
29. Upper body

Exploded view of control valve assembly (©Toyo Kogyo Co. Ltd.)

Assembly

1. Assemble the valves and springs into the valve body bores as were removed.

2. Install the two steel balls and springs into their positions in the valve body, along with the orifice check valve. Install the separator plate and the upper valve body.

VALVE BODY SPRING TENSION SPECIFICATIONS

Name of spring	Outer diameter	Free length
Throttle backup	7.3mm (0.287 in)	36.0mm (1.417 in)
Downshift	5.55mm (0.218 in)	22.0mm (0.866 in)
Pressure modifier	8.4mm (0.331 in)	18.5mm (0.728 in)
2-3 shift	6.9mm (0.272 in)	41.0mm (1.614 in)
1-2 shift	6.55mm (0.258 in)	32.0mm (1.260 in)
Second lock	5.55mm (0.218 in)	33.5mm (1.319 in)
Pressure regulator	11.7mm (0.461 in)	43.0mm (1.693 in)
Steel ball	6.5mm (0.256 in)	26.8mm (1.516 in)
Orifice check	5.0mm (0.197 in)	21.5mm (0.846 in)

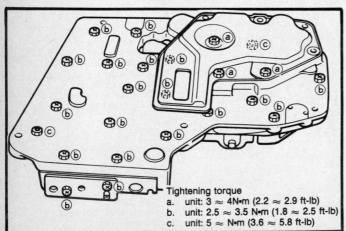

Tightening torque
a. unit: 3 ≈ 4N•m (2.2 ≈ 2.9 ft-lb)
b. unit: 2.5 ≈ 3.5 N•m (1.8 ≈ 2.5 ft-lb)
c. unit: 5 ≈ N•m (3.6 ≈ 5.8 ft-lb)

Control valve bodies attaching screw torque (©Toyo Kogyo Co. Ltd.)

DIFFERENTIAL

Disassembly, Inspection and Assembly

1. The differential is disassembled in the conventional manner, with the removal of the ring gear and pinion gears from the carrier housing.

2. The inspection of the components consists of checking for broken teeth, worn gears and thrust washers, or a cracked carrier housing.

3. The roller bearing must be pressed from the carrier housing and new ones pressed back on. New races must be used with new bearings.

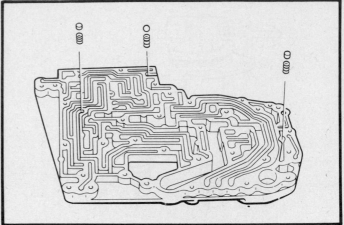

Location of steelballs and orifice check valve (©Toyo Kogyo Co. Ltd.)

4. The backlash of the pinion gears is 0.0-0.039 in. (0.0-0.1mm).

5. If the backlash of the pinions are not correct, replace all the thrust washers with new ones and recheck. If excessive clearance still exists, check the carrier for wear.

OUTPUT GEAR

Disassembly, Inspection and Assembly

1. The bearings must be removed from the shaft with the use of a puller or press.

2. The use of a press is required during the installation of the bearings.

3. Inspect the shaft for broken or worn gear teeth or splines.

IDLER GEAR

Disassembly, Inspection and Assembly

1. Remove the locknut and remove the components on the shaft with the use of a puller or press as required.

2. Do not lose the adjusting shims as the components are removed.

3. Replace the components as required.

4. Check and adjust the idler gear bearing preload as follows:

   a. Secure the assembly in a vise and tighten the locknut to the lower limit of its tightening torque which is 94 ft. lbs. (130 N•m).

   b. Measure the preload while tightening the locknut, using special measuring tools and a spring scale.

   c. If the specified preload cannot be obtained within the specified tightening torque, adjust by selecting the proper adjusting shims.

   d. The preload can be reduced by increasing the thickness of the shims. A total of allowable shims to be used is seven.

   e. The tightening torque specification is 94-130 ft. lbs. (130-180 N•m).

   f. The preload specification is 0.3-7.8 inch lb. (0.03-0.9 N•cm).

   g. The value indicated on the spring scale should be 0.07-2.0 lbs. (30-900 grams).

Transaxle Assembly

Assembly

1. With the converter housing secured, install the oil seals, bearings outer races and bearings into the housing.

2. Install the output gear assembly and the bearing housing assembly. Install the idler gear assembly.

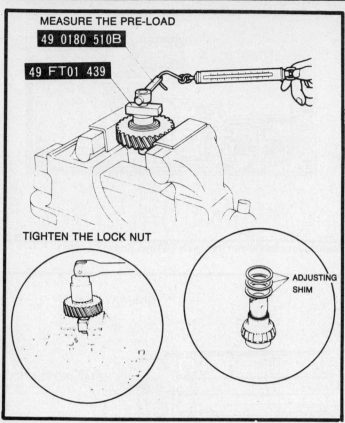

MEASURE THE PRE-LOAD

49 0180 510B

49 FT01 439

TIGHTEN THE LOCK NUT

ADJUSTING SHIM

Adjusting idler gear preload (©Toyo Kogyo Co. Ltd.)

3. Install the differential assembly.

4. Install the seal into the side bearing housing and install the bearing outer race, and adjusting shims onto the transaxle case.

NOTE: The transaxle manufacturer has designed special tools for use during the assembly of the final drive unit. This repair procedure should not be attempted unless these tools or their equivalents, along with their use instructions are present. It is suggested the special tools be obtained before the transaxle is overhauled.

5. The tolerances for the final drive are as follows:

a. Side bearing tightening torque—13.7-18.8 ft. lbs. (19-26 N•m).

b. Output gear bearing preload—0.3-7.8 in. lbs. (0.03-0.9 N•m).

c. Reading on spring scale for preload—0.07-2.0 lbs. (30-900 grams).

d. The differential side gear bearing preload—1.8-2.5 inch lbs. (2.1-2.9 N•m).

e. The reading on the spring scale—4.6-6.4 lbs. (2.1-2.9 Kg.).

OUTPUT GEAR BEARING SHIM SPECIFICATIONS

Part Number			Thickness of Shim
FT01	19	224	0.10mm (0.004 in)
FT01	19	225	0.12mm (0.005 in)
FT01	19	226	0.14mm (0.006 in)
FT01	19	227	0.16mm (0.007 in)
FT01	19	228	0.20mm (0.008 in)
FT01	19	229	0.50mm (0.020 in)

6. If the manual shaft, actuator support, control rod, detent ball and spring have been removed previously, install the components in their proper order.

DIFFERENTIAL SIDE BEARING SHIM SPECIFICATIONS

Part Number			Thickness of Shim
G001	27	401	0.10mm (0.004 in)
G001	27	411	0.12mm (0.005 in)
G001	27	412	0.14mm (0.006 in)
G001	27	413	0.16mm (0.007 in)
G001	27	402	0.20mm (0.008 in)
G991	27	405	0.50mm (0.020 in)

7. With the seals on the low and reverse brake piston, install the piston into the transaxle case, being careful not to damage or cut the lubricated oil seals.

8. Install the low and reverse brake hub and secure with the snapring.

9. Install the dished plate so that the protruding side faces the driven plates.

10. Starting with a steel plate, install the clutch plate pack into the transaxle case, alternating steel to lined and lined to steel, until a total of four steel and four lined plates have been installed.

11. Install the retaining plate and the one-way clutch. Push the one-way clutch down with the use of a compressing tool and install the snapring into its groove.

12. Measure the clearance of the low and reverse brake clutch pack between the retaining plate and the one-way clutch with a feeler gauge blade. The clearance should be 0.032-0.041 in. (0.8-1.05mm).

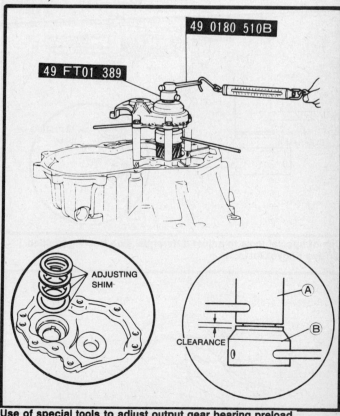

49 0180 510B

49 FT01 389

ADJUSTING SHIM

CLEARANCE

A

B

Use of special tools to adjust output gear bearing preload (©Toyo Kogyo Co. Ltd.)

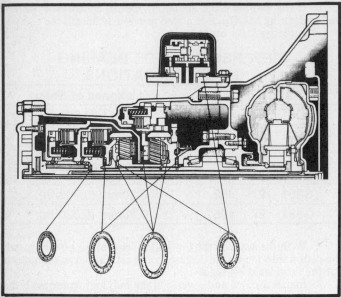

Needle bearing location within transaxle (©Toyo Kogyo Co. Ltd.)

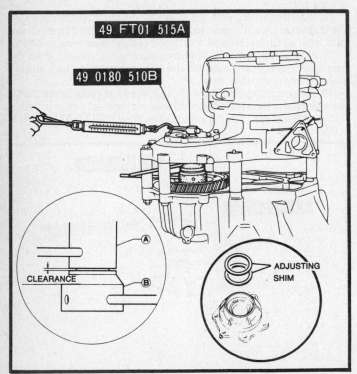

Use of special tools to adjust differential side bearing preload
(©Toyo Kogyo Co. Ltd.)

49 FT01 515A

49 0180 510B

CLEARANCE

A

B

ADJUSTING SHIM

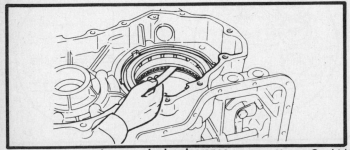

Measuring low and reverse brake clearance (©Toyo Kogyo Co. Ltd.)

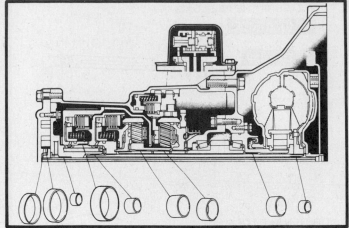

Bushing location within transaxle (©Toyo Kogyo Co. Ltd.)

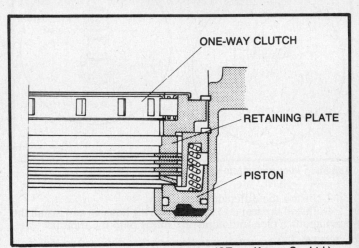

ONE-WAY CLUTCH

RETAINING PLATE

PISTON

Assembly of low and reverse brake set (©Toyo Kogyo Co. Ltd.)

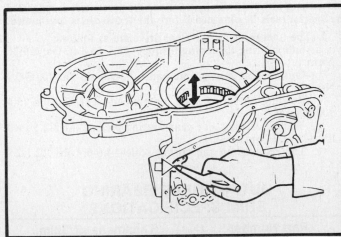

Checking low and reverse brake operation with air pressure
(©Toyo Kogyo Co. Ltd.)

13. If the clearance is not within the specified tolerance, adjust it by selecting a different sized retaining plate.

14. Check the operation of the low and reverse brake by blowing compressed air into the apply port of the case.

15. Install the one-way clutch inner race assembly and the drum hub assembly. Slight movement may have to be accomplished to fit the units properly.

16. Install the parking pawl assembly and the oil pipes.

17. Install the governor assembly into the case. Tighten the governor retaining bolts to 3.6-5.8 ft. lbs. (5-8 N•m).

NOTE: Mount the governor so that the sleeve projection on the governor is aligned with the mating mark on the transaxle case.

18. Apply a thin coat of sealant to the surface of the clutch housing which faces the transaxle case. Mount the case to the converter housing and install the retaining bolts. Tighten the bolts to a torque of 26.8-40 ft. lbs. (37-40 N•m).

─────────── **CAUTION** ───────────

The preload adaptor tool or its equivalent, must be installed into the driveshaft coupling hole and secured by using wire, to prevent the side differential gear from turning the top of the pinion gear inside the differential gear case. Should this occur, the drive shaft coupling of the side gear will move and the transaxle may have to be disassembled again to correct the problem.

19. Install new seals on the servo components and install into the case. Install the snap ring and cover with the help of a compressing tool.

20. Install the connecting shell, the sun gear and spacer, the planetary carrier and the rear clutch hub.

21. Install the thrust washer and bearing. Install the rear clutch assembly and its thrust bearing.

22. Install the front clutch and the brake band.

23. Install the anchor end bolt and the locknut for the brake band.

24. The total end play must be checked in the following manner:

    a. Remove the pump cover from the oil pump.

    b. Install the bearing into the rear clutch drum.

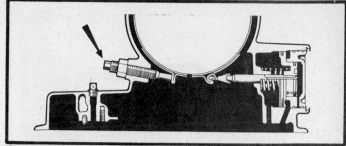

Correct assembly of servo and anchor end bolt
(©Toyo Kogyo Co. Ltd.)

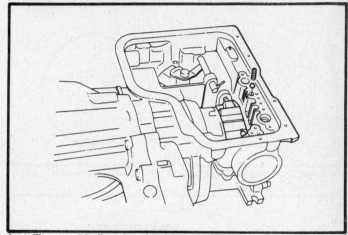

Installing steel ball and spring in case (©Toyo Kogyo Co. Ltd.)

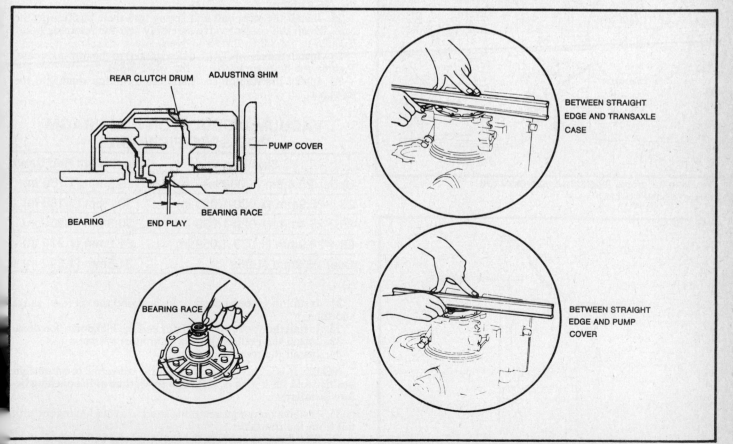

Measuring for total end play (©Toyo Kogyo Co. Ltd.)

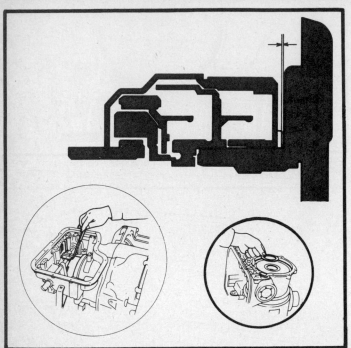

Measuring for front clutch drum end play (©Toyo Kogyo Co. Ltd.)

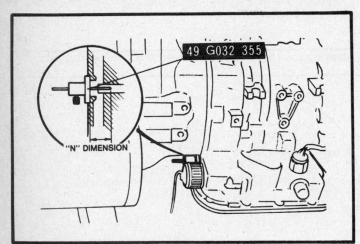

Checking for proper lengthened modulator rod
(©Toyo Kogyo Co. Ltd.)

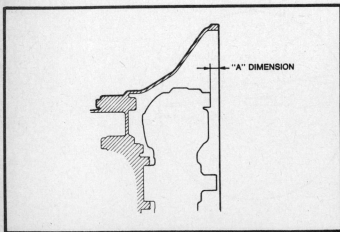

Dimension A = 0.79 in. (20mm) (©Toyo Kogyo Co. Ltd.)

c. Mount the bearing race to the pump cover and then install this inside the rear clutch drum.

d. Note that adjusting shims are not to be used between the pump cover and the brake drum.

e. Position a straight edge on the transaxle case and measure the clearance between the straight edge and either the pump cover or the transaxle case.

Between the straight edge and the pump cover—less than 0.004 in. (0.1mm).

Between the straight edge and the transaxle case—less than 0.006 in. (0.15mm).

CAUTION

Do not position the straight edge on the screws for mounting the oil pump to the case.

f. The total end play must be 0.010-0.020 in. (0.25-0.5mm). If the end play does not agree with the standard value, adjust it by selecting a suitable bearing thrust race.

25. Assemble the oil pump assembly and install it onto the transaxle case with the correct bearing thrust race. Tighten the bolts to 10.8-15.9 ft. lbs. (15-22 N•m).

26. With oil pump installed, check the front clutch drum end play. This is accomplished in the following manner.

a. Push the front clutch drum towards the oil pump with a prybar.

b. Measure the clearance between the front clutch drum and the connecting shell. This is considered front clutch drum end play. The standard end play is 0.020-0.031 in. (0.5-0.8mm).

c. If the end play is not specified, adjust it by selecting a proper adjusting shim.

27. Tighten the anchor end bolt to a torque of 8.7-10.8 ft. lbs. (12-15 N•m) and loosen it two complete turns. While holding the end bolt securely, tighten the locknut to a torque of 40.5-59.3 ft. lbs. (56-82 N•m).

28. Install the steel ball and spring into their position in the case. Install the control valve assembly and the retaining bolts. Tighten to 5.8-8.0 ft. lbs. (8-11 N•m).

29. Install the oil pan (with a new gasket) to the transaxle case. Tighten the bolts to 5.8-8.0 ft. lbs. (8-11 N•m).

30. Install the turbine shaft and the oil pump shaft into the transaxle.

VACUUM MODULATOR DIAPHRAGM ROD SPECIFICATIONS

Size N	Diaphragm Rod Used
Under 25.4mm (1.000 in)	29.5mm (1.160 in)
25.4-25.9mm (1.000-1.020 in)	30.0mm (1.180 in)
25.9-26.4mm (1.020-1.039 in)	30.5mm (1.200 in)
26.4-26.9mm (1.039-1.059 in)	31.0mm (1.220 in)
Over 26.9mm (1.059 in)	31.5mm (1.240 in)

31. Install the speedometer drive gear and the oil level gauge and tube.

32. Install the vacuum modulator and the kickdown solenoid.

33. Install the neutral starting (inhibitor) switch.

34. Install the torque converter.

NOTE: It is a good policy to have the converter in an upright position and fill it with A/T fluid to the bottom of the opening before installation.

35. Install a converter retaining strap to avoid having the unit fall from the transaxle.

36. The distance between the converter end and the end of the converter housing should be approximately 0.79 in. (20.0mm).

S SPECIFICATIONS

SPECIFICATIONS
Jatco F3A Transaxle

Item	Transaxle	Specification
Model		F3A
Gear Ratio	1st	2.842
	2nd	1.541
	3rd	1.000
	Reverse	2.400
Oil capacity liters (U.S. qts.)		5.7 (6.0)
Fluid type		A.T.F. type F (M2C33F)
Fluid level *Engine idling condition at "P" position		Between "F" and "L" marks on gauge

STALL REVOLUTION

Before brake in	rpm	2,150-2,400
After brake in	rpm	2,200-2,450

LINE PRESSURE

"R"	Idling condition	kPa (psi)	400-700 (57-100)
	Stall condition	kPa (psi)	1,600-1,900 (228-270)
"D"	Idling condition	kPa (psi)	300-400 (43-57)
	Stall condition	kPa (psi)	900-1,100 (128-156)
"2"	Idling condition	kPa (psi)	800-1,200 (114-171)
	Stall condition	kPa (psi)	800-1,200 (114-171)
"1"	Idling condition	kPa (psi)	300-400 (43-57)
	Stall condition	kPa (psi)	900-1,100 (128-156)

CUT BACK POINT

Vacuum of vacuum pump	Governor pressure kPa (psi)
0 mm-Hg (0 in-Hg)	100-160 (14-23)
200 mm-Hg (7.87 in-Hg)	40-100 (6-14)

GOVERNOR PRESSURE

Driving speed mph	Governor pressure kPa (psi)
20	80-120 (11-17)
35	140-200 (20-28)
55	270-340 (38-48)

SHIFT POINT SPEED

Throttle condition		Shift point km/h (mph)
Wide open throttle	$D^1 \rightarrow D^2$	54-76 (33-47)
	$D^2 \rightarrow D^3$	100-131 (62-81)
	$D^3 \rightarrow D^2$	87-115 (55-71)
	$D^2 \rightarrow D^1$	25-50 (15-31)
Half throttle 200 mm-Hg (7.87 in-Hg)	$D^1 \rightarrow D^2$	17-36 (10-32)
	$D^2 \rightarrow D^3$	28-67 (17-41)

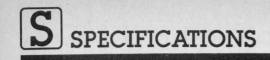

SPECIFICATIONS

SPECIFICATIONS
Jatco F3A Transaxle

Item	Transaxle	Specification
SHIFT POINT SPEED		
Fully closed throttle	$D^3 \rightarrow D^1$	9-20 (5-12)
	$1_2 \rightarrow 1_1$	41-56 (25-34)
TORQUE CONVERTER		
Stall torque ratio		2,100
Bushing diameter	Standard	33.00-33.025 (1.299-1.300)
mm (in)	Wear limit	33.075
OIL PUMP		
Clearance		
Gear end float	Standard	0.02-0.04 (0.0008-0.0016)
mm (in)	Limit	0.08 (0.0031)
Outer gear and crest	Standard	0.14-0.21 (0.0055-0.0083)
mm (in)	Limit	0.25 (0.0098)
Outer gear and housing	Standard	0.05-0.20 (0.002-0.0079)
mm (in)	Limit	0.25 (0.0098)
Oil seal ring and ring groove	Standard	0.04-0.16 (0.0016-0.0063)
mm (in)	Limit	0.40 (0.0157)
Pump housing sleeve diameter	Standard	37.950-37.975 (1.4941-1.4951)
mm (in)	Limit	37.900 (1.4922)
Inner gear bushing inner diameter	Standard	38.0-38.025 (1.4961-1.4971)
mm (in)	Limit	38.075 (1.499)
FRONT CLUTCH		
Number of driven and drive plates		3
Front clutch clearance	mm (in)	1.6-1.8 (0.063-0.071)
Clearance adjusting retaining plate	mm (in)	5.2(0.205) 5.4(0.213) 5.6(0.220) 5.8(0.228) 6.0(0.236) 6.2(0.244)
Return spring free length	mm (in)	25.2-27.2 (0.996-1.075)
Drum bushing inner diameter	Standard	44.0-44.025 (1.7322-1.7331)
mm (in)	Limit	44.075 (1.7354)
Front clutch drum end prary mm (in) Clearance between drum and connecting shell.		0.5-0.8 (0.020-0.032)
End play adjusting shim	mm (in)	1.3(0.051) 1.5(0.059) 1.7(0.067) 1.9(0.075) 2.1(0.083) 2.3(0.091) 2.5(0.098) 2.7(0.106)
REAR CLUTCH		
Number of driven and drive plates		4
Rear clutch clearance	mm (in)	0.8-1.5 (0.031-0.059)
Return spring free length	mm (in)	25.2-27.2 (0.992-1.071)
LOW AND REVERSE BRAKE		
Number of friction and steel plates		4
Clearance mm (in) Total clearance measured between retaining plate and stopper.		0.8-1.05 (0.031-0.041)

SPECIFICATIONS
Jatco F3A Transaxle

Item	Transaxle	Specification
LOW AND REVERSE BRAKE		
Clearance adjusting retaining plates mm (in)		4.6(0.181) 4.8(0.189) 5.0(0.197) 5.2(0.205) 5.4(0.213) 5.6(0.221)
Free length of return spring mm (in)		26.7-28.7 (1.051-1.130)
SERVO		
Free length of return spring mm (in)		47.0-49.0 (1.85-1.929)
GOVERNOR		
Primary spring	Outer diameter	8.7-9.3 (0.343-0.366)
mm (in)	Free length	16.5-18.5 (0.65-0.728)
Secondary spring	Outer diameter	8.95-9.55 (0.352-0.376)
mm (in)	Free length	12.4-14.4 (0.488-0.567)
ONE-WAY CLUTCH		
Bushing diameter	Standard	12.987-130.013 (5.1177-5.1187)
mm (in)	Limit	130.063 (5.1207)
GEAR ASSEMBLY		
Total end play mm (in)		0.25-0.50 (0.010-0.020)
End play adjusting race mm (in)		1.2(0.047) 1.4(0.055) 1.6(0.063) 1.8(0.071) 2.0(0.079) 2.2(0.087)
Idle gear bearing preload kg (in-lb)		0.03-0.09 (0.3-7.8)
Preload adjusting shims mm (in)		0.10(0.004) 0.12(0.005) 0.14(0.006) 0.16(0.007) 0.50(0.020) 0.20(0.008)
Output gear bearing preload kg (in-lb)		0.03-0.9 (0.3-7.8)
CONTROL VALVE		
Throttle backup valve spring	Diameter	7.3 (0.287)
mm (in)	Free length	36.0 (1.417)
Down shift valve spring	Diameter	5.55 (0.219)
mm (in)	Free length	22.0 (0.866)
Pressure modifier valve spring	Diameter	8.4 (0.331)
mm (in)	Free length	18.5 (0.728)
2 → 3 shift valve spring	Diameter	6.9 (0.272)
mm (in)	Free length	41.0 (1.614)
1 → 2 shift valve spring	Diameter	6.55 (6.258)
mm (in)	Free length	32.0 (1.260)
Second lock valve spring	Diameter	5.55 (0.219)
mm (in)	Free length	33.5 (1.319)
Pressure regulator valve spring	Diameter	11.7 (0.461)
mm (in)	Free length	43.0 (1.693)
Steel ball spring	Diameter	6.5 (0.256)
mm (in)	Free length	26.8 (1.055)
Orifice check valve spring	Diameter	5.0 (0.197)
mm (in)	Free length	21.5 (0.846)
VACUUM DIAPHRAGM		
Available diaphragm rods mm (in)		29.0(1.142) 29.5(1.161) 30.0(1.181) 30.5(1.200) 31.0(1.220)

S SPECIFICATIONS

SPECIFICATIONS
Jatco F3A Transaxle

Item	Transaxle	Specification
DRIVE AND DIFFERENTIAL		
Final gear	Type	Helical gear
	Reduction ratio	3.450
Side bearing preload	kg (in-lb)	2.1-2.9 (4.62-6.39)
Preload adjusting shims	mm (in)	0.1(0.004) 0.2(0.008) 0.3(0.012) 0.4(0.016) 0.5(0.020) 0.6(0.024) 0.7(0.028) 0.8(0.031) 0.9(0.035) 0.12(0.0047) 0.14(0.0055) 0.16(0.0063)
Backlash of side gear and pinion	mm (in)	0-0.1 (0-0.004)
Backlash adjusting thrust washers	mm (in)	2.0(0.079) 2.1(0.083) 2.2(0.087)

TIGHTENING TORQUE SPECIFICATIONS
Jatco F3A Transaxle

Item	Nm (ft. lb.)
Drive plate to crankshaft	98-105 (70-75)
Drive plate to torque converter	35-50 (25.3-36.2)
Converter housing to engine	91-119 (65-86)
Converter housing to transaxle case	37-55 (26.8-39.8)
Bearing housing to converter housing	19-26 (13.7-18.8)
Side bearing housing to transaxle case	19-26 (13.7-18.8)
Bearing cover to transaxle case	11-14 (8.0-10.1)
Oil pump to transaxle case	19-26 (13.7-18.8)
Governor coker to transaxle case	5-8 (3.6-5.8)
Oil pan	5-8 (3.6-5.8)
Anchor end bolt (when adjusting band brake)	12-15 (8.7-10.8)
Anchor end bolt lock nut	56-82 (41-59)
Control valve body to transaxle case	8-11 (5.8-8.0)
Lower valve body to upper valve body	2.5-3.5 (1.8-2.5)
Side plate to control valve body	2.5-3.5 (1.8-2.5)
Reamer bolt of control valve body	5-7 (3.6-5.1)
Oil strainer of control valve	3-4 (2.2-2.9)
Governor valve body to governor shaft	8-11 (5.8-8.0)
Oil pump cover	11-14 (8.0-10.1)
Inhibitor switch	19-26 (13.7-18.8)
Neutral switch	10-15 (7.2-8.0)
Manual shaft lock nut	30-40 (21.7-29.0)
Oil cooler pipe set bolt	16-24 (11.6-17.4)
Actuator for parking rod to transaxle case	12-16 (8.7-11.6)
Idle bear bearing lock nut	130-180 (94-130)

SPECIAL TOOLS

SPECIAL TOOL APPLICATION

Tool Number	Identification
49 FT01 377	Replacer Lo. & Rev. Piston
49 FT01 439	Holder Idle Gear Shaft
49 FT01 361	Remover Bearing
38MM or 1½"	Socket Wrench
4MM 3.2MM	Pin Punch
49 B001 795	Installer Oil Seal
49 FT01 376	Lifter Servopiston
49 FT01 377	Replacer Lo. Rev. Piston
49 0839 425	Bearing Puller Set
49 F401 330	Bearing Installer Set
49 F401 365	Bearing Remover
49 FT01 380	Shim Selector Set
49 F401 380	Shim Selector Set

SPECIAL TOOL APPLICATION

Tool Number	Identification
49 FT01 515	Preload Adaptor
49 0180 510A	Preload Adaptor
Welding Rod	Drive Shaft Hanger

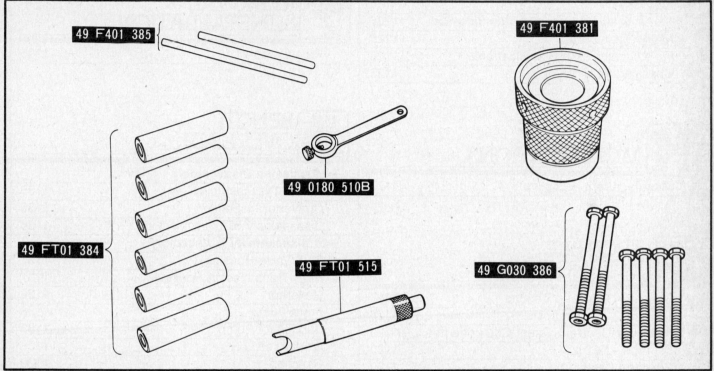

Differential side bearing preload tool set (©Toyo Kogyo Co. Ltd.)

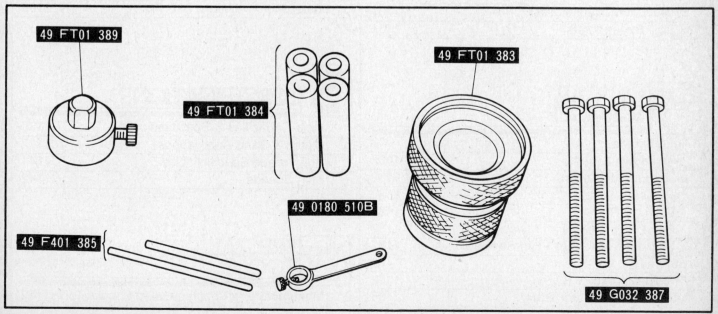

Output gear bearing preload tool set (©Toyo Kogyo Co. Ltd.)

INDEX

MERCEDES-BENZ
W4A040

APPLICATIONS

TRANSMISSION APPLICATION CHART
W4A-040, W4A-020

Year	Model	Transmission
'81 and later	300D Turbodiesel	W4A-040
'81 and later	300CD Turbodiesel	W4A-040
'81 and later	300TD Turbodiesel	W4A-040
'81 and later	300SD Turbodiesel	W4A-040
'81-'82	380SLC	W4A-040
'81-later	380SL	W4A-040
'81-'83	380SEL	W4A-040
'81-'83	380SEC	W4A-040
'84 and later	380SE	W4A-040
'84 and later	500SEC	W4A-040
'84 and later	500SEL	W4A-040
'84 and later	190E	W4A-020
'84 and later	190D	W4A-020

GENERAL DESCRIPTION

The W4A-040 transmission is a fully automatic four-speed unit consisting primarily of a three element welded torque converter and a compound planetary gear set. Two multiple disc clutches, one overrunning clutch, and three bands provide friction ele-

ments required to obtain desired function of the planetary gear set. A hydraulic system, pressurized by a primary gear type pump and secondary piston type pump provides working pressure required to operate friction elements and automatic controls.

The W4A-020 is very similar to the W4A-040. The similarities apply to the layout of the planetary gear sets, brake bands and clutches and the shift valves. It is a 5-speed converter type transmission with an input torque of 147.5 ft. lbs. (200 N•m).

On vehicles equipped with the gas engine, with the shift lever in positions "D" and "3", the transmission starts in second gear

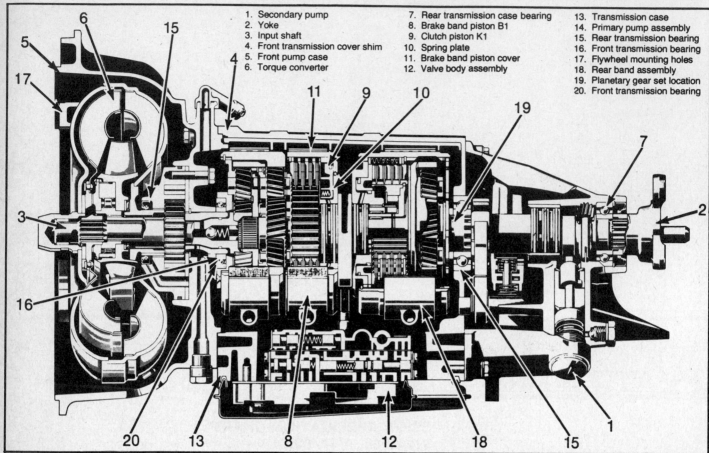

1. Secondary pump
2. Yoke
3. Input shaft
4. Front transmission cover shim
5. Front pump case
6. Torque converter
7. Rear transmission case bearing
8. Brake band piston B1
9. Clutch piston K1
10. Spring plate
11. Brake band piston cover
12. Valve body assembly
13. Transmission case
14. Primary pump assembly
15. Rear transmission bearing
16. Front transmission bearing
17. Flywheel mounting holes
18. Rear band assembly
19. Planetary gear set location
20. Front transmission bearing

Typical automatic transmission (© Mercedes-Benz of America)

when driving in the lower load range and in first gear when in the higher load range.

On vehicles equipped with the diesel engine, the transmission starts in first gear in all forward driving positions. When the vehicle is stopped the transmission will remain in second gear to prevent creeping. The ratio in first gear has been changed to 4.25:1 to accommodate the lower rear axle ratio.

Transmission and Converter Identification

TRANSMISSION

The W4A-040 and W4A-020 transmissions can be identified by a tag that is attached to the transmission case, near the center servo cover. The lower line of the tag shows the transmission build number and the top line of the tag shows the transmission assembly part number.

CONVERTER

The torque converter used with the Mercedes-Benz automatic transmission is a sealed unit and cannot be disassembled for service. If the hub of the converter is scored, or if metal particles are found in the transmission fluid, replace the torque converter.

A smaller torque converter is used on the W4A-020 with the pump gear diameter being 9.6 in. (245mm.).

Transmission Fasteners

Metric bolts and fasteners are used in attaching the transmission to the engine and also in attaching the transmission to the chassis crossmember mount.

The metric fastener dimensions are very close to the dimensions of the familiar inch system fasteners, and for this reason, replacement fasteners must have the same measurement and strength as those removed.

Do not attempt to interchange metric fasteners for inch system fasteners. Mismatched or incorrect fasteners can result in damage to the transmission unit through malfunctions, breakage or possible personal injury.

Care should be taken to reuse the fasteners in the same locations as removed, whenever possible.

NOTE: At an oil temperature of 20-30 degrees C the maximum fluid level is 30mm below the lower dipstick mark. This information is provided as an aid during an oil change, which is generally made at this temperature.

Wipe the dipstick with a clean lint free cloth, immerse it fully for measuring, pull the dipstick out again and read the oil level.

Fluid Type Specifications

Only type A, Dexron® or Dexron® II automatic transmission fluid should be used in the Mercedes-Benz automatic transmission. Failure to use the proper grade and type automatic transmission fluid could result in serious internal transmission damage.

Checking Transmission Fluid Level

Check the automatic transmission fluid level at least every 6,000 miles. This fluid check is made with the engine running, the parking brake on, and the selector lever in the "P" position. The vehicle must also be on level ground and in an unloaded condition. The automatic transmission must also be at operating temperature which is about 80 degrees centigrade. Prior to inspection run the engine for about 1-2 minutes at idling speed so that the torque converter can fill up.

Fill the transmission as required. Actuate the service brake, when the upper dipstick mark is attained after adding transmission fluid. Move the selector lever in all range positions. Then move it back to position "P", so that the working pistons of the servo members are charged with transmission fluid. Check the transmission fluid once again and make corrections if necessary.

NOTE: A fully cooled down transmission will show an oil level below the bottom dipstick mark even when correctly filled with oil.

If the oil level is too low the oil pump will suck up air which can be clearly heard. The oil will foam and provide wrong results during an oil level checkup. Wait unitl the oil foam is down (for approx. 2 minutes), add oil and check oil level.

Excessive transmission fluid must be drained otherwise the transmission gears would be splashing in oil. The temperature will increase unnecessarily until the foaming oil will be ejected through breather. Continuous operation under such circumstances will lead to transmission damage.

Fluid Capacity

All W4A-020 and W4A-040 automatic transmissions have a fluid capacity of 12.9 pts.

MODIFICATIONS

Brake Band B3 Adjusting Bolt

The adjusting bolt for brake band B3 has been modified. On the modified version, the bolt head is "sheared off" after the brake band adjustment has been made. This prevents a subsequent alteration of the brake band setting (no readjustment is possible). The previous version adjusting bolt should be replaced by the modified version only during the course of any transmission repairs that might be performed requiring the removal of the automatic transmission from the vehicle.

TROUBLE DIAGNOSIS

NOTE: On all automatic transmissions, this brake band may now only be adjusted on transmissions removed from the vehicle.

Adjust brake band B3 using the procedure below.
1. Remove the transmission.
2. Remove the valve body.
3. Remove solenoid from transmission if solenoid is installed in an inclined position.
4. Remove the previous version adjusting bolt and replace with the modified version.
5. Tighten the adjusting bolt to 3.6 ft. lbs.
6. Measure the brake band gap and record the measurement.
7. Back off the adjusting bolt by 1¾ turns and tighten the lock nut, making sure in doing so that the adjusting bolt is not turned.
8. Measure the gap again. It must be 0.118 in. (3mm) wider than the gap measured previously.
9. Twist off (shear off) the head of the adjusting bolt.
10. Install the solenoid and the valve body and install the transmission.

Brake Band Piston B2

The seal ring for the brake band piston B2 is made out of teflon. It has a very wide sealing surface and because of this the piston is not in direct contact with the housing and cannot seize.

Fluid Line Connection Bore Relocation

The connection bore of the right transmission fluid line to the transmission fluid cooler has been relocated by 0.43 in. On transmissions with a wide fluid pan the connection to the transmission has been changed to an inlet union fitting (banjo fitting) and is fastened directly to the transmission with the inlet union screw. The previously used elbow fitting is now being omitted from production. Replacement transmissions are being supplied with the previous as well as with the relocated fitting bores. Should the transmission require replacement the following should be noted.

On transmissions with narrow oil pans, the oil line must be slightly rebent if installing a replacement transmission with relocated connection bore. On transmissions with wide oil pans and when a previous version is replaced by a modified version transmission, a new oil line with an inlet union fitting must be installed. Also, when a modified version is replaced by the previous version transmission, an oil line with an elbow fitting and a nut must be installed.

CLUTCH AND BAND APPLICATION CHART
W4A-040, W4A-020

Gear Range	Front Brake	Center Brake	Rear Brake	Front Clutch	Rear Clutch	Overdrive Clutch
First gear		X			X	X
Second gear	X	X				
Third gear		X		X		
Fourth gear				X	X	
Reverse			X		X	X
Neutral/Park						

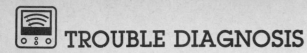

CHILTON'S THREE "C's" TRANSMISSION DIAGNOSIS CHART
Mercedes-Benz Model W4A-040

Condition	Cause	Correction
Slips in all selector positions	a) Incorrect modulating pressure b) Modulating pressure control valve or pressure relief	a) Adjust modulator or replace b) Clean or replace problem valve
Rough jerking when changing gear	a) Check modulating and line pressure b) Vacuum lines or connections leaking or broken c) Control pressure linkage out of adjustment d) Control valve converter adjustment incorrect	a) Adjust pressure as necessary; if line pressure is to high replace valve body assembly b) Replace as necessary c) Adjust control pressure linkage as required d) Correct problem as required
Rough jerk on 3-2 downshift	a) Rear servo piston sealing ring worn or damaged b) Defective rear servo piston	a) Replace defective component as required b) Replace as required
No upshifts	a) Incorrect governor pressure b) Defective governor assembly c) Valve body dirty or valves sticking	a) Correct pressure as necessary b) Repair or replace governor c) Repair or replace components as necessary
Upshifts only in upper speed range of gears	a) Control pressure linkage out of adjustment b) Defective governor assembly	a) Adjust linkage as required b) Repair or replace governor
Upshifts only in lower speed range of gears	a) Control speed linkage damaged or out of adjustment b) Accelerator linkage out of adjustment c) Defective governor assembly	a) Repair or adjust linkage as necessary b) Adjust linkage as required c) Repair or replace governor
No kickdown shifts	a) Fuse for power supply to the solenoid valve blown b) Defective solenoid valve c) Control pressure linkage damaged or out of adjustment d) Kickdown control valve in the valve body sticking	a) Replace fuse b) Replace solenoid valve c) Repair or adjust control pressure linkage d) Repair or replace control valve as required
No engine braking on downshifts	a) Control pressure linkage out of adjustment b) Defective servo piston(s) c) Defective valve body assembly	a) Adjust control pressure linkage as required b) Repair or replace piston(s) as necessary c) Repair or replace valve body as required
Slips in all selector positions	valve for modulating pressure dirty or sticking c) Line to transmission vacuum unit clogged or leaking d) Line pressure control valve dirty or sticking e) Defective primary pump	 c) Clean or replace vacuum line d) Clean or replace line pressure control valve e) Repair or replace pump
Transmission grabs or vehicle shakes when starting off from a complete stop	a) Incorrective modulating pressure b) Check transmission vacuum unit	a) Correct pressure as required b) If fluid is found replace the unit; if fuel is found check and adjust the injection system

CHILTON'S THREE "C's" TRANSMISSION DIAGNOSIS CHART
Mercedes-Benz Model W4A-040

Condition	Cause	Correction
Transmission slips in 1st gear	a) Dirty or sticking valves in valve body b) Defective center servo piston or piston sealing ring damage c) Defective center band or thrust body d) Bleed valves for the front clutch supporting flange sticking	a) Correct as required b) Repair servo piston and sealing ring as required c) Repair center band or thrust body as required d) Correct or replace components as necessary
Transmission slips on upshifts	a) Incorrect modulator or line pressure b) Faulty valve body assembly c) Defective front or rear clutch d) Oil distribution sleeve damage	a) Correct modulator and/or line pressure as required b) Replace sealing bushings on plug pipes c) Repair or replace front or rear clutch, as required d) Repair as necessary
Transmission slips in 3rd gear	a) Valve body sealing bushings worn or damaged b) Defective rear clutch assembly c) Oil distributing sleeve damaged	a) Replace valve body or sealing bushings as required b) Repair or replace as required c) Repair as necessary
Transmission slips in 1st and 2nd gears	a) Rear band worn or damaged b) Adjust brake band	a) Replace rear band as required b) Install a longer thrust pin
Transmission slips in all gears	a) Incorrect modulating pressure b) Defective modulator pressure relief valve or control valve	a) Correct pressure as required b) Replace problem valve
No positive engagement in Reverse	a) Front band out of adjustment b) Front servo piston sealing ring worn or damaged c) Defective one-way clutch in gear unit assembly	a) Correct front band adjustment b) Replace front servo piston sealing ring as required c) Repair or replace one-way clutch as required
Rough jerk when engaging selector lever in "D" position	a) Engine idle speed too high b) Incorrect modulating and/or line pressure c) Defective pressure receiving piston located in the extension housing	a) Correct as required b) Correct modulating and/or line pressure as required c) Correct the pressure receiving piston as necessary

Hydraulic Control System

TORQUE CONVERTER

The torque converter operates as an automatic clutch, a variable torque converter, and as a vibration damper between the engine and the transmission at the same time.

CLUTCHES AND BANDS

Two multiple-disc clutches, one overrunning clutch, and three brake bands provide the friction elements required to obtain the desired function of the planetary gear set.

OIL PUMP

This particular automatic transmission uses a conventional gear-type oil pump, which is mounted just behind the torque converter. The oil pump draws filtered oil from the fluid pan and sends it under pressure to the main pressure valve and the manual valve in the control valve body.

The hydraulic system is also composed of a secondary piston-type pump, which provides, along with the primary pump, the line pressure to operate the friction elements and the automatic controls of the automatic transmission. The secondary pump is located in the rear transmission extension housing.

GOVERNOR ASSEMBLY

The governor is a conventional design in that it has weights and springs, and is mounted on the output shaft. In this way, the governor only turns when the vehicle is moving. It produces an oil pressure in relation to the road speed of the vehicle. This pressure is then directed into the valve body and used to control gearshift timing and operation. The main pressure coming from the oil pump acts against the centrifugal force until the proper governor pressure is set between the different valve surfaces. During moderate speeds, the increasing centrifugal force from the governor valve alone accounts for more increase in pressure. In this way, the governor can provide an exact amount of pressure at low road speeds, and prevent high pressure at high road speeds.

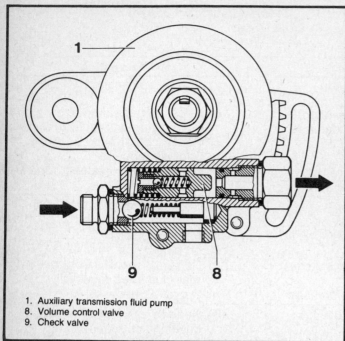

Cross section of auxiliary pump and check valves
(© Mercedes-Benz of America)

1. Auxiliary transmission fluid pump
8. Volume control valve
9. Check valve

AUXILIARY OIL PUMP

An auxiliary oil pump is used to insure proper cooling and adequate lubrication of the internal components of the transmission. It is installed in the transmission fluid circuit between the transmission and the oil cooler which is located within the radiator. The auxiliary pump is driven by the air conditioning pulley and also serves as an idler pulley for the compressor.

Should the auxiliary pump fail, check valves are used to route the fluid through the normal cooling and lubrication circuits to prevent fluid and transmission overheating.

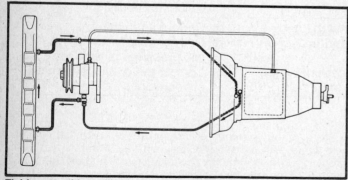

Fluid route with auxiliary pump inoperative
(© Mercedes-Benz of America)

VALVE BODY

The main valve body is located in the lower part of the transmission. The valve body is a two piece design, using two separator plates as well as an oil distributing plate. The separator plates serve as a seal between the upper and lower valve bodies, as well as a connection for the different oil passages and openings. There are a number of different valves in the valve body, each with a specific function.

Diagnosis Tests

To troubleshoot automatic transmissions, it is important that several basic points be understood to save the technician's time.

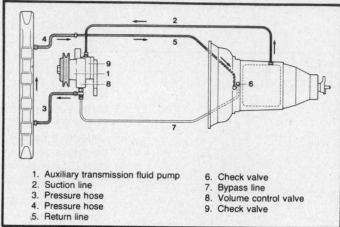

1. Auxiliary transmission fluid pump
2. Suction line
3. Pressure hose
4. Pressure hose
5. Return line
6. Check valve
7. Bypass line
8. Volume control valve
9. Check valve

Fluid route with auxiliary pump operating
(© Mercedes-Benz of America)

A road test should be performed if the vehicle's condition allows it. Use care so that more damage is not done on the road test than has already occurred. Inspect carefully for leaks and other signs of obvious damage. Make sure that all the cable and linkages are attached. Pull out the dipstick and check the color and smell of the fluid. Be sure that the engine is in at least a reasonable state of tune. When road testing, pick a route that will show all the transmission operations, and try the unit in each range, including kickdown and reverse. If the trouble cannot be pinpointed after using the Clutch and Band Application Chart in conjunction with the road test, then further testing will be required. This means that the shift points, stall speed and oil pressure will have to be checked.

CONTROL LINE (WORKING) PRESSURE

NOTE: Before making any hydraulic pressure tests, be sure that the transmission fluid level and fluid condition are up to specification. Also, make sure that manual and throttle linkages, EGR system, and neutral safety/back-up light switch are checked and adjusted as required.

The working pressure of the automatic transmission is not adjustable. Line pressure is automatically established when the vacuum modulator is correctly adjusted. To check the line pressure, drive the vehicle in the indicated range and speed that is shown in the chart. Record the pressure readings on the gauge.

GOVERNOR PRESSURE TEST

NOTE: Before making and hydraulic pressure tests, be sure that the transmission fluid level and fluid condition are up to specification. Also, make sure that manual and throttle linkages, EGR system, and neutral safety/back-up light switch are checked and adjusted as required.

The governor pressure is a partial pressure of the line pressure and is set to the required value by the centrifugal governor, which is attached to the output shaft of the transmission. The governor pressure can never exceed the line pressure and for this reason the upper pressure valves can be measured only while driving at full throttle. In measuring the governor pressure, an accurate oil pressure gauge is required.

THROTTLE VALVE CONTROL PRESSURE TEST

NOTE: Before making any hydraulic pressure tests, be sure that the transmission fluid level and fluid condition are up to specification. Also, make sure that manual and throttle linkages, EGR system, and neutral safety/back-up light switch are checked and adjusted as required.

The throttle valve control pressure is a partial pressure of the modulating pressure. It is mechanically controlled by the position of the accelerator pedal. If the control pressure rod linkage is adjusted correctly the control pressure will be correct.

For correct control rod linkage adjustment follow the following procedure.

Four Cylinder Models

1. Remove the vacuum control unit from the carburetor.
2. Disconnect the automatic choke connecting rod so the throttle valve rests against the idle stop.
3. Loosen the screw and turn the levers against each other so the control rod rests against the idle stop.
4. Tighten the screw and depress the accelerator to the kickdown position. The throttle valve must rest against the full throttle stop.
5. Install the vacuum control unit on the distributor and connect the automatic choke rod.

Five Cylinder Models

1. Disconnect the control pressure rod.
2. Push the angle lever toward the front of the vehicle.
3. Push the control pressure rod rearward against the stop and adjust its length so there is no binding.
4. Tighten the counter nut after adjustment.

Eight Cylinder Models

1. Remove the air filter and disconnect the control pressure linkage.
2. The throttle valve should rest against the idle speed stop.
3. Push the regulating lever and angle lever to the idle position.
4. Push the control pressure rod completely rearward against the stop and adjust the length of the rod so there is no tension.
5. When checking the rod for length, hold it to the left of the socket, not above to compensate for rotary motion of the linkage.

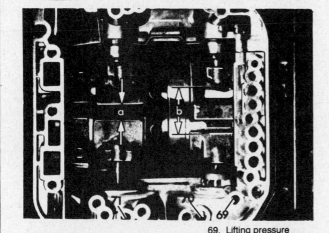

A. Free play measurement
B. Free play measurement
69. Lifting pressure
70. Shift pressure B2
71. Shift pressure B1

Measurement of band free-play (© Mercedes-Benz of America)

AIR PRESSURE TEST

Air pressure is used to determine free play of the center and rear bands. To check the rear band free play, introduce air pressure into the rear band release pressure passage located inside the transmission case. Mark the position of the band end on the drum. Apply air pressure to the rear band apply pressure passage in the transmission case. Mark the position of the band end on the drum. Measure the distance between the two marks; measurement is the rear band free play. To find the center band free play,

measure the position of the band end on the drum in its released position. Apply air pressure to the center servo apply passage in the transmission case. Mark the position of the band end on the drum. The distance between the two marks is the center band free play.

NOTE: This free play should be 3 or 4mm. If not, install a pressure pin of the correct length to bring the free play within its required specification.

STALL SPEED TEST

NOTE: Before making any hydraulic pressure tests, be sure that the transmission fluid level and fluid condition are up to specification. Also, make sure that manual and throttle linkages, EGR system, and neutral safety back-up light switch are checked and adjusted as required.

A stall speed test is a quick test of the torque converter but since it is a demanding test on the transmission, it should only be done if the vehicle accelerates poorly or it fails to reach high speed. A tachometer will be required that is compatible with the ignition system that is used on the vehicle. Never perform this test any longer than the time it takes to look at the gauges and record the reading. When making the test, do not hold the throttle open longer than five seconds or severe transmission damage may result from the heat that is generated. If engine speed exceeds maximum limits, release the accelerator immediately as this is an indication of clutch or band slippage. With the engine at normal operating temperature, vacuum line disconnected, tachometer installed, and parking brake applied firmly, stall test the transmission by pushing the accelerator pedal to the floor and noting the engine speed on the tachometer. If the stall speed is higher than specified, general transmission problems are indicated and hydraulic pressure tests should be made to locate the faulty internal parts of the transmission. If the stall speed is lower than specified, the torque converter roller clutch is at fault.

NOTE: Make sure that the engine performance is adequate before concluding that the torque converter is the problem. The torque converter is a sealed unit and cannot be taken apart for repair.

MODULATOR PRESSURE TEST

NOTE: Before making any hydraulic pressure tests, be sure that the transmission fluid level and fluid condition are up to specification. Also make sure that manual and throttle linkages, EGR system, and neutral safety/back-up light switch are checked and adjusted as required.

Modulator pressure must be measured and corrected before making line pressure and governor pressure tests. To check the modulator pressure, accelerate the vehicle on the road or on a dynamometer to 40 mph. Read the regulating pressure on the gauge, which is attached to the modulating pressure take-off point on the transmission. The pressure reading should be 40 psi in "D" for the W4A-040 transmission. As transmission oil temperature increases, a bimetallic spring attached to the modulating sleeve housing (on rear face of case, inside extension housing) applies pressure to the modulator valve stem. This will move it toward the full load position. This increases modulator pressure and stabilizes the line pressure at high fluid temperatures. To insure that the spring does not influence the modulator pressure, the test must be performed with the fluid temperature between 140°F and 195°F. Pressure may be adjusted by removing the vacuum line from the vacuum unit and turning the adjusting screw in or out using a 4mm Allen wrench. One complete turn of the adjusting screw changes the modulating pressure about 3 psi. It may be necessary to remove the vacuum modulator cover and the locking plate before performing the adjustment procedure.

ON CAR SERVICES

Adjustments

KICKDOWN SWITCH ADJUSTMENT

The kickdown position of the solenoid valve is controlled by the accelerator pedal. Push the accelerator pedal against the kickdown limit stop. In this position the throttle lever should rest against the full load stop of the venturi control unit. Adjustments are made by loosening the clamping screw on the return lever which is on the accelerator pedal shaft and turning the shaft. Tighten the clamping screw again.

VACUUM MODULATOR ADJUSTMENT

Original equipment modulators are not adjustable on this unit. Often, aftermarket replacements have a set screw in the vacuum pipe so that the shifting quality can be "fine-tuned." Modulator service is generally confined to replacement.

On transmission models having an adjustable modulator, remove the vacuum line from the modulator and insert a 4mm Allen wrench into the modulator nipple and engage the adjusting screw. One complete turn of the adjusting screw changes the modulating pressure approximately 3 psi.

Whenever the modulator is inspected, always check the rubber hose connector for cracks or other deterioration.

PRESSURE CONTROL CABLE

The pressure control cable can be replaced without removing the valve body. It is secured to the transmission housing by a locking lever. To remove, push the locking lever toward the sleeve and turn counterclockwise. Pull out in an upward direction.

CONTROL PRESSURE ROD ADJUSTMENT

Four Cylinder Models

1. Remove the vacuum control unit from the carburetor.
2. Disconnect the automatic choke connecting rod so the throttle valve rests against the idle stop.
3. Loosen the screw and turn the levers against each other so the control rod rests against the idle stop.
4. Tighten the screw and depress the accelerator to the kickdown position. The throttle valve must rest against the full throttle stop.
5. Install the vacuum control unit on the distributor and connect the automatic choke rod.

Five Cylinder Models

1. Disconnect the control pressure rod.
2. Push the angle lever toward the front of the vehicle.
3. Push the control pressure rod rearward against the stop and adjust its length so there is not binding.
4. Tighten the counter nut after adjustment.

Eight Cylinder Models

1. Remove the air filter and disconnect the control pressure linkage.
2. The throttle valve should rest against the idle speed stop.
3. Push the regulating lever and angle lever to the idle position.
4. Push the control pressure rod completely rearward against the stop and adjust the length of the rod so there is no tension.
5. When checking the rod for length, hold it to the left of the socket, not above to compensate for rotary motion of the linkage.

SELECTOR ROD LINKAGE ADJUSTMENT

NOTE: The vehicle must be standing with the weight normally distributed on all four wheels. No jacks may be used.

1. Disconnect the selector rod from the selector lever.
2. Set the selector lever in Neutral and make sure that there is approximately 1mm clearance between the selector lever and the N stop of the selector gate.
3. Adjust the length of the selector rod so that it can be attached free of tension.
4. Retighten the counternut.

BAND ADJUSTMENT AND INTERVAL

The adjusting bolt for brake band B3 has been modified. The bolt head is "sheared off" after the brake band adjustment is made. Brake band B3 can only be adjusted when the transmission has been removed from the vehicle.

1. Remove the transmission.
2. Remove the valve body.
3. Remove solenoid from transmission if solenoid is installed in an inclined position.
4. Remove the previous version adjusting bolt and replace with the modified version.
5. Tighten the adjusting bolt to 3.6 ft. lbs.
6. Measure the brake band gap and record the measurement.
7. Back off the adjusting bolt by 1¾ turns and tighten the lock nut, making sure in doing so that the adjusting bolt is not turned.
8. Measure the gap again. It must be 0.118 in. (3mm) wider than the gap measured previously.
9. Twist off (shear off) the head of the adjusting bolt.
10. Install the solenoid and the valve body and install the transmission.

STARTER LOCKOUT & BACK-UP LIGHT SWITCH ADJUSTMENT

1. Disconnect the selector rod and move the selector lever on the transmission to the Neutral position.
2. Tighten the clamping screw prior to making adjustments.
3. Loosen the adjusting screw and insert the locating pin through the driver into the locating hole in the shift housing.
4. Tighten the adjusting screw and remove the locating pin.
5. Move the selector lever to position N and connect the selector rod so that there is no tension.
6. Check to be sure that the engine cannot be started in Neutral or Park.
7. On the W4A-020, the starter lockout and back-up light switch can be adjusted from below. A gasket prevents water from reaching the electrical connections.

Services

FLUID CHANGE

Transmission and Converter

Mercedes-Benz recommends periodic fluid changes at intervals of 27,000 miles. Type A, Dexron® or Dexron® II automatic transmission fluid meeting Mercedes-Benz quality standard must be used in the automatic transmission. Failure to use the proper grade and type fluid could cause serious internal automatic transmission damage.

For vehicles that are subjected to aggravated conditions (such as taxis, trailer pulling vehicles, or vehicles used on mountain roads) additional fluid change is necessary.

NOTE: The miles given for fluid change are average. Each vehicle operated under severe driving conditions should be treated individually.

When the automatic transmission has been removed for repairs, the unit should be drained completely. The converter, cooler and cooler lines should be flushed to remove any particles or dirt that might have entered the components as a result of transmission malfunction or failure.

VACUUM DIAPHRAGM

Removal

1. Raise the vehicle on a hoist and support it safely.
2. Disconnect the vacuum line from the vacuum modulator.

NOTE: As the vacuum line is being disconnected from the modulator, the modulator unit must be held steady.

3. Remove the vacuum modulator and thrust pin from the transmission case.

Installation

1. Install the vacuum modulator unit in the transmission case.
2. Screw the vacuum line to the modulator, using care so as not to turn the modulator.
3. Lower the vehicle from the hoist. Road test the vehicle as required.

OIL PAN DRAINING

Removal

1. Raise the vehicle on a hoist and support it safely.
2. Drain the automatic transmission fluid by loosening the dipstick tube.
3. Remove the transmission fluid pan.
4. If you are going to replace the transmission fluid filter, remove the bolts that retain the fluid filter to the transmission and remove the fluid filter.

Installation

1. Install the new transmission fluid filter in its place.
2. Clean the old gasket material from the transmission case and the transmission fluid pan.
3. Install the transmission fluid pan to the transmission case using a new pan gasket. Install the dipstick tube.
4. Lower the vehicle from the hoist. Fill the transmission with the proper grade transmission fluid.
5. Start the engine and check for leaks. Correct as required.

SHIFT VALVE HOUSING

Removal

1. Raise the vehicle on a hoist and support it safely. Drain the transmission fluid.
2. Remove the transmission fluid pan and the old pan gasket. Remove the fluid filter.
3. Move the selector lever to position "P". Remove the shift valve housing bolts. Remove the shift valve housing from the case.
4. Remove the plug pipes with the sealing bushings and pull the sealing bushings from the plug pipes.

Installation

1. Install new sealing bushings on the plug pipes and insert them into the transmission case.
2. Insert a locating pin for the control pressure valve into the shift valve housing.
3. Carefully install the shift valve housing into the transmission.

NOTE: Make sure that the range selector valve enters correctly into the detent plate.

4. Install the shift valve housing bolts with the spring washers and torque the bolts to 9.4 foot pounds.

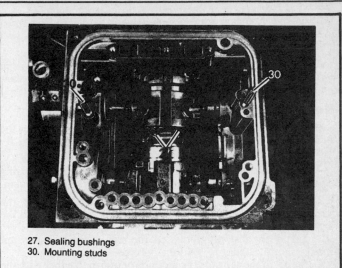

27. Sealing bushings
30. Mounting studs

Location of sealing bushing (© Mercedes-Benz of America)

5. Remove the locating pin.
6. Install a new fluid filter. Install the transmission fluid pan using a new pan gasket. Torque the pan bolts 5.1 foot pounds. Install the fluid filler pipe to the transmission pan.
7. Lower the vehicle from the hoist. Fill the transmission with the proper grade transmission fluid.
8. Start the engine and check for leaks. Road test the vehicle and check the shifting pattern. Correct as required.
9. Check the transmission fluid level at normal operating temperature. Correct as needed.

EXTENSION HOUSING

Removal

1. Raise the vehicle on a hoist and support it safely. Drain the transmission fluid.
2. Slightly raise the engine/transmission unit. Remove both the bolts for the rear engine mount. Remove the 12 tunnel closing plate bolts and remove the tunnel closing plate. On models with the W4A-040 automatic transmission, remove the rear engine mount along with the engine carrier and also remove the mounting bracket for the front exhaust pipe.
3. Loosen the speedometer shaft on the rear of the transmission case and pull it off.
4. Disconnect the selector rod on the range selector lever and move the range selector lever to position "P".
5. Loosen both fastening bolts of the universal shaft intermediate bearing, but do not screw them out. Loosen the universal shaft clamping nut. Unscrew the universal shaft on the transmission, but leave the universal plate on the universal shaft.
6. Slide the universal shaft to the rear, as far as the center bearing and the clamping piece permit.
7. Place a piece of wood under the front of the universal shaft in such a way that the shaft is completely pushed up.
8. Unlock and remove the slotted nut on the three-legged flange. Remove the three-legged flange.
9. Disconnect the vacuum line on the vacuum modulator. If equipped, remove the vacuum modulator mounting bracket. Remove the vacuum modulator.
10. Unscrew the plug for the secondary pump and remove the compression spring.
11. Lower the transmission enough to remove the bolts from the rear transmission housing.
12. Pull off the rear transmission housing using Mercedes-Benz tool No. 115-589-03-33-00, or equivalent.

NOTE: On the W4A-020, the three legged flange is attached with a double hex nut instead of the slot nut used on the W4A-040

transmission. A socket with ¾ inch drive is available from Mercedes-Benz as a special tool for this double hex. It carries the part number 126 589 02 09 00.

NOTE: The centrifugal governor should remain on the output shaft, that is, when pulling off the housing, also pull the governor from the guide of the rear transmission housing at the same time.

Installation

1. Install a new rear transmission housing gasket. Center the gasket on the sealing surface of the transmission housing by means of two screws.

NOTE: In order to install the new transmission rear housing gasket, you must remove the modulating pressure valve housing.

2. Mount the rear transmission housing while moving the speedometer drive with a suitable tool until it is in mesh with the worm gear.

3. Install the fastening bolts on the rear of the transmission housing. Torque them to 9.4 foot pounds.

4. Screw in the plug for the secondary pump together with the compression spring.

5. Coat the vacuum modulator with sealing compound and screw it into the rear of the transmission housing. Connect the vacuum line to the modulator. Install the mounting bracket, if equipped.

6. Place the range selector lever in the "P" position.

7. Place the three-legged flange on the output shaft and torque the slotted nut to 86.2 foot pounds.

8. Attach the selector rod to the range selector lever. Connect the speedometer shaft to the transmission housing.

9. Lift the engine/transmission unit as required. Remove the wooden support from under the propeller shaft and install the propeller shaft to the transmission.

10. Check the rubber mount and screw to the transmission. Install the rear end of the tunnel closing plate. Install the fastening bolts for the rubber mount on the end plate.

11. Lower the vehicle and move it back and forth and tighten the propeller shaft clamping nut. Torque the fastening bolts on the propeller shaft intermediate bearing to 14.5 foot-pounds.

12. Fill the transmission with the proper grade and type auto-

matic transmission fluid. Shift through all gears and correct the fluid level.

13. Check the modulating pressure and adjust, if necessary. Screw on the front end of the tunnel closing plate.

Governor

Removal

1. Raise the vehicle on a hoist and support it safely.
2. Remove the transmission extension housing.
3. Remove the plate spring, worm gear of the speedometer drive, eccentric ring for the secondary pump and the governor from the output shaft.

Installation

1. Attach the governor, eccentric ring, worm gear of the speedometer drive and the plate spring to the output shaft.

NOTE: The flange of the worm gear should face the governor and the curvature of the plate spring should face the worm gear.

2. Reinstall the rear transmission housing.
3. Lower the vehicle from the hoist and fill with the proper grade transmission fluid.
4. Start the engine and check for any leaks. Correct as required.

NOTE: The drive gears on the W4A-020 transmission are made of plastic. A lock ring holds the drive gears in the axial direction. The drive gear of the output shaft is driven by two lugs.

PARKING LOCK

Removal

1. Raise the vehicle on a hoist and support it safely.
2. Remove the transmission extension housing along with the governor.
3. Unscrew the fastening bolt from the holder and remove the holder together with the leaf spring. Remove the resilient linkage.
4. Remove the parking pawl together with the clamping spring.
5. Pull the parking lock gear from the output shaft.

Installation

1. Attach the parking lock gear to the output shaft and slide the parking lock with the clamping spring on the bearing pin.
2. Install the resilient linkage.
3. Install the leaf spring. Install the needle bearing supported roller and holder. Torque the bolts to 7.2 ft. lbs.
4. Place the range selector lever in the "P" position to check if the parking lock engages correctly.
5. Install the governor and the rear transmission housing.
6. Lower the vehicle from the hoist. Fill the transmission with the proper grade fluid.
7. Start the engine and check for leaks. Correct as required.

STARTER LOCK AND BACK-UP LIGHT SWITCH

Removal

1. Raise the vehicle on a hoist and support it safely.
2. Disconnect the selector rod at the range selector lever. Remove the range selector lever from the shaft by loosening the clamping screw.
3. Remove the screws from the starter locking switch. Remove the switch from the shaft.

Installation

1. Install the starter locking switch to the transmission housing.

15. Worm gear of speedometer drive
16. Eccentric ring for the secondary pump
17. Governor assembly
85. Plate spring
19. Parking lock pawl
18. Parking lock gear
20. Modulator pressure housing

Governor and attaching parts (© Mercedes-Benz of America)

2. Place the range selector lever on the switch and tighten it with the clamping screw. Adjust the switch as indicated in the adjustment section of this chapter.

3. Attach the selector rod to the range selector lever and secure it.

4. Lower the vehicle from the hoist and road test as required.

REMOVAL & INSTALLATION

REMOVAL

1. Disconnect the negative battery cable. Raise the vehicle and support it safely.

2. Drain the automatic transmission fluid.

NOTE: To do this, unscrew the fluid filler pipe on the sump of the transmission fluid pan. Also remove the fluid drain plug which is located on the torque converter.

3. Remove the mounting bracket for the front exhaust pipes.

4. Remove the oil cooler pipes and cap them with plastic plugs to prevent leakage.

5. Loosen the fastening bolts on the propeller shaft intermediate bearing, but do not remove them.

6. Loosen the propeller shaft clamping nut. Unscrew the fastening bolts from the engine mounting and remove the engine carrier.

7. Unscrew the propeller shaft on the transmission. Leave the universal plate on the propeller shaft. Slide the propeller shaft toward the rear, as far as the center bearing and clamping piece will permit. Place a suitable piece of wood underneath the propeller shaft at the front of the tunnel, in such a way that the propeller shaft is completely pushed upwards.

8. Pull out the plug for the starter lock and the back-up light switch. Unscrew the clamping screw from the lever-for-control pressure and pull the lever from the shaft.

9. Remove the cable from the kickdown solenoid valve. Disconnect the shift rod on the range selector lever and set the range selector lever to the "P" position. Disconnect the speedometer shaft on the transmission.

NOTE: During removal and installation of the W4A-020, when the vehicle is equipped with a diesel engine, the torque converter must be retained to the transmission. Insert the holding device into the cutout of the vent grille in the converter housing. Remove the holding device before starting the engine.

10. Unscrew the vacuum line from the vacuum diaphragm, while holding a suitable tool on the vacuum diaphragm unit. Unscrew the fastening clips from the mounting bracket.

11. Pull the covering plug from the intermediate flange. Separate the hydraulic clutch from the driven plate by removing the plate bolts.

12. Slightly raise the engine-transmission unit. Remove all the bolts attaching the transmission to the intermediate flange. The two lateral bolts should be removed last.

13. Push the transmission with the torque converter in the direction of the rear axle until the bearing journal of the hydraulic clutch can no longer touch the intermediate flange.

14. Carefully lower the automatic transmission unit with the torque converter. Pull the unit out of the vehicle in the forward direction.

15. Place the transmission in a vertical position. Screw on the holding plate (Mercedes-Benz tool No. 116-589-02-62-00) on the torque converter and pull the torque converter out in an upward direction.

INSTALLATION

1. Install the torque converter to the transmission using the holding tool (Mercedes-Benz tool No. 116-589-02-62-00). Grease the centering pin and the drive flange of the torque converter with molly lube or equivalent.

NOTE: If the torque converter is properly installed, dimension "K" should be approximately 0.157 in. (4mm). Also make sure that when installing the torque converter, the sealing lip of the radial sealing ring in the primary pump housing is not damaged. Check dimension "K" again prior to flanging-on transmission.

2. Place the automatic transmission on the transmission jack. Turn the torque converter in such a manner that the two fastening bores are at the bottom.

3. Rotate the engine until the two bores in the driven plate for fastening the engine to the torque converter are at the bottom.

4. Move the transmission until the bolts of the clutch housing are in alignment with the bores in the intermediate flange. Push the transmission forward until the clutch housing is well seated. Do not use force.

5. After installing the engine and the transmission to the round centering of the clutch bowl, force the torque converter, using a suitable tool, through the cooling slots on the clutch bowl in a forward direction so that distance "A" is eliminated. Install the six bolts into the torque converter.

6. Connect the vacuum modulator to the vacuum line. Connect the fastening clips to the mounting bracket. Connect the speedometer hook-up to the transmission.

7. Attach the selector rod to the range selector lever. Connect the cable to the kickdown solenoid valve. Slide the control pressure lever on the shaft and attach it with the clamping screw. Attach the plug for the starter lock and the back-up light switch.

8. Remove the wooden support from under the universal shaft and screw the universal shaft to the transmission.

9. Bolt the rear engine mount to the transmission. Install the rear engine mounting bolts. Install the rear engine carrier, then install the mounting bracket for the front exhaust pipes.

10. Tighten the universal shaft clamping nut. Tighten the fastening bolts of the universal shaft intermediate bearing.

11. Remove the plastic plugs from the oil cooler pipes and install them. Use the fastening clips to secure the pipes to their proper location.

12. Install the fluid filler pipe to the sump of the transmission. Install the fluid drain plug into the torque converter.

13. Lower the vehicle and connect the negative battery cable.

14. Fill the transmission with the proper type automatic transmission fluid.

15. Start the engine and check for leaks. Correct as required. Road test the vehicle.

BENCH OVERHAUL

Before Disassembly

1. Clean the exterior of the automatic transmission unit before any attempt is made to disassemble it. This procedure is done to prevent dirt and other foreign material from entering the automatic transmission and damaging any internal parts.

2. Handle all automatic transmission parts carefully to avoid nicking or burring the bearing or mating surfaces.

3. Lubricate all internal parts of the automatic transmission with fresh automatic transmission fluid before assembling the automatic transmission unit.

4. Use new gaskets and seals when assembling the automatic transmission.

5. Tighten all bolts and screws to their recommended torque specification.

NOTE: If steam cleaning is done to the exterior of the automatic transmission unit, immediate disassembly should be done to avoid rusting from condensation which has formed on the internal parts of the unit.

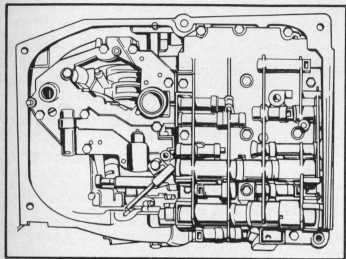

Valve body assembly (© Mercedes-Benz of America)

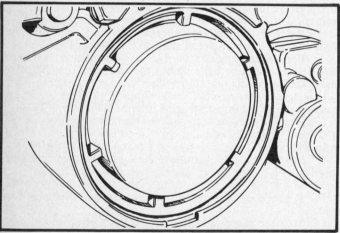

Brake band piston cover (© Mercedes-Benz of America)

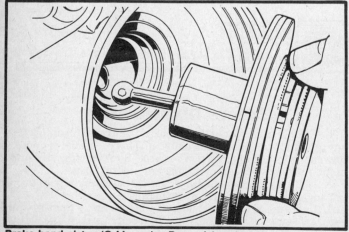

Brake band piston (© Mercedes-Benz of America)

Converter Inspection

1. If the fluid in the torque converter is discolored but does not contain metal bits or particles, the torque converter is not damaged and need not be replaced, as long as trouble-shooting does not point to an internal failure.

2. Color is no longer a good indicator of the transmission fluid condition. In the past, dark color was associated with overheated transmission fluid. It is not considered a positive sign of transmission failure today because of the newer fluids that are available in today's market.

3. If fluid from the torque converter contains metal particles, the torque converter is damaged internally and must be replaced.

4. If the cause of fluid contamination was burned clutch plates or overheated fluid, the torque converter is contaminated and should, in most cases, be replaced.

Transmission Disassembly

1. Mount the automatic transmission unit in a suitable automatic transmission holding fixture.

2. Remove the transmission fluid pan and gasket. Remove the fluid filter.

3. Unscrew the valve body bolts and remove the valve body. Unbolt, the shift lever mechanism and remove with the retaining spring.

4. Remove the lower cover with the intermediate plate and oil pipe. Remove the one-way valve with the brake band guide (B2).

5. Push in the brake band piston cover (B2) and remove the locking ring. Pull out the brake band piston (B2).

6. Using a suitable tool unclamp the B1 brake band locking ring, and remove the B1 brake piston with the cover and the back pressure springs.

7. Pull out the B1 brake band guide.

8. Unscrew the thrust bolt closing plug and remove the range selector lever. Remove the starter lockout switch.

9. Remove the vacuum control unit and the modulating pressure control valve. Detach the kickdown solenoid valve.

10. Unscrew the slotted nut and pull off the three legged flange from the output shaft. Remove the rear transmission extension housing.

11. Remove the plate spring with the worm gear of the speedometer drive. Remove the eccentric ring for the secondary pump and the governor assembly from the output shaft. Remove the secondary pump.

12. Remove the parking lock gear with the parking lock pawl and the expanding spring.

13. Remove the resilient linkage lock ring and remove the resilient linkage.

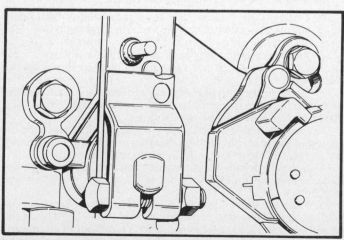

Range selector lever (© Mercedes-Benz of America)

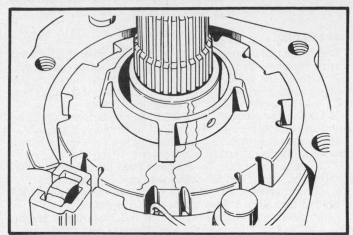

Parking lock pawl with parking lock gear (© Mercedes-Benz of America)

Secondary pump intermediate plate (© Mercedes-Benz of America)

14. Remove the needle bearing. Remove the starter lock and back-up light assembly.

15. Unlock brake band piston cover B3. Remove the locking ring and pull off the cover. Remove brake band piston B3 and the truncated or blunt cone spring.

16. Pull out the clip for the bearing pin from brake band lever B3 and knock the bearing pin out in the forward direction. Remove brake band lever B3 from the transmission housing.

17. Remove the locking clip for thrust body B1 and B2. Remove both of these thrust bodies.

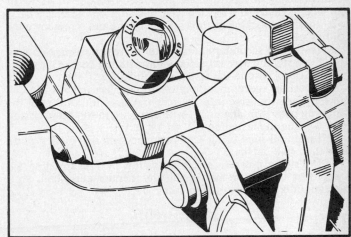

Resilient linkage (© Mercedes-Benz of America)

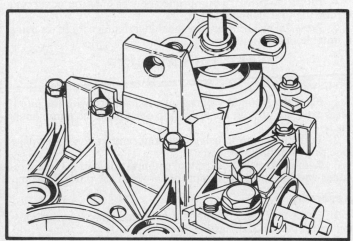

Three legged flange (© Mercedes-Benz of America)

Unit Disassembly

NOTE: After disassembly of each unit, wash all parts in cleaning solvent. Blow dry with compressed air. Inspect all parts for excessive wear or damage and replace parts as needed.

SHIFT VALVE HOUSING

Disassembly

NOTE: The shift valve housing has 18 valve balls. During disassembly make sure that the balls do not roll around. Wash all parts in unused cleaning solvent. Blow dry with compressed air.

1. Remove the bolts from the bottom of the shift valve housing assembly, except for two bolts opposite each other. Position the shift valve housing on an assembly fixture or another suitable disassembly device.

2. Remove the two remaining bolts from the bottom of the shift valve housing and lift off the top together with the intermediate plate.

3. Remove the intermediate plate from the top of the unit. Remove the filter along with its spring from inside the top of the shift valve housing.

4. Lift the bottom of the shift valve housing from the assembly fixture and remove the filter modulating pressure screen. Remove all the valve balls.

Assembly

1. Insert the valve balls into their proper location. Install the filter modulating pressure screen and shift pin.

2. Install the filter with its spring in the top of the shift valve housing. Install the intermediate plate on the shift valve housing.

3. Place the top of the shift valve housing on the intermediate plate and insert two opposite bolts and tighten slightly.

4. Insert the remaining bolts. Torque the bolts to 5.8 ft. lbs. (8 N•m).

REAR TRANSMISSION HOUSING

Disassembly

1. Remove the bolt from the cover plate of the locking piston and remove the locking piston together with the spring. Remove the spring plate along with its two springs. Remove the pressure receiving piston from the rear of the transmission case cover.

2. Remove the bolt for the speedometer drive. Pull the speed-

ometer drive out of the rear transmission case. Remove the speedometer pinion from the bearing body.

3. Remove the bolt for the secondary pump. This bolt is located inside the rear transmission housing. Remove the secondary pump from the transmission case.

NOTE: If the thrust pin (plastic pin) binds or drops out, be sure to replace it. New transmission covers are already provided with the thrust pin (plastic pin), compression spring, ball, and the closing plug.

4. Remove the rear transmission housing seal with a suitable seal removal tool. Remove the locking ring and press out the ball bearing.

5. Unscrew all measuring screw connections and closing plugs with their ball valves.

6. Unscrew the closing plug and remove the steel ball. Check the thrust pin (plastic pin) for smooth operation.

Assembly

1. Press a new ball bearing into the rear transmission case housing, using Mercedes-Benz tool No. 108-589-02-43-00 or equivalent. Install the locking ring. Install a new sealing ring.

2. Insert the locking piston with the spring and screw down the holding plate.

3. Install the secondary pump into the rear transmission case until the fastening bore is in alignment with the bore in the transmission case. Torque the fastening bolt to 5.8 ft. lbs.

4. Insert the speedometer pinion into the bearing body. Install the speedometer drive into the rear transmission case until the fastening bore is in alignment with the bore in the transmission case. Torque the fastening bolt to 5.8 ft. lbs.

5. Install all measuring screw connections and closing plugs with their ball valves.

6. Insert the pressure receiving piston by first inserting the compression spring into the piston and then installing both components into the transmission case.

GOVERNOR

Disassembly

1. Replace the sealing rings as required by disconnecting them and removing them from the governor body.

2. Remove the bolts that hold the unit together. Remove the shift valve housing and the governor housing from the flange.

3. Remove the lock washer, compression spring and the shift valve from the shift valve housing.

4. Remove the spring plate, centrifugal weight and the compression spring in the upward direction from the governor housing.

5. Remove the compression spring with the compensating washers and the control valve in the downward direction from the governor housing.

Assembly

1. Insert the control valve into the governor housing. Install the centrifugal weight with the compression spring in the control valve. Insert the compression washers with compression spring into the control valve.

NOTE: Do not change the number of compensating washers.

2. Attach the spring plate making sure it seats properly. Insert the shift valve with the compression spring and push on the lock washer.

3. Position the shift housing on the flange making sure that the outer oil slots are facing the oil seal rings and the oil ducts are in alignment.

4. Insert the strainer into the seat provided in the oil duct and mount the governor housing. Replace the oil sealing rings if they were dislodged during removal. Torque the bolts to 5.8 ft. lbs. (7.5 N•m).

FRONT PUMP

Disassembly

1. Pull the ball bearing from the front of the transmission cover using Mercedes-Benz tool No. 116-589-07-33-00 or equivalent.

2. Remove the four fastening bolts. Install two bolts approximately 50mm long, opposite each other, in two of the four bolt holes that you removed the fastening bolts from.

3. Loosen the primary pump from the transmission cover by means of tapping the two 50mm bolts lightly with a hammer.

4. Remove the primary pump housing with the intermediate plate from the front transmission cover.

5. Remove the primary pump gears from the pump housing. Remove the O-ring and the radial sealing ring if necessary.

6. The pump housing on the W4A-020 transmission has a roller bearing instead of a bushing for the drive flange.

7. To reduce possible leaks from the roller bearing, a sealing plate is to be installed behind the bearing and is held in place with a steel disc.

Assembly

1. Install a new O-ring and radial sealing ring into the primary pump housing. Lubricate the primary pump gears and insert them into the pump housing.

NOTE: The bevelled outer edge of the pump gear should face the bronze bushing.

2. Insert the intermediate plate in such a manner that the fastening bores for the primary pump are in alignment.

3. Place the installation sleeve, Mercedes-Benz tool No. 116-589-19-61-00 or equivalent, onto the stator shaft and screw in the two studs for guiding the primary pump into place.

4. Insert the primary pump into the transmission cover and torque the four bolts to 14.5 ft. lbs.

5. Press the ball bearing into the transmission case cover using a suitable installation tool.

SECONDARY PUMP

Disassembly

1. Place the secondary pump on a flat surface with the pump gears exposed. Lift out the two pump gears from the pump housing.

2. Turn the pump housing over and remove the cover plate lock ring and the cover plate.

3. Remove the shut-off piston, compression spring, spring retainer and the check ball from the inside of the pump housing.

Assembly

1. Check the O-rings in the shut-off piston and the pump housing and replace if damaged.

2. Insert the shut-off piston into the pump housing.

3. Install the compression spring with the spring retainer and the check ball into the shut-off piston.

4. Install the cover plate and insert the lock ring.

5. Turn the pump unit over and insert the pump gears making sure of gear engagement.

GEAR ASSEMBLY

Disassembly

1. Remove the output shaft together with the rear planetary gear carrier. Place the gear assembly with the input shaft in an upward direction on the assembly stand.

2. Remove the circlip and lift off the planetary gear set. Remove the axial bearing and input shaft.

3. Remove the output shaft radial bearing and the axial bearing and lift out the output shaft.

4. Remove the sun gear bearing and the sun gear. Remove the

plate carrier snap ring and lift the plate carrier and one-way clutch out of the connecting carrier.

5. Detach the supporting disc and remove the compensating ring and O-ring.

6. Turn the one-way clutch in an anticlockwise direction and pull out. Remove the cylindrical rollers.

Assembly

1. Insert the cylindrical rollers into the compensating ring and install the locking plates.

2. Install the inner race of the one-way clutch while rotating in anticlockwise direction. Pull out the locking plates and insert the compensating ring and O-ring.

3. Mount the supporting plate making sure that the pin on the back side of the plate enters into bore of the one-way clutch outer race.

4. Insert the compensating washer into the connecting carrier and place the one-way clutch into connecting carrier.

5. Install the circlip into the outside groove and check for end play of the one-way clutch.

6. Install the sun gear in the roller clutch and insert the axial bearing on the sun gear. Install the output shaft into the roller clutch.

7. Install the axial bearing and the radial bearing on the output shaft. Mount the input shaft and the input shaft axial bearing.

8. Install the front gear set and lock with a circlip. Install the axial bearing on the input shaft.

CLUTCH K1

Disassembly

1. Push the circlip out of the groove with a suitable tool and remove it from the assembly. Remove the plate assembly by tilting the supporting flange.

2. Place a press on the spring retainer in such a manner that the pressure ring is uniformly seated. Push the spring retainer down with the press until the circlip is exposed and can be removed. Carefully release the press and remove the spring retainer and its springs.

3. Hold the piston with a pair of pliers and pull it out of the supporting flange, until it can be held manually.

4. Lift the piston with the lip sealing ring out of the supporting flange. Check the condition of the seal.

Assembly

1. Install a new lip sealing ring, if necessary. Do not use a sharp edged tool when installing, as damage could result.

NOTE: The lip sealing ring should be correctly resting in the groove with the lip pointing in the downward direction.

2. Insert the introducing ring into the supporting flange. Install a new lip sealing ring, if necessary. The lip sealing ring should point in the downward direction. Lubricate the piston and the lip sealing rings. Install and push on the housing bottom without canting.

NOTE: Do not use force since this might damage the lip sealing ring.

3. Insert the piston return spring into the piston. Position the spring retainer in such a manner that each spring is centered in one prominence of the spring retainer.

NOTE: Do not confuse the springs with those of clutch K2.

4. Push the spring retainer carefully without canting, down under the press until the circlip can be installed. Carefully release the press and check for the correct seating of the circlip.

5. Assemble the plate assembly for clutch K1. Soak the new lining plates in clean automatic transmission fluid for a short time before installing them.

6. Insert the plate assembly into the outer plate carrier. Insert

the undulated circlip into the groove and push down into the groove with a suitable tool to secure the clip.

NOTE: The resilient circlips of clutches K1 and K2 are different in spring force and should not be interchanged. The circlip of K1 has six undulations (waves).

CLUTCH K2

Disassembly

1. Push down on the supporting flange, until the circlip can be removed.

2. Remove the plate package by tilting the outside plate carrier.

3. Remove the spring retainer circlip using a suitable tool. Remove the spring retainer along with the compression springs.

4. Remove the piston from the outside of the plate carrier.

Assembly

1. Insert the sealing ring into the piston making sure it is not twisted. Install the lip sealing ring to the inside of the piston.

2. Insert the installation sleeve on the outside of the plate carrier and lubricate the sleeve and the sealing rings with automatic transmission fluid.

3. Place the piston into the outside of the plate carrier. Remove the installation sleeve.

4. Install the compression springs and compress them using a suitable tool until the spring retainer can be inserted. Secure with a circlip and remove the compression tool.

5. Insert the plate package into the outside of the plate carrier. Install the circlip and push into the circlip groove.

Transmission Assembly

1. Mount the transmission unit in a suitable automatic transmission holding fixture.

2. Screw in the closing plug with a new aluminum sealing ring and torque to 2-3 ft. lbs. (10 N•m).

3. Place the O-ring and the sealing ring into the transmission casing.

NOTE: Lubricate all rings and clutch discs with automatic transmission fluid prior to assembling.

4. Install the Teflon rings in the rear clutch supporting flange. Install the supporting flange in accordance with the hole pattern of the fastening bore.

5. Insert the thrust body with the thrust body plate in an upward direction. Insert and tighten the end casing bolts to 8 ft. lbs. (11 N•m).

Placement of sealing rings and O-rings
(© Mercedes-Benz of America)

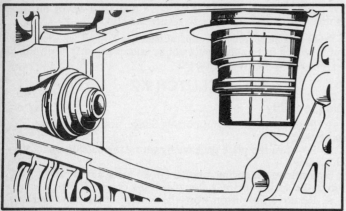

Supporting flange location (© Mercedes-Benz of America)

6. Install the thrust washer into the casing and position it so that the plate for the torsion lock is secured within the transmission casing.

7. Compress the rear brake assembly and install in the transmission casing.

8. Place the rear brake assembly and install in the transmission casing.

NOTE: Check the installation of the gear set by making sure the upper edge of the connecting carrier is lower than the supportive surface of the outside plate.

9. Place the axial bearing into the planetary gear carrier and insert the pressure ring in the groove located on the input shaft.

10. Install the front brake (B1) band in a manner that the assembly lock pin is facing the thrust body.

11. Install the Teflon rings on the front cover and install the front cover with gasket. Tighten to 10 ft. lbs. (13 N•m).

12. Turn the transmission in its holder so that the output shaft is facing up and slip the circlip up to the output shaft groove.

NOTE: To reduce noise on the W4A-020 automatic transmission, the output shaft has an additional bearing. It is a one piece needle bearing with a plastic cage. It is open which will help ease installation.

13. Install the helical gear on the output shaft. Install the axial holder on the shaft directly next to the output shaft.

14. Install a new O-ring in the governor housing and insert the governor. Insert the axial holder in the governor shaft groove.

15. Install the governor cover and secure with the locking ring.

16. Install the secondary pump and torque to 5.9 ft. lbs. (8 N•m). Check the axial holder for proper position.

17. Install the oil pipe and the detent plate with the shaft and torque to 6 ft. lbs. (8.5 N•m).

18. Mount the resilient linkage roller on the resilient linkage and install the linkage on the detent plate. Install lock ring.

19. Install the compensating washers on the helical gear and mount the parking lock pawl with the expanding spring.

Gearset with input shaft (© Mercedes-Benz of America)

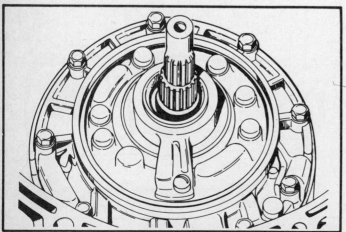

Location of front cover on input shaft (© Mercedes-Benz of America)

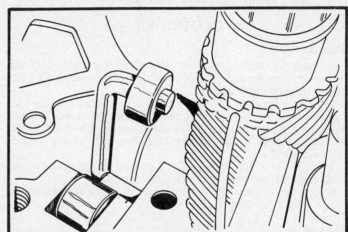

Resilient linkage roller (© Mercedes-Benz of America)

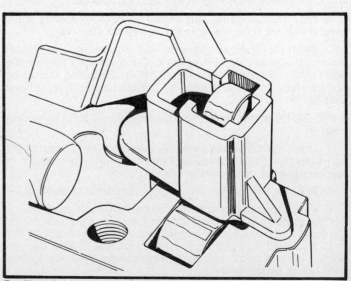

Resilient linkage guide (© Mercedes-Benz of America)

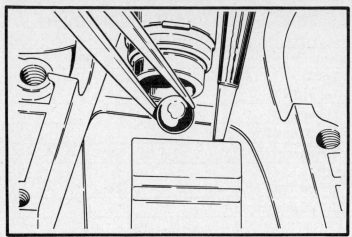

Thrust pin (© Mercedes-Benz of America)

20. Install the parking lock wheel on the output shaft and slip on the shaft sleeve. Torque the slotted nut to 73.8 ft. lbs. (100 N•m).

21. Install rear cover with the washer and torque to 14.8 ft. lbs. (20 N•m).

22. Insert the O-ring into the three legged flange and mount the three legged flange to the output shaft. Torque the slot nut to 88.5 ft. lbs. (120 N•m).

23. Screw in the kick down solenoid and torque to 14.8 ft. lbs. (20 N•m).

24. Insert the thrust pin into the thrust body and install a new O-ring. Install the thrust body assembly along with the modulating pressure control valve in the transmission casing.

25. Mount the vacuum control unit with the holding plate and torque to 5.9 ft. lbs. (8 N•m). Install the starter lockout switch.

26. Mount the range selector lever and place in position "N". Tighten to 5.9 ft. lbs. (8 N•m).

27. Install the front brake band guide and install the front brake (B1). A compression tool to compress the springs can be used.

NOTE: During assembling make sure that the thrust pin of the brake band piston (B1) enters the brake band and that the sealing ring is not damaged.

28. Using the compression tool, squeeze the piston in and insert the locking ring. Insert the thrust pin with the larger diameter towards the brake band B2.

29. Install the brake band B2 making sure that the thrust pin is engaged with the thrust pin.

30. Install the brake band piston cover and secure with a locking ring.

31. Install the one-way valve and the brake band guide B2.

32. Install a new O-ring on the control pressure cable and attach to the connecting rod. Push the plastic sleeve of the control cable into the transmission casing until it engages.

33. Assemble the lower cover, making sure it engages. Center the valve body and torque to 6 ft. lbs. (8 N•m).

34. Install the oil filter and torque to 3 ft. lbs. (4 N•m).

35. Install the oil pan and torque to 5.9 ft. lbs. (8 N•m).

S SPECIFICATIONS

TORQUE SPECIFICATIONS
W4A-040

Item		Foot Pounds	N•m
Valve body to case		5.9	8
Oil pan to case		5.9	8
Oil pan drain plug		10.5	14
Lower cover bolts		5.9	8
Oil filter		3.0	4
Universal shaft clamping nut		22.1	30
Three legged flange nut		88.5	120
Rear cover bolts		14.8	20
Governor bolts		5.9	8
Secondary pump bolts		5.9	8
Axial holder nut		5.9	8
Converter housing to case		30.5	42
Torque converter drain plug		12.0	14
Transmission to engine fastening bolts	M10	33.0	55
	M12	48.0	65
Primary pump, front cover bolts		15.0	21
Detent plate		5.9	8
Kickdown solenoid		14.8	20

S SPECIFICATIONS

SHIFT SPEED CHART—MINIMUM THROTTLE
W4A-040

Selector Position	Approx. MPH
In "D"	
2-3 upshift	14
3-4 upshift	20
3-2 downshift	10
4-3 downshift	14
In "S"	
1-2 upshift	8
2-3 upshift	14
2-1 downshift	—
3-2 downshift	10
In "L"	
1-2 upshift	28
2-1 downshift	8

SHIFT SPEED CHART—FULL THROTTLE
W4A-040

Selector Position	Approx. MPH
In "D"	
2-3 upshift	40
3-4 upshift	80
3-2 downshift	14
4-3 downshift	45
In "S"	
1-2 upshift	26
2-3 upshift	50
2-1 downshift	7
3-2 downshift	14
In "L"	
1-2 upshift	28
2-1 downshift	12

SHIFT SPEED CHART—KICKDOWN
W4A-040

Selector Position	Approx. MPH
In "D"	
1-2 upshift	28
2-3 upshift	50
3-4 upshift	80
2-1 downshift	12
3-2 downshift	38
4-3 downshift	75

SHIFT SPEED CHART—KICKDOWN
W4A-040

Selector Position	Approx. MPH
In "S"	
1-2 upshift	28
2-3 upshift	50
2-1 downshift	12
3-2 downshift	38
In "L"	
1-2 upshift	28
2-1 downshift	18

SPECIAL TOOLS

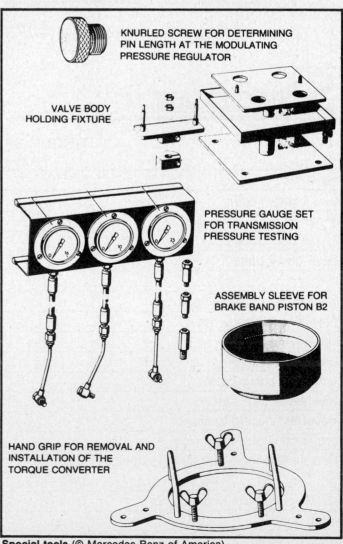

KNURLED SCREW FOR DETERMINING PIN LENGTH AT THE MODULATING PRESSURE REGULATOR

VALVE BODY HOLDING FIXTURE

PRESSURE GAUGE SET FOR TRANSMISSION PRESSURE TESTING

ASSEMBLY SLEEVE FOR BRAKE BAND PISTON B2

HAND GRIP FOR REMOVAL AND INSTALLATION OF THE TORQUE CONVERTER

Special tools (© Mercedes-Benz of America)

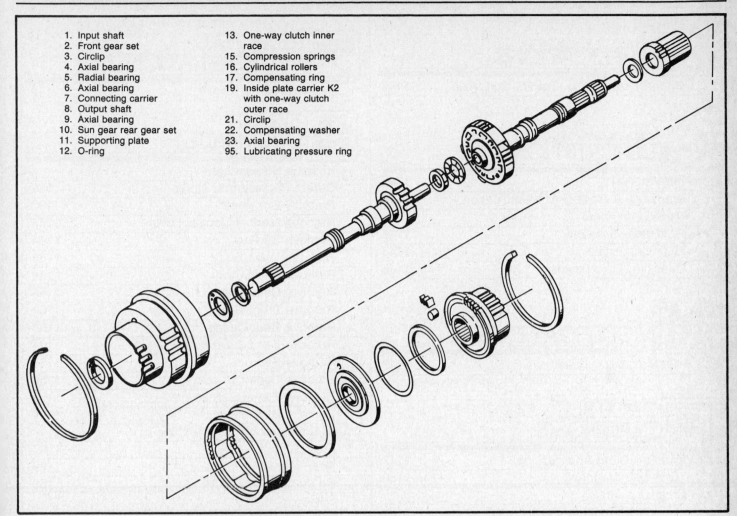

1. Input shaft
2. Front gear set
3. Circlip
4. Axial bearing
5. Radial bearing
6. Axial bearing
7. Connecting carrier
8. Output shaft
9. Axial bearing
10. Sun gear rear gear set
11. Supporting plate
12. O-ring
13. One-way clutch inner race
15. Compression springs
16. Cylindrical rollers
17. Compensating ring
19. Inside plate carrier K2 with one-way clutch outer race
21. Circlip
22. Compensating washer
23. Axial bearing
95. Lubricating pressure ring

Gear assembly—exploded view (© Mercedes-Benz of America)

INDEX

MITSUBISHI
KM-171 • 172
Automatic Transaxle

APPLICATIONS

APPLICATION CHART

Year/Model	Engine Size	Transaxle Model
1982-83 Dodge Colt	1.4 Litre	KM-171
1983-84 Mitsubishi Cordia (L)	1.8 Litre	KM-171
1983-84 Mitsubishi Cordia (LS)	1.8 Litre	KM-171
1983-84 Mitsubishi Tredia	1.8 Litre	KM-171
1983-84 Dodge Colt Vista	1.4 Litre	KM-172

GENERAL DESCRIPTION

The KM-171, 172 is also referred to as the KM-170-1 and the KM-170-2 transaxles. The KM-171, 172 models use an electronically controlled torque converter coupled to a fully automatic 3 speed transmission, including transfer gearing and differential into a compact front wheel transaxle unit.

There are four centers of rotation in the KM-171, 172:
1. Main center line plus valve body
2. Idler gear center line
3. Transfer shaft center line
4. Differential center line

The center distances between these main rotating parts are held precisely to maintain a low noise level through smooth accurate mesh of connecting the center lines.

The transaxle consists of two multiple disc clutches, an overrunning clutch, a hydraulic accumulator, multiple disc brakes, band brake, and planetary gearset. The unit provides three forward ratios and one reverse ratio. The reverse sun gear of the planetary gearsets is connected to the front clutch by a kickdown drum which is splined to the sun gear and to the front clutch retainer. The forward sun gear is connected to the rear clutch by the clutch hub which is splined to the sun gear. The planetary gearset carries a parking sprag on the outside surface of the annulus (ring) gear.

The hydraulic system consists of an oil pump and a valve body which contains all of the valves except the governor valve assembly.

Venting of the transmission sump is done through a vent hole located in the top of the oil pump.

Output torque from the main center line is delivered through helical gears to the transfer shaft. This transfer shaft carries the governor.

An integral helical gear on the transfer shaft drives the differential drive gear; these gears are factors of the final drive ratio. The gear ratio's for the KM-171-172 transaxle are the same except for the final drive gear ratio.

Lever Position	KM-171 Gear Ratio	KM-172 Gear Ratio
1st	2.846	2.846
2nd	1.581	1.581
3rd	1.000	1.000
Reverse	2.176	2.176
Final drive gear	2.800	3.187

NOTE: On the 1982 Colt 1st and 2nd gear ratio's on the KM-170-2 have been changed. 1st speed is 2.551 and 2nd speed is 1.488.

The torque converter, transmission area, and differential are housed in an aluminum die-cast housing and transmission case.

NOTE: The transmission oil sump is common with the differential sump.

The torque converter is attached to the crankshaft through a flexible driving plate. The assembly is of metric design and special tools will be required to service and overhaul the unit. The converter cooling is through an oil to coolant cooler located in the radiator lower tank. The torque converter is a sealed unit and can not be disassembled by the average repair shop.

Transmission and Converter Identification

TRANSMISSION

The transmission can be identified by the 12th digit in the vehicle identification number located on the left top side of the instrument panel and visible through the windshield. The transaxle model can be found on the vehicle information plate riveted onto the headlight support panel. The plate shows model code, engine model, transaxle model, and body color code. The KM-171, 172 3 speed automatic transmission 12th digit code is as follows:

1. 49 states—code 7
2. California—code 8
3. Canada—code 9

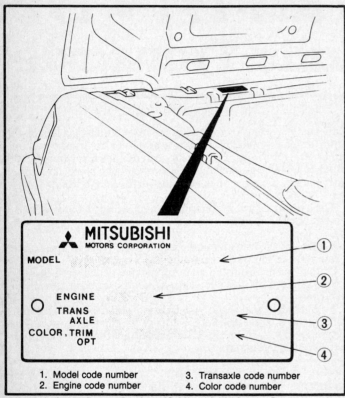

1. Model code number
2. Engine code number
3. Transaxle code number
4. Color code number

Vehicle information code plate (© Mitsubishi Motors Corp.)

CONVERTER

The torque converter is the integral damper clutch type.

Transmission Fasteners

Metric bolt sizes and thread pitches are used for all fasteners on the KM-171, 172 transmissions. The metric fasteners dimensions are very close to the dimensions of the familiar inch system fasteners, and for this reason, replacement fasteners must have the same measurement and strength as those removed.

Do not attempt to interchange metric fasteners for inch system fasteners. Care should be taken to reuse the fasteners in the same locations as removed, whenever possible. Mismatched or incorrect fasteners can result in damage to the transmission unit through malfunctions, breakage or possible personal injury.

Fluid Specifications

Use only automatic transmission fluids of the type marked

Dexron® or Dexron® II or their equivalent. Chrysler corporation does not recommend the use of any additives other than the use of a dye to aid in the determination of fluid leaks.

Capacity

CAPACITIES CHART

Transaxle	U.S. (qts)	Imp. (qts)	Liter
Automatic	5.8	6.1	5.1
Differential	1.0	1.2	1.1

Checking Fluid Levels

1980-84

Place the selector in "PARK" and allow engine to idle. Run the engine at idle speed (minimum operating time of six minutes) to bring the vehicle to normal operating temperature. Then place the vehicle on a level surface with the parking brakes applied. Move selector sequentially to every position to fill the torque converter and hydraulic circuit with fluid, then place lever in "N" Neutral position. This operation is necessary to be sure that the fluid level check is accurate.

Remove the dipstick, wipe it clean and reinsert it into the dipstick hole. Then pull the dipstick out and check to see if the level is on the "HOT" range on the dipstick.

NOTE: Make sure the fluid is at normal operating temperature 50-80°C (120-180°F). If the fluid is low, add ATF until level reaches "HOT" range.

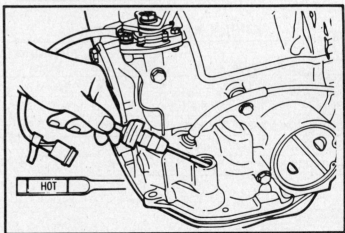

Checking the fluid level (© Chrysler Corp.)

Low fluid level can cause a variety of conditions because it allows pump to take in air along with fluid. Air trapped in hydraulic circuit forms bubbles which make fluid spongy. Therefore, pressures will be erratic. Improper filling can also raise fluid level too high. When transaxle has too much fluid, gears churn up foam and cause same conditions which occur with low fluid level, resulting in accelerated deterioration of ATF. In either case, air bubbles can cause overheating, fluid oxidation, and varnishing, which can interfere with normal valve, clutch, and servo operation. Foaming can also result in fluid escaping from transaxle vent where it may be mistaken for a leak.

Along with fluid level, it is important to check the condition of the fluid. When fluid smells burned, and is contaminated with metal bushing or friction material particles, a complete transaxle overhaul is needed. Be sure to examine fluid on dipstick closely. If there is any doubt about its condition, drain out sample for double check. After fluid has been checked, seat dipstick fully to seal out water and dirt.

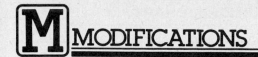 MODIFICATIONS

Reduction ratio	KM-170-2	KM-170-1
1st speed	2.551	2.846
2nd speed	1.488	1.581

The 1982 Colt with the KM-170-1 automatic transaxle has been revised into the KM-170-2 transaxle. The main changes are in the 1st and 2nd gear ratios.

 TROUBLE DIAGNOSIS

CLUTCH AND BAND APPLICATION CHART
KM-171 and 172 Transaxle

Lever Position	Front Clutch	Rear Clutch	One-Way Clutch	Kickdown Band	Low-Reverse Band
P—Parking	—	—	—	—	—
R—Reverse	Applied	—	—	—	Applied
N—Neutral	—	—	—	—	—
D—Drive					
First	—	Applied	Holding	—	—
Second	—	Applied	—	Applied	—
Third (Direct)	Applied	Applied	—	—	—
2—Second					
First	—	Applied	Holding	—	—
Second	—	Applied	—	Applied	—
L—Lockup (First)	—	Applied	—	—	Applied

CHILTON'S THREE "C's" TRANSMISSION DIAGNOSIS CHART
KM-171 and 172 Transaxle

Condition	Cause	Correction
No starter action in Park or Neutral	a) Faulty or maladjusted safety switch b) Manual linkage out of adjustment	a) Adjust or replace safety switch b) Adjust manual linkage
Abnormal shock in selection of Drive, Second, Low or Reverse	a) Engine idle speed too high b) Throttle control cable out of adjustment c) Line pressure too high	a) Adjust engine idle speed to specification b) Adjust throttle control cable c) Adjust regulator valve and/or repair or replace line pressure relief valve
Noise originating within transaxle case	a) Worn or broken gears or other rotating parts	a) Replace parts as needed
Clutch slips in Drive (high stall rpm)	a) Throttle control cable out of adjustment b) Low fluid level c) Manual linkage out of adjustment	a) Adjust throttle control cable b) Correct fluid level c) Adjust manual linkage

CHILTON'S THREE "C's" TRANSMISSION DIAGNOSIS CHART
KM-171 and 172 Transaxle

Condition	Cause	Correction
Clutch slips in Drive (high stall rpm)	d) Line pressure too low	d) Adjust regulator valve and/or repair or replace oil pump
	e) Faulty rear clutch and piston	e) Repair or replace rear clutch and piston
	f) Faulty planetary overrunning clutch	f) Replace planetary overrunning clutch
	g) Valve body malfunction	g) Repair or replace valve body
Clutch slips in Reverse	a) Throttle control cable out of adjustment	a) Adjust throttle control cable
	b) Low fluid level	b) Correct fluid level
	c) Manual linkage out of adjustment	c) Adjust manual linkage
	d) Line pressure too low	d) Adjust regulator valve. Repair or replace oil pump
	e) Valve body malfunction	e) Repair or replace valve body
	f) Faulty front clutch and piston	f) Replace front clutch and/or piston
	g) Faulty low-reverse brake and piston	g) Replace low-reverse brake and/or piston
	h) Absence of O-ring in front clutch circuit, between valve body and case	h) Replace O-ring
Low stall rpm	a) Throttle control cable out of adjustment	a) Adjust throttle control cable
	b) Lack of engine output	b) Repair engine as needed
	c) Faulty torque converter	c) Replace torque converter
No drive in Drive	a) Throttle control cable out of adjustment	a) Adjust throttle control cable
	b) Low fluid level	b) Correct fluid level
	c) Manual linkage out of adjustment	c) Adjust manual linkage
	d) Line pressure too low	d) Adjust pressure regulator Repair or replace oil pump
	e) Faulty rear clutch and piston	e) Replace rear clutch and/or piston
	f) Faulty planetary overrunning clutch	f) Replace planetary overrunning clutch
	g) Valve body malfunction	g) Repair or replace valve body
No drive in Reverse	a) Throttle control cable out of adjustment	a) Adjust throttle control cable
	b) Low fluid level	b) Correct fluid level
	c) Manual linkage out of adjustment	c) Adjust manual linkage
	d) Line pressure too low	d) Adjust pressure regulator Repair or replace oil pump
	e) Valve body malfunction	e) Repair or replace valve body
	f) Faulty front clutch and piston	f) Replace front clutch and/or piston
	g) Faulty low-reverse brake and piston	g) Replace low-reverse brake and/or piston
	h) Absence of O-ring in front clutch circuit between valve body and case	h) Replace O-ring

CHILTON'S THREE "C's" TRANSMISSION DIAGNOSIS CHART
KM-171 and 172 Transaxle

Condition	Cause	Correction
1-2 upshift at wrong speed or no upshift to 2nd gear	a) Throttle control cable out of adjustment b) Low fluid level c) Line pressure too low d) Valve body malfunction e) Governor valve malfunction f) Faulty kickdown band or servo g) Kickdown band out of adjustment	a) Adjust throttle control cable b) Correct fluid level c) Adjust pressure regulator Repair or replace oil pump d) Repair or replace valve body e) Repair or replace governor valve f) Replace kickdown band and/or repair or replace kickdown servo g) Adjust kickdown band servo
Slips in 1-2 upshift (delayed upshift)	a) Throttle control cable out of adjustment b) Low fluid level c) Line pressure too low d) Valve body malfunction e) Faulty kickdown band or servo f) Kickdown band out of adjustment	a) Adjust throttle control cable b) Correct fluid level c) Adjust pressure regulator Repair or replace oil pump d) Repair or replace valve body e) Replace kickdown band and/or replace kickdown servo f) Adjust kickdown band
2-3 shift at wrong vehicle speeds or no upshift to 3rd gear	a) Throttle control cable out of adjustment b) Low fluid level c) Line pressure too low d) Valve body malfunction e) Faulty front clutch and piston f) Governor valve malfunction	a) Adjust throttle control cable b) Correct fluid level c) Adjust pressure regulator Repair or replace oil pump d) Repair or replace valve body e) Replace front clutch and repair or replace piston f) Repair or replace governor valve
Slips in 2-3 upshift (delayed upshift)	a) Throttle control cable out of adjustment b) Low fluid level c) Line pressure too low d) Valve body malfunction e) Faulty front clutch and piston	a) Adjust throttle control cable b) Correct fluid level c) Adjust pressure regulator Repair or replace oil pump d) Repair or replace valve body e) Replace front clutch and/or piston
Poor performance or overheat in Drive 3rd gear	a) Faulty torque converter	a) Replace torque converter
No downshift in Drive 3rd to Low	a) Manual linkage out of adjustment b) Valve body malfunction c) Faulty kickdown band or servo d) Kickdown band out of adjustment	a) Adjust manual linkage b) Repair or replace valve body c) Replace kickdown band and repair or replace kickdown servo d) Adjust kickdown band
Slip or shudder on start up in low	a) Throttle control cable out of adjustment b) Low fluid level c) Manual linkage out of adjustment d) Valve body malfunction	a) Adjust throttle control cable b) Correct fluid level c) Adjust manual linkage d) Repair or replace valve body

CHILTON'S THREE "C's" TRANSMISSION DIAGNOSIS CHART
KM-171 and 172 Transaxle

Condition	Cause	Correction
Upshift in Low	a) Manual linkage out of adjustment	a) Adjust manual linkage
Severe shock in Drive 3-2 kickdown	a) Throttle control cable out of adjustment	a) Adjust throttle control cable
	b) Low fluid level	b) Correct fluid level
	c) Line pressure too low	c) Adjust pressure regulator Repair or replace oil pump
	d) Valve body malfunction	d) Repair or replace valve body
	e) Kickdown band out of adjustment	e) Adjust kickdown band
No lock-up in Park	a) Manual linkage out of adjustment	a) Adjust manual linkage
	b) Faulty parts in parking mechanism	b) Replace parts as needed
Converter housing groan with increases in engine rpm	a) Defective operation of oil pump	a) Repair or replace oil pump
	b) Interference of oil pump gear teeth and wear of bushing	b) Replace oil pump parts as needed
Metallic noises (chatter) from converter housing	a) Cracked or warped drive plate	a) Replace drive plate
	b) Loose drive plate bolt	b) Retorque all drive plate bolts
Hard to put control lever in P position	a) Worn dog of parking sprag	a) Replace
KM-171 Transaxle slips due to excessive wear of sprag (KM-172)	a) Broken ribbon spring of sprag clutch	a) Replace
LOCK-UP TORQUE CONVERTER PROBLEMS		
No drive at any position due to lock-up torque converter engaged	a) Abnormal signal slippage in lock-up torque converter system	a) Replace
	b) Malfunctioning sealing in solenoid valve torque converter	b) Repair or replace as required
Excessive vibration	a) Decreased signal slippage from C.P.U. (Computer Processing Unit)	a) Replace
Inoperative lock-up torque converter system	a) No signal lock-up from C.P.U.	a) Replace
	b) Lock-up line pressure low	b) Restore to proper pressure
	c) Opened or shorted circuit of solenoid valve	c) Replace
Increased fuel consumption	a) Lock-up torque converter does not engage because of a stuck valve	a) Clean up
Lock-up torque converter does not release	a) Decreased driving effort in facing of clutch plate	a) Replace
	b) Burn out clutch disc	b) Release
	c) Lock-up torque converter system solenoid valve stuck open	c) Repair or replace as required
Increased vibration due to no control of slipping ratio	a) Sticking shaft in throttle opening sensor	a) Repair or replace as required

CHILTON'S THREE "C's" TRANSMISSION DIAGNOSIS CHART
KM-171 and 172 Transaxle

Condition	Cause	Correction
No drive at any position	a) Seized or stuck thrust bearing in torque converter	a) Replace
	b) Deformed crankshaft bushing in torque converter	b) Replace
	c) Broken or cracked drive plate	c) Replace
	d) Low oil level	d) Refill with fluid
Increased noise due to in-operative lock-up torque converter	a) Deformed or worn locking-ring in torque converter	a) Replace
Excessive slips when starting	a) Low oil level	a) Refill with fluid
	b) Worn over-running clutch in torque converter	b) Replace
Hunting	a) Oil leakage from valve body	a) Repair or replace as required

TROUBLE DIAGNOSIS

In order to properly diagnose transmission problems and avoid making second repairs for the same problem, all of the available information and knowledge must be used. Included is a list of the components of the transmission and their functions. Also, test procedures and their accompanying specification charts aid in finding solutions to problems. Further answers are found by road testing vehicles and comparing results of the above KM-171-172 Transaxle Diagnosis Chart. This chart gives conditions, cause and correction to most possible trouble conditions in the KM-171, 172 transaxle.

In order to diagnose transmission trouble, the hydraulic control circuits (passages) must be traced. The main components of the hydraulic system are the oil pump, the governor and the valve body assembly.

The oil pump delivers the hydraulic fluid to the torque converter, lubricates the planetary gearsets, overrunning clutch, and friction elements, and produces a pressure for hydraulic control.

This oil pump uses a gear within a ring gear. The pump drive gear is driven by two pawls of the pump drive hub welded to the center of the torque converter shell. Therefore hydraulic pressure is produced throughout engine operation.

The governor is a centrifugal hydraulic unit designed to turn with the rotation of the transfer shaft. The governor valve receives main line pressure and produces governor pressure. Governor pressure increases when transfer shaft (vehicle) speed increases. Governor pressure acts on the 1-2 shift valve, 2-3 shift valve, range control valve, and shuttle valve. The governor body incorporates a filter in order to prevent "valve sticking" caused by foreign material in the fluid.

The valve body assembly consists of a valve body, separating plate, transfer plate, and various valves.

The functions of the valves are

1. The regulator valve controls oil pump pressure to produce regulated main line pressure. The valve operates by varying throttle pressures opposing set spring pressure in the valve. Thus throttle opening changes cause changes in main line pressure. There is an adjusting screw on the end of the regulator valve. The procedure for adjusting the valve is covered in the On Car Services section.

2. The torque converter control valve maintains constant fluid pressure to the torque converter. Fluid coming out of the torque converter flows through the oil cooler and is used to lubri-

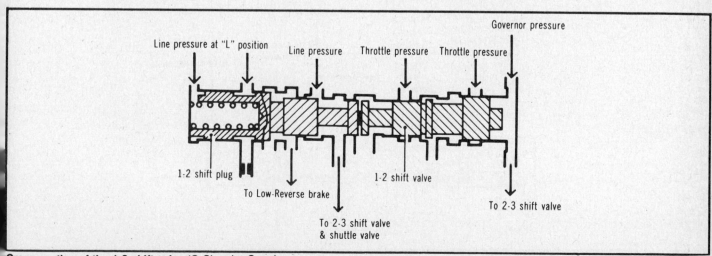

Cross section of the 1-2 shift valve (© Chrysler Corp.)

cate the planetary gearsets, overrunning clutch, and friction elements.

3. The throttle valve controls throttle pressure depending on carburetor throttle opening. Throttle pressure is directed to the regulator valve, 1-2 shift valve, 2-3 shift valve and shuttle valve. Depending on which valve is affected this causes increases in main line pressure, thereby changing shift points and shift timing.

4. The kickdown valve operates in sequence with the throttle valve. This valve is moved by the throttle control cable connected to accelerator linkage. At W.O.T. (wide open throttle) line pressure is directed to each shift valve, delaying the shift points.

5. Manual valve operation is connected to the selector lever in the vehicle. The valve receives main line pressure and delivers it to various valves and elements according to selector lever position.

6. 1-2 shift valve movement is controlled by spring pressure, governor pressure and throttle pressure. This valve controls 1-2 upshift and 2-1 downshifts.

7. The range control valve determines the vehicle speed for downshifting to first gear when "L" range is selected.

8. The 2-3 shift valve shifts the transmission from second to third or from third to second depending on governor pressure and throttle pressure.

9. Shuttle valve operation controls the feed and discharge pressure to the kickdown servo and front clutch to ensure smooth shifting.

Diagnosis Tests

Automatic transmission failures may be caused by four basic conditions; hydraulic malfunctions, poor engine performance, improper adjustments, and mechanical failures. Diagnosis of these problems should always begin by checking easily accessible variables; fluid level and condition, throttle control cable adjustment, and manual control cable adjustment. After all these conditions are checked, perform a road test to see if the problems have been corrected. If the problem still exists after the road test and checks are completed, then hydraulic pressure tests should be performed.

CONTROL PRESSURE TEST

Before performing the control pressure test do the following procedures, bring the engine and transaxle up to normal operating temperature, and install an engine tachometer. Raise the vehicle so that the front wheels can turn and position the tachometer so it can be read. Disconnect the linkage from the manual control lever on the transmission and also the throttle control cable from the carburetor so they can be controlled from outside the vehicle.

Low Reverse Brake Pressure Test With Selector In "L"

1. Attach oil pressure gauge and oil pressure gauge adapter to low-reverse brake and line pressure takeoff ports.

2. Operate engine at 2,500 rpm for test, with the manual control lever all the way rearward to the "L" position.

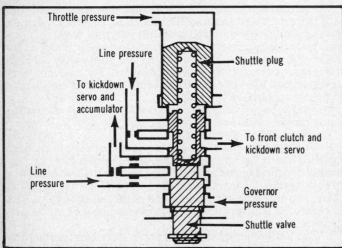

Cross section of the shuttle valve (© Chrysler Corp.)

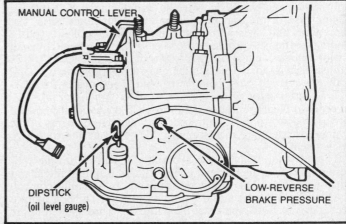

Transaxle right side pressure ports (© Chrysler Corp.)

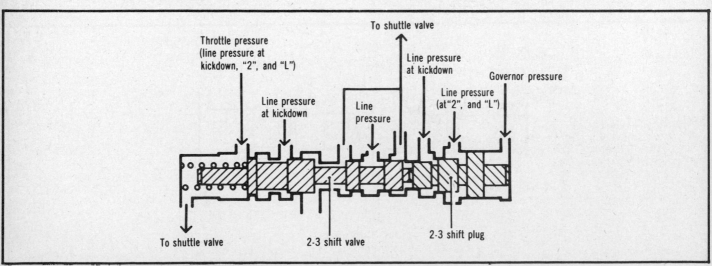

Cross section of the 2-3 shift valve (© Chrysler Corp.)

3. Read the pressures on the gauge as the throttle control cable is pulled from idle to wide open throttle position.

4. When throttle cable is in idle position the line pressure should read between 58-67 psi. and when the throttle cable is pulled to wide open position the line pressure should increase between 98-100 psi.

5. Low-reverse brake pressure should read between 24-33 psi.

6. This test pump output, pressure regulation, condition of the rear clutch and low-reverse hydraulic brake circuit.

Low-Reverse Brake Pressure Test With Selector In "R"

1. Attach oil pressure gauge to low reverse brake pressure take-off port.

2. With engine operating at 2,500 rpm move manual control lever forward to the "R" position.

3. Low-reverse brake pressure should read between 199-284 psi. regardless of throttle opening.

4. This tests pump output, pressure regulation, condition of front clutch and low reverse brake hydraulic circuit.

Line Pressure Test With Selector In "D"

1. Attach oil pressure gauge to line pressure posts.

2. With engine operating at 2,500 rpm, move manual control lever to the "D" position.

3. Read pressure on gauge as throttle control cable is pulled from idle position to the wide-open position.

4. Line pressure should read between 58-67 psi. with cable in idle position and gradually increased, as the throttle cable is pulled toward the wide-open position.

5. This tests pump output, pressure regulation, condition of front and rear clutches and hydraulic circuit.

Lubrication Pressure Test With Selector In "2"

1. Attach oil pressure gauge to line pressure takeoff port and tee (3-way joint) into cooler line (transaxle cooler) fitting to read lubrication pressure.

2. With engine operating at 2,500 rpm move the manual control lever to the 2 position.

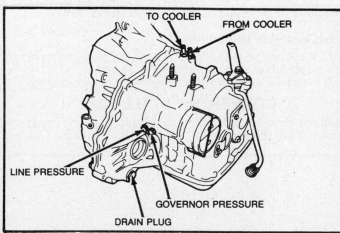

Transaxle left side pressure ports (© Chrysler Corp.)

3. Read pressure on gauge as throttle control cable is pulled from idle to wide-open position.

4. Line pressure should read between 58-67 psi. with throttle cable in idle position and 98-100 psi. in the wide-open position.

5. Lubrication pressure should read 7-21 psi. regardless of the throttle position.

6. This tests pump output, pressure regulation, condition of rear clutch and lubrication hydraulic circuit.

Governor Pressure Test

Governor pressure test should be taken if the transaxle shifts at the wrong vehicle speeds when the control cable is adjusted properly. After the other pressure test are completed, be sure to reconnect the manual linkage and the control cable and properly adjust both.

1. Connect the oil pressure gauge to the governor pressure port.

2. Operate the vehicle in third gear to read the pressures and compare the vehicle speeds shown in the chart.

3. If governor pressures are incorrect at given speeds the governor valve is sticking or the filter in the governor body is clogged.

GOVERNOR PRESSURE ①

Pressure	Vehicle Speed
14 psi	16-18 MPH
43 psi	32-40 MPH
71 psi	53-62 MPH

① Governor pressure should be from 0 to 3 psi when the vehicle stands still. Changes in tire size will cause shift points to occur at corresponding higher or lower vehicle speeds.

4. Governor pressure should respond smoothly to changes in vehicle speeds and should return to 0-2.8 psi when the vehicle is stopped.

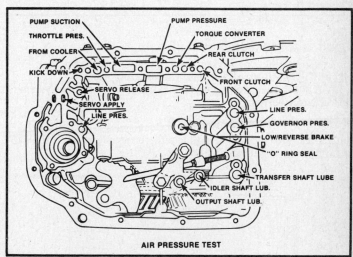

Air pressure test ports (© Chrysler Corp.)

OVERALL PRESSURE TEST
RESULT INDICATIONS

1. Low pressure in "D", "L" and "2", but correct pressure in "R" indicates rear clutch circuit leakage.

2. Low pressure in "D" and "R" but correct pressure in "L" indicates front clutch circuit leakage.

3. Low pressure in "R" and "L" but correct pressure in "2" indicates low-reverse brake circuit leakage.

4. Low line pressure in all selector positions indicates a defective pump, a clogged filter, or a stuck pressure regulator valve.

5. If proper line pressure, minimum to maximum, is found in any test, the pump and pressure regulator are working properly.

ROAD TEST

Before starting a road test, check to see that the fluid level condition and the control cable adjustments are correct. During a road test the transaxle should be operated in each position to check for slipping and hard shifting. Approximate shift speeds for various modes of operation are shown in the Automatic shift speed chart below.

AUTOMATIC SHIFT SPEEDS CHART
KM-171, 172

Engine	1.8 liter
Axle ratio	3.166
Standard tire	155SR13
	km/h (mph)
Closed throttle 1-2	12-19 (7-12)
Closed throttle 2-3	17-23 (11-14)
Part throttle 1-2	26-33 (16-21)
Part throttle 2-3	38-51 (23-32)
Wide open throttle 1-2	44-54 (27-34)
Wide open throttle 2-3	88-89 (54-60)
Kickdown limit 3-2	80-90 (49-56)
Kickdown limit 2-1	33-44 (20-27)
Closed throttle 3-1	9-15 (6-9)

Road test with selector in "P"

1. With vehicle parked on a small grade, put the selector lever in the "P" position and release the parking brake.
2. If the vehicle does not roll backwards, the parking system is working properly.

Road test with selector in "R"

1. Start the engine and stall test the transaxle to see if the friction element is slipping or not.

Selector lever in "P" position (© Mitsubishi Motors Corp.)

Road test with selector In "D"

1. Increase speed of vehicle and while holding the accelerator pedal steady check to see if transaxle makes 1-2 and 2-3 upshift at correct vehicle speeds. Also check for hard shifting or slipping at this time.
2. While driving in third gear, check for noise and vibration.
3. With selector lever in second or third gear, check to see if 2-1, 3-1 and 3-2 kickdown shifts occur properly at specified kickdown limit vehicle speeds.
4. Drive in third gear, and select "2" range, than "L" range to check if engine brake is effective.
5. Drive in third gear at 31 mph. or higher speeds, and select

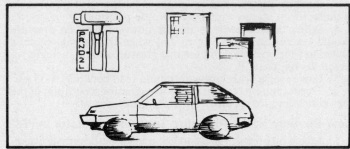

Selector lever in "D" position (© Mitsubishi Motors Corp.)

"L" range to check if 2-1 downshift occurs at proper vehicle speed.

Road test with selector in "2"

1. While driving with selector lever in "2" position increase vehicle speed. Make sure that the transaxle makes 1-2 upshift at the proper vehicle speed. Also check for noise and shock at the time of shifting.
2. Check to see if 2-1 kickdown occurs at correct limit vehicle speed.

Selector lever in "2" position (© Mitsubishi Motors Corp.)

Road test with selector in "L"

1. While driving with selector lever in "L" position, make certain no upshift to second or third gear occurs.
2. Check for noise in either acceleration or deceleration.

CONVERTER STALL TEST

Stall test consists of determining maximum engine speed obtained at full throttle in the "D" and "R" positions. This test

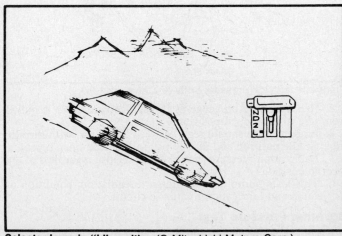

Selector lever in "L" position (© Mitsubishi Motors Corp.)

checks torque converter stator overrunning clutch operation, and holding ability of transaxle clutches and low-reverse brake.

CAUTION

During this test let no one stand in front of or behind the vehicle.

1. Check the transmission fluid level at normal transmission and engine operating temperatures.
2. Apply chocks to both front and rear wheels.
3. Attach engine tachometer.
4. Apply parking and service brakes fully.
5. Start the engine.
6. With the selector in Drive position, depress the accelerator pedal fully and read the maximum engine rpm.

CAUTION

Do not hold the throttle wide open any longer than is necessary to obtain a maximum engine rpm reading, and never longer than 10 seconds at a time. If more than one stall test is required, operate the engine at approximately 1,000 rpms in neutral to cool the transmission fluid between tests.

7. Follow the same procedure in Reverse position.

NOTE: The stall speed for the KM-171 is 2,100 ± 200 rpm. and the stall speed for the KM-172 is 2,200 ± 200 rpm.

INTERPRETATION OF STALL TEST RESULTS

Stall speed above specification in "D"

1. Rear clutch or overrunning clutch is slipping.

Stall speed above specification in "R"

1. Front clutch or low-reverse brake is slipping.

NOTE: If the stall speed is higher than specification in "D" and "R" position, perform a hydraulic test to locate the cause of slippage.

Stall speed below specification in "D" and "R"

1. If stall speed is lower than specification, poor engine performance or a defective torque converter is the suspected problem.
2. Check for engine misfiring, ignition timing and other engine related problems. If these are good then the torque converter is defective.

LOCK-UP TORQUE CONVERTER

The new 3-speed automatic transaxle incorporates a new Mitsubishi development known as ELC (Electronic Control). The system has a built-in damper clutch that operates in 2nd and 3rd gears to keep the torque converter's slip ratio very low, thus helping to improve fuel economy.

The lock-up feature on the automatic transmissions produced by other manufactures operates only at speeds over 25-35 mph, because of vibration problems. One of the design features of the ELC system is that it works at a very low speed. The damper clutch in the ELC system is so effective that it functions without perceptible vibration at speeds as low as 12 mph.

NOTE: The lock-up torque converter will not operate when the coolant temperature is below 50°C (122°F) or when the vehicle is travelling in 1st gear. It also will not operate when in the "R" position.

The ELC computer continuously processes all important information such as engine speed, kickdown drum speed, output shaft speed, throttle position and the coolant temperature. With this information, the ELC computer then provides instructions to the oil pressure valve that controls the damper clutch.

NOTE: Tests done by the manufacturer indicates that a vehicle with the ELC lock-up torque converter uses about 10% less fuel than one without ELC.

A comparison of slip ratios between automatic transaxles without ELC, and transaxles with ELC is shown below:

COMPARISON OF SLIP RATIOS
At a constant speed of—

	25 mph	35 mph	55 mph
Automatic with ELC	2.5:1	1.1:1	1.0:1
Automatic without ELC	9.0:1	5.0:1	3.0:1
ACCELERATION AT 50% THROTTLE:			
Automatic with ELC	4.0:1	1.1:1	1.0:1
Automatic without ELC	30.0:1	13.0:1	5.0:1

DIAGNOSIS OF THE LOCK-UP TORQUE CONVERTER

Lock-Up Torque Converter Operations Test

1. Engage the parking brake and position the selector lever in the "P" or "N" position and start the engine.
2. With the vehicle at normal operating temperature of 122°F (50°C), firmly depress the brake pedal and shift the selector lever to "D" or "R" position. Check to see if the engine stays running or stalls.
3. If the engine stays running then the torque converter is operating correctly.

Engine Stalls

1. Replace the solenoid valve if the valve is not completely closed.
2. Overhaul the valve body when the lock-up torque converter control valve is stuck.
3. Replace the torque converter assembly when the lock-up torque converter is seized (heat seized).
4. Adjust the idle if the idle is incorrectly adjusted.

Lock-Up Solenoid Valve Test

1. With the engine running at normal operating temperature and the selector lever in "N" position, disconnect the connector of the lock-up solenoid valve.
2. Connect a 12 volt battery between the valve connector and the transaxle case.

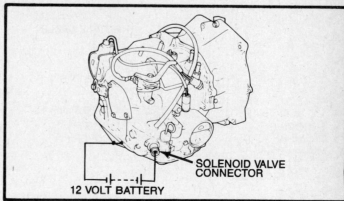

Battery connection for lock-up solenoid test
(© Mitsubishi Motors Corp.)

CAUTION

Do not apply voltage to the solenoid over 5 seconds because the solenoid will burn out.

3. Firmly depress the brake pedal and shift the selector lever into the "D" or "R" position. If the engine stalls, the lock-up clutch operates correctly.

Engine Running

1. Check and repair any broken wires on solenoid valve. If the wires are not broken and incorrect solenoid valve operation still occurs replace the solenoid valve.
2. Overhaul the valve body when the lock-up torque converter control valve is stuck.
3. Replace the torque converter assembly due to abnormal abrasion of lock-up converter.

Lock-Up Torque Converter Circuit Tester

1. Find the inspection connector located in the engine compartment and connect the circuit tester to it.
2. Operate the vehicle in the "2" position at 14 mph and shift to the "D" position at 28 mph.
3. If the circuit tester shows the same voltage as the battery, the lock-up torque converter control system is operating correctly.
4. If the circuit tester shows no value, there is a malfunction in the lock-up torque converter control system.

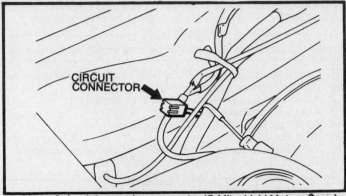

Location of circuit inspection connector (© Mitsubishi Motors Corp.)

3. Turn switch body until the wide end (A) of the manual control lever ovelaps the switch body flange.
4. While keeping the switch body flange and manual lever aligned, torque the two attaching bolts to 10-11.5 N•m (7.5-8.5 ft. lbs.).

ON CAR SERVICES

Adjustments

Proper adjustment of the manual linkage, neutral (inhibitor) safety switch, throttle control cable, kickdown band and line pressure will ensure proper operation and normal service life of the KM-171, 172 transaxle.

NEUTRAL SAFETY (INHIBITOR) SWITCH

1. Place the manual control lever in neutral position.
2. Loosen the two switch attaching bolts.

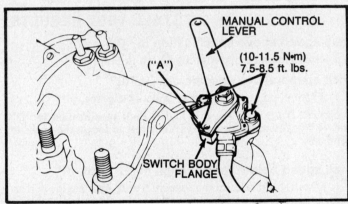

Inhibitor switch adjustment (© Mitsubishi Motors Corp.)

THROTTLE CONTROL CABLE

1. With engine at normal operating temperature, place carburetor throttle lever in the curb idle position.
2. Raise cover (B) of the throttle cable upward to expose the nipple.
3. Loosen lower cable bracket mounting bolt.
4. Move lower cable bracket until distance between nipple and top of cover (A) on throttle cable is adjusted to 0.04 ±0.02 in.
5. Torque lower cable bracket mounting bolt to 9-10.5 ft. lbs.
6. Check the cable for freedom of movement. With the carburetor at wide open throttle, pull the control cable upward away from the transaxle.
7. If the cable is binding or sticking, it may need repair or replacement.

KICKDOWN BAND

1. Wipe all dirt and other contamination from the kickdown servo cover and surrounding area.
2. Remove the snap ring and then the cover.
3. Loosen the lock nut.
4. Holding the kickdown servo piston from turning tighten the adjusting screw to 7 ft. lbs. and then back it off. Repeat the tightening and backing off two times in order to ensure seating of the band on the drum.
5. Tighten the adjusting screw to 3.5 ft. lbs. and back it off 3.5 turns (counterclockwise).

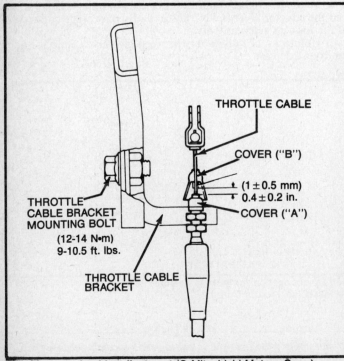

Throttle control cable adjustment (© Mitsubishi Motors Corp.)

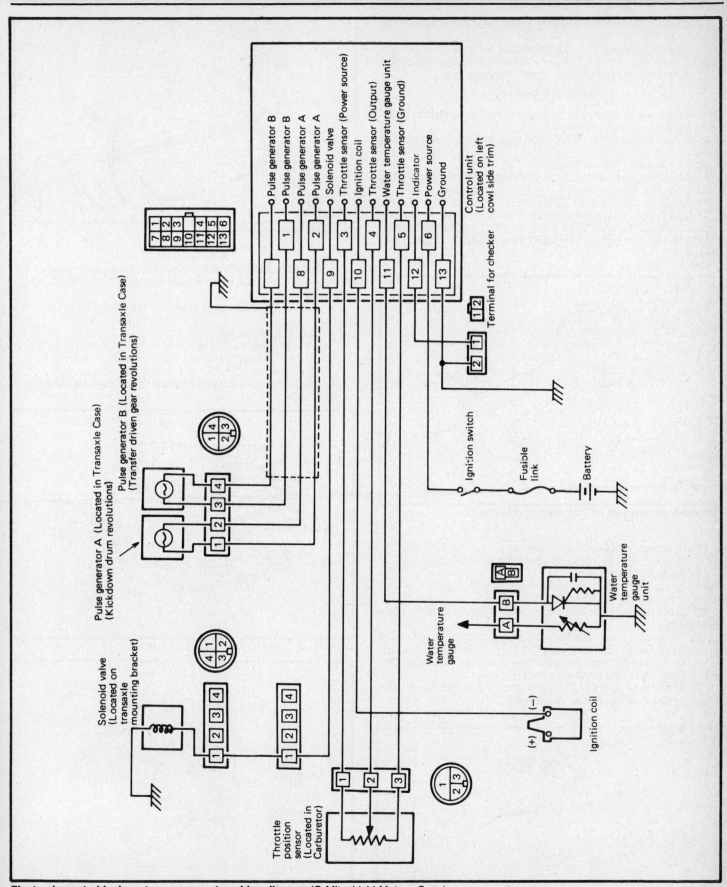

Electronic control lock-up torque converter wiring diagram (© Mitsubishi Motors Corp.)

6. Holding the adjusting screw against rotation, tighten the lock nut to 11-15 ft. lbs.

7. Install a new seal ring (D-shaped) in the groove in the outside surface of the cover. Use care not to distort the seal ring.

8. Install the cover and then install the snap ring.

LINE PRESSURE

Before checking line pressure the engine and transmission should be at normal operating temperature.

1. Position the selector lever in Neutral and apply the parking brake.

2. Attach an engine tachometer.

3. Attach an oil pressure gauge to the line pressure port on the left side of the transmission.

4. Check line pressure at 2,500 rpm.

5. Line pressure should read from 98-100 psi with the throttle control cable in the wide open position. (Pull the throttle control cable to wide open position by hand from inside the engine compartment.)

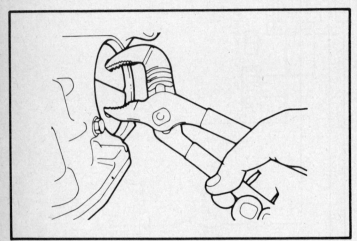

Kickdown servo cover (© Mitsubishi Motors Corp.)

If line pressure is out of specification, it can be adjusted.

1. Remove the oil pan and allow the fluid to drain.

2. Remove the oil pan.

3. Disconnect the throttle from the throttle cam.

4. Remove the oil filter and filter plate.

5. Remove the valve body being careful not to drop the manual valve.

6. Adjust the line pressure by turning the screw on the end of the regulator valve. To increase pressure turn the screw counterclockwise and to decrease pressure turn the screw clockwise. One turn changes the line pressure about 3.7 psi.

7. Make sure that the O-ring is installed in the low-reverse brake passage on top of the valve body.

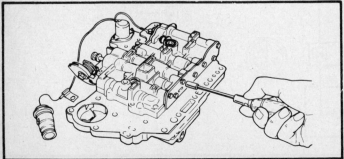

Line pressure adjustment (© Mitsubishi Motors Corp.)

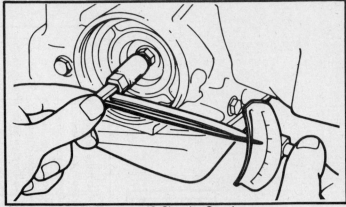

Kickdown band adjustment (© Chrysler Corp.)

8. Install valve body assembly, and at the same time fit the groove of the manual valve on the manual control shaft detent plate pin.

9. Torque the valve body assembly mounting bolts to 7.5-8.5 ft. lbs.

10. Bolt Size (head mark 7):
   a. A bolt 20mm (.787 in.) long
   b. B bolt 28mm (1.102 in.) long
   c. C bolt 45 mm (1.772 in.) long.

11. Install filter plate, gasket and oil filter. Tighten flange bolts to 4-5 ft. lbs.

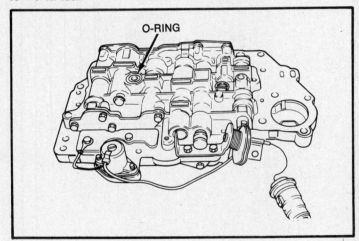

Location of O-ring (© Mitsubishi Motors Corp.)

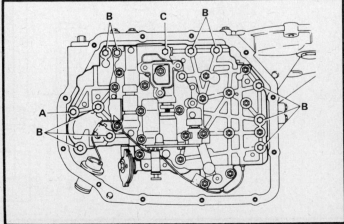

Valve body mounting bolts (© Mitsubishi Motors Corp.)

12. Reconnect throttle control cable to throttle cam.

13. Install a new oil pan gasket and reinstall the oil pan. Then tighten the bolt washer assemblies to 7.5-8.5 ft. lbs. of torque.

14. Refill the transaxle to the proper level with Dexron® or Dexron® II ATF.

MANUAL LINKAGE

The transaxle manual control linkage removal, inspection, installation and adjustment are covered in this section.

Removal

1. Remove the selector handle from the selector lever.
2. Remove the console box.
3. Remove the indicator panel and disconnect the connector for the position indicator light.
4. Disconnect the control cable from the lever.
5. Remove the control cable from the transaxle and the transaxle mount bracket.
2. Check for detent plate wear.
3. Check for worn contact surface of the pushbutton and the sleeve.
4. Check the pin at the end of the selector lever for wear or damage.

Installation

1. Apply grease to all sliding parts.
2. With the selector lever in the "N" position turn the selector handle while pressing downward, so that clearance (0.008-0.035 in.) between the detent plate and the selector lever end pin is within the standard value range.

NOTE: Make sure the selector handle is attached to selector lever so that the pushbutton is at the driver side.

3. After making the adjustment, check to see that the pushbutton free play is within standard value range.

NOTE: The free play range is 0.008-0.063 in.

4. Move the selector lever and the inhibitor switch to the "N" position, and install the control cable.

6. Raise the vehicle, and then remove the bolt mounting the control cable to the floor and the plate assembly mounting nuts.

7. Remove the plate assembly from inside the vehicle, and remove the control cable from underneath the vehicle.

Inspection

1. Check the control cable for excessive bend or damage.

NOTE: Make sure that the tooth washer is in the correct position when connecting the control cable to the transaxle mounting bracket.

5. Turn the adjusting nut to remove the slack from the manual control cable.

6. Place the selector lever in the "N" position, and then mount the indicator panel so that the "N" indication is properly aligned.

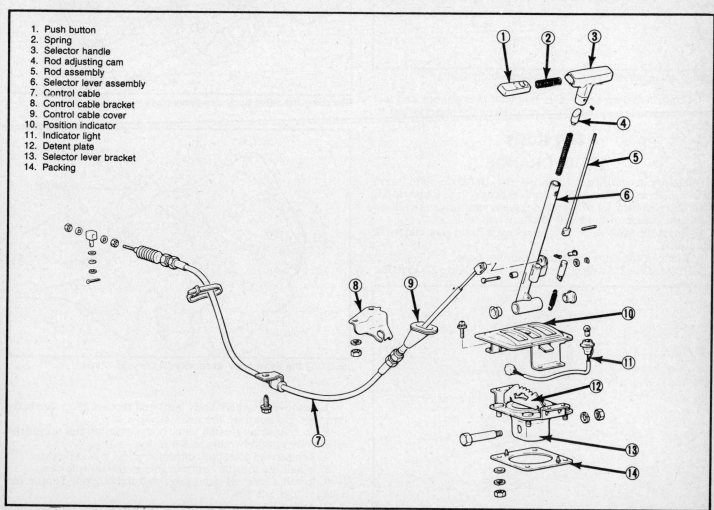

1. Push button
2. Spring
3. Selector handle
4. Rod adjusting cam
5. Rod assembly
6. Selector lever assembly
7. Control cable
8. Control cable bracket
9. Control cable cover
10. Position indicator
11. Indicator light
12. Detent plate
13. Selector lever bracket
14. Packing

Manual shift control parts (© Chrysler Corp.)

1159

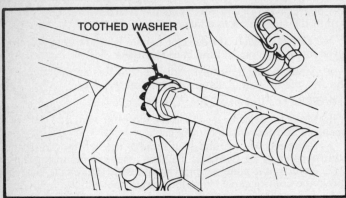

Control cable lock washer (© Mitsubishi Motors Corp.)

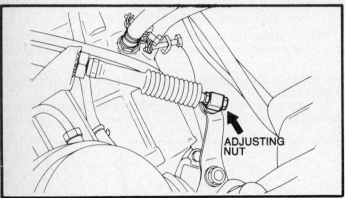

Control cable adjusting nut (© Mitsubishi Motors Corp.)

7. Confirm that the selector lever operation is smooth, and that the correct gear is selected at each position on the indicator panel.

Services

FLUID CHANGE

The factory recommends changing the transaxle fluid every 30,000 miles using Dexron® II fluid. Whenever the transaxle has been disassembled for any reason, adjustment of the kickdown band and change of fluid and filter are required.

1. Raise the vehicle on a hoist. Place a drain pan under the drain plug.
2. Remove the drain plug and drain the fluid.
3. Replace the drain plug. Torque the drain plug to 22-25 ft. lbs.

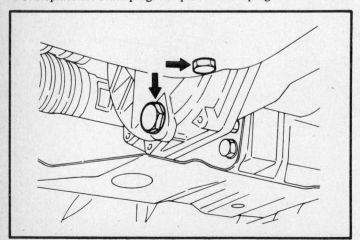

Transaxle fluid drain plugs (© Mitsubishi Motors Corp.)

4. Refill the transaxle with 4.2 qts of Dexron® II fluid (approximately 1.8 qts remains in the torque converter).
5. Start the engine and allow to idle for at least two minutes. With the parking brake applied, move the selector lever to each position, ending in Neutral.
6. Add sufficient fluid to bring the lever to the lower mark. Recheck the fluid level after the transaxle is up to normal operating temperature.

VALVE BODY

Removal and Installation

1. Drain ATF fluid and remove the oil pan.
2. Disconnect the throttle control cable from the throttle cam.
3. Remove the solenoid connector from transaxle case.
4. Remove oil filter and filter plate.

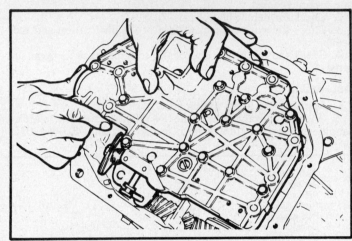

Removing the valve body assembly (© Chrysler Corp.)

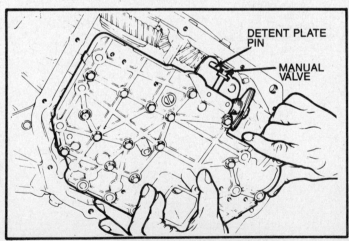

Installing the valve body assembly (© Chrysler Corp.)

5. Remove the valve body bolts and remove the valve body assembly. Do not drop the manual valve.
6. To reassemble, install valve body assembly and torque the valve body assembly bolts to 3-4 ft. lbs.
7. Replace the solenoid connector to the transaxle case.
8. Install the throttle control cable to the throttle cam.
9. Install a new oil pan gasket and the oil pan. Torque the bolts to 7.5-8.5 ft. lbs.
10. Add 4.2 quarts of recommended ATF into the transaxle case through the dipstick hole.

ACCUMULATOR

Removal and Installation

To remove the accumulator, first drain the ATF fluid and remove the oil pan and valve body assembly as previously outlined. With the valve body assembly removed, proceed as follows:

1. Remove the snap ring and accumulator plug.
2. Remove the accumulator springs and piston from the trans-axle case.
3. Assembly is reverse, being sure to lube the seals with ATF or petroleum jelly.

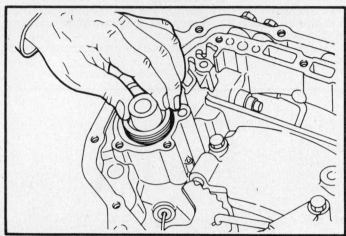

Removing accumulator (© Chrysler Corp.)

KICKDOWN SERVO

Removal and Installation

1. Drain ATF fluid and remove kickdown servo cover snap ring.
2. Remove kickdown servo cover.
3. Using special tool (MD 998303 or its equivalent), push in kickdown servo and remove snap ring.
4. Remove kickdown servo piston, sleeve and spring.
5. Assembly is reverse, being sure to lube the seals with ATF or petroleum jelly.

SPEEDOMETER GEAR

Removal and Installation

1. Drain ATF fluid.
2. Disconnect the speedometer cable and remove the speedometer gear assembly.
3. Drive spring pin out to disassemble the gear and the sleeve (do not reuse O-rings and spring pin).
4. Install new O-rings to the speedometer driven gear sleeve, inner and outer diameters and insert sleeve onto drive gear.

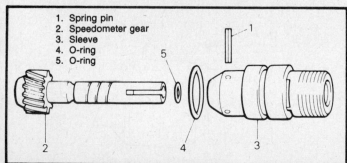

1. Spring pin
2. Speedometer gear
3. Sleeve
4. O-ring
5. O-ring

Speedometer assembly (© Chrysler Corp.)

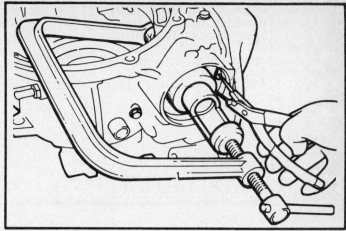

Removing the kickdown servo snap ring (© Chrysler Corp.)

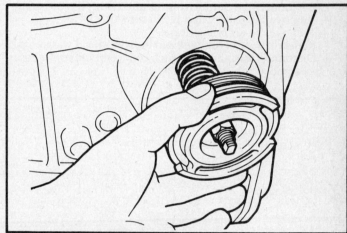

Removing kickdown servo (© Chrysler Corp.)

5. Align pin hole in sleeve with pin slot in gear shaft, and drive in spring pin.
6. Replace the speedometer gear assembly into the transaxle case, and connect speedometer cable.
7. Add recommended ATF fluid.

PULSE GENERATORS "A" AND "B"

Removal and Installation

The pulse "A" generator is located in the transaxle case and monitors the kickdown drum revolutions in the transaxle, for the ELC system.

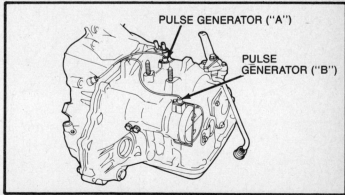

PULSE GENERATOR ("A")

PULSE GENERATOR ("B")

Locations of pulse generators "A" and "B" (© Chrysler Corp.)

The pulse "B" generator is located in the transaxle case and monitors the Transfer driven gear revolutions for the ELC (Electronic Control System) system. This system controls the lock-up torque converter.

1. Find the locations of the pulse generators "A" or "B" and disconnect the lead wire to the generator.

2. With lead wire disconnected, remove the generator from the transaxle case.

3. Install the new pulse generator and connect the lead wire to the generator.

REMOVAL & INSTALLATION

Removal from Vehicle

1. Disconnect the control cable from the transaxle.
2. Disconnect the throttle control cable from the carburetor.
3. Remove the battery and the battery tray.
4. Remove the air cleaner case.
5. Remove the reservoir tank and the windshield washer tank.
6. Disconnect the inhibitor switch connector, oil cooler hoses, and speedometer cable from transaxle.

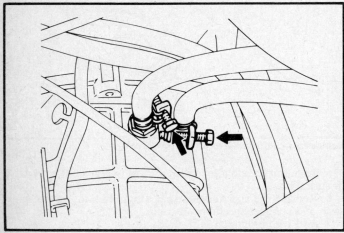

Oil cooler hoses (© Mitsubishi Motors Corp.)

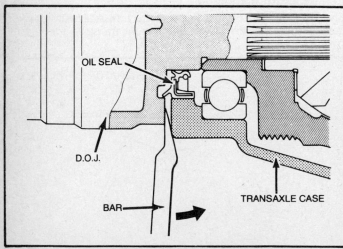

Removal of drive shaft from transaxle (© Chrysler Corp.)

NOTE: Be sure to plug the oil cooler lines, so that no foreign matter enters the lines. It will also keep the oil from draining out of the oil cooler.

7. Remove the starter motor.

8. Raise the vehicle and remove the front wheels and drain the transmission fluid.

9. Remove the strut bars and the stabilizer bar from the lower arms.

10. Remove the right and left driveshafts from the transaxle and place them in a safe place.

11. Remove the bell housing cover and then remove the three bolts connecting the torque converter to the drive plate.

12. After removing the bolts, turn and force the torque converter toward the transaxle to prevent the converter from remaining on the engine side.

13. Remove the five upper bolts connecting the transaxle with the engine.

Upper five connecting bolts (© Mitsubishi Motors Corp.)

14. Using a transmission jack or equivalent, support the lower part of the transaxle and remove the remaining bolts that connect the engine to the transaxle.

NOTE: Support a wide area of the transaxle so that the oil pan is not distorted when supported.

15. Remove the transaxle mount insulator bolts and the mount bracket.

16. Remove the blank cap from inside the right fender shield and remove installation bolts.

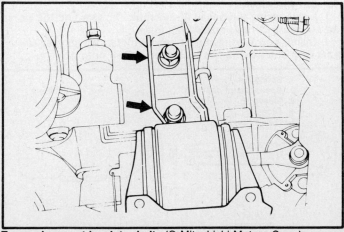

Transaxle mount insulator bolts (© Mitsubishi Motors Corp.)

17. Slide the transaxle assembly to the right and lower it to remove it. Do not allow the converter to fall from the unit.

Installation

The transaxle and converter should be installed as a unit. Connecting the torque converter to engine first could cause damage to the oil seal on the transaxle and the drive plate.

1. Place the transaxle on the removing jack or equivalent and raise it into position in the vehicle.

2. Replace the transaxle mounting bolts and torque them to 32-39 ft. lbs., if the bolts are marked 7 on the head. Torque to 22-25 ft. lbs., if the bolts are marked 10 on the head.

3. Install the 3 bolts that connect the torque converter to the drive plate and torque to 25-30 ft. lbs.

4. Reinstall the bell housing cover and torque bolts to 7.5-8.5 ft. lbs.

5. Install starter motor and torque bolts to 16-23 ft. lbs.

6. Install the speedometer cable at the transaxle, and reinstall the oil cooler lines.

7. Reinstall the strut bars and the stabilizer bar.

8. Fill the transaxle with Dexron® II ATF fluid.

9. Reinstall the inhibitor switch connector.

10. Reinstall the throttle control cable to the carburetor. Adjust the cable per adjustment section.

11. Install the control cable to the transaxle, and adjust the slack out of the cable.

12. Install the battery, the battery tray and the air cleaner case.

13. Reinstall the reservoir tank and the windshield washer tank.

14. Confirm ignition switch starter action in the "P" and "N" positions. Make sure that the starter does not engage in any other positions.

15. Check to see that the selector lever operates smoothly and is properly shifting into every selector position.

16. Check the transmission fluid level again.

BENCH OVERHAUL

Before Disassembly

1. Prior to disassembling the transaxle, thoroughly remove all dirt from the exterior to prevent the dirt from entering the transmission.

2. The automatic transaxle consists of many precision parts. Care should be taken not to scratch, nick or impair the parts during overhaul of the transmission.

3. Make sure bench work areas are clean.

4. Do not use cloth gloves or shop towels during overhaul operations. Use nylon cloth or paper waste if necessary.

5. Clean all metal parts in suitable solvent and dry with compressed air.

6. Clean all clutch discs, plastic thrust plates and rubber parts in automatic transmission fluid.

7. All rubber gaskets and oil seals should be replaced with new at every re-installation.

NOTE: The rubber seal at the oil level dipstick need not be replaced.

8. Do not use grease other than pertroleum jelly.

9. Apply Dexron® II fluid to the friction elements, rotating parts and sliding parts before installation.

10. Do not apply a sealer on adhesive to gaskets.

11. A new clutch disc should be immersed in fluid for more than two hours before installation.

12. When replacing a bushing replace the complete bushing assembly.

Disassembly

Disassembly of Unit

1. Remove the torque converter.

2. Measure and record the input shaft end play. Attach the dial indicator to the converter housing and adjust it to measure input shaft end play.

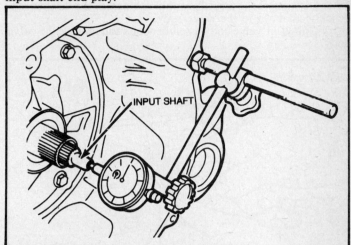
Measure input shaft end play (© Chrysler Corp.)

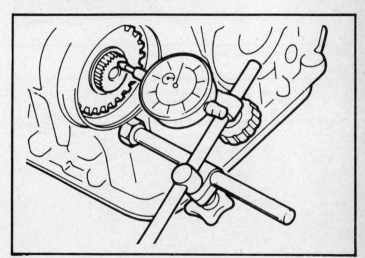
Measure transfer shaft end play (© Chrysler Corp.)

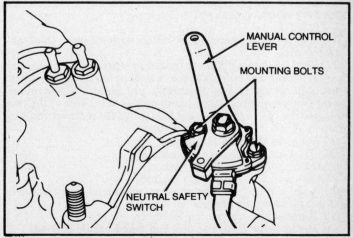
Remove the neutral safety (inhibitor) switch (© Chrysler Corp.)

3. Remove the transfer shaft cover holder and cover.

4. Measure and record the transfer shaft end play.

5. Remove the manual control lever and then the neutral safety switch.

6. Take out 13 bolts to remove the converter housing.

7. Remove the oil pan and gasket.

8. Remove the oil filter.

9. Disconnect the throttle control cable from the throttle cam which is attached to the valve body.

10. Unbolt 11 valve body assembly bolts and remove the valve body.

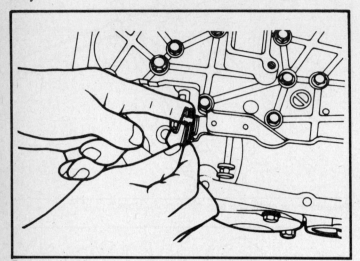

Remove throttle control cable (© Chrysler Corp.)

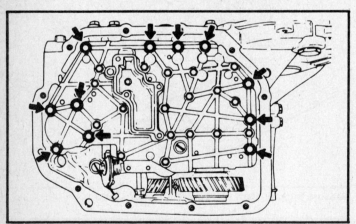

Valve body mounting bolts (© Chrysler Corp.)

11. Set the transmission on the bench, with the input shaft facing upwards.

12. Remove the six oil pump mounting bolts. Screw the special pump remover tool bolts into the two oil pump removing holes. Turn both removers simultaneously and uniformly to remove the oil pump assembly. If the pump moves to the side of the two tools, tap the case lightly on that side or tilt the remover tools to compensate for their off center position.

13. Remove the oil pump gasket.

14. Take out the differential assembly.

15. Detach the fiber thrust washers.

16. Remove the front clutch assembly.

17. Take out the one fiber washer, two metal thrust washers and the caged needle bearing.

18. Remove the rear clutch assembly.

19. Remove the thrust washer and caged needle bearing.

20. Lift out the clutch hub.

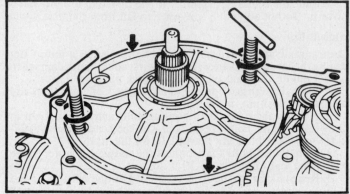

Remove oil pump (© Chrysler Corp.)

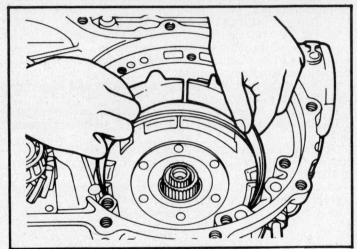

Remove kickdown band (© Chrysler Corp.)

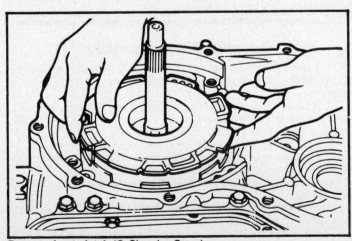

Remove front clutch (© Chrysler Corp.)

21. Take out the next two thrust washers and the needle bearing.

22. Remove the kickdown drum.

23. Take out the kickdown band.

24. Remove the kickdown servo cover snap ring.

25. Pull out the kickdown servo cover.

26. Using special tool, servo spring compressor (MD998303 or equivalent), push in the kickdown servo and remove the snap ring.

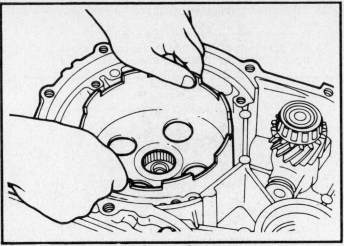

Remove kickdown drum (© Chrysler Corp.)

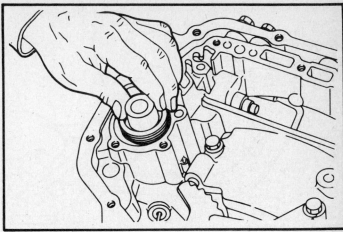

Remove accumulator (© Chrysler Corp.)

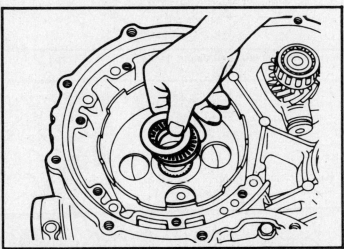

Remove kickdown drum washer and bearing (© Chrysler Corp.)

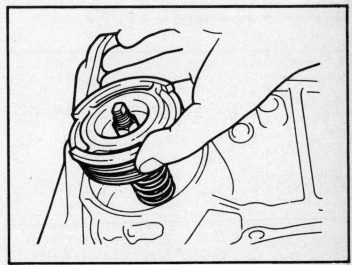

Remove kickdown servo (© Chrysler Corp.)

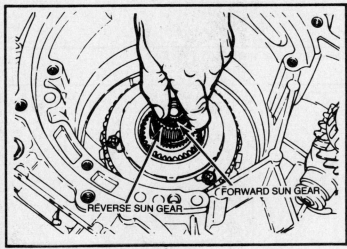

REVERSE SUN GEAR FORWARD SUN GEAR

Remove sun gears (© Chrysler Corp.)

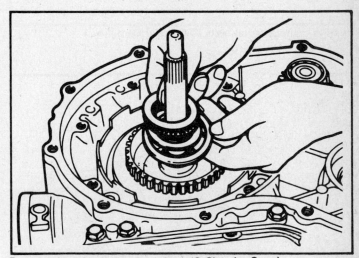

Remove rear clutch thrust washers (© Chrysler Corp.)

27. Remove the kickdown servo piston, sleeve, and spring.

— CAUTION —

Do not turn transaxle upside down as planetary thrust washers could fall out of place.

28. Remove accumulator piston and spring from transmission case.

29. Remove two center support bolts.

30. Attach special tool, center support remover and installer, to the center support. Holding the handle of the tool, pull out the center support straight upward.

31. Take out the reverse sun gear and forward sun gear together.
32. Remove the planet carrier assembly.
33. Lift out the thrust bearing and thrust race.
34. Remove the idler shaft lock plate.

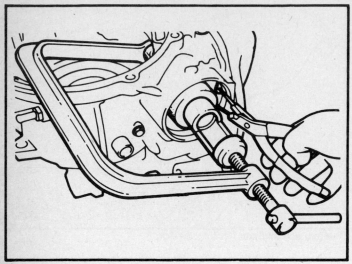

Remove kickdown servo snap ring (© Chrysler Corp.)

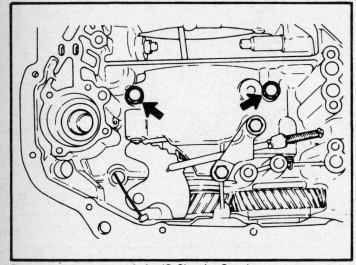

Remove center support bolts (© Chrysler Corp.)

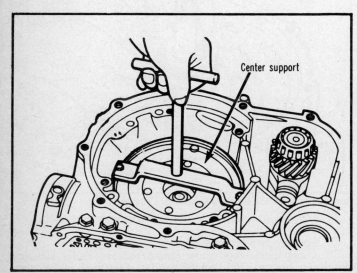

Remove center support (© Chrysler Corp.)

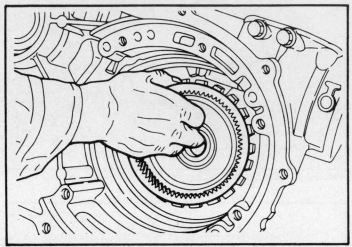

Remove internal gear and output flange (© Chrysler Corp.)

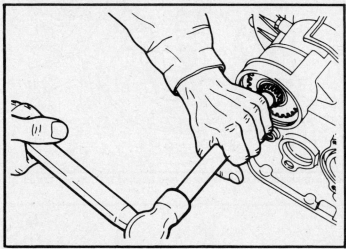

Remove transfer shaft (© Chrysler Corp.)

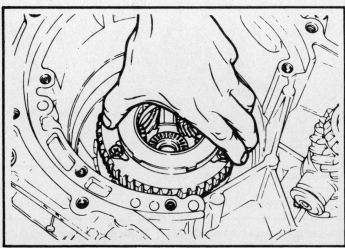

Remove planet carrier (© Chrysler Corp.)

35. Using special tool, wrench adapter (MD998344 or equivalent) loosen the transfer idler shaft.

36. Draw out the transfer idler shaft. Remove the transfer idler gear, bearing inner races (2 pieces), and spacer from inside the case. Use special tool L-4518 or equivalent to remove each bearing outer race. Use special tool C-4628 with handle C-4171 (or equivalent) to install each bearing outer race.

37. Remove the bearing retainer.

38. Remove the snap ring from the bearing.

39. Draw out the internal (ring) gear, output flange, transfer drive gear, and bearing as an assembly, from the case.

40. Remove the transfer shaft rear end snap ring.

41. Using a brass drift on the rear end of the transfer shaft, drive out the transfer shaft toward the engine mounting surface. The transfer driven gear comes off.

42. Remove the snap ring from the transmission case, then remove the taper roller bearing inner and outer races.

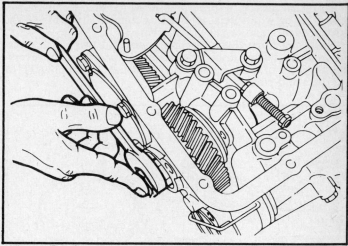

Loosen idler shaft (© Chrysler Corp.)

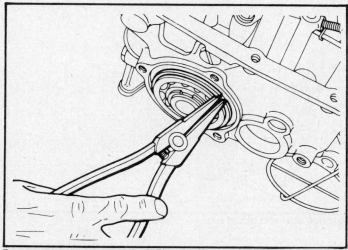

Remove bearing snap ring (© Chrysler Corp.)

Unit Disassembly and Assembly
FRONT CLUTCH

Disassembly and Assembly

1. Remove the snap ring, then remove three clutch reaction plates and two clutch discs. When the clutch reaction plates and clutch discs are to be reused, keep the order and direction of their installation straight.

2. With the return spring compressed with special tool, spring compressor (MD-998337 or equivalent), remove the snap ring, then the spring retainer and return spring.

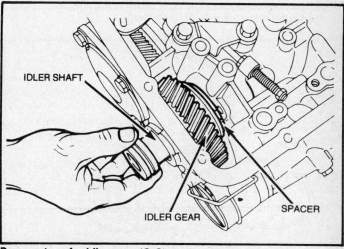

IDLER SHAFT

IDLER GEAR

SPACER

Remove transfer idler gear (© Chrysler Corp.)

3. Remove the piston.

4. Remove the D-section rings from the outside of the piston and the front clutch retainer.

5. Install the D-section ring in the groove in the outside surface of the piston with its round side out. Install another D-section ring to the front clutch retainer.

6. With ATF applied to the surface of the D-section rings, push the piston into the front clutch retainer by hand.

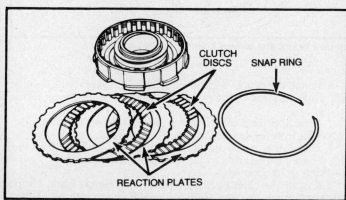

CLUTCH DISCS

SNAP RING

REACTION PLATES

Remove reaction clutches (© Chrysler Corp.)

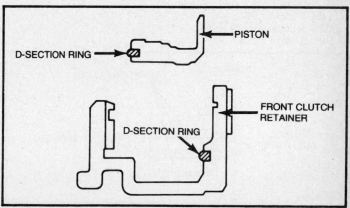

PISTON

D-SECTION RING

FRONT CLUTCH RETAINER

D-SECTION RING

Install D-section rings (© Chrysler Corp.)

7. Install the return spring and spring retainer. Compress the return spring with special tool, spring compressor (DM-998337 or equivalent), and install the snap ring.

8. Install three clutch reaction plates and two clutch discs. When the plates and discs are removed, reinstall them by reversing the order of disassembly. Prior to installation apply ATF to the discs and plates.

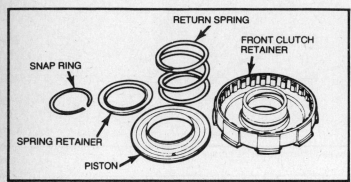

Remove piston and spring (© Chrysler Corp.)

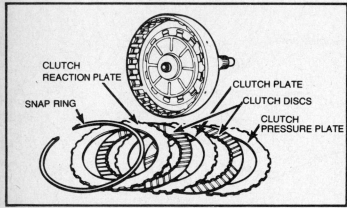

Remove clutch discs (© Chrysler Corp.)

— CAUTION —

When new clutch discs are used, they should be soaked in ATF for more than two hours before installation.

9. After installing the snap ring, check to see if there is a 0.4-0.6mm (.0156-.0234 in.) clearance between the snap ring and the clutch reaction plate. To check clearance, hold the entire clutch reaction plate down with 11 lbs. of force. If the clearance is out of specification, select a snap ring for correct clearance.

10. Sizes of snap rings available:
   a) 1.6mm (.0629 in.)
   b) 1.8mm (.0709 in.)
   c) 2.0mm (.0787 in.)

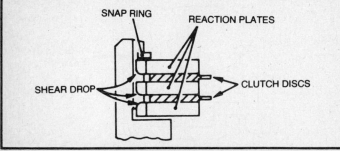

Install front clutches (© Chrysler Corp.)

   d) 2.2mm (.0866 in.)
   e) 2.4mm (.0945 in.)
   f) 2.6mm (.1024 in.)
   g) 2.8mm (.1102 in.)
   h) 3.0mm (.1181 in.)

REAR CLUTCH

Disassembly and Assembly

1. Remove the snap ring. Remove the clutch reaction plate, two clutch discs, clutch plate, and clutch pressure plate.

2. After removing the seal ring, remove the snap ring and then remove the thrust race.

3. Using an appropriate pry bar, remove the waved spring.

4. Remove the return spring and piston.

5. Remove two D-section rings from the piston.

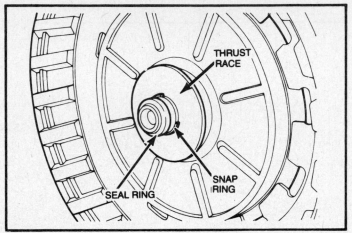

Remove seal and thrust race (© Chrysler Corp.)

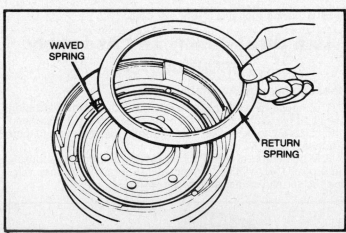

Remove return and waved springs (© Chrysler Corp.)

6. Install the new D-section rings in the grooves in the outside and inside surfaces of the piston (rounded edge of D-ring to the outside).

7. After applying ATF to the outside of piston and seals, push the piston into the rear clutch retainer by hand.

8. Install the return spring, then compress the return spring with the waved snap ring by pushing down and seating the waved snap ring in its groove.

9. Install the clutch pressure plate, two clutch discs, clutch plate, and clutch reaction plate to the rear clutch retainer. When reaction plate, clutch plate, and clutch discs are removed, rein-

stall them by reversing the order of disassembly. Prior to installing, apply ATF to plates and discs.

CAUTION

When new clutch discs are used, soak them in ATF for more than two hours before installation.

10. Install the snap ring. Check to see that the clearance between the snap ring and the clutch reaction plate is 0.3-0.5mm (.0118-.020 in.). To check the clearance, hold the entire clutch reaction plate down with 11 lbs. of force. If the clearance is out of specifications, adjust it by selecting the proper size snap ring. The snap rings are common to those used for the front clutch.

11. Install the thrust race, then the snap ring. Always use a new seal ring.

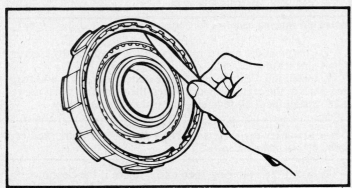

Measure snap ring to reaction plate clearance (© Chrysler Corp.)

OIL PUMP

Disassembly and Assembly

1. Remove the five bolts to separate the pump housing from the reaction shaft support.

2. Take the oil pump drive and driven gears from the pump housing. When the gears are to be reused, draw mating marks (with a felt pen) on the side surfaces of the gears so that they can be reinstalled in their original positions.

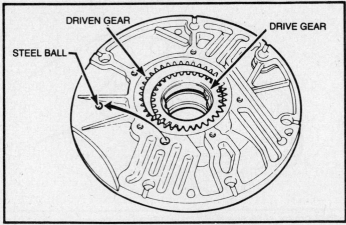

Remove oil pump drive gear (© Chrysler Corp.)

3. Remove the steel ball from the pump housing.
4. Take the two seal rings out of the reaction shaft support.
5. Using an appropriate tool pry out the pump housing oil seal.
6. Using special tool (MD-998334 or equivalent) install the oil seal to the pump housing. Apply a thin coat of transmission fluid to the oil seal lip before installation.

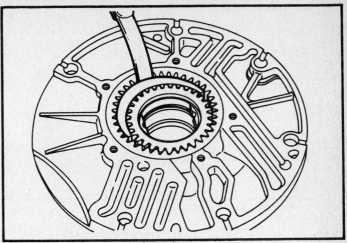

Measure oil pump clearance (© Chrysler Corp.)

7. After coating the drive and driven gears with transmission fluid, install them in the pump housing. When reusing the gears, install them with the mating marks properly aligned.

8. Measure the following clearances:

a. Driven gear O.D.-to-housing clearance	0.08-0.15mm .0031-.0059 in.
b. Driven gear tooth top-to-crescent clearance	0.11-0.24mm .0043-.0094 in.
c. Driven gear side clearance	0.025-0.05mm .001-.002 in.
d. Drive gear tooth top-to-crescent clearance	0.22-0.34mm .0087-.0118 in.
e. Drive gear side clearance	0.025-0.05mm .001-.002 in.

9. Put the steel ball in the 9mm (.354 in.) diameter hole in the pump housing.

10. Install two seal rings coated with ATF to the reaction support shaft.

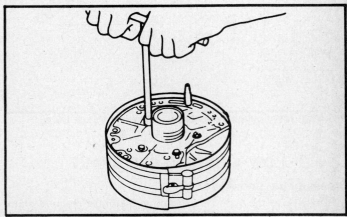

Assemble oil pump (© Chrysler Corp.)

11. Temporarily install the reaction shaft support on the pump housing. Tighten the five bolts fingertight.

12. With the reaction shaft support properly positioned on the pump housing using special tools, oil pump band (C-3759 or equivalent) and guide pin (MD-998336 or equivalent), torque the five bolts to 7.5-8.5 ft. lbs.

13. Make sure that the oil pump gear turns freely.

14. Install a new O-ring in the groove provided in the outer edge of the pump housing. Before installing apply petroleum jelly on the O-ring.

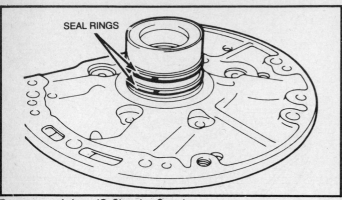

Remove seal rings (© Chrysler Corp.)

KICKDOWN SERVO PISTON

Disassembly and Assembly

1. Remove the jam nut and the adjusting screw.
2. Remove the sleeve and the piston, removing the O-ring from the sleeve and the D-rings from the piston.
3. Apply ATF to the new D-rings and the O-ring.
4. Install new D-rings to the piston and a new O-ring to the sleeve.
5. Install the piston into the sleeve, then insert the adjusting screw into the piston and screw the jam nut on to secure the unit.

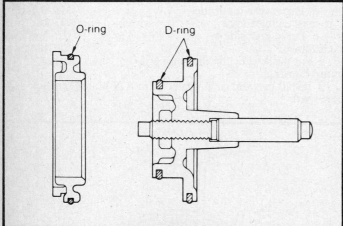

Kickdown servo piston assembly (© Mitsubishi Motors Corp.)

LOW AND REVERSE BRAKE

Disassembly and Assembly

1. Remove the snap ring. Remove the brake reaction plate, four discs, three plates, and pressure plate. Keep the discs and plates in order for purposes of reassembly.
2. Using an appropriate pry bar, remove the snap ring.
3. Remove the return spring and waved spring.
4. Remove the piston. If the piston is hard to remove, place the center support on the bench with the piston side down, and blow air into the oil passage to force the piston out.
5. Remove the D-section rings from the piston.
6. Install new D-section rings on the piston with rounded side of each seal directed to the outside.
7. Apply ATF to the piston and rings, and install the piston into the center support by hand.
8. Install the waved spring over the return spring.

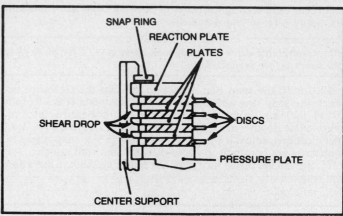

Install low-reverse clutches (© Chrysler Corp.)

9. Compress the return spring with the snap ring by pushing down and seating the snap ring in its groove.
10. Install the pressure plate, three plates, four discs, and reaction plate to the center support. When the discs and plates are reused, install them by reversing the order of diassembly.

―――――――――― CAUTION ――――――――――

When new discs are used, soak them in AFT for more than two hours before installation.

11. Install the snap ring, then check to see if the clearance between the snap ring and the brake reaction plate is 0.8-1.0mm (.0315-.0394 in.). To check the clearance, hold the entire clutch reaction plate down with 11 lbs. force. If the clearance is out of specification, adjust by selecting a proper size snap ring.
12. Sizes of snap rings available:
   a) 1.6mm (.0629 in.).
   b) 1.8mm (.0709 in.).
   c) 2.0mm (.0787 in.).
   d) 2.2mm (.0866 in.).
   e) 2.4mm (.0945 in.).
   f) 2.6mm (.1024 in.).
   g) 2.8mm (.1102 in.).
   h) 3.0mm (.1181 in.).

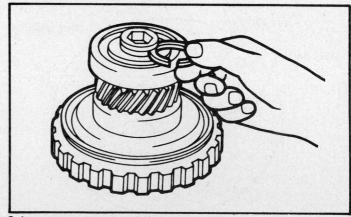

Select proper snap ring (© Chrysler Corp.)

PLANET CARRIER ASSEMBLY

Disassembly and Assembly

1. Pry the tabs of the stopper plate straight to remove the stopper plate.
2. Remove two bearing end plates and the overrunning clutch.

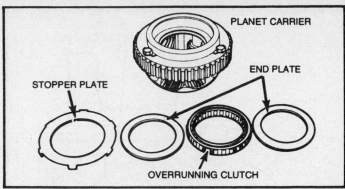

Disassemble overrunning clutch (© Chrysler Corp.)

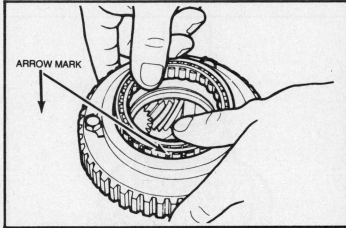

Install overrunning clutch (© Chrysler Corp.)

3. Prior to installing the overrunning clutch, check the sprag, ribbon spring, and the outer race, for damage.

4. Insert the end plate into the carrier assembly.

5. Press the overrunning clutch into the carrier assembly, in the direction of the arrow stamped on the outside surface of the cage.

6. Install the end plate.

7. Install the stopper plate, then bend the tabs to secure the stopper plate to the planet carrier.

INTERNAL GEAR AND TRANSFER DRIVE GEAR

Disassembly and Assembly

1. Remove the snap ring from the rear end of the output flange.

2. Using special tool, bearing and gear puller (MD-998348 or its equivalent) pull off the ball bearings and remove the transfer drive gear from the output flange.

Removal of snap ring from internal gear (© Mitsubishi Motors Corp.)

3. Remove the snap ring and separate the internal gear from the output flange.

4. Using special tool (MD-998349 or its equivalent) press fit the two ball bearings and the transfer drive gear onto the output flange.

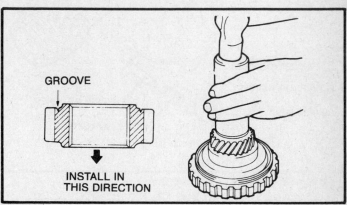

Installation of transfer drive gear (© Mitsubishi Motors Corp.)

— CAUTION —
Replace the output flange and the transfer drive gear as a set.

5. Install transfer drive gear in the proper direction with attention paid to groove on the side of the gear surface.

6. Select a snap ring, that will be the thickest one that can be installed in the groove.

TRANSFER SHAFT AND GOVERNOR

Disassembly and Assembly

1. Remove three seal rings.

2. Loosen the governor set screws to remove the governor assembly.

3. Remove the snap ring, and disassemble the governor into governor weight, spring retainer, governor valve and governor spring.

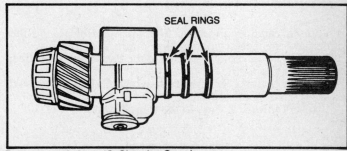

Remove seal rings (© Chrysler Corp.)

4. Pull off the governor filter. Replace the filter if clogged with dirt.

5. Use special tools, bearing puller (MD-998354 or its equivalent) and bearing installer (MD-998322 or its equivalent) to replace the taper roller bearing inner race assembly.

— CAUTION —
Replace the taper roller bearing inner and outer races as a set.

6. Install the taper roller bearing inner race assembly using special tool (MD-998322 or its equivalent).

7. Install the governor valve, spring, spring retainer, and governor weight to the governor body, then install the snap ring.

8. Install the governor filter. When the removed governor fil-

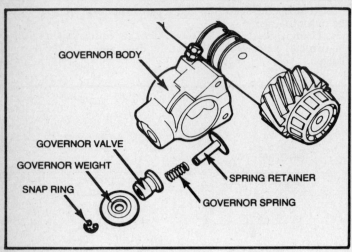

Disassemble governor (© Chrysler Corp.)

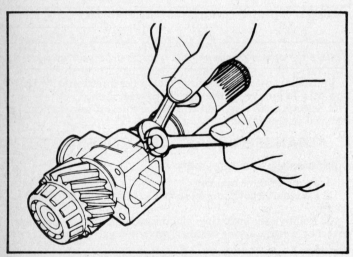

Remove governor (© Chrysler Corp.)

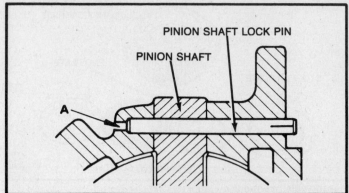

Removal location of pinion shaft lock pin (© Mitsubishi Motors Corp.)

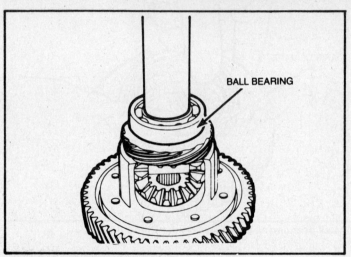

Install ball bearing (© Chrysler Corp.)

ter is reused, carefully inspect the filter interior. Replace the filter with a new one if the contamination of dirt is present.

9. Install the governor assembly to the transfer shaft. Tighten the set screws to 6-7 ft. lbs.

10. After tightening the set screws, tighten the jam nut to 3-4 ft. lbs. while holding the set screw.

11. Install three seal rings to the transfer shaft.

DIFFERENTIAL

Disassembly and Assembly

1. Using special tool (MD-998329 or its equivalent) remove the ball bearings from the differential.

2. Using a punch, drive out the pinion shaft lock pin.

3. Remove the pinion shaft, then remove the pinion gear and the washer.

4. Remove the eight bolts and lock washers from the differential drive gear and remove the drive gear.

5. Press ball bearings in both ends of the differential housing.

NOTE: When pressing the bearings, apply the load to the inner race. Do not apply load to outer race.

6. Install spacer to the back of each side gear and install the side gears in the differential housing. When reusing the side gears and the spacers, be sure that they are in their original position.

NOTE: If using new differential side gears, install spacers of medium thickness 1.0-0.07mm (0.039-0.003 in.).

7. Put a washer on the back of the pinion gear and install the pinion gear. Turn the pinion gear to bring it into mesh with the side gears.

8. Insert the pinion shaft.

9. Measure the backlash between the side gear and the pinion gear. The backlash should be 0-0.076mm (0-.0030 in.), and the right and left-hand gear pairs should have an equal backlash. If

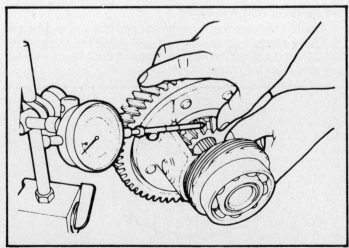

Measure backlash (pinion-to-side gear) (© Chrysler Corp.)

the backlash is out of specification disassemble the gears and re-assemble them using the spacers selected for correct backlash.

10. Install the pinion shaft lock pin, and after installation check to see that projection of the lock pin is less than 3mm (0.118 in.).

NOTE: Do not reuse the lock pin, install a new lock pin at reassembly.

11. Install differential drive gear.

12. After applying ATF to their threads, temporarily tighten down the drive gear bolts.

13. Torque the drive gear bolts to 47-54 ft. lbs. in the sequence shown below.

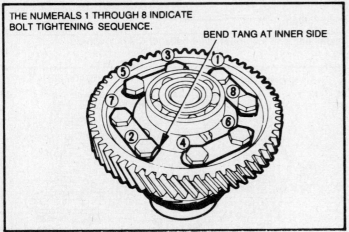

THE NUMERALS 1 THROUGH 8 INDICATE BOLT TIGHTENING SEQUENCE.

BEND TANG AT INNER SIDE

Tightening sequence (drive gear bolts) (© Chrysler Corp.)

VALVE BODY

Disassembly and Assembly

NOTE: Do not place any parts of the valve body or the transfer plate in a vise or any other form of clamp. The slightest distortion of the valve body or the transfer plate will cause sticking valves, excessive leakage or both.

1. Remove the throttle cam assembly.

2. Remove the 13 bolts (one is shorter) to separate the transfer plate and separating plate from the valve body.

3. Take off the stiffener plate, then the separating plate. Remove the two steel balls and two springs.

4. Remove the manual valve.

5. Remove the kickdown valve, throttle valve and two springs.

6. Remove two regulator plugs.

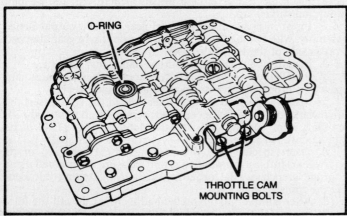

O-RING

THROTTLE CAM MOUNTING BOLTS

Remove throttle cam (© Chrysler Corp.)

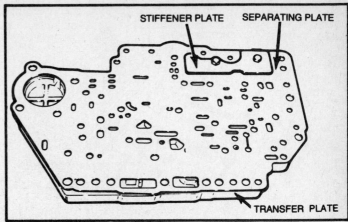

STIFFENER PLATE   SEPARATING PLATE

TRANSFER PLATE

Remove stiffener plate (© Chrysler Corp.)

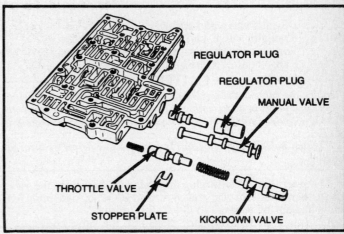

REGULATOR PLUG

REGULATOR PLUG

MANUAL VALVE

THROTTLE VALVE

STOPPER PLATE

KICKDOWN VALVE

Remove valves (© Chrysler Corp.)

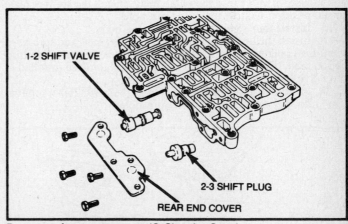

1-2 SHIFT VALVE

2-3 SHIFT PLUG

REAR END COVER

Remove valves—rear cover (© Chrysler Corp.)

7. Take off the rear end cover and gasket.

8. Pull out the 1-2 shift valve and the 2-3 shift plug.

9. Remove the front end cover. Remove each valve, spring and plug. Remove the shuttle valve after removal of the snap ring.

10. Install the valves, springs, and plugs shown below to the valve body. Then install the front end plate by tightening seven bolts to 3-4 ft. lbs.

a. 2-3 shift valve and spring.

b. Shuttle valve, spring, shuttle plug, and snap ring.

1173

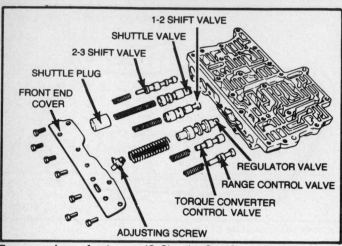

Remove valves—front cover (© Chrysler Corp.)

c. 1-2 shift valve and spring.
d. Regulator valve, spring, and adjusting screw.
e. Torque converter control valve and spring.
f. Range control valve and spring.

——————————— CAUTION ———————————

Replace the valve body, separator plate, transfer plate and various valves and plugs as an assembly. Be careful that no impurities enter the valve body. Prior to installation, wash each part thoroughly in ATF.

Tighten bolts to specification using a torque driver or a torque wrench.

————————————————————————————

11. Insert the 2-3 shift plug and 1-2 shift valve into the valve body, then install the rear end cover and gasket by tightening four bolts and spring washers to 2-4 ft. lbs. torque.
12. Insert the two regulator plugs into the valve body.
13. Insert the manual valve into the valve body.
14. Place the kickdown spring, throttle valve, throttle spring, and kickdown valve into the valve body. Install the stopper plate to the position next to the guide pin hole.
15. Install four steel balls in the valve body.
16. Install the line relief and low relief steel balls and springs to the transfer plate. For spring identification see the spring identification table. The four steel balls are identical to those installed in the valve body.
17. Insert two guide pins special tools (MD-998266 or equivalent) into the transfer plate guide pin holes.

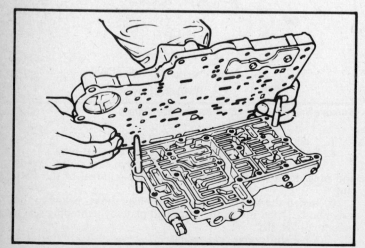

Assemble transfer plate and valve body (© Chrysler Corp.)

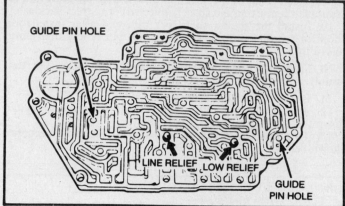

Install line and low-relief steel balls (© Chrysler Corp.)

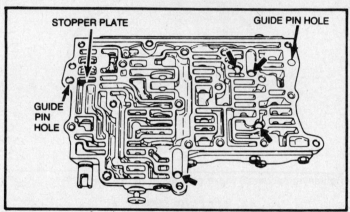

Stopper plate and steel ball location (© Chrysler Corp.)

18. Using the guide pins to align the plates, install the separator plate.
19. Install the stiffener plate, and then temporarily tighten two bolts. Pull off pin.
20. Insert two guide pins (MD-998266 or equivalent) into guide pin holes in the valve body. Using the guide pins as a guide, install the transfer plate and separating plate as a unit to the valve body.
21. Torque the 19 bolts (one shorter) to 3-4 ft. lbs.

Reassembly

Assembly of Unit

1. Place the transaxle case on the bench with the oil pan mounting surface up.
2. Insert in position the internal gear and the output flange assembly, with two ball bearings and transfer drive gear attached from inside of the transaxle case.
3. Install snap ring on the output flange rear bearing.
4. Install the two bearing outer races, two inner races and spacer, in proper directions, to the transfer idler gear.
5. Install assembled transfer idler gear in the case. Insert the idler shaft from outside the case, then screw in and tighten the idler shaft using special tool, wrench adapter (MD-998344 or its equivalent). Also install a new O-ring on the idler shaft.
6. Insert special tool, wrench adapter (MD-998343 or its equivalent) into the output flange and measure the preload using a torque wrench. Set the torque at 1 ft. lb. by tightening or loosening the transfer idler shaft.
7. After completing the preload adjustment, install the idler shaft lock plate. Tighten the lock plate bolt to 15-19 ft. lbs. of torque.

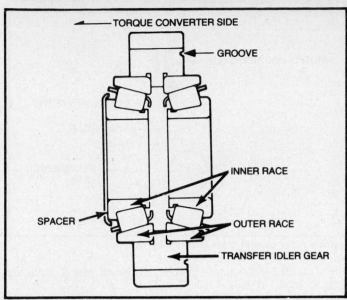

Direction to install transfer idler gear (© Chrysler Corp.)

Labels in figure: TORQUE CONVERTER SIDE, GROOVE, INNER RACE, SPACER, OUTER RACE, TRANSFER IDLER GEAR

8. Install a new O-ring in the groove in the rear end of the transaxle case (output flange area).

9. Install the transfer shaft bearing retainer and tighten the three bolts to 11-15 ft. lbs.

10. Insert transfer shaft (with governor and taper bearing inner race) into the case.

11. Install special tool, transfer shaft retainer (MD-998351 or its equivalent) to the converter mating surface of the transaxle case.

12. Using special tool, bearing installer (MD998350 or equivalent), fit the bearing inner race on the transfer shaft.

13. Install the taper roller bearing outer race, then install the snap ring.

14. Using special tool, bearing installer (MD998350 or equivalent), install the transfer driven gear on the transfer shaft.

15. Install the snap ring to the end of the transfer shaft. Turn the transaxle so that the engine side is up.

16. Apply petroleum jelly to the thrust race and affix it to the output flange.

17. After attaching the thrust races and needle roller bearings to the front and rear of the planet carrier assembly, install the assembly, being careful not to drop the bearings out of place.

18. After attaching the thrust bearing to the forward sun gear

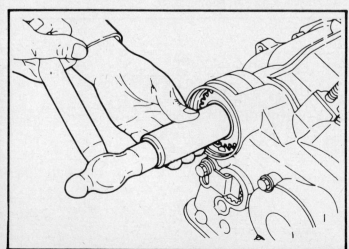

Install transfer driven gear (© Chrysler Corp.)

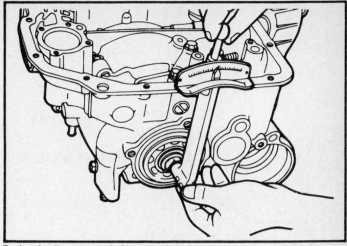

Preload adjustment (© Chrysler Corp.)

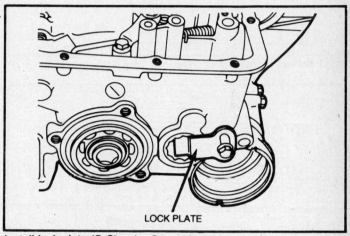

Install lock plate (© Chrysler Corp.)

Label in figure: LOCK PLATE

with petroleum jelly, assemble the forward sun gear with the reverse sun gear, and then install both sun gears in the planet carrier assembly.

19. Check the position of the tooth area of the reverse sun gear to see that it is nearly level with the planet gear long pinion.

20. Attach special tool, center support remover and installer (MD998340 or equivalent) to the center support.

21. Apply ATF to the overrunning clutch inner race fitting area of the center support. Insert the center support (low and reverse brake) assembly into the case by holding the handle of the tool.

22. Install the two center support locking bolts. Tighten the bolts to 15-19 ft. lbs. while pressing the center support firmly with about 22 lbs. of pressure.

CAUTION

Do not turn transaxle upside down as planetary gearset thrust washers could fall out of place.

23. Install special tool (MD-998345 or its equivalent) to retain reverse sun gear firmly.

24. Insert the manual control shaft into the transaxle case and push it fully toward the manual control lever. At this time, do not install the O-ring (larger of two) on the manual control shaft. If the O-ring is installed before inserting the shaft, it can be damaged by the set screw hole.

25. Install the new O-ring on the manual shaft from the outside of the case. Draw the shaft back into the case and install the

1175

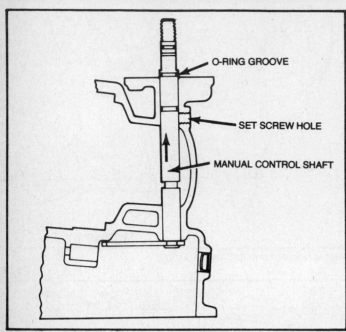

Install manual control shaft (© Chrysler Corp.)

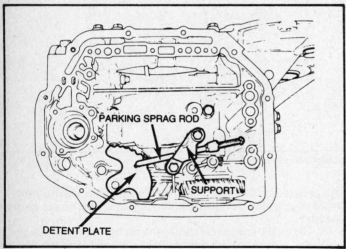

Install parking sprag rod (© Chrysler Corp.)

set screw and gasket. Also install the detent steel ball and spring at this time.

26. Place the case with oil pan mounting surface up.

27. Install the parking sprag rod to the detent plate (manual control shaft).

28. Install the sprag rod support and torque the two bolts to 15-19 ft. lbs.

29. Install the accumulator piston and spring.

30. Install the O-ring at the center of the top of the valve body assembly (low-reverse brake passage).

31. Install the valve body assembly to the case, fitting the detent plate (manual control shaft) pin in the slot of the manual valve.

32. Torque the valve body bolts (11 pieces) to 7.5-8.5 ft. lbs. (one bolt is shorter).

33. Firmly install the throttle control assembly into the transaxle case.

34. Connect the throttle control cable inner cable to the throttle cam.

35. Install the oil filter. Torque bolts to 4-5 ft. lbs.

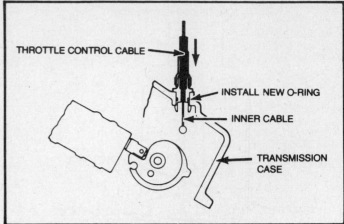

Install throttle control cable (© Chrysler Corp.)

36. Install a new oil pan gasket and the oil pan. Torque the bolts to 7.5-8.5 ft. lbs.

37. Place the case with converter housing mounting surface up.

38. Install the kickdown servo spring, piston and sleeve into the transaxle case. Install one large and one small new D-section ring on the piston and a new O-ring in the groove of the sleeve before installation into the case.

39. Using a special tool, servo spring compressor (MD-998303 or its equivalent), push in the kickdown servo piston and sleeve, then install the snap ring.

40. Install the kickdown band; attach the ends of the band to the ends of the anchor rod and servo piston adjusting screw.

41. Install the kickdown drum with its splines in mesh with the reverse sun gear. Place the kickdown band on the kickdown drum and tighten the kickdown servo adjusting screw to keep the band in position.

42. Apply petroleum jelly to the thrust races and thrust bearings and attach them to the kickdown drum.

43. Attach the thrust races with petroleum jelly to both ends of the clutch hub. Attach the thrust bearing to the engine side thrust race. Install the clutch hub to the forward sun gear splines.

44. Install the rear clutch assembly.

45. Attach the plastic thrust washer with petroleum jelly to the rear clutch retainer. Next, attach the thrust race and thrust bearing with petroleum jelly, to the rear clutch retainer.

46. Install the front clutch assembly.

47. Install the differential assembly.

48. Install a new oil pump gasket.

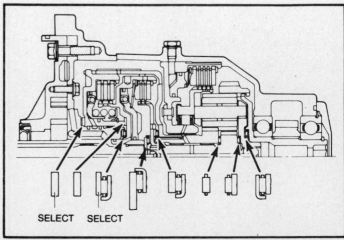

Location of thrust bearings, races and washers (© Chrysler Corp.)

49. Attach the fiber thrust washer with petroleum jelly to the rear end of the oil pump assembly. If the end play which was measured and recorded at the time of disassembly is out of specifications, bring the end play into specification by using the proper size thrust washer and race. Install the correct size thrust race and washer in pairs.

50. When the thrust race is replaced with a race of a different thickness, also replace the thrust washer located between the oil pump and the front clutch. Be sure to use a thrust washer of the proper thickness corresponding to the thrust race.

51. Attach the thrust washer to the front clutch.

52. Install a new O-ring in the groove of the oil pump housing, and apply ATF lightly on the outside surface of the O-ring.

53. Install the oil pump assembly by tightening the six bolts evenly to 11-15 ft. lbs. When installing this oil pump assembly, be careful that the thrust washer will not drop.

54. Prior to installation of the converter housing, make certain that transfer shaft end play measured and recorded at the time of disassembly is the same. If the measurement is out of specification, pull off the taper roller bearing outer race from the converter housing, and replace the spacer with a spacer that will correct the end play. Transfer shaft end play should fall between 0.025mm (0.0010 in.) tight and loose.

55. Place spacer on the differential bearing outer race.

56. Install a new transaxle case gasket on the case.

57. Install the converter housing and torque the 13 bolts to 14-16 ft. lbs.

58. Check the input shaft for correct end play and also the transfer shaft end play and the differential case end play. Readjust if it is necessary.

    a. Input shaft end play—0.5-1.4mm (0.020-0.055 in.)

    b. Transfer shaft end play—0.025mm (0.0010 in.) tight or loose.

    c. Differential end play—0-0.15mm (0-0.006 in.)

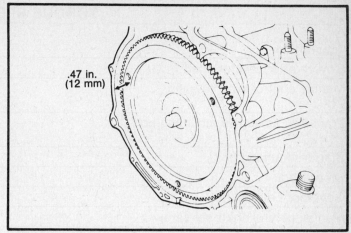

Install torque converter (© Mitsubishi Motors Corp.)

59. Install transfer shaft cover, then the cover holder.

60. Using special tool, oil seal installer (MD-998325 or its equivalent), drive two drive shaft oil seals into the transaxle case and converter housing.

61. Install the neutral (inhibitor) safety switch and the manual lever. Adjust the neutral safety switch (see Adjustments).

62. After applying ATF to the outside surface of the oil pump-side cylindrical portion of the torque converter, install the torque converter carefully so as not to damage the oil seal lip. Make certain the torque converter is in mesh with the oil pump drive gear. Measure the distance betwen the ring gear end to the converter housing end. The torque converter has been properly installed when the measurement is about 12mm (0.47 in.).

S SPECIFICATIONS

TORQUE SPECIFICATIONS

Description	Head Mark	Torque N•m (ft-lbs.)
Drive plate to ring gear	—	35-41 (26-30)
Transaxle to engine	7	43-53 (32-39)
	10	30-34 (22-25)
Bell housing cover	7	10-11.5 (7.5-8.5)
Drain plug on transaxle case	—	30-34 (22-25)
Drain plug on oil pan	—	25-29 (18-21)
Pressure check plug	—	8-9.5 (6-7)
Bearing retainer to transaxle case	7	15-21 (11-15)
Oil cooler connector	—	15-21 (11-15)
Converter housing to transaxle case	7	19-22 (14-16)
Oil pan to transaxle case	7	10-11.5 (7.5-8.5)
Kickdown servo	—	15-21 (11-15)
Center support to transaxle case	8	20-26 (15-19)
Lock plate to transaxle case	7	20-26 (15-19)
Differential drive gear to differential case	10	64-73 (47-54)

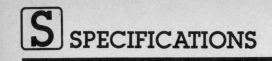

TORQUE SPECIFICATIONS

Description	Head Mark	Torque N•m (ft-lbs.)
Governor to transfer shaft	7	8-9.5 (6-7)
Manual control lever to shaft	—	4-5.5 (3-4)
	—	17-20 (13-15)
Transaxle assembly mounting bolt	7	43-53 (32-39)
	10	30-34 (22-25)
Starter mounting bolt	—	22-32 (16-23)
Oil pan bolt	—	10-11 (7.5-8.5)
Governor bolt locknut	—	4.0-5.5 (3-4)
Manual control shaft set screw	—	8-9.5 (6-7)
Inhibitor switch to transaxle case	7	10-11.5 (7.5-8.5)
Sprag rod support to transmission case	7	20-26 (15-19)
Oil pump housing to reaction shaft support	7	10-11.5 (7.5-8.5)
Oil pump assembly to transmission case	7	15-21 (11-15)
End plate to valve body	7	4-5.5 (3-4)
Valve body to transfer plate	7	4-5.5 (3-4)
Stiffener plate to transfer plate	—	4-5.5 (3-4)
Throttle cam bracket to transfer plate	—	4-5.5 (3-4)
Throttle cam to bracket	—	8-9.5 (6-7)
Valve body assembly to transfer case	7	10-11.5 (7.5-8.5)
Oil filter to transfer plate	7	5-6.5 (4-5)
Speedometer gear sleeve locking plate to converter housing	4	3-4.5 (2.5-3.5)

AUTOMATIC SHIFT SPEEDS CHART
KM-171, 172 Automatic Transaxles

Throttle Position	Gear Shift	Vehicle Speed
Minimum	1-2 upshift	7-12 MPH
	2-3 upshift	11-14 MPH
	3-1 downshift	6-9 MPH
Wide Open	1-2 upshift	27-24 MPH
	2-3 upshift	54-60 MPH
Wide Open Throttle Kickdown	3-2 downshift	49-56 MPH
Part Throttle Kickdown	3-2 downshift	32-40 MPH
Wide Open Throttle Kickdown	3-1 downshift	24-29 MPH

SELECT RACE AND WASHER CHART
Input Shaft End Play ①

Symbol	Thickness mm (in.)	Part number
THRUST WASHER (FIBER)		
K	1.8 (.071)	MD707290
L	2.2 (.087)	MD707291
M	2.6 (.102)	MD707292
N	3.0 (.118)	MD707293
THRUST RACE (METAL)		
E	0.8 (.031)	MD707265
F	1.2 (.047)	MD707266
G	1.6 (.063)	MD707267
H	2.0 (.079)	MD707268

① Select in pairs (race and washer on the same line).

SPRING IDENTIFICATION TABLE

Location of Spring	O.D. mm (in.)	Free Length mm (in.)
Throttle	9.5 (.374)	32.4 (1.276)
Kickdown	6.4 (.252)	26.1 (1.028)
Torque converter control	8.4 (.331)	24.1 (0.949)
Range control	8.4 (.331)	24.1 (0.949)
Regulator	15.4 (.606)	51.4 (2.024)
1-2 shift	7.6 (.299)	39.0 (1.535)
Shuttle	6.6 (.260)	59.5 (2.343)
2-3 shift	6.8 (.268)	30.2 (1.189)
Low relief	6.6 (.260)	16.8 (0.661)
Line relief	7.0 (.276)	24.4 (0.961)

SPECIAL TOOLS

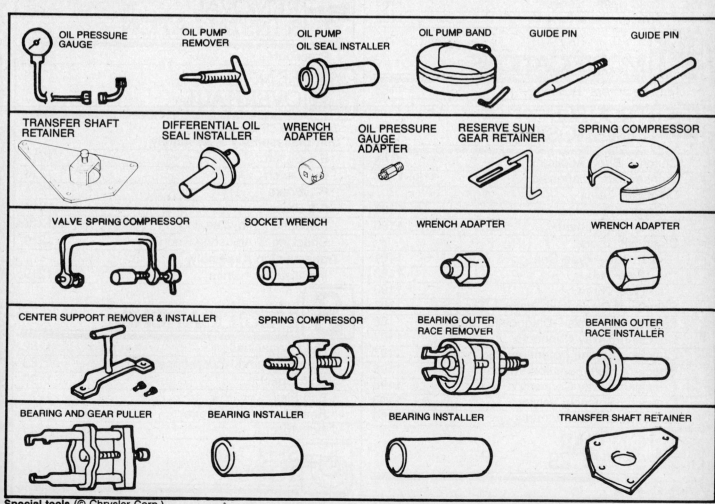

Special tools (© Chrysler Corp.)

INDEX

RENAULT
MB1 • MJ
Automatic Transaxle

 APPLICATIONS

Model MB-1   Renault Alliance
Model MJ-1, 3   Renault 18 and 18i
                               Renault Fuego

 GENERAL DESCRIPTION

The model MB-1 automatic transaxle and engine are mounted in a transverse position while the models MJ-1 and MJ-3 automatic transaxles are mounted in a longitudinal position in their respective vehicles. Each transaxle has three forward speeds and one reverse. The forward speeds are controlled in their upshifting and downshifting by mechanical, hydraulic and electrical controls.

Transaxle and Converter Identification

TRANSAXLE

The identification plates, located under external bolt heads on both the MB and MJ transaxles, are stamped with information for the model and type, the type suffix and the fabrication (serial) number. The plates can be oval or rectangular in appearance.

CONVERTER

No known markings are present on the converters.

Metric Fasteners

The transaxles are designed and assembled using metric fasteners. Metric measurements are used to determine clearances with-

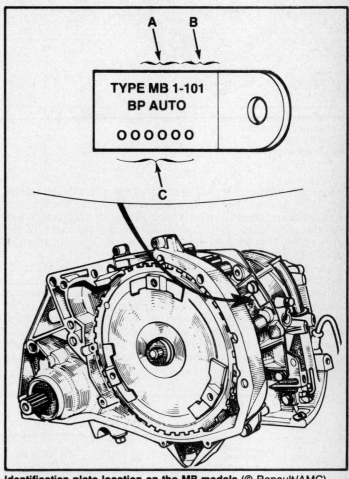

Identification plate location on the MB models (© Renault/AMC)
A-Automatic Transaxle Type
B-Type Suffix
C-Fabrication Number

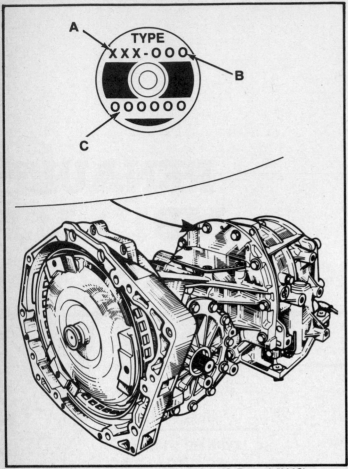

Identification plate location on MJ models (© Renault/AMC)
A-Automatic Transaxle Type
B-Type Suffix
C-Fabrication Number

Fluid Capacities

Transaxle Model	Car line	Dry Fill Qts. (Liter)	Refill Qts. (Liter)
MB-1	Alliance	4.5 (4.3)	3.7 (3.5)
MJ-1, MJ-3	18, 18i, Fuego	5.6 (5.3)	3.7 (3.5)

RECOMMENDED CHANGE INTERVAL AND RECOMMENDED FLUID TYPE

The recommended change interval is 30,000 mile (48,000 KM) or every 24 month. The only fluid types recommended for the MB and MJ models are Dexron® II, Mobil 220 ATF or AMC/Jeep/Renault ATF. It is recommended by the manufacturer that AMC/Jeep/Renault ATF or Mobil 220 ATF be used as the initial fill for new replacement automatic transaxles of the MB and MJ models.

Checking Fluid Levels

The automatic transaxle dipstick is located on the left side of the vehicle, in the engine compartment. Check the fluid level with the engine/transaxle at normal operating temperature and the engine idling. Have the vehicle on a level surface.

1. Remove the dipstick and determine the temperature of the fluid. Wipe the dipstick clean and reinsert it into the fill tube.

2. Remove the dipstick and read the indicated level of the fluid. Again, determine the temperature of the fluid.

3. If the dipstick is too hot to hold, the transaxle is at its normal operating temperature of 160°-170°F. (71°-77°C.) and the level should be between the ADD to FULL marks on the dipstick.

4. If the dipstick is warm, room temperature to 100°F. (38°C.). The fluid level should be in the ADD range of the dipstick.

5. Add enough transmission fluid to fill the transaxle to its proper level. With the transaxle at normal operating temperature, one-half pint of fluid is needed to raise the level from the ADD (B) mark to the FULL (A) mark. Do not overfill.

Precautions

Overfilling of the transaxle can cause any of the following:
   a. Foaming of the fluid.
   b. Loss of fluid.
   c. Damage to the transaxle.
Low fluid level can cause the following:
   a. Slipping of the transaxle internal components.
   b. Loss of drive.
   c. Damage to the transaxle.
The correct fluid level cannot be obtained if:
   a. The vehicle has been driven for a long period of time at high speed.
   b. The vehicle has been driven in city traffic in hot weather for a long period of time.
   c. The vehicle has stopped after towing a trailer and the fluid is immediately checked.

in the units. Metric tools will be required to service the transaxles and due to the number of alloy parts used, torque specifications must be strictly observed when noted. Before installing capscrews into the aluminum parts, always dip the threaded part of the screw or bolt into oil, preventing the threads from galling the aluminum threads in the case and components.

The metric fastener dimensions are extremely close to the dimensions of the familiar inch system fasteners. For this reason, replacement fasteners must have the same measurement and strength as those removed. Do not attempt to interchange metric fasteners for inch system fasteners. Mismatched or incorrect fasteners can result in damage to the transaxle unit through malfunctions, breakage, looseness or possible personal injury. Care should be exercised to use the fasteners in the same locations as removed.

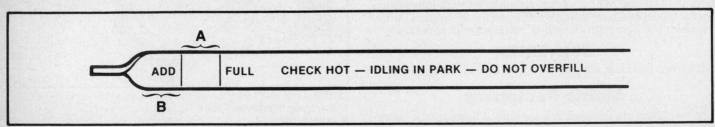

Dipstick indicator (© Renault/AMC)

d. If any of the above has occurred, wait 30 minutes until the fluid has cooled and stabilized at an even temperature before checking.

To check the fluid level:

a. Apply the parking brake.

b. Place the transaxle in the P position and start the engine.

c. With the vehicle stationary, move the selector lever through all the gear ranges and return it to the P position.

d. Check the fluid level as outlined in the Checking Fluid Level section.

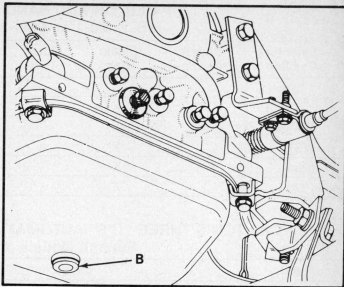

Drain plug (B) location on oil pan (© Renault/AMC)

voltage to ensure proper Electronic Control Unit operation, resulting in loss of 1st and 2nd gears.

Torque Converter Removal and Installation

Before removing the transaxle from the engine, mark the converter and drive plate for assembly alignment. These components must be properly aligned to ensure the correct operation and function of the ignition system. The ignition control module input is dependent upon the correct signal from the converter circumference and TDC sensor.

Rear Case Locator Bolt "O" Ring

When overhauling the transaxle, the rear case locator bolt "O" ring must be replaced with a new one during the assembly.

Differential Case Snapring Slot

Two different width snapring slots are used on the differential cases to retain the small bearings. The early production cases have a slot which measures 0.069 inch (1.75mm) in width. The later production cases have a slot which measures 0.099 inch (2.5mm) in width. It is most important to install the correct sized snapring.

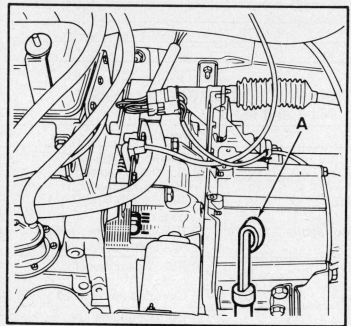

Dipstick location (A) on Alliance (© Renault/AMC)

Electrical System Inspection

When inspecting and checking for electrical problems in the transaxle electrical components, the battery must be fully charged, since a low-charged battery may not produce enough

CLUTCH AND BAND APPLICATION CHART
MB-1, MJ-1 and MJ-3 Automatic Transaxles

Selector Position	Clutch Freewheel	Clutch One	Clutch Two	Brake One	Brake Two	Solenoid EL-1	Solenoid EL-2
P							X
R		X	X				X

CLUTCH AND BAND APPLICATION CHART
MB-1, MJ-1 and MJ-3 Automatic Transaxles

Selector Position		Clutch Freewheel	Clutch One	Clutch Two	Brake One	Brake Two	Solenoid EL-1	Solenoid EL-2
N								X
A	1	X	X					X
	2		X			X	X	X
(D)	3		X	X				
2nd			X			X	X	X
1st			X		X			X

CHILTON'S THREE "C'S" AUTOMATIC TRANSMISSION DIAGNOSIS CHART
Renault Models MB-1, MJ-1 and MJ-3

Condition	Cause	Correction
Engine Stalls and has uneven idle	a) Engine idle b) Ignition System c) Accelerator control d) Vacuum modulator and/or hoses	a) Correct engine Idle b) Correct ignition system malfunction c) Repair accelerator control d) Repair or renew vacuum modulator and/or hoses
Creeps in "N" position	a) Gear selector lever b) E-1/E-2 Clutches	a) Adjust gear selector lever b) Overhaul as required
Excessive creep in "D"	a) Engine Idle b) Accelerator control c) Converter	a) Correct engine idle b) Correct accelerator control c) Renew converter assembly
Slippage when starting in "D" or "R"	a) Fluid level b) Fluid pressure c) Valve body d) Converter	a) Correct fluid level b) Adjust fluid pressure c) Clean, repair or renew valve body assembly d) Renew converter assembly
Slippage when starting off in "D" only	a) Fluid level b) E-1/E-2 clutches c) Overrunning clutch	a) Correct fluid level b) Correct or renew clutches c) Renew overrunning clutch
Slippage during shift	a) Fluid pressure b) Modulator c) Valve body d) Oil pump screen e) E-1/E-2 or overrunning clutches	a) Correct fluid pressure b) Adjust or renew modulator assembly c) Clean, repair or renew valve body d) Clean or renew oil pump screen e) Overhaul and renew as required
No 1st gear hold	a) Selector lever b) Harness, plugs, grounds c) Computer control unit d) Multifunction switch	a) Adjust selector lever b) Clean, repair, or renew components as required c) Test and/or renew computer control unit d) Clean, repair or renew components as required

CHILTON'S THREE "C'S" AUTOMATIC TRANSMISSION DIAGNOSIS CHART
Renault Models MB-1, MJ-1 and MJ-3

Condition	Cause	Correction
No 1st gear hold	e) Valve body	e) Clean, repair or renew valve body assembly
No 2nd gear hold	a) Selector lever	a) Adjust selector lever
	b) Harness, plugs, grounds	b) Clean, repair, or renew components as required
	c) Computer control unit	c) Test and/or renew computer control unit
	d) Multifunction switch	d) Clean, repair or renew components as required
	e) Valve body	e) Clean, repair or renew valve body assembly
Remains in 1st gear when in "D" position	a) Harness, plugs grounds	a) Clean, repair or renew components as required
	b) Computer control unit	b) Test and/or renew computer control unit
	c) Solenoid valves	c) Clean, repair or renew solenoid valves
	d) Road speed indicator	d) Test, repair or renew indicator assembly
	e) Valve body	e) Clean, repair or renew valve body assembly
Remains in 3rd gear	a) Fuses	a) Test circuits and renew fuses
	b) Harness, plugs, grounds	b) Clean, repair, or renew components as required
	c) Computer control assembly	c) Test and/or renew computer control unit
	d) Oil pump	d) Repair or renew oil pump
	e) Valve body	e) Clean, repair or renew valve body assembly
Some gear ratios unobtainable and selector lever out of position	a) Selector lever	a) Adjust selector lever
	b) Selector control	b) Adjust or repair selector control
	c) Manual valve mechanical control	c) Repair or renew components as required
Park position not operating	a) Selector lever	a) Adjust selector lever
	b) Broken or damaged components	b) Repair or renew components as required
Starter not operating and/or back-up lights not operating	a) Selector lever	a) Adjust selector lever
	b) Selector control	b) Adjust or repair selector control
	c) Harness, plugs, grounds	c) Clean, repair, or renew components as required
	d) Computer control unit	d) Test and/or renew computer control unit
	e) Multifunction switch	e) Clean, repair or renew components as required
No 1st in "D" position, operates—2nd to 3rd to 2nd	a) El-1 solenoid ball valve stays open	a) Test and/or renew El-1 solenoid ball valve

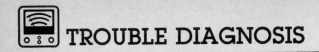

CHILTON'S THREE "C'S" AUTOMATIC TRANSMISSION DIAGNOSIS CHART
Renault Models MB-1, MJ-1 and MJ-3

Condition	Cause	Correction
No 2nd in "D" position, operates—1st to 3rd to 1st	a) EI-1 solenoid ball valve stays closed b) Solenoid ball valves reversed	a) Test and/or renew EI-1 solenoid ball valve b) Reverse solenoid ball valves
Operates in 3rd only	a) EI-2 solenoid ball valve stays open	a) Test and/or renew EI-2 solenoid ball valve
No 3rd, operates 1st to 2nd to 1st	a) EI-2 solenoid ball valve stays closed	a) Test and/or renew EI-2 solenoid ball valve
Surge when starting off	a) Idle speed b) Accelerator controls c) Fluid level	a) Correct idle speed b) Correct the accelerator controls c) Correct fluid level
Surge during shifting	a) Modulator valve and/or hoses b) Valve body assembly	a) Adjust or renew modulator assembly and/or hoses b) Clean, repair or renew valve body assembly
Incorrect shifting speeds	a) Accelerator controls b) Load Potentiometer setting c) Harness, plugs or grounds d) Kickdown switch e) Computer control units f) Road speed	a) Correct accelerator controls b) Adjust setting of load potentiometer c) Clean, repair or renew components as required d) Adjust or renew kickdown switch e) Test and/or renew computer control f) Bring vehicle to correct road speed.
No drive	a) Selector lever ad b) Fluid level c) Valve body d) Oil pump e) Oil pump screen f) Oil pump shaft broken g) Turbine shaft broken h) Final Drive i) Converter drive plate broken j) Converter k) E-1/E-2 clutches	a) Adjust selector lever b) Correct fluid level c) Clean, repair or renew valve body assembly d) Repair or renew oil pump d) Clean or renew oil pump screen f) Renew oil pump shaft g) Replace turbine shaft h) Correct final drive malfunction i) Replace converter drive plate j) Renew converter k) Correct or renew clutches
No drive in 1st gear hold or in "D" position	a) Valve body b) E-1/E-2 Clutches c) Overrunning clutch	a) Clean, repair or renew valve body assembly b) Correct or renew clutches c) Renew overrunning clutch

CHILTON'S THREE "C'S" AUTOMATIC TRANSMISSION DIAGNOSIS CHART
Renault Models MB-1, MJ-1 and MJ-3

Condition	Cause	Correction
No drive in "R" or 3rd gear	a) Valve body	a) Clean, repair or renew valve body assembly
	b) E-1/E-2 clutches	b) Correct or renew clutches
No reverse or engine braking in 1st gear hold	a) Multifunction switch	a) Test, repair or renew multifunction switch
	b) Valve Body	b) Clean, repair or renew valve body assembly
	c) F-1 Brake	c) Correct or renew brake
No 1st gear in "D" position	a) Harness, plugs or grounds	a) Clean, repair or renew components as required
	b) Solenoid valves	b) Clean, repair or renew solenoid valves
	c) Overrunning clutch	c) Renew overrunning clutch
No 2nd gear in "D" position	a) Harness, plugs or grounds	a) Clean, repair or renew components as required
	b) Valve body assembly	b) Clean, repair or renew valve body assembly
	c) F-2 brake	c) Correct or renew brake
No 3rd gear in "D" position	a) Harness, plugs or grounds	a) Clean, repair or renew components as required
	b) Computer control unit	b) Test and/or renew computer control
	c) Solenoid valves	c) Clean, repair or renew solenoid valves
	d) Multifunction switch	d) Test, repair or renew multifunction switch
	e) Valve body	e) Clean, repair or renew valve body assembly

HYDRAULIC AND ELECTRICAL CONTROLS

Hydraulic Controls

OIL PUMP

The oil pump is driven directly from the engine and supplies fluid to the transaxle hydraulic system. Pressure is directed to the converter assembly, to the brakes and clutches and for lubricating the internal components of the transaxle. The oil pump has internally toothed gears and is located at the rear of the transaxle.

VALVE BODY

The hydraulic valve body regulates the fluid pressure according to the engine load, through the pressure regulator and the vacuum modulator. The valve body components routes the fluid to operate the clutches and the brake clutches, through varied passages. Gear ratio changes are determined by the operation of the two solenoid valves, E-1 and E-2, called the solenoid ball valves. The electrical signal to operate the solenoid ball valves are routed from the governor and computer assemblies.

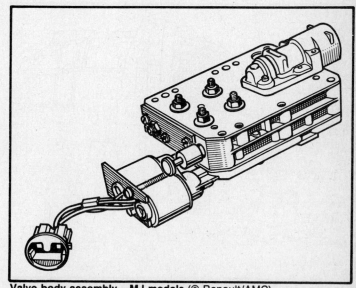

Valve body assembly—MJ models (© Renault/AMC)

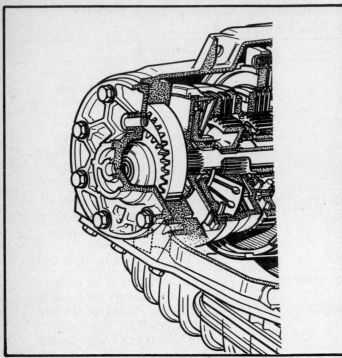

Oil pump location—MJ models (© Renault/AMC)

VACUUM MODULATOR AND PRESSURE REGULATOR

To produce the circuit pressure, the vacuum modulator and the pressure regulator are used to determine the pressure to the varied components and control valves, depending upon engine load and the vehicle speed. Both units control the quality of the transaxle shift, both up and down.

Electrical Controls

GOVERNOR

The governor is a small low-wattage alternator which supplies to the computer an alternating current (AC) which varies accordingly to the engine load, dependent upon the accelerator pedal position, and the vehicle speed.

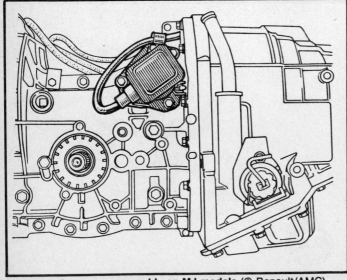

Location of governor assembly on MJ models (© Renault/AMC)

COMPUTER

The computer transmits electrical impulses to the solenoid ball valves according to the strength of the alternating current (AC) supplied by the governor through vehicle speed and engine load. The position of the gear selector lever allows current to flow to pre-designated areas of the transaxle. The computer is made up of electronic and mechanical components.

KICKDOWN SWITCH

The kickdown switch is activated by the accelerator pedal at the end of its travel. It grounds a circuit in the computer to allow a lower gear ratio to be selected in certain conditions.

SOLENOID BALL VALVES

Upon an electrical signal, the ball valves open or close hydraulic circuits to allow the gear shifting.

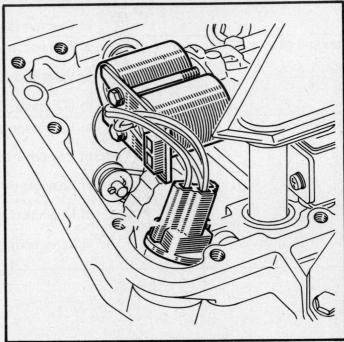

Solenoid ball valves mounted on valve body (© Renault/AMC)

MULTIFUNCTION SWITCH

This switch is driven by the gear shift linkage and allows the opening and closing of different electrical circuits, depending upon the linkage position. It controls the engine start-up circuit when the selector lever is in the "P" or "N" position, the back-up light circuit when the selector lever is in the "R" position and also controls the initial operation of the EL-1 and EL-2 solenoid ball valves.

IGNITION SWITCH

The transaxle electrical components are energized when the ignition switch is turned on.

KICKDOWN CONTROL

A kickdown position is provided for command downshifting.

ENGINE LOAD POTENTIOMETER

This is a unit that provides variable voltage based on the throttle position to the computer control unit.

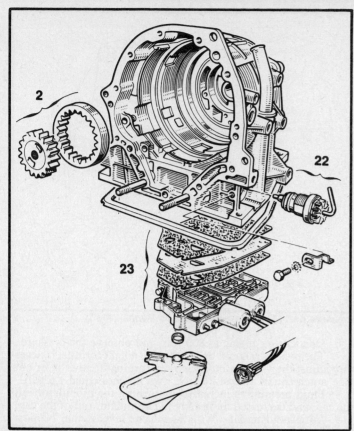

Oil pump (2), Vacuum Diaphragm Capsule (22), Valve body (23) on MB models (© Renault/AMC)

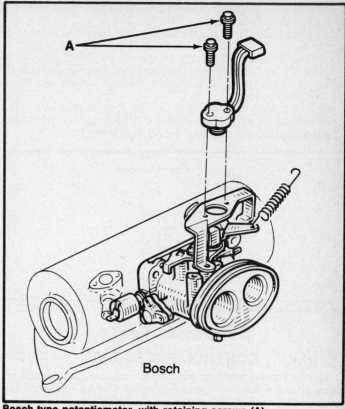

Bosch

Bosch type potentiometer, with retaining screws (A)
(© Renault/AMC)

ROAD SPEED SENSOR

The road speed sensor is a magnetic unit, fitted opposite the "park" ring with signals sent to the computer control unit.

SELECTOR LEVER

The selector lever has six positions for controlling the transaxle operation.

Park (P)—The transaxle is mechanically locked. The starter can be operated to start the engine.

Reverse (R)—The vehicle may be driven backward and the back-up lights are illuminated.

Neutral (N)—No power flow through the transaxle. The starter can be operated to start the engine.

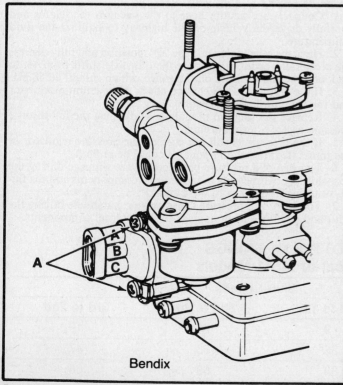

Bendix

Bendix type potentiometer. (A) screws are used for adjustment
(© Renault/AMC)

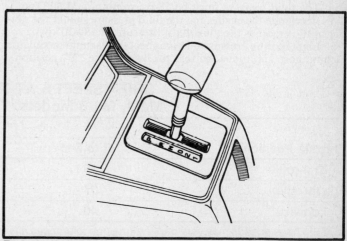

Typical selector lever (© Renault/AMC)

1189

Drive (D)—Automatic (A)—The three forward gears shift up and down automatically. 1 to 2 to 3 to 2 to 1.

2nd Gear Hold (2)—Only the 1st and 2nd gears are available. 1 to 2 to 1.

1st Gear Hold (1)—Only the 1st gear is available.

In the "D" or "A" position, the computer determines the ideal shift points based on the information received and the data from the computer memory.

An interlocking mechanism is used to prevent positions 1, R, and P from being selected accidently. The selector lever pad must be squeezed in order to move the selector lever.

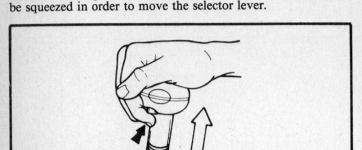

Use of interlock mechanism on the gear shift lever (© Renault/AMC)

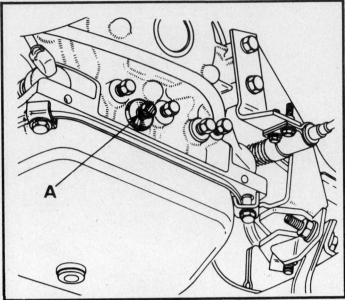

Pressure port (A) on transaxle case (© Renault/AMC)

Diagnosis Tests

CONTROL PRESSURE

To test the control pressure, a 0-300 psi pressure gauge should be attached to the transaxle pressure test port and a calibrated tachometer attached to the engine.

The transaxle fluid must be at 176°F (80°C.) or above. The vacuum modulator and the vacuum circuits must be in good condition. Regulated fluid pressure varies with the fluid temperature. It is therefore normal to fluid pressures higher than the indicated value if the fluid temperature has not reached its normal checking temperature.

CHECKING OF THE FLUID PRESSURE

The fluid pressure is checked in two steps:
1. Initial adjustment in the shop.
2. Road testing at full throttle.

Initial Adjustment

1. Connect the pressure gauge to the transaxle and correct the fluid level as required. Install a tachometer to the engine.
2. Lock the parking and service brakes, start the engine.
3. High pressure test—Move the selector lever to the "P" position. The fluid pressure must be 58 psi minimum at 800 rpm.
4. Accelerate the engine and the fluid pressure should rise rapidly until it reaches the maximum pressure of 189-203 psi.
5. Light throttle pressure—Disconnect the vacuum modulator vacuum hose and move the selector lever to the "N" position.

6. Operate the engine at 800 rpm and observe the pressure.
7. The pressure should be 36-39 psi at a light throttle. If necessary adjust the vacuum modulator by turning it either in or out. One notch equals 1.5 psi. (MB-1, Two notches equal 1.5 psi).
8. Fluid pressure is increased by turning the modulator into the case and decreased by turning the modulator out of the case.
9. Initial adjustment—With the selector lever in the "N" position, run the engine at 3800 rpm. The fluid pressure must be close to the full throttle pressure. The final tests and adjustments must be made during the road test.

Road Testing

1. Connect the vacuum hose to the vacuum modulator and carefully drive the vehicle on the highway to stabilize the fluid temperature.
2. Have the selector lever in the "D" position and fully depress the accelerator pedal. Just before the transaxle shifts from 1st to 2nd, observe the pressure on the gauge, which should be 58 psi.
3. If the pressure is not correct, check the vacuum modulator and the vacuum hose routing.
4. Replace the vacuum modulator and adjust the full throttle pressure as previously outlined.
5. If the pressure is still not correct, the pressure regulator or the transaxle internal components could be at fault.
6. Too low of a pressure produces severe slippage during the gear shifting, overheating of the internal components and the fluid, resulting in damage to the transaxle.
7. Too high of a pressure causes severe harshness during the shift and could result in damage to the internal components.

SHIFT SPEEDS AT THROTTLE OPENINGS
MJ-1, MJ-3 Models, Typical of MB-1 Models

Throttle Position	Shift Speeds			
	1st to 2nd	2nd to 1st	2nd to 3rd	3rd to 2nd
Light throttle	15	9	28	19
Full throttle	37	25	65	47
Kickdown	40	34	68	65

NOTE: These speeds may vary depending upon tolerances allowed in the various units, such as the governor, computer, speedometer and size of tires.

DIAGNOSIS TOOLS

Should the transaxle operation suggest a malfunction of the internal components, three test boxes are available through the manufacturer, to test the electrical components and their affect upon the hydraulic components, while the vehicle is operating.

Type One

Type one test box (B.VI. 454-06, B.VI. 797) contains an electrical circuit assembly connected to indicator lights, a dial, switches and a storage compartment for the required test wiring.

INDICATOR LIGHTS

The indicator lights operate as follows:

1. The red indicator light represents current from the battery and is on when the test box is operating.

2. The blue light represents current being applied to the solenoid ball valve EL-1.

3. The white light represents current being applied to the solenoid ball valve EL-2.

4. The green light represents the activation of the emission control system, if equipped (not used in U.S.).

5. The orange light represents current being applied to the kickdown switch.

C-1 SWITCH

This switch has two positions for test purposes.

Position A—Allows the transaxle to be operated in the normal manner with the use of the selector lever.

Position 1-2-3—Move the selector lever to the "A" ("D" or Drive) position. By turning the switch knob to the number 1, 2 or 3 position, the transaxle gear ratio can be controlled.

C-2 SWITCH

This switch allows the checking of the battery current at position one, current through the solenoid ball valves (EL-1 and EL-2) at position two, the fluid temperature at position six, while positions four and five are not used.

GALVANOMETER

The dial has scales that allows successive readings of the following:

1. Transmission fluid temperature.
2. Battery voltage with the engine stopped or operating.
3. Current passing through the solenoid ball valves in amperes.

TEST CABLE

A special test cable is used to plug into the diagnostic socket of the automatic transaxle and to the test cable of the test box.

THERMOMETER

A special thermometer replaces the transaxle dipstick in its tube. A connector wire is used between the thermometer and the test box.

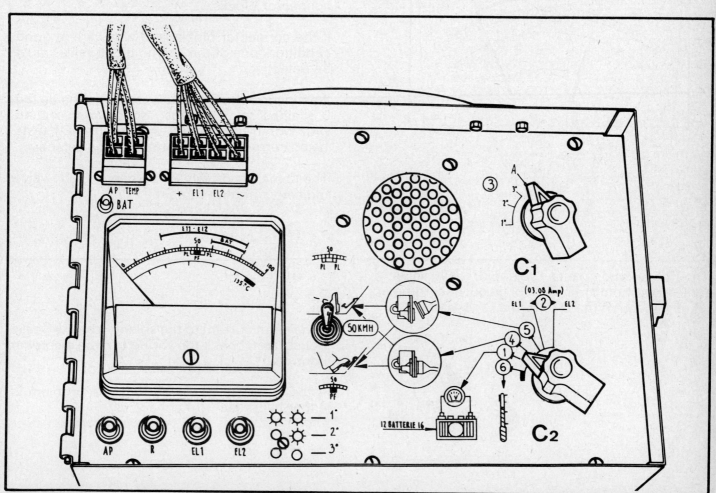

Test box type one (B.VI. 454-06, B.VI. 797) (© Renault/AMC)

READING	REMARKS
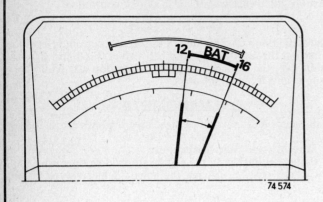 74 574	Incorrect battery voltage (outside the 12 volt to 16 volt range) may cause the automatic transmission to malfunction.
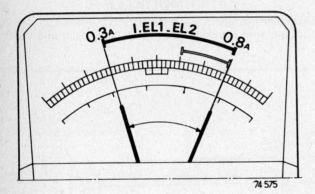 74 575	If the current is normal (between 0.3 amps and 0.8 amps), the solenoid ball valves are in good electrical condition. If the current is abnormal, check the wires and connector blocks. If the connector blocks and wires are in good condition, one of the solenoid ball valves must be defective. If an incorrect reading is obtained (outside the 0.3 amps to 0.8 amps range) when testing with switch C1 in the A position (the C1 tests being correct) the computer may be defective. The blue and white solenoid ball valve indicators should remain lit.

The blue and white solenoid ball valve indicators should remain lit or go out according to the selection made with the C1 switch.

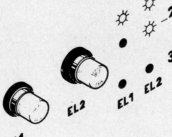

If the input current to the solenoid ball valves is not correct, check the wiring and the electrical controls.

If the input current is correct, the problem is either hydraulic or mechanical.

Type Two

The type two test box (B.VI. 797-01, B.VI. 797-02) contains function indicator lights, a potentiometer, a galvanometer dial, a digital display, switches, two leads for connection to the vehicle and three safety fuses.

INDICATOR LIGHTS

1. The EL-1 yellow indicator light represents current being applied to the solenoid ball valve EL-1.
2. The EL-2 yellow light indicator represents current being applied to the solenoid ball valve EL-2.
3. The red AP indicator light indicates current to the emission control system, if used (Not in U.S.).
4. The RC green indicator light indicates current to the kickdown switch and that it is operating.

DIGITAL DISPLAY

The digital display indicates multifunction switch operation and the computer condition.

POTENTIOMETER

The potentiometer is not used while testing the transaxle units.

CIRCUIT BREAKER

The circuit breaker is not used while testing the transaxle units.

GALVANOMETER

The galvanometer has four scales to allow successive readings of the following:
1. Battery voltage with the engine stopped or operating.
2. Measurement of current passing through the solenoid ball valves.
3. The third is not used during the tests.
4. Measures the transaxle fluid temperature. A red zone is indicated and the transaxle fluid temperature must not exceed it.

SWITCH

The switch is used to select the test modes that can be performed with the test instrument.
1. Position 0—indicates battery voltage with the engine stopped or operating.
2. Position 1—Measures the current in EL-1 and its input.
3. Position 2—Measures the current in EL-2 and its input.
4. Position 3—Places the vehicle in the third gear ratio when the selector lever is in the "D" position (EL-1 and EL-2 are not activated).
5. Position 4—Not used.
6. Position 5—Not used.
7. Position 6—Not used.
8. Position 7—Allows transaxle fluid temperature to be measured.

FUSES

1. Fuse a—Protects test box input (1A).
2. Fuse b—Protects EL-1 current (1A).
3. Fuse c—Protects EL-2 current (1A).

THERMOMETER

A special thermometer replaces the transaxle dipstick in its tube. A connector wire is used between the thermometer and the test box.

TEST CABLE

A special test cable is used between the diagnostic socket of the transaxle and the test box.

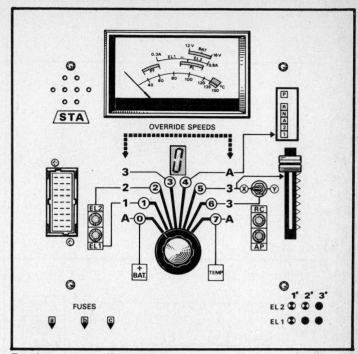

Test box type two (B.VI. 797-01 or B.VI. 797-2) (© Renault/AMC)

Type Three

The type three test box (B.VI. 958) has a self checking feature. By connecting terminal 14 to the battery and switching the I1 switch to the TEST position, test lights 1, 2, 3, 4, 5, 6, 7, 8 and the positive (+) red zone should illuminate. If they do not illuminate, the test box is defective.

DESCRIPTION

Zone A is used to test MB and MJ transaxles.
1. Solenoid valves
2. Road speed sensor
3. Potentiometer
4. 2nd gear hold switch   gear selector
4 & 5. 1st gear hold switch   lever position
6. Multifunction switch
15. Diagnostic socket
14. Control box feed
RAZ. Return to zero for check lights 1 to 6
TEST. B.VI. 958 check
DIAG. Instrument panel check light

Zone B is used to measure the solenoid valve windings and voltage and to test the multifunction switch on all RENAULT automatic transaxles.
7-8. Reading control lights
P. Control harnesses
P1. Control input sockets

Zone C is used to check types 4139 and 4141 transaxles. Additional wiring is required.

Zone D is used to check and adjust the load potentiometer on MB and MJ transaxles.
12. Inverter
9. Adjustment check light
+. Feed light (MB-MJ)
F. Fuse (3.15A)
16. Test harness connectors

READING	REMARKS
	Incorrect battery voltage (outside the 12 volt to 16 volt range) can cause the automatic transmission to malfunction. **Note:** This test may also be performed with the vehicle moving. If there is no voltage, check test box fuses a, b, and c.
	If the current is normal (between 0.3 amps. and 0.8 amps.), the solenoid ball valves are in good electrical condition. If the current is abnormal: • check the wires and the connector blocks • if the wires and blocks are in good condition, one of the solenoid ball valves must be defective. If there is no current, check test box fuses a, b, and c.
	If the current is normal (between 0.3 amps. and 0.8 amps.), the solenoid ball valves are in good electrical condition. If the current is abnormal: • check the wires and the connector blocks • if the wires and blocks are in good condition, one of the solenoid ball valves must be defective. If there is no current, check test box fuses a, b, and c.
	If the input current to the solenoid ball valves is not correct, check the leads and the electrical controls. If the input current is correct, the problem is either hydraulic or mechanical.

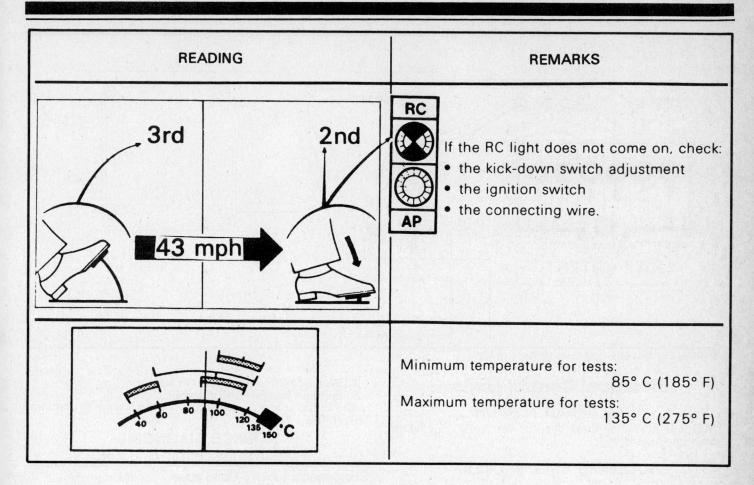

READING	REMARKS
3rd · 43 mph → 2nd	**RC** / **AP** — If the RC light does not come on, check: • the kick-down switch adjustment • the ignition switch • the connecting wire.
(temperature gauge 40 60 80 100 120 135 150 °C)	Minimum temperature for tests: 85° C (185° F) Maximum temperature for tests: 135° C (275° F)

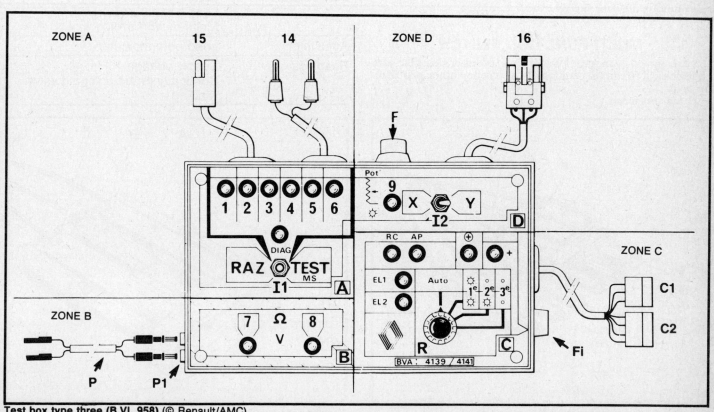

Test box type three (B.VI. 958) (© Renault/AMC)

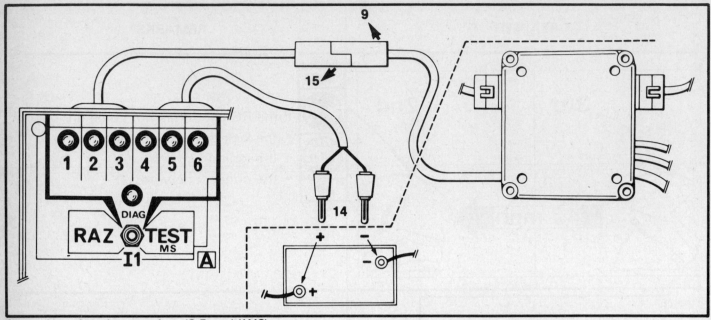

Connections of test box type three (© Renault/AMC)

Electrical Control Units

ROAD SPEED SENSOR

1. This is a winding fitted opposite the "park" ring which senses vehicle speed.

SOLENOID BALL VALVES

1. These are solenoid-operated ball valves which open or close hydraulic channels to change gears.
2. They are controlled by the computer.

MULTI-FUNCTION SWITCH

Its cam, moved by the gear selector lever, opens or closes the various electrical circuits depending on the position of the gear selector lever:

1. Starter circuit.

2. Back up lights circuit (lever in R).
3. Solenoid ball valves EL1 and EL2.
4. The starter is only activated when the lever is in positions "N" or "P".

SERVICE DIAGNOSIS
Diagnostic Tester B.VI.958

Components which may be tested	Road speed sensor Solenoid valves Load potentiometer Multifunction switch
Adjustment	Load potentiometer
Readings	Supply voltage Continuity in the solenoid valve winding

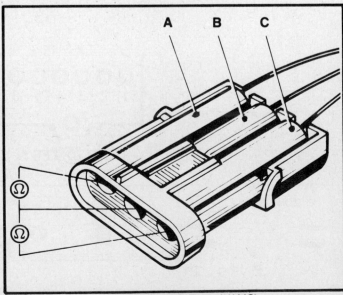

Checking the 6-way connector (© Renault/AMC)

Checking the load potentiometer (© Renault/AMC)

COMPUTER

This is an electronic calculator which interprets information from the following sources:
1. The road speed sensor.
2. The engine load potentiometer.
3. The multifunction switch.

The computer then changes the information into electrical instructions to the solenoid ball valves to change the gear ratios.

ENGINE LOAD POTENTIOMETER

1. It is a simple potentiometer which provides variable voltage based on throttle position.

CHECKING THE 6-WAY CONNECTOR

Unplug connector from the computer and make the following checks.

Action on vehicle	Check	Diagnosis
Ignition switched off	B-Ground = 4 ohm ± 3	Backup lamps
Ignition switched off	A-Ground = 12V ± 2	Backup lamps
Ignition switched on	E-Ground = 0 ohm	Ground
Ignition switched on	F-Ground = 12V ± 2	Current feed to module
Operate starter	C-Ground = 12V ± 2	Starter

CHECKING ENGINE LOAD POTENTIOMETER

(Unplug connector)

Check	Diagnosis
C to B = 4k ohm ± 1 A to B = 2,5k ohm ± 1	If the readings are different the potentiometer is faulty or incorrectly adjusted.
A to B: open throttle slowly; the ohmmeter should never show infinite resistance (∞)	

RESULTS OF THE READINGS
Diagnostic Tester B.VI.958

(Road test the vehicle, but do not shut the engine off after the test.)
Vehicle Stopped (Engine Running)

Checks	Check light(s)	Good	Bad	Faulty components	Oper-ation
Solenoid Valves	1	O	★	Solenoid valves Harness	IX-X-XI
Road Speed Sensor	2	O	★	Faulty road speed sensor	
Potentio-meter	3	O	★	Load potentiometer harness	XII-XV

Engine Not Running—Ignition Switch On

Position of the control lever	Check light(s)	Good		Faulty components	Oper-ation
2nd hold	4	4 ★	5 O	If bad, multifunction switch and harness	V-XIV
1st hold	4 and 5	4 ★	5 ★	If bad, check multifunction switch and harness	V-XIV
P L N D	4 and 5	4 O	5 O	If bad, check multifunction switch and harness	III-IV XIII-XIV
P—N	6	★		If bad, check selector lever adjustment and multifunction switch operation	II

1197

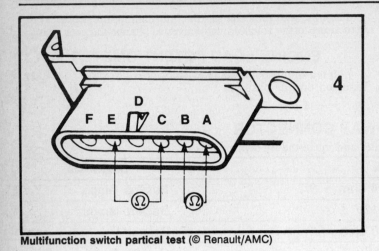

Multifunction switch partical test (© Renault/AMC)

CONTROL OF THE POTENTIOMETER

Test	Check
	light
Press accelerator to floor	9
Good	★
Bad or badly adjusted	O

PARTIAL CHECK OF MULTI-FUNCTION SWITCH
(Unplug the 6-way connector and check computer socket.)

Check	Diagnosis
A to B = 0 ohm (selector in R) E to C = 0 ohm (selector in P or N)	Replace multifunction switch

CHECKING THE 3-WAY CONNECTOR

Action on vehicle	Check	Diagnosis
Ignition switched on	B-Ground = 4.3 V ± 0.5	If this check proves a problem exists, check 6 way connector. Replace the computer if connector is satisfactory. Replace computer.

CHECKING THE SOLENOID VALVES AND HARNESS
(Unplug connector from the computer.)

Check	Diagnosis	
A to C = 30 ohm ± 10	If 0 ohm	:Replace wiring or solenoid valves
	60 ohm ± 20	:Poor connection
B to C = 30 ohm ± 10		:Replace wiring or solenoid valves
C to Ground = ∞	If not ∞: There is a short circut between the solenoid valve windings and ground: Replace the wiring or solenoid valves	

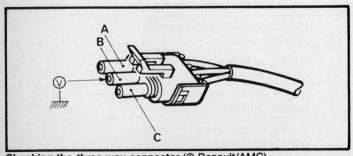

Checking the three way connector (© Renault/AMC)

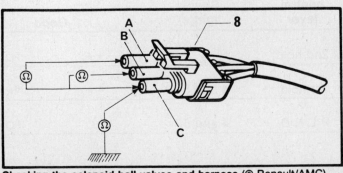

Checking the solenoid ball valves and harness (© Renault/AMC)

CHECKING THE SOLENOID VALVES

Test points		Diagnosis
A - C = 30 ohm ± 10	Si 0 ohm	:Replace the Solenoid Valves
	60 ohm ± 20	:Bad connection
B - C = 30 ohm ± 10	∞	:Replace the Solenoid Valves
C - Ground = ∞		:If different from ∞
		—Solenoid valves short between ground and windings. Replace the solenoid valves.

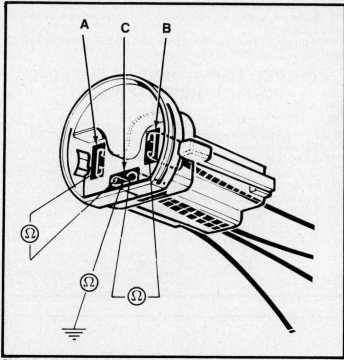

Checking the solenoid valves (© Renault/AMC)

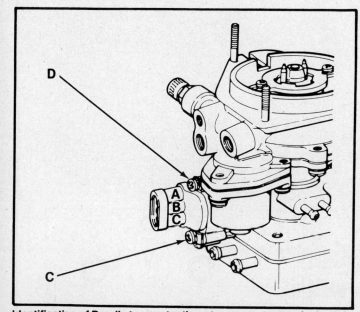

Identification of Bendix type potentiometer connector terminals and adjusting screws (C & D) (© Renault/AMC)

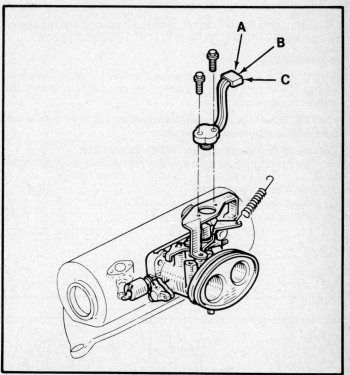

Identification of Bosch type potentiometer connector terminal (© Renault/AMC)

Adjustment of The Potentiometer

1. Partially unscrew the 2 screws attaching the potentiometer (on the throttle plate housing).
2. Keep the throttle plate fully open and slowly rotate the potentiometer until check light 9 comes on. Tighten the 2 screws V in the position when 9 is on.
3. If check light 9 does not come on, check the potentiometer wiring or replace the potentiometer.
4. Each time the potentiometer is removed or replaced, it has to be adjusted.

CONTROL OF THE MULTIFUNCTION SWITCH (ZONE B)

Backup lights not working test

NOTE: Be sure to check that the governor cable is correctly adjusted.

1. Vehicle stopped.
2. Ignition switch off.
3. B.Vi. 958 connected to battery.
4. Disconnect 6 wire connector from the auto trans computer.
5. Connect control harness to B.Vi 958 (male red connector to red terminal).

6. If backup light not working, readings to be taken between A and B.

Gear Selector	Check Lights	
	7	8
D/1/2/N/P	○	○
R	○	★

If check lights 7 and 8 do not give exact results as given above, refer to MULTIFUNCTION SWITCH REPLACEMENT.

Replacement

This operation consists of replacing the multifunction switch by cutting the wire harness connecting the computer and the multifunction switch.

NOTE: Always test the multifunction switch to be certain it is faulty before replacing the switch.

Contents of the Multifunction Switch Repair Kit:

1. one multifunction switch with a wire harness and male connector.
2. one female connector.
3. six male terminals.
4. six seals.

Removal and Installation

1. Remove the multifunction switch from the transaxle.
2. Cut the harness the same length as the replacement harness.
3. On the computer side, remove 65mm (2.6 in.) of outer insulation from the cable end.
4. Remove 5mm (0.20 in.) of insulation from each wire.
5. Install a seal on each wire.
6. Install and crimp the six male terminals on the wire ends.

NOTE: When installing the wires in the connector, be sure the wire color codes are not mismatched.

7. Install the connector locking device.
8. Some computers are connected to the multifunction switch with eight wires.
9. If this is the case, cut the yellow wire on the computer side of the harness flush with the protective sleeve.

CONTROL/ADJUSTMENT OF THE LOAD POTENTIOMETER (ZONE D)

Test

Be sure to check that accelerator cable is correctly adjusted.
1. Vehicle stopped
2. Ignition switch off
3. Disconnect 3 wire connector from the harness connecting the computer to the throttle plate
4. Connect 3 wire connector to connector on B.Vi. 958
5. Connect terminals to the battery

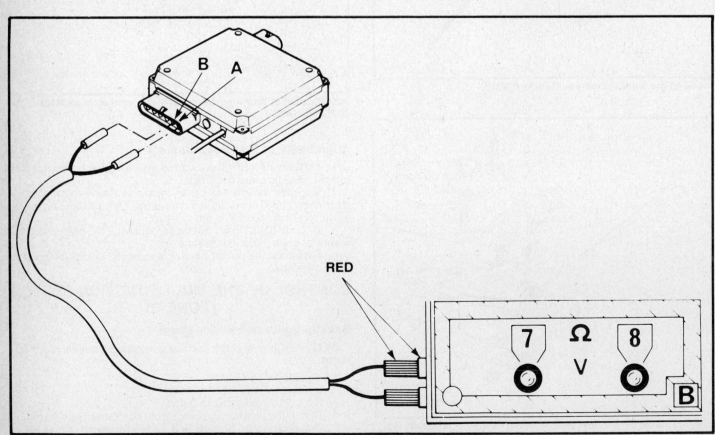

Control of the multifunction switch with the type three test box in zone "B" (© Renault/AMC)

Press accelerator to floor	Check light 9
Good	✪
Bad or badly adjusted	○

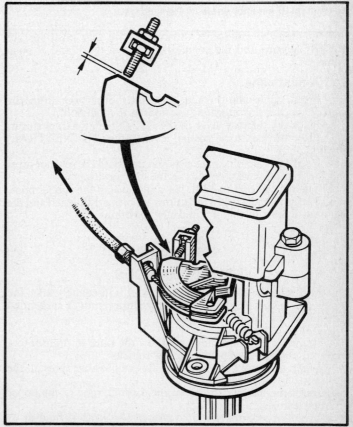

Control adjustment of the load potentiometer with the type three test box in zone "D" (© Renault/AMC)

ON CAR SERVICES

Adjustments

GOVERNOR CABLE

1. Before adjusting the governor cable, inspect the accelerator cable to be sure it is adjusted properly.

    a. Depress the accelerator to the fully wide open position.

    b. Measure the compression on the cable spring which should be 0.080 in. (2 mm) from the released position.

    c. Check for proper kickdown switch operation.

2. When adjusting the governor, cable, complete the following:

    a. Adjust the cable locknuts on both the governor and throttle sides to the midway position.

    b. Adjust the cable stop to obtain a clearance of 0.008-0.028 in. (0.2-0.7mm) between the screw and the lever with the throttle fully open.

    c. Tighten the locknuts.

d. Verify that the length of the governor cable is approximately 0.788 in. (20mm) between the wide open throttle position and the closed position.

CAUTION

The screw has been preset at the time of manufacture and must not be adjusted under any circumstances.

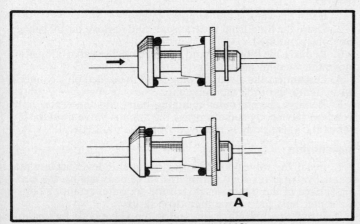

Accelerator cable adjustment (© Renault/AMC)

Governor cable adjustment (© Renault/AMC)

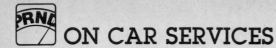

KICKDOWN SWITCH

NOTE: Adjustment is made with the accelerator cable.

1. Be sure the accelerator cable has sufficient play to allow about 1/16 inch (3-4mm) movement in the stop sleeve when the accelerator pedal is completely depressed.
2. Properly install the sealing cover in position to prevent corrosion of the contacts.

─────────── **CAUTION** ───────────

Accelerator cable/pedal travel, kickdown switch adjustment and the governor control cable adjustments are all closely related. Be sure each is properly adjusted whenever any of the adjustments are changed.

MANUAL LINKAGE

Cable Adjustment

1. Place the transaxle manual lever in the P (PARK) position.
2. Place the selector lever in the P (PARK) position.
3. Adjust the cable assembly by loosening the adjusting yoke nuts and sliding the cable and the yoke forward to remove the slack in the cable.

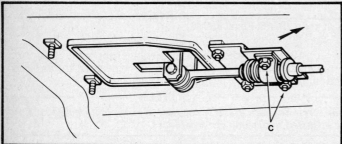

Adjustment of selector cable (© Renault/AMC)

4. Tighten the yoke nuts. Be sure all six gear positions are properly aligned and the engine will start in the P and N positions.

Rod Adjustment

1. From under the vehicle, pull the rubber boot from the lockbolt on the shifting shaft and loosen the lockbolt.
2. Place the selector lever in the "N" (NEUTRAL) position.
3. Place the transaxle manual lever in the "N" (NEUTRAL) position.
4. Verify that no binding exists and that both the selector lever and the manual lever remains in the "N" position.
5. Tighten the bolt to 13 ft. lbs. and reinstall the rubber boot.
6. Verify that all six gear positions are properly aligned and the engine will start in the "P" and "N" positions.

Services

FLUID CHANGES

The fluid must be drained when hot and immediately after the engine has been turned off. This procedure removes suspended particles in the fluid.

1. Remove the dipstick.
2. Remove the drain plug and allow the fluid to drain into a waste oil container, after raising the vehicle.
3. When the fluid has drained as long as possible, reinstall the drain plug.
4. Refill the transaxle through the dipstick tube or the upper drain plug hole.
5. Install approximately 2⅔ quarts of Dexron® II fluid or its equivalent.

6. Start the engine and allow it to idle. Check the fluid level after running the selector lever through all the gear positions.
7. Correct the fluid level as necessary.

OIL PAN

Removal and Installation

1. Raise the vehicle and support safely.
2. Drain the transmission as previously outlined. Reinstall the drain plug. Remove transaxle mount bolt and raise the assembly to gain clearance for pan removal, as required (Alliance).
3. Remove the retaining bolts from the oil pan and bump the oil pan to loosen.
4. Remove the oil pan and the gasket.
5. Clean the gasket from the oil pan and the mating surface of the transaxle.

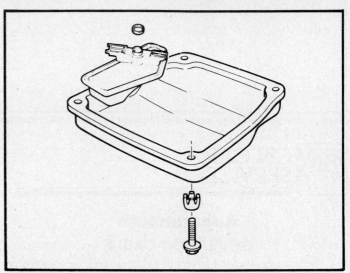

Typical oil pan and filter assembly (© Renault/AMC)

6. Install a new gasket on the oil pan and fit into position on the mating surface of the transaxle.
7. Install the retaining bolts and tighten to 54 *inch* lbs. Install mount bolt, if removed.
8. Install fluid as outlined previously.

NOTE: With the oil pan off the transaxle, the filter unit can be changed.

VALVE BODY

Removal

1. Raise the vehicle and support safely.
2. Drain the fluid from the transaxle and remove the oil pan as previously outlined.
3. Remove the fluid filter and its seal from the valve body. Remove the vacuum modulator.
4. Disconnect the electrical plug from the sealed plug connector by removal of the retaining clip.
5. Remove the six outer retaining bolts and the center bolt from the valve body and disengage the manual valve from the lever as the valve body is removed from the transaxle.

Installation

1. Install the valve body by engaging the shift lever lug into the manual valve groove and seating the valve body against the mating surface of the transaxle. Install the six outer retaining bolts, the center bolt and torque them to 5 ft. lbs.
2. Install the fluid filter and seal to the valve body by first lubricating the "O" ring for the filter suction pipe and installing it

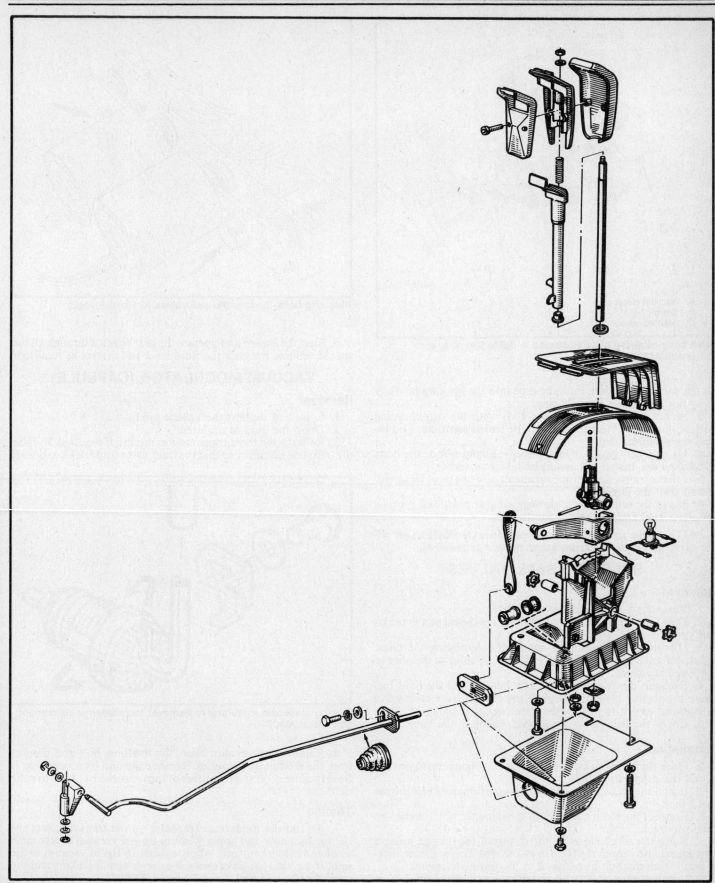

Exploded view of shift lever and linkage—18 series (© Renault/AMC)

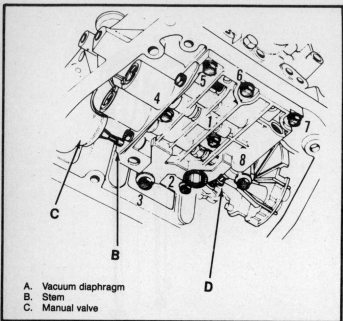

A. Vacuum diaphragm
B. Stem
C. Manual valve

Valve body retaining bolts illustrated in tightening sequence
(© Renault/AMC)

on the suction pipe end. Push the pipe into the housing carefully so as not to damage the "O" ring.

3. Secure the filter to the valve body with the two retaining bolts. Connect the electrical plug to the sealed connector and install the retaining clip.

4. Using a new gasket, install the oil pan and torque the bolts to 54 *inch* lbs. Install the mount bolt, if removed.

5. Fill the transaxle with approximately 2⅔ quarts of Dexron® II and start the engine.

6. Move the selector lever through all gear positions, recheck the fluid level and correct as required.

NOTE: Some transaxles may use a transaxle shield as an under-carriage protector. Remove and replace as required.

SOLENOID BALL VALVES

Removal

1. Raise the vehicle and support safely.

2. Drain the transaxle of fluid and remove the oil pan as previously outlined.

3. Disconnect the electrical wires after removing the clips. Mark the solenoid ball valves to indicate the color of the wire to each was attached.

4. Remove the two retaining bolts holding the solenoid ball valve supporting plate and remove the valves. Note each valve position so as not to reverse them during the installation.

5. Check the ball valves for proper sealing of the balls.

Installation

1. Place the solenoid ball valves in their original position and install the supporting plate.

2. Install the retaining bolts in the supporting plate and torque to 12 *inch* lbs.

3. Connect the electrical wires to the same terminals as before their removal.

4. Raise the transaxle as required, install the oil pan using a new gasket and torque the bolts to 54 *inch* lbs. Lower the transaxle and install the bolt as required in the transaxle mount.

5. Install approximately 2⅔ quarts of Dexron® II fluid or its equivalent, into the transaxle.

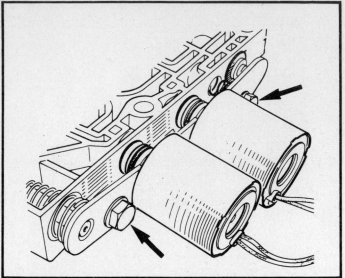

Retaining bolts for solenoid ball valves (© Renault/AMC)

6. Start the engine and operate the gear selector through all the gear selections. Recheck the fluid level and correct as required.

VACUUM MODULATOR (CAPSULE)

Removal

1. Raise and support the vehicle safely.

2. Drain the fluid as required.

3. Remove the front transmission mount, if required, to raise the transaxle assembly so that the modulator (capsule) is exposed.

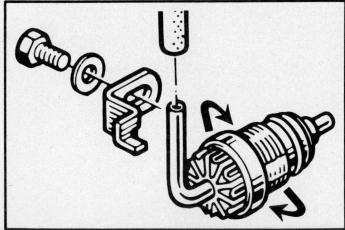

Turning of vacuum modulator for removal, installation or adjustment
(© Renault/AMC)

4. Remove the vacuum hose, the retaining bolt and bracket from the modulator (capsule). Remove the unit by unscrewing it from the case. Count the number of turns necessary to remove the unit.

Testing

1. To test the modulator (capsule) on the transaxle, remove the vacuum hose and apply vacuum from a vacuum source such as a hand held pump unit. Apply at least 16 Hg. of vacuum to the unit. If the vacuum leaks away, the diaphragm is leaking and the unit must be replaced.

2. With the modulator (capsule) off the transaxle, the same

test can be performed. If the vacuum cannot be held or the operating pin does not move, the unit is defective and must be replaced.

Installation

1. Install the modulator (capsule) into the transaxle by screwing the unit in the same number of turns as was counted when the unit was removed.
2. Install the retaining bracket and bolt. Attach the vacuum hose to the unit.
3. Lower the transaxle, if raised, and install the front mount bolt.
4. Lower the vehicle and install 2⅔ quarts of Dexron® II or its equivalent, into the transaxle. Start the engine, operate the gear selector lever through all of the gear positions and recheck the level of the fluid. Correct as required.

SPEEDOMETER DRIVE SHAFT SEAL

Removal

1. Disconnect the speedometer cable at the transaxle and remove.
2. Insert a special tool, part number B.VI. 905 or its equivalent into the case opening.
3. Insert the end of the tool into the seal and by turning part of the tool and holding the second part, the seal can be removed from the case bore.

Installation

1. Lubricate the seal and push it downward into the case bore, until it seats squarely at the bottom.
2. Install the speedometer cable and tighten the assembly.

SELECTOR LEVER

Removal

FUEGO AND 18i

1. Position the selector lever at the "N" position.
2. Working under the vehicle, remove the circlip from the transaxle lever, remove the protective cover at the bracket, remove the bracket retaining bolt and remove the bracket arm.
3. From inside the vehicle, remove the selector lever grille by sliding it out.
4. Remove the selector lever housing. The lever can then be disassembled by removing a drift pin from its bottom.

Installation

1. Install the selector lever to its base and install the drift pin.
2. Check to be sure the transaxle lever and the selector lever is set at the "N" position.
3. Mount the boot and selector lever housing onto the rod and insert the control rod in the bearing at the control end.
4. Attach the control rod at the transaxle side and install the circlip.
5. Reconnect the arm and tighten the bolt to 13 ft. lbs.
6. Install the protective cover and secure it to the rod.
7. Complete the assembly inside the vehicle for the gear selector housing.

ALLIANCE

Removal

1. Disconnect the negative battery cable, raise the vehicle and support safely.
2. Disconnect the selector lever cable from the selector lever and lower the vehicle.
3. Remove the selector lever grille, the console bezel, the radio and the console itself.
4. Remove the two selector lever bracket retaining bolts and spacers. Remove the selector lever assembly.

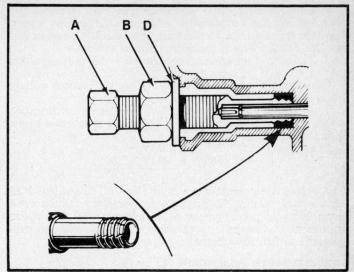

Use of special tool (A-extractor, B-nut and D-spacer) to remove speedometer drive shaft oil seal (© Renault/AMC)

Installation

1. Install the following in this order, the selector lever assembly, the spacers and retaining bolts, the console, the radio, the control bezel and the selector lever grille.
2. Raise the vehicle and support safely. Connect the selector lever cable.
3. Lower the vehicle and connect the battery cable.
4. Check the gear selector lever operation and make adjustments as required.

THROTTLE POSITION POTENTIOMETER

Removal

VEHICLES WITH BENDIX TBI AND BOSCH FI

1. Remove the air filter assembly (vehicles equipped with Bendix TBI only).
2. Separate the wire connector from the potentiometer.
3. Remove the two retaining screws and the potentiometer.

Installation

1. Install the potentiometer and the two retaining screws.
2. Install the wire connector.
3. If the vehicle is equipped with the Bendix TBI, install the air filter assembly.

Adjustment.

1. On vehicles equipped with Bendix TBI, remove the air filter assembly.
2. Turn the ignition to the "ON" position.
3. Using a digital volt-ohm meter, insert the negative (−) voltmeter lead into the terminal "C" of the potentiometer.

NOTE: Do not disconnect the connector. Insert the voltmeter lead (−) into the back of the connector and push it in to contact the terminal.

4. Insert the positive (+) voltmeter lead into terminal "B" of the throttle position sensor.
5. Move the throttle plate to the wide open throttle position by hand. Be sure the throttle contacts the stop.

—————— CAUTION ——————
Do not have the engine operating.

6. Note the exact voltmeter reading. This is input voltage and should be approximately 4.3 volts.

7. Remove the positive voltmeter lead from terminal "B" and insert it in the Terminal "A" of the throttle position sensor. Open the throttle plate to the wide open throttle position and note the voltage. This is considered output voltage.

8. The output voltage must be adjusted so that output voltage is 4% ± 0.5% of the input voltage.

Example: If the input voltage is 5 volts, then output voltage equals 5V x 4% = 0.20V ± 0.03 V.

9. At supply voltages less than 5V, the potentiometer setting should be 4% of supply voltage ± voltage in proportion to the 5V/0.2V setting.

Example: 5V .200V ± 30MV

4V .160V ± $\dfrac{30MV \times .160}{0.2}$

10. Adjust the potentiometer (both Bendix TBI and Bosch FI vehicles) by loosening the bottom potentiometer retaining screw and pivoting the potentiometer on the adjusting slot for a coarse adjustment. Loosen the top retaining screw and pivot the potentiometer for a fine adjustment.

On Work Bench Adjustment

1. Using a regulated power source, such as the vehicle battery, connect a lead between the positive (+) terminal of the power source and the terminal "B" of the potentiometer.

2. Connect a lead from the negative (−) terminal of the power source and terminal "C" of the potentiometer.

3. Open the throttle to the wide open position.

4. Using a digital volt/ohm meter, read the input voltage between terminals "B" and "C." Close the throttle.

5. Remove the positive (+) lead from terminal "B" and insert it in terminal "A."

6. Open the throttle plate to its wide open position.

7. Read the voltage on the voltmeter. This is output voltage and should be 4% ± 0.5% of the input voltage. Close the throttle.

Example: 12.5V x 4% = 0.5V ± .062V

KICKDOWN SWITCH

Adjustment

1. The kickdown switch must operate with the accelerator pedal fully depressed.

2. Be sure the accelerator cable has approximately 1/16 inch (3–4mm) movement in the stop sleeve when the accelerator pedal is completely depressed. The switch is adjusted by the cable setting.

3. Be certain the electrical connector cover is properly positioned to prevent corrosion.

Removal

1. Remove the accelerator cable and electrical wire.
2. Disconnect the wire from the kickdown switch.
3. Remove the switch retaining bolts and remove the switch.

Installation

1. Install the switch and the retaining bolts.
2. Install the electrical wire.
3. Install the accelerator cable and adjust the cable and switch.

CONVERTER OIL SEAL

Removal

The converter oil seal can be removed after the transaxle has been removed from the vehicle and the converter removed from the transaxle. The seal is pryed from the housing bore and with the use of a special seal installer tool, the seal can be reinstalled to its proper depth.

DIFFERENTIAL BEARING NUT AND OIL SEAL

NOTE: The differential bearing nut may be removed with the transaxle in the vehicle.

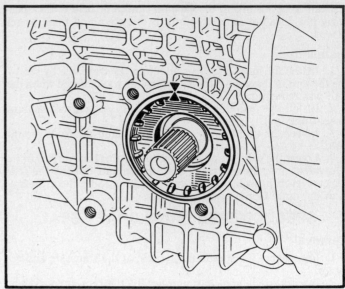

Matchmarking position of differential bearing nut (© Renault/AMC)

Removal

1. Raise the vehicle and support safely.
2. Drain the transaxle of fluid.
3. Insert a special spacer tool or its equivalent, between the lower shock absorber attaching base and the lower suspension arm pivot shaft.
4. Remove the brake caliper and punch out the drive shaft roll pins.
5. With appropriate tools, loosen the steering tie rod ends, the upper suspension ball joints and tilt the stub axle carriers to disengage the drive shafts from the side gears.
6. Match mark the position of the differential bearing nut with respect to the housing. Remove the "O" ring from the side gear.
7. Remove the lockstop and unscrew the nut, counting the number of turns required to remove it.
8. Remove the oil seal and "O" ring from the differential nut.

Installation

1. Lubricate the seal and "O" ring. Install both on the differential nut.

NOTE: The seal is positioned in the differential nut with the seal lip pointing inward.

2. Carefully install the differential nut and tighten it the same number of turns as required to remove it.

NOTE: A seal protector cannot be used on vehicles equipped with automatic transaxles.

3. Install the lockstop and install the "O" ring onto the side gear.
4. Position the drive shaft to line up the roll pin holes. Insert the roll pins and seal the holes.
5. Install the steering and upper suspension ball joints. Tighten the nuts securely to a torque of 48 ft. lbs. on the upper suspension ball joint nuts; 26 ft. lbs. on the steering tie rod ball joint nuts; 59 ft. lbs. on the wheel lugs and 45 ft. lbs. on the brake caliper bolts.
6. Install the brake caliper and road wheels. Tighten the bolts to the above torque.
7. Remove the special tool spacer from the suspension and lower the vehicle.
8. Fill the transaxle with Dexron® II fluid or its equivalent to its correct level.
9. Apply the brakes several times before driving off to road test.

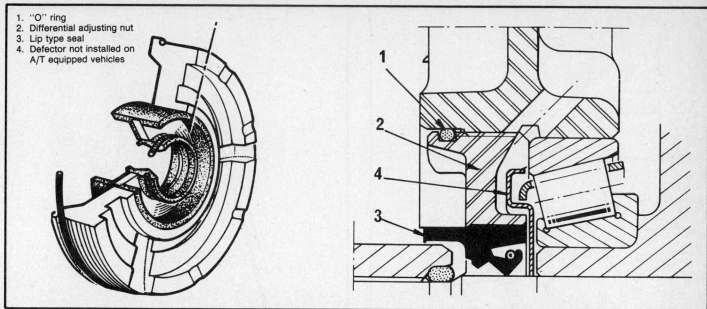

1. "O" ring
2. Differential adjusting nut
3. Lip type seal
4. Defector not installed on A/T equipped vehicles

Seal installation in differential bearing nut (© Renault/AMC)

MOLDED WIRE HARNESS

The wiring used to control the varied electrical components has molded sockets and most require the complete replacement of the wire assembly, should a malfunction occur within the wire assembly.

The governor/computer/multifunction switches and wiring can be removed separately, therefore, not requiring the removal of the lower unit housing of the transaxle when the solenoid valve wiring or the sealed plugs are not the cause of the malfunction.

REMOVAL & INSTALLATION

Transaxle Removal

FUEGO, 18i MODELS

NOTE: The transaxle can either be removed with the engine from above or can be removed separately from under the vehicle. The procedures outlines are directed to the removal of the transaxle separately.

1. Disconnect the battery cables.
2. Raise the vehicle and support safely. Drain the fluid from the transaxle unit.
3. Disconnect the vacuum hose to the vacuum modulator.
4. Disconnect the transaxle electrical wiring connectors and remove the support.
5. Insert the suspension spacers between the lower shock absorber fixing base and the lower control arm pivot shaft.
6. Have the vehicle in a position or on a lift to raise the vehicle as required.
7. Drive the roll pins out of the drive shafts.
8. Remove the suspension upper ball joints and the steering tie rod ends.
9. Tilt the stub axles to free the drive shafts from the side gears.

10. Remove the selector linkage from the transaxle selector lever.
11. Remove the fluid dipstick tube.
12. Remove the converter protective plate and remove the three retaining bolts.
13. Remove the exhaust pipe bracket nut which is attached to the transaxle.
14. If not already positioned, place the transmission jack assembly under the rear of the transaxle. Remove the two supports and gently lower the transaxle from the installed position, enough to remove the speedometer and governor cables.
15. Remove the engine to transaxle bolts and slowly lower the transaxle from under the vehicle.
16. As soon as the converter is exposed, install a converter retaining strap to hold the converter in place.

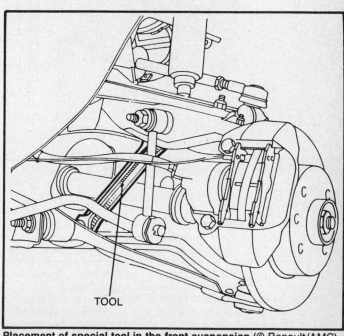

TOOL

Placement of special tool in the front suspension (© Renault/AMC)

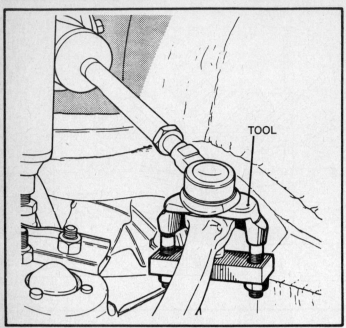

Separating the tie rod end—typical (© Renault/AMC)

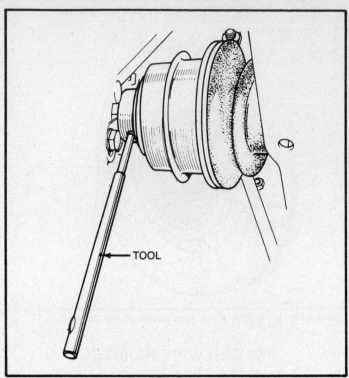

Removing the pins from the axle (© Renault/AMC)

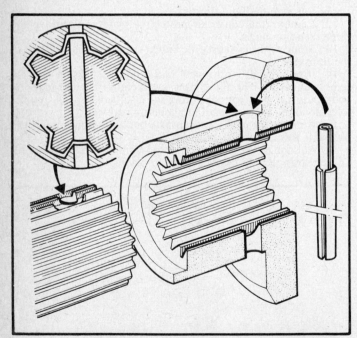

Location of pins in the stub axle and drive shaft (© Renault/AMC)

Installation

1. The transaxle is replaced in the reverse order of its removal with the following points that must be noted:

a. The converter drive plate has a sharp cornered edge marked with a daub of paint and the converter has one of the three fixing bosses which is located opposite the hole used as a reference point when setting the distributor timing.

b. When installing the transaxle, place the boss that is located opposite the timing hole in line with the sharp cornered edge on the converter drive plate which is marked by the daub of paint.

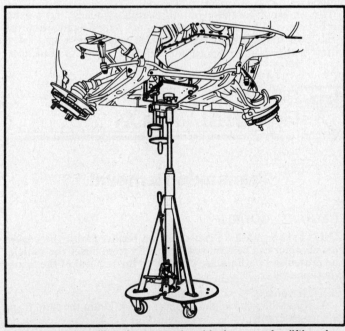

Removing or installing the transaxle with the use of a lifting device—typical (© Renault/AMC)

c. Install new lock washers during the installation.

d. Tighten the converter bolts gradually and to a torque of 30 ft. lbs.

e. If the vehicle is equipped with a TDC sensor, position the sensor approximately 0.039 in. (1mm) from the engine flywheel. If a new sensor is used, three pegs are on the sensor which allows the position of the sensor to be set correctly.

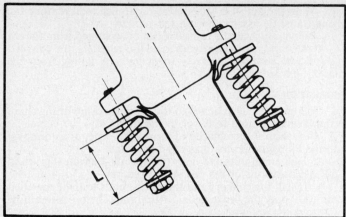

Exhaust pipe to manifold retaining bolts and springs
(© Renault/AMC)

f. Adjust the selector lever and the governor cable as previously outlined.

g. Be sure the computer and governor connections are correctly made and the grounding wires are in place.

h. Fill the unit with Dexron® II fluid and start the engine.

i. After the engine has operated a short time, move the selector lever through all the gear positions and recheck the fluid level. Correct as required.

j. Road test the vehicle and correct any malfunctions as required.

Removal

ALLIANCE, ENCORE

1. Disconnect the battery cables.
2. Raise the vehicle and support safely.
3. Drain the transaxle fluid, the engine oil, the cooling system, both the radiator and the block.
4. Remove the air intake assembly and the radiator.
5. Disconnect the wire harness connectors, the vacuum hoses, the accelerator cable and the heater house.

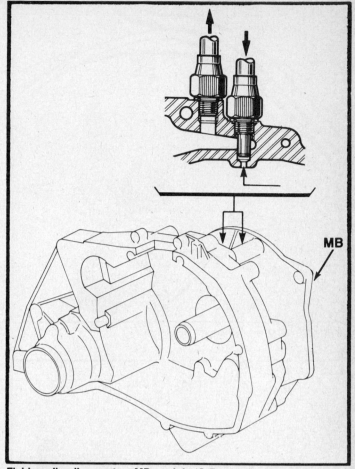

Fluid cooling line ports—MB models (© Renault/AMC)

NOTE: Mark the wiring, vacuum hoses and heater hoses to aid in the assembly.

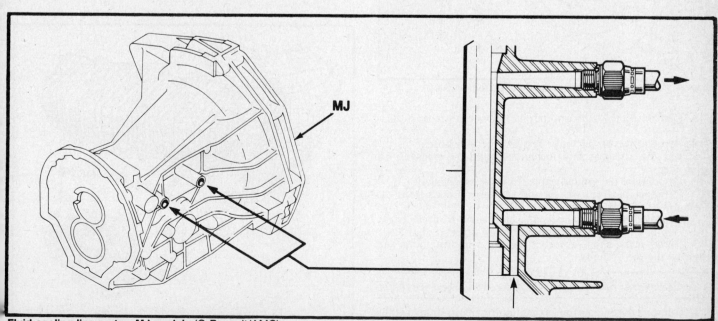

Fluid cooling line ports—MJ models (© Renault/AMC)

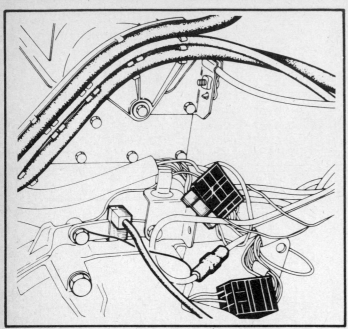

Wiring connections—typical (© Renault/AMC)

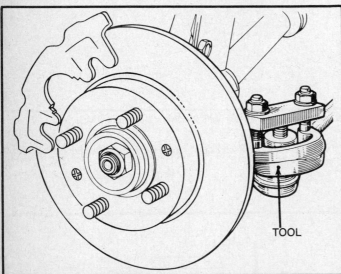

TOOL

Removal of tie rod end—Alliance models (© Renault/AMC)

6. Disconnect the exhaust pipe clamp from the exhaust manifold.

7. Remove the power brake booster vacuum hose.

8. Remove the gear shift mechanism and the transaxle oil cooler hoses.

9. Disconnect the ground cable from the transaxle.

10. Remove the front wheels and the tie rod ends from the steering links.

11. Remove the brake calipers and hang them from the body.

12. Remove the drive shaft retaining roll pins.

13. Remove the shock absorber bottom mounting bolts and withdraw the drive shafts.

CAUTION

Do not damage the rubber boot at the outer end of the drive shafts.

14. Remove the engine/transaxle mounting bolts or nuts at the front mounting and at the rear mounting.

15. With the aid of a lifing chain or similar tool, remove the engine/transaxle assembly from the vehicle.

16. Upon removal, the transaxle can be separated from the engine. If the unit is not to be overhauled immediately, the converter should be strapped securely to prevent its falling from the transaxle assembly.

Installation

1. The transaxle is attached to the engine and the lifting chain or similar tool is used to lower the assembly into the vehicle.

2. The assembly is replaced in the reverse order of its removal with the following points that must be noted:

   a. Tighten all nuts and bolts to a specified torque if given in the specifications or the outline procedures.

   b. Install the calipers and torque the bolts to their specified torque. Apply the brake pedal several times before attempting to move the vehicle.

   c. Fill the engine and the transaxle with oil and fluid.

   d. Fill the cooling system with proper coolant.

   e. New bolts must be used when installing the exhaust pipe clamp.

NOTE: With the springs installed on the exhaust pipe clamp, the distance between the clamp and the lower part of the hex bolt head should be 1.71 in. (43.5mm).

   f. After the roll pins have been installed in the drive shafts, the holes must be plugged with a sealer.

   g. Be certain the rubber boots on the drive shafts are in good condition and not torn or damaged.

BENCH OVERHAUL

MJ-1, MJ-3 TRANSAXLE MODELS

Before Disassembly

1. Remove the converter from the transaxle.
2. Remove the dipstick tube and the wiring.

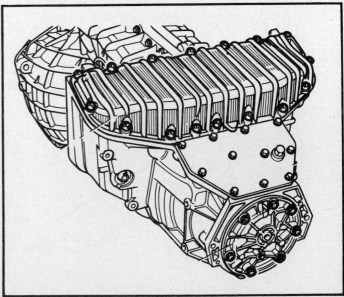

Inverted MJ transaxle models (© Renault/AMC)

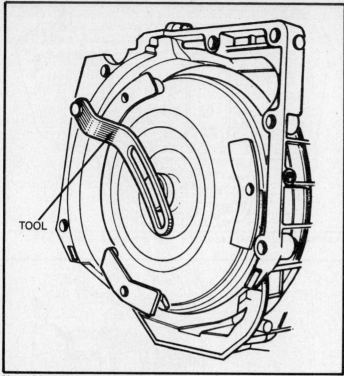

Use of bracket tool to hold torque converter (© Renault/AMC)

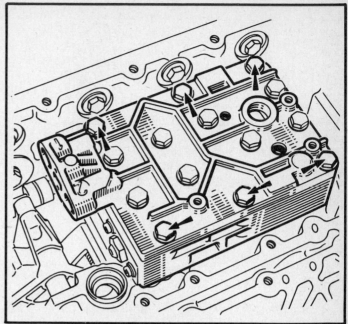

Valve body attaching bolts—MJ models (© Renault/AMC)

3. Remove the governor-computer from the assembly by the removal of the three upper bolts.

4. Remove the multifunction switch, leaving only the sealed plug on the housing.

5. Remove the vacuum modulator (capsule).

Disassembly.

1. Invert the transaxle and remove the oil pan retaining bolts, the oil pan, the bottom cover and the gasket.

2. Remove the filter and seal. Do not discard the suction tube seal.

3. Disconnect the sealed plug socket and remove the moulded wiring.

4. Remove the outer valve body bolts from each side and remove the valve body assembly. Disengage the manual valve from the inner selector lever.

NOTE: A center retaining bolt may be encountered on some transaxle models.

5. From the outer end, remove the pump cover and remove the pump drive shaft. Inspect for wear on the slots for the lugs of the drive pump gear.

6. Remove the driven pump gear, marking its direction, if to be used again by the direction of the chamfer.

7. Remove the four inner differential assembly bolts from inside the transmission case.

8. Remove the two roll pins, the bolt and the parking gear latch from the gear control linkage.

9. Remove the connecting arm without separating the ball joints. Remove the gear control linkage.

10. Pull the shaft, but do not remove the toothed quadrant.

CAUTION

The socket containing the locking ball must not be removed unless it is to be replaced.

---

11. Set the transaxle on the transmission at the pump housing end. Remove the transaxle/transmission case assembly bolts.

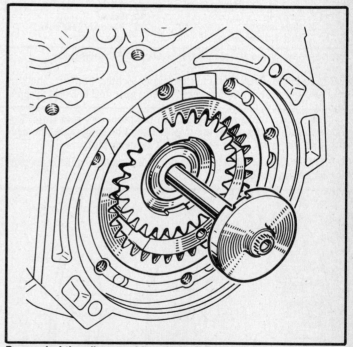

Removal of the oil pump drive shaft (© Renault/AMC)

12. Separate the differential and transmission cases.

13. Remove the parking latch by taking out the centering pin. A slide hammer type tool is used for this operation.

14. Remove the parking latch shaft, the parking latch and the return spring.

15. Remove the brake mechanism retaining bolts (10) and remove the drive train while holding the turbine shaft. Leave the needle thrust bearing inside the case.

16. Position the drive train on a support. Remove the planetary gear train, the sun gear (P-1), the F-1 and F-2 brake assemblies, clutch E-2, clutch E-1 and the turbine shaft.

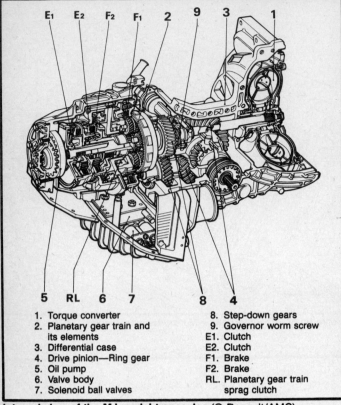

1. Torque converter
2. Planetary gear train and its elements
3. Differential case
4. Drive pinion—Ring gear
5. Oil pump
6. Valve body
7. Solenoid ball valves
8. Step-down gears
9. Governor worm screw
E1. Clutch
E2. Clutch
F1. Brake
F2. Brake
RL. Planetary gear train sprag clutch

Internal view of the MJ model transaxles (© Renault/AMC)

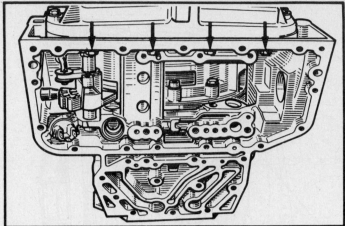

Location of four inner case bolts—MJ models (© Renault/AMC)

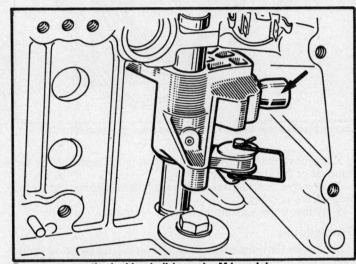

Do not remove the locking ball (arrow)—MJ models (© Renault/AMC)

17. Keep the needle thrust bearings located between the sun gear and E-1 clutch and between the sun gear and E-2 clutch separated.

18. Remove the sprag clutch from the planetary gear train. Remove the adjusting shim, the needle thrust bearing plate, the needle thrust bearing, the needle thrust bearing plate.

NOTE: The thrust bearing inside the planetary gear train cannot be disassembled.

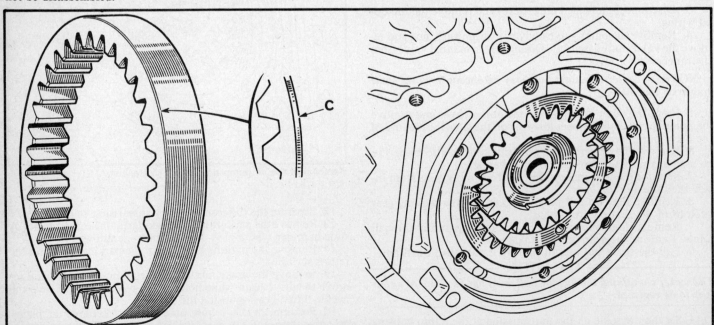

Removal or installation of the oil pump gears. Note beveled edge (C) (© Renault/AMC)

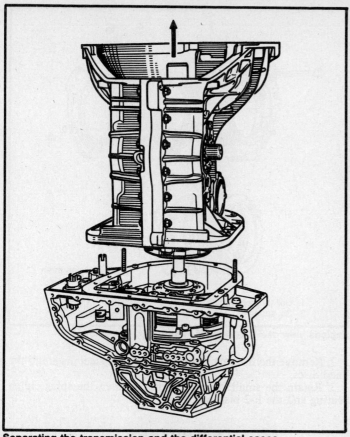

Separating the transmission and the differential cases
(© Renault/AMC)

Component Disassembly

E-1 CLUTCH

Disassembly

1. Remove the compression ring from the needle thrust bearing before removing the needle thrust bearing plate.

2. The turbine shaft and the hub are one piece and cannot be disassembled.

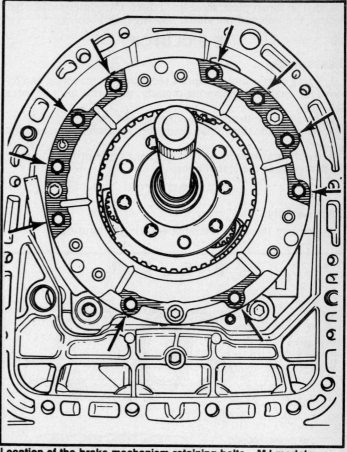

Location of the brake mechanism retaining bolts—MJ models
(© Renault/AMC)

3. Push downward on the E-1 piston housing and remove the retaining ring.

4. Disassemble the following after the retaining ring removal:
   a. The housing, and shaft.
   b. Apply compressed air to the piston housing input orifice and remove the piston.
   c. The diaphragm spring.

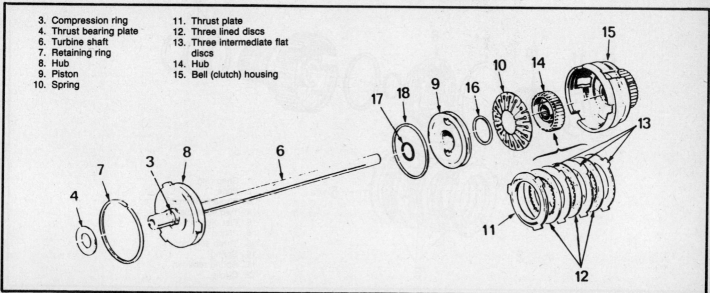

3. Compression ring	11. Thrust plate
4. Thrust bearing plate	12. Three lined discs
6. Turbine shaft	13. Three intermediate flat
7. Retaining ring	discs
8. Hub	14. Hub
9. Piston	15. Bell (clutch) housing
10. Spring	

Exploded view of E-1 clutches—MJ models (© Renault/AMC)

d. The thrust plate, three lined discs, three intermediate flat discs, the hub and the clutch housing (bell housing).

E-2 CLUTCH

Disassembly

1. Using a press tool, compress the clutch return spring and remove the snapring, the spring retainer, the spring and the three seal rings.
2. Remove the thrust plate snapring and the plate.
3. Remove the three lined discs, the two waved discs and the flat disc.
4. Apply compressed air to the bearing input orifice and push the piston from the clutch housing.

F-1 BRAKE

Disassembly

1. Remove the three retaining bolts in the housing.

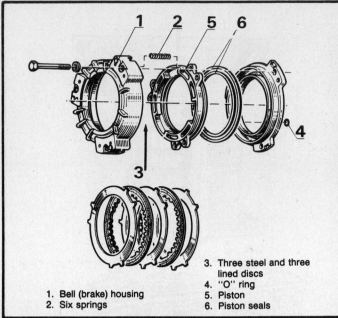

3. Three steel and three lined discs
4. "O" ring
5. Piston
6. Piston seals

1. Bell (brake) housing
2. Six springs

Explode view of F-2 brake—MJ models (© Renault/AMC)

2. Remove the housing, the six springs, the steel discs and the lined discs.
3. Retain the small "O" ring from between the sprag clutch bearing and the F-2 piston housing.

F-2 BRAKE

Disassembly

1. Remove the three retaining bolts in the housing.
2. Remove the housing, the six springs the steel and lined discs.
3. Retain the "O" ring located between the sprag clutch bearing and the F-1 piston housing.
4. Push the pistons out of the housings with compressed air. Remove the piston seals.

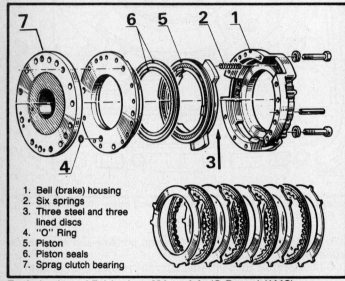

1. Bell (brake) housing
2. Six springs
3. Three steel and three lined discs
4. "O" Ring
5. Piston
6. Piston seals
7. Sprag clutch bearing

Explode view of F-1 brake—MJ models (© Renault/AMC)

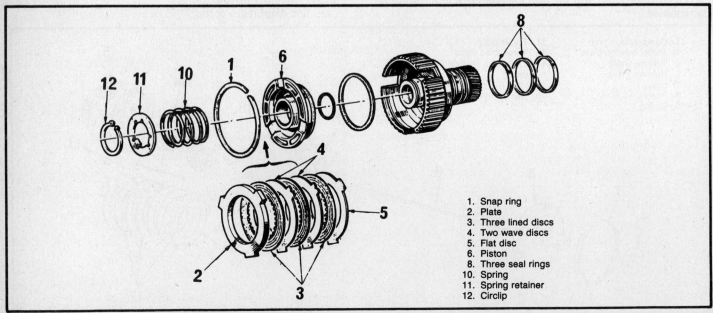

1. Snap ring
2. Plate
3. Three lined discs
4. Two wave discs
5. Flat disc
6. Piston
8. Three seal rings
10. Spring
11. Spring retainer
12. Circlip

Exploded view of E-2 clutches—MJ models (© Renault/AMC)

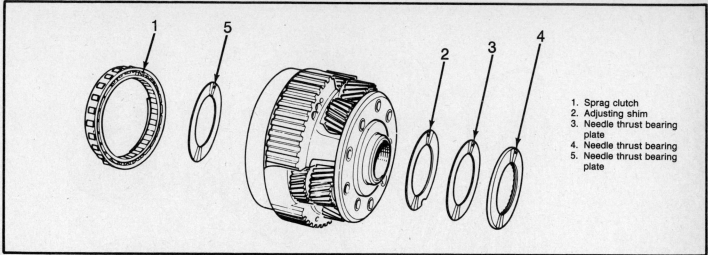

Sprag and thrust bearings and washers—MJ models (© Renault/AMC)

1. Sprag clutch
2. Adjusting shim
3. Needle thrust bearing plate
4. Needle thrust bearing
5. Needle thrust bearing plate

MB-1 MODELS

Disassembly

1. Place the transaxle on a clean work bench area and remove the converter.

2. Remove the four bolts on the step-down drive case and the remaining bolts on the converter and differential case. Separate the cases.

3. Remove the oil pan assembly.

4. Remove the sealed connection and its retaining clip from the valve body area.

5. Remove the valve body assembly from the case. Remove the two seals and plate.

NOTE: The center valve body bolts on the pressure outlet side and the bolt next to the inlet screen tube are locator bolts and must be replaced in the same location during the reassembly.

6. Remove the "Park" latch shaft and spring.

7. Remove the needle roller thrust bearing, snapring, reverse drive train, overrunning clutch and the F-1 clutch disc pack as a unit.

8. Remove the F-1 piston with air pressure applied through the apply port in the valve body case channels.

9. Remove the friction washer, the E-2 bell (clutch) housing the 1.5 mm thrust friction washer, the forward drive train and the E-1, E-2 clutch packs.

NOTE: The E-1 and E-2 clutch assemblies cannot be disassembled and must be replaced as a unit. Only the needle roller bearing can be replaced.

10. Remove the snapring, the F-1 piston holder sleeve, the F-2 clutch disc pack, the needle roller thrust bearing, the feed hub support and the F-2 cup assembly.

11. Remove the F-2 piston assembly and the oil pump gears.

12. The shift linkage and remaining parking linkage can be removed as required.

INSPECTION AND CLEANING

ALL TRANSAXLE MODELS

CAUTION

Do not use Trichlorethylene to clean the transaxle case and components. Harmful deposits can be left on the oil seals. Do not use rags with lint, only lint free shop rags.

1. Use alcohol, mineral spirits or a professional cleaning agent to clean the case and components.

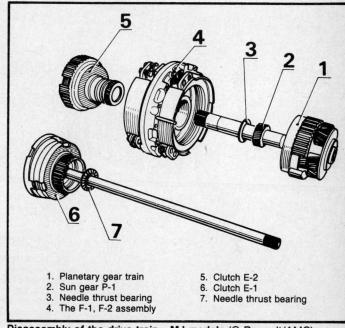

1. Planetary gear train
2. Sun gear P-1
3. Needle thrust bearing
4. The F-1, F-2 assembly
5. Clutch E-2
6. Clutch E-1
7. Needle thrust bearing

Disassembly of the drive train—MJ models (© Renault/AMC)

2. Use compressed air to dry the case and components after the cleaning process has been completed.

3. Use compressed air to blow out all the holes and channels in the following components;

  a. The transaxle case.
  b. The sprag clutch bearing.
  c. The forward sun gear.
  d. The reverse sun gear.
  e. The E-2 bell housing (ball valves).
  f. The E-1 piston (ball valves).
  g. The E-1 hub.
  h. The pump cover.
  i. The pump shaft.
  j. The turbine shaft.
  k. The stator support.
  l. The Converter oil return calibrating jet.
  m. The planetary gear carrier.

4. It is a normal overhaul procedure to replace the lined and unlined clutch discs during the disassembly and assembly of the transaxle.

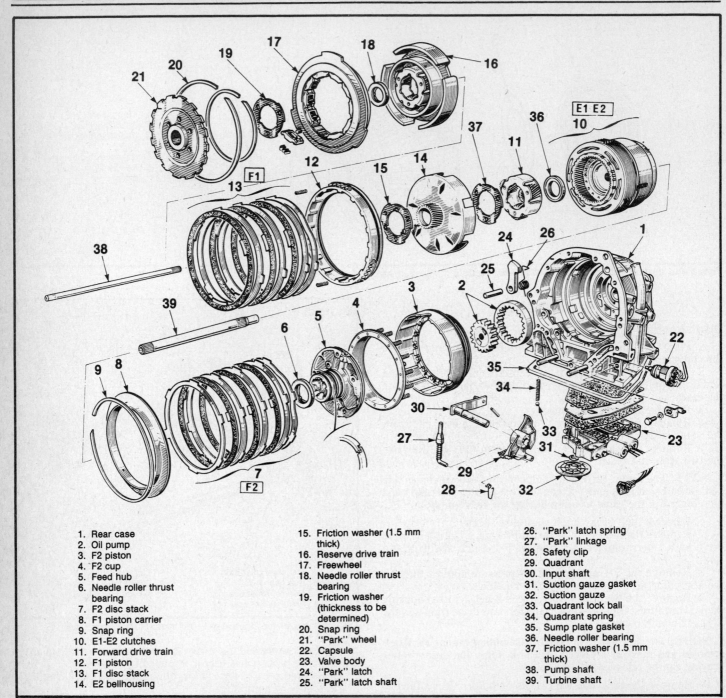

Exploded view of MB type rear case assembly (© Renault/AMC)

1. Rear case
2. Oil pump
3. F2 piston
4. F2 cup
5. Feed hub
6. Needle roller thrust bearing
7. F2 disc stack
8. F1 piston carrier
9. Snap ring
10. E1-E2 clutches
11. Forward drive train
12. F1 piston
13. F1 disc stack
14. E2 bellhousing

15. Friction washer (1.5 mm thick)
16. Reserve drive train
17. Freewheel
18. Needle roller thrust bearing
19. Friction washer (thickness to be determined)
20. Snap ring
21. "Park" wheel
22. Capsule
23. Valve body
24. "Park" latch
25. "Park" latch shaft

26. "Park" latch spring
27. "Park" linkage
28. Safety clip
29. Quadrant
30. Input shaft
31. Suction gauze gasket
32. Suction gauze
33. Quadrant lock ball
34. Quadrant spring
35. Sump plate gasket
36. Needle roller bearing
37. Friction washer (1.5 mm thick)
38. Pump shaft
39. Turbine shaft

5. After the cleaning of the components, lubricate the parts immediately with fluid to prevent rusting of metal components.

6. Inspect all sealing ring and "O" ring grooves for the condition of the seating areas. Replace any component showing worn or damaged grooves.

7. Check the condition of the gear teeth on the planetary gear unit and the gear cluster on their shafts.

8. To clean the converter without a professional cleaner, fill the converter with the proper grade of fluid. Invert the converter and allow it to drain for a period of time. Again, place the converter upright and remove the remaining fluid with a syringe from the center of the turbine hub.

9. Check the sealing surfaces on the converter, the stator support housing and the housing breather.

10. Inspect the condition of the oil pump gears and their housing. Be sure the drive shaft is re-useable, along with the cover.

11. The transmission case, the oil pump and ring gear wheel assembly are matched and the changing of one part always entails the replacement of the whole assembly.

12. Inspect the white metal sleeve on the E-1 clutch, the ring groove, the contact surfaces on the sealed junction box, the engagement shaft and all the sealing surfaces.

13. Check the condition of the intermediate clutch discs and that they slide easily on the hub splines and in the clutch housings (bell housings).

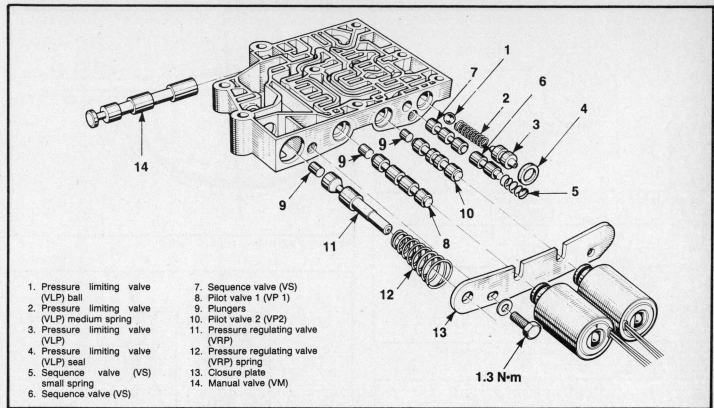

1. Pressure limiting valve (VLP) ball
2. Pressure limiting valve (VLP) medium spring
3. Pressure limiting valve (VLP)
4. Pressure limiting valve (VLP) seal
5. Sequence valve (VS) small spring
6. Sequence valve (VS)
7. Sequence valve (VS)
8. Pilot valve 1 (VP 1)
9. Plungers
10. Pilot valve 2 (VP2)
11. Pressure regulating valve (VRP)
12. Pressure regulating valve (VRP) spring
13. Closure plate
14. Manual valve (VM)

Exploded view of valve body components—typical (© Renault/AMC)

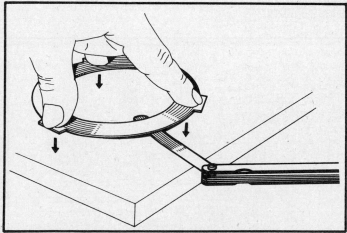

Checking the wave clearance of disc (© Renault/AMC)

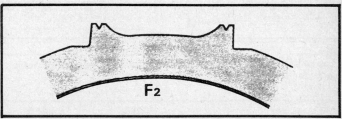

Identification of brake disc (© Renault/AMC)

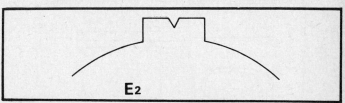

Identification of clutch disc (© Renault/AMC)

14. When installing the new steel wave plates, check the wave with a feeler gauge. Lay the disc flat on a flat surface and without exerting pressure on the disc, slip a feeler gauge blade between the disc and the flat surface. The clearance must be between 0.010-0.018 in. (0.25-0.45mm).

15. Change any bearing plates and thrust plates showing signs of overheating, poor surface conditions, run-out or taper.

CAUTION

If one of the assemblies has overheated, all needle bearings or thrust bearings must be replaced.

16. Be sure the oil seals fit tightly in their grooves. Measure the seal diameter at two points at right angles to each other, but do not squeeze the seal. Take an average of the two readings and compare it with the seal groove dimension.

17. The seal groove dimension should be 0.008-0.028 in. (0.2-0.7mm).

18. Change the seals without hesitation during the reassemble to avoid internal leak problems.

19. Check the clutch pistons for free movement of their relief check balls. Each ball should move freely in its socket and should not stick to its seat or to the crimped side. The ball travel should be approximately 0.0039 in. (1mm). Should the check balls not operate properly, the entire piston must be replaced.

20. The E-1 clutch bearing and the E-2 clutch bell housing have seal rings. Check the amount of wear on the ring sides, the condition of the bottoms of the ring grooves and the fit of the ring gaps, which must fit together in a flat manner. The gap play should be between 0.002-0.014 in. (0.05-0.35mm).

21. In addition to the checks as outlined in Step 20, inspect the

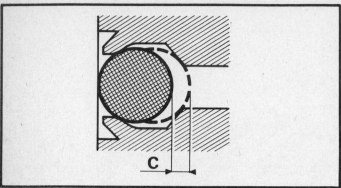

Piston check ball clearance (© Renault/AMC)

Incorrect and correct fitting of seal ring (© Renault/AMC)

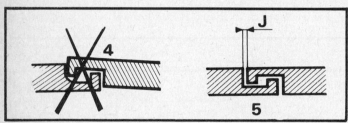

Incorrect (4) and correct (5) fittings of rings. J represents allowable tolerance (© Renault/AMC)

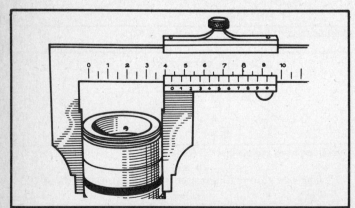

Measuring of white metal sleeve (© Renault/AMC)

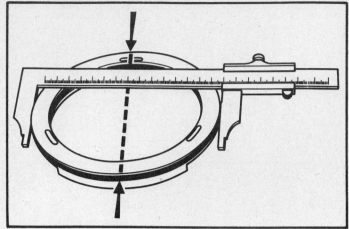

Measuring piston seal rings (© Renault/AMC)

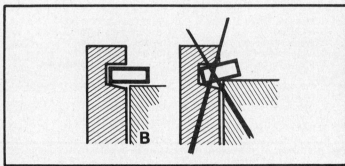

Correct (B) installation of snaprings and incorrect fitting (© Renault/AMC)

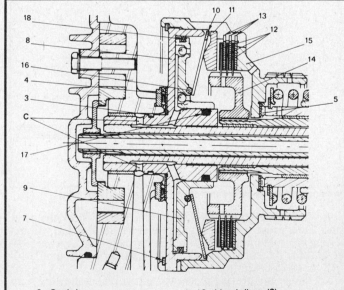

Assembly of E-1 clutch unit—typical (© Renault/AMC)

3. Seal ring
4. Needle thrust bearing plate
5. Needle thrust bearing
7. Circlip
8. Piston housing
9. Piston
10. Diaphragm spring
11. Thrust plate
12. Lined discs (3)
13. Flat intermediate discs (3)
14. Hub
15. Connecting bell housing
16. Diaphragm thrust ring
17. O ring
18. Rectangular seal
C. E1 piston oil feed hole

surface condition of the piston bore, the diaphragm spring for breakage, the hub, the fit of the two sleeves in the piston housing and the fit of the turbine shaft on the E-1 clutch assembly.

22. On the E-2 clutch assembly, check the piston bore, the return spring, spring retainer and the snapring.

23. In addition to checking the gears on the planetary gear assembly, check the condition of the white metal sleeves, the sprag clutch, its race surface, the needle bearing and its bearing plate.

NOTE: The sprag clutch can be replaced if necessary, but the planetary gear assembly must be replaced as a unit.

24. The valve body and regulator assembly must not be disassembled, according to the manufacturer. Only the solenoid balls can be changed. Should poor quality of shifting or damage to the clutches and brakes occur, the valve body and its regulator assembly must be changed.

Assembly of Components

MJ-1, MJ-3, MB-1 MODELS

E-1 CLUTCH

Assembly

1. Place the thrust ring on the piston.
2. Lubricate and install the two piston seals. Install the rectangular seal on the piston and the "O" ring on the E-1 piston sleeve.

NOTE: Lightly lubricate the bore and the part of the hub in which the piston will slide.

3. Place the piston into its housing with the flange upward, by pushing it in with the thumbs while tilting it back and forth.
4. Assemble the following into the housing, in their proper order;
   a. The hub with the recessed part facing upward.
   b. A lubricated steel disc followed by a lubricated lined disc, continuing until a total of three each have been installed.
   c. The thrust plate with the smooth side towards the lined disc.
   d. The diaphragm spring.
5. Install the piston into the connecting bell housing.
6. Install the snapring, positioning the ends between the two lugs on the piston housing. Be sure the snapring is properly seated in its groove.
7. Install the bearing plate for the needle thrust bearing. Install the seal ring after checking the ring gap play.
8. Check the operation of the E-1 components by applying air pressure to the piston through the apply hole in the hub.

E-2 CLUTCH

Assembly

1. After checking the ring gap play and the condition of the three grooves in the bell housing, install the three seal rings on the E-2 bell housing.
2. Lubricate the two piston seals and install the rectangular seal on the piston and the "O" ring on the piston hub in the E-2 bell housing.

NOTE: Be sure the seals fit properly in their grooves.

3. Install the piston into the bell housing and using a press, compress the spring to install the snapring. Guide the spring retainer during the compression.
4. Align the slots in the piston with the slots in the bell housing. Install in the following order, the following components:
   a. The thrust plate.
   b. A lubricated steel disc, followed by a lubricated lined disc, until a total of three steel discs and three lined discs are installed.
   c. Install the thrust plate with the punched mark surface towards the outside of the housing.
5. Install the snapring with the ends fully engaged with its groove.
6. Check the operation of the E-2 components by applying compressed air to the piston through the apply hole in the hub.

CHECKING AND ADJUSTING THE OPERATING ENDPLAY OF THE E-2 CLUTCH

Assembly

1. Place the assembly on a flat surface. The end play is checked

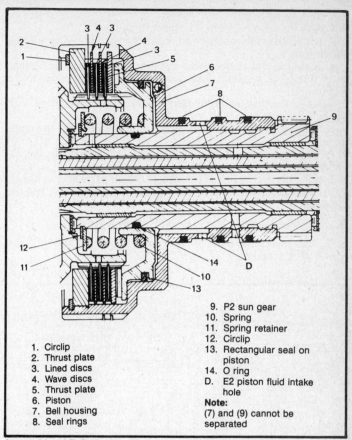

1. Circlip
2. Thrust plate
3. Lined discs
4. Wave discs
5. Thrust plate
6. Piston
7. Bell housing
8. Seal rings
9. P2 sun gear
10. Spring
11. Spring retainer
12. Circlip
13. Rectangular seal on piston
14. O ring
D. E2 piston fluid intake hole

Note:
(7) and (9) cannot be separated

Assembly of E-2 clutch unit—typical (© Renault/AMC)

with either a dial indicator and a special plate or with the use of a feeler gauge blade.

2. The clearance to be checked is between the piston and the steel disc, with the clutch pack against the snapring, without compressing the wave discs.
3. The play should be between 0.043-0.083 in. (1.1-2.1mm)
4. If the play is greater than specifications, a thicker thrust plate must be used.

Checking and Adjusting F-2 Operating Endplay

1. Install the piston without its seal into the F-2 piston housing.
2. Install in order:
   a. A flat disc 0.059 in. (1.5mm) thick.
   b. A lined disc.
   c. A waved disc, marked with two notches, 0.079 in. (2.0mm) thick.

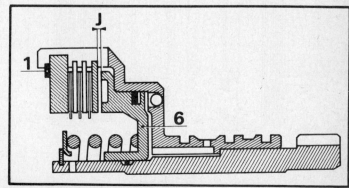

Checking operating clearance (J) between clutch disc and piston (G)—typical (© Renault/AMC)

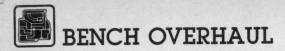
d. A lined disc.

e. A flat disc 0.059 in. (1.5mm) thick.

3. Install the bell housing and attach the assembly to the sprag clutch hub.

4. Install a dial indicator to the housing and with the gauge point resting on a spline of the first lined disc, set the gauge to the zero mark.

5. Raise the disc assembly pack so that it makes contact with the bell housing top.

6. Take measurements at several points and average the readings.

7. The end play should be between 0.028-0.067 in. (0.70-1.70mm).

8. If the play is outside this range, check all parts that would affect the tolerance, such as the piston, wave disc, lined disc and the housing.

Reassembly of the F-1 and F-2 Clutch brakes

1. Disassemble the previously assembled brake and hold the clutch pack together.

2. Lubricate the four seals for the F-1 and F-2 pistons and install them on the pistons and housings. Be sure the seals fit tightly into their grooves.

3. Place the "O" ring between the sprag clutch hub and the F-1 housing.

4. Install the F-1 piston into its housing carefully so as not to damage the seals.

5. Install the steel discs 0.059 in. (1.5mm) thick and the lined discs.

6. Place the six springs in the housing and cap the assembly with the F-1 bell housing.

7. Install the three F-1 assembly bolts into the sprag clutch hub.

NOTE: F-1 operating clearance is between 0.043-0.122 in. (1.1-3.1mm).

8. Invert the assembly and rest it on the F-1 bell housing.

9. Place the "O" ring between the sprag clutch hub and the F-2 housing.

10. Install the F-2 piston into its housing being careful not to damage the seals.

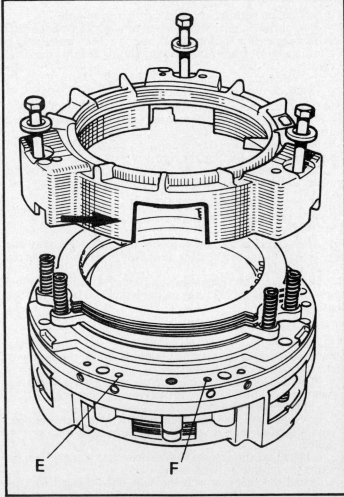

Air applied to E port to check F-1 piston operation and air applied to F port to check F-2 piston operation (© Renault/AMC)

11. Install the clutch pack previously selected, into the F-2 housing.

12. Place the six springs in their housings and cap the assembly with the F-2 bell housing. Install the three bolts into the F-1 sprag clutch assembly.

Assembly of F-1 and F-2 brake units (© Renault/AMC)

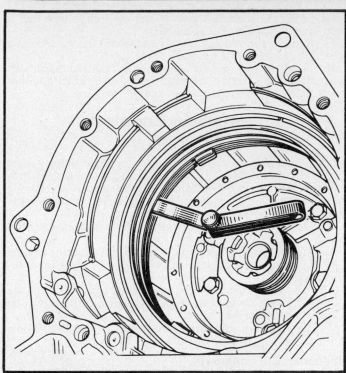

Checking the F-2 brake operating clearance—typical
(© Renault/AMC)

13. Check the F-1 and F-2 components with air pressure.
14. The air pressure is applied to the apply ports on the clutch housing.

PLANETARY GEAR

Assembly

1. Install the sprag clutch on the planetary gear train. The shoulder of the cage should face towards inside or bottom of the carrier.
2. Correctly install the thrust bearing plate.
3. Install the sun gear so that it centers and holds the inner thrust bearing.

Assembly of the Units into the Transaxle

MJ-1, MJ-3, MODELS

1. Place the E-1 assembly and the turbine shaft on a tube or pipe approximately 4 inches (100mm) in diameter.
2. Place the needle thrust bearing between the E-1 and P-2, with the pins facing towards P-2.
3. Roughly center the E-2 discs and slide the assembly onto the splines in the E-1 connecting bell housing.
4. Gently turn the assembly, without forcing, to avoid damaging the discs.
5. When all the discs have been properly placed, a play of approximately ⅛ in. (4mm) should exist between E-1 and E-2.

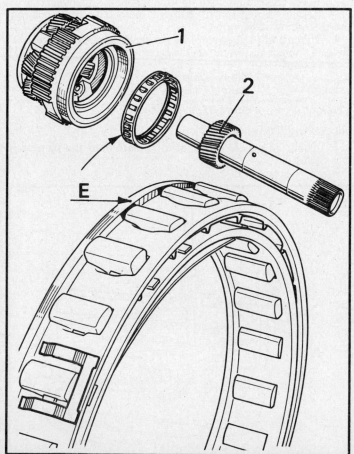

Assembly of sprag (E) in planetary gear train (1) along with P1 sun gear (2) (© Renault/AMC)

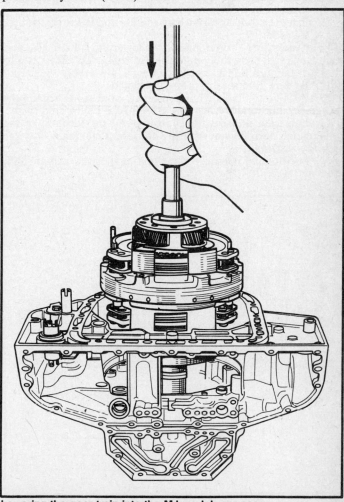

Lowering the gear train into the MJ model rear case
(© Renault/AMC)

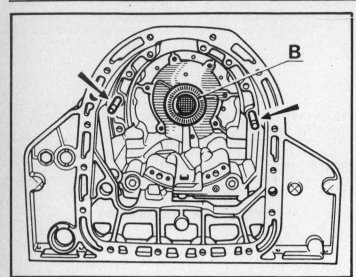

Location of needle thrust bearing (B) and use of the two guide bolts
(© Renault/AMC)

6. Lubricate the E-2 rings and their bearing surfaces on the sprag clutch hub.

7. Roughly center the F-2 discs and slowly lower the brake assembly onto E-2.

8. Proceed in the same manner for the E-2 unit.

9. Place the thrust bearing between P-2 and P-1, with the pins facing towards P-2.

10. Center the F-1 discs and slowly lower the P-1 sun gear and planetary carrier assembly onto the F-1 brake. To aid in assembly, turn the unit but do not force it.

11. Be sure all discs are properly aligned.

12. Install into the transmission case the thrust washer and the two guide stud to allow the unit assembly to be lowered easily.

13. Lubricate the seal ring housing and the location of the sprag clutch hub. Be sure there is no burrs that might interfere with the assembly.

14. Position the assembly while holding it by the turbine shaft.

Slowly lower the assembly, making sure the sprag clutch hub is lined up with the E-1, E-2 assemblies.

15. Remove the two guide studs and install the ten retaining bolts. Torque them to 15 ft. lbs.

16. Install the parking latch spring on the shaft and then install the parking latch. Install the shaft with the threaded hole upwards. Install the centering dowel and the snapring.

Transaxle Endplay
MJ MODELS

Before assembling the two-housings, the transaxle endplay must be checked and adjusted. The operating endplay must be 0.016-0.031 in. (0.4-0.8mm). The adjustment consists of determining the overall endplay and reducing it to within the acceptable tolerance by installing a shim of the appropriate thickness.

To determine the endplay, measurements must be made as follows:

a. The dimension between the needle thrust bearing and the differential housing contact surface. This will be known as dimension C.

b. The dimension between the planetary gear carrier and the transmission housing contact surface. This dimension will be known as dimension D.

c. The difference between dimensions D and C gives the overall endplay dimension, known as JT.

Measuring Dimension (C):

1. Install main shaft needle thrust bearing.

2. Using a straight edge and a depth gauge, measure dimension (A) between the output shaft and the housing contact surface.

3. Measure dimension (B) between the needle thrust bearing and the output shaft.

4. Dimension (C) between the needle thrust bearing and the housing contact surface is, therefore: C = A − B.

5. Example:

$$A = 72.10mm \ (2.839 \ in.)$$
$$minus \ B = 57.15mm \ (2.250 \ in.)$$

therefore C = 14.95mm (0.589 in.)

Measuring Dimension (D):

1. Install the needle thrust bearing plate onto the planetary gear carrier.

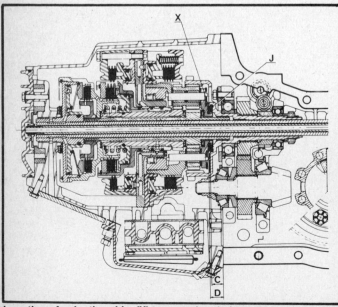

Location of selective shim (X) to control end play tolerance (J)—MJ models (© Renault/AMC)

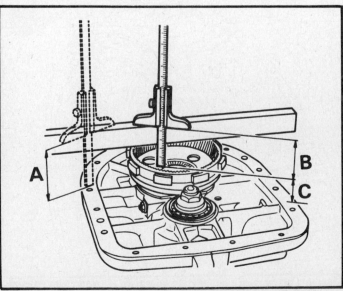

Measuring dimension A, B and C—MJ models (© Renault/AMC)

1222

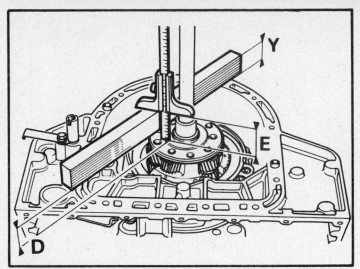

Measuring dimension D and Y—MJ models (© Renault/AMC)

2. Measure dimension (E) on the transmission case between the straight edge and the plate on the planetary gear carrier: D=E−Y
3. Y is the thickness of the straight edge.
4. Example:

E = 41.85mm (1.648 in.)
minus Y = 25.00mm (0.984 in.)

therefore D = 16.85mm (0.664 in.)

Overall End Play:

1. Overall end play (JT) between the planetary gear carrier and the needle thrust bearing is: JT=D−C.
2. Example:

D = 16.85mm (0.664 in.)
minus C = 14.95mm (0.589 in.)

therefore JT = 1.90mm (0.075 in.)

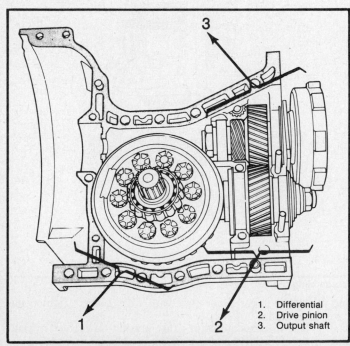

1. Differential
2. Drive pinion
3. Output shaft

Differential assembly—MJ models (© Renault/AMC)

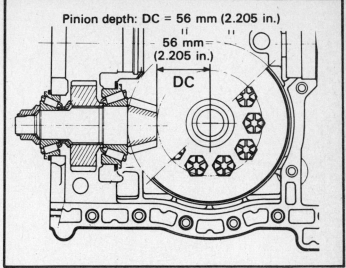

Pinion depth: DC = 56 mm (2.205 in.)

56 mm (2.205 in.)

DC

Pinion depth—MJ models (© Renault/AMC)

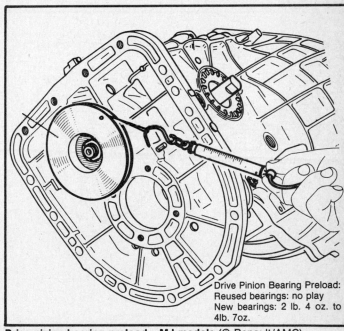

Drive Pinion Bearing Preload:
Reused bearings: no play
New bearings: 2 lb. 4 oz. to 4lb. 7oz.

Drive pinion bearing preload—MJ models (© Renault/AMC)

Determining Shim Thickness:

1. The desired operating end play, lets say 0.6mm (0.024 in.), will be obtained by inserting a shim (X) which will be equal to: X=JT−0.6mm (0.024 in.).
2. Example: X = 1.90mm −0.6mm = 1.30mm

(X = 0.075 in. −0.024 in. = 0.051 in.)

3. Shims are available in the following thicknesses:
0.25, 0.50, 0.80, 1.00, 1.30, 1.50, 1.75, 2.00, 2.25, 2.50mm
4. So as not to be confused with the needle thrust bearing plate, the adjustment shims are brown and have a notch.
5. If the shim calculation comes out to zero or greater than 2.5mm (0.098 in.), check that:

    a. all needle thrust bearings are in position
    b. the sun gears are properly meshed
    c. the discs are properly seated on the splines.

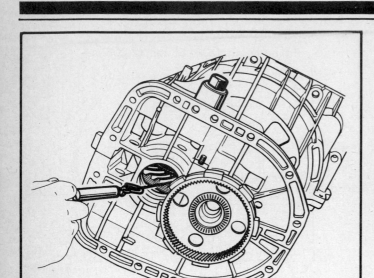

Differential Bearing Preload:
Reused bearings: no play

New bearings: 2 lb. 4 oz. to 4lb. 7oz.

Differential bearing preload—MJ models (© Renault/AMC)

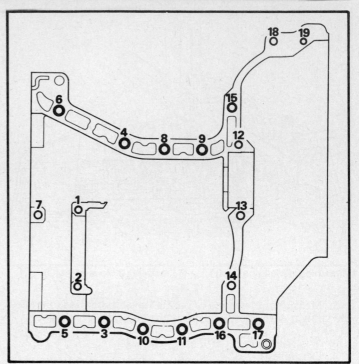

Sequence of bolt tightening to 14 ft. lbs. torque —MJ models (© Renault/AMC)

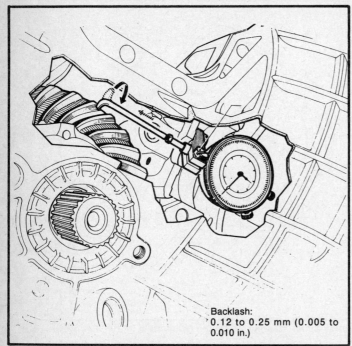

Backlash:
0.12 to 0.25 mm (0.005 to 0.010 in.)

Ring and pinion back lash—MJ models (© Renault/AMC)

Assembling the Two Cases

1. Install the needle thrust bearing on the output shaft in the differential case.

2. Install the endplay adjusting shim that was previously selected. Shim should have a notch.

3. Install the needle thrust plate.

4. Be sure the oil seal is correctly installed on the transmission case.

5. Install the 0.276 in. (7.0mm) diameter guide studs on the transmission case.

6. Install the centering dowels and coat the sealing surface with gasket sealer. Install the gasket.

7. Lubricate the turbine shaft and slowly lower the differential case onto the transmission case. Tighten the attaching bolts

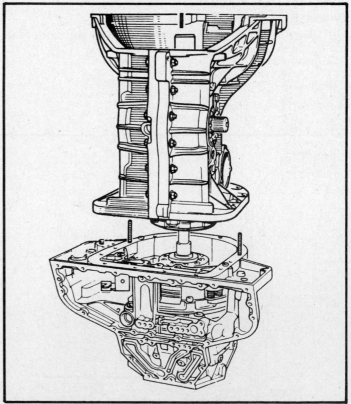

Assembling the two cases—MJ models (© Renault/AMC)

and install the lower cover plate with a dry gasket. Tighten the cover plate bolts.

8. Place the dial indicator gauge bracket on the cover plate and set the point of the gauge on the E-1 shaft.

9. Pull on the turbine shaft and set the gauge to zero.

10. Push the turbine shaft back into the unit and read the endplay on the dial indicator gauge. The endplay should be 0.016-0.032 in. (0.4-0.8mm).

11. When the endplay is correct, finish assembling the two housings and arrange the wiring clips correctly.

12. Install the sealed junction plug equipped with a new "O" ring.

13. Install the assembled sector and control shaft, being sure the "O" ring is in place. Install the assembled parking rod with its end in its housing and the control sector. Install the roll pin.

14. Install the valve body, being sure that both centering dowels are positioned on the valve body and that the two toothed quadrants are properly meshed when the selector lever is in *park* position.

15. Install the valve body on the housing and engage the manual valve on its ball joint. Tighten the bolts to their proper torque.

16. Connect the sealed junction plug and check that the marks on the valve body, the solenoid ball valves and on the plugs all match. Position the magnet on the solenoid ball valve retaining clamp.

17. Lubricate and install the inner and outer gears, aligning the marks made during the disassembly. Chamfer face downward into housing.

18. Install the pump drive shaft and engage the drive shaft lugs to the inner gear lugs.

19. Lubricate the "O" ring for the filter suction pipe and a slip it over the end of the pipe. Push the pipe into the housing carefully to avoid damage to the "O" ring.

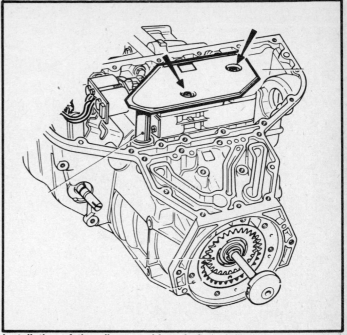

Installation of the oil pump drive shaft and filter assembly—MJ models (© Renault/AMC)

25. Install the governor/computer with its seal, the vacuum diaphragm (capsule), the wiring and the dipstick.

Assembly

MB-1 MODELS

1. Install the oil pump gears and make sure they rotate freely in the case.

2. Install the clutches and brakes into their housings in the same manner as outlined in the Assembly of Component Section.

3. Install the F-2 piston and the piston cup into the case. Be sure the springs enter their seats properly.

4. Using guide bolts, install the feed support hub with its rings installed, into the case. Install the bolts and tighten alternately and evenly.

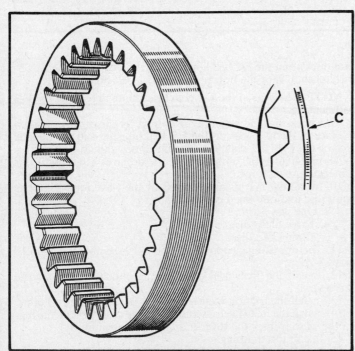

Chamfer on pump gear edge is to be placed downward into the housing—MJ models (© Renault/AMC)

20. Install the oil filter and secure it with its two bolts.

21. Install the oil pan and retain it with the retaining bolts.

22. Install the stator support with the aid of a guide bolt in one of the bolt holes. Lubricate the turbine shaft and install the stator support.

23. Lubricate the converter oil seal and install the seal with a seal installer tool.

24. Lubricate the converter white metal sleeve, the turbine shaft and the pump shaft splines. Install the converter assembly and install a converter holding tool.

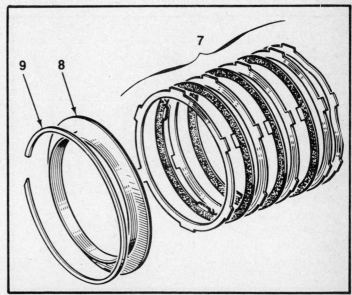

Assembly of the F-2 discs (7), piston carrier (8) and snapring (9)—MB models (© Renault/AMC)

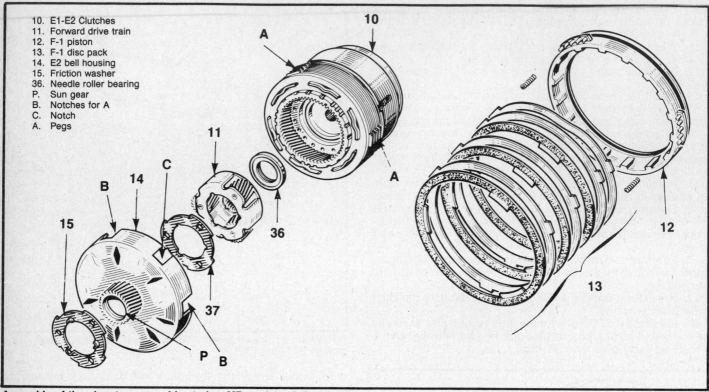

10. E1-E2 Clutches
11. Forward drive train
12. F-1 piston
13. F-1 disc pack
14. E2 bell housing
15. Friction washer
36. Needle roller bearing
P. Sun gear
B. Notches for A
C. Notch
A. Pegs

Assembly of the planetary gear drive train—MB models (© Renault/AMC)

5. Install the needle roller bearing and the F-2 brake steel clips. Install one wave form disc, one plain disc and one lined disc alternately as follows:

    a. One wave form disc.
    b. Four plain discs.
    c. Three lined discs.

6. Install the F-1 piston sleeve and the snapring.

7. Check the F-2 operating clearance which should be 0.050-0.130 in. (1.3-3.2mm). Check and replace the disc assembly if the clearance is incorrect.

8. Assemble the E-1, E-2 clutches, install the needle roller bearing, the forward drive train, the friction thrust washer (1.5

mm thick), and the E-2 bell housing. The three pegs of the E-1, E-2 clutches fit into the notches of the E-2 bell housing.

NOTE: The pegs of the F-2 clutches fit into notches of the E-2 bell housing.

9. Check that the assembly is correct by measuring between the face of the hub gear on the E-2 bell housing and the outside face of the E-1, E-2 clutches. The clearance should be 1.598 ± 0.028 in. (40.6 ± 0.07mm). Check the order of assembly if this dimension is incorrect.

10. Install the F-1 piston followed by the wave form disc, one plain disc and one lined disc as follows:

    a. One wave disc.
    b. Three plain discs.
    c. Three lined discs.

11. The operating clearance for the F-1 assembly is 0.03-0.10 in. (0.8-2.7mm).

12. Install the freewheel overrunning clutch on the reverse drive train.

13. Install the friction washer which is 0.05 in. (1.5mm) thick.

14. Install the freewheel assembly into the case. Be sure the lugs on the washer inter the reverse drive train assembly.

15. Install the snapring.

16. Install the sealed junction box and its clip.

17. Install the manual valve of the valve body into the toothed quadrant. Position the valve body in position with the two seals and the plate.

18. Hand tighten the remaining valve body bolts in sequence to their proper torque.

19. The oil pan and gasket can be installed along with the other outside components.

Adjustment of the Rear Case

Before Attachment To the Differential Assembly

NOTE: If any of the internal components of the transmission assembly have been replaced, the following two adjustments outlined must be performed with the use of a special measured tool.

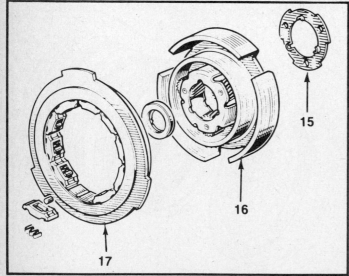

Assembly of freewheel (17) into the reverse drive train (16) with thrust washer (15) (© Renault/AMC)

MB-1 Transaxle

REVERSE GEAR TRAIN ADJUSTMENT

1. Shim 19 is used for adjustment.
2. 18 is the needle roller thrust bearing.
3. 16 is the reverse drive train.
4. Measure dimensions A and B. Subtract B from A. X = A-B
5. Overall clearance: JT = X + C

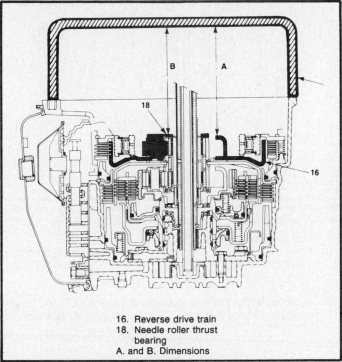

16. Reverse drive train
18. Needle roller thrust bearing
A. and B. Dimensions

Reverse gear train adjustment with special tool to find A and B dimensions—MB models (© Renault/AMC)

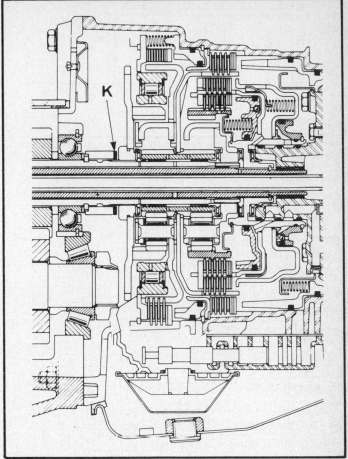

Location of shim "K"—MB models (© Renault/AMC)

6. The average reverse gear train operating clearance is 0.4mm (.016 in.).
7. The shim (19) thickness is: JT—0.4mm (.016 in.)
8. Example:
   A = 158.2mm (6.228 in.)
   B = 156.9mm (6.177 in.)
   C = 1.3mm (0.051 in.)
   X = A-B = 158.2mm (6.228 in.)-156.9mm (6.177 in.) = 1.3mm (0.015 in.)
   JT = X + C = 1.3mm (0.015 in.) + 1.3mm (0.015 in.) = 2.6mm (0.102 in.)
9. Shim thickness required: 2.6mm (0.102 in.)-0.4mm (0.016 in.) = 2.2mm (0.086 in.)
10. Shim thicknesses available: 1.5 (0.059 in.)-2 (0.079 in.)-2.6 (0.102 in.) and 3.2mm (0.126 in.).
11. In the above example, a shim is selected which gives an operating clearance as close to the ideal as possible, in this case one of 2mm (0.079 in.)
12. Measure dimension (C) on "park" wheel (21).

END PLAY ADJUSTMENT

1. Shim (K) is used for end play adjustment.
2. Measure dimension G. It equals F-H.
3. Measure dimension E. It equals H-D.
4. Over end play equals G-E.
5. Average operating clearance equals 0.8 mm (0.031 in.).
6. Based on the information above, the thickness of shim (K). = overall end play—0.8 mm (0.031 in.)

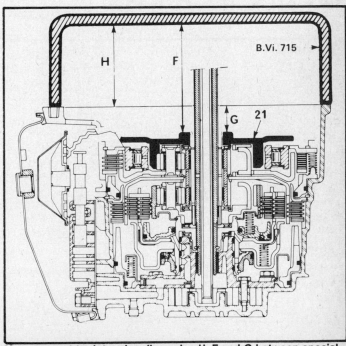

Measurement to determine dimension H, F and G between special tool and the park gear—MB models (© Renault/AMC)

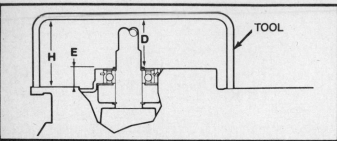

Measurement to determine dimension H, E and D, using special tool—MB models (© Renault/AMC)

7. **Example:**
   H = 120mm (4.724 in.)
   F = 145.3mm (5.720 in.)
   D = 97.6mm (3.843 in.)

   $$\frac{\begin{array}{l}F = 145.3mm\ (5.720\ in.)\\ H = 120mm\ (4.724\ in.)\end{array}}{G = 25.3mm\ (0.996\ in.)}$$

   $$\frac{\begin{array}{l}H = 120mm\ (4.725\ in.)\\ D = 97.6mm\ (3.843\ in.)\end{array}}{E = 22.4mm\ (0.882\ in.)}$$

   $$\frac{\begin{array}{l}G = 25.3mm\ (.996\ in.)\\ E = 22.4mm\ (.882\ in.)\end{array}}{\text{overall endplay} = 2.9mm\ (.114\ in.)}$$

   $$\frac{\begin{array}{l}\text{overall endplay} = 2.9mm\ (.114\ in.)\\ \text{desired endplay} = 0.8mm\ (.032\ in.)\end{array}}{\text{required shim} = 2.1mm\ (.082\ in.)}$$

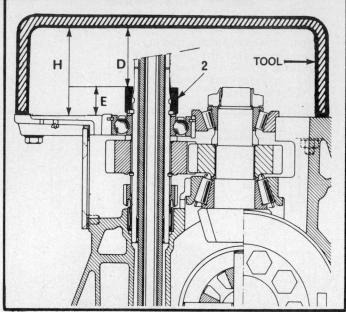

Measurement to determine dimension H, D and E between special tool and bearing spacer (2)—MB models (© Renault/AMC)

8. Shim thickness available:

0.25mm (0.010 in.)	1.7mm (0.066 in.)
0.7mm (0.003 in.)	2.3mm (0.090 in.)
1.1mm (0.043 in.)	

9. In the example shown, a shim, 2.3mm (0.090 in.) thick would be selected to provide the nearest to ideal clearance of 0.3mm (0.031 in.).

S SPECIFICATIONS

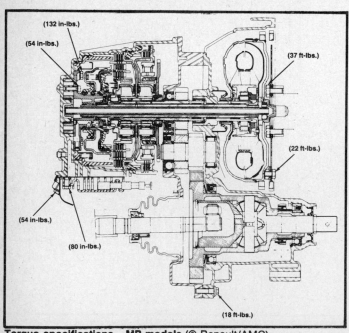

Torque specifications—MB models (© Renault/AMC)

Labels: (132 in-lbs.), (54 in-lbs.), (37 ft-lbs.), (22 ft-lbs.), (54 in-lbs.), (80 in-lbs.), (18 ft-lbs.)

SPECIAL TOOLS

Mot. 50—Torque wrench or equivalent beam type torque wrench

Mot. 593—Drain plug wrench (8 mm square drive)

B.Vi. 466-04—Oil pressure gauge

B.Vi. 31-01—Set of 3 roll pin drifts

B.Vi. 465—Converter oil seal replacement tool and converter holding lug

B.Vi. 883—Differential outside band installer

B.Vi. 905—Speedometer shaft seal replacement tool

B.Vi. 945—Planetary oil seal installing mandrel

B.Vi. 946—Planetary snap ring installer

B.Vi. 947—Intermediary case bearing installer

B.Vi. 955—Differential pinion bearing preload measuring tool

B.Vi. 951—Differential oil seal installer

B.Vi. 958—Diagnostic Tester

B.Vi. 959—Output shaft circlip installing tool

B.Vi. 952—Feed hub aligning dowels and front piston removing tool

B.Vi. 953—Step down driven gear holding tool

B.Vi. 961—Differential pinion bearing race installing tool

B.Vi. 715—Tool from B.Vi. 710 kit

B.Vi. 962—Converter oil seal installing tool

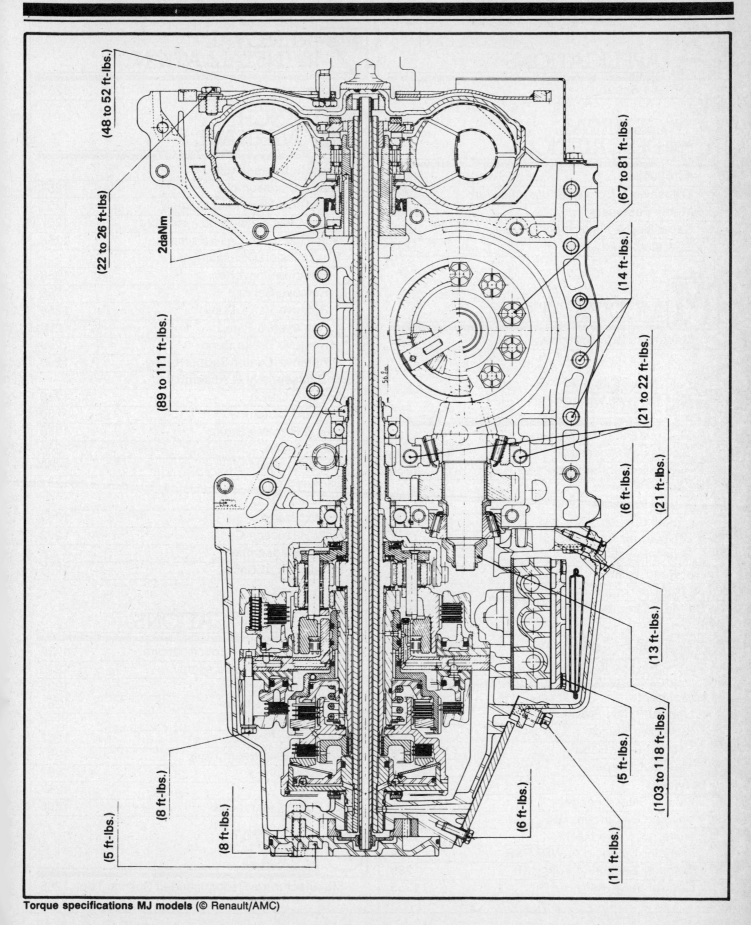

Torque specifications MJ models (© Renault/AMC)

INDEX

SUBARU
3 SPEED • 4 SPEED
Automatic Transaxle

APPLICATIONS

1981-84 SUBARU

GENERAL DESCRIPTION

The 4WD automatic transmission is basically composed of the conventional Subaru front wheel drive automatic transmission. The basic construction is unchanged from the current automatic transmission. Along with the adoption of the 4WD system, the final reduction case and transmission case have been changed thoroughly, and an oil seal holder has been newly introduced in the reduction drive gear portion. The hydraulic clutch, planetary gear, control valve and other elementary components of the automatic transmission section are unchanged from those of the current automatic transmission.

The centrifugal lockup torque converter and the transfer clutch are the main differences on the 4WD automatic transmission. The transfer clutch is operated by a transfer valve and a solenoid. When the solenoid is not energized, the transfer valve is closed and there is no line pressure to the transfer clutch circuit. When the transfer clutch is not engaged the vehicle will be in front wheel drive (FWD). When the solenoid is energized by depressing the 4WD selector switch, the transfer valve is opened allowing the line pressure to flow to the transfer clutch circuit. This will engage the transfer clutch and put the vehicle in 4WD.

The automatic transmission can be separated into two assemblies, the transmission assembly, and the differential and reduction assemblies. Each assembly can be replaced as an assembly and each may be disassembled or assembled independently of the other.

Some of the easy servicing features that are mentioned are as follows.

1. The governor valve which may cause trouble is installed on the outside of the transmission. It can easily be removed and installed.

2. The brake band can be adjusted from the outside of the transmission.

3. The number of adjusting points has been decreased through the use of multi-disc clutches instead of brake bands.

4. Use of only one oil pump and a greater number of efficient needle bearings reduces transmission internal loss to a minimum.

5. The throttle pressure in the control valve assembly, which varies with the accelerator opening, is controlled by intake-manifold vacuum. This eliminates the need of linkage or control cables and makes accelerator operation easy.

6. As automatic transmission fluid cannot be used as a lubricating oil for the hypoid gear, this circuit has been simplified by making the transmission fluid pass through the hollow oil pump drive shaft.

The differential mechanism with a final reduction system is installed between the torque converter and the automatic transmission. The differential case contains the first reduction gear and the governor and speedometer drive gear, which can be removed as an assembly.

Since hypoid gears are used for the final reduction system, hypoid gear oil must be used for proper lubrication. For this reason the final reduction system is separated by oil seals from the other parts of the transmission where an automatic transmission fluid is used.

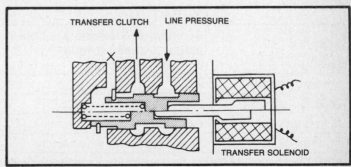

Transfer valve (©Fuji Heavy Industries Ltd.)

1231

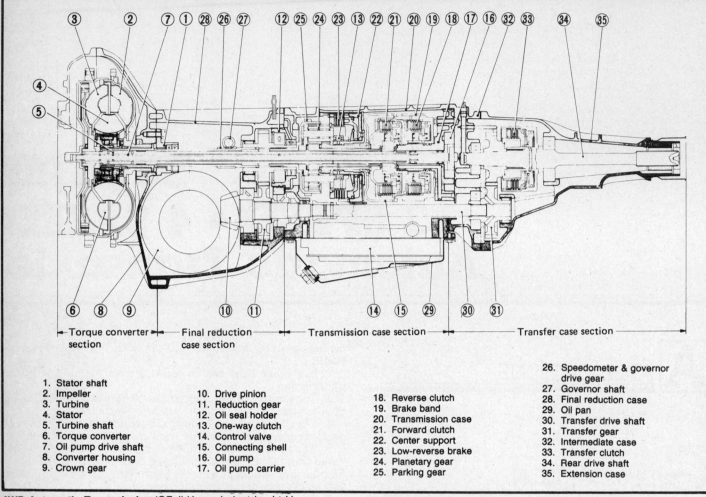

4WD Automatic Transmission (©Fuji Heavy Industries Ltd.)

1. Stator shaft	10. Drive pinion	18. Reverse clutch
2. Impeller	11. Reduction gear	19. Brake band
3. Turbine	12. Oil seal holder	20. Transmission case
4. Stator	13. One-way clutch	21. Forward clutch
5. Turbine shaft	14. Control valve	22. Center support
6. Torque converter	15. Connecting shell	23. Low-reverse brake
7. Oil pump drive shaft	16. Oil pump	24. Planetary gear
8. Converter housing	17. Oil pump carrier	25. Parking gear
9. Crown gear		

26. Speedometer & governor drive gear
27. Governor shaft
28. Final reduction case
29. Oil pan
30. Transfer drive shaft
31. Transfer gear
32. Intermediate case
33. Transfer clutch
34. Rear drive shaft
35. Extension case

Section labels: Torque converter section · Final reduction case section · Transmission case section · Transfer case section

Transmission and Converter Identification

TRANSMISSION

The transmission can be identified by the 11th letter in the vehicle identification number located on the bulkhead panel of the engine compartment. The automatic transmission 11th letter code is as follows.

C. Gunma manufacture—Automatic transmission
F. Gunma manufacture—4WD Automatic transmission

CONVERTER

Type	Symmetric, 3-element, single stage, 2-phase torque converter coupling
Stall torque ratio	2:1
Nominal diameter	236mm (9.29 in.)
Stall speed	2,300-2,500 rpm
One-way clutch	Sprag type one-way clutch

NOTE: The stall speed for the 4WD automatic transmission with a turbo charged engine is 2,700-2,900 rpm.

Metric Fasteners

The metric fastener dimensions are very close to the dimensions of the familiar inch system fasteners. For this reason, replacement fasteners must have the same measurement and strength as those removed.

Do not attempt to interchange metric fasteners for inch system fasteners. Mismatched or incorrect fasteners can result in damage to the transmission unit through malfunctions, breakage or possible personal injury.

Care should be taken to reuse the fasteners in the same location as removed.

Capacities

The conventional Subaru automatic transmission has a fluid capacity of 5.9-6.3 US qts. (5.6-6.0 liters). The 4WD automatic transmission has a fluid capacity of 6.3-6.8 US qts. (6.0-6.4 liters).

FLUID SPECIFICATIONS

Texaco: Texamatic Fluid 6673—Dexron®
Caltex: Texamatic Fluid 6673—Dexron®
Castrol: Castrol TQ—Dexron®
BP: BP Autran—Dexron®
Mobil: Mobil ATF—220

Checking Fluid Level

Checking ATF level and quality is essential to prevent various kinds of transmission trouble resulting from lack or deterioration of fluid.

1. If fluid level in the transmission is too low, clutches and band will slip and ultimatley be damaged. This is because the air sucked by the oil pump and mixed into the fluid will deteriorate the quality of fluid by producing sludge.

2. Too much fluid causes the same problem as to little fluid, because excessive fluid is stirred up by gears to generate air bubbles.

PROCEDURE FOR CHECKING FLUID LEVEL

1. Warm the transmission up until the fluid temperature comes into the range of from 60-80°C (140-176°F). Generally, this will be attained after 5-10 km (3-6 miles) running.

2. Stop the car on level ground.

3. Shift the selector lever to the "P" position and check the fluid level while the engine is kept idling.

4. If necessary, refill the recommended fluid up to the upper level mark on the level gauge with the engine idling and selector lever in "P" position. Be careful not to add fluid beyond the upper level mark. The capacity difference between the lower and upper marks on the level gauge corresponds to a fluid capacity of 0.4 liter.

5. Change fluid at the specified intervals.

NOTE: Use a nylon rag to wipe the dipstick so that the level gauge is kept free from waste threads. Push the level gauge all the way into the filler tube and quickly pull it out before it is splashed with fluid beyond the true indication of fluid level. If it becomes necessary to frequently refill the fluid it is an indication of a leak in the transmission. Immediate repair is required to prevent damage to the transmission. The amount of fluid that can be changed is usually 2.5-3.0 liters (2.6-3.2 US qt, 2.2-2.6 Imp qt).

DIFFERENTIAL

The kind of oil is API classification GL-5 and the SAE viscosity number is 75W-80. The capacity is 0.8-1.2 liter (1.3 US qt, 1.1 Imp qt). Inspect oil level at the specified intervals and, if necessary, refill with the recommended oil, up to the upper level mark on the level gauge. The capacity difference between the lower and upper marks on the level gauge corresponds to an oil capacity of 0.4 liter. Replace the differential gear oil at the specified intervals.

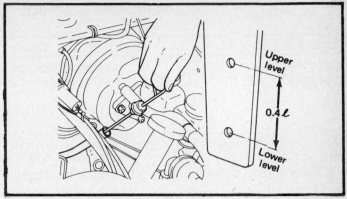

Checking the fluid levels (©Fuji Heavy Industries Ltd.)

NOTE: When replenishing the gear oil, always fill it up to the upper level mark (1.2 liter) on the level gauge. When replenishing or checking the gear oil, always keep the car in level.

The Governor Driven Gear

The 1979 governor driven gear is being incorrectly installed in the 1980 and later vehicles. The problem with this procedure is that this gear will last approximately 700-1,000 miles due to improper contact with the drive gears. The major difference between these two gears is the diameter. The 1979 governor driven gear (part no.# 440-847-000) is easily recognized by a groove cut in the metal portion of the governor shaft. The difference between these two gears are as follow: The 1977-79 governor driven gear (part no.# 440-847-000) diameter is 0.690 in. and the diameter for the 1980 and later governor driven gear (part no.# 440-847-100) is 0.765 in. The length for both of these gears is 1.683 in.

CLUTCH AND BAND APPLICATION CHART
Subaru 2WD and 4WD

Selector Position	Reverse Clutch	Forward Clutch	Brake Band	Low/Reverse Brake	One-Way Clutch
Neutral	Off	Off	Off	Off	Off
Park	Off	Off	Off	On	Off
Reverse	On	Off	Off	On	Off
D (1st gear)	Off	On	Off	Off	On
D (2nd gear)	Off	On	On	Off	Off
D (3rd gear)	On	On	Off	Off	Off
D (kickdown)	Off	On	On	Off	Off
2 range	Off	On	On	Off	Off
1 range	Off	On	Off	On	Off

CHILTON'S THREE "C's" DIAGNOSIS CHART
Subaru

Condition	Cause	Correction
Car does not move in "D" (but runs in "2", "1" and "R")	a) Manual linkage adjustment b) Oil pressures low c) Control valve assembly	a) Adjust as required b) Check pressure readings to make determination c) Clean or overhaul control valve assembly
Card does not move in "D", "2" and "1" (but runs in "R"), slips easily or is difficult to accelerate	a) Manual linkage b) Oil level flow c) Low oil pressure d) Control valve assembly malfunction e) Engine performance poor	a) Adjust manual linkage b) Check and add fluid c) Check pressure readings to make determination d) Clean or overhaul valve body e) Tune up engine
Car does not move in "R" (but runs in "D", "2" and "1"), slips easily or is difficult to accelerate	a) Manual linkage adjustment b) Low oil pressure c) Control valve assembly malfunction	a) Adjust manual linkage b) Check pressure readings to make determination c) Clean or overhaul valve body
Car does not move in all speed ranges or car moves sluggishly	a) Transmission fluid level b) Manual linkage c) Low oil pressure d) Control valve assembly malfunction	a) Check fluid level and add as required b) Adjust manual linkage c) Check pressures to make determination d) Clean or overhaul valve body
Maximum speed too low or insufficient acceleration	a) Transmission fluid level b) Manual linkage c) Low oil pressure d) Stall speed e) Brake band adjustment f) Control valve assembly malfunction g) Engine performance poor	a) Check fluid level and add as required b) Adjust manual linkage c) Check pressures to make determination d) Check and adjust stall speed e) Adjust brake band f) Clean or overhaul valve body g) Tune up engine
Car is braked when shifted to "R"	a) Oil condition b) Brake band adjustment	a) Check oil, add if necessary; change and clean oil screen if necessary b) Adjust brake band
Failure to shift automatically from 1st to 2nd speed	a) Manual linkage b) Vacuum diaphragm c) Downshift solenoid, kickdown switch	a) Adjust manual linkage b) Check and replace vacuum diaphragm c) Check and adjust, or replace downshift solenoid or kickdown switch
Failure to shift automatically from 2nd to 3rd speed	a) Manual linkage b) Vacuum diaphragm c) Downshift solenoid, kickdown switch d) Control valve assembly malfunction e) Governor valve f) Brake band adjustment g) Low oil pressure	a) Adjust manual linkage b) Check and replace vacuum diaphragm c) Check and adjust or replace downshift solenoid or kickdown switch d) Clean or overhaul valve body e) Replace governor valve f) Adjust brake band g) Check oil pressure to make determination

CHILTON'S THREE "C's" DIAGNOSIS CHART
Subaru

Condition	Cause	Correction
Running speed at which shifting occurs from 1st to 2nd or 2nd to 3rd is too high	a) Vacuum diaphragm	a) Check and replace vacuum diaphragm
	b) Downshift solenoid, kickdown switch	b) Check and adjust or replace downshift solenoid or kickdown switch
	c) Low oil pressure	c) Check pressures to make determination
	d) Control valve assembly malfunction	d) Clean or overhaul valve body
	e) Governor valve	e) Check and replace governor valve
Shifting straight from 1st to 3rd	a) Ignition switch and starter motor	a) Check ignition switch and starter motor operation
	b) Control valve assembly malfunction	b) Clean or overhaul valve body
	c) Governor valve	c) Check and replace governor valve
	d) Brake band	d) Adjust brake band
	e) Servo feed pipes	e) Check and replace servo feed pipes
Excessive shock is felt when shifting from 1st to 2nd or from 2nd to 3rd	a) Vacuum diaphragm	a) Check and replace vacuum diaphragm
	b) Low oil pressure	b) Check pressure to make determination
	c) Stall speed	c) Check and adjust stall speed
	d) Control valve assembly	d) Clean or overhaul valve body
	e) Brake band	e) Adjust brake band
Failure to shift from 3rd to 2nd	a) Vacuum diaphragm	a) Check and replace vacuum diaphragm
	b) Control valve assembly	b) Clean or overhaul valve body
	c) Governor valve	c) Check and replace governor valve
	d) Low oil pressure	d) Check pressures to make determination
Failure to shift from 2nd to 1st or from 3rd to 1st	a) Vacuum diaphragm	a) Check and replace vacuum diaphragm
	b) Control valve assembly	b) Clean or overhaul valve body
	c) Governor valve	c) Check and replace governor valve
	d) Brake band	d) Adjust brake band
Occurrence of downshifting from 2nd to 1st or upshifting from 2nd to 3rd when selector lever is placed in "2" position	a) Manual linkage	a) Check and adjust manual linkage
	b) Low oil pressure	b) Check pressures to make determination
	c) Control valve assembly	c) Clean or overhaul valve body
Failure to shift down from 3rd to 2nd when selector lever is shifted to "1"	a) Fluid level	a) Check and add fluid as necessary
	b) Manual linkage	b) Check and adjust manual linkage
	c) Control valve assembly	c) Clean or overhaul valve body
	d) Governor valve	d) Check and replace governor valve
	e) Brake band	e) Adjust brake band

CHILTON'S THREE "C's" DIAGNOSIS CHART
Subaru

Condition	Cause	Correction
Downshifting from 2nd to 1st is accomplished by excessive shock when selector lever is placed in "1" position	a) Vacuum diaphragm b) Stall speed c) Control valve assembly d) Governor valve	a) Check and replace vacuum diaphragm b) Check and adjust stall speed c) Clean or overhaul valve body d) Check and replace governor valve
Excessive chatter in "P" or "N" position of selector lever, excessive chatter in "D", "2", "1" or "R" positions	a) Fluid level low b) Low oil pressure c) Control valve assembly	a) Check and add fluid as necessary b) Check pressures and make determination c) Clean or overhaul valve body
Oil spurts or exhaust contains whitish smoke while car is running	a) Fluid level too high or too low b) Vacuum diaphragm c) Low or high oil pressure d) Stall speed e) Control valve assembly	a) Check and add fluid or drain fluid as necessary b) Check and replace vacuum diaphragm c) Check oil pressures and make determination d) Check and adjust stall speed e) Clean or overhaul valve body

Hydraulic Control System

Signals of the selector lever position, driving speed, and accelerator pedal operation are all conveyed to the control valve assembly, which distributed hydraulic pressure to the forward clutch, reverse clutch, transfer clutch, low & reverse brake, or brake band according to the current driving conditions, thereby achieving automatic transmission control.

LINE PRESSURE

The pressure of oil discharge from the oil pump is regulated by the pressure regulating valve. This is the line pressure and works as the basic oil pressure for the hydraulic controls which govern the operation of the transmission clutches, brake band, etc.

THROTTLE PRESSURE

The throttle pressure is produced and regulated by the vacuum throttle valve, which is actuated by the vacuum diaphragm to which the intake manifold vacuum is applied. Thus, the throttle pressure varies according to the intake manifold vacuum that varies with the carburetor throttle opening and engine speed. The oil is directed to the 2-3 shift valve, in which it performs gear shift in conjunction with the governor pressure. It is also delivered to the pressure regulating valve to control the line pressure.

GOVERNOR PRESSURE

The governor pressure is generated by the governor valve and varies according to car speed. It is directed to the 1-2 shift valve and the 2-3 shift valve, which control gear shifting, and also the pressure regulating valve, which controls the line pressure.

TRANSFER VALVE

The transfer valve is a valve which opens and closes the line pressure circuit to the transfer clutch, and is operated by a solenoid. When the transfer valve is closed, the transfer clutch is not engaged. When the transfer valve is opened, the transfer clutch is engaged and the vehicle will be in 4WD.

TRANSFER CLUTCH

When the line pressure is applied to the transfer clutch, the clutch capacity varies, like the other hydraulic clutches, with the throttle opening and the vehicle speed.

TRANSFER CLUTCH CONTROL CIRCUIT

The transfer clutch circuit and transfer valve have been added to the line pressure circuit between the oil pump discharge side and the control valve.

Major Components

OIL PUMP

The oil pump is installed at the rear end of the transmission. It pressurizes the oil to be delivered to the torque converter and the transmission through the control valve.

The oil pump is an internal gear drive involute gear pump. It is driven at the same speed as the engine by the hollow oil pump drive shaft splined to the converter cover of the torque converter assembly.

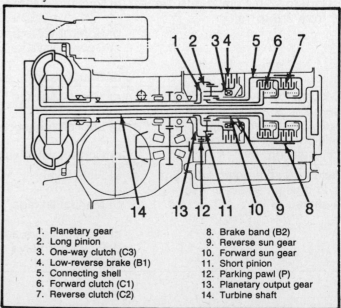

1. Planetary gear
2. Long pinion
3. One-way clutch (C3)
4. Low-reverse brake (B1)
5. Connecting shell
6. Forward clutch (C1)
7. Reverse clutch (C2)
8. Brake band (B2)
9. Reverse sun gear
10. Forward sun gear
11. Short pinion
12. Parking pawl (P)
13. Planetary output gear
14. Turbine shaft

Hydraulic and mechanical power transmitting mechanism
(©Fuji Heavy Industries Ltd.)

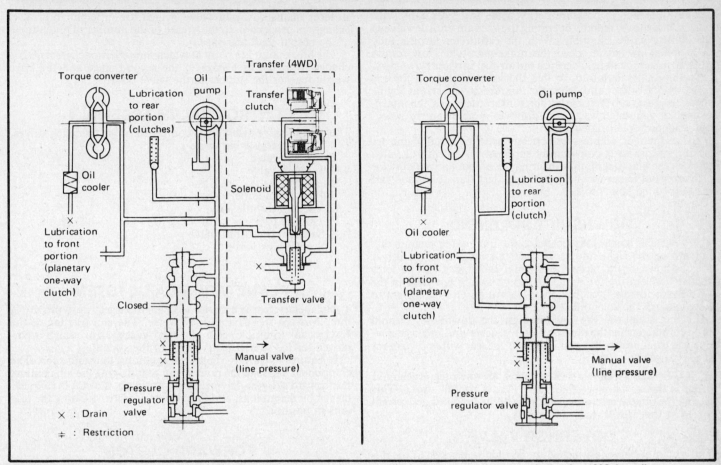

Comparison of hydraulic circuits (A) 4WD automatic transmission for 1983-84 (B) FWD automatic transmission for 1982 & earlier (©Fuji Heavy Industries Ltd.)

Oil admitted from the inlet port flows into part A is directed to part B through the rotation of the inner and outer gears and is then discharged from the outlet port.

Discharged oil from the oil pump is used for functioning the torque converter, for lubricating the parts, and for actuating the friction elements (the clutches and brake band) and the control system.

MANUAL LINKAGE

The movement of the selector lever, mechanically transmitted through the manual linkage, turns the selector arm on the left center of the transmission case, by which the manual plate inside the

case is turned through the manual shaft. When the selector lever is in the "P" and "N" range, the inhibitor switch closes the starter circuit and enables the engine to start. With the lever in the "R" range, the switch closes the back-up light circuit, turning the back-up light on.

VACUUM DIAPHRAGM

The vacuum diaphragm is installed in the right center of the transmission. It is actuated by intake-manifold vacuum to operate the vacuum throttle valve. The vacuum diaphragm has a rubber diaphragm, on one side of which the engine intake-manifold vacuum and the force of the diaphragm spring act, while on the other side atmospheric pressure acts.

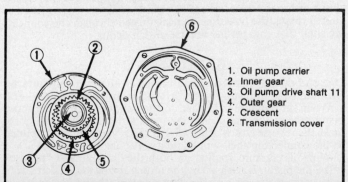

1. Oil pump carrier
2. Inner gear
3. Oil pump drive shaft 11
4. Outer gear
5. Crescent
6. Transmission cover

Oil pump (©Fuji Heavy Industries Ltd.)

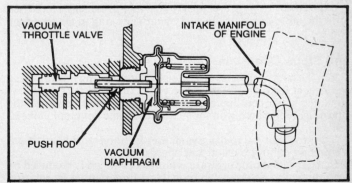

Vacuum diaphragm (©Fuji Heavy Industries Ltd.)

The difference in pressure between the two sides causes the push rod to move, thereby operating the vacuum throttle valve in the control valve assembly. With the carburetor throttle fully open and at low engine speed, the intake-manifold is low, (draws to atmospheric pressure) because the air-fuel mixture flows slowly in the intake-manifold, so that the vacuum reaction force is great. On the other hand, when the mixture flows faster as engine speed increases or when the carburetor throttle closes, the intake-manifold vacuum grows greater (draws to vacuum) and the vacuum reaction force smaller.

In this manner, oil pressure perfectly matched to the engine operating condition is consistently supplied to the control valve through the diaphragm, thus insuring the proper line pressure for providing sufficient torque capacity against transfer torque and the best-suited shift timing.

DOWNSHIFT SOLENOID

The downshift solenoid is located to the front of the vacuum diaphragm on the right side of the transmission. When the driver presses down on the accelerator pedal as far as it will go for a greater accelerating force, the kickdown switch provided in the accelerator linkage switches on to permit an electric current to flow through the solenoid.

In this situation, the push rod in the downshift solenoid projects and pushes the downshift valve, achieving forced gear reduction from 3rd to 2nd gear or 2nd to 1st gear within certain car speed range.

NOTE: The kickdown switch comes on when the accelerator pedal is depressed more than 7/8 or 15/16 of its full stroke. This means that the accelerator pedal should be installed and/or adjusted so that it will travel full stroke.

GOVERNOR VALVE

The governor valve is attached to the right upper side of the differential housing. It is driven by the speedometer and governor drive gear on the reduction drive gear shaft.

The governor valve regulates the line pressure in response to car speed. It also produces the governor pressure that exerts effect on the 1-2 and 2-3 shift valves for automatic gear shifting.

When the car is at a stop and the centrifugal force acting on the valve is zero, the large weight is pushed toward the center of the governor housing by the spring. In this case, the force of the spring is zero.

1st Stage Operation

As car and governor speeds increase, the centrifugal force acting on the large weight is transmitted to the governor valve through the spring, and centrifugal force also acts on the small weight and the governor valve itself.

In this condition, the governor pressure acting on the two annular surfaces of the governor valve, which are different in area, is regulated by the above combined centrifugal force. In this manner, the governor pressure rapidly increases as car speed increases until the large weight is blocked by the snap ring in the governor body.

2nd Stage Operation

When the large weight is prevented by the snap ring from exerting centrifugal force on the governor valve, the governor pressure is regulated by the combined force of the compressed spring and the centrifugal force acting on the small weight and governor valve itself.

The governor valve has two phases for the 1st and 2nd stages for precise control even at low speeds.

Since the governor pressure is a pressure which is produced by the interaction between the centrifugal force caused by rotation and the thrust caused by oil pressure acting on the two annular

surfaces of the governor valve, which are different in area, it changes in proportion to the square of the number of revolutions of the output shaft (car speed).

The break point is a point at which the governor characteristics change from the first stage to the second stage and the large weight reaches the stopper in the valve body.

CONTROL VALVE ASSEMBLY

The control valve assembly is composed of the following valves.
1. Pressure regulating valve
2. Manual valve
3. 1-2 shift valve
4. 2-3 shift valve
5. Pressure modifier valve
6. Vacuum throttle valve
7. Throttle back-up valve
8. Solenoid downshift valve
9. Second lock valve

PLANETARY GEAR SYSTEM

The planetary gear is a device to change the gear ratio providing three forward speeds and one reverse. The construction of the Ravigneaux (multiple) type planetary-gear system, which is employed for the shorter axial length of the system.

It features two kinds of planetary pinions, long and short. The component parts are the reverse sun gear driving the long pinion, the forward sun gear driving the short pinion, the output ring gear driven by the pinions, and the planetary carrier locating the pinions in position.

FORWARD CLUTCH

The forward clutch is always engaged during forward driving.

When the forward clutch has the piston released and the clutch plates are slipping due to clearance between them, no power is transmitted.

When the forward clutch applies hydraulic pressure to the piston so that the clutch plates are held tightly against each other, the drum rotation is transmitted to the clutch hub. When the hydraulic pressure applied to the piston is released, the return spring acts to return the clutch assembly to the original position. When the forward clutch piston is moved by hydraulic pressure to connect the clutch plates, the forward sun gear connected to the clutch hub begins to rotate, providing input to the planetary gears.

REVERSE CLUTCH

The reverse clutch engages in the 3rd forward gear position and reverse gear position, its function being the same as that of the forward clutch. When hydraulic pressure is applied to the reverse clutch piston to connect the clutch plates, the reverse sun gear begins to rotate, the power being transmitted through the connecting shell that engages the reverse clutch drum.

BAND SERVO

One end of the brake band is attached to the transmission case with the band adjusting screw serving as an anchor.

When oil pressure is applied to the "apply" side of the servo piston, the piston rod pushes the band strut and the band brake locks the reverse clutch drum so that the reverse sun gear splined to the connecting shell will be held stationary. (2nd gear)

With oil pressure applied on both the "apply" and "release" sides, the piston is released by the return spring and difference in active area of the servo piston, thus releasing the brake band. (3rd gear)

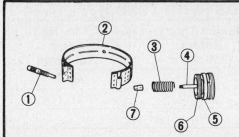

1. Adjusting screw
2. Brake band
3. Return spring
4. Servo piston rod
5. Servo piston cover
6. Servo piston
7. Band strut

Exploded view of band servo (©Fuji Heavy Industries Ltd.)

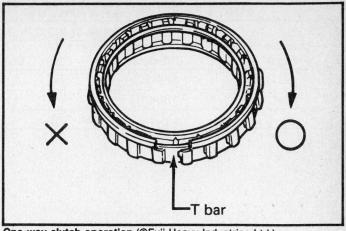

T bar

One-way clutch operation (©Fuji Heavy Industries Ltd.)

LOW AND REVERSE BRAKE

When oil pressure acts on the piston of the low & reverse brake, the multi-disc brake is engaged, and the planetary carrier united with the one-way clutch outer race is locked by the transmission case (D_1 and reverse gears). The return spring in the low & reverse brake is a slit diaphragm spring instead of coil springs as used in the forward and reverse clutches.

ONE-WAY CLUTCH

A sprag type one-way clutch is installed between the planetary carrier and the center support. The clutch prevents the planetary carrier from turning counterclockwise as viewed from the engine side.

It rotates or freewheels in the clockwise direction and does not rotate, locks up, in the counterclockwise direction.

Diagnosis Tests

MAIN LINE PRESSURE

Checking the main line pressure with an appropriate gauge while the transmission is being operated, will give indications of normal and abnormal operation.

A main line pressure plug is located on the rear of the transmission cover, nearly centered on the early models and located at the bottom of the cover on later models.

Line Pressure Test

1. Temporarily attach a oil pressure gauge to a suitable place in the driver's compartment, remove the blind plug located in the front floorboard and pass the hose of the oil pressure gauge to the engine compartment.
2. Remove the pressure check plug from the transmission cover.
3. Attach the oil pressure gauge adapter to the pressure check plug hole in the transmission cover.
4. Connect the oil pressure gauge to the gauge adapter.
5. Run the engine and check the line pressures with the engine at a full-throttle and a minimum throttle. Refer to the accompanying chart for the proper oil pressure reading.

OVERALL LINE PRESSURE TEST RESULT INDICATIONS IN FWD

1. Low pressure with the engine at idle speed indicates, a worn oil pump or clearance not adjusted to specs, a leak in the oil pressure circuit or a inoperative pressure regulator valve.
2. High line pressure with the engine at idle speed indicates, a leak in a vacuum hose or in the vacuum diaphragm or the diaphragm rod is too long, and the pressure regulator valve could be jamming.
3. When the line pressure will not rise with the engine at full throttle, check to see if the vacuum diaphragm rod has been installed or not.
4. If the line pressure does rise but will not come up to specified range, the vacuum throttle valve is jamming or the pressure regulator valve or the pressure regulator is plugged up.

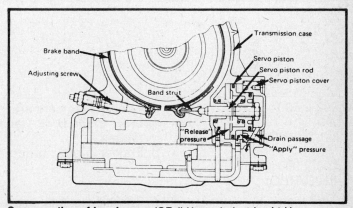

Cross section of band servo (©Fuji Heavy Industries Ltd.)

LINE PRESSURE AT VARIOUS THROTTLE OPENINGS (NON-TURBO)

| Throttle Range | Full Throttle (1.2-2.0 in. Hg.) | | Minimum Throttle (16.9-17.7 in. Hg.) | |
	Before Cut-down	After Cut-down	Before Cut-down	After Cut-down
D	121-142	78-92.5	43-57	43-57
2	145-168	84-98	145-168	84-98
R	200-227		67-81	

NOTE: Line pressure in drive ranges of D, 2 and Reverse will change in steps when the pressure modifier valve operates. These points are called "cut-down points." Before cut-down points denotes slow driving and after cut-down denotes vehicle speed of more than 22 MPH.

TROUBLE DIAGNOSIS

LINE PRESSURE AT VARIOUS THROTTLE OPENINGS (WITH TURBO)

| Throttle Range | Full Throttle (1.2-2.0 in. Hg.) | | Minimum Throttle (16.9-17.7 in. Hg.) | |
	Before Cut-down	After Cut-down	Before Cut-down	After Cut-down
D	188-202	114-128	43-57	43-57
2	188-202	114-128	97-114	97-114
R	284-313		81-95	

STALL TEST RESULTS

Stall Speed	Results	Possible Cause
Higher than 2,500 rpm (Non-TURBO) or 2,900 rpm (TURBO)	a. Splippage of automatic transmission clutch, brake band, etc. (Further stall tests are not necessary.)	a. Low line pressure (If stall speed is higher than specified range at any shift position). b. One-way clutch spliggage. (If stall speed is higher than specified range only in the D range). c. Brake band slippage (If stall speed is higher than specified range only in the 2 range.) d. Slippage of low & reverse brake or reverse brake (If stall speed is higher than specified range only in the R range.)
2,300-2,500 rpm (Non-TURBO) or 2,700-2,900 rpm (TURBO)	a. Control members are in good order in the D, 2, 1 and R ranges. b. Engine in good order.	
Lower than 2,300 rpm (Non-TURBO) or 2,700 rpm (TURBO)	a. Throttle not fully opened. b. Erroneous engine operation or one-way clutch slippage.	
Road test	a. Acceleration is not properly made up to 50 km/h (31 MPH). b. Car speed does not attain more than 80 km/h (50 MPH). c. Operation is not proper at all car speeds.	a. One-way clutch slippage. b. One-way clutch jamming. c. Erroneous engine operation.

OVERALL LINE PRESSURE TEST RESULT INDICATIONS IN 4WD

1. With the engine at idle speed if the line pressure difference between 4WD and FWD is more than 4 psi. Then the transfer pipe is disconnected or the rear shaft seal ring has not been installed.

2. If the line pressure difference between the 4WD and FWD at engine idle speed is less than 4 psi., the solenoid or transfer valve is not working.

GOVERNOR PRESSURE

The governor pressure reading should be taken if a malfunction of the governor pressure system is indicated.

Governor Pressure Test

1. Remove the test plug from the right side of the final reduction case and install the oil pressure gauge adapter and the oil pressure gauge.

2. Warm up the engine by letting the engine idle for several minutes until the oil reaches operating temperature.

3. With the vehicle moving shift to the "2" range and check the governor pressure. Refer to the accompanying chart for the proper governor pressure readings.

GOVERNOR PRESSURE AT VEHICLE SPEED

Speed (mph)	PSI
6 mph	0 psi
25 mph	18-27 psi
50 mph	53-67 psi

AIR PRESSURE TESTS

Air pressure tests can be made to the various fluid passages, located within the transmission unit, separately or with the unit assembled, depending upon the exposed passage.

CHANGE OF LINE PRESSURE WITH INTAKE MANIFOLD VACUUM CHANGES (N AND D RANGES)

Intake Manifold Vacuum (in. HG)	Line Pressure (PSI)
11	74-85
12	70-81
13	64-75
14	60-71
15	53-64
16	48-60
17	46-53
18	46-47

STALL TEST

The purpose of the stall test is to check the clutch and band slippage, the engine performance and to determine if the torque converter is functioning properly.

Procedure

1. Have the engine and the transaxle running at normal operating temperature.

2. Block all four wheels and apply hand brake.

3. Attach a tachometer to the engine and place it in a position to been seen.

NOTE: It is advisable to temporarily mark the specified stall speed (2,300-2,500 rpm) on the meter face.

4. Apply the foot brake and shift the selector lever to the "D" position.

5. With the foot brake applied gradually depress the accelerator pedal until the engine reaches full throttle.

6. When the engine speed is stabilized, read that speed quickly and release the accelerator pedal.

7. Shift the selector valve to the "N" neutral position, and cool down the engine by letting the engine idle for 2-5 minutes.

8. Record the stall speed and perform the stall tests with the selector lever in "2", "1" and "R" positions.

--- CAUTION ---

Do not hold the stall test longer than 5 seconds as damage to the band and clutches can occur. Allow at least two to five minutes before attempting further stall tests.

NOTE: If a relatively high stall speed is noted and internal transmission damages are suspected, that would necessitate tranmission removal and repair, do not continue the stall tests.

ROAD TEST

The following descriptions concerning the road test should be observed correctly to make an accurate diagnosis of the automatic transmission.

Gear Shift Feeling

The feeling of gear shifting as well as running speeds should be carefully checked, whether either of the following abnormalities is remarkable or not.

1. Shifting is not smooth but accompanied with a considerable shock.

2. Shifting is not sharp but accompanied with dragging.

These abnormalities indicate the presence of inaccurate throttle pressure or other related defects.

Checking for Normal Shifting Conditions

1. Running speeds should be stepped up in the sequence of D1 to D2 to D3 when the selector lever is kept in the D position. No up-shifting should arise in the R position of the lever.

2. Kickdown operation should be achieved normally.

3. Running speeds should be stepped down in the sequence of D3 to 2 (1_2) to 1_1 when the selector lever is shifted from the D to 1 position through 2 position.

The engine brake should be in effect throughout the 1_2 and 1_1 gears.

4. No up-shifting should arise in the 1 position of the selector lever.

5. Running speeds should be fixed to the second gear speed when the selector lever is shifted to the 2 position.

6. The car should be locked sufficiently from movement when the selector lever is shifted to the P position.

If any abnormal condition is felt on the second gear speed during the road test, the brake band should be adjusted.

If the defect still remains even through the brake band is in normally adjusted condition, oil leakage from the servo piston sealing parts should be checked.

Checking The 4WD Operation

With the vehicle operating in 4WD, turn the vehicle in a circle while lightly depressing the accelerator pedal, and then shift the vehicle into the FWD position. When the vehicle is shifted into FWD a light shock should be felt. This shock is normal and will be felt everytime this operation takes place. Whenever the transfer clutch facing is replaced with a new one, the above test should be conducted, for the run-in purpose, two or three times with the vehicle set in the 4WD mode and the steering wheel fully turned.

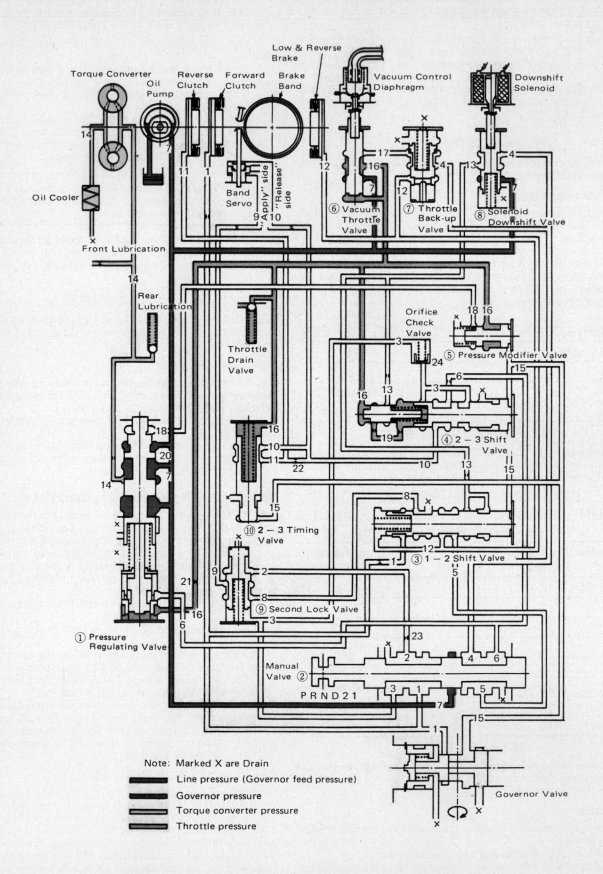

Torque Converter

Oil Pump

Reverse Clutch

Forward Clutch

Low & Reverse Brake

Brake Band

Vacuum Control Diaphragm

Downshift Solenoid

Oil Cooler

Front Lubrication

Note: Marked X are Drain

Line pressure (Governor feed pressure)

Governor pressure

Torque converter pressure

Throttle pressure

FWD automatic transmission in neutral (©Fuji Heavy Industries Ltd.)

NEUTRAL

When the transmission is in the N range, the clutches are released, as pressure oil is not delivered from the oil controlling mechanism to the speed controlling elements (clutches and brake band). Therefore, the power from the input shaft (turbine shaft) is not transmitted to the output shaft.

The pressure of the oil discharged from the oil pump is regulated by the pressure regulating valve ① and the pressurized oil, called line pressure 7, is delivered to the manual valve ②, vacuum throttle valve ⑥, and solenoid downshift valve ⑧. The oil then travels to the torque converter as torque converter oil 14, and, on the way to the converter, part of the oil is supplied to the forward and reverse clutches as rear lubricating oil. Other part of the oil is directed as front lubricating oil to the planetary gears, one-way clutch and low & reverse brake through the oil pump shaft. Since the oil pump is rotating at the same speed as the engine, the volume of oil from the oil pump increases with engine speed, excess oil being returned through the pressure regulating valve ① directly to the oil pan.

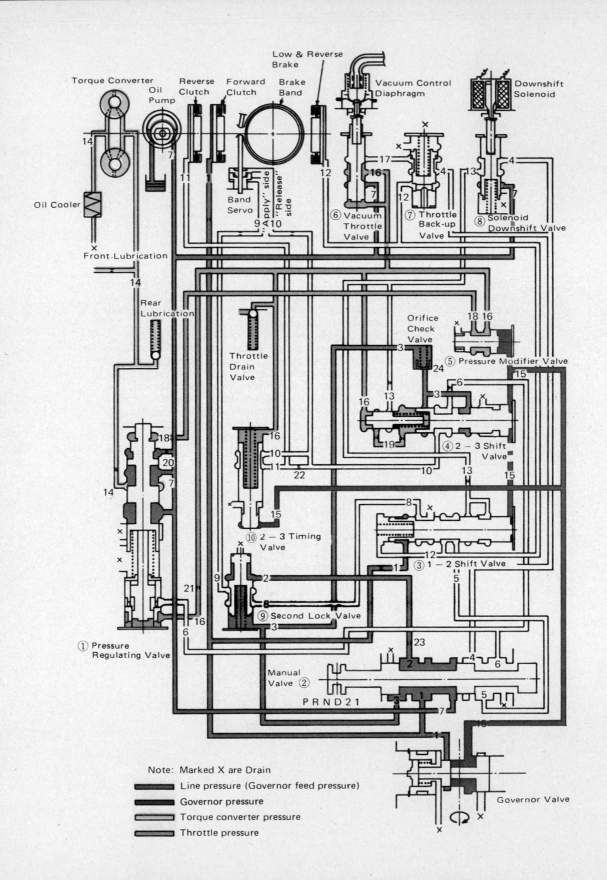

FWD automatic transmission in drive—1st gear (©Fuji Heavy Industries Ltd.)

DRIVE—1ST GEAR

When the transmission is the D (1st gear) range, the forward clutch is engaged and power from the turbine shaft is transmitted to the forward sun gear. The planetary carrier is locked to the transmission case through the one-way clutch outer race, one-way clutch and center support.

The planetary gear system in this range provides a ratio of 2.6:1. Since the planetary carrier tends to turn clockwise when the car is coasting, the one-way clutch is released and runs idle. In this condition, no reverse drive is transmitted to the engine so that the engine brake will not be applied.

With the manual valve ② in the D position, the line pressure 7 admitted into the manual valve ② flows through the line pressure passages 1, 2 and 3. The line pressure passing through the passage 1 acts on the forward clutch, the governor, and the 1-2 shift valve ③ to achieve gear shifting.

The line pressure through the passage 2, enters the second lock valve ⑨. The line pressure through the passage 3, acts on the 2-3 shift valve ④ to perform 2-3 gear shifting and locks the second lock valve ⑨ as well.

The throttle pressure 16, which varies with accelerator pedal depression, acts on the pressure regulating valve ①, pushing the regulating valve ① to cause a rise in the pressure 7.

With an increase in car speed, the governor pressure 15 derived from the line pressure passage 1 actuates the 1-2 shift valve ③, 2-3 shift valve ④, and pressure modifier valve ⑤.

With high governor pressure, the pressure modifier valve ⑤ operates to compress its spring, and the throttle pressure 16 is carried to the passage 18 to act against the spring of the pressure regulating valve ① and the throttle pressure 16, so that the line pressure 7 will drop.

As car speed increases, the governor pressure 15 increases and pushes one side of the 1-2 shift valve ③ counteracting the throttle pressure 19, line pressure 1 and spring. When the governor pressure overcomes these forces, the gear changes from 1st to 2nd.

When the throttle pressure 19 is higher, or the accelerator pedal is depressed farther, the governor pressure rises higher, moving the shifting point to the higher speed side.

NOTE: When the selector lever is placed in the "1" range, the forward clutch is engaged and the planetary gear is locked by the low and reverse clutch brake, instead of being locked by the one-way clutch.

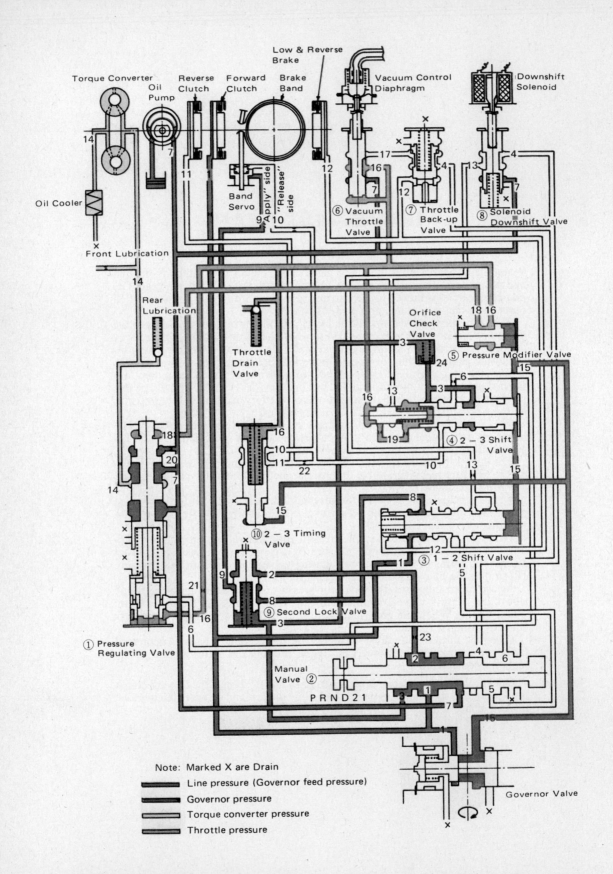

FWD automatic transmission in drive 2nd gear and manual 2—2nd gear (©Fuji Heavy Industries Ltd.)

DRIVE—2ND GEAR AND MANUAL 2—2ND GEAR

When the transmission is in the D (2nd gear) range, the forward clutch is engaged and power from the turbine shaft is transmitted to the forward sun gear. Also, the brake band is applied to hold stationary the reverse clutch drum interlocked with the reverse sun gear and connecting shell.

The power also flows in the same manner with the transmission in the 2 and 1 (2nd gear) range. With the reverse sun gear held stationary, the planetary carrier rotates clockwise as the pinions circle around the reverse sun gear. Thus, the one-way clutch outer race runs idle and a gear ratio of 1.505 to 1 is obtained in this gear position.

When the governor pressure 15 increases with an increase in car speed while traveling in the D (1st gear) range, the 1-2 shift valve ③ moves to permit the line pressure 1 to run through the valve to the line pressure passage 8. The line pressure 8 is delivered to the line pressure passage 9 through the second lock valve ⑨, applying the band servo to shift up to the 2nd gear.

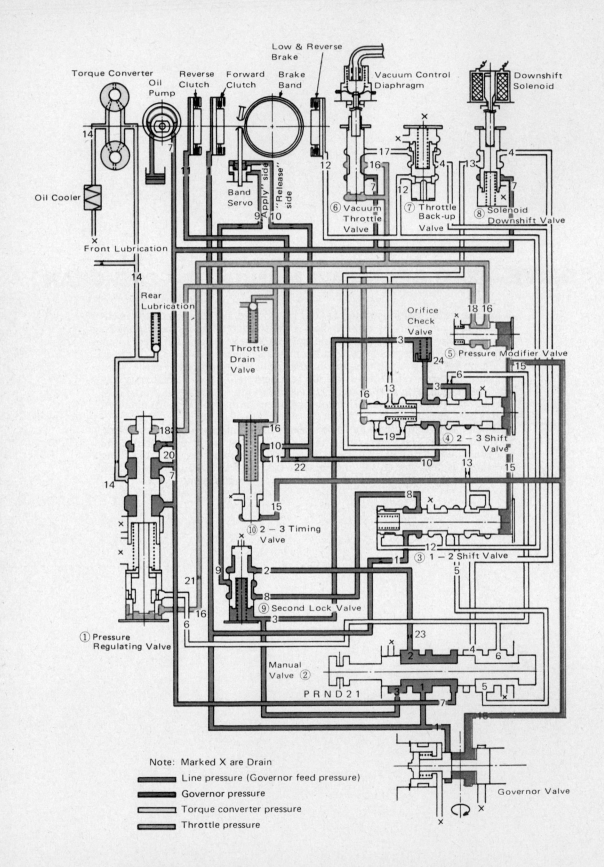

FWD automatic transmission in drive—3rd gear (©Fuji Heavy Industries Ltd.)

DRIVE—3RD GEAR

With the transmission in the D (3rd gear) range, the forward clutch and the reverse clutch are engaged. Although oil pressure is applied to the servo piston on both the "apply" and "release" sides, the brake band is released as the servo piston is released by the combined releasing force which consists of the return spring force and the thrust caused by oil pressure acting on the annular surfaces of the governor valve which are different in area.

The power transmitted from the turbine shaft to the forward clutch drum is divided into two streams; one is transmitted from the forward clutch to the forward sun gear and the other from the reverse clutch to the reverse sun gear through the connecting shell.

Since the forward sun gear and the reverse sun gear make the rotation, the planetary-gear system turns as a unit and the output ring gear also turns in the same diretion at the same speed. Hence, there is no gear reduction in the transmission and a gear ratio of 1 to 1 is achieved.

As car speed increases while traveling in the D (2nd gear) range, the governor pressure 15 grows greater than the spring force of the 2-3 shift valve ④ and the throttle pressure 19. When this takes place, the 2-3 shift valve ④ moves to apply the line pressure 3 to the reverse clutch and the "release" side of the band servo through the line pressure passage 10.

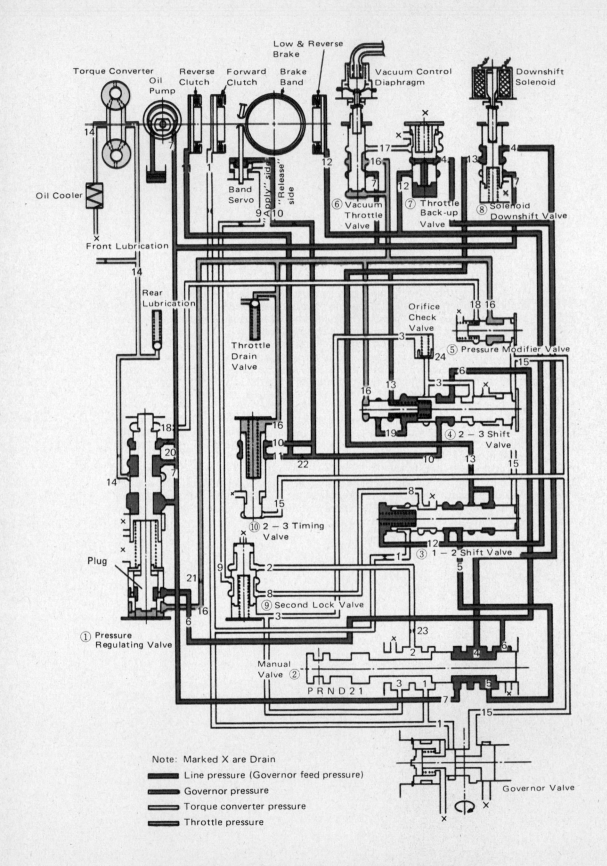

Torque Converter • Oil Pump • Reverse Clutch • Forward Clutch • Brake Band • Low & Reverse Brake • Vacuum Control Diaphragm • Downshift Solenoid

Oil Cooler

Front Lubrication

Rear Lubrication

Band Servo • "Apply" side • "Release" side

⑥ Vacuum Throttle Valve • ⑦ Throttle Back-up Valve • ⑧ Solenoid Downshift Valve

Throttle Drain Valve

Orifice Check Valve

⑤ Pressure Modifier Valve

④ 2 – 3 Shift Valve

⑩ 2 – 3 Timing Valve

③ 1 – 2 Shift Valve

Plug

⑨ Second Lock Valve

① Pressure Regulating Valve

Manual Valve ②

P R N D 2 1

Governor Valve

Note: Marked X are Drain

- Line pressure (Governor feed pressure)
- Governor pressure
- Torque converter pressure
- Throttle pressure

FWD automatic transmission in reverse (©Fuji Heavy Industries Ltd.)

REVERSE

The reverse clutch and the low & reverse brake are engaged when the transmission is in the R range. The power flow is from the turbine shaft, through the reverse clutch, and from the connecting shell to the reverse sun gear. As the planetary carrier is held stationary by the low & reverse brake, the reverse sun gear turns clockwise. This causes the output ring gear to turn counterclockwise at a reduced speed, providing a gear ratio of 2.167 to 1.

With the manual valve ② in the R position, the line pressure 7 entering the manual valve ② flows in the line pressure passages 5, 6. The line pressure flowing through the passage 5 is diverted to the line pressure passage 12 through the 1-2 shift valve ③ to act on the low & reverse brake.

The oil running in the passage 6 passes through the 2-3 shift valve ④ to the line pressure passage 10 and acts on the "release" side of the band servo and the reverse clutch. The throttle pressure 16 and line pressure 6, which vary according to pedal depression, are applied to the plug in the pressure regulating valve ① to push the valve ① to cause a rise in the line pressure 7.

Since there is no governor pressure in the R range, the 1-2 shift valve ③, 2-3 shift valve ④, and the pressure modifier valve ⑤ are not functioning as a valve.

LOCK-UP TORQUE CONVERTER

This lock-up torque converter has a centrifugal lock up clutch built into the torque converter assembly. The lock up clutch has a very simple construction, consisting of five components: shoes and weights with paper facing pasted on their outer surfaces, two leaf springs (main and retractor springs) and pins. A total of eight shoes are used. The lock up clutch transmits torque by the centrifugal force acting on the shoes that slide along the inner circumference of the turbine cover. The shoes rotate at the same speed as the torque converter turbine. The shoes sometimes become completely engaged with the turbine cover, however they usually slide in a half clutch condition. The engine torque is transmitted from the turbine cover through the shoes to the reaction plate and then to the output shaft. The weight's primary job is to increase the transfer torque capacity in the medium and low-speed ranges. The centrifugal force acting on the weight is transmitted to the shoes through the main spring. The retractor spring always function to pull the shoe inward, which, in the low-speed range where the centrifugal force is small, prevents the shoes from touching the turbine drum. The pin holds the shoes in place so that the shoes will not come off the reaction plate, and also serves as a weight stopper.

NOTE: The lock-up torque converter is a sealed unit and can not be disassembled by the average repair shop.

Diagnosis of the Lock-Up Torque Converter

If the following problems frequently occur with the transmission, the problem could be contributed to the torque converter. If the problem is found with the torque converter it should be removed and replaced.

1. Low maximum speed or poor acceleration.
2. Transmission overheating.
3. ATF fluid spills out while the vehicle is running.
4. Vehicle exhaust emits white smoke while running.

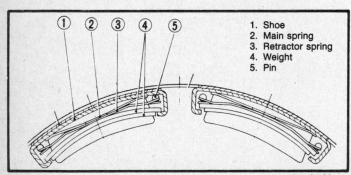

1. Shoe
2. Main spring
3. Retractor spring
4. Weight
5. Pin

Exploded view of the lock-up clutch (©Fuji Heavy Industries Ltd.)

Adjustments

NEUTRAL SAFETY (INHIBITOR) SWITCH

Adjustment

If the manual valve detent position is not aligned with the guide plate groove position, perform the adjustment as follows.
1. Set the selector lever to the "N" position.
2. Loosen the adjusting nut of the linkage rod.

3. Set the detent position so the selector arm is aligned with the "N" location mark of the transmission case (within the range of a 0.24 in. (6mm diameter).
4. Adjust the rod so that the "N" mark of the guide plate is aligned correctly with this detent position.
5. If the indicator needle does not line up with the guide plate marking, remove the console box, loosen the four indicator mounting screws and adjust the position of the indicator assembly.

KICKDOWN SWITCH AND DOWNSHIFT SOLENOID

Testing

An audible click should be heard from the solenoid on the right side of the transmission, when the accelerator pedal is pushed down all the way with the engine off and the ignition switch on. The switch is operated by the upper part of the accelerator lever inside the car. The position of the switch can be varied to give quicker or slower kickdown response.

SECOND GEAR BAND

Adjustment

1. Hold the adjusting screw above the pan on the left side of the transmission.
2. Loosen the locknut.
3. Tighten the adjusting screw to a torque of 6.5 ft. lbs. and back off two complete turns.
4. Tighten the locknut, while holding the screw.

MANUAL LINKAGE

The transmission manual control linkage removal, inspection, installation and adjustments are covered in this section.

Removal

1. Remove the selector handle from the selector lever.
2. Remove the parking brake cover and the console box.
3. Disconnect the electrical connectors for the inhibitor switch and the position indicator light.
4. Remove the adjusting rod from transmission selector arm.
5. Remove the mounting screws and take out the selector lever assembly.

NOTE: Be sure that the selector lever is in the "N" position before removing the selector lever assembly.

Disassembly

1. Remove the selector rod, position indicator and the inhibitor switch from the selector lever assembly.
2. Drive out the spring pin to the position where it is detached from the guide plate.
3. Remove the selector lever installing bolt and detach the boot by pushing it from underneath, then disconnect the selector lever from the plate.
4. Install the selector lever handle and release button to the selector lever temporarily, and drive the spring pin out from the selector rod, making sure not to damage the connected parts.

Inspection

1. Check the selector lever rod for excessive bends or damage.
2. Check the detent plate for wear.
3. Check for worn contact surface of the pushbutton and the sleeve.
4. Check the pin at the end of the selector lever rod for wear or damage.

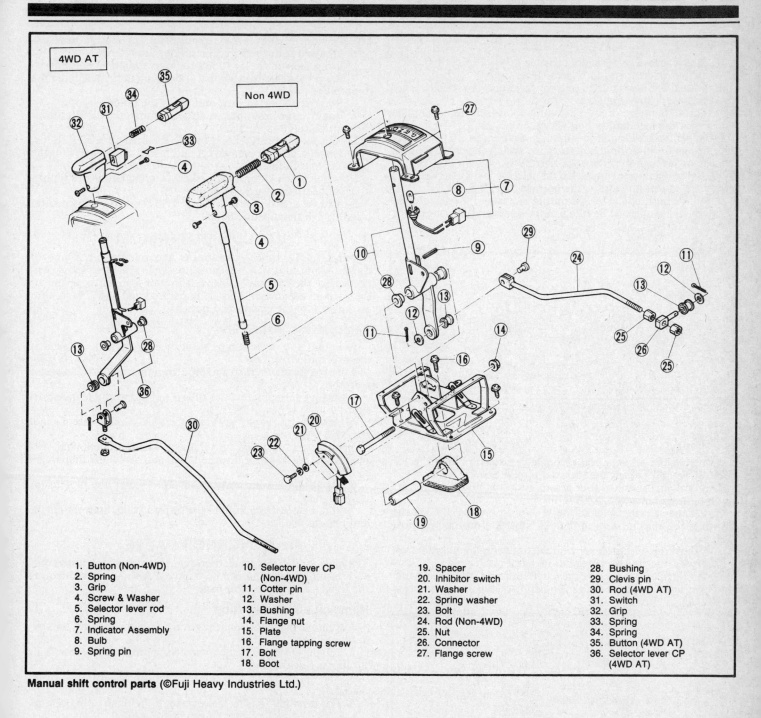

Manual shift control parts (©Fuji Heavy Industries Ltd.)

1. Button (Non-4WD)
2. Spring
3. Grip
4. Screw & Washer
5. Selector lever rod
6. Spring
7. Indicator Assembly
8. Bulb
9. Spring pin

10. Selector lever CP (Non-4WD)
11. Cotter pin
12. Washer
13. Bushing
14. Flange nut
15. Plate
16. Flange tapping screw
17. Bolt
18. Boot

19. Spacer
20. Inhibitor switch
21. Washer
22. Spring washer
23. Bolt
24. Rod (Non-4WD)
25. Nut
26. Connector
27. Flange screw

28. Bushing
29. Clevis pin
30. Rod (4WD AT)
31. Switch
32. Grip
33. Spring
34. Spring
35. Button (4WD AT)
36. Selector lever CP (4WD AT)

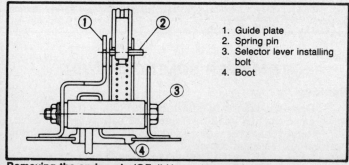

1. Guide plate
2. Spring pin
3. Selector lever installing bolt
4. Boot

Removing the spring pin (©Fuji Heavy Industries Ltd.)

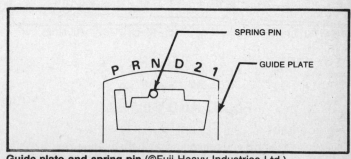

SPRING PIN

GUIDE PLATE

P R N D 2 1

Guide plate and spring pin (©Fuji Heavy Industries Ltd.)

1253

Assembly

1. Apply grease to all sliding parts.
2. Install selector rod to selector lever.
3. Match the holes on the selector lever and the selector lever rod and insert the spring pin.
4. Install the selector lever assembly to the selector lever plate and insert the installation bolt. Torque the bolt to 9-14 ft. lbs.
5. When assembling the inhibitor switch, insert a 0.08 in. drill bit through the knock pin hole, turn the switch slightly so that the bit passes through into the back part of the switch.
6. Bolt the inhibitor switch to the selector lever assembly and remove the drill bit (torque the bolts to 2.9-5.8 ft. lbs.)
7. While pushing the release button in, install the selector handle to the selector lever. Be sure that the release button is installed facing the driver's side.

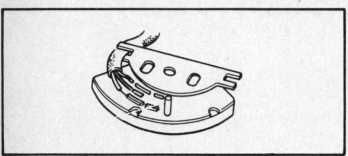

Inhibitor switch (©Fuji Heavy Industries Ltd.)

Installation

1. Install the selector rod through the transmission selector connection and tighten the lock nut temporarily.
2. Install the selector lever assembly to the body and torque the mounting bolts to 3.3-5.4 ft. lbs.
3. Set the selector lever in the "N" position and also set the transmission selector arm in the "N" position on the transmission case.
4. Adjust the selector lever with the transmission selector arm.
5. Install the console box and the hand brake cover.
6. Confirm that the selector lever operation is smooth and that the correct gear is selected at each position on the indicator panel.

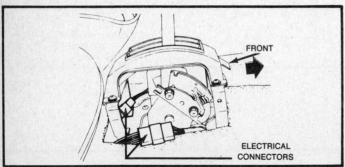

Installing the selector lever assembly (©Fuji Heavy Industries Ltd.)

Services

FLUID AND FILTER

Replacement

The factory recommends changing the transmission fluid and filter every 30,000 miles using the recommended ATF fluid. When-

ever the transmission is disassembled for any reason, band adjustments and change of fluid and filter are required.

1. Bring the vehicle up to normal operating temperature.
2. Raise the vehicle on a hoist, and place a drain pan under the drain plug.
3. Remove the drain plug and drain the fluid.
4. Remove the drain pan and then remove the oil filter from the control valve assembly.
5. Replace the oil filter and torque the bolts to 2.2-2.9 ft. lbs.
6. Install a new oil pan gasket and install oil pan, and torque the bolts to 8 ft. lbs.
7. Install a new drain plug gasket, then install the drain plug. Torque the drain plug to 18 ft. lbs.
8. Add 4.2 quarts of recommended ATF into the transmission case through the dipstick hole.

VACUUM DIAPHRAGM

If rough idling, shifting harshness and undetermined loss of transmission fluid is experienced, possible cracks or loose connections of the vacuum lines may allow air to enter the engine or the vacuum diaphragm may be punctured and allowing fluid to be drawn into the engine and burned.

Removal and Installation

1. Loosen the vacuum pipe at the engine/transaxle bolt and at the governor cover.
2. Pull the vacuum tube and pipe from the vacuum diaphragm assembly.
3. Drain approximately two quarts of fluid from the transmission.
4. Unscrew the diaphragm from the transmission case. Do not drop the push-rod.
5. Install the push-rod into the new vacuum diaphragm, seat the rod on the vacuum throttle valve and screw the diaphragm into place.
6. Install the vacuum tubes and pipe. Secure the pipe to the transmission.
7. Add the necessary fluid to the transmission. Start the engine and recheck the level.

GOVERNOR VALVE

The govenor valve is located on the right side of the differential and reduction case and can be removed without the removal of the transmission or the oil pan.

Removal and Installation

1. Remove the bolts from the governor cover and turn the cover 90 degrees.
2. Pull the governor assembly from the transmission case while turning it clockwise.
3. The valve, sleeve and sealing ring can be inspected or replaced.
4. The installation is in the reverse of the removal procedure.

CAUTION

Do not damage the seal ring, gear or the O-ring when installing the governor assembly. Lubricate the assembly with fluid before installation.

TRANSFER SOLENOID (4WD)

Removal

1. Drain off 1 quart of transmission fluid.
2. Open the hood and disconnect the battery ground cable.
3. Remove the spare tire and loosen the pitching stopper to a position just before it comes off.
4. Disconnect the 4WD selector solenoid harness and keep the harness suspended.

5. Remove the upper cover, the cover must be removed in order to remove the exhaust pipe.

6. Remove the exhaust pipe.

7. Remove the intermediate side cable clamp.

8. Remove the rear crossmember, to ensure safety support the oil pan with a transmission jack or its equivalent.

9. Remove the side cable from the body clip.

10. Push the transmission to the left and insert a piece of wood between the clearance just achieved.

11. Remove the solenoid valve.

12. Installation of the transfer solenoid is just the reverse sequence of the removal procedures.

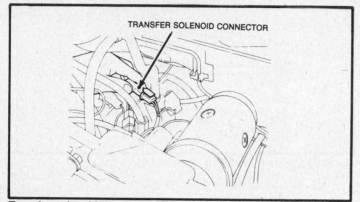

Transfer solenoid connector (©Fuji Heavy Industries Ltd.)

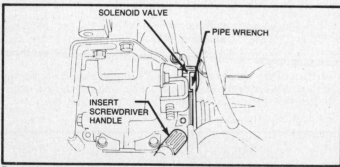

Removing the solenoid valve (©Fuji Heavy Industries Ltd.)

TRANSFER SECTION (4WD)

Removal and Installation

1. Completely drain the ATF from the transmission.

2. Remove the transfer solenoid (see transfer solenoid removal and installation for details).

3. Remove the temperature switch harness from the harness clamp.

4. Remove the 8 mounting bolts and remove the transfer section and the extension assembly as a unit from the intermediate case.

5. Installation of the transfer section is the reverse sequence of the removal procedures.

6. Refill the transmission with the recommended ATF and check the fluid level.

CONTROL VALVE ASSEMBLY

Removal

1. Raise the vehicle with a jack or a hoist and drain the ATF from the transmission.

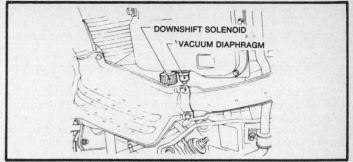

Removing the vacuum diaphragm (©Fuji Heavy Industries Ltd.)

2. Disconnect the vacuum hose and remove the downshift solenoid and the vacuum diaphragm together with the diaphragm rod.

3. Remove the oil pan and disconnect the servo pipes.

4. Remove the 6 mounting bolts and remove the control valve assembly.

NOTE: Be careful not to drop the manual valve or damage the oil strainer.

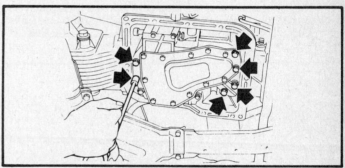

Control valve removal (©Fuji Heavy Industries Ltd.)

Installation

1. Install the control valve assembly and torque the 6 mounting bolts equally at 4.3-5.8 ft. lbs.

2. Install the servo pipes (always use new servo pipes).

3. Install a new oil pan gasket and then install the oil pan.

4. Install the vacuum diaphragm.

5. Install the downshift solenoid and connect the vacuum hose.

NOTE: Make sure to install a new O-ring on the downshift solenoid and the vacuum diaphragm.

6. Refill with the recommended ATF and check the fluid level (approximately 4.2 quarts).

REMOVAL & INSTALLATION

Transmission Removal

1. Open the hood as far as possible and secure it. Remove the spare wheel and disconnect the battery.

2. Remove all fluid lines, vacuum lines and tubes. Mark the lines and tubes for later installation.

3. Disconnect all wiring connections.

4. Disconnect the speedometer cable and unfasten the clip on the speedometer cable.

5. Remove the four bolts connecting the torque converter to the drive plate through the timing hole.

NOTE: Be careful not to drop the bolts into the converter housing.

6. Disconnect and plug the oil cooler hose from the transmission.

7. Remove the starter with the battery cable attached.

8. Remove the upper bolts which secure engine to transmission and loosen the lower nuts.

9. Loosen nut (10mm-0.39 in.) which retains the pitching stopper to the transmission side and slightly tilt the engine backward in order to remove transmission.

10. Disconnect the O_2 sensor harness and unclamp it.

11. Raise the front end of the vehicle and remove the exhaust assembly.

NOTE: Do not strike the O_2 sensor against any parts during removal and a helper is needed to assist in removing the exhaust, due to the weight of the system.

12. Drain the transmission fluid and then disconnect the oil supply pipe.

13. Move the selector to the "P" position and mark the location of the connector nut and separate the manual lever from the linkage rod.

14. Remove the stabilizer.

15. Remove the bolts which secure the left and right transverse links to the front crossmember, and lower the transverse links.

16. Drive both left and right spring pins out of axle shaft.

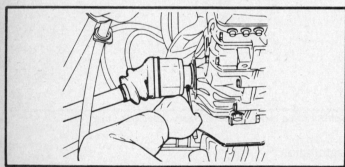

Installing the axle shaft (©Fuji Heavy Industries Ltd.)

NOTE: Use new spring pins, do not reuse the old spring pins.

17. While pushing the wheels toward the outer side, separate the axle shaft from the drive shaft.

18. Remove the mount retaining nut from the rear crossmember.

19. Support the transmission by placing a transmission jack or its equivalent, under the transmission.

20. Remove the crossmember.

21. Remove the two lower nuts that secure the engine to the transmission, and move the transmission away from the engine far enough so that the mainshaft of the transmission does not interfere with the engine.

22. Lower the transmission jack or its equivalent, and remove the transmission from the vehicle.

Transmission Installation

1. Place the transmission on the removing jack and raise into position in the vehicle.

2. When the transmission is aligned with the engine, secure the transmission to the engine.

3. Install the rear crossmember on the vehicle body.

4. Remove the jack from under the transmission.

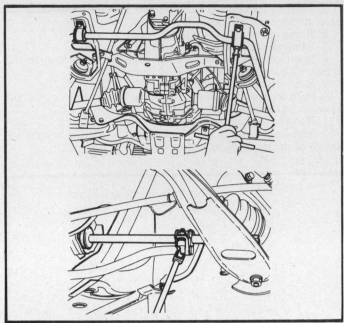

Installing the stabilizer (©Fuji Heavy Industries Ltd.)

5. Clamp the parking brake cable to the body.

6. Align the spring pin holes on the axle shaft and the drive shaft, and drive the spring pin into the holes (always use a new spring pin).

7. Using a punch or its equivalent, line up the bolt holes on the left and the right transverse links with the crossmember, and insert the bolts into the holes from the front side. Torque the bolts to 43-51 ft. lbs.

8. Install the stabilizer and position the two center bushings with their slits facing the rear side of the vehicle and the two outer bushings with their slits facing the inside of the vehicle.

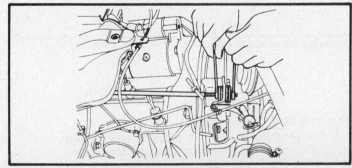

Adjusting the pitching stopper (©Fuji Heavy Industries Ltd.)

9. With the selector in the "P" position, insert the linkage rod into the manual lever, then set the selector at the "N" position, and torque the nut to 7-13 ft. lbs.

10. Connect the oil supply pipe (wipe ATF around the O-ring first).

11. Install the exhaust pipe assembly.

12. Connect the O_2 sensor harness to the O_2 sensor and clamp it.

13. Connect the hot air intake hose and lower the vehicle.

14. Tighten the bolts and nuts which retain the engine to the transmission (torque is 34-40 ft. lbs.). Also install the starter at this time.

15. With the bolt holes on the torque converter and the drive plate properly aligned, install the converter to the drive plate and torque the bolts to 17-20 ft. lbs.

16. Adjust the pitching stopper to 0.071-0.087 in. (1.8-2.2 mm) and torque the adjusting nuts to 7-13 ft. lbs.

17. Connect the speedometer cable and route the cable under the pitching stopper and then clamp it to the pitching stopper.

18. Make all necessary wire connections.

19. Connect the vacuum diaphragm hose and the oil cooler hose.

20. Connect the battery ground cable.

21. Refill the transmission with the recommended ATF.

22. Start the engine and check the exhaust system for any leaks.

23. Check to see that the selector lever operates smoothly and is properly shifting into every selector position.

24. Check the transmission fluid again and if it is low, add ATF until the fluid is at the proper level.

25. Install the spare tire and complete installation.

BENCH OVERHAUL

Before Disassembly

All Models

When disassembling or assembling the automatic transmission, select a place that is clean and free from dust. Clean the exterior of the unit with steam or solvent.

During disassembly or assembly check the condition of each part. Apply a coat of automatic transmission fluid to parts before assembling. Torque all bolts and screw to their specified torque valves. Use petroleum jelly if necessary to hold parts in position when assembling. Be certain to use all new seals and gaskets.

The automatic transmission is divided into two sections, the transmission section and the differential and reduction sections. When replacing or overhauling the transmission separate the transmission from the differential.

Transfer Section

Disassembly

4WD MODELS

1. Remove the rear engine mount and put the transfer unit on a work bench with the oil pan facing down.

2. Remove the solenoid from the transfer unit by turning the solenoid counter-clockwise by hand.

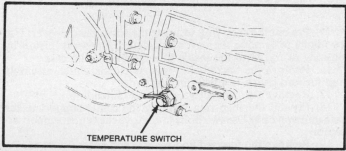

Removing the temperature switch (©Fuji Heavy Industries Ltd.)

3. Remove the temperature switch.

4. Remove the 8 mounting bolts and remove the transfer section together with extension assembly.

NOTE: Make sure to remove the washer from the bearing bore on the upper side of the intermediate case. Do not place the opening of the extension assembly face down, because this may cause the rear shaft assembly to drop.

5. Remove the extension assembly from the transmission section.

6. Remove the rear shaft assembly from the extension housing.

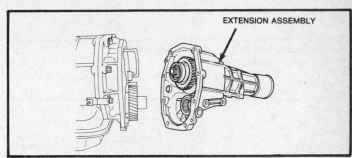

Removing the extension assembly (©Fuji Heavy Industries Ltd.)

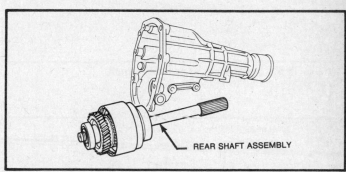

Removing the rear shaft assembly (©Fuji Heavy Industries Ltd.)

NOTE: Be sure not to damage the oil seal in the rear of the extension housing.

7. Remove the seal ring.

8. Using a bearing remover or its equivalent, drive out the ball bearing, washer and transfer driven gear.

9. Using the same bearing remover or its equivalent, remove the transfer clutch assembly drum and ball bearing.

10. Disassemble the transfer clutch assembly by, prying off the inner snap ring, removing the front pressure plate, the three clutch drive plates, the two clutch driven plates and the rear pressure plate.

Transmission Case Section

Disassembly

4WD MODELS

1. With all the ATF drained remove the rear extension assembly.

2. Remove the turbine output shaft and the oil pump drive shaft (pull them straight out).

NOTE: If the shafts cannot be pulled out by hand, wrap a nylon cloth around their splines and use a pair of pliers to remove the shafts. Do not damage the splines in any way.

3. Remove the oil cooler pipe from the transmission case.

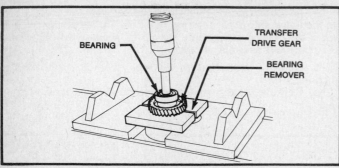

Removing the ball bearing and driven gear
(©Fuji Heavy Industries Ltd.)

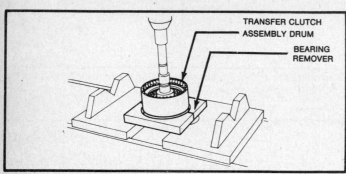

Removal of the transfer clutch assembly drum
(©Fuji Heavy Industries Ltd.)

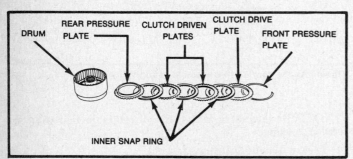

Parts of the transfer clutch assembly (©Fuji Heavy Industries Ltd.)

4. Remove the nuts which secure the transmission case to the final reduction case, and remove the downshift solenoid, transfer solenoid and temperature switch lead wire clips.

5. Remove the vacuum pipe and the ground lead wire.

6. Remove the oil supply pipe.

7. Drain the differential gear oil completely.

8. Place the transmission on a work bench with the housing face down.

Final Reduction Case Section

Disassembly

4WD MODEL

1. With the extension assembly removed, remove the oil pan and the control valve assembly.

2. Wrap a nylon cloth around the spline portion of the drive pinion rear end in order not to damage the oil seal.

3. Remove the transmission case section from the final reduction case section.

Transmission Disassembly

FWD Models

NOTE: Before separating the cases, be sure to drain the differential gear oil.

1. Remove the torque converter assembly from the converter housing.

2. Remove the turbine shaft and oil pump drive shaft. Be careful not to damage the splines when removing the shaft.

3. Remove the nuts securing the transmission case to the differential and reduction case, and detach the downshift solenoid wire.

4. Remove the oil cooler pipes.

5. Remove the vacuum pipe and governor cover.

6. Separate the transmission from the differential and reduction section. Remove the washer located on the planetary output gear.

7. Place the transmission on a stand, drain the transmission fluid and remove the oil pan.

8. Remove the downshift solenoid valve and vacuum diaphragm by turning them with hand. Also remove the diaphragm rod and two O-rings.

9. Carefully pry out the servo apply and release pipes. Note that these pipes are aluminum and must be handled carefully.

10. Remove the six control valve body retaining bolts and lift off the valve body. Be certain not to drop out the manual valve.

11. Remove the transfer valve and loosen the brake band adjusting screw.

12. Remove the rear mounting rubber from the bracket.

13. Take out the bolts securing the transmission cover, turn the cover slightly while tapping rear mounting bucket. Remove the cover and the oil pump carrier as an assembly.

14. Move the transfer drive shaft upward and remove transfer coupling from the rear spline of the drive pinion. Remove the transfer drive shaft and remove the strut band.

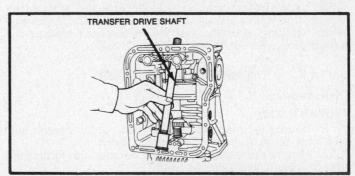

Removing the transfer drive shaft (©Fuji Heavy Industries Ltd.)

15. Pry out the snap ring securing the servo piston cover. Use two bolts to remove the cover and detach the servo piston by pushing its rod from the inside of the transmission case.

16. Remove the brake band, reverse clutch, clutch assembly and forward clutch assembly in that order.

17. Remove the connective shell and clutch hub.

18. Pry out the snap ring securing the center support to the transmission case. Use two bolts to remove the center support assembly.

19. Remove the forward and reverse sun gears.

20. Remove the planetary gear assembly and low and reverse brake plates as an assembly.

21. Remove the low and reverse brake retaining plate.

22. Take out the planetary gear output shaft.

23. Remove the nut and bolts securing the selector arm and neutral safety switch and remove them.

24. Remove the clip and lock nut from the manual shaft and remove the manual shaft and manual plate.
25. Remove the parking rod and lever.
26. Remove the clip from the parking pawl shaft, remove the pawl, the pawl return spring and parking rod support plate.

TRANSFER SECTION

Assembly 4WD Model

1. Apply a coat of recommended ATF to all parts and assemble the transfer clutch.
2. To assemble the transfer clutch, first install the transfer clutch assembly drum and bearing to the rear shaft. Install the rear pressure plate, the two clutch driven plates, the three clutch drive plates and the front pressure plate.

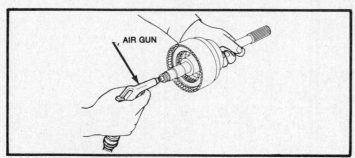

Checking the piston for proper movement
(©Fuji Heavy Industries Ltd.)

NOTE: Apply compressed air into the oil hole to check proper piston movement. Pay attention to the directions of the front and rear pressure plates.

3. After the transfer clutch has been assembled, measure the clearance between the outer snap ring and the front pressure plate. Install a suitable pressure plate to bring the clearance within specifications (transfer clutch clearance 0.4-0.8mm, 0.016-0.031 in.).

PRESSURE PLATES

Plate Thickness mm (in.)	Part Number
4.7 (0.185)	447677000
5.0 (0.197)	447677001
5.3 (0.209)	447677002
5.6 (0.220)	447677003
5.9 (0.232)	447677004

4. Using a bearing installer or its equivalent, install the transfer drive gear, the washer and the ball bearing.
5. Install the seal ring onto the rear drive shaft.
6. Install the rear shaft assembly into the extension housing.
7. Install a suitable washer so that the clearance between the rear shaft assembly and the intermediate case is 0-0.012 in. (0-0.3mm)—standard clearance.
8. Measure dimension "M" using a depth gauge and low-reverse brake gauge made by the manufacture (or use a flat piece of metal).
   a. Place the low-reverse brake gauge or its equivalent, from the rear shaft assembly to the extension mounting surface.

b. Using the depth gauge measure the distance (depth) between the low-reverse brake gauge or its equivalent, to the extension housing mounting surface.

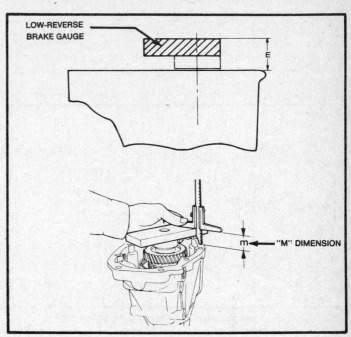

Measuring the "M" dimension (©Fuji Heavy Industries Ltd.)

c. The distance (depth) between the gauge and the extension mounting surface ("M" dimension) will determine what washer thickness to choose, so that the clearance between the rear shaft assembly and the intermediate case will be within specifications.

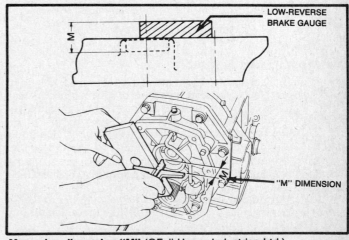

Measuring dimension "M" (©Fuji Heavy Industries Ltd.)

WASHER THICKNESS

Thickness—mm (in.)	Part Number
0.2 (0.008)	803242010
0.5 (0.020)	803242011

9. Install the rear drive gear thrust plate and transfer gear onto the intermediate case.

Unit Disassembly and Assembly

REVERSE CLUTCH

Disassembly and Assembly

1. Pry off the snap ring and remove the retaining plate, drive plates, driven plates, and dish plates. Use a spring compression tool, compress clutch piston and remove the snap ring from the coil spring retainer and remove. Apply air pressure to oil hole to remove piston.

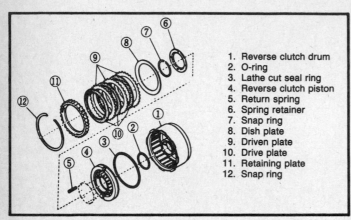

1. Reverse clutch drum
2. O-ring
3. Lathe cut seal ring
4. Reverse clutch piston
5. Return spring
6. Spring retainer
7. Snap ring
8. Dish plate
9. Driven plate
10. Drive plate
11. Retaining plate
12. Snap ring

Reverse clutch components (©Fuji Heavy Industries Ltd.)

2. To assemble, reverse the order of disassembly. Be sure to coat all parts with automatic transmission fluid when installing.
3. Install the driven plates to the clutch drum and align the driven plate missing tooth portion with the oil hole in the clutch drum.
4. Check the clearance between the snap ring and retaining plate to ensure it is within specifications 0.063-0.071 in. If not, change the retaining plate with a proper one.
5. Install the reverse clutch assembly to the oil pump carrier. Apply air into oil to see that the reverse clutch moves properly.

FORWARD CLUTCH

Disassembly and Assembly

1. Pry off the snap ring and remove the retaining plate, drive plates, driven plates, and dish plates. Use a spring compressor tool to compress coil spring retainer and remove snap ring and retainer. Apply air pressure to oil hole to remove piston.
2. To assemble, reverse the order of disassembly. Be sure to coat all parts with automatic transmission fluid when installing.
3. After assembly, check the clearance between the snap ring and retaining plate to see that it is within specifications of 0.039-0.059 in.
4. Install the forward and reverse clutch assemblies to the oil pump carrier. Apply air pressure to the oil hole to see that the forward clutch moves properly.

RETAINING PLATES

Thickness—mm (in.)	Part Number
10.6 (0.417)	453710100
10.8 (0.425)	453710101
11.0 (0.433)	453710102
11.2 (0.441)	453710103
11.4 (0.449)	453710104

PRESSURE PLATES

Plate Thickness mm (in.)	Part Number
11.6 (0.457)	453710105

NOTE: Retaining plates are available in six different sizes.

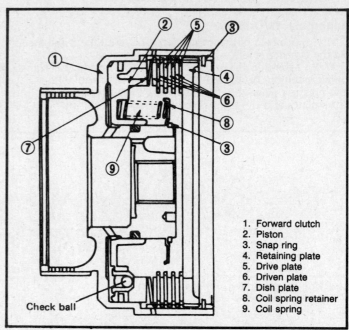

1. Forward clutch
2. Piston
3. Snap ring
4. Retaining plate
5. Drive plate
6. Driven plate
7. Dish plate
8. Coil spring retainer
9. Coil spring

Check ball

Sectional view of forward clutch (©Fuji Heavy Industries Ltd.)

LOW AND REVERSE BRAKE

Disassembly and Assembly

1. Use the necessary tools to remove the snap ring from the center support. Remove the low and reverse brake piston by applying air pressure into the oil hole in the center support.
2. Replace any damaged parts.
3. To assemble, reverse the order of disassembly. Be sure to coat all parts with automatic transmission fluid when installing.

SERVO PISTON

Disassembly and Assembly

1. Pry out the snap ring securing the servo piston cover and use two bolts to remove the cover. Detach the servo piston by pushing its rod from inside the transmission case.
2. To assembly, reverse the order of disassembly. Be sure to coat all parts with automatic transmission fluid when installing.
3. Before assembling the servo piston parts install the two O-rings coated with ATF.

GOVERNOR VALVE

Disassembly and Assembly

1. Remove the screws securing the governor shaft to the governor body.
2. Remove the two snap rings and clip, and disassemble the governor valve assembly. Remove the governor valve, small weight, spring and large weight from the governor body.
3. To assemble reverse the order of disassembly and tighten the governor shaft screw to 3.3-4.0 ft. lbs.

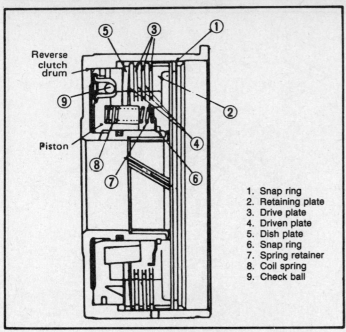

1. Snap ring
2. Retaining plate
3. Drive plate
4. Driven plate
5. Dish plate
6. Snap ring
7. Spring retainer
8. Coil spring
9. Check ball

Sectional view of reverse clutch (©Fuji Heavy Industries Ltd.)

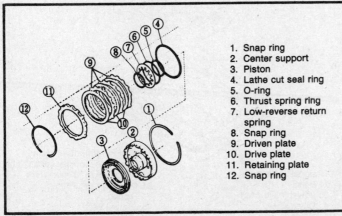

1. Snap ring
2. Center support
3. Piston
4. Lathe cut seal ring
5. O-ring
6. Thrust spring ring
7. Low-reverse return spring
8. Snap ring
9. Driven plate
10. Drive plate
11. Retaining plate
12. Snap ring

Low and reverse brake components (©Fuji Heavy Industries Ltd.)

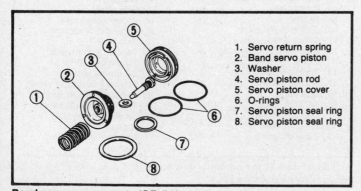

1. Servo return spring
2. Band servo piston
3. Washer
4. Servo piston rod
5. Servo piston cover
6. O-rings
7. Servo piston seal ring
8. Servo piston seal ring

Band servo components (©Fuji Heavy Industries Ltd.)

OIL PUMP

Disassembly and Assembly

NOTE: When disassembling the oil pump note the positions of the side faces of inner gear and outer gear so that they may be installed with their faces facing the same way.

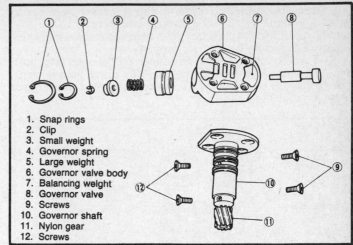

1. Snap rings
2. Clip
3. Small weight
4. Governor spring
5. Large weight
6. Governor valve body
7. Balancing weight
8. Governor valve
9. Screws
10. Governor shaft
11. Nylon gear
12. Screws

Governor valve assembly components (©Fuji Heavy Industries Ltd.)

1. Remove the bolts and disassemble the oil pump carrier and transmission cover.
2. Remove the inner and outer gears from the pump carrier.
3. Check gears and pump carrier bushings. If they are damaged, replace them. Also inspect needle bearings and replace if necessary.
4. When replacing inner or outer gear adjust clearance by selecting its thickness.
5. Check clearances of the gears. Clearance should be 0.08-0.0016 in. between inner/outer gear and transmission cover. Clearance between crescent and tooth tip of outer gear should be 0.0055-0.0083 in. Radial clearance between outer gear and oil pump carrier should be 0.0020-0.0079 in. Clearance between seal ring and groove should be 0.0016-0.0063 in.
6. After installing the gears place the oil pump drive shaft into the pump carrier.
7. When installing the transmission cover, tighten the cover bolts to 4.3-5.8 ft. lbs.

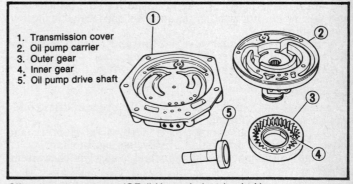

1. Transmission cover
2. Oil pump carrier
3. Outer gear
4. Inner gear
5. Oil pump drive shaft

Oil pump components (©Fuji Heavy Industries Ltd.)

PLANETARY GEAR

Disassembly and Assembly

1. Remove the bolts securing the one-way clutch outer race to the planetary carrier.
2. Push the pinion pin out toward the one-way clutch side, and detach the short pinions, long pinions, thrust washers, needle roller bearings and spacers.
3. Remove the one-way clutch from the outer race.
4. Check all parts and bushings for damage and wear; replace if necessary.

5. Check the planetary carrier-to-thrust washer clearance to see if it is within specifications 0.0059-0.0236 in.

6. To assemble the planetary gear, reverse the disassembly sequence. Be certain all parts face properly.

7. When installing the one-way clutch on the outer race, push the T-bar with finger to insert the one-way clutch until it snaps. Then secure the one-way clutch retainer in the outer race. Torque outer race bolts to 11 ft. lb.

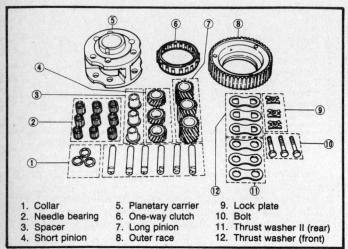

1. Collar
2. Needle bearing
3. Spacer
4. Short pinion
5. Planetary carrier
6. One-way clutch
7. Long pinion
8. Outer race
9. Lock plate
10. Bolt
11. Thrust washer II (rear)
12. Thrust washer (front)

Planetary gear components (©Fuji Heavy Industries Ltd.)

CONTROL VALVE BODY

Disassembly

The control valve is composed of parts which are accurately machined to a high degree and should be handled carefully. Make sure that the valves are clean and free from any foreign material before assembly.

1. Remove the bolts and nut securing the oil strainer and lift off.

2. Remove the bolts and separate the lower valve body, plate, and upper valve body. Be careful not to lose the orifice check valve spring, throttle relief spring and steel ball located in the lower valve body.

3. Remove the manual valve, 1-2 shift and 2-3 shift valves and pressure modifier valve. Remove the side plate.

4. Remove the side plate valves and springs.

Assembly

To assemble the control valve, reverse the order of disassembly and observe the following.

1. When assembling minor parts, such as valve springs and valves, refer to the description of valve springs in chart.

2. Apply automatic transmission fluid to all parts when assembling.

3. When tightening all parts do not force them into place, but lightly push into place with hand.

4. Install the side plates and torque to 1.8-2.5 ft. lbs.

5. Install the orifice check valve and spring, throttle relief spring and steel ball to lower valve body.

6. Assemble the upper and lower valve bodies and torque bolts to 1.8-2.5 ft. lbs.

7. Install the oil strainer and torque bolt to 1.8-2.5 ft. lbs.

FINAL REDUCTION CASE SECTION

Disassembly

1. Place the final reduction assembly on a differential stand or its equivalent, and remove the ten bolts that secure the final reduction housing to the converter housing.

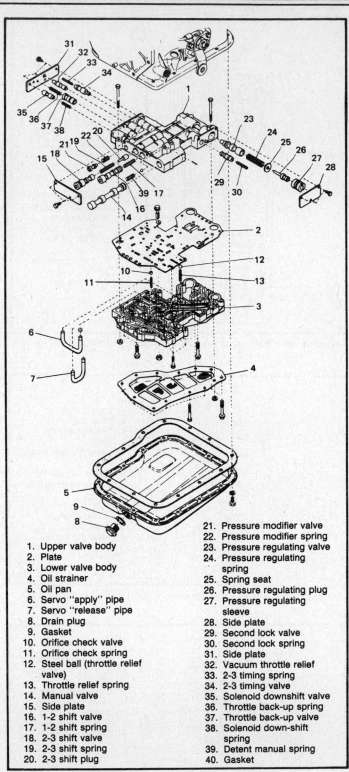

1. Upper valve body
2. Plate
3. Lower valve body
4. Oil strainer
5. Oil pan
6. Servo "apply" pipe
7. Servo "release" pipe
8. Drain plug
9. Gasket
10. Orifice check valve
11. Orifice check spring
12. Steel ball (throttle relief valve)
13. Throttle relief spring
14. Manual valve
15. Side plate
16. 1-2 shift valve
17. 1-2 shift spring
18. 2-3 shift valve
19. 2-3 shift spring
20. 2-3 shift plug
21. Pressure modifier valve
22. Pressure modifier spring
23. Pressure regulating valve
24. Pressure regulating spring
25. Spring seat
26. Pressure regulating plug
27. Pressure regulating sleeve
28. Side plate
29. Second lock valve
30. Second lock spring
31. Side plate
32. Vacuum throttle relief
33. 2-3 timing spring
34. 2-3 timing valve
35. Solenoid downshift valve
36. Throttle back-up spring
37. Throttle back-up valve
38. Solenoid down-shift spring
39. Detent manual spring
40. Gasket

Exploded view of the control valve body
(©Fuji Heavy Industries Ltd.)

2. Remove the bolts that secure the governor cover, and remove the governor body assembly.

NOTE: While removing the governor assembly, slowly turn it to the right.

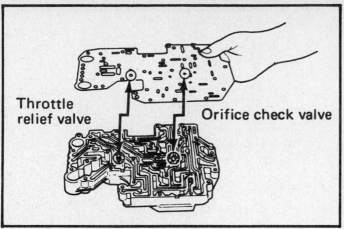

Throttle relief valve

Orifice check valve

Installation of orifice, check and throttle relief valves
(©Fuji Heavy Industries Ltd.)

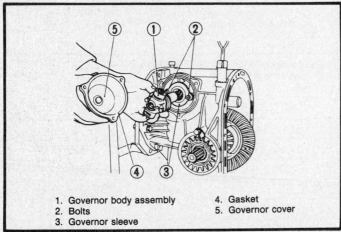

1. Governor body assembly
2. Bolts
3. Governor sleeve
4. Gasket
5. Governor cover

Removal of governor valve assembly (©Fuji Heavy Industries Ltd.)

3. Remove the parking actuator.

4. Remove the three bolts securing the reduction gear oil seal holder.

5. Remove the snap rings from the axle drive shafts in the differential housing.

6. Remove the lock plates, then remove the axle shaft oil seal holders and the axle drive shafts as an assembly.

7. After moving the differential assembly to one side, remove the final reduction housing.

8. Remove the drive pinion lock nut and press out the drive pinion.

9. Remove the snap ring from the end of the speedometer shaft, and remove the speedometer driven gear and the steel ball.

10. Remove the reduction gear.

11. Remove the stator shaft.

12. Check the gears, bearings, seals, O-rings, and gaskets. If they are damaged, replace them.

Installation

1. Press the thrust bearing retainer assembly and the reduction driven gear into the final reduction housing.

NOTE: Be sure that the projection of the retainer flange is aligned with the groove of the final reduction housing.

2. Install the transmission case front gasket and reduction drive gear on the final reduction housing, and snugly tighten the 8 mounting bolts.

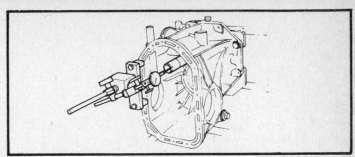

Measuring of run-out (©Fuji Heavy Industries Ltd.)

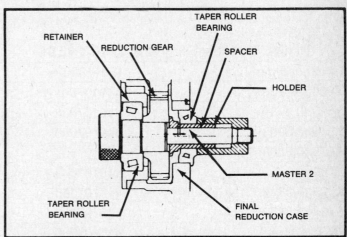

TAPER ROLLER BEARING

RETAINER

REDUCTION GEAR

SPACER

HOLDER

MASTER 2

TAPER ROLLER BEARING

FINAL REDUCTION CASE

Preload adjustment of the drive pinion (©Fuji Heavy Industries Ltd.)

3. With the final reduction housing secured to the differential stand or its equivalent, install the speedometer drive gear.

4. Be sure that the run-out at the tip of the reduction drive gear shaft is 0-0.0031 in. (0-0.08mm). With a dial indicator connected to the drive gear shaft, turn the shaft and watch the dial indicator to get the run-out reading.

5. Install the drive pinion assembly into the final reduction housing.

6. After the drive pinion assembly is installed, a pre-load adjustment of the drive pinion bearings must be performed.

7. Attach the preload check pulley or its equivalent, to the head of the final reduction case holder. Then tighten the holder so that the tension of the spring balance reads 7-9 ft. lbs. to give the specified preload.

NOTE: The torque on the holder to give the specified preload is 7-9 ft. lbs. (10-12 N•m).

8. Measure the clearance between the spacer and the rear bearing (which is preloaded). Slide the spacer rearward and install a dial indicator.

9. Once the clearance has been measured, select a combination of a shim and spacer to ensure a proper preload adjustment.

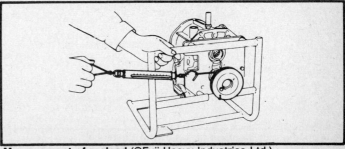

Measurement of preload (©Fuji Heavy Industries Ltd.)

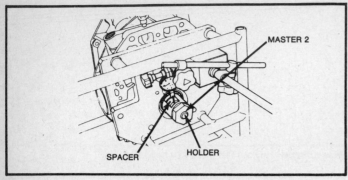

Measurement of clearance (©Fuji Heavy Industries Ltd.)

DRIVE PINION SPACER THICKNESS

Thickness-mm (in)	Part Number
9.600 (0.3780)	446107001
9.625 (0.3789)	446107002
9.650 (0.3799)	446107003
9.675 (0.3809)	446107004
9.700 (0.3819)	446107005
9.725 (0.3829)	446107006
9.750 (0.3839)	446107007
9.775 (0.3848)	446107008

DRIVE PINION SHIM THICKNESS

Thickness-mm (in)	Part Number
0.6 (0.024)	441967001
0.8 (0.031)	441967002
1.0 (0.039)	441967003

10. After the preload adjustments have been made, the drive pinion height adjustment must be made.

11. The drive pinion height adjustment is made by inserting shims between the front bearing cone and the back face of the pinion gear.

12. Set the master drive pinion tool or its equivalent, and the low-reverse brake tool or its equivalent, to measure the clearance (N) between the master and the gauge using a thickness gauge (feeler gauge).

13. To ensure the correct pinion height adjustment select the proper size adjusting shim.

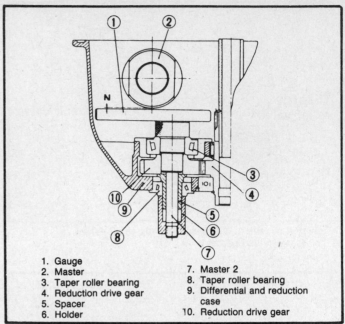

1. Gauge
2. Master
3. Taper roller bearing
4. Reduction drive gear
5. Spacer
6. Holder
7. Master 2
8. Taper roller bearing
9. Differential and reduction case
10. Reduction drive gear

Exploded view of drive pinion height adjustment
(©Fuji Heavy Industries Ltd.)

ADJUSTING SHIM THICKNESS

Thickness-mm (in)	Part Number
0.150 (0.0059)	442182511
0.175 (0.0069)	442182512
0.200 (0.0079)	442182513
0.225 (0.0089)	442182514
0.250 (0.0098)	442182515
0.275 (0.0108)	442182516
0.300 (0.0118)	442182517
0.500 (0.0197)	442182518

14. With the drive pinion installed and the reduction gear in place, install the shim and spacer determined during the preload adjustment, and install the rear bearing cone onto the drive pinion.

15. Install the drive pinion lock nut and lock washer and torque the nut to 87 ft. lbs.

16. Recheck the preload.

17. Install the differential assembly.

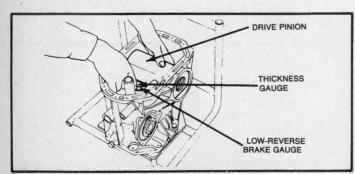

Measurement of the drive pinion height clearance
(©Fuji Heavy Industries Ltd.)

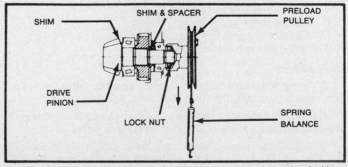

Rechecking the preload adjustment (©Fuji Heavy Industries Ltd.)

18. Install the right and left axle shafts and secure them with the snap rings.

NOTE: Check to see if the clearance between the differential pinion shaft and the axle shaft is within specifications. (Specified clearance 0-0.2mm 0-0.008 in).

19. There are two snap rings available for the adjustment of the clearance between the differential pinion shaft and the axle shaft.

SNAP RING THICKNESS

Thickness—mm (in)	Part Number
1.00-1.10 (0.0394-0.0433)	805026010
1.15-1.25 (0.0453-0.0492)	031526000

20. Install the axle shaft oil seal holder.

21. Install the governor assembly and the governor cover, torque the governor cover bolts to 10-12 ft. lbs.

NOTE: Before installing the governor cover, attach the washer to the cover with vaseline and replace the old gasket with a new one.

22. Install the stator shaft to the converter housing with the new gasket in place and with the flange of the shaft facing upward (torque the flange bolts to 17-20 ft. lbs.).

23. Apply a coat of differential gear oil to the reduction drive gear shaft assembly and install a new mating surface gasket. Install the final reduction case to the converter housing and torque the mounting bolts to 17-20 ft. lbs.

24. Install the parking actuator with the spacer on the final reduction case and torque the parking actuator support bolt to 5.8-8.0 ft. lbs.

Transmission Assembly

Clean and thoroughly check all parts and replace all seals and gaskets during assembly.

To assemble transmission, reverse the disassembly procedures and observe the following points.

1. Install the parking rod support plate and return spring to the case, set the clip to the parking pawl shaft and install the parking rod.

2. Check the one-way clutch for proper operation. It should turn clockwise only, as viewed from the front with the planetary carrier assembly assembled to the center support.

3. When installing the low and reverse brake parts into the case, install the snap ring, retaining plate, drive plates, driven plates, center support assembly and snap ring. There are three drive plates and three driven plates.

NOTE: Before installing low and reverse brake, use a special gauge and select a proper retaining plate so that distance "H" shown in illustration is within specifications (2.778-2.801 in.).

NOTE: When installing the center support, screw two bolts into the center support, then install it into the transmission case while turning the center support gradually.

4. After assembly, measure the clearance between the snap ring and retaining plate. The clearance should be within specifications, 0.0020-0.047 in.

5. The center support is engaged with the transmission case by splines at one position. When installing the center support, be careful not to damage the one-way clutch and bushing.

6. Apply air into the oil hole in the low and reverse brake to see that the piston moves properly.

7. Install the connecting shell and clutch hub as an assembly to the transmission case.

8. Install the forward clutch assembly to the clutch hub.

9. Install the reverse clutch assembly to the forward clutch assembly.

10. Match the projected portions of the brake band with the notches in the transmission case to install the brake band.

11. Select a proper washer to be used at the end of the oil pump carrier until the total end play is within specifications, 0.01-0.02 in.

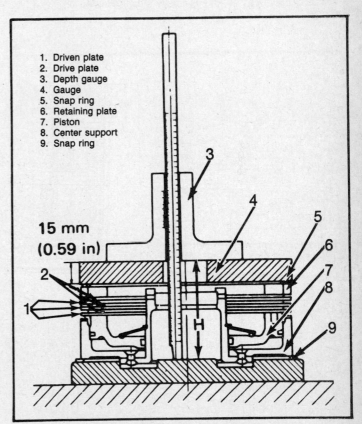

1. Driven plate
2. Drive plate
3. Depth gauge
4. Gauge
5. Snap ring
6. Retaining plate
7. Piston
8. Center support
9. Snap ring

15 mm (0.59 in)

Selection of retaining plate (©Fuji Heavy Industries Ltd.)

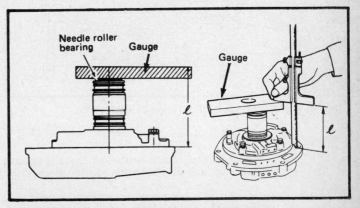

Needle roller bearing — Gauge

Gauge

Measuring distance "L" (©Fuji Heavy Industries Ltd.)

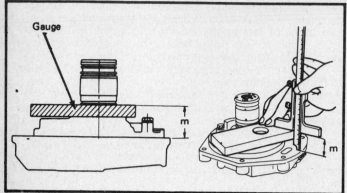

Measuring distance "M" (©Fuji Heavy Industries Ltd.)

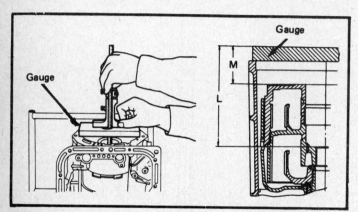

Measuring end play "L" and "M" (©Fuji Heavy Industries Ltd.)

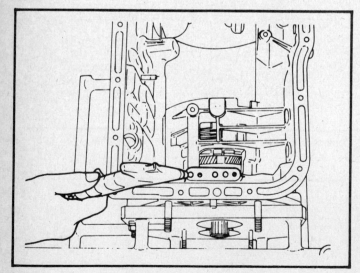

Testing with air pressure (©Fuji Heavy Industries Ltd.)

12. Select a proper reverse clutch washer so that the reverse drum-to-oil pump carrier end play is within specifications, 0.02-0.03 in.

13. Apply petroleum jelly to the washer and pump carrier end, and put the washer on the pump carrier side before installing.

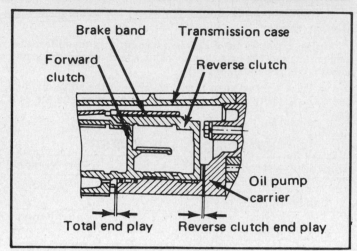

Measuring position of end plays (©Fuji Heavy Industries Ltd.)

NOTE: Do not forget to install the needle bearing.

14. Insert the servo piston cover assembly into the case, using the piston rod as a guide.

NOTE: Two O-rings of the same size are used on the servo piston cover. An O-ring which is used for inner end of servo piston cover must be inserted into the transmission case side in advance.

15. Install the band strut properly. Tighten the adjusting screw to 6.5 ft. lbs. torque, then turn it back 2 turns. Tighten the locknut to 18-1 ft. lbs. torque.

16. Adjust the clearance between the manual plate and the spacer by shims until it is within 0.012 in. Install the safety switch.

17. Install the manual valve groove to the manual plate pin and install to the transmission case. Torque valve body attaching bolts to 4.3-5.8 ft. lbs.

18. Push the vacuum throttle valve in and measure the distance from the rod end to the outer face of the case. Then select a diaphragm rod of the proper length and install it with the vacuum diaphragm. Install the solenoid.

19. Make sure that the servo apply and release pipes are properly installed. Check the height of the pipes above the mating surface of the oil pan to insure that it is 0.83 in. or less.

20. Install oil pan and torque pan retaining bolts to 2.53-3.25 ft. lbs.

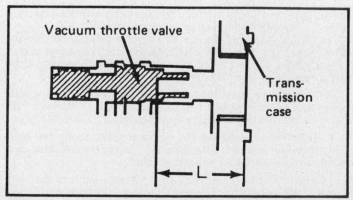

Measurement of throttle valve depth (©Fuji Heavy Industries Ltd.)

S SPECIFICATIONS

GEAR SPECIFICATIONS

		Backlash ①
Planetary gear	Forward sun gear to short pinion	0.15-0.22mm (0.0059-0.0087 in)
	Reverse sun gear to long pinion	0.15-0.22mm (0.0059-0.0087 in)
	Short pinion to long pinion	0.15-0.22mm (0.0059-0.0087 in)
	Long pinion to planetary output gear	0.18-0.25mm (0.0071-0.0098 in)
1st reduction gears		0.05-0.12mm (0.0020-0.0047 in)
2nd reduction gears		0.13-0.18mm (0.0051-0.0071 in)
Governor gears and Speedometer gears		0.30-0.81mm (0.0118-0.0319 in)
Transfer gears		0.051-0.125mm (0.0020-0.0049 in)

①Units: mm (in)

VACUUM DIAPHRAGM ROD

Measurement "L" ①	Part No.	Length ①
25.55 (1.0059) or less	493210103	29 (1.14)
25.65 to 26.05 (1.0098 to 1.0256)	493210104	29.5 (1.16)
26.15 to 26.55 (1.0295 to 1.0453)	493210100	30 (1.18)
26.65 to 27.05 (1.0492 to 1.0650)	493210102	30.5 (1.20)
27.15 (1.0689) or more	493210101	21 (1.22)

① Units: mm (in.)

REVERSE CLUTCH THRUST WASHER

Part No.	Thickness ①
452810100	1.9 (0.075)
452810101	2.1 (0.083)
452810102	2.3 (0.091)
452810103	2.5 (0.098)
452810104	2.7 (0.106)
452810105	1.5 (0.059)
452810106	1.7 (0.067)

① Units: mm (in)

SPRING SPECIFICATIONS
(Low-Reverse Return Spring)

Part No.	465110101
Plate thickness	1.27 (0.050)①
Free height	5.54 (0.218)①
Outer diameter	93.98 (3.70)①
Inner diameter	55.88 (2.20)①

① Units: mm (in)

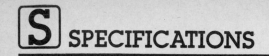

S SPECIFICATIONS

RETAINING PLATE

Part No.	Thickness ①
344268701	7.2 (0.2834)
344268702	7.4 (0.2913)
344268703	7.6 (0.2992)
344268704	7.8 (0.3070)
344268705	8.0 (0.3149)
344268706	8.2 (0.3228)

① Units: mm (in)

WASHER

Part No.	Thickness ①
803021048	1.0 (0.039)
803021049	1.2 (0.047)
803021040	1.4 (0.055)
803021044	1.6 (0.061)
803021045	1.8 (0.171)
803021046	2.0 (0.079)
803021047	2.2 (0.087)

① Units: mm (in)

OIL PUMP CLEARANCES

Inner gear, Part Number	434610100	434610101	434610102
Outer gear, Part Number	434710100	434710101	434710102
Thickness mm,	16-15.99	15.99-15.98	15.98-15.97
in	0.6299-0.6295	0.6295-0.6291	0.6291-0.6287

SPECIAL TOOLS

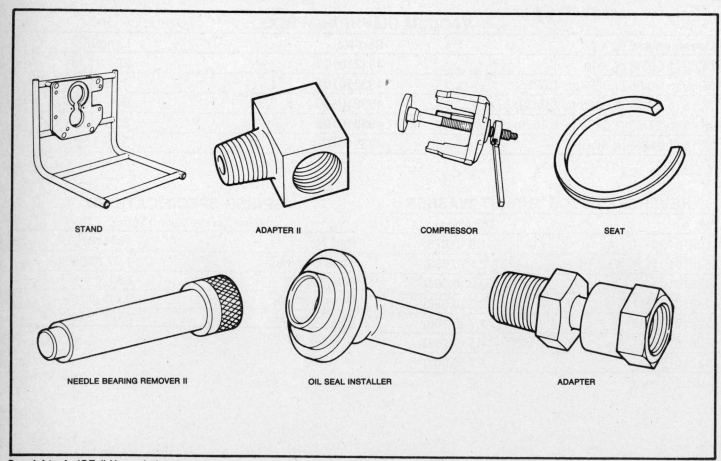

STAND   ADAPTER II   COMPRESSOR   SEAT

NEEDLE BEARING REMOVER II   OIL SEAL INSTALLER   ADAPTER

Special tools (©Fuji Heavy Industries Ltd.)

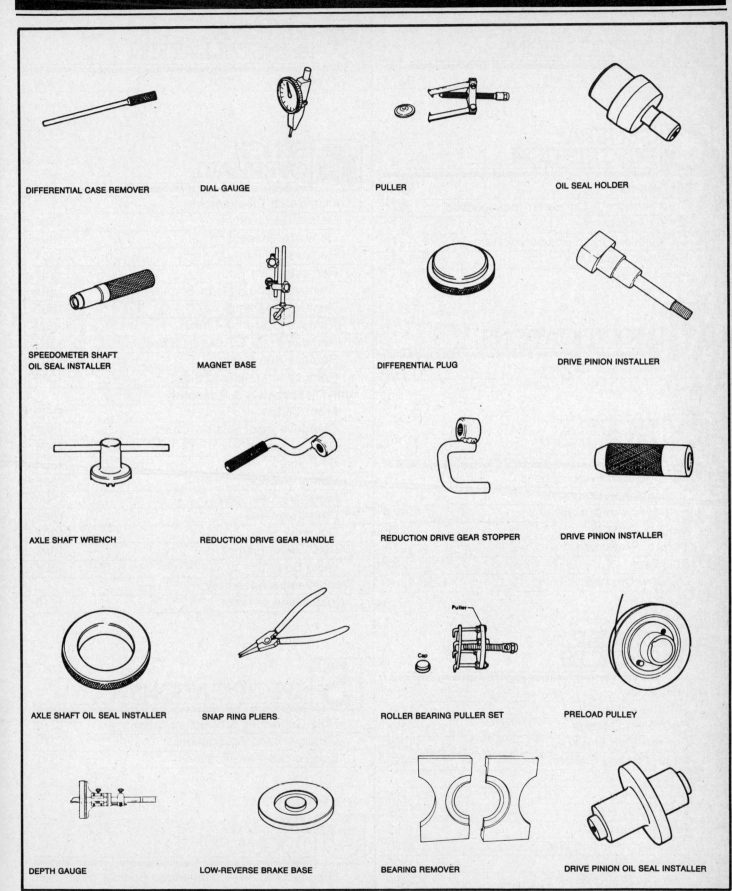

DIFFERENTIAL CASE REMOVER

DIAL GAUGE

PULLER

OIL SEAL HOLDER

SPEEDOMETER SHAFT OIL SEAL INSTALLER

MAGNET BASE

DIFFERENTIAL PLUG

DRIVE PINION INSTALLER

AXLE SHAFT WRENCH

REDUCTION DRIVE GEAR HANDLE

REDUCTION DRIVE GEAR STOPPER

DRIVE PINION INSTALLER

AXLE SHAFT OIL SEAL INSTALLER

SNAP RING PLIERS

ROLLER BEARING PULLER SET

PRELOAD PULLEY

DEPTH GAUGE

LOW-REVERSE BRAKE BASE

BEARING REMOVER

DRIVE PINION OIL SEAL INSTALLER

Special tools (©Fuji Heavy Industries Ltd.)

INDEX

TOYOTA A40, A43D, A43DL, A43DE

APPLICATIONS

Toyoglide 4-Speed Automatic Transmissions
A-40D   A-43D   A-43DL   A-43DE

TRANSMISSION APPLICATION
A-40D, A-43D, A-43DL, A-43DE

Model	Year	Engine Number	Transmission Number
Corolla	'82	3T-C	A-40D
Corolla	'83	4A-C	A-40D
Corona	'80-'82	22R	A-40D
Celica	'80-'81	22R	A-40D
Celica	'82-'84	22R & 22R-E	A-40D
Supra	'80-'81	5M-E	A-40D
Supra	'83-'84	5M-GE	A-43DE & A-43DL
Cressida	'83-'84	5M-GE	A-43DE
Trucks	'83-'84	22R & 22R-E	A-40D, A-43D & A-43DL

GENERAL DESCRIPTION

The A-40D, A-43D, A-43DL and the A-43DE transmissions all consist of the following major units: the torque converter, the clutches, bands, and the planetary gear set and the hydraulic control system.

The torque converter is filled with transmission fluid pressure.

It transforms engine torque automatically and continuously to conform with vehicle torque resistance.

The planetary gear unit serves as an auxiliary transmission. It is located behind the torque converter. The planetary gear unit is controlled by the hydraulic pressure with the help of the operation of the front and rear multiple disc clutches, front and rear bands and the one-way clutch.

The hydraulic control system consists of the front oil pump, the torque converter, the governor and the cooler and lubrication circuits. Further main components are the valve body and the applying clutches and bands.

The selector lever has six ranges, which include "P", "R", "N", "D", "2", and "L". All shifting is automatic and regulated by engine load and vehicle speed.

In the A-43DE there is a solenoid that is electronically controlled which permits more precise control of shift points and torque converter lock-up operation. It will also allow improved response to road changes, engine conditions, driver demands and will improve fuel economy.

The electronically controlled transmission system measures the vehicle speed and the angle of the fuel injection throttle valve. These measurements are then fed to the electronically controlled transmission computer where they are analyzed. The computer then selects the best gear and shift speed to match the driving condition. The computer also monitors engine temperature, brake pedal position, shift lever position and the shift pattern select switches which are located on the dash. This monitoring allows for slight modifications in the "shifting programs."

The A-43DL has a lock up torque converter which automatically engages in third gear to provide a 1 to 1 gear ratio. The lock up torque converter also eliminates any slippage between the engine and the transmission. This action improves fuel economy whenever the lock up converter is engaged.

Transmission and Converter Identification

TRANSMISSION

An identification plate is located on the left side of the transmission, with the model and serial number stamped on the plate. Should a transmission be encountered without an identification plate, examine the case for identifying code letters or digits. Also, obtain the vehicle model and serial number before obtaining replacement parts.

CONVERTER

The converter is a welded unit and cannot be disassembled. The torque converter is a fluid drive coupling between the engine and transmission. It is designed to slip at low speeds, such as when the engine is idling. As engine speed increases, the torque converter will engage the engine to the transmission. There is also a hydraulically controlled mechanical clutch inside the torque converter. This clutch locks the transmission to the engine with almost no slippage. The clutch is controlled by the electronically controlled transmission computer. This clutch is applied in second, third and fourth gears.

Metric Fasteners

Metric bolt sizes and thread pitches are used for all fasteners on the A-40D, A-43D, A-43DL and A-43DE automatic transmissions. Do not attempt to interchange metric fasteners for inch system fasteners. Mismatched or incorrect fasteners can result in damage to the transmission unit through malfunctions, breakage or personal injury.

The metric fasteners dimensions are very close to the inch system fasteners, and for this reason replacement fasteners must have the same measurement and strength as those removed.

Care should be taken to reuse the fasteners in the same locations as removed, whenever possible.

Fluid Specifications

The fluid used in the A-40, A-43D, A-43DL and the A-43DE transmissions is Dexron® II. This applies to all units starting with July 1983 production. Transmissions used prior to July 1983, use Type F automatic transmission fluid.

NOTE: The drain plugs on certain models using Dexron® II have been marked with "DII." All others use Type F automatic transmission fluid. The drain plug change is for the A-40 series transmissions only.

FLUID CAPACITY CHART

Model	Liter	US Qts.	Imp. Qts.
A-43D, A-43DE, A-43DL	6.5	6.9	5.7
A-40D	4.0	4.2	3.5

Checking Fluid Level

The A-40D, A-43D, A-43DL and A-43DE transmissions are designed to operate with the fluid level between the "Add" and "Full" marks on the dipstick indicator. The fluid level should be checked with the transmission at normal operating temperature.

1. With the vehicle on a level surface, engine idling, foot brake applied, wheels blocked move the transmission gear selector through the gear positions to engage each gear and to fill the oil passages with fluid.

2. Place the selector lever in the Park position and apply the parking brake. Do not turn off the engine.

3. Clean the dipstick area of dirt and remove the dipstick from the filler tube. Wipe the dipstick clean and replace in the filler tube making sure to seat it firmly.

4. Again remove the dipstick from the filler tube and check the fluid level as indicated on the dipstick. The level should be between the "Add" and "Full" marks. If needed, add fluid through the filler tube to bring the fluid level to its proper height.

5. When the fluid level is correct, fully seat the dipstick in the filler tube.

Adjustable Line Pressure Sleeve

The A-40D, A-43D, A-43DL and the A-43DE have had an adjustable line pressure sleeve added beginning in February 1983. This sleeve permits fine tuning of the line pressure, during assembly, by the factory. When disassembling and assembling the unit, make sure that the pre-set position is maintained. When adjusting the sleeve, a quarter of a turn in the counterclockwise direction will lower line pressure approximately four pounds per square inch.

1-2 Shift Valve A-40 Series

The 1-2 shift valve has been replaced with a new two piece type. This will eliminate sticking when cold. The two piece valve became effective in the A-40D, A-43D and A-43DL in October of 1981.

Valve Body Design Change (A-40D only)

Beginning February 1983, the valve body of the A-40D automatic transmission has been modified. These modifications will allow the 3-4 upshift at wide open throttle to occur. It will also eliminate the delayed engagement of the neutral/reverse shift when the engine is hot.

Governor Line Pressure Strainer (A-40 series)

A strainer has been added to the line pressure circuit of the automatic transmission. This will prevent the governor valve from sticking.

Governor Valve (A-40 series)

A lock plate and bolt have been added to the governor valve. This will reduce fluid leakage.

PART NUMBER INFORMATION:

Transmission	Previous P/N	New P/N	Part Name
A40	35480-30051	35480-26010	Governor assy
A40D	35480-22010	35480-30060	Governor assy
A40/A40D	35770-22012	35770-14010	Output Shaft
A40/A40D	—	90101-05417	Bolt
A40/A40D	—	90215-11001	Washer, screw location

Detent Spring Retaining Bolt (A-40 series)

Begninning in July of 1981, the detent spring retaining bolt has been lengthened from 1.377 in. (35mm) to 1.574 in (40mm).

Extension Housing Modification (A-40 series)

Effective July 1981, the inside extension housing ribs have been extended. The extension housing bushing oil grooves have been repositioned. This will improve lubrication of the bushing.

Coasting Downshift Shock (A-40D)

When coasting to a stop in drive range, the transmission may exhibit a clunking type noise. The transmission is designed to shift from third to first gear when coasting, but may shift into second gear and then first gear. This is caused by the B-1 brake engaging at the third to second gear downshift. In some transmissions this is caused by an improperly adjusted transmission throttle cable or high throttle pressure. Adjust as required.

Clutch Piston Outer "O" Ring (A-40, A-40D, A-43D, A-43DL)

As of August 1981 the "O" ring for the front clutch (C1), overdrive clutch (C0), and rear clutch has had the cross-sectional diameter increased.

Clutch Piston Return Spring (A-40)

Beginning August of 1981, the return spring for the front clutch (C1) and the rear clutch (C2) has been modified from a single spring type to a multiple spring type. This improves the return action of the clutch piston.

Clutch Cylinder Oil Seal Ring (A-40, A-40D, A-43D, A-43DL)

The cylinder bore, ring groove diameters and oil seal ring grooves have been increased in diameter. This improves performance of the overdrive clutch (C0), front clutch (C1) and the rear clutch.

Clutch Discs and Clutch Plates (A-40)

Due to the change in automatic transmission fluid, clutch discs and clutch plates have been modified. Automatic transmission overhaul gasket kits have also been changed. The new gasket kits can be used in old and new automatic transmissions while rebuilding.

GASKET KIT PART NUMBERS
A-40 series

Previous Part Number	New Part Number	Transmission Type
04351-22022 ①	04351-22023	A-40
04351-22031 ②	04351-22032	A-40D
04351-30070 ①	04351-30071	A-43D
04351-14011 ①	04351-14012	A-43DL

① Parts may be used on previous vehicles
② Parts not interchangeable to previous vehicles

Clutch Hub (multiple disc clutch only)

As of April 1984, the spline length of the clutch hub has been changed from 0.843 in. (21.4mm) to 0.901 in. (22.9mm). The new part number is 35631-30050 and it is interchangeable with previous parts.

Lock-Up Relay Valve Sleeve (A-43D and A-43DE)

Effective June 1983, in order to reduce torque converter lock-up shock, the drain hole diameter in the lock-up valve sleeve has been changed from 0.007 in. (2mm) to 0.059 in. (1.5mm) the new part number is 35215-30012 and it is changeable with the old part.

NOTE: When rebuilding any of the A-40 or A-43 series automatic transmissions, be sure to order the correct gasket rebuilding kit. When ordering replacement parts, be sure of the part number.

TROUBLE DIAGNOSIS

In order to properly diagnose transmission problems and avoid making second repairs for the same problem, all of the available information and knowledge must be used. Included is a working order of the components of the transmission. Test procedures and the accompanying specification charts aid in finding solutions to problems. Further answers are found by road testing the vehicle and comparing all of the results to the Chilton's Three "C's" Transmission Diagnostic Chart. The diagnostic chart gives condition, cause and correction to most possible trouble conditions in the Toyota A-40D, A-43D, A-43DL and A-43DE transmissions.

Hydraulic Control System

The main parts of the hydraulic control system are the oil pump, valve body, governor and the various servo systems, together with the fluid passages connecting these units. The end result of the fluid pressure is to move the clutches and bands of the transmission. The clutches and bands control the planetary gear units which determine the gear ratio of the transmission.

MAJOR COMPONENTS

The major components of the A-40D, A-43D, A-43DL and the A-43DE hydraulic system are the oil pump, the torque converter, governor, cooler and lubrication circuits, valve body and the applying clutches and bands.

The oil pump has the high output necessary to operate the low and reverse gears. The converter pump impeller which is driven by engine rotation is attached to the oil pump. The oil pump provides pressure to shift control valves and apply clutches and bands.

The torque converter consists of three main units; the pump impeller, turbine runner and the stator. The torque converter is a sealed unit and cannot be repaired. It must be replaced as a complete unit when found to be defective.

The pump impeller is driven by the engine crankshaft through the flywheel. The flywheel is bolted to the engine crankshaft.

The turbine, which is mounted to the input shaft, is driven by the pump impeller. The stator is mounted on a one-way clutch. All of these parts are enclosed and operate in a fluid filled housing which is part of the impeller.

The governor valve is installed on the output shaft and operates to produce fluid pressure in relation to vehicle speed. At low vehicle speed, the outer and inner weights act together as a single unit. The centrifugal force on these weights equals the fluid pressure.

CLUTCH APPLICATION CHART
A-43D, A-43DE and A-43DL

Selector Position	Overdrive Clutch (CO)	Clutch 1	Clutch 2		Overdrive Brake (BO)	Brake 1	Brake 2	Brake 3		One-way Clutch (F0)	One-way Clutch (F1)	One-way Clutch (F2)
			I.P.	O.P.				I.P.	O.P.			
Park	Applied											
Reverse	Applied		Applied	Applied				Applied	Applied			
Neutral	Applied											
Drive-1st	Applied	Applied								Applied		Applied
Drive-2nd	Applied	Applied					Applied			Applied	Applied	
Drive-3rd	Applied	Applied	Applied				Applied			Applied		
Overdrive		Applied	Applied		Applied		Applied					
Manual 2	Applied	Applied	Applied			Applied	Applied				Applied	
Low	Applied	Applied					Applied			Applied		Applied

CLUTCH APPLICATION CHART

Selector Position	Overdrive Clutch (CO)	Clutch 1	Clutch 2		Overdrive Brake (BO)	Brake 1	Brake 2	Brake 3		One-way Clutch (F0)	One-way Clutch (F1)
			I.P.	O.P.				I.P.	O.P.		
Park	Applied							Applied	Applied		
Reverse	Applied		Applied	Applied				Applied	Applied		
Neutral	Applied										
Drive-1st	Applied	Applied								Applied	
Drive-2nd		Applied				Applied				Applied	Applied
Drive-3rd	Applied	Applied	Applied								
Overdrive		Applied	Applied		Applied	Applied					
Manual 2	Applied	Applied				Applied					Applied
Low	Applied	Applied						Applied	Applied		

CHILTON'S THREE "C's" TRANSMISSION DIAGNOSIS CHART
Toyota A-40 Series

Condition	Cause	Correction
Vehicle fails to move in any forward range	a) Extremely low oil discharge pressure from front oil pump b) Pressure regulator valve frozen c) Improper operation of manual shift linkage d) Locked by parking lock pawl e) Fluid insufficient f) Front clutch does not operate	a) Repair or replace front oil pump b) Repair valve or replace valve body assembly c) Adjust or repair manual shift linkage d) Repair or replace parking linkage as needed e) Add fluid f) Replace front clutch discs
Vehicle fails to move in "R" range	a) Rear clutch does not operate b) Rear band does not operate	a) Replace rear clutch discs b) Replace rear band or repair rear band servo
Fails to downshift from 2nd to 1st gear	a) Extremely high governor pressure b) 1-2 shift valve does not operate c) Governor valve does not operate d) Throttle valve does not operate	a) Overhaul governor valve assembly b) Repair 1-2 valve or replace valve body assembly c) Overhaul governor valve assembly d) Repair throttle valve or replace valve body assembly

CHILTON'S THREE "C's" TRANSMISSION DIAGNOSIS CHART
Toyota A-40 Series

Condition	Cause	Correction
Improper shifting point	a) Fluid insufficient	a) Add fluid
	b) 1-2 shift valve does not operate	b) Repair 1-2 shift valve or replace valve body assembly
	c) 2-3 shift valve does not operate	c) Repair 2-3 valve or replace valve body assembly
	d) Throttle modulator valve does not operate	d) Repair throttle modulator valve or replace valve body assembly
	e) Throttle connecting rod out of adjustment	e) Adjust throttle connecting rod
	f) Governor pressure is abnormal	f) Overhaul governor valve assembly
	g) Throttle modulator pressure is abnormal	g) Repair throttle modulator valve or replace valve body assembly
Fails to upshift from 1st to 2nd gear	a) 1-2 shift valve does not operate	a) Repair 1-2 shift valve or replace valve body assembly
	b) Governor valve does not operate	b) Overhaul governor valve assembly
	c) Throttle valve does not operate	c) Repair throttle valve or replace valve body assembly
	d) Front band does not operate	d) Replace front band or repair front band servo
Fails to upshift from 2nd to 3rd gear	a) 2-3 shift valve does not operate	a) Repair 2-3 valve or replace valve body assembly
	b) Governor valve does not operate	b) Overhaul governor valve assembly
	c) Throttle valve does not operate	c) Repair throttle valve or replace valve assembly
	d) Extremely high throttle modulator pressure	d) Repair throttle modulator valve or replace valve body assembly
	e) Rear clutch does not operate	e) Replace rear clutch discs
Fails to downshift from 3rd to 2nd gear	a) Extremely high governor pressure	a) Overhaul governor valve assembly
	b) 2-3 shift valve does not operate	b) Repair 2-3 shift valve or replace valve body assembly
	c) Governor valve does not operate	c) Overhaul governor valve assembly
	d) Throttle valve does not operate	d) Repair throttle valve or replace valve body assembly
	e) Front band does not operate	e) Replace front band or repair front band servo
	f) Extremely low throttle modulator pressure	f) Repair throttle modulator valve or replace valve body assembly

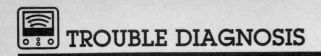

CHILTON'S THREE "C's" TRANSMISSION DIAGNOSIS CHART
Toyota A-40 Series

Condition	Cause	Correction
Oil pressure system noise	a) Air in oil pump suction side is mixing with oil b) Pressure regulator valve vibrates and causes resonance c) Oil leakage in line pressure passage	a) Overhaul oil pump b) Replace pressure regulator valve or replace valve body assembly c) Correct failed part as diagnosed by inspection and air pressure tests
Poor acceleration	a) Engine misses b) Throttle connecting out of adjustment c) Improper operation of one-way clutch d) Wrong type of transmission fluid	a) Repair engine as needed b) Adjust throttle connecting rod c) Replace one-way clutch d) Drain and replace transmission fluid
Oil leakage from front transmission housing	a) Front oil pump body O-ring damaged b) Front oil pump body Type "T" oil seal damaged c) Improper installation of front oil pump body d) Engine rear oil seal damaged e) Torque converter damaged	a) Replace front oil pump body O-ring b) Replace front oil pump body Type "T" oil seal c) Remove front oil pump body and reinstall per procedure d) Replace rear engine oil seal e) Replace torque converter
Slips during engine braking	a) Improper operation of rear band b) Improper operation of front band	a) Replace rear band or repair rear band servo b) Replace front band or repair front band servo
Slips during rapid acceleration	a) Fluid insufficient b) Low throttle pressure c) Improper operation of throttle relay valve d) Shift control rod out of adjustment	a) Add fluid b) Repair throttle valve or replace valve body assembly c) Repair throttle relay valve or replace valve body assembly d) Adjust shift control rod
Mechanical noise	a) Excessive play due to worn planetary gears b) Excessive wear of oil pump gears and other related parts c) Turbine tube converter clearance d) Parking rod out of adjustment	a) Replace planetary gears b) Replace oil pump gears and other related parts c) Replace torque converter d) Adjust parking linkage
Oil leakage from transmission housing	a) Loose bolts and nuts b) Damaged gasket c) Improper installation of union bolts and test plugs d) Damaged oil seal e) Excessive fluid	a) Torque bolts and nuts to specifications b) Replaced gasket c) Remove, reseal, and reinstall bolts and plugs d) Replace oil seal e) Remove excess fluid

CHILTON'S THREE "C's" TRANSMISSION DIAGNOSIS CHART
Toyota A-40 Series

Condition	Cause	Correction
Grinding shifts from 2nd to 3rd gear	a) Rear clutch slips b) Throttle cable disengaged or maladjusted c) Oil level too low d) Oil pressure too low e) Throttle pressure valve stuck f) No. 1 one-way clutch defective	a) Replace rear clutch b) Connect or adjust throttle cable c) Correct oil level d) Disassemble transmission e) Replace valve body f) Disassemble transmission
3rd gear slips	a) Rear clutch slips b) Throttle cable disengaged or maladjusted c) Oil level too low d) Oil pressure too low e) Throttle pressure valve stuck	a) Disassemble transmission b) Connect or adjust throttle cable c) Correct oil level d) Disassemble transmission e) Replace valve body
Stall speed too high	a) Oil level too low b) Engaged clutch slips c) No. 1 or no. 2 one-way clutch slips	a) Correct oil level b) Disassemble transmission c) Disassemble transmission
Stall speed too low	a) Torque converted defective b) Engine output insufficient	a) Replace torque converter b) Test engine
Drive in 2nd gear only	a) 1-2 and 2-3 shift valves stuck	a) Replace valve body
Drive in 3rd gear only	a) 1-2 and 2-3 shift valves stuck b) Governor bushing seized	a) Replace valve body b) Clean or replace governor
Grinding shifts	a) Throttle cable disengaged or maladjusted b) Oil level too low c) Throttle pressure valve stuck d) Front clutch defective	a) Connector or adjust throttle cable b) Correct oil level c) Replace valve body d) Disassemble transmission
Grinding shifts from 1st to 2nd gear	a) Brake 1 and brake 2 slip b) Clutch valve and damper malfunction c) Throttle cable disengaged or maladjusted d) Oil level too low e) Throttle pressure valve stuck f) One-way clutch F defective	a) Disassemble transmission b) Disassemble transmission c) Connect or adjust throttle cable d) Correct oil level e) Replace valve body f) Disassemble transmission
Hard engagement jolt or definite double knock when engaging Reverse gear	a) Damper defective or wrong cover parts	a) Replace valve body
Car cannot be started in "N"	a) Transmission switch defective	a) Replace transmission switch
Car creeps or runs in "N"	a) Selector rod setting wrong b) Front clutch defective (bonded)	a) Adjust selector rod b) Disassemble transmission
Drive in 1st gear only when in "D"	a) 1-2 shift valve stuck b) Governor bushing seized	a) Replace valve body b) Clean or replace governor
Drive in 1st and 2nd gear only when in "D"	a) 2-3 shift valve stuck	a) Replace valve body
No kickdown shifts	a) Throttle cable setting wrong b) Control unit setting wrong c) Throttle pressure valve sticks d) Plastic balls in transfer plate leak	a) Adjust throttle cable b) Adjust valve body c) Replace valve body d) Replace valve body

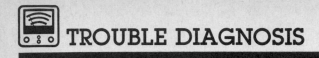

CHILTON'S THREE "C's" TRANSMISSION DIAGNOSIS CHART
Toyota A-40 Series

Condition	Cause	Correction
Selector lever cannot be moved to "P"	a) Selector linkage setting wrong b) Locking device defective	a) Adjust selector linkage b) Repair locking device
Parking position will not disengage	a) Parking lock pawl caught in teeth of output shell b) Excessive friction in parking lock device	a) Replace parking lock pawl b) Repair parking lock device
Parking position does not hold (slips)	a) Selector rod setting wrong	a) Adjust selector rod
Shift points too high	a) Throttle cable setting wrong b) Governor bushing seized c) Governor piston rings defective or worn d) Throttle pressure valve malfunctions e) Shift valves jammed	a) Adjust throttle cable b) Clean or replace governor c) Replace piston rings d) Replace valve body e) Replace valve body
Shift points too low	a) Throttle cable setting wrong b) Governor bushing seized c) Throttle pressure valve malfunctions d) Plastic balls in transfer plate leak	a) Adjust throttle cable b) Clean or replace governor c) Replace valve body d) Replace valve body
Shift points too high or too low and shift movements too long and too soft	a) Brake 1 and brake 2 are damaged by 1-2 gear shifts b) Rear clutch damaged by 2-3 gear shifts	a) Replace brakes b) Replace clutch
No drive in Reverse and 2nd gear	a) Shift valve stuck in 3rd gear position	a) Replace valve body Disassemble transmission if metal particles or abrasion are found in oil sump
No braking effect from 1st gear when in "2" and "1"	a) Clutch valve and damper defective b) Brake 3 defective	a) Replace valve body b) Replace brake 3
No braking effect from 2nd gear when in "2" and "1"	a) Brake 2 defective	a) Replace brake 2
Rattling noise in Neutral	a) Drive plate broken b) Welded drive tabs on converter damaged	a) Replace drive plate b) Replace converter
Growling noise in Neutral, eliminated when accelerating in "N"	a) Valve chatter in control unit b) Oil pump draws in air	a) Correct oil level b) Tighten valve body mounting screws, check gaskets
Harsh downshift to 1st gear	a) Improper operation of the one-way clutch	a) Repair or replace the one-way clutch
Slips when starting to move in "D", "2" and "L" range	a) Fluid insufficient b) Improper operation of front oil pump c) Improper operation of pressure regulator valve d) Improper operation of front clutch e) Improper operation of one-way clutch in "D" or "2" range	a) Add fluid b) Overhaul or replace front oil pump c) Repair or replace pressure regulator valve d) Replace front clutch e) Replace one-way clutch

The oil pump supplies pressure to the regulator valves which will direct fluid to the torque converter. Fluid from the torque converter flows through the oil cooler to lubricate the planetary gear components.

The valve body assembly consists of the manual valve, pressure regulator valve, check valves and the automatic shift control valves. The automatic shift control valves are provided to actuate the upshift or downshift automatically.

Diagnosis Tests

OIL PRESSURE TEST

Certain general precautions should be taken when doing oil pressure testing.

1. The transmission should be filled with the specified transmission fluid to the proper level.
2. Be sure to have all four wheels blocked.
3. Perform the tests with the transmission warmed up to operating temperature.

LINE PRESSURE TESTS

1. Block the front and rear wheels.
2. Apply the parking brake.
3. Make sure the throttle lever will move to the point marked on the transmission case when the carburetor is fully opened.
4. Connect a pressure gauge to the line pressure port.
5. Start the engine.
6. Shift to "D" range and move the throttle valve to the wide open position. Record the pressure.
7. Shift into "2" range and move the throttle valve to wide open position. Record the pressure.
8. Shift to "L" range and move the throttle valve to wide open position. Record the pressure.

— CAUTION —

Do not run the tests longer than 5 seconds at a time. Never make range shifts when the throttle valve is wide open.

With the pressure gauge still connected to the line pressure port, run the tests in the "R", "N" and "P" ranges.

Run the engine at 1,000 rpm and stall rpm in "D" and "R" ranges. Read the oil pressures in each range and record them when done.

Evaluation

When all ranges show higher than specified pressures:
1. Pressure regulator valve defective.
2. Throttle valve defective.
3. Throttle cable out of adjustment. When all ranges show lower than specified pressures:
1. Defective oil pump.
2. Throttle valve defective.
3. Pressure regulator valve defective.

When the pressure at either range is too low, it is usually due to fluid leakage in the said range hydraulic circuit.

1. When the pressure is low in the "D" range, it is an indication of a defective front clutch or overdrive clutch.
2. When the pressure is low in the "R" range, it indicates a defective rear clutch, overdrive clutch or brake number three.

GOVERNOR PRESSURE TESTS

Connect a pressure gauge to the governor pressure port and attach a tachometer to the engine. Shift into "D" range and measure the governor pressure.

— CAUTION —

Decision can be reached with 1000 rpm test. But, if tests are to be made at 1800 and 3500 rpm, it would be safer to test on road or chassis dynamometer, as on-stand test could be hazardous.

When the governor pressure is low or high:
1. Line pressure is defective.
2. Fluid leakage in the governor circuit.
3. The governor valve is defective.

TIME LAG TEST

1. Check the transmission fluid level and adjust if necessary.
2. Block the front and rear wheels.
3. Apply the parking brake. Start the engine.
4. Check the idling speed. Adjust if needed.
5. Move the shift lever from "N" to "D" range. Measure the time it takes from shifting the lever until the shock is felt using a stopwatch. The lag time should be less than 1.2 seconds.
6. In the same fashion, check the lag time for the "N" to "D" range. The lag time should be less than 1.5 seconds.

Evaluation

1. If the "N" to "D" lag time is longer than specified, then the front clutch or the overdrive clutch is defective. Line pressure could also be low.
2. If the "N" to "R" lag time is longer than specified, then the rear clutch, overdrive clutch, or number three brake is defective. Line pressure could also be excessively low.

STALL TEST

The purpose of the stall test is to check transmission and engine performance. This is done by measuring maximum engine rpm against the transmission in "D", "2", "L", and "R" ranges.

1. Check the transmission fluid at normal operating temperature and adjust if necessary.
2. Check the accelerator and throttle linkage and adjust if necessary.
3. Apply the parking brake and block all four wheels.
4. Attach a tachometer to engine.
5. Apply foot brake and accelerator to floor until highest rpm reading is obtained.
6. Compare reading to specifications.

Evaluation

If the stall speed is the same at all ranges but lower than specified:
1. The engine lacks sufficient power.
2. Stator one-way clutch is not operating.

NOTE: If test results show a drop of more than 600 rpm below the specified value, the torque converter could be defective.

When the stall speed at the "D" range is higher than specified:
1. The overdrive one-way clutch is not operating properly.
2. The line pressure is too low.
3. The front clutch is not operating properly.
4. The one-way clutch number 2 is not operating properly.

If the stall speed in the "R" range is higher than specified:
1. The rear clutch or brake number 3 is slipping.
2. Low line pressure.
3. Overdrive one-way clutch defective.

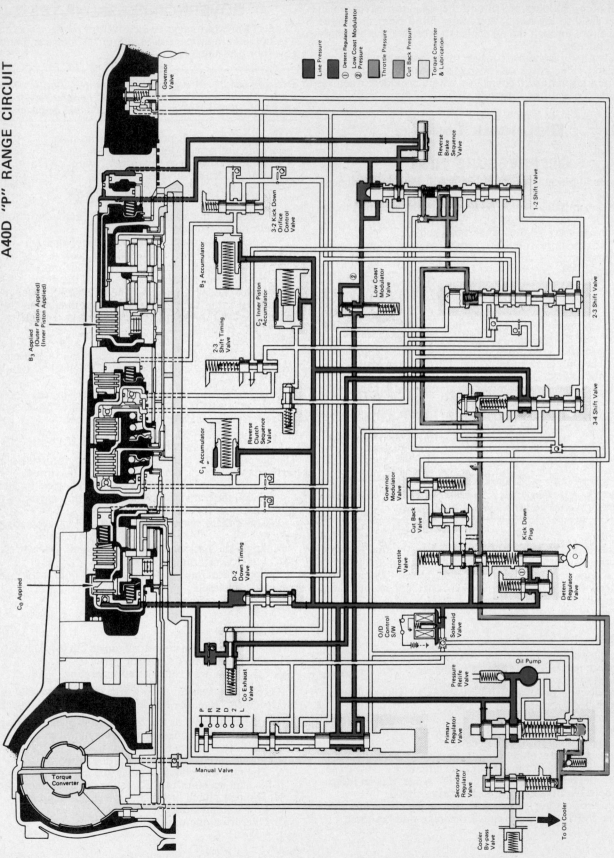

Oil flow circuit park range A-40D automatic transmission

A40D "P" RANGE CIRCUIT

A40D "N" RANGE CIRCUIT

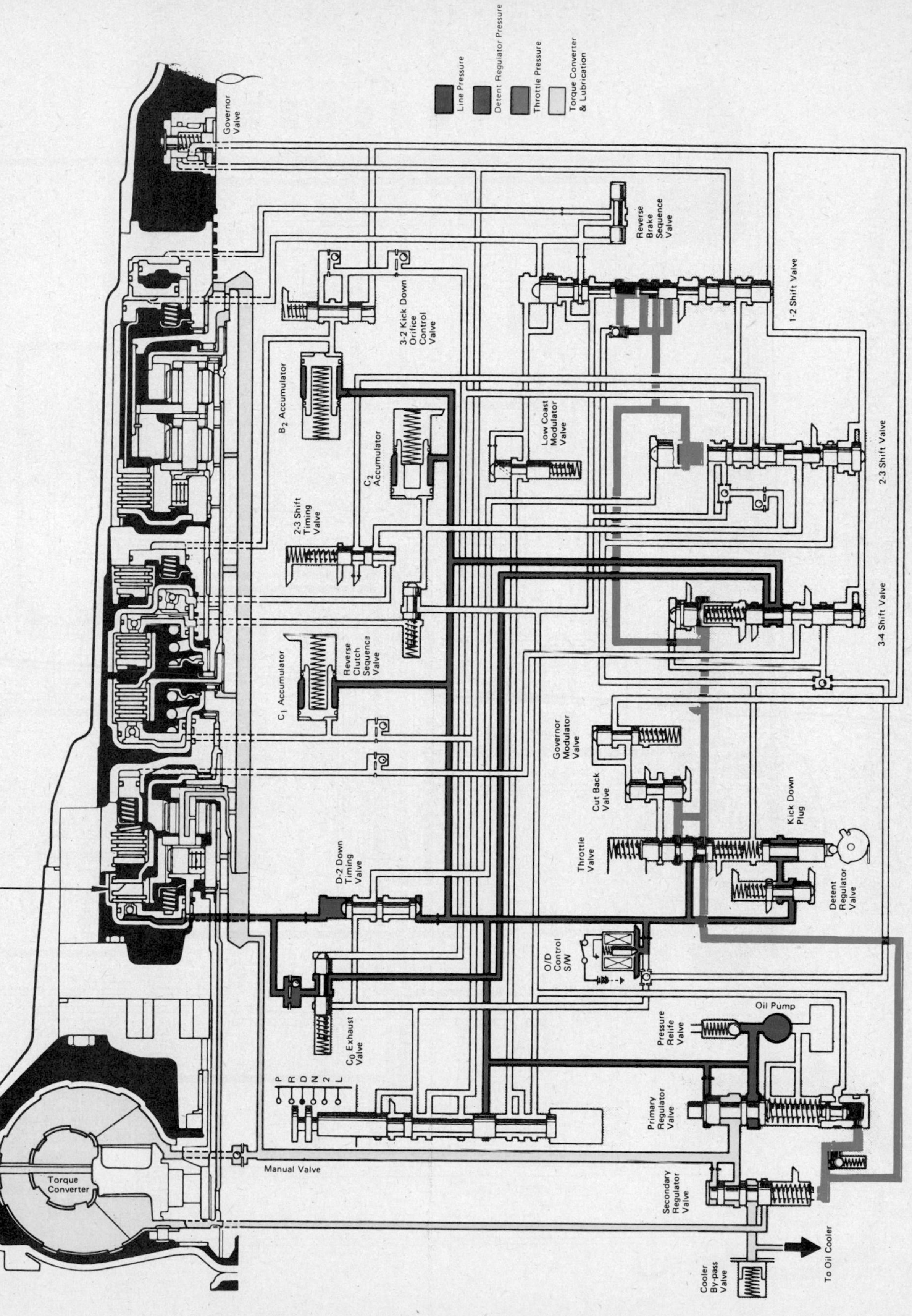

Line Pressure
Detent Regulator Pressure
Throttle Pressure
Torque Converter & Lubrication

Governor Valve

Reverse Brake Sequence Valve

1-2 Shift Valve

3-2 Kick Down Orifice Control Valve

B₂ Accumulator

C₂ Accumulator

Low Coast Modulator Valve

2-3 Shift Valve

2-3 Shift Timing Valve

C₁ Accumulator

Reverse Clutch Sequence Valve

3-4 Shift Valve

Governor Modulator Valve

Cut Back Valve

Kick Down Plug

Throttle Valve

Detent Regulator Valve

D-2 Down Timing Valve

C₀ Applied

O/D Control S/W

Oil Pump

Pressure Relife Valve

C₀ Exhaust Valve

P R D N 2 L

Primary Regulator Valve

Manual Valve

Torque Converter

Secondary Regulator Valve

Cooler By-pass Valve

To Oil Cooler

Oil flow circuit neutral range A-40D automatic transmission

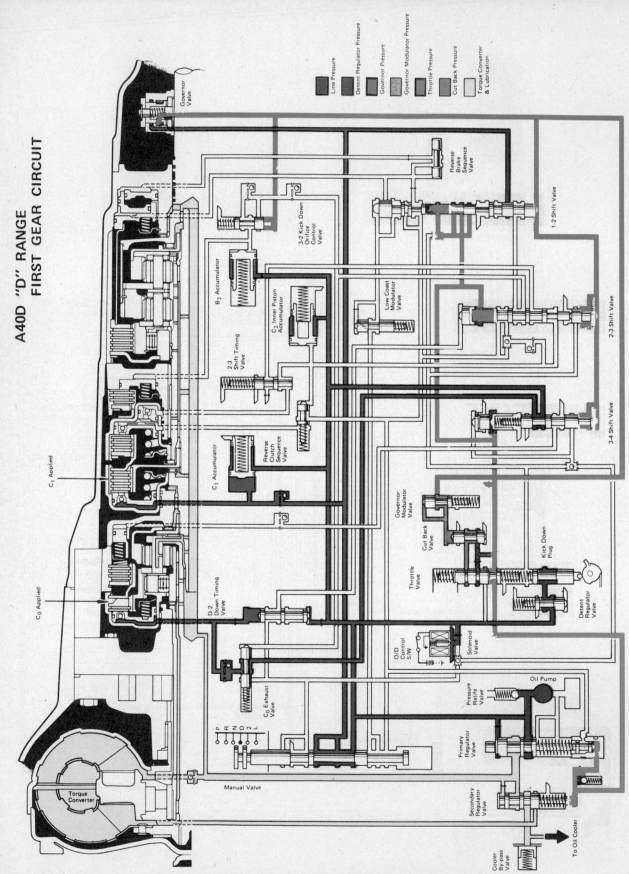

A40D "D" RANGE
FIRST GEAR CIRCUIT

Line Pressure
Detent Regulator Pressure
Governor Pressure
Governor Modulator Pressure
Throttle Pressure
Cut Back Pressure
Torque Converter & Lubrication

Governor Valve

Reverse Brake Sequence Valve

1-2 Shift Valve

3-2 Kick Down Orifice Control Valve

B₂ Accumulator

Low Coast Modulator Valve

2-3 Shift Valve

C₂ Inner Piston Accumulator

2-3 Shift Timing Valve

3-4 Shift Valve

Reverse Clutch Sequence Valve

C₁ Accumulator

C₁ Applied

Governor Modulator Valve

Cut Back Valve

Kick Down Plug

C₀ Applied

D-2 Down Timing Valve

Throttle Valve

Detent Regulator Valve

C₀ Exhaust Valve

O/D Control S/W

Solenoid Valve

P R N D 2 L

Pressure Relife Valve

Oil Pump

Primary Regulator Valve

Manual Valve

Torque Converter

Secondary Regulator Valve

To Oil Cooler

Cooler By-pass Valve

Oil flow circuit drive range 1st gear A-40D automatic transmission

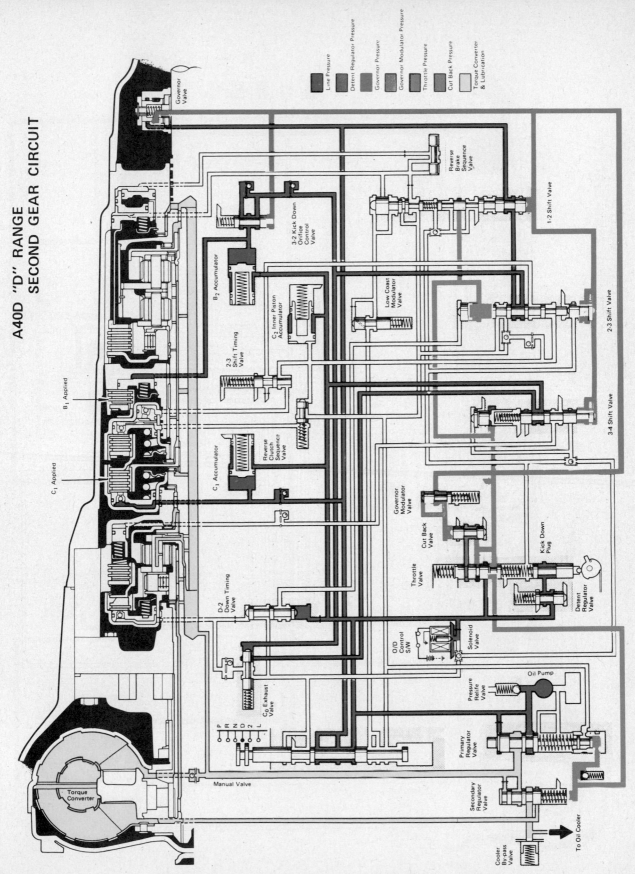

A40D "D" RANGE SECOND GEAR CIRCUIT

Line Pressure · Detent Regulator Pressure · Governor Pressure · Governor Modulator Pressure · Throttle Pressure · Cut Back Pressure · Torque Converter & Lubrication

Oil flow circuit drive range 2nd gear A-40D automatic transmission

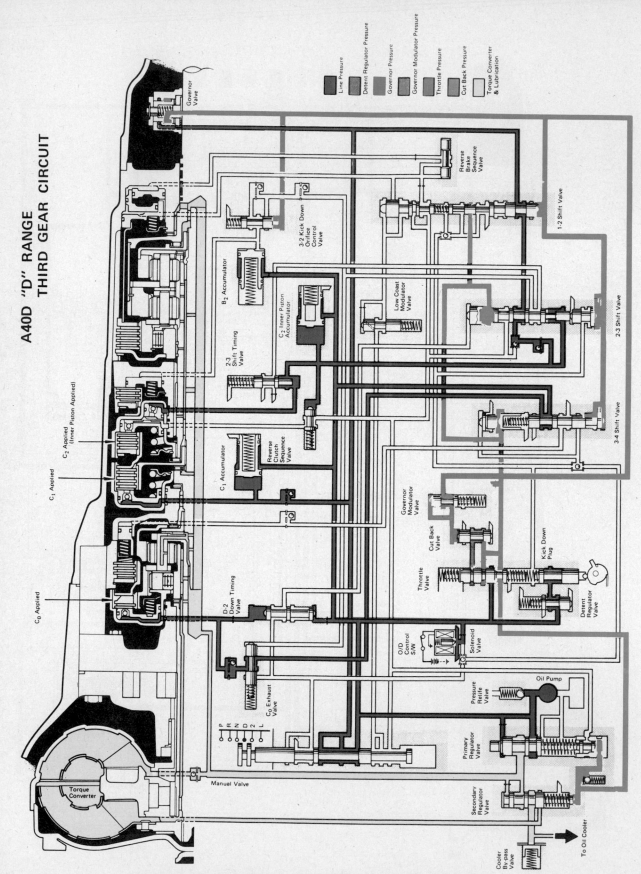

Oil flow circuit drive range 3rd gear A-40D automatic transmission

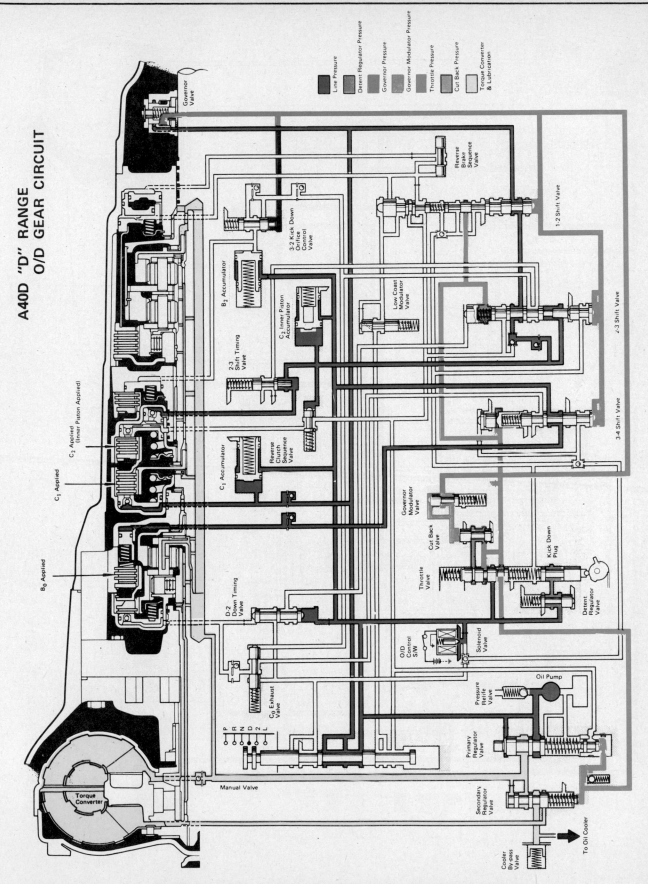

A40D "D" RANGE O/D GEAR CIRCUIT

Line Pressure
Detent Regulator Pressure
Governor Pressure
Governor Modulator Pressure
Throttle Pressure
Cut Back Pressure
Torque Converter & Lubrication

Governor Valve

Reverse Brake Sequence Valve

1-2 Shift Valve

3-2 Kick Down Orifice Control Valve

B₂ Accumulator

C₂ Inner Piston Accumulator

Low Coast Modulator Valve

2-3 Shift Timing Valve

2-3 Valve

3-4 Shift Valve

C₂ Applied (Inner Piston Applied)

C₁ Accumulator

Reverse Clutch Sequence Valve

C₁ Applied

Governor Modulator Valve

B₀ Applied

Cut Back Valve

Kick Down Plug

Throttle Valve

Detent Regulator Valve

D-2 Down Timing Valve

O/D Control S/W

Solenoid Valve

C₀ Exhaust Valve

Oil Pump

Pressure Relife Valve

P R N D 2 L

Primary Regulator Valve

Manual Valve

Torque Converter

Secondary Regulator Valve

To Oil Cooler

Cooler By-pass Valve

Oil flow circuit drive range overdrive gear A-40D automatic transmission

1285

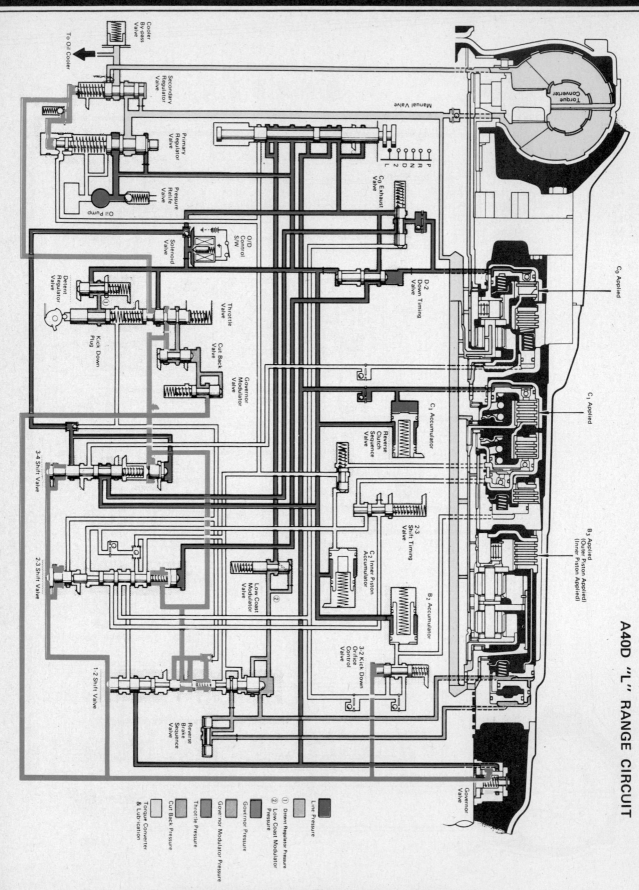

A40D "L" RANGE CIRCUIT

Oil flow circuit low range A-40D automatic transmission

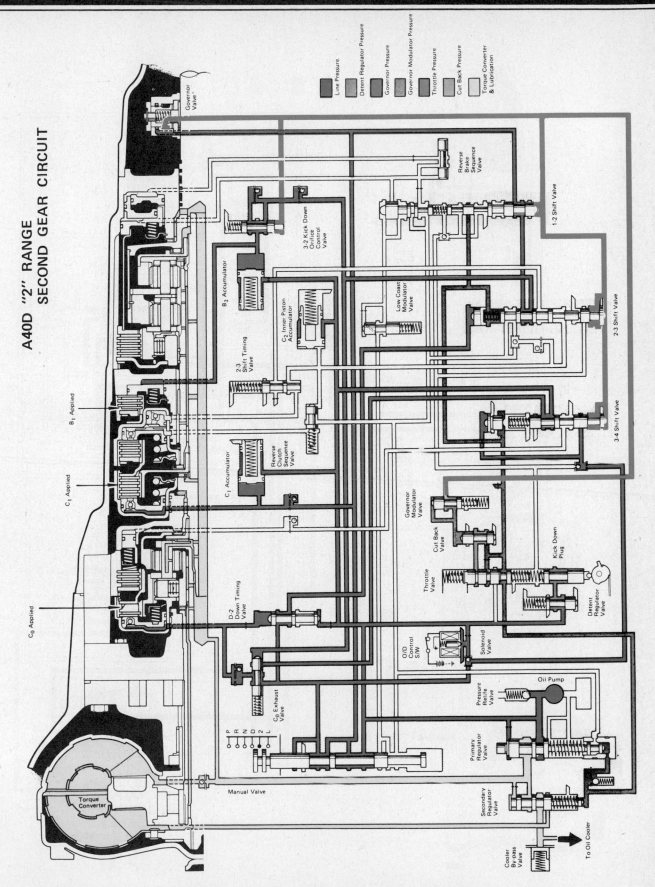

A40D "2" RANGE SECOND GEAR CIRCUIT

Oil flow circuit manual 2 range A-40D automatic transmission

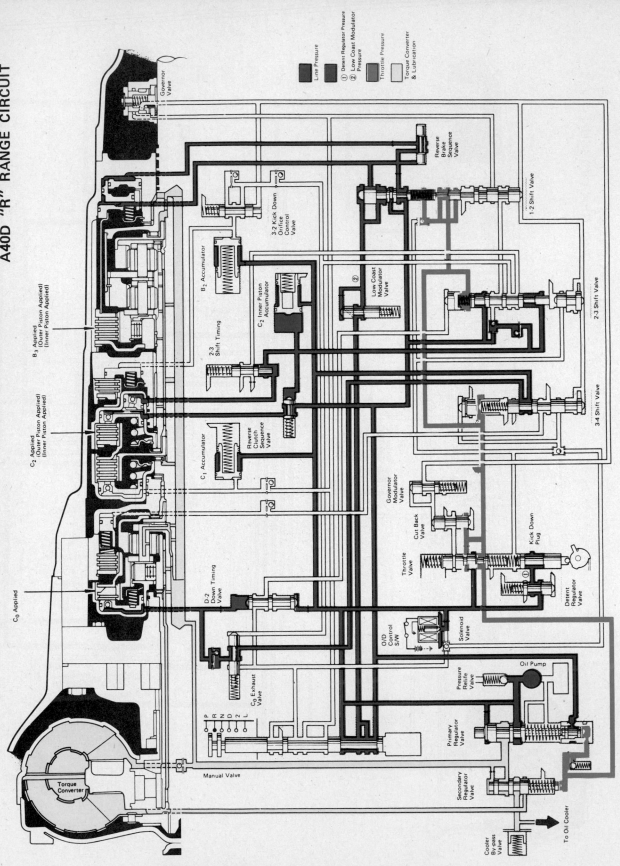

A40D "R" RANGE CIRCUIT

	Line Pressure
①	Detent Regulator Pressure
②	Low Coast Modulator Pressure
	Throttle Pressure
	Torque Converter & Lubrication

Oil flow circuit reverse range A-40D automatic transmission

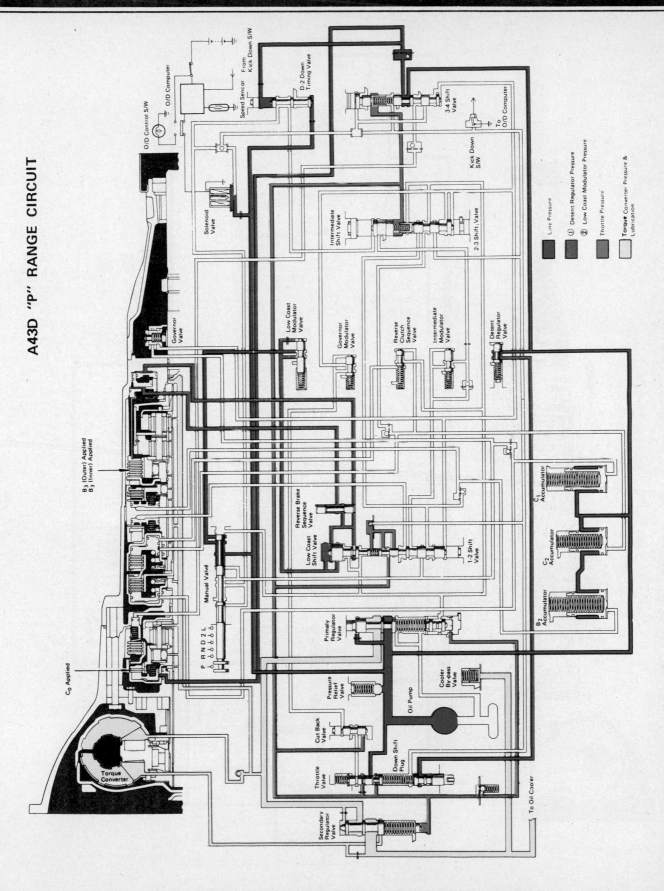

Oil flow circuit park range A-43D, A-43DL and A-43DE automatic transmission

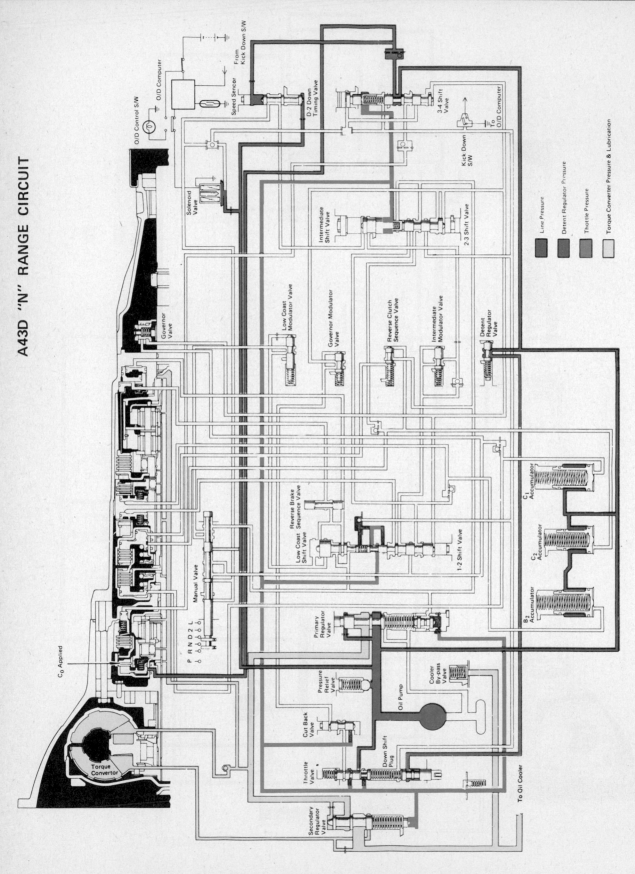

A43D "N" RANGE CIRCUIT

Oil flow circuit neutral range A-43D, A-43DL and A-43DE automatic transmission

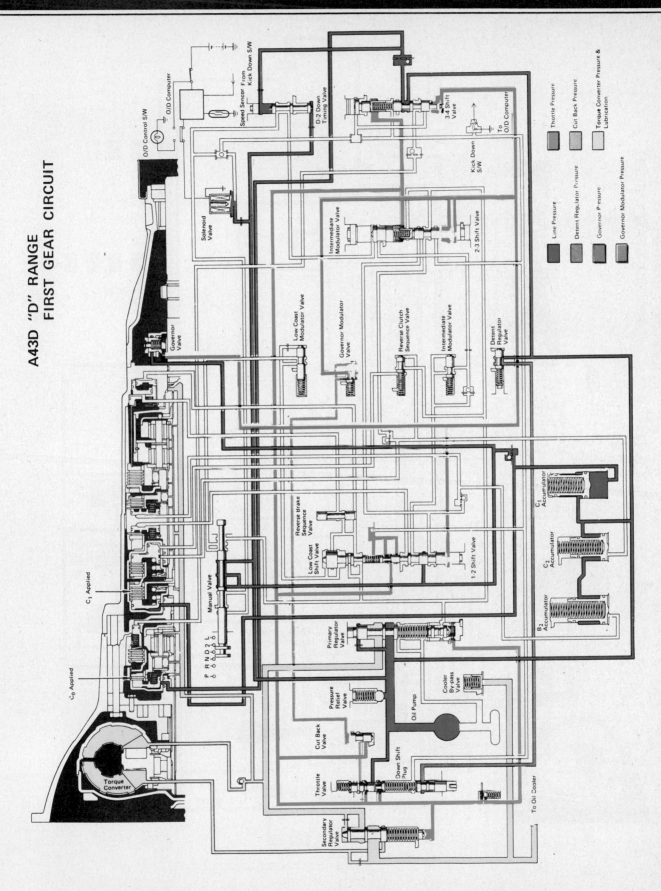

Oil flow circuit drive range 1st gear A-43D, A-43DL and A-43DE automatic transmission

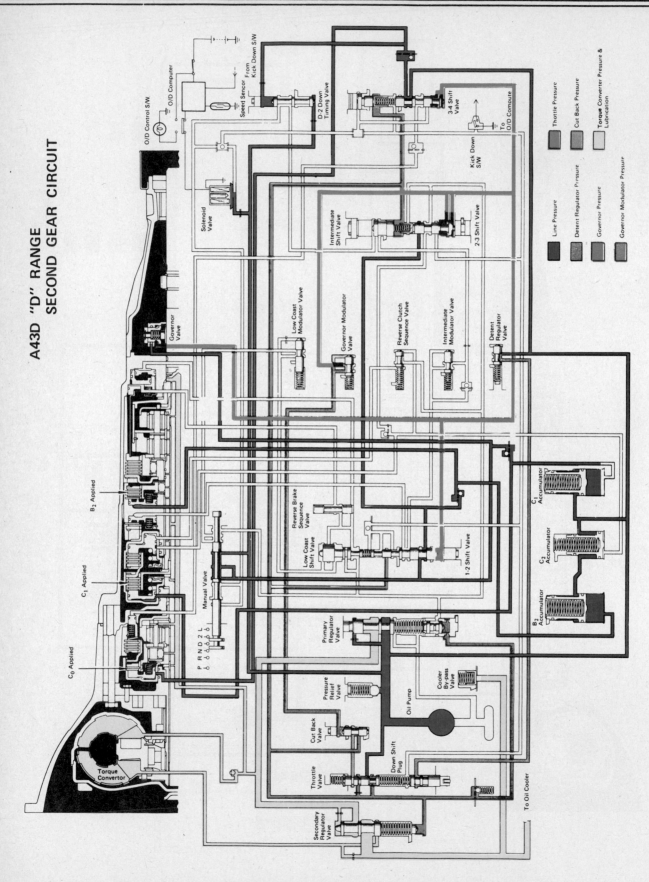

A43D "D" RANGE
SECOND GEAR CIRCUIT

Oil flow circuit drive range 2nd gear A-43D, A-43DL and A-43DE automatic transmission

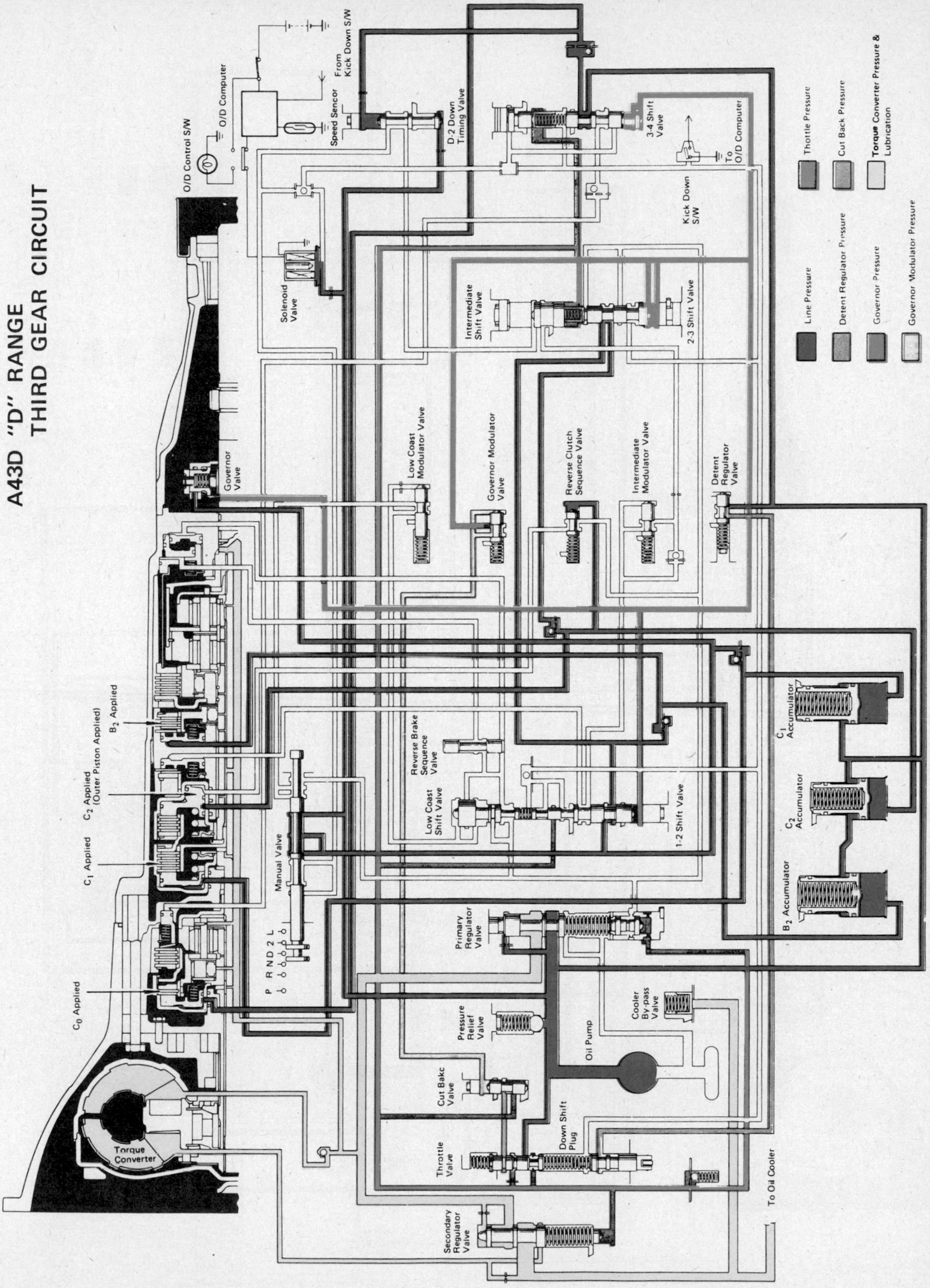

A43D "D" RANGE
THIRD GEAR CIRCUIT

O/D Control S/W

From Kick Down S/W

Speed Sencor

O/D Computer

D-2 Down Timing Valve

3-4 Shift Valve

To O/D Computer

Kick Down S/W

Solenoid Valve

Intermediate Shift Valve

2-3 Shift Valve

Throttle Pressure

Cut Back Pressure

Torque Converter Pressure & Lubrication

Line Pressure

Detent Regulator Pressure

Governor Pressure

Governor Modulator Pressure

Governor Valve

Low Coast Modulator Valve

Governor Modulator Valve

Reverse Clutch Sequence Valve

Intermediate Modulator Valve

Detent Regulator Valve

B2 Applied

C1 Applied C2 Applied (Outer Piston Applied)

Reverse Brake Sequence Valve

Low Coast Shift Valve

1-2 Shift Valve

C1 Accumulator

C2 Accumulator

B2 Accumulator

Manual Valve

P R N D 2 L

C0 Applied

Primary Regulator Valve

Pressure Relief Valve

Cooler By-pass Valve

Oil Pump

Torque Converter

Cut Bakc Valve

Throttle Valve

Down Shift Plug

To Oil Cooler

Secondary Regulator Valve

Oil flow circuit drive range 3rd gear A-43D, A-43DL and A-43DE automatic transmission

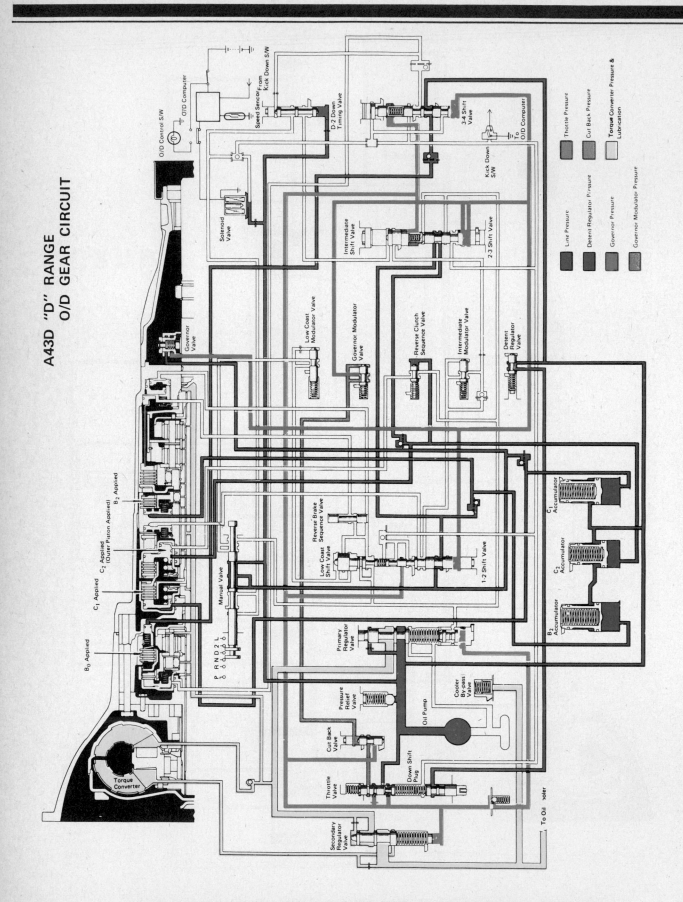

A43D "D" RANGE O/D GEAR CIRCUIT

Oil flow circuit drive range overdrive gear A-43D, A-43DL and A-43DE automatic transmission

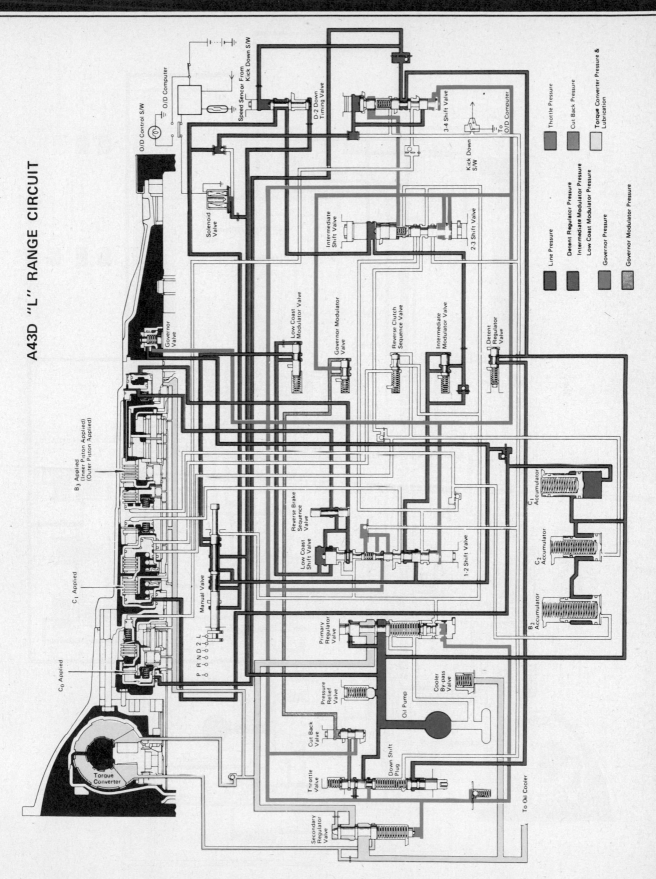

Oil flow circuit low range A-43D, A-43DL and A-43DE automatic transmission

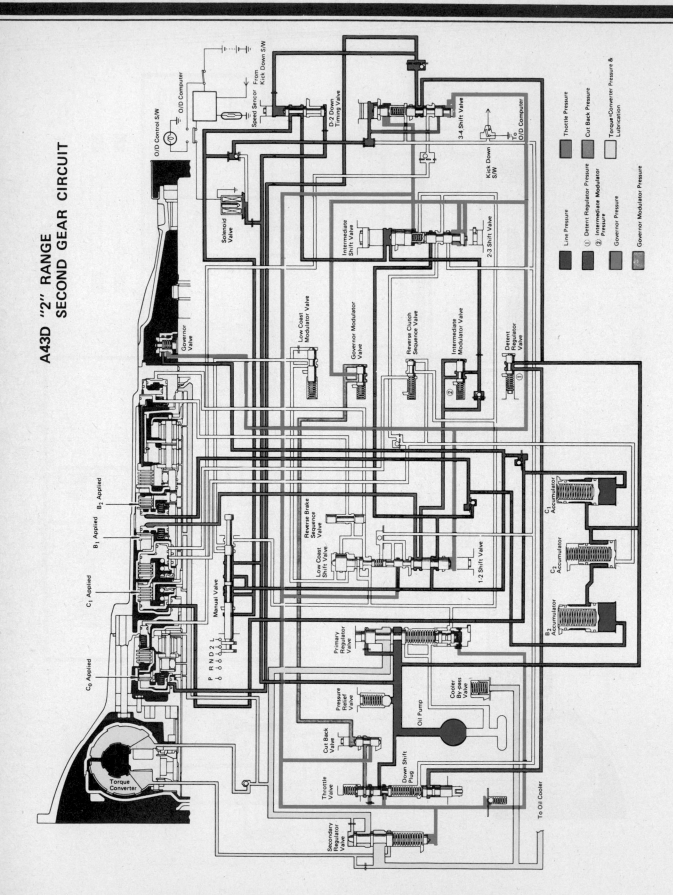

Oil flow circuit manual 2 range A-43D, A-43DL and A-43DE automatic transmission

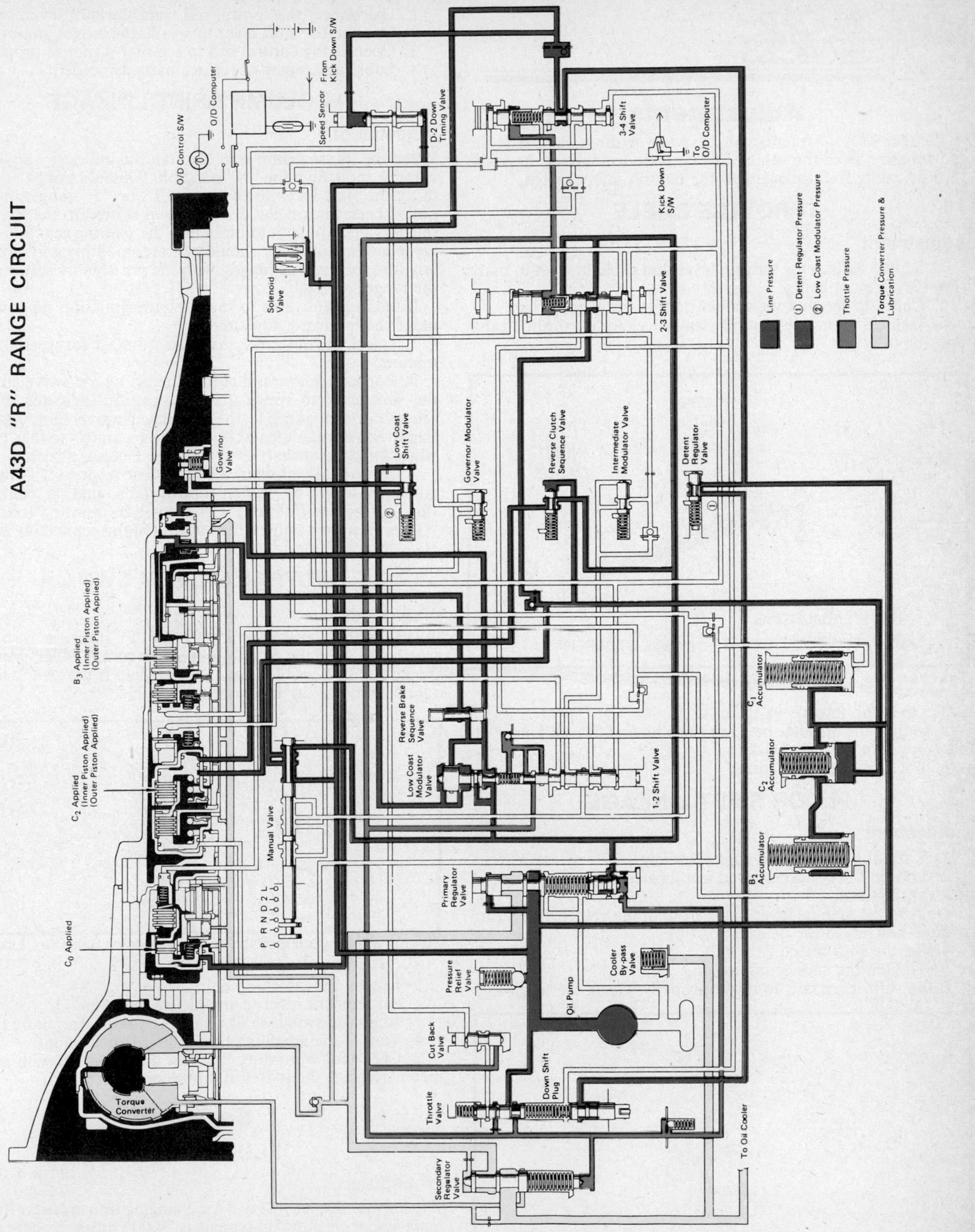

A43D "R" RANGE CIRCUIT

O/D Control S/W

O/D Computer

Speed Sensor

From Kick Down S/W

D-2 Down Timing Valve

3-4 Shift Valve

To O/D Computer

Kick Down S/W

Solenoid Valve

2-3 Shift Valve

Line Pressure

① Detent Regulator Pressure

② Low Coast Modulator Pressure

Throttle Pressure

Torque Converter Pressure & Lubrication

Governor Valve

Low Coast Shift Valve

Governor Modulator Valve

Reverse Clutch Sequence Valve

Intermediate Modulator Valve

Detent Regulator Valve

B₃ Applied (Inner Piston Applied) (Outer Piston Applied)

C₂ Applied (Inner Piston Applied) (Outer Piston Applied)

Manual Valve

P R N D 2 L

Reverse Brake Sequence Valve

Low Coast Modulator Valve

1-2 Shift Valve

C₁ Accumulator

C₂ Accumulator

B₂ Accumulator

C₀ Applied

Primary Regulator Valve

Pressure Relief Valve

Cooler By-pass Valve

Oil Pump

Cut Back Valve

Down Shift Plug

To Oil Cooler

Throttle Valve

Torque Converter

Secondary Regulator Valve

Oil flow circuit reverse range A-43D, A-43DL and A-43DE automatic transmission

ON CAR SERVICES

Adjustments

A number of adjustments can be made without removing the transmission from the vehicle. These include adjustments to the throttle cable, shift linkage and the neutral safety switch.

THROTTLE CABLE

Adjustment

1. Set the carburetor throttle lever and cable bracket to make sure they are not bent.
2. Check to see that the rubber boot is installed correctly.
3. Depress the accelerator fully and check for the throttle valve opening fully.

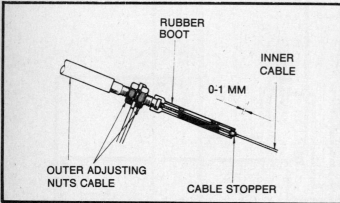

Throttle cable (© Toyota Motor Sales Co. Ltd.)

4. Open the throttle valve fully.
5. Adjust the distance between the boot end face and inner cable stopper or painted mark to 0.04 in.
6. Lock the adjusting nuts.

FLOOR SHIFT LINKAGE

Adjustment

1. Raise the vehicle and support safely.
2. Loosen the connecting rod nut located on the right side of the transmission.
3. Push the manual lever to the front of the vehicle and return it three notches to the neutral position.
4. Set the shift selector to "N".
5. Tighten the connecting rod nut.
If the shift lever fails to move properly, check the following:

Connecting rod location (© Toyota Motor Sales Co. Ltd.)

1. Disconnect the control rod from the shift lever.
2. Operate the shift lever to see that it moves smoothly.
3. Operate the control rod to see that it moves properly.
4. Lubricate, repair or replace parts as needed.

COLUMN SHIFT LINKAGE

Adjustment

When the transmission is in Neutral, the indicator should be accurately indicating the "N" position. It should not be possible to bring the shift lever to the "L", "R" or "P" range unless it is pulled back toward the driver. When shifted to the Park range, the parking pawl should mesh into the parking gear and lock the vehicle. The shift lever should operate smoothly and move properly into the various ranges, with the position indicator showing the ranges correctly.

If the indicator fails to show the transmission range correctly make the following adjustments.

1. Check the bushings, shafts, and linkage for wear and deformation.
2. Loosen the lock nut at the connecting rod swivel and move the shift lever to verify that the position indicator shows the ranges corresponding to the shift lever movement. Also verify that the position indicator is pointing accurately to the "N" range when the control shaft lever is at the Neutral position.
3. Set the transmission manual valve lever to "N" range and adjust the length of the first control rod so that the control position indicator in front of the driver will be pointing accurately to "N" range. Then tighten the lock nut at the connecting rod swivel.

NEUTRAL SAFETY SWITCH

Adjustment

When the shift lever is at the "N" or "P" position, it should be possible to start the engine. But, when at any other position, it should not be possible to start the engine. If the switch is out of adjustment, use the following procedures.

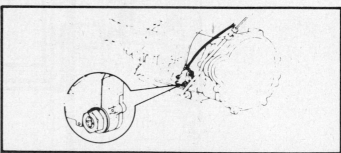

Neutral start switch location (© Toyota Motor Sales Co. Ltd.)

1. Loosen the attaching bolt.
2. Set the shift lever in the neutral position.
3. Align the switch shaft groove to the neutral basic line.
4. Torque the attaching bolt to 35-61 inch pounds.
5. Check for continuity between the terminals with an ohmmeter. Replace the switch if a problem is detected.

Services

FLUID CHANGE

Procedure

The normal service interval for changing transmission fluid and replacing or cleaning oil screens is 24,000 miles. Under more severe operating conditions, the services should be done more often. With heavy city mileage, hill climbing or trailer pulling, the fluid should be checked frequently for blackness or burned smelled. When these conditions occur, change fluid and service the transmission immediately.

1. Raise the vehicle and support safely.
2. Position a suitable drain pan under the transmission.
3. Remove the drain plug and allow the fluid to drain.

— CAUTION —

If the vehicle has been driven recently, the transmission fluid will be hot.

4. Remove the oil pan bolts and remove the pan and gasket. Discard the gasket.
5. Take out the oil tubes by prying gently on them using a suitable tool. Inspect and clean the tubes.
6. Unbolt the five oil strainer retainer bolts and remove the oil strainer. Inspect the strainer and clean or replace it.
7. Install the oil strainer. Torque the five bolts to 43-52 inch pounds.
8. Install the oil tubes by gently tapping them into place with a suitable tool.
9. Install a new pan gasket on the pan and install the pan. Torque them to 34-44 inch pounds.

NOTE: When tightening the bolts, torque them by skipping every other one. Repeat procedure to complete tightening sequence.

10. Replace the drain plug. Torque to 14-16 ft. lbs.
11. Add two quarts of the specified fluid and start the engine. Check the fluid level and correct as required.

SERVICING THE VALVE BODY AND SOLENOID

ALL MODELS

The valve body can be cleaned and serviced without removing the transmission from the vehicle on the transmission models. The Disassembly of the valve body can be accomplished by referring to the "Transmission Disassembly and Assembly" section.

Removal

1. Raise the vehicle and support safely. Drain the fluid and remove the oil pan.
2. Gently remove the oil tubes from the valve body and transmission case area.
3. Loosen the oil strainer bolts; remove the bolts and the oil strainer.

NOTE: At this point the solenoids can be replaced on A-43DE automatic transmission. Disconnect the solenoid connections. Remove the solenoid retaining bolts. Remove the solenoid with the gasket.

4. Loosen the valve body retaining bolts and lower the valve body. Disconnect the throttle wire nipple from the throttle pan and take out the valve body.
5. Remove the second clutch accumulator piston spring.

Installation

1. Install the second clutch accumulator piston spring into the valve body.
2. Connect the throttle cable nipple to the pan.
3. Align the manual valve lever with the manual valve and install the valve body. Torque the bolts to 70-104 inch pounds.
4. Make sure that the oil strainer is clean. Install the oil strainer and torque the bolts to 44-52 inch pounds.

NOTE: Install the solenoids into their proper locations. Make sure that the gaskets are seated, and the valve springs are installed correctly. Torque the bolts to 4-7 ft. lbs. Make all wire connections.

5. Install the oil tubes into their proper bores.

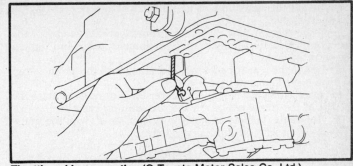

Throttle cable connection (© Toyota Motor Sales Co. Ltd.)

— CAUTION —

Make sure that the oil tubes are inserted in the bores far enough so as not to interfere with the oil pan.

6. Inspect the oil pan to make sure of the location of the two magnets. Install the oil pan with a new pan gasket. Torque the bolts evenly to 35-45 inch pounds.
7. Install the drain plug. Torque to 14-16 ft. lbs.
8. Fill the transmission with the specified fluid. Start the engine and shift through all the gears. Correct the fluid level as necessary.

PARKING PAWL

Removal

1. Raise the vehicle and support safely.
2. Remove the valve body.
3. Loosen the two bolts on the parking lock pawl bracket and remove the bracket.
4. Remove the spring from the pivot pin.
5. Remove the pivot pin and the parking pawl.

Installation

1. Install the parking pawl and the pivot pin.
2. Insert the pivot spring on the pivot pin.
3. Push the lock rod into the forward position and loosely install the two bolts into the parking lock pawl bracket.
4. Check the pawl for smooth operation and torque the bolts 53-78 inch pounds.
5. Install the valve body. Fill the transmission with the specified fluid and correct as necessary.

Extension Housing

Removal

1. Raise the vehicle and support safely. Position a suitable drain pan under the transmission to catch any fluid that may drip.
2. Remove the propeller shaft. Place a block of wood under the transmission oil pan and jack up the transmission enough to remove the weight from the rear support member.
3. Loosen the serrated collar and disconnect the speedometer cable. Be sure not to lose the felt dust protector and washer.
4. Take out the speedometer driven gear.
5. Remove the rear support member along with the rubber exhaust hanger and ground strap.
6. Remove the extension housing and gasket. Discard the gasket.

Installation

1. Install a new gasket on the extension housing. Install the extension housing on the transmission. Install the extension housing bolts and torque to 20-30 ft. lbs.

NOTE: The two lower bolts are shorter than the upper bolts.

2. Install the speedometer driven gear with a new O-ring on the shaft sleeve.

3. Place the felt dust protector and washer on the end of the speedometer cable. Connect the speedometer cable and tighten the serrated collar.

4. Install the rear support member along with the ground strap and rubber exhaust hanger.

5. Install the propeller shaft. Lower the jack so as to place the weight of the transmission on the rear support member.

6. Lower the vehicle and check the fluid level with the transmission in park. Add fluid as needed.

GOVERNOR

Removal

1. Raise the vehicle and support safely.
2. Remove the extension housing.
3. Using snap ring pliers, remove the speedometer drive gear snap ring. Slide the speedometer gear off.
4. Remove the other snap ring and lock ball.
5. Remove the governor lock bolt. Using a suitable tool, loosen the governor retaining clip. Slide the governor off of the shaft.

Installation

1. Using a suitable tool, lift the governor retaining clip and slide the governor onto the shaft.

NOTE: When installing the governor, make sure that the retaining ring faces the end of the shaft. Position the governor in a fashion so that the retaining clip seats properly in the hole in the output shaft.

2. Install the governor lock bolt. Torque to 27-43 inch pounds.
3. Install the lock ball and snap ring on the output shaft. Slip the speedometer drive gear on the shaft.
4. Install the outer snapring.
5. Install the extension housing.

REAR OIL SEAL

Removal

1. Raise the vehicle and support safely.
2. Remove the drive shaft.
3. Take out the oil seal using tool SST 09308-10010 or its equivalent. Remove the dust seal.

Installation

1. Lubricate the new seal with multi-purpose grease and install it.
2. Lubricate the new dust seal with transmission fluid. Install it flush with the housing.
3. Install the drive shaft.
4. Lower the vehicle. Check the transmission fluid. Adjust it to the proper level if necessary.

Removal

1. Disconnect the negative battery cable.
2. Disconnect the upper radiator hose.
3. Drain out some of the coolant.
4. Loosen the transmission throttle cable adjusting nuts. Disconnect the cable housing from the bracket.
5. Disconnect the throttle cable from the throttle linkage.
6. Raise the vehicle and support safely.
7. Drain out the transmission fluid.

8. Disconnect the wiring connections for the back-up lights and the neutral safety switch.
9. Disconnect the starter motor wires. Remove the starter mounting bolts. Pull the starter to the front of the vehicle.
10. Remove the drive shaft. Remove the center bearing if applicable.
11. Disconnect the front exhaust pipe clamp and remove the front exhaust pipe.
12. Remove the oil cooler lines from the radiator.
13. Remove the manual linkage from the transmission.
14. Disconnect the speedometer cable.
15. Remove the right and left stiffener plates from the front of the transmission.
16. Jack up the transmission and remove the rear engine support crossmember.

NOTE: If a transmission jack is not available, place a block of wood between the oil pan and the jack to act as a buffer.

17. Remove the engine under cover plate if so equipped.
18. Disconnect the six torque converter mounting bolts through the service hole at the front side of the drive plate and ring gear.

NOTE: A rubber plug is installed in the service hole and will have to be removed before disconnecting the torque converter mounting bolts.

19. Using one of the bolt holes as access, install a guide pin in the torque converter.
20. Remove the transmission mounting bolts and remove the transmission and torque converter together.
21. Place a suitable container under the converter housing and pull the torque converter straight off its hub.
22. Remove the transmission oil filler tube.

Installation

1. If the torque converter was removed, check to see that it has been properly inserted in the transmission case. Measure the distance between the installed surface of the torque converter to the front surface of the transmission case. The correct distance should be 1.02 in. (26mm).

2. Install a guide pin in one of the lower torque converter mounting holes.
3. Install the transmission oil filler tube.
4. Mount the transmission to the engine so that the guide bolt will pass through a drive plate hole.

—— CAUTION ——

Do not allow the transmission to tilt forward during installation as the torque converter can slip out.

5. Install the transmission housing mounting bolts. Torque to 37-57 ft. lbs. (500-800 kg. cm.).
6. Install the starter. Remove the guide pin.
7. Install the six torque converter bolts. Torque to 11-15 ft. lbs. (150-220 kg. cm.).
8. Install the engine under cover plate.
9. Install the rear transmission support member on the body. Connect the ground strap.
10. Lower the transmission onto the crossmember and install the remaining mounting bolts.
11. Install the converter cover and any exhaust pipe clamps that were removed earlier.
12. Attach the right and left stiffener plates to the front of the transmission.
13. Connect the manual shift linkage and the speedometer cable.
14. Attach the oil cooler lines and torque to 21-28 ft. lbs. (300-400 kg. cm.).
15. Connect the oil cooling line brackets.
16. Install the front exhaust pipe clamp and the front exhaust pipe.

17. Install the drive shaft and the center bearing if equipped.

18. Make the wiring connections for the neutral safety switch and the back-up lights.

19. Connect the transmission throttle cable to the throttle linkage. Install the throttle cable to the throttle cable bracket.

20. Lower the vehicle and connect the upper radiator hose. Fill the radiator with coolant.

21. Connect the negative battery cable.

22. Fill the transmission with approximately 4 quarts of the specified automatic transmission fluid.

23. Start the engine and shift into each gear. Check the fluid level and correct if necessary.

24. Road test the vehicle and check for slippage or other abnormal noises.

BENCH OVERHAUL

Before Disassembly

Before removing any subassemblies, thoroughly clean the outside of the transmission to prevent dirt from contaminating parts during repair. Handle all transmission parts carefully to avoid nicking or burring the bearing or mating surfaces. Lubricate all internal parts before assembly with clean automatic transmission fluid. Do not use any other fluid or lubricants except on gaskets or thrust washers which may be coated with petroleum jelly. Always install new gaskets when assembling the transmission. Torque all bolts to specification.

Converter

Inspection and Removal

1. Make certain that the transmission is held securely.

2. Pull the converter straight out of the transmission. Be careful since the converter contains a large amount of oil. There is no drain plug on the converter so the converter should be drained through the hub.

The fluid drained from the torque converter can help diagnose transmission problems.

1. If the oil in the converter is discolored but does not contain metal bits or particles, the converter is not damaged and need not be replaced. Remember that color is no longer a good indicator of transmission fluid condition. In the past, dark color was associated with overheated transmission fluid. It is not a positive sign of transmission failure with the newer fluids.

2. If the oil in the converter contains metal particles, the converter is damaged internally and must be replaced. The oil may have an "aluminum paint" appearance.

3. If the cause of oil contamination was due to burned clutch plates or overheated oil, the converter is contaminated and should be replaced.

Transmission Disassembly

OIL PAN

Removal

1. With the transmission resting on a flat surface, remove the oil pan bolts.

2. In order to remove the oil pan, lift the transmission from the pan.

NOTE: The transmission is lifted from the oil pan so as not to contaminate the valve body with any foreign materials located in the oil pan.

3. Remove the discard the gasket. Using a suitable tool remove any remaining gasket material left on the transmission case.

4. Remove the oil pan magnet. Examine any particles found in the oil pan. Magnetic particles (brass) will indicate bushing wear, while nonmagnetic particles (steel) will show evidence of gear, bearing and clutch plate wear.

Solenoid

Removal (A-43DE only)

1. Place the transmission in a suitable holding fixture. Turn the transmission so that the oil tubes are facing up.

2. Using a suitable tool remove the oil tubes from the valve body. The solenoid wiring will now be visible.

3. Remove the solenoid grommet from the transmission case.

4. Disconnect the wiring from the number one, two and three solenoid. Remove the solenoids from the transmission case.

5. Remove the solenoid valve from the left side of the transmission.

Solenoid location circled (© Toyota Motor Sales Co. Ltd.)

VALVE BODY

Removal

1. Turn the transmission so that the oil tubes are facing up. Using a suitable tool remove the oil tubes.

2. Loosen the oil strainer bolts; remove the bolts and the oil strainer.

3. Remove the valve body retaining bolts and remove the valve body.

4. Remove the second clutch accumulator piston. Remove the accumulator springs.

NOTE: By using compressed air, the pistons can be dislodged more easily. Force the air into the air holes located in the transmission case.

5. Detach the throttle cable from the throttle cable cam. Remove the plastic throttle cable cam.

6. Remove the parking lock rod bolt and remove the parking lock rod. Detach the parking lock pawl, spring and pivot pin.

MANUAL LEVER SHAFT (OPTIONAL)

Removal

1. Using an appropriate tool, remove the manual lever shaft pin.

2. Slide the shaft out of the transmission case.

3. Remove the detent plate.

GOVERNOR

REMOVAL

1. Remove the extension housing.

2. Remove the speedometer drive gear snap ring.

3. Detach the lock ball and the next snap ring.

4. Remove the governor lock bolt.

5. Using a suitable tool, loosen the governor retaining clip. Remove the governor from the output shaft.

OIL PUMP

Removal

1. Remove the oil pump housing bolts.

2. Using Toyota tool number SST 09610-20012 or its equivalent, remove the oil pump from the transmission case.

CAUTION

Care must be exercised during the oil pump removal so as not to crack the oil pump housing.

3. Remove the oil pump bearing which is located behind the oil pump.

4. Remove the six converter housing bolts. Lift off the converter housing.

OVERDRIVE CLUTCH

Removal

1. Place a straight edge across the overdrive case and measure the distance between the straight edge and the front clutch. Record the measurement for use during reassembly.

2. Grip the input shaft and remove the overdrive clutch assembly.

3. Remove the bearing races located on both sides of the assembly.

4. Remove the overdrive case by pulling it out of the transmission case. Check for bearing races on both sides of the overdrive assembly.

FRONT CLUTCH

Removal

1. Place a straight edge across the transmission case and the front clutch and measure the distance between the straight edge and the front clutch. Record the figure for use during reassembly.

2. Grasp the input shaft and pull out the front clutch assembly.

3. Check for bearings and races on both sides of the assembly.

Front clutch (© Toyota Motor Sales Co. Ltd.)

REAR CLUTCH

Removal

1. Carefully grasp the rear clutch hub.

2. Pull the rear clutch assembly from the transmission case.

3. The rear clutch hub and the rear clutch assembly are removed from the transmission case as one unit.

Rear clutch (© Toyota Motor Sales Co. Ltd.)

CENTER SUPPORT AND SUN GEAR

Removal

1. Turn the transmission over in the stand and remove the two center support bolts.

2. Grasp the center support assembly and pull the assembly towards the front of the case.

3. Using a suitable tool remove the reaction plate retaining ring.

4. Check the end of the sun gear for the bearing races and any needle bearings.

Center support bolt removal (© Toyota Motor Sales Co. Ltd.)

Center support and sun gear removal
(© Toyota Motor Sales Co. Ltd.)

INTERMEDIATE SHAFT

Removal

1. Carefully grasp the rear intermediate shaft.

2. Pull the rear intermediate shaft out of the transmission case.

3. The intermediate shaft and the rear parts group will be removed from the transmission as one unit.

4. Remove the brake apply tube. Remove the rear thrust bearings from the transmission case.

NOTE: The transmission case should be inspected for internal case damage. Check for wear, scoring or any other internal damage that might affect the operation of the transmission after assembly is complete.

Unit Disassembly and Assembly
FRONT CLUTCH

Disassembly

1. From both sides of the clutch, remove the thrust bearings and races.

2. Remove the snap ring from the front clutch hub and remove the front and rear clutch hub.

3. Remove the thrust bearings and races along with the clutch plate.

4. Remove the snap ring and lift out the remaining clutch plates and discs.

5. Using a suitable tool, compress the piston return springs and remove the snap ring.

6. Remove the spring retainer and the return springs.

7. Place the front clutch on the overdrive case and using compressed air, blow out the piston. Remove the O-rings from the piston.

Inspection

1. Make sure that the check ball is free in the front clutch piston. Shake the piston and listen for the check ball moving.

2. Wash all parts in cleaning solvent and blow dry using compressed air.

3. Inspect the piston for nicks, burrs, scores and wear. Inspect the piston springs for distortion.

4. Repair or replace any damaged parts as required.

Assembly

1. Install new O-rings on the front clutch piston. Install the piston in the front clutch drum with the cup side up.

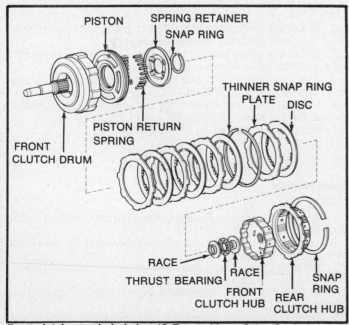

PISTON   SPRING RETAINER   SNAP RING

THINNER SNAP RING
PLATE   DISC

PISTON RETURN SPRING

FRONT CLUTCH DRUM

RACE
THRUST BEARING   RACE
FRONT CLUTCH HUB   REAR CLUTCH HUB   SNAP RING

Front clutch—exploded view (© Toyota Motor Sales Co. Ltd.)

2. Install the piston return springs and the spring retainer.

3. Compress the return springs and retainer using a suitable tool and install the snap ring.

4. Install the clutch discs and plates and install the snap ring. Be sure that the clutch discs and the plates are assembled in the same manner as they were disassembled.

5. Place the front clutch drum onto the overdrive case and with a dial indicator or its equivalent measure the piston stroke. Maxmum piston stroke should be 0.0917 in. (2.33mm).

6. Install the inner snap ring in the clutch drum.

7. Install the clutch plate (A-40D) or the clutch disc (A-43D and A-43DE) into the clutch drums.

8. Install the inner thrust bearings and races.

9. Install the front clutch hub and the rear clutch hub. Make sure that the hub teeth align with the disc lugs.

10. Install the outer snap ring. Install the thrust bearings and races.

OVERDRIVE INPUT SHAFT AND CLUTCH

Disassembly

1. Remove the thrust bearings and races from the overdrive input shaft.

2. Remove the snap ring and hub from the overdrive clutch assembly. Remove the overdrive clutch assembly from the input shaft.

3. Remove the thin snapring, disc, flange and plate from the hub assembly.

4. Using a piston spring compressor or its equivalent, compress the piston return springs and remove the snapring.

5. Remove the spring retainer and the return springs.

6. Remove the overdrive clutch piston from the overdrive clutch assembly. Remove the clutch piston O-rings.

7. Remove the snapring from the overdrive planetary gear assembly and remove the thrust washers and one-way clutch.

8. Remove the four plugs located in the overdrive planetary gear assembly.

Inspection

1. Wash all parts in cleaning solvent and blow dry using compressed air.

2. Inspect all parts for nicks, scores, burrs and wear. Inspect the piston springs for distortion.

3. Make sure that the check ball can be heard when shaking the piston.

4. Repair or replace any damaged parts as required.

Assembly

1. Install the four plugs in the overdrive planetary gear assembly.

2. Install the thrust washer and bearing on the input shaft.

3. Install the one-way clutch and the thrust washer on the input shaft. Secure with the snapring.

4. Lubricate the new O-ring with automatic transmission fluid and install the O-ring on the overdrive clutch piston.

5. Install the overdrive clutch piston in the overdrive clutch drum. Make sure that the cup side is facing up.

6. Install the piston return springs and secure them with the spring retainer and snap ring.

7. Install the plate, disc and flange without inserting the thinner snapring.

8. With a dial indicator or its equivalent, measure the piston stroke of the overdrive clutch. Maximum piston stroke should be 0.0898 in. (2.28mm).

9. Install the thinner snapring. Install the hub and outer snapring.

10. Install the overdrive clutch assembly onto the input shaft along wiith the thrust bearings and races.

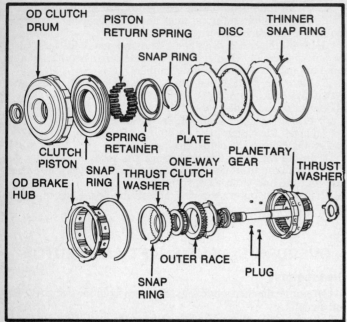

Overdrive input shaft and clutch—exploded view
(© Toyota Motor Sales Co. Ltd.)

NOTE: At this point, check the operation of the one-way clutch by holding the clutch drum with the right hand and turning the input shaft with the left hand. The input shaft should turn clockwise but not turn counterclockwise.

REAR CLUTCH

Disassembly

1. Remove the outer snapring which holds the outer clutch pack to the drum.
2. Remove the clutch discs, plates and flange.
3. Using a suitable tool, compress the piston spring retainer and remove the snapring. Remove the return springs.
4. Remove the rear clutch piston from the rear clutch drum.

NOTE: All A-40D automatic transmissions will have two rear clutch pistons, while the A-43D, A-43DL and A-43DE automatic transmissions will have only one piston.

5. Remove the O-rings from the rear clutch piston. Discard the O-rings.

Inspection

1. Wash all parts in cleaning solvent and blow dry using compressed air.
2. Inspect the piston return springs for distortion. Inspect all parts for burrs, scoring or other wear.
3. Make sure that the check ball can be heard when shaking the piston.
4. Repair or replace any damaged parts as required.

Assembly

1. Install new O-rings on the rear clutch piston.
2. Install the clutch pistons into the rear clutch drum.
3. Install the piston return springs with the piston return spring retainer and set in place with the snap ring.
4. Install the plate, discs and flange in the following order: plate-disc-plate-disc-plate-disc-flange.
5. Install the snapring making sure that the snapring ends are not aligned with a cutout in the rear clutch piston.

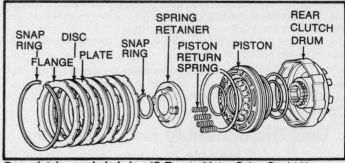

Rear clutch—exploded view (© Toyota Motor Sales Co. Ltd.)

6. Install a dial indicator or its equivalent, measure the piston stroke of the rear clutch. Maximum piston for the A-40D should be 0.059 in. (1.5mm). Maximum piston stroke for the A-43D, A-43DL and A-43DE should be 0.0835 in. (2.12mm).

OIL PUMP

Disassembly

1. Using the torque converter as a work stand, remove the two oil seal rings from the pump cover.
2. Remove the pump cover. Remove the O-ring from the pump.
3. Remove the oil pump drive gear and the oil pump driven gear.

Inspection

1. Wash all parts in cleaning solvent and blow dry using compressed air.
2. Inspect the front oil seal for damage or other signs of wear. Replace if necessary.
3. Measure the body side clearance to a limit of 0.012 in. (0.3mm).
4. Measure the tip of the driven gear to the crescent for a clearance to a limit of 0.012 in. (0.3mm).
5. Measure the pump to side clearance to a limit of 0.004 in. (0.1mm).

Assembly

1. Install the drive gear and the driven gear on the pump body. Place the pump body on the torque converter.
2. Install the pump cover and align the bolt holes. Install the bolts with the wave washers finger tight.
3. Align the pump cover and the pump and torque the pump cover bolts to 53-78 inch lbs. (0.6-0.9 kg-m).
4. Lubricate the two oil seal rings with petroleum jelly and install on the pump cover. Wipe off any excess jelly.
5. Install a new O-ring on the oil pump.

CENTER SUPPORT

Disassembly

A-40D

1. Remove the snap ring and take the sun gear out of the center support.
2. Remove the snap ring and take out the clutch flange, clutch discs and clutch plates.
3. Take out the next snap ring and remove the return spring retainer and the return springs.
4. Remove the No. 1 brake piston from the center support using compressed air.
5. Remove the center support oil seal rings along with the sun gear oil seal rings.

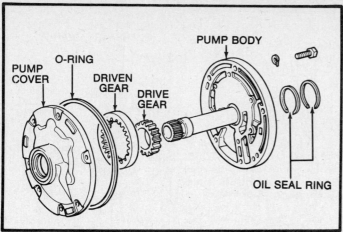

Oil pump—exploded view (© Toyota Motor Sales Co. Ltd.)

Inspection

1. Wash all parts in cleaning solvent and blow dry using compressed air.
2. Inspect the return springs for distortion or other signs of wear.
3. Inspect the sun gear and the center support for any scores, nicks or burrs.
4. Repair or replace any defective parts as needed.
5. Lubricate any new clutch discs with automatic transmission fluid.

Assembly

1. Install new oil seal rings on the center support and the sun gear. Install new O-rings on the brake piston and the center support.

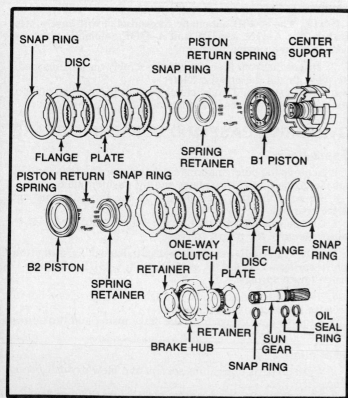

Center support assembly—exploded view
(© Toyota Motor Sales Co. Ltd.)

2. Install the No. 1 brake piston in the center support being careful not do damage the O-rings and with the cup side facing up.
3. Install the piston return springs and hold in place with the return spring retainer and snapring.
4. Install the No. 1 brake plates, clutch discs and clutch flange.
5. Install the snapring on the center support.
6. Check the piston stroke of the No. 1 brake piston by applying 57-114 psi of compressed air into the side oil hole of the center support. Piston stroke should be between 0.0394-0.0472 in. (1.00-1.20mm).
7. Install the center support on the sun gear shaft and install the snapring on the end of the sun gear shaft.

CENTER SUPPORT

Disassembly

A-43D, A-43DL AND A-43DE

1. Remove the snapring from the sun gear shaft and remove the center support from the shaft.
2. Remove the snapring from the front of the center support assembly.
3. Remove the clutch flange, clutch disc and clutch plates from the center support.
4. Using a suitable tool, compress the piston return spring retainer and remove the piston return spring, snapring and the piston return springs.
5. Using compressed air blown through the center support oil hole, remove the No. 1 brake piston. Remove the brake piston O-rings.
6. Turn the center support assembly over and remove the No. 2 brake snapring. Remove the clutch flange clutch discs and clutch plates from the No. 2 brake.
7. Using a suitable tool, compress the piston return spring retainer and remove the piston return spring snapring and the piston return springs.
8. Using compressed air blown through the center support oil hole, remove the No. 2 brake piston. Remove the brake piston O-rings.
9. Remove the one-way clutch assembly.
10. Remove the oil seal rings from the sun gear and the center support.

Inspection

1. Wash all parts in cleaning solvent and blow dry using compressed air.
2. Inspect the return springs for distortion or other signs of wear.
3. Inspect the sun gear and the center support for any scores, nicks or burrs.
4. Check the function of the one-way clutch by holding it and turning the sun gear. The sun gear should turn freely counter-clockwise, and should lock in the clockwise direction.
5. Repair or replace any defective parts as needed.
6. Lubricate any new clutch discs with automatic transmission fluid.

Assembly

1. Install the new oil seal rings on the center support and the sun gear. Install new O-rings on the brake piston.
2. Install the one-way clutch on the sun gear. Install the No. 1 brake piston in the center support.
3. Install the piston return springs and using the snapring, secure the retainer in place.
4. Install the new O-rings on the center support and the piston.
5. Turn the center support over and install the No. 2 brake piston. Install the piston return springs and the return spring retainer with the snapring.

6. Turn the center support over again and install the No. 1 brake piston plate, disc and flange. Install the snapring in the center support.

7. Check the piston stroke of the No. 1 brake piston by applying 57-114 psi of compressed air into the side oil hole of the center support. Piston stroke should be between 0.0256-0.0512 in. (0.65-1.30mm).

8. Turn the center support over and install the No. 2 brake plates, discs and flange. Install the snapring in the center support.

9. Check the piston stroke of the No. 2 brake. Using a dial indicator or its equivalent, measure the piston stroke while applying compressed air (57-114 psi) to the center support oil hole. Piston strokes should measure between 0.0488-0.0835 in. (1.24-2.12mm).

10. Install the center support on the sun gear shaft and install the snapring on the end of the sun gear shaft.

PLANETARY GEAR OUTPUT SHAFT

Disassembly

1. Remove the reaction plate snapring and remove the No. 3 brake disc/plate pack and the front planetary pinion gears.

2. Remove the thrust washer from the planetary gears and lift out the brake discs and plates. Remove the reaction plate.

3. Remove the snapring from the front planetary pinion case and lift out the one-way clutch. Remove the nylon thrust washer from the front planetary pinion gears.

4. Remove the clutch pressure plate and the clutch apply tube.

5. Remove the snapring from the front planetary ring gear and remove the ring gear. Remove the washer inside of the ring gear.

NOTE: THE A-40D automatic transmission will have a steel washer. The A-43D, A-43DL and A-43DE automatic transmission will have a nylon washer.

6. Remove the output shaft from the intermediate shaft assembly. Remove the thrust bearings and races from the output shaft.

7. Remove the oil seal rings from the output shaft.

8. Remove the thrust bearings and races from the intermediate shaft.

9. Remove the rear planetary ring gear and bearing race from the intermedaite shaft along with the rear set ring.

10. Remove and discard all oil seal rings from the output shaft.

Inspection

1. Wash all parts in cleaning solvent and blow dry using compressed air.

2. Inspect all discs and plates and replace any that are excessively worn.

3. Check all gears and shafts for any scoring, wears or burrs.

4. Repair or replace any defective parts as needed.

5. Lubricate new clutch discs with automatic transmission fluid.

Assembly

1. Install the thrust bearing race and rear planetary ring gear on the intermediate shaft. Install the rear set ring.

2. Turn the intermediate shaft over and install the thrust bearing and race on the inside of the ring gear. Install the pinion gear assembly thrust washer on the rear planetary gear carrier.

3. Install the oil seal rings on the output shaft. Install the thrust bearing and race on the output shaft.

4. Install the intermediate shaft in the output shaft. Install the rear planetary gear carrier in the output shaft. Install the snapring.

5. Install the front planetary ring gear. Make sure that the notches align with the lugs. Install the snapring.

6. Install the washer in front of the planetary ring gear and install the front planetary pinion gear. Install the nylon washer, one-way clutch and the snapring.

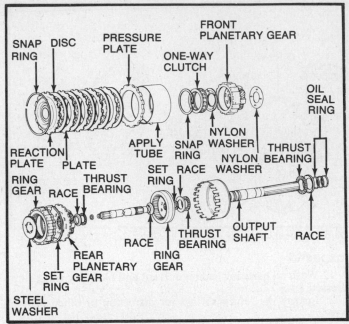

Planetary gear output shaft—exploded view
(© Toyota Motor Sales Co. Ltd.)

7. Install the reaction plate without the disc/plate pack to check the operation of the one-way clutch. The planetary gear must lock in the counterclockwise direction, but must rotate freely in the clockwise direction. If the clutch does not work properly, it must be replaced. Remove the reaction plate.

8. Install the thrust washer on the front planetary gear carrier. Petroleum jelly can be used to hold the washer in place during assembly.

NOTE: The A-40D automatic transmission will have a steel washer. The A-43D, A-43DL and A-43DE automatic transmissions will have a nylon washer.

9. Install the front planetary gear assembly on the intermediate shaft. Install the pressure plate.

10. Install the No. 3 brake clutch pack in the same manner as removed. Install the reaction plate and the snapring.

OVERDRIVE CASE AND OVERDRIVE BRAKE

Disassembly

1. Remove the outer snapring from the overdrive case and lift out the clutch flange, disc plates and the cushion plate.

2. Remove the ring gear along with the thrust washer and thrust bearings.

3. Using a suitable tool, remove the snapring and the spring retainer. Remove the return springs.

NOTE: The A-40D automatic transmission will have 16 piston return springs. The A-43D, A-43DL and A-43DE will have 12 piston return springs.

4. Use compressed air blown through an overdrive case hole to dislodge the overdrive brake piston.

5. Remove the O-rings from the brake piston and the oil seal rings form the overdrive case.

Inspection

1. Wash all parts in cleaning solvent and blow dry using compressed air.

2. Inspect the overdrive case for nicks, burrs or other damage.

3. Check the piston return springs for any distortion.

4. Replace or repair defective parts as needed.

Assembly

1. Install new oil seal rings on the overdrive case and new O-rings on the brake piston.

2. Install the return springs with the spring retainer and insert the snapring.

3. Install the thrust bearing and races on the ring gear and install the ring gear in the overdrive case.

4. Install the cushion plate, discs, plates and flange. Install the snapring.

NOTE: Lubricate new clutch discs and plates with automatic transmission fluid before installing. Install the cushion plate with the rounded end down.

5. Using a feeler gauge or its equivalent, measure the distance between the snapring and the flange. Maximum clearance should be 0.083 in. (2.1mm).

NOTE: The thrust washer not used during reassembly of the overdrive case and overdrive brake will be used during the transmission assembly.

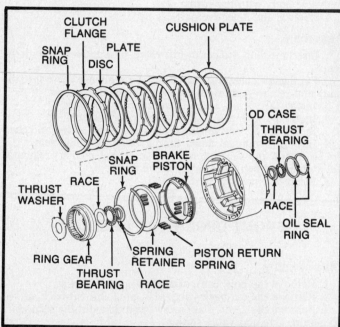

Overdrive case and overdrive brake—exploded view
(© Toyota Motor Sales Co. Ltd.)

GOVERNOR

Disassembly

1. Remove the E-ring and the governor weight from the governor body.

2. Slide the governor valve, spring and the governor valve shaft through the governor bore. Remove from the bottom.

3. Remove the retaining clip from the governor body being careful not to scrap the governor body.

4. Remove the lock plate and bolt from the side of the governor body.

Inspection

1. Wash all parts in a cleaning solvent and blow dry using compressed air.

2. Check all parts for burrs, wear or other signs of excessive damage.

3. Check the oil passages for clogging.

4. Replace any parts that are found to be defective.

Assembly

1. Install the lock plate and bolt to the side of the governor body.

2. Install the retaining clip being careful not to scrape the governor body.

3. Assemble the governor valve shaft, spring and the governor valve and install into the governor body.

4. Install the governor weight and the E-ring in the governor body.

REAR BRAKE PISTONS

Disassembly

1. Using a suitable tool, compress the return spring retainer and remove the snapring. Remove the return spring retainer and the piston return springs.

2. Apply compressed air to the outer and inner piston oil holes. This will dislodge the reaction sleeve and the outer piston. If the piston and sleeve do not come out using the compressed air, lift these units out using needle-nose pliers.

3. Remove the O-rings from the inner and outer pistons and the reaction sleeve.

Inspection

1. Wash all parts in cleaning solvent and blow dry using compressed air.

2. Check return springs for any distortion.

3. Inspect all parts for any burrs, scoring and other signs of damage.

4. Remove the manual shaft oil seals with a suitable tool and install new right and left oil seals with a drift, making sure that they are flush with the transmission case.

5. Repair or replace any defective parts as needed.

Assembly

1. Install new O-rings on the reaction sleeve and the inner and outer pistons. Install the inner and outer pistons in the reaction sleeve.

2. Install the reaction sleeve in the transmission with the spring seats facing up. Be careful not to damage the O-rings.

3. Install the piston return springs and the piston spring retainer. Using a suitable tool, compress the piston return springs and install the snapring.

4. Check the snapring to make sure it is seated on the piston spring retainer.

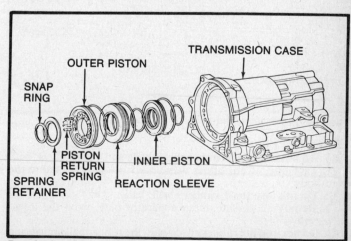

Rear brake piston—exploded view (© Toyota Motor Sales Co. Ltd.)

VALVE BODY

Disassembly

A-40D

1. Invert the transmission case so the valve body is in a horizontal position. Remove the necessary oil delivery tubes.
2. Remove the oil strainer by taking out five mounting bolts.
3. Remove the 17 valve body mounting bolts.

— CAUTION —

Since there are five different lengths of mounting bolts, be sure to keep them in the same order as they came out.

4. Carefully remove the valve body. After disconnecting the throttle wire nipple from the throttle pan, take out the valve body.

— CAUTION —

When removing the valve body, prevent the number one accumulator piston from falling out.

5. Remove the 9 bolts from the valve body cover and separate cover from valve body.
6. Do not lose the 4 rubber check balls.
7. Remove the 5 rear upper valve body bolts and take off the rear upper body.
8. Turn the valve body over and remove the remaining lower bolts.
9. Separate the lower valve body from the rear upper valve body.

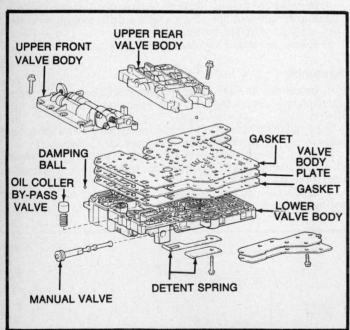

UPPER REAR VALVE BODY

UPPER FRONT VALVE BODY

DAMPING BALL

OIL COLLER BY-PASS VALVE

GASKET

VALVE BODY PLATE

GASKET

LOWER VALVE BODY

MANUAL VALVE

DETENT SPRING

Valve body—exploded view (© Toyota Motor Sales Co. Ltd.)

10. Do not lose the 4 rubber check balls and 1 steel check ball.
11. Take out 5 front upper valve body bolts and separate the front body.
12. Do not lose the 1 rubber check ball.
13. Remove 2 gaskets and a separator plate from the lower valve body.
14. Do not lose the rubber check ball, the rubber ball and spring set, and the check valve and spring set.

LOWER VALVE BODY

Disassembly

1. Remove the manual valve.
2. Remove the valve seat, valve sleeve, primary regulator valve, spring and pressure regulator valve.
3. Remove the seat, plug and manual down timing valve.
4. Remove the seat, spring and overdrive clutch exhaust valve.
5. Remove the seat, plug, 3-4 shift valve and spring.
6. Remove the seat, plug, 1-2 shift valve and spring.
7. Remove the 2 screws from the end plate and pull out the sequence valve and low coast shift valve.
8. Remove the seat, plug, 3rd coast shift valve and plug.
9. Remove the spring seat, spring and pressure relief ball.

Inspection

1. Wash all parts in cleaning solvent and blow dry using compressed air.
2. Inspect all parts for damage and excessive wear.
3. Inspect the pressure relief spring and ball and secure them in the valve body with the spring seat.
4. Replace any defective parts as needed.

Assembly

1. Insert the plug, 3rd coast shift valve, plug and secure with the seat.
2. Put the low coast shift valve and the sequence valve into the body and secure them with the end plate and 2 screws.
3. Install the spring, 1-2 shift valve, plug and seat.
4. Insert the spring, 3-4 shift valve, plug and seat.
5. Install the overdrive clutch exhaust valve, spring and seat.
6. Install the manual down timing valve, plug and seat.
7. Insert the pressure regulator valve, spring, primary regulator valve, pressure regulator valve sleeve and seat.
8. Insert the manual valve into the valve body.

FRONT UPPER VALVE BODY

Disassembly

1. Remove the bolt, cam, cam pin and cam spring.
2. Remove the cut-back valve seat, plug and cut-back valve.
3. Remove the 2 end plate screws and take out the secondary regulator valve and valve spring.
4. Remove the downshift plug, spring, clip, throttle valve, E-ring and spring.

NOTE: Count the number of E-rings because they are used as spacers.

Inspection

1. Wash all parts in cleaning solvent and blow dry using compressed air.
2. Inspect all parts for any signs of excessive wear or damage.
3. Inspect the valve spring for any rust or compressed coils.
4. Replace any defective parts as required.

Assembly

5. Hook the end of the cam spring over the valve body and install cam pin, cam and bolt.
6. Hook the other end of the cam spring into the hole in the cam.
7. Install the cut-back valve with the larger diameter land toward the outside of the valve body.
8. Install the secondary regulator valve and valve spring and secure it with the end plate and 2 screws.
9. Replace the E-rings, throttle valve, spring, clip and downshift plug.

REAR UPPER VALVE BODY

Disassembly

1. Remove the rear upper valve body end plate and pull out the detent valve seat, valve and spring.
2. Remove the 2-3 timing valve, plug and spring.
3. Remove the sequence valve spring and sequence valve.
4. Remove the governor modulator valve and spring and valve.
5. Remove the low modulator valve spring and valve.
6. Remove the 2-3 shift valve retaining spring, plugs, spring and the 2-3 shift valve.
7. Remove the lower 2-3 shift valve plug, seat and valve.
8. Remove the 3-2 kickdown orifice control valve seat, plug, valve and spring.

Inspection

1. Wash all parts in cleaning solvent and blow dry using compressed air.
2. Inspect the valve springs for any signs of rust or excessive wear. Inspect for any collapsed coils.
3. Inspect the valve body housing for any warping or other damage.
4. Replace any defective parts as required.

Assembly

1. Reinstall the 3-2 kickdown orifice control valve spring, valve, plug and seat.
2. Put in the 2-3 shift valve, plug and seat.
3. Install the 2-3 shift valve, spring, plugs and retaining seat.
4. Put the low modulator and governor modulator valves and springs in the upper valve body.
5. Install the 2-3 timing valve and sequence valve with their springs.
6. Install the upper valve body end plate with 2 screws.
7. Install the detent valve, spring and valve seat.

Assembly of the Valve Body

1. Install the check balls in the area under the valve body cover, place the cover on the body and fasten with the 7 bolts.
2. Install the rubber ball, rubber ball and spring and valve and spring into the upper side of the lower valve body.
3. Install the 2 gaskets and separator plate on the lower valve body. Temporarily bolt it down with several bolts.
4. Install 1 rubber check ball and 1 steel check ball into the rear upper valve body. Bolt the lower valve body onto the rear upper valve body.
5. Turn the valve body over and install 5 bolts into the rear upper valve body.
6. Remove the temporary bolts and install 1 rubber check ball in the front upper valve body.
7. Install the lower valve body onto the front upper valve body and fasten it with 3 bolts.
8. Turn the valve body over and install 5 bolts into the front upper valve body.
9. Turn the valve body over and install the final 2 bolts into the valve cover.

NOTE: Torque all valve body bolts to 3.6-4.3 ft. lbs.

VALVE BODY

Disassembly

A-43D, A-43DL AND A-43DE

1. Invert the transmission case so that the valve body is in a horizontal position. Remove the necessary oil delivery tubes.
2. Remove the detent spring along with the manual valve. Remove the oil strainer.
3. Remove the lower valve body bolts.

4. Turn the assembly over and remove the bolts from the upper rear valve body and the upper front valve body.
5. Carefully remove the valve body components. Separate the lower valve body from the upper valve body.
6. Do not lose any of the rubber check balls during disassembly. Remove and discard all of the gasket material.

LOWER VALVE BODY

Disassembly

1. Disconnect and remove the lower valve body plate and gaskets. Remove the cooler by-pass check valve and spring.
2. Turn the assembly over and remove the 7 set bolts and remove the lower body cover, plate and gaskets. Remove the check balls being careful not to scratch the grooves.
3. Remove the pressure relief spring retainer and take out the pressure relief spring and ball.
4. Remove the plate and gasket along with the primary regulator valve. Remove the plunger, spring and sleeve from the primary regulator valve bore.
5. Remove the D-2 down timing valve.
6. Remove the locating pin for the 3-4 shift valve and take out the 3-4 shift valve and spring.
7. Remove the 1-2 shift valve retainer and take out the 1-2 shift valve and spring.
8. Remove the reverse brake plug along with the cover plate and the low coast shift valve.
9. Remove the third coast shift valve and the 3-4 shift control valve.

Inspection

1. Wash all parts in cleaning solvent and blow dry using compressed air.
2. Inspect the valve springs for compressed coils and any distortion.
3. Inspect the valve body housing for any warping or other damage.
4. Replace any defective parts as required.

Assembly

1. Install the low coast shift valve with the small end in first. Install the 3-4 shift control valve in the housing bore with the cup side first.
2. Install the third coast shift valve with the small end first. Install the cover plate.
3. Assemble the 1-2 shift valve and install with the 1-2 shift valve retainer plug.
4. Install the D-2 down timing valve and plug. Install the down timing valve retainer.
5. Install the primary regulator valve and spring. Install the gasket and plate.
6. Install the pressure relief ball, spring and retainer. Make sure that the retainers and pins are installed correctly.
7. Turn the valve body over and install the check balls. Install the gasket, plate and lower body cover.

FRONT UPPER VALVE BODY

Disassembly

1. Remove the check ball and the cut back valve retainer. Remove the cut back valve.
2. Remove the secondary regulator valve and spring. Be careful not to lose the valve since it is spring loaded.
3. Depress the down shift plug into the valve body and while holding in the throttle valve, remove the throttle cam. Remove the down shift plug and spring.
4. Pull out the throttle valve retainer and remove the throttle valve. Remove the throttle valve spring and adjusting rings.

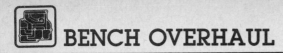

Inspection

1. Wash all parts in cleaning solvent and blow dry using compressed air.
2. Inspect the valve springs for compressed coils and any other noticeable distortion.
3. Inspect the valve body housing for any warping or cracks.
4. Replace any defective parts as required.

Assembly

1. Install the throttle valve and the retainer. Place the adjusting rings on the throttle valve shaft. Install the small spring on the throttle valve shaft.
2. Install the spring on the down shift plug and insert the down shift plug into the valve body.
3. Assemble the throttle cam and insert it into the front upper valve body. Torque the throttle cam bolt to 53-78 inch lbs.
4. Install the secondary regulator valve into its bore on the valve body. Depress the valve and place the cover plate over it. Install the cover plate bolt and torque to 44-52 inch lbs.
5. Install the cut back valve, plug and retainer.

NOTE: Retainers can be coated with petroleum jelly during assembly to hold them in place.

REAR UPPER VALVE BODY

Disassembly

1. Remove the check balls from the valve body along with intermediate shift valve retainer.
2. Remove the plug, intermediate shift valve and spring.
3. Remove the 2-3 shift valve retainer and the 2-3 shift valve assembly.
4. From the side of the valve body, remove one bolt and slide the valve cover to one side. Remove the low coast modulator valve and the governor modulator valve.
5. Slide the valve cover further and remove the rear clutch valve assembly.
6. Remove the cover plate and take out the intermediate modulator valve assembly.
7. Remove the detent regulator valve retainer and the detent regulator valve assembly.

Inspection

1. Wash all parts in cleaning solvent and blow dry using compressed air.
2. Inspect the valve springs for collapsed coils or other damage.
3. Inspect the valve body housing for any warping or cracks.
4. Inspect the remaining parts for any rust, burrs or nicks.
5. Replace any defective parts as required.

Assembly

1. Install the detent regulator valve assembly. Make sure that the retainer fully covers the spring.
2. Install the intermediate modulator valve and spring. Insert the valve with the round end in first.
3. Install the valve body side cover using one bolt. Install the rear sequence valve and spring.
4. Install the governor modulator valve, round end first, then insert the spring.
5. Install the low modulator valve and spring. Place the cover over the valve and install the second bolt through the cover. Torque to 44-52 inch lbs.
6. Install the 2-3 shift valve and insert the 2-3 shift valve plug. Depress the plug and install the intermediate shift valve retainer in the valve body.
7. Install the check balls in the valve body.

Assembly of the Valve Body

1. Place a new gasket on the upper rear valve body.
2. Place the lower valve body with the plate on top of the upper rear valve body.
3. Install the lower valve body bolts to hold the upper rear valve body. Finger tighten only.
4. Turn the valve body over and install the 5 upper rear valve body bolts. Finger tighten only.
5. Position the lower and upper rear valve body assembly on top of the upper front valve body.
6. Install the 4 valve body bolts and finger tighten only.
7. Turn the assembly over and finger tighten the 5 bolts in the upper front valve body.
8. Check the alignment of the gasket and torque the upper front and upper rear valve body bolts to 44-52 inch lbs.
9. Turn the valve body assembly over and check the alignment of the gasket. Torque the lower valve body bolts to 44-52 inch lbs.
10. Install the manual valve and the detent spring.

Transmission Assembly

Soak all new clutches and discs in transmission fluid, use new gaskets and O-rings. Apply transmission fluid on all sliding and rotating surfaces before assembly. Petroleum jelly should be used to hold the thrust washers and needle bearings in their proper location.

1. Place the transmission on a suitable fixture and make sure it is properly secured.
2. Install the thrust washer and bearing in the transmission case. Make sure the thrust washer is installed with the cup facing down.
3. Install the apply tube in the transmission case making sure that the locking tabs align with the transmission case.
4. Install the output shaft assembly into the transmission case aligning the clutch plate notches with the slot in the transmission case.

NOTE: The A-40D automatic transmission does not have the clutch plate notches.

5. Check the clutch pack clearance against the transmission case ledge. Maximum clearance for the A-40D, A-43D, A-43DL and the A-43DE should be 0.0866 in. (2.20mm).
6. Install the reaction plate with the notched tooth facing the valve body. Install the snap ring.
7. Install the center support assembly into the transmission case and install the center support bolts. Torque the bolts to 18-20 ft. lbs. (2.4-2.8 kg-m.).
8. Install the rear clutch in the transmission case. Rotate the clutch to engage the hub with the center support.

NOTE: The rear clutch is installed correctly if the splined center of the clutch is flush with the end of the sun gear shaft.

9. Install the needle bearing race using petroleum jelly to hold it in place.
10. Using petroleum jelly, install the thrust bearing and race on the front clutch. Install the front clutch in the transmission case.
11. Place a straight edge across the transmission case and the front clutch. Measure the distance between the straight edge and the front clutch. Maximum distance for the A-40D should be 1.34 in. (34mm). Distance for the A-43D, A-43DL and A-43DE should be 0.08 in. (2mm).
12. Install the thrust bearing on the front clutch. Use petroleum jelly to hold the thrust washer in place.
13. Install the guide bolts on the transmission case and finger tighten.
14. Install the thrust washer on the end of the overdrive case and install the overdrive case.

15. Install one thrust washer on the overdrive clutch and one washer on the overdrive case. The washer lugs are to be inserted in the clutch holes.

16. Install the overdrive clutch in the transmission case. Place a straight edge across the top of the transmission case and measure the distance between the overdrive clutch and the straight edge. Approximate distance for the A-40D automatic transmission should be 0.08 in. (2mm). Distance for the A-43D and the A-43DE automatic transmissions should be 0.138 in. (3.5mm).

17. Install the O-ring on the outside of the overdrive case.

18. Set the converter housing on the transmission case and secure it with 6 bolts. Torque the short bolts to 20-30 ft. lbs. (2.7-4.2 kg-m.) and the long bolts to 35-49 ft. lbs. (4.8-6.8 kg-m.).

19. Install the thrust washer and bearing on the overdrive clutch.

20. Install the thrust washer on the front of the oil pump and install the oil pump. Remove the guide bolts from the transmission case. Torque the oil pump bolts to 14-18 ft. lbs. (1.8-2.5 kg-m.).

21. Drive in a new pin to hold the manual shaft on the manual lever.

22. Install the parking lock pawl, pin and spring into the case. Install the parking pawl bracket on the case. Torque the 2 bolts to 53-78 in. lbs. (0.6-0.9 kg-m.).

23. Install a new O-ring on the throttle cable and install the throttle cable in the transmission case.

24. Insert the accumulator pistons and springs into the transmission case. Insert the valve body to case O-rings with the rounded edge towards the case.

25. Install the valve body and torque the bolts in 2 or 3 stages to 70-104 in. lbs. (0.8-1.2 kg-m.). Install the oil screen and oil tubes.

26. Install the magnet in the oil pan and install the oil pan with a new gasket. Install the oil pan drain plug.

27. Slide the governor onto the output shaft while prying up on the retaining ring.

28. Install the speedometer drive gear and snap ring on the output shaft.

29. Using a new gasket, install the extension housing. Torque the bolts to 20-30 ft. lbs.

30. Install the neutral safety switch and the shift handle.

31. Install the kick down switch. Install the solenoid switch with new O-rings.

S SPECIFICATIONS

TORQUE SPECIFICATIONS

Bolt Class	Basic Diameter	Thread Pitch	Torque Limit m-kg	(ft-lb)
4T	6	1	0.4– 0.7 (	2.9– 5.0)
	8	1.25	1.0– 1.6 (	7.3– 11.6)
	10	1.25	1.9– 3.1 (	13.7– 22.4)
	10	1.5	1.8– 3.0 (	13.0– 21.7)
	10	1.25	3.5– 5.5 (	25.3– 39.8)
	12	1.5	3.5– 5.0 (	25.3– 36.2)
	12	1.75	3.0– 5.0 (	21.7– 36.2)
	13	1.5	4.5– 7.0 (	32.5– 50.6)
	14	1.5	5.0– 8.0 (	36.2– 57.8)
	14	2	4.7– 7.7 (	34.0– 55.7)
	16	1.5	7.5–11.0 (	54.2– 79.6)
	16	2	7.1–10.6 (	51.3– 76.7)

TORQUE SPECIFICATIONS

Bolt Class	Basic Diameter	Thread Pitch	Torque Limit m-kg	(ft-lb)
5T	6	1	0.6– 0.9 (	4.4– 6.5)
	8	1.25	1.5– 2.2 (	10.9– 15.9)
	10	1.25	3.0– 4.5 (	21.7– 32.5)
	10	1.5	2.7– 4.2 (	19.5– 30.4)
	12	1.25	5.0– 8.0 (	36.2– 57.8)
	12	1.5	5.0– 7.0 (	36.2– 50.6)
	12	1.75	4.8– 6.8 (	34.7– 49.2)
	13	1.5	6.5– 9.0 (	47.0– 65.1)
	14	1.5	7.5–11.0 (	54.2– 79.6)
	14	2	7.0–10.5 (	50.6– 75.9)
	16	1.5	12.0–17.0 (	86.8–123.0)
	16	2	11.5–16.5 (	83.2–119.2)
6T	6	1	0.6– 0.9 (	4.4– 6.5)
	8	1.25	1.5– 2.2 (	10.9– 15.9)
	10	1.25	3.0– 4.5 (	21.7– 32.5)
	10	1.5	2.7– 4.2 (	19.5– 30.4)
	12	1.25	5.0– 8.0 (	36.2– 57.8)
	12	1.5	5.0– 7.0 (	36.2– 50.6)
	12	1.75	4.8– 6.8 (	34.7– 49.2)
7T	6	1	0.8– 1.2 (	5.8– 8.6)
	8	1.25	2.0– 3.0 (	14.5– 21.7)
	10	1.25	4.0– 5.5 (	28.9– 39.8)
	10	1.5	3.7– 5.2 (	26.8– 37.6)
	12	1.25	7.5–10.5 (	54.2– 75.9)
	12	1.5	7.0– 9.0 (	50.6– 65.1)
	12	1.75	6.0– 8.5 (	43.3– 61.4)
	13	1.5	8.0–12.0 (	57.8– 86.8)
	14	1.5	10.0–15.0 (	72.3–108.5)
	14	2	9.5–14.0 (	68.7–101.2)
	16	1.5	15.0–23.0 (	108.5–166.2)
	16	2	14.0–22.0 (	101.2–159.0)

1311

INDEX

TOYOTA AW55 AUTOMATIC TRANSAXLE

APPLICATIONS

Model	Year	Engine Number	Transmission Number
Tercel	1980	1AC	A-55
Tercel	1981-84	3AC	A-55

GENERAL DESCRIPTION

The Toyota A-55 transaxle is a fully automatic 3 speed transmission consisting of a torque converter, two sets of clutches, three sets of disc brakes, two sets of one-way clutches, valve body, oil pump and planetary gears. The A-55 transaxle is a six detent position type having the following shift positions, "P", "R", "N", "D", "2", "L". The torque converter consists of a pump and a turbine with a stator located in between, and all encased in a common housing. The planetary gear unit is provided with a wet type multiple disc clutch and disc brake for the purpose of controlling the speed ratio. Control of the power flow to attain first, second, and third speeds is effected by hydraulic pressure. In order to determine the required hydraulic pressure circuits, the passages for the ATF fluid have been collected in the valve body and the flow controlled by numerous valves. This part of the transaxle is called the hydraulic control system. These valves are controlled in accordance with the engine output condition and the vehicle speed. When the engine output condition changes, the throttle valve opening at that time is converted into hydraulic pressure signal.

When the vehicle speed changes, the speed of the governor turning together with the output shaft is converted into a hydraulic pressure signal. The transaxle has been made to automatically change speed to conform with these hydraulic pressure signals.

Factors causing the speed change are governor pressure produced in accordance with the vehicle speed and throttle pressure produced by changes in the carburetor throttle valve opening or accelerator pedal travel. This throttle pressure is controlled by the throttle valve cam connected to the carburetor by a cable.

Transmission and Converter Identification

TRANSMISSION

An identification plate is normally located on the left side of the transaxle case, with the model and serial number stamped on the plate. Should a transaxle be encountered without an identification plate, check the identification information plate on the firewall in the engine compartment and also the plate on the top of the instrument panel and driver's door post. If there is still no transaxle model number found, examine the transaxle case for identifying code letters or digits. Also, obtain the vehicle model and serial number before ordering replacment parts.

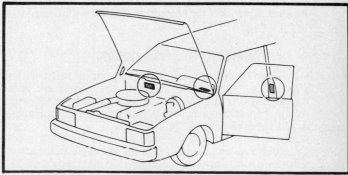

Identification information plate (© Toyota Motor Corporation)

CONVERTER

The torque converter is a 3 element, single stage, 2 phase type. The converter is a welded unit and cannot be disassembled by the average repair shop.

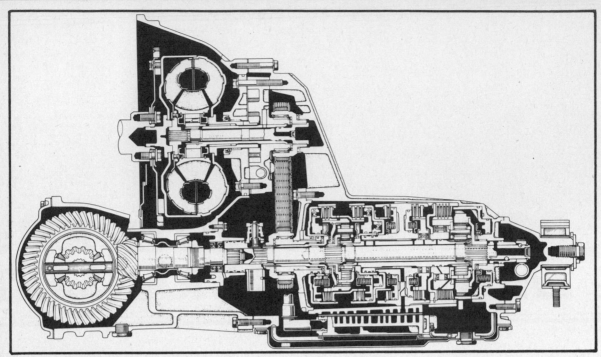

A-55 transaxle (© Toyota Motor Corporation)

FLUID CAPACITY CHART

	Liters	US Qts.	Imp. Qts.
Drain and refill	2.2	2.3	1.9
Dry refill	4.5	4.8	4.0

Checking Fluid Level

The fluid level should be checked when the transaxle is at normal operating temperature.

1. With the engine idling and the parking brake engaged, depress the brake pedal and shift the selector into each position from park to low and then return to park.
2. Now pull out the transaxle dipstick and wipe it clean.
3. With the dipstick clean push it back fully into the dipstick tube.
4. Pull the dipstick out again and check to see if the fluid is in the "HOT" range.
5. If the fluid is low, add the recommended ATF fluid until the fluid level reaches the "HOT" range.

Metric Fasteners

Metric bolt sizes and thread pitches are used for all fasteners on the A-55 transaxle. The metric fasteners dimensions are very close to the dimensions of the familiar inch system fasteners, and for this reason, replacement fasteners must have the same measurement and strength as those removed.

Do not attempt to interchange metric fasteners for inch system fasteners. Care should be taken to reuse the fasteners in the same locations as removed, whenever possible. Mismatched or incorrect fasteners can result in damage to the transmission unit through malfunctions, breakage or possible personal injury.

Fluid Specifications

The fluid used in the 1980-82 A-55 transaxle is ATF type F. The fluid used in the 1983-84 A-55 transaxle is Dexron® II. No other fluid should be used in this transaxle, unless specified by the manufacturer.

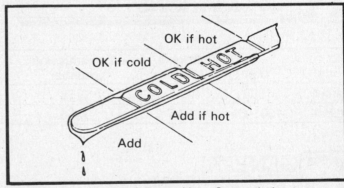

Checking the fluid level (© Toyota Motor Corporation)

M MODIFICATIONS

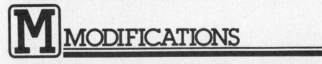

There have been no major modifications to the A-55 transaxle at the time of this printing.

TROUBLE DIAGNOSIS

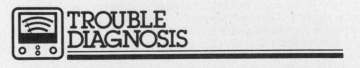

In order to properly diagnose transmission problems and avoid making second repairs for the same problem, all of the available information and knowledge must be used. Included is a list of the components of the transaxle and their functions. Also, test procedures and their accompanying specification charts aid in finding solutions to problems. Further answers are found by road testing vehicles and comparing results of the above A-55 transaxle diagnosis chart. This chart gives conditions, cause and correction to most possible trouble conditions in the A-55 transaxle.

CLUTCH APPLICATION CHART
Toyota A-55

Gear	Clutch 1	Clutch 2	Brake 1	Brake 2	Brake 3	One-way Clutch 1	One-way Clutch 2
P	—	—	—	—	—	—	—
R	—	Applied	—	—	Applied	—	—
N	—	—	—	—	—	—	—
D 1st	Applied	—	—	—	—	—	Holding
D 2nd	Applied	—	—	Applied	—	Holding	—
D 3rd	Applied	Applied	—	Applied	—	—	—
D 3-2 Kickdown	Applied	—	—	Applied	—	—	—
(2) 1st	Applied	—	—	—	—	—	Holding
(2) 2nd	Applied	—	Applied	Applied	—	—	Holding
L (low)	Applied	—	—	—	Applied	—	Holding

CHILTON'S THREE "C's" DIAGNOSIS CHART
Toyota A-55 Transaxle

Condition	Cause	Correction
Harsh down-shift	a) Throttle linkage out of adjustment b) Accumulator pistons faulty c) Valve body faulty d) Transmission faulty	a) Adjust throttle linkage b) Inspect accumulator pistons c) Inspect valve body d) Disassemble and inspect transmission
No down-shift when coasting	a) Governor faulty b) Valve body faulty	a) Inspect governor b) Inspect valve body
Down-shift occurs too quick or too late while coasting	a) Throttle linkage out of adjustment b) Governor faulty c) Valve body faulty d) Transmission faulty	a) Adjust throttle linkage b) Inspect governor c) Inspect valve body d) Disassemble and inspect transmission
No 3-2 or 2-1 kickdown	a) Throttle linkage out of adjustment b) Governor faulty c) Valve body faulty	a) Adjust throttle linkage b) Inspect governor c) Inspect valve body
No engine braking in "2" range	a) Valve body faulty b) Transmission faulty	a) Inspect valve body b) Disassemble and inspect transmission
Harsh engagement into any drive range	a) Throttle linkage out of adjustment b) Valve body or primary regulator faulty c) Accumulator pistons faulty d) Transmission faulty	a) Adjust throttle linkage b) Inspect valve body c) Inspect accumulator pistons d) Disassemble and inspect transmission
Delayed 1-2 or 2-3 up-shift, or down-shifts from 3-2 then shifts back to 3	a) Throttle linkage out of adjustment b) Governor faulty c) Valve body faulty	a) Adjust throttle linkage b) Inspect governor c) Inspect valve body
Slips on 1-2 or 2-3 up-shift, or slips or shudders on take-off	a) Manual linkage out of adjustment b) Throttle linkage out of adjustment c) Transmission faulty	a) Adjust linkage b) Adjust throttle linkage c) Disassemble and inspect transmission

CHILTON'S THREE "C's" DIAGNOSIS CHART
Toyota A-55 Transaxle

Condition	Cause	Correction
Drag, binding or tie-up on 1-2 or 2-3 up-shift	a) Manual linkage out of adjustment b) Valve body faulty c) Transmission faulty	a) Adjust linkage b) Inspect valve body c) Disassemble and inspect transmission
Fluid discolored or smells burnt	a) Fluid contamination b) Torque converter faulty c) Transmission is faulty	a) Replace the fluid b) Replace the torque converter c) Disassemble and inspect the transmission
Vehicle does not move in any forward range or reverse	a) Manual linkage out of adjustment b) Valve body or primary regulator faulty c) Transmission faulty	a) Adjust the linkage b) Inspect valve body c) Disassemble and inspect transmission
Vehicle does not move in any range	a) Park lock pawl faulty b) Valve body or primary regulator faulty c) Torque converter faulty d) Broken converter drive plate e) Oil pump intake screen blocked f) Transmission faulty	a) Inspect park pawl b) Inspect valve body c) Replace the torque converter d) Replace the torque converter e) Clean the screen f) Disassemble and inspect transmission
Shift lever position is incorrect	a) Manual linkage out of adjustment b) Manual valve and lever faulty c) Transmission faulty	a) Adjust linkage b) Inspect valve body c) Disassemble and inspect transmission
Vehicle does not hold in "P"	a) Manual linkage out of adjustment b) Parking lock pawl cam and spring faulty	a) Adjust linkage b) Inspect cam and spring

HYDRAULIC CONTROL SYSTEM

The main parts of the hydraulic control system for the A-55 trans-axle are the torque converter, oil pump, governor, cooler and lubrication circuits, valve body and applying clutches and brakes.

Major Components

OIL PUMP

The oil pump is used to send the ATF fluid to the torque converter, to lubricate the planetary gear units, and to supply the operating (line) pressure for hydraulic control. The oil pump drive gear, together with the torque converter impeller, is constantly driven by the engine. The pump has the capacity to supply the necessary hydraulic pressure for operating from low speed to high speed and when reversing.

VALVE BODY

The valve body distributes the hydraulic pressure delivered by the oil pump to the various parts, and to perform automatic gear changes by regulating the hydraulic pressure in accordance with the throttle valve opening and vehicle speed.

1. The manual valve is linked to the shift lever in the driver's compartment and is used to charge the fluid passages, according to the movement of the shift lever.

2. The control valve check ball prevents loss of fluid from the torque converter when the engine is not running.

3. The primary regulator valve automatically controls the hydraulic pressure to the other valves and units of the transaxle as required by changing speed and torque conditions in the transaxle.

4. The oil pump safety relief check ball limits the maximum pressure output of the oil pump.

5. The detent regulator valve controls pressure passing through the downshift plug and acting on the 1-2 and 2-3 shift valves at kickdown.

6. The accumulators lessen the shock when the rear clutch and the number 2 brake are applied.

7. The cut-back valve regulates the cut-back pressure acting on the throttle valve by applying cut-back pressure to the throttle valve. The throttle pressure is lowered to prevent any unnecessary power loss from the oil pump.

8. The throttle valve operates in relation to engine load and creates the throttle pressure corresponding to the load. This valve is connected to the accelerator linkage. The throttle valve inner lever pushes the downshift plug in relation to accelerator pedal travel. Two springs on the inner valve oppose the inner lever pressure. When the throttle valve is partially closed a passage on the discharge side is closed and a passage for line pressure is opened to produce throttle pressure. Throttle pressure passing through the throttle modulator valve is routed to the shift valves. This pressure opposes governor pressure at the shift valves.

9. When the accelerator pedal is depressed fully, the downshift plug pushes strongly against the throttle valve to open the line pressure passage, causing throttle pressure to equal line pressure.

10. The 1-2 shift valve provides automatic shifting from 1st to 2nd and from 2nd to 1st. This valve is controlled by governor pressure, throttle modulator pressure and line pressure. When

governor pressure is high and throttle modulator pressure is low, the 1-2 shift valve is moved, which causes the brake number 2 passage to open. This results in the transmission shifting to 2nd gear. When governor pressure is low and throttle pressure is high, the 1-2 shift valve moves to close the brake number 2 passage, resulting in the transmission downshifting to 1st gear.

11. The 2-3 shift valve provides automatic shifting from 2nd to 3rd gear and from 3rd to 2nd gear. The valve is controlled by governor pressure, line pressure, throttle pressure and spring tension. When governor pressure is high and overcomes spring tension and throttle pressure the valve opens the line pressure passage to the rear clutch shifting to 3rd gear. When governor pressure is low, the 2-3 shift valve moves to close the line pressure passage to the rear clutch downshifting to 2nd gear.

Diagnosis Tests

TIME LAG TEST

When the shift lever is shifted while the engine is idling, there will be a certain time delay (lag) before the shock on the transaxle can be felt. This time delay (lag) is used for checking the condition of the front clutch, rear clutch and brake number 3.

Measuring Lag Time

1. Start the vehicle and bring the engine and transaxle up to normal operating temperature.
2. With the parking brake fully engaged, shift the shift lever from "N" to "D" range.
3. Using a stop watch or a wrist watch, measure the time it takes from shifting the lever until the shock is felt (average lag time is less than 1.2 seconds).
4. Now shift the shift lever from "N" to "R" range and measure the time lag (average lag time is less than 1.5 seconds).

NOTE: Allow at least one minute intervals between tests. Make three measurements and then calculate the average lag time.

Time Lag Test Result Indications

If the shift from "N" to "D" time lag is longer than specified, the problems could be:
1. The line pressure is too low.
2. The front clutch could be badly worn.
If the shift from "N" to "R" time lag is longer than specified, the problems could be:
1. The rear clutch is worn.
2. Brake number could be worn.
3. The line pressure is too low.

Hydraulic Tests

Governor Pressure Test

1. Engage the parking brake and chock all four wheels.
2. Connect a oil pressure gauge to the governor pressure port on the transaxle.
3. Start the engine and bring it up to normal operating temperature.
4. Shift the shift lever into the "D" range and measure the governor pressure at the speeds specified in the chart below:

GOVERNOR PRESSURE AT VEHICLE SPEED

Speed (mph)	PSI
19 mph	17-26 psi
31 mph	26-34 psi
63 mph	54-71 psi

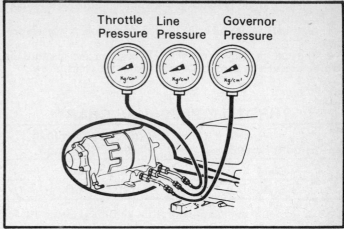

Pressure test plug location (© Toyota Motor Corporation)

Governor Pressure Test Result Indications

If the governor pressure is not within specifications:
1. The line pressure could be too low.
2. A possible fluid leakage in the governor pressure circuit.
3. The governor valve is not operating correctly.

Line Pressure Test

1. Engage the parking brake and chock all four wheels.
2. Connect an oil pressure gauge to the line pressure port on the transaxle.
3. Start the engine and bring it up to normal operating temperature.
4. Shift the shift lever into the "D" position and measure the line pressure at the speeds specified in the chart below:

LINE PRESSURE CHART

Engine Speed	Line Pressure (psi)	
	"D" Range	"R" Range
Idling	57-65	95-107
Stall	132-161	223-259

5. In the same manner, perform the line pressure test for the "R" range.

NOTE: If the measured line pressures are not within specifications, recheck the throttle link adjustment and retest.

Line Pressure Test Result Indications

1. If the line pressure is higher than specified:
   a. Regulator valve is not operating correctly.
   b. Throttle link is out of adjustment.
   c. The throttle valve is not operating correctly.
2. If the line pressure is lower than specified:
   a. The oil pump may be defective.
   b. The throttle link is out of adjustment.
   c. The throttle valve is not operating correctly.
   d. The regulator valve is not operating correctly.
3. If the line pressure is low in the "D" range only:
   a. The front clutch is not operating correctly.
   b. There is a possible fluid leakage in the "D" range circuit.
4. If the line pressure is low in the "R" range only:
   a. The rear clutch is not operating correctly.
   b. Brake number 3 is not operating correctly.
   c. There is a possible fluid leakage in the "R" range circuit.

Throttle Pressure Test

1. Engage the parking brake and chock all four wheels.

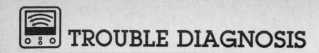
2. Connect an oil pressure gauge to the throttle pressure port on the transaxle.

3. Start the engine and bring it up to normal operating temperature.

4. Shift the shift lever into the "D" position and measure the throttle pressure at the speeds specified in the chart below:

THROTTLE PRESSURE CHART

Engine Speed	Throttle Pressure (psi) "D" and "R" Range
Idling	0-4.3 psi
Stall	110-118 psi

5. In the same manner, perform the throttle pressure test for the "R" range.

NOTE: If the measured throttle pressures are not within specifications, recheck the throttle link adjustment and retest.

Throttle Pressure Test Result Indications

1. If the throttle pressure is higher than specified:
   a. The throttle valve is not operating correctly.
   b. The throttle circuit orifice could be clogged.
2. If the throttle pressure is lower than specified:
   a. Oil pump may be defective.
   b. The regulator valve is not operating correctly.
   c. The throttle valve is not operating correctly.

ROAD TEST

Road Test With Selector in "P"

1. With the vehicle parked on a small grade, put the selector lever in the "P" position and release the parking brake.
2. If the vehicle does not roll backwards, the parking system is working properly.

Road Test With Selector in "R"

1. Start the engine and while running at full throttle, check the transaxle for slipping.

Road Test With Selector in "D"

1. Increase speed of vehicle and while holding the accelerator pedal steady, check to see if transaxle makes 1-2 and 2-3 upshifts at correct vehicle speeds. Also check for hard shifting or slipping at this time.
2. While driving in third gear, check for noise and vibration.
3. With selector lever in second or third gear, check to see if 2-1, 3-1 and 3-2 kickdown shifts occur properly at specified kickdown limit vehicle speeds.
4. Drive in third gear, and select 2 range, than L range to check if engine brake is effective.
5. While driving in the "D" range, shift the selector to the "L" range to check if the 3-2 and the 2-1 downshift occurs at the proper vehicle speed.

Road Test with Selector in "2"

1. While driving with the selector lever in the "2" position, increase the vehicle speed and check to see that the transaxle makes the 1-2 upshift at the proper vehicle speed. Also check for noise and shock at the time of shifting.
2. Check to see if the 2-1 kickdown occurs at correct vehicle speed limit.

Road Test With Selector in "L"

1. While running in the "L" range, check to see that there is no up-shift to 2nd gear.
2. Check for noise in either acceleration or deceleration.

AUTOMATIC VEHICLE SPEED SHIFT CHART (MPH) km/h

"D" Range (throttle valve full open)				"L" Range
1-2	2-3	3-2	2-1	2-1
(26-36)	(59-68)	(54-64)	(20-30)	(22-31)
42-58	96-110	88-103	33-49	35-51

STALL TEST

The object of this test is to check the overall performance of the transaxle and the engine by measuring the maximum engine speeds at the "D" and "R" ranges.

Measuring Stall Speed

1. Engage the parking brake and chock all four wheels.
2. Attach a tachometer to the engine and place it in a position to be seen by the operator.
3. Start the engine and bring the vehicle up to normal operating temperature.
4. Apply the foot brake and shift the selector lever to the "D" position.
5. With foot brake applied, gradually depress the accelerator pedal until the engine reaches full throttle.
6. When the engine speed is stabilized, read the engine speed quickly and release the accelerator pedal. Hold no longer than 5 seconds. Stall speed should be 2,200 ± 150 rpm.
7. Shift the selector lever to the "N" position, and cool down the transaxle fluid by letting the engine run for 2-5 minutes at fast idle speed.
8. Record the stall speed and perform the stall test with the selector lever in the "R" position.

NOTE: Do not perform the stall test longer than 5 seconds as damage to the transaxle can occur.

Interpretation of Stall Test Results

1. If the stall speed is lower than specified:
   a. Engine output could be insufficient.
   b. Stator one-way is not operating correctly.

NOTE: If the stall speed is more than 600 rpm below the specified stall speed, the torque converter could be defective.

2. If the stall speed in the "D" position is higher than specified:
   a. The front clutch could be slipping.
   b. One-way clutch number 2 is not operating correctly.
   c. The line pressure could be too low.
3. If the stall speed in the "R" position is higher than specified:
   a. The rear clutch could be slipping.
   b. Brake number 3 could be slipping.
   c. The line pressure could be too low.

STATOR ONE-WAY CLUTCH TEST

(CONVERTER REMOVED)

1. Fill the torque converter with the recommended ATF up to the top of the stator splines.
2. Insert the one-way clutch test tool or its equivalent into the stator spline.
3. Turn the one-way clutch tool rapidly to the left, the one-way clutch is not functioning and the stator is turning, creating resistance against the ATF fluid.
4. Now turn the one-way clutch tool rapidly to the right. At this time there should be no resistance felt when turning the one-way clutch to the right.
5. If there is resistance when turning the one-way clutch to the right, the one-way clutch is not sliding freely and therefore not operating correctly.

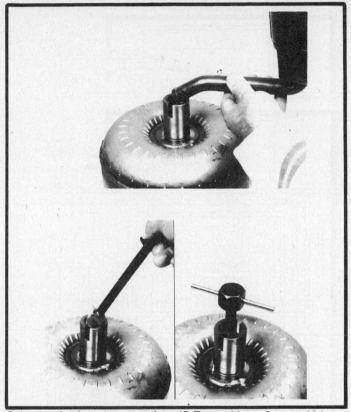

One-way clutch test preparations (© Toyota Motor Corporation)

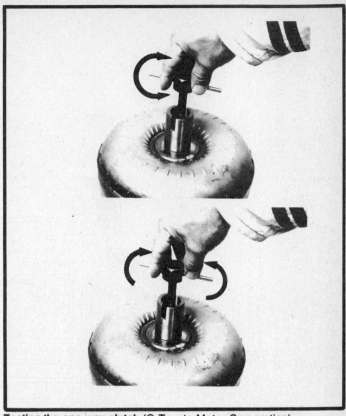

Testing the one-way clutch (© Toyota Motor Corporation)

Installing the oil filter (© Toyota Motor Corporation)

Drain plug removal (© Toyota Motor Corporation)

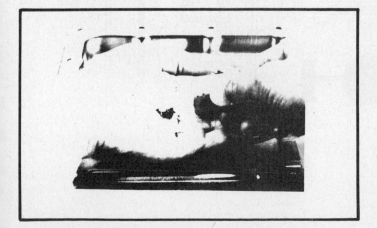

Checking the magnetic particles (© Toyota Motor Corporation)

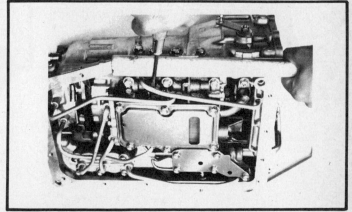

Oil tube removal (© Toyota Motor Corporation)

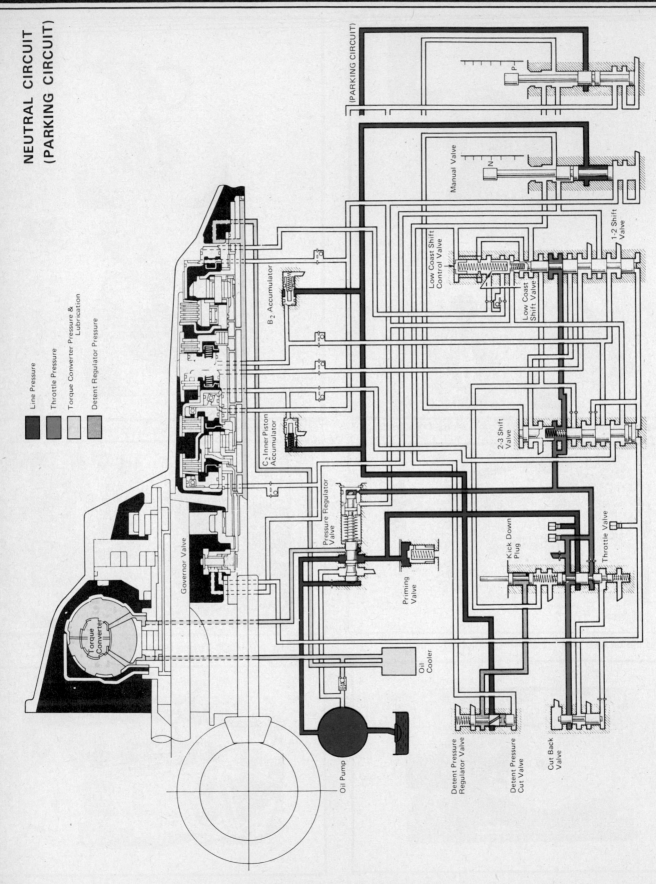

NEUTRAL CIRCUIT (PARKING CIRCUIT)

(PARKING CIRCUIT)

Line Pressure

Throttle Pressure

Torque Converter Pressure & Lubrication

Detent Regulator Pressure

Manual Valve

Low Coast Shift Control Valve

Low Coast Shift Valve

1-2 Shift Valve

B_2 Accumulator

2-3 Shift Valve

C_2 Inner Piston Accumulator

Pressure Regulator Valve

Kick Down Plug

Throttle Valve

Governor Valve

Priming Valve

Torque Converter

Oil Cooler

Oil Pump

Detent Pressure Regulator Valve

Detent Pressure Cut Valve

Cut Back Valve

Automatic transaxle in "N" neutral range

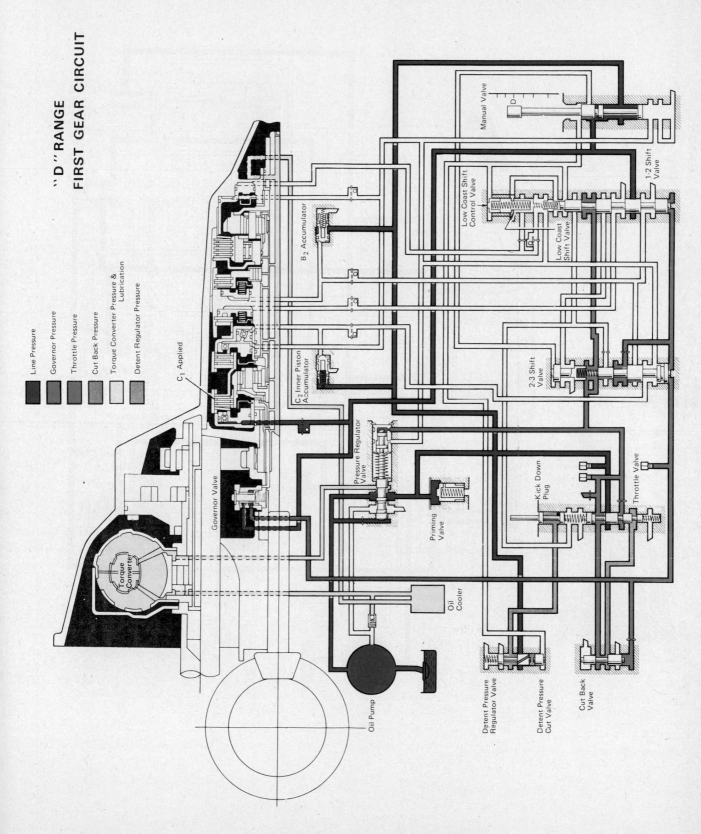

"D" RANGE FIRST GEAR CIRCUIT

Line Pressure
Governor Pressure
Throttle Pressure
Cut Back Pressure
Torque Converter Pressure & Lubrication
Detent Regulator Pressure

Torque Converter

Governor Valve

C₁ Applied

B-2 Accumulator

C₂ Inner Piston Accumulator

Pressure Regulator Valve

Priming Valve

Oil Cooler

Oil Pump

Detent Pressure Regulator Valve

Detent Pressure Cut Valve

Cut Back Valve

Kick Down Plug

Throttle Valve

2-3 Shift Valve

Low Coast Shift Control Valve

Low Coast Shift Valve

1-2 Shift Valve

Manual Valve

Automatic transaxle in "D" range 1st gear

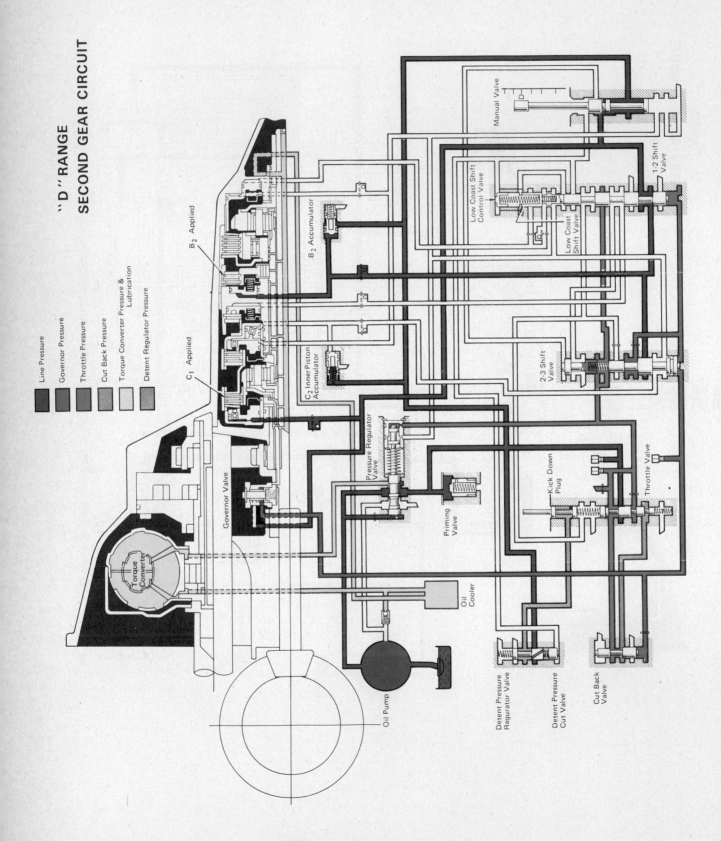

"D" RANGE
SECOND GEAR CIRCUIT

Line Pressure
Governor Pressure
Throttle Pressure
Cut Back Pressure
Torque Converter Pressure & Lubrication
Detent Regulator Pressure

Manual Valve

B₂ Applied

B₂ Accumulator

C₁ Applied

C₂ Inner Piston Accumulator

Low Coast Shift Control Valve

Low Coast Shift Valve

1-2 Shift Valve

2-3 Shift Valve

Governor Valve

Pressure Regulator Valve

Priming Valve

Kick Down Plug

Throttle Valve

Torque Converter

Oil Cooler

Oil Pump

Detent Pressure Regurator Valve

Detent Pressure Cut Valve

Cut Back Valve

Automatic transaxle in "D" range 2nd gear

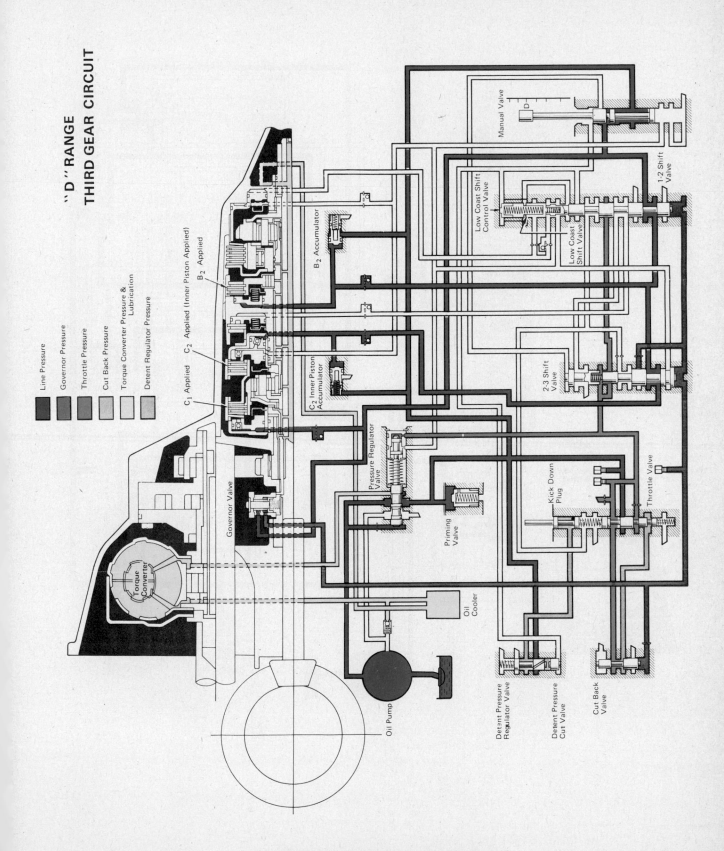

"D" RANGE
THIRD GEAR CIRCUIT

Line Pressure
Governor Pressure
Throttle Pressure
Cut Back Pressure
Torque Converter Pressure & Lubrication
Detent Regulator Pressure

Manual Valve

Low Coast Shift Control Valve

1-2 Shift Valve

Low Coast Shift Valve

2-3 Shift Valve

B₂ Accumulator

B₂ Applied

C₂ Applied (Inner Piston Applied)

B₂ Applied

C₂ Applied

C₂ Inner Piston Accumulator

C₁ Applied

Governor Valve

Pressure Regulator Valve

Kick Down Plug

Throttle Valve

Priming Valve

Torque Converter

Oil Cooler

Oil Pump

Detent Pressure Regulator Valve

Detent Pressure Cut Valve

Cut Back Valve

Automatic transaxle in "D" range 3rd gear

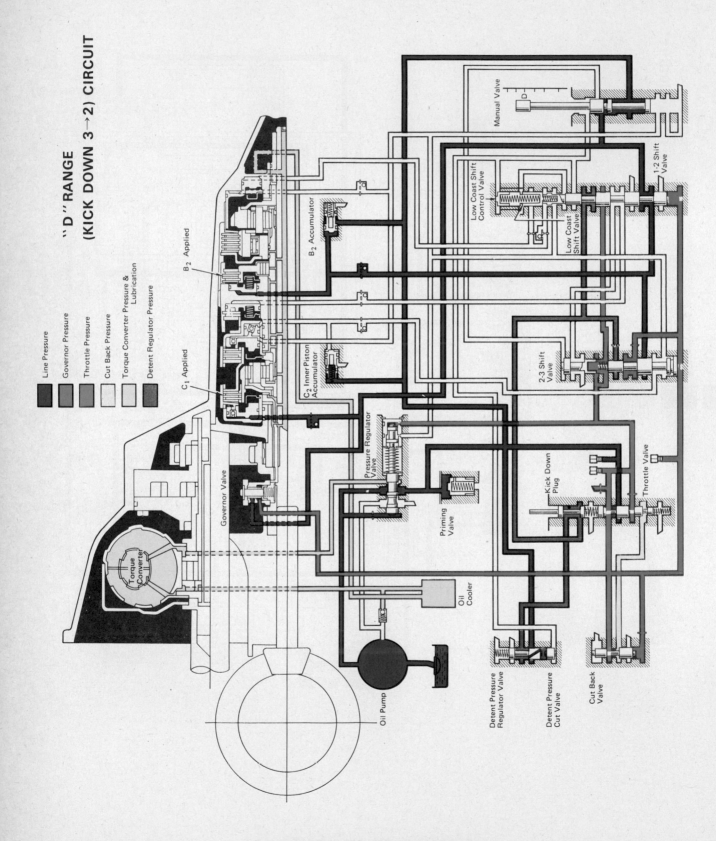

"D" RANGE (KICK DOWN 3→2) CIRCUIT

Line Pressure
Governor Pressure
Throttle Pressure
Cut Back Pressure
Torque Converter Pressure & Lubrication
Detent Regulator Pressure

Torque Converter

Governor Valve

B_2 Accumulator

B_2 Applied

B_2

C_1 Applied

C_2 Inner Piston Accumulator

Pressure Regulator Valve

Priming Valve

Oil Cooler

Oil Pump

Detent Pressure Regulator Valve

Detent Pressure Cut Valve

Kick Down Plug

Throttle Valve

Cut Back Valve

Manual Valve

Low Coast Shift Control Valve

Low Coast Shift Valve

1-2 Shift Valve

2-3 Shift Valve

Automatic transaxle in "D" range kickdown

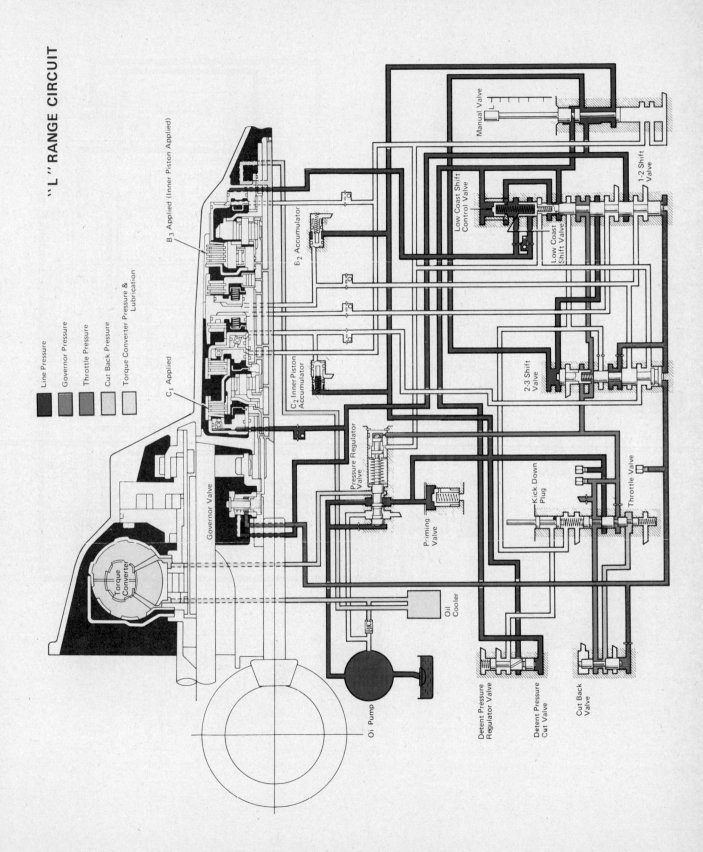

"L" RANGE CIRCUIT

Line Pressure

Governor Pressure

Throttle Pressure

Cut Back Pressure

Torque Converter Pressure & Lubrication

B₃ Applied (Inner Piston Applied)

B₂ Accumulator

C₁ Applied

C₂ Inner Piston Accumulator

Governor Valve

Torque Converter

Pressure Regulator Valve

Priming Valve

Oil Cooler

Oil Pump

Manual Valve

Low Coast Shift Control Valve

Low Coast Shift Valve

1-2 Shift Valve

2-3 Shift Valve

Kick Down Plug

Throttle Valve

Detent Pressure Regulator Valve

Detent Pressure Cut Valve

Cut Back Valve

Automatic transaxle in "L" low range

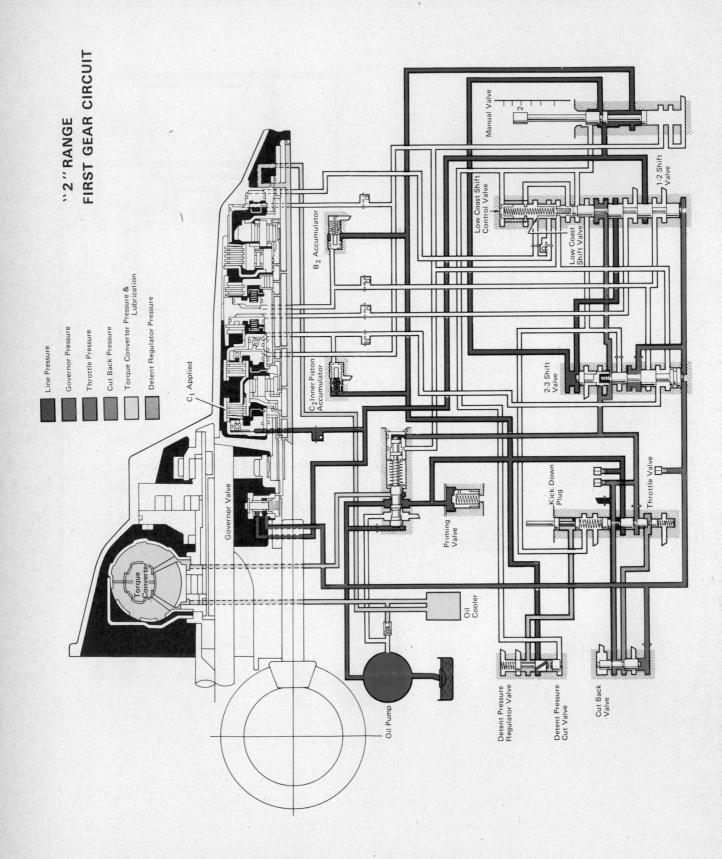

"2" RANGE FIRST GEAR CIRCUIT

Line Pressure
Governor Pressure
Throttle Pressure
Cut Back Pressure
Torque Converter Pressure & Lubrication
Detent Regulator Pressure

Torque Converter

Governor Valve

C_1 Applied

C_2 Inner Piston Accumulator

B_2 Accumulator

Oil Pump

Priming Valve

Oil Cooler

Manual Valve

Low Coast Shift Control Valve

Low Coast Shift Valve

1-2 Shift Valve

2-3 Shift Valve

Kick Down Plug

Throttle Valve

Detent Pressure Regulator Valve

Detent Pressure Cut Valve

Cut Back Valve

Automatic transaxle in "2" range 1st gear

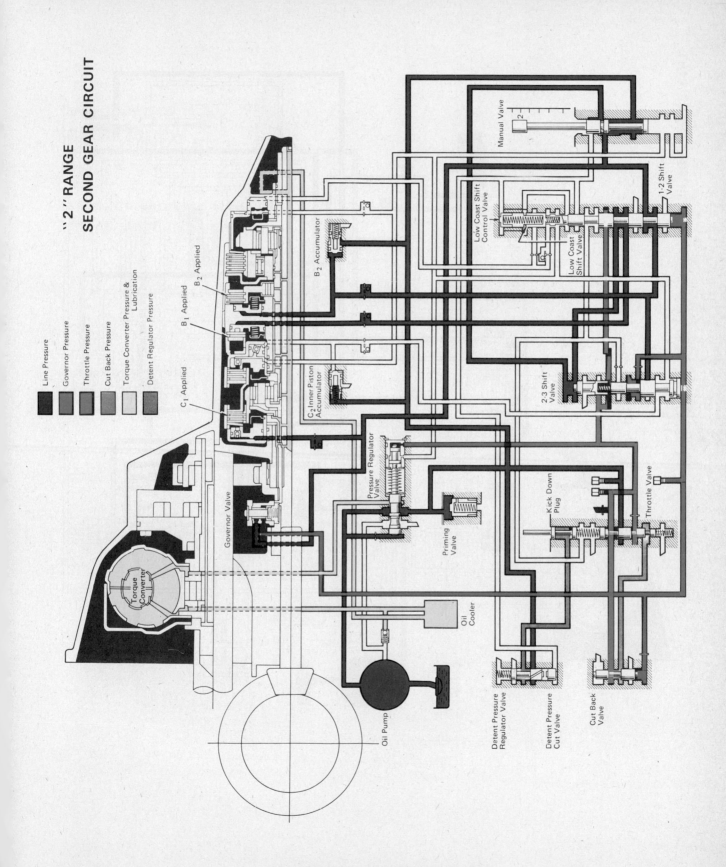

"2" RANGE
SECOND GEAR CIRCUIT

Line Pressure
Governor Pressure
Throttle Pressure
Cut Back Pressure
Torque Converter Pressure & Lubrication
Detent Regulator Pressure

C₁ Applied
B₁ Applied
B₂ Applied
B₂ Accumulator
C₂ Inner Piston Accumulator
Governor Valve
Torque Converter
Pressure Regulator Valve
Priming Valve
Oil Pump
Oil Cooler
Kick Down Plug
Throttle Valve
Detent Pressure Regulator Valve
Detent Pressure Cut Valve
Cut Back Valve
Manual Valve
Low Coast Shift Control Valve
Low Coast Shift Valve
1-2 Shift Valve
2-3 Shift Valve

Automatic transaxle in "2" range 2nd gear

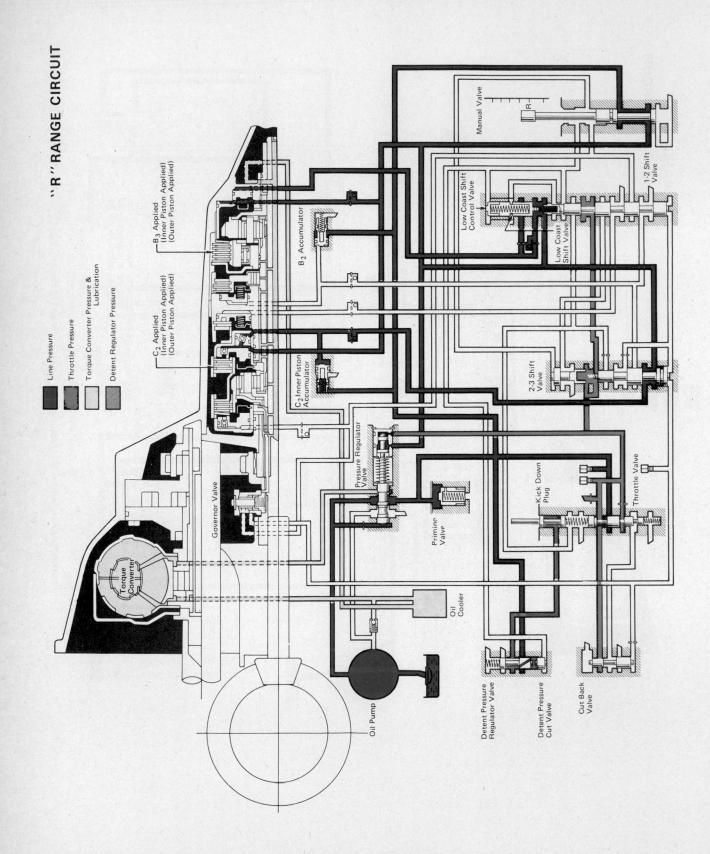

"R" RANGE CIRCUIT

Line Pressure
Throttle Pressure
Torque Converter Pressure & Lubrication
Detent Regulator Pressure

Manual Valve

Low Coast Shift Control Valve
Low Coast Shift Valve
1-2 Shift Valve

B₃ Applied (Inner Piston Applied) (Outer Piston Applied)
B₂ Accumulator

C₂ Applied (Inner Piston Applied) (Outer Piston Applied)
C₂ Inner Piston Accumulator

2-3 Shift Valve

Pressure Regulator Valve

Priming Valve

Kick Down Plug

Throttle Valve

Governor Valve

Torque Converter

Oil Cooler

Oil Pump

Detent Pressure Regulator Valve

Detent Pressure Cut Valve

Cut Back Valve

Automatic transaxle in "R" reverse

ON CAR SERVICES

Adjustments

THROTTLE LINK

Adjustment

1. Remove the air cleaner and check to see if the throttle lever and the throttle link are bent or damaged.
2. Push on the throttle lever and see if the throttle valve opens fully.
3. Using a pedal jack or its equivalent, fully depress and hold the accelerator pedal to the floor.
4. Loosen the turnbuckle lock nut and adjust the throttle linkage length by turning the turnbuckle.
5. The adjustment will be correct when the throttle valve lever indicator lines up with the mark on the transaxle case.
6. Now tighten the turnbuckle lock nut and recheck the adjustment.
7. Install the air cleaner and remove the pedal jack from the accelerator pedal.

FLOOR SHIFT LINKAGE

Adjustment

1. From underneath the vehicle check the shift linkage connecting rod bushing for wear or deformation.
2. Loosen the lock nut on the connecting rod.
3. Move the manual shift lever all the way forward and return the shift lever to the "N" neutral position (3 notches).
4. Set the shift selector to the "N" position.

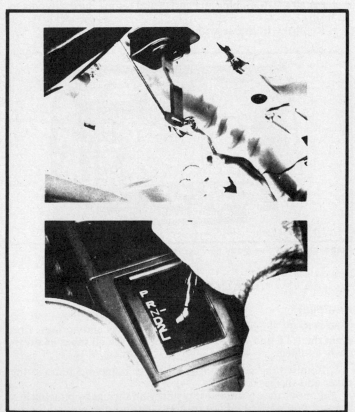

Floor shift linkage adjustment (© Toyota Motor Corporation)

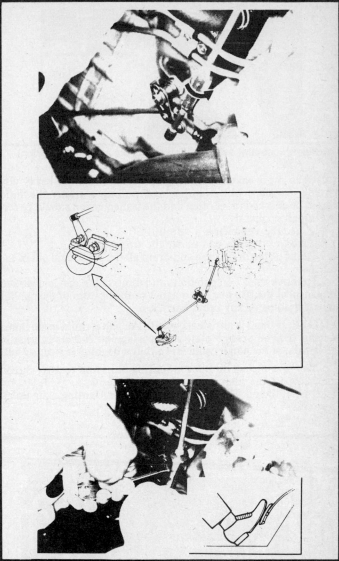

Adjusting the throttle linkage (© Toyota Motor Corporation)

5. While holding the selector slightly toward the "R" position, tighten the connecting rod lock nut.

NEUTRAL SAFETY SWITCH

Adjustment

Whenever it is possible to start the engine with the shift selector in any position other than the "P" or "N" positions, adjustment of the neutral safety switch is required.

1. Loosen the neutral safety switch hold down bolt.
2. Set the shift selector lever to the "N" position.
3. Align the switch shaft groove with the neutral base line on the transaxle.
4. Hold the switch in the align position and torque the hold down bolt to 9 ft. lbs.

Services

OIL PAN, FLUID AND FILTER

Removal and Change

The normal service interval for changing transmission fluid and replacing or cleaning oil filters is 24,000 miles. When the vehicle

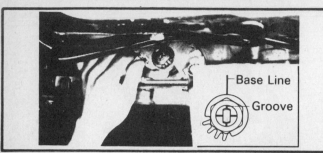

Installing the neutral safety switch (© Toyota Motor Corporation)

is used in more severe operating conditions such as, heavy city driving, constant hill climbing and pulling a trailer the fluid should be checked more often and the transmission should be service more frequently.

1. Raise the vehicle on a safe lift.
2. Place a oil drain pan under the transaxle.
3. Remove the drain plug and drain all the ATF fluid out of the transaxle.
4. Remove the 17 oil pan bolts and remove the pan and gasket.
5. Inspect the pan and the magnet in the bottom of the pan for any steel chips or any other particles.

NOTE: If there is any steel chips in the pan it could mean that a bearing, gear or a clutch plate are wearing out. If there is brass in the bottom of the pan it could mean that a bushing is wearing out.

6. Remove the six oil filter mounting bolts and remove the oil filter. Inspect the filter and clean or replace it.
7. Install the oil filter and torque the six mounting bolts to 53-78 in. lbs.

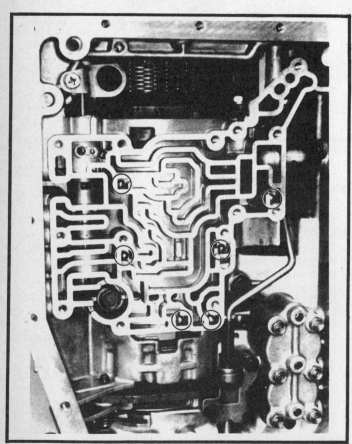

Location of the steel balls (© Toyota Motor Corporation)

Installation

1. Install the oil pan with a new gasket to the transaxle case. Torque the 17 oil pan bolts to 65 in. lbs.
2. Install the drain plug with a new gasket and torque the drain plug to 22 ft. lbs.
3. Refill the transaxle with 2.3 U.S. quarts of the recommended ATF fluid. Start the engine and run it at idle. Check the fluid level and if the level is low add the necessary fluid to bring the level up to the "HOT" range on the dipstick.

VALVE BODY

Removal

The valve body can be removed from the transaxle while the transaxle is still attached to the vehicle. This procedure is not advisable because during removal, some of the valves and the steel check balls may fall out of the valve body, becoming lost or maybe installed in the wrong position in the valve body during installation.

1. Raise the vehicle and support safely. Drain the ATF from the transaxle.
2. Pry up both ends of the oil pressure tubes with a screwdriver and remove the six oil tubes.

NOTE: When removing the valve body, be careful not to lose the pin and shift valve plug seat. Also try to keep the valve body gasket and separator plate attached to the transaxle, because this will hold the six steel balls in place in the upper valve body.

Installation

1. Install the valve body assembly and torque the 14 valve body bolts to 48 in. lbs.
2. Install the oil tubes by pressing the tubes into position by hand (do not bend or damage the tubes).
3. Install a new oil pan gasket and the oil pan, torque the oil pan bolts to 65 in. lbs.
4. Install the drain plug and gasket and torque the drain plug to 22 ft. lbs.
5. Refill the transaxle with the recommended ATF.

Removing the valve body (© Toyota Motor Corporation)

ACCUMULATOR

Removal

NOTE: To remove the accumulator pistons and springs, first drain the ATF and remove the oil pan and the oil tubes as previously outlined.

1. Remove the six accumulator cover bolts and remove the cover and the gasket.
2. Remove the accumulator pistons and springs by blowing low pressure compressed air (14 psi) into the air holes around the accumulator cylinders.

Accumulator piston removal (© Toyota Motor Corporation)

Inspecting the accumulator pistons (© Toyota Motor Corporation)

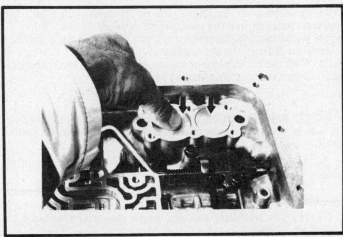

Installing the accumulator pistons (© Toyota Motor Corporation)

Installing the accumulator cover (© Toyota Motor Corporation)

3. Position a rag under the accumulator pistons to catch the pistons as they come out of the cylinders.

NOTE: Do not use high pressure air to remove the accumulator pistons and keep face away from pistons to avoid injury.

Installation

Before installing the accumulator pistons and springs, check the pistons, springs, cover and cylinder for wear or damage.

1. Install new O-rings around the accumulator pistons and coat the O-rings with ATF.

2. Press the accumulator pistons and springs into the accumulator cylinder by hand.

NOTE: Be sure to install the accumulator pistons and springs in the same cylinder that they came out of.

3. Install a new accumulator cover gasket and then the cover and the six bolts. Torque the bolts to 30-60 in. lbs.

4. Install the oil tubes and oil pan. Add the recommended ATF to the transaxle and recheck level.

SPEEDOMETER GEARS

Removal

1. Place a drain pan under the extension housing to catch any ATF that might drain out.

2. Remove the speedometer cable.

3. Remove the bolt and lock plate that hold the speedometer driven gear to the extension housing and remove the driven gear.

4. Remove the extension housing and gasket.

Installing the extension housing (© Toyota Motor Corporation)

5. Remove the snap ring from the output shaft sleeve and remove the speedometer drive gear.

Installation

1. Install the speedometer drive gear and snap ring.

2. Install the extension housing with a new gasket and torque the housing bolts to 14 ft. lbs.

3. Install new O-rings and bushings to the speedometer driven gear shaft sleeve.

4. Install the speedometer driven gear assembly into the extension housing and install the lock plate and bolt.

5. Install the speedometer cable.

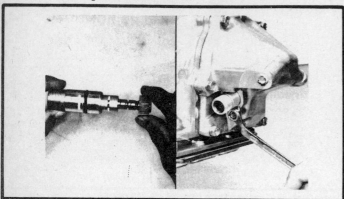

Installing the speedometer driven gear with housing
(© Toyota Motor Corporation)

TRANSAXLE REMOVAL AND INSTALLATION

Removal

1. Disconnect the positive battery cable.
2. Drain out some of the coolant from the radiator.
3. Remove the upper radiator hose from the engine.
4. Disconnect the electrical connectors to the neutral safety switch and the back-up light switch.
5. Remove the air cleaner assembly.
6. Remove the throttle link.
7. Remove the oil cooler pipe clamp.
8. Using two wrenches disconnect the oil cooler inlet pipe.
9. Remove the upper transaxle set bolts.
10. Raise the vehicle and support it safely. Drain the ATF.
11. Remove both drive shafts.
12. Remove the exhaust flange nuts and the clamp on the side of the transaxle. Remove the front exhaust pipe.
13. Remove the stiffener plate.
14. Disconnect the control link at the rear connection.
15. Disconnect the speedometer cable.
16. Remove the engine under cover.
17. Remove the three torque converter cover bolts and remove the converter cover.
18. Remove the six torque converter set bolts by turning the crankshaft to gain access to each bolt.
19. Disconnect the oil cooler outlet pipe.

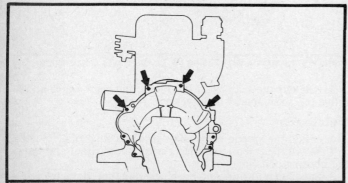

Location of the upper transaxle bolts (© Toyota Motor Corporation)

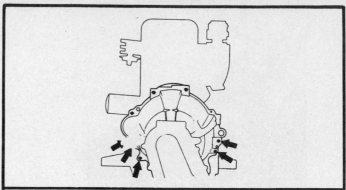

Location of the lower transaxle bolts (© Toyota Motor Corporation)

20. Remove the 5 transaxle mounting bolts.
21. Disconnect the rear bond cable.
22. Place a wooden block between the engine and the firewall panel.
23. Position a transmission jack or its equivalent under the transaxle and remove the rear engine support.
24. While turning the crankshaft, pry on the torque converter to separate it from the drive plate.
25. With the transaxle free of any obstructions, lower the jack and remove the transaxle from the vehicle.

INSTALLATION

NOTE: Before installing the transaxle, apply grease to the center hub of the torque converter and the pilot hole in the crankshaft.

1. Insert a guide pin in the most outward converter mounting hole.
2. With the transaxle on the removing jack, raise the transaxle into position in the vehicle.

NOTE: The transaxle and the torque converter should be installed as a unit.

3. Align the guide pin with one of the holes in the drive plate and install the transaxle to the engine.

NOTE: The transaxle should be installed to the engine so that the tip of the converter goes into the hole in the end of the crankshaft.

4. Remove the guide pin and install two torque converter set bolts about half way in and tighten them evenly.
5. Install the 5 transaxle mounting bolts and torque the bolts to 47 ft. lbs.
6. Install the rear support member and torque the bolts to 70 ft. lbs.
7. Loosen the temporarily installed torque converter set bolts and install the other four bolts by turning the crankshaft to gain access to the bolt holes. After tightening the bolts evenly, torque the bolts to 13 ft. lbs.
8. Install the torque converter cover.
9. Using two wrenches, connect the oil cooler outlet pipe. The torque for the nuts is 16 ft. lbs.
10. Install the engine under cover and install the stiffener plate.
11. Install the exhaust clamp on the side of the transaxle and the exhaust flange nuts and install the front exhaust pipe.
12. Connect the speedometer cable and the rear bond cable.
13. Align the shift lever and control lever at the "N" position and connect the control link.
14. Install both drive shafts.
15. Lower the vehicle and install the upper transaxle set bolts. Torque the set bolts to 47 ft. lbs.
16. Using two wrenches, connect the oil cooler inlet pipe.
17. Install the oil cooler pipe clamp.
18. Connect the throttle link.

19. Connect the electrical connectors to the neutral safety switch and the back-up light switch.
20. Install the upper radiator hose and refill the cooling system with coolant.
21. Adjust the throttle link (see adjustment section).
22. Install the air cleaner assembly and connect the positive battery cable.
23. Refill the transaxle with 2.3 U.S. quarts of the recommended ATF.

NOTE: If the torque converter has been drained, then the transaxle should be refilled with 4.8 U.S. quarts of the recommended ATF.

24. Perform a road test to check the operation of the transaxle.
25. Check for fluid leaks and for differential gear oil leaks.

BENCH OVERHAUL

Before Disassembly

1. Before disassembling the transaxle, thoroughly remove all dirt from the exterior to prevent the dirt from entering the transaxle.
2. The transaxle consists of many precision parts. Care should be taken not to scratch, nick or damage the parts during the overhaul of the transaxle.
3. Make sure that the bench work area is clean.
4. Clean all metal parts in a suitable solvent and dry with compressed air.
5. Clean all clutch discs, thrust plates and rubber parts in automatic transmission fluid.
6. All rubber gaskets and oil seals should be replaced with new at every reinstallation.
7. Apply automatic transmission fluid to the friction elements, rotating parts and sliding parts prior to installation.
8. During disassembly, always keep the parts in order.
9. A new clutch disc should be immersed in fluid for more than two hours before installation.
10. When replacing a bushing, replace the complete bushing assembly.

Disassembly

1. Remove the torque converter.
2. Remove the transmission case from the transaxle.
3. Remove the neutral safety switch.
4. Remove the speedometer driven gear and remove the extension housing.

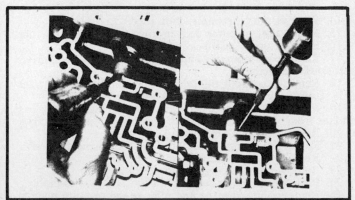
Manual lever shaft removal (© Toyota Motor Corporation)

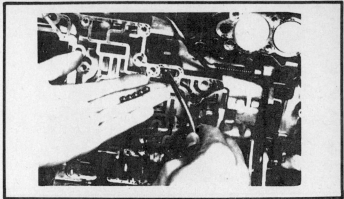
Removing the steel balls (© Toyota Motor Corporation)

Removal of the park lock rod (© Toyota Motor Corporation)

5. Remove the speedometer drive gear and the output shaft sleeve (do not lose the locking ball on the shaft sleeve).
6. With the transaxle oil pan face down on the bench, remove the oil pan bolts and lift the transaxle up to separate the transaxle from the oil pan.
7. Turn the transaxle over and remove the oil tubes.
8. Remove the oil filter and the valve body assembly.
9. Remove the six steel balls and the valve vibrating stopper from the valve body and set them aside.
10. Remove the accumulator pistons and springs.
11. Remove the parking lock rod, spring, pivot pin and parking lock pawl.
12. Remove the spacer and turn the ring 90 degrees.
13. With a hammer and punch, drive out the slotted spring pin and remove the manual valve shaft lever.

Oil pump delivery & pressure tube removal
(© Toyota Motor Corporation)

Removal of the oil pump (© Toyota Motor Corporation)

Removing the center support bolts (© Toyota Motor Corporation)

Input shaft and sprocket removal (© Toyota Motor Corporation)

Center support and sun gear removal (© Toyota Motor Corporation)

Front clutch removal (© Toyota Motor Corporation)

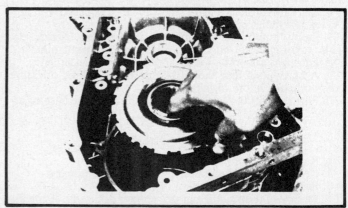

No. 2 one-way clutch removal (© Toyota Motor Corporation)

Rear clutch removal (© Toyota Motor Corporation)

14. Remove the oil pump suction tube.
15. Remove the oil pump delivery tube and the pressure tube.
16. Remove the oil pump.
17. Remove the snap ring and pull out the input shaft, driven sprockets and chain.
18. Remove the front transaxle support and place the transaxle standing up on a wooden block.
19. Measure the distance between the top of the transaxle case and the front clutch (make a note of the distance for reassembly).
20. Remove the front clutch and bearings.
21. Remove the output shaft and the front planetary gear.
22. Remove the rear clutch.
23. Remove the two center support bolts.
24. Remove the center support and the sun gear assembly.
25. Remove the snap ring and remove the reaction plate retaining ring.

Brake No. 3 disc removal (© Toyota Motor Corporation)

Planetary ring gear removal (© Toyota Motor Corporation)

26. Remove the rear number 2 one-way clutch and the rear planetary gear.
27. Remove the brake number 3 disc, plate and cushion plate.
28. Remove the rear planetary ring gear.
29. The basic disassembly is complete.

Unit Disassembly and Assembly

OIL PUMP

Disassembly and Assembly

1. Remove the three oil pump cover bolts and remove the pump cover.
2. Remove the check ball, priming valve and spring.
3. Remove the pressure regulator valve assembly.
4. Remove the two oil seal rings from the front support.

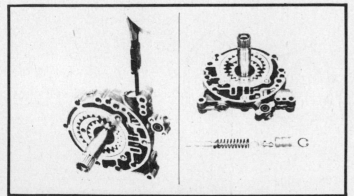

Removing the pressure regulator assembly
(© Toyota Motor Corporation)

Measuring the body clearance (© Toyota Motor Corporation)

Measuring the tip clearance (© Toyota Motor Corporation)

5. Pull the driven gear to one side of the pump body and using a feeler gauge, measure the body clearance of the driven gear. Standard clearance is 0.0028-0.0059 in. (0.07-0.15mm).
6. Measure between the gear teeth and crescent shaped part of the pump, to check the tip clearance of both gears. Standard tip clearance is 0.0043-0.0055 in. (0.11-0.14mm).
7. Using a steel straightedge and a feeler gauge, measure the side clearance of both gears. Standard side clearance is 0.0008-0.0020 in. (0.02-0.05mm).
8. Remove and replace the front oil seal on the pump.
9. After checking to see that the measurments of the oil pump gears are within specifications, install the priming valve and the check ball valve.
10. Install the oil pump cover and torque the pump cover bolts to 13 ft. lbs. (19 N•m).
11. Install the pressure regulator valve assembly.
12. Apply petroleum jelly to the oil seal rings and install the oil seal rings on the front support on the pump.

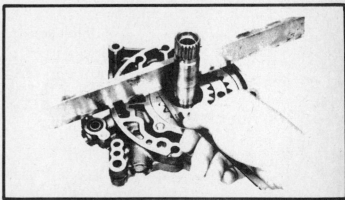

Measuring the side clearance (© Toyota Motor Corporation)

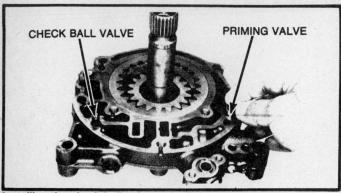

Installing the check ball valve and priming valve
(© Toyota Motor Corporation)

Measuring front clutch clearance (© Toyota Motor Corporation)

13. After applying ATF to the O-ring, install the new O-ring on the pump.

FRONT CLUTCH

Disassembly and Assembly

1. Remove the thrust bearing and race from the front side of the clutch.

2. Remove the snap ring from the front clutch drum and also remove the planetary ring gear, the rear clutch hub, the thrust bearing and races (note the position of the races) and the clutch plate and disc.

3. Remove the thinner snap ring and remove the remaining clutch plates and discs.

4. Compress the piston return spring using special Toyota tool SST 09350-20013 or its equivalent, in a press. Then remove the snap ring with an appropriate snap ring removing tool.

5. Remove the piston by inserting air pressure into the piston apply hole of the clutch drum.

6. Inspect the front clutch piston, disc, plate, return spring and clutch drum.

7. Install new O-rings on the piston and install the piston in the front clutch drum (apply ATF to the O-rings).

8. Place the clutch drum in an arbor press.

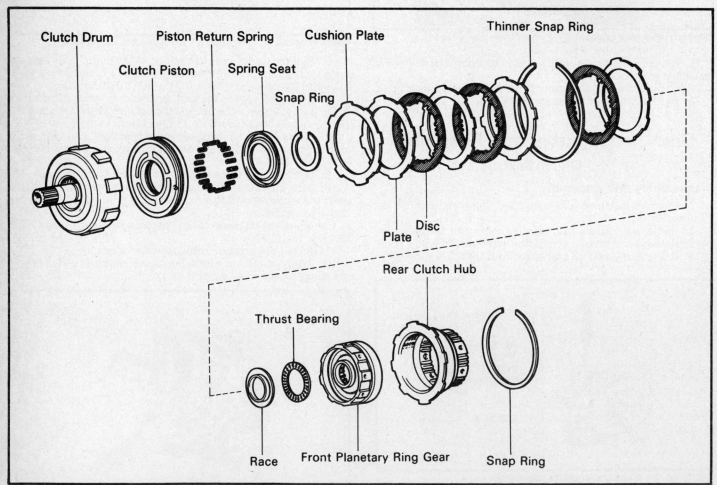

Front clutch components (© Toyota Motor Corporation)

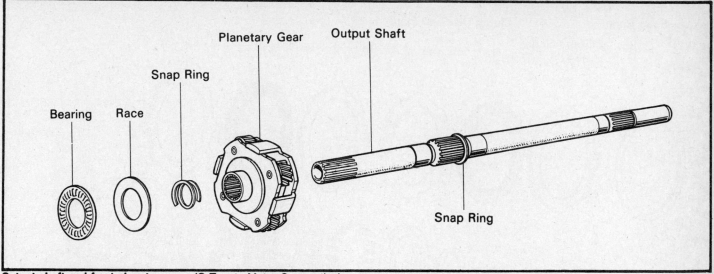

Output shaft and front planetary gear (© Toyota Motor Corporation)

Bearing   Race   Snap Ring   Planetary Gear   Output Shaft   Snap Ring

9. Install the piston return springs, spring seat and snap ring in place.

10. Using the special Toyota tool SST 09350-20013 or its equivalent, compress the return springs and install the snap ring in the groove.

11. Install the clutch discs and plates and measure the clearance of the front clutch. Standard clearance is 0.0118-0.0587 in. (0.30-1.49mm).

12. Install the thinner snap ring and the inner bearing and race. Coat the parts with petroleum jelly to keep them in place. Face the lip of the race towards the front clutch body.

13. Install the planetary gear and make sure the hub meshes with all the discs and is fully inserted.

14. Install the rear clutch hub and the outer snap ring.

OUTPUT SHAFT AND FRONT PLANETARY GEAR

Disassembly and Assembly

1. Remove the thrust bearing and race from the front side of the planetary gear.

2. Remove the planetary gear snap ring and pull the planetary gear off the output shaft.

3. Measure the planetary gear thrust clearance. The standard clearance is 0.0079-0.0197 in. (0.20-0.50mm).

4. Position the planetary gear assembly on the output shaft and install the planetary gear snap ring.

5. Install the thrust bearing and race.

REAR CLUTCH

Disassembly and Assembly

1. Remove the outer clutch pack retaining snap ring from the clutch drum and remove the clutch flange, discs and plates from the drum. If the clutch plates and discs are to be reused, they must be kept in the original order for assembly.

2. Compress the piston return spring using special Toyota tool SST 09350-20013 or its equivalent, in a press. Then remove the snap ring with an appropriate snap ring removal tool.

3. Remove the piston by inserting compressed air into the center support. If the piston does not come out completely, use a pair of pliers to remove it.

4. Remove the rear clutch from the center support and remove the O-rings from the rear clutch piston.

5. Inspect the rear clutch piston, discs, plates, return springs and clutch drum.

6. Install new O-rings and install the inner and outer piston in the clutch drum.

7. Install the piston return springs, spring seat and snap ring in place.

8. Using special Toyota tool SST 09350-20013 or its equivalent, compress the return spring and install the snap ring.

9. Install the clutch discs, plates and flange and install the snap ring.

10. Install the rear clutch onto the center support and using a dial indicator, measure the piston stroke of the rear clutch while applying and releasing compressed air. The standard piston stroke is 0.0386-0.0748 in. (0.98-1.90mm).

NOTE: If the piston stroke is higher than the limit, the clutch pack is probably worn. If the stroke is less than the limit, the parts may be assembled wrong or there may be excess ATF on the clutch discs.

CENTER SUPPORT ASSEMBLY

Disassembly and Assembly

1. Remove the center support assembly from the sun gear.

2. Remove the snap ring from the front of the center support assembly and remove the clutch flange, disc and plate (No. 1 brake).

Measuring the piston stroke (© Toyota Motor Corporation)

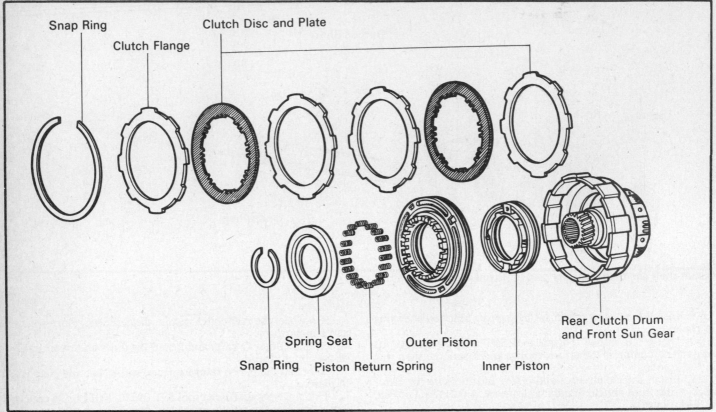

Rear clutch components (© Toyota Motor Corporation)

Labels in figure: Snap Ring, Clutch Flange, Clutch Disc and Plate, Spring Seat, Snap Ring, Piston Return Spring, Outer Piston, Inner Piston, Rear Clutch Drum and Front Sun Gear

3. Compress the piston return springs using special Toyota tool SST 09350-20013 or its equivalent, in a press. Remove the snap ring with an appropriate snap ring removal tool.

4. Remove the No. 1 brake piston by inserting compressed air into the center support. If the piston does not pop out, use a pair of pliers to remove the piston.

5. Remove the No. 1 brake piston O-rings.

6. Turn the center support assembly over and remove the rear snap ring on No. 2 brake.

7. Disassemble the No. 2 brake assembly in the same manner as the procedure for the No. 1 brake assembly.

8. Remove the three oil seal rings from the center support.

9. Remove the one-way clutch assembly and oil seal rings from the sun gear.

10. Check the operation of the one-way clutch by holding the No. 2 brake hub and turning the sun gear. The sun gear should turn freely counter clockwise and should lock clockwise. If the one-way clutch does not work properly, replace it.

11. Install the two oil seal rings and one-way clutch assembly on the sun gear.

12. Install three oil seal rings on the center support.

13. Install new O-rings on the piston and install No. 1 brake piston in the center support.

14. Install the piston return springs and seat the retainer with snap ring, in place.

15. Using special tool SST 09350-20013 or its equivalent, compress the return spring and install the snap ring.

16. Install new O-rings on the piston and center support.

17. Turn center support over and install No. 2 brake piston in the same manner as No. 1 brake piston was installed.

18. Check the piston stroke of No. 1 brake. Standard piston stroke is 0.0256-0.0512 in. (0.65-1.30mm). The maximum piston stroke is 0.0512 in. (1.30mm).

19. Check the piston stroke of No. 2 brake. Standard piston stroke is 0.0366-0.0677 in. (0.93-1.72mm). The maximum piston stroke is 0.0677 in. (1.72mm).

20. Assemble the center support and sun gear shaft.

REAR NO. 2 ONE-WAY CLUTCH AND PLANETARY GEAR

Disassembly and Assembly

1. Remove the snap ring and remove the one-way clutch.

2. Remove No. 2 thrust washer from rear planetary gear.

3. Install No. 2 thrust washer in front of the planetary pinion gear. Be sure to face the lugs downward and match them with the slots in the back of the planetary gear.

4. Install the one-way clutch into the outer race facing the spring cage toward the front.

5. Make sure that the one-way clutch operates properly and then install the reaction plate on the planetary.

TRANSAXLE CASE AND REAR BRAKE PISTON

Disassembly and Assembly

1. Using special tool 09350-20013 or its equivalent, compress the return springs and remove the spring retainer snap ring, spring retainer and the eighteen springs.

2. Insert compressed air into the oil hole in the transaxle case to remove the outer piston and reaction sleeve.

3. Inspect the transaxle case and remove and replace the manual shaft oil seals.

4. Install new O-rings on the piston and install the piston into the transaxle case.

5. Align the portion of the piston marked "A" with the groove on the transaxle case marked "B".

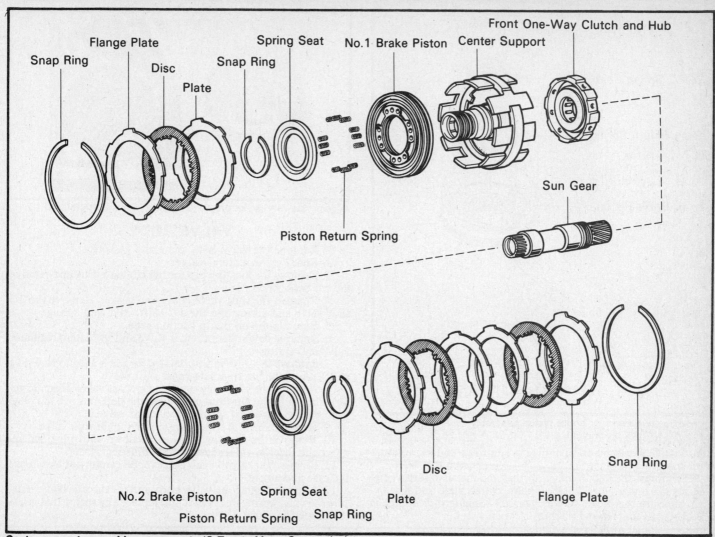

Snap Ring
Flange Plate
Disc
Plate
Snap Ring
Spring Seat
No.1 Brake Piston
Center Support
Front One-Way Clutch and Hub
Sun Gear
Piston Return Spring

No.2 Brake Piston
Piston Return Spring
Spring Seat
Snap Ring
Plate
Disc
Flange Plate
Snap Ring

Center support assembly components (© Toyota Motor Corporation)

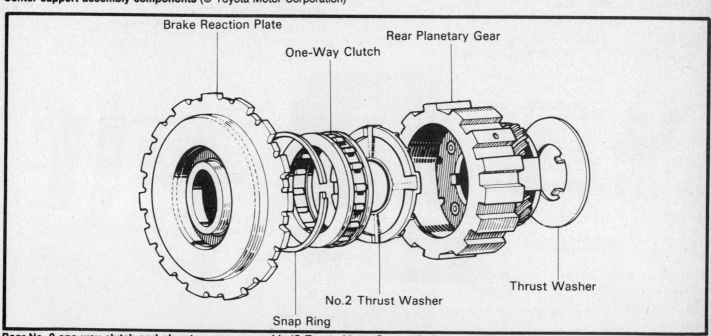

Brake Reaction Plate
One-Way Clutch
Rear Planetary Gear
Thrust Washer
No.2 Thrust Washer
Snap Ring

Rear No. 2 one-way clutch and planetary gear assembly (© Toyota Motor Corporation)

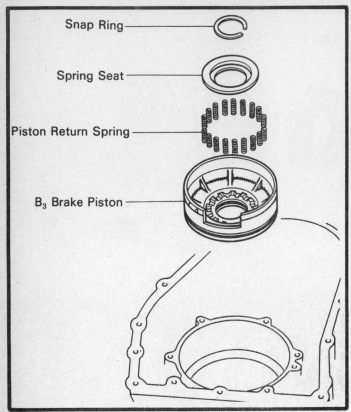

Transaxle case and rear brake piston assembly
(© Toyota Motor Corporation)

6. Install the eighteen piston return springs and set retainer with snap ring in place.

7. Compress the piston return springs and install the snap ring.

8. Install brake No. 3 cushion plate, clutch plate and disc.

9. Measure the No. 3 brake clearance. Standard clearance is 0.3953-0.449 in. (10.04-11.30mm).

Aligning the rear brake piston (© Toyota Motor Corporation)

VALVE BODY

1. Remove the valve body plate and gaskets.

2. Remove the manual valve.

3. Remove the locating pin for the cut back plug and remove the cut back valve.

4. Remove the shift valve cover and gasket. Remove the 2-3 shift valve and spring and the 1-2 shift valve and spring.

5. Remove the oil pump suction tube.

6. Remove detent pressure cut valve and the detent regulator valve and spring.

7. Remove the shift valve plug seat for the 2-3 shift valve plug and remove the intermediate-coast shift valve.

8. Remove the snap ring on the low-coast valve plug and insert a bolt into the plug and pulling on the bolt, remove the plug. Remove the low-coast spring, sleeve and valve.

9. Remove the vibrating stopper for the throttle valve.

10. Remove the locating pin for the down shift plug and remove the throttle valve, spring and adjusting spacer.

11. Remove the throttle valve sleeve. Be careful not to damage the case and sleeve.

12. After inspecting the valve body and the throttle body, measure the valve spring free height and replace any spring that is less than specifications:

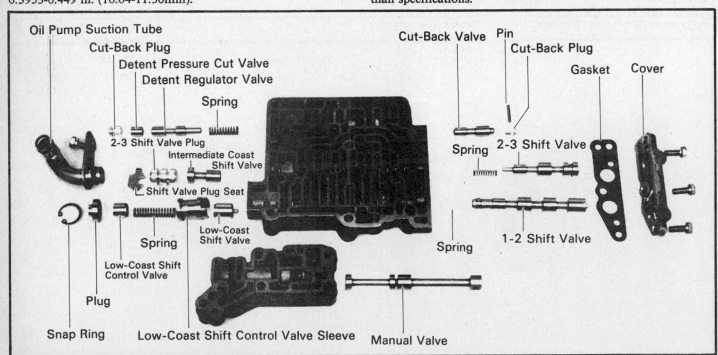

Valve body assembly (© Toyota Motor Corporation)

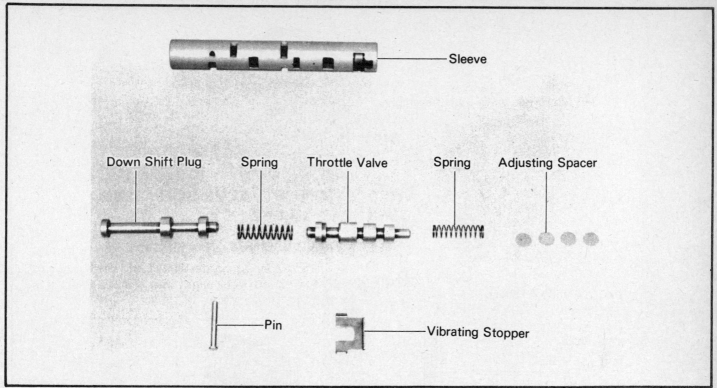

Labels in figure: Sleeve, Down Shift Plug, Spring, Throttle Valve, Spring, Adjusting Spacer, Pin, Vibrating Stopper

Throttle valve assembly (© Toyota Motor Corporation)

VALVE SPRING FREE LENGTH

Valve Spring	Free Length in. (mm)
Throttle valve spring (Rear)	1.0827 (27.50)
Throttle valve spring (Front)	1.1823 (30.03)
Detent regulator valve spring	1.0787 (27.40)
2-3 shift valve spring	0.8701 (22.10)
1-2 shift valve spring	1.0236 (26.00)
Low-coast shift valve	1.4370 (36.50)

13. Install the low-coast shift valve and the low-coast shift control valve.

14. Install the 1-2 shift valve plug and snap ring.

15. Install the intermediate-coast shift valve.

16. Install the 2-3 shift valve plug and the 2-3 shift valve plug seat.

17. Install detent regulator valve with spring and the detent pressure cut valve.

18. Install the oil pump suction tube.

19. Install the 1-2 shift valve and spring and the 2-3 shift valve and spring.

20. Install the shift valve cover and gasket. Torque the bolts to 48 in. lbs. (5.4 N•m).

21. Install the cut-back valve with plug and the cutback retainer. Coat the pin with petroleum jelly to keep it in place.

22. When assembling the throttle valve, be sure to use the same amount of adjusting spacers that were removed at disassembly.

23. Install the throttle valve and spring into the throttle sleeve and assemble the sleeve to the transaxle case.

24. Push down shift plug forward and install the location pin.

25. Install the valve vibrating stopper. Apply petroleum jelly to keep it in place and check to see that the throttle valve slides smoothly.

GOVERNOR

Disassembly and Assembly

1. Remove the snap ring and remove the governor body support.

2. Remove the retaining ring and pull the governor body from the governor support.

3. Remove the E-ring and the governor weight.

4. Slide it down through the bore and remove the governor valve.

5. Measure the governor spring free-height and replace it if it is less than specifications. Standard free-height 0.7717 in. (19.60mm).

6. Check the governor body and support and oil seal ring for wear or damage.

7. Check the governor pressure adapter and oil seal for wear or damage. Remove and replace the oil seal.

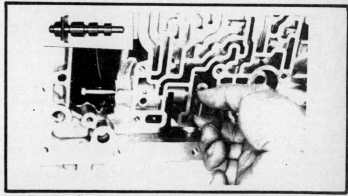

Installing the vibrating stopper (© Toyota Motor Corporation)

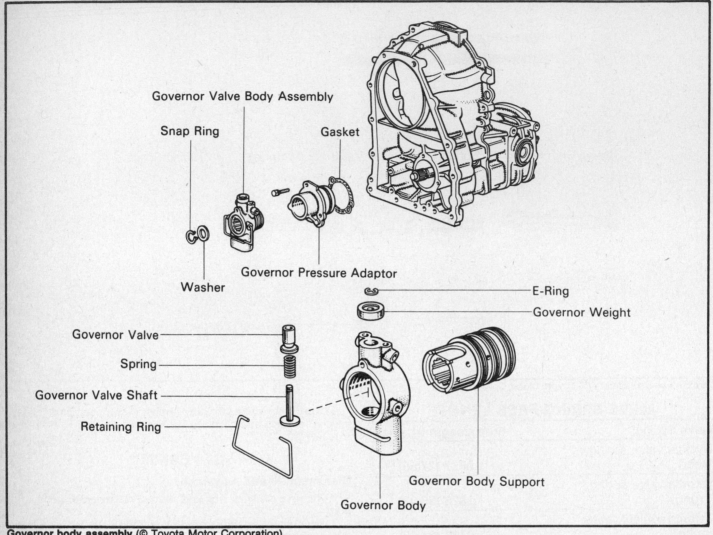

Governor body assembly (© Toyota Motor Corporation)

8. Install the governor valve, spring and shaft to the governor body.

9. Compress the governor valve spring and install the governor weight and E-ring on the governor shaft.

10. Install the governor body to the governor support.

11. Install a new O-ring on the governor pressure adapter and coat the O-ring and the drive pinion with grease. Install the governor pressure adapter.

12. Insert the oil strainer into the adapter and torque the adapter mounting bolts to 48 in. lbs. (5.4 N•m).

13. Install the governor valve assembly and check to see that the governor assembly is operating smoothly.

Transaxle Assembly

1. Install the thrust washer, facing the cup side downward, and the bearing. Use petroleum jelly to keep the small parts in place.

2. Install the rear planetary ring gear and No. 3 brake cushion plate, disc and plate.

3. Install the thrust bearing and coat the race with petroleum jelly and attach it to the ring gear.

4. After aligning the notch and the tab, install the rear planetary gear and thrust washer.

5. With the disc flukes aligned, install the rear planetary gear.

6. Measure the clearance of No. 3 brake. Standard clearance is 0.3953-0.4449 in. (10.04-11.30mm).

7. Align the portion of the reaction plate marked "A" with the portion of the transaxle case marked "B" and install the reaction plate and snap ring.

8. Align the oil hole and the bolt hole of the center support with those of the body side and insert the center support assembly into the transaxle case.

9. Install the two center support bolts and washers. Torque the bolts to 19 ft. lbs. (25 N•m).

10. Install the rear clutch assembly into the transaxle case and install the thrust bearing race.

11. Install the output shaft and the front planetary gear. Install the thrust bearing and race.

12. Install the front clutch assembly into the transaxle case.

13. Using a clutch drum height gauge or its equivalent, measure the distance between the top surface of the transaxle case and the front clutch assembly. If the distance is within specifications, the front clutch is installed correctly.

NOTE: Also use the measurement found at disassembly. Height: 0.024-0.063 in. (0.6-1.6mm).

14. Install the thrust bearing and race. Install an O-ring on the transaxle case.

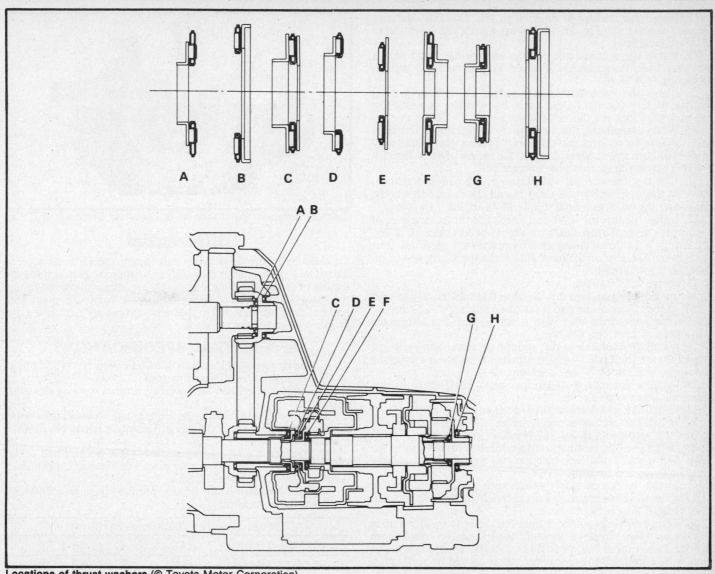

Locations of thrust washers (© Toyota Motor Corporation)

15. Install the thrust washer on the front support and install the front support on the transaxle case.

NOTE: If there is a clearance between the surfaces of the front support and the transaxle case when installing the front support, the front clutch is not completely installed.

16. Tighten the front support bolts in a diagonal order a little at a time, with the final torque being 14 ft. lbs. (19 N•m).

17. Check the front clutch input shaft thrust play. Thrust play: 0.0094-0.0378 in. (0.24-0.96mm).

18. Check the front clutch output shaft thrust play. Thrust play: 0.0122-0.0602 in. (0.31-1.53mm).

19. Install the bearing on the drive sprocket and install the thrust race on the transaxle case.

20. Install input shaft, drive sprocket chain and driven sprocket and install the snap ring.

21. Check the thrust clearance between the snap ring and the driven sprocket. Thrust clearance is 0.0043-0.0272 in. (0.11-0.69mm).

22. Install the thrust race on the oil pump and install the oil pump. Torque the oil pump bolts gradually to 13 ft. lbs. (18 N•m).

23. Check to see that the oil pump drive gear rotates smoothly and then check the input shaft thrust play. Thrust play is 0.0039-0.0276 in. (0.10-0.70mm).

24. Install the oil pump delivery tube and the oil pump pressure tubes.

25. Install the manual lever shaft into the transaxle case and drive in the slotted spring pin. After assembly, turn the spacer 90° degrees and stake it.

NOTE: Always replace the spacer and the slotted spring pin with a new one. Never reuse a slotted spring pin.

26. Install the park pawl, pivot pin and spring into the transaxle case.

Measuring the thrust clearance (© Toyota Motor Corporation)

27. Install the park pawl bracket on the transaxle case and torque the bolts to 65 in. lbs. (7.4 N•m). Check the operation of the park lock pawl.

28. Install the accumulator pistons and springs and install a new gasket and the accumulator cover. Torque the cover bolts to 48 in. lbs. (5.4 N•m).

29. Install the valve body plate, gasket, valve body and oil strainer (before assembling the valve body, make sure that the cut-back plug lock pin did not fall out).

30. When assembling the valve body to the upper transaxle case, be sure to connect the oil pump suction pipe. Gradually torque the bolts in a diagonal order to the torque of 48 in. lbs. (5.4 N•m). Tighten the suction pipe bracket bolt.

31. Connect the manual valve connecting rod and manual valve to the front valve body and install the front valve body, tightening the bolts to a final torque of 48 in. lbs. (5.4 N•m).

32. Install the throttle lever and check the thrust clearance of the throttle lever. Thrust clearance should be less than 0.0197 in. (0.50mm). If the thrust clearance is more than the specified clearance, insert a washer on the outer side of the throttle lever and install the throttle cover.

33. Install the oil tubes.

34. Install the magnets in the oil pan and install the oil pan with a new gasket. Torque the pan bolts to 65 in. lbs. (7.4 N•m).

35. Install the drain plug with a new gasket and torque the drain plug to 22 ft. lbs. (29 N•m).

36. Install the transaxle gasket and the governor apply gaskets. Assemble the transaxle to the transmission case and torque the mounting bolts to 14 ft. lbs. (19 N•m).

37. Install a new oil seal ring to the output shaft sleeve and install the output shaft sleeve.

38. Install the speedometer drive gear and snap ring.

39. Install the rear extension housing with a new gasket and torque the bolts to 14 ft. lbs. (19 N•m).

40. Install O-rings, bushing and speedometer driven gear to the shaft sleeve and install the speedometer driven gear assembly into the extension housing.

41. Install the neutral safety switch with the slit in the switch and the neutral base line match up and tighten the bolt and nut.

42. Install the oil filler tube.

43. Temporarily install the torque converter to the drive plate and set up a dial indicator. Measure the torque converter sleeve runout. If the runout exceeds 0.0118 in. (0.30mm) and the runout cannot be corrected, the torque converter should be replaced.

44. If the torque converter has been drained, then refill the converter with 1.1 U.S. quarts of the recommended ATF and install the converter in the transaxle.

45. Check the torque converter installation by using calipers and a straight edge. Measure from the installed converter center piece surface to the front surface of the transaxle housing. Correct distance is more than 0.31 in. (8mm).

Checking converter installation (© Toyota Motor Corporation)

Differential

To reassemble the final drive unit, many special tools are required and are available through varied sources. Instructions on the use of the tools during reassembly are usually included in the tool packs. The required specifications for bearing preload and gear backlash are included in the outline to aid in determining the proper tolerances and preloads.

DIFFERENTIAL SPECIFICATIONS

1. The ring gear backlash is 0.0039-0.0059 in. (0.10-0.15mm).

2. The maximum ring gear run out is 0.0028 in. (0.07mm). If the runout is greater than the specified runout, install a new ring gear.

3. Before disassembling the differential, measure the total preload on the drive pinion bearing. The total preload (starting) is 5.2-8.7 in. lbs. (0.6-1.0 N•m).

4. Measure the side gear backlash while holding the other side gear towards the differential case. The standard backlash is 0.0016-0.0094 in. (0.04-0.24mm).

5. If the backlash is not within specifications, use a different thickness thrust washer.

Thrust Washer Thickness in. (mm)	
0.0583-0.0598	(1.48-1.52)
0.0602-0.0618	(1.53-1.57)
0.0622-0.0638	(1.58-1.62)
0.0642-0.0657	(1.63-1.67)
0.0661-0.0667	(1.68-1.72)
0.0681-0.0697	(1.73-1.77)

Measuring the sleeve run-out (© Toyota Motor Corporation)

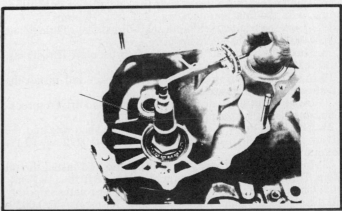

Measuring the preload (© Toyota Motor Corporation)

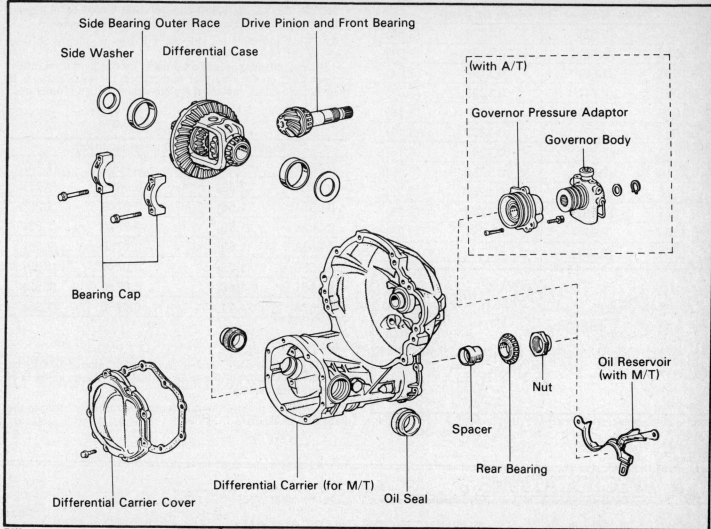

Differential components (© Toyota Motor Corporation)

6. The torque for the ring gear set bolts is 67-75 ft. lbs. (91-102 N•m).

7. The torque for the drive pinion lock nut is 108 ft. lbs. (147 N•m).

8. Drive pinion bearing preload:
   New bearing: 4.3-8.7 in. lbs. (0.5-1.0 N•m).
   Reused bearing: 2.6-4.3 in. lbs. (0.3-0.5 N•m).

9. Push the side bearing boss on the teeth surface of the ring gear and measure the backlash: 0.0039 in. (0.10mm).

10. Select a ring gear back side washer using the backlash as reference.

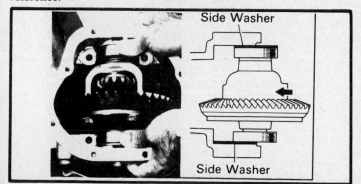

Location of the side washers (© Toyota Motor Corporation)

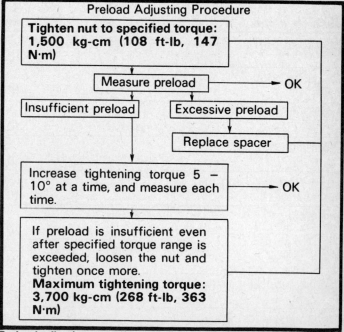

Preload adjusting procedures (© Toyota Motor Corporation)

Side Washer Thickness in. (mm)			
0.1031	(2.62)	0.1173	(2.98)
0.1043	(2.65)	0.1185	(3.01)
0.1055	(2.68)	0.1197	(3.04)
0.1067	(2.71)	0.1209	(3.07)
0.1079	(2.74)	0.1220	(3.10)
0.1091	(2.77)	0.1232	(3.13)
0.1102	(2.80)	0.1244	(3.16)
0.1114	(2.83)	0.1256	(3.19)
0.1126	(2.86)	0.1268	(3.22)
0.1138	(2.89)	0.1280	(3.25)
0.1150	(2.92)	0.1291	(3.28)
0.1161	(2.95)		

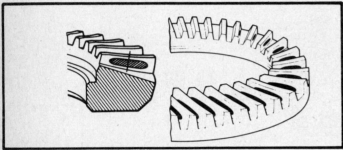

Proper teeth contact (© Toyota Motor Corporation)

NOTE: The backlash will change about 0.0008 in. (0.02mm) with a 0.0012 in. (0.03mm) variation of the side washer.

11. When installing the side bearing caps, torque the bolts to 33-39 ft. lbs. (45-53 N•m).

12. Coat red paint or lead on three or four teeth at three different positions on the ring gear and inspect the teeth pattern. If there is toe contact, replace the plate washer with a thinner one.

Plate Washer Thickness in. (mm)			
0.0591	(1.50)	0.0685	(1.74)
0.0602	(2.53)	0.0697	(1.77)
0.0614	(1.56)	0.0709	(1.80)
0.0626	(1.59)	0.0720	(1.83)
0.0638	(1.62)	0.0732	(1.86)
0.0650	(1.65)	0.0744	(1.89)
0.0661	(1.68)	0.0756	(1.92)
0.0673	(1.71)	0.0768	(1.95)

NOTE: If the plate washer thickness is altered 0.0039 in. (0.10mm), the center of the teeth contact will change about ⅛ of the total teeth surface.

12. When installing the differential carrier cover torque the bolts to 8-11 ft. lbs. (10-15 N•m).

S SPECIFICATIONS

BUSHING BORE CHART MM (IN.)

Bushing name		Length mm (in.)	Finished bore mm (in.)	Bore limit mm (in.)
Stator support	Front	9.75 (0.3839)	16.000–16.018 (0.6299–0.6306)	16.068 (0.6326)
Oil pump body		13.46 (0.5299)	38.125–38.150 (1.5010–1.5020)	38.200 (1.5039)
Front support		10.75 (0.4232)	31.038–31.063 (1.2220–1.2230)	31.113 (1.2249)
Front clutch drum		9.75 (0.3839)	22.025–22.046 (0.8671–0.8680)	22.096 (0.8699)
Front planetary ring gear flange		6.55 (0.2579)	30.025–30.051 (1.1821–1.1831)	30.101 (1.1851)
Sun gear	Front	9.75 (0.3839)	22.025–22.046 (0.8671–0.8680)	22.096 (0.8699)
	Rear	9.75 (0.3839)	22.025–22.046 (0.8671–0.8680)	22.096 (0.8699)
Center support		65.68 (2.5858)	36.386–36.411 (1.4325–1.4335)	36.461 (1.4355)
Transmission case		10.75 (0.4232)	32.025–32.050 (1.2608–1.2618)	32.100 (1.2638)

SPRING SPECIFICATIONS
Coil Spring

Item	Piston Return Spring (Forward-Reverse Clutch) in. (mm)	Brake Piston Return Spring (B1,B2) in. (mm)	(B3)
Free Length	1.1378 (28.90)	0.6346 (16.12)	1.0303 (26.17)
Coil Outside Diameter	0.315 (8.00)	0.0315 (8.00)	0.3110 (7.90)
Number of Coils	12	6	9

SPECIFICATION OF SPRINGS IN THE VALVE BODY ASSEMBLY

Item	Free length mm (in.)	Coil outside diameter mm (in.)	No. coils	Wire Diameter mm (in.)
Regulator valve	55.80 (2.1968)	18.10 (0.7126)	8.5	1.6 (0.063)
Valve body				
1-2 shift valve	26.00 (1.0236)	5.15 (0.2028)	14.5	0.5 (0.020)
Low-coast valve	36.50 (1.4370)	8.60 (0.3386)	16	1.2 (0.047)
2-3 shift valve	22.10 (0.8701)	6.40 (0.2520)	9.5	0.6 (0.024)
Detent regulator	27.40 (1.0787)	8.00 (0.3150)	10	1.0 (0.039)
Throttle valve				
Front	30.03 (1.1823)	8.55 (0.3366)	8.9	0.9 (0.035)
Rear	27.50 (1.0827)	7.40 (0.2913)	10.25	0.6 (0.024)
Accumulator				
Front	67.00 (2.6378)	17.80 (0.7008)	12.5	2.3 (0.091)
Rear	38.42 (1.5126)	14.03 (0.5524)	10	2.03 (0.0799)
Governor valve	19.60 (0.7717)	9.40 (0.3701)	6	0.80 (0.0315)
T/C check ball valve	26.20 (1.0315)	6.60 (0.2598)	14	0.60 (0.0236)
Priming valve	19.20 (0.7559)	6.30 (0.2480)	9	0.65 (0.0256)

TORQUE SPECIFICATIONS

Description	Torque
Transaxle mount bolts	14 ft. lbs. (19 N•m)
Extension housing bolts	14 ft. lbs. (19 N•m)
Neutral safety swtich	9 ft. lbs. (13 N•m)
Drive plate bolts	47 ft. lbs. (64 N•m)
Torque converter bolts	13 ft. lbs. (18 N•m)
Oil pump bolts	13 ft. lbs. (18 N•m)
Center support	19 ft. lbs. (25 N•m)
Valve body bolts	48 in. lbs. (5.4 N•m)
Oil pan bolts	65 in. lbs. (7.4 N•m)

TORQUE SPECIFICATIONS

Description	Torque
Oil pump cover bolts	13 ft. lbs. (18 N•m)
Front support bolts	14 ft. lbs. (19 N•m)
No. 3 valve body cover bolt	48 in. lbs. (5.4 N•m)
Accumulator piston cover	48 in. lbs. (5.4 N•m)
Governor pressure adapter	48 in. lbs. (5.4 N•m)
Oil cooler pipe nut	25 ft. lbs. (34 N•m)
Pressure testing plug	65 in. lbs. (7.4 N•m)
Parking lock pawl bracket	65 in. lbs. (7.4 N•m)
Oil pan drain plug	22 ft. lbs. (29 N•m)

INDEX

TOYOTA A140E AUTOMATIC TRANSAXLE

APPLICATIONS

Model	Year	Engine Number	Transmission Number
Camry	1983-84	2S-E	A-140-E

GENERAL DESCRIPTION

The Toyota A-140-E transaxle is housed in a one piece aluminum die-cast case. The oil sump is divided by two oil seals on the transfer shaft to maintain a proper oil level in the transfer area and for efficient lubrication of the differential gear area. The transaxle is composed of a simple planetary gear set, an overdrive direct clutch disengaging in 4th gear, a one-way clutch and an overdrive brake engaging in 4th gear. The 4th gear unit and the transfer drive gear are arranged on the output shaft of the 3-speed unit in a compact package. It is supported by a long span of the ball bearing and the needle bearing. This transaxle also incorporates a electro-hydraulic control system and a electronically controlled torque converter. The electro-hydraulic control system is intended to improve fuel economy, performance and shift quality by precise control of the shift points and timing according to the signals from nine sensors through a preprogrammed microprocessor, located on the fire wall on the passenger side of the vehicle. The lock-up torque converter is also controlled by the electro-hydraulic control system and is applied in second, third and fourth gears.

Transmission and Converter Identification

TRANSMISSION

An identification plate is normally located on the left side of the transaxle case, with the model and serial number stamped on the plate. Should a transaxle be encountered without an identification plate, check the identification information plate on the firewall in the engine compartment and also this plate is on the top of the instrument panel and driver's door post. If there is still no transaxle model number found, examine the transaxle case for identifying code letters or digits. Also, obtain the vehicle model and serial number before ordering replacement parts.

CONVERTER

The converter is a welded unit and cannot be disassembled by the average repair shop. This converter incorporates a lock up clutch which is controlled by the electro-hydraulic control system. If internal malfunctions occur, the converter must be replaced. No specific identification is given for quick identification by the repairman. Should converter replacement be necessary, order from the information given on the model and the serial number plate.

Metric Fasteners

Metric bolt sizes and thread pitches are used for all fasteners on the A-55 transaxle. The metric fasteners dimensions are very close to the dimensions of the familiar inch system fasteners, and for this reason, replacement fasteners must have the same measurement and strength as those removed.

Do not attempt to interchange metric fasteners for inch system fasteners. Care should be taken to reuse the fasteners in the same locations as removed, whenever possible. Mismatched or incorrect fasteners can result in damage to the transmission unit through malfunctions, breakage or possible personal injury.

Fluid Specifications

The fluid used in the 1983-84 A-140-E transaxle is Dexron® II. No other fluids should be used in this transaxle, unless specified by the manufacturer.

FLUID CAPACITY CHART

	Liters	U.S. Qts.	Imp. Qts.
Drain and refill	2.4	2.5	2.1
Dry refill	6.0	6.3	5.3

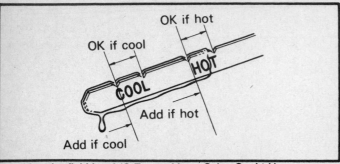

Checking the fluid level (© Toyota Motor Sales Co. Ltd.)

Checking Fluid Level

The fluid level should be checked when the transaxle is at normal operating temperature.

1. With the engine idling and the parking brake engaged, depress the brake pedal and shift the selector into each position from park to low and then return to park.

2. Pull out the transaxle dipstick and wipe it clean.

3. With the dipstick clean, push it back fully into the dipstick tube.

4. Pull the dipstick out again and check to see if the fluid is in the "HOT" range.

5. If the fluid is low, add the recommended ATF fluid until the fluid level reaches the "HOT" range.

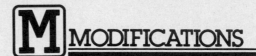

M MODIFICATIONS

There have been no major modifications to the A-140-E transaxle at the time of this printing.

TROUBLE DIAGNOSIS

CLUTCH APPLICATION CHART
Toyota A-140-E

Gear	Clutch 0	Clutch 1	Clutch 2	Brake 0	Brake 1	Brake 2	Brake 3	One-way Clutch 1	One-way Clutch 2
P	Off	Off	Off	Off	Off	Off	Off	Off	Off
R	On	Off	On	Off	Off	Off	On	Off	Off
N	Off	Off	Off	Off	Off	Off	Off	Off	Off
D-1st	On	On	Off	Off	Off	Off	Off	Off	Holding
D-2nd	On	On	Off	Off	On	Off	Off	Holding	Off
D-3rd	On	On	On	Off	Off	On	Off	Off	Off
O-D Lock-up	Off	On	On	On	Off	On	Off	Off	Off
2-1st	On	On	Off	Off	Off	Off	Off	Off	Holding
2-2nd	On	On	Off	Off	On	On	Off	Holding	Off
2-3rd	On	On	On	Off	Off	On	Off	Off	Off
L-1st	On	On	Off	Off	Off	Off	On	Off	Holding

CHILTON'S THREE "CS" DIAGNOSIS CHART
Toyota A-140-E

Condition	Cause	Correction
Fluid discolored or smells burnt	a) Fluid contamination b) Torque converter faulty c) Transmission is faulty	a) Replace the fluid b) Replace the torque converter c) Disassemble and inspect the transmission
Vehicle does not move in any forward range or reverse	a) Manual linkage out of adjustment b) Valve body or primary regulator faulty c) Transmission faulty	a) Adjust the linkage b) Inspect valve body c) Disassemble and inspect transmission

CHILTON'S THREE "CS" DIAGNOSIS CHART
Toyota A-140-E

Condition	Cause	Correction
Vehicle does not move in any range	a) Park lock pawl faulty b) Valve body or primary regulator faulty c) Torque converter faulty d) Broken converter drive plate e) Oil pump intake screen blocked f) Transmission faulty	a) Inspect park pawl b) Inspect valve body c) Replace the torque converter d) Replace the torque converter e) Clean the screen f) Disassemble and inspect transmission
Shift lever position is incorrect	a) Manual linkage out of adjustment b) Manual valve and lever faulty c) Transmission faulty	a) Adjust linkage b) Inspect valve body c) Disassemble and inspect transmission
Slips on 1-2, 2-3 or 3-OD up-shift, or slips or shudders on take-off	a) Control cable out of adjustment b) Throttle cable out of adjustment c) Valve body faulty d) Solenoid valve faulty e) Transmission faulty	a) Adjust control cable b) Adjust throttle cable c) Inspect valve body d) Inspect valve body e) Disassemble and inspect transmission
Drag, binding or tie-up on 1-2, 2-3 or 3-OD up-shift	a) Control cable out of adjustment b) Valve body faulty c) Transmission faulty	a) Adjust control cable b) Inspect valve body c) Disassemble and inspect transmission
No lock-up in 2nd, 3rd or OD	a) Electric control faulty b) Valve body faulty c) Solenoid valve faulty d) Transmission faulty	a) Inspect electric control b) Inspect valve body c) Inspect valve body d) Disassemble and inspect transmission
Harsh down-shift	a) Throttle cable out of adjustment b) Throttle cable and cam faulty c) Accumulator pistons faulty d) Valve body faulty e) Transmission faulty	a) Adjust throttle cable b) Inspect throttle cable and cam c) Inspect accumulator pistons d) Inspect valve body e) Disassemble and inspect transmission
No down-shift when coasting	a) Valve body faulty b) Solenoid valve faulty c) Electric control faulty	a) Inspect valve body b) Inspect solenoid valve c) Inspect electric control
Down-shift occurs too quick or too late while coasting	a) Throttle cable faulty b) Valve body faulty c) Transmission faulty d) Solenoid valve faulty e) Electric control faulty	a) Inspect throttle cable b) Inspect valve body c) Disassemble and inspect transmission d) Inspect solenoid valve e) Inspect electric control
No OD-3, 3-2 or 2-1 kickdown	a) Solenoid valve faulty b) Electric control faulty c) Valve body faulty	a) Inspect solenoid valve b) Inspect electric control c) Inspect valve body
Harsh engagement into any drive range	a) Throttle linkage out of adjustment b) Valve body or primary regulator faulty c) Accumulator pistons faulty d) Transmission faulty	a) Adjust throttle linkage b) Inspect valve body c) Inspect accumulator pistons d) Disassemble and inspect transmission

CHILTON'S THREE "CS" DIAGNOSIS CHART
Toyota A-140-E

Condition	Cause	Correction
No engine braking in "2" or "L" range	a) Solenoid valve faulty b) Electric control faulty c) Valve body faulty d) Transmission faulty	a) Inspect the solenoid valve b) Inspect the electric control c) Inspect the valve body d) Disassemble and inspect the transmission
Vehicle does not hold in "P"	a) Control cable is out of adjustment b) Parking lock pawl cam and spring faulty	a) Adjust the control cable b) Inspect the cam and spring

In order to properly diagnose transmission problems and avoid making second repairs for the same problem, all of the available information and knowledge must be used. Included is a list of the components of the transaxle and their functions. Also, test procedures and their accompanying specification charts aid in finding solutions to problems. Further answers are found by road testing vehicles and comparing results of the above A-140-E transaxle diagnosis chart. This chart gives conditions, cause and correction to most possible trouble conditions in the A-140-E transaxle.

ELECTRONICALLY CONTROLLED TRANSMISSION

When trouble occurs with the ECT system, the trouble can be caused by either the engine, ECT electronic control or the automatic transmission itself. These areas should be distinctly isolated before proceeding with troubleshooting the ECT system. Troubleshoot the ECT system as follows:

1. Remove the instrument panel box and the right side speaker box.
2. Turn the ignition switch to the on position.
3. Using the proper circuit tester measure the voltage at each electrical terminal.

Hydraulic Control System

The main parts of the hydraulic control system for the A-140-E transaxle are the, torque converter, oil pump, cooler and lubrication circuits, valve body and applying clutches and brakes. The system is controlled by the Electro-hydraulic control system. This

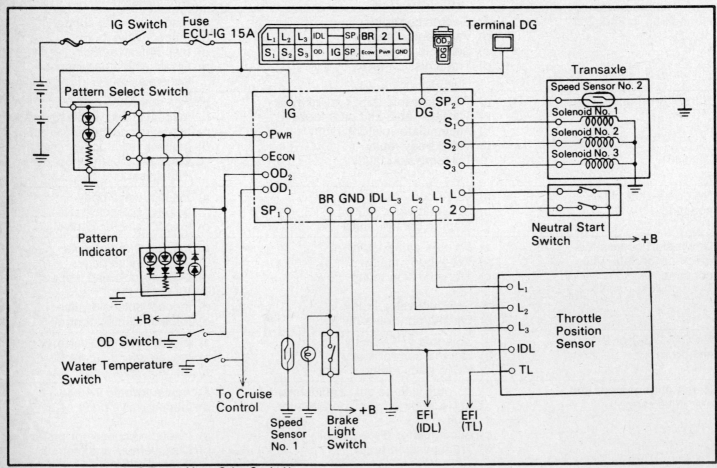

Electronic control circuit (© Toyota Motor Sales Co. Ltd.)

ELECTRONIC CONTROL CIRCUIT TROUBLESHOOTING CHART
Toyota A-140-E

Terminal	Measuring condition	Voltage (V)	
		DENSO type computer	AISIN type computer
L₁-GND	Throttle valve fully closed	5	12
	Throttle valve fully closed full open	5 to 0	12 to 0
	Throttle valve fully open	0	0
L₂-GND	Throttle valve fully closed	5	12
	Throttle valve fully closed to full open	5 to 0 to 5	12 to 0 to 12
	Throttle valve fully open	5	12
L₃-GND	Throttle valve fully closed	5	12
	Throttle valve fully closed to full open	5 to 0 to 5 to 0 to 5	12 to 0 to 12 to 0 to 12
	Throttle valve fully open	5	12
IDL-GND	Standing still	0	12
	Throttle valve opening above 1.5°	4	4
SP₁-GND	Standing still	12 or 0	12 or 0
	Engine running, vehicle moving	6	6
BR-GND	Brake pedal depressed	12	12
	Brake pedal not depressed	0	0
2-GND	2 range	9 to 16	9 to 16
	Except 2 range	0 to 2	0 to 2
L-GND	L range	9 to 16	9 to 16
	Except L range	0 to 2	0 to 2
S₁-GND	—	12	12
S₂, S₃-GND	—	0	0
OD₁-GND	Coolant temp. below 70°C	0	0
	Coolant temp. above 70°C	5	12
OD₂-GND	OD switch turn ON	12	12
	OD switch turn OFF	0	0
IG-GND	Standing still	12	12
SP₂-GND	Standing still	5 or 0	12 or 0
	Engine running	4	10
PWR-GND	PWR pattern	12	12
	Except PWR pattern	1	1
ECON-GND	ECON pattern	12	12
	Except ECON pattern	1	1

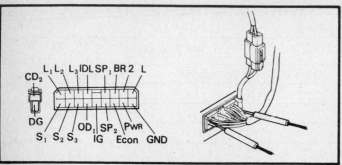

Measuring the voltage (© Toyota Motor Sales Co. Ltd.)

system incorporates nine sensors and electronic signals, from these nine sensors are inputted into an ECU (Electronic Control Unit), which outputs its computation results into three solenoid valves. Two of these three valves control the transmission clutch and one controls the lock-up clutch inside the torque converter. These three shift valves are a simple straight type. They operate by solenoid and clutch pressures, both of which acts as a signal pressure in the normal drive "D" range. The lock-up clutch engages in 2nd, 3rd and 4th gears. These engagements are controlled by the solenoid switching clutch pressure which is generated as a signal pressure of the lock-up relay valve in 2nd, 3rd and 4th gears.

The oil pump is used to send the ATF fluid to the torque converter, to lubricate the inner working parts of the transaxle and to supply the operating pressure for the hydraulic control. The oil pump drive gear has a special tooth profile, this tooth profile is originated from the hypocychloid curve instead of the involute curve. Since the gear features an enlarged displacement per tooth, its width is narrowed to approximately two-thirds of that of a

conventional involute gear pump. The pump has the capacity to supply the necessary hydraulic pressure for operating from low speed to high speed and when reversing.

Diagnosis Tests
TIME LAG TEST

When the shift lever is shifted while the engine is idling, there will be a certain time delay (lag) before the shock on the transaxle can be felt. This time delay (lag) is used for checking the condition of the overdrive clutch, forward clutch, direct clutch and first and reverse brake.

Measuring Lag Time

1. Start the vehicle and bring the engine and transaxle up to normal operating temperature.
2. With the parking brake fully engaged, shift the shift lever from "N" to "D" range.
3. Using a stop watch or a wrist watch, measure the time it takes from shifting the lever until the shock is felt, (average lag time is less than 1.2 seconds).
4. Now shift the shift lever from "N" to "R" range and measure the time lag, (average lag time is less than 1.5 seconds).

NOTE: Allow at least one minute intervals between tests. Make three measurements and then calculate the average lag time.

TIME LAG TEST RESULT INDICATIONS
If the shift from "N" to "D" time lag is longer than specified, the problems could be,
1. The line pressure is too low.
2. The front clutch could be badly worn.
3. The OD one-way clutch is not operating properly.

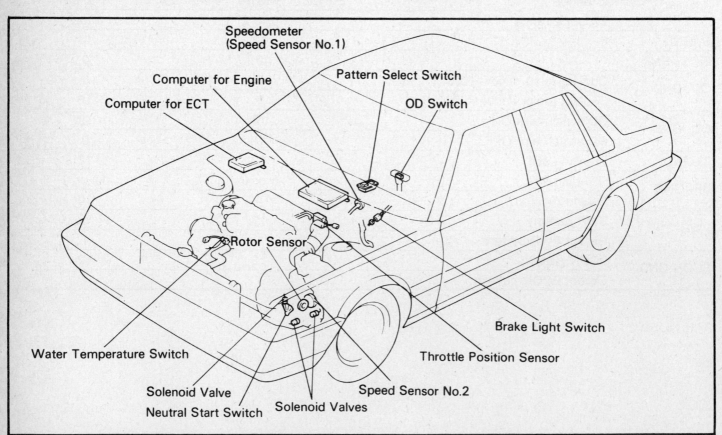

Electronic control circuit components (© Toyota Motor Sales Co. Ltd.)

If the shift from "N" to "R" time lag is longer than specified, the problems could be,
1. The line pressure is too low.
2. The direct clutch is badly worn.
3. The OD one-way clutch is not operating properly.

HYDRAULIC TESTS

Line Pressure Test

1. Engage the parking brake and chock all four wheels.
2. Connect an oil pressure gauge to the line pressure port on the transaxle.
3. Start the engine and bring it up to normal operating temperature.
4. Shift the shift lever into the "D" position and measure the line pressure at the speeds specified in the chart below:

LINE PRESSURE CHART

Engine Speed	Line Pressure "D" Range	PSI "R" Range
Idling	53-61	77-102
Stall	131-152	205-239

5. In the same manner, perform the line pressure test for the "R" range.

NOTE: If the measured line pressures are not within specifications, recheck the throttle cable adjustment and retest.

LINE PRESSURE TEST RESULT INDICATIONS

If the line pressure is higher than specified,
1. The throttle cable is out of adjustment.
2. The throttle valve is defective.
3. The regulator valve is not operating properly.

If the line pressure is lower than specified,
1. The throttle valve is defective.
2. The throttle cable is out of adjustment.
3. The regulator valve is not operating properly.
4. The oil pump could be defective.
5. The over-drive clutch is not operating properly.

If the line pressure is low in the "D" range only.
1. There is a possible fluid leakage in the "D" range circuit.
2. The forward clutch is defective.

If the line pressure is low in the "R" range only.
1. There is a possible fluid leakage in the "R" range circuit.
2. The first and reverse brake is not operating properly.
3. The direct clutch is defective.

ROAD TEST

Road Test With Selector in "P"

1. With the vehicle parked on a small grade, put the selector lever in the "P" position and release the parking brake.
2. If the vehicle does not roll backwards then the parking system is working properly.

Road Test With Selector in "R"

1. Start the engine and while running at full throttle check the transaxle for slipping.

Road Test With Selector in "D"

1. Increase speed of the vehicle and while holding the accelerator pedal steady check to see if the transaxle makes the 1-2, 2-3, 3-OD and lock-up upshifts at the correct vehicle speed.
2. If there is no 1-2 upshift:
   a. The No. 2 solenoid is stuck.
   b. The 1-2 shift valve is not operating properly.

3. If there is no 2-3 upshift:
   a. The No. 1 solenoid is stuck.
   b. The 2-3 shift valve is not operating properly.
4. If there is no 3-OD upshift:
   a. The 3-OD shift valve is not operating properly.
5. If the lock-up is defective:
   a. The No. 3 solenoid is stuck.
   b. The lock-up relay valve is stuck.
6. While running in the "D" range, 2nd and 3rd gears and overdrive check to see if the 2-1, 3-1, 3-2, OD-3 and OD-2 kickdown shifts occur properly at the specified kickdown limit vehicle speeds.
7. Drive in third gear, and select "2" range than the "L" range to check if the engine brake is effective. Also check for hard shifting and slipping at this time.
8. While driving in the "D" range shift the selector to the "L" range to check if the OD-3, 3-2 and 2-1 downshifts occur at the proper vehicle speed.

Road Test With Selector in "2"

1. While driving with the selector lever in the "2" position increase the vehicle speed, and check to see that the transaxle makes the 1-2 upshift at the proper vehicle speed. Also check for noise and shock at the time of shifting.
2. Check to see if the 2-1 kickdown occurs at correct vehicle speed limit.

Road Test With Selector in "L"

1. While running in the "L" range, check to see that there is no up-shift to 2nd gear.
2. Check for noise in either acceleration or deceleration.

Converter Stall Test

The object of this test is to check to the overall performance of the transaxle and the engine by measuring the maximum engine speeds at the "D" and "R" ranges.

Measuring Stall Speed

1. Engage the parking brake and chock all four wheels.
2. Attach a tachometer to the engine and place it in a position to be seen.
3. Start the engine and bring the vehicle up to normal operating temperature.
4. Apply the foot brake and shift the selector lever to the "D" position.
5. With foot brake applied gradually depress the accelerator pedal until the engine reaches full throttle.
6. When the engine speed is stabilized, read that speed quickly and release the accelerator pedal.
7. Shift the selector lever to the "N" position, and cool down the engine by letting the engine idle for 2 to 5 minutes (specified stall speed 2,200 ± 150 rpm).
8. Record the stall speed and perform the stall test with the selector lever in the "R" position.

NOTE: Do not perform the stall test longer than 5 seconds as damage to the transaxle can occur.

Interpretation of Stall Test Results

If the stall speed is lower than specified.
1. Engine output could be insufficient.
2. Stator one-way is not operating correctly.

NOTE: If the stall speed is more than 600 rpm below the specified stall speed, the torque converter could defective.

If the stall speed in the "D" position is higher than specified.
1. The front clutch could be slipping.
2. One-way clutch number 2 is not operating correctly.
3. The line pressure could be too low.

4. The over-drive one-way clutch is not operating properly.

If the stall speed in the "R" position is higher than specified.

1. The line pressure could be too low.
2. Improper fluid level.
3. The over-drive one-way clutch is not operating properly.

THE LOCK-UP TORQUE CONVERTER

To eliminate power loss and fuel waste, Toyota has added a mechanical clutch inside the torque converter. It firmly locks the engine to the transaxle with virtually no slippage, and that means less fuel waste. The lock-up clutch is controlled by the ECT system, which applies the clutch in 2nd, 3rd, and 4th gears. Along with the lock-up torque converter there's the ECT shift pattern select switches. Located on the dash or console in the Camry, the switches allows the driver to select normal, power and economy shift patterns to suit the drivers immediate driving needs. In the normal pattern the ECT shifts according to a computer program developed by the manufacture. In the economy pattern the computer is instructed to introduce a modified lock-up torque converter schedule, causing the torque converter to lock-up at a lower speed. In this way less slippage occurs during city driving, result-

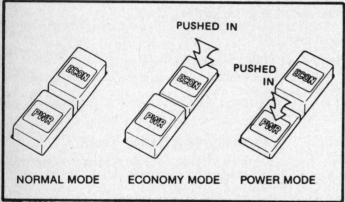

Shift pattern select switches (© Toyota Motor Sales Co. Ltd.)

ing in better fuel economy. In the power pattern the ECT computer adopts an entirely different shift pattern, instead of concentrating on vehicle speed the computer concentrates on the driver's demand on the throttle pedal. Lock-up operation occurs just as in the normal pattern and the result is later upshifts and more responsive downshifts to better respond to the driver's commands.

NOTE: The ETC provides identical fuel economy in all three patterns when driving on the open highway. Its effect is only noticeable during around-town and city driving.

Adjustments

NEUTRAL SAFETY SWITCH

Adjustment

1. Connect an Ohmmeter between the two electrical terminals on the neutral safety switch.
2. Shift the selector lever into the "N" position.
3. Adjust the switch to the point where there is continuity between the terminals.
4. Lock down the switch with the two mounting bolts.

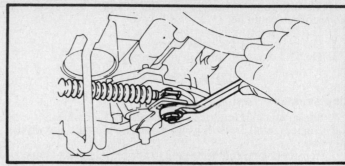

Adjusting the shift linkage (© Toyota Motor Sales Co. Ltd.)

TRANSAXLE SHIFT LINKAGE

Adjustment

1. Loosen the swivel nut on the shift linkage lever.
2. Push the manual lever fully forward toward the right side of the vehicle and return the lever two notches to the neutral position.
3. Set the shift lever to the "N" position and while holding the lever lightly toward the "R" position, tighten the swivel nut.

THROTTLE LINK

Adjustment

1. Remove the air cleaner and check to see if the throttle lever and the throttle link are not bent or damaged.
2. Push on the throttle lever and see if the throttle valve opens fully.
3. Using a pedal jack or its equivalent, fully depress and hold the accelerator pedal to the floor.
4. Loosen the turnbuckle lock nut and adjust the throttle linkage length by turning the turnbuckle.
5. The adjustment will be correct when the throttle valve lever indicator lines up with the mark on the transaxle case.
6. Now tighten the turnbuckle lock nut and recheck the adjustment.
7. Install the air cleaner and remove the pedal jack from the accelerator pedal.

THROTTLE CABLE

Adjustment

1. Remove the air cleaner hose, then depress the accelerator pedal all the way to see if the throttle valve opens fully.
2. Fully depress the accelerator pedal and loosen the adjustment nuts on the throttle cable.
3. Adjust the throttle cable so that the distance between the end of the cable boot and the stopper on the cable is 0.04 in. (0-1mm).
4. Tighten the adjusting nuts, recheck the adjustments and install the air cleaner hose.

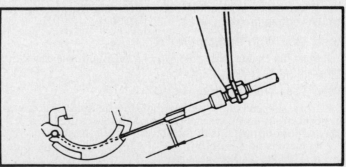

Adjusting the throttle cable (© Toyota Motor Sales Co. Ltd.)

Services

FLUID AND FILTER CHANGE

The normal service interval for changing transmission fluid and replacing or cleaning oil filters is 24,000 miles. When the vehicle is used in more severe operating conditions such as, heavy city driving, constant hill climbing and pulling a trailer the fluid should be check more often and the transmission should be service more frequently.

Procedure

1. Raise the vehicle on a safe lift.
2. Place a oil drain pan under the transaxle.
3. Remove the drain plug and drain all the ATF fluid out of the transaxle.
4. Remove the 15 oil pan bolts and remove the pan and gasket.
5. Inspect the pan and the magnet in the bottom of the pan for any steel chips or any other particles.

NOTE: If there is any steel chips in the pan it could mean that a bearing, gear or a clutch plate are wearing out. If there is brass in the bottom of the pan it could mean that a bushing is wearing out.

6. Remove the three oil filter mounting bolts and remove the oil filter. Inspect the filter and clean or replace it.
7. Install the oil filter and torque the three mounting bolts to 7 ft. lbs. (10 N•m).
8. Install the oil pan with a new gasket to the transaxle case. Torque the 15 oil pan bolts to 43 inch lbs. (4.9 N•m).
9. Install the drain plug with a new gasket and torque the drain plug to 22 ft. lbs.
10. Refill the transaxle with 2.5 U.S. quarts of the recommended ATF fluid. Start the engine and run it at idle. Check the fluid level and if the level is low add the necessary fluid to bring the level up to the "HOT" range on the dipstick.

VALVE BODY

Removal & Installation

1. Raise the vehicle on a safe hoist, drain the ATF and remove the oil pan.
2. Remove the oil filter and disconnect the solenoid connectors.
3. Pry up both ends of the oil pressure tubes with a screwdriver and remove the oil tubes.
4. Remove the manual detent valve, manual valve and valve body.
5. Disconnect the throttle cable from the cam, remove the 12 valve body bolts and remove the valve body.
6. Remove the second brake apply gasket.
7. Install the second brake apply gasket and place the valve body on the transaxle.
8. Connect the throttle cable to the cam and with the valve body in position install the 12 valve body bolts. Torque the bolts to 7 ft. lbs.

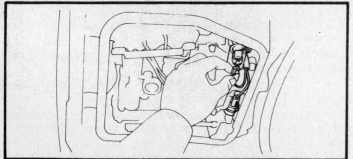

Disconnecting the solenoid (© Toyota Motor Sales Co. Ltd.)

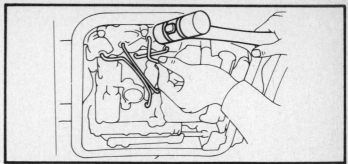

Installing the oil tubes (© Toyota Motor Sales Co. Ltd.)

9. Connect the two solenoid connectors to each solenoid.
10. Align the manual valve with the pin on the manual shift lever and torque the manual valve body bolts to 7 ft. lbs. (10 N•m).
11. Instal lthe detent spring and torque the hold down bolts to 7 ft. lbs. (10 N•m).
12. Using a plastic hammer install the oil tubes in their proper positions.
13. Install the oil filter and the oil pan with a new gasket to the transaxle case, torque the oil pan bolts to 43 inch lbs. (4.9 N•m).
14. Refill the transaxle with 2.5 U.S. quarts of the recommended ATF fluid. Start the engine and run it at idle, check the fluid level and if the level is low add the necessary fluid to bring the level up to the "HOT" range on the dipstick.

ACCUMULATOR

Removal and Installation

To remove the accumulator pistons and springs, first drain the ATF and remove the oil pan and the oil tubes as previously outlined.

1. Remove the five accumulator cover bolts one turn at a time until the spring tension is released, then remove the cover and the gasket.
2. Remove the accumulator pistons and springs by blowing low pressure compressed air (14 psi) into the air holes around the accumulator cylinders.
3. Position a rag under the accumulator pistons to catch the pistons as they come out of the cylinders.

NOTE: Do not use high pressure to remove the accumulator pistons and keep face away from pistons to avoid injury.

Before installing the accumulator pistons and springs, check the pistons, springs, cover and cylinder for wear or damage.

4. Install new O-rings around the accumulator pistons and coat the O-rings with ATF.
5. Install the springs and pistons into their bores, and install the cover with a new gasket. Torque the bolts gradually to 7 ft. lbs. (10 N•m).
6. Install the oil tubes and oil pan and refill the transaxle with the recommended ATF.

SPEED SENSOR

Removal and Installation

1. Remove the left front drive shaft and remove the transaxle dust cover.
2. Remove the two bolts and the support bracket and remove the speed sensor and O-ring.
3. Inspect the speed sensor by connecting an ohmmeter to the speed sensor and check that the meter deflects when the sensor is brought close to a magnet and removed from it.
4. Install the speed sensor with a new O-ring and coat the O-ring with ATF.

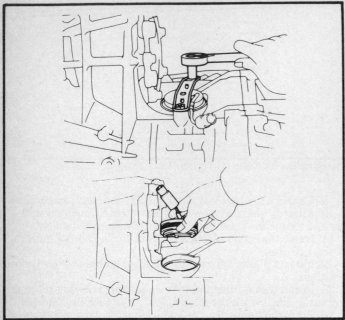

Speed sensor removal or installation (© Toyota Motor Sales Co. Ltd.)

5. Install the support bracket and the bracket bolts and torque the bolts to 9 ft. lbs. (13 N•m).
6. Install the transaxle dust cover and the left front drive shaft.

THROTTLE CABLE

Removal and Installation

1. Disconnect the throttle cable from the bracket and the throttle linkage.
2. Remove the clip and disconnect the transaxle control cable from the manual shift lever and remove the shift lever.
3. Remove the neutral safety switch.
4. Drain the ATF and remove the valve body as previously outlined.
5. Remove the one bolt retaining plate and pull the cable out of the transaxle case.
6. Push the new throttle cable all the way in the transaxle and install the one bolt retaining plate.
7. Install the valve body (as previously outlined).
8. Connect the throttle bracket to the throttle linkage and to the housing bracket. Adjust the throttle cable (see adjustment section.)
9. Install the neutral safety switch and the manual shift lever. Adjust the neutral safety switch (see adjustment section).
10. Connect the transaxle control cable and adjust the cable (see adjustment section), then test drive the vehicle.

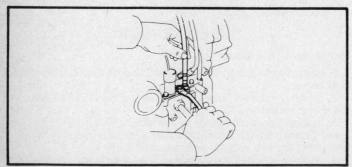

Installing the retainer plate (© Toyota Motor Sales Co. Ltd.)

 ## REMOVAL & INSTALLATION

REMOVAL

1. Disconnect the positive battery cable.
2. Disconnect the electrical connectors to the neutral safety switch and the back-up light switch.
3. Remove the air cleaner assembly.
4. Remove the throttle link.
5. Remove the oil cooler pipe clamp.
6. Using two wrenches disconnect the oil cooler inlet pipe.
7. Remove the upper transaxle set bolts.
8. Raise the vehicle and support it safely, and drain the ATF.
9. Position a transmission jack or its equivalent under the transaxle and remove the front and rear transaxle mounts.
10. Remove the left side dust cover and mounting bracket.
11. Remove the side gear shaft, intermediate shaft and universal joint from the transaxle.
12. Remove the transaxle control cable bracket and stiffener plate.
13. Remove the torque converter dust cover and locking plate, then remove the six torque converter mounting bolts (turn the crankshaft to gain access to each bolt).
14. Remove the starter motor and the lower transaxle mounting bolts.
15. While turning the crankshaft, pry on the torque converter to separate it from the drive plate.
16. With the transaxle free of any obstructions, lower the jack and remove the transaxle from the vehicle.

Installation

Before installing the transaxle, apply grease to the center hub of the torque converter and the pilot hole in the crankshaft.
1. Insert a guide pin in the most outward converter mounting hole.

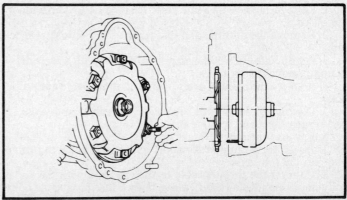

Installing the guide pin (© Toyota Motor Sales Co. Ltd.)

2. With the transaxle on the removing jack, raise the transaxle into position in the vehicle.

NOTE: The transaxle and the torque converter should be installed as a unit.

3. Align the guide pin with one of the holes in the drive plate and install the transaxle to the engine.

NOTE: The transaxle should be installed to the engine so that the tip of the converter goes into the hole in the end of the crankshaft.

4. Remove the guide pin and install two torque converter set bolts about half way in and tighten them evenly.

5. Install the 5 transaxle mounting bolts and torque the bolts to 47 ft. lbs.

6. Install the starter motor and the other four torque converter mounting bolts (do not forget to remove the guide pin) torque the bolts to 13 ft. lbs. (18 N•m).

7. Install the torque converter cover.

8. Using two wrenches connect the oil cooler outlet pipe, the torque for the nuts is 16 ft. lbs., and install the stiffener plate.

9. Install the control cable bracket.

10. Install the side gear shaft, intermediate shaft and universal joint.

11. Install the left side dust cover and mounting bracket.

12. Install the front and rear transaxle mounting and remove the removing jack.

13. Lower the vehicle and install the upper transaxle mounting bolts, torque the bolts to 47 ft. lbs.

14. Using two wrenches connect the oil cooler inlet pipe and install oil cooler pipe clamp.

15. Connect the throttle link and the electrical connectors to the neutral safety switch and the back-up light switch.

16. Adjust the throttle link (see adjustment section).

17. Install the air cleaner assembly and connect the positive battery cable.

18. Refill the transaxle with 2.5 U.S. quarts of the recommended ATF.

NOTE: If the torque converter has been drained, then the transaxle should be filled with 6.3 U.S. quarts of the recommended ATF.

19. Perform a road test to check the operation of the transaxle and to check the front end alignment.

20. Check for fluid leaks and for differential gear oil leaks.

Unit Disassembly and Assembly

OIL PUMP

When disassembling and assembling the oil pump be sure to replace all O-rings and seals. Inspect all oil pump gears and check the gear clearances. Driven gear body clearance: 0.0028-0.0059 (0.07-0.15mm). Gear tip clearance: 0.0043-0.0055 in. (0.11-0.14mm). Gear side clearance: 0.0008-0.0020 in. (0.02-0.05mm).

DIRECT CLUTCH

Replace all O-rings with new ones and apply ATF to the O-rings when installing them. Using a feeler gauge measure the clearance of the direct clutch. Direct Clutch Clearance: 0.0173-0.0437 in. (0.44-1.11mm).

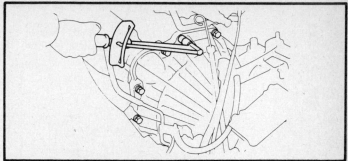

Installing the transaxle mounting bolts
(© Toyota Motor Sales Co. Ltd.)

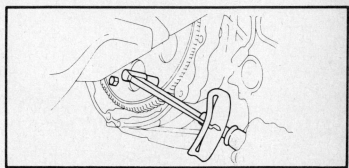

Installing the torque converter (© Toyota Motor Sales Co. Ltd.)

FORWARD CLUTCH

When reassembling the forward clutch make sure that the check ball in the clutch piston is free by shaking the piston and check to see if the valve leaks, by applying low pressure compressed air. Also measure the clearance of the forward clutch. Forward Clutch Clearance: 0.0163-0.0429 in. (0.414-1.090mm).

NO. 1 ONE-WAY CLUTCH AND SUN GEAR

When disassembling and assembling the one-way clutch and sun gear, check the operation of the one-way clutch by holding the sun

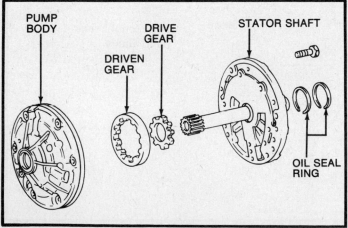

Exploded view of the oil pump (© Toyota Motor Sales Co. Ltd.)

PUMP BODY
DRIVEN GEAR
DRIVE GEAR
STATOR SHAFT
OIL SEAL RING

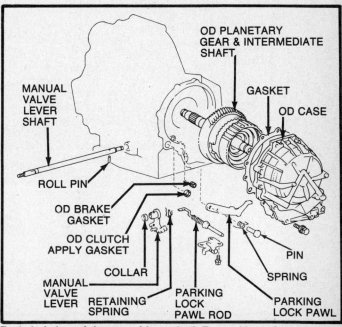

Exploded view of the over drive unit (© Toyota Motor Sales Co. Ltd.)

OD PLANETARY GEAR & INTERMEDIATE SHAFT
GASKET
OD CASE
MANUAL VALVE LEVER SHAFT
ROLL PIN
OD BRAKE GASKET
OD CLUTCH APPLY GASKET
MANUAL VALVE LEVER
COLLAR
RETAINING SPRING
PARKING LOCK PAWL ROD
PIN
SPRING
PARKING LOCK PAWL

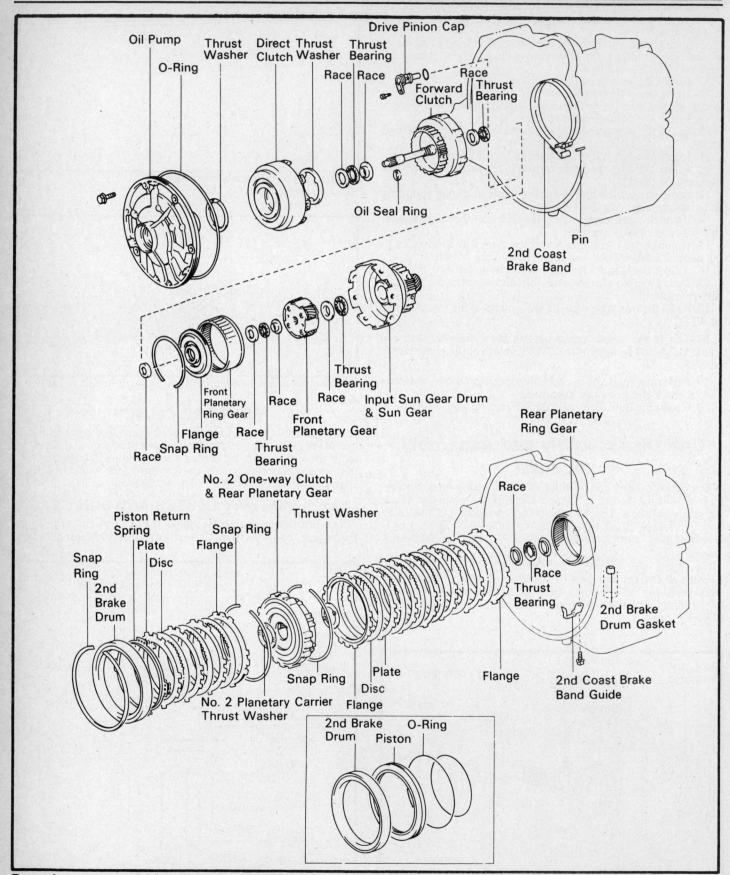

Transaxle components (© Toyota Motor Sales Co. Ltd.)

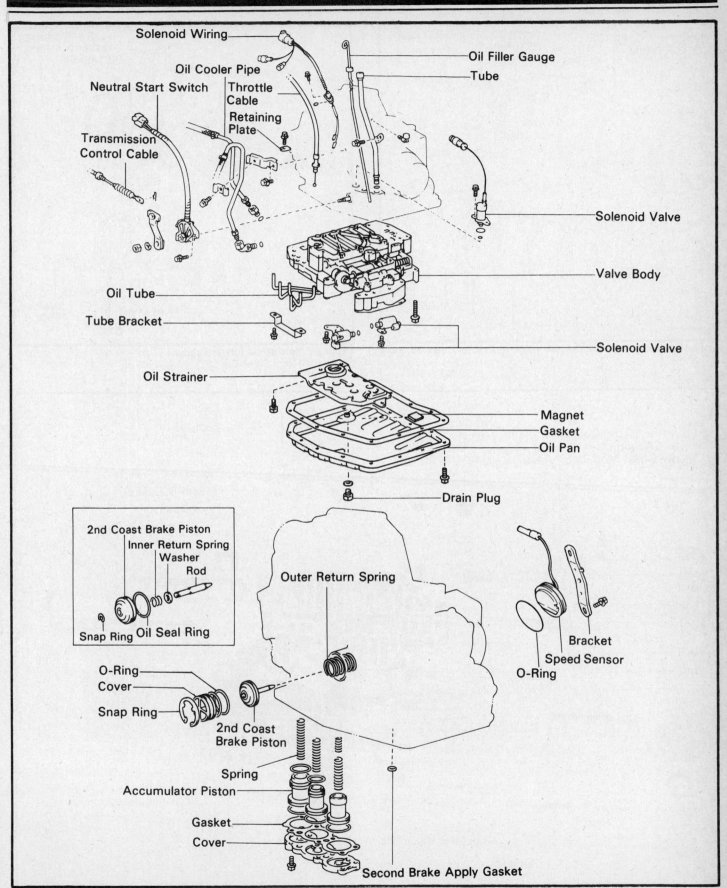

Solenoid Wiring

Oil Cooler Pipe

Neutral Start Switch

Throttle Cable

Retaining Plate

Transmission Control Cable

Oil Filler Gauge

Tube

Solenoid Valve

Valve Body

Oil Tube

Tube Bracket

Solenoid Valve

Oil Strainer

Magnet

Gasket

Oil Pan

Drain Plug

2nd Coast Brake Piston

Inner Return Spring

Washer

Rod

Snap Ring   Oil Seal Ring

Outer Return Spring

Bracket

Speed Sensor

O-Ring

O-Ring

Cover

Snap Ring

2nd Coast Brake Piston

Spring

Accumulator Piston

Gasket

Cover

Second Brake Apply Gasket

Transaxle components (© Toyota Motor Sales Co. Ltd.)

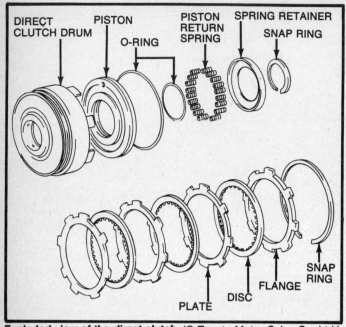

Exploded view of the direct clutch (© Toyota Motor Sales Co. Ltd.)

DIRECT CLUTCH DRUM — PISTON — O-RING — PISTON RETURN SPRING — SPRING RETAINER — SNAP RING

PLATE — DISC — FLANGE — SNAP RING

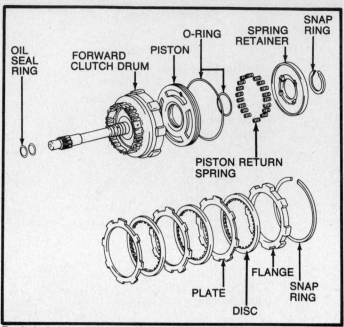

Exploded view of the forward clutch
(© Toyota Motor Sales Co. Ltd.)

OIL SEAL RING — FORWARD CLUTCH DRUM — PISTON — O-RING — SPRING RETAINER — SNAP RING

PISTON RETURN SPRING

PLATE — DISC — FLANGE — SNAP RING

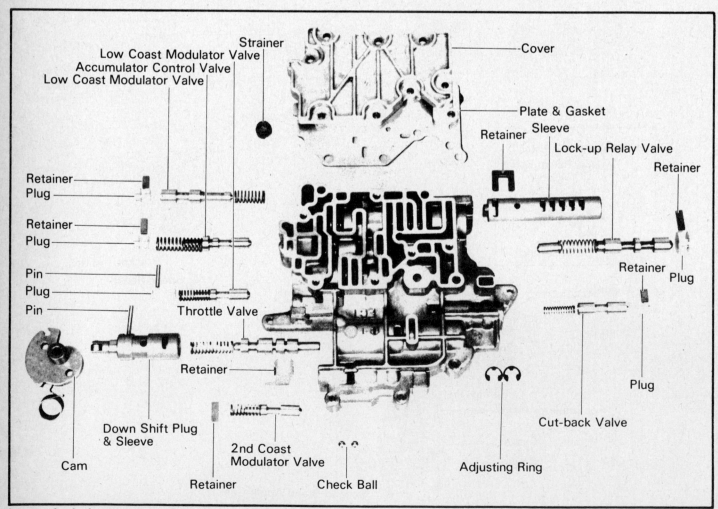

Lower valve body components (© Toyota Motor Sales Co. Ltd.)

Low Coast Modulator Valve
Accumulator Control Valve
Low Coast Modulator Valve
Strainer
Cover
Plate & Gasket
Sleeve
Retainer
Lock-up Relay Valve
Retainer
Retainer
Plug
Retainer
Plug
Pin
Plug
Pin
Throttle Valve
Retainer
Plug
Retainer
Cut-back Valve
Down Shift Plug & Sleeve
Cam
2nd Coast Modulator Valve
Retainer
Check Ball
Adjusting Ring
Plug

gear input drum and turning the hub. The hub should turn freely clockwise and should lock-up when turned counterclockwise. If the one-way clutch does not operate properly, it should be replaced.

NO. 2 ONE-WAY CLUTCH AND REAR PLANETARY GEAR

Check the operation of the No. 2 one-way clutch in the same manner as the No. 1 one-way clutch was checked. When assembling the one-way clutch, be sure to install the one-way clutch into the outer race, facing the flange cage toward the oil pump side.

FIRST AND REVERSE BRAKE PISTON

When removing the piston from the transaxle case compressed air must be applied to the oil passage of the transaxle case in order to remove the piston. If the piston does not pop out with the compressed air, use needle nose pliers to remove it. Install new O-rings and apply ATF when installing them.

OVERDRIVE UNIT

When disassembling and assembling the overdrive unit be sure to measure the clearance of the overdrive brake. To measure the clearance, use a feeler gauge and check the clearance between the cushion plate and the piston. Clearance: 0.0201-0.0661 in. (0.51-1.68mm). Again using a feeler gauge measure the clearance of the overdrive clutch, measure the clearance between the piston and the end of the plate. Clearance: 0.0283-0.0661 in. (0.72-1.68mm). Install all new O-rings and coat the O-rings with ATF. The pre-load for the counter drive bearing is, 2.0-3.4 ft. lbs. (9-15 N•m). If the overdrive gear assembly is properly installed to the overdrive case, the clearance between them will be about 0.138 in. (3.5mm).

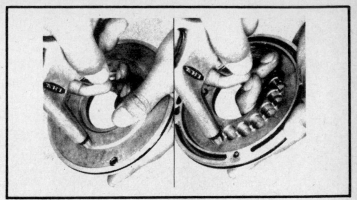

Checking the clutch piston check ball (© Toyota Motor Sales Co. Ltd.)

Checking one-way clutch operation (© Toyota Motor Sales Co. Ltd.)

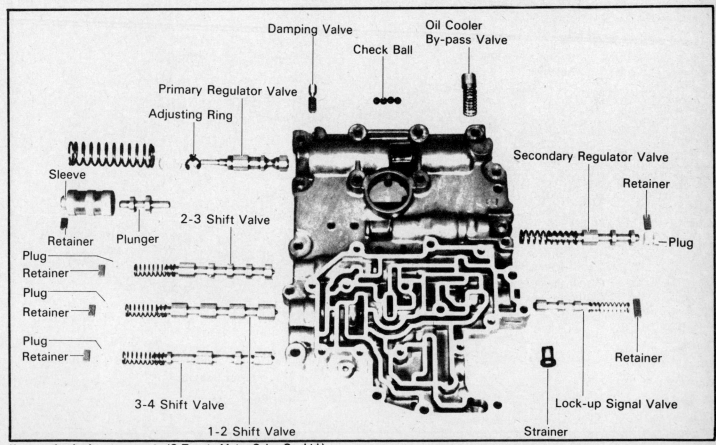

Upper valve body components (© Toyota Motor Sales Co. Ltd.)

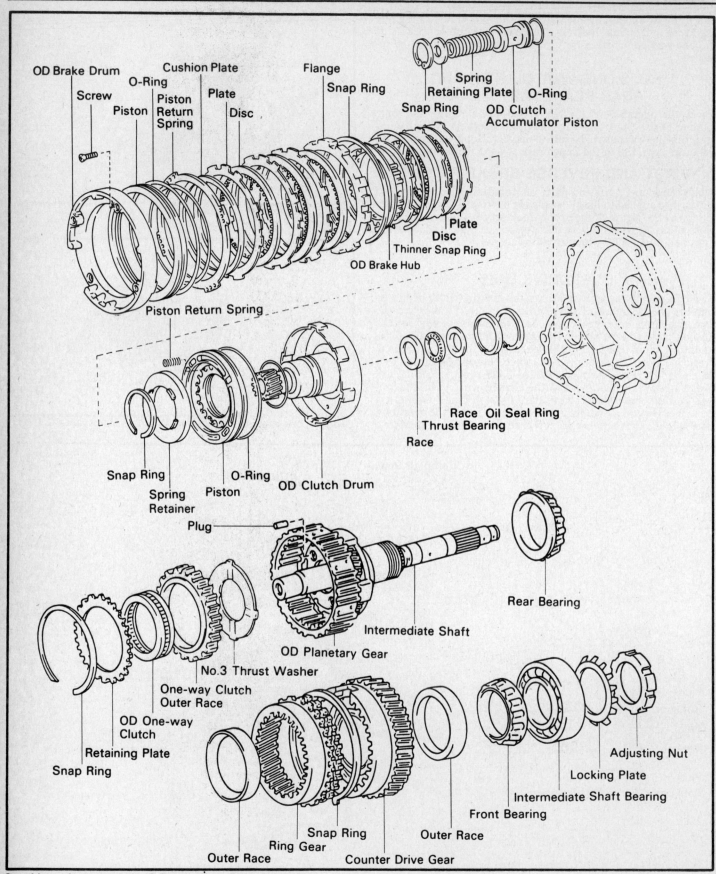

Overdrive unit components (© Toyota Motor Sales Co. Ltd.)

Installing the one-way clutch (© Toyota Motor Sales Co. Ltd.)

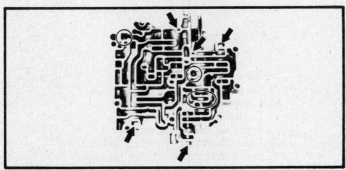

Location of the steel check balls (© Toyota Motor Sales Co. Ltd.)

S PECIFICATIONS

DIFFERENTIAL SPECIFICATIONS
Toyota A-140-E

	In. lbs.	N•m
SIDE BEARING PRELOAD		
New bearing	8.7-13.9	1.0-1.6
Reused bearing	4.3-6.9	0.5-0.8
DRIVE PINION PRELOAD		
New bearing	8.7-13.9	1.0-1.6
Reused bearing	4.3-6.9	0.5-0.8
TOTAL PRELOAD		
New bearing	2.5-3.6	0.3-0.4
Reused bearing	1.2-1.7	0.1-0.2
BACKLASH		
Pinion to side gear	0.0020-0.0079	0.05-0.20mm

TORQUE SPECIFICATIONS CHART
Toyota A-140E

Description	ft-lb	N•m
Transmission case x Transaxle case	22	29
Transmission case x Case cover	13	18
Transmission case protector	13	18
Rear bearing retainer	13	18
Output shaft bearing lock plate	13	18
Input shaft oil receiver	65 in.-lb	7.4
5th driven gear lock nut	90	123
Reverse idler shaft lock bolt	18	25
Control shaft cover	27	37
Reverse shift arm bracket	13	18
Reverse shift arm pivot	13	18
Shift fork No. 3	9	13
Ring gear x Differential case	71	97
Lock ball assembly	27	37
Control shift lever	56 in.-lb	6.4
Filler plug	36	49
Drain plug	36	49
Back-up light switch	33	39
Side bearing retainer	13	18
Clutch release bearing retainer	65 in.-lb	7.4
Speedometer driven gear lock plate	48 in.-lb	5.4
Transaxle case x Lock plate	18	25
Straight screw plug (Shift fork shaft No. 2)	9	13
(Reverse restrict pin holder)	9	13
Transaxle case x Engine 12 mm	47	64
10 mm	25	34
Bolt locking plate x transaxle	18	25
Stiffener plate x Engine	27	37
Stiffener plate x Transaxle case	27	37
Drive plate	61	37
Torque converter	13	18
Oil pump x Transaxle case	16	22
Oil pump body x Stator shaft	7	10
Second coast brake band guide	48 in.-lb	5.4
Upper valve body x Lower valve body	48 in.-lb	5.4
Valve body	7	10
Accumulator cover	7	10
Oil strainer	7	10
Oil pan	43 in.-lb	4.9
Oil pan drain plug	22	29
Cooler pipe union nut	25	34
Testing plug	65 in.-lb	7.4
Parking lock pawl bracket	65 in.-lb	7.4
Overdrive case x Transaxle case	18	25
Overdrive brake drum x Overdrive case	48 in.-lb	5.4

SPECIAL TOOLS

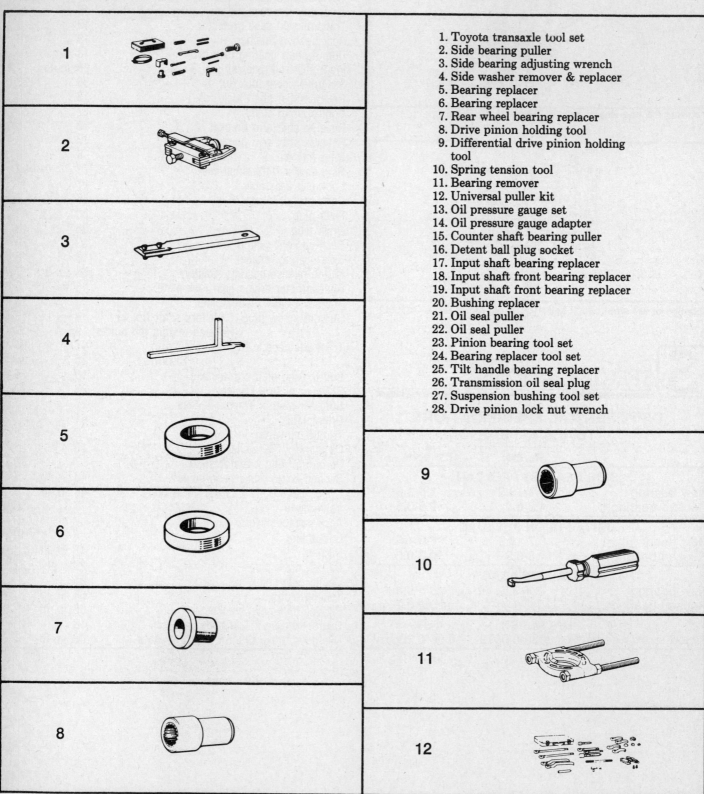

1. Toyota transaxle tool set
2. Side bearing puller
3. Side bearing adjusting wrench
4. Side washer remover & replacer
5. Bearing replacer
6. Bearing replacer
7. Rear wheel bearing replacer
8. Drive pinion holding tool
9. Differential drive pinion holding tool
10. Spring tension tool
11. Bearing remover
12. Universal puller kit
13. Oil pressure gauge set
14. Oil pressure gauge adapter
15. Counter shaft bearing puller
16. Detent ball plug socket
17. Input shaft bearing replacer
18. Input shaft front bearing replacer
19. Input shaft front bearing replacer
20. Bushing replacer
21. Oil seal puller
22. Oil seal puller
23. Pinion bearing tool set
24. Bearing replacer tool set
25. Tilt handle bearing replacer
26. Transmission oil seal plug
27. Suspension bushing tool set
28. Drive pinion lock nut wrench

Special tools (© Toyota Motor Corporation)

13		21	
14		22	
15		23	
16		24	
17		25	
18		26	
19		27	
20		28	

INDEX

VOLVO
AW70 • AW71

APPLICATIONS

Year	Model Usage	Transmission
82 and later	Volvo GLT Turbo	AW71
82 and later	Volvo GLT, GL, DL	AW70

GENERAL DESCRIPTION

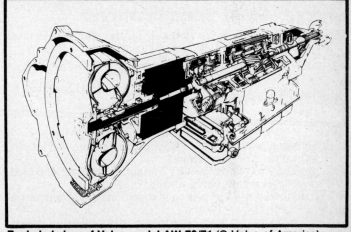

Exploded view of Volvo model AW-70/71 (© Volvo of America)

The AW70 and AW71 are both three speed automatics with overdrive as the fourth speed. The AW71 is used for somewhat heavier duty applications than the AW70, such as with the higher torque B21F Turbo engine.

The following major components are used:

1. Hydrodynamic torque converter.

2. Hydraulically controlled planetary gear transmission, which includes the overdrive and is located ahead of the three speed planetary gear transmission. The overdrive gear is automatically engaged when a controlling switch is energized.

3. Gear Selector—The sequence being P-R-N-D-2-1.

The entire transmission is contained in a single housing which is bolted to the rear of the engine, and operated using a single mechanical hookup. A starter inhibitor switch and reverse light switch is also provided. Valve bodies on both units are located on the bottom. The overdrive gear ratio of 0.69:1 is obtained in fourth gear.

Transmission and Converter Identification

TRANSMISSION

The AW70 automatic transmission model is used in the Volvo models DL, GL, and GLT when equipped with the B21F engine. The AW71 transmission model is used in the Volvo model GLT when equipped with the B21F Turbo engine.

A plate carrying the letter reference and serial number is fixed to the left-hand side of the transmission case.

CONVERTER

The effective diameter is 9.764 in. (248mm). The converter acts as an automatic clutch. It also multiplies engine torque to an extent determined by throttle position, engine speed and driving conditions. Additional torque multiplication is provided by the planetary gearsets, located within the transmission, when first, second, or reverse gears are in use.

Torque multiplication by the converter reaches a maximum of approximately 2 to 1 when the engine is running at full throttle and the turbine is "stalled", i.e. is prevented from turning by holding the car on the brakes with one of the gears engaged. Under running conditions the multiplication of torque varies with the speed ratio between the impeller and turbine and responds automatically to the input from the engine and the output needed to propel the car. When the rotational speed of the turbine approaches 90 per cent of the impeller speed, the input and output torque become equalized, the stator starts to revolve in unison (as permitted by the one-way clutch) and the converter acts as a fluid coupling.

Energy is transmitted from a vaned impeller, driven by the engine, to a vaned turbine (which drives the gearset) by the rapid circulation of fluid which then returns to the impeller through the vanes of a central stator carried on a fixed hub. A sprag—or one-way clutch—prevents the stator from rotating backwards under fluid pressure. All three elements (impeller, turbine and stator) are completely enclosed in a circular impeller cover which carries the mounting bosses (or ring) and contains the fluid. Fluid from the converter is circulated through a cooling element installed in the main radiator and releases heat to the engine cooling system, the capacity of which may need up-rating to carry the extra duty.

Metric Fasteners

The metric fastener dimensions are very close to the dimensions of the familiar inch sytem fasteners, and for this reason, replacement fasteners must have the same measurement and strength as those removed.

Do not attempt to interchange metric fasteners for inch system fasteners. Mismatched or incorrect fasteners can result in damage to the transmission unit through malfunctions, breakage or possible person injury.

Care should be taken to reuse the fasteners in the same locations as removed.

Fluid Specifications

Use only ATF type F or G automatic transmission fluid in these units, when adding fluid or changing completely.

FLUID CAPACITIES

	Litres	U.S. Quarts
AW70 & AW71	7.5	7.9

Checking Fluid Level

1. Shift gear selector into "P" Park. Start engine and let idle.
2. Shift into various positions.
3. Shift back to "P" Park. Wait 2 minutes, then check oil level.
4. If oil level is low, check unit for oil leak.
5. If oil level is too high, check to determine if oil contains water.
6. Fill oil to correct level. Note that the distance between Max. and Min. marks corresponds to only 0.2 qt. of oil. Use only ATF type F or G automatic transmission fluid.

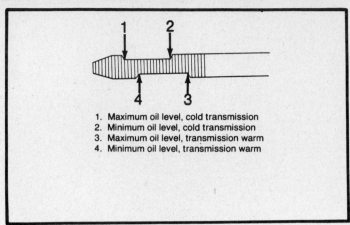

1. Maximum oil level, cold transmission
2. Minimum oil level, cold transmission
3. Maximum oil level, transmission warm
4. Minimum oil level, transmission warm

Oil level indicator (© Volvo of America)

M MODIFICATIONS

Tightening Center Support Bolts

When servicing or rebuilding the AW-70 or AW-71 models, the following procedure is necessary for tightening the center support bolts. Failure to do so may result in the bolts becoming loose in service.

1. Assemble center support bolts in main case. Align bolt holes and finger tighten the bolts. Do not torque the bolts at this stage.
2. Assemble clutches and pump to the main case and torque the pump bolts.
3. Torque the center support location bolt to a torque of 17-20 ft. lbs. Then tighten the opposite bolt to the same torque.

Selector Lever/Cross Shaft Nut

When assembling the cross shaft lever to the transmission, the cross shaft nut must not be overtightened or internal damage to the transmission may result. The correct procedure is to place the transmission in the Neutral position and, with the opposite end of the cross shaft held, assemble the lever, washer, and nut and tighten.

TROUBLE DIAGNOSIS

CLUTCH APPLICATION CHART
AW-70 and AW71 Automatic Transmission

Selector Position	Clutch OD	Forward C-1	Direct C-2	Brake OD	Brake B-1	Brake B-2	Brake B-3	One-way Clutch (OD)	One-way Clutch (1)	One-way Clutch (2)
Park	X						X			
Reverse	X		X				X	X		
Neutral	X									
Drive										
1st	X	X						X		X
2nd	X	X				X		X	X	
3rd	X	X	X			X		X		
4th		X	X	X		X				
Manual 2										
1st	X	X						X		X
2nd	X	X			X	X		X	X	
Manual 1										
1st	X	X					X	X		X

CHILTON'S THREE C's TRANSMISSION DIAGNOSIS CHART
AW-70 and AW-71

Condition	Cause	Correction
Shift points too high	a) Accelerator cable setting wrong b) Governor bushing seized c) Governor piston rings defective or worn d) Throttle pressure valve malfunctions e) Shift valves jammed	a) Adjust accelerator cable b) Clean or replace governor c) Replace piston rings d) Replace valve body control unit e) Replace valve body control unit
Shift points too low	a) Accelerator cable setting wrong b) Governor bushing seized c) Throttle pressure valve malfunctions d) Plastic balls in transfer plate leak	a) Adjust accelerator cable b) Clean or replace governor c) Replace valve body control unit d) Replace valve body control unit
Shift points too high or too low and shift movements too long and too soft	a) Clutch C + C damaged by 1-2 gear shifts b) Clutch B damaged by 2-3 gear shifts	a) Replace clutches b) Replace clutch B
No kickdown shifts	a) Accelerator cable setting wrong b) Control unit setting wrong c) Throttle pressure valve sticks d) Plastic balls in transfer plate leak	a) Adjust accelerator cable b) Adjust valve body control unit c) Replace valve body control unit d) Replace valve body control unit
Selector lever cannot be moved to "P"	a) Selector linkage setting wrong b) Locking device defective	a) Adjust selector linkage b) Repair locking device
Parking position will not disengage	a) Parking lock pawl caught in teeth of output shell b) Excessive friction in parking lock device	a) Replace parking lock pawl b) Repair parking lock device

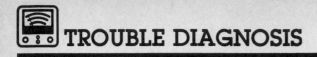

CHILTON'S THREE C's TRANSMISSION DIAGNOSIS CHART
AW-70 and AW-71

Condition	Cause	Correction
Parking position does not hold (slips)	a) Selector rod setting wrong b) Lock pin defective	a) Adjust selector rod b) Replace lock pin
Car cannot be started in 0 or N	a) Transmission switch defective	a) Replace transmission switch
Car creeps or runs in 0 or N	a) Selector rod setting wrong b) Clutch A released too slowly c) Clutch A defective (bonded)	a) Adjust selector rod b) Disassemble transmission c) Disassemble transmission
Drive in 1st and 2nd gear only when in A or D	a) 2nd-3rd shift valves stuck	a) Replace valve body control unit
Drive in 2nd gear only	a) 1st-2nd and 2nd-3rd shift valves stuck	a) Replace valve body control unit
Drive in 3rd gear only	a) 1st-2nd and 2nd-3rd shift valves stuck b) Governor bushing seized	a) Replace valve body control unit b) Clean or replace governor
No forward or reverse drive	a) Oil level insufficient b) Pump drive defective c) Drive plate broken d) Parking lock pawl stuck e) Clutches A and B defective	a) Correct oil level b) Replace converter and pump c) Replace drive plate d) Replace pawl e) Disassemble transmission
No forward drive	a) Selector linkage setting wrong b) Clutch OD defective or oil lost through leak in supply line	a) Adjust selector linkage b) Replace clutch OD
No reverse drive	a) Selector linkage setting wrong b) Clutch B or D defective c) Brake B3 defective d) Oil level too low, pump cannot draw in oil	a) Adjust selector linkage b) Disassemble transmission c) Disassemble transmission d) Correct oil level
Hard engagement jolt or definite double knock when engaging reverse gear	a) Damper B defective or wrong cover parts	a) Replace valve body control unit
Slipping or shaking in Reverse gear	a) Clutch B or D damaged b) Serious loss of oil in supply line to B or D	a) Disassemble transmission b) Disassemble transmission
No drive in Reverse and 2nd gear	a) Shift valve stuck in 3rd gear position	a) Replace valve body control unit Disassemble transmission if metal particles or abrasion are found in oil sump
Grinding shifts	a) Accelerator cable disengaged or maladjusted b) Oil level too low c) Throttle pressure valve stuck d) Clutch A defective	a) Connect or adjust accelerator cable b) Correct oil level c) Replace valve body control unit d) Disassemble transmission
Grinding shifts from 1st to 2nd gear	a) Clutches C and C' slip b) Clutch valve and damper C malfunction c) Accelerator cable disengaged or maladjusted d) Oil level too low e) Throttle pressure valve stuck f) One-way clutch F defective	a) Disassemble transmission b) Disassemble transmission c) Connect or adjust accelerator cable d) Correct oil level e) Replace valve body control unit f) Disassemble transmission

CHILTON'S THREE C's TRANSMISSION DIAGNOSIS CHART
AW-70 and AW-71

Condition	Cause	Correction
Grinding shifts from 2nd to 3rd gear	a) Clutch B slips b) Accelerator cable disengaged or maladjusted	a) Replace clutch B b) Connect or adjust accelerator cable
Rattling noise in Neutral	a) Drive plate broken b) Welded drive dogs on converter damaged	a) Replace drive plate b) Replace converter
Growling noise in Neutral, eliminated when accelerating in 0 or N	a) Valve chatter in control unit b) Oil pump draws in air	a) Correct oil level b) Tighten valve body mounting screws, check gasket
Oil on torque converter bell housing	a) Shaft seal shot b) Primary pump body O-ring shot c) Converter leaks at welded seams d) Plug leaks	a) Replace shaft seal b) Replace O-ring c) Replace converter d) Replace seal
Oil on output flange	a) Shaft seal shot	a) Replace shaft seal
Oil on speedometer drive	a) O-ring shot b) Shaft seal in speedometer bushing shot	a) Replace O-ring b) Replace speedometer bushing
Grinding shifts from 2nd to 3rd gear	c) Oil level too low d) Oil pressure too low e) Throttle pressure valve stuck f) One-way clutch E defective	c) Correct oil level d) Disassemble transmission e) Replace valve body control unit f) Disassemble transmission
3rd gear slips	a) Clutch B slips b) Accelerator cable disengaged or maladjusted c) Oil level too low d) Oil pressure too low e) Throttle pressure valve stuck	a) Disassemble transmission b) Connect or adjust accelerator cable c) Correct oil level d) Disassemble transmission e) Replace valve body control unit
Stall speed too high	a) Oil level too low b) Engaged clutch slips c) One-way clutch (F or G) slips	a) Correct oil level b) Disassemble transmission c) Disassemble transmission
Stall speed too low	a) Torque converter defective b) Engine output insufficient	a) Replace torque converter b) Test engine
No braking effect from 2nd gear when in 2 and 1	a) Clutch C'' defective	a) Replace clutch C'
Transmission shifts too early when downshifting from 2nd to 1st gear manually	a) Locking valve pressure too high b) Loss of pressure in governor supply line between governor and shift valves	a) Replace valve body control unit b) Disassemble transmission
Transmission shifts too late when downshifting from 2nd to 1st gear manually	a) Locking valve pressure too low b) Governor pressure too high	a) Replace valve body control unit b) Disassemble transmission
Transmission vibrates at fast move-offs	a) Clutch A defective b) Propeller shaft center bearing defective c) One-way clutch F or G defective	a) Replace clutch A b) Replace center bearing c) Disassemble transmission
Transmission shifts hard or down	a) Accelerator cable setting wrong b) Clutch A defective	a) Adjust accelerator cable
Drive in 0 or N	a) Selector linkage setting wrong b) Clutch A (forward) bonded c) Clutch B (reverse) bonded	a) Adjust selector linkage b) Disassemble transmission c) Disassemble transmission

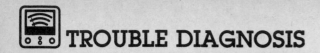

CHILTON'S THREE C's TRANSMISSION DIAGNOSIS CHART
AW-70 and AW-71

Condition	Cause	Correction
No braking effect from 1st gear when in 2 and 1	a) Clutch valve and damper D defective b) Clutch D defective	a) Replace valve body body control unit b) Replace clutch D
Stall speed in forward too high	a) Clutch A or 1st gear one-way clutch slips	a) Disassemble transmission
Stall speed in forward too low	a) Engine output not sufficient b) Converter one-way clutch defective	a) Check engine tuning b) Replace converter
Whining depending on speed	a) Center bearing of propeller shaft defective	a) Replace center bearing
Vehicle does not hold in park position	a) Linkage play excessive b) Rod length needs adjustment c) Damaged lock pin d) Damaged valve body e) Locking device defective f) Parking pawl, spring defective	a) Replace bushings b) Adjust sleeve c) Replace lock pin d) Replace valve body e) Repair locking device f) Replace defective parts
Oil on torque converter bell housing	a) Shaft seal shot b) Primary pump body O-ring shot c) Converter leaks at welded seams d) Plug leaks	a) Replace shaft seal b) Replace O-ring a) Replace converter d) Replace seal
Oil on output flange	a) Shaft seal shot	a) Replace shaft seal
Oil on speedometer drive	a) O-ring shot b) Shaft seal in speedometer bushing shot	a) Replace O-ring b) Replace speedometer bushing

POWER FLOW

Neutral/Park

UNITS APPLIED—OVERDRIVE CLUTCH, REAR BRAKE

When the selector lever is in the park position, a lock pawl engages with the front ring gear, which prevents the output shaft from rotating and thus immobilizes the vehicle.

Reverse

UNITS APPLIED—OVERDRIVE CLUTCH, REAR CLUTCH, ONE-WAY CLUTCH, REAR BRAKE

Planet pinions drive their ring gear in a counterclockwise direction, which transmits power to the output shaft at a speed ratio of 2.21:1, in reverse.

Drive, First Gear

UNITS APPLIED—OVERDRIVE CLUTCH, FRONT CLUTCH, ONE-WAY OD CLUTCH, ONE-WAY CLUTCH 2

Planet pinions of the rear train drive their carrier in a clockwise direction, and also drives the sun gear counterclockwise, at a speed controlled by the front planetary train.

Drive, Second Gear

UNITS APPLIED—OVERDRIVE CLUTCH, FRONT CLUTCH, BRAKE B2, ONE-WAY OD CLUTCH, ONE-WAY CLUTCH 2

The front clutch is applied and transmits power from the input shaft to the rear ring gear. The sun gear is held against counterclockwise rotation by brake B2 and the front brake. Planet pinions then transmit power to the output shaft at a speed ratio of 1.45:1.

Drive, Third Gear

UNITS APPLIED—OVERDRIVE CLUTCH, FRONT CLUTCH, REAR CLUTCH, REAR BRAKE, ONE-WAY OD CLUTCH

Front and rear clutches are both applied. The entire planetary gear assembly rotates as a unit. The rear brake is applied to assist in gear changing. Ratio will be 1:1.

Drive, Fourth Gear (Overdrive)

UNITS APPLIED—FRONT CLUTCH, REAR CLUTCH, OVERDRIVE BRAKE, BRAKE B2

The overdrive engages automatically to provide a fourth gear. The overdrive brake is applied which will cause the sun gear to stop rotating. Power is then transmitted to the front clutch and then transferred to the output shaft. Drive ratio is reduced from 1:1 to 0.69:1.

Second Gear, Position 2

UNITS APPLIED—OVERDRIVE CLUTCH, FRONT BRAKE, BRAKE B2, ONE-WAY OVERDRIVE CLUTCH, ONE-WAY CLUTCHES 1 AND 2

The difference in comparison to gear selector position "D", is the fact that the front brake is also applied. Brake B2 prevents the sun gear from rotating counterclockwise. First gear is not locked out.

First Gear, Position 1

UNITS APPLIED—OVERDRIVE CLUTCH, FRONT CLUTCH, REAR BRAKE, ONE-WAY OVERDRIVE CLUTCH

The difference in this position as opposed to "D" is that the rear brake is also applied and the planetary gear is prevented from rotating. Power is then transferred from the output shaft to the input shaft.

Hydraulic Control System

The power required to apply and hold the clutches and brakes which control the action of the planetary gears is provided by an engine-driven pump which draws fluid from the oil pan through a strainer and delivers it, under regulated pressure, to a system of valves, ports and passages. The pump also supplies fluid to the torque converter, a cooler, and the lubrication system of the gearset. Most of the hydraulic circuits and all valves (except the governor) are contained in the valve bodies assembly which is attached to the base of the transmission case and can be removed as a complete unit.

In addition to the primary function of automatic gearshifting, the hydraulic system is designed to make the shifts smoothly and to vary the hydraulic loading applied to the clutches and brakes in a manner appropriate to the torque which is imposed on them under a wide range of operating conditions. These requirements are met by using a variety of automatic valves which respond to variations in hydraulic pressure. The refinement in control obtained in this way is an important operational advantage.

The hydraulic system is controlled by the following basic controls:

1. Primary and secondary regulator valves automatically determine the pressure of the fluid in various parts of the system in relation to a number of operational requirements.

2. Governor valve, carried by the output shaft, provides a variable pressure signal (governor pressure) which is regulated in relation to car speed.

3. Throttle valve provides a variable pressure signal (throttle pressure) primarily dependent on the extent to which the carburetor throttle is opened.

4. Manual valve, operated by a selector lever, enables the driver to choose various modes of operation, including neutral and park.

GOVERNOR

The governor is mounted on the output shaft which is, at all times connected to the road wheels which drive the vehicle and therefore revolves at a speed proportional to the speed of the vehicle. In all forward gears, fluid at line pressure is routed to the governor by the manual valve. From the governor, fluid is directed to the shift valves, the governor modulator valve and the cut-back valve at a regulated governor pressure which rises as the speed of the vehicle increases.

A two-stage governor mechanism is used which controls governor pressure through the speed range.

When the vehicle is at rest, the output shaft is stationary and an inlet port is closed by the valve. At low vehicle speeds the valve moves to an intermediate position in which it is cracked open to admit fluid at line pressure against the opposition of the centrifugal force produced by the governor weight, valve and spring acting in unison. Fluid is directed to the outlet port at a regulated governor pressure which increases as the speed of the shaft rises in response to the rapid build-up of centrifugal force.

When a pre-determined speed is reached, a disc, which is part of the stem to which the governor weight is attached, makes contact with the governor body. From this stage onwards, regulation is maintained by a balance between governor pressure acting on the differential areas of the valve and the spring load (plus the small centrifugal force of the valve itself), with the net result that governor pressure continues to rise with vehicle speed and can approach (but never reach) the level of line pressure. Excess pressure will force the valve towards the shaft, so opening an exhaust port and closing the supply port.

PRIMARY REGULATOR VALVE

1. Valve closed by spring load, cutting off line 1 from line 1A.
2. Valve in regulating position, allowing fluid to reach circuits

supplying secondary regulator valve, lubrication system and torque converter-coupling.

3. At high speeds, valve permits any surplus fluid to return to pump inlet circuit.

SECONDARY REGULATOR VALVE

1. Valve closed by spring load, cutting off return circuit from torque converter-coupling.
2. Valve in intermediate position, allowing hot fluid from torque converter-coupling to flow to cooler.
3. Valve fully opened, allowing surplus fluid to reach cooler circuit.

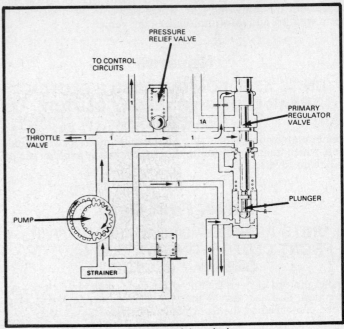

Primary regulator valve (© Volvo of America)

MANUAL VALVE

The manual valve is linked mechanically to the gear selector lever (operated by the driver) and is precisely located, relative to a series of ports, by a local detent device which must not be over-ridden by the operating linkage. One port receives fluid at line pressure from the primary regulator valve. The other ports are connected to various parts of the hydraulic system.

PRIMARY REGULATOR VALVE

The primary regulator valve receives fluid from the engine-driven pump and directs it, at a regulated line pressure, to the manual valve, throttle valve, second speed brake (B.2) accumulator and direct clutch (C.2) accumulator. Also directs fluid to the lubrication system of the planetary gearset, the torque converter, the secondary regulator valve and to the cooler. Fluid surplus to requirements is re-circulated through the primary regulator valve to the suction port of the pump when the demand is low.

The primary regulating function provides for an increase in line pressure when the engine torque is high and a reduction at normal driving speeds. Line pressure is also increased to a suitably high value when reverse gear is engaged manually.

THROTTLE VALVE AND KICKDOWN VALVE

Fluid is fed at line pressure to the throttle valve from the primary regulator valve and is directed at regulated throttle pressure to the primary and secondary regulator valves, the shift valves, the cutback valve, and the kickdown valve. A damping valve is included in the line which serves the primary regulator valve.

The primary function of the throttle valve is to send a pressure signal to the shift valves which acts in opposition to governor pressure. An upshift or a downshift takes place when hydraulic unbalance allows governor pressure to overcome throttle pressure, or vice versa.

A cable connects the carburetor throttle lever to a cam which is in contact with a roller mounted at one end of a kickdown valve, located in tandem with the throttle valve in the valve bodies assembly.

General Arrangement of the Gear Set

Various rotating parts of the transmission are arranged in groups that always turn in unison. Some are permanently connected by welding and others by the interlocking of splines (or castellations) which enable the parts to be separated during dismantling and re-engaged on assembly. The rotating parts which are grouped in these various ways are listed below:

1. Torque converter turbine, input shaft, forward clutch cylinder and direct clutch (inner member).
2. Forward clutch (inner member), intermediate shaft and rear ring gear.
3. Direct clutch cylinder, brake hub (B.1) and sun gear.
4. Front planet carrier and brake hub (B.3.)
5. Front planet ring gear, rear planet carrier, cover and output shaft.

Power enters the transmission through the input shaft and forward clutch cylinder assembly. This cylinder is the outer (driving) member of the forward clutch and is coupled to the inner member of the neighbouring direct clutch assembly by shallow, interlocking projections or keys.

The gear set consists of two planetary trains which are located end to end at the rear of the transmission case. Each train consists of four planet pinions, located in a carrier, which are in mesh with the internal teeth of a ring gear. Both sets of planet pinions are in mesh with a single, lengthy sun gear, the teeth of which are integral with the rear end of a hollow shaft within which the intermediate shaft is located. Helical involute tooth forms are used throughout.

When the forward clutch is engaged, power is transmitted through its inner member to the intermediate shaft and thence to the ring gear of the rear planetary train. Engagement of the direct clutch transmits power to the sun gear through the hollow shaft of which it is an intergral part. These are the two routes through which power can flow into the transmission. No matter which gear is in use, power leaves the transmission through the output shaft which passes through the extension housing and is connected to the front universal joint of the propeller shaft.

Three forward speed ratios, one reverse speed ratio and a neutral condition are obtained by the selective engagement of two clutches and three brakes, all of which are of the multi-disc type, running in oil. One-way sprag clutches act in association with two of the brakes to permit rotation in one direction only.

Fluid supplied under pressure from a pump, through a control system, operates the multi-disc clutches and brakes by means of pistons which are retracted by springs when the pressure is released. As the pump is driven from the impellor member of the torque converter, hydraulic pressure is generated whenever the engine is running. A manual valve, and a large number of automatic valves, direct the hydraulic pressure selectively to the clutches and brakes and so determine the action of the gearing.

The overdrive unit is located ahead of the 3-speed transmission, between the oil pump and the front clutch (C.1), within the transmission casing. This is essentially a fourth gear and will automatically engage when driving in third gear with a throttle opening less than 85 percent. Overdrive can be disengaged, by a push button on the gear selector, to obtain a three speed unit. This

is indicated to the driver by a light on the instrument panel which reads "OD-OFF". The overdrive will remain disengaged until the button on the gear selector is pushed again or the ignition switch is turned off. The transmission will always return to the fourth speed range when the ignition is switched off.

BY-PASS VALVE

The by-pass valve protects the oil cooler from excessive pressure.

PRESSURE RELIEF VALVE

The pressure relief valve is located immediately after the oil pump. It will open automatically at a preset pressure.

CUTBACK VALVE

The cutback valve on the AW-70 and AW-71 is acted on by pressure from the governor modulator valve. The cutback valve on both transmissions have the same function: to lower the throttle pressure and the line pressure at normal and high speeds. This causes a reduction in line pressure which is needed to drive the oil pump. It also improves the gear changing qualities.

Shift Valves—Operating Principles

The function of a shift valve is to signal changes of gear (upshifts and downshifts) in response to variations in governor pressure and throttle pressure. Each valve has only two operative positions so that two valves are required in a three-speed transmission (1-2 and 2-3). A "snap" action is essential in order that the valve does not hesitate, or "hunt" between the two gears that it controls.

1-2 SHIFT VALVE

This valve controls the oil flow to engage gears 1 and 2. The throttle pressure, which varies with the throttle opening, acts on one end of this valve. On the other end, the governor pressure acts. At the middle of the valve there are passages leading to the clutches and brakes which controls the planetary gear operation when in first and second gears. Which gear is used depends on line, throttle and governor pressure.

2-3 SHIFT VALVE

The 2-3 shift valve occupies the downshift position when the vehicle is driven in 1st, 2nd and reverse gear. There is no governor pressure in reverse.

In 2nd gear, throttle pressure, spring tension, and governor pressure are applied to the 2-3 shift valve. Fluid received from the 1-2 shift valve is able to pass to the intermediate coast modulator valve through adjacent ports. Other intermediate ports provide a fluid route for the direct clutch. In the middle of the valve there are passages that lead to the clutch and brakes. These clutch and brakes control the planetary gear operation in second and third speeds. The position of the 2-3 shift valve is determined by line, throttle and governor pressure.

3-4 SHIFT VALVE (AW-71)

Throttle pressure, which varies with the throttle opening acts on one end of this valve. On the other end acts the governor pressure, which varies with the vehicle speed. In the middle of the valve are two oil passages. These passages direct oil to the overdrive clutch (CO) and overdrive brake (BO). Which passage is used depends on the strength of the line pressure.

LOW COAST SHIFT VALVE

The low cost shift valve is acted on by modulated line pressure.

The low coast shift valve is located above, and in alignment with, the 1-2 shift valve, a compressed coil spring is placed between them and normally holds the low-coast shift valve in its upper position where it acts as a stop to limit the upshift travel of the 1-2 shift valve.

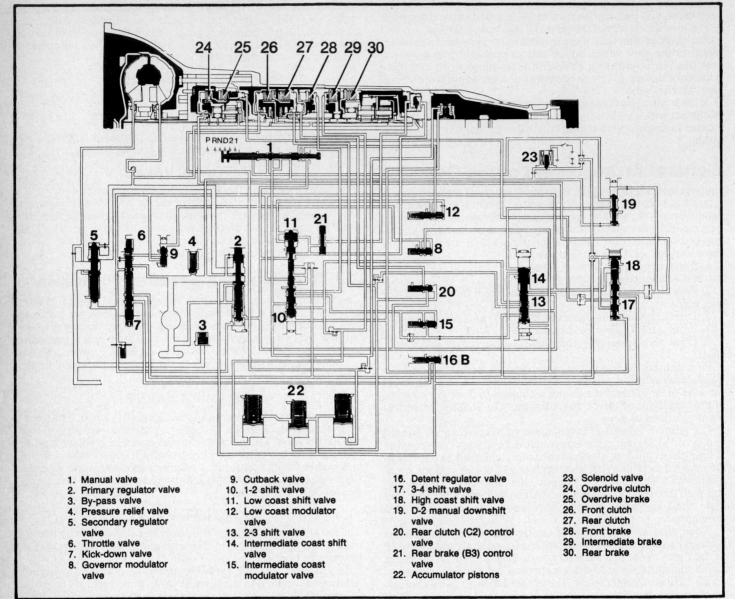

1. Manual valve
2. Primary regulator valve
3. By-pass valve
4. Pressure relief valve
5. Secondary regulator valve
6. Throttle valve
7. Kick-down valve
8. Governor modulator valve

9. Cutback valve
10. 1-2 shift valve
11. Low coast shift valve
12. Low coast modulator valve
13. 2-3 shift valve
14. Intermediate coast shift valve
15. Intermediate coast modulator valve

16. Detent regulator valve
17. 3-4 shift valve
18. High coast shift valve
19. D-2 manual downshift valve
20. Rear clutch (C2) control valve
21. Rear brake (B3) control valve
22. Accumulator pistons

23. Solenoid valve
24. Overdrive clutch
25. Overdrive brake
26. Front clutch
27. Rear clutch
28. Front brake
29. Intermediate brake
30. Rear brake

Location of valves in valve body assembly (© Volvo of America)

When the manual valve is placed in first gear, fluid at directed line pressure passes through the low coast modulator valve and acts upon unequal areas of the low coast shift valve. If the vehicle is stationary, or being operated in 1st gear, the low coast shift valve will move downwards into contact with the 1-2 shift valve, which is then in the downshift position. Ports are opened which allow this pressurized fluid to apply both pistons of brake B3, the former feed being controlled by the orifice shown on the schematic drawings.

If the manual valve is placed in 1st gear while the vehicle is being operated in 2nd gear (1-2 shift valve in upper position) the hydraulic pressure acting on the top of the low coast shift valve is opposed by governor pressure acting on the bottom of the 1-2 shift valve. The large and small pistons of brake B3 are both open to exhaust. As the vehicle speed falls, modulated line pressure overcomes governor pressure, at a pre-determined value, and forces both the low coast and 1-2 shift valves down to their low positions. Ports are opened to allow fluid at modulated line pressure to apply both pistons of brake B3.

When the manual valve is placed in reverse gear, fluid passes directly to the low coast shift valve. If this valve is in its upper position the pressurized fluid has direct access, through ports, to brake B3. If the manual valve is shifted directly from 1st to reverse, the pressurized fluid overcomes the modulated line pressure and forces the low coast shift valve into its upper position. This shift does not involve "stroking" the pistons of brake B3, but increases the pressure already acting on them.

INTERMEDIATE COAST SHIFT VALVE

The intermediate coast shift valve is located above, and in alignment with, the 2-3 shift valve. A compressed coil spring is placed between them and normally holds the intermediate coast shift valve in its upper position where it acts as a stop to limit the upshift travel of the 2-3 shift valve.

When the manual valve is placed either in 1st gear or 2nd gear, (vehicle stationary), fluid at directed line pressure acts directly on the large upper surface of the intermediate coast shift valve and imposes an hydraulic load which forces the valve downwards to its lower position and thus prevents the 2-3 shift valve from moving upwards to engage top gear, regardless of vehicle speed.

If the vehicle is being operated in 3rd gear when the manual valve is placed either in 1st gear or 2nd gear, a similar action takes place, almost regardless of vehicle speed or throttle opening. The intermediate coast shift valve forcing the 2-3 shift valve downwards to the 2nd gear position. For all practical purposes there is no inhibition on obtaining this manually activated 3-2 shift. This is because the line pressure which acts downwards on a large area of the intermediate cost shift valve, is higher than the governor pressure which acts upwards on the smaller area of the 2-3 shift valve.

HIGH COAST SHIFT VALVE

The high coast shift valve is manually controlled by a push button on the gear selector, or automatically when the electric kickdown switch is engaged. When switching the overdrive unit off manually, the high coast shift valve will depress the 3-4 shift valve to its lower position. This will disengage the fourth gear. The high coast shift valve will remain in the lower position until the solenoid valve is disengaged. In both cases, the high coast shift valve is acted on by line pressure.

DETENT REGULATOR VALVE

The detent regulator valve is located ahead of the kick down valve and is under constant line pressure. It reduces line pressure to a point where it can act on the kick down valve. The detent regulator valve receives fluid at throttle pressure from the kick down valve and regulates the detent pressure at which fluid is applied to the 2-3 shift valve. Detent pressure increases the vehicle speed at which a 3-2 shift can occur.

INTERMEDIATE COAST MODULATOR VALVE

The intermediate coast modulator valve modulates line pressure to a lower value before it is applied to brake B1 when second gear is engaged (either automatically or manually) in order to ensure a smooth shift. Brake B1 is used at all times, in second gear, and supplements the thermal capacity of brake B2 on an automatic 1-2 shift. Total torque capacity would be higher than necessary if full line pressure were applied to brake B1.

If the vehicle is being driven in third gear when the gear selector is moved to position 2, the downshift to second gear will occur, regardless of the throttle opening or vehicle speed.

D-2 MANUAL DOWNSHIFT VALVE

This valve controls manual downshifting from fourth gear to second gear. Third gear is used only for a short time. This eliminates the risk of the engine over-revving during the braking period. Downshift valve D-2 is influenced by pressures at both ends; control pressure from the high coast shift valve at one end, and pressure for overdrive clutch (CO) at the other end.

REAR CLUTCH (C2) CONTROL VALVE

Rear clutch (C2) is composed of two piston surfaces. When engaging third gear, the smaller of the two surfaces is used. In position "R," both surfaces must be used to prevent the clutch from slipping. This valve provides a smooth engagement of reverse gear by applying the rear clutches.

REAR BRAKE B-3) CONTROL VALVE

This valve provides smooth engagement of the reverse gear, by using two hydraulic pistons. These pistons are applied in stages and are fed by separate oil passages. This valve serves as a restrictor in the piston oil passages. This valve also divides the oil flow to the pistons. The front piston is applied before the rear piston which results in B3 being applied for an additional period of time. The reverse gear engagement is therefore smooth.

ACCUMULATOR PISTONS

Accumulator pistons are found in all oil circuits for the front clutch, rear clutch, and brake B2.

SOLENOID VALVE

The solenoid valve controls the engagement and disengagement of the fourth gear (overdrive). It is engaged by a switch on the gear selector. When engaged, the solenoid relieves line pressure from one end of the 3-4 shift valve. When disengaged, the solenoid then supplies, the end of the 3-4 shift valve with line pressure. The solenoid valve does not return to the engaged position until it receives a new impulse from the gear selector switch or the ignition is switched off/on.

Diagnostic Tests
LINE PRESSURE
Excessive Pressure

Usually caused by a seizing valve (provided the throttle cable is correctly adjusted).
It might be one of the following two valves.
a. Throttle Valve
b. Primary Regulator Valve

THROTTLE VALVE

As the throttle valve influences line pressure, it is possible to check the throttle valve operation as follows.
1. Let engine idle, gear selector position "N."
2. Pull the transmission cable by hand, not influencing throttle opening (and engine speed).
3. Pressure should increase. If not, the throttle valve seizes.

PRIMARY REGULATOR VALVE

Increase engine speed. If the primary regulator valve seizes, the normal control of the pressure will fail. Pressure will vary directly in proportion to the oil pump speed (engine speed).

Test Procedure

1. Remove front plug and connect nipple. Attach the pressure gauge to the door window. Route the hose behind the splash guard, over the steering control rod and between oil pipes to transmission. Connect to the pressure nipple.
2. Start engine and let idle. Gear selector in position "N" and idle speed approx. 900 rpm.
3. Depress the brake pedal and shift gear selector into "D". Note reading.
4. Shift gear selector into "R." Note reading.

TOO LOW PRESSURE

Too low pressures may be caused by seizing primary regulator valve or throttle valve. Test as described under "Excessive Pressure".
If these two tests verify that the too low pressure is not caused by any of these valves, the fault may be:
1. Defective pressure relief valve (only early versions).
2. Defective oil pump.
NOTE: A defective oil pump usually makes noise.

GOVERNOR PRESSURE

The governor pressure is a modified line pressure. So governor pressure will be incorrect if line pressure is incorrect. Therefore, an incorrect line pressure must be corrected before governor pressure is checked.

Procedures

1. Attach pressure gauge to the door window. Route the hose behind splash shield, over control arm and into transmission. Remove rear plug on transmission and connect nipple.

2. Test drive the vehicle in "D" and note readings. Pressure should be 0 when vehicle is standing still, also in position "R."

LOW GOVERNOR PRESSURE
1. Governor leaks or jams.
2. Oil leak at cover for governor oil ducts.
3. Governor seals on output shaft are defective.

EXCESSIVE GOVERNOR PRESSURE
Govenor jams. Remove and check governor.

LINE PRESSURE CHART

Selector Position	Model AW-70	Model AW-71
D	50-63 psi	65-77 psi
R	71-91 psi	106-117 psi

STALL SPEED TEST

Prepare Vehicle for Stall Test

Install an engine tachometer and connect a 0 to 300 psi test pressure gauge to line pressure fitting on transmission. Install chocks in front of and behind both front wheels and set hand brake.

CAUTION

Do not maintain stall rpm longer than five seconds

Perform Stall Test in "D" Range

Start engine and set selector lever to "D". Firmly apply the foot brake, and press the accelerator pedal to full throttle position. Quickly read the highest line pressure and engine rpm obtained. AW-70 stall speed should fall between 1,800-2,300 rpm with the line pressure between 137-160 psi. AW-71 stall speed should fall between 2,000-2,500 rpm with the line pressure between 140-205 psi.

Perform Stall Test In "R" Range

Set selector lever to "R". Firmly apply foot brake and press accelerator pedal to full throttle position. Quickly read the highest line pressure and engine rpm obtained. Stall rpm for the AW-70 should fall between 1,800-2,300 and line pressure 195-242 psi. AW-71 stall rpm should fall between 2,000-2,500 and line pressure should be between 213-270 psi.

Perform Time Lag Test

Obtain a stop watch. With engine idling and selector lever in "N", simultaneously shift to "D" and start stop watch. Stop the watch when transmission engagement shock is felt. Time should be less than 1.2 seconds.

Set selector back to "N" and repeat test for shift from "N" to "R". Time should be less than 1.5 seconds.

Perform Hydraulic Pressure Tests

Using an engine tachometer, and a 0-100 psi test gauge for governor pressure port for governor pressure test, and a 0-300 psi test gauge to line pressure port for line pressure test. Ensure chocks are in front of and behind both front wheels.

LINE PRESSURE CHECK IN "D" RANGE

Set the parking brake. Set the selector lever to "D". Apply the foot brake and allow the engine to idle (900 rpm). Line pressure for the AW-70 should be 50-63 psi. Line pressure for the AW-71 should be 65-77 psi.

LINE PRESSURE CHECK IN "R" RANGE

Set the parking brake. Set the selector lever in "R". Apply the foot brake and allow the engine to idle (900 rpm). Line pressure for the

STALL TEST EVALUATION

Malfunction	Action
Grinding or grating noise from transmission	Troubleshoot noise problems
Stall speed higher than specified maximum with clutch or brake squawk in "D" range	Troubleshoot front clutch
Stall speed higher than specified maximum with no apparent clutch or brake slippage	Check torque converter
Stall speed higher than specified maximum with clutch or brake in squawk in "R" range	Troubleshoot reverse range elements
Time lag in shift from "N" to "D" is longer than specified	Troubleshoot valve body
Time lag in shift from "N" to "R" is longer than specified	Troubleshoot valve body
Incorrect governor pressure	Troubleshoot governor
Line pressure higher than specified in all ranges	Troubleshoot valve body
Line pressure lower than specified in all ranges	Troubleshoot valve body
Line pressure lower than specified in "D" range	Troubleshoot front clutch
Line pressure lower than specified in "R" range	Troubleshoot "R" range elements

AW-70 should be 106-117 psi. be 71-91 psi. Line pressure for the AW-71 should.

Perform Governor Pressure Test

Jack up rear of vehicle and install stands so rear wheels are free to rotate. Release hand brake. Start engine and set selector to "D". Operate vehicle to obtain speedometer readings equal to 1,400 and 2,400 output shaft rpm, when governor pressure test readings should be 13-21 and 58-75 psi.

ROAD TEST

Check Upshift Points at Full Throttle in "D" Range

Set selector lever to "D" Drive vehicle at full throttle from standing start and observe road speeds at shift points. Speeds at shift points should be specified.

Check Upshift Points at Half Throttle in "D" Range

With selector in "D" range, drive vehicle at approximately half throttle and observe road speeds at shift points. Speeds at shift points should be near nominal speeds specified.

Check Coast Downshift Speed

With vehicle running in 3rd gear, release accelerator and allow speed to decrease. Engine rpm should decrease in direct relation to vehicle speed, and a downshift from 3rd to 2nd, 2nd to 1st should occur as specified.

ROAD TEST EVALUATION

Malfunction	Action
Shift lever position indicator incorrect	Troubleshoot manual linkage
Vehicle moves forward with shift lever in "N"	Troubleshoot manual linkage
Vehicle moves backward with shift lever in "N"	Troubleshoot manual linkage
Harsh engagement into any drive ranges	Troubleshoot for pressure surges
Noise in transmission when engine is running	Troubleshoot for noise problems
Delayed 1-2 upshift	Troubleshoot "D" range
Delayed 2-3 upshift	Troubleshoot "D" range
Delayed 3-4 upshift	Troubleshoot "D" range
Downshifts from 3rd speed to 2nd speed, then shifts back to 3rd speed	Troubleshoot "D" range
Slip on 1-2 upshift	Troubleshoot 2nd speed
Slip on 2-3 upshift	Troubleshoot 3rd speed
Drag, binding, or tie-up on 1-2 shift	Troubleshoot 1st speed
Drag, binding, or tie-up on 2-3 shift	Troubleshoot 2nd speed
Slip, squawk, or shudder on full throttle take-off in forward ranges	Troubleshoot 1st speed
Transmission noisy during operation	Troubleshoot noise problems
Slip, squawk, or shudder on take-off in "R" range	Troubleshoot "R" range
Harsh downshifts	Troubleshoot valve body
No coast downshift	Troubleshoot governor
Noisy during coastdown	Troubleshoot noise problems
No 4-3 kickdown	Troubleshoot throttle valve
No 3-2 kickdown	Troubleshoot throttle valve
No 2-1 kickdown	Troubleshoot throttle valve
No downshift	Inspect governor

ROAD TEST EVALUATION

Malfunction	Action
Downshift to first speed occurs above specified maximum speed when "1" range is manually selected	Inspect governor
No engine braking in "2" range	Troubleshoot coast brake
Automatic 2-3 upshift in "2" range	Inspect valve body
Coast downshift occurs above specified maximum speed	Troubleshoot valve body
Coast downshift occurs below specified minimum speed	Troubleshoot valve body

Check Kickdown Speeds in "D" Range

With vehicle decelerating from high speed in 3rd gear, attempt kickdown (press accelerator to full throttle) at 5 mph (8 kph) intervals. Record highest speed at which kickdown from third to second occurs, then repeat for kickdown from second to first. Kickdown speeds should be as specified.

Check Manual Downshift Points

— CAUTION —

Manual 3-2 downshift is possible at any speed. Shifting into "2" range at speeds in excess of 90 mph may cause damage to transmission.

While in 3rd gear in "D" range, manually shift into "2" range. A 3-2 downshift should occur immediately, and engine braking should decelerate vehicle. Manually shift into "1" range. A 2-1 downshift should occur after vehicle has decelerated to speed specified and engine braking should continue.

Check Automatic Upshift Point at Half Throttle in "2" Range

With range selector lever in "2", drive vehicle at approximately half throttle. Observe road speed at 1-2 upshift. Upshift should occur near nominal speed specified.

Check "1" Range Operation

With selector lever in "1", drive vehicle and accelerate to approximately 40 mph. Transmission should remain in first gear. Release accelerator and check for engine braking effect.

Check "R" Range Operation

Set selector lever to "R". Drive vehicle in reverse and check for slipping.

Check Parking Lock

Stop vehicle on a hill with a grade of at least 5°. Set selector lever to "P" and release brake. Vehicle should not move when brake is released. Check parking lock with vehicle heading uphill and downhill.

Check Converter Function

Inability to start on steep grades combined with poor acceleration from rest indicates that the converter stator one-way clutch is slipping or that the stator support is fractured. This condition permits the stator to rotate in an opposite direction to the turbine and torque multiplication cannot occur. Check the stall speed, and if it is more than 50% below normal, the converter assembly must be renewed.

Below standard acceleration in top gear above 30 mph combined with a substantially reduced maximum speed indicates that the stator one-way clutch has locked in the engaged condition.

The stator will then not rotate with the turbine and impeller, therefore the fluid flywheel phase of the converter performance cannot occur. This condition will also be indicated by severe overheating of the transmission, although the stall speed will remain normal. The converter assembly must be replaced.

ON CAR SERVICES

Adjustments

SHIFT LEVER LINKAGE

Adjustment

Start engine and release hand brake. Hold foot on foot brake. Set selector lever to "N". Vehicle should not attempt to move. Set selector lever to "R". Vehicle should attempt to move backward.

Set selector lever to "D", "2", and to "1". Vehicle should attempt to move forward in each range.

THROTTLE CABLE AND KICKDOWN CABLE

Adjustment

1. Disconnect link and cable at throttle control pulley.
2. Loosen locknut screw out throttle shaft adjusting screw, then turn in the screw until it just touches the boss and make one additional turn. Lock with the locknut. Check that throttle valve does not seize or bind.
3. Adjust the throttle control link until it fits on pulley ball and does not influence pulley position.
4. Attach cable to pulley. Adjust cable sheath. The cable should be stretched but not influence pulley position.
5. Depress throttle pedal to full throttle position. The pulley should touch the full throttle abutment.
6. Adjust the cable to the transmission. At idle there should be 0.40" clearance between clip and adjusting sheath. The clip must not touch the sheath.

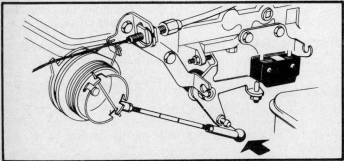

Throttle control link adjustment (© Volvo of America)

NEUTRAL SAFETY SWITCH

The neutral safety switch is located at and directly controlled by the gear shift control lever.

1. Select gear shift position "P". Adjust switch to set P-mark at the center of the switch lever.

2. Select gearshift position "N". Check that the N mark is at the center of the switch lever.
3. Move gearshift selector from "P" to "1" and back again. Check that the control pin does not slide out of the switch lever.
4. Check that engine starts in gearshift positions "P" and "N" only; and that back-up lights operate in position "R".

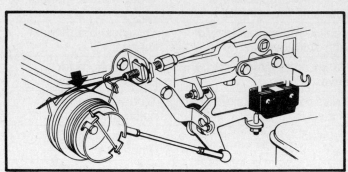

Throttle cable adjustment (© Volvo of America)

Services

FLUID CHANGE

1. If transmission has been overhauled or completely drained, fill with 9.8 qts. of type F or G automatic transmission fluid.
2. Shift gear selector to position "P", start engine and let idle. If converter has been emptied or a new converter has been installed add 2.6 qts. of ATF.
3. Shift gear selector to various positions.
4. Place gear selector in "P", wait 2 minutes and then check transmission oil level. Use measuring range "COLD" and dipstick.
5. Add oil as necessary. Note that distance between "Max." and "Min." marks on dipstick corresponds to only 0.2 qt. of oil.
6. Recheck oil level.

OIL PAN

Removal

1. Raise the vehicle and support safely, disconnect oil filler pipe from oil pan and drain fluid.
2. Remove the oil pan retaining bolts and carefully remove the pan from the case. Remove and clean the oil strainer.

Installation

1. Clean the oil pan.
2. Install the oil strainer.
3. Place a new gasket and the oil pan in place and install the oil pan retaining bolts.
4. Connect the oil filler pipe to the oil pan, and fill the transmission with the recommended automatic transmission fluid.

OVERDRIVE SOLENOID VALVE

Removal

1. Raise the vehicle and support safely.
2. It may be necessary to drain a certain amount of transmission fluid from the unit.
3. Remove the shift lever linkage as required.
4. Disconnect the electrical connector at the gear selector.
5. Clean the area around the solenoid. Remove the solenoid retaining bolts and O-rings.
6. Check the solenoid with an ohmmeter. The resistance should be 13 ohms. When electrical current is disconnected, the air passage on the face of the valve should be blocked. If this does not occur, replace the valve.

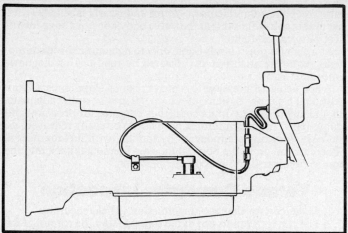

Location of solenoid valve on transmission (© Volvo of America)

Installation

1. Lubricate the O-rings with clean automatic transmission fluid before installation. This will hold the O-rings in place.
2. Install the solenoid assembly. Torque the retaining bolts to 9 ft. lbs. (13 N•m).
3. Connect the electrical connector at the gear selector.
4. Install the shift lever linkage as required.
5. Lower the vehicle and check the fluid level. Replace lost fluid as required.
6. Start the engine and check for leaks.
7. Road test the vehicle, and check for positive engagement of the overdrive gear.

VALVE BODY

Removal

1. Raise the vehicle and support safely, disconnect the oil filler pipe from the oil pan and drain the fluid.
2. Remove the oil pan and oil strainer.
3. Remove all the valve body retaining bolts except the one behind the detent spring for the manual valve.
4. Loosen the final bolt and install the plate retaining tool which holds the accumulator pistons in place. Otherwise the accumulator pistons will drop out.
5. Remove remaining bolt, disconnect the throttle cable from the cam and remove the valve body assembly.

Installation

1. Hold the valve body assembly in place and connect the throttle cable to the cam.
2. Position the selector cam pin within the recess on the manual valve.
3. Position the valve body and install retaining bolts finger tight. Remove the plate retaining tool and tighten bolts to the specified torque: 3.5-6 ft. lbs. Install particle magnet.
4. Install oil strainer bolts.
5. Place oil pan with new gasket in position and install pan retaining bolts.
6. Connect oil filler pipe and fill transmission with the recommended automatic transmission fluid.

EXTENSION HOUSING/GOVERNOR

Removal

1. Raise vehicle and support safely.
2. Disconnect propeller shaft at rear drive flange and remove shaft.

3. Remove exhaust pipe clamps as necessary.
4. Support engine and remove the bolts securing transmission support member. Pull back, twist and lift out.
5. Remove rear engine mount and bracket for exhaust pipes.
6. Use a puller and pull off drive flange, after removing retaining nut.
7. Disconnect speedometer cable at drive gear.
8. Remove the extension housing to case bolts and lift off extension housing. Replace extension housing oil seal.
9. Remove speedometer drive gear and spacer ring.
10. Unhook drive spring and slide governor off output shaft.
11. Remove cover for governor oil ducts.

Installation

1. Place governor on output shaft and hold out lock spring in order to position governor on shaft.
2. Slide speedometer drive gear spacer and drive gear on shaft.
3. With new oil seal installed in extension housing, place housing with new gasket against rear of case and install retaining bolts.
4. Connect speedometer cable at drive gear.
5. Push drive flange onto output shaft and install and tighten retaining nut.
6. Install rear engine mount and hook up exhaust pipe bracket.
7. Place transmission support member into position and install retaining bolts.
8. Install exhaust pipe clamps as necessary.
9. Slide propeller shaft into place and connect at rear flange with retaining bolts.
10. Lower vehicle, check transmission fluid level and road test.

Removing governor spring clip (© Volvo of America)

REMOVAL & INSTALLATION

Removal

1. Remove carburetor air cleaner.
2. Disconnect throttle cable at pulley and cable sheath at bracket.
3. Remove the two upper converter housing to engine bolts.
4. Disconnect transmission oil filler pipe from the engine.
5. Raise the vehicle and support safely. Disconnect oil filler pipe from oil pan and drain transmission oil.
6. Remove the retaining bolts and take off the splash guard.
7. Pry off the rubber suspension rings from the front muffler.
8. Mark the flanges and disconnect the drive shaft at the rear flange. Remove drive shaft.

9. Remove the exhaust pipe clamps.

10. Remove the bolts securing the transmission support member. Pull support member back, twist and lift out.

11. Remove the rear engine mount securing bolts. Remove attachment and bracket.

12. Disconnect speedometer cable at transmission extension.

13. Remove transmission oil cooler pipes.

14. Remove transmission neutral safety switch. On later models the switch is located at, and directly controlled by the gearshift control lever.

15. Disconnect gearshift control rod.

16. Remove cover plate between engine and transmission, remove starter motor blind cover and remove starter motor.

17. Remove bolts attaching converter to drive plate.

18. Position a transmission fixture under transmission and remove the lower retaining bolts and separate the converter from the drive plate.

19. Lower the transmission assembly and slide it out from under vehicle.

Installation

1. Position the transmission and converter assembly on a transmission fixture. Raise and position the transmission behind the engine.

2. Line up and install the lower transmission retaining bolts, adjust the plate-between the starter motor and casing and install the starter motor.

3. Connect the oil filler pipe at the lower end.

4. Install the upper transmission to the engine bolts.

5. Install the converter to the drive plate bolts and torque to 30-36 ft. lbs.

6. Install the starter motor blind plate and lower cover plate.

7. Move gear selector lever into position "2".

8. Attach the control rod at the front end, and adjustable clevis to the gear selector lever.

9. Check control adjustment. The clearance from "D" stop should be approximately the same as from "2" to stop. Move lever to position "1" and then to "P". Recheck clearance in position "D" and "2". Readjust if necessary.

10. Install starter neutral safety switch. Torque to 4-7 ft. lbs.

11. Install oil cooler pipes. Torque to 14-22 ft. lbs.

12. Install drive shaft and attach at rear flange.

13. Install exhaust pipe brackets, rear engine mount and the speedometer cable.

14. Install transmission support member and torque bolts to 30-37 ft. lbs.

15. Install exhaust pipe clamps and muffler hanger.

16. Install engine splash guard.

17. Attach throttle cable to bracket and adjust cable.

18. Fill the transmission with the recommended transmission fluid.

19. Install carburetor air cleaner.

20. Road test vehicle and recheck the fluid level.

Before Disassembly

Prior to the removal of any components, the outside of the transmission must be thoroughly cleaned. High standards of cleanliness are required when handling or storing components and care is necessary to avoid damage to light-alloy parts. Bench surfaces and tools must be scrupulously clean.

Unless requiring replacement, clutch and brake plate packs should be kept in their correct relationships.

When dismantling sub-assemblies, particularly the valve body

parts, keep the components in groups and clearly labelled. To assist in this you will find that the valve body housings have identifications cast on them.

As a general rule it is advisable only to dismantle those components requiring attention as indicated by road test or diagnosis procedure.

When using air pressure to remove pistons from bores a "conventional" supply system of up to 80 psi is quite adequate. Should any piston tip in its bore (thus releasing air pressure) and still remain far enough into its bore not to be easily removed, do not risk damaging components by forcibly withdrawing piston. Square piston up in the bore again, even pressing it back into the bore if necessary, and reapply air pressure.

Torque Converter Inspection

1. Make certain that the transmission is held securely.

2. The converter pulls out of the transmission. Be careful of the weight since the converter contains a large amount of oil. There is no drain plug on the converter so the converter should be drained through the hub.

The transmission fluid drained from the converter can help diagnose transmission problems.

1. If the oil in the converter is discolored but does not contain metal bits or particles, the converter is not damaged and need not be replaced. Remember that color is no longer a good indicator of transmission fluid condition. In the past, dark color was associated with overheated transmission fluid. It is not a positive sign of transmission failure with the newer fluids that are being used today.

2. If the oil in the converter contains metal particles, the converter is damaged internally and must be replaced. The oil may have an "aluminum paint" appearance.

3. If the cause of oil contamination was burned clutch plates or overheated oil, the converter is contaminated and should be replaced.

EXTENSION HOUSING AND GOVERNOR

Removal

1. With the transmission mounted in a secure fixture, remove the propeller shaft and coupling flange.

2. Remove the speedometer cable and rear extension housing. Discard the housing gasket.

3. Loosen the large speedometer driven gear and the spacer. Remove these and place aside.

4. Unsnap the drive ring and remove the screw and lock plate.

5. Withdraw the governor from the shaft. It may be necessary to use a puller to remove it.

OIL PAN AND OIL TUBES

Removal

1. Position the transmission in order to gain access to the oil pan retaining bolts.

2. Remove the pan bolts and discard the pan gasket.

3. Carefully remove the oil pipes and check for blockage with compressed air. Discard the oil filter.

VALVE BODY

Removal

1. Remove all valve body retaining bolts except one behind cam spring.

2. Loosen the final bolt and install special tool retainer plate to hold accumulator pistons in place. Otherwise the accumulator pistons will drop out.

3. Remove the valve body assembly and remove the final bolt.

4. Remove the kick down cable from the throttle cam and lift away the valve body assembly.

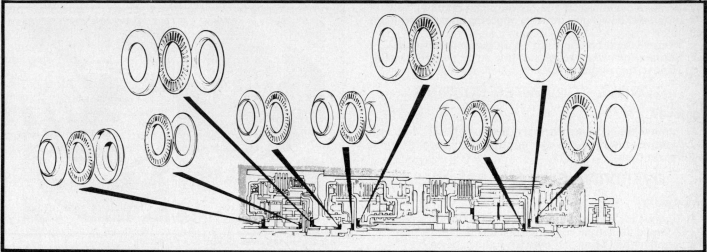

Thrust bearing locations (© Volvo of America)

Oil pipe locations (© Volvo of America)

Feed hole locations (© Volvo of America)

ACCUMULATOR PISTONS

Removal

1. Remove the retainer plate and lift out the accumulator pistons.

2. If removal is difficult, compressed air can be used to dislodge the accumulator pistons.

3. Clean and check the pistons for scoring or other damage. Replace if damaged.

GEAR SELECTOR MECHANISM (OPTIONAL)

Removal

1. Loosen the lock plate bolts (2) and remove with the thrust rod. Remove the parking pawl.

2. Remove the lock ring that holds the cam and tap out the pin with a punch.

3. Remove the oil seals that surround the gear selector shaft and remove the shaft.

OIL PUMP

Removal

1. Turn transmission on the fixture so that the oil pump faces up.

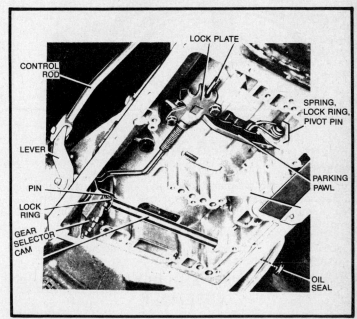

Gear selector mechanism and related components
(© Volvo of America)

2. Remove the hub seals and the oil pump retaining bolts.

3. Install two dowel pins into two opposing oil pump retaining bolt holes.

4. Remove the oil pump using an oil pump removal tool.

5. Remove the two dowel pins. Using an oil pump seal puller tool, remove the oil pump seal.

TORQUE CONVERTER HOUSING

Removal

1. Remove the oil pump assembly. Remove the oil pump seal.

2. Remove the torque converter housing by pulling and turning at the same time.

OVERDRIVE CLUTCH ASSEMBLY

Removal

1. Remove the oil pump assembly. Remove the oil pump seal.

2. Remove the torque converter housing.

3. Remove the O-ring and overdrive clutch assembly.

4. Remove the overdrive housing by lifting out with both hands.

FRONT CLUTCH

Removal

1. Remove the oil pump assembly, oil pump seal, and the torque converter housing.

2. Remove the "O"-ring and overdrive clutch assembly. Remove the overdrive housing.

3. Lift out the front clutch assembly, with the bearing race and needle bearing in place.

Rear clutch removal (© Volvo of America)

Center support removal (© Volvo of America)

Front clutch removal (© Volvo of America)

REAR CLUTCH

Removal

1. Remove the oil pump assembly, oil pump seal, and the torque converter housing.

2. Remove the "O"-ring and overdrive clutch assembly and housing.

3. Remove the front clutch bearing race and needle bearings.

4. Remove the rear clutch bearing races and needle bearing.

5. Lift out the rear clutch assembly.

CENTER SUPPORT AND PLANETARY GEAR ASSEMBLY

Removal

1. Remove the 2 bolts securing the center support to the case.

Planetary gearset removal (© Volvo of America)

2. Remove center support assembly by gripping and pulling on the "nose" on which the sealing rings are fitted.

NOTE: The planetary sun gear will come out with the center support.

3. Retrieve the thrust race and plates between rear of planetary sun gear and rear carrier assembly ring gear.

REAR BRAKE AND COUNTERSHAFT

Removal

1. Remove the countershaft retaining ring and lift out the rear brake countershaft. Remove the needle bearing and bearing race.
2. Remove lock ring which holds the rear brake return springs. A press tool is used to release the tension of the return springs.
3. Remove the return spring thrust plate and the 16 return springs.
4. Remove the pistons with a suitable tool. It may be necessary to use compressed air (maximum 14 psi) to loosen the pistons.
5. Remove the nipples for the tubes which lead to the oil cooler.

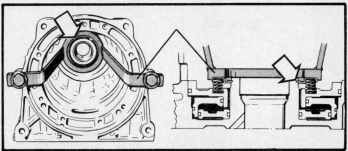

Press tool location for removal of return springs (© Volvo of America)

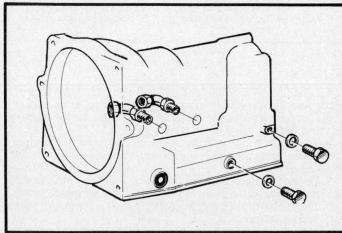

Location of oil cooler tubes (© Volvo of America)

Unit Disassembly and Assembly

GOVERNOR

Disassembly

1. Remove the drive ring, governor weight, shaft, spring and governor.
2. Inspect all parts for signs of wear, abrasions, and cracks.
3. Clean all parts with unused solvent.

Assembly

1. Lubricate all parts with automatic transmission fluid.
2. Install the shaft, spring and governor in the body.
3. Check that the governor does not bind.

EXTENSION HOUSING

Disassembly

1. Remove the oil seal with a suitable tool.

2. Clean the extension housing with the proper solvent and inspect for scoring. If the unit is damaged it must be replaced.
3. Remove the bushing with a drift or punch.

Assembly

1. Install the new bushing with a drift or punch.
2. Install the oil seal in the extension housing.

Governor parts (© Volvo of America)

VALVE BODY

Disassembly—Lower Valve Body

1. Place valve body on a clean bench, lower valve body uppermost. Remove detent spring and lower valve body cover.
2. Remove 5 screws partly securing upper valve bodies to lower.
3. Turn assembly over and remove 5 screws securing rear upper valve body to lower valve body and put body aside; retrieve the nylon balls.
4. Loosen 5 screws securing front upper valve body, then holding against spring pressure, remove screws.
5. Allow spring pressure to release, and lift off valve body.
6. Remove separator plate and gasket, the nylon balls, one spring and by pass valve and spring.
7. Compress pressure relief valve and spring. Remove retainer, spring and ball. Take out the manual valve.
8. Compress primary regulator valve sleeve and remove retainer. Remove sleeve, plunger, spring and primary regulator valve.
9. Take out 2 screws securing low coast shift valve cover and remove cover. Remove low coast shift valve and 1-2 shift valve spring. Remove 1-2 shift valve retainer plug and 1-2 shift valve.

Disassembly—Upper Rear Valve Body

1. Remove 2 screws securing rear valve cover and remove cover.
2. Remove 4 valves and their springs, intermediate coast modulator, reverse sequence, governor modulator and low coast modulator valves.

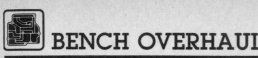
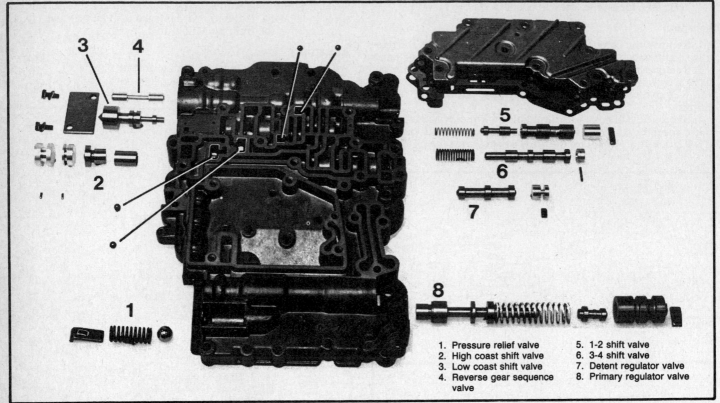

1. Pressure relief valve
2. High coast shift valve
3. Low coast shift valve
4. Reverse gear sequence valve
5. 1-2 shift valve
6. 3-4 shift valve
7. Detent regulator valve
8. Primary regulator valve

Valve location in lower valve body (© Volvo of America)

3. Remove detent regulator valve retainer, valve spring and valve.

4. Take out the 2-3 shift valve retainer plug, the 2-3 shift valve and spring.

5. Remove the intermediate coast shift valve retainer, plug and valve.

NOTE: On some installations the intermedaite coast valve will be working within a sleeve.

Disassembly—Upper Front Valve Body

1. Remove screw securing downshift cam to valve body; remove cam, spacer and spring.

2. Withdraw kickdown valve and spring, and throttle valve.

NOTE: A small quantity of clips will be found on the spring stem of the throttle valve. These clips are fitted when the valve body is built. If they are removed, the same quantity must be replaced or the transmission will malfunction.

3. Remove cut-back valve retainer plug, valve and spring.

4. Remove 2 screws securing secondary regulator valve cover, and remove cover, valve and spring.

Assembly—Lower Valve Body

1. Assemble pressure relief ball and spring and secure with retainer.

2. Install primary regulator valve and spring. Assemble plunger to sleeve and locate sleeve behind primary regulator valve spring. Press sleeve into bore to compress spring, and install retainer.

3. Install low coast shift valve, cover and plate. Secure with 2 screws and washers.

4. Assemble 1-2 shift valve spring, valve and plug. Press plug into bore to compress spring and secure with retainer.

5. Install manual valve.

6. Install the nylon balls, and one ball and spring into their respective pockets. Install by-pass valve and spring in its pocket.

7. Carefully lay separator plate and gaskets on the lower valve body and line up valve block securing holes.

8. Press down on separator plate to compress the springs. Place upper front valve body into position on separator plate and install 5 screws.

9. Locate the nylon balls in position on separator plate gasket. Place upper rear valve body in position and assemble 5 screws.

10. Turn valve block over and install 5 screws. Torque all valve block screws to specifications.

11. Assemble lower valve body cover with 2 screws and assemble detent spring with 1 screw. Be sure spring fits into machined step in lower valve body.

NOTE: Do not use petroleum jelly or any form of grease to assist in the assembly of the balls. Grease will cause balls to stick and the transmission will not function properly.

Assembly—Upper Rear Valve Body

1. Assemble detent regulator valve and retainer.

2. Assemble intermediate coast modulator, reverse sequence, governor modulator, and low coast modulator valves and springs. Fit cover plate and secure with 2 screws and washers.

3. Assemble 2-3 shift valve, plug and retainer. Install 2-3 shift valve spring from opposite end of bore, and assemble intermediate coast shift valve sleeve (if equipped). Install intermediate coast shift valve and plug. Push plug into bore to compress spring and install retainer.

NOTE: Spring specifications can be used only to identify new springs. Do not use the free length of a spring as a measurement on condition. Only a special measuring device can decide whether a spring is faulty or not.

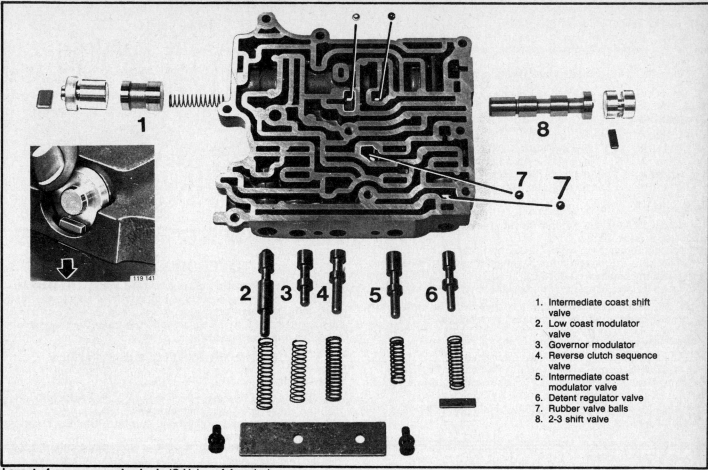

Layout of upper rear valve body (© Volvo of America)

1. Intermediate coast shift valve
2. Low coast modulator valve
3. Governor modulator
4. Reverse clutch sequence valve
5. Intermediate coast modulator valve
6. Detent regulator valve
7. Rubber valve balls
8. 2-3 shift valve

NOTE: Valve retainers can easily be removed with a magnet. Force must not be used at any time.

Assembly—Upper Front Valve Body

1. Locate spring in cup end of cut-back valve and assemble the valve upward into its bore. Place the plug into position and hold it against spring tension to install its retaining ring.

2. Place secondary regulator valve spring into bore. Assemble valve and install cover.

3. Remove the clips from the spring end of the throttle valve and place valve in its bore.

4. Locate the valve spring in position and install the same number of clips removed. Assemble kickdown valve and spring.

5. Assemble washers, cam spring and spacer to hex-headed screw.

NOTE: Hooked leg of spring to engage in cam, compress kickdown valve and assemble cam to valve block. Position cam so that straight leg of spring will lie on unmachined surface of valve block, with slight tension on the spring, the step of the cam will lie against the kickdown valve roller when it is released. Roller of kickdown valve must run squarely on profile of cam.

6. Fit keep plate to throttle valve.

ACCUMULATOR PISTONS

Disassembly

1. Remove the valve body assembly using the accumulator piston retaining tool.

2. Lift out the accumulator pistons and remove the retaining tool. If the pistons are difficult to remove, compressed air (maximum 14 psi), applied to the feed hole can be used to dislodge them.

3. Remove the accumulator piston springs.

Inspection

1. The pistons are constructed of either white metal or aluminum, and can be cleaned with the springs in unused solvent.

2. Check the pistons for scoring, burrs and any other damage or wearing. Replace any parts that are found to be defective.

3. Blow dry all parts with compressed air.

Assembly

1. Install new O-rings on the pistons.
2. Install the accumulator pistons in the valve body. The short spring and the smallest piston are to be installed in the center of the valve body.
3. Install the accumulator piston retaining tool.

OIL PUMP

Disassembly

1. Remove the hub seals.
2. Take out the 6 bolts and separate the pump.
3. Remove the O-ring and the pump gears. Note gears should be marked with a color pen before removing.
4. Remove the housing oil seal.

Inspection

1. Clean all parts with unused cleaning solvent. Blow dry parts with compressed air.
2. Check all parts for wear, cracks, and scoring.
3. Check the torque converter bushing for outward movement. If the bushing has moved outward, it will block a drain channel and cause leakage. Replace if damaged.

NOTE: Pump parts are accurately matched, therefore if any parts are defective, all the parts must be replaced.

Assembly

1. Install oil seal on torque converter shaft.
2. Assemble pump loosely; install 6 bolts finger tight.
3. Install centering tool, tighten bolts. Torque bolts to 4.4-6.6 ft. lbs.
4. Install O-ring in groove on pump body. Lubricate seals and install on hub.

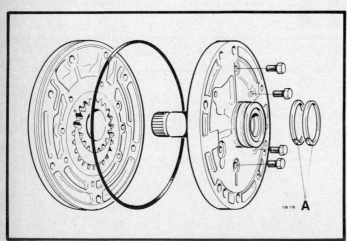

Oil pump disassembled (© Volvo of America)

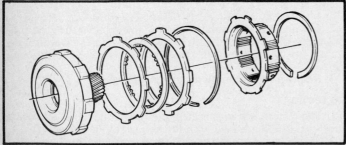

Layout of overdrive clutch (© Volvo of America)

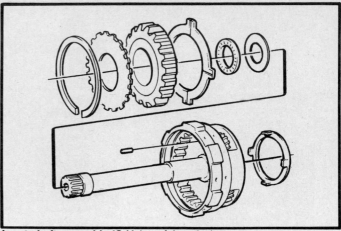

Input shaft assembly (© Volvo of America)

OVERDRIVE UNIT

NOTE: The overdrive unit is composed of three separate components. These components are the overdrive clutch, the input shaft with the planetary gear carrier and one-way overdrive clutch, and the overdrive housing which contains the ring gear and overdrive brake assemblies.

OVERDRIVE CLUTCH ASSEMBLY

Disassembly

1. Remove the overdrive lock ring and the brake hub along with the clutch pack lock ring and the clutches.
2. Unclip the retaining rings and compress the return springs with a spring compressor.
3. Remove the lock ring, the spring compressor, the ring cage and the retaining rings.
4. Remove the clutch piston from its housing. Blow compressed air through the feed hole on the inside of the housing to dislodge the piston.
5. Remove the O-rings from the piston.

Inspection

1. Clean all parts, except the clutches, with cleaning solvent. Blow dry all parts with compressed air.
2. Check all parts for wear, cracks or other damage. Replace as necessary.
3. Check the clutch piston by shaking. The piston ball should move freely.
4. Check that the friction discs are flat and not damaged. Replace any that are damaged.

Assembly

1. Lubricate all parts with automatic transmission fluid prior to assembly.
2. Install the new O-rings on the clutch piston. The O-rings should not be turned in the grooves during assembly.
3. Insert the clutch piston into its housing being careful not to damage or dislodge the O-rings.
4. Install the return springs and their retainer, making sure the rings are vertical.
5. Using the spring compressor, load the springs and install the lock ring.
6. Install the unlined clutch disc at the bottom, the friction lining and the steel bevelled disc outermost.

NOTE: Minimum disc thickness is 0.82 in. (2.1mm) for used discs. New disc thickness is 0.91 in. (2.3mm).

7. Install the clutch pack lock ring, the brake hub and the brake hub lock ring.

8. Check the piston function by blowing compressed air (maximum 14 psi) through the feed hole located on the inside of the clutch drum. Block the opposite hole. A click should be heard when air passes through. This indicates that the piston is functioning.

INPUT SHAFT ASSEMBLY

Disassembly

1. Remove the pressure plate lock ring, the pressure plate, and the one-way clutch.
2. Remove the thrust washer with the needle bearing and bearing race.
3. Remove the oil passage plugs located in the planetary gear shaft.
4. Remove the other thrust washer from the planetary gear carrier. Keep all parts in their correct order.

Inspection

1. Clean all parts with cleaning solvent and dry using compressed air.
2. Inspect all parts for cracks, scoring or other signs of wear.
3. Check the gear teeth and splines for burrs and wear.
4. Replace any damaged parts as needed.

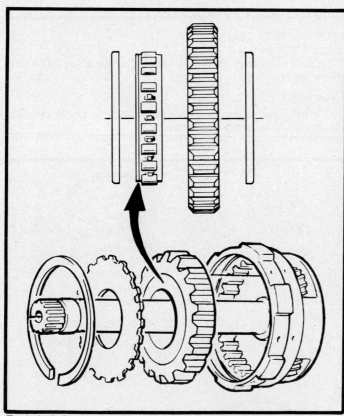

Exploded view of one-way clutch and bearing race
(© Volvo of America)

Assembly

1. Lubricate all parts with automatic transmission fluid prior to assembly.
2. Install the oil passage plugs in the planetary gear shaft.
3. Install the bearing race, needle bearing and thrust washer. The grooves on the thrust washer are to be facing up.
4. Place the bearing race in the one-way clutch and assemble with the outer race.
5. Install the one-way clutch and outer race in the planetary gear carrier.

NOTE: The collar part on the one-way clutch must face outward and away from the planetary gear carrier.

6. Install the pressure plate and lock ring.
7. Assemble the overdrive clutch to the input shaft of the planetary gear carrier, making sure that the carrier fits properly into the clutch pack.

NOTE: At this point check the function of the one-way clutch by holding the carrier and turning the input shaft. The shaft should be able to turn clockwise but not counterclockwise.

8. Install the thrust washer in the rear of the planetary gear carrier.
9. Install the bearing race and the needle bearing on the input shaft, with any washer plugs facing out.

NOTE: Two types of bearing washers are being used for the AW-70 and AW-71.

OVERDRIVE ASSEMBLY

Disassembly

1. Remove the brake pack lock ring and thrust plate.
2. Disassemble the brake pack with the thrust ring and remove the bearing race from the ring gear.
3. Remove the ring gear along with the bearing races and needle bearing.
4. Remove the brake piston lock ring.
5. Remove the spring retainer and the return springs.
6. Dislodge the brake piston by blowing compressed air (maximum 14 psi) through the feed hole located in the overdrive housing.
7. Remove the O-rings from the piston and unclip the sealing rings from the overdrive housing.

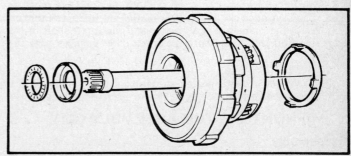

Thrust washer, bearing race and needle bearing location
(© Volvo of America)

Inspection

1. Clean all parts with cleaning solvent and blow dry with compressed air.
2. Inspect all parts for scoring, or other damage and replace if necessary.
3. Check the return springs and piston ring groove.
4. Check all discs for warping and replace if found to be distorted. Minimum thickness is 0.83 in. (2.1mm)
5. Check that the overdrive housing plugs are mounted properly.

Assembly

1. Install new sealing rings in the overdrive housing. These rings should slide smoothly once they are in the groove.
2. If needed install new needle bearings in the overdrive housing. Do this with the housing in a vise and tap the bearings in with a 29mm socket.
3. Install new O-rings on the piston.
4. Lubricate the remaining parts with automatic transmission fluid.

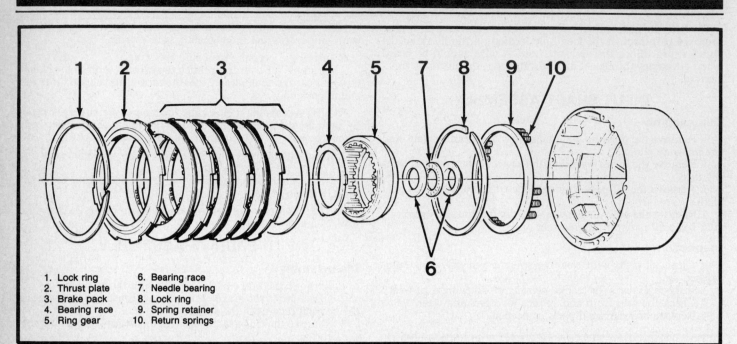

1. Lock ring
2. Thrust plate
3. Brake pack
4. Bearing race
5. Ring gear
6. Bearing race
7. Needle bearing
8. Lock ring
9. Spring retainer
10. Return springs

Exploded view of overdrive (© Volvo of America)

5. Install the piston in the overdrive housing, being careful not to damage the O-rings.

6. Install the return springs, retainer and the lock ring.

7. Press the lock ring into position making sure that the gap is not in one of the recesses of the body.

8. Check the clearance between the lock ring and the pressure plate. The clearance should be 0.014-0.063 in. (0.35-1.60mm).

9. Install the planetary gear carrier and the input shaft in the overdrive housing. Make sure the input shaft engages with the ring gear.

NOTE: When properly seated, the clutch drum should measure 0.14 in. (3.5mm) below the edge of the overdrive housing.

FRONT CLUTCH ASSEMBLY (C1)

Disassembly

1. Remove the snap ring from C-1 clutch cylinder and remove C-2 clutch input hub.

2. Remove C-1 clutch hub from inside clutch pack by pulling on splined center flange.

3. Take out the thrust bearing and race plate between input shaft end and C-1 clutch hub.

4. Remove the clutch plates.

5. Using a spring compressor tool, compress clutch spring sufficiently to remove snap ring; carefully release spring compressor tool and remove 18 springs.

6. Using air pressure blow through drilling in inside wall of piston, while holding fingers over other holes, piston will be blown out.

7. Remove O-rings from piston. Do not disturb ball valve inserted in piston.

Inspection

1. Wash all parts, except the clutch discs, with cleaning solvent. Blow all parts dry with compressed air.

2. Check that the clutch discs are not distorted or damaged. Minimum thickness is 0.83 in. (2.1mm). Replace if necessary.

3. Inspect the return springs, input shaft, hub and clutch drum for any signs of damage or unusual wearing, such as scoring or burrs. Replace any damaged components.

4. Check the clutch piston by shaking to see if the ball valve moves freely.

Assembly

1. Fit O-rings to piston and install piston in clutch cylinder with spring locations facing upwards.

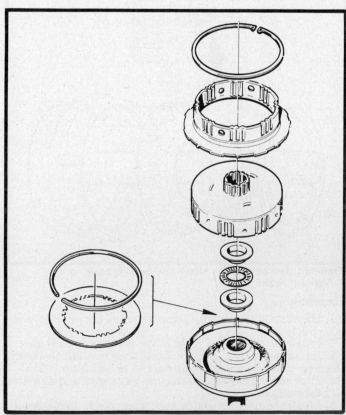

Exploded view front clutch (© Volvo of America)

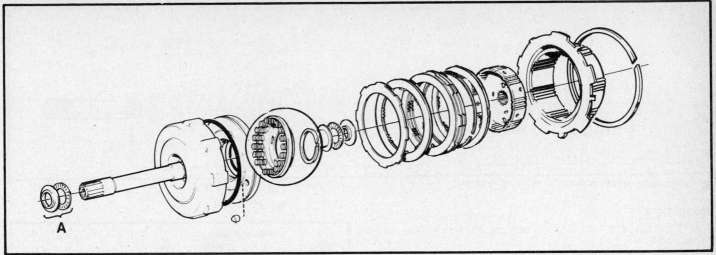

Exploded view clutch pack (© Volvo of America)

2. Place 8 springs in locations in piston and stand retainer plate and snap ring in top of piston.

3. Use spring compressor tool to compress spring, then install snap ring.

4. Place the bearing, then the race plate with flange protruding through bearing to locate input shaft counter bore, to end face of input shaft.

5. Assemble clutch pack into cylinder: start with unlined plate, then alternate with lined and unlined plates.

6. Locate clutch hub into center of clutch pack onto thrust bearing.

7. Finish assembling clutch with direct clutch hub then install retaining ring.

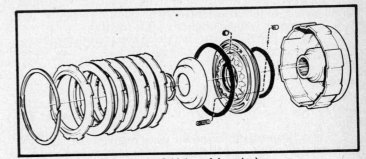

Exploded view rear clutch (© Volvo of America)

REAR CLUTCH ASSEMBLY (C2)

Disassembly

1. Remove snap ring from clutch cylinder.
2. Invert cylinder and shake or tap out clutch plates.
3. Use a spring compressor tool to compress clutch spring and remove snap ring.
4. Remove 18 springs.
5. Apply air pressure to the drilling and cylinder inside wall while holding fingers over other drillings; the piston will blow out.
6. Remove O-rings from piston. Do not disturb the ball valve assemblies inserted in pistons.

Inspection

1. Wash all parts, except the clutches, with cleaning solvent. Blow dry with compressed air.
2. Check that the clutch discs are flat and not distorted. Minimum thickness is 0.82 in. (2.1mm).
3. Inspect the return springs and the clutch drum for any scoring, burrs or other damage. Replace as needed.
4. Check the clutch piston by shaking; make sure the ball valve moves freely.

Assembly

1. Fit O-rings to front and rear of piston and assemble piston in clutch cylinder. Rear (smaller) piston diameter is entered first.
2. Place 18 springs in place and stand retainer and snap ring on top of springs.
3. Use a spring compressor tool to compress springs and retainer, then install snap ring.

4. Assemble clutch pack starting with unlined plate against piston, then alternate with lined and unlined plates, finishing with thicker backing plate.

CENTER SUPPORT

Disassembly

1. Remove 3 sealing rings from forward nose of center support.
2. Remove retaining ring from forward rim of center support and remove B-1 brake pack.
3. Use a spring compressor tool to compress brake springs, then remove the snap ring.
4. Apply air pressure to brake apply hole in outside wall of center support to blow out piston.
5. Remove O-rings from piston and remove brake hub complete with one-way clutch assembly.
6. Remove retaining ring from rear rim of center support and remove B-2 brake pack.
7. Use a spring compressor tool to compress brake spring, then remove snap ring.
8. Unload spring compressor tool to release 12 coil springs.
9. Apply air pressure to brake feed hole in outside wall of center support and blow out B-2 brake piston.

— **CAUTION** —

When removing pistons with air pressure, do not remove both retainer rings and then blow out pistons. Holding the center support with a heavy clutch is a wise precaution.

10. Remove O-rings from pistons.

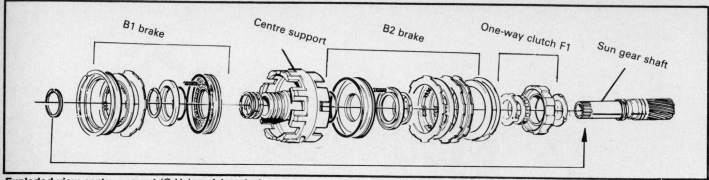

Exploded view center support (© Volvo of America)

Inspection

1. Wash all parts with cleaning solvent. Blow dry using compressed air.

2. Check the clutch discs for warping, distortion, or other damage. Minimum thickness is 0.83 in. (2.1mm). Replace as needed.

3. Check the one-way clutch while its on the sun gear. The shaft should be able to turn counter-clockwise but not clockwise. Replace if the clutch is loose or grinds while rotating.

4. Check the remaining parts for nicks, burrs or other damage. Replace any damaged parts.

Assembly

1. Fit new O-rings on brake piston; assemble piston to center support rear bore (over shorter hub) with spring locations upward.

2. Stand 12 springs in locations; place retainer and snap ring over springs, compress the springs and install the snap ring.

3. Assemble B-2 brake pack, unlined plate to piston first, then alternating with lined and unlined plates. Finish with thicker backing plate, then install snap ring.

4. Fit O-rings to B-1 brake piston, assemble piston to center support front bore (over hub with sealing ring grooves, with spring locations uppermost).

5. Stand 12 springs in locations, place retainer and snap ring over springs, compress springs and install snap ring.

6. Assemble B-1 brake pack, unlined plate to piston first then alternating with a lined and unlined plate. Finish with a thicker (backing) plate, then install snap ring.

PLANETARY GEAR ASSEMBLY

Disassembly

1. Remove the rear brake discs (B3), one-way clutch (F2) and the front planetary gear. Place the planetary gear assembly on the intermediate shaft and remove the front brake pack with the front planetary gear assembly.

2. Compress the front ring gear lock ring and remove the front ring gear.

3. Remove the rear planetary gear thrust washer. Leave the front planetary gear washer in place.

4. Separate the input shaft from the output shaft and remove the needle bearing and the bearing race from the output shaft.

5. Remove the rear planetary gear assembly from the rear ring gear. Remove the bearing washer and needle bearing.

6. Unclip the rear ring gear lock and remove the rear ring gear.

7. Remove the bearing race from the output shaft.

8. Remove three oil sealing rings from the output shaft. Unclip the retaining rings and lift of the hub.

9. Remove the thrust washer from the front planetary gear carrier, along with the brake pack.

10. Divide the front planetary gear carrier from the brake pack thrust/reaction plate.

Brake disc and one-way clutch (© Volvo of America)

Bearing washer and needle bearing locations (© Volvo of America)

11. Remove the lock that holds the bearing cages and one-way clutch and remove these. The thrust washer should now be free to come out.

Inspection

1. Wash all parts, except the brake discs, with cleaning solvent. Blow dry with compressed air.

2. Check that the clutch discs are not damaged or warped. Minimum thickness should be 0.83 in. (2.1mm).

3. Inspect all remaining parts for burrs, cracks or other damage. Replace any damaged parts.

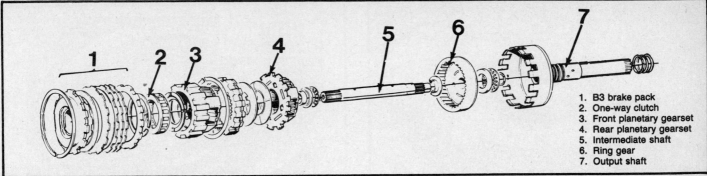

1. B3 brake pack
2. One-way clutch
3. Front planetary gearset
4. Rear planetary gearset
5. Intermediate shaft
6. Ring gear
7. Output shaft

Planetary gear assembly (© Volvo of America)

Assembly

1. Lubricate all parts with automatic transmission fluid prior to assembly.
2. Install the thrust washer with the lugs facing down. Washer can only be installed one way.
3. Install the lower bearing cage.
4. Install the one-way clutch, using hand pressure to seat it.

NOTE: The arrow on the outside of the clutch must point down. This indicates that the flange is facing up.

5. Install the upper bearing cage and lock ring.
6. Assemble the brake pack reaction plate to the front of the planetary gear carrier.
7. Place the rear brake (B3) on the front planetary gear carrier. Thrust disc should be outermost.
8. Install new oil seal rings on the output shaft.
9. Install the rear bearing race and ring gear on the intermediate shaft. Secure with the lock ring.
10. Place the needle bearing and bearing race on the intermediate shaft.
11. Install the rear planetary gear carrier in the rear ring gear.
12. Position the needle bearing and bearing race on the output shaft. Assemble the intermediate shaft to the output shaft.
13. Place the front ring gear above the rear ring gear and install the thrust washer on the rear planetary gear.
14. Place the thrust washer on the front planetary gear and assemble the front and rear planetary gears.

REAR BRAKE

Disassembly

1. Separate the three pistons from each other by hand and lay aside.
2. Remove the O-rings and discard them.

Inspection

1. Wash all parts with cleaning solvent. Blow dry using compressed air.
2. Check the pistons for scoring or any other signs of damage.
3. Replace any damaged parts with new parts.

Assembly

1. Lubricate all parts with automatic transmission fluid.
2. Install new O-rings in the piston grooves.
3. Assemble the piston by hand in the reverse order as disassembly.

Transmission Assembly

Check all parts before assembling, making sure that all needle bearings and thrust washers are secure and located properly. Soak any new discs in automatic transmission fluid before installing.

Three brake pistons (© Volvo of America)

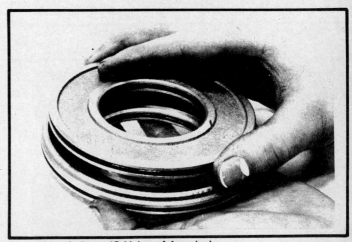

Assembly of piston (© Volvo of America)

Petroleum jelly may be used only to keep needle bearings and thrust washers in place during assembly.

Whenever possible use new O-rings, gaskets and sealing rings during assembly. Do not use gasket sealer in place of a regular gasket.

Dry all parts using compressed air. Do not use rags or any other material which can leave lint behind. This could cause a malfunction later.

1. Turn the transmission casing to a vertical position for assembling. Clean the casing prior to assembling.

Rear brake piston (© Volvo of America)

Rear clutch lying flush with sun gear (© Volvo of America)

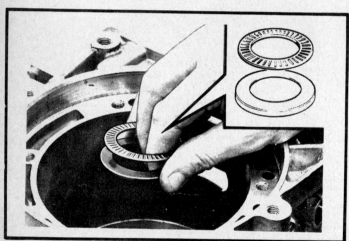

Rear bearing and bearing race (© Volvo of America)

Needle bearings and bearing races on the front clutch
(© Volvo of America)

Location of compressed air feed hole (© Volvo of America)

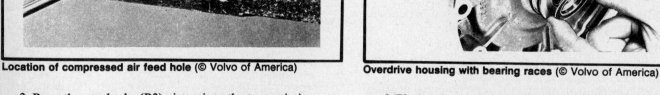

Overdrive housing with bearing races (© Volvo of America)

2. Press the rear brake (B3) piston into the transmission gear case. A spring compressor can be used if needed.

3. Install the return springs and retainer.

4. Off load the return springs with a spring compressor and install the retaining ring.

5. Tighten the screws crosswise using the proper wrench, while making sure the retaining plate is installed square.

6. Fit the rear bearing and bearing race onto the intermediate shaft and place the shaft in the rear brake piston.

7. Lower the planetary gear carrier with the rear brake pack (B3) into the gear case, making sure the recess in the brake pack faces the oil pan.

8. Install the lock, making sure that the gap in the lock ring is between two recesses in the casing.

NOTE: Apply compressed air (maximum 14 psi) to the feed hole located in the casing. If a clear click is heard then the piston is installed properly. If not, then remove and check the rear brake assembly.

9. Install the center support assembly by lowering into the casing above the rear brake pack. Move the center support around to engage the sun gear in the planetary gears and to line up the front one-way clutch.

10. Install the center support retaining bolts. These bolts should be installed loosely while moving the center support around. This will ensure correct alignment of the center support. Do not torque bolts at this time.

11. Carefully assemble the rear clutch assembly (C2) to the nose of the center support. Rotate to be sure all the brake plates are engaged by their hub.

NOTE: When fully engaged, face of clutch hub (outer spline) will lie flush with, or just rearward of, front and middle sun gear assembly splines (externally splined tube).

12. Assemble the needle bearing and the bearing races to the hub of the front clutch assembly (C1). Petroleum jelly can be used to help hold them in place.

13. Assemble the front clutch (C1) and input shaft to the transmission. Turn slowly to ensure engagement of the splines in the front clutch (C1) and the rear clutch (C2) which both connect to the direct clutch plates.

14. Install the bearing race in the rear of the overdrive housing. A small amount of petroleum jelly can be used to hold the bearing race in place.

15. Install the guide pins in the overdrive. The guide pins will centralize the overdrive during installation.

16. Place the overdrive in the transmission casing and check that the overdrive clutch (CO) is approximately 0.14 in. (3.5mm) beneath the edge of the overdrive housing. Install the O-ring making sure it seats properly.

17. Lubricate the overdrive surfaces with petroleum jelly and install the torque converter casing. Torque the 4 upper bolts to 25 ft. lbs. (35 N•m). Torque the 2 lower bolts to 43 ft. lbs. (60 N•m).

18. Fit thrust bearing to input shaft and its race plate to pump with flange lip locating in bore of stator support.

19. Install 2 sealing rings to nose of pump cover; be certain rings are free.

20. Install O-ring to O.D. of pump assembly and smear with petroleum jelly.

21. Fit pump to transmission; orientate pump by aligning suction and delivery ports between pump and maincase.

22. Assemble pump part way over input shaft. Carefully ease pump inwards up to rubber O-ring while turning input shaft by hand.

23. Install 7 pump to case bolts and hand tighten.

24. Using hand pressure, work pump into case bore. Use a blunt "pusher" to work O-ring into its groove.

25. Once fully seated the pump flange will project approximately 6mm behind case. Torque pump retaining bolts to specifications.

26. Torque center support bolts to 5 ft. lbs. at a time until proper torque reading is obtained.

27. Check that both input and output shafts are free to rotate and have end float.

NOTE: The input and output shafts will not necessarily each have the same amount of end float. Both shafts will offer a little resistance to turning, particularly the output shaft in the overrun direction.

28. Install the gear selector shaft and cam. A new pivot is required to hold it in place.

29. Install the gear selector lock ring, making sure it seats properly.

30. Install the gear selector shaft oil seals with a suitable tool.

31. Locate the pivot end of the parking brake pawl in the case and fit the pivot pin through the spring and pawl and secure with a snap ring.

32. Install the thrust rod to the gear selector cam and install the lock plate. Torque the bolts to 5 ft. lbs. (7 N•m).

33. Connect the kick down cable to the gear case. The type of kick down cable may vary with the type of engine.

Center support assembly being lowered into the casing (© Volvo of America)

Fitting race to pump (© Volvo of America)

Gear selector shaft and cam (© Volvo of America)

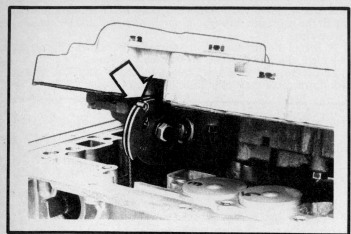

Kick-down cable running through cam groove (© Volvo of America)

Checking converter for fit. Distance should be 0.64-0.77 in. (© Volvo of America)

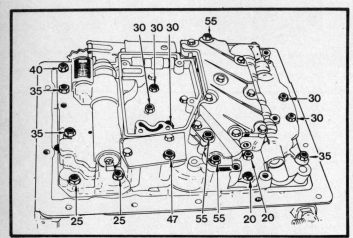

Location of valve body bolts. Numbers refer to length in millimeters (© Volvo of America)

Free play on kick-down cable (© Volvo of America)

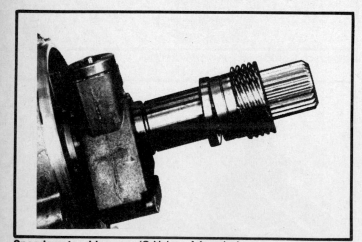

Speedometer drive gear (© Volvo of America)

34. Once through the gear case, connect the cable to the cam. The cable must run through the cam groove.

35. Lower the valve body down into position on the case. Be certain that the accumulators and springs close properly.

36. Install the valve body bolts in their proper locations as to length. Check that the valve body is sitting flush on all its mating surfaces, then tighten the bolts to 7 ft. lbs. (10 N•m).

37. Install the gasket, spacer and oil filter and tighten the bolts to 3.6 ft. lbs. (5 N•m).

38. Install the oil pipes into their proper position in the valve body.

39. Carefully pull the kick down cable until the cam barely moves and install the cable clip 0.04 in. (1.0mm) from the end of the bolt thread.

40. Install the oil pan magnet in the oil pan directly under the oil filter.

41. Install a new gasket on the oil pan and install the oil pan. Torque the bolts to 3.6 ft. lbs. (5 N•m).

42. Fit gasket, cover plate and screws to rear face of case to close off governor feed and return ports in case and torque retaining bolts to specifications.

43. Install governor retaining and drive ring to governor body by first inserting lower leg of clip into tapered "through" hole in governor body. Then insert short leg into blind hole on opposite side of governor body.

44. Carefully slide governor over output shaft while holding

clip leg out to allow governor to seat. Clip leg has to be located in small drilling in shaft opposite the governor feed and return drilling. It may be necessary to ease governor to and fro on shaft to engage clip leg in its hole in the shaft.

45. Install speedometer drive gear with drive ball, retaining clip and spacers. If drive gear is press fit, use a special driving tool to install it on shaft.

46. Install new gasket to rear face of case and a new seal in transmission extension housing.

47. Assemble extension housing to case and install the retaining bolts. Torque bolts to specifications.

48. Fit coupling flange and install retaining bolt/nut.

49. Using new O-rings, install the nipples for the oil cooler tubes.

50. Place new O-rings on the plugs for the pressure gauge connections. Install these in the transmission casing and tighten to 5.8 ft. lbs. (8 N•m).

51. Place the torque converter on the input shaft and turn it slowly until it engages with the output shaft splines.

52. Install the gear shift selector lever and torque to 10 ft. lbs. (14 N•m).

NOTE: When placing torque converter on the transmission take care so as not to damage the oil pump seal or bushing.

53. Lubricate the solenoid O-rings with petroleum jelly and install the solenoid. Torque to 9.4 ft. lbs. (13 N•m).

54. Reconnect the solenoid wire, and secure the wire to the transmission case with the proper fasteners.

SPECIFICATIONS

REDUCTION RATIOS

1st speed	2.45:1
2nd speed	1.45:1
3rd speed	1:1
Overdrive	0.69:1
Reverse	2.21:1
Converter ratio	1-2:1
Converter size	9.764 in (248 mm)
Lubricant	ATF Type F or G

TORQUE CHART

Description		ft. lbs.	N•m
Converter casing-engine		25-36	35-50
Drive plate to torque converter		30-36	41-50
Center support to gear case		17-20	24-28
Pump cover to pump body		4-6	6-9
Pump assembly to gear case		13-18	18-25
Parking pawl plate		4-6	6-9
Converter casing to gear case	M 10	19-34	26-47
	M 12	35-49	48-68
Rear extension housing to gear case		20-30	27-42
Valve bodies for cam	M 6	4-6	6-9
	M 5	3.5-4	5-6
Oil strainer to lower valve body		3.5-4	5-6
Cover plate to gear case		4-6	6-9
Valve body to gear case		6-9	8-12
Oil pan to gear case		3-3.5	4-5

TORQUE CHART

Description	ft. lbs.	N•m
Coupling flange to output shaft	30-36	40-50
Blind plug for pressure test	3.5-6	5-9
Oil cooler nut to gear case	14-22	20-30
Speedometer drive	3-4	4-6
Oil dipstick nut	58-72	80-100
Solenoid valve	7-12	10-16
Oil pan drain plug	13-17	18-23

SHIFT SPEEDS
km/h (mph)

Limits for shift points	AW 70 (3.73)	AW 70 (3.91)	AW 71 (3.73)	AW 71 (3.91)	Throttle opening %
1-2	65 (41)	62 (39)	63 (40)	60 (38)	100 ① (63)
2-3	108 (68)	103 (65)	105 (66)	100 (63)	100 ① (63)
3-4	114 (72)	109 (69)	111 (70)	105 (66)	75 (47)
4-3	40 (25)	38 (24)	39 (25)	37 (23)	0 (0)
3-2	102 (64)	97 (61)	99 (62)	94 (59)	100 ① (63)
2-1	51 (32)	49 (31)	50 (32)	48 (30)	100 ① (63)

① Kick-down position

CLEARANCES

Component	Clearance in. (mm)
Oil pump: pump body-outer gear wheel	0.083 (2.1)
arc segment-large gear wheel	0.0043-0.0055 (0.11-0.14)
axial clearance	0.0008-0.0019 (0.02-0.05)
Brake BO: between clutch pressure plate and lock ring	0.0138-0.063 (0.35-1.60)
Clutch C2, brakes B1 & B2: between clutch pressure plate and lock ring	0.0118-0.0472 (0.3-1.2)
Input shaft, clutch CO: axial clearance	0.0118-0.0354 (0.3-0.9)
Output shaft: axial clearance	0.0118-0.0354 (0.3-0.9)

SPRING IDENTIFICATION CHART
AW70, AW71

Spring	Free length mm (in.)	Active coils	Wire dia mm (in.)	Spring OD mm (in.)	Remarks
Accumulator B2	66.68 (2.625)	14.00	2.80 (0.110)	17.34 (0.682)	AW70: 020, 033
	68.35 (2.691)	13.00	2.60 (0.102)	17.91 (0.705)	AW70: 055
	66.68 (2.625)	12.00	3.20 (0.126)	20.4 (0.803)	AW71
Accumulator C2	61.21 (2.410)	11.5	2.50 (0.098)	16.54 (0.651)	AW70
	55.18 (2.172)	8.5	2.00 (0.079)	15.87 (0.625)	AW71
Accumulator C1	68.56 (2.700)	15.5	2.03 (0.080)	17.53 (0.690)	AW70, AW71
	64.80 (2.551)	13.0	2.00 (0.079)	17.20 (0.677)	AW70: 053
Governor	20.63 (0.812)	1.5	0.90 (0.035)	9.05 (0.356)	
Throttle valve, secondary	21.94 (0.864)	8	0.71 (0.028)	8.58 (0.338)	
Throttle valve, primary	43.0 (1.693)	15.5	1.19 (0.047)	10.80 (0.429)	
Detent regulator valve	31.39 (1.236)	13.5	0.90 (0.035)	8.85 (0.348)	
Intermediate coast modulator valve type 1	25.6 (1.008)	11.5	1.14 (0.045)	9.00 (0.354)	AW70
type 2	27.26 (1.073)	9.5	1.10 (0.043)	9.04 (0.356)	AW71
Reverse clutch sequence valve	37.55 (1.478)	14.5	1.17 (0.046)	9.17 (0.361)	
Governor modulator valve	36.07 (1.420)	12.0	0.71 (0.028)	9.09 (0.358)	Yellow
Intermediate coast modulator valve	42.35 (1.667)	15.0	0.84 (0.033)	9.24 (0.364)	
Intermediate coast shift valve	35.10 (1.382)	12.5	0.76 (0.030)	8.96 (0.353)	
Low coast shift valve	34.62 (1.363)	13.0	0.56 (0.022)	7.56 (0.298)	
Line pressure relief valve	32.14 (1.265)	9.0	2.03 (0.080)	13.14 (0.517)	
Pressure relief valve	33.32 (1.312)	7.0	1.32 (0.052)	13.82 (0.544)	
Shift valve 3-4, type 1	37.88 (1.491)	14.5	1.10 (0.043)	10.60 (0.417)	AW70
type 2	33.65 (1.325)	14.5	1.10 (0.043)	10.60 (0.417)	AW71
Primary regulator valve, type 1	73.30 (2.886)	15	1.588 (0.063)	16.72 (0.658)	AW70
type 2	61.20 (2.409)	13	1.80 (0.071)	17.2 (0.677)	AW71 (AW70 transmission: 055)
Secondary regulator valve	71.27 (2.806)	15	1.93 (0.076)	17.43 (0.686)	

SPECIAL TOOLS

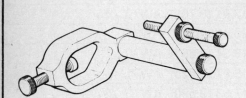

END-FLOAT CHECKING GAUGE

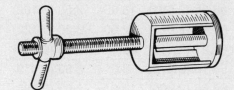

CLUTCH SPRING COMPRESSOR

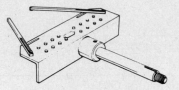

TRANSMISSION MOUNTING BRACKET

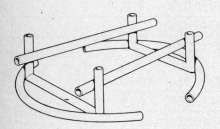

BENCH CRADLE

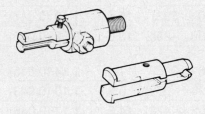

BUSH AND NEEDLE
BEARING REMOVER

PRESSURE TEST EQUIPMENT

CLUTCH SPRING COMPRESSOR

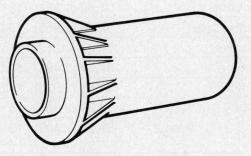

FRONT PUMP SEAL INSTALLER

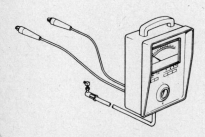

TACHOMETER AND PRESSURE
TEST EQUIPMENT

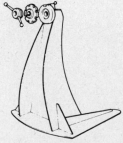

ENGINE STAND

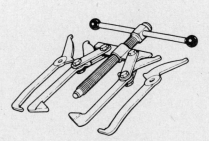

TWO LEGGED PULLER

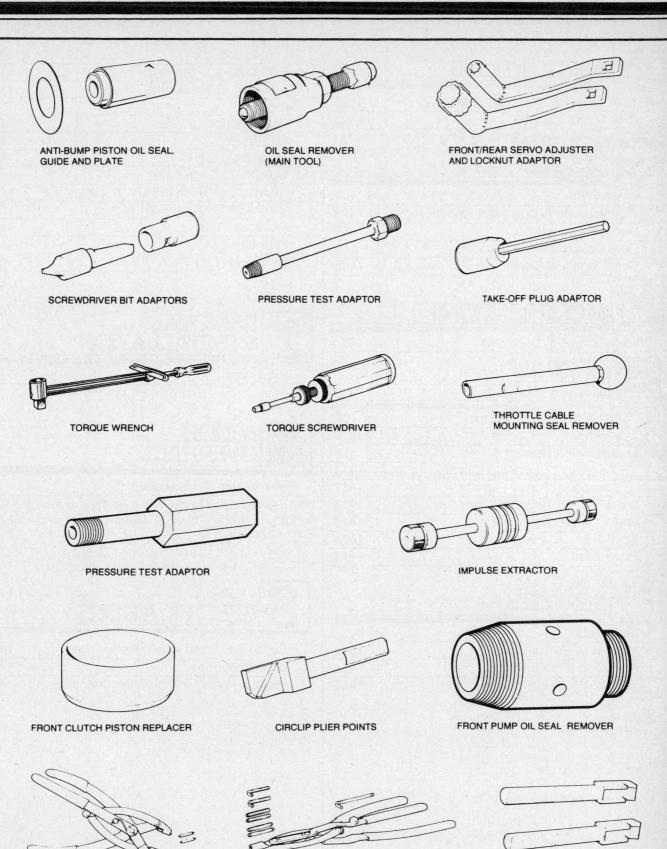

ANTI-BUMP PISTON OIL SEAL,
GUIDE AND PLATE

OIL SEAL REMOVER
(MAIN TOOL)

FRONT/REAR SERVO ADJUSTER
AND LOCKNUT ADAPTOR

SCREWDRIVER BIT ADAPTORS

PRESSURE TEST ADAPTOR

TAKE-OFF PLUG ADAPTOR

TORQUE WRENCH

TORQUE SCREWDRIVER

THROTTLE CABLE
MOUNTING SEAL REMOVER

PRESSURE TEST ADAPTOR

IMPULSE EXTRACTOR

FRONT CLUTCH PISTON REPLACER

CIRCLIP PLIER POINTS

FRONT PUMP OIL SEAL REMOVER

CIRCLIP PLIERS, LARGE

CIRCLIP PLIERS

CIRCLIP PLIER POINTS

INDEX

ZF
4HP-22

A APPLICATIONS

1984 Lincoln Continental, Mark VII W/2.4L Turbocharged Diesel Engine
1984 Volvo 760 GLE W/D24T Diesel Engine

G GENERAL DESCRIPTION

The ZF 4HP22 automatic transmission is a four speed transmission incorporating a lock-up clutch, located in the torque converter and is engaged only when the transmission is operating in the fourth gear range. The fourth gear is an overdrive ratio. This transmission is only available coupled to a diesel engine at the present time.

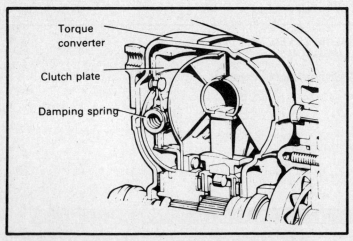

Cross section of converter components (© Volvo of America)

**ZF 4HP 22 AUTOMATIC
TRANSMISSION IDENTIFICATION TAG
(ADJACENT TO MANUAL LEVER)**

```
22-XXX              SERIAL NO.     ZF
1043 010 008   MODEL NO.
4HP-22          ◯
FORD ASSY.    ZF Getriebe GmbH
NO. E4LP-CA              Saarbrucken
```

**PART NO. PREFIX AND SUFFIX
ALSO USED AS MODEL NUMBER**

ZF transmission identification tag (© Ford Motor Co.)

Transmission and Converter Identification

TRANSMISSION

The transmission identification tag is located adjacent to the manual lever on the left side of the unit. Both Volvo and Ford Motor Company have part numbers and model identifications stamped on the tag. The prefix and suffix of the part number is used as the model number for the Ford Motor Company's parts identifications program.

CONVERTER

The torque converter is a 10¼ inch diameter unit with a 2.55:1 ratio at full stall speed. Identification numbers or symbols are either stamped into the cover or inkstamped on the cover surface.

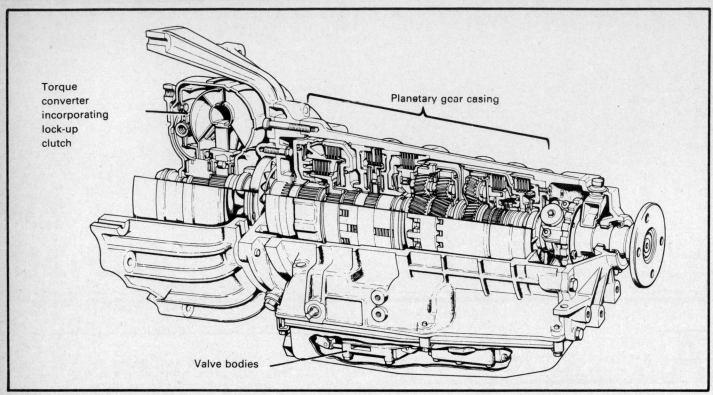

Cutaway view of ZF 4HP22 automatic transmission (© Volvo of America)

Metric Fasteners

The ZF 4HP22 transmission models are designed and assembled using metric fasteners. Metric measurements are used to determine clearances within the unit during the initial assembly. Metric tools are required to service the unit and torque specifications must be strictly adhered to. Before installing capscrews into aluminum parts, always dip the threaded part of the screw or bolt into oil or anti-seize compound to prevent the threads from galling the aluminum threads in the case or component.

The metric thread is extremely close to the dimensions of the familiar inch system threads and for this reason, extreme care must be exercised to prevent the interchanging of inch system bolts or screws to that of the metric type. Mismatched or incorrect fasteners can result in damage to the transmission unit through malfunctions, breakage, looseness or possible personal injury. The fasteners should be used in the same location as removed from, or with fasteners of the same measurement and strength as the ones removed.

Fluid Capacities and Fluid Specifications

The fluid fill capacity with the transmission dry, is 8 quarts (US) or 7.7 Liters. The fluid type to be used is Dexron® II or its equivalent.

FLUID LEVEL INSPECTION

Pre-Road Test Check

The fluid level should ideally be checked with the transmission at operating temperatures. Test conditions are:
1. Engine at hot curb idle.
2. Shift selector in Park (after moving through all the ranges to fill clutch cavities).

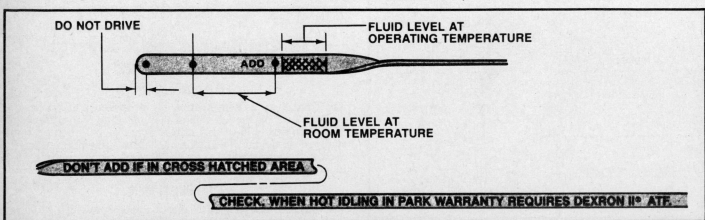

Fluid level dipstick indicator rod markings (© Ford Motor Co.)

For road testing, a cold check can be made. The fluid level should be between the inner holes. If the level is at or below the lowest hole, the vehicle should **not** be driven without adding fluid.

Hot Fill

After the vehicle is driven some 20 minutes, the fluid temperature should be close to 150 degrees Fahrenheit (65°C). The final fill should be in the cross-hatched area at operating temperature. DO NOT OVERFILL. DO NOT ADD FLUID IF IT IS IN THE CROSS-HATCHING.

Leak Check

If the fluid is low, check for and repair any repairable leak.

Fluid Condition

If the fluid is burnt or discolored, or if it has clutch residue, the transmission should be replaced. Be sure to note the fluid condition on the warranty return Diagnostic Form.

MODIFICATIONS

No transmission modifications have been published by the manufacturer at time of this publication.

TROUBLE DIAGNOSIS

The ZF 4HP22 Automatic transmission torque converter and gear train are not to be serviced by the manufacturers' new car dealerships at this time. If diagnosis determines damages or malfunctions are present in the converter or drive train, the entire transmission assembly must be removed from the vehicle and re-placed through the dealership parts department exchange program. As the supply of transmissions become more plentiful, the overhaul by the independent repair shops will be required to fulfill the requirements of the motoring public.

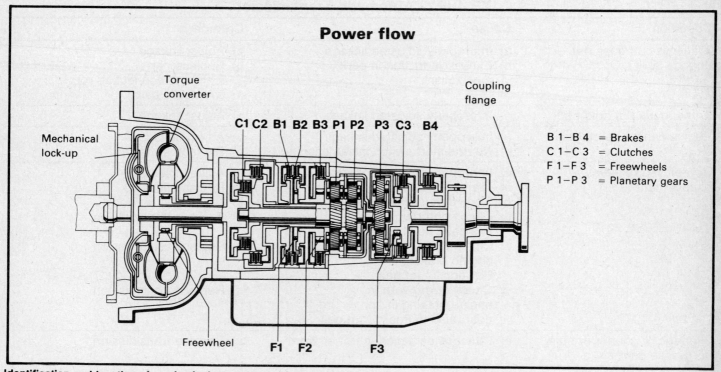

Power flow

Identification and location of mechanical components (© Volvo of America)

CLUTCH AND BRAKE APPLICATION CHART
ZF 4HP22 Automatic Transmission

Gear Selector Position and Gear	Clutch			Brake				Overrunning Clutch			Parking Pawl
	C-1	C-2	C-3	B-1	B-2	B-3	B-4	F-1	F-2	F-3	
P			ON								ON
R		ON	ON			ON					
N			ON								

CLUTCH AND BRAKE APPLICATION CHART
ZF 4HP22 Automatic Transmission

Gear Selector Position and Gear		Clutch			Brake				Overrunning Clutch			Parking
		C-1	C-2	C-3	B-1	B-2	B-3	B-4	F-1	F-2	F-3	Pawl
D	1st	ON		ON						ON	ON	
	2nd	ON		ON	ON	ON			ON		ON	
	3rd	ON	ON	ON		ON					ON	
	4th	ON	ON			ON		ON				
3	1st	ON		ON						ON	ON	
	2nd	ON		ON	ON	ON			ON		ON	
	3rd	ON	ON	ON		ON					ON	
2	1st	ON		ON						ON	ON	
	2nd	ON		ON	ON	ON			ON		ON	
1	1st	ON		ON			ON				ON ①	

① Only transfers power when engine is pulling

CHILTONS THREE "C's" TRANSMISSION DIAGNOSIS CHART
ZF 4HP22 Automatic Transmission

Condition	Cause	Correction
Transmission does not engage park	a) Improperly adjusted linkage b) Excessive friction in park mechanism	a) Adjust linkage b) Replace parts (cam and connection rod, eventually pawl)
Trans. does not hold park	a) Improperly adjusted linkage	a) Adjust linkage
Engine cannot be started	a) Improperly adjusted linkage b) Neutral start switch malfunctioning	a) Adjust linkage b) Replace switch
No/delayed reverse engagement	a) Improperly adjusted linkage b) Transmission filter plugged c) Body dirty/sticking valves d) Clutch burnt/worn, in this case no 3rd gear e) Clutch burnt/worn, no engine braking in Position 1, 1st gear f) Clutch burnt/worn, no engine braking in 2nd + 3rd gear, also in Pos. 1, 1st gear	a) Adjust linkage b) Replace filter c) Replace valve body d) Replace transmission e) Replace transmission f) Replace transmission
Slippage or chatter at start in reverse gear	a) Clutches damaged, burnt or worn	a) Replace transmission
Harsh engagement P-R or N-R, or distinct double jerk at P-R or N-R (below 1500 RPM engine speed)	a) Valve body malfunction (will give the same symptoms when changing from 2nd to 3rd gear)	a) Replace valve body
Back-up lights do not operate, Bulbs, wiring and fuses O.K.	a) Improperly adjusted linkage b) Neutral start switch malfunctioning	a) Adjust the linkage b) Replace switch
Engine cannot be started in the "N" position	a) Improperly adjusted linkage b) Neutral start switch malfunctioning	a) Adjust linkage b) Replace switch

CHILTONS THREE "C's" TRANSMISSION DIAGNOSIS CHART
ZF 4HP22 Automatic Transmission

Condition	Cause	Correction
Vehicle moves in Position N	a) Improperly adjusted linkage b) Clutch seized	a) Adjust linkage b) Replace transmission
No drive in "D" position	a) Improperly adjusted linkage b) Transmission filter plugged c) Clutch burnt/worn d) One way clutch 1st gear slips	a) Adjust linkage b) Replace filter c) Replace transmission d) Replace transmission
Slipping or chatter at driveway	a) Clutch burnt/worn	a) Replace transmission
Strong jerk N-D (below 1500 RPM engine speed)	a) Clutch damper malfunction b) Clutch burnt/worn	a) Replace valve body b) Replace transmission
No or erratic shifts No 1-2/2-1 No 1-2 No 2-3/3-2 No 2-3 No 3-4/4-3 No 3-4	a) Governor valve sticking b) Shift valve 1-2 sticking a) Clutches burnt/worn a) Governor valve sticking b) Shift valve 2-3 sticking a) Clutch burnt/worn a) Governor valve sticking b) Shift valve 3-4 sticking a) Clutch burnt/worn	a) Replace governor b) Replace valve body a) Replace transmission a) Replace governor b) Replace valve body a) Replace transmission a) Replace governor b) Replace valve body a) Replace transmission
Vehicle starts in 2nd gear Vehicle starts in 3rd gear Shifts 1-3 in ⓓ , D ranges	a) Sticking governor b) 1-2 Shift valve sticking a) Sticking governor b) 1-2, 2-3 Shift valves sticking a) 2-3 Shift valve sticking	a) Replace governor b) Replace valve body a) Replace governor b) Replace valve body a) Replace valve body

Shift Speeds
 No upshifts
 	
 Shift points incorrect
 at full throttle
 No 1-2/2-1 shift at kickdown
 	
 No 2-3/3-2 shift at kickdown
 	
 No 4-3 shift at kickdown
	a) Stuck governor
	b) Shift valves sticking
	a) Throttle cable
	  setting incorrect
	a) Throttle cable
	  setting incorrect
	a) Throttle cable
	  setting incorrect
	a) 4-3 Kickdown valve sticking
		a) Replace governor
		b) Replace valve body
		a) Re-adjust throttle cable
		
		a) Re-adjust throttle cable
		
		a) Re-adjust throttle cable
		
		a) Replace valve body

Shift quality Harsh shifts at light throttle Harsh shifts at full throttle and kickdown Soft shifts at full throttle and kickdown	a) Valve body malfunction a) Valve body malfunction b) Clutch plates burnt/worn a) Valve body malfunction b) Clutch plates burnt/worn	a) Replace valve body a) Replace valve body b) Replace transmission a) Replace valve body b) Replace transmission
Position D 3rd Gear No engine braking	a) Clutch burnt/worn	a) Replace transmission
Position L No manual 2-1 downshift	a) Dirty/sticking valve body b) Governor sticking	a) Replace valve body b) Replace governor
No engine braking	a) Clutch burnt/worn	a) Replace transmission
Torque Converter Lockup points incorrect for lockup clutch	a) Valve body malfunction b) Governor pressure incorrect	a) Replace valve body b) Replace governor

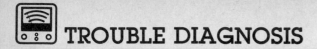

CHILTONS THREE "C's" TRANSMISSION DIAGNOSIS CHART
ZF 4HP22 Automatic Transmission

Condition	Cause	Correction
Shift too harsh	a) Damper malfunction b) Torque converter malfunction	a) Replace valve body b) Replace transmission
No lockup	a) Valve body malfunction b) Torque converter malfunction	a) Replace valve body b) Replace transmission
Throttle cable sticking	a) Too much friction in sleeve of throttle cable b) Throttle pressure valve sticking	a) Replace cable b) Replace valve body
Noisy and no drive after long journey	a) Oil filter on valve body dirty	a) If there is no burnt clutch plate lining in oil sump, then replace filter, otherwise replace transmission
Very noisy and no drive	a) Flex plate is damaged b) Pump drive worn	a) Replace flex plate or transmission b) Replace transmission
Oil dripping from converter housing	a) Seal ring in pump housing damaged b) Pump housing porous c) Converter leaking from welded seam	a) Replace seal b) Replace transmission c) Replace transmission
Leakage between transmission and oil pan	a) Incorrect torque of bolts b) Pan gasket damaged	a) Tighten bolts b) Replace gasket
Leakage between intermediate plate and main housing (esp. at pump pressure point)	a) Converter housing bolts have worked loose	a) Tighten bolts
Oil loss at speedo	a) Damaged O-ring on speedo	a) Replace O-ring
Oil leak at throttle connection cable	a) O-ring connection damaged	a) Replace O-ring or complete cable
Oil leak at extension housing	a) Output oil seal damaged	a) Replace seal
Loss of oil through breather	a) Oil level too high b) No breather cap c) O-ring breather damaged d) Securing clip broken/damaged	a) Check and correct oil level b) Replace cap or change breather c) Remove extension housing and replace O-ring d) Replace clip
Leakage in cooler lines	a) Loose connections	a) Re-tighten
Oil leak at intermediate	a) Plugs loose	a) Tighten plugs, replace washers
Leakage between main case and extension housing	a) Loose bolts b) Gasket damaged	a) Re-tighten b) Replace gasket
High pitched noise in all positions, esp. if oil is cold	a) Low oil level b) Leaking valve body	a) Top off as required b) Replace valve body
High-pitched squeaking noise (dependent on engine RPM) in all gears when oil is warm, accompanied by intermittent no drive after long journey	a) Dirty filter	a) If no debris in sump, just replace filter, otherwise replace transmission
Loud noise when in lockup	a) Torsional damper malfunction	a) Replace transmission
Torsional vibrations from engine when in lockup	a) Engine RPM is too low, lockup shift point incorrect	a) Replace valve body

TRANSMISSION OPERATION

Torque Converter With Lock-up Clutch

The torque converter serves as both a clutch and a hydraulic gear, linking the engine to the gearbox. Due to the slip between the impeller and turbine there is always some power loss in the torque converter when it is operating hydraulically. The lock-up unit, which is very similar to a manual gearbox clutch, makes it possible to mechanically transfer power and thereby eliminate this power loss. This has the added benefit of lowering engine rpm, fuel consumption and oil temperature.

The lock-up function can only be engaged when cruising at high speed in 4th gear. Moreover the transmission oil temperature must exceed 20°C (68°F).

The mechanical lock-up unit consists of a lined clutch plate and damping spring. The plate is pressed against the torque converter casing when the clutch is engaged.

A special valve in the valve body system beneath the transmission, controls the engagement and disengagement of the clutch. To the driver, lock-up engagement feels like a gear change.

DISENGAGED LOCK-UP CLUTCH

Power is transferred from the impeller by the turbine to the transmission input shaft. Hydraulic oil under pressure, directed by a valve in the valve body, passes through the hollow input shaft and grooves in the front thrust washer, to the front side of the clutch plate. This prevents the plate from contacting the torque converter front face. The oil returns through grooves at the bottom of the stator.

ENGAGED LOCK-UP CLUTCH

The oil flow is reversed when lock-up is engaged. Oil flows through the stator grooves and pushes the lock-up clutch plate forwards so that its friction face is pressed against the torque converter body.

Springs on the clutch plate take up the shock of engagement, and the engine torque is now transferred mechanically to the input shaft. Surplus oil returns through the hollow input shaft.

Transmission Mechanical Power Flow

1ST SPEED, GEAR SELECTOR IN D

1. C1 front clutch is applied.
2. C3 clutch for 4th gear is applied.
3. P1 planetary gear carrier is locked against gear case through F2 freewheel when engine is pulling. But is overrun when engine is coasting.
4. P3 planetary gear rotates with planetary gear carrier.
5. F3 freewheel is engaged.

GEAR SELECTOR IN POSITION 1

1. B3 brake is applied and engine braking is obtained.

2ND SPEED, GEAR SELECTOR IN D

1. C1 front clutch is applied.
2. C3 clutch for 4th gear is applied.
3. B1 and B2 brakes are applied.
4. F2 freewheel is not locked.
5. Intermediate shaft, which is splined to sun gear shaft for P1 and P2 planetary gears is locked. P3 planetary gear rotates as a solid block.

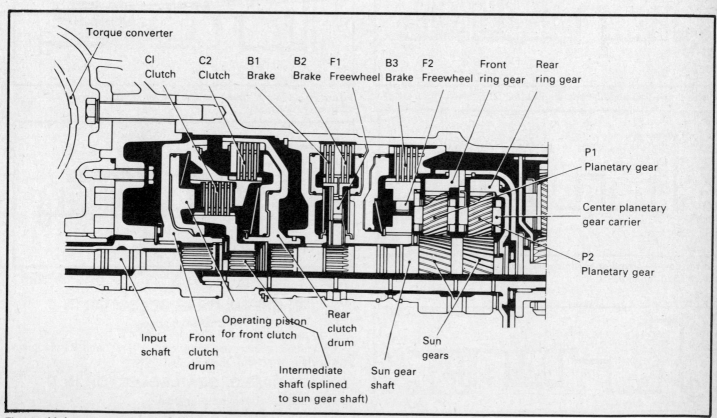

First to third gear components (© Volvo of America)

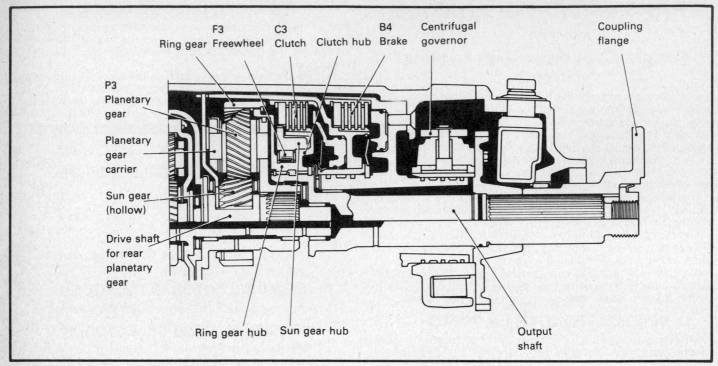

Overdrive components (© Volvo of America)

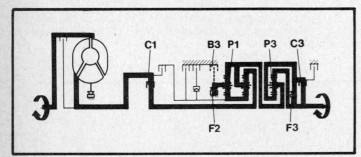

Power flow—first speed, selector lever in "D" (© Volvo of America)

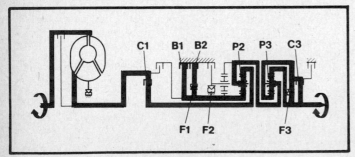

Power flow—second speed, selector lever in "D"
(© Volvo of America)

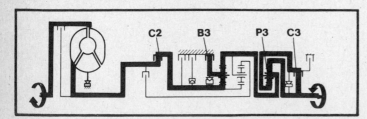

Power flow— selector lever in reverse (© Volvo of America)

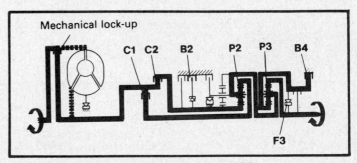

Power flow—fourth speed, selector lever in "D"
(© Volvo of America)

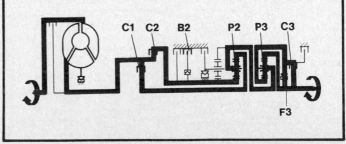

Power flow—third speed, selector lever in "D" (© Volvo of America)

3RD SPEED, GEAR SELECTOR IN D

1. C1, C2 and C3 clutches are applied.
2. B2 brake is applied.
3. F1 and F2 freewheels are overrun. P1, P2 and P3 planetary gears rotate as a solid block so that ratio is 1:1.

4TH SPEED, GEAR SELECTOR IN D

1. C1 and C2 clutches are applied.
2. B2 and B4 brakes are applied.
3. No freewheels are locked.

4. B4 brake prevents P3 planetary gear sun wheel from rotating. Planetary gear, driven by planetary gear carrier, transfers power via ring gear to output shaft, achieving a reduction ratio 0.73:1.

5. At speeds above a preset value the torque converter is locked to prevent slipping.

REVERSE

1. C2 and C3 clutches are applied.
2. B3 brake is applied.
3. Front planetary gear carrier is locked and the output shaft rotates counter clockwise. P3 planetary gear rotates as a solid block.

SHIFT SELECTOR POSITIONS AND OPERATION

FORD MOTOR CO.

The ZF transmission is fully automatic in either the Ⓓ (overdrive) or D (overdrive lockout) positions. Manual upshifting and downshifting is available through the forward drive positions Ⓓ, D, L.

Ⓓ(Overdrive)—This is the normal driving position for an automatic overdrive transmission. In this position the transmission starts in first gear and as the vehicle accelerates, automatically upshifts to second, third and fourth gears. The transmission will automatically downshift as vehicle speed decreases.

NOTE: The transmission will not shift into or remain in overdrive (fourth) gear when the accelerator is pushed to the floor.

D (Overdrive Lockout)—In this position the transmission operates as in Ⓓ(OVERDRIVE) except there will be no shift into the overdrive gear and no converter clutch lockup. This position may be used when driving up or down mountainous roads to provide better performance and greater engine braking than the overdrive position. The transmission may be shifted from Ⓓ to D or D to Ⓓ at any vehicle speed.

L (Low)—This position can be used when maximum engine braking is desired. To help brake the vehicle on hilly roads where D (Overdrive Lockout) does not provide enough braking, shift the selector lever to L (Low). At vehicle speeds above approximately 20 mph the transmission will shift to second gear, and remain in second gear. When vehicle speed drops below approximately 20 mph the transmission will downshift to first gear, and remain in first gear. Upshifts from L (Low) can be made by manually shifting to Ⓓ (Overdrive) or D (Overdrive Lockout). When the L (Low) position is selected for initial driveaway, the transmission will remain in the selected gear range until the selector is moved into another gear position.

P, R AND N—These positions operate the same as other Ford automatics.

Reverse Inhibitor—If the selector is moved to R with the vehicle moving forward at 19 mph or more, the transmission will not shift to reverse gear.

FORCED DOWNSHIFTS

1. At vehicle speeds from approximately 50 mph to 20 mph in Ⓓ(Overdrive) or D (Overdrive Lockout) the transmission will downshift to second gear when the accelerator is pushed to the floor.
2. At vehicle speeds above approximately 50 mph the transmission will not downshift to second gear.
3. At vehicle speeds below approximately 20 mph the transmission will downshift to first gear when the accelerator is pushed to the floor.
4. At most vehicle speeds in Ⓓ(Overdrive) the transmission will downshift from fourth gear to third gear when the accelerator is pushed for moderate to heavy acceleration.

GEAR SELECTOR

VOLVO

1. The gear selector has 7 positions. The overdrive fourth gear and the lock-up clutch are only available when the lever is placed in "D".
2. The start inhibitor switch is located in the housing. It is an electrical switch which prevents the engine from starting unless "N" or "P" is selected.
3. There is no electrical selection of overdrive (4th) gear, all gear selections are made through a linkage rod.
4. Adjustment of the linkage rod is done in same way as on the AW71 gearbox.

GENERAL DIAGNOSIS SEQUENCE

The general diagnosis sequence is the same as for Ford automatics, except that there is *no line pressure test:*

1. Fluid level and condition
2. Injection pump linkage adjustment
3. Free movement of T.V. cable/cable adjustment
4. Manual linkage check
5. Road test
6. Stall test
7. Visual inspection (as appropriate)
8. Do not drive the vehicle unless:
   a. Fluid level is correct.
   b. Manual selector lever is in synchronization with detents in the transmission.
   c. Kickdown (T.V.) cable moves free of all obstructions.

NOTE: Experienced technicians can use the operation of a C3 or C5 automatic transmission with an added gear set for fourth

STALL SPEED DIAGNOSIS
ZF 4HP22 Automatic Transmission

Selector Positions	Stall Speed(s) High (Slip)	Stall Speeds Low
Forward Ranges Ⓓ, D, L	Clutch Slippage: Replace Transmission	1. Check engine for proper tune-up. 2. Check injector pump linkage for proper adjustment.
All Driving Ranges	Check T.V. Adjustment; if okay Replace Transmission	3. If okay, replace transmission asssembly due to torque converter one-way clutch slip.
R Only	Clutch Slippage: Replace Transmission	

gear in the diagnosis. A major difference is the hydraulic application of the converter clutch, which can be definitely felt coming on. Most conditions that would lead to overhaul of a C5 or C3 would lead to replacement of the ZF transmission.

STALL TEST

The stall test checks for clutch slippage, for engine performance and for torque converter operation. It should be done only with the engine coolant and transmission fluid at proper levels and at operating temperature, and with the T.V. cable set properly. Apply the service and parking brakes firmly for each stall test.

1. Look up the specified stall RPM for the vehicle (minimum 2600 RPM, maximum 2900 RPM). Use a grease pencil to mark the RPM on the dial of a diesel tachometer.

2. Connect the tachometer to the engine and position it for easy reading from the driver's seat.

3. In each of the driving ranges, press the accelerator to the floor and hold it just long enough to let the engine get to full RPM.

CAUTION

If the needle goes past the mark, something is slipping. Release the accelerator immediately.

4. Record the results in each range on the Diagnosis Check Sheet.

5. Run the engine at fast idle, in neutral, between each test to cool the fluid.

6. Refer to the diagnosis chart for further checks or corrective action to take.

ROAD TEST

Before Road Test

KICKDOWN (T.V.) CABLE

1. Bead must be tightly crimped to cable.

2. Cable must move freely both ways when accelerator is depressed and released.

3. Clearance must be as specified between bead and barrel end.

CAUTION

If the shifts are mushy, do not drive the vehicle until the adjustment is correct.

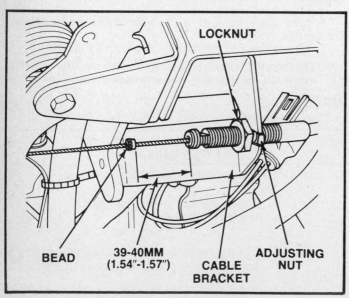

Kickdown (T.V.) cable adjustment (© Ford Motor Co.)

MANUAL LINKAGE

Check before road test. Engine can be off.

1. Pull the column shift lever toward you to "ungate" it. On vehicles with a floor shift, depress the button the "T" handle. Move it through all the ranges.

2. Feel the detents in the transmission. Are they synchronized with the markings on the shift selector?

3. Shift to the Ⓓ(overdrive) position detent and let the lever drop into position.

4. Check if the shift gate pawl is against the Ⓓstop by trying to move the lever toward position Ⓓwithout ungating it.

If there is free movement to the Ⓓstop; or if the pawl is up on the D land; an adjustment is required.

CAUTION

Do not drive the car if the adjustment is not correct.

ROAD TEST

Drive the vehicle in all ranges and through all gears. Use the Diagnosis Check Sheet and check for:

1. Proper Engagement

2. Correct Upshift and Downshift Speeds

3. Any Signs of Slip, Harshness, Mushiness or other Shift Feel Condition

4. Engagement and Disengagement of Converter Clutch

ON CAR SERVICES

Adjustments

FORD MOTOR COMPANY VEHICLES

MANUAL LEVER LINKAGE

Adjustment

1. Put the selector lever in the Ⓓ position, tight against the stop and retain it with a weight. With floor shift, block the lever rearward.

2. Disconnect the linkage at the manual lever on the transmission or the bellcrank.

3. Shift the lever fully counterclockwise; then back three detents to Overdrive Ⓓ.

NOTE: The ZF transmission has an extra detent position, marked "X" on the illustration. This detent position is not used on Ford vehicle applications. It is equivalent to Manual low.

4. Connect the linkage; check the selector is still in Ⓓ; tighten the nut securely.

KICKDOWN (T.V.) CABLE

Installation and Adjustment

NOTE: If a new cable is used, the reference bead will be loose on the cable. Proceed as follows:

NEW CABLE

1-A. With cable reconnected at transmission and transmission bolted up to engine, follow steps B4-B5 and set adjusting nuts approximately in the center of the threaded barrel.

2-A. Pull the "T" head until you feel the wide-open throttle "full" stop, (about 6.4mm or .25 inch before maximum cable travel). Do not pull any farther.

3-A. Slide the bead along the cable until there is a gap of 39-40mm (1.54 to 1.57 inch) between the end of the threaded barrel and the end of the bead closest to the barrel.

4-A. Crimp the bead to the braided cable core with a wire ter-

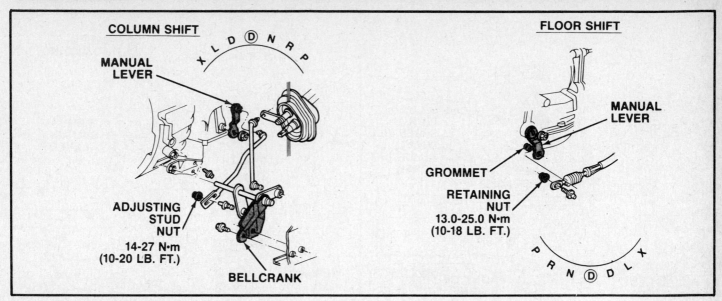

COLUMN SHIFT

MANUAL LEVER

ADJUSTING STUD NUT

14-27 N•m (10-20 LB. FT.)

BELLCRANK

FLOOR SHIFT

MANUAL LEVER

GROMMET

RETAINING NUT

13.0-25.0 N•m (10-18 LB. FT.)

Adjustment of manual shift linkage (© Ford Motor Co.)

minal crimper. Be careful to distort the bead as little as possible.

5-A. Remove the cable from the bracket and proceed to B.

WITH A USED CABLE, REFERENCE BEAD CRIMPED TIGHT TO CABLE

1-B. Rest the braided cable core wire on the split in the white plastic lever insert (7L109) with the "T" head on the trunnion side and pull it through.

2-B. Snap the "T" head into the insert trunnions.

3-B. Snap the insert into the lower rectangular hole in the injector pump side lever after threading the braided cable core through the slot.

4-B. Spin the rearward adjusting nut back to end of the threaded barrel and place the threaded barrel through the slot in the cable bracket.

5-B. Pull the threaded barrel into the 10.2mm diameter hole in the bracket.

Cable Adjustment

6-C. Set the injector pump top lever at the full throttle position.

7-C. Tighten the rear adjusting nut on the threaded barrel until

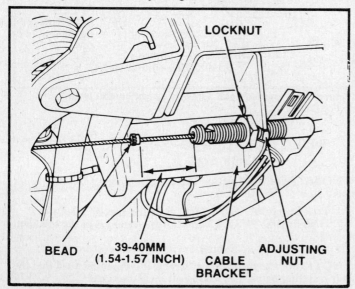

LOCKNUT

BEAD

39-40MM (1.54-1.57 INCH)

CABLE BRACKET

ADJUSTING NUT

Bead clearance on kickdown (T.V.) cable (© Ford Motor Co.)

a gap of 39-40mm (1.54-1.57 inch) exists between the edge of the crimped bead on the cable closest to the barrel and the end of the threaded barrel.

8-C. Tighten the forward adjusting nut to lock the cable assembly to the bracket. Torque to 9-12 N•m (80-106 lb-in).

9-C. Recheck 39-40mm (1.54-1.57 inch) dimension and reset if necessary.

INJECTOR PUMP LINKAGE

Adjustment

Three adjustments affect the transmission performance and the transmission shift speeds: Low-Speed Idle Adjustment, High Engine "W.O.T." (Wide Open Throttle) Speed Adjustment and Injector Pump Operating Lever Linkage Setting. All these adjustments are performed on the injector pump. The Low-Speed Idle Adjustment and the High Engine "W.O.T." Speed Adjustment must be performed before the Injector Pump Operating Lever Linkage Setting. All three adjustments must be performed prior to adjusting the Kickdown (T.V.) Cable.

Before proceeding with any of these adjustments the following must be verified:

1. The engine must be at the normal operating temperature.

2. The valve clearance must be at the specified dimensions.

3. All electrical equipment must be in the OFF position.

4. A tachometer, such as the Diesel Tach/Timing Meter, Rotunda 78-0116 or equivalent, must be attached to the diagnostic plug connector of the diesel engine.

LOW-SPEED IDLE

Adjustment

1. Start the engine.

2. Loosen the locknut on the low-speed idle adjusting screw (located on the top inboard side of the injector pump). Adjust the idle speed by turning the low-speed adjusting screw until 750-800 rpm is obtained.

3. Turn the knurled head screw until the clearance between the knurled head and the speed control lever is 0.5-1.0mm (0.020-0.040 inch).

4. Check, and if required, adjust the High Engine "W.O.T." Speed and the Injector Pump Operating Lever Setting.

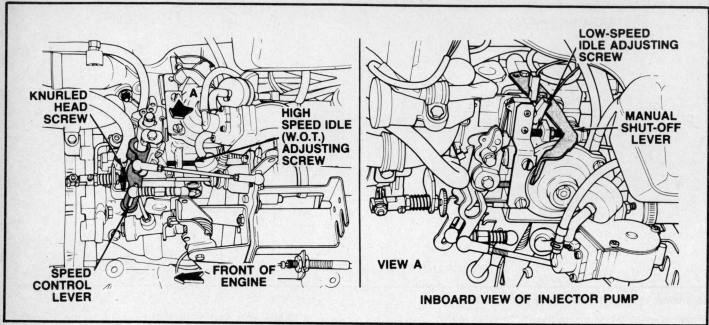

Speed controls on diesel engine injector pump (© Ford Motor Co.)

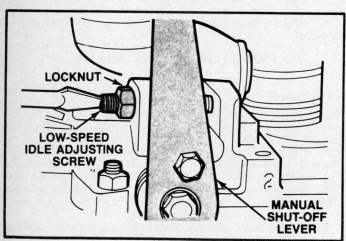

Low speed adjusting screw location (© Ford Motor Co.)

HIGH ENGINE "W.O.T." (WIDE OPEN THROTTLE) SPEED

Adjustment

NOTE: Before adjusting the High Engine "W.O.T." speed, make sure the engine is at normal operating temperature.

1. Start the engine.
2. Move the speed control lever to the full load or "W.O.T." (Wide Open Throttle) position.
3. Loosen the locknut and turn the engine high idle speed ("W.O.T.") adjusting screw (located on the outboard side of the injector pump) until 5350 ± 100 rpm is obtained.
4. Check the throttle cable so that the stop on the speed control lever rests on the engine high idle speed ("W.O.T.") adjusting screw when the lever is in the full load or "W.O.T." position
5. Check to verify that the speed control lever is at the full load or "W.O.T." position when the accelerator is depressed fully to the floor.

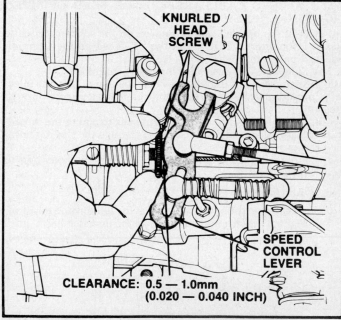

Clearance for knurled head screw to speed control lever (© Ford Motor Co.)

INJECTOR PUMP OPERATING LEVER LINKAGE SETTING

NOTE: Prior to adjusting the injector pump operating lever, make sure of the following:

1. Low-Speed Idle Adjustment is at the specified setting.
2. High Engine "W.O.T." Speed Adjustment is at the specified setting.
3. The engine is at normal operating temperature.

NOTE: For the purpose of accuracy, it is recommended that the metric setting be used in taking all measurements.

1. Measure distance "A" from the front face of the pump brack-

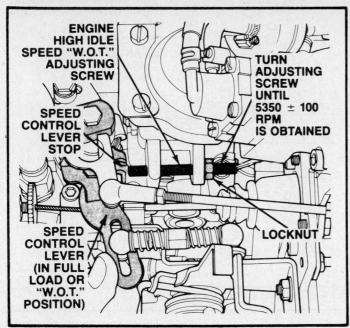

Wide open throttle (W.O.T.) speed adjustment (© Ford Motor Co.)

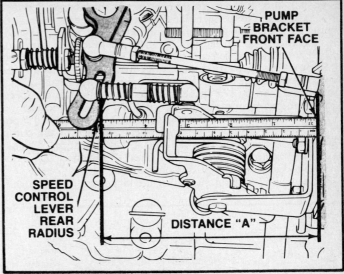

Measuring dimension "A" (© Ford Motor Co.)

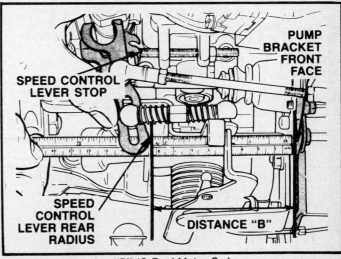

Measuring dimension "B" (© Ford Motor Co.)

et to the rear radius of the speed control lever Record distance "A".

2. Push the speed control lever against the full load or the "W.O.T." stop and measure distance "B" from the front face of the pump bracket to the rear radius of the speed control lever, Record distance "B".

3. Subtract distance "B" from distance "A" to find distance "Y" ("A" − "B" = "Y"). For example: if distance "A" is 128mm (5.03 inches) and distance "B" is 81.0mm (3.18 inches), then by subtracting distance "B" from distance "A", distance "Y" is 47.0mm (1.85 inches) (128mm − 81mm = 47.0mm or 5.03 inches − 3.18 inches = 1.85 inches).

4. Find distance "C" by finding distance "Y" in the appropriate chart. For example: if distance "Y" is 47.0mm (1.85 inches) then distance "C" is 67.0mm (2.64 inches).

5. Disconnect the linkage from the lower stud on the speed control lever and measure distance "C" from the centerline of the lever shaft (on top of the injector pump) to the centerline of the

DISTANCE "C" ADJUSTING TABLE CHARTS
Ford Motor Company

Measurements in Inches

Y (in.)	1.61	1.63	1.65	1.67	1.69	1.71	1.73	1.75	1.77	1.79	1.81	1.83
C (in.)	3.07	3.03	3.00	2.94	2.90	2.87	2.83	2.79	2.76	2.73	2.70	2.66
Y (in.)	1.85	1.87	1.89	1.91	1.93	1.95	1.97	1.99	2.01	2.03	2.05	2.07
C (in.)	2.64	2.61	2.58	2.55	2.53	2.50	2.47	2.45	2.42	2.40	2.38	2.35
Y (in.)	2.09	2.11	2.13	2.15	2.17	2.19	2.20					
C (in.)	2.33	2.31	2.29	2.27	2.26	2.24	2.22					

Measurements in MM

Y (mm)	41	41.5	42	42.5	43	43.5	44	44.5	45	45.5	46	46.5
C (mm)	78.1	77.0	76.0	74.9	73.9	73.0	72.0	71.1	70.3	69.4	68.6	67.8
Y (mm)	47	47.5	48	48.5	49	49.5	50	50.5	51	51.5	52	52.5
C (mm)	67.0	66.3	65.6	64.9	64.2	63.5	62.9	62.3	61.6	61.0	60.5	59.9
Y (mm)	53	53.5	54	54.5	55	55.5	56					
C (mm)	59.4	58.8	58.3	57.8	57.3	56.8	56.4					

lower ball stud. If the measurement is not to the specified distance "C", adjust to the specified distance by loosening the nut retaining the lower stud to the lever and moving the nut to the specified distance. Tighten the nut. Connect the linkage to the stud.

6. Make sure the speed control lever rests against the low-speed idle stop screw. Measure distance "X" from the front face of the pump bracket to the end of the rear ball stud socket Distance "X" should be 68.0mm (2.68 inches). If required, adjust to the specified dimension by turning the nut between the ball sockets.

7. Place the speed control lever in the full load or "W.O.T." position. Measure distance "Z" from the front face of the pump bracket to the end of the rear ball stud socket. Distance "Z" must be 29.0 ± 0.5mm (1.14 ± 0.020 inches). If distance "Z" is not correct, repeat Steps 1-4 of this procedure.

8. Check, and if required, adjust the kickdown (T.V.) cable.

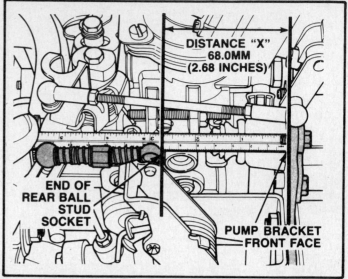

Measuring dimension "X" (© Ford Motor Co.)

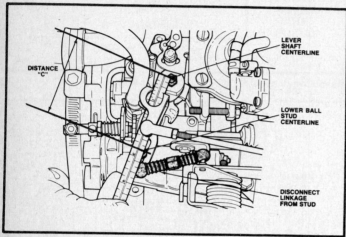

Measuring dimension "C" (© Ford Motor Co.)

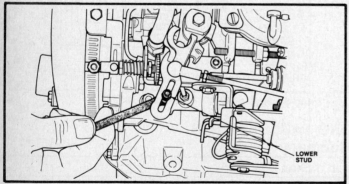

Adjusting dimension "C" (© Ford Motor Co.)

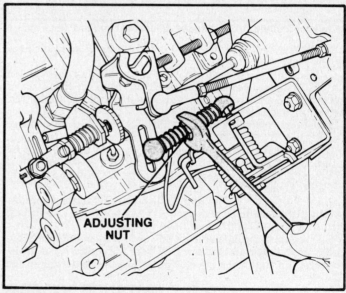

Adjusting dimension "X" (© Ford Motor Co.)

Services

FLUID CHANGE

1. Change fluid at 30,000 miles. Remove and clean oil pan.
2. Remove and inspect screen; replace if damaged or clogged.
3. Use only DEXRON® II fluid. Fill with approximately 3 or 4 quarts (does not include converter) and check fluid level (see Diagnosis section) with transmission hot.

OIL PAN AND SCREEN

Removal

1. Remove drain plug to drain out most of the fluid.
2. Remove the bolt attaching the filler stub tube to the converter housing.
3. Disconnect the stub tube from the oil pan.
4. Remove (6) bolts and clamps with 10mm socket.
5. Use Torx bit 27 to remove three bolts attaching oil screen to valve body.

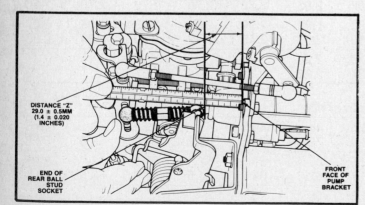

Checking dimension "Z" (© Ford Motor Co.)

Installation

1. Install new screen O-ring.
2. Pan gasket is reusable if it is not damaged. Gasket should be installed onto oil pan.
3. Tighten bolts at assembly:
4. Screen: 8 N•m (71 <u>inch</u> pounds).
5. Pan: 8 N•m (71 <u>inch</u> pounds).

B7390BP11-Transmission-Copy 11-15-Galley 3

NOTE: Two identical clamps without inner radius mount on sides of oil pan. Four long clamps with radius mount on corners. Corner clamps and bolts are to be installed first.

6. Connect the filler stub tube to the oil pan and the converter housing. Tighten the tube bracket bolt to 23 N•m (17 ft. lbs.) and the pan nut to 100-110 N•m (74-85 ft. lbs.)

VALVE BODY (MAIN CONTROL ASSEMBLY)

Removal

1. Drain and remove oil pan.
2. Remove oil pan screen bolts (3) with Torx bit 27.
3. Remove 13 more attaching bolts to remove valve body.

NOTE: Remove only the large head bolts with Torx bit 27

4. Clean case and valve body mating surfaces. Inspect for burrs and distortion.

Installation

1. Position valve body under case to engage detent plate pin in manual valve Ⓐ
2. Pull on kickdown cable to position accelerator cam so that roller on throttle piston clears the cam Ⓑ
3. Then install valve body against the case.
4. Install 13 valve body bolts finger tight to hold the valve body to the case for alignment length identification.

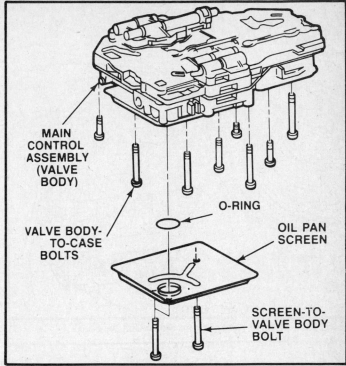

Valve body and screen assembly (© Ford Motor Co.)

Alignment of Valve Body

1. Align the valve body by inserting the valve body gauge (special service tool #T84P-77003-A) between the throttle piston pin and the valve body housing. If the piston pin interferes with the gauge and does not allow it to pass through, use the notch in the gauge handle to grip the pin and draw the throttle piston farther out of its bore.

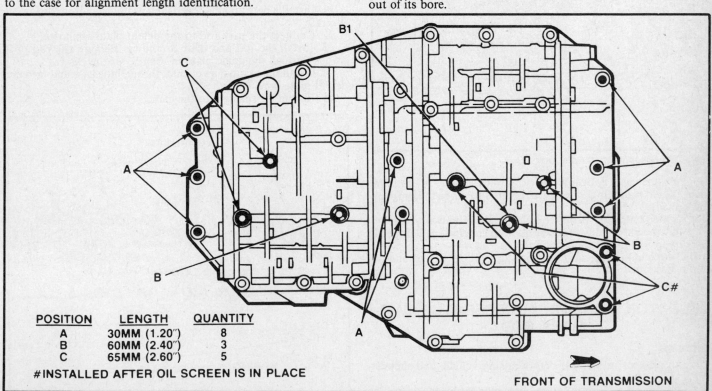

POSITION	LENGTH	QUANTITY
A	30MM (1.20″)	8
B	60MM (2.40″)	3
C	65MM (2.60″)	5

#INSTALLED AFTER OIL SCREEN IS IN PLACE

FRONT OF TRANSMISSION

Valve body retaining bolt location (© Ford Motor Co.)

1419

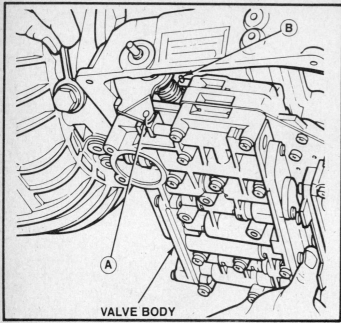

Installation of valve body (© Ford Motor Co.)

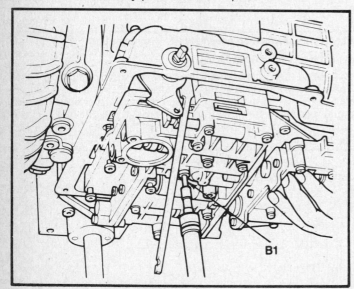

Valve body alignment (© Ford Motor Co.)

2. Push the valve body forward (toward the converter) until the gauge is held snug. (Light pressure required to move the gauge up and down.)

3. Tighten bolt "B1" firmly to hold the valve body in place. Do not allow the valve body to move after this operation. Torque all 13 bolts to 8 N•m (71 inch pounds.)

4. Complete this operation by installing oil pan screen and oil pan as described earlier.

SELECTOR LINKAGE, ACCELERATOR CAM, PARK ROD

Removal

1. Put selector in Neutral before raising vehicle and support safely.

2. Disconnect and remove the outer manual lever.

3. Remove the oil pan, sump screen and valve body.

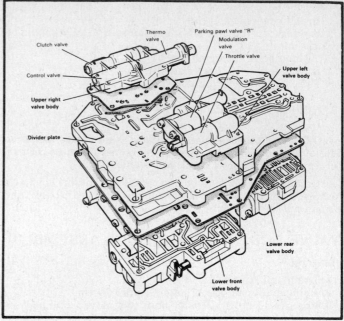

Valve body assembly (© Volvo of America)

4. Disconnect the T-bar end of the kickdown cable from its seat in the accelerator cam.

5. Punch out the roll pin from the detent plate and manual lever shaft.

6. Pull out the shaft to remove the leg spring, cam and detent plate.

7. Unhook the parking pawl rod and pull it out of the case.

8. Remove and discard the shaft seal.

Installation

1. Install a new manual lever shaft seal. Drive it in flush with the case.

2. Connect the park rod to the detent plate as shown.

3. Install the rod and plate as shown. Be sure the rod protrudes through the guide plate in the rear of the case.

4. Install the manual lever shaft through the case and into the detent plate bore.

5. Fit the leg spring into the cam.

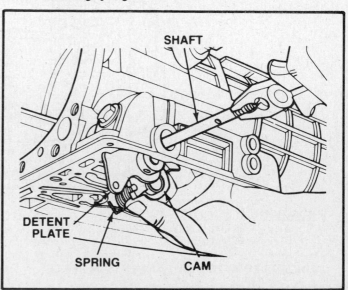

Removing manual lever shaft (© Ford Motor Co.)

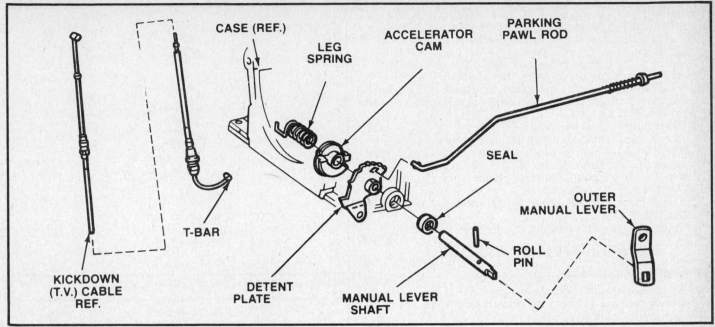

Exploded view of selector internal linkage (© Ford Motor Co.)

6. Install the cam and spring in the case, with the leg of the spring on the cast support.

7. Push the shaft in until it stops.

8. Align the holes in the shaft and detent plate.

9. Install a new roll pin with the slot to the rear of the transmission.

10. Revolve the cam once to tension the leg spring; then seat the T-bar end of the cable in the cam.

11. Install the valve body, screen and oil pan.

NEUTRAL START SWITCH

1. The switch is located just forward of the manual lever, near the cooler return line fitting.

2. There is no switch adjustment.

Replacement

1. Disconnect the electrical connector and remove the bolt, washer and retainer plate to remove the switch. Reverse the procedure to install it. Tighten the bolt to 10 N•m (88 inch pounds) torque.

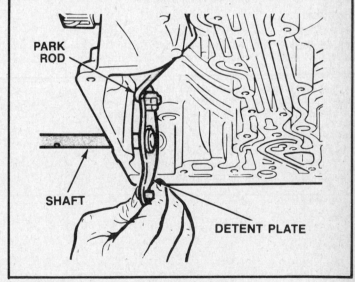

Installing the manual lever shaft (© Ford Motor Co.)

EXTENSION HOUSING

Removal

1. Raise the vehicle and support safely.

2. Remove the driveshaft. To maintain initial driveshaft balance, mark the rear driveshaft yoke and axle companion flange so they can be installed in their original position.

3. Position a transmission jack to support the transmission.

4. Remove the speedometer cable from the extension housing.

5. Remove the engine rear support to crossmember attaching nuts.

6. Raise the transmission and remove the rear support to body bracket through bolts. Remove the crossmember.

7. Loosen the extension housing attaching bolts and allow the transmission to drain.

8. Remove the nine extension housing-to-case attaching bolts and remove housing.

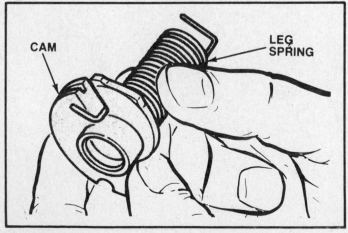

Fitting the spring leg to the cam (© Ford Motor Co.)

Installation

1. Install a new extension housing gasket on the case. Install the extension housing. Install and tighten nine attaching bolts to 23 N•m (17 ft. lbs.).
2. Position the crossmember and install the through bolts. Tighten the attaching nuts to 48-88 N•m (36-50 ft. lbs.).
3. Lower the transmission and install the engine rear support-to-crossmember attaching nuts. Tighten the attaching nuts to 48-68 N•m (30-50 ft. lbs.).
4. Remove the transmission jack.
5. Install the speedometer cable in the extension housing.
6. Install the driveshaft in the transmission. Connect the driveshaft to the rear axle flange so that the index marks, made during disassembly, are aligned. Lubricate the slip yoke splines with C1AZ-19590-B grease or equivalent.
7. Lower the vehicle and fill the transmission with fluid (DEXRON® II).
8. Check the extension housing area for fluid leakage.

BREATHER (VENT) ASSEMBLY

Removal and Installation

1. Remove extension housing.
2. Remove locking washer with channel lock pliers.
3. Remove breather from inside extension housing.
4. Use new O-ring and new locking washer for assembly.

GOVERNOR

Removal

1. Remove driveshaft and extension housing.
2. Remove interlocking snap ring behind parking gear; and slide parking gear and governor off of shaft and hub of rear clutch housing.

NOTE: If necessary, pry split driver spline rings out from between parking gear and shaft: one at a time. Use a plastic hammer at installation, if needed, to tap rings into place.

Installation

1. Replace any of the following that are damaged.
   a. O-ring on output shaft forward of park gear splines.
   b. Steel ring on output shaft forward of O-ring.

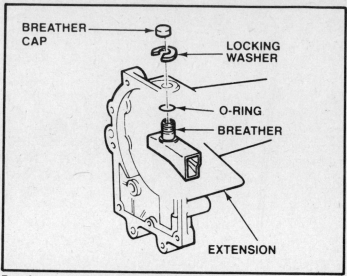

Breather assembly location (© Ford Motor Co.)

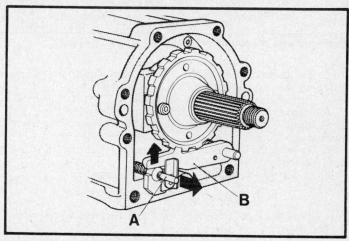

Parking pawl mechanism (© Volvo of America)

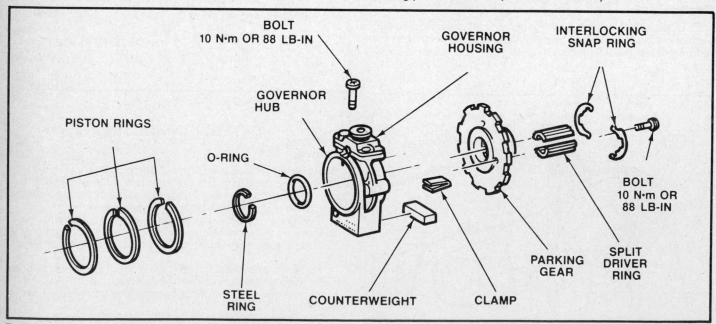

Exploded view of governor assembly (© Ford Motor Co.)

c. Piston rings on hub of rear clutch housing.

2. Unbolt parking gear if necessary for access to clamp and counterweight. Governor housing may be unbolted from hub for inspection. Torque governor housing and parking gear bolts to 10 N•m (88 inch lbs.).

PARK LOCK

Removal and Installation

1. Remove extension housing and parking gear/governor assembly.
2. Unbolt guide plates from case and remove.
3. Pull pawl and spring off shaft; remove shaft from case.
4. Reverse procedure to install. Set the spring tension by placing the 90° leg of the spring into the hole in the pawl (twist clockwise).

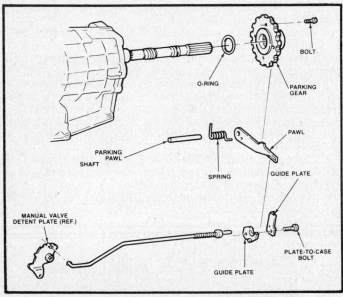

Exploded view of park lock components (© Ford Motor Co.)

KICKDOWN (T.V.) CABLE

Removal and Installation

1. In the engine compartment, remove the cable and insert from the injector pump side lever and cable bracket.
2. Raise the vehicle and support safely.
3. Remove the oil pan, sump screen and valve body as described earlier.
4. Carefully pry the cable out of the case with two screwdrivers as shown. (Push in by hand when reinstalling the cable.)
5. Unhook the T-bar end of the cable from the accelerator cam and remove the cable.
6. Reverse the above procedure to connect the cable.

NOTE: Before installing and adjusting the kickdown (T.V.) cable, perform the Injector Pump Linkage Adjustment.

 REMOVAL & INSTALLATION

Removal

FORD MOTOR COMPANY VEHICLES

1. Remove the Kickdown (T.V.) Cable and insert from the injector pump side lever and cable bracket to the engine compartment.
2. Place the transmission selector lever in N (Neutral). Raise the vehicle and support safely.

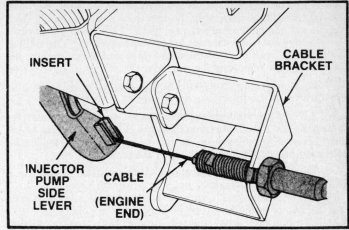

Engine compartment end of kickdown (T.V.) cable (© Ford Motor Co.)

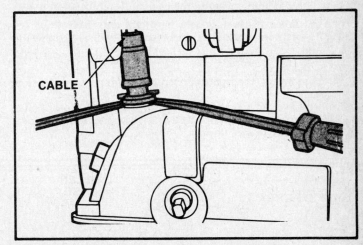

Removing cable housing from case (© Ford Motor Co.)

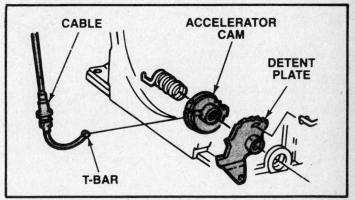

Removal of "T" bar from the accelerator cam (© Ford Motor Co.)

3. Remove the outer manual lever and nut from the transmission selector shaft.
4. Remove the engine brace from the lower end of the converter housing and engine block.
5. Place a transmission jack under the transmission.
6. Remove the converter-to-flywheel attaching nuts. Place a wrench on the crankshaft pulley attaching bolt to turn the converter to gain access to the nuts.

NOTE: The converter studs are installed in the converter with Loc-Tite. During disassembly the nuts may override the Loc-Tite and the nut and stud come out as a "bolt." This poses no concern. The stud and converter threads are to be cleaned, Loc-Tite applied and the "bolt" can be reinstalled and tightened to normal specifications without removing the nut from the stud.

7. Disconnect the driveshaft from the rear axle and slide shaft rearward from the transmission.

NOTE: To maintain driveshaft balance, mark the rear drive-shaft yoke and axle companion flange so the driveshaft can be installed in its original position. Install a seal installation tool in the extension housing to prevent fluid leakage.

8. Disconnect the neutral start switch electrical connector.
9. Remove the extension housing damper.
10. Remove the rear mount-to-crossmember attaching nuts and the two crossmember-to-side support attaching bolts.
11. Remove the two engine rear support-to-extension housing attaching bolts and remove the rear mount from the exhaust system.
12. On Continental with column shift, remove the two bolts securing the bellcrank bracket to the engine to transmission brace.

NOTE: Some exhaust system hardware may have to be removed to facilitate removal of crossmember and transmission.

13. Disconnect each oil line from the fittings on the transmission.
14. Disconnect the speedometer cable from the extension housing.
15. Remove the (2) converter housing to starter motor bolts.
16. Secure the transmission to the jack with the chain and lower it slightly.

17. Remove the (4) converter housing-to-cylinder block attaching bolts.
18. Remove the filler tube and dipstick.
19. Carefully move the transmission and converter assembly away from the engine and, at the same time, lower the jack to clear the underside of the vehicle.

Installation

1. Place the transmission on the jack. Secure the transmission to the jack with a chain.
2. Rotate the converter until the studs are in alignment with the holes in the flywheel and flexplate.
3. Move the converter and transmission assembly forward into position, using care not to damage the flywheel, flexplate, and the converter pilot. The converter face must rest squarely against the flexplate. This indicates that the converter pilot is not binding in the engine crankshaft.
4. Install the filler tube and dipstick, position bracket over the upper right housing to engine bolt hole.
5. Install and tighten the (4) converter housing-to-engine attaching bolts to 52-65 N•m (38-48 ft. lbs.).
6. Remove the safety chain from around the transmission.
7. Connect the oil cooler lines by pushing them into the fittings on the transmission (located on the intermediate plate).
8. Connect the speedometer cable to the extension housing.
9. Install the extension housing damper. Torque the bolts to 24-34 N•m (18-25 ft. lbs.).
10. Secure the crossmember on the side support and install the attaching bolts and nuts. Position the rear mount on the crossmember and tighten nuts to specification.
11. Install the rear mount on to the exhaust system. Secure the

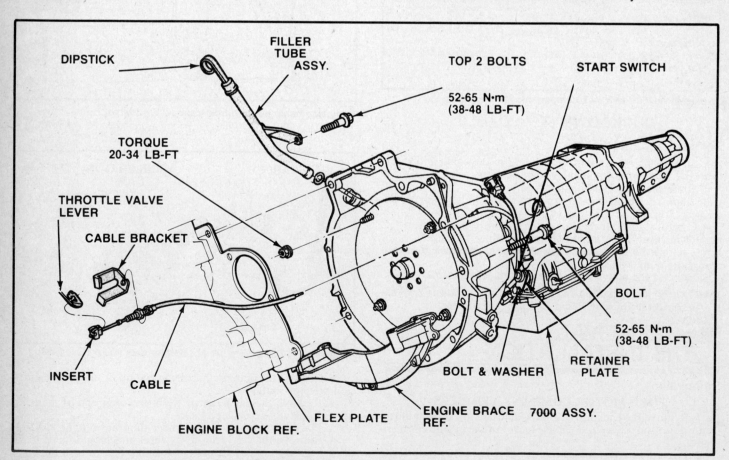

Removal or installation of transmission and converter assembly (© Ford Motor Co.)

engine rear support to the extension housing and tighten the bolts to specification.

12. If removed, install exhaust system hardware.

13. Lower the transmission and remove the jack.

14. On Continental column shift, position the bellcrank to the engine to transmission brace and install the two attaching bolts. Torque the bolts to 14-27 N•m (10-20 ft. lbs.).

15. Guide the Kickdown (T.V.) Cable up into the engine compartment.

16. Install the outer manual lever on the transmission selector shaft. Torque the nut to 14-27 N•m (10-20 ft. lbs.).

17. Install the converter to flywheel attaching nuts (or "bolts") and torque them to 27-46 N•m (20-34 ft. lbs.)

18. Install the engine brace on the lower end of the converter housing and engine block. Torque the bolts to 20-24 N•m (15-18 ft. lbs.).

19. Connect the neutral start switch harness at the transmission.

20. Connect the driveshaft to the rear axle. Install the driveshaft so the index marks, made during removal, are correctly aligned.

NOTE: Lubricate the yoke splines.

21. Adjust the manual shift linkage.

22. Lower the vehicle and adjust the Kickdown (T.V.) Cable.

23. Fill the transmission to the correct level with the specified fluid (Dexron® II). Start the engine and shift the transmission to all ranges, then recheck the fluid level.

CONVERTER HOUSING AND INTERMEDIATE PLATE GASKET

Removal

Remove transmission and converter assembly from car as just described. (If the studs come out of the converter cover, screw them back in.)

Use tool handles to remove converter assembly from the transmission.

NOTE: Oil will be running out of converter. Handle carefully to avoid damage to pump bushing and oil seal lip.

Place transmission on work bench.

To Service Gasket Only

Remove 12 long 17mm bolts closest to pump shaft. Pull converter housing and intermediate plate assembly away as a unit. Be careful not to disturb input shaft and clutch cylinder.

To install, be sure thrust washers and thrust bearing are properly positioned as in inset view. Use petroleum jelly to hold in place while plate is assembled to transmission.

To Replace Converter Housing

Remove 6 short 17mm bolts farthest from pump shaft.

Tighten all bolts to 46 N•m (34 ft. lbs.)

With the transmission in a horizontal position, use handles to install converter. Guide it carefully onto pump shaft until it seats.

Removal
VOLVO MODELS

1. Remove air cleaner.

2. Disconnect throttle cable at pulley and cable sheath at bracket.

3. Remove the two upper converter housing to engine bolts.

4. Disconnect tranmission oil filler pipe from the engine.

5. Raise the vehicle and support safely. Disconnect oil filler pipe from oil pan and drain transmission oil.

6. Remove the retaining bolts and take off the splash guard.

7. Pry off the rubber suspension rings from the front muffler.

8. Mark the flanges and disconnect the drive shaft at the rear flange. Remove drive shaft.

9. Remove the exhaust pipe clamps.

10. Remove the bolts securing the transmission support member. Pull support member back, twist and lift out.

11. Remove the rear engine mount securing bolts. Remove attachment and bracket.

12. Disconnect speedometer cable at transmission extension.

13. Remove transmission oil cooler pipes.

14. Remove transmission neutral safety switch. On later models the switch is located at, and directly controlled by the gearshift control lever.

15. Disconnect gearshift control rod.

16. Remove cover plate between engine and transmission, remove starter motor blind cover and remove starter motor.

17. Remove bolts attaching converter to drive plate.

18. Position a transmission fixture under transmission and remove the lower retaining bolts and separate the converter from the drive plate.

19. Lower the transmission assembly and slide it out from under vehicle.

Installation

1. Position the transmission and converter assembly on a transmission fixture. Raise and position the transmission behind the engine.

2. Line up and install the lower transmission retaining bolts, adjust the plate between the starter motor and casing and install the starter motor.

3. Connect the oil filler pipe at the lower end.

4. Install the upper transmission to the engine bolts.

5. Install the converter to the drive plate bolts and torque to 30-36 ft. lbs.

6. Install the starter motor blind plate and lower cover plate.

7. Move gear selector lever into position 2.

8. Attach the control rod at the front end, and adjustable clevis to the gear selector lever.

9. Check control adjustment. The clearance from "D" stop should be approximately the same as from "2" to stop. Move lever to position "1" and then to "P". Recheck clearance in position "D" and "2". Readjust if necessary.

10. Install starter neutral safety switch. Torque to 4-7 ft. lbs.

11. Install oil cooler pipes. Torque to 14-22 ft. lbs.

12. Install drive shaft and attach at rear flange.

13. Install exhaust pipe brackets, rear engine mount and the speedometer cable.

14. Install transmission support member and torque bolts to 30-37 ft. lbs.

15. Install exhaust pipe clamps and muffler suspender.

16. Install engine splash guard.

17. Attach throttle cable to bracket and adjust cable.

18. Fill the transmission with the recommended transmission fluid.

19. Install air cleaner.

20. Road test vehicle and recheck the fluid level.

AUTOMATIC TRANSMISSION THROTTLE CABLE

Adjust

1. Check for wear.

2. Depress accelerator pedal to floor. Do not move throttle control by hand as incorrect adjustment may result.

3. With accelerator pedal fully depressed measurement between cable sheath and clip should be 50.4-52.6mm (1.98-2.07 in.).

INDEX

MODIFICATIONS

CHANGES AND/OR MODIFICATION SECTION

This section includes the known and available change or modification information, pertaining to the automatic transmissions/transaxles covered in the first Chilton's Automatic Transmission Manual, and remaining in use from 1980 to present.

Included in this section are numerous late changes and/or modifications for the transmissions/transaxles covered in this second Chilton's Automatic Transmission Manual, that could not be added to the individual sections before the manual publication date. Although many changes and modifications are covered, others have been published by the manufacturer that have not reached our segment of the transmission industry. Therefore, it behooves the repairman to continually update his knowledge through attendance at the numerous technical seminars, sponsored by Transmission Associations, Parts and Supply Firms and other Vocational and Trade groups. Many monthly publications are available to update the rebuilding process of particular units, while Technical and Trade Associations have visual and/or sound products, both for rent or sale.

CHRYSLER CORPORATION
AMERICAN MOTORS CORPORATION/JEEP

Torque Command, TorqueFlite
A-904, A-998, A-999, A-727

1980 Changes and/or Modifications

REAR CLUTCH RETAINER (A-904 FAMILY)

Snap ring groove diameter increased by .110 snap ring free diameter also increased by .110 and radial section decreased to provide clearance with wide ratio annulus gear. 1979 retainers will be serviced with packages including the new retainers and snap rings.

	1980 P/N	1979 P/N
Rear Clutch Retainer (4-Plate)	4130765	4130195
Rear Clutch Retainer (3-Plate)	4202046	4130461
Snap Ring (thin)	4130761	1942421
Snap Ring (medium)	4130762	1942423
Snap Ring (thick)	4130763	2538617

KICKDOWN BAND ASSEMBLIES
(A-904 FAMILY)

New design flex-band P/N 4058863 replaces standard band 2204792 and the A-999 wide band 3681921. New part will service prior models.

VALVE BODY ASSEMBLIES (A-904 & A-727)

The following changes to the valve body assemblies were effective at the start of 1980 model year.

The lockup valve was changed to a two-diameter valve to provide a snap action valve in order to eliminate lockup valve buzz and to decrease lockup shudder. The lockup speed was also increased for most applications in order to eliminate lockup shudder and vibrations.

The part throttle kickdown limit for A-904 6-cylinder applications was increased approximately 10 mph for better driveability.

The switch valve was changed to eliminate switch valve buzz when in reverse. A .005 deep x .06 wide step on one land was added. This change was effective at S/N 6595-0000. The new valve body components will be used to service prior models.

GOVERNORS (A-904 & A-727)

The outer governor weights were increased 0.070 on the O.D. This was done in order to create a new governor weight for wide ratio transmissions and to maintain common tooling for all governor bodies. The new weights and body assemblies can be used together to service prior models.

AMC-JEEP 4-WHEEL DRIVE TRANSMISSIONS

Three new transmissions were introduced for 4-wheel drive usage—A-998 transmission for 258 AMC passenger car, A-999 for CJ-7 Jeep and A-727 for the Senior Jeep. New parts involved are two (2) output shafts, output shaft bearing, bearing snap ring, adapter seal and three (3) adapters. The transfer case hole mounting pattern on the two Jeep adapters is rotated 3° counterclockwise from the passenger car version.

AMC 2.5 LITRE 4-CYLINDER (A-904)

New case with revised bell housing configuration to fit the Pontiac 4-cylinder engine. Not interchangeable with prior models.

TRUCK 4-WHEEL DRIVE TRANSMISSIONS (A-727)

New die cast aluminum adapter (P/N 4130675) to replace cast iron adapter 3743285. Over-all length of new adapter was increased by 1.84", which requires a new output shaft P/N 4130677. Lockup feature was also added to most 4-wheel drive units. New parts and transmissions are not interchangeable with prior model.

MEDIUM TRUCK EXTENSION (A-727)

Casting and machining of the brake attaching boss was modified to accept 9 x 3 parking brake for 18,000# GVW motor home. New extension will service prior model year.

DODGE TRUCK WITH 446-IHC ENGINE (A-727)

New transmission similar to 1979 440-engine except uses case P/N 3743105. Adapter plate is used to mate transmission bell with back of block of the International Harvester engine.

MMC TRANSMISSION (Colt & Arrow)

New shift quality package developed for the 1980 MMC transmissions. Modifications include V-8 type valve body with provisions for rear servo feed check ball, elimination of bleed hole in case accumulator bore, longer accumulator spring and 2-disc front clutch with thicker pressure plate for use with 1.6 and 2.0 litre engines. New parts are not interchangeable with prior models.

Effective with transmission serial #4202084-6604-9994, the 1.6 and 2.0 litre front clutch packs were modified to improve clutch life. The separator plate (P/N 1942403) between the two friction discs was replaced by 2801969 and the thick pressure plate P/N 4202090) was replaced by the standard plate 2801969. Transmissions built before date code "6604" should be repaired with the revised clutch pack.

1980 Model Year Running Changes
VALVE BODY ASSEMBLIES (A-998 & A-999)

Valve body assemblies for 318 wide ratio and 360 engine applications were revised by adding an orifice in the steel plate to improve 1-2 shift quality and adding a check ball in the rear clutch circuit to improve neutral to drive shift. Kickdown spring loads were increased and the top accumulators spring removed in these transmissions at the same time.

Part	New P/N	Old P/N
Valve Body Assy. (318 Wide Ratio)	4203667	4202215
Valve Body Assy. (360)	4202668	4202213
Steel Plate	4202567	4202071
Kickdown Spring	4058885	4058781
Top Accumulator Spring	—	3515114

New valve body assemblies will service the old by changing springs as noted above.

VALVE BODY ASSEMBLIES (LOCK-UP)

Lockup speed was increased to 40 MPH for Chrysler 6-cylinder applications by using a 6.2# lockup spring. New valve body assembly will service the old.

Part	New P/N	Old P/N
Valve Body Assembly	4202780	4202214
Lockup Spring	4202672	4202642

Lockup speeds were increased during the model year on all other transmissions by increasing the lockup spring loads.

1981 Changes and/or Modifications
VALVE BODY ASSEMBLIES (A-904 AND A-727)

Part throttle 3-2 kickdown limits were increased by either increasing load of limit valve spring or by eliminating the limit body. Elimination of the limit body required changes to the steel plates and transfer plates.

Check ball added to the rear servo circuit of A-904 6-cylinder to improve neutral to reverse shift quality. Can be used to service prior models if counterbore is added to Rear Servo Feed passage of Case (½").

TRANSMISSION CASE (A-904)

Counterbore added to rear servo feed passage to allow use of check ball in this circuit to improve neutral to reverse shift quality. New case will service prior models.

	New P/N	Supersedes
Case (Chrysler 6-Cylinder)	4202774	3743111
Case Assy. (Chrysler 6-Cylinder)	4202777	3743125
Case (AMC 6-Cylinder Pass.)	4202776	3743113
Case Assy. (AMC 6-Cylinder Pass.)	4202778	3743127

TRANSMISSION CASE (A-904T)

New case added for 6-cylinder truck usage incorporates double-wrap reverse band and A-999 servo piston bores. Also used in heavy-duty 6-cylinder passenger car applications. 4130663 case-4202047 case assembly.

TRANSMISSION CASE (A-727 JEEP)

Casting revised to provide clearance with lockup valve body. New case will service prior models.

	New P/N	Supersedes
Case	4202577	3743105
Case Assembly	4202576	3743120

1981 Model Year Running Changes

INPUT SHAFT (A-904 FOUR-CYLINDER)

The turbine hub spline was lengthened by .540" to eliminate possible strip-out of hub spline. The new shaft should be used to service all 1979 through 1981 transmissions used with 2.0 and 2.6 litre MMC engines and 2.0 and 2.5 litre AMC and AM General engines. The old shaft with ground pilot will continue to be used with the 1.6 litre MMC engine.

NEW P/N: 4269140
OLD P/N: 4130788

OVERFILLING AUTOMATIC TRANSMISSIONS 1981 AND LATER

Automatic transmissions are frequently overfilled because the fluid level is checked when it is not "HOT" and the dipstick indicates that fluid should be added. However, the low reading is normal since the level will rise as the fluid temperature increases. Therefore, as a running change in the 1981 model year, all automatic transmission dipsticks have been revised with improved labeling and dimples added for checking oil level warm (85°F-125°F). These new dipstick part numbers are:

New P/N	Old P/N	Models Affected
4202951	2466302	J,E,T and Truck
4202952	4117465	Truck
4202953	4028908	B,F,G,X,S, and Y
4202971	[5224068] [4207049]	M,Z,P, and D

NOTE: Fluid level should not be checked when it is cold to the touch. "Warm" is fluid between 85°-125°F (29°-52°C).

If the fluid level checks low, add sufficient fluid to bring the level to within the marks indicated for the appropriate temperature.

─────── CAUTION ───────
DO NOT OVERFILL THE TRANSMISSION.

Overfilling may cause leakage out the RWD vent which may be misdiagnosed as a pump seal leak. In addition, overfilling causes aeration or foaming due to the oil being picked up by the rotating gear train. This significantly reduces the life of the oil and may cause a transmission failure.

─────── CAUTION ───────
On front wheel drive vehicles, the dipstick is located just behind the radiator electric cooling fan. Caution should be taken so as not to allow your hand or fingers to be caught in the fan.

All Chrysler built transmissions use DEXRON® or DEXRON® II Automatic Transmission Fluid.

1982 Changes and/or Modifications

REAR SERVO PISTON SEAL (A-904)

New Viton seal 4202864 released for fleet usage to replace 2464462 on designated assemblies that require high temperature endurance. New seal can also be used in all other applications.

WIDE RATIO GEAR SET (A-904 FAMILY)

AMC 6 and 8-cylinder and MMC 4-cylinder transmissions were changed to the wide ratio gear set, making wide ratio common across the board for 1982. New case, valve body assemblies, governors, kickdown lever and springs, accumulator springs, and some front clutch assemblies are required in the above transmissions to match shift quality with the ratio change.

TRANSMISSION ASSEMBLY (A-900 TRUCK)

The A-904 transmission was introduced for some 1981 model trucks equipped with 225 and 318 engines up to 6000 GVW. The usage has been expanded up to 8500 GVW for the 1982 Model Year.

EXTENSION SEAL (A-904)

New Vamac extension seal with improved high temperature material, P/N 4058047. This seal must be used in 1982 B3 vans and wagons equipped with A-900 transmissions. The new seal can be used in place of old part 3515384 in all other applications.

CASE (A-904 MMC)

The MMC case has an added orifice in the accumulator servo bore. New case assembly 4269141 is not interchangeable with 1981 part 4202116. The new assembly can be used in place of 3878521 for 1974 through 1979 Model Years.

VALVE BODY ASSEMBLY (A-904)

The MMC valve body has an added drilled orifice. Various springs were also changed to match shift quality to the wide ratio gear set. Miscellaneous valve body changes were also made for AMC and Jeep six-cylinder usages.

1983 Changes and/or Modifications

INNER OIL PUMP ROTOR (A-904 FOUR-CYLINDER)

To improve wear and brinelling on the inner rotor lugs in all 4-cylinder applications, the lug shape becomes dovetailed. The mating broached slot in the torque converter is also revised. Rotors are not interchangeable. The new 1983 torque converters can be used with prior model transmissions. The new 1983 transmissions with revised rotor lugs *cannot* be used with prior model torque converters. New service oil pump assemblies are also required for 4-cylinder applications:

Part	1983	1982 & Prior
Oil pump assembly w/rotors	4269948	4130192
Oil pump and support Assy. w/rotors	4269935	4202371

4X4 ADAPTERS (AMC AND JEEP)

The bearing shoulder area in the adapters was increased which reduced the seal bore by .123 in. The seals are not interchangeable.

Past model units can be serviced by using the new 1983 adapters in conjunction with the new seal. Part numbers involved are:

Part	1983 P/N	1982 P/N
Adapter (AMC Pass)	4269952	4130540
Adapter (A-999 Jeep)	4269953	4130730
Adapter (A-727 Jeep)	4269957	4130734
Seal-Adapter	4269956	4130539

MMC 4-WHEEL DRIVE (A-904)

A new transmission is being introduced for Mitsubishi built 4X4 trucks. It is similar to that used in 2.6 litre passenger car except for transfer case adapter and related parts. A 4-disc rear clutch will also be used in place of 3-disc for durability.

REAR SERVO PISTON SEAL (A-904 MMC)

The material of the rear servo seal is changed to VITON to improve resistance to high temperature. This seal is common with A-404 family and can be used to service prior models.

STEADY DRIVING SURGE AT 30-40 MPH FOLLOWING CONVERTER LOCK-UP

1981-83 TRUCKS AND VANS, w/318 2V AND LIGHT DUTY FEDERAL EMISSIONS ASPIRATOR WITH LOCK-UP CONVERTER.

Road test the vehicle and verify the condition. If surge is still present at steady speeds between 30 and 40 mph with the engine fully warmed up and after all warm driveability diagnostic procedures have been followed, do the following:

Repair Procedure

Parts Required:

1-Spring	PN 4202672
1-Lock-Up Body	PN 4202209

1. Remove transmission oil pan
2. Remove valve body and inspect the lock-up valve body.
   a. If lock-up valve body is the *old* style lock-up body, replace it with new style Lock-Up Body PN 4202209 *and* replace the present lock-up spring with a new Lock-Up Spring PN 4202672. Reuse the existing lock-up valve, fail safe valve and spring, cover, and screws.
   b. If the lock-up valve body is the *new* style lock-up body install only the new Lock-Up Spring PN 4202672.
3. Install the valve body and torque screws to 35 inch pounds (4 N•m).
4. Install the transmission oil pan and fill with ATF fluid.
5. Adjust shift and throttle linkage as necessary.

CHRYSLER CORPORATION, AMERICAN MOTORS CORPORATION/JEEP

Updated Modifications From 1978 to 1980

NOTE: Because of the importance of the modifications for the affected transmissions, the following updates are included.

RECURRING TRANSMISSION PROBLEMS FROM A CLOGGED FLUID COOLER

Recurring transmission problems may be a direct result of a clogged transmission cooler. A clogged transmission cooler may result in overheated transmission fluid and a loss or reduction in lubrication resulting in a transmission failure.

The transmission oil cooler can be clogged by particles of the lock-up clutch friction material or other foreign material, as the transmission oil cooler has an inner mesh design to help distribute the heat to the radiator lower tank coolant.

When a transmission repair requires transmission and/or torque converter removal, cooler line flow at the transmission must be checked. This is accomplished by:

1. Disconnect the fluid return line at the rear of the transmission and place a collecting container under the disconnected line.
2. Run the engine at *curb idle speed*, with the transmission in neutral.

If fluid flow is intermittent or if it takes longer than 20 seconds to collect a quart of ATF, the cooler lines and radiator cooler must be reverse flushed.

--- CAUTION ---

With transmission fluid level at specification, fluid collection should not exceed one (1) quart of automatic transmission fluid (ATF), or internal transmission damage may occur.

Whenever friction material is found in the transmission cooler inlet, it is necessary to replace the torque converter and clean and repair the transmission as required.

When reverse flushing of the cooler system fails to clear all the obstructions from the system, the radiator transmission cooler must be repaired by an approved repair facility or the radiator replaced.

REVERSE FLUSH PROCEDURE

When reverse flushing an automatic transmission fluid cooler, the following procedure should be used:

1. Disconnect the cooler lines at the transmission.
2. Disconnect the cooler lines at the radiator and remove the inlet fitting from the oil cooler connection on the radiator. In all operations use a back-up wrench to prevent damage.
3. Carefully dislodge any material that may be collected at the inlet of the cooler with a small screwdriver or other suitable tool and intermittent spurts of compressed air in the outlet of the cooler.
4. Using a hand suction gun filled with mineral spirits, reverse flush the cooler by pumping in mineral spirits and clearing with intermittent spurts of compressed air.
5. Using the method in Step 4, flush the cooler lines separately to ensure they are free flowing.
6. Reinstall the brass fitting in the cooler and reinstall the cooler lines.
7. To remove all remaining mineral spirits from the cooler and lines, one (1) quart of ATF should be pumped through the cooler and cooler lines prior to connecting the lines to the transmission.

When the reverse flushing of the cooler is completed, fill the transmission to the specified level and check the system for leaks.

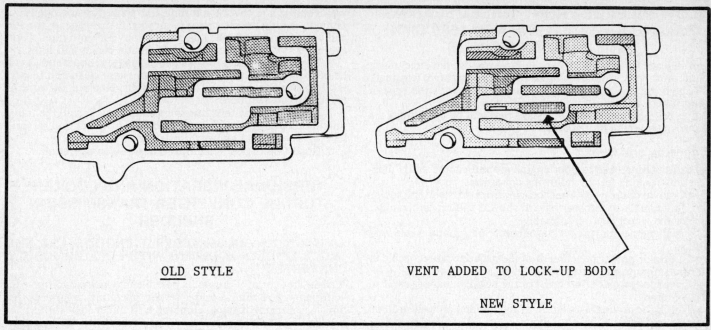

OLD STYLE

VENT ADDED TO LOCK-UP BODY

NEW STYLE

Comparison of old style and new style lock-up converter valve bodies (© Chrysler Corp.)

If reverse flushing of the cooler system fails to clear all obstructions from the system, the radiator cooler assembly must be replaced.

TORQUE CONVERTER LOCK-UP CLUTCH DRAG IN REVERSE GEAR AND IMPROVED TRANSMISSION PERFORMANCE—1978-79 A-904 and LA-904 (A-998 and A-999)

Some 1978 and 1979 vehicles equipped with a lock-up transmission may exhibit a condition of the torque converter lock-up clutch engaging when the vehicle transmission is shifted into reverse.

Torque converter lock-up clutch engagement can be easily diagnosed when one or more of the following conditions exist:

a. The engine hesitates and/or feels extremely sluggish when accelerating in reverse.

b. The torque converter stall speed is lower in reverse than in drive by 200 rpm or more.

In normal reverse operation, the torque converter lock-up clutch should not be applied. A lock-up clutch drag condition may be caused by a hydraulic pressure build up due to a restricted transmission oil cooler or by oil leakage into the lock-up circuit at the inner face of the pump assembly.

To correct this condition, the transmission oil cooler system must first be reversed flushed to ensure proper transmission oil cooling and fluid flow. If the transmission continues to exhibit the lock-up drag condition after the cooler has been reverse flushed and fluid flow checked, it will be necessary to replace the pump assembly with a new service pump assembly which includes:

1. Pump housing
2. Select Fit Pump Gears
3. Reaction Shaft Support Assembly
4. Pump-Torque Converter Oil Seal
5. All Steel Seal Rings

Part Number	Application
4202089	Lock-Up Transmission
4202298	Non-Lock-Up Transmission

These pumps will provide improved transmission performance.

These pump assemblies have select fit components and must not be disassembled or modified.

The pump assemblies are not interchangeable, and should only be used on the transmission for which they were released. The seal and gasket package for both pump assemblies is P/N 4131042, which includes:

1. Torque Converter Impeller Hub Seal
2. Pump Housing Seal
3. Reaction Shaft Support Gasket
4. Reaction Shaft Support Seal Rings (2)
5. Front Input Shaft Seal Ring
6. Rear Clutch Retainer Seal Ring

It is important gear selector and throttle linkage be adjusted properly and transmission fluid level is correct to ensure proper transmission performance.

A-727 OVERRUNNING CLUTCH FAILURES

Overrunning clutch failure may be the result of poor retention of the output shaft bearing by the bearing snap ring under a high load condition. This results in rearward movement of the output shaft which may cause the overrunning clutch to bear against the case and carry the full gear train thrust load. This in turn causes excessive wear of the race into the case and overrunning clutch failure.

The output shaft bearing may have an improperly machined snap ring groove in the outside diameter of the bearing outer race, which allows the snap ring to spread and release during heavy throttle operation.

All known overrunning clutch failures have resulted from bearings date coded with "□". If the transmission output shaft bearing has the date code shown; the bearing, snap ring, and case must be replaced.

Part	Part Number
Output Shaft Bearing	2466224
Output Shaft Bearing Snap Ring	2400320

MODIFICATIONS

LOW MILEAGE FRONT WHEEL BEARING FAILURES—1978, 1979, AND 1980 OMNI AND HORIZON MODELS

Low mileage front wheel bearing failures may be the direct result of an improperly grounded engine to battery (negative terminal).

A high pitch whining sound from a bearing with this type of wear pattern (electrostatic) is characteristic.

The ball bearings on the outboard race will be black from the electrostatic arcing on the race.

Diagnosis and Repair

A bearing failure due to poor engine ground can be easily diagnosed by looking for the following conditions:

• Removal of the noisy wheel bearing from the steering knuckle and disassembly of the bearing will show a pattern on the outer race of the wheel bearing assembly.

Check engine for proper installation of ground cable and straps.

• Check for proper attachment of the negative battery cable to the transmission mounting bolt.

• Check for proper attachment of the negative battery cable to body ground.

• Check for proper installation of the braided ground strap on the right side engine mount.

• Check for proper installation of the braided ground strap on the right rear side of the engine to the firewall.

If all ground cables and straps are properly installed, a check of the battery ground cable may be necessary.

To check the ground cable, use the following procedure:

1. Disconnect the negative battery cable from the transmission.

2. Using a test lamp, connect one lead to the positive battery terminal and the other end to the battery ground cable eyelet from the transmission. Firmly tug (not yanking), straighten out the cable and move the cable up and down and sideways. If the test light does not stay lit, the cable is defective and should be replaced.

3. Repeat the procedure in Step 2 and test the body ground cable from the negative battery terminal.

4. Clean cables and connections of all corrosion.

5. Reconnect the battery cable to the transmission and torque to 70 ft. lbs. (95 N•m). Also, reconnect the body ground wire, torque to 65 inch lbs. (7 N•m).

Replace the defective wheel bearing.

NO DRIVE IN ANY GEAR CONDITION—A-904 (1978-79)

In many instances, an automatic transmission failure, reported as *A NO DRIVE CONDITION,* may be mis-diagnosed. To ensure proper diagnosis and repair, the following procedure should be used when a "No Drive in any Gear" condition exists:

1. Check to verify the "No Drive in any Gear" condition.

NOTE: To save time and possibly unnecessary work; first, perform those operations that do not require transmission removal.

2. If after performing all diagnostic in-vehicle tests, the condition still exists, remove the transmission and torque converter from the vehicle.

3. Drain the transmission and torque converter as best as possible.

NOTE: Remove as much oil as possible from the torque converter. This will enable you to inspect the torque converter turbine hub inner-drive splines.

4. Before you begin any major disassembly, disassemble the transmission only to the point of removing the input shaft.

5. Insert the input shaft into the torque converter turbine hub spline until the shaft bottoms against the front of the torque converter and then pull the shaft back a ½ in. Rotate the input shaft slowly and firmly so as to drive the torque converter turbine. This will enable you to check the turbine hub spline for a stripped condition by noting the resistance to turning. If strippage is found, it will be necessary to replace the torque converter and input shaft, as well as clean and flush the transmission cooler and lines.

6. If torque converter turbine hub strippage is not found, it will be necessary to disassemble the transmission, clean and inspect the transmission for worn or failed parts. Replace all worn or failed parts as required.

7. Reassemble the transmission as necessary. Install the transmission. Check the transmission cooler flow. Check and set fluid level and check and adjust throttle and shift linkage.

8. Road test vehicle for proper transmission operation.

TORSIONAL VIBRATION AND LOCK-UP TORQUE CONVERTER TRANSMISSION SHUDDER

All 1978-79 225, 318, 360 FEDERAL ENGINES, CAR AND TRUCK MODELS EQUIPPED WITH LOCK-UP TORQUE CONVERTER

A slight amount of vibration is possible in a lock-up torque converter equipped vehicle under certain operating conditions (i.e. direct gear engine lugging, climbing hills under light throttle, or accelerating in direct gear, etc.). This occurs when the hydraulic drive through the torque converter is changed to a direct drive when the lock-up clutch is applied. In these instances, no repairs should be attempted. When an abnormal driveline disturbance is experienced on these vehicles, it can best be described as either torsional vibration or lock-up shudder. These conditions can be identified and corrected as follows:

Torsional Vibration

A continuous drumming or groaning sound emitted by the drive train, especially at low lock-up speeds. This condition may occur at the minimum lock-up speed up through approximately 45 mph. This condition can best be described as being similar to lugging a manual transmission vehicle in high gear.

If the condition experienced is abnormal torsional vibration, a new lock-up spring should be installed. This will increase the minimum lock-up speed.

Before installing a new lock-up spring, advise the customer that raising the lock-up speed may slightly reduce fuel economy and the torsional vibration is not harmful to the transmission. Once properly informed the customer may decide *not* to have the lock-up spring changed.

To ensure the proper lock-up spring and valve body end cover are used with the proper transmission application, check the list below:

1978 Transmissions

1. Transmission with a serial number up to 5911-xxxx, install Lock-up Valve Spring and Cover Package, P/N 4186185.

2. Transmissions with a serial number 5911-xxxx to 6093-xxxx, install lock-up spring from Package P/N 4186185, and retain the original valve body end cover.

3. Transmissions with a serial number after 6093-xxxx, install Lock-up Spring, P/N 4130478 (orange color code) and retain the original valve body end cover.

1979 Transmissions

1. 1979 transmissions, install Lock-up Spring, P/N 4130478 (orange color code) and retain the original valve body end cover.

Lock-Up Shudder

A vertical shaking of the instrument panel and steering column induced by faulty operation of the lock-up clutch, similar to driving over toll booth speed warning strips.

These disturbances may be caused by any one or a combination of the following items:
1. Rough Road Conditions
2. Poor Engine Performance
3. Poor Driveability
4. Defective Torque Converter
5. Defective Transmission or Pump

A road test should be performed, preferably with the owner, as he can best verify the condition when it occurs. Many times poor engine performance, roughness, cold engine bucking, or surge are misdiagnosed as lock-up shudder and/or torsional vibration.

In some instances, a new engine (under 300 miles) may affect engine and transmission performance. If a lock-up shudder or vibration condition is encountered on a new engine vehicle, no transmission repairs should be attempted until the vehicle has accumulated a minimum of 300 miles. The condition may clear up with mileage.

If the condition experienced is lock-up shudder, the following procedure should be used:

To ensure proper diagnosis and repair, if engine performance is suspected, check engine tune (timing, propane idle adjustment, and scope check). Also, check transmission fluid level and throttle linkage adjustment.

If after ensuring the above items are satisfactory and lock-up shudder still exists, proceed as follows:

1. Transmission oil cooler flow should be checked. Inadequate flow is an intermittent flow of less than 1 quart in 20 seconds (in neutral, transmission at operating temperature, engine at curb idle). If inadequate flow is found, inspect the cooler lines for kinks and sharp bends, then disconnect the transmission cooler line at the cooler inlet and remove the brass fitting. Inspect the inlet of the cooler for lock-up clutch friction material. If friction material is found or cooler flow is low, the transmission cooling system should be reverse flushed as described in the same Technical Service Bulletin. When reverse flushing fails to clear any obstruction from the system and flow remains inadequate, the radiator should be repaired or replaced.

Whenever friction material is found in the cooler inlet, it will be necessary to replace the torque converter and clean and repair the transmission as necessary.

If no friction material is found and cooler flow is adequate, proceed to Step 2.

2. Replace the lock-up valve body assembly with Service Stepped Lock-up Valve Body, P/N 4202219. This lock-up valve body is designed to provide a more positive lock-up shift. If the shudder condition persists, proceed to Step 3.

3. Replace the torque converter with a new Service Unit, P/N 4058489 for 318 CID and P/N 4058287 for 360 CID A-904-LA Torqueflite transmissions. These torque converters are easily identified by yellow paint on the torque converter ring gear. The transmission pump assembly on all A-904 series transmissions should also be replaced with Service Pump Assembly, P/N 4202089. When replacing a torque converter in an A-904 225 CID application or all A-727 applications, use a standard service unit.

When replacing the pump assembly, inspect the input shaft seal rings for cracking or sticking and lube the rings prior to pump installation. Input shaft end-play should also be checked after the new pump assembly is installed to ensure proper input shaft end-play.

After the replacement of these components is completed, a short break-in period may be necessary to achieve maximum improvement. No further major repairs to improve transmission performance, other than adjustment, should be attempted until at least 300 miles have been accumulated on these new components.

This information pertains to ALL 1978 225, 318, and 360 engine applications and 1979 225, 318, and 360 Federal engine applications *only*, and not for use on 1979 California engine applications.

OIL PUMP NOISES, REVERSE MOAN, BUZZ, ENGINE RUNAWAY, OIL BURPING FROM DIPSTICK OR VENT

1978-79 A-904 TORQUEFLITE TRANSMISSIONS

Some hydraulic-mechanical noise (low pitch moan) is normal when shifting a transmission into "Reverse," especially after parking overnight. Noise is caused by air being purged from the transmission.

When transmission performance is suspect, first inspect transmission oil level and correct if required. At this time, inspect the transmission and cooler lines for any leaks and/or obstructions. Also, check for proper adjustment and operation of the throttle and gearshift linkage.

Pump Noises—"Moan" or "Buzzing" in Reverse Gear

When shifting a vehicle into reverse gear (primarily cold) or when the shift lever is between "Park" and "Reverse" position, a loud moan or buzz may be heard from the transmission for a time period longer than 10 seconds.

If the noise continues for more than 10 seconds, the following diagnostic procedure should be used:
1. Set the parking brake and apply the service brake with your left foot. Shift the transmission into "Reverse."
2. With your right foot depress the accelerator pedal slowly, raising the engine rpm until the "Moan" or "Buzzing" noise is heard. Hold the engine rpm at the point of the loudest moan for approximately 1-2 minutes, return to idle, shift into "Park," and immediately check the transmission oil dipstick for foamy oil.

—————————— CAUTION ——————————

Do not hold engine rpm at or near torque converter stall speed for more than five seconds.

a. If foaming is not present, replace the transmission valve body switch valve with a new Valve, P/N 4202474. This new valve has an undercut land to eliminate "buzz" or "moan."

b. If foam is present, replace the transmission pump assembly.

NOTE: If the buzzing noise is still present after replacement of the valve and foaming is not present, an inspection of the transmission oil cooler is required. A plugged cooler may cause switch valve buzz.

Intermittent Engine Runaway and/or Transmission Slippage

Engine runaway, especially when stopping after initial start, or transmission slippage that is not consistent and does not occur during heavy throttle application may be another indication of a transmission pump deficiency.

When either/or both conditions occur, check the transmission oil for aeration. If aeration is present, replace the transmission pump assembly. In all repairs, follow the procedures for transmission and torque converter removal and installation and transmission pump replacement.

Oil Burping from Transmission Vent and/or Dipstick Tube Due to Pump Aeration

Oil burping from the vent on the transmission pump may be misdiagnosed as a front pump seal leak. Also, in more severe cases, oil may leak out the dipstick tube. Both of these conditions may also be due to a transmission pump defect causing oil aeration. If either of these conditions are present:
1. Check the transmission fluid level and condition.
a. If the oil level is above specification, correct the fluid level and retest

After every repair, make certain the following are correct:
a. Transmission Fluid Level
b. Shift Linkage Adjustment
c. Throttle Linkage Adjustment

MODIFICATIONS

THM125/125C Transaxles

CASE COVER CHANGE

Starting mid October 1980, a new design transaxle case cover went into production for some THM 125 automatic transaxles. Both the new and old design transaxle case covers are being used in current production.

The new design case cover has a larger manual valve plug bore. Also, a section of the transaxle case casting has been removed. The changes made in the new design transaxle case cover require a larger manual bore plug and a six lobe socket head screw.

Regardless of design, when servicing the transaxle case cover order service package number 8631957. The old design transaxle case cover uses manual bore plug part number 8631165 and retaining bolt number 11503562. The new design transaxle case cover uses manual bore plug part number 8637091 and retaining bolt part number 8637087. Also, the new design six lobe socket head screw requires a number 40 internal six lobe socket head bit and holder.

DRIVEN SPROCKET WASHER

A new service driven sprocket to driven sprocket support thrust washer has been released for the first design driven sprocket support assembly. This revision is incorporated in all THM 125 automatic transaxles now being built. This design change also affects the transaxle case cover gaskets.

When reassembling the transaxle unit with the first design driven sprocket support, use the second design gaskets and the first design service driven sprocket to driven sprocket support thrust washer. The part number is 8631981 and the color of the required component is red.

NOTE: The first design washer is white. The second design is black. The first design service washer is red.

The second design driven sprocket support and case to case cover gaskets must be used, as the first design driven sprocket support and case to case cover gaskets are not available for service.

Incorrect combination of these parts may result in gasket distortion, oil leaks, loss of bolt torque or needle bearing damage.

DRIVEN SPROCKET SUPPORT

When diagnosing a THM 125 automatic transaxle for lack of drive, slipping shifts or erratic shift points check the driven sprocket support for wear.

If present, the wear pattern is caused by the bearing sleeve on the outside hub of the driven sprocket moving and wearing into the driven sprocket support. As this wear condition reaches an advanced state the oil feed passages in the driven sprocket support are exposed, allowing an oil pressure cross leak.

The bearing sleeve on the driven sprocket may, after causing the described wear pattern groove, move back to its proper location and appear to be normal. If this condition is suspected, be

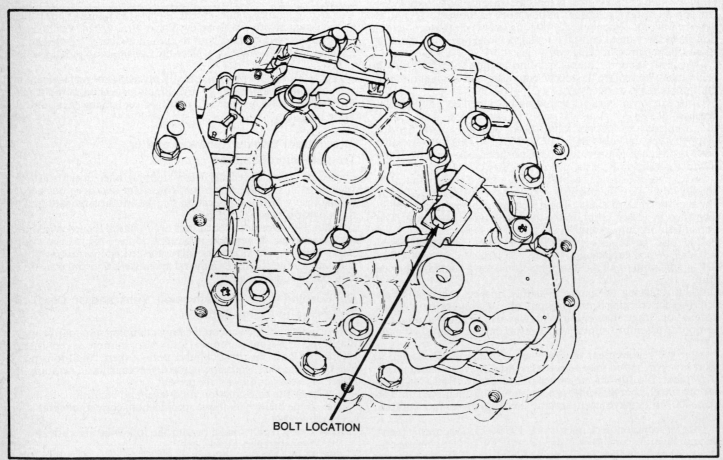

BOLT LOCATION

Pump cover bolt location THM 125 automatic transaxle (© General Motors Corp.)

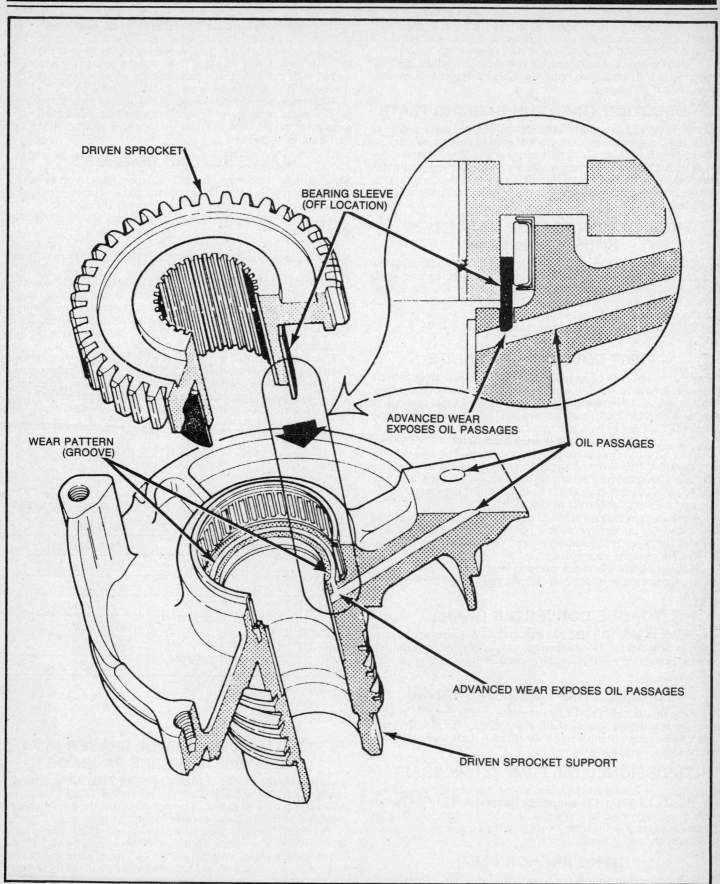

Driven sprocket support—cross section THM 125 transaxle (© General Motors Corp.)

sure to check the driven sprocket support for the wear pattern groove. If this condition exists, replace the driven sprocket, driven sprocket support and any other damaged parts.

Check the direct clutch assembly and the intermediate band for wear. Repair or replace as required. Check the torque converter and flush if necessary.

PRODUCTION TRIAL RUN BACKING PLATE

On all THM 125 automatic transaxles built around the middle of July 1981, a production trial run was started using a new design direct clutch backing plate, part number 8631764. The new design backing plate has a raised side for identification, and a flat side, which when assembled, should face toward the clutch plates. When servicing the transaxle use the current backing plate, part number 8631027.

NEW DESIGN TORQUE CONVERTER HOUSING OIL SEAL

Due to the usage of a new turbine shaft and oil pump drive shaft a new design torque converter housing oil seal is being used in all units produced after December 1981. The new oil seal can be identified by the part number 8637420 stamped on the front face of the seal. The old design seal will have either the part number 8631158 stamped on it, or no part identification at all.

PUMP COVER BOLT CHANGE

Starting at the end of May, 1981, some THM 125 automatic transaxles were being built with a substitute pump cover to transaxle case bolt. The standard pump cover to transaxle case bolt is an M8X1.25X105 bolt, part number 8637266. The substitute bolt is an M8X1.25X110 bolt, part number 11501048 and is used with two standard steel washers that are 1.5mm thick.

If the substitute pump cover to transaxle case bolt and washers are removed from any transaxle, be sure to use the two washers during reassembly. Failure to use the two washers on the M8X1.25X110 bolt may result in interference between the converter and the pump cover to case bolt.

After reassembling a THM 125 automatic transaxle containing the substitute pump cover to case bolt, install the torque converter and check for interference between the torque converter and the pump cover to case bolts.

When installing the pump cover to transaxle case bolt, be sure to use thread sealer on the bolt threads and torque the bolt to 15 ft. lbs.

TORQUE CONVERTER CHANGE

Beginning in 1982 all THM 125 automatic transaxles will be built with a new design 245 millimeter torque converter. This new torque converter will replace the present 254mm torque converter.

TURBINE SHAFT DESIGN CHANGE

Starting in 1982 all THM 125 automatic transaxles will be built using a new design turbine shaft. The spline of the new shaft will be 5.1mm longer than the old style turbine shaft, and will incorporate an O-ring seal groove.

REDESIGNED OIL PUMP DRIVE SHAFT

Beginning in January 1982 a new style oil pump drive shaft will be used in all THM 125 automatic transaxles. The new shaft is 23.7mm longer and has 15 teeth on the oil pump spline rather than the old shaft which has 20 teeth on the oil pump spline and is 23.7mm shorter in length.

BAND ANCHOR PLUG

Starting around the middle of June, 1981, all THM 125 automatic transaxles are being built with a new design band anchor plug. This new anchor plug has a tab which holds the part in place. All automatic transaxles built prior to mid June 1981 have the old design style band anchor plug. A staking operation was required to hold the old plug in place. This staking operation is not required with the new design band anchor plug, as due to the tab extension, it is held in place by the reverse oil pipe.

When replacing the new design band anchor plug the reverse oil pipe must be removed first. When repairing automatic transaxles prior to mid June 1981 use the new style band anchor plug, part number 8637640.

VALVE BUZZING DIAGNOSIS

Some X body vehicles, Citation, Skylark, Omega and Phoenix, equipped with the THM 125 automatic transaxle may experience a buzzing noise which can only be detected at curb idle.

When diagnosing a buzzing noise problem, follow the procedure below:

1. Be sure that the buzzing noise is coming from the automatic transaxle assembly, not from the engine or any other part of the vehicle.

2. Check for engine coolant in the transaxle fluid. Check and correct the transaxle fluid level. Recheck for the buzzing noise.

3. If the buzzing noise is not corrected, remove the oil pan and check for a plugged or damaged oil strainer. Also, check for a missing or damaged O-ring seal. Replace parts as required. Recheck for the buzzing noise.

4. If the noise is still present, check the automatic transaxle serial number. If the transaxle was built prior to the break point serial numbers in the chart below, the buzzing noise may be coming from the pressure regulator valve, which is located in the valve body. To correct the noise replace the valve body unit, according to the valve body service package chart.

VALVE BODY SERVICE PACKAGE CHART
THM 125 Automatic Transaxle

Break point serial number	Part Number
1980 CV	8637958
1980 PZ	8637957
1981 CD	8637961
1981 CV	8637960
1981 CT	8637960
1981 PZ	8637959

REVISED VALVE CONTROL SPACER PLATE AND GASKET SERVICE PACKAGE

Starting with the month of March 1982, all THM 125 automatic transaxles are being built with a revised version of the valve control spacer plate and gasket. It is important that the proper spacer plate and gasket be used when servicing the unit.

The revised design spacer plate package will include the proper gasket, and can be identified with a yellow stripe. Be sure to use the old design gasket with the old design spacer plate and the revised design gasket with the revised spacer plate, as these parts are not interchangeable. Use the following charts to determine proper usage.

BURNT BAND AND DIRECT CLUTCH ASSEMBLY CONDITION

Some THM 125 automatic transaxle equipped vehicles may experience a burnt band and direct clutch condition. A possible cause of the burnt band and direct drive condition might be the third accumulator check valve not seating properly. This condition allows the intermediate band to drag while the direct clutch is applied causing excessive friction. If the third accumulator is found to be defective order service package part number 8643964, which contains a new dual land third accumulator check valve and a conical spring. Refer to the following procedure to replace the accumulator assembly:

1. Remove the intermediate servo cover and gasket.
2. Remove the third accumulator check valve and spring. Inspect the third accumulator valve bore for wear and damage to the valve seat and also for the presence of the valve seat.
3. Plug both the feed and exhaust holes in the bore using petroleum jelly.
4. Replace the third accumulator check valve with the new dual land check valve. Center the valve to be sure that it is seated properly.
5. Leak test the valve seat by pouring solvent into the accumulator check valve bore. Check for a leak on the inside of the case. A small amount of leakage is acceptable.
6. If the valve leaks tap the assembly with a brass drift and rubber mallet in order to try and reseat the valve.
7. Repeat the leak test procedure. If the valve still leaks it may be necessary to replace the transaxle case.
8. If the valve does not leak, remove the check valve and install the new conical valve spring onto the valve. Be sure that the small end goes on first. Install the valve into the transaxle case bore.
9. Using a new gasket, install the servo cover.

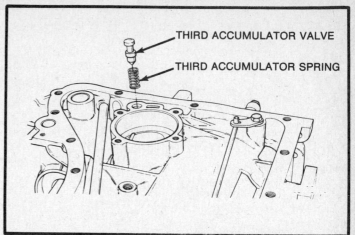

Third accumulator assembly—THM 125 automatic transaxle (© General Motors Corp.)

OIL WEIR USAGE

During the month of September 1981 all THM 125 automatic transaxles were assembled with a new part called an oil weir. This part was used by General Motors for one month as a production trial run. The oil weir is located in the rear case oil pan area. Its function is to revise the lubrication flow around the differential assembly.

The oil weir part number is 8637836 and is held in position by a retaining clip part number 8637837. Both of these parts are available for service. Automatic transaxles built without an oil weir do not require the addition of the part during service.

NO REVERSE WHEN HOT

When diagnosing a THM 125 automatic transaxle for a no reverse when hot condition, first check the line pressure. If after checking the line pressure it is okay, carefully check the following list of possible causes in addition to those listed in the Chilton Three C's diagnostic section in the proper Chilton manual.

1. Be sure that the transaxle case to low and reverse clutch housing cup plug assembly is fully seated and not restricted.
2. Check for a damaged or missing low and reverse pipe washer and O-ring.
3. Check and retorque all driven sprocket support bolts to 18 ft. lbs. If the bolt torque is found to be low, use Loctite® on the bolt threads.
4. Check the transaxle case cover (valve body and driven sprocket mating surfaces) and the driven sprocket support sealing surface for possible damage, porosity, leaks and flatness.
5. Check for the correct transaxle case to transaxle case cover gasket and the transaxle case to transaxle cover center gasket.
6. Make certain that the low and reverse clutch inner and outer piston lip seals are installed correctly. The lip seals must be installed with the lip facing down and away from the clutch apply ring. With the low and reverse clutch piston installed into the low & reverse clutch housing, the lip of the lip seal must contact the walls of the low and reverse clutch housing to form a proper seal. Installation of these seals in any other manner may cause the no reverse condition.

LOW-REVERSE CLUTCH ASSEMBLY— DESIGN CHANGE

Starting around the middle of July, 1981, some 1982 vehicles produced with the THM 125 automatic transaxle were assembled with a new design low and reverse clutch assembly. This design change produces a more desirable neutral to reverse shift. The new design assembly consists of a modified low and reverse piston which eliminates the need for an apply ring. A smaller low and reverse clutch housing feed orifice is also used, as is a waved steel clutch plate located next to the low and reverse piston. The new waved steel clutch plate eliminates the one flat steel clutch plate.

INTERMEDIATE BAND/DIRECT CLUTCH HOUSING ASSEMBLY SERVICE PACKAGE

A new intermediate band and direct clutch housing service package has been assembled and released to repair all THM 125 automatic transaxles. This new service package, part number 8643941 consists of a direct clutch housing and drum assembly, and an intermediate band assembly. Both of these parts must be used together as a complete unit. These two items are no longer available individually and can only be obtained as a set.

PRESSURE REGULATOR VALVE RETAINING PIN

When diagnosing the 125C automatic transaxle for no drive or harsh shifts (high line pressure), check the control valve assembly for a worn or missing pressure regulator valve retaining pin.

If after checking the pressure regulator valve retaining pin it is found to be either missing or worn the following repair must be performed.

1. Position the control valve and oil pump assembly with the machined portion face down. Be certain that the machined face is protected in order to prevent damage to its surface.
2. Using a ⅜ in. drift punch and hammer close the pressure regulator valve retaining pin hole. Close the pin hole only enough to hold the new retaining pin in place after assembly.
3. Reassemble the pressure regulator and reverse boost valve train assembly.

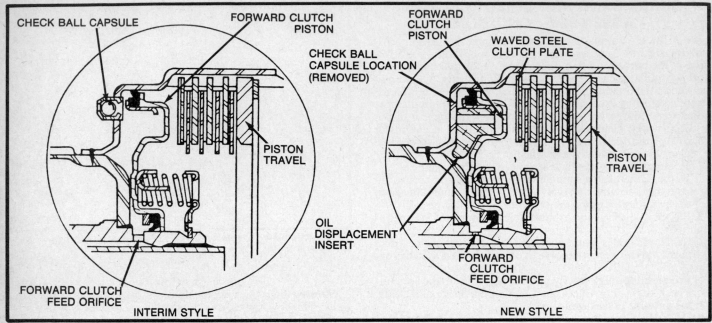

Forward clutch assembly—125 automatic transaxle (© General Motors Corp.)

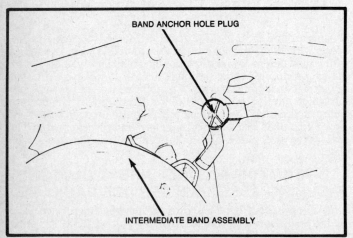

Band anchor plug location—THM 125 automatic transaxle
(© General Motors Corp.)

4. Retain the valve train with a new steel retaining pin, part number 112496. Be sure that the new pin is inserted from and flush with the machined face of the control valve and oil pump assembly.

FORWARD CLUTCH CHANGES

Beginning July, 1981 some changes were made in the forward clutch assembly to produce a more desirable neutral to drive engagement and eliminate the check ball capsule. These changes were accomplished in two phases. Phase one began in July of 1981 and phase two in September of the same year.

PHASE ONE—INTERIM STYLE

The forward clutch was redesigned, eliminating the apply ring. The backing plate was made selective to control piston travel.

PHASE TWO—NEW STYLE

The forward clutch feed orifice was reduced in size and an oil displacement insert was added. These two changes will produce a more desirable neutral to drive engagement.

The check ball capsule was removed and two exhaust holes were added to the new forward clutch piston. When the piston is applied the exhaust holes will seal against the waved steel clutch plate. When the piston is released, apply oil will exhaust between the waved steel clutch plate and the piston. Also, a selective backing plate is used to control piston travel.

FORWARD CLUTCH SELECTION PROCEDURE

When servicing the individual parts that make up the forward clutch assembly in the THM 125 automatic transaxle, first identify the forward clutch assembly style and then select only those parts specified in the chart below for each style.

When replacing the selective backing plate, check the end play in the following manner.

1. Insert a feeler gauge between the selective backing plate and the snap ring.
2. The end play should be 0.040–0.070 in., without compressing the waved clutch plate.
3. If the end play is not within specification, select the proper backing plate from the forward clutch end play chart. For positive identification measure the thickness of the selective backing plate.
4. Use of a new style forward clutch housing without proper end play will cause excessive clutch plate wear.

FRONT BAND CHANGE

THM 125 automatic transaxles produced late in 1981, were being built with a wider intermediate band which conforms with the wider band surface on the direct clutch drums. The new wider band cannot be used with the early model THM 125 automatic transaxle equipped with the narrow band area. The early design band will fit the late model transaxle, but this is not recommended. The early design band is 1.49 inches wide. The new design band is 1.74 inches wide.

LATE OR DELAYED UPSHIFTS

Some THM 125 automatic transaxles may experience late or delayed upshifts (1-2 shift 30-35 mph, 2-3 shift 50-55 mph) this will occur if the line boost lever cannot lift the line boost valve off its

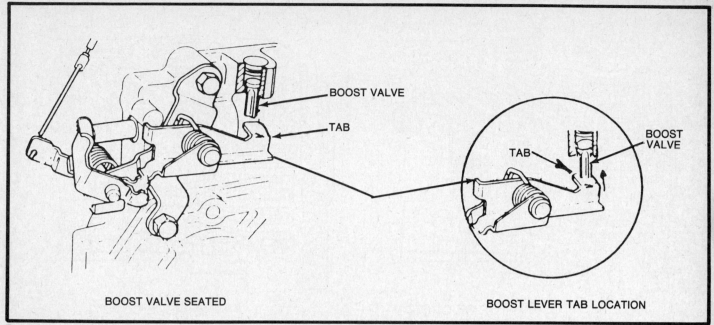

Boost lever and related components—THM 125 transaxle (© General Motors Corp.)

seat. To correct the problem, check and adjust the T.V. linkage. If the linkage adjustment does not correct the condition, connect a pressure gauge and check the transaxle line pressure. If the line pressure is high, remove the valve body cover and check the position of the line boost lever. With the T.V. linkage set and the throttle linkage on the idle stop. The boost lever should be holding the boost valve off its seat. If not, and the linkage is correctly adjusted and the linkage springs properly positioned, bend the tab on the boost lever to hold the boost valve completely off its seat.

GOVERNOR COVER AND BEARING ASSEMBLY CHANGE

Beginning late March, 1981, some THM 125 automatic transaxles were built with a new design governor cover bearing in place of the old design thrust washer. This new bearing will be in either one of two designs. The first design is a three piece thrust bearing assembly and the second design is a one piece bearing. For service, only the first design bearing will be used.

A new design governor cover was also put into production. The height of the governor hub was reduced to allow clearance for the increased thickness of the bearing.

This design change was made to reduce friction between the speedometer gear and governor cover during high speed, long distance driving.

ROUGH NEUTRAL-TO-DRIVE GEAR ENGAGEMENT 1982 THROUGH 1984 THM 125/125C TRANSAXLES

Some 1982 through 1984 THM 125/125C transaxles may exhibit a rough neutral to drive gear engagement condition. A new forward clutch wave plate went into production, beginning in December of 1983, to prevent this condition. When servicing any 1982 through 1984 THM 125/125C transaxles for this condition, order and install part number 8652126, forward clutch wave plate.

NEW AUXILIARY VALVE BODY AND AUXILIARY VALVE BODY GASKET ALL THM 125C TRANSAXLES

During September, 1983 all THM 125C transmissions were built with a new auxiliary valve body and valve body gasket. The new auxiliary valve body does not have an orifice plug hole. The auxiliary valve body gasket is made out of a new material and has three holes made larger.

The changes to the gasket eliminate a no torque converter clutch release (TCC) or no TCC apply condition that resulted from incorrect cup plug, mispositioned cup plug or eroding gasket.

NOTE: The only interchangeable part is the auxiliary valve body cover. The new auxiliary valve body gasket must be used with the new auxiliary valve body. The past auxiliary valve body gasket must be used with the past auxiliary valve body.

When servicing any model THM 125C transmission auxiliary valve body, refer to the following procedure:

1. Identify the auxiliary valve body being serviced (past or new).

2. If the past auxiliary valve body is being serviced, refer to Chart 1. If the new auxiliary valve body is being serviced, refer to Chart 2.

CHART 1

Part Being Replaced	Part Number
Auxiliary Valve Body Cover Gasket	8653947
Auxiliary Valve Body Cover	8643645
Auxiliary Valve Body Orifice Plug	8623796
Auxiliary Valve Body (past design not serviced)	New auxiliary valve body must be used, order Service Package 8653946.

MODIFICATIONS

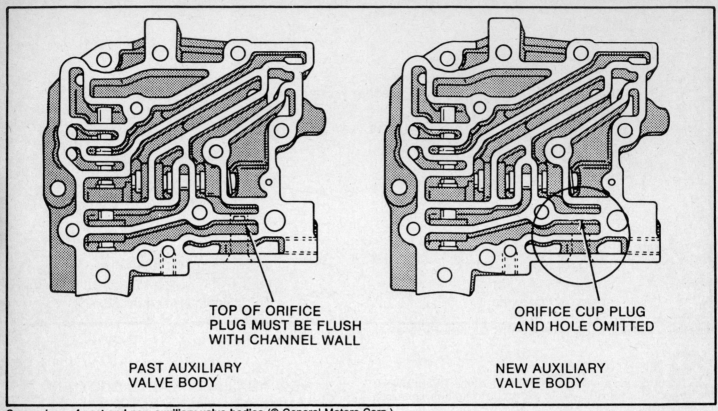

TOP OF ORIFICE
PLUG MUST BE FLUSH
WITH CHANNEL WALL

ORIFICE CUP PLUG
AND HOLE OMITTED

PAST AUXILIARY
VALVE BODY

NEW AUXILIARY
VALVE BODY

Comparison of past and new auxiliary valve bodies (© General Motors Corp.)

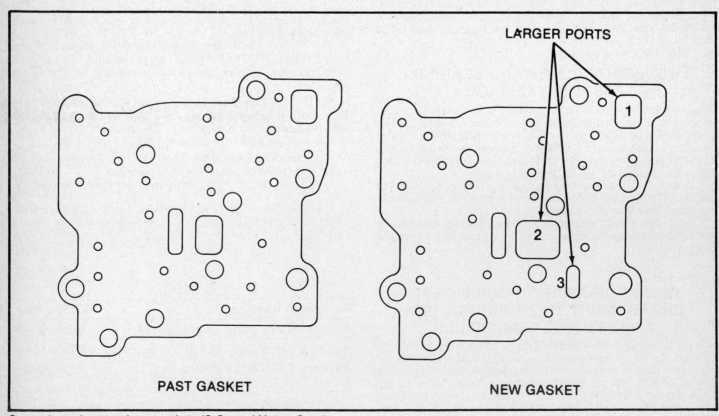

LARGER PORTS

1

2

3

PAST GASKET

NEW GASKET

Comparison of past and new gaskets (© General Motors Corp.)

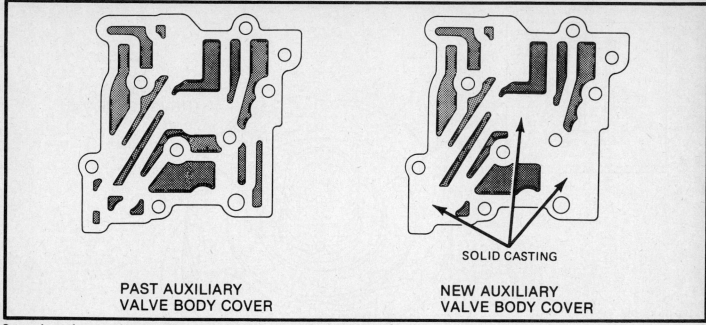

PAST AUXILIARY
VALVE BODY COVER

NEW AUXILIARY
VALVE BODY COVER

SOLID CASTING

Comparison of past and new auxiliary valve body covers (© General Motors Corp.)

CHART 2

Part Being Replaced	Part Number
Auxiliary Valve Body Cover Gasket	8643863
Auxiliary Valve Body Cover	8643645
Auxiliary Valve Body Models BF, BL, CE, CA, CB, CF, CL, CK, CT, CC, PE, PD, PG, PJ, PW, PF	8653946 Service Package
EM, EN, EW, HC, HS, HV, HY, OP	8653945 Service Package

Service Package 8653946 contains:

1	8643865	Auxiliary Valve Body
1	8643863	Gasket Aux. Valve Body
1	8643645	Cover Aux. Valve Body

Service Package 8653945 contains:

1	8643864	Body Auxiliary Valve
1	8643863	Gasket Aux. Valve Body Cover
1	8643645	Cover Aux. Valve Body

Only the Auxiliary Valve Body Cover, Auxiliary Valve Body Cover Gasket, and Auxiliary Valve Body Orifice Plug can be ordered separately.

When servicing any auxiliary valve body inspect it for erosion around the hole number 1. If the gasket is eroded, then replace the auxiliary valve body cover along with the required gasket.

If the auxiliary valve body being serviced needs the orifice plug replaced due to damage or missing follow the procedure listed below.

    a. If the orifice plug is still in the auxiliary valve body, remove it with a $7/32$ in. screw extractor.

    b. Install a new orifice plug (Part Number 8623796) using a $5/16$ in. punch to start the orifice plug in the hole. Then use a $3/8$ in. punch and seat the plug flush with the wall.

WHINING NOISE AND SLOW ENGAGEMENT THM 180C AUTOMATIC TRANSMISSIONS (CHEVETTE AND 1000 MODELS)

The vehicles referenced may exhibit the following condition:

Whining noise which increases with engine rpm in all ranges and slow or slipping engagement. The whining noise is similar to noise caused from the steering wheel being turned to its maximum travel.

If the above condition exists check the transmission oil line pressure. If the line pressure is low, refer to the following service procedure.

1. Remove the oil filter and visually inspect for restriction.
2. If the oil filter is restricted remove the transmission from vehicle, and remove the pump.
3. After removing the pump inspect the selective end-play washer for wear especially on the inside diameter of the washer. If the washer is worn replacement is necessary.
4. Remove any burrs that may be present around the lube hole on the Pump Tower.
5. Inspect washer thrust surface for damage. Remove any high spot that may be present by stoning the thrust surface.
6. Thoroughly wash the Pump Body with solvent before reassembly.
7. Select the correct end-play washer and assemble pump to the transmission, replace oil screen and install transmission into vehicle.

NEW THIRD OIL PRESSURE SWITCH— THM 200-C 01 MODEL TRANSMISSION 5.0L BONNEVILLE AND GRAND PRIX

Beginning November 1, 1983 a new third oil pressure switch and bracket assembly went into production for all 1984 THM 200-C 01 model transmissions.

When servicing any 1984 THM 200-C 01 model transmission that necessitates that the third oil pressure switch be replaced

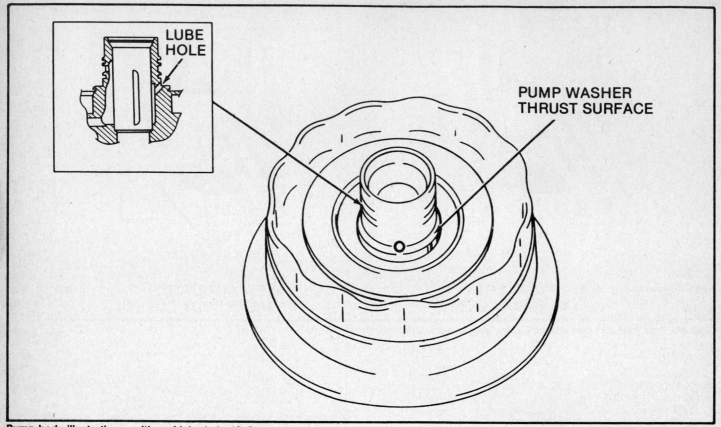

Pump body illustrating position of lube hole (© General Motors Corp.)

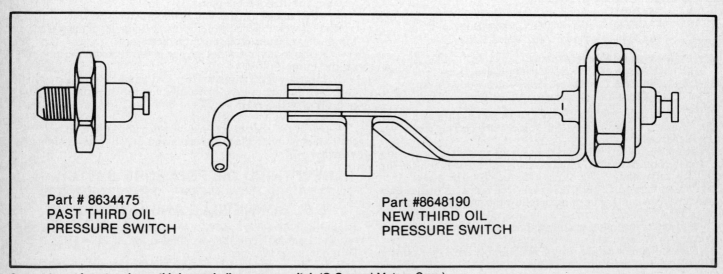

Comparison of past and new third speed oil pressure switch (© General Motors Corp.)

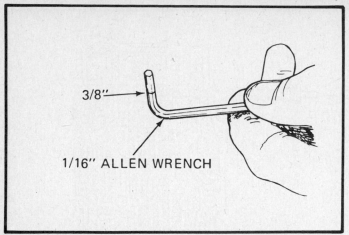

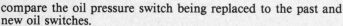

Marking of Allen wrench (© General Motors Corp.)

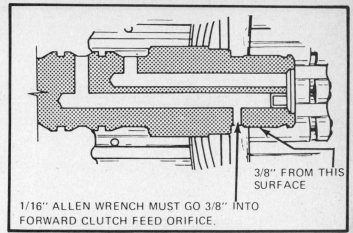

Measurement for Allen wrench insertion (© General Motors Corp.)

compare the oil pressure switch being replaced to the past and new oil switches.

If the oil switch required is the past switch, order Part Number 8634475. If the oil switch required is the new switch, order Part Number 8648190.

THM 200C LATE ENGAGEMENT OR SLIPPING IN DRIVE

Some early 1984 model THM 200C transmissions may experience a late engagement or slipping in drive range. This condition is usually detected while the transmission is cold, and could be caused by a blocked forward clutch feed orifice hole.

Other causes for late engagement or slipping in drive are low transmission oil level, cut or nicked forward clutch piston seals and/or cut or nicked Teflon® turbine shaft seals.

Refer to the list below and verify serial and model numbers. If the serial number is prior to the number on the chart then follow this procedure:

MODEL SERIAL NUMBER

BH	54628
OI	21738
OR	1119
OU	1727

SERVICE PROCEDURE

1. Check transmission oil level and correct if required.
2. Visually inspect the forward clutch piston seals and turbine shaft Teflon® seals for cuts and nicks.
3. Use a 1/16 in. Allen wrench marked on the short end as illustrated in Fig. 8. Using the Allen wrench as a gage, insert the small end into the forward clutch feed orifice hole and make sure the Allen wrench goes into the orifice hole (without any drag) until the mark on the wrench is flush with the ground diameter.

The part numbers for the Housing Assembly Forward Clutch is 8638944 and 8628924 for the Forward Clutch Piston Seals. The Turbine Shaft Teflon® Seals are part number 8628090.

PRESSURE REGULATOR BUSHING PIN DESIGN CHANGE—THM 325-4L

Beginning early in April, 1983 production the THM 325-4L transmission case was changed along with the coiled spring pin used to retain the pressure regulator valve bushing in the case. A larger solid steel pin is now used. This change was made to eliminate the possibility of case face distortion during assembly. Due to different sizes, these two pins cannot be used interchangeably. Furthermore, the new solid pin is a slip fit in the transmission case and may fall out if the transmission is rolled over; loss of this pin would enable the pressure regulator bushing to lose proper orientation, resulting in the loss of proper pressure regulator valve operation.

If replacement of either pin is required, use the following numbers to order the correct pin.

Coiled Spring	P/N 9437415
Solid Pin	P/N 141202

HIGH SHIFT POINTS—1982 "C" CARS WITH 5.7L DIESEL AND 350C TRANSMISSION

1982 "C" cars equipped with the 5.7 liter diesel engine and 350 C transmission may experience higher than normal or delayed transmission shift points. This condition may be caused by low vacuum at the modulator due to a disconnected or damaged EGR valve vacuum hose on the underside of the air cleaner.

Modifications and Changes Made to More Than One THM Model Transmission/Transaxle Assemblies

SERVICING OF THE TORQUE CONVERTER CLUTCH VALVE TRAIN IN THM 200-4R AND 325-4L TRANSMISSIONS

Early production 1982 Cadillacs equipped with gasoline engines and THM 200-4R or 325-4L transmissions were built with a Torque Converter Clutch (TCC) valve train installed in the control valve assembly of the transmission. This original design control valve assembly contains a hollow bushing as well as converter clutch throttle and shift valves and a calibration spring.

Beginning late in 1982 production, the TCC valve train was eliminated from the control valve assembly. This second design control valve assembly contains only a bushing to direct TCC signal oil flow. The converter clutch apply valve and solenoid continues to be used as the control for TCC operation.

When servicing the THM 200-4R or 325-4L Transmission, it is essential that the proper gasket and spacer plate be used to assure proper transmission operation. On THM 200-4R applications, incorrect parts can result in poor fuel economy, and a hard diagnostic code 39 on HT4100 equipped vehicles. On THM 325-4L applications, incorrect parts can result in poor shift quality.

MODIFICATIONS

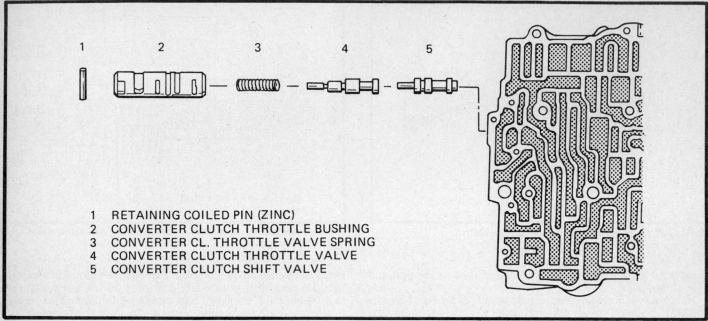

1 RETAINING COILED PIN (ZINC)
2 CONVERTER CLUTCH THROTTLE BUSHING
3 CONVERTER CL. THROTTLE VALVE SPRING
4 CONVERTER CLUTCH THROTTLE VALVE
5 CONVERTER CLUTCH SHIFT VALVE

Past design control valve assembly with T.C.C. Valve train (© General Motors Corp.)

THM 200-4R (DEVILLE AND BROUGHAM SERIES VEHICLES)

1. Service Information

a. First and second design control valve assemblies and spacer plates are not interchangeable. Care must be taken to ensure the correct spacer plate is used with the correct control valve assembly. Second design gaskets can be used to service both first and second design components.

b. First design parts are no longer available through GMWDD. Second design parts must be used to service these applications. Refer to the following parts information chart for the proper second design part numbers to be used when servicing first design applications:

THM 325-4L (ELDORADO AND SEVILLE)

2. Service Information

a. On 4.1L V-6 applications, the complete service package must be used when replacing a first design control valve assembly. The first design spacer plate is currently available but must not be used on the second design control valve assembly. On HT4100 applications, the second design control valve assembly is compatible with the existing first design spacer plate. The gasket package will service both first and second applications.

b. First design control valve assemblies are no longer available through GMWDD. Second design parts must be used to service these applications. Refer to the following parts information chart for the proper second design part numbers to be used when servicing first design applications.

THM 325-4L, FIRST DESIGN TCC VALVE TRAIN SERVICE PARTS INFORMATION

Engine	Trans Code	Control Valve Assembly	Gasket Package	Spacer Plate	Service Package
4.1L V-6	AM	N/A	8635919	8635648①	8635938②
HT4100	AJ	8635955	8635919	8635640	N/A

① First design spacer plate, not to be used on second design control valve assembly.
② Contains second design control valve assembly, spacer plate and gasket package.

THM 200-4R, FIRST DESIGN TCC VALVE TRAIN SERVICE PARTS INFORMATION

Engine	Trans Code	Control Valve Assembly	Gasket Package	Spacer Plate	Service Package
4.1L V-6	BY	N/A	8634969	N/A	8639133①
HT4100	AA & AP	N/A	8634969	8639027②	8634981①

① Contains second design control valve assembly, spacer plate, and gasket package.
② Second design spacer plate, not to be used on first design control valve assembly.

NOTE: If disassembly of a second design control valve assembly on either model transmission is performed, location of the solid bushing during reassembly is important. Locate the bushing so that the coiled pin fits into the groove in the bushing. Failure to do so could result in a loss of TCC operation.

NO REVERSE, FIRST GEAR ONLY IN FORWARD
THM 200, 200C, 200-4R, 325 and 325-4L TRANSMISSIONS/TRANSAXLES 1979-84 CADILLACS

1979-1984 Cadillacs equipped with THM 200, 200C, 200-4R, 325 and 325-4L transmissions may experience a lack of engagement in reverse, second, third and fourth gear while operating properly in first gear. This condition can be caused by stripped input drum to rear sun gear splines and does not affect line pressure readings or cause worn clutch plates or bands.

Inform technicians performing overhaul procedures for this condition that careful inspection of the input drum splines and planetary gear assemblies is necessary. Spline wear may not be completely obvious during disassembly since the splines may hold with hand torque but not with engine torque.

To inspect the splines properly, remove the snap ring used to retain the input drum to the sum gear shaft and remove the input drum from the sun gear. If any wear is present, replace the sun gear shaft along with the input drum.

DIAGNOSING OIL LEAKS ON 125C, 200C, 325-4L, AND 200-4R TRANSMISSIONS

When any THM transmission oil leak is detected, it is very important that they are diagnosed properly, as to the location and type of leak.

The following procedure will help in diagnosing the type and location of the leak and will suggest a correction method.

DIAGNOSIS PROCEDURE: (ALL MODELS)
The following procedure can be performed on car.

1. Clean all residual oil from the transmission, concentrating on the transmission oil pan to case mating areas (all models), TV cable connector (all models), transmission oil pan to sprocket cover interface area (325-4L model), final drive to case connection (325-4L model), and valve body cover to transmission oil pan interface area (125C model) (CRC's electramotive cleaner, or equivalent is recommended).

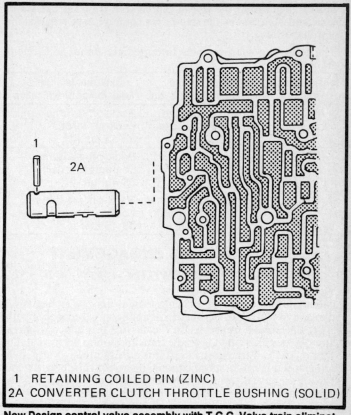

1   RETAINING COILED PIN (ZINC)
2A CONVERTER CLUTCH THROTTLE BUSHING (SOLID)

New Design control valve assembly with T.C.C. Valve train eliminated (© General Motors Corp.)

2. Dust the entire transmission with a white powder (e.g., Leak Tracing Powder or Foot Powder Spray).

3. After normal operating temperature (170°F) has been obtained, let the transmission stand for at least (30) thirty minutes.

4. Inspect the transmission for leakage by following red oil traces left in the powder. (If residual oil is left on the transmission oil pan or sprocket cover, it will be necessary for the cleaning and dusting procedure to be repeated.)

5. Once the leak has been diagnosed as to location and type (wetness, moist, damp, etc.), refer to the following repair procedure:

MODIFICATIONS

Ford Motor Company

OVERSENSITIVE 3-2 DOWNSHIFT

1982 CAR LINES EQUIPPED WITH C-3 A/T AND 2.3L ENGINE

If an oversensitive 3-2 downshift is encountered prior to servicing the main control valve assembly, inspect the modulator vacuum line for engine fuel.

If gasoline is found in the line or modulator, drain the line and replace the modulator. Route the vacuum hose from the vacuum tree on the fire wall to a higher elevation than the vacuum tree. Use a clamp and a self-tapping screw to hold the hose in place. If no fuel is encountered, proceed with the normal valve body repair.

CHANGE OF THREAD SPECIFICATIONS ON INTERMEDIATE BAND ADJUSTING SCREW AND LOCKNUT

1981-82 CAR LINES USING C-4 AND EARLY C-5 AUTOMATIC TRANSMISSIONS

During 1981 model C4 transmission production, a change of intermediate band adjustment screw and nut was incorporated—from coarse to fine thread.

The adjustment specifications are different for the intermediate band on C4 transmissions depending on the thread of the adjustment screw and nut.

Prior to any intermediate band adjustment or service, always examine the threads of the adjustment screw to determine the type of threads—fine or coarse.

MODIFICATIONS

NOTE: Enough of the thread can be seen from the outside of the transmission case so the screw does not have to be removed for visual inspection.

The following chart denotes Intermediate Band Adjustment Specifications:

Transmission Type	Pitch on Thread Adjustment Screw & Nut	Intermediate Band Adjustment Specification
C4	Fine pitch thread (C4 trans W/C5 case)	Back-off 3 turns. Locknut torque 35-45 lbs.-ft
C4	Coarse pitch thread	Back-off 1¾ turns. Locknut torque 35-45 lbs.-ft.
C5	Fine pitch thread only	Back-off 4¼ turns. Locknut torque 35-45 lbs.-ft.

HARSH REVERSE ENGAGEMENT

1981 CAR LINES EQUIPPED WITH C-4 (PEN) AND 3.3L ENGINE

A harsh neutral to reverse idle engagement may be encountered on the above 1981 3.3L passenger car applications equipped with a C-4 (PEN) model transmission. To service this concern, check the model identification tag on the transmission to verify that it is a PEN model C-4 transmission. If it is a PEN model, verify that the idle speed is set to specifications, if the concern persists, the following are instructions to rework the main control valve body assembly and the low-reverse servo piston assembly:

NOTE: This rework may cause slight delay in reverse engagement.

1. Remove the low-reverse servo assembly. Mustang and Capri vehicle applications require lowering the transmission to remove the low-reverse servo. To lower the transmission, remove the engine support-to-crossmember nuts, loosen the right-hand crossmember nut, remove the left hand crossmember bolt and nut, and then swing the crossmember to the right side. The transmission can be lowered with a jack sufficiently to gain access to the low-reverse servo cover.

2. After removing the low-reverse servo piston, drill a 0.031 ± 0.002 in. (#68 Drill) diameter hole through the piston top surface. This can be facilitated by inserting the servo in a vise. Allow the top of the servo to be supported by the vise not clamped in the jaws. Clean the metal shavings from the drilled hole and from the piston.

Drilling Servo piston (© Ford Motor Co.)

3. Reinstall the piston into the case as outlined in the low-reverse servo shop manual procedure. Follow Steps 5-7. No special orientation of the hole is necessary when installing the servo assembly into the case.

4. Adjust the low-reverse band.

Step II Main Control Valve Body Assembly Modification

1. Remove the main control valve body assembly from the transmission.

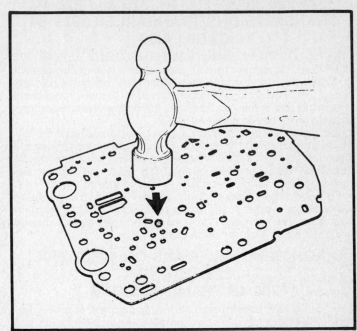

Seating ball bearing in separator plate orifice (© Ford Motor Co.)

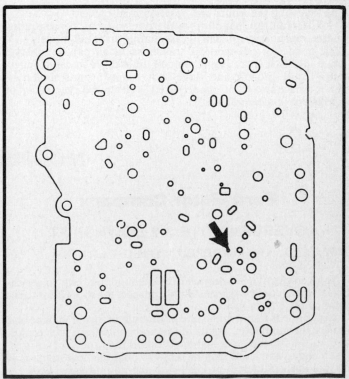

Location of reworked orifice in separator plate (© Ford Motor Co.)

2. Remove the seperator plate from the main control valve body be careful not to lose the upper valve body shuttle valve and check valve when seperating the upper and lower valve bodies.

3. Rework the seperator plate as follows: Place the seperator plate on a hard flat surface such as a steel block. Using a steel ball approximately ¼ in. diameter, rework hole #76 by placing the ball in the hole and striking the ball with a hammer until the hole is reduced to a diameter of slightly less than 0.040 in. where a #60 drill will not quite pass through the hole. Then size the hole to 0.040 in. by drilling with a #60 drill. Clean-up metal burrs from the hole after the operation.

4. Reassemble the main control valve body assembly.

5. Reinstall the main control valve body assembly in the transmission.

INTERMEDIATE BAND ADJUSTMENT SPECIFICATION CHANGE

1981 C-4 A/T WITH FINE THREAD ADJUSTING SCREWS

All C-4 automatic transmissions built from January 5, 1981 and after are equipped with a new intermediate band adjuster screw and nut using a fine pitch ½-28 thread.

Whenever a band adjustment is required, the following new procedure is required:

Intermediate Band Adjustment

1. Remove and discard the lock nut.

2. Install a new lock nut on the adjusting screw. With the special tool, tighten the adjusting screw until the handle clicks. The tool is a pre-set torque wrench which clicks and breaks when the torque on the adjusting screw reaches 10 ft. lbs.

3. Back off the adjusting screw exactly 3 turns.

4. Hold the adjusting screw from turning and tighten the lock nut to 40 ft. lbs.

This change is being incorporated concurrently with new cases bearing a yellow trademark. The fine adjusting screw can be identified by an identification rib on the strut end.

Transmissions built prior to the above date will continue to use the old band adjustment procedure.

New Model Numbers Affected

PEJ-	AC4	PEB-	N11	Pen-	A1	PEM-	W1
	AD4		P9		B1		C6
			Z1				D6
			U5				E6
PEA-	CP1	PEE-	FL6				AC1
	CE10		GB1				AD1
							AE1
							AL1
							AM1
							AN1
							AK1

SHIFT HUNTING CONDITION DURING 1-2 UPSHIFT

1980 AND EARLIER C-4 MODELS

To service the condition of shift hunting (rapid progressional first-to-second, second-to-first gear shift) occurring during the 1-2 shift period at minimum throttle (approximately 10 mph), replace the production primary valve with service primary valve part no. D70Z-7C054-A as follows:

1. Remove the transmission extension.

2. Remove the governor from the transmission output shaft.

3. Remove the governor primary valve snap ring, washer and spring. Remove the governor primary valve from the body and discard.

4. Install the new service primary valve reinstall the spring washer and snap ring in the governor body.

5. Reinstall the governor to the oil collector body.

6. Reinstall the extension assembly.

7. Lower the vehicle and fill the transmission to proper level.

8. Test drive vehicle.

PART NUMBER	PART NAME
D70Z-7C054-A	Primary Valve

NOTE: C4 automatic transmission use transmission fluid meeting Ford Specification ESP-M2C 138-CJ or Dexron® II, Series D.

HARSH 1-2 UPSHIFTS AND/OR 3-2 DOWNSHIFTS

1981 CAR LINES EQUIPPED WITH 3.3L ENGINES AND C-4 A/T, MODELS PEN-A, PEN-B, PEN-M and PEN-N ONLY

Customer concerns of harsh 1-2 upshifting and/or 3-2 downshifts, may be resolved by reinstalling the following shift feel revision kit—E1DZ-7D371-A.

Shift feel revision kit consists of:

1-Intermediate servo cover

1-Main intermediate servo cover gasket

1-Intermediate servo piston

1-Intermediate servo piston seal (small)

1-Intermediate servo piston seal (large)

1-Intermediate servo piston return spring (orange)

1-Main control intermediate servo accumulator spring (yellow)

DESCRIPTION OF CHANGES AND INTERCHANGEABILITY

1984 CAR AND TRUCK LINES EQUIPPED WITH C-5 AUTOMATIC TRANSMISSIONS

NOTE: Information arrived to late to include with the C-5 testing and overhaul section.

C-5 transmission will have the following changes incorporated for 1984 model vehicles.

Approximately eight (8) models of C-5 automatic transmissions are currently released for the 1984 five (5) passenger car models and three (3) truck models. The truck models are two (2) F-150 applications and one (1) Ranger/Bronco II 2.8L 4x4 application.

Vehicle and/or engine combinations dropped for 1984 include the 3.3L (200 CID) engine with the C-5 transmission; the 2.3L Ranger with the C-5 transmission; and the 3.8L F-100 C-5 truck model. the 2.3L Ranger will be released with the C-3 transmission. New to C-5 will be the F-150 4.9L and 5.0L truck applications.

MAJOR DESIGN CHANGES FOR INCORPOATION OF THE 4.9L AND THE 5.0L F-150 APPLICATIONS

1. Micro-finish change to the forward planet assembly for durability. This planet will be the service replacement for all C-5 model transmissions.

2. The reverse clutch pack will have one more steel plate (3 to 4) and one more friction plate (3 to 4).

3. The converter is a 12 in. non-converter clutch 110 type converter. It is as deep as the converter clutch type converter because the clutch assembly has been replaced by a spacer.

4. Two new flywheels (flywheels were used on other vehicle/engine applications).

5. Transmission fluid capacity is 11.5 U.S. quarts.

C-5 PASSENGER CAR HIGHLIGHTS

1. All passsenger car applications have 12 in. converter clutch type converters.

2. All converters will have an orange special balance mark on a converter stud. If a flywheel bolt has a special balance mark, align the marks to avoid powertrain imbalance.

3. Fleet applications with the auxiliary cooler option will have an "H" fitting that bypasses some of the auxiliary cooler flow, especially during cold weather operation to ensure lubrication flow to the transmission.

INTERCHANGEABILITY:

The following 1984 transmission and main control are carryover 1983 and can be used on the 1983 model if service replacement is necessary:

For 1983 Ranger/Bronco II 2.8L 4x4:
Use 1984:
PEJ-AJ E37P-7000-EA
Main Control E37P-7A100-AA

NO OR DELAYED UPSHIFTS/DOWNSHIFTS

1982 ECONOLINE AND BRONCO WITH C-6 A/T WITH BUILD DATE OF 10-1-81 to 2-28-82

No or delayed upshift or downshift may be caused by forward and reverse planet assembly bearing spacer and thrust washer deterioration.

No or delayed upshift or downshift in vehicles with transmissions built between 10-1-81 and 2-28-82 may be caused by forward and reverse planet assembly bearing spacer and thrust washer deterioration. The transmission build date can be determined from the metal I.D. tag that is bolted to the intermediate servo cover.

This condition is characterized by fine scoring of the pump gear cavities and/or converter impeller hub and excessive magnetic metallic contamination in the main control, oil pan, and oil filter screen.

When servicing a transmission built between 10-1-81 and 2-28-82 that exhibits no or delayed upshift or downshift, remove the transmission oil pan to inspect for excessive magnetic contamination. If such contamination is present in the oil pan or oil pick-up screen, remove the transmission and replace the forward and reverse planet assemblies. Replace other components as necessary. Replacement of the planet assemblies is required because deterioration of the spacer and thrust washer is not readily apparent by visual inspection.

SLIPPING 3RD GEAR PERFORMANCE AND/ OR NO 4-3 DOWNSHIFT

1981-82 CAR LINES EQUIPPED WITH AOD TRANSMISSION

Slipping 3rd gear, lack of 3rd gear performance, or no 4-3 downshift may be caused by a blocked hydraulic passageway in the transmission case.

The blockage of this particular transmission case passageway feeds both the overdrive servo for release of the overdrive band and forward clutch circuit in 3rd gear. Therefore, if this passageway is blocked, the overdrive band may drag resulting in a lack of 3rd gear performance. Eventually, the overdrive band material may deteriorate and require replacement.

To identify cases that have a portion of the case hydraulic passageway blocked, visually check the die numbers located on the top of the case in the converter housing area. With the transmission in the vehicle, it is necessary to use a long-handled flexible mirror with a flashlight to read the numbers.

If the case is identified with the die numbers 31 or 32, remove the oil pan, filter, and main control valve body. Identify the passageway and the portion that maybe blocked. If the passageway is blocked, replace the case.

HARSH 2-3 SHIFT

1980-81 CAR LINES EQUIPPED WITH AOD TRANSMISSION

The following is a procedure to resolve harsh 2-3 shift concerns.

Check for a Missing Check Ball

1. Remove the valve body from the transmission.
2. Disassemble the valve body.
3. Refer to the illustration for the proper location of the number 3 check ball.
4. If the check ball is present, proceed to the check the 2-3 capacity modulator valve.

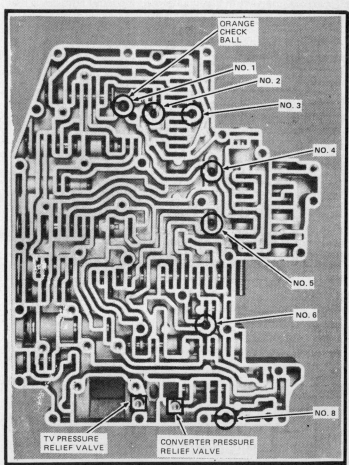

Location of Check balls. Check ball number seven was eliminated in later production years (© Ford Motor Co.)

5. If the check ball is not present, install the check ball and reassemble the valve body.
6. Reassemble the transmission fluid level following the "Fluid Level Check" procedure.

Check the 2-3 Capacity Modulator Valve

1. Follow the valve body disassembly procedure for both the location of the 2-3 capacity modulator valve and for the removal and installation of the valve.

2. If the valve does not move freely, remove any obstructions. If necessary, replace the main control valve body.

3. If the valve moves freely, reassemble the valve body and proceed to the check for a blocked 2-3 accumulator case feed passage.

4. When reassembling the valve body, follow the assembly instructions which includes replacing the gaskets, using the valve body alignment pins when installing the separator plate on the valve body and when installing the valve body on the case. Also, properly torque the valve body to avoid repeat servicing.

Check the 2-3 Accumulator Case Feed Passage

1. With the transmission in the vehicle and the main control valve body removed, air pressure test the 2-3 accumulator piston. Apply air to the 2-3 accumulator passage. Use service tool T80L-77030-B or equivalent in order to seal the apply passage. Check for a free flow of air to the accumulator bore.

2. If there is not free flow air, drill the passage free by using a 6 in. long ¼ in. diameter (.250) drill bit. Drill into the passage 3 in. To indicate when a 3 in. depth has been reached, wrap a thin piece of black electrical tape around the drill 3 in. from the drill tip. Drill into the passage until the black tape meets the case valve body surface. After this operation, it is important to remove all metal particles and shavings from the passageway and the bore. Use regulated air pressure and blow into both the passageway and accumulator bore to remove all particles thoroughly.

3. Check with air to insure the passageway is clear. If there is still no free flow of air to the accumulator bore, replace the case.

4. If there is free flow of air to the accumulator bore, reinstall the 2-3 accumulator assembly into the case. Reinstall the valve body using the alignment pins. Finish assembling the transmission.

5. Check the transmission fluid level.

ERRATIC 4-3 AND 3-4 SHIFTS

1981-82 CAR LINES EQUIPPED WITH AOD TRANSMISSION

Erratic 4-3 and 3-4 shifts at vehicle speeds of 45 mph or more may be the result of the governor body restricting line pressure to the governor valve and/or areas in the transmission allowing leakage in the governor pressure circuit.

This condition may be recognized by a 4-3 downshift as the throttle is released followed by a 3-4 upshift as the throttle is applied even though the vehicle speed remains nearly constant.

To service, first verify the transmission build date. On 1981 and 1982 vehicles with transmissions built prior to November 16, 1981, check the governor casting vendor symbol located on the casting back below the body casting number. If the vendor symbol   appears, replace the governor.

If the transmission has a build date after November 16, 1981, or if the governor body casting does not have the specified vendor symbol, or if the vehicle is not corrected by replacing the governor, check for areas that may cause leakage in the governor pressure circuit. Such areas include: a broken or unseated governor retaining ring, worn or damaged output shaft seal rings, a worn or damaged case bore at the output shaft seal rings, an oversize counterweight bore or an undersized output shaft at the counterweight bore, case porosity, leakage between the main control and case due to out of flatness or loose main control valve body bolts.

REVISED OVERDRIVE BAND PIN

1980-81 CAR LINE EQUIPPED WITH AOD TRANSMISSIONS

Overdrive premature band wear may be caused by movement of the overdrive anchor pin. For anchor pin movement inboard more than ³/32″ (2.38mm) from machined face of the case boss, replace the anchor pin with the revised anchor pin—(E2AZ-7F295-A).

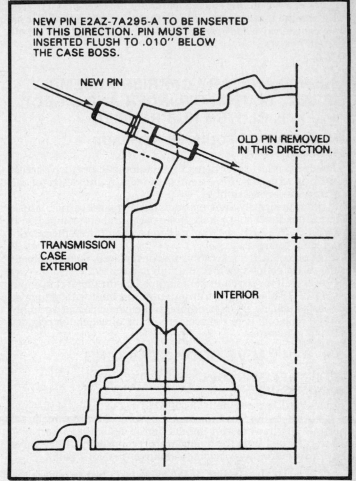

NEW PIN E2AZ-7A295-A TO BE INSERTED IN THIS DIRECTION. PIN MUST BE INSERTED FLUSH TO .010″ BELOW THE CASE BOSS.

Installation of new band anchor pin (© Ford Motor Co.)

NOTE: During transmission overhaul verify anchor pin movement-replace if movement is in excess of ³/32″ (2.38mm).

CAUTION

Exercise care not to cock the pin in the case. By driving the old pin out with new pin, the old pin will help to align the service pin to prevent the service pin from cocking in the transmision case hole. If the pin digs into the case, leakage, case cranks or metal contamination may result.

WHISTLING NOISE ON ACCELERATION

1981-82 CAR LINES EQUIPPED WITH AOD TRANSMISSION

A high frequency "whistle" noise may be emitted on vehicles equipped with the AOD transmission. This noise may be caused by converter pressure relief valve oscillation.

This "whistle" type noise is reported to occur in first, second and reverse gears during light throttle with a cold transmission and/or heavier throttle with a warm transmission. The "whistle" noise is approximately the same pitch in all three gears. Usually, the "whistle" stops one or two seconds before the 2-3 shift occurs. Because of the throttle openings involved, it may not be possible to find the "whistle" noise in reverse.

If the "whistle" noise is identified, change, only the converter pressure relief valve with the new design valve (E2AZ-7E217-A) and not the throttle pressure relief valve.

NOTE: Prior to this change, both the converter pressure relief valve and the throttle pressure relief valve were identical. For any main control valve body service involving disassembly, do not mix the relief valves.

NEW PLANETARY CARRIER ASSEMBLY, DIRECT CLUTCH CYLINDER AND DIRECT CLUTCH HUB REVISED

1980-81 CARLINES EQUIPPED WITH AOD TRANSMISSIONS

In the event internal servicing of an automatic overdrive transmission is required, it is essential to identify the design of the planetary carrier assembly.

In order to identify transmission's design planet carrier, visually check the direct clutch hub. If the part numbers stamped on it are EOAZ-7F236-AB, the transmission was built with the new design planet carrier assembly.

If the planet carrier assembly must be replaced, no replacement of the direct clutch cylinder and hub is required.

However, if the part numbers stamped on the direct clutch hub are EOAZ-7F236-AA, the transmission was built with the previous design planet carrier assembly. If the planet carrier assembly must be replaced, then replacement of the direct clutch cylinder and hub is required.

VALVE BODY SERVICING

1980-81 CARLINES EQUIPPED WITH AOD TRANSMISSIONS

The No. 7 ball was originally installed to insure the 3-4 shift, however, further testing has indicated the No. 7 ball is not required. During AOD transmission production in May 1981, the No. 7 ball was omitted from the main control (valve body). If the valve body is apart for any servicing—remove the No. 7 ball.

NOTE: The disassembly of the valve body just to remove the No. 7 ball is not recommended.

ASSEMBLY INTERCHANGE, CHANGES AND MODIFICATIONS

1981-83 CAR LINES EQUIPPED WITH AOD TRANSMISSION 1981-82

In the event an entire automatic overdrive transmission assembly is to be replaced in a 1981 vehicle, the following chart lists the 1982 AOD transmissions that can be used to service the 1981 models/applications:

NOTE: 1981 models not listed are to be serviced by individual components only.

1982 Models	1981 Models	1982 Model Applicatons
PKA-AS5 E2AP-7000-KA	PKA-AS E1AP-7000-ACA	5.8L Ford/Mercury Police 49S/Can. 2.73 axle
PKA-M13 E2VP-7000-AA	PKA-M8 E1VP-7000-BA	5.9L Lincoln/Mark 50S/Unq. Can. 3.08 axle
PKA-AG5 E2AP-7000-CA	PKA-AL E1AP-7000-JA	5.0L Ford/Mercury (Sedan) and Ford/Mercury Police W/O Low Gear Lockout 50S/Unq. Can. 3.08 axle
PKA-AG5 E2AP-7000-CA	PKA-AG E1AP-7000-HA	5.0L Ford/Mercury (SW) 50S/Unq. Can. 3.08 axle
PKA-AU5 E2AP-7000-HA	PKA-AU E1AP-7000-AEA	5.0L Ford/Mercury Police 50S 3.08 axle

1982 Models	1981 Models	1982 Model Applicatons
PKA-AH5 E2SP-7000-AA	PKA-AH E1SP-7000-BA	4.2L T'Bird/XR-7 50S/Can. 3.08 axle
PKA-AF5 E2AP-7000-AA	PKA-AF E1AP-7000-GA	4.2L Ford/Mercury Sedan and Ford/Mercury Police W/O Low Gear Lockout 50S/Can: 3.08 axle
PKA-AT5 E2AP-7000-CA	PKA-AT E1AP-7000-ADA	4.2L Ford/Mercury Police 50S/Can. 3.08 axle
PKB-A6 E2TP-7000-AA	PKB-A1 E1TP-7000-AAC	5.0L F-100/150 3.25 axle, F-250 3.54/3.73 axle 49S/Can.
PKB-A6 E2TP-7000-AA	PKB-A E1TP-7000-AAA	5.0L F-100/150 3.25 axle, F-250 3.54/3.73 alxe 49S/Can.

1982-83

Fifteen (15) models are currently released for the 1983 Automatic Overdrive Transmission (AOD) program; eleven (11) passenger car models and four (4) truck models.

New to AOD for 1983 is the 4.9L engine, the LTD/Marquis, and the Econoline Series applications. There are two (2) new transmission calibrations for the 4.9L applications and one (1) new transmission for the 5.0L

C. New cable TV linkage. The TV linkage adjustment can be checked and reset, but there is no fine adjustment capability as with the TV rod type linkage (4.9L E and F Series application).

INTERCHANGEABILITY:

The following chart lists the 1983 AOD transmissions that can be used to service the 1982 models and applications listed:

1983 Models	Replaces 1982 Models		1982 Model Applications
		PASSENGER CARS	
PKA-AU17 ① E3AP-7000-CA	—	PKA-AU7 E2AP-7000-HA	5.0L Ford/Mercury Police 3.08 A/R
PKA-AS17 ① E3AP-7000-BA	—	PKA-AS7 E2AP-7000-KA	5.8L H.O. Ford/Mercury Police 2.73 A/R
PKA-AG17 ① E3AP-7000-AA	—	PKA-AG7 E2AP-7000-CA	5.0L Ford/Mercury and Police 3.08 A/R with Low Gear Lockout Delete
PKA-AY12 ① E3AP-7000-DA	—	PKA-AY2 E2AP-7000-DA	5.0L Ford/Mercury Altitude and Police 3.42 A/R with Low Gear Lockout Delete
PKA-BC5 ① E3VP-7000-BA	—	PKA-BC3① E2VP-7000-BB	5.0L Lincoln/Mark 3.42 A/R
PKA-BD12 ① E35P-7000-CB	—	PKA-BD3① E25P-7000-AB	5.0L Continental 3.08 A/R
PKA-BB12 ① E35AP-7000-EA	—	PKA-BB2 E2AP-7000-JA	5.0L Ford/Mercury Police 3.42 A/R
PKA-C25 ① E3AP-7000-FA	—	PKA-C15 E2AP-7000-NA	5.8L Ford/Mercury Police 2.73 A/R
PKA-M25 ① E3VP-7000-AB	—	PKA-M16① E2VP-7000-AB	5.0L Lincoln/Mark 3.08 A/R

Truck			
PKB-A20	—	PKB-A10	5.0L F100/150/250
E3TP-7000-MA		E2TP-7000-AB	3.25, 3.54, 3.73, A/R

① Push connect cooler line fittings. Replace with ¼ in. pipe fitting where applicable for 1982 usage.

The following 1982-83 main control valve body assembly can be used to service the 1982 main control listed:

Main Control	Replaces	1982 Main Control
E25P-7A100-AA (PVG)	—	E2SP-7A100-CA (SWG, SVG)
E2AP-7A100-DA (OVH)	—	E2AP-7A100-FA (RWH, RVH)
E2AP-7A100-HA (OCH)	—	E2AP-7A100-JA (RBH, RCH)
E3SP-7A100-CA (UVR)	—	E2SP-7A100-DB, DA (NWM, NVM)

There are four (4) new main control assemblies for 1983.

USE OF ANAEROBIC SEALANT ON EXTENSION HOUSING BOLTS

1983 CAR LINES EQUIPPED WITH AOD TRANSMISSIONS

The #3, #4 and #5 extension housing bolts are now pre-coated with Dri-Loc Anaerobic Sealant in production. Revised service procedures are provided for reinstalling these extension housing to main case bolts—removal and recoating of thread sealant.

In the event service requires removing and reinstalling the extension housing bolts (#3, #4, and #5 bolts).

The following is the revised procedure:
1. Wire brush the bolts and case bolt holes.
2. Remove as much loose sealant as possible.
3. Recoat the bolt with either Threadlock and Sealer (EOAZ-19554-A), Pipe Sealant with Teflon (D8AZ-19554-A), or Teflon Tape.
4. Torque the bolts to specifications (16-20 ft. lbs. or 22-27 N•m).

FLUID LEAKAGE AT LEFT SIDE OF PAN GASKET AREA

1983 CAR LINES EQUIPPED WITH AOD TRANSMISSION

Fluid leakage in the left (driver's) side area of the oil pan may be caused by an undertorqued pipe plugs(s).

Some vehicles built before February 7, 1983, may exhibit a fluid leakage at the left side area of transmission oil pan gasket. Prior to servicing the suspect oil pan gasket:
1. Clean off all traces of transmission fluid.
2. Test drive vehicle and then observe the concern area.
3. If fluid leakage is occurring from a pipe plug(s), the following service procedure should be performed:
   a. Remove the suspect plug(s).
   b. Clean plug threads and reinstall to proper torque specifications (8-16 N•m—6-12 ft. lbs.) and road test.

NEW 3-4 SHIFT VALVE AND SPRING

1983½ CAR LINES EQUIPPED WITH AOD TRANSMISSION

A new 3-4 shift valve configuration and spring was incorporated in production mid-March, 1983 which moves the 3-4 shift to a

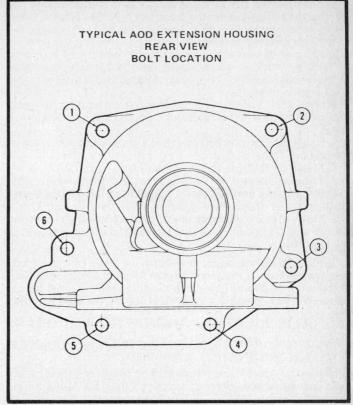

TYPICAL AOD EXTENSION HOUSING
REAR VIEW
BOLT LOCATION

Rear extension housing retaining bolt locations (© Ford Motor Co.)

higher vehicle speed and provides for 4-3 downshifts with less throttle and at higher speeds.

The new shift valve is comprised of two parts and the bore plug has been replaced by a sleeve.

The new shift valve configuration will change the 3-4/4-3 shift pattern. The new 3-4 shift will feel delayed if compared directly with the old design. This condition may be more evident prior to engine break-in. The old design would upshift to fourth gear even during fairly heavy throttle acceleration. The new design will not upshift to fourth gear until the vehicle approaches the desired speed and the driver eases up on the accelerator pedal.

The new 4-3 downshift pattern feels more responsive than the old design. At moderate to heavy throttle, the transmission will downshift to third gear easier and at higher speeds.

Easier downshifts or delayed 3-4 shifts is the intent of the new shift pattern and it should not be interpreted as a transmission concern. Proper explanation to the customer of this as normal vehicle operation is required.

REVISED FRONT OIL PUMP GASKET

1983½ CAR LINES EQUIPPED WITH AOD TRANSMISSION

A new front pump gasket was incorporated in May, 1983 on all AOD transmissions. The pump gasket is notched matching a recessed area in the pump body. This will allow transmission fluid to drainback at a higher point into the case, alleviating some transmission pump case leakage concerns.

The AOD transmission case will also be changed removing the drainback hole in the case casting. Refer to Figure 17 for the location of the case drainback hole. The hole allowed transmission fluid in the pump area to drainback to the oil pan. Instead, the notched gasket will provide a path for the fluid to vent at a higher point into the case.

MODIFICATIONS

For service, the transmission service case will be changed to the new level which deletes the drainback hole. The service case is interchangeable for all model years and all AOD applications.

The new notched pump gasket can be used on both type transmission cases. However, the original design gasket cannot be used on the new level case which has the drainback hole deleted since there is no provision for drainback of transmission fluid with this combination of parts.

Service stock with the original design front pump gasket may be used on a case with no drainback hole; modify the gasket as follows:

1. Using the new notched gasket as a template, lay it on top of the original design gasket.
2. Match all feed passages and bolt holes.
3. Trace the notched portion on the original design level gasket.
4. Remove the notched gasket and cut out the portion traced on the original design level gasket.
5. Verify that the modification was done correctly by comparing the modified gasket with the notched gasket that was used as the template.

NOTE: Do not use sealer or adhesive on pump case or gasket-to-pump surface. If the pump gasket notch is blocked, no fluid drainback is possible. This could result in the fluid pressure unseating the front pump O-ring or fluid coming out the filler tube.

ERRATIC SHIFTING AND/OR NO 4TH GEAR

1983½ THUNDERBIRD, COUGAR CAR LINES EQUIPPED WITH 5.0L ENGINE (CFI 3-22W-ROO)

The transmission TV rod return may be restricted by the rubber hose and nylon fittings protruding from the back of the rubber connector block (—9E455—). This connector block is attached to the 3-port PVS valve, at the rear left hand side of the intake manifold. Potential kinking of the canister purge hose is also possible due to incorrect orientation of the nylon elbow on the rubber block connector.

On a customer concern basis, the following procedure is recommended:

1. Remove the rubber connector block from the 3-port PVS.
2. With an appropriate deep well socket (slotted), rotate the 3-port PVS (located on rear left hand side of intake manifold) clockwise, until the ports are aimed toward the upper rear rocker cover attaching bolt (approximately 15-20° from original position).
3. Rotate the middle and lower nylon elbow 180° from original position. The middle elbow should face the left side of the engine and the lower elbow should face the right side of the engine.
   a. Route the middle vacuum hose from the connector block in front of the PVS valve and under the kickdown (TV-rod) rod. The upper and middle hoses should be tucked down.
   b. Route the lower vacuum hose to the purge control valve under the kickdown rod.
4. Ensure that any other hoses that are routed in area of kickdown rod (TV rod) are placed under or away from rod to eliminate any potential interference.

REVISED THROTTLE VALVE (TV) LINKAGE ADJUSTMENT PROCEDURE USING TV CONTROL PRESSURE

1980-84 CAR AND TRUCK LINES EQUIPPED WITH AOD TRANSMISSION

This revised method of setting TV linkage on all AOD transmissions is the only way to adjust the linkage to the middle of the specification curve. This method sets the linkage to the most sensitive point.

The new procedure attached uses a TV control pressure gage block service tool D84P-70332-A. If that tool is not available, alternates are listed in the procedure. Highlights of the new procedure include setting the TV linkage at idle with the gage block installed to 35 ± 5 PSI.

The "TV pressure method for adjusting the TV linkage" procedure is recommended for transmission shift concerns while the "Linkage Adjusted at the Carburetor" procedure is recommended when the idle speed is changed by 50 rpm.

LINKAGE ADJUSTMENT USING TV CONTROL PRESSURE TV ROD SYSTEMS ONLY

The following procedure may be used to check and/or adjust the throttle valve (TV) rod linkage using the TV control pressure.

1. Check/adjust the engine curb idle speed to specification required.
2. Attach a 0-100 PSI pressure gage, T73L-6600-A, with the adapter fitting D80L-77001-A, or equivalent to the TV port on the transmission with sufficient flexible hose to make gage accessible while operating the engine.
3. Obtain a TV control pressure gage block, service tool no. D84P-70332-A, or fabricate a block .397 ± .007 inch thick. The following drill bit shanks may also be used in order of preference: Letter X (.397 in.), 10mm (.3937 in.) or 25/64 (.3906 in.).
4. Operate the engine until normal operating temperature is reached and the throttle lever is off fast idle or the Idle Speed Control plunger (if equipped) is at its normal idle position. The transmission fluid temperature should be approximately 100-150°F. Do not make pressure check if transmission fluid is cold or too hot to touch.
5. Set parking brake, place shift selector in N (neutral), remove air cleaner, shut off air conditioner. If equipped with a Vacuum Operated Throttle Modulator, disconnect and plug the vacuum line to this unit. If equipped with a Throttle Solenoid Positioner or an Idle Speed Control, do not disconnect either of these units.

—————— CAUTION ——————
Do not make pressure check in Park.

6. With engine idling in neutral, and no accessory load on engine, insert gage block (or drill shank) between the carburetor throttle lever and adjustment screw on the TV linkage lever at the carburetor. The TV pressure should be 35 psi ± 5 psi. For best transmission function, use the adjusting screw to set the pressure as close as possible to 35 psi. Turning the screw in will raise the pressure 1.5 psi per turn. Backing out the screw will lower the pressure. If equipped with Idle Speed Control, some "hunting" may occur and an average pressure reading will have to be determined. If the adjusting screw does not have enough adjustment range to bring TV pressure within specification, first adjust rod at the transmission.
7. Remove gage block, allowing TV lever to return to idle. With engine still idling in neutral, TV pressure must be at or near zero (less than 5 psi). If not, back out adjusting screw until TV pressure is less than 5 psi. Reinstall gage block and check that TV pressure is still 35 psi ± 5 psi.

DESCRIPTION OF CHANGES AND INTERCHANGEABILITY FOR 1984

1984 CAR AND TRUCK LINES EQUIPPED WITH AOD TRANSMISSIONS

AOD transmissions will have the following changes incorporated for 1983½ and 1984 model vehicles.

Twenty (20) models are currently released for the 1984 Automatic Overdrive Transmission (AOD) Program: Sixteen (16) passenger car models and four (4) F-Series/E-Series models. This is an increase of three (3) transmission models from the 17 models in 1983.

New to AOD for 1984 is the Mustang/Capri vehicle line equipped with either the 3.8L or the 5.0L H.O. engine both scheduled as a running change after Job #1. The 5.0L H.O. engine is a new power plant application with the AOD transmission. The

Mark VII for 1984 will have the console floor shift (cable type) transmission shift controls. The F-100 truck has been replaced by the Range application.

MAJOR DESIGN CHANGES FOR INCORPORATION OF THE 3.8L AND 5.0L H.O. MUSTANG/CAPRI APPLICATION:

1. Two (2) new transmission models.
2. One (1) new main control valve body calibration.
3. New manual lever (oriented down).
4. Both 3.8L and 5.0L H.O. packages will have the cable type floor shift with the shift brackets installed on the rear of the transmission on two extension housing stud bolts.
5. 13mm hex head extension housing bolts will be used in holes No. 1 and No. 6 (maybe No. 2 also) to provide bearing surface for the floor shift bracket. 10mm hex head bolts will be used in the remainder of the extension housing holes.
6. TV levers will be curved similar to truck lever.
7. Converter has a higher stall ratio (165K) for improved performance.

MARK VII APPLICATIONS:

1. 13mm hex head extension housing bolts will be used in holes No. 1 and No. 6 (maybe No. 2 also) to provide bearing surface for the floor shift bracket. 10mm hex head bolts will be used in the remainder of the extension housing holes.

AOD DESIGN CHANGES AFFECTING ALL PASSENGER CAR AND TRUCK APPLICATIONS:

1. The dipstick full mark for operating temperature (hot) fluid fill has been changed to a cross-hatched area instead of arrows. Do not add fluid if level is in the cross-hatched area.
2. The following AOD hardware changes were incorporated on all model AOD transmissions with build dates of July 19, 1983, and later. These hardware changes will affect past model serviceability.
   a. Common forward and reverse clutch friction plates and pressure plates which result in new internal snap ring locations for both the reverse clutch drum and the forward clutch cylinder. (The forward clutch cylinder friction plate usage will be expanded to the reverse clutch drum and the reverse clutch pressure plate usage will be expanded to the forward clutch cylinder.)
   b. A new external retaining ring for the intermediate one-way clutch which results in a deeper snap ring groove on the reverse clutch drum.

SERVICEABILITY REVISIONS:

The new reverse clutch drums (no change to number of plates; passenger car—3 plate drum, 4 plate drum and truck drum; and no change to clutch pack clearance specification) will have an internal identification groove adjacent to the clutch pack snap ring groove. This internal identification groove indicates that the 7E311 friction plates and the new intermediate one-way clutch snap ring must be used with this drum.

When service stock is exhausted on the original reverse clutch drum, the new reverse clutch drum will be the replacement drum for all past model service.

The new intermediate one-way clutch retaining ring will replace all stock in the depot and will be used on all past model service, but must be used with the new level reverse clutch drum. Therefore, whenever the original design level drum is replaced on past model applications, the intermediate one-way clutch retaining ring must be replaced with the new level retaining ring.

The new forward clutch cylinder (same number of plates as before—4 plate cylinder and 5 plate cylinder; and no change to clutch pack clearance specification) will be identified by a reduced chamfer ($1/32$ in. x 45° O.D.) vs. the previous forward clutch cylinder ($1/8$ in. x 45° O.D.). The reduced chamfer identification indicates that 7F278 pressure plate must be used.

1. All converters will have an orange special balance mark on a converter stud. If a flywheel bolt hole has a special balance mark, align the marks to avoid powertrain imbalance.
2. Passenger cars with auxiliary oil coolers will have an "H" fitting that bypasses some of the auxiliary cooler flow, especially during cold weather operation to ensure lubrication flow to the transmission.

CARBURETOR DESIGN CHANGES AFFECTING TV LINKAGE ADJUSTMENT PROCEDURE:

Passenger Cars with 3.8L CFI

1. A new idle speed control motor (ISC) will be incorporated on the carburetor replacing other conventional throttle positioners. The ISC will have the capability of varying the throttle plate opening via signals from the EEC IV system. Before TV linkage is checked and adjusted, the ISC motor plunger must be retracted.

E and F-Series 4.9L YFA-FBC

1. A new idle speed control motor (ISC) (same as 3.8L CFI passenger car) will be incorporated on the carburetor replacing other throttle positioners. The ISC motor plunger must be retracted before checking and adjusting the TV linkage. But, in addition, there is a fast idle cam lever and that must be de-cammed before the TV linkage is adjusted.

INTERCHANGEABILITY

The following chart lists the 1984 AOD transmissions that can be used to service the 1983 models and applications listed.

1984 Model	Replaces	1983 Models	1983 Model Applications
		PASSENGER CARS	
PKA-AS23 E4AP-7000-JA	—	PKA-AS21 E3AP-7000-BA	5.8L H.O. Ford police 2.73 Axle with low gear lockout.
PKA-C31 E4AP-7000-KA	—	PKA-C29 E3AP-7000-FA	5.8L H.O. Ford/Mercury (Sedan) Canada, Ford Police (50S/Can/Alt) 2.73 Axle without low gear lockout.
PKA-BD18 E45P-7000-DA	—	PKA-BD16 E35P-7000-CB	5.0L Continental (50S/Can) 3.08 Axle, (Alt/Calif.) 3.27 Axle.
PKA-AG23 E4AP-7000-HA	—	PKA-AG21 E3AP-7000-AA	5.0L Ford/Mercury (Passenger Car) Ford Police (50S/Unique Canada) 3.08 Axle without low gear lockout.

MODIFICATIONS

INTERCHANGEABILITY

The following chart lists the 1984 AOD transmissions that can be used to service the 1983 models and applications listed.

1984 Model	Replaces	1983 Models	1983 Model Applications
		PASSENGER CARS	
PKA-AY18 E4AP-7000-FA	—	PKA-AY16 E3AP-7000-DA	5.0L Ford/Mercury (Passenger Car) Ford Police (Alt/Unique Canada) 3.55 Axle without low gear lockout.
PKA-BB18 E4AP-7000-EA	—	PKA-BB16 E3AP-7000-EA	5.0L Ford Police (Alt/Unique Canada) 3.55 Axle with low gear lockout.
PKA-AU23 E4AP-7000-GA	—	PKA-AU21 E3AP-7000-CA	5.0L Ford Police (50S/Unique Canada) 3.08 Axle without low gear lockout.
PKA-M31 E4VP-7000-DA	—	PKA-M29 E3VP-7000-AB	5.0L Lincoln/Mark VI (50S) 3.08 Axle.
PKA-BC12 E4VP-7000-CA	—	PKA-BC10 E3VP-7000-CA	5.0L Lincoln/Mark VI (50S/Can/Alt) 3.55 Axle.
PKA-K6 E4SP-7000-DA	—	PKA-K4 E3SP-7000-FA	5.0L T-Bird/Cougar (50S/Can) 3.08 Axle, (Alt) 3.27 Axle.
*PKA-CB6 E4DP-7000-HA	—	PKA-CB3 E3DP-7000-EA PKA-BR3 E3SP-7000-BA	3.8L T-Bird/Cougar (50S/Can) 3.08 Axle. 3.8L T-Bird/Cougar (50S/Can) 3.08 Axle.
PKA-BT6 E4SP-7000-CA	—	PKA-BT4 E3SP-7000-EA	3.8L T-Bird/Cougar (Alt), LTD/Marquis (49S/Can/Alt) 3.45 Axle.
		LIGHT TRUCKS	
PKB-A26 E3TP-7000-MA	—	PKB-A24 E3TP-7000-MA	5.0L E100/150 3.50 Axle, F100/150, 3.55 Axle, F250 3.54/3.55/3.73 Axle, E250 3.54/3.55 Axle (50S/Can/Alt).
PKB-E5 E3TP-7000-NA	—	PKB-E4 E3TP-7000-NA	4.9L F100/150 (50S/Can) 3.08 Axle.
PKB-F4 E3TP-7000-PA	—	PKB-F3 E3TP-7000-PA	4.9L E100/150 3.50 Axle, E250 3.54/3.55 Axle (50S/Can/Alt), F100/150 3.55 Axle (40S/Can/Alt).
PKB-G5 E3UP-7000-SA	—	PKB-G4 E3UP-7000-SA	5.0L (50S/Can/Alt) 4.10 Axle.

*Use speedometer driven gear C7SP-17271-B 18T gray when using transmission on a 1983 model vehicle.
Main control valve body interchangeabillty:
All the 1984 main control valve bodies are pull-ahead 1983 and, therefore, are interchangeable.

OIL LEAKAGE REPAIR PROCEDURE

Key	Location	Leak Cause	Correction
		200C AND 200-4R ONLY	
⑭	Pump Assembly	Pump Bolts Loose	Retorque Bolts and Recheck
		Pump "O" Ring Cut or Damaged	Remove "O" Ring and Replace
		Pump Porosity	Replace Pump
⑮	Rear Extension Seal	Torn or Damaged	Remove Seal and Replace
		125C ONLY	
⑯	Valve Body Cover to Case Assembly	Low Bolt Torque	Retorque Bolt and Recheck
		RTV Bead Broken	Remove Cover and Reseal with RTV Gasket
		Gasket Leak	Remove Gasket and Replace
⑰	Axle Shaft Seals	Seals Damaged	Remove Seals and Replace

1454

OIL LEAKAGE REPAIR PROCEDURE

Key	Location	Leak Cause	Correction
		ALL MODELS	
②	Transmission Oil Pan	Low Bolt Torque Gasket Leak Broken RTV Bead	Retorque and Recheck Bolts Remove and Replace Gasket Remove Cover and Reseal with RTV
③	TV Cable Connector "C"	Connector Cocked and interferring with mount	Remove Connector and Reinstall
		Seal Damaged	Remove and Replace Seal
		Connector Cracked	Remove and Replace Cable
	Fill Tube "D"	Seal Missing or Damaged	Remove Fill Tube and Replace Seal
	Electrical Connector "E"	"O" Ring Missing or Damaged	Remove Connector and Replace Seal
		Connector Missing or Damaged	Remove and Replace Connector
④	Manual Shaft	Seal Assembly Damaged	Remove and Replace Seal
⑤	Governor Cover	"O" Ring Damaged	Remove and Replace "O" Ring
		Low Bolt Torque	Retorque Bolts and Recheck
⑥	Speedo Fitting	Low Bolt Torque	Retorque Bolt and Recheck
		Seal Damaged	Remove and Replace Seal
⑦	Servo Cover	"O" Ring Damaged	Remove and Replace "O" Ring
⑧	Cooler Fittings	Low Fitting Torque Cracked Fitting	Retorque Fitting and Recheck Replace and Retorque Fitting
⑪	Converter Assembly	Hub or Seam Weld Leak	Remove and Replace Converter
⑫	Converter Seal	Seal Damaged	Remove and Replace Seal
⑬	Vent	Leaking	Check for the following and correct as necessary: A. Oil Overfill B. Blocked Drainback hole in sprocket support C. Engine Coolant in oil
		325-4L ONLY	
①	Sprocket Cover	RTV Bead Broken	Remove Cover and Reseal with RTV
		Cracked Cover	Replace Cover
	Corner "A"	Leak	Past Design Case-Drill through and Add Nut, Bolt and Lock Washer
	Corner "B"	Leak	Remove Cover and Reseal with RTV
⑨	Case Face to Final Drive	Low Bolt Torque	Retorque Bolts and Recheck
⑩	Case Face to Final Drive Governor Cover	Plug Loose (Leaking)	Remove Plug and Replace (Loctite Plug)
		Plug High	Drive Plug into Case Below Face Surface

THM 200C

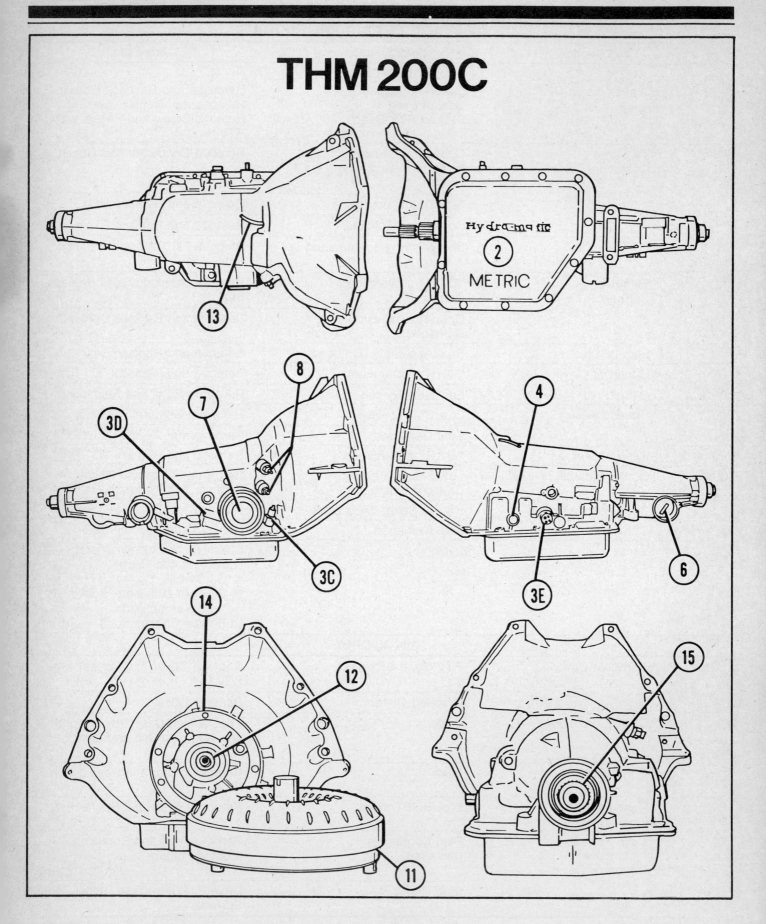

THM 125C

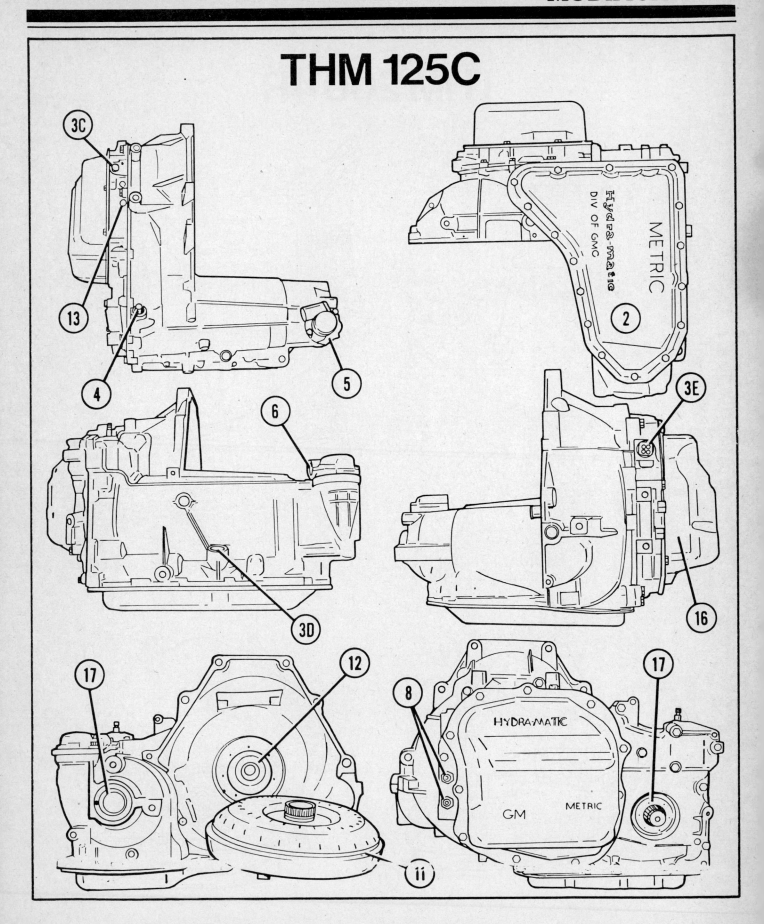

THM 200 4R

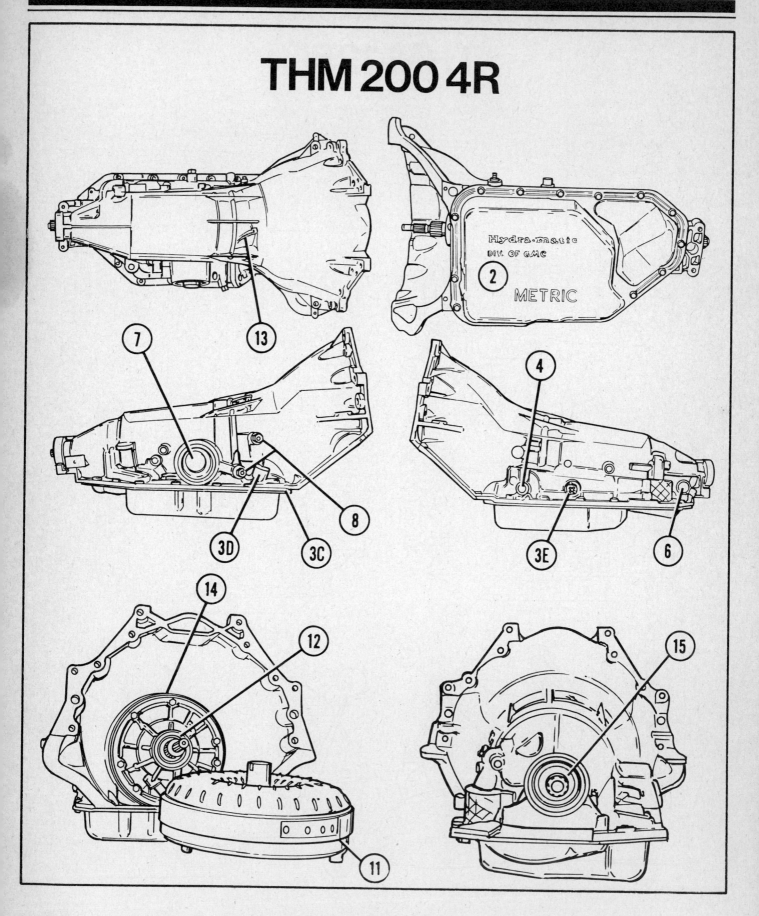

THM 325 4L

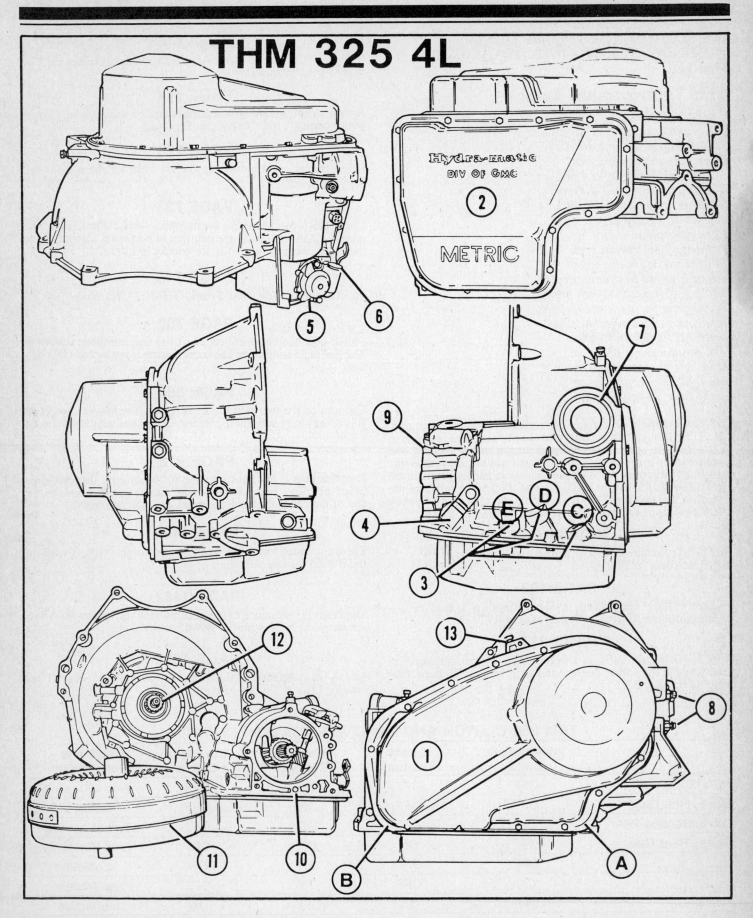

CORRECTION SECTION

CORRECTIONS FOR VOLUME I OF THE
PROFESSIONAL AUTOMATIC TRANSMISSION
MANUAL

The Typographic Error

The typographic error
Is a slippery thing and sly.
You can hunt till you are dizzy,
But it somehow will get by.
Till the forms are off the presses,
It is strange how still it keeps;
It shrinks down in a corner
And never stirs or peeps.
The typographic error,
Too small for human eyes,
Till the ink is on the paper
When it grows to mountain size.
The boss, who stares with horror,
Then grabs the page and groans,
The copy reader drops his head
Upon his hands and moans.
The remainder of the issue
May be clean as clean can be.
But that typographic error
Is the only thing you see.

When our first Automatic Transmission Manual was published, we thought all irregularities that were found in the text, charts and art work were corrected during the typesetting and page make-up operations. However, such was not the case. Some mistakes had slipped by. With the help of our manual users in the field and research by our staff, a list of the known mistakes are noted, so that owners of our first manual can make the necessary page corrections to have an up-to-date manual.

INDEX PAGE

PAGE 103

Gasket outline designation reversed. Caption should read—"Gasket outline A904 (B), Gasket outline A727 (A)"

PAGE 217

Step 5—Delete the band specification and refer to the specification pages at the end of the section for correct applications. (Beginning on page 248).

Page 444

THM 250 Clutch and Band Application Chart is incorrect. The correct chart is as follows;

PAGE 574

Art work caption wrong. The correct caption should read; "Front pump casting", not "Drive clutch piston".

PAGE 726

Detent shown upside down in the art work for removal of the manual linkage.

PAGE 733

Check ball locations wrong for numbers 4 and 5 check balls. The arrows for the two balls are pointing to bolt holes instead of the ball seats. Refer to page 721 for correct locations.

PAGE 745

Head at top of page should read "THM 125 Transaxle".

PAGE 750

Clutch and band application chart has one component wrong. The low band is *off* when the transmission is in the 2nd (D) position.

PAGE 880

Captions on the two pictures are reversed. The low/reverse band adjustment is on top and the intermediate band adjustment is on the bottom.

PAGE 978

Specifications is not split into the ft. lbs. and in. lbs. columns. From the entry "End plates-to-body" torque specifications to the end of the chart, the measurements are inch pounds.

PAGE 1435

The front clutch assembly, as shown in the art work, is used on the BW 65 models only.

PAGE 1482

The assembly sequence of the accumulator springs, as shown in the art work, is used on the BW 65 models only.

PAGE 1523

Add to Units Applied, along with the "Front clutch", the "Overrunning Clutch".

THM 250 CLUTCH AND BAND APPLICATION CHART

	Intermediate Band	Direct Clutch	Forward Clutch	Low/Rev. Clutch	Low and Roller Clutch
NEUTRAL	OFF	OFF	OFF	OFF	Free-Wheeling
Drive, First Gear	OFF	OFF	ON	OFF	Locked
Drive, Second Gear	ON	OFF	ON	OFF	Free-Wheeling
Drive, Third Gear	OFF	ON	ON	OFF	Free-Wheeling
L$_1$	OFF	OFF	ON	ON	Locked
L$_2$	ON	OFF	ON	OFF	Free-Wheeling
REVERSE	OFF	ON	OFF	ON	Ineffective

NOTES

NOTES

Metric Tables

SI METRIC TABLES

The following tables are given in SI (International System) metric units. SI units replace both customary (English) and the older gavimetric units. The use of SI units as a new worldwide standard was set by the International Committee of Weights and Measures in 1960. SI has since been adopted by most countries as their national standard.

These tables are general conversion tables which will allow you to convert customary units, which appear in the text, into SI units.

The following are a list of SI units and the customary units, used in this book, which they replace:

To measure:	Use SI units:	Which replace (customary units):
mass	kilograms (kg)	pounds (lbs)
temperature	Celsius (°C)	Fahrenheit (°F)
length	millimeters (mm)	inches (in.)
force	newtons (N)	pounds force (lbs)
capacities	liters (l)	pints/quarts/gallons (pts/qts/gals)
torque	newton-meters (N-m)	foot pounds (ft lbs)
pressure	kilopascals (kPa)	pounds per square inch (psi)
volume	cubic centimeters (cm³)	cubic inches (cu in.)
power	kilowatts (kW)	horsepower (hp)

If you have had any prior experience with the metric system, you may have noticed units in this chart which are not familiar to you. This is because, in some cases, SI units differ from the older gravimetric units which they replace. For example, newtons (N) replace kilograms (kg) as a force unit, kilopascals (kPa) replace atmospheres or bars as a unit of pressure, and, although the units are the same, the name Celsius replaces centigrade for temperature measurement.

If you are not using the SI tables, have a look at them anyway; you will be seeing a lot more of them in the future.

METRIC INFORMATION

ENGLISH TO METRIC CONVERSION: MASS (WEIGHT)

Current **mass** measurement is expressed in pounds and ounces (lbs. & ozs.). The metric unit of mass (or weight) is the kilogram (kg). Even although this table does not show conversion of masses (weights) larger than 15 lbs, it is easy to calculate larger units by following the data immediately below.

To convert ounces (oz.) to grams (g): multiply th number of ozs. by 28
To convert grams (g) to ounces (oz.): multiply the number of grams by .035

To convert pounds (lbs.) to kilograms (kg): multiply the number of lbs. by .45
To convert kilograms (kg) to pounds (lbs.): multiply the number of kilograms by 2.2

lbs	kg	lbs	kg	oz	kg	oz	kg
0.1	0.04	0.9	0.41	0.1	0.003	0.9	0.024
0.2	0.09	1	0.4	0.2	0.005	1	0.03
0.3	0.14	2	0.9	0.3	0.008	2	0.06
0.4	0.18	3	1.4	0.4	0.011	3	0.08
0.5	0.23	4	1.8	0.5	0.014	4	0.11
0.6	0.27	5	2.3	0.6	0.017	5	0.14
0.7	0.32	10	4.5	0.7	0.020	10	0.28
0.8	0.36	15	6.8	0.8	0.023	15	0.42

ENGLISH TO METRIC CONVERSION: TEMPERATURE

To convert Fahrenheit (F) to Celsius (°C): take number of °F and subtract 32; multiply result by 5; divide result by 9

To convert Celsius (°C) to Fahrenheit (°F): take number of °C and multiply by 9; divide result by 5; add 32 to total

Fahrenheit (F)		Celsius (C)		Fahrenheit (F)		Celsius (C)		Fahrenheit (F)		Celsius (C)	
°F	°C	°C	°F	°F	°C	°C	°F	°F	°C	°C	°F
−40	−40	−38	−36.4	80	26.7	18	64.4	215	101.7	80	176
−35	−37.2	−36	−32.8	85	29.4	20	68	220	104.4	85	185
−30	−34.4	−34	−29.2	90	32.2	22	71.6	225	107.2	90	194
−25	−31.7	−32	−25.6	95	35.0	24	75.2	230	110.0	95	202
−20	−28.9	−30	−22	100	37.8	26	78.8	235	112.8	100	212
−15	−26.1	−28	−18.4	105	40.6	28	82.4	240	115.6	105	221
−10	−23.3	−26	−14.8	110	43.3	30	86	245	118.3	110	230
−5	−20.6	−24	−11.2	115	46.1	32	89.6	250	121.1	115	239
0	−17.8	−22	−7.6	120	48.9	34	93.2	255	123.9	120	248
1	−17.2	−20	−4	125	51.7	36	96.8	260	126.6	125	257
2	−16.7	−18	−0.4	130	54.4	38	100.4	265	129.4	130	266
3	−16.1	−16	3.2	135	57.2	40	104	270	132.2	135	275
4	−15.6	−14	6.8	140	60.0	42	107.6	275	135.0	140	284
5	−15.0	−12	10.4	145	62.8	44	112.2	280	137.8	145	293
10	−12.2	−10	14	150	65.6	46	114.8	285	140.6	150	302
15	−9.4	−8	17.6	155	68.3	48	118.4	290	143.3	155	311
20	−6.7	−6	21.2	160	71.1	50	122	295	146.1	160	320
25	−3.9	−4	24.8	165	73.9	52	125.6	300	148.9	165	329
30	−1.1	−2	28.4	170	76.7	54	129.2	305	151.7	170	338
35	1.7	0	32	175	79.4	56	132.8	310	154.4	175	347
40	4.4	2	35.6	180	82.2	58	136.4	315	157.2	180	356
45	7.2	4	39.2	185	85.0	60	140	320	160.0	185	365
50	10.0	6	42.8	190	87.8	62	143.6	325	162.8	190	374
55	12.8	8	46.4	195	90.6	64	147.2	330	165.6	195	383
60	15.6	10	50	200	93.3	66	150.8	335	168.3	200	392
65	18.3	12	53.6	205	96.1	68	154.4	340	171.1	205	401
70	21.1	14	57.2	210	98.9	70	158	345	173.9	210	410
75	23.9	16	60.8	212	100.0	75	167	350	176.7	215	414

METRIC INFORMATION

ENGLISH TO METRIC CONVERSION: LENGTH

To convert inches (ins.) to millimeters (mm): multiply number of inches by 25.4

To convert millimeters (mm) to inches (ins.): multiply number of millimeters by .04

Inches	Decimals	Milli-meters	inches to millimeters (inches)	inches to millimeters (mm)	Inches	Decimals	Milli-meters	inches to millimeters (inches)	inches to millimeters (mm)
1/64	0.051625	0.3969	0.0001	0.00254	33/64	0.515625	13.0969	0.6	15.24
1/32	0.03125	0.7937	0.0002	0.00508	17/32	0.53125	13.4937	0.7	17.78
3/64	0.046875	1.1906	0.0003	0.00762	35/64	0.546875	13.8906	0.8	20.32
1/16	0.0625	1.5875	0.0004	0.01016	9/16	0.5625	14.2875	0.9	22.86
5/64	0.078125	1.9844	0.0005	0.01270	37/64	0.578125	14.6844	1	25.4
3/32	0.09375	2.3812	0.0006	0.01524	19/32	0.59375	15.0812	2	50.8
7/64	0.109375	2.7781	0.0007	0.01778	39/64	0.609375	15.4781	3	76.2
1/8	0.125	3.1750	0.0008	0.02032	5/8	0.625	15.8750	4	101.6
9/64	0.140625	3.5719	0.0009	0.02286	41/64	0.640625	16.2719	5	127.0
5/32	0.15625	3.9687	0.001	0.0254	21/32	0.65625	16.6687	6	152.4
11/64	0.171875	4.3656	0.002	0.0508	43/64	0.671875	17.0656	7	177.8
3/16	0.1875	4.7625	0.003	0.0762	11/16	0.6875	17.4625	8	203.2
13/64	0.203125	5.1594	0.004	0.1016	45/64	0.703125	17.8594	9	228.6
7/32	0.21875	5.5562	0.005	0.1270	23/32	0.71875	18.2562	10	254.0
15/64	0.234375	5.9531	0.006	0.1524	47/64	0.734375	18.6531	11	279.4
1/4	0.25	6.3500	0.007	0.1778	3/4	0.75	19.0500	12	304.8
17/64	0.265625	6.7469	0.008	0.2032	49/64	0.765625	19.4469	13	330.2
9/32	0.28125	7.1437	0.009	0.2286	25/32	0.78125	19.8437	14	355.6
19/64	0.296875	7.5406	0.01	0.254	51/64	0.796875	20.2406	15	381.0
5/16	0.3125	7.9375	0.02	0.508	13/16	0.8125	20.6375	16	406.4
21/64	0.328125	8.3344	0.03	0.762	53/64	0.828125	21.0344	17	431.8
11/32	0.34375	8.7312	0.04	1.016	27/32	0.84375	21.4312	18	457.2
23/64	0.359375	9.1281	0.05	1.270	55/64	0.859375	21.8281	19	482.6
3/8	0.375	9.5250	0.06	1.524	7/8	0.875	22.2250	20	508.0
25/64	0.390625	9.9219	0.07	1.778	57/64	0.890625	22.6219	21	533.4
13/32	0.40625	10.3187	0.08	2.032	29/32	0.90625	23.0187	22	558.8
27/64	0.421875	10.7156	0.09	2.286	59/64	0.921875	23.4156	23	584.2
7/16	0.4375	11.1125	0.1	2.54	15/16	0.9375	23.8125	24	609.6
29/64	0.453125	11.5094	0.2	5.08	61/64	0.953125	24.2094	25	635.0
15/32	0.46875	11.9062	0.3	7.62	31/32	0.96875	24.6062	26	660.4
31/64	0.484375	12.3031	0.4	10.16	63/64	0.984375	25.0031	27	690.6
1/2	0.5	12.7000	0.5	12.70					

ENGLISH TO METRIC CONVERSION: TORQUE

To convert foot-pounds (ft. lbs.) to Newton-meters: multiply the number of ft. lbs. by 1.3

To convert inch-pounds (in. lbs.) to Newton-meters: multiply the number of in. lbs. by .11

in lbs	N-m	in lbs	N-m	in lbs	N-m	in lbs	N-m	in lbs	N-m
0.1	0.01	1	0.11	10	1.13	19	2.15	28	3.16
0.2	0.02	2	0.23	11	1.24	20	2.26	29	3.28
0.3	0.03	3	0.34	12	1.36	21	2.37	30	3.39
0.4	0.04	4	0.45	13	1.47	22	2.49	31	3.50
0.5	0.06	5	0.56	14	1.58	23	2.60	32	3.62
0.6	0.07	6	0.68	15	1.70	24	2.71	33	3.73
0.7	0.08	7	0.78	16	1.81	25	2.82	34	3.84
0.8	0.09	8	0.90	17	1.92	26	2.94	35	3.95
0.9	0.10	9	1.02	18	2.03	27	3.05	36	4.0/